Edited By: Robert Kiesling, kiesling@lsl.com
Published By: Linux Systems Labs, www.lsl.com

Printed in Canada

6th edition.

Copyright

The Linux Documentation Project
The original, unaltered edition of LDP
documents are on line at http://sunsite.unc.edu/LDP/.

Introduction to the Linux Documentation Project

Greg Hankins and Michael K. Johnson

v1.0, 25 November 1997

The Linux Documentation Project (LDP) is working on developing good, reliable documentation for the Linux operating system. The overall goal of the LDP authors is to write documents in various formats that cover installing, configuring, and using Linux. The LDP produces documents in a variety of formats: plain text that you can read anywhere, HTML documents you can read with a browser, man pages that can be read online or in a book, and typeset documentation that can be printed and read in books.

The LDP's "home" is its web page, found at `http://sunsite.unc.edu/LDP/` and countless mirrors listed at `http://sunsite.unc.edu/LDP/hmirrors.html`. This is the place to check for updates, news, and some documents that only exist online. A few documents that exist only online are;

- *Linux Gazette*, a monthly collection of unedited articles and letters from Linux users everywhere.
- *The Linux Kernel Hackers' Guide*, an interactive, edited forum where Linux kernel developers talk about kernel development issues.
- Special HOWTOs, HOWTO documents that rely on things that cannot be supported in plain text versions.

In addition to the LDP web pages, there are four basic types of documentation produced by the LDP: Guides, HOWTOs and mini-HOWTOs, man pages, and FAQs.

- Guides
  Entire books on complex topics.
- HOWTOs and Mini-HOWTOs
  Documents with full coverage of a fairly well-defined topic or simple coverage, usually of a single task.
- Manual pages
  Documentation for single programs, file formats, and library functions in standard UNIX reference format.
- FAQs
  Frequently Asked Questions on various topics, including the Linux FAQ.

If you have comments about any particular document in this set, feel free to send it to the author. All documents have the author's email address to send comments to, and while the authors may not always have time to respond, they do read and consider thoughtful comments on their work. Your comments help make the next versions of these documents better. If you have comments or questions about the LDP in general, please contact Greg Hankins via email at gregh@sunsite.unc.edu.

The Linux Information Sheet

Michael K. Johnson

v4.13, 24 October 1997

Abstract

This document provides basic information about the Linux operating system, including an explanation of Linux, a list of features, some requirements, and some resources.

Introduction to Linux

Linux is a completely free re-implementation of the POSIX specification, with SYSV and BSD extensions (which means it looks like Unix, but does not come from the same source code base), which is available in both source code and binary form. Its copyright is owned by Linus Torvalds <torvalds@transmeta.com> and other contributors, and is freely redistributable under the terms of the GNU General Public License (GPL). A copy of the GPL is included with the Linux source; you can also get a copy from `(ftp://prep.ai.mit.edu/pub/gnu/COPYING)`

Linux is *not* public domain, nor is it 'shareware'. It is 'free' software, commonly called **freeware**, and you may give away or sell copies, but you must include the source code or make it available in the same way as any binaries you give or sell. If you distribute any modifications, you are legally bound to distribute the source for those modifications. See the GNU General Public License for details.

Linux is still free as of version 2.0, and will continue to be free. Because of the nature of the GPL to which Linux is subject, it would be illegal for it to be made not free. Note carefully: the 'free' part involves access to the source code rather than money; it is perfectly legal to charge money for distributing Linux, so long as you also distribute the source code. This is a generalization; if you want the fine points, read the GPL.

Linux runs on 386/486/Pentium machines with ISA, EISA, PCI and VLB busses. MCA (IBM's proprietary bus) is not well-supported in 2.0.x and earlier versions, but support has been added to the current development tree, 2.1.x. If you are interested, see `(http://glycerine.itsmm.uni.edu/mca)`

There is a port to multiple Motorola 680x0 platforms (currently running on some Amigas, Ataris, and VME machines), which now works quite well. It requires a 68020 with an MMU, a 68030, 68040, or a 68060, and also requires an FPU. Networking and X now work. See `(news:comp.os.linux.m68k)`

Linux runs well on DEC's Alpha CPU, currently supporting the "Jensen," "NoName," "Cabriolet," "Universal Desktop Box" (better known as the Multia), and many other platforms. For more information, see `(http://www.azstarnet.com/ axplinux/FAQ.html)`

Linux runs well on Sun SPARCs; most sun4c and sun4m machines now run Linux, with support for sun4 and sun4u in active development. Red Hat Linux is (as of this writing) the only Linux distribution available for SPARCs; see `(http://www.redhat.com/support/docs/rhl-sparc/)`

Linux is being actively ported to the PowerPC architecture, including PowerMac (Nubus and PCI), Motorola, IBM, and Be machines. See `(http://www.cs.nmt.edu/ linuxppc/)` and `(http://www.linuxppc.org/)`

Ports to other machines, including MIPS and ARM, are under way and showing various amounts of progress. Don't hold your breath, but if you are interested and able to contribute, you may well find other developers who wish to work with you.

Linux is no longer considered to be in beta testing, as version 1.0 was released on March 14, 1994. There are still bugs in the system, and new bugs will creep up and be fixed as time goes on. Because Linux follows the "open development model", all new versions will be released to the public, whether or not they are considered "production quality". However, in order to help people tell whether they are getting a stable version or not, the following scheme has been implemented: Versions 1.x.y, where x is an even number, are stable versions, and only bug fixes will be applied as y is incremented. So from version 1.2.2 to 1.2.3, there were only bug fixes, and no new features. Versions 1.x.y, where x is an odd number, are beta-quality releases for developers only, and may be unstable and may crash, and are having new features added to them all the time. From time to time, as the current development kernel stabilizes, it will be frozen as the new "stable" kernel, and development will continue on a new development version of the kernel.

The current stable version is 2.0.31 (this will continue to change as new device drivers get added and bugs fixed), and development has also started on the experimental 2.1.x kernels. If 2.0.x is too new for you, you may want to stick with 1.2.13 for the time being. However, the latest releases of 2.0 have proved quite stable. Do note that in order to upgrade from 1.2 to 2.0, you need to upgrade some utilities as well; you may wish to upgrade to the latest version of your Linux distribution in order to obtain those utilities. The Linux kernel source code also contains a file, Documentation/Changes, which explains these changes and more.

Most versions of Linux, beta or not, are quite stable, and you can keep using those if they do what you need and you don't want to be on the bleeding edge. One site had a computer running version 0.97p1 (dating from the summer of 1992) for over 136 days without an error or crash. (It would have been longer if the back hoe operator hadn't mistaken a main power transformer for a dumpster...) Others have posted uptimes in excess of a year. One site still had a computer running Linux 0.99p15s over 600 days at last report.

One thing to be aware of is that Linux is developed using an open and distributed model, instead of a closed and centralized model like much other software. This means that the current development version is always public (with up to a week or two of delay) so that anybody can use it. The result is that whenever a version with new functionality is released, it almost always contains bugs, but it also results in a very rapid development so that the bugs are found and corrected quickly, often in hours, as many people work to fix them.

In contrast, the closed and centralized model means that there is only one person or team working on the project, and they only release software that they think is working well. Often this leads to long intervals between releases, long waiting for bug fixes, and slower development. The latest release of such software to the public is sometimes of higher quality, but the development speed is generally much slower.

As of October 24, 1997, the current stable version of Linux is 2.0.31, and the latest development version is 2.1.59.

Linux Features

- multitasking: several programs running at once.
- multiuser: several users on the same machine at once (and no two-user licenses!).
- multi-platform: runs on many different CPUs, not just Intel.
- multiprocessor: SMP support is available on the Intel and SPARC platforms (with work currently in progress on other platforms), and Linux is used in several loosely-coupled MP applications, including Beowulf systems (see `(http://cesdis.gsfc.nasa.gov/linux-web/beowulf/beowulf.html)`) and the Fujitsu AP1000+ SPARC-based supercomputer.
- runs in protected mode on the 386.
- has memory protection between processes, so that one program can't bring the whole system down.
- demand loads executables: Linux only reads from disk those parts of a program that are actually used.

- shared copy-on-write pages among executables. This means that multiple process can use the same memory to run in. When one tries to write to that memory, that page (4KB piece of memory) is copied somewhere else. Copy-on-write has two benefits: increasing speed and decreasing memory use.
- virtual memory using paging (not swapping whole processes) to disk: to a separate partition or a file in the file system, or both, with the possibility of adding more swapping areas during runtime (yes, they're still called swapping areas). A total of 16 of these 128 MB swapping areas can be used at once, for a theoretical total of 2 GB of usable swap space. It is simple to increase this if necessary, by changing a few lines of source code.
- a unified memory pool for user programs and disk cache, so that all free memory can be used for caching, and the cache can be reduced when running large programs.
- dynamically linked shared libraries (DLL's), and static libraries too, of course.
- does core dumps for post-mortem analysis, allowing the use of a debugger on a program not only while it is running but also after it has crashed.
- mostly compatible with POSIX, System V, and BSD at the source level.
- through an iBCS2-compliant emulation module, mostly compatible with SCO, SVR3, and SVR4 at the binary level.
- all source code is available, including the whole kernel and all drivers, the development tools and all user programs; also, all of it is freely distributable. Plenty of commercial programs are being provided for Linux without source, but everything that has been free, including the entire base operating system, is still free.
- POSIX job control.
- pseudo terminals (pty's).
- 387-emulation in the kernel so that programs don't need to do their own math emulation. Every computer running Linux appears to have a math coprocessor. Of course, if your computer already contains an FPU, it will be used instead of the emulation, and you can even compile your own kernel with math emulation removed, for a small memory gain.
- support for many national or customized keyboards, and it is fairly easy to add new ones dynamically.
- multiple virtual consoles: several independent login sessions through the console, you switch by pressing a hot-key combination (not dependent on video hardware). These are dynamically allocated; you can use up to 64.
- Supports several common file systems, including minix, Xenix, and all the common system V file systems, and has an advanced file system of its own, which offers file systems of up to 4 TB, and names up to 255 characters long.
- transparent access to MS-DOS partitions (or OS/2 FAT partitions) via a special file system: you don't need any special commands to use the MS-DOS partition, it looks just like a normal Unix file system (except for funny restrictions on filenames, permissions, and so on). MS-DOS 6 compressed partitions do not work at this time without a patch (dmsdosfs). VFAT (WNT, Windows 95) support is available in Linux 2.0
- special file system called UMSDOS which allows Linux to be installed on a DOS file system.
- read-only HPFS-2 support for OS/2 2.1
- HFS (Macintosh) file system support is available separately as a module.

- CD-ROM file system which reads all standard formats of CD-ROMs.
- TCP/IP networking, including ftp, telnet, NFS, etc.
- AppleTalk server
- Netware client and server
- Lan Manager (SMB) client and server
- Many networking protocols: the base protocols available in the latest development kernels include TCP, IPv4, IPv6, AX.25, X.25, IPX, DDP (AppleTalk), NetBEUI, Netrom, and others. Stable network protocols included in the stable kernels currently include TCP, IPv4, IPX, DDP, and AX.25.

Hardware Issues

Minimal configuration

The following is probably the smallest possible configuration that Linux will work on: 386SX/16, 1 MB RAM, 1.44 MB or 1.2 MB floppy, any supported video card (+ keyboards, monitors, and so on of course). This should allow you to boot and test whether it works at all on the machine, but you won't be able to do anything useful. See `(http://rsphy1.anu.edu.au/ gpg109/mem.html)` for minimal Linux configurations

In order to do something, you will want some hard disk space as well, 5 to 10 MB should suffice for a very minimal setup (with only the most important commands and perhaps one or two small applications installed, like, say, a terminal program). This is still very, very limited, and very uncomfortable, as it doesn't leave enough room to do just about anything, unless your applications are quite limited. It's generally not recommended for anything but testing if things work, and of course to be able to brag about small resource requirements.

Usable configuration

If you are going to run computationally intensive programs, such as gcc, X, and TeX, you will probably want a faster processor than a 386SX/16, but even that should suffice if you are patient.

In practice, you will want at least 4 MB of RAM if you don't use X, and 8 MB if you do. Also, if you want to have several users at a time, or run several large programs (compilations for example) at a time, you may want more than 4 MB of memory. It will still work with a smaller amount of memory (should work even with 2 MB), but it will use virtual memory (using the hard drive as *slow* memory) and that will be so slow as to be unusable. If you use many programs at once, 16 MB will reduce swapping considerably. If you don't want to swap appreciably under any normal load, 32 MB will probably suffice. Of course, if you run memory-hungry applications, you may want more.

The amount of hard disk you need depends on what software you want to install. The normal basic set of Unix utilities, shells, and administrative programs should be comfortable in less than 10 MB, with a bit of room to spare for user files. For a more complete system, get Red Hat, Debian, or another distribution, and assume that you will need 60 to 300 MB, depending on what you choose to install and what distribution you get. Add whatever space you want to reserve for user files to these totals. With today's prices on hard drives, if you are buying a new system, it makes no sense to buy a drive that is too small. Get at least 500 MB, preferably 1GB or more, and you will not regret it.

Add more memory, more hard disk, a faster processor and other stuff depending on your needs, wishes and budget to go beyond the merely usable. In general, one big difference from DOS is that with Linux, adding memory makes a large difference, whereas with DOS, extra memory doesn't make that much difference. This of course has something to do with MS-DOS's 640KB limit, which is completely nonexistent under Linux.

Supported hardware

CPU:

Anything that runs 386 protected mode programs (all models of 386's 486's, 586's, and 686's should work. 286s and below may someday be supported on a smaller kernel called ELKS (Embeddable Linux Kernel Subset), but don't expect the same capabilities). A version for the 680x0 CPU (for $x = 2$ with external MMU, 3, 4, and 6) which runs on Amigas and Ataris can be found at tsx-11.mit.edu in the 680x0 directory. Many DEC Alphas, SPARCs, and PowerPC machines are supported. Ports are also being done to the ARM, StrongARM, and MIPS architectures. More details are available elsewhere.

Architecture:

ISA or EISA bus. MCA (mostly true, blue PS/2's) support is incomplete but improving (see above). Local busses (VLB and PCI) work. Linux puts higher demands on hardware than DOS, Windows, and in fact most operating systems. This means that some marginal hardware that doesn't fail when running less demanding operating system may fail when running Linux. Linux is an excellent memory tester...

RAM:

Up to 1 GB on Intel; more on 64-bit platforms. Some people (including Linus) have noted that adding ram without adding more cache at the same time has slowed down their machine extremely, so if you add memory and find your machine slower, try adding more cache. Some machines can only cache certain amounts of memory regardless of how much RAM is installed (64 MB is the most one popular chip set can cache). Over 64 MB of memory will require a boot-time parameter, as the BIOS cannot report more than 64MB, because it is "broken as designed."

Data storage:

Generic AT drives (EIDE, IDE, 16 bit HD controllers with MFM or RLL, or ESDI) are supported, as are SCSI hard disks and CD-ROMs, with a supported SCSI adaptor. Generic XT controllers (8 bit controllers with MFM or RLL) are also supported. Supported SCSI adaptors: Advansys, Adaptec 1542, 1522, 1740, 27xx, and 29xx (with some exceptions) series, Buslogic MultiMaster and Flashpoint, NCR53c8xx-based controllers, DPT controllers, Qlogic ISP and FAS controllers, Seagate ST-01 and ST-02, Future Domain TMC-88x series (or any board based on the TMC950 chip) and TMC1660/1680, Ultrastor 14F, 24F and 34F, Western Digital wd7000, and others. SCSI, QIC-02, and some QIC-80 tapes are also supported. Several CD-ROM devices are also supported, including Matsushita/Panasonic, Mitsumi, Sony, Soundblaster, Toshiba, ATAPI (EIDE), SCSI, and others. For exact models, check the hardware compatibility HOWTO.

Video:

VGA, EGA, CGA, or Hercules (and compatibles) work in text mode. For graphics and X, there is support for (at least) normal VGA, some super-VGA cards (most of the cards based on ET3000, ET4000, Paradise, and some Trident chip sets), S3, 8514/A, ATI MACH8/32/64, and Hercules. (Linux uses the Xfree86 X server, so that determines what cards are supported. A full list of supported chip sets alone takes over a page.)

Networking:

Ethernet support includes 3COM 503/509/579/589/595/905 (501/505/507 are supported but not recommended), AT&T GIS (neé NCR) WaveLAN, most WD8390-based cards, most WD80x3-based cards, NE1000/2000 and most clones, AC3200, Apricot 82596, AT1700, ATP, DE425/434/435/500, D-Link DE-600/620, DEPCA, DE100/101, DE200/201/202 Turbo, DE210, DE422, Cabletron E2100 (not recommended), Intel EtherExpress (not recommended), DEC EtherWORKS 3, HP LAN, HP PCLAN/plus, most AMD LANCE-based cards, NI5210, ni6510, SMC Ultra, DEC 21040 (tulip), Zenith Z-Note ethernet, All Zircom cards and all Cabletron cards other than the E2100 are unsupported, due to the manufacturers unwillingness to release programming information freely.

FDDI support currently includes the DEF*xx* cards from DEC.

Point-to-Point networking support include PPP, SLIP, CSLIP, and PLIP.

Limited Token Ring support is available.

Serial:

Most 16450 and 16550 UART-based boards, including AST Fourport, the Usenet Serial Card II, and others. Intelligent boards supported include Cyclades Cyclom series (supported by the manufacturer), Comtrol Rocketport series (supported by the manufacturer), Stallion (most boards; supported by the manufacturer), and Digi (some boards; supported by the manufacturer). Some ISDN, frame relay, and leased line hardware is supported.

Other hardware:

SoundBlaster, ProAudio Spectrum 16, Gravis Ultrasound, most other sound cards, most (all?) flavors of bus mice (Microsoft, Logitech, PS/2), etc.

An Incomplete List of Ported Programs and Other Software

Most of the common Unix tools and programs have been ported to Linux, including almost all of the GNU stuff and many X clients from various sources. Actually, ported is often too strong a word, since many programs compile out of the box without modifications, or only small modifications, because Linux tracks POSIX quite closely. Unfortunately, there are not as many end-user applications yet as we would like, but this is changing rapidly. Contact the vendor of your favorite commercial Unix application and ask if they have ported it to Linux.

Here is an incomplete list of software that is known to work under Linux:

Basic Unix commands:

`ls`, `tr`, `sed`, `awk` and so on (you name it, Linux probably has it).

Development tools:

`gcc`, `gdb`, `make`, `bison`, `flex`, `perl`, `rcs`, `cvs`, `prof`.

Languages and Environments:

C, C++, Objective C, Java, Modula-3, Modula-2, Oberon, Ada95, Pascal, Fortran, ML, scheme, Tcl/tk, Perl, Python, Common Lisp, and many others.

Graphical environments:

X11R5 (XFree86 2.x), X11R6 (XFree86 3.x), MGR.

Editors:

GNU Emacs, XEmacs, Micro Emacs, `jove`, ez, `epoch`, `elvis` (GNU vi), `vim`, `vile`, `joe`, `pico`, `jed`, and others.

Shells:

`bash` (POSIX sh-compatible), `zsh` (includes `ksh` compatibility mode), `pdksh`, `tcsh`, `csh`, `rc`, `es`, `ash` (mostly sh-compatible shell used as `/bin/sh` by BSD), and many more.

Telecommunication:

Taylor (BNU-compatible) UUCP, SLIP, CSLIP, PPP, `kermit`, `szrz`, `minicom`, `pcomm`, `xcomm`, `term` (runs multiple shells, redirects network activity, and allows remote X, all over one modem line), Seyon (popular X-windows communications program), and several fax and voice-mail (using ZyXEL and other modems) packages are available. Of course, remote serial logins are supported.

News and mail:

C-news, `innd`, `trn`, `nn`, `tin`, `smail`, `elm`, `mh`, `pine`, etc.

Text processing:

TEX, LATEX `groff`, `doc`, `ez`, LyX, Lout, Linuxdoc-SGML, and others.

Games:

Nethack, several Muds and X games, and lots of others. One of those games is looking through all the games available at tsx-11 and sunsite.

Suites:

AUIS, the Andrew User Interface System. ez is part of this suite.

All of these programs (and this isn't even a hundredth of what is available) are freely available. Commercial software is becoming widely available; ask the vendor of your favorite commercial software if they support Linux.

Who uses Linux?

Linux is freely available, and no one is required to register their copies with any central authority, so it is difficult to know how many people use Linux. Several businesses now survive solely on selling and supporting Linux (and relatively few Linux users purchase products from those businesses), and the Linux newsgroups are some of the most heavily read on the Internet, so the number is likely in the millions, but concrete numbers are hard to come by.

However, one brave soul, Harald T. Alvestrand <Harald.T.Alvestrand@uninett.no>, has decided to try. If you are willing to be counted as a Linux user, please use the web forms available at `(http://counter.li.org/)` Alternatively, you can send a message to linux-counter@uninett.no with one of the following subjects: 'I use Linux at home', 'I use Linux at work', or 'I use Linux at home and at work'. He will also accept 'third-party' registrations; ask him for details.

He posts his counts to `(news:comp.os.linux.misc)` each month; they are also available from `(http://counter.li.org/)`.

Getting Linux

Anonymous FTP

For freely-redistributable Linux documentation, see the Linux Documentation Project sites at `(ftp://sunsite.unc.edu/pub/Linux/docs/LDP/)` and `(http://sunsite.unc.edu/LDP/)`

Stay tuned to the `(news:comp.os.linux.announce)` newsgroup for further developments.

At least the following anonymous ftp sites carry Linux.

```
Textual name                   Numeric address  Linux directory
============================== ===============  ===============
tsx-11.mit.edu                 18.172.1.2       /pub/linux
sunsite.unc.edu                152.2.22.81      /pub/Linux
ftp.funet.fi                   128.214.248.6    /pub/Linux
net.tamu.edu                   128.194.177.1    /pub/linux
ftp.mcc.ac.uk                  130.88.203.12    /pub/linux
src.doc.ic.ac.uk               146.169.2.1      /packages/linux
fgb1.fgb.mw.tu-muenchen.de     129.187.200.1    /pub/linux
ftp.informatik.tu-muenchen.de  131.159.0.110    /pub/comp/os/linux
ftp.dfv.rwth-aachen.de         137.226.4.111    /pub/linux
ftp.informatik.rwth-aachen.de  137.226.225.3    /pub/Linux
ftp.Germany.EU.net             192.76.144.75    /pub/os/Linux
```

ftp.ibp.fr	132.227.60.2	/pub/linux
ftp.uu.net	137.39.1.9	/systems/unix/linux
wuarchive.wustl.edu	128.252.135.4	mirrors/linux
ftp.win.tue.nl	131.155.70.100	/pub/linux
ftp.stack.urc.tue.nl	131.155.2.71	/pub/linux
srawgw.sra.co.jp	133.137.4.3	/pub/os/linux
cair.kaist.ac.kr		/pub/Linux
ftp.denet.dk	129.142.6.74	/pub/OS/linux
NCTUCCCA.edu.tw	140.111.1.10	/Operating-Systems/Linux
nic.switch.ch	130.59.1.40	/mirror/linux
sunsite.cnlab-switch.ch	193.5.24.1	/mirror/linux
cnuce_arch.cnr.it	131.114.1.10	/pub/Linux
ftp.monash.edu.au	130.194.11.8	/pub/linux
ftp.dstc.edu.au	130.102.181.31	/pub/linux
ftp.sydutech.usyd.edu.au	129.78.192.2	/pub/linux

tsx-11.mit.edu and fgb1.fgb.mw.tu-muenchen.de are the official sites for Linux's GCC. Some sites mirror other sites. Please use the site closest (network-wise) to you whenever possible.

At least sunsite.unc.edu and ftp.informatik.tu-muenchen.de offer ftpmail services. Mail ftpmail@sunsite.unc.edu or ftp@informatik.tu-muenchen.de for help.

If you are lost, try looking at `(ftp://sunsite.unc.edu/pub/Linux/distributions/)`, where several distributions are offered. Red Hat Linux and Debian appear to be the most popular distributions at the moment, at least in the U.S.

CDROM

Many people now install Linux from Cd-ROMs. The distributions have grown to hundreds of MBs of Linux software, and downloading that over even a 28.8 modem takes a *long* time.

There are essentially two ways to purchase a Linux distribution on CDROM: as part of an archive of FTP sites, or directly from the manufacturer. If you purchase an archive, you will almost always get several different distributions to choose from, but usually support is not included. When you purchase a distribution directly from the vendor, you usually only get one distribution, but you usually get some form of support, usually installation support.

Other methods of obtaining Linux

There are many BBS's that have Linux files. A list of them is occasionally posted to comp.os.linux.announce. Ask friends and user groups, or order one of the commercial distributions. A list of these is contained in the Linux distribution HOWTO, available as `(ftp://sunsite.unc.edu/pub/Linux/docs/HOWTO/distribution-HOWTO)`, and posted regularly to the `(news:comp.os.linux.announce)` newsgroup.

Getting started

As mentioned at the beginning, Linux is not centrally administered. Because of this, there is no "official" release that one could point at, and say "That's Linux." Instead, there are various "distributions," which are more or less complete collections of software configured and packaged so that they can be used to install a Linux system.

The first thing you should do is to get and read the list of Frequently Asked Questions (FAQ) from one of the FTP sites, or by using the normal Usenet FAQ archives (e.g. rtfm.mit.edu). This document has plenty of instructions on what to do to get started, what files you need, and how to solve most of the common problems (during installation or otherwise).

Legal Status of Linux

Although Linux is supplied with the complete source code, it is copyrighted software, not public domain. However, it is available for free under the GNU General Public License, sometimes referred to as the "copyleft". See the GPL for more information. The programs that run under Linux each have their own copyright, although many of them use the GPL as well. X uses the MIT X copyright, and some utilities are under the BSD copyright. In any case, all of the software on the FTP site is freely distributable (or else it shouldn't be there).

News About Linux

A monthly magazine, called *Linux Journal*, was launched over three years ago. It includes articles intended for almost all skill levels, and is intended to be helpful to all Linux users. One-year subscriptions are $22 in the U.S., $27 in Canada and Mexico, and $32 elsewhere, payable in US currency. Subscription inquiries can be sent via email to subs@ssc.com, or faxed to +1-206-782-7191, or phoned to +1-206-782-7733, or mailed to Linux Journal, PO Box 85867, Seattle, WA 98145-1867 USA. SSC has a PGP public key available for encrypting your mail to protect your credit card number; finger info@ssc.com to get the key.

There are several Usenet newsgroups for Linux discussion, and also several mailing lists. See the Linux FAQ for more information about the mailing lists (you should be able to find the FAQ either in the newsgroup or on the FTP sites).

The newsgroup `(news:comp.os.linux.announce)` is a moderated newsgroup for announcements about Linux (new programs, bug fixes, etc).

The newsgroup `(news:comp.os.linux.answers)` is a moderated newsgroup to which the Linux FAQ, HOWTO documents, and other documentation postings are made.

The newsgroup `(news:comp.os.linux.admin)` is an unmoderated newsgroup for discussion of administration of Linux systems.

The newsgroup `(news:comp.os.linux.development.system)` is an unmoderated newsgroup specifically for discussion of Linux *kernel* development. The only application development questions that should be discussed here are those that are intimately associated with the kernel. All other development questions are probably generic Unix development questions and should be directed to a comp.unix group instead, unless they are very Linux-specific applications questions, in which case they should be directed at comp.os.linux.development.apps.

The newsgroup `(news:comp.os.linux.development.apps)` is an unmoderated newsgroup specifically for discussion of Linux-related applications development. It is not for discussion of where to get applications for Linux, nor a discussion forum for those who would like to see applications for Linux.

The newsgroup `(news:comp.os.linux.hardware)` is for Linux-specific hardware questions.

The newsgroup `(news:comp.os.linux.networking)` is for Linux-specific networking development and setup questions.

The newsgroup `(news:comp.os.linux.x)` is for Linux-specific X Windows questions.

The newsgroup `(news:comp.os.linux.misc)` is the replacement for comp.os.linux, and is meant for any discussion that doesn't belong elsewhere.

In general, *do not* cross post between the Linux newsgroups. The *only* cross posting that is appropriate is an occasional posting between one unmoderated group and `(news:comp.os.linux.announce)`. The whole point of splitting the old comp.os.linux group into many groups is to reduce traffic in each group. Those that do not follow this rule will be flamed without mercy...

Linux is on the web at the URL `(http://sunsite.unc.edu/LDP/)`

The Future

After Linux 1.0 was released, work was done on several enhancements. Linux 1.2 included disk access speedups, TTY improvements, virtual memory enhancements, multiple platform support, quotas, and more. Linux 2.0, the current stable version, has even more enhancements, including many performance improvements, several new networking protocols, one of the fastest TCP/IP implementations in the world, and far more. Even higher performance, more networking protocols, and more device drivers will be available in Linux 2.2.

Even with over 3/4 million lines of code in the kernel, there is plenty of code left to write, and even more documentation. Please join the linux-doc@vger.rutgers.edu mailing list if you would like to contribute to the documentation. Send mail to majordomo@vger.rutgers.edu with a single line containing the word "help" in the body (*not* the subject) of the message.

This document

This document is maintained by Michael K. Johnson <johnsonm@redhat.com>. Please mail me with any comments, no matter how small. I can't do a good job of maintaining this document without your help. A more-or-less current copy of this document can always be found at `(http://sunsite.unc.edu/LDP/)`

Legalese

The Linux *Meta*-FAQ

Michael K. Johnson

v4.7, 25 October 1997

Abstract

This is the Meta-FAQ for Linux. It is mainly a list of valuable sources of information. Check these sources out if you want to learn more about Linux, or have problems and need help.

Introduction

What is Linux?

Linux is an independent implementation of the POSIX operating system specification, with SYSV and BSD extensions, that has been written entirely from scratch (this means it looks and acts just like Unix). It has no proprietary code in it. Linux is freely distributable under the GNU General Public License.

Linux works on IBM PC compatibles with an ISA or EISA bus (including local bus variants VLB and PCI) and a 386 or higher processor. Some Amiga and Atari computers with MMU's are also supported. This means 68020 with an external MMU, 68030, 68040, or 68060. Support for the Digital Alpha is now stable. Red Hat and Craftworks have Alpha distributions of Linux. Support for Sparc is stable, and Red Hat Linux is available for Sparc. Support for PowerPC is in development for multiple platforms, including Nubus and PCI Macintosh, Motorola Powerstack, IBM 830 and 850, and other platforms. Support for ARM, StrongARM, and MIPS is in various stages of completion, but don't hold your breath. Read comp.os.linux.announce instead.

See the Linux INFO-SHEET for more technical information on these ports, and the Hardware Compatibility HOWTO for more exact hardware requirements.

The Linux kernel is written by Linus Torvalds <torvalds@transmeta.com> and other volunteers. Most of the programs running under Linux are generic Unix freeware, many of them from the GNU project.

The Linux INFO-SHEET

More specific technical information on Linux. Includes pointers to information on the various ports, a feature list, information about how to get Linux, and more.

The Linux HOWTO's

These are somewhat like FAQ's, but instead of answering common questions, they explain how to do common tasks, like ordering a release of Linux, setting up print services under Linux, setting up a basic UUCP feed, etc. See

```
http://sunsite.unc.edu/LDP/HOWTO/HOWTO-INDEX.html
```

or

```
ftp://sunsite.unc.edu/pub/Linux/docs/HOWTO/
```

for the definitive versions of all the HOWTO's. Other sites with up-to-date copies of the HOWTOs are ftp.cc.gatech.edu and tsx-11.mit.edu.

In addition, there are many short, free-form documents called "Mini-HOWTOs." These documents cover very specific subjects, such as BogoMIPS or Color-ls. These are available at

```
ftp://sunsite.unc.edu/pub/Linux/docs/HOWTO/mini/
```

and at

```
http://sunsite.unc.edu/LDP/HOWTO/HOWTO-INDEX.html
```

Linux newsgroups

There are several Usenet newsgroups for Linux. It is a good idea to follow at least comp.os.linux.announce if you use Linux. comp.os.linux.announce is moderated by Lars Wirzenius. To make submissions to the newsgroup, send mail to linux-announce@news.ornl.gov. You may direct questions about comp.os.linux.announce to Lars Wirzenius, wirzeniu@iki.fi.

The newsgroup comp.os.linux.announce is a moderated newsgroup for announcements about Linux (new programs, bug fixes, etc).

The newsgroup comp.os.linux.answers is a moderated newsgroup to which the Linux FAQ, HOWTO documents, and other documentation postings are made.

The newsgroup comp.os.linux.setup is an unmoderated newsgroup for discussion of issues and problems involved in setting up Linux systems.

The newsgroup comp.os.linux.admin is an unmoderated newsgroup for discussion of administration of Linux systems.

The newsgroup comp.os.linux.development.system is an unmoderated newsgroup specifically for discussion of Linux *kernel* development. The only application development questions that should be discussed here are those that are intimately associated with the kernel. All other development questions are probably generic Unix development questions and should be directed to a comp.unix group instead, unless they are very Linux-specific applications questions, in which case they should be directed at comp.os.linux.development.apps.

The newsgroup comp.os.linux.development.apps is an unmoderated newsgroup specifically for discussion of Linux-related applications development. It is not for discussion of where to get applications for Linux, nor a discussion forum for those who would like to see applications for Linux.

The newsgroup comp.os.linux.hardware is for Linux-specific hardware questions.

The newsgroup comp.os.linux.networking is for Linux-specific networking development and setup questions.

The newsgroup comp.os.linux.x is for Linux-specific X Windows questions.

The newsgroup comp.os.linux.misc is an unmoderated newsgroup for any Linux discussion that doesn't belong anywhere else.

In general, *do not* cross post between the Linux newsgroups. The *only* cross posting that is appropriate is an occasional posting between one unmoderated group and comp.os.linux.announce. The whole point of splitting the old comp.os.linux group into many groups was to reduce traffic in each. Those that do not follow this rule will be flamed without mercy...

Other newsgroups

Do not assume that all your questions are appropriate for a Linux newsgroup just because you are running Linux. Is your question really about shell programming under any Unix or Unix clone? Then ask in comp.unix.shell. Is it about GNU Emacs? Then try asking in gnu.emacs.help. Also, if you don't know another group to ask in, but think there might be, politely ask in your post if there is another group that would be more appropriate for your question. At least the groups comp.unix.{questions,shell,programming,bsd,admin} and comp.windows.x.i386unix should be useful for a Linux user.

The World-Wide Web

Greg Hankins, (gregh@cc.gatech.edu), maintains the home WWW page for the Linux project. The URL is (`http://sunsite.unc.edu/LDP/`)

The Linux Software Map

Information on free software available for Linux can be found in the Linux Software Map, which can be found at http://www.execpc.com/ lsm/.

Getting Linux

Linux FTP sites

A more complete list of Linux FTP sites is in the Linux INFO-SHEET, which can always be found at

```
http://sunsite.unc.edu/LDP/HOWTO/INFO-SHEET.html
```

The most important sites are listed here; please see the INFO-SHEET for a site nearer to you (there are many mirrors).

```
textual name             numeric addr    Linux directory
=======================  ==============  ===============
tsx-11.mit.edu           18.86.0.44      /pub/linux
sunsite.unc.edu          152.2.22.81     /pub/Linux
ftp.kernel.org           206.184.214.34  /pub/linux
```

These sites are the main "home" sites for Linux where most uploads take place. There are many mirror sites; please use the closest (network-wise) site to you.

Linux on physical media

Linux is distributed on physical media, mainly CD-ROM, by several commercial vendors. Please read the distribution HOWTO, posted regularly to comp.os.linux.announce, and available at

```
http://sunsite.unc.edu/LDP/HOWTO/Distribution-HOWTO.html
```

AFS

Linux is available over AFS by mounting the volume project.linux from sipb.mit.edu

Commercial networks

Compuserve has some Linux archives.

Mailservers and such

Sunsite offers ftp-mail service—mail ftpmail@sunsite.unc.edu.

Linux distributions

Linux is distributed by its author only as a kernel. Other people have put together "distributions" that pair the Linux kernel with utilities and application software to make a complete working package.

There are several distributions of Linux, which are available at various sites. Sunsite mirrors many of the distributions at

```
ftp://sunsite.unc.edu/pub/Linux/distributions/
```

The most commonly recommended, freely-available distributions are Red Hat (http://www.redhat.com), Slackware (ftp://ftp.cdrom.com), and Debian (http://www.debian.org).

These are available for free over the Internet, and are also sold on CD-ROM.

There are other distributions of Linux as well. Most commercial distributors of Linux advertise in *Linux Journal*.

Linux mailing-lists

Used mostly for discussion between developers of new features and testers of pre-release versions. See addresses in the FAQ. Send mail to majordomo@vger.rutgers.edu with the single word `help` in the body of the message , and you will get mail explaining how to subscribe to the many Linux mailing lists there. Save this mail, as it tells you how to unsubscribe from the lists, and if you post annoying messages to the list complaining about not being able to get off the list (because you didn't follow instructions and save the mail telling you how to unsubscribe), you will likely be flamed for wasting international bandwidth and money.

Documentation for various programs

Many programs come with some sort of documentation, often in a file called README or something similar. It is a *very* good idea to read them with care. It is boring to see (and answer) questions that are answered in the documentation. Most programs also have "man pages"; use the command `man programname` to get documentation on a program named `programname`. To get help using the man program, use `man man`.

Most distributions put other documentation about programs in the directory `/usr/doc/`; your distribution should include documentation on how to access that documentation.

More Documentation

The Linux Documentation Project is working on a lot of documentation. Already, over 3000 pages of book-style documentation has been released to the general public, and another 2000 or so printed pages of man pages have also been released, with more to follow. Check

```
http://sunsite.unc.edu/LDP/
```

for documents written by the LDP.

Keeping track of current releases

Important new releases, programs, and ports are usually announced in comp.os.linux.announce.

This Document

The latest version of this document should always be available from

```
http://sunsite.unc.edu/LDP/HOWTO/META-FAQ.html
```

Legalese

Lars Wirzenius, wirzeniu@iki.fi, wrote the first version of this document; it is now maintained by Michael K. Johnson, johnsonm@redhat.com. Mail me if you have any questions about this document.

Documentation Conventions

We have attempted to use the following documentation conventions in this guide:

Bold — Used to mark **new concepts**, **WARNINGS**, and **keywords** in a language.

italics — Used for *emphasis* in text, and occasionally for quotes or introductions at the beginnings of sections.

⟨*slanted*⟩ — Used to mark **meta-variables** in the text, especially in command lines. For example, in

`ls -l` ⟨*foo*⟩

⟨*foo*⟩ represents a file name, such as `/bin/cp`.

`Typewriter` — Used to represent screen interaction, as in

```
$ ls -l /bin/cp
-rwxr-xr-x  1 root    wheel    12104 Sep 25 15:53 /bin/cp
```

Also used for code examples, whether C code, shell scripts, or to display files like configuration files. When necessary for the sake of clarity, these examples or figures are enclosed in thin boxes.

[Key] — Represents a key to press, such as in this example

Press [Return] to continue.

◇ — A diamond in the margin, like a black diamond on a ski hill, marks "danger" or "caution". Carefully read the paragraphs so marked.

Contents

Part I

Linux Installation and Getting Started Guide 3.1
by Matt Welsh

Contents

Preface

Linux Installation and Getting Started (LIGS) has been the shepherding work for countless new users of the Linux operating system. Linux continues to evolve and so, too, must this guide.

Matt Welsh, the original author, has turned the book over to the care and management of Specialized Systems Consultants, Inc. (SSC), publishers of *Linux Journal*, computer books, and references. *Linux Installation and Getting Started* is still covered by the GNU General Public License—it is still freely redistributable, like the operating system it describes. This new version becomes a collaborative effort of individuals separated by geography but brought together on the Internet, much like Linux itself. If you believe you could expand or update a section of *Linux Installation and Getting Started* or have something new and wonderful to add, please send e-mail to `ligs@ssc.com` and tell us how you'd like to contribute.

For this edition, we've added distribution-specific instructions for obtaining and installing S.u.S.E. Linux, Debian GNU/Linux, Linux Slackware, Caldera OpenLinux, and Red Hat Linux. Please read through the acknowledgements, and if you should meet someone named there on line or in person, thank them for the help.

Specialized Systems Consultants, Inc. (SSC)
August, 1997

Preface to the previous edition.

"You are in a maze of twisty little passages, all alike."

Before you looms one of the most complex and utterly intimidating systems ever written. Linux, the free UNIX clone for the personal computer, produced by a mish mash team of UNIX gurus, hackers, and the occasional loon. The system itself reflects this complex heritage, and although the development of Linux may appear to be a disorganized volunteer effort, the system is powerful, fast, and free. It is a true 32-bit operating system solution.

My own experiences with Linux began several years ago when I sat down to figure out how to install the only "distribution" available at the time—a couple of diskettes made available by H. J. Lu. I downloaded a slew of files and read page upon page of loosely-organized installation notes. Somehow, I managed to install this basic system and get everything to work together. This was long before you could buy the Linux software on CD-ROM from worldwide distributors; before, in fact, Linux was able to access a CD-ROM drive. This was before XFree86, before Emacs, before commercial software support, and before Linux became a true rival to MS-DOS, Microsoft Windows, and OS/2 in the personal computer market.

You hold in your hands a map and guidebook to the world of Linux. It is my hope that this book will help you get rolling with what I consider to be the fastest, most powerful operating system for the personal computer. Setting up your own Linux system can be great fun—so grab a cup of coffee, sit back, and read on.

Matt Welsh
January 1994

Hints for UNIX novices.

Getting started with your own Linux system does not require a great deal of UNIX background. Many UNIX novices have successfully installed Linux on their systems. This is a worthwhile learning experience, but keep in mind that it can be frustrating. Moreover, once you are ready to delve into the more complex tasks of running Linux—installing new software, recompiling the kernel, and so forth—having background knowledge in UNIX is necessary.

However, simply by running your own Linux system you will learn the essentials of UNIX. This book helps you get started—Chapter 3 is a tutorial covering UNIX basics. Chapter 4 has information on Linux system administration. You may wish to read these chapters before attempting to install Linux at all—the information will prove to be invaluable should you run into problems.

Nobody can expect to go from UNIX novice to UNIX system administrator overnight. No implementation of UNIX is expected to be maintenance free. You must be prepared for the journey that lies ahead. Otherwise, if you're new to UNIX, you may very well become frustrated with the system.

Hints for UNIX gurus.

Someone with years of experience in UNIX programming and system administration may still need assistance before he or she is able to pick up and install Linux. UNIX wizards must be familiar with certain aspects of the system before they dive in. Linux is neither a commercial UNIX system, nor attempts to uphold the same standards. While stability is an important factor in Linux development, it is not the only factor.

Perhaps more important is functionality. In many cases, new code becomes part of the standard kernel while it is still buggy and not functionally complete. The Linux development model assumes that it is more important to release code for users to test and use, than delay a release until it is complete. WINE (the Microsoft Windows Emulator for Linux) had an official alpha release before it was completely tested. The Linux community at large had a chance to work with the code, and those who found the alpha code good enough for their needs could use it. Commercial UNIX vendors rarely, if ever, release software this way.

If you have been a UNIX systems administrator for more than a decade, and have used every commercial UNIX system under the Sun (pun intended), Linux may take some getting used to. The system is very modern and dynamic. A new kernel is released every few weeks. New software is constantly being released. One day, your system may be completely up-to-date, and the next day the system may be in the Stone Age.

With all of this activity, how does one keep up with the ever-changing Linux world? For the most part, it is best to upgrade only those parts of the system which need upgrading, and only when you think it is necessary. For example, if you never use Emacs, there is little reason to continuously install new releases of Emacs on your system. Furthermore, even if you are an avid Emacs user, there is usually no reason to upgrade unless you need a feature that is present only in the next release. There is little or no reason to always be on top of the newest software versions.

We hope that Linux will meet or exceed your expectations for a home brew UNIX system. At the very core of Linux is the spirit of free software, of constant development and growth. The Linux community favors expansion over stability, which is a difficult concept to swallow, especially after being steeped in the world of commercial UNIX. Expecting Linux to be perfect is unrealistic; nothing in the free software world ever is. We believe, however, that Linux is as complete and useful as any other implementation of UNIX.

Audience.

This book is for personal computer users who want to install and use Linux. We assume that you have basic knowledge about personal computers and operating systems like MS-DOS, but no previous knowledge of Linux or UNIX.

Despite this, we strongly suggest that UNIX novices invest in one of the many good UNIX books out there. You still need UNIX know-how to install and run a complete system. No distribution of Linux is completely bug-free. You may be required to fix small problems by hand. Running a UNIX system is not an easy task, even with commercial versions of UNIX. If you're serious about Linux, bear in mind that it takes considerable effort and attention to keep the system running. This is true of any UNIX system. Because of the diversity of the Linux community and the many needs which the software attempts to meet, not everything can be taken care of for you all of the time.

Organization.

This book contains the following chapters:

Chapter 1, *Introduction to Linux*, is a general introduction to Linux, its capabilities, and requirements for running it on your system. It also provides hints for getting help and reducing your stress level.

Chapter 2, *Obtaining and Installing Linux*, explains how to obtain and install Linux software, beginning with drive repartitioning, creating filesystems, and installing software packages. The chapter contains instructions that are meant to be general for any Linux distribution and relies for specifics on the documentation provided by your particular release.

Chapter 3, *Linux Tutorial*, is a complete introduction for UNIX novices. If you have previous UNIX experience, most of this material should be familiar.

Chapter 4, *System Administration*, introduces important concepts for system administration under Linux. This will be of interest to UNIX system administrators who want to know about the Linux-specific issues for running a system.

Chapter 5, *Advanced Features*, introduces a number of advanced that Linux supports, like the X Window System and TCP/IP networking. We also provide a complete guide to configuring XFree86-3.1.

Appendix A, *Sources of Linux Information*, is a list of further documentation sources like newsgroups, mailing lists, on-line documents, and books.

Appendix C, *FTP Tutorial and Site List*, is a tutorial for downloading files from the Internet with FTP. This appendix also lists FTP archive sites that carry Linux software.

Appendix D, *The GNU General Public License*, is the license agreement under which Linux is distributed. It is important that Linux users understand the GPL. Many disagreements over the terms in describes have been raised.

Acknowledgments.

This edition builds on the work of those who have gone before, and they are thanked below in Matt Welsh's original acknowledgement. Additionally, we owe thanks to Larry Ayers, Boris Beletsky, Sean Dreilinger, Evan Leibovitch, and Henry Pierce for contributing the information in Chapter 2 on S.u.S.E. Linux, Debian GNU/Linux, Linux Slackware, Caldera OpenLinux, and Red Hat Linux, respectively. David Bandel updated Chapter 2 and added a section describing a generic Linux installation. Vernard Martin updated and added to Chapter 5. Thanks are also due to Belinda Frazier for editing and to Jay Painter for the update to Chapter 4 on systems administration.

Acknowledgments from the previous edition.

This book has been long in the making, and many people have contributed to the outcome. In particular, I would like to thank Larry Greenfield and Karl Fogel for their work on the first version of Chapter 3, and to Lars Wirzenius for his work on Chapter 4. Thanks to Michael K. Johnson for his assistance with the LDP and the LaTeX conventions used in this manual, and to Ed Chi, who sent me a printed copy of the book.

Thanks to Melinda A. McBride at SSC, Inc., who did an excellent job of completing the index for Chapters 3, 4, and 5. I would also like to thank Andy Oram, Lar Kaufman, and Bill Hahn at O'Reilly and Associates for their assistance with the Linux Documentation Project.

Thanks to Linux Systems Labs, Morse Telecommunications, and Yggdrasil Computing for their support of the Linux Documentation Project through sales of this book and other works.

Much thanks to the many Linux activists, including (in no particular order) Linus Torvalds, Donald Becker, Alan Cox, Remy Card, Ted T'so, H. J. Lu, Ross Biro, Drew Eckhardt, Ed Carp, Eric Youngdale, Fred van Kempen, and Steven Tweedie, for devoting so much time and energy to this project, and without whom there wouldn't be anything to write a book about.

Finally, special thanks to the myriad of readers who have sent their helpful comments and corrections; they are far too many to list here.

Credits and legalese.

The Linux Documentation Project consists of a loose team of writers, proofreaders, and editors who are working on a set of definitive Linux manuals.

This manual is one of several which are distributed by the Linux Documentation Project. Other manuals include the *Linux User's Guide, System Administrator's Guide, Network Administrator's Guide,* and *Kernel Hacker's Guide.* These manuals are all available in LaTeX source and PostScript output format for anonymous FTP access at `sunsite.unc.edu`, in the directory `/pub/Linux/docs/LDP`.

CHAPTER 1

Introduction to Linux

Linux is quite possibly the most important free software achievement since the original Space War, or, more recently, Emacs. It has developed into an operating system for business, education, and personal productivity. Linux is no longer only for UNIX wizards who sit for hours in front of a glowing console (although we assure you that many users fall into this category). This book will help you get the most from Linux.

Linux (pronounced with a short *i*, as in *LIH-nucks*) is a UNIX operating system clone which runs on a variety of platforms, especially personal computers with Intel 80386 or better processors. It supports a wide range of software, from TEX, to the X Window System, to the GNU C/C++ compiler, to TCP/IP. It's a versatile, bona fide implementation of UNIX, freely distributed under the terms of the GNU General Public License (see Appendix D).

Linux can turn any 80386 (or better) personal computer into a workstation that puts the full power of UNIX at your fingertips. Businesses install Linux on entire networks of machines, and use the operating system to manage financial and hospital records, distributed computing environments, and telecommunications. Universities worldwide use Linux to teach courses on operating system programming and design. Computing enthusiasts everywhere use Linux at home for programming, productivity, and all-around hacking.

What makes Linux so different is that it is a free implementation of UNIX. It was and still is developed cooperatively by a group of volunteers, primarily on the Internet, who exchange code, report bugs, and fix problems in an open-ended environment. Anyone is welcome to join the Linux development effort. All it takes is interest in hacking a free UNIX clone, and some programming know-how. The book in your hands is your tour guide.

About this book.

This book is an installation and entry-level guide to Linux. The purpose is to get new users up and running by consolidating as much important material as possible into one book. Instead of covering volatile technical details which tend to change with rapid development, we give you the straight background to find out more on your own.

Linux is not difficult to install and use. However, as with any implementation of UNIX, there is often black magic involved to get everything working correctly. We hope that this book will get you on the Linux tour bus and show you how great an operating system can be.

In this book, we cover the following topics:

- What is Linux? The design and philosophy of this unique operating system, and what it can do for you.
- Details of running Linux, including suggestions on recommended hardware configuration.
- Specific instructions to install various Linux distributions, including Debian, Red Hat Software, and Slackware.

- A brief, introductory UNIX tutorial for users with no previous UNIX experience. This tutorial should provide enough material for novices to find their way around the system.
- An introduction to system administration under Linux. This covers the most important tasks that Linux administrators need to perform, like creating user accounts and managing file systems.
- Information on configuring more advanced features of Linux, like the X Window System, TCP/IP networking, and electronic mail and news.

This book is for the personal computer user who wishes to get started with Linux. We don't assume previous UNIX experience but do expect novices to refer to other material along the way. For those unfamiliar with UNIX, a list of useful references is given in Appendix A. In general, this book is meant to be read in addition to another book on basic UNIX concepts.

A brief history of Linux.

UNIX is one of the most popular operating systems worldwide because of its large support base and distribution. It was originally developed as a multitasking system for minicomputers and mainframes in the mid-1970's, but has since grown to become one of the most widely-used operating systems anywhere, despite its sometimes confusing interface and lack of central standardization.

Many hackers feel that UNIX is the Right Thing—the One True Operating System. Hence, the development of Linux by an expanding group of UNIX hackers who want to get their hands dirty with their own system.

Versions of UNIX exist for many systems, from personal computers to supercomputers like the Cray Y-MP. Most versions of UNIX for personal computers are expensive and cumbersome. At the time of this writing, a one-machine version of AT&T's System V for the 386 runs about US$1500.

Linux is a free version of UNIX developed primarily by Linus Torvalds at the University of Helsinki in Finland, with the help of many UNIX programmers and wizards across the Internet. Anyone with enough know-how and gumption can develop and change the system. The Linux kernel uses no code from AT&T or any other proprietary source, and much of the software available for Linux was developed by the GNU project of the Free Software Foundation in Cambridge, Massachusetts, U.S.A. However, programmers from all over the world have contributed to the growing pool of Linux software.

Linux was originally developed as a hobby project by Linus Torvalds. It was inspired by Minix, a small UNIX system developed by Andy Tanenbaum. The first discussions about Linux were on the Usenet newsgroup, `comp.os.minix`. These discussions were concerned mostly with the development of a small, academic UNIX system for Minix users who wanted more.

The very early development of Linux mostly dealt with the task-switching features of the 80386 protected-mode interface, all written in assembly code. Linus writes,

> "After that it was plain sailing: hairy coding still, but I had some devices, and debugging was easier. I started using C at this stage, and it certainly speeds up development. This is also when I started to get serious about my megalomaniac ideas to make 'a better Minix than Minix.' I was hoping I'd be able to recompile `gcc` under Linux someday...
>
> "Two months for basic setup, but then only slightly longer until I had a disk driver (seriously buggy, but it happened to work on my machine) and a small file system. That was about when I made 0.01 available (around late August of 1991): it wasn't pretty, it had no floppy driver, and it couldn't do much of anything. I don't think anybody ever compiled that version. But by then I was hooked, and didn't want to stop until I could chuck out Minix."

No announcement was ever made for Linux version 0.01. The 0.01 sources weren't even executable. They contained only the bare rudiments of the kernel source and assumed that you had access to a Minix machine to compile and experiment with them.

On October 5, 1991, Linus announced the first "official" version of Linux, which was version 0.02. At that point, Linus was able to run `bash` (the GNU Bourne Again Shell) and `gcc` (the GNU C compiler), but not much else. Again, this was intended as a hacker's system. The primary focus was kernel development—user support, documentation, and distribution had not yet been addressed. Today, the Linux community still seems to treat these issues as secondary to "real programming"—kernel development.

As Linus wrote in `comp.os.minix`,

> "Do you pine for the nice days of Minix-1.1, when men were men and wrote their own device drivers? Are you without a nice project and just dying to cut your teeth on an OS you can try to modify for your needs? Are you finding it frustrating when everything works on Minix? No more all-nighters to get a nifty program working? Then this post might be just for you.
>
> "As I mentioned a month ago, I'm working on a free version of a Minix look alike for AT-386 computers. It has finally reached the stage where it's even usable (though may not be, depending on what you want), and I am willing to put out the sources for wider distribution. It is just version 0.02... but I've successfully run `bash`, `gcc`, `gnu-make`, `gnu-sed`, `compress`, etc. under it."

After version 0.03, Linus bumped up the version number to 0.10, as more people started to work on the system. After several further revisions, Linus increased the version number to 0.95 in March, 1992, to reflect his expectation that the system was ready for an "official" release soon. (Generally, software is not assigned the version number 1.0 until it is theoretically complete or bug-free.). Almost a year and a half later, in late December of 1993, the Linux kernel was still at version 0.99.pl14—asymptotically approaching 1.0. At the time of this writing, the current stable kernel version is 2.0 patch level 31, and version 2.1 is under development.

Most of the major, free UNIX software packages have been ported to Linux, and commercial software is becoming available. More hardware is supported than in the original kernel versions. Many people have executed benchmarks on 80486 Linux systems and found them comparable with mid-range workstations from Sun Microsystems and Digital Equipment Corporation. Who would have ever guessed that this "little" UNIX clone would have grown up to take on the entire world of personal computing?

System features.

Linux supports features found in other implementations of UNIX, and many which aren't found elsewhere. In this section, we'll take a nickel tour of the features of the Linux kernel.

Linux is a complete multitasking, multiuser operating system, as are all other versions of UNIX. This means that many users can log into and run programs on the same machine simultaneously.

The Linux system is mostly compatible with several UNIX standards (inasmuch as UNIX has standards) at the source level, including IEEE POSIX.1, System V Unix from AT&T, and Berkeley System Distribution Unix. Linux was developed with source code portability in mind, and it's easy to find commonly used features that are shared by more than one platform. Much of the free UNIX software available on the Internet and elsewhere compiles under Linux "right out of the box." In addition, all of the source code for the Linux system, including the kernel, device drivers, libraries, user programs, and development tools, is freely distributable.

Other specific internal features of Linux include POSIX job control (used by shells like `csh` and `bash`), pseudo terminals (`pty` devices), and support for dynamically loadable national or customized keyboard drivers. Linux supports **virtual consoles** that let you switch between login sessions on the same system console. Users of the `screen` program will find the Linux virtual console implementation familiar.

The kernel can emulate 387-FPU instructions, and systems without a math coprocessor can run programs that require floating-point math capability.

Linux supports various file systems for storing data, like the ext2fs file system, which was developed specifically for Linux. The System V Unix and Xenix file systems are also supported, as well as the Microsoft MS-DOS and Windows 95 VFAT file systems on a hard drive or floppy. The ISO 9660 CD-ROM file system is also supported. We'll talk more about file systems in chapters 2 and 4.

Linux provides a complete implementation of TCP/IP networking software. This includes device drivers for many popular Ethernet cards, SLIP (Serial Line Internet Protocol) and PPP (Point-to-Point Protocol), which provide access to a TCP/IP network via a serial connection, PLIP (Parallel Line Internet Protocol), and

NFS (Network File System). The complete range of TCP/IP clients and services is also supported, which includes FTP, `telnet`, NNTP, and SMTP. We'll talk more about networking in Chapter 5.

The Linux kernel is developed to use protected-mode features of Intel 80386 and better processors. In particular, Linux uses the protected-mode, descriptor based, memory-management paradigm, and other advanced features. Anyone familiar with 80386 protected-mode programming knows that this chip was designed for multitasking systems like UNIX (or, actually, Multics). Linux exploits this functionality.

The kernel supports demand-paged, loaded executables. Only those segments of a program which are actually in use are read into memory from disk. Also, copy-on-write pages are shared among executables. If several instances of a program are running at once, they share physical memory, which reduces overall usage.

In order to increase the amount of available memory, Linux also implements disk paging. Up to 128 megabytes of **swap space**[1] may be allocated on disk. When the system requires more physical memory, it swaps inactive pages to disk, letting you run larger applications and support more users. However, swapping data to disk is no substitute for physical RAM, which is much faster.

The Linux kernel also implements a unified memory pool for user programs and disk cache. All free memory is used by the cache, which is reduced when running large programs.

Executables use dynamically linked, shared libraries: code from a single library on disk. This is not unlike the SunOS shared library mechanism. Executable files occupy less disk space, especially those which use many library functions. There are also statically linked libraries for object debugging and maintaining "complete" binary files when shared libraries are not installed. The libraries are dynamically linked at run time, and the programmer can use his or her own routines in place of the standard library routines.

To facilitate debugging, the kernel generates core dumps for post-mortem analysis. A core dump and an executable linked with debugging support allows a developer to determine what caused a program to crash.

Software features.

Virtually every utility one would expect of a standard UNIX implementation has been ported to Linux, including basic commands like `ls`, `awk`, `tr`, `sed`, `bc`, and `more`. The familiar working environment of other UNIX systems is duplicated on Linux. All standard commands and utilities are included. (Novice UNIX or Linux users should see Chapter 3 for an introduction to basic UNIX commands.)

Many text editors are available, including `vi`, `ex`, `pico`, `jove`, and GNU `emacs`, and variants like Lucid `emacs`, which incorporates extensions of the X Window System, and `joe`. The text editor you're accustomed to using has more than likely been ported to Linux.

The choice of a text editor is an interesting one. Many UNIX users prefer "simple" editors like `vi`. (The original author wrote this book with `vi`.) But `vi` has many limitations due to its age, and modern editors like `emacs` have gained popularity. `emacs` supports a complete, Lisp based macro language and interpreter, powerful command syntax, and other extensions. There are `emacs` macro packages which let you read electronic mail and news, edit directory contents, and even engage in artificially intelligent psychotherapy sessions (indispensable for stressed-out Linux hackers).

Most of the basic Linux utilities are GNU software. GNU utilities support advanced features that are not found in the standard versions of BSD and AT&T UNIX programs. For example, the GNU `vi` clone, `elvis`, includes a structured macro language that differs from the original AT&T implementation. However, GNU utilities are intended to remain compatible with their BSD and System V counterparts. Many people consider the GNU versions to be superior to the originals.

A **shell** is a program which reads and executes commands from the user. In addition, many shells provide features like **job control,** managing several processes at once, input and output redirection, and a command language for writing **shell scripts**. A shell script is a program in the shell's command language and is analogous to a MS-DOS batch file.

Many types of shells are available for Linux. The most important difference between shells is the command language. For example, the C Shell (`csh`) uses a command language similar to the C programming language. The classic Bourne Shell `sh` uses another command language. The choice of a shell is often

[1] Swap space is inappropriately named; entire processes are not swapped, but rather individual pages. Of course, in many cases, entire processes will be swapped out, but this is not always true.

based on the command language it provides, and determines, to a large extent, the qualities of your working environment under Linux.

The GNU Bourne Again Shell (`bash`) is a variation of the Bourne Shell which includes many advanced features like job control, command history, command and filename completion, an `emacs`-like interface for editing command lines, and other powerful extensions to the standard Bourne Shell language. Another popular shell is `tcsh`, a version of the C Shell with advanced functionality similar to that found in `bash`. Other shells include `zsh`, a small Bourne-like shell; the Korn Shell (`ksh`); BSD's `ash`; and `rc`, the Plan 9 shell.

If you're the only person using the system and prefer to use `vi` and `bash` exclusively as your editor and shell, there's no reason to install other editors or shells. This "do it yourself" attitude is prevalent among Linux hackers and users.

Text processing and word processing.

Almost every computer user needs a method of preparing documents. In the world of personal computers, **word processing** is the norm: editing and manipulating text in a "What-You-See-Is-What-You-Get" (WYSIWYG) environment and producing printed copies of the text, complete with graphics, tables, and ornamentation.

Commercial word processors from Corel, Applix, and Star Division are available in the UNIX world, but **text processing,** which is quite different conceptually, is more common. In text processing systems, text is entered in a **page-description language,** which describes how the text should be formatted. Rather than enter text within a special word processing environment, you can modify text with any editor, like `vi` or `emacs`. Once you finish entering the source text (in the typesetting language), a separate program converts the source to a format suitable for printing. This is somewhat analogous to programming in a language like C, and "compiling" the document into printable form.

Many text processing systems are available for Linux. One is `groff`, the GNU version of the classic `troff` text formatter originally developed by Bell Labs and still used on many UNIX systems worldwide. Another modern text processing system is TeX, developed by Donald Knuth of computer science fame. Dialects of TeX, like LaTeX, are also available.

Text processors like TeX and `groff` differ mostly in the syntax of their formatting languages. The choice of one formatting system over another is based upon what utilities are available to satisfy your needs, as well as personal taste.

Many people consider `groff`'s formatting language to be a bit obscure and use find TeX more readable. However, `groff` produces ASCII output which can be viewed on a terminal more easily, while TeX is intended primarily for output to a printing device. Various add-on programs are required to produce ASCII output from TeX formatted documents, or convert TeX input to `groff` format.

Another program is `texinfo`, an extension to TeX which is used for software documentation developed by the Free Software Foundation. `texinfo` can produce printed output, or an online-browsable hypertext "Info" document from a single source file. Info files are the main format of documentation used in GNU software like `emacs`.

Text processors are used widely in the computing community for producing papers, theses, magazine articles, and books. (This book is produced using LaTeX.) The ability to process source language as a text file opens the door to many extensions of the text processor itself. Because a source document is not stored in an obscure format that only one word processor can read, programmers can write parsers and translators for the formatting language, and thus extend the system.

What does a formatting language look like? In general, a formatted source file consists mostly of the text itself, with **control codes** to produce effects like font and margin changes, and list formatting.

Consider the following text:

> Mr. Torvalds:
>
> We are very upset with your current plans to implement *post-hypnotic suggestions* in the **Linux** terminal driver code. We feel this way for three reasons:
>
> 1. Planting subliminal messages in the terminal driver is not only immoral, it is a waste of time;

2. It has been proven that "post-hypnotic suggestions" are ineffective when used upon unsuspecting UNIX hackers;
3. We have already implemented high-voltage electric shocks, as a security measure, in the code for `login`.

We hope you will reconsider.

This text might appear in the LaTeX formatting language as the following:

```
\begin{quote}
Mr. Torvalds:

We are very upset with your current plans to implement
{\em post-hypnotic suggestions\/} in the {\bf Linux} terminal
driver code. We feel this way for three reasons:
\begin{enumerate}
\item Planting subliminal messages in the kernel driver is not only
    immoral, it is a waste of time;
\item It has been proven that ''post-hypnotic suggestions''
    are ineffective when used upon unsuspecting UNIX hackers;
\item We have already implemented high-voltage electric shocks, as
    a security measure, in the code for {\tt login}.
\end{enumerate}
We hope you will reconsider.
\end{quote}
```

The author enters the text using any text editor and generates formatted output by processing the source with LaTeX. At first glance, the typesetting language may appear to be obscure, but it's actually quite easy to understand. Using a text processing system enforces typographical standards when writing. All the enumerated lists within a document will look the same, unless the author modifies the definition of an enumerated list. The goal is to allow the author to concentrate on the text, not typesetting conventions.

When writing with a text editor, one generally does not think about how the printed text will appear. The writer learns to visualize the finished text's appearance from the formatting commands in the source.

WYSIWYG word processors are attractive for many reasons. They provide an easy-to-use visual interface for editing documents. But this interface is limited to aspects of text layout which are accessible to the user. For example, many word processors still provide a special format language for producing complicated expressions like mathematical formulae. This is text processing, albeit on a much smaller scale.

A not-so-subtle benefit of text processing is that you specify exactly which format you need. In many cases, the text processing system requires a format specification. Text processing systems also allow source text to be edited with any text editor, instead of relying on format codes which are hidden beneath a word processor's opaque user interface. Further, the source text is easily converted to other formats. The tradeoff for this flexibility and power is the lack of WYSIWYG formatting.

Some programs let you preview the formatted document on a graphics display device before printing. The `xdvi` program displays a "device independent" file generated by the TeX system under X. Applications like `xfig` and `gimp` provide WYSIWYG graphics interfaces for drawing figures and diagrams, which are subsequently converted to text processing language for inclusion in your document.

Text processors like `troff` were around long before WYSIWYG word processing was available. Many people still prefer their versatility and independence from a graphics environment.

Many text-processing-related utilities are available. The powerful METAFONT system, which is used to design fonts for TeX, is included in the Linux port of TeX. Other programs include `ispell`, an interactive spelling checker and corrector; `makeindex`, which generates indices in LaTeX documents; and many other `groff` and TeXbased macro packages which format many types of technical and mathematical texts. Conversion programs that translate between TeX or `groff` source to a myriad of other formats are also available.

A newcomer to text formatting is YODL, written by Karel Kubat. YODL is an easy-to-learn language with filters to produce various output formats, like LaTeX, SGML, and HTML.

Programming languages and utilities.

Linux provides a complete UNIX programming environment which includes all of the standard libraries, programming tools, compilers, and debuggers which you would expect of other UNIX systems.

Standards like POSIX.1 are supported, which allows software written for Linux to be easily ported to other systems. Professional UNIX programmers and system administrators use Linux to develop software at home, then transfer the software to UNIX systems at work. This not only saves a great deal of time and money, but also lets you work in the comfort of your own home. (One of the authors uses his system to develop and test X Window System applications at home, which can be directly compiled on workstations elsewhere.) Computer Science students learn UNIX programming and explore other aspects of the system, like kernel architecture.

With Linux, you have access to the complete set of libraries and programming utilities and the complete kernel and library source code.

Within the UNIX software world, systems and applications are often programmed in C or C++. The standard C and C++ compiler for Linux is GNU `gcc`, which is an advanced, modern compiler that supports C++, including AT&T 3.0 features, as well as Objective-C, another object-oriented dialect of C.

Besides C and C++, other compiled and interpreted programming languages have been ported to Linux, like Smalltalk, FORTRAN, Java, Pascal, LISP, Scheme, and Ada (if you're masochistic enough to program in Ada, we aren't going to stop you). In addition, various assemblers for writing protected-mode 80386 code are available, as are UNIX hacking favorites like Perl (the script language to end all script languages) and Tcl/Tk (a shell-like command processing system which has support for developing simple X Window System applications).

The advanced `gdb` debugger can step through a program one line of source code at a time, or examine a core dump to find the cause of a crash. The `gprof` profiling utility provides performance statistics for your program, telling you where your program spends most of its execution time. As mentioned above, the `emacs` text editor provides interactive editing and compilation environments for various programming languages. Other tools include GNU `make` and `imake`, which manage compilation of large applications, and RCS, a system for source code locking and revision control.

Finally, Linux supports dynamically linked, shared libraries (DLLs), which result in much smaller binaries. The common subroutine code is linked at run-time. These DLLs let you override function definitions with your own code. For example, if you wish to write your own version of the `malloc()` library routine, the linker will use your new routine instead of the one in the libraries.

The X Window System.

The X Window System, or simply X, is a standard graphical user interface (GUI) for UNIX machines and is a powerful environment which supports many applications. Using the X Window System, you can have multiple terminal windows on the screen at once, each having a different login session. A pointing device like a mouse is often used with X, although it isn't required.

Many X-specific applications have been written, including games, graphics and programming utilities, and documentation tools. Linux and X make your system a bona fide workstation. With TCP/IP networking, your Linux machine can display X applications running on other machines.

The X Window System was originally developed at the Massachusetts Institute of Technology and is freely distributable. Many commercial vendors have distributed proprietary enhancements to the original X Window System as well. The version of X for Linux is XFree86, a port of X11R6 which is freely distributable. XFree86 supports a wide range of video hardware, including VGA, Super VGA, and accelerated video adaptors. XFree86 is a complete distribution of the X Windows System software, and contains the X server itself, many applications and utilities, programming libraries, and documents.

Standard X applications include `xterm`, a terminal emulator used for most text-based applications within a window, `xdm`, which handles logins, `xclock`, a simple clock display, `xman`, a X-based manual page reader, and `xmore`. The many X applications available for Linux are too numerous to mention here, but their number includes spreadsheets, word processors, graphics programs, and web browsers like the Netscape Navigator. Many other applications are available separately. Theoretically, any application written for X should compile cleanly under Linux.

The interface of the X Window System is controlled largely by the **window manager**. This user-friendly program is in charge of the placement of windows, the user interface for resizing and moving them, changing windows to icons, and the appearance of window frames, among other tasks. XFree86 includes `twm`, the classic MIT window manager, and advanced window managers like the Open Look Virtual Window Manager (`olvwm`) are available. Popular among Linux users is `fvwm`—a small window manager that requires less than half the memory of `twm`. It provides a 3-dimensional appearance for windows and a virtual desktop. The user moves the mouse to the edge of the screen, and the desktop shifts as though the display were much larger than it really is. `fvwm` is greatly customizable and allows access to functions from the keyboard as well as mouse. Many Linux distributions use `fvwm` as the standard window manager. A version of `fvwm` called `fvwm95-2` offers Microsoft Windows 95-like look and feel.

The XFree86 distribution includes programming libraries for wily programmers who wish to develop X applications. Widget sets like Athena, Open Look, and Xaw3D are supported. All of the standard fonts, bitmaps, manual pages, and documentation are included. PEX (a programming interface for 3-dimensional graphics) is also supported.

Many X application programmers use the proprietary Motif widget set for development. Several vendors sell single and multiple user licenses for binary versions of Motif. Because Motif itself is relatively expensive, not many Linux users own it. However, binaries statically linked with Motif routines can be freely distributed. If you write a program using Motif, you may provide a binary so users without the Motif libraries can use the program.

A major caveat to using the X Window System is its hardware requirements. A 80386-based CPU with 4 megabytes of RAM is capable of running X, but 16 megabytes or more of physical RAM is needed for comfortable use. A faster processor is nice to have as well, but having enough physical RAM is much more important. In addition, to achieve really slick video performance, we recommend getting an accelerated video card, like a VESA Local Bus (VLB) S3 chip set card. Performance ratings in excess of 300,000 xstones have been achieved with Linux and XFree86. Using adequate hardware, you'll find that running X and Linux is as fast, or faster, than running X on other UNIX workstations.

In Chapter 5 we discuss how to install and use X on your system.

Networking.

Would you like to communicate with the world? Linux supports two primary UNIX networking protocols: TCP/IP and UUCP. TCP/IP (Transmission Control Protocol/Internet Protocol) is the networking paradigm which allows systems all over the world to communicate on a single network, the **Internet.** With Linux, TCP/IP, and a connection to the Internet, you can communicate with users and machines via electronic mail, Usenet news, and FTP file transfer.

Most TCP/IP networks use Ethernet as the physical network transport. Linux supports many popular Ethernet cards and interfaces for personal computers, including pocket and PCMCIA Ethernet adaptors.

However, because not everyone has an Ethernet connection at home, Linux also supports **SLIP** (Serial Line Internet Protocol) and **PPP** (Point-to-Point Protocol), which provide Internet access via modem. Many businesses and universities provide SLIP and PPP servers. In fact, if your Linux system has an Ethernet connection to the Internet and a modem, your system can become a SLIP or PPP server for other hosts.

NFS (Network File System) lets your system seamlessly share file systems with other machines on the network. FTP (File Transfer Protocol) lets you transfer files with other machines. `sendmail` sends and receives electronic mail via the SMTP protocol; C-News and INN are NNTP based new systems; and `telnet`, `rlogin`, and `rsh` let you log in and execute commands on other machines on the network. `finger` lets you get information about other Internet users.

Linux also supports Microsoft Windows connectivity via Samba, and Macintosh connectivity with AppleTalk and LocalTalk. Support for Novell's IPX protocol is also included.

The full range of mail and news readers is available for Linux, including `elm`, `pine`, `rn`, `nn`, and `tin`. Whatever your preference, you can configure a Linux system to send and receive electronic mail and news from all over the world.

The system provides a standard UNIX socket programming interface. Virtually any program that uses TCP/IP can be ported to Linux. The Linux X server also supports TCP/IP, and applications running on other systems may use the display of your local system.

In Chapter 5, we discuss the installation of TCP/IP software, including SLIP and PPP.

UUCP (UNIX-to-UNIX Copy) is an older mechanism to transfer files, electronic mail, and electronic news between UNIX machines. Historically, UUCP machines are connected over telephone lines via modem, but UUCP is able to transfer data over a TCP/IP network as well. If you do not have access to a TCP/IP network or a SLIP or PPP server, you can configure your system to send and receive files and electronic mail using UUCP. See Chapter 5 for more information.

Telecommunications and BBS software.

If you have a modem, you'll be able to communicate with other machines via telecommunications packages available for Linux. Many people use telecommunications software to access bulletin board systems (BBS's) as well as commercial, online services like Prodigy, CompuServe, and America Online. People use modems to connect to UNIX systems at work or school. Modems can send and receive faxes.

A popular communications package for Linux is `seyon`, which provides a customizable, ergonomic interface under X and has built-in support for the Kermit and ZModem file transfer protocols. Other telecommunications programs include C-Kermit, `pcomm`, and `minicom`. These are similar to communications programs found on other operating systems, and are quite easy to use.

If you do not have access to a SLIP or PPP server (see the previous section), you can use `term` to multiplex your serial line. The `term` program allows you to open more than one login session over a modem connection. It lets you redirect X client connections to your local X server via a serial line. Another software package, KA9Q, implements a similar, SLIP-like interface.

Operating a Bulletin Board System (BBS) is a favorite hobby and means of income for many people. Linux supports a wide range of BBS software, most of which is more powerful than that available for other operating systems. With a phone line, modem, and Linux, you can turn your system into a BBS and provide dial-in access for users worldwide. BBS software for Linux includes XBBS and UniBoard BBS packages.

Most BBS software locks the user into a menu based system where only certain functions and applications are available. An alternative to BBS access is full UNIX access, which lets users dial into your system and log in normally. This requires a fair amount of maintenance by the system administrator, but providing public UNIX access is not difficult. In addition to TCP/IP networking, you can make electronic mail and news access available on your system.

If you do not have access to a TCP/IP network or UUCP feed, Linux lets you communicate with BBS networks like FidoNet, which let you exchange electronic news and mail over a telephone line. You can find more information on telecommunications and BBS software under Linux in Chapter 5.

World Wide Web.

It is worth noting that Linux includes web server software as well as web browsers. The most common server is Apache. Thousands of Linux systems run Apache on the Internet today.

Linux distributions include different web browsers, and other browsers can be downloaded from the Internet. Available browsers include Lynx, Mosaic, Netscape, Arena, and Amaya.

Linux provides complete support for Java and CGI applets, and Perl is a standard tool in the Linux programming environment.

Interfacing with MS-DOS.

Various utilities exist to interface with MS-DOS. The most well-known application is the Linux MS-DOS Emulator, which lets you run MS-DOS applications directly from Linux. Although Linux and MS-DOS are completely different operating systems, the 80386 protected-mode environment allows MS-DOS applications to behave as if they were running in their native 8086 environment.

The MS-DOS emulator is still under development, but many popular applications run under it. Understandably, MS-DOS applications that use bizarre or esoteric features of the system may never be supported, because of the limitations inherent in any emulator. For example, you shouldn't expect to run programs that use 80386 protected-mode features, like Microsoft Windows (in 386 enhanced mode, that is).

Standard MS-DOS commands and utilities like `PKZIP.EXE` work under the emulators, as do 4DOS, a `COMMAND.COM` replacement, FoxPro 2.0, Harvard Graphics, MathCad, Stacker 3.1, Turbo Assembler, Turbo C/C++, Turbo Pascal, Microsoft Windows 3.0 (in real mode), and WordPerfect 5.1.

The MS-DOS Emulator is meant mostly as an ad-hoc solution for those who need MS-DOS for only a few applications and use Linux for everything else. It's not meant to be a complete implementation of MS-DOS. Of course, if the Emulator doesn't satisfy your needs, you can always run MS-DOS as well as Linux on the same system. Using the LILO boot loader, you can specify at boot time which operating system to start. Linux can also coexist with other operating systems, like OS/2.

Linux provides a seamless interface to transfer files between Linux and MS-DOS. You can mount a MS-DOS partition or floppy under Linux, and directly access MS-DOS files as you would any file.

Currently under development is **WINE**—a Microsoft Windows emulator for the X Window System under Linux. Once WINE is complete, users will be able to run MS-Windows applications directly from Linux. This is similar to the commercial WABI Windows emulator from Sun Microsystems, which is also available for Linux.

In Chapter 5, we talk about the MS-DOS tools available for Linux.

Other applications.

A host of miscellaneous programs and utilities exist for Linux, as one would expect of such a hodgepodge operating system. Linux's primary focus is UNIX personal computing, but this is not the only field where it excels. The selection of business and scientific software is expanding, and commercial software vendors have begun to contribute to the growing pool Linux applications.

Several relational databases are available for Linux, including Postgres, Ingres, and Mbase. These are full-featured, professional, client/server database applications, similar to those found on other UNIX platforms. Many commercial database systems are available as well.

Scientific computing applications include FELT (finite element analysis); `gnuplot` (data plotting and analysis); Octave (a symbolic mathematics package similar to MATLAB); `xspread` (a spreadsheet calculator); `xfractint` (an X-based port of the popular Fractint fractal generator); and `xlispstat` (statistics). Other applications include SPICE (circuit design and analysis) and Khoros (image and digital signal processing and visualization). Commercial packages like Maple and MathLab are available.

Many more applications have been ported to Linux. If you absolutely cannot find what you need, you can attempt to port the application from another platform to Linux yourself. Whatever your field, porting standard UNIX applications to Linux is straightforward. Linux's complete UNIX programming environment is sufficient to serve as the base for any scientific application.

Linux also has its share of games. These include classic text based dungeon games like Nethack and Moria; **MUDs** (multi-user dungeons, which allow many users to interact in a text-based adventure) like DikuMUD and TinyMUD; and a slew of X games like `xtetris`, `netrek`, and `xboard`, the X11 version of `gnuchess`. The popular shoot-em-up, arcade-style game, Doom, has also been ported to Linux.

For audiophiles, Linux supports various sound cards and related software, like CDplayer, which makes a CD-ROM drive into an audio CD player, MIDI sequencers and editors, which let you compose music for playback through a synthesizer or other MIDI controlled instrument, and sound editors for digitized sounds.

Can't find the application you're looking for? The Linux Software Map, described in Appendix A, lists software packages which have been written or ported to Linux. Another way to find Linux applications is to look at the `INDEX` files found on Linux FTP sites, if you have Internet access.

Most freely-distributable, UNIX based software will compile on Linux with little difficulty. If all else fails, you can write the application yourself. If you're looking for a commercial application, there may be a free "clone" available. Or, you can encourage the software company to consider releasing a binary version for Linux. Several individuals have contacted software companies and asked them to port their applications to Linux, with various degrees of success.

Copyright issues.

Linux is covered by what is known as the GNU *General Public License*, or **GPL**. The GPL was developed for the GNU project by the Free Software Foundation and specifies several provisions for the distribution and modification of free software. *Free,* in this sense, refers to distribution, not cost. The GPL has always been subject to misinterpretation. We hope that this summary will help you understand the extent and goals of the GPL and its effect on Linux. A complete copy of the GPL is printed in Appendix D.

Originally, Linus Torvalds released Linux under a license more restrictive than the GPL, which allowed the software to be freely distributed and modified, but prevented any money from changing hands for its distribution and use. On the other hand, the GPL allows people to sell and profit from free software, but does not allow them to restrict another's right to distribute the software in any way.

First, it should be explained that free software that is covered by the GPL is not in the public domain. Public domain software by definition is not copyrighted and is literally owned by the public. Software covered by the GPL, on the other hand, is copyrighted by the author. The software is protected by standard international copyright laws, and the author is legally defined. The GPL provides for software which may be freely distributed but is not in the public domain.

GPL-licensed software is also not shareware. Generally, shareware is owned and copyrighted by an author who requires users to send in money for its use. Software covered by the GPL may be distributed and used free of charge.

The GPL also lets people take, modify, and distribute their own versions of the software. However, any derived works of GPL software must also be covered by the GPL. In other words, a company may not take Linux, modify it, and sell it under a restrictive license. If the software is derived from Linux, that software must be covered under the GPL also.

The GPL allows free software to be distributed and used free of charge. It also lets a person or organization distribute GPL software for a fee, and even make a profit from its sale and distribution. However, a distributor of GPL software cannot take those rights away from a purchaser. If you purchase GPL software from a third-party source, you may distribute the software for free, and sell it yourself as well.

This may sound like a contradiction. Why sell software when the GPL allows you to get it for free? Let's say that a company decided to bundle a large amount of free software on a CD-ROM and distribute it. That company would need to charge for the overhead of producing and distributing the CD-ROM, and may even decide to profit from the sales of the software. This is allowed by the GPL.

Organizations that sell free software must follow certain restrictions set forth in the GPL. They cannot restrict the rights of users who purchase the software. If you buy a CD-ROM that contains GPL software, you can copy and distribute the CD-ROM free of charge, or resell it yourself. Distributors must make obvious to users that the software is covered by the GPL. Distributors must also provide, free of charge, the complete source code to the software distributed. This permits anyone who purchases GPL software to make modifications to that software.

Allowing a company to distribute and sell free software is a good thing. Not everyone has access to the Internet and the ability to download software for free. Many organizations sell Linux on diskette, tape, or CD-ROM via mail order, and profit from the sales. Linux developers may never see any of this profit; that is the understanding reached between the developer and the distributor when software is licensed by the GPL. In other words, Linus Torvalds knew that companies may wish to sell Linux, and that he might not see a penny of the profits.

In the free software world, the important issue is not money. The goal of free software is always to develop and distribute fantastic software and allow anyone to obtain and use it. In the next section, we'll discuss how this applies to the development of Linux.

The design and philosophy of Linux.

New users often have a few misconceptions and false expectations about Linux. It is important to understand the philosophy and design of Linux in order to use it effectively. We'll start by describing how Linux is *not* designed.

In commercial UNIX development houses, the entire system is developed under a rigorous quality assurance policy that utilizes source and revision control systems, documentation, and procedures to report and resolve bugs. Developers may not add features or change key sections of code on a whim. They must validate the change as a response to a bug report and subsequently "check in" all changes to the source control system, so that the changes may be reversed if necessary. Each developer is assigned one or more parts of the system code, and only that developer can alter those sections of the code while it is "checked out" (that is, while the code is under his or her control).

Organizationally, a quality assurance department runs rigorous tests on each new version of the operating system and reports any bugs. The developers fix these bugs as reported. A complex system of statistical analysis is used to ensure that a certain percentage of bugs are fixed before the next release, and that the operating system as a whole passes certain release criteria.

The software company, quite reasonably, must have quantitative proof that the next revision of the operating system is ready to be shipped; hence, the gathering and analysis of statistics about the performance of the operating system. It is a big job to develop a commercial UNIX system, often large enough to employ hundreds, if not thousands, of programmers, testers, documenters, and administrative personnel. Of course, no two commercial UNIX vendors are alike, but that is the general picture.

The Linux model of software development discards the entire concept of organized development, source code control systems, structured bug reporting, and statistical quality control. Linux is, and likely always will be, a hacker's operating system. (By *hacker,* I mean a feverishly dedicated programmer who enjoys exploiting computers and does interesting things with them. This is the original definition of the term, in contrast to the connotation of *hacker* as a computer wrongdoer, or outlaw.)

There is no single organization responsible for developing Linux. Anyone with enough know-how has the opportunity to help develop and debug the kernel, port new software, write documentation, and help new users. For the most part, the Linux community communicates via mailing lists and Usenet newsgroups. Several conventions have sprung up around the development effort. Anyone who wishes to have their code included in the "official" kernel, mails it to Linus Torvalds. He will test and include the code in the kernel as long as it doesn't break things or go against the overall design of the system.

The system itself is designed using an open-ended, feature-minded approach. The number of new features and critical changes to the system has recently diminished, and the general rule is that a new version of the kernel will be released every few weeks. Of course, this is a rough figure. New release criteria include the number of bugs to be fixed, feedback from users testing pre-release versions of the code, and the amount of sleep Linus Torvalds has had this week.

Suffice it to say that not every bug is fixed, nor is every problem ironed out between releases. As long as the revision appears to be free of critical or recurring bugs, it is considered to be stable, and the new version is released. The thrust behind Linux development is not to release perfect, bug-free code: it is to develop a free UNIX implementation. Linux is for the developers, more than anyone else.

Anyone who has a new feature or software application generally makes it available in an **alpha version**—that is, a test version, for those brave users who want to hash out problems in the initial code. Because the Linux community is largely based on the Internet, alpha software is usually uploaded to one or more Linux FTP sites (see Appendix C), and a message is posted to one of the Linux Usenet newsgroups about how to obtain and test the code. Users who download and test alpha software can then mail results, bug fixes, and questions to the author.

After the initial bugs have been fixed, the code enters a **beta test** stage, in which it is usually considered stable but not complete. It works, but not all of the features may be present. The software may also go directly to a final stage, in which the software is considered complete and usable.

Keep in mind that these are only conventions—not rules. Some developers may feel so confident of their software that they decide it isn't necessary to release alpha or test versions. It is always up to the developer to make these decisions.

You might be amazed at how such an unstructured system of volunteers who program and debug a complete UNIX system gets anything done at all. As it turns out, this is one of the most efficient and motivated development efforts ever employed. The entire Linux kernel is written *from scratch*, without code from proprietary sources. It takes a huge amount of work to port all the free software under the sun to Linux. Libraries are written and ported, file systems are developed, and hardware drivers are written for many popular devices—all due to the work of volunteers.

Linux software is generally released as a **distribution**, a set of prepackaged software which comprises an entire system. It would be difficult for most users to build a complete system from the ground up, starting with the kernel, adding utilities, and installing all of the necessary software by hand. Instead, many software distributions are available which include everything necessary to install and run a complete system. There is no single, standard distribution—there are many, and each has its own advantages and disadvantages. We describe installation of the various Linux distributions starting on page 39.

Differences between Linux and other operating systems.

It is important to understand the differences between Linux and other operating systems, like MS-DOS, OS/2, and the other implementations of UNIX for personal computers. First of all, Linux coexists happily with other operating systems on the same machine: you can run MS-DOS and OS/2 along with Linux on the same system without problems. There are even ways to interact between various operating systems, as we'll see.

Why use Linux? Why use Linux, instead of a well known, well tested, and well documented commercial operating system? We could give you a thousand reasons. One of the most important, however, is that Linux is an excellent choice for personal UNIX computing. If you're a UNIX software developer, why use MS-DOS at home? Linux allows you to develop and test UNIX software on your PC, including database and X Window System applications. If you're a student, chances are that your university computing systems run UNIX. You can run your own UNIX system and tailor it to your needs. Installing and running Linux is also an excellent way to learn UNIX if you don't have access to other UNIX machines.

But let's not lose sight. Linux isn't only for personal UNIX users. It is robust and complete enough to handle large tasks, as well as distributed computing needs. Many businesses—especially small ones—have moved their systems to Linux in lieu of other UNIX based, workstation environments. Universities have found that Linux is perfect for teaching courses in operating systems design. Large, commercial software vendors have started to realize the opportunities which a free operating system can provide.

Linux vs. MS-DOS. It's not uncommon to run both Linux and MS-DOS on the same system. Many Linux users rely on MS-DOS for applications like word processing. Linux provides its own analogs for these applications, but you might have a good reason to run MS-DOS as well as Linux. If your dissertation is written using WordPerfect for MS-DOS, you may not be able to convert it easily to TEX or some other format. Many commercial applications for MS-DOS aren't available for Linux yet, but there's no reason that you can't use both.

MS-DOS does not fully utilize the functionality of 80386 and 80486 processors. On the other hand, Linux runs completely in the processor's protected mode, and utilizes all of its features. You can directly access all of your available memory (and beyond, with virtual RAM). Linux provides a complete UNIX interface which is not available under MS-DOS. You can easily develop and port UNIX applications to Linux, but under MS-DOS you are limited to a subset of UNIX functionality.

Linux and MS-DOS are different entities. MS-DOS is inexpensive compared to other commercial operating systems and has a strong foothold in the personal computer world. No other operating system for the personal computer has reached the level of popularity of MS-DOS, because justifying spending $1,000 for other operating systems alone is unrealistic for many users. Linux, however, is free, and you may finally have the chance to decide for yourself.

You can judge Linux vs. MS-DOS based on your expectations and needs. Linux is not for everybody. If you always wanted to run a complete UNIX system at home, without the high cost of other UNIX implementations for personal computers, Linux may be what you're looking for.

Linux vs. The Other Guys. A number of other advanced operating systems have become popular in the PC world. Specifically, IBM's OS/2 and Microsoft Windows have become popular for users upgrading from MS-DOS.

Both OS/2 and Windows NT are full featured multitasking operating systems, like Linux. OS/2, Windows NT, and Linux support roughly the same user interface, networking, and security features. However, the real difference between Linux and The Other Guys is the fact that Linux is a version of UNIX, and benefits from contributions of the UNIX community at large.

What makes UNIX so important? Not only is it the most popular operating system for multiuser machines, it is a foundation of the free software world. Much of the free software available on the Internet is written specifically for UNIX systems.

There are many implementations of UNIX from many vendors. No single organization is responsible for its distribution. There is a large push in the UNIX community for standardization in the form of open systems, but no single group controls this design. Any vendor (or, as it turns out, any hacker) may develop a standard implementation of UNIX.

OS/2 and Microsoft operating systems, on the other hand, are proprietary. The interface and design are controlled by a single corporation, which develops the operating system code. In one sense, this kind of organization is beneficial because it sets strict standards for programming and user interface design, unlike those found even in the open systems community.

Several organizations have attempted the difficult task of standardizing the UNIX programming interface. Linux, in particular, is mostly compliant with the POSIX.1 standard. As time goes by, it is expected that the Linux system will adhere to other standards, but standardization is not the primary goal of Linux development.

Linux vs. other implementations of UNIX. Several other implementations of UNIX exist for 80386 or better personal computers. The 80386 architecture lends itself to UNIX, and vendors have taken advantage of this.

Other implementations of UNIX for the personal computer are similar to Linux. Almost all commercial versions of UNIX support roughly the same software, programming environment, and networking features. However, there are differences between Linux and commercial versions of UNIX.

Linux supports a different range of hardware than commercial implementations. In general, Linux supports most well-known hardware devices, but support is still limited to hardware which the developers own. Commercial UNIX vendors tend to support more hardware at the outset, but the list of hardware devices which Linux supports is expanding continuously. We'll cover the hardware requirements for Linux in Section 1.

Many users report that Linux is at least as stable as commercial UNIX systems. Linux is still under development, but the two-pronged release philosophy has made stable versions available without impeding development.

The most important factor for many users is price. Linux software is free if you can download it from the Internet or another computer network. If you do not have Internet access, you can still purchase Linux inexpensively via mail order on diskette, tape, or CD-ROM (see Appendix B).

Of course, you may copy Linux from a friend who already has the software, or share the purchase cost with someone else. If you plan to install Linux on a large number of machines, you need only purchase a single copy of the software—Linux is not distributed with a "single machine" license.

The value of commercial UNIX implementations should not be demeaned. In addition to the price of the software itself, one often pays for documentation, support, and quality assurance. These are very important factors for large institutions, but personal computer users may not require these benefits. In any case, many businesses and universities have found that running Linux in a lab of inexpensive personal computers is preferable to running a commercial version of UNIX in a lab of workstations. Linux can provide workstation functionality on a personal computer at a fraction of the cost.

Linux systems have traveled the high seas of the North Pacific, and manage telecommunications and data analysis for an oceanographic research vessel. Linux systems are used at research stations in Antarctica. Several hospitals maintain patient records on Linux systems.

Other free or inexpensive implementations of UNIX are available for the 80386 and 80486. One of the best known is 386BSD, an implementation of BSD UNIX for the 80386. The 386BSD package is comparable to Linux in many ways, but which one is better depends on your needs and expectations. The only strong distinction we can make is that Linux is developed openly, and any volunteer can aid in the development process, while 386BSD is developed by a closed team of programmers. Because of this, serious philosophical and design differences exist between the two projects. The goal of Linux is to develop a complete UNIX system from scratch (and have a lot of fun in the process), and the goal of 386BSD is in part to modify the existing BSD code for use on the 80386.

NetBSD is another port of the BSD NET/2 distribution to several machines, including the 80386. NetBSD has a slightly more open development structure, and is comparable to 386BSD in many respects.

Another project of note is HURD, an effort by the Free Software Foundation to develop and distribute a free version of UNIX for many platforms. Contact the Free Software Foundation (the address is given in Appendix D) for more information about this project. At the time of this writing, HURD is still under development.

Other inexpensive versions of UNIX exist as well, like Minix, an academic but useful UNIX clone upon which early development of Linux was based. Some of these implementations are mostly of academic interest, while others are full fledged systems.

Hardware requirements.

You must be convinced by now of how wonderful Linux is, and of all the great things it can do for you. However, before you rush out and install Linux, you need to be aware of its hardware requirements and limitations.

Keep in mind that Linux is developed by users. This means, for the most part, that the hardware supported by Linux is that which the users and developers have access to. As it turns out, most popular hardware and peripherals for personal computers are supported. Linux supports more hardware than some commercial implementations of UNIX. However, some obscure devices aren't supported yet.

Another drawback of hardware support under Linux is that many companies keep their hardware interfaces proprietary. Volunteer Linux developers can't write drivers for the devices because the manufacturer does not make the technical specifications public. Even if Linux developers could develop drivers for proprietary devices, they would be owned by the company which owns the device interface, which violates the GPL. Manufacturers that maintain proprietary interfaces write their own drivers for operating systems like MS-DOS and Microsoft Windows. Users and third-party developers never need to know the details of the interface.

In some cases, Linux programmers have attempted to write hackish device drivers based on assumptions about the interface. In other cases, developers work with the manufacturer and try to obtain information about the device interface, with varying degrees of success.

In the following sections, we attempt to summarize the hardware requirements for Linux. The Linux Hardware HOWTO (see page 25) contains a more complete listing of hardware supported by Linux.

◇ **Disclaimer:** Much hardware support for Linux is in the development stage. Some distributions may or may not support experimental features. This section lists hardware which has been supported for some time and is known to be stable. When in doubt, consult the documentation of your Linux distribution. See Section 2 for more information about Linux distributions.

Linux is available for many platforms in addition to Intel 80x86 systems. These include Macintosh, Amiga, Sun SparcStation, and Digital Equipment Corporation Alpha based CPU's. In this book, however, we focus on garden-variety Intel 80386, 80486, and Pentium processors, and clones by manufacturers like AMD, Cyrix, and IBM.

Motherboard and CPU requirements. Linux currently supports systems with the Intel 80386, 80486, or Pentium CPU, including all variations like the 80386SX, 80486SX, 80486DX, and 80486DX2. Non-Intel clones work with Linux as well. Linux has also been ported to the DEC Alpha and the Apple PowerMac.

If you have an 80386 or 80486SX, you may also wish to use a math coprocessor, although one isn't required. The Linux kernel can perform FPU emulation if the machine doesn't have a coprocessor. All standard FPU couplings are supported, including IIT, Cyrix FasMath, and Intel.

Most common PC motherboards are based on the PCI bus but also offer ISA slots. This configuration is supported by Linux, as are EISA and VESA-bus systems. IBM's MicroChannel (MCA) bus, found on most IBM PS/2 systems, is significantly different, and support has been recently added.

Memory requirements. Linux requires very little memory, compared to other advanced operating systems. You should have 2 megabytes of RAM at the very least, and 4 megabytes is strongly recommended. The more memory you have, the faster the system will run. Some distributions require more RAM for installation.

Linux supports the full 32-bit address range of the processor. In other words, it uses all of your RAM automatically.

Linux will run with only 4 megabytes of RAM, including bells and whistles like the X Window System and `emacs`. However, having more memory is almost as important as having a faster processor. For general use, 16 megabytes is enough, and 32 megabytes, or more, may be needed for systems with a heavy user load.

Most Linux users allocate a portion of their hard drive as swap space, which is used as **virtual RAM**. Even if your machine has more than 16 megabytes of physical RAM, you may wish to use swap space. It is no replacement for physical RAM, but it can let your system run larger applications by swapping inactive portions of code to disk. The amount of swap space that you should allocate depends on several factors; we'll come back to this question in the next chapter.

Hard drive controller requirements. It is possible to run Linux from a floppy diskette, or, for some distributions, a live file system on CD-ROM, but for good performance you need hard disk space. Linux can co-exist with other operating systems—it only needs one or more disk partitions.

Linux supports all IDE and EIDE controllers as well as older MFM and RLL controllers. Most, but not all, ESDI controllers are supported. The general rule for non-SCSI hard drive and floppy controllers is that if you can access the drive from MS-DOS or another operating system, you should be able to access it from Linux.

Linux also supports a number of popular SCSI drive controllers. This includes most Adaptec and Buslogic cards based on the NCR chip set.

Hard drive space requirements. Of course, to install Linux, you need to have some amount of free space on your hard drive. Linux will support more than one hard drive on the same machine; you can allocate space for Linux across multiple drives if necessary.

How much hard drive space depends on your needs and the software you're installing. Linux is relatively small, as UNIX implementations go. You could run a system in 20 megabytes of disk space. However, for expansion and larger packages like X, you need more space. If you plan to let more than one person use the machine, you need to allocate storage for their files. Realistic space requirements range from 200 megabytes to one gigabyte or more.

Also, you will likely want to allocate disk space as virtual RAM. We will discuss installing and using swap space in the next chapter.

Each Linux distribution comes with literature to help you gauge the precise amount of storage required for your software configuration. Look at the information which comes with your distribution or the appropriate installation section in Chapter 2.

Monitor and video adaptor requirements. Linux supports standard Hercules, CGA, EGA, VGA, IBM monochrome, Super VGA, and many accelerated video cards, and monitors for the default, text-based interface. In general, if the video card and monitor work under an operating system like MS-DOS, the combination should work fine under Linux. However, original IBM CGA cards suffer from "snow" under Linux, which is not pleasant to view.

Graphical environments like X have video hardware requirements of their own. Rather than list them here, we relegate that discussion to page 147. Popular video cards are supported and new card support is added regularly.

Miscellaneous hardware. You may also have devices like a CD-ROM drive, mouse, or sound card, and may be interested in whether or not this hardware is supported by Linux.

Mice and other pointing devices. Typically, a mouse is used only in graphical environments like X. However, several Linux applications that are not associated with a graphical environment also use mice.

Linux supports standard serial mice like Logitech, MM series, Mouseman, Microsoft (2-button), and Mouse Systems (3-button). Linux also supports Microsoft, Logitech, and ATIXL bus mice, and the PS/2 mouse interface.

Pointing devices that emulate mice, like track balls, should work also.

CD-ROM drives. Many common CD-ROM drives attach to standard IDE controllers. Another common interface for CD-ROM is SCSI. SCSI support includes multiple logical units per device so you can use CD-ROM "juke boxes." Additionally, a few proprietary interfaces, like the NEC CDR-74, Sony CDU-541 and CDU-31a, Texel DM-3024, and Mitsumi are supported.

Linux supports the standard ISO 9660 file system for CD-ROMs, and the High Sierra file system extensions.

Tape drives. Any SCSI tape drive, including quarter inch, DAT, and 8MM are supported, if the SCSI controller is supported. Devices that connect to the floppy controller like floppy tape drives are supported as well, as are some other interfaces, like QIC-02.

Printers. Linux supports the complete range of parallel printers. If MS-DOS or some other operating system can access your printer from the parallel port, Linux should be able to access it, too. Linux printer software includes the UNIX standard `lp` and `lpr` software. This software allows you to print remotely via a network, if you have one. Linux also includes software that allows most printers to handle PostScript files.

Modems. As with printer support, Linux supports the full range of serial modems, both internal and external. A great deal of telecommunications software is available for Linux, including Kermit, `pcomm`, `minicom`, and `seyon`. If your modem is accessible from another operating system on the same machine, you should be able to access it from Linux with no difficulty.

Ethernet cards. Many popular Ethernet cards and LAN adaptors are supported by Linux. Linux also supports some FDDI, frame relay, and token ring cards, and all ArcNet cards. A list of supported network cards is included in the kernel source of your distribution.

Sources of Linux information.

Many other sources of information about Linux are available. In particular, a number of books about UNIX in general will be of use, especially for readers unfamiliar with UNIX. We suggest that you peruse one of these books before attempting to brave the jungles of Linux.

Information is also available online in electronic form. You must have access to an online network like the Internet, Usenet, or Fidonet to access the information. If you do not, you might be able to find someone who is kind enough to give you hard copies of the documents.

Online documents.

Many Linux documents are available via anonymous FTP from Internet archive sites around the world and networks like Fidonet and CompuServe. Linux CD-ROM distributions also contain the documents mentioned here. If you are can send mail to Internet sites, you may be able to retrieve these files using one of the FTP e-mail servers that mail you the documents or files from the FTP sites. See Appendix C for more information on using FTP e-mail servers.

A list of well-known Linux archive sites is given in Appendix C. To reduce network traffic, you should use a FTP site that is geographically close to you.

Appendix A contains a partial list of the Linux documents available via anonymous FTP. The filenames vary depending on the site. Most sites keep Linux-related documents in the `docs` subdirectory of their Linux archive. For example, the FTP site `sunsite.unc.edu`, keeps Linux files in `/pub/Linux`, with Linux-related documentation in `/pub/Linux/docs`.

Examples of available online documents are *Linux Frequently Asked Questions with Answers,* a collection of frequently asked questions about Linux; Linux HOWTO documents, which describe specific aspects of the system, like the Installation HOWTO, Printing HOWTO, and Ethernet HOWTO; and the *Linux META-FAQ,* which is a list of information sources on the Internet.

Many of these documents are also regularly posted to one or more Linux-related Usenet newsgroups; see page 26 below.

Linux on the World Wide Web.

The Linux Documentation Project Home Page is on the World Wide Web at

`http://sunsite.unc.edu/LDP`

This web page lists many HOWTOs and other documents in HTML format, as well as pointers to other sites of interest to Linux users, like `ssc.com`, home of the *Linux Journal,* a monthly magazine. You can find the home page at

`http://www.ssc.com/linux/`

Books and other published works.

The books of the Linux Documentation Project are the result of an effort carried out over the Internet to write and distribute a bona fide set of manuals for Linux, analogs of the documentation which comes with commercial UNIX versions and covers installation, operation, programming, networking, and kernel development.

Linux Documentation Project manuals are available via anonymous FTP and by mail order. Appendix A lists the manuals available and describes how to obtain them.

Many large publishers, including MIS:Press, Digital Press, O'Reilly & Associates, and SAMS have jumped onto the Linux bandwagon. Check with computer bookstores or SSC's web page at

`http://www.ssc.com/`

A large number of books about UNIX in general are applicable to Linux. In its use and programming interface, Linux does not differ greatly from other implementations of UNIX. Almost everything you would like to know about using and programming Linux can be found in general UNIX texts. In fact, this book is meant to supplement the library of UNIX books currently available. Here, we present the most important Linux-specific details and hope that you will look to other sources for in-depth information.

Armed with good books about UNIX as well as this book, you should be able to tackle just about anything. Appendix A lists several UNIX books which are recommended highly for UNIX newcomers and wizards.

The *Linux Journal* magazine is distributed worldwide, and is an excellent way to keep in touch with the goings-on of the Linux community, especially if you do not have access to Usenet news (see below). See Appendix A for information on subscribing to the *Linux Journal*.

Usenet newsgroups.

Usenet is a worldwide electronic news and discussion forum with a diverse selection of **newsgroups,** which are discussion areas devoted to specific topics. Much discussion about Linux development occurs over the Internet and Usenet. Not surprisingly, a number of Usenet newsgroups are dedicated to Linux.

The original Linux newsgroup, `alt.os.linux`, was created to move some of the discussion about Linux from `comp.os.minix` and various mailing lists. Soon, the traffic on `alt.os.linux` grew large enough that a newsgroup in the `comp` hierarchy was warranted. A vote was taken in February, 1992, and `comp.os.linux` was created.

`comp.os.linux` quickly became one of the most popular (and loudest) of the Usenet groups, more popular than any other group in the `comp.os` hierarchy. In December, 1992, a vote was taken to split the newsgroup to reduce traffic; only `comp.os.linux.announce` passed this vote. In July, 1993, the group was finally split into a new hierarchy. Almost 2,000 people voted in the `comp.os.linux` reorganization, making it one of the largest Usenet Calls For Votes ever.

If you do not have Usenet, there are mail-to-news gateways available for each of the newsgroups below.

`comp.os.linux.announce`
: A moderated newsgroup for announcements about Linux, including bug reports and important patches to software. If you read any Linux newsgroup at all, read this one. Often, the important postings in this group are not cross posted. This group also contains many periodic postings about Linux, including the online documents described in the last section and listed in Appendix A.

  Postings to these newsgroups must be approved by the moderators, Matt Welsh and Lars Wirzenius. If you wish to submit an article, you simply post the article as you normally would; the news software will forward the article to the moderators for approval. However, if your news system is not set up correctly, you may need to mail the article directly to `linux-announce@tc.cornell.edu`.

`comp.os.linux.development.system`
: An unmoderated newsgroup for discussions about the development of the Linux system related to the kernel, device drivers, and loadable modules.

`comp.os.linux.help`
: An unmoderated newsgroup which is devoted to assisting Linux newcomers.

`comp.os.linux.development.apps`
: An unmoderated newsgroup for questions and discussion regarding the writing of applications for Linux and the porting of applications to Linux.

`comp.os.linux.hardware`
: Questions and discussion specific to a particular piece of hardware.

comp.os.linux.m68k
: This is to further interest in and development of the port of Linux to Motorola 680x0 architecture.

comp.os.linux.networking
: Discussion relating to networking and communications including Ethernet boards, SLIP, and PPP.

comp.os.linux.x
: Discussion of X Window System features unique to Linux, including servers, clients, fonts, and libraries.

comp.os.linux.setup
: Questions and discussion relating to Linux installation and system administration.

comp.os.linux.misc
: All discussion which doesn't quite fit into the other available Linux groups. Any nontechnical or meta-discourse about Linux should occur in comp.os.linux.misc.

Internet mailing lists.

If you have access to Internet electronic mail, you can participate in several mailing lists, even if you do not have Usenet access. If you are not directly on the Internet, you can join one of these mailing lists if you can exchange electronic mail with the Internet (for example, through UUCP, Fidonet, CompuServe, or other networks which exchange Internet mail).

For more information about the Linux mailing lists, send e-mail to

majordomo@vger.rutgers.edu

Include a line with the word help in the body of the message, and a message will be returned to you which describes how to subscribe and unsubscribe to various mailing lists. The word lists on a line by itself will retrieve the names of mailing lists which are accessible through the majordomo.vger.rutgers.edu server.

There are several special-purpose mailing lists for Linux as well. The best way to find out about these is to watch the Linux Usenet newsgroups for announcements, as well as to read the list of publicly-available mailing lists, which is posted to the Usenet news.answers group.

Getting help.

You will undoubtedly need assistance during your adventures in the Linux world. Even UNIX wizards are occasionally stumped by some quirk or feature of Linux. It's important to know how, where, and when to find help.

The primary means of obtaining help is through Internet mailing lists and newsgroups as discussed in Section 1. If you don't have access to these sources, you may be able to find comparable Linux discussion forums on online services, like BBS's and CompuServe.

Several businesses provide commercial support for Linux. These services allow you to pay a subscription fee that lets you call consultants for help with your Linux problems.

Keeping the following suggestions in mind will greatly improve your experience with Linux and guarantee more success in finding help.

Consult all available documentation...first! You should do this when you first encounter a problem. Various sources of information are listed in Section 1 and Appendix A. These documents are laboriously written for people who need help with the Linux system, like you. As mentioned above, books written for UNIX are applicable to Linux, and you should use them, too.

If you have access to Usenet news, or any of the Linux-related mailing lists, be sure to read the information there before posting. Often, solutions to common problems that are not easy to find in the documentation are well-covered in newsgroups and mailing lists. If you only post to these groups but don't read them, you are asking for trouble.

Learn to appreciate self-reliance. You asked for it by running Linux in the first place. Remember, Linux is all about hacking and fixing problems. It is not a commercial operating system, nor does it try to be one. Hacking won't kill you. In fact, it will be enlightening to investigate and solve problems yourself—you may even one day call yourself a Linux guru. Learn to appreciate the full value of hacking the system and fixing problems yourself. You shouldn't expect to run a complete, home brew Linux system without some handiwork.

Remain calm. Nothing is earned by taking an axe—or worse, a powerful electromagnet—to your Linux box. A large punching bag or a long walk is a good way to relieve occasional stress attacks. As Linux matures and distributions become more reliable, we hope this problem will disappear. However, even commercial UNIX implementations can be tricky. When all else fails, sit back, take a few deep breaths, and return to the problem when you feel relaxed. Your mind and conscience will be clearer.

Refrain from posting spuriously. Many people make the mistake of posting or mailing messages pleading for help prematurely. When encountering a problem, do not rush immediately to the nearest terminal and post a message to one of the Linux Usenet groups. First try to resolve the problem yourself, and be absolutely certain what the problem is. Does your system not respond when switched on? Perhaps it is unplugged.

When you post for help, make it worthwhile. Remember that people who read your post are not necessarily there to help you. Therefore, it is important to remain as polite, terse, and informative as possible.

How does one accomplish this? First, you should include as much relevant information about your system and your problem as possible. Posting the simple request, "I cannot seem to get e-mail to work" will probably get you nowhere unless you include information about your system, what software you're using, what you have attempted to do so far, and what the results were. When you include technical information, it is also a good idea to include general information about the version of your software (the Linux kernel version, for example), as well as a brief summary of your hardware configuration. But don't over do it—your monitor type and brand is probably irrelevant if you're trying to configure network software.

CHAPTER 2

Obtaining and Installing Linux

David Bandel rewrote and revised the first section on installing Linux. Parts of the work by the following authors of the different sections on Linux distributions were also added to this first section.

Boris Beletsky wrote the Debian section. Sean Dreilinger wrote the section on Slackware. Henry Pierce wrote the section on Red Hat Linux. Evan Leibovitch wrote the section on Caldera OpenLinux. Larry Ayers Pierce wrote the section on S.u.S.E. Linux.

Generic installation.

Unlike most other operating systems, Linux can be obtained free of charge. Due to the GNU General Public License under which Linux is distributed (see Appendix D), no one can sell you a license for the software. You can use Linux at no charge and are encouraged to make it available to others.

But that doesn't mean companies aren't entitled to reimbursement for copying costs plus a profit. They may also add software that is not free that runs on the system.

This gives you the freedom to choose. If purchasing a CD-ROM is not within your budget, you may simply borrow a friend's copy or download the source from the Internet. Whether purchased from a major Linux distributor or downloaded from their FTP site (see Appendix C), you get the same operating system and the software packages that they offer. In fact, you can get more free software from one of the FTP sites than the companies can distribute on CD, due to restrictions some authors place on the distribution of their software.

Major Linux distributions.

An in-depth look at some of the Linux distributions begins on page 39. These distributions are: Debian, Red Hat, Caldera, Slackware, and S.u.S.E. Each section has more information on where to obtain that distribution. But remember, Linux is the kernel. The software is part of the distribution, not Linux. Most of the software is freely available and can be ported between various UNIX platforms. After taking into account what the kernel itself will support, the biggest difference comes in what the libraries (software called from within the applications) support.

Each distribution has its own installation and maintenance utilities that ease installation and system administration. Each is apparently aimed at a different audience. Any distribution will get you started and keep you running. So I recommend that you read about each distribution and talk to any knowledgeable friends. Most large cities have a Linux User Group, most with experienced users, who argue at length over which distribution is the best, and why. I suggest that you listen to some of their arguments and then decide. You can also join mailing lists (I recommend joining only one at a time) and reading user posts and answers from the list gurus. As different as each distribution is, so too are the mailing lists that provide assistance. Making the right choice for yourself is important, because changing distributions generally means reinstalling from scratch.

Common concerns.

This section makes the assumptions that the average newcomer to Linux:

- has a computer with MS-DOS and Windows or OS/2;
- has a basic understanding of MS-DOS but not UNIX;
- knows or can find out what kind of hardware the computer has installed;
- has a desire to "try out" Linux for whatever reason, though probably not switch to it exclusively (yet); and
- has neither a spare machine nor second disk drive available, but several hundred megabytes on an existing drive free for use.

These assumptions are not extreme, and may even be a bit conservative. Some say that if your VCR still blinks 12:00, Linux isn't for you, but then that would leave me out as well. My VCR still blinks 12:00.

Before we begin, we must know where we are going. While it is certainly possible to get from New York to California (eventually) by striking out in almost any random direction, most of us would opt to go in a more or less direct route. So it is with installing Linux.

Hardware.

This section explains all of the installation steps necessary short of the actual install. Each distribution handles this preparation slightly differently. While the installs look different, they accomplish the same things and have more in common than not. All require:

- planning;
- gathering system hardware information;
- backing up your old system (optional, but strongly recommended);
- preparing Linux partitions;
- deciding on a boot loader (for dual boot systems);
- booting a Linux kernel;
- installing the kernel;
- choosing and installing software packages;
- loading the software;
- making final configuration adjustments; and
- rebooting into a running system.

Now that I've sufficiently oversimplified the process, let's go down the list. Hang on, it's not that bad when you learn from others' mistakes.

Planning.

I can't overemphasize this step. Any pilot will tell you that the landing is only as good as the approach. The same goes for Linux installation.

First, determine what kind of hardware you have. A checklist has been included to assist you. Be as precise as possible, but don't get carried away. For example, if you have an Ethernet card, you need to know what kind (e.g., SMC-Ultra, 3Com 3C509, etc.), base I/O (e.g., io=0x300), interrupt (IRQ 10), but not the hardware address (00 00 a6 27 bf 3c). Not all information will be needed for your hardware. If you have Windows 95 or Windows NT running, you can copy the values from the system hardware device information screen. Otherwise, consult the hardware manuals or the hardware company's Web site. Since it is important, we'll review this worksheet here.

System planning worksheet.

General

Processor:	Type:	386 486 Pentium PPro	
Speed (optional):			
	Mfg:		
	Intel AMD Cyrix		
	Motherboard:	Make:	Chip Set:
Example:	Make: unknown	Chip Set: triton II	
Mouse:	Mfg:	Type: bus PS/2 serial port	
If serial:	COM1 (ttyS0) COM2 (ttyS1)		
Hard disk drive(s):	Type:	IDE/MFM/RLL/ESDI SCSI	
size: (list each drive):			
If SCSI: Controller	make:	model:	
example:	make: BusLogic	model: 948	
disk	partition:	size:	
boot:	Linux DOS/Windows OS/2 other		
disk	partition:	size:	boot:
disk	partition:	size:	boot:
disk	partition:	size:	boot:
disk	partition:	size:	boot:
CD-ROM:	IDE/ATAPI SCSI Proprietary		
mfg (proprietary only):	model		

X-Windows:

Video Card:	mfg:	model:	
RAM:			
> 1Mb 1Mb 2Mb 4Mb >4Mb			
Monitor:	mfg:	model:	max scan rate:

Networking:

Modem:	mfg:	model:	
serial port:	COM1 COM2 COM3 COM4		
(ttyS0)	(ttyS1)	(ttyS2)	(ttyS3)

Computer hostname: (example: rainier)

The following answers are only needed if using network interface card (NIC): (do not configure networking if you do not have a NIC installed)

NIC type:	ethernet token ring FDDI other
NIC mfg:	model:
network domain name:	(example: mountains.net)
IP address:	(ex: 192.168.1.2)
network address:	(ex: 192.168.1.0)
netmask:	(ex. 255.255.255.0)
broadcast address:	(ex: 192.168.1.255)
gateway(s):	(ex: none or 192.168.1.1)
DNS(s):	(ex: 192.168.1.2)

Some of the General Section is there for future reference. Specifically, we don't need to know right now our CPU processor type. We can also do without ever knowing what chip set we have on the motherboard. But if the information is available, it is good to have.

Mice.

Other information, beginning with the mouse, we do need, if we expect to use the mouse. We need to know the mouse manufacturer, because different brands implement internal signal functions differently. Here, attention to detail is everything. If you have a mouse with a Microsoft brand on it, it may have a serial or PS/2 interface. Looking at the connector for the computer won't help, either. A number of computers come with mice that look like serial mice and have a serial-type connector, but are connected to the motherboard internally as a PS/2 mouse.

Read the print on the bottom of the mouse carefully before deciding. Also, if you have a mouse with three buttons, but it has a switch on the bottom which you can change between, say, Microsoft and Mouse System, choose Mouse System. The Microsoft setting doesn't implement the middle button, which is useful in UNIX. For manufacturer, choose the switch setting, since that is the signaling protocol used. No drivers exist for a "Cutie" mouse, but do exist for the switch settings of Microsoft and Mouse System found on the bottom of the mouse.

While not specifically asked for, the only additional information you may want to add is the device through which the system accesses the mouse. Linux must know how the device is referred to. If you have a PS/2 mouse, you will normally use either `/dev/psaux`, the auxiliary port for a PS/2 pointing device, or `/dev/psmouse`, a synonym sometimes available for use. Bus mice are accessed through a file specifically created for that proprietary mouse, like `/dev/atibm` ATI bus mice, `/dev/logibm` for Logitech bus mice, `/dev/inportbm` for InPort bus mice, or their respective synonyms of `atimouse`, `logimouse`, and so on. For serial mice, if you know the MS-DOS `COM:` port, substitute `/dev/ttyS0` for `COM1:` and `/dev/ttyS1` for `COM2:`. I'll refrain from explaining the origins of the `tty` name of `ttyS0` since that will take up several paragraphs and is already explained in many UNIX references

Hard drives and CD-ROMs.

Before you begin installation, you need to take stock of how much hard disk real estate you will dedicate to Linux versus how much you have. Deciding during installation how you want to divide up your hard disk is only asking for problems and will probably end up in lost time, lost data, and a reinstall.

Your hard drive will be one of several kinds. For our purposes, IDE, MFM, RLL, and ESDI are equivalent, and I will use the term IDE. This also encompasses EIDE, the most common interface in home computer systems on the market currently and favored for its low price.

If the hard drive has a SCSI interface, this will be evident during booting. You will need to know the make and model of the SCSI controller. The most common are the Adaptec and BusLogic controllers, but by no means are they the only ones. These also have specific models, like the AHA-1572 or BTC-958. This information is often displayed during system initialization.

To allocate space, we need to assess the hard drive size. Under OS/2, you can use the entire hard disk for OS/2, then install Microsoft Windows on the partition with OS/2 and run Microsoft Windows under OS/2. This is not true of Linux. If you have MS-DOS and Microsoft Windows, or OS/2 on your computer, Linux needs its own partition. It cannot be loaded on a MS-DOS or OS/2 partition. And while Linux has DOS emulators and can read and even run some DOS programs, DOS cannot "see" what is on a Linux partition.

If you have and want to keep MS-DOS (assumed), you must determine how much space to reserve for it. Subtract this number from the hard disk total and that is what you have to work with. For now, annotate the total size of the drive(s) you have and the second number with how much to dedicate to Linux.

For your CD-ROM drive(s) you need similar information. A CD-ROM drive is either IDE/ATAPI, the most common in home systems marketed today; SCSI; or an older, proprietary drive, like those connected to sound cards. If you have an IDE or SCSI drive, so much the better. If you have a proprietary drive, you must know the make and model because Linux identifies proprietary CD-ROM drives by manufacturer and the specific drive.

Disk drives under Linux.

For newcomers to Linux who are familiar only with MS-DOS, and for those who come from other UNIX platforms, devices under Linux have have peculiar references. These references are used almost from the start, and some understanding of them is necessary.

Under Linux, as under any UNIX, **devices** are special files. Hard drives are treated as files and are referred to by name, as are modems, your monitor screen, and other hardware devices. UNIX treats them as files to be read from and written to. Since Linux sees them as files, they will all be located in a directory dedicated to devices. After installation you will be able to see them under the directory `/dev`, for *devices*.

Even though these devices are seen by Linux as files, they are special. They come in two flavors, under one general heading. This general heading is **named pipes**, so called because they act as funnels for data flowing between the software and the hardware. The "flavors," as I call them, are **block** and **character**, which refer to the way the device communicates, in blocks of data or individual characters. They are created automatically during installation.

These naming conventions are discussed on page 127.

The X Window System

I've included on your worksheet information regarding your video card and monitor. While this is not absolutely necessary, most of those who come from the Microsoft Windows or OS/2 world want to install and configure a **graphical user interface** (GUI) for use. Some distributions walk you through this set up, others point you to post-installation programs. This information will be important then.

You must know the manufacturer and specific model of your video card. Some cards can be probed for RAM or chip sets, others can't. In either case, knowing how much RAM is on the card and the chips used, like the S3 or S3-Virge, is important. This information saves much time and grief. The most difficult and frustrating part of any Linux installation and setup is the X Window System.

The data for your monitor is often more difficult to obtain. If you have one of the more obscure brands of monitors, you may need to supply vertical and horizontal scan rates yourself.

◇ If in doubt, always err on the conservative side. Overdriving your system can result in damage to the monitor or video card.

We already have most of the information that we need for the mouse, the only other subsystem the X server needs. The information that Linux needs to know about your mouse is described on page 32.

Networking.

This section is not as significant yet as the worksheet suggests. Networking is explained in detail in Chapter 5. But if you have a **network interface card** (NIC), be it Ethernet, token ring, or other system, you must read up on the card before proceeding. This information is needed during installation to use the NIC.

During initial Linux installation, if you do not have a NIC, you can skip over some of the networking part. However, all computers must have a name under Linux. The example on the worksheet assumes you've chosen a theme, like mountains, and will name your computers after names of mountains, but any scheme your concoct is fine.

If you have a modem, you must know where it is connected. This is a serial port, `/dev/ttyS0` through `/dev/ttyS3`, corresponding to MS-DOS `COM:` ports 1–4. ISDN is treated similarly, but is normally set up post-installation with special, multiple device designations.

That finishes our worksheet and about half of the planning that we need to do. One notation that is not on our worksheet is the amount of random access memory (RAM) the system has. Linux runs happily on a system with less than 4 MB of RAM, but this has a significant impact on installation and subsequent system usage. If you have 4 MB of RAM or less, then you must follow special procedures for low memory machines where applicable. With the current low price of RAM and with few machines being sold today with less than 8MB of RAM, this generally isn't an issue. If it is, be sure to check your distribution for special instructions.

Planning, Part 2.

Portions of the following section, particularly the disk partitioning strategies, are highly contentious among seasoned installers, but I will give you my thoughts on it. You are welcome to deviate as you see fit. Most differences in opinion, though, come from a difference in the ultimate purpose for the system; i.e., as a workstation, Web server, News server, or other function.

Partitioning strategies.

Few seasoned Linux users will tell you to make one Linux native partition and one swap partition and start installation. There are several reasons for this, and I subscribe to most of them, so I have several Linux native partitions. But to me, the most compelling reason of all, is that one day you will want to upgrade, and that will require reformatting the file system(s). In fact, the Slackware distribution has, at last look, no means to even attempt an "in-place" upgrade, or any indication that it will in the future. Upgrading from kernel 0.99 to 1.2.13 required me to reformat, as did the upgrade from 1.2.13 to 2.0.0, and I suspect that another will be required for 2.2.0 (or whatever the next stable kernel is). What I don't ever want to do is lose the files that I have accumulated in my home directory. Yes, I have a backup. But keeping my `/home` directory intact is easier, especially since I moved all my special files to a subdirectory there.

◇ Another reason is that any bootable partition must be within the first 1024 sectors (about 512 MB) of the hard drive. When any PC boots up, a sequence of events occurs which ends in the loading of the operating system. Due to limitations in the BIOS (Basic Input/Output System), until the operating system is loaded, only the first 1024 sectors of the first or second hard disk can be accessed. This is important, so mark this section and remember this.

To get a feel for exactly what we're talking about, I'm going to describe a standard Linux file system and how Linux handles partitions.

Under MS-DOS, every partition is usually a different drive, and little distinction is made between whether that is a physical drive or a logical drive (partition). Under Linux, physical and logical drives are much less rigidly designated

During installation, you must choose a partition as your root partition. The root partition is designated as "/". When we refer to "`/dev`", this is really two directories, "`/`" and "`dev`". Your Linux kernel will be located on the root partition, but can be in a subdirectory as long as that subdirectory resides on the root partition. For example, some distributions use `/boot` to hold the kernel, system map, and boot up files. So the following structure (as a minimum) will be set up on your root partition during install:

```
/bin
/dev
/etc
/home
/lib
/lost+found
/proc
/root
/sbin
/usr
/var
```

You may see others like `/boot`, `/mnt`, `/cdrom`, `/floppy`, `/opt`, and so on, but the above are essential.

So, if this is the root partition, and if all those directories are in the root partition, then what about any other partitions? Well, Linux can use a directory name (say `/usr`) as a **mount point**. That is, the other partition on the disk (or on another disk) is mounted under it (in this case `/usr`).

If you unmount the other partition and look in the subdirectory Linux uses as a mount point, you will (or should) see nothing—no files or directories. When the other partition is mounted, you will see files and directories which are on that partition under the mount point. So if you have two drives, one with 120 MB and another with 840 MB, you can make one partition on the 120MB drive (let's say it's the root partition) and mount any partitions you have created on the 840MB drive (this could be one big partition, or several smaller partitions) under their respective mount points, one partition per mount point, creating, in effect, one, 960-MB file system.

The one restriction is that you cannot use certain directories on the root drive as mount points, because they contain files that are needed to either boot the system or mount other systems. Obviously if the command used to mount other partitions is located on another partition and you can't access that partition until you've mounted it, you'll be like the dog chasing its tail.

◇ The directories you will *not* be using as mount points are: /bin, /dev, /etc, /lib, /lost+found, /proc, /root, and /sbin.

A detailed description of what files are contained in these standard system directories is given on page 97.

Let's look at a small example. You are an aspiring Internet Service Provider (ISP). You have four machines, and each has a 1-gigabyte drive. So, you decide to allocate space as follows:

```
machine A:  / = 120MB
/usr = remainder of drive (exported)
/home = 0 - mount point (mounted from B)
/var/news = 0 - mount point (mounted from C)
/var/spool/mail = 0 - mount point (mounted from D)

machine B: / = 120MB
/usr = 0 - mount point (mounted from A)
/home = remainder of drive (exported)
/var/news = 0 - mount point (mounted from C)
/var/spool/mail = 0 - mount point (mounted from D)

machine C: / = 120MB
/usr = 0 - mount point (mounted from A)
/home = 0 - mount point (mounted from B)
/var/news = remainder of drive (exported)
/var/spool/mail = 0 - mount point (mounted from D)

machine D:  (reader exercise)
```

You probably noticed that I arbitrarily assigned the root partition 120MB, and allocated the rest to whatever (/usr, /home, /var/spool/mail and so forth). I also didn't allocate any space to a swap partition. So, let's look at what we will likely need, understanding that "it depends," is key. I will discuss this from the perspective of a home situation with only a few users, lots of programs, and no other remarkable needs.

The best place to start is to tell you what my primary home computer looks like. I have two drives, /dev/hda (1.2 Gb) and /dev/hdb (540 MB). df (disk free) displays

```
File system        1024-blocks  Used Available Capacity Mounted on
/dev/hda1            150259    69605    72894     49%   /
/dev/hda3            723923   615452    71075     90%   /usr
/dev/hda2            150291    93326    49204     65%   /usr/X11R6
/dev/hdb1            499620   455044    18773     96%   /home
```

You can see that I have a half-used 150-MB root (/) partition, a nearly full /usr partition, a largely used /usr/X11R6 partition, and a large, but cramped, 500-MB /home partition. The remainder of the drive, /dev/hdb, is a swap partition.

At a realistic minimum, I would suggest reserving 80–100 MB for your root partition, about 10 MB per user on your /home partition, as much space as you can reserve for swap, within reason (see the next section), and the rest to /usr. I have a five-user system at home, but I personally have over 400 MB of the /home directory tied up, much of that in graphics—a photo album of family and friends. Your /usr partition should probably be at least 250 MB, but the minimum will depend on what you decide to install. As you can see, it can rapidly fill with over 800 MB of programs, libraries, and data. Also remember that partitions give you flexibility that you lose with one, giant partition.

◇ As of this writing, at least one distribution, Caldera OpenLinux (Lite, Base, and Standard), fails to install if your root partition is larger than 2 GB.

The swap partition.

You must give thought to a swap partition. Unlike Microsoft Windows, Linux uses a dedicated swap partition for speed. Although it is possible to create a swap file, it is not recommended. Linux can use up to 128 MB of swap space, but more than that is wasted. I recommend a practical minimum of 16 MB. The optimum is probably as much as you can spare between 32 and 64MB—the more, the better.

One last consideration before you decide to how best to carve up the disk. Remember that I said the BIOS cannot "see" past sector 1024 on the hard drive (about 512MB). So, the Linux kernel (a file probably called `vmlinuz` on your boot disk), or any OS kernel for that matter, must reside entirely on one of the first two disk drives (`/dev/hda` or `/dev/hdb`) and within the first 1024 sectors, or the BIOS will be unable to load it. To insure that it can, plan to make your root partition (as well as any other boot partition) fall entirely within this limitation on either the first or second hard drive.

Repartitioning.

At the beginning of this chapter I said I'd make a few assumptions. One was that you would want to keep your comfortable MS-DOS and Microsoft Windows operating system around. And since the computer you bought only has MS-DOS on it, it doesn't make sense to have multiple partitions, so the one drive you have is probably entirely dedicated to MS-DOS.

One way or another, then, we will have two operating systems on this computer. If you currently have nothing on your disk (lucky you), that is great, but you're not quite ready to skip ahead. Linux is comfortable wherever you put it. Your BIOS may not be capable of booting it, but once running, it will not complain if it's relegated to the fourth partition of the fourth hard drive. But MS-DOS and Microsoft Windows aren't so forgiving. They want the first drive and the first partition and may refuse to boot from any other position. I have seen MS-DOS boot from the first partition on the second hard drive, but the first hard drive did not have any MS-DOS partitions, so MS-DOS didn't recognize the drive. The best strategy is often the path of least resistance. If at all possible, put MS-DOS on the first drive and the first partition.

A second consideration in a multiple OS situation is which operating system to load first. If you're tempted to partition the hard disk and install Linux first (reserving `/dev/hda1` for MS-DOS, then installing MS-DOS second, don't. Windows 95 is the worst offender, but Microsoft products in general will delete any previous boot loader you had installed on the master boot record (what the BIOS uses to point to bootable kernels). In fact, you may even hear this referred to as the "Microsoft virus". This is not a virus in the true sense of the word, just arrogance on the part of Microsoft, that one would only want a Microsoft operating system to boot. Linux does not cause such problems, and in fact provides a way to choose the default boot image. It also allows you to intervene during the boot process to specify which operating system to boot. This is a standard part of Linux installation procedures.

Backing up your old system.

Before we actually get to work on the partition table, I will walk through procedures to protect the data that you have on the hard disk. These procedures assume that you have a DOS partition. Other operating systems may or may not have a way to accomplish the same thing.

◇ The first thing that you should do is perform a complete backup. The tools that you will use work as they should. But these procedures are inherently dangerous. Any time you work with a hard disk partition table, you can easily lose all the data contained on the drive. **Back up your hard disk before you proceed.**

Once you have your disk backed up, create a boot floppy disk for the system. You can either use the MS-DOS command

```
C:> format a:  /s
```

which formats the floppy and puts the required system files on it, or, using a formatted disk, issue the command

```
C:>sys a:
```

Once you have created a boot floppy and tested it to insure that it works, copy the following files from your MS-DOS system to the boot floppy: `FDISK.EXE`, `SCANDISK.EXE`, and `SYS.COM`. Also copy the file `RESTORRB.EXE` from a Linux distribution CD or Linux FTP archive. (See Appendix C).

Run a defragmentation program on your DOS drive to defragment and group the files together at the front of the disk. If defragmenter encounters any errors, you need to run `SCANDISK.EXE` to fix the problems. Once you have defragmented the disk and ensured that the files are compressed toward the front of the drive (as indicated in the graphical portrayal of your disk), you're ready to run `FIPS.EXE` to shrink the MS-DOS partition.

`FIPS.EXE`

On your Linux distribution CD (or an Internet distribution site), you'll find a copy of `FIPS.EXE`, which can shrink the MS-DOS partition. Note that `FIPS.EXE` only works for MS-DOS partitions. If you have other partitions that you need to shrink, the program Partition Magic may help, but is not free. Copy `FIPS.EXE` to your boot floppy and reboot using this floppy. This accomplishes two things: it insures that the boot floppy works, and insures that you are booted into MS-DOS Real Mode and are not running Microsoft Windows.

At the `A:>` prompt, type `FIPS` (upper or lower case). You will be greeted and asked which drive you want to operate on (if you have more than one). Select the drive to shrink. Once you confirm your choice, let `FIPS.EXE` make a copy of your boot and root sectors to the floppy in case something untoward happens.

You will then be asked if all of the free space on your partition should be used to create a second partition. If you say, "yes," you will not have any free space on the MS-DOS partition to save data to, so say, "no." You will then be able to alter the amount of space allocated between the first and second partitions. Note that if you didn't properly defragment your drive, you won't have much to work with on the second partition. Also, if you use MS-DOS mirroring software, a file is created at the very end of the partition, and `FIPS.EXE` tells you that you have no space to create a second partition. Exit and correct the problem by deleting the `MIRROR.FIL` file, then restart `FIPS.EXE`.

You can edit and re-edit the table until you are satisfied. Once you are happy with the distribution of space between the partitions, confirm your changes and write out the table.

Once `FIPS.EXE` has finished, remove the boot floppy and reboot your computer. In this example, we'll destroy and recreate the second partition during installation to create at least two partitions for Linux: a swap partition and a Linux native partition. But you can create as many as you like.

Preparing to boot Linux.

In order to install Linux, we must begin by booting the Linux kernel. This is accomplished in exactly the same manner as if you wanted to reload MS-DOS: we need a boot disk. But most distributions come only with a CD-ROM, and even if we had a running Linux system, the command to create boot disks for Linux is different than for MS-DOS. If you bought a new computer with a bootable CD-ROM, some distributions allow you to boot in this manner. But we'll go through the process of creating a boot disk for the rest of us.

Creating a Linux boot disk under DOS.

Each distribution CD contains a MS-DOS program that allows you to write a raw disk image to a formatted floppy disk. You must have a high density floppy, and some distributions require this to be a 3.5-inch, 1.44 Mb floppy. Insert the floppy in the drive. On the CD (or on your disk drive if you downloaded it) find `RAWRITE2.EXE` (you may have the older `RAWRITE.EXE`).

Then `cd` to the directory that has the disk image(s) that you need to boot with. There may be only one, or as many as seven which are configured for different hardware. You will have to consult the distribution documentation. Running `RAWRITE2.EXE` with no arguments results in your having to answer two questions: the path name of the disk image file to write. and the destination disk drive, either `A:` or `B:`. To shortcut the prompts with `RAWRITE.EXE` or `RAWRITE2.EXE`, issue the arguments on the MS-DOS command line

`C:> rawrite` ⟨*diskimage*⟩ ⟨*drive*⟩

Repeat this step for any additional disk images your system needs.

◇ If you can check the floppy disks with `SCANDISK.EXE` and do a surface scan before writing the images to the floppy, you may save yourself some time later. Most initial install failures come from boot disks that are bad, and `RAWRITE2.EXE` doesn't verify the disks.

◇ This is also true if you create boot disks under Linux. he `badblocks(1)` manual page describes how to check disks for errors.

Label the disks that you create for future use.

Creating a Linux boot disk under Linux.

If you have an operational Linux system; for example, if you upgrade and want to create the disk images with Linux, you change to the directory with the disk images and issue the command

```
# dd if=⟨diskimage⟩ of=⟨boot floppy device⟩ bs=512 conv=sync ; sync
```

Substitute the disk image name for *diskimage* and the correct floppy device (almost always `/dev/fd0`), and repeat for each disk that you need. The `dd` arguments are: `if` for input file; `of` for output file, and here we want to use the floppy device; `bs` for block size, in this case 512 bytes; `conv=sync` ensures that the output file is exactly the same size as the input file. The trailing "`sync`" insures that we flush the buffers to disk immediately.

An alternate method that works, though will often be shunned by "real" Linux administrators, is the `cp` (copy) command

```
cp ⟨diskimage⟩ ⟨boot floppy device⟩ ; sync
```

Again, substitute the disk image file name for *diskimage*, the correct *boot floppy device*, and repeat the step for each disk that you need. You may receive a message asking if you want to replace the boot floppy device with *diskimage*. Obviously this won't happen, since the floppy diskette is not a true file but a device, but Linux doesn't pay attention to that detail. Just say, "yes," if you are asked.

With the Linux installation boot disks in hand, you're ready to install our system. Most distributions invoke `fdisk`, the Linux version, so you can create a native Linux partition and a swap partition. The install programs continue by creating the file system (the equivalent of formatting a MS-DOS disk) for both the Linux and swap partitions, and initialize the swap partition and mount the Linux partition.

One question that you will be asked is whether you want to check your hard disk for bad blocks. If you are using a SCSI drive, answer "no." SCSI drives have built-in error checking and correcting. IDE and similar drives don't have this and need to map out bad blocks. If you have an older drive you want to do this. If you say, "yes," the installation program will invoke the `badblocks` program to maps out all of the bad blocks it finds. This takes time. If in doubt, say, "yes."

Partitioning the hard disk: `fdisk` and `cfdisk`.

Every operating system, be it MS-DOS and Microsoft Windows, or Linux, has its own version of `fdisk`. If you want to create a partition for use by MS-DOS, use the MS-DOS version, `FDISK.EXE`, to create the partition and write the table. If you are going to create a partition for Linux, you must create it with the Linux version, `fdisk`.

Under Linux, two disk partitioning programs are available: the original `fdisk`, and a friendlier `cfisk`. The difference between the two is that in `fdisk` you issue all commands via the keyboard with letters and numbers. With `cfdisk`, you use the arrow keys to highlight the options you want, and press `Enter` to execute the command. The only time you use anything but the arrow and `Enter` keys is when you specify a number for the size of the partition.

For starters, all Linux boot disks are created essentially equal. Reboot the computer with the boot floppy in the boot drive. You will be greeted with a screen with some instructions and a prompt

```
LILO boot:
```

and a flashing cursor. If you use the `Tab` key, you should see a list of names. The names differ depending on the distribution, but look for one that says "rescue" or "expert." The "install" label starts the installation program after loading the kernel, so if you want to let the installation program walk you through the partitioning and file system initialization process, you can use the "install" label; otherwise, choose a different label. You may also need to provide Linux some boot parameters. For our purposes, this should not be necessary, but you'll soon find out if this is the case.

Enter a label name and press return. When the Linux kernel finishes the boot up process, you may be presented with any of a number of prompts, depending on the distribution. If you have a shell prompt, like the pound sign (`#`) or a dollar sign (`$`), you're where you need to be. If not, hold down `Alt` and press `F2`. You should be able to activate one of the system's virtual consoles.

Once you have a prompt (you should not need to log in), you will be working as "`root`" (more on this in Chapter 4). Enter the command

```
# fdisk
```

If an error is returned, try `cfdisk`. This is the disk partition utility. It defaults to `/dev/hda`, so if you need to work on the second hard drive, use the command

```
# fdisk /dev/hdb
```

In `fdisk`, press `m` to see a menu. The commands you will use are: `n` to create a new partition; `d` to destroy a partition; `t` to change the partition type (83 is Linux Native, 82 is Linux Swap); `p` prints to the screen the partition information currently in memory (not what's on the disk); `w` writes the partition table to disk; and `q` quits.

◇ Until you issue the `w` command, you are not committed and can make changes or quit without making any changes.

◇ Pay attention to prefixes and suffixes of the partition size. With the partition size you need to specify "+" if the size will be other than the ending partition number, and a suffix of "k" or "M" to specify kb or MB.

One final note on partitions: you can create up to four primary partitions. If you need more than four partitions, you will create three primary partitions and then extended partitions. The extended partition numbers begin with 5, so you may have `/dev/hda1`, `/dev/hda2`, `/dev/hda3`, `/dev/hda5`, and `/dev/hda6` if you need five partitions.

As a final check before you write the partition table, ensure that your partitions do not overlap. As long as the start and end segments don't overlap with any other start and end segments, you can be sure the partition boundaries are okay. A beginning number may be listed as 1024 for partitions with numbers starting higher than that. For now, just consider that a reminder that the BIOS will not be able to read (or boot from) that partition.

`cfdisk` does exactly the same thing as `fdisk`, but displays on the screen the state of the partition table in memory (but not on the disk) at all times. Use the Up and Down arrow keys to select a partition to work on, and the Right and Left arrow keys to select the action to be performed. Then press `Enter` to perform the action. You will have to input numbers for the size you want to make the partition, but all information is given on the screen, just follow the instructions. `cfdisk` defaults to `/dev/hda`, so you must to give it the argument `/dev/hdb` if you want to change the partition table on a second disk drive. Remember to write the table before you quit. This is the hardest part of `cfdisk`. It doesn't ask for confirmation before exiting. So select Write and press `Enter` before you select Quit and press `Enter`.

Linux distributions.

You are now faced with the task of deciding which particular distribution of Linux suits your needs. Not all distributions are alike. Many of them come with just about all of the software you'd need to run a complete system—and then some. Other Linux distributions are "small" distributions intended for users without copious amounts of disk space. Many distributions contain only the core Linux software, and you are expected to install larger software packages, such as the X Window System, yourself. (In Chapter 5 we'll show you how.)

The Linux *Distribution HOWTO* contains a list of Linux distributions available on the Internet as well as by mail order.

If you have access to USENET news, or another computer conferencing system, you might want to ask there for personal opinions from people who have installed Linux. Also, *Linux Journal* maintains a table of features comparing Linux Distributions and periodically publishes software reviews of distributions (check `http://www.ssc.com/lj/selected.html` for on-line versions of the table and articles). Even better, if you know someone who installed Linux, ask them for help and advice. There are many factors to consider when choosing a distribution; however, everyone's needs and opinions are different. In actuality, most of the popular Linux distributions contain roughly the same set of software, so the distribution you select is more or less arbitrary.

Debian GNU/Linux.

This section on Debian GNU/Linux was written by Boris Beletsky.

Debian GNU/Linux installation features.

Dependencies:	yes
Install boot methods:	floppy
Install methods:	CD, hard disk, NFS, FTP
System initialization:	Sys V `init`
Ease of installation:	challenging
Graphical administration tools:	no
Installation utility:	`dselect`
Package maintenance utility:	`dselect/dpkg`

Getting floppy images.

If you have fast, cheap Internet access, the best way to get Debian is via anonymous FTP (see Appendix C). The home ftp site of Debian is located at `ftp.debian.org` in the `/pub/debian` directory. The structure of Debian archive is described in the table on page 40.

For a base installation of Debian you need about 12 megabytes of disk space and some floppies. First, you need boot and driver floppy images. Debian provides two sets of boot floppy images, for 1.2 and 1.44 Mb floppy disks, and one set of the base images which work with either type of floppy. Check what floppy drive your system boots from, and download the appropriate disk set.

Choose the appropriate floppy set for your hardware from the table on page 41 and write the images to floppy as described on page 37.

Downloading the packages.

To install and use Debian, you need more than the base system. To decide what packages you want, download the file `Packages` from:

```
ftp://ftp.debian.org/pub/debian/stable/Packages
```

This file is a current list of Debian packages available in the stable Debian distribution. The file comes in a special format; every package has its own entry separated by a blank line. Each package's information is broken up into fields. The table on page 47 describes the fields and their possible values. It should give you an idea of how to build your personal download list. When you have the list of the packages you want, you need to decide how to download them. If you are an experienced user, you may want to download the `netbase` package—and SLIP and PPP, if necessary—so you can download packages later, via Linux. Otherwise, you can download all of the packages with your current operating system and install them later from a mounted partition.

Booting from floppies and installing Debian GNU/Linux.

The Rescue floppy. Place the Rescue floppy in the boot drive and reboot. In a minute or two, you should see a screen introduce the Rescue floppy and the `boot` prompt.

Directory	Contents
`./stable/`	Latest stable Debian release.
`./stable/binary-i386`	Debian packages for Intel i386 architecture.
`./stable/disks-i386`	Boot and root disks needed for Debian installation.
`./stable/disks-i386/current`	The current boot floppy set.
`./stable/disks-i386/special-kernels`	Special kernels and boot floppy disks, for hardware. Configurations that refuse to work with our regular boot floppies.
`./stable/msdos-i386`	DOS short file names for Debian packages.

Table 2.1: Debian GNU/Linux archive structure.

File Name	**Label**	**Description**
`rsc1440.bin`	Rescue Floppy	
`drv1440.bin`	Device Drivers	
`base-1.bin`	Base 1	Floppy set for systems with 1.44MB floppy drive and at least 5MB RAM.
`base-2.bin`	Base 2	
`base-3.bin`	Base 3	
`base-4.bin`	Base 4	
`base-5.bin`	Base 5	
`root.bin`	Root Disk	
`rsc1440r.bin`	Rescue Floppy	Optional Rescue Disk image for low memory systems (less then 5MB of RAM).
`rsc1200r.bin`	Rescue Floppy	
`drv1200.bin`	Device Drivers	
`base-1.bin`	Base 1	Floppy set for systems with 1.2MB floppy drive.
`base-2.bin`	Base 2	
`base-3.bin`	Base 3	
`base-4.bin`	Base 4	
`root.bin`	Root Disk	

Table 2.2: Debian GNU/Linux installation floppies.

It's called the *Rescue* floppy because you can use it to boot your system and perform repairs if there is a problem that makes your hard disk unbootable. Save this floppy after you install the system.

You can do two things at the `boot:` prompt: press the function keys `F1` through `F10` to view a few pages of helpful information, or boot the system. If you have any hardware devices that Linux doesn't access correctly at boot time, you may find a parameter to add to the boot command line in the screens you see by pressing `F3`, `F4`, and `F5`.

If you add parameters to the boot command line, be sure to type the word "`linux`" and a space before the first parameter. If you simply press `Enter`, that's the same as typing "`linux`" without any special parameters.

If this is the first time you're booting the system, press `Enter` and see if it works correctly. It probably will. If not, you can reboot later and look for any special parameters that inform the system about your hardware.

Once you press `Enter`, you should see the messages

```
Loading...
Uncompressing Linux...
```

then there is a page or so of cryptic information about the hardware in the system. There may be many messages in the form of, "`can't find` *something*," "*something* `not present`," "`can't initialize` *something*," or even "`this driver release depends on` *something*," Most of these are harmless. The installation boot disk is built to run on computers with many different peripheral devices. Obviously, no computer will have every possible peripheral device, and the operating system may emit a few complaints while it looks for peripherals you don't own. You may also see the system pause for a while. This happens if it is waiting for a device to respond that is not present on your system. If you find that the time it takes to boot the system unacceptably long, you can create a custom kernel after you install the system which doesn't have the drivers for non-existent devices.

Low memory systems. If your system has 4MB of RAM, you may see a paragraph about low memory and a text menu with three choices. If your system has enough RAM, you won't see this at all, and you'll go directly to the color or monochrome dialog box. If you get the low-memory menu, you should go through its selections in order. Partition your disk, activate the swap partition, and start the graphical installation system.

The program that is used to partition your disk is called `cfdisk`, and you should see the manual page for `cfdisk` and the instructions on page 38 for assistance.

`cfdisk` is used to create a Linux Swap partition (type 82) on the hard drive. You need the swap partition for virtual memory during installation, because the procedure likely uses more memory than you have physical RAM for. Select the amount of virtual memory that you intend to use once your system is installed. It is exactly equal to the amount of disk space required. Sixteen megabytes is probably the smallest practical amount, but use 32 megabytes if you can spare the disk space, and 64 megabytes if the disk is large enough and you won't miss the space.

The color or monochrome dialog box. Once the system finishes booting, you should see the color or monochrome dialog box. If your monitor displays black and white (monochrome), press `Enter` and continue with the installation. Otherwise, use the arrow key to move the cursor to the `Color` menu item and then press `Enter`. The display should change from black and white to color. Press `Enter` again to continue with the installation.

The Main Menu You may see a dialog box that says,

```
The installation program is determining the current state of your system.
```

On some systems, this message flashes by too quickly to read. It is displayed between steps in the installation process. The installation program checks the state of the system after each step. This allows you to restart the installation without losing the work that you have already done, if you halt the system in the middle of the installation. If you need to restart an installation, you will be prompted to select color or monochrome again, configure the keyboard, reactivate the swap partition, and remount any disks that have been initialized. Any other installation on the system will be saved.

During the entire process, you are presented with the main menu. The choices at the top of the menu change to indicate your progress in installing the system. Phil Hughes wrote in *Linux Journal* that you could teach a chicken to install Debian. He meant that the installation process was mostly just pecking at the `Enter` key. The first choice on the installation menu is the next action you should perform according to what the system detects you have already done. It should say `Next`, and, at this point, the next item should be

```
Configure the Keyboard
```

Configuring the keyboard. Make sure that the highlight is on the `Next` item, and press `Enter` for the keyboard configuration menu. Select a keyboard that conforms to the layout used for your national language, or select something close to it if the keyboard layout you want isn't shown. After installation you can select a keyboard layout from a wider range of choices. Move the highlight to the keyboard selection and press `Enter`. Use the arrow keys to move the highlight—they are in the same place on all national language keyboard layouts and are independent of the keyboard configuration.

The shell. If you are an experienced UNIX or Linux user, press `LeftAlt` and `F2` in unison for the second virtual console. That's the `Alt` key on the left-hand side of the `Space` bar and the `F2` function key. You'll see a separate window running a Bourne shell clone called `ash`. At this point, the root file system is on the RAM disk, and there is a limited set of UNIX utilities available for your use. You can see what programs are available with the command

```
ls /bin /sbin /usr/bin /usr/sbin
```

◇ The shell and commands are there only in case something goes wrong. In particular, you should always use the menus, not the shell, to activate your swap partition, because the menu software can't detect whether you've done this from the shell. Press `LeftAlt`-`F1` to get back to menus. Linux provides up to 64 virtual consoles, but the Rescue floppy only uses a few of them.

◇ **Last chance!** Have you backed up your disks? Here's your first chance to wipe out all of the data on your disks, and your last chance to save your old system. If you haven't backed up all of your disks, remove the floppy from the drive, reset the system, and create a backup.

Partition your hard disks. If you have not already partitioned your disks for Linux Native and Linux Swap file systems, the menu item `Next` will be

```
Partition a Hard Disk
```

If you have already created at least one Linux Native and one Linux Swap disk partition, the `Next` menu selection will be

```
Initialize and Activate the Swap Disk Partition
```

or you may even skip that step if your system has little RAM and the installation software asked you to activate the swap partition as soon as the system started. Whatever the `Next` menu selection is, you can use the down-arrow key to select

```
Partition a Hard Disk
```

The `Partition a Hard Disk` menu item presents you with a list of disk drives you can partition and runs the `cfdisk` program (see page 38), which allows you to create and edit disk partitions. You must create at least one Linux (type 83) disk partition.

Your swap partition will be used to provide virtual memory for the system and should be between 16 and 128 megabytes in size, depending on how much disk space you have and how many large programs you want to run. Linux will not use more than 128 megabytes of swap, so there's no reason to make your swap partition larger than that. A swap partition is strongly recommended, but you can do without one if you insist and system has more than 16 Mb of RAM.

`Initialize and Activate the Swap Disk Partition`**.** This is the `Next` menu item after you create one disk partition. You have the choice of initializing and activating a new swap partition, activating a previously initialized partition, and doing without a swap partition. It's always permissible to re-initialize a swap partition, so select `Initialize and Activate the Swap Disk Partition` unless you are sure that you know what you are doing. This menu choice will give you the option to scan the entire partition for unreadable disk blocks caused by defects on the surface of the hard disk platters. This is useful if you have MFM, RLL, or older IDE disks, and checking the disk never hurts. Properly working SCSI disks don't need to be scanned. They have their own internal mechanism for mapping out bad disk blocks.

The swap partition provides virtual memory to supplement the RAM in your system, and it's even used while the system is being installed. That's why we initialize it first.

Initialize a Linux disk partition. At this point, the `Next` menu item should be

```
Initialize a Linux Disk Partition
```

If it isn't, you haven't completed the disk partitioning process, or you haven't made one of the menu choices dealing with your swap partition.

You can initialize a Linux disk partition, or alternately you can mount a previously initialized partition.

◇ The boot floppies will not upgrade an old system without removing the files—Debian provides a different procedure than using the boot floppies for upgrading existing Debian systems. Thus, if you are using old disk partitions that are not empty, you should initialize them, which erases all of the files. You must initialize any partition that you created in the disk partitioning step. About the only reason to mount a partition without initializing it at this point would be to mount a partition upon which you have user files, like `/home`, that you don't want deleted.

Select the `Next` menu item, to initialize and mount the root (the "/" directory) disk partition. The first partition you mount or initialize, after the swap partition, if you're using it, is the partition mounted as root. You will be offered the choice to scan the disk partition for bad blocks, as when you initialized the swap partition. It never hurts to scan for bad blocks. Keep in mind that this step can take 10 minutes or more if you have a large disk.

Install the base system. Once you've mounted the root partition, the `Next` menu item will be

```
Install the Base System
```

unless you already performed some of the installation steps. You can use the arrow keys to select the menu items to initialize or mount disk partitions if you have additional partitions to set up. If you have created separate partitions for `/var`, `/usr`, or other file systems, you should initialize and mount them now.

There will be a pause while the system looks for a local copy of the base system. This search is for CD-ROM installations and will not succeed. You are then offered a menu of drives from which to read the base floppies. Select the appropriate drive. Feed in the Base 1, Base 2, Base 3, and Base 4 floppies—and Base 5 if you are using 1.2MB floppies—as requested by the program. If one of the base floppies is unreadable, you need to create a replacement floppy and feed all five floppies into the system again. After the floppies have been read, the system installs the files. This can take ten minutes or more on a slow system.

Install the operating system kernel. At this point, the `Next` menu item should be

```
Install the Operating System Kernel
```

Select it, and you will be prompted to select a floppy drive and insert the Rescue floppy. This copies the kernel onto the hard disk. This kernel is used later to create a custom boot floppy for your system and make the hard disk bootable without a floppy.

Install the device drivers. Select the menu item to install the device drivers. You will be prompted to insert the Device Drivers floppy, and the drivers will be copied onto your hard disk. Select the

```
Configure Device Drivers
```

menu item and look for devices which are on your system. Configure those device drivers, so they will be loaded whenever your system boots.

There is a menu selection for PCMCIA device drivers, but you do not need to use it. After installation you can install the `pcmcia-cs` package. This detects PCMCIA cards automatically and configures those it finds. It also recognizes cards that are hot swapped when the system is running—they will all be configured as they are plugged in, and de-configured when unplugged.

Configure the base system. At this point the system read in all of the files that make up a minimal Debian system, but you must perform some configuration before the system will run. Select

```
Configure the Base System
```

This asks you to select your time zone. Look for your time zone or region of the world in the menu, and type it at the prompt. This may lead to another menu where you can select more specific information.

Next, you are asked if your system clock should be set to Greenwich Mean Time (GMT) or local time. Select GMT if are running only Linux or another UNIX on your system. Select local time if you use another operating system like MS-DOS or Microsoft Windows. UNIX systems keep GMT time on the system clock and use software which converts it to the local time. This allows them to keep track of daylight savings time and leap years, and even allows users who are logged in from other time zones to individually set the time zone on their terminal. If you run the system clock on GMT and your locality uses daylight savings time, the system adjusts for daylight savings time properly on the days it starts and ends.

Configure the network. You must configure the network even if you don't have one, but you only have to answer the first two questions:

```
What is the name of your computer?
Is your system connected to a network?
```

If you are connected to a network, check with your system administrator or ISP vendor if you don't know the following information:

- your computer's host name;
- your computer's or ISP's domain name;

- your computer's IP address;
- the netmask to use with your network;
- the IP address of your network;
- the broadcast address to use on your network;
- if your network has a gateway, the IP address of the default gateway system to which you should route packets;
- the system on your network to use for Domain Name Service (DNS); and
- whether you connect to the network using Ethernet.

The program will guess that the network IP address is the bitwise AND of your system's IP address and netmask. It will guess that the broadcast address is the bitwise OR of your system's IP address with the bitwise negation of the netmask. It will guess that your gateway system is also your DNS server. If you can't find any of these answers, use the system's guesses—if necessary, you can alter them after installation by editing the `/etc/init.d/network` file.

Make the hard disk bootable. If you choose to make the hard disk boot directly to Linux, you are asked to install a master boot record. If you aren't using a boot manager (this is probably the case if you don't know what a boot manager is), answer "yes" to this question. The next question is whether you want to boot Linux automatically from the hard disk when you turn on the system. This sets Linux to be the bootable partition—the one that will be loaded from the hard disk. If you answer "no" to this question, you can set the bootable partition later using the MS-DOS `FDISK.EXE` program, or the Linux `fdisk` or `activate` programs.

Make a boot floppy. You should make a boot floppy even if you intend to boot the system from the hard disk. The reason for this is that it's possible for the hard disk bootstrap to be installed incorrectly. A boot floppy will almost always work. Select

```
Make a Boot Floppy
```

from the menu and feed the system a blank floppy as directed. Make sure that the floppy isn't write protected. The software attempts to format and write it. Mark this diskette the "Custom Boot" floppy and write-protect it once it has been written.

The moment of truth. This is what electrical engineers call the "smoke test"—what happens when you power up a new system for the first time. Remove the floppy disk from the floppy drive and select

```
Reboot the System
```

from the menu. If the Linux system doesn't start up, insert the Custom Boot floppy you created in the previous step and reset the system. Linux should boot. You should see the same messages as when you first booted the installation boot floppy, followed by some new messages.

Add a user account and password. After you've added logins, (Chapter 4 discusses this in some detail), you are dropped into `dselect`, the Debian package management program.

◇ You should read the tutorial before attempting to install packages with `dselect`.

`dselect` allows you to select the packages that you want installed on your system. The Debian package management software is described in detail starting on page 46. If you have a CD-ROM or hard disk with the additional Debian packages or are connected to the Internet, you may want to read that section now. Otherwise, exit `dselect`. You can use the package management software after you have transferred the Debian package files to your system.

◇ You must be the superuser (root) to use `dselect`.

◇ If you install the X Window System and do not use a US keyboard, read the X11 Release note for non-US keyboards.

Log in. After you exit `dselect`, you are at the `login:` prompt. Log in using the personal login and password you selected. Your system is ready to use.

Running Debian GNU/Linux.

This section describes the Debian packaging system and Debian-specific utilities. The Debian/GNU Linux `Packages` file format is shown in the table on page 47.

Debian distributions come in archives called **packages**. Every package is a collection of files (programs, usually) that can be installed using `dpkg` or `dselect`. In addition, the package contains some information about itself that is read by the installation utilities.

Package classifications. The packages that are included with Debian GNU/Linux are classified according to how essential they are (priority) and their functionality (section).

The *priority* of a package indicates how essential or necessary it is. Debian GNU/Linux classifies all packages into four different priority levels:

Required. These packages must be installed for the system to operate correctly and have been installed as part of the base system.

◇ Never remove a required package from the system unless you are absolutely sure of what you are doing. This bears repeating: **Never, never, never remove a required package from the system unless you are absolutely sure of what you are doing.** It is likely that doing so will render your system completely unusable.

Required packages are abbreviated in `dselect` as `Req`.

Important. Important packages are found on almost all UNIX-like operating systems. These packages include `cron`, `man`, and `vi`.

Important packages are abbreviated in `dselect` as `Imp`.

Standard. Standard packages are packages that, more or less, comprise the "standard," character based, Debian GNU/Linux system. The Standard system includes a fairly complete software development environment and GNU Emacs.

Standard packages are abbreviated in `dselect` as `Std`.

Optional. Optional packages comprise a fairly complete system. The Optional system includes TEX and the X Window System.

Optional packages are abbreviated in `dselect` as `Opt`.

Extra Extra packages are only useful to a small or select group of people, or are installed for a specific purpose. Extra packages might include such programs as electronics and ham radio applications.

Extra packages are abbreviated in `dselect` as `Xtr`.

By default, `dselect` automatically selects the Standard system if the user doesn't want to individually select the packages to be installed.

The *section* of a package indicates its functionality or use. Packages on the CD-ROM and in FTP archives are arranged in subdirectories according to function. The directory names are fairly self-explanatory: for example, the directory `admin` contains packages for system administration and the directory `devel` contains packages for software development and programming. Unlike priority levels, there are many sections, and more may be added in the future, so we do not individually describe them in this guide.

Package relationships. Each package includes information about how it relates to the other packages included with the system. There are four package relationships in Debian GNU/Linux: conflicts, dependencies, recommendations, and suggestions.

A *conflict* occurs when two or more packages cannot be installed on the same system at the same time. A good example of conflicting packages are mail transfer agents (MTAs). A MTA is a program that delivers electronic mail to users on the system and other machines on the network. Debian GNU/Linux has two mail transfer agents: `sendmail` and `smail`.

Only one mail transfer agent may be installed at a time. They both do the same job and are not designed to coexist. Therefore, the `sendmail` and `smail` packages conflict. If you try to install `sendmail` when `smail` is already installed, the Debian GNU/Linux package maintenance system will refuse to install it. Likewise, if you try to install `smail` when `sendmail` is already installed, `dselect` (or `dpkg`; see below) will refuse to install it.

A *dependency* occurs when one package requires another package to function properly. Using our electronic mail example, users read mail with programs called mail user agents (MUAs). Popular MUAs include

Package	Package Name	
Priority	**Package Importance**	
	Required	Should be installed for proper system operation.
	Important	Not required but important.
	Optional	Not necessary but useful.
	Extra	Package may conflict with other packages with higher priorities.
Section	**General Category**	
	Base	Base system.
	Devel	Development tools.
	X11	Packages for the X Window System.
	Admin	Administration utilities.
	Doc	Documentation.
	Comm	Various communication utilities.
	Editors	Various editors.
	Electronics	Electronics utilities.
	Games	Games. (You knew that, didn't you?)
	Graphics	Graphics utilities.
	Hamradio	Utilities for Internet radio.
	Mail	Email clients and servers.
	Math	Mathematics utilities. (Like calculators, etc....)
	Net	Various tools to connect to the network (usually TCP/IP).
	News	Servers and clients for Internet news (NNTP).
	Shells	Shells, such as `tcsh` and `bash`.
	Sound	Any sound application (like audio CD players).
	TeX	Anything that can read, write, and convert TeX.
	Text	Applications to manipulate texts (like `nroff`).
	Misc	Everything else that doesn't fit above.
Maintainer	Name of the person who maintains the package and his or her e-mail address.	
Version	Version of the package in the format *upstream-version–debian-version*.	
Depends	A list of other packages upon which the current package depends and will not function without.	
Recommends	Another level of package dependencies—it is strongly recommended the packages listed in this field be installed if this package is to be used.	
Suggests	Packages listed in this field may be useful to the packages this entry describes.	
Filename	File name of the package via FTP or CD-ROM.	
MS-DOS-Filename	File name of the package in short DOS format.	
Size	Size of the package after the installation.	
Md5sum	The md5sum check, made to insure this package is official.	
Description	This field will tell you about the package—*do not* download the package without reading it.	

Table 2.3: Fields in a Debian/GNU Linux `Packages` file record.

elm, pine, and emacs RMAIL mode. It is normal to install several MUAs at once because they do not conflict. But MUAs do not deliver mail—that is the job of the MTA. So all mail user agent packages *depend* on a mail transfer agent.

A package can also *recommend* or *suggest* other related packages.

dselect.

This section is a brief tutorial on Debian dselect. For more detailed information, refer to the dselect manual at

ftp://ftp.debian.org/debian/Debian-1.2/disks-i386/current/dselect.beginner.6.html

dselect is simple, menu-driven interface which helps install packages. It takes you through the package installation process in the order of the on-screen menu:

```
Debian Linux dselect package handling front end.
0.  [A]ccess Choose the access method to use.
1.  [U]pdate Update list of available packages, if possible.
2.  [S]elect Request which packages you want on your system.
3.  [I]nstall Install and upgrade wanted packages.
4.  [C]onfig Configure any packages that are unconfigured.
5.  [R]emove Remove unwanted software.
6.  [Q]uit Quit dselect.
```

There are two ways to select an option from the menu: choose it with arrows, or press the key of the corresponding letter in brackets.

Access. In this menu you choose the method to obtain and install the packages.

Abbreviation	Description
cdrom	install from a CD-ROM
nfs	install from an NFS server (not yet mounted)
harddisk	install from a hard disk partition (not yet mounted)
mounted	install from a file system which is already mounted
floppy	install from a pile of floppy disks
ftp	install using ftp

Update. dselect reads the Packages database (described above) and creates a database of the packages available on your system.

Select. This section of the program selects the packages. Choose your the package you want and press Enter. If you have a slow machine, the screen may clear and remain blank for 15 seconds. The first thing that appears is Page 1 of the Help file. You can view this screen by pressing "?" at any point in the Select screens, and you can page through the help screens by pressing the . (period) key.

To exit the Select screen after all of the selections are complete, press Enter. This returns you to the main screen *if* there are no problems with your selection. You must resolve those problems first. When you are satisfied with any given screen, press Enter.

Dependency conflicts are quite normal and to be expected. If you select package A and that package requires the unselected package B in order to run, dselect warns you of the problem and will most likely suggest a solution. If package A conflicts with package B, you must decide between them.

Install dselect runs through the entire 800 packages and installs the ones that are selected. You will need to make decisions during this process. It is often useful to switch to a different shell to compare, for example, an old configuration file with a new one. If the old file is called conf.modules, for example the new file will be called conf.modules.dpkg-new.

The screen scrolls by fairly quickly on faster machines. You can halt the display is by pressing Control-S and restart it with Control-Q. At the end of the run, there will be a list of any uninstalled packages.

Configure. Most packages are configured in Step 3, but anything remaining can be configured here.

Remove. Remove packages that are no longer needed.

Quit. *Au revoir.*

dpkg.

This is a command line tool that installs and manipulates Debian packages. It has several options that allow you to install, configure, update, remove, and perform other operations on Debian packages. You can even build your own packages. dpkg also allows you to list the available packages, files "owned" by packages, which package owns a file, and so on.

Installing or updating new or existing packages. Type the following command:

```
# dpkg -i ⟨filename⟩.deb
```

where *filename* is the name of the file containing a Debian package, like tcsh_6.06-11_i386.deb. dpkg is partly interactive; during the installation it may ask additional questions, like whether to install the new version of a configuration file or keep the old version.

You may also unpack a package without configuring it by entering:

```
# dpkg -unpack ⟨filename⟩
```

If a package depends on an uninstalled package or a newer version of a package you already have, or if any other dependency problem occurs during the installation, dpkg will exit without configuring it.

Configuring installed packages. If dpkg aborts during installation and leaves a package installed, the package is left unconfigured. The Debian packaging system requires the package to be configured to avoid dependency problems. Some packages also require configuration to work properly.

To configure a package, type:

```
dpkg -configure ⟨package⟩
```

where *package* is the name of the package, like tcsh. (Notice that this is not the original name of the file from which tcsh was installed, which was longer, included a version number, and ended in .deb.)

Removing installed packages. In the Debian package system, there are two ways to eliminate packages: remove and purge. The remove option removes the specified package; the purge option removes both the specified package and its configuration files. The usage is:

```
# dpkg -r ⟨package⟩
# dpkg -purge ⟨package⟩
```

If there are any installed packages that depend on the one you wish to remove, the package will *not* be removed, and dpkg will abort with an error message.

Reporting package status. To report the status of the package (e.g., installed, not installed, or unconfigured), enter:

```
# dpkg -s ⟨package⟩
```

Listing available packages. To list the installed packages that match some pattern, type:

```
# dpkg -l ⟨package-name-pattern⟩
```

where *package-name-pattern* is an optional argument specifying a pattern for the package names to match, like *sh. Normal shell wildcards are allowed. If you don't specify the pattern, all of the installed packages are listed.

Listing files owned by packages. To list all the files owned by a particular package, simply type:

```
# dpkg -L ⟨package⟩
```

However, this does not list files created by package-specific installation scripts.

Finding the package that owns a file. To find the package which owns a particular file, type the following command:

```
# dpkg -S ⟨filename-pattern⟩
```

where *filename-pattern* is the pattern with which to search the package names for a match. Again, normal shell wild cards are allowed.

Summary. `dpkg` is simple to use and is preferred over `dselect` when all that you need to do is install, upgrade, or remove a small number of packages. It also has some functionality that `dselect` (an interface to `dpkg`) doesn't have, like finding which package owns a file. For the full list of options, refer to the `dpkg(8)` manual page.

About Debian GNU/Linux.

The Debian GNU/Linux Project was created by Ian Murdock in 1993, initially under the sponsorship of the Free Software Foundation's GNU project. Later, Debian separated from FSF. Debian is the result of a volunteer effort to create a free, high-quality UNIX-compatible operating system based on the Linux kernel, complete with a suite of applications.

The Debian community is a group of more than 150 unpaid volunteers from all over the world who collaborate via the Internet. The founders of the project have formed the organization Software in the Public Interest (SPI) to sponsor Debian GNU/Linux development.

Software in the Public Interest is a non-profit organization formed when the FSF withdrew their sponsorship of Debian. The purpose of the organization is to develop and distribute free software. Its goals are very much like those of FSF, and it encourages programmers to use the GNU General Public License on their programs. However, SPI has a slightly different focus in that it is building and distributing a Linux system that diverges in many technical details from the GNU system planned by FSF. SPI still communicates with FSF and cooperates in sending them changes to GNU software and in asking its users to donate to FSF and the GNU project.

SPI can be reached by post at:

Software in the Public Interest
P.O. Box 70152
Pt. Richmond, CA 94807-0152

Mailing lists.

There are several Debian-related mailing lists:

`debian-announce@lists.debian.org`
: Moderated. Major system announcements. Usually about one message per month.

`debian-changes@lists.debian.org`
: Announcements of new package releases for the stable distribution. Usually several messages per day.

`debian-devel-changes@lists.debian.org`
: Announcements of new package releases for the unstable distribution. Usually several messages per day.

`debian-user@lists.debian.org`
: A mailing list where users of Debian ask for and get support. Usually about 50 packages per day.

`debian-sparc@lists.debian.org`

`debian-alpha@lists.debian.org`

`debian-68k@lists.debian.org`
: Lists for those who are involved in porting Debian software to the SPARC, DEC Alpha, and Motorolla 680x0 platforms.

There are also several mailing lists for Debian developers.

You can subscribe to those mailing list by mail or the World Wide Web. For more information, please visit `http://www.debian.org/`.

Bug tracking system.

The Debian project has a bug tracking system that handles bug reports by users. As soon as the bug is reported, it is given a number and all of the information provided on the particular bug is stored in a file and mailed to the maintainer of the package. When the bug is fixed, it must be marked as done ("closed") by the maintainer. If it was closed by mistake, it may be reopened.

To receive more information on the bug tracing system, send e-mail to `request@bugs.debian.org` with `help` in the body of the message.

Acknowledgments.

Many thanks to Bruce Perens and the other authors of Debian related materials that were used to write this chapter. Thanks also to Vadik Vygonets, my beloved cousin, who helped me quite a bit. Lastly, thanks are also due to the members of Debian community for their hard work. Let's hope that Debian GNU/Linux becomes even better.

Last note.

Debian GNU/Linux changes very quickly, and many facts can change more quickly than this book. The source text of this section is updated regularly. You can find it at

```
http://www.cs.huji.ac.il/~borik/debian/ligs/
```

Red Hat Linux.

This section on Red Hat Linux was written by Henry Pierce.

Red Hat Linux installation features.

Dependencies:	yes
Install boot methods:	CD, floppy,loadin (from DOS)
Install methods:	CD, hard disk, NFS, FTP, SMB
System initialization:	Sys V init
Ease of installation:	easy
Graphical administration tools:	numerous
Installation utility:	install script that calls RPM
Package maintenance utility:	RPM, glint

The RPM package management system.

Red Hat Linux's RPM package management system manages software by defining how a software package is built for installation and collects information about its components and installation methods during the build process. A RPM package has an organized packet of data in the header of *package*.`rpm` which can be added to a database that describes where the package belongs, what supporting packages are required, whether the required packages are installed, and provides a means to determine software dependencies.

RPM gives system administrators the ability to: upgrade individual components or entire systems while preserving the configuration of the system or package; query the database for the location of files, packages, or related information; perform package verification so packages can be installed properly, or at all; keep source packages "pristine" (provide the package author's original source and second-party patches separately) so that porting issues can be tracked. Because RPM does this, you can install, upgrade, or remove packages with a single command line in text mode or a few clicks of the mouse in X Package Management Tool. Examples of using RPM from the command line are:

```
# rpm -install ⟨package⟩.rpm # this installs ⟨package⟩
# rpm -upgrade ⟨package⟩.rpm # this upgrades ⟨package⟩
# rpm -erase ⟨package⟩.rpm # this removes or erases ⟨package⟩
```

Package naming conventions. A properly built *package*.rpm has the following characteristics: its name identifies the package, the version, the build revision, the architecture, and the extension .rpm, which identifies it as a RPM package.

Take, for example, bash-1.14.7-1.i386.rpm. The name itself contains useful information: the package is bash (the Bourne Again SHell), it is version 1.14.7, and it is build 1 of the current version for Red Hat Linux. It was built for Intel or compatible 80386 or higher CPUs, and it is in RPM format. So, if you see a package named bash-1.14.7-2.i386.rpm, you know that it is the second build of bash version 1.14.7, and probably contains fixes for problems of the previous build and is more current. While the internal organization of a *.rpm file is beyond the scope of this section, a properly built package contains an executable file, any configuration files, the documentation (at least manual pages), any miscellaneous files directly related to the package, a record of where the packages files are to be installed, and a record of any required packages. After successful installation, information about the package is registered in the system's RPM database. A more thorough discussion of RPM package management system may be found in the RPM HOWTO on page 1270. It is also available at

```
http://www.redhat.com/support/docs/rpm/RPM-HOWTO/RPM-HOWTO.html
```

A note about upgrading Red Hat Linux.

Only upgrades from version 2.0 of Red Hat Linux and onward are supported due to major changes in Linux's binary format. Otherwise, upgrades can be performed from the same installation methods of CD-ROM, NFS, FTP, and hard disk. As of Red Hat Linux version 4.0, the upgrade option is incorporated into the Boot diskette instead of a separate program. If you upgrade from v2.1 to v3.0.3 and want to upgrade again to version 4.0, you need to create the Boot diskette instead of looking for an upgrade script, the same as Red Hat 4.*x* installation from scratch. This method does not reformat your partitions nor delete your configuration files.

Creating the installation floppies.

To create an Installation Floppy Kit, you need the following:

1. The Red Hat Boot diskette image, boot.img, which is available at:

   ```
   ftp//ftp.redhat.com/pub/redhat/current/i386/images/boot.img
   ```

   or in the images directory of a Red Hat CD-ROM.

2. The Red Hat Supplemental diskette image, supp.img, which is available at

   ```
   ftp://ftp.redhat.com/pub/redhat/current/i386/images/supp.img
   ```

   or in the images directory of a Red Hat CD-ROM. This diskette is required if your method of installation is not CD-ROM based, or you need PCMCIA support for any device, like a CD-ROM on a laptop, to install properly. This diskette can also be used with the Boot diskette as an emergency start disk for an installed system.

3. The program RAWRITE.EXE, which is available at:

   ```
   ftp://ftp.redhat.com/pub/redhat/current/i386/dosutils/rawrite.exe
   ```

   or in the DOS directory of a Red Hat CD-ROM.

4. MS-DOS and Windows 95 users installing Red Hat Linux for the first time on a machine that will have Linux installed as a second operating system should also obtain:

```
ftp://ftp.redhat.com/pub/redhat/dos/fdips11.zip
```

and unzip the files into: `C:\FIPS` if you need to free space on your hard drive.

5. An Emergency Boot diskette for an existing operating system on the target machine on which Linux will be installed as a second operating system must be created.

Installation media.

After you create the Installation floppies using `RAWRITE.EXE` or `dd` as described on page 37, insure that your installation method is properly set up for the Red Hat installation diskettes. For CD-ROM, NFS, FTP, and hard drive installation methods, the source must have the directory `/RedHat` on the "top level" with the directories `/base` and `/RPMS` underneath:

```
/RedHat
    |----> /RPMS (contains binary the .rpm s to be installed)
    |----> /base (contains a base system and files to set up \\
             the hard drive)
```

NFS installation. For NFS installation, you will either need a Red Hat CD-ROM on a machine (such as an existing Linux box) that can support and export an ISO-9660 file system with Rockridge Extensions, or you need to mirror one of the Red Hat distributions with the directory tree organized as described above—and of course, the proper files in each directory. The directory `/RedHat` needs to be exported to the machines on the network that are to have Red Hat Linux installed or upgraded. This machine must be on an Ethernet; you can not do an NFS install via dialup link.

Hard drive installation. Hard drive installations must have the `/RedHat` directory created relative to the root directory of the partition (it doesn't matter which partition) that will contain the Red Hat distribution obtained either from CD-ROM or an FTP site. For example, on the primary DOS partition, the path to `\RedHat` should be `C:\RedHat`. On a MS-DOS file system, it does not matter that the *package*`.rpm` names are truncated. All you need to do is make sure the `\RedHat\base` directory contains the base files from a CD-ROM or FTP site and the `\RedHat\RPMS` directory contains all of the *package*`.rpm` files from the CD-ROM or FTP site. Then you can install or upgrade from that partition. If you have an existing Linux partition that is not needed for an installation or upgrade, you can set it up as outlined here and use it.

FTP installation. To install via FTP over the Internet, all you need is the IP address of the FTP server and the root directory path for the Red Hat Linux system you wish to install. See Appendix C for a list of Linux FTP sites and mirrors. If you intend to do an FTP installation over a low-bandwidth connection (anything slower than a 128K ISDN link), it is highly recommended you copy the files to an existing MS-DOS hard drive partition and then install from the hard drive. The total size of the packages in the `/RedHat/RPMS` directory is approximately 170MB and will take many hours to install. If something goes wrong with the installation, such as the link going down, you need to start from the beginning. If you get the files first and set up your hard drive to install Linux, it is then less work and less confusing to recover from a failed installation. You don't even need to download all of the files in `/RedHat/RPMS` to successfully install a minimal system which can grow with your needs. See the next section for details.

Customizing your NFS or hard drive installation.

One of the interesting things that you can do with Red Hat Linux is customize the installation process. This is not for the faint of heart—only those already familiar with Red Linux or Linux in general should attempt it. As of Red Hat Linux version 4.x, the `/RedHat/RPMS` directory contains approximately 170MB of `.rpm` files. RPM compresses these packages and assumes that the packages need an average of 2 to 3MB of hard drive space for every 1MB of RPM package volume. If *package*`.rpm` is 6MB in size, you need between 12 and 18MB of free space to install the package.

Customizing which packages are available for installation is an option when installing the system via FTP, NFS, and hard drive. CD-ROMs (typically) cannot be written to, but you can copy the files to the hard drive and install from there with the customized package list. FTP and NFS installations can only be designed if you have root access to the server(s) on your network or your system administrator is willing to work with you. The following installation situations make custom installation desirable: when obtaining Red Hat Linux via FTP over a low-bandwidth connection or when designing a suite of software to be used by all Red Hat Linux workstations on a network.

To customize the installation, you must obtain the `/base/comps` file which provides you with the list of packages that a full installation would normally include. Then, the packages you actually want to install from `/base/comps` need to be downloaded. The `/base/comps` file must be edited to reflect the packages that you obtained and are going to install.

◇ If you have local RPM packages, you can add them to the `comps` file as well.

The `comps` file. The Red Hat installation program uses the file `/RedHat/base/comps` (the file here is an example from Red Hat Linux version 4.0) to determine what packages are available in the `/RedHat/RPMS` directory for each category to be installed. The file is organized by category, and each category contains a list of packages Red Hat believes are the minimum required for that section. NOTE: only the *package* part of a package's name (`package-version-build.rpm`) is listed in the file. This means the `comps` file is generally usable from one version of Red Hat to the next. A section in this file has the structure:

number category
package
`...`
`end`

That is a tag to identify the category number, the category, a list of the package names in the category, and the tag "end" to mark the end of the category.

Without exception, everyone needs all of the software packages listed in the **Base** section of the file. The other sections, though, can generally be customized or eliminated to suit a particular need. For example, there are three types of **Networked Stations**: "plain", management, and dial-up. An examination of these sections shows that many of the software packages are listed in all three categories, but some software packages are specific to the category. If you are creating a **Dial-up Networked Station**, then you can safely eliminate the "Plain" and "Management" sections and any software unique to those categories. Conversely, if you only need basic networking capability for networked work stations, the other sections can be eliminated from the file as well as the software unique to those sections. All you need to do is make sure that you have all of the software packages listed in that category. If you have local custom packages (those not provided by Red Hat Software), you should add them to an existing category that is appropriate rather than creating a new category.

Because the list of packages in each category only contains the name of the package (i.e., not the entire `package-name-version-build.rpm`), you can substitute any updates Red Hat has made available in the `updates` directory on:

```
ftp://ftp.redhat.com/pub/redhat/current/updates
```

or one of Red Hat's mirror sites for the original package found in the distribution's original `/RedHat/RPMS` directory. The installation program is relatively version-insensitive. The only warning here is to insure that package dependencies are met. When an RPM package is built, RPM itself tries to determine what packages must be installed for the package to work (the RPM developer also has direct control of this as well—he or she can add dependencies that RPM might not ordinarily detect). This is where a little experimentation or research may be needed. For example, one way to determine package dependencies (if you have user access to your NFS server on an existing Red Hat Linux box) is to `telnet` or `login` into it (or if you have the CD-ROM, mount it and go to the `RedHat/RPMS` directory) and query the package for its dependencies:

```
[root@happy RPMS] rpm -q -p -R bash-1.14.7-1.i386.rpm

libc.so.5

libtermcap.so.2
```

The "-q" puts rpm in query mode, the "-p" tells rpm to query an uninstalled package, and the "-R" tells rpm to list the target package's dependencies. In this example, we see libc.so.5 and libtermcap.so.2 are required. Since libc and termcap are part of the base of required software (as is bash), you must insure that the libc and libtermcap packages (the dependency packages) are present to be able to install bash (the target). As long as you get the entire base system installed, you can boot the system when the installation program completes. You can add additional packages to Red Hat Linux as required even if the installation program reports that a package failed to install because its dependencies were not met.

The table on page 56 describes the categories of software found in /base/comps in Red Hat v4.0:

Recommended minimal installation.

It is difficult to determine how much space an installation will require. However, someone installing via FTP should get the **Base** system and the **Dialup Networked Station** and install these. Then, additional software can be obtained and added as the need arises. Of course, if you want to do C programming, you should get the relevant packages and edit the comps file appropriately.

◇ If you encounter a package during the installation which requires another package that you don't have available, or you make a mistake in the comps file, you can generally finish the installation and have a bootable, working system. You can correct the problem by manually adding the failed packages and their dependencies later. Overall, get the entire **Base** system and one of the **Networked Station** packages installed, and you can add anything you need or want later.

2.0.1 How much space do you really need?

The table on page 57 gives approximate disk space requirements Red Hat Linux and various subsystems.

Installation.

By now, you should have created the Installation Floppy Kit, prepared your hard drive, and have your installation media ready. The details of the installation follow. You first begin by booting your system and configuring the installation program to install from your selected medium. After this the installation proceeds with the same steps for everyone. You need to begin by booting your computer with the diskette labeled "Boot diskette".

Installation media revisited.

As the boot diskette starts up, the kernel attempts to detect any hardware for which the boot kernel has drivers compiled directly into it. Once booting is complete, a message appears which asks if you have a color screen (if you do, select "OK"). Next comes the Red Hat Welcome screen. Choose "OK" to continue. The next question asks if you need PCMCIA support. You must answer "yes" if you are installing to a laptop, inserting the Supplemental diskette when prompted. Once PCMCIA support is enabled if necessary, you are presented with a screen that asks what type of installation method to use. Follow the instructions in the following sections for the method you chose.

CD-ROM installation. To install from CD-ROM, highlight "Local CD-ROM" from the list of installation types. Then click "OK". You will be asked if you have a SCSI, IDE/ATAPI, or proprietary CD-ROM. This is where some of the hardware research pays off: if you have 4X or faster CD-ROM drive that was made recently and bundled with a Sound Blaster or other sound card, you most likely have an IDE/ATAPI type drive. This is one of the most confusing issues facing you.

If you choose SCSI, you must know what kind of SCSI card you have and will be presented a list. Scroll down the list until you find your SCSI card. After you select it, you will be asked if you wish to AUTOPROBE for it or SPECIFY OPTIONS. Most people should choose AUTOPROBE, which causes the program to scan for your SCSI card and enable the SCSI support for your card when found.

After the Installation Program has successfully located the Red Hat CD-ROM, you should read the next section.

RPM Category	Required?	Comments
BASE	Yes	Should not be customized.
C Development	Highly Recommend	Need the minimal system to compile a kernel.
Development Libs	Highly Recommend	Need the minimal system to compile a kernel.
C++ Development	Optional	C++ Development.
Networked Workstation	Recommend; Required for other network software	Whether you are on an Ethernet or going to dialup networking, you need to install this package suite; You shouldn't customize this.
Anonymous FTP/Gopher Server	Optional	If your Linux box is going to serve files via FTP or Gopher.
Web Server	Optional	Useful for Web Developers for local development, required if you serve Web pages.
Network Management Workstation	Optional	Has additional tools useful for dialup as well as Ethernet network.
Dialup Workstation	Recommended	Required if you are going to dialup.
Game Machine	Optional	Need I say more? Fortunes are required for humor.
Multimedia Machine	Optional	If you have supported hardware.
X Window System	Optional	If you want to run X.
X Multimedia Support	Optional	If you have supported hardware.
TEX Document Formatting	Optional	Installation of the *entire* package is recommended.
`emacs`	Recommended	The One True Editing Environment.
`emacs` with X support	Recommended	Requires X
MS-DOS and Microsoft Windows Connectivity	Optional	Huh?
Extra Documentation	Required	Manual pages should *always* be installed.

Table 2.4: Important Red Hat Linux packages.

Hard drive installation. To install from a hard drive, highlight this option and choose "`OK`". If you have not already chosen PCMCIA support, you will be prompted to insert the Supplemental diskette.

NFS installation. To install via NFS, highlight this option and choose "`OK`". You must choose the Ethernet card installed on the target machine so the Installation Program can load the correct driver. Highlight the appropriate card from the list, and then select "`OK`", allowing the Installation Program to `AUTOPROBE` for your card.

◇ If your machine locks up, you must press `Ctrl`-`Alt`-`Delete` to reboot the system. Most of the time, when this happens, it is because the probing interferes with a non-Ethernet card. If this happens, try again and choose `SPECIFY OPTIONS`, and give the data about your card in this form:

```
ether=⟨IRQ⟩,⟨IO_PORT⟩,eth0
```

This instructs the probe to look at the location specified by the values *IRQ* and *IO_PORT* for the Ethernet card. If your Ethernet card is configured for IRQ 11 and IO_PORT 0x300, specify:

```
ether=11,0x300,eth0
```

After the card has been successfully found, you will be prompted for TCP/IP information about your machine and the NFS server with the Linux installation packages. First, you will be asked to provide the target machine's *IP Address, Netmask, Default Gateway*, and *Primary Name Server*. For example:

Use of Partition	Recommend	Size Comments
Swap	2 x Physical RAM	If less than 16MB of RAM installed, 16MB is a must. If space is tight, and 16MB RAM installed, 1 x Physical RAM is the minimum recommended.
Root system, no X	100 - 200MB	Depends on tools, like compilers, that are needed.
Root system, with X	250-350MB	Depends on tools like compilers, that are needed.
/home	5 - Infinite MB	Depends on being single or multiple users and needs.
/var	5 Infinite	Depends on news feeds, number of users, etc.
/usr/local	25 - 200MB	Used for programs not in RPM format or to be kept separate from the rest of Red Hat.
/usr	350+ MB	

Table 2.5: Typical Red Hat Linux disk space requirements.

```
IP Address:          192.168.181.21
Netmask:             255.255.255.0
Default Gateway:     192.168.181.1
Primary Nameserver:  192.168.181.2
```

After you select `OK`, you are prompted for the target machine's *Domain name* and *Host name*. For example, if your domain name is `infomagic.com` and host name is `vador`, enter:

```
Domainname:                  infomagic.com
Host name:                   vador.infomagic.com
Secondary nameserver IP:     Enter if needed
Tertiary nameserver IP:      Enter if needed
```

The last screen prompts you for the NFS server and the exported directory containing the Red Hat distribution. For example, if your NFS server is `redhat.infomagic.com`, enter:

```
NFS Server name:     redhat.infomagic.com
Red Hat Directory:   /pub/mirrors/linux/RedHat
```

If you do not know these values, ask your system administrator. After you enter the values, select `OK` to continue. If the installation program reports an error locating the Red Hat distribution, make sure that you have the correct values filled in above and that your network administrator has given you export permission for the target machine.

FTP installation. FTP installation is similar to the NFS installation described above. You are prompted for the Ethernet card and your machine's TCP/IP information. However, you will be asked for the *FTP site name* and *Red Hat directory* on the Red Hat mirror site, instead of NFS server information. One warning about performing an FTP installation: find the closest and least busy FTP site to your location. See Appendix C for a list of Linux FTP sites.

◇ If your hardware isn't detected, you may need to provide an override for the hardware to be enabled properly. You may also want to check:

http://www.redhat.com/pub/redhat/updates/***version***/images

to see if Red Hat has updated boot diskettes for your hardware.

Walking through the rest of the installation.

1. Next, you are asked if you are installing to a New System or Upgrading Red Hat Linux 2.0 or greater. If upgrading, you will not be offered the chance to partition your hard drive or configure anything with your system except LILO. Select either `INSTALL` or `UPGRADE` to continue.

2. If you are upgrading, you will be asked for the root partition of your existing Red Hat system. Highlight the appropriate partition and press `OK`. If you are installing for the first time, you need to partition your hard disk with the free space determined above.

3. After you create the necessary Linux Native and Linux Swap partitions, you must initialize and enable the swap partition. You will then be asked to which partition(s) you intend to install Linux If upgrading, select the root partition. You must configure and choose at least one partition, which will be the root partition. Highlight the root partition. Then, unless you are upgrading, you are presented with a table of other available partitions. Choose the appropriate partitions and `EDIT` to indicate which partitions will be used for which directories. If you have more than one partition for the Linux installation, now is the time to designate those as well.

4. Next, a list of software categories to install is presented, followed by a chance to customize which software packages from each category are to be installed. If you have not installed Red Hat or other distributions of Linux before, simply choose the category of software to install and let the setup program install the defaults for each category. If you need a package that wasn't installed originally, you can always install it later. While the software is installing, you will see a progress indicator and you should get a cup or two of coffee. Installation can take thirty minutes to an hour or more, depending on software choices and hardware configuration.

5. After the software installation is done, you will be asked to configure your mouse. A discussion of mouse protocols and devices starts on page 31.

6. Next is the X Window System configuration. It is recommend you wait until after you boot your system for the first time to configure X. If something goes wrong with the X configuration, you may need to start the installation procedure from the beginning if the Installation Program isn't able to recover.

7. If you do not have an Ethernet card, *do not* configure your network at this time. If you have a network card and didn't configure it earlier, you should configure it now. Configuration for a dialup network should be done after the installation is complete.

8. Next, you need to configure the system clock. UTC is a good choice if you are on a network and want daylight savings time handled properly. Local Time is okay if the computer is a stand-alone machine.

9. If you do not have a US keyboard, you will need specify the configuration for your keyboard.

10. You are prompted for the `root` system password. Write it down, and don't forget it. Recovering the password is not a trivial matter. You will need the password to access the system when you first reboot.

11. Finally, you will be asked to configure LILO.

◇ If you have not installed a root partition that begins and ends between cylinder 0-1023, *do not install LILO.* If, when you reboot the system for the first time, LILO does not allow you to boot your system correctly, use the Emergency MS-DOS and Windows 95 boot diskette and, at `A:\>` enter `FDISK /mbr`. This allows your system to boot into an existing MS-DOS or Windows 95 system as it did before LILO was installed. You can then use the Red Hat Boot diskette with the following parameters at the `boot:` prompt to boot your system on the hard drive:

```
boot:  rescue root=/dev/⟨xxxx⟩ ro load_ramdisk=0
```

Where *xxxx* is the root partition.

After the installation procedure is complete, you are ready to reboot your system and use Linux.

After installation.

Now that you have installed Linux and booted your system for the first time, there are some useful things to know about using your system

Understanding the LILO prompt. When you power up or reboot the system, you may see the LILO prompt, which you hopefully configured for a 30-second or so delay before it boots the system. When LILO appears on the screen, if you do nothing, the default operating system will boot at the prescribed timeout period. However, from LILO, you can control several aspects of how Linux boots, or tell LILO to boot an alternative operating system. If you wish to override the default behavior of LILO, pressing the `Shift` key at the appearance of LILO will cause a "boot:" prompt to appear. Pressing `Tab` at this prompt will produce a list of available operating systems:

```
LILO boot:
dos linux
boot:
```

This tells us that "`dos`" is the default operating system, which will boot if nothing is typed; to boot Linux, type "`linux`". However, LILO lets you pass parameters to the Linux kernel which override the default behavior. For example, you may have been experimenting with start-up configuration files and did something to prevent the system from coming up properly. If so, you want to boot the system up to the point where it reads the configuration files and no further . The override for this is "`single`":

```
boot:  linux single
```

boots the system in single user mode so you can take corrective action. This is also useful if your system doesn't boot all the way to the `login:` prompt for some reason.

Logging in the first time. Now that you are faced with the `login:` prompt for the first time, you may be wondering how to get into the system. At this point on a newly installed system, there is only one account to log in to—the administrative account, "`root`". This account is used to manage your system and do things like configure the system, add and remove users, software, and so on. To login into the account, enter "`root`" at the `login:` prompt and press `Enter`. You are asked for the password you entered during installation. Enter that password at the `password:` prompt. The system prompt `[root@locahost] #` appears after you have successfully negotiated the login. The system prompt tells you two things: you are logged in as `root`, and in this case, your machine is called `localhost`. If you named your machine during the installation process, your host name will appear instead of `localhost`.

Caldera OpenLinux

This section on Caldera OpenLinux was written by Evan Leibovitch.

This section is intended to be a complement to the Getting Started Guides that Caldera ships with all of its Linux-based products. References to the Getting Started Guide for Caldera OpenLinux Base is indicated throughout this section as "the Guide".

Obtaining Caldera OpenLinux.

Unlike most other Linux distributions, Caldera OpenLinux is not available for downloading from the Internet, nor can it be distributed freely, nor passed around. This is because of the commercial packages which are part of COL; while most of the components of COL are under the GNU Public License, the commercial components, such as Looking Glass and Metro-X, are not. In the list of packages included on the COL media starting on page 196 of the Guide, the commercial packages are noted by an asterisk.

COL is available directly from Caldera, or through a network of Partners around the world who have committed to supporting Caldera products. These Partners can usually provide professional assistance, configuration and training for Caldera users. For a current list of Partners, check the Caldera web site.

Preparing to install Caldera OpenLinux.

Caldera supports the same hardware as any other release based on Linux 2.0 kernels. Appendix A of the Guide (p. 145) lists mosts of the SCSI hosts supported and configuration parameters necessary for many hardware combinations.

Taking a page out of the Novell manual style, Caldera's Guide provides an installation worksheet that assists you in having at hand all the details of your system that you'll need for installation. It is highly recommended you complete this before starting installation; while some parameters, such as setting up your network, are not required for installation, doing it all at one time is usually far easier than having to come back to it. Sometimes this can't be avoided, but do as much at installation time as possible.

Creating boot/modules floppies.

The COL distribution does not come with the floppy disks required for installation. There are two floppies involved; one is used for booting, and the other is a "modules" disk which contains many hardware drivers.

While the Guide recommends that you create the floppies by copying them from the CD-ROM, it is better to get newer versions of the disks from the Caldera web site. The floppy images on some CD-ROMs have errors that cause problems, especially with installations using SCSI disks and large partitions.

To get newer versions of the floppy images, download them from Caldera's FTP site. In directory `pub/col-1.0/updates/Helsinki`, you'll find a bunch of numbered directories. Check out the directories in descending order—that will make sure you get the latest versions.

If you find one of these directories has a subdirectory called `bootdisk`, the contents of that directory are what you want.

You should find two files:

```
install-2.0.25-⟨XXX⟩.img
modules-2.0.25-⟨XXX⟩.img
```

The *XXX* is replaced by the version number of the disk images. At the time of writing, the current images are `034` and located in the `001` directory.

After you have these images, transfer them onto two floppies as described for generic installations on page 37, using the MS-DOS program `RAWRITE.EXE` from the Caldera CD-ROM or dd from a Linux system.

Caldera's CD-ROM is bootable if your system's BIOS allows it, but use the downloaded floppies if possible. They are newer and will contain bug-fixes that won't be in the CD versions.

Preparing the hard disks.

This procedure is no different than other Linux distributions. You must use `fdisk` on your booted hard disk to allocate at least two Linux partitions, one for the swap area and one for the root file system. If you are planning to make your system dual-boot COL with another operating system, like Microsoft Windows or MS-DOS, or even OS/2, it's usually preferable to install COL last. The Linux `fdisk` programs recognizes "foreign" OS types better than the disk partitioning tools of most other operating systems.

To run the Linux `fdisk`, you must start your system with the boot (and maybe the modules) floppy described above. You must tell COL what kind of disk and disk controller you have. You can't even get as far as entering `fdisk` if Linux doesn't recognize your hard disk!

To do this, follow the boot up instructions in the Guide, from step 2 on pages 33–36. Don't bother going through the installation or detection of Cd-ROMs or network cards at this time; all that matters at this point is that Linux "sees" the boot hard disk so you can partition it with `fdisk`. A brief description of the use of the Linux `fdisk` is provided on page 28 of the Guide.

Remember that when running `fdisk`, you need to set up both your root file system as Linux Native (type 83) and your Swap space (type 82) as new partitions. A brief discussion of how much swap space to allocate is offered on page 10 of the Guide.

◇ As soon as you have allocated the partitions and written the partition table information to make it permanent, you must reboot.

Slackware

This section on Linux Slackware was written by Sean Dreilinger.

Slackware is not for you. (Or maybe it is.)

Welcome to the Slackware distribution of Linux! This chapter aims to help the new Linux user or administrator evaluate Slackware, plan a Slackware system, and install Slackware Linux.

Whether or not to choose Slackware as the flavor of Linux you will use is a serious consideration. It may seem like a trivial decision now, but Linux boxes have a way of taking on more and more responsibility in organizational computing environments. Plenty of Linux *experiments* have evolved in their first year to become mission-critical machines serving many more users and purposes than originally intended. Slackware is one of the most widely used distributions of Linux. When it comes to finding the newest, easiest, or most carefully planned distribution of Linux, Slackware may be "none of the above". Some background on the life and times of Slackware put things into perspective.

A quick history.

In 1993, Soft Landing System created one of the first organized distributions of Linux. Although it was a great start, the SLS distribution had many shortcomings (it didn't exactly work, for starters). Slackware, a godsend from Patrick Volkerding, solved most of these issues, was mirrored via FTP and pressed onto CD-ROMs worldwide, and quickly became the most widely used flavor of Linux. For a while, Slackware was the only full featured Linux "solution." Other Linux distribution maintainers, both commercial and nonprofit, have gradually developed distributions that are also well worth your consideration.

According to statistics maintained by the Linux Counter Project, Slackware inhabits about 69% of all machines that run Linux. Slackware is typically obtained via FTP or CD-ROM and installed on a 80486-class computer running at 66 MHz with about 16 MB of memory and 1050 MB of storage. More information about Linux use and the Linux Counter Project is available on the World Wide Web.

```
http://domen.uninett.no/~hta/linux/counter.html
```

By January 1994, Slackware had achieved such widespread use that it earned a popular notoriety normally reserved for rock stars and cult leaders. Gossip spread through the Usenet suggesting that the entire Slackware project was the work of witches and devil-worshipers!

"Linux, the free OS....except for your SOUL! MOUHAHAHAHA!"

```
From:  cajho@uno.edu
Date:  7 Jan 1994 15:48:07 GMT
```

```
Jokes alluding to RFC 666, demonic daemons, and speculation that Pat Volkerding was
actually L. Ron Hubbard in disguise were rampant in the threads that followed. The
whole amusing incident probably helped Slackware gain some market share:

I LOVE THIS!!
I was browsing here to figure which version of Linux to install, but after this,
I think that I hve no choice but to install Slackware now.

From:  widsith@phantom.com (David Devejian)
Date:  10 Jan 1994 04:57:41 GMT

All folklore and kidding aside, Slackware is a wise and powerful choice for
your adventures in Linux, whether you are a hobbyist, student, hacker, or
system-administrator-in-the-making.
```

Why, then?

If you are a system administrator, you may already be dealing with one or more key servers running Slackware. Unless you have time to experiment at work, sticking to the tried-and-true distribution may be the easiest way to go. If you expect to get help from UNIX literate friends and colleagues, you had better make sure they're running something compatible—odds are they're running Slackware. Its shortcomings are widely acknowledged, for the most part discovered, documented, and patched whenever possible. You can put together a Slackware box, close the known security holes, and install some complementary tools from the other Linux distributions to create an excellent UNIX server or desktop workstation, all in about half a day.

Have a look also at the Buyer's Guide published in the *Linux Journal*, which gives a thorough comparison and evaluation of each major distribution. For a straightforward listing of Linux flavors, have a look at the Linux Distribution HOWTO at

```
http://sunsite.unc.edu/LDP/HOWTO/Distribution-HOWTO.html
```

Upgrade? Think twice!

```
24-Aug-95 NOTE: Trying to upgrade to ELF Slackware from a.out Slackware will
undoubtedly cause you all kinds of problems.  Don't do it.

Patrick Volkerding
```

One thing we don't hear too often with Slackware is the U-word. Slackware's setup program is designed to put a fresh operating system onto empty hard disks or empty disk partitions. Installing on top of a previous Slackware installation can erase your custom applications and cause compatibility problems between updated applications and older files on the same system. When Slackware was first put together, everyone was a first-time Linux user, and the system was always experimental—reinstalling the entire operating system and applications was the norm in a developmental system. Today, many institutions and businesses run mission-critical applications on Slackware Linux. In such environment, a simple reboot is a planned activity and taking down the system and overwriting all the user files or custom applications is absolutely unacceptable.

Teaching you how to finagle a Slackware upgrade is beyond the scope of this chapter, but it is workable if you are an experienced UNIX administrator and you've taken precautions to preserve your local modifications and user files. There is an Internet resource that claims to analyze your distribution and bring it up to date across the Internet. you might want to have a look at this URL if you're facing an upgrade situation:

```
ftp://ftp.wsc.com/pub/freeware/linux/update.linux/
```

Or read, weep, and learn from the upgrade expertise of Greg Louis in his mini HOWTO document: *Upgrading Your Linux Distribution* available where finer LDP publications are mirrored:

```
http://sunsite.unc.edu/LDP/
```

Select an installation method.

Slackware can be installed from a variety of media and network sources to fit your needs and budget. Every installation method requires you to have at least three floppy diskettes available to get started.

CD-ROM. Installation from CD-ROM is fast, popular, and convenient. Although someone has to break down and pay for the initial purchase of a CD-ROM, sharing CD's is *encouraged.* Because Linux and the Slackware distribution are copylefted, you may make as many copies as you like. CD-ROM installation is also a bit better practice in terms of netiquette, since you're not hogging bandwidth for an all-day FTP transfer. Finally, you may be grateful for the extra utilities and documentation that accompany the CD-ROM, especially if you run into installation hassles or need to add components in the future.

Party! If you're a hobbyist (or want to watch a few dozen Slackware installs before taking on the task at work), see if there is a LUG (Linux User Group) in your area that sponsors install parties. Imagine a roomful of generous and knowledgeable hackers uniting to share CD-ROMs and expertise with other enthusiasts.

FTP. According to the Linux Counter Project, FTP is still the most popular way to obtain Linux by a narrow margin. Once you transfer Slackware from the closest possible FTP mirror, you'll still need to put the Slackware 'disk sets' onto installation media such as a hard drive partition or laboriously copy them onto 50-odd floppy diskettes.

NFS. In a networked environment, it is possible to install Slackware on a shared file system and allow everyone on the Local net to attach to this shared location and install. If you have the technical know-how or a geeked out system administrator who is Linux-literate, this is a great way to go. The initial distribution of Slackware can be added to the network via CD-ROM, FTP, loading floppies, tape, or even via a remote NFS share across the Internet! For details on such a remote share, see these URLs:

```
http://sunsite.doc.ic.ac.uk/sunsite/access/nfs.html
ftp://ftp.cdrom.com/pub/linux/slackware/MIRRORS.TXT
http://www.cs.us.es/archive/nfs.html
```

Floppy. It's time consuming, but it works—you can buy or create the pile of floppies needed to install Slackware and then feed them into your box one-by-one when prompted. Slackware "disk sets" are actually designed and arranged to fit floppy diskettes. If you happen to have a huge stack of recycled, high-density floppy diskettes at your disposal, this can be the most economical way to go.

Hard disk. This is the way to do it if you've transferred the Slackware distribution across the Internet via FTP—you'll escape the floppy trap by merely creating boot, root, and rescue diskettes. It requires you to have an extra disk or disk partition with extra space to hold the Slackware files during installation (you can erase them afterwards). Installation from the hard drive is also a workaround if you bought the CD but your CD-ROM drive is not supported by any of the Linux kernels that come with the Slackware CD. You can use your present operating system to transfer the Slackware files onto spare hard disk space, then boot into the Slackware installation.

Tape. Still experimental as of this writing, tape offers a great compromise of speed and economy when installing Slackware—worth considering if a friend with compatible tape drive can dupe a CD or FTP archive for you. Get the latest details from the Tape section of the `INSTALL.TXT` file that accompanies your Slackware distribution.

Boot disks: always a good thing.

Even if you're gifted with a direct T-3 Internet connection that allows you to suck up a new distribution of Slackware right off the 'Net, you'll be wise to start by building the two Slackware setup disks (boot and root) before proceeding. In the event of an unfortunate accident (power outage, feline friends traversing the keyboard, or even human error), these two little disks may be able to revive your system or at least rescue your personal files.

Slackware setup worksheet.

After the files are all copied, Slackware can go on to do most of the system and network configuration, if you're ready. To help you plan your decisions, this section consists of a worksheet derived from the text-based Slackware setup program. You can use this worksheet to record answers in advance (while your computer is still working!), so you'll be ready with the necessary details-partitions, IP addresses, modem and mouse IRQs, host and domain names, and others that you're required to provide during setup.

1. **Keyboard:** Slackware `setup` will want to know if you need to remap your keyboard to something other than a standard USA 101 key layout?

   yes or no

2. **Swap Configuration:** Do you have one or more partitions prepared as type 82 (Linux Swap)?

   yes or no

   Do you want `setup` to use `mkswap` on your swap partitions? Most likely "yes", unless you have less than 4MB of RAM and have already done this to help `setup` work better.

   yes or no

3. **Prepare Main Linux Partition:** `setup` will list any partitions marked as type 83 (Linux Native) and ask which one to use for the root (/) of the Linux file system. Use a format like `/dev/hda3` or whatever the device name is.

   partition name

◇ Last chance to back out! When using the install from scratch option, you must install to a blank partition. If you have not already formatted it manually, then you must format it when prompted. Enter "`I`" to install from scratch, or "`a`" to add software to your existing system.

   [i]nstall or [a]dd

   (Re)format the main Linux partition. Would you like to format this partition?

   [y]es, [n]o, or [c]heck sectors, too

   `ext2fs` defaults to one inode per 4096 bytes of drive space. If you're going to have many small files on your drive, you may need more inodes (one is used for each file entry). You can change the density to one inode per 2048 bytes, or even per 1024 bytes. Enter `2048` or `1024`, or just hit `Enter` to accept the default of 4096.

   4096 (default). 2048, or 1024

4. **Prepare Additional Linux Partitions:** You can mount some other partitions for `/usr` or `/usr/X11` or whatever (`/tmp`—you name it). Would you like to use some of the other Linux partitions to mount some of your directories?

   [y]es or [n]o

   These are your Linux partitions (*partition list displayed*). These partitions are already in use (*partition list displayed*). Enter the partition you would like to use, or type `q` to quit adding new partitions. Use a format such as: `/dev/hda3` or whatever the device name is.

   Partition name or [q]uit

   Would you like to format this partition?

   [y]es, [n]o, or [c]heck sections, too

   Now this new partition must be mounted somewhere in your new directory tree. For example, if you want to put it under `/usr/X11R6`, then respond: `/usr/X11R6` Where would you like to mount this new partition?

   Mount point

   Would you like to mount some more additional partitions?

   [y]es or [n]o

5. **DOS and OS/2 Partition Setup:** The following DOS FAT or OS/2 HPFS partitions were found: (*partition list displayed*). Would you like to set up some of these partitions to be visible from Linux?

   [y]es or [n]o

Please enter the partition you would like to access from Linux, or type `q` to quit adding new partitions. Use a format such as: /dev/hda3 or whatever the device name is.

Partition name or [q]uit

Now this new partition must be mounted somewhere in your directory tree. Please enter the directory under which you would like to put it. for instance, you might want to reply /dosc, /dosd, or something like that. Where would you like to mount this partition?

Mount point

6. **Source Media Selection:**

```
(a) Install from a hard drive partition.
(b) Install from floppy disks.
(c) Install via NFS.
(d) Install from a pre-mounted directory.
(e) Install from CD-ROM.
```

1, 2, 3, 4, or 5

7. **Install from a hard drive partition:** To install directly from the hard disk, you must have a partition with a directory containing the Slackware distribution such that each disk other than the boot disk is contained in a subdirectory. For example, if the distribution is in /stuff/slack, then you need to have directories named /stuff/slack/a1, /stuff/slack/a2, and so on, each containing the files that would be on that disk. You may install from DOS, HPFS, or Linux partitions. Enter the partition where the Slackware sources can be found, or `p` to see a partition list.

Partition name or [p]artition list

What directory on this partition can the Slackware sources be found. In the example above, this would be: /stuff/slack. What directory are the Slackware sources in?

Directory name

What type of file system does your Slackware source partition contain?

```
(a) FAT (MS-DOS, DR-DOS, OS/2)
(b) Linux Second Extended File System
(c) Linux Xiafs
(d) Linux MINIX
(e) OS/2 HPFS
```

1, 2, 3, 4, or 5

8. **Install from a pre-mounted directory:** Okay, we will install from a directory that is currently mounted. This can be mounted normally or through NFS. You need to specify the name of the directory that contains the subdirectories for each source disk. Which directory would you like to install from?

Directory name

9. **Install from floppy disks:** The base Slackware series (A) can be installed from 1.2M or 1.44M media. Most of the other disks will not fit on 1.2M media, but can be downloaded to your hard drive and installed from there later. Which drive would you like to install from (1/2/3/4)?

```
/dev/fd0u1440 (1.44M drive a:)
/dev/fd1u1440 (1.44M drive b:)
/dev/fd0h1200 (1.2M drive a:)
/dev/fd1h1200 (1.2M drive b:)
```

1, 2, 3, or 4

10. **Install via NFS:** You're running off the hard drive file system. Is this machine currently running on the network you plan to install from? If so, we won't try to reconfigure your ethernet card. Are you up and running on the network?

    [y]es or [n]o

    You will need to enter the IP address you wish to assign to this machine. Example: 111.112.113.114. What is your IP address?

    IP address

    Now we need to know your netmask. Typically this will be 255.255.255.0. What is your netmask?

    IP address

    Do you have a gateway (y/n)?

    [y]es or [n]o

    What is your gateway address?

    IP address

    Good! We're all set on the local end, but now we need to know where to find the software packages to install. First, we need the IP address of the machine where the Slackware sources are stored. Since you're already running on the network, you should be able to use the hostname instead of an IP address if you wish. What is the IP address of your NFS server?

    IP address

    There must be a directory on the server with the Slackware sources for each disk in subdirectories beneath it. `setup` needs to know the name of the directory on your server that contains the disk subdirectories. For example, if your A3 disk is found at `/slackware/a3`, then you would respond: `/slackware`. What is the Slackware source directory?

    Directory name

11. **Install from CD-ROM:** What type of CD-ROM drive do you have?

```
(a) Works with most ATAPI/IDE CD drives (/dev/hd*)
(b) SCSI (/dev/scd0 or /dev/scd1)
(c) Sony CDU31A/CDU33A (/dev/sonycd)
(d) Sony 531/535 (/dev/cdu535)
(e) Mitsumi, proprietary interface--not IDE (/dev/mcd)
(f) New Mitsumi, also not IDE (/dev/mcdx0)
(g) Sound Blaster Pro/Panasonic (/dev/sbpcd)
(h) Aztech/Orchid/Okano/Wearnes (/dev/aztcd)
(i) Phillips and some ProAudioSpectrum16 (/dev/cm206cd)
(j) Goldstar R420 (/dev/gscd)
(k) Optics Storage 8000 (/dev/optcd)
(l) Sanyo CDR-H94 + ISP16 soundcard (/dev/sjcd)
(m) Try to scan for your CD drive
```

1, 2, 3, 4, 5, 6, 7 8, 9, 10, 11, 12, or 13

IDE CD-ROM: Enter the device name that represents your IDE CD-ROM drive. This will probably be one of these (in the order of most to least likely): `/dev/hdb /dev/hdc /dev/hdd /dev/hde /dev/hdf /dev/hdg /dev/hdh /dev/hda`

Device name

SCSI CD-ROM: Which SCSI CD-ROM are you using? If you're not sure, select `/dev/scd0`.

1. /dev/scd0
2. /dev/scd1

installation method: With the Slackware CD, you can run most of the system from the CD if you're short of drive space or if you just want to test Linux without going through a complete installation. Which type of installation do you want (slakware or slaktest)?

slakware Normal installation to hard drive

slaktest Link `/usr->/cdrom/live/usr` to run mostly from CD-ROM

slakware or slaktext

12. **Series Selection:** Identify which Packages you plan to install. You may specify any combination of disk sets at the prompt which follows. For example, to install the base system, the base X Window System, and the Tcl toolkit, you would enter: `a x tcl`. Which disk sets do you want to install?

```
A Base Linux system
AP Various applications that do not need X
D Program Development (C, C++, Kernel source, Lisp, Perl, etc.)
E GNU Emacs
F FAQ lists
K Linux kernel source
N Networking (TCP/IP, UUCP, Mail)
Q Extra kernels with special drivers (needed for non-SCSI CD)
T TeX
TCL Tcl/Tk/TclX, Tcl language, and Tk toolkit for developing X apps
X Xfree86 Base X Window System
XAP X Window Applications
XD Xfree86 X11 server development system
XV Xview (OpenLook virtual Window Manager, apps)
Y Games (that do not require X)
```

Any combination of a ap d e f k n q t tcl x xap xd xv y and other disk sets offered, separated by spaces

13. **Software Installation:** Next, software packages are going to be transferred on to your hard drive. If this is your first time installing Linux, you should probably use PROMPT mode. This will follow a defaults file on the first disk of each series you install that will ensure that required packages are installed automatically. You will be prompted for the installation of other packages. If you don't use PROMPT mode, the install program will just go ahead and install everything from the disk sets you have selected. Do you want to use PROMPT mode (y/n)?

    [y]es or [n]o

    These defaults are user definable—you may set any package to be added or skipped automatically by editing your choices into a file called `TAGFILE` that will be found on the first disk of each series. There will also be a copy of the original tagfile called `TAGFILE.ORG` available in case you want to restore the default settings. The tagfile contains all the instructions needed to completely automate your installation. Would you like to use a special tagfile extension? You can specify an extension consisting of a "." followed by any combination of 3 characters other than `tgz`. For instance, I specify '.pat', and then whenever any tagfiles called 'tagfile.pat' are found during the installation they are used instead of the default "tagfile" files. If the install program does not find tagfiles with the custom extension, it will use the default tagfiles. Enter your custom tagfile extension (including the leading "."), or just press `Enter` to continue without a custom extension.

    Tagfile extension `Enter`

14. **Extra Configuration:** If you wish, you may now go through the options to reconfigure your hardware, make a boot disk, and install LILO. If you've installed a new kernel image, you should go through these steps again. Otherwise, it's up to you.

    [y]es or [n]o

15. **Boot Disk Creation:** It is recommended that you make a boot disk. Would you like to do this?

    [y]es or [n]o

    Now put a formatted floppy in your boot drive. This will be made into your Linux boot disk. Use this to boot Linux until LILO has been configured to boot from the hard drive. Any data on the target disk will be destroyed. Insert the disk and press `Return`, or `s` if you want to skip this step.

    `Enter` *or [s]kip*

16. **Modem Setup:** A link in `/dev` will be created from your call-out device (`cua0`, `cua1`, `cua2` , `cua3`) to `/dev/modem`. You can change this link later if you put your modem on a different port. Would you like to set up your modem?

    [y]es or [n]o

    These are the standard serial I/O devices, Which device is your modem attached to (0, 1, 2, 3)?

    ```
    0 /dev/ttyS0 (or COM1:  under DOS)
    1 /dev/ttyS1 (or COM2:  under DOS)
    2 /dev/ttyS2 (or COM3:  under DOS)
    3 /dev/ttyS3 (or COM4:  under DOS)
    ```

0, 1, 2, or 3

17. **Mouse Setup:** A link will be created in `/dev` from your mouse device to `/dev/mouse`. You can change this link later if you switch to a different type of mouse. Would you like to set up your mouse?

[y]es or [n]o

These types are supported. Which type of mouse do you have (1, 2, 3, 4, 5, 6, 7)?

```
(a) Microsoft compatible serial mouse
(b) QuickPort or PS/2 style mouse (Auxiliary port)
(c) Logitech Bus Mouse
(d) ATI XL Bus Mouse
(e) Microsoft Bus Mouse
(f) Mouse Systems serial mouse
(g) Logitech (MouseMan) serial mouse
```

1, 2, 3, 4, 5, 6, or 7

These are the standard serial I/O devices. Which device is your mouse attached to (0, 1, 2, 3)?

```
0 /dev/ttyS0 (or COM1:  under DOS)
1 /dev/ttyS1 (or COM2:  under DOS)
2 /dev/ttyS2 (or COM3:  under DOS)
3 /dev/ttyS3 (or COM4:  under DOS)
```

0, 1, 2, or 3

18. **Network Configuration:** Now we will attempt to configure your mail and TCP/IP. This process probably won't work on all possible network configurations, but should give you a good start. You will be able to reconfigure your system at any time by typing `netconfig`. First, we'll need the name you'd like to give your host. Only the base host name is needed right now (not the domain). Enter the host name.

Host name

Now, we need the domain name. Do not supply a leading "." Enter the domain name.

Domain name

If you only plan to use TCP/IP through loopback, then your IP address will be 127.0.0.1, and we can skip a lot of the following questions. Do you plan to *only* use loopback?

[y]es or [n]o

Enter your IP address for the local machine. Example: 111.112.113.114. Enter the IP address for this machine (aaa.bbb.ccc.ddd).

IP address

Enter your gateway address, such as 111.112.113.1. If you don't have a gateway, you can edit `/etc/rc.d/rc.inet1` later,or you can probably get away with entering your own IP address here. Enter the gateway address (aaa.bbb.ccc.ddd).

IP address

Enter your netmask. This will generally look something like this: 255.255.255.0. Enter the netmask (aaa.bbb.ccc.ddd).

IP address

Will you be accessing a name server?

[y]es or [n]o

Please give the IP address of the name server to use. You can add more Domain Name Servers by editing `/etc/resolv.conf`. Name server for your domain (aaa.bbb.ccc.ddd)?

IP address

You may now reboot your computer by pressing `Ctrl`-`Alt`-`Delete`. If you installed LILO, remove the boot disk from your computer before rebooting. Don't forget to create your `/etc/fstab` if you don't have one (see page 126)!

Making Slackware happen.

If you've taken the time to plot and plan as recommended in the preceding sections, then the actual installation is a piece of cake. There isn't much writing needed to explain the actual process of loading Slackware on your computer(s). Follow the steps to build boot and root diskettes, then answer a long series of questions asked by the menu driven Slackware installation program. If you've completed the Slackware Installation Worksheet, these questions will be familiar and everything will run smoothly.

Build some boot disks.

Choose your kernel! When installing Slackware Linux, you must create a boot diskette with a Linux kernel that is specially prepared to recognize your system hardware. For example, to install Slackware from an IDE CD-ROM drive onto a SCSI hard drive, the kernel that you put onto the boot diskette will need to have drivers for your SCSI card and your IDE CD-ROM drive.

The kernels are stored as compressed *binary image* files that you can access from most any operating system to create a Slackware Boot diskette. On the Slackware FTP site, CD-ROM, or NFS mount, you'll find a subdirectory called `bootdsks.144`, containing 1.44 MB kernel images for creating boot disks on 1.44MB high density 3.5" floppy diskettes. If you're working from a 5.25" floppy diskette drive, look in a directory called `bootdsks.12` for kernel images that will fit the smaller diskette format.

The table on page 71 provides a quick reference of the kernel images available as we went to press. Information and up-to-date boot disk image information is available from this URL:

```
ftp://ftp.cdrom.com/pub/linux/slackware/bootdsks.144/README.TXT
```

Boot into action.

Here's the big anti-climax. After all of this planning, preparation, and partitioning, you're in the home stretch. Make sure that the boot floppy is in the diskette drive, and restart your computer. Now is a good time to go get some coffee (or whatever you like to keep you company) and return to the machine ready to play the part of a button-pushing drone, answering yes-no questions for an hour or so.

Log in as root (no password) and type `setup` or `setup.tty`.

File	IDE Slackware bootdisks:
aztech.i	CD-ROM drives: Aztech CDA268-01A, Orchid CD-3110, Okano/Wearnes CDD110, Conrad TXC, CyCDROM CR520, CR540.
bare.i	IDE support only.
cdu31a.i	Sony CDU31/33a CD-ROM.
cdu535.i	Sony CDU531/535 CD-ROM.
cm206.i	Philips/LMS cm206 CD-ROM with cm260 adapter card.
goldstar.i	Goldstar R420 CD-ROM (sometimes sold in a Reveal "Multimedia Kit").
mcd.i	NON-IDE Mitsumi CD-ROM support.
mcdx.i	Improved NON-IDE Mitsumi CD-ROM support.
net.i	Ethernet support.
optics.i	Optics Storage 8000 AT CD-ROM (the "DOLPHIN" drive).
sanyo.i	Sanyo CDR-H94A CD-ROM support.
sbpcd.i	Matsushita, Kotobuki, Panasonic, CreativeLabs (Sound Blaster), Longshine and Teac NON-IDE CD-ROM support.
xt.i	MFM hard drive support.

Table 2.6: Slackware IDE boot disk images.

The Slackware `setup` program.

Slackware comes with two versions of an excellent `setup` program. One is a colorful, dialog-based, menu-driven version. An alternative, `setup.tty`, is a text-only version that you may actually prefer, because detailed diagnostics and error messages stay on the screen and are not covered up by the next dialog box. If you're attempting a Slackware installation on sketchy hardware, I strongly recommend the less colorful `setup.tty` routine. If you don't know much about UNIX and would feel more comfortable with an attractive, "clean" interface to the same process, then by all means go for the beautiful setup.

```
============== Slackware96 Linux Setup (version HD-3.1.0) =============

  Welcome to Slackware Linux Setup.

  Hint: If you have trouble using the arrow keys on your keyboard,
  you can use '+', '-', and TAB instead. Which option would you like?
  ===============================================================
        HELP       Read the Slackware Setup HELP file
        KEYMAP     Remap your keyboard
        MAKE TAGS  Tagfile customization program
        TARGET     Select target directory [now: / ]
        SOURCE     Select source media
        DISK SETS  Decide which disk sets you wish to install
        INSTALL    Install selected disk sets
        CONFIGURE  Reconfigure your Linux system
        PKGTOOL    Install or remove packages with Pkgtool
        EXIT       Exit Slackware Linux Setup
  ===============================================================
=================================================================
```

File	**SCSI/IDE Slackware boot disks:**
`7000fast.s`	Western Digital 7000FASST SCSI support.
`Advansys.s`	AdvanSys SCSI support.
`Aha152x.s`	Adaptec 152x SCSI support.
`Aha1542.s`	Adaptec 1542 SCSI support.
`Aha1740.s`	Adaptec 1740 SCSI support.
`Aha2x4x.s`	Adaptec AIC7xxx SCSI support (For these cards: AHA-274x, AHA-2842, AHA-2940, AHA-2940W, AHA-2940U, AHA-2940UW, AHA-2944D, AHA-2944WD, AHA-3940, AHA-3940W, AHA-3985, AHA-3985W).
`Am53c974.s`	AMD AM53/79C974 SCSI support.
`Aztech.s`	All supported SCSI controllers, plus CD-ROM support for Aztech CDA268-01A, Orchid CD-3110, Okano/Wearnes CDD110, Conrad TXC, CyCDROM CR520, CR540.
`Buslogic.s`	Buslogic MultiMaster SCSI support.
`Cdu31a.s`	All supported SCSI controllers, plus CD-ROM support for Sony CDU31/33a.
`Cdu535.s`	All supported SCSI controllers, plus CD-ROM support for Sony CDU531/535.
`Cm206.s`	All supported SCSI controllers, plus Philips/LMS cm206 CD-ROM with cm260 adapter card.
`Dtc3280.s`	DTC (Data Technology Corp) 3180/3280 SCSI support.
`Eata_dma.s`	DPT EATA-DMA SCSI support. (Boards like PM2011, PM2021, PM2041, PM3021, PM2012B, PM2022, PM2122, PM2322, PM2042, PM3122, PM3222, PM3332, PM2024, PM2124, PM2044, PM2144, PM3224, PM3334.)
`Eata_isa.s`	DPT EATA-ISA/EISA SCSI support. (Boards like PM2011B/9X, PM2021A/9X, PM2012A, PM2012B, PM2022A/9X, PM2122A/9X, PM2322A/9X).
`Eata_pio.s`	DPT EATA-PIO SCSI support (PM2001 and PM2012A).
`Fdomain.s`	Future Domain TMC-16x0 SCSI support.
`Goldstar.s`	All supported SCSI controllers, plus Goldstar R420 CD-ROM (sometimes sold in a Reveal "Multimedia Kit").
`In2000.s`	Always IN2000 SCSI support.
`Iomega.s`	IOMEGA PPA3 parallel port SCSI support (also supports the parallel port version of the ZIP drive).
`Mcd.s`	All supported SCSI controllers, plusstandard non-IDE Mitsumi CD-ROM support.
`Mcdx.s`	All supported SCSI controllers, plus enhanced non-IDE Mitsumi CD-ROM support.
`N53c406a.s`	NCR 53c406a SCSI support.
`N_5380.s`	NCR 5380 and 53c400 SCSI support.
`N_53c7xx.s`	NCR 53c7xx, 53c8xx SCSI support (Most NCR PCI SCSI controllers use this driver).
`Optics.s`	All supported SCSI controllers, plus support for the Optics Storage 8000 AT CDROM (the "DOLPHIN" drive).
`Pas16.s`	Pro Audio Spectrum/Studio 16 SCSI support.
`Qlog_fas.s`	ISA/VLB/PCMCIA Qlogic FastSCSI! support (also supports the Control Concepts SCSI cards based on the Qlogic FASXXX chip).
`Qlog_isp.s`	Supports all Qlogic PCI SCSI controllers, except the PCI-basic, which the AMD SCSI driver supports.
`Sanyo.s`	All supported SCSI controllers, plus Sanyo CDR-H94A CD-ROM support.
`Sbpcd.s`	All supported SCSI controllers, plus Matsushita, Kotobuki, Panasonic, CreativeLabs (Sound Blaster), Longshine and Teac NON-IDE CDROM support.
`Scsinet.s`	All supported SCSI controllers, plus full ethernet support.
`Seagate.s`	Seagate ST01/ST02, Future Domain TMC-885/950 SCSI support.
`Trantor.s`	Trantor T128/T128F/T228 SCSI support.
`Ultrastr.s`	UltraStor 14F, 24F, and 34F SCSI support.
`Ustor14f.s`	UltraStor 14F and 34F SCSI support

Table 2.7: Slackware SCSI/IDE boot disk images.

```
                 <  OK  >      <Cancel>
=======================================================================
```

Transferring Slackware onto your system from here should involve little more than selecting what you want from the menus. By filling out Section 3 of the worksheet in advance, you should be able progress quickly through each menu in order, until you reach the INSTALL option, at which point things may s l o w down: you are advised to select the PROMPT feature and *read* about each software package, deciding whether or not you'd like it to end up on your Slackware system. The last part of a regular setup is the CONFIGURE section on the setup menu, and the questions you must answer bear a striking resemblance to the second half of the Section 3 worksheet.

Is that all?

Definitely not! At this point, you either have some annoying obstacle that is preventing the setup from completing, or more likely, you're looking at the `root` prompt

```
darkstar~#
```

and wondering "What Next?"

Well, if you're plagued by problems, you'll want to proceed directly to the next section on troubleshooting. If things appear to be in working order, you've still got some details to attend to. It's sort of like purchasing a new automobile—after you select and pay for a car, there are still some things that you need before you can drive it with confidence—insurance, a steering wheel club, and perhaps some luxuries that make the driving experience closer to Fahrvergnügen than FAQ!

Troubleshooting difficult deliveries.

Not every Slackware installation is born on cue to expecting system administrators. I've pulled a few all-nighters, sitting down after work one evening to upgrade a Slackware box and still there struggling to get the damn thing back online at dawn, before people start bitching about their missing mail and news. This section will look at a few common Slackware setup problems, solutions, and where to look for additional assistance.

Slackware installation FAQs. Patrick Volkerding, the father of Slackware, has dealt with many questions of new users by listening, answering, and anticipating repeat queries. To catch the new Slackware users before they ask the same question for the 5,000th time, Patrick has kindly created documentation and included it with the Slackware distribution. Three files that you may find very helpful in answering your initial questions are `FAQ.TXT`, `INSTALL.TXT`, and `BOOTING.TXT`.

Web Support For Slackware. The easiest way to access finding Linux documents in general is the Linux Documentation Project Home Page. See page 25 for a description of the LDP Home Page.

At this time, the Slackware-specific help you'll find on the Internet tends to be highly customized—like how to NFS-mount the distribution on computers within a certain university or how to wire your dorm room into a particular residential WAN using Slackware.

Usenet Groups For Slackware. The `comp.os.linux.*` hierarchy of Usenet is a treasure trove of Linux information, not necessarily Slackware-specific. At present, 11 separate Linux forums handle a high volume of discussion in this hierarchy, which is described on page 26.

Mailing lists for Slackware. At this time, there are no electronic mail discussions devoted to Slackware per se. You can participate in some excellent Linux-related talk via e-mail, try `http://www.linux.org`, and ask in the Usenet newsgroups for a few good subscription lists.

There is a general Linux mailing list server, `majordomo@vger.rutgers.edu`. See page 27 for a description of how to subscribe to mailing lists via this server.

You get what you pay for (commercial support). Commercial support for Linux is available from some of the CD-ROM vendors and a long list of Linux Consultants, who can be contacted through the Linux Commercial and Consultants HOWTO documents:

```
http://sunsite.unc.edu/LDP/HOWTO/Consultants-HOWTO.html
http://sunsite.unc.edu/LDP/HOWTO/Commercial-HOWTO.html
```

Basking in the afterglow.

Don't rest on your laurels quite yet, especially if your Slackware machine is a shared computer or lives in a networked environment. Grooming a computer for community and network use is a bit more demanding than just running the setup program and then forgetting about it. We'll leave you with a few pointers to securing and sharing your new Slackware system.

Consider reinstalling!

I know you just sat through what may have been a long and perplexing installation session. But before you move into the house you just built, consider tearing it down and starting over again. Friedrich Nietzsche had a quote:

> A man learns what he needs to know about building his house only after he's finished.

If, in the process of installing the system, you had some thoughts about how you might do it differently, now is the time. If your Slackware Linux box will be a multi-user machine or a network server, there may never be such a convenient opportunity to re-install or reconfigure the system in radical ways.

Secure the system.

Get off the LAN at once. Out of the box, Slackware is an insecure system. Although Patrick Volkerding does his best to create a secure distribution, a few inevitable holes become known, and patches or workarounds are made available in the system administration (and cracker) communities. If you installed Slackware from a network source like a NFS-mounted drive, you should temporarily disconnect your box from the LAN after a successful installation, while you plug a few holes.

Give `root` a password. By default, a new Slackware box will not require a password for the root user. When you're comfortable that your new Slackware system is stable (after a few hours, not days or weeks), add a password to protect the root account. Login as root and type:

```
# passwd root
```

Give yourself an account. On large, shared systems, the super-user `root` account is not used as a working `login` account by any individual. If you're interested in system administration or are running a networked machine, this is a good precedent to follow. Use the `/sbin/adduser` program and make yourself a `login` account, rather than working out of the `root` login. I always smile when I see students and hobbyists posting proudly to the Usenet as `root@mymachine.mydomain`. Be humble and safe: create another `login` account for your daily work and use `su` (rather than `login`) to enter the `root` account sparingly.

Read Chapter 4 for a discussion of what you should do with the `root` account (or shouldn't).

Deny `root` logins. Not only is it uncommon to *work* as the root user, it is *not considered secure to* `login` *as root across the network.* Administrative users usually connect to a UNIX box as their regular, user-name `login`, then `su` to `root` as needed. To prevent crackers, hackers, and ignorant users from logging in directly as `root`, edit the file `/etc/securetty` and comment out (prepend a pound (#) sign before) all but the local terminals:

```
console

tty1
tty2
# ttyS0
# ttyS1
```

After this fix, users who attempt to login in as `root` across the network will be denied:

```
Linux 2.0.29 (durak.interactivate.com) (ttyp4)

durak login:  root
root login refused on this terminal.
durak login:
```

Apply the simple fixes. Slackware installs itself with some very real security problems. Rather than master UNIX security and sleuth out these vulnerabilities yourself, you can jump start the hole-patching process by visiting a Web resource maintained for just this purpose, called *Slackware SimpleFixes*:

```
http://cesdis.gsfc.nasa.gov/linux-web/simplefixes/simplefixes.html
```

Check for patches on `ftp.cdrom.com` As an actively maintained Linux distribution, Slackware updates and patches are available from:

```
ftp://ftp.cdrom.com/pub/linux/slackware/patches/
```

Stay current. You might like to subscribe to one or more electronic mailing lists that alert users to issues in Linux administration, such as:

```
linux-alert-request@tarsier.cv.nrao.edu
linux-security-request@redhat.com
```

Back up.

Like how things are running? Save it for a rainy day by backing up. Amanda (the Advanced Maryland Automatic Network Disk Archiver) is one of several backup options for Linux installations. You can learn more about Amanda from:

```
http://www.cs.umd.edu/projects/amanda/index.html
```

S.u.S.E.

This section on S.u.S.E. Linux was written by Larry Ayers.

The S.u.S.E distribution began a few years ago as an adaptation of Slackware. Patrick Volkerding of Slackware helped the S.u.S.E developers at first, but before too long, the distribution began to assume an identity of its own. Several new features intended to aid the first-time user increase the probability an installation won't need to be immediately redone. Given the cross-pollination endemic in the free software world, I wouldn't be surprised to learn some of these features have shown up in newer Slackware releases.

Beginning the installation.

When booting your machine from the single installation disk, you are really booting a miniature Linux system designed for this purpose. A colored screen appears, ready to ask a series of questions which with any luck will guide you through the process. YAST (Yet Another Set-up Tool) shows its Slackware ancestry inasmuch as it uses the `dialog` program. This tool enables shell scripts to present dialog boxes, radio buttons, and check lists which allow a user to make choices and direct the course of an installation.

While no distribution can guarantee a painless installation, the developers at GmbH have managed to anticipate several problems that new Linux users are liable to have. One of the more frustrating problems is finding that your CD-ROM drive isn't recognized. Copying the packages needed to get started to a hard drive and installing them from there is a solution, but it's awkward and time-consuming. Rather than provide a selection of several disk images, one of which probably has the CD-ROM drive support you need, the single S.u.S.E. boot disk contains a small, basic kernel with all drivers available–if needed–in the form of modules. The kernel daemon is a background process which ensures the relevant module will be loaded if a modular function is needed. This helps to eliminate one stumbling block. Another common trap is underestimating the disk space which you need. This forces the installation to abort itself due to lack of room. When this happens, the crucial final steps (like LILO installation) haven't yet been reached, and starting over is usually necessary. Script-based installations are necessarily sequential in nature; you may know that skipping one step won't hurt anything, but it's hard to anticipate every eventuality in a shell script, and if things go awry the script usually aborts.

During the S.u.S.E. installation, a running tally of partition space remaining is displayed on the YAST screen; while selecting packages, you can try various combinations while keeping in mind how much free disk space you would prefer to remain free. Partitioning and formatting disks, as well as creation and activation of a swap partition, are processes that aren't much different than in other distributions. They all use the same underlying tools; the procedure has become more or less standardized.

Dependencies. The use of **dependencies**, which consist of information included in a software package concerning what other packages are necessary for it to run, has spread rapidly among Linux distributions. Unfortunately no universal format for dependencies has arisen. Each distribution uses a different format. Red Hat's RPM format, used in several distributions, is powerful and effective, but it has a few drawbacks. It works best on an all-RPM system, as the dependency checking done by the RPM program only knows about RPM packages. S.u.S.E. uses an adaptation of Slackware's `*.tar.gz` format, which has the advantage of flexibility. The dependencies are only checked if a package is installed from within the YAST program, allowing the option (for a skilled user) of unarchiving a package in another location, then checking out the files and configuration before final installation. Dependencies are most useful during the initial setup and while becoming familiar with a new installation. Once you've used the system for a while, you'll have an idea of what libraries and programs are available. Most software packages for Linux also contain information as to what needs to be present on a system in order for the package to function. It is wise to read through the entire `rc.config` file before running `SuSEconfig` and committing any changes you may have made. Some of the default actions the script will take you may prefer to handle yourself, but they are easily disabled by editing the file.

Users familiar with the Slackware layout of initialization files will need to make some adjustments; the files usually found in `/etc/rc.d` are instead in `/sbin/init.d`.

Post-installation.

YAST is also intended to be used after installation for routine system maintenance. The multiplicity of resource files necessary for Linux to boot and run can be bewildering to beginners. YAST offers a menu-driven interface to these files, including the `sendmail` configuration file, the `cron` (scheduling) files, initialization scripts, and various networking files. The changes made within the YAST session are written to a single file in the `/etc` directory, `rc.config`, which can also be edited directly. These changes are then written to the various "real" configuration files by a script called `SuSEconfig`. This script is automatically run by YAST at the end of a YAST session; if `/etc/rc.config` is edited directly, `SuSEconfig` must be started manually. This sounds like a complicated procedure, but it's much easier than tracking down the individual files, learning the correct syntax needed to edit them, and making them do what you want.

After you have S.u.S.E. Linux up and running, it's a good idea to install the kernel source (available on the CD-ROM, it's an optional package which can be installed during initial set-up). S.u.S.E. installs a generic kernel, and you probably need only a few of of the accompanying modules. This is an excellent opportunity to familiarize yourself with the mechanics of source code compilation, and you'll end up with a smaller customized kernel with only the capabilities you need. The `gcc` compiler and accompanying tools must be installed in order to compile a kernel; these tools are a near-necessity on a Linux system even if you're not a programmer. The YAST dependency checking will help insure that all of the required compilation tools are installed.

Kernel compilation can seem daunting to a beginner, but it is a fairly intuitive process. Three interfaces are available for the initial configuration step. The first (and oldest) is a console-mode script invoked via the command `make config`. This script asks a series of questions and uses the results to write a file which guides the compiler in its work. You need to know some basic facts about your hardware such as what type of hard disk and CD-ROM drive you have. If you want sound support you'll need to know the IRQ your card uses, as well as a few other parameters that can be gathered from the card's manual or the output of the MS-DOS `msd` utility.

The other two interfaces are `menuconfig` and `xconfig`. The first uses a modified version of the `dialog` program mentioned above, which runs on a virtual console or a `xterm` and resembles the YAST setup tool. `xconfig` is a Tk-based version, designed to run in a X window. All three accomplish the same task. The latter two let you make choices without typing much. The kernel sources are well-documented. The `README` file in the top-level directory contains enough information to nearly guarantee a successful build.

Getting X up and running.

Successfully configuring the X Window System (specifically XFree86, which is included with S.u.S.E. and most other distributions) can be a stumbling block. There is such a multiplicity of monitors and video cards that each installation of X must be individually configured. The difficulty has been eased somewhat with the release of XFree86 3.2, which is included with the most recent S.u.S.E. release. A `dialog` based configuration tool can now be used in place of the previous `xf86config`. Both are based on shell scripts similar to the one that is used to configure the Linux kernel. Nonetheless, you will still need to know your monitor's horizontal and vertical refresh rates as well as the chip set installed on your video card. It helps to initially set your sites low, i.e., get X functioning at a low resolution first before attempting to make full use of your video card's capabilities.

The S.u.S.E. developers have taken some pains in configuring the various window managers, for example, `fvwm95`. The first time you start X, many of the applications you elected for installation will be available from the mouse activated root window menu. Another entry on the menu allows you to change the window background.

Many well-designed icons are supplied with the S.u.S.E. distribution. This gives new users something of a reprieve. After getting Linux and X running finally, there is enough to do just learning the system without feeling compelled to customize the environment, in order to make it tolerable to view!

Later upgrades.

The minute you finish installing even the most up-to-date distribution, it begins to incrementally become outdated. This is a slow process, but eventually you will feel the need to upgrade some part of the system. Some distributions work best when the native format of upgrade file is used, but S.u.S.E. works well using the standard `*.tar.gz` format. S.u.S.E. follows in Slackware's footsteps in this respect. The majority of software packages will compile and install well (on a reasonably current Linux system) from the `tar`'ed and `gzip`'ed format most developers use. There are a few tricky packages out there. In these cases RPM can be used. The dependency checking won't work, but RPM allows you to take advantage of a more experienced user's `makefile` editing and configuration skills.

Post-installation procedures.

At this point it's a good idea to explain how to reboot and shutdown the system as you're using it. You should never reboot or shutdown your Linux system by pressing the reset switch or with the old "Vulcan Nerve Pinch"—that is, by pressing `Ctrl`-`Alt`-`Del` in unison. On most Linux systems, however, this causes the system to shut down gracefully, as if you had used the `shutdown` command. You shouldn't simply switch off the power, either. As with most UNIX systems, Linux caches disk writes in memory. Therefore, if you suddenly reboot the system without shutting down "cleanly", you can corrupt the data on your drives, causing untold damage.

The easiest way to shut down the system is with the `shutdown` command. As an example, to shutdown and reboot the system immediately, use the following command as `root`:

```
# shutdown -r now
```

This cleanly reboots your system. The manual page for `shutdown` describes the other command-line arguments that are available. Use the command `man shutdown` to see the manual page for `shutdown`.

Note, however, that many Linux distributions do not provide the `shutdown` command on the installation media. This means that the first time you reboot your system after installation, you may need to use the `Ctrl`-`Alt`-`Del` combination after all. Thereafter, you should always use the `shutdown` command.

After you have a chance to explore and use the system, there are several configuration chores that you should undertake. The first is to create a user account for yourself (and, optionally, any other users that might have access to the system). Creating user accounts is described in Chapter 4. Usually, all that you have to do is `login` as `root`, and run the `adduser` (sometimes `useradd`) program. This leads you through several prompts to create new user accounts.

If you create more than one file system for Linux, or if you're using a swap partition, you may need to edit the file `/etc/fstab` in order for those file systems to be available automatically after rebooting. If you're using a separate file system for `/usr`, and none of the files that should be in `/usr` appear to be present, you may simply need to mount that file system. See page 126 for a description of the `/etc/fstab` file.

Running into trouble.

Almost everyone runs into some kind of snag or hang up when attempting to install Linux the first time. Most of the time, the problem is caused by a simple misunderstanding. Sometimes, however, it can be something more serious, like an oversight by one of the developers, or a bug.

If your installation appears to be successful, but you received unexpected error messages, these are described here as well.

Problems with booting the installation media

When attempting to boot the installation media for the first time, you may encounter a number of problems. These are listed below. Note that the following problems are *not* related to booting your newly installed Linux system. See page 84 for information on these kinds of pitfalls.

- **Floppy or media error when attempting to boot.**

  The most popular cause for this kind of problem is a corrupt boot floppy. Either the floppy is physically damaged, in which case you should re-create the disk with a *brand new* floppy, or the data on the floppy is bad, in which case you should verify that you downloaded and transferred the data to the floppy correctly. In many cases, simply re-creating the boot floppy will solve your problems. Retrace your steps and try again.

  If you received your boot floppy from a mail order vendor or some other distributor, instead of downloading and creating it yourself, contact the distributor and ask for a new boot floppy—but only after verifying that this is indeed the problem.

- **System hangs during boot or after booting.**

  After the installation media boots, you will see a number of messages from the kernel itself, indicating which devices were detected and configured. After this, you will usually be presented with a login prompt, allowing you to proceed with installation (some distributions instead drop you right into an installation program of some kind). The system may appear to hang during several of these steps. Be patient: loading software from floppy is comparatively slow. In many cases, the system has not hung at all but is merely taking a long time. Verify that there is no drive or system activity for at least several minutes before assuming that the system is hung.

  1. After booting from the `LILO` prompt, the system must load the kernel image from floppy. This may take several seconds; you will know that things are going well if the floppy drive light is still on.

  2. While the kernel boots, SCSI devices must be probed for. If you do not have any SCSI devices installed, the system will hang for up to 15 seconds while the SCSI probe continues; this usually occurs after the line

     ```
     lp_init: lp1 exists (0), using polling driver
     ```

     appears on your screen.

  3. After the kernel is finished booting, control is transferred to the system boot-up files on the floppy. Finally, you will be presented with a `login` prompt, or be dropped into an installation program. If you are presented with a login prompt such as

     ```
     Linux login:
     ```

you should then `login` (usually as `root` or `install`—this varies with each distribution). After entering the user name, the system may pause for 20 seconds or more while the installation program or shell is being loaded from floppy. Again, the floppy drive light should be on. Don't assume that the system is hung.

Any of the above items may be the source of your problem. However, it is possible that the system actually may hang while booting, which can be due to several causes. First of all, you may not have enough available RAM to boot the installation media. (See the following item for information on disabling the RAM disk to free up memory.)

The cause of many system hangs is hardware incompatibility. The last chapter presented an overview of supported hardware under Linux. Even if your hardware is supported, you may run into problems with incompatible hardware configurations which are causing the system to hang. See page 79, below, for a discussion of hardware incompatibilities.

- **System reports out-of-memory errors while attempting to boot or install the software.**

  This item deals with the amount of RAM that you have available. On systems with 4 megabytes of RAM or less, you may run into trouble booting the installation media or installing the software itself. This is because many distributions use a RAM disk, a file system loaded directly into RAM, for operations while using the installation media. The entire image of the installation boot floppy, for example, may be loaded into a RAM disk, which may require more than a megabyte of RAM.

  You may not see an "out of memory" error when attempting to boot or install the software; instead, the system may unexpectedly hang, or fail to boot. If your system hangs, and none of the explanations in the previous section seem to be the cause, try disabling the RAM disk. See your distribution's documentation for details.

  Keep in mind that Linux itself requires at least 2 megabytes of RAM to run at all; most modern distributions of Linux require 4 megabytes or more.

- **The system reports an error like "`permission denied`" or "`file not found`" while booting.**

  This is an indication that your installation boot up media is corrupt. If you try to boot from the installation media (and you're sure that you're doing everything correctly), you should not see any errors like this. Contact the distributor of your Linux software and find out about the problem, and perhaps obtain another copy of the boot media if necessary. If you downloaded the boot disk yourself, try re-creating it and see if this solves the problem.

- **The system reports the error "`VFS: Unable to mount root`" when booting.**

  This error message means that the root file system (found on the boot media itself), could not be found. This means that either your boot media is corrupt in some way, or that you are not booting the system correctly.

  For example, many CD-ROM distributions require that you have the CD-ROM in the drive when booting. Be sure that the CD-ROM drive is on and check for any activity. It's also possible that the system is not locating your CD-ROM drive at boot time; see page 79 for more information.

Hardware problems.

The most common form of problem when attempting to install or use Linux is an incompatibility with hardware. Even if all of your hardware is supported by Linux, a misconfiguration or hardware conflict can sometimes cause strange results—your devices may not be detected at boot time, or the system may hang.

It is important to isolate these hardware problems if you suspect that they may be the source of your trouble.

Isolating hardware problems If you experience a problem that you believe to be hardware-related, the first thing that you should to do is attempt to isolate the problem. This means eliminating all possible variables and (usually) taking the system apart, piece-by-piece, until the offending piece of hardware is isolated.

This is not as frightening as it may sound. Basically, you should remove all nonessential hardware from your system, and then determine which device is causing the trouble—possibly by reinserting each device, one at a time. This means that you should remove all hardware other than the floppy and video controllers, and of course the keyboard. Even innocent-looking devices such as mouse controllers can wreak unknown havoc on your peace of mind unless you consider them nonessential.

For example, let's say that the system hangs during the Ethernet board detection sequence at boot time. You might hypothesize that there is a conflict or problem with the Ethernet board in your machine. The quick and easy way to find out is to pull the Ethernet board, and try booting again. If everything goes well, then you know that either (a) the Ethernet board is not supported by Linux (see page 23), or (b) there is an address or IRQ conflict with the board.

"Address or IRQ conflict?" What on earth does that mean? All devices in your machine use an **IRQ**, or *interrupt request line*, to tell the system that they need something done on their behalf. You can think of the IRQ as a cord that the device tugs when it needs the system to take care of some pending request. If more than one device is tugging on the same cord, the kernel won't be able to determine which device it needs to service. Instant mayhem.

Therefore, be sure that all of your installed devices use unique IRQ lines. In general, the IRQ for a device can be set by jumpers on the card; see the documentation for the particular device for details. Some devices do not require the use of an IRQ at all, but it is suggested that you configure them to use one if possible. (The Seagate ST01 and ST02 SCSI controllers are good examples).

In some cases, the kernel provided on your installation media is configured to use certain IRQs for certain devices. For example, on some distributions of Linux, the kernel is preconfigured to use IRQ 5 for the TMC-950 SCSI controller, the Mitsumi CD-ROM controller, and the bus mouse driver. If you want to use two or more of these devices, you'll need to first install Linux with only one of these devices enabled, then recompile the kernel in order to change the default IRQ for one of them. (See Chapter 4 for information on recompiling the kernel.)

Another area where hardware conflicts can arise is with DMA (direct memory access) channels, I/O addresses, and shared memory addresses. All of these terms describe mechanisms through which the system interfaces with hardware devices. Some Ethernet boards, for example, use a shared memory address as well as an IRQ to interface with the system. If any of these are in conflict with other devices, then the system may behave unexpectedly. You should be able to change the DMA channel, I/O or shared memory addresses for your various devices with jumper settings. (Unfortunately, some devices don't allow you to change these settings.)

The documentation for various hardware devices should specify the IRQ, DMA channel, I/O address, or shared memory address that the devices use, and how to configure them. Again, the simple way to get around these problems is to temporarily disable the conflicting devices until you have time to determine the cause of the problem.

The table below is a list of IRQ and DMA channels used by various "standard" devices on most systems. Almost all systems have some of these devices, so you should avoid setting the IRQ or DMA of other devices in conflict with these values.

Problems recognizing hard drive or controller. When Linux boots, you should see a series of messages on your screen such as:

```
Console:  color EGA+ 80x25, 8 virtual consoles
Serial driver version 3.96 with no serial options enabled
tty00 at 0x03f8 (irq = 4) is a 16450
tty03 at 0x02e8 (irq = 3) is a 16550A
lp_init:  lp1 exists (0), using polling driver
...
```

Here, the kernel is detecting the various hardware devices present on your system. At some point, you should see the line

Device	I/O address	IRQ	DMA
ttyS0 (COM1)	3f8	4	n/a
ttyS1 (COM2)	2f8	3	n/a
ttyS2 (COM3)	3e8	4	n/a
ttyS3 (COM4)	2e8	3	n/a
lp0 (LPT1)	378 - 37f	7	n/a
lp1 (LPT2)	278 - 27f	5	n/a
fd0, fd1 (floppies 1 and 2)	3f0 - 3f7	6	2
fd2, fd3 (floppies 3 and 4)	370 - 377	10	3

Table 2.8: Common device settings.

```
Partition check:
```

followed by a list of recognized partitions, for example:

```
Partition check:
hda:  hda1 hda2
hdb:  hdb1 hdb2 hdb3
```

If, for some reason, your drives or partitions are not recognized, then you will not be able to access them in any way.

There are several things that can cause this to happen:

- **Hard drive or controller not supported.** If you have a hard drive controller (IDE, SCSI, or otherwise) that is not supported by Linux, the kernel will not recognize your partitions at boot time.
- **Drive or controller improperly configured.** Even if your controller is supported by Linux, it may not be configured correctly. (This is particularly a problem for SCSI controllers. Most non-SCSI controllers should work fine without any additional configuration).

  Refer to the documentation for your hard drive and/or controller. In particular, many hard drives need to have a jumper set to be used as a slave drive (the second device on either the primary or secondary IDE bus). The acid test of this kind of condition is to boot MS-DOS or some other operating system that is known to work with your drive and controller. If you can access the drive and controller from another operating system, then it is not a problem with your hardware configuration.

  See page 80, above, for information on resolving possible device conflicts, and page 82, below, for information on configuring SCSI devices.
- **Controller properly configured, but not detected.** Some BIOS-less SCSI controllers require the user to specify information about the controller at boot time. A description of how to force hardware detection for these controllers begins on page 82.
- **Hard drive geometry not recognized.** Some systems, like the IBM PS/ValuePoint, do not store hard drive geometry information in the CMOS memory, where Linux expects to find it. Also, certain SCSI controllers need to be told where to find drive geometry in order for Linux to recognize the layout of your drive.

  Most distributions provide a boot up option to specify the drive geometry. In general, when booting the installation media, you can specify the drive geometry at the LILO boot prompt with a command such as:

  boot: *linux hd=*⟨*cylinders*⟩,⟨*heads*⟩,⟨*sectors*⟩

  where ⟨*cylinders*⟩, ⟨*heads*⟩, and ⟨*sectors*⟩ correspond to the number of cylinders, heads, and sectors per track for your hard drive.

After installing Linux, you will be able to install LILO, allowing you to boot from the hard drive. At that time, you can specify the drive geometry to LILO, making it unnecessary to enter the drive geometry each time you boot. See Chapter 4 for more information about LILO.

Problems with SCSI controllers and devices. Presented here are some of the most common problems with SCSI controllers and devices like CD-ROMs, hard drives, and tape drives. If you have problems getting Linux to recognize your drive or controller, read on.

The Linux SCSI HOWTO (see Appendix A) contains much useful information on SCSI devices in addition to that listed here. SCSI can be particularly tricky to configure at times.

- **A SCSI device is detected at all possible IDs.** This is caused by strapping the device to the same address as the controller. You need to change the jumper settings so that the drive uses a different address than the controller.

- **Linux reports sense errors, even if the devices are known to be error-free.** This can be caused by bad cables or bad termination. If your SCSI bus is not terminated at both ends, you may have errors accessing SCSI devices. When in doubt, always check your cables.

- **SCSI devices report timeout errors.** This is usually caused by a conflict with IRQ, DMA, or device addresses. Also check that interrupts are enabled correctly on your controller.

- **SCSI controllers that use BIOS are not detected.** Detection of controllers that use BIOS will fail if the BIOS is disabled, or if your controller's signature is not recognized by the kernel. See the Linux SCSI HOWTO (page 1285) for more information about this.

- **Controllers using memory mapped I/O do not work.** This is caused when the memory-mapped I/O ports are incorrectly cached. Either mark the board's address space as uncacheable in the XCMOS settings, or disable cache altogether.

- **When partitioning, you get a warning that "cylinders > 1024", or you are unable to boot from a partition using cylinders numbered above 1023.** BIOS limits the number of cylinders to 1024, and any partition using cylinders numbered above this won't be accessible from the BIOS. As far as Linux is concerned, this affects only booting; once the system has booted you should be able to access the partition. Your options are to either boot Linux from a boot floppy, or boot from a partition using cylinders numbered below 1024.

- **CD-ROM drive or other removable media devices are not recognized at boot time.** Try booting with a CD-ROM (or disk) in the drive. This is necessary for some devices.

If your SCSI controller is not recognized, you may need to force hardware detection at boot time. This is particularly important for BIOS-less SCSI controllers. Most distributions allow you to specify the controller IRQ and shared memory address when booting the installation media. For example, if you are using a TMC-8xx controller, you may be able to enter

```
boot:  linux tmx8xx=⟨interrupt⟩,⟨memory-address⟩
```

at the LILO boot prompt, where *interrupt* is the IRQ of controller, and *memory-address* is the shared memory address. Whether or not this is possible depends on the distribution of Linux; consult your documentation for details.

Problems installing the software.

Actually installing the Linux software should be quite trouble-free, if you're lucky. The only problems that you might experience would be related to corrupt installation media or lack of space on your Linux file systems. Here is a list of these common problems.

- **System reports** "`Read error`", "`file not found`", **or other errors while attempting to install the software.** This indicates a problem with the installation media. If you install from floppy, keep in mind that floppies are quite susceptible to media errors of this type. Be sure to use brand-new, newly formatted floppies. If you have an MS-DOS partition on your drive, many Linux distributions allow you to install the software from the hard drive. This may be faster and more reliable than using floppies.

  If you use a CD-ROM, be sure to check the disc for scratches, dust, or other problems that may cause media errors.

  The cause of the problem may be that the media is in the incorrect format. Many Linux distributions require that the floppies be formatted in high-density MS-DOS format. (The boot floppy is the exception; it is not in MS-DOS format in most cases.) If all else fails, either obtain a new set of floppies, or recreate the floppies (using new diskettes) if you downloaded the software yourself.

- **System reports errors such as** "`tar: read error`" **or** "`gzip: not in gzip format`". This problem is usually caused by corrupt files on the installation media. In other words, your floppy may be error-free, but the data on the floppy is in some way corrupted. If you downloaded the Linux software using text mode, rather than binary mode, then your files will be corrupt, and unreadable by the installation software.

- **System reports errors like** "`device full`" **while installing.** This is a clear-cut sign that you have run out of space when installing the software. Not all Linux distributions can pick up the mess cleanly; you shouldn't be able to abort the installation and expect the system to work.

  The solution is usually to re-create your file systems (with `mke2fs`) which deletes the partially installed software. You can attempt to re-install the software, this time selecting a smaller amount of software to install. In other cases, you may need to start completely from scratch, and rethink your partition and file system sizes.

- **System reports errors such as** "`read_intr: 0x10`" **while accessing the hard drive.** This usually indicates bad blocks on your drive. However, if you receive these errors while using `mkswap` or `mke2fs`, the system may be having trouble accessing your drive. This can either be a hardware problem (see page 79), or it might be a case of poorly specified geometry. If you used the

  `hd=`⟨*cylinders*⟩`,`⟨*heads*⟩`,`⟨*sectors*⟩

  option at boot time to force detection of your drive geometry, and incorrectly specified the geometry, you could be prone to this problem. This can also happen if your drive geometry is incorrectly specified in the system CMOS.

- **System reports errors like** "`file not found`" **or** "`permission denied`". This problem can occur if not all of the necessary files are present on the installation media (see the next paragraph) or if there is a permissions problem with the installation software. For example, some distributions of Linux have been known to have bugs in the installation software itself. These are usually fixed very rapidly, and are quite infrequent. If you suspect that the distribution software contains bugs, and you're sure that you have not done anything wrong, contact the maintainer of the distribution to report the bug.

If you have other strange errors when installing Linux (especially if you downloaded the software yourself), be sure that you actually obtained all of the necessary files when downloading. For example, some people use the FTP command

```
mget *.*
```

when downloading the Linux software via FTP. This will download only those files that contain a "`.`" in their filenames; if there are any files without the "`.`", you will miss them. The correct command to use in this case is

```
mget *
```

The best advice is to retrace your steps when something goes wrong. You may think that you have done everything correctly, when in fact you forgot a small but important step somewhere along the way. In many cases, re-downloading and re-installing the software can solve the problem. Don't beat your head against the wall any longer than you have to!

Also, if Linux unexpectedly hangs during installation, there may be a hardware problem of some kind. See page 79 for hints.

Problems after installing Linux.

You've spent an entire afternoon installing Linux. In order to make space for it, you wiped your MS-DOS and OS/2 partitions, and tearfully deleted your copies of SimCity and Wing Commander. You reboot the system, and nothing happens. Or, even worse, *something* happens, but it's not what should happen. What do you do?

On page 78, we cover some of the most common problems that can occur when booting the Linux installation media—many of those problems may apply here. In addition, you may be victim to one of the following maladies.

Problems booting Linux from floppy. If you use a floppy to boot Linux, you may need to specify the location of your Linux root partition at boot time. This is especially true if you are using the original installation floppy itself, and not a custom boot floppy that was created during installation.

While booting the floppy, hold down `Shift` or `Ctrl`. This should present you with a boot menu. Press `Tab` to see a list of available options. For example, many distributions allow you to type

```
boot: linux hd=⟨partition⟩
```

at the boot menu, where *partition* is the name of the Linux root partition, like `/dev/hda2`. Consult the documentation for your distribution for details.

Problems booting Linux from the hard drive. If you opted to install LILO instead of creating a boot floppy, you should be able to boot Linux from the hard drive. However, the automated LILO installation procedure used by many distributions is not always perfect. It may make incorrect assumptions about your partition layout, and you will need to re-install LILO to get everything correct. LILO installation is covered in Chapter 4.

- **System reports** "`Drive not bootable--Please insert system disk.`" The hard drive's master boot record is corrupt in some way. In most cases, it's harmless, and everything else on your drive is still intact. There are several ways around this:

  1. While partitioning your drive using `fdisk`, you may have deleted the partition that was marked as "active". MS-DOS and other operating systems attempt to boot the "active" partition at boot time (Linux pays no attention to whether the partition is "active" or not). You may be able to boot MS-DOS from floppy and run `FDISK.EXE` to set the active flag on your MS-DOS paritition, and all will be well.

     Another command to try (with MS-DOS 5.0 and higher) is

     ```
     FDISK /MBR
     ```

     This command attempts to rebuild the hard drive master boot record for booting MS-DOS, by overwriting LILO. If you no longer have MS-DOS on your hard drive, you need to boot Linux from floppy and attempt to install LILO later.

  2. If you created a MS-DOS partition using Linux's version of `fdisk`, or vice versa, you may get this error. You should create MS-DOS partitions only using MS-DOS's version, `FDISK.EXE`. (This applies to operating systems other than MS-DOS.) The best solution is either to start from scratch and repartition the drive correctly, or to merely delete and re-create the offending partitions with the correct version of `fdisk`.

  3. The LILO installation procedure may have failed. In this case, you should either boot from your Linux boot floppy (if you have one), or from the original installation media. Either of these should provide options for specifying the Linux root partition to use when booting. Hold down `Shift` or `Ctrl` at boot time, and press `Tab` from the boot menu for a list of options.

- **When booting the system from the hard drive, MS-DOS (or another operating system) starts instead of Linux.** First of all, be sure that you actually installed LILO when installing the Linux software. If not, then the system still boots MS-DOS (or whatever other operating system you may have) when you attempt to boot from the hard drive. In order to boot Linux from the hard drive, you need to install LILO (see Chapter 4).

  On the other hand, if you *did* install LILO, and another operating system boots instead of Linux, then you have LILO configured to boot that other operating system by default. While the system is booting, hold down `Shift` or `Ctrl`, and press `Tab` at the boot prompt. This should present you with a list of possible operating systems to boot; select the appropriate option (usually "`linux`") to boot Linux.

  If you wish to select Linux as the default operating system, you must re-install LILO. See Chapter 4.

  It may also be possible that you attempted to install LILO, but the installation procedure failed in some way. See the previous item.

Problems logging in After booting Linux, you should be presented with a `login` prompt, like

```
linux login:
```

At this point, either the distribution's documentation or the system itself will tell you what to do. For many distributions, you simply log in as `root`, with no password. Other possible user names to try are `guest` or `test`.

Most newly installed Linux systems should not require a password for the initial log in. However, if you are asked to enter a password, there may be a problem. First, try using a password equivalent to the username; that is, if you are logging in as `root`, use "`root`" as the password.

If you simply can't log in, there may be a problem. First, consult your distribution's documentation; the user name and password to use may be buried in there somewhere. The user name and password may have been given to you during the installation procedure, or they may be printed on the `login` banner.

One cause may be a problem with installing the Linux `login` program and initialization files. You may need to reinstall (at least parts of) the Linux software, or boot your installation media and attempt to fix the problem by hand—see Chapter 4 for hints.

Problems using the system. If logging in is successful, you should be presented with a shell prompt (like "`#`" or "`$`") and can happily roam around your system. However, there are some initial problems with using the system that sometimes creep up.

The most common initial configuration problem is incorrect file or directory permissions. This can cause the error message

```
Shell-init:  permission denied
```

to be printed after logging in (in fact, any time you see the message "`permission denied`" you can be fairly certain that it is a problem with file permissions).

In many cases, it's a simple matter of using `chmod` to fix the permissions of the appropriate files or directories. For example, some distributions of Linux once used the (incorrect) file mode 0644 for the root directory (/). The fix was to issue the command

```
# chmod 755 /
```

as `root`. However, in order to issue this command, you needed to boot from the installation media and mount your Linux root filesystem by hand—a hairy task for most newcomers.

As you use the system, you may run into places where file and directory permissions are incorrect, or software does not work as configured. Welcome to the world of Linux! While most distributions are quite trouble-free, very few of them are perfect. We don't want to cover all of those problems here. Instead, throughout the book we help you to solve many of these configuration problems by teaching you how to find them and fix them yourself. In Chapter 1 we discussed this philosophy in some detail. In Chapter 4, we give hints for fixing many of these common configuration problems.

When booting the system from the hard drive, MS-DOS (or another operating system) starts instead of Linux. First of all, be sure that you actually installed LILO when installing the Linux software. If not, then the system still boots MS-DOS (or whatever other operating system you may have) when you attempt to boot from the hard drive. In order to boot Linux from the hard drive, you need to install LILO (see [illegible]).

On the other hand, if you did install LILO, and another operating system boots instead of Linux, then you have LILO configured to boot that other operating system by default. While the system is booting, hold down the [illegible] key and press Tab at the boot prompt. This should present you with a list of possible operating systems to boot; select the appropriate option (usually just linux) to boot Linux.

If you wish to select Linux as the default operating system, you must reinstall LILO. See Chapter 5.

It may also be possible that you attempted to install LILO, but the installation procedure failed in some way. See the previous item.

Problems logging in. After booting Linux, you should be presented with a login prompt, like:

```
[illegible] login:
```

At this prompt, enter the [illegible] the system itself will tell you what to enter. For many distributions, you simply log in as root with no password. Other possible usernames to try are guest or test.

Most newly installed Linux systems should not require a password for the initial login. However, if you are asked to enter a password, there may be a problem. First, try using a password equivalent to the username; that is, if you are logging in as root, use "root" as the password.

If you simply can't log in, there may be a problem. First, consult your distribution's documentation; the username and password to use may be buried in there somewhere. The username and password may have been given to you during the installation procedure, or they may be printed on the login banner.

One cause may be a problem with installing the Linux login program and initialization files. You may need to reinstall (at least parts of) the Linux software, or boot your installation media and attempt to fix the problem by hand—see Chapter 8 for hints.

Problems using the system. If your login is successful, you should be presented with a shell prompt (such as # or $) and can happily roam around your system. However, there are some initial problems with using the system that sometimes creep up.

The most common initial configuration problem is incorrect file or directory permissions. This can cause the error message

```
[illegible]: Permission denied
```

to be printed after logging in (in fact, any time you see the message Permission denied, you can be fairly certain that it is a problem with file permissions).

In many cases, it's a simple matter of using chmod to fix the permissions of the appropriate files or directories. For example, some distributions of Linux once used the (incorrect) file mode 0644 for the root directory (/). The fix was to issue the command

```
# chmod 755 /
```

as root. However, in order to issue this command, you needed to boot from the installation media and mount the Linux root filesystem by hand—a hairy task for most newcomers.

As you use the system, you may run into places where file and directory permissions are incorrect, or software does not work as configured. Welcome to the world of Linux! While most distributions are quite trouble-free, very few of them are perfect. We don't want to cover all of those problems here. Instead, throughout the book we help you to solve many of these configuration problems by teaching you how to find and fix them yourself. In Chapter 1, we discussed this philosophy in some detail. In Chapter 5, we give hints for fixing many of these common configuration problems.

CHAPTER 3

Linux Tutorial

Introduction.

If you're new to UNIX and Linux, you may be a bit intimidated by the size and apparent complexity of the system before you. There are many good books on using UNIX out there for all levels of expertise from novice to expert. However, none of these books presents an introduction to using Linux. While 95% of using Linux is exactly like using other UNIX systems, the most straightforward way to get going on your new system is with a tutorial tailored for Linux.

This chapter does not go into great detail or cover advanced topics. Instead, we want you to hit the ground running, so that you may then read a more general book about UNIX and understand the basic differences between other UNIX systems and Linux.

We assumed very little here about your background, except perhaps that you have some familiarity with personal computer systems, and MS-DOS. However, even if you're not an MS-DOS user, you should be able to understand everything here. At first glance, UNIX looks a lot like MS-DOS—after all, parts of MS-DOS were modeled on the CP/M operating system, which in turn was modeled on UNIX. However, only the most superficial features of UNIX resemble MS-DOS. Even if you're completely new to the PC world, this tutorial should help.

And, before we begin: don't be afraid to experiment. The system won't bite you. You can't destroy anything by working on the system. UNIX has built-in security features to prevent "normal" users from damaging files that are essential to the system. Even so, the worst thing that can happen is that you may delete some or all of your files and you'll have to re-install the system. So, at this point, you have nothing to lose.

Basic UNIX concepts.

UNIX is a multitasking, multiuser operating system, which means that many people can run many different applications on one computer at the same time. This differs from MS-DOS, where only one person can use the system at any one time. Under UNIX, to identify yourself to the system, you must **log in**, which entails entering your **login name** (the name the system uses to identify you), and entering your **password**, which is your personal key for logging in to your account. Because only you know your password, no one else can log in to the system under your user name.

On traditional UNIX systems, the system administrator assigns you a user name and an initial password when you are given an account on the system. However, because in Linux you are the system administrator, you must set up your own account before you can log in. For the following discussions, we'll use the imaginary user name, "`larry`."

In addition, each UNIX system has a **host name** assigned to it. It is this host name that gives your machine a name, gives it character and charm. The host name is used to identify individual machines on a network, but even if your machine isn't networked, it should have a host name. For our examples below, the system's host name is "`mousehouse`."

Creating an account.

Before you can use a newly installed Linux system, you must set up a user account for yourself. It's usually not a good idea to use the `root` account for normal use; you should reserve the `root` account for running privileged commands and for maintaining the system, as discussed in the next chapter.

In order to create an account for yourself, log in as `root` and use the `useradd` or `adduser` command. See page 129 for information on this procedure.

Logging in.

At login time, you'll see a prompt resembling the following:

```
mousehouse login:
```

Enter your user name and press the `Return` key. Our hero, `larry`, would type:

```
mousehouse login:  larry
Password:
```

Next, enter your password. The characters you enter won't be echoed to the screen, so type carefully. If you mistype your password, you'll see the message

```
Login incorrect
```

and you'll have to try again.

Once you have correctly entered the user name and password, you are officially logged in to the system, and are free to roam.

Virtual consoles.

The system's **console** is the monitor and keyboard connected directly to the system. (Because UNIX is a multiuser operating system, you may have other terminals connected to serial ports on your system, but these would not be the console.) Linux, like some other versions of UNIX, provides access to **virtual consoles** (or VCs), that let you have more than one login session on the console at one time.

To demonstrate this, log in to your system. Next, press `Alt-F2`. You should see the `login:` prompt again. You're looking at the second virtual console. To switch back to the first VC, press `Alt-F1`. *Voila!* You're back to your first `login` session.

A newly-installed Linux system probably lets you to access only the first half-dozen or so VCs, by pressing `Alt-F1` through `Alt-F4`, or however many VCs are configured on your system. It is possible to enable up to 12 VCs—one for each function key on your keyboard. As you can see, use of VCs can be very powerful because you can work in several different sessions at the same time.

While the use of VCs is somewhat limiting (after all, you can look at only one VC at a time), it should give you a feel for the multiuser capabilities of UNIX. While you're working on the first VC, you can switch over to the second VC and work on something else.

Shells and commands.

For most of your explorations in the world of UNIX, you'll be talking to the system through a **shell**, a program that takes the commands you type and translates them into instructions to the operating system. This can be compared to the `COMMAND.COM` program under MS-DOS, which does essentially the same thing. A shell is just one interface to UNIX. There are many possible interfaces—like the X Window System, which lets you run commands by using the mouse and keyboard.

As soon as you log in, the system starts the shell, and you can begin entering commands. Here's a quick example. Larry logs in and is waiting at the shell **prompt**.

```
mousehouse login:  larry
Password:  larry's password
Welcome to Mousehouse!

/home/larry#
```

The last line of this text is the shell's prompt, indicating that it's ready to take commands. (More on what the prompt itself means later.) Let's try telling the system to do something interesting:

```
/home/larry# make love
make:  *** No way to make target 'love'.  Stop.
/home/larry#
```

Well, as it turns out, make is the name of an actual program on the system, and the shell executed this program when given the command. (Unfortunately, the system was being unfriendly.)

This brings us to the burning question: What is a command? What happens when you type "make love?" The first word on the command line, "make," is the name of the command to be executed. Everything else on the command line is taken as arguments to this command. Example:

```
/home/larry# cp foo bar
```

The name of this command is "cp," and the arguments are "foo" and "bar."

When you enter a command, the shell does several things. First, it checks the command to see if it is internal to the shell. (That is, a command which the shell knows how to execute itself. There are a number of these commands, and we'll go into them later.) The shell also checks to see if the command is an alias, or substitute name, for another command. If neither of these conditions apply, the shell looks for a program, on disk, having the specified name. If successful, the shell runs the program, sending the arguments specified on the command line.

In our example, the shell looks for a program called make, and runs it with the argument love. Make is a program often used to compile large programs, and takes as arguments the name of a "target" to compile. In the case of "make love," we instructed make to compile the target love. Because make can't find a target by this name, it fails with a humorous error message, and returns us to the shell prompt.

What happens if we type a command to a shell and the shell can't find a program having the specified name? Well, we can try the following:

```
/home/larry# eat dirt
eat:  command not found
/home/larry#
```

Quite simply, if the shell can't find a program having the name given on the command line (here, "eat"), it prints an error message. You'll often see this error message if you mistype a command (for example, if you had typed "mkae love" instead of "make love").

Logging out.

Before we delve much further, we should tell you how to log out of the system. At the shell prompt, use the command

```
/home/larry# exit
```

to log out. There are other ways of logging out, but this is the most foolproof one.

Changing your password.

You should also know how to change your password. The command passwd prompts you for your old password, and a new password. It also asks you to reenter the new password for validation. Be careful not to forget your password—if you do, you will have to ask the system administrator to reset it for you. (If you are the system administrator, see page 129.)

Files and directories.

Under most operating systems (including UNIX), there is the concept of a **file**, which is just a bundle of information given a name (called a **filename**). Examples of files might be your history term paper, an e-mail message, or an actual program that can be executed. Essentially, anything saved on disk is saved in an individual file.

Files are identified by their file names. For example, the file containing your history paper might be saved with the file name `history-paper`. These names usually identify the file and its contents in some form that is meaningful to you. There is no standard format for file names as there is under MS-DOS and some other operating systems; in general, a file name can contain any character (except the / character—see the discussion of path names, below) and is limited to 256 characters in length.

With the concept of files comes the concept of directories. A **directory** is a collection of files. It can be thought of as a "folder" that contains many different files. Directories are given names, with which you can identify them. Furthermore, directories are maintained in a tree-like structure; that is, directories may contain other directories.

Consequently, you can refer to a file by its **path name**, which is made up of the filename, preceded by the name of the directory containing the file. For example, let's say that Larry has a directory called `papers`, which contains three files: `history-final`, `english-lit`, and `masters-thesis`. Each of these three files contains information for three of Larry's ongoing projects. To refer to the `english-lit` file, Larry can specify the file's pathname, as in:

```
papers/english-lit
```

As you can see, the directory and filename are separated by a single slash (/). For this reason, filenames themselves cannot contain the / character. MS-DOS users will find this convention familiar, although in the MS-DOS world the backslash (\) is used instead.

As mentioned, directories can be nested within each other as well. For example, let's say that there is another directory within `papers`, called `notes`. The `notes` directory contains the files `math-notes` and `cheat-sheet`. The pathname of the file `cheat-sheet` would be

```
papers/notes/cheat-sheet
```

Therefore, a path name is really like a path to the file. The directory that contains a given subdirectory is known as the **parent directory**. Here, the directory `papers` is the parent of the `notes` directory.

The directory tree.

Most UNIX systems use a standard layout for files so that system resources and programs can be easily located. This layout forms a directory tree, which starts at the "/" directory, also known as the "root directory". Directly underneath / are important subdirectories: `/bin`, `/etc`, `/dev`, and `/usr`, among others. These directories in turn contain other directories which contain system configuration files, programs, and so on.

In particular, each user has a **home directory**, which is the directory set aside for that user to store his or her files. In the examples above, all of Larry's files (like `cheat-sheet` and `history-final`) are contained in Larry's home directory. Usually, user home directories are contained under `/home`, and are named for the user owning that directory. Larry's home directory is `/home/larry`.

The diagram on page 91 shows a sample directory tree, which should give you an idea of how the directory tree on your system is organized.

The current working directory.

At any moment, commands that you enter are assumed to be relative to your **current working directory**. You can think of your working directory as the directory in which you are currently "located." When you first log in, your working directory is set to your home directory—`/home/larry`, in our case. Whenever you refer to a file, you may refer to it in relationship to your current working directory, rather than specifying the full pathname of the file.

Here's an example. Larry has the directory `papers`, and `papers` contains the file `history-final`. If Larry wants to look at this file, he can use the command

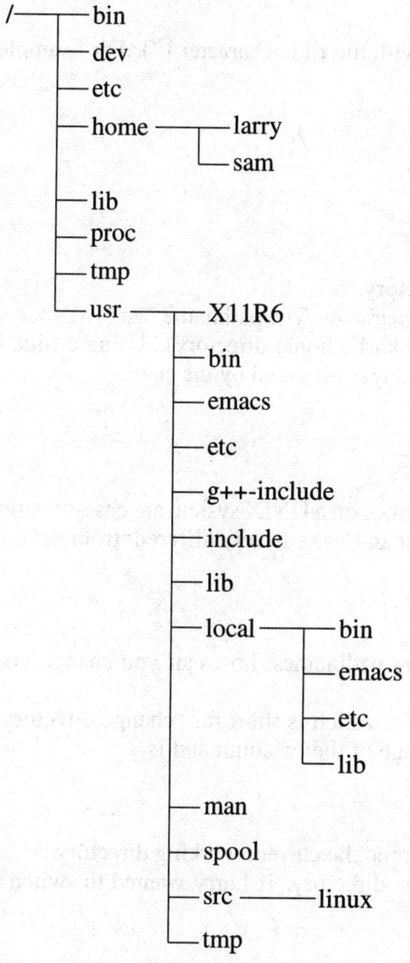

Figure 3.1: A typical (abridged) UNIX directory tree.

```
/home/larry# more /home/larry/papers/history-final
```

The `more` command simply displays a file, one screen at a time. However, because Larry's current working directory is `/home/larry`, he can instead refer to the file relative to his current location by using the command

```
/home/larry# more papers/history-final
```

If you begin a filename (like `papers/final`) with a character other than `/`, you're referring to the file in terms relative to your current working directory. This is known as a **relative path name**.

On the other hand, if you begin a file name with a `/`, the system interprets this as a full path name—that is, a path name that includes the entire path to the file, starting from the root directory, `/`. This is known as an **absolute path name**.

Referring to home directories.

Under both `tcsh` and `bash`[1] you can specify your home directory with the tilde character (~). For example, the command

```
/home/larry# more ~/papers/history-final
```

is equivalent to

```
/home/larry# more /home/larry/papers/history-final
```

The shell replaces the ~ character with the name of your home directory.

You can also specify other user's home directories with the tilde character. The pathname `~karl/letters` translates to `/home/karl/letters` by the shell (if `/home/karl` is karl's home directory). Using a tilde is simply a shortcut; there is no directory named ~—it's just syntactic sugar provided by the shell.

First steps into UNIX.

Before we begin, it is important to know that all file and command names on a UNIX system are case-sensitive (unlike operating systems such as MS-DOS). For example, the command `make` is very different from `Make` or `MAKE`. The same is true for file and directory names.

Moving around.

Now that you can log in, and you know how to refer to files using pathnames, how can you change your current working directory, to make life easier?

The command for moving around in the directory structure is `cd`, which is short for "change directory". Many often-used UNIX commands are two or three letters. The usage of the `cd` command is

cd ⟨*directory*⟩

where *directory* is the name of the directory which you wish to become the current working directory.

As mentioned earlier, when you log in, you begin in your home directory. If Larry wanted to switch to the `papers` subdirectory, he'd use the command

```
/home/larry# cd papers
/home/larry/papers#
```

As you can see, Larry's prompt changes to reflect his current working directory (so he knows where he is). Now that he's in the `papers` directory, he can look at his history final with the command

```
/home/larry/papers# more history-final
```

Now, Larry is stuck in the `papers` subdirectory. To move back up to the next higher (or parent) directory, use the command

```
/home/larry/papers# cd ..
/home/larry#
```

(Note the space between the "cd" and the "`..`".) Every directory has an entry named "`..`" which refers to the parent directory. Similarly, every directory has an entry named "`.`" which refers to itself. Therefore, the command

```
/home/larry/papers# cd .
```

[1] `tcsh` and `bash` are two **shells** that run under Linux. The shell is a program that reads user commands and executes them; most Linux systems enable either `tcsh` or `bash` for new user accounts.

gets us nowhere.

You can also use absolute pathnames with the cd command. To cd into Karl's home directory, we can use the command

```
/home/larry/papers# cd /home/karl
/home/karl#
```

Also, using cd with no argument will return you to your own home directory.

```
/home/karl# cd
/home/larry#
```

Looking at the contents of directories.

Now that you know how to move around directories, you might think, "So what?" Moving around directories is fairly useless by itself, so let's introduce a new command, ls. The ls command displays a listing of files and directories, by default from your current directory. For example:

```
/home/larry# ls
Mail
letters
papers
/home/larry#
```

Here we can see that Larry has three entries in his current directory: Mail, letters, and papers. This doesn't tell us much—are these directories or files? We can use the -F option of the ls command to get more detailed information.

```
/home/larry# ls -F
Mail/
letters/
papers/
/home/larry#
```

From the / appended to each filename, we know that these three entries are in fact subdirectories.

Using ls -F may also append "*" to the end of a filename in the resulting list which would indicate that the file is an **executable**, or a program which can be run. If nothing is appended to the filename using ls -F, the file is a "plain old file," that is, it's neither a directory nor an executable.

In general, each UNIX command may take a number of options in addition to other arguments. These options usually begin with a "-," as demonstrated above with the -F option. The -F option tells ls to give more information about the type of the files involved—in this case, printing a / after each directory name.

If you give ls a directory name, the system will print the contents of that directory.

```
/home/larry# ls -F papers
english-lit
history-final
masters-thesis
notes/
/home/larry#
```

Or, for a more interesting listing, let's see what's in the system's /etc directory.

```
/home/larry# ls /etc

Images        ftpusers      lpc           rc.new        shells
adm           getty         magic         rc0.d         startcons
bcheckrc      gettydefs     motd          rc1.d         swapoff
```

```
brc            group          mount          rc2.d          swapon
brc~           inet           mtab           rc3.d          syslog.conf
csh.cshrc      init           mtools         rc4.d          syslog.pid
csh.login      init.d         pac            rc5.d          syslogd.reload
default        initrunlvl     passwd         rmt            termcap
disktab        inittab        printcap       rpc            umount
fdprm          inittab.old    profile        rpcinfo        update
fstab          issue          psdatabase     securetty      utmp
ftpaccess      lilo           rc             services       wtmp
/home/larry#
```

If you're a MS-DOS user, you may notice that the filenames can be longer than 8 characters, and can contain periods in any position. You can even use more than one period in a filename.

Let's move to the top of the directory tree, and then down to another directory with the commands

```
/home/larry# cd ..
/home# cd ..
/# cd usr
/usr# cd bin
/usr/bin#
```

You can also move into directories in one step, as in `cd /usr/bin`.

Try moving around various directories, using `ls` and `cd`. In some cases, you may run into the foreboding "`Permission denied`" error message. This is simply UNIX security kicking in: in order to use the `ls` or `cd` commands, you must have permission to do so. We talk more about this starting on page 105.

Creating new directories.

It's time to learn how to create directories. This involves the use of the `mkdir` command. Try the following:

```
/home/larry# mkdir foo
/home/larry# ls -F
Mail/
foo/
letters/
papers/
/home/larry# cd foo
/home/larry/foo# ls
/home/larry/foo#
```

Congratulations! You made a new directory and moved into it. Since there aren't any files in this new directory, let's learn how to copy files from one place to another.

Copying files.

To copy files, use the command `cp`, as shown here:

```
/home/larry/foo# cp /etc/termcap  .
/home/larry/foo# cp /etc/shells  .
/home/larry/foo# ls -F
shells    termcap
/home/larry/foo# cp shells bells
/home/larry/foo# ls -F
bells    shells    termcap
/home/larry/foo#
```

The `cp` command copies the files listed on the command line to the file or directory given as the last argument. Notice that we use "." to refer to the current directory.

Moving files.

The mv command moves files, rather than copying them. The syntax is very straightforward:

```
/home/larry/foo# mv termcap sells
/home/larry/foo# ls -F
bells    sells    shells
/home/larry/foo#
```

Notice that the termcap file has been renamed sells. You can also use the mv command to move a file to a completely new directory.

◇ **Note:** mv and cp will overwrite a destination file having the same name without asking you. Be careful when you move a file into another directory. There may already be a file having the same name in that directory, which you'll overwrite!

Deleting files and directories.

You now have an ugly rhyme developing with the use of the ls command. To delete a file, use the rm command, which stands for "remove," as shown here:

```
/home/larry/foo# rm bells sells
/home/larry/foo# ls -F
shells
/home/larry/foo#
```

We're left with nothing but shells, but we won't complain. Note that rm by default won't prompt you before deleting a file—so be careful.

A related command to rm is rmdir. This command deletes a directory, but only if the directory is empty. If the directory contains any files or subdirectories, rmdir will complain.

Looking at files.

The commands more and cat are used for viewing the contents of files. more displays a file, one screenful at a time, while cat displays the whole file at once.

To look at the file shells, use the command

```
/home/larry/foo# more shells
```

In case you're interested what shells contains, it's a list of valid shell programs on your system. On most systems, this includes /bin/sh, /bin/bash, and /bin/csh. We'll talk about these different types of shells later.

While using more, press Space to display the next page of text, and b to display the previous page. There are other commands available in more as well, these are just the basics. Pressing q will quit more.

Quit more and try cat /etc/termcap. The text will probably fly by too quickly for you to read it all. The name "cat" actually stands for "concatenate," which is the real use of the program. The cat command can be used to concatenate the contents of several files and save the result to another file. This will be again in section 3.

Getting online help.

Almost every UNIX system, including Linux, provides a facility known as **manual pages**. These manual pages contain online documentation for system commands, resources, configuration files and so on.

The command used to access manual pages is man. If you're interested in learning about other options of the ls command, you can type

```
/home/larry# man ls
```

and the manual page for `ls` will be displayed.

Unfortunately, most manual pages are written for those who already have some idea of what the command or resource does. For this reason, manual pages usually contain only the technical details of the command, without much explanation. However, manual pages can be an invaluable resource for jogging your memory if you forget the syntax of a command. Manual pages will also tell you about commands that we don't cover in this book.

I suggest that you try `man` for the commands that we've already gone over and whenever I introduce a new command. Some of these commands won't have manual pages, for several reasons. First, the manual pages may not have been written yet. (The Linux Documentation Project is responsible for manual pages under Linux as well. We are gradually accumulating most of the manual pages available for the system.) Second, the the command might be an internal shell command, or an alias (discussed on page 88), which would not have a manual page of its own. One example is `cd`, which is an internal shell command. The shell itself actually processes the `cd`—there is no separate program that implements this command.

Summary of basic UNIX commands.

This section introduces some of the most useful basic commands of a UNIX system, including those that are covered in the previous section.

Note that options usually begin with "-," and in most cases you can specify more than one option with a single "-." For example, rather than use the command `ls -l -F`, you can use `ls -lF`.

Rather than listing every option for each command, we only present useful or important commands at this time. In fact, most of these commands have many options that you'll never use. You can use `man` to see the manual pages for each command, which list all of the available options.

Also note that many of these commands take as arguments a list of files or directories, denoted in this table by "*file1* ... *fileN*." For example, the `cp` command takes as arguments a list of files to copy, followed by the destination file or directory. When copying more than one file, the destination must be a directory.

`cd` Change the current working directory.
Syntax: `cd` ⟨*directory*⟩
Where *directory* is the directory which you want to change to. ("`.`" refers to the current directory, "`..`" the parent directory.)
Example: `cd ../foo` sets the current directory up one level, then back down to `foo`.

`ls` Displays information about the named files and directories.
Syntax: `ls` ⟨*file1*⟩ ⟨*file2*⟩ ...⟨*fileN*⟩
Where *file1* through *fileN* are the filenames or directories to list. The most commonly used options are `-F` (to display the file type), and `-l` (to give a "long" listing including file size, owner, permissions, and so on).
Example: `ls -lF /home/larry` displays the contents of the directory `/home/larry`.

`cp` Copies one or more file to another file or directory.
Syntax: `cp` ⟨*file1*⟩ ⟨*file2*⟩ ...⟨*fileN*⟩ ⟨*destination*⟩
Where *file1* through *fileN* are the files to copy, and *destination* is the destination file or directory.
Example: `cp ../frog joe` copies the file `../frog` to the file or directory `joe`.

`mv` Moves one or more file to another file or directory. This command does the equivalent of a copy followed by the deletion of the original file. You can use this to rename files, like in the MS-DOS command `RENAME`.
Syntax: `mv` ⟨*file1*⟩ ⟨*file2*⟩ ...⟨*fileN*⟩ ⟨*destination*⟩
Where *file1* through *fileN* are the files to move, and *destination* is the destination file or directory.
Example: `mv ../frog joe` moves the file `../frog` to the file or directory `joe`.

`rm` Deletes files. Note that when you delete a file under UNIX, they are unrecoverable (unlike MS-DOS, where you can usually "undelete" the file).

	Syntax: `rm` ⟨*file1*⟩ ⟨*file2*⟩ ...⟨*fileN*⟩ Where *file1* through *fileN* are the filenames to delete. The `-i` option prompts for confirmation before deleting the file. Example: `rm -i /home/larry/joe /home/larry/frog` deletes the files `joe` and `frog` in `/home/larry`.
`mkdir`	Creates new directories. Syntax: `mkdir` ⟨*dir1*⟩ ⟨*dir2*⟩ ...⟨*dirN*⟩ Where *dir1* through *dirN* are the directories to create. Example: `mkdir /home/larry/test` creates the directory `test` in `/home/larry`.
`rmdir`	Deletes empty directories. When using `rmdir`, the current working directory must not be within the directory to be deleted. Syntax: `rmdir` ⟨*dir1*⟩ ⟨*dir2*⟩ ...⟨*dirN*⟩ Where *dir1* through *dirN* are the directories to delete. Example: `rmdir /home/larry/papers` deletes the directory `/home/larry/papers`, if empty.
`man`	Displays the manual page for the given command or resource (that is, any system utility that isn't a command, such as a library function.) Syntax: `man` ⟨*command*⟩ Where *command* is the name of the command or resource to get help on. Example: `man ls` gives help on the `ls` command.
`more`	Displays the contents of the named files, one screenful at a time. Syntax: `more` ⟨*file1*⟩ ⟨*file2*⟩ ...⟨*fileN*⟩ Where *file1* through *fileN* are the files to display. Example: `more papers/history-final` displays the file `papers/history-final`.
`cat`	Officially used to concatenate files, `cat` is also used to display the contents of a file on screen. Syntax: `cat` ⟨*file1*⟩ ⟨*file2*⟩ ...⟨*fileN*⟩ Where *file1* through *fileN* are the files to display. Example: `cat letters/from-mdw` displays the file `letters/from-mdw`.
`echo`	Displays the given arguments on the screen. Syntax: `echo` ⟨*arg1*⟩ ⟨*arg2*⟩ ...⟨*argN*⟩ Where *arg1* through *argN* are the arguments to echo. Example: `echo "Hello world"` displays the string "`Hello world`."
`grep`	Display every line in one or more files that match the given pattern. Syntax: `grep` ⟨*pattern*⟩ ⟨*file1*⟩ ⟨*file2*⟩ ...⟨*fileN*⟩ Where *pattern* is a regular expression pattern, and *file1* through *fileN* are the files to search. Example: `grep loomer /etc/hosts` displays every line in the file `/etc/hosts` that contains the pattern "`loomer`."

Exploring the file system.

A **file system** is the collection of files and the hierarchy of directories on a system. The time has now come to escort you around the file system.

You now have the skills and the knowledge to understand the Linux file system, and you have a road map. (Refer to diagram on page 91).

First, change to the root directory (`cd /`), and then enter `ls -F` to display a listing of its contents. You'll probably see the following directories[2]: `bin`, `dev`, `etc`, `home`, `install`, `lib`, `mnt`, `proc`, `root`, `tmp`, `user`, `usr`, and `var`.

[2]You may see others, and you might not see all of them. Every release of Linux differs in some respects.

Now, let's take a look at each of these directories.

/bin — /bin is short for "binaries," or executables, where many essential system programs reside. Use `ls -F /bin` to list the files here. If you look down the list you may see a few commands that you recognize, such as cp, ls, and mv. These are the actual programs for these commands. When you use the cp command, for example, you're running the program /bin/cp.

Using `ls -F`, you'll see that most (if not all) of the files in /bin have an asterisk ("*") appended to their filenames. This indicates that the files are executables, as described on page 93.

/dev — The "files" in /dev are **device drivers**— they access system devices and resources like disk drives, modems, and memory. Just as your system can read data from a file, it can also read input from the mouse by accessing /dev/mouse.

Filenames that begin with fd are floppy disk devices. fd0 is the first floppy disk drive, and fd1 is the second. You may have noticed that there are more floppy disk devices than the two listed above: these represent specific types of floppy disks. For example, fd1H1440 accesses high-density, 3.5" diskettes in drive 1.

The following is a list of some of the most commonly used device files. Even though you may not have some of the physical devices listed below, chances are that you'll have drivers in /dev for them anyway.

- /dev/console refers to the system's console—that is, the monitor connected directly to your system.
- The various /dev/ttyS and /dev/cua devices are used for accessing serial ports. /dev/ttyS0 refers to "COM1" under MS-DOS. The /dev/cua devices are "call-out" devices, and used with a modem.
- Device names beginning with hd access hard drives. /dev/hda refers to the *whole* first hard disk, while /dev/hda1 refers to the first *partition* on /dev/hda.
- Device names that begin with sd are SCSI drives. If you have a SCSI hard drive, instead of accessing it through /dev/hda, you would access /dev/sda. SCSI tapes are accessed via st devices, and SCSI CD-ROM via sr devices.
- Device names that begin with lp access parallel ports. /dev/lp0 is the same as "LPT1" in the MS-DOS world.
- /dev/null is used as a "black hole"—data sent to this device is gone forever. Why is this useful? Well, if you wanted to suppress the output of a command appearing on your screen, you could send that output to /dev/null. We'll talk more about this later.
- Device names that begin with /dev/tty refer to the "virtual consoles" on your system (accessed by pressing Alt-F1, Alt-F2, and so on). /dev/tty1 refers to the first VC, /dev/tty2 refers to the second, and so on.
- Device names beginning with /dev/pty are **pseudo-terminals**, which are used to provide a "terminal" to remote login sessions. For example, if your machine is on a network, incoming telnet logins would use one of the /dev/pty devices.

/etc — /etc contains a number of miscellaneous system configuration files. These include /etc/passwd (the user database), /etc/rc (the system initialization script), and so on.

/sbin — /sbin contains essential system binaries that are used for system administration.

/home — /home contains user's home directories. For example, /home/larry is the home directory for the user "larry." On a newly installed system, there may not be any users in this directory.

`/lib` — `/lib` contains **shared library images**, which are files that contain code which many programs share in common. Rather than each program using its own copy of these shared routines, they are all stored in one common place, in `/lib`. This makes executable files smaller, and saves space on your system.

`/proc` — `/proc` supports a "virtual file system," where the files are stored in memory, not on disk. These "files" refer to the various **processes** running on the system, and let you get information about the programs and processes that are running at any given time. This is discussed in more detail starting on page 108.

`/tmp` — Many programs store temporary information and in a file that is deleted when the program has finished executing. The standard location for these files is in `/tmp`.

`/usr` — `/usr` is a very important directory which contains subdirectories that contain some of the most important and useful programs and configuration files used on the system.

The various directories described above are essential for the system to operate, but most of the items found in `/usr` are optional. However, it is these optional items that make the system useful and interesting. Without `/usr`, you'd have a boring system that supports only programs like `cp` and `ls`. `/usr` contains most of the larger software packages and the configuration files that accompany them.

`/usr/X11R6` — `/usr/X11R6` contains The X Window System, if you installed it. The X Window System is a large, powerful graphical environment that provides a large number of graphical utilities and programs, displayed in "windows" on your screen. If you're at all familiar with the Microsoft Windows or Macintosh environments, X will look familiar. The `/usr/X11R6` directory contains all of the X executables, configuration files, and support files. This is covered in more detail in Chapter 5.

`/usr/bin` — `/usr/bin` is the real warehouse for software on any UNIX system, containing most of the executables for programs not found in other places, like `/bin`.

`/usr/etc` — Just as `/etc` contains essential miscellaneous system programs and configuration files, `/usr/etc` contains miscellaneous utilities and files, that in general, are not essential to the system.

`/usr/include` — `/usr/include` contains **include files** for the C compiler. These files (most of which end in `.h`, for "header") declare data structure names, subroutines, and constants used when writing programs in C. Files in `/usr/include/sys` are generally used when programming on the UNIX system level. If you are familiar with the C programming language, here you'll find header files like `stdio.h`, which declare functions like `printf()`.

`/usr/g++-include` — `/usr/g++-include` contains include files for the C++ compiler (much like `/usr/include`).

`/usr/lib` — `/usr/lib` contains the "stub" and "static" library equivalents for the files found in `/lib`. When compiling a program, the program is "linked" with the libraries found in `/usr/lib`, which then directs the program to look in `/lib` when it needs the actual code in the library. In addition, various other programs store configuration files in `/usr/lib`.

`/usr/local` — `/usr/local` is much like `/usr`—it contains various programs and files not essential to the system, but which make the system fun and exciting. In general, programs in `/usr/local` are specialized for your system—consequently, `/usr/local` differs greatly between UNIX systems.

Here, you might find large software packages like TeX and `emacs`, if you installed them.

`/usr/man` — This directory contains manual pages. There are two subdirectories in it for every manual page "section" (use the command `man man` for details). For example, `/usr/man/man1` contains the source (that is, the unformatted original) for manual pages in section 1, and

	/usr/man/cat1 contains the formatted manual pages for section 1.
/usr/src	/usr/src contains the source code (the uncompiled instructions) for various programs on your system. The most important directory here is /usr/src/linux, which contains the source code for the Linux kernel.
/var	/var holds directories that often change in size or tend to grow. Many of those directories used to reside in /usr, but since those who support Linux are trying to keep it relatively unchangeable, the directories that change often have been moved to /var. Some Linux distributions maintain their software package databases in directories under /var.
/var/adm	/var/adm contains various files of interest to the system administrator, specifically system logs, which record errors or problems with the system. Other files record logins to the system as well as failed login attempts. This will be covered in Chapter 4.
/var/spool	/var/spool contains files which are "spooled" to another program. For example, if your machine is connected to a network, incoming mail is stored in /var/spool/mail until you read or delete it. Outgoing or incoming news articles are in /var/spool/news, and so on.

Types of shells.

As mentioned before, UNIX is a multitasking, multiuser operating system. Multitasking is very useful, and once you understand it, you'll use it all of the time. Before long, you'll run programs in the background, switch between tasks, and pipeline programs together to achieve complicated results with a single command.

Many of the features we'll cover in this section are features provided by the shell itself. Be careful not to confuse UNIX (the actual operating system) with a shell—a shell is just an interface to the underlying system. The shell provides functionality in addition to UNIX itself.

A shell is not only an interpreter for the interactive commands you type at the prompt, but also a powerful programming language. It lets you to write **shell scripts**, to "batch" several shell commands together in a file. If you know MS-DOS you'll recognize the similarity to "batch files." Shell scripts are a very powerful tool, that will let you automate and expand your use of UNIX. See page 117 for more information.

There are several types of shells in the UNIX world. The two major types are the "Bourne shell" and the "C shell." The Bourne shell uses a command syntax like the original shell on early UNIX systems, like System III. The name of the Bourne shell on most UNIX systems is /bin/sh (where sh stands for "shell"). The C shell (not to be confused with sea shell) uses a different syntax, somewhat like the programming language C, and on most UNIX systems is named /bin/csh.

Under Linux, several variations of these shells are available. The two most commonly used are the Bourne Again Shell, or "Bash" (/bin/bash), and "Tcsh" (/bin/tcsh). bash is a form of the Bourne shell that includes many of the advanced features found in the C shell. Because bash supports a superset of the Bourne shell syntax, shell scripts written in the standard Bourne shell should work with bash. If you prefer to use the C shell syntax, Linux supports tcsh, which is an expanded version of the original C shell.

The type of shell you decide to use is mostly a religious issue. Some folks prefer the Bourne shell syntax with the advanced features of bash, and some prefer the more structured C shell syntax. As far as normal commands such as cp and ls are concerned, the shell you use doesn't matter—the syntax is the same. Only when you start to write shell scripts or use advanced features of a shell do the differences between shell types begin to matter.

As we discuss the features of the various shells, we'll note differences between Bourne and C shells. However, for the purposes of this manual most of those differences are minimal. (If you're really curious at this point, read the man pages for bash and tcsh.)

Wild cards.

A key feature of most UNIX shells is the ability to refer to more than one file by name using special characters. These **wild cards** let you refer to, say, all file names that contain the character "n".

The wild card "*" specifies any character or string of characters in a file name. When you use the character "*" in a file name, the shell replaces it with all possible substitutions from file names in the directory you're referencing.

Here's a quick example. Suppose that Larry has the files `frog`, `joe`, and `stuff` in his current directory.

```
/home/larry# ls
frog     joe     stuff
/home/larry#
```

To specify all files containing the letter "o" in the filename, use the command

```
/home/larry# ls *o*
frog     joe
/home/larry#
```

As you can see, each instance of "*" is replaced with all substitutions that match the wild card from filenames in the current directory.

The use of "*" by itself simply matches all filenames, because all characters match the wild card.

```
/home/larry# ls *
frog     joe     stuff
/home/larry#
```

Here are a few more examples:

```
/home/larry# ls f*
frog
/home/larry# ls *ff
stuff
/home/larry# ls *f*
frog     stuff
/home/larry# ls s*f
stuff
/home/larry#
```

The process of changing a "*" into a series of filenames is called **wild card expansion** and is done by the shell. This is important: an individual command, such as `ls`, never sees the "*" in its list of parameters. The shell expands the wild card to include all filenames that match. So, the command

```
/home/larry# ls *o*
```

is expanded by the shell to

```
/home/larry# ls frog joe
```

One important note about the "*" wild card: it does not match file names that begin with a single period ("`.`"). These files are treated as **hidden** files—while they are not really hidden, they don't show up on normal `ls` listings and aren't touched by the use of the "*" wild card.

Here's an example. We mentioned earlier that each directory contains two special entries: "`.`" refers to the current directory, and "`..`" refers to the parent directory. However, when you use `ls`, these two entries don't show up.

```
/home/larry# ls
frog     joe     stuff
/home/larry#
```

If you use the `-a` switch with `ls`, however, you can display filenames that begin with '`.`'. Observe:

```
/home/larry# ls -a
.   ..   .bash_profile   .bashrc   frog   joe   stuff
/home/larry#
```

The listing contains the two special entries, '.' and '..', as well as two other "hidden" files—.bash_profile and .bashrc. These two files are startup files used by bash when larry logs in. They are described starting on page 120.

Note that when you use the "*" wild card, none of the filenames beginning with "." are displayed.

```
/home/larry# ls *
frog    joe    stuff
/home/larry#
```

This is a safety feature: if the "*" wild card matched filenames beginning with '.', it would also match the directory names '.' and '..'. This can be dangerous when using certain commands.

Another wild card is "?". The "?" wild card expands to only a single character. Thus, ls ? displays all one-character filenames. And ls termcap? would display termcap but not "termcap.backup." Here's another example:

```
/home/larry# ls j?e
joe
/home/larry# ls f??g
frog
/home/larry# ls ????f
stuff
/home/larry#
```

As you can see, wild cards lets you specify many files at one time. In the command summary that starts on page 96, we said that the cp and mv commands actually can copy or move more than one file at a time. For example,

```
/home/larry# cp /etc/s* /home/larry
```

copies all filenames in /etc beginning with "s" to the directory /home/larry. The format of the cp command is really

cp ⟨*file1*⟩ ⟨*file2*⟩ ⟨*file3*⟩ ... ⟨*fileN*⟩ ⟨*destination*⟩

where *file1* through *fileN* is a list of filenames to copy, and *destination* is the destination file or directory. mv has an identical syntax.

If you are copying or moving more than one file, the *destination* must be a directory. You can only copy or move a single file to another file.

UNIX plumbing.

Standard input and standard output.

Many UNIX commands get input from what is called **standard input** and send their output to **standard output** (often abbreviated as stdin and stdout). Your shell sets things up so that standard input is your keyboard, and standard output is the screen.

Here's an example using the cat command. Normally, cat reads data from all of the files specified by the command line, and sends this data directly to stdout. Therefore, using the command

```
/home/larry/papers# cat history-final masters-thesis
```

displays the contents of the file history-final followed by masters-thesis.

However, if you don't specify a filename, cat reads data from stdin and sends it back to stdout. Here's an example:

```
/home/larry/papers# cat
Hello there.
Hello there.
Bye.
Bye.
Ctrl-D
/home/larry/papers#
```

Each line that you type is immediately echoed back by cat. When reading from standard input, you indicate the input is "finished" by sending an EOT (end of text) signal, in general, generated by pressing Ctrl-D.

Here's another example. The sort command reads lines of text (again, from stdin, unless you specify one or more filenames) and sends the sorted output to stdout. Try the following.

```
/home/larry/papers# sort
bananas
carrots
apples
Ctrl-D
apples
bananas
carrots
/home/larry/papers#
```

Now we can alphabetize our shopping list... isn't UNIX useful?

Redirecting input and output.

Now, let's say that you want to send the output of sort to a file, to save our shopping list on disk. The shell lets you **redirect** standard output to a filename, by using the ">" symbol. Here's how it works:

```
/home/larry/papers# sort > shopping-list
bananas
carrots
apples
Ctrl-D
/home/larry/papers#
```

As you can see, the result of the sort command isn't displayed, but is saved to the file named shopping-list. Let's look at this file:

```
/home/larry/papers# cat shopping-list
apples
bananas
carrots
/home/larry/papers#
```

Now you can sort your shopping list, and save it, too! But let's suppose that you are storing the unsorted, original shopping list in the file items. One way of sorting the information and saving it to a file would be to give sort the name of the file to read, in lieu of standard input, and redirect standard output as we did above, as follows:

```
/home/larry/papers# sort items > shopping-list
/home/larry/papers# cat shopping-list
apples
bananas
carrots
/home/larry/papers#
```

However, there's another way to do this. Not only can you redirect standard output, you can redirect standard input as well, using the "<" symbol.

```
/home/larry/papers# sort < items
apples
bananas
carrots
/home/larry/papers#
```

Technically, `sort < items` is equivalent to `sort items`, but lets you demonstrate the following point: `sort < items` behaves as if the data in the file `items` was typed to standard input. The shell handles the redirection. `sort` wasn't given the name of the file (`items`) to read; as far as `sort` is concerned, it still reads from standard input as if you had typed the data from your keyboard.

This introduces the concept of a **filter**. A filter is a program that reads data from standard input, processes it in some way, and sends the processed data to standard output. Using redirection, standard input and standard output can be referenced from files. As mentioned above, `stdin` and `stdout` default to the keyboard and screen respectively. `sort` is a simple filter. It sorts the incoming data and sends the result to standard output. `cat` is even simpler. It doesn't do anything with the incoming data, it simply outputs whatever is given to it.

Using pipes.

We already demonstrated how to use `sort` as a filter. However, these examples assume that you have data stored in a file somewhere or are willing to type the data from the standard input yourself. What if the data that you wanted to sort came from the output of another command, like `ls`?

The `-r` option to `sort` sorts the data in reverse-alphabetical order. If you want to list the files in your current directory in reverse order, one way to do it is follows:

```
/home/larry/papers# ls
english-list
history-final
masters-thesis
notes
```

Now redirect the output of the `ls` command into a file called `file-list`:

```
/home/larry/papers# ls > file-list
/home/larry/papers# sort -r file-list
notes
masters-thesis
history-final
english-list
/home/larry/papers#
```

Here, you save the output of `ls` in a file, and then run `sort -r` on that file. But this is unwieldy and uses a temporary file to save the data from `ls`.

The solution is **pipelining**. This is a shell feature that connects a string of commands via a "pipe." The `stdout` of the first command is sent to the `stdin` of the second command. In this case, we want to send the `stdout` of `ls` to the `stdin` of `sort`. Use the "|" symbol to create a pipe, as follows:

```
/home/larry/papers# ls | sort -r
notes
masters-thesis
history-final
english-list
/home/larry/papers#
```

This command is shorter and easier to type.

Here's another useful example, the command

```
/home/larry/papers# ls /usr/bin
```

displays a long list of files, most of which fly past the screen too quickly for you to read. So, let's use `more` to display the list of files in `/usr/bin`.

```
/home/larry/papers# ls /usr/bin | more
```

Now you can page down the list of files at your leisure.

But the fun doesn't stop here! You can pipe more than two commands together. The command `head` is a filter that displays the first lines from an input stream (in this case, input from a pipe). If you want to display the last filename in alphabetical order in the current directory, use commands like the following:

```
/home/larry/papers# ls | sort -r | head -1
notes
/home/larry/papers#
```

where `head -1` displays the first line of input that it receives (in this case, the stream of reverse-sorted data from `ls`).

Non-destructive redirection.

Using ">" to redirect output to a file is destructive: in other words, the command

```
/home/larry/papers# ls > file-list
```

overwrites the contents of the file `file-list`. If instead, you redirect with the symbol ">>," the output is appended to (added to the end of) the named file instead of overwriting it. For example,

```
/home/larry/papers# ls >> file-list
```

appends the output of the `ls` command to `file-list`.

Keep in mind that redirection and pipes are features of the shell—which supports the use of ">", "»" and "|". It has nothing to do with the commands themselves.

File permissions.

Concepts of file permissions.

Because there is typically more than one user on a UNIX system, UNIX provides a mechanism known as **file permissions**, which protect user files from tampering by other users. This mechanism lets files and directories be "owned" by a particular user. For example, because Larry created the files in his home directory, Larry owns those files and has access to them.

UNIX also lets files be shared between users and groups of users. If Larry desired, he could cut off access to his files so that no other user could access them. However, on most systems the default is to allow other users to read your files but not modify or delete them in any way.

Every file is owned by a particular user. However, files are also owned by a particular **group**, which is a defined group of users of the system. Every user is placed into at least one group when that user's account is created. However, the system administrator may grant the user access to more than one group.

Groups are usually defined by the type of users who access the machine. For example, on a university UNIX system users may be placed into the groups `student`, `staff`, `faculty` or `guest`. There are also a few system-defined groups (like `bin` and `admin`) which are used by the system itself to control access to resources—very rarely do actual users belong to these system groups.

Permissions fall into three main divisions: read, write, and execute. These permissions may be granted to three classes of users: the owner of the file, the group to which the file belongs, and to all users, regardless of group.

Read permission lets a user read the contents of the file, or in the case of directories, list the contents of the directory (using `ls`). Write permission lets the user write to and modify the file. For directories, write permission lets the user create new files or delete files within that directory. Finally, execute permission lets the user run the file as a program or shell script (if the file is a program or shell script). For directories, having execute permission lets the user `cd` into the directory in question.

Interpreting file permissions.

Let's look at an example that demonstrates file permissions. Using the `ls` command with the `-l` option displays a "long" listing of the file, including file permissions.

```
/home/larry/foo# ls -l stuff

  -rw-r--r--   1 larry      users          505 Mar 13 19:05 stuff

  /home/larry/foo#
```

The first field in the listing represents the file permissions. The third field is the owner of the file (`larry`) and the fourth field is the group to which the file belongs (`users`). Obviously, the last field is the name of the file (`stuff`). We'll cover the other fields later.

This file is owned by `larry`, and belongs to the group `users`. The string `-rw-r-r-` lists, in order, the permissions granted to the file's owner, the file's group, and everybody else.

The first character of the permissions string ("`-`") represents the type of file. A "`-`" means that this is a regular file (as opposed to a directory or device driver). The next three characters ("`rw-`") represent the permissions granted to the file's owner, `larry`. The "`r`" stands for "read" and the "`w`" stands for "write". Thus, `larry` has read and write permission to the file `stuff`.

As mentioned, besides read and write permission, there is also "execute" permission—represented by an "`x`." However, a "`-`" is listed here in place of an "`x`," so Larry doesn't have execute permission on this file. This is fine, as the file `stuff` isn't a program of any kind. Of course, because Larry owns the file, he may grant himself execute permission for the file if he so desires. (This will be covered shortly.)

The next three characters, ("`r-`"), represent the group's permissions on the file. The group that owns this file is `users`. Because only an "`r`" appears here, any user who belongs to the group `users` may read this file.

The last three characters, also ("`r-`"), represent the permissions granted to every other user on the system (other than the owner of the file and those in the group `users`). Again, because only an "`r`" is present, other users may read the file, but not write to it or execute it.

Here are some other examples of permissions:

`-rwxr-xr-x` The owner of the file may read, write, and execute the file. Users in the file's group, and all other users, may read and execute the file.

`-rw-----` The owner of the file may read and write the file. No other user can access the file.

`-rwxrwxrwx` All users may read, write, and execute the file.

Dependencies.

The permissions granted to a file also depend on the permissions of the directory in which the file is located. For example, even if a file is set to `-rwxrwxrwx`, other users cannot access the file unless they have read and execute access to the directory in which the file is located. For example, if Larry wanted to restrict access to all of his files, he could set the permissions to his home directory `/home/larry` to `-rwx----`. In this way, no other user has access to his directory, and all files and directories within it. Larry doesn't need to worry about the individual permissions on each of his files.

In other words, to access a file at all, you must have execute access to all directories along the file's pathname, and read (or execute) access to the file itself.

Typically, users on a UNIX system are very open with their files. The usual set of permissions given to files is `-rw-r-r-`, which lets other users read the file but not change it in any way. The usual set of permissions given to directories is `-rwxr-xr-x`, which lets other users look through your directories, but not create or delete files within them.

However, many users wish to keep other users out of their files. Setting the permissions of a file to `-rw-----` will prevent any other user from accessing the file. Likewise, setting the permissions of a directory to `-rwx----` keeps other users out of the directory in question.

Changing permissions.

The command `chmod` is used to set the permissions on a file. Only the owner of a file may change the permissions on that file. The syntax of `chmod` is

```
chmod {a,u,g,o}{+,-}{r,w,x} ⟨filenames⟩
```

Briefly, you supply one or more of **a**ll, **u**ser, **g**roup, or **o**ther. Then you specify whether you are adding rights (+) or taking them away (-). Finally, you specify one or more of **r**ead, **w**rite, and e**x**ecute. Some examples of legal commands are:

`chmod a+r stuff`
: Gives all users read access to the file.

`chmod +r stuff`
: Same as above—if none of `a`, `u`, `g`, or `o` is specified, `a` is assumed.

`chmod og-x stuff`
: Remove execute permission from users other than the owner.

`chmod u+rwx stuff`
: Let the owner of the file read, write, and execute the file.

`chmod o-rwx stuff`
: Remove read, write, and execute permission from users other than the owner and users in the file's group.

Managing file links.

Links let you give a single file more than one name. Files are actually identified by the system by their **inode number**, which is just the unique file system identifier for the file. A directory is actually a listing of inode numbers with their corresponding filenames. Each filename in a directory is a **link** to a particular inode.

Hard links.

The `ln` command is used to create multiple links for one file. For example, let's say that you have a file called `foo` in a directory. Using `ls -i`, you can look at the inode number for this file.

```
/home/larry# ls -i foo
22192 foo
/home/larry#
```

Here, `foo` has an inode number of 22192 in the file system. You can create another link to `foo`, named `bar`, as follows:

```
/home/larry# ln foo bar
```

With `ls -i`, you see that the two files have the same inode.

```
/home/larry# ls -i foo bar
22192 bar   22192 foo
/home/larry#
```

Now, specifying either `foo` or `bar` will access the same file. If you make changes to `foo`, those changes appear in `bar` as well. For all purposes, `foo` and `bar` are the same file.

These links are known as **hard links** because they create a direct link to an inode. Note that you can hard-link files only when they're on the same file system; symbolic links (see below) don't have this restriction.

When you delete a file with `rm`, you are actually only deleting one link to a file. If you use the command

```
/home/larry# rm foo
```

then only the link named foo is deleted, bar will still exist. A file is only truly deleted on the system when it has no links to it. Usually, files have only one link, so using the rm command deletes the file. However, if a file has multiple links to it, using rm will delete only a single link; in order to delete the file, you must delete all links to the file.

The command `ls -l` displays the number of links to a file (among other information).

```
/home/larry# ls -l foo bar
-rw-r--r--   2 root     root            12 Aug  5 16:51 bar
-rw-r--r--   2 root     root            12 Aug  5 16:50 foo
/home/larry#
```

The second column in the listing, "2", specifies the number of links to the file.

As it turns out, a directory is actually just a file containing information about link-to-inode associations. Also, every directory contains at least two hard links: "." (a link pointing to itself), and ".." (a link pointing to the parent directory). The root directory (/) ".." link just points back to /. (In other words, the parent of the root directory is the root directory itself.)

Symbolic links.

Symbolic links, or symlinks, are another type of link, which are somewhat different from hard links. A symbolic link lets you give a file another name, but doesn't link the file by inode.

The command `ln -s` creates a symbolic link to a file. For example, if you use the command

```
/home/larry# ln -s foo bar
```

you will create a symbolic link named bar that points to the file foo. If you use `ls -i`, you'll see that the two files have different inodes, indeed.

```
/home/larry# ls -i foo bar
22195 bar   22192 foo
/home/larry#
```

However, using `ls -l`, we see that the file bar is a symlink pointing to foo.

```
/home/larry# ls -l foo bar
lrwxrwxrwx   1 root     root             3 Aug  5 16:51 bar -> foo
-rw-r--r--   1 root     root            12 Aug  5 16:50 foo
/home/larry#
```

The file permissions on a symbolic link are not used (they always appear as rwxrwxrwx). Instead, the permissions on the symbolic link are determined by the permissions on the target of the symbolic link (in our example, the file foo).

Functionally, hard links and symbolic links are similar, but there are differences. For one thing, you can create a symbolic link to a file that doesn't exist; the same is not true for hard links. Symbolic links are processed by the kernel differently than are hard links, which is just a technical difference but sometimes an important one. Symbolic links are helpful because they identify the file they point to; with hard links, there is no easy way to determine which files are linked to the same inode.

Links are used in many places on the Linux system. Symbolic links are especially important to the shared library images in /lib. See page 143 for more information.

Job control.

Jobs and processes.

Job control is a feature provided by many shells (including bash and tcsh) that let you control multiple running commands, or **jobs**, at once. Before we can delve much further, we need to talk about **processes**.

Every time you run a program, you start what is called a "process." The command ps displays a list of currently running processes, as shown here:

```
/home/larry# ps

  PID TT STAT  TIME COMMAND
   24  3 S     0:03 (bash)
  161  3 R     0:00 ps

/home/larry#
```

The PID listed in the first column is the **process ID**, a unique number given to every running process. The last column, COMMAND, is the name of the running command. Here, we're looking only at the processes which Larry himself is currently running. (There are many other processes running on the system as well—"ps -aux" lists them all.) These are bash (Larry's shell), and the ps command itself. As you can see, bash is running concurrently with the ps command. bash executed ps when Larry typed the command. After ps has finished running (after the table of processes is displayed), control is returned to the bash process, which displays the prompt, ready for another command.

A running process is also called a "job." The terms "process" and "job" are interchangeable. However, a process is usually referred to as a "job" when used in conjunction with job control—a feature of the shell that lets you switch between several independent jobs.

In most cases users run only a single job at a time—whatever command they last typed to the shell. However, using job control, you can run several jobs at once, and switch between them as needed.

How might this be useful? Let's say you are editing a text file and want to interrupt your editing and do something else. With job control, you can temporarily suspend the editor, go back to the shell prompt and start to work on something else. When you're done, you can switch back to the editor and be back where you started, as if you didn't leave the editor. There are many other practical uses of job control.

Foreground and background.

Jobs can either be in the **foreground** or in the **background**. There can only be one job in the foreground at a time. The foreground job is the job with which you interact—it receives input from the keyboard and sends output to your screen, unless, of course, you have redirected input or output, as described starting on page 102). On the other hand, jobs in the background do not receive input from the terminal—in general, they run along quietly without the need for interaction.

Some jobs take a long time to finish and don't do anything interesting while they are running. Compiling programs is one such job, as is compressing a large file. There's no reason why you should sit around being bored while these jobs complete their tasks; just run them in the background. While jobs run in the background, you are free to run other programs.

Jobs may also be **suspended**. A suspended job is a job that is temporarily stopped. After you suspend a job, you can tell the job to continue in the foreground or the background as needed. Resuming a suspended job does not change the state of the job in any way—the job continues to run where it left off.

Suspending a job is not equal to interrupting a job. When you **interrupt** a running process (by pressing the interrupt key, which is usually Ctrl-C)[3], the process is killed for good. Once the job is killed, there's no hope of resuming it. You'll must run the command again. Also, some programs trap the interrupt, so that pressing Ctrl-C won't immediately kill the job. This is to let the program perform any necessary cleanup operations before exiting. In fact, some programs don't let you kill them with an interrupt at all.

Backgrounding and killing jobs.

Let's begin with a simple example. The command yes is a seemingly useless command that sends an endless stream of y's to standard output. (This is actually useful. If you piped the output of yes to another command which asked a series of yes and no questions, the stream of y's would confirm all of the questions.)

Try it out:

[3] You can set the interrupt key with the stty command.

```
/home/larry# yes
    y
    y
    y
    y
    y
```

The y's will continue *ad infinitum*. You can kill the process by pressing the interrupt key, which is usually `Ctrl-C`. So that we don't have to put up with the annoying stream of y's, let's redirect the standard output of yes to /dev/null. As you may remember, /dev/null acts as a "black hole" for data. Any data sent to it disappears. This is a very effective method of quieting an otherwise verbose program.

```
/home/larry# yes > /dev/null
```

Ah, much better. Nothing is printed, but the shell prompt doesn't come back. This is because yes is still running, and is sending those inane y's to /dev/null. Again, to kill the job, press the interrupt key.

Let's suppose that you want the yes command to continue to run but wanted to get the shell prompt back so that you can work on other things. You can put yes into the background, allowing it to run, without need for interaction.

One way to put a process in the background is to append an "&" character to the end of the command.

```
/home/larry# yes > /dev/null &
[1] 164
/home/larry#
```

As you can see, the shell prompt has returned. But what is this "[1] 164"? And is the yes command really running?

The "[1]" represents the **job number** for the yes process. The shell assigns a job number to every running job. Because yes is the one and only job we're running, it is assigned job number 1. The "164" is the process ID, or PID, number given by the system to the job. You can use either number to refer to the job, as you'll see later.

You now have the yes process running in the background, continuously sending a stream of y's to /dev/null. To check on the status of this process, use the internal shell command jobs.

```
/home/larry# jobs
[1]+  Running                    yes >/dev/null  &
/home/larry#
```

Sure enough, there it is. You could also use the ps command as demonstrated above to check on the status of the job.

To terminate the job, use the kill command. This command takes either a job number or a process ID number as an argument. This was job number 1, so using the command

```
/home/larry# kill %1
```

kills the job. When identifying the job with the job number, you must prefix the number with a percent ("%") character.

Now that you've killed the job, use jobs again to check on it:

```
/home/larry# jobs

[1]+  Terminated                 yes >/dev/null

/home/larry#
```

The job is in fact dead, and if you use the jobs command again nothing should be printed.

You can also kill the job using the process ID (PID) number, displayed along with the job ID when you start the job. In our example, the process ID is 164, so the command

```
/home/larry# kill 164
```

is equivalent to

```
/home/larry# kill %1
```

You don't need to use the "%" when referring to a job by its process ID.

Stopping and restarting jobs.

There is another way to put a job into the background. You can start the job normally (in the foreground), **stop** the job, and then restart it in the background.

First, start the `yes` process in the foreground, as you did before:

```
/home/larry# yes > /dev/null
```

Again, because `yes` is running in the foreground, you shouldn't get the shell prompt back.

Now, rather than interrupt the job with `Ctrl-C`, **suspend** the job. Suspending a job doesn't kill it: it only temporarily stops the job until you restart it. To do this, press the suspend key, which is usually `Ctrl-Z`.

```
/home/larry# yes > /dev/null
ctrl-Z
[1]+  Stopped                    yes >/dev/null
/home/larry#
```

While the job is suspended, it's simply not running. No CPU time is used for the job. However, you can restart the job, which causes the job to run again as if nothing ever happened. It will continue to run where it left off.

To restart the job in the foreground, use the `fg` command (for "foreground").

```
/home/larry# fg
yes >/dev/null
```

The shell displays the name of the command again so you're aware of which job you just put into the foreground. Stop the job again with `Ctrl-Z`. This time, use the `bg` command to put the job into the background. This causes the command to run just as if you started the command with "&" as in the last section.

```
/home/larry# bg
[1]+ yes >/dev/null &
/home/larry#
```

And you have your prompt back. `Jobs` should report that `yes` is indeed running, and you can kill the job with `kill` as we did before.

How can you stop the job again? Using `Ctrl-Z` won't work, because the job is in the background. The answer is to put the job in the foreground with `fg`, and then stop it. As it turns out, you can use `fg` on either stopped jobs or jobs in the background.

There is a big difference between a job in the background and a job that is stopped. A stopped job is not running—it's not using any CPU time, and it's not doing any work (the job still occupies system memory, although it may have been swapped out to disk). A job in the background is running and using memory, as well as completing some task while you do other work.

However, a job in the background may try to display text on your terminal, which can be annoying if you're trying to work on something else. For example, if you used the command

```
/home/larry# yes &
```

without redirecting stdout to /dev/null, a stream of y's would be displayed on your screen, without any way for you to interrupt it. (You can't use `Ctrl-C` to interrupt jobs in the background.) In order to stop the endless y's, use the fg command to bring the job to the foreground, and then use `Ctrl-C` to kill it.

Another note. The fg and bg commands normally affect the job that was last stopped (indicated by a "+" next to the job number when you use the jobs command). If you are running multiple jobs at once, you can put jobs in the foreground or background by giving the job ID as an argument to fg or bg, as in

```
/home/larry# fg %2
```

(to put job number 2 into the foreground), or

```
/home/larry# bg %3
```

(to put job number 3 into the background). You can't use process ID numbers with fg or bg.

Furthermore, using the job number alone, as in

```
/home/larry# %2
```

is equivalent to

```
/home/larry# fg %2
```

Just remember that using job control is a feature of the shell. The fg, bg and jobs commands are internal to the shell. If for some reason you use a shell that doesn't support job control, don't expect to find these commands available.

In addition, there are some aspects of job control that differ between bash and tcsh. In fact, some shells don't provide job control at all—however, most shells available for Linux do.

Using the vi editor.

A **text editor** is a program used to edit files that are composed of text: a letter, C program, or a system configuration file. While there are many such editors available for Linux, the only editor that you are guaranteed to find on any UNIX system is vi— the "visual editor." vi is not the easiest editor to use, nor is it very self-explanatory. However, because vi is so common in the UNIX world, and sometimes necessary, it deserves discussion here.

Your choice of an editor is mostly a question of personal taste and style. Many users prefer the baroque, self-explanatory, and powerful emacs—an editor with more features than any other single program in the UNIX world. For example, Emacs has its own built-in dialect of the LISP programming language, and has many extensions (one of which is an Eliza-like artificial intelligence program). However, because Emacs and its support files are relatively large, it may not be installed on some systems. vi, on the other hand, is small and powerful but more difficult to use. However, once you know your way around vi, it's actually very easy.

This section presents an introduction to vi—we won't discuss all of its features, only the ones you need to know to get started. You can refer to the man page for vi if you're interested in learning more about this editor's features. Alternatively, you can read the book, *Learning the* vi *Editor* from O'Reilly and Associates. See Appendix A for information.

Concepts.

While using vi, at any one time you are in one of three modes of operation. These modes are called **command mode**, **insert mode**, and **last line mode**.

When you start up vi, you are in **command mode**. This mode lets you use commands to edit files or change to other modes. For example, typing "x" while in command mode deletes the character underneath the cursor. The arrow keys move the cursor around the file you're editing. Generally, the commands used in command mode are one or two characters long.

You actually insert or edit text within **insert mode**. When using vi, you'll probably spend most of your time in this mode. You start insert mode by using a command such as "i" (for "insert") from command mode.

While in insert mode, you can insert text into the document at the current cursor location. To end insert mode and return to command mode, press `Esc`.

Last line mode is a special mode used to give certain extended commands to `vi`. While typing these commands, they appear on the last line of the screen (hence the name). For example, when you type ":" in command mode, you jump into last line mode and can use commands like "`wq`" (to write the file and quit `vi`), or "`q!`" (to quit `vi` without saving changes). Last line mode is generally used for `vi` commands that are longer than one character. In last line mode, you enter a single-line command and press `Enter` to execute it.

Starting vi.

The best way to understand these concepts is to fire up `vi` and edit a file. The example "screens" below show only a few lines of text, as if the screen were only six lines high instead of twenty-four.

The syntax for `vi` is

vi ⟨*filename*⟩

where *filename* is the name of the file to edit.

Start up `vi` by typing

```
/home/larry# vi test
```

to edit the file `test`. You should see something like

```
_
~
~
~
~
~
"test" [New file]
```

The column of "~" characters indicates you are at the end of the file. The _ represents the cursor.

Inserting text.

The `vi` program is now in command mode. Insert text into the file by pressing `i`, which places the editor into insert mode, and begin typing.

```
Now is the time for all good men to come to the aid of the party_
~
~
~
~
~
```

Type as many lines as you want (pressing `Return` after each). You may correct mistakes with the `Backspace` key.

To end insert mode and return to command mode, press `Esc`.

In command mode you can use the arrow keys to move around in the file. (If you have only one line of text, trying to use the up- or down-arrow keys will probably cause `vi` to beep at you.)

There are several ways to insert text other than the `i` command. The `a` command inserts text beginning after the current cursor position, instead of at the current cursor position. For example, use the left arrow key to move the cursor between the words "good" and "men."

```
Now is the time for all good_men to come to the aid of the party.
~
~
~
~
~
```

Press a to start insert mode, type "wo," and then press Esc to return to command mode.

```
Now is the time for all good women to come to the aid of the party.
~
~
~
~
~
```

To begin inserting text at the next line, use the o command. Press o and enter another line or two:

```
Now is the time for all good humans to come to the aid of the party.
Afterwards, we'll go out for pizza and beer.
~
~
~
~
```

Deleting text.

From command mode, the x command deletes the character under the cursor. If you press x five times, you'll end up with:

```
Now is the time for all good humans to come to the aid of the party.
Afterwards, we'll go out for pizza and_
~
~
~
~
```

Now press a and insert some text, followed by esc:

```
Now is the time for all good humans to come to the aid of the party.
Afterwards, we'll go out for pizza and Diet Coke.
~
~
~
~
```

You can delete entire lines using the command dd (that is, press d twice in a row). If the cursor is on the second line and you type dd, you'll see:

```
Now is the time for all good humans to come to the aid of the party.
~
~
~
~
~
```

To delete the word that the cursor is on, use the dw command. Place the cursor on the word "good," and type dw.

```
Now is the time for all humans to come to the aid of the party.
~
~
~
~
~
```

Changing text.

You can replace sections of text using the `R` command. Place the cursor on the first letter in "party," press `R`, and type the word "hungry."

```
Now is the time for all humans to come to the aid of the hungry.
~
~
~
~
~
```

Using `R` to edit text is like the `i` and `a` commands, but `R` overwrites, rather than inserts, text.

The `r` command replaces the single character under the cursor. For example, move the cursor to the beginning of the word "Now," and press `r` followed by `C`, you'll see:

```
Cow is the time for all humans to come to the aid of the hungry.
~
~
~
~
~
```

The "~" command changes the case of the letter under the cursor from upper to lowercase, and back. For example, if you place the cursor on the "o" in "Cow" above and repeatedly press `~`, you'll end up with:

```
COW IS THE TIME FOR ALL WOMEN TO COME TO THE AID OF THE HUNGRY.
~
~
~
~
~
```

Commands for moving the cursor.

You already know how to use the arrow keys to move around the document. In addition, you can use the `h`, `j`, `k`, and `l` commands to move the cursor left, down, up, and right, respectively. This comes in handy when (for some reason) your arrow keys aren't working correctly.

The `w` command moves the cursor to the beginning of the next word; the `b` command moves it to the beginning of the previous word.

The `0` command (that's the zero key) moves the cursor to the beginning of the current line, and the `$` command moves it to the end of the line.

When editing large files, you'll want to move forwards or backwards through the file a screenful at a time. Pressing `Ctrl-F` moves the cursor one screenful forward, and `Ctrl-B` moves it a screenful back.

To move the cursor to the end of the file, press `G`. You can also move to an arbitrary line; for example, typing the command `10G` would move the cursor to line 10 in the file. To move to the beginning of the file, use `1G`.

You can couple moving commands with other commands, such as those for deleting text. For example, the `d$` command deletes everything from the cursor to the end of the line; `dG` deletes everything from the cursor to the end of the file, and so on.

Saving files and quitting `vi`.

To quit `vi` without making changes to the file, use the command `:q!`. When you press the ":," the cursor moves to the last line on the screen and you'll be in last line mode.

```
COW IS THE TIME FOR ALL WOMEN TO COME TO THE AID OF THE HUNGRY.
~
~
~
~
~

:_
```

In last line mode, certain extended commands are available. One of them is `q!`, which quits `vi` without saving. The command `:wq` saves the file and then exits `vi`. The command `ZZ` (from command mode, without the ":") is equivalent to `:wq`. Remember that you must press [Enter] after a command entered in last line mode.

To save the file without quitting vi, use `:w`.

Editing another file.

To edit another file, use the `:e` command. For example, to stop editing `test` and edit the file `foo` instead, use the command

```
COW IS THE TIME FOR ALL WOMEN TO COME TO THE AID OF THE HUNGRY.
~
~
~
~
~
~
:e foo_
```

If you use `:e` without saving the file first, you'll get the error message

```
No write since last change (":edit!" overrides)
```

which means that `vi` doesn't want to edit another file until you save the first one. At this point, you can use `:w` to save the original file, and then use `:e`, or you can use the command

```
COW IS THE TIME FOR ALL WOMEN TO COME TO THE AID OF THE HUNGRY.
~
~
~
~
~

:e! foo_
```

The "`!`" tells `vi` that you really mean it—edit the new file without saving changes to the first.

Including other files.

If you use the `:r` command, you can include the contents of another file in the current file. For example, the command

```
:r foo.txt
```

inserts the contents of the file `foo.txt` in the text at the location of the cursor.

Running shell commands.

You can also run shell commands within `vi`. The `:r!` command works like `:r`, but rather than read a file, it inserts the output of the given command into the buffer at the current cursor location. For example, if you use the command

```
:r! ls -F
```

you'll end up with

```
COW IS THE TIME FOR ALL WOMEN TO COME TO THE AID OF THE HUNGRY.
letters/
misc/
papers/_
~
~
```

You can also "shell out" of vi, in other words, run a command from within vi, and return to the editor when you're done. For example, if you use the command

```
:! ls -F
```

the ls -F command will be executed and the results displayed on the screen, but not inserted into the file you're editing. If you use the command

```
:shell
```

vi starts an instance of the shell, letting you temporarily put vi "on hold" while you execute other commands. Just log out of the shell (using the exit command) to return to vi.

Getting help.

vi doesn't provide much in the way of interactive help (most UNIX programs don't), but you can always read the man page. vi is a visual front-end to the ex editor; which handles many of the last-line mode commands in vi. So, in addition to reading the man page for vi, see ex as well.

Customizing your environment.

A shell provides many mechanisms to customize your work environment. As mentioned above, a shell is more than a command interpreter—it is also a powerful programming language. Although writing shell scripts is an extensive subject, we'd like to introduce you to some of the ways that you can simplify your work on a UNIX system by using these advanced features of the shell.

As mentioned before, different shells use different syntaxes when executing shell scripts. For example, Tcsh uses a C-like syntax, while Bourne shells use another type of syntax. In this section, we won't be encountering many differences between the two, but we will assume that shell scripts are executed using the Bourne shell syntax.

Shell scripts.

Let's say that you use a series of commands often and would like to save time by grouping all of them together into a single "command". For example, the three commands

```
/home/larry# cat chapter1 chapter2 chapter3 > book
/home/larry# wc -l book
/home/larry# lp book
```

concatenates the files chapter1, chapter2, and chapter3 and places the result in the file book. The second command displays a count of the number of lines in book, and the third command lp book prints book.

Rather than type all these commands, you can group them into a **shell script**. The shell script used to run all these commands might look like this:

```
#!/bin/sh
# A shell script to create and print the book
cat chapter1 chapter2 chapter3 > book
wc -l book
lp book
```

Shell scripts are just plain text files; you can create them with an editor such as emacs or vi, which is described starting on page 112.

Let's look at this shell script. The first line, "#!/bin/sh," identifies the file as a shell script and tells the shell how to execute the script. It instructs the shell to pass the script to /bin/sh for execution, where /bin/sh is the shell program itself. Why is this important? On most UNIX systems, /bin/sh is a Bourne-type shell, like bash. By forcing the shell script to run using /bin/sh, you ensure that the script will run under a Bourne-syntax shell (rather than a C shell). This will cause your script to run using the Bourne syntax even if you use tcsh (or another C shell) as your login shell.

The second line is a **comment**. Comments begin with the character "#" and continue to the end of the line. Comments are ignored by the shell—they are commonly used to identify the shell script to the programmer and make the script easier to understand.

The rest of the lines in the script are just commands, as you would type them to the shell directly. In effect, the shell reads each line of the script and runs that line as if you had typed it at the shell prompt.

Permissions are important for shell scripts. If you create a shell script, make sure that you have execute permission on the script in order to run it. When you create text files, the default permissions usually don't include execute permission, and you must set them explicitly. See the discussion of file permissions on page 105 for details. Briefly, if this script were saved in the file called makebook, you could use the command

```
/home/larry# chmod u+x makebook
```

to give yourself execute permission for the shell script makebook.

You can use the command

```
/home/larry# makebook
```

to run all the commands in the script.

Shell variables and the environment.

A shell lets you define **variables**, as do most programming languages. A variable is just a piece of data that is given a name.

◇ tcsh, as well as other C-type shells, use a different mechanism for setting variables than is described here. This discussion assumes the use of a Bourne shell like bash. See the tcsh manual page for details.

When you assign a value to a variable (using the "=" operator), you can access the variable by prepending a "$" to the variable name, as demonstrated below.

```
/home/larry# foo="hello there"
```

The variable foo is given the value "hello there." You can then refer to this value by the variable name prefixed with a "$" character. For example, the command

```
/home/larry# echo $foo
hello there
/home/larry#
```

produces the same results as

```
/home/larry# echo "hello there"
hello there
/home/larry#
```

These variables are internal to the shell, which means that only the shell can access them. This can be useful in shell scripts; if you need to keep track of a filename, for example, you can store it in a variable, as above. Using the set command displays a list of all defined shell variables.

However, the shell lets you **export** variables to the **environment**. The environment is the set of variables that are accessible by all commands that you execute. Once you define a variable inside the shell, exporting it makes the variable part of the environment as well. Use the export command to export a variable to the environment.

◇ Again, here we differ between bash and tcsh. If you use tcsh, another syntax is used for setting environment variables (the setenv command). See the tcsh manual page for more information.

The environment is very important to the UNIX system. It lets you configure certain commands just by setting variables the commands know about.

Here's a quick example. The environment variable PAGER is used by the man command. It specifies the command to use to display manual pages one screenful at a time. If you set PAGER to the name of a command, it uses that command to display the man pages, instead of more (which is the default).

Set PAGER to "cat". This causes output from man to be displayed to the screen all at once, without pausing between pages.

```
/home/larry# PAGER="cat"
```

Now, export PAGER to the environment.

```
/home/larry# export PAGER
```

Try the command man ls. The man page should fly past your screen without pausing for you.

Now, if we set PAGER to "more", the more command is used to display the man page.

```
/home/larry# PAGER="more"
```

Note that we don't have to use the export command after we change the value of PAGER. We only need to export a variable once; any changes made to it thereafter will automatically be propagated to the environment.

The manual pages for a particular command tell you if the command uses any environment variables. For example, the man man page explains that PAGER is used to specify the pager command.

Some commands share environment variables. For example, many commands use the EDITOR environment variable to specify the default editor to use when one is needed.

The environment is also used to keep track of important information about your login session. An example is the HOME environment variable, which contains the name of your home directory.

```
/home/larry/papers# echo $HOME
/home/larry
```

Another interesting environment variable is PS1, which defines the main shell prompt. For example,

```
/home/larry# PS1="Your command, please:  "
Your command, please:
```

To set the prompt back (which contains the current working directory followed by a "#" symbol),

```
Your command, please:  PS1="\w# "
/home/larry#
```

The bash manual page describes the syntax used for setting the prompt.

The PATH environment variable. When you use the ls command, how does the shell find the ls executable itself? In fact, ls is in /bin on most systems. The shell uses the environment variable PATH to locate executable files for commands you type.

For example, your PATH variable may be set to

```
/bin:/usr/bin:/usr/local/bin:.
```

This is a list of directories for the shell to search, each directory separated by a ":". When you use the command ls, the shell first looks for /bin/ls, then /usr/bin/ls, and so on.

Note that the PATH has nothing to do with finding regular files. For example, if you use the command

```
/home/larry# cp foo bar
```

the shell does not use PATH to locate the files foo and bar—those filenames are assumed to be complete. The shell only uses PATH to locate the cp executable.

This saves you time, and means that you don't have to remember where all the command executables are stored. On many systems, executables are scattered about in many places, such as /usr/bin, /bin, or /usr/local/bin. Rather than give the command's full pathname (such as /usr/bin/cp), you can set PATH to the list of directories that you want the shell to automatically search.

Notice that PATH contains '.', which is the current working directory. This lets you create a shell script or program and run it as a command from your current directory without having to specify it directly (as in ./makebook). If a directory isn't in your PATH, then the shell will not search it for commands to run; this also includes the current directory.

Shell initialization scripts.

In addition to the shell scripts that you create, there are a number of scripts that the shell itself uses for certain purposes. The most important of these are **initialization scripts**, which are scripts executed by the shell when you log in.

The initialization scripts themselves are simply shell scripts. However, they initialize your environment by executing commands automatically when you log in. If you always use the mail command to check your mail when you log in, you place the command in the initialization script so it will execute automatically.

Both bash and tcsh distinguish between a **login shell** and other invocations of the shell. A login shell is a shell invoked when you log in. Usually, it's the only shell you'll use. However, if you "shell out" of another program like vi, you start another instance of the shell, which isn't your login shell. In addition, whenever you run a shell script, you automatically start another instance of the shell to execute the script.

The initialization files used by bash are: /etc/profile (set up by the system administrator and executed by all bash users at login time), $HOME/.bash_profile (executed by a login bash session), and $HOME/.bashrc (executed by all non-login instances of bash). If .bash_profile is not present, .profile is used instead.

tcsh uses the following initialization scripts: /etc/csh.login (executed by all tcsh users at login time), $HOME/.tcshrc (executed at login time and by all new instances of tcsh), and $HOME/.login (executed at login time, following .tcshrc). If .tcshrc is not present, .cshrc is used instead.

A complete guide to shell programming is beyond the scope of this book. See the manual pages for bash or tcsh to learn more about customizing the UNIX environment.

CHAPTER 4

System Administration

This chapter covers the most important things that you need to know about system administration under Linux in sufficient detail to start using the system comfortably. In order to keep the chapter manageable, it covers just the basics and omits many important details. The *Linux System Administrator's Guide*, by Lars Wirzenius (see page 208) provides considerably more detail on system administration topics. It will help you understand better how things work and hang together. At least, skim through the SAG so that you know what it contains and what kind of help you can expect from it.

The `root` account.

UNIX differentiates between different users. What they can do to each other and the system is regulated. File permissions are arranged so that normal users can't delete or modify files in directories like `/bin` and `/usr/bin`. Most users protect their own files with the appropriate permissions so that other users can't access or modify them. (One wouldn't want anybody to be able to read one's love letters.) Each user is given an **account** which includes a user name and home directory. In addition, there are special, system defined accounts which have special privileges. The most important of these is the **root account**, which is used by the system administrator. By convention, the system administrator is the user, `root`.

There are no restrictions on `root`. He or she can read, modify, or delete any file on the system, change permissions and ownerships on any file, and run special programs like those which partition a hard drive or create file systems. The basic idea is that a person who cares for the system logs in as `root` to perform tasks that cannot be executed as a normal user. Because `root` can do anything, it is easy to make mistakes that have catastrophic consequences.

If a normal user tries inadvertently to delete all of the files in `/etc`, the system will not permit him or her to do so. However, if `root` tries to do the same thing, the system doesn't complain at all. It is very easy to trash a UNIX system when using `root`. The best way to prevent accidents is:

- Sit on your hands before you press `Return` for any command that is non-reversible. If you're about to clean out a directory, re-read the entire command to make sure that it is correct.
- Use a different prompt for the `root` account. `root`'s `.bashrc` or `.login` file should set the shell prompt to something different than the standard user prompt. Many people reserve the character "#" in prompts for `root` and use the prompt character "$" for everyone else.
- Log in as `root` only when absolutely necessary. When you have finished your work as `root`, log out. The less you use the `root` account, the less likely you are to damage the system. You are less likely to confuse the privileges of `root` with those of a normal user.

If you picture the `root` account as a special, magic hat that gives you lots of power, you can, by waving your hands, destroy entire cities. It is a good idea to be a bit careful about what you do with your hands.

Because it is easy to wave your hands in a destructive manner, it is not a good idea to wear the magic hat when it is not needed, despite the wonderful feeling.

We'll talk in greater detail about the system administrator's responsibilities starting on page 129.

Booting the system.

Some people boot Linux with a floppy diskette that contains a copy of the Linux kernel. This kernel has the Linux root partition coded into it, so it knows where to look for the root file system. This is the type of floppy created by Slackware during installation, for example.

To create your own boot floppy, locate the kernel image on your hard disk. It should be in the file `/vmlinuz`, or `/vmlinux`. In some installations, `/vmlinuz` is a soft link to the actual kernel, so you may need to track down the kernel by following the links.

Once you know where the kernel is, set the root device of the kernel image to the name of your Linux root partition with the `rdev` command. The format of the command is

`rdev` ⟨*kernel-name*⟩ ⟨*root-device*⟩

where *kernel-name* is the name of the kernel image, and *root-device* is the name of the Linux root partition. For example, to set the root device in the kernel `/vmlinuz` to `/dev/hda2`, use the command

```
# rdev /vmlinuz /dev/hda2
```

`rdev` can set other options in the kernel, like the default SVGA mode to use at boot time. The command

```
# rdev -h
```

prints a help message on the screen. After setting the root device, simply copy the kernel image to the floppy. Before copying data to any floppy, however, it's a good idea to use the MS-DOS `FORMAT.COM` or the Linux `fdformat` program to format the diskette. This lays down the sector and track information that is appropriate to the floppy's capacity.

Floppy diskette formats and their device driver files are discussed further starting on page 136.

Device driver files, as mentioned earlier, reside in the `/dev` directory. To copy the kernel in the file `/etc/Image` to the floppy in `/dev/fd0`, use the command

```
# cp /vmlinuz /dev/fd0
```

This floppy should now boot Linux.

Using LILO.

LILO is a separate boot loader that resides on your hard disk. It is executed when the system boots from the hard drive and can automatically boot Linux from a kernel image stored there.

LILO can also be used as a first-stage boot loader for several operating systems, which allows you to select the operating system you to boot, like Linux or MS-DOS. With LILO, the default operating system is booted unless you press `Shift` during the boot-up sequence, or if the `prompt` directive is given in the `lilo.conf` file. In either case, you will be provided with a boot prompt, where you type the name of the operating system to boot (such as "`linux`" or "`msdos`"). If you press `Tab` at the boot prompt, a list of operating systems that the system knows about will be provided.

The easy way to install LILO is to edit the configuration file, `/etc/lilo.conf`. The command

```
# /sbin/lilo
```

rewrites the modified `lilo.conf` configuration to the boot sector of the hard disk, and must be run every time you modify `lilo.conf`.

The LILO configuration file contains a "stanza" for each operating system that you want to boot. The best way to demonstrate this is with an example. The `lilo.conf` file below is for a system which has a Linux root partition on `/dev/hda1` and a MS-DOS partition on `/dev/hda2`.

```
# Tell LILO to modify the boot record on /dev/hda (the first
# non-SCSI hard drive). If you boot from a drive other than
# /dev/hda,  change the following line.
boot = /dev/hda

# Set a sane videomode
vga = normal

# Set the delay in milli-seconds.  This is the time you have to
# press the 'SHIFT' key to bring up the LILO: prompt if you
# haven't specified the 'prompt' directive.
delay = 60

# Name of the boot loader. No reason to modify this unless you're
# doing some serious hacking on LILO.
install = /boot/boot.b

# This forces LILO to prompt you for the OS you want to boot.
# A 'TAB' key at the LILO: prompt will display a list of the OS's
# available to boot according to the names given in the 'label='
# directives below.
prompt

# Have LILO perform some optimization.
compact

# Stanza for Linux root partition on /dev/hda1.
image = /vmlinuz         # Location of kernel
   label = linux         # Name of OS (for the LILO boot menu)
   root = /dev/hda1      # Location of root partition
   read-only             # Mount read only

# Stanza for MS-DOS partition on /dev/hda2.
other = /dev/hda2        # Location of partition
   table = /dev/hda      # Location of partition table for /dev/hda2
   label = msdos         # Name of OS (for boot menu)
```

The first operating system stanza is the default operating system for LILO to boot. Also note that if you use the "`root =`" line, above, there's no reason to use `rdev` to set the root partition in the kernel image. LILO sets it at boot time.

The Microsoft Windows '95 installer will overwrite the LILO boot manager. If you are going to install Windows '95 on your system after installing LILO, make sure to create a boot disk first (see Section 4). With the boot disk, you can boot Linux and re-install LILO after the Windows '95 installation is completed. This is done simply by typing, as root, the command `/sbin/lilo`, as in the step above. Partitions with Windows '95 can be configured to boot with LILO using the same `lilo.conf` entries that are used to boot the MS-DOS partition.

The *Linux FAQ* (see Appendix A) provides more information on LILO, including how to use LILO to boot with the OS/2 Boot Manager.

Shutting down.

Shutting down a Linux system can be tricky. You should never simply turn off the power or press the reset switch. The kernel keeps track of the disk read/write data in memory buffers. If you reboot the system without giving the kernel a chance to write its buffers to disk, you can corrupt the file systems.

Other precautions are taken during shutdown as well. All processes are sent a signal that allows them to die gracefully (by first writing and closing all files, for example). File systems are unmounted for safety. If you wish, the system can also alert users that the system is going down and give them a chance to log off.

The easiest way to shut down is with the `shutdown` command. The format of the command is

shutdown ⟨*time*⟩ ⟨*warning-message*⟩

The *time* argument is the time to shut down the system (in the format *hh:mm:ss*), and *warning-message* is a message displayed on all user's terminals before shutdown. Alternately, you can specify the *time* as "now," to shut down immediately. The `-r` option may be given to `shutdown` to reboot the system after shutting down.

For example, to shut down and reboot the system at 8:00 pm, use the command

```
# shutdown -r 20:00
```

The command `halt` may be used to force an immediate shutdown without any warning messages or grace period. `halt` is useful if you're the only one using the system and want to shut down and turn off the machine.

◇ Don't turn off the power or reboot the system until you see the message:

```
The system is halted
```

It is very important that you shut down the system, "cleanly," using the `shutdown` or `halt` command. On some systems, pressing Ctrl-Alt-Del will be trapped and cause a `shutdown`. On other systems, using the "Vulcan nerve pinch" will reboot the system immediately and cause disaster.

The /etc/inittab file.

Immediately after Linux boots and the kernel mounts the root file system, the first program that the system executes is `init`. This program is responsible for starting the system startup scripts, and modifies the system operating from its initial boot-up state to its standard, multiuser state. `init` also spawns the `login:` shells for all of the tty devices on the system, and specifies other startup and shutdown procedures.

After startup, `init` remains quietly in the background, monitoring and if necessary altering the running state of the system. There are many details that the `init` program must see to. These tasks are defined in the `/etc/inittab` file. A sample `/etc/inittab` file is shown below.

◇ Modifying the `/etc/inittab` file incorrectly can prevent you from logging in to your system. At the very least, when changing the `/etc/inittab` file, keep on hand a copy of the original, correct file, and a boot/root emergency floppy in case you make a mistake.

```
#
# inittab This file describes how the INIT process should set up
# the system in a certain run-level.
#
# Version: @(#)inittab 2.04 17/05/93 MvS
#                               2.10    02/10/95        PV
#
# Author: Miquel van Smoorenburg, <miquels@drinkel.nl.mugnet.org>
# Modified by: Patrick J. Volkerding, <volkerdi@ftp.cdrom.com>
# Minor modifications by:
# Robert Kiesling, <kiesling@terracom.net>
#
# Default runlevel.
id:3:initdefault:

# System initialization (runs when system boots).
si:S:sysinit:/etc/rc.d/rc.S

# Script to run when going single user (runlevel 1).
su:1S:wait:/etc/rc.d/rc.K

# Script to run when going multi user.
rc:23456:wait:/etc/rc.d/rc.M
```

```
# What to do at Ctrl-Alt-Del
ca::ctrlaltdel:/sbin/shutdown -t5 -rfn now

# Runlevel 0 halts the system.
l0:0:wait:/etc/rc.d/rc.0

# Runlevel 6 reboots the system.
l6:6:wait:/etc/rc.d/rc.6

# What to do when power fails (shutdown to single user).
pf::powerfail:/sbin/shutdown -f +5 "THE POWER IS FAILING"

# If power is back before shutdown, cancel the running shutdown.
pg:0123456:powerokwait:/sbin/shutdown -c "THE POWER IS BACK"

# If power comes back in single user mode, return to multi user mode.
ps:S:powerokwait:/sbin/init 5

# The getties in multi user mode on consoles an serial lines.
#
# NOTE NOTE NOTE adjust this to your getty or you will not be
#           able to login !!
#
# Note: for 'agetty' you use linespeed, line.
# for 'getty_ps' you use line, linespeed and also use 'gettydefs'
c1:1235:respawn:/sbin/agetty 38400 tty1 linux
c2:1235:respawn:/sbin/agetty 38400 tty2 linux
c3:1235:respawn:/sbin/agetty 38400 tty3 linux
c4:1235:respawn:/sbin/agetty 38400 tty4 linux
c5:1235:respawn:/sbin/agetty 38400 tty5 linux
c6:12345:respawn:/sbin/agetty 38400 tty6 linux

# Serial lines
# s1:12345:respawn:/sbin/agetty -L 9600 ttyS0 vt100
s2:12345:respawn:/sbin/agetty -L 9600 ttyS1 vt100

# Dialup lines
d1:12345:respawn:/sbin/agetty -mt60 38400,19200,9600,2400,1200 ttyS0 vt100
#d2:12345:respawn:/sbin/agetty -mt60 38400,19200,9600,2400,1200 ttyS1 vt100

# Runlevel 4 used to be for an X-window only system, until we discovered
# that it throws init into a loop that keeps your load avg at least 1 all
# the time. Thus, there is now one getty opened on tty6. Hopefully no one
# will notice. ;^)
# It might not be bad to have one text console anyway, in case something
# happens to X.
x1:4:wait:/etc/rc.d/rc.4

# End of /etc/inittab
```

At startup, this /etc/inittab starts six virtual consoles, a login: prompt on the modem attached to /dev/ttyS0, and a login: prompt on a character terminal connected via a RS-232 serial line to /dev/ttyS1.

Briefly, init steps through a series of **run levels**, which correspond to various operating states of the system. Run level 1 is entered immediately after the system boots, run levels 2 and 3 are the normal, multiuser operation modes of the system, run level 4 starts the X Window System via the X display manager xdm, and run level 6 reboots the system. The run level(s) associated with each command are the second item in each line of the /etc/inittab file.

For example, the line

```
s2:12345:respawn:/sbin/agetty -L 9600 ttyS1 vt100
```

will maintain a login prompt on a serial terminal for runlevels 1–5. The "s2" before the first colon is a symbolic identifier used internally by init. respawn is an init keyword that is often used in conjunction with serial terminals. If, after a certain period of time, the agetty program, which spawns the terminal's login: prompt, does not receive input at the terminal, the program times out and terminates execution. "respawn" tells init to re-execute agetty, ensuring that there is always a login: prompt at the terminal, regardless of whether someone has logged in. The remaining parameters are passed directly to agetty and instruct it to spawn the login shell, the data rate of the serial line, the serial device, and the terminal type, as defined in /etc/termcap or /etc/terminfo.

The /sbin/agetty program handles many details related to terminal I/O on the system. There are several different versions that are commonly in use on Linux systems. They include mgetty, psgetty, or simply, getty.

In the case of the /etc/inittab line

```
d1:12345:respawn:/sbin/agetty -mt60 38400,19200,9600,2400,1200 ttyS0 vt100
```

which allows users to log in via a modem connected to serial line /dev/ttyS0, the /sbin/agetty parameters "-mt60" allow the system to step through all of the modem speeds that a caller dialing into the system might use, and to shut down /sbin/agetty if there is no connection after 60 seconds. This is called **negotiating** a connection. The supported modem speeds are enumerated on the command line also, as well as the serial line to use, and the terminal type. Of course, both of the modems must support the data rate which is finally negotiated by both machines.

Many important details have been glossed over in this section. The tasks that /etc/inittab maintains would comprise a book of their own. For further information, the manual pages of the init and agetty programs, and the Linux Documentation Project's Serial HOWTO (page 1374), are starting points.

Managing file systems.

Another task of the system administrator is caring for file systems. Most of this job entails periodically checking the file systems for corrupted files or other damage. Many Linux systems also automatically check the file systems at boot time.

Mounting file systems.

Before a file system is accessible to the system, it must be **mounted** on a directory. For example, if you have a file system on a floppy, you must mount it under a directory like /mnt in order to access the files on the floppy (see page 138). After mounting the file system, all of the files in the file system appear in that directory. After unmounting the file system, the directory (in this case, /mnt) will be empty.

The same is true of file systems on the hard drive. The system automatically mounts file systems on your hard drive at boot up time. The so-called "root file system" is mounted on the directory /. If you have a separate file system for /usr, it is mounted on /usr. If you only have a root file system, all files (including those in /usr) exist on that file system.

mount and umount (not *unmount*) are used to mount and unmount file systems. The command

```
mount -av
```

is executed automatically by the file /etc/rc at boot time, or by the file /etc/rc.d/boot (see page 144) on some Linux systems. The file /etc/fstab provides information on file systems and mount points. An example /etc/fstab file is

```
# device     directory     type     options
/dev/hda2    /             ext2     defaults
/dev/hda3     /usr          ext2    defaults
/dev/hda4    none          swap     sw
/proc        /proc         proc     none
```

The first field, `device`, is the name of the partition to mount. The second field is the mount point. The third field is the file system type, like `ext2` (for ext2fs) or `minix` (for Minix file systems). Table 4.1 lists the various file system types that are mountable under Linux.[1] Not all of these file system types may be available on your system, because the kernel must have support for them compiled in. See page 139 for information on building the kernel.

File system	Type name	Comment
Second Extended File system	`ext2`	Most common Linux file system.
Extended File system	`ext`	Superseded by `ext2`.
Minix File system	`minix`	Original Minix file system; rarely used.
Xia File system	`xia`	Like `ext2`, but rarely used.
UMSDOS File system	`umsdos`	Used to install Linux on an MS-DOS partition.
MS-DOS File system	`msdos`	Used to access MS-DOS files.
`/proc` File system	`proc`	Provides process information for `ps`, etc.
ISO 9660 File system	`iso9660`	Format used by most CD-ROMs.
Xenix File system	`xenix`	Used to access files from Xenix.
System V File system	`sysv`	Used to access files from System V variants for the x86.
Coherent File system	`coherent`	Used to access files from Coherent.
HPFS File system	`hpfs`	Read-only access for HPFS partitions (DoubleSpace).

Table 4.1: Linux File system Types

The last field of the `fstab` file are the `mount` options. This is normally set to `defaults`.

Swap partitions are included in the `/etc/fstab` file. They have a mount directory of `none`, and type `swap`. The `swapon -a` command, which is executed from `/etc/rc` or `/etc/init.d/boot`, is used to enable swapping on all of the swap devices that are listed in `/etc/fstab`.

The `/etc/fstab` file contains one special entry for the `/proc` file system. As described on page 108, the `/proc` file system is used to store information about system processes, available memory, and so on. If `/proc` is not mounted, commands like `ps` will not work.

◇ The `mount` command may be used only by root. This ensures security on the system. You wouldn't want regular users mounting and unmounting file systems on a whim. Several software packages are available which allow non-root users to mount and unmount file systems, especially floppies, without compromising system security.

The `mount -av` command actually mounts all of the file systems other than the root file system (in the table above, `/dev/hda2`). The root file system is automatically mounted at boot time by the kernel.

Instead of using `mount -av`, you can mount a file system by hand. The command

```
# mount -t ext2 /dev/hda3 /usr
```

is equivalent to mounting the file system with the entry for `/dev/hda3` in the example `/etc/fstab` file, above.

Device driver names.

In addition to the partition names listed in the `/etc/fstab` file, Linux recognizes a number of fixed and removable media devices. They are classified by type, interface, and the order they are installed. For example, the first hard drive on your system, if it is an IDE or older MFM hard drive, is controlled by the `/dev/hda` device driver. The first partition on the hard drive is `/dev/hda1`, the second partition is `/dev/hda2`, the

[1] This table is current as of kernel version 1.1.37.

third partition is `/dev/hda3`, and so on. The first partition of the second IDE drive is often `/dev/hdb1`, the second partition `/dev/hdb2`, and so on. The naming scheme for the most commonly installed IDE drives for Intel-architecture, ISA and PCI bus machines, is given in Table 4.2.

Device driver	Drive
/dev/hda	Master IDE drive, primary IDE bus.
/dev/hdb	Slave IDE drive, primary IDE bus.
/dev/hdc	Master IDE drive, secondary IDE bus.
/dev/hdd	Slave IDE drive, secondary IDE bus.

Table 4.2: IDE device driver names.

CD-ROM and tape drives which use the extended IDE/ATAPI drive interface also use these device names.

Many machines, however, including high-end personal computer workstations, and machines based on Digital Equipment Corporation's Alpha processor, use the Small Computer System Interface (SCSI). The naming conventions for SCSI devices are somewhat different than that given above, due the greater flexibility of SCSI addressing. The first SCSI hard drive on a system is `/dev/sda`, the second SCSI drive is `/dev/sdb`, and so on. A list of common SCSI devices is given in Table 4.3.

Device driver	Drive
/dev/sda	First SCSI hard drive.
/dev/sdb	Second SCSI hard drive.
/dev/st0	First SCSI tape drive.
/dev/st1	Second SCSI tape drive.
/dev/scd0	First SCSI CD-ROM drive.
/dev/scd1	Second SCSI CD-ROM drive.

Table 4.3: SCSI device drivers

Note that SCSI CD-ROM and tape drives are named differently than SCSI hard drives. Removable SCSI media, like the Iomega Zip drive, follow naming conventions for non-removable SCSI drives. The use of a Zip drive for making backups is described starting on page 136

Streaming tape drives, like those which read and write QIC-02, QIC-40, and QIC-80 format magnetic tapes, have their own set of device names, which are described on page 137.

Floppy disk drives use still another naming scheme, which is described on page 136.

Checking file systems.

It is usually a good idea to check your file systems for damaged or corrupted files every now and then. Some systems automatically check their file systems at boot time (with the appropriate commands in `/etc/rc` or `/etc/init.d/boot`).

The command used to check a file system depends on the type of the file system. For ext2fs file systems (the most commonly used type), this command is `e2fsck`. For example, the command

```
# e2fsck -av /dev/hda2
```

checks the ext2fs file system on `/dev/hda2` and automatically corrects any errors.

It is usually a good idea to unmount a file system before checking it, and necessary, if `e2fsck` is to perform any repairs on the file system. The command

```
# umount /dev/hda2
```

unmounts the file system on `/dev/hda2`. The one exception is that you cannot unmount the root file system. In order to check the root file system when it's unmounted, you should use a maintenance boot/root diskette (see page 145). You also cannot unmount a file system if any of the files which it contains are "busy"—that is, in use by a running process. For example, you cannot unmount a file system if any user's current working directory is on that file system. You will instead receive a "`Device busy`" error message.

Other file system types use different forms of the `e2fsck` command, like `efsck` and `xfsck`. On some systems, you can simply use the command `fsck`, which automatically determines the file system type and executes the appropriate command.

◇ If e2fsck reports that it performed repairs on a mounted file system, you must reboot the system immediately. You should give the command `shutdown -r` to perform the reboot. This allows the system to re-synchronize the information about the file system after `e2fsck` modifies it.

The `/proc` file system never needs to be checked in this manner. `/proc` is a memory file system and is managed directly by the kernel.

Using a swap file.

Instead of reserving a separate partition for swap space, you can use a swap file. However, you need to install Linux and get everything running before you create the swap file.

With Linux installed, you can use the following commands to create a swap file. The command below creates a swap file of size 8208 blocks (about 8 Mb).

```
# dd if=/dev/zero of=/swap bs=1024 count=8208
```

This command creates the swap file, `/swap`. The "`count=`" parameter is the size of the swap file in blocks.

```
# mkswap /swap 8208
```

This command initializes the swap file. Again, replace the name and size of the swap file with the appropriate values.

```
# /etc/sync
# swapon /swap
```

Now the system is swapping on the file `/swap`. The `/etc/sync` command ensures that the file has been written to disk.

One major drawback to using a swap file is that all access to the swap file is done through the file system. This means the blocks which make up the swap file may not be contiguous. Performance may not be as good as a swap partition, where the blocks are always contiguous and I/O requests are made directly to the device.

Another drawback of large swap files is the greater chance that the file system will be corrupted if something goes wrong. Keeping the regular file systems and swap partitions separate prevents this from happening.

Swap files can be useful if you need to use more swap space temporarily. If you're compiling a large program and would like to speed things up somewhat, you can create a temporary swap file and use it in addition to the regular swap space.

To remove a swap file, first use `swapoff`, as in

```
# swapoff /swap
```

Then the file can be deleted.

```
# rm /swap
```

Each swap file or partition may be as large as 16 megabytes, but you may use up to 8 swap files or partitions on your system.

Managing users.

Even if you're the only user on your system, it's important to understand the aspects of user management under Linux. You should at least have an account for yourself (other than `root`) to do most of your work.

Each user should have his or her own account. It is seldom a good idea to have several people share the same account. Security an issue, and accounts uniquely identify users to the system. You must be able to keep track of who is doing what.

User management concepts.

The system keeps track of the following information about each user:

user name This identifier is unique for every user. Example user names are `larry`, `karl`, and `mdw`. Letters and digits may be used, as well as "_" and "." (period). User names are usually limited to 8 characters in length.

user ID This number, abbreviated UID, is unique for every user. The system generally keeps track of users by UID, not user name.

group ID This number, abbreviated GID, is the user's default group. On page 105, we discuss group permissions. Each user belongs to one or more groups as defined by the system administrator.

password This is the user's encrypted password. The `passwd` command is used to set and change user passwords.

full name The user's "real name," or "full name," is stored along with the user name. For example, the user `schmoj` may be "Joe Schmo" in real life.

home directory
This is the directory the user is initially placed in at login, and where his or her personal files are stored. Every user is given a home directory, which is commonly located under `/home`.

login shell The shell that is started for the user at login. Examples are `/bin/bash` and `/bin/tcsh`.

This information is stored in the file `/etc/passwd`. Each line in the file has the format

```
user name:encrypted password:UID:GID:full name:home directory:login shell
```

An example might be

```
kiwi:Xv8Q981g71oKK:102:100:Laura Poole:/home/kiwi:/bin/bash
```

In this example, the first field, "`kiwi`," is the user name.

The next field, "`Xv8Q981g71oKK`", is the encrypted password. Passwords are not stored on the system in human-readable format. The password is encrypted using itself as the secret key. In other words, one must know the password in order to decrypt it. This form of encryption is reasonably secure.

Some systems use "shadow passwords," in which password information is stored in the file `/etc/shadow`. Because `/etc/passwd` is world-readable, `/etc/shadow` provides some degree of extra security because its access permissions are much more restricted. Shadow passwords also provide other features, like password expiration.

The third field, "`102`," is the UID. This must be unique for each user. The fourth field, "`100`," is the GID. This user belongs to the group numbered 100. Group information is stored in the file `/etc/group`. See page 132 for more information.

The fifth field is the user's full name, "`Laura Poole`". The last two fields are the user's home directory (`/home/kiwi`), and login shell (`/bin/bash`), respectively. It is not required that the user's home directory be given the same name as the user name. It simply helps identify the directory.

Adding users.

When adding users, several steps must be taken. First, the user is given an entry in `/etc/passwd`, with a unique user name and UID. The GID, full name, and other information must be specified. The user's home directory must be created, and the permissions on the directory set so that the user owns the directory. Shell initialization files must be installed in the home directory, and other files must be configured system-wide (for example, a spool for the user's incoming e-mail).

It is not difficult to add users by hand, but when you are running a system with many users, it is easy to forget something. The easiest way to add users is to use an interactive program which updates all of the system files automatically. The name of this program is `useradd` or `adduser`, depending on what software is installed.

The `adduser` command takes its information from the file `/etc/adduser.conf`, which defines a standard, default configuration for all new users.

A typical `/etc/adduser.conf` file is shown below.

```
# /etc/adduser.conf: 'adduser' configuration.
# See adduser(8) and adduser.conf(5) for full documentation.

# The DSHELL variable specifies the default login shell on your
# system.
DSHELL=/bin/bash

# The DHOME variable specifies the directory containing users' home
# directories.
DHOME=/home

# If GROUPHOMES is "yes", then the home directories will be created as
# /home/groupname/user.
GROUPHOMES=no

# If LETTERHOMES is "yes", then the created home directories will have
# an extra directory - the first letter of the user name. For example:
# /home/u/user.
LETTERHOMES=no

# The SKEL variable specifies the directory containing "skeletal" user
# files; in other words, files such as a sample .profile that will be
# copied to the new user's home directory when it is created.
SKEL=/etc/skel

# FIRST_SYSTEM_UID to LAST_SYSTEM_UID inclusive is the range for UIDs
# for dynamically allocated administrative and system accounts.
FIRST_SYSTEM_UID=100
LAST_SYSTEM_UID=999

# FIRST_UID to LAST_UID inclusive is the range of UIDs of dynamically
# allocated user accounts.
FIRST_UID=1000
LAST_UID=29999

# The USERGROUPS variable can be either "yes" or "no".  If "yes" each
# created user will be given their own group to use as a default, and
# their home directories will be g+s.  If "no", each created user will
# be placed in the group whose gid is USERS_GID (see below).
USERGROUPS=yes

# If USERGROUPS is "no", then USERS_GID should be the GID of the group
# 'users' (or the equivalent group) on your system.
USERS_GID=100

# If QUOTAUSER is set, a default quota will be set from that user with
# 'edquota -p QUOTAUSER newuser'
QUOTAUSER=""
```

In addition to defining preset variables for the `adduser` command, `/etc/adduser.conf` also specifies where default system configuration files for each user are located. In this example, they are located in the directory `/etc/skel`, as defined by the `SKEL=` line, above. Files which are placed in this directory, like a system-wide, default .profile, .tcshrc, or .bashrc file, will be automatically installed in a new user's home directory by the adduser command.

Deleting users.

Deleting users can be accomplished with the commands userdel or deluser, depending on the software installed on the system.

If you'd like to temporarily "disable" a user from logging in to the system without deleting his or her account, simply prepend an asterisk ("*") to the password field in /etc/passwd. For example, changing kiwi's /etc/passwd entry to

```
kiwi:*Xv8Q981g71oKK:102:100:Laura Poole:/home/kiwi:/bin/bash
```

prevents kiwi from logging in.

Setting user attributes.

After you have created a user, you may need to change attributes for that user, like the home directory or password. The easiest way to do this is to change the values directly in /etc/passwd. To set a user's password, use passwd. The command

```
# passwd larry
```

will change larry's password. Only root may change other users' passwords in this manner. Users can change their own passwords, however.

On some systems, the commands chfn and chsh allow users to set their own full name and login shell attributes. If not, the system administrator must change these attributes for them.

Groups.

As mentioned above, each user belongs to one or more groups. The only real importance of group relationships pertains to file permissions. As you'll recall from page 105, each file has a "group ownership" and a set of permissions that define how users in that group may access the file.

There are several system-defined groups, like bin, mail, and sys. Users should not belong to any of these groups; they are used for system file permissions. Instead, users should belong to an individual group like users. You can also maintain several groups for users, like student, staff, and faculty.

The file /etc/group contains information about groups. The format of each line is

```
group name:password:GID:other members
```

Some example groups might be:

```
root:*:0:
users:*:100:mdw,larry
guest:*:200:
other:*:250:kiwi
```

The first group, root, is a special system group reserved for the root account. The next group, users, is for regular users. It has a GID of 100. The users mdw and larry are given access to this group. Remember that in /etc/passwd each user was given a default GID. However, users may belong to more than one group, by adding their user names to other group lines in /etc/group. The groups command lists what groups you are given access to.

The third group, guest, is for guest users, and other is for "other" users. The user kiwi is given access to this group as well.

The "password" field of /etc/group is sometimes used to set a password on group access. This is seldom necessary. To protect users from changing into privileged groups (with the newgroup command), set the password field to '*'.

The commands addgroup or groupadd may be used to add groups to your system. Usually, it's easier just to add entries in /etc/group yourself, as no other configuration needs to be done to add a group. To delete a group, simply delete its entry in /etc/group.

System administration responsibilities.

Because the system administrator has so much power and responsibility, when some users have their first opportunity to login as `root`. either on a Linux system or elsewhere, the tendency is to abuse `root`'s privileges. I have known so-called "system administrators" who read other users' mail, delete users' files without warning, and generally behave like children when given such a powerful "toy."

Because the administrator has such power on the system, it takes a certain amount of maturity and self-control to use the `root` account as it was intended—to run the system. There is an unspoken code of honor which exists between the system administrator and the users on the system. How would you feel if your system administrator was reading your e-mail or looking over your files? There is still no strong legal precedent for electronic privacy on time-sharing computer systems. On UNIX systems, the `root` user has the ability to forego all security and privacy mechanisms on the system. It is important that the system administrator develop a trusting relationship with his or her users. I can't stress that enough.

Coping with users.

UNIX security is rather lax by design. Security on the system is an afterthought—the system was originally developed in an environment where users intruding upon other users had been simply unheard of. Because of this, even with security measures, there is still the ability for normal users to do harm.

System administrators can take two stances when dealing with abusive users: they can be either paranoid or trusting. The paranoid system administrator usually causes more harm than he or she prevents. One of my favorite sayings is, "Never attribute to malice anything which can be attributed to stupidity." Put another way, most users don't have the ability or knowledge to do real harm on the system. Ninety percent of the time, when a user is causing trouble on the system (for instance, by filling up the user partition with large files, or running multiple instances of a large program), the user is simply unaware that he or she is creating a problem. I have come down on users who were causing a great deal of trouble, but they were simply acting out of ignorance—not malice.

When you deal with users who cause potential trouble, don't be accusatory. The burden of proof is on you; that is, the rule of "innocent until proven guilty" still holds. It is best to simply talk to the user and question him or her about the trouble instead of being confrontational. The last thing you want is to be on the user's bad side. This will raise a lot of suspicion about you—the system administrator—running the system correctly. If a user believes that you distrust or dislike them, they might accuse you of deleting files or breaching privacy on the system. This is certainly not the kind of position you want to be in.

If you find that a user is attempting to "crack," or otherwise intentionally do harm to the system, don't return the malicious behavior with malice of your own. Instead, provide a warning, but be flexible. In many cases, you may catch a user "in the act" of doing harm to the system. Give them a warning. Tell them not to let it happen again. However, if you *do* catch them causing harm again, be absolutely sure that it is intentional. I can't even begin to describe the number of cases where it appeared as though a user was causing trouble, when in fact it was either an accident or a fault of my own.

Setting the rules.

The best way to run a system is not with an iron fist. That may be how you run the military, but UNIX is not designed for such discipline. It makes sense to lay down a few simple and flexible guidelines. The fewer rules you have, the less chance there is of breaking them. Even if your rules are perfectly reasonable and clear, users will still at times break them without intending to. This is especially true of new users learning the ropes of the system. It is not patently obvious that you shouldn't download a gigabyte of files and mail them to everyone on the system. Users need help to understand the rules and why they are there.

If you do specify usage guidelines for your system, make sure also that the rationale for a particular guideline is clear. If you don't, users will find all sorts of creative ways to get around the rule, and not know that they are breaking it.

What it all means.

We don't tell you how to run your system down to the last detail. That depends on how you're using the system. If you have many users, things are much different than if you have only a few users, or if you're the only user on the system. However, it's always a good idea—in any situation—to understand what being the system administrator really means.

Being the system administrator doesn't make a UNIX wizard. There are many administrators who know very little about UNIX. Likewise, many "normal" users know more about UNIX than any system administrator. Also, being the system administrator does not allow one to use malice against users. Just because the system gives administrators the ability to mess with user files does not mean that he or she has a right to do so.

Being the system administrator is not a big deal. It doesn't matter if your system is a tiny '386 or a Cray supercomputer. Running the system is the same, regardless. Knowing the `root` password isn't going to earn you money or fame. It will allow you to maintain the system and keep it running. That's it.

Archiving and compressing files.

Before we can talk about backups, we need to introduce the tools to archive files on UNIX systems.

Using `tar`.

`tar` is most often used to archive files. Its command syntax is

`tar` ⟨*options*⟩ ⟨*file1*⟩ ⟨*file2*⟩ ... ⟨*fileN*⟩

where *options* is the list of commands and options for `tar`, and *file1* through *fileN* is the list of files to add or extract from the archive.

For example, the command

```
# tar cvf backup.tar /etc
```

packs all of the files in `/etc` into the tar archive `backup.tar`. The first argument to `tar`, "`cvf`," is the `tar` "command." "`c`" tells `tar` to create a new archive file. "`v`" forces `tar` to use verbose mode, printing each file name as it is archived. The "`f`" option tells `tar` that the next argument, `backup.tar`, is the name of the archive to create. The rest of the arguments to `tar` are the file and directory names to add to the archive.

The command

```
# tar xvf backup.tar
```

will extract the tar file `backup.tar` in the current directory.

◇ Old files with the same name are overwritten when extracting files into an existing directory.

Before extracting tar files, it is important to know where the files should be unpacked. Let's say that you archive the following files: `/etc/hosts`, `/etc/group`, and `/etc/passwd`. If you use the command

```
# tar cvf backup.tar /etc/hosts /etc/group /etc/passwd
```

the directory name `/etc/` is added to the beginning of each file name. In order to extract the files to the correct location, use

```
# cd /
# tar xvf backup.tar
```

because files are extracted with the path name saved in the archive file.

However, if you archive the files with the command

```
# cd /etc
# tar cvf hosts group passwd
```

the directory name is not saved in the archive file. Therefore, you need to "`cd /etc`" before extracting the files. As you can see, how the tar file is created makes a large difference in where you extract it. The command

```
# tar tvf backup.tar
```

can be used to display a listing of the archive's files without extracting them. You can see what directory the files in the archive are stored relative to, and extract the archive in the correct location.

`gzip` and `compress`.

Unlike MS-DOS archiving programs, `tar` does not automatically compress files as it archives them. If you are archive two, 1-megabyte files, the resulting file is two megabytes in size. The `gzip` command compresses a file (it need not be a `tar` file). The command

```
# gzip -9 backup.tar
```

compresses `backup.tar` and leaves you with `backup.tar.gz`, a compressed version of the file. The `-9` switch tells `gzip` to use the highest compression factor.

The `gunzip` command may be used to uncompress a gzipped file. Equivalently, you may use "`gzip -d`".

`gzip` is a relatively new tool in the UNIX community. For many years, the `compress` command was used instead. However, because of several factors, including a software patent dispute against the `compress` data compression algorithm and the fact that `gzip` is much more efficient, `compress` is being phased out.

Files that are output by `compress` end in "`.Z`." `backup.tar.Z` is the compressed version of `backup.tar`, while `backup.tar.gz` is the gzipped version[2]. The `uncompress` command is used to expand a `compressed` file. It is equivalent to "`compress -d`." `gunzip` knows how to handle `compressed` files as well.

Putting them together.

To archive a group of files and compress the result, use the commands:

```
# tar cvf backup.tar /etc
# gzip -9 backup.tar
```

The result is `backup.tar.gz`. To unpack this file, use the reverse commands:

```
# gunzip backup.tar.gz
# tar xvf backup.tar
```

Always make sure that you are in the correct directory before unpacking a tar file.

You can use some UNIX cleverness to do this on one command line.

```
# tar cvf - /etc | gzip -9c > backup.tar.gz
```

Here, we send the tar file to '`-`', which stands for `tar`'s standard output. This is piped to `gzip`, which compresses the incoming tar file. The result is saved in `backup.tar.gz`. The `-c` option tells `gzip` to send its output to standard output, which is redirected to `backup.tar.gz`.

A single command to unpack this archive would be:

```
# gunzip -c backup.tar.gz | tar xvf -
```

Again, `gunzip` uncompresses the contents of `backup.tar.gz` and sends the resulting tar file to standard output. This is piped to `tar`, which reads '`-`', this time referring to `tar`'s standard input.

Happily, the `tar` command also includes the `z` option to automatically compress/uncompress files on the fly, using the `gzip` compression algorithm.

The command

```
# tar cvfz backup.tar.gz /etc
```

is equivalent to

```
# tar cvf backup.tar /etc
# gzip backup.tar
```

Just as the command

```
# tar xvfz backup.tar.Z
```

may be used instead of

```
# uncompress backup.tar.Z
# tar xvf backup.tar
```

Refer to the `tar` and `gzip` manual pages for more information.

---

[2]For some time, the extension `.z` (lowercase "z") was used for gzipped files. The conventional `gzip` extension is now `.gz`.

Using floppies and making backups.

Floppies are often used as backup media. If you don't have a tape drive connected to your system, floppy disks can be used (although they are slower and somewhat less reliable).

As mentioned earlier, floppy diskettes must be formatted with the MS-DOS `FORMAT.COM` or Linux `fdformat` program. This lays down the sector and track information that is appropriate to the floppy's capacity.

A few of the device names and formats of floppy disks which are accessible by Linux are given in Table 4.4.

Floppy device driver	Format
/dev/fd0d360	Double density, 360 Kb, 5.25 inch.
/dev/fd0h1200	High density, 1.2 MB, 5.25 inch.
/dev/fd0h1440	High density, 1.44 MB, 3.5 inch.

Table 4.4: Linux floppy disk formats.

Devices which begin with `fd0` are the first floppy diskette drive, which is named the `A:` drive under MS-DOS. The driver file names of second floppy device begin with `fd1`. Generally, the Linux kernel can detect the format of a diskette that has already been formatted—you can simply use `/dev/fd0` and let the system detect the format. But when you first use completely new, unformatted floppy disks, you may need to use the driver specification if the system can't detect the diskette's type.

A complete list of Linux devices and their device driver names is given in *Linux Allocated Devices,* by H. Peter Anvin (see Appendix A).

You can also use floppies to hold individual file systems and `mount` the floppy to access the data on it. See page 138.

Using floppies for backups.

The easiest way to make a backup using floppies is with `tar`. The command

```
# tar cvfzM /dev/fd0 /
```

will make a complete backup of your system using the floppy drive `/dev/fd0`. The "`M`" option to `tar` allows the backup to span multiple volumes; that is, when one floppy is full, `tar` will prompt for the next. The command

```
# tar xvfzM /dev/fd0
```

restores the complete backup. This method can also be used with a tape drive connected to your system. See section 4.

Several other programs exist for making multiple-volume backups; the `backflops` program found on `tsx-11.mit.edu` may come in handy.

Making a complete backup of the system with floppies can be time- and resource-consuming. Many system administrators use an **incremental backup** policy. Every month, a complete backup is made, and every week only those files which have been modified in the last week are backed up. In this case, if you trash your system in the middle of the month, you can simply restore the last full monthly backup, and then restore the last weekly backups as needed.

The `find` command is useful for locating files which were modified after a certain date. Several scripts for managing incremental backups can be found on `sunsite.unc.edu`.

Backups with a Zip drive.

Making backups to a Zip drive is similar to making floppy backups, but because Zip disks commonly have a capacity of 98 Kb, it is feasible to use a single, mounted Zip disk for a single backup archive.

Zip drives are available with two different hardware interfaces: a SCSI interface and a parallel port PPA interface. Zip drive support is generally not included as a pre-compiled Linux option, but it can be specified when building a custom kernel for your system. Page 140 describes the installation of an Iomega Zip device driver.

Zip drives of either interface and follow the naming conventions for SCSI devices, which are described on page 127.

Zip disks are commonly pre-formatted with a MS-DOS file system. You can either use the existing MS-DOS file system, which must be supported by your Linux kernel, or use `mke2fs` or a similar program to write a Linux file system to the disk.

A Zip disk, when mounted as the first SCSI device, is `/dev/sda4`.

```
# mount /dev/sda4 /mnt
```

It is often convenient to provide a separate mount point for Zip file systems; for example, `/zip`. The following steps, which must be executed as `root`, would create the mount point:

```
# mkdir /zip
# chmod 0755 /zip
```

Then you can use `/zip` for mounting the Zip file system.

Writing archives to Zip disks is similar to archiving to floppies. To archive and compress the `/etc` directory to a mounted Zip drive, the command used would be

```
# tar zcvf /zip/etc.tgz /etc
```

This command could be executed from any directory because it specifies absolute path names. The archive name `etc.tgz` is necessary if the Zip drive contains a MS-DOS file system, because any files written to the disk must have names which conform to MS-DOS's 8+3 naming conventions; otherwise, the file names will be truncated.

Similarly, extracting this archive requires the commands

```
# cd /
# tar zxvf /zip/etc.tgz
```

To create, for example, an ext2 file system on a Zip drive, you would give the command (for an *unmounted* Zip disk)

```
# mke2fs /dev/sda4
```

With a Zip drive mounted in this manner, with an ext2 file system, it is possible to back up entire file systems with a single command.

```
# tar zcvf /zip/local.tar.gz /usr/local
```

Note that backing up with `tar` is still preferable in many cases to simply making an archival copy with the `cp -a` command, because `tar` preserves the original files' modification times.

Making backups to tape devices.

Archiving to a streaming tape drive is similar to making a backup to a floppy file system, only to a different device driver. Tapes are also formatted and handled differently that floppy diskettes. Some representative tape device drivers for Linux systems are listed in Table 4.5.

Floppy tape drives use the floppy drive controller interface and are controlled by the ftape device driver, which is covered below. Installation of the ftape device driver module is described on page 142. SCSI tape devices are listed in Table 4.3.

To archive the `/etc` directory a tape device with `tar`, use the command

```
# tar cvf /dev/qft0 /etc
```

Similarly, to extract the files from the tape, use the commands

Tape device driver	Format
/dev/rft0	QIC-117 tape, rewind on close.
/dev/nrft0	QIC-117 tape, no rewind on close.
/dev/tpqic11	QIC-11 tape, rewind on close.
/dev/ntpqic11	QIC-11 tape, no rewind on close.
/dev/qft0	Floppy tape drive, rewind on close.
/dev/nqft0	Floppy tape drive, no rewind on close.

Table 4.5: Tape device drivers.

```
# cd /
# tar xvf /dev/qft0
```

Tapes, like diskettes, must be formatted before they can be used. The ftape driver can format tapes under Linux. To format a QIC-40 format tape, use the command

```
# ftformat -format-parameter qic40-205ft -mode-auto -omit-erase -discard-header
```

Other tape drives have their own formatting software. Check the hardware documentation for the tape drive or the documentation of the Linux device driver associated with it.

Before tapes can be removed from the drive, they must be rewound and the I/O buffers written to the tape. This is analogous to unmounting a floppy before ejecting it, because the tape driver also caches data in memory. The standard UNIX command to control tape drive operations is `mt`. Your system may not provide this command, depending on whether it has tape drive facilities. The ftape driver has a similar command, `ftmt`, which is used to control tape operations.

To rewind a tape before removing it, use the command

```
# ftmt -f /dev/qft0 rewoffl
```

Of course, substitute the correct tape device driver for your system.

It is also a good idea to retension a tape after writing to it, because magnetic tapes are susceptible to stretch. The following command accomplishes this.

```
# ftmt -f /dev/qft0 retension
```

To obtain the status of the tape device, with a formatted tape in the drive, give the command

```
# ftmt -f /dev/qft0 status
```

Using floppies as file systems.

You can create a file system on a floppy as you would on a hard drive partition. For example,

```
# mke2fs /dev/fd0 1440
```

creates a file system on the floppy in `/dev/fd0`. The size of the file system must correspond to the capacity of the floppy. High-density 3.5" disks are 1.44 megabytes, or 1440 blocks, in size. High-density 5.25" disks are 1200 blocks. It is necessary to specify the size of the file system in blocks if the system cannot automatically detect the floppy's capacity.

In order to access the floppy, you must mount the file system contained on it. The command

```
# mount /dev/fd0 /mnt
```

will mount the floppy in `/dev/fd0` on the directory `/mnt`. Now, all of the files on the floppy will appear under `/mnt` on your drive.

The **mount point**, the directory where you're mounting the file system, must exist when you use the `mount` command. If it doesn't exist, create it with `mkdir` as described on page 136.

See page 126 for more information on file systems, mounting, and mount points.

◇ Note that any I/O to the floppy is buffered the same as hard disk I/O is. If you change data on the floppy, you may not see the drive light come on until the kernel flushes its I/O buffers. It's important that you not remove a floppy before you unmount it with the command

```
# umount /dev/fd0
```

Do not simply switch floppies as you would on a MS-DOS system. Whenever you change floppies, `umount` the first floppy and `mount` the next.

Upgrading and installing new software.

Another duty of the system administrator is the upgrading and installation of new software.

Linux system development is rapid. New kernel releases appear every few weeks, and other software is updated nearly as often. Because of this, new Linux users often feel the need to upgrade their systems constantly to keep up with the rapidly changing pace. This is unnecessary and a waste of time. If you kept pace with all of the changes in the Linux world, you would spend all of your time upgrading and none of your time using the system.

Some people feel that you should upgrade when a new distribution release is made; for example, when Slackware comes out with a new version. Many Linux users completely reinstall their system with the newest Slackware release every time.

The best way to upgrade your system depends on the Linux distribution you have. Debian/GNU Linux and Red Hat Linux both have intelligent package management software which allows easy upgrades by installing a new package. For example, the C compiler, `gcc`, comes in a pre-built binary package. When it is installed, all of the files of the older version are overwritten or removed.

For the most part, senselessly upgrading to "keep up with the trend" is not important at all. This isn't MS-DOS or Microsoft Windows. There is no important reason to run the newest version of all of the software. If you find that you would like or need features that a new version offers, then upgrade. If not, don't upgrade. In other words, upgrade only what you must, when you must. Don't upgrade for the sake of upgrading. This wastes a lot of time and effort.

Upgrading the kernel

Upgrading the kernel is a a matter of obtaining the kernel sources and compiling them. This is generally a painless procedure, but you can run into problems if you try to upgrade to a development kernel, or upgrade to a new kernel version. The version of a kernel has two parts, the kernel version and patch level. As of the time of this writing, the latest stable kernel is version `2.0.30`. The `2.0` is the kernel version and `30` is the patch level. Odd-numbered kernel versions like `2.1` are development kernels. Stay away from development kernels unless you want to live dangerously! As a general rule, you should be able to upgrade easily to another patch level, but upgrading to a new version requires the upgrade of system utilities which interact closely with the kernel.

The Linux kernel sources may be retrieved from any of the Linux FTP sites (see Section C for a list). On `sunsite.unc.edu`, for instance, the kernel sources are found in `/pub/Linux/kernel`, organized into subdirectories by version number.

Kernel sources are released as a gzipped tar file. For example, the file containing the 2.0.30 kernel sources is `linux-2.0.30.tar.gz`.

Kernel sources are unpacked in the `/usr/src` directory, creating the directory `/usr/src/linux`. It is common practice for `/usr/src/linux` to be a soft link to another directory which contains the version number, like `/usr/src/linux-2.0.30`. This way, you can install new kernel sources and test them out before removing the old kernel sources. The commands to create the kernel directory link are

```
# cd /usr/src
# mkdir linux-2.0.30
# rm -r linux
```

```
# ln -s linux-2.0.30 linux
# tar xzf linux-2.0.30.tar.gz
```

When upgrading to a newer patch level of the same kernel version, kernel patch files can save file transfer time because the kernel source is around 7MB after being compressed by `gzip`. To upgrade from kernel 2.0.28 to kernel 2.0.30, you would download the patch files `patch-2.0.29.gz` and `patch-2.0.30.gz`, which can be found at the same FTP site as the kernel sources. After you have placed the patches in the `/usr/src` directory, apply the patches to the kernel in sequence to update the source. One way to do this would be

```
# cd /usr/src
# gzip -cd patch-2.0.29.gz | patch -p0
# gzip -cd patch-2.0.20.gz | patch -p0
```

After the sources are unpacked and any patches have been applied, you need to make sure that three symbolic links in `/usr/include` are correct for your kernel distribution. To create these links use the commands

```
# cd /usr/include
# rm -rf asm linux scsi
# ln -s /usr/src/linux/include/asm-i386 asm
# ln -s /usr/src/linux/include/linux linux
# ln -s /usr/src/linux/include/scsi scsi
```

After you create the links, there is no reason to create them again when you install the next kernel patch or a newer kernel version. (See page 107 for more about symbolic links.)

In order to compile the kernel, you must have the `gcc` C compiler installed on your system. `gcc` version 2.6.3 or a more recent version is required to compile the 2.0 kernel.

First `cd` to `/usr/src/linux`. The command `make config` prompts you for a number of configuration options. This is the step where you select the hardware that your kernel will support. The biggest mistake to avoid is not including support for your hard disk controller. Without the correct hard disk support in the kernel, the system won't even boot. If you are unsure about what a kernel option means, a short description is available by pressing `?` and `Return`.

Next, run the command `make dep` to update all of the source dependencies. This is an important step. `make clean` removes old binary files from the kernel source tree.

The command `make zImage` compiles the kernel and writes it to `/usr/src/linux/arch/i386/boot/zImage`. Linux kernels on Intel systems are always compressed. Sometimes the kernel you want to compile is too large to be compressed with the compression system that `make zImage` uses. A kernel which is too large will exit the kernel compile with the error message: `Kernel Image Too Large`. If this happens, try the command `make bzImage`, which uses a compression system that supports larger kernels. The kernel is written to `/usr/src/linux/arch/i386/boot/bzImage`.

Once you have the kernel compiled, you need to either copy it to a boot floppy (with a command like "`cp zImage /dev/fd0`") or install the image so LILO will boot from your hard drive. See page 122 for more information.

Adding a device driver to the kernel.

Page 136 describes how to use an Iomega Zip drive to make backups. Support for the Iomega Zip drive, like many other devices, is not generally compiled into stock Linux distribution kernels—the variety of devices is simply too great to support all of them in a usable kernel. However, the source code for the Zip parallel port device driver is included as part of the kernel source code distribution. This section describes how to add support for an Iomega Zip parallel port drive and have it co-exist with a printer connected to a different parallel port.

You must have installed and successfully built a custom Linux kernel, as described in the previous section.

Selecting the Zip drive `ppa` device as a kernel option requires that you answer `Y` to the appropriate questions during the `make config` step, when you determine the configuration of the custom kernel. In particular, the `ppa` device requires answering "`Y`" to three options:

```
SCSI support?  [Y/n/m] Y
SCSI disk support?  [Y/n/m] Y
IOMEGA Parallel Port Zip Drive SCSI support?  [Y/n/m] Y
```

After you have successfully run `make config` with all of the support options you want included in the kernel, then run `make dep`, `make clean`, and `make zImage` to build the kernel, you must tell the kernel how to install the driver. This is done via a command line to the LILO boot loader. As described on page 122, the LILO configuration file, `/etc/lilo.conf` has "stanzas" for each operating system that it knows about, and also directives for presenting these options to the user at boot time.

Another directive that LILO recognizes is "`append=`", which allows you to add boot-time information required by various device drivers to the command line. In this case, the Iomega Zip `ppa` driver requires an unused interrupt and I/O port address. This is exactly analogous to specifying separate printer devices like `LPT1:` and `LPT2:` under MS-DOS.

For example, if your printer uses the hexadecimal (base 16) port address `0x378` (see the installation manual for your parallel port card if you don't know what the address is) and is polled (that is, it doesn't require an IRQ line, a common Linux configuration), you would place the following line in your system's `/etc/lilo.conf` file:

```
append="lp=0x378,0"
```

It is worth noting that Linux automatically recognizes one `/dev/lp` port at boot time, but when specifying a custom port configurations, the boot-time instructions are needed.

The "`0`" after the port address tells the kernel *not* to use a IRQ (interrupt request) line for the printer. This is generally acceptable because printers are much slower than CPUs, so a slower method of accessing I/O devices, known as **polling**, where the kernel periodically checks the printer status on its own, still allows the computer to keep up with the printer.

However, devices that operate at higher speeds, like serial lines and disks, each require an **IRQ,** or **interrupt request,** line. This is a hardware signal sent by the device to the processor whenever the device requires the processor's attention; for example, if the device has data waiting to be input to the processor. The processor stops whatever it is doing and handles the interrupt request of the device. The Zip drive `ppa` device requires a free interrupt, which must correspond to the interrupt that is set on the printer card that you connect the Zip drive to. At the time of this writing, the Linux `ppa` device driver does not support "chaining" of parallel port devices, and separate parallel ports must be used for the Zip `ppa` device and each printer.

To determine which interrupts are already in use on your system, the command

```
# cat /proc/interrupt
```

displays a list of devices and the IRQ lines they use. However, you also need to be careful not to use any automatically configured serial port interrupts as well, which may not be listed in the `/proc/interrupt` file. The Linux Documentation Project's Serial HOWTO (see page 1374), describes in detail the configuration of serial ports.

◇ You should also check the hardware settings of various interface cards on your machine by opening the machine's case and visually checking the jumper settings if necessary, to ensure that you are not co-opting an IRQ line that is already in use by another device. Multiple devices fighting for an interrupt line is perhaps the single most common cause of non-functioning Linux systems.

A typical `/proc/interrupt` file looks like

```
0:  6091646 timer
1:  40691 keyboard
2:  0 cascade
4:  284686 + serial
13:  1 math error
14:  192560 + ide0
```

The first column is of interest here. These are the numbers of the IRQ lines that are in use on the system. For the ppa driver, we want to choose a line which is *not* listed. IRQ 7 is often a good choice, because it is seldom used in default system configurations. We also need to specify the port address which the ppa device will use. This address needs to be physically configured on the interface card. Parallel I/O ports are assigned specific addresses, so you will need to read the documentation for your parallel port card. In this example, we will use the I/O port address 0x278, which corresponds to the LPT2: printer port under MS-DOS. Adding both the IRQ line and port address to our boot-time command line, above, yields the following statement as it would appear in the appropriate stanza of the /etc/lilo.conf file:

```
append="lp=0x378,0 ppa=0x278,7"
```

These statements are appended to the kernel's start-up parameters at boot time. They ensure that any printer attached to the system does not interfere with the Zip drive's operation. Of course, if your system does not have a printer installed, the "lp=" directive can, and should, be omitted.

After you have installed the custom kernel itself, as described on page 122, and before you reboot the system, be sure to run the command

```
# /sbin/lilo
```

to install the new LILO configuration on the hard drive's boot sector.

Installing a device driver module.

Page 137 describes how to back up files to a tape drive. Linux provides support for a variety of tape drives with IDE, SCSI, and some proprietary interfaces. Another common type of tape drive connects directly to the floppy drive controller. Linux provides the ftape device driver as a module.

You can retrieve the ftape package from the sunsite.unc.edu FTP archive (see Appendix C for instructions). The ftape archive is located in /pub/Linux/kernel/tapes. Be sure to get the most recent version. At the time of this writing, this is ftape-3.04d.tar.gz.

After unpacking the ftape archive in the /usr/src directory, typing make install in the top-level ftape directory will compile the ftape driver modules and utilities, if necessary, and install them. If you experience compatibility problems with the ftape executable distribution files and your system kernel or libraries, executing the commands make clean, make install make modules, and make modules_install will ensure that the modules are compiled and installed on your system.

◇ To use this version of the ftape driver, you must have module support compiled into the kernel, as well as support for the kerneld kernel daemon. However, you must *not* include the kernel's built-in ftape code as a kernel option, as the more recent ftape module completely replaces this code.

make modules_install also installs the device driver modules in the correct directories. On standard Linux systems, modules are located in the directory

/lib/modules/⟨*kernel-version*⟩

If your kernel version is 2.0.30, the modules on your system are located in /lib/modules/2.0.30. The make modules_install step also insures that these modules are locatable by adding the appropriate statements to the modules.dep file, located in the top-level directory of the module files, in this case /lib/modules/2.0.30. The ftape installation adds the following modules to your system (using kernel version 2.0.30 in this example):

```
/lib/modules/2.0.30/misc/ftape.o
/lib/modules/2.0.30/misc/zft-compressor.o
/lib/modules/2.0.30/misc/zftape.o
```

The instructions to load the modules also need to be added to the system-wide module configuration file. This is the file /etc/conf.modules on many systems. To automatically load the ftape modules on demand, add the following lines to the /etc/conf.modules file:

```
alias char-major-27 zftape
pre-install ftape /sbin/swapout 5
```

The first statement loads all of the ftape related modules if necessary when a device with the major number 27 (the ftape device) is accessed by the kernel. Because support for the zftape module (which provides automatic data compression for tape devices) requires the support of the other ftape modules, all of them are loaded on demand by the kernel. The second line specifies load-time parameters for the modules. In this case, the utility `/sbin/swapout`, which is provided with the ftape package, ensures that sufficient DMA memory is available for the ftape driver to function.

To access the ftape device, you must first place a formatted tape in the drive. Instructions for formatting tapes and operation of the tape drive are given in page 137.

Upgrading the libraries.

As mentioned before, most of the software on the system is compiled to use shared libraries, which contain common subroutines shared among different programs.

If you see the message

```
Incompatible library version
```

when attempting to run a program, then you need to upgrade to the version of the libraries which the program requires. Libraries are backwardly compatible. A program compiled to use an older version of the libraries should work with the new version of the libraries installed. However, the reverse is not true.

The newest version of the libraries can be found on Linux FTP sites. On `sunsite.unc.edu`, they are located in `/pub/Linux/GCC`. The "release" files there should explain what files you need to download and how to install them. Briefly, you should get the files `image-`*`version`*`.tar.gz` and `inc-`*`version`*`.tar.gz` where *version* is the version of the libraries to install, such as `4.4.1`. These are tar files compressed with `gzip`. The `image` file contains the library images to install in `/lib` and `/usr/lib`. The `inc` file contains include files to install in `/usr/include`

The `release-`*`version`*`.tar.gz` should explain the installation procedure in detail (the exact instructions vary with each release). In general, you need to install the library's `.a` and `.sa` files in `/usr/lib`. These are the libraries used at compilation time.

In addition, the shared library image files, `libc.so.`*`version`* are installed in `/lib`. These are the shared library images loaded at run time by programs using the libraries. Each library has a symbolic link using the major version number of the library in `/lib`.

The `libc` library version 4.4.1 has a major version number of `4`. The file containing the library is `libc.so.4.4.1`. A symbolic link of the name `libc.so.4` is also placed in `/lib` pointing to the library. You must change this symbolic link when upgrading the libraries. For example, when upgrading from `libc.so.4.4` to `libc.so.4.4.1`, you need to change the symbolic link to point to the new version.

◇ You must change the symbolic link in one step, as described below. If you delete the symbolic link `libc.so.4`, then programs which depend on the link (including basic utilities like `ls` and `cat`) will stop working. Use the following command to update the symbolic link `libc.so.4` to point to the file `libc.so.4.4.1`:

```
# ln -sf /lib/libc.so.4.4.1 /lib/libc.so.4
```

You also need to change the symbolic link `libm.so.`*`version`* in the same manner. If you are upgrading to a different version of the libraries, substitute the appropriate file names, above. The library release notes should explain the details. (See page 107 for more information about symbolic links.)

Upgrading `gcc`.

The `gcc` C and C++ compiler is used to compile software on your system, most importantly the kernel. The newest version of `gcc` is found on the Linux FTP sites. On `sunsite.unc.edu`, it is found in the directory `/pub/Linux/GCC` (along with the libraries). There should be a `release` file for the `gcc` distribution detailing what files you need to download and how to install them. Various distributions like Debian/GNU Linux, Slackware, and Red Hat Linux, have upgrade versions that work with their package management software. In general, these packages are much easier to install than "generic" distributions.

Upgrading other software.

Upgrading other software is often simply a matter of downloading the appropriate files and installing them. Most software for Linux is distributed as compressed tar files that include sources, binaries, or both. If binaries are not included in the release, you may need to compile them yourself. This means at least typing make in the directory where the sources are located.

Reading the USENET newsgroup comp.os.linux.announce for announcements of new software releases is the easiest way to find out about new software. Whenever you are looking for software on an FTP site, downloading the ls-lR index file from the FTP site and using grep to find the files you want is the easiest way to locate software. If you have archie available to you, it can be of assistance as well[3]. There are also other Internet resources which are devoted specifically to Linux. See Appendix A for more details.

Miscellaneous tasks.

There are a number of housekeeping tasks for the system administrator which don't fall into any major category.

System startup files.

When the system boots, a number of scripts are executed automatically by the system before any user logs in. Here is a description of what happens.

At boot-up time, the kernel spawns the process /etc/init. Init is a program which reads its configuration file, /etc/inittab, and spawns other processes based on the contents of this file. One of the important processes started from inittab is the /etc/getty process started on each virtual console. The getty process grabs the VC for use, and starts a login process on the VC. This allows you to login on each VC. If /etc/inittab does not contain a getty process for a certain VC, you will not be able to login on that VC.

Another process executed from /etc/inittab is /etc/rc, the main system initialization file. This file is a simple shell script which executes any initialization commands needed at boot time, such as mounting the file systems (see page 126) and initializing swap space. On some systems, init executes the file /etc/init.d/rc.

Your system may execute other initialization scripts as well. For example /etc/rc.local which usually contains initialization commands specific to your own system, such as setting the host name (see the next section). rc.local may be started from /etc/rc or from /etc/inittab directly.

Setting the host name.

In a networked environment, the host name is used to uniquely identify a particular machine, while on a stand-alone machine, the host name simply gives the system personality and charm. It's like naming a pet: you can always address to your dog as "The dog," but it's much more interesting to assign the dog a name such as Spot or Woofie.

Setting the system's host name is a simple matter of using the hostname command. If you are on a network, your host name should be the full host name of your machine, such as goober.norelco.com. If you are not on a network of any kind, you can choose an arbitrary host and domain name, such as loomer.vpizza.com, shoop.nowhere.edu, or floof.org.

The host name must appear in the file /etc/hosts, which assigns an IP address to each host. Even if your machine is not on a network, you should include your own host name in /etc/hosts. If you are not on a TCP/IP network, and your host name is floof.org, simply include the following line in /etc/hosts:

```
127.0.0.1        floof.org localhost
```

This assigns your host name, floof.org, to the loopback address 127.0.0.1. The loopback interface is present whether the machine is connected to a network or not. The localhost alias is always assigned to this address.

[3]If you don't have archie, you can telnet to an archie server such as archie.rutgers.edu, login as "archie" and use the command "help"

If you are on a TCP/IP network, your actual IP address and host name should appear in /etc/hosts. For example, if your host name is goober.norelco.com, and your IP address is 128.253.154.32, add the following line to /etc/hosts:

```
128.253.154.32        goober.norelco.com
```

To set your host name, simply use the hostname command. For example, the command

```
# hostname -S goober.norelco.com
```

sets the host name to goober.norelco.com. In most cases, the hostname command is executed from one of the system startup files, like /etc/rc or /etc/rc.local. Edit these two files and change the hostname command found there to set your own host name. Upon rebooting, the system will use the new name.

What to do in an emergency.

On some occasions, the system administrator will be faced with the problem of recovering from a complete disaster, such as forgetting the root password or trashing file systems. The best advice is, *don't panic.* Everyone makes stupid mistakes—that's the best way to learn about system administration: the hard way.

Linux is not an unstable version of UNIX. In fact, I have had fewer problems with system hangs than with commercial versions of UNIX on many platforms. Linux also benefits from a strong complement of wizards who can help you out of a bind. (The *double entendre* is intended.)

The first step to fixing any problem yourself is finding out what it is. Poke around, and see how things work. Much of the time, a system administrator posts a desperate plea for help before he or she looks into the problem at all. You'll find that fixing problems yourself is actually very easy. It is the path to enlightenment and guruhood.

There are a few times when reinstalling the system from scratch is necessary. Many new users accidentally delete some essential system file, and immediately reach for the installation disks. This is not a good idea. Before taking such drastic measures, investigate the problem and ask others for help. In many cases, you can recover your system from a maintenance diskette.

Recovery with a maintenance diskette.

One indispensable tool of the system administrator is the so-called "boot/root disk," a floppy that can be booted for a complete Linux system, independent of your hard drive. Boot/root disks are actually very simple—you create a root file system on the floppy, place all of the necessary utilities on it, and install LILO and a bootable kernel on the floppy. Another technique is to use one floppy for the kernel and another for the root file system. In any case, the result is the same: you are running a Linux system completely from the floppy drive.

The canonical example of a boot/root disk is the Slackware boot disks. These diskettes contain a bootable kernel and a root file system, all on floppy. They are intended to be used to install the Slackware distribution, but come in handy when doing system maintenance.

The H.J Lu boot/root disk, available from /pub/Linux/GCC/rootdisk on sunsite.unc.edu, is another example of a maintenance disk. If you're ambitious, you can create your own. In most cases, however, a ready-made boot/root disk is much easier to use and probably will be more complete.

Using a boot/root disk is very simple. Boot the disk on your system, and login as root (usually with no password). In order to access the files on the hard drive, you will need to mount the file systems by hand. For example, the command

```
# mount -t ext2 /dev/hda2 /mnt
```

will mount an ext2fs file system on /dev/hda2 under /mnt. Remember that / is now on the boot/root disk itself; you need to mount your hard drive file systems under some directory in order to access the files. Therefore, /etc/passwd on your hard drive is now /mnt/etc/passwd if you mount your root file system on /mnt.

Fixing the root password.

If you forget your root password, this is not a problem, surprisingly. Boot the boot/root disk, mount the root file system on `/mnt`, and blank out the password field for `root` in `/mnt/etc/passwd`, as in this example:

```
root::0:0:root:/:/bin/sh
```

Now `root` has no password. When you reboot from the hard drive you should be able to login as `root` and reset the password using `passwd`.

Aren't you glad that you learned how to use `vi`? On your boot/root disk, editors like Emacs probably aren't available, but `vi` should be.

Trashed file systems.

If you somehow trash a file systems, you can run `e2fsck` or the appropriate form of `fsck` for the file system type. (See page 128.) In most cases, it is safest to correct any damaged data on the hard drive file systems from floppy.

One common cause of file system damage is a damaged super block. The **super block** is the "header" of the file system that contains information about its status, size, free blocks, and so forth. If you damage the super block, by accidentally writing data directly to the file system's partition table for example, the system probably will not recognize the file system at all. Attempt to mount the file system will fail, and `e2fsck` won't be able to fix the problem.

Happily, an ext2fs file system type saves copies of the superblock at "block group" boundaries on the drive, usually every 8K blocks. To tell `e2fsck` to use a copy of the superblock, use a command like

```
# e2fsck -b 8193 ⟨partition⟩
```

where *partition* is the partition on which the file system resides. The `-b 8193` option tells `e2fsck` to use the copy of the superblock stored at block 8193 in the file system.

Recovering lost files.

If you accidentally delete an important file on your system, there's no way to "undelete" it. However, you can copy the relevant files from the floppy to your hard drive. If you delete `/bin/login`, for example, which allows you to login, simply boot the boot/root floppy, mount the root file system on `/mnt`, and use the command

```
# cp -a /bin/login /mnt/bin/login
```

The `-a` option tells `cp` to preserve the permissions on the file(s) being copied.

Of course, if the files you deleted aren't essential system files that have counterparts on the boot/root floppy, you're out of luck. If you make backups however, you can always restore them.

Trashed libraries.

If you accidentally trash your libraries or symbolic links in `/lib`, more than likely the commands which depend on the libraries will no longer work (see page 143). The easiest solution is to boot your boot/root floppy, mount your root file system, and fix the libraries in `/mnt/lib`. Page 143 describes how install run time libraries and their symbolic links.

CHAPTER 5

Advanced Features

This chapter introduces some of the more advanced and, to the authors' minds, interesting features of Linux. You must have at least basic UNIX experience to implement these techniques, and understand the information contained in the previous chapters.

The X Window System.

The X Window System is a graphical user interface (GUI) that was originally developed at the Massachusetts Institute of Technology. Commercial vendors have since made X the industry standard GUI for UNIX platforms. Virtually every UNIX workstation in the world now runs some form of X.

A free port of the MIT X Window System version 11, release 6 (X11R6) for 80386, 80486, and Pentium UNIX systems was developed by a team of programmers that was originally headed by David Wexelblat. This release, known as XFree86[1], is available for System V/386, 386BSD, and other Intel x86 UNIX implementations, including Linux. It provides all of the binaries, support files, libraries, and tools required for installation.

Some features offered by this release are:

- complete inclusion of the X Consortium's X11R6.3 release;
- a new DPMS extension, donated by Digital Equipment Corporation;
- the Low Bandwidth X (LBX) extension in all X servers;
- Microsoft IntelliMouse support;
- support for `gzip` font compression.

To the use the X Window System, you are encouraged to read *The X Window System: A User's Guide* (see Appendix A). Here, we describe step-by-step an XFree86 installation under Linux. You still need to fill in some of the details by reading the XFree86 documentation, which is discussed below. The Linux XFree86 HOWTO is another good information source.

Hardware requirements.

Video display. The documentation for your video adaptor should specify the chip set. If you are in the market for a new video card, or are buying a machine that comes with a video card, ask the vendor to find out exactly what make, model, and chip set the video card comes with. The vendor may need to call the manufacturer's technical support department. Many personal computer hardware vendors state their video card is a "standard SVGA card," that "should work," with your system. Explain that your software (mention Linux and XFree86!) does not support all video chip sets, and that you must have detailed information.

[1] XFree86 is a trademark of The XFree86 Project, Inc.

You can also determine your video card chip set by running the `SuperProbe` program which is included with the XFree86 distribution. This is described below.

Video cards using these chip sets are supported on all bus types, including VLB and PCI. Many of the cards support 256-color graphics modes. In addition, some of the cards support color modes like monochrome, 15-bit, 16-bit, and 24-bit. For color depths greater than 256 (8-bit), you must have the requisite amount of video dynamic RAM (DRAM) installed. However, the usual configuration is 8 bits per pixel (256 colors).

The monochrome server also supports generic VGA cards, the Hercules monochrome card, the Hyundai HGC1280, Sigma LaserView, and Apollo monochrome cards.

The release notes for the current version of XFree86 should contain the complete list of supported video chip sets. The XFree86 distribution has chip set specific README files that give detailed information on the state of support for each chip set.

One problem faced by the XFree86 developers is that some video card manufacturers use non-standard mechanisms to determine the clock frequencies that are used to drive their card. They either don't release specifications which describe how to program the card or require developers to sign non-disclosure statements to get the information. This practice restricts the free distribution of XFree86, and the XFree86 development team is unwilling to accept it. This has been a problem with certain video cards manufactured by Diamond, but as of release 3.3, Diamond actively supports the XFree86 Project, Inc.

We also suggest using an accelerated card, like a S3 chip set card. You should check the XFree86 documentation and verify that your particular card is supported before you take the plunge and purchase expensive hardware. Benchmark comparisons of video cards under XFree86 are posted routinely to the USENET news groups `comp.windows.x.i386unix` and `comp.os.linux.misc`.

It is important to note that the average accelerated video card is significantly faster than the standard graphics card of most workstations. An 80486DX2, 66-MHz Linux System with 20 megabytes of RAM, equipped with a VESA Local Bus (VLB) S3-864 chip set card with 2 megabytes of DRAM, will consistently be about 7 times as fast a Sun Sparc IPX workstation on X benchmarks with the XFree86 server version 3.1. Version 3.3 is even faster. In general, a Linux system with an accelerated SVGA card will give you much greater performance than commercial UNIX workstations, which usually employ simple frame buffers for graphics.

Memory, CPU, and disk space. The suggested setup for XFree86 under Linux is a 80486 machine with at least 8 megabytes of RAM. Your machine needs at least 4 megabytes of physical RAM and 16 megabytes of virtual RAM (for example, 8 megabytes of physical RAM and 8 megabytes of swap space). The more physical RAM installed, the less the system must swap to and from the disk when memory is low. Because swapping is inherently slow (disks are very slow compared to memory), having 8 megabytes of RAM or more is necessary to run XFree86 comfortably. A system with 4 megabytes of physical RAM could run 10 times more slowly than one with 8 megabytes or more.

A stock, out-of-the-box XFree86 installation requires 60–80 megabytes of disk space, at a minimum. This includes space for the X server(s), fonts, libraries, and standard utilities. If you plan to add applications, you can probably run XFree86 comfortably in 120–150 megabytes of disk space.

XFree86 installation.

The Linux binary distribution of XFree86 can be found at a number of FTP sites. On `sunsite.unc.edu`, it is found in the directory `/pub//X11/XFree86`. At of the time of this writing, the current version is 3.3.1. Newer versions are released periodically. If you obtain XFree86 as part of a Linux distribution, downloading the software separately is not necessary.

These files are included in the XFree86-3.3.1 distribution.

One of the following servers is required:

File	Description
X338514.tgz	Server for 8514-based boards.
X33AGX.tgz	Server for AGX-based boards.
X33I128.tgz	Server for the Imagine I128 boards.
X33Ma64.tgz	Server for Mach64-based boards.
X33Ma32.tgz	Server for Mach32-based boards.
X33Ma8.tgz	Server for Mach8-based boards.
X33Mono.tgz	Server for monochrome video modes.
X33P9K.tgz	Server for P9000-based boards.
X33S3.tgz	Server for S3-based boards.
X33S3V.tgz	Server for S3/Virge-based boards.
X33SVGA.tgz	Server for Super VGA-based boards.
X33VGA16.tgz	Server for VGA/EGA-based boards.
X33W32.tgz	Server for ET4000/W32-based boards.

All of the following files are required:

File	Description
preinst.sh	Pre-installation script.
postinst.sh	Post-installation script.
X33bin.tgz	Clients, run-time libs, and app-defaults files.
X33doc.tgz	Documentation.
X33fnts.tgz	75dpi, misc and PEX fonts.
X33lib.tgz	Data files required at run-time.
X33man.tgz	Manual pages.
X33set.tgz	XF86Setup utility.
X33VG16.tgz	16-color VGA server (XF86Setup needs this server).

The following is required for new installations, and optional for existing installations:

File	Description
X33cfg.tgz	sample config files for xinit, xdm.

◇ Do not install X33cfg.tgz over an existing XFree86 installation without first backing up the configuration files. Unpacking X33cfg.tgz overwrites these and other files. If you have customized configuration files, there is no need to install this package anyway.

◇ The bit mapped fonts distributed with release 3.3.1 are compressed with the gzip program rather than compress. You will probably want to remove the old fonts after you back them up. The X servers and font servers in previous releases cannot read fonts compressed by gzip, so keep a copy of the old fonts if you want to use older servers.

The following files are optional:

File	Description
X33f100.tgz	100dpi fonts.
X33fcyr.tgz	Cyrillic fonts.
X33fnon.tgz	Other fonts (Chinese, Japanese, Korean, Hebrew).
X33fscl.tgz	Scalable fonts (Speedo and Type1).
X33fsrv.tgz	Font server and config files.
X33prog.tgz	X header files, config files and compile-time libs.
X33nest.tgz	Nested X server.
X33vfb.tgz	Virtual frame buffer X server.
X33prt.tgz	X Print server.
X33ps.tgz	PostScript version of the documentation.
X33html.tgz	HTML version of the documentation.
X33jdoc.tgz	Documentation in Japanese (for version 3.2).
X33jhtm.tgz	HTML version of the documentation in Japanese (3.2).
X33lkit.tgz	X server Link Kit.

The XFree86 directory should contain README files and installation notes for the current version.

Next, as root, create the directory /usr/X11R6 if it doesn't already exist. Then run the pre-installation script, preinst.sh. You should copy the script, and all of the archive files for your system to the /var/tmp directory before you run preinst.sh. /usr/X11R6 must be your current directory when you run the pre-installation script and unpack the archives.

```
# cd /usr/X11R6
# sh /var/tmp/preinst.sh
```

You should then unpack the files from /var/tmp to /usr/X11R6 with a command like:

```
# gzip -d < /var/tmp/X33prog.tgz | tar vxf -
```

◇ These tar files are packed relative to /usr/X11R6. You must unpack the files there. On some Linux distributions, the parent directory is /var/X11R6 instead.

After you have unpacked the required files and any optional files you selected, run the post-installation script postinst.sh.

```
# cd /usr/X11R6
# sh /var/tmp/postinst.sh
```

Now link the file /usr/X11R6/bin/X to the server that supports your video card. For example, the SVGA color server, /usr/bin/X11/X should be linked to /usr/X11R6/bin/XF86_SVGA. To use the monochrome server instead, relink X to XF86_MONO with the command

```
# ln -sf /usr/X11R6/bin/XF86_MONO  /usr/X11R6/bin/X
```

The same holds true for the other servers.

You also need to ensure that the directory, /usr/X11R6/bin, is on your path. This can be done by editing your system default /etc/profile or /etc/csh.login (based on the shell that you, or other users on your system, use). Or you can simply add the directory to your personal path by modifying /etc/.bashrc or /etc/.cshrc, based on your shell.

Finally, ensure that /usr/X11R6/lib can be located by ld.so, the run time linker. To do this, add the line

```
/usr/X11R6/lib
```

to the file /etc/ld.so.conf, and run /sbin/ldconfig, as root.

Probing the hardware configuration.

If you aren't sure which server to use or don't know the video card's chip set, the SuperProbe program, which is found in /usr/X11R6/bin, can attempt to determine the video chip set and other information. Write down its output for later reference.

To run SuperProbe from the command line, simply enter

```
# SuperProbe
```

◇ It is possible that SuperProbe will confuse hardware that uses I/O port addresses that might be used by video cards. To prevent SuperProbe from checking these addresses, use the excl argument, followed by a list of addresses that SuperProbe should not examine. For example:

```
# SuperProbe -excl 0x200-0x230,0x240
```

The addresses are given as hexadecimal numbers that are prefixed by 0x.

To display a list of video devices that SuperProbe knows about, use the command

```
# SuperProbe -info
```

SuperProbe can print lots of information if you provide it with the -verbose argument. You can redirect the output to a file:

```
# SuperProbe -verbose >superprobe.out
```

◇ Running SuperProbe can cause the system to hang. Make certain that any non-essential applications are not running, or at least have all of their data safely saved to disk, and ensure that any users are logged off. Also, a loaded system (one that is printing in the background, for example), can skew the output of software like SuperProbe or an X server that is trying to measure the video card's timing specifications.

Automatically generating the XF86Config file.

Creating the XF86Config file by hand is an arduous task, but it is not impossible. Several tools in the XFree86 version 3.3.1 distribution can assist you. One of them, the XF86Setup program, can automatically generate an XF86Config file in the correct format. You must know the exact specifications of your video board and the Vertical and Horizontal refresh values of your monitor. Most of the information can be found in the owner's manuals.

Several other configuration programs are available as well, depending on the Linux distribution. The most common ones are Xconfigurator and xf86config. The latter program is an older version of XF86Setup and is included in older releases of XFree86. You should always use XF86Setup if both it and xf86config are available.

Configuring XFree86.

In this section, we describe how to create and edit the XF86Config file, which configures the XFree86 server. In many cases, it is best to start with an XFree86 configuration that uses a low resolution, like 640x480, which is supported by nearly all video cards and monitors. Once XFree86 works at a lower, standard resolution, you can tweak the configuration to exploit the capabilities of your video hardware. This ensures that XFree86 works on your system, and that the installation is essentially correct, before you attempt the sometimes difficult task of setting up XFree86 for high-performance use.

In addition to the information listed here, you should read the following documents:

- The XFree86 documentation in /usr/X11R6/lib/X11/doc (from the XFree86-3.1-doc package). You should especially see the file README.Config, which is an XFree86 configuration tutorial.
- Several video chip sets have separate README files in the above directory (like README.Cirrus and README.S3). Read the file that applies to your video card.
- The manual page for XFree86.
- The manual page for XF86Config.
- The manual page for the server that you are using, like XF86_SVGA or XF86_S3.

The main XFree86 configuration file is /usr/X11R6/lib/X11/XF86Config. This file contains information for your mouse, video card parameters, and so on. The file XF86Config.eg is provided with the XFree86 distribution as an example. Copy this file to XF86Config and edit it as a starting point.

The XF86Config manual page explains the format of the XF86Config file. Read the manual page if you have not done so already.

We are going to describe a sample XF86Config file, a section at a time. This file may not look exactly like the sample file included in the XFree86 distribution, but the structure is the same.

◇ Note that the XF86Config file format may change with each version of XFree86. See your distribution's release notes for errata.

◇ **Do not copy the configuration file listed here to your system and try to use it.** A configuration file that does not correspond to your hardware can drive the monitor at a frequency that is too high. There have been reports of damage to monitors, especially fixed-frequency monitors, that has been caused by incorrectly configured XF86Config files. **Make absolutely sure that your XF86Config file corresponds to your hardware before you use it.**

Each section of the `XF86Config` file is surrounded by a pair of lines with the syntax, `Section "`⟨*section-name*⟩`"...EndSection`.

The first section of the `XF86Config` file is `Files`, which looks like this:

```
Section "Files"
    RgbPath     "/usr/X11R6/lib/X11/rgb"
    FontPath    "/usr/X11R6/lib/X11/fonts/misc/"
    FontPath    "/usr/X11R6/lib/X11/fonts/75dpi/"
EndSection
```

The `RgbPath` line sets the path to the X11R6 RGB color database, and each `FontPath` line sets the path to a directory containing X11 fonts. You shouldn't have to modify these lines. Simply ensure that a `FontPath` entry exists for each font type that you have installed; that is, for each directory in `/usr/X11R6/lib/X11/fonts`.

The next section is `ServerFlags`, which specifies several global flags for the server. In general this section is empty.

```
Section "ServerFlags"
# Uncomment this to cause a core dump at the spot where a signal is
# received.  This may leave the console in an unusable state, but may
# provide a better stack trace in the core dump to aid in debugging
#    NoTrapSignals

# Uncomment this to disable the <Crtl><Alt><BS> server abort sequence
#    DontZap
EndSection
```

In this `ServerFlags` section, all of the lines are commented out.

The next section is `Keyboard`. This example shows a basic configuration that should work on most systems. The `XF86Config` file describes how to modify the configuration.

```
Section "Keyboard"
    Protocol     "Standard"
    AutoRepeat  500 5
    ServerNumLock
EndSection
```

The next section is `Pointer`, which specifies parameters for the mouse device:

```
Section "Pointer"

    Protocol     "MouseSystems"
    Device       "/dev/mouse"

# Baudrate and SampleRate are only for some Logitech mice
#    BaudRate    9600
#    SampleRate 150

# Emulate3Buttons is an option for 2-button Microsoft mice
#    Emulate3Buttons

# ChordMiddle is an option for some 3-button Logitech mice
#    ChordMiddle

EndSection
```

For the moment, the only options that should concern you are `Protocol` and `Device`. `Protocol` specifies the mouse protocol, which is not necessarily the same as the manufacturer. XFree86 under Linux recognizes these mouse protocols:

- BusMouse;
- Logitech;
- Microsoft;
- MMSeries;
- Mouseman;
- MouseSystems;
- PS/2;
- MMHitTab.

BusMouse should be used for the Logitech bus mice. Older Logitech mice use Logitech, and newer Logitech serial mice use either Microsoft or Mouseman protocols.

Device specifies the device file by which the mouse can be accessed. On most Linux systems, this is /dev/mouse, which is usually a link to the appropriate serial port, like /dev/cua0 for serial mice and the appropriate bus mouse device for bus mice. At any rate, be sure that the device file exists.

The next section is Monitor, which specifies the characteristics of your monitor. As with other sections in the XF86Config file, there may be more than one Monitor section. This is useful if you have multiple monitors connected to a system, or use the same XF86Config file for multiple hardware configurations.

```
Section "Monitor"

    Identifier  "CTX 5468 NI"

    # These values are for a CTX 5468NI only! Don't attempt to use
    # them with your monitor (unless you have this model)

    Bandwidth    60
    HorizSync    30-38,47-50
    VertRefresh  50-90

    # Modes: Name       dotclock  horiz                vert

    ModeLine "640x480"   25       640 664 760 800      480 491 493 525
    ModeLine "800x600"   36       800 824 896 1024     600 601 603 625
    ModeLine "1024x768"  65       1024 1088 1200 1328  768 783 789 818

EndSection
```

Identifier is an arbitrary name for the Monitor entry. This can be any string and is used to refer to the Monitor entry later in the XF86Config file.

HorizSync specifies the valid horizontal sync frequencies for your monitor, in kHz. Multisync monitors may have a range of values, or several, comma separated ranges. Fixed-frequency monitors require a list of discrete values; for example:

```
    HorizSync    31.5, 35.2, 37.9, 35.5, 48.95
```

The monitor manual should list these values in the technical specifications section. If it does not, contact the manufacturer or vendor of your monitor to obtain it.

VertRefresh specifies the valid vertical refresh rates (or vertical synchronization frequencies) for your monitor, in kHz. Like HorizSync, this can be a range or a list of discrete values. Your monitor manual should list them.

HorizSync and VertRefresh are used only to double-check that the monitor resolutions are in valid ranges. This reduces the chance that you will damage your monitor by driving it at a frequency it was not designed for.

The ModeLine directive is used to specify resolution modes for your monitor. The format is

```
ModeLine ⟨name⟩ ⟨clock⟩ ⟨horiz-values⟩ ⟨vert-values⟩
```

name is an arbitrary string which you will use to refer to the resolution mode later in the file. *dot-clock* is the driving clock frequency, or "dot clock" associated with the resolution mode. A dot clock is usually specified in MHz. It is the rate at which the video card must send pixels to the monitor at this resolution. *horiz-values* and *vert-values* are four numbers each that specify when the electron gun of the monitor should fire, and when the horizontal and vertical sync pulses fire during a sweep.

The file VideoModes.doc, included with the XFree86 distribution, describes in detail how to determine the ModeLine values for each resolution mode that your monitor supports. *clock* must correspond to one of the dot clock values that your video card supports. Later in the XF86Config file, you will specify these clocks.

Two files, modeDB.txt and Monitors, may have ModeLine information for your monitor. They are located in /usr/X11R6/lib/X11/doc.

Start with ModeLine values for VESA-standard monitor timings, because most monitors support them. ModeDB.txt includes the timing values for VESA-standard resolutions. For example, this entry,

```
# 640x480@60Hz Non-Interlaced mode
# Horizontal Sync = 31.5kHz
# Timing: H=(0.95us, 3.81us, 1.59us), V=(0.35ms, 0.064ms, 1.02ms)
#
# name         clock    horizontal timing      vertical timing      flags
 "640x480"      25.175  640  664  760  800     480  491  493  525
```

is the VESA-standard timing for a 640x480 video mode. It has a dot clock of 25.175, which your video card must support. This is described below. To include this entry in the XF86Config file, use the line

```
ModeLine "640x480" 25.175  640 664 760 800  480 491 493 525
```

The *name* argument to ModeLine ("640x480") is an arbitrary string. By convention modes are named by their resolutions, but *name* can, technically, be any descriptive label.

For each ModeLine, the server checks the mode specifications and ensures that they fall in the range of values specified for Bandwidth, HorizSync, and VertRefresh. If they do not, the server complains when you attempt to start X. For one thing, the dot clock used by the mode should not be greater than the value used for Bandwidth. However, in many cases, it is safe to use a mode that has a slightly higher bandwidth than your monitor can support.

If the VESA standard timings do not work, (you'll know after you try to use them), then look in the files modeDB.txt and Monitors, which include specific mode values for many monitor types. You can create ModeLine entries from these values as well. Be sure only to use values for your specific monitor. Many 14 and 15-inch monitors do not support higher resolution modes, and often resolutions of 1024x768 at low dot clocks. If you can't find high-resolution modes for your monitor in these files, then your monitor probably does not support them.

If you are completely at a loss and can't find ModeLine values for your monitor, follow the instructions in the VideoModes.doc file, which is included in the XFree86 distribution, and generate values from the specifications in your monitor's manual. Your mileage will certainly vary when you attempt to generate ModeLine values by hand. But this is a good place to look if you can't find the values that you need. VideoModes.doc also describes the format of the ModeLine directive, and other aspects of the XFree86 server in gory detail.

Lastly, if you do obtain ModeLine values that are almost but not exactly right, you may possibly be able to modify the values a little to obtain the desired result. For example, if the XFree86 display image is shifted slightly, or the image seems to "roll," then follow the instructions in the VideoModes.doc file and fix the values. Be sure to check the controls on the monitor itself. In many cases, you must change the horizontal or vertical size of the display after XFree86 starts, to center and size the image.

◇ Don't use monitor timing values or ModeLine values for monitors other than your model. If you try to drive a monitor at a frequency for which it was not designed, you can damage or even destroy it.

The next section of the XF86Config file is Device, which specifies parameters for your video card. Here is an example.

```
Section "Device"
        Identifier "#9 GXE 64"

        # Nothing yet; we fill in these values later.

EndSection
```

This section defines properties for a particular video card. `Identifier` is an arbitrary, descriptive string. You will use this string to refer to the card later.

Initially, you don't need to include anything in the `Device` section except the `Identifier`. We will use the X server itself to probe for the properties of the video card and enter them into the `Device` section later. The XFree86 server is capable of probing for the video chip set, clocks, RAMDAC, and amount of video RAM on the board. This is described on page 156.

Before we do this, however, we need to finish writing the `XF86Config` file. The next section is `Screen`, which specifies the monitor/video card combination to use for a particular server.

```
Section "Screen"
    Driver      "Accel"
    Device      "#9 GXE 64"
    Monitor     "CTX 5468 NI"
    Subsection "Display"
        Depth       16
        Modes       "1024x768" "800x600" "640x480"
        ViewPort    0 0
        Virtual     1024 768
    EndSubsection
EndSection
```

The `Driver` line specifies the X server that you will be using. Valid `Driver` values are:

- `Accel`: For the `XF86_S3`, `XF86_Mach32`, `XF86_Mach8`, `XF86_8514`, `XF86_P9000`, `XF86_AGX`, and `XF86_W32` servers;
- `SVGA`: For the `XF86_SVGA` server;
- `VGA16`: For the `XF86_VGA16` server;
- `VGA2`: For the `XF86_Mono` server;
- `Mono`: For the non-VGA monochrome drivers in the `XF86_Mono` and `XF86_VGA16` servers.

Be sure that `/usr/X11R6/bin/X` is a symbolic link to this server.

The `Device` line specifies the `Identifier` of the `Device` section that corresponds to the video card to use for this server. Above, we created a `Device` section with the line

```
Identifier "#9 GXE 64"
```

Therefore, we use `"#9 GXE 64"` on the `Device` line here.

Similarly, the `Monitor` line specifies the name of the `Monitor` section to be used with this server. Here, `"CTX 5468 NI"` is the `Identifier` used in the `Monitor` section described above.

`Subsection "Display"` defines several properties of the XFree86 server corresponding to your monitor/video card combination. The `XF86Config` file describes all of these options in detail. Most of them are not necessary to get the system working.

The options that you should know about are:

- `Depth`. Defines the number of color planes; that is, the number of bits per pixel. Usually, `Depth` is set to 8. For the `VGA16` server, you would use a depth of 4, and for the monochrome server a depth of 1. If you use an accelerated video card with enough memory to support more bits per pixel, you can set `Depth` to 16, 24, or 32. If you have problems with depths higher than 8, set it back to 8 and attempt to debug the problem later.

- `Modes`. This is the list of mode names which have been defined using the `ModeLine` directive(s) in the `Monitor` section. In the above section, we used `ModeLines` named `"1024x768"`, `"800x600"`, and `"640x48"`. Therefore, we use a `Modes` line of

  ```
  Modes    "1024x768" "800x600" "640x480"
  ```

  The first mode listed on this line is the default when XFree86 starts. After XFree86 is running, you can switch between the modes listed here using the keys `Ctrl`-`Alt`-`Numeric +` and `Ctrl`-`Alt`-`Numeric -`.

  It might be best, when you initially configure XFree86, to use lower resolution video modes like 640x480, which tend to work with most systems. Once you have the basic configuration working, you can modify `XF86Config` to support higher resolutions.

- `Virtual`. Set the virtual desktop size. XFree86 can use additional memory on your video card to extend the size of the desktop. When you move the mouse pointer to the edge of the display, the desktop scrolls, bringing the additional space into view. Even if you run the server at a lower video resolution like 800x600, you can set `Virtual` to the total resolution that your video card can support. A 1-megabyte video card can support 1024x768 at a depth of 8 bits per pixel; a 2-megabyte card 1280x1024 at depth 8, or 1024x768 at depth 16. Of course, the entire area will not be visible at once, but it can still be used.

  The `Virtual` feature is rather limited. If you want to use a true virtual desktop, `fvwm` and similar window managers allow you to have large, virtual desktops by hiding windows and using other techniques, instead of storing the entire desktop in video memory. See the manual pages for `fvwm` for more details about this. Many Linux systems use `fvwm` by default.

- `ViewPort`. If you are using the `Virtual` option which is described above, `ViewPort` sets the coordinates of the upper-left-hand corner of the virtual desktop when XFree86 starts up. `Virtual 0 0` is often used. If this is unspecified, then the desktop is centered on the virtual desktop display, which may be undesirable to you.

Many other options for this section exist; see the `XF86Config` manual page for a complete description. In practice, these options are not necessary to get XFree86 working initially.

Filling in video card information.

Your `XF86Config` file is now ready, with the exception of complete information on the video card. We'll use the X server to probe for this information, and add it to `XF86Config`.

Instead of probing for this information with the X server, `XF86Config` values for many cards are listed in the files `modeDB.txt`, `AccelCards`, and `Devices`. These files are all found in `/usr/X11R6/lib/X11/doc`. In addition, there are various `README` files for certain chip sets. You should look at these files for information on your video card and use that information (the clock values, chip set type, and any options) in the `XF86Config` file. If any information is missing, you can probe for it.

In most of these examples we demonstrate configuration of a #9 GXE 64 video card, which uses the `XF86_S3` chipset. First, determine the video chip set on the card. Running `SuperProbe` (found in `/usr/X11R6/bin`) tells you this information, but you need to know the chip set name as it is known to the X server.

To do this, run the command

```
X -showconfig
```

This gives the chip set names known to the X server. (The manual pages for each X server list these, too.) For example, with the accelerated `XF86_S3` server, we get:

```
XFree86 Version 3.1 / X Window System
(protocol Version 11, revision 0, vendor release 6000)
Operating System: Linux
```

```
Configured drivers:
  S3: accelerated server for S3 graphics adaptors (Patchlevel 0)
      mmio_928, s3_generic
```

The valid chip set names for this server are `mmio_928` and `s3_generic`. The `XF86_S3` man page describes these chip sets and video cards that use them. In the case of the #9 GXE 64 video card, `mmio_928` is appropriate.

If you don't know which chip set is in use, the X server can probe it for you. To do this, run the command

```
X -probeonly > /tmp/x.out 2>&1
```

if you use `bash` as your shell. If you use `csh`, try:

```
X -probeonly &> /tmp/x.out
```

You should run this command while the system is unloaded; that is, while no other activity occurs on the system. This command also probes for your video card dot clocks (as seen below), and system load can throw off this calculation.

The output from the above, in `/tmp/x.out`, should contain lines like:

```
XFree86 Version 3.1 / X Window System
(protocol Version 11, revision 0, vendor release 6000)
Operating System: Linux
Configured drivers:
  S3: accelerated server for S3 graphics adaptors (Patchlevel 0)
      mmio_928, s3_generic
Several lines deleted...
(--) S3: card type: 386/486 localbus
(--) S3: chipset:   864 rev. 0
(--) S3: chipset driver: mmio_928
```

Here, we see that the two valid chip sets for this server (in this case, `XF86_S3`) are `mmio_928` and `s3_generic`. The server probed for and found a video card that has the `mmio_928` chipset.

In the `Device` section of the `XF86Config` file, add a `Chipset` line that has the name of the chip set as determined above. For example,

```
Section "Device"
        # We already had Identifier here...
        Identifier "#9 GXE 64"
        # Add this line:
        Chipset "mmio_928"
EndSection
```

Now, we need to determine the driving clock frequencies used by the video card. A driving clock frequency, or dot clock, is simply a rate at which the video card can send pixels to the monitor. As described above, each monitor resolution has a dot clock associated with it. We need to determine which dot clocks are made available by the video card.

First, you should look at the documentation mentioned above and see if the card's clocks are listed there. The dot clocks are usually a list of 8 or 16 values, all of which are in MHz. For example, when looking at `modeDB.txt`, we see an entry for the Cardinal ET4000 video card, which looks like:

```
# chip    ram   virtual   clocks                                default-mode  flags
 ET4000   1024  1024 768   25  28  38  36  40  45  32   0  "1024x768"
```

The dot clocks for this card are 25, 28, 38, 36, 40, 45, 32, and 0 MHz.

In the `Devices` section of the `XF86Config` file, add a `Clocks` line containing the list of dot clocks for your card. For example, for the clocks above, add the line

```
Clocks 25 28 38 36 40 45 32 0
```

to the `Devices` section of the file, after `Chipset`.

◇ **The order of the dot clocks is important.** Don't re-sort the list or remove duplicates.

If you cannot find the dot clocks associated with your card, the X server can probe for these, too. Use `X -probeonly` as described above. The output should contain lines which look like the following:

```
(--) S3: clocks:  25.18  28.32  38.02  36.15  40.33  45.32  32.00  00.00
```

We can then add a `Clocks` line which contains all of these values, as printed. You can use more than one `Clocks` line in `XF86Config` if all of the values (sometimes there are more than 8 clock values printed) do not fit onto one line. Again, be sure to keep the list of clocks in the order that they are displayed.

◇ Be sure that there is no `Clocks` line (or that it is commented out) in the `Devices` section of the file when using `X -probeonly`. If there is a `Clocks` line present, the server does not probe for the clocks—it uses the values given in `XF86Config`.

Some video boards use a programmable clock chip. See the manual page for your X server or the XFree86 `README` file that describes your video card. The chip essentially allows the X server to tell the card the dot clocks to use. For video cards that have clock chips, you may not find a list of dot clocks for the card in any of the above files. Or, the list of dot clocks printed when using `X -probeonly` will only contain one or two discrete clock values, with the rest being duplicates or zero. Or, the X server may provide an explicit warning that the video card has a programmable clock chip, like:

```
(--) SVGA: cldg5434: Specifying a Clocks line makes no sense for this driver
```

This example is taken from a `XF86_SVGA` server running a Cirrus Logic PCI card.

For boards which use programmable clock chips, you use a `ClockChip` line instead of a `Clocks` line in the `XF86Config` file. `ClockChip` is the name of the clock chip as used by the video card; the manual pages for each server describe them. For example, in the file `README.S3`, we see that several S3-864 video cards use an "ICD2061A" clock chip, and that we should use the line

```
ClockChip "icd2061a"
```

instead of `Clocks` in the `XF86Config` file. As with `Clocks`, this line goes in the `Devices` section, after `Chipset`.

Similarly, some video cards require that you specify the RAMDAC chip type in the `XF86Config` file. This is done with a `Ramdac` line. The `XF86_Accel` man page describes this option. Often the X server will correctly probe for the RAMDAC.

Some video card types require that you specify several options in the `Devices` section of `XF86Config`. These options are described in the manual page for your server, as well as in the various files like `README.cirrus` and `README.S3`. These options are enabled using an `Option` line. For example, the #9 GXE 64 card requires two options:

```
Option "number_nine"
Option "dac_8_bit"
```

An X server may work without the `Option` lines, but they are necessary to get the best performance out of the card. There are too many options to list here. They are different for each card. If you must use one, the X server manual pages and various files in `/usr/X11R6/lib/X11/doc` will tell you what they are.

When you finish, you should have a `Devices` section that looks something like:

```
Section "Device"
        # Device section for the #9 GXE 64 only !
        Identifier "#9 GXE 64"
        Chipset "mmio_928"
        ClockChip "icd2061a"
        Option "number_nine"
        Option "dac_8_bit"
EndSection
```

There are other options which you can include in the `Devices` entry. The X server manual pages provide the gritty details.

Running XFree86.

With your `XF86Config` file configured, you can fire up the X server and give it a spin. Again, be sure that the `/usr/X11R6/bin` directory is on your path.

The command to start XFree86 is

```
startx
```

This is a front end to `xinit` (if you run `xinit` directly on other UNIX systems). It starts the X server and executes the commands in the file `.xinitrc` in your home directory. `.xinitrc` is a shell script that contains the command lines of the X clients to run when the X server starts. If this file does not exist, the system default `/usr/X11R6/lib/X11/xinit/xinitrc` is used.

A simple `.xinitrc` file looks like this:

```
#!/bin/sh

xterm -fn 7x13bold -geometry 80x32+10+50 &
xterm -fn 9x15bold -geometry 80x34+30-10 &
oclock -geometry 70x70-7+7 &
xsetroot -solid midnightblue &

exec twm
```

This script starts two `xterm` clients and an `oclock`, and sets the root window (background) color to `midnightblue`. It starts `twm`, the window manager. `twm` is executed with the shell's `exec` statement. This causes the `xinit` process to be replaced by `twm`. After the `twm` process exits, the X server shuts down. You can cause `twm` to exit by using the root menu. Depress mouse button 1 on the desktop background. This displays a pop-up menu that allows you to `Exit Twm`.

Be sure that the last command in `.xinitrc` is started with `exec`, and that it is not placed into the background (no ampersand at the end of the line). Otherwise the X server will shut down immediately after it starts the clients in the `.xinitrc` file.

Alternately, you can exit X by pressing `Ctrl`-`Alt`-`Backspace` in combination. This kills the X server directly, exiting the window system.

The above is a only a simple desktop configuration. Again, we suggest that you read a book like *The X Window System: A User's Guide* (see Appendix A). The possible variations of X usage and configuration are too many to describe here. The `xterm`, `oclock`, and `twm` manual pages will provide you clues on how to begin.

When you run into trouble.

Often, something will not be quite right when you first start the X server. This is nearly always caused by something in your `XF86Config` file. Usually, the monitor timing values or the video card dot clocks are set incorrectly. If the display seems to roll, or the edges are fuzzy, this indicates that the monitor timing values or dot clocks are wrong. Also, be sure that you correctly specified the video card chip set and options in the `Device` section of `XF86Config`. Be absolutely sure that you are using the correct X server and that `/usr/X11R6/bin/X` is a symbolic link to it.

If all else fails, try to start X "bare"; that is, with a command like:

```
X > /tmp/x.out 2>&1
```

You can then kill the X server (using `Ctrl`-`Alt`-`Backspace`) and examine the contents of `/tmp/x.out`. The X server reports any warnings or errors—for example, if your video card doesn't have a dot clock corresponding to a mode supported by your monitor.

The file `VideoModes.doc`, which is included in the XFree86 distribution, contains many hints for adjusting the values in your `XF86Config` file.

Remember that you can use `Ctrl`-`Alt`-`Numeric +` and `Ctrl`-`Alt`-`Numeric -` to switch between the video modes listed on the `Modes` line of the `Screen` section of `XF86Config`. If the highest resolution mode doesn't look right, try switching to a lower resolution. This lets you know, at least, that those parts of your X configuration are working correctly.

Also, adjust the vertical and horizontal size/hold knobs on your monitor. In many cases, it is necessary to adjust these when starting up X. For example, if the display seems to be shifted slightly to one side, you can usually correct this using the monitor controls.

Again, the USENET newsgroup `comp.windows.x.i386unix` is devoted to discussions about XFree86. It might be a good idea to read the newsgroups for postings related to video configuration. You might run across someone with the same problem.

There are also sample `XF86Config` files which have been contributed by users. Some of these are available on the `sunsite.unc.edu` archive in the `/pub/Linux/X11` directory, and elsewhere. You might find a configuration file that somebody has already written for your hardware.

Accessing MS-DOS files.

If, for some twisted and bizarre reason, you want to access files from MS-DOS, it's easily done under Linux.

The usual way to access MS-DOS files is to mount an MS-DOS partition or floppy under Linux, allowing you to access the files directly through the file system. For example, if you have an MS-DOS floppy in `/dev/fd0`, the command

```
# mount -t msdos /dev/fd0 /mnt
```

will mount it under `/mnt`. See Section 4 for more information on mounting floppies.

You can also mount an MS-DOS partition of your hard drive for access under Linux. If you have an MS-DOS partition on `/dev/hda1`, the command

```
# mount -t msdos /dev/hda1 /mnt
```

mounts it. Be sure to `umount` the partition when you're done using it. You can have a MS-DOS partition automatically mounted at boot time if you include the entry in `/etc/fstab`. See Section 4 for details. The following line in `/etc/fstab` will mount an MS-DOS partition on `/dev/hda1` on the directory `/dos`.

```
/dev/hda1     /dos     msdos     defaults
```

You can also mount the VFAT file systems that are used by Windows 95:

```
# mount -t vfat /dev/hda1 /mnt
```

This allows access to the long filenames of Windows 95. This only applies to partitions that actually have the long filenames stored. You can't mount a normal FAT16 file system and use this to get long filenames.

The Mtools software may also be used to access MS-DOS files. The commands `mcd`, `mdir`, and `mcopy` all behave like their MS-DOS counterparts. If you install Mtools, there should be manual pages available for these commands.

Accessing MS-DOS files is one thing; running MS-DOS programs is another. There is an MS-DOS Emulator under development for Linux; it is widely available, and included in most distributions. It can also be retrieved from a number of locations, including the various Linux FTP sites listed in Appendix C. The MS-DOS Emulator is reportedly powerful enough to run a number of applications, including WordPerfect, from Linux. However, Linux and MS-DOS are vastly different operating systems. The power of any MS-DOS emulator under UNIX is limited. In addition, a Microsoft Windows emulator that runs under X Windows is under development.

Networking with TCP/IP.

Linux supports a full implementation of the TCP/IP (Transport Control Protocol/Internet Protocol) networking protocols. TCP/IP has become the most successful mechanism for networking computers worldwide. With Linux and an Ethernet card, you can network your machine to a local area network, or (with the proper network connections) to the Internet—the worldwide TCP/IP network.

Hooking up a small LAN of UNIX machines is easy. It simply requires an Ethernet controller in each machine and the appropriate Ethernet cables and other hardware. Or, if your business or university provides access to the Internet, you can easily add your Linux machine to this network.

The current implementation of TCP/IP and related protocols for Linux is called "NET-3," and before that, "NET-2." This has no relationship to the so-called NET-2 release of BSD UNIX; instead, "NET-3" in this context means the second implementation of TCP/IP for Linux.

Linux NET-3 also supports SLIP—Serial Line Internet Protocol. SLIP allows you to have dialup Internet access using a modem. If your business or university provides SLIP access, you can dial in to the SLIP server and put your machine on the Internet over the phone line. Alternately, if your Linux machine also has Ethernet access to the Internet, you can set up your Linux box as a SLIP server.

For complete information on setting up TCP/IP under Linux, we encourage you to read the Linux NET-3 HOWTO, available via anonymous FTP from `sunsite.unc.edu`. The NET-3 HOWTO is a complete guide to configuring TCP/IP, including Ethernet and SLIP connections, under Linux. The Linux Ethernet HOWTO is a related document that describes configuration of various Ethernet card drivers for Linux. The *Linux Network Administrator's Guide*, from the Linux Documentation Project, is also available. See Appendix A for more information on these documents.

Also of interest is the book *TCP/IP Network Administration*, by Craig Hunt. It contains complete information on using and configuring TCP/IP on UNIX systems.

Hardware requirements.

You can use Linux TCP/IP without any networking hardware at all—configuring "loopback" mode allows you to talk to yourself. This is necessary for some applications and games which use the "loopback" network device.

However, if you want to use Linux with an Ethernet TCP/IP network, you need one of the following Ethernet cards: 3com 3c503, 3c503/16; Novell NE1000, NE2000; Western Digital WD8003, WD8013; Hewlett Packard HP27245, HP27247, HP27250.

The following clones are reported to work: WD-80x3 clones: LANNET LEC-45; NE2000 clones: Alta Combo, Artisoft LANtastic AE-2, Asante Etherpak 2001/2003, D-Link Ethernet II, LTC E-NET/16 P/N 8300-200-002, Network Solutions HE-203, SVEC 4 Dimension Ethernet, 4-Dimension FD0490 EtherBoard 16, and D-Link DE-600, SMC Elite 16.

There are a few common situations that you should watch out for concerning supported cards: 1) Several cards are supported but offer shoddy performance or have other restrictions. Examples are the 3Com 3C501 which works but gives absolutely horrible performance and the Racal-Interlan NI6510 using the AM7990 LANCE chip which doesn't work with more than 16 megabytes of RAM. In the same vein, many cards are NE1000/NE2000 compatible clones and can have various problems. See the Linux Ethernet HOWTO for a more complete discussion of Linux Ethernet hardware compatibility.

Linux also supports SLIP and PPP, which allows you to use a modem to access the Internet over the phone line. In this case, you'll need a modem compatible with your SLIP or PPP server—most servers require a 14.4bps V.32bis modem at a minimum . Performance is greatly improved with a 33.6bps or higher modem.

Configuring TCP/IP on your system.

In this section we're going to discuss how to configure an Ethernet TCP/IP connection on your system. Note that this method should work for many systems, but certainly not all. This discussion should be enough to get you on the right path to configuring the network parameters of your machine, but there are numerous caveats and fine details not mentioned here. We direct you to the *Linux Network Administrators' Guide* and the NET-3-HOWTO for more information.[2]

[2]Some of this information is adapted from the NET-3-HOWTO by Terry Dawson and Matt Welsh.

First of all, we assume that you have a Linux system that has the TCP/IP software installed. This includes basic clients such as `telnet` and `ftp`, system administration commands such as `ifconfig` and `route` (usually found in `/etc`), and networking configuration files (such as `/etc/hosts`). The other Linux-related networking documents described above explain how to go about installing the Linux networking software if you do not have it already.

We also assume that your kernel has been configured and compiled with TCP/IP support enabled. See Section 4 for information on compiling your kernel. To enable networking, you must answer "yes" to the appropriate questions during the `make config` step, and rebuild the kernel.

Once this has been done, you must modify a number of configuration files used by NET-3. For the most part this is a simple procedure. Unfortunately, however, there is wide disagreement between Linux distributions as to where the various TCP/IP configuration files and support programs should go. Much of the time, they can be found in `/etc`, but in other cases may be found in `/usr/etc`, `/usr/etc/inet`, or other bizarre locations. In the worst case you'll have to use the `find` command to locate the files on your system. Also note that not all distributions keep the NET-3 configuration files and software in the same location—they may be spread across several directories.

The following information applies primarily to Ethernet connections. If you're planning to use SLIP or PPP, read this section to understand the concepts, and follow the more specific instructions in the following sections.

Your network configuration. Before you can configure TCP/IP, you need to determine the following information about your network setup. In most cases, your local network administrator can provide you with this information.

- IP address. This is the unique machine address in dotted-decimal format. An example is 128.253.153.54. Your network administrators will provide you with this number.

  If you're only configuring loopback mode (i.e. no SLIP, no Ethernet card, just TCP/IP connections to your own machine) then your IP address is 127.0.0.1.

- Your network mask ("netmask"). This is a dotted quad, similar to the IP address, which determines which portion of the IP address specifies the subnetwork number, and which portion specifies the host on that subnet. (If you're shaky on these TCP/IP networking terms, we suggest reading some introductory material on network administration.) The network mask is a pattern of bits, which when overlaid onto an address on your network, will tell you which subnet that address lives on. This is very important for routing, and if you find, for example, that you can happily talk to people outside your network, but not to some people within your network, there is a good chance that you have an incorrect mask specified.

  Your network administrators will have chosen the netmask when the network was designed, and therefore they should be able to supply you with the correct mask to use. Most networks are class C subnetworks which use 255.255.255.0 as their netmask. Other Class B networks use 255.255.0.0. The NET-3 code will automatically select a mask that assumes no subnetting as a default if you do not specify one.

  This applies as well to the loopback port. Since the loopback port's address is always 127.0.0.1, the netmask for this port is always 255.0.0.0. You can either specify this explicitly or rely on the default mask.

- Your network address. This is your IP address masked bitwise-ANDed with the netmask. For example, if your netmask is 255.255.255.0, and your IP address is 128.253.154.32, your network address is 128.253.154.0. With a netmask of 255.255.0.0, this would be 128.253.0.0.

  If you're only using loopback, you don't have a network address.

- Your broadcast address. The broadcast address is used to broadcast packets to every machine on your subnet. Therefore, if the host number of machines on your subnet is given by the last byte of the IP address (netmask 255.255.255.0), your broadcast address will be your network address ORed with 0.0.0.255.

For example, if your IP address is 128.253.154.32, and your netmask is 255.255.255.0, your broadcast address is 128.253.154.255.

Note that for historical reasons, some networks are set up to use the network address as the broadcast address. If you have any doubt, check with your network administrators. (In many cases, it will suffice to duplicate the network configuration of other machines on your subnet, substituting your own IP address, of course.)

If you're only using loopback, you don't have a broadcast address.

- Your gateway address. This is the address of the machine which is your "gateway" to the outside world (i.e., machines not on your subnet). In many cases the gateway machine has an IP address identical to yours but with a ".1" as its host address; e.g., if your IP address is 128.253.154.32, your gateway might be 128.253.154.1. Your network administrators will provide you with the IP address of your gateway.

  In fact, you may have multiple gateways. A *gateway* is simply a machine that lives on two different networks (has IP addresses on different subnets), and routes packets between them. Many networks have a single gateway to "the outside world" (the network directly adjacent to your own), but in some cases you will have multiple gateways—one for each adjacent network.

  If you're only using loopback, you don't have a gateway address. The same is true if your network is isolated from all others.

- Your name server address. Most machines on the net have a name server which translates host names into IP addresses for them. Your network admins will tell you the address of your name server. You can also run a server on your own machine by running `named`, in which case the name server address is 127.0.0.1. Unless you absolutely must run your own name server, we suggest using the one provided to you on the network (if any). Configuration of `named` is another issue altogether; our priority at this point is to get you talking to the network. You can deal with name resolution issues later.

  If you're only using loopback, you don't have a name server address.

SLIP users: You may or may not require any of the above information, except for a name server address. When using SLIP, your IP address is usually determined in one of two ways: Either (a) you have a "static" IP address, which is the same every time you connect to the network, or (b) you have a "dynamic" IP address, which is allocated from a pool available addresses when you connect to the server. In the following section on SLIP configuration, this is covered in more detail.

NET-3 supports full routing, multiple routes, subnetworking (at this stage on byte boundaries only), the whole nine yards. The above describes most basic TCP/IP configurations. Yours may be quite different: when in doubt, consult your local network gurus and check out the man pages for `route` and `ifconfig`. Configuring TCP/IP networks is very much beyond the scope of this book; the above should be enough to get most people started.

The networking `rc` files. `rc` files are systemwide configuration scripts executed at boot time by `init`, which start up all of the basic system daemons (such as `sendmail`, `cron`, etc.) and configure things such as the network parameters, system host name, and so on. `rc` files are usually found in the directory `/etc/rc.d` but on other systems may be in `/etc`. In general Slackware distributions use the files `rc.inet1, etc` in `/etc/rc.d` whereas the Red Hat distributions use a series of directories

Here, we're going to describe the `rc` files used to configure TCP/IP. There are two of them: `rc.inet1` and `rc.inet2`. `rc.inet1` is used to configure the basic network parameters (such as IP addresses and routing information). `rc.inet2` fires up the TCP/IP daemons (`telnetd`, `ftpd`, and so forth).

Many systems combine these two files into one, usually called `rc.inet` or `rc.net`. The names given to your `rc` files doesn't matter, as long as they perform the correct functions and are executed at boot time by `init`. To ensure this, you may need to edit `/etc/inittab` and uncomment lines to execute the appropriate `rc` file(s). In the worst case you will have to create the `rc.inet1` and `rc.inet2` files from scratch and add entries for them to `/etc/inittab`.

As we said, `rc.inet1` configures the basic network interface. This includes your IP and network address, and the routing table information for your network. The routing tables are used to route outgoing (and incoming) network datagrams to other machines. On most simple configurations, you have three routes: One for sending packets to your own machine, another for sending packets to other machines on your network, and another for sending packets to machines outside of your network (through the gateway machine). Two programs are used to configure these parameters: `ifconfig` and `route`. Both of these are usually found in `/etc`.

`ifconfig` is used for configuring the network device interface with the parameters it requires to function, such as the IP address, network mask, broadcast address and the like. `Route` is used to create and modify entries in the routing table.

For most configurations, an `rc.inet1` file that looks like the following should work. You will, of course, have to edit this for your own system. Do *not* use the sample IP and network addresses listed here for your own system; they correspond to an actual machine on the Internet.

```
#!/bin/sh
# This is /etc/rc.d/rc.inet1 -- Configure the TCP/IP interfaces

# First, configure the loopback device

HOSTNAME='host name'

/etc/ifconfig lo 127.0.0.1       # uses default netmask 255.0.0.0
/etc/route add 127.0.0.1         # a route to point to the loopback device

# Next, configure the ethernet device. If you're only using loopback or
# SLIP, comment out the rest of these lines.

# Edit for your setup.
IPADDR="128.253.154.32"          # REPLACE with YOUR IP address
NETMASK="255.255.255.0"          # REPLACE with YOUR netmask
NETWORK="128.253.154.0"          # REPLACE with YOUR network address
BROADCAST="128.253.154.255"      # REPLACE with YOUR broadcast address, if you
                                 # have one. If not, leave blank and edit below.
GATEWAY="128.253.154.1"          # REPLACE with YOUR gateway address!

/etc/ifconfig eth0 ${IPADDR} netmask ${NETMASK} broadcast ${BROADCAST}

# If you don't have a broadcast address, change the above line to just:
# /etc/ifconfig eth0 ${IPADDR} netmask ${NETMASK}

/etc/route add ${NETWORK}

# The following is only necessary if you have a gateway; that is, your
# network is connected to the outside world.
/etc/route add default gw ${GATEWAY} metric 1

# End of Ethernet Configuration
```

Again, you may have to tweak this file somewhat to get it to work. The above should be sufficient for the majority of simple network configurations, but certainly not all.

`rc.inet2` starts up various servers used by the TCP/IP suite. The most important of these is `inetd`. `Inetd` sits in the background and listens to various network ports. When a machine tries to make a connection to a certain port (for example, the incoming `telnet` port), `inetd` forks off a copy of the appropriate daemon for that port (in the case of the `telnet` port, `inetd` starts `in.telnetd`). This is simpler than running many separate, stand-alone daemons (e.g., individual copies of `telnetd`, `ftpd`, and so forth)—`inetd` starts up the daemons only when they are needed.

`Syslogd` is the system logging daemon—it accumulates log messages from various applications and stores them into log files based on the configuration information in `/etc/syslogd.conf`. `routed` is a server used to maintain dynamic routing information. When your system attempts to send packets to another network, it may require additional routing table entries in order to do so. `routed` takes care of manipulating the routing table without the need for user intervention.

Our example `rc.inet2`, below, only starts up the bare minimum of servers. There are many other servers as well—many of which have to do with NFS configuration. When attempting to setup TCP/IP on your system, it's usually best to start with a minimal configuration and add more complex pieces (such as NFS) when you have things working.

Note that in the below file, we assume that all of the network daemons are held in `/etc`. As usual, edit this for your own configuration.

```
#! /bin/sh
# Sample /etc/rc.d/rc.inet2

# Start syslogd
if [ -f /etc/syslogd ]
then
        /etc/syslogd
fi

# Start inetd
if [ -f /etc/inetd ]
then
        /etc/inetd
fi

# Start routed
if [ -f /etc/routed ]
then
        /etc/routed -q
fi

# Done!
```

Among the various additional servers that you may want to start in `rc.inet2` is `named`, a name server—it is responsible for translating (local) IP addresses to names, and vice versa. If you don't have a name server elsewhere on the network, or want to provide local machine names to other machines in your domain, it may be necessary to run `named`. (For most configurations it is not necessary, however.) `named` configuration is somewhat complex and requires planning; we refer interested readers to a good book on TCP/IP network administration.

The `/etc/hosts` file. `/etc/hosts` contains a list of IP addresses and the host names that they correspond to. In general, `/etc/hosts` only contains entries for your local machine, and perhaps other "important" machines (such as your name server or gateway). Your local name server will provide address-to-name mappings for other machines on the network, transparently.

For example, if your machine is `loomer.vpizza.com` with the IP address 128.253.154.32, your `/etc/hosts` would look like:

```
127.0.0.1              localhost
128.253.154.32         loomer.vpizza.com loomer
```

If you're only using loopback, the only line in `/etc/hosts` should be for 127.0.0.1, with both `localhost` and your host name after it.

The `/etc/networks` file. The `/etc/networks` file lists the names and addresses of your own, and other, networks. It is used by the `route` command, and allows you to specify a network by name, should you so desire.

Every network you wish to add a route to using the `route` command (generally called from `rc.inet1`—see above) must have an entry in `/etc/networks`.

As an example,

```
default 0.0.0.0 # default route    - mandatory
loopnet 127.0.0.0 # loopback network - mandatory
mynet 128.253.154.0 # Modify for your own network address
```

The /etc/host.conf **file.** This file is used to specify how your system will resolve host names. It should contain the two lines:

```
order hosts,bind
multi on
```

These lines tell the resolve libraries to first check the /etc/hosts file for any names to lookup, and then to ask the name server (if one is present). The multi entry allows you to have multiple IP addresses for a given machine name in /etc/hosts.

The /etc/resolv.conf **file.** This file configures the name resolver, specifying the address of your name server (if any) and your domain name. Your domain name is your fully-qualified host name (if you're a registered machine on the Internet, for example), with the host name chopped off. That is, if your full host name is loomer.vpizza.com, your domain name is just vpizza.com.

For example, if your machine is goober.norelco.com, and has a name server at the address 128.253.154.5, your /etc/resolv.conf would look like:

```
domain      norelco.com
nameserver  127.253.154.5
```

You can specify more than one name server—each must have a nameserver line of its own in resolv.conf.

Setting your host name. You should set your system host name with the hostname command. This is usually called from /etc/rc or /etc/rc.local; simply search your system rc files to determine where it is invoked. For example, if your (full) host name is loomer.vpizza.com, edit the appropriate rc file to execute the command:

```
/bin/hostname loomer.vpizza.com
```

Note that the hostname executable may not be found in /bin on your system.

Trying it out. Once you have all of these files set up, you should be able to reboot your new kernel and attempt to use the network. There are many places where things can go wrong, so it's a good idea to test individual aspects of the network configuration (e.g., it's probably not a good idea to test your network configuration by firing up Mosaic over a network-based X connection).

You can use the netstat command to display your routing tables; this is usually the source of the most trouble. The netstat man page describes the exact syntax of this command in detail. In order to test network connectivity, we suggest using a client such as telnet to connect to machines both on your local subnetwork and external networks. This will help to narrow down the source of the problem. (For example, if you're unable to connect to local machines, but can connect to machines on other networks, more than likely there is a problem with your netmask and routing table configuration). You can also invoke the route command directly (as root) to play with the entries in your routing table.

You should also test network connectivity by specifying IP addresses directly, instead of host names. For example, if you have problems with the command

```
$ telnet shoop.vpizza.com
```

the cause may be incorrect name server configuration. Try using the actual IP address of the machine in question; if that works, then you know your basic network setup is (more than likely) correct, and the problem lies in your specification of the name server address.

Debugging network configurations can be a difficult task, and we can't begin to cover it here. If you are unable to get help from a local guru we strongly suggest reading the *Linux Network Administrators' Guide* from the LDP.

SLIP configuration.

SLIP (Serial Line Internet Protocol) allows you to use TCP/IP over a serial line, be that a phone line, with a dialup modem, or a leased asynchronous line of some sort. Of course, to use SLIP you'll need access to a dial-in SLIP server in your area. Many universities and businesses provide SLIP access for a modest fee.

There are two major SLIP-related programs available—`dip` and `slattach`. Both of these programs are used to initiate a SLIP connection over a serial device. It is necessary to use one of these programs in order to enable SLIP—it will not suffice to dial up the SLIP server (with a communications program such as `kermit`) and issue `ifconfig` and `route` commands. This is because `dip` and `slattach` issue a special *ioctl()* system call to seize control of the serial device to be used as a SLIP interface.

`dip` can be used to dial up a SLIP server, do some handshaking to login to the server (exchanging your user name and password, for example) and then initiate the SLIP connection over the open serial line. `slattach`, on the other hand, does very little other than grab the serial device for use by SLIP. It is useful if you have a permanent line to your SLIP server and no modem dialup or handshaking is necessary to initiate the connection. Most dialup SLIP users should use `dip`, on the other hand.

`dip` can also be used to configure your Linux system as a SLIP server, where other machines can dial into your own and connect to the network through a secondary Ethernet connection on your machine. See the documentation and man pages for `dip` for more information on this procedure.

SLIP is quite unlike Ethernet, in that there are only two machines on the "network"—the SLIP host (that's you) and the SLIP server. For this reason, SLIP is often referred to as a "point-to-point" connection. A generalization of this idea, known as PPP (Point to Point Protocol) has also been implemented for Linux.

When you initiate a connection to a SLIP server, the SLIP server will give you an IP address based on (usually) one of two methods. Some SLIP servers allocate "static" IP addresses—in which case your IP address will be the same every time you connect to the server. However, many SLIP servers allocate IP addresses dynamically—in which case you receive a different IP address each time you connect. In general, the SLIP server will print the values of your IP and gateway addresses when you connect. `dip` is capable of reading these values from the output of the SLIP server login session and using them to configure the SLIP device.

Essentially, configuring a SLIP connection is just like configuring for loopback or ethernet. The main differences are discussed below. Read the previous section on configuring the basic TCP/IP files, and apply the changes described below.

Static IP address SLIP connections using `dip`. If you are using a static-allocation SLIP server, you may want to include entries for your IP address and host name in `/etc/hosts`. Also, configure these files listed in the above section: `rc.inet2`, `host.conf`, and `resolv.conf`.

Also, configure `rc.inet1`, as described above. However, you only want to execute `ifconfig` and `route` commands for the loopback device. If you use `dip` to connect to the SLIP server, it will execute the appropriate `ifconfig` and `route` commands for the SLIP device for you. (If you're using `slattach`, on the other hand, you *will* need to include `ifconfig`/`route` commands in `rc.inet1` for the SLIP device—see below.)

`dip` should configure your routing tables appropriately for the SLIP connection when you connect. In some cases, however, `dip`'s behavior may not be correct for your configuration, and you'll have to run `ifconfig` or `route` commands by hand after connecting to the server with `dip` (this is most easily done from within a shell script that runs `dip` and immediately executes the appropriate configuration commands). Your gateway is, in most cases, the address of the SLIP server. You may know this address before hand, or the gateway address will be printed by the SLIP server when you connect. Your `dip` chat script (described below) can obtain this information from the SLIP server.

`ifconfig` may require use of the `pointopoint` argument, if `dip` doesn't configure the interface correctly. For example, if your SLIP server address is 128.253.154.2, and your IP address is 128.253.154.32, you may need to run the command

```
ifconfig sl0 128.253.154.32 pointopoint 128.253.154.2
```

as `root`, after connecting with `dip`. The man pages for `ifconfig` will come in handy.

Note that SLIP device names used with the `ifconfig` and `route` commands are `sl0`, `sl1` and so on (as opposed to `eth0`, `eth1`, etc. for Ethernet devices).

On page 168, below, we explain how to configure `dip` to connect to the SLIP server.

Static IP address SLIP connections using slattach. If you have a leased line or cable running directly to your SLIP server, then there is no need to use dip to initiate a connection. slattach can be used to configure the SLIP device instead.

In this case, your /etc/rc.inet1 file should look something like the following:

```
#!/bin/sh
IPADDR="128.253.154.32"           # Replace with your IP address
REMADDR="128.253.154.2" # Replace with your SLIP server address

# Modify the following for the appropriate serial device for the SLIP
# connection:
slattach -p cslip -s 19200 /dev/ttyS0
/etc/ifconfig sl0 $IPADDR pointopoint $REMADDR up
/etc/route add default gw $REMADDR
```

slattach allocates the first unallocated SLIP device (sl0, sl1, etc.) to the serial line specified.

Note that the first parameter to slattach is the SLIP protocol to use. At present the only valid values are slip and cslip. slip is regular SLIP, as you would expect, and cslip is SLIP with datagram header compression. In most cases you should use cslip; however, if you seem to be having problems with this, try slip.

If you have more than one SLIP interface then you will have routing considerations to make. You will have to decide what routes to add, and those decisions can only be made on the basis of the actual layout of your network connections. A book on TCP/IP network configuration, as well as the man pages to route, will be of use.

Dynamic IP address SLIP connections using dip. If your SLIP server allocates an IP address dynamically, then you certainly don't know your address in advance—therefore, you can't include an entry for it in /etc/hosts. (You should, however, include an entry for your host with the loopback address, 127.0.0.1.)

Many SLIP servers print your IP address (as well as the server's address) when you connect. For example, one type of SLIP server prints a string such as,

```
Your IP address is 128.253.154.44.
Server address is 128.253.154.2.
```

dip can capture these numbers from the output of the server and use them to configure the SLIP device.

See page 167, above, for information on configuring your various TCP/IP files for use with SLIP. Below, we explain how to configure dip to connect to the SLIP server.

Using dip.

dip can simplify the process of connecting to a SLIP server, logging in, and configuring the SLIP device. Unless you have a leased line running to your SLIP server, dip is the way to go.

To use dip, you'll need to write a "chat script" which contains a list of commands to communicate with the SLIP server at login time. These commands can automatically send your user name and password to the server, as well as get information on your IP address from the server.

Here is an example dip chat script, for use with a dynamic IP address server. For static servers, you will need to set the variables $local and $remote to the values of your local IP address and server IP address, respectively, at the top of the script. See the dip man page for details.

```
main:
  # Set Maximum Transfer Unit. This is the maximum size of packets
  # transmitted on the SLIP device. Many SLIP servers use either 1500 or
  # 1006; check with your network admins when in doubt.
  get $mtu 1500

  # Make the SLIP route the default route on your system.
  default
```

```
    # Set the desired serial port and speed.
    port cua03
    speed 38400

    # Reset the modem and terminal line. If this causes trouble for you,
    # comment it out.
    reset

    # Prepare for dialing. Replace the following with your
    # modem initialization string.
    send ATT&C1&D2\\N3&Q5%M3%C1N1W1L1S48=7\r
    wait OK 2
    if $errlvl != 0 goto error
    # Dial the SLIP server
    dial 2546000
    if $errlvl != 0 goto error
    wait CONNECT 60
    if $errlvl != 0 goto error

    # We are connected.  Login to the system.
login:
    sleep 3
    send \r\n\r\n
    # Wait for the login prompt
    wait login: 10
    if $errlvl != 0 goto error

    # Send your user name
    send USERNAME\n

    # Wait for password prompt
    wait ord: 5
    if $errlvl != 0 goto error

    # Send password.
    send PASSWORD\n

    # Wait for SLIP server ready prompt
    wait annex: 30
    if $errlvl != 0 goto error

    # Send commands to SLIP server to initiate connection.
    send slip\n
    wait Annex 30

    # Get the remote IP address from the SLIP server. The 'get...remote'
    # command reads text in the form xxx.xxx.xxx.xxx, and assigns it
    # to the variable given as the second argument (here, $remote).
    get $remote remote
    if $errlvl != 0 goto error
    wait Your 30

    # Get local IP address from SLIP server, assign to variable $local.
    get $local remote
    if $errlvl != 0 goto error

    # Fire up the SLIP connection
done:
```

```
    print CONNECTED to $remote at $rmtip
    print GATEWAY address $rmtip
    print LOCAL address $local
    mode SLIP
    goto exit
  error:
    print SLIP to $remote failed.

  exit:
```

dip automatically executes ifconfig and route commands based on the values of the variables $local and $remote. Here, those variables are assigned using the get...remote command, which obtains text from the SLIP server and assigns it to the named variable.

If the ifconfig and route commands that dip runs for you don't work, you can either run the correct commands in a shell script after executing dip, or modify the source for dip itself. Running dip with the -v option will print debugging information while the connection is being set up, which should help you to determine where things might be going awry.

Now, in order to run dip and open the SLIP connection, you can use a command such as:

```
/etc/dip/dip -v /etc/dip/mychat 2>&1
```

Where the various dip files, and the chat script (mychat.dip), are stored in /etc/dip.

The above discussion should be enough to get you well on your way to talking to the network, either via Ethernet or SLIP. Again, we strongly suggest looking into a book on TCP/IP network configuration, especially if your network has any special routing considerations, other than those mentioned here.

Dial-up networking with PPP.

Linux supports a full implementation of the PPP (Point-to-Point) networking protocols. PPP is a mechanism for creating and running IP (the Internet Protocol) and other network protocols over a serial connection (using a null modem cable), over a telnet link or a link using modems and telephone lines (and of course using digital lines such as ISDN). This section only covers configuring PPP as a client connecting via an analog modem to a remote machine that provides PPP dialup service.

For complete information on setting up PPP under Linux, we encourage you to read the Linux PPP HOWTO, available via anonymous FTP from sunsite.unc.edu. The PPP HOWTO is a complete guide to configuring PPP, including modem, ISDN, and null modem cables, under Linux. Much of the information in this section was gleaned from this document. The *Linux Network Administrator's Guide*, from the Linux Documentation Project, is also available. See Appendix A for more information on these documents.

What you need to get started.

We assume that your kernel has been configured and compiled with TCP/IP support enabled. See Section 4 for information on compiling your kernel. To enable networking, you must answer "yes" to the appropriate questions during the make config step, and rebuild the kernel. We also assume that ppp has been compiled and installed on your system as well. We assume that you are using a Linux 1.2.x kernel with the PPP 2.1.2 software or Linux 1.3.X/2.0.x and PPP 2.2.0. At the time of writing, the latest official version of PPP available for Linux is ppp-2.2f. Please see the kerneld mini-HOWTO if you plan to use modules to load ppp into your kernel. *It is highly recommended that you use a version of the Linux kernel and the appropriate PPP version that are known to be stable together.*

You should also read

- the documentation that comes with the PPP package;
- the pppd and chat manual pages (use man chat and man pppd to explore these);
- the Linux Network Administration Guide (NAG);

- the Net-2/3 HOWTO;
- Linux kernel documentation installed in /usr/src/linux/Documentation when you install the Linux source code;
- The modem setup information page—see Modem Setup Information (http://www.in.net/info/modems/index.html)
- The excellent Unix and Linux books published by O'Reilly and Associates. See O'Reilly and Associates' on-Line catalog (`http://www.ora.com/`). If you are new to Unix or Linux, run (don't walk) to your nearest computer book shop and invest in a number of these immediately!
- The PPP FAQ (available from ftp://sunsite.unc.edu/pub/Linux/docs/faqs; see Appendix C). This contains a great deal of useful information in question/answer format that is very useful when working out why PPP is not working (properly).

An overview of the steps involved.

There are several steps to setting up your system to use PPP. We recommend that you read through all of these steps thoroughly before attempting to actually bring up a PPP connection. Each of these steps will be discussed in detail later.

1. Make sure that TCP/IP support is compiled into your kernel.
2. Make sure that PPP support is compiled into your kernel either statically or as a loadable module.
3. Make sure that PPP software is compiled and installed on your systems.
4. Make sure that you have a modem attached and configured for your computer, and that you know which serial port the modem is assigned to.
5. Make sure you have the following information from your PPP dialup server provider (usually an ISP)
   - The phone number you will dial to connect to the remote PPP dialup service provider.
   - Whether or not you are using dynamic or static IP assignment. If the latter, you will need to know that static IP number.
   - The IP address of the DNS (Domain Name Service) server that you will be using to resolve host names when connected

Make sure that the kernel has TCP/IP support. Linux PPP operations come in two parts: 1) the PPP daemon and kernel support for PPP. Most distributions seem to provide PPP kernel support in their default installation kernels, but others do not. You should make sure that TCP/IP is compiled into your kernel. You can do this by issuing the following command:

```
grep -i "TCP/IP" /var/adm/messages
```

If you get a line similar to

```
Jun  8 09:52:08 gemini kernel: Swansea University Computer Society TCP/IP for NET3.019
```

then you have TCP/IP support compiled in. You can also look for the above information on the console while Linux is booting. On many fast machines, this scrolls by too quickly. You can use `Shift`-`PageUp` to scroll the screen up and see this.

Make sure that the kernel has PPP support. If at boot your kernel reports messages like

```
PPP Dynamic channel allocation code copyright 1995 Caldera, Inc.
PPP line discipline registered.
```

then your kernel has PPP support. You can also issue the command

```
# grep -i "PPP" /var/adm/messages
```

If you get a line similar to

```
Jun  8 09:52:08 gemini kernel: PPP: version 0.2.7 (4 channels) NEW_TTY_DRIVERS O PTIMIZE_FLAGS
```

that means PPP support is present.

Make sure that you have a modem configured. You should make sure that your modem is correctly set up and that you know which serial port it is connected to.

- DOS COM1: = Linux /dev/cua0 (and /dev/ttyS0).
- DOS COM2: = Linux /dev/cua1 (and /dev/ttyS1), et cetera.

Historically, Linux used `/dev/cua`*x* devices for dial out and `/dev/ttyS`*x* devices for dial in. The kernel code that required this was changed in kernel version 2.0.*x* and you should now use `/dev/ttyS`*x* for both dial in and dial out. The `/dev/cua`*x* device names may well disappear in future kernel versions.

If you are using a high speed (external) modem (14,400 Baud or above), your serial port needs to be capable of handling the throughput that such a modem is capable of producing, particularly when the modems are compressing the data.

This requires your serial port to have a modern UART (Universal Asynchronous Receiver Transmitter) such as a 16550(A). If you are using an old machine (or old serial card), it is quite possible that your serial port has only an 8250 UART, which will cause you considerable problems when used with a high speed modem.

Use the command

```
# setserial -a /dev/ttyS⟨x⟩
```

to get Linux to report to you the type of UART you have. If you do not have a 16550A type UART, invest in a new serial card (available for under $50).

◇ You will need to configure your modem correctly for PPP—to do this **Read your modem manual!** Most modems come with a factory default setting that selects the options required for PPP. The recommended configuration specifies (in standard Hayes commands):

- Hardware flow control (RTS/CTS) (&K3 on many Hayes modems);
- E1 Command/usr/src/linux-2.0.27/include/linux/serial.h Echo ON (required for chat to operate);
- Q0 Report result codes (required for chat to operate);
- S0=0 Auto Answer OFF (unless you want your modem to answer the phone);
- &C1 Carrier Detect ON only after connect;
- &S0 Data Set Ready (DSR) always ON;
- (depends) Data Terminal Ready.

There is a site offering sample configurations for a growing variety of modem makes and models at http://www.in.net/info/modems/index.html which may assist you in this.

Use your communications software (e.g. `minicom` or `seyon`) to find out about your modem configuration and set it to what is required for PPP. Many modems report their current settings in response to AT&V, but you should consult your modem manual.

If you completely mess up the settings, you can return to sanity (usually) by issuing an AT&F—return to factory settings. (For most modem modems I have encountered, the factory settings include all you need for PPP—but you should check).

Once you have worked out the modem setup string, write it down. You now have a decision: you can store these settings in your modem non-volatile memory so they can be recalled by issuing the appropriate AT command, you can pass the correct settings to your modem as part of the PPP dialing process.

If you only use your modem from Linux to call into your ISP or corporate server, the simplest set up will have you save your modem configuration in non-volatile RAM.

If on the other hand, your modem is used by other applications and operating systems, it is safest to pass this information to the modem as each call is made so that the modem is guaranteed to be in the correct state for the call. (This has the added advantage also of recording the modem setup string in case the modem looses the contents of its NV-RAM, which can indeed happen).

ISP information. Before you can establish your PPP connection with a remote server, you need to obtain the following information from the system administrator or technical support people of the ISP.

- The telephone number(s) to dial for the service If you are behind a PABX, you also need the PABX number that gives you an outside dial tone—this is frequently digit zero (0) or nine (9).

- Does the server use dynamic or static IP numbers? If the server uses static IP numbers, then you may need to know what IP number to use for your end of the PPP connection. If your ISP is providing you with a subnet of valid IP numbers, you will need to know the IP numbers you can use and the network mask (netmask).

  Most Internet Service Providers use dynamic IP numbers. As mentioned above, this has some implications in terms of the services you can use.

  However, even if you are using static IP numbers, most PPP servers will never (for security reasons) allow the client to specify an IP number as this is a security risk. You do still need to know this information.

- What are the IP numbers of the ISP's Domain Name Servers? There should be at least two although only one is needed.

  There could be a problem here. The MS Windows 95 PPP setup allows the DNS address to be passed to the client as part of its connection process. So your ISP (or corporate help desk) may well tell you you don't need the IP address of the DNS server(s).

  For Linux, you do need the address of at least one DNS. The Linux implementation of PPP does not allow the setting of the DNS IP number dynamically at connection time—and quite possibly will never do so.

- Does the server require the use of PAP/CHAP? If this is the case you need to know the "id" and "secret" you are to use in connecting. (These are probably your user name and password at your ISP).

- Does the server automatically start PPP or do you need to issue any commands to start PPP on the server once you are logged in? If you must issue a command to start PPP, what is it?

- Is the server a Microsoft Windows NT system and, if so, is it using the MS PAP/CHAP system? Many corporate LAN's seem to use MS Windows NT this way for increased security.

Every device that connects to the Internet must have its own, unique IP number. These are assigned centrally by a designated authority for each country. Therefore to use a PPP connection, you must have an IP assigned to you. Due to the increased number of machines on the Internet (partly do the large number of

PPP users), a dynamic scheme has been developed for PPP that provides an IP on the fly to your machine when it first establishes the PPP connection. This means that you will have a different IP address every time you connect to the remote PPP dialup service. This is the most common method for most ISP's. The other method is to use a static IP. You cannot just choose an IP to use. It must be assigned by the centralized agency in charge of issuing IP numbers. This prevents two computers from having the same IP address and causing problems on the Internet. The remote PPP dialup service provider will be able to tell you if you are using a static or dynamic IP and also provide you with the actual IP number if you are using the static method.

It is important to note that if you are using dynamic IP assignment, it will be very very difficult to provide any permanent Internet services such as World Wide Web servers, gopher services, or Internet Relay Chat servers. You can still use such services that are on other machines but cannot offer such services on your machine without going through an extreme amount of effort. Doing this beyond the scope of this document.

PAP and CHAP are different, commonly used authentication methods. Linux supports both of them.

Testing your modem and remote service. Now that you have sorted out the serial port and modem settings, it is a good idea to make sure that these settings do indeed work by dialing your ISP and seeing if you can connect.

Using you terminal communications package (`minicom` or `seyon`), set up the modem initialization required for PPP and dial into the PPP server you want to connect to with a PPP session.

(Note: at this stage we are not trying to make a PPP connection—just establishing that we have the right phone number and also to find out exactly what the server sends to us in order to get logged in and start PPP).

During this process, either capture (log to a file) the entire login process or carefully (very carefully) write down exactly what prompts the server gives to let you know it is time to enter your user name and password (and any other commands needed to establish the PPP connection).

If your server uses PAP, you should not see a login prompt, but should instead see the (text representation) of the link control protocol (which looks like garbage) starting on your screen.

A few words of warning:-

- Some servers are quite intelligent: you can log in using text based user name/passwords or using PAP. So if your ISP or corporate site uses PAP but you do not see the garbage start up immediately, this may not mean you have done something wrong.
- Some servers require you to enter some text initially and then start a standard PAP sequence.
- Some PPP servers are passive—that is they simply sit there sending nothing until the client that is dialing in sends them a valid link control protocol (LCP) packet. If the PPP server you are connecting to operates in passive mode, you will never see the garbage.
- Some servers do not start PPP until you press Enter—so it is worth trying this if you correctly log in and do not see the garbage!

It is worth dialing in at least twice—some servers change their prompts (e.g. with the time!) every time you log in. The two critical prompts your Linux box needs to be able to identify every time you dial in are:

- the prompt that requests you to enter your user name;
- the prompt that requests you to enter your password.

If you have to issue a command to start PPP on the server, you will also need to find out the prompt the server gives you once you are logged in to tell you that you can now enter the command to start PPP.

If your server automatically starts PPP, once you have logged in, you will start to see garbage on your screen—this is the PPP server sending your machine information to start up and configure the PPP connection.

This should look something like this :

```
y}#.!}!}!} }8}!}}U}"}\&} } } } }}\& ...}'}"}(}"} .~~y}
```

On some systems, PPP must be explicitly started on the server. This is usually because the server has been set up to allow PPP logins and shell logins using the same user name and password pair. If this is the case, issue this command once you have logged in. Again, you will see the garbage as the server end as the PPP connection starts up.

If you do not see this immediately after connecting (and logging in and starting the PPP server if required), press Enter to see if this starts the PPP server...

At this point, you can hang up your modem (usually, type +++ quickly and then issue the ATH0 command once your modem responds with OK).

If you can't get your modem to work, read your modem manual, the man pages for your communications software, and the Serial HOWTO. Once you have this sorted out, carry on as above.

Using Internet servers with dynamic IP numbers. If you use dynamic IP numbers (and many service providers will only give you a dynamic IP number unless you pay significantly more for your connection), then you have to recognize the limitations this imposes.

First of all, outbound service requests will work just fine. That is, you can send email using sendmail (provided you have correctly set up sendmail), FTP files from remote sites, finger users on other machines, browse the web etc.

In particular, you can answer email that you have brought down to your machine while you are off line. Mail will simply sit in your mail queue until you dial back into your ISP.

However, your machine is not connected to the Internet 24 hours a day, nor does it have the same IP number every time it is connected. So it is impossible for you to receive email directed to your machine, and very difficult to set up a Web or FTP server that your friends can access. As far as the Internet is concerned your machine does not exist as a unique, permanently contactable machine as it does not have a unique IP number (remember—other machines will be using the IP number when they are allocated it on dial in).

If you set up a WWW (or any other server), it is totally unknown by any user on the Internet unless they know that your machine is connected and its actual (current) IP number. There are a number of ways they can get this info, ranging from you ringing them, sending them email to tell them or cunning use of "`.plan`" files on a shell account at your service provider (assuming that your provider allows shell and finger access).

For most users, this is not a problem—all that most people want is to send and receive e-mail (using your account on your service provider) and make outbound connections to WWW, FTP and other servers on the Internet. If you must have inbound connections to your server, you should really get a static IP number.

PPP connection files. You now need to be logged in as root to create the directories and edit the files needed to set up PPP. PPP uses a number of files to connect and set up a PPP connection. These differ in name and location between PPP 2.1.2 and 2.2.

For PPP 2.1.2 the files are:

```
/usr/sbin/pppd          # the PPP binary.
/usr/sbin/ppp-on        # the dialer and connection script.
/usr/sbin/ppp-off       # the disconnection script.
/etc/ppp/options        # the options pppd uses for all connections.
/etc/ppp/options.ttyXX  # options specific to connections on this port.
```

For PPP 2.2 the files are:

```
/usr/sbin/pppd                    # the PPP binary
/etc/ppp/scripts/ppp-on           # the dialer/connection script
/etc/ppp/scripts/ppp-on-dialer    # part 1 of the dialer script
/etc/ppp/scripts/ppp-off          # the actual chat script itself
/etc/ppp/options                  # the options pppd uses for all connections
/etc/ppp/options.ttyXX            # the options specific to a connection on this port
```

Red Hat Linux users should note that the standard Red Hat 4.x installation places these scripts in `/usr/doc/ppp-2.2.0f-2/scripts`.

In your `/etc` directory there should be a ppp directory:-

```
drwxrwxr-x   2 root     root          1024 Oct  9 11:01 ppp
```

If it does not exist—create it with these ownerships and permissions.

If the directory already existed, it should contain a template options file called `options.tpl`. This file is included below.

It contains an explanation of nearly all the PPP options (these are useful to read in conjunction with the `pppd` manual pages). While you can use this file as the basis of your `/etc/ppp/options` file, it is probably better to create your own options file that does not include all the comments in the template— it will be much shorter and easier to read/maintain.

Some distributions of PPP seem to have lost the `options.tpl` file. You should examine the PPP HOWTO for the complete version.

What options should I use? Well, as in all things that depends (sigh). The options specified here should work with most servers.

However, if it does not work, read the template file (`/etc/ppp/options.tpl`) and the `pppd` manual pages and speak to the system administrator or user support people who run the server to which you are connecting.

You should also note that the connect scripts presented here use some command line options to `pppd` to make things a bit easier to change.

```
# /etc/ppp/options (no PAP/CHAP support)
#
# Prevent pppd from forking into the background -detach
#
# use the modem control lines
modem
# use uucp style locks to ensure exclusive access to the serial device
lock
# use hardware flow control
crtscts
# create a default route for this connection in the routing table
defaultroute
# do NOT set up any "escaped" control sequences
asyncmap 0
# use a maximum transmission packet size of 552 bytes
mtu 552
# use a maximum receive packet size of 552 bytes
mru 552
#
#-------END OF SAMPLE /etc/ppp/options (no PAP/CHAP support)
```

Setting up the PPP connection manually. Now that you have created your `/etc/ppp/options` and `/etc/resolv.conf files` (and, if necessary, the `/etc/ppp/pap|chap-secrets` file), you can test the settings by manually establishing a PPP connection. (Once we have the manual connection working, we will automate the process).

To do this, your communications software must be capable of quitting without resetting the modem. `minicom` can do this with the sequence `Control`-`A`-`Q`

- Make sure you are logged in as root.
- Fire up you communications software (`minicom` or `seyon`), dial into the PPP server, and log in as normal. If you need to issue a command to start up PPP on the server, do so. You will now see the garbage you saw before.
- If you are using PAP or CHAP, then merely connecting to the remote system should start PPP on the remote and you will see the garbage without logging in. Although this may not happen for some servers— try pressing Enter and see if the garbage starts up.
- Now quit the communications software without resetting the modem and at the Linux prompt (as root) type

```
# pppd -d /dev/ttyS0 38400 &
```

Substituting the name of the device your modem is connected to, of course.

The `-d` option enables debugging—the PPP connection start-up conversation will be logged to your system log—which is useful for tracing problems later.

- Your modem lights should now flash as the PPP connection is established. It will take a short while for the PPP connection to be made.

At this point you can look at the PPP interface, by issuing the command

```
# ifconfig
```

In addition to any Ethernet and loop back devices you have, you should see something like :-

```
ppp0      Link encap:Point-Point Protocol
          inet addr:10.144.153.104  P-t-P:10.144.153.51 Mask:255.255.255.0
          UP POINTOPOINT RUNNING  MTU:552  Metric:1
          RX packets:0 errors:0 dropped:0 overruns:0
          TX packets:0 errors:0 dropped:0 overruns:0
```

Where

- inet addr:10.144.153.10 is the IP number of your end of the link.
- P-t-P:10.144.153.5 is the server's IP number.

(`ifconfig` will not report these IP numbers, but the ones used by your PPP server.) Note: `ifconfig` also tells you that the link is up and running.

You should also be able to see a route to the the remote host (and beyond). To do this, issue the command

```
# route -n
```

You should see something like:-

```
Kernel routing table
Destination     Gateway         Genmask         Flags MSS    Window Use Iface
10.144.153.3    *               255.255.255.255 UH    1500   0        1 ppp0
127.0.0.0       *               255.0.0.0       U     3584   0       11 lo
10.0.0.0        *               255.0.0.0       U     1500   0       35 eth0
default         10.144.153.3    *               UG    1500   0        5 ppp0
```

Of particular importance here, notice we have two entries pointing to our PPP interface.

The first is a host route (indicated by the H flag) and that allows us to see the host to which we are connected to—but no further.

The second is the default route, established by giving `pppd` the option `defaultroute`. This is the route that tells our Linux PC to send any packets not destined for the local Ethernet(s)—to which we have specific network routes—to the PPP server itself. The PPP server then is responsible for routing our packets out onto the Internet and routing the return packets back to us.

◇ If you do not see a routing table with two entries, something is wrong. In particular, if your syslog shows a message telling you `pppd` is not replacing an existing default route, then you have a default route pointing at your Ethernet interface—which MUST be replaced by a specific network route. You can only have one default route.

You will need to explore your system initialization files to find out where this default route is being set up (it will use a `route add default` command). Change this command to something like `route add net`.

Now test the link by pinging the server at its IP number as reported by the `ifconfig` output; i.e.:

```
# ping 10.144.153.51
```

You should receive output like

```
PING 10.144.153.51 (10.144.153.51): 56 data bytes
64 bytes from 10.144.153.51: icmp_seq=0 ttl=255 time=328.3 ms
64 bytes from 10.144.153.51: icmp_seq=1 ttl=255 time=190.5 ms
64 bytes from 10.144.153.51: icmp_seq=2 ttl=255 time=187.5 ms
64 bytes from 10.144.153.51: icmp_seq=3 ttl=255 time=170.7 ms
```

This listing will go on for ever—to stop it press Ctrl-C, at which point you will receive some more information:

```
--- 10.144.153.51 ping statistics ---
4 packets transmitted, 4 packets received, 0% packet loss
round-trip min/avg/max = 170.7/219.2/328.3 ms
```

Now try pinging a host by name (not the name of the PPP server itself) but a host at another site that you know is probably going to be up and running. For example

```
# ping sunsite.unc.edu
```

This time there will be a bit of a pause as Linux obtains the IP number for the fully qualified host name you have pinged from the DNS you specified in `/etc/resolv.conf`—so don't worry (but you will see your modem lights flash). Shortly you will receive output like

```
 PING sunsite.unc.edu (152.2.254.81): 56 data bytes
64 bytes from 152.2.254.81: icmp_seq=0 ttl=254 time=190.1 ms
64 bytes from 152.2.254.81: icmp_seq=1 ttl=254 time=180.6 ms
64 bytes from 152.2.254.81: icmp_seq=2 ttl=254 time=169.8 ms
64 bytes from 152.2.254.81: icmp_seq=3 ttl=254 time=170.6 ms
64 bytes from 152.2.254.81: icmp_seq=4 ttl=254 time=170.6 ms
```

Again, stop the output by pressing Ctrl-C and get the statistics:

```
--- sunsite.unc.edu ping statistics ---
5 packets transmitted, 5 packets received, 0% packet loss
round-trip min/avg/max = 169.8/176.3/190.1 ms
```

If you don't get any response, try pinging the IP address of the DNS server at your ISP's site. If you get a result from this, then it looks like you have a problem with `/etc/resolv.conf`.

If this doesn't work, you have a routing problem, or your ISP has a problem routing packets back to you. Check your routing table as shown above and if that is okay, contact your ISP. A good test of the ISP is to use another operating system to connect. If you can get beyond your ISP with that, then the problem is at your end.

If everything works, shut down the connection by typing

```
# ppp-off
```

After a short pause, the modem should hang itself up.

If that does not work, either turn off your modem or fire up your communications software and interrupt the modem with +++ and then hang up with ATH0 when you receive the modem's OK prompt.

You may also need to clean up the lock file created by pppd by typing

```
# rm -f /var/lock/LCK..ttySx
```

Creating the connection scripts.

You can continue to log in by hand as shown above, but it is much neater to set up some scripts to do this automatically for you.

A set of scripts automates the log in and PPP start up, so all you have to do (as root or as a member of the PPP group) is issue a single command to fire up your connection.

If your ISP does not require the use of PAP/CHAP, these are the scripts for you.

If the PPP package installed correctly, you should have two example files. For PPP 2.1.2, they are in /usr/sbin and for PPP 2.2, they are in `/etc/ppp/scripts`. They are called

for PPP-2.1.2

```
ppp-on
ppp-off
```

and for PPP-2.2

```
ppp-off
ppp-on
ppp-on-dialer
```

If you are using PPP 2.1.2, I strongly urge you to delete the sample files. There are potential problems with these—and don't tell me they work fine—I used them for ages too, and recommended them in the first version of this document.

For the benefit of PPP 2.1.2 users, here are better template versions, taken from the PPP 2.2 distribution. I suggest that you copy and use these scripts instead of the old PPP-2.1.2 scripts.

The ppp-on **script.** This is the first of a pair of scripts that actually fire up the connection.

```
#!/bin/sh
#
# Script to initiate a PPP connection. This is the first part of the
# pair of scripts. This is not a secure pair of scripts as the codes
# are visible with the 'ps' command.  However, it is simple.
#
# These are the parameters. Change as needed.
TELEPHONE=555-1212        # The telephone number for the connection
ACCOUNT=george            # The account name for logon (as in 'George Burns')
PASSWORD=gracie           # The password for this account (and 'Gracie Allen')
LOCAL_IP=0.0.0.0          # Local IP address if known. Dynamic = 0.0.0.0
REMOTE_IP=0.0.0.0         # Remote IP address if desired. Normally 0.0.0.0
NETMASK=255.255.255.0     # The proper netmask if needed
#
# Export them so that they will be available to 'ppp-on-dialer'
export TELEPHONE ACCOUNT PASSWORD
#
# This is the location of the script which dials the phone and logs
# in.  Please use the absolute file name as the $PATH variable is not
# used on the connect option.  (To do so on a 'root' account would be
# a security hole so don't ask.)
#
DIALER_SCRIPT=/etc/ppp/ppp-on-dialer
#
# Initiate the connection
#
#
exec /usr/sbin/pppd debug /dev/ttySx 38400 \
        $LOCAL_IP:$REMOTE_IP \
        connect $DIALER_SCRIPT
```

Here is the ppp-on-dialer script:

```
#!/bin/sh
#
# This is part 2 of the ppp-on script. It will perform the connection
# protocol for the desired connection.
#
/usr/sbin/chat -v                                                   \
        TIMEOUT         3                                   \
        ABORT           '\nBUSY\r'                          \
        ABORT           '\nNO ANSWER\r'                     \
        ABORT           '\nRINGING\r\n\r\nRINGING\r'        \
        ''              \rAT                                \
        'OK-+++\c-OK'   ATH0
```

```
        TIMEOUT           30                        \
        OK                ATDT$TELEPHONE            \
        CONNECT           ''                        \
        ogin:--ogin:      $ACCOUNT                  \
        assword:          $PASSWORD
```

For PPP-2.2, the `ppp-off` script looks like:

```
#!/bin/sh
######################################################################
#
# Determine the device to be terminated.
#
if [ "$1" = "" ]; then
        DEVICE=ppp0
else
        DEVICE=$1
fi

######################################################################
#
# If the ppp0 pid file is present then the program is running. Stop it.
if [ -r /var/run/$DEVICE.pid ]; then
        kill -INT 'cat /var/run/$DEVICE.pid'
#
# If the kill did not work then there is no process running for this
# pid. It may also mean that the lock file will be left. You may wish
# to delete the lock file at the same time.
        if [ ! "$?" = "0" ]; then
                rm -f /var/run/$DEVICE.pid
                echo "ERROR: Removed stale pid file"
                exit 1
        fi
#
# Success. Let pppd clean up its own junk.
        echo "PPP link to $DEVICE terminated."
        exit 0
fi
#
# The ppp process is not running for ppp0
echo "ERROR: PPP link is not active on $DEVICE"
exit 1
```

Editing the supplied PPP startup scripts.

As the new scripts come in two parts, and we will edit them in turn.

The `ppp-on` **script.** You will need to edit the `ppp-on` script to reflect your user name at your ISP, your password at your ISP, the telephone number of your ISP.

Each of the lines like TELEPHONE= actually set up shell variables that contain the information to the right of the '=' (excluding the comments of course). So edit each of these lines so it is correct for your ISP and connection.

Also, as you are setting the IP number (if you need to) in the `/etc/ppp/options` file, delete the line that says

```
$LOCAL_IP:$REMOTE_IP \
```

Also, make sure that the shell variable DIALER_SCRIPT points at the full path and name of the dialer script that you are actually going to use. So, if you have moved this or renamed the script, make sure you edit this line correctly in the `ppp-on` script.

The `ppp-on-dialer` **script.** This is the second of the scripts that actually brings up our PPP link.

Note: a chat script is normally all on one line. the backslashes are used to allow line continuations across several physical lines (for human readability) and do not form part of the script itself.

However, it is very useful to look at it in detail so that we understand what it is actually (supposed) to be doing!

A chat script is a sequence of "expect string" "send string" pairs. In particular, note that we always expect something before we send something.

If we are to send something without receiving anything first, we must use an empty expect string (indicated by "") and similarly for expecting something without sending anything! Also, if a string consists of several words, (e.g. NO CARRIER), you must quote the string so that it is seen as a single entity by chat.

The chat line in our template is:

```
exec /usr/sbin/chat -v
```

Invoke `chat`. The `-v` tells `chat` to copy all its I/O into the system log (usually `/var/log/messages`). Once you are happy that the `chat` script is working reliably, edit this line to remove the `-v` to save unnecessary clutter in your syslog.

```
TIMEOUT         3
```

This sets the timeout for the receipt of expected input to three seconds. You may need to increase this to 5 or 10 seconds if you are using a really slow modem.

```
ABORT           '\nBUSY\r'
```

If the string BUSY is received, abort the operation.

```
ABORT           '\nNO ANSWER\r'
```

If the string NO ANSWER is received, abort the operation

```
  ABORT           '\nRINGING\r\n\r\nRINGING\r'
\begin{verbatim} \end{tscreen}

  If the (repeated) string RINGING is received, abort the operation.
  This is because someone is ringing your phone line!

\begin{tscreen} \begin{verbatim}
  ''              \rAT
```

Expect nothing from the modem and send the string AT.

```
OK-+++\c-OK   ATH0
```

This one is a bit more complicated as it uses some of chat's error recovery capabilities.

What is says is...Expect OK, if it is NOT received (because the modem is not in command mode) then send +++ (the standard Hayes-compatible modem string that returns the modem to command mode) and expect OK. Then send ATH0 (the modem hang up string). This allows your script to cope with the situation of your modem being stuck on-line.

```
TIMEOUT         30
```

Set the timeout to 30 seconds for the remainder of the script. If you experience trouble with the chat script aborting due to timeouts, increase this to 45 seconds or more.

```
OK              ATDT$TELEPHONE
```

Expect OK (the modem's response to the ATH0 command) and dial the number we want to call.

```
CONNECT         ''
```

Expect CONNECT (which our modem sends when the remote modem answers) and send nothing in reply.

```
ogin:--ogin:    $ACCOUNT
```

Again, we have some error recovery built in here. Expect the `login` prompt (`ogin:`), but if we don't receive it by the timeout, send a return and then look for the login prompt again. When the prompt is received, send the user name (stored in the shell variable `$ACCOUNT`).

```
assword:        $PASSWORD
```

Expect the password prompt and send our password (again, stored in a shell variable).

This chat script has reasonable error recovery capability. `chat` has considerably more features than demonstrated here. For more information consult the `chat` manual page (`man 8 chat`).

Starting PPP at the server end.

While the `ppp-on-dialer` script is fine for servers that automatically start `pppd` at the server end once you have logged in, some servers require that you explicitly start PPP on the server.

If you need to issue a command to start up PPP on the server, you do need to edit the `ppp-on-dialer` script.

At the end of the script (after the password line) add an additional expect-send pair—this one would look for your login prompt (beware of characters that have a special meaning in the Bourne shell, like

```
$[]
```

Once chat has found the shell prompt, chat must issue the ppp start up command required for your ISPs PPP server.

In one author's case, the PPP server uses the standard Linux `bash` prompt

```
[hartr@kepler hartr]$
```

which requires the response

```
# ppp
```

to start up PPP on the server.

It is a good idea to allow for a bit of error recovery here, so use

```
hartr-hartr ppp
```

This says, if we don't receive the prompt within the timeout, send a carriage return and looks for the prompt again.

Once the prompt is received, then send the string "ppp."

Note: don't forget to add a to the end of the previous line so chat still thinks the entire chat script is on one line!

Unfortunately, some servers produce a very variable set of prompts! You may need to log in several times using minicom to understand what is going on and pick the stable "expect" strings.

If your PPP server uses PAP (Password Authentication Protocol).

If the server to which you are connecting requires PAP or CHAP authentication, you have a little bit more work.

To the above options file, add the following lines

```
#
# force pppd to use your ISP user name as your 'host name' during the
# authentication process
name <your ISP user name>       # you need to edit this line
#
```

```
# If you are running a PPP *server* and need to force PAP or CHAP
# uncomment the appropriate one of the following lines. Do NOT use
# these is you are a client connecting to a PPP server (even if it uses PAP
# or CHAP) as this tells the SERVER to authenticate itself to your
# machine (which almost certainly can't do---and the link will fail).
#+chap
#+pap
#
# If you are using ENCRYPTED secrets in the /etc/ppp/pap-secrets
# file, then uncomment the following line.
# Note: this is NOT the same as using MS encrypted passwords as can be
# set up in MS RAS on Windows NT.
#+papcrypt
```

Using MSCHAP.

Microsoft Windows NT RAS can be set up to use a variation on CHAP (Challenge/Handshake Authentication Protocol). In your PPP sources you will find a file called `README.MSCHAP80` that discusses this. You can determine if the server is requesting authentication using this protocol by enabling debugging for pppd. If the server is requesting MSCHAP authentication, you will see lines like

```
rcvd [LCP ConfReq id=0x2 <asyncmap 0x0> <auth chap 80> <magic 0x46a3>]
```

The critical information here is `auth chap 80`.

In order to use MS CHAP, you will need to recompile `pppd` to support this. Please see the instructions in the `README.MSCHAP80` file in the PPP source file for instructions on how to compile and use this variation.

If you are using PAP or CHAP authentication, then you also need to create the secrets files. These are `/etc/ppp/pap-secrets` and `/etc/ppp/chap-secrets`.

They must be owned by user root, group root and have file permissions 740 for security. The first point to note about PAP and CHAP is that they are designed to authenticate computer systems not users. In other words, once your computer has made its PPP connection to the server, ANY user on your system can use that connection—not just you.

PAP can (and for CHAP does) require bidirectional authentication—that is a valid name and secret is required on each computer for the other computer involved. However, this is not the way most PPP servers offering dial up PPP PAP authenticated connections operate.

Your ISP will probably have given you a user name and password to allow you to connect to their system and thence the Internet. Your ISP is not interested in your computer's name at all, so you will probably need to use the user name at your ISP as the name for your computer. This is done using the name user name option to `pppd`. So, if you are to use the user name given you by your ISP, add the line

```
name your_user name_at_your_ISP
```

to your `/etc/ppp/options` file.

Technically, you should really use `user our_user name_at_your_ISP` for PAP, but `pppd` is sufficiently intelligent to interpret name as user if it is required to use PAP. The advantage of using the name option is that this is also valid for CHAP.

As PAP is for authenticating computers, technically you need also to specify a remote computer name. However, as most people only have one ISP, you can use a wild card (*) for the remote host name in the secrets file.

The `/etc/ppp/pap-secrets` file looks like

```
# Secrets for authentication using PAP
# client        server        secret     acceptable_local_IP_addresses
```

The four fields are white space delimited and the last one can be blank (which is what you want for a dynamic and probably static IP allocation from your ISP).

Suppose your ISP gave you a user name of `fred` and a password of `flintstone` you would set the name `fred` option in `/etc/ppp/options` and set up your `/etc/ppp/pap-secrets` file as follows

```
# Secrets for authentication using PAP
# client        server  secret          acceptable local IP addresses
fred            *       flintstone
```

This says for the local machine name fred (which we have told pppd to use even though it is not our local machine name) and for any server, use the password (secret) of flintstone.

Note that we do not need to specify a local IP address, unless we are required to force a particular local, static IP address. Even if you try this, it is unlikely to work as most PPP servers (for security reasons) do not allow the remote system to set the IP number they are to be given.

This requires that you have mutual authentication methods—that is, you must allow for both your machine to authenticate the remote server and the remote server to authenticate your machine.

So, if your machine is fred and the remote is barney, your machine would set name fred remotename barney and the remote machine would set name barney remotename fred in their respective /etc/ppp/options.ttyS*x* files.

The /etc/chap-secrets file for fred would look like

```
# Secrets for authentication using CHAP
# client        server  secret          acceptable local IP addresses
fred            barney  flintstone
barney          fred    wilma
```

and for barney

```
# Secrets for authentication using CHAP
# client        server  secret          acceptable local IP addresses
barney          fred    flintstone
fred            barney  wilma
```

Note in particular that both machines must have entries for bidirectional authentication. This allows the local machine to authenticate itself to the remote and the remote machine to authenticate itself to the local machine.

A chat script for PAP/CHAP authenticated connections. If your ISP is using PAP/CHAP, then your chat script is much simpler. All your chat script needs to do is dial the telephone, wait for a connect and then let pppd handle the logging in!

```
#!/bin/sh
#
# This is part 2 of the ppp-on script. It will perform the connection
# protocol for the desired connection.
#
exec /usr/sbin/chat -v                                          \
        TIMEOUT         3                                       \
        ABORT           '\nBUSY\r'                              \
        ABORT           '\nNO ANSWER\r'                         \
        ABORT           '\nRINGING\r\n\r\nRINGING\r'            \
        ''              \rAT                                    \
        'OK-+++\c-OK'   ATH0                                    \
        TIMEOUT         30                                      \
        OK              ATDT$TELEPHONE                          \
        CONNECT         ''                                      \
```

As we have already seen, you can turn on debug information logging with the -d option to pppd. The debug option is equivalent to this.

As we are establishing a new connection with a new script, leave in the debug option for now. (Warning: if your disk space is tight, logging pppd exchanges can rapidly extend your syslog file and run you into trouble—but to do this you must fail to connect and keep on trying for quite a few minutes).

Once you are happy that all is working properly, then you can remove this option.

```
exec /usr/sbin/pppd debug file options.myserver /dev/ttyS0 38400 \
```

Testing the connection script. Open a new root Xterm (if you are in X) or open a new virtual console and log in as root.

In this new session, issue the command

```
# tail -f /var/log/messages
```

Many systems log output to /var/log/messages. If it has a different name on your system, substitute the name of your system log file in the command above.

In the first window (or virtual console) issue the command

```
# ppp-on &
```

(or whatever name you have called your edited version of /usr/sbin/ppp-on). If you do not put the script into the background by specifying & at the end of the command, you will not get your terminal prompt back until PPP exits (when the link terminates).

Now switch back to the window that is tracking your system log.

Shutting down the PPP link.

When you have finished with the PPP link, use the standard ppp-off command to shut it down (remember that you must be root or a member of the ppp group!).

Troubleshooting common problems once the link is working.

One problem you will find is that many service providers will only support the connection software package that they distribute to new accounts. This is (typically) Microsoft Windows, and many service provider help desks seem to know nothing about Unix (or Linux). So, be prepared for limited assistance from them.

You could, of course, do the individual a favor and educate them about Linux (any ISP help desk person should be reasonably "with it" in Internet terms and that means they should have a home Linux box—of course it does).

Address resolution problems. OK—your PPP connection is up and running and you can ping the PPP server by IP number (the second or "remote" IP number shown by ifconfig ppp0), but you can't reach anything beyond this.

First of all, try pinging the IP numbers you have specified in /etc/resolv.conf as name servers. If this works, you can see beyond your PPP server (unless this has the same IP number as the "remote" IP number of your connection). So now try pinging the full Internet name of your service provider

```
ping my.isp.net
```

Substituting, of course, the name of your actual ISP. If this does not work, you have a problem with name resolution. This is probably because of a typo in your /etc/resolv.conf file.

If it still doesn't work (and your service provider confirms that his name servers are up and running), you have a problem somewhere else—and check carefully through your Linux installation (looking particularly at file permissions).

If you still can't ping your service provider's IP name servers by IP number, either they are down (give them a voice call and check) or there is a routing problem at your service provider's end.

One possibility is that the "remote end" is a Linux PPP server where the IP forwarding option has not been specified in the kernel.

Debugging a failed attempt. There are any number of reasons that your connection does not work—chat has failed to complete correctly, you have a dirty line, etc. So check your syslog for indications.

A very common problem is that people compile PPP support into the kernel and yet when they try to run pppd, the kernel complains that it does not support PPP. There are a variety of reasons this can occur.

- You failed to boot the new kernel that you compiled with PPP support.
- You failed to install the PPP module that you compiled.
- You expected modules to be loaded automatically, but they aren't.

- You are using the incorrect version of PPP for your kernel.
- You are not running pppd as root.
- You mistyped something in your startup scripts.
- You are not correctly logging into the server.
- You are not starting PPP on the server.
- The remote PPP process is slow to start.
- Default route not set.

And a host of others. Look in the PPP FAQ (which is really a series of questions and answers). This is a very comprehensive document and the answers are there. If the answer to your problems is not there, the problem is not PPP's fault.

Getting help when totally stuck. If you can't get your PPP link to work, go back through this document and check everything—in conjunction with the output created by "chat-v" and "pppd -d" in you system log.

Also consult the PPP documentation and FAQ plus the other documents mentioned above.

If you are still stuck, try the comp.os.linux.misc and comp.os.linux.networking newsgroups. These are reasonably regularly scanned by people that can help you with PPP, as is comp.protocols.ppp.

If you do choose to seek help in the USENET newsgroups, please don't post a very long message consisting of debugging output. This wastes huge amounts of network bandwidth. It is much better to describe the problem and perhaps include a few lines of debugging output (definitely no more than one screenful).

Networking with UUCP.

UUCP (UNIX-to-UNIX Copy) is an older mechanism used to transfer information between UNIX systems. Using UUCP, UNIX systems dial each other up (using a modem) and transfer mail messages, news articles, files, and so on. If you don't have TCP/IP or SLIP access, you can use UUCP to communicate with the world. Most of the mail and news software (see page 186) can be configured to use UUCP to transfer information to other machines. In fact, if there is an Internet site nearby, you can arrange to have Internet mail sent to your Linux machine via UUCP from that site.

The *Linux Network Administrator's Guide* contains complete information on configuring and using UUCP under Linux. Also, the Linux UUCP HOWTO, available via anonymous FTP from sunsite.unc.edu, should be of help. Another source of information on UUCP is the book *Managing UUCP and USENET*, by Tim O'Reilly and Grace Todino. See Appendix A for more information.

Electronic mail.

Like most UNIX systems, Linux provides a number of software packages for using electronic mail. E-mail on your system can either be local (that is, you only mail other users on your system), or networked (that is, you mail, using either TCP/IP or UUCP, users on other machines on a network). E-mail software usually consists of two parts: a *mailer* and a *transport*. The mailer is the user-level software which is used to actually compose and read e-mail messages. Popular mailers include elm and mailx. The transport is the low-level software which actually takes care of delivering the mail, either locally or remotely. The user never sees the transport software; they only interact with the mailer. However, as the system administrator, it is important to understand the concepts behind the transport software and how to configure it.

The most popular transport software for Linux is smail. This software is easy to configure, and is able to send both local and remote TCP/IP and UUCP e-mail. The more powerful sendmail transport is used on UNIX systems, however.

Most of the Linux mail software can be retrieved via anonymous FTP from sunsite.unc.edu in the directory /pub/Linux/system/Mail.

News and USENET.

Linux also provides a number of facilities for managing electronic news. You may choose to set up a local news server on your system, which will allow users to post "articles" to various "news groups" on the system, a lively form of discussion. However, if you have access to a TCP/IP or UUCP network, then you will be able to participate in USENET—a worldwide network news service.

There are two parts to the news software—the **server** and the **client**. The news server is the software which controls the news groups and handles delivering articles to other machines (if you are on a network). The news client, or **news reader**, is the software which connects to the server to allow users to read and post news.

There are several forms of news servers available for Linux. They all follow the same basic protocols and design. The two primary versions are "C News" and "INN." There are many types of news readers, as well, such as `rn` and `tin`. The choice of news reader is more or less a matter of taste; all news readers should work equally well with different versions of the server software. That is, the news reader is independent of the server software, and vice versa.

If you only want to run news locally (that is, not as part of USENET), then you will need to run a server on your system, as well as install a news reader for the users. The news server will store the articles in a directory such as `/usr/spool/news`, and the news reader will be compiled to look in this directory for news articles.

However, if you wish to run news over the network, there are several options open to you. TCP/IP network-based news uses a protocol known as NNTP (Network News Transmission Protocol). NNTP allows a news reader to read news over the network, on a remote machine. NNTP also allows news servers to send articles to each other over the network—this is the software upon which USENET is based. Most businesses and universities have one or more NNTP servers set up to handle all of the USENET news for that site. Every other machine at the site runs a NNTP-based news reader to read and post news over the network via the NNTP server. This means that only the NNTP server actually stores the news articles on disk.

Here are some possible scenarios for news configuration.

- You run news locally. That is, you have no network connection, or no desire to run news over the network. In this case, you need to run C News or INN on your machine, and install a news reader to read the news locally.

- You have access to a TCP/IP network and a NNTP server. If your organization has an NNTP news server set up, you can read and post news from your Linux machine by simply installing an NNTP-based news reader. (Most news readers available can be configured to run locally or use NNTP). In this case, you do not need to install a news server or store news articles on your system. The news reader will take care of reading and posting news over the network. Of course, you will need to have TCP/IP configured and have access to the network (see Section 5).

- You have access to a TCP/IP network but have no NNTP server. In this case, you can run an NNTP news server on your Linux system. You can install either a local or an NNTP-based news reader, and the server will store news articles on your system. In addition, you can configure the server to communicate with other NNTP news servers to transfer news articles.

- You want to transfer news using UUCP. If you have UUCP access (see Section 5), you can participate in USENET as well. You will need to install a (local) news server and a news reader. In addition, you will need to configure your UUCP software to periodically transfer news articles to another nearby UUCP machine (known as your "news feed"). UUCP does not use NNTP to transfer news; simply, UUCP provides its own mechanism for transferring news articles.

The one downside of most news server and news reader software is that it must be compiled by hand. Most of the news software does not use configuration files; instead, configuration options are determined at compile time.

Most of the "standard" news software (available via anonymous FTP from `ftp.uu.net` in the directory `/news`) will compile out-of-the box on Linux. Necessary patches can be found on `sunsite.unc.edu` in

/pub/Linux/system/Mail (which is, incidentally, also where mail software for Linux is found). Other news binaries for Linux may be found in this directory as well.

For more information, refer to the Linux News HOWTO from sunsite.unc.edu in /pub/Linux/docs/HOWTO. Also, the LDP's *Linux Network Administrator's Guide* contains complete information on configuring news software for Linux. The book *Managing UUCP and Usenet*, by Tim O'Reilly and Grace Todino, is an excellent guide to setting up UUCP and news software. Also of interest is the USENET document "How to become a USENET site," available from ftp.uu.net, in the directory /usenet/news.announce.newusers.

APPENDIX A

Sources of Linux Information

This appendix contains information on various sources of Linux information, such as online documents, books, and more. Many of these documents are available either in printed form, or electronically from the Internet or BBS systems. Many Linux distributions also include much of this documentation in the distribution itself, so after you have installed Linux these files may be present on your system.

Online documents.

These documents should be available on any of the Linux FTP archive sites (see Appendix C for a list). If you do not have direct access to FTP, you may be able to locate these documents on other online services (such as CompuServe, local BBS's, and so on). If you have access to Internet mail, you can use the `ftpmail` service to receive these documents. See Appendix C for more information.

In particular, the following documents may be found on `sunsite.unc.edu` in the directory `/pub/Linux/docs`. Many sites mirror this directory; however, if you're unable to locate a mirror site near you, this is a good one to fall back on.

You can also access Linux files and documentation using `gopher`. Just point your `gopher` client to port 70 on `sunsite.unc.edu`, and follow the menus to the Linux archive. This is a good way to browse Linux documentation interactively.

The Linux Frequently Asked Questions with Answers
: The Linux Frequently Asked Questions list, or "FAQ," is a list of common questions (and answers) about Linux. This document is meant to provide a general source of information about Linux, common problems and solutions, and a list of other sources of information. Every new Linux user should read this document. It is available in a number of formats, including plain ASCII, PostScript, and HTML. The Linux FAQ is maintained by Robert Kiesling, `kiesling@terracom.net`.

The Linux META-FAQ
: The META-FAQ is a collection of "metaquestions" about Linux; that is, sources of information about the Linux system, and other general topics. It is a good starting place for the Internet user wishing to find more information about the system. It is maintained by Michael K. Johnson, `johnsonm@sunsite.unc.edu`.

The Linux INFO-SHEET
: The Linux INFO-SHEET is a technical introduction to the Linux system. It gives an overview of the system's features and available software, and also provides a list of other sources of Linux information. The format and content is similar in nature to the META-FAQ; incidentally, it is also maintained by Michael K. Johnson.

Linux Journal
: *Linux Journal* makes selected articles available in electronic form from their web site, specifically in `http://www.ssc.com/lj/selected.html`. Articles cover topics for be-

ginning to advanced users, include features about Linux being used in the "real world," and the frequently referenced Linux distribution comparison articles and tables.

Linux Gazette A free, on-line publication found at `http://www.ssc.com/lg/`, *Linux Gazette* offers answers and entertainment, "making Linux just a little more fun."

The Linux Software Map
The Linux Software Map is a list of many applications available for Linux, where to get them, who maintains them, and so forth. It is far from complete—to compile a complete list of Linux software would be nearly impossible. However, it does include many of the most popular Linux software packages. If you can't find a particular application to suit your needs, the LSM is a good place to start. It is maintained by Lars Wirzenius, `lars.wirzenius@helsinki.fi`.

The Linux HOWTO Index
The Linux HOWTOs are a collection of "how to" documents, each describing in detail a certain aspect of the Linux system. They are maintained by Matt Welsh, `mdw@sunsite.unc.edu`. The `HOWTO-Index` lists the HOWTO documents which are available.

Other online documents
If you browse the `docs` subdirectory of any Linux FTP site, you'll see many other documents which are not listed here: A slew of FAQ's, interesting tidbits, and other important information. This miscellany is difficult to categorize here; if you don't see what you're looking for on the list above, just take a look at one of the Linux archive sites listed in Appendix C.

Linux Documentation Project manuals.

The Linux Documentation Project is working on developing a set of manuals and other documentation for Linux, including man pages. These manuals are in various stages of development, and any help revising and updating them is greatly appreciated. If you have questions about the LDP, please contact Matt Welsh (`mdw@sunsite.unc.edu`).

These books are available via anonymous FTP from a number of Linux archive sites, including `sunsite.unc.edu` in the directory `/pub/Linux/docs/LDP`. A number of commercial distributors are selling printed copies of these books; in the future, you may be able to find the LDP manuals on the shelves of your local bookstore.

Linux Installation and Getting Started, by Matt Welsh
A new user's guide for Linux, covering everything the new user needs to know to get started. You happen to hold this book in your hands.

The Linux System Administrators' Guide, by Lars Wirzenius
This is a complete guide to running and configuring a Linux system. There are many issues relating to systems administration which are specific to Linux, such as needs for supporting a user community, file system maintenance, backups, and more. This guide covers them all.

The Linux Network Administrators' Guide, by Olaf Kirch
An extensive and complete guide to networking under Linux, including TCP/IP, UUCP, SLIP, and more. This book is a very good read; it contains a wealth of information on many subjects, clarifying the many confusing aspects of network configuration.

The Linux Kernel Hackers' Guide, by Michael Johnson
The gritty details of kernel hacking and development under Linux. Linux is unique in that the complete kernel source is available. This book opens the doors to developers who wish to add or modify features within the kernel. This guide also contains comprehensive

coverage of kernel concepts and conventions used by Linux.

Books and other published works.

Linux Journal is a monthly magazine for and about the Linux community, written and produced by a number of Linux developers and enthusiasts. It is distributed worldwide, and is an excellent way to keep in touch with the dynamics of the Linux world, especially if you don't have access to USENET news.

At the time of this writing, subscriptions to *Linux Journal* are US$22/year in the United States, US$27 in Canada, and US$32 elsewhere. To subscribe, or for more information, write to Linux Journal, PO Box 55549, Seattle, WA, 98155-0549, USA, or call +1 206 782-7733. Their FAX number is +1 206 782-7191, and e-mail address is `linux@ssc.com`. You can also find a *Linux Journal* FAQ and sample articles via anonymous FTP on `sunsite.unc.edu` in `/pub/Linux/docs/linux-journal`.

As we have said, not many books have been published dealing with Linux specifically. However, if you are new to the world of UNIX, or want more information than is presented here, we suggest that you take a look at the following books which are available.

Using UNIX.

Title: *Learning the UNIX Operating System*
Author: Grace Todino & John Strang
Publisher: O'Reilly and Associates, 1987
ISBN: 0-937175-16-1, $9.00

A good introductory book on learning the UNIX operating system. Most of the information should be applicable to Linux as well. I suggest reading this book if you're new to UNIX and really want to get started with using your new system.

Title: *Learning the* `vi` *Editor*
Author: Linda Lamb
Publisher: O'Reilly and Associates, 1990
ISBN: 0-937175-67-6, $21.95

This is a book about the `vi` editor, a powerful text editor found on every UNIX system in the world. It's often important to know and be able to use `vi`, because you won't always have access to a "real" editor such as Emacs.

System Administration.

Title: *Essential System Administration*
Author: Æleen Frisch
Publisher: O'Reilly and Associates, 1991
ISBN: 0-937175-80-3, $29.95

From the O'Reilly and Associates Catalog, "Like any other multi-user system, UNIX requires some care and feeding. *Essential System Administration* tells you how. This book strips away the myth and confusion surrounding this important topic and provides a compact, manageable introduction to the tasks faced by anyone responsible for a UNIX system." I couldn't have said it better myself.

Title: *TCP/IP Network Administration*
Author: Craig Hunt
Publisher: O'Reilly and Associates, 1990
ISBN: 0-937175-82-X, $24.95

A complete guide to setting up and running a TCP/IP network. While this book is not Linux-specific, roughly 90% of it is applicable to Linux. Coupled with the Linux NET-2-HOWTO and *Linux Network Administrator's Guide*, this is a great book discussing the concepts and technical details of managing TCP/IP.

Title: *Managing UUCP and Usenet*
Author: Tim O'Reilly and Grace Todino
Publisher: O'Reilly and Associates, 1991
ISBN: 0-937175-93-5, $24.95

This book covers how to install and configure UUCP networking software, including configuration for USENET news. If you're at all interested in using UUCP or accessing USENET news on your system, this book is a must-read.

The X Window System.

Title: *The X Window System: A User's Guide*
Author: Niall Mansfield
Publisher: Addison-Wesley
ISBN: 0-201-51341-2, N/A

A complete tutorial and reference guide to using the X Window System. If you installed X windows on your Linux system, and want to know how to get the most out of it, you should read this book. Unlike some windowing systems, a lot of the power provided by X is not obvious at first sight.

Programming.

Title: *The C Programming Language*
Author: Brian Kernighan and Dennis Ritchie
Publisher: Prentice-Hall, 1988
ISBN: 0-13-110362-8, $25.00

This book is a must-have for anyone wishing to do C programming on a UNIX system. (Or any system, for that matter.) While this book is not ostensibly UNIX-specific, it is quite applicable to programming C under UNIX.

Title: *The Unix Programming Environment*
Author: Brian Kernighan and Bob Pike
Publisher: Prentice-Hall, 1984
ISBN: 0-13-937681-X, $40.00

An overview to programming under the UNIX system. Covers all of the tools of the trade; a good read to get acquainted with the somewhat amorphous UNIX programming world.

Title: *Advanced Programming in the UNIX Environment*
Author: W. Richard Stevens
Publisher: Addison-Wesley
ISBN: 0-201-56317-7, $50.00

This mighty tome contains everything that you need to know to program UNIX at the system level—file I/O, process control, interprocess communication, signals, terminal I/O, the works. This book focuses on various UNI standards, including POSIX.1, which Linux mostly adheres to.

Kernel hacking.

Title: *Inside Linux: A Look at Operating System Development*
Author: Randolph Bentson
Publisher: Specialized Systems Consultants
ISBN: 0-916151-89-1, $22.00

This book provides an informal introduction to a number of operating system issues by looking at the history of operating systems, by looking at how they are used, and by looking at the details of one operating system. The contents are a conscious effort to braid discussion of history, theory and practice so that the reader can see what goes on inside the system.

Title: *The Design of the UNIX Operating System*
Author: Maurice J. Bach
Publisher: Prentice-Hall, 1986
ISBN: 0-13-201799-7, $70.00

This book covers the algorithms and internals of the UNIX kernel. It is not specific to any particular kernel, although it does lean towards System V-isms. This is the best place to start if you want to understand the inner tickings of the Linux system.

Title: *The Magic Garden Explained*
Author: Berny Goodheart and James Cox
Publisher: Prentice-Hall, 1994
ISBN: 0-13-098138-9, $53.00

This book describes the System V R4 kernel in detail. Unlike Bach's book, which concentrates heavily on the algorithms which make the kernel tick, this book presents the SVR4 implementation on a more technical level. Although Linux and SVR4 are distant cousins, this book can give you much insight into the workings of an actual UNIX kernel implementation. This is also a very modern book on the UNIX kernel—published in 1994.

APPENDIX B
Linux Vendor List

This appendix lists contact information for a number of vendors which sell Linux on diskette, tape, and CD-ROM. Many of them provide Linux documentation, support, and other services as well. This is by no means a complete listing; if you purchased this book in printed form, it's very possible that the vendor or publishing company also provides Linux software and services.

The author makes no guarantee as to the accuracy of any of the information listed in this Appendix. This information is included here only as a service to readers, not as an advertisement for any particular organization.

Caldera, Inc.
633 South 550 East
Provo, Utah 84606 USA
Tel: 800-850-7779 Fax: 801-377-8752
`info@caldera.com`

Fintronic Linux Systems
1360 Willow Rd., Suite 205
Menlo Park, CA 94025 USA
Tel: 415 325-4474
Fax: 415 325-4908
`linux@fintronic.com`

InfoMagic, Inc.
PO Box 30370
Flagstaff, AZ 86003-0370 USA
Tel: 800 800-6613, 602 526-9565
Fax: 602 526-9573
`Orders@InfoMagic.com`

Lasermoon Ltd
2a Beaconsfield Road, Fareham,
Hants, England. PO16 0QB.
Tel: +44 (0) 329 826444.
Fax: +44 (0) 329 825936.
`info@lasermoon.co.uk`

Linux Journal
P.O. Box 85867
Seattle, WA 98145-1867 USA
Tel: 206 782-7733
Fax: 206 782-7191
`linux@ssc.com`

Linux Systems Labs
250 Huron Ave.
Port Huron, MI 48061 USA
Tel: 810 987 8807
Fax: 810 987 3562 `info@lsl.com`

Nascent Technology
Linux from Nascent CDROM
P.O. Box 60669
Sunnyvale CA 94088-0669 USA
Tel: 408 737-9500
Fax: 408 241-9390
`nascent@netcom.com`

Red Hat Software
P.O. Box 4325
Chapel Hill, NC 27515 USA
Tel: 919 309-9560
`redhat@redhat.com`

SW Technology
251 West Renner Suite 229
Richardson, TX 75080 USA
Tel: 214 907-0871
`swt@netcom.com`

Takelap Systems Ltd.
The Reddings, Court Robin Lane,
Llangwm, Usk, Gwent, United Kingdom NP5 1ET.
Tel: +44 (0)291 650357
Fax: +44 (0)291 650500
`info@ddrive.demon.co.uk`

Trans-Ameritech Enterprises, Inc.
2342A Walsh Ave
Santa Clara, CA 95051 USA
Tel: 408 727-3883
`roman@trans-ameritech.com`

Unifix Software GmbH
Postfach 4918
D-38039 Braunschweig
Germany
Tel: +49 (0)531 515161
Fax: +49 (0)531 515162

Yggdrasil Computing, Incorporated
4880 Stevens Creek Blvd., Suite 205
San Jose, CA 95129-1034 USA
Tel: 800 261-6630, 408 261-6630
Fax: 408 261-6631
`info@yggdrasil.com`

APPENDIX C

FTP Tutorial and Site List

The File Transfer Protocol (FTP) is the set of programs used for transferring files between systems on the Internet. Most Unix, VMS, and MS-DOS systems on the Internet have a program called `ftp` which you use to transfer these files, and if you have Internet access, the best way to download the Linux software is by using `ftp`. This appendix covers basic `ftp` usage—of course, there are many more functions and uses of `ftp` than are given here.

At the end of this appendix there is a listing of FTP sites where Linux software can be found. Also, if you don't have direct Internet access but are able to exchange electronic mail with the Internet, information on using the `ftpmail` service is included below.

If you're using an MS-DOS, Unix, or VMS system to download files from the Internet, then `ftp` is a command-driven program. However, there are other implementations of `ftp` out there, such as the Macintosh version (called `Fetch`) with a nice menu-driven interface, which is quite self-explanatory. Even if you're not using the command-driven version of `ftp`, the information given here should help.

`ftp` can be used to both upload (send) or download (receive) files from other Internet sites. In most situations, you're going to be downloading software. On the Internet there are a large number of publicly-available **FTP archive sites**, machines which allow anyone to `ftp` to them and download free software. One such archive site is `sunsite.unc.edu`, which has a lot of Sun Microsystems software, and acts as one of the main Linux sites. In addition, FTP archive sites **mirror** software to each other—that is, software uploaded to one site will be automatically copied over to a number of other sites. So don't be surprised if you see the exact same files on many different archive sites.

Starting `ftp`

Note that in the example "screens" printed below I'm only showing the most important information, and what you see may differ. Also, commands in *italics* represent commands that you type; everything else is screen output.

To start `ftp` and connect to a site, simply use the command

```
ftp ⟨hostname⟩
```

where ⟨*hostname*⟩ is the name of the site you are connecting to. For example, to connect to the mythical site `shoop.vpizza.com` we can use the command

```
ftp shoop.vpizza.com
```

Logging In

When `ftp` starts up we should see something like

```
Connected to shoop.vpizza.com.
220 Shoop.vpizza.com FTPD ready at 15 Dec 1992 08:20:42 EDT
Name (shoop.vpizza.com:mdw):
```

Here, ftp is asking us to give the user name that we want to login as on shoop.vpizza.com. The default here is mdw, which is my user name on the system I'm using FTP from. Since I don't have an account on shoop.vpizza.com I can't login as myself. Instead, to access publicly-available software on an FTP site you login as anonymous, and give your Internet e-mail address (if you have one) as the password. So, we would type

```
Name (shoop.vpizza.com:mdw):  anonymous
331-Guest login ok, send e-mail address as password.
Password:  mdw@sunsite.unc.edu
230- Welcome to shoop.vpizza.com.
230- Virtual Pizza Delivery[tm]:  Download pizza in 30 cycles or less
230- or you get it FREE!
ftp>
```

Of course, you should give your e-mail address, instead of mine, and it won't echo to the screen as you're typing it (since it's technically a "password"). ftp should allow us to login and we'll be ready to download software.

Poking Around

Okay, we're in. ftp> is our prompt, and the ftp program is waiting for commands. There are a few basic commands you need to know about. First, the commands

ls ⟨*file*⟩

and

dir ⟨*file*⟩

both give file listings (where ⟨*file*⟩ is an optional argument specifying a particular file name to list). The difference is that ls usually gives a short listing and dir gives a longer listing (that is, with more information on the sizes of the files, dates of modification, and so on).

The command

cd ⟨*directory*⟩

will move to the given directory (just like the cd command on Unix or MS-DOS systems). You can use the command

cdup

to change to the parent directory[1].

The command

help ⟨*command*⟩

will give help on the given ftp ⟨*command*⟩ (such as ls or cd). If no command is specified, ftp will list all of the available commands.

If we type dir at this point we'll see an initial directory listing of where we are.

[1] The directory above the current one.

```
ftp> dir
200 PORT command successful.
150 Opening ASCII mode data connection for /bin/ls.
total 1337

dr-xr-xr-x  2 root     wheel          512 Aug 13 13:55 bin
drwxr-xr-x  2 root     wheel          512 Aug 13 13:58 dev
drwxr-xr-x  2 root     wheel          512 Jan 25 17:35 etc
drwxr-xr-x 19 root     wheel         1024 Jan 27 21:39 pub
drwxrwx-wx  4 root     ftp-admi      1024 Feb  6 22:10 uploads
drwxr-xr-x  3 root     wheel          512 Mar 11  1992 usr

226 Transfer complete.
921 bytes received in 0.24 seconds (3.7 Kbytes/s)
ftp>
```

Each of these entries is a directory, not an individual file which we can download (specified by the d in the first column of the listing). On most FTP archive sites, the publicly available software is under the directory /pub, so let's go there.

```
ftp> cd pub
ftp> dir
200 PORT command successful.
150 ASCII data connection for /bin/ls (128.84.181.1,4525) (0 bytes).
total 846

-rw-r--r--   1 root      staff        1433 Jul 12  1988 README
-r--r--r--   1 3807      staff       15586 May 13  1991 US-DOMAIN.TXT.2
-rw-r--r--   1 539       staff       52664 Feb 20  1991 altenergy.avail
-r--r--r--   1 65534     65534       56456 Dec 17  1990 ataxx.tar.Z
-rw-r--r--   1 root      other     2013041 Jul  3  1991 gesyps.tar.Z
-rw-r--r--   1 432       staff       41831 Jan 30  1989 gnexe.arc
-rw-rw-rw-   1 615       staff       50315 Apr 16  1992 linpack.tar.Z
-r--r--r--   1 root      wheel       12168 Dec 25  1990 localtime.o
-rw-r--r--   1 root      staff        7035 Aug 27  1986 manualslist.tblms
drwxr-xr-x   2 2195      staff         512 Mar 10 00:48 mdw
-rw-r--r--   1 root      staff        5593 Jul 19  1988 t.out.h

226 ASCII Transfer complete.
2443 bytes received in 0.35 seconds (6.8 Kbytes/s)
ftp>
```

Here we can see a number of (interesting?) files, one of which is called README, which we should download (most FTP sites have a README file in the /pub directory).

Downloading files

Before downloading files, there are a few things that you need to take care of.

- **Turn on hash mark printing.** Hash marks are printed to the screen as files are being transferred; they let you know how far along the transfer is, and that your connection hasn't hung up (so you don't sit for 20 minutes, thinking that you're still downloading a file). In general, a hash mark appears as a pound sign (#), and one is printed for every 1024 or 8192 bytes transferred, depending on your system.

  To turn on hash mark printing, give the command hash.

```
ftp> hash
Hash mark printing on (8192 bytes/hash mark).
ftp>
```

- **Determine the type of file which you are downloading.** As far as FTP is concerned, files come in two flavors: **binary** and **text**. Most of the files which you'll be downloading are binary files: that is, programs, compressed files, archive files, and so on. However, many files (such as `README`s and so on) are text files.

  Why does the file type matter? Only because on some systems (such as MS-DOS systems), certain characters in a text file, such as carriage returns, need to be converted so that the file will be readable. While transferring in binary mode, no conversion is done—the file is simply transferred byte after byte.

  The commands `bin` and `ascii` set the transfer mode to binary and text, respectively. When in doubt, always use binary mode to transfer files. If you try to transfer a binary file in text mode, you'll corrupt the file and it will be unusable. (This is one of the most common mistakes made when using FTP.) However, you can use text mode for plain text files (whose file names often end in `.txt`).

  For our example, we're downloading the file `README`, which is most likely a text file, so we use the command

```
ftp> ascii
200 Type set to A.
ftp>
```

- **Set your local directory.** Your **local directory** is the directory on your system where you want the downloaded files to end up. Whereas the `cd` command changes the remote directory (on the remote machine which you're FTP'ing to), the `lcd` command changes the local directory.

  For example, to set the local directory to `/home/db/mdw/tmp`, use the command

```
ftp> lcd /home/db/mdw/tmp
Local directory now /home/db/mdw/tmp
ftp>
```

Now you're ready to actually download the file. The command

`get` ⟨*remote-name*⟩ ⟨*local-name*⟩

is used for this, where ⟨*remote-name*⟩ is the name of the file on the remote machine, and ⟨*local-name*⟩ is the name that you wish to give the file on your local machine. The ⟨*local-name*⟩ argument is optional; by default, the local file name is the same as the remote one. However, if for example you're downloading the file `README`, and you already have a `README` in your local directory, you'll want to give a different ⟨*local-filename*⟩ so that the first one isn't overwritten.

For our example, to download the file `README`, we simply use

```
ftp> get README
200 PORT command successful.
150 ASCII data connection for README (128.84.181.1,4527) (1433 bytes).
#
226 ASCII Transfer complete.
local:  README remote:  README
1493 bytes received in 0.03 seconds (49 Kbytes/s)
ftp>
```

Quitting FTP

To end your FTP session, simply use the command

```
quit
```

The command

```
close
```

can be used to close the connection with the current remote FTP site; the open command can then be used to start a session with another site (without quitting the FTP program altogether).

```
ftp> close
221 Goodbye.
ftp> quit
```

Using ftpmail

ftpmail is a service which allows you to obtain files from FTP archive sites via Internet electronic mail. If you don't have direct Internet access, but are able to send mail to the Internet (from a service such as CompuServe, for example), ftpmail is a good way to get files from FTP archive sites. Unfortunately, ftpmail can be slow, especially when sending large jobs. Before attempting to download large amounts of software using ftpmail, be sure that your mail spool will be able to handle the incoming traffic. Many systems keep quotas on incoming electronic mail, and may delete your account if your mail exceeds this quota. Just use common sense.

sunsite.unc.edu, one of the major Linux FTP archive sites, is home to an ftpmail server. To use this service, send electronic mail to

```
ftpmail@sunsite.unc.edu
```

with a message body containing only the word:

```
help
```

This will send you back a list of ftpmail commands and a brief tutorial on using the system.

For example, to get a listing of Linux files found on sunsite.unc.edu, send mail to the above address containing the text

```
open sunsite.unc.edu
cd /pub/Linux
dir
quit
```

You may use the ftpmail service to connect to any FTP archive site; you are not limited to sunsite.unc.edu. The next section lists a number of Linux FTP archives.

Linux FTP Site List

The table on page 202 is a listing of the most well-known FTP archive sites which carry the Linux software. Keep in mind that many other sites mirror these, and more than likely you'll run into Linux on a number of sites not on this list.

tsx-11.mit.edu, sunsite.unc.edu, and nic.funet.fi are the "home sites" for the Linux software, where most of the new software is uploaded. Most of the other sites on the list mirror some combination of these three. To reduce network traffic, choose a site that is geographically closest to you.

Site Name	IP Address	Directory
tsx-11.mit.edu	18.172.1.2	/pub/linux
sunsite.unc.edu	152.2.22.81	/pub/Linux
nic.funet.fi	128.214.6.100	/pub/OS/Linux
ftp.mcc.ac.uk	130.88.200.7	/pub/linux
fgb1.fgb.mw.tu-muenchen.de	129.187.200.1	/pub/linux
ftp.informatik.tu-muenchen.de	131.159.0.110	/pub/Linux
ftp.dfv.rwth-aachen.de	137.226.4.105	/pub/linux
ftp.informatik.rwth-aachen.de	137.226.112.172	/pub/Linux
ftp.ibp.fr	132.227.60.2	/pub/linux
kirk.bu.oz.au	131.244.1.1	/pub/OS/Linux
ftp.uu.net	137.39.1.9	/systems/unix/linux
wuarchive.wustl.edu	128.252.135.4	/systems/linux
ftp.win.tue.nl	131.155.70.100	/pub/linux
ftp.ibr.cs.tu-bs.de	134.169.34.15	/pub/os/linux
ftp.denet.dk	129.142.6.74	/pub/OS/linux

Table C.1: Linux FTP Sites

APPENDIX D

The GNU General Public License

Printed below is the GNU General Public License (the *GPL* or *copyleft*), under which Linux is licensed. It is reproduced here to clear up some of the confusion about Linux's copyright status—Linux is *not* shareware, and it is *not* in the public domain. The bulk of the Linux kernel is copyright ©1993 by Linus Torvalds, and other software and parts of the kernel are copyrighted by their authors. Thus, Linux *is* copyrighted, however, you may redistribute it under the terms of the GPL printed below.

GNU GENERAL PUBLIC LICENSE

Version 2, June 1991

Copyright ©1989, 1991 Free Software Foundation, Inc. 675 Mass Ave, Cambridge, MA 02139, USA Everyone is permitted to copy and distribute verbatim copies of this license document, but changing it is not allowed.

PREAMBLE

The licenses for most software are designed to take away your freedom to share and change it. By contrast, the GNU General Public License is intended to guarantee your freedom to share and change free software–to make sure the software is free for all its users. This General Public License applies to most of the Free Software Foundation's software and to any other program whose authors commit to using it. (Some other Free Software Foundation software is covered by the GNU Library General Public License instead.) You can apply it to your programs, too.

When we speak of free software, we are referring to freedom, not price. Our General Public Licenses are designed to make sure that you have the freedom to distribute copies of free software (and charge for this service if you wish), that you receive source code or can get it if you want it, that you can change the software or use pieces of it in new free programs; and that you know you can do these things.

To protect your rights, we need to make restrictions that forbid anyone to deny you these rights or to ask you to surrender the rights. These restrictions translate to certain responsibilities for you if you distribute copies of the software, or if you modify it.

For example, if you distribute copies of such a program, whether gratis or for a fee, you must give the recipients all the rights that you have. You must make sure that they, too, receive or can get the source code. And you must show them these terms so they know their rights.

We protect your rights with two steps: (1) copyright the software, and (2) offer you this license which gives you legal permission to copy, distribute and/or modify the software.

Also, for each author's protection and ours, we want to make certain that everyone understands that there is no warranty for this free software. If the software is modified by someone else and passed on, we want its recipients to know that what they have is not the original, so that any problems introduced by others will not reflect on the original authors' reputations.

Finally, any free program is threatened constantly by software patents. We wish to avoid the danger that redistributors of a free program will individually obtain patent licenses, in effect making the program proprietary. To prevent this, we have made it clear that any patent must be licensed for everyone's free use or not licensed at all.

The precise terms and conditions for copying, distribution and modification follow.

GNU GENERAL PUBLIC LICENSE

TERMS AND CONDITIONS FOR COPYING, DISTRIBUTION AND MODIFICATION

0. This License applies to any program or other work which contains a notice placed by the copyright holder saying it may be distributed under the terms of this General Public License. The "Program", below, refers to any such program or work, and a "work based on the Program" means either the Program or any derivative work under copyright law: that is to say, a work containing the Program or a portion of it, either verbatim or with modifications and/or translated into another language. (Hereinafter, translation is included without limitation in the term "modification".) Each licensee is addressed as "you".

   Activities other than copying, distribution and modification are not covered by this License; they are outside its scope. The act of running the Program is not restricted, and the output from the Program is covered only if its contents constitute a work based on the Program (independent of having been made by running the Program). Whether that is true depends on what the Program does.

1. You may copy and distribute verbatim copies of the Program's source code as you receive it, in any medium, provided that you conspicuously and appropriately publish on each copy an appropriate copyright notice and disclaimer of warranty; keep intact all the notices that refer to this License and to the absence of any warranty; and give any other recipients of the Program a copy of this License along with the Program.

   You may charge a fee for the physical act of transferring a copy, and you may at your option offer warranty protection in exchange for a fee.

2. You may modify your copy or copies of the Program or any portion of it, thus forming a work based on the Program, and copy and distribute such modifications or work under the terms of Section 1 above, provided that you also meet all of these conditions:

   a. You must cause the modified files to carry prominent notices stating that you changed the files and the date of any change.

   b. You must cause any work that you distribute or publish, that in whole or in part contains or is derived from the Program or any part thereof, to be licensed as a whole at no charge to all third parties under the terms of this License.

   c. If the modified program normally reads commands interactively when run, you must cause it, when started running for such interactive use in the most ordinary way, to print or display an announcement including an appropriate copyright notice and a notice that there is no warranty (or else, saying that you provide a warranty) and that users may redistribute the program under these conditions, and telling the user how to view a copy of this License. (Exception: if the Program itself is interactive but does not normally print such an announcement, your work based on the Program is not required to print an announcement.)

   These requirements apply to the modified work as a whole. If identifiable sections of that work are not derived from the Program, and can be reasonably considered independent and separate works in themselves, then this License, and its terms, do not apply to those sections when you distribute them as separate works. But when you distribute the same sections as part of a whole which is a work based on the Program, the distribution of the whole must be on the terms of this License, whose permissions for other licensees extend to the entire whole, and thus to each and every part regardless of who wrote it.

   Thus, it is not the intent of this section to claim rights or contest your rights to work written entirely by you; rather, the intent is to exercise the right to control the distribution of derivative or collective works based on the Program.

   In addition, mere aggregation of another work not based on the Program with the Program (or with a work based on the Program) on a volume of a storage or distribution medium does not bring the other work under the scope of this License.

3. You may copy and distribute the Program (or a work based on it, under Section 2) in object code or executable form under the terms of Sections 1 and 2 above provided that you also do one of the following:

    a. Accompany it with the complete corresponding machine-readable source code, which must be distributed under the terms of Sections 1 and 2 above on a medium customarily used for software interchange; or,

    b. Accompany it with a written offer, valid for at least three years, to give any third party, for a charge no more than your cost of physically performing source distribution, a complete machine-readable copy of the corresponding source code, to be distributed under the terms of Sections 1 and 2 above on a medium customarily used for software interchange; or,

    c. Accompany it with the information you received as to the offer to distribute corresponding source code. (This alternative is allowed only for noncommercial distribution and only if you received the program in object code or executable form with such an offer, in accord with Subsection b above.)

    The source code for a work means the preferred form of the work for making modifications to it. For an executable work, complete source code means all the source code for all modules it contains, plus any associated interface definition files, plus the scripts used to control compilation and installation of the executable. However, as a special exception, the source code distributed need not include anything that is normally distributed (in either source or binary form) with the major components (compiler, kernel, and so on) of the operating system on which the executable runs, unless that component itself accompanies the executable.

    If distribution of executable or object code is made by offering access to copy from a designated place, then offering equivalent access to copy the source code from the same place counts as distribution of the source code, even though third parties are not compelled to copy the source along with the object code.

4. You may not copy, modify, sublicense, or distribute the Program except as expressly provided under this License. Any attempt otherwise to copy, modify, sublicense or distribute the Program is void, and will automatically terminate your rights under this License. However, parties who have received copies, or rights, from you under this License will not have their licenses terminated so long as such parties remain in full compliance.

5. You are not required to accept this License, since you have not signed it. However, nothing else grants you permission to modify or distribute the Program or its derivative works. These actions are prohibited by law if you do not accept this License. Therefore, by modifying or distributing the Program (or any work based on the Program), you indicate your acceptance of this License to do so, and all its terms and conditions for copying, distributing or modifying the Program or works based on it.

6. Each time you redistribute the Program (or any work based on the Program), the recipient automatically receives a license from the original licensor to copy, distribute or modify the Program subject to these terms and conditions. You may not impose any further restrictions on the recipients' exercise of the rights granted herein. You are not responsible for enforcing compliance by third parties to this License.

7. If, as a consequence of a court judgment or allegation of patent infringement or for any other reason (not limited to patent issues), conditions are imposed on you (whether by court order, agreement or otherwise) that contradict the conditions of this License, they do not excuse you from the conditions of this License. If you cannot distribute so as to satisfy simultaneously your obligations under this License and any other pertinent obligations, then as a consequence you may not distribute the Program at all. For example, if a patent license would not permit royalty-free redistribution of the Program by all those who receive copies directly or indirectly through you, then the only way you could satisfy both it and this License would be to refrain entirely from distribution of the Program.

If any portion of this section is held invalid or unenforceable under any particular circumstance, the balance of the section is intended to apply and the section as a whole is intended to apply in other circumstances.

It is not the purpose of this section to induce you to infringe any patents or other property right claims or to contest validity of any such claims; this section has the sole purpose of protecting the integrity of the free software distribution system, which is implemented by public license practices. Many people have made generous contributions to the wide range of software distributed through that system in reliance on consistent application of that system; it is up to the author/donor to decide if he or she is willing to distribute software through any other system and a licensee cannot impose that choice.

This section is intended to make thoroughly clear what is believed to be a consequence of the rest of this License.

8. If the distribution and/or use of the Program is restricted in certain countries either by patents or by copyrighted interfaces, the original copyright holder who places the Program under this License may add an explicit geographical distribution limitation excluding those countries, so that distribution is permitted only in or among countries not thus excluded. In such case, this License incorporates the limitation as if written in the body of this License.

9. The Free Software Foundation may publish revised and/or new versions of the General Public License from time to time. Such new versions will be similar in spirit to the present version, but may differ in detail to address new problems or concerns.

   Each version is given a distinguishing version number. If the Program specifies a version number of this License which applies to it and "any later version", you have the option of following the terms and conditions either of that version or of any later version published by the Free Software Foundation. If the Program does not specify a version number of this License, you may choose any version ever published by the Free Software Foundation.

10. If you wish to incorporate parts of the Program into other free programs whose distribution conditions are different, write to the author to ask for permission. For software which is copyrighted by the Free Software Foundation, write to the Free Software Foundation; we sometimes make exceptions for this. Our decision will be guided by the two goals of preserving the free status of all derivatives of our free software and of promoting the sharing and reuse of software generally.

NO WARRANTY

11. BECAUSE THE PROGRAM IS LICENSED FREE OF CHARGE, THERE IS NO WARRANTY FOR THE PROGRAM, TO THE EXTENT PERMITTED BY APPLICABLE LAW. EXCEPT WHEN OTHERWISE STATED IN WRITING THE COPYRIGHT HOLDERS AND/OR OTHER PARTIES PROVIDE THE PROGRAM "AS IS" WITHOUT WARRANTY OF ANY KIND, EITHER EXPRESSED OR IMPLIED, INCLUDING, BUT NOT LIMITED TO, THE IMPLIED WARRANTIES OF MERCHANTABILITY AND FITNESS FOR A PARTICULAR PURPOSE. THE ENTIRE RISK AS TO THE QUALITY AND PERFORMANCE OF THE PROGRAM IS WITH YOU. SHOULD THE PROGRAM PROVE DEFECTIVE, YOU ASSUME THE COST OF ALL NECESSARY SERVICING, REPAIR OR CORRECTION.

12. IN NO EVENT UNLESS REQUIRED BY APPLICABLE LAW OR AGREED TO IN WRITING WILL ANY COPYRIGHT HOLDER, OR ANY OTHER PARTY WHO MAY MODIFY AND/OR REDISTRIBUTE THE PROGRAM AS PERMITTED ABOVE, BE LIABLE TO YOU FOR DAMAGES, INCLUDING ANY GENERAL, SPECIAL, INCIDENTAL OR CONSEQUENTIAL DAMAGES ARISING OUT OF THE USE OR INABILITY TO USE THE PROGRAM (INCLUDING BUT NOT LIMITED TO LOSS OF DATA OR DATA BEING RENDERED INACCURATE OR LOSSES SUSTAINED BY YOU OR THIRD PARTIES OR A FAILURE OF THE PROGRAM TO OPERATE WITH ANY OTHER PROGRAMS), EVEN IF SUCH HOLDER OR OTHER PARTY HAS BEEN ADVISED OF THE POSSIBILITY OF SUCH DAMAGES.

END OF TERMS AND CONDITIONS

APPENDIX: HOW TO APPLY THESE TERMS TO YOUR NEW PROGRAMS

If you develop a new program, and you want it to be of the greatest possible use to the public, the best way to achieve this is to make it free software which everyone can redistribute and change under these terms.

To do so, attach the following notices to the program. It is safest to attach them to the start of each source file to most effectively convey the exclusion of warranty; and each file should have at least the "copyright" line and a pointer to where the full notice is found.

> ⟨*one line to give the program's name and a brief idea of what it does.*⟩ Copyright ©19yy ⟨*name of author*⟩
>
> This program is free software; you can redistribute it and/or modify it under the terms of the GNU General Public License as published by the Free Software Foundation; either version 2 of the License, or (at your option) any later version.
>
> This program is distributed in the hope that it will be useful, but WITHOUT ANY WARRANTY; without even the implied warranty of MERCHANTABILITY or FITNESS FOR A PARTICULAR PURPOSE. See the GNU General Public License for more details.
>
> You should have received a copy of the GNU General Public License along with this program; if not, write to the Free Software Foundation, Inc., 675 Mass Ave, Cambridge, MA 02139, USA.

Also add information on how to contact you by electronic and paper mail.

If the program is interactive, make it output a short notice like this when it starts in an interactive mode:

```
Gnomovision version 69, Copyright (C) 19yy name of author Gnomovision comes with
ABSOLUTELY NO WARRANTY; for details type 'show w'. This is free software, and you
are welcome to redistribute it under certain conditions; type 'show c' for details.
```

The hypothetical commands 'show w' and 'show c' should show the appropriate parts of the General Public License. Of course, the commands you use may be called something other than 'show w' and 'show c'; they could even be mouse-clicks or menu items–whatever suits your program.

You should also get your employer (if you work as a programmer) or your school, if any, to sign a "copyright disclaimer" for the program, if necessary. Here is a sample; alter the names:

> Yoyodyne, Inc., hereby disclaims all copyright interest in the program 'Gnomovision' (which makes passes at compilers) written by James Hacker.
>
> *signature of Ty Coon*, 1 April 1989
> Ty Coon, President of Vice

This General Public License does not permit incorporating your program into proprietary programs. If your program is a subroutine library, you may consider it more useful to permit linking proprietary applications with the library. If this is what you want to do, use the GNU Library General Public License instead of this License.

Part II

Linux System Administrator's Guide 0.6
by Lars Wirzenius

Contents

Linux System Administrators' Guide 0.6

Lars Wirzenius

The Linux Documentation Project

This is version 0.6 of the Linux System Administrators' Guide.
Published November 15, 1997.

The LaTeX source code and other machine readable formats can be found on the Internet via anonymous ftp on `sunsite.unc.edu`, in the directory `/pub/Linux/docs/LDP`. Also available are at least Postscript and TeX .DVI formats. The official home page for the book is `http://www.iki.fi/liw/linux/sag/`. The current version can always be found at that location.

This page is dedicated to a future dedication.

In the mean time... I'd like someone who knows him let Terry Pratchett know that his way of using footnotes is rather inspiring.

CHAPTER 1

Introduction

In the beginning, the file was without form, and void; and emptiness was upon the face of the bits. And the Fingers of the Author moved upon the face of the keyboard. And the Author said, Let there be words, and there were words.

This manual, the Linux System Administrators' Guide, describes the system administration aspects of using Linux. It is intended for people who know next to nothing about system administration (as in "what is it?"), but who have already mastered at least the basics of normal usage. This manual also doesn't tell you how to install Linux; that is described in the Installation and Getting Started document. See below for more information about Linux manuals.

System administration is all the things that one has to do to keep a computer system in a useable shape. It includes things like backing up files (and restoring them if necessary), installing new programs, creating accounts for users (and deleting them when no longer needed), making certain that the file system is not corrupted, and so on. If a computer were, say, a house, system administration would be called maintenance, and would include cleaning, fixing broken windows, and other such things. System administration is not called maintenance, because that would be too simple.[1]

The structure of this manual is such that many of the chapters should be usable independently, so that if you need information about, say, backups, you can read just that chapter.[2] This hopefully makes the book easier to use as a reference manual, and makes it possible to read just a small part when needed, instead of having to read everything. However, this manual is first and foremost a tutorial, and a reference manual only as a lucky coincidence.

This manual is not intended to be used completely by itself. Plenty of the rest of the Linux documentation is also important for system administrators. After all, a system administrator is just a user with special privileges and duties. A very important resource are the manual pages, which should always be consulted when a command is not familiar.

While this manual is targeted at Linux, a general principle has been that it should be useful with other UNIX based operating systems as well. Unfortunately, since there is so much variance between different versions of UNIX in general, and in system administration in particular, there is little hope to cover all variants. Even covering all possibilities for Linux is difficult, due to the nature of its development.

There is no one official Linux distribution, so different people have different setups, and many people have a setup they have built up themselves. This book is not targeted at any one distribution, even though I use the Debian GNU/Linux system almost exclusively. When possible, I have tried to point out differences, and explain several alternatives.

I have tried to describe how things work, rather than just listing "five easy steps" for each task. This means that there is much information here that is not necessary for everyone, but those parts are marked as

[1] There are some people who *do* call it that, but that's just because they have never read this manual, poor things.

[2] If you happen to be reading a version that has a chapter on backups, that is.

such and can be skipped if you use a preconfigured system. Reading everything will, naturally, increase your understanding of the system and should make using and administering it more pleasant.

Like all other Linux related development, the work was done on a volunteer basis: I did it because I thought it might be fun and because I felt it should be done. However, like all volunteer work, there is a limit to how much effort I have been able to spend, and also on how much knowledge and experience I have. This means that the manual is not necessarily as good as it would be if a wizard had been paid handsomely to write it and had spent a few years to perfect it. I think, of course, that it is pretty nice, but be warned.

One particular point where I have cut corners is that I have not covered very thoroughly many things that are already well documented in other freely available manuals. This applies especially to program specific documentation, such as all the details of using `mkfs`). I only describe the purpose of the program, and as much of its usage as is necessary for the purposes of this manual. For further information, I refer the gentle reader to these other manuals. Usually, all of the referred to documentation is part of the full Linux documentation set.

While I have tried to make this manual as good as possible, I would really like to hear from you if you have any ideas on how to make it better. Bad language, factual errors, ideas for new areas to cover, rewritten sections, information about how various UNIX versions do things, I am interested in all of it. My contact information is available via the World Wide Web at `http://www.iki.fi/liw/mail-to-lasu.html`. You need to read this web page to bypass my junkmail filters.

Many people have helped me with this book, directly or indirectly. I would like to especially thank Matt Welsh for inspiration and LDP leadership, Andy Oram for getting me to work again with much-valued feedback, Olaf Kirch for showing me that it can be done, and Adam Richter at Yggdrasil and others for showing me that other people can find it interesting as well.

Stephen Tweedie, H. Peter Anvin, Rémy Card, Theodore Ts'o, and Stephen Tweedie have let me borrow their work[3] (and thus make the book look thicker and much more impressive). I am most grateful for this, and very apologetic for the earlier versions that sometimes lacked proper attribution.

In addition, I would like to thank Mark Komarinski for sending his material in 1993 and the many system administration columns in Linux Journal. They are quite informative and inspirational.

Many useful comments have been sent by a large number of people. My miniature black hole of an archive doesn't let me find all their names, but some of them are, in alphabetical order: Paul Caprioli, Ales Cepek, Marie-France Declerfayt, Dave Dobson, Olaf Flebbe, Helmut Geyer, Larry Greenfield and his father, Stephen Harris, Jyrki Havia, Jim Haynes, York Lam, Timothy Andrew Lister, Jim Lynch, Michael J. Micek, Jacob Navia, Dan Poirier, Daniel Quinlan, Jouni K Seppänen, Philippe Steindl, G.B. Stotte. My apologies to anyone I have forgotten.

[3] A comparison between the xia and ext2 file systems, the device list and a description of the ext2 file system. These aren't part of the book any more.

The LDP Rhyme[4]

A wondrous thing,
and beautiful,
'tis to write,
a book.

I'd like to sing,
of the sweat,
the blood and tear,
which it also took.

It started back in,
nineteen-ninety-two,
when users whined,
"we can nothing do!"

They wanted to know,
what their problem was,
and how to fix it
(by yesterday).

We put the answers in,
a Linux f-a-q,
hoped to get away,
from any more writin'.

"That's too long,
it's hard to search,
and we don't read it,
any-which-way!"

Then a few of us,
joined together
(virtually, you know),
to start the LDP.

We started to write,
or plan, at least,
several books,
one for every need.

The start was fun,
a lot of talk,
an outline,
then a slew.

Then silence came,
the work began,
some wrote less,
others more.

A blank screen,
oh its horrible,
it sits there,
laughs in the face.

We still await,
the final day,
when everything,
will be done.

Until then,
all we have,
is a draft,
for you to comment on.

[4]The author wishes to remain anonymous. It was posted to the LDP mailing list by Matt Welsh.

CHAPTER 2

Overview of a Linux System

God looked over everything he had made,
and saw that it was very good.
Genesis 1:31

This chapter gives an overview of a Linux system. First, the major services provided by the operating system are described. Then, the programs that implement these services are described with a considerable lack of detail. The purpose of this chapter is to give an understanding of the system as a whole, so that each part is described in detail elsewhere.

2.1 Various parts of an operating system

A UNIX operating system consists of a **kernel** and some **system programs**. There are also some **application programs** for doing work. The kernel is the heart of the operating system[1]. It keeps track of files on the disk, starts programs and runs them concurrently, assigns memory and other resources to various processes, receives packets from and sends packets to the network, and so on. The kernel does very little by itself, but it provides tools with which all services can be built. It also prevents anyone from accessing the hardware directly, forcing everyone to use the tools it provides. This way the kernel provides some protection for users from each other. The tools provided by the kernel are used via **system calls**; see manual page section 2 for more information on these.

The system programs use the tools provided by the kernel to implement the various services required from an operating system. System programs, and all other programs, run 'on top of the kernel', in what is called the **user mode**. The difference between system and application programs is one of intent: applications are intended for getting useful things done (or for playing, if it happens to be a game), whereas system programs are needed to get the system working. A word processor is an application; `telnet` is a system program. The difference is often somewhat blurry, however, and is important only to compulsive categorizers.

An operating system can also contain compilers and their corresponding libraries (GCC and the C library in particular under Linux), although not all programming languages need be part of the operating system. Documentation, and sometimes even games, can also be part of it. Traditionally, the operating system has been defined by the contents of the installation tape or disks; with Linux it is not as clear since it is spread all over the FTP sites of the world.

[1] In fact, it is often mistakenly considered to be the operating system itself, but it is not. An operating system provides many more services than a plain kernel.

2.2 Important parts of the kernel

The Linux kernel consists of several important parts: process management, memory management, hardware device drivers, file system drivers, network management, and various other bits and pieces. Figure 2.1 shows some of them.

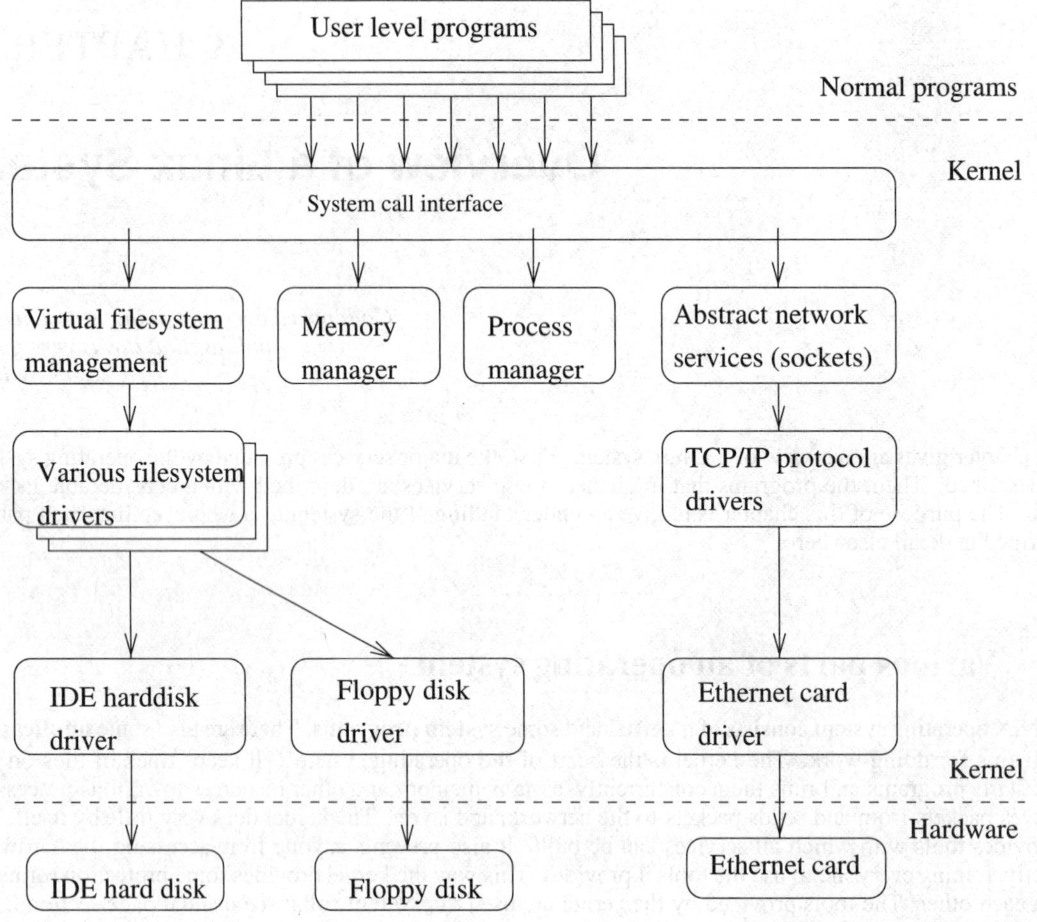

Figure 2.1: Some of the more important parts of the Linux kernel.

Probably the most important parts of the kernel (nothing else works without them) are memory management and process management. Memory management takes care of assigning memory areas and swap space areas to processes, parts of the kernel, and for the buffer cache. Process management creates processes, and implements multitasking by switching the active process on the processor.

At the lowest level, the kernel contains a hardware device driver for each kind of hardware it supports. Since the world is full of different kinds of hardware, the number of hardware device drivers is large. There are often many otherwise similar pieces of hardware that differ in how they are controlled by software. The similarities make it possible to have general classes of drivers that support similar operations; each member of the class has the same interface to the rest of the kernel but differs in what it needs to do to implement them. For example, all disk drivers look alike to the rest of the kernel, i.e., they all have operations like 'initialize the drive', 'read sector N', and 'write sector N'.

Some software services provided by the kernel itself have similar properties, and can therefore be abstracted into classes. For example, the various network protocols have been abstracted into one programming interface, the BSD socket library. Another example is the **virtual file system** (VFS) layer that abstracts the file system operations away from their implementation. Each file system type provides an implementation of each file system operation. When some entity tries to use a file system, the request goes via the VFS, which routes the request to the proper file system driver.

2.3 Major services in a UNIX system

This section describes some of the more important UNIX services, but without much detail. They are described more thoroughly in later chapters.

2.3.1 `init`

The single most important service in a UNIX system is provided by `init`. `init` is started as the first process of every UNIX system, as the last thing the kernel does when it boots. When `init` starts, it continues the boot process by doing various startup chores (checking and mounting file systems, starting daemons, etc).

The exact list of things that `init` does depends on which flavor it is; there are several to choose from. `init` usually provides the concept of **single user mode**, in which no one can log in and `root` uses a shell at the console; the usual mode is called **multiuser mode**. Some flavors generalize this as **run levels**; single and multiuser modes are considered to be two run levels, and there can be additional ones as well, for example, to run X on the console.

In normal operation, `init` makes sure `getty`s are working (to allow users to log in), and to adopt orphan processes (processes whose parent has died; in UNIX *all* processes *must* be in a single tree, so orphans must be adopted).

When the system is shut down, it is `init` that is in charge of killing all other processes, unmounting all file systems and stopping the processor, along with anything else it has been configured to do.

2.3.2 Logins from terminals

Logins from terminals (via serial lines) and the console (when not running X) are provided by the `getty` program. `init` starts a separate instance of `getty` for each terminal for which logins are to be allowed. `getty` reads the user name and runs the `login` program, which reads the password. If the user name and password are correct, `login` runs the shell. When the shell terminates, i.e., the user logs out, or when `login` terminated because the user name and password didn't match, `init` notices this and starts a new instance of `getty`. The kernel has no notion of logins, this is all handled by the system programs.

2.3.3 Syslog

The kernel and many system programs produce error, warning, and other messages. It is often important that these messages can be viewed later, even much later, so they should be written to a file. The program doing this is `syslog`. It can be configured to sort the messages to different files according to writer or degree of importance. For example, kernel messages are often directed to a separate file from the others, since kernel messages are often more important and need to be read regularly to spot problems.

2.3.4 Periodic command execution: `cron` and `at`

Both users and system administrators often need to run commands periodically. For example, the system administrator might want to run a command to clean the directories with temporary files (`/tmp` and `/var/tmp`) from old files, to keep the disks from filling up, since not all programs clean up after themselves correctly.

The `cron` service is set up to do this. Each user has a `crontab`, where he lists the commands he wants to execute and the times they should be executed. The `cron` daemon takes care of starting the commands when specified.

The `at` service is similar to `cron`, but it is once only: the command is executed at the given time, but it is not repeated.

2.3.5 Graphical user interface

UNIX and Linux don't incorporate the user interface into the kernel; instead, they let it be implemented by user level programs. This applies for both text mode and graphical environments.

This arrangement makes the system more flexible, but has the disadvantage that it is simple to implement a different user interface for each program, making the system harder to learn.

The graphical environment primarily used with Linux is called the X Window System (X for short). X also does not implement a user interface; it only implements a window system, i.e., tools with which a graphical user interface can be implemented. The three most popular user interface styles implemented over X are Athena, Motif, and Open Look.

2.3.6 Networking

Networking is the act of connecting two or more computers so that they can communicate with each other. The actual methods of connecting and communicating are slightly complicated, but the end result is very useful.

UNIX operating systems have many networking features. Most basic services—file systems, printing, backups, etc—can be done over the network. This can make system administration easier, since it allows centralized administration, while still reaping in the benefits of microcomputing and distributed computing, such as lower costs and better fault tolerance.

However, this book merely glances at networking; see the Linux Network Administrators' Guide for more information, including a basic description of how networks operate.

2.3.7 Network logins

Network logins work a little differently than normal logins. There is a separate physical serial line for each terminal via which it is possible to log in. For each person logging in via the network, there is a separate virtual network connection, and there can be any number of these[2]. It is therefore not possible to run a separate `getty` for each possible virtual connection. There are also several different ways to log in via a network, `telnet` and `rlogin` being the major ones in TCP/IP networks.

Network logins have, instead of a herd of `getty`s, a single daemon per way of logging in (`telnet` and `rlogin` have separate daemons) that listens for all incoming login attempts. When it notices one, it starts a new instance of itself to handle that single attempt; the original instance continues to listen for other attempts. The new instance works similarly to `getty`.

2.3.8 Network file systems

One of the more useful things that can be done with networking services is sharing files via a **network file system**. The one usually used is called the Network File System, or NFS, developed by Sun.

With a network file system any file operations done by a program on one machine are sent over the network to another computer. This fools the program to think that all the files on the other computer are actually on the computer the program is running on. This makes information sharing extremely simple, since it requires no modifications to programs.

2.3.9 Mail

Electronic mail is usually the most important method for communicating via computer. An electronic letter is stored in a file using a special format, and special mail programs are used to send and read the letters.

Each user has an **incoming mailbox** (a file in the special format), where all new mail is stored. When someone sends mail, the mail program locates the receiver's mailbox and appends the letter to the mailbox file. If the receiver's mailbox is in another machine, the letter is sent to the other machine, which delivers it to the mailbox as it best sees fit.

The mail system consists of many programs. The delivery of mail to local or remote mailboxes is done by one program (the **mail transfer agent** or **MTA**, e.g., `sendmail` or `smail`), while the programs users use

[2]Well, at least there can be many. Network bandwidth still being a scarce resource, there is still some practical upper limit to the number of concurrent logins via one network connection.

are many and varied (**mail user agent** or **MUA**, e.g., `pine` or `elm`). The mailboxes are usually stored in `/var/spool/mail`.

2.3.10 Printing

Only one person can use a printer at one time, but it is uneconomical not to share printers between users. The printer is therefore managed by software that implements a **print queue**: all print jobs are put into a queue and whenever the printer is done with one job, the next one is sent to it automatically. This relieves the users from organizing the print queue and fighting over control of the printer.[3]

The print queue software also **spools** the printouts on disk, i.e., the text is kept in a file while the job is in the queue. This allows an application program to spit out the print jobs quickly to the print queue software; the application does not have to wait until the job is actually printed to continue. This is really convenient, since it allows one to print out one version, and not have to wait for it to be printed before one can make a completely revised new version.

2.4 The file system layout

The file system is divided into many parts; usually along the lines of a root file system with `/bin`, `/lib`, `/etc`, `/dev`, and a few others; a `/usr` file system with programs and unchanging data; a `/var` file system with changing data (such as log files); and a `/home` file system for everyone's personal files. Depending on the hardware configuration and the decisions of the system administrator, the division can be different; it can even be all in one file system.

Chapter 3 describes the file system layout in some detail; the Linux Filesystem Standard covers it in somewhat more detail.

[3]Instead, they form a new queue *at* the printer, waiting for their printouts, since no one ever seems to be able to get the queue software to know exactly when anyone's printout is really finished. This is a great boost to intra-office social relations.

CHAPTER 3

Overview of the Directory Tree

Two days later, there was Pooh,
sitting on his branch, dangling his
legs, and there, beside him, were four
pots of honey…
(A.A. Milne)

This chapter describes the important parts of a standard Linux directory tree, based on the FSSTND file system standard. It outlines the normal way of breaking the directory tree into separate file systems with different purposes and gives the motivation behind this particular split. Some alternative ways of splitting are also described.

3.1 Background

This chapter is loosely based on the Linux file system standard, FSSTND, version 1.2, [1], which attempts to set a standard for how the directory tree in a Linux system is organized. Such a standard has the advantage that it will be easier to write or port software for Linux, and to administer Linux machines, since everything will be in their usual places. There is no authority behind the standard that forces anyone to comply with it, but it has got the support of most, if not all, Linux distributions. It is not a good idea to break with the FSSTND without very compelling reasons. The FSSTND attempts to follow Unix tradition and current trends, making Linux systems familiar to those with experience with other Unix systems, and vice versa.

This chapter is not as detailed as the FSSTND. A system administrator should also read the FSSTND for a complete understanding.

This chapter does not explain all files in detail. The intention is not to describe every file, but to give an overview of the system from a file system point of view. Further information on each file is available elsewhere in this manual or the manual pages.

The full directory tree is intended to be breakable into smaller parts, each on its own disk or partition, to accommodate to disk size limits and to ease backup and other system administration. The major parts are the root, `/usr`, `/var`, and `/home` file systems (see figure 3.1). Each part has a different purpose. The directory tree has been designed so that it works well in a network of Linux machines which may share some parts of the file systems over a read-only device (e.g., a CD-ROM), or over the network with NFS.

The roles of the different parts of the directory tree are described below.

- The root file system is specific for each machine (it is generally stored on a local disk, although it could be a ram disk or network drive as well) and contains the files that are necessary for booting the system up, and to bring it up to such a state that the other file systems may be mounted. The contents of the

[1] *Linux Filesystem Structure—Release 1.2,* by Daniel Quinlan, March, 1995

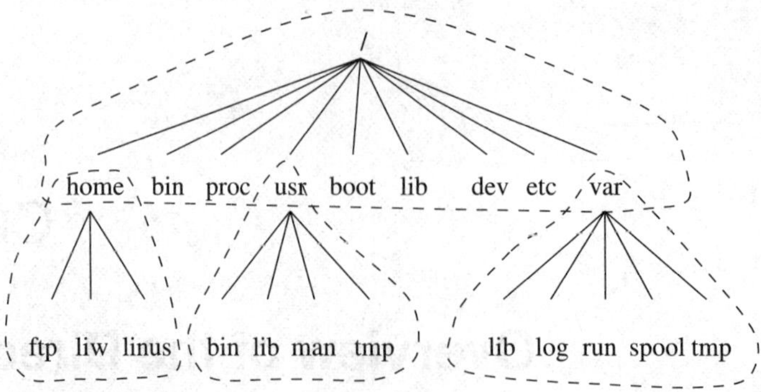

Figure 3.1: Parts of a Unix directory tree. Dashed lines indicate partition limits.

root file system will therefore be sufficient for the single user state. It will also contain tools for fixing a broken system, and for recovering lost files from backups.

- The `/usr` file system contains all commands, libraries, manual pages, and other unchanging files needed during normal operation. No files in `/usr` should be specific for any given machine, nor should they be modified during normal use. This allows the files to be shared over the network, which can be cost-effective since it saves disk space (there can easily be hundreds of megabytes in `/usr`), and can make administration easier (only the master `/usr` needs to be changed when updating an application, not each machine separately). Even if the file system is on a local disk, it could be mounted read-only, to lessen the chance of file system corruption during a crash.

- The `/var` file system contains files that change, such as spool directories (for mail, news, printers, etc), log files, formatted manual pages, and temporary files. Traditionally everything in `/var` has been somewhere below `/usr`, but that made it impossible to mount `/usr` read-only.

- The `/home` file system contains the users' home directories, i.e., all the real data on the system. Separating home directories to their own directory tree or file system makes backups easier; the other parts often do not have to be backed up, or at least not as often (they seldom change). A big `/home` might have to be broken on several file systems, which requires adding an extra naming level below `/home`, e.g., `/home/students` and `/home/staff`.

Although the different parts have been called file systems above, there is no requirement that they actually be on separate file systems. They could easily be kept in a single one if the system is a small single-user system and the user wants to keep things simple. The directory tree might also be divided into file systems differently, depending on how large the disks are, and how space is allocated for various purposes. The important part, though, is that all the standard *names* work; even if, say, `/var` and `/usr` are actually on the same partition, the names `/usr/lib/libc.a` and `/var/adm/messages` must work, for example by moving files below `/var` into `/usr/var`, and making `/var` a symlink to `/usr/var`.

The Unix file system structure groups files according to purpose, i.e., all commands are in one place, all data files in another, documentation in a third, and so on. An alternative would be to group files files according to the program they belong to, i.e., all Emacs files would be in one directory, all TEX in another, and so on. The problem with the latter approach is that it makes it difficult to share files (the program directory often contains both static and shareable and changing and non-shareable files), and sometimes to even find the files (e.g., manual pages in a huge number of places, and making the manual page programs find all of them is a maintenance nightmare).

3.2 The root file system

The root file system should generally be small, since it contains very critical files and a small, infrequently modified file system has a better chance of not getting corrupted. A corrupted root file system will generally mean that the system becomes unbootable except with special measures (e.g., from a floppy), so you don't want to risk it.

The root directory generally doesn't contain any files, except perhaps the standard boot image for the system, usually called `/vmlinuz`. All other files are in subdirectories in the root file systems:

`/bin` Commands needed during bootup that might be used by normal users (probably after bootup).

`/sbin` Like `/bin`, but the commands are not intended for normal users, although they may use them if necessary and allowed.

`/etc` Configuration files specific to the machine.

`/root` The home directory for user `root`.

`/lib` Shared libraries needed by the programs on the root file system.

`/lib/modules` Loadable kernel modules, especially those that are needed to boot the system when recovering from disasters (e.g., network and file system drivers).

`/dev` Device files.

`/tmp` Temporary files. Programs running after bootup should use `/var/tmp`, not `/tmp`, since the former is probably on a disk with more space.

`/boot` Files used by the bootstrap loader, e.g., LILO. Kernel images are often kept here instead of in the root directory. If there are many kernel images, the directory can easily grow rather big, and it might be better to keep it in a separate file system. Another reason would be to make sure the kernel images are within the first 1024 cylinders of an IDE disk.

`/mnt` Mount point for temporary mounts by the system administrator. Programs aren't supposed to mount on `/mnt` automatically. `/mnt` might be divided into subdirectories (e.g., `/mnt/dosa` might be the floppy drive using an MS-DOS file system, and `/mnt/exta` might be the same with an ext2 file system).

`/proc`, `/usr`, `/var`, `/home` Mount points for the other file systems.

3.2.1 The `/etc` directory

The `/etc` directory contains a lot of files. Some of them are described below. For others, you should determine which program they belong to and read the manual page for that program. Many networking configuration files are in `/etc` as well, and are described in the Networking Administrators' Guide.

`/etc/rc` or `/etc/rc.d` or `/etc/rc?.d` Scripts or directories of scripts to run at startup or when changing the run level. See the chapter on `init` for further information.

`/etc/passwd` The user database, with fields giving the user name, real name, home directory, encrypted password, and other information about each user. The format is documented in the *passwd* manual page.

`/etc/fdprm` Floppy disk parameter table. Describes what different floppy disk formats look like. Used by `setfdprm`. See the *setfdprm* manual page for more information.

`/etc/fstab` Lists the file systems mounted automatically at startup by the `mount -a` command (in `/etc/rc` or equivalent startup file). Under Linux, also contains information about swap areas used automatically by `swapon -a`. See section 4.8.5 and the *mount* manual page for more information.

`/etc/group` Similar to `/etc/passwd`, but describes groups instead of users. See the *group* manual page for more information.

`/etc/inittab` Configuration file for `init`.

`/etc/issue` Output by `getty` before the login prompt. Usually contains a short description or welcoming message to the system. The contents are up to the system administrator.

`/etc/magic` The configuration file for `file`. Contains the descriptions of various file formats based on which `file` guesses the type of the file. See the *magic* and *file* manual pages for more information.

`/etc/motd` The **message of the day**, automatically output after a successful login. Contents are up to the system administrator. Often used for getting information to every user, such as warnings about planned down times.

`/etc/mtab` List of currently mounted file systems. Initially set up by the scripts, and updated automatically by the `mount` command. Used when a list of mounted file systems is needed, e.g., by the `df` command.

`/etc/shadow` Shadow password file on systems with shadow password software installed. Shadow passwords move the encrypted password from `/etc/passwd` into `/etc/shadow`; the latter is not readable by anyone except `root`. This makes it harder to crack passwords.

`/etc/login.defs` Configuration file for the `login` command.

`/etc/printcap` Like `/etc/termcap`, but intended for printers. Different syntax.

`/etc/profile`, `/etc/csh.login`, `/etc/csh.cshrc` Files executed at login or startup time by the Bourne or C shells. These allow the system administrator to set global defaults for all users. See the manual pages for the respective shells.

`/etc/securetty` Identifies secure terminals, i.e., the terminals from which `root` is allowed to log in. Typically only the virtual consoles are listed, so that it becomes impossible (or at least harder) to gain superuser privileges by breaking into a system over a modem or a network.

`/etc/shells` Lists trusted shells. The `chsh` command allows users to change their login shell only to shells listed in this file. `ftpd`, the server process that provides FTP services for a machine, will check that the user's shell is listed in `/etc/shells` and will not let people log in unless the shell is listed there.

`/etc/termcap` The terminal capability database. Describes by what "escape sequences" various terminals can be controlled. Programs are written so that instead of directly outputting an escape sequence that only works on a particular brand of terminal, they look up the correct sequence to do whatever it is they want to do in `/etc/termcap`. As a result most programs work with most kinds of terminals. See the *termcap*, *curs_termcap*, and *terminfo* manual pages for more information.

3.2.2 The `/dev` directory

The `/dev` directory contains the special device files for all the devices. The device files are named using special conventions; these are described in the Device list.[2] The device files are created during installation, and later with the `/dev/MAKEDEV` script. The `/dev/MAKEDEV.local` is a script written by the system administrator that creates local-only device files or links (i.e., those that are not part of the standard `MAKEDEV`, such as device files for some non-standard device driver).

3.3 The `/usr` file system

The `/usr` file system is often large, since all programs are installed there. All files in `/usr` usually come from a Linux distribution; locally installed programs and other stuff goes below `/usr/local`. This makes it possible to update the system from a new version of the distribution, or even a completely new distribution,

[2] *Linux Device List,* by Peter Anvin

without having to install all programs again. Some of the subdirectories of /usr are listed below (some of the less important directories have been dropped; see the FSSTND for more information).

/usr/X11R6 The X Window System, all files. To simplify the development and installation of X, the X files have not been integrated into the rest of the system. There is a directory tree below /usr/X11R6 similar to that below /usr itself.

/usr/X386 Similar to /usr/X11R6, but for X11 Release 5.

/usr/bin Almost all user commands. Some commands are in /bin or in /usr/local/bin.

/usr/sbin System administration commands that are not needed on the root file system, e.g., most server programs.

/usr/man, /usr/info, /usr/doc Manual pages, GNU Info documents, and miscellaneous other documentation files, respectively.

/usr/include Header files for the C programming language. This should actually be below /usr/lib for consistency, but the tradition is overwhelmingly in support for this name.

/usr/lib Unchanging data files for programs and subsystems, including some site-wide configuration files. The name lib comes from library; originally libraries of programming subroutines were stored in /usr/lib.

/usr/local The place for locally installed software and other files.

3.4 The /var file system

The /var contains data that is changed when the system is running normally. It is specific for each system, i.e., not shared over the network with other computers.

/var/catman A cache for man pages that are formatted on demand. The source for manual pages is usually stored in /usr/man/man*; some manual pages might come with a pre-formatted version, which is stored in /usr/man/cat*. Other manual pages need to be formatted when they are first viewed; the formatted version is then stored in /var/man so that the next person to view the same page won't have to wait for it to be formatted. (/var/catman is often cleaned in the same way temporary directories are cleaned.)

/var/lib Files that change while the system is running normally.

/var/local Variable data for programs that are installed in /usr/local (i.e., programs that have been installed by the system administrator). Note that even locally installed programs should use the other /var directories if they are appropriate, e.g., /var/lock.

/var/lock Lock files. Many programs follow a convention to create a lock file in /var/lock to indicate that they are using a particular device or file. Other programs will notice the lock file and won't attempt to use the device or file.

/var/log Log files from various programs, especially login (/var/log/wtmp, which logs all logins and logouts into the system) and syslog (/var/log/messages, where all kernel and system program message are usually stored). Files in /var/log can often grow indefinitely, and may require cleaning at regular intervals.

/var/run Files that contain information about the system that is valid until the system is next booted. For example, /var/run/utmp contains information about people currently logged in.

/var/spool Directories for mail, news, printer queues, and other queued work. Each different spool has its own subdirectory below /var/spool, e.g., the mailboxes of the users are in /var/spool/mail.

/var/tmp Temporary files that are large or that need to exist for a longer time than what is allowed for /tmp. (Although the system administrator might not allow very old files in /var/tmp either.)

3.5 The /proc file system

The /proc file system contains a illusionary file system. It does not exist on a disk. Instead, the kernel creates it in memory. It is used to provide information about the system (originally about processes, hence the name). Some of the more important files and directories are explained below. The /proc file system is described in more detail in the *proc* manual page.

/proc/1 A directory with information about process number 1. Each process has a directory below /proc with the name being its process identification number.

/proc/cpuinfo Information about the processor, such as its type, make, model, and perfomance.

/proc/devices List of device drivers configured into the currently running kernel.

/proc/dma Shows which DMA channels are being used at the moment.

/proc/file systems File systems configured into the kernel.

/proc/interrupts Shows which interrupts are in use, and how many of each there have been.

/proc/ioports Which I/O ports are in use at the moment.

/proc/kcore An image of the physical memory of the system. This is exactly the same size as your physical memory, but does not really take up that much memory; it is generated on the fly as programs access it. (Remember: unless you copy it elsewhere, nothing under /proc takes up any disk space at all.)

/proc/kmsg Messages output by the kernel. These are also routed to syslog.

/proc/ksyms Symbol table for the kernel.

/proc/loadavg The 'load average' of the system; three meaningless indicators of how much work the system has to do at the moment.

/proc/meminfo Information about memory usage, both physical and swap.

/proc/modules Which kernel modules are loaded at the moment.

/proc/net Status information about network protocols.

/proc/self A symbolic link to the process directory of the program that is looking at /proc. When two processes look at /proc, they get different links. This is mainly a convenience to make it easier for programs to get at their process directory.

/proc/stat Various statistics about the system, such as the number of page faults since the system was booted.

/proc/uptime The time the system has been up.

/proc/version The kernel version.

Note that while the above files tend to be easily readable text files, they can sometimes be formatted in a way that is not easily digestible. There are many commands that do little more than read the above files and format them for easier understanding. For example, the free program reads /proc/meminfo and converts the amounts given in bytes to kilobytes (and adds a little more information, as well).

CHAPTER 4

Using Disks and Other Storage Media

On a clear disk you can seek forever.

When you install or upgrade your system, you need to do a fair amount of work on your disks. You have to make file systems on your disks so that files can be stored on them and reserve space for the different parts of your system.

This chapter explains all these initial activities. Usually, once you get your system set up, you won't have to go through the work again, except for using floppies. You'll need to come back to this chapter if you add a new disk or want to fine-tune your disk usage.

The basic tasks in administering disks are:

- Format your disk. This does various things to prepare it for use, such as checking for bad sectors. (Formatting is nowadays not necessary for most hard disks.)
- Partition a hard disk, if you want to use it for several activities that aren't supposed to interfere with one another. One reason for partitioning is to store different operating systems on the same disk. Another reason is to keep user files separate from system files, which simplifies back-ups and helps protect the system files from corruption.
- Make a file system (of a suitable type) on each disk or partition. The disk means nothing to Linux until you make a file system; then files can be created and accessed on it.
- Mount different file systems to form a single tree structure, either automatically, or manually as needed. (Manually mounted file systems usually need to be unmounted manually as well.)

Chapter 5 contains information about virtual memory and disk caching, of which you also need to be aware when using disks.

This chapter explains what you need to know for hard disks, floppies, CD-ROM's, and tape drives.

4.1 Two kinds of devices

UNIX, and therefore Linux, recognizes two different kinds of device: random-access block devices (such as disks), and character devices (such as tapes and serial lines), some of which may be serial, and some random-access. Each supported device is represented in the file system as a **device file**. When you read or write a device file, the data comes from or goes to the device it represents. This way no special programs (and no special application programming methodology, such as catching interrupts or polling a serial port) are necessary to access devices; for example, to send a file to the printer, one could just say

```
$ cat filename > /dev/lp1
$
```

and the contents of the file are printed (the file must, of course, be in a form that the printer understands). However, since it is not a good idea to have several people cat their files to the printer at the same time, one usually uses a special program to send the files to be printed (usually `lpr`). This program makes sure that only one file is being printed at a time, and will automatically send files to the printer as soon as it finishes with the previous file. Something similar is needed for most devices. In fact, one seldom needs to worry about device files at all.

Since devices show up as files in the file system (in the `/dev` directory), it is easy to see just what device files exist, using `ls` or another suitable command. In the output of `ls -l`, the first column contains the type of the file and its permissions. For example, inspecting a serial device gives on my system

```
$ ls -l /dev/cua0
crw-rw-rw-   1 root     uucp       5,  64 Nov 30  1993 /dev/cua0
$
```

The first character in the first column, i.e., '`c`' in `crw-rw-rw-` above, tells an informed user the type of the file, in this case a character device. For ordinary files, the first character is '`-`', for directories it is '`d`', and for block devices '`b`'; see the `ls` man page for further information.

Note that usually all device files exist even though the device itself might be not be installed. So just because you have a file `/dev/sda`, it doesn't mean that you really do have an SCSI hard disk. Having all the device files makes the installation programs simpler, and makes it easier to add new hardware (there is no need to find out the correct parameters for and create the device files for the new device).

4.2 Hard disks

This subsection introduces terminology related to hard disks. If you already know the terms and concepts, you can skip this subsection.

See figure 4.1 for a schematic picture of the important parts in a hard disk. A hard disk consists of one or more circular **platters**,[1] of which either or both **surfaces** are coated with a magnetic substance used for recording the data. For each surface, there is a **read-write head** that examines or alters the recorded data. The platters rotate on a common axis; a typical rotation speed is 3600 rotations per minute, although high-performance hard disks have higher speeds. The heads move along the radius of the platters; this movement combined with the rotation of the platters allows the head to access all parts of the surfaces.

The processor (CPU) and the actual disk communicate through a **disk controller**. This relieves the rest of the computer from knowing how to use the drive, since the controllers for different types of disks can be made to use the same interface towards the rest of the computer. Therefore, the computer can say just "hey disk, gimme what I want", instead of a long and complex series of electric signals to move the head to the proper location and waiting for the correct position to come under the head and doing all the other unpleasant stuff necessary. (In reality, the interface to the controller is still complex, but much less so than it would otherwise be.) The controller can also do some other stuff, such as caching, or automatic bad sector replacement.

The above is usually all one needs to understand about the hardware. There is also a bunch of other stuff, such as the motor that rotates the platters and moves the heads, and the electronics that control the operation of the mechanical parts, but that is mostly not relevant for understanding the working principle of a hard disk.

The surfaces are usually divided into concentric rings, called **tracks**, and these in turn are divided into **sectors**. This division is used to specify locations on the hard disk and to allocate disk space to files. To find a given place on the hard disk, one might say "surface 3, track 5, sector 7". Usually the number of sectors is the same for all tracks, but some hard disks put more sectors in outer tracks (all sectors are of the same physical size, so more of them fit in the longer outer tracks). Typically, a sector will hold 512 bytes of data. The disk itself can't handle smaller amounts of data than one sector.

Each surface is divided into tracks (and sectors) in the same way. This means that when the head for one surface is on a track, the heads for the other surfaces are also on the corresponding tracks. All the corresponding tracks taken together are called a **cylinder**. It takes time to move the heads from one track (cylinder) to another, so by placing the data that is often accessed together (say, a file) so that it is within one

[1] The platters are made of a hard substance, e.g., aluminum, which gives the hard disk its name.

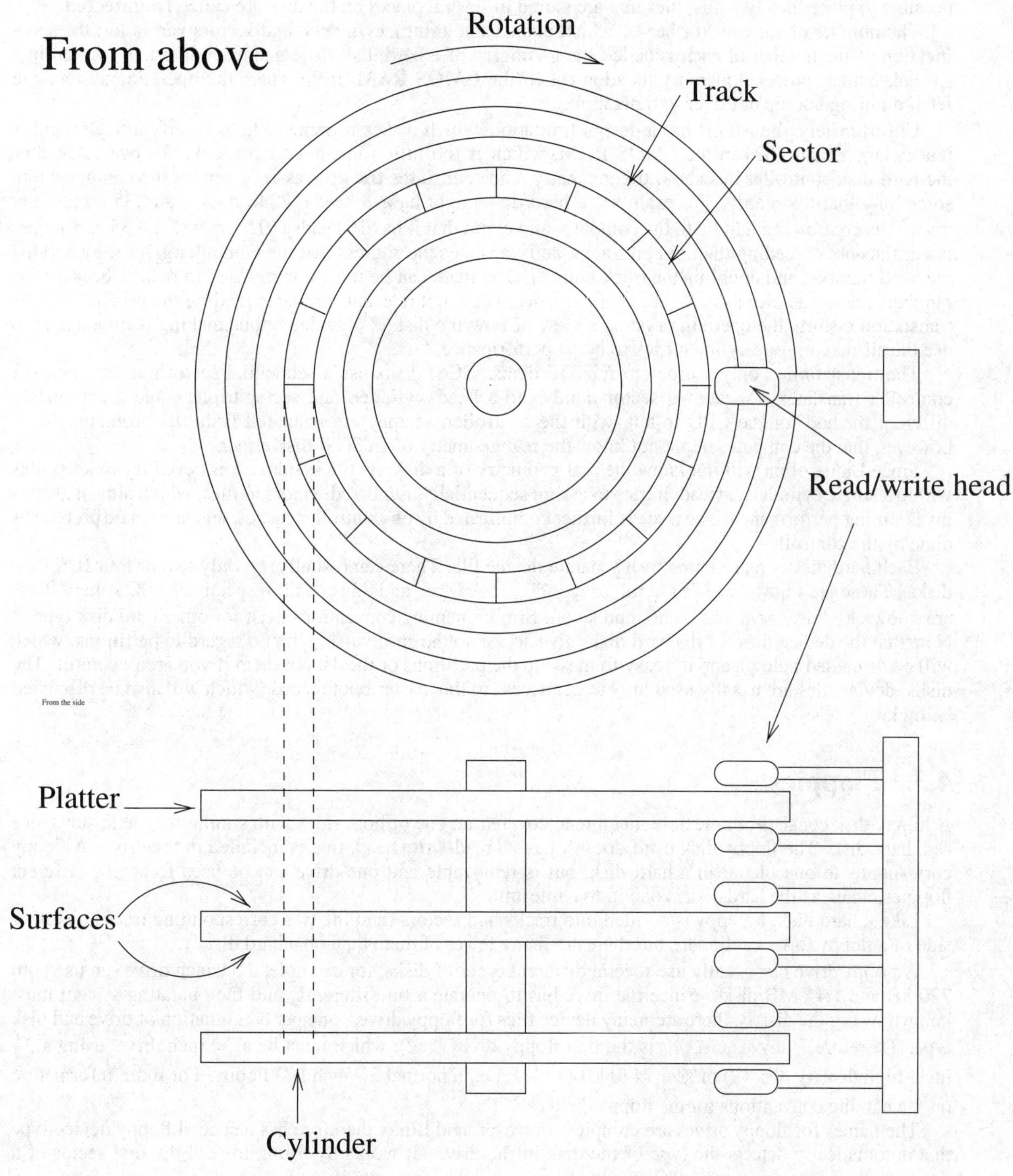

Figure 4.1: A schematic picture of a hard disk.

cylinder, it is not necessary to move the heads to read all of it. This improves performance. It is not always possible to place files like this; files that are stored in several places on the disk are called **fragmented**.

The number of surfaces (or heads, which is the same thing), cylinders, and sectors vary a lot; the specification of the number of each is called the **geometry** of a hard disk. The geometry is usually stored in a special, battery-powered memory location called the **CMOS RAM**, from where the operating system can fetch it during bootup or driver initialization.

Unfortunately, the BIOS[2] has a design limitation, which makes it impossible to specify a track number that is larger than 1024 in the CMOS RAM, which is too little for a large hard disk. To overcome this, the hard disk controller lies about the geometry, and **translates the addresses** given by the computer into something that fits reality. For example, a hard disk might have 8 heads, 2048 tracks, and 35 sectors per track[3]. Its controller could lie to the computer and claim that it has 16 heads, 1024 tracks, and 35 sectors per track, thus not exceeding the limit on tracks, and translates the address that the computer gives it by halving the head number, and doubling the track number. The math can be more complicated in reality, because the numbers are not as nice as here (but again, the details are not relevant for understanding the principle). This translation distorts the operating system's view of how the disk is organized, thus making it impractical to use the all-data-on-one-cylinder trick to boost performance.

The translation is only a problem for IDE disks. SCSI disks use a sequential sector number (i.e., the controller translates a sequential sector number to a head, cylinder, and sector triplet), and a completely different method for the CPU to talk with the controller, so they are insulated from the problem. Note, however, that the computer might not know the real geometry of an SCSI disk either.

Since Linux often will not know the real geometry of a disk, its file systems don't even try to keep files within a single cylinder. Instead, it tries to assign sequentially numbered sectors to files, which almost always gives similar performance. The issue is further complicated by on-controller caches, and automatic prefetches done by the controller.

Each hard disk is represented by a separate device file. There can (usually) be only two or four IDE hard disks. These are known as `/dev/hda`, `/dev/hdb`, `/dev/hdc`, and `/dev/hdd`, respectively. SCSI hard disks are known as `/dev/sda`, `/dev/sdb`, and so on. Similar naming conventions exist for other hard disk types.[4] Note that the device files for the hard disks give access to the entire disk, with no regard to partitions (which will be discussed below), and it's easy to mess up the partitions or the data in them if you aren't careful. The disks' device files are usually used only to get access to the master boot record (which will also be discussed below).

4.3 Floppies

A floppy disk consists of a flexible membrane covered on one or both sides with similar magnetic substance as a hard disk. The floppy disk itself doesn't have a read-write head, that is included in the drive. A floppy corresponds to one platter in a hard disk, but is removable and one drive can be used to access different floppies, whereas the hard disk is one indivisible unit.

Like a hard disk, a floppy is divided into tracks and sectors (and the two corresponding tracks on either side of a floppy form a cylinder), but there are many fewer of them than on a hard disk.

A floppy drive can usually use several different types of disks; for example, a $3\frac{1}{2}$ inch drive can use both 720 kB and 1.44 MB disks. Since the drive has to operate a bit differently and the operating system must know how big the disk is, there are many device files for floppy drives, one per combination of drive and disk type. Therefore, `/dev/fd0H1440` is the first floppy drive (`fd0`), which must be a $3\frac{1}{2}$ inch drive, using a $3\frac{1}{2}$ inch, high density disk (`H`) of size 1440 kB (`1440`), i.e., a normal $3\frac{1}{2}$ inch HD floppy. For more information on the naming conventions for the floppy devices.[5]

The names for floppy drives are complex, however, and Linux therefore has a special floppy device type that automatically detects the type of the disk in the drive. It works by trying to read the first sector of a

[2]The BIOS is some built-in software stored on ROM chips. It takes care, among other things, of the initial stages of booting.

[3]The numbers are completely imaginary.

[4]*Linux Device List,* by Peter Anvin.

[5]*Linux Device List,* by Peter Anvin.

newly inserted floppy using different floppy types until it finds the correct one. This naturally requires that the floppy is formatted first. The automatic devices are called `/dev/fd0`, `/dev/fd1`, and so on.

The parameters the automatic device uses to access a disk can also be set using the program `setfdprm`. This can be useful if you need to use disks that do not follow any usual floppy sizes, e.g., if they have an unusual number of sectors, or if the autodetecting for some reason fails and the proper device file is missing.

Linux can handle many nonstandard floppy disk formats in addition to all the standard ones. Some of these require using special formatting programs. We'll skip these disk types for now, but in the mean time you can examine the `/etc/fdprm` file. It specifies the settings that `setfdprm` recognizes.

The operating system must know when a disk has been changed in a floppy drive, for example, in order to avoid using cached data from the previous disk. Unfortunately, the signal line that is used for this is sometimes broken, and worse, this won't always be noticeable when using the drive from within MS-DOS. If you are experiencing weird problems using floppies, this might be the reason. The only way to correct it is to repair the floppy drive.

4.4 CD-ROMs

A CD-ROM drive uses an optically read, plastic coated disk. The information is recorded on the surface of the disk[6] in small 'holes' aligned along a spiral from the center to the edge. The drive directs a laser beam along the spiral to read the disk. When the laser hits a hole, the laser is reflected in one way; when it hits smooth surface, it is reflected in another way. This makes it easy to code bits, and therefore information. The rest is easy, mere mechanics.

CD-ROM drives are slow compared to hard disks. Whereas a typical hard disk will have an average seek time less than 15 milliseconds, a fast CD-ROM drive can use tenths of a second for seeks. The actual data transfer rate is fairly high at hundreds of kilobytes per second. The slowness means that CD-ROM drives are not as pleasant to use instead of hard disks (some Linux distributions provide 'live' file systems on CD-ROM's, making it unnecessary to copy the files to the hard disk, making installation easier and saving a lot of hard disk space), although it is still possible. For installing new software, CD-ROM's are very good, since it maximum speed is not essential during installation.

There are several ways to arrange data on a CD-ROM. The most popular one is specified by the international standard ISO 9660. This standard specifies a very minimal file system, which is even more crude than the one MS-DOS uses. On the other hand, it is so minimal that every operating system should be able to map it to its native system.

For normal UNIX use, the ISO 9660 file system is not usable, so an extension to the standard has been developed, called the Rock Ridge extension. Rock Ridge allows longer filenames, symbolic links, and a lot of other goodies, making a CD-ROM look more or less like any contemporary UNIX file system. Even better, a Rock Ridge file system is still a valid ISO 9660 file system, making it usable by non-UNIX systems as well. Linux supports both ISO 9660 and the Rock Ridge extensions; the extensions are recognized and used automatically.

The file system is only half the battle, however. Most CD-ROM's contain data that requires a special program to access, and most of these programs do not run under Linux (except, possibly, under dosemu, the Linux MS-DOS emulator).

A CD-ROM drive is accessed via the corresponding device file. There are several ways to connect a CD-ROM drive to the computer: via SCSI, via a sound card, or via EIDE. The hardware hacking needed to do this is outside the scope of this book, but the type of connection decides the device file.[7]

4.5 Tapes

A tape drive uses a tape, similar[8] to cassettes used for music. A tape is serial in nature, which means that in order to get to any given part of it, you first have to go through all the parts in between. A disk can be

[6] That is, the surface inside the disk, on the metal disk inside the plastic coating.

[7] *Linux Device List,* by Peter Anvin.

[8] But completely different, of course.

accessed randomly, i.e., you can jump directly to any place on the disk. The serial access of tapes makes them slow.

On the other hand, tapes are relatively cheap to make, since they do not need to be fast. They can also easily be made quite long, and can therefore contain a large amount of data. This makes tapes very suitable for things like archiving and backups, which do not require large speeds, but benefit from low costs and large storage capacities.

4.6 Formatting

Formatting is the process of writing marks on the magnetic media that are used to mark tracks and sectors. Before a disk is formatted, its magnetic surface is a complete mess of magnetic signals. When it is formatted, some order is brought into the chaos by essentially drawing lines where the tracks go, and where they are divided into sectors. The actual details are not quite exactly like this, but that is irrelevant. What is important is that a disk cannot be used unless it has been formatted.

The terminology is a bit confusing here: in MS-DOS, the word formatting is used to cover also the process of creating a file system (which will be discussed below). There, the two processes are often combined, especially for floppies. When the distinction needs to be made, the real formatting is called **low-level formatting**, while making the file system is called **high-level formatting**. In UNIX circles, the two are called formatting and making a file system, so that's what is used in this book as well.

For IDE and some SCSI disks the formatting is actually done at the factory and doesn't need to be repeated; hence most people rarely need to worry about it. In fact, formatting a hard disk can cause it to work less well, for example because a disk might need to be formatted in some very special way to allow automatic bad sector replacement to work.

Disks that need to be or can be formatted often require a special program anyway, because the interface to the formatting logic inside the drive is different from drive to drive. The formatting program is often either on the controller BIOS, or is supplied as an MS-DOS program; neither of these can easily be used from within Linux.

During formatting one might encounter bad spots on the disk, called **bad blocks** or **bad sectors**. These are sometimes handled by the drive itself, but even then, if more of them develop, something needs to be done to avoid using those parts of the disk. The logic to do this is built into the file system; how to add the information into the file system is described below. Alternatively, one might create a small partition that covers just the bad part of the disk; this approach might be a good idea if the bad spot is very large, since file systems can sometimes have trouble with very large bad areas.

Floppies are formatted with `fdformat`. The floppy device file to use is given as the parameter. For example, the following command would format a high density, $3\frac{1}{2}$ inch floppy in the first floppy drive:

```
$ fdformat /dev/fd0H1440
Double-sided, 80 tracks, 18 sec/track. Total capacity 1440 kB.
Formatting ... done
Verifying ... done
$
```

Note that if you want to use an autodetecting device (e.g., `/dev/fd0`), you *must* set the parameters of the device with `setfdprm` first. To achieve the same effect as above, one would have to do the following:

```
$ setfdprm /dev/fd0 1440/1440
$ fdformat /dev/fd0
Double-sided, 80 tracks, 18 sec/track. Total capacity 1440 kB.
Formatting ... done
Verifying ... done
$
```

It is usually more convenient to choose the correct device file that matches the type of the floppy. Note that it is unwise to format floppies to contain more information than what they are designed for.

fdformat will also validate the floppy, i.e., check it for bad blocks. It will try a bad block several times (you can usually hear this, the drive noise changes dramatically). If the floppy is only marginally bad (due to dirt on the read/write head, some errors are false signals), fdformat won't complain, but a real error will abort the validation process. The kernel will print log messages for each I/O error it finds; these will go to the console or, if syslog is being used, to the file /usr/adm/messages. fdformat itself won't tell where the error is (one usually doesn't care, floppies are cheap enough that a bad one is automatically thrown away).

```
$ fdformat /dev/fd0H1440
Double-sided, 80 tracks, 18 sec/track. Total capacity 1440 kB.
Formatting ... done
Verifying ... read: Unknown error
$
```

The badblocks command can be used to search any disk or partition for bad blocks (including a floppy). It does not format the disk, so it can be used to check even existing file systems. The example below checks a $3\frac{1}{2}$ inch floppy with two bad blocks.

```
$ badblocks /dev/fd0H1440 1440
718
719
$
```

badblocks outputs the block numbers of the bad blocks it finds. Most file systems can avoid such bad blocks. They maintain a list of known bad blocks, which is initialized when the file system is made, and can be modified later. The initial search for bad blocks can be done by the mkfs command (which initializes the file system), but later checks should be done with badblocks and the new blocks should be added with fsck. We'll describe mkfs and fsck later.

Many modern disks automatically notice bad blocks, and attempt to fix them by using a special, reserved good block instead. This is invisible to the operating system. This feature should be documented in the disk's manual, if you're curious if it is happening. Even such disks can fail, if the number of bad blocks grows too large, although chances are that by then the disk will be so rotten as to be unusable.

4.7 Partitions

A hard disk can be divided into several **partitions**. Each partition functions as if it were a separate hard disk. The idea is that if you have one hard disk, and want to have, say, two operating systems on it, you can divide the disk into two partitions. Each operating system uses its partition as it wishes and doesn't touch the other one's. This way the two operating systems can co-exist peacefully on the same hard disk. Without partitions one would have to buy a hard disk for each operating system.

Floppies are not partitioned. There is no technical reason against this, but since they're so small, partitions would be useful only very rarely. CD-ROM's are usually also not partitioned, since it's easier to use them as one big disk, and there is seldom a need to have several operating systems on one.

4.7.1 The MBR, boot sectors and partition table

The information about how a hard disk has been partitioned is stored in its first sector (that is, the first sector of the first track on the first disk surface). The first sector is the **master boot record** (MBR) of the disk; this is the sector that the BIOS reads in and starts when the machine is first booted. The master boot record contains a small program that reads the partition table, checks which partition is active (that is, marked bootable), and reads the first sector of that partition, the partition's **boot sector** (the MBR is also a boot sector, but it has a special status and therefore a special name). This boot sector contains another small program that reads the first part of the operating system stored on that partition (assuming it is bootable), and then starts it.

The partitioning scheme is not built into the hardware, or even into the BIOS. It is only a convention that many operating systems follow. Not all operating systems do follow it, but they are the exceptions. Some operating systems support partitions, but they occupy one partition on the hard disk, and use their internal partitioning method within that partition. The latter type exists peacefully with other operating systems (including Linux), and does not require any special measures, but an operating system that doesn't support partitions cannot co-exist on the same disk with any other operating system.

As a safety precaution, it is a good idea to write down the partition table on a piece of paper, so that if it ever corrupts you don't have to lose all your files. (A bad partition table can be fixed with `fdisk`). The relevant information is given by the `fdisk -l` command:

```
$ fdisk -l /dev/hda

Disk /dev/hda: 15 heads, 57 sectors, 790 cylinders
Units = cylinders of 855 * 512 bytes

   Device Boot  Begin    Start      End  Blocks   Id  System
/dev/hda1           1        1       24   10231+  82  Linux swap
/dev/hda2          25       25       48   10260   83  Linux native
/dev/hda3          49       49      408  153900   83  Linux native
/dev/hda4         409      409      790  163305    5  Extended
/dev/hda5         409      409      744  143611+  83  Linux native
/dev/hda6         745      745      790   19636+  83  Linux native
$
```

4.7.2 Extended and logical partitions

The original partitioning scheme for PC hard disks allowed only four partitions. This quickly turned out to be too little in real life, partly because some people want more than four operating systems (Linux, MS-DOS, OS/2, Minix, FreeBSD, NetBSD, or Windows/NT, to name a few), but primarily because sometimes it is a good idea to have several partitions for one operating system. For example, swap space is usually best put in its own partition for Linux instead of in the main Linux partition for reasons of speed (see below).

To overcome this design problem, **extended partitions** were invented. This trick allows partitioning a **primary partition** into sub-partitions. The primary partition thus subdivided is the extended partition; the subpartitions are **logical partitions**. They behave like primary[9] partitions, but are created differently. There is no speed difference between them.

The partition structure of a hard disk might look like that in figure 4.2. The disk is divided into three primary partitions, the second of which is divided into two logical partitions. Part of the disk is not partitioned at all. The disk as a whole and each primary partition has a boot sector.

4.7.3 Partition types

The partition tables (the one in the MBR, and the ones for extended partitions) contain one byte per partition that identifies the type of that partition. This attempts to identify the operating system that uses the partition, or what it uses it for. The purpose is to make it possible to avoid having two operating systems accidentally using the same partition. However, in reality, operating systems do not really care about the partition type byte; e.g., Linux doesn't care at all what it is. Worse, some of them use it incorrectly; e.g., at least some versions of DR-DOS ignore the most significant bit of the byte, while others don't.

There is no standardization agency to specify what each byte value means, but some commonly accepted ones are included in in table 4.1. The same list is available in the Linux `fdisk` program.

4.7.4 Partitioning a hard disk

There are many programs for creating and removing partitions. Most operating systems have their own, and it can be a good idea to use each operating system's own, just in case it does something unusual that the others can't. Many of the programs are called `fdisk`, including the Linux one, or variations thereof. Details on using the Linux `fdisk` are given on its man page. The `cfdisk` command is similar to `fdisk`, but has a nicer (full screen) user interface.

[9] Illogical?

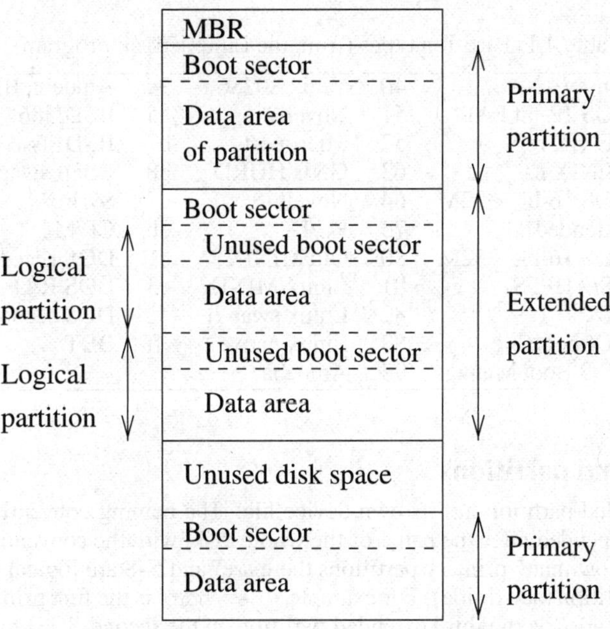

Figure 4.2: A sample hard disk partitioning.

When using IDE disks, the boot partition (the partition with the bootable kernel image files) must be completely within the first 1024 cylinders. This is because the disk is used via the BIOS during boot (before the system goes into protected mode), and BIOS can't handle more than 1024 cylinders. It is sometimes possible to use a boot partition that is only partly within the first 1024 cylinders. This works as long as all the files that are read with the BIOS are within the first 1024 cylinders. Since this is difficult to arrange, it is *a very bad idea* to do it; you never know when a kernel update or disk defragmentation will result in an unbootable system. Therefore, make sure your boot partition is completely within the first 1024 cylinders.

Some newer versions of the BIOS and IDE disks can, in fact, handle disks with more than 1024 cylinders. If you have such a system, you can forget about the problem; if you aren't quite sure of it, put it within the first 1024 cylinders.

Each partition should have an even number of sectors, since the Linux file systems use a 1 kB block size, i.e., two sectors. An odd number of sectors will result in the last sector being unused. This won't result in any problems, but it is ugly, and some versions of `fdisk` will warn about it.

Changing a partition's size usually requires first backing up everything you want to save from that partition (preferably the whole disk, just in case), deleting the partition, creating new partition, then restoring everything to the new partition. If the partition is growing, you may need to adjust the sizes (and backup and restore) of the adjoining partitions as well.

Since changing partition sizes is painful, it is preferable to get the partitions right the first time, or have an effective and easy to use backup system. If you're installing from a media that does not require much human intervention (say, from CD-ROM, as opposed to floppies), it is often easy to play with different configuration at first. Since you don't already have data to back up, it is not so painful to modify partition sizes several times.

There is a program for MS-DOS, called `fips`, which resizes an MS-DOS partition without requiring the backup and restore, but for other file systems it is still necessary.

Table 4.1: Partition types (from the Linux `fdisk` program).

0	Empty	40	Venix 80286	94	Amoeba BBT
1	DOS 12-bit FAT	51	Novell?	a5	BSD/386
2	XENIX root	52	Microport	b7	BSDI fs
3	XENIX usr	63	GNU HURD	b8	BSDI swap
4	DOS 16-bit <32M	64	Novell	c7	Syrinx
5	Extended	75	PC/IX	db	CP/M
6	DOS 16-bit ≥32M	80	Old MINIX	e1	DOS access
7	OS/2 HPFS	81	Linux/MINIX	e3	DOS R/O
8	AIX	82	Linux swap	f2	DOS secondary
9	AIX bootable	83	Linux native	ff	BBT
a	OS/2 Boot Manag	93	Amoeba		

4.7.5 Device files and partitions

Each partition and extended partition has its own device file. The naming convention for these files is that a partition's number is appended after the name of the whole disk, with the convention that 1–4 are primary partitions (regardless of how many primary partitions there are) and 5–8 are logical partitions (regardless of within which primary partition they reside). For example, `/dev/hda1` is the first primary partition on the first IDE hard disk, and `/dev/sdb7` is the third extended partition on the second SCSI hard disk. The device list gives more information.[10]

4.8 File systems

4.8.1 What are file systems?

A **file system** is the methods and data structures that an operating system uses to keep track of files on a disk or partition; that is, the way the files are organized on the disk. The word is also used to refer to a partition or disk that is used to store the files or the type of the file system. Thus, one might say "I have two file systems" meaning one has two partitions on which one stores files, or that one is using the "extended file system", meaning the type of the file system.

The difference between a disk or partition and the file system it contains is important. A few programs (including, reasonably enough, programs that create file systems) operate directly on the raw sectors of a disk or partition; if there is an existing file system there it will be destroyed or seriously corrupted. Most programs operate on a file system, and therefore won't work on a partition that doesn't contain one (or that contains one of the wrong type).

Before a partition or disk can be used as a file system, it needs to be initialized, and the bookkeeping data structures need to be written to the disk. This process is called **making a file system**.

Most UNIX file system types have a similar general structure, although the exact details vary quite a bit. The central concepts are **superblock**, **inode**, **data block**, **directory block**, and **indirection block**. The superblock contains information about the file system as a whole, such as its size (the exact information here depends on the file system). An inode contains all information about a file, except its name. The name is stored in the directory, together with the number of the inode. A directory entry consists of a filename and the number of the inode which represents the file. The inode contains the numbers of several data blocks, which are used to store the data in the file. There is space only for a few data block numbers in the inode, however, and if more are needed, more space for pointers to the data blocks is allocated dynamically. These dynamically allocated blocks are indirect blocks; the name indicates that in order to find the data block, one has to find its number in the indirect block first.

UNIX file systems usually allow one to create a **hole** in a file (this is done with `lseek`; check the manual page), which means that the file system just pretends that at a particular place in the file there is just zero

[10] *Linux Device List,* by Peter Anvin.

bytes, but no actual disk sectors are reserved for that place in the file (this means that the file will use a bit less disk space). This happens especially often for small binaries, Linux shared libraries, some databases, and a few other special cases. (Holes are implemented by storing a special value as the address of the data block in the indirect block or inode. This special address means that no data block is allocated for that part of the file, ergo, there is a hole in the file.)

Holes are moderately useful. On the author's system, a simple measurement showed a potential for about 4 MB of savings through holes of about 200 MB total used disk space. That system, however, contains relatively few programs and no database files. The measurement tool is described in appendix A.

4.8.2 File systems galore

Linux supports several types of file systems. As of this writing the most important ones are:

minix
: The oldest, presumed to be the most reliable, but quite limited in features (some time stamps are missing, at most 30 character filenames) and restricted in capabilities (at most 64 MB per file system).

xia
: A modified version of the minix file system that lifts the limits on the filenames and file system sizes, but does not otherwise introduce new features. It is not very popular, but is reported to work very well.

ext2
: The most featureful of the native Linux file systems, currently also the most popular one. It is designed to be easily upwards compatible, so that new versions of the file system code do not require re-making the existing file systems.

ext
: An older version of `ext2` that wasn't upwards compatible. It is hardly ever used in new installations any more, and most people have converted to `ext2`.

In addition, support for several foreign file system exists, to make it easier to exchange files with other operating systems. These foreign file systems work just like native ones, except that they may be lacking in some usual UNIX features, or have curious limitations, or other oddities.

msdos
: Compatibility with MS-DOS (and OS/2 and Windows NT) FAT file systems.

umsdos
: Extends the `msdos` file system driver under Linux to get long filenames, owners, permissions, links, and device files. This allows a normal `msdos` file system to be used as if it were a Linux one, thus removing the need for a separate partition for Linux.

iso9660
: The standard CD-ROM file system; the popular Rock Ridge extension to the CD-ROM standard that allows longer file names is supported automatically.

nfs
: A networked file system that allows sharing a file system between many computers to allow easy access to the files from all of them.

hpfs
: The OS/2 file system.

sysv
: SystemV/386, Coherent, and Xenix file systems.

The choice of file system to use depends on the situation. If compatibility or other reasons make one of the non-native file systems necessary, then that one must be used. If one can choose freely, then it is probably wisest to use ext2, since it has all the features but does not suffer from lack of performance.

There is also the `proc` file system, usually accessible as the `/proc` directory, which is not really a file system at all, even though it looks like one. The `proc` file system makes it easy to access certain kernel data structures, such as the process list (hence the name). It makes these data structures look like a file system, and that file system can be manipulated with all the usual file tools. For example, to get a listing of all processes one might use the command

```
$ ls -l /proc
total 0
dr-xr-xr-x   4 root     root           0 Jan 31 20:37 1
dr-xr-xr-x   4 liw      users          0 Jan 31 20:37 63
dr-xr-xr-x   4 liw      users          0 Jan 31 20:37 94
```

```
dr-xr-xr-x   4 liw      users           0 Jan 31 20:37 95
dr-xr-xr-x   4 root     users           0 Jan 31 20:37 98
dr-xr-xr-x   4 liw      users           0 Jan 31 20:37 99
-r--r--r--   1 root     root            0 Jan 31 20:37 devices
-r--r--r--   1 root     root            0 Jan 31 20:37 dma
-r--r--r--   1 root     root            0 Jan 31 20:37 filesystems
-r--r--r--   1 root     root            0 Jan 31 20:37 interrupts
-r--------   1 root     root      8654848 Jan 31 20:37 kcore
-r--r--r--   1 root     root            0 Jan 31 11:50 kmsg
-r--r--r--   1 root     root            0 Jan 31 20:37 ksyms
-r--r--r--   1 root     root            0 Jan 31 11:51 loadavg
-r--r--r--   1 root     root            0 Jan 31 20:37 meminfo
-r--r--r--   1 root     root            0 Jan 31 20:37 modules
dr-xr-xr-x   2 root     root            0 Jan 31 20:37 net
dr-xr-xr-x   4 root     root            0 Jan 31 20:37 self
-r--r--r--   1 root     root            0 Jan 31 20:37 stat
-r--r--r--   1 root     root            0 Jan 31 20:37 uptime
-r--r--r--   1 root     root            0 Jan 31 20:37 version
$
```

(There will be a few extra files that don't correspond to processes, though. The above example has been shortened.)

Note that even though it is called a file system, no part of the `proc` file system touches any disk. It exists only in the kernel's imagination. Whenever anyone tries to look at any part of the `proc` file system, the kernel makes it look as if the part existed somewhere, even though it doesn't. So, even though there is a multi-megabyte `/proc/kcore` file, it doesn't take any disk space.

4.8.3 Which file system should be used?

There is usually little point in using many different file systems. Currently, ext2fs is the most popular one, and it is probably the wisest choice. Depending on the overhead for bookkeeping structures, speed, (perceived) reliability, compatibility, and various other reasons, it may be advisable to use another file system. This needs to be decided on a case-by-case basis.

4.8.4 Creating a file system

File systems are created, i.e., initialized, with the `mkfs` command. There is actually a separate program for each file system type. `mkfs` is just a front end that runs the appropriate program depending on the desired file system type. The type is selected with the `-t fstype` option.

The programs called by `mkfs` have slightly different command line interfaces. The common and most important options are summarized below; see the manual pages for more.

- `-t` *fstype* Select the type of the file system.
- `-c` Search for bad blocks and initialize the bad block list accordingly.
- `-l` *filename* Read the initial bad block list from the file *filename*.

To create an ext2 file system on a floppy, one would give the following commands:

```
$ fdformat -n /dev/fd0H1440
Double-sided, 80 tracks, 18 sec/track. Total capacity 1440 kB.
Formatting ... done
$ badblocks /dev/fd0H1440 1440 > bad-blocks
$ mkfs -t ext2 -l bad-blocks /dev/fd0H1440
mke2fs 0.5a, 5-Apr-94 for EXT2 FS 0.5, 94/03/10
360 inodes, 1440 blocks
72 blocks (5.00%) reserved for the super user
```

```
First data block=1
Block size=1024 (log=0)
Fragment size=1024 (log=0)
1 block group
8192 blocks per group, 8192 fragments per group
360 inodes per group

Writing inode tables: done
Writing superblocks and file system accounting information: done
$
```

First, the floppy was formatted (the `-n` option prevents validation, i.e., bad block checking). Then bad blocks were searched with `badblocks`, with the output redirected to a file, `bad-blocks`. Finally, the file system was created, with the bad block list initialized by whatever `badblocks` found.

The `-c` option could have been used with `mkfs` instead of `badblocks` and a separate file. The example below does that.

```
$ mkfs -t ext2 -c /dev/fd0H1440
mke2fs 0.5a, 5-Apr-94 for EXT2 FS 0.5, 94/03/10
360 inodes, 1440 blocks
72 blocks (5.00%) reserved for the super user
First data block=1
Block size=1024 (log=0)
Fragment size=1024 (log=0)
1 block group
8192 blocks per group, 8192 fragments per group
360 inodes per group

Checking for bad blocks (read-only test): done
Writing inode tables: done
Writing superblocks and file system accounting information: done
$
```

The `-c` is more convenient than a separate use of `badblocks`, but `badblocks` is necessary for checking after the file system has been created.

The process to prepare file systems on hard disks or partitions is the same as for floppies, except that the formatting isn't needed.

4.8.5 Mounting and unmounting

Before one can use a file system, it has to be **mounted**. The operating system then does various bookkeeping things to make sure that everything works. Since all files in UNIX are in a single directory tree, the mount operation will make it look like the contents of the new file system are the contents of an existing subdirectory in some already mounted file system.

For example, figure 4.3 shows three separate file systems, each with their own root directory. When the last two file systems are mounted below `/home` and `/usr`, respectively, on the first file system, we can get a single directory tree, as in figure 4.4.

The mounts could be done as in the following example:

```
$ mount /dev/hda2 /home
$ mount /dev/hda3 /usr
$
```

The `mount` command takes two arguments. The first one is the device file corresponding to the disk or partition containing the file system. The second one is the directory below which it will be mounted. After these commands the contents of the two file systems look just like the contents of the `/home` and `/usr`

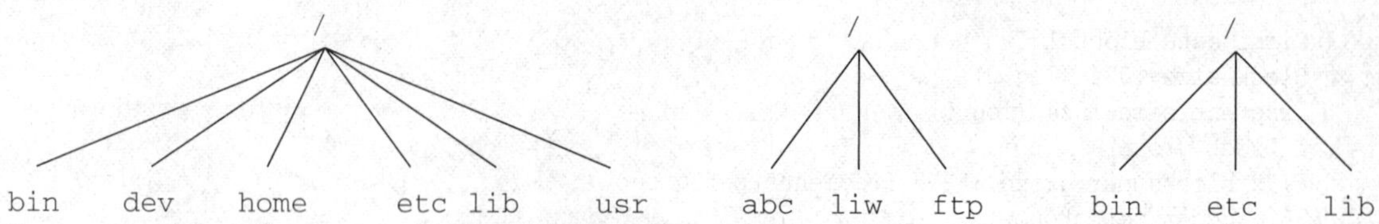

Figure 4.3: Three separate file systems.

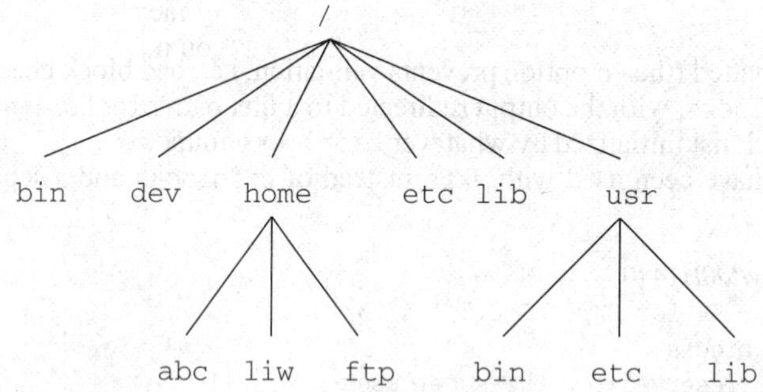

Figure 4.4: `/home` and `/usr` have been mounted.

directories, respectively. One would then say that "`/dev/hda2` **is mounted on** `/home`", and similarly for `/usr`. To look at either file system, one would look at the contents of the directory on which it has been mounted, just as if it were any other directory. Note the difference between the device file, `/dev/hda2`, and the mounted-on directory, `/home`. The device file gives access to the raw contents of the disk, the mounted-on directory gives access to the files on the disk. The mounted-on directory is called the **mount point**.

Linux supports many file system types. `mount` tries to guess the type of the file system. You can also use the `-t` *fstype* option to specify the type directly; this is sometimes necessary, since the heuristics `mount` uses do not always work. For example, to mount an MS-DOS floppy, you could use the following command:

```
$ mount -t msdos /dev/fd0 /floppy
$
```

The mounted-on directory need not be empty, although it must exist. Any files in it, however, will be inaccessible by name while the file system is mounted. (Any files that have already been opened will still be accessible. Files that have hard links from other directories can be accessed using those names.) There is no harm done with this, and it can even be useful. For instance, some people like to have `/tmp` and `/var/tmp` synonymous, and make `/tmp` be a symbolic link to `/var/tmp`. When the system is booted, before the `/usr` file system is mounted, a `/var/tmp` directory residing on the root file system is used instead. When `/usr` is mounted, it will make the `/var/tmp` directory on the root file system inaccessible. If `/var/tmp` didn't exist on the root file system, it would be impossible to use temporary files before mounting `/var`.

If you don't intend to write anything to the file system, use the `-r` switch for `mount` to do a **readonly mount**. This will make the kernel stop any attempts at writing to the file system, and will also stop the kernel from updating file access times in the inodes. Read-only mounts are necessary for unwritable media, e.g., CD-ROM's.

The alert reader has already noticed a slight logistical problem. How is the first file system (called the **root file system**, because it contains the root directory) mounted, since it obviously can't be mounted on another file system? Well, the answer is that it is done by magic.[11] The root file system is magically mounted at boot time, and one can rely on it to always be mounted—if the root file system can't be mounted, the system does

[11] For more information, see the kernel source or the Kernel Hackers' Guide.

not boot. The name of the file system that is magically mounted as root is either compiled into the kernel, or set using LILO or `rdev`.

The root file system is usually first mounted readonly. The startup scripts will then run `fsck` to verify its validity, and if there are no problems, they will **re-mount** it so that writes will also be allowed. `fsck` must not be run on a mounted file system, since any changes to the file system while `fsck` is running *will* cause trouble. Since the root file system is mounted readonly while it is being checked, `fsck` can fix any problems without worry, since the remount operation will flush any metadata that the file system keeps in memory.

On many systems there are other file systems that should also be mounted automatically at boot time. These are specified in the `/etc/fstab` file; see the *fstab* man page for details on the format. The details of exactly when the extra file systems are mounted depend on many factors, and can be configured by each administrator if need be. When the chapter on booting is finished, you may read all about it there.

When a file system no longer needs to be mounted, it can be unmounted with `umount`[12]. `umount` takes one argument: either the device file or the mount point. For example, to unmount the directories of the previous example, one could use the commands

```
$ umount /dev/hda2
$ umount /usr
$
```

See the man page for further instructions on how to use the command. It is imperative that you always unmount a mounted floppy. *Don't just pop the floppy out of the drive!* Because of disk caching, the data is not necessarily written to the floppy until you unmount it, so removing the floppy from the drive too early might cause the contents to become garbled. If you only read from the floppy, this is not very likely, but if you write, even accidentally, the result may be catastrophic.

Mounting and unmounting requires super user privileges, i.e., only `root` can do it. The reason for this is that if any user can mount a floppy on any directory, then it is rather easy to create a floppy with, say, a Trojan horse disguised as `/bin/sh`, or any other often used program. However, it is often necessary to allow users to use floppies, and there are several ways to do this:

- Give the users the `root` password. This is obviously bad security, but is the easiest solution. It works well if there is no need for security anyway, which is the case on many non-networked, personal systems.
- Use a program such as `sudo` to allow users to use mount. This is still bad security, but doesn't directly give super user privileges to everyone.[13]
- Make the users use `mtools`, a package for manipulating MS-DOS file systems, without mounting them. This works well if MS-DOS floppies are all that is needed, but is rather awkward otherwise.
- List the floppy devices and their allowable mount points together with the suitable options in `/etc/fstab`.

The last alternative can be implemented by adding a line like the following to the `/etc/fstab` file:

```
/dev/fd0 /floppy msdos user,noauto 0 0
```

The columns are: device file to mount, directory to mount on, file system type, options, backup frequency (used by `dump`), and `fsck` pass number (to specify the order in which file systems should be checked upon boot; 0 means no check).

The `noauto` option stops this mount to be done automatically when the system is started (i.e., it stops `mount -a` from mounting it). The `user` option allows any user to mount the file system, and, because of security reasons, disallows execution of programs (normal or setuid) and interpretation of device files from the mounted file system. After this, any user can mount a floppy with an `msdos` file system with the following command:

[12] It should of course be `unmount`, but the `n` mysteriously disappeared in the 70's, and hasn't been seen since. Please return it to Bell Labs, NJ, if you find it.

[13] It requires several seconds of hard thinking on the users' behalf.

```
$ mount /floppy
$
```

The floppy can (and needs to, of course) be unmounted with the corresponding `umount` command.

If you want to provide access to several types of floppies, you need to give several mount points. The settings can be different for each mount point. For example, to give access to both MS-DOS and ext2 floppies, you could have the following to lines in `/etc/fstab`:

```
/dev/fd0    /dosfloppy    msdos   user,noauto  0  0
/dev/fd0    /ext2floppy   ext2    user,noauto  0  0
```

For MS-DOS file systems (not just floppies), you probably want to restrict access to it by using the `uid`, `gid`, and `umask` file system options, described in detail on the *mount* manual page. If you aren't careful, mounting an MS-DOS file system gives everyone at least read access to the files in it, which is not a good idea.

4.8.6 Checking file system integrity with `fsck`

File systems are complex creatures, and as such, they tend to be somewhat error-prone. A file system's correctness and validity can be checked using the `fsck` command. It can be instructed to repair any minor problems it finds, and to alert the user if there any non-repairable problems. Fortunately, the code to implement file systems is debugged quite effectively, so there are seldom any problems at all, and they are usually caused by power failures, failing hardware, or operator errors; for example, by not shutting down the system properly.

Most systems are setup to run `fsck` automatically at boot time, so that any errors are detected (and hopefully corrected) before the system is used. Use of a corrupted file system tends to make things worse: if the data structures are messed up, using the file system will probably mess them up even more, resulting in more data loss. However, `fsck` can take a while to run on big file systems, and since errors almost never occur if the system has been shut down properly, a couple of tricks are used to avoid doing the checks in such cases. The first is that if the file `/etc/fastboot` exists, no checks are made. The second is that the ext2 file system has a special marker in its superblock that tells whether the file system was unmounted properly after the previous mount. This allows `e2fsck` (the version of `fsck` for the ext2 file system) to avoid checking the file system if the flag indicates that the unmount was done (the assumption being that a proper unmount indicates no problems). Whether the `/etc/fastboot` trick works on your system depends on your startup scripts, but the ext2 trick works every time you use `e2fsck`—it has to be explicitly bypassed with an option to `e2fsck` to be avoided. (See the *e2fsck* man page for details on how.)

The automatic checking only works for the file systems that are mounted automatically at boot time. Use `fsck` manually to check other file systems, e.g., floppies.

If `fsck` finds non-repairable problems, you need either in-depth knowledge of how file systems work in general, and the type of the corrupt file system in particular, or good backups. The latter is easy (although sometimes tedious) to arrange, the former can sometimes be arranged via a friend, the Linux newsgroups and mailing lists, or some other source of support, if you don't have the know-how yourself. I'd like to tell you more about it, but my lack of education and experience in this regard hinders me. The `debugfs` program by Theodore T'so should be useful.

`fsck` must only be run on unmounted file systems, never on mounted file systems (with the exception of the read-only root during startup). This is because it accesses the raw disk, and can therefore modify the file system without the operating system realizing it. There *will* be trouble, if the operating system is confused.

4.8.7 Checking for disk errors with `badblocks`

It can be a good idea to periodically check for bad blocks. This is done with the `badblocks` command. It outputs a list of the numbers of all bad blocks it can find. This list can be fed to `fsck` to be recorded in the file system data structures so that the operating system won't try to use the bad blocks for storing data. The following example will show how this could be done.

```
$ badblocks /dev/fd0H1440 1440 > bad-blocks
$ fsck -t ext2 -l bad-blocks /dev/fd0H1440
Parallelizing fsck version 0.5a (5-Apr-94)
```

```
e2fsck 0.5a, 5-Apr-94 for EXT2 FS 0.5, 94/03/10
Pass 1: Checking inodes, blocks, and sizes
Pass 2: Checking directory structure
Pass 3: Checking directory connectivity
Pass 4: Check reference counts.
Pass 5: Checking group summary information.

/dev/fd0H1440: ***** FILE SYSTEM WAS MODIFIED *****
/dev/fd0H1440: 11/360 files, 63/1440 blocks
$
```

If badblocks reports a block that was already used, e2fsck will try to move the block to another place. If the block was really bad, not just marginal, the contents of the file may be corrupted.

4.8.8 Fighting fragmentation

When a file is written to disk, it can't always be written in consecutive blocks. A file that is not stored in consecutive blocks is **fragmented**. It takes longer to read a fragmented file, since the disk's read-write head will have to move more. It is desirable to avoid fragmentation, although it is less of a problem in a system with a good buffer cache with read-ahead.

The ext2 file system attempts to keep fragmentation at a minimum, by keeping all blocks in a file close together, even if they can't be stored in consecutive sectors. Ext2 effectively always allocates the free block that is nearest to other blocks in a file. For ext2, it is therefore seldom necessary to worry about fragmentation. There is a program for defragmenting an ext2 file system.[14]

There are many MS-DOS defragmentation programs that move blocks around in the file system to remove fragmentation. For other file systems, defragmentation must be done by backing up the file system, re-creating it, and restoring the files from backups. Backing up a file system before defragmenting is a good idea for all file systems, since many things can go wrong during the defragmentation.

4.8.9 Other tools for all file systems

Some other tools are also useful for managing file systems. df shows the free disk space on one or more file systems; du shows how much disk space a directory and all its files contain. These can be used to hunt down disk space wasters.

sync forces all unwritten blocks in the buffer cache (see section 5.6) to be written to disk. It is seldom necessary to do this by hand; the daemon process update does this automatically. It can be useful in catastrophes, for example if update or its helper process bdflush dies, or if you must turn off power now and can't wait for update to run.

4.8.10 Other tools for the ext2 file system

In addition to the file system creator (mke2fs) and checker (e2fsck) accessible directly or via the file system type independent front ends, the ext2 file system has some additional tools that can be useful.

tune2fs adjusts file system parameters. Some of the more interesting parameters are:

- A maximal mount count. e2fsck enforces a check when file system has been mounted too many times, even if the clean flag is set. For a system that is used for developing or testing the system, it might be a good idea to reduce this limit.

- A maximal time between checks. e2fsck can also enforce a maximal time between two checks, even if the clean flag is set, and the file system hasn't been mounted very often. This can be disabled, however.

- Number of blocks reserved for root. Ext2 reserves some blocks for root so that if the file system fills up, it is still possible to do system administration without having to delete anything. The reserved amount is by default 5%, which on most disks isn't enough to be wasteful. However, for floppies there is no point in reserving any blocks.

[14] *Linux file system defragmenter,* by Stephen Tweedie and Alexei Vovenko.

See the *tune2fs* manual page for more information.

`dumpe2fs` shows information about an ext2 file system, mostly from the superblock. Figure 4.5 shows a sample output. Some of the information in the output is technical and requires understanding of how the file system works, but much of it is readily understandable even for layadmins.

`debugfs` is a file system debugger. It allows direct access to the file system data structures stored on disk and can thus be used to repair a disk that is so broken that `fsck` can't fix it automatically. It has also been known to be used to recover deleted files. However, `debugfs` very much requires that you understand what you're doing; a failure to understand can destroy all your data.

`dump` and `restore` can be used to back up an ext2 file system. They are ext2 specific versions of the traditional UNIX backup tools. See page 277 for more information on backups.

4.9 Disks without file systems

Not all disks or partitions are used as file systems. A swap partition, for example, will not have a file system on it. Many floppies are used in a tape-drive emulating fashion, so that a `tar` or other file is written directly on the raw disk, without a file system. Linux boot floppies don't contain a file system, only the raw kernel.

Avoiding a file system has the advantage of making more of the disk usable, since a file system always has some bookkeeping overhead. It also makes the disks more easily compatible with other systems: for example, the `tar` file format is the same on all systems, while file systems are different on most systems. You will quickly get used to disks without file systems if you need them. Bootable Linux floppies also do not necessarily have a file system, although that is also possible.

One reason to use raw disks is to make image copies of them. For instance, if the disk contains a partially damaged file system, it is a good idea to make an exact copy of it before trying to fix it, since then you can start again if your fixing breaks things even more. One way to do this is to use `dd`:

```
$ dd if=/dev/fd0H1440 of=floppy-image
2880+0 records in
2880+0 records out
$ dd if=floppy-image of=/dev/fd0H1440
2880+0 records in
2880+0 records out
$
```

The first `dd` makes an exact image of the floppy to the file `floppy-image`, the second one writes the image to the floppy. (The user has presumably switched the floppy before the second command. Otherwise the command pair is of doubtful usefulness.)

4.10 Allocating disk space

4.10.1 Partitioning schemes

It is not easy to partition a disk in the best possible way. Worse, there is no universally correct way to do it; there are too many factors involved.

The traditional way is to have a (relatively) small root file system, which contains `/bin`, `/etc`, `/dev`, `/lib`, `/tmp`, and other stuff that is needed to get the system up and running. This way, the root file system (in its own partition or on its own disk) is all that is needed to bring up the system. The reasoning is that if the root file system is small and is not heavily used, it is less likely to become corrupt when the system crashes, and you will therefore find it easier to fix any problems caused by the crash. Then you create separate partitions or use separate disks for the directory tree below `/usr`, the users' home directories (often under `/home`), and the swap space. Separating the home directories (with the users' files) in their own partition makes backups easier, since it is usually not necessary to backup programs (which reside below `/usr`). In a networked environment it is also possible to share `/usr` among several machines (e.g., by using NFS), thereby reducing the total disk space required by several tens or hundreds of megabytes times the number of machines.

```
dumpe2fs 0.5b, 11-Mar-95 for EXT2 FS 0.5a, 94/10/23
Filesystem magic number:  0xEF53
Filesystem state:         clean
Errors behavior:          Continue
Inode count:              360
Block count:              1440
Reserved block count:     72
Free blocks:              1133
Free inodes:              326
First block:              1
Block size:               1024
Fragment size:            1024
Blocks per group:         8192
Fragments per group:      8192
Inodes per group:         360
Last mount time:          Tue Aug  8 01:52:52 1995
Last write time:          Tue Aug  8 01:53:28 1995
Mount count:              3
Maximum mount count:      20
Last checked:             Tue Aug  8 01:06:31 1995
Check interval:           0
Reserved blocks uid:      0 (user root)
Reserved blocks gid:      0 (group root)

Group 0:
  Block bitmap at 3, Inode bitmap at 4, Inode table at 5
  1133 free blocks, 326 free inodes, 2 directories
  Free blocks: 307-1439
  Free inodes: 35-360
```

Figure 4.5: Sample output from `dumpe2fs`

The problem with having many partitions is that it splits the total amount of free disk space into many small pieces. Nowadays, when disks and (hopefully) operating systems are more reliable, many people prefer to have just one partition that holds all their files. On the other hand, it can be less painful to back up (and restore) a small partition.

For a small hard disk (assuming you don't do kernel development), the best way to go is probably to have just one partition. For large hard disks, it is probably better to have a few large partitions, just in case something does go wrong. (Note that 'small' and 'large' are used in a relative sense here; your needs for disk space decide what the threshold is.)

If you have several disks, you might wish to have the root file system (including `/usr`) on one, and the users' home directories on another.

It is a good idea to be prepared to experiment a bit with different partitioning schemes (over time, not just while first installing the system). This is a bit of work, since it essentially requires you to install the system from scratch several times, but it is the only way to be sure you do it right.

4.10.2 Space requirements

The Linux distribution you install will give some indication of how much disk space you need for various configurations. Programs installed separately may also do the same. This will help you plan your disk space usage, but you should prepare for the future and reserve some extra space for things you will notice later that you need.

The amount you need for user files depends on what your users wish to do. Most people seem to need as much space for their files as possible, but the amount they will live happily with varies a lot. Some people do only light text processing and will survive nicely with a few megabytes, others do heavy image processing and will need gigabytes.

By the way, when comparing file sizes given in kilobytes or megabytes and disk space given in megabytes, it can be important to know that the two units can be different. Some disk manufacturers like to pretend that a kilobyte is 1000 bytes and a megabyte is 1000 kilobytes, while all the rest of the computing world uses 1024 for both factors. Therefore, my 345 MB hard disk is really a 330 MB hard disk.[15]

Swap space allocation is discussed on page 255.

4.10.3 Examples of hard disk allocation

I used to have a 109 MB hard disk. Now I am using a 330 MB hard disk. I'll explain how and why I partitioned these disks.

The 109 MB disk I partitioned in a lot of ways, when my needs and the operating systems I used changed; I'll explain two typical scenarios. First, I used to run MS-DOS together with Linux. For that, I needed about 20 MB of hard disk, or just enough to have MS-DOS, a C compiler, an editor, a few other utilities, the program I was working on, and enough free disk space to not feel claustrophobic. For Linux, I had a 10 MB swap partition, and the rest, or 79 MB, was a single partition with all the files I had under Linux. I experimented with having separate root, `/usr`, and `/home` partitions, but there was never enough free disk space in one piece to do much interesting.

When I didn't need MS-DOS anymore, I repartitioned the disk so that I had a 12 MB swap partition, and again had the rest as a single file system.

The 330 MB disk is partitioned into several partitions, like this:

5 MB	root file system
10 MB	swap partition
180 MB	`/usr` file system
120 MB	`/home` file system
15 MB	scratch partition

The scratch partition is for playing around with things that require their own partition, e.g., trying different Linux distributions, or comparing speeds of file systems. When not needed for anything else, it is used as swap space (I like to have a *lot* of open windows).

4.10.4 Adding more disk space for Linux

Adding more disk space for Linux is easy, at least after the hardware has been properly installed (the hardware installation is outside the scope of this book). You format it if necessary, then create the partitions and file system as described above, and add the proper lines to `/etc/fstab` so that it is mounted automatically.

4.10.5 Tips for saving disk space

The best tip for saving disk space is to avoid installing unnecessary programs. Most Linux distributions have an option to install only part of the packages they contain, and by analyzing your needs you might notice that you don't need most of them. This will help save a lot of disk space, since many programs are quite large. Even if you do need a particular package or program, you might not need all of it. For example, some on-line documentation might be unnecessary, as might some of the Elisp files for GNU Emacs, some of the fonts for X11, or some of the libraries for programming.

If you cannot uninstall packages, you might look into compression. Compression programs such as `gzip` or `zip` will compress (and uncompress) individual files or groups of files. The `gzexe` system will compress and uncompress programs invisibly to the user (unused programs are compressed, then uncompressed as they are used). The experimental `DouBle` system will compress all files in a file system, invisibly to the programs that use them. (If you are familiar with products such as Stacker for MS-DOS, the principle is the same.)

[15] Sic transit discus mundi.

CHAPTER 5

Memory Management

Minnet, jag har tappat mitt minne,
är jag svensk eller finne
kommer inte ihåg...
(Bosse Österberg)

This section describes the Linux memory management features, i.e., virtual memory and the disk buffer cache. The purpose and workings and the things the system administrator needs to take into consideration are described.

5.1 What is virtual memory?

Linux supports **virtual memory**, that is, using a disk as an extension of RAM so that the effective size of usable memory grows correspondingly. The kernel will write the contents of a currently unused block of memory to the hard disk so that the memory can be used for another purpose. When the original contents are needed again, they are read back into memory. This is all made completely transparent to the user; programs running under Linux only see the larger amount of memory available and don't notice that parts of them reside on the disk from time to time. Of course, reading and writing the hard disk is slower (on the order of a thousand times slower) than using real memory, so the programs don't run as fast. The part of the hard disk that is used as virtual memory is called the **swap space**.

Linux can use either a normal file in the file system or a separate partition for swap space. A swap partition is faster, but it is easier to change the size of a swap file (there's no need to repartition the whole hard disk, and possibly install everything from scratch). When you know how much swap space you need, you should go for a swap partition, but if you are uncertain, you can use a swap file first, use the system for a while so that you can get a feel for how much swap you need, and then make a swap partition when you're confident about its size.

You should also know that Linux allows one to use several swap partitions and/or swap files at the same time. This means that if you only occasionally need an unusual amount of swap space, you can set up an extra swap file at such times, instead of keeping the whole amount allocated all the time.

A note on operating system terminology: computer science usually distinguishes between swapping (writing the whole process out to swap space) and paging (writing only fixed size parts, usually a few kilobytes, at a time). Paging is usually more efficient, and that's what Linux does, but traditional Linux terminology talks about swapping anyway.[1]

[1]Thus quite needlessly annoying a number of computer scientists something horrible.

5.2 Creating a swap space

A swap file is an ordinary file; it is in no way special to the kernel. The only thing that matters to the kernel is that it has no holes, and that it is prepared for use with `mkswap`. It must reside on a local disk, however; it can't reside in a file system that has been mounted over NFS due to implementation reasons.

The bit about holes is important. The swap file reserves the disk space so that the kernel can quickly swap out a page without having to go through all the things that are necessary when allocating a disk sector to a file. The kernel merely uses any sectors that have already been allocated to the file. Because a hole in a file means that there are no disk sectors allocated (for that place in the file), it is not good for the kernel to try to use them.

One good way to create the swap file without holes is through the following command:

```
$ dd if=/dev/zero of=/extra-swap bs=1024 count=1024
1024+0 records in
1024+0 records out
$
```

where `/extra-swap` is the name of the swap file and the size of is given after the `count=`. It is best for the size to be a multiple of 4, because the kernel writes out **memory pages**, which are 4 kilobytes in size. If the size is not a multiple of 4, the last couple of kilobytes may be unused.

A swap partition is also not special in any way. You create it just like any other partition; the only difference is that it is used as a raw partition, that is, it will not contain any file system at all. It is a good idea to mark swap partitions as type 82 (Linux swap); this will the make partition listings clearer, even though it is not strictly necessary to the kernel.

After you have created a swap file or a swap partition, you need to write a signature to its beginning; this contains some administrative information and is used by the kernel. The command to do this is `mkswap`, used like this:

```
$ mkswap /extra-swap 1024
Setting up swapspace, size = 1044480 bytes
$
```

Note that the swap space is still not in use yet: it exists, but the kernel does not use it to provide virtual memory.

You should be very careful when using `mkswap`, since it does not check that the file or partition isn't used for anything else. *You can easily overwrite important files and partitions with* `mkswap`*!* Fortunately, you should only need to use `mkswap` when you install your system.

The Linux memory manager limits the size of each swap space to about 127 MB (for various technical reasons, the actual limit is $(4096-10)\times 8\times 4096 = 133890048$ bytes, or 127.6875 megabytes). You can, however, use up to 16 swap spaces simultaneously, for a total of almost 2 GB.[2]

5.3 Using a swap space

An initialized swap space is taken into use with `swapon`. This command tells the kernel that the swap space can be used. The path to the swap space is given as the argument, so to start swapping on a temporary swap file one might use the following command.

```
$ swapon /extra-swap
$
```

Swap spaces can be used automatically by listing them in the `/etc/fstab` file.

```
/dev/hda8     none     swap     sw     0     0
/swapfile     none     swap     sw     0     0
```

[2]A gigabyte here, a gigabyte there, pretty soon we start talking about real memory.

The startup scripts will run the command `swapon -a`, which will start swapping on all the swap spaces listed in `/etc/fstab`. Therefore, the `swapon` command is usually used only when extra swap is needed.

You can monitor the use of swap spaces with `free`. It will tell the total amount of swap space used.

```
$ free
              total       used       free     shared    buffers
Mem:          15152      14896        256      12404       2528
-/+ buffers:             12368       2784
Swap:         32452       6684      25768
$
```

The first line of output (`Mem:`) shows the physical memory. The total column does not show the physical memory used by the kernel, which is usually about a megabyte. The used column shows the amount of memory used (the second line does not count buffers). The free column shows completely unused memory. The shared column shows the amount of memory shared by several processes; the more, the merrier. The buffers column shows the current size of the disk buffer cache.

That last line (`Swap:`) shows similar information for the swap spaces. If this line is all zeroes, your swap space is not activated.

The same information is available via `top`, or using the `proc` file system in file `/proc/meminfo`. It is currently difficult to get information on the use of a specific swap space.

A swap space can be removed from use with `swapoff`. It is usually not necessary to do it, except for temporary swap spaces. Any pages in use in the swap space are swapped in first; if there is not sufficient physical memory to hold them, they will then be swapped out (to some other swap space). If there is not enough virtual memory to hold all of the pages Linux will start to thrash; after a long while it should recover, but meanwhile the system is unusable. You should check (e.g., with `free`) that there is enough free memory before removing a swap space from use.

All the swap spaces that are used automatically with `swapon -a` can be removed from use with `swapoff -a`; it looks at the file `/etc/fstab` to find what to remove. Any manually used swap spaces will remain in use.

Sometimes a lot of swap space can be in use even though there is a lot of free physical memory. This can happen for instance if at one point there is need to swap, but later a big process that occupied much of the physical memory terminates and frees the memory. The swapped-out data is not automatically swapped in until it is needed, so the physical memory may remain free for a long time. There is no need to worry about this, but it can be comforting to know what is happening.

5.4 Sharing swap spaces with other operating systems

Virtual memory is built into many operating systems. Since they each need it only when they are running, i.e., never at the same time, the swap spaces of all but the currently running one are being wasted. It would be more efficient for them to share a single swap space. This is possible, but can require a bit of hacking. The Tips-HOWTO contains some advice on how to implement this.

5.5 Allocating swap space

Some people will tell you that you should allocate twice as much swap space as you have physical memory, but this is a bogus rule. Here's how to do it properly:

1. Estimate your total memory needs. This is the largest amount of memory you'll probably need at a time, that is the sum of the memory requirements of all the programs you want to run at the same time. This can be done by running at the same time all the programs you are likely to ever be running at the same time.

   For instance, if you want to run X, you should allocate about 8 MB for it, gcc wants several megabytes (some files need an unusually large amount, up to tens of megabytes, but usually about four should do), and so on. The kernel will use about a megabyte by itself, and the usual shells and other small utilities perhaps a few hundred kilobytes (say a megabyte together). There is no need to try to be exact, rough estimates are fine, but you might want to be on the pessimistic side.

Remember that if there are going to be several people using the system at the same time, they are all going to consume memory. However, if two people run the same program at the same time, the total memory consumption is usually not double, since code pages and shared libraries exist only once.

The `free` and `ps` commands are useful for estimating the memory needs.

2. Add some security to the estimate in step 1. This is because estimates of program sizes will probably be wrong, because you'll probably forget some programs you want to run, and to make certain that you have some extra space just in case. A couple of megabytes should be fine. (It is better to allocate too much than too little swap space, but there's no need to over-do it and allocate the whole disk, since unused swap space is wasted space; see later about adding more swap.) Also, since it is nicer to deal with even numbers, you can round the value up to the next full megabyte.

3. Based on the computations above, you know how much memory you'll be needing in total. So, in order to allocate swap space, you just need to subtract the size of your physical memory from the total memory needed, and you know how much swap space you need. (On some versions of UNIX, you need to allocate space for an image of the physical memory as well, so the amount computed in step 2 is what you need and you shouldn't do the subtraction.)

4. If your calculated swap space is very much larger than your physical memory (more than a couple times larger), you should probably invest in more physical memory, otherwise performance will be too low.

It's a good idea to have at least some swap space, even if your calculations indicate that you need none. Linux uses swap space somewhat aggressively, so that as much physical memory as possible can be kept free. Linux will swap out memory pages that have not been used, even if the memory is not yet needed for anything. This avoids waiting for swapping when it is needed—the swapping can be done earlier, when the disk is otherwise idle.

Swap space can be divided among several disks. This can sometimes improve performance, depending on the relative speeds of the disks and the access patterns of the disks. You might want to experiment with a few schemes, but be aware that doing the experiments properly is quite difficult. You should not believe claims that any one scheme is superior to any other, since it won't always be true.

5.6 The buffer cache

Reading from a disk[3] is very slow compared to accessing (real) memory. In addition, it is common to read the same part of a disk several times during relatively short periods of time. For example, one might first read an e-mail message, then read the letter into an editor when replying to it, then make the mail program read it again when copying it to a folder. Or, consider how often the command `ls` might be run on a system with many users. By reading the information from disk only once and then keeping it in memory until no longer needed, one can speed up all but the first read. This is called **disk buffering**, and the memory used for the purpose is called the **buffer cache**.

Since memory is, unfortunately, a finite, nay, scarce resource, the buffer cache usually cannot be big enough (it can't hold all the data one ever wants to use). When the cache fills up, the data that has been unused for the longest time is discarded and the memory thus freed is used for the new data.

Disk buffering works for writes as well. On the one hand, data that is written is often soon read again (e.g., a source code file is saved to a file, then read by the compiler), so putting data that is written in the cache is a good idea. On the other hand, by only putting the data into the cache, not writing it to disk at once, the program that writes runs quicker. The writes can then be done in the background, without slowing down the other programs.

[3] Except a RAM disk, for obvious reasons.

Most operating systems have buffer caches (although they might be called something else), but not all of them work according to the above principles. Some are **write-through**: the data is written to disk at once (it is kept in the cache as well, of course). The cache is called **write-back** if the writes are done at a later time. Write-back is more efficient than write-through, but also a bit more prone to errors: if the machine crashes, or the power is cut at a bad moment, or the floppy is removed from the disk drive before the data in the cache waiting to be written gets written, the changes in the cache are usually lost. This might even mean that the file system (if there is one) is not in full working order, perhaps because the unwritten data held important changes to the bookkeeping information.

Because of this, you should never turn off the power without using a proper shutdown procedure (see chapter 6), or remove a floppy from the disk drive until it has been unmounted (if it was mounted) or after whatever program is using it has signaled that it is finished and the floppy drive light doesn't shine anymore. The `sync` command **flushes** the buffer, i.e., forces all unwritten data to be written to disk, and can be used when one wants to be sure that everything is safely written. In traditional UNIX systems, there is a program called `update` running in the background which does a `sync` every 30 seconds, so it is usually not necessary to use `sync`. Linux has an additional daemon, `bdflush`, which does a more imperfect sync more frequently to avoid the sudden freeze due to heavy disk I/O that `sync` sometimes causes.

Under Linux, `bdflush` is started by `update`. There is usually no reason to worry about it, but if `bdflush` happens to die for some reason, the kernel will warn about this, and you should start it by hand (`/sbin/update`).

The cache does not actually buffer files, but blocks, which are the smallest units of disk I/O (under Linux, they are usually 1 kB). This way, also directories, super blocks, other file system bookkeeping data, and non-file system disks are cached.

The effectiveness of a cache is primarily decided by its size. A small cache is next to useless: it will hold so little data that all cached data is flushed from the cache before it is reused. The critical size depends on how much data is read and written, and how often the same data is accessed. The only way to know is to experiment.

If the cache is of a fixed size, it is not very good to have it too big, either, because that might make the free memory too small and cause swapping (which is also slow). To make the most efficient use of real memory, Linux automatically uses all free RAM for buffer cache, but also automatically makes the cache smaller when programs need more memory.

Under Linux, you do not need to do anything to make use of the cache, it happens completely automatically. Except for following the proper procedures for shutdown and removing floppies, you do not need to worry about it.

CHAPTER 6

Boots And Shutdowns

Start me up
Ah. . . you've got to. . . you've got to
Never, never never stop
Start it up
Ah. . . start it up, never, never, never
You make a grown man cry,
you make a grown man cry
(Rolling Stones)

This section explains what goes on when a Linux system is brought up and taken down, and how it should be done properly. If proper procedures are not followed, files might be corrupted or lost.

6.1 An overview of boots and shutdowns

The act of turning on a computer system and causing its operating system to be loaded[1] is called **booting**. The name comes from an image of the computer pulling itself up from its bootstraps, but the act itself slightly more realistic.

During bootstrapping, the computer first loads a small piece of code called the **bootstrap loader**, which in turn loads and starts the operating system. The bootstrap loader is usually stored in a fixed location on a hard disk or a floppy. The reason for this two step process is that the operating system is big and complicated, but the first piece of code that the computer loads must be very small (a few hundred bytes), to avoid making the firmware unnecessarily complicated.

Different computers do the bootstrapping differently. For PC's, the computer (its BIOS) reads in the first sector (called the **boot sector**) of a floppy or hard disk. The bootstrap loader is contained within this sector. It loads the operating system from elsewhere on the disk (or from some other place).

After Linux has been loaded, it initializes the hardware and device drivers, and then runs `init`. `init` starts other processes to allow users to log in, and do things. The details of this part will be discussed below.

In order to shut down a Linux system, first all processes are told to terminate (this makes them close any files and do other necessary things to keep things tidy), then file systems and swap areas are unmounted, and finally a message is printed to the console that the power can be turned off. If the proper procedure is not followed, terrible things can and will happen; most importantly, the file system buffer cache might not be flushed, which means that all data in it is lost and the file system on disk is inconsistent, and therefore possibly unusable.

[1] On early computers, it wasn't enough to merely turn on the computer, you had to manually load the operating system as well. These new-fangled thing-a-ma-jigs do it all by themselves.

6.2 The boot process in closer look

You can boot Linux either from a floppy or from the hard disk. The installation section in *Installation and Getting Started*[2] tells you how to install Linux so you can boot it the way you want to.

When a PC is booted, the BIOS will do various tests to check that everything looks all right,[3] and will then start the actual booting. It will choose a disk drive (typically the first floppy drive, if there is a floppy inserted, otherwise the first hard disk, if one is installed in the computer; the order might be configurable, however) and will then read its very first sector. This is called the **boot sector**; for a hard disk, it is also called the **master boot record**, since a hard disk can contain several partitions, each with their own boot sectors.

The boot sector contains a small program (small enough to fit into one sector) whose responsibility is to read the actual operating system from the disk and start it. When booting Linux from a floppy disk, the boot sector contains code that just reads the first few hundred blocks (depending on the actual kernel size, of course) to a predetermined place in memory. On a Linux boot floppy, there is no file system, the kernel is just stored in consecutive sectors, since this simplifies the boot process. It is possible, however, to boot from a floppy with a file system, by using LILO, the LInux LOader.

When booting from the hard disk, the code in the master boot record will examine the partition table (also in the master boot record), identify the active partition (the partition that is marked to be bootable), read the boot sector from that partition, and then start the code in that boot sector. The code in the partition's boot sector does what a floppy disk's boot sector does: it will read in the kernel from the partition and start it. The details vary, however, since it is generally not useful to have a separate partition for just the kernel image, so the code in the partition's boot sector can't just read the disk in sequential order, it has to find the sectors wherever the file system has put them. There are several ways around this problem, but the most common way is to use LILO. (The details about how to do this are irrelevant for this discussion, however; see the LILO documentation for more information; it is most thorough.)

When booting with LILO, it will normally go right ahead and read in and boot the default kernel. It is also possible to configure LILO to be able to boot one of several kernels, or even other operating systems than Linux, and it is possible for the user to choose which kernel or operating system is to be booted at boot time. LILO can be configured so that if one holds down the `Alt`, `Shift`, or `Ctrl` key at boot time (when LILO is loaded), LILO will ask what is to be booted and not boot the default right away. Alternatively, LILO can be configured so that it will always ask, with an optional timeout that will cause the default kernel to be booted.

With LILO, it is also possible to give a **kernel command line argument**, after the name of the kernel or operating system.

Booting from floppy and from hard disk have both their advantages, but generally booting from the hard disk is nicer, since it avoids the hassle of playing around with floppies. It is also faster. However, it can be more troublesome to install the system to boot from the hard disk, so many people will first boot from floppy, then, when the system is otherwise installed and working well, will install LILO and start booting from the hard disk.

After the Linux kernel has been read into the memory, by whatever means, and is started for real, roughly the following things happen:

- The Linux kernel is installed compressed, so it will first uncompress itself. The beginning of the kernel image contains a small program that does this.
- If you have a super-VGA card that Linux recognizes and that has some special text modes (such as 100 columns by 40 rows), Linux asks you which mode you want to use. During the kernel compilation, it is possible to preset a video mode, so that this is never asked. This can also be done with LILO or `rdev`.
- After this, the kernel checks what other hardware there is (hard disks, floppies, network adapters...), and configures some of its device drivers appropriately; while it does this, it outputs messages about its findings. For example, when I boot, I it looks like this:

---

[2] *Installation and Getting Started Guide* by Matt Welsh.

[3] This is called the **power on self test**, or **POST** for short.

```
LILO boot:
Loading linux.
Console: color EGA+ 80x25, 8 virtual consoles
Serial driver version 3.94 with no serial options enabled
tty00 at 0x03f8 (irq = 4) is a 16450
tty01 at 0x02f8 (irq = 3) is a 16450
lp_init: lp1 exists (0), using polling driver
Memory: 7332k/8192k available (300k kernel code, 384k reserved, 176k data)
Floppy drive(s): fd0 is 1.44M, fd1 is 1.2M
Loopback device init
Warning WD8013 board not found at i/o = 280.
Math coprocessor using irq13 error reporting.
Partition check:
  hda: hda1 hda2 hda3
VFS: Mounted root (ext filesystem).
Linux version 0.99.pl9-1 (root@haven) 05/01/93 14:12:20
```

The exact texts are different on different systems, depending on the hardware, the version of Linux being used, and how it has been configured.

- Then the kernel will try to mount the root file system. The place is configurable at compilation time, or any time with rdev or LILO. The file system type is detected automatically. If the mounting of the root file system fails, for example because you didn't remember to include the corresponding file system driver in the kernel, the kernel panics and halts the system (there isn't much it can do, anyway).

  The root file system is usually mounted read-only (this can be set in the same way as the place). This makes it possible to check the file system while it is mounted; it is not a good idea to check a file system that is mounted read-write.

- After this, the kernel starts the program init (located in /sbin/init) in the background (this will always become process number 1). init does various startup chores. The exact things it does depends on how it is configured; see chapter 7 for more information (not yet written). It will at least start some essential background daemons.

- init then switches to multi-user mode, and starts a getty for virtual consoles and serial lines. getty is the program which lets people log in via virtual consoles and serial terminals. init may also start some other programs, depending on how it is configured.

- After this, the boot is complete, and the system is up and running normally.

6.3 More about shutdowns

It is important to follow the correct procedures when you shut down a Linux system. If you fail do so, your file systems probably will become trashed and the files probably will become scrambled. This is because Linux has a disk cache that won't write things to disk at once, but only at intervals. This greatly improves performance but also means that if you just turn off the power at a whim the cache may hold a lot of data and that what is on the disk may not be a fully working file system (because only some things have been written to the disk).

Another reason against just flipping the power switch is that in a multi-tasking system there can be lots of things going on in the background, and shutting the power can be quite disastrous. By using the proper shutdown sequence, you ensure that all background processes can save their data.

The command for properly shutting down a Linux system is shutdown. It is usually used in one of two ways.

If you are running a system where you are the only user, the usual way of using shutdown is to quit all running programs, log out on all virtual consoles, log in as root on one of them (or stay logged in as root if you already are, but you should change to the root directory, to avoid problems with unmounting), then give the command `shutdown -h now` (substitute `now` with a plus sign and a number in minutes if you want a delay, though you usually don't on a single user system).

Alternatively, if your system has many users, use the command `shutdown -h` *+time message*, where *time* is the time in minutes until the system is halted, and *message* is a short explanation of why the system is shutting down.

```
# shutdown -h +10 'We will install a new disk.  System should
> be back on-line in three hours.'
#
```

This will warn everybody that the system will shut down in ten minutes, and that they'd better get lost or lose data. The warning is printed to every terminal on which someone is logged in, including all `xterms`:

```
Broadcast message from root (ttyp0) Wed Aug 2 01:03:25 1995...

We will install a new disk.  System should
be back on-line in three hours.
The system is going DOWN for system halt in 10 minutes !!
```

The warning is automatically repeated a few times before the boot, with shorter and shorter intervals as the time runs out.

When the real shutting down starts after any delays, all file systems (except the root one) are unmounted, user processes (if anybody is still logged in) are killed, daemons are shut down, all file system are unmounted, and generally everything settles down. When that is done, `init` prints out a message that you can power down the machine. Then, *and only then*, should you move your fingers towards the power switch.

Sometimes, although rarely on any good system, it is impossible to shut down properly. For instance, if the kernel panics and crashes and burns and generally misbehaves, it might be completely impossible to give any new commands, hence shutting down properly is somewhat difficult, and just about everything you can do is hope that nothing has been too severely damaged and turn off the power. If the troubles are a bit less severe (say, somebody hit your keyboard with an axe), and the kernel and the `update` program still run normally, it is probably a good idea to wait a couple of minutes to give `update` a chance to flush the buffer cache, and only cut the power after that.

Some people like to shut down using the command `sync`[4] three times, waiting for the disk I/O to stop, then turn off the power. If there are no running programs, this is about equivalent to using `shutdown`. However, it does not unmount any file systems and this can lead to problems with the ext2fs "clean file system" flag. The triple-sync method is *not recommended*.

(In case you're wondering: the reason for *three* syncs is that in the early days of UNIX, when the commands were typed separately, that usually gave sufficient time for most disk I/O to be finished.)

6.4 Rebooting

Rebooting means booting the system again. This can be accomplished by first shutting it down completely, turning power off, and then turning it back on. A simpler way is to ask `shutdown` to reboot the system, instead of merely halting it. This is accomplished by using the `-r` option to shutdown, for example, by giving the command `shutdown -r now`.

Most Linux systems run `shutdown -r now` when Ctrl-Alt-Del is pressed on the keyboard. This reboots the system. The action on Ctrl-Alt-Del is configurable, however, and it might be better to allow for some delay before the reboot on a multiuser machine. Systems that are physically accessible to anyone might even be configured to do nothing when Ctrl-Alt-Del is pressed.

[4] `sync` flushes the buffer cache.

6.5 Single user mode

The shutdown command can also be used to bring the system down to single user mode, in which no one can log in, but `root` can use the console. This is useful for system administration tasks that can't be done while the system is running normally.

6.6 Emergency boot floppies

It is not always possible to boot a computer from the hard disk. For example, if you make a mistake in configuring LILO, you might make your system unbootable. For these situations, you need an alternative way of booting that will always work (as long as the hardware works). For typical PC's, this means booting from the floppy drive.

Most Linux distributions allow one to create an **emergency boot floppy** during installation. It is a good idea to do this. However, some such boot disks contain only the kernel, and assume you will be using the programs on the distribution's installation disks to fix whatever problem you have. Sometimes those programs aren't enough; for example, you might have to restore some files from backups made with software not on the installation disks.

Thus, it might be necessary to create a custom root floppy as well. The *Bootdisk HOWTO* by Graham Chapman contains instructions for doing this. You must, of course, remember to keep your emergency boot and root floppies up to date.

You can't use the floppy drive you use to mount the root floppy for anything else. This can be inconvenient if you only have one floppy drive. However, if you have enough memory, you can configure your boot floppy to load the root disk to a RAM disk (the boot floppy's kernel needs to be specially configured for this). Once the root floppy has been loaded into the RAM disk, the floppy drive is free to mount other disks.

Chapter 7

init

Uuno on numero yksi

This chapter describes the init process, which is the first user level process started by the kernel. init has many important duties, such as starting getty (so that users can log in), implementing run levels, and taking care of orphaned processes. This chapter explains how init is configured and how you can make use of the different run levels.

7.1 init comes first

init is one of those programs that are absolutely essential to the operation of a Linux system, but that you still can mostly ignore. A good Linux distribution will come with a configuration for init that will work for most systems, and on these systems there is nothing you need to do about init. Usually, you only need to worry about init if you hook up serial terminals, dial-in (not dial-out) modems, or if you want to change the default run level.

When the kernel has started itself (has been loaded into memory, has started running, and has initialized all device drivers and data structures and such), it finishes its own part of the boot process by starting a user level program, init. Thus, init is always the first process (its process number is always 1).

The kernel looks for init in a few locations that have been historically used for it, but the proper location for it (on a Linux system) is /sbin/init. If the kernel can't find init, it tries to run /bin/sh, and if that also fails, the startup of the system fails.

When init starts, it finishes the boot process by doing a number of administrative tasks, such as checking file systems, cleaning up /tmp, starting various services, and starting a getty for each terminal and virtual console where users should be able to log in (see chapter 8).

After the system is properly up, init restarts getty for each terminal after a user has logged out (so that the next user can log in). init also adopts orphan processes: when a process starts a child process and dies before its child, the child immediately becomes a child of init. This is important for various technical reasons, but it is good to know it, since it makes it easier to understand process lists and process tree graphs.[1]

There are a few variants of init available. Most Linux distributions use sysvinit (written by Miquel van Smoorenburg), which is based on the System V init design. The BSD versions of Unix have a different init. The primary difference is run levels: System V has them, BSD does not (at least traditionally). This difference is not essential. We'll look at sysvinit only.

[1] init itself is not allowed to die. You can't kill init even with SIGKILL.

7.2 Configuring `init` to start `getty`: the `/etc/inittab` file

When it starts up, `init` reads the `/etc/inittab` configuration file. While the system is running, it will re-read it, if sent the HUP signal;[2] this feature makes it unnecessary to boot the system to make changes to the `init` configuration take effect.

The `/etc/inittab` file is a bit complicated. We'll start with the simple case of configuring `getty` lines. Lines in `/etc/inittab` consist of four colon-delimited fields:

id:runlevels:action:process

The fields are described below. In addition, `/etc/inittab` can contain empty lines, and lines that begin with a number sign ('#'); these are both ignored.

id — This identifies the line in the file. For `getty` lines, it specifies the terminal it runs on (the characters after `/dev/tty` in the device file name). For other lines, it doesn't matter (except for length restrictions), but it should be unique.

runlevels — The run levels the line should be considered for. The run levels are given as single digits, without delimiters. (Run levels are described in the next section.)

action — What action should be taken by the line, e.g., `respawn` to run the command in the next field again, when it exits, or `once` to run it just once.

process — The command to run.

To start a `getty` on the first virtual terminal (`/dev/tty1`), in all the normal multi-user run levels (2–5), one would write the following line:

```
1:2345:respawn:/sbin/getty 9600 tty1
```

The first field says that this is the line for `/dev/tty1`. The second field says that it applies to run levels 2, 3, 4, and 5. The third field means that the command should be run again, after it exits (so that one can log in, log out, and then log in again). The last field is the command that runs `getty` on the first virtual terminal.[3]

If you wanted to add terminals or dial-in modem lines to a system, you'd add more lines to `/etc/inittab`, one for each terminal or dial-in line. For more details, see the manual pages *init*(8), *inittab*(5), and *getty*(8).

If a command fails when it starts, and `init` is configured to `restart` it, it will use a lot of system resources: `init` starts it, it fails, `init` starts it, it fails, `init` starts it, it fails, and so on, ad infinitum. To prevent this, `init` will keep track of how often it restarts a command, and if the frequency grows to high, it will delay for five minutes before restarting again.

7.3 Run levels

A **run level** is a state of `init` and the whole system that defines what system services are operating. Run levels are identified by numbers, see table 7.1. There is no consensus of how to use the user defined run levels (2 through 5). Some system administrators use run levels to define which subsystems are working, e.g., whether X is running, whether the network is operational, and so on. Others have all subsystems always running or start and stop them individually, without changing run levels, since run levels are too coarse for controlling their systems. You need to decide for yourself, but it might be easiest to follow the way your Linux distribution does things.

Run levels are configured in `/etc/inittab` by lines like the following:

```
12:2:wait:/etc/init.d/rc 2
```

The first field is an arbitrary label, the second one means that this applies for run level 2. The third field means that `init` should run the command in the fourth field once, when the run level is entered, and that `init` should

[2] Using the command `kill -HUP 1` as root, for example

[3] Different versions of `getty` are run differently. Consult your manual page—and make sure it is the correct manual page.

Table 7.1: Run level numbers

0	Halt the system.
1	Single-user mode (for special administration).
2–5	Normal operation (user defined).
6	Reboot.

wait for it to complete. The /etc/init.d/rc command runs whatever commands are necessary to start and stop services to enter run level 2.

The command in the fourth field does all the hard work of setting up a run level. It starts services that aren't already running, and stops services that shouldn't be running in the new run level any more. Exactly what the command is, and how run levels are configured, depends on the Linux distribution.

When init starts, it looks for a line in /etc/inittab that specifies the default run level:

```
id:2:initdefault:
```

You can ask init to go to a non-default run level at startup by giving the kernel a command line argument of single or emergency.[4] This allows you to choose the single user mode (run level 1), which is described in section 7.5.

While the system is running, the telinit command can change the run level. When the run level is changed, init runs the relevant command from /etc/inittab.

7.4 Special configuration in /etc/inittab

The /etc/inittab has some special features that allow init to react to special circumstances. These special features are marked by special keywords in the third field. Some examples:

powerwait
: Allows init to shut the system down, when the power fails. This assumes the use of a UPS, and software that watches the UPS and informs init that the power is off.

ctrlaltdel
: Allows init to reboot the system, when the user presses Ctrl-Alt-Del on the console keyboard. Note that the system administrator can configure the reaction to Ctrl-Alt-Del to be something else instead, e.g., to be ignored, if the system is in a public location.[5]

sysinit
: Command to be run when the system is booted. This command usually cleans up /tmp, for example.

The list above is not exhaustive. See your *inittab*(5) manual page for all possibilities, and for details on how to use the above ones.

7.5 Booting in single user mode

An important run level is **single user mode** (run level 1), in which only the system administrator is using the machine and as few system services—including logins—as possible are running. Single user mode is necessary for a few administrative tasks,[6] such as running fsck on a /usr partition—this requires that the partition be unmounted, and that can't happen, unless just about all system services are killed.

A running system can be taken to single user mode by using telinit to request run level 1. At bootup, it can be entered by giving the word single or emergency on the kernel command line: the kernel gives the command line to init as well, and init understands from that word that it shouldn't use the default run level. (The kernel command line is entered in a way that depends on how you boot the system.)

---

[4]Kernel command line arguments can be given via LILO, for example. See section 7.5.

[5]Or to start nethack.

[6]It probably shouldn't be used for playing nethack.

Booting into single user mode is sometimes necessary so that one can run fsck by hand, before anything mounts or otherwise touches a broken /usr partition (any activity on a broken file system is likely to break it more, so fsck should be run as soon as possible).

The bootup scripts init runs will automatically enter single user mode, if the automatic fsck at bootup fails. This is an attempt to prevent the system from using a file system that is so broken that fsck can't fix it automatically. Such breakage is relatively rare, and usually involves a broken hard disk or an experimental kernel release, but it's good to be prepared.

As a security measure, a properly configured system will ask for the root password before starting the shell in single user mode. Otherwise, it would be simple to just enter a suitable line to LILO to get in as root. (This will break if /etc/passwd has been broken by file system problems, of course, and in that case you'd better have a boot floppy handy.)

CHAPTER 8

Logging In And Out

This chapter needs a quote. Suggestions, anyone?

This section describes what happens when a user logs in or out. The various interactions of background processes, log files, configuration files, and so on are described in some detail.

8.1 Logins via terminals

Figure 8.1 shows how logins happen via terminals. First, `init` makes sure there is a `getty` program for the terminal connection (or console). `getty` listens at the terminal and waits for the user to notify that he is ready to login in (this usually means that the user must type something). When it notices a user, `getty` outputs a welcome message (stored in `/etc/issue`), and prompts for the user name, and finally runs the `login` program. `login` gets the user name as a parameter, and prompts the user for the password. If these match, `login` starts the shell configured for the user; else it just exits and terminates the process (perhaps after giving the user another chance at entering the user name and password). `init` notices that the process terminated, and starts a new `getty` for the terminal.

Note that the only new process is the one created by `init` (using the `fork` system call); `getty` and `login` only replace the program running in the process (using the `exec` system call).

A separate program, for noticing the user, is needed for serial lines, since it can be (and traditionally was) complicated to notice when a terminal becomes active. `getty` also adapts to the speed and other settings of the connection, which is important especially for dial-in connections, where these parameters may change from call to call.

There are several versions of `getty` and `init` in use, all with their good and bad points. It is a good idea to learn about the versions on your system, and also about the other versions (you could use the Linux Software Map to search them). If you don't have dial-in's, you probably don't have to worry about `getty`, but `init` is still important.

8.2 Logins via the network

Two computers in the same network are usually linked via a single physical cable. When they communicate over the network, the programs in each computer that take part in the communication are linked via a **virtual connection**, a sort of imaginary cable. As far as the programs at either end of the virtual connection are concerned, they have a monopoly on their own cable. However, since the cable is not real, only imaginary, the operating systems of both computers can have several virtual connections share the same physical cable. This way, using just a single cable, several programs can communicate without having to know of or care about the other communications. It is even possible to have several computers use the same cable; the virtual connections exist between two computers, and the other computers ignore those connections that they don't take part in.

That's a complicated and over-abstracted description of the reality. It might, however, be good enough to understand the important reason why network logins are somewhat different from normal logins. The virtual connections are established when there are two programs on different computers that wish to communicate. Since it is in principle possible to login from any computer in a network to any other computer, there is a huge number of potential virtual communications. Because of this, it is not practical to start a `getty` for each potential login.

There is a single process inetd (corresponding to `getty`) that handles *all* network logins. When it notices an incoming network login (i.e., it notices that it gets a new virtual connection to some other computer), it starts a new process to handle that single login. The original process remains and continues to listen for new logins.

To make things a bit more complicated, there is more than one communication protocol for network logins. The two most important ones are `telnet` and `rlogin`. In addition to logins, there are many other virtual connections that may be made (for FTP, Gopher, HTTP, and other network services). It would be ineffective to have a separate process listening for a particular type of connection, so instead there is only one listener that can recognize the type of the connection and can start the correct type of program to provide the service. This single listener is called `inetd`; see the "Linux Network Administrators' Guide" for more information.

8.3 What `login` does

The `login` program takes care of authenticating the user (making sure that the user name and password match), and of setting up an initial environment for the user by setting permissions for the serial line and starting the shell.

Part of the initial setup is outputting the contents of the file `/etc/motd` (short for message of the day) and checking for electronic mail. These can be disabled by creating a file called `.hushlogin` in the user's home directory.

If the file `/etc/nologin` exists, logins are disabled. That file is typically created by `shutdown` and relatives. `login` checks for this file, and will refuse to accept a login if it exists. If it does exist, `login` outputs its contents to the terminal before it quits.

`login` logs all failed login attempts in a system log file (via `syslog`). It also logs *all* logins by `root`. Both of these can be useful when tracking down intruders.

Currently logged in people are listed in `/var/run/utmp`. This file is valid only until the system is next rebooted or shut down; it is cleared when the system is booted. It lists each user and the terminal (or network connection) he is using, along with some other useful information. The `who`, `w`, and other similar commands look in `utmp` to see who are logged in.

All successful logins are recorded into `/var/log/wtmp`. This file will grow without limit, so it must be cleaned regularly, for example by having a weekly `cron` job to clear it.[1] The `last` command browses `wtmp`.

Both `utmp` and `wtmp` are in a binary format (see the *utmp* manual page); it is unfortunately not convenient to examine them without special programs.

8.4 Access control

The user database is traditionally contained in the `/etc/passwd` file. Some systems use **shadow passwords**, and have moved the passwords to `/etc/shadow`. Sites with many computers that share the accounts use NIS or some other method to store the user database; they might also automatically copy the database from one central location to all other computers.

The user database contains not only the passwords, but also some additional information about the users, such as their real names, home directories, and login shells. This other information needs to be public, so that

[1] Good Linux distributions do this out of the box.

anyone can read it. Therefore the password is stored encrypted. This does have the drawback that anyone with access to the encrypted password can use various cryptographical methods to guess it, without trying to actually log into the computer. Shadow passwords try to avoid this by moving the password into another file, which only `root` can read (the password is still stored encrypted). However, installing shadow passwords later onto a system that did not support them can be difficult.

With or without passwords, it is important to make sure that all passwords in a system are good, i.e., not easily guessable. The `crack` program can be used to crack passwords; any password it can find is by definition not a good one. While `crack` can be run by intruders, it can also be run by the system administrator to avoid bad passwords. Good passwords can also be enforced by the `passwd` program; this is in fact more effective in CPU cycles, since cracking passwords requires quite a lot of computation.

The user group database is kept in `/etc/group`; for systems with shadow passwords, there can be a `/etc/shadow.group`.

`root` usually can't login via most terminals or the network, only via terminals listed in the `/etc/securetty` file. This makes it necessary to get physical access to one of these terminals. It is, however, possible to log in via any terminal as any other user, and use the `su` command to become `root`.

8.5 Shell startup

When an interactive login shell starts, it automatically executes one or more pre-defined files. Different shells execute different files; see the documentation of each shell for further information.

Most shells first run some global file, for example, the Bourne shell (`/bin/sh`) and its derivatives execute `/etc/profile`; in addition, they execute `.profile` in the user's home directory. `/etc/profile` allows the system administrator to have set up a common user environment, especially by setting the PATH to include local command directories in addition to the normal ones. On the other hand, `.profile` allows the user to customize the environment to his own tastes by overriding, if necessary, the default environment.

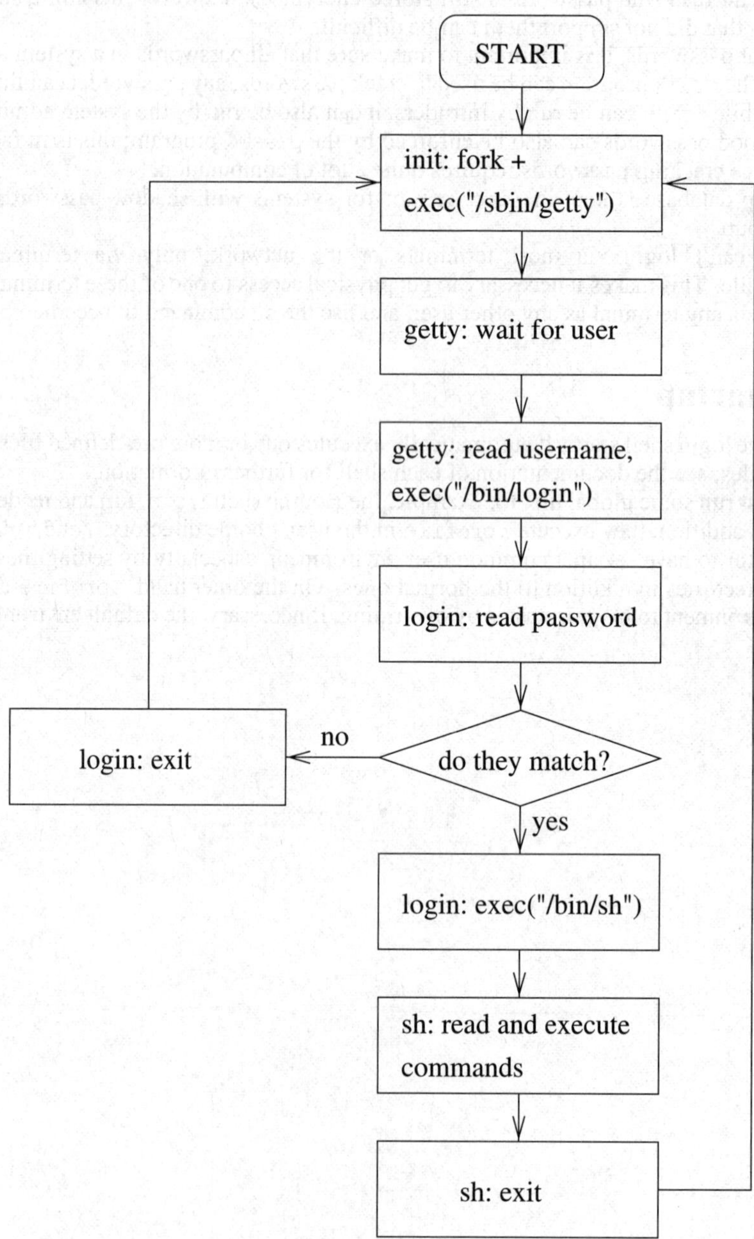

Figure 8.1: Logins via terminals: the interaction of `init`, `getty`, `login`, and the shell.

Chapter 9

Managing user accounts

The similarities of sysadmins and drug dealers:
both measure stuff in K's, and both have users.
(Old, tired computer joke.)

This chapter explains how to create new user accounts, how to modify the properties of those accounts, and how to remove the accounts. Different Linux systems have different tools for doing this.

9.1 What's an account?

When a computer is used by many people it is usually necessary to differentiate between the users, for example, so that their private files can be kept private. This is important even if the computer can only be used by a single person at a time, as with most microcomputers.[1] Thus, each user is given a unique user name, and that name is used to log in.

There's more to a user than just a name, however. An **account** is all the files, resources, and information belonging to one user. The term hints at banks, and in a commercial system each account usually has some money attached to it, and that money vanishes at different speeds depending on how much the user stresses the system. For example, disk space might have a price per megabyte and day, and processing time might have a price per second.

9.2 Creating a user

The Linux kernel itself treats users are mere numbers. Each user is identified by a unique integer, the **user id** or **uid**, because numbers are faster and easier for a computer to process than textual names. A separate database outside the kernel assigns a textual name, the **user name**, to each user id. The database contains additional information as well.

To create a user, you need to add information about the user to the user database, and create a home directory for him. It may also be necessary to educate the user, and set up a suitable initial environment for him.

Most Linux distributions come with a program for creating accounts. There are several such programs available. Two command line alternatives are `adduser` and `useradd`; there may be a GUI tool as well. Whatever the program, the result is that there is little if any manual work to be done. Even if the details are many and intricate, these programs make everything seem trivial. However, section 9.2.4 describes how to do it by hand.

[1] It might be quite embarrassing if my sister could read my love letters.

9.2.1 /etc/passwd and other informative files

The basic user database in a Unix system is the text file, /etc/passwd (called the **password file**), which lists all valid user names and their associated information. The file has one line per user name, and is divided into seven colon-delimited fields:

1. User name.
2. Password, in an encrypted form.
3. Numeric user id.
4. Numeric group id.
5. Full name or other description of account.
6. Home directory.
7. Login shell (program to run at login).

The format is explained in more detail in *passwd*(5).

Any user on the system may read the password file, so that they can, for example, learn the name of another user. This means that the password (the second field) is also available to everyone. The password file encrypts the password, so in theory there is no problem. However, the encryption is breakable, especially if the password is weak (e.g., it is short or it can be found in a dictionary). Therefore it is not a good idea to have the password in the password file.

Many Linux systems have **shadow passwords**. This is an alternative way of storing the password: the encrypted password is stored in a separate file, /etc/shadow, which only root can read. The /etc/passwd file only contains a special marker in the second field. Any program that needs to verify a user is setuid, and can therefore access the shadow password file. Normal programs, which only use the other fields in the password file, can't get at the password.[2]

9.2.2 Picking numeric user and group IDs

On most systems it doesn't matter what the numeric user and group IDs are, but if you use the Network file system (NFS), you need to have the same uid and gid on all systems. This is because NFS also identifies users with the numeric UIDs. If you aren't using NFS, you can let your account creation tool pick them automatically.

If you are using NFS, you'll have to be invent a mechanism for synchronizing account information. One alternative is the NIS system.[3]

9.2.3 Initial environment: /etc/skel

When the home directory for a new user is created, it is initialized with files from the /etc/skel directory. The system administrator can create files in /etc/skel that will provide a nice default environment for users. For example, he might create a /etc/skel/.profile that sets the EDITOR environment variable to some editor that is friendly towards new users.

However, it is usually best to try to keep /etc/skel as small as possible, since it will be next to impossible to update existing users' files. For example, if the name of the friendly editor changes, all existing users would have to edit their .profile. The system administrator could try to do it automatically, with a script, but that is almost certain going to break someone's file.

Whenever possible, it is better to put global configuration into global files, such as /etc/profile. This way it is possible to update it without breaking users' own setups.

[2] Yes, this means that the password file has all the information about a user *except* his password. The wonder of development.

[3] *Linux Network Administrators' Guide,* by Olaf Kirch.

9.2.4 Creating a user by hand

To create a new account manually, follow these steps:

1. Edit /etc/passwd with vipw(8) and add a new line for the new account. Be careful with the syntax. *Do not edit directly with an editor!* vipw locks the file, so that other commands won't try to update it at the same time. You should make the password field be '*', so that it is impossible to log in.

2. Similarly, edit /etc/group with vigr, if you need to create a new group as well.

3. Create the home directory of the user with mkdir.

4. Copy the files from /etc/skel to the new home directory.

5. Fix ownerships and permissions with chown and chmod. The -R option is most useful. The correct permissions vary a little from one site to another, but usually the following commands do the right thing:

```
cd /home/newusername
chown -R username.group .
chmod -R go=u,go-w .
chmod go= .
```

6. Set the password with passwd(1).

After you set the password in the last step, the account will work. You shouldn't set it until everything else has been done, otherwise the user may inadvertently log in while you're still copying the files.

It is sometimes necessary to create dummy accounts[4] that are not used by people. For example, to set up an anonymous FTP server (so that anyone can download files from it, without having to get an account first), you need to create an account called ftp. In such cases, it is usually not necessary to set the password (last step above). Indeed, it is better not to, so that no-one can use the account, unless they first become root, since root can become any user.

9.3 Changing user properties

There are a few commands for changing various properties of an account (i.e., the relevant field in /etc/passwd):

chfn	Change the full name field.
chsh	Change the login shell.
passwd	Change the password.

The super-user may use these commands to change the properties of any account. Normal users can only change the properties of their own account. It may sometimes be necessary to disable these commands (with chmod) for normal users, for example in an environment with many novice users.

Other tasks need to be done by hand. For example, to change the user name, you need to edit /etc/passwd directly (with vipw, remember). Likewise, to add or remove the user to more groups, you need to edit /etc/group (with vigr). Such tasks tend to be rare, however, and should be done with caution: for example, if you change the user name, e-mail will no longer reach the user, unless you also create a mail alias.[5]

---

[4] Surreal users?

[5] The user's name might change due to marriage, for example, and he might want to have his user name reflect his new name.

9.4 Removing a user

To remove a user, you first remove all his files, mailboxes, mail aliases, print jobs, `cron` and `at` jobs, and all other references to the user. Then you remove the relevant lines from `/etc/passwd` and `/etc/group` (remember to remove the user name from all groups it's been added to). It may be a good idea to first disable the account (see below), before you start removing stuff, to prevent the user from using the account while it is being removed.

Remember that users may have files outside their home directory. The `find` command can find them:

```
find / -user username
```

However, note that the above command will take a *long* time, if you have large disks. If you mount network disks (see section 2.3.8), you need to be careful so that you won't trash the network or the server.

Some Linux distributions come with special commands to do this; look for `deluser` or `userdel`. However, it is easy to do it by hand as well, and the commands might not do everything.

9.5 Disabling a user temporarily

It is sometimes necessary to temporarily disable an account, without removing it. For example, the user might not have paid his fees, or the system administrator may suspect that a cracker has got the password of that account.

The best way to disable an account is to change its shell into a special program that just prints a message. This way, whoever tries to log into the account, will fail, and will know why. The message can tell the user to contact the system administrator so that any problems may be dealt with.

It would also be possible to change the user name or password to something else, but then the user won't know what is going on. Confused users mean more work.[6]

A simple way to create the special programs is to write 'tail scripts':

```
#!/usr/bin/tail +2
This account has been closed due to a security breach.
Please call 555-1234 and wait for the men in black to arrive.
```

The first two characters ('`#!`') tell the kernel that the rest of the line is a command that needs to be run to interpret this file. The `tail` command in this case outputs everything except the first line to the standard output.

If `billg` is suspected of a security breach, the system administrator would do something like this:

```
# chsh -s /usr/local/lib/no-login/security billg
# su - tester
This account has been closed due to a security breach.
Please call 555-1234 and wait for the men in black to arrive.
#
```

The purpose of the `su` is to test that the change worked, of course.

Tail scripts should be kept in a separate directory, so that their names don't interfere with normal user commands.

[6] But they can be *so* fun, if you're a BOFH.

CHAPTER 10

Backups

Hardware is indeterministically reliable.
Software is deterministically unreliable.
People are indeterministically unreliable.
Nature is deterministically reliable.

This chapter explains about why, how, and when to make backups, and how to restore things from backups.

10.1 On the importance of being backed up

Your data is valuable. It will cost you time and effort re-create it, and that costs money or at least personal grief and tears; sometimes it can't even be re-created, e.g., if it is the results of some experiments. Since it is an investment, you should protect it and take steps to avoid losing it.

There are basically four reasons why you might lose data: hardware failures, software bugs, human action, or natural disasters.[1] Although modern hardware tends to be quite reliable, it can still break seemingly spontaneously. The most critical piece of hardware for storing data is the hard disk, which relies on tiny magnetic fields remaining intact in a world filled with electromagnetic noise. Modern software doesn't even tend to be reliable; a rock solid program is an exception, not a rule. Humans are quite unreliable, they will either make a mistake, or they will be malicious and destroy data on purpose. Nature might not be evil, but it can wreak havoc even when being good. All in all, it is a small miracle that anything works at all.

Backups are a way to protect the investment in data. By having several copies of the data, it does not matter as much if one is destroyed (the cost is only that of the restoration of the lost data from the backup).

It is important to do backups properly. Like everything else that is related to the physical world, backups will fail sooner or later. Part of doing backups well is to make sure they work; you don't want to notice that your backups didn't work.[2] Adding insult to injury, you might have a bad crash just as you're making the backup; if you have only one backup medium, it might destroyed as well, leaving you with the smoking ashes of hard work.[3] Or you might notice, when trying to restore, that you forgot to back up something important, like the user database on a 15 000 user site. Best of all, all your backups might be working perfectly, but the last known tape drive reading the kind of tapes you used was the one that now has a bucketful of water in it.

When it comes to backups, paranoia is in the job description.

[1] The fifth reason is "something else".
[2] Don't laugh. This has happened to several people.
[3] Been there, done that…

10.2 Selecting the backup medium

The most important decision regarding backups is the choice of backup medium. You need to consider cost, reliability, speed, availability, and usability.

Cost is important, since you should preferably have several times more backup storage than what you need for the data. A cheap medium is usually a must.

Reliability is extremely important, since a broken backup can make a grown man cry. A backup medium must be able to hold data without corruption for years. The way you use the medium affects it reliability as a backup medium. A hard disk is typically very reliable, but as a backup medium it is not very reliable, if it is in the same computer as the disk you are backing up.

Speed is usually not very important, if backups can be done without interaction. It doesn't matter if a backup takes two hours, as long as it needs no supervision. On the other hand, if the backup can't be done when the computer would otherwise be idle, then speed is an issue.

Availability is obviously necessary, since you can't use a backup medium if it doesn't exist. Less obvious is the need for the medium to be available even in the future, and on computers other than your own. Otherwise you may not be able to restore your backups after a disaster.

Usability is a large factor in how often backups are made. The easier it is to make backups, the better. A backup medium mustn't be hard or boring to use.

The typical alternatives are floppies and tapes. Floppies are very cheap, fairly reliable, not very fast, very available, but not very usable for large amounts of data. Tapes are cheap to somewhat expensive, fairly reliable, fairly fast, quite available, and—depending on the size of the tape—quite comfortable.

There are other alternatives. They are usually not very good on availability, but if that is not a problem, they can be better in other ways. For example, magneto-optical disks can have good sides of both floppies (they're random access, making restoration of a single file quick) and tapes (contain a lot of data).

10.3 Selecting the backup tool

There are many tools that can be used to make backups. The traditional UNIX tools used for backups are `tar`, `cpio`, and `dump`. In addition, there are large number of third party packages (both freeware and commercial) that can be used. The choice of backup medium can affect the choice of tool.

`tar` and `cpio` are similar, and mostly equivalent from a backup point of view. Both are capable of storing files on tapes, and retrieving files from them. Both are capable of using almost any media, since the kernel device drivers take care of the low level device handling and the devices all tend to look alike to user level programs. Some UNIX versions of `tar` and `cpio` may have problems with unusual files (symbolic links, device files, files with very long pathnames, and so on), but the Linux versions should handle all files correctly.

`dump` is different in that it reads the file system directly and not via the file system. It is also written specifically for backups; `tar` and `cpio` are really for archiving files, although they work for backups as well.

Reading the file system directly has some advantages. It makes it possible to back files up without affecting their time stamps; for `tar` and `cpio`, you would have to mount the file system read-only first. Directly reading the file system is also more effective, if everything needs to be backed up, since it can be done with much less disk head movement. The major disadvantage is that it makes the backup program specific to one file system type; the Linux `dump` program understands the ext2 file system only.

`dump` also directly supports backup levels (which we'll be discussing below); with `tar` and `cpio` this has to be implemented with other tools.

A comparison of the third party backup tools is beyond the scope of this book. The Linux Software Map lists many of the freeware ones.

10.4 Simple backups

A simple backup scheme is to back up everything once, then back up everything that has been modified since the previous backup. The first backup is called a **full backup**, the subsequent ones are **incremental backups**. A full backup is often more laborious than incremental ones, since there is more data to write to the tape and a full backup might not fit onto one tape (or floppy). Restoring from incremental backups can be many times more work than from a full one. Restoration can be optimized so that you always back up everything since the previous full backup; this way, backups are a bit more work, but there should never be a need to restore more than a full backup and an incremental backup.

If you want to make backups every day and have six tapes, you could use tape 1 for the first full backup (say, on a Friday), and tapes 2 to 5 for the incremental backups (Monday through Thursday). Then you make a new full backup on tape 6 (second Friday), and start doing incremental ones with tapes 2–5 again. You don't want to overwrite tape 1 with until you've got a new full backup, lest something happens while you're making the full backup. After you've made a full backup to tape 6, you want to keep tape 1 somewhere else, so that when your other backup tapes are destroyed in the fire, you still have at least something left. When you need to make the next full backup, you fetch tape 1 and leave tape 6 in its place.

If you have more than six tapes, you can use the extra ones for full backups. Each time you make a full backup, you use the oldest tape. This way you can have full backups from several previous weeks, which is good if you want to find an old, now deleted file, or an old version of a file.

10.4.1 Making backups with `tar`

A full backup can easily be made with `tar`:

```
# tar -create -file /dev/ftape /usr/src
tar:  Removing leading / from absolute path names in the archive
#
```

The example above uses the GNU version of `tar` and its long option names. The traditional version of `tar` only understands single character options. The GNU version can also handle backups that don't fit on one tape or floppy, and also very long paths; not all traditional versions can do these things. (Linux only uses GNU `tar`.)

If your backup doesn't fit on one tape, you need to use the `-multi-volume` (`-M`) option:

```
# tar -cMf /dev/fd0H1440 /usr/src
tar:  Removing leading / from absolute path names in the archive
Prepare volume #2 for /dev/fd0H1440 and hit return:
#
```

Note that you should format the floppies before you begin the backup, or else use another window or virtual terminal and do it when `tar` asks for a new floppy.

After you've made a backup, you should check that it is OK, using the `-compare` (`-d`) option:

```
# tar -compare -verbose -f /dev/ftape
usr/src/
usr/src/linux
usr/src/linux-1.2.10-includes/
....
#
```

Failing to check a backup means that you will not notice that your backups aren't working until after you've lost the original data.

An incremental backup can be done with `tar` using the `-newer` (`-N`) option:

```
# tar -create -newer '8 Sep 1995' -file /dev/ftape /usr/src -verbose
tar:  Removing leading / from absolute path names in the archive
usr/src/
usr/src/linux-1.2.10-includes/
usr/src/linux-1.2.10-includes/include/
usr/src/linux-1.2.10-includes/include/linux/
usr/src/linux-1.2.10-includes/include/linux/modules/
```

```
usr/src/linux-1.2.10-includes/include/asm-generic/
usr/src/linux-1.2.10-includes/include/asm-i386/
usr/src/linux-1.2.10-includes/include/asm-mips/
usr/src/linux-1.2.10-includes/include/asm-alpha/
usr/src/linux-1.2.10-includes/include/asm-m68k/
usr/src/linux-1.2.10-includes/include/asm-sparc/
usr/src/patch-1.2.11.gz
#
```

Unfortunately, `tar` can't notice when a file's inode information has changed, for example, that it's permission bits have been changed, or when its name has been changed. This can be worked around using `find` and comparing current file system state with lists of files that have been previously backed up. Scripts and programs for doing this can be found on Linux FTP sites.

10.4.2 Restoring files with `tar`

The `-extract` (`-x`) option for `tar` extracts files:

```
# tar -extract -same-permissions -verbose -file /dev/fd0H1440
usr/src/
usr/src/linux
usr/src/linux-1.2.10-includes/
usr/src/linux-1.2.10-includes/include/
usr/src/linux-1.2.10-includes/include/linux/
usr/src/linux-1.2.10-includes/include/linux/hdreg.h
usr/src/linux-1.2.10-includes/include/linux/kernel.h
...
#
```

You also extract only specific files or directories (which includes all their files and subdirectories) by naming on the command line:

```
# tar xpvf /dev/fd0H1440 usr/src/linux-1.2.10-includes/include/linux/hdreg.h
usr/src/linux-1.2.10-includes/include/linux/hdreg.h
#
```

Use the `-list` (`-t`) option, if you just want to see what files are on a backup volume:

```
# tar -list -file /dev/fd0H1440
usr/src/
usr/src/linux
usr/src/linux-1.2.10-includes/
usr/src/linux-1.2.10-includes/include/
usr/src/linux-1.2.10-includes/include/linux/
usr/src/linux-1.2.10-includes/include/linux/hdreg.h
usr/src/linux-1.2.10-includes/include/linux/kernel.h
...
#
```

Note that `tar` always reads the backup volume sequentially, so for large volumes it is rather slow. It is not possible, however, to use random access database techniques when using a tape drive or some other sequential medium.

`tar` doesn't handle deleted files properly. If you need to restore a file system from a full and an incremental backup, and you have deleted a file between the two backups, it will exist again after you have done the restore. This can be a big problem, if the file has sensitive data that should no longer be available.

10.5 Multilevel backups

The simple backup method outlined in the previous section is often quite adequate for personal use or small sites. For more heavy duty use, multilevel backups are more appropriate.

The simple method has two backup levels: full and incremental backups. This can be generalized to any number of levels. A full backup would be level 0, and the different levels of incremental backups levels 1, 2, 3, ... At each incremental backup level you back up everything that has changed since the previous backup at the same or a previous level.

The purpose for doing this is that it allows a longer **backup history** cheaply. In the example in the previous section, the backup history went back to the previous full backup. This could be extended by having more tapes, but only a week per new tape, which might be too expensive. A longer backup history is useful, since deleted or corrupted files are often not noticed for a long time. Even a version of a file that is not very up to date is better than no file at all.

With multiple levels the backup history can be extended more cheaply. For example, if we buy ten tapes, we could use tapes 1 and 2 for monthly backups (first Friday each month), tapes 3 to 6 for weekly backups (other Fridays; note that there can be five Fridays in one month, so we need four more tapes), and tapes 7 to 10 for daily backups (Monday to Thursday). With only four more tapes, we've been able to extend the backup history from two weeks (after all daily tapes have been used) to two months. It is true that we can't restore every version of each file during those two months, but what we can restore is often good enough.

Figure 10.1 shows which backup level is used each day, and which backups can be restored from at the end of the month.

Backup levels can also be used to keep file system restoration time to a minimum. If you have many incremental backups with monotonously growing level numbers, you need to restore all of them if you need to rebuild the whole file system. Instead you can use level numbers that aren't monotonous, and keep down the number of backups to restore.

To minimize the number of tapes needed to restore, you could use a smaller level for each incremental tape. However, then the time to make the backups increases (each backup copies everything since the previous full backup). A better scheme is suggested by the `dump` manual page and described by the table 10.2. Use the following succession of backup levels: 3, 2, 5, 4, 7, 6, 9, 8, 9... This keeps both the backup and restore times low. The most you have to backup is two day's worth of work. The number of tapes for a restore depends on how long you keep between full backups, but it is less than in the simple schemes.

A fancy scheme can reduce the amount of labor needed, but it does mean there are more things to keep track of. You must decide if it is worth it.

`dump` has built-in support for backup levels. For `tar` and `cpio` it must be implemented with shell scripts.

10.6 What to back up

You want to back up as much as possible. The major exception is software that can be easily reinstalled,[4] but even they may have configuration files that it is important to back up, lest you need to do all the work to configure them all over again. Another major exception is the `/proc` file system; since that only contains data that the kernel always generates automatically, it is *never* a good idea to back it up. Especially the `/proc/kcore` file is unnecessary, since it is just an image of your current physical memory; it's pretty large as well.

Gray areas include the news spool, log files, and many other things in `/var`. You must decide what you consider important.

The obvious things to back up are user files (`/home`) and system configuration files (`/etc`, but possibly other things scattered all over the file system).

[4] You get to decide what's easy. Some people consider installing from dozens of floppies easy.

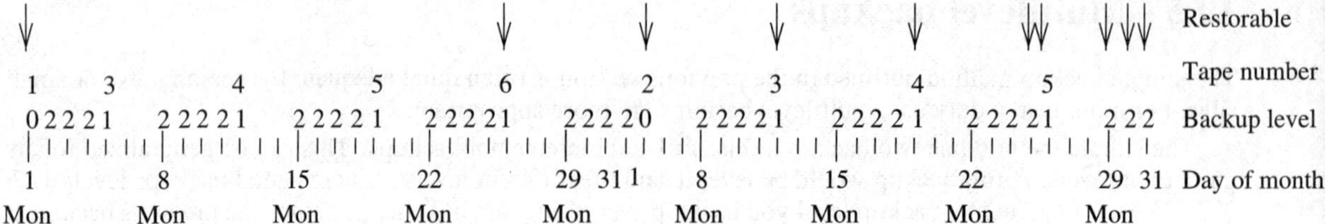

Figure 10.1: A sample multilevel backup schedule.

Figure 10.2: Efficient backup scheme using many backup levels

Tape	Level	Backup (days)	Restore tapes
1	0	n/a	1
2	3	1	1, 2
3	2	2	1, 3
4	5	1	1, 2, 4
5	4	2	1, 2, 5
6	7	1	1, 2, 5, 6
7	6	2	1, 2, 5, 7
8	9	1	1, 2, 5, 7, 8
9	8	2	1, 2, 5, 7, 9
10	9	1	1, 2, 5, 7, 9, 10
11	9	1	1, 2, 5, 7, 9, 10, 11
…	9	1	1, 2, 5, 7, 9, 10, 11, …

10.7 Compressed backups

Backups take a lot of space, which can cost quite a lot of money. To reduce the space needed, the backups can be compressed. There are several ways of doing this. Some programs have support for for compression built in; for example, the `-gzip` (`-z`) option for GNU `tar` pipes the whole backup through the `gzip` compression program, before writing it to the backup medium.

Unfortunately, compressed backups can cause trouble. Due to the nature of how compression works, if a single bit is wrong, all the rest of the compressed data will be unusable. Some backup programs have some built in error correction, but no method can handle a large number of errors. This means that if the backup is compressed the way GNU `tar` does it, with the whole output compressed as a unit, a single error makes all the rest of the backup lost. Backups must be reliable, and this method of compression is not a good idea.

An alternative way is to compress each file separately. This still means that the one file is lost, but all other files are unharmed. The lost file would have been corrupted anyway, so this situation is not much worse than not using compression at all. The `afio` program (a variant of `cpio`) can do this.

Compression takes some time, which may make the backup program unable to write data fast enough for a tape drive.[5] This can be avoided by buffering the output (either internally, if the backup program if smart enough, or by using another program), but even that might not work well enough. This should only be a problem on slow computers.

[5] If a tape drive doesn't write data fast enough, it has to stop; this makes backups even slower, and can be bad for the tape and the drive.

CHAPTER 11

Keeping Time

Time is an illusion. Lunchtime double so.
(Douglas Adams.)

This chapter explains how a Linux system keeps time, and what you need to do to avoid causing trouble. Usually, you don't need to do anything about time, but it is good to understand it.

11.1 Time zones

Time measurement is based on mostly regular natural phenomena, such as alternating light and dark periods caused by the rotation of the planet. The total time taken by two successive periods is constant, but the lengths of the light and dark period vary. One simple constant is noon.

Noon is the time of the day when the Sun is at its highest position. Since the Earth is round,[1] noon happens at different times in different places. This leads to the concept of **local time**. Humans measure time in many units, most of which are tied to natural phenomena like noon. As long as you stay in the same place, it doesn't matter that local times differ.

As soon as you need to communicate with distant places, you'll notice the need for a common time. In modern times, most of the places in the world communicate with most other places in the world, so a global standard for measuring time has been defined. This time is called **universal time** (UT or UTC, formerly known as Greenwich Mean Time or GMT, since it used to be local time in Greenwich, England). When people with different local times need to communicate, they can express times in universal time, so that there is no confusion about when things should happen.

Each local time is called a time zone. While geography would allow all places that have noon at the same time have the same time zone, politics makes it difficult. For various reasons, many countries use **daylight savings time**, that is, they move their clocks to have more natural light while they work, and then move the clocks back during winter. Other countries do not do this. Those that do, do not agree when the clocks should be moved, and they change the rules from year to year. This makes time zone conversions definitely non-trivial.

Time zones are best named by the location or by telling the difference between local and universal time. In the US and some other countries, the local time zones have a name and a three letter abbreviation. The abbreviations are not unique, however, and should not be used unless the country is also named. It is better to talk about the local time in, say, Helsinki, than about East European time, since not all countries in Eastern Europe follow the same rules.

Linux has a time zone package that knows about all existing time zones, and that can easily be updated when the rules change. All the system administrator needs to do is to select the appropriate time zone. Also, each user can set his own time zone—this is important since many people work with computers in different

[1] According to recent research.

countries over the Internet. When the rules for daylight savings time change in your local time zone, make sure you'll upgrade at least that part of your Linux system. Other than setting the system time zone and upgrading the time zone data files, there is little need to bother about time.

11.2 The hardware and software clocks

A personal computer has a battery driven hardware clock. The battery ensures that the clock will work even if the rest of the computer is without electricity. The hardware clock can be set from the BIOS setup screen or from whatever operating system is running.

The Linux kernel keeps track of time independently from the hardware clock. During the boot, Linux sets its own clock to the same time as the hardware clock. After this, both clocks run independently. Linux maintains its own clock because looking at the hardware is slow and complicated.

The kernel clock always shows universal time. This way, the kernel does not need to know about time zones at all—the simplicity results in higher reliability and makes it easier to update the time zone information. Each process handles time zone conversions itself (using standard tools that are part of the time zone package).

The hardware clock can be in local time or in universal time. It is usually better to have it in universal time, because then you don't need to change the hardware clock when daylight savings time begins or ends (UTC does not have DST). Unfortunately, some PC operating systems—including MS-DOS, Windows, OS/2—assume the hardware clock shows local time. Linux can handle either, but if the hardware clock shows local time, then it must be modified when daylight savings time begins or ends (otherwise it wouldn't show local time).

11.3 Showing and setting time

In the Debian system, the system time zone is determined by the symbolic link `/etc/localtime`. This link points at a time zone data file that describes the local time zone. The time zone data files are stored in `/usr/lib/zoneinfo`. Other Linux distributions may do this differently.

A user can change his private time zone by setting the TZ environment variable. If it is unset, the system time zone is assumed. The syntax of the TZ variable is described in the *tzset*(3) manual page.

The `date` command shows the current date and time.[2] For example:

```
$ date
Sun Jul 14 21:53:41 EET DST 1996
$
```

That time is Sunday, 14th of July, 1996, at about ten before ten at the evening, in the time zone called "EET DST" (which might be East European Daylight Savings Time). `date` can also show the univeral time:

```
$ date -u
Sun Jul 14 18:53:42 UTC 1996
$
```

`date` is also used to set the kernel's software clock:

```
# date 07142157
Sun Jul 14 21:57:00 EET DST 1996
# date
Sun Jul 14 21:57:02 EET DST 1996
#
```

[2]Beware of the `time` command, which does *not* show the current time.

See the `date` manual page for more details—the syntax is a bit arcane. Only `root` can set the time. While each user can have his own time zone, the clock is the same for everyone.

`date` only shows or sets the software clock. The `clock` commands synchronizes the hardware and software clocks. It is used when the system boots, to read the hardware clock and set the software clock. If you need to set both clocks, you first set the software clock with `date`, and then the hardware clock with `clock -w`.

The `-u` option to `clock` tells it that the hardware clock is in universal time. You *must* use the `-u` option correctly. If you don't, your computer will be quite confused about what the time is.

The clocks should be changed with care. Many parts of a Unix system require the clocks to work correctly. For example, the `cron` daemon runs commands periodically. If you change the clock, it can be confused of whether it needs to run the commands or not. On one early Unix system, someone set the clock twenty years into the future, and `cron` wanted to run all the periodic commands for twenty years all at once. Current versions of `cron` can handle this correctly, but you should still be careful. Big jumps or backward jumps are more dangerous than smaller or forward ones.

11.4 When the clock is wrong

The Linux software clock is not always accurate. It is kept running by a periodic **timer interrupt** generated by PC hardware. If the system has too many processes running, it may take too long to service the timer interrupt, and the software clock starts slipping behind. The hardware clock runs independently and is usually more accurate. If you boot your computer often (as is the case for most systems that aren't servers), it will usually keep fairly accurate time.

If you need to adjust the hardware clock, it is usually simplest to reboot, go into the BIOS setup screen, and do it from there. This avoids all trouble that changing system time might cause. If doing it via BIOS is not an option, set the new time with `date` and `clock` (in that order), but be prepared to reboot, if some part of the system starts acting funny.

A networked computer (even if just over the modem) can check its own clock automatically, by comparing it to some other computer's time. If the other computer is known to keep very accurate time, then both computers will keep accurate time. This can be done by using the `rdate` and `netdate` commands. Both check the time of a remote computer (`netdate` can handle several remote computers), and set the local computer's time to that. By running one these commands regularly, your computer will keep as accurate time as the remote computer.

APPENDIX A

Measuring Holes

This appendix contains the interesting part of the program used to measure the potential for holes in a filesystem. The source distribution of the book contains the full source code (sag/measure-holes/measure-holes.c).

```
int process(FILE *f, char *filename) {
        static char *buf = NULL;
        static long prev_block_size = -1;
        long zeroes;
        char *p;

        if (buf == NULL || prev_block_size != block_size) {
                free(buf);
                buf = xmalloc(block_size + 1);
                buf[block_size] = 1;
                prev_block_size = block_size;
        }
        zeroes = 0;
        while (fread(buf, block_size, 1, f) == 1) {
                for (p = buf; *p == '\0'; )
                        ++p;
                if (p == buf+block_size)
                        zeroes += block_size;
        }
        if (zeroes > 0)
                printf("%ld %s\n", zeroes, filename);
        if (ferror(f)) {
                errormsg(0, -1, "read failed for '%s'", filename);
                return -1;
        }
        return 0;
}
```

Part III

"The Linux Network Administrators' Guide 1.0" by Olaf Kirch

Contents

Preface

With the Internet much of a buzzword recently, and otherwise serious people joyriding along the "Informational Superhighway," computer networking seems to be moving toward the status of TV sets and microwave ovens. The Internet is recently getting an unusually high media coverage, and social science majors are descending on Usenet newsgroups to conduct researches on the "Internet Culture." Carrier companies are working to introduce new transmission techniques like ATM that offer many times the bandwidth the average network link of today has.

Of course, networking has been around for a long time. Connecting computers to form local area networks has been common practice even at small installations, and so have been long-haul links using public telephone lines. A rapidly growing conglomerate of world-wide networks has, however, made joining the global village a viable option even for small non-profit organizations of private computer users. Setting up an Internet host with mail and news capabilities offering dial-up access has become affordable, and the advent of ISDN will doubtlessly accelerate this trend.

Talking of computer networks quite frequently means talking about UNIX. Of course, UNIX is neither the only operating system with network capabilities, nor will it remain a front-runner forever, but it has been in the networking business for a long time, and will surely continue to do so for some time to come.

What makes it particularly interesting to private users is that there has been much activity to bring free UNIXoid operating systems to the PC, being 386BSD, FreeBSD — and Linux. However, Linux is *not* UNIX. That is a registered trademark of whoever currently holds the rights to it (Univel, while I'm typing this), while Linux is an operating system that strives to offer all functionality the POSIX standards require for UNIX-like operating systems, but is a complete reimplementation.

The Linux kernel was written largely by Linus Torvalds, who started it as a project to get to know the Intel i386, and to "make MINIX better." MINIX was then another popular PC operating system offering vital ingredients of UNIX functionality, and was written by Prof. Andrew S. Tanenbaum.

Linux is covered by the GNU General Public License (GPL), which allows free distribution of the code (please read the GPL ,page 203, for a definition of what "free software" means). Outgrowing its child's diseases, and drawing from a large and ever-growing base of free application programs, it is quickly becoming the oprating system of choice for many PC owners. The kernel and C library have become that good that most standard software may be compiled with no more effort than is required on any other mainstream UNIXish system, and a broad assortment of packaged Linux distributions allows you to almost drop it onto your hard disk and start playing.

Documentation on Linux

One of the complaints that are frequently levelled at Linux (and free software in general) is the sorry state or complete lack of documentation. In the early days it was not unusual for a package to come with a handful of *READMEs* and installation notes. They gave the moderately experienced UNIX wizard enough information to successfully install and run it, but left the average newbie out in the cold.

Back in late 1992, Lars Wirzenius and Michael K. Johnson suggested to form the Linux Documentation Project, or LDP, which aims at providing a coherent set of manuals. Stopping short of answering questions like "How?", or "Why?", or "What's the meaning of life, universe, and all the rest?", these manuals attempt to cover most aspects of running and using a Linux system users without requiring a prior degree in UNIX.

Among the achievements of the LDP are the *Installation and Getting Started Guide*, written by Matt Welsh, the *Kernel Hacker's Guide* by Michael K. Johnson, and the manpage project coordinated by Rik Faith, which so far supplied a set of roughly 450 manual pages for most system and C library calls. The *System Administrators' Guide*, written by Lars Wirzenius, is still at the Alpha stage. A User's Guide is being prepared.

This book, the *Linux Network Administrators' Guide*, is part of the LDP series, too. As such, it may be copied and distributed freely under the LDP copying license which is reproduced on the second page.

However, the LDP books are not the only source of information on Linux. At the moment, there are more than a dozen HOWTOs that are posted to **comp.os.linux.announce** regularly and archived at various FTP sites. HOWTOs are short documents of a few pages that give you a brief introduction into topics such as Ethernet support under Linux, or the configuration of Usenet news software, and answer frequently asked questions. They usually provide the most accurate and up-to-date information avaliable on the topic. A list of available HOWTOs is produced in the "Annotated Bibliography" toward the end of this book.

About This Book

When I joined the Linux Documentation Project in 1992, I wrote two small chapters on UUCP and *smail*, which I meant to contribute to the System Administrator's Guide. Development of TCP/IP networking was just beginning, and when those "small chapters" started to grow, I wondered aloud if it wouldn't be nice to have a Networking Guide. "Great", everyone said, "I'd say, go for it!" So I went for it, and wrote a first version of the Networking Guide, which I released in September 1993.

The new Networking Guide you are reading right now is a complete rewrite that features several new applications that have become available to Linux users since the first release.

The book is organized roughly in the sequence of steps you have to take to configure your system for networking. It starts by discussing basic concepts of networks, and TCP/IP-based networks in particular. We then slowly work our way up from configuring TCP/IP at the device level to the setup of common applications such as *rlogin* and friends, the Network File System, and the Network Information System. This is followed by a chapter on how to set up your machine as a UUCP node. The remainder of the book is dedicated to two major applications that run on top of both TCP/IP and UUCP: electronic mail and news.

The email part features an introduction of the more intimate parts of mail transport and routing, and the myriads of addressing schemes you may be confronted with. It describes the configuration and management of *smail*, a mail transport agent commonly used on smaller mail hubs, and *sendmail*, which is for people who have to do more complicated routing, or have to handle a large volume of mail. The *sendmail* chapter has been written and contributed by Vince Skahan.

The news part attempts to give you an overview of how Usenet news works, covers C news, the most widely used news transport software at the moment, and the use of NNTP to provide newsreading access to a local network. The book closes with a short chapter on the care and feeding of the most popular newsreaders on Linux.

The Official Printed Version

In autumn 1993, Andy Oram, who has been around the LDP mailing list from almost the very beginning, asked me about publishing my book at O'Reilly and Associates. I was excited about this; I had never imagined my book being that successful. We finally agreed that O'Reilly would produce an enhanced Official Printed Version of the Networking Guide with me, while I retained the original copyright so that the source of the book could be freely distributed.[1] This means that you can choose freely: you can get the LaTeX source distributed on the network (or the preformatted DVI or PostScript versions, for that matter), and print it out. Or you can purchase the official printed version from O'Reilly, which will be available some time later this year.

Then, why would you want to pay money for something you can get for free? Is Tim O'Reilly out of his mind for publishing something everyone can print and even sell herself?[2] Or is there any difference between these versions?

The answers are "it depends," "no, definitely not," and "yes and no." O'Reilly and Associates do take a risk in publishing the Networking Guide, but I hope it will finally pay off for them. If it does, I believe this project can serve as an example how the free software world and companies can cooperate to produce something both benefit from. In my view, the great service O'Reilly is doing to the Linux community (apart from the book being readily available in your local bookstore) is that it may help Linux being recognized as something to be taken seriously: a viable and useful alternative to commercial PC UNIX operating systems.

So what about the differences between the printed version and the online one? Andy Oram has made great efforts at transforming my early ramblings into something actually worth printing. (He has also been reviewing the other books put out by the Linux Documentation Project, trying to contribute whatever professional skills he can to the Linux community.)

Since Andy started reviewing the Networking Guide and editing the copies I sent him, the book has improved vastly over what it was half a year ago. It would be nowhere close to where it is now without his contributions. All his edits have been fed back into online version, as will any changes that will be made to the Networking Guide during the copy-editing phase at O'Reilly. So there will be no difference in content. Still, the O'Reilly version *will* be different: On one hand, people at O'Reilly are putting a lot of work into the look and feel, producing a much more pleasant layout than you could ever get out of standard LaTeX. On the other hand, it will feature a couple of enhancements like an improved index, and better and more figures.

More Information

If you follow the instructions in this book, and something does not work nevertheless, please be patient. Some of your problems may be due to stupid mistakes on my part, but may also be caused by changes in the networking software. Therefore, you should probably ask on **comp.os.linux.help** first. There's a good chance that you are not alone with your problems, so that a fix or at least a proposed workaround is likely to be known. If you have the opportunity, you should also try to get the latest kernel and network release from one of the Linux FTP sites, or a BBS near you. Many problems are caused by software from different stages of development, which fail to work together properly. After all, Linux is "work in progress".

Another good place to inform yourself about current development is the Networking HOWTO. It is maintained by Terry Dawson[3]. It is posted to **comp.os.linux.announce** once a month, and contains the most up-to-date information. The current version can also be obtained (among others) from **tsx-11.mit.edu**, in */pub/linux/doc*. For problems you can't solve in any other way, you may also contact the author of this book at the address given in the preface. However, please, refrain from asking developers for help. They are already devoting a major part of their spare time to Linux anyway, and occasionally even have a life beyond the net :-)

On the Authors

Olaf has been a UNIX user and part-time administrator for a couple of years while he was studying mathematics. At the moment, he's working as a UNIX programmer and is writing a book. One of his favorite

[1] The copyright notice is reproduced on the page immediately following the title page.

[2] Note that while you are allowed to print out the online version, you may *not* run the O'Reilly book through a photocopier, and much less sell any of those (hypothetical) copies.

[3] Terry Dawson can be reached at **terryd@extro.ucc.su.oz.au**.

sports is doing things with *sed* that other people would reach for their *perl* interpreter for. He has about as much fun with this as with mountain hiking with a backpack and a tent.

Vince Skahan has been administering large numbers of UNIX systems since 1987 and currently runs sendmail+IDA on approximately 300 UNIX workstations for over 2000 users. He admits to losing considerable sleep from editing quite a few *sendmail.cf* files 'the hard way' before discovering sendmail+IDA in 1990. He also admits to anxiously awaiting the delivery of the first perl-based version of sendmail for even more obscure fun[4]...

[4]Don't you think we could do it with *sed*, Vince?

Olaf can be reached at the following address:

Olaf Kirch
Kattreinstr. 38
64295 Darmstadt
Germany **okir@monad.swb.de**

Vince can be reached at:

Vince Skahan
vince@victrola.wa.com

We are open to your questions, comments, postcards, etc. However, we ask you *not* to telephone us unless it's really important.

Thanks

Olaf says: This book owes very much to the numerous people who took the time to proofread it and helped iron out many mistakes, both technical and grammatical (never knew that there's such a thing as a dangling participle). The most vigorous among them was Andy Oram at O'Reilly and Associates.

I am greatly indebted to Andres Sepúlveda, Wolfgang Michaelis, Michael K. Johnson, and all developers who spared the time to check the information provided in the Networking Guide. I also wish to thank all those who read the first version of the Networking Guide and sent me corrections and suggestions. You can find hopefully complete list of contributors in the file *Thanks* in the online distribution. Finally, this book would not have been possible without the support of Holger Grothe, who provided me with the critical Internet connectivity.

I would also like to thank the following groups and companies who printed the first edition of the Networking Guide and have donated money either to me, or to the Linux Documentation Project as a whole.

- Linux Support Team, Erlangen, Germany
- S.u.S.E. GmbH, Fuerth, Germany
- Linux System Labs, Inc., United States

Vince says: Thanks go to Neil Rickert and Paul Pomes for lots of help over the years regarding the care and feeding of sendmail+IDA and to Rich Braun for doing the initial port of sendmail+IDA to Linux. The biggest thanks by far go to my wife Susan for all the support on this and other projects.

Typographical Conventions

In writing this book, a number of typographical conventions were employed to mark shell commands, variable arguments, etc. They are explained below.

Bold Font Used to mark hostnames and mail addresses, as well as new concepts and warnings.

Italics Font Used to mark file names, UNIX commands, and keywords in configuration files. Also used for *emphasis* in text.

`Typewriter Font` Used to represent screen interaction, such as user interaction when running a program. Also used for code examples, whether it is a configuration file, a shell script, or something else.

Typewriter Slanted Font Used to mark meta-variables in the text, especially in representations of the command line. For example,

```
$ ls -l foo
```

where *foo* would "stand for" a filename, such as */tmp*.

`Key` Represents a key to press. You will often see it in this form:

Press `return` to continue.

◇ A diamond in the margin, like a black diamond on a ski hill, marks "danger" or "caution." Read paragraphs marked this way carefully.

`$` and `#` When preceding a shell command to be typed, these denote the shell prompt. The '`$`' symbol is used when the command may be executed as a normal user; '`#`' means that the command requires super user privilieges.

The Linux Documentation Project

The Linux Documentation Project, or LDP, is a loose team of writers, proofreaders, and editors who are working together to provide complete documentation for the Linux operating system. The overall coordinator of the project is Matt Welsh, who is heavily aided by Lars Wirzenius and Michael K. Johnson.

This manual is one in a set of several being distributed by the LDP, including a Linux Users' Guide, System Administrators' Guide, Network Administrators' Guide, and Kernel Hackers' Guide. These manuals are all available in LaTeX source format, `.dvi` format, and postscript output by anonymous FTP from `nic.funet.fi`, in the directory `/pub/OS/Linux/doc/doc-project`, and from `tsx-11.mit.edu`, in the directory `/pub/linux/docs/guides`.

We encourage anyone with a penchant for writing or editing to join us in improving Linux documentation. If you have Internet e-mail access, you can join the `DOC` channel of the `Linux-Activists` mailing list by sending mail to

```
linux-activists-request@niksula.hut.fi
```

with the line

```
X-Mn-Admin:  join DOC
```

in the header or as the first line of the message body. An empty mail without the additional header line will make the mail-server return a help message. To leave the channel, send a message to the same address, including the line

```
X-Mn-Admin:  leave DOC
```

Filesystem Standards

Throughout the past, one of the problems that afflicted Linux distributions as well as separate packages was that there was no single accepted file system layout. This resulted in incompatibilities between different packages, and confronted users and administrators alike with the task to locate various files and programs.

To improve this situation, in August 1993, several people formed the Linux File System Standard Group, or FSSTND Group for short, coordinated by Daniel Quinlan. After six months of discussion, the group presented a draft that presents a coherent file sytem structure and defines the location of most essential programs and configuration files.

This standard is supposed to be implemented by most major Linux distributions and packages. Throughout this book, we will therefore assume that any files discussed reside in the location specified by the standard; only where there is a long tradition that conflicts with this specification will alternative locations be mentioned.

The Linux File System Standard can be obtained from all major Linux FTP sites and their mirrors; for instance, you can find it on **sunsite.unc.edu** below */pub/linux/docs*. Daniel Quinlan, the coordinator of the FSSTND group can be reached at **quinlan@bucknell.edu**.

CHAPTER 1

Introduction to Networking

1.1 History

The idea of networking is probably as old as telecommunications itself. Consider people living in the stone age, where drums may have been used to transmit messages between individuals. Suppose caveman A wants to invite caveman B for a game of hurling rocks at each other, but they live too far apart for B to hear A banging his drum. So what are A's options? He could 1) walk over to B's place, 2) get a bigger drum, or 3) ask C, who lives halfway between them, to forward the message. The last is called networking.

Of course, we have come a long way from the primitive pursuits and devices of our forebears. Nowadays, we have computers talk to each other over vast assemblages of wires, fiber optics, microwaves, and the like, to make an appointment for Saturday's soccer match.[1] In the following, we will deal with the means and ways by which this is accomplished, but leave out the wires, as well as the soccer part.

We will describe two types of networks in this guide: those based on UUCP, and those based on TCP/IP. These are protocol suites and software packages that supply means to transport data between two computers. In this chapter, we will look at both types of networks, and discuss their underlying principles.

We define a network as a collection of *hosts* that are able to communicate with each other, often by relying on the services of a number of dedicated hosts that relay data between the participants. Hosts are very often computers, but need not be; one can also think of X-terminals or intelligent printers as hosts. Small agglomerations of hosts are also called *sites*.

Communication is impossible without some sort of language or code. In computer networks, these languages are collectively referred to as *protocols*. However, you shouldn't think of written protocols here, but rather of the highly formalized code of behavior observed when heads of state meet, for instance. In a very similar fashion, the protocols used in computer networks are nothing but very strict rules for the exchange of messages between two or more hosts.

1.2 UUCP Networks

UUCP is an abbreviation for Unix-to-Unix Copy. It started out as a package of programs to transfer files over serial lines, schedule those transfers, and initiate execution of programs on remote sites. It has undergone major changes since its first implementation in the late seventies, but is still rather spartan in the services it offers. Its main application is still in wide-area networks based on dial-up telephone links.

UUCP was first developed by Bell Laboratories in 1977 for communication between their Unix-development sites. In mid-1978, this network already connected over 80 sites. It was running email as an application, as well as remote printing. However, the system's central use was in distributing new software and bugfixes.[2] Today, UUCP is not confined to the UNIX environment any more. There are both free and commercial ports available for a variety of platforms, including AmigaOS, DOS, Atari's TOS, etc.

[1] The original spirit of which (see above) still shows on some occasions in Europe.

[2] Not that the times had changed that much…

One of the main disadvantages of UUCP networks is their low bandwidth. On one hand, telephone equipment places a tight limit on the maximum transfer rate. On the other hand, UUCP links are rarely permanent connections; instead, hosts rather dial up each other at regular intervals. Hence, most of the time it takes a mail message to travel a UUCP network it sits idly on some host's disk, awaiting the next time a connection is established.

Despite these limitations, there are still many UUCP networks operating all over the world, run mainly by hobbyists, which offer private users network access at reasonable prices. The main reason for the popularity of UUCP is that it is dirt cheap compared to having your computer connected to The Big Internet Cable. To make your computer a UUCP node, all you need is a modem, a working UUCP implementation, and another UUCP node that is willing to feed you mail and news.

1.2.1 How to Use UUCP

The idea behind UUCP is rather simple: as its name indicates, it basically copies files from one host to another, but it also allows certain actions to be performed on the remote host.

Suppose your machine is allowed to access a hypothetical host named **swim**, and have it execute the *lpr* print command for you. Then you could type the following on your command line to have this book printed on **swim**:[3]

```
$ uux -r swim!lpr !netguide.dvi
```

This makes *uux*, a command from the UUCP suite, schedule a *job* for **swim**. This job consists of the input file, *netguide.dvi*, and the request to feed this file to *lpr*. The `-r` flag tells *uux* not to call the remote system immediately, but to rather store the job away until a connection is established at a later occasion. This is called *spooling*.

Another property of UUCP is that it allows to forward jobs and files through several hosts, provided they cooperate. Assume that **swim** from the above examples has a UUCP link with **groucho**, which maintains a large archive of UNIX applications. To download the file *tripwire-1.0.tar.gz* to your site, you might issue

```
$ uucp -mr swim!groucho!~/security/tripwire-1.0.tar.gz trip.tgz
```

The job created will request **swim** to fetch the file from **groucho**, and send it to your site, where UUCP will store it in *trip.tgz* and notify you via mail of the file's arrival. This will be done in three steps. First, your site sends the job to **swim**. When **swim** establishes contact with **groucho** the next time, it downloads the file. The final step is the actual transfer from **swim** to your host.

The most important services provided by UUCP networks these days are electronic mail and news. We will come back to these later, so we will give only a brief introduction here.

Electronic mail – email for short – allows you to exchange messages with users on remote hosts without actually having to know how to access these hosts. The task of directing a message from your site to the destination site is performed entirely by the mail handling system. In a UUCP environment, mail is usually transported by executing the *rmail* command on a neighboring host, passing it the recipient address and the mail message. *rmail* will then forward the message to another host, and so on, until it reaches the destination host. We will look at this in detail in chapter 13.

News may best be described as sort of a distributed bulletin board system. Most often, this term refers to Usenet News, which is by far the most widely known news exchange network with an estimated number of 120,000 participating sites. The origins of Usenet date back to 1979, when, after the release of UUCP with the new Unix V7, three graduate students had the idea of a general information exchange within the Unix community. They put together some scripts, which became the first netnews system. In 1980, this network connected **duke**, **unc**, and **phs**, at two Universities in North Carolina. Out of this, Usenet eventually grew. Although it originated as a UUCP-based network, it is no longer confined to one single type of network.

The basic unit of information is the article, which may be posted to a hierarchy of newsgroups dedicated to specific topics. Most sites receive only a selection of all newsgroups, which carry an average of 60MB worth of articles a day.

[3] When using *bash*, the GNU Bourne Again Shell, you might have to escape the exclamation mark, because it uses it as its history character.

In the UUCP world, news is generally sent across a UUCP link by collecting all articles from the groups requested, and packing them up in a number of *batches*. These are sent to the receiving site, where they are fed to the *rnews* command for unpacking and further processing.

Finally, UUCP is also the medium of choice for many dial-up archive sites which offer public access. You can usually access them by dialing them up with UUCP, logging in as a guest user, and download files from a publicly accessible archive area. These guest accounts often have a login name and password of **uucp/nuucp** or something similar.

1.3 TCP/IP Networks

Although UUCP may be a reasonable choice for low-cost dial-up network links, there are many situations in which its store-and-forward technique proves too inflexible, for example in Local Area Networks (LANs). These are usually made up of a small number of machines located in the same building, or even on the same floor, that are interconnected to provide a homogeneous working environment. Typically, you would want to share files between these hosts, or run distributed applications on different machines.

These tasks require a completely different approach to networking. Instead of forwarding entire files along with a job description, all data is broken up in smaller chunks (packets), which are forwarded immediately to the destination host, where they are reassembled. This type of network is called a *packet-switched* network. Among other things, this allows to run interactive applications over the network. The cost of this is, of course, a greatly increased complexity in software.

The solution that UNIX system — and many non-UNIX sites — have adopted is known as TCP/IP. In this section, we will have a look at its underlying concepts.

1.3.1 Introduction to TCP/IP-Networks

TCP/IP traces its origins to a research project funded by the United States DARPA (Defense Advanced Research Projects Agency) in 1969. This was an experimental network, the ARPANET, which was converted into an operational one in 1975, after it had proven to be a success.

In 1983, the new protocol suite TCP/IP was adopted as a standard, and all hosts on the network were required to use it. When ARPANET finally grew into the Internet (with ARPANET itself passing out of existence in 1990), the use of TCP/IP had spread to networks beyond the Internet itself. Most notable are UNIX local area networks, but in the advent of fast digital telephone equipment, such as ISDN, it also has a promising future as a transport for dial-up networks.

For something concrete to look at as we discuss TCP/IP throughout the following sections, we will consider Groucho Marx University (GMU), situated somewhere in Fredland, as an example. Most departments run their own local area networks, while some share one, and others run several of them. They are all interconnected, and are hooked to the Internet through a single high-speed link.

Suppose your Linux box is connected to a LAN of UNIX hosts at the Mathematics Department, and its name is **erdos**. To access a host at the Physics Department, say **quark**, you enter the following command:

```
$ rlogin quark.physics
Welcome to the Physics Department at GMU
(ttyq2) login:
```

At the prompt, you enter your login name, say **andres**, and your password. You are then given a shell on **quark**, to which you can type as if you were sitting at the system's console. After you exit the shell, you are returned to your own machine's prompt. You have just used one of the instantaneous, interactive applications that TCP/IP provides: remote login.

While being logged into **quark**, you might also want to run an X11-based application, like a function plotting program, or a PostScript previewer. To tell this application that you want to have its windows displayed on your host's screen, you have to set the *DISPLAY* environment variable:

```
$ export DISPLAY=erdos.maths:0.0
```

If you now start your application, it will contact your X server instead of **quark**'s, and display all its windows on your screen. Of course, this requires that you have X11 runnning on **erdos**. The point here is that TCP/IP allows **quark** and **erdos** to send X11 packets back and forth to give you the illusion that you're on a single system. The network is almost transparent here.

Another very important application in TCP/IP networks is NFS, which stands for *Network File System*. It is another form of making the network transparent, because it basically allows you to mount directory hierarchies from other hosts, so that they appear like local file systems. For example, all users' home directories can be on a central server machine, from which all other hosts on the LAN mount the directory. The effect of this is that users can log into any machine, and find themselves in the same home directory. Similarly, it is possible to install applications that require large amounts of disk space (such as TEX) on only one machine, and export these directories to other machines. We will come back to NFS in chapter 11.

Of course, these are only examples of what you can do over TCP/IP networks. The possibilities are almost limitless.

We will now have a closer look at the way TCP/IP works. You will need this to understand how and why you have to configure your machine. We will start by examining the hardware, and slowly work our way up.

1.3.2 Ethernets

The type of hardware most widely used throughout LANs is what is commonly known as *Ethernet*. It consists of a single cable with hosts being attached to it through connectors, taps or transceivers. Simple Ethernets are quite inexpensive to install, which, together with a net transfer rate of 10 Megabits per second accounts for much of its popularity.

Ethernets come in three flavors, called *thick* and *thin*, respectively, and *twisted pair*. Thin and thick Ethernet each use a coaxial cable, differing in width and the way you may attach a host to this cable. Thin Ethernet uses a T-shaped "BNC" connector, which you insert into the cable, and twist onto a plug on the back of your computer. Thick Ethernet requires that you drill a small hole into the cable, and attach a transceiver using a "vampire tap". One or more hosts can then be connected to the transceiver. Thin and thick Ethernet cable may run for a maximum of 200 and 500 meters, respectively, and are therefore also called 10base-2 and 10base-5. Twisted pair uses a cable made of two copper wires which is also found in ordinary telephone installations, but usually requires additional hardware. It is also known as 10base-T.

Although adding a host to a thick Ethernet is a little hairy, it does not bring down the network. To add a host to a thinnet installation, you have to disrupt network service for at least a few minutes because you have to cut the cable to insert the connector.

Most people prefer thin Ethernet, because it is very cheap: PC cards come for as little as US$ 50, and cable is in the range of a few cent per meter. However, for large-scale installations, thick Ethernet is more appropriate. For example, the Ethernet at GMU's Mathematics Department uses thick Ethernet, so traffic will not be disrupted each time a host is added to the network.

One of the drawbacks of Ethernet technology is its limited cable length, which precludes any use of it other than for LANs. However, several Ethernet segments may be linked to each other using repeaters, bridges or routers. Repeaters simply copy the signals between two or more segments, so that all segments together will act as if it was one Ethernet. timing requirements, there may not be more than four repeaters any two hosts on the network. Bridges and Routers are more sophisticated. They analyze incoming data and forward it only when the recipient host is not on the local Ethernet.

Ethernet works like a bus system, where a host may send packets (or *frames*) of up to 1500 bytes to another host on the same Ethernet. A host is addressed by a six-byte address hardcoded into the firmware of its Ethernet board. These addresses are usually written as a sequence of two-digit hex numbers separated by colons, as in **aa:bb:cc:dd:ee:ff**.

A frame sent by one station is seen by all attached stations, but only the destination host actually picks it up and processes it. If two stations try to send at the same time, a *collision* occurs, which is resolved by the two stations aborting the send, and reattempting it a few moments later.

1.3.3 Other Types of Hardware

In larger installations, such as Groucho Marx University, Ethernet is usually not the only type of equipment used. At Groucho Marx University, each department's LAN is linked to the campus backbone, which is a fiber optics cable running FDDI (*Fiber Distributed Data Interface*). FDDI uses an entirely different approach to transmitting data, which basically involves sending around a number of *tokens*, with a station only being allowed to send a frame if it captures a token. The main advantage of FDDI is a speed of up to 100 Mbps, and a maximum cable length of up to 200 km.

For long-distance network links, a different type of equipment is frequently used, which is based on a standard named X.25. Many so-called Public Data Networks, like Tymnet in the U.S., or Datex-P in Germany, offer this service. X.25 requires special hardware, namely a Packet Assembler/Disassembler or *PAD*. X.25 defines a set of networking protocols of its own right, but is nevertheless frequently used to connect networks running TCP/IP and other protocols. Since IP packets cannot simply be mapped onto X.25 (and vice versa), they are simply encapsulated in X.25 packets and sent over the network.

Frequently, radio amateurs use their equipment to network their computers; this is called *packet radio* or *ham radio*. The protocol used by ham radios is called AX.25, which was derived from X.25.

Other techniques involve using slow but cheap serial lines for dial-up access. These require yet another protocol for transmission of packets, such as SLIP or PPP, which will be described below.

1.3.4 The Internet Protocol

Of course, you wouldn't want your networking to be limited to one Ethernet. Ideally, you would want to be able to use a network regardless of what hardware it runs on and how many subunits it is made up of. For example, in larger installations such as Groucho Marx University, you usually have a number of separate Ethernets that have to be connected in some way. At GMU, the maths department runs two Ethernets: one network of fast machines for professors and graduates, and another one with slow machines for students. Both are linked to the FDDI campus backbone.

This connection is handled by a dedicated host, a so-called *gateway*, which handles incoming and outgoing packets by copying them between the two Ethernets and the fiber optics cable. For example, if you are at the Maths Department, and want to access **quark** on the Physics Deparment's LAN from your Linux box, the networking software cannot send packets to **quark** directly, because it is not on the same Ethernet. Therefore, it has to rely on the gateway to act as a forwarder. The gateway (name it **sophus**) then forwards these packets to its peer gateway **niels** at the Physics Department, using the backbone, with **niels** delivering it to the destination machine. Data flow between **erdos** and **quark** is shown in figure 1.1 (With apologies to Guy L. Steele).

This scheme of directing data to a remote host is called *routing*, and packets are often referred to as *datagrams* in this context. To facilitate things, datagram exchange is governed by a single protocol that is independent of the hardware used: IP, or *Internet Protocol*. In chapter 2, we will cover IP and the issues of routing in greater detail.

The main benefit of IP is that it turns physically dissimilar networks into one apparently homogeneous network. This is called internetworking, and the resulting "meta-network" is called an *internet*. Note the subtle difference between *an* internet and *the* Internet here. The latter is the official name of one particular global internet.

Of course, IP also requires a hardware-independent addressing scheme. This is achieved by assigning each host a unique 32-bit number, called the *IP address*. An IP address is usually written as four decimal numbers, one for each 8-bit portion, separated by dots. For example, **quark** might have an IP address of **0x954C0C04**, which would be written as **149.76.12.4**. This format is also called *dotted quad* notation.

You will notice that we now have three different types of addresses: first there is the host's name, like **quark**, then there are IP addresses, and finally, there are hardware addresses, like the 6-byte Ethernet address. All these somehow have to match, so that when you type *rlogin quark*, the networking software can be given **quark**'s IP address; and when IP delivers any data to the Physics Department's Ethernet, it somehow has to find out what Ethernet address corresponds to the IP address. Which is rather confusing.

We will not go into this here, and deal with it in chapter 2 instead. For now, it's enough to remember that these steps of finding addresses are called *hostname resolution*, for mapping host names onto IP addresses, and *address resolution*, for mapping the latter to hardware addresses.

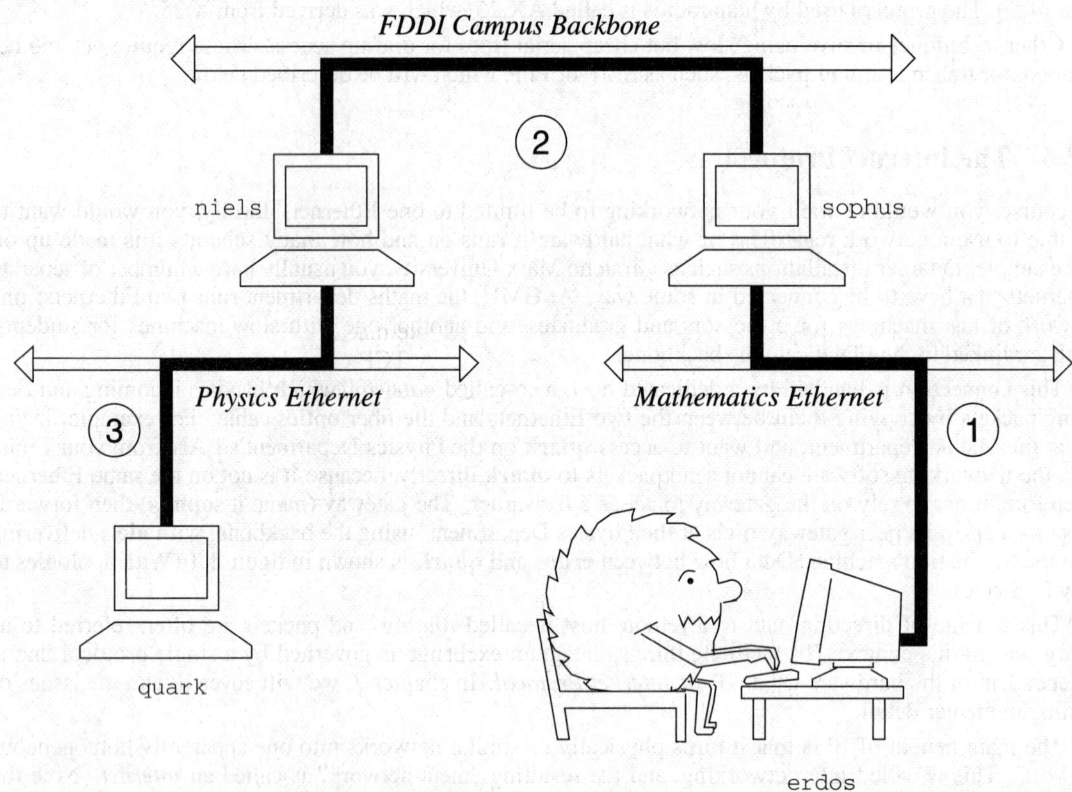

Figure 1.1: The three steps of sending a datagram from **erdos** to **quark**.

1.3.5 IP over Serial Lines

On serial lines, a "de facto" standard known as SLIP or *Serial Line IP* is frequently used. A modification of SLIP is known as CSLIP, or *compressed SLIP*, and performs compression of IP headers to make better use of the relatively low bandwidth provided by serial links.[4] A different serial protocol is PPP, or *Point-to-Point Protocol*. PPP has many more features than SLIP, including a link negotiation phase. Its main advantage over SLIP is, however, that it isn't limited to transporting IP datagrams, but that it was designed to allow for any type of datagrams to be transmitted.

1.3.6 The Transmission Control Protocol

Now, of course, sending datagrams from one host to another is not the whole story. If you log into **quark**, you want to have a reliable connection between your *rlogin* process on **erdos** and the shell process on **quark**. Thus, the information sent to and fro must be split up into packets by the sender, and reassembled into a character stream by the receiver. Trivial as it seems, this involves a number of hairy tasks.

A very important thing to know about IP is that, by intent, it is not reliable. Assume that ten people on your Ethernet started downloading the latest release of XFree86 from GMU's FTP server. The amount of traffic generated by this might be too much for the gateway to handle, because it's too slow, and it's tight on memory. Now if you happen to send a packet to **quark**, **sophus** might just be out of buffer space for a moment and therefore unable to forward it. IP solves this problem by simply discarding it. The packet is irrevocably lost. It is therefore the responsibility of the communicating hosts to check the integrity and completeness of the data, and retransmit it in case of an error.

This is performed by yet another protocol, TCP, or *Transmission Control Protocol*, which builds a reliable service on top of IP. The essential property of TCP is that it uses IP to give you the illusion of a simple connection between the two processes on your host and the remote machine, so that you don't have to care about how and along which route your data actually travels. A TCP connection works essentially like a two-way pipe that both processes may write to and read from. Think of it as a telephone conversation.

TCP identifies the end points of such a connection by the IP addresses of the two hosts involved, and the number of a so-called *port* on each host. Ports may be viewed as attachment points for network connections. If we are to strain the telephone example a little more, one might compare IP addresses to area codes (numbers map to cities), and port numbers to local codes (numbers map to individual people's telephones).

In the *rlogin* example, the client application (*rlogin*) opens a port on **erdos**, and connects to port 513 on **quark**, which the *rlogind* server is known to listen to. This establishes a TCP connection. Using this connection, *rlogind* performs the authorization procedure, and then spawns the shell. The shell's standard input and output are redirected to the TCP connection, so that anything you type to *rlogin* on your machine will be passed through the TCP stream and be given to the shell as standard input.

1.3.7 The User Datagram Protocol

Of course, TCP isn't the only user protocol in TCP/IP networking. Although suitable for applications like *rlogin*, the overhead involved is prohibitve for applications like NFS. Instead, it uses a sibling protocol of TCP called UDP, or *User Datagram Protocol*. Just like TCP, UDP also allows an application to contact a service on a certain port on the remote machine, but it doesn't establish a connection for this. Instead, you may use it to send single packets to the destination service – hence its name.

Assume you have mounted the TeX directory hierarchy from the department's central NFS server, *galois*, and you want to view a document describing how to use LaTeX. You start your editor, who first reads in the entire file. However, it would take too long to establish a TCP connection with *galois*, send the file, and release it again. Instead, a request is made to *galois*, who sends the file in a couple of UDP packets, which is much faster. However, UDP was not made to deal with packet loss or corruption. It is up to the application – NFS in this case – to take care of this.

1.3.8 More on Ports

Ports may be viewed as attachment points for network connections. If an application wants to offer a certain service, it attaches itself to a port and waits for clients (this is also called *listening* on the port). A client that

[4] SLIP is described in RFC 1055. The header compression CSLIP is based in is described in RFC 1144.

wants to use this service allocates a port on its local host, and connects to the server's port on the remote host.

An important property of ports is that once a connection has been established between the client and the server, another copy of the server may attach to the server port and listen for more clients. This permits, for instance, several concurrent remote logins to the same host, all using the same port 513. TCP is able to tell these connections from each other, because they all come from different ports or hosts. For example, if you twice log into **quark** from **erdos**, then the first *rlogin* client will use the local port 1023, and the second one will use port 1022. Both however, will connect to the same port 513 on **quark**.

This example shows the use of ports as rendezvous points, where a client contacts a specific port to obtain a specific service. In order for a client to know the proper port number, an agreement has to be reached between the administrators of both systems on the assignment of these numbers. For services that are widely used, such as *rlogin*, these numbers have to be administered centrally. This is done by the IETF (or *Internet Engineering Task Force*), which regularly releases an RFC titled *Assigned Numbers*. It describes, among other things, the port numbers assigned to *well-known services*. Linux uses a file mapping service names to numbers, called */etc/services*. It is described in section 9.3.

It is worth noting that although both TCP and UDP connections rely on ports, these numbers do not conflict. This means that TCP port 513, for example, is different from UDP port 513. In fact, these ports serve as access points for two different services, namely *rlogin* (TCP) and *rwho* (UDP).

1.3.9 The Socket Library

In UNIX operating systems, the software performing all the tasks and protocols described above is usually part of the kernel, and so it is in Linux. The programming interface most common in the UNIX world is the *Berkeley Socket Library*. Its name derives from a popular analogy that views ports as sockets, and connecting to a port as plugging in. It provides the (*bind(2)*) call to specifiy a remote host, a transport protocol, and a service which a program can connect or listen to (using *connect(2)*, *listen(2)*, and *accept(2)*). The socket library is however somewhat more general, in that it provides not only a class of TCP/IP-based sockets (the *AF_INET* sockets), but also a class that handles connections local to the machine (the *AF_UNIX* class). Some implementations can also handle other classes as well, like the XNS (*Xerox Networking System*) protocol, or X.25.

In Linux, the socket library is part of the standard *libc* C library. Currently, it only supports *AF_INET* and *AF_UNIX* sockets, but efforts are made to incorporate support for Novell's networking protocols, so that eventually one or more socket classes for these would be added.

1.4 Linux Networking

Being the result of a concerted effort of programmers around the world, Linux wouldn't have been possible without the global network. So it's not surprising that already in early stages of development, several people started to work on providing it with network capabilities. A UUCP implementation was running on Linux almost from the very beginning, and work on TCP/IP-based networking started around autumn 1992, when Ross Biro and others created what now has become known as Net-1.

After Ross quit active development in May 1993, Fred van Kempen began to work on a new implementation, rewriting major parts of the code. This ongoing effort is known as Net-2. A first public release, Net-2d, was made in Summer 1992 (as part of the 0.99.10 kernel), and has since been maintained and expanded by several people, most notably Alan Cox, as Net-2Debugged. After heavy debugging and numerous improvements to the code, he changed its name to Net-3 after Linux 1.0 was released. This is the version of the networking code currently included in the official kernel releases.

Net-3 offers device drivers for a wide variety of Ethernet boards, as well as SLIP (for sending network traffic over serial lines), and PLIP (for parallel lines). With Net-3, Linux has a TCP/IP implementation that behaves very well in a local area network environment, showing uptimes that beat some of the commercial PC Unices. Development currently moves toward the necessary stability to reliably run it on Internet hosts.

Beside these facilities, there are several projects going on that will enhance the versatility of Linux. A driver for PPP (the point-to-point protocol, another way to send network traffic over serial lines), is at Beta stage currently, and an AX.25 driver for ham radio is at Alpha stage. Alan Cox has also implemented a driver for Novell's IPX protocol, but the effort for a complete networking suite compatible with Novell's has been put on hold for the moment, because of Novell's unwillingness to provide the necessary documentation. Another very promising undertaking is *samba*, a free NetBIOS server for Unices, written by Andrew Tridgell.[5]

1.4.1 Different Streaks of Development

In the meanwhile, Fred continued development, going on to Net-2e, which features a much revised design of the networking layer. At the time of writing, Net-2e is still Beta software. Most notable about Net-2e is the incorporation of DDI, the *Device Driver Interface*. DDI offers a uniform access and configuration method to all networking devices and protocols.

Yet another implemtation of TCP/IP networking comes from Matthias Urlichs, who wrote an ISDN driver for Linux and FreeBSD. For this, he integrated some of the BSD networking code in the Linux kernel.

For the foreseeable future, however, Net-3 seems to be here to stay. Alan currently works on an implementation of the AX.25 protocol used by ham radio amateurs. Doubtlessly, the yet to be developed "module" code for the kernel will also bring new impulses to the networking code. Modules allow you to add drivers to the kernel at run time.

Although these different network implementations all strive to provide the same service, there are major differences between them at the kernel and device level. Therefore, you will not be able to configure a system running a Net-2e kernel with utilities from Net-2d or Net-3, and vice versa. This only applies to commands that deal with kernel internals rather closely; applications and common networking commands such as *rlogin* or *telnet* run on either of them.

Nevertheless, all these different network version should not worry you. Unless you are participating in active development, you will not have to worry about which version of the TCP/IP code you run. The official kernel releases will always be accompanied by a set of networking tools that are compatible with the networking code present in the kernel.

1.4.2 Where to Get the Code

The latest version of the Linux network code can be obtained by anonymous FTP from various sites. The official FTP site for Net-3 is **sunacm.swan.ac.uk**, mirrored by **sunsite.unc.edu** below *system/Network/sunacm*. The latest Net-2e patch kit and binaries are available from **ftp.aris.com**. Matthias Urlichs' BSD-derived networking code can be gotten from **ftp.ira.uka.de** in */pub/system/linux/netbsd*.

The latest kernels can be found on **nic.funet.fi** in */pub/OS/Linux/PEOPLE/Linus*; **sunsite** and **tsx-11.mit.edu** mirror this directory.

1.5 Maintaining Your System

Throughout this book, we will mainly deal with installation and configuration issues. Administration is, however, much more than that — after setting up a service, you have to keep it running, too. For most of them, only little attendance will be necessary, while some, like mail and news, require that you perform routine tasks to keep your system up-to-date. We will discuss these tasks in later chapters.

The absolute minimum in maintenance is to check system and per-application log files regularly for error conditions and unusual events. Commonly, you will want to do this by writing a couple of administrative shell scripts and run them from *cron* periodically. The source distribution of some major applications, like *smail* or C News, contain such scripts. You only have to tailor them to suit your needs and preferences.

The output from any of your *cron* jobs should be mailed to an administrative account. By default, many applications will send error reports, usage statistics, or logfile summaries to the **root** account. This only makes sense if you log in as **root** frequently; a much better idea is to forward **root**'s mail to your personal account setting up a mail alias as described in chapter 14.

However carefully you have configured your site, Murphy's law guarantees that some problem *will* surface eventually. Therefore, maintaining a system also means being available for complaints. Usually, people expect that the system administrator can at least be reached via email as **root**, but there are also other addresses that are commonly used to reach the person responsible for a specific aspect of maintenence. For instance,

[5] NetBIOS is the protocol on which applications like *lanmanager* and Windows for Workgroups are based.

complaints about a malfunctioning mail configuration will usually be addressed **postmaster**; and problems with the news system may be reported to **newsmaster** or **usenet**. Mail to **hostmaster** should be redirected to the person in charge of the host's basic network services, and the DNS name service if you run a name server.

1.5.1 System Security

Another very important aspect of system administration in a network environment is protecting your system and users from intruders. Carelessly managed systems offer malicious people many targets: attacks range from password guessing to Ethernet snooping, and the damage caused may range from faked mail messages to data loss or violation of your users' privacy. We will mention some particular problems when discussing the context they may occur in, and some common defenses against them.

This section will discuss a few examples and basic techniques in dealing with system security. Of course, the topics covered can not treat all security issues you may be faced with exhaustively; they merely serve to illustrate the problems that may arise. Therefore, reading a good book on security is an absolute must, especially in a networked system. Simon Garfinkel's "Practical UNIX Security" (see [Spaf93]) is highly recommendable.

System security starts with good system administration. This includes checking the ownership and permissions of all vital files and directories, monitoring use of privileged accounts, etc. The COPS program, for instance, will check your file system and common configuration files for unusual permissions or other anomalies. It is also wise to use a password suite that enforces certain rules on the users' passwords that make them hard to guess. The shadow password suite, for instance, requires a password to have at least five letters, and contain both upper and lower case numbers and digits.

When making a service accessible to the network, make sure to give it "least privilege," meaning that you don't permit it to do things that aren't required for it to work as designed. For example, you should make programs setuid to **root** or some other privileged account only when they really need this. Also, if you want to use a service for only a very limited application, don't hesitate to configure it as restrictively as your special application allows. For instance, if you want to allow diskless hosts to boot from your machine, you must provide the TFTP (trivial file transfer service) so that they can download basic configuration files from the */boot* directory. However, when used unrestricted, TFTP allows any user anywhere in the world to download any world-readable file from your system. If this is not what you want, why not restrict TFTP service to the */boot* directory?[6]

Along the same line of thought, you might want to restrict certain services to users from certain hosts, say from your local network. In chapter 9, we introduce *tcpd* which does this for a variety of network applications.

Another important point is to avoid "dangerous" software. Of course, any software you use can be dangerous, because software may have bugs that clever people might exploit to gain access to your system. Things like these happen, and there's no complete protection against this. This problem affects free software and commercial products alike.[7] However, programs that require special privilege are inherently more dangerous than others, because any loophole can have drastic consequences.[8] If you install a setuid program for network purposes be doubly careful that you don't miss anything from the documentation, so that you don't create a security breach by accident.

You can never rule out that your precautions might fail, regardless how careful you have been. You should therefore make sure you detect intruders early. Checking the system log files is a good starting point, but the intruder is probably as clever, and will delete any obvious traces he or she left. However, there are tools like *tripwire*[9] that allow you to check vital system files to see if their contents or permissions have been changed. *tripwire* computes various strong checksums over these files and stores them in a database. During subsequent runs, the checksums are re-computed and compared to the stored ones to detect any modifications.

---

[6] We will come back to this in chapter 9.

[7] There have been commercial Unices you have to pay lots of money for that came with a setuid-**root** shell script which allowed users to gain **root** privilege using a simple standard trick.

[8] In 1988, the RTM worm brought much of the Internet to a grinding halt, partly by exploiting a gaping hole in some *sendmail* programs. This hole has long been fixed since.

[9] Written by Gene Kim and Gene Spafford.

1.6 Outlook on the Following Chapters

The next few chapters will deal with configuring Linux for TCP/IP networking, and with running some major applications. Before getting our hands dirty with file editing and the like, we will examine IP a little closer in chapter 2. If you already know about the way IP routing works, and how address resolution is performed, you might want to skip this chapter.

Chapter 3 deals with the very basic configuration issues, such as building a kernel and setting up your Ethernet board. The configuration of your serial ports is covered in a separate chapter, because the discussion does not apply to TCP/IP networking only, but is also relevant for UUCP.

Chapter 5 helps you to set up your machine for TCP/IP networking. It contains installation hints for standalone hosts with only loopback enabled, and hosts connected to an Ethernet. It will also introduce you to a few useful tools you can use to test and debug your setup. The next chapter discusses how to configure hostname resolution, and explains how to set up a name server.

This is followed by two chapters featuring the configuration and use of SLIP and PPP, respectively. Chapter 7 explains how to establish SLIP connections, and gives a detailed reference of *dip*, a tool that allows you to automate most of the necessary steps. Chapter 8 covers PPP and *pppd*, the PPP daemon you need for this.

Chapter 9 gives a short introduction to setting up some of the most important network applications, such as *rlogin* and *rcp*. This also covers how services are managed by the *inetd* super, and how you may restrict certain security-relevant services to a set of trusted hosts.

The next two chapters discuss NIS, the Network Information System, and NFS, the Network File System. NIS is a useful tool to distribute administrative information such as user passwords in a local area network. NFS allows you to share file systems between several hosts in your network.

Chapter 12 gives you an extensive introduction to the administration of Taylor UUCP, a free implementation of the UUCP suite.

The remainder of the book is taken up by a detailed tour of electronic mail and Usenet News. Chapter 13 introduces you to the central concepts of electronic mail, like what a mail address looks like, and how the mail handling system manages to get your message to the recipient.

Chapters 14 and 15 each cover the setup of *smail* and *sendmail*, two mail transport agents you can use for Linux. This book explains both of them, because *smail* is easier to install for the beginner, while *sendmail* is more flexible.

Chapters 16 and 17 explain the way news are managed in Usenet, and how you install and use C news, a popular software package for managing Usenet news. Chapter 18 briefly covers how to set up an NNTP daemon to provide news reading access for your local network. Chapter 19 finally shows you how to configure and maintain various newsreaders.

CHAPTER 2

Issues of TCP/IP Networking

We will now turn to the details you'll come in touch with when connecting your Linux machine to a TCP/IP network including dealing with IP addresses, host names, and sometimes routing issues. This chapter gives you the background you need in order to understand what your setup requires, while the next chapters will cover the tools to deal with these.

2.1 Networking Interfaces

To hide the diversity of equipment that may be used in a networking environment, TCP/IP defines an abstract *interface* through which the hardware is accessed. This interface offers a set of operations which is the same for all types of hardware and basically deals with sending and receiving packets.

For each periphereal device you want to use for networking, a corresponding interface has to be present in the kernel. For example, Ethernet interfaces in Linux are called *eth0* and *eth1*, and SLIP interfaces come as *sl0*, *sl1*, etc. These interface names are used for configuration purposes when you want to name a particular physical device to the kernel. They have no meaning beyond that.

To be useable for TCP/IP networking, an interface must be assigned an IP address which serves as its identifcation when communicating with the rest of the world. This address is different from the interface name mentioned above; if you compare an interface to door, then the address is like the name-plate pinned on it.

Of course, there are other device parameters that may be set; one of these is the maximum size of datagrams that can be processed by that particular piece of hardware, also called *Maximum Transfer Unit*, or MTU. Other attributes will be introduced later.

2.2 IP Addresses

As mentioned in the previous chapter, the addresses understood by the IP networking protocol are 32-bit numbers. Every machine must be assigned a number unique to the networking environment. If you are running a local network that does not have TCP/IP traffic with other networks, you may assign these numbers according to your personal preferences. However, for sites on the Internet, numbers are assigned by a central authority, the Network Information Center, or NIC.[1]

For easier reading, IP addresses are split up into four, 8-bit numbers called *octets*. For example, **quark.physics.groucho.edu** has an IP address of **0x954C0C04**, which is written as **149.76.12.4**. This format is often referred to as the *dotted quad notation*.

Another reason for this notation is that IP addresses are split into a *network* number, which is contained in the leading octets, and a *host* number, which is the remainder. When applying to the NIC for IP addresses,

[1]Frequently, IP addresses will be assigned to you by the provider you buy your IP connectivity from. However, you may also apply to NIC directly for an IP address for your network by sending a mail to **hostmaster@internic.net**.

you are not assigned an address for each single host you plan to use. Instead, you are given a network number, and are allowed to assign all valid IP addresses within this range to hosts on your network according to your preferences.

Depending on the size of the network, the host part may need to be smaller or larger. To accomodate different needs, there are several classes of networks, defining different splits of IP addresses.

Class A — Class A comprises networks **1.0.0.0** through **127.0.0.0**. The network number is contained in the first octet. This provides for a 24 bit host part, allowing roughly 1.6 million hosts.

Class B — Class B contains networks **128.0.0.0** through **191.255.0.0**; the network number is in the first two octets. This allows for 16320 nets with 65024 hosts each.

Class C — Class C networks range from **192.0.0.0** through **223.255.255.0**, with the network number being contained in the first three octets. This allows for nearly 2 million networks with up to 254 hosts.

Classes D, E, and F — Addresses falling into the range of **224.0.0.0** through **254.0.0.0** are either experimental, or are reserved for future use and don't specify any network.

If we go back to the example in the previous chapter, we find that **149.76.12.4**, the address of **quark**, refers to host **12.4** on the class B network **149.76.0.0**.

You may have noticed that in the above list not all possible values were allowed for each octet in the host part. This is because host numbers with octets all **0** or all **255** are reserved for special purposes. An address where all host part bits are zero refers to the network, and one where all bits of the host part are 1 is called a broadcast address. This refers to all hosts on the specified network simultaneously. Thus, **149.76.255.255** is not a valid host address, but refers to all hosts on network **149.76.0.0**.

There are also two network addresses that are reserved, **0.0.0.0** and **127.0.0.0**. The first is called the *default route*, the latter the *loopback address*. The default route has something to do with the way IP routes datagrams, which will be dealt with below.

Network **127.0.0.0** is reserved for IP traffic local to your host. Usually, address **127.0.0.1** will be assigned to a special interface on your host, the so-called *loopback interface*, which acts like a closed circuit. Any IP packet handed to it from TCP or UDP will be returned to them as if it had just arrived from some network. This allows you to develop and test networking software without ever using a "real" network. Another useful application is when you want to use networking software on a standalone host. This may not be as uncommon as it sounds; for instance, many UUCP sites don't have IP connectivity at all, but still want to run the INN news system nevertheless. For proper operation on Linux, INN requires the loopback interface.

2.3 Address Resolution

Now that you've seen how IP addresses are made up, you may be wondering how they are used on an Ethernet to address different hosts. After all, the Ethernet protocol identifies hosts by a six-octet number that has absolutely nothing in common with an IP address, doesn't it?

Right. That's why a mechanism is needed to map IP addresses onto Ethernet addresses. This is the so-called *Address Resolution Protocol*, or ARP. In fact, ARP is not confined to Ethernets at all, but is used on other types networks such as ham radio as well. The idea underlying ARP is exactly what most people do when they have to find Mr. X. Ample in a throng of 150 people: they go round, calling out his name, confident that he will respond if he's there.

When ARP wants to find out the Ethernet address corresponding to a given IP address, it uses a feature of Ethernet known as "broadcasting," where a datagram is addressed to all stations on the network simultaneously. The broadcast datagram sent by ARP contains a query for the IP address. Each receiving host compares this to its own IP address, and if it matches, returns an ARP reply to the inquiring host. The inquiring host can now extract the sender's Ethernet address from the reply.

Of course you might wonder how a host may know on which of the zillions of Ethernets throughout the world it is to find the desired host, and why this should even be an Ethernet. These questions all involve what is called routing, namely finding out the physical location of a host in a network. This will be the topic of the following section.

For a moment, let's talk about ARP a little longer. Once a host has discovered an Ethernet address, it stores it in its ARP cache, so that it doesn't have to query for it the next time it wants to send a datagram to the host in question. However, it is unwise to keep this information forever; for instance, the remote host's Ethernet card may be replaced because of technical problems, so the ARP entry becomes invalid. To force another query for the IP address, entries in the ARP cache are therefore discarded after some time.

Sometimes, it is also necessary to find out the IP address associated with a given Ethernet address. This happens when a diskless machine wants to boot from a server on the network, which is quite a common situation on local area networks. A diskless client, however, has virtually no information about itself – except for its Ethernet address! So what it basically does is broadcast a message containing a plea for boot servers to tell it its IP address. There's another protocol for this, named *Reverse Address Resolution Protocol*, or RARP. Along with the BOOTP protocol, it serves to define a procedure for bootstrapping diskless clients over the network.

2.4 IP Routing

2.4.1 IP Networks

◇ When you write a letter to someone, you usually put a complete address on the envelope, specifying the country, state, zip code, etc. After you put it into the letter box, the postal service will deliver it to its destination: it will be sent to the country indicated, whose national service will dispatch it to the proper state and region, etc. The advantage of this hierarchical scheme is rather obvious: Wherever you post the letter, the local postmaster will know roughly the direction to forward the letter to, but doesn't have to care which way the letter will travel by within the destination country.

IP networks are structured in a similar way. The whole Internet consists of a number of proper networks, called *autonomous systems*. Each such system performs any routing between its member hosts internally, so that the task of delivering a datagram is reduced to finding a path to the destination host's network. This means, as soon as the datagram is handed to *any* host that is on that particular network, further processing is done exclusively by the network itself.

2.4.2 Subnetworks

This structure is reflected by splitting IP addresses into a host and network part, as explained above. By default, the destination network is derived from the network part of the IP address. Thus, hosts with identical IP network numbers should be found within the same network, and vice versa.[2]

It makes sense to offer a similar scheme *inside* the network, too, since it may consist of a collection of hundreds of smaller networks itself, with the smallest units being physical networks like Ethernets. Therefore, IP allows you to subdivide an IP network into several *subnets*.

A subnet takes over responsibility for delivering datagrams to a certain range of IP addresses from the IP network it is part of. As with classes A, B, or C, it is identified by the network part of the IP addresses. However, the network part is now extended to include some bits from the host part. The number of bits that are interpreted as the subnet number is given by the so-called *subnet mask*, or *netmask*. This is a 32-bit number, too, which specifies the bit mask for the network part of the IP address.

The campus network of Groucho Marx University is an example of such a network. It has a class B network number of **149.76.0.0**, and its netmask is therefore **255.255.0.0**.

Internally, GMU's campus network consists of several smaller networks, such as the LANs of various departments. So the range of IP addresses is broken up into 254 subnets, **149.76.1.0** through **149.76.254.0**. For example, the Department of Theoretical Physics has been assigned **149.76.12.0**. The campus backbone is a network by its own right, and is given **149.76.1.0**. These subnets share the same IP network number, while the third octet is used to distinguish between them. Thus they will use a subnet mask of **255.255.255.0**.

Figure 2.1 shows how **149.76.12.4**, the address of **quark**, is interpreted differently when the address is taken as an ordinary class B network, and when used with subnetting.

[2]Autonomous systems are slightly more general, however. They may comprise more than one IP network.

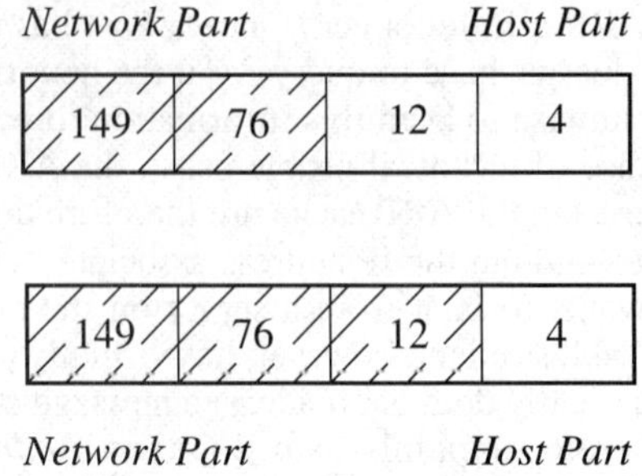

Figure 2.1: Subnetting a class B network

It is worth noting that subnetting (as the technique of generating subnets is called) is only an *internal division* of the network. Subnets are generated by the network owner (or the administrators). Frequently, subnets are created to reflect existing boundaries, be they physical (between two Ethernets), administrative (between two departments), or geographical, and authority over these subnets is delegated to some contact person. However, this structure affects only the network's internal behavior, and is completely invisible to the outside world.

2.4.3 Gateways

Subnetting is not only an organizational benefit, it is frequently a natural consequence of hardware boundaries. The viewpoint of a host on a given physical network, such as an Ethernet, is a very limited one: the only hosts it is able to talk to directly are those of the network it is on. All other hosts can be accessed only through so-called *gateways*. A gateway is a host that is connected to two or more physical networks simultaneously and is configured to switch packets between them.

For IP to be able to easily recognize if a host is on a local physical network, different physical networks have to belong to different IP networks. For example the network number **149.76.4.0** is reserved for hosts on the mathematics LAN. When sending a datagram to **quark**, the network software on **erdos** immediately sees from the IP address, **149.76.12.4**, that the destination host is on a different physical network, and therefore can be reached only through a gateway (**sophus** by default).

sophus itself is connected to two distinct subnets: the Mathematics Department, and the campus backbone. It accesses each through a different interface, *eth0* and *fddi0*, respectively. Now, what IP address do we assign it? Should we give it one on subnet **149.76.1.0**, or on **149.76.4.0**?

The answer is: both. When talking to a host on the Maths LAN, **sophus** should use an IP address of **149.76.4.1**, and when talking to a host on the backbone, it should use **149.76.1.4**.

Thus, a gateway is assigned one IP address per network it is on. These addresses — along with the corresponding netmask — are tied to the interface the subnet is accessed through. Thus, the mapping of interfaces and addresses for **sophus** would look like this:

iface	address	netmask
eth0	**149.76.4.1**	**255.255.255.0**
fddi0	**149.76.1.4**	**255.255.255.0**
lo	**127.0.0.1**	**255.0.0.0**

The last entry describes the loopback interface *lo*, which was introduced above.

Figure 2.2 shows a part of the network topology at Groucho Marx University (GMU). Hosts that are on two subnets at the same time are shown with both addresses.

Generally, you can ignore the subtle difference between attaching an address to a host or its interface. For hosts that are on one network only, like **erdos**, you would generally refer of the host as having this-and-that IP address although strictly speaking, it's the Ethernet interface that has this IP address. However, this distinction is only really important when you refer to a gateway.

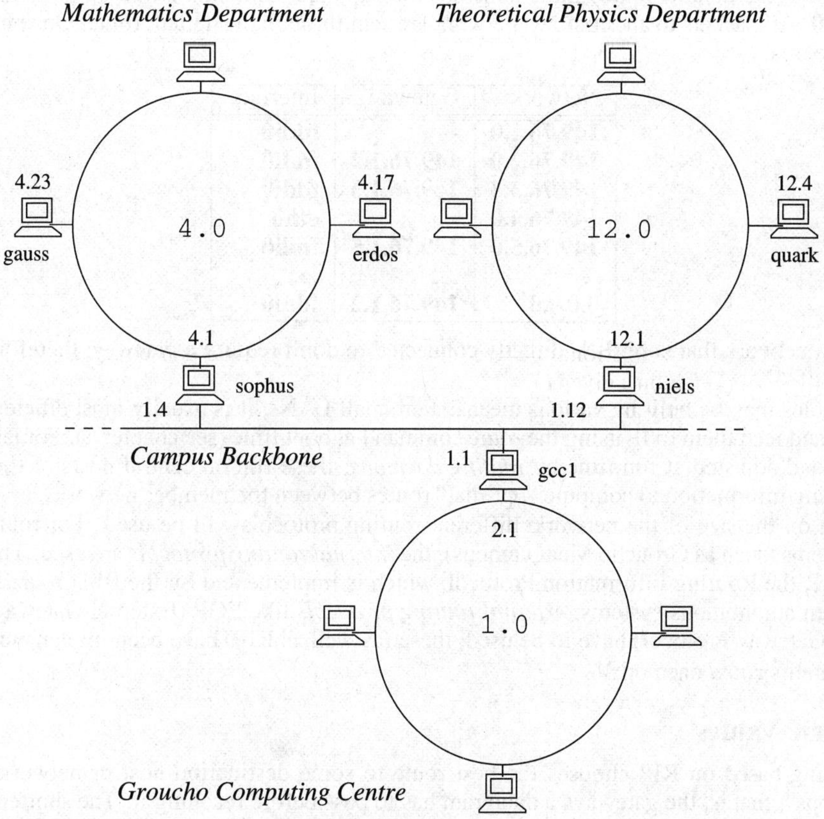

Figure 2.2: A part of the net topology at Groucho Marx Univ.

2.4.4 The Routing Table

We are now focusing our attention on how IP chooses a gateway to use when delivering a datagram to a remote network.

We have seen before that **erdos**, when given a datagram for **quark**, checks the destination address and finds it is not on the local network. It therefore sends it to the default gateway, **sophus**, which is now basically faced with the same task. **sophus** recognizes that **quark** is not on any of the networks it is connected to directly, so it has to find yet another gateway to forward it through. The correct choice would be *niels*, the gateway to the Physics Department. **sophus** therefore needs some information to associate a destination network with a suitable gateway.

The routing information IP uses for this is basically a table linking networks to gateways that reach them. A catch-all entry (the *default route*) must generally be supplied, too; this is the gateway associated with network **0.0.0.0**. All packets to an unknown network are sent through the default route. On **sophus**, this table might look like this:

Network	Gateway	Interface
149.76.1.0	-	**fddi0**
149.76.2.0	**149.76.1.2**	**fddi0**
149.76.3.0	**149.76.1.3**	**fddi0**
149.76.4.0	-	**eth0**
149.76.5.0	**149.76.1.5**	**fddi0**
...	...	...
0.0.0.0	**149.76.1.2**	**fddi0**

Routes to a network that **sophus** is directly connected to don't require a gateway; therefore they show a gateway entry of "-".

Routing tables may be built by various means. For small LANs, it is usually most efficient to construct them by hand and feed them to IP using the *route* command at boot time (see chapter 5). For larger networks, they are built and adjusted at run-time by *routing daemons*; these run on central hosts of the network and exchange routing information to compute "optimal" routes between the member networks.

Depending on the size of the network, different routing protocols will be used. For routing inside autonomous systems (such as Groucho Marx campus), the *internal routing protocols* are used. The most prominent one is RIP, the Routing Information Protocol, which is implemented by the BSD *routed* daemon. For routing between autonomous systems, *external routing protocols* like EGP (External Gateway Protocol), or BGP (Border Gateway Protocol) have to be used; these (as well as RIP) have been implemented in the University of Cornell's *gated* daemon.[3]

2.4.5 Metric Values

Dynamic routing based on RIP chooses the best route to some destination host or network based on the number of "hops", that is, the gateways a datagram has to pass before reaching it. The shorter a route is, the better RIP rates it. Very long routes with 16 or more hops are regarded as unusable, and are discarded.

To use RIP to manage routing information internal to your local network, you have to run *gated* on all hosts. At boot time, *gated* checks for all active network interfaces. If there is more than one active interface (not counting the loopback interface), it assumes the host is switching packets between several networks, and will actively exchange and broadcast routing information. Otherwise, it will only passively receive any RIP updates and update the local routing table.

When broadcasting the information from the local routing table, *gated* computes the length of the route from the so-called *metric value* associated with the routing table entry. This metric value is set by the system administrator when configuring the route and should reflect the actual cost of using this route. Therefore, the metric of a route to a subnet the host is directly connected to should always be zero, while a route going through two gateways should have a metric of two. However, note that you don't have to bother about metrics when you don't use *RIP* or *gated*.

[3] *routed* is considered broken by many people. Since *gated* supports RIP as well, it is better to use that instead.

2.5 The Internet Control Message Protocol

IP has a companion protocol that we haven't talked about yet. This is the *Internet Control Message Protocol* (ICMP) and is used by the kernel networking code to communicate error messages and the like to other hosts. For instance, assume that you are on **erdos** again and want to *telnet* to port 12345 on **quark**, but there's no process listening on that port. When the first TCP packet for this port arrives on **quark**, the networking layer will recognize this and immediately return an ICMP message to **erdos** stating "Port Unreachable".

There are quite a number of messages ICMP understands, many of which deal with error conditions. However, there is one very interesting message called the Redirect message. It is generated by the routing module when it detects that another host is using it as a gateway, although there is a much shorter route. For example, after booting the routing table of **sophus** may be incomplete, containing the routes to the Mathematics network, to the FDDI backbone, and the default route pointing at the Groucho Computing Center's gateway (**gcc1**). Therefore, any packets for **quark** would be sent to **gcc1** rather than to **niels**, the gateway to the Physics Department. When receiving such a datagram, **gcc1** will notice that this is a poor choice of route, and will forward the packet to **niels**, at the same time returning an ICMP Redirect message to **sophus** telling it of the superior route.

Now, this seems a very clever way to avoid having to set up any but the most basic routes manually. However be warned that relying on dynamic routing schemes, be it RIP or ICMP Redirect messages, is not always a good idea. ICMP Redirect and RIP offer you little or no choice in verifying that some routing information is indeed authentic. This allows malicious good-for-nothings to disrupt your entire network traffic, or do even worse things. For this reason, there are some versions of the Linux networking code that treat Redirect messages that affect network routes, as if they were only Redirects for host routes.

2.6 The Domain Name System

2.6.1 Hostname Resolution

◇ As described above, addressing in TCP/IP networking revolves around 32-bit numbers. However, you will have a hard time remembering more than a few of these. Therefore, hosts are generally known by "ordinary" names such as **gauss** or **strange**. It is then the application's duty to find the IP address corresponding to this name. This process is called *host name resolution*.

An application that wants to find the IP address of a given host name does not have to provide its own routines for looking up a hosts and IP adresses. Instead, it relies on number of library functions that do this transparently, called *gethostbyname(3)* and *gethostbyaddr(3)*. Traditionally, these and a number of related procedures were grouped in a separate library called the resolver library; on Linux, these are part of the standard *libc*. Colloquially, this collection of functions are therefore referred to as "the resolver."

Now, on a small network like an Ethernet, or even a cluster of them, it is not very difficult to maintain tables mapping host names to addresses. This information is usually kept in a file named */etc/hosts*. When adding or removing hosts, or reassigning addresses, all you have to do is update the *hosts* on all hosts. Quite obviously, this will become burdensome with networks than comprise more than a handful of machines.

One solution to this problem is NIS, the *Network Information System* developed by Sun Microsystems, colloquially called YP, or *Yellow Pages*. NIS stores the *hosts* file (and other information) in a database on a master host, from which clients may retrieve it as needed. Still, this approach is only suitable for medium-sized networks such as LANs, because it involves maintaining the entire *hosts* database centrally, and distributing it to all servers.

On the Internet, address information was initially stored in a single *HOSTS.TXT* database, too. This file was maintained at the Network Information Center, or NIC, and had to be downloaded and installed by all participating sites. When the network grew, several problems with this scheme arose. Beside the administrative overhead involved in installing *HOSTS.TXT* regularly, the load on the servers that distributed it became too high. Even more severe was the problem that all names had to be registered with the NIC, which had to make sure that no name was issued twice.

This is why, in 1984, a new name resolution scheme has been adopted, the *Domain Name System*. DNS was designed by Paul Mockapetris, and addresses both problems simultaneously.

2.6.2 Enter DNS

DNS organizes host names in a hierarchy of domains. A domain is a collection of sites that are related in some sense — be it because they form a proper network (e.g. all machines on a campus, or all hosts on BITNET), because they all belong to a certain organization (like the U.S. government), or because they're simply geographically close. For instance, universities are grouped in the **edu** domain, with each University or College using a separate *subdomain* below which their hosts are subsumed. Groucho Marx University might be given the **groucho.edu** domain, with the LAN of the Mathematics Department being assigned **maths.groucho.edu**. Hosts on the departmental network would have this domain name tacked onto their host name; so **erdos** would be known as **erdos.maths.groucho.edu**. This is called the *fully qualified domain name*, or FQDN, which uniquely identifies this host world-wide.

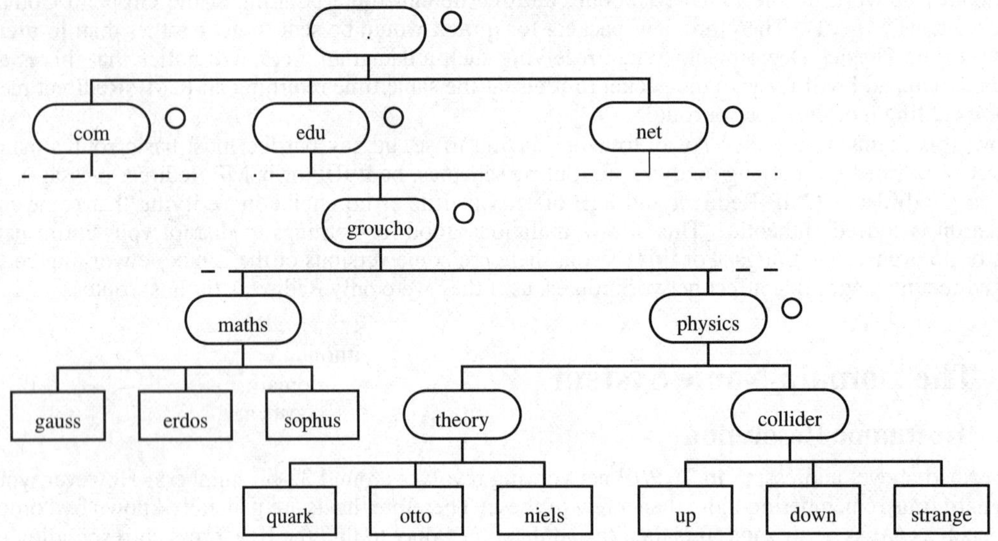

Figure 2.3: A part of the domain name space

Figure 2.3 shows a section of the name space. The entry at the root of this tree, which is denoted by a single dot, is quite appropriately called the *root domain*, and encompasses all other domains. To indicate that a host name is a fully qualified domain name, rather than a name relative to some (implicit) local domain, it is sometimes written with a trailing dot. This signifies that the name's last component is the root domain.

Depending on its location in the name hierarchy, a domain may be called top-level, second-level, or third-level. More levels of subdivision occur, but are rare. These are a couple of top-level domains you may see frequently:

edu (Mostly US) educational institutions like universities, etc.

com Commercial organizations, companies.

org Non-commercial organizations. Often private UUCP networks are in this domain.

net Gateways and other administrative host on a network.

mil US military institutions.

gov US government institutions.

uucp Officially, all site names formerly used as UUCP names without domain, have been moved to this domain.

Technically, the first four of these belong to the US part of the Internet, but you may also see non-US sites in these domains. This is especially true of the **net** domain. However, **mil** and **gov** are used exclusively in the US.

Outside the US, each country generally uses a top-level domain of its own named after the two-letter country code defined in ISO-3166. Finland, for instance, uses the **fi** domain, **fr** is used by France, **de** by Germany, or **au** by Australia. Below this top-level domain, each country's NIC is free to organize host names in whatever way they want. Australia, for example, has second-level domain similar to the international top-level domains, named **com.au**, **edu.au**, and so on. Others, like Germany, don't use this extra level, but rather have slightly longish names that refer directly to the organizations running a particular domain. For example, it's not uncommon to see host names like **ftp.informatik.uni-erlangen.de**. Chalk that up to German efficiency.

Of course, these national domains do not imply that a host below that domain is actually located in that country; it only signals that the host has been registered with that country's NIC. A Swedish manufacturer might have a branch in Australia, and still have all its hosts registered with the **se** top-level domain.

Now, organizing the name space in a hierarchy of domain names nicely solves the problem of name uniqueness; with DNS, a host name has to be unique only within its domain to give it a name different from all other hosts world-wide. Furthermore, fully qualified names are quite easy to remember. Taken by themselves, these are already very good reasons to split up a large domain into several subdomains.

But DNS does even more for you than than this: it allows you to delegate authority over a subdomain to its administrators. For example, the maintainers at the Groucho Computing Center might create a subdomain for each department; we already encountered the **maths** and **physics** subdomains above. When they find the network at the Physics Department too large and chaotic to manage from outside (after all, physicists are known to be an unruly bunch of people), they may simply pass control over the **physics.groucho.edu** domain to the administrators of this network. These are then free to use whatever host names they like, and assign them IP addresses from their network in whatever fashion the like, without outside interference.

To this end, the name space is split up into *zones*, each rooted at a domain. Note the subtle difference between a zone and a domain: the *domain* **groucho.edu** encompasses all hosts at the Groucho Marx University, while the *zone* **groucho.edu** includes only the hosts that are managed by the Computing Center directly, for example those at the Mathematics Department. The hosts at the Physics Department belong to a different zone, namely **physics.groucho.edu**. In figure 2.3, the start of a zone is marked by a small circle to the right of the domain name.

2.6.3 Name Lookups with DNS

At first glance, all this domain and zone fuss seems to make name resolution an awfully complicated business. After all, if no central authority controls what names are assigned to which hosts, then how is a humble application supposed to know?

Now comes the really ingenuous part about DNS. If you want to find out the IP address of **erdos**, then, DNS says, go ask the people that manage it, and they will tell you.

In fact, DNS is a giant distributed database. It is implemented by means of so-called name servers that supply information on a given domain or set of domains. For each zone, there are at least two, at most a few, name servers that hold all authoritative information on hosts in that zone. To obtain the IP address of **erdos**, all you have to do is contact the name server for the **groucho.edu** zone, which will then return the desired data.

Easier said than done, you might think. So how do I know how to reach the name server at Groucho Marx University? In case your computer isn't equipped with an address-resolving oracle, DNS provides for this, too. When your application wants to look up information on **erdos**, it contacts a local name server, which conducts a so-called iterative query for it. It starts off by sending a query to a name server for the root domain, asking for the address of **erdos.maths.groucho.edu**. The root name server recognizes that this name does not belong to its zone of authority, but rather to one below the **edu** domain. Thus, it tells you to contact an **edu** zone name server for more information, and encloses a list of all **edu** name servers along with their addresses. Your local name server will then go on and query one of those, for instance **a.isi.edu**. In a manner similar to the root name server, **a.isi.edu** knows that the **groucho.edu** people run a zone of their own, and point you to their servers. The local name server will then present its query for **erdos** to one of these, which will finally recognize the name as belonging to its zone, and return the corresponding IP address.

Now, this looks like a lot of traffic being generated for looking up a measly IP address, but it's really only miniscule compared to the amount of data that would have to be transferred if we were still stuck with *HOSTS.TXT*. But there's still room for improvement with this scheme.

To improve response time during future queries, the name server will store the information obtained in its local *cache*. So the next time anyone on your local network wants to look up the address of a host in the **groucho.edu** domain, your name server will not have to go through the whole process again, but will rather go to the **groucho.edu** name server directly.[4]

Of course, the name server will not keep this information forever, but rather discard it after some period. This expiry interval is called the *time to live*, or TTL. Each datum in the DNS database is assigned such a TTL by administrators of the responsible zone.

2.6.4 Domain Name Servers

Name servers that hold all information on hosts within a zone are called *authoritative* for this zone, and are sometimes referred to as *master name servers*. Any query for a host within this zone will finally wind down at one of these master name servers.

To provide a coherent picture of a zone, its master servers must be fairly well synchronized. This is achieved by making one of them the *primary* server, which loads its zone information from data files, and making the others *secondary* servers who transfer the zone data from the primary server at regular intervals.

One reason to have several name servers is to distribute work load, another is redundance. When one name server machine fails in a benign way, like crashing or losing its network connection, all queries will fall back to the other servers. Of course, this scheme doesn't protect you from server malfunctions that produce wrong replies to all DNS requests, e.g. from software bugs in the server program itself.

Of course, you can also think of running a name server that is not authoritative for any domain.[5] This type of server is useful nevertheless, as it is still able to conduct DNS queries for the applications running on the local network, and cache the information. It is therefore called a *caching-only* server.

2.6.5 The DNS Database

We have seen above that DNS does not only deal with IP addresses of hosts, but also exchanges information on name servers. There are in fact a whole bunch of different types of entries the DNS database may have.

A single piece of information from the DNS database is called a *resource record*, or RR for short. Each record has a type associated with it, describing the sort of data it represents, and a class specifying the type of network it applies to. The latter accomodates the needs of different addressing schemes, like IP addresses (the IN class), or addresses of Hesiod networks (used at MIT), and a few more. The prototypical resource record type is the A record which associates a fully qualified domain name with an IP address.

Of course, a host may have more than one name. However, one of these names must be identified as the official, or *canonical host name*, while the others are simply aliases referring to the former. The difference is that the canocical host name is the one with an A record associated, while the others only have a record of type CNAME which points to the canonical host name.

We will not go through all record types here, but save them for a later chapter, but rather give you a brief example here. Figure 2.4 shows a part of the domain database that is loaded into the name servers for the **physics.groucho.edu** zone.

Apart from A and CNAME records, you can see a special record at the top of the file, stretching several lines. This is the SOA resource record, signalling the *Start of Authority*, which holds general information on the zone the server is authoritative for. This comprises, for instance, the default time-to-live for all records.

Note that all names in the sample file that do not end with a dot should be interpreted relative to the **groucho.edu** domain. The special name "@" used in the SOA record refers to the domain name by itself.

We have seen above that the name servers for the **groucho.edu** domain somehow have to know about the **physics** zone so that they can point queries to their name servers. This is usually achieved by a pair of records: the NS record that gives the server's FQDN, and an A record associating an address with that name. Since these records are what holds the name space together, they are frequently called the *glue records*. They

[4] If it didn't, then DNS would be about as bad as any other method, because each query would involve the root name servers.

[5] Well, almost. A name server at least has to provide name service for **localhost** and reverse lookups of **127.0.0.1**.

```
;
; Authoritative Information on physics.groucho.edu
@                       IN    SOA         {
                       niels.physics.groucho.edu.
                       hostmaster.niels.physics.groucho.edu.
                       1034             ; serial no
                       360000           ; refresh
                       3600             ; retry
                       3600000          ; expire
                       3600             ; default ttl
                     }
;
; Name servers
                        IN    NS        niels
                        IN    NS        gauss.maths.groucho.edu.
gauss.maths.groucho.edu. IN A           149.76.4.23
;
; Theoretical Physics (subnet 12)
niels                   IN    A         149.76.12.1
                        IN    A         149.76.1.12
nameserver              IN    CNAME     niels
otto                    IN    A         149.76.12.2
quark                   IN    A         149.76.12.4
down                    IN    A         149.76.12.5
strange                 IN    A         149.76.12.6
...
; Collider Lab. (subnet 14)
boson                   IN    A         149.76.14.1
muon                    IN    A         149.76.14.7
bogon                   IN    A         149.76.14.12
...
```

Figure 2.4: An excerpt from the *named.hosts* file for the Physics Department.

are the only instances of records where a parent zone actually holds information on hosts in the subordinate zone. The glue records pointing to the name servers for **physics.groucho.edu** are shown in figure 2.5.

```
;
; Zone data for the groucho.edu zone.
@                   IN      SOA          {
                     vax12.gcc.groucho.edu.
                     hostmaster.vax12.gcc.groucho.edu.
                     233                ; serial no
                     360000             ; refresh
                     3600               ; retry
                     3600000            ; expire
                     3600               ; default ttl
                   }
....
;
; Glue records for the physics.groucho.edu zone
physics             IN      NS          niels.physics.groucho.edu.
                    IN      NS          gauss.maths.groucho.edu.
niels.physics       IN      A           149.76.12.1
gauss.maths         IN      A           149.76.4.23
...
```

Figure 2.5: An excerpt from the *named.hosts* file for GMU.

2.6.6 Reverse Lookups

Beside looking up the IP address belonging to a host, it is sometimes desirable to find out the canonical host name corresponding to an address. This is called *reverse mapping* and is used by several network services to verify a client's identity. When using a single *hosts* file, reverse lookups simply involve searching the file for a host that owns the IP address in question. With DNS, an exhaustive search of the name space is out of the question, of course. Instead, a special domain, **in-addr.arpa**, has been created which contains the IP addresses of all hosts in a reverted dotted-quad notation. For instance, an IP address of **149.76.12.4** corresponds to the name **4.12.76.149.in-addr.arpa**. The resource record type linking these names to their canonical host names is PTR.

Creating a zone of authority usually means that its administrators are given full control over how they assign addresses to names. Since they usually have one or more IP networks or subnets at their hands, there's a one-to-many mapping between DNS zones and IP networks. The Physics Department, for instance, comprises the subnets **149.76.8.0**, **149.76.12.0**, and **149.76.14.0**.

As a consequence, new zones in the **in-addr.arpa** domain have to be created along with the **physics** zone and delegated to the network administrators at the department: **8.76.149.in-addr.arpa**, **12.76.149.in-addr.arpa**, and **14.76.149.in-addr.arpa**. Otherwise, installing a new host at the Collider Lab would require them to contact their parent domain to have the new address entered into their **in-addr.arpa** zone file.

The zone database for subnet 12 is shown in figure 2.6. The corresponding glue records in the database of their parent zone is shown in figure 2.7.

One important consequence of this is that zones can only be created as supersets of IP networks, and, even more severe, that these network's netmasks have to be on byte boundaries. All subnets at Groucho Marx University have a netmask of **255.255.255.0**, whence an **in-addr.arpa** zone could be created for each subnet. However, if the netmask was **255.255.255.128** instead, creating zones for the subnet **149.76.12.128** would be impossible, because there's no way to tell DNS that the **12.76.149.in-addr.arpa** domain has been split in two zones of authority, with host names ranging from **1** through **127**, and **128** through **255**, respectively.

```
;
; the 12.76.149.in-addr.arpa domain.
@               IN      SOA    {
                    niels.physics.groucho.edu.
                    hostmaster.niels.physics.groucho.edu.
                    233 360000 3600 3600000 3600
                  }
2               IN      PTR         otto.physics.groucho.edu.
4               IN      PTR         quark.physics.groucho.edu.
5               IN      PTR         down.physics.groucho.edu.
6               IN      PTR         strange.physics.groucho.edu.
```

Figure 2.6: An excerpt from the *named.rev* file for subnet 12.

```
;
; the 76.149.in-addr.arpa domain.
@                     IN        SOA          {
                        vax12.gcc.groucho.edu.
                        hostmaster.vax12.gcc.groucho.edu.
                        233 360000 3600 3600000 3600
                      }
...
; subnet 4: Mathematics Dept.
1.4             IN      PTR       sophus.maths.groucho.edu.
17.4            IN      PTR       erdos.maths.groucho.edu.
23.4            IN      PTR       gauss.maths.groucho.edu.
...
; subnet 12: Physics Dept, separate zone
12              IN      NS        niels.physics.groucho.edu.
                IN      NS        gauss.maths.groucho.edu.
niels.physics.groucho.edu. IN  A 149.76.12.1
gauss.maths.groucho.edu. IN  A   149.76.4.23
...
```

Figure 2.7: An excerpt from the *named.rev* file for network **149.76**.

CHAPTER 3

Configuring the Networking Hardware

3.1 Devices, Drivers, and all that

Up to now, we've been talking quite a bit about network interfaces and general TCP/IP issues, but didn't really cover exactly *what* happens when "the networking code" in the kernel accesses a piece of hardware. For this, we have to talk a little about the concept of interfaces and drivers.

First, of course, there's the hardware itself, for example an Ethernet board: this is a slice of Epoxy, cluttered with lots of tiny chips with silly numbers on them, sitting in a slot of your PC. This is what we generally call a device.

For you to be able to use the Ethernet board, special functions have to be present in your Linux kernel that understand the particular way this device is accessed. These are the so-called device drivers. For example, Linux has device drivers for several brands of Ethernet boards that are very similar in function. They are known as the "Becker Series Drivers", named after their author, Donald Becker. A different example is the D-Link driver that handles a D-Link pocket adaptor attached to a parallel port.

But, what do we mean when we say a driver "handles" a device? Let's go back to that Ethernet board we examined above. The driver has to be able to communicate with the peripheral's on-board logic somehow: it has to send commands and data to the board, while the board should deliver any data received to the driver.

In PCs, this communication takes place through an area of I/O memory that is mapped to on-board registers and the like. All commands and data the kernel sends to the board have to go through these registers. I/O memory is generally described by giving its starting or *base address*. Typical base addresses for Ethernet boards are `0x300`, or `0x360`.

Usually, you don't have to worry about any hardware issues such as the base address, because the kernel makes an attempt at boot time to detect a board's location. This is called autoprobing, which means that the kernel reads several memory locations and compares the data read with what it should see if a certain Ethernet board was installed. However, there may be Ethernet boards it cannot detect automatically; this is sometimes the case with cheap Ethernet cards that are not-quite clones of standard boards from other manufacturers. Also, the kernel will attempt to detect only one Ethernet device when booting. If you're using more than one board, you have to tell the kernel about this board explicitly.

Another such parameter that you might have to tell the kernel about is the interrupt request channel. Hardware components usually interrupt the kernel when they need care taken of them, e.g. when data has arrived, or a special condition occurs. In a PC, interrupts may occur on one of 15 interrupt channels numbered 0, 1, and 3 through 15. The interrupt number assigned to a hardware component is called its *interrupt request number*, or IRQ.[1]

As described in chapter 2, the kernel accesses a device through a so-called interface. Interfaces offer an abstract set of functions that is the same across all types of hardware, such as sending or receiving a datagram.

Interfaces are identified by means of names. These are names defined internally in the kernel, and are not device files in the */dev* directory. Typical names are *eth0*, *eth1*, etc, for Ethernet interfaces. The assignment

[1] IRQs 2 and 9 are the same because the PC has two cascaded interrupt processors with eight IRQs each; the secondary processor is connected to IRQ 2 of the primary one.

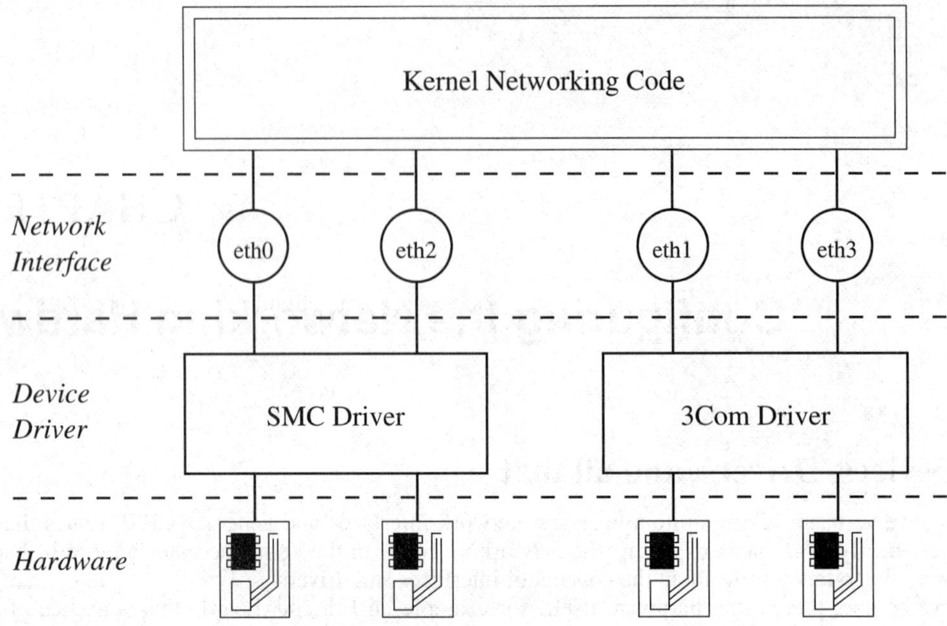

Figure 3.1: The relationship between drivers, interfaces, and the hardware.

of interfaces to devices usually depends on the order in which devices are configured; for instance the first Ethernet board installed will become *eth0*, the next will be *eth1*, and so on. One exception from this rule are SLIP interfaces, which are assigned dynamically; that is, whenever a SLIP connection is established, an interface is assigned to the serial port.

The picture given in figure 3.1 tries to show the relationship between the hardware, device drivers and interfaces.

When booting, the kernel displays what devices it detects, and what interfaces it installs. The following is an excerpt of a typical boot screen:

```
.
.
This processor honours the WP bit even when in supervisor mode. Good.
Floppy drive(s): fd0 is 1.44M
Swansea University Computer Society NET3.010
IP Protocols: ICMP, UDP, TCP
PPP: version 0.2.1 (4 channels) OPTIMIZE_FLAGS
TCP compression code copyright 1989 Regents of the University of California
PPP line discipline registered.
SLIP: version 0.7.5 (4 channels)
CSLIP: code copyright 1989 Regents of the University of California
dl0: D-Link DE-600 pocket adapter, Ethernet Address: 00:80:C8:71:76:95
Checking 386/387 coupling... Ok, fpu using exception 16 error reporting.
Linux version 1.1.11 (okir@monad) #3 Sat May 7 14:57:18 MET DST 1994
```

This shows that the kernel has been compiled with TCP/IP enabled, and drivers for SLIP, CSLIP, and PPP included. The third line from below says that a D-Link pocket adaptor was detected, and installed as interface *dl0*. If you have a different type of Ethernet card, the kernel will usually print a line starting with *eth0*, followed by the type of card detected. If you have an Ethernet card installed but don't see any such message, this means that the kernel is unable to detect your board properly. This is dealt with in a later section.

3.2 Kernel Configuration

Most Linux distributions come along with boot disks that work for all common types of PC hardware. This means that the kernel on those disks has all sorts of drivers configured in that you will never need, but which waste precious system memory because parts of the kernel cannot be swapped out. Therefore, you will generally roll your own kernel, including only those drivers you actually need or want.

When running a Linux system, you should be familiar with building a kernel. The basics of this are explained in Matt Welsh's "Installation and Getting Started" Guide, which is also part of the Linux Documentation Project's series. In this section, we will therefore discuss only those configuration options that affect networking.

When running `make config`, you will first be asked general configurations, for instance whether you want kernel math emulation or not, etc. One of these asks you whether you want TCP/IP networking support. You must answer this with `y` to get a kernel capable of networking.

3.2.1 Kernel Options in Linux 1.0 and Higher

After the general option part is complete, the configuration will go on to ask you for various features such as SCSI drivers, etc. The subsequent list questions deal with networking support. The exact set of configuration options is in constant flux because of the ongoing development. A typical list of options offered by most kernel versions around 1.0 and 1.1 looks like this (comments are given in italics):

```
*
* Network device support
*
Network device support? (CONFIG_ETHERCARDS) [y]
```

Despite the macro name displayed in brackets, you must answer this question with `y` if you want to use *any* type of networking devices, regardless of whether this is Ethernet, SLIP, or PPP. When answering this question with `y`, support for Ethernet-type devices is enabled automatically. Support for other types of network drivers must be enabled separately:

```
SLIP (serial line) support? (CONFIG_SLIP) [y]
  SLIP compressed headers (SL_COMPRESSED) [y]
PPP (point-to-point) support (CONFIG_PPP) [y]
PLIP (parallel port) support (CONFIG_PLIP) [n]
```

These questions concern the various link layer protocols supported by Linux. SLIP allows you to transport IP datagrams across serial lines. The compressed header option provides support for CSLIP, a technique that compresses TCP/IP headers to as little as three bytes. Note that this kernel option does not turn on CSLIP automatically, it merely provides the necessary kernel functions for it.

PPP is another protocol to send network traffic across serial lines. It is much more flexible than SLIP, and is not limited to IP, but will also support IPX once it is implemented. As PPP support has been completed only lately, this option may not be present in your kernel.

PLIP provides for a way to send IP datagrams across a parallel port connection. It is mostly used to communicate with PCs running DOS.

The following questions deal with Ethernet boards from various vendors. As more drivers are being developed, you are likely to see questions added to this section. If you want to build a kernel you can use on a number of different machines, you can enable more than one driver.

```
NE2000/NE1000 support (CONFIG_NE2000) [y]
WD80*3 support (CONFIG_WD80x3) [n]
SMC Ultra support (CONFIG_ULTRA) [n]
3c501 support (CONFIG_EL1) [n]
3c503 support (CONFIG_EL2) [n]
3c509/3c579 support (CONFIG_EL3) [n]
HP PCLAN support (CONFIG_HPLAN) [n]
AT1500 and NE2100 (LANCE and PCnet-ISA) support (CONFIG_LANCE) [n]
AT1700 support (CONFIG_AT1700) [n]
```

```
DEPCA support (CONFIG_DEPCA) [n]
D-Link DE600 pocket adaptor support (CONFIG_DE600) [y]
AT-LAN-TEC/RealTek pocket adaptor support (CONFIG_ATP) [n]
*
* CD-ROM drivers
*
...
```

Finally, in the filesystem section, the configuration script will ask you whether you want support for NFS, the networking filesystem. NFS lets you export filesystems to several hosts, which makes the files appear as if they were on an ordinary hard disk attached to the host.

```
NFS filesystem support (CONFIG_NFS_FS) [y]
```

3.2.2 Kernel Options in Linux 1.1.14 and Higher

Starting with Linux 1.1.14, which added alpha support for IPX, the configuration procedure changed slightly. The general options section now asks whether you want networking support in general. It is immediately followed by a couple of question on miscellaneous networking options.

```
*
* Networking options
*
TCP/IP networking (CONFIG_INET) [y]
```

To use TCP/IP networking, you must answer this question with `y`. If you answer with `n`, however, you will still be able to compile the kernel with IPX support.

```
IP forwarding/gatewaying (CONFIG_IP_FORWARD) [n]
```

You have to enable this option if your system acts as a gateway between two Ethernets, or between and Ethernet and a SLIP link, etc. Although it doesn't hurt to enable this by default, you may want to disable this to configure a host as a so-called firewall. Firewalls are hosts that are connected to two or more networks, but don't route traffic between them. They are commonly used to provide users from a company network with Internet access at a minimal risk to the internal network. Users will be allowed to log into the firewall and use Internet services, but the company's machines will be protected from outside attacks because any incoming connections can't cross the firewall.

```
*
* (it is safe to leave these untouched)
*
PC/TCP compatibility mode (CONFIG_INET_PCTCP) [n]
```

This option works around an incompatibility with some versions of PC/TCP, a commercial TCP/IP implementation for DOS-based PCs. If you enable this option, you will still be able to communicate with normal UNIX machines, but performance may be hurt over slow links.

```
Reverse ARP (CONFIG_INET_RARP) [n]
```

This function enables RARP, the Reverse Address Resolution Protocol. RARP is used by diskless clients and X terminals to inquire their IP address when booting. You should enable RARP only when you plan to serve this sort of clients. The latest package of network utilities (*net-0.32d*) contains a small utility named *rarp* that allows you to add systems to the RARP cache.

```
Assume subnets are local (CONFIG_INET_SNARL) [y]
```

When sending data over TCP, the kernel has to break up the stream into several packets before giving it to IP. For hosts that can be reached over a local network such as an Ethernet, larger packets will be used than for hosts where data has to go through long-distance links.[2] If you don't enable *SNARL*, the kernel will assume only those networks are local that it actually has an interface to. However, if you look at the class B network at Groucho Marx University, the whole class B network is local, but most hosts interface to only one or two subnets. If you enable *SNARL*, the kernel will assume *all* subnets are local and use large packets when talking to all hosts on campus.

If you do want to use smaller packet sizes for data sent to specific hosts (because, for instance, the data goes through a SLIP link), you can do so using the *mtu* option of *route*, which is briefly discussed at the end of this chapter.

```
Disable NAGLE algorithm (normally enabled) (CONFIG_TCP_NAGLE_OFF) [n]
```

Nagle's rule is a heuristic to avoid sending particularly small IP packets, also called tinygrams. Tinygrams are usually created by interactive networking tools that transmit single keystrokes, such as *telnet* or *rsh*. Tinygrams can become particularly wasteful on low-bandwidth links like SLIP. The Nagle algorithm attempts to avoid them by holding back transmission of TCP data briefly under some circumstances. You might only want to disable Nalge's algorithm if you have severe problems with packets getting dropped.

```
The IPX protocol (CONFIG_IPX) [n]
```

This enables support for IPX, the transport protocol used by Novell Networking. It is still under development, and isn't really useful yet. One benefit of this will be that you can exchange data with IPX-based DOS utilities one day, and route traffic between your Novell-based networks through a PPP link. Support for the high-level protocols of Novell networking is however not in sight, as the specifications for these are available only at horrendous cost and under a non-disclosure agreement.

Starting in the 1.1.16 kernel, Linux supports another driver type, the dummy driver. The following question appears toward the start of the device driver section.

```
Dummy net driver support (CONFIG_DUMMY) [y]
```

The dummy driver doesn't really do much, but is quite useful on standalone or SLIP hosts. It is basically a masqueraded loopback interface. The reason to have this sort of interface is that on hosts that do SLIP but have no Ethernet, you want to have an interface that bears your IP address all the time. This is discussed in a little more detail in section 5.7.7 in chapter 5.

3.3 A Tour of Linux Network Devices

The Linux kernel supports a number of hardware drivers for various types of equipment. This section gives a short overview of the driver families available, and the interface names used for them.

There are a number of standard names for interfaces in Linux, which are listed below. Most drivers support more than one interface, in which case the interfaces are numbered, as in *eth0*, *eth1*, etc.

lo The local loopback interface. It is used for testing purposes, as well as a couple of network applications. It works like a closed circuit in that any datagram written to it will be immediately returned to the host's networking layer. There's always one loopback device present in the kernel, and there's little sense in having fewer or more.

ethn The *n*-th Ethernet card. This is the generic interface name for most Ethernet boards.

dln These interfaces access a D-Link DE-600 pocket adapter, another Ethernet device. It is a little special in that the DE-600 is driven through a parallel port.

sln The *n*-th SLIP interface. SLIP interfaces are associated with serial lines in the order in which they are allocated for SLIP; i.e., the first serial line being configured for SLIP becomes *sl0*, etc. The kernel supports up to four SLIP interfaces.

pppn The *n*-th PPP interface. Just like SLIP interfaces, a PPP interface is associated with a serial line once it is converted to PPP mode. At the moment, up to four interfaces are supported.

[2]This is to avoid fragmentation by links that have a very small maximum packet size.

plipn The *n*-th PLIP interface. PLIP transports IP datagrams over parallel lines. Up to three PLIP interfaces are supported. They are allocated by the PLIP driver at system boot time, and are mapped onto parallel ports.

For other interface drivers that may be added in the future, like ISDN, or AX.25, other names will be introduced. Drivers for IPX (Novell's networking protocol), and AX.25 (used by ham radio amateurs) are under development, but are at alpha stage still.

During the following sections, we will discuss the details of using the drivers described above.

3.4 Ethernet Installation

The current Linux network code supports various brands of Ethernet cards. Most drivers were written by Donald Becker
(**becker@cesdis.gsfc.nasa.gov**), who authored a family of drivers for cards based on the National Semiconductor 8390 chip; these have become known as the Becker Series Drivers. There are also drivers for a couple of products from D-Link, among them the D-Link pocket adaptor that allows you to access an Ethernet through a parallel port. The driver for this was written by Bjørn Ekwall (**bj0rn@blox.se**). The DEPCA driver was written by David C. Davies (**davies@wanton.lkg.dec.com**).

3.4.1 Ethernet Cabling

If you're installing an Ethernet for the first time in your life, a few words about the cabling may be in order here. Ethernet is very picky about proper cabling. The cable must be terminated on both ends with a 50-Ohm resistor, and you must not have any branches (i.e. three cables connected in a star-shape). If you are using a thin coax cable with T-shaped BNC junctions, these junctions must be twisted on the board's connector directly; you should not insert a cable segment.

If you connect to a thicknet installation, you have to attach your host through a transceiver (sometimes called Ethernet Attachment Unit). You can plug the transceiver into the 15-pin AUI port on your board directly, but may also use a shielded cable.

3.4.2 Supported Boards

A complete list of supported boards is available in the Ethernet HOWTO (page 843) posted monthly to **comp.os.linux.announce** by Paul Gortmaker. [3]

Here's a list of the more widely-known boards supported by Linux. The actual list in the HOWTO is about three times longer. However, even if you find your board in this list, check the HOWTO first; there are sometimes important details about operating these cards. A case in point is the case of some DMA-based Ethernet boards that use the same DMA channel as the Adaptec 1542 SCSI controller by default. Unless you move either of them to a different DMA channel, you will wind up with the Ethernet board writing packet data to arbitrary locations on your hard disk.

3Com EtherLink Both 3c503 and 3c503/16 are supported, as are 3c507 and 3c509. The 3c501 is supported, too, but is too slow to be worth buying.

Novell Eagle NE1000 and NE2000, and a variety of clones. NE1500 and NE2100 are supported, too.

Western Digital/SMC WD8003 and WD8013 (same as SMC Elite and SMC Elite Plus) are supported, and also the newer SMC Elite 16 Ultra.

Hewlett Packard HP 27252, HP 27247B, and HP J2405A.

D-Link DE-600 pocket adaptor, DE-100, DE-200, and DE-220-T. There's also a patch kit for the DE-650-T, which is a PCMCIA card.[4]

DEC DE200 (32K/64K), DE202, DE100, and DEPCA rev E.

Allied Teliesis AT1500 and AT1700.

[3] Paul can be reached at **gpg109@rsphysse.anu.edu.au**.

[4] It can be gotten – along with other Laptop-related stuff – from **tsx-11.mit.edu** in *packages/laptops*.

To use one of these cards with Linux, you may use a precompiled kernel from one of the major Linux distributions. These generally have drivers for all of them built in. In the long term, however, it's better to roll your own kernel and compile in only those drivers you actually need.

3.4.3 Ethernet Autoprobing

At boot time, the Ethernet code will try to locate your board and determine its type. Cards are probed for at the following addresses and in the following order:

Board	Addresses probed for
WD/SMC	0x300, 0x280, 0x380, 0x240
SMC 16 Ultra	0x300, 0x280
3c501	0x280
3c503	0x300, 0x310, 0x330, 0x350, 0x250, 0x280, 0x2a0, 0x2e0
NEx000	0x300, 0x280, 0x320, 0x340, 0x360
HP	0x300, 0x320, 0x340, 0x280, 0x2C0, 0x200, 0x240
DEPCA	0x300, 0x320, 0x340, 0x360

There are two limitations to the autoprobing code. For one, it may not recognize all boards properly. This is especially true for some of the cheaper clones of common boards, but also for some WD80x3 boards. The second problem is that the kernel will not auto-probe for more than one board at the moment. This is a feature, because it is assumed you want to have control about which board is assigned which interface.

If you are using more than one board, or if the autoprobe should fail to detect your board, you have to tell the kernel explicitly about the card's base address and name.

In Net-3, you have can use two different schemes to accomplish this. One way is to change or add information in the *drivers/net/Space.c* file in the kernel source code that contains all information about drivers. This is recommended only if you are familiar with the networking code. A much better way is to provide the kernel with this information at boot time. If you use *lilo* to boot your system, you can pass parameters to the kernel by specifying them through the *append* option in *lilo.conf*. To inform the kernel about an Ethernet device, you can pass the following parameter:

`ether=`*irq*, *base_addr*, *param1*, *param2*, *name*

The first four parameters are numerical, while the last is the device name. All numerical values are optional; if they are omitted or set to zero, the kernel will try to detect the value by probing for it, or use a default value.

The first parameter sets the IRQ assigned to the device. By default, the kernel will try to auto-detect the device's IRQ channel. The 3c503 driver has a special feature that selects a free IRQ from the list 5, 9, 3, 4, and configures the board to use this line.

The *base_addr* parameter gives the I/O base address of the board; a value of zero tells the kernel to probe the addresses listed above.

The remaining two parameters may be used differently by different drivers. For shared-memory boards such as the WD80x3, they specify start and end addresses of the shared memory area. Other cards commonly use *param1* to set the level of debugging information that is being displayed. Values of 1 through 7 denote increasing levels of verbosity, while 8 turns them off altogether; 0 denotes the default. The 3c503 driver uses *param2* to select the internal transceiver (default) or an external transceiver (a value of 1). The former uses the board's BNC connector; the latter uses its AUI port.

If you have two Ethernet boards, you can have Linux autodetect one board, and pass the second board's parameters with *lilo*. However, you must make sure the driver doesn't accidentally find the second board first, else the other one won't be registered at all. You do this by passing *lilo* a `reserve` option, which explicitly tells the kernel to avoid probing the I/O space taken up by the second board.

For instance, to make Linux install a second Ethernet board at `0x300` as *eth1*, you would pass the following parameters to the kernel:

```
reserve=0x300,32 ether=0,0x300,eth1
```

The *reserve* option makes sure no driver accesses the board's I/O space when probing for some device. You may also use the kernel parameters to override autoprobing for *eth0*:

```
reserve=0x340,32 ether=0,0x340,eth0
```

To turn off autoprobing altogether, you can specify a *base_addr* argument of -1:

```
ether=0,-1,eth0
```

3.5 The PLIP Driver

PLIP stands for *Parallel Line IP* and is a cheap way to network when you want to connect only two machines. It uses a parallel port and a special cable, achieving speeds of 10kBps to 20kBps.

PLIP was originally developed by Crynwr, Inc. Its design is rather ingenuous (or, if you prefer, hackish): for a long time, the parallel ports on PCs used to be only uni-directional printer ports; that is, the eight data lines could only be used to send from the PC to the peripheral device, but not the other way round. PLIP works around this by using the port's five status line for input, which limits it to transferring all data as nibbles (half bytes) only. This mode of operation is called mode zero PLIP. Today, these uni-directional ports don't seem to be used much anymore. Therefore, there is also a PLIP extension called mode 1 that uses the full 8 bit interface.

Currently, Linux only supports mode 0. Unlike earlier versions of the PLIP code, it now attempts to be compatible with the PLIP implementations from Crynwr, as well as the PLIP driver in NCSA *telnet*.[5] To connect two machines using PLIP, you need a special cable sold at some shops as "Null Printer" or "Turbo Laplink" cable. You can, however, make one yourself fairly easily. Appendix A shows you how.

The PLIP driver for Linux is the work of almost countless persons. It is currently maintained by Niibe Yutaka. If compiled into the kernel, it sets up a network interface for each of the possible printer ports, with *plip0* corresponding to parallel port *lp0*, *plip1* corresponding to *lp1*, etc. The mapping of interface to ports is currently this:

Interface	I/O Port	IRQ
plip0	0x3BC	7
plip1	0x378	7
plip2	0x278	5

If you have configured your printer port in a different way, you have to change these values in *drivers/net/Space.c* in the Linux kernel source, and build a new kernel.

This mapping does not mean, however, that you cannot use these parallel ports as usual. They are accessed by the PLIP driver only when the corresponding interface is configured *up*.

3.6 The SLIP and PPP Drivers

SLIP (Serial Line IP), and PPP (Point-to-Point Protocol) are a widely used protocol for sending IP packets over a serial link. A number of institutions offer dialup SLIP and PPP access to machines that are on the Internet, thus providing IP connectivity to private persons (something that's otherwise hardly affordable).

To run SLIP or PPP, no hardware modifications are necessary; you can use any serial port. Since serial port configuration is not specific to TCP/IP networking, a separate chapter has been devoted to this. Please refer to chapter 4 for more information.

---

[5] NCSA *telnet* is a popular program for DOS that runs TCP/IP over Ethernet or PLIP, and supports *telnet* and FTP.

CHAPTER 4

Setting up the Serial Hardware

There are rumors that there are some people out there in netland who only own one PC and don't have the money to spend on a T1 Internet link. To get their daily dose of news and mail nevertheless, they are said to rely on SLIP links, UUCP networks, and bulletin board systems (BBS's) that utilize public telephone networks.

This chapter is intended to help all those people who rely on modems to maintain their link. However, there are many details that this chapter cannot go into, for instance how to configure your modem for di-alin. All these topics will be covered in the upcoming Serial HOWTO by Greg Hankins,[1] to be posted to **comp.os.linux.announce** on a regular basis.

4.1 Communication Software for Modem Links

There are a number of communication packages available for Linux. Many of them are *terminal programs* which allow a user to dial into another computer as if she was sitting in front of a simple terminal. The traditional terminal program for Unices is *kermit*. It is, however, somewhat Spartan. There are more comfortable programs available that support a dictionary of telephone numers, script languages for calling and logging into remote computer systems, etc. One of them is *minicom*, which is close to some terminal programs former DOS users might be accustomed to. There are also X-based communications packages, e.g. *seyon*.

Also, a number of Linux-based BBS packages are available for people that want to run a bulletin board system. Some of these packages can be found at **sunsite.unc.edu** in */pub/Linux/system/Network*.

Apart from terminal programs, there is also software that uses a serial link non-interactively to transport data to or from your computer. The advantage of this technique is that it takes much less time to download a few dozen kilobytes automatically, than it might take you to read your mail on-line in some mailbox and browse a bulletin board for interesting articles. On the other hand, this requires more disk storage because of the loads of useless information you usually get.

The epitome of this sort of communications software is UUCP. It is a program suite that copies files from one host to another, executes programs on a remote host, etc. It is frequently used to transport mail or news in private networks. Ian Taylor's UUCP package, which also runs under Linux, is described in the following chapter. Other non-interactive communication software is, for example, used throughout Fidonet. Ports of Fidonet applications like *ifmail* are also available.

SLIP, the serial line Internet protocol, is somewhat inbetween, allowing both interactive and non-interactive use. Many people use SLIP to dial up their campus network or some other sort of public SLIP server to run FTP sessions, etc. SLIP may however also be used over permanent or semi-permanent connections for LAN-to-LAN coupling, although this is really only interesting with ISDN.

[1] To be reached at **gregh@cc.gatech.edu**.

4.2 Introduction to Serial Devices

The devices a UNIX kernel provides for accessing serial devices are typically called *ttys*. This is an abbreviation for *Teletype*™, which used to be one of the major manufacturers of terminals in the early days of Unix. The term is used nowadays for any character-based data terminal. Throughout this chapter, we will use the term exclusively to refer to kernel devices.

Linux distinguishes three classes of ttys: (virtual) consoles, pseudo-terminals (similar to a two-way pipe, used by application such as X11), and serial devices. The latter are also counted as ttys, because they permit interactive sessions over a serial connection; be it from a hard-wired terminal or a remote computer over a telephone line.

Ttys have a number of configurable parameters which can be set using the *ioctl(2)* system call. Many of them apply only to serial devices, since they need a great deal more flexibility to handle varying types of connections.

Among the most prominent line parameters are the line speed and parity. But there are also flags for the conversion between upper and lower case characters, of carriage return into line feed, etc. The tty driver may also support various *line disciplines* which make the device driver behave completely different. For example, the SLIP driver for Linux is implemented by means of a special line discipline.

There is a bit of ambiguity about how to measure a line's speed. The correct the term is *Bit rate*, which is related to the line's transfer speed measured in bits per second (or bps for short). Sometimes, you hear people refer to it as the *Baud rate*, which is not quite correct. These two terms are, however, not interchangeable. The Baud rate refers to a physical characteristic of some serial device, namely the clock rate at which pulses are transmitted. The bit rate rather denotes a current state of an existing serial connection between two points, namely the average number of bits transferred per second. It is important to know that these two values are usually different, as most devices encode more than one bit per electrical pulse.

4.3 Accessing Serial Devices

Like all devices in a UNIX system, serial ports are accessed through device special files, located in the */dev* directory. There are two varieties of device files related to serial drivers, and for each port, there is one device file from each of them. Depending on the file it is accessed by, the device will behave differently.

The first variety is used whenever the port is used for dialing in; it has a major number of 4, and the files are named *ttyS0*, *ttyS1*, etc. The second variety is used when dialing out through a port; the files are called *cua0*, etc, and have a major number of 5.

Minor numbers are identical for both types. If you have your modem on one of the ports *COM1* through *COM4*, its minor number will be the *COM* port number plus 63. If your setup is different from that, for example when using a board supporting multiple serial lines, please refer to the Serial Howto.

Assume your modem is on *COM2*. Thus its minor number will be 65, and its major number will be 5 for dialing out. There should be a device *cua1* which has these numbers. List the serial ttys in the */dev* directory. Columns 5 and 6 should show major and minor numbers, respectively:

```
$ ls -l /dev/cua*
crw-rw-rw-   1 root     root         5,  64 Nov 30 19:31 /dev/cua0
crw-rw-rw-   1 root     root         5,  65 Nov 30 22:08 /dev/cua1
crw-rw-rw-   1 root     root         5,  66 Oct 28 11:56 /dev/cua2
crw-rw-rw-   1 root     root         5,  67 Mar 19  1992 /dev/cua3
```

If there is no such device, you will have to create one: become super-user and type

```
# mknod -m 666 /dev/cua1 c 5 65
# chown root.root /dev/cua1
```

Some people suggest making */dev/modem* a symbolic link to your modem device, so that casual users don't have to remember the somewhat unintuitive *cua1*. However, you cannot use *modem* in one program, and the real device file name in another. This is because these programs use so-called *lock files* to signal that the device is used. By convention, the lock file name for *cua1*, for instance, is *LCK..cua1*. Using different device files for the same port means that programs will fail to recognize each other's lock files, and will both use the device at the same time. As a result, both applications will not work at all.

4.4 Serial Hardware

Linux currently supports a wide variety of serial boards which use the RS-232 standard. RS-232 is currently the most common standard for serial communcications in the PC world. It uses a number of circuits for transmitting single bits as well as for synchronization. Additional lines may be used for signaling the presence of a carrier (used by modems), and handshake.

Although hardware handshake is optional, it is very useful. It allows either of the two stations to signal whether it is ready to receive more data, or if the other station should pause until the receiver is done processing the incoming data. The lines used for this are called "Clear to Send" (CTS) and "Ready to Send" (RTS), respectively, which accounts for the colloquial name of hardware handshake, namely "RTS/CTS".

In PCs, the RS-232 interface is usually driven by a UART chip derived from the National Semiconductor 16450 chip, or a newer version thereof, the NSC 16550A[2]. Some brands (most notably internal modems equipped with the Rockwell chipset) also use completely different chips that have been programmed to behave as if they were 16550's.

The main difference between 16450's and 16550's that the latter have a FIFO buffer of 16 Bytes, while the former only have a 1-Byte buffer. This makes 16450's suitable for speeds up to 9600 Baud, while higher speeds require a 16550-compatible chip. Besides these chips, Linux also supports the 8250 chip, which was the original UART for the PC-AT.

In the default configuration, the kernel checks the four standard serial ports *COM1* through *COM4*. These will be assigned device minor numbers 64 through 67, as described above.

If you want to configure your serial ports properly, you should install Ted Tso's *setserial* command along with the *rc.serial* script. This script should be invoked from */etc/rc* at system boot time. It uses *setserial* to configure the kernel serial devices. A typical *rc.serial* script looks like this:

```
# /etc/rc.serial - serial line configuration script.
#
# Do wild interrupt detection
/sbin/setserial -W /dev/cua*

# Configure serial devices
/sbin/setserial /dev/cua0 auto_irq skip_test autoconfig
/sbin/setserial /dev/cua1 auto_irq skip_test autoconfig
/sbin/setserial /dev/cua2 auto_irq skip_test autoconfig
/sbin/setserial /dev/cua3 auto_irq skip_test autoconfig

# Display serial device configuration
/sbin/setserial -bg /dev/cua*
```

Please refer to the documentation that comes along with *setserial* for an explanation of the parameters.

If your serial card is not detected, or the *setserial -bg* command shows an incorrect setting, you will have to force the configuration by explicitly supplying the correct values. Users with internal modems equipped with the Rockwell chipset are reported to experience this problem. If, for example, the UART chip is reported to be a NSC 16450, while in fact it is NSC 16550-compatible, you have to change the configuration command for the offending port to

```
/sbin/setserial /dev/cua1 auto_irq skip_test autoconfig uart 16550
```

Similar options exist to force *COM* port, base address, and IRQ setting. Please refer to the *setserial(8)* manual page.

[2] There was also a NSC 16550, but it's FIFO never really worked.

If your modem supports hardware handshake, you should make sure to enable it. Surprising as it is, most communication programs do not attempt to enable this by default; you have to set it manually instead. This is best performed in the *rc.serial* script, using the *stty* command:

```
$ stty crtscts < /dev/cua1
```

To check if hardware handshake is in effect, use

```
$ stty -a < /dev/cua1
```

This gives you the status of all flags for that device; a flag shown with a preceding minus as in `-crtscts` means that the flag has been turned off.

CHAPTER 5

Configuring TCP/IP Networking

In this chapter, we will go through all the steps necessary to setting up TCP/IP networking on your machine. Starting with the assignment of IP addresses, we will slowly work our way through the configuration of TCP/IP network interfaces, and introduce a few tools that come quite handy when hunting down problems with your network installation.

Most of the tasks covered in this chapter you will generally have to do only once. Afterwards, you have to touch most configuration files only when adding a new system to your network, or when you reconfigure your system entirely. Some of the commands used to configure TCP/IP, however, have to be executed each time the system is booted. This is usually done by invoking them from the system */etc/rc* scripts.

Commonly, the network-specific part of this procedure is contained in a script called *rc.net* or *rc.inet*. Sometimes, you will also see two scripts named *rc.inet1* and *rc.inet2*, where the former initializes the kernel part of networking, while the latter starts basic networking services and applications. Throughout the following, I will adhere to the latter concept.

Below, I will discuss the actions performed by *rc.inet1*, while applications will be covered in later chapters. After finishing this chapter, you should have established a sequence of commands that properly configure TCP/IP networking on your computer. You should then replace any sample commands in *rc.inet1* with your commands, make sure *rc.inet1* is executed at startup time, and reboot your machine. The networking *rc* scripts that come along with your favorite Linux distribution should give you a good example.

5.1 Setting up the *proc* Filesystem

Some of the configuration tools of the Net-2 release rely on the *proc* filesystem for communicating with the kernel. This is an interface that permits access to kernel run-time information through a filesystem-like mechanism. When mounted, you can list its files like any other filesystem, or display their contents. Typical items include the *loadavg* file that contains the system load average, or *meminfo*, which shows current core memory and swap usage.

To this, the networking code adds the *net* directory. It contains a number of files that show things like the kernel ARP tables, the state of TCP connections, and the routing tables. Most network administration tools get their information from these files.

The *proc* filesystem (or *procfs* as it is also known) is usually mounted on */proc* at system boot time. The best method is to add the following line to */etc/fstab*:

```
# procfs mont point:
none /proc proc defaults
```

and execute "`mount /proc`" from your */etc/rc* script.

The *procfs* is nowadays configured into most kernels by default. If the *procfs* is not in your kernel, you will get a message like "`mount: fs type procfs not supported by kernel`". You will then have to recompile the kernel and answer "yes" when asked for *procfs* support.

5.2 Installing the Binaries

If you are using one of the pre-packaged Linux distributions, it will most probably contain the major networking applications and utilities along with a coherent set of sample files. The only case where you might have to obtain and install new utilities is when you install a new kernel release. As they occasionally involve changes in the kernel networking layer, you will need to update the basic configuration tools. This at least involves recompiling, but sometimes you may also be required to obtain the latest set of binaries. These are usually distributed along with the kernel, packaged in an archive called *net-XXX.tar.gz*, where *XXX* is the version number. The release matching Linux 1.0 is 0.32b, the latest kernel as of this writing (1.1.12 and later) require 0.32d.

If you want to compile and install the standard TCP/IP network applications yourself, you can obtain the sources from most Linux FTP servers. These are more or less heavily patched versions of programs from Net-BSD or other sources. Other applications, such as *Xmosaic*, *xarchie*, or Gopher and IRC clients must be obtained separately. Most of them compile out of the box if you follow the instructions.

The official FTP site for Net-3 is **sunacm.swan.ac.uk**, mirrored by **sunsite.unc.edu** below *system/Network/sunacm*. The latest Net-2e patch kit and binaries are available from **ftp.aris.com**. Matthias Urlichs' BSD-derived networking code can be gotten from **ftp.ira.uka.de** in */pub/system/linux/netbsd*.

5.3 Another Example

For the remainder of this book, let me introduce a new example that is less complex than Groucho Marx University, and may be closer to the tasks you will actually encounter. Consider the Virtual Brewery, a small company that brews, as the name indicates, virtual beer. To manage their business more efficiently, the virtual brewers want to network their computers, which all happen to be PCs running a bright and shiny Linux 1.0.

On the same floor, just across the hall, there's the Virtual Winery, who work closely with the brewery. They run an Ethernet of their own. Quite naturally, the two companies want to link their networks once they are operational. As a first step, they want to set up a gateway host that forwards datagrams between the two subnets. Later, they also want to have a UUCP link to the outside world, through which they exchange mail and news. In the long run, the also want to set up a SLIP connection to connect to the Internet occasionally.

5.4 Setting the Hostname

Most, if not all, network applications rely on the local host's name having been set to some reasonable value. This is usually done during the boot procedure by executing the *hostname* command. To set the hostname to *name*, it is invoked as

```
# hostname name
```

It is common practice to use the unqualified hostname without any domain name for this. For instance, hosts at the Virtual Brewery might be called **vale.vbrew.com**, **vlager.vbrew.com**, etc. These are their official, fully qualified domain names. Their local hostnames would be only the first component of the name, such as **vale**. However, as the local hostname is frequently used to look up the host's IP address, you have to make sure that the resolver library is able to look up the host's IP address. This usually means that you have to enter the name in */etc/hosts* (see below).

Some people suggest to use the *domainname* command to set the kernel's idea of a domain name to the remaining part of the FQDN. In this way you could combine the output from *hostname* and *domainname* to get the FQDN again. However, this is at best only half correct. *domainname* is generally used to set the host's NIS domain, which may be entirely different from the DNS domain your host belongs to. NIS is covered in chapter 10.

5.5 Assigning IP Addresses

If you configure the networking software on your host for standalone operation (for instance, to be able to run the INN netnews software), you can safely skip this section, because you will need an IP address just for the loopback interface, which is always **127.0.0.1**.

Things are a little more complicated with real networks like Ethernets. If you want to connect your host to an existing network, you have to ask its administrators to give you an IP address on this network. When setting up the network all by yourself, you have to assign IP addresses yourself as described below.

Hosts within a local network should usually share addresses from the same logical IP network. Hence you have to assign an IP network address. If you have several physical networks, you either have to assign them different network numbers, or use subnetting to split your IP address range into several subnetworks.

If your network is not connected to the Internet, you are free to choose any (legal) network address. You only have to make sure to choose one from classes A, B, or C, else things will most likely not work properly. However, if you intend to get on the Internet in the near future, you should obtain an official IP address *now*. The best way to proceed is to ask your network service provider to help you. If you want to obtain a network number just in case you might get on the Internet someday, request a Network Address Application Form from **hostmaster@internic.net**.

To operate several Ethernets (or other networks, once a driver is available), you have to split your network into subnets. Note that subnetting is required only if you have more than one *broadcast network*; point-to-point links don't count. For instance, if you have one Ethernet, and one or more SLIP links to the outside world, you don't need to subnet your network. The reason for this will be explained in chapter 7.

As an example, the brewery's network manager applies to the NIC for a class B network number, and is given **191.72.0.0**. To accomodate the two Ethernets, she decides to use eight bits of the host part as additional subnet bits. This leaves another eight bits for the host part, allowing for 254 hosts on each of the subnets. She then assigns subnet number 1 to the brewery, and gives the winery number 2. Their respective network addresses are thus **191.72.1.0** and **191.72.2.0**. The subnet mask is **255.255.255.0**.

vlager, which is the gateway between the two networks, is assigned a host number of 1 on both of them, which gives it the IP addresses **191.72.1.1** and **191.72.2.1**, respectively. Figure 5.1 shows the two subnets, and the gateway.

Note that in this example I am using a class B network to keep things simple; a class C network would be more realistic. With the new networking code, subnetting is not limited to byte boundaries, so even a class C network may be split into several subnets. For instance, you could use 2 bits of the host part for the netmask, giving you four possible subnets with 64 hosts on each.[1]

5.6 Writing *hosts* and *networks* Files

After you have subnetted your network, you should prepare for some simple sort of hostname resolution using the */etc/hosts* file. If you are not going to use DNS or NIS for address resolution, you have to put all hosts in the *hosts* file.

Even if you want to run DNS or NIS during normal operation, you want to have some subset of all hostnames in */etc/hosts* nevertheless. For one, you want to have some sort of name resolution even when no network interfaces are running, for example during boot time. This is not only a matter of convenience, but also allows you to use symbolic hostnames in your *rc.inet* scripts. Thus, when changing IP addresses, you only have to copy an updated *hosts* file to all machines and reboot, rather than having to edit a large number of *rc* files separately. Usually, you will put all local hostnames and addresses in *hosts*, adding those of any gateways and NIS servers if used.[2]

Also, during intial testing, you should make sure your resolver only uses information from the *hosts* file. Your DNS or NIS software may come with sample files that may produce strange results when being used. To make all applications use */etc/hosts* exclusively when looking up the IP address of a host, you have to edit

[1] The last number on each subnet is reserved as the broadcast address, so it's in fact 63 hosts per subnet.

[2] You will need the address of any NIS servers only if you use Peter Eriksson's NYS. Other NIS implementations locate their servers at run-time only by using *ypbind*.

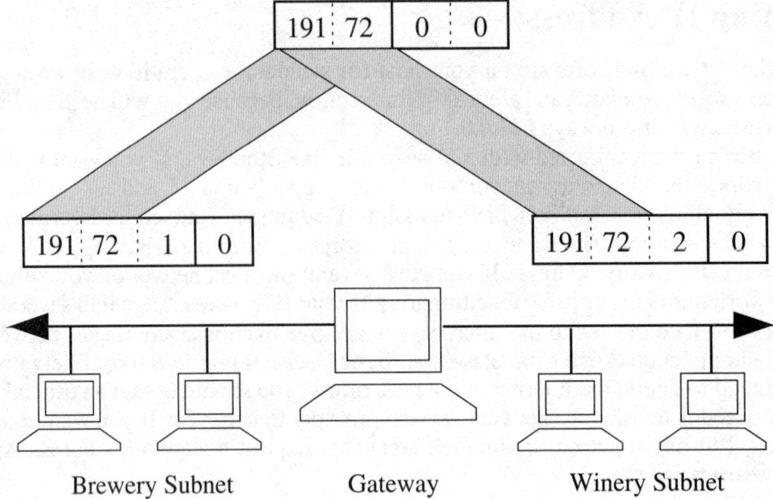

Figure 5.1: Virtual Brewery and Virtual Winery – the two subnets.

the */etc/host.conf* file. Comment out any lines that begin with the keyword *order* by preceding them with a hash sign, and insert the line

```
order hosts
```

The configuration of the resolver library will be covered in detail in chapter 6.

The *hosts* file contains one entry per line, consisting of an IP address, a hostname, and an optional list of aliases for the hostname. The fields are separated by spaces or tabs, and the address field must begin in column one. Anything following a hash sign (#) is regarded as a comment and is ignored.

Hostnames can be either fully qualified, or relative to the local domain. For **vale**, you would usually enter the the fully qualified name, **vale.vbrew.com**, and **vale** by itself in the *hosts* file, so that it is known by both its official name and the shorter local name.

This is an example how a *hosts* file at the Virtual Brewery might look. Two special names are included, **vlager-if1** and **vlager-if2** that give the addresses for both interfaces used on **vlager**.

```
#
# Hosts file for Virtual Brewery/Virtual Winery
#
# IP            local         fully qualified domain name
#
127.0.0.1       localhost
#
191.72.1.1      vlager        vlager.vbrew.com
191.72.1.1      vlager-if1
191.72.1.2      vstout        vstout.vbrew.com
191.72.1.3      vale          vale.vbrew.com
#
191.72.2.1      vlager-if2
191.72.2.2      vbeaujolais   vbeaujolais.vbrew.com
191.72.2.3      vbardolino    vbardolino.vbrew.com
191.72.2.4      vchianti      vchianti.vbrew.com
```

Just as with a host's IP address, you sometimes would like to use a symbolic name for network numbers, too. Therefore, the *hosts* file has a companion called */etc/networks* that maps network names to network numbers and vice versa. At the Virtual Brewery, we might install a *networks* file like this:[3]

```
# /etc/networks for the Virtual Brewery
brew-net        191.72.1.0
wine-net        191.72.2.0
```

5.7 Interface Configuration for IP

After setting up your hardware as explained in the previous chapter, you have to make these devices known to the kernel networking software. A couple of commands are used to configure the network interfaces, and initialize the routing table. These tasks are usually performed from the *rc.inet1* script each time the system is booted. The basic tools for this are called *ifconfig* (where "if" stands for interface), and *route*.

ifconfig is used to make an interface accessible to the kernel networking layer. This involves the assignment of an IP address and other parameters, and activating the interface, also known as "taking up." Being active here means that the kernel will send and receive IP datagrams through the interface. The simplest way to invoking it is

```
ifconfig interface ip-address
```

which assigns *ip-address* to *interface* and activates it. All other parameters are set to default values. For instance, the default subnet mask is derived from the network class of the IP address, such as **255.255.0.0** for a class B address. *ifconfig* is described in detail at the end of this chapter.

route allows you to add or remove routes from the kernel routing table. It can be invoked as

```
route [add|del] target
```

where the add and del arguments determine whether to add or delete the route to *target*.

5.7.1 The Loopback Interface

The very first interface to be activated is the loopback interface:

```
# ifconfig lo 127.0.0.1
```

Occasionally, you will also see the dummy hostname **localhost** being used instead of the IP address. *ifconfig* will look up the name in the *hosts* file where an entry should declare it as the hostname for **127.0.0.1**:

```
# Sample /etc/hosts entry for localhost
localhost       127.0.0.1
```

To view the configuration of an interface, you invoke *ifconfig* giving it the interface name as argument:

```
$ ifconfig lo
lo        Link encap Local Loopback
          inet addr 127.0.0.1  Bcast [NONE SET]  Mask 255.0.0.0
          UP BROADCAST LOOPBACK RUNNING  MTU 2000  Metric 1
          RX packets 0 errors 0 dropped 0 overrun 0
          TX packets 0 errors 0 dropped 0 overrun 0
```

As you can see, the loopback interface has been assigned a netmask of **255.0.0.0**, since **127.0.0.1** is a class A address. As you can see, the interface doesn't have a broadcast address set, which isn't normally very useful for the loopback anyway. However, if you run the *rwhod* daemon on your host, you may have to set the loopback device's broadcast address in order for *rwho* to function properly. Setting the broadcast is explained in section "All About *ifconfig*" below.

Now, you can almost start playing with your mini-"network." What is still missing is an entry in the routing table that tells IP that it may use this interface as route to destination **127.0.0.1**. This is accomplished by typing

[3]Note that names in *networks* must not collide with hostnames from the *hosts* file, else some programs may produce strange results.

```
# route add 127.0.0.1
```

Again, you can use **localhost** instead of the IP address.

Next, you should check that everything works fine, for example by using *ping*. *ping* is the networking equivalent of a sonar device[4] and is used to verify that a given address is actually reachable, and to measure the delay that occurs when sending a datagram to it and back again. The time required for this is often referred to as the round-trip time.

```
# ping localhost
PING localhost (127.0.0.1): 56 data bytes
64 bytes from 127.0.0.1: icmp_seq=0 ttl=32 time=1 ms
64 bytes from 127.0.0.1: icmp_seq=1 ttl=32 time=0 ms
64 bytes from 127.0.0.1: icmp_seq=2 ttl=32 time=0 ms
^C

--- localhost ping statistics ---
3 packets transmitted, 3 packets received, 0% packet loss
round-trip min/avg/max = 0/0/1 ms
```

When invoking *ping* as shown here, it will go on emitting packets forever unless interrupted by the user. The `^C` above marks the place where we pressed Ctrl-C.

The above example shows that packets for **127.0.0.1** are properly delivered and a reply is returned to *ping* almost instantaneously. This shows you have succeeded in setting up your first network interface.

If the output you get from *ping* does not resemble that shown above, you are in trouble. Check any error if they indicate some file hasn't been installed properly. Check that the *ifconfig* and *route* binaries you use are compatible with the kernel release you run, and, above all, that the kernel has been compiled with networking enabled (you see this from the presence of the */proc/net* directory). If you get an error message saying "Network unreachable," then you probably have got the *route* command wrong. Make sure you use the same address as you gave to *ifconfig*.

The steps described above are enough to use networking applications on a standalone host. After adding the above lines to *rc.inet1* and making sure both *rc.inet* scripts are executed from */etc/rc*, you may reboot your machine and try out various applications. For instance, "*telnet localhost*" should establish a *telnet* connection to your host, giving you a login prompt.

However, the loopback interface is useful not only as an example in networking books, or as a testbed during development, but is actually used by some applications during normal operation.[5] Therefore, you always have to configure it, regardless of whether your machine is attached to a network or not.

5.7.2 Ethernet Interfaces

Configuring an Ethernet interface goes pretty much the same as with the loopback interface, it just requires a few more parameters when you are using subnetting.

At the Virtual Brewery, we have subnetted the IP network, which was originally a class B network, into class C subnetworks. To make the interface recognize this, the *ifconfig* incantation would look like this:

```
# ifconfig eth0 vstout netmask 255.255.255.0
```

This assigns the *eth0* interface the IP address of **vstout (191.72.1.2)**. If we had omitted the netmask, *ifconfig* would have deduced the the netmask from the IP network class, which would have resulted in a netmask of **255.255.0.0**. Now a quick check shows:

```
# ifconfig eth0
eth0      Link encap 10Mps Ethernet HWaddr  00:00:C0:90:B3:42
          inet addr 191.72.1.2 Bcast 191.72.1.255 Mask 255.255.255.0
          UP BROADCAST RUNNING  MTU 1500  Metric 1
          RX packets 0 errors 0 dropped 0 overrun 0
          TX packets 0 errors 0 dropped 0 overrun 0
```

[4] Anyone remember Pink Floyd's "Echoes"?

[5] For instance, all applications based on RPC use the loopback interface to register themselves with the *portmapper* daemon at startup.

You can see that *ifconfig* automatically set the broadcast address (the Bcast field above) to the usual value, which is the hosts network number with the host bits all set. Also, the message transfer unit (the maximum size of Ethernet frames the kernel will generate for this interface) has been set to the maximum value of 1500 bytes. All these values can be overidden with special options that will be described later.

Quite similar to the loopback case, you now have to install a routing entry that informs the kernel about the network that can be reached through *eth0*. For the Virtual Brewery, you would invoke *route* as

```
# route add -net 191.72.1.0
```

At first, this looks a little like magic, because it's not really clear how *route* detects which interface to route through. However, the trick is rather simple: the kernel checks all interfaces that have been configured so far and compares the destination address (**191.72.1.0** in this case) to the network part of the interface address (that is, the bitwise and of the interface address and the netmask). The only interface that matches is *eth0*.

Now, what's that -net option for? This is used because *route* can handle both routes to networks and routes to single hosts (as you have seen above with **localhost**). When being given an address in dotted quad notation, it attempts to guess whether it is a network or a hostname by looking at the host part bits. If the address' host part is zero, *route* assumes it denotes a network, otherwise it takes it as a host address. Therefore, *route* would think that **191.72.1.0** is a host address rather than a network number, because it cannot know that we use subnetting. We therefore have to tell it explicitly that it denotes a network, giving it the -net flag.

Of course, the above *route* command is a little tedious to type, and it's prone to spelling mistakes. A more convenient approach is to use the network names we have defined in */etc/networks* above. This makes the command much more readable; even the -net flag can now be omitted, because *route* now knows that **191.72.1.0** denotes a network.

```
# route add brew-net
```

Now that you've finished the basic configuration steps, we want to make sure your Ethernet interface is indeed running happily. Choose a host from your Ethernet, for instance **vlager**, and type

```
# ping vlager
PING vlager: 64 byte packets
64 bytes from 191.72.1.1: icmp_seq=0. time=11. ms
64 bytes from 191.72.1.1: icmp_seq=1. time=7. ms
64 bytes from 191.72.1.1: icmp_seq=2. time=12. ms
64 bytes from 191.72.1.1: icmp_seq=3. time=3. ms
^C

----vstout.vbrew.com PING Statistics----
4 packets transmitted, 4 packets received, 0% packet loss
round-trip (ms)  min/avg/max = 3/8/12
```

If you don't see any output similar to this, then something is broken, obviously. If you encounter unusual packet loss rates, this hints at a hardware problem, like bad or missing terminators, etc. If you don't receive any packets at all, you should check the interface configuration with *netstat*. The packet statistics displayed by *ifconfig* should tell you whether any packets have been sent out on the interface at all. If you have access to the remote host, too, you should go over to that machine and check the interface statistics, too. In this way, you can determine exactly where the packets got dropped. In addition, you should display the routing information with *route* to see if both hosts have the correct routing entry. *route* prints out the complete kernel routing table when invoked without any arguments (the -n option only makes it print addresses as dotted quad instead of using the hostname):

```
# route -n
Kernel routing table
Destination     Gateway          Genmask         Flags Metric Ref Use    Iface
127.0.0.1       *                255.255.255.255 UH    1      0      112 lo
191.72.1.0      *                255.255.255.0   U     1      0       10 eth0
```

The detailed meaning of these fields is explained below in section 5.9. The `Flag` column contains a list of flags set for each interface. `U` is always set for active interfaces, and `H` says the destination address denotes a host. If the `H` flag is set for a route that you meant to be a network route, then you have to specify the `-net` option with the *route* command. To check whether a route you have entered is used at all, check if the `Use` field in the second to last column increases between two invocations of *ping*.

5.7.3 Routing through a Gateway

In the previous section, I covered only the case of setting up a host on a single Ethernet. Quite frequently, however, one encounters networks connected to one another by gateways. These gateways may simply link two or more Ethernets, but may provide a link to the outside world, the Internet, as well. In order to use the service of a gateway, you have to provide additional routing information to the networking layer.

For instance, the Ethernets of the Virtual Brewery and the Virtual Winery are linked through such a gateway, namely the host **vlager**. Assuming that **vlager** has already been configured, we only have to add another entry to **vstout**'s routing table that tells the kernel it can reach all hosts on the Winery's network through **vlager**. The appropriate incantation of *route* is shown below; the `gw` keyword tells it that the next argument denotes a gateway.

```
# route add wine-net gw vlager
```

Of course, any host on the Winery network you wish to talk to must have a corresponding routing entry for the Brewery's network, otherwise you would only be able to send data from **vstout** to **vbardolino**, but any response returned by the latter would go into the great bit bucket.

This example describes only a gateway that switches packets between two isolated Ethernets. Now assume that **vlager** also has a connection to the Internet (say, through an additional SLIP link). Then we would want datagrams to *any* destination network other than the Brewery to be handed to **vlager**. This can be accomplished by making it the default gateway for **vstout**:

```
# route add default gw vlager
```

The network name **default** is a shorthand for **0.0.0.0**, which denotes the default route. You do not have to add this name to */etc/networks*, because it is built into *route*.

When you see high packet loss rates when *ping*ing a host behind one or more gateways, this may hint at a very congested network. Packet loss is not so much due to technical deficiencies as due to temporary excess loads on forwarding hosts, which makes them delay or even drop incoming datagrams.

5.7.4 Configuring a Gateway

Configuring a machine to switch packets between two Ethernets is pretty straightforward. Assume we're back at **vlager**, which is equipped with two Ethernet boards, each being connected to one of the two networks. All you have to do is configure both interfaces separately, giving them their respective IP address, and that's it.

It is quite useful to add information on the two interfaces to the *hosts* file in the way shown below, so we have handy names for them, too:

```
191.72.1.1      vlager      vlager.vbrew.com
191.72.1.1      vlager-if1
191.72.2.1      vlager-if2
```

The sequence of commands to set up the two interfaces is then:

```
# ifconfig eth0 vlager-if1
# ifconfig eth1 vlager-if2
# route add brew-net
# route add wine-net
```

5.7.5 The PLIP Interface

When using a PLIP link to connect two machines, things are a little different from what you have to do when using an Ethernet. The former are so-called *point-to-point* links, because they involve ony two hosts ("points"), as opposed to broadcast networks.

As an example, we consider the laptop computer of some employee at the Virtual Brewery that is connected to **vlager** via PLIP. The laptop itself is called **vlite**, and has only one parallel port. At boot time, this port will be registered as *plip1*. To activate the link, you have to configure the *plip1* interface using the following commands:[6]

```
# ifconfig plip1 vlite pointopoint vlager
# route add default gw vlager
```

The first command configures the interface, telling the kernel that this is a point-to-point link, with the remote side having the address of **vlager**. The second installs the default route, using **vlager** as gateway. On **vlager**, a similar *ifconfig* command is necessary to activate the link (a *route* invocation is not needed):

```
# ifconfig plip1 vlager pointopoint vlite
```

The interesting point is that the *plip1* interface on **vlager** does not have to have a separate IP address, but may also be given the address **191.72.1.1**.[7]

Now, we have configured routing from the laptop to the Brewery's network; what's still missing is a way to route from any of the Brewery's hosts to **vlite**. One particularly cumbersome way is to add a specific route to every host's routing table that names **vlager** as a gateway to **vlite**:

```
# route add vlite gw vlager
```

A much better option when faced with temporary routes is to use dynamic routing. One way to do so is to use *gated*, a routing daemon, which you would have to install on each host in the network in order to distribute routing information dynamically. The easiest way, however, is to use *proxy* ARP. With proxy ARP, **vlager** will respond to any ARP query for **vlite** by sending its own Ethernet address. The effect of this is that all packets for **vlite** will wind up at **vlager**, which then forwards them to the laptop. We will come back to proxy ARP in section 5.10 below.

Future Net-3 releases will contain a tool called *plipconfig* which will allow you to set the IRQ of the printer port to use. Later, this may even be replaced by a more general *ifconfig* command.

5.7.6 The SLIP and PPP Interface

Although SLIP and PPP links are only simple point-to-point links like PLIP connections, there is much more to be said about them. Usually, establishing a SLIP connection involves dialing up a remote site through your modem, and setting the serial line to SLIP mode. PPP is used in a similar fashion. The tools required for setting up a SLIP or PPP link will be described in chapters 7 and 8.

5.7.7 The Dummy Interface

The dummy interface is really a little exotic, but rather useful nevertheless. Its main benefit is with standalone hosts, and machines whose only IP network connection is a dial-up link. In fact, the latter are standalone hosts most of the time, too.

The dilemma with standalone hosts is that they only have a single network device active, the loopback device, which is usually assigned the address **127.0.0.1**. On some occasions, however, you need to send data to the 'official' IP address of the local host. For instance, consider the laptop **vlite**, that has been disconnected from any network for the duration of this example. An application on **vlite** may now want to send some data to another application on the same host. Looking up **vlite** in */etc/hosts* yields an IP address of **191.72.1.65**, so the application tries to send to this address. As the loopback interface is currently the only active interface

[6]Note that `pointopoint` is not a typo. It's really spelt like this.

[7]Just as a matter of caution, you should however configure a PLIP or SLIP link only after you have completely set up the routing table entries for your Ethernets. With some older kernels, your network route might otherwise end up pointing at the point-to-point link.

on the machine, the kernel has no idea that this address actually refers to itself! As a consequence, the kernel discards the datagram, and returns an error to the application.

This is where the dummy device steps in. It solves the dilemma by simply serving as the alter ego of the loopback interface. In the case of **vlite**, you would simply give it the address **191.72.1.65** and add a host route pointing to it. Every datagram for **191.72.1.65** would then be delivered locally. The proper invocation is:

```
# ifconfig dummy vlite
# route add vlite
```

5.8 All About *ifconfig*

There are a lot more parameters to *ifconfig* than we have described above. Its normal invocation is this:

```
ifconfig interface [[-net|-host] address [parameters]]
```

interface is the interface name, and *address* is the IP address to be assigned to the interface. This may either be an IP address in dotted quad notation, or a name *ifconfig* will look up in */etc/hosts* and */etc/networks*. The `-net` and `-host` options force *ifconfig* to treat the address as network number or host address, respectively.

If *ifconfig* is invoked with only the interface name, it displays that interface's configuration. When invoked without any parameters, it displays all interfaces you configured so far; an option of `-a` forces it to show the inactive ones as well. A sample invocation for the Ethernet interface *eth0* may look like this:

```
# ifconfig eth0
eth0      Link encap 10Mbps Ethernet  HWaddr 00:00:C0:90:B3:42
          inet addr 191.72.1.2 Bcast 191.72.1.255 Mask 255.255.255.0
          UP BROADCAST RUNNING  MTU 1500  Metric 0
          RX packets 3136 errors 217 dropped 7 overrun 26
          TX packets 1752 errors 25 dropped 0 overrun 0
```

The `MTU` and `Metric` fields show the current MTU and metric value for that interface. The metric value is traditionally used by some operating systems to compute the cost of a route. Linux doesn't use this value yet, but defines it for compatibility nevertheless.

The RX and TX lines show how many packets have been received or transmitted error free, how many errors occurred, how many packets were dropped, probably because of low memory, and how many were lost because of an overrun. Receiver overruns usually happen when packets come in faster than the kernel can service the last interrupt. The flag values printed by *ifconfig* correspond more or less to the names of its command line options; they will be explained below.

The following is a list of parameters recognized by *ifconfig* with the corresponding flag names are given in brackets. Options that simply turn on a feature also allow it to be turned off again by preceding the option name by a dash (-).

`up`
: This marks an interface "up", i.e. accessible to the IP layer. This option is implied when an *address* is given on the command line. It may also be used to re-eenable an interface that has been taken down temporarily using the `down` option.
(This option corresponds to the flags `UP RUNNING`.)

`down`
: This marks an interface "down", i.e. inaccessible to the IP layer. This effectively disables any IP traffic through the interface. Note that this does not delete all routing entries that use this interface automatically. If you take the interface down permanently, you should to delete these routing entries and supply alternative routes if possible.

`netmask` *mask*
: This assigns a subnet mask to be used by the interface. It may be given as either a 32-bit hexadecimal number preceded by 0x, or as a dotted quad of decimal numbers.

`pointopoint` *address*
: This option is used for point-to-point IP links that involve only two hosts. This option is needed to configure, for example, SLIP or PLIP interfaces.
(If a point-to-point address has been set, *ifconfig* displays the `POINTOPOINT` flag.)

`broadcast` *address* The broadcast address is usually made up from the network number by setting all bits of the host part. Some IP implementations use a different scheme; this option is there to adapt to these strange environments.

(If a broadcast address has been set, *ifconfig* displays the `BROADCAST` flag.)

`metric` *number* This option may be used to assign a metric value to the routing table entry created for the interface. This metric is used by the Routing Information Protocol (RIP) to build routing tables for the network.[8] The default metric used by *ifconfig* is a value of zero. If you don't run a RIP daemon, you don't need this option at all; if you do, you will rarely need to change the metric value.

`mtu` *bytes* This sets the Maximum Transmission Unit, which is the maximum number of octets the interface is able to handle in one transaction. For Ethernets, the MTU defaults to 1500; for SLIP interfaces, this is 296.

`arp` This is an option specific to broadcast networks such as Ethernets or packet radio. It enables the use of ARP, the Address Resolution Protocol, to detect the physical addresses of hosts attached to the network. For broadcast networks, is on by default.

(If ARP is disabled, *ifconfig* displays the flag `NOARP`.)

`-arp` Disables the use of ARP on this interface.

`promisc` Puts the interface in promiscuous mode. On a broadcast network, this makes the interface receive all packets, regardless of whether they were destined for another host or not. This allows an analysis of network traffic using packet filters and such, also called *Ethernet snooping*. Usually, this is a good technique of hunting down network problems that are otherwise hard to come by.

On the other hand, this allows attackers to skim the traffic of your network for passwords and do other nasty things. One protection against this type of attack is not to let anyone just plug in their computers in your Ethernet. Another option is to use secure authentication protocols, such as Kerberos, or the SRA login suite.[9]

(This option corresponds to the flag `PROMISC`.)

`-promisc` Turns off promiscuous mode.

`allmulti` Multicast addresses are some sort of broadcast to a group of hosts who don't necessarily have to be on the same subnet. Multicast addresses are not yet supported by the kernel.

(This option corresponds to the flag `ALLMULTI`.)

`-allmulti` Turns off multicast addresses.

5.9 Checking with *netstat*

Next, I will turn to a useful tool for checking your network configuration and activity. It is called *netstat* and is, in fact, rather a collection of several tools lumped together. We will discuss each of its functions in the following sections.

5.9.1 Displaying the Routing Table

When invoking *netstat* with the `-r` flag, it displays the kernel routing table in the way we've been doing this with *route* above. On **vstout**, it produces:

```
# netstat -nr
```

[8] RIP chooses the optimal route to a given host based on the "length" of the path. It is computed by summing up the individual metric values of each host-to-host link. By default, a hop has length 1, but this may be any positive integer less than 16. (A route length of 16 is equal to infinity. Such routes are considered unusable.) The `metric` parameter sets this hop cost, which is then broadcast by the routing daemon.

[9] SRA can be obtained from **ftp.tamu.edu** in */pub/sec/TAMU*.

```
Kernel routing table
Destination     Gateway         Genmask         Flags Metric Ref Use    Iface
127.0.0.1       *               255.255.255.255 UH    1      0       50 lo
191.72.1.0      *               255.255.255.0   U     1      0      478 eth0
191.72.2.0      191.72.1.1      255.255.255.0   UGN   1      0      250 eth0
```

The `-n` option makes *netstat* print addresses as dotted quad IP numbers rather than the symbolic host and network names. This is especially useful when you want to avoid address lookups over the network (e.g. to a DNS or NIS server).

The second column of *netstat*'s output shows the gateway the routing entry points to. If no gateway is used, an asterisk is printed instead. Column three shows the "generality" of the route. When given an IP address to find a suitable route for, the kernel goes through all routing table entries, taking the bitwise AND of the address and the genmask before comparing it to the target of the route.

The fourth column displays various flags that describe the route:

G — The route uses a gateway.

U — The interface to be used is up.

H — Only a single host can be reached through the route. For example, this is the case for the loopback entry **127.0.0.1**.

D — This is set if the table entry has been generated by an ICMP redirect message (see section 2.5).

M — This is set if the table entry was modified by an ICMP redirect message.

The `Ref` column of *netstat*'s output shows the number of references to this route, that is, how many other routes (e.g. through gateways) rely on the presence of this route. The last two columns show the number of times the routing entry has been used, and the interface that datagrams are passed to for delivery.

5.9.2 Displaying Interface Statistics

When invoked with the `-i` flag, *netstat* will display statistics for the network interfaces currently configured. If, in addition, the `-a` option is given, it will print *all* interfaces present in the kernel, not only those that have been configured currently. On **vstaout**, the output from *netstat* will look like this:

```
$ netstat -i
Kernel Interface table
Iface   MTU Met  RX-OK RX-ERR RX-DRP RX-OVR  TX-OK TX-ERR TX-DRP TX-OVR Flags
lo        0   0   3185      0      0      0   3185      0      0      0 BLRU
eth0   1500   0 972633     17     20    120 628711    217      0      0 BRU
```

The MTU and Met fields show the current MTU and metric value for that interface. The RX and TX columns show how many packets have been received or transmitted error free (RX-OK/TX-OK), damaged (RX-ERR/TX-ERR), how many were dropped (RX-DRP/TX-DRP), and how many were lost because of an overrun (RX-OVR/TX-OVR).

The last column shows the flags that have been set for this interface. These are one-character versions of the long flag names the are printed when you display the interface configuration with *ifconfig*.

B — A broadcast address has been set.

L — This interface is a loopback device

M — All packets are received (promiscuous mode).

N — Trailers are avoided.

O — ARP is turned off for this interface.

P — This is a point-to-point connection.

R — Interface is running.

U — Interface is up.

5.9.3 Displaying Connections

netstat supports a set of options to display active or passive sockets. The options -t, -u, -w, and -x show active TCP, UDP, RAW, or UNIX socket connections. If you provide the -a flag in addition, sockets that are waiting for a connection (i.e. listening) are displayed as well. This will give you a list of all servers that are currently running on your system.

Invoking *netstat -ta* on **vlager** produces

```
$ netstat -ta
Active Internet connections
Proto Recv-Q Send-Q Local Address      Foreign Address      (State)
tcp        0      0 *:domain           *:*                  LISTEN
tcp        0      0 *:time             *:*                  LISTEN
tcp        0      0 *:smtp             *:*                  LISTEN
tcp        0      0 vlager:smtp        vstout:1040          ESTABLISHED
tcp        0      0 *:telnet           *:*                  LISTEN
tcp        0      0 localhost:1046     vbardolino:telnet    ESTABLISHED
tcp        0      0 *:chargen          *:*                  LISTEN
tcp        0      0 *:daytime          *:*                  LISTEN
tcp        0      0 *:discard          *:*                  LISTEN
tcp        0      0 *:echo             *:*                  LISTEN
tcp        0      0 *:shell            *:*                  LISTEN
tcp        0      0 *:login            *:*                  LISTEN
```

This shows most servers simply waiting for an incoming connection. However, the fourth line shows an incoming SMTP connection from **vstout**, and the sixth line tells you there is an outgoing *telnet* connection to **vbardolino**.[10]

Using the -a flag all by itself will display all sockets from all families.

5.10 Checking the ARP Tables

On some occasions, it is useful to view or even alter the contents of the kernel's ARP tables, for example when you suspect a duplicate Internet address is the cause for some intermittent network problem. The *arp* tool was made for things like these. Its command line options are

```
arp [-v] [-t hwtype] -a [hostname]
arp [-v] [-t hwtype] -s hostname hwaddr
arp [-v] -d hostname [hostname...]
```

All *hostname* arguments may be either symbolic host names or IP addresses in dotted quad notation.

The first invocation displays the ARP entry for the IP address or host specified, or all hosts known if no *hostname* is given. For example, invoking *arp* on **vlager** may yield

```
# arp -a
IP address        HW type                      HW address
191.72.1.3        10Mbps Ethernet              00:00:C0:5A:42:C1
191.72.1.2        10Mbps Ethernet              00:00:C0:90:B3:42
191.72.2.4        10Mbps Ethernet              00:00:C0:04:69:AA
```

which shows the Ethernet addresses of **vlager**, **vstout** and **vale**.

Using the -t option you can limit the display to the hardware type specified. This may be *ether*, *ax25*, or *pronet*, standing for 10Mbps Ethernet, AMPR AX.25, and IEEE 802.5 token ring equipment, respectively.

The -s option is used to permanently add *hostname*'s Ethernet address to the ARP tables. The *hwaddr* argument specifies the hardware address, which is by default expected to be an Ethernet address, specified

[10] You can tell whether a connection is outgoing or not from the port numbers involved. The port number shown for the *calling* host will always be a simple integer, while on the host being called, a well-known service port will be in use, for which *netstat* uses the symbolic name found in */etc/services*.

as six hexadecimal bytes separated by colons. You may also set the hardware address for other types of hardware, too, using the `-t` option.

One problem which may require you to manually add an IP address to the ARP table is when for some reasons ARP queries for the remote host fail, for instance when its ARP driver is buggy or there is another host in the network that erroneously identifies itself with that host's IP address. Hard-wiring IP addresses in the ARP table is also a (very drastic) measure to protect yourself from hosts on your Ethernet that pose as someone else.

Invoking *arp* using the `-d` switch deletes all ARP entries relating to the given host. This may be used to force the interface to re-attempt to obtain the Ethernet address for the IP address in question. This is useful when a misconfigured system has broadcast wrong ARP information (of course, you have to reconfigure the broken host before).

The `-s` option may also be used to implement *proxy* ARP. This is a special technique where a host, say **gate**, acts as a gateway to another host named **fnord**, by pretending that both addresses refer to the same host, namely **gate**. It does so by publishing an ARP entry for **fnord** that points to its own Ethernet interface. Now when a host sends out an ARP query for **fnord**, **gate** will return a reply containing its own Ethernet address. The querying host will then send all datagrams to **gate**, which dutyfully forwards them to **fnord**.

These contortions may be necessary, for instance, when you want to access **fnord** from a DOS machine with a broken TCP implementation that doesn't understand routing too well. When you use proxy ARP, it will appear to the DOS machine as if **fnord** was on the local subnet, so it doesn't have to know about how to route through a gateway.

Another very useful application of proxy ARP is when one of your hosts acts as a gateway to some other host only temporarily, for instance through a dial-up link. In a previous example, we already encountered the laptop **vlite** which was connected to **vlager** through a PLIP link only from time to time. Of course, this will work only if the address of the host you want to provide proxy ARP for is on the same IP subnet as your gateway. For instance, **vstout** could proxy ARP for any host on the Brewery subnet (**191.72.1.0**), but never for a host on the Winery subnet (**191.72.2.0**).

The proper invocation to provide proxy ARP for **fnord** is given below; of course, the Ethernet address given must be that of **gate**.

```
# arp -s fnord 00:00:c0:a1:42:e0 pub
```

The proxy ARP entry may be removed again by invoking:

```
# arp -d fnord
```

5.11 The Future

Linux networking is still evolving. Major changes at the kernel layer will bring a very flexible configuration scheme that will allow you to configure the network devices at run time. For instance, the *ifconfig* command will take arguments that set the IRQ line and DMA channel.

Another change to come soon is the additional `mtu` flag to the *route* command which will set the Maximum Transmission Unit for a particular route. This route-specific MTU overrides the MTU specified for the interface. You will typically use this option for routes through a gateway, where the link between the gateway and the destination host requires a very low MTU. For instance, assume host **wanderer** is connected to **vlager** through a SLIP link. When sending data from **vstout** to **wanderer**, the networking layer on **wanderer** would would use packets of up to 1500 bytes, because packets are sent across the Ethernet. The SLIP link, on the other hand, is operated with an MTU of 296, so the network layer on **vlager** would have to break up the IP packets into smaller fragments that fit into 296 bytes. If instead, you would have configured the route on **vstout** to use a MTU of 296 right from the start, this relatively expensive fragmentation could be avoided:

```
# route add wanderer gw vlager mtu 296
```

Note that the `mtu` option also allows you to selectively undo the effects of the 'Subnets Are Local' Policy (SNARL). This policy is a kernel configuration option and is described in chapter 3.

Chapter 6

Name Service and Resolver Configuraton

As discussed in chapter 2, TCP/IP networking may rely on different schemes to convert names into addresses. The simplest way, which takes no advantage of the way the name space has been split up into zones is a host table stored in */etc/hosts*. This is useful only for small LANs that are run by one single administrator, and otherwise have no IP traffic with the outside world. The format of the *hosts* file has already been described in chapter 5.

Alternatively, you may use BIND – the Berkeley Internet Name Domain Service – for resolving host names to IP addresses. Configuring BIND may be a real chore, but once you've done it, changes in the network topology are easily made. On Linux, as on many other UNIXish systems, name service is provided through a program called *named*. At startup, it loads a set of master files into its cache, and waits for queries from remote or local user processes. There are different ways to set up BIND, and not all require you to run a name server on every host.

This chapter can do little more but give a rough sketch of how to operate a name server. If you plan to use BIND in an enviroment with more than just a small LAN and probably an Internet uplink, you should get a good book on BIND, for instance Cricket Liu's "DNS and BIND" (see [AlbitzLiu92]). For current information, you may also want to check the release notes contained in the BIND sources. There's also a newsgroup for DNS questions called **comp.protocols.tcp-ip.domains**.

6.1 The Resolver Library

When talking of "the resolver", we do not mean any special application, but rather refer to the *resolver library*, a collection of functions that can be found in the standard C library. The central routines are *gethostbyname(2)* and *gethostbyaddr(2)* which look up all IP addresses belonging to a host, and vice versa. They may be configured to simply look up the information in *hosts*, query a number of name servers, or use the *hosts* database of NIS (Network Information Service). Other applications, like *smail*, may include different drivers for any of these, and need special care.

6.1.1 The *host.conf* File

The central file that controls your resolver setup is *host.conf*. It resides in */etc* and tells the resolver which services to use, and in what order.

Options in *host.conf* must occur on separate lines. Fields may be separated by white space (spaces or tabs). A hash sign (#) introduces a comment that extends to the next newline.

The following options are available:

order — This determines the order in which the resolving services are tried. Valid options are *bind* for querying the name server, *hosts* for lookups in */etc/hosts*, and *nis* for NIS lookups. Any or all of them may be specified. The order in which they appear on the line detemines the order in which the respective services are tried.

multi Takes *on* or *off* as options. This detemines if a host in */etc/hosts* is allowed to have several IP addresses, which is usually referred to as being "multi-homed". This flag has no effect on DNS or NIS queries.

nospoof As explained in the previous chapter, DNS allows you to find the hostname belonging to an IP address by using the **in-addr.arpa** domain. Attempts by name servers to supply a false hostname are called "*spoofing*". To guard against this, the resolver may be configured to check if the original IP address is in fact associated with the hostname obtained. If not, the name is rejected and an error returned. This behavior is turned on by setting *nospoof on*.

alert This option takes *on* or *off* as arguments. If it is turned on, any spoof attempts (see above) will cause the resolver to log a message to the *syslog* facility.

trim This option takes a domain name as an argument, which will be removed from hostnames before lookup. This is useful for *hosts* entries, where you might only want to specify hostnames without local domain. A lookup of a host with the local domain name appended will have this removed, thus allowing the lookup in */etc/hosts* to succeed.

trim options accumulate, making it possible to consider your host as being local to several domains.

A sample file for **vlager** is shown below:

```
# /etc/host.conf
# We have named running, but no NIS (yet)
order   bind hosts
# Allow multiple addrs
multi   on
# Guard against spoof attempts
nospoof on
# Trim local domain (not really necessary).
trim    vbrew.com.
```

6.1.2 Resolver Environment Variables

The settings from *host.conf* may be overridden using a number of environment variables. These are

`RESOLV_HOST_CONF` This specifies a file to be read instead of */etc/host.conf*.

`RESOLV_SERV_ORDER` Overrides the *order* option given in *host.conf*. Services are given as *hosts*, *bind*, and *nis*, separated by a space, comma, colon, or semicolon.

`RESOLV_SPOOF_CHECK` Determines the measures taken against spoofing. It is completely disabled by *off*. The values *warn* and *warn off* enable spoof checking, but turn logging on and off, respectively. A value of * turns on spoof checks, but leaves the logging facility as defined in *host.conf*.

`RESOLV_MULTI` A value of *on* or *off* may be used to override the *multi* options from tt host.conf.

`RESOLV_OVERRIDE_TRIM_DOMAINS` This environment specifies a list of trim domains which override those given in *host.conf*.

`RESOLV_ADD_TRIM_DOMAINS` This environment specifies a list of trim domains which are added to those given in *host.conf*.

6.1.3 Configuring Name Server Lookups — *resolv.conf*

When configuring the resolver library to use the BIND name service for host lookups, you also have to tell it which name servers to use. There is a separate file for this, called *resolv.conf*. If this file does not exist or is empty, the resolver assumes the name server is on your local host.

If you run a name server on your local host, you have to set it up separately, as will be explained in the following section. If your are on a local network and have the opportunity to use an existing nameserver, this should always be preferred.

The most important option in *resolv.conf* is *nameserver*, which gives the IP address of a name server to use. If you specifiy several name servers by giving the *nameserver* option several times, they are tried in the order given. You should therefore put the most reliable server first. Currently, up to three name servers are supported.

If no *nameserver* option is given, the resolver attempts to connect to the name server on the local host.

Two other options, *domain* and *search* deal with default domains that are tacked onto a hostname if BIND fails to resolve it with the first query. The *search* option specifies a list of domain names to be tried. The list items are separated by spaces or tabs.

If no *search* option is given, a default search list is constructed from the local domain name by using the domain name itself, plus all parent domains up to the root. The local domain name may be given using the *domain* statement; if none is given, the resolver obtains it through the *getdomainname(2)* system call. If this sounds confusing to you, consider this sample *resolv.conf* file for the Virtual Brewery:

```
# /etc/resolv.conf
# Our domain
domain          vbrew.com
#
# We use vlager as central nameserver:
nameserver      191.72.1.1
```

When resolving the name **vale**, the resolver would look up **vale**, and failing this, **vale.vbrew.com**, and **vale.com**.

6.1.4 Resolver Robustness

If you are running a LAN inside a larger network, you definitely should use central name servers if they are available. The advantage of this is that these will develop rich caches, since all queries are forwarded to them. This scheme, however has a drawback: when a fire recently destroyed the backbone cable at our university, no more work was possible on our department's LAN, because the resolver couldn't reach any of the name servers anymore. There was no logging in on X terminals anymore, no printing, etc.

Although it is not very common for campus backbones to go down in flames, one might want to take precautions against cases like these.

One option is to set up a local name server that resolves hostnames from your local domain, and forwards all queries for other hostnames to the main servers. Of course, this is applicable only if you are running your own domain.

Alternatively, you can maintain a backup host table for your domain or LAN in */etc/hosts*. In */etc/host.conf* you would then include "*order bind hosts*" to make the resolver fall back to the hosts file if the central name server is down.

6.2 Running *named*

The program that provides domain name service on most UNIX machines is usually called *named* (pronounced *name-dee*). This is a server program originally developed for BSD providing name service to clients, and possibly to other name servers. The version currently used on most Linux installations seems to be BIND-4.8.3. The new version, BIND-4.9.3, is being Beta-tested at the moment, and should be available on Linux soon.

This section requires some understanding of the way the Domain Name System works. If the following discussion is all Greek to you, you may want to re-read chapter 2, which has some more information on the basics of DNS.

named is usually started at system boot time, and runs until the machine goes down again. It takes its information from a configuration file called */etc/named.boot*, and various files that contain data mapping domain names to addresses and the like. The latter are called *zone files*. The formats and semantics of these files will be explained in the following section.

To run *named*, simply enter

```
# /usr/sbin/named
```

at the prompt. *named* will come up, read the *named.boot* file and any zone files specified therein. It writes its process id to */var/run/named.pid* in ASCII, downloads any zone files from primary servers, if necessary, and starts listening on port 53 for DNS queries.[1]

6.2.1 The *named.boot* File

The *named.boot* file is generally very small and contains little else but pointers to master files containing zone information, and pointers to other name servers. Comments in the boot file start with a semicolon and extend to the next newline. Before we discuss the format of *named.boot* in more detail, we will take a look at the sample file for **vlager** given in figure 6.1.[2]

```
;
; /etc/named.boot file for vlager.vbrew.com
;
directory       /var/named
;
;               domain                    file
;-----------------------------------------------------
cache           .                         named.ca
primary         vbrew.com                 named.hosts
primary         0.0.127.in-addr.arpa      named.local
primary         72.191.in-addr.arpa       named.rev
```

Figure 6.1: The *named.boot* file for *vlager*.

The *cache* and *primary* commands shown in this example load information into *named*. This information is taken from the master files specified in the second argument. They contain textual representations of DNS resource records, which we will look at below.

In this example, we configured *named* as the primary name server for three domains, as indicated by the *primary* statements at the end of the file. The first of these lines, for instance, instructs *named* to act as a primary server for **vbrew.com**, taking the zone data from the file *named.hosts*. The *directory* keyword tells it that all zone files are located in */var/named*.

The *cache* entry is very special and should be present on virtually all machines running a name server. Its function is two-fold: it instructs *named* to enable its cache, and to load the *root name server hints* from the cache file specified (*named.ca* in our example). We will come back to the name server hints below.

Here's a list of the most important options you can use in *named.boot*:

directory This specifies a directory in which zone files reside. Names of files may be given relative to this directory. Several directories may be specified by repeatedly using *directory*. According to the Linux filesystem standard, this should be */var/named*.

primary This takes a *domain name* and a *file name* as an argument, declaring the local server authoritative for the named domain. As a primary server, *named* loads the zone information from the given master file.

Generally, there will always be at least one *primary* entry in every boot file, namely for reverse mapping of network **127.0.0.0**, which is the local loopback network.

secondary This statement takes a *domain name*, an *address list*, and a *file name* as an argument. It declares the local server a secondary master server for the domain specified.

A secondary server holds authoritative data on the domain, too, but it doesn't gather it from files, but tries to download it from the primary server. The IP address of at least one primary

[1] There are various *named* binaries floating around Linux FTP sites, each configured a little differently. Some have their pid file in */etc*, some store it in */tmp* or */var/tmp*.

[2] Note that the domain names in this example are given *without* trailing dot. Earlier versions of *named* seem to treat trailing dots in *named.boot* as an error, and silently discards the line. BIND-4.9.3 is said to fix this.

server must thus be given to *named* in the address list. The local server will contact each of them in turn until it successfully transfers the zone database, which is then stored in the backup file given as the third argument. If none of the primary servers responds, the zone data is retrieved from the backup file instead.

named will then attempt to refresh the zone data at regular intervals. This is explained below along in connection with the SOA resource record type.

cache This takes a *domain* and a *file name* as arguments. This file contains the root server hints, that is a list of records pointing to the root name servers. Only NS and A records will be recognized. The *domain* argument is generally the root domain name ".".

This information is absolutely crucial to *named*: if the *cache* statement does not occur in the boot file, *named* will not develop a local cache at all. This will severely degrade performance and increase network load if the next server queried is not on the local net. Moreover, *named* will not be able to reach any root name servers, and thus it won't resolve any addresses except those it is authoritative for. An exception from this rule is when using forwarding servers (cf. the *forwarders* option below).

forwarders This statement takes an *address list* as an argument. The IP addresses in this list specify a list of name servers that *named* may query if it fails to resolve a query from its local cache. They are tried in order until one of them responds to the query.

slave This statement makes the name server a *slave* server. That is, it will never perform recursive queries itself, but only forwards them to servers specified with the *forwarders* statement.

There are two options which we will not describe here, being *sortlist* and *domain*. Additionally, there are two directives that may be used inside the zone database files. These are *$INCLUDE* and *$ORIGIN*. Since they are rarely needed, we will not describe them here, either.

6.2.2 The DNS Database Files

Master files included by *named*, like *named.hosts*, always have a domain associated with them, which is called the *origin*. This is the domain name specified with the *cache* and *primary* commands. Within a master file, you are allowed to specify domain and host names relative to this domain. A name given in a configuration file is considered *absolute* if it ends in a single dot, otherwise it is considered relative to the origin. The origin all by itself may be referred to using "@".

All data contained in a master file is split up in *resource records*, or RRs for short. They make up the smallest unit of information available through DNS. Each resource record has a type. A records, for instance, map a hostname to an IP address, and a CNAME record associates an alias for a host with its official hostname. As an example, take a look at figure 6.3 on page 360, which shows the *named.hosts* master file for the virtual brewery.

Resource record representations in master files share a common format, which is

[*domain*] [*ttl*] [*class*] *type rdata*

Fields are separated by spaces or tabs. An entry may be continued across several lines if an opening brace occurs before the first newline, and the last field is followed by a closing brace. Anything between a semicolon and a newline is ignored.

domain This is the domain name to which the entry applies. If no domain name is given, the RR is assumed to apply to the domain of the previous RR.

ttl In order to force resolvers to discard information after a certain time, each RR is associated a "*time to live*", or *ttl* for short. The *ttl* field specifies the time in seconds the information is valid after it has been retrieved from the server. It is a decimal number with at most eight digits.

If no *ttl* value is given, it defaults to the value of the *minimum* field of the preceding SOA record.

class This is an address class, like IN for IP addresses, or HS for objects in the Hesiod class. For TCP/IP networking, you have to make this IN.

If no *class* field is given, the class of the preceding RR is assumed.

type This describes the type of the RR. The most common types are A, SOA, PTR, and NS. The following sections describe the various types of RR's.

rdata This holds the data associated with the RR. The format of this field depends on the type of the RR. Below, it will be described for each RR separately.

The following is an incomplete list of RRs to be used in DNS master files. There are a couple more of them, which we will not explain. They are experimental, and of little use generally.

SOA This describes a zone of authority (SOA means "Start of Authority"). It signals that the records following the SOA RR contain authoritative information for the domain. Every master file included by a *primary* statement must contain an SOA record for this zone. The resource data contains the following fields:

origin This is the canonical hostname of the primary name server for this domain. It is usually given as an absolute name.

contact This is the email address of the person responsible for maintaining the domain, with the '@' character replaced by a dot. For instance, if the responsible person at the Virtual Brewery is **janet**, then this field would contain *janet.vbrew.com.*

serial This is the version number of the zone file, expressed as a single decimal number. Whenever data is changed in the zone file, this number should be incremented.

The serial number is used by secondary name servers to recognize when zone information has changed. To stay up to date, secondary servers request the primary server's SOA record at certain intervals, and compare the serial number to that of the cached SOA record. If the number has changed, the secondary servers transfers the whole zone database from the primary server.

refresh This specifies the interval in seconds that the secondary servers should wait between checking the SOA record of the primary server. Again, this is a decimal number with at most eight digits.

Generally, the network topology doesn't change too often, so that this number should specify an interval of roughly a day for larger networks, and even more for smaller ones.

retry This number determines the intervals at which a secondary server should retry contacting the primary server if a request or a zone refresh fails. It must not be too low, or else a temporary failure of the server or a network problem may cause the secondary server to waste network resources. One hour, or perhaps one half hour, might be a good choice.

expire This specifies the time in seconds after which the server should finally discard all zone data if it hasn't been able to contact the primary server. It should normally be very large. Craig Hunt ([Hunt92]) recommends 42 days.

minimum This is the default ttl value for resource records that do not explicitly specify one. This requires other name servers to discard the RR after a certain amount of time. It has however nothing to do with the time after which a secondary server tries to update the zone information.

minimum should be a large value, especially for LANs where the network topology almost never changes. A value of around a week or a month is probably a good choice. In the case that single RRs may change more frequently, you can still assign them different ttl's.

A
: This associates an IP address with a hostname. The resource data field contains the address in dotted quad notation.

For each host, there must be only one A record. The hostname used in this A record is considered the official or *canonical* hostname. All other hostnames are aliases and must be mapped onto the canonical hostname using a CNAME record.

NS
: This points to a master name server of a subordinate zone. For an explanation why one has to have NS records, see section 2.6. The resource data field contains the hostname of the name server. To resolve the hostname, an additional A record is needed, the so-called *glue record* which gives the name server's IP address.

CNAME
: This associates an alias for a host with its *canonical hostname*. The canonical hostname is the one the master file provides an A record for; aliases are simply linked to that name by a CNAME record, but don't have any other records of their own.

PTR
: This type of record is used to associate names in the **in-addr.arpa** domain with hostnames. This is used for reverse mapping of IP addresses to hostnames. The hostname given must be the canonical hostname.

MX
: This RR announces a *mail exchanger* for a domain. The reasons to have mail exchangers are discussed in section 13.4.1 in chapter 13. The syntax of an MX record is

```
[domain] [ttl] [class] MX preference host
```

host names the mail exchanger for *domain*. Every mail exchanger has an integer *preference* associated with it. A mail transport agent who desires to deliver mail to *domain* will try all hosts who have an MX record for this domain until it succeeds. The one with the lowest preference value is tried first, then the others in order of increasing preference value.

HINFO
: This record provides information on the system's hardware and software. Its syntax is

```
[domain] [ttl] [class] HINFO hardware software
```

The *hardware* field identifies the hardware used by this host. There are special conventions to specify this. A list of valid names is given in the "Assigned Numbers" (RFC 1340). If the field contains any blanks, it must be enclosed in double quotes. The *software* field names the operating system software used by the system. Again, a valid name from the "Assigned Numbers" RFC should be chosen.

6.2.3 Writing the Master Files

Figures 6.2, 6.3, 6.4, and 6.5 give sample files for a name server at the brewery, located on *vlager*. Owing to the nature of the network discussed (a single LAN), the example is pretty straightforward. If your requirements are more complex, and you can't get *named* going, get "DNS and BIND" by Cricket Liu and Paul Albitz ([AlbitzLiu92]).

The *named.ca* cache file shown in figure 6.2 shows sample hint records for a root name server. A typical cache file usually describes about a dozen name servers, or so. You can obtain the current list of name servers for the root domain using the *nslookup* tool described toward the end of this chapter.[3]

[3]Note that you can't query your name server for the root servers if you don't have any root server hints installed: Catch 22! To escape this dilemma, you can either make *nslookup* use a different name server, or you can use the sample file in figure 6.2 as a starting point, and then obtain the full list of valid servers.

```
;
; /var/named/named.ca          Cache file for the brewery.
;                    We're not on the Internet, so we don't need
;                    any root servers. To activate these
;                    records, remove the semicolons.
;
; .                99999999   IN   NS  NS.NIC.DDN.MIL
; NS.NIC.DDN.MIL   99999999   IN   A   26.3.0.103
; .                99999999   IN   NS  NS.NASA.GOV
; NS.NASA.GOV      99999999   IN   A   128.102.16.10
```

Figure 6.2: The *named.ca* file.

```
;
; /var/named/named.hosts        Local hosts at the brewery
;                                Origin is vbrew.com
;
@                   IN  SOA   vlager.vbrew.com. (
                              janet.vbrew.com.
                              16          ; serial
                              86400       ; refresh: once per day
                              3600        ; retry:   one hour
                              3600000     ; expire:  42 days
                              604800      ; minimum: 1 week
                              )
                    IN  NS    vlager.vbrew.com.
;
; local mail is distributed on vlager
                    IN  MX    10 vlager
;
; loopback address
localhost.          IN  A     127.0.0.1
; brewery Ethernet
vlager              IN  A     191.72.1.1
vlager-if1          IN  CNAME vlager
; vlager is also news server
news                IN  CNAME vlager
vstout              IN  A     191.72.1.2
vale                IN  A     191.72.1.3
; winery Ethernet
vlager-if2          IN  A     191.72.2.1
vbardolino          IN  A     191.72.2.2
vchianti            IN  A     191.72.2.3
vbeaujolais         IN  A     191.72.2.4
```

Figure 6.3: The *named.hosts* file.

```
;
; /var/named/named.local        Reverse mapping of 127.0.0
;                                Origin is 0.0.127.in-addr.arpa.
;
@                   IN  SOA  vlager.vbrew.com. (
                             joe.vbrew.com.
                             1         ; serial
                             360000    ; refresh: 100 hrs
                             3600      ; retry:   one hour
                             3600000   ; expire:  42 days
                             360000    ; minimum: 100 hrs
                             )
                    IN  NS   vlager.vbrew.com.
1                   IN  PTR  localhost.
```

Figure 6.4: The *named.local* file.

```
;
; /var/named/named.rev          Reverse mapping of our IP addresses
;                                Origin is 72.191.in-addr.arpa.
;
@                   IN  SOA  vlager.vbrew.com. (
                             joe.vbrew.com.
                             16         ; serial
                             86400      ; refresh: once per day
                             3600       ; retry:   one hour
                             3600000    ; expire:  42 days
                             604800     ; minimum: 1 week
                             )
                    IN  NS   vlager.vbrew.com.
; brewery
1.1                 IN  PTR  vlager.vbrew.com.
2.1                 IN  PTR  vstout.vbrew.com.
3.1                 IN  PTR  vale.vbrew.com.
; winery
1.2                 IN  PTR  vlager-if1.vbrew.com.
2.2                 IN  PTR  vbardolino.vbrew.com.
3.2                 IN  PTR  vchianti.vbrew.com.
4.2                 IN  PTR  vbeaujolais.vbrew.com.
```

Figure 6.5: The *named.rev* file.

6.2.4 Verifying the Name Server Setup

There's a fine tool for checking the operation of your name server setup. It is called *nslookup*, and may be used both interactively and from the command line. In the latter case, you simply invoke it as

```
nslookup hostname
```

and it will query the name server specified in *resolv.conf* for *hostname*. (If this file names more than one server, *nslookup* will choose one at random).

The interactive mode, however, is much more exciting. Besides looking up individual hosts, you may query for any type of DNS record, and transfer the entire zone information for a domain.

When invoked without argument, *nslookup* will display the name server it uses, and enter interactive mode. At the '>' prompt, you may type any domain name it should query for. By default, it asks for class A records, those containing the IP address relating to the domain name.

You may change this type by issuing "`set type=`*type*", where *type* is one of the resource record names described above in section 6.2, or ANY.

For example, you might have the following dialogue with it:

```
$ nslookup
Default Name Server:  rs10.hrz.th-darmstadt.de
Address:  130.83.56.60

> sunsite.unc.edu
Name Server:  rs10.hrz.th-darmstadt.de
Address:  130.83.56.60

Non-authoritative answer:
Name:    sunsite.unc.edu
Address:  152.2.22.81
```

If you try to query for a name that has no IP address associated, but other records were found in the DNS database, *nslookup* will come back with an error message saying "`No type A records found`". However, you can make it query for records other than type A by issuing the "`set type`" command. For example, to get the SOA record of **unc.edu**, you would issue:

```
> unc.edu
*** No address (A) records available for unc.edu
Name Server:  rs10.hrz.th-darmstadt.de
Address:  130.83.56.60

> set type=SOA
> unc.edu
Name Server:  rs10.hrz.th-darmstadt.de
Address:  130.83.56.60

Non-authoritative answer:
unc.edu
        origin = ns.unc.edu
        mail addr = shava.ns.unc.edu
        serial = 930408
        refresh = 28800 (8 hours)
        retry   = 3600 (1 hour)
        expire  = 1209600 (14 days)
        minimum ttl = 86400 (1 day)

Authoritative answers can be found from:
UNC.EDU nameserver = SAMBA.ACS.UNC.EDU
SAMBA.ACS.UNC.EDU       internet address = 128.109.157.30
```

In a similar fashion you can query for MX records, and so forth. Using a type of ANY returns all resource records associated with a given name.

```
> set type=MX
> unc.edu
Non-authoritative answer:
unc.edu preference = 10, mail exchanger = lambada.oit.unc.edu
lambada.oit.unc.edu      internet address = 152.2.22.80

Authoritative answers can be found from:
UNC.EDU nameserver = SAMBA.ACS.UNC.EDU
SAMBA.ACS.UNC.EDU        internet address = 128.109.157.30
```

A practical application of *nslookup* beside debugging is to obtain the current list of root name servers for the *named.ca* file. You can do this by querying for all type NS records associated with the root domain:

```
> set typ=NS
> .
Name Server:  fb0430.mathematik.th-darmstadt.de
Address:  130.83.2.30

Non-authoritative answer:
(root)  nameserver = NS.INTERNIC.NET
(root)  nameserver = AOS.ARL.ARMY.MIL
(root)  nameserver = C.NYSER.NET
(root)  nameserver = TERP.UMD.EDU
(root)  nameserver = NS.NASA.GOV
(root)  nameserver = NIC.NORDU.NET
(root)  nameserver = NS.NIC.DDN.MIL

Authoritative answers can be found from:
(root)  nameserver = NS.INTERNIC.NET
(root)  nameserver = AOS.ARL.ARMY.MIL
(root)  nameserver = C.NYSER.NET
(root)  nameserver = TERP.UMD.EDU
(root)  nameserver = NS.NASA.GOV
(root)  nameserver = NIC.NORDU.NET
(root)  nameserver = NS.NIC.DDN.MIL
NS.INTERNIC.NET internet address = 198.41.0.4
AOS.ARL.ARMY.MIL         internet address = 128.63.4.82
AOS.ARL.ARMY.MIL         internet address = 192.5.25.82
AOS.ARL.ARMY.MIL         internet address = 26.3.0.29
C.NYSER.NET     internet address = 192.33.4.12
TERP.UMD.EDU    internet address = 128.8.10.90
NS.NASA.GOV     internet address = 128.102.16.10
NS.NASA.GOV     internet address = 192.52.195.10
NS.NASA.GOV     internet address = 45.13.10.121
NIC.NORDU.NET   internet address = 192.36.148.17
NS.NIC.DDN.MIL  internet address = 192.112.36.4
```

The complete set of commands available with *nslookup* may be obtained by the `help` command from within *nslookup*.

6.2.5 Other Useful Tools

There are a few tools that can help you with your tasks as a BIND administrator. I will briefly describe two of them here. Please refer to the documentation that comes with these tools for information on how to use them.

hostcvt is a tool that helps you with your initial BIND configuration by converting your */etc/hosts* file into master files for *named*. It generates both the forward (A) and reverse mapping (PTR) entries, and takes care of aliases and the like. Of course, it won't do the whole job for you, as you may still want to tune the timeout values in the SOA record, for instance, or add MX records and the like. Still, it may help you save a few aspirins. *hostcvt* is part of the BIND source, but can also be found as a standalone package on a few Linux FTP servers.

After setting up your name server, you may want to test your configuration. The ideal (and, to my knowledge) only tool for this is *dnswalk*, a *perl*-based package that walks your DNS database, looking for common mistakes and verifying that the information is consistent. *dnswalk* has been released on **comp.sources.misc** recently, and should be available on all FTP sites that archive this group (**ftp.uu.net** should be a safe bet if you don't know of any such site near you).

CHAPTER 7

Serial Line IP

The serial line protocols, SLIP and PPP, provide the Internet connectivity for the poor. Apart from a modem and a serial board equipped with a FIFO buffer, no hardware is needed. Using it is not much more complicated than a mailbox, and an increasing number of private organizations offer dial-up IP at an affordable cost to everyone.

There are both SLIP and PPP drivers available for Linux. SLIP has been there for quite a while, and works fairly reliably. A PPP driver has been developed recently by Michael Callahan and Al Longyear. It will be described in the next chapter.

7.1 General Requirements

To use SLIP or PPP, you have to configure some basic networking features as described in the previous chapters, of course. At the least, you have to set up the looback interface, and provide for name resolution. When connecting to the Internet, you will of course want to use DNS. The simplest option is to put the address of some name server into your *resolv.conf* file; this server will be queried as soon as the SLIP link is activated. The closer this name server is to the point where you dial in, the better.

However, this solution is not optimal, because all name lookups will still go through your SLIP/PPP link. If you worry about the bandwidth this consumes, you can also set up a *caching-only* name server. It doesn't really serve a domain, but only acts as a relay for all DNS queries produced on your host. The advantage of this scheme is that it builds up a cache, so that most queries have to be sent over the serial line only once. A *named.boot* file for a caching-only server looks like this:

```
; named.boot file for caching-only server
directory                          /var/named

primary     0.0.127.in-addr.arpa   db.127.0.0 ; loopback net
cache       .                      db.cache   ; root servers
```

In addition to this *name.boot* file, you also have to set up the *db.cache* file with a valid list of root name servers. This is described toward the end of the Resolver Configuration chapter.

7.2 SLIP Operation

Dial-up IP servers frequently offer SLIP service through special user accounts. After logging into such an account, you are not dropped into the common shell; instead a program or shell script is executed that enables the server's SLIP driver for the serial line and configures the appropriate network interface. Then you have to do the same at your end of the link.

On some operating systems, the SLIP driver is a user-space program; under Linux, it is part of the kernel, which makes it a lot faster. This requires, however, that the serial line be converted to SLIP mode explicitly.

This is done by means of a special tty line discipline, SLIPDISC. While the tty is in normal line discipline (DISC0), it will exchange data only with user processes, using the normal *read(2)* and *write(2)* calls, and the SLIP driver is unable to write to or read from the tty. In SLIPDISC, the roles are reversed: now any user-space processes are blocked from writing to or reading from the tty, while all data coming in on the serial port will be passed directly to the SLIP driver.

The SLIP driver itself understands a number of variations on the SLIP protocol. Apart from ordinary SLIP, it also understands CSLIP, which performs the so-called Van Jacobson header compression on outgoing IP packets.[1] This improves throughput for interactive sessions noticeably. Additionally, there are six-bit versions for each of these protocols.

A simple way to convert a serial line to SLIP mode is by using the *slattach* tool. Assume you have your modem on */dev/cua3*, and have logged into the SLIP server successfully. You will then execute:

```
# slattach /dev/cua3 &
```

This will switch the line discipline of *cua3* to SLIPDISC, and attach it to one of the SLIP network interfaces. If this is your first active SLIP link, the line will be attached to *sl0*; the second would be attached to *sl1*, and so on. The current kernels support up to eight simultaneous SLIP links.

The default encapsulation chosen by *slattach* is CSLIP. You may choose any other mode using the `-p` switch. To use normal SLIP (no compression), you would use

```
# slattach -p slip /dev/cua3 &
```

Other modes are `cslip`, `slip6`, `cslip6` (for the six-bit version of SLIP), and `adaptive` for adaptive SLIP. The latter leaves it to the kernel to find out which type of SLIP encapsulation the remote end uses.

Note that you must use the same encapsulation as your peer does. For example, if **cowslip** uses CSLIP, you have to do so, too. The symptoms of a mismatch will be that a *ping* to the remote host will not receive any packets back. If the other host *ping*s you, you may also see messages like "`Can't build ICMP header`" on your console. One way to avoid these difficulties is to use adaptive SLIP.

In fact, *slattach* does not only allow you to enable SLIP, but other protocols that use the serial line as well, like PPP or KISS (another protocol used by ham radio people). For details, please refer to the *slattach(8)* manual page.

After turning over the line to the SLIP driver, you have to configure the network interface. Again, we do this using the standard *ifconfig* and *route* commands. Assume that from **vlager**, we have dialed up a server named **cowslip**. You would then execute

```
# ifconfig sl0 vlager pointopoint cowslip
# route add cowslip
# route add default gw cowslip
```

The first command configures the interface as a point-to-point link to **cowslip**, while the second and third add the route to **cowslip** and the default route using **cowslip** as a gateway.

When taking down the SLIP link, you first have to remove all routes through **cowslip** using *route* with the `del` option, take the interface down, and send *slattach* the hangup signal. Afterwards you have to hang up the modem using your terminal program again:

```
# route del default
# route del cowslip
# ifconfig sl0 down
# kill -HUP 516
```

7.3 Using *dip*

Now, that was rather simple. Nevertheless, you might want to automate the above steps so that you only have to invoke a simple command that performs all steps shown above. This is what *dip* is for.[2] The current

[1] Van Jacobson header compression is described in RFC 1441.

[2] *dip* means *Dialup IP*. It was written by Fred van Kempen.

release as of this writing is version 3.3.7. It has been patched very heavily by a number of people, so that you can't speak of *the dip* program anymore. These different strains of development will hopefully be merged in a future release.

dip provides an interpreter for a simple scripting language that can handle the modem for you, convert the line to SLIP mode, and configure the interfaces. This is rather primitive and restrictive, but sufficient for most cases. A new release of *dip* may feature a more versatile language one day.

To be able to configure the SLIP interface, *dip* requires root privilege. It would now be tempting to make *dip* setuid to **root**, so that all users can dial up some SLIP server without having to give them root access. This is very dangerous, because setting up bogus interfaces and default routes with *dip* may disrupt routing on your network badly. Even worse, this will give your users the power to connect to *any* SLIP server, and launch dangerous attacks on your network. So if you want to allow your users to fire up a SLIP connection, write small wrapper programs for each prospective SLIP server, and have these wrappers invoke *dip* with the specific script that establishes the connection. These programs can then safely be made setuid **root**.[3]

7.3.1 A Sample Script

A sample script is produced in figure 7.1. It can be used to connect to **cowslip** by invoking *dip* with the script name as argument:

```
# dip cowslip.dip
DIP: Dialup IP Protocol Driver version 3.3.7 (12/13/93)
Written by Fred N. van Kempen, MicroWalt Corporation.

connected to cowslip.moo.com with addr 193.174.7.129
#
```

After connecting to **cowslip** and enabling SLIP, *dip* will detach from the terminal and go to the background. You can then start using the normal networking services on the SLIP link. To terminate the connection, simply invoke **dip** with the `-k` option. This sends a hangup signal to *dip* process, using the process id *dip* records in */etc/dip.pid*:[4]

```
# kill -k
```

In *dip*'s scripting language, keywords prefixed with a dollar symbol denote variable names. *dip* has a predefined set of variables which will be listed below. *$remote* and *$local*, for instance, contain the hostnames of the local and remote host involved in the SLIP link.

The first two statements in the sample script are *get* commands, which is *dip*'s way to set a variable. Here, the local and remote hostname are set to **vlager** and **cowslip**, respectively.

The next five statements set up the terminal line and the modem. The *reset* sends a reset string to the modem; for Hayes-compatible modems, this is the *ATZ* command. The next statement flushes out the modem response, so that the login chat in the next few lines will work properly. This chat is pretty straight-forward: it simply dials 41988, the phone number of **cowslip**, and logs into the account *Svlager* using the password *hey-jude*. The *wait* command makes *dip* wait for the string given as its first argument; the number given as second argument make the wait time out after that many seconds if no such string is received. The *if* commands interspersed in the login procedure check that no error has occurred while executing the command.

The final commands executed after logging in are *default*, which makes the SLIP link the default route to all hosts, and *mode*, which enables SLIP mode on the line and configures the interface and routing table for you.

7.3.2 A *dip* Reference

Although widely used, *dip* hasn't been very well documented yet. In this section, we will therefore give a reference for most of *dip*'s commands. You can get an overview of all commands it provides by invoking *dip* in test mode, and entering the *help* command. To find out about the syntax of a command, you may enter it without any arguments; of course this does not work with commands that take no arguments.

[3] *diplogin* can (and must) be run setuid, too. See the section at the end of this chapter.

[4] See the newsgroup **alt.tla** for more palindromic fun with three-letter acronyms.

```
# Sample dip script for dialing up cowslip

# Set local and remote name and address
get $local vlager
get $remote cowslip

port cua3                    # choose a serial port
speed 38400                  # set speed to max
modem HAYES                  # set modem type
reset                        # reset modem and tty
flush                        # flush out modem response

# Prepare for dialing.
send ATQ0V1E1X1\r
wait OK 2
if $errlvl != 0 goto error
dial 41988
if $errlvl != 0 goto error
wait CONNECT 60
if $errlvl != 0 goto error

# Okay, we're connected now
sleep 3
send \r\n\r\n
wait ogin: 10
if $errlvl != 0 goto error
send Svlager\n
wait ssword: 5
if $errlvl != 0 goto error
send hey-jude\n
wait running 30
if $errlvl != 0 goto error

# We have logged in, and the remote side is firing up SLIP.
print Connected to $remote with address $rmtip
default                      # Make this link our default route
mode SLIP                    # We go to SLIP mode, too
# fall through in case of error

error:
print SLIP to $remote failed.
```

Figure 7.1: A sample *dip* script

```
$ dip -t
DIP: Dialup IP Protocol Driver version 3.3.7 (12/13/93)
Written by Fred N. van Kempen, MicroWalt Corporation.

DIP> help
DIP knows about the following commands:

databits default  dial     echo     flush
get      goto     help     if       init
mode     modem    parity   print    port
reset    send     sleep    speed    stopbits
term     wait

DIP> echo
Usage: echo on|off
DIP> _
```

Throughout the following, examples that display the `DIP>` prompt show how to enter a command in test mode, and what output it produces. Examples lacking this prompt should be taken as script excerpts.

7.3.2.1 The Modem Commands

There is a number of commands *dip* provides to configure your serial line and modem. Some of these are obvious, such as *port*, which selects a serial port, and *speed*, *databits*, *stopbits*, and *parity*, which set the common line parameters.

The *modem* command selects a modem type. Currently, the only type supported is *HAYES* (capitalization required). You have to provide *dip* with a modem type, else it will refuse to execute the *dial* and *reset* commands. The *reset* command sends a reset string to the modem; the string used depends on the modem type selected. For Hayes-compatible modems, this is *ATZ*.

The *flush* code can be used to flush out all responses the modem has sent so far. Otherwise a chat script following the *reset* might be confused, because it reads the *OK* responses from earlier commands.

The *init* command selects an initialization string to be passed to the modem before dialling. The default for Hayes modems is "*ATE0 Q0 V1 X1*", which turns on echoing of commands and long result codes, and selects blind dialing (no checking of dial tone).

The *dial* command finally sends the initialization string to the modem and dials up the remote system. The default dial command for Hayes modems is *ATD*.

7.3.2.2 *echo* and *term*

The *echo* command serves as a debugging aid, in that using *echo on* makes *dip* echo to the console everything sends to the serial device. This can be turned off again by calling *echo off*.

dip also allows you to leave script mode temporarily and enter terminal mode. In this mode, you can use *dip* just like any ordinary terminal program, writing to the serial line and reading from it. To leave this mode, enter `Ctrl-]`.

7.3.2.3 The *get* Command

The *get* command is *dip*'s way of setting a variable. The simplest form is to set a variable to a constant, as used throughout the above example. You may, however, also prompt the user for input by specifying the keyword *ask* instead of a value:

```
DIP> get $local ask
Enter the value for $local: _
```

A third method is to try to obtain the value from the remote host. Bizarre as it seems first, this is very useful in some cases: Some SLIP servers will not allow you to use your own IP address on the SLIP link, but will rather assign you one from a pool of addresses whenever you dial in, printing some message that informs you about the address you have been assigned. If the message looks something like this "`Your address: 193.174.7.202`", then the following piece of *dip* code would let you pick up the address:

```
... login chat ....
wait address: 10
get $locip remote
```

7.3.2.4 The *print* Command

This is the command to echo text to the console *dip* was started from. Any of *dip*'s variables may be used in print commands, such as

```
DIP> print Using port $port at speed $speed
Using port cua3 at speed 38400
```

7.3.2.5 Variable Names

dip only understands a predefined set of variables. A variable name always begins with a dollar symbol and must be written in lower-case letters.

The *$local* and *$locip* variables contain the local host's name and IP address. Setting the hostname makes *dip* store the canonical hostname in *$local*, at the same time assigning *$locip* the corresponding IP address. The analogous thing happens when setting the *$locip*.

The *$remote* and *$rmtip* variables do the same for the remote host's name and address. *$mtu* contains the MTU value for the connection.

These five variables are the only ones that may be assigned values directly using the *get* command. A host of other variables can only be set through corresponding commands, but may be used *print* statements; these are *$modem*, *$port*, and *$speed*.

$errlvl is the variable through which you can access the result of the last command executed. An error level of 0 indicates success, while a non-zero value denotes an error.

7.3.2.6 The *if* and *goto* Commands

The *if* command is rather a conditional branch than what one usually calls an if. Its syntax is

`if` *var op number* `goto` *label*

where the expression must be a simple comparison between one of the variables *$errlvl*, *$locip*, and *$rmtip*. The second operand must be an integer number; the operator *op* may be one of `==`, `!=`, `<`, `>`, `<=`, and `>=`.

The *goto* command makes the execution of the script continue at the line following that bearing the label. A label must occur as the very first token on the line, and must be followed immediately by a colon.

7.3.2.7 *send*, *wait* and *sleep*

These commands help implement simple chat scripts in *dip*. *send* outputs its arguments to the serial line. It does not support variables, but understands all C-style backslash character sequences such as *n* and *b*. The tilde character (~) is used as an abbreviation for carriage return/newline.

wait takes a word as an argument, and scans all input on the serial line until it recognizes this word. The word itself may not contain any blanks. Optionally, you may give *wait* a timeout value as second argument; if the expected word is not received within that many seconds, the command will return with an *$errlvl* value of one.

The *sleep* statement may be used to wait for a certain amount of time, for instance to patiently wait for any login sequence to complete. Again, the interval is specified in seconds.

7.3.2.8 *mode* and *default*

These commands are used to flip the serial line to SLIP mode and configure the interface.

The *mode* command is the last command executed by *dip* before going into daemon mode. Unless an error occurs, the command does not return.

mode takes a protocol name as argument. *dip* currently recognizes *SLIP* and *CSLIP* as valid names. The current version of *dip* does not understand adaptive SLIP, however.

After enabling SLIP mode on the serial line, *dip* executes *ifconfig* to configure the interface as a point-to-point link, and invokes *route* to set the route to the remote host.

If, in addition, the script executes the *default* command before *mode*, *dip* will also make the default route point to the SLIP link.

7.4 Running in Server Mode

Setting up your SLIP client was the hard part. Doing the opposite, namely configuring your host to act as a SLIP server, is much easier.

One way to do this is to to use *dip* in server mode, which can be achieved by invoking it as *diplogin*. Its main configuration file is */etc/diphosts*, which associates login names with the address this host is assigned. Alternatively, you can also use *sliplogin*, a BSD-derived tool that features a more flexible configuration scheme that lets you execute shell scripts whenever a host connects and disconnects. It is currently at Beta.

Both programs require that you set up one login account per SLIP client. For instance, assume you provide SLIP service to Arthur Dent at **dent.beta.com**, you might create an account named **dent** by adding the following line to your *passwd* file:

```
dent:*:501:60:Arthur Dent's SLIP account:/tmp:/usr/sbin/diplogin
```

Afterwards, you would set **dent**'s password using the *passwd* utility.

Now, when **dent** logs in, *dip* will start up as a server. To find out if he is indeed permitted to use SLIP, it will look up the user name in */etc/diphosts*. This file details the access rights and connection parameter for each SLIP user. A sample entry for **dent** could look like this:

```
dent::dent.beta.com:Arthur Dent:SLIP,296
```

The first of the colon-separated fields is the name the user must log in as. The second field may contain an additional password (see below). The third is the hostname or IP address of the calling host. Next comes an informational field without any special meaning (yet). The last field describes the connection parameters. This is a comma-separated list specifying the protocol (currently one of *SLIP* or *CSLIP*), followed by the MTU.

When **dent** logs in, *diplogin* extracts the information on him from the *diphosts* file, and, if the second field is not empty, prompts for an "external security password". The string entered by the user is compared to the (unencrypted) password from *diphosts*. If they do not match, the login attempt is rejected.

Otherwise, *diplogin* proceeds by flipping the serial line to CSLIP or SLIP mode, and sets up the interface and route. This connection remains established until the user disconnects and the modem drops the line. *diplogin* will then return the line to normal line discipline, and exit.

diplogin requires super-user privilege. If you don't have *dip* running setuid **root**, you should make *diplogin* a separate copy of *dip* instead of a simple link. *diplogin* can then safely be made setuid, without affecting the status of *dip* itself.

7.4 Running in Server Mode

CHAPTER 8

The Point-to-Point Protocol

8.1 Untangling the P's

Just like SLIP, PPP is a protocol to send datagrams across a serial connection, but addresses a couple of deficiencies of the former. It lets the communicating sides negotiate options such as the IP address and the maximum datagram size at startup time, and provides for client authorization. For each of these capabilities, PPP has a separate protocol. Below, we will briefly cover these basic building blocks of PPP. This discussion is far from complete; if you want to know more about PPP, you are urged to read its specification in RFC 1548, as well as the dozen or so companion RFCs.[1]

At the very bottom of PPP is the *High-Level Data Link Control* Protocol, abbreviated HDLC,[2] which defines the boundaries around the individual PPP frames, and provides a 16-bit checksum. As opposed to the more primitive SLIP encapsulation, a PPP frame is capable of holding packets from other protocols than IP, such as Novell's IPX, or Appletalk. PPP achieves this by adding a protocol field to the basic HDLC frame that identifies the type of packet is carried by the frame.

LCP, the Link Control Protocol, is used on top of HDLC to negotiate options pertaining to the data link, such as the Maximum Receive Unit (MRU) that states the maximum datagram size one side of the link agrees to receive.

An important step at the configuration stage of a PPP link is client authorization. Although it is not mandatory, it is really a must for dial-up lines. Usually, the called host (the server) asks the client to authorize itself by proving it knows some secret key. If the caller fails to produce the correct secret, the connection is terminated. With PPP, authorization works both ways; that is, the caller may also ask the server to authenticate itself. These authentication procedures are totally independent of each other. There are two protocols for different types of authorization, which we will discuss further below. They are named Password Authentication Protocol, or PAP, and Challenge Handshake Authentication Protocol, or CHAP.

Each network protocol that is routed across the data link, like IP, AppleTalk, etc, is configured dynamically using a corresponding Network Control Protocol (NCP). For instance, to send IP datagrams across the link, both PPPs must first negotiate which IP address each of them uses. The control protocol used for this is IPCP, the Internet Protocol Control Protocol.

Beside sending standard IP datagrams across the link, PPP also supports Van Jacobson header compression of IP datagrams. This is a technique to shrink the headers of TCP packets to as little as three bytes. It is also used in CSLIP, and is more colloquially referred to as VJ header compression. The use of compression may be negotiated at startup time through IPCP as well.

[1] The relevant RFCs are listed in the Annoted Bibiliography at the end of this book.

[2] In fact, HDLC is a much more general protocol devised by the International Standards Organization (ISO).

8.2 PPP on Linux

On Linux, PPP functionality is split up in two parts, a low-level HDLC driver located in the kernel, and the user space *pppd* daemon that handles the various control protocols. The current release of PPP for Linux is *linux-ppp-1.0.0*, and contains the kernel PPP module, *pppd*, and a program named *chat* used to dial up the remote system.

The PPP kernel driver was written by Michael Callahan. *pppd* was derived from a free PPP implementation for Sun and 386BSD machines, which was written by Drew Perkins and others, and is maintained by Paul Mackerras. It was ported to Linux by Al Longyear.[3] *chat* was written by Karl Fox.[4]

Just like SLIP, PPP is implemented by means of a special line discipline. To use some serial line as a PPP link, you first establish the connection over your modem as usual, and subsequently convert the line to PPP mode. In this mode, all incoming data is passed to the PPP driver, which checks the incoming HDLC frames for validity (each HDLC frame carries a 16 bit checksum), and unwraps and dispatches them. Currently, it is able to handle IP datagrams, optionally using Van Jacobson header compression. As soon as Linux supports IPX, the PPP driver will be extended to handle IPX packets, too.

The kernel driver is aided by *pppd*, the PPP daemon, which performs the entire initialization and authentication phase that is necessary before actual network traffic can be sent across the link. *pppd*'s behavior may be fine-tuned using a number of options. As PPP is rather complex, it is impossible to explain all of them in a single chapter. This book therefore cannot cover all aspects of *pppd*, but only give you an introduction. For more information, refer to the manual pages and *README*s in the *pppd* source distribution, which should help you sort out most questions this chapter fails to discuss. If your problems persist even after reading all documentation, you should turn to the newsgroup **comp.protocols.ppp** for help, which is the place where you will reach most of the people involved in the development of *pppd*.

8.3 Running *pppd*

When you want to connect to the Internet through a PPP link, you have to set up basic networking capabilities such as the loopback device, and the resolver. Both have been covered in the previous chapters. There are some things to be said about using DNS over a serial link; please refer to the SLIP chapter for a discussion of this.

As an introductory example of how to establish a PPP connection with *pppd*, assume you are at **vlager** again. You have already dialed up the PPP server, **c3po**, and logged into the **ppp** account. **c3po** has already fired up its PPP driver. After exiting the communications program you used for dialing, you execute the following command:

```
# pppd /dev/cua3 38400 crtscts defaultroute
```

This will flip the serial line *cua3* to PPP mode and establish an IP link to **c3po**. The transfer speed used on the serial port will be 38400 bps. The *crtscts* option turns on hardware handshake on the port, which is an absolute must at speeds above 9600 bps.

The first thing *pppd* does after starting up is to negotiate several link characteristics with the remote end, using LCP. Usually, the default set of options *pppd* tries to negotiate will work, so we won't go into this here. We will return to LCP in more detail in some later section.

For the time being, we also assume that **c3po** doesn't require any authentication from us, so that the configuration phase is completed successfully.

pppd will then negotiate the IP parameters with its peer using IPCP, the IP control protocol. Since we didn't specify any particular IP address to *pppd* above, it will try to use the address obtained by having the resolver look up the local hostname. Both will then announce their address to each other.

Usually, there's nothing wrong with these defaults. Even if your machine is on an Ethernet, you can use the same IP address for both the Ethernet and the PPP interface. Nevertheless, *pppd* allows you to use a

[3]Both authors have said they will be very busy for some time to come. If you have any questions on PPP in general, you'd best ask the people on the NET channel of the Linux activists mailing list.

[4]**karl@morningstar.com**.

different address, or even to ask your peer to use some specific address. These options are discussed in a later section.

After going through the IPCP setup phase, *pppd* will prepare your host's networking layer to use the PPP link. It first configures the PPP network interface as a point-to-point link, using *ppp0* for the first PPP link that is active, *ppp1* for the second, and so on. Next, it will set up a routing table entry that points to the host at the other end of the link. In the example shown above, *pppd* will make the default network route point to **c3po**, because we gave it the *defaultroute* option.[5] This causes all datagrams to hosts not on your local network to be sent to **c3po**. There are a number of different routing schemes *pppd* supports, which we will cover in detail later in this chapter.

8.4 Using Options Files

Before *pppd* parses its command line arguments, it scans several files for default options. These files may contain any valid command line arguments, spread out across an arbitrary number of lines. comments are introduced by has signs.

The first options file is */etc/ppp/options*, which is always scanned when *pppd* starts up. Using it to set some global defaults is a good idea, because it allows you to keep your users from doing several things that may compromise security. For instance, to make *pppd* require some kind of authentication (either PAP or CHAP) from the peer, you would add the `auth` option to this file. This option cannot be overridden by the user, so that it becomes impossible to establish a PPP connection with any system that is not in our authentication databases.

The other option file, which is read after */etc/ppp/options*, is *.ppprc* in the user's home directory. It allows each user to specify her own set of default options.

A sample */etc/ppp/options* file might look like this:

```
# Global options for pppd running on vlager.vbrew.com
auth                    # require authentication
usehostname             # use local hostname for CHAP
lock                    # use UUCP-style device locking
domain vbrew.com        # our domain name
```

The first two of these options apply to authentication and will be explained below. The `lock` keyword makes *pppd* comply to the standard UUCP method of device locking. With this convention, each process that accesses a serial device, say */dev/cua3*, creates a lock file named *LCK..cua3* in the UUCP spool directory to signal that the device is in use. This is necessary to prevent any other programs such as *minicom* or *uucico* to open the serial device while used by PPP.

The reason to provide these options in the global configuration file is that options such as those shown above cannot be overridden, and so provide for a reasonable level of security. Note however, that some options can be overridden later; one such an example is the *connect* string.

8.5 Dialing out with *chat*

One of the things that may have struck you as inconvenient in the above example is that you had to establish the connection manually before you could fire up *pppd*. Unlike *dip*, *pppd* does not have its own scripting language for dialing the remote system and logging in, but rather relies on some external program or shell script to do this. The command to be executed can be given to *pppd* with the *connect* command line option. *pppd* will redirect the command's standard input and output to the serial line. One useful program for this is *expect*, written by Don Libes. It has a very powerful language based on Tcl, and was designed exactly for this sort of application.

The *pppd* package comes along with a similar program called *chat*, which lets you specify a UUCP-style chat script. Basically, a chat script consists of an alternating sequence of strings that we expect to receive from

[5] The default network route is only installed if none is present yet.

the remote system, and the answers we are to send. We will call the expect and send strings, respectively. This is a typical excerpt from a chat script;

```
ogin: b1ff ssword: s3kr3t
```

This tells *chat* to wait for the remote system to send the login prompt, and return the login name **b1ff**. We only wait for `ogin:` so that it doesn't matter if the login prompt starts with an uppercase or lowercase l, or if it arrives garbled. The following string is an expect-string again that makes *chat* wait for the password prompt, and send our password in response.

This is basically all that chat scripts are about. A complete script to dial up a PPP server would, of course, also have to include the appropriate modem commands. Assume your modem understands the Hayes command set, and the server's telephone number was 318714. The complete *chat* invocation to establish a connection with **c3po** would then be

```
$ chat -v '' ATZ OK ATDT318714 CONNECT '' ogin: ppp word: GaGariN
```

By definition, the first string must be an expect string, but as the modem won't say anything before we have kicked it, we make *chat* skip the first expect by specifying an empty string. We go on and send `ATZ`, the reset command for Hayes-compatible modems, and wait for its response (`OK`). The next string sends the dial command along with the phone number to *chat*, and expects the `CONNECT` message in response. This is followed by an empty string again, because we don't want to send anything now, but rather wait for the login prompt. The remainder of the chat script works exactly as described above.

The `-v` option makes *chat* log all activities to the *syslog* daemon's *local2* facility.[6]

Specifying the chat script on the command line bears a certain risk, because users can view a process' command line with the *ps* command. You can avoid this by putting the chat script in a file, say *dial-c3po*. You make *chat* read the script from the file instead of the command line by giving it the `-f` option, followed by the file name. The complete *pppd* incantation would now look like this:

```
# pppd connect "chat -f dial-c3po" /dev/cua3 38400 -detach \
        crtscts modem defaultroute
```

Beside the *connect* option that specifies the dial-up script, we have added two more options to the command line: *-detach*, which tells *pppd* not to detach from the console and become a background process. The *modem* keyword makes it perform some modem-specific actions on the serial device, like hanging up the line before and after the call. If you don't use this keyword, *pppd* will not monitor the port's DCD line, and will therefore not detect if the remote end hangs up unexpectedly.

The examples shown above were rather simple; *chat* allows for much more complex chat scripts. One very useful feature is the ability to specify strings on which to abort the chat with an error. Typical abort strings are messages like `BUSY`, or `NO CARRIER`, that your modem usually generates when the called number is busy, or doesn't pick up the phone. To make *chat* recognize these immediately, rather than timing out, you can specify them at the beginning of the script using the `ABORT` keyword:

```
$ chat -v ABORT BUSY ABORT 'NO CARRIER' '' ATZ OK ...
```

In a similar fashion, you may change the timeout value for parts of the chat scripts by inserting `TIMEOUT` options. For details, please check the *chat(8)* manual page.

Sometimes, you'd also want to have some sort of conditional execution of parts of the chat script. For instance, when you don't receive the remote end's login prompt, you might want to send a BREAK, or a carriage return. You can achieve this by appending a sub-script to an expect string. It consists of a sequence of send- and expect-strings, just like the overall script itself, which are separated by hyphens. The sub-script is executed whenever the expected string they are appended to is not received in time. In the example above, we would modify the chat script as follows:

```
ogin:-BREAK-ogin: ppp ssword: GaGariN
```

Now, when *chat* doesn't see the remote system send the login prompt, the sub-script is executed by first sending a BREAK, and then waiting for the login prompt again. If the prompt now appears, the script continues as usual, otherwise it will terminate with an error.

[6] If you edit *syslog.conf* to redirect these log messages to a file, make sure this file isn't world readable, as *chat* also logs the entire chat script by default – including passwords and all.

8.6 Debugging Your PPP Setup

By default, *pppd* will log any warnings and error messages to *syslog*'s *daemon* facility. You have to add an entry to *syslog.conf* that redirects this to a file, or even the console, otherwise *syslog* simply discards these messages. The following entry sends all messages to */var/log/ppp-log*:

```
daemon.*                /var/log/ppp-log
```

If your PPP setup doesn't work at once, looking into this log file should give you a first hint of what goes wrong. If this doesn't help, you can also turn on extra debugging output using the `debug` option. This makes *pppd* log the contents of all control packets sent or received to *syslog*. All messages will go to the *daemon* facility.

Finally, the most drastic feature is to enable kernel-level debugging by invoking *pppd* with the *kdebug* option. It is followed by a numeric argument that is the bitwise OR of the following values: 1 for general debug messages, 2 for printing the contents of all incoming HDLC frames, and 4 to make the driver print all outgoing HDLC frames. To capture kernel debugging messages, you must either run a *syslogd* daemon that reads the */proc/kmsg* file, or the *klogd* daemon. Either of them directs kernel debugging to *syslog*'s *kernel* facility.

8.7 IP Configuration Options

IPCP is used to negotiate a couple of IP parameters at link configuration time. Usually, each peer may send an IPCP Configuration Request packet, indicating which values it wants to change from the defaults, and to what value. Upon receipt, the remote end inspects each option in turn, and either acknowledges or rejects it.

pppd gives you a lot of control about which IPCP options it will try to negotiate. You can tune this through various command line options we will discuss below.

8.7.1 Choosing IP Addresses

In the example above, we had *pppd* dial up **c3po** and establish an IP link. No provisions were taken to choose a particular IP address on either end of the link. Instead, we picked **vlager**'s address as the local IP address, and let **c3po** provide its own. Sometimes, however, it is useful to have control over what address is used on one or the other end of the link. *pppd* supports several variations of this.

To ask for particular addresses, you generally provide *pppd* with the following option:

local_addr: *remote_addr*

where *local_addr* and *remote_addr* may be specified either in dotted quad notation, or as hostnames.[7] This makes *pppd* attempt to use the first address as its own IP address, and the second as the peer's. If the peer rejects either of them during IPCP negotiation, no IP link will be established.[8]

If you want to set only the local address, but accept any address the peer uses, you simply leave out the *remote_addr* part. For instance, to make **vlager** use the IP address **130.83.4.27** instead of its own, you would give it `130.83.4.27:` on the command line. Similarly, to set the remote address only, you would leave the *local_addr* field blank. By default, *pppd* will then use the address associated with your hostname.

Some PPP servers that handle a lot of client sites assign addresses dynamically: addresses are assigned to systems only when calling in, and are claimed after they have logged off again. When dialing up such a server, you must make sure that *pppd* doesn't request any particular IP address from the server, but rather accept the address the server asks you to use. This means that you mustn't specify a *local_addr* argument. In addition, you have to use the `noipdefault` option, which makes *pppd* wait for the peer to provide the IP address instead of using the local host's address.

---

[7] Using hostnames in this option has consequences on CHAP authentication. Please refer to the section on CHAP below.

[8] You can allow the peer PPP to override your ideas of IP addresses by giving *pppd* the `ipcp-accept-local` and `ipcp-accept-remote` options. Please refer to the manual page for details.

8.7.2 Routing Through a PPP Link

After setting up the network interface, *pppd* will usually set up a host route to its peer only. If the remote host is on a LAN, you certainly want to be able to connect to hosts "behind" your peer as well; that is, a network route must be set up.

We have already seen above that *pppd* can be asked to set the default route using the `defaultroute` option. This option is very useful if the PPP server you dialed up will act as your Internet gateway.

The reverse case, where your system acts as a gateway for a single host, is also relatively easy to accomplish. For example, take some employee at the Virtual Brewery whose home machine is called **loner**. When connecting to **vlager** through PPP, he uses an address on the Brewery's subnet. At **vlager**, we can now give *pppd* the `proxyarp` option, which will install a proxy ARP entry for **loner**. This will automatically make **loner** accessible from all hosts at the Brewery and the Winery.

However, things aren't always as easy as that, for instance when linking two local area networks. This usually requires adding a specific network route, because these networks may have their own default routes. Besides, having both peers use the PPP link as the default route would generate a loop, where packets to unknown destinations would ping-pong between the peers until their time-to-live expired.

As an example, suppose the Virtual Brewery opens a branch in some other city. The subsidiary runs an Ethernet of their own using the IP network number **191.72.3.0**, which is subnet 3 of the Brewery's class B network. They want to connect to the Brewery's main Ethernet via PPP to update customer databases, etc. Again, **vlager** acts as the gateway; its peer is called **sub-etha** and has an IP address of **191.72.3.1**..

When **sub-etha** connects to **vlager**, it will make the default route point to **vlager** as usual. On **vlager**, however, we will have to install a network route for subnet 3 that goes through **sub-etha**. For this, we use a feature of *pppd* not discussed so far – the *ip-up* command. This is a shell script or program located in */etc/ppp* that is executed after the PPP interface has been configured. When present, it is invoked with the following parameters:

`ip-up` *iface device speed local_addr remote_addr*

where *iface* names the network interface used, *device* is the pathname of the serial device file used (*/dev/tty* if stdin/stdout are used), and *speed* is the device's speed. *local_addr* and *remote_addr* give the IP addresses used at both ends of the link in dotted quad notation. In our case, the *ip-up* script may contain the following code fragment:

```
#!/bin/sh
case $5 in
191.72.3.1)             # this is sub-etha
        route add -net 191.72.3.0 gw 191.72.3.1;;
...
esac
exit 0
```

In a similar fashion, */etc/ppp/ip-down* is used to undo all actions of *ip-up* after the PPP link has been taken down again.

However, the routing scheme is not yet complete. We have set up routing table entries on both PPP hosts, but so far, all other hosts on both networks don't know anything about the PPP link. This is not a big problem if all hosts at the subsidiary have their default route pointing at **sub-etha**, and all Brewery hosts route to **vlager** by default. If this is not the case, your only option will usually be to use a routing daemon like *gated*. After creating the network route on **vlager**, the routing daemon would broadcast the new route to all hosts on the attached subnets.

8.8 Link Control Options

Above, we already encountered LCP, the Link Control Protocol, which is used to negotiate link characteristics, and to test the link.

The two most important options that may be negotiated by LCP are the maximum receive unit, and the Asynchronous Control Character Map. There are a number of other LCP configuration options, but they are far too specialized to discuss here. Please refer to RFC 1548 for a description of those.

The Asynchronous Control Character Map, colloquially called the async map, is used on asynchronous links such as telephone lines to identify control characters that must be escaped (replaced by a specific two-character sequence). For instance, you may want to avoid the XON and XOFF characters used for software handshake, because some misconfigured modem might choke upon receipt of an XOFF. Other candidates include `Ctrl-]` (the *telnet* escape character). PPP allows you to escape any of the characters with ASCII codes 0 through 31 by specifying them in the async map.

The async map is a bitmap 32 bits wide, with the least significant bit corresponding to the ASCII NUL character, and the most significant bit corrsponding to ASCII 31. If a bit is set, it signals that the corresponding character must be escaped before sending it across the link. Initially, the async map is set to *0xffffffff*, that is, all control characters will be esaped.

To tell your peer that it doesn't have to escape all control characters but only a few of them, you can specify a new asyncmap to *pppd* using the `asyncmap` option. For instance, if only `^S` and `^Q` (ASCII 17 and 19, commonly used for XON and XOFF) must be escaped, use the following option:

```
asyncmap 0x000A0000
```

The Maximum Receive Unit, or MRU, signals to the peer the maximum size of HDLC frames we want to receive. Although this may remind you of the MTU value (Maximum Transfer Unit), these two have little in common. The MTU is a parameter of the kernel networking device, and describes the maximum frame size the interface is able to handle. The MRU is more of an advice to the remote end not to generate any frames larger than the MRU; the interface must nevertheless be able to receive frames of up to 1500 bytes.

Choosing an MRU is therefore not so much a question of what the link is capable of transferring, but of what gives you the best throughput. If you intend to run interactive applications over the link, setting the MRU to values as low as 296 is a good idea, so that an occasional larger packet (say, from an FTP session) doesn't make your cursor "jump." To tell *pppd* to request an MRU of 296, you would give it the option `mru 296`. Small MRUs, however, only make sense if you don't have VJ header compression disabled (it is enabled by default).

pppd understands also a couple of LCP options that configure the overall behavior of the negotiation process, such as the maximum number of configuration requests that may be exchanged before the link is terminated. Unless you kow exactly what you are doing, you should leave these alone.

Finally, there are two options that apply to LCP echo messages. PPP defines two messages, Echo Request and Echo Response. *pppd* uses this feature to check if a link is still operating. You can enable this by using the `lcp-echo-interval` option together with a time in seconds. If no frames are received from the remote host within this interval, *pppd* generates an Echo Request, and expects the peer to return an Echo Response. If the peer does not produce a response, the link is terminated after a certain number of requests sent. This number can be set using the `lcp-echo-failure` option. By default, this feature is disabled altogether.

8.9 General Security Considerations

A misconfigured PPP daemon can be a devastating security breach. It can be as bad as letting anyone plug in their machine into your Ethernet (and that is very bad). In this section, we will discuss a few measures that should make your PPP configuration safe.

One problem with *pppd* is that to configure the network device and the routing table, it requires **root** privilege. You will usually solve this by running it setuid **root**. However, *pppd* allows users to set various security-relevant options. To protect against any attacks a user may launch by manipulating these options, it is suggested you set a couple of default values in the global */etc/ppp/options* file, like those shown in the sample file in section 8.4. Some of them, such as the authentication options, cannot be overridden by the user, and so provide a reasonable protection against manipulations.

Of course, you have to protect yourself from the systems you speak PPP with, too. To fend off hosts posing as someone else, you should always some sort of authentication from your peer. Additionally, you should not allow foreign hosts to use any IP address they choose, but restrict them to at least a few. The following section will deal with these topics.

8.10 Authentication with PPP

8.10.1 CHAP versus PAP

With PPP, each system may require its peer to authenticate itself using one of two authentication protocols. These are the Password Authentication Protocol (PAP), and the Challenge Handshake Authentication Protocol (CHAP). When a connection is established, each end can request the other to authenticate itself, regardless of whether it is the caller or the callee. Below I will loosely talk of 'client' and 'server' when I want to distinguish between the authenticating system and the authenticator. A PPP daemon can ask its peer for authentication by sending yet another LCP configuration request identifying the desired authentication protocol.

PAP works basically the same way as the normal login procedure. The client authenticates itself by sending a user name and an (optionally encrypted) password to the server, which the server compares to its secrets database. This technique is vulnerable to eavesdroppers who may try to obtain the password by listening in on the serial line, and to repeated trial and error attacks.

CHAP does not have these deficiencies. With CHAP, the authenticator (i.e. the server) sends a randomly generated "challenge" string to the client, along with its hostname. The client uses the hostname to look up the appropriate secret, combines it with the challenge, and encrypts the string using a one-way hashing function. The result is returned to the server along with the client's hostname. The server now performs the same computation, and acknowledges the client if it arrives at the same result.

Another feature of CHAP is that it doesn't only require the client to authenticate itself at startup time, but sends challenges at regular intervals to make sure the client hasn't been replaced by an intruder, for instance by just switching phone lines.

pppd keeps the secret keys for CHAP and PAP in two separate files, called */etc/ppp/chap-secrets* and *pap-secrets*, respectively. By entering a remote host in one or the other file, you have a fine control over whether CHAP or PAP is used to authenticate ourselves with our peer, and vice versa.

By default, *pppd* doesn't require authentication from the remote, but will agree to authenticate itself when requested by the remote. As CHAP is so much stronger than PAP, *pppd* tries to use the former whenever possible. If the peer does not support it, or if *pppd* can't find a CHAP secret for the remote system in its *chap-secrets* file, it reverts to PAP. If it doesn't have a PAP secret for its peer either, it will refuse to authenticate altogether. As a consequence, the connection is closed down.

This behavior can be modified in several ways. For instance, when given the `auth` keyword, *pppd* will require the peer to authenticate itself. *pppd* will agree to use either CHAP or PAP for this, as long as it has a secret for the peer in its CHAP or PAP database, respectively. There are other options to turn a particular authentication protocol on or off, but I won't describe them here. Please refer to the *pppd(8)* manual page for details.

If all systems you talk PPP with agree to authenticate themselves with you, you should put the `auth` option in the global */etc/ppp/options* file and define passwords for each system in the *chap-secrets* file. If a system doesn't support CHAP, add an entry for it to the *pap-secrets* file. In this way, you can make sure no unauthenticated system connects to your host.

The next two sections discuss the two PPP secrets files, *pap-secrets* and *chap-secrets*. They are located in */etc/ppp* and contain triples of clients, servers and passwords, optionally followed by a list of IP addresses. The interpretation of the client and server fields is different for CHAP and PAP, and also depends on whether we authenticate ourselves with the peer, or whether we require the server to authenticate itself with us.

8.10.2 The CHAP Secrets File

When it has to authenticate itself with some server using CHAP, *pppd* searches the *pap-secrets* file for an entry with the client field equal to the local hostname, and the server field equal to the remote hostname sent in the CHAP Challenge. When requiring the peer to authenticate itself, the roles are simply reversed:

pppd will then look for an entry with the client field equal to the remote hostname (sent in the client's CHAP Response), and the server field equal to the local hostname.

The following is a sample *chap-secrets* file for **vlager**:[9]

```
# CHAP secrets for vlager.vbrew.com
#
# client            server            secret                   addrs
#---------------------------------------------------------------------
vlager.vbrew.com  c3po.lucas.com    "Use The Source Luke"  vlager.vbrew.com
c3po.lucas.com    vlager.vbrew.com  "riverrun, pasteve"    c3po.lucas.com
*                 vlager.vbrew.com  "VeryStupidPassword"   pub.vbrew.com
```

When establishing a PPP connection with **c3po**, **c3po** asks **vlager** to authenticate itself using CHAP by sending a CHAP challenge. *pppd* then scans *chap-secrets* for an entry with the client field equal to **vlager.vbrew.com** and the server field equal to **c3po.lucas.com**,[10] and finds the first line shown above. It then produces the CHAP Response from the challenge string and the secret (`Use The Source Luke`), and sends it off to **c3po**.

At the same time, *pppd* composes a CHAP challenge for **c3po**, containing a unique challenge string, and its fully qualified hostname **vlager.vbrew.com**. **c3po** constructs a CHAP Response in the manner we just discussed, and returns it to **vlager**. *pppd* now extracts the client hostname (**c3po.vbrew.com**) from the Response, and searches the *chap-secrets* file for a line matching **c3po** as a client, and **vlager** as the server. The second line does this, so *pppd* combines the CHAP challenge and the secret `riverrun, pasteve`, encrypts them, and compares the result to **c3po**'s CHAP respnose.

The optional fourth field lists the IP addresses that are acceptable for the clients named in the first field. The addresses may be given in dotted quad notation or as hostnames that are looked up with the resolver. For instance, if **c3po** requests to use an IP address during IPCP negotiation that is not in this list, the request will be rejected, and IPCP will be shut down. In the sample file shown above, **c3po** is therefore limited to using its own IP address. If the address field is empty, any addresses will be allowed; a value of - prevents the use of IP with that client altogether.

The third line of the sample *chap-secrets* file allows any host to establish a PPP link with **vlager** because a client or server field of * matches any hostname. The only requirement is that it knows the secret, and uses the address of **pub.vbrew.com**. Entries with wildcard hostnames may appear anywhere in the secrets file, since *pppd* will always use the most specific entry that applies to a server/client pair.

There are some words to be said about the way *pppd* arrives at the hostnames it looks up in the secrets file. As explained before, the remote hostname is always provided by the peer in the CHAP Challenge or Response packet. The local hostname will be derived by calling the *gethostname(2)* function by default. If you have set the system name to your unqualified hostname, such you have to provide *pppd* with the domain name in addition using the `domain` option:

```
# pppd \ldots domain vbrew.com
```

This will append the Brewery's domain name to **vlager** for all authentication-related activities. Other options that modify progpppd's idea of the local hostname are `usehostname` and `name`. When you give the local IP address on the command line using "*local*: varremote", and *local* is a name instead of a dotted quad, *pppd* will use this as the local hostname. For details, please refer to the *pppd(8)* manual page.

8.10.3 The PAP Secrets File

The PAP secrets file is very similar to that used by CHAP. The first two fields always contain a user name and a server name; the third holds the PAP secret. When the remote sends an authenticate request, *pppd* uses the entry that has a server field equal to the local hostname, and a user field equal to the user name sent in the request. When authenticating itself with the peer, *pppd* picks the secret to be sent from the line with the user field equal to the local user name, and the server field equal to the remote hostname.

A sample PAP secrets file might look like this:

[9] The double quotes are not part of the password, they merely serve to protect the white space within the password.

[10] This hostname is taken from the CHAP challenge.

```
# /etc/ppp/pap-secrets
#
# user          server          secret          addrs
vlager-pap      c3po            cresspahl       vlager.vbrew.com
c3po            vlager          DonaldGNUth     c3po.lucas.com
```

The first line is used to authenticate ourselves when talking to **c3po**. The second line describes how a user named **c3po** has to authenticate itself with us.

The name **vlager-pap** in column one is the user name we send to **c3po**. By default, *pppd* will pick the local hostname as the user name, but you can also specify a different name by giving the `user` option, followed by that name.

When picking an entry from the *pap-secrets* file for authentication with the peer, *pppd* has to know the remote host's name. As it has no way of finding that out, you have to specify it on the command line using the `remotename` keyword, followed by the peer's hostname. For instance, to use the above entry for authentication with **c3po**, we have to add the following option to *pppd*'s command line:

```
\#{} pppd ... remotename c3po user vlager-pap
```

In the fourth field (and all fields following), you may specify what IP addresses are allowed for that particular host, just as in the CHAP secrets file. The peer may then only request addresses from that list. In the sample file, we require **c3po** to use its real IP address.

Note that PAP is a rather weak authentication method, and it is suggested you use CHAP instead whenever possible. We will therefore not cover PAP in greater detail here; if you are interested in using PAP, you will find some more PAP features in the *pppd(8)* manual page.

8.11 Configuring a PPP Server

Running *pppd* as a server is just a matter of adding the appropriate options to the command line. Ideally, you would create a special account, say **ppp**, and give it a script or program as login shell that invokes *pppd* with these options. For instance, you would add the following line to */etc/passwd*:

```
ppp:*:500:200:Public PPP Account:/tmp:/etc/ppp/ppplogin
```

Of course, you may want to use different uids and gids than those shown above. You would also have to set the password for the above account using the *passwd* command.

The *ppplogin* script might then look like this:

```
#!/bin/sh
# ppplogin - script to fire up pppd on login
mesg n
stty -echo
exec pppd -detach silent modem crtscts
```

The *mesg* command disables other users to write to the tty using, for instance, the *write* command. The *stty* command turns off character echoing. The is necessary, because otherwise everything the peer sends would be echoed back to it. The most important *pppd* option given above is `-detach`, because it prevents *pppd* drom detaching from the controlling tty. If we didn't specify this option, it would go to the background, making the shell script exit. This would in turn would cause the serial line to be hung up and the connection to be dropped. The *silent* option causes *pppd* to wait until it receives a packet from the calling system before it starts sending. This prevents transmit timeouts to occur when the calling system is slow in firing up its PPP client. The `modem` makes *pppd* watch the DTR line to see if the peer has dropped the connection, and `crtscts` turns on hardware handshake.

Beside these options, you might want to force some sort of authentication, for example by specifying `auth` on *pppd*'s command line, or in the global options file. The manual page also discusses more specific options for turning individual authentication protocols on and off.

CHAPTER 9

Various Network Applications

After successfully setting up IP and the resolver, you have to turn to the services you want to provide over the network. This chapter covers the configuration of a few simple network applications, including the *inetd* server, and the programs from the *rlogin* family. The Remote Procedure Call interface that services like the Network File System (NFS) and the Network Information System (NIS) are based upon will be dealt with briefly, too. The configuration of NFS and NIS, however, takes up more room, will be described in separate chapters. This applies to electronic mail and netnews as well.

Of course, we can't cover all network applications in this book. If you want to install one that's not discussed here, like *talk*, *gopher*, or *Xmosaic* please refer to its manual pages for details.

9.1 The *inetd* Super-Server

Frequently, services are performed by so-called *daemons*. A daemon is a program that opens a certain port, and waits for incoming connections. If one occurs, it creates a child process which accepts the connection, while the parent continues to listen for further requests. This concept has the drawback that for every service offered, a daemon has to run that listens on the port for a connection to occur, which generally means a waste of system resources like swap space.

Thus, almost all UNIX installations run a "super-server" that creates sockets for a number of services, and listens on all of them simultaneously using the *select(2)* system call. When a remote host requests one of the services, the super-server notices this and spawns the server specified for this port.

The super-server commonly used is *inetd*, the Internet Daemon. It is started at system boot time, and takes the list of services it is to manage from a startup file named */etc/inetd.conf*. In addition to those servers invoked, there are a number of trivial services which are performed by *inetd* itself called *internal services*. They include *chargen* which simply generates a string of characters, and *daytime* which returns the system's idea of the time of day.

An entry in this file consists of a single line made up of the following fields:

service type protocol wait user server cmdline

The meaning of each field is as follows:

service gives the service name. The service name has to be translated to a port number by looking it up in the */etc/services* file. This file will be described in section 9.3 below.

type specifies a socket type, either *stream* (for connection-oriented protocols) or *dgram* (for datagram protocols). TCP-based services should therefore always use *stream*, while UDP-based services should always use *dgram*.

protocol names the transport protocol used by the service. This must be a valid protocol name found in the *protocols* file, also explained below.

wait This option applies only to *dgram* sockets. It may be either *wait* or *nowait*. If *wait* is specified, *inetd* will only execute one server for the specified port at any time. Otherwise, it will immediately continue to listen on the port after executing the server.

This is useful for "single-threaded" servers that read all incoming datagrams until no more arrive, and then exit. Most RPC servers are of this type and should therefore specify *wait*. The opposite type, "multi-threaded" servers, allow an unlimited number of instances to run concurrently; this is only rarely used. These servers should specify *nowait*.

stream sockets should always use *nowait*.

user This is the login id of the user the process is executed under. This will frequently be the **root** user, but some services may use different accounts. It is a very good idea to apply the principle of least privilege here, which states that you shouldn't run a command under a privileged account if the program doesn't require this for proper functioning. For example, the NNTP news server will run as **news**, while services that may pose a security risk (such as *tftp* or *finger*) are often run as **nobody**.

server gives the full path name of the server program to be executed. Internal services are marked by the keyword *internal*.

cmdline This is the command line to be passed to the server. This includes argument 0, that is the command name. Usually, this will be the program name of the server, unless the program behaves differently when invoked by a different name.

This field is empty for internal services.

```
#
# inetd services
ftp       stream tcp nowait root   /usr/sbin/ftpd     in.ftpd -l
telnet    stream tcp nowait root   /usr/sbin/telnetd in.telnetd -b/etc/issue
#finger    stream tcp nowait bin    /usr/sbin/fingerd in.fingerd
#tftp     dgram  udp wait   nobody /usr/sbin/tftpd    in.tftpd
#tftp     dgram  udp wait   nobody /usr/sbin/tftpd    in.tftpd /boot/diskless
login     stream tcp nowait root   /usr/sbin/rlogind in.rlogind
shell     stream tcp nowait root   /usr/sbin/rshd     in.rshd
exec      stream tcp nowait root   /usr/sbin/rexecd  in.rexecd
#
#        inetd internal services
#
daytime   stream tcp nowait root internal
daytime   dgram  udp nowait root internal
time      stream tcp nowait root internal
time      dgram  udp nowait root internal
echo      stream tcp nowait root internal
echo      dgram  udp nowait root internal
discard   stream tcp nowait root internal
discard   dgram  udp nowait root internal
chargen   stream tcp nowait root internal
chargen   dgram  udp nowait root internal
```

Figure 9.1: A sample */etc/inetd.conf* file.

A sample *inetd.conf* file is shown in figure 9.1. The *finger* service commented out, so that it is not available. This is often done for security reasons, because may be used by attackers to obtain names of users on your system.

The *tftp* is shown commented out as well. *tftp* implements the *Primitive File Transfer Protocol* that allows to transfer any world-readable files from your system without password checking etc. This is especially harmful with the */etc/passwd* file, even more so when you don't use shadow password.

TFTP is commonly used by diskless clients and X terminals to download their code from a boot server. If you need to run *tftpd* for this reason, make sure to limit its scope to those directories clients will retrieve files from by adding those directory names to *tftpd*'s command line. This is shown in the second *tftp* line in the example.

9.2 The *tcpd* access control facility

Since opening a computer to network access involves many security risks, applications are designed to guard against several types of attacks. Some of these, however, may be flawed (most drastically demonstrated by the RTM Internet worm), or do not distinguish between secure hosts from which requests for a particular service will be accepted, and insecure hosts whose requests should be rejected. We already briefly discussed the *finger* and *tftp* services above. Thus, one would want to limit access to these services to "trusted hosts" only, which is impossible with the usual setup, where *inetd* either provides this service to all clients, or not at all.

A useful tool for this is *tcpd*,[1] a so-called daemon wrapper. For TCP services you want to monitor or protect, it is invoked instead of the server program. *tcpd* logs the request to the *syslog* daemon, checks if the remote host is allowed to use that service, and only if this succeeds will it executes the real server program. Note that this does not work with UDP-based services.

For example, to wrap the *finger* daemon, you have to change the corresponding line in *inetd.conf* to

```
# wrap finger daemon
finger  stream  tcp     nowait  root    /usr/sbin/tcpd   in.fingerd
```

Without adding any access control, this will appear to the client just as a usual *finger* setup, except that any requests are logged to *syslog*'s *auth* facility.

Access control is implemented by means of two files called */etc/hosts.allow* and */etc/hosts.deny*. They contain entries allowing and denying access, respectively, to certain services and hosts. When *tcpd* handles a request for a service such as *finger* from a client host named **biff.foobar.com**, it scans *hosts.allow* and *hosts.deny* (in this order) for an entry matching both the service and client host. If a matching entry is found in *hosts.allow*, access is granted, regardless of any entry in *hosts.deny*. If a match is found in *hosts.deny*, the request is rejected by closing down the connection. If no match is found at all, the request is accepted.

Entries in the access files look like this:

servicelist: *hostlist* [: *shellcmd*]

servicelist is a list of service names from */etc/services*, or the keyword *ALL*. To match all services except *finger* and *tftp*, use "*ALL EXCEPT finger, tftp*".

hostlist is a list of host names or IP addresses, or the keywords *ALL*, *LOCAL*, or *UNKNOWN*. *ALL* matches any host, while *LOCAL* matches host names not containing a dot.[2] *UNKNOWN* matches any hosts whose name or address lookup failed. A name starting with a dot matches all hosts whose domain is equal to this name. For example, **.foobar.com** matches **biff.foobar.com**. There are also provisions for IP network addresses and subnet numbers. Please refer to the *hosts_access(5)* manual page for details.

To deny access to the *finger* and *tftp* services to all but the local hosts, put the following in */etc/hosts.deny*, and leave */etc/hosts.allow* empty:

```
in.tftpd, in.fingerd:  ALL EXCEPT LOCAL, .your.domain
```

The optional *shellcmd* field may contain a shell command to be invoked when the entry is matched. This is useful to set up traps that may expose potential attackers:

```
in.ftpd: ALL EXCEPT LOCAL, .vbrew.com : \
      echo "request from %d@%h" >> /var/log/finger.log; \
      if [ %h != "vlager.vbrew.com" ]; then \
          finger -l @%h >> /var/log/finger.log \
      fi
```

[1] Written by Wietse Venema, **wietse@wzv.win.tue.nl**.

[2] Usually only local host names obtained from lookups in */etc/hosts* contain no dots.

The *%h* and *%d* arguments are expanded by *tcpd* to the client host name and service name, respectively. Please refer to the *hosts_access(5)* manual page for details.

9.3 The *services* and *protocols* Files

The port numbers on which certain "standard" services are offered are defined in the "Assigned Numbers" RFC. To enable server and client programs to convert service names to these numbers, at least a part of the list is kept on each host; it is stored in a file called */etc/services*. An entry is made up like this:

service port/*protocol* [*aliases*]

Here, *service* specifies the service name, *port* defines the port the service is offered on, and *protocol* defines which transport protocol is used. Commonly, this is either *udp* or *tcp*. It is possible for a service to be offered for more than one protocol, as well as offering different services on the same port, as long as the protocols are different. The *aliases* field allows to specify alternative names for the same service.

Usually, you don't have to change the services file that comes along with the network software on your Linux system. Nevertheless, we give a small excerpt from that file below.

```
# The services file:
#
# well-known services
echo          7/tcp                     # Echo
echo          7/udp                     #
discard       9/tcp   sink null         # Discard
discard       9/udp   sink null         #
daytime      13/tcp                     # Daytime
daytime      13/udp                     #
chargen      19/tcp   ttytst source     # Character Generator
chargen      19/udp   ttytst source     #
ftp-data     20/tcp                     # File Transfer Protocol (Data)
ftp          21/tcp                     # File Transfer Protocol (Control)
telnet       23/tcp                     # Virtual Terminal Protocol
smtp         25/tcp                     # Simple Mail Transfer Protocol
nntp        119/tcp   readnews          # Network News Transfer Protocol
#
# UNIX services
exec        512/tcp                     # BSD rexecd
biff        512/udp   comsat            # mail notification
login       513/tcp                     # remote login
who         513/udp   whod              # remote who and uptime
shell       514/tcp   cmd               # remote command, no passwd used
syslog      514/udp                     # remote system logging
printer     515/tcp   spooler           # remote print spooling
route       520/udp   router routed     # routing information protocol
```

Note that, for example, the *echo* service is offered on port 7 for both TCP and UDP, and that port 512 is used for two different services, namely the COMSAT daemon (which notifies users of newly arrived mail, see *xbiff(1x)*), over UDP, and for remote execution (*rexec(1)*), using TCP.

Similar to the services file, the networking library needs a way to translate protocol names — for example, those used in the services file — to protocol numbers understood by the IP layer on other hosts. This is done by looking up the name in the */etc/protocols* file. It contains one entry per line, each containing a protocol name, and the associated number. Having to touch this file is even more unlikely than having to meddle with */etc/services*. A sample file is given below:

```
#
# Internet (IP) protocols
#
```

```
ip      0       IP              # internet protocol, pseudo protocol number
icmp    1       ICMP            # internet control message protocol
igmp    2       IGMP            # internet group multicast protocol
tcp     6       TCP             # transmission control protocol
udp     17      UDP             # user datagram protocol
raw     255     RAW             # RAW IP interface
```

9.4 Remote Procedure Call

A very general mechanism for client-server applications is provided by RPC, the *Remote Procedure Call* package. RPC was developed by Sun Micrsystems, and is a collection of tools and library functions. Important applications built on top of RPC are NFS, the Network Filesystem, and NIS, the Network Information System, both of which will be introduced in later chapters.

An RPC server consists of a collection of procedures that client may call by sending an RPC request to the server, along with the procedure parameters. The server will invoke the indicated procedure on behalf of the client, handing back the return value, if there is any. In order to be machine-independent, all data exchanged between client and server is converted to a so-called *External Data Representation* format (XDR) by the sender, and converted back to the machine-local representation by the receiver.

Sometimes, improvements to an RPC application introduce incompatible changes in the procedure call interface. Of course, simply changing the server would crash all application that still expect the original behavior. Therefore, RPC programs have version numbers assigned to them, usually starting with 1, and with each new version of the RPC interface this counter will be bumped. Often, a server may offer several versions simultaneously; clients then indicate by the version number in their requests which implementation of the service they want to use.

The network communication between RPC servers and clients is somewhat peculiar. An RPC server offers one or more collections of procedures; each set is being called a *program*, and is uniquely identified by a *program number*. A list mapping service names to program numbers is usually kept in */etc/rpc*, an excerpt of which is reproduced below in figure 9.2.

```
#
# /etc/rpc - miscellaenous RPC-based services
#
portmapper      100000  portmap sunrpc
rstatd          100001  rstat rstat_svc rup perfmeter
rusersd         100002  rusers
nfs             100003  nfsprog
ypserv          100004  ypprog
mountd          100005  mount showmount
ypbind          100007
walld           100008  rwall shutdown
yppasswdd       100009  yppasswd
bootparam       100026
ypupdated       100028  ypupdate
```

Figure 9.2: A sample */etc/rpc* file.

In TCP/IP networks, the authors of RPC were faced with the problem of mapping program numbers to generic network services. They chose to have each server provide both a TCP and a UDP port for each program and each version. Generally, RPC applications will use UDP when sending data, and only fall back to TCP when the data to be transferred doesn't fit into a single UDP datagram.

Of course, client programs have to have a way to find out which port a program number maps to. Using a configuration file for this would be too unflexible; since RPC applications don't use reserved ports, there's no guarantee that a port originally meant to be used by our database application hasn't been taken by some other process. Therefore, RPC applications pick any port they can get, and register it with the so-called *portmapper daemon*. The latter acts as a service broker for all RPC servers running on its machine: a client that wishes to contact a service with a given program number will first query the portmapper on the server's host which returns the TCP and UDP port numbers the service can be reached at.

This method has the particular drawback that it introduces a single point of failure, much like the *inetd* daemon does for the standard Berkeley services. However, this case is even a little worse, because when the portmapper dies, all RPC port information is lost; this usually means you have to restart all RPC servers manually, or reboot the entire machine.

On Linux, the portmapper is called *rpc.portmap* and resides in */usr/sbin*. Other than making sure it is started form *rc.inet2*, the portmapper doesn't require any configuration work.

9.5 Configuring the *r* Commands

There are a number of commands for executing commands on remote hosts. These are *rlogin*, *rsh*, *rcp* and *rcmd*. They all spawn a shell on the remote host and allow the user to execute commands. Of course, the client needs to have an account on the host where the commmand is to be executed. Thus all these commands perform an authorization procedure. Usually, the client will tell the user's login name to the server, which in turn requests a password that is validated in the usual way.

Sometimes, however, it is desirable to relax authorization checks for certain users. For instance, if you frequently have to log into other machines on your LAN, you might want to be admitted without having to type your password every time.

Disabling authorization is advisable only on a small number of hosts whose password databases are synchronized, or for a small number of privileged users who need to access many machines for administrative reasons. Whenever you want to allow people to log into your host without having to specify a login id or password, make sure that you don't accidentally grant access to anybody else.

There are two ways to disable authorization checks for the *r* commands. One is for the super user to allow certain or all users on certain or all hosts (the latter definitely being a bad idea) to log in without being asked for a password. This access is controlled by a file called */etc/hosts.equiv*. It contains a list of host and user names that are considered equivalent to users on the local host. An alternative option is for a user to grant other users on certain hosts access to her account. These may be listed in the file *.rhosts* in the user's home directory. For security reasons, this file must be owned by the user or the super user, and must not be a symbolic link, otherwise it will be ignored.[3]

When a client requests an *r* service, her host and user name are searched in the */etc/hosts.equiv* file, and then in the *.rhosts* file of the user she wants to log in as. As am example, assume **janet** is working on **gauss** and tries to log into **joe**'s account on **euler**. Throughout the following, we will refer to Janet as the *client* user, and to Joe as the *local* user. Now, when Janet types

```
$ rlogin -l joe euler
```

on **gauss**, the server will first check *hosts.equiv*[4] if Janet should be granted free access, and if this fails, it will try to look her up in *.rhosts* in **joe**'s home directory.

The *hosts.equiv* file on **euler** looks like this:

```
gauss
euler
-public
quark.physics.groucho.edu      andres
```

An entry consists of a host name, optionally followed by a user name. If a host name appears all by itself, all users from that host will be admitted to their local accounts without any checks. In the above example,

[3]In an NFS environment, you may need to give it a protection of 444, because the super user is often very restricted in accessing files on disks mounted via NFS.

[4]Note that the *hosts.equiv* file is *not* searched when someone attempts to log in as **root**.

Janet would be allowed to log into her account **janet** when coming from **gauss**, and the same applies to any other user except **root**. However, if Janet wants to log in as **joe**, she will be prompted for a password as usual.

If a host name is followed by a user name, as in the last line of the above sample file, this user is given password-free access to *all* accounts except the **root** account.

The host name may also be preceded by a minus sign, as in the entry "**-public**". This requires authorization for all accounts on **public**, regardless of what rights individual users grant in their *.rhosts* file.

The format of the *.rhosts* file is identical to that of *hosts.equiv*, but its meaning is a little different. Consider Joe's *.rhosts* file on **euler**:

```
chomp.cs.groucho.edu
gauss       janet
```

The first entry grants **joe** free acess when logging in from **chomp.cs.groucho.edu**, but does not affect the rights of any other account on **euler** or **chomp**. The second entry is a slight variation of this, in that it grants **janet** free access to Joe's account when logging in from **gauss**.

Note that the client's host name is obtained by reverse mapping the caller's address to a name, so that this feature will fail with hosts unknown to the resolver. The client's host name is considered to match the name in the hosts files in one of the following cases:

- The client's canonical host name (not an alias) literally matches the host name in the file.
- If the client's host name is a fully qualified domain name (such as returned by the resolver when you have DNS running), and it doesn't literally match the host name in the hosts file, it is compared to that host name expanded with the local domain name.

CHAPTER 10

The Network Information System

When you are running a local area network, your overall goal is usually to provide an environment to your users that makes the network transparent. An important stepping stone to this end is to keep vital data such as user account information synchronized between all hosts. We have seen before that for host name resolution, a powerful and sophisticated service exists, being DNS. For others tasks, there is no such specialized service. Moreover, if you manage only a small LAN with no Internet connectivity, setting up DNS may not seem worth the trouble for many administrators.

This is why Sun developed NIS, the *Network Information System*. NIS provides generic database access facilities that can be used to distribute information such as that contained in the *passwd* and *groups* files to all hosts on your network. This makes the network appear just as a single system, with the same accounts on all hosts. In a similar fashion, you can use NIS to distribute the hostname information form */etc/hosts* to all machines on the network.

NIS is based on RPC, and comprises a server, a client-side library, and several administrative tools. Originally, NIS was called *Yellow Pages*, or YP, which is still widely used to informally refer this service. On the other hand, Yellow Pages is a trademark of British Telecom, which required Sun to drop that name. As things go, some names stick with people, and so YP lives on as a prefix to the names of most NIS-related commands such as *ypserv*, *ypbind*, etc.

Today, NIS is available for virtually all Unices, and there are even free implementations of it. One is from the BSD Net-2 release, and has been derived from a public domain reference implementation donated by Sun. The library client code from this release has been in the GNU *libc* for a long time, while the administrative programs have only recently been ported to Linux by Swen Thümmler.[1] An NIS server is missing from the reference implementation. Tobias Reber has written another NIS package including all tools and a server; it is called *yps*.[2]

Currently, a complete rewrite of the NIS code called NYS is being done by Peter Eriksson,[3] which supports both plain NIS and Sun's much revised NIS+. NYS not only provides a set of NIS tools and a server, but also adds a whole new set of library functions which will most probably make it into the standard *libc* eventually. This includes a new configuration scheme for hostname resolution that replaces the current scheme using *host.conf*. The features of these functions will be discussed below.

This chapter will focus on NYS rather than the other two packages, to which I will refer as the "traditional" NIS code. If you do want to run any of these packages, the instructions in this chapter may or may not be enough. To obtain additional information, please get a standard book on NIS, such as Hal Stern's *NFS and NIS* (see [Stern92]).

For the time being, NYS is still under development, and therefore standard Linux utilities such as the network programs or the *login* program are not yet aware of the NYS configuration scheme. Until NYS is merged into the mainstream *libc* you therefore have to recompile all these binaries if you want to make them

[1] To be reached at **swen@uni-paderborn.de**. The NIS clients are available as `yp-linux.tar.gz` from **sunsite.unc.edu** in *system/Network*.

[2] The current version (as of this writing) is `yps-0.21` and can be obtained from **ftp.lysator.liu.se** in the */pub/NYS* directory.

[3] To be reached at **pen@lysator.liu.se**.

use NYS. In any of these applications' *Makefiles*, specify *-lnsl* as the last option before *libc* to the linker. This links in the relevant functions from *libnsl*, the NYS library, instead of the standard C library.

10.1 Getting Acquainted with NIS

NIS keeps database information is in so-called *maps* containing key-value pairs. Maps are stored on a central host running the NIS server, from which clients may retrieve the information through various RPC calls. Quite frequently, maps are stored in DBM files.[4]

The maps themselves are usually generated from master text files such as */etc/hosts* or */etc/passwd*. For some files, several maps are created, one for each search key type. For instance, you may search the *hosts* file for a host name as well as for an IP address. Accordingly, two NIS maps are derived from it, called *hosts.byname* and *hosts.byaddr*, respectively. Table 10.1 lists common maps and the files they are generated form.

Master File	Map(s)	
/etc/hosts	*hosts.byname*	*hosts.byaddr*
/etc/networks	*networks.byname*	*networks.byaddr*
/etc/passwd	*passwd.byname*	*passwd.byuid*
/etc/group	*group.byname*	*group.bygid*
/etc/services	*services.byname*	*services.bynumber*
/etc/rpc	*rpc.byname*	*rpc.bynumber*
/etc/protocols	*protocols.byname*	*protocols.bynumber*
/usr/lib/aliases	*mail.aliases*	

Table 10.1: Some standard NIS maps and the corresponding files.

There are other files and maps you may find support for in some NIS package or other. These may contain information for applications not discussed in this book, such as the *bootparams* map that may used by some BOOTP servers, or which currently don't have any function in Linux (like the *ethers.byname* and *ethers.byaddr* maps).

For some maps, people commonly use *nicknames*, which are shorter and therefore easier to type. To obtain a full list of nicknames understood by your NIS tools, run the following command:

```
$ ypcat -x
NIS map nickname translation table:
        "passwd" -> "passwd.byname"
        "group" -> "group.byname"
        "networks" -> "networks.byaddr"
        "hosts" -> "hosts.byname"
        "protocols" -> "protocols.bynumber"
        "services" -> "services.byname"
        "aliases" -> "mail.aliases"
        "ethers" -> "ethers.byname"
        "rpc" -> "rpc.bynumber"
        "netmasks" -> "netmasks.byaddr"
        "publickey" -> "publickey.byname"
        "netid" -> "netid.byname"
        "passwd.adjunct" -> "passwd.adjunct.byname"
        "group.adjunct" -> "group.adjunct.byname"
        "timezone" -> "timezone.byname"
```

[4] DBM is a simple database management library that uses hashing techniques to speed up search operations. There's a free DBM implementation from the GNU project called *gdbm*, which is part of most Linux distributions.

The NIS server is traditionally called *ypserv*. For an average network, a single server usually suffices; large networks may choose to run several of these on different machines and different segments of the network to relieve the load on the server machines and routers. These servers are synchronized by making one of them the *master server*, and the others *slave servers*. Maps will be created only on the master server's host. From there, they are distributed to all slaves.

You will have noticed that we have been talking about "networks" very vaguely all the time; of course there's a distinctive concept in NIS that refers to such a network, that is the collection of all hosts that share part of their system configuration data through NIS: the *NIS domain*. Unfortunately, NIS domains have absolutely nothing in common with the domains we encountered in DNS. To avoid any ambiguity throughout this chapter, I will therefore always specify which type of domain I mean.

NIS domains have a purely administrative function only. They are mostly invisible to users, except for the sharing of passwords between all machines in the domain. Therefore, the name given to a NIS domain is relevant only to the administrators. Usually, any name will do, as long as it is different from any other NIS domain name on your local network. For instance, the administrator at the Virtual Brewery may choose to create two NIS domains, one for the Brewery itself, and one for the Winery, which she names **brewery** and **winery**, respectively. Another quite common scheme is to simply use the DNS domain name for NIS as well. To set and display the NIS domain name of your host, you can use the *domainname* command. When invoked without any argument, it prints the current NIS domain name; to set the domain name, you must become super user and type:

```
# domainname brewery
```

NIS domains determine which NIS server an application will query. For instance, the *login* program on a host at the Winery should, of course, only query the Winery's NIS server (or one of them, if there were several) for a user's password information; while an application on a Brewery host should stick with the Brewery's server.

One mystery now remains to be solved, namely how a client finds out which server to connect to. The simplest approach would be to have a configuration file that names the host on which to find the server. However, this approach is rather inflexible, because it doesn't allow clients to use different servers (from the same domain, of course), depending on their availability. Therefore, traditional NIS implementations rely on a special daemon called *ypbind* to detect a suitable NIS server in their NIS domain. Before being able to perform any NIS queries, any application first finds out from *ypbind* which server to use.

ypbind probes for servers by broadcasting to the local IP network; the first to respond is assumed to be the potentially fastest one and will be used in all subsequent NIS queries. After a certain interval has elapsed, or if the server becomes unavailable, *ypbind* will probe for active servers again.

Now, the arguable point about dynamic binding is that you rarely need it, and that it introduces a security problem: *ypbind* blindly believes whoever answers, which could be a humble NIS server as well as a malicious intruder. Needless to say this becomes especially troublesome if you manage your password databases over NIS. To guard against this, NYS does *not* use *ypbind* by default, but rather picks up the server host name from a configuration file.

10.2 NIS versus NIS+

NIS and NIS+ share little more than their name and a common goal. NIS+ is structured in an entirely different way. Instead of a flat name space with disjoint NIS domains, it uses a hierarchical name space similar to that of DNS. Instead of maps, so called *tables* are used that are made up of rows and columns, where each row represents an object in the NIS+ database, while the columns cover those properties of the objects that NIS+ knows and cares about. Each table for a given NIS+ domain comprises those of its parent domains. In addition, an entry in a table may contain a link to another table. These features make it possible to structure information in many ways.

Traditional NIS has an RPC version number of 2, while NIS+ is version 3.

NIS+ does not seem to be very widely used yet, and I don't really know that much about it. (Well, almost nothing). For this reason, we will not deal with it here. If you are interested in learning more about it, please refer to Sun's NIS+ administration manual ([NISPlus]).

10.3 The Client Side of NIS

If you are familiar with writing or porting network applications, you will notice that most NIS maps listed above correspond to library functions in the C library. For instance, to obtain *passwd* information, you generally use the *getpwnam(3)* and *getpwuid(3)* functions which return the account information associated with the given user name or numerical user ID, repsectively. Under normal circumstances, these functions will perform the requested lookup on the standard file, such as */etc/passwd*.

A NIS-aware implementation of these functions, however, will modify this behavior, and place an RPC call to have the NIS server look up the user name or ID. This happens completely transparent to the application. The function may either "append" the NIS map to or "replace" the original file with it. Of course, this does not refer to a real modification of the file, it only means that it *appears* to the application as if the file had been replaced or appended to.

For traditional NIS implementations, there used to be certain conventions as to which maps replaced, and which were appended to the original information. Some, like the *passwd* maps, required kludgy modifications of the *passwd* file which, when done wrong, would open up security holes. To avoid these pitfalls, NYS uses a general configuration scheme that determines whether a particular set of client functions uses the original files, NIS, or NIS+, and in which order. It will be described in a later section of this chapter.

10.4 Running a NIS Server

After so much theoretical techno-babble, it's time to get our hands dirty with actual configuration work. In this section, we will cover the configuration of a NIS server. If there's already a NIS server running on your network, you won't have to set up your own server; in this case, you may safely skip this section.

◇ Note that if you are just going to experiment with the server, make sure you don't set it up for a NIS domain name that is already in use on your network. This may disrupt the entire network service and make a lot of people very unhappy, and very angry.

There are currently two NIS servers freely available for Linux, one contained in Tobias Reber's *yps* package, and the other in Peter Eriksson's *ypserv* package. It shouldn't matter which one you run, regardless of whether you use NYS or the standard NIS client code that is in *libc* currently. At the time of this writing, the code for the handling of NIS slave servers seems to be more complete in *yps*. So if you have to deal with slave servers, *yps* might be a better choice.

After installing the server program (*ypserv*) in */usr/sbin*, you should create the directory that is going to hold the map files your server is to distribute. When setting up a NIS domain for the **brewery** domain, the maps would go to */var/yp/brewery*. The server determines if it is serving a particular NIS domain by checking if the map directory is present. If you are disabling service for some NIS domain, make sure to remove the directory as well.

Maps are usually stored in DBM files to speed up lookups. They are created from the master files using a program called *makedbm* (for Tobias' server) or *dbmload* (for Peter's server). These may not be interchangeable. Transforming a master file into a form parseable by *dbmload* usually requires some *awk* or *sed* magic, which tend to be a little tedious to type and hard to remember. Therefore, Peter Eriksson's *ypserv* package contains a Makefile (called *ypMakefile*) that does all these jobs for you. You should install it as *Makefile* in your map directory, and edit it to reflect the maps you want to distribute. Towards the top of the file, you find the *all* target that lists the services *ypserv* is to offer. By default, the line looks something like this:

```
all: ethers hosts networks protocols rpc services passwd group netid
```

If you don't want to produce the *ethers.byname* and *ethers.byaddr* maps, for example, simply remove the *ethers* prerequisite from this rule. To test your setup, it may suffice to start with just one or two maps, like the *services.** maps.

After editing the *Makefile*, while in the map directory, type "`make`". This will automatically generate and install the maps. You have to make sure to update the maps whenever you change the master files, otherwise the changes will remain invisible to the network.

The next section explains how to configure the NIS client code. If your setup doesn't work, you should try to find out whether any requests arrive at your server or not. If you specify the `-D` command line flag to the NYS server, it prints debugging messages to the console about all incoming NIS queries, and the results returned. These should give you a hint as to where the problem lies. Tobias' server has no such option.

10.5 Setting up a NIS Client with NYS

Throughout the remainder of this chapter, we will cover the configuration of a NIS client.

Your first step should be to tell NYS which server to use for NIS service, setting it in the */etc/yp.conf* configuration file. A very simple sample file for a host on the Winery's network may look like this:

```
# yp.conf - YP configuration for NYS library.
#
domainname winery
server vbardolino
```

The first statement tells all NIS clients that they belong to the **winery** NIS domain. If you omit this line, NYS will use the domain name you assigned your system through the *domainname* command. The *server* statement names the NIS server to use. Of course, the IP address corresponding to **vbardolino** must be set in the *hosts* file; alternatively, you may use the IP address itself with the *server* statement.

In the form shown above, the *server* command tells NYS to use the named server whatever the current NIS domain may be. If, however, you are moving your machine between different NIS domains frequently, you may want to keep information for several domains in the *yp.conf* file. You can have information on the servers for various NIS domains in *yp.conf* by adding the NIS domain name to the *server* statement. For instance, you might change the above sample file for a laptop to look like this:

```
# yp.conf - YP configuration for NYS library.
#
server vbardolino winery
server vstout     brewery
```

This allows you to bring up the laptop in any of the two domains by simply setting the desired NIS domain at boot time through the *domainname* command.

After creating this basic configuration file and making sure it is world-readable, you should run your first test to check if you can connect to your server. Make sure to choose any map your server distributes, like *hosts.byname*, and try to retrieve it by using the *ypcat* utility. *ypcat*, like all other administrative NIS tools, should live in */usr/sbin*.

```
# ypcat hosts.byname
191.72.2.2      vbeaujolais  vbeaujolais.linus.lxnet.org
191.72.2.3      vbardolino   vbardolino.linus.lxnet.org
191.72.1.1      vlager       vlager.linus.lxnet.org
191.72.2.1      vlager       vlager.linus.lxnet.org
191.72.1.2      vstout       vstout.linus.lxnet.org
191.72.1.3      vale         vale.linus.lxnet.org
191.72.2.4      vchianti     vchianti.linus.lxnet.org
```

The output you get should look somthing like that shown above. If you get an error message instead that says "" or something similar, then either the NIS domain name you've set doesn't have a matching server defined in *yp.conf*, or the server is unreachable for some reason. In the latter case, make sure that a *ping* to the host yields a positive result, and that it is indeed running a NIS server. You can verify the latter by using *rpcinfo*, which should produce the following output:

```
# rpcinfo -u serverhost ypserv
program 100004 version 2 ready and waiting
```

10.6 Choosing the Right Maps

Having made sure you can reach the NIS server, you have to decide which configuration files to replace or augment with NIS maps. Commonly, you will want use NIS maps for the host and password lookup functions. The former is especially useful if you do not run BIND. The latter permits all users to log into their account from any system in the NIS domain; this usually requires sharing a central */home* directory between all hosts via NFS. It is explained detail in section 10.7 below. Other maps, like *services.byname*, aren't such a dramatic gain, but save you some editing work if you install any network applications that use a service name that's not in the standard *services* file.

Generally, you want to have some freedom of choice when a lookup function uses the local files, and when it queries the NIS server. NYS allows you to configure the order in which a function accesses these services. This is controlled through the */etc/nsswitch.conf* file, which stands for *Name Service Switch* but of course isn't limited to the name service. For any of the data lookup functions supported by NYS, it contains a line naming the services to use.

The right order of services depends on the type of data. It is unlikely that the *services.byname* map will contain entries differing from those in the local *services* file; it may only contain more. So a good choice may be to query the local files first, and check NIS only if the service name wasn't found. Hostname information, on the other hand, may change very frequently, so that DNS or the NIS server should always have the most accurate account, while the local *hosts* file is only kept as a backup if DNS and NIS should fail. In this case, you would want to check the local file last.

The example below shows how to configure *gethostbyname(2)*, *gethostbyaddr(2)*, and *getservbyname(2)* functions as described above. They will try the listed services in turn; if a lookup succeeds, the result is returned, otherwise the next service is tried.

```
# small sample /etc/nsswitch.conf
#
hosts:      nis dns files
services:   files nis
```

The complete list of services that may be used with an entry in the *nsswitch.conf* file is shown below. The actual maps, files, servers and objects being queried depend on the entry name.

nisplus or *nis+* — Use the NIS+ server for this domain. The location of the server is obtained from the */etc/nis.conf* file.

nis — Use the current NIS server of this domain. The location of the server queried is configured in the *yp.conf* file as shown in the previous section. For the *hosts* entry, the maps *hosts.byname* and *hosts.byaddr* are queried.

dns — Use the DNS name server. This service type is only useful with the *hosts* entry. The name servers queried are still determined by the standard *resolv.conf* file.

files — Use the local file, such as the */etc/hosts* file for the *hosts* entry.

dbm — Look up the information from DBM files located in */var/dbm*. The name used for the file is that of the corresponding NIS map.

Currently, NYS supports the following *nsswitch.conf* entries: *hosts*, *networks*, *passwd*, *group*, *shadow*, *gshadow*, *services*, *protocols*, *rpc*, and *ethers*. More entries are likely to be added.

Figure 10.1 shows a more complete example which introduces another feature of *nsswitch.conf*: the *[NOTFOUND=return]* keyword in the *hosts* entry tells NYS to return if the desired item couldn't be found in the NIS or DNS database. That is, NYS will continue and search the local files *only* if calls to the NIS and DNS servers failed for some other reason. The local files will then only be used at boot time and as a backup when the NIS server is down.

```
# /etc/nsswitch.conf
#
hosts:      nis dns [NOTFOUND=return] files
networks:   nis [NOTFOUND=return] files

services:   files nis
protocols:  files nis
rpc:        files nis
```

Figure 10.1: Sample *nsswitch.conf* file.

10.7 Using the *passwd* and *group* Maps

One of the major applications of NIS is in synchronizing user and account information on all hosts in a NIS domain. To this end, you usually keep only a small local */etc/passwd* file, to which the site-wide information from the NIS maps is appended. However, simply enabling NIS lookups for this service in *nsswitch.conf* is not nearly enough.

When relying on the password information distributed by NIS, you first have to make sure that the numeric user ID's of any users you have in your local *passwd* file match the NIS server's idea of user ID's. You will want this for other purposes as well, like mounting NFS volumes from other hosts in your network.

If any of the numeric ids in */etc/passwd* or */etc/group* deviate from those in the maps, you have to adjust file ownerships for all files that belong to that user. First you should change all uids and gids in *passwd* and *group* to the new values; then find all files that belong to the users just changed, and finally change their ownership. Assume **news** used to have a user ID of 9, and **okir** had a user id of 103, which were changed to some other value; you could then issue the following commands:

```
# find / -uid   9 -print >/tmp/uid.9
# find / -uid 103 -print >/tmp/uid.103
# cat /tmp/uid.9   | xargs chown news
# cat /tmp/uid.103 | xargs chown okir
```

It is important that you execute these commands with the *new passwd* file installed, and that you collect all file names before you change the ownership of any of them. To update the group ownerships of files, you will use a similar command.

Having done this, the numerical UID's and GID's on your system will agree with those on all other hosts in your NIS domain. The next step will be to add configuration lines to *nsswitch.conf* that enables NIS lookups for user and group information:

```
#/etc/nsswitch.conf - passwd and group treatment
passwd: nis files
group:  nis files
```

This makes the *login* command and all its friends first query the NIS maps when a user tries to log in, and if this lookup fails, fall back to the local files. Usually, you will remove almost all users from your local files, and only leave entries for **root** and generic accounts like **mail** in it. This is because some vital system tasks may require to map UID's to user names or vice versa. For example, administrative *cron* jobs may execute the *su* command to temporarily become **news**, or the UUCP subsystem may mail a status report. If **news** and **uucp** don't have entries in the local *passwd* file, these jobs will fail miserably during a NIS brownout.

There are two big caveats in order here: on one hand, the setup as described up to here only works for login suites that don't use shadow password, like those included in the *util-linux* package. The intricacies of using shadow passwords with NIS will be covered below. On the other hand, the login commands are not the only ones that access the *passwd* file – look at the *ls* command, which most people use almost constantly. Whenever doing a long listing, *ls* will display the symbolic names for user and group owners of a file; that is, for each UID and GID it encounters, it will have to query the NIS server once. This will slow things down rather badly if your local network is clogged, or, even worse, when the NIS server is not on the same physical network, so that datagrams have to pass through a router.

Still, this is not the whole story yet. Imagine what happens if a user wants to change her password. Usually, she will invoke *passwd*, which reads the new password and updates the local *passwd* file. This is impossible with NIS, since that file isn't available locally anymore, but having users log into the NIS server whenever they want to change their password is not an option either. Therefore, NIS provides a drop-in replacement for *passwd* called *yppasswd*, which does the analoguous thing in the presence of NIS. To change the password on the server host, it contacts the *yppasswdd* daemon on that host via RPC, and provides it with the updated password information. Usually, you install *yppasswd* over the normal program by doing something like this:

```
# cd /bin
# mv passwd passwd.old
# ln yppasswd passwd
```

At the same time you have to install *rpc.yppasswdd* on the server and start it from *rc.inet2*. This will effectively hide any of the contortions of NIS from your users.

10.8 Using NIS with Shadow Support

There is no NIS support yet for sites that use the shadow login suite. John F. Haugh, the author of the shadow suite, recently released a version of the shadow library functions covered by the GNU Library GPL to **comp.sources.misc**. It already has some support for NIS, but it isn't complete, and the files haven't been added to the standard C library yet. On the other hand, publishing the information from */etc/shadow* via NIS kind of defeats the purpose of the shadow suite.

Although the NYS password lookup functions don't use a *shadow.byname* map or anything likewise, NYS supports using a local */etc/shadow* file transparently. When the NYS implementation of *getpwnam* is called to look up information related to a given login name, the facilities specified by the *passwd* entry in *nsswitch.conf* are queried. The *nis* service will simply look up the name in the *passwd.byname* map on the NIS server. The *files* service, however, will check if */etc/shadow* is present, and if so, try to open it. If none is present, or if the user doesn't have **root** privilege, if reverts to the traditional behavior of looking up the user information in */etc/passwd* only. However, if the *shadow* file exists and can be opened, NYS will extract the user password from *shadow*. The *getpwuid* function is implemented accordingly. In this fashion, binaries compiled with NYS will deal with a local shadow suite installation transparently.

10.9 Using the Traditional NIS Code

If you are using the client code that is in the standard *libc* currently, configuring a NIS client is a little different. On one hand, it uses a *ypbind* daemon to broadcast for active servers rather than gathering this information from a configuration file. You therefore have to make sure to start *ypbind* at boot time. It must be invoked after the NIS domain has been set and the RPC portmapper has been started. Invoking *ypcat* to test the server should then work as shown above.

Recently, there have been numerous bug reports that NIS fails with an error message saying "`clntudp_create: RPC: portmapper failure - RPC: unable to receive`". These are due to an incompatible change in the way *ypbind* communicates the binding information to the library functions. Obtaining the latest sources for the NIS utilities and recompiling them should cure this problem.[5]

Also, the way traditional NIS decides if and how to merge NIS information with that from the local files deviates from that used by NYS. For instance, to use the NIS password maps, you have to include the following line somewhere in your */etc/passwd* map:

```
+:*:0:0:::
```

[5] The source for *yp-linux* can be gotten from **ftp.uni-paderborn.de** in directory */pub/Linux/LOCAL*.

This marks the place where the password lookup functions "insert" the NIS maps. Inserting a similar line (minus the last two colons) into */etc/group* does the same for the *group.** maps. To use the *hosts.** maps distributed by NIS, change the *order* line in the *host.conf* file. For instance, if you want to use NIS, DNS, and the */etc/hosts* file (in that order), you need to change the line to

```
order yp bind hosts
```

The traditional NIS implementation does not support any other maps at the moment.

CHAPTER 11

The Network File System

NFS, the network filesystem, is probably the most prominent network services using RPC. It allows to access files on remote hosts in exactly the same way as a user would access any local files. This is made possible by a mixture of kernel functionality on the client side (that uses the remote file system) and an NFS server on the server side (that provides the file data). This file access is completely transparent to the client, and works across a variety of server and host architectures.

NFS offers a number of advantages:

- Data accessed by all users can be kept on a central host, with clients mounting this directory at boot time. For example, you can keep all user accounts on one host, and have all hosts on your network mount */home* from that host. If installed alongside with NIS, users can then log into any system, and still work on one set of files.

- Data consuming large amounts of disk space may be kept on a single host. For example, all files and programs relating to LaTeX and METAFONT could be kept and maintained in one place.

- Administrative data may be kept on a single host. No need to use *rcp* anymore to install the same stupid file on 20 different machines.

Linux NFS is largely the work of Rick Sladkey,[1] who wrote the NFS kernel code and large parts of the NFS server. The latter is derived from the *unfsd* user-space NFS server originally written by Mark Shand, and the *hnfs* Harris NFS server written by Donald Becker.

Let's have a look now at how NFS works: A client may request to mount a directory from a remote host on a local directory just the same way it can mount a physical device. However, the syntax used to specify the remote directory is different. For example, to mount */home* from host **vlager** to */users* on **vale**, the administrator would issue the following command on **vale**:[2]

```
# mount -t nfs vlager:/home /users
```

mount will then try to connect to the *mountd* mount daemon on **vlager** via RPC. The server will check if **vale** is permitted to mount the directory in question, and if so, return it a file handle. This file handle will be used in all subsequent requests to files below */users*.

When someone accesses a file over NFS, the kernel places an RPC call to *nfsd* (the NFS daemon) on the server machine. This call takes the file handle, the name of the file to be accessed, and the user's user ID and group ID as parameters. These are used in determining access rights to the specified file. In order to prevent unauthorized users from reading or modifying files, user and group ids must be the same on both hosts.

On most UNIX implementations, the NFS functionality of both client and server are implemented as kernel-level daemons that are started from user space at system boot. These are the NFS daemon (*nfsd*) on

[1] Rick can be reached at **jrs@world.std.com**.

[2] Note that you can omit the `-t nfs` argument, because *mount* sees from the colon that this specifies an NFS volume.

the server host, and the *Block I/O Daemon* (*biod*) running on the client host. To improve throughput, *biod* performs asynchronous I/O using read-ahead and write-behind; also, several *nfsd* daemons are usually run concurrently.

The NFS implementation of Linux is a little different in that the client code is tightly integrated in the virtual file system (VFS) layer of the kernel and doesn't require additional control through *biod*. On the other hand, the server code runs entirely in user space, so that running several copies of the server at the same time is almost impossible because of the synchronization issues this would involve. Linux NFS currently also lacks read-ahead and write-behind, but Rick Sladkey plans to add this someday.[3]

The biggest problem with the Linux NFS code is that the Linux kernel as of version 1.0 is not able to allocate memory in chunks bigger than 4K; as a consequence, the networking code cannot handle datagrams bigger than roughly 3500 bytes after subtracting header sizes, etc. This means that transfers to and from NFS daemons running on systems that use large UDP datagrams by default (e.g. 8K on SunOS) need to be downsized artificially. This hurts performance badly under some circumstances.[4] This limit is gone in late Linux-1.1 kernels, and the client code has been modified to take advantage of this.

11.1 Preparing NFS

Before you can use NFS, be it as server or client, you must make sure your kernel has NFS support compiled in. Newer kernels have a simple interface on the proc filesystem for this, the */proc/filesystems* file, which you can display using *cat*:

```
$ cat /proc/filesystems
minix
ext2
msdos
nodev proc
nodev nfs
```

If *nfs* is missing from this list, then you have to compile your own kernel with NFS enabled. Configuring the kernel network options is explained in section "Kernel Configuration" in chapter 3.

For older kernels prior to Linux 1.1, the easiest way to find out whether your kernel has NFS support enabled is to actually try to mount an NFS file system. For this, you could create a directory below */tmp*, and try to mount a local directory on it:

```
# mkdir /tmp/test
# mount localhost:/etc /tmp/test
```

If this mount attempt fails with an error message saying "`fs type nfs no supported by kernel`", you must make a new kernel with NFS enabled. Any other error messages are completely harmless, as you haven't configured the NFS daemons on your host yet.

11.2 Mounting an NFS Volume

NFS volumes[5] are mounted very much the way usual file systems are mounted. You invoke *mount* using the following syntax:

```
# mount -t nfs nfs_volume local_dir options
```

[3]The problem with write-behind is that the kernel buffer cache is indexed by device/inode pairs, and therefore can't be used for NFS-mounted file systems.

[4]As explained to me by Alan Cox: The NFS specification requires the server to flush each write to disk before it returns an acknowledgement. As BSD kernels are only capable of page-sized writes (4K), writing a 4 chunks of 1K each to a BSD-based NFS server results in 4 write operations of 4K each.

[5]One doesn't say file system, because these are not proper file systems.

nfs_volume is given as *remote_host:remote_dir*. Since this notation is unique to NFS file systems, you can leave out the `-t nfs` option.

There are a number of additional options that you may specify to *mount* upon mounting an NFS volume. These may either be given following the `-o` switch on the command line, or in the options field of the */etc/fstab* entry for the volume. In both cases, multiple options are separated from each other by commas. Options specified on the command line always override those given in the *fstab* file.

A sample entry in */etc/fstab* might be

```
# volume              mount point       type  options
news:/usr/spool/news  /usr/spool/news   nfs   timeo=14,intr
```

This volume may then be mounted using

```
# mount news:/usr/spool/news
```

In the absence of a *fstab* entry, NFS *mount* invocations look a lot uglier. For instance, suppose you mount your users' home directories from a machine named **moonshot**, which uses a default block size of 4K for read/write operations. You might decrease block size to 2K to suit Linux' datagram size limit by issuing

```
# mount moonshot:/home /home -o rsize=2048,wsize=2048
```

The list of all valid options is described in its entirety in the *nfs(5)* manual page that comes with Rick Sladkey's NFS-aware *mount* tool which can be found in Rik Faith's *util-linux* package). The following is an incomplete list of those you would probably want to use:

rsize=n and *wsize=n* These specify the datagram size used by the NFS clients on read and write requests, respectively. They currently default to 1024 bytes, due to the limit on UDP datagram size described above.

timeo=n This sets the time (in tenths of a second) the NFS client will wait for a request to complete. The default values is 0.7 seconds.

hard Explicitly mark this volume as hard-mounted. This is on by default.

soft Soft-mount the driver (as opposed to hard-mount).

intr Allow signals to interrupt an NFS call. Useful for aborting when the server doesn't respond.

Except for *rsize* and *wsize*, all of these options apply to the client's behavior if the server should become inaccessible temporarily. They play together in the following way: whenever the client sends a request to the NFS server, it expects the operation to have finished after a given interval (specified in the *timeout* option). If no confirmation is received within this time, a so-called *minor timeout* occurs, and the operation is retried with the timeout interval doubled. After reaching a maximum timeout of 60 seconds, a *major timeout* occurs.

By default, a major timeout will cause the client to print a message to the console and start all over again, this time with an initial timeout interval twice that of the previous cascade. Potentially, this may go on forever. Volumes that stubbornly retry an operation until the server becomes available again are called *hard-mounted*. The opposite variety, *soft-mounted* volumes gerenates an I/O error for the calling process whenever a major timeout occurs. Because of the write-behind introduced by the buffer cache, this error condition is not propagated to the process itself before it calls the *write(2)* function the next time, so a program can never be sure that a write operation to a soft-mounted volume has succeded at all.

Whether you hard- or soft-mount a volume is not simply a question of taste, but also has to do with what sort of information you want to access from this volume. For example, if you mount your X programs by NFS, you certainly would not want your X session to go berserk just because someone brought the network to a grinding halt by firing up seven copies of *xv* at the same time, or by pulling the Ethernet plug for a moment. By hard-mounting these, you make sure that your computer will wait until it is able to re-establish contact with your NFS-server. On the other hand, non-critical data such as NFS-mounted news partititons or FTP archives may as well be soft-mounted, so it doesn't hang your session in case the remote machine should be temporarily unreachable, or down. If your network connection to the server is flakey or goes through a loaded router, you may either increase the initial timeout using the *timeo* option, or hard-mount the volumes, but allow for signals interrupting the NFS call so that you may still abort any hanging file access.

Usually, the *mountd* daemon will in some way or other keep track of which directories have been mounted by what hosts. This information can be displayed using the *showmount* program, which is also included in the NFS server package. The Linux *mountd*, however, does not do this yet.

11.3 The NFS Daemons

If you want to provide NFS service to other hosts, you have to run the *nfsd* and *mountd* daemons on your machine. As RPC-based programs, they are not managed by *inetd*, but are started up at boot time, and register themselves with the portmapper. Therefore, you have to make sure to start them only after *rpc.portmap* is running. Usually, you include the following two lines in your *rc.inet2* script:

```
if [ -x /usr/sbin/rpc.mountd ]; then
        /usr/sbin/rpc.mountd; echo -n " mountd"
fi
if [ -x /usr/sbin/rpc.nfsd ]; then
        /usr/sbin/rpc.nfsd; echo -n " nfsd"
fi
```

The ownership information of files a NFS daemon provides to its clients usually contains only numerical user and group ID's. If both client and server associate the same user and group names with these numerical id's, they are said to share the same uid/gid space. For example, this is the case when you use NIS to distribute the *passwd* information to all hosts on your LAN.

On some occasions, however, they do not match. Rather updating the UID's and GID's of the client to match those of the server, you can use the *ugidd* mapping daemon to work around this. Using the *map_daemon* option explained below, you can tell *nfsd* to map the server's UID/GID space to the client's UID/GID space with the aid of the *ugidd* on the client.

ugidd is an RPC-based server, and is started from *rc.inet2* just like *nfsd* and *mountd*.

```
if [ -x /usr/sbin/rpc.ugidd ]; then
        /usr/sbin/rpc.ugidd; echo -n " ugidd"
fi
```

11.4 The *exports* File

While the above options applied to the client's NFS configuration, there is a different set of options on the server side that configure its per-client behavior. These options must be set in the */etc/exports* file.

By default, *mountd* will not allow anyone to mount directories from the local host, which is a rather sensible attitude. To permit one or more hosts to NFS-mount a directory, it must *exported*, that is, must be specified in the *exports* file. A sample file may look like this:

```
# exports file for vlager
/home           vale(rw) vstout(rw) vlight(rw)
/usr/X386       vale(ro) vstout(ro) vlight(ro)
/usr/TeX        vale(ro) vstout(ro) vlight(ro)
/               vale(rw,no_root_squash)
/home/ftp       (ro)
```

Each line defines a directory, and the hosts allowed to mount it. A host name is usually a fully qualified domain name, but may additionally contain the * and *?* wildcard, which act the way they do with the Bourne shell. For instance, **lab*.foo.com** matches **lab01.foo.com** as well as **laber.foo.com**. If no host name is given, as with the */home/ftp* directory in the example above, any host is allowed to mount this directory.

When checking a client host against the *exports* file, *mountd* will look up the client's hostname using the *gethostbyaddr(2)* call. With DNS, this call returns the client's canonical hostname, so you must make sure not to use aliases in *exports*. Without using DNS, the returned name is the first hostname found in the *hosts* file that matches the client's address.

The host name is followed by an optional, comma-separated list of flags, enclosed in brackets. These flags may take the following values:

insecure Permit non-authenticated access from this machine.

unix-rpc Require UNIX-domain RPC authentication from this machine. This simply requires that requests originate from a reserved internet port (i.e. the port number has to be less than 1024). This option is on by default.

secure-rpc Require secure RPC authentication from this machine. This has not been implemented yet. See Sun's documentation on Secure RPC.

kerberos Require Kerberos authentication on accesses from this machine. This has not been implemented yet. See the MIT documentation on the Kerberos authentication system.

root_squash This is a security feature that denies the super user on the specified hosts any special access rights by mapping requests from UID 0 on the client to uid 65534 (-2) on the server. This UID should be associated with the user **nobody**.

no_root_squash Don't map requests from UID 0. This option is on by default.

ro Mount file hierarchy read-only. This option is on by default.

rw Mount file hierarchy read-write.

link_relative Convert absolute symbolic links (where the link contents start with a slash) into relative links by prepending the necessary number of *../*'s to get from the directory containing the link to the root on the server. This option only makes sense when a host's entire file system is mounted, else some of the links might point to nowhere, or even worse, files they were never meant to point to.

This option is on by default.

link_absolute Leave all symbolic link as they are (the normal behavior for Sun-supplied NFS servers).

map_identity The *map_identity* option tells the server to assume that the client uses the same uid's and gid's as the server. This option is on by default.

map_daemon This option tells the NFS server to assume that client and server do not share the same uid/gid space. *nfsd* will then build a list mapping id's between client and server by querying the client's *ugidd* daemon.

An error parsing the *exports* file is reported to *syslogd*'s *daemon* facility at level *notice* whenever *nfsd* or *mountd* is started up.

Note that host names are obtained from the client's IP address by reverse mapping, so you have to have the resolver configured properly. If you use BIND and are very security-conscious, you should enable spoof checking in your *host.conf* file.

11.5 The Linux Automounter

Sometimes, it is wasteful to mount all NFS volumes users might possibly want to access; either because of the sheer number of volumes to be mounted, or because of the time this would take at startup. A viable alternative to this is a so-called *automounter*. This is a daemon that automatically and transparently mounts any NFS volume as needed, and unmounts them after they have not been used for some time. One of the clever things about an automounter is that it is able to mount a certain volume from alternative places. For instance, you may keep copies of your X programs and support files on two or three hosts, and have all other hosts mount them via NFS. Using an automounter, you may specify all three of them to be mounted on */usr/X386*; the automounter will then try to mount any of these until one of the mount attempts succeeds.

The automounter commonly used with Linux is called *amd*. It was originally written by Jan-Simon Pendry and has been ported to Linux by Rick Sladkey. The current version is *amd-5.3*.

Explaining *amd* is beyond the scope of this chapter; for a good manual please refer to the sources; they contain a texinfo file with very detailed information.

CHAPTER 12

Managing Taylor UUCP

12.1 History

UUCP was designed in the late seventies by Mike Lesk at AT&T Bell Laboratories to provide a simple dial-up network over public telephone lines. Since most people that want to have email and Usenet News on their home machine still communicate through modems, UUCP has remained very popular. Although there are many implementations running on a wide variety of hardware platforms and operating systems, they are compatible to a high degree.

However, as with most software that has somehow become "standard" over the years, there is no UUCP which one would call *the* UUCP. It has undergone a steady process of evolution since the first version which was implemented in 1976. Currently, there are two major species which differ mainly in their support of hardware and their configuration. Of these, various implementations exist, each varying slightly from its siblings.

One species is the so-called "Version 2 UUCP", which dates back to a 1977 implementation by Mike Lesk, David A. Novitz, and Greg Chesson. Although it is fairly old, it is still in frequent use. Recent implementations of Version 2 provide much of the comfort of the newer UUCP species.

The second species was developed in 1983, and is commonly referred to as BNU (Basic Networking Utilities), HoneyDanBer UUCP, or HDB for short. The name is derived from the authors' names, P. Honeyman, D. A. Novitz, and B. E. Redman. HDB was conceived to eliminate some of Version 2 UUCP's deficiencies. For example, new transfer protocols were added, and the spool directory was split so that now there is one directory for each site you have UUCP traffic with.

The implementation of UUCP currently distributed with Linux is Taylor UUCP 1.04,[1] which is the version this chapter is based upon. Taylor UUCP Version 1.04 was released in February 1993. Apart from traditional configuration files, Taylor UUCP may also be compiled to understand the new-style – a.k.a. "Taylor" – configuration files.

Version 1.05 has been released recently, and will soon make its way into most distributions. The differences between these versions mostly affect features you will never use, so you should be able to configure Taylor UUCP 1.05 using the information form this book.

As included in most Linux distributions, Taylor UUCP is usually compiled for BNU compatibility, or the Taylor configuiration scheme, or both. As the latter is much more flexible, and probably easier to understand than the often rather obscure BNU configuration files, I will describe the Taylor scheme below.

The purpose of this chapter is not to give you an exhaustive description of what the command line options for the UUCP commands are and what they do, but to give you an introduction on how to set up a working UUCP node. The first section gives a hopefully gentle introduction about how UUCP implements remote execution and file transfers. If you are not entirely new to UUCP, you might want to skip this and move on to section 12.3, which explains the various files used to set up UUCP.

[1] Written and copyrighted by Ian Taylor, 1993.

We will however assume that you are familiar with the user programs of the UUCP suite. These are *uucp* and *uux*. For a description, please refer to the on-line manual pages.

Besides the publicly accessible programs, *uux* and *uucp*, the UUCP suite contains a number of commands used for administrative purposes only. They are used to monitor UUCP traffic across your node, remove old log files, or compile statistics. None of these will be described here, because they're peripheral to the main tasks of UUCP. Besides, they're well documented and fairly easy to understand. However, there is a third category, which comprise the actual UUCP "work horses." They are called *uucico* (where cico stands for copy-in copy-out), and *uuxqt*, which executes jobs sent from remote systems.

12.1.1 More Information on UUCP

Those who don't find everything they need in this chapter should read the documentation that comes along with the package. This is a set of texinfo files that describe the setup using the Taylor configuration scheme. Texinfo can be converted to DVI and to GNU info files using *tex* and *makeinfo*, respectively.

If you want to use BNU or even (shudder!) Version 2 configuration files, there is a very good book, "Managing UUCP and Usenet" ([OReilly89]). I find it very useful. Another good source for information about UUCP on Linux is Vince Skahan's UUCP-HOWTO, which is posted regularly to **comp.os.linux.announce**.

There's also a newsgroup for the discussion of UUCP, called **comp.mail.uucp**. If you have questions specific to Taylor UUCP, you may be better off asking them there, rather than on the **comp.os.linux** groups.

12.2 Introduction

12.2.1 Layout of UUCP Transfers and Remote Execution

Vital to the understanding of UUCP is the concept of *jobs*. Every transfer a user initiates with *uucp* or *uux* is called a job. It is made up of a *command* to be executed on a remote system, and a collection of *files* to be transferred between sites. One of these parts may be missing.

As an example, assume you issued the following command on your host, which makes UUCP copy the file *netguide.ps* to host **pablo**, and makes it execute the *lpr* command to print the file.

```
$ uux -r pablo!lpr !netguide.ps
```

UUCP does not generally call the remote system immediately to execute a job (else you could make do with *kermit*). Instead, it temporarily stores the job description away. This is called *spooling*. The directory tree under which jobs are stored is therefore called the *spool directory* and is generally located in */var/spool/uucp*. In our example, the job description would contain information about the remote command to be executed (*lpr*), the user who requested the execution, and a couple of other items. In addition to the job description, UUCP has to store the input file, *netguide.ps*.

The exact location and naming of spool files may vary, depending on some compile-time options. HDB-compatible UUCP's generally store spool files in a directory named */var/spool/uucp/site*, where *site* is the name of the remote site. When compiled for Taylor configuration, UUCP will create subdirectories below the site-specific spool directory for different types of spool files.

At regular intervals, UUCP dials up the remote system. When a connection to the remote machine is established, UUCP transfers the files describing the job, plus any input files. The incoming jobs will not be executed immediately, but only after the connection terminates. This is done by *uuxqt*, which also takes care of forwarding any jobs if they are designated for another site.

To distinguish between important and less important jobs, UUCP associates a *grade* with each job. This is a single letter, ranging from 0 through 9, A though Z, and a through z, in decreasing precedence. Mail is customarily spooled with grade B or C, while news is spooled with grade N. Jobs with higher grade are transferred earlier. Grades may be assigned using the `-g` flag when invoking *uucp* or *uux*.

You can also disallow the transfer of jobs below a given grade at certain times. This is also called the *maximum spool grade* allowed during a conversation and defaults to z. Note the terminological ambiguity here: a file is transferred only if it is *equal or above* the maximum spool grade.

12.2.2 The Inner Workings of *uucico*

◇ To understand why *uucico* needs to know certain things, a quick description of how it actually connects to a remote system might be in order here.

When you execute *uucico -s system* from the command line, it first has to connect physically. The actions taken depend on the type of connection to open – e.g. when using telephone line, it has to find a modem, and dial out. Over TCP, it has to call *gethostbyname(3)* to convert the name to a network address, find out which port to open, and bind the address to the corresponding socket.

After this connection has been established, an authorization procedure has to be passed. It generally consists of the remote system asking for a login name, and possibly a password. This is commonly called the *login chat*. The authorization procedure is performed either by the usual *getty/login* suite, or – on TCP sockets – by *uucico* itself. If authorization succeeds, the remote end fires up *uucico*. The local copy of *uucico* which initiated the connection is referred to as *master*, the remote copy as *slave*.

Next follows the *handshake phase*: the master now sends its hostname, plus several flags. The slave checks this hostname for permission to log in, send and receive files, etc. The flags describe (among other things) the maximum grade of spool files to transfer. If enabled, a conversation count, or *call sequence number* check takes place here. With this feature, both sites maintain a count of successful connections, which are compared. If they do not match, the handshake fails. This is useful to protect yourself against impostors.

Finally, the two *uucico*'s try to agree on a common *transfer protocol*. This protocol governs the way data is transferred, checked for consistency, and retransmitted in case of an error. There is a need for different protocols because of the differing types of connections supported. For example, telephone lines require a "safe" protocol which is pessimistic about errors, while TCP transmission is inherently reliable and can use a more efficient protocol that foregoes most extra error checking.

After the handshake is complete, the actual transmission phase begins. Both ends turn on the selected protocol driver. The drivers possibly perform a protocol-specific initialization sequence.

First, the master sends all files queued for the remote system whose spool grade is high enough. When it has finished, it informs the slave that it is done, and that the slave may now hang up. The slave now can either agree to hang up, or take over the conversation. This is a change of roles: now the remote system becomes master, and the local one becomes slave. The new master now sends its files. When done, both *uucico*'s exchange termination messages, and close the connection.

We will not go into this in greater detail: please refer to either the sources or any good book on UUCP for this. There is also a really antique article floating around the net, written by David A. Novitz, which gives a detailed description of the UUCP protocol. The Taylor UUCP FAQ also disucsses some details of the way UUCP is implemented. It is posted to **comp.mail.uucp** regularly.

12.2.3 *uucico* Command Line Options

This section describes the most important command line options for *uucico*. For a complete list, please refer to the *uucico(1)* manual page.

`-s` *system* Call the named *system* unless prohibited by call time restrictions.

`-S` *system* Call the named *system* unconditionally.

`-r1` Start *uucico* in master mode. This is the default when `-s` or `-S` is given. All by itself, the `-r1` option causes *uucico* to try to call all systems in *sys*, unless prohibited by call or retry time restrictions.

`-r0` Start *uucico* in slave mode. This is the default when no `-s` or `-S` is given. In slave mode, either standard input/output are assumed to be connected to a serial port, or the TCP port specified by the `-p` option is used.

`-x` *type*, `-X` *type* Turn on debugging of the specified type. Several types may be given as a comma-separated list. The following types are valid: *abnormal*, *chat*, *handshake*, *uucp-proto*, *proto*, *port*, *config*, *spooldir*, *execute*, *incoming*, *outgoing*. Using *all* turns on all options. For compatibility with other UUCP implementations, a number may be specified instead, which turns on debugging for the first *n* items from the above list.

Debugging messages will be logged to the file *Debug* below */var/spool/uucp*.

12.3 UUCP Configuration Files

In contrast to simpler file transfer programs, UUCP was designed to be able to handle all transfers automatically. Once it is set up properly, interference by the administrator should not be necessary on a day-to-day basis. The information required for this is is kept in a couple of *configuration files* that reside in the directory */usr/lib/uucp*. Most of these files are used only when dialing out.

12.3.1 A Gentle Introduction to Taylor UUCP

To say that UUCP configuration is hard would be an understatement. It is really a hairy subject, and the sometimes terse format of the configuration files doesn't make things easier (although the Talyor format is almost easy reading compared to the older formats in HDB or Version 2).

To give you a feel how all these files interact, we will introduce you to the most important ones, and have a look at sample entries of these files. We won't explain everything in detail now; a more accurate account is given in separate sections below. If you want to set up your machine for UUCP, you had best start with some sample files, and adapt them gradually. You can pick either those shown below, or those included in your favorite Linux distribution.

All files described in this section are kept in */usr/lib/uucp* or a subdirectory thereof. Some Linux distributions contain UUCP binaries that have support for both HDB and Taylor configuration enabled, and use different subdirectories for each configuration file set. There will usually be a *README* file in */usr/lib/uucp*.

For UUCP to work properly, these files must be owned by the **uucp** user. Some of them contain passwords and telephone numbers, and therefore should have permissions of 600.[2]

The central UUCP configuration file is */usr/lib/uucp/config*, and is used to set general parameters. The most important of them (and for now, the only one), is your host's UUCP name. At the Virtual Brewery, they use **vstout** as their UUCP gateway:

```
# /usr/lib/uucp/config - UUCP main configuration file
hostname        vstout
```

The next important configuration file is the *sys* file. It contains all system-specific information of sites you are linked to. This includes the site's name, and information on the link itself, such as the telephone number when using a modem link. A typical entry for a modem-connected site called **pablo** would be

```
# /usr/lib/uucp/sys - name UUCP neighbors
# system: pablo
system          pablo
time            Any
phone           123-456
port            serial1
speed           38400
chat            ogin: vstout ssword: lorca
```

The *port* names a port to be used, and *time* specifies the times at which it may be called. *chat* describes the login chat scripts – the sequence of strings that must be exchanged between to allow *uucico* to log into **pablo**. We will get back to chat scripts later. The *port* command does not name a device special file such as */dev/cua1*, but rather names an entry in the *port* file. You can assign these names as you like as long as they refer to a valid entry in *port*.

The *port* file holds information specific to the link itself. For modem links, it describes the device special file to be used, the range of speeds supported, and the type of dialing equipment connected to the port. The entry below describes */dev/cua1* (a.k.a. COM 2), to which a NakWell modem is connected that is capable of running at speeds up to 38400bps. The entry's name way chosen to match the port name given in the *sys* file.

[2]Note that although most UUCP commands must be setuid to **uucp**, you must make sure the *uuchk* program is *not*. Otherwise, users will be able to display passwords even though they have mode 600.

```
# /usr/lib/uucp/port - UUCP ports
# /dev/cua1 (COM2)
port            serial1
type            modem
device          /dev/cua1
speed           38400
dialer          nakwell
```

The information pertaining to the dialers itself is kept in yet another file, called – you guessed it: *dial*. For each dialer type, it basically contains the sequence of commands to be issued to dial up a remote site, given the telephone number. Again, this is specified as a chat script. For example, the entry for the above NakWell might look like this:

```
# /usr/lib/uucp/dial - per-dialer information
# NakWell modems
dialer          nakwell
chat            "" ATZ OK ATDT\T CONNECT
```

The line starting with *chat* specifies the modem chat, which is the sequence of commands sent to and received from the modem to initialize it and make it dial the desired number. The "*\T*" sequence will be replaced with the phone number by *uucico*.

To give you a rough idea how *uucico* deals with these configuration files, assume you issued the command

```
$ uucico -s pablo
```

on the command line. The first thing *uucico* does is look up **pablo** in the *sys* file. From the *sys* file entry for **pablo** it sees that it should use the *serial1* port to establish the connection. The *port* file tells it that this is a modem port, and that it has a NakWell modem attached.

uucico now searches *dial* for the entry describing the NakWell modem, and having found one, opens the serial port */dev/cua1* and executes the dialer chat. That is, it sends "`ATZ`", waits for the "`OK`" response, etc. When encountering the string "*\T*", it substitutes the phone number (123–456) extracted from the *sys* file.

After the modem returns `CONNECT`, the connection has been established, and the modem chat is complete. *uucico* now returns to the *sys* file and executes the login chat. In our example, it would wait for the "`login:`" prompt, then send its user name (`neruda`), wait for the "`password:`" prompt, and send its password, "`lorca`".

After completing authorization, the remote end is assumed to fire up its own *uucico*. The two will then enter the handshake phase described in the previous section.

The way the configuration files depend on each other is also shown in figure 12.1.

12.3.2 What UUCP Needs to Know

Before you start writing the UUCP configuration files, you have to gather some information it needs to know.

First, you will have to figure out what serial device your modem is attached to. Usually, the (DOS) ports COM1 through COM4 map to the device special files */dev/cua0* through */dev/cua3*. Most distributions, such as Slackware, create a link */dev/modem* as a link to the appropriate *cua** device file, and configure *kermit*, *seyon*, etc, to use this generic file. In this case, you should use */dev/modem* in your UUCP configuration, too.

The reason for this is that all dial-out programs use so-called *lock files* to signal when a serial port is in use. The names of these lock files are a concatenation of the string *LCK..* and the device file name, for instance *LCK..cua1*. If programs use different names for the same device, they will fail to recognize each other's lock files. As a consequence, they will disrupt each other's session when started at the same time. This is not an unlikely event when you schedule your UUCP calls using a *crontab* entry.

For details of setting up your serial ports, please refer to chapter 4.

Next, you must find out at what speed your modem and Linux will communicate. You will have to set this to the maximum effective transfer rate you expect to get. The effective transfer rate may be much higher than the raw physical transfer rate your modem is capable of. For instance, many modems send and receive data at 2400bps (bits per second). Using compression protocols such as V.42bis, the actual transfer rate may climb up to 9600bps.

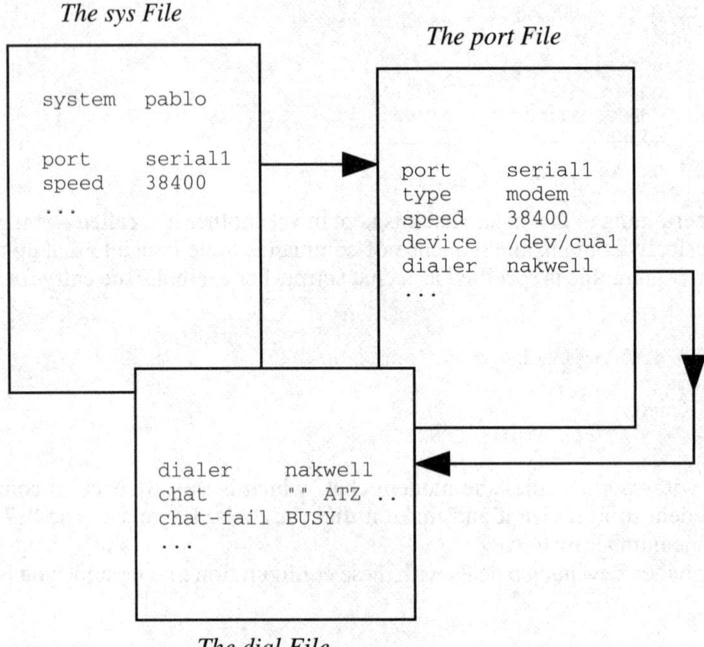

Figure 12.1: Interaction of Taylor UUCP Configuration Files.

Of course, if UUCP is to do anything, you will need the phone number of a system to call. Also, you will need a valid login id and possibly a password for the remote machine.[3]

You will also have to know *exactly* how to log into the system. E.g., do you have to press the BREAK key before the login prompt appears? Does it display `login:` or `user:`? This is necessary for composing the *chat script*, which is a recipe telling *uucico* how to log in. If you don't know, or if the usual chat script fails, try to call the system with a terminal program like *kermit* or *minicom*, and write down exactly what you have to do.

12.3.3 Site Naming

As with TCP/IP-based networking, your host has to have a name for UUCP networking. As long as you simply want to use UUCP for file transfers to or from sites you dial up directly, or on a local network, this name does not have to meet any standards.[4]

However, if you use UUCP for a mail or news link, you should think about having the name registered with the UUCP Mapping project. The UUCP Mapping Project is described in chapter 13. Even if you participate in a domain, you might consider having an official UUCP name for your site.

Frequently, people choose their UUCP name to match the first component of their fully qualified domain name. Suppose your site's domain address is **swim.twobirds.com**, then your UUCP host name would be **swim**. Think of UUCP sites as knowing each other on a first-name basis. Of course, you can also use a UUCP name completely unrelated to your fully qualified domain name.

However, make sure not to use the unqualified site name in mail addresses unless you have registered it

[3]If you're just going to try out UUCP, get the number of an archive site near you. Write down the login and password – they're public to make anonymous downloads possible. In most cases, they're something like **uucp/uucp** or **nuucp/uucp**.

[4]The only limitation is that it shouldn't be longer than 7 characters, so as to not confuse hosts with filesystems that impose a narrow limit on file names.

as your official UUCP name.[5] At the very best, mail to an unregistered UUCP host will vanish in some big black bit bucket. If you use a name already held by some other site, this mail will be routed to that site, and cause its postmaster no end of headaches.

By default, the UUCP suite uses the name set by *hostname* as the site's UUCP name. This name is commonly set in the */etc/rc.local* script. If your UUCP name is different from what you set your host name to, you have to use the *hostname* option in the *config* file to tell *uucico* about your UUCP name. This is described below.

12.3.4 Taylor Configuration Files

We now return to the configuration files. Taylor UUCP gets its information from the following files:

config This is the main configuration file. You can define your site's UUCP name here.

sys This file describes all sites known to you. For each site, it specifies its name, at what times to call it, which number to dial (if any), what type of device to use, and how to log on.

port Contains entries describing each port available, together with the line speed supported and the dialer to be used.

dial Describes dialers used to establish a telephone connection.

dialcode Contains expansions for symbolic dialcodes.

call Contains the login name and password to be used when calling a system. Rarely used.

passwd Contains login names and passwords systems may use when logging in. This file is used only when *uucico* does its own password checking.

Taylor configuration files are generally made up of lines containing keyword-value pairs. A hash sign introduces a comment that entends to the end of the line. To use a hash sign by itself, you may escape it with a backslash.

There are quite a number of options you can tune with these configuration files. We can't go into all parameters here, but will only cover the most important ones. They you should be able to configure a modem-based UUCP link. Additional sections will describe the modifications necessary if you want to use UUCP over TCP/IP or over a direct serial line. A complete reference is given in the Texinfo documents that accompany the Taylor UUCP sources.

When you think you have configured your UUCP system completely, you can check your configuration using the *uuchk* tool (located in */usr/lib/uucp*). *uuchk* reads your configuration files, and prints out a detailed report of the configuration values used for each system.

12.3.5 General Configuration Options – the *config* File

You won't generally use this file to describe much beside your UUCP hostname. By default, UUCP will use the name you set with the *hostname* command, but it is generally a good idea to set the UUCP name explicitly. A sample file is shown below:

```
# /usr/lib/uucp/config - UUCP main configuration file
hostname        vstout
```

Of course, there are a number of miscellaneous parameters that may be set here, too, such as the name of the spool directory, or access rights for anonymous UUCP. The latter will be described in a later section.

12.3.6 How to Tell UUCP about other Systems – the *sys* File

The *sys* file describes the systems your machine knows about. An entry is introduced by the *system* keyword; the subsequent lines up to the next *system* directive detail the parameters specific to that site. Commonly, a system entry will define parameters such as the telephone number and the login chat.

[5]The UUCP Mapping Project registers all UUCP hostnames world-wide and makes sure they are unique. To register your UUCP name, ask the maintainers of the site that handles your mail; they will be able to help you with it.

Parameters before the very first *system* line set default values used for all systems. Usually, you will set protocol paramters and the like in the defaults section.

Below, the most prominent fields are discussed in some detail.

12.3.6.1 System Name

The *system* command names the remote system. You must specify the correct name of the remote system, not an alias you invented, because *uucico* will check it against what the remote system says it is called when you log on.[6]

Each system name may appear only once. If you want to use several sets of configurations for the same system (such as different telephone numbers *uucico* should try in turn), you can specify *alternates*. Alternates are described below.

12.3.6.2 Telephone Number

If the remote system is to be reached over a telephone line, the *phone* field specifies the number the modem should dial. It may contain several tokens interpreted by *uucico*'s dialing procedure. An equal sign means to wait for a secondary dial tone, and a dash generates a one-second pause. For instance, some telephone installations will choke when you don't pause between dialing the prefix code and telephone number.

Any embedded alphabetic string may be used to hide site-dependent information like area codes. Any such string is translated to a dialcode using the *dialcode* file. Suppose you have the following *dialcode* file:

```
# /usr/lib/uucp/dialcode - dialcode translation
Bogoham         024881
Coxton          035119
```

With these translations, you can use a phone number such as *Bogoham7732* in the *sys* file, which makes things probably a little more legible.

12.3.6.3 Port and Speed

The *port* and *speed* options are used to select the device used for calling the remote system, and the maximum speed to which the device should be set.[7] A *system* entry may use either option alone, or both options in conjunction. When looking up a suitable device in the *port* file, only those ports are selected that have a matching port name and/or speed range.

Generally, using the *speed* option should suffice. If you have only one serial device defined in *port*, *uucico* will always pick the right one, anyway, so you only have to give it the desired speed. If you have several modems attached to your systems, you still often don't want to name a particular port, because if *uucico* finds that there are several matches, it tries each device in turn until it finds an unused one.

12.3.6.4 The Login Chat

Above, we already encountered the login chat script, which tells *uucico* how to log into the remote system. It consists of a list of tokens, specifying strings expected and sent by the local *uucico* process. The intention is to make *uucico* wait until the remote machine sends a login prompt, then return the login name, wait for the remote system to send the password prompt, and send the password. Expect and send strings are given in alternation. *uucico* automatically appends a carriage return character (*\r*) to any send string. Thus, a simple chat script would look like

```
ogin:  vstout ssword:  catch22
```

[6]Older Version 2 UUCP's don't broadcast their name when being called; however, newer implementations often do, and so does Taylor UUCP.

[7]The Baud rate of the tty must be at least as high as the maximum transfer speed.

You will notice that the expect fields don't contain the whole prompts. This is to make sure that the login succeeds even if the remote system broadcasts `Login:` instead of `login:`.

uucico also allows for some sort of conditional execution, for example in the case that the remote machine's *getty* needs to be reset before sending a prompt. For this, you can attach a sub-chat to an expect string, offset by a dash. The sub-chat is executed only if the main expect fails, i.e. a timeout occurs. One way to use this feature is to send a BREAK if the remote site doesn't display a login prompt. The following example gives an allround chat script that should also work in case you have to hit return before the login appears. `""` tells UUCP to not wait for anything and continue with the next send string immediately.

```
"" \n\r\d\r\n\c ogin:-BREAK-ogin: vstout ssword: catch22
```

There are a couple of special strings and escape characters which may occur in the chat script. The following is an incomplete list of characters legal in expect strings:

`""` The empty string. It tells *uucico* not to wait for anything, but proceed with the next send string immediately.

\t Tab character.

\r Carriage return character.

\s Space character. You need this to embed spaces in a chat string.

\n Newline character.

** Backslash character.

On send strings, the following escape characters and strings are legal in addition to the above:

EOT End of transmission character (`^D`).

BREAK Break character.

\c Suppress sending of carriage return at end of string.

\d Delay sending for 1 second.

\E Enable echo checking. This requires *uucico* to wait for the echo of everything it writes to be read back from the device before it can continue with the chat. It is primarily useful when used in modem chats (which we will encounter below). Echo checking is off by default.

\e Disable echo checking.

\K Same as *BREAK*.

\p Pause for fraction of a second.

12.3.6.5 Alternates

Sometimes it is desirable to have multiple entries for a single system, for instance if the system can be reached on different modem lines. With Taylor UUCP, you can do this by defining a so-called *alternate*.

An alternate entry retains all settings from the main system entry, and and specifies only those values that should be overridden in the default system entry, or added to it. An alternate is offset from the system entry by a line containing the keyword *alternate*.

To use two phone numbers for **pablo**, you would modify its *sys* entry in the following way:

```
system        pablo
phone         123-456
... entries as above ...
alternate
phone         123-455
```

When calling **pablo**, *uucico* will now first dial 123-456, and if this fails, try the alternate. The alternate entry retains all settings from the main system entry, and overrides only the telephone number.

12.3.6.6 Restricting Call Times

Taylor UUCP provides a number of ways you may restrict the times when calls can be placed to a remote system. You might do this either because of limitations the remote host places on its services during business hours, or simply to avoid times with high call rates. Note that it is always possible to override call time restrictions by giving *uucico* the `-S` or `-f` option.

By default, Taylor UUCP will disallow connections at any time, so you *have* to use some sort of time specification in the *sys* file. If you don't care about call time restrictions, you can specify the *time* option with a value of *Any* in your *sys* file.

The simplest way to restrict call time is the *time* entry, which is followed by a string made up of a day and a time subfield. Day may be any of *Mo, Tu, We, Th, Fr, Sa, Su* combined, or *Any*, *Never*, or *Wk* for weekdays. The time consists of two 24-hour clock values, separated by a dash. They specify the range during which calls may be placed. The combination of these tokens is written without white space in between. Any number of day and time specifications may be grouped together with commas. For example,

```
time            MoWe0300-0730,Fr1805-2000
```

allows calls on Monday and Wednesdays from 3 a.m. to 7.30, and on Fridays between 18.05 and 20.00. When a time field spans midnight, say *Mo1830-0600*, it actually means Monday, between midnight and 6 a.m., and between 6.30 p.m. and midnight.

The special time strings *Any* and *Never* mean what they say: Calls may be placed at any or no time, respectively.

The *time* command takes an optional second argument that describes a retry time in minutes. When an attempt to establish a connection fails, *uucico* will not allow another attempt to dial up the remote host within a certain interval. By default, *uucico* uses an exponential backoff scheme, where the retry interval increases with each repeated failure. For instance, when you specify a retry time of 5 minutes, *uucico* will refuse to call the remote system within 5 minutes after the last failure.

The *timegrade* command allows you to attach a maximum spool grade to a schedule. For instance, assume you have the following *timegrade* commands in a *system* entry:

```
timegrade       N Wk1900-0700,SaSu
timegrade       C Any
```

This allows jobs with a spoolgrade of C or higher (usually, mail is queued with grade B or C) to be transferred whenever a call is established, while news (usually queued with grade N) will be transferred only during the night and at weekends.

Just like *time*, the *timegrade* command takes a retry interval in minutes as an optional third argument.

However, a caveat about spool grades is in order here: First, the *timegrade* option applies only to what *your* systems sends; the remote system may still transfer anything it likes. You can use the *call-timegrade* option to explicitly request it to send only jobs above some given spool grade; but there's no guarantee it will obey this request.[8]

Similarly, the *timegrade* field is not checked when a remote system calls in, so any jobs queued for the calling system will be sent. However, the remote system can explicitly request your *uucico* to restrict itself to a certain spool grade.

12.3.7 What Devices there are – the *port* File

The *port* file tells *uucico* about the available ports. These may be modem ports, but other types such as direct serial lines and TCP sockets are supported as well.

Like the *sys* file, *port* consists of separate entries starting with the keyword *port*, followed by the port name. This name may be used by in the *sys* file's *port* statement. The name need not be unique; if there are several ports with the same name, *uucico* will try each in turn until it finds one that is not currently being used.

---

[8] If the remote system runs Talyor UUCP, it will obey.

The *port* command should be immediately followed by the *type* statement that describes what type of port is described. Valid types are *modem*, *direct* for direct connections, and *tcp* for TCP sockets. If the *port* command is missing, the port type defaults to modem.

In this section, we will cover only modem ports; TCP ports and direct lines are discussed in a later section.

For modem and direct ports, you have to specify the device for calling out using the *device* directive. Usually, this is the name of a device special file in the */dev* directory, like */dev/cua1*.[9]

In the case of a modem device, the port entry also determines what type of modem is connected to the port. Different types of modems have to be configured differently. Even modems that claim to be Hayes-compatible needn't be really compatible with each other. Therefore, you have to tell *uucico* how to initialize the modem and how to make it dial the desired number. Taylor UUCP keeps the descriptions of all dialers in a file named *dial*. To use any of these, you have to specify the dialer's name using the *dialer* command.

Sometimes, you will want to use a modem in different ways, depending on which system you call. For instance, some older modems don't understand when a high-speed modem attempts to connect at 14400bps; they simply drop the line instead of negotiating a connect at, say, 9600bps. When you know site **drop** uses such a dumb modem, you have to set up your modem differently when calling them. For this, you need an additional port entry in the *port* file that specifies a different dialer. Now you can give the new port a different name, such as *serial1-slow*, and use the *port* directive in **drop** system entry in *sys*.

A better way is to distinguish the ports by the speeds they support. For instance, the two port entries for the above situation may look like this:

```
# NakWell modem; connect at high speed
port            serial1         # port name
type            modem           # modem port
device          /dev/cua1       # this is COM2
speed           38400           # supported speed
dialer          nakwell         # normal dialer

# NakWell modem; connect at low speed
port            serial1         # port name
type            modem           # modem port
device          /dev/cua1       # this is COM2
speed           9600            # supported speed
dialer          nakwell-slow    # don't attempt fast connect
```

The system entry for site **drop** would now give *serial1* as port name, but request to use it at 9600bps only. *uucico* will then automatically use the second port entry. All remaining sites that have a speed of 38400bps in the system entry will be called using the first port entry.

12.3.8 How to Dial a Number – the *dial* File

The *dial* file describes the way various dialers are used. Traditionally, UUCP talks of dialers rather than modems, because in earlier times, it was usual practice to have one (expensive) automatic dialing device serve a whole bank of modems. Today, most modems have dialing support built in, so this distinction gets a little blurred.

Nevertheless, different dialers or modems may require a different configuration. You can describe each of them in the *dial* file. Entries in *dial* start with the *dialer* command that gives the dialer's name.

The most important entry beside this is the modem chat, specified by the *chat* command. Similar to the login chat, it consists of a sequence of strings *uucico* sends to the dialer and the responses it expects in return. It is commonly used to reset the modem to some known state, and dial the number. The following sample dialer entry shows a typical modem chat for a Hayes-compatible modem:

```
# NakWell modem; connect at high speed
dialer          nakwell         # dialer name
chat            "" ATZ OK\r ATH1E0Q0 OK\r ATDT\T CONNECT
chat-fail       BUSY
```

[9] Some people use the *ttyS** devices instead, which are intended for dial-in only.

```
chat-fail       ERROR
chat-fail       NO\sCARRIER
dtr-toggle      true
```

The modem chat begins with `""`, the empty expect string. *uucico* will therefore send the first command (`ATZ`) right away. `ATZ` is the Hayes command to reset the modem. It then waits until the modem has sent `OK`, and sends the next command which turns off local echo, and the like. After the modem returns `OK` again, *uucico* sends the dialing command (`ATDT`). The escape sequence `\T` in this string is replaced with the phone number taken from the system entry *sys* file. *uucico* then waits for the modem to return the string `CONNECT`, which signals that a connection with the remote modem has been established successfully.

Often, the modem fails to connect to the remote system, for instance if the other system is talking to someone else and the line is busy. In this case, the modem will return some error message indicating the reason. Modem chats are not capable to detect such messages; *uucico* will continue to wait for the expected string until it times out. The UUCP log file will therefore only show a bland "timed out in chat script" instead of the true reason.

However, Taylor UUCP allows you to tell *uucico* about these error messages using the *chat-fail* command as shown above. When *uucico* detects a chat-fail string while executing the modem chat, it aborts the call, and logs the error message in the UUCP log file.

The last command in the example shown above tells UUCP to toggle the DTR line before starting the modem chat. Most modems can be configured to go on-hook when detecting a change on the DTR line, and enter command mode.[10]

12.3.9 UUCP Over TCP

Absurd as it may sound at the first moment, using UUCP to transfer data over TCP not that bad an idea, especially when transferring large amount of data such as Usenet news. On TCP-based links, news is generally exchanged using the NNTP protocol, where articles are requested and sent individually, without compression or any other optimization. Although adequate for large sites with several concurrent newsfeeds, this technique is very unfavorable for small sites that receive their news over a slow connection such as ISDN. These sites will usually want to combine the qualities of TCP with the advantages of sending news in large batches, which can be compressed and thus transferred with very low overhead. A standard way to transfer these batches is to use UUCP over TCP.

In *sys*, you would specify a system to be called via TCP in the following way:

```
system          gmu
address         news.groucho.edu
time            Any
port            tcp-conn
chat            ogin: vstout word: clouseau
```

The *address* command gives the IP address of the host, or its fully qualified domain name. The corresponding *port* entry would read:

```
port            tcp-conn
type            tcp
service         540
```

The entry states that a TCP connection should be used when a *sys* entry references *tcp-conn*, and that *uucico* should attempt to connect to the TCP network port 540 on the remote host. This is the default port number of the UUCP service. Instead of the port number, you may also give a symbolic port name to the *service* command. The port number corresponding to this name will be looked up in */etc/services*. The common name for the UUCP service is *uucpd*.

[10] You can also configure some modems to reset themselves when detecting a transition on DTR. Some of them, however, don't seem to like this, and occasionally get hung.

12.3.10 Using a Direct Connection

Assume you use a direct line connecting your system **vstout** to **tiny**. Very much like in the modem case, you have to write a system entry in the *sys* file. The *port* command identifies the serial port *tiny* is hooked up to.

```
system          tiny
time            Any
port            direct1
speed           38400
chat            ogin: cathcart word: catch22
```

In the *port* file, you have to describe the serial port for the direct connection. A *dialer* entry is not needed, because there's no need for dialing.

```
port            direct1
type            direct
speed           38400
```

12.4 The Do's and Dont's of UUCP – Tuning Permissions

12.4.1 Command Execution

UUCP's task is to copy files from one system to another, and to request execution of certain commands on remote hosts. Of course, you as an administrator would want to control what rights you grant other systems – allowing them to execute any command on your system is definitely not a good idea.

By default, the only commands Taylor UUCP allows other systems to execute on your machine are *rmail* and *rnews*, which are commonly used to to exchange email and Usent news over UUCP. The default search path used by *uuxqt* is a compile-time option, but should usually contain */bin*, */usr/bin*, and */usr/local/bin*. To change the set of commands for a particular system, you can use the *commands* keyword in the *sys* file. Similarly, the search path can be changed with the *command-path* statement. For instance, you may want to allow system **pablo** to execute the *rsmtp* command in addition to *rmail* and *rnews*:[11]

```
system          pablo
...
commands        rmail rnews rsmtp
```

12.4.2 File Transfers

Taylor UUCP also allows you to fine-tune file transfers in great detail. At one extreme, you can disable transfers to and from a particular system. Just set *request* to *no*, and the remote system will not be able either to retrieve files from your system or send it any files. Similarly, you can prohibit your users from transferring files to or from a system by setting *transfer* to *no*. By default, users on both the local and the remote system are allowed to up- and download files.

In addition, you can configure the directories to and from which files may be copied. Usually, you will want to restrict access from remote systems to a single directory hierarchy, but still allow your users to send files from their home directory. Commonly, remote users will be allowed to receive files only from the public UUCP directory, */var/spool/uucppublic*. This is the traditional place to make files publicly available; very much like FTP servers on the Internet. It is commonly referred to using the tilde character.

Therefore, Taylor UUCP provides four different commands to configure the directories for sending and receiving files. They are *local-send*, which specifies the list of directories a user may ask UUCP to send files from; *local-receive*, which gives the the list of directories a user may ask to receive files to; and *remote-send* and *remote-receive*, which do the analogous for requests from a foreign system. Consider the following example:

---

[11] *rsmtp* is used to deliver mail with batched SMTP. This is described in the mail chapters.

```
system          pablo
...
local-send      /home ~
local-receive   /home ~/receive
remote-send     ~ !~/incoming !~/receive
remote-receive  ~/incoming
```

The *local-send* command allows users on your host to send any files below */home* and from the public UUCP directory to **pablo**. The *local-receive* command allows them to receive files either to the world-writable *receive* directory in the *uucppublic*, or any world-writable directory below */home*. The *remote-send* directive allows **pablo** to request files from */var/spool/uucppublic*, except for files below the *incoming* and *receive* directories. This is signaled to *uucico* by preceding the directory names with exclamation marks. Finally, the last line allows **pablo** to upload any files to **incoming**.

One of the biggest problems with file transfers using UUCP is that will only receive files to directories that are world-writable. This may tempt some users to set up traps for other users, etc. However, there's no way escaping this problem except disabling UUCP file transfers altogether.

12.4.3 Forwarding

UUCP provides a mechanism to have other systems execute file transfers on your behalf. For instance, this allows you to make **seci** retrieve a file from **uchile** for you, and send it to your system. The following command would achieve this:

```
$ uucp -r seci!uchile!~/find-ls.gz ~/uchile.files.gz
```

This technique of passing a job through several systems is called *forwarding*. In the above example, the reason to use forwarding may be that **seci** has UUCP access to **uchile**, but your host doesn't. However, if you run a UUCP system, you would want to limit the forwarding service to a few hosts you trust not to run up a horrendous phone bill by making you download the latest X11R6 source release for them.

By default, Taylor UUCP disallows forwarding altogether. To enable forwarding for a particular system, you can use the *forward* command. This command specifies a list of sites the system may request you to forward jobs to and from. For instance, the UUCP administrator of **seci** would have to add the following lines to the *sys* file to allow **pablo** to request files from **uchile**:

```
####################
# pablo
system          pablo
...
forward         uchile
####################
# uchile
system          uchile
...
forward-to      pablo
```

The *forward-to* entry for **uchile** is necessary so that any files returned by it are actually passed on to **pablo**. Otherwise UUCP would drop them. This entry uses a variation of the *forward* command that permits **uchile** only to send files to **pablo** through **seci**; not the other way round.

To permit forwarding to any system, use the special keyword *ANY* (capital letters required).

12.5 Setting up your System for Dialing in

If you want to set up your site for dialing in, you have to permit logins on your serial port, and customize some system files to provide UUCP accounts. This will be the topic of the current section.

12.5.1 Setting up *getty*

If you want to use a serial line as a dialin port, you have to enable a *getty* process on this port. However, some *getty* implementations aren't really suitable for this, because you usually want to use a serial port for dialing in and out. You therefore have to make sure to use a *getty* that is able to share the line with other programs like *uucico*, or *minicom*. One program that does this is *uugetty* from the *getty_ps* package. Most Linux distributions have it; check for *uugetty* in your */sbin* directory. Another program I am aware of is Gert Doering's *mgetty*, which also supports reception of facsimiles. You can also obtain the latest versions of these from **sunsite.unc.edu** as either binary or source.

Explaining the differences in the way *uugetty* and *mgetty* handle logins is beyond the scope of this little section; for more information, please refer to the Serial HOWTO by Grag Hankins, as well as the documentation that comes along with *getty_ps* and *mgetty*.

12.5.2 Providing UUCP Accounts

Next, you have to set up user accounts that let remote sites log into your system and establish a UUCP connection. Generally, you will provide a separate login name to each system that polls you. When setting up an account for system **pablo**, you would probably give it **Upablo** as the user name.

For systems that dial in through the serial port, you usually have to add these accounts to the system password file, */etc/passwd*. A good practice is to put all UUCP logins in a special group such as **uuguest**. The account's home directory should be set to the public spool directory */var/spool/uucppublic*; its login shell must be *uucico*.

If you have the shadow password suite installed, you can do this with the *useradd* command:

```
# useradd -d /var/spool/uucppublic -G uuguest -s /usr/lib/uucp/uucico Upablo
```

If you don't use the shadow password suite, you probably have to edit */etc/passwd* by hand, adding a line like that shown below, where 5000 and 150 are the numerical uid and gid assigned to user **Upablo** and group **uuguest**, respectively.

```
Upablo:x:5000:150:UUCP Account:/var/spool/uucppublic:/usr/lib/uucp/uucico
```

After installing the account, you have to activate it by setting its password with the *passwd* command.

To serve UUCP systems that connect to your site over TCP, you have to set up *inetd* to handle incoming connections on the *uucp* port. You do this by adding the following line to */etc/inetd.conf*:[12]

```
uucp   stream  tcp   nowait  root  /usr/sbin/tcpd  /usr/lib/uucp/uucico -l
```

The `-l` option makes *uucico* perform its own login authorization. It will prompt for a login name and a password just like the standard *login* program, but will rely on its private password database instead of */etc/passwd*. This private password file is named */usr/lib/uucp/passwd* and contains pairs of login names and passwords:

```
Upablo  IslaNegra
Ulorca  co'rdoba
```

Of course, this file must be owned by **uucp** and have permissions of 600.

If this database sounds like such a good idea you would like to use on normal serial logins, too, you will be disappointed to hear that this isn't possible at the moment without major contortions. First off, you need Taylor UUCP 1.05 for this, because it allows *getty* to pass the login name of the calling user to *uucico* using the `-u` option.[13] Then, you have to trick the *getty* you are using into invoking *uucico* instead of the usual */bin/login*. With *getty_ps*, you can do this by setting the *LOGIN* option in the configuration file. However, this disables interactive logins altogether. *mgetty*, on the other hand, has a nice feature that allows you to invoke different login commands based on the name the user provided. For instance, you can tell *mgetty* to

[12] Note that usually, *tcpd* has mode 700, so that you must invoke it as user **root**, not **uucp** as you would usually do.

[13] The `-u` option is present in 1.04, too, but is only a no-op.

use *uucico* for all users that provide a login name beginning with a capital U, but let everyone else be handled by the standard *login* command.

To protect your UUCP users from callers giving a false system name and snarfing all their mail, you should add *called-login* commands to each system entry in the *sys* file. This is described in section 12.5.3 above.

12.5.3 Protecting Yourself Against Swindlers

One of the biggest problems about UUCP is that the calling system can lie about its name; it announces its name to the called system after logging in, but the server doesn't have a way to check this. Thus, an attacker could log into his or her own UUCP account, pretend to be someone else, and pick up that other site's mail. This is particularly troublesome if you offer login via anonymous UUCP, where the password is made public.

Unless you know you can trust all sites that call your system to be honest, you *must* guard against this sort of impostors. The cure against this disease is to require each system to use a particular login name by specifying a *called-login* in *sys*. A sample system entry may look like this:

```
system          pablo
... usual options ...
called-login    Upablo
```

The upshot of this is that whenever a system logs in and pretends it is **pablo**, *uucico* will check whether it has logged in as **Upablo**. If it hasn't, the calling system will be turned down, and the connection is dropped. You should make it a habit to add the *called-login* command to every system entry you add to your *sys* file. It is important that you do this for *all* sytems, regardless of whether they will ever call your site or not. For those sites that never call you, you should probably set *called-login* to some totally bogus user name, such as **neverlogsin**.

12.5.4 Be Paranoid – Call Sequence Checks

Another way to fend off and detect impostors is to use call sequence checks. Call sequence checks help you protect against intruders that somehow managed to find out the password you log into your UUCP system with.

When using call sequence checks, both machines keep track of the number of connections established so far. It is incremented with each connection. After logging in, the caller sends its call sequence number, and the callee checks it against its own number. If they don't match, the connection attempt will be rejected. If the initial number is chosen at random, attackers will have a hard time guessing the correct call sequence number.

But call sequence checks do more for you than this: even if some very clever person should detect your call sequence number as well as your password, you will find this out. When the attacker call your UUCP feed and steals your mail, this will increase the feeds call sequence number by one. The next time *you* call your feed and try to log in, the remote *uucico* will refuse you, because the numbers don't match anymore!

If you have enabled call sequence checks, you should check your log files regularly for error messages that hint at possible attacks. If your system rejects the call sequence number the calling system offers it, *uucico* will put a message into the log file saying something like "Out of sequence call rejected". If your system is rejected by its feed because the sequence numbers are out of sync, it will put a message in the log file saying "Handshake failed (RBADSEQ)".

To enable call sequence checks, you have to add following command to the system entry:

```
# enable call sequence checks
sequence        true
```

Beside this, you have to create the file containing the sequence number itself. Taylor UUCP keeps the sequence number is in a file called *.Sequence* in the remote site's spool directory. It *must* be owned by **uucp**, and must be mode 600 (i.e. readable and writeable only by **uucp**). It is best to initialize this file with an arbitrary, agreed-upon start value. Otherwise, an attacker might manage to guess the number by trying out all values smaller than, say, 60.

```
# cd /var/spool/uucp/pablo
# echo 94316 > .Sequence
# chmod 600 .Sequence
# chown uucp.uucp .Sequence
```

Of course, the remote site has to enable call sequence checks as well, and start by using exactly the same sequence number as you.

12.5.5 Anonymous UUCP

If you want to provide anonymous UUCP access to your system, you first have to set up a special account for it as described above. A common practive is to give it a login name and a password of **uucp**.

In addition, you have to set a few of the security options for unknown systems. For instance, you may want to prohibit them from executing any commands on your system. However, you cannot set these parameters in a *sys* file entry, because the *system* command requires the system's name, which you don't have. Taylor UUCP solves this dilemma through the *unknown* command. *unknown* can be used in the *config* file to specify any command that can usually appear in a system entry:

```
unknown         remote-receive ~/incoming
unknown         remote-send ~/pub
unknown         max-remote-debug none
unknown         command-path /usr/lib/uucp/anon-bin
unknown         commands rmail
```

This will restrict unknown systems to downloading files from below the *pub* directory and uploading files to the *incoming* directory below */var/spool/uucppublic*. The next line will make *uucico* ignore any requests from the remote system to turn on debugging locally. The last two lines permit unknown systems to execute *rmail*; but the command path specified makes *uucico* look for the *rmail* command in a private directory named *anon-bin* only. This allows you to provide some special *rmail* that, for instance, forwards all mail to the super-user for examination. This allows anonymous users to reach the maintainer of the system, but prevents them at the same time from injecting any mail to other sites.

To enable anonymous UUCP, you must specify at least one *unknown* statement in *config*. Otherwise *uucico* will reject any unknown systems.

12.6 UUCP Low-Level Protocols

To negotiate session control and file transfers with the remote end, *uucico* uses a set of standardized messages. This is often referred to as the high-level protocol. During the initialization phase and the hangup phase these are simply sent across as strings. However, during the real transfer phase, an additional low-level protocol is employed which is mostly transparent to the higher levels. This is to make error checks possible when using unreliable lines, for instance.

12.6.1 Protocol Overview

As UUCP is used over different types of connections, such as serial lines or TCP, or even X.25, specific low-level protocols are needed. In addition, several implementations of UUCP have introduced different protocols that do roughly the same thing.

Protocols can be divided into two categories: streaming and packet-oriented protocols. Protocols of the latter variety transfer a file as a whole, possibly computing a checksum over it. This is nearly free of any overhead, but requires a reliable connection, because any error will cause the whole file to be retransmitted. These protocols are commonly used over TCP connections, but are not suitable for use over telephone lines. Although modern modems do quite a good job at error correction, they are not perfect, nor is there any error detection between your computer and the modem.

On the other hand, packet protocols split up the file into several chunks of equal size. Each packet is sent and received separately, a checksum is computed, and an acknowledgement is returned to the sender. To make this more efficient, sliding-window protocols were invented, which allow for a limited number (a window) of outstanding acknowledgements at any time. This greatly reduces the amount of time *uucico* has to wait during a transmission. Still, the relatively large overhead compared to a streaming protocol make packet protocls inefficient for use over TCP.

The width of the data path also makes a difference. Sometimes, sending eight-bit characters over a serial connection is impossible, for instance if the connection goes through a stupid terminal server. In this case, characters with the eighth bit set have to be quoted on transmission. When you transmit eight-bit characters over a seven-bit connection, they have to be under worst-case assumptions, this doubles the amount of data to be transmitted, although compression done by the hardware may compensate for this. Lines that can transmit arbitrary eight-bit characters are usually called eight-bit clean. This is the case for all TCP connections, as well as for most modem connections.

The following protocols are available with Taylor UUCP 1.04:

g
: This is the most common protocol and should be understood by virtually all *uucico*'s. It does thorough error checking and is therefore well-suited for noisy telephone links. *g* requires an eight-bit clean connection. It is a packet-oriented protocol which uses a sliding-window technique.

i
: This is a bidirectional packet protocol which can send and receive files at the same time. It requires a full-duplex connection and an eight-bit clean data path. It is currently understood only by Taylor UUCP.

t
: This is a protocol intended for use over a TCP connection, or other truly error-free networks. It uses packets of 1024 bytes and requires an eight-bit clean connection.

e
: This should basically do the same as *t*. The main difference is that *e* is a streaming protocol.

f
: This is intended for use with reliable X.25 connections. It is a streaming protocol and expects a seven-bit data path. Eight-bit characters are quoted, which can make it very inefficient.

G
: This is the System V Release 4 version of the *g* protocol. It is also understood by some other versions of UUCP.

a
: This protocol is similiar to ZMODEM. It requires an eight bit connection, but quotes certain control characters like XON and XOFF.

12.6.2 Tuning the Transmission Protocol

All protocols allow for some variation in packet sizes, timeouts, and the like. Usually, the defaults provided work well under standard circumstances, but may not be optimal for your situation. The *g* protocol, for instance, uses window sizes from 1 to 7, and packet sizes in powers of 2 ranging from 64 through 4096.[14] If your telephone line is usually so noisy that it drops more than 5 percent all packets, you should probably lower the packet size and shrink the window. On the other hand, on very good telephone lines the protocol overhead of sending ACKs for every 128 bytes may prove wasteful, so that you might increase the packet size to 512 or even 1024.

Taylor UUCP provides a meachanism to suit your needs by tuning these parameters with the *protocol-parameter* command in the *sys* file. For instance, to set the *g* protocol's packet size to 512 when talking to **pablo**, you have to add:

```
system          pablo
...
protocol-parameter g  packet-size  512
```

The tunable parameters and their names vary from protocol to protocol. For a complete list of them please refer to the documentation enclosed in the Taylor UUCP source.

---

[14]Most binaries included in Linux distributions default to a window size of 7 and 128-byte packets.

12.6.3 Selecting Specific Protocols

Not every implementation of *uucico* speaks and understand each protocol, so during the initial handshake phase, both processes have to agree on a common protocol. The master *uucico* offers the slave a list of supported protocols by sending `P`*protlist*, from which the slave may pick one.

Based on the type of port used (modem, TCP, or direct), *uucico* will compose a default list of protocols. For modem and direct connections, this list usually comprises *i*, *a*, *g*, *G*, and *j*. For TCP connections, the list is *t*, *e*, *i*, *a*, *g*, *G*, *j*, and *f*. You can override this default list with the *protocols* command, which may be specified in a system entry as well as a port entry. For instance, you might edit the *port* file entry for your modem port like this:

```
port            serial1
...
protocols       igG
```

This will require any incoming or outgoing connection through this port to use *i*, *g*, or *G*. If the remote system does not support any of these, the conversation will fail.

12.7 Troubleshooting

This section describes what may go wrong with your UUCP connection, and makes suggestions where to look for the error. However, the questions were compiled off the top of my head. There's much more that can go wrong.

In any case, enable debugging with `-xall`, and take a look at the output in *Debug* in the spool directory. It should help you to quickly recognize where the problem lies. Also, I have always found it helpful to turn on my modem's speaker when it didn't connect. With Hayes-compatible modems, this is accomplished by adding "`ATL1M1 OK`" to the modem chat in the *dial* file.

The first check always should be whether all file permissions are set correctly. *uucico* should be setuid **uucp**, and all files in */usr/lib/uucp*, */var/spool/uucp* and */var/spool/uucppublic* should be owned by **uucp**. There are also some hidden files[15] in the spool directory which must be owned by **uucp** as well.

***uucico* keeps saying "Wrong time to call"**: This probably means that in the system entry in *sys*, you didn't specify a *time* command that details when the remote system may be called, or you gave one which actually forbids calling at the current time. If no call schedule is given, *uucico* assumes that the system may never be called.

***uucico* complains that the site is already locked**: This means that *uucico* detected a lock file for the remote system in */var/spool/uucp*. The lock file may be from an earlier call to the system that crashed, or was killed. However, it's also likely that there's another *uucico* process sitting around that is trying to dial the remote system and got stuck in a chat script, etc. If this *uucico* process doesn't succeed in connecting to the remote system, kill it with a hangup signal, and remove any lock files it left lying around.

I can connect to the remote site, but the chat script fails: Look at the text you receive from the remote site. If it's garbled, this might be a speed-related problem. Otherwise, confirm if it really agrees with what your chat script expects. Remember, the chat script starts with an expect string. If you receive the login prompt, then send your name, but never get the password prompt, insert some delays before sending it, or even in-between the letters. You might be too fast for your modem.

My modem does not dial: If your modem doesn't indicate that the DTR line has been raised when *uucico* calls out, you possibly haven't given the right device to *uucico*. If your modem recognizes DTR, check with a terminal program that you can write to it. If this works, turn on echoing with *\E* at the start of the modem chat. If it doesn't echo your commands during the modem chat, check if your line speed is too high or low for your modem. If you see the echo, check if you have disabled modem responses, or set them to number codes. Verify that the chat script itself is correct. Remember that you have to write two backslashes to send one to the modem.

My modem tries to dial, but doesn't get out: Insert a delay into the phone number. This is especially useful when dialing out from a company's internal telephone net. For people in Europe, who usually dial

[15] That is, files whose name begins with a dot. Such files aren't normally displayed by the *ls* command.

pulse-tone, try touch-tone. In some countries, postal services have been upgrading their nets recently. Touch-tone sometimes helps.

I log file says I have extremely high packet loss rates: This looks like a speed problem. Maybe the link between computer and modem is too slow (remember to adapt it to the highest effective rate possible)? Or is it your hardware that is too slow to service interrupts in time? With a NSC 16550A chipset on your serial port, 38kbps are said to work reasonably well; however, without FIFOs (like 16450 chips), 9600 bps is the limit. Also, you should make sure hardware handshake is enabled on the serial line.

Another likely cause is that hardware handshake isn't enabled on the port. Taylor UUCP 1.04 has no provisions for turning on RTS/CTS handshake. You have to enable this explicitly from *rc.serial* using the following command:

```
$ stty crtscts < /dev/cua3
```

I can log in, but handshake fails: Well, there can be a number of problems. The output in the log file should tell you a lot. Look at what protocols the remote site offers (It sends a string P*protlist* during the handshake). Maybe they don't have any in common (did you select any protocols in *sys* or *port*?).

If the remote system sends `RLCK`, there is a stale lockfile for you on the remote system. If it's not because you're already connected to the remote system on a different line, ask to have it removed.

If it sends `RBADSEQ`, the other site has conversation count checks enabled for you, but numbers didn't match. If it sends `RLOGIN`, you were not permitted to login under this id.

12.8 Log Files

When compiling the UUCP suite to use Taylor-style logging, you have only three global log files, all of which reside in the spool directory. The main log file is named *Log* and contains all information about connections established and files transferred. A typical excerpt looks like this (after a little reformatting to make it fit the page):

```
uucico pablo - (1994-05-28 17:15:01.66 539) Calling system pablo (port cua3)
uucico pablo - (1994-05-28 17:15:39.25 539) Login successful
uucico pablo - (1994-05-28 17:15:39.90 539) Handshake successful
               (protocol 'g' packet size 1024 window 7)
uucico pablo postmaster (1994-05-28 17:15:43.65 539) Receiving D.pabloB04aj
uucico pablo postmaster (1994-05-28 17:15:46.51 539) Receiving X.pabloX04ai
uucico pablo postmaster (1994-05-28 17:15:48.91 539) Receiving D.pabloB04at
uucico pablo postmaster (1994-05-28 17:15:51.52 539) Receiving X.pabloX04as
uucico pablo postmaster (1994-05-28 17:15:54.01 539) Receiving D.pabloB04c2
uucico pablo postmaster (1994-05-28 17:15:57.17 539) Receiving X.pabloX04c1
uucico pablo - (1994-05-28 17:15:59.05 539) Protocol 'g' packets: sent 15,
               resent 0, received 32
uucico pablo - (1994-05-28 17:16:02.50 539) Call complete (26 seconds)
uuxqt pablo postmaster (1994-05-28 17:16:11.41 546) Executing X.pabloX04ai
               (rmail okir)
uuxqt pablo postmaster (1994-05-28 17:16:13.30 546) Executing X.pabloX04as
               (rmail okir)
uuxqt pablo postmaster (1994-05-28 17:16:13.51 546) Executing X.pabloX04c1
               (rmail okir)
```

The next important log file is *Stats*, which lists file transfer statistics. The section of *Stats* corresponding to the above transfer looks like this:

```
postmaster pablo (1994-05-28 17:15:44.78)
                    received 1714 bytes in 1.802 seconds (951 bytes/sec)
postmaster pablo (1994-05-28 17:15:46.66)
                    received 57 bytes in 0.634 seconds (89 bytes/sec)
postmaster pablo (1994-05-28 17:15:49.91)
                    received 1898 bytes in 1.599 seconds (1186 bytes/sec)
```

```
postmaster pablo (1994-05-28 17:15:51.67)
                 received 65 bytes in 0.555 seconds (117 bytes/sec)
postmaster pablo (1994-05-28 17:15:55.71)
                 received 3217 bytes in 2.254 seconds (1427 bytes/sec)
postmaster pablo (1994-05-28 17:15:57.31)
                 received 65 bytes in 0.590 seconds (110 bytes/sec)
```

Again, the lines have been split to make it fit the page.

The third file if *Debug*. This is the place where debugging information is written. If you use debugging, you should make sure that this file has a protection mode of 600. Depending on the debug mode you selected, it may contain the login and password you use to connect to the remote system.

Some UUCP binaries included in Linux distributions have been compiled to use HDB-style logging. HDB UUCP uses a whole bunch of log files stored below */var/spool/uucp/.Log*. This directory contains three more directories, named *uucico*, *uuxqt*, and *uux*. They contain the logging output generated by each of the corresponding commands, sorted into different files for each site. Thus, output from *uucico* when calling site **pablo** will go into *.Log/uucico/pablo*, while the subsequent *uuxqt* run will write to *.Log/uuxqt/pablo*. The lines written to the various lofiles are however the same as with Taylor logging.

When you enable debugging output with HDB-style logging compiled in, it will go to the *.Admin* directory below */var/spool/uucp*. During outgoing calls, debugging information will be sent to *.Admin/audit.local*, while the output from *uucico* when someone calls in will go to *.Admin/audit*.

CHAPTER 13

Electronic Mail

One of the most prominent uses of networking since the first networks were devised, has been eletronic mail. It started as a simple service that copied a file from one machine to another, and appended it to the recipient's *mailbox* file. Basically, this is still what email is all about, although an ever growing net with its complex routing requirements and its ever increasing load of messages has made a more elaborate scheme necessary.

Various standards of mail exchange have been devised. Sites on the Internet adhere to one laid out in RFC 822, augmented by some RFCs that describe a machine-independent way of transferring special characters, and the like. Much thought has also been given recently to "multi-media mail", which deals with including pictures and sound in mail messages. Another standard, X.400, has been defined by CCITT.

Quite a number of mail transport programs have been implemented for UNIX systems. One of the best-known is the University of Berkeley's *sendmail*, which is used on a number of platforms. The original author was Eric Allman, who is now actively working on the *sendmail* team again. There are two Linux ports of *sendmail-5.56c* available, one of which will be described in chapter 15. The *sendmail* version currently being developed is 8.6.5.

The mail agent most commonly used with Linux is *smail-3.1.28*, written and copyrighted by Curt Landon Noll and Ronald S. Karr. This is the one included in most Linux distributions. In the following, we will refer to it simply as *smail*, although there are other versions of it which are entirely different, and which we don't describe here.

Compared to *sendmail*, *smail* is rather young. When handling mail for a small site without complicated routing requirements, their capabilities are pretty close. For large sites, however, *sendmail* always wins, because its configuration scheme is much more flexible.

Both *smail* and *sendmail* support a set of configuration files that have to be customized. Apart from the information that is required to make the mail subsystem run (such as the local hostname), there are many more parameters that may be tuned. *sendmail*'s main configuration file is very hard to understand at first. It looks as if your cat had taken a nap on your keyboard with the shift key pressed. *smail* configuration files are more structured and easier to understand than *sendmail*'s, but don't give the user as much power in tuning the mailer's behavior. However, for small UUCP or Internet sites the work required in setting up any of them is roughly the same.

In this chapter, we will deal with what email is and what issues you as an administrator will have to deal with. Chapters 14 and 15 will give instructions on setting up *smail* and *sendmail* for the first time. The information provided there should suffice to get smaller sites operational, but there are many more options, and you can spend many happy hours in front of your computer configuring the fanciest features.

Toward the end of the current chapter we will briefly cover setting up *elm*, a very common mail user agent on many UNIXish systems, including Linux.

For more information about issues specific to electronic mail on Linux, please refer to the Electronic Mail HOWTO by Vince Skahan, which is posted to **comp.os.linux.announce** regularly. The source distributions of *elm*, *smail* and *sendmail* also contain very extensive documentation that should answer most of your questions on setting them up. If you are looking for information on email in general, a number of RFCs deal with this topic. They are listed in the bibliography at the end of the book.

13.1 What is a Mail Message?

A Mail message generally consists of a message body, which is the text the sender wrote, and special data specifying recipients, transport medium, etc., very much like what you see when you look at a letter's envelope.

This administrative data falls into two categories; in the first category is any data that is specific to the transport medium, like the address of sender and recipient. It is therefore called *the envelope*. It may be transformed by the transport software as the message is passed along.

The second variety is any data necessary for handling the mail message, which is not particular to any transport mechanism, such as the message's subject line, a list of all recipients, and the date the message was sent. In many networks, it has become standard to prepend this data to the mail message, forming the so-called *mail header*. It is offset from the *mail body* by an empty line.[1]

Most mail transport software in the UNIX world uses a header format outlined in a RFC 822. Its original purpose was to specify a standard for use on the ARPANET, but since it was designed to be independent from any environment, it has been easily adapted to other networks, including many UUCP-based networks.

RFC 822 however is only the greatest common denominator. More recent standards have been conceived to cope with growing needs as, for example, data encryption, international character set support, and multimedia mail extensions (MIME).

In all these standards, the header consists of several lines, separated by newline characters. A line is made up of a field name, beginning in column one, and the field itself, offset by a colon and white space. The format and semantics of each field vary depending on the field name. A header field may be continued across a newline, if the next line begins with a TAB. Fields can appear in any order.

A typical mail header may look like this:

```
From brewhq.swb.de!ora.com!andyo Wed Apr 13 00:17:03 1994
Return-Path: <brewhq.swb.de!ora.com!andyo>
Received: from brewhq.swb.de by monad.swb.de with uucp
        (Smail3.1.28.1 #6) id m0pqqlT-00023aB; Wed, 13 Apr 94 00:17 MET DST
Received: from ora.com (ruby.ora.com) by brewhq.swb.de with smtp
        (Smail3.1.28.1 #28.6) id <m0pqoQr-0008qhC>; Tue, 12 Apr 94 21:47 MEST
Received: by ruby.ora.com (8.6.8/8.6.4) id RAA26438;
Tue, 12 Apr 94 15:56 -0400
Date: Tue, 12 Apr 1994 15:56:49 -0400
Message-Id: <199404121956.PAA07787@ruby>
From: andyo@ora.com (Andy Oram)
To: okir@monad.swb.de
Subject: Re: Your RPC section
```

Usually, all necessary header fields are generated by the mailer interface you use, like *elm*, *pine*, *mush*, or *mailx*. Some however are optional, and may be added by the user. *elm*, for example, allows you to edit part of the message header. Others are added by the mail transport software. A list of common header fields and their meaning are given below:

`From:` This contains the sender's email address, and possibly the "real name". A complete zoo of formats is used here.

`To:` This is the recipient's email address.

`Subject:` Describes the content of the mail in a few words. At least that's what it *should* do.

`Date:` The date the mail was sent.

`Reply-To:` Specifies the address the sender wants the recipient's reply directed to. This may be useful if you have several accounts, but want to receive the bulk of mail only on the one you use most frequently. This field is optional.

---

[1] It is customary to append a *signature* or *.sig* to a mail message, usually containing information on the author, along with a joke or a motto. It is offset from the mail message by a line containing "-- ".

`Organization:` The organization that owns the machine from which the mail originates. If your machine is owned by you privately, either leave this out, or insert "private" or some complete nonsense. This field is optional.

`Message-ID:` A string generated by mail transport on the originating system. It is unique to this message.

`Received:` Every site that processes your mail (including the machines of sender and recipient) inserts such a field into the header, giving its site name, a message id, time and date it received the message, which site it is from, and which transport software was used. This is so that you can trace which route the message took, and can complain to the person responsible if something went wrong.

`X-`*anything:* No mail-related programs should complain about any header which starts with `X-`. It is used to implement additional features that have not yet made it into an RFC, or never will. This is used by the Linux Activists mailing list, for example, where the channel is selected by the `X-Mn-Key:` header field.

The one exception to this structure is the very first line. It starts with the keyword `From` which is followed by a blank instead of a colon. To distinguish it from the ordinary `From:` field, it is frequently referred to as `From_`. It contains the route the message has taken in UUCP bang-path style (explained below), time and date when it was received by the last machine having processed it, and an optional part specifying which host it was received from. Since this field is regenerated by every system that processes the message, it is somtimes subsumed under the envelope data.

The `From_` field is there for backward compatibilty with some older mailers, but is not used very much anymore, except by mail user interfaces that rely on it to mark the beginning of a message in the user's mailbox. To avoid potential trouble with lines in the message body that begin with "From ", too, it has become standard procedure to escape any such occurence by preceding it with ">".

13.2 How is Mail Delivered?

Generally, you will compose mail using a mailer interface like *mail* or *mailx*; or more sophisticated ones like *elm*, *mush*, or *pine*. These programs are called *mail user agents*, or MUA's for short. If you send a mail message, the interface program will in most cases hand it to another program for delivery. This is called the *mail transport agent*, or MTA. On some systems, there are different mail transport agents for local and remote delivery; on others, there is only one. The command for remote delivery is usually called *rmail*, the other is called *lmail* (if it exists).

Local delivery of mail is, of course, more than just appending the incoming message to the recipient's mailxbox. Usually, the local MTA will understand aliasing (setting up local recipient addresses pointing to other addresses), and forwarding (redirecting a user's mail to some other destination). Also, messages that cannot be delivered must usually be *bounced*, that is, returned to the sender along with some error message.

For remote delivery, the transport software used depends on the nature of the link. If the mail must be delivered over a network using TCP/IP, SMTP is commonly used. SMTP stands for Simple Mail Transfer Protocol, and is defined in RFC 788 and RFC 821. SMTP usually connects to the recipient's machine directly, negotiating the message transfer with the remote side's SMTP daemon.

In UUCP networks, mail will usually not be delivered directly, but rather be forwarded to the destination host by a number of intermediate systems. To send a message over a UUCP link, the sending MTA will usually execute *rmail* on the forwarding system using *uux*, and feed it the message on standard input.

Since this is done for each message separately, it may produce a considerable work load on a major mail hub, as well as clutter the UUCP spool queues with hundreds of small files taking up an unproportional amount of disk space.[2] Some MTAs therefore allow you to collect several messages for a remote system in a single batch file. The batch file contains the SMTP commands that the local host would normally issue if a direct SMTP connection was used. This is called BSMTP, or *batched* SMTP. The batch is then fed to the *rsmtp* or *bsmtp* program on the remote system, which will process the input as if a normal SMTP connection had occurred.

[2]This is because disk space is usually allocated in blocks of 1024 Bytes. So even a message of at most 400 Bytes will eat a full KB.

13.3 Email Addresses

For electronic mail, an address is made up of at least the name of a machine handling the person's mail, and a user identification recognized by this system. This may be the recipient's login name, but may also be anything else. Other mail addressing schemes, like X.400, use a more general set of "attributes" which are used to look up the recipient's host in an X.500 directory server.

The way a machine name is interpreted, i.e. at which site your message will finally wind up, and how to combine this name with the recipient's user name greatly depends on the network you are on.

Internet sites adhere to the RFC 822 standard, which requires a notation of **user@host.domain**, where **host.domain** is the host's fully qualified domain name. The middle thing is called an "at" sign. Because this notation does not involve a route to the destination host but gives the (unique) hostname instead, this is called an *absolute* address.

In the original UUCP environment, the prevalent form was **path!host!user**, where **path** described a sequence of hosts the message had to travel before reaching the destination **host**. This construct is called the *bang path* notation, because an exclamation mark is loosely called a "bang". Today, many UUCP-based networks have adopted RFC 822, and will understand this type of address.

Now, these two types of addressing don't mix too well. Assume an address of **hostA!user@hostB**. It is not clear whether the '@' sign takes precedence over the path, or vice versa: do we have to send the message to **hostB**, which mails it to **hostA!user**, or should it be sent to **hostA**, which fowards it to **user@hostB**?

Addresses that mix different types of address operators are called *hybrid addresses*. Most notorious is the above example. It is usually resolved by giving the '@' sign precedence over the path. In the above example, this means sending the message to **hostB** first.

However, there is a way to specify routes in RFC 822-conformant ways: **<@hostA,@hostB:user@hostC>** denotes the address of **user** on **hostC**, where **hostC** is to be reached through **hostA** and **hostB** (in that order). This type of address is freqeuently called a *route-addr address*.

Then, there is the '%' address operator: **user%hostB@hostA** will first be sent to **hostA**, which expands the rightmost (in this case, only) percent sign to an '@' sign. The address is now **user@hostB**, and the mailer will happily forward your message to **hostB** which delivers it to **user**. This type of address is sometimes referred to as "Ye Olde ARPANET Kludge", and its use is discouraged. Nevertheless, many mail transport agents generate this type of address.

Other networks have still different means of addressing. DECnet-based networks, for example, use two colons as an address separator, yielding an address of *host::user.*[3] Lastly, the X.400 standard uses an entirely different scheme, by describing a recipient by a set of attribute-value pairs, like country and organization.

On FidoNet, each user is identified by a code like **2:320/204.9**, consisting of four numbers denoting zone (2 is for Europe), net (320 being Paris and Banlieue), node (the local hub), and point (the individual user's PC). Fidonet addresses can be mapped to RFC 822; the above would be written as **Thomas.Quinot@p9.f204.n320.z2.fidonet.org**. Now didn't I say domain names are easy to remember?

There are some implications to using these different types of addressing which will be described throughout the following sections. In a RFC 822 environment, however, you will rarely use anything else than absolute addresses like *user@host.domain*.

13.4 How does Mail Routing Work?

The process of directing a message to the recipient's host is called *routing*. Apart from finding a path from the sending site to the destination, it involves error checking as well as speed and cost optimization.

There is a big difference between the way a UUCP site handles routing, and the way an Internet site does. On the Internet, the main job of directing data to the recipient host (once it is known by it's IP address) is done by the IP networking layer, while in the UUCP zone, the route has to be supplied by the user, or generated by the mail transfer agent.

---

[3]When trying to reach a DECnet address from an RFC 822 environment, you may use "*host::user*"@*relay*, where *relay* is the name of a known Internet-DECnet relay.

13.4.1 Mail Routing on the Internet

On the Internet, it depends entirely on the destination host whether any specific mail routing is performed at all. The default is to deliver the message to the destination host directly by looking up its IP address, and leave the actual routing of the data to the IP transport layer.

Most sites will usually want to direct all inbound mail to a highly available mail server that is capable of handling all this traffic, and have it distribute this mail locally. To announce this service, the site publishes a so-called MX record for their local domain in the DNS database. MX stands for *Mail Exchanger* and basically states that the server host is willing to act as a mail forwarder for all machines in this domain. MX records may also be used to handle traffic for hosts that are not connected to the Internet themselves, like UUCP networks, or company networks with hosts carrying confidential information.

MX records also have a *preference* associated with them. This is a positive integer. If several mail exchangers exist for one host, the mail transport agent will try to transfer the message to the exchanger with the lowest preference value, and only if this fails will it try a host with a higher value. If the local host is itself a mail exchanger for the destination address, it must not forward messages to any MX hosts with a higher preference than its own; this is a safe way of avoiding mail loops.

Suppose that an organization, say Foobar Inc., want all their mail handled by their machine called **mailhub**. They will then have an MX record like this in the DNS database:

```
foobar.com          IN    MX      5    mailhub.foobar.com
```

This announces **mailhub.foobar.com** as a mail exchanger for **foobar.com** with a preference value of 5. A host that wishes to deliver a message to **joe@greenhouse.foobar.com** will check DNS for **foobar.com**, and finds the MX record pointing at **mailhub**. If there's no MX with a preference smaller than 5, the message will be delivered to **mailhub**, which then dispatches it to **greenhouse**.

The above is really only a sketch of how MX records work. For more information on the mail routing on the Internet, please refer to RFC 974.

13.4.2 Mail Routing in the UUCP World

Mail routing on UUCP networks is much more complicated than on the Internet, because the transport software does not perform any routing itself. In earlier times, all mail had to be addressed using bang paths. Bang paths specified a list of hosts through which to forward the message, separated by exclamation marks, and followed by the user's name. To address a letter to Janet User on a machine named **moria**, you would have used the path **eek!swim!moria!janet**. Whis would have sent the mail from your host to **eek**, from there on to **swim** and finally to **moria**.

The obvious drawback of this technique is that it requires you to remember much about the network topology, fast links, etc. Much worse than that, changes in the network topology — like links being deleted or hosts being removed — may cause messages to fail simply because you weren't aware of the change. And finally, in case you move to a different place, you will most likely have to update all these routes.

One thing, however, that made the use of source routing necessary was the presence of ambiguous hostnames: For instance, assume there are two sites named **moria**, one in the U.S., and one in France. Which site now does **moria!janet** refer to? This can be made clear by specifying what path to reach **moria** through.

The first step in disambiguating hostnames was the founding of *The UUCP Mapping Project*. It is located at Rutgers University, and registers all official UUCP hostnames, along with information on their UUCP neighbors and their geographic location, making sure no hostname is used twice. The information gathered by the Mapping Project is published as the *Usenet Maps*, which are distributed regularly through Usenet.[4] A typical system entry in a Map (after removing the comments) looks like this.

```
moria
            bert(DAILY/2),
            swim(WEEKLY)
```

[4]Maps for sites registered with The UUCP Mapping Project are distributed through the newsgroup **comp.mail.maps**; other organizations may publish separate maps for their network.

This entry says that **moria** has a link to **bert**, which it calls twice a day, and **swim**, which it calls weekly. We will come back to the Map file format in more detail below.

Using the connectivity information provided in the maps, you can automatically generate the full paths from your host to any destination site. This information is usually stored in the *paths* file, also called *pathalias database* sometimes. Assume the Maps state that you can reach **bert** through **ernie**, then a pathalias entry for **moria** generated from the Map snippet above may look like this:

```
moria           ernie!bert!moria!%s
```

If you now give a destination address of **janet@moria.uucp**, your MTA will pick the route shown above, and send the message to **ernie** with an envelope address of **bert!moria!janet**.

Building a *paths* file from the full Usenet maps is however not a very good idea. The information provided in them is usually rather distorted, and occasionally out of date. Therefore, only a number of major hosts use the complete UUCP world maps to build their *paths* file. Most sites only maintain routing information for sites in their neighborhood, and send any mail to sites they don't find in their databases to a smarter host with more complete routing information. This scheme is called *smart-host routing*. Hosts that have only one UUCP mail link (so-called *leaf sites*) don't do any routing of their own; they rely entirely on their smart-host.

13.4.3 Mixing UUCP and RFC 822

The best cure against the problems of mail routing in UUCP networks so far is the adoption of the domain name system in UUCP networks. Of course, you can't query a name server over UUCP. Nevertheless, many UUCP sites have formed small domains that coordinate their routing internally. In the Maps, these domains announce one or two host as their mail gateways, so that there doesn't have to be a map entry for each host in the domain. The gateways handle all mail that flows into and out of the domain. The routing scheme inside the domain is completely invisible to the outside world.

This works very well with the smart-host routing scheme described above. Global routing information is maintained by the gateways only; minor hosts within a domain will get along with only a small hand-written *paths* file that lists the routes inside their domain, and the route to the mail hub. Even the mail gateways do not have to have routing information for every single UUCP host in the world anymore. Beside the complete routing information for the domain they serve, they only need to have routes to entire domains in their databases now. For instance, the pathalias entry shown below will route all mail for sites in the **sub.org** domain to **smurf**:

```
.sub.org         swim!smurf!%s
```

Any mail addressed to **claire@jones.sub.org** will be sent to **swim** with an envelope address of **smurf!jones!claire**.

The hierarchical organization of the domain name space allows mail servers to mix more specific routes with less specific ones. For instance, a system in France may have specific routes for subdomains of **fr**, but route any mail for hosts in the **us** domain toward some system in the U.S. In this way, domain-based routing (as this technique is called) greatly reduces the size of routing datbases as well as te administrative overhead needed.

The main benefit of using domain names in a UUCP environment, however, is that compliance with RFC 822 permits easy gatewaying between UUCP networks and the Internet. Many UUCP domains nowadays have a link with an Internet gateway that acts as their smart-host. Sending messages across the Internet is faster, and routing information is much more reliable because Internet hosts can use DNS instead of the Usenet Maps.

In order to be reachable from the Internet, UUCP-based domains usually have their Internet gateway announce an MX record for them (MX records were described above). For instance, assume that **moria** belongs to the **orcnet.org** domain. **gcc2.groucho.edu** acts as their Internet gateway. **moria** would therefore use **gcc2** as its smart-host, so that all mail for foreign domains is delivered across the Internet. On the other hand, **gcc2** would announce an MX record for **orcnet.org**, and deliver all incoming mail for **orcnet** sites to **moria**.

The only remaining problem is that the UUCP transport programs can't deal with fully qualified domain names. Most UUCP suites were designed to cope with site names of up to eight characters, some even less, and using non-alphanumeric characters such as dots is completely out of the question for most.

Therefore, some mapping between RFC 822 names and UUCP hostnames is needed. The way this mapping is done is completely implementation-dependent. One common way of mapping FQDNs to UUCP names is to use the pathalias file for this:

```
moria.orcnet.org  ernie!bert!moria!%s
```

This will produce a pure UUCP-style bang path from an address that specifies a fully qualified domain name. Some mailers provide a special files for this; *sendmail*, for instance, uses the *uucpxtable* for this.

The reverse transformation (colloquially called domainizing) is sometimes required when sending mail from a UUCP network to the Internet. As long as the mail sender uses the fully qualified domain name in the destination address, this problem can be avoided by not removing the domain name from the envelope address when forwarding the message to the smart-host. However, there are still some UUCP sites that are not part of any domain. They are usually domainized by appending the pseudo-domain **uucp**.

13.5 Pathalias and Map File Format

The pathalias database provides the main routing information in UUCP-based networks. A typical entry looks like this (site name and path are separated by TABs):

```
moria.orcnet.org  ernie!bert!moria!%s
moria             ernie!bert!moria!%s
```

This makes any message to **moria** be delivered via **ernie** and **bert**. Both **moria**'s fully qualified name and its UUCP name have to be given if the mailer does not have a separate way to map between these name spaces.

If you want to direct all messages to hosts inside some domain to its mail relay, you may also specify a path in the pathalias database, giving the domain name as target, preceded by a dot. For example, if all hosts in the **sub.org** may be reached through **swim!smurf**, the pathalias entry might look like this:

```
.sub.org        swim!smurf!%s
```

Writing a pathalias file is acceptable only when you are running a site that does not have to do much routing. If you have to do routing for a large number of hosts, a better way is to use the *pathalias* command to create the file from map files. Maps can be maintained much easier, because you may simply add or remove a system by editing the system's map entry, and re-create the map file. Although the maps published by the Usenet Mapping Project aren't used for routing very much anymore, smaller UUCP networks may provide routing information in their own set of maps.

A map file mainly consists of a list of sites, listing the sites each system polls or is polled by. The system name begins in column one, and is followed by a comma-separated list of links. The list may be continued across newlines if the next line begins with a tab. Each link consists of the name of the site, followed by a cost given in brackets. The cost is an arithmetic expression, made up of numbers and symbolic costs. Lines beginning with a hash sign are ignored.

As an example, consider **moria**, which polls **swim.twobirds.com** twice a day, and **bert.sesame.com** once per week. Moreover, the link to **bert** only uses a slow 2400bps modem. **moria**'s would publish the following maps entry:

```
moria.orcnet.org
        bert.sesame.com(DAILY/2),
        swim.twobirds.com(WEEKLY+LOW)

moria.orcnet.org = moria
```

The last line would make it known under its UUCP name, too. Note that it must be *DAILY/2*, because calling twice a day actually halves the cost for this link.

Using the information from such map files, *pathalias* is able to calculate optimal routes to any destination site listed in the paths file, and produce a pathalias database from this which can then be used for routing to these sites.

pathalias provides a couple of other features like site-hiding (i.e. making sites accessible only through a gateway) etc. See the manual page for *pathalias* for details, as well as a complete list of link costs.

Comments in the map file generally contain additional information on the sites described in it. There is a rigid format in which to specify this, so that it can be retrieved from the maps. For instance, a program called *uuwho* uses a database created from the map files to display this information in a nicely formatted way.

When you register your site with an organization that distributes map files to its members, you generally have to fill out such a map entry.

Below is a sample map entry (in fact, it's the one for my site):

```
#N      monad, monad.swb.de, monad.swb.sub.org
#S      AT 486DX50; Linux 0.99
#O      private
#C      Olaf Kirch
#E      okir@monad.swb.de
#P      Kattreinstr. 38, D-64295 Darmstadt, FRG
#L      49 52 03 N / 08 38 40 E
#U      brewhq
#W      okir@monad.swb.de (Olaf Kirch); Sun Jul 25 16:59:32 MET DST 1993
#
monad   brewhq(DAILY/2)
# Domains
monad = monad.swb.de
monad = monad.swb.sub.org
```

The white space after the first two characters is a TAB. The meaning of most of the fields is pretty obvious; you will receive a detailed description from whichever domain you register with. The *L* field is the most fun to find out: it gives your geographical position in latitude/longitude and is used to draw the postscript maps that show all sites for each country, as well as world-wide.[5]

13.6 Configuring *elm*

elm stands for "electronic mail" and is one of the more reasonably named UNIX tools. It provides a full-screen interface with a good help feature. We won't discuss here how to use *elm*, but only dwell on its configuration options.

Theoretically, you can run *elm* unconfigured, and everything works well — if you are lucky. But there are a few options that must be set, although only required on occasions.

When it starts, *elm* reads a set of configuration variables from the *elm.rc* file in */usr/lib/elm*. Then, it will attempt to read the file *.elm/elmrc* in your home directory. You don't usually write this file yourself. It is created when you choose "save options" from *elm*'s options menu.

The set of options for the private *elmrc* file is also available in the global *elm.rc* file. Most settings in your private *elmrc* file override those of the global file.

13.6.1 Global *elm* Options

In the global *elm.rc* file, you must set the options that pertain to your host's name. For example, at the Virtual Brewery, the file for **vlager** would contain the following:

```
#
# The local hostname
```

[5]They are posted regularly in **news.lists.ps-maps**. Beware. They're HUGE.

```
hostname = vlager
#
# Domain name
hostdomain = .vbrew.com
#
# Fully qualified domain name
hostfullname = vlager.vbrew.com
```

These options set *elm*'s idea of the local hostname. Although this information is rarely used, you should set these options nevertheless. Note that these options only take effect when giving them in the global configuration file; when found in your private *elmrc*, they will be ignored.

13.6.2 National Character Sets

Recently, there have been proposals to amend the RFC 822 standard to support various types of messages, such as plain text, binary data, Postscript files, etc. The set of standards and RFCs covering these aspects are commonly referred to as MIME, or Multipurpose Internet Mail Extensions. Among other things, this also lets the recipient know if a character set other than standard ASCII has been used when writing the message, for example using French accents, or German umlauts. This is supported by *elm* to some extent.

The character set used by Linux internally to represent characters is usually referred to as ISO-8859-1, which is the name of the standard it conforms to. It is also known as Latin-1. Any message using characters from this character set should have the following line in its header:

```
Content-Type:  text/plain; charset=iso-8859-1
```

The receiving system should recognize this field and take appropriate measures when displaying the message. The default for *text/plain* messages is a *charset* value of *us-ascii*.

To be able to display messages with character sets other than ASCII, *elm* must know how to print these characters. By default, when *elm* receives a message with a *charset* field other than *us-ascii* (or a content type other than *text/plain*, for that matter), it tries to display the message using a command called *metamail*. Messages that require *metamail* to be displayed are shown with an 'M' in the very first column in the overview screen.

Since Linux' native character set is ISO-8859-1, calling *metamail* is not necessary to display messages using this character set. If *elm* is told that the display understands ISO-8859-1, it will not use *metamail* but will display the message directly instead. This can be done by setting the following option in the global *elm.rc*:

```
displaycharset = iso-8859-1
```

Note that you should set this options even when you are never going to send or receive any messages that actually contain characters other than ASCII. This is because people who do send such messages usually configure their mailer to put the proper `Content-Type:` field into the mail header by default, whether or not they are sending ASCII-only messages.

However, setting this option in *elm.rc* is not enough. The problem is that when displaying the message with its builtin pager, *elm* calls a library function for each character to determine whether it is printable or not. By default, this function will only recognize ASCII characters as printable, and display all other characters as "^?". You may overcome this by setting the environment variable *LC_CTYPE* to *ISO-8859-1*, which tells the library to accept Latin-1 characters as printable. Support for this and other features is available since *libc-4.5.8*.

When sending messages that contain special characters from ISO-8859-1, you should make sure to set two more variables in the *elm.rc* file:

```
charset = iso-8859-1
textencoding = 8bit
```

This makes *elm* report the character set as ISO-8859-1 in the mail header, and send it as an 8-bit value (the default is to strip all characters to 7 bit).

Of course, any of these options can also be set in the private *elmrc* file instead of the global one.

CHAPTER 14

Getting *smail* Up and Running

This chapter will give you a quick introduction to setting up *smail*, and an overview of the functionality it provides. Although *smail* is largely compatible with *sendmail* in its behaviour, their configuration files are completely different.

The main configuration file is the */usr/lib/smail/config*. You always have to edit this file to reflect values specific to your site. If you are only a UUCP leaf site, you will have relatively little else to do, ever. Other files that configure routing and transport options may also be used; they will be dealt with briefly, too.

By default, *smail* processes and delivers all incoming mail immediately. If you have relatively high traffic, you may instead have *smail* collect all messages in the so-called *queue*, and process it at regular intervals only.

When handling mail within a TCP/IP network, *smail* is frequently run in daemon mode: at system boot time, it is invoked from *rc.inet2*, and puts itself in the background where it waits for incoming TCP connections on the SMTP port (usually port 25). This is very beneficial whenever you expect to have a significant amount of traffic, because *smail* isn't started up separately for every incoming connection. The alternative would be to have *inetd* manage the SMTP port, and have it spawn *smail* whenever there is a connection on this port.

smail has a lot a flags that control it behavior; describing them in detail here wouldn't help you much. Fortunately, *smail* supports a number of standard modes of operation that are enabled when you invoke it by a special command name, like *rmail*, or *smtpd*. Usually, these aliases are symbolic links to the *smail* binary itself. We will encounter most of them when discussing the various features of *smail*.

There are two links to *smail* you should have under all circumstances; namely */usr/bin/rmail* and */usr/sbin/sendmail*.[1] When you compose and send a mail message with a user agent like *elm*, the message will be piped into *rmail* for delivery, with the recipient list given to it on the command line. The same happens with mail coming in via UUCP. Some versions of *elm*, however, invoke */usr/sbin/sendmail* instead of *rmail*, so you need both of them. For example, if you keep *smail* in */usr/local/bin*, type the following at the shell prompt:

```
# ln -s /usr/local/bin/smail /usr/bin/rmail
# ln -s /usr/local/bin/smail /usr/sbin/sendmail
```

If you want to dig further into the details of configuring *smail*, please refer to the manual pages *smail(1)* and *smail(5)*. If it isn't included in your favorite Linux distribution, you can get it from the source to *smail*.

14.1 UUCP Setup

To use *smail* in a UUCP-only environment, the basic installation is rather simple. First, you must make sure you have the two symbolic links to *rmail* and *sendmail* mentioned above. If you expect to receive SMTP batches from other sites, you also have to make *rsmtp* a link to *smail*.

[1] This is the new standard location of *sendmail* according to the Linux File System Standard. Another common location is */usr/lib*.

In Vince Skahan's *smail* distribution, you will find a sample configuration file. It is named *config.sample* and resides in */usr/lib/smail*. You have to copy it to *config* and edit it to reflect values specific to your site.

Assume your site is named *swim.twobirds.com*, and is registered in the UUCP maps as *swim*. Your smarthost is *ulysses*. Then your *config* file should look like this:

```
#
# Our domain names
visible_domain=two.birds:uucp
#
# Our name on outgoing mails
visible_name=swim.twobirds.com
#
# Use this as uucp-name as well
uucp_name=swim.twobirds.com
#
# Our smarthost
smart_host=ulysses
```

The first statement tells *smail* about the domains your site belongs to. Insert their names here, separated by colons. If your site name is registered in the UUCP maps, you should also add *uucp*. When being handed a mail message, *smail* determines your host's name using the *hostname(2)* system call, and checks the recipient's address against this hostname, tacking on all names from this list in turn. If the address matches any of these names, or the unqualified hostname, the recipient is considered local, and *smail* attempts to deliver the message to a user or alias on the local host. Otherwise, the recipient is considered remote, and delivery to the destination host is attempted.

visible_name should contain a single, fully qualified domain name of your site that you want to use on outgoing mails. This name is used when generating the sender's address on all outgoing mail. You must make sure to use a name that *smail* recognizes as referring to the local host (i.e. the hostname with one of the domains listed in the *visible_domain* attribute). Otherwise, replies to your mails will bounce off your site.

The last statement sets the path used for smart-host routing (described in section 13.4). With this sample setup, *smail* will forward any mail for remote addresses to the smart host. The path specified in the *smart_path* attribute will be used as a route to the smart host. Since messages will be delivered via UUCP, the attribute must specify a system known to your UUCP software. Please refer to chapter 12 on making a site known to UUCP.

There's one option used in the above file that we haven't explained yet; this is *uucp_name*. The reason to use the option is this: By default, *smail* uses the value returned by *hostname(2)* for UUCP-specific things such as the return path given in the *From_* header line. If your hostname is *not* registered with the UUCP mapping project, you should tell *smail* to use your fully qualified domain name instead.[2] This can be done by adding the *uucp_name* option to the *config* file.

There is another file in */usr/lib/smail*, called *paths.sample*. It is an example of what a *paths* file might look like. However, you will not need one unless you have mail links to more than one site. If you do, however, you will have to write one yourself, or generate one from the Usenet maps. The *paths* file will be described later in this chapter.

14.2 Setup for a LAN

If you are running a site with two or more hosts connected by a LAN, you will have to designate one host that handles your UUCP connection with the outside world. Between the hosts on your LAN, you will most probably want to exchange mail with SMTP over TCP/IP. Assume we're back at the Virtual Brewery again, and **vstout** is set up as the UUCP gateway.

[2]The reason is this: Assume your hostname is *monad*, but is not registered in the maps. However, there is a site in the maps called *monad*, so every mail to *monad!root*, even sent from a direct UUCP neighbor of yours, will wind up on the other *monad*. This is a nuisance for everybody.

In a networked environment, it is best to keep all user mailboxes on a single file system, which is NFS-mounted on all other hosts. This allows users to move from machine to machine, without having to move their mail around (or even worse, check some three or four machines for newly-arrived mail each morning). Therefore, you also want to make sender addresses independent from the machine the mail was written on. It is common practice to use the domain name all by itself in the sender address, instead of a hostname. Janet User, for example, would specify **janet@vbrew.com** instead of **janet@vale.vbrew.com**. We will explain below how to make the server recognize the domain name as a valid name for your site.

A different way of keeping all mailboxes on a central host is to use POP or IMAP. POP stands for *Post Office Protocol* and lets users access their mailboxes over a simple TCP/IP conection. IMAP, the *Interactive Mail Access Protocol*, is similar to POP, but more general. Both clients and servers for IMAP and POP have been ported to Linux, and are available from **sunsite.unc.edu** below */pub/Linux/system/Network*.

14.2.1 Writing the Configuration Files

The configuration for the Brewery works as follows: all hosts except the mail server **vstout** itself route all outgoing mail to the server, using smart host routing. **vstout** itself sends all outgoing mail to the real smart host that routes all of the Brewery's mail; this host is called **moria**.

The standard *config* file for all hosts other than **vstout** looks like this:

```
#
# Our domain:
visible_domain=vbrew.com
#
# What we name ourselves
visible_name=vbrew.com
#
# Smart-host routing: via SMTP to vstout
smart_path=vstout
smart_transport=smtp
```

This is very similar to what we used for a UUCP-only site. The main difference is that the transport used to send mail to the smart host is, of course, SMTP. The *visible_domain* attribute makes *smail* use the domain name instead of the local hostname on all outgoing mail.

On the UUCP mail gateway **vstout**, the *config* file looks a little different:

```
#
# Our hostnames:
hostnames=vbrew.com:vstout.vbrew.com:vstout
#
# What we name ourselves
visible_name=vbrew.com
#
# in the uucp world, we're known as vbrew.com
uucp_name=vbrew.com
#
# Smart transport: via uucp to moria
smart_path=moria
smart_transport=uux
#
# we're authoritative for our domain
auth_domains=vbrew.com
```

This *config* file uses a different scheme to tell *smail* what the local host is called. Instead of giving it a list of domains and letting it find the hostname with a system call, it specifies a list explicitly. The above list contains both the fully qualified and the unqualified hostname, and the domain name all by itself. This makes *smail* recognize **janet@vbrew.com** as a local address, and deliver the message to **janet**.

The *auth_domains* variable names the domains for which **vstout** is considered to be authoritative. That is, if *smail* receives any mail addressed to *host*.**vbrew.com** where *host* does not name an existing local machine, it rejects the message and returns it to the sender. If this entry isn't present, any such message will be sent to the smart-host, who will return it to **vstout**, and so on until it is discarded for exceeding the maximum hop count.

14.2.2 Running *smail*

First, you have to decide whether to run *smail* as a separate daemon, or whether to have *inetd* manage the SMTP port and invoke *smail* only whenever an SMTP connection is requested from some client. Usually, you will prefer daemon operation on the mail server, because this loads the machine far less than spawning *smail* over and over again for each single connection. As the mail server also delivers most incoming mail directly to the users, you will choose *inetd* operation on most other hosts.

Whatever mode of operation you choose for each individual host, you have to make sure you have the following entry in your */etc/services* file:

```
smtp        25/tcp          # Simple Mail Transfer Protocol
```

This defines the TCP port number that *smail* should use for SMTP conversations. 25 is the standard defined by the Assigned Numbers RFC.

When run in daemon mode, *smail* will put itself in the background, and wait for a connection to occur on the SMTP port. When a connection occurs, it forks and conducts an SMTP conversation with the peer process. The *smail* daemon is usually started by invoking it from the *rc.inet2* script using the following command:

```
/usr/local/bin/smail -bd -q15m
```

The `-bd` flag turns on daemon mode, and `-q15m` makes it process whatever messages have accumulated in the message queue every 15 minutes.

If you want to use *inetd* instead, your */etc/inetd.conf* file should contain a line like this:

```
smtp   stream  tcp nowait  root   /usr/sbin/smtpd smtpd
```

smtpd should be a symbolic link to the *smail* binary. Remember you have to make *inetd* re-read *inetd.conf* by sending it a *HUP* signal after making these changes.

Daemon mode and *inetd* mode are mutually exclusive. If you run *smail* in deamon mode, you should make sure to comment out any line in *inetd.conf* for the *smtp* service. Equivalently, when having *inetd* manage *smail*, make sure that *rc.inet2* does not start the *smail* daemon.

14.3 If You Don't Get Through...

If something goes wrong with your installation, there are a number of features that may help you to find what's at the root of the problem. The first place to check are *smail*'s log files. They are kept in */var/spool/smail/log*, and are named *logfile* and *paniclog*, respectively. The former lists all transactions, while the latter is only for error messages related to configuration errors and the like.

A typical entry in *logfile* looks like this:

```
04/24/94 07:12:04: [m0puwU8-00023UB] received
|             from: root
|          program: sendmail
|             size: 1468 bytes
04/24/94 07:12:04: [m0puwU8-00023UB] delivered
|              via: vstout.vbrew.com
|               to: root@vstout.vbrew.com
|          orig-to: root@vstout.vbrew.com
|           router: smart_host
|        transport: smtp
```

This shows that a message from **root** to **root@vstout.vbrew.com** has been properly delivered to host **vstout** over SMTP.

Messages *smail* could not deliver generate a similar entry in the log file, but with an error message instead of the `delivered` part:

```
04/24/94 07:12:04: [m0puwU8-00023UB] received
|       from: root
|    program: sendmail
|       size: 1468 bytes
04/24/94 07:12:04: [m0puwU8-00023UB] root@vstout.vbrew.com ... deferred
  (ERR_148) transport smtp: connect: Connection refused
```

The above error is typical for a situation in which *smail* properly recognizes that the message should be delivered to **vstout** but was not able to connect to the SMTP service on **vstout**. If this happens, you either have a configuration problem, or TCP support is missing from your *smail* binaries.

This problem is not as uncommon as one might think. There have been precompiled *smail* binaries around, even in some Linux distributions, without support for TCP/IP networking. If this is the case for you, you have to compile *smail* yourself. Having installed *smail*, you can check if it has TCP networking support by telnetting to the SMTP port on your machine. A successful connect to the SMTP server is shown below (your input is marked *like this*):

```
$ telnet localhost smtp
Trying 127.0.0.1...
Connected to localhost.
Escape character is '^]'.
220 monad.swb.de Smail3.1.28.1 #6 ready at Sun, 23 Jan 94 19:26 MET
QUIT
221 monad.swb.de closing connection
```

If this test doesn't produce the SMTP banner (the line starting with the 220 code), first make sure that your configuration is *really* correct before you go through compiling *smail* yourself, which is described below.

If you encounter a problem with *smail* that you are unable to locate from the error message *smail* generates, you may want to turn on debugging messages. You can do this using the `-d` flag, optionally followed by a number specifying the level of verbosity (you may not have any space between the flag and the numerical argument). *smail* will then print a report of its operation to the screen, which may give you more hints about what is going wrong.

[Don't know,...Maybe people don't find this funny:] If nothing else helps, you may want to invoke *smail* in Rogue mode by giving the `-bR` option on the command line. The manpage says on this option: "Enter the hostile domain of giant mail messages, and RFC standard scrolls. Attempt to make it down to protocol level 26 and back." Although this option won't solve your problems, it may provide you some comfort and consolation.[3]

14.3.1 Compiling *smail*

If you know for sure that *smail* is lacking TCP network support, you have to get the source. It is probably included in your distribution, if you got it via CD-ROM, otherwise you may get it from the net via FTP.[4]

When compiling *smail*, you had best start with the set of configuration files from Vince Skahan's *newspak* distribution. To compile in the TCP networking driver, you have to set the *DRIVER_CONFIGURATION* macro in the *conf/EDITME* file to either *bsd-network* or *arpa-network*. The former is suitable for LAN installations, but the Internet requires *arpa-network*. The difference between these two is that the latter has a special driver for BIND service that is able to recognize MX records, which the former doesn't.

[3]Don't use this if you're in a really bad mood.

[4]If you bought this with a Linux distribution from a vendor, you are entitled to the source code "for a nominal shipping charge", according to *smail*'s copying conditions.

14.4 Mail Delivery Modes

As noted above, *smail* is able to deliver messages immediately, or queue them for later processing. If you choose to queue messages, *smail* will store away all mail in the *messages* directory below */var/spool/smail*. It will not process them until explicitly told so (this is also called "running the queue").

You can select one of three delivery modes by setting the *delivery_mode* attribute in the *config* file to either of *foreground*, *background*, or *queued*. These select delivery in the foreground (immediate processing of incoming messages), in the background, (message is delivered by a child of the receiving process, with the parent process exiting immediately after forking), and queued. Incoming mail will always be queued regardless of this option if the boolean variable *queue_only* is set in the *config* file.

If you turn on queuing, you have to make sure the queues are checked regularly; probably every 10 or 15 minutes. If you run *smail* in daemon mode, you have to add the option `-q10m` on the command line to process the queue every 10 minutes. Alternatively, you can invoke *runq* from *cron* at these intervals. *runq* should be a link to *smail*.

You can display the current mail queue by invoking *smail* with the `-bp` option. Equivalently, you can make *mailq* a link to *smail*, and invoke *mailq*:

```
$ mailq -v
m0pvB1r-00023UB From: root  (in /var/spool/smail/input)
                Date: Sun, 24 Apr 94 07:12 MET DST
                Args: -oem -oMP sendmail root@vstout.vbrew.com
Log of transactions:
 Xdefer: <root@vstout.vbrew.com> reason: (ERR_148) transport smtp:
 connect: Connection refused
```

This shows a single message sitting in the message queue. The transaction log (which is only displayed if you give *mailq* the `-v` option) may give an additional reason why it is still waiting for delivery. If no attempt has been made yet to deliver the message, no transaction log will be displayed.

Even when you don't use queuing, *smail* will occasionally put messages into the queue when it finds immediate delivery fails for a transient reason. For SMTP connections, this may be an unreachable host; but messages may also be deferred when the file system is found to be full. You should therefore put in a queue run every hour or so (using *runq*), else any deferred message will stick around the queue forever.

14.5 Miscellaneous *config* Options

There are quite a number of options you may set in the *config* file, which, although useful, are not essential to running *smail*, and which we will not discuss here. Instead, we will only mention a few that you might find a reason to use:

error_copy_postmaster If this boolean variable is set, any error will generate a message to the postmaster. Usually, this is only done for errors that are due to a faulty configuration. The variable can be turned on by putting it in the *config* file, preceded by a plus (+).

max_hop_count If the hop count for a message (i.e. the number of hosts already traversed) equals or exceeds this number, attempts at remote delivery will result in an error message being returned to the sender. This is used to prevent messages from looping forever. The hop count is generally computed from the number of *Received:* fields in the mail header, but may also be set manually using the `-h` option on the command line.

This variable defaults to 20.

postmaster The postmaster's address. If the address **Postmaster** cannot be resolved to a valid local address, then this is used as the last resort. The default is **root**.

14.6 Message Routing and Delivery

smail splits up mail delivery into three different tasks, the router, director, and transport module.

The router module resolves all remote addresses, determining to which host the message should be sent to next, and which transport must be used. Depending on the nature of the link, different transports such as UUCP or SMTP may be used.

Local addresses are given to the director task which resolves any forwarding or aliasing. For example, the address might be an alias or a mailing list, or the user might want to forward her mail to another address. If the resulting address is remote, it is handed to the router module for additional routing, otherwise it is assigned a transport for local delivery. By far the most common case will be delivery to a mailbox, but messages may also be piped into a command, or appended to some arbitrary file.

The transport module, finally, is responsible for whatever method of delivery has been chosen. It tries to deliver the message, and in case of failure either generates a bounce message, or defers it for a later retry.

With *smail*, you have much freedom in configuring these tasks. For each of them, a number of drivers are available, from which you can choose those you need. You describe them to *smail* in a couple of files, namely *routers*, *directors*, and *transports*, located in */usr/lib/smail*. If these files do not exist, reasonable defaults are assumed that should be suitable for many sites that either use SMTP or UUCP for transport. If you want to change *smail*'s routing policy, or modify a transport, you should get the sample files from the *smail* source distribution,[5] copy the sample files to */usr/lib/smail*, and modify them according to your needs. Sample configuration files are also given in Appendix B.

14.7 Routing Messages

When given a message, *smail* first checks if the destination is the local host, or a remote site. If the target host address is one of the local hostnames configured in *config*, the message is handed to the director module. Otherwise, *smail* hands the destination address to a number of router drivers to find out which host to forward a message to. They can be described in the *routers* file; if this file does not exist, a set of default routers are used.

The destination host is passed to all routers in turn, and the one finding the most specific route is selected. Consider a message addressed to **joe@foo.bar.com**. Then, one router might know a default route for all hosts in the **bar.com** domain, while another one has information for **foo.bar.com** itself. Since the latter is more specific, it is chosen over the former. If there are two routers that provide a "best match," the one coming first in the *routers* file is chosen.

This router now specifies the transport to be used, for instance UUCP, and generates a new destination address. The new address is passed to the transport along with the host to forward the message to. In the above example, *smail* might find out that **foo.bar.com** is to be reached via UUCP using the path **ernie!bert**. It will then generate a new target of **bert!foo.bar.com!user**, and have the UUCP transport use this as the envelope address to be passed to **ernie**.

When using the default setup, the following routers are available:

- If the destination host address can be resolved using the *gethostbyname(3)* or *gethostbyaddr(3)* library call, the message will be delivered via SMTP. The only exception is if the address is found to refer to the local host, it is handed to the director module, too.

  smail also recognizes IP addresses written as dotted quad as a legal hostname, as long as they can be resolved through a *gethostbyaddr(3)* call. For example, **scrooge@[149.76.12.4]** would be a valid although highly unusual mail address for **scrooge** on **quark.physics.groucho.edu**.

  If your machine is on the Internet, these routers are not what you are looking for, because they do not support MX records. See below for what to do in this case.

- If */usr/lib/smail/paths*, the pathalias database, exists, *smail* will try to look up the target host (minus any trailing **.uucp**) in this file. Mail to an address matched by this router will be delivered using UUCP, using the path found in the database.

[5] The default configuration files can be found in *samples/generic* below the source directory.

- The host address (minus any trailing **.uucp**) will be compared to the output of the *uuname* command to check if the target host is in fact a UUCP neighbor. If this is the case, the message will be delivered using the UUCP transport.
- If the address has not been matched by any of the above routers, it will be delivered to the smart host. The path to the smart host as well as the transport to be used are set in the *config* file.

These defaults work for many simple setups, but fail if routing requirements get a little more complicated. If you are faced with any of the problems discussed below, you will have to install your own *routers* file to override the defaults. A sample *routers* file you might start with is given in appendix B. Some Linux distributions also come with a set of configuration files that are tailored to work around these difficulties.

Probably the worst problems arise when your host lives in a dual universe with both dialup IP and UUCP links. You will then have hostnames in your *hosts* file that you only talk occasionally to through your SLIP link, so *smail* will attempt to deliver any mail for these hosts via SMTP. This is usually not what you want, because even if the SLIP link is activated regularly, SMTP is much slower than sending the mail over UUCP. With the default setup, there's no way escaping *smail*.

You can avoid this problem by having *smail* check the *paths* file before querying the resolver, and put all hosts you want to force UUCP delivery to into the *paths* file. If you don't want to send any messages over SMTP *ever*, you can also comment out the resolver-based routers altogether.

Another problem is that the default setup doesn't provide for true Internet mail routing, because the resolver-based router does not evaluate MX records. To enable full support for Internet mail routing, comment out this router, and uncomment the one that used BIND instead. There are, however, *smail* binaries included in some Linux distributions that don't have BIND support compiled in. If you enable BIND, but get a message in the *paniclog* file saying "`router inet_hosts: driver bind not found`", then you have to get the sources and recompile *smail* (see section 14.2 above).

Finally, it is not generally a good idea to use the *uuname* driver. For one, it will generate a configuration error when you don't have UUCP installed, because no *uuname* command will be found. The second is when you have more sites listed in your UUCP *Systems* file than you actually have mail links with. These may be sites you only exchange news with, or sites you occasionally download files from via anonymous UUCP, but have no traffic with otherwise.

To work around the first problem, you can substitute a shell script for *uuname* which does a simple *exit 0*. The more general solution is, however, to edit the *routers* file and remove this driver altogether.

14.7.1 The *paths* database

smail expects to find the pathalias database in the *paths* file below */usr/lib/smail*. This file is optional, so if you don't want to perform any pathalias routing at all, simply remove any existing *paths* file.

paths must be a sorted ASCII file that contains entries which map destination site names to UUCP bang paths. The file has to be sorted because *smail* uses a binary search for looking up a site. Comments are not allowed in this file, and the site name must be separated from the path using a TAB. Pathalias databases are discussed in somewhat greater detail in chapter 13.

If you generate this file by hand, you should make sure to include all legal names for a site. For example, if a site is known by both a plain UUCP name and a fully qualified domain name, you have to add an entry for each of them. The file can be sorted by piping it through the *sort(1)* command.

If your site is only a leaf site, however, then no *paths* file should be necessary at all: just set up the smart host attributes in your *config* file, and leave all routing to your mail feed.

14.8 Delivering Messages to Local Addresses

Most commonly, a local address is just a user's login name, in which case the message is delivered to her mailbox, */var/spool/mail/user*. Other cases include aliases and mailing list names, and mail forwarding by the user. In these cases, the local address expands to a new list of addresses, which may be either local or remote.

Apart from these "normal" addresses, *smail* can handle other types of local message destinations, like file names, and pipe commands. These are not addresses in their own right, so you can't send mail to, say, **/etc/passwd@vbrew.com**; they are only valid if they have been taken from forwarding or alias files.

A *file name* is anything that begins with a slash (/) or a tilde (~). The latter refers to the user's home directory, and is possible only if the filename was taken from a *.forward* file or a forwarding entry in the mailbox (see below). When delivering to a file, *smail* appends the messages to the file, creating it if necessary.

A *pipe command* may be any UNIX command preceded by the pipe symbol (`|`). This causes *smail* to hand the command to the shell along with its arguments, but without the leading '`|`'. The message itself is fed to this command on standard input.

For example, to gate a mailing list into a local newsgroup, you might use a shell script named *gateit*, and set up a local alias which delivers all messages from this mailing list to the script using "|*gateit*".

If the invocation contains white space, it has to be enclosed in double quotes. Due to the security issues involved, care is taken not to execute the command if the address has been obtained in a somewhat dubious way (for example, if the alias file from which the address was taken was writable by everyone).

14.8.1 Local Users

The most common case for a local address is to denote a user's mailbox. This mailbox is located in */var/spool/mail* and has the name of the user. It is owned by her, with a group of **mail**, and has mode 660. If it does not exist, it is created by *smail*.

Note that although */var/spool/mail* is currently the standard place to put the mailbox files, some mail software may have different paths compiled in, for example */usr/spool/mail*. If delivery to users on your machine fails consistently, you should try if it helps to make this a symbolic link to */var/spool/mail*.

There are two addresses *smail* requires to exist: **MAILER-DAEMON** and **Postmaster**. When generating a bounce message for an undeliverable mail, a carbon copy is sent to the **postmaster** account for examination (in case this might be due to a configuration problem). The **MAILER-DAEMON** is used as the sender's address on the bounce message.

If these addresses do not name valid accounts on your system, *smail* implicitly maps **MAILER-DAEMON** to **postmaser**, and **postmaster** to **root**, respectively. You should usually override this by aliasing the **postmaster** account to whoever is responsible for maintaining the mail software.

14.8.2 Forwarding

A user may redirect her mail by having it forwarded to an alternative address using one of two methods supported by *smail*. One option is to put

```
Forward to recipient, ...
```

in the first line of her mailbox file. This will send all incoming mail to the specified list of recipients. Alternatively, she might create a *.forward* file in her home directory, which contains the comma-separated list of recipients. With this variety of forwarding, all lines of the file are read and interpreted.

Note that any type of address may be used. Thus, a practical example of a *.forward* file for vacations might be

```
janet, "|vacation"
```

The first address delivers the incoming message to **janet**'s mailbox nevertheless, while the *vacation* command returns a short notification to the sender.

14.8.3 Alias Files

smail is able to handle alias files compatible with those known by Berkeley's *sendmail*. Entries in the alias file may have the form

```
alias: recipients
```

recipients is a comma-separated list of addresses that will be substituted for the alias. The recipient list may be continued across newlines if the next line begins with a TAB.

There is a special feature that allows *smail* to handle mailing lists from the alias file: if you specify "`:include:`*filename*" as recipient, *smail* will read the file specified, and substitute its contents as a list of recipients.

The main aliases file is */usr/lib/aliases*. If you choose to make this file world-writable, *smail* wil not deliver any messages to shell commands given in this file. A sample file is shown below:

```
# vbrew.com /usr/lib/aliases file
hostmaster: janet
postmaster: janet
usenet: phil
# The development mailing list.
development: joe, sue, mark, biff
        /var/mail/log/development
owner-development: joe
# Announcements of general interest are mailed to all
# of the staff
announce: :include: /usr/lib/smail/staff,
        /var/mail/log/announce
owner-announce: root
# gate the foobar mailing list to a local newsgroup
ppp-list: "|/usr/local/lib/gateit local.lists.ppp"
```

If an error occurs while delivering to an address generated from the *aliases* file, *smail* will attempt to send a copy of the error message to the "alias owner." For example, if delivery to **biff** fails when delivering a message to the **development** mailing list, a copy of the error message will be mailed to the sender, as well as to **postmaster** and **owner-development**. If the owner address does not exist, no additional error message will be generated.

When delivering to files or when invoking programs given in the *aliases* file, *smail* will become the **nobody** user to avoid any security hassles. Especially when delivering to files, this can be a real nuisance. In the file given above, for instance, the log files must be owned and writable by **nobody**, or delivery to them will fail.

14.8.4 Mailing Lists

Instead of using the *aliases* file, mailing lists may also be managed by means of files in the */usr/lib/smail/lists* directory. A mailing list named *nag-bugs* is described by the file *lists/nag-bugs*, which should contain the members' addresses, separated by commas. The list may be given on multiple lines, with comments being introduced by a hash sign.

For each mailing list, a user (or alias) named **owner-***listname* should exist; any errors occurring when resolving an address are reported to this user. This address is also used as the sender's address on all outgoing messages in the `Sender:` header field.

14.9 UUCP-based Transports

There are a number of transports compiled into *smail* that utilize the UUCP suite. In a UUCP environment, messages are usually passed on by invoking *rmail* on the next host, giving it the message on standard input and the envelope address on the command line. On your host, *rmail* should be a link to the *smail* command.

When handing a message to the UUCP transport, *smail* converts the target address to a UUCP bang path. For example, **user@host** will be transformed to **host!user**. Any occurrence of the '**%**' address operator is preserved, so **user%host@gateway** will become **gateway!user%host**. However, *smail* will never generate such addresses itself.

Alternatively, *smail* can send and receive BSMTP batches via UUCP. With BSMTP, one or more messages are wrapped up in a single batch that contains the commands the local mailer would issue if a real SMTP connection had be established. BSMTP is frequently used in store-and-forward (e.g. UUCP-based) networks to save disk space. The sample *transports* file in appendix B contains a transport dubbed *bsmtp* that generates partial BSMTP batches in a queue directory. They must be combined into the final batches later, using a shell script that adds the appropriate *HELO* and *QUIT* command.

To enable the *bsmtp* transport for specific UUCP links you have to use so-called *method* files (please refer to the *smail(5)* manual page for details). If you have only one UUCP link, and use the smart host router, you enable sending SMTP batches by setting the *smart_transport* configuration variable to *bsmtp* instead of *uux*.

To receive SMTP batches over UUCP, you must make sure that you have the unbatching command the remote site sends its batches to. If the remote site uses *smail*, too, you need to make *rsmtp* a link to *smail*. If the remote site runs *sendmail*, you should additionally install a shell script named */usr/bin/bsmtp* that does a simple "*exec rsmtp*" (a symbolic link won't work).

14.10 SMTP-based Transports

smail currently supports an SMTP driver to deliver mail over TCP connections.[6] It is capable of delivering a message to any number of addresses on one single host, with the hostname being specified as either a fully qualified domain name that can be resolved by the networking software, or in dotted quad notation enclosed in square brackets. Generally, addresses resolved by any of the BIND, *gethostbyname(3)*, or *gethostbyaddr(3)* router drivers will be delivered to the SMTP transport.

The SMTP driver will attempt to connect to the remote host immediately through the *smtp* port as listed in */etc/services*. If it cannot be reached, or the connection times out, delivery will be reattempted at a later time.

Delivery on the Internet requires that routes to the destination host be specified in the *route-addr* format described in chapter 13, rather than as a bang path.[7] *smail* will therefore transform **user%host@gateway**, where **gateway** is reached via **host1!host2!host3**, into the source-route address **<@host2,@host3:user%host@gateway>** which will be sent as the message's envelope address to **host1**. To enable these transformations (along with the built-in BIND driver), you have to edit the entry for the *smtp* driver in the *transports* file. A sample *transports* file is given in Appendix B.

14.11 Hostname Qualification

Sometimes it is desirable to catch unqualified hostnames (i.e. those that don't have a domain name) specified in sender or recipient addresses, for example when gatewaying between two networks, where one requires fully qualified domain names. On an Internet-UUCP relay, unqualifed hostnames should be mapped to the **uucp** domain by default. Other address modifications than these are questionable.

The */usr/lib/smail/qualify* file tells *smail* which domain names to tack onto which hostnames. Entries in the *qualify* file consists of a hostname beginning in column one, followed by domain name. Lines containing a hash sign as its first non-white character are considered comments. Entries are searched in the order they appear in.

If no *qualify* file exists, no hostname qualification is performed at all.

A special hostname of * matches any hostnames, thus enabling you to map all hosts not mentioned before into a default domain. It should be used only as the last entry.

At the Virtual Brewery, all hosts have been set up to use fully qualified domain names in the sender's addresses. Unqualified recipient addresses are considered to be in the **uucp** domain, so only a single entry in the *qualify* file is needed.

```
# /usr/lib/smail/qualify, last changed Feb 12, 1994 by janet
#
*           uucp
```

[6]The authors call this support "simple". For a future version of *smail*, they advertise a complete backend which will handle this more efficiently.

[7]However, the use of routes in the Internet is discouraged altogether. Fully qualified domain names should be used instead.

CHAPTER 15

Sendmail+IDA

15.1 Introduction to Sendmail+IDA

It's been said that you aren't a *real* Unix system administrator until you've edited a *sendmail.cf* file. It's also been said that you're crazy if you've attempted to do so twice.

Sendmail is an incredibly powerful program. It's also incredibly difficult to learn and understand for most people. Any program whose definitive reference (*Sendmail*, published by O'Reilly and Associates) is 792 pages long quite justifiably scares most people off.

Sendmail+IDA is different. It removes the need to edit the always cryptic *sendmail.cf* file and allows the administrator to define the site-specific routing and addressing configuration through relatively easy to understand support files called *tables*. Switching to sendmail+IDA can save you many hours of work and stress.

Compared to the other major mail transport agents, there is probably nothing that can't be done faster and simpler with sendmail+IDA. Typical things that are needed to run a normal UUCP or Internet site become simple to accomplish. Configurations that normally are extremely difficult are simple to create and maintain.

At this writing, the current version of *sendmail5.67b+IDA1.5* is available via anonymous FTP from **vixen.cso.uiuc.edu**. It compiles without any patching required under Linux.

All the configuration files required to get sendmail+IDA sources to compile, install, and run under Linux are included in *newspak-2.2.tar.gz* which is available via anonymous FTP on **sunsite.unc.edu** in the directory */pub/Linux/system/Mail*.

15.2 Configuration Files — Overview

Traditional sendmail is set up through a system configuration file (typically */etc/sendmail.cf* or */usr/lib/sendmail.cf*), that is not anything close to any language you've seen before. Editing the *sendmail.cf* file to provide customized behavior can be a humbling experience.

Sendmail+IDA makes such pain essentially a thing of the past by having all configuration options table-driven with rather easy to understand syntax. These options are configured by running *m4* (a macro processor) or *dbm* (a database processor) on a number of data files via Makefiles supplied with the sources.

The *sendmail.cf* file defines only the default behavior of the system. Virtually all special customization is done through a number of optional tables rather than by directly editing the *sendmail.cf* file. A list of all *sendmail* tables is given in figure 15.1.

15.3 The *sendmail.cf* File

The *sendmail.cf* file for sendmail+IDA is not edited directly, but is generated from an *m4* configuration file provided by the local system administrator. In the following, we will refer to it as *sendmail.m4*.

mailertable defines special behavior for remote hosts or domains.

uucpxtable forces UUCP delivery of mail to hosts that are in DNS format.

pathtable defines UUCP bang-paths to remote hosts or domains.

uucprelays short-circuits the pathalias path to well-known remote hosts.

genericfrom converts internal addresses into generic ones visible to the outside world.

xaliases converts generic addresses to/from valid internal ones.

decnetxtable converts RFC-822 addresses to DECnet-style addresses.

Figure 15.1: *sendmail* Support Files.

This file contains a few definitions and otherwise merely points to the tables where the real work gets done. In general, it is only necessary to specify:

- the pathnames and filenames used on the local system.
- the name(s) the site is known by for e-mail purposes.
- which default mailer (and perhaps smart relay host) is desired.

There are a large variety of parameters that can be defined to establish the behavior of the local site or to override compiled-in configuration items. These configuration options are identified in the file *ida/cf/OPTIONS* in the source directory.

A *sendmail.m4* file for a minimal configuration (UUCP or SMTP with all non-local mail being relayed to a directly connected smart-host) can be as short as 10 or 15 lines excluding comments.

15.3.1 An Example *sendmail.m4* File

A *sendmail.m4* file for **vstout** at the Virtual Brewery is shown below. **vstout** uses SMTP to talk to all hosts on the Brewery's LAN, and sends all mail for other destinations to **moria**, its Internet relay host, via UUCP.

15.3.2 Typically Used *sendmail.m4* Parameters

A few of the items in the *sendmail.m4* file are required all the time; others can be ignored if you can get away with defaults. The following sections describe each of the items in the example *sendmail.m4* file in more detail.

15.3.2.1 Items that Define Paths

```
dnl #define(LIBDIR,/usr/local/lib/mail)dnl  # where all support files go
```

LIBDIR defines the directory where sendmail+IDA expects to find configuration files, the various dbm tables, and special local definitions. In a typical binary distribution, this is compiled into the sendmail binary and does not need to be explicitly set in the sendmail.m4 file.

The above example has a leading *dnl* which means that this line is essentially a comment for information only.

To change the location of the support files to a different location, remove the leading *dnl* from the above line, set the path to the desired location, and rebuild and reinstall the *sendmail.cf* file.

15.3.2.2 Defining the Local Mailer

```
define(LOCAL_MAILER_DEF, mailers.linux)dnl  # mailer for local delivery
```

```
dnl #------------------ SAMPLE SENDMAIL.M4 FILE ------------------
dnl # (the string 'dnl' is the m4 equivalent of commenting out a line)
dnl # you generally don't want to override LIBDIR from the compiled in paths
dnl #define(LIBDIR,/usr/local/lib/mail)dnl        # where all support files go
define(LOCAL_MAILER_DEF, mailers.linux)dnl       # mailer for local delivery
define(POSTMASTERBOUNCE)dnl                       # postmaster gets bounces
define(PSEUDODOMAINS, BITNET UUCP)dnl             # don't try DNS on these
dnl #---------------------------------------------------------------
dnl #
define(PSEUDONYMS, vstout.vbrew.com  vstout.UUCP vbrew.com)
dnl                                               # names we're known by
define(DEFAULT_HOST, vstout.vbrew.com)dnl         # our primary 'name' for mail
define(UUCPNAME, vstout)dnl                       # our uucp name
dnl #
dnl #---------------------------------------------------------------
dnl #
define(UUCPNODES, |uuname|sort|uniq)dnl           # our uucp neighbors
define(BANGIMPLIESUUCP)dnl                        # make certain that uucp
define(BANGONLYUUCP)dnl                           #  mail is treated correctly
define(RELAY_HOST, moria)dnl                      # our smart relay host
define(RELAY_MAILER, UUCP-A)dnl                   # we reach moria via uucp
dnl #
dnl #--------------------------------------------------------------------
dnl #
dnl # the various dbm lookup tables
dnl #
define(ALIASES, LIBDIR/aliases)dnl                # system aliases
define(DOMAINTABLE, LIBDIR/domaintable)dnl        # domainize hosts
define(PATHTABLE, LIBDIR/pathtable)dnl            # paths database
define(GENERICFROM, LIBDIR/generics)dnl           # generic from addresses
define(MAILERTABLE, LIBDIR/mailertable)dnl        # mailers per host or domain
define(UUCPXTABLE, LIBDIR/uucpxtable)dnl          # paths to hosts we feed
define(UUCPRELAYS, LIBDIR/uucprelays)dnl          # short-circuit paths
dnl #
dnl #--------------------------------------------------------------------
dnl #
dnl # include the 'real' code that makes it all work
dnl # (provided with the source code)
dnl #
include(Sendmail.mc)dnl                             # REQUIRED ENTRY !!!
dnl #
dnl #----------- END OF SAMPLE SENDMAIL.M4 FILE -------
```

Figure 15.2: A sample *sendmail.m4* file for **vstout**.

Most operating systems provide a program to handle local delivery of mail. Typical programs for many of the major variants of Unix are already built into the sendmail binary.

In Linux, it is necessary to explicitly define the appropriate local mailer since a local delivery program is not necessarily present in the distribution you've installed. This is done by specifying *LOCAL_MAILER_DEF* in the *sendmail.m4* file.

For example, to have the commonly used *deliver* program[1] provide this service, you would set *LOCAL_MAILER_DEF* to *mailers.linux*.

The following file should then be installed as *mailers.linux* in the directory pointed to by *LIBDIR*. It explicitly defines the *deliver* program in the internal *Mlocal* mailer with the proper parameters to result in *sendmail* correctly delivering mail targeted for the local system. Unless you are a sendmail expert, you probably do not want to alter the following example.

```
# -- /usr/local/lib/mail/mailers.linux --
#     (local mailers for use on Linux )
Mlocal, P=/usr/bin/deliver, F=SlsmFDMP, S=10, R=25/10, A=deliver $u
Mprog,  P=/bin/sh,          F=lsDFMeuP,  S=10, R=10, A=sh -c $u
```

There is a also built-in default for *deliver* in the *Sendmail.mc* file that gets included into the *sendmail.cf* file. To specify it, you would not use the mailers.linux file and would instead define the following in your *sendmail.m4* file:

```
dnl --- (in sendmail.m4) ---
define(LOCAL_MAILER_DEF, DELIVER)dnl       # mailer for local delivery
```

Unfortunately, *Sendmail.mc* assumes deliver is installed in */bin*, which is not the case with Slackware1.1.1 (which installs it in */usr/bin*). In that case you'd need to either fake it with a link or rebuild deliver from sources so that it resides in */bin*.

15.3.2.3 Dealing with Bounced Mail

```
define(POSTMASTERBOUNCE)dnl                # postmaster gets bounces
```

Many sites find that it is important to ensure that mail is sent and received with close to a 100% success rate. While examining *syslogd(8)* logs is helpful, the local mail administrator generally needs to see the headers on bounced mail in order to determine if the mail was undeliverable because of user error or a configuration error on one of the systems involved.

Defining *POSTMASTERBOUNCE* results in a copy of each bounced message being set to the person defined as **Postmaster** for the system.

Unfortunately, setting this parameter also results in the *text* of the message being sent to the Postmaster, which potentially has related privacy concerns for people using mail on the system.

Site postmasters should in general attempt to discipline themselves (or do so via technical means through shell scripts that delete the text of the bounce messages they receive) from reading mail not addressed to them.

15.3.2.4 Domain Name Service Related Items

```
define(PSEUDODOMAINS, BITNET UUCP)dnl       # don't try DNS on these
```

There are several well known networks that are commonly referenced in mail addresses for historical reasons but that are not valid for DNS purposes. Defining *PSEUDODOMAINS* prevents needless DNS lookup attempts that will always fail.

---

[1] *deliver* was written by Chip Salzenberg (**chip%tct@ateng.com**). It is part of several Linux distributions and can be found in the usual anonymous FTP archives such as **ftp.uu.net**.

15.3.2.5 Defining Names the Local System is Known by

```
define(PSEUDONYMS, vstout.vbrew.com  vstout.UUCP vbrew.com)
dnl                                       # names we're known by
define(DEFAULT_HOST, vstout.vbrew.com)dnl # our primary 'name' for mail
```

Frequently, systems wish to hide their true identity, serve as mail gateways, or receive and process mail addressed to 'old' names by which they used to be known.

PSEUDONYMS specifies the list of all hostnames for which the local system will accept mail.

DEFAULT_HOST specifies the hostname that will appear in messages originating on the local host. It is important that this parameter be set to a valid value or all return mail will be undeliverable.

15.3.2.6 UUCP-Related Items

```
define(UUCPNAME, vstout)dnl               # our uucp name
define(UUCPNODES, |uuname|sort|uniq)dnl   # our uucp neighbors
define(BANGIMPLIESUUCP)dnl                # make certain that uucp
define(BANGONLYUUCP)dnl                   #  mail is treated correctly
```

Frequently, systems are known by one name for DNS purposes and another for UUCP purposes. *UUCPNAME* permits you to define a different hostname that appears in the headers of outgoing UUCP mail.

UUCPNODES defines the commands that return a list of hostnames for the systems we are connected directly to via UUCP connections.

BANGIMPLIESUUCP and *BANGONLYUUCP* ensure that mail addressed with UUCP 'bang' syntax is treated according to UUCP behavior rather than the more current Domain Name Service behavior used today on Internet.

15.3.2.7 Relay Systems and Mailers

```
define(RELAY_HOST, moria)dnl              # our smart relay host
define(RELAY_MAILER, UUCP-A)dnl           # we reach moria via UUCP
```

Many system administrators do not want to be bothered with the work needed to ensure that their system is able to reach all the networks (and therefore systems) on all networks worldwide. Instead of doing so, they would rather relay all outgoing mail to another system that is known to be indeed "smart."

RELAY_HOST defines the UUCP hostname of such a smart neighboring system.

RELAY_MAILER defines the mailer used to relay the messages there.

It is important to note that setting these parameters results in your outgoing mail being forwarded to this remote system, which will affect the load of their system. Be certain to get explicit agreement from the remote Postmaster before you configure your system to use another system as a general purpose relay host.

15.3.2.8 The Various Configuration Tables

```
define(ALIASES, LIBDIR/aliases)dnl           # system aliases
define(DOMAINTABLE, LIBDIR/domaintable)dnl   # domainize hosts
define(PATHTABLE, LIBDIR/pathtable)dnl       # paths database
define(GENERICFROM, LIBDIR/generics)dnl      # generic from addresses
define(MAILERTABLE, LIBDIR/mailertable)dnl   # mailers per host or domain
define(UUCPXTABLE, LIBDIR/uucpxtable)dnl     # paths to hosts we feed
define(UUCPRELAYS, LIBDIR/uucprelays)dnl     # short-circuit paths
```

With these macros, you can change the location where sendmail+IDA looks for the various dbm tables that define the system's "real" behavior. It is generally wise to leave them in *LIBDIR*.

15.3.2.9 The Master *Sendmail.mc* File

```
include(Sendmail.mc)dnl                    # REQUIRED ENTRY !!!
```

The authors of sendmail+IDA provide the *Sendmail.mc* file which contains the true "guts" of what becomes the sendmail.cf file. Periodically, new versions are released to fix bugs or add functionality without requiring a full release and recompilation of sendmail from sources.

It is important *not* to edit this file.

15.3.2.10 So Which Entries are Really Required?

When not using any of the optional dbm tables, sendmail+IDA delivers mail via the *DEFAULT_MAILER* (and possibly *RELAY_HOST* and *RELAY_MAILER*) defined in the *sendmail.m4* file used to generate *sendmail.cf*. It is easily possible to override this behavior through entries in the *domaintable* or *uucpxtable*.

A generic site that is on Internet and speaks Domain Name Service, or one that is UUCP-only and forwards all mail via UUCP through a smart *RELAY_HOST*, probably does not need any specific table entries at all.

Virtually all systems should set the *DEFAULT_HOST* and *PSEUDONYMS* macros, which define the canonical site name and aliases it is known by, and *DEFAULT_MAILER*. If all you have is a relay host and relay mailer, you don't need to set these defaults since it works automagically.

UUCP hosts will probably also need to set *UUCPNAME* to their official UUCP name. They will also probably set *RELAY_MAILER*, and *RELAY_HOST* which enable smart-host routing through a mail relay. The mail transport to be used is defined in *RELAY_MAILER* and should usually be *UUCP-A* for UUCP sites.

If your site is SMTP-only and talks 'Domain Name Service', you would change the *DEFAULT_MAILER* to *TCP-A* and probably delete the *RELAY_MAILER* and *RELAY_HOST* lines.

15.4 A Tour of Sendmail+IDA Tables

Sendmail+IDA provides a number of tables that allow you to override the default behavior of sendmail (specified in the *sendmail.m4* file) and define special behavior for unique situations, remote systems, and networks. These tables are post-processed with *dbm* using the Makefile provided with the distribution.

Most sites will need few, if any, of these tables. If your site does not require these tables, the easiest thing is probably to make them zero length files (with the *touch* command) and use the default Makefile in *LIBDIR* rather than editing the Makefile itself.

15.4.1 *mailertable*

The *mailertable* defines special treatment for specific hosts or domains based on the remote host or network name. It is frequently used on Internet sites to select an intermediate mail relay host or gateway to reach a remote network through, and to specify a particular protocol (UUCP or SMTP) to be used. UUCP sites will generally not need to use this file.

Order is important. Sendmail reads the file top-down and processes the message according to the first rule it matches. So it is generally wise to place the most explicit rules at the top of the file and the more generic rules below.

Suppose you want to forward all mail for the Computer Science department at Groucho Marx University via UUCP to a relay host **ada**. To do so, you would have a *mailertable* entry that looked like the following:

```
# (in mailertable)
#
# forward all mail for the domain .cs.groucho.edu via UUCP to ada
UUCP-A,ada          .cs.groucho.edu
```

Suppose you want all mail to the larger **groucho.edu** domain to go to a different relayhost **bighub** for address resolution and delivery. The expanded mailertable entries would look quite similar.

```
# (in mailertable)
#
# forward all mail for the domain cs.groucho.edu via UUCP to ada
UUCP-A,ada          .cs.groucho.edu
#
# forward all mail for the domain groucho.edu via UUCP to bighub
UUCP-A,bighub       .groucho.edu
```

As mentioned above, order is important. Reversing the order of the two rules shown above will result in all mail to **.cs.groucho.edu** going through the more generic **bighub** path instead of the explicit **ada** path that is really desired.

```
# (in mailertable)
#
# forward all mail for the domain .groucho.edu via UUCP to bighub
UUCP-A,bighub      .groucho.edu
#
# (it is impossible to reach the next line because
#    the rule above will be matched first)
UUCP-A,ada         .cs.groucho.edu
#
```

In the mailertable examples above, the *UUCP-A* mailer makes *sendmail* use UUCP delivery with domainized headers.

The comma between the mailer and remote system tells it to forward the message to **ada** for address resolution and delivery.

Mailertable entries are of the format:

mailer delimiter relayhost *host_or_domain*

There are a number of possible mailers. The differences are generally in how they treat addresses. Typical mailers are *TCP-A* (TCP/IP with Internet-style addresses), *TCP-U* (TCP/IP with UUCP-style addresses), and *UUCP-A* (UUCP with Internet-style addresses).

The character that separates the mailer from the host portion on the left-hand-side of a mailertable line defines how the address is modified by the mailertable. The important thing to realize is that this only rewrites the envelope (to get the mail into the remote system). Rewriting anything other than the envelope is generally frowned upon due to the high probability of breaking the mail configuration.

! An exclamation point strips off the recipient hostname before forwarding to the mailer. This can be used when you want to wish to essentially force mail into a misconfigured remote site.

, A comma does not change the address in any way. The message is merely forwarded via the specified mailer to the specified relay host.

: A colon removes the recipient hostname only if there are intermediate hosts between you and the destination. Thus, **foo!bar!joe** will have **foo** removed, while **xyzzy!janet** will remain unchanged.

15.4.2 *uucpxtable*

Usually, mail to hosts with fully-qualified domain names is delivered via Internet style (SMTP) delivery using Domain Name Service (DNS), or via the relay host. The *uucpxtable* forces delivery via UUCP routing by converting the domainized name into a UUCP-style un-domainized remote hostname.

It is frequently used when you're a mail forwarder for a site or domain or when you wish to send mail via a direct and reliable UUCP link rather than potentially multiple hops through the default mailer and any intermediate systems and networks.

UUCP sites that talk to UUCP neighbors who use domainized mail headers would use this file to force delivery of the mail through the direct UUCP point-to-point link between the two systems rather than using the less direct route through the *RELAY_MAILER* and *RELAY_HOST* or through the *DEFAULT_MAILER*.

Internet sites who do not talk UUCP probably would not use the *uucpxtable*.

Suppose you provide mail forwarding service to a system called **sesame.com** in DNS and **sesame** in the UUCP maps. You would need the following *uucpxtable* entry to force mail for their host to go through your direct UUCP connection.

```
#============== /usr/local/lib/mail/uucpxtable ============
# Mail sent to joe@sesame.com is rewritten to sesame!joe and
# therefore delivered via UUCP
#
sesame    sesame.com
#
#-----------------------------------------------------------
```

15.4.3 *pathtable*

The *pathtable* is used to define explicit routing to remote hosts or networks. The *pathtable* file should be in pathalias-style syntax, sorted alphabetically. The two fields on each line must be separated by a real TAB, else *dbm* might complain.

Most systems will not need any *pathtable* entries.

```
#================ /usr/local/lib/mail/pathtable ================
#
# this is a pathalias-style paths file to let you kick mail to
# UUCP neighbors to the direct UUCP path so you don't have to
# go the long way through your smart host that takes other traffic
#
# you want real tabs on each line or m4 might complain
#
# route mail through one or more intermediate sites to a remote
# system using UUCP-style addressing.
#
sesame!ernie!%s            ernie
#
# forwarding to a system that is a UUCP neighbor of a reachable
# internet site.
#
swim!%s@gcc.groucho.edu     swim
#
# The following sends all mail for two networks through different
# gateways (see the leading '.' ?).
# In this example, "uugate" and "byte" are specific systems that serve
# as mail gateways to the .UUCP and .BITNET pseudo-domains respectively
#
%s@uugate.groucho.edu            .UUCP
byte!%s@mail.shift.com           .BITNET
#
#=================== end of pathtable ======================
```

15.4.4 *domaintable*

The *domaintable* is generally used to force certain behavior after a DNS lookup has occurred. It permits the administrator to make shorthand names available for commonly referenced systems or domains by replacing the shorthand name with the proper one automatically. It can also be used to replace incorrect host or domain names with the "correct" information.

Most sites will not need any *domaintable* entries.

The following example shows how to replace an incorrect address people are attempting to mail to with the correct address:

```
#============= /usr/local/lib/mail/domaintable ================
#
#
brokenhost.correct.domain        brokenhost.wrong.domain
#
#
#=================== end of domaintable ======================
```

15.4.5 *aliases*

Aliases permit a number of things to happen:

- They provide a shorthand or well-known name for mail to be addressed to in order to go to one or more persons.
- They invoke a program with the mail message as the input to the program.
- They send mail to a file.

All systems require aliases for **Postmaster** and **MAILER-DAEMON** to be RFC-compliant.

Always be extremely aware of security when defining aliases that invoke programs or write to programs since sendmail generally runs setuid-root.

Changes to the *aliases* file do not take effect until the command

```
# /usr/lib/sendmail -bi
```

is executed to build the required dbm tables. This can also be done by executing the *newaliases* command, usually from cron.

Details concerning mail aliases may be found in the *aliases(5)* manual page.

```
#--------------------- /usr/local/lib/mail/aliases ------------------
#
# demonstrate commonly seen types of aliases
#
usenet:         janet                       # alias for a person
admin:          joe,janet                   # alias for several people
newspak-users:  :include:/usr/lib/lists/newspak
                                            # read recipients from a file
changefeed:     | /usr/local/lib/gup        # alias that invokes a program
complaints:     /var/log/complaints         # alias that writes mail to a file
#
# The following two aliases must be present to be RFC-compliant.
# It is important to have them resolve to 'a person' who reads mail routinely.
#
postmaster:     root                        # required entry
MAILER-DAEMON:  postmaster                  # required entry
#
#-----------------------------------------------------------------
```

15.4.6 Rarely Used Tables

The following tables are available, but rather infrequently used. Consult with the documentation that comes with the sendmail+IDA sources for details.

uucprelays The *uucprelays* file is used to "short-circuit" the UUCP path to especially well known sites rather than using a multi-hop or unreliable path generated by processing the UUCP maps with *pathalias*.

genericfrom and *xaliases* The *genericfrom* file hides local usernames and addresses from the outside world by automatically converting local usernames to generic sender addresses that do not match internal usernames.

The associated *xalparse* utility automates the generation of the genericfrom and aliases file so that both incoming and outgoing username translations occur from a master xaliases file.

decnetxtable The *decnetxtable* rewrites domainized addresses into decnet-style addresses much like the domaintable can be used to rewrite undomainized addresses into domainized SMTP-style addresses.

15.5 Installing *sendmail*

In this section, we'll take a look at how to install a typical binary distribution of sendmail+IDA, and walk through what needs to be done to make it localized and functional.

The current binary distribution of sendmail+IDA for Linux can be gotten from **sunsite.unc.edu** in */pub/Linux/system/Mail*. Even if you have an earlier version of *sendmail* I strongly recommend you go to the *sendmail5.67b+IDA1.5* version since all required Linux-specific patches are now in the vanilla sources and several significant security holes have been plugged that were in versions prior to about December 1, 1993.

If you are building *sendmail* from the sources, you should follow the instructions in the *README*s included in the source distribution. The current sendmail+IDA source is available from **vixen.cso.uiuc.edu**. To build sendmail+IDA on Linux, you also need the Linux-specific configuration files from *newspak-2.2.tar.gz*, which is available on **sunsite.unc.edu** in the */pub/Linux/system/Mail* directory.

If you have previously installed *smail* or another mail delivery agent, you'll probably want to remove (or rename) all the files from smail to be safe.

15.5.1 Extracting the binary distribution

First, you have to unpack the archive file in some safe location:

```
$ gunzip -c sendmail5.65b+IDA1.5+mailx5.3b.tgz | tar xvf -
```

If you have a "modern" *tar*, for example from a recent Slackware Distribution, you can probably just do a `tar -zxvf` *filename*`.tgz` and get the same results.

Unpacking the archive creates a directory named *sendmail5.65b+IDA1.5+mailx5.3b*. In this directory, you find a complete installation of sendmail+IDA plus a binary of the *mailx* user agent. All file paths below this directory reflect the location where the files should be installed, so it's safe to work up a *tar* command to move 'em over:

```
# cd sendmail5.65b+IDA1.5+mailx5.3b
# tar cf - . | (cd /; tar xvvpoof -)
```

15.5.2 Building *sendmail.cf*

To build a *sendmail.cf* file customized for your site, you have to write a *sendmail.m4* file, and process it with *m4*. In */usr/local/lib/mail/CF*, you find a sample file called *sample.m4*. Copy it to *yourhostname.m4*, and edit it to reflect the situation of your site.

The sample file is set up for a UUCP-only site that has domainized headers and talks to a smart host. Sites like this only need to edit a few items.

In the current section, I will only give a short overview of the macros you have to change. For a complete description of what they do, please refer to the earlier discussion of the *sendmail.m4*.

LOCAL_MAILER_DEF Define define the file that defines the mailers for local mail delivery. See section "Defining the Local Mailer" above for what goes in here.

PSEUDONYMS Define all the names your local host is known by.

DEFAULT_HOST Put in your fully qualified domain name. This name will appear as your hostname in all outgoing mail.

UUCPNAME Put in your unqualified hostnmae.

RELAY_HOST and *RELAY_MAILER* If you talk UUCP to a smart-host, set *RELAY_HOST* to the UUCP name of your 'smart relay' uucp neighbor. Use the UUCP-A mailer if you want domainized headers.

DEFAULT_MAILER If you are on Internet and talk DNS, you should set this to *TCP-A*. This tells sendmail to use the *TCP-A* mailer, which delivers mail via SMTP using normal RFC style addressing for the envelope. Internet sites probably do not need to define *RELAY_HOST* or *RELAY_MAILER*.

To create the *sendmail.cf* file, execute the command

```
# make yourhostname.cf
```

This processes the *yourhostname.m4* file and creates *yourhostname.cf* from it.

Next, you should test whether the configuration file you've created does what you expect it to do. This is explained in the following two sections.

Once you're happy with its behavior, copy it into place with the command:

```
# cp yourhostname.cf /etc/sendmail.cf
```

At this point, your sendmail system is ready for action. Put the following line in the appropriate startup file (generally */etc/rc.inet2*). You can also execute it by hand to have the process start up now.

```
# /usr/lib/sendmail -bd -q1h
```

15.5.3 Testing the *sendmail.cf* file

To put sendmail into 'test' mode, you invoke it with the `-bt` flag. The default configuration file is the sendmail.cf file that is installed on the system. You can test an alternate file by using the `-C`*filename* option.

In the following examples, we test *vstout.cf*, the configuration file generated from the *vstout.m4* file shown in figure 15.2.

```
# /usr/lib/sendmail -bt -Cvstout.cf
ADDRESS TEST MODE
Enter <ruleset> <address>
[Note: No initial ruleset 3 call]
>
```

The following tests ensure that *sendmail* is able to deliver all mail to users on your system. In all cases the result of the test should be the same and point to the local system name with the *LOCAL* mailer.

First test how a mail to a local user would be delivered.

```
# /usr/lib/sendmail -bt -Cvstout.cf
ADDRESS TEST MODE
Enter <ruleset> <address>
[Note: No initial ruleset 3 call]
> 3,0 me
rewrite: ruleset  3   input: me
rewrite: ruleset  7   input: me
rewrite: ruleset  9   input: me
rewrite: ruleset  9 returns: < me >
rewrite: ruleset  7 returns: < > , me
rewrite: ruleset  3 returns: < > , me
rewrite: ruleset  0   input: < > , me
rewrite: ruleset  8   input: < > , me
```

```
rewrite: ruleset 20  input: < > , me
rewrite: ruleset 20 returns: < > , @ vstout . vbrew . com , me
rewrite: ruleset  8 returns: < > , @ vstout . vbrew . com , me
rewrite: ruleset 26  input: < > , @ vstout . vbrew . com , me
rewrite: ruleset 26 returns: $# LOCAL $@ vstout . vbrew . com $: me
rewrite: ruleset  0 returns: $# LOCAL $@ vstout . vbrew . com $: me
```

The output shows how *sendmail* processes the address internally. It is handed to various rulesets which analyze it, invoke other rulesets in turn, and break it up into its components.

In our example, we passed the address **me** to rulesets 3 and 0 (this is the meaning of the `3,0` entered before the address). The last line shows the parsed address as returned by ruleset 0, containing the mailer the message would be delivered by, and the host and user name given to the mailer.

Next, test mail to a user on your system with UUCP syntax.

```
# /usr/lib/sendmail -bt -Cvstout.cf
ADDRESS TEST MODE
Enter <ruleset> <address>
[Note: No initial ruleset 3 call]
> 3,0 vstout!me
rewrite: ruleset  3   input: vstout ! me
[...]
rewrite: ruleset  0 returns: $# LOCAL $@ vstout . vbrew . com  $: me
>
```

Next, test mail addressed to a user on your system with Internet syntax to your fully qualified hostname.

```
# /usr/lib/sendmail -bt -Cvstout.cf
ADDRESS TEST MODE
Enter <ruleset> <address>
[Note: No initial ruleset 3 call]
> 3,0 me@vstout.vbrew.com
rewrite: ruleset  3   input: me @ vstout . vbrew . com
[...]
rewrite: ruleset  0 returns: $# LOCAL $@ vstout . vbrew . com $: me
>
```

You should repeat the above two tests with each of the names you specified in the *PSEUDONYMS* and *DEFAULT_NAME* parameters in your *sendmail.m4* file.

Lastly, test that you can mail to your relay host.

```
# /usr/lib/sendmail -bt -Cvstout.cf
ADDRESS TEST MODE
Enter <ruleset> <address>
[Note: No initial ruleset 3 call]
> 3,0 fred@moria.com
rewrite: ruleset  3   input: fred @ moria . com
rewrite: ruleset  7   input: fred @ moria . com
rewrite: ruleset  9   input: fred @ moria . com
rewrite: ruleset  9 returns: < fred > @ moria . com
rewrite: ruleset  7 returns: < @ moria . com > , fred
rewrite: ruleset  3 returns: < @ moria . com > , fred
rewrite: ruleset  0   input: < @ moria . com > , fred
rewrite: ruleset  8   input: < @ moria . com > , fred
rewrite: ruleset  8 returns: < @ moria . com > , fred
```

```
rewrite: ruleset 29   input: < @ moria . com > , fred
rewrite: ruleset 29 returns: < @ moria . com > , fred
rewrite: ruleset 26   input: < @ moria . com > , fred
rewrite: ruleset 25   input: < @ moria . com > , fred
rewrite: ruleset 25 returns: < @ moria . com > , fred
rewrite: ruleset  4   input: < @ moria . com > , fred
rewrite: ruleset  4 returns: fred @ moria . com
rewrite: ruleset 26 returns: < @ moria . com > , fred
rewrite: ruleset  0 returns: $# UUCP-A $@ moria $: < @ moria . com > , fred
>
```

15.5.4 Putting it all together – Integration Testing *sendmail.cf* and the tables

At this point, you've verified that mail will have the desired default behavior and that you'll be able to both send and received validly addressed mail. To complete the installation, it may be necessary to create the appropriate dbm tables to get the desired final results.

After creating the table(s) that are required for your site, you must process them through *dbm* by typing *make* in the directory containing the tables.

If you are UUCP-only, you do *not* need to create any of the tables mentioned in the *README.linux* file. You'll just have to touch the files so that the Makefile works.

If you're UUCP-only and you talk to sites in addition to your smart-host, you'll need to add *uucpxtable* entries for each (or mail to them will also go through the smart host) and run *dbm* against the revised *uucpxtable*.

First, you need to make certain that mail through your *RELAY_HOST* is sent to them via the *RELAY_MAILER*.

```
# /usr/lib/sendmail -bt -Cvstout.cf
ADDRESS TEST MODE
Enter <ruleset> <address>
[Note: No initial ruleset 3 call]
> 3,0 fred@sesame.com
rewrite: ruleset  3   input: fred @ sesame . com
rewrite: ruleset  7   input: fred @ sesame . com
rewrite: ruleset  9   input: fred @ sesame . com
rewrite: ruleset  9 returns: < fred > @ sesame . com
rewrite: ruleset  7 returns: < @ sesame . com > , fred
rewrite: ruleset  3 returns: < @ sesame . com > , fred
rewrite: ruleset  0   input: < @ sesame . com > , fred
rewrite: ruleset  8   input: < @ sesame . com > , fred
rewrite: ruleset  8 returns: < @ sesame . com > , fred
rewrite: ruleset 29   input: < @ sesame . com > , fred
rewrite: ruleset 29 returns: < @ sesame . com > , fred
rewrite: ruleset 26   input: < @ sesame . com > , fred
rewrite: ruleset 25   input: < @ sesame . com > , fred
rewrite: ruleset 25 returns: < @ sesame . com > , fred
rewrite: ruleset  4   input: < @ sesame . com > , fred
rewrite: ruleset  4 returns: fred @ sesame . com
rewrite: ruleset 26 returns: < @ sesame . com > , fred
rewrite: ruleset  0 returns: $# UUCP-A $@ moria $: < @ sesame . com > , fred
>
```

If you have UUCP neighbors other than your *RELAY_HOST*, you need to ensure that mail to them has the proper behavior. Mail addressed with UUCP-style syntax to a host you talk UUCP with should go directly to them (unless you explicitly prevent it with a *domaintable* entry). Assume host **swim** is a direct UUCP neighbor of yours. Then feeding **swim!fred** to *sendmail* should produce the following result:

```
# /usr/lib/sendmail -bt -Cvstout.cf
ADDRESS TEST MODE
Enter <ruleset> <address>
[Note: No initial ruleset 3 call]
> 3,0 swim!fred
rewrite: ruleset  3   input: swim ! fred
[...lines omitted...]
rewrite: ruleset  0 returns: $# UUCP $@ swim $: < > , fred
>
```

If you have *uucpxtable* entries to force UUCP delivery to certain UUCP neighbors who send their mail with Internet style domainized headers, that also needs to be tested.

```
# /usr/lib/sendmail -bt -Cvstout.cf
ADDRESS TEST MODE
Enter <ruleset> <address>
[Note: No initial ruleset 3 call]
> 3,0 dude@swim.2birds.com
rewrite: ruleset  3   input: dude @ swim . 2birds . com
[...lines omitted...]
rewrite: ruleset  0 returns: $# UUCP $@ swim . 2birds $: < > , dude
>
```

15.6 Administrivia and Stupid Mail Tricks

Now that we've discussed the theory of configuring, installing, and testing a sendmail+IDA system, lets take a few moments to look into things that *do* happen routinely in the life of a mail administrator.

Remote systems sometimes break. Modems or phone lines fail, DNS definitions are set incorrectly due to human error. Networks go down unexpectedly. In such cases, mail administrators need to know how to react quickly, effectively, and *safely* to keep mail flowing through alternate routes until the remote systems or service providers can restore normal services.

The rest of this chapter is intended to provide you with the solutions to the most frequently encountered "electronic mail emergencies".

15.6.1 Forwarding Mail to a Relay Host

To forward mail for a particular host or domain to a designated relay system, you generally use the *mailertable*.

For example, to forward mail for **backwood.org** to their UUCP gateway system **backdoor**, you'd put the following entry into *mailertable*:

```
UUCP-A,backdoor    backwood.org
```

15.6.2 Forcing Mail into Misconfigured Remote Sites

Frequently, Internet hosts will have trouble getting mail into misconfigured remote sites. There are several variants of this problem, but the general symptom is that mail is bounced by the remote system or never gets there at all.

These problems can put the local system administrator in a bad position because your users generally don't care that you don't personally administer every system worldwide (or know how to get the remote administrator to fix the problem). They just know that their mail didn't get through to the desired recipient on the other end and that you're a likely person to complain to.

A remote site's configuration is their problem, not yours. In all cases, be certain to *not* break your site in order to communicate with a misconfigured remote site. If you can't get in touch with the Postmaster at the remote site to get them to fix their configuration in a timely manner, you have two options.

- It is generally possible to force mail into the remote system successfully, although since the remote system is misconfigured, replies on the remote end might not work... but then that's the remote administrator's problem.

  You can fix the bad headers in the envelope on your outgoing messages only by using a *domaintable* entry for their host/domain that results in the invalid information being corrected in mail originating from your site:

  ```
  braindead.correct.domain.com        braindead.wrong.domain.com
  ```

- Frequently, misconfigured sites 'bounce' mail back to the sending system and effectively say "that mail isn't for this site" because they do not have their *PSEUDONYMNS* or equivalent set properly in their configuration. It is possible to totally strip off all hostname and domain information from the envelope of messages going from your site to them.

  The *!* in the following *mailertable* delivers mail to their remote site making it appear to their *sendmail* as if it had originated locally on their system. Note that this changes only the envelope address, so the proper return address will still show up in the message.

  ```
  TCP!braindead.correct.domain.com  braindead.wrong.domain.com
  ```

Regardless, even if you get mail into their system, there is no guarantee that they can reply to your message (they're broken, remember...) but then their users are yelling at their administrators rather than your users yelling at you.

15.6.3 Forcing Mail to be Transferred via UUCP

In an ideal world (from the Internet perspective), all hosts have records in the Domain Name Service (DNS) and will send mail with fully qualified domain names.

If you happen to talk via UUCP to such a site, you can force mail to go through the point-to-point UUCP connection rather than through your default mailer by essentially "undomainizing" their hostname through the *uucpxtable*.

To force UUCP delivery to **sesame.com**, you would put the following in your *uucpxtable*:

```
# un-domainize sesame.com to force UUCP delivery
sesame    sesame.com
```

The result is that sendmail will then determine (via *UUCPNODES* in the *sendmail.m4* file) that you are directly connected to the remote system and will queue the mail for delivery with UUCP.

15.6.4 Preventing Mail from Being Delivered via UUCP

The opposite condition also occurs. Frequently, systems may have a number of direct UUCP connections that are used infrequently or that are not as reliable and always available as the default mailer or relay host.

For example, in the Seattle area there are a number of systems that exchange the various Linux distributions via anonymous UUCP when the distributions are released. These systems talk UUCP only when necessary, so it is generally faster and more reliable to send mail through multiple very reliable hops and common (and always available) relay hosts.

It is easily possible to prevent UUCP delivery of mail to a host that you are directly connected to. If the remote system has a fully-qualified domain name, you can add an entry like this to the *domaintable*:

```
# prevent mail delivery via UUCP to a neighbor
snorkel.com          snorkel
```

This will replace any occurence of the UUCP name with the FQDN, and thus prevent a match by the *UUCPNODES* line in the *sendmail.m4* file. The result is generally that mail will go via the *RELAY_MAILER* and *RELAY_HOST* (or *DEFAULT_MAILER*).

15.6.5 Running the Sendmail Queue on Demand

To process queued messages immediately, merely type '/usr/lib/runq'. This invokes sendmail with the appropriate options to cause sendmail to run through the queue of pending jobs immediately rather than waiting for the next scheduled run.

15.6.6 Reporting Mail Statistics

Many site administrators (and the persons they work for) are interested in the volume of mail passing to, from, and through the local site. There are a number of ways to quantify mail traffic.

- Sendmail comes with a utility called *mailstats* that reads a file called */usr/local/lib/mail/sendmail.st* and reports the number of messages and number of bytes transferred by each of the mailers used in the *sendmail.cf* file. This file must be created by the local administrator manually for sendmail logging to occur. The running totals are cleared by removing and recreating the *sendmail.st* file. One way is to do the following:

```
# cp /dev/null /usr/lib/local/mail/sendmail.st
```

- Probably the best way to do quality reporting regarding who uses mail and how much volume passes to, from, and through the local system is to turn on mail debugging with *syslogd(8)*. Generally, this means running the */etc/syslogd* daemon from your system startup file (which you should be doing anyway), and adding a line to */etc/syslog.conf(5)* that looks something like the following:

```
mail.debug                              /var/log/syslog.mail
```

  If you use *mail.debug* and get any medium to high mail volume, the syslog output can get quite large. Output files from *syslogd* generally need to be rotated or purged on a routine basis from *crond(8)*.

  There are a number of commonly available utilities that can summarize the output of mail logging from syslogd. One of the more well known utilities is *syslog-stat.pl*, a *perl* script that is distributed with the sendmail+IDA sources.

15.7 Mixing and Matching Binary Distributions

There is no true standard configuration of electronic mail transport and delivery agents and there is no "one true directory structure."

Accordingly, it is necessary to ensure that all the various pieces of the system (USENET news, mail, TCP/IP) agree on the location of the local mail delivery program (*lmail*, *deliver*, etc.), remote mail delivery program (*rmail*), and the mail transport program (*sendmail* or *smail*). Such assumptions are not generally documented, although use of the *strings* command can help determine what files and directories are expected. The following are some problems we've seen in the past with some of the commonly available Linux binary distributions and sources.

- Some versions of the NET-2 distribution of TCP/IP have services defined for a program called *umail* rather than *sendmail*.

- There are various ports of *elm* and *mailx* that look for a delivery agent of */usr/bin/smail* rather than sendmail.

- Sendmail+IDA has a built-in local mailer for *deliver*, but expects it to be located in */bin* rather than the more typical Linux location of */usr/bin*.

Rather than go through the trouble of building all the mail clients from sources, we generally fake it with the appropriate soft links…

15.8 Where to Get More Information

There are many places you can look for more information on *sendmail*. For a list, see the Linux MAIL Howto posted regularly to **comp.answers**. It is also available for anonymous FTP on **rtfm.mit.edu**. However, the definitive place is in the sendmail+IDA sources. Look in the directory *ida/cf* below the source directory for the files *DBM-GUIDE*, *OPTIONS*, and *Sendmail.mc*.

15.8 Where to Get More Information

There are many places you can look for more information on *sendmail*. For a list, see the Linux MAIL-Howto posted regularly to comp.answers. It is also available for anonymous FTP on rtfm.mit.edu. However, the definitive place is in the sendmail+IDA source. Look in the directory *ida/cf* below the source directory for the files *DBM-GUIDE*, *OPTIONS*, and *Sendmail.mc*.

CHAPTER 16

Netnews

16.1 Usenet History

The idea of network news was born in 1979 when two graduate students, Tom Truscott and Jim Ellis, thought of using UUCP to connect machines for the purpose of information exchange among UNIX users. They set up a small network of three machines in North Carolina.

Initially, traffic was handled by a number of shell scripts (later rewritten in C), but they were never released to the public. They were quickly replaced by "A" news, the first public release of news software.

"A" news was not designed to handle more than a few articles per group and day. When the volume continued to grow, it was rewritten by Mark Horton and Matt Glickman, who called it the "B" release (a.k.a. Bnews). The first public release of Bnews was version 2.1 in 1982. It was expanded continuously, with several new features being added. Its current version is Bnews 2.11. It is slowly becoming obsolete, with its last official maintainer having switched to INN.

Another rewrite was done and released in 1987 by Geoff Collyer and Henry Spencer; this is release "C," or C News. In the time following there have been a number of patches to C News, the most prominent being the C News Performance Release. On sites that carry a large number of groups, the overhead involved in frequently invoking *relaynews*, which is responsible for dispatching incoming articles to other hosts, is significant. The Performance Release adds an option to *relaynews* that allows to run it in *daemon mode*, in which the program puts itself in the background.

The Performance Release is the C News version currently included in most Linux releases.

All news releases up to "C" are primarily targeted for UUCP networks, although they may be used in other environments as well. Efficient news transfer over networks like TCP/IP, DECNet, or related requires a new scheme. This was the reason why, in 1986, the "Network News Transfer Protocol", NNTP, was introduced. It is based on network connections, and specifies a number of commands to interactively transfer and retrieve articles.

There are a number of NNTP-based applications available from the Net. One of them is the *nntpd* package by Brian Barber and Phil Lapsley, which you can use, among other things, to provides newsreading service to a number of hosts inside a local network. *nntpd* was designed to complement news packages such as Bnews or C News to give them NNTP features.

A different NNTP package is INN, or Internet News. It is not merely a front end, but a news system by its own right. It comprises a sophisticated news relay daemon that is capable of maintaining several concurrent NNTP links efficiently, and is therefore the news server of choice for many Internet sites.

16.2 What *is* Usenet, Anyway?

One of the most astounding facts about Usenet is that it isn't part of any organization, or has any sort of centralized network management authority. In fact, it's part of Usenet lore that except for a technical description, you cannot define *what* it is, you can only say what it isn't. If you have Brendan Kehoe's excellent "Zen and the Art of the Internet" (available online or through Prentice-Hall, see [Kehoe92]) at hand, you will find an amusing list of Usenet's non-properties.

At the risk of sounding stupid, one might define Usenet as a collaboration of separate sites who exchange Usenet news. To be a Usenet site, all you have to do is find another site Usenet site, and strike an agreement with its owners and maintainers to exchange news with you. Providing another site with news is also called *feeding* it, whence another common axiom of Usenet philosophy originates: "Get a feed and you're on it."

The basic unit of Usenet news is the article. This is a message a user writes and "posts" to the net. In order to enable news sytems to deal with it, it is prepended with administrative information, the so-called article header. It is very similar to the mail header format laid down in the Internet mail standard RFC 822, in that it consists of several lines of text, each beginning with a field name terminated by a colon, which is followed by the field's value.[1]

Articles are submitted to one or more *newsgroups*. One may consider a newsgroup a forum for articles relating to a common topic. All newsgroups are organized in a hierarchy, with each group's name indicating its place in the hierarchy. This often makes it easy to see what a group is all about. For example, anybody can see from the newsgroup name that **comp.os.linux.announce** is used for announcements concerning a computer operating system named Linux.

These articles are then exchanged between all Usenet sites that are willing to carry news from this group. When two sites agree to exchange news, they are free to exchange whatever newsgroups they like to, and may even add their own local news hierarchies. For example, **groucho.edu** might have a news link to **barnyard.edu**, which is a major news feed, and several links to minor sites which it feeds news. Now, Barnyard College might receive all Usenet groups, while GMU only wants to carry a few major hierarchies like **sci**, **comp**, **rec**, etc. Some of the downstream sites, say a UUCP site called **brewhq**, will want to carry even fewer groups, because they don't have the network or hardware resources. On the other hand, **brewhq** might want to receive newsgroups from the **fj** hierarchy, which GMU doesn't carry. It therefore maintains another link with **gargleblaster.com**, who carry all **fj** groups, and feed them to **brewhq**. The news flow is shown in figure 16.1.

The labels on the arrows originating from **brewhq** may require some explanation, though. By default, it wants all locally generated news to be sent to **groucho.edu**. However, as **groucho.edu** does not carry the **fj** groups, there's no pointing in sending it any messages from those groups. Therefore, the feed from **brewhq** to GMU is labelled **all,!fj**, meaning that all groups except those below **fj** are sent to it.

16.3 How Does Usenet Handle News?

Today, Usenet has grown to enormous proportions. Sites that carry the whole of netnews usually transfer something like a paltry sixty megabytes a day.[2] Of course this requires much more than pushing around files. So let's take a look at the way most UNIX systems handle Usenet news.

News is distributed through the net by various transports. The historical medium used to be UUCP, but today the main traffic is carried by Internet sites. The routing algorithm used is called *flooding*: Each site maintains a number of links (*news feeds*) to other sites. Any article generated or received by the local news system is forwarded to them, unless it has already been seen at that site, in which case it is discarded. A site may find out about all other sites the article has already traversed by looking at the `Path:` header field. This header contains a list of all systems the article has been forwarded by in bang path notation.

To distinguish articles and recognize duplicates, Usenet articles have to carry a message id (specified in the `Message-Id:` header field), which combines the posting site's name and a serial number into "*<serial@site>*". For each article processed, the news system logs this id into a *history* file against which all newly arrived articles are checked.

The flow between any two sites may be limited by two criteria: for one, an article is assigned a distribution (in the `Distribution:` header field) which may be used to confine it to a certain group of sites. On the other hand, the newsgroups exchanged may be limited by both the sending or receiving system. The set of newsgroups and distributions allowed for transmission to a site are usually kept in the *sys* file.

---

[1] The format of Usenet news messages is specified in RFC 1036, "Standard for interchange of USENET messages".

[2] Wait a moment: 60 Megs at 9600 bps, that's 60 million by 1200, that is... mutter, mutter,... Hey! That's 34 hours!

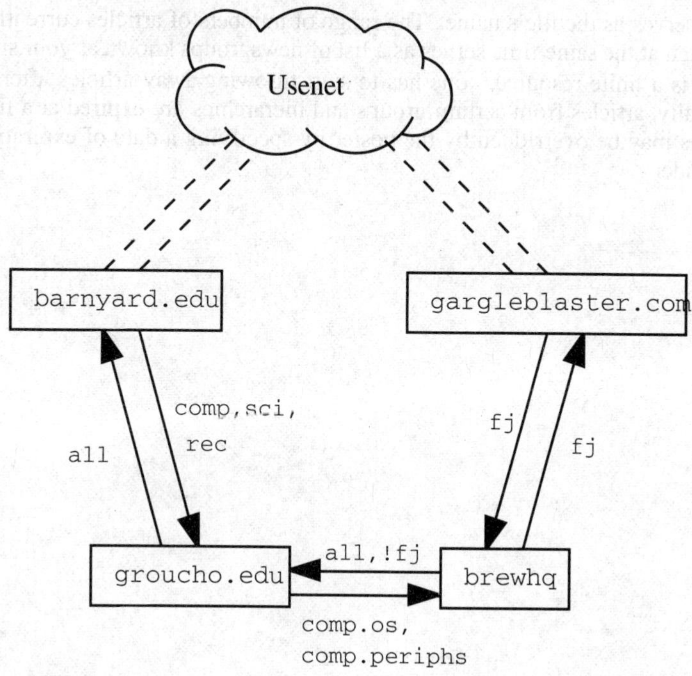

Figure 16.1: Usenet news flow through Groucho Marx University.

The sheer number of articles usually requires that improvements be made to the above scheme. On UUCP networks, the natural thing to do is to collect articles over a period of time, and combine them into a single file, which is compressed and sent to the remote site. This is called *batching*.[3]

An alternative technique is the *ihave/sendme* protocol that prevents duplicate articles from being transferred in the first place, thus saving net bandwidth. Instead of putting all articles in batch files and sending them along, only the message ids of articles are combined into a giant "ihave" message and sent to the remote site. It reads this message, compares it to its history file, and returns the list of articles it wants in a "sendme" message. Only these articles are then sent.

Of course, ihave/sendme only makes sense if it involves two big sites that receive news from several independent feeds each, and who poll each other often enough for an efficient flow of news.

Sites that are on the Internet generally rely on TCP/IP-based software that uses the Network News Transfer Protocol, NNTP.[4] It transfers news between feeds and provides Usenet access to single users on remote hosts.

NNTP knows three different ways to transfer news. One is a real-time version of ihave/sendme, also referred to as *pushing* news. The second technique is called *pulling* news, in which the client requests a list of articles in a given newsgroup or hierarchy that have arrived at the server's site after a specified date, and chooses those it cannot find in its history file. The third mode is for interactive newsreading, and allows you or your newsreader to retrieve articles from specified newgroups, as well as post articles with incomplete header information.

At each site, news are kept in a directory hierarchy below */var/spool/news*, each article in a separate file, and each newsgroup in a separate directory. The directory name is made up of the newsgroup name, with the components being the path components. Thus, **comp.os.linux.misc** articles are kept in */var/spool/news/comp/os/linux/misc*. The articles in a newsgroup are assigned numbers in the order they

[3]The golden rule of netnews, according to Geoff Collyer: "Thou shalt batch thine articles."

[4]Described in RFC 977.

arrive. This number serves as the file's name. The range of numbers of articles currently online is kept in a file called *active*, which at the same time serves as a list of newsgroups known at your site.

Since disk space is a finite resource,[5] one has to start throwing away articles after some time. This is called *expiring*. Usually, articles from certain groups and hierarchies are expired at a fixed number of days after they arrive. This may be overridden by the poster by specifying a date of expiration in the `Expires:` field of the article header.

[5] Some people claim that Usenet is a conspiracy by modem and hard disk vendors.

CHAPTER 17

C News

One of the most popular software packages for Netnews is C News. It was designed for sites that carry news over UUCP links. This chapter will discuss the central concepts of C News, and the basic installation and maintenance tasks.

C News stores its configuration files in */usr/lib/news*, and most of its binaries in the */usr/lib/news/bin* directory. Articles are kept below */var/spool/news*. You should make sure virtually all files in these directories are owned by user **news**, group **news**. Most problems arise from files being inaccessible to C News. Make it a rule for you to become user **news** using *su* before you touch anything in there. The only exceptions is *setnewsids*, which is used to set the real user id of some news programs. It must be owned by **root** and must have the setuid bit set.

In the following, we describe all C News configuration files in detail, and show you what you have to do to keep your site running.

17.1 Delivering News

Articles may be fed to C News in several ways. When a local user posts an article, the newsreader usually hands it to the *inews* command, which completes the header information. News from remote sites, be it a single article or a whole batch, is given to the *rnews* command, which stores it in the */var/spool/newsin.coming* directory, from where it will be picked up at a later time by *newsrun*. With any of these two techniques, however, the article will eventually be handed to the *relaynews* command.

For each article, the *relaynews* command first checks if the article has already been seen at the local site by looking up the message id in the *history* file. Duplicate articles will be dropped. Then, *relaynews* looks at the `Newsgroups:` header line to find out if the local site requests articles from any of these groups. If it does, and the newsgroup is listed in the *active* file, *relaynews* tries to store the article in the corresponding directory in the news spool area. If this directory does not exist, it is created. The article's message id will then be logged to the *history* file. Otherwise, *relaynews* drops the article.

If *relaynews* fails to store an incoming article because a group it has been posted to is not listed in your *active* file, the article will be moved to the **junk** group.[1] *relaynews* will also check for stale or misdated articles and reject them. Incoming batches that fail for any other reason are moved to */var/spool/news/in.coming/bad*, and an error message is logged.

After this, the article will be relayed to all other sites that request news from these groups, using the transport specified for each particular site. To make sure it isn't sent to a site that already has seen it, each destination site is checked against the article's `Path:` header field, which contains the list of sites the article has traversed so far, written in bang path style. Only if the destination site's name does not appear in this list will the article be sent to it.

[1] There may be a difference between the groups that exist at your site, and those that your site is willing to receive. For example, the subscription list may specify **comp.all**, which means all newsgroups below the **comp** hierarchy, but at your site, only a number of **comp** groups are listed in *active*. Articles posted to those groups will be moved to **junk**.

C News is commonly used to relay news between UUCP sites, altough it is also possible to use it in a NNTP environment. To deliver news to a remote UUCP site — either single articles or whole batches — *uux* is used to execute the *rnews* command on the remote site, and feed the article or batch to it on standard input.

When batching is enabled for a given site, C News does not send any incoming article immediately, but appends its path name to a file, usually *out.going/site/togo*. Periodically, a batcher program is executed from a crontab entry,[2] which puts the articles in one or more files, optionally compresses them, and sends them to *rnews* at the remote site.

Figure 17.1 shows the news flow through *relaynews*. Articles may be relayed to the local site (denoted by *ME*), to some site named **ponderosa** via email, and a site named **moria**, for which batching is enabled.

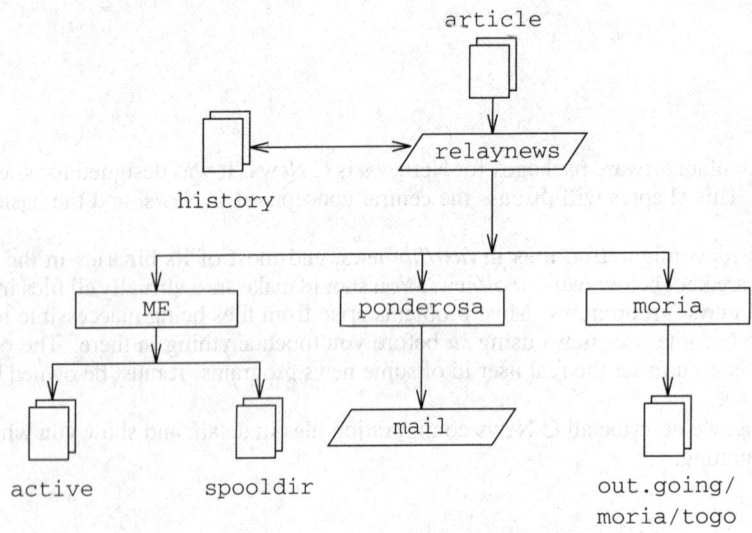

Figure 17.1: News flow through *relaynews*.

17.2 Installation

To install C News, untar the files into their proper places if you haven't done so yet, and edit the configuration files listed below. They are all located in */usr/lib/news*. Their formats will be described in the following sections.

sys
: You probably have to modify the *ME* line that describes your system, although using *all/all* is always a safe bet. You also have to add a line for each site you feed news to.

  If you are a leaf site, you only need a line that sends all locally generated articles to your feed. Assume your feed is **moria**, then your *sys* file should look like this:

```
ME:all/all::
moria/moria.orcnet.org:all/all,!local:f:
```

organization
: Your organization's name. For example, "`Virtual Brewery, Inc.`". On your home machine, enter "private site", or anything else you like. Most people will not call your site properly configured if you haven't customized this file.

newsgroups

mailname
: Your site's mail name, e.g. **vbrew.com**.

[2]Note that this should be the crontab of **news**, in order not to mangle file permissions.

whoami Your site's name for news purposes. Quite often, the UUCP site name is used, for example **vbrew**.

explist You should probably edit this file to reflect your preferred expiry times for some special newsgroups. Disk space may play an important role in it.

To create an initial hierarchy of newsgroups, obtain an *active* and a *newsgroups* file from the site that feeds you, and install them in */usr/lib/news*, making sure they are owned by news and have a mode of 644. Remove all **to.*** groups from the active file, and add **to.***mysite* and **to.***feedsite*, as well as **junk** and **control**. The **to.*** groups are normally used for exchanging ihave/sendme messages, but you should create them regardless of whether you plan to use ihave/sendme or not. Next, replace all article numbers in the second and third field of *active* using the following command:

```
# cp active active.old
# sed 's/ [0-9]* [0-9]* / 0000000000 00001 /' active.old > active
# rm active.old
```

The second command is an invocation of *sed(1)*, one of my favorite UNIX commands. This invocation replaces two strings of digits with a string of zeroes and the string 000001, respectively.

Finally, create the news spool directory and the subdirectories used for incoming and outgoing news:

```
# cd /var/spool
# mkdir news news/in.coming news/out.going
# chown -R news.news news
# chmod -R 755 news
```

If you're using a later release of C News, you may also have to create the *out.master* directory in the news spool directory.

If you're using newsreaders from a different distribution than the C News you have running, you may find that some expect the news spool on */usr/spool/news* rather than in */var/spool/news*. If your newsreader doesn't seem to find any articles, create a symbolic from */usr/spool/news* to */var/spool/news*.

Now, you are ready to receive news. Note that you don't have to create any directories other than those shown above, because each time C News receives an article from a group for which there's no spool directory yet, it will create it.

In particular, this happens to *all* groups an article has been crossposted to. So, after a while, you will find your news spool cluttered with directories for newsgroups you have never subscribed to, like **alt.lang.teco**. You may prevent this by either removing all unwanted groups from *active*, or by regularly running a shell script which removes all empty directories below */var/spool/news* (except *out.going* and *in.coming*, of course).

C News needs a user to send error messages and status reports to. By default, this is **usenet**. If you use the default, you have to set up an alias for it which forwards all of its mail to one or more responsible persons. (Chapters 14 and 15 explain how to do so for *smail* and *sendmail*). You may also override this behavior by setting the environment variable *NEWSMASTER* to the appropriate name. You have to do so in **news**' crontab file, as well as every time you invoke an administrative tool manually, so installing an alias is probably easier.

While you're hacking */etc/passwd*, make sure that every user has her real name in the *pw_gecos* field of the password file (this is the fourth field). It is a question of Usenet netiquette that the sender's real name appears in the From: field of the article. Of course, you will want to do so anyway when you use mail.

17.3 The *sys* file

The *sys* file, located in */usr/lib/news*, controls which hierarchies you receive and forward to other sites. Although there are maintenance tools named *addfeed* and *delfeed*, I think it's better to maintain this file by hand.

The *sys* file contains entries for each site you forward news to, as well as a description of the groups you will accept. An entry looks like

site[/*exclusions*]:*grouplist*[/*distlist*][:*flags*[:*cmds*]]

Entries may be continued across newlines using a backslash (\). A hash sign (#) denotes a comment.

site
: This is the name of the site the entry applies to. One usually chooses the site's UUCP name for this. There has to be an entry for your site in the *sys* file, too, else you will not receive any articles yourself.

The special site name *ME* denotes your site. The *ME* entry defines all groups you are willing to store locally. Articles that aren't matched by the *ME* line will go to the **junk** group.

Since C News checks *site* against the site names in the `Path:` header field, you have to make sure they really match. Some sites use their fully qualified domain name in this field, or an alias like **news.***site.domain*. To prevent any articles from being returned to these sites, you have to add these to the exclusion list, separated by commas.

For the entry applying to site **moria**, for instance, the site field would contain **moria/moria.orcnet.org**.

grouplist
: This is a comma-separated subscription list of groups and hierarchies for that particular site. A hierarchy may be specified by giving the hierarchy's prefix (such as **comp.os** for all groups whose name starts with this prefix), optionally followed by the keyword **all** (e.g. **comp.os.all**).

A hierarchy or group is excluded from forwarding by preceding it with an exclamation mark. If a newsgroup is checked against the list, the longest match applies. For example, if *grouplist* contains

```
!comp,comp.os.linux,comp.folklore.computers
```

no groups from the **comp** hierarchy except **comp.folklore.computers** and all groups below **comp.os.linux** will be fed to that site.

If the site requests to be forwarded all news you receive yourself, enter *all* as *grouplist*.

distlist
: is offset from the *grouplist* by a slash, and contains a list of distributions to be forwarded. Again, you may exclude certain distributions by preceding them with an exclamation mark. All distributions are denoted by *all*. Omitting *distlist* implies a list of *all*.

For example, you may use a distribution list of *all,!local* to prevent news for local use only from being sent to remote sites.

There are usually at least two distributions: *world*, which is often the default distribution used when none is specified by the user, and *local*. There may be other distributions that apply to a certain region, state, country, etc. Finally, there are two distributions used by C News only; these are *sendme* and *ihave*, and are used for the sendme/ihave protocol.

The use of distributions is a subject of debate. For one, some newsreaders create bogus distributions by simply using the top level hierarchy, for example **comp** when posting to **comp.os.linux**. Distributions that apply to regions are often questionable, too, because news may travel outside of your region when sent across the Internet.[3] Distributions applying to an organization, however, are very meaningful, for example to prevent confidential information from leaving the company network. This purpose, however, is generally served better by creating a separate newsgroup or hierarchy.

flags
: This describes certain parameters for the feed. It may be empty, or a combination of the following:

F
: This flag enables batching.

f
: This is almost identical to the *F* flag, but allows C News to calculate the size of outgoing batches more precisely.

[3]It is not uncommon for an article posted in, say Hamburg, to go to Frankfurt via **reston.ans.net** in the Netherlands, or even via some site in the U.S.

I — This flag makes C News produce an article list suitable for use by ihave/sendme. Additional modifications to the *sys* and the *batchparms* file are required to enable ihave/sendme.

n — This creates batch files for active NNTP transfer clients like *nntpxmit* (see chapter 18). The batch files contain the article's filename along with its message id.

L — This tells C News to transmit only articles posted at your site. This flag may be followed by a decimal number *n*, which makes C News only transfer articles posted within *n* hops from your site. C News determines the number of hops from the `Path:` field.

u — This tells C News to batch only articles from unmoderated groups.

m — This tells C News to batch only articles from moderated groups.

You may use at most one of *F*, *f*, *I*, or *n*.

cmds — This field contains a command to be executed for each article, unless batching is enabled. The article will be fed to the command on standard input. This should only be used for very small feeds; otherwise the load on both systems will be too high.

The default command is

```
uux - -r -z system!rnews
```

which invokes *rnews* on the remote system, feeding it the article on standard input.

The default search path for commands given in this field is */bin:/usr/bin:/usr/lib/news/bin/batch*. The latter directory contains a number of shell scripts whose name starts with *via*; they are briefly described later in this chapter.

If batching is enabled using either of the *F* or *f*, *I* or *n* flags, C News expects to find a file name in this field rather than a command. If the file name does not begin with a slash (/), it is assumed to be relative to */var/spool/news/out.going*. If the field is empty, it defaults to *system/togo*.

When setting up C News, you will most probably have to write your own *sys* file. To help you with it, we give a sample file for **vbrew.com** below, from which you might copy what you need.

```
# We take whatever they give us.
ME:all/all::

# We send everything we receive to moria, except for local and
# brewery-related articles. We use batching.
moria/moria.orcnet.org:all,!to,to.moria/all,!local,!brewery:f:

# We mail comp.risks to jack@ponderosa.uucp
ponderosa:comp.risks/all::rmail jack@ponderosa.uucp

# swim gets a minor feed
swim/swim.twobirds.com:comp.os.linux,rec.humor.oracle/all,!local:f:

# Log mail map articles for later processing
usenet-maps:comp.mail.maps/all:F:/var/spool/uumaps/work/batch
```

17.4 The *active* file

The *active* file is located in */usr/lib/news* and lists all groups known at your site, and the articles currently online. You will rarely have to touch it, but we explain it nevertheless for sake of completeness. Entries take the following form:

newsgroup high low perm

newsgroup is, of course, the group's name. *low* and *high* are the lowest and highest numbers of articles currently available. If none are available at the moment, *low* is equal to *high*+1.

At least, that's what the *low* field is meant to do. However, for efficiency reasons, C News doesn't update this field. This wouldn't be such a big loss if there weren't some newsreaders that depend on it. For instance, *trn* checks this field to see if it can purge any articles from its thread database. To update the *low* field, you therefore have to run the *updatemin* command regularly (or, in earlier version of C News, the *upact* script).

perm is a parameter detailing the access users are granted to the group. It takes one of the following values:

y Users are allowed to post to this group.

n Users are not allowed to post to this group. However, the group may still be read.

x This group has been disabled locally. This happens sometimes when news admininistrators (or their superiors) take offense to articles posted to certain groups.

Articles received for this group are not stored locally, although they are forwarded to the sites that request them.

m This denotes a moderated group. When a user tries to post to this group, an intelligent newsreader will notify her of this, and send the article to the moderator instead. The moderator's address is taken from the *moderators* file in */usr/lib/news*.

=real-group This marks *newsgroup* as being a local alias for another group, namely *real-group*. All articles posted to *newsgroup* will be redirected to it.

In C News, you will generally not have to access this file directly. Groups may be added or deleted locally using *addgroup* and *delgroup* (see below in section 17.10). When groups are added or deleted for the whole of Usenet, this is usually done by sending a *newgroup* or *rmgroup* control message, respectively. *Never send such a message yourself!* For instructions on how to create a newsgroup, read the monthly postings in **news.announce.newusers**.

A file closely related to *active* is *active.times*. Whenever a group is created, C News logs a message to this file, containing the name of the group created, the date of creation, whether it was done by a *newgroup* control message or locally, and who did it. This is for the convenience of newsreaders who may notify the user of any recently created groups. It is also used by the *NEWGROUPS* command of NNTP.

17.5 Article Batching

Newsbatches follow a particular format which is the same for Bnews, C News, and INN. Each article is preceded by a line like this:

```
#! rnews count
```

where *count* is the number of bytes in the article. When batch compression is used, the resulting file is compressed as a whole, and preceded by another line, indicated by the message to be used for unpacking. The standard compression tool is **compress**, which is marked by

```
#! cunbatch
```

Sometimes, when having to send batches via mail software that removes the eighth bit from all data, a compressed batch may be protected using what is called c7-encoding; these batches will be marked by *c7unbatch*.

When a batch is fed to *rnews* on the remote site, it checks for these markers and processes the batch appropriately. Some sites also use other compression tools, like *gzip*, and precede their gzipped files with *zunbatch* instead. C News does not recognize non-standard headers like these; you have to modify the source to support them.

In C News, article batching is performed by */usr/lib/news/bin/batch/sendbatches*, which takes a list of articles from the *site/togo* file, and puts them into several newsbatches. It should be executed once per hour or even more frequently, depending on the volume of traffic.

Its operation is controlled by the *batchparms* file in */usr/lib/news*. This file describes the maximum batch size allowed for each site, the batching and optional compression program to be used, and the transport for delivering it to the remote site. You may specify batching parameters on a per-site basis, as well as a set of default parameters for sites not explicitly mentioned.

To perform batching for a specific site, you invoke it as

```
# su news -c "/usr/lib/news/bin/batch/sendbatches site"
```

When invoked without arguments, *sendbatches* handles all batch queues. The interpretation of "all" depends on the presence of a default entry in *batchparms*. If one is found, all directories in */var/spool/news/out.going* are checked, otherwise, it cycles through all entries in *batchparms*. Note that *sendbatches*, when scanning the *out.going* directory, takes only those directories that contain no dot or at sign (@) as site names.

When installing C News, you will most likely find a *batchparms* file in your distribution which contains a reasonable default entry, so there's a good chance that you wouldn't have to touch the file. Just in case, we describe its format nevertheless. Each line consists of six fields, separated by spaces or tabs:

site size max batcher muncher transport

The meaning of these fields is as follows:

site is the name of the site the entry applies to. The *togo* file for this site must reside in *out.going/togo* below the news spool. A site name of */default/* denotes the default entry.

size is the maximum size of article batches created (before compression). For single articles larger than this, C News makes an exception and puts them in a single batch by themselves.

max is the maximum number of batches created and scheduled for transfer before batching stalls for this particular site. This is useful in case the remote site should be down for a long time, because it prevents C News from cluttering your UUCP spool directories with zillions of newsbatches.

C News determines the number of queued batches using the *queulen* script in */usr/lib/news/bin*. Vince Skahan's *newspak* release should contain a script for BNU-compatible UUCPs. If you use a different flavor of spool directories, for example, Taylor UUCP, you might have to write your own.[4]

The *batcher* field contains the command used for producing a batch from the list of articles in the *togo* file. For regular feeds, this is usually *batcher*. For other purposes, alternative batchers may be provided. For instance, the ihave/sendme protocol requires the article list to be turned into ihave or sendme control messages, which are posted to the newsgroup **to.***site*. This is performed by *batchih* and *batchsm*.

The *muncher* field specifies the command used for compression. Usually, this is **compcun**, a script that produces a compressed batch.[5] Alternatively, you might provide a muncher that uses *gzip*, say *gzipcun* (to be clear: you have to write it yourself). You have to make sure that *uncompress* on the remote site is patched to recognize files compressed with *gzip*.

If the remote site does not have an *uncompress* command, you may specify *nocomp* which does not do any compression.

The last field, *transport*, describes the transport to be used. A number of standard commands for different transports are available whose names begin with *via*. *sendbatches* passes them the destination site name on the command line. If the *batchparms* entry was not */default/*, it derives the site name from the *site* field by stripping of anything after and including the first dot or slash. If entry was */default/*, the directory names in *out.going* are used.

There are two commands that use *uux* to execute *rnews* on the remote system; *viauux* and *viauuxz*. The latter sets the `-z` flag for (older versions of) *uux* to keep it from returning success messages for each article

[4] If you don't care about the number of spool files (because you're the only person using your computer, and you don't write articles by the megabyte), you may replace the script's contents by a simple *exit 0* statement.

[5] As shipped with C News, **compcun** uses **compress** with the 12 bit option, since this is the least common denominator for most sites. You may produce a copy of it, say **compcun16**, where you use 16 bit compression. The improvement is not too impressive, though.

delivered. Another command, *viamail*, sends article batches to the user **rnews** on the remote system via mail. Of course, this requires that the remote system somehow feeds all mail for **rnews** to their local news system. For a complete list of these transports, refer to the *newsbatch(8)* manual page.

All commands from the last three fields must be located in either of *out.going/site* or */usr/lib/news/bin/batch*. Most of them are scripts, so that you may easily tailor new tools for your personal needs. They are invoked as a pipe. The list of articles is fed to the batcher on standard input, which produces the batch on standard output. This is piped into the muncher, and so on.

A sample file is given below.

```
# batchparms file for the brewery
# site          | size    |max    |batcher  |muncher     |transport
#---------------+--------+-------+---------+-----------+----------
/default/         100000  22      batcher   compcun     viauux
swim               10000  10      batcher   nocomp      viauux
```

17.6 Expiring News

In Bnews, expiring used to be performed by a program called *expire*, which took a list of newsgroups as arguments, along with a time specification after which articles had to be expired. To have different hierarchies expired at different times, you had to write a script that invoked *expire* for each of them separately. C News offers a more convenient solution to this: in a file called *explist*, you may specify newsgroups and expiration intervals. A command called *doexpire* is usually run once a day from *cron*, and processes all groups according to this list.

Occasionally, you may want to retain articles from certain groups even after they have been expired; for example, you might want to keep programs posted to **comp.sources.unix**. This is called *archiving*. *explist* permits you to mark groups for archiving.

An entry in *explist* looks like this:

grouplist perm times archive

grouplist is a comma-separated list of newsgroups to which the entry applies. Hierarchies may be specified by giving the group name prefix, optionally appended with *all*. For example, for an entry applying to all groups below **comp.os**, you might either enter **comp.os** or **comp.os.all** in *grouplist*.

When expiring news from a group, the name is checked against all entries in *explist* in the order given. The first matching entry applies. For example, to throw away the majority of **comp** after four days, except for **comp.os.linux.announce** which you want to keep for a week, you simply have an entry for the latter, which specifies a seven-day expiration period, followed by that for **comp**, which specifies four days.

The *perm* field details if the entry applies to moderated, unmoderated, or any groups. It may take the values *m*, *u*, or *x*, which denote moderated, unmoderated, or any type.

The third field, *times*, usually contains only a single number. This is the number of days after which articles will be expired if they haven't been assigned an artificial expiration date in an `Expires:` field in the article header. Note that this is the number of days counting from its *arrival* at your site, not the date of posting.

The *times* field may, however, be more complex than that. It may be a combination of up to three numbers, separated from one another by a dash. The first denotes the number of days that have to pass before the article is considered a candidate for expiration. It is rarely useful to use a value other than zero. The second field is the above-mentioned default number of days after which it will be expired. The third is the number of days after which an article will be expired unconditionally, regardless of whether it has an `Expires:` field or not. If only the middle number is given, the other two take default values. These may be specified using the special entry */bounds/*, which is described below.

The fourth field, *archive*, denotes whether the newsgroup is to be archived, and where. If no archiving is intended, a dash should be used. Otherwise, you either use a full path name (pointing to a directory), or an at sign (@). The at sign denotes the default archive directory which must then be given to *doexpire* by using the `-a` flag on the command line. An archive directory should be owned by **news**. When *doexpire* archives an article from, say **comp.sources.unix**, it stores it in the directory **comp/sources/unix** below the archive directory, creating it if not existent. The archive directory itself, however, will not be created.

There are two special entries in your *explist* file that *doexpire* relies on. Instead of a list of newsgroups, they have the keywords */bounds/* and */expired/*. The */bounds/* entry contains the default values for the three values of the *times* field described above.

The */expired/* field determines how long C News will hold on to lines in the *history* file. This is needed because C News will not remove a line from the history file once the corresponding article(s) have been expired, but will hold on to it in case a duplicate should arrive after this date. If you are fed by only one site, you can keep this value small. Otherwise, a couple of weeks is advisable on UUCP networks, depending on the delays you experience with articles from these sites.

A sample *explist* file with rather tight expiry intervals is reproduced below:

```
# keep history lines for two weeks. Nobody gets more than three months
/expired/                        x    14     -
/bounds/                         x    0-1-90 -

# groups we want to keep longer than the rest
comp.os.linux.announce           m     10    -
comp.os.linux                    x     5     -
alt.folklore.computers           u     10    -
rec.humor.oracle                 m     10    -
soc.feminism                     m     10    -

# Archive *.sources groups
comp.sources,alt.sources         x     5     @

# defaults for tech groups
comp,sci                         x     7     -

# enough for a long weekend
misc,talk                        x     4     -

# throw away junk quickly
junk                             x     1     -

# control messages are of scant interest, too
control                          x     1     -

# catch-all entry for the rest of it
all                              x     2     -
```

With expiring in C News, there are a number of potential troubles looming. One is that your newsreader might rely on the third field of the active file, which contains the number of the lowest article on-line. When expiring articles, C News does not update this field. If you need (or want) to have this field represent the real situation, you need to run a program called *updatemiin* after each run of *doexpire*.[6]

Second, C News does not expire by scanning the newsgroup's directory, but simply checks the *history* file if the article is due for expiration.[7] If your history file somehow gets out of sync, articles may be around on your disk forever, because C News has literally forgotten them.[8] You can repair this using the *addmissing* script in */usr/lib/news/bin/maint*, which will add missing articles to the *history* file, or *mkhistory*, which rebuilds the entire file from scratch. Don't forget to become **news** before invoking it, else you will wind up with a *history* file unreadable by C News.

[6]In older versions of C News, this was done by a script called *upact*.

[7]The article's date of arrival is kept in the middle field of the history line, given in seconds since January 1, 1970.

[8]I don't know *why* this happens, but for me, it does from time to time.

17.7 Miscellaneous Files

There are a number of files that control C News' behavior, but are not essential to its functioning. All of them reside in */usr/lib/news*. We will describe them briefly.

newsgroups This is a companion file of *active* which contains a list of newsgroup names, along with a one-line description of its main topic. This file is automatically updated when C News receives a *checknews* control message (see section 17.8).

localgroups If you have a number of local groups that you don't want C News to complain about every time you receive a *checknews* message, put their names and descriptions in this file, just like they would appear in *newsgroups*.

mailpaths This file contains the moderator's address for each moderated group. Each line contains the group name, followed by the moderator's email address (offset by a tab).

Two special entries are provided as default. These are *backbone* and *internet*. Both provide — in bang-path notation — the path to the nearest backbone site, and the site that understands RFC 822-style addresses (**user@host**). The default entries are

```
internet     backbone
```

You will not have to change the *internet* entry if you have *smail* or *sendmail* installed, because they understand RFC 822-addressing.

The *backbone* entry is used whenever a user posts to a moderated group whose moderator is not listed explicitly. If the newsgroup's name is **alt.sewer**, and the *backbone* entry contains *path*!%s, C News will mail the article to *path*!**alt-sewer**, hoping that the backbone machine is able to forward the article. To find out which path to use, ask the news admins at the site that feeds you. As a last resort, you can also use **uunet.uu.net!%s**.

distributions This file is not really a C News file, but it is used by some newsreaders, and *nntpd*. It contains the list of distributions recognized by your site, and a description of its (intended) effect. For example, Virtual Brewery has the following file:

```
world          everywhere in the world
local          Only local to this site
nl             Netherlands only
mugnet         MUGNET only
fr             France only
de             Germany only
brewery        Virtual Brewery only
```

log This file contains a log of all C News activities. It is culled regularly by running *newsdaily*; copies of the old logfiles are kept in *log.o*, *log.oo*, etc.

errlog This is a log of all error messages created by C News. These do not include articles junked due to wrong group, etc. This file is mailed to the newsmaster (**usenet** by default) automatically by *newsdaily* if it is found to be non-empty.

errlog is cleared by *newsdaily*. Old copies are kept in *errlog.o* and companions.

batchlog This logs all runs of *sendbatches*. It is usually of scant interest only. It is also attended by *newsdaily*.

watchtime This is an empty file created each time *newswatch* is run.

17.8 Control Messages

The Usenet news protocol knows a special category of articles which evoke certain responses or actions by the news system. These are called *control* messages. They are recognized by the presence of a `Control:`

field in the article header, which contains the name of the control operation to be performed. There are several types of them, all of which are handled by shell scripts located in */usr/lib/news/ctl*.

Most of these will perform their action automatically at the time the article is processed by C News, without notifying the newsmaster. By default, only *checkgroups* messages will be handed to the newsmaster,[9] but you may change this by editing the scripts.

17.8.1 The *cancel* Message

The most widely known message is *cancel*, with which a user may cancel an article sent by her earlier. This effectively removes the article from the spool directories, if it exists. The *cancel* message is forwarded to all sites that receive news from the groups affected, regardless of whether the article has been seen already or not. This is to take into account the possibility that the original article has been delayed over the cancellation message. Some news systems allow users to cancel other person's messages; this is of course a definite no-no.

17.8.2 *newgroup* and *rmgroup*

Two messages dealing with creation or removal of newsgroups are the *newgroup* and *rmgroup* message. Newsgroups below the "usual" hierarchies may be created only after a discussion and voting has been held among Usenet readers. The rules applying to the **alt** hierarchy allow for something close to anarchy. For more information, see the regular postings in **news.announce.newusers** and **news.announce.newgroups**. Never send a *newgroup* or *rmgroup* message yourself unless you definitely know that you are allowed to.

17.8.3 The *checkgroups* Message

checkgroups messages are sent by news administrators to make all sites within a network synchronize their *active* files with the realities of Usenet. For example, commercial Internet service providers might send out such a message to their customers' sites. Once a month, the "official" *checkgroups* message for the major hierarchies is posted to **comp.announce.newgroups** by its moderator. However, it is posted as an ordinary article, not as a control message. To perform the *checkgroups* operation, save this article to a file, say */tmp/check*, remove everything up to the beginning of the control message itself, and feed it to the *checkgroups* script using the following command:

```
# su news -c "/usr/lib/news/bin/ctl/checkgroups" < /tmp/check
```

This will update your *newsgroups* file, adding the groups listed in *localgroups*. The old *newsgroups* file will be moved to *newsgroups.bac*. Note that posting the message locally will rarely work, because *inews* refuses to accept that large an article.

If C News finds mismatches between the *checkgroups* list and the *active* file, it will produce a list of commands that would bring your site up to date, and mail it to the news administrator. The output typically looks like this:

```
From news Sun Jan 30 16:18:11 1994
Date: Sun, 30 Jan 94 16:18 MET
From: news (News Subsystem)
To: usenet
Subject: Problems with your active file

The following newsgroups are not valid and should be removed.
        alt.ascii-art
        bionet.molbio.gene-org
        comp.windows.x.intrisics
        de.answers

You can do this by executing the commands:
         /usr/lib/news/bin/maint/delgroup alt.ascii-art
         /usr/lib/news/bin/maint/delgroup bionet.molbio.gene-org
```

[9] There's a funny typo in RFC 1036 (p.12): "Implementors and administrators may choose to allow control messages to be carried out automatically, or to queue them for annual processing."

```
        /usr/lib/news/bin/maint/delgroup comp.windows.x.intrisics
        /usr/lib/news/bin/maint/delgroup de.answers

The following newsgroups were missing.
        comp.binaries.cbm
        comp.databases.rdb
        comp.os.geos
        comp.os.qnx
        comp.unix.user-friendly
        misc.legal.moderated
        news.newsites
        soc.culture.scientists
        talk.politics.crypto
        talk.politics.tibet
```

When you receive a message like this from your news system, don't believe it blindly. Depending on who sent the *checkgroups* message, it may lack a few groups or even entire hierarchies; so you should be careful about removing any groups. If you find groups are listed as missing that you want to carry at your site, you have to add them using the *addgroup* script. Save the list of missing groups to a file and feed it to the following little script:

```
#!/bin/sh
cd /usr/lib/news

while read group; do
    if grep -si "^$group[[:space:]].*moderated" newsgroup; then
        mod=m
    else
        mod=y
    fi
    /usr/lib/news/bin/maint/addgroup $group $mod
done
```

17.8.4 *sendsys*, *version*, and *senduuname*

Finally, there are three messages that may be used to find out about the network's topology. These are *sendsys*, *version*, and *senduuname*. They cause C News to return to the sender the *sys* file, a software version string, and the output of *uuname(1)*, respectively. C News is very laconic about *version* messages; it returns a simple, unadorned "C".

Again, you should *never* issue such a message, unless you have made sure that it cannot leave a your (regional) network. Replies to *sendsys* messages can quickly bring down a UUCP network.[10]

17.9 C News in an NFS Environment

A simple way to distribute news within a local network is to keep all news on a central host, and export the relevant directories via NFS, so that newsreaders may scan the articles directly. The advantage of this method over NNTP is that the overhead involved in retrieving and threading articles is significantly lower. NNTP, on the other hand, wins in a heterogeneous network where equipment varies widely among hosts, or where users don't have equivalent accounts on the server machine.

When using NFS, articles posted on a local host have to be forwarded to the central machine, because accessing adminstrative files might otherwise expose the system to race-conditions that leave the files inconsistent. Also, you might want to protect your news spool area by exporting it read-only, which requires forwarding to the central machine, too.

---

[10] I wouldn't try this on the Internet, either.

C News handles this transparently. When you post an article, your newsreader usually invokes *inews* to inject the article into the news system. This command runs a number of checks on the article, completes the header, and checks the file *server* in */usr/lib/news*. If this file exists and contains a hostname different from the local host's name, *inews* is invoked on that server host via *rsh*. Since the *inews* script uses a number of binary commands and support files from C News, you have to either have C News installed locally, or mount the news software from the server.

For the *rsh* invocation to work properly, each user must have an equivalent account on the server system, i.e. one to which she can log in without being asked for a password.

Make sure that the hostname given in *server* literally matches the output of the *hostname(1)* command on the server machine, else C News will loop forever when trying to deliver the article.

17.10 Maintenance Tools and Tasks

Despite the complexity of C News, a news administrator's life can be fairly easy, because C News provides you with a wide variety of maintenance tools. Some of these are intended to be run regularly from *cron*, like *newsdaily*. Using these scripts reduces daily care and feeding requirements of your C News installation greatly.

Unless stated otherwise, these commands are located in */usr/lib/news/bin/maint*. Note that you must become user **news** before invoking these commands. Running them as super-user may render these files inaccessible to C News.

newsdaily The name already says it: runs this once a day. It is an important script that helps you keep log files small, retaining copies of each from the last three runs. It also tries to sense any anomalies, like stale batches in the incoming and outgoing directories, postings to unkown or moderated newsgroups, etc. Resulting error messages will be mailed to the newsmaster.

newswatch This is a script that should be run regularly to look for anomalies in the news system, once an hour or so. It is intended to detect problems that will have immediate effect on the operability of your news system and mail a trouble report to the newsmaster. Things checked include stale lock files that don't get removed, unattended input batches, and disk space shortage.

addgroup Adds a group to your site locally. The proper invocation is

```
addgroup groupname y|n|m|=realgroup
```

The second argument has the same meaning as the flag in the *active* file, meaning that anyone may post to the group (*y*), that no-one may post (*n*), that it is moderated (*m*), or that it is an alias for another group (=*realgroup*).

You might also want to use *addgroup* when the first articles in a newly created group arrive earlier than the *newgroup* control message that is intended to create it.

delgroup Allows you to delete a group locally. Invoke it as

```
delgroup groupname
```

You still have to delete the articles that remain in the newsgroup's spool directory. Alternatively, you might leave it to the natural course of events (a.k.a. *expire*) to make them go away.

addmissing Adds missing articles to the *history* file. Run this script when there are articles that seem to hang around forever.[11]

newsboot This script should be run at system boot time. It removes any lock files left over when news processes were killed at shutdown, and closes and executes any batches left over from NNTP connections that were terminated when shutting down the system.

---

[11] Ever wondered how to get rid of that "Help! I can't get X11 to work with 0.97.2!!!" article?

newsrunning This resides in */usr/lib/news/bin/input*, and may be used to disable unbatching of incoming news, for instance during work hours. You may turn off unbatching by invoking

/usr/lib/news/bin/`input/newsrunning off`

It is turned on by using *on* instead of *off*.

CHAPTER 18

A Description of NNTP

18.1 Introduction

Due to the different network transport used, NNTP provides for a vastly different approach to news exchange from C news. NNTP stands for "Network News Transfer Protocol," and is not a particular software package, but an Internet Standard.[1] It is based on a stream-oriented connection – usually over TCP – between a client anywhere in the network, and a server on a host that keeps netnews on disk storage. The stream connection allows the client and server to interactively negotiate article transfer with nearly no turnaround delay, thus keeping the number of duplicate articles low. Together with the Internet's high transfer rates, this adds up to a news transport that surpasses the original UUCP networks by far. While some years ago it was not uncommon for an article to take two weeks or more before it arrived in the last corner of Usenet, this is now often less than two days; on the Internet itself, it is even within the range of minutes.

Various commands allow clients to retrieve, send, and post articles. The difference between sending and posting is that the latter may involve articles with incomplete header information.[2] Article retrieval may be used by news transfer clients as well as newsreaders. This makes NNTP an excellent tool for providing news access to many clients on a local network without going through the contortions that are necessary when using NFS.

NNTP also provides for an active and a passive way of news transfer, colloquially called "pushing" and "pulling." Pushing is basically the same as the C news ihave/sendme protocol. The client offers an article to the server through the "*IHAVE <varmsgid>*" command, and the server returns a response code that indicates whether it already has the article, or if it wants it. If so, the client sends the article, terminated by a single dot on a separate line.

Pushing news has the single disadvantage that it places a heavy load on the server system, since it has to search its history database for every single article.

The opposite technique is pulling news, in which the client requests a list of all (available) articles from a group that have arrived after a specified date. This query is performed by the *NEWNEWS* command. From the returned list of message ID's, the client selects those articles it does not yet have, using the *ARTICLE* command for each of them in turn.

The problem with pulling news is that it needs tight control by the server over which groups and distributions it allows a client to request. For example, it has to make sure that no confidential material from newsgroups local to the site are sent to unauthorized clients.

There are also a number of convenience commands for newsreaders that permit them to retrieve the article header and body separately, or even single header lines from a range of articles. This lets you keep all news on a central host, with all users on the (presumably local) network using NNTP-based client programs for reading and posting. This is an alternative to exporting the news directories via NFS which is described in chapter 17.

---

[1] Formally specified in RFC 977.

[2] When posting an article over NNTP, the server always adds at least one header field, which is `Nntp-Posting-Host:`. It contains the client's host name.

An overall problem of NNTP is that it allows the knowledgeable to insert articles into the news stream with false sender specification. This is called *news faking*.[3] An extension to NNTP allows to require a user authentication for certain commands.

There are a number of NNTP packages available. One of the more widely known is the NNTP daemon, also known as the *reference implementation*. Originally, it was written by Stan Barber and Phil Lapsley to illustrate the details of RFC 977. Its most recent version is *nntpd-1.5.11*, which will be described below. You may either get the sources and compile it yourself, or use the *nntpd* from Fred van Kempen's *net-std* binary package. No ready-to-go binaries of *nntpd* are provided, because of various site-specific values that must be compiled in.

The *nntpd* package consists of a server and two clients for pulling and pushing news, respectively, as well as an *inews* replacement. They live in a Bnews environment, but with a little tweaking, they will be happy with C news, too. However, if you plan to use NNTP for more than offering newsreaders access to your news server, the reference implementation is not really an option. We will therefore discuss only the NNTP daemon contained in the *nntpd* package, and leave out the client programs.

There is also a package called "InterNet News," or INN for short, that was written by Rich Salz. It provides both NNTP and UUCP-based news transport, and is more suitable for large news hubs. When it comes to news transport over NNTP, it is definitely better than *nntpd*. INN is currently at version *inn-1.4sec*. There is a kit for building INN on a Linux machine from Arjan de Vet; it is available from **sunsite.unc.edu** in the *system/Mail* directory. If you want to set up INN, please refer to the documentation that comes along with the source, as well as the INN FAQ posted regularly to **news.software.b**.

18.2 Installing the NNTP server

The NNTP server is called *nntpd*, and may be compiled in two ways, depending on the expected load on the news system. There are no compiled versions available, because of some site-specific defaults that are hard-coded into the executable. All configuration is done through macro definines in *common/conf.h*.

nntpd may be configured as either a standalone server that is started at system boot time from *rc.inet2*, or a daemon managed by *inetd*. In the latter case you have to have the following entry in */etc/inetd.conf*:

```
nntp    stream  tcp nowait      news    /usr/etc/in.nntpd       nntpd
```

If you configure *nntpd* as standalone, make sure that any such line in *inetd.conf* is commented out. In either case, you have to make sure there's the following line in */etc/services*:

```
nntp    119/tcp     readnews untp       # Network News Transfer Protocol
```

To temporarily store any incoming articles, etc, *nntpd* also needs a *.tmp* directory in your news spool. You should create it using

```
# mkdir /var/spool/news/.tmp
# chown news.news /var/spool/news/.tmp
```

18.3 Restricting NNTP Access

Access to NNTP resources is governed by the file *nntp_access* in */usr/lib/news*. Lines in the file describe the access rights granted to foreign hosts. Each line has the following format:

```
site read|xfer|both|no post|no [!exceptgroups]
```

If a client connects to the NNTP port, *nntpd* attempts to obtain the host's fully qualified domain name from its IP address by reverse lookup. The client's hostname and IP address are checked against the *site* field of each entry in the order in which they appear in the file. Matches may be either partial or exact. If an entry matches exactly, it applies; if the match is partial, it only applies if there is no other match following which is at least as good. *site* may be specified in one of the following ways:

[3] The same problem exists with SMTP, the Simple Mail Transfer Protocol.

hostname This is a fully qualified domain name of a host. If this matches the client's canonical hostname literally, the entry applies, and all following entries are ignored.

IP address This is an IP address in dotted quad notation. If the client's IP address matches this, the entry applies, and all following entries are ignored.

domain name This is a domain name, specified as **.domain*. If the client's hostname matches the domain name, the entry matches.

network name This is the name of a network as specified in */etc/networks*. If the network number of the client's IP address matches the network number associated with the network name, the entry matches.

default The *default* matches any client.

Entries with a more general site specification should be specified earlier, because any matches by these will be overridden by later, more exact matches.

The second and third field describe the access rights granted to the client. The second details the permissions to retrieve news by pulling (*read*), and transmit news by pushing (*xfer*). A value of *both* enables both, *no* denies access altogether. The third field grants the client the right to post articles, that is, deliver articles with incomplete header information which is completed by the news software. If the second field contains *no*, the third field is ignored.

The fourth field is optional, and contains a comma-separated list of groups the client is denied access to. A sample *nntp_access* file is shown below:

```
#
# by default, anyone may transfer news, but not read or post
default                 xfer            no
#
# public.vbrew.com offers public access via modem, we allow
# them to read and post to any but the local.* groups
public.vbrew.com        read            post    !local
#
# all other hosts at the brewery may read and post
*.vbrew.com             read            post
```

18.4 NNTP Authorization

When capitalizing the access tokens like *xfer* or *read* in the *nntp_acces* file, *nntpd* requires the authorization from the client for the respective operations. For instance, when specifying a permission of *Xfer* or *XFER*, *nntpd* will not let the client transfer articles to your site unless it passes authorization.

The authorization procedure is implemented by means of a new NNTP command named *AUTHINFO*. Using this command, the client transmits a user name and a password to the NNTP server. *nntpd* will validate them by checking them against the */etc/passwd* database, and verify that the user belongs to the **nntp** group.

The current implementation of NNTP authorization is only experimental, and has therefore not been implemented very portably. The result of this is that it works only with plain-style password databases; shadow passwords will not be recognized.

18.5 *nntpd* Interaction with C News

When receiving an article, *nntpd* has to deliver it to the news subsystem. Depending on whether it was received as a result of an *IHAVE* or *POST* command, the article is handed to *rnews* or *inews*, respectively. Instead of invoking *rnews*, you may also configure it (at compile time) to batch the incoming articles and move the resulting batches to */var/spool/news/in.coming*, where they are left for *relaynews* to pick them up at the next queue run.

To be able to properly perform the ihave/sendme protocol, *nntpd* has to be able to access the *history* file. At compile time, you therefore have to make sure the path is set correctly. You should also make sure that

C news and *nntpd* agree on the format of your history file. C news uses *dbm* hashing functions to access it; however, there are quite a number of different and slightly incompatible implementations of the *dbm* library. If C news has been linked with the a different *dbm* library than you have in your standard *libc*, you have to link *nntpd* with this library, too.

A typical symptom of *nntpd* and C news disagreeing on the database format are error messages in the system log that *nntpd* could not open it properly, or duplicate articles received via NNTP. A good test is to pick an article from your spool area, telnet to the *nntp* port, and offer it to *nntpd* as shown in the example below (your input is marked *like this*). Of course, you have to replace *<msg@id>* with the message-ID of the article you want to feed to *nntpd* again.

```
$ telnet localhost nntp
Trying 127.0.0.1...
Connected to loalhost
Escape characters is '^]'.
201 vstout NNTP[auth] server version 1.5.11t (16 November 1991) ready at
Sun Feb 6 16:02:32 1194 (no posting)
IHAVE <msg@id>
435 Got it.
QUIT
```

This conversation shows the proper reaction of *nntpd*; the message "`Got it`" tells you that it already has this article. If you get a message of "`335 Ok`" instead, the lookup in the history file failed for some reason. Terminate the conversation by typing Ctrl-D. You can check what has gone wrong by checking the system log; *nntpd* logs all kinds of messages to the *daemon* facility of *syslog*. An incompatible *dbm* library usually manifests itself in a message complaining that *dbminit* failed.

CHAPTER 19

Newsreader Configuration

Newsreaders are intended to offer the user functionality that allows her to access the functions of the news system easily, like posting articles, or skimming the contents of a newsgroup in a comfortable way. The quality of this interface is subject of endless flame wars.

There are a couple of newsreaders available which have been ported to Linux. Below I will describe the basic setup for the three most popular ones, namely *tin*, *trn*, and *nn*.

One of the most effective newsreaders is

```
$ find /var/spool/news -name '[0-9]*' -exec cat {} \; | more
```

This is the way UNIX die-hards read their news.

The majority of newsreaders, however, are much more sophisticated. They usually offer a full-screen interface with separate levels for displaying all groups the user has subscribed to, for displaying an overview of all articles in one group. and for individual articles.

At the newsgroup level, most newsreaders display a list of articles, showing their subject line, and the author. In big groups, it is impossible for the user to keep track of articles relating to each other, although it is possible to identify responses to earlier articles.

A response usually repeats the original article's subject, prepending it with "`Re: `". Additionally, the message ID of the article it is a direct follow-up to may be given in the `References:` header line. Sorting articles by these two criteria generates small clusters (in fact, trees) of articles, which are called *threads*. One of the tasks in writing a newsreader is devising an efficient scheme of threading, because the time required for this is proportional to the square of the number of articles.

Here, we will not dig any further into how the user interfaces are built. All newsreaders currently available for Linux have a good help function, so you ought to get along.

In the following, we will only deal with administrative tasks. Most of these relate to the creation of threads databases and accounting.

19.1 *tin* Configuration

The most versatile newsreader with respect to threading is *tin*. It was written by Iain Lea and is loosely modeled on an older newsreader named *tass*.[1] It does its threading when the user enters the newsgroup, and it is pretty fast at this unless you're doing this via NNTP.

On an 486DX50, it takes roughly 30 seconds to thread 1000 articles when reading directly from disk. Over NNTP to a loaded news server, this would be somewhere above 5 minutes.[2] You may improve this by regularly updating your index file with the `-u` option, or by invoking *tin* with the `-U` option.

[1] Written by Rich Skrenta.

[2] Things improve drastically if the NNTP server does the threading itself, and lets the client retrieve the threads databases; INN-1.4 does this, for instance.

Usually, *tin* dumps its threading databases in the user's home directory below *.tin/index*. This may however be costly in terms of resources, so that you should want to keep a single copy of them in a central location. This may be achieved by making *tin* setuid to **news**, for example, or some entirely unprivileged account.[3] *tin* will then keep all thread databases below */var/spool/news/.index*. For any file access or shell escape, it will reset its effective uid to the real uid of the user who invoked it.[4]

A better solution is to install the *tind* indexing daemon that runs as a daemon and regularly updates the index files. This daemon is however not included in any release of Linux, so you would have to compile it yourself. If you are running a LAN with a central news server, you may even run *tind* on the server and have all clients retrieve the index files via NNTP. This, of course, requires an extension to NNTP. Patches for *nntpd* that implement this extension are included in the *tin* source.

The version of *tin* included in some Linux distributions has no NNTP support compiled in, but most do have it now. When invoked as *rtin* or with the `-r` option, *tin* tries to connect to the NNTP server specified in the file */etc/nntpserver* or in the `NNTPSERVER` environment variable. The *nntpserver* file simply contains the server's name on a single line.

19.2 *trn* Configuration

trn is the successor to an older newsreader, too, namely *rn* (which means *read news*). The "t" in its name stands for "threaded." It was written by Wayne Davidson.

Unlike *tin*, *trn* has no provision for generating its threading database at run-time. Instead, it uses those prepared by a program called *mthreads* that has to be invoked regularly from *cron* to update the index files.

Not running *mthreads*, however, doesn't mean you cannot access new articles, it only means you will have all those "Novell buys out Linix!!" articles scattered across your article selection menu, instead of a single thread you may easily skip.

To turn on threading for particular newsgroups, *mthreads* is invoked with the list of newsgroups on the command line. The list is made up in exactly the same fashion as the one in the *sys* file:

```
mthreads comp,rec,!rec.games.go
```

will enable threading for all of **comp** and **rec**, except for **rec.games.go** (people who play Go don't need fancy threads). After that, you simply invoke it without any option at all to make it thread any newly arrived articles. Threading of all groups found in your *active* file can be turned on by invoking *mthreads* with a group list of **all**.

If you're receiving news during the night, you will customarily run *mthreads* once in the morning, but you can also to do so more frequently if needed. Sites that have very heavy traffic may want to run *mthreads* in daemon mode. When it is started at boot time using the `-d` option, it puts itself in the background, and wakes up every 10 minutes to check if there are any newly-arrived articles, and threads them. To run *mthreads* in daemon mode, put the following line in your *rc.news* script:

```
/usr/local/bin/rn/mthreads -deav
```

The `-a` option makes *mthread* automatically turn on threading for new groups as they are created; `-v` enables verbose log messages to *mthreads*' log file, *mt.log* in the directory where you have *trn* installed.

Old articles no longer available must be removed from the index files regularly. By default, only articles whose number is below the low water mark will be removed.[5] Articles above this number who have been expired nevertheless (because the oldest article has been assigned an long expiry date by an `Expires:` header field) may be removed by giving *mthreads* the `-e` option to force an "enhanced" expiry run. When *mthreads* is running in daemon mode, the `-e` option makes it put in such an enhanced expiry run once a day, shortly after midnight.

19.3 *nn* Configuration

nn, written by Kim F. Storm, claims to be a newsreader whose ultimate goal is not to read news. It's name stands for "No News", and its motto is "No news is good news. *nn* is better."

To achieve this ambitious goal, *nn* comes along with a large assortment of maintenance tools that not only allow generation of threads, but also extensive checks on the consistency of these databases, accounting, gathering of usage

[3] However, do *not* use **nobody** for this. As a rule, no files or commands whatsoever should be associated with this user.

[4] This is the reason why you will get ugly error messages when invoking it as super user. But then, you shouldn't work as **root**, anyway.

[5] Note that C news doesn't update this low water mark automatically; you have to run *updatemin* to do so. Please refer to chapter 17.

statistics, and access restrictions. There is also an administration program called *nnadmin*, which allows you to perform these tasks interactively. It is very intuitive; hence, we will not dwell on these aspects, and only deal with the generation of the index files.

The *nn* threads database manager is called *nnmaster*. It is usually run as a daemon, started from the *rc.news* or *rc.inet2* script. It is invoked as

```
/usr/local/lib/nn/nnmaster -l -r -C
```

This enables threading for all newsgroups present in your *active* file.

Equivalently, you may invoke *nnmaster* periodically from *cron*, giving it a list of groups to act upon. This list is very similar to the subscription list in the *sys* file, except that it uses blanks instead of commas. Instead of the fake group name **all**, an empty argument of `""` should be used to denote all groups. A sample invocation is

```
# /usr/local/lib/nn/nnmaster !rec.games.go rec comp
```

Note that the order is significant here: The leftmost group specification that matches always wins. Thus, if we had put *!rec.games.go* after *rec*, all articles from this group had been threaded nevertheless.

nn offers several methods to remove expired articles from its databases. The first is to update the database by scanning the news group directories and discarding the entries whose corresponding article is no longer available. This is the default operation obtained by invoking *nnmaster* with the `-E` option. It is reasonably fast unless you're doing this via NNTP.

Method 2 behaves exactly like a default expiry run of *mthreads*, in that it only removes those entries that refer to articles whose number is below the low water mark in the *active* file. It may be enabled using the `-e` option.

Finally, a third strategy is to discard the entire database and recollect all articles. This may be done by giving `-E3` to *nnmaster*.

The list of groups to be expired is given by the `-F` option in the same fashion as above. However, if you have *nnmaster* running as daemon, you must kill it (using `-k`) before expiry can take place, and to re-start it with the original options afterwards. Thus the proper command to run expire on all groups using method 1 is:

```
# nnmaster -kF ""
# nnmaster -lrC
```

There are many more flags that may be used to fine-tune the behavior of *nn*. If you are concerned about removing bad articles or digestifying article digests, read the *nnmaster* manual page.

nnmaster relies on a file named *GROUPS*, which is located in */usr/local/lib/nn*. If it does not exist initially, it is created. For each newsgroup, it contains a line that begins with the group's name, optionally followed by a time stamp, and flags. You may edit these flags to enable certain behavior for the group in question, but you may not change the order in which the groups appear.[6] The flags allowed and their effects are detailed in the *nnmaster* manual page, too.

[6] This is because their order has to agree with that of the entries in the (binary) *MASTER* file.

APPENDIX A

A Null Printer Cable for PLIP

To make a Null Printer Cable for use with a PLIP connection, you need two 25-pin connectors (called DB-25) and some 11-conductor cable. The cable must be at most 15 meters long.

If you look at the connector, you should be able to read tiny numbers at the base of each pin, from 1 for the pin top left (if you hold the broader side up) to 25 for the pin bottom right. For the Null Printer cable, you have to connect the following pins of both connectors with each other:

```
D0       2—15  ERROR
D1       3—13  SLCT
D2       4—12  PAPOUT
D3       5—10  ACK
D4       6—11  BUSY
GROUND  25—25  GROUND
ERROR   15— 2  D0
SLCT    13— 3  D1
PAPOUT  12— 4  D2
ACK     10— 5  D3
BUSY    11— 6  D4
```

All remaining pins remain unconnected. If the cable is shielded, the shield should be connected to the DB-25's metallic shell on one end only.

APPENDIX B

Sample *smail* Configuration Files

This section shows sample configuration files for a UUCP leaf site on a local area network. They are based on the sample files included in the source distribution of *smail-3.1.28*. Although I make a feeble attempt to explain how these files work, you are advised to read the very fine *smail(8)* manual page, which discusses these files in great length. Once you've understood the basic idea behind *smail* configuration, it's worthwhile reading. It's easy!

The first file shown is the *routers* file, which describes a set of routers to *smail*. When *smail* has to deliver a message to a given address, it hands the address to all routers in turn, until one of them matches it. Matching here means that the router finds the destination host in its database, be it the *paths* file, */etc/hosts*, or whatever routing mechanism the router interfaces to.

Entries in *smail* configuration files always begin with a unique name identifying the router, transport, or director. They are followed by a list of attributes that define its behavior. This list consists of a set of global attributes, such as the *driver* used, and private attributes that are only understood by that particular driver. Attributes are separated by commas, while the sets of global and private attributes are separated from each other using a semicolon.

To make these fine distinctions clear, assume you want to maintain two separate pathalias files; one containing the routing information for your domain, and a second one containing global routing information, probably generatzed from the UUCP maps. With *smail*, you can now specify two routers in the *routers* file, both of which use the *pathalias* driver. This driver looks up hostnames in a pathalias database. It expects to be given the name of the file in a private attribute:

```
#
# pathalias database for intra-domain routing
domain_paths:
        driver=pathalias,          # look up host in a paths file
        transport=uux;             # if matched, deliver over UUCP

        file=paths/domain,         # file is /usr/lib/smail/paths/domain
        proto=lsearch,             # file is unsorted (linear search)
        optional,                  # ignore if the file does not exist
        required=vbrew.com,        # look up only *.vbrew.com hosts

#
# pathalias database for routing to hosts outside our domain
world_paths:
        driver=pathalias,          # look up host in a paths file
        transport=uux;             # if matched, deliver over UUCP

        file=paths/world,          # file is /usr/lib/smail/paths/world
        proto=bsearch,             # file is sorted with sort(1)
        optional,                  # ignore if the file does not exist
        -required,                 # no required domains
        domain=uucp,               # strip ending ".uucp" before searching
```

The second global attribute given in each of the two *routers* entries above defines the transport that should be used when the router matches the address. In our case, the message will be delivered using the *uux* transport. Transports are defined in the *transports* file, which is exlained below.

You can fine-tune by which transport a message will be delivered if you specify a mathod file instead of the *transports* attribute. Method files provide a mapping from target hostnames to transports. We won't deal with them here.

The following *routers* file defines routers for a local area network that query the resolver library. On an Internet host, however, you would want to use a router that handles MX records. You should therefore uncomment the alternative *inet_bind* router that uses *smail*'s builtin BIND driver.

In an environment that mixes UUCP and TCP/IP, you may encounter the problem that you have hosts in your */etc/hosts* file that you have only occasional SLIP or PPP contact with. Usually, you would still want to send any mail for them over UUCP. To prevent the *inet_hosts* driver from matching these hosts, you have to put them into the *paths/force* file. This is another pathalias-style database, and is consulted before *smail* queries the resolver.

```
# A sample /usr/lib/smail/routers file
#
# force - force UUCP delivery to certain hosts, even when
#         they are in our /etc/hosts
force:
        driver=pathalias,          # look up host in a paths file
        transport=uux;             # if matched, deliver over UUCP

        file=paths/force,          # file is /usr/lib/smail/paths/force
        optional,                  # ignore if the file does not exist
        proto=lsearch,             # file is unsorted (linear search)
        -required,                 # no required domains
        domain=uucp,               # strip ending ".uucp" before searching

# inet_addrs - match domain literals containing literal
#         IP addresses, such as in janet@[191.72.2.1]
inet_addrs:
        driver=gethostbyaddr,      # driver to match IP domain literals
        transport=smtp;            # deliver using SMTP over TCP/IP

        fail_if_error,             # fail if address is malformed
        check_for_local,           # deliver directly if host is ourself

# inet_hosts - match hostnames with gethostbyname(3N)
#         Comment this out if you wish to use the BIND version instead.
inet_hosts:
        driver=gethostbyname,      # match hosts with the library function
        transport=smtp;            # use default SMTP

        -required,                 # no required domains
        -domain,                   # no defined domain suffixes
        -only_local_domain,        # don't restrict to defined domains

# inet_hosts - alternate version using BIND to access the DNS
#inet_hosts:
#       driver=bind,               # use built-in BIND driver
#       transport=smtp;            # use TCP/IP SMTP for delivery
#
#       defnames,                  # use standard domain searching
#       defer_no_connect,          # try again if the nameserver is down
#       -local_mx_okay,            # fail (don't pass through) an MX
#                                  # to the local host

#
# pathalias database for intra-domain routing
domain_paths:
        driver=pathalias,          # look up host in a paths file
```

```
        transport=uux;              # if matched, deliver over UUCP

        file=paths/domain,          # file is /usr/lib/smail/paths/domain
        proto=lsearch,              # file is unsorted (linear search)
        optional,                   # ignore if the file does not exist
        required=vbrew.com,         # look up only *.vbrew.com hosts

#
# pathalias database for routing to hosts outside our domain
world_paths:
        driver=pathalias,           # look up host in a paths file
        transport=uux;              # if matched, deliver over UUCP

        file=paths/world,           # file is /usr/lib/smail/paths/world
        proto=bsearch,              # file is sorted with sort(1)
        optional,                   # ignore if the file does not exist
        -required,                  # no required domains
        domain=uucp,                # strip ending ".uucp" before searching


# smart_host - a partically specified smarthost director
#       If the smart_path attribute is not defined in
#       /usr/lib/smail/config, this router is ignored.
#       The transport attribute is overridden by the global
#       smart_transport variable
smart_host:
        driver=smarthost,           # special-case driver
        transport=uux;              # by default deliver over UUCP

        -path,                      # use smart_path config file variable
```

The handling of mail for local addresses is configured in the *directors* file. It is made up just like the *routers* file, with a list of entries that define a director each. Directors do *not* deliver a message, they merely perform all the redirection that is possible, for instance through aliases, mail forwarding, and the like.

When delivering mail to a local address, such as **janet**, *smail* passes the usr name to all directors in turn. If a director matches, it either specifies a transport the message should be delivered by (for instance, to the user's mailbox file), or generates a new address (for instance, after evaluating an alias).

Because of the security issues involved, directors usually do a lot of checking of whether the files they use may be compromised or not. Addresses obtained in a somewhat dubious way (for instance from a world-writable *aliases* file) are flagged as unsecure. Some transport drivers will turn down such addresses, for instance the transport that delivers a message to a file.

Apart from this, *smail* also *associates a user* with each address. Any write or read operations are performed as the user. For delivery to, say **janet**'s mailbox, the address is of course associated with **janet**. Other addresses, such as those obtained from the *aliases* file, have other users associated from them, for instance, the **nobody** user.

For details of these features, please refer to the *smail(8)* manpage.

```
# A sample /usr/lib/smail/directors file

# aliasinclude - expand ":include:filename" addresses produced
#       by alias files
aliasinclude:
        driver=aliasinclude,        # use this special-case driver
        nobody;                     # access file as nobody user if unsecure

        copysecure,                 # get permissions from alias director
        copyowners,                 # get owners from alias director

# forwardinclude - expand ":include:filename" addrs produced
```

```
#       by forward files
forwardinclude:
        driver=forwardinclude,    # use this special-case driver
        nobody;                   # access file as nobody user if unsecure

        checkpath,                # check path accessibility
        copysecure,               # get perms from forwarding director
        copyowners,               # get owners from forwarding director

# aliases - search for alias expansions stored in a database
aliases:
        driver=aliasfile,         # general-purpose aliasing director
        -nobody,                  # all addresses are associated
                                  # with nobody by default anyway
        sender_okay,              # don't remove sender from expansions
        owner=owner-$user;        # problems go to an owner address

        file=/usr/lib/aliases,    # default: sendmail compatible
        modemask=002,             # should not be globally writable
        optional,                 # ignore if file does not exist
        proto=lsearch,            # unsorted ASCII file

# dotforward - expand .forward files in user home directories
dotforward:
        driver=forwardfile,       # general-purpose forwarding director
        owner=real-$user,         # problems go to the user's mailbox
        nobody,                   # use nobody user, if unsecure
        sender_okay;              # sender never removed from expansion

        file=~/.forward,          # .forward file in home directories
        checkowner,               # the user can own this file
        owners=root,              # or root can own the file
        modemask=002,             # it should not be globally writable
        caution=0-10:uucp:daemon, # don't run things as root or daemons
        # be extra careful of remotely accessible home directories
        unsecure="~ftp:~uucp:~nuucp:/tmp:/usr/tmp",

# forwardto - expand a "Forward to " line at the top of
#       the user's mailbox file
forwardto:
        driver=forwardfile,
        owner=Postmaster,         # errors go to Postmaster
        nobody,                   # use nobody user, if unsecure
        sender_okay;              # don't remove sender from expansion

        file=/var/spool/mail/${lc:user}, # location of user's mailbox
        forwardto,                # enable "Forward to " check
        checkowner,               # the user can own this file
        owners=root,              # or root can own the file
        modemask=0002,            # under System V, group mail can write
        caution=0-10:uucp:daemon, # don't run things as root or daemons

# user - match users on the local host with delivery to their mailboxes
user:   driver=user;              # driver to match usernames

        transport=local,          # local transport goes to mailboxes

# real_user - match usernames when prefixed with the string "real-"
```

```
real_user:
        driver=user;                # driver to match usernames

        transport=local,            # local transport goes to mailboxes
        prefix="real-",             # for example, match real-root

# lists - expand mailing lists stored below /usr/lib/smail/lists
lists:  driver=forwardfile,
        caution,                    # flag all addresses with caution
        nobody,                     # and then associate the nobody user
        sender_okay,                # do NOT remove the sender
        owner=owner-$user;          # the list owner

        # map the name of the mailing list to lower case
        file=lists/${lc:user},
```

After successfully routing or directing a message, *smail* hands the message to the transport specified by the router or director that matched the address. These transports are defined in the *transports* file. Again, a transport is defined by a set of global and private options.

The most important option defined by each entry is driver that handles the transport, for instance the *pipe* driver, which invokes the command specified in the *cmd* attribute. Apart from this, there are a number of global attributes a transport may use, that perform various transformations on the message header, and possibly message body. The *return_path* attribute, for instance, makes the transport insert a *return_path* field in the message header The *unix_from_hack* attribute makes it precede every occurrence of the word `From` at the beginning of a line with a > sign.

```
# A sample /usr/lib/smail/transports file

# local - deliver mail to local users
local:  driver=appendfile,          # append message to a file
        return_path,                # include a Return-Path: field
        from,                       # supply a From_ envelope line
        unix_from_hack,             # insert > before From in body
        local;                      # use local forms for delivery

        file=/var/spool/mail/${lc:user}, # location of mailbox files
        group=mail,                 # group to own file for System V
        mode=0660,                  # group mail can access
        suffix="\n",                # append an extra newline

# pipe - deliver mail to shell commands
pipe:   driver=pipe,                # pipe message to another program
        return_path,                # include a Return-Path: field
        from,                       # supply a From_ envelope line
        unix_from_hack,             # insert > before From in body
        local;                      # use local forms for delivery

        cmd="/bin/sh -c $user",     # send address to the Bourne Shell
        parent_env,                 # environment info from parent addr
        pipe_as_user,               # use user-id associated with address
        ignore_status,              # ignore a non-zero exit status
        ignore_write_errors,        # ignore write errors, i.e., broken pipe
        umask=0022,                 # umask for child process
        -log_output,                # do not log stdout/stderr

# file - deliver mail to files
file:   driver=appendfile,
        return_path,                # include a Return-Path: field
        from,                       # supply a From_ envelope line
```

```
        unix_from_hack,             # insert > before From in body
        local;                      # use local forms for delivery

        file=$user,                 # file is taken from address
        append_as_user,             # use user-id associated with address
        expand_user,                # expand ~ and $ within address
        suffix="\n",                # append an extra newline
        mode=0600,                  # set permissions to 600

# uux - deliver to the rmail program on a remote UUCP site
uux:    driver=pipe,
        uucp,                       # use UUCP-style addressing forms
        from,                       # supply a From_ envelope line
        max_addrs=5,                # at most 5 addresses per invocation
        max_chars=200;              # at most 200 chars of addresses

        cmd="/usr/bin/uux - -r -a$sender -g$grade $host!rmail $(($user)$)",
        pipe_as_sender,             # have uucp logs contain caller
        log_output,                 # save error output for bounce messages
#       defer_child_errors,         # retry if uux returns an error

# demand - deliver to a remote rmail program, polling immediately
demand: driver=pipe,
        uucp,                       # use UUCP-style addressing forms
        from,                       # supply a From_ envelope line
        max_addrs=5,                # at most 5 addresses per invocation
        max_chars=200;              # at most 200 chars of addresses

        cmd="/usr/bin/uux - -a$sender -g$grade $host!rmail $(($user)$)",
        pipe_as_sender,             # have uucp logs contain caller
        log_output,                 # save error output for bounce messages
#       defer_child_errors,         # retry if uux returns an error

# hbsmtp - half-baked BSMTP. The output files must
#       be processed regularly and sent out via UUCP.
hbsmtp: driver=appendfile,
        inet,                       # use RFC 822-addressing
        hbsmtp,                     # batched SMTP w/o HELO and QUIT
        -max_addrs, -max_chars;     # no limit on number of addresses

        file="/var/spool/smail/hbsmtp/$host",
        user=root,                  # file is owned by root
        mode=0600,                  # only read-/writeable by root.

# smtp - deliver using SMTP over TCP/IP
smtp:   driver=tcpsmtp,
        inet,
        -max_addrs, -max_chars;     # no limit on number of addresses

        short_timeout=5m,               # timeout for short operations
        long_timeout=2h,                # timeout for longer SMTP operations
        service=smtp,                   # connect to this service port
# For internet use: uncomment the below 4 lines
#       use_bind,                       # resolve MX and multiple A records
#       defnames,                       # use standard domain searching
#       defer_no_connect,               # try again if the nameserver is down
#       -local_mx_okay,                 # fail an MX to the local host
```

Glossary

An enormous difficulty in networking is to remember what all the abbreviations and terms one encounters really mean. Here's a list of those used frequently throughout the guide, along with a short explanation.

ACU — Automatic Call Unit. A modem.[1]

ARP — Address Resolution Protocol. Used to map IP addresses to Ethernet addresses.

ARPA — Advanced Research Project Agency, later DARPA. Founder of the Internet.

ARPANET — The ancestor of today's Internet; an experimental network funded by the U.S. Defense Advanced Research Project Agency (DARPA).

Assigned Numbers — The title of an *RFC* published regularly that lists the publicly allocated numbers used for various things in TCP/IP networking. For example, it contains the list of all port numbers of well-known services like *rlogin*, *telnet*, etc. The most recent release of this document is RFC 1340.

bang path — In UUCP networks, a special notation for the path from one UUCP site to another. The name derives from the use of exclamation marks ('bangs') to separate the host names. Example: **foo!bar!ernie!bert** denotes a path to host **bert**, travelling (in this order) **foo**, **bar**, and **ernie**.

BBS — Bulletin Board System. A dial-up mailbox system.

BGP — Border Gateway Protocol. A protocol for exchanging routing information between autonomous systems.

BIND — The Berkeley Internet Name Domain server. An implementation of a DNS server.

BNU — Basic Networking Utilities. This is the most common UUCP variety at the moment. It is also known as HoneyDanBer UUCP. This name is derived from the authors' names: P. Honeyman, D.A. Novitz, and B.E. Redman.

broadcast network — A network that allows one station to address a datagram to all other stations on the network simultaneously.

BSD — Berkeley Software Distribution. A UNIX flavor.

canonical hostname — A host's primary name within the Domain Name System. This is the host's only name that has an A record associated with it, and which is returned when performing a reverse lookup.

CCITT — Comiteé Consultatif International de Télégraphique et Téléphonique. An International organization of telephone services, etc.

CSLIP — Compressed Serial Line IP. A protocol for exchanging IP packets over a serial line, using header compression of most TCP/IP datagrams.

DNS — Domain name system. This is a distributed database used on the Internet for mapping of host names to IP addresses.

EGP — External Gateway Protocol. A protocol for exchanging routing information between autonomous systems.

[1] Alternatively: A teenager with a telephone.

Ethernet — In colloquial terms, the name of a sort of network equipment. Technically, Ethernet is part of a set of standards set forth by the IEEE. The Ethernet hardware uses a single piece of cable, frequently coax cable, to connect a number of hosts, and allows transfer rates of up to 10Mbps. The Ethernet protocol defines the manner in which hosts may communicate over this cable.[2]

FQDN — Fully Qualified Domain Name. A hostname with a domain name tacked onto it, so that it is a valid index into the Domain Name database.

FTP — File Transfer Protocol. The protocol one of the best-known file transfer service is based on and named after.

FYI — "For Your Information." Series of documents with informal information on Internet topics.

GMU — Groucho Marx University. Fictitious University used as an example throughout this book.

GNU — GNU's not Unix – this recursive acronym is the name of a project by the Free Software Association to provide a coherent set of UNIX-tools that may be used and copied free of charge. All GNU software is covered by a special Copyright notice, also called the GNU General Public License (GPL), or Copyleft. See page 203.

HoneyDanBer — The name of a UUCP variety. See also BNU.

host — Generally, a network node: something that is able to receive and transmit network messages. This will usually be a computer, but you can also think of X-Terminals, or smart printers.

ICMP — Internet Control Message Protocol. A networking protocol used by IP to return error information to the sending host, etc.

IEEE — Institute of Electrical and Eletronics Engineers. Another standards organization. From a UNIX user's point of view, their most important achievement are probably the POSIX standards which define aspects of a UNIX systems, ranging from system call interfaces and semantics to administration tools.

Apart from this, the IEEE developed the specifications for Ethernet, Token Ring, and Token Bus networks. A widely-used standard for binary representation of real numbers is also due to the IEEE.

IETF — Internet Engineering Task Force.

internet — A computer network formed of a collection of individual smaller networks.

Internet — A particular world-wide internet.

IP — Internet Protocol. A networking protocol.

ISO — International Standards Organization.

ISDN — Integrated Services Digital Network. New telecommunications technology using digital instead of analogue circuitry.

LAN — Local Area Network. A small computer network.

MX — Mail Exchanger. A DNS resource record type used for marking a host as mail gateway for a domain.

network, packet-switched — A variety of networks that provide instantaneous forwarding of data by all data up in small packets, which are tramsported to their destination individually. Packet-switched networks rely on permanent or semi-permanent connections.

network, store-and-forward — They are pretty much the opposite of packet-switched networks. These networks transfer data as entire files, and don't use permanent connections. Instead, hosts conect to each other at certain intervals only, and transfer all data at once. This requires that data be stored intermediately until a connection is established.

NFS — Network File System. A standard networking protocol and software suite for accessing data on remote disks transparently.

NIS — Network Information System. An RPC-based application that allows to share configuration files such as the password file between several hosts. See also the entry under YP.

[2] As an aside, the Ethernet *protocol* commonly used by TCP/IP is *not* exactly the same as IEEE 802.3. Ethernet frames have a type field where IEEE 802.3 frames have a length field.

NNTP — Network News Transfer Protocol. Used to transfer news over TCP network connections.

octet — On the Internet, the technical term referring to a quantity of eight bits. It is used rather than *byte*, because there are machines on the Internet that have byte sizes other than eight bits.

OSI — Open Systems Interconnection. An ISO standard on network software.

path — Often used in UUCP networks as a synonym for *route*. Also see *bang path*.

PLIP — Parallel Line IP. A protocol for exchanging IP packets over a parallel line such as a printer port.

port, TCP or UDP — Ports are TCP's and UDP's abstraction of a service endpoint. Before a process can provide or access some networking service, it must claim (bind) a port. Together with the hosts' IP addresses, ports uniquely identify the two peers of a TCP connection.

portmapper — The portmapper is the mediator between the program numbers used by RPC as an identification of individual RPC servers, and the TCP and UDP port numbers those services are listening to.

PPP — The point-to-point protocol. PPP is a flexible and fast link-layer protocol to send various network protocols such as IP or IPX across a point-to-point connection. Apart from being used on serial (modem) links, PPP can also be employed as the link-level protocol on top of ISDN.

RARP — Reverse Address Resolution Protocol. It permits hosts to find out their IP address at boot time.

resolver — This is a library responsible for mapping hostnames to IP addresses and vice versa.

resource record — This is the basic unit of information in the DNS database, commonly abbreviated as RR. Each record has a certain type and class associated with it, for instance a record mapping a host name to an IP address has a type of A (for address), and a class of IN (for the Internet Protocol).

reverse lookup — The act of looking up a host's name based on a given IP address. Within DNS, this is done by looking up the host's IP address in the **in-addr.arpa** domain.

RFC — Request For Comments. Series of documents describing Internet standards.

RIP — Routing Information Protocol. This is a routing protocol used dynamically adjust routes inside a (small) network.

route — The sequence of hosts a piece of information has to travel from the originating host to the destination host. Finding an appropriate route is also called *routing*.

routing daemon — In larger networks, network topology changes are hard to adapt to manually, so facilities are used to distribute current routing information to the network's member hosts. This is called dynamic routing; the routing information is exchanged by *routing daemons* running on central hosts in the network. The protocols they employ are called *routing protocols*.

RPC — Remote Procedure Call. Protocol for executing procdures inside a process on a remote host.

RR — Short for *resource record*.

RS-232 — This is a very common standard for serial interfaces.

RTS/CTS — A colloquial name for the hardware handshake performed by two devices communicating over RS-232. The name derives from the two cicuits involved, RTS ("Ready To Send"), and CTS ("Clear To Send").

RTM Internet Worm — A Virus-like program that used several flaws in VMS and BSD 4.3 Unix to spread through the Internet. Several "mistakes" in the program caused it to multiply without bound, and so effectively bringing down large parts of the Internet. RTM are the author's initials (Robert T. Morris), which he left in the program.

site — An agglomeration of hosts which, to the outside, behave almost like a single network node. For example, when speaking from an Internet point of view, one would call a Groucho Marx University a site, regardless of the complexity of its interior network.

SLIP — Serial Line IP. This is a protocol for exchanging IP packets over a serial line, see also CSLIP.

SMTP — Simple Mail Transfer Protocol. Used for mail transport over TCP connections, but also for mail batches transported over UUCP links (batched SMTP).

SOA Start of Authority. A DNS resource record type.

System V A UNIX flavor.

TCP Transmission Control Protocol. A networking protocol.

TCP/IP Sloppy description of the Internet protocol suite as a whole.

UDP User Datagram Protocol. A networking protocol.

UUCP Unix to Unix Copy. A suite of network transport commands for dial-up networks.

Version 2 UUCP An aging UUCP variety.

virtual beer Every Linuxer's favorite drink. The first mention of virtual beer I remember was in the release note of the Linux 0.98.X kernel, where Linus listed the "Oxford Beer Trolls" in his credits section for sending along some virtual beer.

well-known services This term is frequently used to refer to common networking services such as *telnet* and *rlogin*. In a more technical sense, it describes all services that have been assigned an official port number in the "Assigned Numbers" RFC.

YP Yellow Pages. An older name for NIS which is no longer used, because Yellow Pages is a trademark of British Telecom. Nevertheless, most NIS utilities have retained names with a prefix of *yp*.

Annotated Bibliography

Books

The following is a list of books you might want to read to if you want to know more about some of the topics covered in the Networking Guide. It is not very complete or systematic, I just happen to have read them and find them quite useful. Any additions to, and enhancement of this list are welcome.

General Books on the Internet

[Kehoe92] Brendan P. Kehoe: *Zen and the Art of the Internet.* .

"Zen" was one of, if not *the* first Internet Guide, introducing the novice user to the various trades, services and the folklore of the Internet. Being a 100-page tome, it covered topics ranging from email to Usenet news to the Internet Worm. It is available via anonymous FTP from many FTP servers, and may be freely distributed and printed. A printed copy is also available from Prentice-Hall.

Administration Issues

[Hunt92] Craig Hunt: *TCP/IP Network Administration*. O'Reilly and Associates, 1992. ISBN 0-937175-82-X.

If the Linux Network Administrators' Guide is not enough for you, get this book. It deals with everything from obtaining an IP address to troubleshooting your network to security issues.

Its focus is on setting up TCP/IP, that is, interface configuration, the setup of routing, and name resolution. It includes a detailed description of the facilities offered by the routing daemons `routed` and `gated`, which supply dynamic routing.

It also describes the configuration of application programs and network daemons, such as `inetd`, the `r` commands, NIS, and NFS.

The appendix has a detailed reference of `gated`, and `named`, and a description of Berkeley's `sendmail` configuration.

[Stern92] Hal Stern: *Managing NIS and NFS*. O'Reilly and Associates, 1992. ISBN 0-937175-75-7.

This is a companion book to Craig Hunt's "TCP/IP Network Administration" book. It covers the use of NIS, the Network Information System, and NFS, the Network File System, in extenso, including the configuration of an automounter, and PC/NFS.

[OReilly89] Tim O'Reilly and Grace Todino: *Managing UUCP and Usenet, 10th ed.* O'Reilly and Associates, 1992. ISBN 0-93717593-5.

This is the standard book on UUCP networking. It covers Version 2 UUCP as well as BNU. It helps you to set up your UUCP node from the start, giving practical tips and solutions for many problems, like testing the connection, or writing good chat scripts. It also deals with more exotic topics, like how to set up a travelling UUCP node, or the subtleties present in different flavors of UUCP.

The second part of the book deals with Usenet and netnews software. It explains the configuration of both Bnews (version 2.11) and C news, and introduces you to netnews maintenance tasks.

[Spaf93] Gene Spafford and Simson Garfinkel: *Practical UNIX Security*. O'Reilly and Associates, 1992. ISBN 0-937175-72-2.

This is a must-have for everyone who manages a system with network access, and for others as well. The book discusses all issues relevant to computer security, ranging the basic security features UNIX offers physical security. Although you should strive to secure all parts of your system, the discussion of networks and security is the most interesting part of the book in our context. Apart from basic security policies that concern the Berkeley services (*telnet*, *rlogin*, etc), NFS and NIS, it also deals with enhanced security features like MIT's Kerberos, Sun's Secure RPC, and the use of firewalls to shield your network from attacks from the Internet.

[AlbitzLiu92] Paul Albitz and Cricket Liu: *DNS and BIND*. O'Reilly and Associates, 1992. ISBN 1-56592-010-4.

This book is useful for all those that have to manage DNS name service. It explains all features of DNS in great detail and give examples that make even those BIND options plausible that appear outright weird at first sight. I found it fun to read, and really learned a lot from it.

[NISPlus] Rick Ramsey: *All about Administering NIS+*. Prentice-Hall, 1993. ISBN 0-13-068800-2.

The Background

The following is a list of books that might be of interest to people who want to know more about *how* TCP/IP and its applications work, but don't want to read RFCs.

[Stevens90] Richard W. Stevens: *UNIX Network Programming*. Prentice-Hall International, 1990. ISBN 0-13-949876-X.

This is probably *the* most widely used book on TCP/IP network programming, which, at the same time, tells you a lot about the nuts and bolts of the Internet Protocols.[3]

[Tanen89] Andrew S. Tanenbaum: *Computer Networks*. Prentice-Hall International, 1989. ISBN 0-13-166836-6[4].

This book gives you a very good insight into general networking issues. Using the OSI Reference Model, it explains the design issues of each layer, and the algorithms that may be used to achieve these. At each layer, the implementations of several networks, among them the ARPAnet, are compared to each other.

The only drawback this book has is the abundance of abbreviations, which sometimes makes it hard to follow what the author says. But this is probably inherent to networking.

---

[3] Note that Stevens has just written a new TCP/IP, called *TCP/IP Illustrated, Volume 1, The Protocols*, published by Addison Wesley. I didn't have the time to look at it, though.

[4] The ISBN under which it is available in North America might be different.

[Comer88] Douglas R. Comer: *Internetworking with TCP/IP: Principles, Protocols, and Architecture*. Prentice-Hall International, 1988.

Miscellaneous and Legalese

RFCs

The following is a list of RFCs mentioned throughout this book. All RFCs are available via anonymous FTP from **nic.ddn.mil**, **ftp.uu.net**. To obtain an RFC via email, send a message to **service@nic.ddn.mil**, putting the request `send RFC-`*number*`.TXT` in the subject header line.

1340 Assigned Numbers, *Postel, J.*, and *Reynolds, J.* The Assigned Numbers RFC defines the meaning of numbers used in various protocols, such as the port numbers standard TCP and UDP servers are known to listen on, and the protocol numbers used in the IP datagram header.

1144 Compressing TCP/IP headers for low-speed serial links, *Jacobson, V.* This document describes the algorithm used to compress TCP/IP headers in CSLIP and PPP. Very worthwhile reading!

1033 Domain Administrators Operations Guide, *Lottor, M.* Together with its companion RFCs, RFC 1034 and RFC 1035, this is the definitive source on DNS, the Domain Name System.

1034 Domain Names - Concepts and Facilities, *Mockapetris, P.V.* A companion to RFC 1033.

1035 Domain names - Implementation and Specification, *Mockapetris, P.V.* A companion to RFC 1033.

974 Mail Routing and the Domain System, *Partridge, C.* This RFC describes mail routing on the Internet. Read this for the full story about MX records...

977 Network News Transfer Protocol, *Kantor, B.*, and *Lapsley, P.* The definition of NNTP, the common news transport used on the Internet.

1094 NFS: Network File System Protocol specification, *Nowicki, B.* The formal specification of the NFS and mount protocols (version 2).

1055 Nonstandard for Transmission of IP Datagrams over Serial Lines: SLIP, *Romkey, J.L.* Describes SLIP, the Serial Line Internet Protocol.

1057 RPC: Remote Procedure Call Protocol Specification: Version 2, *Sun Microsystems, Inc*

1058 Routing Information Protocol, *Hedrick, C.L.* Describes RIP, which is used to exchange dynamic routing information within LANs and MANs.

821 Simple Mail Transfer Protocol, *Postel, J.B.* Defines SMTP, the mail transport protocol over TCP/IP.

1036 Standard for the Interchange of USENET messages, *Adams, R.*, and *Horton, M.R.* This RFC describes the format of Usenet News messages, and how they are exchanged on the Internet as well as on UUCP networks. A revision of this RFC is expected to be released sometime soon.

822 Standard for the Format of ARPA Internet text messages, *Crocker, D.* This is the definitive source of wisdom regarding, well, RFC-conformant mail. Everyone knows it, few have really read it.

968 Twas the Night Before Start-up, *Cerf, V.* Who says the heroes of networking remain unsung?

RFCs

Part IV

"Linux Access HOWTO" by Michael De La Rue,

access-howto@ed.ac.uk

Contents

Abstract

v2.11, 28 March 1997
The Linux Access HOWTO covers the use of adaptive technology with Linux; in particular, using adaptive technology to make Linux accessible to those who could not use it otherwise. It also covers areas where Linux can be used within more general adaptive technology solutions.

1 Introduction

The aim of this document is to serve as an introduction to the technologies which are available to make Linux usable by people who, through some disability would otherwise have problems with it. In other words, the target groups of the technologies are, the blind, the partially sighted, deaf and the physically disabled. As any other technologies or pieces of information are discovered they will be added.

The information here is not just for these people (although that is probably the main aim) but also to allow developers of Linux to become aware of the difficulties involved here. Possibly the biggest problem is that, right now, very few of the developers of Linux are aware of the issues and various simple ways to make life simpler for implementors of these systems. This has, however, changed noticeably since the introduction of this document, and at least to a small extent because of this document, but also to a large extent due to the work of some dedicated developers, many of whom are mentioned in the document's Acknowledgements.

Please send any comments or extra information or offers of assistance to <access-howto@ed.ac.uk> This address might become a mailing list in future, or be automatically handed over to a future maintainer of the HOWTO, so please don't use it for personal email.

I don't have time to follow developments in all areas. I probably won't even read a mail until I have time to update this document. It's still gratefully received. If a mail is sent to the blind-list or the access-list, I *will* eventually read it and put any useful information into the document. Otherwise, please send a copy of anything interesting to the above email address.

Normal mail can be sent to

```
Linux Access HOWTO
23 Kingsborough Gardens
Glasgow G12 9NH
Scotland
U.K.
```

and will gradually make its way round the world to me. Email will be faster by weeks.

I can be personally contacted using <miked@ed.ac.uk>. Since I use mail filtering on all mail I receive, please use the other address except for personal email. This is most likely to lead to an appropriate response.

1.1 Distribution Policy

2 Comparing Linux with other Operating Systems

2.1 General Comparison

The best place to find out about this is in such documents as the 'Linux Info Sheet', 'Linux Meta-FAQ' and 'Linux Frequently Asked Questions with Answers' (see 7.1). Major reasons for a visually impaired person to use Linux would include its inbuilt networking which gives full access to the Internet. More generally, users are attracted by the full development environment included. Also, unlike most other modern GUI environments, the graphical front end to Linux (X Window System) is clearly separated from the underlying environment and there is a complete set of modern programs such as World Wide Web browsers and fax software which work directly in the non graphical environment. This opens up the way to provide alternative access paths to the systems functionality; Emacspeak is a good example.

For other users, the comparison is probably less favorable and less clear. People with very specific and complex needs will find that the full development system included allows properly customized solutions. However, much of the software which exists on other systems is only just beginning to become available. More development is being done however in almost all directions.

2.2 Availability of Adaptive Technology

There is almost nothing commercial available *specifically* for Linux. There is a noticeable amount of free software which would be helpful in adaptation, for example, a free speech synthesizer and some free voice control software. There are also a number of free packages which provide good support for certain Braille terminals, for example.

2.3 Inherent Usability

Linux has the vast advantage over Windows in that most of its software is command line oriented. This is now changing and almost everything is now available with a graphical front end. However, because it is in origin a programmer's operating system, line-oriented programs are still being written covering almost all new areas of interest. For the physically disabled, this means that it is easy to build custom programs to suit their needs. For the visually impaired, this should make use with a speech synthesizer or Braille terminal easy and useful for the foreseeable future.

Linux's multiple virtual consoles system make it practical to use as a multi-tasking operating system by a visually impaired person working directly through Braille.

The windowing system used by Linux (X11) comes with many programming tools, and should be adaptable. However, in practice, the adaptive programs available up till now have been more primitive than those on the Macintosh or Windows. They are, however, completely free (as opposed to hundreds of pounds) and the quality is definitely improving.

In principle it should be possible to put together a complete, usable Linux system for a visually impaired person for about $500 (cheap & nasty PC + sound card). This compares with many thousands of dollars for other operating systems (screen reader software/ speech synthesizer hardware). I have yet to see this. I doubt it would work in practice because the software speech synthesizers available for Linux aren't yet sufficiently good. For a physically disabled person, the limitation will still be the expense of input hardware.

3 Visually Impaired

I'll use two general categories here. People who are partially sighted and need help seeing / deciphering / following the text and those who are unable to use any visual interface whatsoever.

3.1 Seeing the Screen with Low Vision

There are many different problems here. Often magnification can be helpful, but that's not the full story. Sometimes people can't track motion, sometimes people can't find the cursor unless it moves. This calls for a range of techniques, the majority of which are only just being added to X.

3.1.1 SVGATextMode

This program is useful for improving the visibility of the normal text screen that Linux provides. The normal screen that Linux provides shows 80 characters across by 25 vertically. This can be changed (and the quality of those characters improved) using SVGATextMode. The program allows full access to the possible modes of an SVGA graphics card. For example, the text can be made larger so that only 50 by 15 characters appear on the screen. There isn't any easy way to zoom in on sections of a screen, but you can resize when needed.

3.1.2 X Window System

For people who can see the screen there are a large number of ways of improving X. They don't add up to a coherent set of features yet, but if set up correctly could solve many problems.

Different Screen Resolutions The X server can be set up with many different resolutions. A single key press can then change between them allowing difficult to read text to be seen.

In the file `/etc/XF86Config`, you have an entry in the Screen section with a line beginning with modes. If, for example, you set this to

```
Modes        "1280x1024" "1024x768" "800x600" "640x480" "320x240"
```

with each mode set up correctly (which requires a reasonably good monitor for the highest resolution mode), you will be able to have four times screen magnification, switching between the different levels using

`Ctrl+Alt+Keypad-Plus` and `Ctrl+Alt+Keypad-Minus`

Moving the mouse around the screen will scroll you to different parts of the screen. For more details on how to set this up you should see the documentation which comes with the **XFree86** X server.

Screen Magnification There are several known screen magnification programs, `xmag` which will magnify a portion of the screen as much as needed but is very primitive. Another one is `xzoom`. Previously I said that there had to be something better than `xmag`, well this is it. See section 8.6.

Another program which is available is `puff`. This is specifically oriented towards visually impaired users. It provides such features as a box around the pointer which makes it easier to locate. Other interesting features of `puff` are that, if correctly set up, it is able to select and magnify portions of the screen as they are updated. However, there seem to be interactions between `xpuff` and the window manager which could make it difficult to use. When used with my `fvwm` setup, it didn't respond at all to key presses. However using `twm` improved the situation.

The final program which I have seen working is `dynamag`. This again has some specific advantages such as the ability to select a specific area of the screen and monitor it, refreshing the magnified display at regular intervals between a few tenths of a second at twenty seconds. `dynamag` is part of the UnWindows distribution. See 8.8 for more details.

Change Screen Font The screen fonts all properly written X software should be changeable. You can simply make it big enough for you to read. This is generally accomplished by putting a line the file `.Xdefaults` which should be in your home directory. By putting the correct lines in this you can change the fonts of your programs, for example

```
Emacs.font: -sony-fixed-medium-r-normal--16-150-75-75-c-80-iso8859-*
```

To see what fonts are available, use the program `xfontsel` under X.

There should be some way of changing things at a more fundamental level so that everything comes out with a magnified font. This could be done by renaming fonts, and by telling telling font generating programs to use a different level of scaling. If someone gets this to work properly, please send me the details of how you did it.

Cross Hair Cursors etc.. For people that have problems following cursors there are many things which can help;

- cross-hair cursors (horizontal and vertical lines from the edge of the screen)
- flashing cursors (flashes when you press a key)

No software I know of specifically provides a cross hair cursor. `puff`, mentioned in the previous section does however provide a flashing box around the cursor which can make it considerably easier to locate.

For now the best that can be done is to change the cursor bitmap. Make a bitmap file as you want it, and another one which is the same size, but completely black. Convert them to the XBM format and run

```
xsetroot -cursor cursorfile.xbm black-file.xbm
```

actually, if you understand masks, then the black-file doesn't have to be completely black, but start with it like that. The `.Xdefaults` file controls cursors used by actual applications. For much more information, please see the X11-big-cursor Mini-HOWTO, by Joerg Schneider <schneid@ira.uka.de>.

3.1.3 Audio

Provided that the user can hear, audio input can be very useful for making a more friendly and communicative computing environment. For a person with low vision, audio clues can be used to help locate the pointer (see 8.8). For a console mode user using Emacspeak (see 8.1), the audio icons available will provide very many useful facilities.

Setting up Linux audio is covered in the Linux Sound HOWTO (see 7.1). Once sound is set up, sounds can be played with the `play` command which is included with most versions of Linux. This is the way to use my version of UnWindows.

3.1.4 Producing Large Print

Using large print with Linux is quite easy. There are several techniques.

LaTeX / TeX LaTeX is an extremely powerful document preparation system. It may be used to produce large print documents of almost any nature. Though somewhat complicated to learn, many documents are produced using LaTeX or the underlying typesetting program, TeX.

This will produce some reasonably large text

```
\font\magnifiedtenrm=cmr10 at 20pt  \% setup a big font
\magnifiedtenrm
this is some large text
\bye
```

For more details, see the LaTeX book which is available in any computer book shop. There are also a large number of introductions available on the Internet.

3.1.5 Outputting Large Text

Almost all Linux printing uses PostScript, and Linux can drive almost any printer using it. I output large text teaching materials using a standard Epson dot matrix printer.

For users of X, there are various tools available which can produce large Text. These include `LyX`, and many commercial word processors.

3.2 Aids for Those Who Can't Use Visual Output

For someone who is completely unable to use a normal screen there are two alternatives: Braille and Speech. Obviously for people who also have hearing loss, speech isn't always useful, so Braille will always be important.

If you can choose, which should you choose? This is a matter of 'vigorous' debate. Speech is rapid to use, reasonably cheap and especially good for textual applications (e.g. reading a long document like this one). Problems include needing a quiet environment, possibly needing headphones to work without disturbing others and avoid being listened in on by them (not available for all speech synthesizers).

Braille is better for applications where precise layout is important (e.g. spreadsheets). Also it can be somewhat more convenient if you want to check the beginning of a sentence when you get to the end. Braille is, however, much more expensive and slower for reading text. Obviously, the more you use Braille, the faster you get. Grade II Braille is difficult to learn, but is almost certainly worth it since it is much faster. This means that if you don't use Braille for a fair while you can never discover its full potential and decide for yourself. Anyway, enough said on this somewhat controversial topic. (Based on original by James Bowden <jrbowden@bcs.org.uk>)

3.2.1 Braille Terminals

Braille terminals are normally a line or two of Braille. Since these are at most 80 characters wide and normally 40 wide, they are somewhat limited. I know of two kinds:

- Hardware driven Braille terminals.
- Software driven Braille terminals.

The first kind works only when the computer is in text mode and reads the screen memory directly. See section 9.1.

The second kind of Braille terminal is similar, in many ways, to a normal terminal screen of the kind Linux supports automatically. Unfortunately, they need special software to make them usable.

There are two packages which help with these. The first, `BRLTTY`, works with several Braille display types and the authors are keen to support more as information becomes available. Currently `BRLTTY` supports Tieman B.V.'s CombiBraille series, Alva B.V.'s ABT3 series and Telesensory Systems Inc.'s PowerBraille and Navigator series displays. The use of Blazie Engineering's Braille Lite as a Braille display is discouraged, but support may be renewed on demand. See section 9.2.

The other package I am aware of is Braille Enhanced Screen. This is designed to work on other UNIX systems as well as Linux. This should allow user access to a Braille terminal with many useful features such as the ability to run different programs in different 'virtual terminals' at the same time.

3.2.2 Speech Synthesis

Speech Synthesizers take (normally) ASCII text and convert it into actual spoken output. It is possible to have these implemented as either hardware or software. Unfortunately, the free Linux speech synthesizers are, reportedly, not good enough to use as a sole means of output.

Hardware speech synthesizers are the alternative. The main one that I know of that works is DECtalk from Digital, driven by `emacspeak`. However, at this time (March 1997) a driver for the Doubletalk synthesizer has been announced. Using `emacspeak` full access to all of the facilities of Linux is fairly easy. This includes the normal use of the shell, a world wide web browser and many other similar features, such as email. Although, it only acts as a plain text reader (similar to IBM's one for the PC) when controlling programs it doesn't understand, with those that it does, it can provide much more sophisticated control. See section 8.1 for more information about `emacspeak`.

3.2.3 Handling Console Output

When it starts up, Linux at present puts all of its messages straight to the normal (visual) screen. This could be changed if anyone with a basic level of kernel programming ability wants to do it. This means that it is impossible for most Braille devices to get information about what Linux is doing before the operating system is completely working.

It is only at that stage that you can start the program that you need for access. If the BRLTTY program is used and run very early in the boot process, then from this stage on the messages on the screen can be read. Most hardware and software will still have to wait until the system is completely ready. This makes administering a Linux system difficult, but not impossible for a visually impaired person. Once the system is ready however, you can scroll back by pressing (on the default keyboard layout) Shift-PageUp.

There is one Braille system that can use the console directly, called the Braillex. This is designed to read directly from the screen memory. Unfortunately the normal scrolling of the terminal gets in the way of this. If you are using a Kernel newer than 1.3.75, just type `linux no-scroll` at the LILO prompt or configure LILO to do this automatically. If you have an earlier version of Linux, see section 9.1

The other known useful thing to do is to use sounds to say when each stage of the boot process has been reached. (T.V. Raman suggestion)

3.2.4 Optical Character Recognition

There is a free Optical Character Recognition (OCR) program for Linux called `xocr`. In principle, if it is good enough, this program would allow visually impaired people to read normal books to some extent (accuracy of OCR is never high enough..). However, according to the documentation, this program needs training to recognize the particular font that it is going to use and I have no idea how good it is since I don't have the hardware to test it.

3.3 Beginning to Learn Linux

Beginning to learn Linux can seem difficult and daunting for someone who is either coming from no computing background or from a pure DOS background. Doing the following things may help:

- Learn to use Linux (or UNIX) on someone else's system before setting up your own.
- Initially control Linux from your own known speaking/Braille terminal. If you plan to use speech, you may want to learn `emacs` now. You can learn it as you go along though. See below
- If you come from an MS-DOS background, read the DOS2Linux Mini HOWTO for help with converting (see 7.1.4).

The Emacspeak HOWTO written by Jim Van Zandt (<jrv@vanzandt.mv.com>) covers this in much more detail (see 7.1.4).

If you are planning to use Emacspeak, you should know that Emacspeak does not attempt to teach Emacs, so in this sense, prior knowledge of Emacs would always be useful. This said, you certainly do not need to know much about Emacs to start using Emacspeak. In fact, once Emacspeak is installed and running, it provides a fluent interface to the rich set of online documentation including the info pages, and makes learning what you need a lot easier.

"In summary: starting to use Emacspeak takes little learning. Getting the full mileage out of Emacs and Emacspeak, especially if you intend using it as a replacement for X Windows as I do does involve eventually becoming familiar with a lot of the Emacs extensions; but this is an incremental process and does not need to be done in a day." - *T.V.Raman*

One other option which may be interesting are the RNIB training tapes which include one covering UNIX. These can be got from

```
RNIB
Customer Services
PO Box 173
Peterborough
Cambridgeshire PE2 6WS
Tel: 01345 023153 (probably only works in UK)
```

3.4 Braille Embossing

Linux should be the perfect platform to drive a Braille embosser from. There are many formatting tools which are aimed specifically at the fixed width device. A Braille embosser can just be connected to the serial port using the standard Linux printing mechanisms. For more info see the Linux Printing HOWTO.

There is a free software package which acts as a multi-lingual grade two translator available for Linux from the American "National Federation for the Blind". This is called NFBtrans. See section 8.7 for more details.

4 Hearing Problems

For the most part there is little problem using a computer for people with hearing problems. Almost all of the output is visual. There are some situations where sound output is used though. For these, the problem can sometimes be worked round by using visual output instead.

4.1 Visual Bells

By tradition, computers go 'beep' when some program sends them a special code. This is generally used to get attention to the program and for little else. Most of the time, it's possible to replace this by making the entire screen (or terminal emulator) flash. How to do this is very variable though.

xterm (under X)

for xterm, you can either change the setting by pressing the middle mouse button while holding down the control key, or by putting a line with just '`XTerm*visualBell:    true`' (not the quotes of course) in the file `.Xdefaults` in your home directory.

the console (otherwise)

The console is slightly more complex. Please see Alessandro Rubini's Visible bell mini HOWTO for details on this. Available along with all the other Linux documentation (see section 7.1). Mostly the configuration has to be done on a per application basis, or by changing the Linux Kernel itself.

5 Physical Problems

Many of these problems have to be handled individually. The needs of the individual, the ways that they can generate input and other factors vary so much that all that this HOWTO can provide is a general set of pointers to useful software and expertise.

5.1 Unable to Use a Mouse/Pointer

Limited mobility can make it difficult to use a mouse. For some people a tracker ball can be a very good solution, but for others the only possible input device is a keyboard (or even something which simulates a keyboard). For normal use of Linux this shouldn't be a problem (but see the section 5.3), but for users of X, this may cause major problems under some circumstances.

Fortunately, the `fvwm` window manager has been designed for use without a pointer and most things can be done using this. I actually do this myself when I lose my mouse (don't ask) or want to just keep typing. `fvwm` is included with all distributions of Linux that I know of. Actually using other programs will depend on their ability to accept key presses. Many X programs do this for all functions. Many don't. Sticky mouse keys, which are supposedly present in the current release of X, should make this easier.

5.1.1 Unable to Use a Keyboard

People who are unable to use a keyboard normally can sometimes use one through a head stick or a mouth stick. This calls for special setup of the keyboard. Please see also the section 5.3.

Other Input Hardware (X Window System only) For others, the keyboard cannot be used at all and only pointing devices are available. In this case, no solution is available under the standard Linux Console and X will have to be used. If the X-Input extension can be taught to use the device and the correct software for converting pointer input to characters can be found (I haven't seen it yet) then any pointing should be usable without a keyboard.

There are a number of devices worth considering for such input such as touch screens and eye pointers. Many of these will need a 'device driver' written for them. This is not terribly difficult if the documentation is available, but requires someone with good C programming skills. Please see the *Linux Kernel Hackers guide* and other kernel reference materials for more information. Once this is set up, it should be possible to use these devices like a normal mouse.

5.1.2 Controlling Physical Hardware From Linux

The main group of interest here are the Linux Lab Project. Generally, much GPIB (a standard interface to scientific equipment, also known as the IEEE bus) hardware can be controlled. This potentially gives much potential for very ambitious accessibility projects. As far as I know none have yet been attempted.

5.2 Speech Recognition

Speech recognition is a very powerful tool for enabling computer use. There are two recognition systems that I know of for Linux, the first is `ears` which is described as "recognition is not optimal. But it is fine for playing and will be improved", the second is `AbbotDemo` "A speaker independent continuous speech recognition system" which may well be more interesting, though isn't available for commercial use without prior arrangement. See the Linux software map for details (see section 7.1).

5.3 Making the Keyboard Behave

5.3.1 X Window System.

The latest X server which comes with Linux can include many features which assist in input. This includes such features as StickKeys, MouseKeys, RepeatKeys, BounceKeys, SlowKeys, and TimeOut. These allow customization of the keyboard to the needs of the user. These are provided as part of the `XKB`> extension in versions of X after version 6.1. To find out your version and see whether you have the extension installed, you can try.

```
xdpyinfo -queryExtensions
```

5.3.2 Getting Rid of Auto Repeat

To turn off key repeat on the Linux console run this command (I think it has to be run once per console; a good place to run it would be in your login files, `.profile` or `.login` in your home directory).

```
setterm -repeat off
```

To get rid of auto repeat on any X server, you can use the command

```
xset -r
```

which you could put into the file which get runs when you start using X (often `.xsession` or `.xinit` under some setups)

Both of these commands are worth looking at for more ways of changing behavior of the console.

5.3.3 Macros / Much input, few key presses

Often in situations such as this, the biggest problem is speed of input. Here the most important thing to aim for is the most number of commands with the fewest key presses. For users of the shell (`bash` / `tcsh`) you should look at the manual page, in particular command and filename completion (press the tab key and bash tries to guess what should come next). For information on macros which provide sequences of commands for just one key press, have a look at the Keystroke HOWTO.

5.3.4 Sticky Keys

Sticky keys are a feature that allow someone who can only reliably press one button at a time to use a keyboard with all of the various modifier keys such as shift and control. These keys, instead of having to be held on at the same time as the other key instead become like the caps lock key and stay on while the other key is pressed. They may then either switch off or stay on for the next key depending on what is needed. For information about how to set this up please see the Linux Keyboard HOWTO, especially section 'I can use only one finger to type with' (section 15 in the version I have) for more information on this. - Information from Toby Reed.

6 General Programming Issues

Many of the issues worth taking into account are the same when writing software which is designed to be helpful for access as when trying to follow good design.

6.1 Try to Make it Easy to Provide Multiple Interfaces

If your software is only usable through a graphical interface, then it can be very hard to make it usable for someone who can't see. If it's only usable through a line oriented interface, then someone who can't type will have difficulties.

Provide keyboard shortcuts as well as the use of the normal X pointer (generally the mouse). You can almost certainly rely on the user being able to generate key presses to your application.

6.2 Make software configurable.

If it's easy to change fonts then people will be able to change to one they can read. If the color scheme can be changed then people who are color blind will be more likely to be able to use it. If fonts can be changed easily then the visually impaired will find your software more useful.

6.3 Test the Software on Users.

If you have a number of people use your software, each with different access problems, then they will be more likely to point up specific problems. Obviously, this won't be practical for everybody, but you can always ask for feedback.

6.4 Make Output Distinct

Where possible, make it clear what different parts of your program are what. Format error messages in a specific way to identify them. Under X, make sure each pane of your window has a name so that any screen reader software can identify it.

6.5 Licenses

Some software for Linux (though none of the key programs) has a license like 'not for commercial use'. This could be quite bad for a person who starts using the software for their personal work and then possibly begins to be able to do work they otherwise couldn't with it. This could be something which frees them from financial and other dependence on others people. Even if the author of the software is willing to make exceptions, it makes the user vulnerable both to changes of commercial conditions (some company buys up the rights) and to refusal from people they could work for (many companies are overly paranoid about licenses). It is much better to avoid this kind of licensing where possible. Protection from commercial abuse of software can be obtained through more specific licenses like the GNU General Public License or Artistic License where needed.

7 Other Information

7.1 Linux Documentation

The Linux documentation is critical to the use of Linux and most of the documents mentioned here should be included in recent versions of Linux, from any source I know of.

If you want to get the documentation on the Internet, here are some example sites. These should be mirrored at most of the major FTP sites in the world.

- ftp.funet.fi (128.214.6.100) : /pub/OS/Linux/doc/
- tsx-11.mit.edu (18.172.1.2) : /pub/linux/docs/
- sunsite.unc.edu (152.2.22.81) : /pub/Linux/docs/

7.1.1 The Linux Info Sheet

A simple and effective explanation of what Linux is. This is one of the things that you should hand over when you want to explain why you want Linux and what it is good for.

The Linux Info Sheet is available on the World Wide Web from
`(http://sunsite.unc.edu/mdw/HOWTO/INFO-SHEET.html)`
and other mirrors.

7.1.2 The Linux Meta FAQ

A list of other information resources, much more complete than this one. The meta FAQ is available on the World Wide Web from `(http://sunsite.unc.edu/mdw/HOWTO/META-FAQ.html)` and other mirrors

7.1.3 The Linux Software Map

The list of software available for Linux on the Internet. Many of the packages listed here were found through this. The LSM is available in a searchable form from `(http://www.boutell.com/lsm/)`. It is also available in a single text file in all of the FTP sites mentioned in section 7.1.

7.1.4 The Linux HOWTO documents

The HOWTO documents are the main documentation of Linux. This Access HOWTO is an example of one.

The home site for the Linux Documentation Project which produces this information is

`(http://sunsite.unc.edu/mdw/linux.html)`.

There are also many companies producing these in book form. Contact a local Linux supplier for more details.

The Linux HOWTO documents will be in the directory `HOWTO` in all of the FTP sites mentioned in section 7.1.

7.1.5 The Linux FAQ

A list of 'Frequently Asked Questions' with answers which should solve many common questions. The FAQ list is available from `(http://www.cl.cam.ac.uk/users/iwj10/linux-faq/)` as well as all of the FTP sites mentioned in section 7.1.

7.2 Mailing Lists

There are two lists that I know of covering these issues specifically for Linux. There are also others which it is worth researching which cover computer use more generally. Incidentally, if a mail is sent to these lists I *will* read it eventually and include any important information in the Access-HOWTO, so you don't need to send me a separate copy unless it's urgent in some way.

7.2.1 The Linux Access List

This is a general list covering Linux access issues. It is designed 'to service the needs of users and developers of the Linux OS and software who are either disabled or want to help make Linux more accessible'. To subscribe send email to <majordomo@ssv1.union.utah.edu> and in the BODY (not the subject) of the email message put:

```
subscribe linux-access <your-email-address>
```

7.2.2 The Linux Blind List

This is a mailing list covering Linux use for blind users. There is also a list of important and useful software being gathered in the list's archive. To subscribe send mail to <blinux-list-request@redhat.com> with the `subject: help`. This list is now moderated.

7.3 WWW References

The World Wide Web is, by its nature, very rapidly changing. If you are reading this document in an old version, then some of these are likely to be out of date. The original version that I maintain on the WWW shouldn't go more than a month or two out of date, so refer to that please.

Linux Documentation is available from `(http://sunsite.unc.edu/mdw/linux.html)`

Linux Access On the Web `(http://www.tardis.ed.ac.uk/~mikedlr/access/)` with all of the versions of the HOWTO in `(http://www.tardis.ed.ac.uk/~mikedlr/access/HOWTO/)`. Preferably, however, download from one of the main Linux FTP sites. If I get a vast amount of traffic I'll have to close down these pages and move them elsewhere.

The BLINUX Documentation and Development Project `(http://leb.net/blinux/)`. "The purpose of The BLINUX Documentation and Development Project is to serve as a catalyst which will both spur and speed the development of software and documentation which will enable the blind user to run his or her own Linux workstation."

Emacspeak WWW page `(http://cs.cornell.edu/home/raman/emacspeak/emacspeak.html)`

BRLTTY unofficial WWW page `(http://www.sf.co.kr/t.linux/new/brltty.html)`

Yahoo (one of the most major Internet catalogs)
`(http://www.yahoo.com/Society_and_Culture/Disabilities/Adaptive_Technology/)`

The Linux Lab Project `(http://www.fu-berlin.de/~clausi/)`.

The BLYNX pages: Lynx Support Files Tailored For Blind and Visually Handicapped Users

`(http://leb.net/blinux/blynx/)`.

7.4 Suppliers

This is a UK supplier for the Braillex.

```
Alphavision Limited
```

7.5 Manufacturers

7.5.1 Alphavision

I think that they are a manufacturer? RNIB only lists them as a supplier, but others say they make the Braillex.

```
Alphavision Ltd
Seymour House
Copyground Lane
High Wycombe
Bucks HP12 3HE
England
U.K.
```

Phone
: +44 1494-530 555

Linux Supported Alphavision AT Products

- Braillex

7.5.2 Blazie Engineering

The Braille Lite was supported in the original version of `BRLTTY`. That support has now been discontinued. If you have one and want to use it with Linux then that may be possible by using this version of the software.

```
Blazie Engineering
105 East Jarrettsville Rd.
Forest Hill, MD 21050
U.S.A.
```

Phone
: +1 (410) 893-9333

FAX
: +1 (410) 836-5040

BBS
: +1 (410) 893-8944

E-Mail
: <info@blazie.com>

WWW
: (http://www.blazie.com/)

Blazie AT Products

- Braille Lite (support discontinued)

7.5.3 Digital Equipment Corporation

```
Digital Equipment Corporation
P.O. Box CS2008
Nashua
NH 03061-2008
U.S.A
```

Order
: +1 800-722-9332

Tech info
: +1 800-722-9332

FAX
: +1 603-884-5597

WWW
: (http://www.digital.com/)

Linux Supported DEC AT Products

- DECTalk Express

7.5.4 Kommunikations-Technik Stolper GmbH


```
KTS Stolper GmbH
Herzenhaldenweg 10
73095 Albershausen
Germany
```

Phone

+49 7161 37023

Fax

+49 7161 32632

Linux Supported KTG AT Products

- Brailloterm

8 Software Packages

References in this section are taken directly from the Linux Software map which can be found in all standard places for Linux documentation and which lists almost all of the software available for Linux.

8.1 Emacspeak

Emacspeak is the software side of a speech interface to Linux. Any other character based program, such as a WWW browser, or `telnet` or another editor can potentially be used within `emacspeak`. The main difference between it and normal screen reader software for such operating systems as DOS is that it also has a load more extra features. It is based in the emacs text editor.

A text editor is generally just a program which allows you to change the contents of a file, for example, adding new information to a letter. Emacs is in fact far beyond a normal text editor, and so this package is much more useful than you might imagine. You can run any other program from within emacs, getting any output it generates to appear in the emacs terminal emulator.

The reason that emacs is a better environment for Emacspeak is that it can can understand the layout of the screen and can intelligently interpret the meaning of, for example, a calendar, which would just be a messy array of numbers otherwise. The originator of the package manages to look after his own Linux machine entirely, doing all of the administration from within emacs. He also uses it to control a wide variety of other machines and software directly from that machine.

Emacspeak is included within the Debian Linux distribution and is included as contributed software within the Slackware distribution. This means that it is available on many of the CDROM distributions of Linux. By the time this is published, the version included should be 5 or better, but at present I only have version 4 available for examination.

```
Begin3
Title:          emacspeak - a speech output interface to Emacs
Version:        4.0
Entered-date:   30MAY96
Description:    Emacspeak is the first full-fledged speech output
                system that will allow someone who cannot see to work
                directly on a UNIX system. (Until now, the only option
                available to visually impaired users has been to use a
                talking PC as a terminal.) Emacspeak is built on top
                of Emacs. Once you start emacs with emacspeak loaded,
                you get spoken feedback for everything you do. Your
                mileage will vary depending on how well you can use
                Emacs.  There is nothing that you cannot do inside
                Emacs:-)
Keywords:       handicap access visually impaired blind speech emacs
Author:         raman@adobe.com (T. V. Raman)
Maintained-by:  jrv@vanzandt.mv.com (Jim Van Zandt)
```

```
Primary-site:    sunsite.unc.edu apps/sound/speech
                 124kB   emacspeak-4.0.tgz
Alternate-site:
Original-site:   http://www.cs.cornell.edu /pub/raman/emacspeak
                 123kB   emacspeak.tar.gz/Info/People/raman/emacspeak/emacspeak.tar.gz
Platforms:       DECtalk Express or DEC Multivoice speech synthesizer,
                 GNU FSF Emacs 19 (version 19.23 or later) and TCLX
                 7.3B (Extended TCL).
Copying-policy: GPL
End
```

8.2 BRLTTY

This is a program for running a serial port Braille terminal. It has been widely tested and used, and supports a number of different kinds of hardware (see the Linux Software Map entry below).

The maintainer is, Nikhil Nair <nn201@cus.cam.ac.uk>. The other people working on it are Nicolas Pitre <nico@cam.org> and Stephane Doyon <doyons@jsp.umontreal.ca>. Send any comments to all of them.

The authors seem keen to get support in for more different devices, so if you have one you should consider contacting them. They will almost certainly need programming information for the device, so if you can contact your manufacturer and get that they are much more likely to be able to help you.

A brief feature list (from their README file) to get you interested

- Full implementation of the standard screen review facilities.
- A wide range of additional optional features, including blinking cursor and capital letters, screen freezing for leisurely review, attribute display to locate highlighted text, hypertext links, etc.
- 'Intelligent' cursor routing. This allows easy movement of the cursor in text editors etc. without moving the hands from the Braille display.
- A cut & paste function. This is particularly useful for copying long filenames, complicated commands etc.
- An on-line help facility.
- Support for multiple Braille codes.
- Modular design allows relatively easy addition of drivers for other Braille displays, or even (hopefully) porting to other Unix-like platforms.

```
Begin3
Title:           BRLTTY - Access software for Unix for a blind person
                          using a soft Braille terminal
Version:         1.0.2, 17SEP96
Entered-date:    17SEP96
Description:     BRLTTY is a daemon which provides access to a Unix console
                 for a blind person using a soft Braille display (see the
                 README file for a full explanation).

                 BRLTTY only works with text-mode applications.

                 We hope that this system will be expanded to support
                 other soft Braille displays, and possibly even other
                 Unix-like platforms.
Keywords:        Braille console access visually impaired blind
Author:          nn201@cus.cam.ac.uk (Nikhil Nair)
                 nico@cam.org (Nicolas Pitre)
                 doyons@jsp.umontreal.ca (Stephane Doyon)
                 jrbowden@bcs.org.uk (James Bowden)
Maintained-by:   nn201@cus.cam.ac.uk (Nikhil Nair)
Primary-site:    sunsite.unc.edu /pub/Linux/system/Access
                 110kb brltty-1.0.2.tar.gz (includes the README file)
                   6kb brltty-1.0.2.README
                   1kb brltty-1.0.2.lsm
```

```
  Platforms:        Linux (kernel 1.1.92 or later) running on a PC or DEC Alpha.
                    Not X/graphics.
                    Supported Braille displays (serial communication only):
                      - Tieman B.V.: CombiBraille 25/45/85;
                      - Alva B.V.: ABT3xx series;
                      - Telesensory Systems Inc.: PowerBraille 40 (not 65/80),
                        Navigator 20/40/80 (latest firmware version only?).
  Copying-policy: GPL
  End
```

8.3 Screen

Screen is a standard piece of software to allow many different programs to run at the same time on one terminal. It has been enhanced to support some Braille terminals (those from Telesensory) directly.

8.4 Rsynth

This is a speech synthesizer listed in the Linux Software Map. It doesn't apparently work well enough for use by a visually impaired person. Use hardware instead, or improve it.. a free speech synthesizer would be really really useful.

8.5 xocr

`xocr` is a package which implements optical character recognition for Linux. As with `Rsynth`, I don't think that this will be acceptable as a package for use as a sole means of input by a visually impaired person. I suspect that the algorithm used means that it will need to be watched over by someone who can check that it is reading correctly. I would love to be proved wrong.

8.6 xzoom

`xzoom` is a screen magnifier, in the same vein as `xmag`, but sufficiently better to be very useful to a visually impaired person. The main disadvantages of `xzoom` are that it can't magnify under itself, that some of the key controls aren't compatible with `fvwm`, the normal Linux window manager and that it's default configuration doesn't run over a network (this can be fixed at some expense to speed). Apart from that though, it's excellent. It does continuous magnification which allows you to, for example, scroll a document up and down, whilst keeping the section you are reading magnified. Alternatively, you can move a little box around the screen, magnifying the contents and letting you search for the area you want to see. `xzoom` is also available as an rpm from the normal Red Hat sites, making it very easy to install for people using the rpm system (such as Red Hat users).

```
  Begin3
  Title:          xzoom
  Version:        0.1
  Entered-date:   Mar 30 1996
  Description:    xzoom can magnify (by integer value) rotate
                  (by a multiple if 90 degrees) and mirror about
                  the X or Y axes areas on X11 screen
                  and display them in it's window.
  Keywords:       X11 zoom magnify xmag
  Author:         Itai Nahshon <nahshon@best.com>
  Maintained-by:  Itai Nahshon <nahshon@best.com>
  Primary-site:   sunsite.unc.edu
                  probably in /pub/Linux/X11/xutils/xzoom-0.1.tgz
  Platforms:      Linux+11. Support only for 8-bit depth.
                  Tested only in Linux 1.3.* with the XSVGA 3.1.2
  driver.
                                 Needs the XSHM extension.
  Copying-policy: Free
  End
```

8.7 NFBtrans

nfbtrans is a multi-grade Braille translation program distributed by the National Federation for the Blind in the U.S.A. It is released for free in the hope that someone will improve it. Languages covered are USA English, UK English, Spanish, Russian, Esperanto, German, Biblical Hebrew and Biblical Greek, though others could be added just by writing a translation table. Also covered are some computer and math forms. I have managed to get it to compile under Linux, though, not having a Braille embosser available at the present moment I have not been able to test it.

NFBtrans is available from (ftp://nfb.org/ftp/nfb/Braille/nfbtrans/). After downloading it, you will have to compile it.

8.7.1 Compiling NFBtrans on Linux

I have returned this patch to the maintainer of NFBtrans and he says that he has included it, so if you get a version later than 740, you probably won't have to do anything special. Just follow the instructions included in the package.

```
unzip -L NFBTR740.ZIP    \#or whatever filename you have
mv makefile Makefile
```

Next save the following to a file (e.g. patch-file)

```
*** nfbpatch.c.orig     Tue Mar 12 11:37:28 1996
--- nfbpatch.c  Tue Mar 12 11:37:06 1996
***************
*** 185,190 ****
--- 185,193 ----
    return (finfo.st\_size);
  \}              /* filelength */

+ \#ifndef linux
+ /* pretty safe to assume all linux has usleep I think ?? this should be
+ done properly anyway */
  \#ifdef SYSVR4
  void usleep(usec)
    int usec;
***************
*** 195,200 ****
--- 198,204 ----
UKP  \}           /* usleep */

  \#endif
+ \#endif

  void beep(count)
    int count;
```

and run

```
patch < patch-file
```

then type

```
make
```

and the program should compile.

8.8 UnWindows

UnWindows is a package of access utilities for X which provides many useful facilities for the visually impaired (not blind). It includes a screen magnifier and other customized utilities to help locate the pointer. UnWindows can be downloaded from (ftp://ftp.cs.rpi.edu/pub/unwindows).

As it comes by default, the package will not work on Linux because it relies on special features of Suns. However, some of the utilities do work and I have managed to port most of the rest so this package may be interesting to some people. My port will either be incorporated back into the original or will be available in the BLINUX archives (see 7.3). The remaining utility which doesn't yet work is the configuration utility.

In my version the programs, instead of generating sounds themselves, just call another program. The other program could for example be

```
play /usr/lib/games/xboing/sounds/ouch.au
```

which would make the `xboing` ouch noise, for example it could do this as the pointer hit the left edge of the screen.

8.8.1 dynamag

`dynamag` is a screen magnification program. please see the section on Screen magnification (3.1.2). This program worked in the default distribution.

8.8.2 coloreyes

`coloreyes` makes it easy to find the pointer (mouse) location. It consists of a pair of eyes which always look in the direction of the pointer (like xeyes) and change color depending on how far away the mouse is (unlike xeyes). This doesn't work in the default distribution, but the test version, at the same location, seems to work.

8.8.3 border

`border` is a program which detects when the pointer (mouse) has moved to the edge of the screen and makes a sound according to which edge of the screen has been approached. The version which is available uses a SUN specific sound system. I have now changed this so that instead of that, it just runs a command, which could be any Linux sound program.

8.8.4 un-twm

The window manager is a special program which controls the location of all of the other windows (programs) displayed on the X screen. `un-twm` is a special version which will make a sound as the pointer enters different windows. The sound will depend on what window has been entered. The distributed version doesn't work on linux because, like `border` it relies on SUN audio facilities. Again I already have a special version which will be available by the time you read this.

9 Hardware

9.1 Braille terminals driven from Screen Memory

These are Braille terminals that can read the screen memory directly in a normal text mode. It is possible to use it to work with Linux for almost all of the things that a seeing user can do on the console, including installation. However, it has a problem with the scrolling of the normal Linux kernel, so a kernel patch needs to be applied. See 9.1.3.

9.1.1 Braillex

The Braillex is a terminal which is designed to read directly from the Screen memory, thus getting round any problems with MS-DOS programs which don't behave strangely. If you could see it on screen, then this terminal should be able to display it in Braille. In Linux, unfortunately, screen handling is done differently from MS-DOS, so this has to be changed somewhat.

To get this terminal to work, you have to apply the patch given below in section 9.1.3. Once this is done, the Braillex becomes one of the most convenient ways to use Linux as it allows all of the information normally available to a seeing person to be read. Other terminals don't start working until the operating system has completely booted.

The Braillex is available with two arrangements of Braille cells (80x1 or 40x2) and there is a model, called the IB 2-D which also has a vertical bar to show information about all of the lines of the screen (using 4 programmable dots per screen line)

```
Price: 8,995  (pounds sterling) or 11495 UKP for 2-D
Manufacturer: Alphavision Limited (UK)
Suppliers: ????
```

9.1.2 Brailloterm

"What is Brailloterm?"

It's a refreshable display Braille, made by KTS Kommunikations-Technik Stolper GmbH. It has 80 Braille cells in an unique line. Each cell has 8 dots that are combined (up/down) to represent a character. By default, Brailloterm shows me the line in which the screen cursor is. I can use some functions in Brailloterm to see any line in the screen." - *Jose Vilmar Estacio de Souza* <jvilmar@embratel.net.br>

Jose then goes on to say that the terminal can also use the serial port under DOS but that it needs a special program. I don't know if any of the ones for Linux would work.

As with Braillex, this needs a special patch to the kernel work properly. See section 9.1.3.

```
Price: about 23.000,- DM /  \$ 15.000,
Manufacturer: Kommunikations-Technik Stolper GmbH
Suppliers: ????
```

9.1.3 Patching the Kernel for Braillex and Brailloterm

This probably also applies to any other terminals which read directly from screen memory to work under MS-DOS. Mail me to confirm any terminals that you find work. This does not apply and will actually lose some features for terminals driven using the BRLTTY software.

I am told this patch applies to all Kernels version 1.2.X. It should also work on all Kernel versions from 1.1.X to 1.3.72, with just a warning from patch (I've tested that the patch applies to 1.3.68 at least). **From 1.3.75 the patch is no longer needed** because the Kernel can be configured not to scroll using 'linux no-scroll' at the LILO prompt. See the Boot Prompt HOWTO for more details.

```
*** drivers/char/console.c\~{}  Fri Mar 17 07:31:40 1995
--- drivers/char/console.c      Tue Mar  5 04:34:47 1996
***************
*** 601,605 ****
  static void scrup(int currcons, unsigned int t, unsigned int b)
  \{
!       int hardscroll = 1;

        if (b > video\_num\_lines || t >= b)
--- 601,605 ----
  static void scrup(int currcons, unsigned int t, unsigned int b)
  \{
!       int hardscroll = 0;

        if (b > video\_num\_lines || t >= b)
```

To apply it:

1. Save the above text to a file (say patch-file)
2. change to the drivers/char directory of your kernel sources
3. run

   ```
   patch < patch-file
   ```

4. Compile your kernel as normal

Apply those patches and you should be able to use the Braille terminal as normal to read the Linux Console.

Put in words, the patch just means 'change the 1 to a 0 in the first line of the function `scrup` which should be near line 603 in the file drivers/char/console.c'. The main thing about `patch` is that program understands this, and that it knows how to guess what to do when the Linux developers change things in that file.

If you want to use a more modern kernel with completely disabled scrolling, (instead of the boot prompt solution I already mentioned), please use the following patch. **This does not apply to kernels earlier than 1.3.75**.

```
*** console.c       Fri Mar 15 04:01:45 1996
--- console.c   Thu Apr  4 13:29:48 1996
***************
*** 516,520 ****
```

```
        unsigned char has_wrapped;
      /* all of videomem is data of fg_console */
        static unsigned char hardscroll_enabled;
      ! static unsigned char hardscroll_disabled_by_init = 0;

        void no_scroll(char *str, int *ints)
      --- 516,520 ----
        unsigned char has_wrapped;
       /* all of videomem is data of fg_console */
        static unsigned char hardscroll_enabled;
      ! static unsigned char hardscroll_disabled_by_init = 1;

        void no_scroll(char *str, int *ints)
```

9.2 Software Driven Braille Terminals

The principle of operation of these terminal is very close to that of a CRT terminal such as the VT100. They connect to the serial port and the computer has to run a program which sends them output. At present there are two known programs for Linux. `BRLTTY` (see section 8.2) and Braille enhanced screen.

9.2.1 Tieman B.V.

CombiBraille This Braille terminal is supported by the `BRLTTY` software. It comes in three versions with 25, 45 or 85 Braille cells. The extra five cells over a standard display are used for status information.

```
Price: around 4600 UKP for the 45 cell model ...
Manufacturer: Tieman B.V.
Suppliers: Concept Systems, Nottingham, England (voice +44 115 925 5988)
```

9.2.2 Alva B.V.

The ABT3xx series is supported in `BRLTTY`. Only the ABT340 has been confirmed to work at this time. Please pass back information to the `BRLTTY` authors on other models.

```
Price: 20 cell - 2200 UKP; 40 cell 4500 UKP; 80 cell 8000 UKP
Manufacturer: Alva
Suppliers: Professional Vision Services LTD, Hertshire, England
          (+44 1462 677331)
```

9.2.3 Telesensory Systems Inc. displays

Because they have provided programming information to the developers, the Telesensory displays are supported both by `BRLTTY` and `screen`.

PowerBraille There are three models the 40, the 65 and the 80. Only the 40 is known to be supported by `BRLTTY`.

```
Price: 20 cell - 2200 UKP; 40 cell 4500 UKP; 80 cell 8000 UKP
Manufacturer: Alva
Suppliers: Professional Vision Services LTD, Hertshire, England
          (+44 1462 677331)
```

Navigator Again there are three models the 20, the 60 and the 80. Recent versions are all known to work with `BRLTTY` but whether earlier ones (with earlier firmware) also work has not been confirmed.

```
Price: 80 cell 7800 UKP
Manufacturer: Alva
Suppliers: Professional Vision Services LTD, Hertshire, England
          (+44 1462 677331)
```

9.2.4 Braille Lite

This is more a portable computer than a terminal. It could, however, be used with BRLTTY version 0.22 (but not newer versions) as if it was a normal Braille terminal. Unfortunately, many of the features available with the CombiBraille cannot be used with the Braille Lite. This means that it should be avoided for Linux use where possible.

```
Price: \$3,395.00
Manufacturer: Blazie Engineering
```

9.3 Speech Synthesizers

Speech synthesizers normally connect to the serial port of a PC. Useful features include

- Braille labels on parts
- Many voices to allow different parts of document to be spoken differently
- Use with headphones (not available on all models)

The critical problem is that the quality of the speech. This is much more important to someone who is using the speech synthesiser as their main source of information than to someone who is just getting neat sounds out of a game. For this reason T.V. Raman seems to only recommend the DECTalk. Acceptable alternatives would be good.

9.3.1 DECTalk Express

This is a hardware speech synthesizer. It is recommended for use with Emacspeak and in fact the DECTalk range are the only speech synthesizers which work with that package at present. This synthesizer has every useful feature that I know about. The only disadvantage that I know of at present is price.

```
Price: \$1195.00
Manufacturer: Digital Equipment Corporation

Suppliers: Many.  I'd like details of those with Specific Linux
        support / delivering international or otherwise of note only
        please.  Otherwise refer to local organizations.
        Digital themselves or the Emacspeak WWW pages.
```

9.3.2 Accent SA

This is a synthesizer made by Aicom Corporation. An effort has begun to write a driver for it however help is needed. Please see (http://www.cyberspc.mb.ca/ astrope/speak.html) if you think you can help.

9.3.3 SPO256-AL2 Speak and Spell chip.

Some interest has been expressed in using this chip in self built talking circuits. I'd be interested to know if anyone has found this useful. A software package speak-0.2pl1.tar.gz was produced by David Sugar <dyfet@tycho.com>. My suspicion, though, is that the quality of the output wouldn't be good enough for regular use.

10 Acknowledgements

Much of this document was created from various information sources on the Internet, many found from Yahoo and DEC's Alta Vista Search engine. Included in this was the documentation of most of the software packages mentioned in the text. Some information was also gleaned from the Royal National Institute for the Blind's helpsheets.

T.V. Raman, the author of Emacspeak, has reliably contributed comments, information and text as well as putting me in touch with other people who he knew on the Internet.

Kenneth Albanowski <kjahds@kjahds.com> provided the patch needed for the Brailloterm and information about it.

Roland Dyroff of S.u.S.E. GmbH (Linux distributors and makers of S.u.S.E. Linux (English/German)) looked up KTS Stolper GmbH at my request and got some hardware details and information on the Brailloterm.

The most major and careful checks over of this document were done by James Bowden, <jrbowden@bcs.org.uk> and Nikhil Nair <nn201@cus.cam.ac.uk>, the BRLTTY authors who suggested a large number of corrections as well as extra information for some topics.

The contributors to the blinux and linux-access mailing lists have contributed to this document by providing information for me to read.

Mark E. Novak of the Trace R&D center (`http://trace.wisc.edu/`) pointed me in the direction of several packages of software and information which I had not seen before. He also made some comments on the structure of the document which I have partially taken into account and should probably do more about.

Other contributors include Nicolas Pitrie and Stephane Doyon.

A number of other people have contributed comments and information. Specific contributions are acknowledged within the document.

This version was specifically produced for the Dr. Linux book. This is because they provided warning of its impending release to myself and other LDP authors. Their doing this is strongly appreciated since wrong or old information sits around much longer in a book than on the Internet.

No doubt you made a contribution and I haven't mentioned it. Don't worry, it was an accident. I'm sorry. Just tell me and I will add you to the next version.

Part V

"Alpha Miniloader HOWTO" by David Rusling,

david.rusling@reo.mts.dec.com

Contents

Abstract

v0.84, 6th December 1996
This document describes the Miniloader, a program for Alpha based systems that can be used to initialize the machine and load Linux. The Alpha Linux Miniloader (to give it it's full name) is also known as MILO.

1 Introduction

This document describes the Miniloader for Linux on Alpha AXP (MILO). This firmware is used to initialize Alpha AXP based systems, load and start Linux and, finally, provide PALcode for Linux.

1.1 Copyright

1.2 New Versions of this Document

The latest version of this document can be found in

`ftp://gatekeeper.dec.com/pub/Digital/Linux-Alpha/Miniloader/docs`

and David Mosberger-Tang is kind enough to include the html form of it in his excellent Linux Alpha FAQ site

`http://www.azstarnet.com/~axplinux`

2 What is MILO?

On Intel based PC systems, the BIOS firmware sets up the system and then loads the image to be run from the boot block of a DOS file system. This is more or less what MILO does on an Alpha based system, however there are several interesting differences between BIOS firmware and MILO, not least of which is that MILO includes and uses standard Linux device drivers unmodified. MILO is firmware, unlike LILO, which relies on the BIOS firmware to get itself loaded. The main functional parts of MILO are:

1. PALcode,
2. Memory set-up code (builds page tables and turns on virtual addressing),
3. Video code (BIOS emulation code and TGA (21030)),
4. Linux kernel code. This includes real Linux kernel code (for example, the interrupt handling) and ersatz or mock Linux kernel,
5. Linux block device drivers (for example, the floppy driver),
6. File system support (ext2, MS-DOS and ISO9660),
7. User inteface code (MILO),
8. Kernel interface code (sets up the HWRPB and memory map for linux),
9. NVRAM code for managing environment variables.

The following paragraphs describe these functional parts in more detail.

PALcode can be thought of as a tiny software layer that tailors the chip to a particular operating system. It runs in a special mode (PALmode) which has certain restrictions but it uses the standard Alpha instruction set with just five extra instructions. In this way, the Alpha chip can run such diverse operating systems as Windows NT, OpenVMS, Digital Unix and, of course, Linux. The PALcode that MILO uses (and therefore Linux itself) is, like the rest of MILO, freeware. It is derived from Digital's Evaluation Board software example Digital Unix PALcode.. The differences between the different PALcodes are because of differences in address mapping and interrupt handling that exist between the Alpha chips (21066 based systems have a different I/O map to 21064+2107x systems) and different Alpha based systems.

For MILO to operate properly it needs to know what memory is available, where Linux will eventually be running from and it must be able to allocate temporary memory for the Linux device drivers. The code maintains a memory map that has entries for permanent and temporary allocated pages. As it boots, MILO uncompresses itself into the correct place in physical memory. When it passes control to the Linux kernel, it reserves memory for the compressed version of itself, the PALcode (which the kernel needs) and some data structures. This leaves `most` of the memory in the system for Linux itself.

The final act of the memory code is to set up and turn on virtual addressing so that the data structures that Linux expects to see are at the correct place in virtual memory.

MILO contains video code that initialises and uses the video device for the system. It will detect and use a VGA device if there is one, otherwise it will try to use a TGA (21030) video device. Failing that, it will assume that there is no graphics device. The BIOS emulation that the standard, pre-built, images include is Digital's own BIOS emulation which supports most, if not all, of the standard graphics devices available.

Linux device drivers live within the kernel and expect certain services from the kernel. Some of these services are provided directly by Linux kernel code, for example the interrupt handling and some is provided by kernel look-alike routines.

MILO's most powerful feature is that you can embed unaltered Linux device drivers into it. This gives it the potential to support every device that Linux does. MILO includes all of the block devices that are configured into the Linux kernel that it is built against as well as a lot of the block device code (for example, ll_rw_blk()).

MILO loads the Linux kernel from real file systems rather than from boot blocks and other strange places. It understands MSDOS, EXT2 and ISO9660 filesystems. Gzip'd files are supported and these are recommended, particularly if you are loading from floppy which is rather slow. MILO recognises these by their *.gz* suffix.

Built into MILO is a simple keyboard driver which, together with an equally simple video driver allows it to have a simple user interface. That interface allows you to list file systems on configured devices, boot Linux or run flash update utilities and set environment variables that control the system's booting. Like LILO, you can pass arguments to the Kernel.

MILO must tell the Linux kernel what sort of system this is, how much memory there is and which of that memory is free. It does this using the HWRPB (Hardware Restart Parameter Block) data structure and associated memory cluster descriptions. These are placed at the appropriate place in virtual memory just before control is passed to the Linux kernel.

3 Pre-Built Standard MILO Images.

If you are planning to run Linux on a standard Alpha based system, then there are pre-built "standard" MILO images that you might use. These (along with the sources and other interesting stuff) can be found in (`ftp://gatekeeper.dec.com/pub/Digital/Linux-Alpha/Miniloader`).

The `images` subdirectory contains a directory per standard system (eg AlphaPC64) with MILO images having the following naming convention:

1. `MILO` - Miniloader executable image, this image can be loaded in a variety of ways,
2. `fmu.gz` - Flash management utility,
3. `MILO.dd` - Boot block floppy disk image. These should be written using rawrite.exe or `dd` on Linux.

The `test-images`, like the `images` subdirectory contains a directory per standard system. These images are somewhat experimental but tend to contain all the latest features.

4 How To Build MILO

You build MILO separately from the Kernel. As MILO requires parts of the kernel to function (for example interrupt handling) you must first configure and build the kernel that matches with MILO that you want to build. Mostly this means building the kernel with the same version number. So, MILO-2.0.25.tar.gz will build against linux-2.0.25.tar.gz. MILO may build against a higher version of the kernel, but there again it may not. Also, now that ELF shared libraries are fully supported, there are two versions of the MILO sources. To build under an ELF system you must first unpack the standard MILO sources and then patch those sources with the same version numbered ELF patch. In the remainder of this discussion, I assume that your kernel sources and object files are stored in the subtree at `/usr/src/linux` and that the Linux kernel has been fully built with the command `make boot`

To build MILO, change your working directory to the MILO source directory and invoke `make` with:

```
$      make KSRC=/usr/src/linux config
```

Just like the Linux kernel, you will be asked a series of questions

```
Echo output to the serial port (MINI_SERIAL_ECHO) [y]
```

It's a good idea to echo kernel printk to `/dev/ttyS0` if you can. If you can (and want to), then type "y", otherwise "n". All of the standard, pre-built, MILO images include serial port I/O using COM1.

```
Use Digital's BIOS emulation code (not free) (MINI_DIGITAL_BIOS_EMU) [y]
```

This code is included as a library which is freely distributable so long as it is used on an Alpha based system. The sources are not available. If you answer `n` then the freeware alternative BIOS emulation will be built. It's sources are included with MILO. Note that you cannot right now choose build Digital's BIOS emulation code in an ELF system (the library is not yet ready) and so you must answer no to this question.

```
Build PALcode from sources (Warning this is dangerous) (MINI_BUILD_PALCODE_FROM_SOURCES) [n]
```

You should only do this if you have changed the PALcode sources, otherwise use the standard, pre-built PALcode included with MILO.

You are now all set to build the MILO image itself:

```
$      make KSRC=/usr/src/linux
```

When the build has successfully completed, the MILO image is in the file called `milo`. There are a lot of images called `milo.*`, these should be ignored.

5 How To Load MILO

The most commonly supported method of loading MILO is from the Windows NT ARC firmware as most shipping systems support this. However, there are a wide variety of ways to load MILO. It may be loaded from:

- a failsafe boot block floppy,
- the Windows NT ARC firmware,
- Digital's SRM console,
- an Alpha Evaluation Board Debug Monitor,
- flash/ROM.

5.1 Loading MILO from the Windows NT ARC firmware

Most, if not all, Alpha AXP based systems include the Windows NT ARC boot firmware, and this is the prefered method of booting MILO, and thus Linux. Once the Windows NT firmware is running and you have the correct MILO image for your system, this method is completely generic.

The Windows NT ARC firmware is an environment in which programs can run and make callbacks into the firmware to perform actions. The Windows NT OSLoader is a program that does exactly this. linload.exe is a much simpler program which does just enough to load and execute MILO. It loads the appropriate image file into memory at 0x00000000 and then makes a swap-PAL PALcall to it. MILO, like Linux, uses a different PALcode to Windows NT which is why the swap has to happen. MILO relocates itself to 0x200000 and continues on through the PALcode reset entry point as before.

Before you add a Linux boot option, you will need to copy linload.exe and the appropriate MILO that you wish to load to someplace that the Windows NT ARC firmware can read from. In the following example, I assume that you are booting from a DOS format floppy disk:

1. At the boot menu, select `"Supplementary menu..."`
2. At the `"Supplementary menu"`, select `"Set up the system..."`
3. At the `"Setup menu"`, select `"Manage boot selection menu..."`
4. In the `"Boot selections menu"`, choose `"Add a boot selection"`
5. Choose `"Floppy Disk 0"`
6. Enter `"linload.exe"` as the osloader directory and name
7. Say "yes" to the operating system being on the same partition as the osloader
8. Enter "\" as the operating system root directory

9. I usually enter `"Linux"` as the name for this boot selection
10. Say "No" you do not want to initialise the debugger at boot time
11. You should now be back in the `"Boot selections menu"`, choose the `"Change a boot selection option"` and pick the selection you just created as the one to edit
12. Use the down arrow to get `"OSLOADFILENAME"` up and then type in the name of the MILO image that you wish to use, for example `"noname.arc"` followed by return.
13. Press ESC to get back to the `"Boot Selections menu"`
14. Choose `"Setup Menu"` (or hit ESC again) and choose `"Supplementary menu, and save changes"` option
15. ESC will get you back to the `"Boot menu"` and you can attempt to boot MILO. If you do not want Linux as the first boot option, then you can alter the order of the boot options in the `"Boot selections menu"`.

At the end of all this, you should have a boot selection that looks something like:

```
LOADIDENTIFIER=Linux
SYSTEMPARTITION=multi(0)disk(0)fdisk(0)
OSLOADER=multi(0)disk(0)fdisk(0)\linload.exe
OSLOADPARTITION=multi(0)disk(0)fdisk(0)
OSLOADFILENAME=\noname.arc
OSLOADOPTIONS=
```

You can now boot MILO (and then Linux). You can load linload.exe and MILO directly from a file system that Windows NT understands such as NTFS or DOS on a hard disk.

The contents of `OSLOADOPTIONS` are passed to MILO which interprets it as a command. So, in order to boot Linux directly from Windows NT without pausing in MILO, you could pass the following in `OSLOADOPTIONS`:

```
boot sda2:vmlinux.gz root=/dev/sda2
```

See Section 6 for more information on the commands available.

Another (rather sneaky) way of loading of loading MILO via the WNT ARC firmware is to put MILO onto an MS-DOS floppy and call it `fwupdate.exe` and then choose the "Upgrade Firmware" option.

5.2 Loading MILO from the Evaluation Board Debug Monitor

Evaluation boards (and often designs cloned from them) include support for the Alpha Evaluation Board Debug Monitor. Consult your system document before considering this method of booting MILO. The following systems are known to include Debug Monitor support:

- AlphaPC64 (Section 5.6.2),
- EB64+ (Section 5.6.4),
- EB66+ (Section 5.6.3),
- EB164 (Section 5.6.6),
- PC164 (Section 5.6.7).

Before you consider this method, you should note that the early versions of the Evaluation Board Debug Monitor did not include video or keyboard drivers and so you must be prepared to connect another system via the serial port so that you can use the Debug Monitor. Its interface is very simple and typing help shows a whole heap of commands. The ones that are most interesting include the word `boot` or `load` in them.

The Evaluation Board Debug Monitor can load an image either via the network (netboot) or via a floppy (flboot). In either case, set the boot address to 0x200000 (`> bootadr 200000`) before booting the image.

If the image is on floppy (and note that only DOS formatted floppies are supported), then you will need to type the following command:

```
AlphaPC64> flboot <MILO-image-name>
```

5.3 Loading MILO from a Failsafe Boot Block Floppy

Only the AxpPCI33 is known to include failsafe boot block floppy support.

If you do not have a standard pre-built MILO .dd image, then you may need to build a SRM boot block floppy. Once you have built MILO, you need to do the following on Digital Unix box:

```
fddisk -fmt /dev/rfd0a
cat mboot bootm > /dev/rfd0a
disklabel -rw rfd0a 'rx23' mboot bootm
```

Or on a Linux box:

```
cat mboot bootm > /dev/fd0
```

If you have a standard MILO image available (say `MILO.dd`) then you would build a boot block floppy using the following command:

```
dd if=MILO.dd of=/dev/fd0
```

5.4 Loading MILO from Flash

There are a number of systems where MILO can be blown into flash and booted directly (instead of via the Windows NT ARC firmware):

- AlphaPC64 (Section 5.6.2)
- Noname (Section 5.6.1)
- EB66+ (Section 5.6.3)
- EB164 (Section 5.6.6)
- PC164 (Section 5.6.7)

5.5 Loading MILO from the SRM Console

Reference Manual) Console knows nothing about filesystems or disk-partitions, it simply expects that the secondary bootstrap loader occupies a consecutive range of physical disk sectors starting from a given offset. The information describing the secondary bootstrap loader (its size and offset) is given in the first 512 byte block. To load MILO via the SRM you must generate that structure on a device which the SRM can access (such as a floppy disk). This is what `mboot` and `bootm`, `mboot` is the first block (or boot description) and `mboot` is the `MILO` image rounded up to a 512-byte boundary.

To load MILO from a boot block device, either build `mboot` and `bootm` and push them onto the boot device using the following command:

```
$ cat mboot bootm > /dev/fd0
```

Or, grab the appropriate `MILO.dd` from a web site and write it onto the boot device using either `RAWRITE.EXE` or `dd`.

Once you have done that you can boot the SRM console and use one of its many commands to boot MILO. For example, to boot MILO from a boot block floppy you would use the following command:

```
>>>boot dva0
(boot dva0.0.0.0.1 -flags 0)
block 0 of dva0.0.0.0.1 is a valid boot block
reading 621 blocks from dva0.0.0.0.1
bootstrap code read in
base = 112000, image_start = 0, image_bytes = 4da00
initializing HWRPB at 2000
initializing page table at 104000
initializing machine state
setting affinity to the primary CPU
jumping to bootstrap code
MILO Stub: V1.1
Unzipping MILO into position
Allocating memory for unzip
####...
```

The following systems are known to have SRM Console support:

- Noname (Section 5.6.1)

- AlphaPC64 (Section 5.6.2)
- EB164 (Section 5.6.6)
- PC164 (Section 5.6.7)

5.6 System Specific Information

5.6.1 AxpPCI33 (Noname)

The Noname board can load MILO from the Windows NT ARC firmware (Section 5.1), from the SRM Console (Section 5.5). and from a failsafe boot block floppy (Section 5.3). A flash management utility, runnable from MILO is available so that once MILO is running, it can be blown into flash (Section 7). However, be warned that once you have done this you will lose the previous image held there as there is only room for one image.

The way that Noname boots is controlled by a set of jumpers on the board, J29 and J28. These look like:

```
                    4
      J29       2 x x x 6
                1 x x x 5

      J28       2 x x x 6
                1 x x x 5
                    3
```

The two options that we're interested in are J28, pins 1-3 which boots the console/loader from flash and J29, pins 1-3 which boots the console/loader from a boot block floppy. The second option is the one that you need to first boot MILO on the Noname board.

Once you've selected the boot from floppy option via the jumpers, put the SRM boot block floppy containing MILO into the floppy and reboot. In a few seconds (after the floppy light goes out) you should see the screen blank to white and MILO telling you what's going on.

If you are really interested in technical stuff, the Noname loads images off of the floppy into physical address 0x104000 and images from flash into 0x100000. For this reason, MILO is built with its PALcode starting at 0x200000. When it is first loaded, it moves itself to the correct location (see relocate.S).

5.6.2 AlphaPC64 (Cabriolet)

The AlphaPC64 includes the Windows NT ARC firmware (Section 5.1), the SRM Console (Section 5.5) and the Evaluation Debug Monitor (Section 5.2). These images are in flash and there is room to add MILO so that you can boot MILO directly from flash. A flash management utility, runnable from MILO is available so that once MILO is running, it can be blown into flash (Section 7). This system supports MILO environment variables.

You select between the boot options (and MILO when it is been put into flash) using a combination of jumpers and a boot option which is saved in the NVRAM of the TOY clock.

The jumper is J2, SP bits 6 and 7 have the following meanings:

- SP bit 6 should always be out. If this jumper is set then the SROM mini-debugger gets booted,
- SP bit 7 in is boot image selected by the boot option byte in the TOY clock,
- SP bit 7 out is boot first image in flash.

So, with bit 7 out, the Debug Monitor will be booted as it is `always` the first image in flash. With bit 7 in, the image selected by the boot option in the TOY clock will be selected. The Debug Monitor, the Windows NT ARC firmware and MILO all support setting this boot option byte but you must be very careful using it. In particular, you cannot set the boot option so that next time the system boots MILO when you are running the Windows NT ARC firmware, it only allows you to set Debug Monitor or Windows NT ARC as boot options.

To get MILO into flash via the Evaluation Board Debug Monitor, you will need a flashable image. The build proceedures make MILO.rom, but you can also make a rom image using the makerom tool in the Debug Monitor software that comes with the board:

```
> makerom -v -i7 -l200000 MILO -o mini.flash
```

(type makerom to find out what the arguments mean, but 7 is a flash image id used by the srom and -l200000 gives the load address for the image as 0x200000).

Load that image into memory (via the Debug Monitor commands flload, netload, and so on) at 0x200000 and then blow the image into flash:

```
AlphaPC64> flash 200000 8
```

(200000 is where the image to be blown is in memory and 8 is the segment number where you put the image. There are 16 1024*64 byte segments in the flash and the Debug Monitor is at seg 0 and the Windows NT ARC firmware is at seg 4).

Set up the image that the srom will boot by writing the number of the image into the TOY clock.

```
AlphaPC64> bootopt 131
```

(131 means boot the 3rd image, 129 = 1st, 130 = 2nd and so on).

Power off, put jumper 7 on and power on and you should see the MILO burst into life. If you don't then take jumper 7 back off and reboot the Debug Monitor.

5.6.3 EB66+

The EB66+, like all of the Alpha Evaluation Boards built by Digital contains the Evaluation Board Debug Monitor and so this is available to load MILO (Section 5.2). Quite often (although not always) boards whose design is derived from these include the Debug Monitor also. Usually, these boards include the Windows NT ARC firmware (Section 5.1). A flash management utility, runnable from MILO is available so that once MILO is running, it can be blown into flash (Section 7). This system supports MILO environment variables.

These systems have several boot images in flash controlled by jumpers. The two jumper banks are J18 and J16 and are located at the bottom of the board in the middle (if the Alpha chip is at the top). You select between the boot options (and MILO when it is been put into flash) using a combination of jumpers and a boot option which is saved in the NVRAM of the TOY clock.

Jumper 7-8 of J18 in means boot the image described by the boot option. Jumper 7-8 of J18 out means boot the Evaluation Board Debug Monitor.

Blowing an image into flash via the Evaluation Board Debug Monitor is exactly the same proceedure as for the AlphaPC64 (Section 5.6.2).

5.6.4 EB64+/Aspen Alpine

This system is quite like the AlphaPC64 except that it does not contain flash which MILO can be loaded from. The EB64+ has two ROMs, one of which contains the Windows NT ARC firmware (Section 5.1). and the other contains the Evaluation Board Debug Monitor (Section 5.2).

The Aspen Alpine is a little different in that it only has one ROM; this contains the Windows NT ARC firmware.

5.6.5 Universal Desktop Box (Multia)

This is a very compact pre-packaged 21066 based system that includes a TGA (21030) graphics device. Although you can *just* fit a half height PCI graphics card in the box you are better off waiting for full TGA support in XFree86. It includes the Windows NT ARC firmware and so booting from that is the prefered method (Section 5.1).

5.6.6 EB164

The EB164, like all of the Alpha Evaluation Boards built by Digital contains the Evaluation Board Debug Monitor and so this is available to load MILO (Section 5.2). Quite often (although not always) boards whose design is derived from these include the Debug Monitor also. Usually, these boards include the Windows NT ARC firmware (Section 5.1). The SRM console is also available (Section 5.5). A flash management utility, runnable from MILO is available so that once MILO is running, it can be blown into flash (Section 7). This system supports MILO environment variables.

These systems have several boot images in flash controlled by jumpers. The two jumper bank is J1 and is located at the bottom of the board on the left (if the Alpha chip is at the top). You select between the boot options (and MILO when it is been put into flash) using a combination of jumpers and a boot option which is saved in the NVRAM of the TOY clock.

Jumper SP-11 of J1 in means boot the image described by the boot option. Jumper SP-11 of J1 out means boot the Evaluation Board Debug Monitor.

Blowing an image into flash via the Evaluation Board Debug Monitor is exactly the same proceedure as for the AlphaPC64 (Section 5.6.2).

5.6.7 PC164

The PC164, like all of the Alpha Evaluation Boards built by Digital contains the Evaluation Board Debug Monitor and so this is available to load MILO (Section 5.2). Quite often (although not always) boards whose design is derived from these include the Debug Monitor also. Usually, these boards include the Windows NT ARC firmware (Section 5.1). The SRM console is also available (Section 5.5). A flash management utility, runnable from MILO is available so that once MILO is running, it can be blown into flash (Section 7). This system supports MILO environment variables.

These systems have several boot images in flash controlled by jumpers. The main jumper block, J30, contains the system configuration jumpers and jumper CF6 in means that the system will boot the Debug Monitor, the default is out.

Blowing an image into flash via the Evaluation Board Debug Monitor is exactly the same proceedure as for the AlphaPC64 (Section 5.6.2).

5.6.8 XL266

The XL266 is one of a family of systems that are known as Avanti. It has a riser card containing the Alpha chip and cache which plugs into the main board at right angles. This board can replace the equivalent Pentium board.

Some of these systems ship with the SRM console but others, notably the XL266 ship with only the Windows NT ARC firmware (Section 5.1).

Here is my list of compatible systems:

- AlphaStation 400 (Avanti),
- AlphaStation 250,
- AlphaStation 200 (Mustang),
- XL. There are two flavours, XL266 and XL233 with the only difference being in processor speed and cache size.

Note The system that I use to develop and test MILO is an XL266 and so this is the only one that I can guarentee will work. However, technically, all of the above systems are equivalent; they have the same support chipsets and the same interrupt handling mechanisms.

5.6.9 Platform2000

This is a 233Mhz 21066 based system.

6 MILO's User Interface

Once you have correctly installed/loaded/run MILO you will see the MILO (for MIniLOader) prompt displayed on your screen. There is a very simple interface that you must use in order to boot a particular Linux kernel image. Typing "help" is a good idea as it gives a useful summary of the commands.

6.1 The "help" Command

Probably the most useful command that MILO has:

```
MILO> help
MILO command summary:

ls [-t fs] [dev:[dir]]
                    - List files in directory on device
boot [-t fs] [dev:file] [boot string]
                    - Boot Linux from the specified device and file
run [-t fs] dev:file
                    - Run the standalone program dev:file
show                - Display all known devices and file systems
set VAR VALUE       - Set the variable VAR to the specified VALUE
unset VAR           - Delete the specified variable
reset               - Delete all variables
print               - Display current variable settings
help [var]          - Print this help text
```

```
Devices are specified as: fd0, hda1, hda2, sda1...
Use the '-t filesystem-name' option if you want to use
  anything but the default filesystem  ('ext2').
Use the 'show' command to show known devices and filesystems.
Type 'help var' for a list of variables.
```

Note that the `bootopt` command only appears on AlphaPC64 (and similar) systems. Refer to the board's dcoumentation to find out just what it means.

Devices. Until you use a command that needs to make use of a device, no device inititalisation will take place. The first `show`, `ls`, `boot` or `run` commands all cause the devices within MILO to be initialised. Devices are named in the same way (exactly) that Linux itself will name them. So, the first IDE disk will be called 'hda' and its first partition will be 'hda1'. Use the `show` command to show what devices are available.

File Systems. MILO supports three file systems, MS-DOS, EXT2 and ISO 9660. So long as a device is available to it, MILO can `listboot` or `run` an image stored on one of these file systems. MILO's default file system is `EXT2` and so you have tell MILO that the file system is something other than that. All of the commands that use filenames allow you to pass the file system using the `-t [filesystem]` option. So, if you wanted to list the contents of a SCSI CD ROM, you might type the following:

```
MILO> ls -t iso9660 scd0:
```

Variables. MILO contains some settable variables that help the boot process. If you are loading via the Windows NT ARC firmware, then MILO makes use of the boot option environment variables set up by that firmware. For some systems, MILO (for example, the AlphaPC64) maintains its own set of environment variables that do not change from boot to boot. These variables are:

```
MILO> help var
Variables that MILO cares about:
  MEMORY_SIZE      - System memory size in megabytes
  BOOT_DEV         - Specifies the default boot device
  BOOT_FILE        - Specifies the default boot file
  BOOT_STRING      - Specifies the boot string to pass to the kernel
  SCSIn_HOSTID     - Specifies the host id of the n-th SCSI controller.
  AUTOBOOT         - If set, MILO attempts to boot on powerup
                     and enters command loop only on failure.
  AUTOBOOT_TIMEOUT - Seconds to wait before auto-booting on powerup.
```

6.2 Booting Linux

The `boot` command boots a linux kernel from a device. You will need to have a linux kernel image on an EXT2 formated disk (SCSI, IDE or floppy) or an ISO9660 formatted CD available to MILO. The image can be gzip'd and in this case MILO will recognise that it is gzip'd by the .gz suffix.

You should note that the version of MILO does not usually have to match the version of the Linux kernel that you are loading. You boot Linux using the following command syntax:

```
MILO> boot [-t file-system] device-name:file-name [[boot-option] [boot-option] ...]
```

Where `device-name` is the name of the device that you wish to use and `file-name` is the name of the file containing the Linux kernel. All arguments supplied after the file name are passed directly to the Linux kernel.

If you are installing Red Hat, then you will need to specify a root device and so on. So you would use:

```
MILO> boot fd0:vmlinux.gz root=/dev/fd0 load_ramdisk=1
```

MILO will automatically contain the block devices that you configure into your vmlinux. I have tested the floppy driver, the IDE driver and a number of SCSI drivers (for example, the NCR 810), and these work fine. Also, it is important to set the host id of the SCSI controller to a reasonable value. By default, MILO will initialize it to the highest possible value (7) which should normally work just fine. However, if you wish, you can explicitly set the host id of the *n*-th SCSI controller in the system by setting environment variable `SCSIn_HOSTID` to the appropriate value. For example, to set the hostid of the first SCSI controller to 7, you can issue the following command at the MILO prompt:

```
setenv SCSI0_HOSTID 7
```

6.3 Rebooting Linux

You may want to reboot a running Linux system using the `shutdown -r now` command. In this case, the Linux kernel returns control to MILO (via the HALT CallPAL entrypoint). MILO leaves a compressed copy of itself in memory for just this reason and detects that the system is being rebooted from information held in the HWRPB (Hardware Restart Parameter Block). In this case it starts to reboot using exactly the same command that was used to boot the Linux kernel the last time. There is a 30 second timeout that allows you to interrupt this process and boot whatever kernel you wish in whatever way you wish.

6.4 The "bootopt" command

For flash based systems such as the AlphaPC64, EB164 and the EB66+, there are a number of possible boot options and these are changed using the `bootopt` command. This has one argument, a decimal number which is the type of the image to be booted the next time the system is power cycled or reset:

0 Boot the Evaluation Board Debug Monitor,

1 Boot the Windows NT ARC firmware.

In order to tell the boot code to boot the MILO firmware from flash then you need a boot option that means boot the N'th image. For this, you need to 128 plus N, so if MILO is the third image, you would use the command:

```
MILO> bootopt 131
```

Note: be very careful with this command. A good rule is never to set bootopt to 0 (the Evaluation Board Debug Monitor), but instead use the system's jumpers to achieve the same thing.

7 Running the Flash Management Utility

The `run` command is used to run the flash management utility. Before you start you will need a device available to MILO that contains the updateflash program. This (like vmlinux) can be gzip'd. You need to run the flash management utility program from the MILO using the (`run`) command:

```
MILO> run fd0:fmu.gz
```

Once it has loaded and initialised, the flash management utility will tell you some information about the flash device and give you a command prompt. Again the `help` command is most useful.

```
Linux MILO Flash Management Utility V1.0

Flash device is an Intel 28f008SA
  16 segments, each of 0x10000 (65536) bytes
Scanning Flash blocks for usage
Block 12 contains the environment variables
FMU>
```

Note that on systems where environment variables may be stored and where there is more than one flash block (for example, the AlphaPC64) the flash management utility will look for a block to hold MILO's environment variables. If such a block already exists, the flash management utility will tell you where it is. Otherwise, you must use the `environment` command to set a block and initialise it. In the above example, flash block 12 contains MILO's environment variables.

7.1 The "help" command

```
FMU> help
FMU command summary:

list                  - List the contents of flash
program               - program an image into flash
quit                  - Quit
environment           - Set which block should contain the environment variables
bootopt num           - Select firmware type to use on next power up
help                  - Print this help text
FMU>
```

Note that the `environment` and `bootopt` commands are only available on the EB66+, the AlphaPC64, EB164 and PC164 systems (and their clones).

7.2 The "list" command

The "list" command shows the current usage of the flash memory. Where there is more than one flash block, the usage of each flash block is shown. In the example below you can see that Windows NT ARC is using blocks 4:7 and block 15.

```
FMU> list
Flash blocks:  0:DBM  1:DBM  2:DBM  3:WNT  4:WNT  5:WNT  6:WNT  7:WNT  8:MILO
        9:MILO 10:MILO 11:MILO 12:MILO 13:U 14:U 15:WNT
Listing flash Images
  Flash image starting at block 0:
    Firmware Id:  0 (Alpha Evaluation Board Debug Monitor)
    Image size is 191248 bytes (3 blocks)
    Executing at 0x300000
  Flash image starting at block 3:
    Firmware Id:  1 (Windows NT ARC)
    Image size is 277664 bytes (5 blocks)
    Executing at 0x300000
  Flash image starting at block 8:
    Firmware Id:  7 (MILO/Linux)
    Image size is 217896 bytes (4 blocks)
    Executing at 0x200000
FMU>
```

7.3 The "program" command

The flash management utility contains a compressed copy of a flash image of MILO. The "program" command allows you to blow this image into flash. The command allows you to back out, but before you run it you should use the "list" command to see where to put MILO. If MILO is already in flash, then the flash management utility will offer to overwrite it.

```
FMU> program
Image is:
    Firmware Id:  7 (MILO/Linux)
    Image size is 217896 bytes (4 blocks)
    Executing at 0x200000
Found existing image at block 8
Overwrite existing image? (N/y)? y
Do you really want to do this (y/N)? y
Deleting blocks ready to program: 8 9 10 11
Programming image into flash
Scanning Flash blocks for usage
FMU>
```

Wait until it has completed before powering off your system.

`Note:` I cannot emphasise just how careful you must be here not to overwrite an existing flash image that you might need or render your system useless. A very good rule is never to overwrite the Debug Monitor.

7.4 The "environment" command

This selects a flash block to contain MILO's environment variables.

7.5 The "bootopt" command

This is just the same as MILO's "bootopt" command, see (Section 6.4).

7.6 The "quit" command

This is really pretty meaningless. The only way back to MILO (or anything else) once the flash management utility has run is to reboot the system.

8 Restrictions.

Unfortunately this is not a perfect world and there, as always, some restrictions that you should be aware of.

MILO is not meant to load operating systems other than Linux, although it can load images linked to run at the same place in memory as Linux (which is 0xFFFFFC0000310000). This is how the flash management utilities can be run.

The PALcode sources included in `miniboot/palcode/`*blah* are correct, however there are problems when they are built using the latest `gas`. They *do* build if you use the ancient a.out gas that's supplied in the Alpha Evaluation Board toolset (and that's how they were built). I'm trying to get someone to fix the new gas. Meanwhile, as a workaround, I have provided pre-built PALcode for the supported boards and David Mosberger-Tang has a fixed gas on his ftp site.

9 Problem Solving.

Here are some common problems that people have seen, together with the solutions.

Reading MS-DOS floppies from the Evaluation Board Debug Monitor.

Some of the older versions of the Evaluation Board Debug Monitor (pre-version 2.0) have a problem with DOS format flopies generated from Linux. Usually, the Debug Monitor can load the first few sectors all right, but then goes into an endless loop complaining about "bad sectors." Apparently, there is an incompatibility between the DOS file system as expected by the Debug Monitor and the Linux implementation of DOSFS. To make the long story short: if you run into this problem, try using DOS to write the floppy disk. For example, if loading the file `MILO.cab` doesn't work, use a DOS machine, insert the floppy and then do:

```
copy a:MILO.cab c:
copy c:MILO.cab a:
del c:MILO.cab
```

Then try booting from that floppy again. This normally solves the problem.

MILO displays a long sequence of `O>` and does not accept input.

This usually happens when MILO was built to use COM1 as a secondary console device. In such a case, MILO echoes output to COM1 and accepts input from there also. This is great for debugging but not so great if you have a device other than a terminal connected. If this happens, disconnect the device or power it down until the Linux kernel has booted. Once Linux is up and running, everything will work as expected.

MILO complains that the kernel image has the wrong magic number

Older versions of MILO did not support the ELF object file format and so could not recognise an ELF image and this might be your problem. If this is reported, upgrade to the latest MILO that you can find. All 2.0.20 and beyond MILOs support ELF. On the other hand it could be that the image is indeed damaged. You should also note that MILO does not yet automatically distinquish between GZIP'd and non-GZIP'd images; you need to add the ".gz" suffix to the file name.

MILO prints "...turning on virtual addressing and jumping to the Linux Kernel" and nothing else happens

One obvious problem is that the kernel image is wrongly built or is built for another Alpha system altogether. Another is that the video board is a TGA (Zlxp) device and the kernel has been built for a VGA device (or vice versa). It is worth building the kernel to echo to COM1 and then connecting a terminal to that serial port or retrying the kernel that came with the Linux distribution that you installed.

MILO does not recognise the SCSI device

The standard MILO images include as many device drivers as are known to be stable for Alpha (as of now that includes the NCR 810, QLOGIC ISP, Buslogic and Adaptec 2940s and 3940 cards). If your card is not included, it may be that the driver is not stable enough on an Alpha system yet. Again, the latest MILO images are worth trying. You can tell which SCSI devices a MILO image has built into it by using the "show" command.

10 Acknowledgements.

I would like to thank:

- Eric Rasmussen and Eilleen Samberg the authors of the PALcode,
- Jim Paradis for the keyboard driver and the original MILO interface,
- Jay Estabrook for his help and bugfixes,
- David Mosberger-Tang for the freeware BIOS emulation and his support and encouragement,
- Last (and `not` least) Linus Torvalds for the timer code and his kernel.

There are a number of things that still need doing to MILO, if you want to add something yourself, then do let me know `mailto:david.rusling@reo.mts.dec.com` so that we do not duplicate our efforts.

Finally, a big thank you to Digital for producing such a wonderful chip (and paying me to do this).

Part VI

"Assembly HOWTO" by François-René Rideau,

rideau@ens.fr

Contents

Abstract

v0.4l, 16 November 1997
This is the Linux Assembly HOWTO. This document describes how to program in assembly using *free* programming tools, focusing on development for or from the Linux Operating System on i386 platforms. Included material may or may not be applicable to other hardware and/or software platforms. Contributions about these would be gladly accepted.
keywords: assembly, assembler, free, macroprocessor, preprocessor, asm, inline asm, 32-bit, x86, i386, gas, as86, nasm

1 Introduction

1.1 Legal Blurp

1.2 IMPORTANT NOTE

This is expectedly the last release I'll make of this document. There's one candidate new maintainer, but until he really takes the HOWTO over, I'll accept feedback.

You are especially invited to ask questions, to answer to questions, to correct given answers, to add new FAQ answers, to give pointers to other software, to point the current maintainer to bugs or deficiencies in the pages. If you're motivated, you could even *TAKE OVER THE MAINTENANCE OF THE FAQ*. In one word, contribute!

To contribute, please contact whoever appears to maintain the Assembly-HOWTO. Current maintainers are *François-René Rideau* (mailto:rideau@clipper.ens.fr) and now *Paul Anderson* (mailto:paul@geeky1.ebtech.net).

1.3 Foreword

This document aims at answering frequently asked questions of people who program or want to program 32-bit x86 assembly using *free* assemblers, particularly under the Linux operating system. It may also point to other documents about non-free, non-x86, or non-32-bit assemblers, though such is not its primary goal.

Because the main interest of assembly programming is to build to write the guts of operating systems, interpreters, compilers, and games, where a C compiler fails to provide the needed expressivity (performance is more and more seldom an issue), we stress on development of such software.

1.3.1 How to use this document

This document contains answers to some frequently asked questions. At many places, Universal Resource Locators (URL) are given for some software or documentation repository. Please see that the most useful repositories are mirrored, and that by accessing a nearer mirror site, you relieve the whole Internet from unneeded network traffic, while saving your own precious time. Particularly, there are large repositories all over the world, that mirror other popular repositories. You should learn and note what are those places near you (networkwise). Sometimes, the list of mirrors is listed in a file, or in a login message. Please heed the advice. Else, you should ask archie about the software you're looking for...

The most recent version for this documents sits in
(http://www.eleves.ens.fr:8080/home/rideau/Assembly-HOWTO) or (http://www.eleves.ens.fr:8080/home/rid
but what's in Linux HOWTO repositories *should* be fairly up to date, too (I can't know):
(ftp://sunsite.unc.edu/pub/Linux/docs/HOWTO/) (?)
A French translation of this HOWTO can be found around
(ftp://ftp.ibp.fr/pub/linux/french/HOWTO/)

1.3.2 Other related documents

- If you don't know what *free* software is, please do read *carefully* the GNU General Public License, which is used in a lot of free software, and is a model for most of their licenses. It generally comes in a file named COPYING, with a library version in a file named COPYING.LIB. Literature from the FSF (Free Software Foundation) might help you, too.
- Particularly, the interesting kind of free software comes with sources that you can consult and correct, or sometimes even borrow from. Read your particular license carefully, and do comply with it.

- There is a FAQ for comp.lang.asm.x86 that answers generic questions about x86 assembly programming, and questions about some commercial assemblers in a 16-bit DOS environment. Some of it apply to free 32-bit asm programming, so you may want to read this FAQ... (`http://www2.dgsys.com/~raymoon/faq/asmfaq.zip`)
- FAQs and docs exist about programming on your favorite platform, whichever it is, that you should consult for platform-specific issues not directly related to programming in assembler.

1.4 Credits

I would like to thanks the following persons, by order of appearance:

- *Linus Torvalds* (`mailto:buried.alive@in.mail`) for Linux
- *Bruce Evans* (`mailto:bde@zeta.org.au`) for bcc from which as86 is extracted
- *Simon Tatham* (`mailto:anakin@poboxes.com`) and *Julian Hall* (`mailto:jules@earthcorp.com`) for NASM
- *Jim Neil* (`mailto:jim-neil@digital.net`) for Terse
- *Greg Hankins* (`mailto:gregh@sunsite.unc.edu`) for maintaining HOWTOs
- *Raymond Moon* (`mailto:raymoon@moonware.dgsys.com`) for his FAQ
- *Eric Dumas* (`mailto:dumas@excalibur.ibp.fr`) for his translation of the Mini-HOWTO into French (sad thing for the original author to be French and write in English)
- *Paul Anderson* (`mailto:paul@geeky1.ebtech.net`) and *Rahim Azizarab* (`mailto:rahim@megsinet.net`) for helping me, if not for taking over the HOWTO.
- All the people who have contributed ideas, remarks, and moral support.

2 DO YOU NEED ASSEMBLY?

Well, I wouldn't want to interfere with what you're doing, but here are a few opinions from hard-earned experience.

2.1 Pros and Cons

2.1.1 The advantages of Assembly

Assembly can express very low-level things.

- You can access machine-dependent registers and I/O.
- You can control the exact behavior of code in critical sections that might involve hardware or I/O lock-ups
- You can break the conventions of your usual compiler, which might allow some optimizations (like temporarily breaking rules about GC, threading, etc).
- You can get access to unusual programming modes of your processor (e.g. 16 bit code for startup or BIOS interface on Intel PCs)
- You can build interfaces between code fragments using incompatible conventions (e.g. produced by different compilers, or separated by a low-level interface).
- You can produce reasonably fast code for tight loops to cope with a bad non-optimizing compiler (but then, there are free optimizing compilers available!)
- You can produce hand-optimized code that's perfectly tuned for your particular hardware setup, though not to anyone else's.
- You can write some code for your new language's optimizing compiler (that's something few will ever do, and even they, not often).

2.1.2 The disadvantages of Assembly

Assembly is a very low-level language (the lowest above hand-coding the binary instruction patterns). This means

- it's long and tedious to write initially,
- it's very bug-prone,
- your bugs will be very difficult to chase,
- it's very difficult to understand and modify, i.e. to maintain.
- the result is very non-portable to other architectures, existing or future,
- your code will be optimized only for a certain implementation of a same architecture: for instance, among Intel-compatible platforms, each CPU design and variation (bus width, relative speed and size of CPU/caches/RAM/Bus/disks presence of FPU, MMX extensions, etc) implies potentially completely different optimization techniques. CPU designs already include Intel 386, 486, Pentium, PPro, Pentium II; Cyrix 5x86, 6x86; AMD K5, K6. New designs keep appearing, so don't expect either this listing or your code to be up-to-date.
- your code might also be unportable across different OS platforms on the same architecture, by lack of proper tools. (well, GAS seems to work on all platforms; NASM seems to work or be workable on all Intel platforms).
- you spend more time on a few details, and can't focus on small and large algorithmic design, that are known to bring the largest part of the speed up. [e.g. you might spend some time building very fast list/array manipulation primitives in assembly; only a hash table would have sped up your program much more; or, in another context, a binary tree; or some high-level structure distributed over a cluster of CPUs]
- a small change in algorithmic design might completely invalidate all your existing assembly code. So that either you're ready (and able) to rewrite it all, or you're tied to a particular algorithmic design;
- On code that isn't too far from what's in standard benchmarks, commercial optimizing compilers outperform hand-coded assembly (well, that's less true on the x86 architecture than on RISC architectures, and perhaps less true for widely available/free compilers; anyway, for typical C code, GCC is fairly good);
- And in any case, as says moderator John Levine on comp.compilers, "compilers make it a lot easier to use complex data structures, and compilers don't get bored halfway through and generate reliably pretty good code." They will also *correctly* propagate code transformations throughout the whole (huge) program when optimizing code between procedures and module boundaries.

2.1.3 Assessment

All in all, you might find that though using assembly is sometimes needed, and might even be useful in a few cases where it is not, you'll want to:

- minimize the use of assembly code,
- encapsulate this code in well defined interfaces,
- have your assembly code automatically generated, from patterns expressed in a higher-level language than assembly (e.g. GCC inline-assembly macros),
- have automatic tools translate these programs into assembly code,
- have this code be optimized if possible,
- all of the above; i.e., write (an extension to) an optimizing compiler back-end.

Even in cases when Assembly is needed (e.g. OS development), you'll find that not so much of it is, and that the above principles hold.

See the sources for the Linux kernel about it: as little assembly as needed, resulting in a fast, reliable, portable, maintainable OS. Even a successful game like DOOM was almost massively written in C, with a tiny part only being written in assembly for speed up.

2.2 How to not use assembly

2.2.1 General procedure to achieve efficient code

As says Charles Fiterman on comp.compilers about human vs computer-generated assembly code,

"The human should always win and here is why.

- First the human writes the whole thing in a high level language.
- Second he profiles it to find the hot spots where it spends its time.
- Third he has the compiler produce assembly for those small sections of code.
- Fourth he hand tunes them looking for tiny improvements over the machine generated code.

The human wins because he can use the machine."

2.2.2 Languages with optimizing compilers

Languages like ObjectiveCAML, SML, Common LISP, Scheme, ADA, Pascal, C, C++, among others, all have free optimizing compilers that'll optimize the bulk of your programs, and often do better than hand-coded assembly even for tight loops, while allowing you to focus on higher-level details, and without forbidding you to grab a few percent of extra performance in the above-mentioned way, once you've reached a stable design. Of course, there are also commercial optimizing compilers for most of these languages, too.

Some languages have compilers that produce C code, which can be further optimized by a C compiler. LISP, Scheme, Perl, and many other are such. Speed is fairly good.

2.2.3 General procedure to speed your code up

As for speeding code up, you should do it only for parts of a program that a profiling tool has consistently identified as being a performance bottleneck.

Hence, if you identify some code portion as being too slow, you should

- first try to use a better algorithm;
- then try to compile it rather than interpret it;
- then try to enable and tweak optimization from your compiler;
- then give the compiler hints about how to optimize (typing information in LISP; register usage with GCC; lots of options in most compilers, etc);
- then possibly fall back to assembly programming.

Finally, before you end up writing assembly, you should inspect generated code, to check that the problem really is with bad code generation, as this might really not be the case: compiler-generated code might be better than what you'd have written, particularly on modern multi-pipelined architectures! Slow parts of a program might be intrinsically so. Biggest problems on modern architectures with fast processors are due to delays from memory access, cache-misses, TLB-misses, and page-faults; register optimization becomes useless, and you'll more profitably re-think data structures and threading to achieve better locality in memory access. Perhaps a completely different approach to the problem might help, then.

2.2.4 Inspecting compiler-generated code

There are many reasons to inspect compiler-generated assembly code. Here is what you'll do with such code:

- check whether generated code can be obviously enhanced with hand-coded assembly (or by tweaking compiler switches);
- when that's the case, start from generated code and modify it instead of starting from scratch;
- more generally, use generated code as stubs to modify, which at least gets right the way your assembly routines interface to the external world;
- track down bugs in your compiler (hopefully rarer).

The standard way to have assembly code be generated is to invoke your compiler with the `-S` flag. This works with most Unix compilers, including the GNU C Compiler (GCC), but YMMV. As for GCC, it will produce more understandable assembly code with the `-fverbose-asm` command-line option. Of course, if you want to get good assembly code, don't forget your usual optimization options and hints.

3 ASSEMBLERS

3.1 GCC Inline Assembly

The well-known GNU C/C++ Compiler (GCC), an optimizing 32-bit compiler at the heart of the GNU project, supports the x86 architecture quite well, and includes the ability to insert assembly code in C programs, in such a way that register allocation can be either specified or left to GCC. GCC works on most available platforms, notably Linux, *BSD, VSTa, OS/2, *DOS, Win*, etc.

3.1.1 Where to find GCC

The original GCC site is the GNU FTP site `(ftp://prep.ai.mit.edu/pub/gnu/)` together with all the released application software from the GNU project. Linux configured and precompiled versions can be found in `(ftp://sunsite.unc.edu/pub/Linux/GCC/)` There exists a lot of FTP mirrors of both sites, everywhere around the world, as well as CD-ROM copies.

GCC development has split in two branches recently. See more about the experimental version, egcs, at `(http://www.cygnus.com/egcs/)`

Sources adapted to your favorite OS, and binaries precompiled for it, should be found at your usual FTP sites.

For most popular DOS port of GCC is named DJGPP, and can be found in directories of such name in FTP sites. See: `(http://www.delorie.com/djgpp/)`

There is also a port of GCC to OS/2 named EMX, that also works under DOS, and includes lots of UNIX emulation library routines. See:

`(http://www.leo.org/pub/comp/os/os2/gnu/emx+gcc/)`
`(http://warp.eecs.berkeley.edu/os2/software/shareware/emx.html)`
`(ftp://ftp-os2.cdrom.com/pub/os2/emx09c/)`

3.1.2 Where to find docs for GCC Inline Asm

The documentation of GCC includes documentation files in TEXinfo format. You can compile them with TEX and print the result, or convert them to .info, and browse them with emacs, or convert them to .html, or nearly whatever you like. convert (with the right tools) to whatever you like, or just read as is. The .info files are generally found on any good installation for GCC.

The right section to look for is: `C Extensions::Extended Asm::`

Section `Invoking GCC::Submodel Options::i386 Options::` might help too. Particularly, it gives the i386 specific constraint names for registers: abcdSDB correspond to `%eax`, `%ebx`, `%ecx`, `%edx`, `%esi`, `%edi`, `%ebp` respectively (no letter for `%esp`).

The DJGPP Games resource (not only for game hackers) has this page specifically about assembly: `(http://www.rt66.com/~brennan/djgpp/djgpp_asm.html)`

Finally, there is a web page called, "DJGPP Quick ASM Programming Guide", that covers URLs to FAQs, AT&T x86 ASM Syntax, Some inline ASM information, and converting .obj/.lib files: `(http://remus.rutgers.edu/~avly/djasm.html)`

GCC depends on GAS for assembling, and follow its syntax (see below); do mind that inline asm needs percent characters to be quoted so they be passed to GAS. See the section about GAS below.

Find *lots* of useful examples in the `linux/include/asm-i386/` subdirectory of the sources for the Linux kernel.

3.1.3 Invoking GCC to have it properly inline assembly code?

Be sure to invoke GCC with the `-O` flag (or `-O2`, `-O3`, etc), to enable optimizations and inline assembly. If you don't, your code may compile but not run properly. Actually (kudos to Tim Potter, timbo@moshpit.air.net.au), it is enough to use the `-fasm` flag (and perhaps `-finline-functions`) which is part of all the features enabled by `-O`. So if you have problems with buggy optimizations in your particular implementation/version of GCC, you can still use inline asm. Similarly, use `-fno-asm` to disable inline assembly. (Why would you?).

More generally, good compile flags for GCC on the x86 platform are

```
gcc -O2 -fomit-frame-pointer -m386 -Wall
```

`-O2` is the good optimization level. It yields code that is a lot larger, but only a bit faster; such over-optimization might be useful for tight loops only (if any), which you may be doing in assembly anyway; if you need that, do it just for the few routines that need it.

`-fomit-frame-pointer` allows generated code to skip the stupid frame pointer maintenance, which makes code smaller and faster, and frees a register for further optimizations. It precludes the easy use of debugging tools (`gdb`), but when you use these, you just don't care about size and speed anymore anyway.

`-m386` yields more compact code, without any measurable slowdown, note that small code also means less disk I/O and faster execution, but perhaps on the above mentioned tight loops; you might appreciate `-mpentium` for special Pentium-optimizing GCC targeting a specifically Pentium platform.

`-Wall` enables all warnings and helps you catch obvious stupid errors.

To optimize even more, option `-mregparm=2` and/or corresponding function attribute might help, but might pose lots of problems when linking to foreign code.

Note that you can add make these flags the default by editing file `/usr/lib/gcc-lib/i486-linux/2.7.2.2/specs` or wherever that is on your system (better not add -Wall there, though).

3.2 GAS

GAS is the GNU Assembler that GCC relies upon.

3.2.1 Where to find it

Find it at the same place where you found GCC, in a package named binutils.

3.2.2 What is this AT&T syntax

Because GAS was invented to support a 32-bit UNIX compiler, it uses standard "AT&T" syntax, which resembles the syntax for standard m68k assemblers, and is standard in the UNIX world. This syntax is no worse, no better than the "Intel" syntax. It's just different. When you get used to it, you find it much more regular than the Intel syntax, though a bit boring.

Here are the major caveats about GAS syntax:

- Register names are prefixed with `%`, so that registers are `%eax`, `%dl` and such instead of just `eax`, `dl`, etc. This makes it possible to include external C symbols directly in assembly source, without any risk of confusion, or any need for ugly underscore prefixes.
- The order of operands is source(s) first, and destination last, as opposed to the Intel convention of destination first and sources last. Hence, what in Intel syntax is `mov ax,dx` (move contents of register `dx` into register `ax`) will be in AT&T syntax `mov %dx, %ax`.
- The operand length is specified as a suffix to the instruction name. The suffix is `b` for (8-bit) byte, `w` for (16-bit) word, and `l` for (32-bit) long. For instance, the correct syntax for the above instruction would have been `movw %dx,%ax`. However, GAS does not require strict AT&T syntax, so the suffix is optional when length can be guessed from register operands, and else defaults to 32-bit (with a warning).
- Immediate operands are marked with a `$` prefix, as in `addl $5,%eax` (add immediate long value 5 to register `%eax`).
- No prefix to an operand indicates it is a memory-address; hence `movl $foo,%eax` puts the address of variable `foo` in register `%eax`, but `movl foo,%eax` puts the contents of variable `foo` in register `%eax`.
- Indexing or indirection is done by enclosing the index register or indirection memory cell address in parentheses, as in `testb $0x80,17(%ebp)` (test the high bit of the byte value at offset 17 from the cell pointed to by `%ebp`).

A program exists to help you convert programs from TASM syntax to AT&T syntax. See `(ftp://x2ftp.oulu.fi/pub/msdos/programming/convert/ta2asv08.zip)`

GAS has comprehensive documentation in TEXinfo format, which comes at least with the source distribution. Browse extracted .info pages with Emacs or whatever. There used to be a file named gas.doc or as.doc around the GAS source package, but it was merged into the TEXinfo docs. Of course, in case of doubt, the ultimate documents are the sources themselves. A section that will particularly interest you is `Machine Dependencies::i386-Dependent::`

Again, the sources for Linux (the OS kernel), come in as good examples; see under linux/arch/i386, the following files: `kernel/*.S, boot/compressed/*.S, mathemu/*.S`

If you are writing kind of a language, like a thread package, you might as well see how other languages (OCaml, gforth, etc), or thread packages (QuickThreads, MIT pthreads, LinuxThreads, etc), or whatever, do it.

Finally, just compiling a C program to assembly might show you the syntax for the kind of instructions you want. See Section 2, above.

3.2.3 Limited 16-bit mode

GAS is a 32-bit assembler, meant to support a 32-bit compiler. It currently has only limited support for 16-bit mode, which consists in prepending the 32-bit prefixes to instructions, so you write 32-bit code that runs in 16-bit mode on a 32 bit CPU. In both modes, it supports 16-bit register usage, but what is unsupported is 16-bit addressing. Use the directive `.code16` and `.code32` to switch between modes. Note that an inline assembly statement `asm(".code16\n")` will allow GCC to produce 32-bit code that'll run in real mode.

I've been told that most code needed to fully support 16-bit mode programming was added to GAS by Bryan Ford, but at least, it doesn't show up in any of the distributions I tried, up to binutils-2.8.1.x ... more info on this subject would be welcome.

A cheap solution is to define macros (see below) that somehow produce the binary encoding (with `.byte`) for just the 16-bit mode instructions you need (almost nothing if you use code16 as above, and can safely assume the code will run on a 32-bit capable x86 CPU). To find the proper encoding, you can get inspiration from the sources of 16-bit capable assemblers for the encoding.

3.3 GASP

GASP is the GAS Preprocessor. It adds macros and some nice syntax to GAS.

3.3.1 Where to find GASP

GASP comes together with GAS in the GNU binutils archive.

3.3.2 How it works

It works as a filter, much like `cpp` and the like. I have no idea on details, but it comes with its own TEXinfo documentation, so just browse them (in .info), print them, grok them. GAS with GASP looks like a regular macro-assembler to me.

3.4 NASM

The Netwide Assembler project is producing yet another assembler, written in C, that should be modular enough to eventually support all known syntaxes and object formats.

3.4.1 Where to find NASM

`(http://www.cryogen.com/Nasm)`

Binary release on your usual sunsite mirror in `devel/lang/asm/` Should also be available as .rpm or .deb in your usual Red Hat/Debian distributions' contrib.

3.4.2 What it does

At the time this HOWTO is written, the current NASM version is 0.96.

The syntax is Intel-style. Some macroprocessing support is integrated.

Supported object file formats are `bin`, `a.out`, `coff`, `elf`, `as86`, (DOS) `obj`, `win32`, (their own format) `rdf`.

NASM can be used as a back end for the free LCC compiler (support files included).

Surely NASM evolves too fast for this HOWTO to be kept up to date. Unless you're using BCC as a 16-bit compiler (which is out of scope of this 32-bit HOWTO), you should use NASM instead of say AS86 or MASM, because it is actively supported online, and runs on all platforms.

Note: NASM also comes with a disassembler, NDISASM.

Its hand-written parser makes it much faster than GAS, though of course, it doesn't support three bazillion different architectures. For the x86 target, it should be the assembler of choice...

3.5 AS86

AS86 is a 80x86 assembler, both 16-bit and 32-bit, part of Bruce Evans' C Compiler (BCC). It has mostly Intel-syntax, though it differs slightly as for addressing modes.

3.5.1 Where to get AS86

A completely outdated version of AS86 is distributed by H.J. Lu just to compile the Linux kernel, in a package named bin86 (current version 0.4), available in any Linux GCC repository. But I advise no one to use it for anything else but compiling Linux. This version supports only a hacked minix object file format, which is not supported by the GNU binutils or anything, and it has a few bugs in 32-bit mode, so you really should better keep it only for compiling Linux.

The most recent versions by Bruce Evans (bde@zeta.org.au) are published together with the FreeBSD distribution. Well, they were: I could not find the sources from distribution 2.1 on Hence, I put the sources at my place: (http:///www.eleves.ens.fr:8080/home/rideau/files/bcc-95.3.12.src.tgz)

The Linux/8086 (aka ELKS) project is somehow maintaining bcc (though I don't think they included the 32-bit patches). See around (http://www.linux.org.uk/Linux8086.html) (ftp://linux.mit.edu/).

Among other things, these more recent versions, unlike H.J. Lu's, supports Linux GNU a.out format, so you can link you code to Linux programs, or use the usual tools from the GNU binutil package to manipulate your data. This version can co-exist without any harm with the previous one (see according question below).

BCC from 12 March 1995 and earlier version has a misfeature that makes all segment pushing/popping 16-bit, which is quite annoying when programming in 32-bit mode. A patch is published in the Tunes project (http://www.eleves.ens.fr:8080/home/rideau/Tunes/) subpage files/tgz/tunes.0.0.0.25.src.tgz in unpacked subdirectory LLL/i386/ The patch should also be in available directly from (http://www.eleves.ens.fr:8080/home/rideau/files/as86.bcc.patch.gz) Bruce Evans accepted this patch, so if there is a more recent version of BCC somewhere someday, the patch should have been included.

3.5.2 How to invoke the assembler?

Here's the GNU Makefile entry for using BCC to transform .s asm into both GNU a.out .o object and .l listing:

```
%.o %.l:          %.s
        bcc -3 -G -c -A-d -A-l -A$*.l -o $*.o $<
```

Remove the %.l, -A-l, and -A$*.l, if you don't want any listing. If you want something else than GNU a.out, you can see the docs of BCC about the other supported formats, and/or use the objcopy utility from the GNU binutils package.

3.5.3 Where to find docs

The docs are what is included in the bcc package. Man pages are also available somewhere on the FreeBSD site. When in doubt, the sources themselves are often a good docs: it's not very well commented, but the programming style is straightforward. You might try to see how AS86 is used in Tunes 0.0.0.25.

3.5.4 What if I can't compile Linux any more with this new version ?

Linus is buried alive in mail, and my patch for compiling Linux with a Linux a.out as86 didn't make it to him (!). Now, this shouldn't matter: just keep your as86 from the bin86 package in /usr/bin, and let bcc install the good as86 as /usr/local/libexec/i386/bcc/as where it should be. You never need explicitly call this "good" as86, because bcc does everything right, including conversion to Linux a.out, when invoked with the right options; so assemble files exclusively with bcc as a frontend, not directly with as86.

3.6 OTHER ASSEMBLERS

These are other, non-regular, options, in case the previous didn't satisfy you (why?), that I don't recommend in the usual case, but that could prove quite useful if the assembler must be integrated in the software you're designing (i.e. an OS or development environment).

3.6.1 Win32Forth assembler

Win32Forth is a *free* 32-bit ANS FORTH system that successfully runs under Win32s, Win95, Win/NT. It includes a free 32-bit assembler (either prefix or postfix syntax) integrated into the FORTH language. Macro processing is done with the full power of the reflective language FORTH; however, the only supported input and output contexts is Win32For itself (no dumping of .obj file – you could add that yourself, of course). Find it at (ftp://ftp.forth.org/pub/Forth/win32for/)

3.6.2 Terse

Terse is a programming tool that provides the most compact assembler syntax for the x86 family. See http://www.terse.com. It is said that there was a free clone somewhere, that was abandoned after worthless pretenses that the syntax would be owned by the original author, and that I invite you to take over, in case the syntax interests you.

3.6.3 Non-free and/or Non-32bit x86 assemblers.

You may find more about them, together with the basics of x86 assembly programming, in Raymond Moon's FAQ for comp.lang.asm.x86 (`http://www2.dgsys.com/~raymoon/faq/asmfaq.zip`)

Note that all DOS-based assemblers should work inside the Linux DOS Emulator, as well as other similar emulators, so that if you already own one, you can still use it inside a real OS. Recent DOS-based assemblers also support COFF and/or other object file formats that are supported by the GNU BFD library, so that you can use them together with your free 32-bit tools, perhaps using GNU objcopy (part of the binutils) as a conversion filter.

4 METAPROGRAMMING/MACROPROCESSING

Assembly programming is a bore, but for critical parts of programs.

You should use the appropriate tool for the right task, so don't choose assembly when it's not fit; C, OCAML, Perl, Scheme, might be a better choice for most of your programming.

However, there are cases when these tools do not give a fine enough control on the machine, and assembly is useful or needed. In those case, you'll appreciate a system of macroprocessing and metaprogramming that'll allow recurring patterns to be factored each into a one indefinitely reusable definition, which allows safer programming, automatic propagation of pattern modification, etc. A "plain" assembler is often not enough, even when one is doing only small routines to link with C.

4.1 What's integrated into the above

Yes I know this section does not contain much useful up-to-date information. Feel free to contribute what you discover the hard way.

4.1.1 GCC

GCC allows (and requires) you to specify register constraints in your "inline assembly" code, so the optimizer always knows about it; thus, inline assembly code is really made of patterns, not forcibly exact code.

Then, you can make put your assembly into CPP macros, and inline C functions, so anyone can use it in as any C function or macro. Inline functions resemble macros very much, but are sometimes cleaner to use. Beware that in all those cases, code will be duplicated, so only local labels (of `1:` style) should be defined in that assembly code. However, a macro would allow the name for a non-local defined label to be passed as a parameter (or else, you should use additional meta-programming methods). Also, note that propagating inline asm code will spread potential bugs in them, so watch out doubly for register constraints in such inline asm code.

Lastly, the C language itself may be considered as a good abstraction to assembly programming, which relieves you from most of the trouble of assembling.

Beware that some optimizations that involve passing arguments to functions through registers may make those functions unsuitable to be called from external (and particularly hand-written assembly) routines in the standard way; the "asmlinkage" attribute may prevent a routine to be concerned by such optimization flag; see the Linux kernel sources for examples.

4.1.2 GAS

GAS has some macro capability included, as detailed in the TEXinfo docs. Moreover, while GCC recognizes .s files as raw assembly to send to GAS, it also recognizes .S files as files to pipe through CPP before to feed them to GAS. Again and again, see Linux sources for examples.

4.1.3 GASP

It adds all the usual macroassembly tricks to GAS. See its TEXinfo docs.

4.1.4 NASM

NASM has some macro support, too. See according docs. If you have some bright idea, you might wanna contact the authors, as they are actively developing it. Meanwhile, see about external filters below.

4.1.5 AS86

It has some simple macro support, but I couldn't find docs. Now the sources are very straightforward, so if you're interested, you should understand them easily. If you need more than the basics, you should use an external filter (see below).

4.1.6 OTHER ASSEMBLERS

- Win32FORTH: CODE and END-CODE are normal that do not switch from interpretation mode to compilation mode, so you have access to the full power of FORTH while assembling.
- TUNES: it doesn't work yet, but the Scheme language is a real high-level language that allows arbitrary meta-programming.

4.2 External Filters

Whatever is the macro support from your assembler, or whatever language you use (even C!), if the language is not expressive enough to you, you can have files passed through an external filter with a Makefile rule like that:

```
%.s:    %.S other_dependencies
        $(FILTER) $(FILTER_OPTIONS) < $< > $@
```

4.2.1 CPP

CPP is truely not very expressive, but it's enough for easy things, it's standard, and called transparently by GCC.

As an example of its limitations, you can't declare objects so that destructors are automatically called at the end of the declaring block; you don't have diversions or scoping, etc.

CPP comes with any C compiler. If you could make it without one, don't bother fetching CPP (though I wonder how you could).

4.2.2 M4

M4 gives you the full power of macroprocessing, with a Turing equivalent language, recursion, regular expressions, etc. You can do with it everything that CPP cannot.

See macro4th/This4th from (ftp://ftp.forth.org/pub/Forth/) in Reviewed/ ANS/ (?), or the Tunes 0.0.0.25 sources as examples of advanced macroprogramming using m4.

However, its disfunctional quoting and unquoting semantics force you to use explicit continuation-passing tail-recursive macro style if you want to do advanced macro programming. (Which is remindful of TeX—btw, has anyone tried to use TeX as a macroprocessor for anything else than typesetting?) This is not worse than cpp, which does not allow quoting and recursion anyway.

The right version of m4 to get is GNU m4 1.4 (or later if exists), which has the most features and the least bugs or limitations of all. m4 is designed to be slow for anything but the simplest uses, which might still be ok for most assembly programming (you're not writing million-lines assembly programs, are you?).

4.2.3 Macroprocessing with your own filter

You can write your own simple macro-expansion filter with the usual tools: perl, awk, sed, etc. That's quick to do, and you control everything. But of course, any power in macroprocessing must be earned the hard way.

4.2.4 Metaprogramming

Instead of using an external filter that expands macros, one way to do things is to write programs that write part or all of other programs.

For instance, you could use a program outputing source code

- to generate sine/cosine/whatever lookup tables,

- to extract a source-form representation of a binary file,
- to compile your bitmaps into fast display routines,
- to extract documentation, initialization/finalization code, description tables, as well as normal code from the same source files,
- to have customized assembly code, generated from a perl/shell/scheme script that does arbitrary processing,
- to propagate data defined at one point only into several cross-referencing tables and code chunks.

Think about it!

Backends from existing compilers Compilers like SML/NJ, Objective CAML, MIT-Scheme, etc, do have their own generic assembler backend, which you might or not want to use, if you intend to generate code semi-automatically from the according languages.

The New-Jersey Machine-Code Toolkit There is a project, using the programming language Icon, to build a basis for producing assembly-manipulating code. See http://www.cs.virginia.edu/~nr/toolkit/.

Tunes The Tunes OS project is developping its own assembler as an extension to the Scheme language, as part of its development process. It doesn't run at all yet, though help is welcome.

The assembler manipulates symbolic syntax trees, so it could equally serve as the basis for a assembly syntax translator, a disassembler, a common assembler/compiler back-end, etc. Also, the full power of a real language, Scheme, make it unchallenged as for macroprocessing and metaprograming. See http://www.eleves.ens.fr:8080/home/rideau/Tunes/.

5 CALLING CONVENTIONS

5.1 Linux

5.1.1 Linking to GCC

That's the preferred way. Check GCC docs and examples from Linux kernel `.S` files that go through GAS (not those that go through AS86).

32-bit arguments are pushed down stack in reverse syntactic order (hence popped in the right order), above the 32-bit near return address. `%ebp`, `%esi`, `%edi`, `%ebx` are callee-saved, other registers are caller-saved; `%eax` is to hold the result, or `%edx:%eax` for 64-bit results.

FP stack: I'm not sure, but I think it's result in `st(0)`, whole stack caller-saved.

Note that GCC has options to modify the calling conventions by reserving registers, having arguments in registers, not assuming the FPU, etc. Check the i386 .info pages.

Beware that you must then declare the `cdecl` attribute for a function that will follow standard GCC calling conventions (I don't know what it does with modified calling conventions). See in the GCC info pages the section: `C Extensions::Extended Asm::`

5.1.2 ELF vs a.out problems

Some C compilers prepend an underscore before every symbol, while others do not.

Particularly, Linux a.out GCC does such prepending, while Linux ELF GCC does not.

If you need cope with both behaviors at once, see how existing packages do. For instance, get an old Linux source tree, the Elk, qthreads, or OCAML...

You can also override the implicit C->asm renaming by inserting statements like

```
void foo asm("bar") (void);
```

to be sure that the C function foo will be called really bar in assembly.

Note that the utility `objcopy`, from the `binutils` package, should allow you to transform your a.out objects into ELF objects, and perhaps the contrary too, in some cases. More generally, it will do lots of file format conversions.

5.1.3 Direct Linux syscalls

This is specifically *not* recommended, because the conventions change from time to time or from kernel flavor to kernel flavor (cf. L4Linux), plus it's not portable, it's a burden to write, it's redundant with the libc effort, AND it precludes fixes and extensions that are made to the libc, like, for instance the `zlibc` package, that does on-the-fly transparent decompression of gzip-compressed files. The standard, recommended way to call Linux system services is, and will stay, to go through the libc.

Shared objects should keep your stuff small. And if you really want smaller binaries, do use `#!` stuff, with the interpreter having all the overhead you want to keep out of your binaries.

Now, if for some reason, you don't want to link to the libc, go get the libc and understand how it works! After all, you're pretending to replace it, ain't you?

You might also take a look at how my eforth 1.0c

```
ftp://ftp.forth.org/pub/Forth/Linux/linux-eforth-1.0c.tgz
```

does it.

The sources for Linux come in handy, too, particularly the asm/unistd.h header file, that describes how to do system calls.

Basically, you issue an `int $0x80`, with the __NR_syscallname number (from `asm/unistd.h`) in `%eax`, and parameters (up to five) in `%ebx`, `%ecx`, `%edx`, `%esi`, `%edi` respectively. Result is returned in `%eax`, with a negative result being an error whose opposite is what libc would put in errno. The user-stack is not touched, so you needn't have a valid one when doing a syscall.

5.1.4 I/O under Linux

If you want to do direct I/O under Linux, either it's something very simple that doesn't need OS arbitration, and you should see the `IO-Port-Programming` mini-HOWTO; or it needs a kernel device driver, and you should try to learn more about kernel hacking, device driver development, kernel modules, etc, for which there are other excellent HOWTOs and documents from the LDP.

Particularly, if what you want is Graphics programming, then do join the GGI project: http://synergy.caltech.edu/~ggi/, and http://sunserver1.rz.uni-duesseldorf.de/~becka/doc/scrdrv.html

Anyway, in all these cases, you'll be better off using GCC inline assembly with the macros from `linux/asm/*.h` than writing full assembly source files.

5.1.5 Accessing 16-bit drivers from Linux/i386

Such thing is theoretically possible (proof: see how DOSEMU can selectively grant hardware port access to programs),and I heard rumors that someone somewhere did actually do it in the PCI driver. (Some VESA access stuff? ISA PnP? dunno). If you have some more precise information on that, you'll be most welcome. Anyway, good places to look for more information are the Linux kernel sources, DOSEMU sources (and other programs at ftp://tsx-11.mit.edu/pub/linux/ALPHA/dosemu/ and sources for various low-level programs under Linux. (perhaps GGI if it supports VESA.) Basically, you must either use 16-bit protected mode or vm86 mode.

The first is simpler to set up, but only works with well behaved code that won't do any kind of segment arithmetics or absolute segment addressing (particularly addressing segment 0), unless by chance it happens that all segments used can be setup in advance in the LDT.

The later allows for more "compatibility" with vanilla 16-bit environments, but requires more complicated handling.

In both cases, before you can jump to 16-bit code, you must

- mmap any absolute address used in the 16-bit code (such as ROM, video buffers, DMA targets, and memory-mapped I/O) from /dev/mem to your process' address space,
- set up the LDT and/or vm86 mode monitor,
- grab proper I/O permissions from the kernel (see the above section).

Again, carefully read the source for the stuff contributed to the DOSEMU repository above, particularly these mini-emulators for running ELKS or simple .COM programs under Linux/i386.

5.2 DOS

Most DOS extenders come with some interface to DOS services. Read their docs about that, but often, they just simulate `int $0x21` and such, so you do "as if" you were in real mode (I doubt they have more than stubs and extend things to work with 32-bit operands; they most likely will just reflect the interrupt into the real-mode or vm86 handler).

Docs about DPMI and such (and much more) can be found on ftp://x2ftp.oulu.fi/pub/msdos/programming/.

DJGPP comes with its own (limited) glibc derivative/subset/replacement, too.

It is possible to cross-compile from Linux to DOS, see the devel/msdos/ directory of your local FTP mirror for sunsite.unc.edu Also see the MOSS MS-DOS extender from the Flux project in Utah.

Other documents and FAQs are more MS-DOS centered. We do not recommend MS-DOS development.

5.3 Your very own OS

Control being what attract many programmers to assembly, want of OS development is often what leads to or stems from assembly hacking. Note that any system that allows self-development could be qualified an "OS" even though it might run “on top” of an underlying system with multitasking or I/O (much like Linux over Mach or OpenGenera over Unix), etc. Hence, for easier debugging purpose, you might like to develop your “OS” first as a process running on top of Linux (despite the slowness), then use the Flux OS Kit, http://ww.cs.utah.edu/projects/flux/. It grants use of Linux and BSD drivers in your own OS to make it standalone. When your OS is stable, it’s time to write your own hardware drivers if you really love that.

This HOWTO will not itself cover topics such as boot loader code and getting into 32-bit mode, handling interrupts, The basics about Intel “protected mode” or “V86/R86” braindeadness, defining your object format and calling conventions. The main place where to find reliable information about that all is source code of existing OSes and bootloaders. Lots of pointers lie in the following WWW page: (`http://www.eleves.ens.fr:8080/home/rideau/Tunes/Review/OSes.html`)

A few pointers (in addition to those already in the rest of the HOWTO)

- *pentium manuals* (`http://www.intel.com/design/pentium/manuals/`)
- *cpu bugs in the x86 family* (`http://www.xs4all.nl/~feldmann`)
- *hornet.eng.ufl.edu for assembly coders* (`http://www.eng.ufl.edu/ftp`)
- *ftp.luth.se* (`ftp://ftp.luth.se/pub/msdos/demos/code/`)
- *PM FAQ* (`ftp://zfja-gate.fuw.edu.pl/cpu/protect.mod`)
- *80x86 Assembly Page* (`http://www.fys.ruu.nl/~faber/Amain.html`)
- *Courseware* (`http://www.cit.ac.nz/smac/csware.htm`)
- *game programming* (`http://www.ee.ucl.ac.uk/~phart/gameprog.html`)
- *experiments with asm-only linux programming* (`http://bewoner.dma.be/JanW`)

And of course, do use your usual Internet Search Tools to look for more information. Tell me anything interesting you find.

Authors’ .sig:

```
--    ,                                ,              \_ v    \~{}  ^  --
-- Fare -- rideau@clipper.ens.fr -- Francois-Rene Rideau -- +)ang-Vu Ban --
--                              '                      / .            --
Join the TUNES project for a computing system based on computing freedom !
                TUNES is a Useful, Not Expedient System
WWW page at URL: http://www.eleves.ens.fr:8080/home/rideau/Tunes/
```

Part VII

"Linux AX25-HOWTO, Amateur Radio" by Terry Dawson, VK2KTJ, terry@perf.no.itg.telstra.com.au

Contents

Abstract

v1.5, 17 October 1997
The Linux Operating System is perhaps the only operating system in the world that can boast native and standard support for the AX.25 packet radio protocol utilized by Amateur Radio Operators worldwide. This document aims to describe how to install and configure this support.

1 Introduction.

This document was originally an appendix to the HAM-HOWTO, but grew too large to be reasonably managed in that fashion. This document describes how to install and configure the native AX.25, NetRom and Rose support for Linux. A few typical configurations are described that could be used as models to work from.

The Linux implementation of the amateur radio protocols is very flexible. To people relatively unfamiliar with the Linux operating system the configuration process may look daunting and complicated. It will take you a little time to come to understand how the whole thing fits together. You will find configuration very difficult if you have not properly prepared yourself by learning about Linux in general. You cannot expect to switch from some other environment to Linux without learning about Linux itself.

1.1 Changes from the previous version

```
Additions:
        Joerg Reuters Web Page
        "More Information" section
        ax25ipd configuration.

Corrections/Updates:
        Changed pty's to a safer range to prevent possible conflicts
        Updated module and ax25-utils versions.

To Do:
        Fix up the SCC section, this is probably wrong.
        Expand on the programming section.
```

1.2 Where to obtain new versions of this document.

The best place to obtain the latest version of this document is from a Linux Documentation Project archive. The Linux Documentation Project runs a Web Server and this document appears there as *the AX25-HOWTO* (`http://sunsite.unc.edu/LDP/HOWTO/AX25-HOWTO.html`). This document is also available in various formats from *the sunsite.unc.edu ftp archive* (`ftp://sunsite.unc.edu/pub/Linux/docs/howto/`).

You can always contact me, but I pass new versions of the document directly to the LDP HOWTO coordinator, so if it isn't there then chances are I haven't finished it.

1.3 Other related documentation.

There is a lot of related documentation. There are many documents that relate to Linux networking in more general ways and I strongly recommend you also read these as they will assist you in your efforts and provide you with stronger insight into other possible configurations.

They are:
The HAM-HOWTO (`http://sunsite.unc.edu/LDP/HOWTO/HAM-HOWTO.html`),
the NET-3-HOWTO (`http://sunsite.unc.edu/LDP/HOWTO/NET-3-HOWTO.html`),
the Ethernet-HOWTO (`http://sunsite.unc.edu/LDP/HOWTO/Ethernet-HOWTO.html`),
and:
the Firewall-HOWTO (`http://sunsite.unc.edu/LDP/HOWTO/Firewall-HOWTO.html`)

More general Linux information may be found by reference to other *Linux HOWTO* (`http://sunsite.unc.edu/LDP/HOWTO/`) documents.

2 The Packet Radio Protocols and Linux.

The *AX.25* protocol offers both connected and connectionless modes of operation, and is used either by itself for point-point links, or to carry other protocols such as TCP/IP and NetRom.

It is similar to X.25 level 2 in structure, with some extensions to make it more useful in the amateur radio environment.

The NetRom protocol is an attempt at a full network protocol and uses AX.25 at its lowest layer as a data-link protocol. It provides a network layer that is an adapted form of AX.25. The NetRom protocol features dynamic routing and node aliases.

The Rose protocol was conceived and first implemented by Tom Moulton W2VY and is an implementation of the X.25 packet layer protocol and is designed to operate with AX.25 as its data-link layer protocol. It too provides a network layer. Rose addresses take the form of 10 digit numbers. The first four digits are called the Data Network Identification Code (DNIC) and are taken from Appendix B of the CCITT X.121 recommendation. More information on the Rose protocol may be obtained from the *RATS Web server* (`http://www.rats.org/`).

Alan Cox developed some early kernel based AX.25 software support for Linux. Jonathon Naylor `<g4klx@g4klx.demon.co.uk>` has taken up ongoing development of the code, has added NetRom and Rose support and is now the developer of the AX.25 related kernel code. DAMA support was developed by Joerg, DL1BKE, `jreuter@poboxes.com`. Baycom and SoundModem support were added by Thomas Sailer, `<sailer@ife.ee.ethz.ch>`. The AX.25 utility software is now maintained by me.

The Linux code supports KISS based TNC's (Terminal Node Controllers), the Ottawa PI card, the Gracilis PacketTwin card and other Z8530 SCC based cards with the generic SCC driver and both the Parallel and Serial port Baycom modems. Thomas's new sound-modem driver supports Soundblaster and sound cards based on the Crystal chip set.

The User programs contain a simple PMS (Personal Message System), a beacon facility, a line mode connect program, 'listen' an example of how to capture all AX.25 frames at raw interface level and programs to configure the NetRom protocol. Included also are an AX.25 server style program to handle and despatch incoming AX.25 connections and a NetRom daemon which does most of the hard work for NetRom support.

2.1 How it all fits together.

The Linux AX.25 implementation is a brand new implementation. While in many ways it may looks similar to NOS, or BPQ or other AX.25 implementations, it is none of these and is not identical to any of them. The Linux AX.25 implementation is capable of being configured to behave almost identically to other implementations, but the configuration process is very different.

To assist you in understanding how you need to think when configuring this section describes some of the structural features of the AX.25 implementation and how it fits into the context of the overall Linux structure.

Simplified Protocol Layering Diagram

```
----------------------------------------------
| AF_AX25 | AF_NETROM |  AF_INET    | AF_ROSE |
|=========|===========|=============|=========|
|         |           |             |         |
|         |           |    TCP/IP   |         |
|         |           ----------    |         |
|         |   NetRom           |    | Rose    |
|         -------------------------------------
|            AX.25                            |
----------------------------------------------
```

This diagram simply illustrates that NetRom, Rose and TCP/IP all run directly on top of AX.25, but that each of these protocols is treated as a separate protocol at the programming interface. The '`AF_`' names are simply the names given to the '*Address Family*' of each of these protocols when writing programs to use them. The important thing to note here is the implicit dependence on the configuration of your AX.25 devices before you can configure your NetRom, Rose or TCP/IP devices.

Software module diagram of Linux Network Implementation

```
----------------------------------------------------------------------------
User    | Programs |  call         node    ||  Daemons | ax25d  mheardd
        |          |  pms          mheard  ||          | inetd  netromd
----------------------------------------------------------------------------
        | Sockets  | open(), close(), listen(), read(), write(), connect()
        |          |------------------------------------------------------
        |          |   AF\_AX25   |  AF\_NETROM  |   AF\_ROSE   |  AF_INET
        |------------------------------------------------------------------
Kernel  | Protocols |   AX.25     |   NetRom    |     Rose     | IP/TCP/UDP
        |------------------------------------------------------------------
        | Devices  |   ax0,ax1    |  nr0,nr1    | rose0,rose1 | eth0,ppp0
```

```
           |--------------------------------------------------------------
           | Drivers     | Kiss   PI2   PacketTwin   SCC   BPQ    | slip ppp
           |             |      Soundmodem        Baycom          | ethernet
--------------------------------------------------------------------------
Hardware | PI2 Card, PacketTwin Card, SCC card, Serial port, Ethernet Card
--------------------------------------------------------------------------
```

This diagram is a little more general than the first. This diagram attempts to show the relationship between user applications, the kernel and the hardware. It also shows the relationship between the Socket application programming interface, the actual protocol modules, the kernel networking devices and the device drivers. Anything in this diagram is dependent on anything underneath it, and in general you must configure from the bottom of the diagram upwards. So for example, if you want to run the *call* program you must also configure the Hardware, then ensure that the kernel has the appropriate device driver, that you create the appropriate network device, that the kernel includes the desired protocol that presents a programming interface that the *call* program can use. I have attempted to lay out this document in roughly that order.

3 The AX.25/NetRom/Rose software components.

The AX.25 software is comprised of three components, the kernel source, the network configuration tools and the utility programs.

The version 2.0.xx Linux kernels include the AX.25, NetRom, Z8530 SCC, PI card and PacketTwin drivers by default. These have been significantly enhanced in the 2.1.* kernels. Unfortunately, the rest of the 2.1.* kernels makes them fairly unstable at the moment and not a good choice for a production system. To solve this problem Jonathon Naylor has prepared a patch kit which will bring the amateur radio protocol support in a 2.0.28 kernel up to the standard of the 2.1.* kernels. This is very simple to apply, and provides a range of facilities not present in the standard kernel such as Rose support.

3.1 Finding the kernel, tools and utility packages.

3.1.1 The kernel source:

The kernel source can be found in its usual place at: **ftp.kernel.org**

```
/pub/linux/kernel/v2.0/linux-2.0.31.tar.gz
```

The current version of the AX25 upgrade patch is available at: **ftp.pspt.fi**

```
/pub/linux/ham/ax25/ax25-module-14e.tar.gz
```

3.1.2 The network tools:

The latest alpha release of the standard Linux network tools support AX.25 and NetRom and can be found at: **ftp.inka.de**

```
/pub/comp/Linux/networking/net-tools/net-tools-1.33.tar.gz
```

The latest ipfwadm package can be found at: **ftp.xos.nl**

```
/pub/linux/ipfwadm/
```

3.1.3 The AX25 utilities:

There are two different families of AX25-utilities. One is for the `2.0.*` kernels and the other will work with either the `2.1.*` kernels or the `2.0.*+moduleXX` kernels. The ax25-utils version number indicates the oldest version of kernel that they will work with. Please choose a version of the ax25-utils appropriate to your kernel. The following are working combinations. You **must** use one of the following combinations, any other combination will not work, or will not work well.

```
Linux Kernel              AX25 Utility set
----------------------    ------------------------
linux-2.0.29              ax25-utils-2.0.12c.tar.gz **
linux-2.0.28+module12     ax25-utils-2.1.22b.tar.gz **
linux-2.0.30+module14c    ax25-utils-2.1.42a.tar.gz
linux-2.0.31+module14d    ax25-utils-2.1.42a.tar.gz
linux-2.1.22 ++           ax25-utils-2.1.22b.tar.gz
linux-2.1.42 ++           ax25-utils-2.1.42a.tar.gz
```

Note: the `ax25-utils-2.0.*` series (marked above with the '**' symbol) is now obsolete and is no longer supported. This document covers configuration using the versions of software recommended above the table. While there are differences between the releases, most of the information will be relevant to earlier releases of code.

The AX.25 utility programs can be found at: *ftp.pspt.fi* (`ftp://ftp.pspt.fi/pub/linux/ham/ax25/`)
or at: *sunsite.unc.edu* (`ftp://sunsite.unc.edu/pub/Linux/apps/ham/`)

4 Installing the AX.25/NetRom/Rose software.

To successfully install AX.25 support on your Linux system you must configure and install an appropriate kernel and then install the AX.25 utilities.

4.1 Compiling the kernel.

If you are already familiar with the process of compiling the Linux Kernel then you can skip this section, just be sure to select the appropriate options when compiling the kernel. If you are not, then read on.

The normal place for the kernel source to be unpacked to is the `/usr/src` directory into a subdirectory called `linux`. To do this you should be logged in as `root` and execute a series of commands similar to the following:

```
# mv Linux linux.old
# cd /usr/src
# tar xvfz linux-2.0.31.tar.gz
# tar xvfz /pub/net/ax25/ax25-module-14e.tar.gz
# patch -p0 </usr/src/ax25-module-14/ax25-2.0.31-2.1.47-2.diff
# cd linux
```

After you have unpacked the kernel source and applied the upgrade, you need to run the configuration script and choose the options that suit your hardware configuration and the options that you wish built into your kernel. You do this by using the command:

```
# make menuconfig
```

You might also try:

```
# make config
```

I'm going to describe the full screen method (menuconfig) because it is easier to move around, but you use whichever you are most comfortable with.

In either case you will be offered a range of options at which you must answer 'Y' or 'N'. (Note you may also answer 'M' if you are using modules. For the sake of simplicity I will assume you are not, please make appropriate modifications if you are).

The options most relevant to an AX.25 configuration are:

```
Code maturity level options  --->
    ...
    [*] Prompt for development and/or incomplete code/drivers
    ...
General setup  --->
    ...
    [*] Networking support
    ...
Networking options  --->
    ...
    [*] TCP/IP networking
    [?] IP: forwarding/gatewaying
    ...
    [?] IP: tunneling
    ...
    [?] IP: Allow large windows (not recommended if <16Mb of memory)
    ...
    [*] Amateur Radio AX.25 Level 2
    [?] Amateur Radio NET/ROM
    [?] Amateur Radio X.25 PLP (Rose)
    ...
```

```
Network device support  --->
    [*] Network device support
    ...
    [*] Radio network interfaces
    [?] BAYCOM ser12 and par96 driver for AX.25
    [?] Soundcard modem driver for AX.25
    [?] Soundmodem support for Soundblaster and compatible cards
    [?] Soundmodem support for WSS and Crystal cards
    [?] Soundmodem support for 1200 baud AFSK modulation
    [?] Soundmodem support for 4800 baud HAPN-1 modulation
    [?] Soundmodem support for 9600 baud FSK G3RUH modulation
    [?] Serial port KISS driver for AX.25
    [?] BPQ Ethernet driver for AX.25
    [?] Gracilis PackeTwin support for AX.25
    [?] Ottawa PI and PI/2 support for AX.25
    [?] Z8530 SCC KISS emulation driver for AX.25
    ...
```

The options I have flagged with a '*' are those that you **must** must answer 'Y' to. The rest are dependent on what hardware you have and what other options you want to include. Some of these options are described in more detail later on, so if you don't know what you want yet, then read ahead and come back to this step later.

After you have completed the kernel configuration you should be able to cleanly compile your new kernel:

```
# make dep
# make clean
# make zImage
```

make sure you move your `arch/i386/boot/zImage` file wherever you want it and then edit your `/etc/lilo.conf` file and rerun *lilo* to ensure that you actually boot from it.

4.1.1 A word about Kernel modules

I recommend that you **don't** compile any of the drivers as modules. In nearly all installations you gain nothing but additional complexity. Many people have problems trying to get the modularized components working, not because the software is faulty but because modules are more complicated to install and configure.

If you've chosen to compile any of the components as modules, then you'll also need to use:

```
# make modules
# make modules_install
```

to install your modules in the appropriate location.

You will also need to add some entries into your `/etc/conf.modules` file that will ensure that the *kerneld* program knows how to handle the kernel modules. You should add/modify the following:

```
alias net-pf-3     ax25
alias net-pf-6     netrom
alias net-pf-11    rose
alias tty-ldisc-1  slip
alias tty-ldisc-3  ppp
alias tty-ldisc-5  mkiss
alias bc0          baycom
alias nr0          netrom
alias pi0a         pi2
alias pt0a         pt
alias scc0         optoscc    (or one of the other scc drivers)
alias sm0          soundmodem
alias tunl0        newtunnel
alias char-major-4 serial
alias char-major-5 serial
alias char-major-6 lp
```

4.1.2 What's new in 2.0.*+ModuleXX or 2.1.* Kernels ?

The `2.1.*` kernels have enhanced versions of nearly all of the protocols and drivers. The most significant of the enhancements are:

modularized
: the protocols and drivers have all been modularized so that you can *insmod* and *rmmod* them whenever you wish. This reduces the kernel memory requirements for infrequently used modules and makes development and bug hunting much simpler. That being said, it also makes configuration slightly more difficult.

All drivers are now network drivers
: all of the network devices such as Baycom, SCC, PI, Packettwin etc now present a normal network interface, that is they now look like the ethernet driver does, they no longer look like KISS TNC's. A new utility called *net2kiss* allows you to build a KISS interface to these devices if you wish.

bug fixed
: there have been many bug fixes and new features added to the drivers and protocols. The Rose protocol is one important addition.

4.2 The network configuration tools.

Now that you have compiled the kernel you should compile the new network configuration tools. These tools allow you to modify the configuration of network devices and to add routes to the routing table.

The new alpha release of the standard `net-tools` package includes support for AX.25 and NetRom support. I've tested this and it seems to work well for me.

4.2.1 A patch kit that adds Rose support and fixes some bugs.

The standard net-tools-1.33.tar.gz package has some small bugs that affect the AX.25 and NetRom support. I've made a small patch kit that corrects these and adds Rose support to the tools as well.

You can get the patch from

```
ftp://zone.pspt.fi/pub/linux/ham/ax25/net-tools-1.33.rose.tjd.diff.gz
```

4.2.2 Building the standard net-tools release.

Don't forget to read the `Release` file and follow any instructions there. The steps I used to compile the tools were:

```
# cd /usr/src
# tar xvfz net-tools-1.33.tar.gz
# zcat net-tools-1.33.rose.tjd.diff.gz | patch -p0
# cd net-tools-1.33
# make config
```

At this stage you will be presented with a series of configuration questions, similar to the kernel configuration questions. Be sure to include support for all of the protocols and network devices types that you intend to use. If you do not know how to answer a particular question then answer 'Y'.

When the compilation is complete, you should use the:

```
# make install
```

command to install the programs in their proper place.

If you wish to use the IP firewall facilities then you will need the latest firewall administration tool `ipfwadm`. This tool replaces the older `ipfw` tool which will not work with new kernels.

I compiled the `ipfwadm` utility with the following commands:

```
# cd /usr/src
# tar xvfz ipfwadm-2.0beta2.tar.gz
# cd ipfwadm-2.0beta2
# make install
# cp ipfwadm.8 /usr/man/man8
# cp ipfw.4 /usr/man/man4
```

4.3 The AX.25 user and utility programs.

After you have successfully compiled and booted your new kernel, you need to compile the user programs. To compile and install the user programs you should use a series of commands similar to the following:

```
# cd /usr/src
# tar xvfz ax25-utils-2.1.42a.tar.gz
# cd ax25-utils-2.1.42a
# make config
# make
# make install
```

The files will be installed under the /usr directory by default in subdirectories: bin, sbin, etc and man.

If this is a first time installation, that is you've never installed any AX.25 utilities on your machine before you should also use the:

```
# make installconf
```

command to install some sample configuration files into the /etc/ax25/ directory from which to work.

If you get messages something like:

```
gcc -Wall -Wstrict-prototypes -O2 -I../lib -c call.c
call.c: In function 'statline':
call.c:268: warning: implicit declaration of function 'attron'
call.c:268: 'A_REVERSE' undeclared (first use this function)
call.c:268: (Each undeclared identifier is reported only once
call.c:268: for each function it appears in.)
```

then you should double check that you have the *ncurses* package properly installed on your system. The configuration script attempts to locate your ncurses packages in the common locations, but some installations have ncurses badly installed and it is unable to locate them.

5 A note on call signs, addresses and things before we start.

Each AX.25 and NetRom port on your system must have a call sign/ssid allocated to it. These are configured in the configuration files that will be described in detail later on.

Some AX.25 implementations such as NOS and BPQ will allow you to configure the same call sign/ssid on each AX.25 and NetRom port. For somewhat complicated technical reasons Linux does not allow this. This isn't as big a problem in practice as it might seem.

This means that there are things you should be aware of and take into consideration when doing your configurations.

1. Each AX.25 and NetRom port must be configured with a unique call sign/ssid.
2. TCP/IP will use the call sign/ssid of the AX.25 port it is being transmitted or received by, i.e., the one you configured for the AX.25 interface in item 1.
3. NetRom will use the call sign/ssid specified for it in its configuration file, but this call sign is only used when your NetRom is speaking to another NetRom, this is **not** the call sign/ssid that AX.25 users who wish to use your NetRom 'node' will use. More on this later.
4. Rose will, by default, use the call sign/ssid of the AX.25 port, unless the Rose call sign has been specifically set using the rsparms command. If you set a call sign/SSID using the rsparms command then Rose will use this call sign/ssid on all ports.
5. Other programs, such as the ax25d program can listen using any call sign/SSID that they wish and these may be duplicated across different ports.
6. If you are careful with routing you can configure the same IP address on all ports if you wish.

5.1 What are all those T1, T2, N2 and things ?

Not every AX.25 implementation is a TNC2. Linux uses nomenclature that differs in some respects from that you will be used to if your sole experience with packet is a TNC. The following table should help you interpret what each of the configurable items are, so that when you come across them later in this text you'll understand what they mean.

```
-----------------------------------------------------------------
Linux  | TAPR TNC | Description
-----------------------------------------------------------------
T1     | FRACK    | How long to wait before retransmitting an
       |          | unacknowledged frame.
-----------------------------------------------------------------
T2     | RESPTIME | The minimum amount of time to wait for another
       |          | frame to be received before transmitting
       |          | an acknowledgement.
-----------------------------------------------------------------
T3     | CHECK    | The period of time we wait between sending
       |          | a check that the link is still active.
-----------------------------------------------------------------
N2     | RETRY    | How many times to retransmit a frame before
       |          | assuming the connection has failed.
-----------------------------------------------------------------
Idle   |          | The period of time a connection can be idle
       |          | before we close it down.
-----------------------------------------------------------------
Window | MAXFRAME | The maximum number of unacknowledged
       |          | transmitted frames.
-----------------------------------------------------------------
```

5.2 Run time configurable parameters

The `2.1.*` and `2.0.* +moduleXX` kernels have a new feature that allows you to change many previously unchangeable parameters at run time. If you take a careful look at the `/proc/sys/net/` directory structure you will see many files with useful names that describe various parameters for the network configuration. The files in the `/proc/sys/net/ax25/` directory each represents one configured AX.25 port. The name of the file relates to the name of the port.

The structure of the files in `/proc/sys/net/ax25/<portname>/` is as follows:

```
FileName               Meaning             Values                Default
ip_default_mode        IP Default Mode     0=DG 1=VC             0
ax25_default_mode      AX.25 Default Mode  0=Normal 1=Extended   0
backoff_type           Backoff             0=Linear 1=Exponential 1
connect_mode           Connected Mode      0=No 1=Yes            1
standard_window_size   Standard Window     1  <= N <= 7          2
extended_window_size   Extended Window     1  <= N <= 63         32
t1_timeout             T1 Timeout          1s <= N <= 30s        10s
t2_timeout             T2 Timeout          1s <= N <= 20s        3s
t3_timeout             T3 Timeout          0s <= N <= 3600s      300s
idle_timeout           Idle Timeout        0m <= N               20m
maximum_retry_count    N2                  1  <= N <= 31         10
maximum_packet_length AX.25 Frame Length   1  <= N <= 512        256
```

In the table T1, T2 and T3 are given in seconds, and the Idle Timeout is given in minutes. But please note that the values used in the sysctl interface are given in internal units where the time in seconds is multiplied by 10, this allows resolution down to 1/10 of a second. With timers that are allowed to be zero, e.g., T3 and Idle, a zero value indicates that the timer is disabled.

The structure of the files in `/proc/sys/net/netrom/` is as follows:

```
FileName                          Values          Default
default_path_quality                              10
link_fails_count                                  2
network_ttl_initialiser                           16
obsolescence_count_initialiser                    6
routing_control                                   1
transport_acknowledge_delay                       50
transport_busy_delay                              1800
transport_maximum_tries                           3
transport_requested_window_size                   4
```

```
transport_timeout                                    1200
```

The structure of the files in /proc/sys/net/rose/ is as follows:

```
FileName                       Values                Default
acknowledge_hold_back_timeout                        50
call_request_timeout                                 2000
clear_request_timeout                                1800
link_fail_timeout                                    1200
maximum_virtual_circuits                             50
reset_request_timeout                                1800
restart_request_timeout                              1800
routing_control                                      1
window_size                                          3
```

To set a parameter all you need to do is write the desired value to the file itself, for example to check and set the Rose window size you'd use something like:

```
# cat /proc/sys/net/rose/window_size
3
# echo 4 >/proc/sys/net/rose/window_size
# cat /proc/sys/net/rose/window_size
4
```

6 Configuring an AX.25 port.

Each of the AX.25 applications read a particular configuration file to obtain the parameters for the various AX.25 ports configured on your Linux machine. For AX.25 ports the file that is read is the /etc/ax25/axport file. You must have an entry in this file for each AX.25 port you want on your system.

6.1 Creating the AX.25 network device.

The network device is what is listed when you use the ifconfig command. This is the object that the Linux kernel sends and receives network data from. Nearly always the network device has a physical port associated with it, but there are occasions where this isn't necessary. The network device does relate directly to a device driver.

In the Linux AX.25 code there are a number of device drivers. The most common is probably the KISS driver, but others are the SCC driver(s), the Baycom driver and the SoundModem driver.

Each of these device drivers will create a network device when it is started.

6.1.1 Creating a KISS device.

Kernel Compile Options:

```
General setup  --->
    [*] Networking support
Network device support  --->
    [*] Network device support
    ...
    [*] Radio network interfaces
    [*] Serial port KISS driver for AX.25
```

Probably the most common configuration will be for a KISS TNC on a serial port. You will need to have the TNC preconfigured and connected to your serial port. You can use a communications program like minicom or seyon to configure the TNC into KISS mode.

To create a KISS device you use the kissattach program. In it simplest form you can use the kissattach program as follows:

```
# /usr/sbin/kissattach /dev/ttyS0 radio
# kissparms -p radio -t 100 -s 100 -r 25
```

The kissattach command will create a KISS network device. These devices are called 'ax[0-9]'. The first time you use the kissattach command it creates 'ax0', the second time it creates 'ax1' etc. Each KISS device has an associated serial port.

The *kissparms* command allows you to set various KISS parameters on a KISS device.

Specifically the example presented would create a KISS network device using the serial device '/dev/ttyS0' and the entry from the /etc/ax25/axports with a port name of 'radio'. It then configures it with a *txdelay* and *slottime* of 100 milliseconds and a ppersist value of 25.

Please refer to the manual pages for more information.

Configuring for Dual Port TNC's The *mkiss* utility included in the ax25-utils distribution allows you to make use of both modems on a dual port TNC. Configuration is fairly simple. It works by taking a single serial device connected to a single multiport TNC and making it look like a number of devices each connected to a single port TNC. You do this **before** you do any of the AX.25 configuration. The devices that you then do the AX.25 configuration on are pseudo-TTY interfaces, (/dev/ttyq*), and not the actual serial device. Pseudo-TTY devices create a kind of pipe through which programs designed to talk to tty devices can talk to other programs designed to talk to tty devices. Each pipe has a master and a slave end. The master end is generally called '/dev/ptyq*' and the slave ends are called '/dev/ttyq*'. There is a one to one relationship between masters and slaves, so /dev/ptyq0 is the master end of a pipe with /dev/ttyq0 as its slave. You must open the master end of a pipe before opening the slave end. *mkiss* exploits this mechanism to split a single serial device into separate devices.

Example: if you have a dual port TNC and it is connected to your /dev/ttyS0 serial device at 9600 bps, the command:

```
# /usr/sbin/mkiss -s 9600 /dev/ttyS0 /dev/ptyq0 /dev/ptyq1
# /usr/sbin/kissattach /dev/ttyq0 port1
# /usr/sbin/kissattach /dev/ttyq1 port2
```

would create two pseudo-tty devices that each look like a normal single port TNC. You would then treat /dev/ttyq0 and /dev/ttyq1 just as you would a conventional serial device with TNC connected. This means you'd then use the kissattach command as described above, on each of those, in the example for AX.25 ports called port1 and port2. You shouldn't use kissattach on the actual serial device as the mkiss program uses it.

The mkiss command has a number of optional arguments that you may wish to use. They are summarized as follows:

-c

enables the addition of a one byte checksum to each KISS frame. This is not supported by most KISS implementation, it is supported by the G8BPG KISS ROM.

-s <speed>

sets the speed of the serial port.

-h

enables hardware handshaking on the serial port, it is off by default. Most KISS implementation do not support this, but some do.

-l

enables logging of information to the *syslog* logfile.

6.1.2 Creating a Baycom device.

Kernel Compile Options:

```
Code maturity level options  --->
    [*] Prompt for development and/or incomplete code/drivers
General setup  --->
    [*] Networking support
Network device support  --->
    [*] Network device support
    ...
    [*] Radio network interfaces
    [*] BAYCOM ser12 and par96 driver for AX.25
```

Thomas Sailer, <sailer@ife.ee.ethz.ch>, despite the popularly held belief that it would not work very well, has developed Linux support for Baycom modems. His driver supports the Ser12 serial port, Par96 and the enhanced PicPar parallel port modems. Further information about the modems themselves may be obtained from the Baycom Web site, http://www.baycom.de/.

Your first step should be to determine the i/o and addresses of the serial or parallel port(s) you have Baycom modem(s) connected to. When you have these you must configure the Baycom driver with them.

The BayCom driver creates network devices called: `bc0`, `bc1`, `bc2` etc. when it is configured.

The `sethdlc` utility allows you to configure the driver with these parameters, or, if you have only one Baycom modem installed you may specify the parameters on the `insmod` command line when you load the Baycom module.

For example, a simple configuration. Disable the serial driver for COM1: then configure the Baycom driver for a Ser12 serial port modem on COM1: with the software DCD option enabled:

```
# setserial /dev/ttyS0 UART none
# insmod hdlcdrv
# insmod baycom mode="ser12*" iobase=0x3f8 irq=4
```

Par96 parallel port type modem on LPT1: using hardware DCD detection:

```
# insmod hdlcdrv
# insmod baycom mode="par96" iobase=0x378 irq=7 options=0
```

This is not really the preferred way to do it. The `sethdlc` utility works just as easily with one device as with many.

The `sethdlc` manual page has the full details, but a couple of examples will illustrate the most important aspects of this configuration. The following examples assume you have already loaded the Baycom module using:

```
# insmod hdlcdrv
# insmod baycom
```

or that you compiled the kernel with the driver inbuilt.

Configure the `bc0` device driver as a Parallel port Baycom modem on LPT1: with software DCD:

```
# sethdlc -p -i bc0 mode par96 io 0x378 irq 7
```

Configure the `bc1` device driver as a Serial port Baycom modem on COM1:

```
# sethdlc -p -i bc1 mode "ser12*" io 0x3f8 irq 4
```

6.1.3 Configuring the AX.25 channel access parameters.

The AX.25 channel access parameters are the equivalent of the KISS ppersist, txdelay and slottime type parameters. Again you use the `sethdlc` utility for this.

Again the `sethdlc` man page is the source of the most complete information but another example of two won't hurt:

Configure the `bc0` device with TxDelay of 200 mS, SlotTime of 100 mS, PPersist of 40 and half duplex:

```
# sethdlc -i bc0 -a txd 200 slot 100 ppersist 40 half
```

Note that the timing values are in milliseconds.

Configuring the Kernel AX.25 to use the BayCom device The BayCom driver creates standard network devices that the AX.25 Kernel code can use. Configuration is much the same as that for a PI or PacketTwin card.

The first step is to configure the device with an AX.25 call sign. The `ifconfig` utility may be used to perform this.

```
# /sbin/ifconfig bc0 hw ax25 VK2KTJ-15 up
```

will assign the BayCom device `bc0` the AX.25 call sign `VK2KTJ-15`. Alternatively you can use the `axparms` command, you'll still need to use the `ifconfig` command to bring the device up though:

```
# ifconfig bc0 up
# axparms -setcall bc0 vk2ktj-15
```

The next step is to create an entry in the `/etc/ax25/axports` file as you would for any other device. The entry in the `axports` file is associated with the network device you've configured by the call sign you configure. The entry in the `axports` file that has the call sign that you configured the BayCom device with is the one that will be used to refer to it.

You may then treat the new AX.25 device as you would any other. You can configure it for TCP/IP, add it to ax25d and run NetRom or Rose over it as you please.

6.1.4 Creating a SoundModem device.

Kernel Compile Options:

```
Code maturity level options  --->
    [*] Prompt for development and/or incomplete code/drivers
General setup  --->
    [*] Networking support
Network device support  --->
    [*] Network device support
    ...
    [*] Radio network interfaces
    [*] Soundcard modem driver for AX.25
    [?] Soundmodem support for Soundblaster and compatible cards
    [?] Soundmodem support for WSS and Crystal cards
    [?] Soundmodem support for 1200 baud AFSK modulation
    [?] Soundmodem support for 4800 baud HAPN-1 modulation
    [?] Soundmodem support for 9600 baud FSK G3RUH modulation
```

Thomas Sailer has built a new driver for the kernel that allows you to use your sound card as a modem. Connect your radio directly to your sound card to play packet! Thomas recommends at least a 486DX2/66 if you want to use this software as all of the digital signal processing is done by the main CPU.

The driver currently emulates 1200 bps AFSK, 4800 HAPN and 9600 FSK (G3RUH compatible) modem types. The only sound cards currently supported are SoundBlaster and WindowsSoundSystem Compatible models. The sound cards require some circuitry to help them drive the Push-To-Talk circuitry, and information on this is available from *Thomas's SoundModem PTT circuit web page* (`http://www.ife.ee.ethz.ch/ sailer/pcf/ptt_circ/ptt.html`). There are quite a few possible options, they are: detect the sound output from the sound card, or use output from a parallel port, serial port or midi port. Circuit examples for each of these are on Thomas's site.

The SoundModem driver creates network devices called: `sm0`, `sm1`, `sm2` etc when it is configured.

Note: the SoundModem driver competes for the same resources as the Linux sound driver. So if you wish to use the SoundModem driver you must ensure that the Linux sound driver is not installed. You can of course compile them both as modules and insert and remove them as you wish.

Configuring the sound card. The SoundModem driver does not initialize the sound card. The ax25-utils package includes a utility to do this called "`setcrystal`" that may be used for sound cards based on the Crystal chip set. If you have some other card then you will have to use some other software to initialize it. Its syntax is fairly straightforward:

```
setcrystal [-w wssio] [-s sbio] [-f synthio] [-i irq] [-d dma] [-c dma2]
```

So, for example, if you wished to configure a SoundBlaster card at I/O base address 0x388, IRQ 10 and DMA 1 you would use:

```
# setcrystal -s 0x388 -i 10 -d 1
```

To configure a WindowSoundSystem card at I/O base address 0x534, IRQ 5, DMA 3 you would use:

```
# setcrystal -w 0x534 -i 5 -d 3
```

The `[-f synthio]` parameter is the set the synthesizer address, and the `[-c dma2]` parameter is to set the second DMA channel to allow full duplex operation.

Configuring the SoundModem driver. When you have configured the sound card you need to configure the driver telling it where the sound card is located and what sort of modem you wish it to emulate.

The `sethdlc` utility allows you to configure the driver with these parameters, or, if you have only one sound card installed you may specify the parameters on the `insmod` command line when you load the SoundModem module.

For example, a simple configuration, with one SoundBlaster sound card configured as described above emulating a 1200 bps modem:

```
# insmod hdlcdrv
# insmod soundmodem mode="sbc:afsk1200" iobase=0x220 irq=5 dma=1
```

This is not really the preferred way to do it. The `sethdlc` utility works just as easily with one device as with many.

The `sethdlc` man page has the full details, but a couple of examples will illustrate the most important aspects of this configuration. The following examples assume you have already loaded the SoundModem modules using:

```
# insmod hdlcdrv
# insmod soundmodem
```

or that you compiled the kernel with the driver built in.

Configure the driver to support the WindowsSoundSystem card we configured above to emulate a G3RUH 9600 compatible modem as device `sm0` using a parallel port at 0x378 to key the Push-To-Talk:

```
# sethdlc -p -i sm0 mode wss:fsk9600 io 0x534 irq 5 dma 3 pario 0x378
```

Configure the driver to support the SoundBlaster card we configured above to emulate a 4800 bps HAPN modem as device `sm1` using the serial port located at 0x2f8 to key the Push-To-Talk:

```
# sethdlc -p -i sm1 mode sbc:hapn4800 io 0x388 irq 10 dma 1 serio 0x2f8
```

Configure the driver to support the SoundBlaster card we configured above to emulate a 1200 bps AFSK modem as device `sm1` using the serial port located at 0x2f8 to key the Push-To-Talk:

```
# sethdlc -p -i sm1 mode sbc:afsk1200 io 0x388 irq 10 dma 1 serio 0x2f8
```

Configuring the AX.25 channel access parameters. The AX.25 channel access parameters are the equivalent of the KISS ppersist, txdelay and slottime type parameters. You use the `sethdlc` utility for this as well.

Again the `sethdlc` man page is the source of the most complete information but another example of two won't hurt:

Configure the `sm0` device with TxDelay of 100 mS, SlotTime of 50mS, PPersist of 128 and full duplex:

```
# sethdlc -i sm0 -a txd 100 slot 50 ppersist 128 full
```

Note that the timing values are in milliseconds.

Setting the audio levels and tuning the driver. It is very important that the audio levels be set correctly for any radio based modem to work. This is equally true of the SoundModem. Thomas has developed some utility programs that make this task easier. They are called `smdiag` and `smmixer`.

`smdiag`

provides two types of display, either an oscilloscope type display or an eye pattern type display.

`smmixer`

allows you to actually adjust the transmit and receive audio levels.

To start the `smdiag` utility in "eye" mode for the SoundModem device `sm0` you would use:

```
# smdiag -i sm0 -e
```

To start the `smmixer` utility for the SoundModem device `sm0` you would use:

```
# smmixer -i sm0
```

Configuring the Kernel AX.25 to use the SoundModem The SoundModem driver creates standard network devices that the AX.25 Kernel code can use. Configuration is much the same as that for a PI or PacketTwin card.

The first step is to configure the device with an AX.25 call sign. The `ifconfig` utility may be used to perform this.

```
# /sbin/ifconfig sm0 hw ax25 VK2KTJ-15 up
```

will assign the SoundModem device `sm0` the AX.25 call sign `VK2KTJ-15`. Alternatively you can use the `axparms` command, but you still need the `ifconfig` utility to bring the device up:

```
# ifconfig sm0 up
# axparms -setcall sm0 vk2ktj-15
```

The next step is to create an entry in the `/etc/ax25/axports` file as you would for any other device. The entry in the `axports` file is associated with the network device you've configured by the call sign you configure. The entry in the `axports` file that has the call sign that you configured the SoundModem device with is the one that will be used to refer to it.

You may then treat the new AX.25 device as you would any other. You can configure it for TCP/IP, add it to ax25d and run NetRom or Rose over it as you please.

6.1.5 Creating a PI card device.

Kernel Compile Options:

```
General setup  --->
    [*] Networking support
Network device support  --->
    [*] Network device support
    ...
    [*] Radio network interfaces
    [*] Ottawa PI and PI/2 support for AX.25
```

The PI card device driver creates devices named 'pi[0-9][ab]'. The first PI card detected will be allocated 'pi0', the second 'pi1' etc. The 'a' and 'b' refer to the first and second physical interface on the PI card. If you have built your kernel to include the PI card driver, and the card has been properly detected then you can use the following command to configure the network device:

```
# /sbin/ifconfig pi0a hw ax25 VK2KTJ-15 up
```

This command would configure the first port on the first PI card detected with the call sign VK2KTJ-15 and make it active. To use the device all you now need to do is to configure an entry into your /etc/ax25/axports file with a matching call sign/ssid and you will be ready to continue on.

The PI card driver was written by David Perry, <dp@hydra.carleton.edu>

6.1.6 Creating a PacketTwin device.

Kernel Compile Options:

```
General setup  --->
     [*] Networking support
Network device support  --->
     [*] Network device support
     ...
     [*] Radio network interfaces
     [*] Gracilis PackeTwin support for AX.25
```

The PacketTwin card device driver creates devices named 'pt[0-9][ab]'. The first PacketTwin card detected will be allocated 'pt0', the second 'pt1' etc. The 'a' and 'b' refer to the first and second physical interface on the PacketTwin card. If you have built your kernel to include the PacketTwin card driver, and the card has been properly detected then you can use the following command to configure the network device:

```
# /sbin/ifconfig pt0a hw ax25 VK2KTJ-15 up
```

This command would configure the first port on the first PacketTwin card detected with the call sign VK2KTJ-15 and make it active. To use the device all you now need to do is to configure an entry into your /etc/ax25/axports file with a matching call sign/ssid and you will be ready to continue on.

The PacketTwin card driver was written by Craig Small VK2XLZ, <csmall@triode.apana.org.au>.

6.1.7 Creating a generic SCC device.

Kernel Compile Options:

```
General setup  --->
     [*] Networking support
Network device support  --->
     [*] Network device support
     ...
     [*] Radio network interfaces
     [*] Z8530 SCC KISS emulation driver for AX.25
```

Joerg Reuter, DL1BKE, jreuter@poboxes.com has developed generic support for Z8530 SCC based cards. His driver is configurable to support a range of different types of cards and present an interface that looks like a KISS TNC so you can treat it as though it were a KISS TNC.

Obtaining and building the configuration tool package. While the kernel driver is included in the standard kernel distribution, Joerg distributes more recent versions of his driver with the suite of configuration tools that you will need to obtain as well.

You can obtain the configuration tools package from:

Joerg's web page (http://www.rat.de/jr/)

or:

db0bm.automation.fh-aachen.de

/incoming/dl1bke/

or:

insl1.etec.uni-karlsruhe.de

/pub/hamradio/linux/z8530/

or:

ftp.ucsd.edu

```
/hamradio/packet/tcpip/linux
/hamradio/packet/tcpip/incoming/
```

You will find multiple versions, choose the one that best suits the kernel you intend to use:

```
z8530drv-2.4a.dl1bke.tar.gz    2.0.*
z8530drv-utils-3.0.tar.gz     2.1.6 or greater
```

The following commands were what I used to compile and install the package for kernel version 2.0.30:

```
# cd /usr/src
# gzip -dc z8530drv-2.4a.dl1bke.tar.gz | tar xvpofz -
# cd z8530drv
# make clean
# make dep
# make module          # If you want to build the driver as a module
# make for_kernel      # If you want the driver to built into your kernel
# make install
```

After the above is complete you should have three new programs installed in your /sbin directory: gencfg, sccinit and sccstat. It is these programs that you will use to configure the driver for your card.

You will also have a group of new special device files created in your /dev called scc0-scc7. These will be used later and will be the 'KISS' devices you will end up using.

If you chose to 'make for_kErne' then you will need to recompile your kernel. To ensure that you include support for the z8530 driver you must be sure to answer 'Y' to: 'Z8530 SCC kiss emulation driver for AX.25' when asked during a kernel 'make config'.

If you chose to 'make module' then the new scc.o will have been installed in the appropriate /lib/modules directory and you do not need to recompile your kernel. Remember to use the *insmod* command to load the module before your try and configure it.

Configuring the driver for your card. The z8530 SCC driver has been designed to be as flexible as possible so as to support as many different types of cards as possible. With this flexibility has come some cost in configuration.

There is more comprehensive documentation in the package and you should read this if you have any problems. You should particularly look at doc/scc_eng.doc or doc/scc_ger.doc for more detailed information. I've paraphrased the important details, but as a result there is a lot of lower level detail that I have not included.

The main configuration file is read by the *sccinit* program and is called /etc/z8530drv.conf. This file is broken into two main stages: Configuration of the hardware parameters and channel configuration. After you have configured this file you need only add:

```
# sccinit
```

into the rc file that configures your network and the driver will be initialized according to the contents of the configuration file. You must do this before you attempt to use the driver.

Configuration of the hardware parameters. The first section is broken into stanzas, each stanza representing an 8530 chip. Each stanza is a list of keywords with arguments. You may specify up to four SCC chips in this file by default. The #define MAXSCC 4 in scc.c can be increased if you require support for more.

The allowable keywords and arguments are:

chip

the chip keyword is used to separate stanzas. It will take anything as an argument. The arguments are not used.

data_a

this keyword is used to specify the address of the data port for the z8530 channel 'A'. The argument is a hexadecimal number e.g. 0x300

ctrl_a

this keyword is used to specify the address of the control port for the z8530 channel 'A'. The arguments is a hexadecimal number e.g. 0x304

data_b

this keyword is used to specify the address of the data port for the z8530 channel 'B'. The argument is a hexadecimal number e.g. 0x301

ctrl_b

this keyword is used to specify the address of the control port for the z8530 channel 'B'. The arguments is a hexadecimal number e.g. 0x305

irq

this keyword is used to specify the IRQ used by the 8530 SCC described in this stanza. The argument is an integer e.g. 5

pclock

this keyword is used to specify the frequency of the clock at the PCLK pin of the 8530. The argument is an integer frequency in Hz which defaults to 4915200 if the keyword is not supplied.

board

the type of board supporting this 8530 SCC. The argument is a character string. The allowed values are:

PA0HZP

the PA0HZP SCC Card

EAGLE

the Eagle card

PC100

the DRSI PC100 SCC card

PRIMUS

the PRIMUS-PC (DG9BL) card

BAYCOM

BayCom (U)SCC card

escc

this keyword is optional and is used to enable support for the Extended SCC chips (ESCC) such as the 8580, 85180, or the 85280. The argument is a character string with allowed values of 'yes' or 'no'. The default is 'no'.

vector

this keyword is optional and specifies the address of the vector latch (also known as "intack port") for PA0HZP cards. There can be only one vector latch for all chips. The default is 0.

special

this keyword is optional and specifies the address of the special function register on several cards. The default is 0.

option

this keyword is optional and defaults to 0.

Some example configurations for the more popular cards are as follows:

BayCom USCC

```
chip    1
data_a  0x300
ctrl_a  0x304
data_b  0x301
ctrl_b  0x305
irq     5
board   BAYCOM
#
# SCC chip 2
#
chip    2
data_a  0x302
ctrl_a  0x306
data_b  0x303
ctrl_b  0x307
board   BAYCOM
```

PA0HZP SCC card

```
chip 1
data_a 0x153
data_b 0x151
ctrl_a 0x152
ctrl_b 0x150
irq 9
pclock 4915200
board PA0HZP
vector 0x168
escc no
#
#
#
chip 2
data_a 0x157
data_b 0x155
ctrl_a 0x156
ctrl_b 0x154
irq 9
pclock 4915200
board PA0HZP
vector 0x168
escc no
```

DRSI SCC card

```
chip 1
data_a 0x303
data_b 0x301
ctrl_a 0x302
ctrl_b 0x300
irq 7
pclock 4915200
board DRSI
escc no
```

If you already have a working configuration for your card under NOS, then you can use the `gencfg` command to convert the PE1CHL NOS driver commands into a form suitable for use in the z8530 driver configuration file.

To use `gencfg` you simply invoke it with the same parameters as you used for the PE1CHL driver in NET/NOS. For example:

```
# gencfg 2 0x150 4 2 0 1 0x168 9 4915200
```

will generate a skeleton configuration for the OptoSCC card.

Channel Configuration The Channel Configuration section is where you specify all of the other parameters associated with the port you are configuring. Again this section is broken into stanzas. One stanza represents one logical port, and therefore there would be two of these for each one of the hardware parameters stanzas as each 8530 SCC supports two ports.

These keywords and arguments are also written to the `/etc/z8530drv.conf` file and must appear **after** the hardware parameters section.

Sequence is very important in this section, but if you stick with the suggested sequence it should work okay. The keywords and arguments are:

device

This keyword must be the first line of a port definition and specifies the name of the special device file that the rest of the configuration applies to. e.g. `/dev/scc0`

speed

This keyword specifies the speed in bits per second of the interface. The argument is an integer: e.g. `1200`

clock

This keyword specifies where the clock for the data will be sourced. Allowable values are:

dpll

Normal half duplex operation

external

MODEM supplies its own Rx/Tx clock

divider

Use full duplex divider if installed.

mode

This keyword specifies the data coding to be used. Allowable arguments are: `nrzi` or `nrz`

rxbuffers

This keyword specifies the number of receive buffers to allocate memory for. The argument is an integer, e.g. 8.

txbuffers

This keyword specifies the number of transmit buffers to allocate memory for. The argument is an integer, e.g. 8.

bufsize

This keyword specifies the size of the receive and transmit buffers. The arguments is in bytes and represents the total length of the frame, so it must also take into account the AX.25 headers and not just the length of the data field. This keyword is optional and defaults to `384`

txdelay

The KISS transmit delay value, the argument is an integer in mS.

persist

The KISS persist value, the argument is an integer.

slot

The KISS slot time value, the argument is an integer in mS.

tail

The KISS transmit tail value, the argument is an integer in mS.

fulldup

The KISS full duplex flag, the argument is an integer. `1`==Full Duplex, `0`==Half Duplex.

wait

The KISS wait value, the argument is an integer in mS.

min

The KISS min value, the argument is an integer in S.

maxkey

The KISS maximum key-up time, the argument is an integer in S.

idle

The KISS idle timer value, the argument is an integer in S.

maxdef

The KISS maxdef value, the argument is an integer.

group

The KISS group value, the argument is an integer.

txoff

The KISS txoff value, the argument is an integer in mS.

softdcd

The KISS softdcd value, the argument is an integer.

slip

The KISS slip flag, the argument is an integer.

Using the driver. To use the driver you simply treat the `/dev/scc*` devices just as you would a serial tty device with a KISS TNC connected to it. For example, to configure Linux Kernel networking to use your SCC card you could use something like:

```
# kissattach -s 4800 /dev/scc0 VK2KTJ
```

You can also use NOS to attach to it in precisely the same way. From JNOS for example you would use something like:

```
attach asy scc0 0 ax25 scc0 256 256 4800
```

The `sccstat` and `sccparam` tools. To assist in the diagnosis of problems you can use the `sccstat` program to display the current configuration of an SCC device. To use it try:

```
# sccstat /dev/scc0
```

and you will see displayed a very large amount of information relating to the configuration and health of the `/dev/scc0` SCC port.

The `sccparam` command allows you to change or modify a configuration after you have booted. Its syntax is very similar to the NOS `param` command, so to set the `txtail` setting of a device to 100mS you would use:

```
# sccparam /dev/scc0 txtail 0x8
```

6.1.8 Creating a BPQ ethernet device.

Kernel Compile Options:

```
General setup  --->
    [*] Networking support
Network device support  --->
    [*] Network device support
    ...
    [*] Radio network interfaces
    [*] BPQ Ethernet driver for AX.25
```

Linux supports BPQ Ethernet compatibility. This enables you to run the AX.25 protocol over your Ethernet LAN and to internetwork your Linux machine with other BPQ machines on the LAN.

The BPQ network devices are named '`bpq[0-9]`'. The '`bpq0`' device is associated with the '`eth0`' device, the '`bpq1`' device with the '`eth1`' device etc.

Configuration is quite straightforward. You firstly must have configured a standard Ethernet device. This means you will have compiled your kernel to support your Ethernet card and tested that this works. Refer to the Ethernet HOWTO for more information on how to do this.

To configure the BPQ support you need to configure the Ethernet device with an AX.25 call sign. The following command will do this for you:

```
# /sbin/ifconfig bpq0 hw ax25 vk2ktj-14 up
```

Again, remember that the call sign you specify should match the entry in the `/etc/ax25/axports` file that you wish to use for this port.

6.1.9 Configuring the BPQ Node to talk to the Linux AX.25 support.

BPQ Ethernet normally uses a multicast address. The Linux implementation does not, and instead it uses the normal Ethernet broadcast address. The NET.CFG file for the BPQ ODI driver should therefore be modified to look similar to this:

```
LINK SUPPORT

        MAX STACKS 1
        MAX BOARDS 1

LINK DRIVER E2000                    ; or other MLID to suit your card

        INT 10                       ;
        PORT 300                     ; to suit your card
```

```
        FRAME ETHERNET_II

        PROTOCOL BPQ 8FF ETHERNET_II ; required for BPQ - can change PID

BPQPARAMS                            ; optional - only needed if you want
                                     ; to override the default target addr

        ETH_ADDR  FF:FF:FF:FF:FF:FF  ; Target address
```

6.2 Creating the `/etc/ax25/axports` file.

The `/etc/ax25/axports` is a simple text file that you create with a text editor. The format of the `/etc/ax25/axports` file is as follows:

```
portname  callsign  baudrate  paclen  window  description
```

where:

portname
: Is a text name that you will refer to the port by.

callsign
: Is the AX.25 call sign you want to assign to the port.

baudrate
: Is the speed at which you wish the port to communicate with your TNC.

paclen
: Is the maximum packet length you want to configure the port to use for AX.25 connected mode connections.

window
: Is the AX.25 window (K) parameter. This is the same as the `MAXFRAME` setting of many tnc's.

description
: Is a textual description of the port.

In my case, mine looks like:

```
radio    VK2KTJ-15       4800        256     2       4800bps 144.800 MHz
ether    VK2KTJ-14       10000000    256     2       BPQ/ethernet device
```

Remember, you must assign unique callsign/ssid to each AX.25 port you create. Create one entry for each AX.25 device you want to use, this includes KISS, Baycom, SCC, PI, PT and SoundModem ports. Each entry here will describe exactly one AX.25 network device. The entries in this file are associated with the network devices by the callsign/ssid. This is at least one good reason for requiring unique callsign/ssid.

6.3 Configuring AX.25 routing.

You may wish to configure default digipeater's paths for specific hosts. This is useful for both normal AX.25 connections and also IP based connections. The `axparms` command enables you to do this. Again, the manual page offers a complete description, but a simple example might be:

```
# /usr/sbin/axparms -route add radio VK2XLZ VK2SUT
```

This command would set a digipeater entry for `VK2XLZ` via `VK2SUT` on the AX.25 port named `radio`.

7 Configuring an AX.25 interface for TCP/IP.

It is very simple to configure an AX.25 port to carry TCP/IP. If you have KISS interfaces then there are two methods for configuring an IP address. The *kissattach* command has an option that allows you to do specify an IP address. The more conventional method using the `ifconfig` command will work on all interface types.

So, modifying the previous KISS example:

```
# /usr/sbin/kissattach -i 44.136.8.5 -m 512 /dev/ttyS0 radio
# /sbin/route add -net 44.136.8.0 netmask 255.255.255.0 ax0
# /sbin/route add default ax0
```

to create the AX.25 interface with an IP address of `44.136.8.5` and an `MTU` of `512` bytes. You should still use the `ifconfig` to configure the other parameters if necessary.

If you have any other interface type then you use the `ifconfig` program to configure the IP address and netmask details for the port and add a route via the port, just as you would for any other TCP/IP interface. The following example is for a PI card device, but would work equally well for any other AX.25 network device:

```
# /sbin/ifconfig pi0a 44.136.8.5 netmask 255.255.255.0 up
# /sbin/ifconfig pi0a broadcast 44.136.8.255 mtu 512
# /sbin/route add -net 44.136.8.0 netmask 255.255.255.0 pi0a
# /sbin/route add default pi0a
```

The commands listed above are typical of the sort of configuration many of you would be familiar with if you have used NOS or any of its derivatives or any other TCP/IP software. Note that the default route might not be required in your configuration if you have some other network device configured.

To test it out, try a ping or a telnet to a local host.

```
# ping -i 5 44.136.8.58
```

Note the use of the '`-i 5`' arguments to `ping` that tell it to send pings every 5 seconds instead of its default of 1 second.

8 Configuring a NetRom port.

The NetRom protocol relies on, and uses the AX.25 ports you have created. The NetRom protocol rides on top of the AX.25 protocol. To configure NetRom on an AX.25 interface you must configure two files. One file describes the Netrom interfaces, and the other file describes which of the AX.25 ports will carry NetRom. You can configure multiple NetRom ports, each with its own call sign and alias, the same procedure applies for each.

8.1 Configuring `/etc/ax25/nrports`

The first is the `/etc/ax25/nrports` file. This file describes the NetRom ports in much the same way as the `/etc/ax25/axports` file describes the AX.25 ports. Each NetRom device you wish to create must have an entry in the `/etc/ax25/nrports` file. Normally a Linux machine would have only one NetRom device configured that would use a number of the AX.25 ports defined. In some situations you might wish a special service such as a BBS to have a separate NetRom alias and so you would create more than one.

This file is formatted as follows:

```
name callsign  alias  paclen   description
```

Where:

name
Is the text name that you wish to refer to the port by.

callsign
Is the call sign that the NetRom traffic from this port will use. Note, this is **not** that address that users should connect to to get access to a *node* style interface. (The node program is covered later). This callsign/ssid should be unique and should not appear elsewhere in either of the `/etc/ax25/axports` or the `/etc/ax25/nrports` files.

alias
Is the NetRom alias this port will have assigned to it.

paclen
Is the maximum size of NetRom frames transmitted by this port.

description
Is a free text description of the port.

An example would look something like the following:

```
netrom  VK2KTJ-9         LINUX   236     Linux Switch Port
```

This example creates a NetRom port known to the rest of the NetRom network as '`LINUX:VK2KTJ-9`'.

This file is used by programs such as the *call* program.

8.2 Configuring /etc/ax25/nrbroadcast

The second file is the /etc/ax25/nrbroadcast file. This file may contain a number of entries. There would normally be one entry for each AX.25 port that you wish to allow NetRom traffic on.

This file is formatted as follows:

```
axport min_obs def_qual worst_qual verbose
```

Where:

axport
: Is the port name obtained from the /etc/ax25/axports file. If you do not have an entry in /etc/ax25/nrbroadcasts for a port then this means that no NetRom routing will occur and any received NetRom broadcasts will be ignored for that port.

min_obs
: Is the minimum obselesence value for the port.

def_qual
: Is the default quality for the port.

worst_qual
: Is the worst quality value for the port, any routes under this quality will be ignored.

verbose
: Is a flag determining whether full NetRom routing broadcasts will occur from this port or only a routing broadcast advertising the node itself.

An example would look something like the following:

```
radio    1    200    100    1
```

8.3 Creating the NetRom Network device

When you have the two configuration files completed you must create the NetRom device in much the same way as you did for the AX.25 devices. This time you use the nrattach command. The nrattach works in just the same way as the axattach command except that it creates NetRom network devices called "nr[0-9]." Again, the first time you use the nrattach command it creates the nr0 device, the second time it creates the "nr1" network devices etc. To create the network device for the NetRom port we've defined we would use:

```
# nrattach netrom
```

This command would start the NetRom device (nr0) named netrom configured with the details specified in the /etc/ax25/nrports file.

8.4 Starting the NetRom daemon

The Linux kernel does all of the NetRom protocol and switching, but does not manage some functions. The NetRom daemon manages the NetRom routing tables and generates the NetRom routing broadcasts. You start NetRom daemon with the command:

```
# /usr/sbin/netromd -i
```

You should soon see the /proc/net/nr_neigh file filling up with information about your NetRom neighbors.

Remember to put the /usr/sbin/netromd command in your *rc* files so that it is started automatically each time you reboot.

8.5 Configuring NetRom routing.

You may wish to configure static NetRom routes for specific hosts. The nrparms command enables you to do this. Again, the manual page offers a complete description, but a simple example might be:

```
# /usr/sbin/nrparms -nodes VK2XLZ-10 + #MINTO 120 5 radio VK2SUT-9
```

This command would set a NetRom route to #MINTO:VK2XLZ-10 via a neighbor VK2SUT-9 on my AX.25 port called 'radio'.

You can manually create entries for new neighbors using the *nrparms* command as well. For example:

```
# /usr/sbin/nrparms -routes radio VK2SUT-9 + 120
```

This command would create VK2SUT-9 as a NetRom neighbor with a quality of 120 and this will be locked and will not be deleted automatically.

9 Configuring a NetRom interface for TCP/IP.

Configuring a NetRom interface for TCP/IP is almost identical to configuring an AX.25 interface for TCP/IP.

Again you can either specify the ip address and mtu on the *nrattach* command line, or use the `ifconfig` and `route` commands, but you need to manually add `arp` entries for hosts you wish to route to because there is no mechanism available for your machine to learn what NetRom address it should use to reach a particular IP host.

So, to create an `nr0` device with an IP address of `44.136.8.5`, an mtu of `512` and configured with the details from the `/etc/ax25/nrports` file for a NetRom port named `netrom` you would use:

```
# /usr/sbin/nrattach -i 44.136.8.5 -m 512 netrom
# route add 44.136.8.5 nr0
```

or you could use something like the following commands manually:

```
# /usr/sbin/nrattach netrom
# ifconfig nr0 44.136.8.5 netmask 255.255.255.0 hw netrom VK2KTJ-9
# route add 44.136.8.5 nr0
```

Then for each IP host you wish to reach via NetRom you need to set route and arp entries. To reach a destination host with an IP address of `44.136.80.4` at NetRom address `BBS:VK3BBS` via a NetRom neighbor with call sign `VK2SUT-0` you would use commands as follows:

```
# route add 44.136.80.4 nr0
# arp -t netrom -s 44.136.80.4 vk2sut-0
# nrparms -nodes vk3bbs + BBS 120 6 sl0 vk2sut-0
```

The '`120`' and '`6`' arguments to the *nrparms* command are the NetRom *quality* and *obsolescence count* values for the route.

10 Configuring a Rose port.

The Rose packet layer protocol is similar to layer three of the X.25 specification. The kernel based Rose support is a modified version of the FPAC Rose implementation, http://fpac.lmi.ecp.fr/f1oat/f1oat.html.

The Rose packet layer protocol protocol relies on, and uses the AX.25 ports you have created. The Rose protocol rides on top of the AX.25 protocol. To configure Rose you must create a configuration file that describes the Rose ports you want. You can create multiple Rose ports if you wish, the same procedure applies for each.

10.1 Configuring `/etc/ax25/rsports`

The file where you configure your Rose interfaces is the `/etc/ax25/rsports` file. This file describes the Rose port in much the same way as the `/etc/ax25/axports` file describes the AX.25 ports.

This file is formatted as follows:

```
name  address  description
```

Where:

name

is the text name that you wish to refer to the port by.

address

is the 10 digit Rose address you wish to assign to this port.

description

is a free text description of the port.

An example would look something like the following:

```
rose  5050294760  Rose Port
```

Note that Rose will use the default callsign/ssid configured on each AX.25 port unless you specify otherwise.

To configure a separate callsign/ssid for Rose to use on each port you use the *rsparms* command as follows:

```
# /usr/sbin/rsprams -call VK2KTJ-10
```

This example would make Linux listen for and use the callsign/ssid `VK2KTJ-10` on all of the configured AX.25 ports for Rose calls.

10.2 Creating the Rose Network device.

When you have created the /etc/ax25/rsports file you may create the Rose device in much the same way as you did for the AX.25 devices. This time you use the rsattach command. The rsattach command creates network devices named 'rose[0-5]'. The first time you use the rsattach command it create the 'rose0' device, the second time it creates the 'rose1' device etc. For example:

```
# rsattach rose
```

This command would start the Rose device (rose0) configured with the details specified in the /etc/ax25/rsports file for the entry named 'rose'.

10.3 Configuring Rose Routing

The Rose protocol currently supports only static routing. The rsparms utility allows you to configure your Rose routing table under Linux.

For example:

```
# rsparms -nodes add 5050295502 radio vk2xlz
```

would add a route to Rose node 5050295502 via an AX.25 port named "radio" in your /etc/ax25/axports file to a neighbor with the call sign VK2XLZ.

You may specify a route with a mask to capture a number of Rose destinations into a single routing entry. The syntax looks like:

```
# rsparms -nodes add 5050295502/4 radio vk2xlz
```

which would be identical to the previous example except that it would match any destination address that matched the first four digits supplied, in this case any address commencing with the digits 5050. An alternate form for this command is:

```
# rsparms -nodes add 5050/4 radio vk2xlz
```

which is probably the less ambiguous form.

11 Making AX.25/NetRom/Rose calls.

Now that you have all of your AX.25, NetRom and Rose interfaces configured and active, you should be able to make test calls.

The AX25 Utilities package includes a program called "call" which is a split-screen terminal program for AX.25, NetRom and Rose.

A simple AX.25 call would look like:

```
/usr/bin/call radio VK2DAY via VK2SUT
```

A simple NetRom call to a node with an alias of SUNBBS would look like:

```
/usr/bin/call netrom SUNBBS
```

A simple Rose call to HEARD at node 5050882960 would look like:

```
/usr/bin/call rose HEARD 5050882960
```

Note: you must tell call which port you wish to make the call on, as the same destination node might be reachable on any of the ports you have configured.

The call program is a line mode terminal program for making AX.25 calls. It recognizes lines that start with '~' as command lines. The '~.' command will close the connection.

Please refer to the man page in /usr/man for more information.

12 Configuring Linux to accept Packet connections.

Linux is a powerful operating system and offers a great deal of flexibility in how it is configured. With this flexibility comes a cost in configuring it to do what you want. When configuring your Linux machine to accept incoming AX.25, NetRom or Rose connections there are a number of questions you need to ask yourself. The most important of which is: "What do I want users to see when they connect?". People are developing neat little applications that may be used to provide services to callers, a simple example is the pms program included in the AX25 utilities, a more complex example is the node program also included in the AX25 utilities. Alternatively you might want to give users a login prompt so that they can make use of a shell account, or you might even have written your own program, such as a customized database or a game, that you want people to connect to. Whatever you choose, you must tell the AX.25 software about this so that it knows what software to run when it accepts an incoming AX.25 connection.

The `ax25d` program is similar to the `inetd` program commonly used to accept incoming TCP/IP connections on UNIX machines. It sits and listens for incoming connections, when it detects one it goes away and checks a configuration file to determine what program to run and connect to that connection. Since this the standard tool for accepting incoming AX.25, NetRom and Rose connections I'll describe how to configure it.

12.1 Creating the `/etc/ax25/ax25d.conf` file.

This file is the configuration file for the `ax25d` AX.25 daemon which handles incoming AX.25, NetRom and Rose connections.

The file is a little cryptic looking at first, but you'll soon discover it is very simple in practice, with a small trap for you to be wary of.

The general format of the `ax25d.conf` file is as follows:

```
# This is a comment and is ignored by the ax25d program.
[port_name] || <port_name> || {port_name}
<peer1>    window T1 T2 T3 idle N2 <mode> <uid> <cmd> <cmd-name> <arguments>
<peer2>    window T1 T2 T3 idle N2 <mode> <uid> <cmd> <cmd-name> <arguments>
parameters window T1 T2 T3 idle N2 <mode>
<peer3>    window T1 T2 T3 idle N2 <mode> <uid> <cmd> <cmd-name> <arguments>
  ...
default    window T1 T2 T3 idle N2 <mode> <uid> <cmd> <cmd-name> <arguments>
```

Where:

#

At the start of a line marks a comment and is completely ignored by the `ax25d` program.

<port_name>

Is the name of the AX.25, NetRom or Rose port as specified in the `/etc/ax25/axports`, `/etc/ax25/nrports` and `/etc/ax25/rsports` files. The name of the port is surrounded by the '`[]`' brackets if it is an AX.25 port, the '<>' brackets if it is a NetRom port, or the '`{}`' brackets if it is a Rose port. There is an alternate form for this field, and that is use prefix the port name with '`callsign/ssid via`' to indicate that you wish accept calls to the callsign/ssid via this interface. The example should more clearly illustrate this.

<peer>

Is the call sign of the peer node that this particular configuration applies to. If you don't specify an SSID here then any SSID will match.

window

Is the AX.25 Window parameter (K) or MAXFRAME parameter for this configuration.

T1

Is the Frame retransmission (T1) timer in half second units.

T2

Is the amount of time the AX.25 software will wait for another incoming frame before preparing a response in 1 second units.

T3

Is the amount of time of inactivity before the AX.25 software will disconnect the session in 1 second units.

idle

Is the idle timer value in seconds.

N2

Is the number of consecutive retransmissions that will occur before the connection is closed.

<mode>

Provides a mechanism for determining certain types of general permissions. The modes are enabled or disabled by supplying a combination of characters, each representing a permission. The characters may be in either upper or lower case and must be in a single block with no spaces.

u/U

UTMP - currently unsupported.

v/V

Validate call - currently unsupported.

q/Q

Quiet - Don't log connection

n/N

Check NetRom Neighbor - currently unsupported.

d/D

Disallow Digipeaters - Connections must be direct, not digipeated.

l/L

Lockout - Don't allow connection.

***/0**

Marker - place marker, no mode set.

<uid>

Is the user ID that the program to be run to support the connection should be run as.

<cmd>

Is the full pathname of the command to be run, with no arguments specified.

<cmd-name>

Is the text that should appear in a *ps* as the command name running (normally the same as <cmd> except without the directory path information.

<arguments>

Are the command line argument to be passed to the <:cmd> when it is run. You pass useful information into these arguments by use of the following tokens:

%d

Name of the port the connection was received on.

%U

AX.25 call sign of the connected party without the SSID, in uppercase.

%u

AX.25 call sign of the connected party without the SSID, in lowercase.

%S

AX.25 call sign of the connected party with the SSID, in uppercase.

%s

AX.25 call sign of the connected party with the SSID, in lowercase.

%P

AX.25 call sign of the remote node that the connection came in from without the SSID, in uppercase.

%p

AX.25 call sign of the remote node that the connection came in from without the SSID, in lowercase.

%R

AX.25 call sign of the remote node that the connection came in from with the SSID, in uppercase.

%r

AX.25 call sign of the remote node that the connection came in from with the SSID, in lowercase.

You need one section in the above format for each AX.25, NetRom, or Rose interface you want to accept incoming AX.25, NetRom, or Rose connections on.

There are two special lines in the paragraph, one starts with the string 'parameters' and the other starts with the string "default" (yes there is a difference). These lines serve special functions.

The 'default' lines purpose should be obvious, this line acts as a catch-all, so that any incoming connection on the <interface_call> interface that doesn't have a specific rule will match the 'default' rule. If you don't have a 'default' rule, then any connections not matching any specific rule will be disconnected immediately without notice.

The 'parameters' line is a little more subtle, and here is the trap I mentioned earlier. In any of the fields for any definition for a peer you can use the '*' character to say 'use the default value'. The 'parameters' line is what sets those default values. The kernel software itself has some defaults which will be used if you don't specify any using the 'parameters' entry. The trap is that the these defaults apply **only** to those rules **below** the 'parameters' line, not to those above. You may have more than one 'parameters' rule per interface definition, and in this way you may create groups of default configurations. It is important to note that the 'parameters' rule does not allow you to set the 'uid' or 'command' fields.

12.2 A simple example ax25d.conf file.

Okay, an illustrative example:

```
# ax25d.conf for VK2KTJ - 02/03/97
# This configuration uses the AX.25 port defined earlier.

# <peer> Win T1  T2  T3  idl N2 <mode> <uid> <exec> <argv[0]>[<args....>]

[VK2KTJ-0 via radio]
parameters 1    10  *   *   *   *   *
VK2XLZ     *     *  *   *   *   *   *      root  /usr/sbin/axspawn axspawn %u +
VK2DAY     *     *  *   *   *   *   *      root  /usr/sbin/axspawn axspawn %u +
NOCALL     *     *  *   *   *   *   L
default    1    10  5 100 180  5    *      root  /usr/sbin/pms pms -a -o vk2ktj

[VK2KTJ-1 via radio]
default    *     *     *    *   *   0      root /usr/sbin/node node

<netrom>
parameters 1    10  *   *   *   *   *
NOCALL     *     *  *   *   *   *   L
default    *     *  *   *   *   *   0          root /usr/sbin/node node

{VK2KTJ-0 via rose}
parameters 1    10  *   *   *   *   *
VK2XLZ     *     *  *   *   *   *   *      root  /usr/sbin/axspawn axspawn %u +
VK2DAY     *     *  *   *   *   *   *      root  /usr/sbin/axspawn axspawn %u +
NOCALL     *     *  *   *   *   *   L
default    1    10  5 100 180  5    *      root  /usr/sbin/pms pms -a -o vk2ktj

{VK2KTJ-1 via rose}
default    *     *     *    *   *   0      root /usr/sbin/node node radio
```

This example says that anybody attempting to connect to the callsign 'VK2KTJ-0' heard on the AX.25 port called 'radio' will have the following rules applied:

Anyone whose call sign is set to 'NOCALL' should be locked out, note the use of mode 'L'.

The parameters line changes two parameters from the kernel defaults (Window and T1) and will run the /usr/sbin/axspawn program for them. Any copies of /usr/sbin/axspawn run this way will appear as axspawn in a ps listing for convenience. The next two lines provide definitions for two stations who will receive those permissions.

The last line in the paragraph is the "catch all" definition that everybody else will get (including VK2XLZ and VK2DAY using any other SSID other than -1). This definition sets all of the parameters implicitly and will cause the pms program to be run with a command line argument indicating that it is being run for an AX.25 connection, and that the owner call sign is VK2KTJ. (See the 'Configuring the PMS' section below for more details).

The next configuration accepts calls to VK2KTJ-1 via the radio port. It runs the node program for everybody that connects to it.

The next configuration is a NetRom configuration, note the use of the greater-then and less-than braces instead of the square brackets. These denote a NetRom configuration. This configuration is simpler, it simply says that anyone connecting to our NetRom port called 'netrom' will have the node program run for them, unless they have a call sign of 'NOCALL' in which case they will be locked out.

The last two configurations are for incoming Rose connections. The first for people who have placed calls to 'vk2ktj-0' and the second for 'VK2KTJ-1 at the our Rose node address. These work precisely the same way. Not the use of the curly braces to distinguish the port as a Rose port.

This example is a contrived one but I think it illustrates clearly the important features of the syntax of the configuration file. The configuration file is explained fully in the ax25d.conf *man* page. A more detailed example is included in the ax25-utils package that might be useful to you too.

12.3 Starting ax25d

When you have the two configuration files completed you start ax25d with the command:

```
# /usr/sbin/ax25d
```

When this is run people should be able to make AX.25 connections to your Linux machine. Remember to put the ax25d command in your rc files so that it is started automatically when you reboot each time.

13 Configuring the node software.

The node software was developed by Tomi Manninen <tomi.manninen@hut.fi> and was based on the original PMS program. It provides a fairly complete and flexible node capability that is easily configured. It allows users once they are connected to make Telnet, NetRom, Rose, and AX.25 connections out and to obtain various sorts of information such as Finger, Nodes and Heard lists etc. You can configure the node to execute any Linux command you wish fairly simply.

The node would normally be invoked from the ax25d program although it is also capable of being invoked from the TCP/IP inetd program to allow users to telnet to your machine and obtain access to it, or by running it from the command line.

13.1 Creating the /etc/ax25/node.conf file.

The node.conf file is where the main configuration of the node takes place. It is a simple text file, and its format is as follows:

```
# /etc/ax25/node.conf
# configuration file for the node(8) program.
#
# Lines beginning with '#' are comments and are ignored.

# Hostname
# Specifies the hostname of the node machine
hostname        radio.gw.vk2ktj.ampr.org

# Local Network
# allows you to specify what is consider 'local' for the
# purposes of permission checking using nodes.perms.
localnet        44.136.8.96/29

# Hide Ports
# If specified allows you to make ports invisible to users. The
# listed ports will not be listed by the (P)orts command.
hiddenports     rose netrom

# Node Identification.
# this will appear in the node prompt
NodeId          LINUX:VK2KTJ-9

# NetRom port
```

```
# This is the name of the netrom port that will be used for
# outgoing NetRom connections from the node.
NrPort          netrom

# Node Idle Timeout
# Specifies the idle time for connections to this node in seconds.
idletimout      1800

# Connection Idle Timeout
# Specifies the idle timer for connections made via this node in
# seconds.
conntimeout     1800

# Reconnect
# Specifies whether users should be reconnected to the node
# when their remote connections disconnect, or whether they
# should be disconnected complete.
reconnect       on

# Command Aliases
# Provide a way of making complex node commands simple.
alias           CONV    "telnet vk1xwt.ampr.org 3600"
alias           BBS     "connect radio vk2xsb"

# Externam Command Aliases
# Provide a means of executing external commands under the node.
# extcmd <cmdname> <flag> <userid> <command>
# Flag == 1 is the only implemented function.
# <command> is formatted as per ax25d.conf
extcmd          PMS     1       root    /usr/sbin/pms pms -u %U -o VK2KTJ

# Logging
# Set logging to the system log. 3 is the noisiest, 0 is disabled.
loglevel        3

# The escape character
# 20 = (Control-T)
EscapeChar      20
```

13.2 Creating the `/etc/ax25/node.perms` file.

The node allows you to assign permissions to users. These permissions allow you to determine which users should be allowed to make use of options such as the (T)elnet, and (C)onnect commands, for example, and which shouldn't. The `node.perms` file is where this information is stored and contains five key fields. For all fields an asterisk '*' character matches anything. This is useful for building default rules.

user

The first field is the call sign or user to which the permissions should apply. Any SSID value is ignored, so you should just place the base call sign here.

method

Each protocol or access method is also given permissions. For example you might allow users who have connected via AX.25 or NetRom to use the (C)onnect option, but prevent others, such as those who are telnet connected from a non-local node from having access to it. The second field therefore allows you to select which access method this permissions rule should apply to. The access methods allowed are:

```
method  description
------  ------------------------------------------------------------
ampr    User is telnet connected from an amprnet address (44.0.0.0)
ax25    User connected by AX.25
```

```
host    User started node from command line
inet    user is telnet connected from a non-loca, non-ampr address.
local   User is telnet connected from a 'local' host
netrom  User connected by NetRom
rose    User connected by Rose
*       User connected by any means.
```

port

For AX.25 users you can control permissions on a port by port basis too if you choose. This allows you to determine what AX.25 are allowed to do based on which of your ports they have connected to. The third field contains the port name if you are using this facility. This is useful only for AX.25 connections.

password

You may optionally configure the node so that it prompts users to enter a password when they connect. This might be useful to help protect specially configured users who have high authority levels. If the fourth field is set then its value will be the password that will be accepted.

permissions

The permissions field is the final field in each entry in the file. The permissions field is coded as a bit field, with each facility having a bit value which if set allows the option to be used and if not set prevents the facility being used. The list of controllable facilities and their corresponding bit values are:

```
value   description
-----   -------------------------------------------------
  1     Login allowed.
  2     AX25 (C)onnects allowed.
  4     NetRom (C)onnects allowed.
  8     (T)elnet to local hosts allowed.
 16     (T)elnet to amprnet (44.0.0.0) hosts allowed.
 32     (T)elnet to non-local, non-amprnet hosts allowed.
 64     Hidden ports allowed for AX.25 (C)onnects.
128     Rose (C)onnects allowed.
```

To code the permissions value for a rule, simply take each of the permissions you want that user to have and add their values together. The resulting number is what you place in field five.

A sample `nodes.perms` might look like:

```
# /etc/ax25/node.perms
#
# The node operator is VK2KTJ, has a password of 'secret' and
# is allowed all permissions by all connection methods
vk2ktj  *       *       secret  255

# The following users are banned from connecting
NOCALL  *       *       *       0
PK232   *       *       *       0
PMS     *       *       *       0

# INET users are banned from connecting.
*       inet    *       *       0

# AX.25, NetRom, Local, Host and AMPR users may (C)onnect and (T)elnet
# to local and ampr hosts but not to other IP addresses.
*       ax25    *       *       159
*       netrom  *       *       159
*       local   *       *       159
*       host    *       *       159
*       ampr    *       *       159
```

13.3 Configuring node to run from ax25d

The node program would normally be run by the ax25d program. To do this you need to add appropriate rules to the /etc/ax25/ax25d.conf file. In my configuration I wanted users to have a choice of either connecting to the node or connecting to other services. ax25d allows you to do this by cleverly creating creating port aliases. For example, given the ax25d configuration presented above, I want to configure node so that all users who connect to VK2KTJ-1 are given the node. To do this I add the following to my /etc/ax25/ax25d.conf file:

```
[vk2ktj-1 via radio]
default    *     *     *    *    *    0     root /usr/sbin/node node
```

This says that the Linux kernel code will answer any connection requests for the call sign "VK2KTJ-1" heard on the AX.25 port named 'radio', and will cause the node program to be run.

13.4 Configuring node to run from inetd

If you want users to be able to telnet a port on your machine and obtain access to the node you can go this fairly easily. The first thing to decide is what port users should connect to. In this example I've arbitrarily chosen port 4000, though Tomi gives details on how you could replace the normal telnet daemon with the node in his documentation.

You need to modify two files.

To /etc/services you should add:

```
node     3694/tcp          #OH2BNS's node software
```

and to /etc/inetd.conf you should add:

```
node     stream  tcp     nowait  root     /usr/sbin/node node
```

When this is done, and you have restarted the inetd program any user who telnet connects to port 3694 of your machine will be prompted to login and if configured, their password and then they will be connected to the node.

14 Configuring axspawn.

The axspawn program is a simple program that allows AX.25 stations who connect to be logged in to your machine. It may be invoked from the ax25d program as described above in a manner similar to the node program. To allow a user to log in to your machine you should add a line similar to the following into your /etc/ax25/ax25d.conf file:

```
default * * * * * 1 root /usr/sbin/axspawn axspawn %u
```

If the line ends in the + character then the connecting user must hit return before they will be allowed to login. The default is to not wait. Any individual host configurations that follow this line will have the axspawn program run when they connect. When axspawn is run it first checks that the command line argument it is supplied is a legal callsign, strips the SSID, then it checks that /etc/passwd file to see if that user has an account configured. If there is an account, and the password is either "" (null) or + then the user is logged in, if there is anything in the password field the user is prompted to enter a password. If there is not an existing account in the /etc/passwd file then axspawn may be configured to automatically create one.

14.1 Creating the /etc/ax25/axspawn.conf file.

You can alter the behaviour of axspawn in various ways by use of the /etc/ax25/axspawn.conf file. This file is formatted as follows:

```
# /etc/ax25/axspawn.conf
#
# allow automatic creation of user accounts
create    yes
#
# guest user if above is 'no' or everything else fails. Disable with "no"
guest     no
#
# group id or name for autoaccount
group     ax25
#
# first user id to use
first_uid 2001
```

```
#
# maximum user id
max_uid    3000
#
# where to add the home directory for the new users
home       /home/ax25
#
# user shell
shell      /bin/bash
#
# bind user id to call sign for outgoing connects.
associate yes
```

The eight configurable characteristics of *axspawn* are as follows:

#

Indicates a comment.

create

If this field is set to `yes` then `axspawn` will attempt to automatically create a user account for any user who connects and does not already have an entry in the `/etc/passwd` file.

guest

This field names the login name of the account that will be used for people who connect who do not already have accounts if `create` is set to `no`. This is usually `ax25` or `guest`.

group

This field names the group name that will be used for any users who connect and do not already have an entry in the `/etc/passwd` file.

first_uid

This is the number of the first userid that will be automatically created for new users.

max_uid

This is the maximum number that will be used for the userid of new users.

home

This is the home (login) directory of new users.

shell

This is the login shell of any new users.

associate

This flag indicates whether outgoing AX.25 connections made by this user after they login will use their own callsign, or your stations callsign.

15 Configuring `pms`

The `pms` program is an implementation of a simple personal message system. It was originally written by Alan Cox. Dave Brown, N2RJT, <`dcb@vectorbd.com`> has taken on further development of it. At present it is still very simple, supporting only the ability to send mail to the owner of the system and to obtain some limited system information but Dave is working to expand its capability to make it more useful.

After that is done there are a couple of simple files that you should create that give users some information about the system and then you need to add appropriate entries into the `ax25d.conf` file so that connected users are presented with the PMS.

15.1 Create the `/etc/ax25/pms.motd` file.

The `/etc/ax25/pms.motd` file contains the 'message of the day' that users will be presented with after they connect and receive the usual BBS id header. The file is a simple text file, any text you include in this file will be sent to users.

15.2 Create the /etc/ax25/pms.info file.

The /etc/ax25/pms.info file is also a simple text file in which you would put more detailed information about your station or configuration. This file is presented to users in response to their issuing of the Info command from the PMS> prompt.

15.3 Associate AX.25 call signs with system users.

When a connected user sends mail to an AX.25 callsign, the *pms* expects that call sign to be mapped, or associated with a real system user on your machine. This is described in a section of its own.

15.4 Add the PMS to the /etc/ax25/ax25d.conf file.

Adding pms to your ax25d.conf file is very simple. There is one small thing you need to think about though. Dave has added command line arguments to the PMS to allow it to handle a number of different text end-of-line conventions. AX.25 and NetRom by convention expect the end-of-line to be CR/LF while the standard UNIX end-of-line is just newline. So, for example, if you wanted to add an entry that meant that the default action for a connection received on an AX.25 port is to start the PMS then you would add a line that looked something like:

```
default  1  10 5 100 5   0    root  /usr/sbin/pms pms -a -o vk2ktj
```

This simply runs the pms program, telling it that it is an AX.25 connection it is connected to and that the PMS owner is vk2ktj. Check the manual page for what you should specify for other connection methods.

15.5 Test the PMS.

To test the PMS, you can try the following command from the command line:

```
# /usr/sbin/pms -u vk2ktj -o vk2ktj
```

Substitute your own call sign for mine and this will run the pms, telling it that it is to use the unix end-of-line convention, and that user logging in is vk2ktj. You can do all the things connected users can.

Additionally you might try getting some other node to connect to you to confirm that your ax25d.conf configuration works.

16 Configuring the "user_call" programs.

The "user_call" programs are really called: ax25_call and netrom_call. They are very simple programs designed to be called from ax25d to automate network connections to remote hosts. They may of course be called from a number of other places such as shell scripts or other daemons such as the node program.

They are like a very simple call program. They don't do any meddling with the data at all, so the end of line handling you'll have to worry about yourself.

Let's start with an example of how you might use them. Imagine you have a small network at home and that you have one Linux machine acting as your Linux radio gateway and another machine, lets say a BPQ node connected to it via an ethernet connection.

Normally if you wanted radio users to be able to connect to the BPQ node they would either have to digipeat through your Linux node, or connect to the node program on your Linux node and then connect from it. The ax25_call program can simplify this if it is called from the ax25d program.

Imagine the BPQ node has the call sign VK2KTJ-9 and that the linux machine has the AX.25/ethernet port named "bpq." Let us also imagine the Linux gateway machine has a radio port called "radio."

An entry in the /etc/ax25/ax25d.conf that looked like:

```
[VK2KTJ-1 via radio]
default     * * * *    *  *  *
                             root /usr/sbin/ax25_call ax25_call bpq %u vk2ktj-9
```

enables users to connect direct to "VK2KTJ-1" which would actually be the Linux ax25d daemon and then be automatically switched to an AX.25 connection to "VK2KTJ-9" via the bpq interface.

There are all sorts of other possible configurations that you might try. The netrom_call and rose_call utilities work in similar ways. One amateur has used this utility to make connections to a remote BBS easier. Normally the users would have to manually enter a long connection string to make the call so he created an entry that made the BBS appear as though it were on the local network by having his ax25d proxy the connection to the remote machine.

17 Configuring the Rose uplink and downlink commands

If you are familiar with the ROM based Rose implementation you will be familiar with the method by which AX.25 users make calls across a Rose network. If a users local Rose node has the call sign VK2KTJ-5 and the AX.25 user wants to connect to VK5XXX at remote Rose node 5050882960 then they would issue the command:

```
c vk5xxx v vk2ktj-5 5050 882960
```

At the remote node, VK5XXX would see an incoming connection with the local AX.25 users call sign and being digipeated via the remote Rose nodes callsign.

The Linux Rose implementation does not support this capability in the kernel, but there are two application programs called rsuplnk and rsdwnlnk which perform this function.

17.1 Configuring a Rose downlink

To configure your Linux machine to accept a Rose connection and establish an AX.25 connection to any destination call sign that is not being listened for on your machine you need to add an entry to your /etc/ax25/ax25d.conf file. Normally you would configure this entry to be the default behaviour for incoming Rose connections. For example you might have Rose listeners operating for destinations like NODE-0 or HEARD-0 that you wish to handle locally, but for all other destination calls you may want to pass them to the rsdwnlink command and assume they are AX.25 users.

A typical configuration would look like:

```
#
{* via rose}
NOCALL   * * * * * *  L
default  * * * * * *  - root  /usr/sbin/rsdwnlnk rsdwnlnk 4800 vk2ktj-5
#
```

With this configuration any user who established a Rose connection to your Linux nodes address with a destination call of something that you were not specifically listening for would be converted into an AX.25 connection on the AX.25 port named 4800 with a digipeater path of VK2KTJ-5.

17.2 Configuring a Rose uplink

To configure your Linux machine to accept AX.25 connections in the same way that a ROM Rose node would you must add an entry into your /etc/ax25/ax25d.conf file that looks similar to the following:

```
#
[VK2KTJ-5* via 4800]
NOCALL   * * * * * *  L
default  * * * * * *  - root  /usr/sbin/rsuplnk rsuplnk rose
#
```

Note the special syntax for the local callsign. The '*' character indicates that the application should be invoked if the call sign is heard in the digipeater path of a connection.

This configuration would allow an AX.25 user to establish Rose calls using the example connect sequence presented in the introduction. Anybody attempting to digipeat via VK2KTJ-5 on the AX.25 port named 4800 would be handled by the rsuplnk command.

18 Associating AX.25 call signs with Linux users.

There are a number of situations where it is highly desirable to associate a call sign with a Linux user account. One example might be where a number of amateur radio operators share the same Linux machine and wish to use their own call sign when making calls. Another is the case of PMS users wanting to talk to a particular user on your machine.

The AX.25 software provides a means of managing this association of linux user account names with call signs. We've mentioned it once already in the PMS section, but I'm spelling it out here to be sure you don't miss it.

You make the association with the axparms command. An example looks like:

```
# axparms -assoc vk2ktj terry
```

This command associates that AX.25 call sign vk2ktj with the user terry on the machine. So, for example, any mail for vk2ktj on the pms will be sent to Linux account terry.

Remember to put these associations into your rc file so that they are available each time your reboot.

Note you should never associate a call sign with the root account as this can cause configuration problems in other programs.

19 The /proc/ file system entries.

The /proc file system contains a number of files specifically related to the AX25 and NetRom kernel software. These files are normally used by the AX52 utilities, but they are plainly formatted so you may be interested in reading them. The format is fairly easily understood so I don't think much explanation will be necessary.

/proc/net/arp
: Contains the list of Address Resolution Protocol mappings of IP addresses to MAC layer protocol addresses. These can can AX.25, ethernet or some other MAC layer protocol.

/proc/net/ax25
: Contains a list of AX.25 sockets opened. These might be listening for a connection, or active sessions.

/proc/net/ax25_bpqether
: Contains the AX25 over ethernet BPQ style call sign mappings.

/proc/net/ax25_calls
: Contains the Linux userid to callsign mappings set my the *axparms -assoc* command.

/proc/net/ax25_route
: Contains AX.25 digipeater path information.

/proc/net/nr
: Contains a list of NetRom sockets opened. These might be listening for a connection, or active sessions.

/proc/net/nr_neigh
: Contains information about the NetRom neighbors known to the NetRom software.

/proc/net/nr_nodes
: Contains information about the NetRom nodes known to the NetRom software.

/proc/net/rose
: Contains a list of Rose sockets opened. These might be listening for a connection, or active sessions.

/proc/net/rose_nodes
: Contains a mapping of Rose destinations to Rose neighbors.

/proc/net/rose_neigh
: Contains a list of known Rose neighbors.

/proc/net/rose_routes
: Contains a list of all established Rose connections.

20 AX.25, NetRom, Rose network programming.

Probably the biggest advantage of using the kernel based implementations of the amateur packet radio protocols is the ease with which you can develop applications and programs to use them.

While the subject of Unix Network Programming is outside the scope of this document I will describe the elementary details of how you can make use of the AX.25, NetRom and Rose protocols within your software.

20.1 The address families.

Network programming for AX.25, NetRom and Rose is quite similar to programming for TCP/IP under Linux. The major differences being the address families used, and the address structures that need to be mangled into place.

The address family names for AX.25, NetRom and Rose are `AF_AX25`, `AF_NETROM` and `AF_ROSE` respectively.

20.2 The header files.

You must always include the 'ax25.h' header file, and also the 'netrom.h' or 'rose.h' header files if you are dealing with those protocols. Simple top level skeletons would look something like the following:

For AX.25:

```
#include <ax25.h>
int s, addrlen = sizeof(struct full_sockaddr_ax25);
struct full_sockaddr_ax25 sockaddr;
sockaddr.fsa_ax25.sax25_family = AF_AX25
```

For NetRom:

```
#include <ax25.h>
#include <netrom.h>
  int s, addrlen = sizeof(struct full_sockaddr_ax25);
  struct full_sockaddr_ax25 sockaddr;
  sockaddr.fsa_ax25.sax25_family = AF_NETROM;
```

For Rose:

```
#include <ax25.h>
#include <rose.h>
  int s, addrlen = sizeof(struct sockaddr_rose);
  struct sockaddr_rose sockaddr;
  sockaddr.srose_family = AF_ROSE;
```

20.3 Call sign mangling and examples.

There are routines within the `lib/ax25.a` library built in the AX25 utilities package that manage the call sign conversions for you. You can write your own of course if you wish.

The user_call utilities are excellent examples from which to work. The source code for them is included in the AX25 utilities package. If you spend a little time working with those you will soon see that ninety percent of the work is involved in just getting ready to open the socket. Actually making the connection is easy, the preparation takes time.

The example are simple enough to not be very confusing. If you have any questions, you should feel to direct them to the `linux-hams` mailing list and someone there will be sure to help you.

21 Some sample configurations.

Following are examples of the most common types of configurations. These are guides only as there are as many ways of configuring your network as there are networks to configure, but they may give you a start.

21.1 Small Ethernet LAN with Linux as a router to Radio LAN

Many of you may have small local area networks at home and want to connect the machines on that network to your local radio LAN. This is the type of configuration I use at home. I arranged to have a suitable block of addresses allocated to me that I could capture in a single route for convenience and I use these on my Ethernet LAN. Your local IP coordinator will assist you in doing this if you want to try it as well. The addresses for the Ethernet LAN form a subset of the radio LAN addresses. The following configuration is the actual one for my Linux router on my network at home:

```
                                           .    .    .    .    . .
  ---                                   .
  | Network          /---------\     .    Network
  | 44.136.8.96/29|           |    .      44.136.8/24         \ | /
  |                | Linux     |   .                            \|/
  |                |           |  .                              |
  |          eth0 | Router    |  .  /-----\    /----------\      |
  |----------------|           |-----| TNC |----| Radio     |---/
  |    44.136.8.97 |  and      |  .  \-----/    \----------/
  |                |           | sl0
  |                | Server    | 44.136.8.5
  |                |           |   .
  |                |           |    .
  |                \___________/     .
  ---                                      .    .    .    .    . .

#!/bin/sh
# /etc/rc.net
# This configuration provides one KISS based AX.25 port and one
# Ethernet device.

echo "/etc/rc.net"
echo "  Configuring:"
```

```
echo -n "    loopback:"
/sbin/ifconfig lo 127.0.0.1
/sbin/route add 127.0.0.1
echo " done."

echo -n "    ethernet:"
/sbin/ifconfig eth0 44.136.8.97 netmask 255.255.255.248 \
                broadcast 44.136.8.103 up
/sbin/route add 44.136.8.97 eth0
/sbin/route add -net 44.136.8.96 netmask 255.255.255.248 eth0
echo " done."

echo -n "    AX.25: "
kissattach -i 44.136.8.5 -m 512 /dev/ttyS1 4800
ifconfig sl0 netmask 255.255.255.0 broadcast 44.136.8.255
route add -host 44.136.8.5 sl0
route add -net 44.136.8.0 window 1024 sl0

echo -n "    Netrom: "
nrattach -i 44.136.8.5 netrom

echo "  Routing:"
/sbin/route add default gw 44.136.8.68 window 1024 sl0
echo "    default route."
echo done.

# end
```

/etc/ax25/axports

```
# name  call sign         speed   paclen  window  description
4800    VK2KTJ-0         4800    256     2       144.800 MHz
```

/etc/ax25/nrports

```
# name  call sign         alias   paclen  description
netrom  VK2KTJ-9         LINUX   235     Linux Switch Port
```

/etc/ax25/nrbroadcast

```
# ax25_name     min_obs def_qual        worst_qual      verbose
4800            1       120             10              1
```

- You must have IP_FORWARDING enabled in your kernel.
- The AX.25 configuration files are pretty much those used as examples in the earlier sections, refer to those where necessary.
- I've chosen to use an IP address for my radio port that is not within my home network block. I needn't have done so, I could have easily used `44.136.8.97` for that port too.
- `44.136.8.68` is my local IPIP encapsulated gateway and hence is where I point my default route.
- Each of the machines on my Ethernet network have a route:

  ```
  route add -net 44.0.0.0 netmask 255.0.0.0 \
          gw 44.136.8.97 window 512 mss 512 eth0
  ```

  The use of the `mss` and `window` parameters means that I can get optimum performance from both local Ethernet and radio based connections.
- I also run my smail, http, ftp and other daemons on the router machine so that it needs to be the only machine to provide others with facilities.
- The router machine is a lowly 386DX20 with a 20Mb hard drive and a very minimal Linux configuration.

21.2 IPIP encapsulated gateway configuration.

Linux is now very commonly used for TCP/IP encapsulated gateways around the world. The new tunnel driver supports multiple encapsulated routes and makes the older `ipip` daemon obsolete.

A typical configuration would look similar to the following.

```
                                                  .     .     .     .    . .
  ---                                         .
   | Network          /---------\         .      Network
   | 154.27.3/24      |         |       .        44.136.16/24        \ | /
   |                  | Linux   |      .                              \|/
   |                  |         |     .                                |
   |            eth0  | IPIP    |    .  /-----\      /----------\      |
---|------------------|         |-----| TNC |-----| Radio      |---/
   |   154.27.3.20    | Gateway |    .  \-----/      \----------/
   |                  |         | sl0
   |                  |         | 44.136.16.1
   |                  |         |     .
   |                  |         |       .
   |                  \_________/          .
  ---                                             .     .     .     .    . .
```

The configuration files of interest are:

```
# /etc/rc.net
# This file is a simple configuration that provides one KISS AX.25
# radio port, one Ethernet device, and utilizes the kernel tunnel driver
# to perform the IPIP encapsulation/decapsulation
#
echo "/etc/rc.net"
echo "  Configuring:"
#
echo -n "    loopback:"
/sbin/ifconfig lo 127.0.0.1
/sbin/route add 127.0.0.1
echo " done."
#
echo -n "    ethernet:"
/sbin/ifconfig eth0 154.27.3.20 netmask 255.255.255.0 \
                broadcast 154.27.3.255 up
/sbin/route add 154.27.3.20 eth0
/sbin/route add -net 154.27.3.0 netmask 255.255.255.0 eth0
echo " done."
#
echo -n "    AX.25: "
kissattach -i 44.136.16.1 -m 512 /dev/ttyS1 4800
/sbin/ifconfig sl0 netmask 255.255.255.0 broadcast 44.136.16.255
/sbin/route add -host 44.136.16.1 sl0
/sbin/route add -net 44.136.16.0 netmask 255.255.255.0 window 1024 sl0
#
echo -n "    tunnel:"
/sbin/ifconfig tunl0 44.136.16.1 mtu 512 up
#
echo done.
#
echo -n "Routing ... "
source /etc/ipip.routes
echo done.
#
# end.
```

and:

```
# /etc/ipip.routes
# This file is generated using the munge script
#
/sbin/route add -net 44.134.8.0 netmask 255.255.255.0 tunl0 gw 134.43.26.1
/sbin/route add -net 44.34.9.0 netmask 255.255.255.0 tunl0 gw 174.84.6.17
/sbin/route add -net 44.13.28.0 netmask 255.255.255.0 tunl0 gw 212.37.126.3
   ...
   ...
   ...
```

/etc/ax25/axports

```
# name  call sign        speed   paclen  window  description
4800    VK2KTJ-0        4800    256     2       144.800 MHz
```

Some points to note here are:

- The new tunnel driver uses the *gw* field in the routing table in place of the *pointopoint* parameter to specify the address of the remote IPIP gateway. This is why it now supports multiple routes per interface.
- You **can** configure two network devices with the same address. In this example both the `sl0` and the `tunl0` devices have been configured with the IP address of the radio port. This is done so that the remote gateway sees the correct address from your gateway in encapsulated datagrams sent to it.
- The route commands used to specify the encapsulated routes can be automatically generated by a modified version of the *munge* script. This is included below. The route commands would then be written to a separate file and read in using the *bash* `source /etc/ipip.routes` command (assuming you called the file with the routing commands `/etc/ipip.routes`) as illustrated. The source file must be in the NOS route command format.
- Note the use of the `window` argument on the `route` command. Setting this parameter to an appropriate value improves the performance of your radio link.

The new tunnel-munge script:

```
#!/bin/sh
#
# From: Ron Atkinson <n8fow@hamgate.cc.wayne.edu>
#
#  This script is basically the 'munge' script written by Bdale N3EUA
#  for the IPIP daemon and is modified by Ron Atkinson N8FOW. It's
#  purpose is to convert a KA9Q NOS format gateways route file
#  (usually called 'encap.txt') into a Linux routing table format
#  for the IP tunnel driver.
#
#        Usage: Gateway file on stdin, Linux route format file on stdout.
#               eg.  tunnel-munge < encap.txt > ampr-routes
#
# NOTE: Before you use this script be sure to check or change the
#       following items:
#
#     1) Change the 'Local routes' and 'Misc user routes' sections
#        to routes that apply to your own area (remove mine please!)
#     2) On the fgrep line be sure to change the IP address to YOUR
#        gateway Internet address. Failure to do so will cause serious
#        routing loops.
#     3) The default interface name is 'tunl0'. Make sure this is
#        correct for your system.

echo "#"
echo "# IP tunnel route table built by $LOGNAME on 'date'"
echo "# by tunnel-munge script v960307."
echo "#"
echo "# Local routes"
echo "route add -net 44.xxx.xxx.xxx netmask 255.mmm.mmm.mmm dev sl0"
```

```
echo "#"
echo "# Misc user routes"
echo "#"
echo "# remote routes"

fgrep encap | grep "^route" | grep -v " XXX.XXX.XXX.XXX" | \
awk '{
        split($3, s, "/")
        split(s[1], n,".")
        if      (n[1] == "")    n[1]="0"
        if      (n[2] == "")    n[2]="0"
        if      (n[3] == "")    n[3]="0"
        if      (n[4] == "")    n[4]="0"
        if      (s[2] == "1")   mask="128.0.0.0"
        else if (s[2] == "2")   mask="192.0.0.0"
        else if (s[2] == "3")   mask="224.0.0.0"
        else if (s[2] == "4")   mask="240.0.0.0"
        else if (s[2]== "5")    mask="248.0.0.0"
        else if (s[2] == "6")   mask="252.0.0.0"
        else if (s[2] == "7")   mask="254.0.0.0"
        else if (s[2] == "8")   mask="255.0.0.0"
        else if (s[2] == "9")   mask="255.128.0.0"
        else if (s[2] == "10")  mask="255.192.0.0"
        else if (s[2] == "11")  mask="255.224.0.0"
        else if (s[2] == "12")  mask="255.240.0.0"
        else if (s[2]== "13")   mask="255.248.0.0"
        else if (s[2] == "14")  mask="255.252.0.0"
        else if (s[2] == "15")  mask="255.254.0.0"
        else if (s[2] == "16")  mask="255.255.0.0"
        else if (s[2] == "17")  mask="255.255.128.0"
        else if (s[2] == "18")  mask="255.255.192.0"
        else if (s[2] == "19")  mask="255.255.224.0"
        else if (s[2] == "20")  mask="255.255.240.0"
        else if (s[2] == "21")  mask="255.255.248.0"
        else if (s[2] == "22")  mask="255.255.252.0"
        else if (s[2] == "23")  mask="255.255.254.0"
        else if (s[2] == "24")  mask="255.255.255.0"
        else if (s[2] == "25")  mask="255.255.255.128"
        else if (s[2] == "26")  mask="255.255.255.192"
        else if (s[2] == "27")  mask="255.255.255.224"
        else if (s[2] == "28")  mask="255.255.255.240"
        else if (s[2] == "29")  mask="255.255.255.248"
        else if (s[2] == "30")  mask="255.255.255.252"
        else if (s[2] == "31")  mask="255.255.255.254"
        else                    mask="255.255.255.255"

if (mask == "255.255.255.255")
        printf "route add -host %s.%s.%s.%s gw %s dev tunl0\n"\
                ,n[1],n[2],n[3],n[4],$5
else
        printf "route add -net %s.%s.%s.%s gw %s netmask %s dev tunl0\n"\
                ,n[1],n[2],n[3],n[4],$5,mask
 }'

echo "#"
echo "# default the rest of amprnet via mirrorshades.ucsd.edu"
echo "route add -net 44.0.0.0 gw 128.54.16.18 netmask 255.0.0.0 dev tunl0"
echo "#"
```

```
echo "# the end"
```

21.3 AXIP encapsulated gateway configuration

Many Amateur Radio Internet gateways encapsulate AX.25, NetRom and Rose in addition to TCP/IP. Encapsulation of AX.25 frames within IP datagrams is described in RFC-1226 by Brian Kantor. Mike Westerhof wrote an implementation of an AX.25 encapsulation daemon for UNIX in 1991. The ax25-utils package includes a marginally enhanced version of it for Linux.

An AXIP encapsulation program accepts AX.25 frames at one end, looks at the destination AX.25 address to determine what IP address to send them to, encapsulates them in a tcp/ip datagram and then transmits them to the appropriate remote destination. It also accepts TCP/IP datagrams that contain AX.25 frames, unwraps them and processes them as if it had received them directly from an AX.25 port. To distinguish IP datagrams containing AX.25 frames from other IP datagrams which don't, AXIP datagrams are coded with a protocol id of 4 (or 94 which is now deprecated). This process is described in RFC-1226.

The `ax25ipd` program included in the ax25-utils package presents itself as a program supporting a KISS interface across which you pass AX.25 frames, and an interface into the TCP/IP protocols. It is configured with a single configuration file called `/etc/ax25/ax25ipd.conf`.

21.3.1 AXIP configuration options.

The `ax25ipd` program has two major modes of operation, "digipeater" mode and "tnc" mode. In "tnc" mode the daemon is treated as though it were a kiss TNC, you pass KISS encapsulated frames to it and it will transmit them, this is the usual configuration. In "digipeater" mode, you treat the daemon as though it were an AX.25 digipeater. There are subtle differences between these modes.

In the configuration file you configure "routes" or mappings between destination AX.25 call signs and the IP addresses of the hosts that you want to send the AX.25 packets too. Each route has options which will be explained later.

Other options that are configured here are

the tty that the `ax25ipd` daemon will open and its speed (usually one end of a pipe)

what call sign you want to use in "digipeater" mode

beacon interval and text

whether you want to encapsulate the AX.25 frames in IP datagrams or in UDP/IP datagrams. Nearly all AXIP gateways use IP encapsulation, but some gateways are behind firewalls that will not allow IP with the AXIP protocol id to pass and are forced to use UDP/IP. Whatever you choose must match what the TCP/IP host at the other end of the link is using.

21.3.2 A typical `/etc/ax25/ax25ipd.conf` file.

```
#
# ax25ipd configuration file for station floyd.vk5xxx.ampr.org
#
# Select axip transport. 'ip' is what you want for compatibility
# with most other gateways.
#
socket ip
#
# Set ax25ipd mode of operation. (digi or tnc)
#
mode tnc
#
# If you selected digi, you must define a callsign.  If you selected
# tnc mode, the call sign is currently optional, but this may change
# in the future! (2 calls if using dual port kiss)
#
#mycall vk5xxx-4
#mycall2 vk5xxx-5
#
# In digi mode, you may use an alias. (2 for dual port)
```

```
#
#myalias svwdns
#myalias2 svwdn2
#
# Send an ident every 540 seconds ...
#
#beacon after 540
#btext ax25ip -- tncmode rob/vk5xxx -- Experimental AXIP gateway
#
# Serial port, or pipe connected to a kissattach in my case
#
device /dev/ttyq0
#
# Set the device speed
#
speed 9600
#
# loglevel 0 - no output
# loglevel 1 - config info only
# loglevel 2 - major events and errors
# loglevel 3 - major events, errors, and AX25 frame trace
# loglevel 4 - all events
# log 0 for the moment, syslog not working yet ...
#
loglevel 2
#
# If we are in digi mode, we might have a real tnc here, so use param to
# set the tnc parameters ...
#
#param 1 20
#
# Broadcast Address definition. Any of the addresses listed will be forwarded
# to any of the routes flagged as broadcast capable routes.
#
broadcast QST-0 NODES-0
#
# ax.25 route definition, define as many as you need.
# format is route (call/wildcard) (ip host at destination)
# ssid of 0 routes all ssid's
#
# route <destcall> <destaddr> [flags]
#
# Valid flags are:
#         b  - allow broadcasts to be transmitted via this route
#         d  - this route is the default route
#
route vk2sut-0 44.136.8.68 b
route vk5xxx 44.136.188.221 b
route vk2abc 44.1.1.1
#
#
```

21.3.3 Running `ax25ipd`

Create your `/etc/ax25/axports` **entry:**

```
# /etc/ax25/axports
#
axip    VK2KTJ-13       9600    256     AXIP port
```

```
#
```

Run the `kissattach` **command to create that port:**

```
/usr/sbin/kissattach /dev/ptyq0 axip
```

Run the `ax25ipd` **program:**

```
/usr/sbin/ax25ipd &
```

Test the AXIP link:

```
call axip vk5xxx
```

21.3.4 Some notes about the routes and route flags

The "`route`" command is where you specify where you want your AX.25 packets encapsulated and sent to. When the `ax25ipd` daemon receives a packet from its interface, it compares the destination call sign with each of the call signs in its routing table. If it finds a match then the ax.25 packet is encapsulated in an IP datagram and then transmitted to the host at the specified IP address.

There are two flags you can add to any of the route commands in the `ax25ipd.conf` file. The two flags are:

b

Traffic with a destination address matching any of those on the list defined by the "`broadcast`" keyword should be transmitted via this route.

d

Any packets not matching any route should be transmitted via this route.

The broadcast flag is very useful, as it enables informations that is normally destined for all stations to a number of AXIP destinations. Normally axip routes are point-to-point and unable to handle "broadcast" packets.

21.4 Linking NOS and Linux using a pipe device

Many people like to run some version of NOS under Linux because it has all of the features and facilities they are used to. Most of those people would also like to have the NOS running on their machine capable of talking to the Linux kernel so that they can offer some of the Linux capabilities to radio users via NOS.

Brandon S. Allbery, KF8NH, contributed the following information to explain how to interconnect the NOS running on a Linux machine with the kernel code using the Linux pipe device.

Since both Linux and NOS support the SLIP protocol it is possible to link the two together by creating a slip link. You could do this by using two serial ports with a loopback cable between them, but this would be slow and costly. Linux provides a feature that many other Unix-like operating systems provide called "pipes." These are special pseudo-devices that look like a standard tty device to software but in fact loopback to another pipe device. To use these pipes the first program must open the **master** end of the pipe, and the open then the second program can open the **slave** end of the pipe. When both ends are open the programs can communicate with each other simply by writing characters to the pipes in the way they would if they were terminal devices.

To use this feature to connect the Linux kernel and a copy of NOS, or some other program you first must choose a pipe device to use. You can find one by looking in your `/dev` directory. The master end of the pipes are named: `ptyq[1-f]` and the slave end of the pipes are known as: `ttyq[1-f]`. Remember they come in pairs, so if you select `/dev/ptyqf` as your master end then you must use `/dev/ttyqf` as the slave end.

Once you have chosen a pipe device pair to use you should allocate the master end to you Linux kernel and the slave end to the NOS program, as the Linux kernel starts first and the master end of the pipe must be opened first. You must also remember that your Linux kernel must have a different IP address to your NOS, so you will need to allocate a unique address for it if you haven't already.

You configure the pipe just as if it were a serial device, so to create the SLIP link from your Linux kernel you can use commands similar to the following:

```
# /sbin/slattach -s 38400 -p slip /dev/ptyqf &
# /sbin/ifconfig sl0 broadcast 44.255.255.255 pointopoint 44.70.248.67 /
    mtu 1536 44.70.4.88
# /sbin/route add 44.70.248.67 sl0
# /sbin/route add -net 44.0.0.0 netmask 255.0.0.0 gw 44.70.248.67
```

In this example the Linux kernel has been given IP address `44.70.4.88` and the NOS program is using IP address `44.70.248.67`. The `route` command in the last line simply tells your Linux kernel to route all datagrams for the amprnet via the slip link created by the `slattach` command. Normally you would put these commands into your `/etc/rc.d/rc.inet2` file after all your other network configuration is complete so that the slip link is created automatically when you reboot. Note: there is no advantage in using `cslip` instead of `slip` as it actually reduces performance because the link is only a virtual one and occurs fast enough that having to compress the headers first takes longer than transmitting the uncompressed datagram.

To configure the NOS end of the link you could try the following:

```
# you can call the interface anything you want; I use "linux" for convenience.
attach asy ttyqf - slip Linux 1024 1024 38400
route addprivate 44.70.4.88 linux
```

These commands will create a SLIP port named "linux" via the slave end of the pipe device pair to your Linux kernel, and a route to it to make it work. When you have started NOS you should be able to ping and telnet to your NOS from your Linux machine and vice versa. If not, double check that you have made no mistakes especially that you have the addresses configured properly and have the pipe devices around the right way.

22 Where do I find more information about .... ?

Since this document assumes you already have some experience with packet radio, which might not be the case, I've collected a set of references to other information that you might find useful.

22.1 Packet Radio

You can get general information about Packet Radio from these sites:

American Radio Relay League (`http://www.arrl.org/`)

Radio Amateur Teleprinter Society (`http://www.rats.org/`)

Tucson Amateur Packet Radio Group (`http://www.tapr.org/`)

22.2 Protocol Documentation

AX.25, NetRom—Jonathon Naylor has collated a variety of documents that relate to the packet radio protocols themselves. This documentation has been packaged up into `ax25-doc-1.0.tar.gz`, at ftp://ftp.pspt.fi/pub/ham/linux/ax25/.

22.3 Hardware Documentation

Information on the **PI2 Card** is provided by the Ottawa Packet Radio Group, http://hydra.carleton.ca/.

Information on Baycom hardware is available at http://www.baycom.de/.

23 Discussion relating to Amateur Radio and Linux.

There are various places that discussion relating to Amateur Radio and Linux take place. They take place in the `comp.os.linux.*` newsgroups, they also take place on the `HAMS` list on `vger.rutgers.edu`. Other places where they are held include the `tcp-group` mailing list at `ucsd.edu` (the home of amateur radio TCP/IP discussions), and you might also try the `#linpeople` channel on the `linuxnet` irc network.

To join the Linux **linux-hams** channel on the mail list server, send mail to:

```
Majordomo@vger.rutgers.edu
```

with the line:

```
subscribe linux-hams
```

in the message body. The subject line is ignored.

The **linux-hams** mailing list is archived at:

zone.pspt.fi (`http://zone.pspt.fi/archive/linux-hams/`) and *zone.oh7rba.ampr.org* (`http://zone.oh7rba.ampr.org/archive/linux-hams/`). Please use the archives when you are first starting, because many common questions are answered there.

To join the `tcp-group` send mail to:

```
listserver@ucsd.edu
```

with the line:

```
subscribe tcp-group
```

in the body of the text.

Note: Please remember that the `tcp-group` is primarily for discussion of the use of advanced protocols, of which TCP/IP is one, in Amateur Radio. *Linux specific questions should not ordinarily go there.*

24 Acknowledgements.

The following people have contributed to this document in one way or another, knowingly or unknowingly. In no particular order (as I find them): Jonathon Naylor, Thomas Sailer, Joerg Reuter, Ron Atkinson, Alan Cox, Craig Small, John Tanner, Brandon Allbery, Hans Alblas, Klaus Kudielka, Carl Makin.

25 Copyright.

[illegible]

24 Acknowledgements

[illegible]

25 Copyright

[illegible]

This program is free software; you can redistribute it and/or modify it under the terms of the GNU General Public License as published by the Free Software Foundation; either version 2 of the License, or (at your option) any later version.

This program is distributed in the hope that it will be useful, but WITHOUT ANY WARRANTY; without even the implied warranty of MERCHANTABILITY or FITNESS FOR A PARTICULAR PURPOSE. See the GNU General Public License for more details.

You should have received a copy of the GNU General Public License along with this program; if not, write to the Free Software Foundation, Inc., 675 Mass Ave, Cambridge, MA 02139, USA.

Part VIII

"Linux Benchmarking HOWTO" by André D. Balsa,

andrewbalsa@usa.net

Contents

Abstract

v0.12, 15 August 1997
The Linux Benchmarking HOWTO discusses some issues associated with the benchmarking of Linux systems and presents a basic benchmarking toolkit, as well as an associated form, which enable one to produce significant benchmarking information in a couple of hours. Perhaps it will also help diminish the amount of useless articles in comp.os.linux.hardware...

1 Introduction

"What we cannot speak about we must pass over in silence."

Ludwig Wittgenstein (1889-1951), Austrian philosopher.

Benchmarking means **measuring** the speed with which a computer system will execute a computing task, in a way that will allow comparison between different hard/software combinations. It **does not** involve user-friendliness, aesthetic or ergonomic considerations or any other subjective judgment.

Benchmarking is a tedious, repetitive task, and takes attention to details. Very often the results are not what one would expect, and subject to interpretation (which actually may be the most important part of a benchmarking procedure).

Finally, benchmarking deals with facts and figures, not opinion or approximation.

1.1 Why is benchmarking so important?

Apart from the reasons pointed out in the BogoMips Mini-HOWTO (section 7, paragraph 2), one occasionally is confronted with a limited budget and/or minimum performance requirements while putting together a Linux box. In other words, when confronted with the following questions:

- How do I maximize performance within a given budget?
- How do I minimize costs for a required minimum performance level?
- How do I obtain the best performance/cost ratio (within a given budget or given performance requirements)?

One will have to examine, compare and produce benchmarks. Minimizing costs with no performance requirements usually involves putting together a machine with leftover parts (that old 386SX-16 box lying around in the garage will do fine) and does not require benchmarks, and maximizing performance with no cost ceiling is not a realistic situation (unless one is willing to put a Cray box in his or her living room—the leather-covered power supplies around it look nice, don't they?).

Benchmarking per se is senseless, a waste of time and money; it is only meaningful as part of a decision process; i.e., if one has to make a choice between two or more alternatives.

Usually another parameter in the decision process is **cost**, but it could be availability, service, reliability, strategic considerations or any other rational, measurable characteristic of a computer system. When comparing the performance of different Linux kernel versions, for example, **stability** is almost always more important than speed.

1.2 Invalid benchmarking considerations

Very often read in newsgroups and mailing lists, unfortunately:

1. Reputation of manufacturer (unmeasurable and meaningless).
2. Market share of manufacturer (meaningless and irrelevant).
3. Irrational parameters. (For example, superstition or prejudice: would you buy a processor labeled 131313ZAP and painted pink?)
4. Perceived value (meaningless, unmeasurable, and irrational).
5. Amount of marketing hype: this one is the worst, I guess. I personally am fed up with the "XXX inside" or "kkkkkws compatible" logos (now the "aaaaaPowered" has joined the band—what next?). IMHO, the billions of dollars spent on such campaigns would be better used by research teams on the design of new, faster, (cheaper) bug-free processors. No amount of marketing hype will remove a floating-point bug in the FPU of the brand-new processor you just plugged in your motherboard, but an exchange against a redesigned processor will.
6. "You get what you pay for" opinions are just that: opinions. Give me the facts, please.

2 Benchmarking procedures and interpretation of results

A few semi-obvious recommendations:

1. First and foremost, **identify your benchmarking goals**. What is it you are exactly trying to benchmark? In what way will the benchmarking process help later in your decision making? How much time and resources are you willing to put into your benchmarking effort?
2. **Use standard tools**. Use a current, stable kernel version, standard, current GCC and libc and a standard benchmark. In short, use the LBT (see below).
3. Give a **complete description** of your setup (see the LBT report form below).
4. Try to **isolate a single variable**. Comparative benchmarking is more informative than "absolute" benchmarking.**I cannot stress this enough.**
5. **Verify your results**. Run your benchmarks a few times and verify the variations in your results, if any. Unexplained variations will invalidate your results.
6. If you think your benchmarking effort produced meaningful information, **share it** with the Linux community in a **precise** and **concise** way.
7. Please **forget about BogoMips**. I promise myself I shall someday implement a very fast ASIC with the BogoMips loop wired in. Then we shall see what we shall see!

2.1 Understanding benchmarking choices

2.1.1 Synthetic vs. applications benchmarks

Before spending any amount of time on benchmarking chores, a basic choice must be made between "synthetic" benchmarks and "applications" benchmarks.

Synthetic benchmarks are specifically designed to measure the performance of individual components of a computer system, usually by exercising the chosen component to its maximum capacity. An example of a well-known synthetic benchmark is the **Whetstone** suite, originally programmed in 1972 by Harold Curnow in FORTRAN (or was that ALGOL?) and still in widespread use nowadays. The Whestone suite will measure the floating-point performance of a CPU.

The main criticism that can be made of synthetic benchmarks is that they do not represent a computer system's performance in real-life situations. Take, for example, the Whetstone suite: the main loop is very short and will easily fit in the primary cache of a CPU, keeping the FPU pipeline constantly filled and so exercising the FPU to its maximum speed. We cannot really criticize the Whetstone suite if we remember it was programmed 25 years ago (its design dates even earlier than that), but we must make sure we interpret its results with care, when it comes to benchmarking modern microprocessors.

Another very important point to note about synthetic benchmarks is that, ideally, they should tell us something about a **specific** aspect of the system being tested, independently of all other aspects: a synthetic benchmark for Ethernet card I/O throughput should result in the same or similar figures whether it is run on a 386SX-16 with 4 MBytes of RAM or a Pentium 200 MMX with 64 MBytes of RAM. Otherwise, the test will be measuring the overall performance of the CPU/Motherboard/Bus/Ethernet card/Memory subsystem/DMA combination: not very useful since the variation in CPU will cause a greater impact than the change in Ethernet network card. (This of course assumes we are using the same kernel/driver combination, which could cause an even greater variation)!

Finally, a very common mistake is to average various synthetic benchmarks and claim that such an average is a good representation of real-life performance for any given system.

Here is a comment on FPU benchmarks quoted with permission from the Cyrix Corp. Web site:

> *"A Floating Point Unit (FPU) accelerates software designed to use floating point mathematics : typically CAD programs, spreadsheets, 3D games and design applications. However, today's most popular PC applications make use of both floating point and integer instructions. As a result, Cyrix chose to emphasize 'parallelism' in the design of the 6x86 processor to speed up software that intermixes these two instruction types.*
>
> *The x86 floating point exception model allows integer instructions to issue and complete while a floating point instruction is executing. In contrast, a second floating point instruction cannot begin execution while a previous floating point instruction is executing. To remove the performance limitation created by the floating point exception model, the 6x86 can speculatively issue up to four floating point instructions to the on-chip FPU while continuing to issue and execute integer instructions. As an example, in a code sequence of two floating point instructions (FLTs) followed by six integer instructions (INTs) followed by two FLTs, the 6x86*

processor can issue all ten instructions to the appropriate execution units prior to completion of the first FLT. If none of the instructions fault (the typical case), execution continues with both the integer and floating point units completing instructions in parallel. If one of the FLTs faults (the atypical case), the speculative execution capability of the 6x86 allows the processor state to be restored in such a way that it is compatible with the x86 floating point exception model.

Examination of benchmark tests reveals that synthetic floating point benchmarks use a pure floating point-only code stream not found in real-world applications. This type of benchmark does not take advantage of the speculative execution capability of the 6x86 processor. Cyrix believes that non-synthetic benchmarks based on real-world applications better reflect the actual performance users will achieve. Real-world applications contain intermixed integer and floating point instructions and therefore benefit from the 6x86 speculative execution capability."

So, the recent trend in benchmarking is to choose common applications and use them to test the performance of complete computer systems. For example, **SPEC**, the non-profit corporation that designed the well-known SPECINT and SPECFP synthetic benchmark suites, has launched a project for a new applications benchmark suite. But then again, it is very unlikely that such commercial benchmarks will ever include any Linux code.

Summarizing, synthetic benchmarks are valid as long as you understand their purposes and limitations. Applications benchmarks will better reflect a computer system's performance, but none are available for Linux.

2.1.2 High-level vs. low-level benchmarks

Low-level benchmarks will directly measure the performance of the hardware: CPU clock, DRAM and cache SRAM cycle times, hard disk average access time, latency, track-to-track stepping time, etc... This can be useful in case you bought a system and are wondering what components it was built with, but a better way to check these figures would be to open the case, list whatever part numbers you can find and somehow obtain the data sheet for each part (usually on the Web).

Another use for low-level benchmarks is to check that a kernel driver was correctly configured for a specific piece of hardware: if you have the data sheet for the component, you can compare the results of the low-level benchmarks to the theoretical, printed specs.

High-level benchmarks are more concerned with the performance of the hardware/driver/OS combination for a specific aspect of a microcomputer system, for example file I/O performance, or even for a specific hardware/driver/OS/application performance, e.g. an Apache benchmark on different microcomputer systems.

Of course, all low-level benchmarks are synthetic. High-level benchmarks may be synthetic or applications benchmarks.

2.2 Standard benchmarks available for Linux

IMHO a simple test that anyone can do while upgrading any component in his or her Linux box is to launch a kernel compile before and after the hardware or software upgrade and compare compilation times. If all other conditions are kept equal then the test is valid as a measure of compilation performance and one can be confident to say that:

"Changing A to B led to an improvement of x % in the compile time of the Linux kernel under such and such conditions."

No more, no less.

Since kernel compilation is a very usual task under Linux, and since it exercises most functions that get exercised by normal benchmarks (except floating-point performance), it constitutes a rather good **individual** test. In most cases, however, results from such a test cannot be reproduced by other Linux users because of variations in hardware or software configurations and so this kind of test cannot be used as a "yardstick" to compare dissimilar systems (unless we all agree on a standard kernel to compile - see below).

Unfortunately, there are no Linux-specific benchmarking tools, except perhaps the Byte Linux Benchmarks which are a slightly modified version of the Byte Unix Benchmarks dating back from May 1991 (Linux mods by Jon Tombs, original authors Ben Smith, Rick Grehan and Tom Yager).

There is a central Web site for the Byte Linux Benchmarks.

An improved, updated version of the Byte Unix Benchmarks was put together by David C. Niemi. It is called UnixBench 4.01 to avoid confusion with earlier versions. Here is what David wrote about his mods:

"The original and slightly modified BYTE Unix benchmarks are broken in quite a number of ways which make them an unusually unreliable indicator of system performance. I intentionally made my 'index' values look a lot different to avoid confusion with the old benchmarks."

David has set up a majordomo mailing list for discussion of benchmarking on Linux and competing OSs. Join with "subscribe bench" sent in the body of a message to majordomo@wauug.erols.com. The Washington Area Unix User Group is also in the process of setting up a Web site for Linux benchmarks.

Also recently, Uwe F. Mayer, mayer@math.vanderbilt.edu, ported the BYTE Bytemark suite to Linux. This is a modern suite carefully put together by Rick Grehan at BYTE Magazine to test the CPU, FPU, and memory system performance of modern microcomputer systems (these are strictly processor-performance oriented benchmarks, no I/O or system performance is taken into account).

Uwe has also put together a Web site with a database of test results for his version of the Linux BYTEmark benchmarks.

While searching for synthetic benchmarks for Linux, you will notice that sunsite.unc.edu carries few benchmarking tools. To test the relative speed of X servers and graphics cards, the xbench-0.2 suite by Claus Gittinger is available from sunsite.unc.edu, ftp.x.org, and other sites. Xfree86.org refuses (wisely) to carry or recommend any benchmarks.

The XFree86 Benchmarks Survey is a Web site with a database of x-bench results.

For pure disk I/O throughput, the `hdparm` program (included with most distributions, otherwise available from sunsite.unc.edu) will measure transfer rates if called with the `-t` and `-T` switches.

There are many other tools freely available on the Internet to test various performance aspects of your Linux box.

2.3 Links and references

The comp.benchmarks.faq by Dave Sill is the standard reference for benchmarking. It is not Linux specific, but recommended reading for anybody serious about benchmarking. It is available from a number of FTP and web sites and lists **56 different benchmarks**, with links to FTP or Web sites that carry them. Some of the benchmarks listed are commercial, though. (SPEC, for example.)

I will not go through each one of the benchmarks mentioned in the comp.benchmarks.faq, but there is at least one low-level suite which I would like to comment on: the lmbench suite, by Larry McVoy. Quoting David C. Niemi:

> *"Linus and David Miller use this a lot because it does some useful low-level measurements and can also measure network throughput and latency if you have 2 boxes to test with. But it does not attempt to come up with anything like an overall 'figure of merit.'"*

A rather complete FTP site for **freely** available benchmarks was put together by Alfred Aburto. The Whetstone suite used in the LBT can be found at this site.

There is a **multipart FAQ by Eugene Miya** that gets posted regularly to comp.benchmarks; it is an excellent reference.

3 The Linux Benchmarking Toolkit (LBT)

I will propose a basic benchmarking toolkit for Linux. This is a preliminary version of a comprehensive Linux Benchmarking Toolkit, to be expanded and improved. Take it for what it's worth, i.e. as a proposal. If you don't think it is a valid test suite, feel free to email me your criticisms and I will be glad to make the changes and improve it if I can. Before getting into an argument, however, read this HOWTO and the mentioned references: informed criticism is welcomed, empty criticism is not.

3.1 Rationale

This is just common sense:

1. It should not take a whole day to run. When it comes to comparative benchmarking (various runs), nobody wants to spend days trying to figure out the fastest setup for a given system. Ideally, the entire benchmark set should take about 15 minutes to complete on an average machine.
2. All source code for the software used must be freely available on the Net, for obvious reasons.
3. Benchmarks should provide simple figures reflecting the measured performance.
4. There should be a mix of synthetic benchmarks and application benchmarks (with separate results, of course).
5. Each **synthetic** benchmark should exercise a particular subsystem to its maximum capacity.
6. Results of **synthetic** benchmarks should **not** be averaged into a single figure of merit (that defeats the whole idea behind synthetic benchmarks, with considerable loss of information).
7. Applications benchmarks should consist of commonly executed tasks on Linux systems.

3.2 Benchmark selection

I have selected five different benchmark suites, trying as much as possible to avoid overlap in the tests:

1. Kernel 2.0.0 (default configuration) compilation using GCC.
2. Whetstone version 10/03/97 (latest version by Roy Longbottom).
3. xbench-0.2 (with fast execution parameters).
4. UnixBench benchmarks version 4.01 (partial results).
5. BYTE Magazine's BYTEmark benchmarks beta release 2 (partial results).

For tests 4 and 5, "(partial results)" means that not all results produced by these benchmarks are considered.

3.3 Test duration

1. Kernel 2.0.0 compilation: 5–30 minutes, depending on the **real** performance of your system.
2. Whetstone: 100 seconds.
3. Xbench-0.2: < 1 hour.
4. UnixBench benchmarks version 4.01: approximately. 15 minutes.
5. BYTE Magazine's BYTEmark benchmarks: approximately. 10 minutes.

3.4 Comments

3.4.1 Kernel 2.0.0 compilation:

- **What:** it is the only application benchmark in the LBT.
- The code is widely available; (i.e., I finally found some use for my old Linux CD-ROMs).
- Most Linuxers recompile the kernel quite often, so it is a significant measure of overall performance.
- The kernel is large, and GCC uses a large chunk of memory; attenuates L2 cache size bias with small tests.
- It does frequent I/O to disk.
- Test procedure: get a pristine 2.0.0 source, compile with default options (`make config`, press Enter repeatedly). The reported time should be the time spent on compilation i.e. after you type make zImage, not including `make dep`, `make clean`. Note that the default target architecture for the kernel is the i386, so if compiled on another architecture, gcc too should be set to cross-compile, with i386 as the target architecture.
- **Results:** compilation time in minutes and seconds (please don't report fractions of seconds).

3.4.2 Whetstone:

- **What:** measures pure floating point performance with a short, tight loop. The source (in C) is quite readable and it is very easy to see which floating-point operations are involved.
- Shortest test in the LBT.
- It's an "Old Classic" test: comparable figures are available, its flaws and shortcomings are well known.
- Test procedure: the newest C source should be obtained from Aburto's site. Compile and run in double precision mode. Specify `gcc` and `-O2` as precompiler and precompiler options, and define POSIX 1 to specify machine type.
- **Results:** a floating-point performance figure in MWIPS.

3.4.3 Xbench-0.2:

- **What:** measures X server performance.
- The xStones measure provided by xbench is a weighted average of several tests indexed to an old Sun station with a single-bit-depth display. *Hmmm...* it is questionable as a test of modern X servers, but it's still the best tool I have found.
- Test procedure: compile with `-O2`. We specify a few options for a shorter run:`./xbench -timegoal 3 > results/name_of_your_linux_box.out`. To get the xStones rating, we must run an awk script; the simplest way is to type `make summary.ms`. Check the summary.ms file: the xStone rating for your system is in the last column of the line with your machine name specified during the test.
- **Results:** an X performance figure in xStones.
- Note: this test, as it stands, is outdated. It should be re-coded.

3.4.4 UnixBench version 4.01:

- **What:** measures overall Unix performance. This test will exercise the file I/O and kernel multitasking performance.
- I have discarded all arithmetic test results, keeping only the system-related test results.
- Test procedure: make with -O2. Execute with `./Run -1` (run each test once). You will find the results in the ./results/report file. Calculate the geometric mean of the EXECL THROUGHPUT, FILECOPY 1, 2, 3, PIPE THROUGHPUT, PIPE-BASED CONTEXT SWITCHING, PROCESS CREATION, SHELL SCRIPTS and SYSTEM CALL OVERHEAD indexes.
- **Results:** a system index.

3.4.5 BYTE Magazine's BYTEmark benchmarks:

- **What:** provides a good measure of CPU performance. Here is an excerpt from the documentation; *"These benchmarks are meant to expose the theoretical upper limit of the CPU, FPU, and memory architecture of a system. They cannot measure video, disk, or network throughput (those are the domains of a different set of benchmarks). You should, therefore, use the results of these tests as part, not all, of any evaluation of a system."*
- I have discarded the FPU test results since the Whetstone test is just as representative of FPU performance.
- I have split the integer tests in two groups: those more representative of memory-cache-CPU performance and the CPU integer tests.
- Test procedure: `make` with `-O2`. Run the test with `./nbench > myresults.dat` or similar. Then, from myresults.dat, calculate geometric mean of STRING SORT, ASSIGNMENT and BITFIELD test indexes; this is the **memory index**; calculate the geometric mean of NUMERIC SORT, IDEA, HUFFMAN and FP EMULATION test indexes; this is the **integer index**.
- **Results:** a memory index and an integer index calculated as explained above.

3.5 Possible improvements

The ideal benchmark suite would run in a few minutes, with synthetic benchmarks testing every subsystem separately and applications benchmarks providing results for different applications. It would also automatically generate a complete report and eventually email the report to a central database on the Web.

We are not really interested in portability here, but it should at least run on all recent (> 2.0.0) versions and flavors (i386, Alpha, Sparc...) of Linux.

If anybody has any idea about benchmarking network performance in a simple, easy and reliable way, with a short (less than 30 minutes to setup and run) test, please contact me.

3.6 LBT Report Form

Besides the tests, the benchmarking procedure would not be complete without a form describing the setup, so here it is (following the guidelines from comp.benchmarks.faq):

```
LINUX BENCHMARKING TOOLKIT REPORT FORM
```

```
CPU
==
Vendor:
Model:
Core clock:
Motherboard vendor:
Mbd. model:
Mbd. chipset:
Bus type:
Bus clock:
Cache total:
Cache type/speed:
SMP (number of processors):
```

```
RAM
====
Total:
Type:
Speed:
```

```
Disk
====
Vendor:
Model:
Size:
Interface:
Driver/Settings:
```

```
Video board
===========
Vendor:
Model:
Bus:
Video RAM type:
Video RAM total:
X server vendor:
X server version:
X server chipset choice:
Resolution/vert. refresh rate:
Color depth:
```

```
Kernel
=====
Version:
Swap size:
```

```
gcc
===
Version:
Options:
libc version:
```

```
Test notes
==========
```

```
RESULTS
========
Linux kernel 2.0.0 Compilation Time: (minutes and seconds)
Whetstones: results are in MWIPS.
Xbench: results are in xstones.
Unixbench Benchmarks 4.01 system INDEX:
BYTEmark integer INDEX:
BYTEmark memory INDEX:
```

```
Comments*
=========
* This field is included for possible interpretations of the results, and as
such, it is optional. It could be the most significant part of your report,
though, specially if you are doing comparative benchmarking.
```

3.7 Network performance tests

Testing network performance is a challenging task since it involves at least two machines, a server and a client machine, hence twice the time to setup and many more variables to control, etc. On an Ethernet network, I guess your best bet would be the ttcp package.

3.8 SMP tests

SMP tests are another challenge, and any benchmark specifically designed for SMP testing will have a hard time proving itself valid in real-life settings, since algorithms that can take advantage of SMP are hard to come by. It seems later versions of the Linux kernel (> 2.1.30 or around that) will do "fine grained" multiprocessing, but I have no more information than that for the moment.

According to David Niemi, *"... shell8* [part of the Unixbench 4.01 benchmarks]*does a good job at comparing similar hardware/OS in SMP and UP modes."*

4 Example run and results

The LBT was run on my home machine, a Pentium-class Linux box that I put together myself and that I used to write this HOWTO. Here is the LBT Report Form for this system:

```
LINUX BENCHMARKING TOOLKIT REPORT FORM

CPU

==

Vendor: Cyrix/IBM

Model: 6x86L P166+

Core clock: 133 MHz

Motherboard vendor: Elite Computer Systems (ECS)

Mbd. model: P5VX-Be

Mbd. chipset: Intel VX

Bus type: PCI

Bus clock: 33 MHz

Cache total: 256 KB

Cache type/speed: Pipeline burst 6 ns

SMP (number of processors): 1

RAM

====

Total: 32 MB

Type: EDO SIMMs

Speed: 60 ns

Disk

====

Vendor: IBM

Model: IBM-DAQA-33240

Size: 3.2 GB

Interface: EIDE

Driver/Settings: Bus Master DMA mode 2

Video board

===========
```

```
Vendor: Generic S3

Model: Trio64-V2

Bus: PCI

Video RAM type: EDO DRAM

Video RAM total: 2 MB

X server vendor: XFree86

X server version: 3.3

X server chipset choice: S3 accelerated

Resolution/vert. refresh rate: 1152x864 @ 70 Hz

Color depth: 16 bits

Kernel
=====

Version: 2.0.29

Swap size: 64 MB

gcc
===

Version: 2.7.2.1

Options: -O2

libc version: 5.4.23

Test notes
==========

Very light load. The above tests were run with some of the special
Cyrix/IBM 6x86 features enabled with the setx86 program: fast ADS,
fast IORT, Enable DTE, fast LOOP, fast Lin. VidMem.

RESULTS
========

Linux kernel 2.0.0 Compilation Time: 7m12s

Whetstones: 38.169 MWIPS.

Xbench: 97243 xStones.

BYTE Unix Benchmarks 4.01 system INDEX: 58.43

BYTEmark integer INDEX: 1.50

BYTEmark memory INDEX: 2.50

Comments
=========

This is a very stable system with homogeneous performance, ideal
for home use and/or Linux development. I will report results
with a 6x86MX processor as soon as I can get my hands on one!
```

5 Pitfalls and caveats of benchmarking

After putting together this HOWTO I began to understand why the words "pitfalls" and "caveats" are so often associated with benchmarking.

5.1 Comparing apples and oranges

Or should I say Apples and PCs? This is so obvious and such an old dispute that I won't go into any details. I doubt the time it takes to load Word on a Mac compared to an average Pentium is a real measure of anything. Likewise booting Linux and Windows NT, etc... Try as much as possible to compare identical machines with a single modification.

5.2 Incomplete information

A single example will illustrate this very common mistake. One often reads in comp.os.linux.hardware the following or similar statement: "I just plugged in processor XYZ running at nnn MHz and now compiling the linux kernel only takes i minutes" (adjust XYZ, nnn and i as required). This is irritating, because no other information is given, i.e. we don't even know the amount of RAM, size of swap, other tasks running simultaneously, kernel version, modules selected, hard disk type, GCC version, etc. I recommend you use the LBT Report Form, which at least provides a standard information framework.

5.3 Proprietary hardware/software

A well-known processor manufacturer once published results of benchmarks produced by a special, customized version of GCC. Ethical considerations apart, those results were meaningless, since 100% of the Linux community would go on using the standard version of GCC. The same goes for proprietary hardware. Benchmarking is much more useful when it deals with off-the-shelf hardware and free (in the GNU/GPL sensc) software.

5.4 Relevance

We are talking Linux, right? So we should forget about benchmarks produced on other operating systems (this is a special case of the "Comparing apples and oranges" pitfall above). Also, if one is going to benchmark Web server performance, **do not** quote FPU performance and other irrelevant information. In such cases, less is more. Also, you do **not** need to mention the age of your cat, your mood while benchmarking, etc.

6 FAQ

Q1.

Is there any single figure of merit for Linux systems?

A:

No, thankfully nobody has yet come up with a Lhinuxstone (tm) measurement. And if there was one, it would not make much sense: Linux systems are used for many different tasks, from heavily loaded Web servers to graphics workstations for individual use. No single figure of merit can describe the performance of a Linux system under such different situations.

Q2.

Then, how about a dozen figures summarizing the performance of diverse Linux systems?

A:

That would be the ideal situation. I would like to see that come true. Anybody volunteers for a **Linux Benchmarking Project**? With a Web site and an on-line, complete, well-designed reports database?

Q3.

... BogoMips ...?

A:

BogoMips has nothing to do with the performance of your system. Check the BogoMips Mini-HOWTO.

Q4.

What is the "best" benchmark for Linux?

A:

It all depends on which performance aspect of a Linux system one wants to measure. There are different benchmarks to measure the network (Ethernet sustained transfer rates), file server (NFS), disk I/O, FPU, integer, graphics, 3D, processor-memory bandwidth, CAD performance, transaction time, SQL performance, Web server performance, real-time performance, CD-ROM performance, Quake performance (!), etc. AFAIK no benchmark suite exists for Linux that supports all these tests.

Q5.

What is the fastest processor under Linux?

A:

Fastest at what task? If one is heavily number-crunching oriented, a very high clock rate Alpha (600 MHz and going) should be faster than anything else, since Alphas have been designed for that kind of performance. If, on the other hand, one wants to put together a very fast news server, it is probable that the choice of a fast hard disk subsystem and lots of RAM will result in higher performance improvements than a change of processor, for the same amount of $.

Q6.

Let me rephrase the last question, then: is there a processor that is fastest for general-purpose applications?

A:

This is a tricky question but it takes a very simple answer: **NO**. One can always design a faster system even for general-purpose applications, independent of the processor. Usually, all other things being equal, higher clock rates will result in higher performance systems (and more headaches too). Taking out an old 100 MHz Pentium from an (usually not) upgradable motherboard, and plugging in the 200 MHz version, one should feel the extra "hummph." Of course, with only 16 MBytes of RAM, the same investment would have been more wisely spent on extra SIMMs.

Q7.

So clock rates influence the performance of a system?

A:

For most tasks except for NOP empty loops (these get removed by modern optimizing compilers), an increase in clock rate will not give you a linear increase in performance. Very small, processor-intensive programs that will fit entirely in the primary cache inside the processor (the L1 cache, usually 8 or 16 K), will have a performance increase equivalent to the clock rate increase, but most "true" programs are much larger than that, have loops that do not fit in the L1 cache, share the L2 (external) cache with other processes, depend on external components and will give much smaller performance increases. This is because the L1 cache runs at the same clock rate as the processor, whereas most L2 caches and all other subsystems (DRAM, for example) will run asynchronously at lower clock rates.

Q8.

OK, then, one last question on that matter: which is the processor with the best price/performance ratio for general purpose Linux use?

A:

Defining "general purpose Linux use" in not an easy thing. For any particular application, there is always a processor with THE BEST price/performance ratio at any given time, but it changes rather frequently as manufacturers release new processors, so answering Processor XYZ running at n MHz would be a snapshot answer. However, the price of the processor is insignificant when compared to the price of the whole system one will be putting together. So, really, the question should be how can one maximize the price/performance ratio for a given system? And the answer to that question depends heavily on the minimum performance requirements and/or maximum cost established for the configuration being considered. Sometimes, off-the-shelf hardware will not meet minimum performance requirements and expensive RISC systems will be the only alternative. For home use, I recommend a balanced, homogeneous system for overall performance (now go figure what I mean by balanced and homogeneous :-); the choice of a processor is an important decision , but no more than choosing hard disk type and capacity, amount of RAM, video card, etc.

Q9.

What is a "significant" increase in performance?

A:

I would say that anything under 1% is not significant (could be described as "marginal"). We humans will hardly perceive the difference between two systems with a 5% difference in response time. Of course some hard-core benchmarkers are not humans and will tell you that, when comparing systems with 65.9 and 66.5 performance indexes, the later is "definitely faster."

Q10.

How do I obtain "significant" increases in performance at the lowest cost?

A:

Since most source code is available for Linux, careful examination and algorithmic redesign of key subroutines could yield order-of-magnitude increases in performance in some cases. If one is dealing with a commercial project and does not wish to delve deeply in C source code a **Linux consultant should be called in**. See the Consultants-HOWTO.

7 Copyright, acknowledgments and miscellaneous

7.1 How this document was produced

The first step was reading Section 4 "Writing and submitting a HOWTO" of the HOWTO Index by Greg Hankins.

I knew absolutely nothing about SGML or LaTeX, but was tempted to use an automated documentation generation package after reading the various comments about SGML-Tools. However, inserting tags manually in a document reminds me of the days I hand-assembled a 512 byte monitor program for a now defunct 8-bit microprocessor, so I got hold of the LyX sources, compiled it, and used its LinuxDoc mode. Highly recommended combination. **LyX and SGML-Tools**.

7.2 Copyright

The Linux Benchmarking HOWTO is copyright (C) 1997 by André D. Balsa. Linux HOWTO documents may be reproduced and distributed in whole or in part, in any medium physical or electronic, as long as this copyright notice is retained on all copies. Commercial redistribution is allowed and encouraged; however, the author would like to be notified of any such distributions.

All translations, derivative works, or aggregate works incorporating any Linux HOWTO documents must be covered under this copyright notice. That is, you may not produce a derivative work from a HOWTO and impose additional restrictions on its distribution. Exceptions to these rules may be granted under certain conditions; please contact the Linux HOWTO coordinator at the address given below.

In short, we wish to promote dissemination of this information through as many channels as possible. However, we do wish to retain copyright on the HOWTO documents, and would like to be notified of any plans to redistribute the HOWTOs.

If you have questions, please contact Greg Hankins, the Linux HOWTO coordinator, at gregh@sunsite.unc.edu via email, or at +1 404 853 9989.

7.3 New versions of this document

New versions of the Linux Benchmarking-HOWTO will be placed on sunsite.unc.edu and mirror sites. There are other formats, such as a Postscript and dvi version in the other-formats directory. The Linux Benchmarking-HOWTO is also available for WWW clients such as Grail, a Web browser written in Python. It will also be posted regularly to comp.os.linux.answers.

7.4 Feedback

Suggestions, corrections, additions wanted. Contributors wanted and acknowledged. Flames not wanted.

I can always be reached at andrewbalsa@usa.net.

7.5 Acknowledgments

David Niemi, the author of the Unixbench suite, has proved to be an endless source of information and (valid) criticism.

I also want to thank Greg Hankins, the Linux HOWTO coordinator and one of the main contributors to the SGML-tools package, Linus Torvalds and the entire Linux community. This HOWTO is my way of giving back.

7.6 Disclaimer

Your mileage may, and will, vary. Be aware that benchmarking is a touchy subject and a great time-and-energy consuming activity.

7.7 Trademarks

Pentium and Windows NT are trademarks of Intel and Microsoft Corporations respectively.

BYTE and BYTEmark are trademarks of McGraw-Hill, Inc.

Cyrix and 6x86 are trademarks of Cyrix Corporation.

Linux is not a trademark, hopefully never will be.

[illegible]

7 Copyright, acknowledgements and miscellaneous

7.1 How this document was produced

[illegible]

7.2 Copyright

7.3 New versions of this document

New versions of the Linux Benchmarking-HOWTO will be placed on sunsite.unc.edu and mirror sites. There are other formats, such as a Postscript and dvi version in the other-formats directory. The Linux Benchmarking-HOWTO is also available for WWW clients such as Grail, a Web browser written in Python. It will also be posted regularly to comp.os.linux.answers.

7.4 Feedback

Suggestions, corrections, additions wanted. Contributors wanted and acknowledged. Flames not wanted.

[illegible]

7.5 Acknowledgements

David Niemi, the author of the Unixbench suite, has proved to be an endless source of information and (valid) criticism.

I also want to thank Greg Hankins, the Linux HOWTO coordinator and one of the main contributors to the SGML-tools package, Linus Torvalds and the entire Linux community. This HOWTO is my way of giving back.

7.6 Disclaimer

Your mileage may, and will, vary. Be aware that benchmarking is a touchy subject and a great time-and-energy consuming activity.

7.7 Trademarks

Pentium and Windows NT are trademarks of Intel and Microsoft Corporations respectively.

BYTE and BYTEmark are trademarks of McGraw-Hill, Inc.

Cyrix and 6x86 are trademarks of Cyrix Corporation.

Linux is not a trademark, hopefully never will be.

Part IX

"The Linux Bootdisk HOWTO" by Tom Fawcett and Graham Chapman

Contents

Abstract

v2.3, 4 April 1997
This document describes how to create Linux boot, boot/root and utility maintenance disks. These disks could be used as rescue disks or to test new kernels. Note: if you haven't read the Linux FAQ and related documents such as the Linux Installation HOWTO and the Linux Install Guide, then you should not be trying to build boot diskettes.

1 Introduction

1.1 Why Build Boot Disks?

Linux boot disks are useful in a number of situations, such as:

- Testing a new kernel.
- Recovering from disk or system failure. Such a failure can be anything from a lost boot sector to a disk head crash.

There are several ways of obtaining boot disks:

- Use one from a distribution such as Slackware. This will at least allow you to boot.
- Use a rescue package to set up disks designed to be used as rescue disks.
- Learn what is required for each of the various types of disk to operate, then build your own.

I originally chose the last option - learn how it works so that you can do it yourself. That way, if something breaks, you can work out what to do to fix it. Plus you learn a lot about how Linux works along the way.

Experienced Linux users may find little of use in this document. However users new to Linux system administration who wish to protect against root disk loss and other mishaps may find it useful.

A note on versions—this document has been updated to support the following packages and versions:

- Linux 2.0.6
- LILO 0.19

1.2 Feedback and Credits

We welcome any feedback, good or bad, on the content of this document. Please let us know if you find any errors or omissions. Send comments, corrections and questions to Tom Fawcett (`fawcett@nynexst.com`) or Graham Chapman (`grahamc@zeta.org.au`).

We thank the following people for correcting errors and providing useful suggestions for improvement:

```
Randolph Bentson
Grant R. Bowman
Scott Burkett
Cameron Davidson
Bruce Elliot
Javier Ros Ganuza
HARIGUCHI Youichi
Duncan Hill
Bjxrn-Helge Mevik
Lincoln S. Peck
Dwight Spencer
Cameron Spitzer
Johannes Stille
```

2 Disks

2.1 Summary of Disk Types

I classify boot-related disks into four types. The discussion here and throughout this document uses the term "disk" to refer to diskettes unless otherwise specified. Most of the discussion could be equally well applied to hard disks.

A summary of disk types and uses is:

boot A disk containing a kernel which can be booted. The disk can contain a file system and use a boot loader to boot, or it can simply contain the kernel only at the start of the disk. The disk can be used to boot the kernel using a root file system on another disk. This could be useful if you lost your boot loader due to, for example, an incorrect installation attempt.

root A disk with a file system containing everything required to run a Linux system. It does not necessarily contain either a kernel or a boot loader.

This disk can be used to run the system independently of any other disks, once the kernel has been booted. A special kernel feature allows a separate root disk to be mounted after booting, with the root disk being automatically copied to a RAM disk.

You can use this type of disk to check another disk for corruption without mounting it, or to restore another disk after a disk failure or loss of files.

boot/root A disk which is the same as a root disk, but which contains a kernel and a boot loader. It can be used to boot from, and to run the system. The advantage of this type of disk is that it is compact—everything required is on a single disk. However the gradually increasing size of everything means that it won't necessarily always be possible to fit everything on a single diskette, even with compression.

utility A disk which contains a file system, but is not intended to be mounted as a root file system. It is an additional data disk. You use this type of disk to carry additional utilities where you have too much to fit on your root disk. The term "utility" only really applies to diskettes, where you use a utility disk to store additional recovery utility software.

The most flexible approach for rescue diskettes is probably to use separate boot and root diskettes, and one or more utility diskettes to handle the overflow.

2.2 Boot

2.2.1 Overview

All PC systems start the boot process by executing code in ROM to load the sector from sector 0, cylinder 0 of the boot drive and try and execute it. On most bootable disks, sector 0, cylinder 0 contains either:

- code from a boot loader such as LILO, which locates the kernel, loads it and executes it to start the boot proper.
- the start of an operating system kernel, such as Linux.

If a Linux kernel has been written to a diskette as a raw device, then the first sector will be the first sector of the Linux kernel itself, and this sector will continue the boot process by loading the rest of the kernel and running Linux. For a more detailed description of the boot sector contents, see the documentation in lilo-01.5 or higher.

An alternative method of storing a kernel on a boot disk is to create a file system, not as a root file system, but simply as a means of installing LILO and thus allowing boot-time command line options to be specified. For example, the same kernel could then be used to boot using a hard disk root file system, or a diskette root file system. This could be useful if you were trying to rebuild the hard disk file system, and wanted to repeatedly test results.

2.2.2 Setting Pointer to Root

The kernel must somehow obtain a pointer to the drive and partition to be mounted as the root drive. This can be provided in several ways:

- By setting `ROOT_DEV = devicename` in the Linux kernel makefile and rebuilding the kernel (for advice on how to rebuild the kernel, read the Linux FAQ and look in `/usr/src/linux`). Comments in the Linux makefile describe the valid values for `devicename`.
- By running the `rdev` utility:

  ```
  rdev filename devicename
  ```

  This sets the root device of the kernel contained in `filename` to be `devicename`. For example:

```
rdev zImage /dev/sda1
```

This sets the root device in the kernel in `zImage` to the first partition on the first SCSI drive.

There are some alternative ways of issuing the `rdev` command. Try:

```
rdev -h
```

and it will display command usage.

There is usually no need to configure the root device for boot diskette use, because the kernel currently used to boot from probably already points to the root drive device. The need can arise, however, if you obtain a kernel from another machine, for example, from a distribution, or if you want to use the kernel to boot a root diskette. It is probably a good idea to check the current root drive setting, just in case it is wrong. To get rdev to check the current root device in a kernel file, enter the command:

```
rdev <filename>
```

It is possible to change the root device set in a kernel by means other than using rdev. For details, see the FAQ at the end of this document.

2.2.3 Copying Kernel to Boot Diskette

Once the kernel has been configured, it must be copied to the boot diskette.

The commands described below (and throughout the HOWTO) assume that the diskettes have been formatted. If not, then use `fdformat` to format the diskettes before continuing.

If the disk is not intended to contain a file system, then the kernel can be copied using the dd command, as follows:

```
dd if=infilename of=devicename

where   infilename is the name of the kernel
and     devicename is the diskette raw device,
        usually /dev/fd0
```

The `cp` command can also be used:

```
cp filename devicename
```

For example:

```
dd if=zImage of=/dev/fd0
```

or

```
cp zImage /dev/fd0
```

The seek parameter to the `dd` command should not be used. The file must be copied to start at the boot sector (sector 0, cylinder 0), and omitting the seek parameter will do this.

The output device name to be used is usually `/dev/fd0` for the primary diskette drive (i.e. drive "A:" in DOS), and `/dev/fd1` for the secondary. These device names will cause the kernel to auto-detect the attributes of the drives. Drive attributes can be specified to the kernel by using other device names: for example `/dev/fd0H1440` specifies a high density 1.44 Mb drive. It is rare to need to use these specific device names.

Where the kernel is to be copied to a boot disk containing a file system, then the disk is mounted at a suitable point in a currently-mounted file system, then the `cp` command is used. For example:

```
mount -t ext2 /dev/fd0 /mnt
cp zImage /mnt
umount /mnt
```

Note that for almost all operations in this HOWTO, the user should be operating as the superuser.

2.3 Root

2.3.1 Overview

A root disk contains a complete working Linux system, but without necessarily including a kernel. In other words, the disk may not be bootable, but once the kernel is running, the root disk contains everything needed to support a full Linux system. To be able to do this, the disk must include the minimum requirements for a Linux system:

- File system.

- Minimum set of directories—dev, proc, bin, etc, lib, usr, tmp.
- Basic set of utilities—bash (to run a shell), ls, cp, etc.
- Minimum set of configuration files—rc, inittab, fstab, etc.
- Runtime library to provide basic functions used by utilities.

Of course, any system only becomes useful when you can run something on it, and a root diskette usually only becomes useful when you can do something like:

- Check a file system on another drive, for example to check your root file system on your hard drive, you need to be able to boot Linux from another drive, as you can with a root diskette system. Then you can run fsck on your original root drive while it is not mounted.
- Restore all or part of your original root drive from backup using archive and compression utilities including cpio, tar, gzip, and ftape.

2.4 Boot/Root

This is essentially the same as the root disk, with the addition of a kernel and a boot loader such as LILO.

With this configuration, a kernel file is copied to the root file system, and LILO is then run to install a configuration which points to the kernel file on the target disk. At boot time, LILO will boot the kernel from the target disk.

Several files must be copied to the diskette for this method to work. Details of these files and the required LILO configuration, including a working sample, are given below in the section titled "LILO."

2.4.1 RAM Disks and Root File systems on Diskette

For a diskette root file system to be efficient, you need to be able to run it from a RAM disk; i.e. an emulated disk drive in main memory. This avoids having the system run at a snail's pace, which a diskette would impose. The Ftape HOWTO states that a RAM disk will be required when using Ftape because Ftape requires exclusive use of the diskette controller.

There is an added benefit from using a RAM disk—the Linux kernel includes an automatic RAM disk root feature, whereby it will, under certain circumstances, automatically copy the contents of a root diskette to a RAM disk, and then switch the root drive to be the RAM disk instead of the diskette. This has three major benefits:

- The system runs a lot faster.
- The diskette drive is freed up to allow other diskettes to be used on a single-diskette drive system.
- With compression, the RAM disk image on a disk can be substantially smaller than (eg, 40% the size of) the corresponding disk image. This means that a 1.44 Meg floppy disk may hold a root containing roughly 3.6 Meg.

For kernels 1.3.48+, the RAM disk code was substantially rewritten. You have some more options and the commands for using the RAM disk are somewhat different. Section 4, below, discusses how to take advantage of these.

You must configure your kernel to have RAM disk support, but the RAM disk is dynamically expandable so you need not specify the size. rdev -r is no longer used to specify the RAM disk size, but instead sets a RAM disk word in the kernel image. Section 4 discusses this in more detail.

If you have a kernel *before* 1.3.48, the following requirements apply. Note that this applies only to kernels prior to 1.3.48.

- The file system on the diskette drive must be either a minix or an ext2 file system. The ext2 file system is generally the preferred file system to use. Note that if you have a Linux kernel earlier than 1.1.73, then you should see the comments in the section titled "File Systems" to see whether your kernel will support ext2. If your kernel is old then you may have to use minix. This will not cause any significant problems.
- A RAM disk must be configured into the kernel, and it must be at least as big as the diskette drive.

A RAM disk can be configured into the kernel in several ways:

- By uncommenting the RAMDISK macro in the Linux kernel makefile, so that it reads:

  ```
  RAMDISK = -DRAMDISK=1440
  ```

  to define a RAM disk of 1440 1K blocks, the size of a high-density diskette.
- By running the rdev utility, available on most Linux systems. This utility displays or sets values for several things in the kernel, including the desired size for a RAM disk. To configure a RAM disk of 1440 blocks into a kernel in a file named zImage, enter:

```
rdev -r zImage 1440
```

this might change in the future, of course. To see what your version of `rdev` does, enter the command:

```
rdev -h
```

and it should display its options.

- By using the boot loader package LILO to configure it into your kernel at boot time. This can be done using the LILO configuration parameter:

  ```
  ramdisk = 1440
  ```

  to request a RAM disk of 1440 1K blocks at boot time.
- By interrupting a LILO automatic boot and adding `ramdisk=1440` to the command line. For example, such a command line might be:

  ```
  zImage ramdisk=1440
  ```

  See the section on LILO for more details.
- By editing the kernel file and altering the values near the start of the file which record the RAM disk size. This is definitely a last resort, but can be done. See the FAQ near the end of this document for more details.

The easiest of these methods is LILO configuration, because you need to set up a LILO configuration file anyway, so why not add the RAM disk size here?

LILO configuration is briefly described in a section titled "LILO" below, but it is advisable to obtain the latest stable version of LILO from your nearest Linux mirror site, and read the documentation that comes with it.

RAM disks can be made larger than the size of a diskette, and made to contain a file system as large as the RAM disk. This can be useful to load all the software required for rescue work onto a single high-performance RAM disk. The method of doing this is described in the FAQ section under the question "How can I create an oversize RAM disk file system?"

2.5 Utility

Often one disk is not sufficient to hold all the software you need to be able to perform rescue functions of analyzing, repairing and restoring corrupted disk drives. By the time you include `tar`, `gzip`, `e2fsck`, `fdisk`, Ftape and so on, there is enough for a whole new diskette, maybe even more if you want lots of tools.

This means that a rescue set often requires a utility diskette, with a file system containing any extra files required. This file system can then be mounted at a convenient point, such as /usr, on the boot/root system.

Creating a file system is fairly easy, and is described above in the section titled "File Systems" below.

3 Components

3.1 File Systems

The Linux kernel now supports two file system types for root disks to be automatically copied to RAM disk. These are minix and ext2, of which ext2 is the preferred file system. The ext2 support was added sometime between 1.1.17 and 1.1.57, I'm not sure exactly which. If you have a kernel within this range then edit `/usr/src/linux/drivers/block/ramdisk.c` and look for the word "ext2." If it is not found, then you will have to use a Minix file system, and therefore the `mkfs` command to create it. If using ext2, then you may find it useful to use the `-i` option to specify more inodes than the default; `-i 2000` is suggested so that you don't run out of inodes. Alternatively, you can save on inodes by removing lots of unnecessary `/dev` files. `mke2fs` will by default create 360 inodes on a 1.44Mb diskette. I find that 120 inodes is ample on my current rescue root diskette, but if you include all the devices in the `/dev` directory then you will easily exceed 360. Using a compressed root file system allows a larger file system, and hence more inodes by default, but you may still need to either reduce the number of files or increase the number of inodes.

To create an ext2 file system on a diskette on my system, I issue the following command:

```
mke2fs -m 0 /dev/fd0
```

The `mke2fs` command will automatically detect the space available and configure itself accordingly. If desired, the diskette size in 1Kb blocks can be specified to speed up mke2fs operation. The `-m 0` parameter prevents it from reserving space for root, and hence provides more usable space on the disk.

An easy way to test the result is to create a system using the above command or similar, and then attempt to mount the diskette. If it is an ext2 system, then the command:

```
mount -t ext2 /dev/fd0 /<mount point>
```

should work.

3.2 Kernel

3.2.1 Building a Custom Kernel

In most cases it would be possible to copy your current kernel and boot the diskette from that. However there may be cases where you wish to build a separate one.

One reason is size. The kernel is one of the largest files in a minimum system, so if you want to build a boot/root diskette, then you will have to reduce the size of the kernel as much as possible. The kernel now supports changing the diskette after booting and before mounting root, so it is not necessary any more to squeeze the kernel into the same disk as everything else, therefore these comments apply only if you choose to build a boot/root diskette.

There are two ways of reducing kernel size:

- Building it with the minimum set of facilities necessary to support the desired system. This means leaving out everything you don't need. Networking is a good thing to leave out, as well as support for any disk drives and other devices which you don't need when running your boot/root system.
- Compressing it, using the standard compressed-kernel option included in the `makefile`:

  ```
  make zImage
  ```

  Refer to the documentation included with the kernel source for up-to-date information on building compressed kernels. Note that the kernel source is usually in `/usr/src/linux`.

Having worked out a minimum set of facilities to include in a kernel, you then need to work out what to add back in. Probably the most common uses for a boot/root diskette system would be to examine and restore a corrupted root file system, and to do this you may need kernel support.

For example, if your backups are all held on tape using Ftape to access your tape drive, then, if you lose your current root drive and drives containing Ftape, then you will not be able to restore from your backup tapes. You will have to reinstall Linux, download and reinstall Ftape, and then try and read your backups.

It is probably desirable to maintain a copy of the same version of backup utilities used to write the backups, so that you don't waste time trying to install versions that cannot read your backup tapes.

The point here is that, whatever I/O support you have added to your kernel to support backups should also be added into your boot/root kernel.

The procedure for actually building the kernel is described in the documentation that comes with the kernel. It is quite easy to follow, so start by looking in `/usr/src/linux`. Note that if you have trouble building a kernel, then you should probably not attempt to build boot/root systems anyway.

3.3 Devices

A `/dev` directory containing a special file for all devices to be used by the system is mandatory for any Linux system. The directory itself is a normal directory, and can be created with the mkdir command in the normal way. The device special files, however, must be created in a special way, using the mknod command.

There is a shortcut, though—copy your existing `/dev` directory contents, and delete the ones you don't want. The only requirement is that you copy the device special files using the `-R` option. [5] This will copy the directory without attempting to copy the contents of the files. Note that if you use lower case, as in "`-r`," there will be a vast difference, because you will probably end up copying the entire contents of all of your hard disks—or at least as much of them as will fit on a diskette! Therefore, take care, and use the command:

```
cp -dpR /dev /mnt
```

assuming that the diskette is mounted at `/mnt`. The `dp` switches ensure that symbolic links are copied as links (rather than the target file being copied) and that the original file attributes are preserved, thus preserving ownership information.

You can also use the `-p` option of `cpio`, because `cpio` will handle device special files correctly, and not try and copy the contents. For example:

```
cd /dev
find . -print | cpio -pmd /mnt/dev
```

[5] Warning: The `cp` command supplied with the most recent version of fileutils (3.13) is reported not to respect the `-R` flag.

will copy all device special files from `/dev` to `/mnt/dev`. In fact it will copy all files in the directory tree starting at `/dev`, and will create any required subdirectories in the target directory tree.

If you want to do it the hard way, use `ls -l` to display the major and minor device numbers for the devices you want, and create them on the diskette using `mknod`.

Many distributions include a shell script called `MAKEDEV` in the `/dev` directory. This shell script could be used to create the devices, but it is probably easier to just copy your existing ones, especially for rescue disk purposes.

Whichever way the device directory is copied, it is worth checking that any special devices you need have been placed on the rescue diskette. For example, Ftape uses tape devices, so you will need to copy all of these.

Note that an inode is required for each device special file, and inodes can at times be a scarce resource, especially on diskette file systems. It therefore makes sense to remove any device special files that you don't need from the diskette /dev directory. Many devices are obviously unnecessary on specific systems. For example, if you do not have SCSI disks, then you can safely remove all the device files starting with "sd." Similarly, if you don't intend to use your serial port then all the device files starting with "cua" can go.

3.4 Directories

It might be possible to get away with just `/dev`, `/proc`, and `/etc` to run a Linux system. I don't know—I've never tested it. However it will certainly be difficult, because without shared libraries all your executables would have to be statically linked. A reasonable minimum set of directories consists of the following:

/dev

Required to perform I/O with devices.

/proc

Required by the ps command.

/etc

System configuration files.

/bin

Utility executables considered part of the system.

/lib

Shared libraries to provide run-time support.

/mnt

A mount point for maintenance on other disks.

/usr

Additional utilities and applications.

Note that the directory tree presented here is for root diskette use only. Refer to the Linux File System Standard for much better information on how file systems should be structured in "standard" Linux systems.

Four of these directories can be created very easily:

- `/dev` is described above in the section titled DEVICES.
- `/proc` only needs to exist. Once the directory is created using `mkdir`, nothing more is required.
- Of the others, /mnt and /usr are included in this list only as mount points for use after the boot/root system is running. Hence again, these directories only need to be created.

The remaining three directories are described in the following sections.

3.4.1 /etc

This directory must contain a number of configuration files. On most systems, these can be divided into 3 groups:

- Required at all times, e.g. rc, fstab, passwd.
- May be required, but no-one is too sure.
- Junk that crept in.

Files which are not essential can be identified with the command:

```
ls -ltru
```

This lists files in reverse order of date last accessed, so if any files are not being accessed, then they can be omitted from a root diskette.

On my root diskettes, I have the number of config files down to 15. This reduces my work to dealing with three sets of files:

- The ones I must configure for a boot/root system:

```
rc.d/*   system startup and run level change scripts
fstab    list of file systems to be mounted
inittab  parameters for the init process - the
         first process started at boot time.
```

- the ones I should tidy up for a boot/root system:

```
passwd   list of logins
shadow   contains passwords
```

  These should be pruned on secure systems to avoid copying user's passwords off the system, and so that when you boot from diskette, unwanted logins are rejected. [6]

- The rest. They work at the moment, so I leave them alone.

Out of this, I only really have to configure two files, and what they should contain is surprisingly small.

- `/etc/rc` should contain:

```
#!/bin/sh
/etc/mount -av
/bin/hostname boot_root
```

  and I don't really need to run `hostname`— it just looks nicer if I do. Even mount is actually only needed to mount `/proc` to support the `ps` command—Linux will run without it, although rescue operations are rather limited without mount.

- fstab should contain:

```
/dev/ram      /        ext2   defaults
/dev/fd0      /        ext2   defaults
/proc         /proc    proc   defaults
```

  I don't think that the first entry is really needed, but I find that if I leave it out, mount won't mount `/proc`.

`/etc/inittab` should be okay as is, unless you want to ensure that users on serial ports cannot login. To prevent this, comment out all the entries for `/etc/getty` which include a ttys or ttyS device at the end of the line. Leave in the tty ports so that you can login at the console.

`/etc/inittab` defines what the system will run or rerun in various states including startup, move to multi-user mode, power failure, and others. A point to be careful of here is to carefully check that the commands entered in `/etc/inittab` refer to programs which are present and to the correct directory. If you place your command files on your rescue disk using the sample directory listing in this HOWTO as a guide, and then copy your `/etc/inittab` to your rescue disk without checking it, then the probability of failure will be quite high, because half of the `/etc/inittab` entries will refer to missing programs or to the wrong directory.

It is worth noting here as well that some programs cannot be moved from one directory to another or they will fail at runtime because they have hard coded the name of another program which they attempt to run. For example on my system, `/etc/shutdown` has hard coded in it `/etc/reboot`. If I move reboot to /bin/reboot, and then issue a `shutdown` command, it will fail because it can't find the `/etc/reboot` file.

For the rest, just copy all the text files in your /etc directory, plus all the executables in your /etc directory that you cannot be sure you do not need. As a guide, consult the sample ls listing in "Sample Boot/Root ls-lR Directory Listing"—this is what I have, so probably it will be sufficient for you if you copy only those files—but note that systems differ a great deal, so you cannot be sure that the same set of files on your system is equivalent to the files on mine. The only sure method is to start with `inittab` and work out what is required.

Most systems now use an `/etc/rc.d` directory containing shell scripts for different run levels. The absolute minimum is a single rc script, but it will probably be a lot simpler in practice to copy the `/etc/inittab` and `/etc/rc.d` directory from your existing system, and prune the shell scripts in the rc.d directory to remove processing not relevant to a diskette system environment.

[6] Note that there is a reason *not* to prune passwd and shadow. `tar` (and probably other archivers) stores user and group names with files. If you restore files to your hard disk from tape, the files will be restored with their original names. If these names do not exist in passwd/group when they are restored, the UID/GID will not be correct.

3.4.2 /bin

Here is a convenient point to place the extra utilities you need to perform basic operations, utilities like `ls`, `mv`, `cat`, `dd`, etc.

See the section titled "Sample Boot/Root ls-lR Directory Listing" for the list of files that I place in my boot/root /bin directory. You may notice that it does not include any of the utilities required to restore from backup, such as `cpio`, `tar`, `gzip`, etc. That is because I place these on a separate utility diskette, to save space on the boot/root diskette. Once I have booted my boot/root diskette, it then copies itself to the RAM disk leaving the diskette drive free to mount another diskette, the utility diskette. I usually mount this as /usr.

Creation of a utility diskette is described below in the section titled "Adding Utility Diskettes."

3.4.3 /lib

In `/lib` you place necessary shared libraries and loaders. If the necessary libraries are not found in your `/lib` directory then the system will be unable to boot. If you're lucky you may see an error message telling you why.

Nearly every program requires at least the libc library:

```
libc.so.X
```

where X is the current version number. Check your `/lib` directory. Note that `libc.so.4` may be a symlink to a libc library with version number in the filename. If you issue the command:

```
ls -l /lib
```

you will see something like:

```
libc.so.4 -> libc.so.4.5.21
```

In this case, the libc library you want is libc.so.4.5.21. This is an example only—the ELF libc library is currently `libc.so.5.`*xxxx*.

To find other libraries you should go through all the binaries you plan to include and check their dependencies. You can do this with `ldd` command. For example, on my system the command:

```
ldd /bin/mount
```

produces the output:

```
/bin/mount:
        libc.so.5 => /lib/libc.so.5.2.18
```

indicating that `/bin/mount` needs the library `libc.so.5`, which is a symbolic link to `libc.so.5.2.18`.

In `/lib` you must also include one or more loaders to load the libraries. The loader file is either `ld.so` (for a.out libraries) or `ld-linux.so` (for ELF libraries). If you're not sure which you need, run the `file` command on the library. For example, on my system:

```
file /lib/libc.so.5.2.18
```

tells me:

```
/lib/libc.so.5.2.18: ELF 32-bit LSB shared object ...
```

so it needs an ELF loader. If you have an a.out library you'll instead see something like:

```
/lib/libc.so.4.7.2: Linux/i386 demand-paged executable (QMAGIC) ...
```

Copy the specific loader(s) you need.

Libraries and loaders should be checked carefully against the included binaries. If the kernel cannot load a necessary library, the kernel will usually hang with no error message.

3.5 LILO

3.5.1 Overview

For the boot/root to be any use, it must be bootable. To achieve this, the easiest way is to install a boot loader, which is a piece of executable code stored at sector 0, cylinder 0 of the diskette. See the section above titled "Boot Diskette" for an overview of the boot process.

LILO is a tried and trusted boot loader available from any Linux mirror site. It allows you to configure the boot loader, including:

- Which device is to be mounted as the root drive.
- Whether to use a RAM disk.

3.5.2 Sample LILO Configuration

This provides a very convenient place to specify to the kernel how it should boot. My root/boot LILO configuration file, used with LILO 0.15, is:

```
boot = /dev/fd0
install = ./mnt/boot.b
map = ./mnt/lilo.map
delay = 50
message = ./mnt/lilo.msg
timeout = 150
compact
image = ./mnt/zImage
        ramdisk = 1440
        root = /dev/fd0
```

Note that I have not tested this recently, because I no longer use LILO-based boot/root diskettes. There is no reason to suppose that it does not still work, but if you try it and it fails, you must read the LILO documentation to find out why.

Note also that boot/root systems no longer rely on LILO, because since 1.3.48, the kernel supports loading a compressed root file system from the same diskette as the kernel. See section 4 for details.

If you have a kernel later than 1.3.48, the "`ramdisk = 1440`" line is unnecessary and should be removed.

Note that `boot.b`, `lilo.msg` and the kernel must first have been copied to the diskette using a command similar to:

```
cp /boot/boot.b ./mnt
```

If this is not done, then LILO will not run correctly at boot time if the hard disk is not available, and there is little point setting up a rescue disk which requires a hard disk in order to boot.

I run LILO using the command:

```
/sbin/lilo -C <configfile>
```

I run it from the directory containing the `/mnt` directory where I have mounted the diskette. This means that I am telling LILO to install a boot loader on the boot device (`/dev/fd0` in this case), to boot a kernel in the root directory of the diskette.

I have also specified that I want the root device to be the diskette, and I want a RAM disk created of 1440 1K blocks, the same size as the diskette. Since I have created an ext2 file system on the diskette, this completes all the conditions required for Linux to automatically switch the root device to the RAM disk, and copy the diskette contents there as well.

The RAM disk features of Linux are described further in the section above titled "RAM Disks and Boot/Root Systems."

It is also worth considering using the `single` parameter to cause Linux to boot in single-user mode. This could be useful to prevent users logging in on serial ports.

I also use the "`DELAY`," "`MESSAGE`" and "`TIMEOUT`" statements so that when I boot the disk, LILO will give me the opportunity to enter command line options if I wish. I don't need them at present, but I never know when I might want to set a different root device or mount a file system read-only.

The message file I use contains the message:

```
Linux Boot/Root Diskette
========================


Enter a command line of the form:

      zImage [ command-line options]

If nothing is entered, linux will be loaded with
defaults after 15 seconds.
```

This is simply a reminder to myself what my choices are.

Readers are urged to read the LILO documentation carefully before attempting to install anything. It is relatively easy to destroy partitions if you use the wrong "`boot=`" parameter. If you are inexperienced, do not run LILO until you are sure you understand it and you have triple-checked your parameters.

Note that you must re-run LILO every time you change the kernel, so that LILO can set up its map file to correctly describe the new kernel file. It is in fact possible to replace the kernel file with one which is almost identical without rerunning LILO, but it is far better not to gamble—if you change the kernel, re-run LILO.

3.5.3 Removing LILO

One other thing I might as well add here while I'm on the LILO topic: if you mess up LILO on a drive containing DOS, you can always replace the boot sector with the DOS boot loader by issuing the DOS command:

```
FDISK /MBR
```

where MBR stands for "Master Boot Record." Note that some purists disagree with this, and they may have grounds, but it works.

3.5.4 Useful LILO Options

LILO has several useful options which are worth keeping in mind when building boot disks:

- Command line options—you can enter command line options to set the root device, ramdisk size (for kernels less than 1.3.48), special device parameters, or other things. If you include the `DELAY` = *nn* statement in your LILO configuration file, then LILO will pause to allow you to select a kernel image to boot, and to enter, on the same line, any options. For example:

  ```
  zImage aha152x=0x340,11,3,1 ro
  ```

  will pass the aha152x parameters through to the aha152x SCSI disk driver (provided that driver has been included when the kernel was built) and will ask for the root file system to be mounted read-only.
- Command line "`lock`" option—this option asks LILO to store the command line entered as the default command line to be used for all future boots. This is particularly useful where you have a device which cannot be auto-selected. By using "`lock`" you can avoid having to type in the device parameter string every time you boot. For example:

  ```
  zImage aha152x=0x340,11,3,1 root=/dev/sda8 ro lock
  ```

- `APPEND` configuration statement—this allows device parameter strings to be stored in the configuration, as an alternative to using the "`lock`" command line option. Note that any keywords of the form word=value MUST be enclosed in quotes. For example:

  ```
  APPEND = "aha152x=0x340,11,3,1"
  ```

- `DELAY` configuration statement—this pauses for `DELAY` tenths of seconds and allows the user to interrupt the automatic boot of the default command line, so that the user can enter an alternate command line.

4 Advanced Bootdisk Creation

4.1 Overview

Previous sections of this document covered the basics of creating boot/root disks, and are applicable to nearly all kernels up to the present (2.0, the latest stable kernel).

Kernels 1.3.48 and later involved a substantial rewrite of the RAM disk code, adding significant new capabilities. These kernels could automatically detect compressed file systems, uncompress them and load them into the ramdisk on boot-up. Root file systems could be placed on a second disk, and as of kernel 1.3.98 or so, ram disks are dynamically expandable.

Altogether, these new capabilities mean that boot disks can contain substantially more than they used to. With compression, a 1722K disk may now hold up to about 3.5 MB of files. As anyone who has created boot disks knows, much time is spent pruning down the file set and finding trimmed-down versions of files that will all fit in a small file system. With the new capabilities this is no longer such a concern.

Unfortunately, creating boot disks to exploit these new features is slightly more difficult now. To build a compressed file system on a floppy, the file system has to be built on another device and then compressed and transferred to the floppy. This means a few more steps.

The basic strategy is to create a compressed root file system, copy the kernel to the floppy disk, tell the kernel where to find the root file system, then copy the compressed root file system to the floppy.

Here's a simple ASCII drawing of what the disk will look like:

```
|<--- zImage --->|<------ Compressed root filesystem -------->|
|________________|____________________________________________|
                 Floppy disk space
```

Here are the steps to create the boot floppy:

4.2 Creating a root file system

The root file system is created pretty much the same way as outlined in Section 2.3 of this document. The primary difference is that you can no longer create a root file system directly on a floppy—you must create it on a separate device larger than the floppy area it will occupy.

4.2.1 Choosing a device

In order to build such a root file system, you need a spare device that is large enough. There are several choices:

- If you have an unused hard disk partition that is large enough (several megabytes), this is the easiest solution. Alternatively, if you have enough physical RAM you can simply turn off swapping and build the file system in your swap partition.
  However, most people don't have a spare partition and can't afford to turn swapping off, so...
- Use a loopback device. A loopback device allows a disk file on an existing file system to be treated as a device. In order to use loopback devices you need specially modified mount and unmount programs. You can find these at:

  ```
  ftp://ftp.win.tue.nl:/pub/linux/util/mount-2.5X.tar.gz
  ```

  where X is the latest modification letter.
  If you do not have loop devices (`/dev/loop0` and `/dev/loop1`) on your system, you'll have to create them first. The commands:

  ```
  mknod /dev/loop0 b 7 0
  mknod /dev/loop1 b 7 1
  mknod /dev/loop2 b 7 2
  ...
  ```

  will do this. You probably only need `/dev/loop0`. One you've installed these special mount/umount binaries, create a temporary file on a hard disk with enough capacity (e.g., `/tmp/fsfile`). You can use a command like

  ```
  dd if=/dev/zero of=/tmp/fsfile bs=1k count=nnn
  ```

  to create an *nnn*-block file.
  Use the file name in place of *DEVICE* below. When you issue a mount command you must include the option "`-o loop`" to tell `mount` to use a loopback device. For example:

  ```
  mount -o loop -t ext2 /tmp/fsfile /mnt
  ```

  will mount `/tmp/fsfile` (via a loopback device) at the mount point `/mnt`. A `df` will confirm this.
- A final option is to use the RAM disk (`DEVICE = /dev/ram` or `/dev/ramdisk`). In this case, RAM is used to simulate a disk drive. The RAM disk must be large enough to hold a file system of the appropriate size. Check your Lilo configuration file (/etc/lilo.conf) for a line like:

  ```
  RAMDISK_SIZE = nnn
  ```

  which determines how much RAM will be allocated. The default is 4096K.

After you've chosen one of these options, prepare the device with:

```
dd if=/dev/zero of=\cparam{DEVICE} bs=1k count=3000
```

This command zeroes out the device. This step is important because the file system on the device will be compressed later, so all unused portions should be filled with zeroes to achieve maximum compression.

Next, create the file system with:

```
mke2fs -m 0 \cparam{DEVICE}
```

(If you're using a loopback device, the disk file you're using should be supplied in place of this DEVICE. In this case, `mke2fs` will ask if you really want to do this; say yes.)

Then mount the device:

```
mount -t ext2 \cparam{DEVICE} /mnt
```

Proceed as before, copying files into `/mnt`, as specified in Section 2.3.

4.2.2 Compressing the file system

After you're done copying files into the root file system, you need to copy it back out and compress it. First, umount it:

```
umount /mnt
```

(Technically you can copy the file system without unmounting it first, but that's somewhat dangerous, and bad practice.)

Next, copy data off the device to a disk file. Call the disk file `rootfs`:

```
dd if=DEVICE of=rootfs bs=1k
```

Then compress it. Use the '`-9`' option of `gzip` for maximal compression:

```
gzip -9 rootfs
```

This may take several minutes. When it finishes, you'll have a file `rootfs.gz` that is your compressed root file system.

If you're tight on disk space, you can combine `dd` and `gzip`:

```
dd if=DEVICE bs=1k | gzip -9 > rootfs.gz
```

4.3 Calculating the space

At this point, check the space to make sure both the kernel and the root file system will fit on the floppy. An "`ls -l`" will show how many bytes each occupies; divide by 1024 to determine how many blocks each will need. For partial blocks, be sure to round up to the next block.

For example, if the kernel size is 453281 bytes, it will need

```
ceil(453281 / 1024) = 443
```

blocks, so it will occupy blocks 0-442 on the floppy disk. The compressed root file system will begin at block 443. Remember this block number for the commands to follow; call it ROOTBEGIN.

You must tell the kernel where on the floppy to find the root file system. Inside the kernel image is a ramdisk word that specifies where the root file system is to be found, along with other options. The word is defined in `/usr/src/linux/arch/i386/kernel/setup.c` and is interpreted as follows:

```
bits  0-10:  Offset to start of ramdisk, in 1024 byte blocks
             (This is ROOTBEGIN, calculated above)
bits 11-13:  unused
bit     14:  Flag indicating that ramdisk is to be loaded
bit     15:  Flag indicating to prompt for floppy
```

(If bit 15 is set, on boot-up you will be prompted to place a new floppy disk in the drive. This is necessary for a two-disk boot set, discussed below in the section "Making a two-disk set." For now, this will be zero.)

If the root file system is to begin at block 443, the ramdisk word is

```
   1BB (hex)        443 (decimal)      (bits 0-10)
 + 4000 (hex)       Ramdisk load flag  (bit 14)
   ----------
 = 41BB (hex)
 =16827 (decimal)
```

This ramdisk word will be set in the kernel image using the "`rdev -r`" command in the next section.

4.4 Copying files to the floppy

At this point you're ready to create the boot floppy. First copy the kernel:

```
dd if=zImage of=/dev/fd0
```

Next, tell the kernel to find its root file system on the floppy:

```
rdev /dev/fd0 /dev/fd0
```

Next, you have to set the RAM disk word in the kernel image now residing on the floppy. The ramdisk word is set using the "`rdev -r`" command. Using the figure calculated above in the section titled "Calculating the space":

```
rdev -r /dev/fd0 16827
```

Finally, place the root file system on the floppy after the kernel. The `dd` command has a `seek` option that allows you to specify how many blocks to skip:

```
dd if=rootfs.gz of=/dev/fd0 bs=1k seek=443
```

(The value 443 is ROOTBEGIN from the section "Calculating the space" above.)

Wait for the floppy drive to finish writing, and you're done.

4.5 Making a two-disk set

If you want more space, you can make a two-disk boot set. In this case, the first floppy disk will contain the kernel alone, and the second will contain the compressed root file system. With this configuration you can use a compressed file system of up to 1440K.

A two-disk set is created using a simple variation of the instructions above. First, you must set the ramdisk PROMPT flag to 1 to instruct the kernel to prompt and wait for the second floppy. The root file system will begin at byte 0 of the second floppy.

From the section "Calculating the space" above, the ramdisk PROMPT flag (bit 15) will be set to 1, and the ramdisk offset will be zero. In our example the new calculation would be:

```
  4000 (hex)      Ramdisk load flag (bit 14)
+ 8000 (hex)      Ramdisk prompt flag (bit 15)
------------
= C000 (hex)
=49152 (decimal)
```

which would be used in the "`rdev -r`" calculation as before.

Follow the instructions of "Copying files to the floppy" above, but after issuing the "`rdev -r`" command, put a new floppy in the drive and issue the command:

```
dd if=rootfs.gz of=/dev/fd0
```

The `seek` option is not needed since the root file system starts at block zero.

5 Troubleshooting

When building rescue disks, it is not uncommon that the first few tries will not boot. The general approach to building a root disk is to assemble components from your existing system, and try and get the diskette-based system to the point where it displays messages on the console. Once it starts talking to you, the battle is half over, because you can see what it is complaining about, and you can fix individual problems until the system works smoothly. If the system just hangs with no explanation, finding the cause can be difficult. To get a system to boot to the stage where it will talk to you requires several components to be present and correctly configured. The recommended procedure for investigating the problem where the system will not talk to you is as follows:

- Check that the root disk actually contains the directories you think it does. It is easy to copy at the wrong level so that you end up with something like `/root_disk/bin` instead of `/bin` on your root diskette.
- Check that there is a `/lib/libc.so` and `/lib/libtermcap.so`, with the same links as appear in your lib directory on your hard disk.
- check that any symbolic links in your `/dev` directory in your existing system also exist on your root diskette file system, where those links are to devices which you have included in your root diskette. In particular, `/dev/console` links are essential in many cases.
- Check that you have included `/dev/tty1` on your root disk.
- Check that you have included `/dev/null`, `/dev/zero`, `/dev/mem`, `/dev/ram`, and tt /dev/kmem devices.
- Check your kernel configuration—support for all resources required up to login point must be built in, not modules. Also, *RAM disk support must be included.*
- Check that your kernel root device and RAM disk settings are correct. Refer to Section 4 for details.

Once these general aspects have been covered, here are some more specific files to check:

1. Make sure `init` is included as `/sbin/init` or `/bin/init`. Make sure it's executable.
2. Run `ldd init` to check init's libraries. Usually this is just `libc.so`, but check anyway. Make sure you included the libraries.
3. Run `file` on the library(ies) reported by `ldd` to see what type they are. Make sure you have the right loader file on the root disk. The loader file is either `ld.so` (for a.out libraries) or `ld-linux.so` (for ELF libraries).
4. Check the `/etc/inittab` on your bootdisk file system for the calls to `getty` Double-check these against your hard disk inittab. Check the man pages of the program you use to make sure these make sense. Inittab is possibly the trickiest part because its syntax and content depend on the init program used and the nature of the system. The only way to tackle it is to read the man pages for init and inittab and work out exactly what your existing system

is doing when it boots. Check to make sure `/etc/inittab` has a system initialization entry. This should contain a command of the form `/etc/rc.x`, to execute one of the `/etc/rc` scripts. The specific script in the inittab must exist.

5. As with `init`, run `ldd` on `getty` (or `agetty`) to see what it needs, and make sure the necessary library files and loaders were included in your root file system.
6. If you have a `/etc/ld.so.cache` file on your rescue disk, remake it.

If init starts, but you get a message like:

```
Id xxx respawning too fast: disabled for n minutes
```

it's coming from init, usually indicating that your `getty` or `login` is dying as soon as it starts up. Check the `getty` and `login` executables, and the libraries they depend upon. Make sure the invocations in `/etc/inittab` are correct. If you get strange messages from `getty`, it may mean the calling form in `/etc/inittab` is wrong. The options of the `getty` programs are variable; even different versions of `agetty` are reported to have different incompatible calling forms. If you're using a different call or program from what you use in your hard disk `/etc/inittab`, double check it.

If you try to run some executable, such as `df`, which is on your rescue disk but you yields a message like: `df: not found`, check two things:

1. Make sure the directory containing the binary is in your `PATH`.
2. Make sure you have libraries (and loaders) the program needs. Type `ldd file` to see what libraries are needed, and make sure those libraries exist. See the section above on `/lib`

6 Frequently Asked Question (FAQ) List

6.1 Q. I boot from my boot/root disks and nothing happens. What do I do?

This answer has been moved to Section 5, above.

6.2 Q. How can I make a boot disk with a XXX driver?

The easiest way is to obtain a Slackware kernel from your nearest Slackware mirror site. Slackware kernels are generic kernels which attempt to include drivers for as many devices as possible, so if you have a SCSI or IDE controller, chances are that a driver for it is included in the Slackware kernel.

Go to the a1 directory and select either IDE or SCSI kernel depending on the type of controller you have. Check the xxxxkern.cfg file for the selected kernel to see the drivers which have been included in that kernel. If the device you want is in that list, then the corresponding kernel should boot your computer. Download the xxxxkern.tgz file and copy it to your boot diskette as described above in the section on making boot disks.

You must then check the root device in the kernel, using the rdev command:

```
rdev zImage
```

`rdev` will then display the current root device in the kernel. If this is not the same as the root device you want, then use rdev to change it. For example, the kernel I tried was set to `/dev/sda2`, but my root SCSI partition is `/dev/sda8`. To use a root diskette, you would have to use the command:

```
rdev zImage /dev/fd0
```

If you want to know how to set up a Slackware root disk as well, that's outside the scope of this HOWTO, so I suggest you check the Linux Install Guide or get the Slackware distribution. See the section in this HOWTO titled "References."

6.3 Q. How do I update my boot floppy with a new kernel?

Just copy the kernel to your boot diskette using the dd command for a boot diskette without a file system, or the `cp` command for a boot/root disk. Refer to the section in this HOWTO titled "Boot" for details on creating a boot disk. The description applies equally to updating a kernel on a boot disk.

6.4 Q. How do I remove LILO so that I can use DOS to boot again?

This is not really a Bootdisk topic, but it is asked so often, so: the answer is, use the DOS command:

```
FDISK /MBR
```

MBR stands for Master Boot Record, and it replaces the boot sector with a clean DOS one, without affecting the partition table. Some purists disagree with this, but even the author of LILO, Werner Almesberger, suggests it. It is easy, and it works.

You can also use the `dd` command to copy the backup saved by LILO to the boot sector—refer to the LILO documentation if you wish to do this.

6.5 Q. How can I boot if I've lost my kernel AND my boot disk?

If you don't have a boot disk standing by, then probably the easiest method is to obtain a Slackware kernel for your disk controller type (IDE or SCSI) as described above for "How do I make a boot disk with a XXX driver?". You can then boot your computer using this kernel, then repair whatever damage there is.

The kernel you get may not have the root device set to the disk type and partition you want. For example, Slackware's generic SCSI kernel has the root device set to `/dev/sda2`, whereas my root Linux partition happens to be `/dev/sda8`. In this case the root device in the kernel will have to be changed.

You can still change the root device and ramdisk settings in the kernel even if all you have is a kernel, and some other operating system, such as DOS.

Rdev changes kernel settings by changing the values at fixed offsets in the kernel file, so you can do the same if you have a hex editor available on whatever systems you do still have running—for example, Norton Utilities Disk Editor under DOS. You then need to check and if necessary change the values in the kernel at the following offsets:

```
0x01F8  Low byte of RAMDISK size
0x01F9  High byte of RAMDISK size
0x01FC  Root minor device number - see below
0X01FD  Root major device number - see below
```

The ramdisk size is the number of blocks of ramdisk to create. If you want to boot from a root diskette then set this to decimal 1440, which is 0x05A0, thus set offset 0x01F8 to 0xA0 and offset 0x01F9 to 0x05. This will allocate enough space for a 1.4Mb diskette.

Note that the meaning of the ramdisk size word changed in kernel version 1.3.48. This meaning is described in Section 4.

The major and minor device numbers must be set to the device you want to mount your root file system on. Some useful values to select from are:

```
device          major minor
/dev/fd0          2     0   1st floppy drive
/dev/hda1         3     1   partition 1 on 1st IDE drive
/dev/sda1         8     1   partition 1 on 1st scsi drive
/dev/sda8         8     8   partition 8 on 1st scsi drive
```

Once you have set these values then you can write the file to a diskette using either Norton Utilities Disk Editor, or a program called `RAWRITE.EXE`. This program is included in several distributions, including the SLS and Slackware distributions. It is a DOS program which writes a file to the "raw" disk, starting at the boot sector, instead of writing it to the file system. If you use Norton Utilities, then you must write the file to a physical disk starting at the beginning of the disk.

6.6 Q. How can I make extra copies of boot/root diskettes?

It is never desirable to have just one set of rescue disks—two or three should be kept in case one is unreadable.

The easiest way of making copies of any diskettes, including bootable and utility diskettes, is to use the `dd` command to copy the contents of the original diskette to a file on your hard drive, and then use the same command to copy the file back to a new diskette. Note that you do not need to, and should not, mount the diskettes, because `dd` uses the raw device interface.

To copy the original, enter the command:

```
dd if=devicename of=filename
where   devicename the device name of the diskette
        drive
and     filename the name of the file where you
        want to copy to
```

For example, to copy from `/dev/fd0` to a temporary file called `/tmp/diskette.copy`, I would enter the command:

```
dd if=/dev/fd0 of=/tmp/diskette.copy
```

Omitting the *count* parameter, as we have done here, means that the whole diskette of 2880 (for a high-density) blocks will be copied.

To copy the resulting file back to a new diskette, insert the new diskette and enter the reverse command:

```
dd if=filename of=devicename
```

Note that the above discussion assumes that you have only one diskette drive. If you have two of the same type, then you can copy diskettes using a command like:

```
dd if=/dev/fd0 of=/dev/fd1
```

6.7 Q. How can I boot without typing in "ahaxxxx=nn,nn,nn" every time?

Where a disk device cannot be auto-detected it is necessary to supply the kernel with a command device parameter string, such as:

```
aha152x=0x340,11,3,1
```

This parameter string can be supplied in several ways using LILO:

- By entering it on the command line every time the system is booted via LILO. This is boring, though.
- By using the LILO "lock" keyword to make it store the command line as the default command line, so that LILO will use the same options every time it boots.
- By using the `APPEND` statement in the LILO configuration file. Note that the parameter string must be enclosed in quotes.

For example, a sample command line using the above parameter string would be:

```
zImage  aha152x=0x340,11,3,1 root=/dev/sda1 lock
```

This would pass the device parameter string through, and also ask the kernel to set the root device to `/dev/sda1` and save the whole command line and reuse it for all future boots.

A sample APPEND statement is:

```
APPEND = "aha152x=0x340,11,3,1"
```

Note that the parameter string must not be enclosed in quotes on the command line, but it must be enclosed in quotes in the `APPEND` statement.

Note also that for the parameter string to be acted on, the kernel must contain the driver for that disk type. If it does not, then there is nothing listening for the parameter string, and you will have to rebuild the kernel to include the required driver. For details on rebuilding the kernel, `cd` to `/usr/src/linux` and read the `README`, and read the Linux FAQ and Installation HOWTO. Alternatively, you could obtain a generic kernel for the disk type and install that.

Readers are strongly urged to read the LILO documentation before experimenting with LILO installation. Careless use of the "`BOOT`" statement can damage partitions.

6.8 Q. How can I create an oversize ramdisk file system?

For kernels later than 1.3.48, it is best to create a compressed file system as described in Section 4. If your kernel is earlier than this, you can either upgrade, or refer to version 2.0 or below of this HOWTO.

6.9 Q. At boot time, I get error `A: cannot execute B`. Why?

There are several cases of program names being hard coded in various utilities. These cases do not occur everywhere, but they may explain why an executable apparently cannot be found on your system even though you can see that it is there. You can find out if a given program has the name of another hard coded by using the "strings" command and piping the output through `grep`.

Known examples of hard coding are:

- Shutdown in some versions has `/etc/reboot` hard coded, so `reboot` must be placed in the `/etc` directory.
- `init` has caused problems for at least one person, with the kernel being unable to find `init`.

To fix these problems, either move the programs to the correct directory, or change configuration files (e.g. `/etc/inittab`) to point to the correct directory. If in doubt, put programs in the same directories as they are on your hard disk, and use the same `/etc/inittab` and `/etc/rc.d` files as they appear on your hard disk.

6.10 Q. My kernel has ramdisk support, but initializes RAM disks of 0K

Where this occurs, a kernel message similar to:

```
Ramdisk driver initialized : 16 ramdisks of 0K size
```

appears as the kernel is booting. The size should be either the default of 4096K, or the size specified in kernel parameters ramdisk_size or ramdisk. If the size is 0K, it is probably because the size has been set to 0 by kernel parameters at boot time. This could possibly be because of an overlooked LILO configuration file parameter:

```
ramdisk 0
```

This was included in sample LILO configuration files included in some older distributions, and was put there to override any previous kernel setting. Since 1.3.48 it is irrelevant, because the ramdisk_size kernel parameter now sets the maximum ramdisk size, not the size allocated at boot time. No ramdisk memory is allocated at boot time.

The solution is to remove the LILO ramdisk parameter.

Note that if you attempt to use a ramdisk which has been set to 0K, then behaviour can be unpredictable, and can result in kernel panics.

A Resources and Pointers

In this section, vvv is used in package names in place of the version, to avoid referring here to specific versions. When retrieving a package, always get the latest version unless you have good reasons for not doing so.

A.1 Distribution boot disks

These are the primary sources for distribution boot disks.

Please use one of the mirror sites to reduce the load on these machines.

- Slackware boot disks
  (`http://sunsite.unc.edu/pub/Linux/distributions/slackware/bootdsks.144/`)
  Slackware mirror sites
  and (`http://sunsite.unc.edu/pub/Linux/distributions/slackware/MIRRORS.TXT`)
- Red Hat boot disks
  (`http://sunsite.unc.edu/pub/Linux/distributions/redhat/current/i386/images/`)
  and *Red Hat mirror sites* (`http://www.redhat.com/ftp.html`)
- *Debian boot disks* (`ftp://ftp.debian.org/pub/debian/stable/disks-i386`) and *Debian mirror sites* (`ftp://ftp.debian.org/debian/README.mirrors`)

A.2 LILO—Linux Loader

Written by Werner Almesberger. Excellent boot loader, and the documentation includes information on the boot sector contents and the early stages of the boot process.

Ftp from: `tsx-11.mit.edu: /pub/linux/packages/lilo/lilo.vvv.tar.gz` also on sunsite and mirror sites.

A.3 Linux FAQ and HOWTOs

These are available from many sources. Look at the Usenet newsgroups `news.answers` and `comp.os.linux.announce`.

Ftp from: `sunsite.unc.edu:/pub/Linux/docs`

- FAQ is in `/pub/linux/docs/faqs/linux-faq`
- HOWTOs are in `/pub/Linux/docs/HOWTO`

For WWW, start at the Linux documentation home page:

```
http://sunsite.unc.edu/mdw/linux.html
```

If desperate, send mail to:

```
mail-server@rtfm.mit.edu
```

with the word "help" in the message, then follow the mailed instructions.

Note: if you haven't read the Linux FAQ and related documents such as the Linux Installation HOWTO and the Linux Install Guide, then you should not be trying to build boot diskettes.

A.4 Ramdisk Usage

An excellent description of the how the new ramdisk code works may be found with the documentation supplied with the Linux kernel. See `/usr/src/linux/Documentation/ramdisk.txt`. It is written by Paul Gortmaker and includes a section on creating a compressed RAM disk, similar to Section 4 of this HOWTO.

A.5 Rescue Packages

A.5.1 Bootkit

Written by Scott Burkett. Bootkit provides a flexible, menu driven framework for managing rescue disk creation and contents. It uses the Dialog package to provide nice menus, and a straight-forward directory tree to contain definitions of rescue disk contents. The package includes samples of the main files needed. The package aims to provide only the framework; it is up to the user to work out what to put on the disks and set up the config files accordingly. For those users who don't mind doing this, it is a good choice.

FTP from: `sunsite.unc.edu: /pub/Linux/system/Recovery/Bootkit-vvv.tar.gz`

A.5.2 CatRescue

Written by Oleg Kibirev. This package concentrates on saving space on the rescue diskettes by extensive use of compression, and by implementing executables as shells scripts. The documentation includes some tips on what to do in various disaster situations.

FTP from: `gd.cs.csufresno.edu/pub/sun4bin/src/CatRescue100.tgz`

A.5.3 Rescue Shell Scripts

Written by Thomas Heiling. This contains shell scripts to produce boot and boot/root diskettes. It has some dependencies on specific versions of other software such as LILO, and so might need some effort to convert to your system, but it might be useful as a starting point if you wanted more comprehensive shell scripts than are provided in this document.

Ftp from: `sunsite.unc.edu:/pub/Linux/system/Recovery/rescue.tgz`

A.5.4 SAR—Search and Rescue

Written by Karel Kubat. SAR produces a rescue diskette, using several techniques to minimize the space required on the diskette. The manual includes a description of the Linux boot/login process.

FTP from: `ftp.icce.rug.nl:/pub/unix/SAR-vvv.tar.gz`

The manual is available via WWW from:

`http://www.icce.rug.nl/karel/programs/SAR.html`

A.5.5 YARD

Written by Tom Fawcett. Yard produces customized rescue diskettes using the compressed ramdisk option of more recent kernels (later than 1.3.48). Yard was designed to automate most of the instructions in Section 4, above. In addition, Yard checks your file selections (loaders and libraries, and `/etc/fstab`, `rc`, `/etc/passwd`) to make sure you've included everything needed to make a bootable rescue disk. Yard needs Perl 5 and kernel version 1.3.48 or later.

The Yard home page is at `(http://www.cs.umass.edu/~fawcett/yard.html)`, which should always have the latest version, plus notices of any recent bugs. Yard may also be downloaded from `(http://sunsite.unc.edu/pub/Linux/system/Recovery/)`

B Samples

B.1 Disk Directory Listings

This lists the contents of directories from my root and utility diskettes. These lists are provided as an example only of the files included to create a working system. I have added some explanatory notes where it seemed useful.

B.1.1 Root Disk `ls-lR` Directory Listing

```
total 18
drwxr-xr-x   2 root     root        1024 Jul 29 21:16 bin/
drwxr-xr-x   2 root     root        9216 Jul 28 16:21 dev/
drwxr-xr-x   3 root     root        1024 Jul 29 20:25 etc/
drwxr-xr-x   2 root     root        1024 Jul 28 19:53 lib/
drwxr-xr-x   2 root     root        1024 Jul 24 22:47 mnt/
drwxr-xr-x   2 root     root        1024 Jul 24 22:47 proc/
drwxr-xr-x   2 root     root        1024 Jul 28 19:07 sbin/
drwxr-xr-x   2 root     root        1024 Jul 29 20:57 tmp/
drwxr-xr-x   4 root     root        1024 Jul 29 21:35 usr/
drwxr-xr-x   3 root     root        1024 Jul 28 19:52 var/

bin:
total 713
-rwxr-xr-x   1 root     bin         7737 Jul 24 22:16 cat*
-rwxr-xr-x   1 root     bin         9232 Jul 24 22:48 chmod*
-rwxr-xr-x   1 root     bin         8156 Jul 24 22:48 chown*
```

```
-rwxr-xr-x   1 root     bin         19652 Jul 24 22:48 cp*
-rwxr-xr-x   1 root     root         8313 Jul 29 21:16 cut*
-rwxr-xr-x   1 root     bin         12136 Jul 24 22:48 dd*
-rwxr-xr-x   1 root     bin          9308 Jul 24 22:48 df*
-rwxr-xr-x   1 root     root         9036 Jul 29 20:24 dircolors*
-rwxr-xr-x   1 root     bin          9064 Jul 24 22:48 du*
-rwxr-x---   1 root     bin         69252 Jul 24 22:51 e2fsck*
-rwxr-xr-x   1 root     bin          5361 Jul 24 22:48 echo*
-rwxr-xr-x   1 root     bin          5696 Jul 24 22:16 hostname*
-rwxr-xr-x   1 root     bin          6596 Jul 24 22:49 kill*
-rwxr-xr-x   1 root     bin         10644 Jul 24 22:17 ln*
-rwxr-xr-x   1 root     bin         13508 Jul 24 22:17 login*
-rwxr-xr-x   1 root     bin         26976 Jul 24 22:17 ls*
-rwxr-xr-x   1 root     bin          7416 Jul 24 22:49 mkdir*
-rwxr-x---   1 root     bin         34596 Jul 24 22:51 mke2fs*
-rwxr-xr-x   1 root     bin          6712 Jul 24 22:49 mknod*
-rwxr-xr-x   1 root     bin         20304 Jul 24 22:17 more*
-rwxr-xr-x   1 root     bin         24704 Jul 24 22:17 mount*
-rwxr-xr-x   1 root     bin         12464 Jul 24 22:17 mv*
-rwxr-xr-x   1 root     bin         20829 Jul 24 22:50 ps*
-rwxr-xr-x   1 root     bin          9424 Jul 24 22:50 rm*
-rwxr-xr-x   1 root     bin          4344 Jul 24 22:50 rmdir*
-rwxr-xr-x   1 root     root       299649 Jul 27 14:12 sh*
-rwxr-xr-x   1 root     bin          9853 Jul 24 22:17 su*
-rwxr-xr-x   1 root     bin           380 Jul 27 14:12 sync*
-rwxr-xr-x   1 root     bin         13620 Jul 24 22:17 umount*
-rwxr-xr-x   1 root     root         5013 Jul 29 20:03 uname*

dev:
total 0
lrwxrwxrwx   1 root     root           10 Jul 24 22:34 cdrom -> /dev/sbpcd
crw--w--w-   1 root     tty        4,   0 Jul 24 21:49 console
brw-rw----   1 root     floppy     2,   0 Apr 28  1995 fd0
lrwxrwxrwx   1 root     root            4 Jul 24 22:34 ftape -> rft0
crw-rw-rw-   1 root     sys       10,   2 Jul 18  1994 inportbm
crw-rw----   1 root     kmem       1,   2 Jul 28 16:21 kmem
crw-rw----   1 root     kmem       1,   1 Jul 18  1994 mem
lrwxrwxrwx   1 root     root            4 Jul 24 22:34 modem -> cua0
lrwxrwxrwx   1 root     root            4 Jul 24 22:34 mouse -> cua1
crw-rw-rw-   1 root     sys        1,   3 Jul 18  1994 null
brw-rw----   1 root     disk       1,   1 Jul 18  1994 ram
crw-rw----   1 root     disk      27,   0 Jul 18  1994 rft0
brw-rw----   1 root     disk      25,   0 Jul 19  1994 sbpcd
***  I have only included devices for the SCSI partitions I use.
***  If you use IDE, then use /dev/hdxx instead.
brw-rw----   1 root     disk       8,   0 Apr 29  1995 sda
brw-rw----   1 root     disk       8,   6 Apr 29  1995 sda6
brw-rw----   1 root     disk       8,   7 Apr 29  1995 sda7
brw-rw----   1 root     disk       8,   8 Apr 29  1995 sda8
lrwxrwxrwx   1 root     root            7 Jul 28 12:56 systty -> console
***  this link from systty to console is required
crw-rw-rw-   1 root     tty        5,   0 Jul 18  1994 tty
crw--w--w-   1 root     tty        4,   0 Jul 18  1994 tty0
crw--w----   1 root     tty        4,   1 Jul 24 22:33 tty1
crw--w----   1 root     tty        4,   2 Jul 24 22:34 tty2
crw--w--w-   1 root     root       4,   3 Jul 24 21:49 tty3
crw--w--w-   1 root     root       4,   4 Jul 24 21:49 tty4
crw--w--w-   1 root     root       4,   5 Jul 24 21:49 tty5
```

```
crw--w--w-   1 root     root       4,   6 Jul 24 21:49 tty6
crw-rw-rw-   1 root     tty        4,   7 Jul 18  1994 tty7
crw-rw-rw-   1 root     tty        4,   8 Jul 18  1994 tty8
crw-rw-rw-   1 root     tty        4,   9 Jul 19  1994 tty9
crw-rw-rw-   1 root     sys        1,   5 Jul 18  1994 zero

etc:
total 20
-rw-r--r--   1 root     root         2167 Jul 29 20:25 DIR_COLORS
-rw-r--r--   1 root     root           20 Jul 28 12:37 HOSTNAME
-rw-r--r--   1 root     root          109 Jul 24 22:57 fstab
-rw-r--r--   1 root     root          271 Jul 24 22:21 group
-rw-r--r--   1 root     root         2353 Jul 24 22:27 inittab
-rw-r--r--   1 root     root            0 Jul 29 21:02 issue
-rw-r--r--   1 root     root         2881 Jul 28 19:38 ld.so.cache
***  Lots of things get upset at boot time if ld.so.cache is missing, but
***  make sure that ldconfig is included and run from rc.x to
***  update it.
-rw-r--r--   1 root     root           12 Jul 24 22:22 motd
-rw-r--r--   1 root     root          606 Jul 28 19:25 passwd
-rw-r--r--   1 root     root         1065 Jul 24 22:21 profile
drwxr-xr-x   2 root     root         1024 Jul 29 21:01 rc.d/
-rw-r--r--   1 root     root           18 Jul 24 22:21 shells
-rw-r--r--   1 root     root          774 Jul 28 13:43 termcap
-rw-r--r--   1 root     root          126 Jul 28 13:44 ttys
-rw-r--r--   1 root     root            0 Jul 24 22:47 utmp

etc/rc.d:
total 5
*** I didn't bother with shutdown scripts - everthing runs on a
*** ramdisk, so there's not much point shutting it down.
-rwxr-xr-x   1 root     root         1158 Jul 24 22:23 rc.K*
-rwxr-xr-x   1 root     root         1151 Jul 28 19:08 rc.M*
-rwxr-xr-x   1 root     root          507 Jul 29 20:25 rc.S*

lib:
total 588
*** I have an ELF system, so I include the ELF loader ld-linux.so. if
*** you are still on a.out, then you need ld.so. Use the file command to
*** see which libraries you should include.
lrwxrwxrwx   1 root     root           17 Jul 24 23:36 ld-linux.so.1 -> ld-lin
ux.so.1.7.3*
-rwxr-xr-x   1 root     root        20722 Aug 15  1995 ld-linux.so.1.7.3*
lrwxrwxrwx   1 root     root           13 Jul 24 23:36 libc.so.5 -> libc.so.5.
0.9*
-rwxr-xr-x   1 root     root       562683 May 19  1995 libc.so.5.0.9*
***  Must include libtermcap
lrwxrwxrwx   1 root     root           19 Jul 28 19:53 libtermcap.so.2 -> libt
ermcap.so.2.0.0*
-rwxr-xr-x   1 root     root        11360 May 19  1995 libtermcap.so.2.0.0*

mnt:
total 0

proc:
total 0

sbin:
```

```
total 191
***  I use Slackware, which uses agetty. Many systems use getty.
***  Check your /etc/inittab to see which it uses. Note that you
***  need (a)getty and login to be able to start doing much.
-rwxr-xr-x   1 root     bin         11309 Jul 24 22:54 agetty*
-rwxr-xr-x   1 root     bin          5204 Jul 24 22:19 halt*
***  Must have this to boot
-rwxr-xr-x   1 root     bin         20592 Jul 24 22:19 init*
-rwxr-xr-x   1 root     root        86020 Jul 28 19:07 ldconfig*
-rwxr-xr-x   1 root     bin          5329 Jul 27 14:10 mkswap*
-rwxr-xr-x   1 root     root         5204 Jul 24 22:20 reboot*
-rwxr-xr-x   1 root     bin         12340 Jul 24 22:20 shutdown*
-rwxr-xr-x   1 root     root         5029 Jul 24 22:20 swapoff*
-rwxr-xr-x   1 root     bin          5029 Jul 24 22:20 swapon*
-rwxr-xr-x   1 root     root        20592 Jul 27 18:18 telinit*
-rwxr-xr-x   1 root     root         7077 Jul 24 22:20 update*

tmp:
total 0

usr:
total 2
drwxr-xr-x   2 root     root         1024 Jul 29 21:00 adm/
drwxr-xr-x   2 root     root         1024 Jul 29 21:16 lib/

usr/adm:
total 0

usr/lib:
total 0

var:
total 1
***  Several things complained until I included this and
***  the /etc/rc.S code to initialize /var/run/utmp, but this
***  won't necessarily apply to your system.
drwxr-xr-x   2 root     root         1024 Jul 28 19:52 run/

var/run:
total 0
```

B.1.2 Utility Disk `ls-lR` Directory Listing

```
total 579
-rwxr-xr-x   1 root     root        42333 Jul 28 19:05 cpio*
-rwxr-xr-x   1 root     root       103560 Jul 29 21:31 elvis*
-rwxr-xr-x   1 root     root        56401 Jul 28 19:06 find*
-rw-r--r--   1 root     root       128254 Jul 28 19:03 ftape.o
-rwxr-xr-x   1 root     root        64161 Jul 29 20:47 grep*
-rwxr-xr-x   1 root     root        45309 Jul 29 20:48 gzip*
-rwxr-xr-x   1 root     root        23560 Jul 28 19:04 insmod*
-rwxr-xr-x   1 root     root          118 Jul 28 19:04 lsmod*
lrwxrwxrwx   1 root     root            5 Jul 28 19:04 mt -> mt-st*
-rwxr-xr-x   1 root     root         9573 Jul 28 19:03 mt-st*
lrwxrwxrwx   1 root     root            6 Jul 28 19:05 rmmod -> insmod*
-rwxr-xr-x   1 root     root       104085 Jul 28 19:05 tar*
lrwxrwxrwx   1 root     root            5 Jul 29 21:35 vi -> elvis*
```

B.2 Shell Scripts to Build Diskettes

These shell scripts are provided as examples only. I use them on my system to create rescue diskettes. You may find it convenient to use them, but if so, read the instructions carefully—for example, if you specify the wrong swap device, you will find your root file system has been thoroughly and permanently erased. So just be darn sure you have it correctly configured before you use it.

The upside of the scripts are that they provide a quick way to get a rescue set together, by doing the following:

- copy a kernel to a boot disk, and use rdev to configure it, as explained above;
- adjust mkroot to your system and build a root disk. Use the directory listing above as a guide to what to include;
- use mkutil to throw your favorite utilities onto one or more utility disks.

There are two shell scripts:

- `mkroot`—builds a root or boot/root diskette.
- `mkutil`—builds a utility diskette.

Both are currently configured to run in the parent directory of boot_disk and util_disk, each of which contains everything to be copied to it's diskette. Note that these shell scripts will not automatically set up and copy all the files for you—you work out which files are needed, set up the directories and copy the files to those directories. The shell scripts are samples which will copy the contents of those directories. Note that they are primitive shell scripts and are not meant for the novice user.

The scripts both contain configuration variables at the start which allow them to be easily configured to run anywhere. First, set up the model directories and copy all the required files into them. To see what directories and files are needed, have a look at the sample directory listings in the previous sections.

Check the configuration variables in the shell scripts and change them as required before running the scripts.

B.2.1 mkroot - Make Root Diskette

```
# mkroot: make a root disk - creates a root diskette
#         by building a file system on it, then mounting it and
#         copying required files from a model.
#         Note: the model to copy from from must dirst be set up,
#         then change the configuration variables below to suit
#         your system.
#
# usage: mkroot [ -d swap | ram ]
#       where swap means use $SWAPDEV swap device
#       and ram means use $RAMDISKDEV ramdisk device

# Copyright (c) Graham Chapman 1996. All rights reserved.
# Permission is granted for this material to be freely
# used and distributed, provided the source is acknowledged.
# No warranty of any kind is provided. You use this material
# at your own risk.

# Configuration variables - set these to suit your system
#
####  set the device to use to build the root filesystem on.
####  ramdisk is safer - swap is ok only if you have plenty of
####  free memory. If linux can't swap then things get nasty.
USEDEVICE="ramdisk"             # set to either "ramdisk" or "swap"
RAMDISKDEV="/dev/ram"           # ramdisk device <==== CHANGE if using ramdisk
SWAPDEV="/dev/sda7"             # swap device    <==== CHANGE if using swap
FSBLOCKS=3072                   # desired filesystem size in blocks
#
####  set name or directory where you have set up your rootdisk
####  model
ROOTDISKDIR="./root_disk"       # name of root disk directory
MOUNTPOINT="/mnt"               # temporary mount point for diskette
```

```
DISKETTEDEV="/dev/fd0"          # device name of diskette drive
LOGFL="'pwd'/mkroot.log"        # log filename
TEMPROOTFS="/tmp/mkrootfs.gz"   # temp file for compressed filesystem
# End of Configuration variables

# Internal variables
ROOTDISKDEV=

case $USEDEVICE in
swap|ramdisk)   :;;
*)      echo "Invalid setting for USEDEVICE variable"
        exit;;
esac

clear
echo "    ***************** W A R N I N G *****************

Use this script with care. If you don't understand it, then
exit NOW!"

if [ "$USEDEVICE" = "swap" ]
then
        ROOTDISKDEV=$SWAPDEV
        echo -e "\nThis script will temporarily remove the swap file $SWAPDEV"
        echo "and use the space to build a compressed root filesystem from"
        echo "the files in the directory tree below $ROOTDISKDIR. To do this"
        echo "safely you must have 8Mb or more of memory, and you should"
        echo "switch to single user mode via 'init 1'."
        echo -e "\nIf you have used a ramdisk since the last reboot, then"
        echo "reboot NOW before using this script."
        echo -e "\nIf the script fails, you may not have a swap partition.
        echo "Run 'free' and check the total size to see if it is correct. "
        echo "If the swap partition $SWAPDEV is missing, do the following:"
        echo "  umount $MOUNTPOINT"
        echo "  mkswap $SWAPDEV"
        echo "  swapon $SWAPDEV"
        echo "to restore the swap partition $SWAPDEV."
else
        ROOTDISKDEV=$RAMDISKDEV
        echo -e "\nThis script will use a ramdisk of $FSBLOCKS Kb. To do this"
        echo "safely you must have at least 8Mb of memory. If you have only"
        echo "8Mb you should ensure nothing else is running on the machine."
        echo -e "\nWhen the script is complete, the ramdisk will still be"
        echo "present, so you should reboot to reclaim the memory allocated"
echo " to the ramdisk."
fi

echo -e "
Do you want to continue (y/n)? \c"
read ans
if [ "$ans" != "Y" -a $ans != "y" ]
then
        echo "not confirmed - aborting"
        exit
fi

echo "Starting mkroot at 'date'" > $LOGFL
```

```
if [ "$USEDEVICE" = "swap" ]
then
        echo "Unmounting swap device $SWAPDEV" | tee -a $LOGFL
        swapoff $SWAPDEV >> $LOGFL 2>&1
fi

echo "Zeroing device $ROOTDISKDEV" | tee -a $LOGFL
dd if=/dev/zero of=$ROOTDISKDEV bs=1024 count=$FSBLOCKS >> $LOGFL 2>&1
if [ $? -ne 0 ]
then
        echo "dd zeroing $ROOTDISKDEV failed" | tee -a $LOGFL
        exit 1
fi

echo "Creating filesystem on device $ROOTDISKDEV" | tee -a $LOGFL
mke2fs -m0 $ROOTDISKDEV $FSBLOCKS >> $LOGFL 2>&1

echo "Mounting $ROOTDISKDEV filesystem at $MOUNTPOINT" | tee -a $LOGFL
mount -t ext2 $ROOTDISKDEV $MOUNTPOINT >> $LOGFL 2>&1
if [ $? -ne 0 ]
then
        echo "mount failed"
        exit 1
fi

# copy the directories containing files
echo "Copying files from $ROOTDISKDIR to $MOUNTPOINT" | tee -a $LOGFL
currdir='pwd'
cd $ROOTDISKDIR
find . -print | cpio -dpumv $MOUNTPOINT >> $LOGFL 2>&1
if [ $? -ne 0 ]
then
        echo "cpio step failed."
        cd $currdir
        exit 1
fi
cd $currdir

fssize='du -sk $MOUNTPOINT|cut -d"       " -f1'
echo "Uncompressed root filesystem size is $fssize Kb" | tee -a $LOGFL
echo "Unmounting filesystem from $ROOTDISKDEV" | tee -a $LOGFL
umount $MOUNTPOINT >> $LOGFL 2>&1

echo "Compressing filesystem from $ROOTDISKDEV into $TEMPROOTFS
        This may take a few minutes..." | tee -a $LOGFL

#       We don't bother with gzip -9 here - takes more than twice as long
#       and saves less than 1% in space on my root disk...
dd if=$ROOTDISKDEV bs=1024 count=$FSBLOCKS 2>>$LOGFL | gzip -c > $TEMPROOTFS

fssize='du -k $TEMPROOTFS|cut -d"       " -f1'
echo "Compressed root filesystem size is $fssize Kb" | tee -a $LOGFL

echo -e "Insert diskette in $DISKETTEDEV and press any key
        ***  Warning: data on diskette will be overwritten!\c"
read ans

echo "Copying compressed filesystem from $TEMPROOTFS to $DISKETTEDEV" | tee -a $LOGFL
```

```
dd if=$TEMPROOTFS of=$DISKETTEDEV >>$LOGFL 2>&1
if [ $? -ne 0 ]
then
        echo "copy step failed."
        exit 1
fi

if [ "$USEDEVICE" = "swap" ]
then
        echo "Reinitialising swap device $SWAPDEV" | tee -a $LOGFL
        mkswap $SWAPDEV >> $LOGFL 2>&1
        echo "Starting swapping to swap device $SWAPDEV" | tee -a $LOGFL
        swapon $SWAPDEV >> $LOGFL 2>&1
fi

echo "Deleting $TEMPROOTFS" | tee -a $LOGFL
rm $TEMPROOTFS

echo "mkroot completed at 'date'" >> $LOGFL

echo "Root diskette creation complete - please read log file $LOGFL"
```

B.2.2 mkutil—Make Utility Diskette

```
# mkutil: make a utility diskette - creates a utility diskette
#         by building a file system on it, then mounting it and
#         copying required files from a model.
#         Note: the model to copy from from must first be set up,
#         then change the configuration variables below to suit
#         your system.

# Copyright (c) Graham Chapman 1996. All rights reserved.
# Permission is granted for this material to be freely
# used and distributed, provided the source is acknowledged.
# No warranty of any kind is provided. You use this material
# at your own risk.

# Configuration variables...
UTILDISKDIR=./util_disk          # name of directory containing model
MOUNTPOINT=/mnt                  # temporary mount point for diskette
DISKETTEDEV=/dev/fd0             # device name of diskette drive

echo $0: create utility diskette
echo Warning: data on diskette will be overwritten!
echo Insert diskette in $DISKETTEDEV and and press any key...
read anything

mke2fs $DISKETTEDEV
if [ $? -ne 0 ]
then
        echo mke2fs failed
        exit
fi

# Any file system type would do here
mount -t ext2 $DISKETTEDEV $MOUNTPOINT
if [ $? -ne 0 ]
then
```

```
        echo mount failed
        exit
fi

# copy the directories containing files
cp -dpr $UTILDISKDIR/* $MOUNTPOINT

umount $MOUNTPOINT

echo Utility diskette complete
```

Part X

"Brief Introduction to Alpha Systems and Processors" by David Mosberger, Editor

davidm@azstarnet.com

Part X

"Brief Introduction to Alpha Systems and Processors"

by David Mosberger, Editor

davidm@azstarnet.com

Contents

1 Abstract

V0.11, 6 June 1997
This document is a brief overview of existing Alpha CPUs, chip sets, and systems. It has something of a hardware bias, reflecting my own area of expertise. Although I am an employee of Digital Equipment Corporation, this is not an official statement by Digital and any opinions expressed are mine and not Digital's.

2 What is Alpha

"Alpha" is the name given to Digital's 64-bit RISC architecture. The Alpha project in Digital began in mid-1989, with the goal of providing a high-performance migration path for VAX customers. This was not the first RISC architecture to be produced by Digital, but it was the first to reach the market. When Digital announced Alpha, in March 1992, it made the decision to enter the merchant semiconductor market by selling Alpha microprocessors.

Alpha is also sometimes referred to as Alpha AXP, for obscure and arcane reasons that aren't worth perusing. Suffice it to say that they are one and the same.

3 What is Digital Semiconductor

Digital Semiconductor (`http://www.digital.com/info/semiconductor/`) (DS) is the business unit within Digital Equipment Corporation (Digital—We don't like the name DEC.) that sells semiconductors on the merchant market. Digital's products include CPUs, support chip sets, PCI-PCI bridges and PCI peripheral chips for comms and multimedia.

4 Alpha CPUs

There are currently two generations of CPU core that implement the Alpha architecture:

- EV4
- EV5

Opinions differ as to what "EV" stands for (Editor's note: the true answer is of course "Electro Vlassic" 12), but the number represents the first generation of Digital's CMOS technology that the core was implemented in. So, the EV4 was originally implemented in CMOS4. As time goes by, a CPU tends to get a mid-life performance kick by being optically shrunk into the next generation of CMOS process. EV45, then, is the EV4 core implemented in CMOS5 process. There is a big difference between shrinking a design into a particular technology and implementing it from scratch in that technology (but I don't want to go into that now). There are a few other wild cards in here: there is also a CMOS4S (optical shrink in CMOS4) and a CMOS5L.

True technophiles will be interested to know that CMOS4 is a 0.75 micron process, CMOS5 is a 0.5 micron process and CMOS6 is a 0.35 micron process.

To map these CPU cores to chips we get:

21064-150,166
: EV4 (originally), EV4S (now)

21064-200
: EV4S

21064A-233,275,300
: EV45

21066
: LCA4S (EV4 core, with EV4 FPU)

21066A-233
: LCA45 (EV4 core, but with EV45 FPU)

21164-233,300,333
: EV5

21164A-417
: EV56

21264

EV6: http://www.mdronline.com/report/articles/21264/21264.html

The EV4 core is a dual-issue (it can issue 2 instructions per CPU clock) superpipelined core with integer unit, floating point unit, and branch prediction. It is fully bypassed and has 64-bit internal data paths and tightly coupled 8Kbyte caches, one each for Instruction and Data. The caches are write-through (they never get dirty).

The EV45 core has a couple of tweaks to the EV4 core: it has a slightly improved floating point unit, and 16KB caches, one each for Instruction and Data (it also has cache parity). (Editor's note: Neal Crook indicated in a separate mail that the changes to the floating point unit (FPU) improve the performance of the divider. The EV4 FPU divider takes 34 cycles for a single-precision divide and 63 cycles for a double-precision divide (non data-dependent). In contrast, the EV45 divider takes typically 19 cycles (34 cycles max) for single-precision and typically 29 cycles (63 cycles max) for a double-precision division (data-dependent).)

The EV5 core is a quad-issue core, also superpipelined, fully bypassed, and so forth. It has tightly-coupled 8Kbyte caches, one each for I and D. These caches are write-through. It also has a tightly-coupled 96Kbyte on-chip second-level cache (the Scache) which is 3-way set associative and write-back (it can be dirty). The EV4->EV5 performance increase is better than just the increase achieved by clock speed improvements. As well as the bigger caches and quad issue, there are microarchitectural improvements to reduce producer/consumer latencies in some paths.

The EV56 core is fundamentally the same microarchitecture as the EV5, but it adds some new instructions for 8 and 16-bit loads and stores (see Section 9). These are primarily intended for use by device drivers. The EV56 core is implemented in CMOS6, which is a 2.0V process.

The 21064 was announced in March 1992. It uses the EV4 core, with a 128-bit bus interface. The bus interface supports the easy connection of an external second-level cache, with a block size of 256-bits (2 data beats on the bus). The Bcache timing is completely software configurable. The 21064 can also be configured to use a 64-bit external bus, (but I'm not sure if any shipping system uses this mode). The 21064 does not impose any policy on the Bcache, but it is usually configured as a write-back cache. The 21064 does contain hooks to allow external hardware to maintain cache coherence with the Bcache and internal caches, but this is hairy.

The 21066 uses the EV4 core and integrates a memory controller and PCI host bridge. To save pins, the memory controller has a 64-bit data bus (but the internal caches have a block size of 256 bits, just like the 21064, therefore a block fill takes 4 beats on the bus). The memory controller supports an external Bcache and external DRAMs. The timing of the Bcache and DRAMs is completely software configurable, and can be controlled to the resolution of the CPU clock period. Having a 4-beat process to fill a cache block isn't as bad as it sounds because the DRAM access is done in page mode. Unfortunately, the memory controller doesn't support any of the new esoteric DRAMs (SDRAM, EDO or BEDO) or synchronous cache RAMs. The PCI bus interface is fully rev2.0 compliant and runs at up to 33MHz.

The 21164 has a 128-bit data bus and supports split reads, with up to 2 reads outstanding at any time (this allows 100% data bus utilization under best-case dream-on conditions, i.e., you can theoretically transfer 128-bits of data on every bus clock). The 21164 supports easy connection of an external 3rd level cache (Bcache) and has all the hooks to allow external systems to maintain full cache coherence with all caches. Therefore, symmetric multiprocessor designs are easy.

The 21164A was announced in October, 1995. It uses the EV56 core. It is nominally pin-compatible with the 21164, but requires split power rails; all of the power pins that were +3.3V power on the 21164 have now been split into two groups; one group provided 2.0V power to the CPU core, the other group supplies 3.3V to the I/O cells. Unlike older implementations, the 21164 pins are not 5V-tolerant. The end result of this change is that 21164 systems are, in general, not upgradeable to the 21164A (though note that it would be relatively straightforward to design a 21164A system that could also accommodate a 21164). The 21164A also has a couple of new pins to support the new 8 and 16-bit loads and stores. It also improves the 21164 support for using synchronous SRAMs to implement the external Bcache.

5 21064 performance vs 21066 performance

The 21064 and the 21066 have the same (EV4) CPU core. If the same program is run on a 21064 and a 21066, at the same CPU speed, then the difference in performance comes only as a result of system Bcache/memory bandwidth. Any code thread that has a high hit-rate on the *internal* caches will perform the same. There are two big performance killers:

1. Code that is write-intensive. Even though the 21064 and the 21066 have write buffers to swallow some of the delays, code that is write-intensive will be throttled by write bandwidth at the system bus. This arises because the on-chip caches are write-through.

2. Code that wants to treat floats as integers. The Alpha architecture does not allow register-register transfers from integer registers to floating point registers. Such a conversion has to be done via memory (And therefore, because the on-chip caches are write-through, via the Bcache). (Editor's note: it seems that both the EV4 and EV45 can

perform the conversion through the primary data cache (Dcache), provided that the memory is cached already. In such a case, the store in the conversion sequence will update the Dcache and the subsequent load is, under certain circumstances, able to read the updated d-cache value, thus avoiding a costly round trip to the Bcache. In particular, it seems best to execute the `stq/ldt` or `stt/ldq` instructions back-to-back, but it is somewhat counterintuitive.)

If you make the same comparison between a 21064A and a 21066A, there is an additional factor due to the different Icache and Dcache sizes between the two chips.

Now, the 21164 solves both these problems: it achieve much higher system bus bandwidths (despite having the same number of signal pins—yes, I know it's got about twice as many pins as a 21064, but all those extra ones are power and ground. (Yes, really.) And it has write-back caches. The only remaining problem is the answer to the question, "How much does it cost?"

6 A Few Notes On Clocking

All of the current Alpha CPUs use high-speed clocks, because their microarchitectures have been designed as so-called short-tick designs. None of the system busses have to run at horrendous speeds as a result though:

- on the 21066(A), 21064(A), 21164 the off-chip cache (Bcache) timing is completely programmable, to the resolution of the CPU clock. For example, on a 275MHz CPU, the Bcache read access time can be controller with a resolution of 3.6ns;
- on the 21066(A), the DRAM timing is completely programmable, to the resolution of the CPU clock (*not* the PCI clock, the CPU clock);
- on the 21064(A), 21164(A), the system bus frequency is a sub-multiple of the CPU clock frequency. Most of the 21064 motherboards use a 33MHz system bus clock;
- Systems that use the 21066 can run the PCI at any frequency relative to the CPU. Generally, the PCI runs at 33MHz;
- Systems that use the APECs chip set (see Section 7) always have their CPU system bus equal to their PCI bus frequency. This means that both busses tends to run at either 25MHz or 33MHz (since these are the frequencies that scale up to match the CPU frequencies). On APECs systems, the DRAM controller timings are software programmable in terms of the CPU system bus frequency.

Aside: Someone suggested that they were getting bad performance on a 21066 because the 21066 memory controller was only running at 33MHz. Actually, it's the super-fast 21064A systems that have memory controllers that "only" run at 33MHz.

7 The Chip Sets

DS sells two CPU support chip sets. The 2107x chip set (aka APECS) is a 21064(A) support chip set. The 2117x chip set (aka ALCOR) is a 21164 support chip set. There will also be 2117xA chip set (aka ALCOR 2) as a 21164A support chip set.

Both chip sets provide memory controllers and PCI host bridges for their CPU. APECS provides a 32-bit PCI host bridge, ALCOR provides a 64-bit PCI host bridge which (in accordance with the requirements of the PCI spec) can support both 32-bit and 64-bit PCI devices.

APECS consists of 6, 208-pin chips (4, 32-bit data slices (DECADE), 1 system controller (COMANCHE), 1 PCI controller (EPIC)). It provides a DRAM controller (128-bit memory bus) and a PCI interface. It also does all the work to maintain memory coherence when a PCI device DMAs into (or out of) memory.

ALCOR consists of 5 chips (4, 64-bit data slices (Data Switch, DSW)—208-pin PQFP and 1 control (Control, I/O Address, CIA)—a 383 pin plastic PGA). It provides a DRAM controller (256-bit memory bus) and a PCI interface. It also does all the work required to support an external Bcache and to maintain memory coherence when a PCI device DMAs into (or out of) memory.

There is no support chip set for the 21066, since the memory controller and PCI host bridge functionality are integrated onto the chip.

8 The Systems

The applications engineering group in DS produces example designs using the CPUs and support chip sets. These are typically PC-AT size motherboards, with all the functionality that you'd typically find on a high-end Pentium motherboard.

Originally, these example designs were intended to be used as starting points for third-parties to produce motherboard designs from. These first-generation designs were called Evaluation Boards (EBs). As the amount of engineering required to build a motherboard has increased (due to higher-speed clocks and the need to meet RF emission and susceptibility regulations) the emphasis has shifted towards providing motherboards that are suitable for volume manufacture.

Digital's system groups have produced several generations of machines using Alpha processors. Some of these systems use support logic that is designed by the systems groups, and some use commodity chip sets from DS. In some cases, systems use a combination of both.

Various third-parties build systems using Alpha processors. Some of these companies design systems from scratch, and others use DS support chip sets, clone/modify DS example designs or simply package systems using build and tested boards from DS.

The EB64: Obsolete design using 21064 with memory controller implemented using programmable logic. I/O provided by using programmable logic to interface a 486<->ISA bridge chip. On-board Ethernet, SuperI/O (2S, 1P, FD), Ethernet and ISA. PC-AT size. Runs from standard PC power supply.

The EB64+: Uses 21064 or 21064A and APECs. Has ISA and PCI expansion (3 ISA, 2 PCI, one pair are on a shared slot). Supports 36-bit DRAM SIMMs. ISA bus generated by Intel SaturnI/O PCI-ISA bridge. On-board SCSI (NCR 810 on PCI) Ethernet (Digital 21040), KBD, MOUSE (PS2 style), SuperI/O (2S, 1P, FD), RTC/NVRAM. Boot ROM is EPROM. PC-AT size. Runs from standard PC power supply.

The EB66: Uses 21066 or 21066A. I/O sub-system is identical to EB64+. Baby PC-AT size. Runs from standard PC power supply. The EB66 schematic was published as a marketing poster advertising the 21066 as "the first microprocessor in the world with embedded PCI." (For trivia fans: there are actually two versions of this poster—I drew the circuits and wrote the spiel for the first version, and some Americans mauled the spiel for the second version.)

The EB164: Uses 21164 and ALCOR. Has ISA and PCI expansion (3 ISA slots, 2 64-bit PCI slots (one is shared with an ISA slot) and 2 32-bit PCI slots. Uses plus-in Bcache SIMMs. I/O sub-system provides SuperI/O (2S, 1P, FD), KBD, MOUSE (PS2 style), RTC/NVRAM. Boot ROM is Flash. PC-AT-sized motherboard. Requires power supply with 3.3V output.

The AlphaPC64 (aka Cabriolet): derived from EB64+ but now baby-AT with Flash boot ROM, no on-board SCSI or Ethernet. 3 ISA slots, 4 PCI slots (one pair are on a shared slot), uses plug-in Bcache SIMMs. Requires power supply with 3.3V output.

The AXPpci33 (aka NoName), is based on the EB66. This design is produced by Digital's Technical OEM (TOEM) group. It uses the 21066 processor running at 166MHz or 233MHz. It is a baby-AT size, and runs from a standard PC power supply. It has 5 ISA slots and 3 PCI slots (one pair are a shared slot). There are 2 versions, with either PS/2 or large DIN connectors for the keyboard.

Other 21066-based motherboards: most if not all other 21066-based motherboards on the market are also based on EB66—there's really not many system options when designing a 21066 system, because all the control is done on-chip.

Multia (aka the Universal Desktop Box): This is a very compact pedestal desktop system based on the 21066. It includes 2 PCMCIA sockets, 21030 (TGA) graphics, 21040 Ethernet and NCR 810 SCSI disk along with floppy, 2 serial ports and a parallel port. It has limited expansion capability (one PCI slot) due to its compact size. (There is some restriction on when you can use the PCI slot, can't remember what) (Note that 21066A-based and Pentium-based Multia's are also available).

DEC PC 150 AXP (aka Jensen): This is a very old Digital system—one of the first-generation Alpha systems. It is only mentioned here because a number of these systems seem to be available on the second-hand market. The Jensen is a floor-standing tower system which used a 150MHz 21064 (later versions used faster CPUs but I'm not sure what speeds). It used programmable logic to interface a 486 EISA I/O bridge to the CPU.

Other 21064(A) systems: There are 3 or 4 motherboard designs around (I'm not including Digital *systems* here) and all the ones I know of are derived from the EB64+ design. These include:

- EB64+ (some vendors package the board and sell it unmodified); AT form-factor.
- Aspen Systems motherboard: EB64+ derivative; baby-AT form-factor.
- Aspen Systems server board: many PCI slots (includes PCI bridge).
- AlphaPC64 (aka Cabriolet), baby AT form-factor.

Other 21164(A) systems: The only one I'm aware of that isn't simply an EB164 clone is a system made by DeskStation. That system is implemented using a memory and I/O controller proprietary to Desk Station. I don't know what their attitude towards Linux is.

9 Bytes and all that stuff

When the Alpha architecture was introduced, it was unique amongst RISC architectures for eschewing 8-bit and 16-bit loads and stores. It supported 32-bit and 64-bit loads and stores (longword and quadword, in Digital's nomenclature). The co-architects (Dick Sites, Rich Witek) justified this decision by citing the advantages:

1. Byte support in the cache and memory sub-system tends to slow down accesses for 32-bit and 64-bit quantities.
2. Byte support makes it hard to build high-speed error-correction circuitry into the cache/memory sub-system.

Alpha compensates by providing powerful instructions for manipulating bytes and byte groups within 64-bit registers. Standard benchmarks for string operations (e.g., some of the Byte benchmarks) show that Alpha performs very well on byte manipulation.

The absence of byte loads and stores impacts some software semaphores and impacts the design of I/O sub-systems. Digital's solution to the I/O problem is to use some low-order address lines to specify the data size during I/O transfers, and to decode these as byte enables. This so-called Sparse Addressing wastes address space and has the consequence that I/O space is non-contiguous (more on the intricacies of Sparse Addressing when I get around to writing it). Note that I/O space, in this context, refers to all system resources present on the PCI and therefore includes both PCI memory space and PCI I/O space.

With the 21164A introduction, the Alpha architecture was ECO'd to include byte addressing. Executing these new instructions on an earlier CPU will cause an OPCDEC PALcode exception, so that the PALcode will handle the access. This will have a performance impact. The ramifications of this are that use of these new instructions (IMO) should be restricted to device drivers rather than applications code.

These new byte load and stores mean that future support chip sets will be able to support contiguous I/O space.

10 Porting

The ability of any Alpha-based machine to run Linux is really only limited by your ability to get information on the gory details of its innards. Since there are Linux ports for the E66, EB64+ and EB164 boards, all systems based on the 21066, 21064/APECS or 21164/ALCOR should run Linux with little or no modification. The major thing that is different between any of these motherboards is the way that they route interrupts. There are three sources of interrupts:

- on-board devices;
- PCI devices;
- ISA devices.

All the systems use an Intel System I/O bridge (SIO) to act as a bridge between PCI and ISA (the main I/O bus is PCI, the ISA bus is a secondary bus used to support slow-speed and 'legacy' I/O devices). The SIO contains the traditional pair of daisy-chained 8259s.

Some systems (e.g., the Noname) route all of their interrupts through the SIO and thence to the CPU. Some systems have a separate interrupt controller and route all PCI interrupts plus the SIO interrupt (8259 output) through that, and all ISA interrupts through the SIO.

Other differences between the systems include:

- how many slots they have;
- what on-board PCI devices they have;
- whether they have Flash or EPROM.

11 More Information

All of the DS evaluation boards and motherboard designs are license-free and the whole documentation kit for a design costs about $50. That includes all the schematics, programmable parts sources, data sheets for CPU and support chip set. The doc kits are available from Digital Semiconductor distributors. I'm not suggesting that many people will want to rush out and buy this, but I do want to point out that the information is available.

Hope that was helpful. Comments/updates/suggestions for expansion to Neal Crook, neal.crook@reo.mts.digital.com.

12 References

[1] http://www.research.digital.com/wrl/publications/abstracts/TN-13.html. Bill Hamburgen, Jeff Mogul, Brian Reid, Alan Eustace, Richard Swan, Mary Jo Doherty, and Joel Bartlett. *Characterization of Organic Illumination Systems*. DEC WRL, Technical Note 13, April 1989.

Part XI

"Linux Busmouse Howto" by Chris Bagwell,

cbagwell@sprynet.com

The Linux Documentation Project
The original, unaltered edition of this, and other, LDP documents, is on line at http://sunsite.unc.edu/LDP/.

Contents

v1.5, 2 November 1997
Chris Bagwell cbagwell@sprynet.com

1 Introduction.

This document is a guide to getting your bus mouse working with Linux. During early kernel versions it was quite common to see questions come up about how to get bus mice working under Linux. With the more advanced distributions available today the questions do not seem to come up as often but there is still an audience for this FAQ.

Busmouse support has been in the kernel for as long as I can remember, and hasn't changed much in a long time, so this document should be relevant to any version of Linux you're likely to have.

1.1 Disclaimer.

The information in this document is correct to the best of my knowledge, but there's a always a chance I've made some mistakes, so don't follow everything too blindly, especially if it seems wrong. Nothing here should have a detrimental effect on your computer, but just in case I take no responsibility for any damages incurred from the use of the information contained herein.

`Microsoft(R) is a Trademark of Microsoft Corporation.`

[trademark notices for other mice, anyone?]

1.2 Feedback.

If you find any mistakes in this document, have any comments about its contents or an update or addition, send them to me at the address listed at the top of this howto.

1.3 Acknowledgements.

This howto has been, in the spirit of Linux, a community effort. Thanks goes out to Mike Battersby, mib@deakin.edu.au as he started this FAQ and I have since started up-keep on it. Any errors are most likely mine.

Many thanks go to Johan Myreen for the sections on the PS/2 mice, Robert T. Harris for help on the ATI-XL sections and Reuben Sumner for miscellaneous info and constructive criticism.

Thanks also to the multitudes of people who have sent me mouse information, fixes, or words of encouragement.

2 Determining your mouse type.

There are two separate but important characteristics you will need to know about your mouse before you go on: what interface it uses and what protocol it uses. The interface is the hardware aspect of the mouse, taking into account things like which I/O ports it uses and how to check if it is installed. This is the part that the kernel is concerned with, so that it knows how to read data from the mouse. The protocol is the software aspect of the mouse. Applications need to know the protocol to interpret the raw mouse data they receive from the kernel.

2.1 Mouse interfaces.

The Linux kernel currently supports four different kinds of bus mouse interface: Inport (Microsoft); Logitech; PS/2; and ATI-XL. There is no sure-fire way of determining your mouse interface — mouse developers generally do their own thing when it comes to standards. The following sections may help. Otherwise, you'll just have to make it up.

2.2 Inport mice.

This includes most of the old-style Microsoft mice that are shaped like a bar of Dove soap. U.S. users who have purchased Gateway computers should note that the mice that come with them are not Inport mice but PS/2 mice (see below). Inport mice generally connect to an interface card which plugs into the bus on your motherboard. If the plug that connects your mouse cord to the interface card is round, has 9 pins, and a notch in one side, you likely have an Inport mouse.

As far as I can tell, apart from the ATI-XL, all ATI mice (such as those on the Graphics Ultra cards) are plain Inport mice.

2.3 Logitech mice.

Logitech mice in general appear almost exactly the same as Inport mice. They, too, connect to an interface card via a 9-pin, mini-DIN connector. Hopefully, it will have come in a Logitech box or have "Logitech" printed on the connector card so that you can tell that it actually is a Logitech mouse.

There are also some truly ancient Microsoft mice (ones with ball bearings on the bottom as well as the mouse ball and a DB9 connector) which also use the Logitech protocol.

2.4 PS/2 mice.

PS/2 mice aren't really bus mice at all. The PS/2 mouse interface is not on an expansion card, the mouse is connected to the PS/2 Auxiliary Device port on the keyboard controller. A PS/2 mouse port uses a 6-pin mini DIN connector, similar to the keyboard connector. Many laptops also use this kind of interface to their track balls — except for the connector, of course.

2.5 ATI-XL mice.

ATI-XL mice are a variant of Inport mice, with some slight differences. They come on the ATI-XL combined video adaptor/mouse card. Unless you know you have an ATI-XL card (and thus an ATI-XL mouse), you probably don't have one of these. It is possible for ATI-XL mice to use either the ATI-XL or Inport kernel drivers, although the ATI-XL driver should give better results.

2.6 Mouse protocols.

The PC world is full of different and conflicting mouse protocols. Fortunately, the choice for bus mice is considerably smaller than that for serial mice. Most Inport, Logitech and ATI-XL mice use the "BusMouse" protocol, although there are some ancient Logitech mice which use the "MouseSystems" protocol, and some even older Microsoft mice which use the Logitech protocol. PS/2 mice use the "PS/2" protocol.

3 Getting your mouse working.

Once you have figured out your mouse interface and protocol types, you're ready to proceed.

3.1 Setting the mouse interrupt.

Now, you'll need to know which interrupt number your mouse is using, and make sure it doesn't conflict with any other peripherals you have installed.

You should make sure that your mouse is not trying to use the same interrupt as any of your other devices — it is not possible for the mouse to share an interrupt under Linux, even though it may work fine under other operating systems. Check the documentation for all your peripherals to see which interrupt they use. In most cases IRQ4 is used for the first serial port (`/dev/ttyS0`), IRQ3 for the second (`/dev/ttyS1`) (these are assuming you actually have such devices — if you don't you can happily use their IRQ's), and IRQ5 for some SCSI adaptors.

Note that for ATI-XL, Inport, and Logitech mice the kernel default is to use IRQ5, so if you are stuck with a pre-compiled kernel (eg, CD-ROM users) you will have to use that. If you are using an Inport or Logitech mice with a newer kernel you may be able to pass a command line option to the kernel to tell it what interrupt to use without recompiling.

3.2 Inport and Logitech mice.

If you open up your computer's case and look at the card which your mouse plugs into, you should notice a block of jumpers on the card (hopefully labeled "INTERRUPT") with positions for interrupt (otherwise known as IRQ) numbers 2, 3, 4, and 5. To change the interrupt, simply move the jumper from its current position onto the correct pair of pins.

```
***************************************************
***   MAKE SURE YOUR COMPUTER IS TURNED OFF    ***
***     BEFORE CHANGING THE JUMPERS AROUND.     ***
***************************************************
```

3.3 ATI-XL mice.

ATI-XL bus mice have a software selectable IRQ—you should have received with your mouse a MS-DOS program (`VSETUP.EXE`) to set the IRQ. In order to do so you must (temporarily) boot MS-DOS and run this program. Note that `VSETUP.EXE` takes an optional parameter "`/70`" to increase the vertical refresh rate (which results in less flicker). `VSETUP.EXE` program also allows you to select either the primary or secondary mouse address—you should set this to the primary address or the kernel will not be able to detect your mouse.

Once `VSETUP.EXE` has been run, you must perform a hard reset for the new configuration to take effect.

3.4 PS/2 mice.

The PS/2 mouse always uses IRQ12—there is no way of changing this (except with a soldering gun.) In the rare case that some other device is using IRQ12, you'll have to re-jumper that peripheral to use another IRQ number.

3.5 Compiling the kernel.

In order for your bus mouse to operate correctly you will need to compile your kernel with the bus mouse support compiled in. If you are using a pre-compiled kernel then it often comes with support for all three bus mouse included. This may still not be enough. The kernel could be trying to use the wrong interrupt or the detection can get confused and treat your mouse as the wrong type. When in doubt, try recompiling your kernel with only support for your mouse type and set it to use the correct interrupt.

Change to your kernel directory (here assumed to be (`/usr/src/linux`) and do a

```
make config
```

If you are unsure as to your mouse type, the first time you recompile the kernel you may wish to enable all of the bus mouse options in the hope that the kernel will auto-detect your mouse properly. People have mixed success with this: it doesn't always work, but on the other hand it might save you further compiles.

3.5.1 Inport, Logitech and ATI-XL mice

Answer "`y`" to the question pertaining to your type of bus mouse interface and "`n`" to all the other bus mouse questions. For example, if you have an Inport mouse you should answer "`y`" to

```
Microsoft bus mouse support
```

and "`n`" to all other bus mouse questions. Answer the non-mouse related questions as you usually would.

If you have a Logitech or Inport mouse, edit the file `/usr/src/linux/include/linux/busmouse.h` and change the line which says

```
#define MOUSE_IRQ 5
```

to reflect the interrupt number for your mouse (see the section 3.1 for details on finding your interrupt number).

If you have an ATI-XL mouse, edit the file `/usr/src/linux/drivers/char/atixlmouse.c` and change the line which says

```
#define ATIXL_MOUSE_IRQ 5
```

to reflect your mouse's interrupt number.

Due to the vagaries of the PC architecture, if you have set your mouse to use interrupt 2, you must set the `#define` to use interrupt 9.

Examples

For a mouse on interrupt 3, you should change the line to read

```
#define MOUSE_IRQ 3
```

For a mouse on interrupt 2, you should change the line to read

```
#define MOUSE_IRQ 9
```

Next, compile your kernel as per the instructions which come with it, and boot from the new kernel. You should now have the bus mouse support correctly compiled in.

The steps to change the interrupt the kernel uses works with any version of the kernel to date. Newer kernels (starting somewhere in the 2.x's) allow you to pass arguments to the kernel during boot up using something like LILO or LOADLIN to specify the interrupt number for Logitech and Microsoft Inport mice. This can be a real time saver as you do not need to recompile your kernel (or know how to).

You can add the following options to your boot line in LILO to change interrupt:

```
bmouse=3  (Logitech Busmice)
msmouse=3 (for Microsoft Inport mice)
```

Substitute the "3" with your mouse's actual interrupt. An example of using this with lilo is:

```
LILO:linux msmouse=3
```

3.5.2 PS/2 mice

To compile the kernel with PS/2 mouse support, answer "y" to the question.

```
PS/2 mouse (aka "auxiliary device") support
```

The PS/2 mouse driver actually supports two kinds of devices: the standard PS/2 Auxiliary Device controller and a special PS/2 mouse interface chip from Chips & Technologies which is used in the Texas Instruments Travelmate and Gateway Nomad laptops. To compile in support for the trackballs on these computers, answer "y" to the

```
C&T 82C710 mouse port support (as on TI Travelmate)
```

question. Note that you will still have to answer "y" to the question about the standard PS/2 driver to even get a chance to answer this question, since the 82C710 driver is actually an add-on to the standard PS/2 mouse driver.

When configured both for a standard PS/2 mouse device and the 82C710 device, the driver first tries to locate a 82C710 chip at boot time. Failing this, the standard driver is used instead, so using a kernel configured for both types of interface on a machine with a standard PS/2 mouse port should work too. However, there has been one report of a falsely detected 82C710 chip, so to be on the safe side do not configure in support for the 82C710 if you don't need it.

Compile your new kernel and boot from it as you normally would.

3.5.3 Selection

It appears that in older kernels you had to compile in support to use the program Selection (so you can cut and paste from virtual consoles). This option does not appear in modern kernels and the program Selection has generally been replaced with the program gpm (see Section 4.1 for more details).

If you are working with an old kernel then you may wish to set this option to "y" regardless of your mouse type so that you may use the Selection program.

3.6 The mouse devices.

Mice under Linux are accessed via the devices in the /dev directory. The following table gives a list of interface types and which device you should use.

```
INTERFACE         DEVICE          MAJOR     MINOR
--------------------------------------------------
Logitech          /dev/logibm      10         0
PS/2              /dev/psaux       10         1
Inport            /dev/inportbm    10         2
ATI-XL            /dev/atibm       10         3

    Table 1.  Mouse devices.
```

Note:

If you are using your ATI-XL mouse with the Inport driver, you should use the inportbm device, not the /dev/atibm device.

The major and minor entries are the device numbers for that particular device.

If you find that you do not have these devices, you should create them first. To do so, execute the following as root.

```
mknod /dev/logimm     c 10 0
mknod /dev/psaux      c 10 1
mknod /dev/inportbm   c 10 2
mknod /dev/atibm      c 10 3
```

Note:

Some time in the (progressively less) recent history of Linux the names for the bus mouse devices have changed. The following device names have been superseded by those above and should be removed: bmousems, bmouseps2, bmouseatixl, and bmouselogitech.

Many people like to create a symbolic link from their mouse device to `/dev/mouse` so that they don't have to remember which device they need to be using. If you have one of the current Linux distributions you will almost certainly find that you have such a link. If you have such a link, or create one, you should make sure that it is pointing to the correct device for your mouse.

4 Using your mouse.

4.1 `gpm`.

`gpm` is a program which allows you to do mouse based "cut and paste" between virtual consoles under Linux and is a good way of testing your mouse out. The current version of `gpm` is ftp://sunsite.unc.edu/pub/Linux/system/mouse/gpm-1.13.tar.gz and contains instructions for getting it compiled. Some Linux distributions, such as Red Hat, come with a precompiled `gpm` binary.

When invoking gpm, use the `-t` switch to indicate which protocol your mouse is using and the `-m` option to indicate which mouse device you are using. Three protocols useful for most bus mice are `logi`, `bm`, and `ps2`. The default for mouse device is to use `/dev/mouse`, so you can omit the `-m` option if you have the appropriate symbolic link. An example for a Microsoft Inport mouse is:

```
gpm -t bm
```

or if you use the PS/2 protocol:

```
gpm -t ps2
```

You should then be able move your mouse and see a block move around the screen and also be able to cut and paste text between virtual consoles using the mouse buttons. Read the documentation with `gpm`, or do a `man gpm` for more information on how to operate it.

4.2 XFree86.

To use your bus mouse under XFree86, you will need to set your mouse protocol type in your XF86config file. If you have a BusMouse protocol mouse, your Xconfig should contain (including the quotes)

```
Section "Pointer"
  Protocol "Busmouse"
  Device   "/dev/mouse"

  # Any other options such as Emulate3Buttons
EndSection
```

For PS/2 mice change the protocol line to:

```
Protocol      "PS2"
```

If you have a two-button mouse, it should also contain the line

```
Emulate3Buttons
```

which will allow you to emulate the use of the middle mouse button by pressing both mouse buttons simultaneously. All other mouse related lines, such as "BaudRate" and "SampleRate" should be commented out, as these have no effect on bus mice.

4.3 XFree86 and `gpm`.

For a long period of the kernel development, it was not possible to share bus mice between processes. Because of this, it was hard to run both XFree86 and `gpm` at the same time. If you try to run X with `gpm` running and you get errors like the following then you know you are using one of these older kernels.

```
Fatal server error:
Cannot open mouse (Device or resource busy)
```

There are two methods of getting `gpm` working with XFree86 with these kernels. The first is to kill any copy of `gpm` you have running before you start up XFree86. The second is to use `gpm`'s "repeater" option (it takes mouse data and repeats the information to multiple applications).

I would recommend upgrading your kernel if possible so that you can share bus mice between processes. For this document, I will only explain the simplest method of using XFree86 and gpm together with older kernels. Please see `gpm`'s documentation if you would like to use the repeater method.

`gpm` allows you to terminate running copies of itself by executing:

```
gpm -k
```

This should be done before starting up X11. Take whatever script you use to start up your X session, such as `startx`, and add the above command to the top of the script so that `gpm` is shut down automatically. You may wish to also put a command that restarts `gpm` at the bottom of the script so that it restarts upon exiting your X session.

5 Still can't get your mouse going?

So you've read through this HOWTO a dozen times, done everything exactly as you think you should have, and your mouse still doesn't work? The best advice I can give you is this: experiment. Sure, it's a pain in the posterior, but in the end the only way to find out what is going to work with your mouse is to try all of the alternatives until you have success.

As always, if there is something you don't understand, try reading the manual page first and see if that helps. If you have a specific question, or a problem you think I might be able to help with, feel free to contact me at the address listed at the top of this howto, and I'll see if I can help you out or point you to someone who can.

The `comp.os.linux.setup` newsgroup or `comp.os.linux.hardware` is the appropriate forum for discussion and/or questions regarding setup — please don't post questions to other groups, and especially don't cross post questions to two or more of the Linux groups, they are more than cluttered enough as it is! When posting, you will get a much better response (and much fewer flames) if you use appropriate Subject: and Keywords: lines. For example:

```
Subject: BUSMICE - Gateway 2000 mouse wont work.
Keywords: mouse busmouse gateway
```

Part XII

"Linux CD-Writing HOWTO" by Winfried Trümper,

winni@xpilot.org

Contents

Abstract

v2.4.1, 16 December 1997
This document deals with the process of writing CDs under Linux.

1 Introduction

My first experience with CD Writers was guided by the "Linux CD Writer mini-HOWTO" by Matt Cutts <cutts@cs.unc.edu>. Thanks Matt!

Although my intention was only to upgrade his document, I rewrote it from the scratch after I realized how much changed since 1994.

1.1 Disclaimer

I (Winfried Truemper) DISCLAIM ALL WARRANTIES WITH REGARD TO THIS DOCUMENT, INCLUDING ALL IMPLIED WARRANTIES OF MERCHANTABILITY AND FITNESS FOR A CERTAIN PURPOSE; IN NO EVENT SHALL I BE LIABLE FOR ANY SPECIAL, INDIRECT OR CONSEQUENTIAL DAMAGES OR ANY DAMAGES WHATSOEVER RESULTING FROM LOSS OF USE, DATA OR PROFITS, WHETHER IN AN ACTION OF CONTRACT, NEGLIGENCE OR OTHER TORTIOUS ACTION, ARISING OUT OF OR IN CONNECTION WITH THE USE OF THIS DOCUMENT. Short: read and use at your own risk.

1.2 Suggested readings

The CD-R FAQ http://www.cd-info.com/CDIC/Technology/CD-R/FAQ.html is a general FAQ about compact-disk recordables (CD-R).

The Linux CD-ROM HOWTO explains everything one should know about CD-ROM drives under Linux. As a supplement, you may want to take a look at the Linux SCSI HOWTO and the Linux Kernel HOWTO.

1.3 Terminology ... lasers at maximum ... fire!

CD-ROM stands for "Compact Disc Read Only Memory," a storage medium utilizing an optical laser to sense microscopic pits on a silver shimmering disk. (The silver shimmering comes from an aluminized layer which is the carrier.) The pits represent the bits of the information (in some way) and are so petite that some billions of them fit on the disc. Thus, a CD is a mass-storage medium.

The term "CD-R" is a short form of "CD-ROM recordable" and refers to a CD that doesn't have those "microscopic pits" on its surface. Thus, it's empty.

Instead of the aluminum layer (silver) a CD-R has a special film (colored) into which "microscopic pits" can be burned in. This is done by giving the laser which normally only senses the pits a little bit more power so he burns the pits. This action can only be taken **once** on a CD-R.

You can leave out some areas for later writing, though, creating a so called multi-session CD.

This HOWTO deals with the task of writing a CD-R. Welcome on board, captain.

1.4 Supported CD-Writers

The detailed list of models which have been reported (not) to work successfully is available from

http://www.shop.de/cgi-bin/winni/lsc.pl

The list will be included in future versions of this HOWTO. Most SCSI CD writers are supported and the newest version of `cdrecord` even supports ATAPI CD writers.

If your hardware isn't supported, you can still use Linux to create an image of the later CD but then you have to use MS-DOS software to write the image to the CD-R. [You may wish to do so because most MS-DOS software cannot deal with long file names available in Linux.]

In this case you can skip all hardware-related sections (those about generic SCSI devices and `cdwrite and cdrecord`).

1.5 Supported "Features"

Currently the software for burning CDs under Linux does support the following main features:

```
Feature          cdwrite-2.1      cdrecord-1.7
----------------------------------------------

ATAPI support    no               yes
Multisession     only partial     yes

RockRidge        yes (mkisofs)    yes (mkisofs)
El Torito        yes (mkisofs)    yes (mkisofs)
HFS              yes (mkhybrid)   yes (mkhybrid)
Joliet           yes (mkhybrid)   yes (mkhybrid)
```

RockRidge is an extension to allow longer filenames and a deeper directory hierarchy. **El Torito** can be used to produce bootable CDs. Please see the accompanied documentation for further details upon this special features. **HFS** lets a Macintosh read the CD-ROM as if it were an HFS volume. **Joliet** brings long filenames (among other things) to some variants of Windows (95, NT).

Section 2.8 lists the availability of the mentioned software.

1.6 Mailing lists

If you want to join the development team (with the intention to actively help them), send e-mail to

cdwrite-request@pixar.com

and put the word `subscribe` in body of the message.

1.7 Availability

The newest version of this document is always available from

```
(http://www.shop.de/~winni/linux/cdr/)
```

2 Prepare your Linux-box for writing CD-ROMs

Before November 1997, the software for Linux didn't support ATAPI cd writers. As a result, the current release of the HOWTO concentrates on dealing with SCSI devices.

The good news is, that dealing with ATAPI devices is much easier and you can still use this HOWTO if you just forget about the "generic SCSI devices." To find out how to address ATAPI devices you can issue the command `cdrecord -scanbus`.

Future versions of this HOWTO will contain more details of dealing with ATAPI cd writers.

2.1 Set up the hardware

Shut down your computer, switch it off and hook CD writer to the SCSI bus.

Make sure the SCSI bus is properly terminated and choose a free SCSI ID for the writer. Look at the Linux SCSI HOWTO if you're not sure. If you're completely clueless, ask an expert.

Switch the power on again and check the messages that the BIOS of the SCSI controller prints immediately after switching the power on.

2.2 A note on writing CDs under Linux

In contrast to other rumors, the Linux kernel does not require a patch in order to write to CDs. Although the file `drivers/scsi/scsi.c` from the kernel sources contains the lines

```
case TYPE_WORM:
case TYPE_ROM:
  SDpnt->writeable = 0;
```

this does only mean that that CDs and WORMs are not writeable through the standard-devices `/dev/sda`–`/dev/sdh`—which is okay.

Instead of using these devices the writing of CDs is done through the so called "**generic SCSI devices**" which permit nearly everything—even writing to CDs.

2.3 Create the generic devices

The Linux SCSI HOWTO says about generic SCSI devices:

> The Generic SCSI device driver provides an interface for sending SCSI commands to all SCSI devices—disks, tapes, CD-ROMs, media changer robots, etc.

Speaking of the generic devices as interfaces means that they provide an alternate way of accessing SCSI hardware than through the standard devices.

This alternate way is required because the standard devices are designed to read data block-wise from a disk, tape or CD-ROM. Compared to this, driving a cd writer (or a scanner) is more exotic; e.g., commands to position the laser must be transmitted. To have a clean (and therefore fast) implementation of standard devices, all such exotic actions must be done through the generic SCSI devices.

As everthing can be done to SCSI hardware through the generic devices they are not fixed to a certain purpose—therefore the name "generic."

Go to the `/dev` directory and check for generic SCSI devices; `ls` should show sga–sgh:

```
bash> cd /dev
bash> ls -l sg*
crw-------    1 root    sys     21,    0 Jan  1  1970 sga
crw-------    1 root    sys     21,    1 Jan  1  1970 sgb
crw-------    1 root    sys     21,    2 Jan  1  1970 sgc
crw-------    1 root    sys     21,    3 Jan  1  1970 sgd
crw-------    1 root    sys     21,    4 Jan  1  1970 sge
crw-------    1 root    sys     21,    5 Jan  1  1970 sgf
crw-------    1 root    sys     21,    6 Jan  1  1970 sgg
crw-------    1 root    sys     21,    7 Jan  1  1970 sgh
```

If you don't have those device files then create them by using the `/dev/MAKEDEV` script:

```
bash> cd /dev/
bash> ./MAKEDEV sg
```

Now the device files should show up.

2.4 Enable usage of the generic SCSI and loopback devices

The Linux kernel needs a module that lends it the ability to deal with generic SCSI devices. If your running kernel has this feature, it should be listed in the pseudo-file `/proc/devices`:

```
bash> cat /proc/devices
Character devices:
  1 mem
  2 pty
  3 ttyp
  4 ttyp
  5 cua
  7 vcs
 21 sg             <----- stands for "SCSI Generic device"

 30 socksys

Block devices:
  2 fd
  7 loop           <----- we even can use the loop-devices
  8 sd
 11 sr             <----- stands for "SCSI cd-Rom"
```

Maybe you have to issue the commands `insmod sg`, `insmod loop` or `insmod sr_mod` to load the modules into the kernel. Check again after you've tried this.

If one of them doesn't succeed, you must re-configure your kernel and re-compile it.

```
bash> cd /usr/src/linux
bash> make config
```

```
[..]
*
* Additional Block Devices
*
Loopback device support (CONFIG_BLK_DEV_LOOP) [M/n/y/?] M

[..]
*
* SCSI support
*
SCSI support (CONFIG_SCSI) [Y/m/n/?] Y
*
* SCSI support type (disk, tape, CD-ROM)
*
SCSI disk support (CONFIG_BLK_DEV_SD) [Y/m/n/?] Y
SCSI tape support (CONFIG_CHR_DEV_ST) [M/n/y/?] M
SCSI CD-ROM support (CONFIG_BLK_DEV_SR) [M/n/y/?] M
SCSI generic support (CONFIG_CHR_DEV_SG) [M/n/y/?] M

[..]
ISO9660 cdrom filesystem (CONFIG_ISO9660_FS) [Y/m/n/?] M
```

Please note that I omitted the not-so-important questions.

2.5 Build and install the kernel

If you have questions regarding this, the Linux Kernel-HOWTO is the suggested reading. Furthermore your Linux distribution should ship with some documentation about this issue.

[Hint: while re-compiling, you can continue with steps 2.7-2.9]

2.6 Reboot the computer for the changes to take effect.

Don't panic if the Linux kernel prints the messages faster than you can read them, at least the initialization of SCSI devices can be re-displayed with the command `dmesg`:

```
scsi0 : NCR53c{7,8}xx (rel 17)
scsi : 1 host.
scsi0 : target 0 accepting period 100ns offset 8 10.00MHz
scsi0 : setting target 0 to period 100ns offset 8 10.00MHz

  Vendor: FUJITSU   Model: M1606S-512        Rev: 6226
  Type:   Direct-Access                      ANSI SCSI
Detected scsi disk sda at scsi0, channel 0, id 0, lun 0

  Vendor: NEC       Model: CD-ROM DRIVE:84   Rev:  1.0a
  Type:   CD-ROM                             ANSI SCSI
Detected scsi CD-ROM sr0 at scsi0, channel 0, id 4, lun 0

scsi : detected 1 SCSI disk total.
SCSI device sda: hdwr sector= 512 bytes. Sectors= 2131992
```

Shown above is only that part of the initialization messages that report the detection of physically present SCSI devices.

2.7 Create loopback devices

Go to the `/dev` directory and check for loopback devices. It's not critical if you don't have those devices, but it's convenient if you do (see 3.5). If you already have them, `ls` should show `loop0–loop7`:

```
bash> cd /dev
bash> ls -l loop*
brw-rw----   1 root  disk    7,   0 Sep 23 17:15 loop0
brw-rw----   1 root  disk    7,   1 Sep 23 17:15 loop1
brw-rw----   1 root  disk    7,   2 Sep 23 17:15 loop2
```

```
brw-rw----    1 root  disk    7,   3 Sep 23 17:15 loop3
brw-rw----    1 root  disk    7,   4 Sep 23 17:15 loop4
brw-rw----    1 root  disk    7,   5 Sep 23 17:15 loop5
brw-rw----    1 root  disk    7,   6 Sep 23 17:15 loop6
brw-rw----    1 root  disk    7,   7 Sep 23 17:15 loop7
```

If you don't have those device files, then create them by using the /dev/MAKEDEV script:

```
bash> cd /dev/
bash> ./MAKEDEV loop
```

The last command only succeeds if you have the loop-module in your kernel (see 2.4 for handling of modules). If insmod loop does not help, you must wait until the new kernel is properly installed (see 2.5).

2.8 Get the user software for burning CDs

2.8.1 Command line utilities

The following package is required to generate prototypes of CD-ROMs:

(ftp://tsx-11.mit.edu/pub/linux/packages/mkisofs/) (mkisofs)
(ftp://ftp.ge.ucl.ac.uk/pub/mkhfs) (mkhybrid)

Depending on the model of your CD writer (see 1.3), one of the following software for writing prototypes to CD-ROMs is required:

ftp://ftp.fokus.gmd.de/pub/unix/cdrecord/ (cdrecord)
ftp://sunsite.unc.edu/pub/Linux/utils/disk-management/ (cdwrite)

Please use the nearest mirrors of these FTP servers or get them from a CD.

Be absolutely sure you have version 2.0 of cdwrite or newer. No older version and especially no beta-versions will work properly! Don't trust the man-page of (old) mkisofs which states you need version 1.5 of cdwrite.

For information about ports of cdwrite to Irix and AIX visit the URL

http://lidar.ssec.wisc.edu/~forrest/

If you are using a kernel prior to release 2.0.31, you may want to patch mkisofs to get along a bug in the Linux file system code. The Debian distribution ships a patch for release 1.05 of mkisofs (1.11 should work, too) of mkisofs that adds the option '-K' to it (see 3.4); it's available from

ftp://ftp.debian.org/pub/debian/bo/source/otherosfs/mkisofs_1.11-1.diff.gz

This patch is only necessary if you want to mount the CD image via the loopback device (see 3.5.).

2.8.2 A graphical user interface (optional)

X-CD-Roast is full X based CD Writer Program, and it is the successor of the cdwtools-0.93. It's available from

(http://www.fh-muenchen.de/home/ze/rz/services/projects/xcdroast/e_overview.html)

Currently X-CD-Roast is based on a patched version of cdwrite 2.0 and thus comes with exactly the same features (see 1.4). Future versions may be based on the alternate cdrecord software.

3 "If to smoke you turn I shall not cease to fiddle while you burn."

Emperor Nero about burning his own classic-CDs (AD64).
He misunderstood it completely.

Usually the writing of a CD under Linux is done in two steps:

- packaging the desired software into one big file using the mkisofs/mkhybrid-utility
- writing the big file to the CD-R with cdwrite or cdrecord

It is also possible to combine the two steps into one via a pipe, but that is discouraged because it's not reliable. See below.

3.1 Determine which generic SCSI device the writer is attached to

[Please note: the current scheme for naming SCSI devices under Linux is unnecessary complicated and not reliable enough. The fact that I describe it in greater detail here should not be misinterpreted as a confirmation of this scheme. People with an ATAPI cd-writer can try "cdrecord -scanbus" to detect the right device and skip the rest of this section.]

After following all steps of the second chapter your system should be able to deal with the task of writing CDs. This section can be used as a proof that everything works as intended.

Issue the command `dmesg`. It should report the messages of the Linux-kernel including those printed while booting (limitation: only the last 200) and contain some information about the CD writer connected to the SCSI bus.

Simple example:

```
  Vendor: YAMAHA  Model: CDR100           Rev: 1.11
  Type:   WORM                            ANSI SCSI revision: 02
Detected scsi CD-ROM sr1 at scsi0, channel 0, id 3, lun 0
```

This machine has 4 SCSI devices connected to it (you can't see it so I tell you), with SCSI ID's from 0 to 3. The writer is the 4th physically present SCSI device and therefore connected to `/dev/sgd` (the fourth generic SCSI device when counting is started with the letter a). In this case the command

```
cdwrite  --eject  --device /dev/sgd
```

opens the tray and is a test if everything is set up properly. A more complicated example:

```
scsi0 : AdvanSys SCSI 1.5: ISA (240 CDB)
scsi1 : Adaptec 1542
scsi : 2 hosts.

  Vendor: HP      Model: C4324/C4325  Rev: 1.20
  Type:   CD-ROM                      ANSI SCSI revision: 02
Detected scsi CD-ROM sr0 at scsi0, channel 0, id 2, lun 0

  Vendor: IBM     Model: DPES-31080   Rev: S31Q
  Type:   Direct-Access               ANSI SCSI revision: 02
Detected scsi disk sda at scsi1, channel 0, id 0, lun 0

scsi : detected 1 SCSI cdrom 1 SCSI disk total.
SCSI device sda: hdwr sector= 512 bytes.
```

In this example, two SCSI controllers host one SCSI device each. What a waste (they are able to host up to seven devices each). It's not my setup, so stop asking if I have too much money. Anyway, for the purpose of being an overlookable example this setup is just excellent.

In the above example the CD Writer has SCSI ID 2 but it is associated with the first generic SCSI device `/dev/sga` because it's the first physically present SCSI device which Linux has detected. Hopefully this shows clearly that the SCSI ID of a device has nothing to do with the associated generic device.

Two questions are left: what happens if you catch the wrong device? If you neither specify the option "–<MANUFACTURER>" nor write any data to the device, usually a warning message is printed and nothing bad happens:

```
bash> cdwrite --eject --device /dev/sgb

Unknown CD-Writer; if this model is compatible with any
supported type, please use the appropriate command line
flag.

Manufacturer:  IBM
Model:         DPES-31080
Revision:      S31Q
```

In this case the device `/dev/sbg` is a SCSI hard disk (from IBM).

If you write data to the wrong device, you overwrite the original content of it and probably irrecoverably damage your system. Be careful, it already happened to me by accident.

3.2 Collect software

Usually this takes up longer than one expects. Remember that missing files cannot be added once the CD is written.

Also keep in mind that a certain amount of the free space of a CD is used for storing the information of the ISO 9660 filesystem (usually a few MB).

3.3 Storing data on a CD.

The term "**ISO 9660** refers to the format in which data is organized on the CD. To be more precise: it's the file system on the CD.

Of course the appearance of files stored in this format is unified by the Linux kernel as for every other file systems, too. So if you mount a CD into the directory tree, you cannot distinguish it's files from other files ... beside the fact that they are not writeable ... even not for root. The mechanism used to unify the appearance of files is called a **virtual file system** (VFS).

The features of the ISO 9660 file system are not so rich compared to those of the extended-2 file system which is normally used under Linux. On the other hand, the CD is only writable once and some features make no sense anyway. The limitations of the ISO 9660 file system are:

- Only eight levels of sub-directories allowed (counted from the top-level directory of the CD) Use RockRidge Extensions to enlarge this number.
- Maximum length for filenames: 32 characters.
- 650 MB capacity.

3.4 Create an ISO 9660 file system

Before any storage medium (e.g. floppy disk, hard disk or CD) can be used, it must get a file system (DOS speak: get formatted). This file system is responsible for organizing and incorporating the files that should be stored on the medium.

Well, a writable CD is only writable once so if we would write an empty file system to it, it would get formatted—but remain completely empty forever.

So what we need is a tool that creates the filesystem while copying the files to the CD. This tool is called `mkisofs`. A sample usage looks as follows:

```
mkisofs  -r   -o cd_image   private_collection/
               `---------'   `-----------------'
                    |                |
          write output to   take directory as input
```

The option "`-r`" sets the permissions of all files to be publicly readable on the CD and enables Rock Ridge extensions. That is what one usually wants and use of this option is recommended until you know what you're doing (hint: without "`-r`" the mount point gets the permissions of `private_collection`!).

If you are running a Linux kernel prior to 2.0.31, you should add the option "`-K`" to work around a bug in the filesystem code. You need the patched version of `mkisofs` for it. This option is equivalent to the option "`-P`" of `cdwrite`. Please see the manual page of `mkisofs` for details. Users of a more recent version of Linux have to worry about neither.

`mkisofs` will try to map all filenames to the 8.3 format used by MS-DOS to ensure highest possible compatibility. In case of naming conflicts (different files have the same 8.3 name), numbers are used in the filenames and information about the chosen filename is printed via stderr (usually the screen).

DON'T PANIC:

> Under Linux you will never see these 8.3 filenames because Linux makes use of the Rock Ridge extensions which contain the original file information (permissions, file name, etc.).

Now you may wonder why the output of `mkisofs` is not directly sent to the writer device. This has two reasons:

- `mkisofs` knows nothing about driving CD writers (see section 2.3.)
- It would not be reliable (see section 4.)

Because the timing of the CD writer is a critical point, we don't feed it directly from `mkisofs` (remember Linux is not a real time operating system and tasks can be timed badly). Instead it is recommended to store the output of `mkisofs` in a separate file on the hard disk. This file is then an 1:1 image of the later CD and is actually written to the CD with the tool `cdwrite` in a second step.

The 1:1 image gets stored in a huge file so you need the same amount of free disk space that your collected software already eats up. That's a drawback.

One could think of creating an extra partition for that and writing the image to that partition instead to a file. I vote against such a strategy because if you write to the wrong partition (due to a typo), you can lose your complete Linux system. Furthermore, it's a waste of disk space because the CD image is temporary data that can be deleted after writing the CD.

3.5 Test the CD image

Linux has the ability to mount files as if they were disk partitions. This feature is useful to check the directory layout of the CD image is okay. To mount the file `cd_image` created above on the directory `/cdrom`, give the command

```
mount -t iso9660 -o ro,loop=/dev/loop0 cd_image /cdrom
```

Now you can inspect the files under `/cdrom`—they appear exactly as they were on a real CD. To unmount the CD image, just say `umount /cdrom`. Warning: If you did not use the option "`-K`" for `mkisofs` then the last file on `/cdrom` may not be fully readable.

Note:

Some ancient versions of `mount` are not able to deal with loopback devices. If you have such an old version of `mount` it is a hint to upgrade your Linux system.Several people already suggested to put information about how to get the newest mount utilities into this HOWTO. I always refuse this. If your Linux distribution ships with an ancient `mount`: report it as a bug. If your Linux distribution is not easily upgradeable: report it as a bug.

If I included all the information that is necessary to work around bugs in bad designed Linux distributions, this HOWTO would be a lot bigger and harder to read.

3.6 Remarks on the blank CD-recordable discs

The German computer magazine "c't" has a list of tips regarding the blank CDs in their November 1996 issue:

- "no-name" discs are generally not of highest quality and should not be used;
- if a recordable CD is defective, this is likely to apply to the whole batch (if you bought more then one at a time); maybe you are lucky and can at least use the first 500MB of such CDs;
- don't touch the CDs at their shimmering side before writing.

3.7 Write the CD image to a CD

Not much more left to do. Before showing you the last command, let me warn you that CD writers want to be fed with a constant stream of data because they have only small data buffers. So the process of writing the CD image to the CD must not be interrupted or a corrupt CD will be the result.

To be sure nothing can interrupt this process, throw all users of the system and unplug the Ethernet cable ... Read the *Bastard operator from hell* to learn about the right attitude to do so.[7]

If you are mentally prepared, dress up in a black robe, multiply the SCSI ID of the CD writer with its SCSI revision and light as many candles, speak two verses of the ASR-FAQ and finally type

```
cdwrite  --device /dev/sgd  cd_image
```

or

```
cdrecord -v speed=2 dev=4,0 cd_image
```

depending on which software you want to use. Of course, you have to replace the example SCSI device with the device your writer is connected to.

Please note that no writer can reposition its laser and can't continue at the original spot on the CD when it gets disturbed. Therefore any strong vibrations or even a shock will completely destroy the CD you are writing.

3.8 If something goes wrong—

Remember that you can still use corrupt CDs as coasters.

4 Frequently asked questions with answers

4.1 "How sensitive is the burning process?"

Answer: that depends on your writer. Modern ones should have a data buffer of 1MB or so and can live 1–2 seconds without data. See the manuals or ask your manufacturer if you want to know the details.

Regardless of the size of those data buffers you must guarantee a constant throughput of 300kb/s or 600kb/s in the long time run.

Disk intensive processes such as updating the *locate* database lower the maximum flow rate will surely corrupt the CD; you better check such processes are not started via `cron`, `at`, or `anacron` while you burn CD-ROMs. .

[7] Drop carrier. Repeatedly. *They'll get the hint.* —Ed.

On the other hand, people reported that they compiled a kernel while burning a CD without a glitch. Of course you need a fast machine for such experiments.

4.2 "Has fragmentation a bad impact on the throughput?"

Fragmentation is usually so low that it's impact isn't noticed.

If you're uncertain than look at the messages printed while booting, the percentage of fragmentation is reported while checking the file systems. You can check for this value with the very dangerous command

```
bash> e2fsck -n  /dev/sda5          # '-n' is important!
[stuff deleted - ignore any errors]
/dev/sda5: 73/12288 files (12.3% non-contiguous)
```

In this example, the fragmentation seems to be very high—but there are only 73 very small files on this file system (used as /tmp) so the value is *not* alarming.

4.3 "Is it possible to store the CD image on an UMSDOS-file system?"

Yes. The only filesystem that isn't reliable and fast enough for writing CDs from is the network file system (NFS).

I'm using UMSDOS myself to share the disk space between Linux and DOS/Win on a PC (486/66) dedicated for writing CDs.

4.4 "Isn't there some way to get around the ISO 9660 limitations?"

Yes. You can put any file system you like on the CD. But other operating systems than Linux won't be able to deal with this CD.

Here goes the recipe:

- Create an empty file of 650MB size.

```
dd if=/dev/zero of="empty_file" bs=1024k count=650
```

- Create an ext-2 filesystem on this file

```
bash> /sbin/mke2fs  empty_file
empty_file is not a block special device.
Proceed anyway? (y,n) y
```

- Mount this empty file through the loopback devices

```
mount -t ext2 -o loop=/dev/loop1 empty_file /mnt
```

- Copy files to /mnt and umount it afterwards.
- Use cdwrite or cdrecord on empty_file (which is no longer empty) as if it were an ISO 9660 image.

If you want to make an entry in /etc/fstab for such a CD, disable the checking of it, e.g.:

```
/dev/cdrom  /cdrom  ext2  defaults,ro  0 0
```

The first 0 means "don't include in dumps," the second (=important) one means "don't check for errors on startup" (fsck will fail to check the CD for errors).

4.5 "How to read and write audio CDs?"

Please get the packages cdda2wav and sox, available from sunsite and its mirrors:

ftp://sunsite.unc.edu/pub/Linux/apps/sound/cdrom/cdda2wav0.71.src.tar.gz
ftp://sunsite.unc.edu/pub/Linux/apps/sound/convert/sox-11gamma-cb3.tar.gz

cdda2wav enables you to get a specific interval (or a whole track) from your audio CD and converts it into a .wav file. sox converts the wav files back into the (audio CD) cdda format so it can be written to the CD-R using cdwrite.

4.6 "How to probe for SCSI devices after boot?"

The file `drivers/scsi/scsi.c` contains the information

```
/*
 * Usage: echo "scsi add-single-device 0 1 2 3" >/proc/scsi/scsi
 * with  "0 1 2 3" replaced by your "Host Channel Id Lun".
 * Consider this feature BETA.
 *     CAUTION: This is not for hotplugging your peripherals. As
 *     SCSI was not designed for this you could damage your
 *     hardware !
 * However perhaps it is legal to switch on an
 * already connected device. It is perhaps not
 * guaranteed this device doesn't corrupt an ongoing data transfer.
 */
```

4.7 "Is it possible to make a 1:1 copy of a data CD?"

Yes. But you should be aware of the fact that any errors while reading the original (due to dust or scratches) will result in a defective copy.

First case: you have a CD writer and a separate CD-ROM drive. By issuing the command

```
cdwrite -v -D /dev/sgc --pad -b  $(isosize  /dev/scd0) /dev/scd0
```

or

```
cdrecord -v dev=3,0 speed=2 -isosize /dev/scd0
```

you read the data stream from the CD-ROM drive attached as `/dev/scd0` and write it directly through `/dev/sgc` to the CD-R.

Second case: you don't have a seperate CD-ROM drive. You have to use the writer to read out the CD-ROM in this case:

```
dd if=/dev/scd0 of=cdimage bs=1c count='isosize  /dev/scd0'
```

This command is equivalent to the result of `mkisofs`, so you should procede as described in Section 3. Please note that this method will fail on audio CDs.

4.8 "Can Linux read Joliet CDs?"

Yes. But you need to patch the kernel and recompile it. For further details see

http://www-plateau.cs.berkeley.edu/people/chaffee/joliet.html

4.9 "How do I read or mount CD-ROMs with the CD writer?"

Just as you do with regular CD-ROM drives. No tricks at all. Note that you have to use the scd devices (SCSI CD-ROM) to mount CDs for reading. Example entry for `/etc/fstab`:

```
/dev/scd0  /cdrom  iso9660  ro,user,noauto  0  0
```

5 Troubleshooting

5.1 It doesn't work: under Linux

Please check first if the writer works under other operating systems. Concretely:

- Does the controller recognize the writer as a SCSI device?
- Does the driver software recognize the writer?
- Is it possible to make a CD using the accompanied software?

If "it doesn't work" even under other operating systems you have a hardware conflict or defective hardware.

5.2 It doesn't work: under MS-DOS and friends

Try to use Linux. Installation and configuration of SCSI-drivers for DOS is the hell. Linux is too complicated? Ha!

5.3 SCSI errors during the burning phase

Most likely those errors are caused by

- missing dis-/reconnect feature on the SCSI bus
- unsufficiently cooled hardware
- defective hardware (should be detected by 5.1.)

Under various circumstances SCSI devices dis- and reconnect themselves (electronically) from the SCSI bus. If this feature is not available (check controller and kernel parameters) some writers run into trouble during burning or fixating the CD-R.

The NCR 53c7,8xx SCSI driver especially has the feature disabled by default, so you might want to check it first:

```
NCR53c7,8xx SCSI support                     [N/y/m/?] y
   always negotiate synchronous transfers [N/y/?] (NEW) n
   allow FAST-SCSI [10MHz]                    [N/y/?] (NEW) y
   allow DISCONNECT                           [N/y/?] (NEW) y
```

6 Credits

Andreas Erdmann <erdmann@zpr.uni-koeln.de>
Provided the example with the YAMAHA writer.

Art Stone <stone@math.ubc.ca>
Had the idea to put non-ISO 9660 file systems on a CD.

Bartosz Maruszewski <B.Maruszewski@zsmeie.torun.pl>
Reported spelling mistakes.

Bernhard Gubanka <beg@ipp-garching.mpg.de>
Noticed the need of a recent version of mount to utilize the loopback device.

Brian H. Toby
Polished the wording.

Bruce Perens <bruce@pixar.com>
Gave information about the cdwrite mailing list.

Dale Scheetz <dwarf@polaris.net>
Helped improving the section about creating the CD image.

"Don H. Olive" <don@andromeda.campbellsvil.edu>
URL of the mkhybrid tool.

Edwin H. Kribbs
Reported that "`-K`" requires a patch for `mkisofs`.

Gerald C Snyder <gcsnyd@loop.com>
Tested writing of an ext2 CD-ROM (see 4.4).

Ingo Fischenisch <ingo@mi.uni-koeln.de>
Provided the example with 2 controllers hosting 2 devices.

Janne Himanka <shem@oyt.oulu.fi>
Pointer to kernel patch to read Joliet CDs.

Joerg Schilling <schilling@fokus.gmd.de>
Information about cdrecord.

Jos van Geffen <jos@tnj.phys.tue.nl>
Noted the problem in 4.9.

Markus Dickebohm <m.dickebohm@uni-koeln.de>

Pierre Pfister <pp@uplift.fr>
Helped to develop the recipe on 1:1 copies.

Rick Cochran <rick@msc.cornell.edu>
Hint about dis-/reconnect disabled by default in the NCR driver.

Stephan Noy <stnoy@mi.uni-koeln.de>
Information and experience about writing audio CDs.

Stephen Harris <sweh@mpn.com>
Contributed hint about writing audio-CDs.

The Sheepy One <kero@escape.com>
Suggested using defective CDs as coasters for drinks.

Volker Kuhlmann <kuhlmav@elec.canterbury.ac.nz>
Noticed that the "cdwrite" package does not contain `mkisofs`.

End of the Linux CD-Writing mini-HOWTO

Part XIII

"The Linux CD-ROM HOWTO" by Jeff Tranter,

jeff_tranter@pobox.com

Contents

Abstract

v1.12, 1 November 1997
This document describes how to install, configure, and use CD-ROM drives under Linux. It lists the supported hardware and answers a number of frequently asked questions. The intent is to bring new users up to speed quickly and reduce the amount of traffic in the Usenet news groups and mailing lists.

1 Introduction

This is the Linux CD-ROM HOWTO. It is intended as a quick reference covering everything you need to know to install and configure CD-ROM hardware under Linux. Frequently asked questions related to CD-ROM are answered, and references are given to other sources of information related to CD-ROM applications and technology.

1.1 Acknowledgments

Much of this information came from the documentation and source files provided with the Linux kernel, the Internet alt.cdrom newsgroup FAQ, and input from Linux users.

Thanks to the SGML Tools package, this HOWTO is available in several formats, all generated from a common source file.

1.2 New Versions Of This Document

New versions of this document will be periodically posted to the comp.os.linux.answers newsgroup. They will also be uploaded to various anonymous ftp sites that archive such information including ftp://sunsite.unc.edu/pub/Linux/docs/HOWTO/.

Hypertext versions of this and other Linux HOWTOs are available on many World Wide Web sites, including http://sunsite.unc.edu/LDP/HOWTO/. Most Linux CD-ROM distributions include the HOWTOs, often under the `/usr/doc` directory, and you can also buy printed copies from several vendors. Sometimes the HOWTOs available from CD-ROM vendors, FTP sites, and printed format are out of date. If the date on this HOWTO is more than six months in the past, then a newer copy is probably available on the Internet.

A French translation of this document, by Bruno Cornec (cornec@stna7.stna.dgac.fr) is available at ftp://ftp.ibp.fr/pub2/linux/french/docs/HOWTO/.

A Japanese translation by Itsushi Minoura (minoura@uni.zool.s.u-tokyo.ac.jp) is available from http://jf.linux.or.jp/JF/JF.html/.

A Chinese translation (BIG-5 encoding) by Yung-kang Wu (yorkwu@ms4.hinet.net) is available from http://linux.ntcic.edu.tw/ yorkwu/linux/howto/cdrom/.

A Polish translation by Bartosz Maruszewski (b.maruszewski@zsmeie.torun.pl) is available from http://www.jtz.org.pl/Html/CDROM-HOWTO.pl.html.

Most translations of this and other Linux HOWTOs can also be found at http://sunsite.unc.edu/pub/Linux/docs/HOWTO/translations/ and ftp://sunsite.unc.edu/pub/Linux/docs/HOWTO/translations/.

If you make a translation of this document into another language, let me know and I'll include a reference to it here.

1.3 Feedback

I rely on you, the reader, to make this HOWTO useful. If you have any suggestions, corrections, or comments, please send them to me, jeff_tranter@pobox.com, and I will try to incorporate them in the next revision.

I am also willing to answer general questions on CD-ROM under Linux, as best I can. Before doing so, please read all of the information in this HOWTO, and then send me detailed information about the problem. Please do not ask me about using CD-ROM drives under operating systems other than Linux.

If you publish this document on a CD-ROM or in hardcopy form, a complimentary copy would be appreciated; mail me for my postal address. Also consider making a donation to the Linux Documentation Project to help support free documentation for Linux. Contact the Linux HOWTO coordinator, Greg Hankins (gregh@sunsite.unc.edu), for more information.

1.4 Distribution Policy

2 CD-ROM Technology

```
"CD-ROM is read-only memory, and audio compact disc system is
available as package-media of digital data for those purpose. For
playing audio CD, please insert Head-phone jack."
--- from a CD-ROM instruction manual
```

Don't Panic The world of CD-ROM technology is not as confusing as your instruction manual.

CD-ROM stands for "Compact Disc Read-Only Memory," a mass storage medium utilizing an optical laser to read microscopic pits on the aluminized layer of a polycarbonate disc. The same format is used for audio Compact Discs. Because of its high storage capacity, reliability, and low cost, CD-ROM has become an increasingly popular storage media.

The storage capacity of a CD-ROM disc is approximately 650 megabytes, equivalent to over 500 high density 3.5" floppy disks or roughly 250,000 typed pages.

First generation drives (known as **single speed**), provided a transfer rate of approximately 150 kilobytes per second. Hardware manufacturers then introduced double speed (300 kB/sec), quad speed (600 kB/sec), and higher. As I write this, 24 times (24X) drives are readily available and affordable.

Most CD-ROM drives use either the Small Computer Systems Interface (SCSI), ATAPI enhanced IDE interface, or a vendor proprietary interface. They also typically support playing audio CDs via an external headphone jack or line level output. Some CDs also allow reading the frames of data from audio CDs in digital form.

CD-ROMs are usually formatted with an ISO 9660 (formerly called "**High Sierra**)" file system. This format restricts filenames to the MS-DOS style (8+3 characters). The **Rock Ridge Extensions** use undefined fields in the ISO 9660 standard to support longer filenames and additional Unix style information (e.g., file ownership, symbolic links, etc.).

PhotoCD is a standard developed by Kodak for storing photographic images as digital data on a CD-ROM. With appropriate software, you can view the images on a computer, manipulate them, or send them to a printer. Information can be added to a PhotoCD at a later date; this is known as **multi-session** capability.

CD recorders (CD-R) are also available and are becoming increasingly affordable. They use a different media and specialized equipment for recording, but the resulting disc can be read by any CD-ROM drive.

In the future, CD-ROM drive vendors are expected to offer new technologies that will increase storage capacity by an order of magnitude.

3 Supported Hardware

This section lists the CD-ROM drivers and interfaces that are currently supported under Linux. The information here is based on the latest stable Linux kernel, which at time of writing was version 2.0.31. A development kernel (2.1.x versions) is also available but is not guaranteed to be stable.

This information is only valid for Linux on the Intel platform. Much of it should be applicable to Linux on other processor architectures, but I have no first hand experience or information.

3.1 ATAPI CD-ROM Drives

ATAPI (ATA Packet Interface) is a protocol for controlling mass storage devices. It builds on the ATA (AT Attachment) interface, the official ANSI standard name for the IDE interface developed for hard disk drives. ATAPI is commonly used for hard disks, CD-ROM drives, tape drives, and other devices. Currently the most popular type of interface, it offers most of the functionality of SCSI, without the need for an expensive controller or cables.

The Linux kernel has a device driver that should work with any ATAPI compliant CD-ROM drive. Vendors shipping compatible drives include Aztech, Mitsumi, NEC, Sony, Creative Labs, and Vertos. If you have recently purchased a CD-ROM drive, especially if it is quad speed or faster, it is almost guaranteed to be IDE/ATAPI.

3.2 SCSI CD-ROM Drives

SCSI (Small Computer Systems Interface) is a popular format for CD-ROM drives. Its chief advantages are a reasonably fast transfer rate, multi-device capability, and support on a variety of computer platforms. Some disadvantages of SCSI are the need for a relatively expensive controller card and cables.

Any SCSI CD-ROM drive with a block size of 512 or 2048 bytes should work under Linux; this includes the vast majority of CD-ROM drives on the market.

You will also need a supported SCSI controller card; see the SCSI HOWTO for more information on interface hardware.

Note that some CD-ROMs include a proprietary controller with a modified interface that is not fully SCSI compatible (e.g. it may not support adding other SCSI devices on the bus). These will most likely *not* work under Linux.

3.3 Proprietary CD-ROM Drives

Several CD-ROM drives using proprietary interfaces are available; the interface is often provided on a sound card. Simple interface cards equivalent to that provided on the sound card are also available. These drives generally tend to be lower in cost and smaller than SCSI drives. Their disadvantages are the lack of standardization and expandability.

Note that proprietary interfaces are sometimes erroneously referred to as IDE interfaces, because like IDE hard disks, they use a simple interface based on the PC/AT bus. To add to the confusion, some vendors, most notably Creative Labs, have shipped many different types of CD-ROM drives and have offered proprietary, SCSI, and ATAPI interfaces on their sound cards.

The table below lists the proprietary CD-ROM drives that are known to be supported under Linux. Drivers for additional devices may be available in the latest development kernels or as kernel patches. The latter can most often be found at `(ftp://sunsite.unc.edu/pub/Linux/kernel/patches/cdrom/)`. Also check the README files included with the kernel distribution, usually installed in `/usr/src/linux/Documentation/cdrom`, for the latest information.

Proprietary CD-ROM Drives

Vendor	Model	Kernel Driver	Notes
Panasonic	CR-521	sbpcd	Note 1
Panasonic	CR-522	sbpcd	Note 1
Panasonic	CR-523	sbpcd	Note 1
Panasonic	CR-562	sbpcd	Note 1
Panasonic	CR-563	sbpcd	Note 1
Creative Labs	CD-200	sbpcd	
IBM	External ISA	sbpcd	Note 2
Longshine	LCS-7260	sbpcd	
Teac	CD-55A	sbpcd	
Sony	CDU-31A	cdu31a	
Sony	CDU-33A	cdu31a	
Sony	CDU-535	sonycd535	Note 3
Sony	CDU-531	sonycd535	
Aztech	CDA268-01A	aztcd	Note 4
Orchid	CDS-3110	aztcd	
Okano/Wearnes	CDD110	aztcd	
Conrad	TXC	aztcd	
CyCDROM	CR520ie	aztcd	
CyCDROM	CR940ie	aztcd	
GoldStar	R420	gscd	Note 5
Philips/LMS	CM206	cm206	Note 6
Mitsumi	CRMC LU005S	mcd/mcdx	Note 7, 8
Mitsumi	FX001	mcd/mcdx	Note 7, 8
Optics Storage	Dolphin 8000AT	optcd	
Lasermate	CR328A	optcd	
Sanyo	H94A	sjcd	
various	various	isp16	Note 9
MicroSolutions	Backpack	bpcd	

Notes:

1. These drives may be sold under the names Creative Labs, Panasonic, Matsushita, or Kotobuki.
2. This drive is the same as a Panasonic CR-562.
3. May also be sold under the Procomm name.

4. This driver is for the CDA268-01A only. Other models, including the CDA268-03I and CDA269-031SE are not proprietary and should use the IDECD (ATAPI) kernel driver.

5. May also be sold as part of a Reveal Multimedia Kit.

6. The Philips CM205 is not supported by this driver, but there is a separate alpha release driver available from ftp://sunsite.unc.edu in /pub/Linux/kernel/patches/cdrom/lmscd0.4.tar.gz

7. May also be sold under the Radio Shack name.

8. There are two drivers available. "mcd" is the original one, and "mcdx" is a newer driver with more features (but possibly less stable).

9. This driver works with CD-ROM drives that are attached to the interface on an ISP16, MAD16 or Mozart sound card.

If a drive listed here is not supported by your kernel, you probably need to upgrade to a newer version.

If your drive is not one of the models listed here, particularly if it was bought recently and is quad speed or faster, it probably uses the IDE/ATAPI interface listed in a previous section.

◇ The single most common error among Linux CD-ROM users is to assume that any drive connected to a SoundBlaster card should use the SBPCD driver.

Creative Labs and most other vendors are no longer selling proprietary interface drives, they are following the standard ATAPI/IDE interface.

3.4 Parallel Port Drives

Some vendors sell CD-ROM drives that attach via a parallel port. The only drive of this type that is currently supported in the Linux kernel is the MicroSolutions Backpack.

Linux kernel drivers for several more of these drives are available separately as kernel patches or loadable modules. For the latest information check (`http://www.torque.net/linux-pp.html`).

3.5 Alternate Drivers

There is an alternate kernel driver available for Panasonic/Matsushita CR-56x drives written by Zoltan Vorosbaranyi. It can be found at (`ftp://ftp.tarki.hu/pub/linux/pcd/pcd-0.29.tar.gz`).

4 Installation

Installation of a CD-ROM under Linux consists of these steps:

1. Installing the hardware;
2. Configuring and building the Linux kernel;
3. Creating device files and setting boot time parameters;
4. Booting the Linux kernel;
5. Mounting the media.

The next sections will cover each of these steps in detail.

4.1 Installing the Hardware

Follow the manufacturer's instructions for installing the hardware or have your dealer perform the installation. The details will vary depending on whether the drive is internal or external and on the type of interface used. There are no special installation requirements for Linux. You may need to set jumpers on the drive and/or interface card for correct operation; some of the kernel drivers include README files that include this information.

As explained in the file `ide-cd`, ATAPI CD-ROMS should be jumpered as "single" or "master," and not "slave" when only one IDE device is attached to an interface (although this restriction is no longer enforced with recent kernels).

4.2 Configuring and Building the Kernel

When initially installing Linux from CD-ROM you will likely be using a boot and/or root disk provided as part of a Linux distribution. If possible, you should choose a boot disk with the kernel driver for your CD-ROM device type. If you cannot find a boot disk with the necessary CD-ROM driver, you have several options:

1. Install over a network;
2. Boot DOS, and install the Linux files onto your hard disk;
3. Boot DOS, and create a set of floppies to install Linux;
4. Find someone who can build you a boot disk with the needed CD-ROM driver.

The Linux Installation HOWTO http://sunsite.unc.edu/LDP/HOWTO/Installation-HOWTO.html has more information on installing Linux. If you purchased Linux on CD-ROM, it likely also came with some installation instructions (that little booklet inside the jewel case, or files on the CD).

Once Linux has initially been installed, most users will want to compile their own kernel, usually for one of these reasons:

- to support a CD-ROM drive or other hardware;
- to upgrade to a newer kernel release;
- to free up memory resources by minimizing the size of the kernel;

The Kernel HOWTO, http://sunsite.unc.edu/LDP/HOWTO/Kernel-HOWTO.html should be consulted for the details of building a kernel. I will just mention here some issues that are specific to CD-ROM drives.

Obviously, you need to compile in support for your CD-ROM drive when you do a `make config`.

If you have an ATAPI CD-ROM drive, you need to answer `yes` to the questions:

```
Enhanced IDE/MFM/RLL disk/cdrom/tape support (CONFIG_BLK_DEV_IDE) [Y/n/?]
Include IDE/ATAPI CDROM support (CONFIG_BLK_DEV_IDECD) [Y/n/?]
```

For SCSI CD-ROM drives, enable these options:

```
SCSI support (CONFIG_SCSI) [Y/n/m/?]
SCSI CD-ROM support (CONFIG_BLK_DEV_SR) [Y/n/m/?]
```

Also enable support for your SCSI host adapter when prompted, e.g.

```
Adaptec AHA152X support (CONFIG_SCSI_AHA152X) [Y/n/m/?]
```

For proprietary interface CD-ROM drives, enable the appropriate driver. You can use the table listed previously to determine the driver to use for your model.

Virtually all CD-ROMs use the ISO 9660 file system, so you must also enable:

```
ISO9660 cdrom filesystem support (CONFIG_ISO9660_FS) [Y/n/m/?]
```

Although not needed for CD-ROM operation, if you have a sound card that is supported under Linux you might want to enable and configure the kernel sound driver at this time as well. The Sound HOWTO http://sunsite.unc.edu/LDP/HOWTO/Sound-HOWTO.html can be a useful reference here.

You should then follow the usual procedure for building the kernel and installing it. Don't boot with the new kernel until you create the device files and set up any boot time parameters as described in the next section.

The ISO 9660 filesystem and almost all of the CD-ROM drivers can be built as loadable kernel modules. This scheme allows the kernel drivers to be loaded and unloaded without rebooting the kernel, freeing up memory. I recommend you get your CD-ROM installation running using compiled-in drivers first. How to use modules is described in the modules documentation and the Kernel HOWTO, http://sunsite.unc.edu/LDP/HOWTO/Kernel-HOWTO.html.

If a drive type listed here is not supported by your kernel, you likely need to upgrade to a newer version.

It is possible that you need to use a driver that is distributed separately from the kernel source code. This usually involves patching the kernel. Again, the Kernel HOWTO, http://sunsite.unc.edu/LDP/HOWTO/Kernel-HOWTO.html explains how to do this.

Note that there is a menu-based kernel configuration program invoked by `make menuconfig` and an X11-based graphical configuration invoked as `make xconfig`. All three configuration methods offer on-line help.

4.3 Creating Device Files and Setting Boot-time Parameters

The kernel uses device files to identify which device driver to use. If you are running a standard Linux distribution you may have created the necessary device files during installation. Under Slackware Linux, for example, there is a menu-based `setup` tool that includes CD-ROM setup, and most systems have a `/dev/MAKEDEV` script. If you don't use these methods, you can use the more manual procedure listed in this section. Even if you use either of these methods, it is recommended that you at least verify the device files against the information in this section.

You create the device file by running the shell commands indicated for your drive type. This should be done as user `root`. Note that some Linux distributions may use slightly different CD-ROM device names from those listed here.

It is recommended that you also create a symbolic link to the CD-ROM device to make it easier to remember. For example, for an IDE CD-ROM drive that is the second device on the secondary interface, the link would be created using

```
# ln -s /dev/hdd /dev/cdrom
```

If you want to play audio CDs, you will need to set the protection on the device file (the real file, not the symbolic link to it) to allow all users to read, e.g.

```
# chmod 664 /dev/hdd
# ls -l /dev/hdd
brw-rw-r--   1 root     disk      22,  64 Feb  4  1995 /dev/hdd
```

When booting Linux, the device drivers attempt to determine whether the appropriate devices are present, typically by probing specific addresses. Many of the drivers auto-probe at several addresses, but because of differences in configuration, possible device conflicts, and hardware limitations, the drivers sometimes need help identifying the addresses and other parameters. Most drivers support an option on the kernel command line to pass this information to the device driver. This can be done interactively, or more commonly, configured into your boot loader. With LILO, for example, you would add an `append` command such as the following to your `/etc/lilo.conf` file:

```
append = "sbpcd=0x230,SoundBlaster"
```

See the LILO documentation for more information.

In the next section I discuss issues specific to individual device drivers, including device files, boot parameters, and the capabilities of the different drivers. You probably only need to read the section relevant to your drive type. The README files are usually found in the directory `/usr/src/linux/Documentation/cdrom`.

4.3.1 Sbpcd Driver

```
      Principal author: Eberhard Moenkeberg (emoenke@gwdg.de)
 Multi-session support: yes (but not all drives)
Multiple drive support: yes
Loadable module support: yes
  Reading audio frames: yes (CR-562, CR-563, CD-200 only)
          Auto-probing: yes
           Device file: /dev/sbpcd, major 25
    Configuration file: sbpcd.h
  Kernel config option: Matsushita/Panasonic CDROM support?
           README file: sbpcd
```

This driver accepts a kernel command line of the form:

```
sbpcd=<io-address>,<interface-type>
```

where the first parameter is the base address of the device (e.g. 0x230), and <interface-type> is one of "SoundBlaster," "LaserMate," or "SPEA." See the file `sbpcd.h` for hints on what interface type to use. Using `sbpcd=0` disables auto-probing, disabling the driver.

The device file can be created using:

```
# mknod /dev/sbpcd b 25 0
```

Up to four drives per controller are supported. The next three drives on the first controller would use minor device numbers 1 through 3. If you have more than one controller, create devices with major numbers 26, 27, and 28, up to a maximum of 4 controllers (this is 16 CD-ROM drives in total; hopefully enough for most users.

See the file `sbpcd` for more information on this driver.

If you recently bought a CD-ROM drive, don't assume that if it connects to a SoundBlaster card it should use this kernel driver. Most CD-ROM drives being sold by Creative Labs are now EIDE/ATAPI drives.

4.3.2 Sonycdu535 Driver

```
      Principal author: Ken Pizzini (ken@halcyon.com)
  Multi-session support: no
 Multiple drive support: no
Loadable module support: yes
   Reading audio frames: no
           Auto-probing: no
            Device file: /dev/sonycd535, major 24
     Configuration file: sonycd535.h
   Kernel config option: Sony CDU535 CDROM support?
            README file: sonycd535
```

This driver accepts a kernel command line of the form:

```
sonycd535=<io-address>
```

where <io-address> is the base address of the controller (e.g. 0x320). Alternatively you can set the address in the file sonycd535.h and compile it in.

The device file can be created using:

```
# mknod /dev/sonycd535 b 24 0
```

Some Linux distributions use /dev/sonycd for this device. Older versions of the driver used major device number 21; make sure your device file is correct.

This driver was previously distributed as a patch but is now part of the standard kernel. See the file sonycd535 for more information on this driver.

4.3.3 Cdu31a Driver

```
      Principal author: Corey Minyard (minyard@-rch.cirr.com)
  Multi-session support: yes
 Multiple drive support: no
Loadable module support: yes
   Reading audio frames: yes
           Auto-probing: no
            Device file: /dev/cdu31a, major 15
     Configuration file: cdu31a.h
   Kernel config option: Sony CDU31A/CDU33A CDROM support?
            README file: cdu31a
```

This driver accepts a kernel command line of the form:

```
cdu31a=<io-address>,<interrupt>,PAS
```

The first number is the I/O base address of the card (e.g. 0x340). The second is the interrupt number to use (0 means to use polled I/O). The optional third parameter should be "PAS" if the drive is connected to a Pro-Audio Spectrum 16 sound card, otherwise left blank.

If the driver is loaded as a module, it uses a slightly different format. When loading the driver using the modprobe or insmod command, the parameters take the form:

```
cdu31a_port=<io-address> cdu31a_irq=<interrupt>
```

The base I/O-address is required while the interrupt number is optional.

The device file can be created using:

```
# mknod /dev/cdu31a b 15 0
```

See the file cdu31a for more information on this driver.

Also see the Web page put together by Jeffrey Oxenreider (zureal@infinet.com) that covers a lot of common problems with these drives. It can be found at (http://www.infinet.com/ zureal/cdu31a.html).

4.3.4 Aztcd Driver

```
      Principal author: Werner Zimmermann (zimmerma@rz.fht-esslingen.de)
 Multi-session support: yes
Multiple drive support: no
Loadable module support: yes
  Reading audio frames: no
          Auto-probing: no
           Device file: /dev/aztcd0, major 29
    Configuration file: aztcd.h
  Kernel config option: Aztech/Orchid/Okano/Wearnes (non IDE) CDROM support?
           README file: aztcd
```

This driver accepts a kernel command line of the form:

```
aztcd=<io-address>
```

where the parameter is the I/O base address of the card (e.g. 0x340).

The device file can be created using:

```
# mknod /dev/aztcd0 b 29 0
```

Note that this driver is for the CDA268-01A only. Other models, including the CDA268-03I and CDA269-031SE are not proprietary and should use the IDECD (ATAPI) kernel driver.

See the file aztcd for more information on this driver.

4.3.5 Gscd Driver

```
      Principal author: Oliver Raupach (raupach@nwfs1.rz.fh-hannover.de)
 Multi-session support: no
Multiple drive support: no
Loadable module support: yes
  Reading audio frames: no
          Auto-probing: no
           Device file: /dev/gscd0, major 16
    Configuration file: gscd.h
  Kernel config option: Goldstar R420 CDROM support?
           README file: gscd
```

This driver accepts a kernel command line of the form:

```
gscd=<io-address>
```

specifying the I/O base address of the card (e.g. 0x340).

The device file can be created using:

```
# mknod /dev/gscd0 b 16 0
```

See the file gscd and the World-Wide Web site (http://linux.rz.fh-hannover.de/ raupach/) for more information on this driver.

4.3.6 Mcd Driver

```
      Principal author: Martin  (martin@bdsi.com)
 Multi-session support: no
Multiple drive support: no
Loadable module support: yes
  Reading audio frames: no
          Auto-probing: no
           Device file: /dev/mcd, major 23
    Configuration file: mcd.h
  Kernel config option: Standard Mitsumi CDROM support?
           README file: mcd
```

This is the older driver for Mitsumi drivers that has been available for some time. You might want to try the newer `mcdx` driver, which has some new features but is possibly less stable.

This driver accepts a kernel command line of the form:

```
mcd=<io-address>,<irq>
```

specifying the I/O base address of the card (e.g. 0x340) and the IRQ request number used.

The device file can be created using:

```
# mknod /dev/mcd b 23 0
```

See the file `mcd` for more information on this driver.

4.3.7 Mcdx Driver

```
      Principal author: Heiko Schlittermann
  Multi-session support: yes
 Multiple drive support: yes
Loadable module support: yes
   Reading audio frames: no (not supported by hardware)
           Auto-probing: no
            Device file: /dev/mcdx0, major 20
     Configuration file: mcdx.h
   Kernel config option: Experimental Mitsumi support?
            README file: mcdx
```

This is a newer driver for Mitsumi drivers. The older and possibly more stable `mcd` driver is still available.

This driver accepts a kernel command line of the form:

```
mcdx=<io-address>,<irq>
```

specifying the I/O base address of the card (e.g. 0x340) and the IRQ request number used.

The device file can be created using:

```
# mknod /dev/mcdx0 b 20 0
```

If you recently bought a Mitsumi CD-ROM drive, don't assume that it should use this kernel driver. Some Mitsumi models are now EIDE/ATAPI drives and should use the idecd kernel driver.

See the file `mcdx` for more information on this driver.

4.3.8 Cm206 Driver

```
      Principal author: David A. van Leeuwen (david@tm.tno.)
  Multi-session support: yes
 Multiple drive support: no
Loadable module support: yes
   Reading audio frames: no
           Auto-probing: yes
            Device file: /dev/cm206cd, major 32
     Configuration file: cm206.h
   Kernel config option: Philips/LMS CM206 CDROM support?
            README file: cm206
```

The driver accepts a kernel command line of the form:

```
cm206=<io-address>,<interrupt>
```

where the first number is the I/O base address of the card (e.g. 0x340). The second is the interrupt channel.

The device file can be created using:

```
# mknod /dev/cm206cd b 32 0
```

See the file `cm206` for more information on this driver.

4.3.9 Optcd Driver

```
    Principal author: Leo Spiekman (spiekman@dutette.et.tudelft.nl)
  Multi-session support: yes
 Multiple drive support: no
Loadable module support: yes
   Reading audio frames: no
          Auto-probing: no
           Device file: /dev/optcd0, major 17
    Configuration file: optcd.h
  Kernel config option: Experimental Optics Storage ... CDROM support?
           README file: optcd
```

The driver accepts a kernel command line of the form

```
optcd=<io-address>
```

to specify the I/O base address of the card (e.g. 0x340).

The device file can be created using:

```
# mknod /dev/optcd0 b 17 0
```

See the file `optcd` for more information on this driver.

4.3.10 Sjcd Driver

```
    Principal author: Vadim V. Model (vadim@rbrf.msk.su)
  Multi-session support: no
 Multiple drive support: no
Loadable module support: yes
   Reading audio frames: no
          Auto-probing: no
           Device file: /dev/sjcd, major 18
    Configuration file: sjcd.h
  Kernel config option: Experimental Sanyo H94A CDROM support?
           README file: sjcd
```

The driver accepts a kernel command line of the form:

```
sjcd=<io-address>,<interrupt>,<dma>
```

indicating the base address, interrupt, and DMA channel to be used (e.g. sjcd=0x340,10,5).

The device file can be created using:

```
# mknod /dev/sjcd b 18 0
```

See the file `sjcd` for more information on this driver.

4.3.11 Bpcd Driver

```
    Principal author: Grant R. Guenther (grant@torque.net)
  Multi-session support: unknown
 Multiple drive support: no
Loadable module support: yes
   Reading audio frames: no
          Auto-probing: yes
           Device file: /dev/bpcd, major 41
    Configuration file: bpcd.h
  Kernel config option: MicroSolutions backpack CDROM support?
           README file: bpcd
```

The driver accepts a kernel command line of the form:

```
bpcd=<io-address>
```

indicating the base address to be used (e.g. bpcd=0x3bc).

The device file can be created using:

```
# mknod /dev/bpcd b 41 0
```

This driver is included with the 2.1 kernel source distribution. See the file bpcd for more information on this driver.

4.3.12 SCSI Driver

```
      Principal author: David Giller
 Multi-session support: yes (depending on drive)
Multiple drive support: yes
Loadable module support: yes
  Reading audio frames: no
          Auto-probing: yes
           Device file: /dev/scd0, major 11
    Configuration file: cdrom.h
  Kernel config option: SCSI CDROM support?
           README file: none
```

There are kernel command line option specific to each type of SCSI controller. See the SCSI HOWTO for more information.

Multiple drives are supported (up to the limit of the maximum number of devices on the SCSI bus). Create device files with major number 11 and minor numbers starting at zero:

```
# mknod /dev/scd0 b 11 0
# mknod /dev/scd1 b 11 1
```

While the kernel driver itself does not support reading digital audio frames, some SCSI drives have the capability and will work with the cdda2wav program (which uses the generic SCSI kernel interface).

4.3.13 IDECD Driver

```
      Principal author: Scott Snyder (snyder@fnald0.fnal.gov)
 Multi-session support: yes
Multiple drive support: yes
Loadable module support: no
  Reading audio frames: yes (on supported drives)
          Auto-probing: yes
           Device file: /dev/hd{a,b,c,d},  major 22
    Configuration file: cdrom.h
  Kernel config option: Include support for IDE/ATAPI Cd-ROMs?
           README file: ide-cd
```

This is the driver for ATAPI CD-ROMs. The driver accepts a kernel command line of the form

```
hdx=cyls,heads,sects,wpcom,irq
  or
hdx=cdrom
```

where hdx can be any of {hda,hdb,hdc,hdd}, or simply hd, for the "next" drive in sequence. Only the first three parameters are required (cyls,heads,sects). For example hdc=1050,32,64 hdd=cdrom.

Getting the IDE driver to recognize your CD-ROM drive can be tricky, especially if you have more than 2 devices or more than one IDE controller. Usually all that is required is to pass the right command line options from LILO. The file /usr/src/linux/Documentation/ide-cd explains how to do this. Read it carefully.

Recent Linux kernels have better support for multiple IDE devices. If you have problems with an older kernel, upgrading may help.

Some IDE controllers have hardware problems which the kernel driver can work around. You may need to pass additional parameters to the driver to enable this. See the documentation for details.

4.4 Booting the Linux Kernel

You can now reboot with the new kernel. Watch for a message such as the following indicating that the CD-ROM has been found by the device driver (the message will vary depending on the drive type):

```
hdd: NEC CD-ROM DRIVE:282, ATAPI CDROM drive
```

If the boot-up messages scroll by too quickly to read, you should be able to retrieve them using dmesg or tail /var/adm/messages.

If the drive is not found, then a problem has occurred, See the section on troubleshooting.

4.5 Mounting, Unmounting, and Ejecting Devices

To mount a CD-ROM, insert a disc in the drive, and run the mount command as root (this assumes you created a symbolic link to your device file as recommended above and that an empty directory /mnt/cdrom exists):

```
# mount -t iso9660 -r /dev/cdrom /mnt/cdrom
```

The CD can now be accessed under the directory /mnt/cdrom.

There are other options to the mount command that you may wish to use; see the mount(8) man page for details.

You can add an entry to /etc/fstab to automatically mount a CD-ROM when Linux boots or to specify parameters to use when it is mounted; see the fstab(5) man page.

Note that to play audio CDs you should *not* try to mount them.

To unmount a CD-ROM, use the umount command as root:

```
# umount /mnt/cdrom
```

The disc can only be unmounted if no processes are currently accessing the drive (including having their default directory set to the mounted drive). You can then eject the disc. Most drives have an eject button; there is also a standalone eject program that allows ejecting CD-ROMs under software control.

Note that you should not eject a disc while it is mounted (this may or may not be possible depending on the type of drive). Some CD-ROM drivers can automatically eject a CD-ROM when it is unmounted and insert the CD tray when a disc is mounted (you can turn this feature off when compiling the kernel or by using a software command).

Its possible that after playing an audio CD you may not be able to mount a CD-ROM. You need to send a CD audio "stop" command (using a CD player program) before trying the mount. This problem only appears to occur with the SBPCD driver.

Stephen Tweedie (sct@dcs.ed.ac.uk) has written the Supermount package which provides transparent mounting of removable media including CD-ROM. You can find it at ftp://sunsite.unc.edu/pub/Linux/patches/diskdrives/.

4.6 Troubleshooting

If you still encounter problems after following the instructions in the HOWTO, here are some things to check. The checks are listed in increasing order of complexity. If a check fails, solve the problem before moving to the next stage.

4.6.1 Step 1: Make sure you are really running the kernel you compiled

You can check the date stamp on the kernel to see if you are running the one that you compiled with CD-ROM support. You can do this with the uname command:

```
% uname -a
Linux fizzbin 2.0.18 #1 Fri Sep 6 10:10:54 EDT 1996 i586
```

or by displaying the file /proc/version:

```
% cat /proc/version
Linux version 2.0.18 (root@fizzbin) (gcc version 2.7.2) #1 Fri Sep 6 10:10:54 EDT 1996
```

If the date stamp doesn't seem to match when you compiled the kernel, then you are running an old kernel. Did you really reboot? If you use LILO, did you re-install it (typically by running /sbin/lilo)? If booting from floppy, did you create a new boot floppy and use it when booting?

4.6.2 Step 2: Make sure the proper kernel drivers are compiled in

You can see what drivers are compiled in by looking at /proc/devices:

```
% cat /proc/devices
Character devices:
 1 mem
 2 pty
 3 ttyp
 4 ttyS
 5 cua
```

```
  7 vcs

Block devices:
  3 ide0
 22 ide1
```

First look for your CD-ROM device driver. These are all block devices, in this case we can see that the `idecd` driver with major number 22 was present.

Also make sure that ISO 9660 filesystem support was compiled in, by looking at `/proc/filesystems`:

```
% cat /proc/filesystems
        ext2
        msdos
nodev   proc
        iso9660
```

You can also see what I/O port addresses are being used by a driver with the file `/proc/ioports`:

```
howto % cat /proc/ioports
  ...
0230-0233 : sbpcd
  ...
```

If any of the drivers you thought you compiled in are not displayed, then something went wrong with the kernel configuration or build. Start the installation process again, beginning with configuration and building of the kernel.

4.6.3 Step 3: Did the kernel detect your drive during booting?

Make sure that the CD-ROM device was detected when the kernel booted. You should have seen a message on boot up. If the messages scrolled off the screen, you can usually recall them using the `dmesg` command:

```
% dmesg
```

or

```
% tail /var/adm/messages
```

If your drive was not found then something is wrong. Make sure it is powered on and all cables are connected. If your drive has hardware jumpers for addressing, check that they are set correctly (e.g. drive 0 if you have only one drive). ATAPI CD-ROMS must be jumpered as “single” or “master,” and not “slave” when only one IDE device is attached to an interface. If the drive works under MS-DOS, then you can be reasonably confident that the hardware is working.

Many kernel drivers using auto-probing, but some do not, and in any case the probing is not always reliable. Use the kernel command line option listed for your kernel driver type. You may want to try several different values if you are not sure of the I/O address or other parameters. LILO can be (and usually is) configured to allow you to enter the parameters manually when booting.

Another possibility is that you used the wrong kernel driver for your CD-ROM driver. Some documentation may refer to proprietary interfaces as IDE, leading some to mistakenly believe they are ATAPI drives.

Another possibility is that your drive (or interface card) is one of the "compatible" type that requires initialization by the DOS driver. Try booting DOS and loading the vendor supplied DOS device driver. Then soft boot Linux using `Control-Alt-Delete`.

If your drive is not listed in this document, it is possible that there are no drivers for it available under Linux. You can check with some of the references listed at the end of this document for assistance.

4.6.4 Step 4: Can you read data from the drive?

Try reading from the CD-ROM drive. Typing the following command should cause the drive activity light (if present) to come on and no errors should be reported. Use whatever device file is appropriate for your drive and make sure a CD-ROM is inserted; use Control-C to exit.

```
# dd if=/dev/cdrom of=/dev/null bs=2048
^C
124+0 records in
124+0 records out
```

If this works, then the kernel is communicating with the drive and you can move on to step 5.

If not, then a possible cause is the device file. Make sure than the device file in the `/dev` directory has the correct major and minor numbers as listed previously for your drive type. Check that the permissions on the device file allow reading and writing.

A remote possibility is a hardware problem. Try testing the drive under DOS, if possible, to determine if this could be the case.

4.6.5 Step 5: Can you mount the drive?

If you can read from the drive but cannot mount it, first verify that you compiled in ISO 9660 file system support by reading `/proc/filesystems`, as described previously.

Make sure you are mounting the drive with the `-t iso9660` and `-r` options and that a known good ISO 9660 CD-ROM (not Audio CD) is inserted in the drive. You normally must mount drives as user `root`.

Make sure that the mount point exists and is an empty directory.

If you are automatically mounting the CD-ROM on boot up, make sure that you have correct entries in the `/etc/fstab` file.

If you are running the syslog daemon, there may be error messages from the kernel that you are not seeing. Try using the `dmesg` command:

```
% dmesg
SBPCD: sbpcd_open: no disk in drive
```

There may also be errors logged to files in `/var/adm`, depending on how your system is configured.

4.6.6 Debugging Audio Problems

If the drive works with CD-ROMs, but not for playing audio CDs, here are some possible solutions.

You need an application program to play audio CDs. Some applications may be broken or may not be compatible with your drive. Try other applications and/or try recompiling them yourself. A good place to look for software is `(ftp://sunsite.unc.edu/pub/Linux/apps/sound/cdrom/)`.

A few of the CD-ROM drivers do not support playing Audio CDs. Check the README file or source code to see if that is the case.

Check if the audio can be played through the headphone jack. If so, then the problem is likely related to your sound card. Use a mixer program to set the input device and volume levels. Make sure you have installed an audio cable from the CD-ROM drive to the sound card. Make sure that the kernel sound card driver is installed and working (see the Sound HOWTO).

4.6.7 When All Else Fails

If you still have problems, here are some final suggestions for things to try:

- carefully re-read this HOWTO document;
- read the references listed at the end of this document, especially the relevant kernel source README files;
- post a question to one of the `comp.os.linux` or other Usenet newsgroups;
- send a question to the Linux mailing list;
- try using the latest Linux kernel;
- contact your computer dealer;
- contact the CD-ROM manufacturer;
- send mail to the maintainer of the relevant kernel driver (look in the file `/usr/src/linux/MAINTAINERS`);
- send mail to me;
- fire up Emacs and type `Esc-x doctor`.

5 Applications

This section briefly lists some of the key applications related to CD-ROM that are available under Linux. Check the Linux Software Map for the latest versions and archive sites.

5.1 Audio CD Players

Several programs are available for playing audio CDs, either through a headphone jack or an attached sound card.

Workman
: A graphical player running under X11 and supporting a CD database and many other features.

WorkBone
: An interactive text-mode player.

xcdplayer
: A simple X11 based player.

cdplayer
: A very simple command line based player.

Xmcd
: An X11/Motif based player.

xmitsumi
: Another X11 based player for Mitsumi drives.

xplaycd
: Another X11 based player, bundled with sound mixer and VU meter programs.

cdtool
: Command line tools for playing audio CDs.

Some of these programs are coded to use a specific device file for the CD-ROM (e.g. `/dev/cdrom`). You may be able to pass the correct device name as a parameter, or you can create a symbolic link in the `/dev` directory. If sending the CD output to a sound card, you may wish to use a mixer program to set volume settings or select the CD-ROM input for recording.

5.2 PhotoCD

PhotoCDs use an ISO 9660 file system containing image files in a proprietary format. Not all CD-ROM drives support reading PhotoCDs.

The `hpcdtoppm` program by Hadmut Danisch converts PhotoCD files to the portable pixmap format. It can be obtained from `(ftp://ftp.gwdg.de/pub/linux/hpcdtoppm)` or as part of the PBM (portable bit map) utilities, available on many archive sites (look for "pbm" or "netpbm").

The `photocd` program by Gerd Knorr kraxel@cs.tu-berlin.de can convert PhotoCD images into Targa or Windows and OS/2 bitmap files.

The same author has written the program `xpcd`, an X11-based program for handling PhotoCD images. You can select the images with a mouse, preview the image in a small window, and load the image with any of the five possible resolutions. You can also mark a part of the Image and load only the selected part. Look for these packages at `(ftp://ftp.cs.tu-berlin.de/pub/linux/Local/misc/)`.

The ImageMagick image file manipulation program also supports PhotoCD files. It is available from `(ftp://ftp.x.org/contrib/applications/ImageMagick/)`.

5.3 Mkisofs

Eric Youngdale's mkisofs package allows creating an ISO 9660 file system on a hard disk partition. This can then be used to assist in creating and testing CD-ROM file systems before mastering discs.

The tools for actually writing data to writable CD-ROM drives tend to be vendor specific. They also require writing the data with no interruptions, so a multitasking operating system like Linux is not particularly well suited.

5.4 ISO 9660 Utilities

These are some utilities for verifying the format of ISO 9660 formatted discs; you may find them useful for testing suspect CDs. The package can be found at `(ftp://ftp.cdrom.com/pub/cdrom/ptf/)`. They were written by Bill Siegmund and Rich Morin.

6 Answers to Frequently Asked Questions

6.1 How can a non-root user mount and unmount discs?

Most mount commands support the user option. If you make an entry such as the following in /etc/fstab:

```
/dev/sbpcd  /mnt/cdrom   iso9660     user,noauto,ro
```

then an ordinary user will be allowed to mount and unmount the drive using these commands:

```
% mount /mnt/cdrom
% umount /mnt/cdrom
```

The disc will be mounted with some options that help enforce security (e.g. programs cannot executed, device files are ignored); in some cases this may be too restrictive.

Another method is to get the usermount package which allows non-root users to mount and unmount removable devices such as floppies and CD-ROMs, but restricts access to other devices (such as hard disk partitions). It is available on major archive sites.

The archive site ftp.cdrom.com has the source file mount.c which allows mounting an unmounting of CD-ROMs (only) by normal users. It runs as a setuid executable.

6.2 Why do I get device is busy when unmounting a CD-ROM?

The disc cannot be unmounted if any processes are accessing the drive, including having their default directory set to the mounted filesystem. If you cannot identify the processes using the disc, you can use the fuser command, as shown in the following example.

```
% umount /cdrom
umount: /dev/hdd: device is busy
% fuser -v /cdrom
                         USER       PID ACCESS COMMAND
/mnt/cdrom               tranter    133 ..c..  bash
```

6.3 How do I export a CD-ROM to other hosts over NFS?

You need to add an entry to the /etc/exports file. Users on other machines will then be able to mount the device. See the exports(5) man page for details.

6.4 Can I boot Linux from a CD-ROM?

When initially installing Linux the most common method is to use a boot floppy. Some distributions allow booting a Linux kernel on CD directly from DOS.

Michael Fulbright (msf@redhat.com) reports that with the right CD-ROM, ROM BIOS, and ATAPI CD-ROM drive it is possible to boot directly from CD. The latest version of mkisofs also supports creating such disks. He has added some patches to support the El Torito standard for bootable CDs.

6.5 How can I read digital data from audio CDs?

Heiko Eissfeldt (heiko@colossus.escape.de) and Olaf Kindel have written a utility that reads audio data and saves it as .wav format sound files. The package is called cdda2wav.tar.gz and can be found on sunsite.unc.edu.

Because CD-ROM drives are changing very quickly, it is difficult to list which models support reading digital data. You best bet is to get the latest cdda2wav package and read the documentation.

For more information on this subject, see the web site http://www.tardis.ed.ac.uk/ psyche/cdda/ and the alt.cd-rom FAQ listed in the references section.

6.6 Why doesn't the find command work properly?

On ISO 9660 formatted discs without the Rock Ridge Extensions, you need to add the -noleaf option to the find command. See find(1) for details.

(In my experience, virtually all recent Linux CDs use the Rock Ridge extensions, so this problem should occur very rarely.)

6.7 Does Linux support any recordable CD-ROM drives?

The X-CD-Roast package for Linux is a graphical front-end for using CD writers. The package can be found at sunsite.unc.edu in /pub/Linux/utils/disk-management/xcdroast-0.95.tar.gz

Also see the Linux CD-Writing HOWTO document, found at

```
ftp://sunsite.unc.edu/pub/Linux/docs/HOWTO/CD-Writing.html
```

or

```
http://sunsite.unc.edu/LDP/HOWTO/CD-Writing.html
```

6.8 Why do I get mount: Read-only file system when mounting a CD-ROM?

CD-ROM is a read-only media. With some early kernels you could mount a CD-ROM for read/write; attempts to write data to the CD would simple be ignored. As of kernel version 1.1.33 this was corrected so that CD-ROMs must be mounted read only (e.g. using the `-r` option to mount).

6.9 Why does the disc tray open when I shut down the system?

As of the 1.1.38 kernel, the sbpcd driver ejects the CD when it is unmounted. If you shut down the system, a mounted CD will be unmounted, causing it to eject.

This feature is for convenience when changing discs. If the tray is open when you mount or read a CD, it will also automatically be closed.

I found that this caused problems with a few programs (e.g. cdplay and workbone). As of the 1.1.60 kernel you can control this feature under software control. A sample program is included in the sbpcd documentation file (or use the eject program).

6.10 I have a "special" CD that can't be mounted

The "special" CD is likely an XA disc (like all Photo CDs or "one-offs" created using CD-R drives). Most of the Linux kernel CD-ROM drivers do not support XA discs, although you may be able to find a patch to add support on one of the archive sites.

The sbpcd driver supports XA. If you are using this driver you can determine if the disc is XA using the following procedure: go into the file `sbpcd.c` and enable the display of the "Table of Contents" (DBG_TOC). Build and install the new kernel and boot from it. During each mount the TOC info will be written (either to the console or to a log file). If the first displayed value in the TOC header line is "20," then it is an XA disc. That byte is "00" with normal disks. If the TOC display shows different tracks, that is also a sign that it is an XA disc.

(Thanks to Eberhard Moenkeberg for the above information.)

Other possibilities for unreadable CDs are:

1. The disc doesn't use an ISO 9660 file system (e.g. some use SunOS or HFS);
2. It is an audio CD;
3. The CD is damaged or defective;
4. You put it in the drive upside down.

6.11 Do multi-platter CD-ROM drives work with Linux?

Several users have reported success with SCSI multi-disc CD-ROM changers. You probably need to enable the "Probe all LUNs on each SCSI device" kernel configuration option. At least one user also had to increase a SCSI timeout value in the kernel driver. The Nakamichi MBR-7 7 disc changer and Pioneer 12 disc changer have been reported to work.

EIDE/ATAPI multi-disc changers are also available. The 2.0 kernel has rudimentary support for some drives using the CDROM_SELECT_DISC ioctl function. The IDE-CD kernel driver documentation file includes source code for a program to select changer slots, or you can use a recent version of the `eject` program described earlier.

6.12 I get "`/cdrom: Permission denied`" errors

Some CDs have root directory file permissions that only allow user `root` to read them. The March 1995 InfoMagic CD set is one example. This is a real inconvenience.

The following patch, courtesy of Christoph Lameter (clameter@waterf.org) patches the kernel to get around this problem.

```
From: clameter@waterf.org (Christoph Lameter)
Newsgroups: comp.os.linux.setup
Subject: InfoMagic Developers Set: Fix for CD-ROM permissions
Date: 12 Apr 1995 20:32:03 -0700
Organization: The Water Fountain - Mining for streams of Living Water
NNTP-Posting-Host: waterf.org
X-Newsreader: TIN [version 1.2 PL2]

The March 1995 Edition of the InfoMagic Developers CD-ROM Set has
problems because the information stored in the root directory
permissions is causing the following problems with using the CDs

1. Disc1 will always have the owner/group of 5101/51 and has write
access allowed (?)

2. Disc2 and 3 have rwx set for root and no rights at all for any
other group/user. These discs cannot be accessed from any user other
than root! I run a BBS and I need to make them accessible for download
by others.

I have seen several fixes to this problem already floating
around. Trouble is that these fixes usually change the rights for ALL
directories on the CD. This fix here changes ONLY the rights for the
root directory of the CD-ROM. If you want to run parts of Linux
directly off the CD you might run into trouble if all directories are
readable for everyone and if they are all owned by root.

This fix will set the rights for the root directory to r-xr-xr-x and
the owner/group to the values indicated in the uid and gid options to
the mount command.

To apply:
 cd /usr/src/linux/fs/isofs
 patch <**THIS MESSAGE**

and recompile kernel (you may have to fix up the patch by hand
depending on your kernel version).

This fix should probably be incorporated into the kernel. What business
does data on a CD have to mess around with the permissions/owners of the
mount-point anyways?

--- inode.c.ORIG        Wed Apr 12 17:24:36 1995
+++ inode.c     Wed Apr 12 17:59:12 1995
@@ -552,7 +552,15 @@
    these numbers in the inode structure. */

        if (!high_sierra)
-           parse_rock_ridge_inode(raw_inode, inode);
+       {  parse_rock_ridge_inode(raw_inode, inode);
+          /* check for access to the root directory rights/owner CL */
+            if((inode->i_sb->u.isofs_sb.s_firstdatazone) == inode->i_ino)
+             { /* Change owner/rights to the ones demanded by the mount command */
+                inode->i_uid = inode->i_sb->u.isofs_sb.s_uid;
+                inode->i_gid = inode->i_sb->u.isofs_sb.s_gid;
+              inode->i_mode = S_IRUGO | S_IXUGO | S_IFDIR;
+             }
+       }
```

```
 #ifdef DEBUG
        printk("Inode: %x extent: %x\n",inode->i_ino, inode->u.isofs_i.i_first_extent);
@@ -805,4 +813,3 @@
 }

 #endif
-
```

Note that the above patch is somewhat old and probably won't apply cleanly against recent 2.0 kernels. Also see the related question on hidden files later in this document.

6.13 How do I interpret IDE CD kernel error messages?

What does it mean when I get a kernel message from the IDE CD-ROM driver like

```
hdxx:  code:  xx key:  x asc:  xx ascq:  x
```

This is an status or error message from the IDE CD-ROM drive. By default the IDECD driver prints out the raw information instead of wasting kernel space with error messages. You can change the default to display the actual error messages by going into /usr/src/linux/drivers/block/ide-cd.c, changing the value of VERBOSE_IDE_CD_ERRORS to 1, and recompiling the kernel.

6.14 How can I tell what speed CD-ROM I have?

Here's one way. This command measures how long is takes to read 1500K of data from CD:

```
% time -p dd if=/dev/cdrom of=/dev/null bs=1k count=1500
1500+0 records in
1500+0 records out
real 5.24
user 0.03
sys 5.07
```

The transfer rate of single speed drives is 150 kilobytes per second, which should take about 10 seconds. At double speed it would take five seconds, quad speed would take 2.5, etc.

The "real" time above is probably the best number to look at—in this case it indicates a double speed drive. You can increase the amount of data transferred to get a more accurate value (in case you were wondering, the data does not get cached). You should probably run the command a few times and take the average.

6.15 My CD-ROM stopped working after Linux was installed

The usual symptom is that the boot disk used to initially install Linux recognized your CD-ROM drive, but after Linux was installed on the hard drive or floppy and rebooted it no longer recognizes the CD-ROM.

The most common reason for this problem is that with some Linux distributions the kernel that is installed on your hard drive (or floppy) is not necessarily the same one that was on your boot disk. You selected a boot disk that matched your CD-ROM hardware, while the kernel you installed is a "generic" kernel that is lacking CD-ROM support. You can verify this by following the troubleshooting guidelines discussed previously in this document (e.g. start by checking /proc/devices).

The solution is to recompile the kernel, ensuring that the drivers for your CD-ROM drive and any others that are needed (e.g. SCSI controller, ISO 9660 file system) are included. See the Kernel HOWTO, http://sunsite.unc.edu/LDP/HOWTO/Kernel-HOWTO.html if you don't know how to do this.

If you passed any command line options to the boot disk (e.g. hdc=cdrom) you need to add these to your boot program configuration file (typically /etc/lilo.conf).

6.16 There are "hidden" files on a CD which I can't read

Some CDs have files with the "hidden" bit set on them. Normally these files are not visible. If you mount the CD with the "unhide" option then the files should be accessible (this doesn't seem to be documented anywhere).

6.17 Where is the CD-ROM API documented?

If you want to write your own application, such as an audio CD player program, you will need to understand the application programming interface (API) provided by Linux.

Originally the CD-ROM kernel drivers used their own ioctl() functions to support features specific to each drive. Header files such as `/usr/include/linux/sbpcd.h` describe these. Because many of the drivers were based on other drivers, the interfaces, while not identical, have a lot in common.

More recently there has been an initiative headed by David van Leeuwen (david@tm.tno.nl) to standardize the API for CD-ROM drives, putting common code in one place and ensuring that all drivers exhibit the same behaviour. This is documented in the file

```
/usr/src/linux/Documentation/cdrom/cdrom-standard.tex
```

Several kernel drivers support this. I expect that by the next major kernel release (maybe 3.0) all CD-ROM drivers will conform to this API.

My book, *Linux Multimedia Guide*, goes into quite a bit of detail on how to program CD-ROM drives, especially for audio functions. See the end of the References section.

6.18 Why don't I see long filenames on this Windows CD-ROM?

If you have a CD-ROM which has long filenames under Windows but not under Linux, it may be formatted using Microsoft's proprietary Joliet filesystem. See the next question for a solution.

6.19 Is Microsoft's Joliet filesystem supported?

Microsoft has created an extension to the ISO CD-ROM format called Joliet. At the time of writing, support for Joliet was in progress and patches were available from

```
http://www-plateau.cs.berkeley.edu/people/chaffee/joliet.html
```

or

```
ftp://www-plateau.cs.berkeley.edu/pub/multimedia/linux/joliet/
```

7 References

I have already mentioned the README files, typically installed in

```
/usr/src/linux/Documentation/cdrom
```

These can be a gold mine of useful information.

The following USENET FAQs are posted periodically to news.answers and archived at Internet FTP sites such as `(ftp://rtfm.mit.edu/)`:

- alt.cd-rom FAQ;
- comp.periphs.scsi FAQ;
- Enhanced IDE/Fast-ATA/ATA-2 FAQ;

Several other Linux HOWTOs have useful information relevant to CD-ROM:

- *SCSI HOWTO* `(http://sunsite.unc.edu/LDP/HOWTO/SCSI-HOWTO.html)`;
- *Hardware Compatibility HOWTO* `(http://sunsite.unc.edu/LDP/HOWTO/Hardware-HOWTO.html)`;
- *Sound HOWTO* `(http://sunsite.unc.edu/LDP/HOWTO/Sound-HOWTO.html)`;
- *Kernel HOWTO* `(http://sunsite.unc.edu/LDP/HOWTO/Kernel-HOWTO.html)`;
- *Distribution HOWTO* `(http://sunsite.unc.edu/LDP/HOWTO/Distribution-HOWTO.html)`;
- *CD Writing HOWTO* `(http://sunsite.unc.edu/LDP/HOWTO/CD-Writing.html)`.

At least a dozen companies sell Linux distributions on CD-ROM; most of them are listed in the Distribution HOWTO.

The following Usenet news groups cover CD-ROM related topics:

- comp.publish.cdrom.hardware;
- comp.publish.cdrom.multimedia;
- comp.publish.cdrom.software;
- comp.sys.ibm.pc.hardware.cd-rom;

- alt.cd-rom;
- alt.cd-rom.reviews.

The `comp.os.linux` newsgroups are also good sources of Linux specific information.
There is a large archive of CD-ROM information and software at

`ftp://ftp.cdrom.com/pub/cdrom/`

A FAQ document on IDE and ATA devices can be found at

`ftp://rtfm.mit.edu/pub/usenet/news.answers/pc-hardware-faq/enhanced-IDE/`

and at

`http://www.seagate.com/techsuppt/faq/faqlist.html`

Western Digital, the company that started the IDE protocol, has information available on the IDE protocol available on their FTP site at

`ftp://fission.dt.wdc.com/pub/standards/atapi`

A Web site dedicated to multimedia can be found at `(http://viswiz.gmd.de/MultimediaInfo/)`. Creative Labs has a Web site at `(http://www.creaf.com/)`.

The Linux Documentation Project has produced several books on Linux, including *Linux Installation and Getting Started*. These are freely available by anonymous FTP from major Linux archive sites or can be purchased in hardcopy format.

The *Linux Software Map* (LSM) is an invaluable reference for locating Linux software. The LSM can be found on various anonymous FTP sites, including `(ftp://sunsite.unc.edu/pub/Linux/docs/LSM/)`.

The Linux mailing list has a number of "channels" dedicated to different topics. To find out how to join, send a mail message with the word "help" as the message body to majordomo@vger.rutgers.edu (Note: at time of writing these mailing lists were severely overloaded and a replacement was being sought).

Finally, a shameless plug: If you want to learn a lot more about multimedia under Linux (especially CD-ROM and sound card applications and programming), check out my book *Linux Multimedia Guide*, ISBN 1-56592-219-0, published by O'Reilly and Associates. As well as the original English version, French and Japanese translations are now in print. For details, call 800-998-9938 in North America or check the Web page `(http://www.ora.com/catalog/multilinux/noframes.html)` or my home page,http://www.pobox.com/~tranter/.

Part XIV

"Linux Cyrillic HOWTO" by Alexander L. Belikoff, abel@bfr.co.il

Contents

Abstract

v3.15, 14 November 1997 This document describes how to set up your Linux box to typeset, view, and print the documents in the Russian language.

1 General notes

1.1 Introduction

This document covers the things you need to successfully typeset, view, and print documents in Russian under Linux. Although this document assumes you're using Linux as an operating system, most of information presented is equally applicable to many other Unix flavors. I shall try to keep the distinction as visible as possible.

There are a number of popular Linux distributions. As an example system I describe the Red Hat 3.0.3 Linux (Picasso) and the Red Hat 4.1 Linux (Vanderbildt)—the one I am personally using. Nevertheless, I shall try to highlight the differences, if they exist, in the Slackware Linux setup.

Since such setup directly modifies and extends the Operating System, you should understand, what you are doing. Even though I tried to keep things as easy as possible, having some experience with a given piece of software is an advantage. I am not going to describe what the X Window System is or how to typeset the documents with TEX and LATEX, or how to install printer in Linux. Those issues are covered in other documents.

For the same reason, in most cases I describe a system-wide setup, by default requiring root privileges. Still, if there is a possibility for user-level setup, I'll try to mention it.

NOTE: The X Window System, TEX, and other Linux components are complex systems with a sophisticated configuration. If you do something wrong, you can not only fail with Russian setup, but to break the component as well, if not the entire system. This is not to scare you off, but merely to make you understand the seriousness of the process and be careful. Preliminary backup of the configuration files is *highly* recommended. Having a guru around is also advantageous.

1.2 Availability and feedback

This document is available at sunsite.unc.edu or tsx-11.mit.edu as a part of the Linux Document Project. Also, it may be available at various FTP sites containing Linux. Moreover, it may be included as a part of Linux distribution.

If you have any suggestions or corrections regarding this document, please, don't hesitate to contact me as abel@bfr.co.il. Any new and useful information about Cyrillic support in various Unices is highly appreciated. Remember, it will help the others.

1.3 Acknowledgments and copyrights

Many people helped me (and not only me) with valuable information and suggestions. Even more people contributed software to the public community. I am sorry if I forgot to mention somebody.

So, here they go:

- Bas V. de Bakker,
- David Daves,
- Serge Vakulenko,
- Sergei O. Naoumov,
- Winfried Trümper,
- Ilya K. Orehov,
- Michael Van Canneyt,
- Alex Bogdanov,
- ...and the countless helpful people from the relcom.fido.ru.unix and relcom.fido.ru.linux Usenet newsgroups.

2 Characters and code sets

In order to understand and print characters of various languages, the system and software should be able to distinguish them from other characters. That is, each unique character must have a unique representation inside the operating system, or the particular software package. Such collection of all unique characters, that the system is able to represent at once, is called a **code set**.

At the time of the most operating system's creation, nobody cared about software being multilingual. Therefore, the most popular code set was (and actually is) **ASCII** (American Standard Code for Information Interchange).

The **standard ASCII** (aka **7-bit ASCII**) comprises 128 unique codes. Some of them ASCII defines as real, printable characters, and some are so-called **control characters**, which had special meanings in the old communication protocols. Each element of the set is identified by an integer **character code** (0-127). The subset of printable characters represents those found on the typewriter's keyboard with some minor additions. Each character occupies 7 least significant bits of a byte, whereas the most significant one was used for control purposes (say, transmission control in old communication packages).

The 7-bit ASCII concept was extended by 8-bit ASCII (aka **extended ASCII**). In this code set, the characters' codes' range is 0-255. The lower half (0-127) is pure ASCII, whereas the upper one contains 127 more characters. Since this code set is backward compatible with the ASCII (character still occupies 8 bit, the codes correspond the old ASCII), this code set gained wide popularity.

The 8-bit ASCII doesn't define the contents of the upper half of the code set. Therefore the ISO organization took the responsibility of defining a family of standards known as **ISO 8859-X** family. It is a collection of 8-bit code sets, where the lower half of each code set (characters with codes 0-127) matches the ASCII and the upper parts define characters for various languages. For example, the following code sets are defined:

- `8859-1`—Europe, Latin America (also known as *Latin 1*);
- `8859-2`—Eastern Europe;
- `8859-5`—Cyrillic;
- `8859-8`—Hebrew.

In Latin 1, the upper half of the table defines various characters which are not part of the English alphabet, but are present in various European languages (German umlauts, French accents, etc).

Another popular extended ASCII implementation is so-called **IBM code page** (named after some computer company, that developed this code set for its infamous personal computers). This one contains pseudo-graphic characters in the upper half.

Software that doesn't make any assumptions about the 8th bit of the ASCII data is called **8-bit clean**. Some older programs, designed with 7-bit ASCII in mind, are not 8-bit clean and may work incorrectly with your extended ASCII data. Most of packages, however, are able to deal with the extended ASCII by default, or require some very basic setup. **NOTE:** before posting the question "I did all setup right, but I cannot enter/view Cyrillic characters!" please consult the section 8 for the notes on the program, you are using.

For information about making your software 8-bit clean, see section 9.1.2.

Since on most systems character occupies 8 bits, there is no way to extend ASCII more and more. The way to implement new symbols in ASCII-based code sets is creation of other extended ASCII implementations. This is the way, the Cyrillic ASCII set is implemented.

We already mentioned ISO 8859-5 standard as defining the Cyrillic code set. But as it often happens to the standards, this one was developed without taking into account the real practices in the former USSR. Therefore, one thing that standard really achieved was another degree of confusion. I wouldn't say that ISO 8859-5 is widely used anywhere.

Other standards for Cyrillic include the so-called **Alt** code set and **Microsoft CP1251** code page. The former one was developed for MS-DOS quite a while ago. Back then, there was not very buzz yet about internetworking, so the intention was to make it as compatible as possible with the IBM standard. Therefore the Alt code set is effectively the same IBM code page, where all specific European characters in the upper half were replaced with the Cyrillic ones, leaving the pseudo-graphic ones. Therefore, it didn't screw the text windowing facilities and provided Cyrillic characters as well. The Alt standard is still alive and extremely popular in MS-DOS.

The Microsoft CP1251 code page is just an attempt of Microsoft to come up with the new standard for Cyrillic code set in Windows. As far as I know, it is not compatible with anything else. (Not very surprising, huh?)

And finally there is **KOI-8**. This one is also quite old, but it was designed wisely and nowadays the design points of it look really useful.

Again, it is compatible with ASCII, and the Cyrillic characters are located in the upper half. But the main design point of KOI-8 is that the Cyrillic characters' positions must correspond to the English characters with the same phonetics. Namely, if we set the eighth bit of the English character `'a'`, we'll get the Cyrillic `'a'`. This means that, given the Cyrillic text written in KOI-8, we can strip the eighth bit of each character *and we still get a readable text, although written with English characters.* This is very important now, since there are many mailers on the Internet that just strip the eighth bit silently, being sure that every single soul on the face of the Earth speaks English.

Not surprisingly, KOI-8 quickly became a de facto standard for Cyrillic on the Internet. Andrew A. Chernov did a tremendous amount of work to make a standard in this area. He is an author of RFC 1489, (*Registration of a Cyrillic Character Set.*)

These two standards differ only in positions of the Cyrillic characters in the table (that is in Cyrillic character codes).

The principal difference is that the Alt code set is used by MS-DOS users only, whereas KOI-8 is used in Unix, as well as in MS-DOS (though in the latter KOI-8 is much less popular). Since we are doing the right thing (namely working in the Unix operating system), we shall focus mostly on KOI-8.

As for the ISO standard, it is more popular in Europe and the US as a standard for Cyrillic. The leader in Russia is definitely KOI-8.

There are other standards, which are different from ASCII and much more flexible. **Unicode** is best known. However, they are not implemented as good as the basic ones in Unix in general and Linux in particular. Therefore, I am not describing them here.

3 Text mode setup

Generally, the text mode setup is the easiest way to show and input Cyrillic characters. There is one significant complication, however: the text mode fonts and keyboard layout manipulations depend on terminal driver implementation. Therefore, there is no portable way to achieve the goal across different systems.

Right now, I describe the way to deal with the Linux console driver. Thus, if you have another system, don't expect it to work for you. Instead, consult your terminal driver manual. Nevertheless, send me any information you find, so I'll be able to include it in further versions of this document.

3.1 Linux Console

The Linux console driver is quite a flexible piece of software. It is capable of changing fonts as well as keyboard layouts. To achieve it, you'll need the kbd package. Both Red Hat and Slackware install kbd as part of a system.

The kbd package contains keyboard control utilities as well as a big collection of fonts and keyboard layouts.

Cyrillic setup with kbd usually involves two things:

1. Screen font setup. This is performed by the `setfont` program. The fonts files are located in `/usr/lib/kbd/consolefonts`.

   NOTE: Never run the `setfont` program under X because it will hang your system. This is because it works with low-level video card calls which X doesn't like.

2. Load the appropriate keyboard layout with the `loadkeys` program.

NOTE: In Red Hat 3.0.3, `/usr/bin/loadkeys` has too restrictive access permissions, namely 700 (`rwx----`). There are no reasons for that, since everyone may compile his own copy and execute it (the appropriate system calls are not root-only). Thus, just ask your system administrator to set more reasonable permissions for it (for example, 755).

The following is an excerpt from my `cyrload` script, which sets up the Cyrillic mode for Linux console:

```
if [ notset.$DISPLAY != notset. ]; then
    echo "'basename $0': cannot run under X"
    exit
fi

loadkeys /usr/lib/kbd/keytables/ru.map
setfont /usr/lib/kbd/consolefonts/Cyr_a8x16
mapscrn /usr/lib/kbd/consoletrans/koi2alt
echo -ne "\033(K"            # the magic sequence
echo "Use the right Ctrl key to switch the mode..."
```

Let me explain it a bit. You load the appropriate keyboard mapping. Then you load a font corresponding to the Alt code set. Then, in order to be able to display text in KOI8-R correctly, you load a **screen translation table**. What it does is a translation of *some* characters from the upper half of the code set to the Alt encoding. The word "some" is crucial here—not all characters get translated, therefore some of them, like IBM pseudo-graphic characters get unmodified to the screen and display correctly, since they are compatible with the Alt code set, as opposed to KOI8-R. To ensure this, run `mc` and pretend you are back to MS-DOS 3.3...

Finally, the magic sequence is important but I have no idea what on the Earth it does. I stole/borrowed/learned it from German HOWTO back in 1994, when it was like the only national language oriented HOWTO. *If you have any idea about this magic sequence, please tell me.*

Finally, for those purists who don't wont to give the *Alt* code set a chance, I'm attaching yet another version of the script above, using native KOI8-R fonts.

```
if [ notset.$DISPLAY != notset. ]; then
    echo "'basename $0': cannot run under X"
    exit
fi

loadkeys /usr/lib/kbd/keytables/ru.map
setfont /usr/lib/kbd/consolefonts/koi-8x16
echo "Use the right Ctrl key to switch the mode..."
```

However, don't expect nice borders in your text mode-based windowing applications.

Now you probably want to test it. Do the appropriate bash or tcsh setup, rerun it, then press the right Control key and make sure you are getting the Cyrillic characters right. The 'q' key must produce Russian "`short i`" character, 'w' generates "`ts`", etc.

If you've screwed something up, the very best thing to do is to reset to the original (that is, US) settings. Execute the following commands:

```
loadkeys /usr/lib/kbd/keytables/defkeymap.map
setfont /usr/lib/kbd/consolefonts/default8x16
```

NOTE: unfortunately enough, the console driver is not able to preserve its state (at least easily enough), while running the X Window System. Therefore, after you leave the X (or switch from it to a console), you have to reload the console Russian font.

3.2 FreeBSD Console

I am not using FreeBSD so I couldn't test the following information. All data in this section should be treated as just pointers to begin with. The FreeBSD project home page may have some information on the subject. Another good source is the relcom.fido.ru.unix newsgroup. Also, check the resources listed in section 12.

Anyway, this is what Ilya K. Orehov suggests to do in order to make FreeBSD console speak Russian:

1. In `/etc/sysconfig` add:

```
keymap=ru.koi8-r
keyrate=fast
# NOTE: '^[' below is a single control character
keychange="61 ^[[K"
cursor=destructive
scrnmap=koi8-r2cp866
font8x16=cp866b-8x16
```

```
font8x14=cp866-8x14
font8x8=cp866-8x8
```

2. In /etc/csh.login:

```
setenv ENABLE_STARTUP_LOCALE
setenv LANG ru_SU.KOI8-R
setenv LESSCHARSET latin1
```

3. Make analogous changes in /etc/profile

4 The X Window System

Like the console mode, the X environment also requires some setup. This involves setting up the input mode and the X fonts. Both are discussed below.

4.1 The X fonts.

First of all, you have to obtain the fonts having the Cyrillic glyphs at the appropriate positions.

If you are using the most recent X (or XFree86) distribution, chances are, that you already have such fonts. In the late 1995, the X Window System incorporated a set of Cyrillic fonts, created by Cronyx. Ask your system administrator, or, if *you* are the one, check your system, namely:

1. Run `xlsfonts | grep koi8`. If there are fonts listed, your X server is already aware about the fonts.
2. Otherwise, run

   ```
   find -name crox\*.pcf\*
   ```

   to find the location of the Cyrillic fonts in the system. You'll have to `enable` those fonts to the X server, as I explain below.

If you haven't found such fonts installed, you'll have to do it yourself.

There is some ambiguity with the fonts. The XFree86 documentation claims that the Russian fonts collection included in the distribution is developed by Cronyx. Nevertheless, you may find another set of Cronyx Cyrillic fonts on the net (e.g. on ftp.kiae.su), known as the **xrus** package (don't confuse it with the `xrus` program, which is used to set up a Cyrillic keyboard layout. Hopefully, the latter one was renamed to `xruskb` recently). Xrus has fewer fonts than the collection in Xfree86 (38 vs 68), but the latter one didn't go along with my Netscape setup—it gave me some really huge font in the menu bar. The xrus package doesn't have this problem.

I would suggest you to download and try both of them. Pick up the one which you like more. Also, I'm going to create RPM packages soon for both collections and download them both to ftp.redhat.com and to my FTP site.

There are also older stuff, for example the **vakufonts** package, created by Serge Vakulenko, which was the base for the one in the X distribution. There are also a number of others. The important point is that the fonts' names in the old collection did not strictly conform to the standard. The latter is fine in general, but sometimes it may cause various weird errors. For example, I had a bad experience with Maple V for Linux, which crashed mysteriously with the vakufonts package, but ran smoothly with the "standard" ones.

So, let's start with the fonts:

1. Download the appropriate fonts collection. The package for XFree86 may be found at any FTP site, containing the X distribution, for example, directly from the XFree86 FTP site. The **xrus** package may be found on ftp.kiae.su
2. Now when you have the fonts, you create some directory for them. It is generally a bad idea to put new fonts to the already existing font directory. So, place them, to, say, /usr/lib/X11/fonts/cyrillic for a system-wide setup, or just create a private directory for personal use.
3. If the new fonts are in BDF format (`*.bdf` files), you have to compile them. For each font do:

   ```
   bdftopcf -o <font>.pcf <font>.bdf
   ```

   If your server supports compressed fonts, do it, using the *compress* program:

   ```
   compress *.pcf
   ```

   Also, if you do want to put the new fonts to an already existing font directory. you have to concatenate the old and the new files named `fonts.alias` in the case both of them exist.

4. Each font directory in the X must contain a list of fonts in it. This list is stored in the file `fonts.dir`. You don't have to create this list manually. Instead, do:

   ```
   cd <new font directory>
   mkfontdir .
   ```

5. Now you have to make this font directory known to the X server. Here, you have a number of options:

   - System-wide setup for XFree86. If you are running this version of X, then append the new directory to the list of directories in the file `XF86Config`. To find the location of this file, see output of `startx`. Also, see **XF86Config(4/5)** for details.
   - System-wide setup through `xinit`. Add the new directory to the `xinit` startup file. See **xinit(1x)** and the next option for details.
   - Personal setup. You have a special start-up file for the X - `~/.xinitrc` (or `~/.Xclients`, or `~/.xsession` for the Red Hat users). Add the following commands to it:

   ```
   xset +fp <new font directory>
   xset fp rehash
   ```

   It is important to note that "`+fp`" means that the new fonts will be added to the head of the font path list. That is, if an application requests say a `fixed` font, it'll be given the one with Cyrillic characters, which is definitely what we are trying to achieve.

   There are problems, though. The `fixed` font in the Cyrillic fonts distribution doesn't have it's bold and italic counterparts. My font of choice is `6x13`, so, since it also lacks bold and italic typefaces, I cannot use Emacs or XEmacs faces in their full glory. Hopefully somebody will ultimately create those fonts and the situation will change.

6. Now restart your X. If you have done everything right, the tests in the beginning of the section will be successful. Also, play with **xfontsel(1x)** to make sure you are able to select the Cyrillic fonts.

In order to make the X clients use the Cyrillic fonts, you have to set up the appropriate X resources. For example, I make the Russian font the default one in my `~/.Xdefaults`:

```
*font:        6x13
```

Since my Cyrillic fonts are first in the font path (see output of '`xset q`'), the font above is taken from the "cyrillic" directory.

This just a simple case. If you want to set the appropriate part of the X client to a Cyrillic font, you have to figure out the name of the resource (e.g. using **editres(1x)**) and to specify it either in the resource database, or in the command line. Here go some examples:

```
$ xterm -font '-cronyx-*-bold-*-*-*-19-*-*-*-*-*-*-*'
```

will run xterm with some ugly font; and

```
$ xfontsel -xrm '*quitButton.font: -*-times-*-*-*-*-13-*-*-*-*-*-koi8-*'
```

will set a Cyrillic Times font for the **Quit** button in `xfontsel`.

4.2 The input translation

In the newest X releases (X11R61 and higher) there are two "standard" input methods: the original one, working through the `xmodmap` utility, and the new one called `xkb`. The very first thing you have to do is **to disable the xkb method.** Don't be charmed by it's ability to set up a Russian keyboard." It looks like this method is using the Cyrillic keysyms defined in `keysymdef.h`. This file defines keysyms for many languages. The only problem is that those definitions have nothing to do with the extended ASCII code set—the one most programs are only able to operate with. I hardly know any programs being able to grok the `keysymdef.h` keysyms, different from 8-bit ASCII. However, our goal is to get the KOI8-R support to work.

To disable the `xkb` support, browse through the `Keyboard` section of your `XF86Config` file and comment all lines starting with `Xkb` (case doesn't matter). Instead, put the following line:

```
XkbDisable
```

The `xmodmap` program.allows customization of codes emitted by various characters and their combinations. It sets the things up based on the file containing the translation table.

In the previous versions of this document I used to describe the `xmodmap` based setup in a great detail. This proved to be almost useless. The `xmodmap` input translation method is well known as being it is non-portable, inflexible, and incomplete. Your configuration may work with one XFree version and fail with a different one. Even worse, sometimes things differ across different servers in the same distribution.

I strongly suggest that you not play with `xmodmap`, at least for now. Apart from headache and disappointment you'll gain nothing. Instead, I recommend installing the xruskb package, which allows you to configure most of the input translation parameters without having to know about `xmodmap`. Again, the Red Hat Linux users are free to download and install an RPM package.

5 Cyrillic support in TEX and LATEX

In this section I'll describe several ways to make TEX and LATEX typeset Cyrillic texts. There are several ways, which differ in setup sophistication and usage convenience. For example, one possibility is to start without any preliminary setup and use the *Washington AMSTEX Cyrillic fonts*. On the other hand, you may install a LATEX package, providing a very high degree of Cyrillic setup. I have an experience with two such packages. One is the `cmcyralt` package by Vadim V. Zhytnikov (`vvzhy@phy.ncu.edu.tw`) and Alexander Harin (`harin@lourie.und.ac.za`), and the other one is the `LH` package by the *CyrTUG* group with styles and hyphenation for LATEX2e by Sergei O. Naoumov (`serge@astro.unc.edu`). I'll describe both.

Note, that there are two versions of LATEX available - 2.09 is the old one, while 2e is a new pre-3.0 release. If you are using LATEX 2.09, then switch quickly to the 2e. The latter retains compatibility with the old one, but has much more features. Hopefully, version 3 will be released soon. I describe a LATEX 2e setup.

Also, both of these packages require the Cyrillic text to be typeset using the Alt code set, not KOI-8! This is caused by historical reasons, since the creators of these packages used to work with EmTeX—the MS-DOG version of TEX (they didn't know about Linux yet.) Switching to the KOI-8 requires some effort and is being expected to be done soon. So far, use some utility to convert your Russian text from KOI-8 to Alt. See section 10.1.

5.1 Using the Washington Cyrillic

This package was created for the American Mathematical Society to provide documents with Russian references. Therefore, the authors were not very careful and the fonts look quite clumsy. This package is usually referred to as a "really bad Cyrillic package for TEX."

Nevertheless, we'll discuss it, because it is very easy to use and doesn't require any setup - this collection is supplied with most of TEX distributions.

Of course, you won't be able to use such luxuries as automatic hyphenation, but anyway—

1. Prepend your document with the following directives:

```
\input cyracc.def
\font\tencyr=wncyr10
\def\cyr{\tencyr\cyracc}
```

2. Now to type a Cyrillic letter, you enter

```
\cyr
```

and use a corresponding Latin letter or a TEX command. Thus, the lower case of the Russian alphabet is expressed by the following codes:

```
a b v g d e \"e zh z i {\u i} k l m n o p r s t u f kh c ch sh shch
{\cprime} y {\cdprime} \'e yu ya
```

It is extremely inconvenient to convert your Russian texts to such encoding, but you can automate the process. The `translit` program (section 10.1) supports a TEX output option.

5.2 KOI-8 package for teTeX

There is some new teTeX-rus package. It is reported to support KOI-8 character set and have all basic stuff required for TEX and LATEX. I personally haven't tried it yet, although I heard about its successful usage.

◇ **NOTE:** This package requires you to reconfigure and rebuild some parts of your teTeX package (for example the precompiled LATEX macros. Unless you know what you are doing, you shouldn't try it without necessary care. Otherwise, you may be better off by borrowing the precompiled parts from somebody on the 'Net.

5.3 Using the cmcyralt package for LaTeX

The `cmcyralt` package can be found on any CTAN (Comprehensive TeX Archive Network) site like `ftp.dante.de`. You should obtain two pieces: the fonts collection from `fonts/cmcyralt` and the styles and hyphenation rules from `macros/latex/contrib/others/cmcyralt`.

Note: Make sure you have the Sauter font package installed, since `cmcyralt` requires some fonts from it. You can get this package from a CTAN site as well.

Now you should do the following:

1. Put the new fonts to the TeX fonts tree. On my system (Slackware 2.2) I created a `cmcyralt` directory in the `/usr/lib/texmf/fonts/cm/`. Create the `src`, `tfm`, and `vf` subdirectories in it. Put there `.mf`, `.tfm`, and `vf` files respectively.
2. Put the font driver files (`*.fd`) from the styles archive to the appropriate place (in my case it was `/usr/lib/texmf/tex/latex/fd`).
3. Put the style files (`*.sty`) to the appropriate LaTeX styles directory (in my case `/usr/lib/texmf/tex/latex/sty`).

Now the hyphenation setup. This requires remaking the LaTeX base file.

1. The file `hyphen.cfg` contains the directives for both English and Russian hyphenation. Extract the one for Russian and place it to the LaTeX hyphenation config file `lthyphen.ltx`. In my case, that file was in `/usr/lib/texmf/tex/latex/latex-base`.
2. Put the `rhyphen.tex` to the same directory. It is needed for making the new base file. Later, you can remove it.
3. Do 'make' in that directory. Don't for get to make a link from `Makefile` to `Makefile.unx`. During the make process check the output. There should be a message:

   ```
   Loading hyphenation patterns for Russian.
   ```

   If everything goes OK, you will get the new `latex.fmt` in that directory. Put it to the appropriate place, where the previous one was (like `/usr/lib/texmf/ini/`).

   ◇ **Don't forget to save the previous one.**

This is it. The installation is complete. Try processing the examples found in the styles archive. If you are to create the PostScript files without any problems, then everything is OK. Now, to use Cyrillic in LaTeX, place the following line in the document's preamble.

```
\usepackage{cmcyralt}
```

For more details, see the `README` file in the `cmcyralt` styles archive.

Note: if you do have problems with the examples, provided you have installed the things right, then probably your TeX system hasn't been installed correctly. For example, during my first try, every attempt to create the `.pk` files for the Russian fonts failed (`MakeTeXPK` stage). A substantial investigation discovered some implicit conflict between the "localfont" and "ljfour" Metafont configurations. It used to work before, but kept crashing after the `cmcyralt` installation. Contact your local TeX guru—TeX is very (sometimes too much) complicated to reconfigure without any prior knowledge.

5.4 Using the CyrTUG package

You can obtain the CyrTUG package from the Sunsite archive. Get the files `CyrTUGfonts.tar.gz`, `CyrTUGmacro.tar.gz`, and `hyphen.tar.Z`.

The process of installation doesn't differ from too much the previous one.

6 Cyrillic in PostScript

Experts say PostScript is easy. I cannot judge—I've got too many things to learn to spare some time to learn PostScript. So I'll try to use my sad experience with it. **I'll appreciate any feedback from you guys who know more on the subject than I do** (approximately. 99% of the Earth population).

Basically, in order to print a Cyrillic text using PostScript, you have to make sure about the following things:

- Cyrillic font is loaded or included in the document.
- Cyrillic text is included in the document.
- Cyrillic text uses the appropriate character codes which correspond to the font's requirements.

- An appropriate font is selected in order to print Cyrillic text.

There is no solution general enough to be recommended as an ultimate treatment. I'll try to outline various ways to cope with different problems related to the subject.

One way to address Cyrillic setup problems generally enough is to use Ghostscript, (or just `gs` in the Newspeak) is a free (well quasi-free) PostScript interpreter. It has many advantages; among them:

- Ability to run on many platforms (various Unices, Windows etc);
- Support for a wide number of non-PostScript printers;
- Good degree of configurability.

What is important in our particular case, is that once Ghostscript is set up, we can do all printing through it, thus eliminating extra setup for other PostScript devices (for example HP LaserJet IV).

6.1 Adding Cyrillic fonts to Ghostscript

This is important, since you probably don't want to put a responsibility to other programs to insert Cyrillic fonts in the PostScript output. Instead, you add them to `gs` and just make the programs generate Cyrillic output compatible with the fonts.

To add a new font (in `pfa` or `pfb` form) in `gs`, you have to:

1. Put it in the Ghostscript `fonts` directory (i.e. `/usr/lib/ghostscript/fonts`).
2. Add the appropriate names and aliases for the font in the `Fontmap` file in the Ghostscript directory.

Recently a decent set of Cyrillic fonts for Ghostscript appeared. It is located in ftp.kapella.gpi.ru. This one even has a necessary part to add to the `Fontmap` file. You have to download the contents of the `/pub/cyrillic/psfonts` directory. The `README` file describes the necessary details.

7 Print setup

Printing is always tricky. There are different printers from different vendors with different facilities. Even for native printing there is no uniform solution (this applies not only to UNIX, but to other operating systems as well).

Another problem is a variety of requirements to the print services. For example, sometimes you want just to print a piece of a C program, containing comments in Russian, so you don't need any pretty-printing —just a raw ASCII output in a single font. Another time, when you design a postcard for your girlfriend, you'll probably need to typeset some document with different fonts and so forth. This will definitely require more effort to set up Cyrillic support.

To accomplish the former task you just have to make your printer understand one Cyrillic font and (maybe) install some filter program to generate data in appropriate format. To accomplish the latter one, you have to teach your printer different fonts and have a special software.

There is also something in the middle, when you get a program which knows how to generate both the fonts and the appropriate printer input, so you can say do some source code pretty-printing without sophisticated word processing systems.

All these options are more or less covered below.

7.1 Pre-loading Cyrillic fonts into a non-PostScript printer

If you have a good old dot matrix printer and all you need is to print a raw KOI-8 text, try the following:

1. Find a proper KOI-8 font for your printer. Check out the MS-DOSish stuff on the Internet (for example the Simtel Archive, ftp://ftp.simtel.net/.
2. Learn from the manual, how to load such font into your printer and, probably, write a simple program doing that.
3. Run this program from the appropriate `rc` file at a boot time.

Thus, having Cyrillic characters in the upper part of the printer's character set will allow you to print texts in Russian without any hassle.

Alternatively to the KOI-8 fonts, you may try to use the Alt font. There are two reasons for this:

- It may be probably much easier to find an Alt font, since those were very widespread in the MS-DOS culture.
- Having a proper Alt font will allow you to print pseudo-graphic characters as well.

However in this case, you'll have to convert your texts from KOI-8 to Alt before sending them to a printer. This is quite easy, since there are a lot of programs doing that (see 10.1 for example), so you just have to call such program properly in the `if` field in `/etc/printcap` file. For example, with the `translit` program you may specify:

```
if=/usr/bin/translit -t koi8-alt.rus
```

See `printcap(5)` for details.

7.2 Printing with different fonts

One great way to cope with different printers and fonts is to use TEX. Its drivers handle all details, so once you make TEX understand Cyrillic fonts, you are done.

Another possibility is to use PostScript. I decided to devote the entire Section 6 to the subject, since it is not simple.

Finally, there are other word processors, which have printer drivers. I never tried anything apart from TEX, so I cannot suggest anything.

7.3 Converting text to TEX

If all you need is just to print an ASCII text without any additional word processing, you may try to use some programs, which would convert your Cyrillic text to a ready-to-process TEX file. For one of the best programs for such purposes, see section 10.1. In this case, you don't even have to bother about installing the Cyrillic fonts for TEX, since `translit` uses the Washington Cyrillic package.

7.4 Text-to-PostScript converters

Sometimes you have just a plain ASCII KOI-8 text and you want to print it just to get it on the paper. One of the easiest ways to achieve that is to use special programs converting text to PostScript.

There are a number of programs doing such conversion. I personally prefer `a2ps`. Originally developed as a simple text-to-PostScript converter it became a big and highly configurable program with many options and allows you to manage various page layouts, syntax highlighting etc. Another tool (now available as a part of the GNU project) is `enscript`.

The main problem with such programs is that they know nothing about Cyrillic fonts. Right now I am investigating a possibility of including Cyrillic fonts in them in order to understand Cyrillic. Stay in touch.

Nevertheless all the blah-blah above would be pointless without any real advice. So, there we go.

7.4.1 The `a2ps` converter

This text-to-PostScript converter has been around for a while and is one of the most versatile printing tools. The author proved to be very open to suggestions, so since the release 4.9.8, `a2ps` supports Cyrillic right off the shelf. All you need is a PostScript printer.

The command I use is:

```
a2ps -X koi8r --print-anyway  <file>
```

7.4.2 GNU `enscript`

GNU `enscript` program is also designed for converting text to PostScript, and it also has a non-ASCII code set support. It doesn't have Cyrillic PostScript fonts, but it is very easy to get them, as will be explained below (thanks to Michael Van Canneyt):

1. Install the newest `enscript`. As of now, the most recent release is 1.5. You may either get the one from the GNU FTP archive, or take an RPM package from the Redhat site.

2. Now, if you are a lucky Red Hat Linux user, download and install the Cyrillic Textbook font, ftp://ftp.redhat.com/pub/contrib/i386/enscript-fonts-koi8-1.0-1.i386.rpm.

3. If you don't use RPM, download the file `textbook.tar.gz` from the Cyrillic Software collection on sunsite.unc.edu, ftp://sunsite.unc.edu/pub/academic/russian-studies/Software/. it to a directory, where `enscript` fonts are located (usually `/usr/share/enscript`). Now change to that directory and run the following command:

   ```
   mkafmmap *.afm
   ```

4. The setup is finished. Try to print some text in KOI8-R Cyrillic with the following command:

   ```
   enscript --font=Textbook8 --encoding=koi8 some.file
   ```

If you want a really quick and dirty solution and you don't care about the output quality and all you need is just Cyrillic on the paper, try the rtxt2ps package. It is a very simple no-frills text-to-PostScript conversion program. The output quality is not very good (or, to be honest, just *bad*) but it does it's job.

8 Miscellaneous utilities setup

Generally, to set a certain utility up to handle the Cyrillic requires just to allow the 8-bit input. In some cases it is required to tell the application to show the extended ASCII characters in their "native" form.

8.1 bash

Three variables should be set on order to make `bash` understand the 8-bit characters. The best place is `~/.inputrc` file. The following should be set:

```
set meta-flag on
set convert-meta off
set output-meta on
```

8.2 `csh` and `tcsh`

The following should be set in `.cshrc`:

```
setenv LC_CTYPE iso_8859_5
stty pass8
```

If you don't have the POSIX `stty` (impossible for Linux), then replace the last call to the following:

```
stty -istrip cs8
```

8.3 DOSEMU

This seems to be the only application, which may require the Alt Cyrillic character set. The reason is that Alt is native to DOS and most of DOS programs dealing with Cyrillic are Alt oriented.

For the console version (`dos`) you just have to load a keyboard and screen driver. Most of the DOS drivers will work fine. I personally use the rk driver by A. Strakhov, which works for both console and X versions of DOSEMU. Another choice is the `r` driver by V. Kurland (sorry for possible misspelling). It is perfectly customizable and supports many code sets, Alt and KOI-8 among them. However it won't work for X (at least the version 1.14 I'm using).

Both drivers can be found on most Russian Internet sites, for example the Kurchatov Institute FTP server, ftp://ftp.kiae.su/pub/cyrillic/msdos/.

For the X version of DOSEMU you have to provide an appropriate X font as well. Alex Bogdanov sent me such font by e-mail. It is an original VGA font from the DOSEMU distribution, modified for the Alt code set. Unfortunately I don't know who is the creator of this font and where the official site is. I'll put this font in ftp://ftp.netvision.net.il/home/b/belikoff/cyrillic/.

To set up the font for DOSEMU you should

- Introduce this font to the X. This is described in 4.1.
- Introduce this font to DOSEMU. If the font just replaces the original VGA font, then it will be recognized by default. Otherwise, you have to describe it in `/etc/dosemu.conf`:

```
# Font to use (without filename extensions). For example:
X { updatefreq 8 title "MS DOS" icon_name "xdos" font "vga-alt"}
```

Finally, you have to load a keyboard driver. Note, the you don't need a screen driver for the X window. Therefore, not all drivers will work. At least two will: `rk` by A. Strakhov, and `cyrkeyb` by Pete Kvitek.

8.4 emacs

The minimal cyrillic support in `emacs` is done by adding the following calls to one's `.emacs` (provided that the Cyrillic character set support is installed for console or X respectively):

```
(standard-display-european t)

(set-input-mode (car (current-input-mode))
   (nth 1 (current-input-mode))
   0)
```

This allows the user to view and input documents in Russian.

However, such mode is not of a big convenience because emacs doesn't recognize the usual keyboard commands while set in Cyrillic input mode. There are a number of packages which use the different approach. They don't rely on the input mode stuff established by the environment (either X or console. Instead, they allow the user to switch the input mode by the special emacs command and emacs itself is responsible for re-mapping the character set. The author took a chance to look at three of them. The russian.el package, http://www.math.uga.edu/~valery/russian.el, by Valery Alexeev (valery@math.uga.edu) allows the user to switch between cyrillic and regular input mode and to translate the contents of a buffer from one Cyrillic coding standard to another (which is especially useful while reading the texts imported from MS-DOS).

The only inconvenience is that emacs still treats the Russian characters as special ones, so it doesn't recognize Russian words' bounds and case changes. To fix it, you have to modify the syntax and case tables of emacs:

```
;; there is a garbage in the variables below, since SGML doesn't like
;; cyrillic characters. You have to put the uppercase and lowercase
;; parts of the Russian alphabet respectively (see the actual files)

(setq *russian-abc-ucase* "*** SGML SUCKS ***")
(setq *russian-abc-lcase* "*** SGML SUCKS ***")


(let ((i 0)
      (len (length *russian-abc-ucase*)))

     (while (< i len)
       (modify-syntax-entry (elt *russian-abc-ucase* i) "w  ")
       (modify-syntax-entry (elt *russian-abc-lcase* i) "w  ")
       (set-case-syntax-pair (elt *russian-abc-ucase* i)
                             (elt *russian-abc-lcase* i)
                             (standard-case-table))
       (setq i (+ i 1))))
```

For this purpose I created a rusup.el file which does this, as well as a couple handy functions. You have to load it in your ~/.emacs.

Another alternative is the package remap which tries to make such support more generic. This package is written by Per Abrahamsen (abraham@iesd.auc.dk) and is accessible at ftp.iesd.auc.dk.

As for the author's opinion, I would suggest to start using the russian.el package because it is very easy to set up and use.

8.5 ispell

There is an rspell add-on created by Neal Dalton (nrd@cray.com) for the GNU ispell package, but I experienced some problems making it work right away. Try it—maybe you will be luckier.

8.6 joe

Try the -asis option.

8.7 ksh

As for the public domain ksh implementation—pdksh 5.1.3, you can input 8 bit characters only in vi input mode. Use:

```
set -o vi
```

8.8 less

So far, less doesn't support the KOI-8 character set, but the following environment variable will do the job:

```
LESSCHARSET=latin1
```

8.9 lynx

As of version 2.6, you may select the appropriate value for the display Character set option.

8.10 `mc` (The Midnight Commander)

To display Cyrillic text correctly, select the *full 8 bits* item in the **Options/Display** menu.

If your problem is the ugly windows' borders, consult Section 3.1.

As an off-topic, if you want to make `mc` use color in an `xterm` window, set the variable `COLORTERM`:

```
COLORTERM= ; export COLORTERM
```

8.11 Netscape Navigator

Make sure you are using `Netscape` version higher than 3. If your `Netscape` is older, download a new one from www.netscape.com.

8.11.1 Basic setup

To be able to see Cyrillic text in most parts of the HTML document, do the following:

- In menu Options/Document Encoding select Cyrillic(KOI-8).
- In menu Options/General Preferences/Fonts select Cyrillic (KOI-8) encoding, Times(Cronyx) as a proportional font and Courier(Cronyx) as a fixed one.
- save options.

NOTE: This setup works with most parts of the document. However, you won't be able to display Cyrillic text in the window header, menus and some controls. To fix these problems, do an

8.11.2 Cyrillic text in frames and input areas

To fix this, it is usually enough to:

1. Copy the Netscape properties database (usually `Netscape.ad`) to `~/Netscape`.
2. In the latter file, set the following property:

```
*documentFonts.charset*iso8859-1:              koi8-r
```

This will force all frame and input elements to use the fonts with KOI8-R encoding instead of the default ones, therefore you have to make sure you have installed such fonts (see section 4.1).

8.11.3 Advanced setup

Andrew A. Chernov is the one who knows more than others about KOI-8 in general and `netscape` in particular. Visit his excellent KOI-8 page and download a patch for the Netscape resource file to make Netscape speak Russian as much as it is able to.

8.12 `pine`

Set the following directive in `~/.pinerc` for personal configuration, or in `/usr/lib/pine.conf` for a global one:

```
character-set=ISO-8859-5
```

8.13 `rlogin`

Make sure that the shell on the destination site is properly set up. Then, if your `rlogin` doesn't work by default, use `'rlogin -8'`.

8.14 `sendmail` (A.k.a., "The Doom of a Sysadmin")

As of version 8, `sendmail` handles 8-bit data correctly by default. If it doesn't do it for you, check the `EightBitMode` option and option `7` given to mailers in your `/etc/sendmail.cf`. See *Sendmail. Operation and Installation Guide* for details.

8.15 XEmacs

Basically, `xemacs` has a very reasonable default setup. However you will still need the package.

If something doesn't work, see Section 8.4. This may help.

Also, I haven't ported my 8.4 package to `xemacs`, so you will lack that functionality. Hopefully, I'll do the port in the near future.

8.16 zsh

Use the same way as with csh (see Section 8.2). The startup files in this case are .zshrc or /etc/zshrc.

9 Localization and Internationalization

So far, I described how to make various programs understand Cyrillic text. Basically, each program required it's own method, very different from the others. Moreover, some programs had incomplete support of languages other than English. Not to mention their inability to interact using user's mother tongue instead of English.

The problems outlined above are very pressing, since software is rarely developed for home market only. Therefore, rewriting substantial parts of software each time the new international market is approached is very ineffective; and making each program implement it's own proprietary solution for handling different languages is not a great idea in a long term either.

Therefore, a need for standardization arises. And the standard shows up.

Everything related to the problems above is divided by two basic concepts: *localization* and *internationalization*. By localization we mean making programs able to handle different language conventions for different countries. Let me give an example. The way date is printed in the United States is MM/DD/YY. In Russia however, the most popular format is DD.MM.YY. Another issues include time representation, printing numbers and currency representation format. Apart from it, one of the most important aspect of localization is defining the appropriate character classes, that is, defining which characters in the character set are language units (letters) and how they are ordered. On the other hand, localization doesn't deal with fonts.

Internationalization (or *i18n* for brevity) is supposed to solve the problems related to the ability of the program interact with the user in his native language.

Both of the concepts above had to be implemented in a standard, giving programmers a consistent way of making the programs aware of national environments.

Although the standard hasn't been finished yet, many parts actually have; so they can be used without much of a problem.

I am going to outline the general scheme of making the programs use the features above in a standard way. Since this deserves a separate document, I'll just try to give a very basic description and pointers to more thorough sources.

9.1 Locale

One of the main concept of the localization is a *locale*. By locale is meant a set of conventions specific to a certain language in a certain country. It is usually wrong to say that locale is just country-specific. For example, in Canada two locales can be defined—Canada/English language and Canada/French language. Moreover, Canada/English is not equivalent to UK/English or US/English, just as Canada/French is not equivalent to France/French or Switzerland/French.

9.1.1 How to use locale

Each locale is a special database, defining at least the following rules:

1. character classification and conversion,
2. monetary values representation,
3. number representation (ie. the decimal character),
4. date/time formatting.

In Red Hat 4.1, which I am using there are actually *two* locale databases: one for the C library (libc) and one for the X libraries. In the ideal case there should be only one locale database for everything.

To change your default locale, it is usually enough to set the LANG environment variable. For example, in sh:

```
LANG=ru_RU
export LANG
```

Sometimes, you may want to change only one aspect of the locale without affecting the others. For example, you may decide (God knows why) to stick with ru_RU locale, but print numbers according to the standard POSIX one. For such cases, there is a set of environment variables, which you can you to configure specific parts for the current locale. In the last example it would be:

```
LANG=ru_RU
LC_NUMERIC=POSIX
export LANG LC_NUMERIC
```

For the full description of those variables, see `locale(7)`.

Now let's be more Linux-specific. Unfortunately, Linux `libc` version 5.3.12, supplied with Red Hat 4.1, doesn't have a Russian locale. In this case one must be downloaded from the Internet (I don't know the exact address, however).

To check the locale for which languages you have, run '`locale -a`'. It will list all locale databases, available to libc.

Fortunately, Linux community is rapidly moving to the new GNU libc (`glibc` version 2, which is much more POSIX-compliant and has a proper Russian locale. Next "stable" Red Hat system will already use `glibc`.

As for the X libraries, they have their own locale database. In the version I am using (XFree86 3.3), there already is a Russian locale database. I am not sure about the previous versions. In any case, you may check it by looking into `usr/lib/X11/locale/` (on most systems). In my case, there already are subdirectories named `koi8-r` and even `iso8859-5`.

9.1.2 Locale-aware programming

With locale, programs don't have to explicitly implement various character conversion and comparison rules, described above. Instead, they use a special API which make use of the rules defined by locale. Also, it is not necessary for program to use the same locale for all rules—it is possible to handle different rules using different locales (although such technique should be strongly discouraged).

From the `setlocale(3)` manual page:

> A program may be made portable to all locales by calling `setlocale(LC_ALL, "" )` after program initialization, by using the values returned from a `localeconv()` call for locale-dependent information and by using `strcoll()` or `strxfrm()` to compare strings.

SunSoft, for example, defines these levels of program localization:

1. *8-bit clean* software. That is, the program calls `setlocale()`, it doesn't make any assumptions about the 8th bit of each character, it users functions from `ctype.h` and limits from `limits.h`, and it takes care about `signed/unsigned` issues.

   It is very important not to make any assumption about the character set nature and ordering. The following programming practices must be avoided:

   ```
   if (c >= 'A' && c <= 'Z') {
       ...
   ```

   Instead, macros from the `ctype.h` header file are locale-aware and should be used in all such occasions.

2. Formats, sorting methods, paper sizes. The program uses `strcoll()` and `strxfrm()` instead of `strcmp()`. For strings, it uses `time()`, `localtime()`, and `strftime()` for time services, and finally, it uses `localeconv()` for a proper numbers and currency representation.

3. Visible text in message catalogs. The program must isolate all visible text in special *message catalogs*. Those map strings in English to their translation to other languages. Selection of messages in an appropriate for a particular environment language is done in a way which is completely transparent for both the program and it's user. To make use of those facilities, the program must call `gettext()` (Sun/POSIX standard), or `catgets()` (X/Open standard). For more information on that, see Section 9.2.

4. EUC/Unicode support. At this level, the program doesn't use the `char` type. Instead it uses `wchar_t`, which defines entities big enough to contain Unicode characters. ANSI C defines this data type and an appropriate API.

For a more detailed explanation of locale, see, for example (6) or (5).

9.2 Internationalization

While localization describes how to adapt a program to a foreign environment, **internationalization** (or "i18n" for brevity) details the ways to make program communicate with a non-English speaking user.

Before, that was done by developing some abstraction of the messages to output from the program's code. Now, such mechanism is (more or less) standardized. And, of course, there are free implementations of it.

The GNU project has finally adopted the way of making the internationalized applications. Ulrich Drepper (`drepper@ipd.info.uni-karlsruhe.de`) developed a package `gettext`. This package is available at all GNU sites like prep.ai.mit.edu. It allows you to develop programs in a way that you can easily make them support more languages. I don't intend to describe the programming techniques, especially because the `gettext` package is delivered with excellent manual.

Request for collaboration: If you want to learn the `gettext` package and to contribute to the GNU project simultaneously; or even if you just want to contribute, then you can do it. GNU goes international, so all the utilities are being made locale-aware. The problem is to translate the messages from English to Russian (and other languages if you'd like). Basically, what one has to do is to get the special `.po` file consisting of the English messages for a certain utility and to append each message with its equivalent in Russian. Ultimately, this will make the system speak Russian if the user wants it to. For more details and further directions contact Ulrich Drepper (drepper@ipd.info.uni-karlsruhe.de).

10 Useful Tools

10.1 Conversion Utilities

There are a number of programs able to convert from KOI-8 to Alt and back. Look at SovInformBureau or ftp.funet.fi for a list of handy little utilities. You can even use the special mode for `emacs` (see section 8.4).

However, I would especially recommend a translit package. It supports many popular code sets and is even able to produce a TEX input files (see Section 5) from text in Russian. Also, Red Hat users will enjoy an RPM package for `translit`.

11 Bibliography

1. Andrey Chernov. `http://www.nagual.ru/ ache/koi8.html` KOI-8 information and setup.
2. Ulrich Drepper. `http://i44www.info.uni-karlsruhe.de/ drepper/conf96/paper.html` Internationalization in the GNU project. Very thorough description of a GNU approach to i18n.
3. Michael Karl Gschwind. `http://www.vlsivie.tuwien.ac.at/mike/i18n.html` Internationalization. Various resources on i18n.
4. Sergei Naumov. `http://sunsite.oit.unc.edu/sergei/Software/Software.html` Information on Cyrillic Software. Cyrillic setup information.
5. The Open Group `http://www.UNIX-systems.org/online.html` Single UNIX specification.
6. Alec Voropay. `http://www.sensi.org/~alec/locale` Localization as it is. General locale usage in Russian.

12 Summary of the various useful resources

`a2ps` Home Page. `http://www-inf.enst.fr/~demaille/a2ps.html`
General Linux Information. `http://sunsite.unc.edu/mdw/linux.html`
Collection of Cyrillic stuff on `ftp.kiae.su`. `ftp://ftp.kiae.su/cyrillic/`
Collection of Cyrillic stuff on `ftp.relcom.ru`. `ftp://ftp.relcom.ru/cyrillic/`
Collection of cyrilization software. ftp://ftp.funet.fi/pub/culture/russian/comp/
Cronyx—the creators of Cyrillic fonts for the X Window System. `http://www.cronyx.ru`
Cyrillic fonts for Ghostscript. `ftp://ftp.kapella.gpi.ru/pub/cyrillic/psfonts`
Cyrillic fonts for X. `ftp://ftp.kiae.su/cyrillic/x11/fonts/xrus-2.1.1-src.tgz`
Ghostscript. `http://www.cs.wisc.edu/~ghost/index.html`
GNU enscript. `ftp://prep.ai.mit.edu/pub/gnu`
relcom.fido.ru.unix newsgroup.
RFC 1489. `file://ds.internic.net/rfc/rfc1489.txt`
`rspell` for GNU `ispell`. `ftp://sunsite.unc.edu/pub/academic/russian-studies/Software/rspell.tar.gz`
SovInformBureau. `http://www.siber.com/sib/russify/`
teTeX russification package. `ftp://xray.sai.msu.su/pub/outgoing/teTeX-rus/`
The kbd package for Linux. `ftp://sunsite.unc.edu/pub/Linux/system/Keyboards/`
The remap package for Emacs. `ftp://ftp.iesd.auc.dk/`
The `rtxt2ps` package. `http://www.siber.com/sib/russify/converters/`
The `russian.el` package for emacs. `http://www.math.uga.edu/ valery/russian.el`
The `translit` package. `ftp://ftp.osc.edu/pub/russian/translit/translit.tar.Z`
The `xruskb` package. `ftp://ftp.relcom.ru/pub/x11/cyrillic/`
Useful Cyrillic packages. `ftp://sunsite.unc.edu/pub/academic/russian-studies/Software`
X fonts collections. `ftp://ftp.switch.ch/mirror/linux/X11/fonts/`
XFree86 FTP site. `http://www.xfree86.org`

Part XV

“Linux Danish/International HOWTO” by Niels Kristian Bech Jensen,

nkbj@image.dk

The Linux Documentation Project
The original, unaltered edition of this, and other, LDP documents, is on line at http://sunsite.unc.edu/LDP/.

Contents

Abstract

v1.9, 11 November 1997
This document describes how to configure Linux and various Linux applications for Danish locale standards such as keyboard, font, and paper size. It is hoped that Linux users from other places in Western Europe will find this document useful, too.

13 Introduction

All European users of almost any operating system have two problems: The first is to tell the computer that you have a non-American keyboard, and the second is to get the computer to display the special characters. To make matters worse some applications will also consider you an exception if you are not an American and require special options or the setting of environment variables.

Under Linux you change the way your computer interprets the keyboard with the commands `loadkeys` and `xmodmap`. `loadkeys` will modify the keyboard for plain Linux while `xmodmap` makes the modifications necessary when the handshaking between X11 and Linux is imperfect.

To display the characters you need to tell your applications that you use the ISO 8859-1 (a.k.a. Latin-1) international set of glyphs. This is not always necessary, but a number of key applications need special attention.

This HOWTO is intended to tell Danish users how to do this. If you continue to have problems after reading this you can try the German HOWTO, the Linux Keyboard and Console HOWTO or the ISO 8859-1 National Character Set FAQ. Many of the hints contained herein are cribbed from there. See Section 20.1 for pointers to these documents. You should also send me a mail describing your problems.

A final problem is that error-messages, menus and documentation of the applications are mostly in English. There is a GNU project under way to address this problem. You can see what it is all about by downloading the file `ABOUT-NLS` or the package `gettext-0.10.tar.gz` (or any later version) from your favorite mirror of `prep.ai.mit.edu`. This project needs volunteers for the translations. Send a mail to `da-request@li.org` with the body `subscribe` if you want to contribute to the Danish part of the project. The documentation in the `gettext` package describes how to use such translations in your own programs.

14 Keyboard setup

14.1 Loading a keytable

You have two tools for configuring your keyboard. Under plain Linux you have `loadkeys` and under X11 you have `xmodmap`.

To try out `loadkeys` type one of these two commands:

```
loadkeys /usr/lib/kbd/keytables/dk.map
```

or

```
loadkeys /usr/lib/kbd/keytables/dk-latin1.map
```

The difference between the two keymaps is that `dk-latin1.map` enables "dead" keys while `dk.map` does not. Dead keys are explained in section 14.3. The program `loadkeys` and the keymaps are part of the package `kbd-0.??.tar.gz` which (with differing version numbers ??) is available with all Linux distributions.

Usually `loadkeys` is executed at boot-time from one of the scripts under the directory `/etc/rc.d/`. Details vary between distributions.

(Note for non-Danish readers: Support for other languages is enabled in a similar manner. Use `es.map` for Spanish keyboards etc.)

Versions of XFree86 up to and including v3.1.2 will normally follow the keymap used by plain Linux, but you can modify keyboard behavior under X11 with `xmodmap`. Usually the X11 initialization process will run this command automatically if you have a file called `.Xmodmap` in your home directory.

In XFree86 v3.2 and higher you should have the following `Keyboard` section in your `/etc/XF86Config` file (it is made automatically by the program `XF86Setup` if you choose a Danish keytable):

```
Section "Keyboard"
    Protocol        "Standard"
    XkbRules        "xfree86"
    XkbModel        "pc101"
    XkbLayout       "dk"
```

```
    XkbVariant      "nodeadkeys"
  EndSection
```

The only keyboard variant available at the moment is `nodeadkeys`, but dead keys can still be made to work. See section 14.3 for more information on this.

14.2 Getting the AltGr key to work under X11

For versions of XFree86 up to and including v3.1.2, you should edit the file `/etc/X11/XF86Config` (or possibly `/etc/XF86Config`) and make sure the line

```
RightAlt    ModeShift
```

appears in the `Keyboard` section. Usually you can do this by uncommenting the appropriate line. In XFree86 v3.1.2 you can use `AltGr` as an alias for `RightAlt`.

The `AltGr` key should work as expected in XFree86 v3.2 and higher if you choose Danish keyboard support.

14.2.1 Making {, [,], and } work under Metro-X

You can't input the characters "{" (<AltGr> <7>), "[" <AltGr> <8>), "]" (<AltGr> <9>), and "}" (<AltGr> <0>) under the Metro-X server. This bug has been observed under versions 3.1.5 and 3.1.8 of the server.

To correct this bug you have to edit the file `/usr/X11R6/lib/X11/xkb/symbols/dk` and change the lines

```
key <AE07> {    [                 7,          slash     ]       };
key <AE08> {    [                 8,      parenleft     ]       };
key <AE09> {    [                 9,     parenright     ]       };
key <AE10> {    [                 0,          equal     ]       };
```

to

```
key <AE07> {    [                 7,          slash     ],
                [         braceleft,       NoSymbol     ]       };
key <AE08> {    [                 8,      parenleft     ],
                [       bracketleft,       NoSymbol     ]       };
key <AE09> {    [                 9,     parenright     ],
                [      bracketright,       NoSymbol     ]       };
key <AE10> {    [                 0,          equal     ],
                [        braceright,       NoSymbol     ]       };
```

14.3 Dead keys and accented characters

Dead keys are those that does not type anything until you hit another key. Tildes and umlauts are like this by default under plain Linux if you use the `dk-latin1.map` keymap. This is the default behaviour for these keys under Microsoft Windows as well.

14.3.1 Removing dead key functionality

- Removing dead key functionality under plain Linux and XFree86 v3.1.2

  Under plain Linux type

  ```
  loadkeys dk.map
  ```

- Removing dead key functionality under XFree86 v3.2 and higher

  Put the following line in the `Keyboard` section of your `/etc/XF86Config` file:

  ```
  XkbVariant      "nodeadkeys"
  ```

14.3.2 Invoking dead key functionality

- Invoking dead key functionality under plain Linux

  Under plain Linux type

  ```
  loadkeys dk-latin1.map
  ```

- Invoking dead key functionality under X11R6 sessions

  First you must make sure you are running XFree86 v3.1.2 or higher. Download and install everything related to the newest release if you have a lower version number. Neither compose nor dead keys will work in X11R6 applications unless these are compiled with support for accented (8-bit) character input. A useful example of such an application is GNU `emacs` version 19.30 (or higher.)

  Some X11 applications still do not support this input method. Eventually this situation might improve, but until that happens you can either hack your applications or submit polite bug reports to the program authors. The latter approach is often the most efficient. See Section 18 for some advice on what needs to be done.

  Next you will have to map a key to `Multi_key` (`Compose`.) The `Scroll Lock` key is most likely already mapped as such if you use XFree86 v3.1.2 (you can verify this with the program `xev`,) and it is easy to map the right `Control` key by uncommenting the appropriate line in the `Keyboard` section of the XFree86 configuration file (often `/etc/XF86Config`.) If you wish to use some other key, or if you are using XFree86 v3.2 or higher and want to change the default, you should put something like

  ```
  keycode 78 = Multi_key
  ```

  in your `~/.Xmodmap` file. The statement in the example defines `Scroll Lock` as the `Compose` key. The default `Compose` key in XFree86 v3.2 and higher is `<Shift><AltGr>`.

  XFree86 v3.2 and higher comes without support for the dead keys on the standard Danish keyboard. To get this support you have to change a few lines in the `xkb_symbols "basic"` section of the file `/usr/X11R6/lib/X11/xkb/symbols/dk`. The lines

  ```
  key <AE12> {    [          acute,           grave       ],
                  [            bar,    dead_ogonek       ]       };
  key <AD12> {    [      diaeresis,     asciicircum       ],
                  [     asciitilde,     dead_macron       ]       };
  ```

  should be changed to

  ```
  key <AE12> {    [     dead_acute,      dead_grave       ],
                  [            bar,     dead_ogonek       ]       };
  key <AD12> {    [ dead_diaeresis, dead_circumflex       ],
                  [     dead_tilde,     dead_macron       ]       };
  ```

  After these changes you can get support for dead keys by removing the line

  ```
  XkbVariant      "nodeadkeys"
  ```

  from the `Keyboard` section of your `/etc/XF86Config` file.

  (Note for non-Danish readers: `/usr/X11R6/lib/X11/xkb/symbols` contains files for many local keyboards.)

  The available keystroke combinations are compiled in `/usr/X11R6/lib/X11/locale/iso8859-1/Compose`. There are some bugs in that file you will want to fix:

  1. The line reading

     ```
     <dead_tilde> <space>                    : "~"   tilde
     ```

     should be changed to

     ```
     <dead_tilde> <space>                    : "~"   asciitilde
     ```

  2. In several places `asciicircum` is misspelled as `asciicirum`

  Finally make sure your shells and/or applications is set up for ISO 8859-1 compatibility as described in section 15.3 and you should be all set.

14.4 Making $ (the dollar sign), ø (oslash) and Ø (Oslash) work

14.4.1 $ (the dollar sign)

There is a bug in the Danish keymaps causing the dollar sign to be accessed with `<Shift><4>` instead of `<AltGr><4>` by default. If this is a problem for you, determine what keymap you load at boot-time. You can find it by looking around in the directory `/etc/rc.d/` or simply by paying attention to what happens at boot-time. On my computer the relevant keymap is called `/usr/lib/kbd/keytables/dk-latin1.map`. You can fix the problem by changing the line

```
keycode   5 = four              dollar          dollar
```

in the keymap file to

```
keycode   5 = four              currency        dollar
```

and then loading the keytable as described in section 14.1. Currency (dansk: "soltegn") is the default <Shift><4> character on a Danish keyboard.

This should fix the problem for both X11 and plain Linux.

14.4.2 ø (oslash) and Ø (Oslash)

In some older distributions "ø" and "Ø" appear as cent and yen. Find the line for keycode 40 in the keymap file and change it from

```
keycode  40 = cent              yen
```

to

```
keycode  40 = +oslash           +Ooblique
```

Note: This bug appears to have been fixed in `kbd-0.88.tar.gz` and newer versions.

The plus signs are necessary to get Caps Lock working properly. "Oslash" can be used as an alias for "Ooblique" in `kbd-0.90.tar.gz` and newer versions.

15 Display and application setup

Most applications need to be compiled as "8-bit clean" to work well with European characters. Some need a few extra hints to get it right.

15.1 Loading the Latin-1 character set on the console

Execute the following commands under the `bash` shell:

```
setfont lat1-16.psf
mapscrn trivial
echo -ne '\033(K'
```

You could also choose to load the font as Unicode to ensure that lines are displayed correctly in programs such as `mc` and `workbone`. Execute the following commands to do that:

```
setfont lat1-16.psf -m lat1.uni
loadunimap lat1.uni
echo -ne '\033(K'
```

If you use Linux kernels v1.3.1 or higher, you do not need the `echo` command when you load the font as Unicode. Note: This only has effect under plain Linux.

15.2 Characters you can display under Linux

Type `dumpkeys -l | less` at the prompt to find out which characters that are readily available. You can map them to your keyboard via the keymap files mentioned in Section 14.1.

15.3 International character sets in specific applications

A number of applications demand special attention. This section describes how to set up configuration files for them.

bash:

Put the following in your `~/.inputrc` file:

```
set meta-flag on
set convert-meta off
set output-meta on
```

elm:

Put the following definitions in your `~/.elm/elmrc` file:

```
charset = iso-8859-1
displaycharset = iso-8859-1
textencoding = 8bit
```

This may not work on some versions of `elm`.

emacs:

Put the following in your `~/.emacs` or the the system-wide initialization file (probably `/usr/lib/emacs/site-lisp/default.el` or `/usr/share/emacs/site-lisp/default.el`):

```
(standard-display-european t)
(require 'iso-syntax)
(set-input-mode (car (current-input-mode))
        (nth 1 (current-input-mode))
        0)
```

You can leave out the first two of the lines above if you have installed locale support, and your `LC_CTYPE` environment variable includes one of the strings `8859-1` or `88591`. See Section 17 for some information on locales.

Dead keys should work under GNU Emacs provided you use GNU Emacs v19.30 or higher and XFree86 v3.1.2 or higher (it works for me anyway), so do not start researching available Elisp packages implementing "electric keys" or anything like that. If you want to implement European keyboard conventions in emacs without upgrading, the best choice is probably the `remap` package available from the SunSite DK server (see section 20.2.) There are also two packages called `iso-acc.elc` and `iso-trans.elc` included with Emacs that has similar functionality, but they are not nearly as powerful.

groff:

Issue the command as

```
groff -Tlatin1 <your_groff_input_file>
```

Remember to change this in `/etc/man.config` to get latin1 characters working in `man` (don't remove the `-mandoc` switch.)

ispell—Spell checking in Danish:

First make sure that you install version 3.1 instead of version 4.0 of `ispell`. The latter is obsolete and multiple brain-damaged. You can download the sources for `ispell` at the GNU archive at `prep.ai.mit.edu`, and you can get a Danish dictionary via FTP from Aalborg University Center, ftp://ftp.iesd.auc.dk/pub/packages/dkispell/. Follow the compilation instructions and you should have no trouble (One caveat: When defining the variables necessary for compilation you must tell `ispell` that Linux is a SysV type OS by defining the variable `USG`.)

When you have installed the Danish dictionary for `ispell` you can check the spelling of a Danish language file by executing the command:

```
ispell -d danish -T latin1 -w "æøåÆØÅ" <your_danish_text_file>
```

(Note for non-Danish readers: You can find dictionaries for most Western languages by reading the file `Where` included with the sources for `ispell`.)

joe:

Issue the command as

```
joe -asis
```

or put the following in your `~/.joerc` file:

```
-asis
```

The hyphen character must be in the first column.

kermit:

This is as close as I can get, but not completely satisfying yet. Put the following in your `~/.kermrc` file:

```
set terminal bytesize 8
set command bytesize 8
set file bytesize 8
set language danish
set file character-set latin1-iso
set transfer character-set latin1-iso
set terminal character-set latin1-iso
```

I think there are more variables to set, but they are hiding. You would have to modify these settings if the remote system is DOS or OS/2 based.

less:

Set the following environment variable:

```
LESSCHARSET=latin1
```

ls:

Issue the command as

```
ls -N
```

or possibly

```
ls --8bit
```

lynx:

Put the following definition in your `~/.lynxrc` file:

```
character_set=ISO Latin 1
```

This can also be set via the `Options` menu in `lynx`. Type 'o' and set the relevant option.

man:

See entry for `groff` in this section.

metamail:

Set the following environment variable:

```
MM_CHARSET=ISO-8859-1
```

nn:

Put the following in your `~/.nn/init` file:

```
set data-bits 8
```

pine:

Put the following definition in your `~/.pinerc` file:

```
character-set=ISO-8859-1
```

This can also be set via the `Setup`, `Config` menu option in `pine`.

rlogin:

Issue the command as

```
rlogin -8 foo.bar.dk
```

tcsh:

Put the following in your `/etc/csh.login` or `~/.tcshrc` file:

```
setenv LANG C
```

Actually you just have to define one of the environment variables `LANG` or `LC_CTYPE`. The value does not matter. Read the `tcsh` man page for more information.

telnet:

Put one line of the following type in your `~/.telnetrc` file for **each** host you want to log on to using `telnet`:

```
<hostname> set outbinary true
```

Example:

```
localhost set outbinary true
foo.bar.dk set outbinary true
```

TEX and LATEX:

There are several problems with TEX and LATEX: You want LATEX to understand the special characters and you do not want LATEX to put in English words like "Chapter" at the beginning of every chapter or use English typesetting conventions.

Under LATEX 2ε, the header of your input file should look something like this:

```
\documentclass[a4paper]{article}

\usepackage[latin1]{inputenc}
\usepackage{t1enc}
\usepackage[danish]{babel}
```

The first `usepackage` statement ensures that LATEX will interpret European characters correctly, so you do not have to use escape codes for European characters. The second is not strictly necessary; but it is recommended to include it to use the DC fonts (which of course must be installed.) The DC fonts should soon be replaced by the newer EC fonts. These two packages are most likely included in your LATEX distribution. The last `usepackage` statement defines a range of standards for typesetting Danish texts.

If you use the Debian distribution (or older Slackware) you will have to install Danish hyphenation tables yourself (dansk: "hyphenation"="orddeling".) These are available from Aalborg University Center, `ftp://ftp.iesd.auc.dk/pub/packages/`. The files you need are `dkhyphen.tex`, `dkcommon.tex` and `dkspecial.tex`. If you use the teTeX distribution (distributed with e.g. Red Hat and S.u.S.E.) you already have the relevant files. Essentially you need to put these into the directory containing international hyphenation tables, edit the appropriate language dependency file (usually called `language.dat`) and finally rebuild LATEX with `initex`. Before you do anything, please make sure you know what files you are changing and back them up in advance.

If you use NTeX (distributed with the Slackware distribution) you will have a configuration script called `ntm-ltx.cfg` located in `/usr/lib/texmf/tools/`. In that case put the hyphenation tables in the the relevant directory (most likely called `/usr/lib/texmf/tex/hyphenation/`) and run the script. It will guide you through the various steps described below. If you use teTeX there is a somewhat more advanced program called `texconfig` to help you.

Below is a description for enabling Danish hyphenation by hand. If it looks vague it is because TEX and LATEX installations differ very much in their choice of path names.

1. Find out where you have the hyphenation tables. Under NTeX they are in

   ```
   /usr/lib/texmf/tex/hyphenation/
   ```

   under teTeX in

   ```
   /usr/lib/texmf/texmf/tex/generic/hyphen/
   ```

   Try issuing the command

   ```
   find /usr/lib/ -iname '*hyph*' -print
   ```

   if you cannot find the directory.

2. Check if the hyphenation tables are already there. If not put the hyphenation tables mentioned above in this directory.

3. Edit the file (probably) called `language.dat`. In the teTeX distribution you can just uncomment the appropriate line. Otherwise insert a line reading

   ```
   danish dkhyphen.tex
   ```

   If you have difficulty finding `language.dat` try issuing the command `find /usr/lib/ -name language.dat -print`

4. Find and back up the file `latex.fmt`. It could be in a variety of places. Use `find /usr/lib/ -name latex.fmt -print` to find it.

5. Go to the directory where you found `latex.fmt`. Issue the command `initex latex.ltx`. Pray. If everything went well you now have a new version of `latex.fmt`.

6. You can now use

   ```
   \usepackage[danish]{babel}
   ```

in your LaTeX headers. Hyphenation should be reasonably correct, quotation marks follow Danish conventions, chapters are now called "Kapitel" instead of "Chapter" etc.

All new Linux distributions now include LaTeX 2ε.

(Note for non-Danish readers: The process is similar for other Western European languages, and the necessary files are normally included in the Linux distributions.)

In LaTeX 2.09, use

```
\documentstyle[a4,isolatin]{article}
```

to include support for ISO 8859-1 characters and European paper sizes.

`isolatin.sty` is available from all DANTE servers (see Section 20.2) and from Michael Gschwind's FTP site, `ftp://ftp.vlsivie.tuwien.ac.at/pub/8bit`. It should also be included in the standard Linux distributions.

Note: Some people prefer using `emacs` in a special mode which translates "special" letters into TeX escape codes, but this method should be obsolete by now.

`tin`:

Put the following definitions in your `~/.tin/headers` file:

```
Mime-Version: 1.0
Content-Type: text/plain; charset=iso-8859-1
Content-Transfer-Encoding: 8bit
```

Now you can post messages with the proper Danish characters in the message body.

16 Miscellaneous problems

16.1 Time zone

Denmark is placed in the Central European Time zone (CET or MET,) which (in the winter) is equivalent to Greenwich Mean Time plus 1 (GMT+1.) You set the time zone on a Linux system by making a symbolic link between `/usr/lib/zoneinfo/localtime` and the file in `/usr/lib/zoneinfo/` with a name corresponding to your zone or country. Danes will want to execute one of the commands

```
ln -sf /usr/lib/zoneinfo/MET /etc/localtime
```

or

```
ln -sf /usr/lib/zoneinfo/Europe/Copenhagen /etc/localtime
```

This automatically sets Daylight Saving Time (GMT+2) in the summer.

You synchronize the system time with the CMOS clock by issuing the command `clock` as root. If your CMOS clock is set to GMT (a.k.a. UTC — the standard on proper Unix systems) use

```
clock -u -s
```

or if your CMOS clock is set to local time use

```
clock -s
```

16.2 A4 paper size

- `dvips`: Edit the file `/usr/lib/texmf/dvips/config.ps` or `~/.dvips`.
- `ghostscript`: Add the command line option `-sPAPERSIZE=a4`.
- `ghostview`: Define the following Xresource:

```
Ghostview.pageMedia:  A4
```

- `TeX/LaTeX`: See the entry for TeX/LaTeX in Section 15.3.
- `xdvi`: Define the Xresource

```
XDvi.paper:     a4
```

16.3 Text file formats for other platforms

You can translate files between an ISO 8859-1 formatted text file and e.g. a DOS text file using code page 850 with the `recode` package. A DOS file called `foo.txt` would be translated into a proper Unix file with the command

```
recode cp850:latin1 foo.txt
```

`Recode` is available as `recode-3.4.tar.gz` from all mirrors of `prep.ai.mit.edu`.

17 Locale support in libc 5.4.x

The locale support has been updated in `libc 5.4.x`. You can avoid many of the individual programs setups described in section 15.3 if the programs on your system is prepared for locale support. The Debian distribution comes with this support if you install the `wg15-locale` package. Read the Locales mini-HOWTO if you want to set up locale support on a non-Debian system.

To enable support for the Danish locale on a system with locale support you just have to set one of the following environment variables:

```
LANG=da_DK.ISO_8859-1
```

or

```
LC_ALL=da_DK.ISO_8859-1
```

Both environment variables set all the individual locale categories. You can also set a single locale category by using the name of the category as an environment variable. The locale categories are:

```
Locale category         Application
----------------        -----------
LC_COLLATE              Collation of strings (sort order.)
LC_CTYPE                Classification and conversion of characters.
LC_MESSAGES             Translations of yes and no.
LC_MONETARY             Format of monetary values.
LC_NUMERIC              Format of non-monetary numeric values.
LC_TIME                 Date and time formats.
LC_ALL                  Sets all of the above (overrides all of them.)
LANG                    Sets all the categories, but can be overridden
                        by the individual locale categories.
```

A few programs such as `bash` and GNU `emacs` still need specific setup, but most should work without further attention. Programs such as `nvi` which didn't work with 8 bit characters before should work now.

Locale support should be more common as distributions based on the new `GNU libc 2` (`libc 6.x`) become available.

18 Programming tips for X11

Displaying 8-bit characters is easy. You can use them just as you would use 7-bit ASCII. Getting applications to accept input of special characters is an entirely different matter.

If you are using e.g. the Xt toolkit and a widget set like Motif you need only add one line to your program. As your **first** call to Xt use `XtSetLanguageProc`. Like this:

```
int main (int argc, char** argv)
{
    ...
    XtSetLanguageProc (NULL, NULL, NULL);
    top = XtAppInitialize ( ... );
    ...
}
```

Now your program will automagically look up the `LC_CTYPE` variable and interpret dead keys etc. according to the `Compose` tables in `/usr/lib/X11/locale/`. This should work for all Western European keyboard layouts and is entirely portable. As XFree86 multilanguage support gets better your program will also be useful in Eastern Europe and the Middle East.

This method of input is supported by Xt, Xlib and Motif v1.2 (and higher.) According to the information I have available it is only partially supported by Xaw. If you have further information on this subject I would like to hear from you.

This section was adapted from a more extensive discussion in Michael Gschwind's Programming for Internationalization. See Section 20.1 for a pointer to that document.

19 Getting X11 applications to speak Danish

To get Danish texts on menus, buttons, etc. in a well behaved X11 application, you just have to translate the resource strings defining the texts. Jacob Nordfalk has done such translations for a lot of applications including `Netscape` and `Ghostview`. The translations and a description of how to install them can be found on his home page, `http://alf.nbi.dk/~nordfalk/ovs/`.

20 References and FTP sites

20.1 Other documents of relevance

The HOWTOs ought to be available from all mirrors of `sunsite.unc.edu` and `tsx-11.mit.edu`. A Danish mirror at the Web is Sunsite DK, `http://sunsite.auc.dk/ldp/HOWTO/`.

The German HOWTO (in German) by Winfried Trümper. A lot of other national HOWTOs such as Finnish, Spanish and Polish are also available in the native languages.

The Linux Keyboard and Console HOWTO by Andries Brouwer.

The Locales mini-HOWTO by Peeter Joot.

The ISO 8859-1 National Character Set FAQ and Programming for Internationalization (plus much more) by Michael Gschwind is available from his home page, http://www.vlsivie.tuwien.ac.at/mike/i18n.html.

20.2 FTP and Web sites

The Linux Danish/International HOWTO has its own home page http://www.image.dk/~nkbj/. It always has the latest version on line. It also has other informations for Danish users of Linux.

The FTP site at Allborg University Center (AUC), ftp://ftp.iesd.auc.dk/pub/packages/, has Danish hyphenation tables, dictionary for ispell etc. AUC is also the home of Suniste DK, ftp://sunsite.auc.dk/pub/os/linux/, which has the Debian and Red Hat distributions, the latest kernels, the Linux Documentation Project, http://sunsite.auc.dk/LDP/, mirrors of sunsite.unc.edu, ftp://sunsite.auc.dk/pub/os/linux/sunsite/, the GNU archives, ftp://sunsite.auc.dk/pub/gnu/, and the remap package for Emacs, ftp://sunsite.auc.dk/packages/auctex/.

Sunsite, ftp://sunsite.unc.edu/pub/Linux/ and mirrors. `doc/howto` has the HOWTOs mentioned above. `utils/nls` and subdirectories contain files related to National Language Support. Developers should take a look at `locale-tutorial-0.8.txt.gz`, `locale-pack-0.8.tar.gz`, and `cat-pack.tar.gz`.

The GNU archives (`ftp://prep.ai.mit.edu/pub/gnu/`) has the `recode` package for character table conversion, the `ABOUT-NLS` file and the `gettext` package for message translation of some GNU applications and (of course) the latest versions of GNU emacs.

The Dante FTP site, ftp://ftp.dante.de/ has everything needed for TeX and LaTeX support.

21 Post-amble: Acknowledgments and Copyright

Thanks to Peter Dalgaard, Anders Majland, Jon Haugsand, Jacob Nordfalk, the authors of the German HOWTO, Michael Gschwind and numerous others for suggestions and help with several questions. And a big thanks to the people at Aalborg University Center for writing and making available several of the packages described in this document.

21.1 Disclaimer

Although the information given in this document is believed to be correct, the authors will accept no liability for the content of this document. Use the tips and examples given herein at your own risk.

21.2 Copyright

This [illegible] is supported by X, Xlib and Motif. [illegible] Acrobat Reader [illegible] information I have [illegible] available [illegible]. If you have further information [illegible] I'd like to hear from you.

[illegible] see [illegible] Michael Gschwind's [illegible] Section 20 [illegible] that document.

19.5 Getting X applications to speak Danish

[illegible]

20 References and FTP sites

20.1 Other documents of relevance

[illegible]

The [illegible] HOWTO [illegible] and [illegible] HOWTO [illegible]

The [illegible] HOWTO [illegible]

The [illegible] HOWTO [illegible]

The ISO 8859-1 National Character Set FAQ [illegible] by Michael [illegible] is available from [illegible]

20.2 FTP and Web sites

The Linux Danish/International HOWTO has its own home page [illegible]

[illegible]

[illegible]

[illegible]

The Slackware FTP [illegible] TeX and LaTeX support.

21 Postamble: Acknowledgements and Copyright

Thanks to [illegible] for the original HOWTO, Michael [illegible]

21.1 Disclaimer

Although the information given in this document is believed to be correct, the authors will accept no liability for the content of this document. Use the tips and examples given herein at your own risk.

21.2 Copyright

Part XVI

"DNS HOWTO"

Nicolai Langfeldt,
janl@math.uio.no

Contents

Abstract

HOWTO become a totally small time DNS admin.

1 Preamble

Keywords: DNS, bind, named, dialup, ppp, slip, Internet, domain, name, hosts, resolving

1.1 Legal stuff

1.2 Credits and request for help.

I want to thank Arnt Gulbrandsen who read the drafts to this work countless times and provided many useful suggestions. I also want to thank the people that have e-mailed suggestions, and thank you notes. Thank you! You help me keep going at this.

This will never be a finished document, please send me mail about your problems and successes, it can make this a better HOWTO. So please send money, comments and/or questions to janl@math.uio.no. If you send E-mail please *make sure* that the return address is correct, I get *a lot* of E-mail. Also, **please** read the 8 section before mailing me.

If you want to translate this HOWTO please notify me so I can keep track of what languages I have been published in.

1.3 Dedication

This HOWTO is dedicated to Anne Line Norheim. Though she will probably never read it since she's not that kind of girl.

2 Introduction.

What this is and isn't.

For starters, DNS is the Domain Name System. The rules that name machines and software that maps those names to IP numbers. This HOWTO documents how to define such mappings using a Linux system. A mapping is simply an association between two things, in this case a machine name, like ftp.linux.org, and the machine's IP number, 199.249.150.4.

DNS is, to the uninitiated (you), one of the more opaque areas of network administration. This HOWTO will try to make a few things clearer. It describes how to set up a *simple* DNS name server. Starting with a caching only server and going on to setting up a primary DNS server for a domain. For more complex setups you can check Section 8 of this document. If it's not described there you will need to read the Real Documentation. I'll get back to what this Real Documentation consists of in Section 9.

Before you start on this you should configure your machine so that you can Telnet in and out of it, and make successfully make all kinds of connections to the net, and you should especially be able to do `telnet 127.0.0.1` and get your own machine (test it now!). You also need a good `/etc/host.conf` (or `/etc/nsswitch.conf`), `/etc/resolv.conf` and `/etc/hosts` files as a starting point, since I will not explain their function here. If you don't already have all this set up and working, the NET-3-HOWTO (page 1074) explains how to set it up. Read it.

If you're using SLIP or PPP you need that working. Read the PPP HOWTO if it's not.

When I say "your machine" I mean the machine you are trying to set up DNS on. Not any other machine you might have that's involved in your networking effort.

I assume you're not behind any kind of firewall that blocks name queries. If you are, you will need a special configuration, see Section 8.

Name serving on Unix is done by a program called `named`. This is a part of the BIND package which is coordinated by Paul Vixie for The Internet Software Consortium. `named` is included in most Linux distributions and is usually installed as `/usr/sbin/named`. If you have a `named` you can probably use it; if you don't have one you can get a binary off a Linux FTP site, or get the latest and greatest source from `ftp.vix.com:/pub/bind` in either the release or testing subdirectory, whatever fits your lifestyle best.

DNS is a net-wide database. Take care about what you put into it. If you put junk into it, you, and others, will get junk out of it. Keep your DNS tidy and consistent and you will get good service from it. Learn to use it, administer it, debug it and you will be another good administrator keeping the net from falling to its knees overloaded by mismanagement.

In this document I state flatly a couple of things that are not completely true (they are at least half truths though). All in the interest of simplification. Things will (probably) work if you believe what I say.

Tip: Make backup copies of all the files I instruct you to change if you already have them, so if after going through this, nothing works, you can get it back to your old, working state.

3 A caching-only name server.

A first stab at DNS configuration, very useful for dialup users.

A caching only name server will find the answer to name queries and remember the answer the next time you need it. First you need a file called `/etc/named.boot`. This is read when `named` starts. For now it should simply contain:

```
;  Boot file for caching only name server
;
directory /var/named
;
; type          domain                          source file or host
cache           .                               root.cache
primary         0.0.127.in-addr.arpa            pz/127.0.0
```

VERY IMPORTANT: In some versions of this document, the file contents listed here will have a couple of spaces or a tab before the first non-blank character. These are not supposed to be in the file. **Delete any leading space** in the files you cut and paste from this HOWTO.

The "`directory`" line tells named where to look for files. All files named subsequently will be relative to this. `/var/named` is the right directory according to the *Linux File System Standard*. Thus, `pz` is a directory under `/var/named`, i.e., `/var/named/pz`.

The file named `/var/named/root.cache` is named in this. `/var/named/root.cache` should contain this:

```
.        518400  NS      D.ROOT-SERVERS.NET.
.        518400  NS      E.ROOT-SERVERS.NET.
.        518400  NS      I.ROOT-SERVERS.NET.
.        518400  NS      F.ROOT-SERVERS.NET.
.        518400  NS      G.ROOT-SERVERS.NET.
.        518400  NS      A.ROOT-SERVERS.NET.
.        518400  NS      H.ROOT-SERVERS.NET.
.        518400  NS      B.ROOT-SERVERS.NET.
.        518400  NS      C.ROOT-SERVERS.NET.
;
D.ROOT-SERVERS.NET.     3600000 A       128.8.10.90
E.ROOT-SERVERS.NET.     3600000 A       192.203.230.10
I.ROOT-SERVERS.NET.     3600000 A       192.36.148.17
F.ROOT-SERVERS.NET.     3600000 A       192.5.5.241
G.ROOT-SERVERS.NET.     3600000 A       192.112.36.4
A.ROOT-SERVERS.NET.     3600000 A       198.41.0.4
H.ROOT-SERVERS.NET.     3600000 A       128.63.2.53
B.ROOT-SERVERS.NET.     3600000 A       128.9.0.107
C.ROOT-SERVERS.NET.     3600000 A       192.33.4.12
```

Remember what I said about leading spaces!

The file describes the root name servers in the world. This changes over time and *must* be maintained. See Section 6 for how to keep it up to date. This file is described in the `named` manual page, but it is, IMHO, best suited for people that already understand `named`.

The next line in `named.boot` is the `primary` line. I will explain its use in a later section. For now, just make this a file named `127.0.0` in the subdirectory `pz`:

```
@               IN      SOA     ns.linux.bogus. hostmaster.linux.bogus. (
                                1       ; Serial
                                28800   ; Refresh
                                7200    ; Retry
                                604800  ; Expire
                                86400)  ; Minimum TTL
                        NS      ns.linux.bogus.
1                       PTR     localhost.
```

Next, you need a /etc/resolv.conf looking something like this:

```
search subdomain.your-domain.edu your-domain.edu
nameserver 127.0.0.1
```

The "search" line specifies what domains should be searched for any host names you want to connect to. The "nameserver" line specifies the address of your nameserver at, in this case your own machine since that is where your named runs. If you want to list several name servers, put in one "nameserver" line for each. (Note: named never reads this file, the resolver that uses named does.)

To illustrate what this file does: If a client tries to look up foo, foo.subdomain.your-domain.edu is tried first, then foo.your fomain.edu, finally foo. If a client tries to look up sunsite.unc.edu, sunsite.unc.edu.subdomain.your-domain.edu is tried first (yes, it's silly, but that's the way it's gotta be) , then sunsite.unc.edu.your-domain.edu, and finally sunsite.unc.edu. You may not want to put in too many domains in the search line, it takes time to search them.

The example assumes you belong in the domain subdomain.your-domain.edu, your machine then, is probably called your-machine.subdomain.your-domain.edu. The search line should not contain your TLD (Top Level Domain, "edu" in this case). If you frequently need to connect to hosts in another domain you can add that domain to the search line like this:

```
search subdomain.your-domain.edu your-domain.edu other-domain.com
```

and so on. Obviously, you need to put in real domain names instead. Please note the lack of periods at the end of the domain names.

Next, depending on your libc version you either need to fix /etc/nsswitch.conf or /etc/host.conf. If you already have nsswitch.conf that's what we'll fix, if not, we'll fix host.conf.

/etc/nsswitch.conf

This is a long file specifying where to get different kinds of data types, from what file or database. It usually contains helpful comments at the top, which you should consider reading, now. After that, find the line starting with "hosts:", it should read

```
hosts:       files dns
```

If there is no line starting with "hosts:," then put in the one above. It says that programs should first look in the /etc/hosts file, then check DNS according to /etc/resolv.conf.

/etc/host.conf

It probably contains several lines, one starting with order and it should look like this:

```
order hosts,bind
```

If there is no "order" line you should stick one in. It tells the host-name resolving routines to first look in /etc/hosts, then ask the name server (which you in resolv.conf said is at 127.0.0.1). These two latest files are documented in resolv(8) (do "man 8 resolv") in most Linux distributions. That man page is IMHO readable, and everyone, especially DNS admins, should read it. Do it now. If you say to yourself, "I'll do it later," you'll never get around to it.

3.1 Starting named

After all this, it's time to start named. If you're using a dial-up connection, connect first. Type "ndc start," and press Return, no options. If that backfires try "/usr/sbin/ndc start" instead. If that back-fires see Section 8. Now you can test your setup. If you view your syslog message file (usually called /var/adm/messages, but another directory to look in is /var/log and another file to look in is syslog) while starting named (do tail -f /var/adm/messages) you should see something like:

```
Jun 30 21:50:55 roke named[2258]: starting.  named 4.9.4-REL Sun Jun 30 21:29:03 MET DST 1996
Jun 30 21:50:55 roke named[2258]: cache zone "" loaded (serial 0)
Jun 30 21:50:55 roke named[2258]: primary zone "0.0.127.in-addr.arpa" loaded (serial 1)
```

If there are any messages about errors, then there is a mistake. named will name the file it is in (one of /etc/named.boot and /etc/root.cache I hope). Kill named and go back and check the file.

Now it's time to start nslookup to examine your handiwork.

```
$ nslookup
Default Server:  localhost
Address:  127.0.0.1

>
```

If that's what you get, it's working. We hope. Anything else, go back and check everything. Each time you change the `/etc/named.boot` file, you need to restart `named` using the `ndc restart` command.

Now you can enter a query. Try looking up some machine close to you. `pat.uio.no` is close to me, at the University of Oslo:

```
> pat.uio.no
Server:  localhost
Address:  127.0.0.1

Name:    pat.uio.no
Address:  129.240.2.50
```

`nslookup` asked your `named` to look for the machine `pat.uio.no`. It then contacted one of the name server machines named in your `root.cache` file, and asked its way from there. It might take tiny while before you get the result as it searches all the domains you named in `/etc/resolv.conf`.

If you try again you get this:

```
> pat.uio.no
Server:  localhost
Address:  127.0.0.1

Non-authoritative answer:
Name:    pat.uio.no
Address:  129.240.2.50
```

Note the "`Non-authoritative answer:`" line we got this time around. That means that `named` did not go out on the network to ask this time, it instead looked in its cache and found it there. But the cached information might be out of date (stale). So you are informed of this (very slight) danger by it saying "`Non-authorative answer:`". When `nslookup` says this the second time you ask for a host, it's a sure sign that `named` caches the information and that it's working. You exit `nslookup` by giving the command "`exit`".

If you're a dialup (PPP or SLIP) user please read Section 7. There is some advice there for you.

Now you know how to set up a caching `named`. Take a beer, milk, or whatever you prefer to celebrate it.

4 A simple domain.

How to set up your own domain.

4.1 But first some dry theory

Before we really start this section, I'm going to serve you some theory on how DNS works. And you're going to read it because it's good for you. If you don't "wanna" you should at least skim it very quickly. Stop skimming when you get to what should go in your `/etc/named.boot` file.

DNS is a hierarchical system. The top is written "`.`" and pronounced "root." Under `.` there are a number of Top Level Domains (TLDs), the best known ones are ORG, COM, EDU and NET, but there are many more.

When looking for a machine, the query proceeds recursively into the hierarchy starting at the top. If you want to find out the address of `prep.ai.mit.edu`, your name server has to find a name server that serves edu. It asks a `.` server (it already knows the `.` servers, that's what the `root.cache` file is for), the `.` server gives a list of edu servers:

```
$ nslookup
Default Server:  localhost
Address:  127.0.0.1
```

Start asking a root server.

```
> server c.root-servers.net.
Default Server:  c.root-servers.net
Address:  192.33.4.12
```

Set the Query type to NS (name server records).

```
> set q=ns
```

Ask about edu.

```
> edu.
```

The trailing . here is significant, it tells the server we're asking that edu is right under . (this narrows the search somewhat).

```
edu      nameserver = A.ROOT-SERVERS.NET
edu      nameserver = H.ROOT-SERVERS.NET
edu      nameserver = B.ROOT-SERVERS.NET
edu      nameserver = C.ROOT-SERVERS.NET
edu      nameserver = D.ROOT-SERVERS.NET
edu      nameserver = E.ROOT-SERVERS.NET
edu      nameserver = I.ROOT-SERVERS.NET
edu      nameserver = F.ROOT-SERVERS.NET
edu      nameserver = G.ROOT-SERVERS.NET
A.ROOT-SERVERS.NET      internet address = 198.41.0.4
H.ROOT-SERVERS.NET      internet address = 128.63.2.53
B.ROOT-SERVERS.NET      internet address = 128.9.0.107
C.ROOT-SERVERS.NET      internet address = 192.33.4.12
D.ROOT-SERVERS.NET      internet address = 128.8.10.90
E.ROOT-SERVERS.NET      internet address = 192.203.230.10
I.ROOT-SERVERS.NET      internet address = 192.36.148.17
F.ROOT-SERVERS.NET      internet address = 192.5.5.241
G.ROOT-SERVERS.NET      internet address = 192.112.36.4
```

This tells us that `*.root-servers.net` serves `edu.`, so we can go on asking `c`. Now we want to know who serves the next level of the domain name: `mit.edu.`:

```
> mit.edu.
Server:  c.root-servers.net
Address:  192.33.4.12

Non-authoritative answer:
mit.edu nameserver = STRAWB.mit.edu
mit.edu nameserver = W20NS.mit.edu
mit.edu nameserver = BITSY.mit.edu

Authoritative answers can be found from:
STRAWB.mit.edu  internet address = 18.71.0.151
W20NS.mit.edu   internet address = 18.70.0.160
BITSY.mit.edu   internet address = 18.72.0.3
```

`strawb`, `w20ns`, and `bitsy` serve `mit`. Select one and inquire about `ai.mit.edu`:

```
> server W20NS.mit.edu.
```

Host names are not case sensitive, but I use my mouse to cut and paste so it gets copied as-is from the screen.

```
Server:  W20NS.mit.edu
Address:  18.70.0.160

> ai.mit.edu.
Server:  W20NS.mit.edu
Address:  18.70.0.160

Non-authoritative answer:
ai.mit.edu      nameserver = WHEATIES.AI.MIT.EDU
ai.mit.edu      nameserver = ALPHA-BITS.AI.MIT.EDU
ai.mit.edu      nameserver = GRAPE-NUTS.AI.MIT.EDU
ai.mit.edu      nameserver = TRIX.AI.MIT.EDU
ai.mit.edu      nameserver = MUESLI.AI.MIT.EDU

Authoritative answers can be found from:
AI.MIT.EDU      nameserver = WHEATIES.AI.MIT.EDU
AI.MIT.EDU      nameserver = ALPHA-BITS.AI.MIT.EDU
AI.MIT.EDU      nameserver = GRAPE-NUTS.AI.MIT.EDU
AI.MIT.EDU      nameserver = TRIX.AI.MIT.EDU
```

```
AI.MIT.EDU      nameserver = MUESLI.AI.MIT.EDU
WHEATIES.AI.MIT.EDU      internet address = 128.52.32.13
WHEATIES.AI.MIT.EDU      internet address = 128.52.35.13
ALPHA-BITS.AI.MIT.EDU    internet address = 128.52.32.5
ALPHA-BITS.AI.MIT.EDU    internet address = 128.52.37.5
GRAPE-NUTS.AI.MIT.EDU    internet address = 128.52.32.4
GRAPE-NUTS.AI.MIT.EDU    internet address = 128.52.36.4
TRIX.AI.MIT.EDU internet address = 128.52.32.6
TRIX.AI.MIT.EDU internet address = 128.52.38.6
MUESLI.AI.MIT.EDU        internet address = 128.52.32.7
MUESLI.AI.MIT.EDU        internet address = 128.52.39.7
```

So `wheaties.ai.mit.edu` is a nameserver for `ai.mit.edu`:

```
> server WHEATIES.AI.MIT.EDU.
Default Server:  WHEATIES.AI.MIT.EDU
Addresses:  128.52.32.13, 128.52.35.13
```

Now I change query type. We've found the name server, so now we're going to ask about everything `wheaties` knows about `prep.ai.mit.edu`.

```
> set q=any
> prep.ai.mit.edu.
Server:  WHEATIES.AI.MIT.EDU
Addresses:  128.52.32.13, 128.52.35.13

prep.ai.mit.edu CPU = dec/decstation-5000.25    OS = unix
prep.ai.mit.edu
        inet address = 18.159.0.42, protocol = tcp
         #21 #23 #25 #79
prep.ai.mit.edu preference = 1, mail exchanger = life.ai.mit.edu
prep.ai.mit.edu internet address = 18.159.0.42
ai.mit.edu      nameserver = alpha-bits.ai.mit.edu
ai.mit.edu      nameserver = wheaties.ai.mit.edu
ai.mit.edu      nameserver = grape-nuts.ai.mit.edu
ai.mit.edu      nameserver = mini-wheats.ai.mit.edu
ai.mit.edu      nameserver = trix.ai.mit.edu
ai.mit.edu      nameserver = muesli.ai.mit.edu
ai.mit.edu      nameserver = count-chocula.ai.mit.edu
ai.mit.edu      nameserver = life.ai.mit.edu
ai.mit.edu      nameserver = mintaka.lcs.mit.edu
life.ai.mit.edu internet address = 128.52.32.80
alpha-bits.ai.mit.edu    internet address = 128.52.32.5
wheaties.ai.mit.edu      internet address = 128.52.35.13
wheaties.ai.mit.edu      internet address = 128.52.32.13
grape-nuts.ai.mit.edu    internet address = 128.52.36.4
grape-nuts.ai.mit.edu    internet address = 128.52.32.4
mini-wheats.ai.mit.edu   internet address = 128.52.32.11
mini-wheats.ai.mit.edu   internet address = 128.52.54.11
mintaka.lcs.mit.edu      internet address = 18.26.0.36
```

So starting at `.` we found the successive name servers for the next level in the domain name. If you had used your own DNS server instead of using all those other servers, your `named` would of course cache all the information it found while digging this out for you, and it would not have to ask again for a while.

A much less talked about, but just as important domain is `in-addr.arpa`. It too is nested like the "normal" domains. `in-addr.arpa` allows us to get the host's name when we have its address. A important thing here is to note that IP numbers are written in reverse order in the in-addr.arpa domain. If you have the address of a machine: 192.128.52.43 named proceeds just like for the `prep.ai.mit.edu` example: find `arpa.` servers. Find `in-addr.arpa.` servers, find `192.in-addr.arpa.` servers, find `128.192.in-addr.arpa.` servers, find `52.128.192.in-addr.arpa.` servers. Find needed records for `43.52.128.192.in-addr.arpa.` Clever huh? (Say "yes".) The reversion of the numbers can be confusing the first two years.

I have just told a lie. DNS does not work literally the way I just told you. But it's close enough.

4.2 Our own domain

Now to define our own domain. We're going to make the domain *linux.bogus* and define machines in it. I use a totally bogus domain name to make sure we disturb no one Out There.

We've already started this part with this line in /etc/named.boot:

```
primary         0.0.127.in-addr.arpa                    pz/127.0.0
```

Please note the lack of "." at the end of the domain names in this file. The first line names the file pz/127.0.0 as defining 0.0.127.in-addr.arpa. We've already set up this file, it reads:

```
@               IN      SOA     ns.linux.bogus. hostmaster.linux.bogus. (
                                1       ; Serial
                                28800   ; Refresh
                                7200    ; Retry
                                604800  ; Expire
                                86400)  ; Minimum TTL
                        NS      ns.linux.bogus.
1                       PTR     localhost.
```

Please note the "." at the end of all the full domain names in this file, in contrast to the named.boot file above. Some people like to start each zone file with a $ORIGIN directive, but this is superfluous. The origin (where in the DNS hierarchy it belongs) of a zone file is specified in the "domain" column of the named.boot file, in this case it's 0.0.127.in-addr.arpa.

This "zone file" contains three "resource records" (RRs): A SOA RR. A NS RR and a PTR RR. SOA is short for Start Of Authority. The "@" is a special notation meaning the origin, and since the "domain" column for this file says 0.0.127.in-addr.arpa the first line really means

```
0.0.127.IN-ADDR.ARPA. IN      SOA ...
```

NS is the Name Server RR, it tells DNS what machine is the name server of the domain. And finally the PTR record says that 1 (equals 1.0.0.127.IN-ADDR.ARPA, i.e. 127.0.0.1) is named localhost.

The SOA record is the preamble to *all* zone files, and there should be exactly one in each zone file, the very first record. It describes the zone, where it comes from (a machine called linux.bogus), who is responsible for its contents (hostmaster@linux.bogus), what version of the zone file this is (serial: 1), and other things having to do with caching and secondary DNS servers. For the rest of the fields, refresh, retry, expire, and minimum use the numbers used in this HOWTO and you should be safe.

The NS record tells us who does DNS serving for 0.0.127.in-addr.arpa, it is ns.linux.bogus. The PTR record tells us that 1.0.0.127.in-addr.arpa (aka 127.0.0.1) is known as localhost.

Now restart your named (the command is ndc restart) and use nslookup to examine what you've done:

```
$ nslookup

Default Server:  localhost
Address:  127.0.0.1

> 127.0.0.1
Server:  localhost
Address:  127.0.0.1

Name:    localhost
Address:  127.0.0.1
```

so it manages to get localhost from 127.0.0.1, good. Now for our main task, the linux.bogus domain, insert a new primary line in named.boot:

```
primary              linux.bogus                        pz/linux.bogus
```

Note the continued lack of ending "." on the domain name in the named.boot file.

In the linux.bogus zone file we'll put some totally bogus data:

```
;
; Zone file for linux.bogus
;
; Mandatory minimum for a working domain
```

```
;
@       IN      SOA     ns.linux.bogus. hostmaster.linux.bogus. (
                        199511301       ; serial, todays date + todays serial #
                        28800           ; refresh, seconds
                        7200            ; retry, seconds
                        3600000         ; expire, seconds
                        86400 )         ; minimum, seconds
                NS      ns.linux.bogus.
                NS      ns.friend.bogus.
                MX      10 mail.linux.bogus    ; Primary Mail Exchanger
                MX      20 mail.friend.bogus. ; Secondary Mail Exchanger

localhost       A       127.0.0.1
ns              A       127.0.0.2
mail            A       127.0.0.4
```

Two things must be noted about the SOA record. ns.linux.bogus *must* be a actual machine with a A record. It is not legal to have a CNAME record for the machine mentioned in the SOA record. Its name need not be "ns," it could be any legal host name. Next, hostmaster.linux.bogus should be read as hostmaster@linux.bogus, this should be a mail alias, or a mailbox, where the person(s) maintaining DNS should read mail frequently. Any mail regarding the domain will be sent to the address listed here. The name need not be "hostmaster", it can be any legal e-mail address, but the e-mail address "hostmaster" *is* expected to work as well.

There is one new RR type in this file, the MX, or Mail eXchanger RR. It tells mail systems where to send mail that is addressed to `someone@linux.bogus`, namely too `mail.linux.bogus` or `mail.friend.bogus`. The number before each machine name is that MX RRs priority. The RR with the lowest number (10) is the one mail should be sent to primarily. If that fails it can be sent to one with a higher number, a secondary mail handler, i.e. `mail.friend.bogus` which has priority 20 here.

Restart named by running `ndc restart`. Examine the results with nslookup:

```
$ nslookup
> set q=any
> linux.bogus
Server:  localhost
Address:  127.0.0.1

linux.bogus
        origin = linux.bogus
        mail addr = hostmaster.linux.bogus
        serial = 199511301
        refresh = 28800 (8 hours)
        retry   = 7200 (2 hours)
        expire  = 604800 (7 days)
        minimum ttl = 86400 (1 day)
linux.bogus     nameserver = ns.linux.bogus
linux.bogus     nameserver = ns.friend.bogus
linux.bogus     preference = 10, mail exchanger = mail.linux.bogus.linux.bogus
linux.bogus     preference = 20, mail exchanger = mail.friend.bogus
linux.bogus     nameserver = ns.linux.bogus
linux.bogus     nameserver = ns.friend.bogus
ns.linux.bogus  internet address = 127.0.0.2
mail.linux.bogus        internet address = 127.0.0.4
```

Upon careful examination you will discover a bug. The line

```
linux.bogus     preference = 10, mail exchanger = mail.linux.bogus.linux.bogus
```

is all wrong. It should be

```
linux.bogus     preference = 10, mail exchanger = mail.linux.bogus
```

I deliberately made a mistake so you could learn from it. Looking in the zone file, we find that the line

```
@               MX      10 mail.linux.bogus     ; Primary Mail Exchanger
```

is missing a period. Or has a "linux.bogus" too many. If a machine name does not end in a period in a zone file, the origin is added to it's end. So either

```
@               MX      10 mail.linux.bogus.     ; Primary Mail Exchanger
```

or

```
@               MX      10 mail                  ; Primary Mail Exchanger
```

is correct. I prefer the latter form, it's less to type. In a zone file the domain should either be written out and ended with a "." or it should not be included at all, in which case it defaults to the origin. I must stress that in the `named.boot` file there should *not* be "."s after the domain names. You have no idea how many times a "." too many or few have fouled up things and confused the h*ll out of people.

So having made my point, here is the new zone file, with some extra information in it as well:

```
;
; Zone file for linux.bogus
;
; Mandatory minimum for a working domain
;
@       IN      SOA     ns.linux.bogus. hostmaster.linux.bogus. (
                        199511301       ; serial, todays date + todays serial #
                        28800           ; refresh, seconds
                        7200            ; retry, seconds
                        604800          ; expire, seconds
                        86400 )         ; minimum, seconds

                NS      ns              ; Inet Address of name server
                NS      ns.friend.bogus.
                MX      10 mail         ; Primary Mail Exchanger
                MX      20 mail.friend.bogus. ; Secondary Mail Exchanger

localhost       A       127.0.0.1
ns              A       127.0.0.2
mail            A       127.0.0.4
;
; Extras
;
@               TXT     "Linux.Bogus, your DNS consultants"

ns              MX      10 mail
                MX      20 mail.friend.bogus.
                HINFO   "Pentium" "Linux 1.2"
                TXT     "RMS"
richard         CNAME   ns
www             CNAME   ns

donald          A       127.0.0.3
                MX      10 mail
                MX      20 mail.friend.bogus.
                HINFO   "i486"  "Linux 1.2"
                TXT     "DEK"

mail            MX      10 mail
                MX      20 mail.friend.bogus.
                HINFO   "386sx" "Linux 1.0.9"

ftp             A       127.0.0.5
                MX      10 mail
                MX      20 mail.friend.bogus.
                HINFO   "P6" "Linux 1.3.59"
```

You might want to move the first three A records so that they're placed next to their respective other records, instead on top like that.

There are a number of new RRs here: HINFO (Host INFOrmation) has two parts, it's a good habit to quote each. The first part is the hardware or CPU on the machine, and the second part the software or OS on the machine. ns has a Pentium CPU and runs Linux 1.2. The TXT record is a free text record that you can use for anything you like. CNAME (Canonical NAME) is a way to give each machine several names. So richard and www is a alias for ns. It's important to note that A MX, CNAME and SOA record should *never* refer to a CNAME record, they should only refer to something with a A record, so it would wrong to have

```
foobar  CNAME   richard                      ; NO!
```

but correct to have

```
foobar  CNAME   ns                           ; Yes!
```

It's also important to note that a CNAME is not a legal host name for a e-mail address: `webmaster@www.linux.bogus` is an illegal e-mail address given the setup above. You can expect quite a few mail admins Out There to enforce this rule even if it works for you. The way to avoid this is to use A records (and perhaps some others too, like a MX record) instead:

```
www     A       127.0.0.2
```

Paul Vixie, the primary `named` wizard, recommends *not* using CNAME. So consider not using it *very* seriously.

Load the new database by running `ndc reload`. This causes named to read its files again.

```
$ nslookup
Default Server:  localhost
Address:  127.0.0.1

> ls -d linux.bogus
```

This means that all records should be listed.

```
[localhost]
 linux.bogus.                     SOA   ns.linux.bogus hostmaster.linux.bogus. (199511301 28800 7200
 linux.bogus.                     NS    ns.linux.bogus
 linux.bogus.                     NS    ns.friend.bogus
 linux.bogus.                     MX    10   mail.linux.bogus
 linux.bogus.                     MX    20   mail.friend.bogus
 linux.bogus.                     TXT   "Linux.Bogus, your DNS consultants"
 localhost                        A     127.0.0.1
 mail                             A     127.0.0.4
 mail                             MX    10   mail.linux.bogus
 mail                             MX    20   mail.friend.bogus
 mail                             HINFO 386sx       Linux 1.0.9
 donald                           A     127.0.0.3
 donald                           MX    10   mail.linux.bogus
 donald                           MX    20   mail.friend.bogus
 donald                           HINFO i486        Linux 1.2
 donald                           TXT   "DEK"
 www                              CNAME ns.linux.bogus
 richard                          CNAME ns.linux.bogus
 ftp                              A     127.0.0.5
 ftp                              MX    10   mail.linux.bogus
 ftp                              MX    20   mail.friend.bogus
 ftp                              HINFO P6          Linux 1.3.59
 ns                               A     127.0.0.2
 ns                               MX    10   mail.linux.bogus
 ns                               MX    20   mail.friend.bogus
 ns                               HINFO Pentium     Linux 1.2
 ns                               TXT   "RMS"
 linux.bogus.                     SOA   ns.linux.bogus hostmaster.linux.bogus. (199511301 28800 7200
```

That's good. Let's check what it says for www alone:

```
> set q=any
> www.linux.bogus.
Server:  localhost
Address:  127.0.0.1

www.linux.bogus canonical name = ns.linux.bogus
```

In other words, the real name of `www.linux.bogus` is `ns.linux.bogus`

```
linux.bogus      nameserver = ns.linux.bogus
linux.bogus      nameserver = ns.friend.bogus
ns.linux.bogus   internet address = 127.0.0.2
```

and ns.linux.bogus has the address 127.0.0.2. Looks good too.

4.3 Winding down

Of course, this domain is highly bogus, and so are all the addresses in it, and it is perhaps, unfortunately a bit confusing. For a real example of a real domain see the next section.

5 A real domain example

Where we list some *real* zone files

Users have suggested that I include a real example of a working domain, as my explanation of what the differences between a working domain and the bogus example was a bit unclear.

◇ One thing about this example: Do *not* enter it into your name servers. Use it only to read for reference. If you want to experiment do that with the bogus example. I use this example with permission from David Bullock of LAND-5. These files were current 24th of September 1996, and might differ from what you find if you query LAND-5's name servers now. Also, keep in mind: delete the leading spaces.

5.1 `/etc/named.boot` (or `/var/named/named.boot`)

Here we find primary lines for the two reverse zones needed: the 127.0.0 net, as well as LAND-5's 206.6.177 subnet. And a primary line for land-5's forward zone land-5.com. Also note that instead of stuffing the files in a directory called `pz`, as I do in this HOWTO, he puts them in a directory called `zone`.

```
;  Boot file for LAND-5 name server
;
directory /var/named
;
; type          domain                          source file or host
cache           .                               root.cache
primary         0.0.127.in-addr.arpa            zone/127.0.0
primary         177.6.206.in-addr.arpa          zone/206.6.177
primary         land-5.com                      zone/land-5.com
```

5.2 `/var/named/root.cache`

Keep in mind that this file is dynamic, and the one listed here is old. You're better off using one produced now, with `dig`.

```
; <<>> DiG 2.1 <<>>
;; res options: init recurs defnam dnsrch
;; got answer:
;; ->>HEADER<<- opcode: QUERY, status: NOERROR, id: 6
;; flags: qr rd ra; Ques: 1, Ans: 9, Auth: 0, Addit: 9
;; QUESTIONS:
;;      ., type = NS, class = IN

;; ANSWERS:
.        518357  NS      H.ROOT-SERVERS.NET.
.        518357  NS      B.ROOT-SERVERS.NET.
.        518357  NS      C.ROOT-SERVERS.NET.
```

```
.        518357  NS      D.ROOT-SERVERS.NET.
.        518357  NS      E.ROOT-SERVERS.NET.
.        518357  NS      I.ROOT-SERVERS.NET.
.        518357  NS      F.ROOT-SERVERS.NET.
.        518357  NS      G.ROOT-SERVERS.NET.
.        518357  NS      A.ROOT-SERVERS.NET.

;; ADDITIONAL RECORDS:
H.ROOT-SERVERS.NET.     165593  A       128.63.2.53
B.ROOT-SERVERS.NET.     165593  A       128.9.0.107
C.ROOT-SERVERS.NET.     222766  A       192.33.4.12
D.ROOT-SERVERS.NET.     165593  A       128.8.10.90
E.ROOT-SERVERS.NET.     165593  A       192.203.230.10
I.ROOT-SERVERS.NET.     165593  A       192.36.148.17
F.ROOT-SERVERS.NET.     299616  A       192.5.5.241
G.ROOT-SERVERS.NET.     165593  A       192.112.36.4
A.ROOT-SERVERS.NET.     165593  A       198.41.0.4

;; Total query time: 250 msec
;; FROM: land-5 to SERVER: default -- 127.0.0.1
;; WHEN: Fri Sep 20 10:11:22 1996
;; MSG SIZE  sent: 17  rcvd: 312
```

5.3 /var/named/zone/127.0.0

Just the basics, the obligatory SOA record, and a record that maps 127.0.0.1 to `localhost`. Both are required. No more should be in this file. It will probably never need to be updated, unless your nameserver or hostmaster address changes.

```
@               IN      SOA     land-5.com. root.land-5.com. (
                                199609203       ; Serial
                                28800   ; Refresh
                                7200    ; Retry
                                604800  ; Expire
                                86400)  ; Minimum TTL
                        NS      land-5.com.

1                       PTR     localhost.
```

5.4 /var/named/zone/land-5.com

Here we see the mandatory SOA record, the needed NS records. We can see that he has a secondary name server at ns2.psi.net. This is as it should be: *always* have an off-site, secondary server as backup. We can also see that he has a master host called land-5 which takes care of all the different services, and that he's done it with CNAMEs (a alternative is using A records).

As you see from the SOA record, the zone file originates at land-5.com, the contact person is `root@land-5.com`. `hostmaster` is another often used address for the contact person. The serial number is in the customary yyyymmdd format with today's serial number appended; this is probably the sixth version of zone file on the 20th of September, 1996. Remember that the serial number *must* increase monotonically, here there is only *one* digit for today's serial number, so after 9 edits he has to wait until tomorrow before he can edit the file again. Consider using two digits.

```
@       IN      SOA     land-5.com. root.land-5.com. (
                        199609206       ; serial, todays date + todays serial #
                        10800           ; refresh, seconds
                        7200            ; retry, seconds
                        10800           ; expire, seconds
                        86400 )         ; minimum, seconds
                NS      land-5.com.
                NS      ns2.psi.net.
                MX      10 land-5.com.  ; Primary Mail Exchanger
```

```
localhost       A       127.0.0.1

router          A       206.6.177.1

land-5.com.     A       206.6.177.2
ns              CNAME   land-5.com.
ftp             CNAME   land-5.com.
www             CNAME   land-5.com.
mail            CNAME   land-5.com.
news            CNAME   land-5.com.

funn            A       206.6.177.3
illusions       CNAME   funn.land-5.com.
@               TXT     "LAND-5 Corporation"

;
;       Workstations
;
ws_177200       A       206.6.177.200
                MX      10 land-5.com.   ; Primary Mail Host
ws_177201       A       206.6.177.201
                MX      10 land-5.com.   ; Primary Mail Host
ws_177202       A       206.6.177.202
                MX      10 land-5.com.   ; Primary Mail Host
ws_177203       A       206.6.177.203
                MX      10 land-5.com.   ; Primary Mail Host
ws_177204       A       206.6.177.204
                MX      10 land-5.com.   ; Primary Mail Host
ws_177205       A       206.6.177.205
                MX      10 land-5.com.   ; Primary Mail Host
; {Many repetitive definitions deleted - SNIP}
ws_177250       A       206.6.177.250
                MX      10 land-5.com.   ; Primary Mail Host
ws_177251       A       206.6.177.251
                MX      10 land-5.com.   ; Primary Mail Host
ws_177252       A       206.6.177.252
                MX      10 land-5.com.   ; Primary Mail Host
ws_177253       A       206.6.177.253
                MX      10 land-5.com.   ; Primary Mail Host
ws_177254       A       206.6.177.254
                MX      10 land-5.com.   ; Primary Mail Host
```

Another thing to note is that the workstations don't have individual names, but rather a prefix followed by the two last parts of the IP numbers. Using such a convention can simplify maintenance significantly, but can be a bit impersonal.

5.5 /var/named/zone/206.6.177

I'll comment on this file after it.

```
@               IN      SOA     land-5.com. root.land-5.com. (
                                199609206       ; Serial
                                28800   ; Refresh
                                7200    ; Retry
                                604800  ; Expire
                                86400)  ; Minimum TTL
                        NS      land-5.com.
                        NS      ns2.psi.net.
;
;       Servers
;
```

```
1       PTR     router.land-5.com.
2       PTR     land-5.com.
3       PTR     funn.land-5.com.
;
;       Workstations
;
200     PTR     ws_177200.land-5.com.
201     PTR     ws_177201.land-5.com.
202     PTR     ws_177202.land-5.com.
203     PTR     ws_177203.land-5.com.
204     PTR     ws_177204.land-5.com.
205     PTR     ws_177205.land-5.com.
; {Many repetitive definitions deleted - SNIP}
250     PTR     ws_177250.land-5.com.
251     PTR     ws_177251.land-5.com.
252     PTR     ws_177252.land-5.com.
253     PTR     ws_177253.land-5.com.
254     PTR     ws_177254.land-5.com.
```

The reverse zone is the bit of the setup that seems to cause the most grief. It is used to find the host name if you have the IP number of a machine. Example: you are an IRC server and accept connections from IRC clients. However you are a Norwegian IRC server and so you only want to accept connections from clients in Norway and other Scandinavian countries. When you get a connection from a client the C library is able to tell you the IP number of the connecting machine because the IP number of the client is contained in all the packets that are passed over the network. Now you can call a function called `gethostbyaddr` that looks up the name of a host given the IP number. `gethostbyaddr` will ask a DNS server, which will then traverse the DNS looking for the machine. Supposing the client connection is from ws_177200.land-5.com. The IP number the C library provides to the IRC server is 206.6.177.200. To find out the name of that machine, we need to find 200.177.6.206.in-addr.arpa. The DNS server will first find the arpa. servers, then find in-addr.arpa. servers, following the reverse trail through 206, then 6 and at last finding the server for the 177.6.206.in-addr.arpa zone at land-5. From which it will finally get the answer that for 200.177.6.206.in-addr.arpa we have a "PTR ws_177200.land-5.com" record, meaning that the name that goes with 206.6.177.200 is ws_177200.land-5.com. As with the explanation of how prep.ai.mit.edu is looked up, this is slightly fictitious.

Getting back to the IRC server example. The IRC server only accepts connections from the Scandinavian countries, i.e., *.no, *.se, *.dk, the name ws_177200.land-5.com clearly does not match any of those, and the server will deny the connection. If there was *no* reverse mapping of 206.2.177.200 through the in-addr.arpa zone the server would have been unable to find the name at all and would have to settle to comparing 206.2.177.200 with *.no, *.se and *.dk, none of which will match.

Some people will tell you that reverse lookup mappings are only important for servers, or not important at all. Not so: Many FTP, News, IRC, and even some http (WWW) servers will *not* accept connections from machines that they are not able to find the name of. So reverse mappings for machines are in fact mandatory.

6 Maintenance

Keeping it working.

There is one maintenance task that you have to do on `named`s, other than keep them running. That's keeping the `root.cache` file updated. The easiest way is using `dig`, first run `dig` with no arguments. You will get the `root.cache` according to your own server. Then ask one of the listed root servers with

```
dig @rootserver . ns
```

You will note that the output looks terribly like a `root.cache` file except for a couple of extra numbers. Those numbers are harmless. Save it to a file; for example

```
dig @e.root-servers.net . ns > root.cache.new
```

and replace the old `root.cache` with it.

Remember to restart `named` after replacing the cache file.

Al Longyear sent me this script that can be run automatically to update `root.cache`. Install a `crontab` entry to run it once a month and forget it. The script assumes you have mail working and that the mail-alias "hostmaster" is defined. You must hack it to suit your setup.

```
#!/bin/sh
#
# Update the nameserver cache information file once per month.
# This is run automatically by a cron entry.
#
(
 echo "To: hostmaster <hostmaster>"
 echo "From: system <root>"
 echo "Subject: Automatic update of the named.boot file"
 echo

 export PATH=/sbin:/usr/sbin:/bin:/usr/bin:
 cd /var/named

 dig @rs.internic.net . ns >root.cache.new

 echo "The named.boot file has been updated to contain the following
information:"
 echo
 cat root.cache.new

 chown root.root root.cache.new
 chmod 444 root.cache.new
 rm -f root.cache.old
 mv root.cache root.cache.old
 mv root.cache.new root.cache
 ndc restart
 echo
 echo "The nameserver has been restarted to ensure that the update is complete."
 echo "The previous root.cache file is now called
/var/named/root.cache.old."
) 2>&1 | /usr/lib/sendmail -t
exit 0
```

Some of you might have picked up that the `root.cache` file is also available by FTP from Internic. Please *don't* use FTP to update root.cache, the above method is much more friendly to the Net.

7 Automatic setup for dialup connections.

This section explains how I have set things up to automate everything. My way might not suit you at all, but you might get a idea from something I've done. Also, I use PPP for dialup, while many use SLIP or CSLIP, so almost everything in your setup can be different from mine. But SLIP's `dip` program should be able to do many of the things I do.

Normally, when I'm not connected to the net I have a `/etc/resolv.conf` file simply containing the line

```
domain uio.no
```

This ensures that I don't have to wait for the host name resolving library to try to connect to a nameserver that can't help me. But when I connect, I want to start my `named` and have a `/etc/resolv.conf` looking like the one described above. I have solved this by keeping two `/etc/resolv.conf` "template" files named `/etc/resolv.conf.local` and `/etc/resolv.conf.connected`. The latter looks like the `/etc/resolv.conf` described before in this document.

To automatically connect to the Net I run a script called "`ppp-on`:"

```
#!/bin/sh
echo calling...
pppd
```

`pppd` has a file called `options` that tells it the particulars of how to get connected. Once my PPP connection is up, `pppd` starts a script called `ip-up` (this is described in the `pppd` man page). This is part of the script:

```
#!/bin/sh
interface="$1"
```

```
device="$2"
speed="$3"
myip="$4"
upip="$5"
 ...
cp -v /etc/resolv.conf.connected /etc/resolv.conf
 ...
/usr/sbin/named
```

I.e., I start my named there. When PPP is disconnected, pppd runs a script called ip-down:

```
#!/bin/sh
cp /etc/resolv.conf.local /etc/resolv.conf
read namedpid </var/run/named.pid
kill $namedpid
```

So this gets things configured and up when connecting and dis-configured and down when disconnecting.

Some programs, irc and talk come to mind, make a few too many assumptions, and for irc, the dcc features, and talk to work right, you have to fix your hosts file. I insert have this in my ip-up script:

```
cp /etc/hosts.ppp /etc/hosts
echo $myip      roke >>/etc/hosts
```

hosts.ppp simply contains

```
127.0.0.1       localhost
```

and the echo thing inserts the IP number i have received for my host name (roke). You should use the name your host knows itself by instead. This can be found with the hostname command.

It is probably not smart to run named when you are not connected to the net, this is because named will try to send queries to the net and it has a long timeout, and you have to wait for this timeout every time some program tries to resolve a name. If you're using dialup you should start named when connecting and kill it when disconnecting. But please see Section 8 for a tip.

Some people like to use a forwarders directive on slow connections. If your Internet provider has DNS servers at 1.2.3.4 and 1.2.3.5, you can insert the line

```
forwarders 1.2.3.4 1.2.3.5
```

in the named.boot file. Also leave the root.cache file empty. That will decrease the amount of IP traffic your host originates, and possibly speed things up. This especially important if you're paying per byte that goes over the wire. This has the added value of letting you off the one maintenance duty you have as a caching named maintainer; you don't have to update a empty root.cache file.

8 FAQ

In this section I list some of the most frequently asked questions related to DNS and this HOWTO. And the answers. Please read this section before mailing me.

1. How do use DNS from inside a firewall?

   A couple of hints: "forwarders," "slave," and have a look in the literature list at the end of this HOWTO.

2. How do I make DNS rotate through the available addresses for a service, say www.busy.site to obtain a load balancing effect, or similar?

   Make several **A** records for www.busy.site and use BIND 4.9.3 or later. Then BIND will round-robin the answers. It will not work with earlier versions of bind.

3. I want to set up DNS on a (closed) intranet. What do I do?

   You drop the cache file and just do zone files. That also means you don't have to get new cache files all the time.

4. My system does not have the ndc program. What do I do?

   Your system then has an old, somewhat obsolete, BIND installed. If security is important to you: upgrade BIND at once. If not, you can live with it. And instead of running ndc start you run named. ndc reload becomes named.reload and ndc restart becomes named.restart. All of those programs are most likely in /usr/sbin.

5. How do I set up a secondary name server?

   If the primary server has address 127.0.0.1 you put a line like this in the named.boot file of your secondary:

```
secondary     linux.bogus              127.0.0.1       sz/linux.bogus
```

6. I want BIND running when I'm disconnected from the Net.

   I have received this mail from Ian Clark <ic@deakin.edu.au> where he explains his way of doing this:

```
I run named on my ''Masquerading'' machine here. I have
two root.cache files, one called root.cache.real which contains
the real root server names and the other called root.cache.fake
which contains...

--------------
; root.cache.fake
; this file contains no information
--------------

When I go off line I copy the root.cache.fake file to root.cache and
restart named.

When I go online I copy root.cache.real to root.cache and restart
named.

This is done from ip-down & ip-up respectively.

The first time I do a query off line on a domain name named doesn't
have details for it puts an entry like this in messages..

Jan 28 20:10:11 hazchem named[10147]: No root nameserver for class IN

which I can live with.

It certainly seems to work for me. I can use the nameserver for
local machines while off the 'Net without the timeout delay for
external domain names and I while on the 'Net queries for external
domains work normally
```

7. Where does the caching name server store it's cache? Is there any way I can control the size of the cache?

   The cache is completely stored in memory, it is not written to disk at any time. Every time you kill `named` the cache is lost. The cache is not controllable in any way. `named` manages it according to some simple rules and that is it. You cannot control the cache or the cache size in any way for any reason. If you want to you can "fix" this by hacking `named`. This is however not recommended.

8. Does `named` save the cache between restarts? Can I make it save it?

   No, `named` does not save the cache when it dies. That means that the cache must be built anew each time you kill and restart `named`. There is no way to make `named` save the cache in a file. If you want you can "fix" this by hacking named. This is however not recommended.

9 How to become a bigger time DNS admin.

Documentation and tools.

Real documentation exists, online and in print. The reading of several of these is required to make the step from small time DNS admin to a big time one. In print, the standard book is *DNS and BIND* by C. Liu and P. Albitz from O'Reilly & Associates, Sebastopol, CA, ISBN 0-937175-82-X. I read this, and it's excellent. There is also a section in on DNS in *TCP/IP Network Administration*, by Craig Hunt from O'Reilly..., ISBN 0-937175-82-X. Another must for Good DNS administration (or good anything for that matter) is *Zen and the Art of Motorcycle Maintenance* by Robert M. Prisig :-) Available as ISBN 0688052304 and others.

Online you will find stuff on (http://www.dns.net/dnsrd/), (http://www.vix.com/isc/bind/); A FAQ, a reference manual (BOG; Bind Operations Guide) as well as papers and protocol definitions and DNS hacks (these, and most, if not all, of the RFCs mentioned below, are also contained in the BIND distribution). I have not read most of these, but then I'm not a big-time DNS admin either. Arnt Gulbrandsen on the other hand has read BOG and he's ecstatic about it. The newsgroup comp.protocols.tcp-ip.domains is about DNS. In addition there are a number of RFCs about DNS, but the most important are probably these:

RFC 2052 A. Gulbrandsen, P. Vixie, *A DNS RR for specifying the location of services (DNS SRV)*, October 1996

RFC 1918 Y. Rekhter, R. Moskowitz, D. Karrenberg, G. de Groot, E. Lear, *Address Allocation for Private Internets*, 02/29/1996.

RFC 1912 D. Barr, *Common DNS Operational and Configuration Errors*, 02/28/1996.

RFC 1713 A. Romao, *Tools for DNS debugging*, 11/03/1994.

RFC 1712 C. Farrell, M. Schulze, S. Pleitner, D. Baldoni, *DNS Encoding of Geographical Location*, 11/01/1994.

RFC 1183 R. Ullmann, P. Mockapetris, L. Mamakos, C. Everhart, *New DNS RR Definitions*, 10/08/1990.

RFC 1035 P. Mockapetris, *Domain names - implementation and specification*, 11/01/1987.

RFC 1034 P. Mockapetris, *Domain names - concepts and facilities*, 11/01/1987.

RFC 1033 M. Lottor, *Domain administrators operations guide*, 11/01/1987.

RFC 1032 M. Stahl, *Domain administrators guide*, 11/01/1987.

RFC 974 C. Partridge, *Mail routing and the domain system*, 01/01/1986.

Online: You will find on [illegible] and [illegible] a FAQ, a reference manual BIND Operations Guide, as well as papers and protocol definitions and DNS hacks (these, and most if not all of the RFCs mentioned below, are also contained in the BIND distribution). I have not read most of these. [illegible] The newsgroup comp.protocols.tcp-ip.domains is about DNS. In addition there are a number of RFCs about DNS, the most important are probably these:

RFC 2052 A. Gulbrandsen, P. Vixie, *A DNS RR for specifying the location of services (DNS SRV)*, October 1996

RFC 1918 Y. Rekhter, R. Moskowitz, D. Karrenberg, G. de Groot, E. Lear, *Address Allocation for Private Internets*, 02/29/1996.

RFC 1912 D. Barr, *Common DNS Operational and Configuration Errors*, 02/28/1996.

RFC 1713 A. Romao, *Tools for DNS debugging*, 11/03/1994.

RFC 1712 C. Farrell, M. Schulze, S. Pleitner, D. Baldoni, *DNS Encoding of Geographical Location*, 11/01/1994.

RFC 1183 R. Ullmann, P. Mockapetris, L. Mamakos, C. Everhart, *New DNS RR Definitions*, 10/08/1990.

RFC 1035 P. Mockapetris, *Domain names - implementation and specification*, 11/01/1987.

RFC 1034 P. Mockapetris, *Domain names - concepts and facilities*, 11/01/1987.

RFC 1033 M. Lottor, *Domain administrators operations guide*, 11/01/1987.

RFC 1032 M. Stahl, *Domain administrators guide*, 11/01/1987.

RFC 974 C. Partridge, *Mail routing and the domain system*, 01/01/1986.

Part XVII

"From DOS to Linux HOWTO" by Guido Gonzato,

guido@ibogfs.cineca.it

Contents

Abstract

v1.2.2, 31 October 1997
This HOWTO is dedicated to all the (soon to be former?) DOS and Windows users who have just taken the plunge and decided to switch to Linux, the free UNIX clone. Given the similarities between DOS and UNIX, the purpose of this document is to help the reader translate his or her knowledge of DOS and Windows into the Linux environment, so as to be productive ASAP.

1 Introduction

1.1 Is Linux Right for You?

You want to switch from DOS/Windows to Linux? Good idea, but beware: it might not be useful for you. IMHO, there is no such thing as "the best computer" or "the best operating system:" it depends on what one has to do. That's why I don't believe that Linux is the best solution for everyone, even if it's technically superior to many commercial OS's. You're going to benefit immensely from Linux if what you need is software for programming, the Internet, or TeX—technical software in general, but if you mostly need commercial software, or if you don't feel like learning and typing commands, look elsewhere.

Linux is not (for now) as easy to use and configure as Windows or the Mac, so be prepared to hack quite a bit. In spite of these warnings, let me tell you that I'm 100% confident that if you belong to the right user type you'll find in Linux your computer Nirvana. It's up to you. And remember that Linux + DOS/Windows can coexist on the same machine, anyway.

Prerequisites for this HOWTO: I'll assume that

- you know the basic DOS commands and concepts;
- Linux, possibly with X Window System, is properly installed on your PC;
- your shell—the equivalent of `COMMAND.COM`—is `bash`;
- you understand that this guide is only an incomplete primer. For more information, please refer to Matt Welsh's "Linux Installation and Getting Started" or Larry Greenfield's "Linux User Guide," sunsite.unc.edu in /pub/Linux/docs/LDP/.

This HOWTO replaces the old "From DOS to Linux — Quick!" Mini-HOWTO. Also note that, unless specified, all information in this work is aimed at bad ol' MS-DOS. There's a section about Windows, but bear in mind that Windows and Linux are totally different, unlike DOS which is sort of a UNIX poor relation.

1.2 It Is. Tell Me More

You installed Linux and the programs you needed on the PC. You gave yourself an account (if not, type `adduser` *now!*) and Linux is running. You've just entered your name and password, and now you are looking at the screen thinking: "Well, now what?"

Now, don't despair. You're almost ready to do the same things you used to do with DOS, and many more. If you were running DOS instead of Linux, you would be doing some of the following tasks:

- running programs and creating, copying, viewing, deleting, printing, renaming files;
- CD'ing, MD'ing, RD'ing, and DIR'ring your directories;
- formatting floppies and copying files from/to them;
- mending your `AUTOEXEC.BAT` and `CONFIG.SYS`;
- writing your own .BAT files and/or `QBasic` and/or C/Pascal programs;
- the remaining 1%.

You'll be glad to know that these tasks can be accomplished under Linux in a fashion similar to DOS. Under DOS, the average user uses very few of the 100-plus commands available: the same, up to a point, holds for Linux.

A few things to point out before going on:

- first, how to get out. To quit Linux: if you see a text mode screen, press Ctrl-Alt-Del, wait for the system to fix its innards and tell you everything is OK, then switch off the PC. If you are working under X Window System, press Ctrl-Alt-Backspace first, then Ctrl-Alt-Del.

◇ *Never* switch off or reset the PC directly: this could damage the file system;

- unlike DOS, Linux has built-in security mechanisms, due to its multiuser nature. Files and directories have permissions associated to them, and therefore some cannot be accessed by the normal user; (see Section 2.3). Only the user whose login name is "root" has the power. (This guy's the system administrator. If you work on your own PC, you'll be root as well.) DOS, on the contrary, will let you wipe out the entire contents of your hard disk;
- you are strongly encouraged to experiment, play, try by yourself: it surely won't hurt. If you need help, you can do the following:
  - to get some help about the "internal commands" of the shell, type `help`;
  - to get help on a command, type `man command` that invokes the manual ("man") page pertinent to `command`. Alternatively, type `info command` that invokes, if available, the info page pertinent to `command`. Info is a hypertext-based documentation system, perhaps not intuitive to use at first. Finally, you may try `apropos command` or `whatis command` pressing then "q" to exit;
- most of the power and flexibility of UNIX comes from the simple concepts of redirection and piping, more powerful than under DOS. Simple commands can be strung together to accomplish complex tasks. Do use these features!
- conventions: `<...>` means something that must be specified, while `[...]` something optional. Example:

```
$ tar -tf <file.tar> [> redir_file]
```

  `file.tar` must be indicated, but redirection to `redir_file` is optional.
- from now on "RMP" means "please read the man pages for further information".

1.3 For the Impatient

Want to strike out? Have a look at this:

```
DOS                      Linux                  Notes
------------------------------------------------------------------------------

BACKUP                   tar -Mcvf device dir/  completely different
CD dirname\              cd dirname/            almost the same syntax
COPY file1 file2         cp file1 file2         ditto
DEL file                 rm file                beware - no undelete
DELTREE dirname          rm -R dirname/         ditto
DIR                      ls                     not exactly the same syntax
DIR file /S              find . -name file      completely different
EDIT file                vi file                I think you won't like it
                         emacs file             this is better
                         jstar file             feels like dos' edit
FORMAT                   fdformat,
                         mount, umount          quite different syntax
HELP command             man command            same philosophy
MD dirname               mkdir dirname/         almost the same syntax
MOVE file1 file2         mv file1 file2         ditto
NUL                      /dev/null              ditto
PRINT file               lpr file               ditto
PRN                      /dev/lp0,
                         /dev/lp1               ditto
RD dirname               rmdir dirname/         almost the same syntax
REN file1 file2          mv file1 file2         not for multiple files
RESTORE                  tar -Mxpvf device      different syntax
TYPE file                less file              much better
WIN                      startx                 poles apart!
```

If you need more than a table of commands, please refer to the following sections.

2 Files and Programs

2.1 Files: Preliminary Notions

Linux has a file system—meaning by that "the structure of directories and files therein"—very similar to that of DOS. Files have filenames that obey special rules, are stored in directories, some are executable, and among these most have command switches. Moreover, you can use wildcard characters, redirection, and piping. There are only a few minor differences:

- under DOS, file names are in the so-called 8.3 form; e.g. `NOTENOUG.TXT`. Under Linux we can do better. If you installed Linux using a file system like ext2 or umsdos, you can use longer filenames (up to 255 characters), and with more than one dot in them: for example, `This_is.a.VERY_long.filename`. Please note that I used both upper and lower case characters: in fact...
- upper and lower case characters in file names or commands are different. Therefore, `FILENAME.tar.gz` and `filename.tar.gz` are two different files. `ls` is a command, `LS` is a mistake;
- Windows 95 users will want to use long file names under Linux, of course. If a file name contains spaces (not recommended but possible), you must enclose the file in double quotes whenever your refer to it. For example:

  ```
  $ # the following command makes a directory called "My old files"
  $ mkdir "My old files"
  $ ls
  My old files    bin     tmp
  ```

  Some characters shouldn't but can be used: some are `!*$&`. I won't tell you how, though.
- there are no compulsory extensions like .COM and ..EXE for programs, or .BAT for batch files. Executable files are marked by an asterisk '`*`' at the end of their name when you issue the `ls -F` command. For example:

  ```
  $ ls -F
  I_am_a_dir/   cindy.jpg    cjpg*   letter_to_Joe    my_1st_script*  old~
  ```

  The files `cjpg*` and `my_1st_script*` are executable—"programs." Under DOS, backup files end in .BAK, while under Linux they end with a tilde '`~`'. Further, a file whose name starts with a dot is considered as hidden. Example: the file `.I.am.a.hidden.file` won't show up after the `ls` command;
- DOS program switches are obtained with `/switch`, Linux switches with `-switch` or `-switch`. Example: `dir /s` becomes `ls -R`. Note that many DOS programs, like `PKZIP` or `ARJ`, use UNIX-style switches.

You can now jump to Section 2.4, but if I were you I'd read on.

2.2 Symbolic Links

UNIX has a type of file that doesn't exist under DOS: the symbolic link. This can be thought of as a pointer to a file or to a directory, and can be used instead of the file or directory it points to; it's similar to Windows 95 shortcuts. Examples of symbolic links are `/usr/X11`, which points to `/usr/X11R6`; `/dev/modem`, which points to either `/dev/cua0` or `/dev/cua1`.

To make a symbolic link:

```
$ ln -s <file_or_dir> <linkname>
```

Example:

```
$ ln -s /usr/doc/g77/DOC g77manual.txt
```

Now you can refer to `g77manual.txt` instead of `/usr/doc/g77/DOC`. Links appear like this in directory listings:

```
$ ls -F
g77manual.txt@
$ ls -l
(various things...)          g77manual.txt -> /usr/doc/g77/DOC
```

2.3 Permissions and Ownership

DOS files and directories have the following attributes: A (archive), H (hidden), R (read-only), and S (system). Only H and R make sense under Linux: hidden files start with a dot, and for the R attribute, read on.

Under UNIX a file has "permissions" and an owner, who in turn belongs to a "group." Look at this example:

```
$ ls -l /bin/ls
-rwxr-xr-x  1  root  bin  27281 Aug 15 1995 /bin/ls*
```

The first field contains the permissions of the file `/bin/ls`, which belongs to root, group bin. Leaving the remaining information aside (Matt's book is there for that purpose), remember that `-rwxr-xr-x` means, from left to right:

`-` is the file type (- = ordinary file, d = directory, l = link, etc); `rwx` are the permissions for the file owner (read, write, execute); `r-x` are the permissions for the group of the file owner (read, execute); (I won't cover the concept of group, you can survive without it as long as you're a beginner.) `r-x` are the permissions for all other users (read, execute).

This is why you can't delete the file `/bin/ls` unless you are root: you don't have the write permission to do so. To change a file's permissions, the command is:

```
$ chmod <whoXperm> <file>
```

where who is `u` (user, that is owner), `g` (group), `o` (other), X is either `+` or `-`, perm is `r` (read), `w` (write), or `x` (execute). Examples:

```
$ chmod u+x file
```

this sets the execute permission for the file owner. Shortcut: `chmod +x file`.

```
$ chmod go-wx file
```

this removes write and execute permission for everyone but the owner.

```
$ chmod ugo+rwx file
```

this gives everyone read, write, and execute permission.

```
# chmod +s file
```

this makes a so-called "setuid" or "suid" file—a file that everyone can execute with its owner's privileges. Typically, you'll come across root suid files.

A shorter way to refer to permissions is with numbers: `rwxr-xr-x` can be expressed as 755 (every letter corresponds to a bit: `--` is 0, `-x` is 1, `-w-` is 2, `-wx` is 3...). It looks difficult, but with a bit of practice you'll understand the concept.

root, being the so-called superuser, can change everyone's file permissions. There's more to it—RMP.

2.4 Translating Commands from DOS to Linux

On the left, the DOS commands; on the right, their Linux counterpart.

```
COPY:         cp
DEL:          rm
MOVE:         mv
REN:          mv
TYPE:         more, less, cat
```

Redirection and plumbing operators: `< > >> |`
Wildcard: `* ?`
`nul:  /dev/null`
`prn, lpt1:  /dev/lp0 or /dev/lp1; lpr`
- EXAMPLES -

```
DOS                                     Linux
---------------------------------------------------------------------

C:\GUIDO>COPY JOE.TXT JOE.DOC           $ cp joe.txt joe.doc
C:\GUIDO>COPY *.* TOTAL                 $ cat * > total
C:\GUIDO>COPY FRACTALS.DOC PRN          $ lpr fractals.doc
C:\GUIDO>DEL TEMP                       $ rm temp
C:\GUIDO>DEL *.BAK                      $ rm *~
C:\GUIDO>MOVE PAPER.TXT TMP\            $ mv paper.txt tmp/
C:\GUIDO>REN PAPER.TXT PAPER.ASC        $ mv paper.txt paper.asc
C:\GUIDO>PRINT LETTER.TXT               $ lpr letter.txt
```

```
C:\GUIDO>TYPE LETTER.TXT              $ more letter.txt
C:\GUIDO>TYPE LETTER.TXT              $ less letter.txt
C:\GUIDO>TYPE LETTER.TXT > NUL        $ cat letter.txt > /dev/null
        n/a                           $ more *.txt *.asc
        n/a                           $ cat section*.txt | less
```

Notes:

- * is smarter under Linux: * matches all files except the hidden ones; .* matches all hidden files; *.* matches only those that have a '.' in the middle, followed by other characters; p*r matches both 'peter' and 'piper'; *c* matches both 'picked' and 'peck';
- when using `more`, press Space to read through the file, "q" or Ctrl-C to exit. `less` is more intuitive and lets you use the arrow keys;
- there is no `UNDELETE`, so *think twice* before deleting anything;
- in addition to DOS < > >>, Linux has 2> to redirect error messages (stderr); moreover, `2>&1` redirects stderr to stdout, while `1>&2` redirects stdout to stderr;
- Linux has another wildcard: the `[]`. Use: `[abc]*` matches files starting with a, b, c; `*[I-N,1,2,3]` matches files ending with I, J, K, L, M, N, 1, 2, 3;
- there is no DOS-like `RENAME`; that is, `mv` *.xxx *.yyy won't work. You could try this simple script; see Section 7.1 for details.

```
#!/bin/sh
# ren: rename multiple files according to several rules

if [ $# -lt 3 ] ; then
  echo "usage: ren \"pattern\" \"replacement\" files..."
  exit 1
fi

OLD=$1 ; NEW=$2 ; shift ; shift

for file in $*
do
  new='echo ${file} | sed s/${OLD}/${NEW}/g'
  mv ${file} $new
done
```

  Beware: it doesn't behave like DOS `REN`, as it uses "regular expressions" that you still don't know. Shortly, if you simply want to change file extensions, use it as in: `ren "htm$" "html" *htm`. Don't forget the `$` sign.

- use `cp -i` and `mv -i` to be warned when a file is going to be overwritten.

2.5 Running Programs: Multitasking and Sessions

To run a program, type its name as you would do under DOS. If the directory (Section 3) where the program is stored is included in the PATH (Section 6.1), the program will start. Exception: unlike DOS, under Linux a program located in the current directory won't run unless the directory is included in the PATH. Escamotage: being `prog` your program, type `./prog`.

This is what the typical command line looks like:

```
$ command -s1 -s2 ... -sn par1 par2 ... parn < input > output
```

where `-s1`, ..., `-sn` are the program switches, `par1`, ..., `parn` are the program parameters. You can issue several commands on the command line:

```
$ command1 ; command2 ; ... ; commandn
```

That's all about running programs, but it's easy to go a step beyond. One of the main reasons for using Linux is that it is a multitasking OS—it can run several programs (from now on, processes) at the same time. You can launch processes in background and continue working straight away. Moreover, Linux lets you have several sessions: it's like having many computers to work on at once!

- To switch to session 1..6:

```
$ ALT-F1 ... ALT-F6
```

- To start a new session without leaving the current one:

```
$ su - <loginname>
```

Example:

```
$ su - root
```

This is useful, for one, when you need to mount a disk (Section 4): normally, only root can do that.

- To end a session:

```
$ exit
```

If there are stopped jobs (see later), you'll be warned.

- To launch a process in foreground:

```
$ progname [-switches] [parameters] [< input] [> output]
```

- To launch a process in background, add an ampersand '&' at the end of the command line:

```
$ progname [-switches] [parameters] [< input] [> output] &
[1] 123
```

the shell identifies the process with a job number (e.g. [1]; see below), and with a PID (123 in our example).

- To see how many processes there are:

```
$ ps -a
```

This will output a list of currently running processes.

- To kill a process:

```
$ kill <PID>
```

You may need to kill a process when you don't know how to quit it the right way.... Sometimes, a process will only be killed by either of the following:

```
$ kill -15 <PID>
$ kill -9 <PID>
```

In addition to this, the shell allows you to stop or temporarily suspend a process, send a process to background, and bring a process from background to foreground. In this context, processes are called "jobs."

- To see how many jobs there are:

```
$ jobs
```

here jobs are identified by their job number, not by their PID.

- To stop a process running in foreground (it won't always work):

```
$ CTRL-C
```

- To suspend a process running in foreground (ditto):

```
$ CTRL-Z
```

- To send a suspended process into background (it becomes a job):

```
$ bg <job>
```

- To bring a job to foreground:

```
$ fg <job>
```

- To kill a job:

```
$ kill <%job>
```

where <job> may be 1, 2, 3, ... Using these commands you can format a disk, zip a bunch of files, compile a program, and unzip an archive all at the same time, and still have the prompt at your disposal. Try this with DOS! And try with Windows, just to see the difference in performance.

2.6 Running Programs on Remote Computers

To run a program on a remote machine whose IP address is `remote.bigone.edu`, you do:

```
$ telnet remote.bigone.edu
```

After logging in, start your favorite program. Needless to say, you must have an account on the remote machine.

If you have X11, you can even run an X application on a remote computer, displaying it on your X screen. Let `remote.bigone.edu` be the remote X computer and `local.linux.box` be your Linux machine. To run from `local.linux.box` an X program that resides on `remote.bigone.edu`, do the following:

- fire up X11, start an `xterm` or equivalent terminal emulator, then type:

```
$ xhost +remote.bigone.edu
$ telnet remote.bigone.edu
```

- after logging in, type:

```
remote:$ DISPLAY=local.linux.box:0.0
remote:$ progname &
```

(instead of `DISPLAY...`, you may have to write `setenv DISPLAY local.linux.box:0.0`. It depends on the remote shell.)

Et voila! Now `progname` will start on `remote.bigone.edu` and will be displayed on your machine. Don't try this over a PPP line though, for it's too slow to be usable.

3 Using Directories

3.1 Directories: Preliminary Notions

We have seen the differences between files under DOS and Linux. As for directories, under DOS the root directory is \, under Linux / is. Similarly, nested directories are separated by \ under DOS, by / under Linux. Example of file paths:

```
DOS:    C:\PAPERS\GEOLOGY\MID_EOC.TEX
Linux:  /home/guido/papers/geology/mid_eocene.tex
```

As usual, `..` is the parent directory, `.` is the current directory. Remember that the system won't let you `cd`, `rd`, or `md` everywhere you want. Each user starts from his or her own directory called "home," given by the system administrator; for instance, on my PC my home directory is `/home/guido`.

3.2 Directories Permissions

Directories, too, have permissions. What we have seen in Section 2.3 holds for directories as well (user, group, and other). For a directory, `rx` means you can `cd` to that directory, and `w` means that you can delete a file in the directory (according to the file's permissions, of course), or the directory itself.

For example, to prevent other users from snooping in `/home/guido/text`:

```
$ chmod o-rwx /home/guido/text
```

3.3 Translating Commands from DOS to Linux

```
DIR:            ls, find, du
CD:             cd, pwd
MD:             mkdir
RD:             rmdir
DELTREE:        rm -R
MOVE:           mv
```

- EXAMPLES -

```
DOS                                     Linux
---------------------------------------------------------------------

C:\GUIDO>DIR                            $ ls
C:\GUIDO>DIR FILE.TXT                   $ ls file.txt
```

```
C:\GUIDO>DIR *.H *.C                    $ ls *.h *.c
C:\GUIDO>DIR/P                          $ ls | more
C:\GUIDO>DIR/A                          $ ls -l
C:\GUIDO>DIR *.TMP /S                   $ find / -name "*.tmp"
C:\GUIDO>CD                             $ pwd
        n/a - see note                  $ cd
        ditto                           $ cd ~
        ditto                           $ cd ~/temp
C:\GUIDO>CD \OTHER                      $ cd /other
C:\GUIDO>CD ..\TEMP\TRASH               $ cd ../temp/trash
C:\GUIDO>MD NEWPROGS                    $ mkdir newprogs
C:\GUIDO>MOVE PROG ..                   $ mv prog ..
C:\GUIDO>MD \PROGS\TURBO                $ mkdir /progs/turbo
C:\GUIDO>DELTREE TEMP\TRASH             $ rm -R temp/trash
C:\GUIDO>RD NEWPROGS                    $ rmdir newprogs
C:\GUIDO>RD \PROGS\TURBO                $ rmdir /progs/turbo
```

Notes:

1. When using `rmdir`, the directory to remove must be empty. To delete a directory and all of its contents, use `rm -R` (at your own risk).
2. The character '~' is a shortcut for the name of your home directory. The commands `cd` or `cd ~` will take you to your home directory from wherever you are; the command `cd ~/tmp` will take you to `/home/your_home/tmp`.
3. `cd -` "undoes" the last `cd`.

4 Floppies, Hard Disks, and the Like

4.1 Managing Devices

You have never thought about it, but the DOS command `FORMAT A:` does a lot more work than it seems. In fact, when you issue the command `FORMAT` it will: 1) physically format the disk; 2) create the A: directory (= create a filesystem); 3) make the disk available to the user (= mount the disk).

These three steps are addressed separately under Linux. You can use floppies in MS-DOS format, though other formats are available and are better—the MS-DOS format won't let you use long filenames. Here is how to prepare a disk (you'll need to start a session as root):

- To format a standard 1.44 MB floppy disk (A:):

  ```
  # fdformat /dev/fd0H1440
  ```

- To create a filesystem:

  ```
  # mkfs -t ext2 -c /dev/fd0H1440
  ```

  To create an MS-DOS filesystem, use `msdos` instead of `ext2`. Before using the disk, you must mount it.

- To mount the disk:

  ```
  # mount -t ext2 /dev/fd0 /mnt
  ```

  or

  ```
  # mount -t msdos /dev/fd0 /mnt
  ```

  Now you can address the files in the floppy. When you've finished, before extracting the disk you *must* unmount it.

- To unmount the disk:

  ```
  # umount /mnt
  ```

Now you can extract the disk. Obviously, you have to `fdformat` and `mkfs` only unformatted disks, not previously used ones. If you want to use drive B:, refer to `fd1H1440` and `fd1` instead of `fd0H1440` and `fd0` in the examples above.

All you used to do with A: or B: is now done using `/mnt` instead. Examples:

```
DOS                                     Linux
---------------------------------------------------------------------

C:\GUIDO>DIR A:                         $ ls /mnt
C:\GUIDO>COPY A:*.*                     $ cp /mnt/* /docs/temp
C:\GUIDO>COPY *.ZIP A:                  $ cp *.zip /mnt/zip
C:\GUIDO>A:                             $ cd /mnt
A:>_                                    /mnt/$ _
```

If you don't like this mounting/unmounting thing, use the `mtools` suite: it's a set of commands that are perfectly equivalent to their DOS counterpart, but start with an 'm': i.e., `mformat`, `mdir`, `mdel`, and so on. They can even preserve long file names, but not file permissions. Use these commands as you'd use the DOS commands and rest in peace.

Needless to say, what holds for floppies also holds for other devices; for instance, you may want to mount another hard disk or a CD-ROM drive. Here's how to mount the CD-ROM:

```
# mount -t iso9660 /dev/cdrom /mnt
```

This was the "official" way to mount your disks, but there's a trick in store. Since it's a bit of a nuisance having to be root to mount a floppy or a CD-ROM, every user can be allowed to mount them this way:

- as root, do the following:

```
~# mkdir /mnt/a: ; mkdir /mnt/a ; mkdir /mnt/cdrom
~# chmod 777 /mnt/a* /mnt/cd*
~# # make sure that the CD-ROM device is right
~# chmod 666 /dev/hdb ; chmod 666 /dev/fd*
```

- add in `/etc/fstab` the following lines:

```
/dev/cdrom      /mnt/cdrom  iso9660 ro,user,noauto       0       0
/dev/fd0        /mnt/a:     msdos   user,noauto          0       0
/dev/fd0        /mnt/a      ext2    user,noauto          0       0
```

Now, to mount a DOS floppy, an ext2 floppy, and a CD-ROM:

```
$ mount /mnt/a:
$ mount /mnt/a
$ mount /mnt/cdrom
```

`/mnt/a`, `/mnt/a:`, and `/mnt/cdrom` can now be accessed by every user. Remember that allowing everyone to mount disks this way is a gaping security hole, if you care.

4.2 Backing Up

Now that you know how to handle floppies etc., a couple of lines to see how to do your backup. There are several packages to help you, but the very least you can do for a multi-volume backup is (as root):

```
# tar -M -cvf /dev/fd0H1440 dir_to_backup/
```

Make sure to have a formatted floppy in the drive, and several more ready. To restore your stuff, insert the first floppy in the drive and do:

```
# tar -M -xpvf /dev/fd0H1440
```

5 What About Windows?

The "equivalent" of Windows is the graphic system X11. Unlike Windows or the Mac, X11 wasn't designed for ease of use or to look good, but just to provide graphic facilities to UNIX workstations. These are the main differences:

- while Windows looks and feels the same all over the world, X11 doesn't: it's much more configurable. X11's overall look is given by a key component called "window manager"; there are many you can choose from. The most common are `fvwm`, basic but nice and memory efficient, `fvwm2-95` and `The Next Level` that give X11 a Windows 95–like taste, plus several others. Some look really beautiful;
- your window manager can be configured so as a window acts as in, er, Windows: you click on it and it comes to foreground. Another possibility is that it comes to foreground when the mouse is located on it. This feature ("focus") and many others can be altered by editing one or more configuration files. Read the docs of your window manager;

- X applications are written using special libraries ("widget sets"); as several are available, applications look different. The most basic ones are those that use the Athena widgets (2–D look; `xdvi`, `xman`, `xcalc`); others use Motif (`netscape`), others still use Tcl/Tk, XForms, Qt and what have you. Some—not all—of these libraries provide roughly the same look and feel as Windows;
- so much for the look of X11, but what about the feel? Unfortunately, all applications behave differently. For instance, if you select a line of text using the mouse and press BACKSPACE, you'd expect the line to disappear, right? This doesn't work with Athena–based apps, but it does with Motif, Qt, and Tcl/Tk ones;
- scrollbars, resizing, and iconization: these, too, depend on the window manager and the widget set. Too many different things to mention here, just a couple of points. When using Athena–based apps the scrollbars are better moved with the central button. If you don't have a three–button mouse, try pressing the two buttons together;
- applications don't have an icon by default, but they can have many. It depends on the window manager. The desktop is called "root window", and you can change its appearance with apps like `xsetroot` or `xloadimage`;
- the clipboard can only contain text, and behaves strange. Once you've selected text, it's already copied to the clipboard: move elsewhere and press the central button. There's an application, `xclipboard`, that provides for multiple clipboard buffers;
- drag and drop is an option, and is only available if you use X applications that support it.

To save memory, it's better to use applications that use the same libraries, but this is difficult to do in practice. There's a project called the K Desktop Environment that aims at making X11 look and behave as coherently as Windows; it's currently in early beta stage but, believe me, it's awesome. It's going to put Windows' interface to shame. Point your browser to `http://www.kde.org`.

6 Tailoring the System

6.1 System Initialization Files

Two important files under DOS are `AUTOEXEC.BAT` and `CONFIG.SYS`, which are used at boot time to initialize the system, set some environment variables like PATH and FILES, and possibly launch a program or batch file. Under Linux there are several initialization files, some of which you had better not tamper with until you know exactly what you are doing. I'll tell you what the most important are, anyway:

```
FILES                                   NOTES

/etc/inittab                            don't touch for now!
/etc/rc.d/*                             ditto
```

If all you need is setting the `$PATH` and other environment variables, or you want to change the login messages or automatically launch a program after the login, have a look at the following files:

```
FILES                                   NOTES

/etc/issue                              sets pre-login message
/etc/motd                               sets post-login message
/etc/profile                            sets $PATH and other variables, etc.
/etc/bashrc                             sets aliases and functions, etc.
/home/your_home/.bashrc                 sets your aliases + functions
/home/your_home/.bash_profile   or
/home/your_home/.profile                sets environment + starts your progs
```

If the latter file exists (note that it is a hidden file), it will be read after the login and the commands in it will be executed.

Example—look at this `.bash_profile`:

```
# I am a comment
echo Environment:
printenv | less   # equivalent of command SET under DOS
alias d='ls -l'   # easy to understand what an alias is
alias up='cd ..'
echo "I remind you that the path is "$PATH
echo "Today is 'date'"  # use the output of command 'date'
```

```
echo "Have a good day, "$LOGNAME
# The following is a "shell function"
ctgz() # List the contents of a .tar.gz archive.
{
  for file in $*
  do
    gzip -dc ${file} | tar tf -
  done
}
# end of .profile
```

`$PATH` and `$LOGNAME`, you guessed right, are environment variables. There are many others to play with; for instance, RMP for apps like `less` or `bash`.

6.2 Program Initialisation Files

Under Linux, virtually everything can be tailored to your needs. Most programs have one or more initialisation files you can fiddle with, often as a `.prognamerc` in your home dir. The first ones you'll want to modify are:

- `.inputrc`: used by `bash` to define keybindings;
- `.xinitrc`: used by `startx` to initialise X Window System;
- `.fvwmrc`: used by the window manager `fvwm`. A sample is in: `/usr/lib/X11/fvwm/system.fvwmrc`;
- `.Xdefault`: used by `rxvt`, a terminal emulator for X, and other programs.

For all of these and the others you'll come across sooner or later, RMP.

7 A Bit of Programming

7.1 Shell Scripts: .BAT Files on Steroids

If you used .BAT files to create shortcuts of long command lines (I did a lot), this goal can be attained by inserting appropriate alias lines (see example above) in `profile` or `.profile`. But if your .BATs were more complicated, then you'll love the scripting language made available by the shell: it's as powerful as QBasic, if not more. It has variables, structures like while, for, case, if... then... else, and lots of other features: it can be a good alternative to a "real" programming language.

To write a script—the equivalent of a .BAT file under DOS—all you have to do is write a standard ASCII file containing the instructions, save it, then make it executable with the command `chmod +x <scriptfile>`. To execute it, type its name.

A word of warning. The system editor is called `vi`, and in my experience most new users find it very difficult to use. I'm not going to explain how to use it, because I don't like it and don't use it, so there. See Matt Welsh's *Linux Installation and Getting Started* (page 3). (You had better get hold of another editor like `joe`, `jed` or `emacs` for X.) Suffice it here to say that:

- to insert some text, type 'i' then your text;
- to quit `vi` whithout saving, type ESC then :q!
- to save and quit, type ESC then :wq

Writing scripts under `bash` is such a vast subject it would require a book by itself, and I will not delve into the topic any further. I'll just give you an example of shell script, from which you can extract some basic rules:

```
#!/bin/sh
# sample.sh
# I am a comment
# don't change the first line, it must be there
echo "This system is: 'uname -a'" # use the output of the command
echo "My name is $0" # built-in variables
echo "You gave me the following $# parameters: "$*
echo "The first parameter is: "$1
echo -n "What's your name? " ; read your_name
echo notice the difference: "hi $your_name" # quoting with "
```

```
echo notice the difference: 'hi $your_name' # quoting with '
DIRS=0 ; FILES=0
for file in 'ls .' ; do
  if [ -d ${file} ] ; then # if file is a directory
    DIRS='expr $DIRS + 1'  # DIRS = DIRS + 1
  elif [ -f ${file} ] ; then
    FILES='expr $FILES + 1'
  fi
  case ${file} in
    *.gif|*jpg) echo "${file}: graphic file" ;;
    *.txt|*.tex) echo "${file}: text file" ;;
    *.c|*.f|*.for) echo "${file}: source file" ;;
    *) echo "${file}: generic file" ;;
  esac
done
echo "there are ${DIRS} directories and ${FILES} files"
ls | grep "ZxY--!!!WKW"
if [ $? != 0 ] ; then # exit code of last command
  echo "ZxY--!!!WKW not found"
fi
echo "enough... type 'man bash' if you want more info."
```

7.2 C for Yourself

Under UNIX, the system language is C, love it or hate it. Scores of other languages (FORTRAN, Pascal, Lisp, Basic, Perl, awk...) are also available.

Taken for granted that you know C, here are a couple of guidelines for those of you who have been spoilt by Turbo C++ or one of its DOS kin. Linux's C compiler is called gcc and lacks all the bells and whistles that usually accompany its DOS counterparts: no IDE, on-line help, integrated debugger, etc. It's just a rough command-line compiler, very powerful and efficient. To compile your standard hello.c you'll do:

```
$ gcc hello.c
```

which will create an executable file called a.out. To give the executable a different name, do

```
$ gcc -o hola hello.c
```

To link a library against a program, add the switch -l<libname>. For example, to link in the math library:

```
$ gcc -o mathprog mathprog.c -lm
```

(The -l<libname> switch forces gcc to link the library /usr/lib/lib<libname>.a; so -lm links /usr/lib/libm.a).

So far, so good. But when your prog is made of several source files, you'll need to use the utility make. Let's suppose you have written an expression parser: its source file is called parser.c and #includes two header files, parser.h and xy.h. Then you want to use the routines in parser.c in a program, say, calc.c, which in turn #includes parser.h. What a mess! What do you have to do to compile calc.c?

You'll have to write a so-called makefile, which teaches the compiler the dependencies between sources and objects files. In our example:

```
# This is makefile, used to compile calc.c
# Press the <TAB> key at appropriate positions!

calc: calc.o parser.o
<TAB>gcc -o calc calc.o parser.o -lm
# calc depends on two object files: calc.o and parser.o

calc.o: calc.c parser.h
<TAB>gcc -c calc.c
# calc.o depends on two source files

parser.o:  parser.c parser.h xy.h
<TAB>gcc -c parser.c
```

```
# parser.o depends on three source files

# end of makefile.
```

Save this file as `makefile` and type `make` to compile your program; alternatively, save it as `calc.mak` and type `make -f calc.mak`, and of course RMP. You can invoke some help about the C functions, that are covered by man pages, section 3; for example,

```
$ man 3 printf
```

There are lots of libraries available out there; among the first you'll want to use are `ncurses`, to handle textmode effects, and `svgalib`, to do graphics. If you feel brave enough to tackle X programming, get `XForms` (`ftp://bloch.phys.uwm.edu/pub/xforms`) and/or one of the many libraries that make writing X programs a breeze. Have a look at `http://www.xnet.com/ blatura/linapp6.html` .

Many editors can act as an IDE; `emacs` and `jed`, for instance, also feature syntax highlighting, automatic indent and so on. Alternatively, get the package `rhide` from `sunsite.unc.edu:/pub/Linux/devel/debuggers/`. It's a Borland IDE clone, and chances are that you'll like it.

8 The Remaining 1%

8.1 Using `tar` & `gzip`

Under UNIX there are some widely used applications to archive and compress files. `tar` is used to make archives—it's like `PKZIP.EXE`, but it doesn't compress, it only archives. To make a new archive:

```
$ tar -cvf <archive_name.tar> <file> [file...]
```

To extract files from an archive:

```
$ tar -xpvf <archive_name.tar> [file...]
```

To list the contents of an archive:

```
$ tar -tf <archive_name.tar> | less
```

You can compress files using `compress`, which is obsolete and shouldn't be used any more, or `gzip`:

```
$ compress <file>
$ gzip <file>
```

that creates a compressed file with extension .Z (`compress`) or .gz (`gzip`). These programs can compress only one file at a time. To decompress, use:

```
$ compress -d <file.Z>
$ gzip -d <file.gz>
```

RMP.

The `unarj`, `zip` and `unzip` (PK??ZIP nnn-compatible) utilities are also available. Files with extension `.tar.gz` or `.tgz` (archived with `tar`, then compressed with `gzip`) are as common in the UNIX world as .ZIP files are under DOS. Here's how to list the contents of a `.tar.gz` archive:

```
$ gzip -dc <file.tar.gz> | tar tf - | less
```

or, equivalently,

```
$ tar -ztf <file.tar.gz> | less
```

8.2 Installing Applications

First of all: installing packages is root's work. Some Linux applications are distributed as `.tar.gz` or `.tgz` archives, specifically prepared so that they can be decompressed from / typing the following command:

```
# gzip -dc <file.tar.gz> | tar xvf -
```

or, equivalently,

```
$ tar -zxf <file.tar.gz>
```

The files will be decompressed in the right directory, which will be created on the fly. Users of the Slackware distribution have a user-friendly `pkgtool` program; another is `rpm`, which is available on all distributions thanks to Red Hat.

Most programs shouldn't be installed from /; typically, the archive will contain a directory called `pkgname/` and a lot of files and/or subdirectories under `pkgname/`. A good rule is to install those packages from `/usr/local`. Besides, some programs are distributed as C or C++ source files, which you'll have to compile to create the binaries. In most cases, all you have to do is issue `make`. Obviously, you'll need the `gcc` or `g++` compiler.

8.3 Tips You Can't Do Without

Command completion: pressing <TAB> when issuing a command will complete the command line for you. Example: you have to type `gcc this_is_a_long_name.c`; typing `gcc thi<TAB>` will suffice. (If you have other files that start with the same characters, supply enough characters to resolve any ambiguity.)

Backscrolling: pressing Shift + Page Up (the gray key) allows you to backscroll a few pages, depending on how much video memory you have.

Resetting the screen: if you happen to `more` or `cat` a binary file, your screen may end up full of garbage. To fix things, blind type `reset` or this sequence of characters: `echo CTRL-V ESC c RETURN`.

Pasting text: in console, see below; in X, click and drag to select the text in an `xterm` window, then click the middle button (or the two buttons together if you have a two-button mouse) to paste. There is also `xclipboard` (alas, only for text); don't get confused by its very slow response.

Using the mouse: install `gpm`, a mouse driver for the console. Click and drag to select text, then right click to paste the selected text. It works across different VCs.

Messages from the kernel: have a look at `/var/adm/messages` or `/var/log/messages` as root to see what the kernel has to tell you, including bootup messages. The command `dmesg` is also handy.

8.4 Useful Programs and Commands

This list reflects my personal preferences and needs, of course. First of all, where to find them. Since you all know how to surf the Net and how to use `archie` and `ftp`, I'll just give you three of the most important addresses for Linux: `ftp://sunsite.unc.edu`, `ftp://tsx-11.mit.edu`, and `ftp://nic.funet.fi`. Please use your nearest mirror.

- `at` allows you to run programs at a specified time;
- `awk` is a simple yet powerful language to manipulate data files (and not only). For example, being `data.dat` your multi field data file,

  ```
  $ awk '$2 ~ "abc" {print $1, "\t", $4}' data.dat
  ```

  prints out fields 1 and 4 of every line in `data.dat` whose second field contains "abc".
- `cron` is useful to perform tasks periodically, at specified date and time;
- `delete-undelete` do what their name means;
- `df` gives you info about all mounted disk(s);
- `dosemu` allows you to run several (not all) DOS programs—including Windows 3.x, with a bit of hacking;
- `file <filename>` tells you what `filename` is (ASCII text, executable, archive, etc.);
- `find` (see also Section 3.3) is one of the most powerful and useful commands. It's used to find files that match several characteristics and perform actions on them. General use of `find` is:

  ```
  $ find <directory> <expression>
  ```

  where <expression> includes search criteria and actions. Examples:

  ```
  $ find . -type l -exec ls -l {} \;
  ```

  finds all the files that are symbolic links and shows what they point to.

  ```
  $ find / -name "*.old" -ok rm {} \;
  ```

  finds all the files matching the pattern and deletes them, asking for your permission first.

  ```
  $ find . -perm +111
  ```

  finds all the files whose permissions match 111 (executable).

```
$ find . -user root
```

finds all the files that belong to root. Lots of possibilities here—RMP.

- gnuplot is a brilliant program for scientific plotting;
- grep finds text patterns in files. For example,

  ```
  $ grep -l "geology" *.tex
  ```

  lists the files *.tex that contain the word "geology". The variant zgrep works on gzipped files. RMP;
- tcx compresses executable binaries keeping them executable;
- joe is an excellent editor. Invoking it by typing jstar you'll get the same key bindings as WordStar and its offspring, including DOS and Borland's Turbo languages editors;
- less is probably the best text browser, and if properly configured lets you browse gzipped, tarred, and zipped files as well;
- lpr <file> prints a file in background. To check the status of the printing queue, use lpq; to remove a file from the printing queue, use lprm;
- mc is a great file manager;
- pine is a nice e-mailing program;
- script <script_file> copies to script_file what appears on screen until you issue the command exit. Useful for debugging;
- sudo allows users to perform some of root's tasks (e.g. formatting and mounting disks; RMP);
- uname -a gives you info about your system;
- zcat and zless are useful for viewing gzipped text files without ungzipping them. Possible use:

  ```
  $ zless textfile.gz
  $ zcat textfile.gz | lpr
  ```
- The following commands often come in handy: bc, cal, chsh, cmp, cut, fmt, head, hexdump, nl, passwd, printf, sort, split, strings, tac, tail, tee, touch, uniq, w, wall, wc, whereis, write, xargs, znew. RMP.

8.5 Common Extensions and Related Programs

You may come across scores of file extensions. Excluding the more exotic ones (i.e. fonts, etc.), here's a list of who's what:

- 1 ... 8: man pages. Get man.
- arj: archive made with arj. unarj to unpack.
- dvi: output file produced by TEX (see below). xdvi to visualise it; dvips to turn it into a PostScript .ps file.
- gif: graphic file. Get seejpeg or xpaint.
- gz: archive made with gzip.
- info: info file (sort of alternative to man pages). Get info.
- jpg, jpeg: graphic file. Get seejpeg.
- lsm: Linux Software Map file. It's a plain ASCII file containing the description of a package.
- ps: PostScript file. To visualise or print it get gs and, optionally, ghostview.
- rpm: Red Hat package. You can install it on any system using the package manager rpm.
- tgz, tar.gz: archive made with tar and compressed with gzip.
- tex: text file to submit to TEX, a powerful typesetting program. Get the package tex, available in many distributions; but beware of NTeX, which has corrupted fonts and is included in some Slackware versions.
- texi: texinfo file, can produce both TEX and info files (cp. info). Get texinfo.
- xbm, xpm, xwd: graphic file. Get xpaint.
- Z: archive made with compress.
- zip: archive made with zip. Get zip and unzip.

9 The End, for Now

Congratulations! You have now grasped a little bit of UNIX and are ready to start working. Remember that your knowledge of the system is still limited, and that you are expected to do more practice with Linux to use it comfortably. But if all you had to do was get a bunch of applications and start working with them, I bet that what I included here is enough.

I'm sure you'll enjoy using Linux and will keep learning more about it—everybody does. I bet, too, that you'll never go back to DOS! I hope I made myself understood and did a good service to my 3 or 4 readers.

9.1 Copyright

9.2 Disclaimer

"From DOS to Linux HOWTO" was written by Guido Gonzato, `guido@ibogfs.cineca.it`. Many thanks to Matt Welsh, the author of *Linux Installation and Getting Started,* to Ian Jackson, former maintainer of "Linux Frequently Asked Questions with Answers," to Giuseppe Zanetti, the author of *Linux,* to all the folks who emailed me suggestions, and especially to Linus Torvalds and GNU who gave us Linux.

This document is provided "as is." I put great effort into writing it as accurately as I could, but you use the information contained in it at your own risk. In no event shall I be liable for any damages resulting from the use of this work.

Feedback is welcome. For any requests, suggestions, flames, etc., feel free to contact me.

Enjoy Linux and life,

Guido

9 The End, for Now

Congratulations! You have now grasped a little bit of UNIX and are ready to start working. Remember that your knowledge of the system is still limited, and that you are expected to do more practice with Linux to use it comfortably. But if all you wanted to get was a bunch of applications and start working with them, I bet that what I've included here is enough.

I'm sure you'll enjoy using Linux and will keep learning more about it—everybody does. I bet, too, that you'll never go back to DOS! I hope I made myself understood and did a good service to my 3 or 4 readers.

9.1 Copyright

9.2 Disclaimer

From DOS to Linux HOWTO was written by Guido Gonzato, guido@ibogfs.df.unibo.it. Many thanks to Matt Welsh, the author of *Linux Installation and Getting Started*, to Ian Jackson, the author of *Linux frequently asked questions with answers*, to Giuseppe Zanetti, the author of *Linux*, to all the folks who emailed me suggestions, and especially to Linus Torvalds and GNU who gave us Linux.

This document is provided "as is". I put great effort into writing it as accurately as I could, but you use the information contained in it at your own risk. In no event shall I be liable for any damages resulting from the use of this work.

Feedback is welcome. For any requests, suggestions, flames, etc., feel free to contact me.

Enjoy Linux and life,

Guido =8-)

Part XVIII

"DOSEMU HOWTO" by Mike Deisher and Uwe Bonnes

The Linux Documentation Project
The original, unaltered edition of this, and other, LDP documents, is on line at http://sunsite.unc.edu/LDP/.

Contents

Abstract

For dosemu-0.64.4 (in progress), 15 March 1997
This is the "Frequently Asked Questions" (FAQ) and HOWTO document for dosemu. The most up-to-date version of the dosemu-HOWTO may be found at ftp.mathematik.th-darmstadt.de, in `/pub/linux/bonnes/`.

1 The preliminaries

1.1 What is dosemu, anyway?

To quote the manual, "dosemu" is a user-level program which uses certain special features of the Linux kernel and the 80386 processor to run MS-DOS in what we in the biz call a "DOS box." The DOS box, a combination of hardware and software trickery, has these capabilities:

o the ability to virtualize all input/output and processor control instructions

o the ability to support the word size and addressing modes of the iAPX86 processor family's "real mode," while still running within the full protected mode environment

o the ability to trap all DOS and BIOS system calls and emulate such calls as are necessary for proper operation and good performance

o the ability to simulate a hardware environment over which DOS programs are accustomed to having control.

o the ability to provide MS-DOS services through native Linux services; for example, dosemu can provide a virtual hard disk drive which is actually a Linux directory hierarchy.

1.2 Names and numbers

```
(xx/yy/zz) means day zz in month yy in year xx(97/2/9).

winemu mean WinOS/2 running in dosemu(97/2/10).
```

1.3 What version of Dosemu should I use?

Dosemu uses the same numbering scheme as the kernel. Uneven second numbers are for possible unstable developer releases, even second numbers are for releases considered stable. At the time of writing, `0.64.4` is the latest stable release, while `0.65.0.6` is the latest developer's release. So if you want to use dosemu, get the latest `stable` release (97/02/28).

```
(xx/yy/zz) means day zz in month yy in year xx(97/2/9).

winemu mean WinOS/2 running in dosemu(97/2/10).
```

1.4 What's the newest version of dosemu and where can I get it?

The newest version of dosemu as of (97/2/9) is `dosemu0.64.4` and can be FTPed from:

```
tsx-11.mit.edu:/pub/linux/ALPHA/dosemu/

ftp.suse.com:/pub/dosemu/
```

However, pre-release versions are also available for developers and ALPHA testers. They can be retrieved from:

```
http://www.ednet.ns.ca/auto/rddc
```

Remember that this is ALPHA code, however: there may be serious bugs and very little documentation for new features. At present, the development version is known to have bugs. Please use it only if you like to do active development. Don't report bugs in the development version, fix them instead.

1.5 Where can I ask questions?

If you have problems regarding installing and running dosemu after reading the documentation, first try to help yourself: Your question has probably been asked and perhaps answered before. Try some search engine on the Internet to retrieve that information. E.g., you can ask

```
http://www.dejanews.com
```

to find all Usenet articles containing the keywords of your question. Helping yourself will probably be faster than asking a well known question. It too frees up the time of developers from answering trivial question and so helps the further development of dosemu(97/2/9) .

1.6 Where can I report bugs and ask questions?

If you want to ask questions and report bugs regarding dosemu, you should consider subscribing to the linux-msdos-digest mailing list. To subscribe, send mail to majordomo@vger.rutgers.edu with the following command in the body of your email message:

```
subscribe linux-msdos-digest your_username@your.email.address
```

If you ever want to remove yourself from the mailing list, you can send mail with the following command in the body of your email message to majordomo@vger.rutgers.edu:

```
unsubscribe linux-msdos-digest your_username@your.email.address
```

(95/8/11). When you are subscribed to linux-msdos, you can send your report as mail to linux-msdos@vger.rutgers.edu. There is a gate that send mails to linux-msdos@vger.rutgers.edu as postings to the newsgroup named linux.dev.msdos. If your News provider doesn't carry that group, ask her(him) to add that group(97/2/10).

1.7 Where can I follow the development?

If you want to follow the development of dosemu, there is a mailing list for developers. To subscribe, send mail to Majordomo@ednet.ns.ca with the following command in the body of your email message:

```
subscribe msdos-devel your_username@your.email.address
```

If you ever want to remove yourself from the mailing list, you can send mail to Majordomo@ednet.ns.ca with the following command in the body of your email message:

```
unsubscribe dosemu-devel your_username@your.email.address
```

Please, don't use this list for the things linux-dosemu-digest is intended for. Contributions to msdos-devel should concern the further development of dosemu. Normal installation problems shouldn't be reported here, and are normally ignored by those reading that list(97/2/9).

1.8 What documentation is available for dosemu?

The dosemu manual (dosemu.texinfo), written by Robert Sanders, has not been updated in some time but is still a good source of information. It is distributed with dosemu.

The "dosemu Novice's Altering Guide," or DANG, is a road map to the inner workings of dosemu. It is designed for the adventurous, those who wish to modify the source code themselves. The DANG is maintained by Alistair MacDonald (alistair@slitesys.demon.co.uk) and is found in the doc-directory of the dosemu source tree.

The EMU failure list (EMUfailure.txt) is a list of all programs known not to work under dosemu.

And then, of course, there is the dosemu FAQ/HOWTO. But you already know about that, don't you? It is also posted once in a while to the mailing list and found in the doc-directory. The most recent version can be found in ftp.mathematik.th-darmstadt.de:/pub/linux/bonnes/(97/2/9).

1.9 I have a program that fails, not listed in EMUfailure.txt

First check, if the failure of your program is not caused by some of the fundamental incapabilities of dosemu, listed in EMUfailure.txt. If you think you have something new, please report to linux-msdos@vger.rutgers.edu. Perhaps it can be made going with the help others. Give detailed information about your setup, tell the version of kernel, dosemu etc and name the observed errors. You can use xdos to cut and paste the error message into your report. But keep your report in a readable form. We know the content of ../etc/config.dist. So only send the active lines from your dosemu.conf. And scan through your debug output and at first only send those parts you think are relevant. Few people are willing to decode some long attachment to a mail, to do debugging for others. Keep your logs at hand(97/2/10).

1.10 How do I submit changes or additions to the HOWTO?

The preferred method is to edit the file dosemu-HOWTO-xx.x.sgml to incorporate the changes, create a diff file by typing something like

```
diff -uw original-file new-file
```

and send it to bon@elektron.ikp.physik.th-darmstadt.de. If you do not know SGML, that's ok. Changes or new information in any form will be accepted. Creating the diff file just makes it easier on the HOWTO maintainer. (97/2/9)

1.11 Message from Greg—

If you have questions, please contact Greg Hankins, the Linux HOWTO coordinator, at `gregh@cc.gatech.edu`(95/8/11).

2 Compiling and installing dosemu

2.1 Where are the installation instructions?

The installation instructions are in the file, "`QuickStart`," included in the distribution.

2.2 Top ten problems while compiling and installing dosemu.

1. Forgetting to read the `QuickStart` guide.
2. Try to compile some old version of dosemu.
3. Try to compile with a kernel older than 2.0.28 or 2.1.15.
4. Having the wrong linux kernel source sitting in `/usr/src/linux` or missing `/usr/src/linux/include/version.h`
5. Use dosemu with a kernel that does not have `IPC` compiled in.
6. Compile with gcc older than 2.7.2 or libc older than x.x.x.
7. Forget to edit your `/etc/dosemu.conf` file.
8. Run DOSEMU with partition access while they are already mounted.
9. Don't install dosemu with sufficient privileges (i.e., root). (97/04/08)

2.3 How can I use dosemu on an older version of the Linux Kernel.

If you still use 1.2.13 and can't upgrade for some reasons, use `dosemu-0.60.4`. If you use some version of dosemu below 2.0.28 and 2.1.15, Hans Lermen (`lermen@elserv.ffm.fgan.de`) reported (97/1/25 and 97/2/11)

```
> Is the dosemu-0.64.3.tgz version of DOSEMU for the 2.xx.yy > versions > of the
linux kernel ??

Yes, but ...

  if ( ((xx == 0) && (yy >= 28)) || ((xx >= 1) && (yy >= 15)) )
    take_dosemu_0_64_4();
  else {
    if (xx == 1)  exit(1);
    take_dosemu_0_64_2_x();
  }
```

2.4 How do I make a.out format binaries?

Starting with version 0.64.4 there is no a.out support any more. If you absolutely need it, you must use version 0.64.3.1. The configure script then should take care for this, if you setup is a standard setup(97/2/11).

2.5 How do I compile dosemu on a machine with low memory?

Marty Leisner (`leisner@sdsp.mc.xerox.com`) reported (95/4/8) that

If you have problems with running out of swap space you may want to add `CFLAGS+=-fno-inline` after `CFLAGS` is defined in `dpmi/Makefile`. Be careful before you do this and check for the existence of swap space. I found Linux crashes a times when it has no swap space.

2.6 Compilation fails with some strange error regarding "slang"

You probably have installed your own version of the Slang library. Hans Lermen <lermen@elserv.ffm.fgan.de> writes(97/2/11):

```
configure --enable-force-slang
```

2.7 What configurable options are available

Try

```
configure -help
```

to get the list of configurable options listed (97/2/12)

2.8 How can I speed up compilation?

Marty Leisner (leisner@sdsp.mc.xerox.com) reported (95/4/8) that

The default optimization is -O2. You may want edit the makefile to use -O (compiled somewhat faster and smaller).

2.9 More compilation tips from Marty—

Marty Leisner (leisner@sdsp.mc.xerox.com) reported (95/4/8) that

You need to have build the kernel on your system to get the current version. If not, you may want to hand modify KERNEL_VERSION in the top level Makefile. The number is of the form, "nmmmppp", where "n" is the version, "mmm" is the minor version, and "ppp" is the patch level. For example, kernel 1.1.88 corresponds to "1001088" and kernel 1.2.1 to "1002001".

Addition from (lermen@elserv.ffm.fgan.de):

For versions greater 0.64.3 this no longer is true. You need to have a valid <linux/version.h>, which has to be part off your standard /usr/include. If you don't have it, you either did a make clean on your kernel source or your distributor failed to support you with this.

2.10 Do I need to compile dosemu as root?

(95/4/8)

No. You must install it as root, though.

Marty Leisner (leisner@sdsp.mc.xerox.com) adds

In order to access I/O ports (including the console) dosemu needs to run as root. Running dosemu in an xterm or in X and requiring no direct hardware access allows you to run dosemu as a user. The security/setuid implications will be worked on in development releases(95/8/11).

Have a look at ../doc/SECURITY.readme too(97/2/9).

2.11 How to I patch dosemu.

If you do patch dosemu from one version to another, do

```
make pristine;./configure; make
```

If you don't make pristine, at least the version of the new executable will be wrong, if the whole thing compiles at all(97/2/9).

2.12 What versions of DOS are known to run with dosemu.

Caldera's OpenDos (formerly known as DrDOS) is reported to work with dosemu Nicolas St-Pierre (draggy@kosmic.org). OpenDos can be used free of charge for non-commercial use, so it is preferred. However, as of now, redistribution is not allowed. You must get OpenDos yourself from Caldera's site, http://www.caldera.com/dos. Hopefully this will change soon, so dosemu can distribute a bootable hdimage. MSDOS version 6.22 is known to work with dosemu. MSDOS version 7 (aka Win95) works with dosemu if you have the boot logo switched off and don't start the graphic shell at boot up. If you make the hdimage bootable with the so called "Rescue Disk" you are offered to make during MS Windows installation, you get the correct settings. If you use your normal Win95 installation to transfer the system files, have a look at the msdos.sys written on the hdimage and change the settings under the section Options to have entries like

```
Options
Logo=0
BootGUI=0
```

(97/3/7)

2.13 Versions known not to run

DOS 4.01 had problems by itself, do it won't work with dosemu either Mattias Hembruch (`mghembru@ece.uwaterloo.ca`) 97/04/03

3 Hard disk setup

3.1 How do I use my hard disk with dosemu?

First, mount your dos hard disk partition as a Linux subdirectory. For example, you could create a directory in Linux such as /dos (mkdir -m 755 /dos) and add a line like

```
/dev/hda1        /dos      msdos   umask=022
```

to your `/etc/fstab` file. (In this example, the hard disk is mounted read-only. You may want to mount it read/write by replacing "022" with "000" and using the `-m 777` option with `mkdir`). Now `mount /dos`. Now you can add a line like

```
lredir d: linux\fs/dos
```

to the `AUTOEXEC.BAT` file in your hdimage (see the comments on `LREDIR` below). On a multi-user system you may want to use

```
lredir d: linux\fs\${home}
```

where `$home` is the name of a variable that contains the location of the DOS directory (/dos in this example)(95/8/11).

Tim Bird (Tim_R_Bird@Novell.COM) states that `LREDIR` users should be careful when they use `LREDIR` in the `AUTOEXEC.BAT`, because `COMMAND.COM` will continue parsing the `AUTOEXEC.BAT` from the redirected drive as the same file offset where it left off in the `AUTOEXEC.BAT` on the physical drive. For this reason, it is safest to have the `AUTOEXEC.BAT` on the redirected drive and the physical drive (diskimage) be the same(95/8/11).

Robert D. Warren (`rw11258@xx.acs.appstate.edu`) reported (94/4/28) that

```
I boot off a small hdimage file (less than 1 MB - and twice as large
as needs be at that), and the next to last line in my config.sys file
on the hdimage boot image is:


        install=c:\lredir.exe c: LINUX\FS\home/dos

This will execute lredir just before the command interpreter runs. And
I have successfully run it with both {\tt command.com} and 4DOS.  This
eliminates the offset problem using lredir in AUTOEXEC.bat.
```

Uwe Bonnes (`bon@elektron.ikp.physik.th-darmstadt.de`) adds (95/8/11) that
It is usefull to do:

```
install=C:\subst.exe g: c:
```

before that, so you have still access to your hdimage as drive `G:` Another useful hint in that circumstance is to configure dosemu to use `AUTOEXEC.EMU` to keep DOS and dosemu apart.

3.2 How can I access the hdimage from Linux?

Use the recent mtools, version 3.0 at the time of writing. With a line in `/etc/mtools.conf` like

```
drive g:  file="/var/lib/dosemu/hdimage" Offset=8832
```

you can use the mtools on the hdimage, like `mdir g:`. `mcopy g:/config.emu /tmp` copies the `config.emu` file from the hdimage to `/tmp/config.emu`. You can edit it there and copy it back. Use a drive letter you find sensible. `G:` is only an example(07/2/9).

3.3 Can I use my stacked/double-spaced/super-stored disk?

At this time, compressed drives cannot be accessed via the redirector (`LREDIR` or `EMUFS`) on a standard kernel. There is a patch for the kernel to mount compressed files under the name `dmsdosfs`. Find it on sunsite.unc.edu and its mirrors

```
http://sunsite.unc.edu:/pub/Linux/system/Filesystems/dosfs/
```

A good idea is also to look in http://sunsite.unc.edu:/pub/Linux/Incoming for a newer version. However, many people have had success by simply uncommenting the

```
disk { wholedisk "/dev/hda" }          # 1st partition on 1st disk
```

line in their dosemu config file. Others have had success using

```
disk { partition "/dev/hda1" }
```

Do that on the risk of losing data on a dosemu crash(97/2/9).

If your DOS partition is already mounted with write access and you try to run dosemu with partition or whole disk access, dosemu will print a warning message and abort. This prevents DOS and Linux from making independent writes to your disk and trashing the data on your dos partition(95/8/11).

If LILO is installed, the above will not work. However...

Thomas Mockridge (`thomas@aztec.co.za`) reports (94/8/5) that

To boot dosemu with LILO and Stacker 4.0 I did a little work around...

1. `dd` the MBR to a file. (or Norton Utility, etc., first 512 bytes)
2. Boot DOS (a cold boot, not dosemu), do a `FDISK.EXE /MBR`, make your dos partition active with (DOS) `FDISK.EXE`.
3. Copy the new MBR to a file.
4. Replace the original MBR
5. Copy the second MBR to `/var/lib/dosemu/partition.hdax` (Whichever is your DOS partition)
6. Set `dosemu.conf`.

```
disk {partition "/dev/hda? ?"}
```

7. Start dosemu *et voila!* No LILO.

Holger Schemel (`q99492@pbhrzx.uni-paderborn.de`) reported (94/2/10) that

Works even fine under dosemu with MSDOS 6.0. If you have problems, then you have to edit the file `DBLSPACE.INI` manually and change the disk letter to the letter your drive gets under dosemu.

Darren J Moffat (`moffatd@dcs.gla.ac.uk`) also reported (94/3/27)

"...Use 6.2 if you can get it!! Just make sure you have a LILO boot disk on hand since dos 6{.2} will change the MBR of the boot HZ."

4 Parallel ports, serial ports and mice

4.1 Port access worked with older version, but doesn't work now!

Read `../doc/README.port-io` and the port section in `../etc/config.dist`.

4.2 Port access was faster with older versions!

To have a chance to log port access, by default every port access produces an exception out of vm86-mode. This takes some time. If you don't want to log port access, use the keyword `fast` in the appropriate port statement.

4.3 Where are the (Microsoft compatible) mouse drivers?

Tom Kimball (`tk@pssparc2.oc.com`) reported (93/11/24) that

Several people said to use a different mouse driver and suggested some. I found a couple that seem to work fine.

```
oak.oakland.edu:/pub/msdos/mouse/mouse701.zip    (mscmouse)
oak.oakland.edu:/pub/msdos/mouse/gmous102.zip    (gmouse)
```

Normally you can use DOSEMU's internal driver, so you don't need any additional mouse driver in dosemu outside winemu(97/2/10).

4.4 Why doesn't the mouse driver work?

Mark Rejhon (`mdrejhon@magi.com`) reported (95/4/7) that

If you start the mouse driver and it just hangs (it might actually take 30-60s), but if you are waiting longer than a minute for the mouse driver to start, try specifying the COM port that the mouse is on, at the mouse driver command line.

4.5 Why does dosemu clobber `COM4`?

Rob Janssen (`rob@pe1chl.ampr.org`) reported (94/3/24) that

According to `jmorriso@bogomips.ee.ubc.ca`, "dosemu still clobbers `COM4` (0x2e8, IRQ 5). 0x2e8 isn't in ports{} in config. I have to run

```
setserial /dev/cua3 irq 5
```

on it after dosemu exits."

This is caused by your VGA BIOS. I have found that by enabling the IO port trace and seeing where it was clobbered.

Disable the "`allowvideoportaccess on`" line in config and it will work fine. When you then have problems with the video, try to enable more selective ranges of IO addresses (e.g., 40-43).

4.6 How do I use dosemu over the serial ports?

4.7 How can I switch between dosemu and a shell over the serial line?

John Taylor (`taylor@pollux.cs.uga.edu`) reported (94/5/25) that

I am running Linux 1.1.13 and want to point out a great feature that should be protected and not taken out (IMHO). With the 52 version, I can run the program, `screen`. From `screen`, I can invoke `dos -D-a`. What is really great (IMHO) is the screen commands (the CTRL-A cmds) still work. This means I can do a CTRL-A C and add another UNIX shell, and switch between the two (DOS or UNIX). This allows me to use dosemu over the serial line really well, because switching is easy.

4.8 How can I get the parallel ports to work?

`dosemu.conf` has lines at the end to redirect printers to either `/dev/lp`*x* or a file. If you want direct access to the bare metal, comment out these emulation lines, and add the line

```
ports { device /dev/lp0 fast range 0x3bc 0x3bf } # lpt0
```

for the "monitor card" printer port (corresponds to /dev/lp0), or

```
ports { device /dev/lp1 fast range 0x378 0x37f } # lpt1

ports { device /dev/lp1 fast range 0x278 0x27f } # lpt2
```

for LPT1 (`/dev/lp1`) and LPT2 (`/dev/lp2`) respectively(97/2/9).

5 Multiple users and Non-interactive sessions

5.1 Can I use dosemu on a multi-user system?

Corey Sweeney (`corey@amiganet.xnet.com`) reported (93/12/8) that

If you are running dosemu on a system in which more then one person may want to run dosemu, then you may want to change the directory of your hard drive image. Currently in the `/etc/dosemu.conf` file there exists the line saying that the hard drive image is hdimage. If you change this to `/var/lib/dosemu/hdimage` then people do not have to worry about what directory they are in when they run dosemu, and hdimage does not have to be moved each time you upgrade to the next patch level.

If you do do this for multi-user dosemu, then you will want to make the hdimage in `/var/lib/dosemu` read-only for everyone but the dosemu administrator.

Note that you can use the new `emufs.sys` thing to mount a "public" directory or a "private" directory (a sub-directory in each person's home directory).

[Note: Users may also create a personal configuration file named `~/.dosrc` (same format as `/etc/dosemu.conf`) to run their own copy of DOS.]

5.2 How can I run DOS commands non-interactively?

I have been meaning to write an article on this for quite some time but have not gotten around to it. Here are some hints from others:

Dan Newcombe (`newcombe@aa.csc.peachnet.edu`) reported (94/1/27) that

Here is an idea (untested) to be able to run a DOS command from the command line (or menu choice, etc...) without modifying the actual emulator. (Your DOS partition is assumed to be mounted under Linux, already.)

Suppose you wanted to run `WP60.EXE` with the command

```
wp60 d:\doc\paper.txt
```

You would do something like

```
dosrun wp60 d:\doc\paper.txt
```

`dosrun` would be a Linux shell program that would a) edit, modify, or re-create the DOS `AUTOEXEC.BAT` from your DOS partition and b) simply run `DOSEMU` (e.g., `dos -C >/dev/null`). Step a) would somehow keep all the stuff you'd normally want in `AUTOEXEC.BAT` (e.g., `MOUSE.COM`) and the last line would be

```
wp60 d:\doc\paper.txt
```

On the dosemu side, beforehand, you would have to modify the `CONFIG.SYS` file (located in hdimage) so that it 1) uses `EMUFS` to access the DOS partition as `D:`, 2) sets `COMPSEC=D:\` (I think. I don't have a DOS manual around.), and 3) sets `shell=c:\command.com /p`.

The idea is that for each time that you load the DOS emulator, you will recreate an AUTOEXEC.bat that is specific to that session. What makes it specific is that the last line will execute the program you want. The modifications on the hdimage are to tell the emulator/DOS that you want to use (and effectively) boot off of `D:`, which will be the actual DOS partition.

If you do not use hdimage and access the DOS filesystem directly upon boot-up of dosemu, then this will work, and you don't have to go through the hdimage part of this all.

Daniel T. Schwager (`danny@dragon.s.bawue.de`) reported (94/7/2) that

You can use different `dosemu.conf` files (and different HD boot images with different `AUTOEXEC.BAT`s) and call dosemu like

```
$ dos -F my_quicken_q_exe_dosemu.conf
```

Dietmar Braun (`braun@math20.mathematik.uni-bielefeld.de`) reported (94/7/4) that

This is no problem at all when you use the redirector of dosemu. It is possible to redirect a drive letter to a linux path given by an environment variable. So I have a shell script named `DOS` which does something like

```
mkdir /tmp/dos.$$
DOSTMP=/tmp/dos.$$; export DOSTMP
```

and then a little trick to get `"echo $* > $DOSTMP/startup.bat"` really working (actually a small C Program which turns '/' in '\' and terminates lines correctly for messy DOS with CR/LF pairs and adds `^Z` at the end of the file), creates startup files, links and so on in this directory, and then starts dosemu. Within `AUTOEXEC.BAT` drive `C:` is redirected from hdimage to this tmp directory, which has links for `$HOME` and `$PWD`.

So if I want to see my file names shortened to 8.3 I can type "`DOS dir`" and I get my current directory listing. So I have full DOS multi user (I don't have any DOS partition and redirecting to Linux preserves user permissions) and multitasking. (dosemu sessions are completely independent). I did this once to be able to use a dos driver for my printer. My `printcap.df` is actually a DOS program. So you can even make DOS executables act as `lpr` filters.

6 dosemu and Netware

6.1 How do I get Netware access from dosemu?

As always, access through the Linux filesystem is preferred. Mount your Netware drives with Caldera's Netware utilities or Volker Lendecke's free ncpfs utility (`ftp://ftp.gwdg.de:/pub/linux/misc/ncpfs`). If you need real IPX access, e.g. to run Novell's `SYSCON.EXE`, read `../doc/NOVELL-HOWTO.txt`.

7 dosemu and the X Window System(97/2/9).

7.1 Can I run dosemu in console mode while running X?

Ronald Schalk (`R.Schalk@uci.kun.nl`) reported (94/1/17) that

Yes, no problem. Just remember to use Ctrl-Alt-<Fn> to go to a Virtual Console (VC), and you can run any Linux application (dosemu is a linux-application). I've got almost always WP5.1 in a DOS session.

[Note: Use Ctrl-Alt-F7 to switch back to X from dosemu, if X runs on VC7.]

7.2 Is it possible to run dosemu in a window in X-windows?

If you have X installed and you have successfully compiled dosemu and run it successfully outside X-windows, you should be able to run "xdos" or "dos -X" right away to bring up a dosemu window. If this does not work, make sure:

```
1. Dosemu has X support compiled in. This is default, however
   if you you have configured dosemu with
   "./configured --without-x", you don't have X support. So make
   "make pristine; ./configure; make; make install" should build
   you a dosemu-executable with X support, if you have the
   X-libraries installed in /usr/X11R6.
2. Set up your X key-mappings.  In an xterm, type

   xmodmap -e "keycode 22 = 0xff08"
   xmodmap -e "keycode 107 = 0xffff"

   These lines fixes the backspace and delete keys respectively.
3. Configured the X-related configuration options in your
   /etc/dosemu.conf file.
```

Alternatively, you can run dosemu inside a color `xterm`, which is not recommended because many color `xterms` have buggy support for the complex text display capabilities of dosemu. This does not require `X_SUPPORT` to be compiled in to dosemu. However, if you really want to do this, do the following steps:

```
1. Install ansi_xterm.  The recommended package is available as:
   tsx-11.mit.edu:/pub/linux/ALPHA/dosemu/Development/ansi-xterm-R6.tar.gz

2. Set up your X key-mappings.  In an xterm, type

   xmodmap -e "keycode 22 = 0xff08"
   xmodmap -e "keycode 107 = 0xffff"

   These lines fixes the backspace and delete keys, respectively.

3. Configured the terminal-related (not X-related) settings in
   /etc/dosemu.conf
```

(972/9).

Marty Leisner (`leisner@sdsp.mc.xerox.com`) reported (95/3/31) that:

I have `xrdb` log the following resources

```
dosxterm*Font:  vga dosxterm*geometry:  80x25 dosxterm*saveLines:  25
```

or I alias "dosxterm" to "`term -fn vga -title dosxterm -geometry 80x25 -sl 25`"

If you use the `xrdb` method, all you have to do is run "`xterm -name dosxterm`"

7.3 Xdos doesn't work on a remote X-display!

At present, dosemu is set up to use the MIT shared memory extensions. This extension only works on a local display. If you want to run xdos on a remote display, configure dosemu with `./configure -enable-nomitshm` after a `make pristine` or on the clean source tree(97/2/9).

7.4 Xdos doesn't find the VGA font

Check that the VGA fonts you installed are listed in the `font.dir` of the directory you installed the fonts in:

```
hertz:~> grep misc /usr/X11R6/lib/X11/XF86Config
    FontPath     "/usr/X11R6/lib/X11/fonts/misc/"
hertz:~> grep vga /usr/X11R6/lib/X11/fonts/misc/fonts.dir
vga.pcf vga
vga11x19.pcf vga11x19
hertz:~> ls /usr/X11R6/lib/X11/fonts/misc/vga*
/usr/X11R6/lib/X11/fonts/misc/vga.pcf
/usr/X11R6/lib/X11/fonts/misc/vga11x19.bdf
/usr/X11R6/lib/X11/fonts/misc/vga11x19.pcf
```

If you installed some X fonts, like you did when you installed dosemu with X support for the first time, `mkfontdir` and then `xset fp rehash` needs to be run. The dosemu install should take care for `mkfontdir` and tells you about `xset fp rehash`. Tell us if it doesn't work for you. (97/2/13)

7.5 The VGA font is very small on my high resolution display

Look for the VGA 11x19 font. (97/2/13)

7.6 Dosemu compilation fails with some strange error regarding X!

As stated above, dosemu uses the MIT shared memory extensions by default. Under XFree86 they are only available with Version 3.1.2 and above. If you have an older version, consider to upgrade, or configure dosemu to not use this extension (see last section)(97/2/9).

7.7 Does ansi emulation work properly?

Marty Leisner (`leisner@sdsp.mc.xerox.com`) reported (95/3/31) that

Yes. I use `NNANSI.COM` under X windows. I find 25, 43 and 50 line mode work properly; however, 50-line mode is difficult to use on a 1024x768 screen (unless smaller fonts are used a bigger screen. 43 line mode will resize the `xterm` window to use 43 lines.

8 dosemu and MS Windows 3.1

8.1 Is it possible to run MS Windows 3.1 under dosemu?

The `../doc/README.Windows` file says:

```
**************************************************************
*    WARNING!!! WARNING!!! WARNING!!! WARNING!!! WARNING!!!   *
*                                                             *
*  Danger Will Robinson!!!  This is not yet fully supported   *
*  and there are many known bugs!  Large programs will almost *
*  certainly NOT WORK!!!  BE PREPARED FOR SYSTEM CRASHES IF   *
*  YOU TRY THIS!!!                                            *
*                                                             *
*    WARNING!!! WARNING!!! WARNING!!! WARNING!!! WARNING!!!   *
**************************************************************
```

Okay, it is possible to boot WINOS2 (the modified version of Windows 3.1 that OS/2 uses) under DOSEMU. Many kudos to Lutz & Dong.

◇ However, YOU NEED BOTH LICENSES, for WINDOWS 3.1 as well OS/2.

There are many known problems. Windows is prone to crash, could take data with it, large programs will not load, etc. etc. etc. In other words, it is NOT ready for daily use. Many video cards are known to have problems (you may see a nice white screen, however, look below for win31-in-xdos). Your program groups are all likely to disappear. ... Basically, it's a pain.

On the other hand, if you're dying to see the little Windows screen running under Linux and you have read this carefully and promise not to bombard the dosemu developers with "MS Word 6.0 doesn't run" messages.

```
1.  Get DOSEMU & the Linux source distributions.
2.  Unpack DOSEMU.
3.  Configure DOSEMU typing './configure' and do _not_ disable vm86plus.
4.  Compile DOSEMU typing 'make'.
5.  Get the OS2WIN31.ZIP distribution from {\ldots} ????
    {\ldots} oh well, and now you have the first problem.
    It _was_ on ibm.com sometime ago, but has vanished from that site, and
    as long as it was there, we could mirror it. {\ldots} you see the problem?
    However, use 'archie' to find it, it will be around somewhere on the net
    {\ldots} for some time ;-)
5.  Unpack the OS2WIN31 files into your WINDOWS\SYSTEM directory.
    (In fact you only need WINDOWS/SYSTEM/os2k386.exe and the mouse driver)
7.  Startup dosemu (make certain that DPMI is set to a value such as 4096)
8.  Copy the file winemu.bat to your c: drive.
```

9. Cross your fingers.

Good luck!

8.2 Windows 3.x in xdos:

As of version 0.64.3 DOSEMU is able to run Windows in xdos. Of course, this is not recommended at all, but if you really want to try, it is safer than starting Windows 3.1 on the console, because when it crashes, it doesn't block your keyboard or freeze your screen.

Hints:

```
1. Get Dosemu & Linux source.
2. Unpack dosemu.
3. Run "./configure" to configure Dosemu (it will enable vm86plus as a
   default).
4. Type "make" to compile.
5. Get a Trident SVGA drivers for Windows. The files are tvgaw31a.zip
   and/or tvgaw31b.zip. They are available at garbo.uwasa.fi in
   /windows/drivers (any mirrors?).
6. Unpack the Trident drivers.
7. In Windows setup, install the Trident "800x600 256 color for 512K
   boards" driver.
8. Do the things described above to get and install OS2WIN31.
10. Start xdos.
11. In Dosemu, go to windows directory and start winemu.
12. Cross your fingers.
```

8.3 Can I install MS Windows from within dosemu?

No you can't. Dos will tell you something like

```
The XMS driver you have on your system is not compatible with Windows...
```

You need to install MS Windows from DOS. You can copy the MS Windows tree to somewhere on your Linux file system and use `LREDIR` to mount it on the same place as it is in DOS. Example:

```
You have windows in d:\windows
You have d:\ mounted as /dosc in Linux
You copy the windows tree to Linux,
e.g.  "cp -a /dosd/windows /usr/share
Inside dosemu you redirect the copied tree like
lredir d:  linux\fs\dosd
```

Now dosemu can't mess around in your MS Windows directory, but changes in the MS Windows directory aren't seen by dosemu either. If you want to do the same with MS Windows on drive `C:` look in this FAQ how to redirect `C:`.

But you can use `SETUP.EXE` from inside the windows directory to install drivers and change some settings. (97/2/1497)

8.4 Notes for the mouse under win31-in-xdos:

1. Use the mouse driver `MOUSE.DRV` from WinOS2

2. In order to let the mouse properly work you need the following in your `WIN.INI` file:

```
[windows]
MouseThreshold1=0
MouseThreshold2=0
MouseSpeed=0
```

3. The mouse cursor gets painted not by X, but by MS Windows, itself, so it depends on the refresh rate how often it gets updated, though the mouse coordinates movement itself will not get delayed. (In fact you have two cursors, but the X cursor is given an 'invisible' cursor shape while it is within the DOS box.)

4. Because the coordinates passed to windows are interpreted relatively, we need to calibrate the cursor. This is done automatically whenever you enter the DOS box window: The cursor gets forced to 0,0 and then back to its correct coordinates. Hence, if you want to recalibrate the cursor, just move the cursor outside and then inside the DOS box again. (97/2/10)

8.5 Why did my icon disappear from the Program Manager?

MS Windows and WinOS2 handle the program group different. While MS Windows stores the setup in `PROGMAN.INI`, WinOS2 wants the concatenation of `PROGMAN.INI` in `SYSTEM.INI`. Here's a hint from Todd T. Freis (`friest@acm.org`):

```
cat progman.ini >> system.ini
```

Be sure to use > > .

9 Video and sound

9.1 Can I run 32-bit video games under dosemu?

Mark Rejhon (`mdrejhon@magi.com`) reported (95/4/8) that

With the recent DPMI improvements that have gone into 0.60, you can now run some 32-bit video games in dosemu. If the game is compatible in an OS/2 DOS box, there are chances that it will work in dosemu. (Example 32-bit games include Descent, Dark Forces, Mortal Kombat 2, Rise of The Triad, which have all successfully been tested in recent dosemu releases).

Before you attempt to run a video game, you must have the keyboard configured in raw keyboard mode and enabled VGA graphics modes, in the `/etc/dosemu.conf` file. If you have successfully run graphics programs in dosemu, and are prepared to take the risk of a possible system crash (this is because you are letting dosemu run with root access to the video card, and leaves the possibility of putting the video card in a bad state that is difficult to recover from) then you can go ahead and try running the video game.

Note, however, you will have to turn off the sound in the game. (Someone will have to program in sound board emulation before we can avoid this). Note that game timers can be a little bit slow, due to Linux multitasking and lack of high-frequency timer support. So the games may run from anywhere from 5 to 100 percent speed. Typically, the speed is approximately 50 percent in recent dosemu releases and is expected to improve eventually.

Who knows, it might even work. If you can't get it to work, check `EMUfailure.txt` if the program is listed there, or falls in a category of programs that at present don't or probably never work with dosemu. If you think, it should be listed in `EMUfailure.txt`, report to `linux-msdos@vger.rutgers.edu`.

Addition from (`lermen@elserv.ffm.fgan.de`(97/2/11)):

There is a security hole when having enabled DPMI and having dosemu suid root (especially when using dos4gw-based games), the client is able to access the whole user space, hence also can modify the dosemu code itself. Use of the `secure on` option in `/etc/dosemu.conf` disables this, but then you can't run those games.

9.2 Exiting from dosemu gives me a screen full of garbage.

(95/4/8)

The problem is that the font information for the VGA text screen is not being saved. Get a copy of the SVGA lib package. The current source is in

```
sunsite.unc.edu:/pub/Linux/libs/graphics/svgalib125.tar.gz
```

It may also be available as a pre-compiled package in your favorite Linux distribution (e.g., Slackware, etc.). Use `savetextmode` to save the current text mode and font to a file in `/tmp` before running dosemu. Then run `textmode` upon exiting dosemu to restore it.

Addition from (`lermen@elserv.ffm.fgan.de`(97/2/11)):

Have a look also at `src/arch/linux/debugger/README.recover` and `README.dosdebug`. `dosdebug` can aid recovery.

9.3 How do I get dosemu to work with my Trident/Actix/other video card?

[The screen flickers violently, displays the video BIOS startup message, and hangs.]

Andrew Tridgell (`tridge@nimbus.anu.edu.au`) reported (94/1/29) that

I found with early versions it would work if I used:

```
ports { 0x42 }
```

but that sometimes my machine would crash when it was cycling the video BIOS in dosemu. This is because you're allowing the VGA BIOS to re-program your clock, which severely stuffs with Linux.

This prompted me to write the read-only and masking patches for dosemu, which I believe are still in the latest version. I now use:

```
ports { readonly 0x42 }
```

and it boots dosemu more slowly, but more reliably.

Tim Shnaider (`tims@kcbbs.gen.nz`) also reported (94/1/18) that

One way of fixing this is to use the `GETROM` program to dump your video BIOS to a file and edit the config file in the `/etc/dosemu` directory There will be a few video lines. Here is my video line

```
video { vga console graphics chipset trident memsize 1024 vbios_file
/etc/dosemu/vbios }
```

where vbios is the file generated by typing

```
getrom > vbios
```

Douglas Gleichman (`p86884@tcville.edsg.hac.com`) reported (94/9/1) that (with the ATI Graphics Ultra)

For dosemu 0.52 you need to add this line to your `dosemu.conf` file:

```
ports  { 0x1ce 0x1cf 0x238 0x23b 0x23c 0x23f 0x9ae8 0x9ae9 0x9aee 0x9aef }
```

The board self-test will list a failure, but graphics programs will run fine.

9.4 Why doesn't my sound card software work with dosemu?

Hannu Savolainen (`hsavolai@cs.Helsinki.FI`) reported (94/3/21) that

The dosemu and any DOS program with it run under control of a protected mode operating system. This means that the memory is not mapped as the program expects. If it somehow manages to start DMA based recording with SB, the recorded sound doesn't find it's way to the application. It just destroys some data in the memory.

James B. MacLean (`macleajb@ednet.ns.ca`) reported (94/6/19) that

Sorry to disappoint, but at this time dosemu does not support directly the necessary interception of interrupts or DMA generally required for sound card access via dosemu.

It's bound to happen at some future date though.

And `Corey Sweeney (orey@d94.nnb.interaccess.com)` reports (97/2/15)

```
Sound code is being currently being worked on
```

10 Games

10.1 Duke3d doesn't work

Hans Lermen <`lermen@elserv.ffm.fgan.de`> said (97/2/16): duke3d must be "configured" via a setup, within this setup you have to choose "keyboard + mouse," or else it won't work.

11 Other Hardware

11.1 How do I get my xxxxx device working under dosemu?

Corey Sweeney (`corey@bbs.xnet.com`) reported (94/5/30) that

Here is a log of my adventures trying to get devices working under dosemu. So far I've gotten my voice mail system working and my scanner half working. Here's how:

1. Look in your manual and find if your card uses any ports. If your manual gives you some, put them in your config file at the "ports" line. Remember that sometimes you need to have several ports in a row, and the first one might be the only one documented.

2. Try it out. If it doesn't work, or you don't have a manual (or your manual is as bad as my AT&T manual). Then run dosemu with `dos -D+T 2> /tmp/io.debug`. Run your device software, then exit dosemu. Look through `/tmp/io.debug` and find any port numbers it might give you. Try adding those to the port lines and try running dosemu again. Ports below 0x400 with the keyword fast don't get logged(97/2/9)!

3. If you still fail then you may need interrupts.

Find out what interrupt the card uses and verify, that the kernel isn't using the IRQ in question (`cat /proc/interrupts`). Hans Lermen wrote (97/2/17):

```
1. Make sure Linux doesn't use this network card

2. Set 'sillyint { use_sigio 5 }' in /etc/dosemu.conf
```

(some addititions (97/2/11)) and that's about it...

Question: What if my card uses DMA? Answer: Your screwed.

12 Problems and fixes

12.1 Security issues

A full featured dosemu needs to be suid root, e.g to access ports. Dosemu runs as suid "root" only where it is needed, and releases this right thereafter. But with DPMI, the DOS client program can access the whole user space, hence also can modify the dosemu code itself. Use of the `secure on` option in `/etc/dosemu.conf` disables this, but then you can't run some applications like 32-bit video games any more.

(`lermen@elserv.ffm.fgan.de`(97/2/11)). E.g. running a well-known compiler with full access might have smaller security implications than some game, obtained by some obscure source.

12.2 Dosemu dies when booting. I have Win95 installed.

Dosemu depends on having the DOS version on the hdimage and the drive you map to contain `COMMAND.COM` be the same. If not, dosemu will crash sooner or later. With the dual- boot option Win95 offers when pressing the F4,F5 and F8 Keys with the "Starting Win95" text, versions on the Win95 drive may swap. Take special care for `COMMAND.COM`. Let your shell variable in `config.emu` point to the correct static version of `COMMAND.COM`, e.g.:

```
shell=c:\win95\command.com c:\ /P /E:1024
```

(97/02/28)

Learn about `dosdebug` and use it to control a dosemu session(97/2/9)

12.3 Dosemu hangs! How can I kill it?

Learn about `dosdebug` and use it to control a dosemu session(97/2/9)

12.4 Dosemu crashed and now I can't type anything.

Daniel Barlow(`jo95004@sable.ox.ac.uk`) reported (95/4/8) that

If you have no terminal or network access that you can use to log in, you may have to press the reset button. If you can still get a usable shell somehow, run "`kbd_mode -a`" to switch the keyboard out of raw mode, or "`stty sane`" on the console so that you can see what you're typing.

A useful thing to do is to use a script to run dosemu, and run "`kbd_mode -a`" automatically right after dosemu. When dosemu crashes, the script usually will resume running, and execute the "`kbd_mode -a`" command.

12.5 I enabled EMS memory in `dosemu.conf` but it does not help.

Rob Janssen (`rob@pe1chl.ampr.org`) reported (94/7/11)

Don't forget to load the provided `ems.sys` from the `config.sys` file.

12.6 How do I get rid of all those annoying "disk change" messages?

(94/8/11)

Grab and install `klogd`. Try

```
sunsite.unc.edu:/pub/Linux/system/Daemons/sysklogd1.2.tgz
```

12.7 Why won't dosemu run a second time after exiting in console mode?

Aldy Hernandez (`aldy@sauron.cc.andrews.edu`) reported (94/7/8) that

You should disable your video and/or BIOS caching.

12.8 Why will dosemu run in a term but not in the console?

JyiJiin Luo (`jjluo@casbah.acns.nwu.edu`) reported (94/4/19) that

I experienced exactly the same problem before. I figured out all the video shadow in my AMI BIOS must be disabled. Now dosemu runs fine on my system.

12.9 How can I speed up dosemu?

In some cases it is useful to play with the value of the `HogThreshold` variable in your `dosemu.conf` file.

Daniel Barlow(`jo95004@sable.ox.ac.uk`) reported (95/4/8) that

HogThreshold should now be set to approximately half of the BogoMips value that the system reports on boot.

12.10 My CDROM drive has problems reading some files under dosemu.

Vinod G Kulkarni (`vinod@cse.iitb.ernet.in`) reported (94/4/7) that

When a CDROM is mounted from Linux and used from within dosemu (mapped drive), there could be some problems. The CD-ROM driver (ISO 9660) in the kernel tries to find out the type of the file (i.e. binary or text). If it can't find, it tries to guess the type of the file using a heuristic. This heuristic fails under some circumstances when a (almost) text file is to be treated as binary. (I do not know if it is a bug or feature.)

The result of this is that if you copy such a file from CD-ROM (from linux itself, and not necessarily dosemu), the resulting file will be usually bigger than original file. (Blanks get added before `^J,^M`.) So a program running in dosemu gives an error or hangs, which may be mistaken as problem of dosemu.

Rob Janssen (`pe1chl@rabo.nl`) reported (94/8/10) that

The way to solve this is to turn off conversion altogether. Pass the option "`-o conv=binary`" to the mount command mounting the CD-ROM, or use the following in `/etc/fstab`:

```
/dev/cdrom      /cdrom          iso9660 conv=binary,ro
```

No patches to the kernel are necessary.

12.11 How do I see debugging output?

Daniel Barlow(`jo95004@sable.ox.ac.uk`) reported (95/4/8) that

As of dosemu 0.60, debugging output is redirected to a file specified on the command line. Use "`dos -D+a -o /tmp/debug`" to log all debug output to `/tmp/debug`. There should no longer be any need to redirect `stderr`.

12.12 Why are my keystrokes echoed twice?

Nick Holloway (`alfie@dcs.warwick.ac.uk`) reported (94/2/22) that

After running DOS after playing with some `stty` settings, I was getting doubled key presses. I can now reveal what the reason is!

It only happens when DOS is run on the console with `istrip` set. This is (I think) because the raw scancodes are mutilated by the `istrip`, so that key release events look like key press events.

So, the input processing needs to be turned off when using the scan codes on a console (it wouldn't be a good idea to do it for tty lines).

12.13 Dosemu scrambles my screen!

For those graphics cards not fully supported in dosemu, with allowed console graphics a dosemu crash may leave your console in a scrambles and nearly unusable way. To prepare for that situation, Spudgun (`spudgun@earthlight.co.nz`) posted following solution. First save your registers when running on the console:

```
cat /usr/bin/savetextmode
restoretextmode -w /etc/textregs
restorefont -w /etc/fontdata
```

Then, when a crash happened, run following script:

```
restoretextmode -r /etc/textregs
restorefont -r /etc/fontdata
restorepalette
```

`If it doesn't fix it nothing will` I also found having an X server running sometimes put my video cards' registers into a strange state where this script made things worse I think since changing X servers or running `savetextmode` on a vt while X was running helped. (97/04/08)

12.14 MS FoxPro 2.6 won't run

FoxPro 2.6 doesn't run on network drives. Alexey Naidyonov (`growler@growler.tsu.tula.ru`) says of that problem: And I guess your FoxPro files are on `lredir`'ed disk, yeah? The matter is that FoxPro doesn't run on such disk, but when I said disk { partition... } in `/etc/dosemu/conf`, it runs.

13 Contributing to the dosemu project

13.1 Who is responsible for dosemu?

(97/2/9)

Dosemu is built upon the work of Matthias Lautner and Robert Sanders. James B. MacLean (jmaclean@ednet.ns.ca) is responsible for organizing the latest releases of dosemu.

```
                History of dosemu

Version     Date                Person
------------------------------------------------------
0.1         September 3, 1992   Matthias Lautner
0.2         September 13, 1992  Matthias Lautner
0.3         ???                 Matthias Lautner
0.4         November 26, 1992   Matthias Lautner
0.47        January 27, 1993    Robert Sanders
0.47.7      February 5, 1993    Robert Sanders
0.48        February 16, 1993   Robert Sanders
0.48pl1     February 18, 1993   Robert Sanders
0.49        May 20, 1993        Robert Sanders
0.49pl2     November 18, 1993   James MacLean
0.49pl3     November 30, 1993   James MacLean
0.49pl3.3   December 3, 1993    James MacLean
0.50        March 4, 1994       James MacLean
0.50pl1     March 18, 1994      James MacLean
0.52        June 16, 1994       James MacLean
0.60        April 9, 1995       James MacLean
0.64.4      February 9,1997     Hans Lermen
```

13.2 I want to help. Who should I contact?

The dosemu project is a team effort. If you wish to contribute, see the DPR (dosemu Project Registry). A current copy may be found in ../doc/DANG (97/2/9).

Part XIX

"Linux Emacspeak HOWTO" by Jim Van Zandt,

jrv@vanzandt.mv.com

Contents

Abstract

v1.2, 7 October 1997
This document describes how a blind user can use Linux with a speech synthesizer to replace the video display. It describes how to get Linux running on your own PC, and how to set it up for speech output. It suggests how to learn about Unix.

1 Introduction

Emacspeak is an Emacs subsystem that allows the user to get feedback using synthesized speech.

Screen reading programs allow a visually impaired user to get feedback using synthesized speech. Such programs have been commercially available for well over a decade. Most of them run on PC's under DOS, and there are now a few screen-readers for the Windows platform. However, screen-readers for the UNIX environment have been conspicuous in their absence.

This means that most visually impaired computer users face the additional handicap of being DOS impaired—a far more serious problem.

Emacspeak is an emacs subsystem that provides basic speech access. Emacspeak will always have the shortcoming that it will only work under Emacs. This said, there is very little that cannot be done inside Emacs, so it's not a real shortcoming. Within Emacs, you can open a "shell window" where you run commands and examine their output, even output that has scrolled out of the window. Emacs provides special modes for running certain commands. For example, it can parse error messages printed by a compiler and open a separate edit window with the cursor at the point of the error. It can also run a debugger and keep a separate edit window open at the point in the source code corresponding to the program counter.

Emacspeak does have a significant advantage: since it runs inside Emacs, a structure-sensitive, fully customizable editor, Emacspeak often has more context-specific information about what it is speaking than its commercial counterparts. In this sense, Emacspeak is not a "screenreader," it is a subsystem that produces speech output. A traditional screen-reader speaks the content of the screen, leaving it to the user to interpret the visually laid-out information. Emacspeak, on the other hand, treats speech as a first-class output mode; it speaks the information in a manner that is easy to comprehend when listening.

This initial version provides a basic speech subsystem for Emacs; using Emacs' power and flexibility, it has proven straightforward to add modules that customize how things are spoken, e.g. depending on the major/minor mode of a given buffer. Note that the basic speech functionality provided by Emacspeak is sufficient to use most Emacs packages effectively; adding package-specific customizations makes the interaction much smoother. This is because package-specific extensions can take advantage of the current context.

Emacspeak will only work with emacs. However, emacs can be used to run any program that has a command-line interface (ls, cd, rm, adduser, etc.). You can even run those like less or lynx which use escape sequences to control the appearance of the screen. The key to this is eterm mode, which you get with the emacs command M-x term.

Emacs must be running, and it is a large program, but it does not literally have to be in RAM. Linux has virtual memory, so you can designate a swap partition, so that programs (or parts of programs) that are not being used at present can be swapped out. You can comfortably run emacs with 8 MB of ram plus 8 MB of swap space.

This document is limited to the following:

- Linux (not Free BSD)
- The Slackware distribution (not Red Hat, Debian, etc.)
- Speech output only (not Braille—see the Access HOWTO)
- Dectalk (Dectalk Express and MultiVoice), DoubleTalk, and LiteTalk synthesizers (not the Accent, SmarTalk, a sound card, etc.)
- Use of Emacs, with T. V. Raman's Emacspeak package, to drive the synthesizer.

The use of adaptive technology with Linux, and in particular, using adaptive technology to make Linux accessible to those who could not use it otherwise, is covered in the Linux Access HOWTO.

If you would like to help extend this document to cover one or more of the other alternatives, or point me to a discussion somewhere else, please contact me.

Emacspeak was written by T. V. Raman `raman@adobe.com`. Emacspeak has a Web page at (`http://www.cs.cornell.edu/Info/People/raman/emacspeak/emacspeak.html`).

Computer hardware, Unix user commands, Unix system administration, Emacs, and Emacspeak are each substantial systems. Attempting to learn all of them at once is likely to lead to frustration. Instead, I suggest that the new user go through a sequence of stages, learning about only one system at a time.

2 Stage 1. DOS with speech

Most blind computer users have speech synthesizers with a screen reader program like JAWS [6.1]. (References in this format refer to entries in the "Footnotes and References" section below.) Using this setup, install and become familiar with some terminal emulator like Telix [6.2] or Commo [6.3], which are available from the SimTel archive [6.4] among others.

2.1 Getting Linux on CDROM

If you have or can borrow a CDROM drive, I recommend you get one of the many good distributions of Linux on that medium. The instructions below are for the Slackware distribution. I am most familiar with disks from InfoMagic [6.5]. Another source is Walnut Creek [6.6] (where the whole idea of inexpensive CD-ROMS full of programs from Internet archives got its start). Distributions other than Slackware are available from Red Hat [6.7], Craftwork [6.8], and Yggdrasil [6.9]. As a rule, these CD-ROMS use the "ISO 9660" format, which can be read under DOS. (They also use the "Rock Ridge extensions" which add extra files in each directory. Linux uses the extra information to give you long filenames, both upper and lower case characters in filenames, and file permissions.)

2.2 Getting Linux by FTP

Another way to get Linux and its documentation is by FTP over the Internet. The home site for the Slackware distribution is Walnut Creek [6.6]. It is also carried by sunsite and many of it mirror sites. Here is a partial list:

- USA (home site) (`ftp://ftp.cdrom.com/pub/linux/slackware`)
- UK/Europe (`ftp://src.doc.ic.ac.uk/public/Mirrors/ftp.cdrom.com/pub/linux/slackware-3.1`)
- Japan (`ftp://ftp.cs.titech.ac.jp/pub/os/linux/slackware`)
- Taiwan (`ftp://NCTUCCCA.edu.tw/OS/Linux/Slackware`)
- Hong Kong (`ftp://ftp.cs.cuhk.hk/pub/slackware`)
- USA (`ftp://sunsite.unc.edu/pub/Linux/distributions/slackware`)
- USA (`ftp://uiarchive.cso.uiuc.edu/pub/systems/linux/sunsite/distributions/slackware`)

More sites are listed in the INFO-SHEET (`ftp://sunsite.unc.edu/pub/Linux/docs/HOWTO/INFO-SHEET`) or (`ftp://uiarchive.cso.uiuc.edu/pub/systems/linux/sunsite/docs/HOWTO/INFO-SHEET`). Sunsite can also be reached using a Web browser: (`http://sunsite.unc.edu/pub/Linux/welcome.html`).

2.3 Linux Documentation

Read the Linux documentation. I will quote here the file names and locations on the first disk of InfoMagic's December 1996 "Developer's Resource" set of six CD-ROMS, as seen under DOS. Other CDROM sets should have similar information, though perhaps differently arranged. The Slackware distribution is on disk 2 of the set. Matt Welsh's step by step guide to installing Linux is in `\doc\install-\install-.002`. (This is a 245 page book.)

More general information is in the Linux "Frequently Asked Questions" list in `\docs\linux.faq\linux-fa.asc`. Longer descriptions are in HOWTO documents (of which this is one). They are found in `\docs`. Note particularly `\docs\hardware`, which lists which kinds of hardware are supported by Linux, `\docs\meta-faq`, which points to sources of information (that is, a more extensive version of this paragraph), and `\help\index`, which is a list of the HOWTO documents with short descriptions. The Linux installation HOWTO, `\docs\installation`, is another (much shorter, somewhat older) version of Matt Welsh's installation instructions.

One note on reading the documentation. You may run into files with ASCII highlighting, where character-backspace-character stands for "bold," and underscore-backspace-character stands for "italics." One way to handle this is to use the `less` program, which displays these sequences in alternate colors. A DOS screenreader can, for example, search for such highlighted text. A DOS version of `less` can be obtained by FTP from the SimTel archive [6.4]. Within the SimTel collection, look for directory msdos/textutil. For example, try (`ftp://ftp.coast.net/pub/SimTel/msdos/textutil`).

I will suggest four alternatives for learning Emacs commands (see section [3.2]). The first option is to install Emacs under DOS and learn it while using the DOS screen reader. Where to get Emacs for DOS is a "frequently asked question" [6.10].

The source code for Emacs (about 10 MB) can be gotten from (`ftp://prep.ai.mit.edu/pub/gnu/`) (look for emacs-19.34b.tar.gz or similar), or from one of many mirrors of the GNU collection [6.11].

3 Stage 2. Terminal to remote UNIX system

Arrange for what is called a "shell account" on some Unix system. Most Internet Service Providers (ISP's) can provide this service. Use the terminal emulator program and a modem to dial in. Learn the basic Unix commands. If the system has Emacs installed, or you can persuade the system administrator to install it, this is your second chance to learn it. It is probably best to learn it at this point, because administering a Unix system (the next stage) will call for you to edit files. Therefore, I include here my suggestions for learning both Unix and Emacs.

3.1 Learning Unix

When you arrange for a shell account, or set up a new account on your own machine, you will have to decide on a user name and a password. Your user name will also be used in your email address, so try to find something short and memorable. Your password is important, and should be hard to guess. That usually means at least six characters, including at least one non-alphanumeric character.

When a Unix system is ready for you to log in, it normally displays a prompt ending with "`login:`." At this point you should type in your user name. It will then prompt you for your password, and will turn off command echoing while you type it in.

The command to finish a terminal session is `logout`.

To learn about a command, use the `man` command to type its manual page ("man page" for short). For example, to learn more about the `cp` command by typing `man cp`. Of course, this helps only if you know or can guess the command name. However, each man page has a line near the beginning with the command name and a short description of what the command does. You can search a database of these lines using the command `apropos`. Thus, typing `apropos working` will list lines that include the word "working."

Under Unix, commands normally accept options starting with a minus sign rather than the forward slash used under DOS. In a path, directory names are separated by forward slashes rather than backward slashes. Both operating systems have a "standard input," by default the keyboard, and a "standard output," by default the display screen. You can redirect the standard input using "<," and redirect the output using ">." You can use the output from one command as the input of another by separating the two commands with "`|`." This is called the "pipe" symbol.

The program that interprets your command is a "shell." Under DOS, COMMAND.COM is the shell. Most Unix shells are descendents of either the Bourne shell `sh` or the C shell `csh`. The shell most commonly used with Linux is the "Bourne again shell," or `bash`. It has several features which can reduce the need for typing. You can use the cursor up key key to bring previous commands to the command line. The cursor will be at the end of the command. You can use cursor left and right to move the cursor within the command, and edit it with Emacs style commands (Control-D or DEL to delete the character to the right, et cetera). Also, you can insert the last word in the previous command with ESC-. (Escape period). You can learn about these and other commands from the bash manual page, in the section entitled "READLINE."

If a program gets "stuck," here is a sequence of keystrokes to try:

- Control-Q. You may have sent a control-S, which halts all output, without realizing it. The control-Q will restart it.
- Control-D, which signals "end of file" under Unix (similar to Control-Z under MS-DOS), in case the program expects input which you are not prepared to supply.
- Control-C is an interrupt, which may halt the program.
- Control-Z puts the program in the background. At this point you may simply log out, although you will be warned about the background process and will have to repeat the `logout` command. You can instead kill the process, as follows: Run `ps` with no arguments. It will list a header line, then one line for each of your processes. The first item on each line is the process id number, or PID. The command used to start the process (or at least the beginning of it) appears at the end of the line. If the PID were 117, you would kill the process with the command `kill -9 117`.
- If running Linux from the console, Alt-2, or some other Alt-number combination, will switch to a different virtual console. You can log in there just as if you had sat down to a different terminal.
- Control-Alt-Del should reboot the computer nondestructively.
- As a last resort, you can hit "reset" or cycle the power. This will leave the filesystems in an invalid state, since some buffers will not have been written to disk. The kernel will discover this while booting, and will take time to check and repair the filesystems. Actual data loss is unlikely unless you had something else going on at the time.

Guido Gonzato `Guido@ibogfs.cineca.it` has written an excellent guide to Linux for (former) DOS users, the DOS2Linux mini-HOWTO. You can probably find it in the same directory as this document, or else at

```
ftp://sunsite.unc.edu/pub/Linux/docs/HOWTO/mini/
```

You can find general Unix information, including manual pages for several systems at

```
http://www.cis.ohio-state.edu/hypertext/man_pages.html
```

There is a tutorial entitled "Beginning Unix and the C Shell" at

```
http://www.eng.hawaii.edu:80/Courses/C.unix/page-03.html.
```

You can get general help from

```
http://www.nova.edu/Inter-Links/UNIXhelp/TOP_.html}
```

or

```
http://www.eecs.nwu.edu/unix.html
```

You can find a list of books on UNIX at

```
http://www.eskimo.com/~cher/eskimospace/booklist.html
```

3.2 Learning Emacs

When you start Emacs, you will normally list on the command line one or more files which you will be editing. To edit a file named "foobar" with Emacs, you would enter the command `emacs foobar`. If you enter the command `emacs` with no arguments, GNU Emacs will assume you are a new user, and print out an introduction which includes the first five commands you need to learn, approximately as follows:

```
Type C-h for help;   ('C-' means use CTRL key.)
Type C-x u to undo changes.
Type C-h t for a tutorial on using Emacs.
Type C-h i to enter Info, which you can use to read GNU documentation.
To kill the Emacs job, type C-x C-c.
```

Note the way Emacs documentation refers to key combinations. C-h means hold the control key down while typing "h." You will also run into key combinations like M-v, which is pronounced "meta v." The tutorial suggests holding down the key labeled "edit" or "meta" then typing "v." I have never run across a keyboard with those keys, so I always use the escape key instead: typing "Esc" then "v" (two separate keystrokes). After using Emacs for a long time, I discovered that under Linux, the left "Alt" key works like a "meta" key. You may want to use this. On the other hand, some of these key combinations may conflict with your screen reader or communications program under MS-DOS. Using the Escape key is more reliable.

Three of the above commands start with C-h, which may be treated as a backspace by your communications program. In that case, you may access the help command using the long form M-x help. Conversely, you may find that pressing the backspace key starts the help command. This issue is treated in the Emacs FAQ, which is available within Emacs using C-h F or M-x help F. Look for the question "Why does the 'Backspace' key invoke help?." In the meantime, you can end the help session with the command C-g. (This is the keyboard-quit command, which cancels any prefix keys you have typed.)

You may also find that C-s and C-q are unavailable because they are used for flow control (XON and XOFF). You should look at the question "How do I handle C-s and C-q being used for flow control?" in the FAQ. For the particular command C-x C-s (save buffer), you may substitute the command C-x s (save-some-buffers). The former command saves the current buffer, while the latter asks the user about each of the modified buffers.

Note in particular the command "C-h t" to start the tutorial. That is one the first things you will want to try. I will only make a couple of comments on the tutorial. To move the cursor, it gives the four commands C-f, C-b, C-p, and C-n (for forward, back, previous line, and next line). These commands always work. However, with a properly installed Emacs, the regular arrow keys should also work. Try them out and use them if you are more comfortable with them. Similarly, you may be able to use home, end, page down, and page up keys in place of the standard commands C-a, C-e, C-v, and M-v. Finally, all Emacspeak commands begin with C-e. Once you start using Emacspeak, you will have to type it twice to get the end of line function. (The "End" key should be unaffected by Emacspeak.)

4 Stage 3. Terminal to local Linux system

This arrangement again requires a MS-DOS machine with a speech synthesizer and a terminal emulator program. However, instead of dialing up a remote computer, it is used as a terminal to a local computer running Linux. To get to this point, you need to install Linux on a machine. You may be able to prevail on a knowledgeable friend to help you with this. However, it is also possible to install it yourself with speech feedback for almost the whole procedure.

4.1 Installing Linux

First, some background. Even the simplest Unix system requires a program called the kernel and a root file system. The kernel has all the device drivers and resource management functions. One normally thinks of a "file system" as residing on a hard disk or floppy disk, but during an installation it is usually in RAM. Linux is normally installed by writing a kernel image to a floppy disk, called the "boot floppy," configuring it to reserve a section of RAM for a ramdisk, then filling that ramdisk with data from a second floppy disk, called the "root floppy." As soon as both floppies have been read in, the user can log in as "root" and complete the installation. The sighted user logs in on the "system console," that is, the computer's own keyboard and video display. However, remember that Unix has been a multiprocessing operating system from the very beginning. Even this very primitive Unix system, running out of a small ramdisk, also supports logins from a terminal connected to a serial port. This is what a blind user can use.

To connect the two computers, you can use a "null modem," a serial cable that connects ground to ground, and transmit on each end to receive on the other. The cable that comes with the DOS application LapLink will work fine. It is particularly handy, in fact, because it has both a 9 pin and a 25 pin connector on each end. If you want to check a cable or have one made, here are the required connections:

For two 9 pin connectors, connect pin 2 (receive data) to pin 3, pin 3 (transmit data) to pin 2, and pin 5 (signal ground) to pin 5.

For two 25 pin connectors, connect pin 2 (receive data) to pin 3, pin 3 (transmit data) to pin 2, and pin 7 (signal ground) to pin 7.

For a 9 pin connector (first) to a 25 pin connector (second), connect pin 2 (receive data) to pin 2 (transmit data), pin 3 (transmit data) to pin 3 (receive data), and pin 5 (signal ground) to pin 7 (signal ground).

You may have noted that I have included no connections for the "handshaking" signals. During login, the serial port is handled by the program `agetty`. Recent versions of this program accept a -L switch which tells it not to expect modem control signals. The version in Slackware 3.0 does, but the one on the 3.0 (and earlier) installation root disks does not. However, Pat Volkerding has assured me that the root disks in the next release of Slackware will have the updated version of `agetty`. It is also possible to use the earlier root disks [6.12].

Consult the documentation on your CDROM, or downloaded from an FTP site, and choose a boot disk with the proper kernel features for your hardware (IDE or SCSI, CDROM driver, etc.). I have the InfoMagic September 1996 "Developer's Resource" set of six CD-ROMS. Slackware 3.1 is on disk 1 of that set, mostly in the two directories slackwar and slakware. (Note the difference in spelling. You will access them in alphabetical order: first slackwar, then slakware.)

Documentation on the boot floppies is in \bootdsks.144\which.one. A copy of the DOS program for writing boot images to a floppy, RAWRITE.EXE, is in the same directory. Assuming the CD-ROM is the M drive under DOS, one might use these commands to write to a floppy disk in the A drive:

```
C>m:
M>cd \bootdsks.144
M>rawrite scsinet.s a:
```

Similarly, to write the "text" root disk:

```
C>m:
M>cd \rootdsks
M>rawrite text.gz a:
```

If you install from floppies, you should also copy the Emacspeak package onto a floppy with a command like this:

```
C>copy m:\contrib\emacspea.tgz a:
```

For the actual installation, proceed as follows: Use the null modem to connect the computer running DOS and equipped with speech output (which I will call the "DOS machine") to the computer into which you want to install Linux (the "Linux machine").

Boot the DOS machine, and start your terminal emulation program. Set it up for 9600 baud, no parity, eight data bits, 1 stop bit.

On the Linux machine, insert the "boot" disk and boot (power up, Crtl-Alt-Del, or hit the reset switch). It should read the disk for five seconds or so, beep, and stop with the following text:

(Note: in the following, the large blocks of text quoted from the installation disks are preceded by "– begin quote" and followed by "– end quote." To skip to the end of a quote, you may search for two dashes starting in the first column. I have word wrapped some sections to limit the line lengths.)

```
-- begin quote
```

```
Welcome to the Slackware96 Linux (v. 3.1.0) boot kernel disk!

If you have any extra parameters to pass to the kernel, enter them at
the prompt below after one of the valid configuration names (ramdisk,
mount, drive2)

Here are some examples (and more can be found in the BOOTING file):

  ramdisk hd=cyl,hds,secs     (Where ''cyl,'' ''hds,'' and ''secs'' are the
                              number of cylinders, sectors, and heads
                              on the drive.  Most machines won't need
                              this.)

In a pinch, you can boot your system with a command like:
  mount root=/dev/hda1

On machines with low memory, you can use mount root=/dev/fd1 or mount
root=/dev/fd0 to install without a ramdisk.  See LOWMEM.TXT for
details.

If you would rather load the root/install disk from your second
floppy drive: drive2 (or even this: ramdisk root=/dev/fd1)

DON'T SWITCH ANY DISKS YET!  This prompt is just for entering extra
parameters.  If you don't need to enter any parameters, hit ENTER to
continue.

boot:
```

-- end quote

I have almost always been able to just hit "Enter" at this point.

After your entry, the Linux machine should read the floppy for another twenty seconds or so, then boot the kernel. The first thing it prints is "Loading ramdisk...," which is somewhat misleading. In this case, "ramdisk" is actually the name of the kernel configuration.

Each device driver in the kernel displays a line or two. The particular disk I'm using (the "bare.i" boot disk) displays more than one screen's worth. It is possible to type shift-page up to scroll the text back. On my machine, the boot messages are as follows:

-- begin quote

```
Loading ramdisk.....
Uncompressing Linux...done.
Now booting the kernel
Console: color VGA+ 80x25, 1 virtual console (max 63)
Calibrating delay loop.. ok - 35.94 BogoMIPS
Memory: 23028k/24768k available (688k kernel code, 384k reserved,
 668k data)
Swansea University Computer Society NET3.035 for Linux 2.0
NET3: Unix domain sockets 0.12 for Linux NET3.035.
Swansea University Computer Society TCP/IP for NET3.034
IP Protocols: ICMP, UDP, TCP
VFS: Diskquotas version dquot_5.6.0 initialized
Checking 386/387 coupling... Ok, fpu using exception 16 error reporting.
Checking 'hlt' instruction... Ok.
Linux version 2.0.0 (root@darkstar) (gcc version 2.7.2) #1 Mon Jun 10
21:11:56 CDT 1996
Serial driver version 4.13 with no serial options enabled
tty00 at 0x03f8 (irq = 4) is a 16550A
PS/2 auxiliary pointing device detected -- driver installed.
```

```
Ramdisk driver initialized : 16 ramdisks of 49152K size
hda: IBM-DBOA-2720, 689MB w/64KB Cache, LBA, CHS=700/32/63
ide0: at 0x1f0-0x1f7,0x3f6 on irq 14
Floppy drive(s): fd0 is 1.44M
Started kswapd v 1.4.2.2
FDC 0 is a 8272A
Partition check:
  hda: hda1 hda2 hda3
VFS: Insert root floppy disk to be loaded into ramdisk and press ENTER
```

-- end quote

Some messages will of course be different on a machine with different hardware. Now, insert the "text" root disk and press ENTER. After it is read, the following is displayed on the console:

-- begin quote

```
RAMDISK: Compressed image found at block 0
JAVA Binary support v1.01 for Linux 1.3.98 (C)1996 Brian A. Lantz
VFS: Mounted root (minix filesystem).
INIT: version 2.60 booting
none on /proc type proc (rw)
INIT: Entering runlevel: 4


Welcome to the Slackware Linux installation disk ,version 3.1.0-text!
### READ THE INSTRUCTIONS BELOW CAREFULLY! ###

You will need one or more partitions of type ''Linux native''
prepared. It is also recommended that you create a swap partition
(type ''Linux swap'') prior to installation. Most users can use the
Linux ''fdisk'' utility to create and tag the types of all these
partitions. OS/2 Boot Manager users, however, should create their
Linux partitions with OS/2 ''fdisk,'' add the bootable (root) partition
to the Boot Manager menu, and then use the Linux ''fdisk" to tag the
partitions as type ''Linux native.''

If you have 4 megabytes or less of RAM, you MUST ACTIVATE a swap
partition before running setup. After making the partition with fdisk,
use:

mkswap /dev/<partition> <number of blocks> ; swapon /dev/<partition>

Once you have prepared the disk partitions for Linux, type ''setup'' to
begin the installation process.

You may now login as ''root.''

slackware login:
```

-- end quote

The program that prints the login prompt is called agetty. The Slackware 3.1 root disks are set up to allow logins only from the computer's own keyboard. You will have to reconfigure it to also allow logins from a serial port. This requires typing four lines on the Linux machine keyboard, with no voice feedback. If you realize you have made a mistake before hitting the carriage return, you can erase it with the backspace key. You can also discard what you have typed on a line with Control-C. Here is what you type:

```
root
cat >>/etc/inittab
s1:45:respawn:/sbin/agetty 9600 ttyS0
control-D
```

```
init q
```

I will repeat that with explanations of what is going on.

First, type "root" and a single carriage return to log in (no password is needed). Next, you need to append one line to /etc/inittab. Type the following two lines:

```
cat >>/etc/inittab
s1:45:respawn:/sbin/agetty 9600 ttyS0
```

Finish each line with the "enter" key. Then type a control-D, which signals end of file to a Unix program. (Note: In the second line, the next to last character is an upper case "S." Everything else is in lower case.) This adds a line to the configuration file of the program init, to instruct it to use agetty to watch for logins on the first serial port on the Linux machine, called "COM1" under DOS, or "/dev/ttyS0" under Linux. To use the second port instead, change the last item on the above line to "ttyS1."

Then type

```
init q
```

which causes init to reread /etc/inittab. At this point the DOS machine should display the login prompt (the third of the blocks of text quoted above). On the DOS machine, type root, and finish the installation. (The next thing you should do is create and enable a swap partition.)

If you don't get the Slackware installation disk prompt, try the following:

- Type a single carriage return on the DOS machine.
- Recheck the terminal setup (9600 baud, no parity, eight data bits, 1 stop bit).
- Disconnect the null modem from the DOS machine. In its place, connect a modem which supports the Hayes "AT" commands. Type AT and a carriage return. You should get a reply of "OK" from the modem.

Once you get the above prompt on the DOS machine, you may type root and a carriage return to log in, and complete the installation like any other user. Of course, you must remember to include these packages: emacs, tcl, and tclX.

The installation script will offer to prepare a boot floppy. You should do this, since it is the most foolproof way to boot Linux. You will probably also want to install lilo (which is an abbreviation for "Linux loader") or loadlin (which is an abbreviation for "load Linux"). The installation script can install lilo. Loadlin is a DOS program that will let you boot from DOS to Linux. Install it on a DOS partition, and copy a compressed kernel file (usually named zImage) to the same partition. While running DOS, you may boot Linux with a command like loadlin zimage root=/dev/hda3 ro/. (I have assumed here that the kernel image is in the same directory as the loadlin program. You may find it more convenient to store kernel images in subdirectories named for the kernel version.)

After the Slackware setup script finishes the main installation, it will tell you to restart by pressing Ctrl-Alt-Del. Before doing that, you should install emacspeak. It can be found with the other "contributed" software. In the InfoMagic set, it is in slackwar/contrib. Assuming you are installing Linux directly from a CD-ROM, the setup script will mount the CD-ROM under /CDROM, and you may install emacspeak with the following command:

```
# installpkg /CDROM/slackwar/contrib/emacspeak.tgz
```

If you install from floppies, insert the floppy you made earlier and type this:

```
# mount -tmsdos /dev/fd0 /floppy
# cp /floppy/emacspea.tgz /tmp/emacspeak.tgz
# installpkg /tmp/emacspeak.tgz
```

You should not install the package directly off the floppy disk, because the DOS filesystem will not allow the full filename, so the installpkg program will think the package name is "emacspea" and will store its records under that name.

If you have a DoubleTalk or LiteTalk speech synthesizer, you should also install the emacspeak-dt package.

Reboot the Linux machine with the new boot floppy, with the DOS machine still connected. You should get a login prompt on the DOS machine. Celebrate! After getting this system working, you need to learn emacs (third option) and Unix system administration.

4.2 Learning Unix System Administration

Mostly you will learn system administration as the need arises. First adding a user (yourself), then installing programs, and so forth. The exception to this is making backups, which you should learn **before** you need them.

Among the many programs you will need to learn are these:

adduser

Register a new user, including creating a home directory and adding an entry in /etc/passwd.

tar

Create and unpack `.tar` files, which are collections of files (something like `.zip` files). To list the contents of an archive, use `tar -tf foobar.tar`. For a more verbose listing, use `tar -tvf foobar.tar`. To unpack an archive, use `tar -xf foobar.tar`.

chmod

Change permissions of a file or directory.

chown

Change ownership of a file or directory.

find

Search directories recursively. For example, the command `find . -name '*alpha*' -print` means: search starting in the current directory (`.`) for a file whose name contains the string "alpha" (`-name '*alpha*'`), and print its path and name (`-print`). (With GNU find, the `-print` is optional.)

du

Display the amount of space occupied by files or subdirectories. For a file with "holes," this may be much less than the length of the file.

df

Display filesystem capacities, free space, and where they are mounted.

mount

Display filesystems, where they are mounted, and the mount flags.

ifconfig

Configure and check internet protocol (IP) network interfaces, including Ethernet cards, SLIP links, and PLIP links.

route

Configure and check IP network routing, after the interface is configured.

ping

Check IP network connectivity, after the interfaces and routes are configured.

ftp

Transfer files across the Internet.

Here are some programs you may want to install:

agrep

Approximate grep searches for approximate, not exact, string matches (also called "fuzzy string searches").

archie

Search Internet archives for files.

flip

Convert text files between Unix and DOS formats.

glimpse

Fuzzy string searches in large collection of files (uses agrep).

lynx

Text mode web browser.

Here are some Web pages related to Unix system administration:
General information

```
http://www.ensta.fr/internet/unix/sys_admin/
```

or

```
http://www.sai.msu.su/sysadm.html
```

There is a Unix system administration tutorial at

```
http://www.iem.ac.ru/sysadm.html
```

UnixWorld Online Magazine Home Page

http://www.wcmh.com/uworld/

Internet Essentials for UNIX System Administrators Tutorial

http://www.greatcircle.com/tutorials/ieusa.html

Pointers to Unix goodies available on the Internet

http://www.ensta.fr/internet/unix/

Pointers to Unix system administration "goodies" available on the Internet

http://www.ensta.fr/internet/unix/sys_admin/

5 Stage 4. Emacspeak under Linux

The Slackware setup script for Emacspeak should create the needed environment variables and install a script `emacspeak` that starts emacs with emacspeak. This is your fourth option for learning Emacs. This is the first time you will be able to actually use Emacspeak. A short tutorial appears below. Within Emacs, you may type C-h C-e to get a list of the commands. To search for a command, use C-h a. To get an explanation for a key sequence, use C-h k. There is also an info file which is part of the Emacspeak distribution. Within emacs, you may type C-u C-h i, then enough backspaces to delete the default path (that is, until the beep), then `/usr/info/emacspeak.info`. If you have the stand-alone info program installed, you can consult the info file with the command `info Emacspeak`.

5.1 Emacspeak Introduction—Speech Enabled Normal Commands

All of the normal Emacs movement commands will speak the relevant information after moving. Here are some of the cursor movement functions that have been speech enabled. Note that this list only enumerates a few of these speech enabled commands; the purpose of emacspeak is to speech-enable all of emacs and provide you spoken feedback as you work. Thus, this list is here only as a representative example of the kind of speech-enabling extensions Emacspeak provides.

'C-n' or 'M-x next-line' or 'down' Moves the cursor to the next line and speaks it.

'C-p' or 'M-x previous-line' or 'up' Moves the cursor to the previous line and speaks it.

'M-f' or 'M-x forward-word' or Moves the cursor to the next word and speaks it. Places point on the first character of the next work, rather than on the space preceding it (This is my personal preference).

'M-b' or 'M-x backward-word' Moves the cursor to the previous word and speaks it.

'M-C-b' or 'M-x backward-sexp' Moves the cursor to the previous sexp and speaks it. If the sexp spans more than a line, only the first line is spoken.

'M-<' or 'M-x beginning-of-buffer' Speaks line moved to.

'M->' or 'M-x end-of-buffer' Speaks line moved to.

'M-m' or 'M-x back-to-indentation' Speaks entire current line. A useful way of hearing the current line.

5.2 Emacspeak Introduction—New Commands

Emacspeak provides a number of commands for reading portions of the current buffer, getting status information, and modifying Emacspeak's state.

All of the commands are documented in the subsequent sections. They can be classified into types:

Emacspeak commands for listening to chunks of information. The names of these commands all start with the common prefix 'emacspeak-'. All Emacspeak commands are bound to the keymap EMACSPEAK-KEYMAP and are accessed with the key 'Control e'. Thus, the Emacspeak command "emacspeak-speak-line" is bound to 'l' in keymap EMACSPEAK-KEYMAP and can be accessed with the keystroke 'Control-e l'.

Here are some of the commands for reading text:

'C-e c' or 'M-x emacspeak-speak-char' Speak current character, using the phonetic alphabet.

'C-e w' or 'M-x emacspeak-speak-word' Speak current word.

'C-e l' or 'M-x emacspeak-speak-line' Speak current line. With prefix 'C-u', speaks the rest of the line from point. With negative prefix 'C-u -', speaks from start of line to point. Voicifies if voice-lock-mode is on. Indicates indentation with a tone if audio indentation is in use. Indicates position of point with an aural highlight if option emacspeak-show-point is turned on –see command 'M-x emacspeak-show-point'.

'C-e .' or 'M-x emacspeak-speak-sentence' Speak the current sentence.

'C-e C-c' or 'M-x emacspeak-speak-current-window' Speak everything in the current window.

'C-e =' or 'M-x emacspeak-speak-current-column' State the column where point is.

The second category of commands provided by Emacspeak manipulate the state of the speech device. The names of these commands start with the common prefix 'dtk-'. You can access these commands via the prefix 'Control-e d'. Thus, the command “dtk-set-rate” is bound to ‘r’ in keymap EMACSPEAK-DTK-SUBMAP and can be executed by pressing ‘Control e d r’.

‘C-e s’ or ‘M-x dtk-stop’ Stop speech now. In addition, any command that causes speech output will discard anything in the speech buffer.

‘C-e d I’ or ‘M-x dtk-toggle-stop-immediately-while-typing’ Toggle state of variable dtk-stop-immediately-while-typing. As the name implies, if true then speech flushes immediately as you type.

‘C-e d i’ or ‘M-x emacspeak-toggle-audio-indentation’ Toggle state of Emacspeak audio indentation. Specifying the method of indentation as ‘tone’ results in the DECtalk producing a tone whose length is a function of the line’s indentation. Specifying ‘speak’ results in the number of initial spaces being spoken.

‘C-e d k’ or ‘M-x emacspeak-toggle-character-echo’ Toggle state of Emacspeak character echo (that is, whether typed characters are echoed).

‘C-e d w’ or ‘M-x emacspeak-toggle-word-echo’ Toggle state of Emacspeak word echo (initially on).

‘C-e d l’ or ‘M-x emacspeak-toggle-line-echo’ Toggle state of Emacspeak line echo (that is, whether typed text is echoed after typing enter).

‘C-e d p’ or ‘M-x dtk-set-punctuations’ Set punctuation state. Possible values are ‘some’, ‘all’, or ‘none’.

‘C-e d q’ or ‘M-x dtk-toggle-quiet’ Toggle state of the speech device between being quiet and talkative. Useful if you want to continue using an emacs session that has emacspeak loaded but wish to make the speech shut up.

‘C-e d R’ or ‘M-x dtk-reset-state’ Restore sanity to the Dectalk. Typically used after the Dectalk has been power cycled.

‘C-e d Space’ or ‘M-x dtk-toggle-splitting-on-white-space’ Toggle state of emacspeak that decides if we split text purely by clause boundaries, or also include whitespace.

‘C-e d r’ or ‘M-x dtk-set-rate’ Set speaking rate for the dectalk.

‘C-e d s’ or ‘M-x dtk-toggle-split-caps’ Toggle split caps mode. In split caps mode, a transition from lower case to upper case is treated like the beginning of a new word. This is useful when reading Hungarian notation in program source code.

‘C-e d v’ or ‘M-x voice-lock-mode’ Toggle Voice Lock mode (initially off). When Voice Lock mode is enabled, text is voiceified as you type it, as follows:

- Comments are spoken in `voice-lock-comment-personality`; (That is a variable whose value should be a personality name.)
- Strings are spoken in `voice-lock-string-personality`.
- Documentation strings are spoken in `voice-lock-doc-string-personality`.
- Function and variable names in their defining forms are spoken in `voice-lock-function-name-personality`.
- Certain other expressions are spoken in other personalities according to the value of the variable `voice-lock-keywords`.

‘C-e d V’ or ‘M-x emacspeak-dtk-speak-version’ Use this to find out which version of the Dectalk firmware you have.

5.3 Emacspeak Introduction—Using the Help System

When you press C-h to get the help index, the screen will appear, but Emacspeak will not speak the window. The only thing spoken is “Type one of the options listed or Space to scroll:.”

Here is the menu that Emacspeak is not speaking:

– begin quote

You have typed C-h, the help character. Type a Help option: (Use Space or Del to scroll through this text. Type “q” to exit the Help command.)

a command-apropos. Give a substring, and see a list of commands (functions interactively callable) that contain that substring. See also the apropos command. b describe-bindings. Display table of all key bindings. c describe-key-briefly. Type a command key sequence; it prints the function name that sequence runs. f describe-function. Type a function name and get documentation of it. C-f Info-goto-emacs-command-node. Type a function name; it takes you to the Info node for that command. F view-emacs-FAQ. Shows emacs frequently asked questions file. i info. The info documentation reader. k describe-key. Type a command key sequence; it displays the full documentation. C-k Info-goto-emacs-key-command-node. Type a command key sequence; it takes you to the Info node for the command bound to that key. l view-lossage. Shows last 100 characters you typed. m describe-mode. Print documentation of current major mode, which describes the commands peculiar to it. n view-emacs-news. Shows emacs news file. p finder-by-keyword. Find packages matching a given topic keyword. s describe-syntax. Display contents of syntax table, plus explanations t help-with-tutorial. Select the Emacs learn-by-doing tutorial. v describe-variable. Type name of a variable; it displays the variable’s documentation and value. w where-is. Type command name; it prints which keystrokes invoke that command. C-c print Emacs copying permission (General Public License). C-d print Emacs ordering information. C-n print news of recent Emacs changes. C-p print information about the GNU project. C-w print information on absence of warranty for GNU Emacs.

– end quote

Suppose you type "a," for command-apropos.

The next spoken prompt is "Apropos command (regexp):"

Now you type some word you think is part of an emacs command, like "visit."

The help system will display the first section of the help, but will leave the cursor in the other window. The spoken text is "Type C-x 1 to remove help window. M-C-v to scroll the help." At this point, I think it's more helpful to move point to the other window with C-x o, then you can use regular navigation commands to speak the help text. You can delete the help window with C-x 0, which will also put point back where it was.

The complete menu displayed by help-for-help is also visible if you do a describe function on help-for-help. In a future version of Emacspeak, Raman plans to add a message to that effect when the user presses C-h ?

6 Footnotes and References

6.1 JAWS

Job Access With Speech (JAWS) is a screen reader which runs under Microsoft MSDOS. It is a product of Henter-Joyce, Inc., 2100 62nd Avenue North, St. Petersburg, FL 33702, telephone: 800-336-5658. A demo of JAWS for DOS is available at (`ftp://ftp.hj.com/pub/jh/dosdemos/JAWS231D.EXE`).

6.2 TELIX

TELIX is a shareware terminal emulator for MSDOS. It can be obtained by FTP from the SimTel archive [6.4]. Within the SimTel collection, look for directory msdos/telix. For example, try (`ftp://ftp.coast.net/pub/SimTel/msdos/telix`). The latest version of the program itself is in the four files tlx322-1.zip, tlx322-2.zip, tlx322-3.zip, and tlx322-4.zip.

6.3 COMMO

COMMO is another shareware terminal emulator for DOS. In the SimTel archive [6.4], it is in directory msdos/commprog, file `commo66.zip`. For example, try (`ftp://ftp.coast.net/pub/SimTel/msdos/commprog/commo66.zip`).

6.4 SimTel

The SimTel archive is maintained by Keith Petersen `w8sdz@Simtel.Net`. CD-ROM copies of Simtel.Net collections are available from Walnut Creek CDROM [6.6]. The primary ftp sites are (`ftp://ftp.simtel.net/pub/simtelnet`), and (`oak.oakland.edu://pub/simtelnet`).

6.5 InfoMagic

InfoMagic is at 11950 N. Highway 89, Flagstaff AZ 86004, telephone 800-800-6613 or 520-526-9565, fax 520-526-9573, email: info@infomagic.com, web: (`http://www.infomagic.com`).

6.6 Walnut Creek

Walnut Creek CDROM has many useful CDROMs. They are at 4041 Pike Lane, Ste D-Simtel, Concord, CA 94520, USA. Telephone (800) 786-9907 or (510) 674-0783, or FAX (510) 674-0821. email: orders@cdrom.com. Web: (`http://www.cdrom.com/`)

6.7 Red Hat

Red Hat Software: telephone 800-454-5502 or 203-454-5500, fax: 203-454-2582, email: sales@redhat.com. Web: (`http://www.redhat.com`).

6.8 Craftwork

CraftWork Solutions, 4320 Stevens Creek Blvd, Suite 170, San Jose CA 95129, telephone 800-985-1878, email: info@craftwork.com, web: (`http://www.craftwork.com`).

6.9 Yggdrasil

Yggdrasil Computing, 4880 Stevens Creek Blvd., Suite 205, San Jose CA 95129-1024, telephone 800-261-6630 or 408-261-6630, fax: 408-261-6631, email: info@yggdrasil.com, web: (`http://www.yggdrasil.com`).

6.10 Emacs for DOS

From the Emacs FAQ of November 11, 1996:

`--begin quote`

93: Where can I get Emacs for my PC running MS-DOS?

A pre-built binary distribution of Emacs 19.34 should be available by the beginning of November 1996 from the Simtel archives, the main site of which is at

`(ftp://ftp.simtel.net/pub/simtelnet/gnu/djgpp/v2gnu/)`

If you prefer to compile Emacs for yourself, you will need a 386 (or better) processor, and are running MS-DOS 3.0 or later. According to Eli Zaretskii `eliz@is.elta.co.il` and Darrel Hankerson `hankedr@dms.auburn.edu`, you will need the following:

Compiler: djgpp version 1.12 maint 1 or later. Djgpp 2.0 or later is recommended, since 1.x is being phased out. Djgpp 2 supports long filenames under Windows 95.

You can get the latest release of djgpp by retrieving all of the files in

`(ftp://ftp.simtel.net/pub/simtelnet/gnu/djgpp)`

Gunzip and tar:

The easiest way is to use "djtar" which comes with djgpp v2.x, because it can open gzip'ed tarfiles (i.e., those ending with ".tar.gz") in one step. Djtar comes in "djdev201.zip," from the URL mentioned above.

Utilities: make, mv, sed, rm.

All of these utilities are available at

`(ftp://ftp.simtel.net/pub/simtelnet/gnu/djgpp/v2gnu)`

16-bit utilities can be found in GNUish:

`(ftp://ftp.simtel.net/pub/simtelnet/gnu/gnuish)`

The file INSTALL in the top-level directory of the Emacs source contains some additional information regarding Emacs under MS-DOS. In addition, the file etc/MSDOS contains some information on the differences between the Unix and MS-DOS versions of Emacs.

For the most comprehensive information on running GNU Emacs on a PC, see the file prepared by Michael Ernst `mernst@theory.lcs.mit.edu` at

`(ftp://theory.lcs.mit.edu/pub/emacs/pc-emacs.gz)`

For a list of other MS-DOS implementations of Emacs (and Emacs look-alikes), consult the list of "Emacs implementations and literature," available at

`(ftp://rtfm.mit.edu/pub/usenet/comp.emacs/)`

Note that while many of these programs look similar to Emacs, they often lack certain features, such as the Emacs Lisp extension language.

`--end quote`

6.11 GNU Mirror Sites

The GNU collection at `(ftp://prep.ai.mit.edu/pub/gnu)` is mirrored at many sites.

6.12 Emacspeak with Earlier Slackware Releases

If you want to install Slackware 3.0 or earlier, you will need to prepare a full null modem cable, including modem control signals.

For two DB25 (25 pin) connectors, the required connections are:

- 1 (Frame Ground) - 1 (Frame Ground)
- 2 (Receive Data) - 3 (Transmit Data)
- 3 (Transmit Data) - 2 (Receive Data)
- 4 (Request To Send) - 5 (Clear To Send)
- 5 (Clear To Send) - 4 (Request To Send)
- 6 (Data Set Ready) - 20 (Data Terminal Ready)
- 7 (Signal Ground) - 7 (Signal Ground)
- 8 (Carrier Detect) - 20 (Data Terminal Ready)
- 20 (Data Terminal Ready) - 6 (Data Set Ready)
- 20 (Data Terminal Ready) - 8 (Carrier Detect)

For two DB9 connectors, the connections are:

- 1 (Carrier Detect) - 4 (Data Terminal Ready)
- 2 (Receive Data) - 3 (Transmit Data)
- 3 (Transmit Data) - 2 (Receive Data)
- 4 (Data Terminal Ready) - 6 (Data Set Ready)
- 4 (Data Terminal Ready) - 1 (Carrier Detect)
- 5 (Signal Ground) - 5 (Signal Ground)
- 6 (Data Set Ready) - 4 (Data Terminal Ready)
- 7 (Request To Send) - 8 (Clear To Send)
- 8 (Clear To Send) - 7 (Request To Send)
- 9 (Ring Indicator) not connected

For a DB9 (listed first) to a DB25 (second), the connections are:

- 1 (Carrier Detect) - 20 (Data Terminal Ready)
- 2 (Receive Data) - 2 (Transmit Data)
- 3 (Transmit Data) - 3 (Receive Data)
- 4 (Data Terminal Ready) - 6 (Data Set Ready)
- 4 (Data Terminal Ready) - 8 (Carrier Detect)
- 5 (Signal Ground) - 7 (Signal Ground)
- 6 (Data Set Ready) - 20(Data Terminal Ready)
- 7 (Request To Send) - 5 (Clear To Send)
- 8 (Clear To Send) - 4 (Request To Send)
- 9 (Ring Indicator) not connected

7 Frequently Asked Questions (FAQ)

7.1 Why does it say "space" after each character?

Your DECtalk Express has old firmware. Use the Emacspeak command 'C-e d V' to find out your version. You should be running a version no older than 4.2bw from March 1995. If you have an earlier version, you can find an updated version at `(http://www.ultranet.com/ rongemma/tips_upd.htm)`, a WWW site maintained by Ron Jemma of the Dectalk Group at DEC. Alternatively, you can send email to Anne Nelson at DEC`nelson@dectlk.enet.dec.com`. The most recent version at this writing is 4.3 release AA X01 May 20 1996.

7.2 On occasion when reading the DECtalk will produce high pitch tones that last for several words or more, if this happens in a buffer it will often repeat within the same buffer.

The problem is due to remaining bugs in the DECtalk firmware. When emacspeak produces tones, especially when split caps is on, the dtk sometime goes into squealing mode.

If you notice this happening in particular text documents, just turn off split caps mode locally with 'C-e d s'.

8 Legalese

All trademarks used in this document are acknowledged as being owned by their respective owners. (Spot the teeth-gritting irony there...)

The right of James R. Van Zandt to be identified as the author of this work is hereby asserted in accordance with sections 77 and 78 of the Copyright Designs and Patents Act 1988.

copies. Commercial redistribution is allowed and encouraged; however, the author would like to be notified of any such distributions.

All translations, derivative works, or aggregate works incorporating any Linux HOWTO documents must be covered under this copyright notice. That is, you may not produce a derivative work from a HOWTO and impose additional restrictions on its distribution. Exceptions to these rules may be granted under certain conditions; please contact the Linux HOWTO coordinator at the address given below.

In short, we wish to promote dissemination of this information through as many channels as possible. However, we do wish to retain copyright on the HOWTO documents, and would like to be notified of any plans to redistribute the HOWTOs.

If you have questions, please contact Greg Hankins, the Linux HOWTO coordinator, at `gregh@sunsite.unc.edu` via email.

Part XX

"Linux Ethernet-HOWTO" by Paul Gortmaker, Editor

Paul.Gortmaker@anu.edu.au

Contents

Abstract

v2.64, 15 November 1997
This is the Ethernet-HOWTO, which is a compilation of information about which Ethernet devices can be used for Linux, and how to set them up. It hopefully answers all the frequently asked questions about using Ethernet cards with Linux. Note that this HOWTO is focused on the hardware and low-level driver aspect of the Ethernet cards, and does not cover the software end of things like `ifconfig` and `route`. See the Network HOWTO for that stuff.

1 Introduction

The Ethernet-HOWTO covers what cards you should and shouldn't buy; how to set them up, how to run more than one, and other common problems and questions. It contains detailed information on the current level of support for all of the most common Ethernet cards available.

It does *not* cover the software end of things, as that is covered in the NET-2 HOWTO. Also note that general non-Linux specific questions about Ethernet are not (or at least they should not be) answered here. For those types of questions, see the excellent amount of information in the *comp.dcom.lans.ethernet* FAQ. You can FTP it from `rtfm.mit.edu` just like all the other newsgroup FAQs.

This present revision covers distribution kernels up to and including (pre-)2.0.31. Some information pertaining to development kernels up to version 2.1.6x is also included.

The Ethernet-HOWTO is edited and maintained by:

Paul Gortmaker, `Paul.Gortmaker@anu.edu.au`

The primary source of information for the initial ASCII version of the Ethernet-HOWTO was:

Donald J. Becker, `becker@cesdis.gsfc.nasa.gov`

who we should thank for writing the vast majority of Ethernet card drivers that are presently available for Linux. He also is the original author of the NFS server. Thanks Donald!

Net-surfers may wish to check out the following Donald Becker's URL:

`http://cesdis.gsfc.nasa.gov/pub/people/becker/whoiam.html`

Please see the Disclaimer and Copying information at the end of this document for information about redistribution of this document and the usual 'we are not responsible for what you do...' legal type mumblings.

1.1 New Versions of this Document

New versions of this document can be retrieved via anonymous FTP from the Sunsite HOWTO Archive, ftp://sunsite.unc.edu/pub/Linux/docs/HOWTO/ and various Linux FTP mirror sites. Updates will be made as new information and/or drivers becomes available. If this copy that you are reading is more than six months old, it is either out of date, or it means that I have been lazy and haven't updated it.

If you have sent me an update and it is not included in the next release, it probably means I've lost it amongst the ton of junk mail I get. Please re-send it along with an abusive message, and I will try and make sure it gets included in the next release.

This document was produced by using the SGML system that was specifically set up for the Linux HOWTO project, and there are various output formats available, including, PostScript, dvi, ASCII, html, and soon TeXinfo.

I would recommend viewing it in the html (via a WWW browser) or the PostScript/dvi format. Both of these contain cross-references that are lost in the ASCII translation.

If you want to get the official copy from sunsite, here is URL.

`http://sunsite.unc.edu/mdw/HOWTO/Ethernet-HOWTO.html`

1.2 Using the Ethernet-HOWTO

As this guide is getting bigger and bigger, you probably don't want to spend the rest of your afternoon reading the whole thing. And the good news is that you don't *have* to read it all.

Chances are you are reading this document because you can't get things to work and you don't know what to do or check. The next section (1.3) is aimed at newcomers to linux and will point you in the right direction.

Typically the same problems and questions are asked *over and over* again by different people. Chances are your specific problem or question is one of these frequently asked questions, and is answered in the FAQ portion of this document . (3). Everybody should have a look through this section before posting for help.

If you haven't got an Ethernet card, then you will want to start with deciding on a card. (2)

If you have already got an Ethernet card, but are not sure if you can use it with Linux, then you will want to read the section which contains specific information on each manufacturer, and their cards. (5)

If you are interested in some of the technical aspects of the Linux device drivers, then you can have a browse of the section with this type of information. (8)

1.3 HELP—It doesn't work!

Okay, don't panic. This will lead you through the process of getting things working, even if you have no prior background in Linux or Ethernet hardware.

The first thing you need to do is figure out what model your card is so you can determine if Linux has a driver for that particular card. Different cards typically have different ways of being controlled by the host computer, and the Linux driver (if there is one) contains this control information in a format that allows Linux to use the card.

If you don't have any manuals or anything of the sort that tell you anything about the card model, then you can either see the section on helping with mystery cards (5.39), or just try a "kitchen sink" kernel with nearly every driver built in and hope one of the drivers recognizes your card.

Now that you know what type of card you have, read through the details of your particular card in the card-specific section (5) which lists in alphabetical order, card manufacturers, individual model numbers and whether it has a Linux driver or not. If it lists it as "Not Supported," you can pretty much give up here. If you can't find your card in that list, then check to see if your card manual lists it as being 'compatible' with another known card type. For example there are hundreds, if not thousands of different cards made to be compatible with the original Novell NE2000 design.

Assuming you have found out that your card does have a Linux driver, you now need to go back to the CD-ROM or whatever you installed from, and find the list of pre-built kernels that comes with it. The kernel is the core operating system that is first loaded at boot, and contains drivers for various pieces of hardware, among other things. Just because Linux has a driver for your card does *not* mean that it is built into every kernel. Depending on who made the CD-ROM, there may be only a few pre-built kernels, and a whole bunch of drivers as smaller separate modules, or there may be a whole lot of kernels, covering a vast combination of built-in driver combinations. Hopefully there will also be a text file with them that lists what drivers are included in which kernels. Try and find a kernel that is listed as having the driver you need as built into it, or try and find a module with the name of the driver you need.

If you found a pre-built kernel that has your driver in it, you will want to boot that kernel instead of the one you are presently using. Most Linux systems use LILO to boot, and will have installed the LILO documentation on your system. Follow the instructions in that for booting another kernel, as they are beyond the scope of this document.

If you instead found a small module that contains the driver, you will need to attach this module to the kernel after it has booted up. See the information that came with your distribution on installing and using modules, along with the module section in this document. (10.2)

If you didn't find either a pre-built kernel with your driver, or a module form of the driver, chances are you have a typically uncommon card, and you will have to build your own kernel with that driver included. Once you have Linux installed, building a custom kernel is not difficult at all. You essentially answer yes or no to what you want the kernel to contain, and then tell it to build it. There is a Kernel HOWTO that will help you along.

At this point, you should have somehow managed to be booting a kernel with your driver built in, or be loading it as a module. About half of the problems people have are related to not having driver loaded one way or another, so you may find things work now.

If it still doesn't work, then you need to verify that the kernel is indeed detecting the card. To do this, you need to type `dmesg | more` when logged in after the system has booted and all modules have been loaded. This will allow you to review the boot messages that the kernel scrolled up the screen during the boot process. If the card has been detected, you should see somewhere in that list a message from your card's driver that starts with `eth0`, mentions the driver name and the hardware parameters (interrupt setting, input/output port address, etc) that the card is set for. If you don't see a message like this, then the driver didn't detect your card, and that is why things aren't working. See the FAQ (3) for what to do if your card is not detected. If you have a NE2000 compatible, there is also some NE2000 specific tips on getting a card detected in the FAQ section as well.

If the card is detected, but the detection message reports some sort of error, like a resource conflict, then the driver probably won't have initialized properly and the card still won't be usable. Most common error messages of this sort are also listed in the FAQ section, along with a solution.

If the detection message seems okay, then double-check the card resources reported by the driver against those that the card is physically set for (either by little black jumpers on the card, or by a software utility supplied by the card manufacturer.) These must match exactly. For example, if you have the card jumpered or configured to IRQ 15 and the driver reports IRQ 10 in the boot messages, things will not work. The FAQ section discusses the most common cases of drivers incorrectly detecting the configuration information of various cards.

At this point, you have managed to get you card detected with all of the correct parameters, and hopefully everything is working. If not, then you either have a software configuration error, or a hardware configuration error. A software configuration error is not setting up the right network addresses for the `ifconfig` and `route` commands, and details of how to do that are fully described in the Network HOWTO and the *Network Administrator's Guide,* which both probably came on the CD-ROM you installed from.

A hardware configuration error is when some sort of resource conflict or mis-configuration (that the driver didn't detect at boot) that stops the card from working properly. This typically can be observed in one of three different ways. (1) You get an error message when `ifconfig` tries to open the device for use, such as "SIOCSFFLAGS: Try again". (2) The driver reports `eth0` error messages (viewed by `dmesg | more`) or strange inconsistencies for each time it tries to send or receive data. (3) Typing `cat /proc/net/dev` shows non-zero numbers in one of the errs, drop, fifo, frame or carrier columns for `eth0`. Most of the typical hardware configuration errors are also discussed in the FAQ section.

Well, if you have got to this point and things still aren't working, read the FAQ section of this document, read the vendor specific section detailing your particular card, *and if it still doesn't work* then you may have to resort to posting to an appropriate newsgroup for help. If you do post, please detail all relevant information in that post, such as the card brand, the kernel version, the driver boot messages, the output from `cat /proc/net/dev`, a clear description of the problem, and of course what you have already tried to do in an effort to get things to work.

You would be surprised at how many people post useless things like "Can someone help me? My Ethernet doesn't work." and nothing else. Readers of the newsgroups tend to ignore such silly posts, whereas a detailed and informational problem description may allow a Linux guru to spot your problem right away.

2 What card should I buy for Linux?

The answer to this question depends heavily on exactly what you intend on doing with your Net connection, and how much traffic it will see.

If you only expect a single user to be doing the occasional FTP session or WWW connection, then an old 8-bit card will probably keep you happy.

If you intend to set up a server, and you require the CPU overhead of Rx'ing and Tx'ing ether packets to be kept at a minimum, you probably want to look at one of the newer PCI cards with the DEC 21040 chip, or the AMD PCnet-PCI chip.

If you fall somewhere in the middle of the above, then any one of the 16-bit ISA cards with stable drivers will do the job for you.

2.1 So What Drivers are Stable?

Of the 16-bit ISA cards, the following drivers are very mature, and you shouldn't have any problems if you buy a card that uses these drivers.

SMC-Ultra/EtherEZ, WD80x3, 3c509, 3c503/16, LANCE, NE2000.

This is not to say that all the other drivers are unstable. It just happens that the above are the oldest and most used of all the Linux drivers, making them the safest choice.

Note that some el-cheapo motherboards can have trouble with the bus mastering that the LANCE cards do, and some el-cheapo NE2000 clones can have trouble getting detected at boot.

As for PCI cards, the PCnet-PCI cards that use the LANCE driver are a safe choice (except for the Boca cards as they have hardware flaws). The Allied Telsyn AT2450 is a PCnet-PCI implementation that is known to work well.

The DEC 21040 "Tulip" driver and the 3c59x "Vortex" driver are relatively new drivers, but have proven themselves to be quite stable already.

2.2 8-bit vs 16-bit Cards

You probably can't buy a new 8-bit ISA Ethercard anymore, but you will find lots of them turning up at computer swap meets and the like for the next few years, at very low prices. This will make them popular for "home Ethernet" systems.

Some 8-bit cards that will provide adequate performance for light to average use are the WD8003, the 3c503 and the NE1000. The 3c501 provides poor performance, and these poor 12-year-old relics of the XT days should be avoided.

The 8-bit data path doesn't hurt performance that much, as you can still expect to get about 500 to 800kB/s FTP download speed to an 8-bit WD8003 card (on a fast ISA bus) from a fast host. And if most of your net-traffic is going to remote sites, then the bottleneck in the path will be elsewhere, and the only speed difference you will notice is during net activity on your local subnet.

2.3 32-Bit / VLB / PCI Ethernet Cards

There aren't many 32-bit Ethercard device drivers because there aren't that many 32-bit Ethercards. There aren't many 32-bit Ethercards out there because a 10Mbs network doesn't justify spending a large price increment for the 32-bit interface. Now that 100Mbs networks are becoming more common, this is changing though.

See Section 2.6 as to why having a 10Mbps Ethercard on an 8MHz ISA bus is really not a bottleneck. Even though having the Ethercard on a fast bus won't necessarily mean faster transfers, it will usually mean reduced CPU overhead, which is good for multi-user systems.

AMD has the 32-bit PCnet-VLB and PCnet-PCI chips. See 5.4.3 for info on the 32-bit versions of the LANCE / PCnet-ISA chip.

The DEC 21040 PCI chip is another option (see 5.17.4) for power users. Many manufacturers produce cards that use this chip, and the prices of such no-name cards are usually quite cheap.

3Com's "Vortex" and "Boomerang" PCI cards are also another option, and the price is quite cheap if you can get one under their evaluation deal while it lasts. (see 5.1.13)

Various clone manufacturers have started making PCI NE2000 clones based on the RealTek 8029 chip. These cards are also supported by the linux NE2000 driver for v2.0 kernels. However you only benefit from the faster bus interface, as the card is still using the age-old NE2000 driver interface.

2.4 Available 100Mbs Cards and Drivers

The present list of supported 100Mbs hardware is as follows: cards with the DEC 21140 chip; the 3c595 Vortex card; and the HP 100VG ANY-LAN. The drivers for the first two are quite stable, but feedback on the HP driver has been low so far as it has only been around since early 1.3.x kernels.

The EtherExpressPro10/100B is finally supported. However you will have to obtain the driver separately from Donald's FTP or WWW site (see below) for v2.0 kernels.

The 21140 100Base-? chip is supported with the same driver as its 10Mbs counterpart, the 21040. SMC's 100Mbs EtherPower PCI card uses this chip. As with the 21040, you have a choice of two drivers to pick from.

Also have a look at the information on Donald's WWW site, at the following URL:
100Mbs Ethernet (`http://cesdis.gsfc.nasa.gov/linux/misc/100mbs.html`)

Donald had done a fair bit of work with the SMC EtherPower-10/100 cards, and reported getting about 4.6MB/s application to application with TCP on P5-100 Triton machines.

(See 5.1.13 and 5.17.4 for more details.)

For 100VG information, see the following section, and this URL on Donald's Site:
Donald's 100VG Page (`http://cesdis.gsfc.nasa.gov/linux/drivers/100vg.html`)

You may also be interested in looking at:
Dan Kegel's Fast Ethernet Page (`http://alumni.caltech.edu/~dank/fe/`)

2.5 100VG versus 100BaseT

The following blurb from yet another one of Donald's informative comp.os.linux postings summarizes the situation quite well:

"For those not in the know, there are two competing 100Mbs ethernet standards, 100VG (aka 100baseVG and 100VG-AnyLAN) and 100baseT (with 100baseTx, 100baseT4 and 100baseFx cable types).

100VG was on the market first, and I feel that it is better engineered than 100baseTx. I was rooting for it to win, but it clearly isn't going to. HP et al. made several bad choices:

1) Delaying the standard so that they could accommodate IBM and support token ring frames. It "seemed like a good idea at the time," since it would enable token ring shops to upgrade without the managers having to admit they made a very expensive mistake committing to the wrong technology. But there was nothing to be gained, as the two frame types couldn't coexist on a network, token ring is a morass of complexity, and IBM went with 100baseT anyway.

2) Producing only ISA and EISA cards. (A PCI model was only recently announced.) The ISA bus is too slow for 100mbs, and relatively few EISA machines exist. At the time VLB was common, fast, and cheap with PCI a viable choice. But "old-timer" wisdom held that servers would stay with the more expensive EISA bus.

3) Not sending me a data book. Yes, this action was the real reason for the 100VGs downfall. I called all over for programming info, and all I could get was a few page color glossy brochure from AT&T describing how wonderful the Regatta chipset was."

2.6 Programmed I/O vs. Shared Memory vs. DMA

Ethernet is 10Mbs. (Don't be pedantic, 3Mbs and 100Mbs don't count.) If you can already send and receive back-to-back packets, you just can't put more bits over the wire. Every modern Ethercard can receive back-to-back packets. The Linux DP8390 drivers (WD80X3, SMC-Ultra, 3c503, NE2000, etc) come pretty close to sending back-to-back packets (depending on the current interrupt latency) and the 3c509 and AT1500 hardware have no problem at all automatically sending back-to-back packets.

The ISA bus can do 5.3MB/sec (42Mb/sec), which sounds like more than enough. You can use that bandwidth in several ways, listed below.

2.6.1 Programmed I/O (e.g. NE2000, 3c509)

Pro: Doesn't use any constrained system resources, just a few I/O registers, and has no 16M limit.

Con: Usually the slowest transfer rate, the CPU is waiting the whole time, and interleaved packet access is usually difficult to impossible.

2.6.2 Shared memory (e.g. WD80x3, SMC-Ultra, 3c503)

Pro: Simple, faster than programmed I/O, and allows random access to packets. The Linux drivers compute the checksum of incoming IP packets as they are copied off the card, resulting in a further reduction of CPU usage vs. an equivalent PIO card.

Con: Uses up memory space (a big one for DOS users, essentially a non-issue under Linux), and it still ties up the CPU.

2.6.3 Slave (normal) Direct Memory Access (e.g. none for Linux.)

Pro: Frees up the CPU during the actual data transfer.

Con: Checking boundary conditions, allocating contiguous buffers, and programming the DMA registers makes it the slowest of all techniques. It also uses up a scarce DMA channel, and requires aligned low memory buffers.

2.6.4 Bus Master Direct Memory Access (e.g. LANCE, DEC 21040)

Pro: Frees up the CPU during the data transfer, can string together buffers, can require little or no CPU time lost on the ISA bus.

Con: Requires low-memory buffers and a DMA channel. Any bus master will have problems with other bus masters that are bus hogs, such as some primitive SCSI adaptors. A few badly designed motherboard chip sets have problems with bus masters. And a reason for not using *any* type of DMA device is using a 486 processor designed for plug-in replacement of a 386: these processors must flush their cache with each DMA cycle. (This includes the Cx486DLC, Ti486DLC, Cx486SLC, Ti486SLC, etc.)

2.7 Type of cable that your card should support

If you are setting up a small "personal" network, you will probably want to use thinnet or thin ethernet cable. This is the style with the standard BNC connectors. See Section 6 for other concerns with different types of Ethernet cable.

Most Ethercards also come in a "Combo" version for only $10-$20 more. These have both twisted pair and thinnet transceiver built-in, allowing you to change your mind later.

The twisted pair cables, with the RJ-45 (giant phone jack) connectors is technically called 10BaseT. You may also hear it called UTP (Unshielded Twisted Pair).

The thinnet, or thin ethernet cabling, (RG-58 coaxial cable) with the BNC (metal push and turn-to-lock) connectors is technically called 10Base2.

The older, thick Ethernet (10mm coaxial cable). which is only found in older installations, is called 10Base5.

Large, corporate installations will most likely use 10BaseT instead of 10Base2. 10Base2 does not offer an easy upgrade path to the new upcoming 100Base-whatever.

3 Frequently Asked Questions

Here are some of the more frequently asked questions about using Linux with an Ethernet connection. Some of the more specific questions are sorted on a "per manufacturer basis." However, since this document is basically "old" by the time you get it, any "new" problems will not appear here instantly. For these, I suggest that you make efficient use of your news reader. For example, nn users would type

```
nn -xX -s'3c'
```

to get all the news articles in your subscribed list that have "3c" in the subject. (ie. 3com, 3c509, 3c503, etc.) The moral: Read the manual page for your news reader.

3.1 Alpha Drivers—Getting and Using them

I heard that there is an updated or alpha driver available for my card. Where can I get it?

The newest of the "new" drivers can be found on Donald's new FTP site, cesdis.gsfc.nasa.gov in the `/pub/linux/` area. Things change here quite frequently, so just look around for it.

Now, if it really is an alpha, or pre-alpha driver, then please treat it as such. In other words, don't complain because you can't figure out what to do with it. If you can't figure out how to install it, then you probably shouldn't be testing it. Also, if it brings your machine down, don't complain. Instead, send us a well documented bug report, or even better, a patch.

Note that some of the "usable" experimental or alpha drivers have been included in the standard kernel source tree. When running `make config`, one of the first things you will be asked is whether to "Prompt for development and/or incomplete code/drivers." You will have to answer "Y" here to get asked about including any alpha or experimental drivers.

People reading this while net-surfing may want to check out Don's Linux Home Page, http://cesdis.gsfc.nasa.gov/pub/linux/linux.html, for the latest dirt on what is new and upcoming.

3.2 Using More than one Ethernet Card per Machine

What needs to be done so that Linux can run two Ethernet cards?

The hooks for multiple Ethercards are all there. However, note that at the moment only *one* Ethercard is auto-probed for by default. This helps to avoid possible boot time hangs caused by probing sensitive cards.

There are two ways that you can enable auto-probing for the second (and third, and...) card. The easiest method is to pass boot-time arguments to the kernel, which is usually done by LILO. Probing for the second card can be achieved by using a boot-time argument as simple as `ether=0,0,eth1`. In this case `eth0` and `eth1` will be assigned in the order that the cards are found at boot. Say if you want the card at `0x300` to be `eth0` and the card at `0x280` to be `eth1` then you could use

```
LILO: linux ether=5,0x300,eth0 ether=15,0x280,eth1
```

The `ether=` command accepts more than the IRQ + I/O + name shown above. Please have a look at Section 10.1 for the full syntax, card specific parameters, and LILO tips.

These boot-time arguments can be made permanent so that you don't have to re-enter them every time. See the LILO configuration option `append` in the LILO manual.

The second way (not recommended) is to edit the file `Space.c` and replace the `0xffe0` entry for the I/O address with a zero. The `0xffe0` entry tells it not to probe for that device—replacing it with a zero will enable auto-probing for that device.

Note that if you are intending to use Linux as a gateway between two networks, you will have to re-compile a kernel with IP forwarding enabled. Usually using an old AT/286 with something like the 'kbridge' software is a better solution.

If you are viewing this while net-surfing, you may wish to look at a Mini-HOWTO Donald has on his WWW site. Check out http://cesdis.gsfc.nasa.gov/linux/misc/multicard.html.

For module users with 8390 based cards, you can have a single module control multiple cards of the same brand. Please see Section 10.2.1 for module specific information about using multiple cards.

3.3 Poor NE2000 Clones

Here is a list of some of the NE2000 clones that are known to have various problems. Most of them aren't fatal. In the case of the ones listed as "bad clones"—this usually indicates that the cards don't have the two NE2000 identifier bytes. NEx000-clones have a Station Address PROM (SAPROM) in the packet buffer memory space. NE2000 clones have `0x57,0x57` in bytes `0x0e,0x0f` of the SAPROM, while other supposed NE2000 clones must be detected by their SA prefix.

This is not a comprehensive list of all the NE2000 clones that don't have the `0x57,0x57` in bytes `0x0e,0x0f` of the SAPROM. There are probably hundreds of them. If you get a card that causes the driver to report an "invalid signature" then you will have to add your cards signature to the driver. The process for doing this is described below.

Accton NE2000 – might not get detected at boot, see below.
Aritsoft LANtastic AE-2 – OK, but has flawed error-reporting registers.
AT-LAN-TEC NE2000 – clone uses Winbond chip that traps SCSI drivers
ShineNet LCS-8634 – clone uses Winbond chip that traps SCSI drivers
Cabletron E10, E20**, E10**-x, E20**-x** – bad clones, but the driver checks for them. See 5.11.1.
D-Link Ethernet II – bad clones, but the driver checks for them. See 5.15.1.
DFI DFINET-300, DFINET-400 – bad clones, but the driver checks for them. See 5.16.1
EtherNext UTP8, EtherNext UTP16 – bad clones, but the driver checks for them.

3.4 Problems with NE1000 / NE2000 cards (and clones)

Problem: PCI NE2000 clone card is not detected at boot with v2.0.x.

Reason: The `ne.c` driver up to v2.0.30 only knows about the PCI ID number of RealTek 8029 based clone cards. Since then, Winbond and Compex have also released PCI NE2000 clone cards, with different PCI ID numbers, and hence the driver doesn't detect them.

Solution: The easiest solution is to upgrade to a v2.0.31 version of the Linux kernel. It knows the ID numbers of about five different NE2000-PCI chips, and will detect them automatically at boot or at module loading time.

Alternatively, after booting, you can get the I/O address (and interrupt) that the card will use from a "`cat /proc/pci`." Say, for example, that it reports IRQ 9 and I/O at `0xffe0`, then at the LILO boot prompt you can add `ether=9,0xffe0,eth0` which will point the driver right at your card and avoid the PCI based probing altogether. (Future v2.1 kernels will know about the PCI IDs of Winbond and Compex NE2000 clones as well, so this won't be necessary then.)

Problem: PCI NE2000 clone card is reported as an NE1000 (8-bit card!) at boot or when I load the ne.o module for v2.0.x, and hence doesn't work.

Reason: Some PCI clones don't implement byte-wide access (and hence are not truly 100% NE2000 compatible). This causes the probe to think they are NE1000 cards if the PCI probing wasn't used (which isn't when an explicit I/O address is given with the module or at boot.)

Solution: You can upgrade to v2.0.31 as described above, or manually make the following change to `drivers/net/ne.c`:

```
-       if (pci_irq_line)
+       if (pci_irq_line || ioaddr >= 0x400)
            wordlength = 2;    /* Catch broken PCI cards mentioned above. */
```

and then recompile the module (or the kernel). Note that v2.0.31 and recent v2.1.x revisions do not require an I/O address for detecting most PCI cards at boot or with the ne.o module—it is best to let it auto-detect the card with these versions.

Problem: PCI NE2000 card gets terrible performance, even when reducing the window size as described in the Performance Tips section.

Reason: The spec sheets for the original 8390 chip, designed and sold over ten years ago, noted that a dummy read from the chip was required before the write operation for maximum reliability. The driver has the facility to do this but it has been disabled by default since the v1.2 days, once the real problem causing the crashes back then was located. One user has reported that re-enabling this "mis-feature" helped their performance with a cheap PCI NE2000 clone card.

Solution: Since it has only been reported as a solution by one person, don't get your hopes up. Re-enabling the read before write fix is done by simply editing the file `linux/drivers/net/ne.c`, uncommenting the line containing `NE_RW_BUGFIX` and then rebuilding the kernel or module as appropriate. Please send an e-mail describing the performance difference and type of card or chip if this helps you.

Problem: NE*000 card hangs machine, sometimes with a "DMA conflict" message, sometimes completely silently.

Reason: There were some bugs in the driver and the upper networking layers that caused this. They have been fixed long ago, in kernels v1.2.9 and above. Upgrade your kernel.

Problem: NE*000 card hangs machine during NE probe, or can not read station address properly.

Reason: Kernels previous to v1.3.7 did not fully reset the card after finding it at boot. Some cheap cards are not left in a reasonable state after power-up and need to be fully reset before any attempt is made to use them. Also, a previous probe may have upset the NE card prior to the NE probe taking place. In that case, look in to using the "reserve=" boot keyword to protect the card from other probes.

Problem: NE*000 driver reports "not found (no reset ack)" during boot probe.

Reason: This is related to the above change. After the initial verification that an 8390 is at the probed I/O address, the reset is performed. When the card has completed the reset, it is supposed to acknowledge that the reset has completed. Your card doesn't, and so the driver assumes that no NE card is present.

Solution: You can tell the driver that you have a bad card by using an otherwise unused mem_end hexadecimal value of 0xbad at boot time. You have to also supply a non-zero I/O base for the card when using the `0xbad` override. For example, a card that is at `0x340` that doesn't acknowledge the reset would use something like:

```
LILO: linux ether=0,0x340,0,0xbad,eth0
```

This will allow the card detection to continue, even if your card doesn't ACK the reset. If you are using the driver as a module, then you can supply the option `bad=0xbad` just like you supply the I/O address. Note that v2.0.x modules won't understand the `bad=` option, as it was added during the v2.1 development.

Problem: NE*000 card hangs machine at first network access.

Reason: This problem has been reported for kernels as old as 1.1.57 to the present. It appears confined to a few software configurable clone cards. It appears that they expect to be initialized in some special way.

Solution: Several people have reported that running the supplied DOS software config program and/or the supplied DOS driver prior to warm booting (i.e. LOADLIN.EXE or the "three-finger-salute") into Linux allowed the card to work. This would indicate that these cards need to be initialized in a particular fashion, slightly different than what the present Linux driver does.

Problem: NE*000 Ethercard at `0x360` doesn't get detected anymore.

Reason: Recent kernels (> 1.1.7X) have more sanity checks with respect to overlapping i/o regions. Your NE2000 card is `0x20` wide in i/o space, which makes it hit the parallel port at `0x378`. Other devices that could be there are the second floppy controller (if equipped) at `0x370` and the secondary IDE controller at `0x376-0x377`. If the port(s) are already registered by another driver, the kernel will not let the probe happen.

Solution: Either move your card to an address like `0x280, 0x340, 0x320` or compile without parallel printer support.

Problem: Network "goes away" every time I print something (NE2000)

Reason: Same problem as above, but you have an older kernel that doesn't check for overlapping I/O regions. Use the same fix as above, and get a new kernel while you are at it.

Problem: NE*000 Ethercard probe at 0xNNN: 00 00 C5 ... not found. (invalid signature yy zz)

Reason: First off, do you have a NE1000 or NE2000 card at the addr. 0xNNN? And if so, does the hardware address reported look like a valid one? If so, then you have a poor NE*000 clone. All NE*000 clones are supposed to have the value `0x57` in bytes 14 and 15 of the SA PROM on the card. Yours doesn't—it has "yy zz" instead.

Solution: There are two ways to get around this. The easiest is to use an `0xbad mem_end` value as described above for the "no reset ack" problem. This will bypass the signature check, as long as a non-zero I/O base is also given. This way no recompilation of the kernel is required.

The second method involves changing the driver itself, and then recompiling your kernel. The driver (`/usr/src/linux/drivers/net/ne.c`) has a "Hall of Shame" list at about line 42. This list is used to detect poor clones. For example, the DFI cards use 'DFI' in the first 3 bytes of the PROM, instead of using 0x57 in bytes 14 and 15, like they are supposed to.

You can determine what the first 3 bytes of your card PROM are by adding a line like:

```
printk("PROM prefix: %2.2x %2.2x %2.2x\n",SA_prom[0],SA_prom[1],SA_prom[2]);
```

into the driver, right after the error message you got above, and just before the "return ENXIO" at line 227.

Reboot with this change in place, and after the detection fails, you will get the three bytes from the PROM like the DFI example above. Then you can add your card to the bad_clone_list[] at about line 43. Say the above line printed out:

```
PROM prefix: 0x3F 0x2D 0x1C
```

after you rebooted. And say that the 8-bit version of your card was called the "FOO-1k" and the 16-bit version the "FOO-2k." Then you would add the following line to the bad_clone_list[]:

```
{"FOO-1k", "FOO-2k", {0x3F, 0x2D, 0x1C,}},
```

Note that the two name strings you add can be anything—they are just printed at boot, and not matched against anything on the card. You can also take out the "printk()" that you added above, if you want. It shouldn't hit that line anymore anyway. Then recompile once more, and your card should be detected.

Problem: Errors like `DMA address mismatch`

Is the chip a real National Semiconductor 8390? (DP8390, DP83901, DP83902 or DP83905)? If not, some clone chips don't correctly implement the transfer verification register. MS-DOS drivers never do error checking, so it doesn't matter to them. (Note: The DMA address check is not done by default as of v1.2.4 for performance reasons. Enable it with the "NE_SANITY" define in `ne.c` if you want the check done.)

Are most of the messages off by a factor of 2? If so: Are you using the NE2000 in a 16-bit slot? Is it jumpered to use only 8-bit transfers?

The Linux driver expects a NE2000 to be in a 16 bit slot. A NE1000 can be in either size slot. This problem can also occur with some clones, notably older D-Link 16-bit cards, that don't have the correct ID bytes in the station address PROM.

Are you running the bus faster than 8MHz? If you can change the speed (faster or slower), see if that makes a difference. Most NE2000 clones will run at 16MHz, but some may not. Changing speed can also mask a noisy bus.

What other devices are on the bus? If moving the devices around changes the reliability, then you have a bus noise problem – just what that error message was designed to detect. Congratulations, you've probably found the source of other problems as well.

Problem: The machine hangs during boot right after the "8390...' or "WD..." message. Removing the NE2000 fixes the problem.

Solution: Change your NE2000 base address to something like `0x340`. Alternatively, you can use the "`reserve=`" boot argument in conjunction with the "`ether=`" argument to protect the card from other device driver probes.

Reason: Your NE2000 clone isn't a good enough clone. An active NE2000 is a bottomless pit that will trap any driver auto-probing in its space. Changing the NE2000 to a less-popular address will move it out of the way of other auto probes, allowing your machine to boot.

Problem: The machine hangs during the SCSI probe at boot.

Reason: It's the same problem as above, change the Ethercard's address, or use the reserve/ether boot arguments.

Problem: The machine hangs during the sound card probe at boot.

Reason: No, that's really during the silent SCSI probe, and it's the same problem as above.

Problem: NE2000 not detected at boot— no boot messages at all

Solution: There is no "magic solution" as there can be a number of reasons why it wasn't detected. The following list should help you walk through the possible problems.

1) Build a new kernel with only the device drivers that you need. Verify that you are indeed booting the fresh kernel. Forgetting to run lilo, etc. can result in booting the old one. (Look closely at the build time/date reported at boot.) Sounds obvious, but we have all done it before. Make sure the driver is in fact included in the new kernel, by checking the `System.map` file for names like `ne_probe`.

2) Look at the boot messages carefully. Does it ever even mention doing a ne2k probe such as "NE*000 probe at 0xNNN: not found (blah blah)" or does it just fail silently. There is a big difference. Use `dmesg|more` to review the boot messages after logging in, or hit Shift-PgUp to scroll the screen up after the boot has completed and the login prompt appears.

3) After booting, do a `cat /proc/ioports` and verify that the full I/O space that the card will require is vacant. If you are at `0x300` then the ne2k driver will ask for `0x300-0x31f`. If any other device driver has registered even one port anywhere in that range, the probe will not take place at that address and will silently continue to the next of the probed addresses. A common case is having the lp driver reserve `0x378` or the second IDE channel reserve `0x376` which stops the NE driver from probing `0x360-0x380`.

4) Same as above for `cat /proc/interrupts`. Make sure no other device has registered the interrupt that you set the Ethercard for. In this case, the probe will happen, and the ether driver will complain loudly at boot about not being able to get the desired IRQ line.

5) If you are still stumped by the silent failure of the driver, then edit it and add some printk() to the probe. For example, with the ne2k you could add/remove lines (marked with a '+' or '-') in `net/ne.c` like:

```
    int reg0 = inb_p(ioaddr);

+       printk("NE2k probe - now checking %x\n",ioaddr);
-       if (reg0 == 0xFF)
+       if (reg0 == 0xFF) {
+           printk("NE2k probe - got 0xFF (vacant i/o port)\n");
            return ENODEV;
+       }
```

Then it will output messages for each port address that it checks, and you will see if your card's address is being probed or not.

6) You can also get the `ne2k` diagnostic from Don's FTP site (mentioned in the HOWTO as well) and see if it is able to detect your card after you have booted into Linux. Use the '`-p 0xNNN`' option to tell it where to look for the card. (The default is `0x300` and it doesn't go looking elsewhere, unlike the boot-time probe.) The output from when it finds a card will look something like:

```
Checking the Ethercard at 0x300.
  Register 0x0d (0x30d) is 00
  Passed initial NE2000 probe, value 00.
8390 registers: 0a 00 00 00 63 00 00 00 01 00 30 01 00 00 00 00
SA PROM  0: 00 00 00 00 c0 c0 b0 b0 05 05 65 65 05 05 20 20
SA PROM 0x10: 00 00 07 07 0d 0d 01 01 14 14 02 02 57 57 57 57

        NE2000 found at 0x300, using start page 0x40 and end page 0x80.
```

Your register values and PROM values will probably be different. Note that all the PROM values are doubled for a 16-bit card, and that the Ethernet address (00:00:c0:b0:05:65) appears in the first row, and the double `0x57` signature appears at the end of the PROM.

The output from when there is no card installed at `0x300` will look something like this:

```
Checking the Ethercard at 0x300.
  Register 0x0d (0x30d) is ff
```

```
 Failed initial NE2000 probe, value ff.
8390 registers: ff ff ff ff ff ff ff ff ff ff ff ff ff ff ff ff
SA PROM       0: ff ff ff ff ff ff ff ff ff ff ff ff ff ff ff ff
SA PROM 0x10: ff ff ff ff ff ff ff ff ff ff ff ff ff ff ff ff

 Invalid signature found, wordlength 2.
```

The `0xff` values arise because that is the value that is returned when one reads a vacant I/O port. If you happen to have some other hardware in the region that is probed, you may see some non `0xff` values as well.

7) Try warm booting into Linux from a DOS boot floppy (via LOADLIN.EXE) after running the supplied DOS driver or configuration program. It may be doing some extra (i.e. non-standard) magic to initialize the card.

8) Try Russ Nelson's `NE2000.COM` packet driver to see if even it can see your card—if not, then things do not look good. Example:

```
A:> ne2000 0x60 10 0x300
```

The arguments are software interrupt vector, hardware IRQ, and I/O base. You can get it from any MS-DOS archive in `PKTDRV11.ZIP`—The current version may be newer than 11.

3.5 Problems with SMC Ultra/EtherEZ and WD80*3 cards

Problem: You get messages such as the following:

```
eth0:  bogus packet size:  65531, status=0xff, nxpg=0xff
```

Reason: There is a shared memory problem.

Solution: The most common reason for this is PCI machines that are not configured to map in ISA memory devices. Hence you end up reading the PC's RAM (all `0xff` values) instead of the RAM on the card that contains the data from the received packet.

Other typical problems that are easy to fix are board conflicts, having cache or "shadow ROM" enabled for that region, or running your ISA bus faster than 8Mhz. There are also a surprising number of memory failures on Ethernet cards, so run a diagnostic program if you have one for your Ethercard.

Problem: SMC EtherEZ doesn't work in non-shared memory (PIO) mode.

Reason: Older versions of the Ultra driver only supported the card in the shared memory mode of operation.

Solution: The driver in kernel version 2.0 and above also supports the programmed I/O mode of operation. Upgrade to v2.0, or get the drop-in replacement for kernel v1.2.13 from Donald's FTP or WWW site.

Problem: Old WD8003 or jumper settable WD8013 always get the IRQ wrong.

Reason: The old WD8003 cards and jumper settable WD8013 clones don't have the EEPROM that the driver can read the IRQ setting from. If the driver can't read the IRQ, then it tries to auto-IRQ to find out what it is. And if auto-IRQ returns zero, then the driver just assigns IRQ 5 for an 8-bit card or IRQ 10 for a 16-bit card.

Solution: Avoid the auto-IRQ code, and tell the kernel what the IRQ that you have jumpered the card to is via a boot-time argument. For example, if you are using IRQ 9, using the following should work.

```
LILO: linux ether=9,0,eth0
```

Problem: SMC Ultra card is detected as WD8013, but the IRQ and shared memory base is wrong.

Reason: The Ultra card looks a lot like a WD8013, and if the Ultra driver is not present in the kernel, the WD driver may mistake the ultra as a WD8013. The Ultra probe comes before the WD probe, so this usually shouldn't happen. The Ultra stores the IRQ and mem base in the EEPROM differently than a WD8013, hence the bogus values reported.

Solution: Recompile with only the drivers you need in the kernel. If you have a mix of WD and Ultra cards in one machine, and are using modules, then load the Ultra module first.

3.6 Problems with 3Com cards

Problem: The 3c503 picks IRQ N, but this is needed for some other device which needs IRQ N. (eg. CD ROM driver, modem, etc.) Can this be fixed without compiling this into the kernel?

Solution: The 3c503 driver probes for a free IRQ line in the order {5, 9/2, 3, 4}, and it should pick a line which isn't being used. Very old drivers used to pick the IRQ line at boot-time, and the current driver (0.99pl12 and newer) chooses when the card is open()/ifconfig'ed.

Alternately, you can fix the IRQ at boot by passing parameters via LILO. The following selects IRQ9, base location 0x300, <ignored value>, and if_port #1 (the external transceiver).

```
LILO: linux ether=9,0x300,0,1,eth0
```

The following selects IRQ3, probes for the base location, <ignored value>, and the default if_port #0 (the internal transceiver)

```
LILO: linux ether=3,0,0,0,eth0
```

Problem: 3c503: configured interrupt X invalid, will use auto-IRQ.

Reason: The 3c503 card can only use one of IRQ{5, 2/9, 3, 4} (These are the only lines that are connected to the card.) If you pass in an IRQ value that is not in the above set, you will get the above message. Usually, specifying an interrupt value for the 3c503 is not necessary. The 3c503 will auto-IRQ when it gets ifconfig'ed, and pick one of IRQ{5, 2/9, 3, 4}.

Solution: Use one of the valid IRQs listed above, or enable auto-IRQ by not specifying the IRQ line at all.

Problem: The supplied 3c503 drivers don't use the AUI (thicknet) port. How does one choose it over the default thinnet port?

Solution: The 3c503 AUI port can be selected at boot-time with 0.99pl12 and later. The selection is overloaded onto the low bit of the currently-unused dev->rmem_start variable, so a boot-time parameter of:

```
LILO: linux ether=0,0,0,1,eth0
```

should work. A boot line to force IRQ 5, port base 0x300, and use an external transceiver is:

```
LILO: linux ether=5,0x300,0,1,eth0
```

With kernels 1.3.42 and newer, you can specify the AUI port when loading as a module as well. Just append `xcvr=1` to the `insmod` command line along with your I/O and IRQ values.

3.7 FAQs Not Specific to Any Card.

3.7.1 Ethercard is Not Detected at Boot.

The usual reason for this is that people are using a kernel that does not have support for their particular card built in. If you are using a pre-compiled kernel that is part of a distribution set, then check the documentation to see which kernel you installed, and if it was built with support for your particular card. If it wasn't, then your options are to try and get one that has support for your card, or build your own.

It is usually wise to build your own kernel with only the drivers you need. This cuts down on the kernel size (saving your precious RAM for applications!) and reduces the number of device probes that can upset sensitive hardware. Building a kernel is not as complicated as it sounds. You just have to answer, "yes," or, "no," to a bunch of questions about what drivers you want, and it does the rest.

The next main cause is having another device using part of the I/O space that your card needs. Most cards are 16 or 32 bytes wide in I/O space. If your card is set at 0x300 and 32 bytes wide, then the driver will ask for 0x300-0x31f. If any other device driver has registered even one port anywhere in that range, the probe will not take place at that address and the driver will silently continue to the next of the probed addresses. So, after booting, do a `cat /proc/ioports` and verify that the full I/O space that the card will require is vacant.

Another problem is having your card jumpered to an I/O address that isn't probed by default. There is a list in Section 8.1 for each card in this document. Even if the I/O setting of your card is not in the list of probed addresses, you can supply it at boot with the `ether=` command as described in Section 10.1

3.7.2 `ifconfig` reports the wrong I/O address for the card.

No it doesn't. You are just interpreting it incorrectly. This is *not* a bug, and the numbers reported are correct. It just happens that some 8390 based cards (WD80X3, SMC-Ultra, etc.) have the actual 8390 chip living at an offset from the first assigned I/O port. Try `cd /usr/src/linux/drivers/net;grep NIC_OFFSET *.c|more` to see what is going on. This is the value stored in `dev->base_addr`, and is what `ifconfig` reports. If you want to see the full range of ports that your card uses, then try `cat /proc/ioports` which will give the numbers you expect.

3.7.3 Shared Memory ISA cards in PCI Machine don't work (0xffff)

This will usually show up as reads of lots of `0xffff` values. No shared memory cards of any type will work in a PCI machine unless you have the PCI ROM BIOS/CMOS SETUP configuration set properly. You have to set it to allow shared memory access from the ISA bus for the memory region that your card is trying to use. If you can't figure out which settings are applicable then ask your supplier or local computer guru. For AMI BIOS, there is usually a "Plug and Play" section where there will be an "ISA Shared Memory Size" and "ISA Shared Memory Base" setting. For cards like the WD8013 and SMC Ultra, change the size from the default of 'Disabled' to 16kB, and change the base to the shared memory address of your card.

3.7.4 NexGen machine gets "mismatched read page pointers" errors.

A quirk of the NexGen CPU caused all users with 8390 based cards (WD80X3, 3c503, SMC Ultra/EtherEZ, NE2000, etc.) to get these error messages. Kernel versions 2.0 and above do not have these problems. Upgrade your kernel.

3.7.5 Asynchronous Transfer Mode (ATM) Support

Werner Almesberger has been working on ATM support for Linux. He has been working with the Efficient Networks ENI155p board (*Efficient Networks* (`http://www.efficient.com/`)) and the Zeitnet ZN1221 board (*Zeitnet* (`http://www.zeitnet.com/`)).

Werner says that the driver for the ENI155p is rather stable, while the driver for the ZN1221 is presently unfinished. Check the latest/updated status at the following URL.

Linux ATM Support (`http://lrcwww.epfl.ch/linux-atm/`)

3.7.6 FDDI Support

Is there FDDI support for Linux?

Yes. Larry Stefani has written a driver for v2.0 with DEC's DEFEA and DEFPA cards. This was included into the v2.0.24 kernel. Currently no other cards are supported, though.

3.7.7 Full Duplex Support

Will Full Duplex give me 20MBps? Does Linux support it?

Cameron Spitzer writes the following about full duplex 10Base-T cards: "If you connect it to a full duplex switched hub, and your system is fast enough and not doing much else, it can keep the link busy in both directions. There is no such thing as full duplex 10BASE-2 or 10BASE-5 (thin and thick coax). Full Duplex works by disabling collision detection in the adapter. That's why you can't do it with coax; the LAN won't run that way. 10BASE-T (RJ45 interface) uses separate wires for send and receive, so it's possible to run both ways at the same time. The switching hub takes care of the collision problem. The signalling rate is 10 Mbps."

So as you can see, you still will only be able to receive or transmit at 10Mbps, and hence don't expect a 2x performance increase. As to whether it is supported or not, that depends on the card and possibly the driver. Some cards may do auto-negotiation, some may need driver support, and some may need the user to select an option in a card's EEPROM configuration. Only the serious or heavy user would notice the difference between the two modes anyway.

3.7.8 Ethernet Cards for Linux on Alpha/AXP PCI Boards

As of v2.0, only the 3c509, DEPCA, DE4X5 LANCE32, and all of the 8390 drivers (WD, SMC-Ultra, NE, 3c503, etc.) have been made "architecture independent," so as to work on the DEC Alpha CPU based systems.

Note that the changes that are required aren't that complicated. You only need to do the following.

- Multiply all `jiffies` related values by HZ/100 to account for the different HZ value that the Alpha uses. (i.e `timeout=2;` becomes `timeout=2*HZ/100;`)
- Replace any I/O memory (640k to 1MB) pointer dereferences with the appropriate readb() writeb() readl() writel() calls, as shown in this example.

```
-       int *mem_base = (int *)dev->mem_start;
-       mem_base[0] = 0xba5eba5e;
+       unsigned long mem_base = dev->mem_start;
+       writel(0xba5eba5e, mem_base);
```

- Replace all memcpy() calls that have I/O memory as source or target destinations with the appropriate one of `memcpy_fromio()` or `memcpy_toio()`.

Details on handling memory accesses in an architecture-independent fashion are documented in the file `linux/Documentation/IO-mapping.txt` that comes with recent kernels.

3.7.9 Linking 10BaseT without a Hub

Can I link 10BaseT (RJ45) based systems together without a hub?

You can link two machines easily, but no more than that, without extra devices or gizmos. See Section 6.2—it explains how to do it. And no, you can't hack together a hub just by crossing a few wires and stuff. It's pretty much impossible to do the collision signal right without duplicating a hub.

3.7.10 SIOCSIFxxx: No such device

I get a bunch of "SIOCSIFxxx: No such device" messages at boot, followed by a "SIOCADDRT: Network is unreachable" What is wrong?

Your Ethernet device was not detected at boot, and when `ifconfig` and `route` are run, they have no device to work with. Use `dmesg | more` to review the boot messages and see if there are any messages about detecting an Ethernet card.

3.7.11 SIOCSFFLAGS: Try again

I get "SIOCSFFLAGS: Try again" when I run `ifconfig`—Huh?

Some other device has taken the IRQ that your Ethercard is trying to use, and so the Ethercard can't use the IRQ. You don't necessarily need to reboot to resolve this, as some devices only grab the IRQs when they need them and then release them when they are done. Examples are some sound cards, serial ports, and the floppy disk driver. You can type `cat /proc/interrupts` to see which interrupts are presently in use. Most of the Linux Ethercard drivers only grab the IRQ when they are opened for use via `ifconfig`. If you can get the other device to "let go" of the required IRQ line, then you should be able to "Try again" with `ifconfig`.

3.7.12 Using `ifconfig` and Link UNSPEC with HW-addr of 00:00:00:00:00:00

When I run `ifconfig` with no arguments, it reports that LINK is UNSPEC (instead of 10Mbs Ethernet) and it also says that my hardware address is all zeros.

This is because people are running a newer version of the `ifconfig` program than their kernel version. This new version of `ifconfig` is not able to report these properties when used in conjunction with an older kernel. You can either upgrade your kernel, "downgrade" `ifconfig`, or simply ignore it. The kernel knows your hardware address, so it really doesn't matter if `ifconfig` can't read it.

You may also get strange information if the `ifconfig` program you are using is a lot older than the kernel you are using.

3.7.13 Huge Number of RX and TX Errors

When I run `ifconfig` with no arguments, it reports that I have a huge error count in both rec'd and transmitted packets. It all seems to work ok—What is wrong?

Look again. It says `RX packets` *big number* **PAUSE** `errors 0` **PAUSE** `dropped 0` **PAUSE** `overrun 0`. And the same for the `TX` column. Hence the big numbers you are seeing are the total number of packets that your machine received and transmitted. If you still find it confusing, try typing `cat /proc/net/dev` instead.

3.7.14 Entries in `/dev/` for Ethercards

I have `/dev/eth0` as a link to `/dev/`*xxx*. Is this right?

Contrary to what you have heard, the files in `/dev/*` are not used. You can delete any `/dev/wd0`, `/dev/ne0`, and similar entries.

3.7.15 Linux and "trailers"

Should I disable trailers when I `ifconfig` my Ethercard?

You can't disable trailers, and you shouldn't want to. "Trailers" are a hack to avoid data copying in the networking layers. The idea was to use a trivial fixed-size header of size 'H', put the variable-size header info at the end of the packet, and allocate all packets 'H' bytes before the start of a page. While it was a good idea, it turned out to not work well in practice. If someone suggests the use of "-trailers," note that it is the equivalent of sacrificial goat blood. It won't do anything to solve the problem, but if problem fixes itself then someone can claim deep magical knowledge.

3.7.16 Access to the raw Ethernet Device

How do I get access to the raw Ethernet device in Linux, without going through TCP/IP and friends?

```
int s=socket(AF_INET,SOCK_PACKET,htons(ETH_P_ALL));
```

This gives you a socket receiving every protocol type. Do `recvfrom()` calls to it and it will fill the sockaddr with device type in sa_family and the device name in the sa_data array. I don't know who originally invented SOCK_PACKET for Linux (its been in for ages) but its superb stuff. You can use it to send stuff raw, too, via `sendto()` calls. You have to have root access to do either of course.

4 Performance Tips

Here are some tips that you can use if you are suffering from low Ethernet throughput, or to gain a bit more speed on those FTP transfers.

The `ttcp.c` program is a good test for measuring raw throughput speed. Another common trick is to do a `ftp> get large_file /dev/null` where `large_file` is > 1MB and residing in the buffer cache on the Tx'ing machine. (Do the "get" at least twice, as the first time will be priming the buffer cache on the Tx'ing machine.) You want the file in the buffer cache because you are not interested in combining the file access speed from the disk into your measurement. Which is also why you send the incoming data to `/dev/null` instead of onto the disk.

4.1 General Concepts

Even an 8-bit card is able to receive back-to-back packets without any problems. The difficulty arises when the computer doesn't get the Rx'd packets off the card quickly enough to make room for more incoming packets. If the computer does not quickly clear the card's memory of the packets already received, the card will have no place to put the new packet.

In this case the card either drops the new packet, or writes over top of a previously received packet. Either one seriously interrupts the smooth flow of traffic by causing and requesting re-transmissions, and can seriously degrade performance by up to a factor of 5!

Cards with more on-board memory are able to "buffer" more packets, and thus can handle larger bursts of back-to-back packets without dropping packets. This in turn means that the card does not require as low a latency from the the host computer with respect to pulling the packets out of the buffer to avoid dropping packets.

Most 8-bit cards have an 8kB buffer, and most 16-bit cards have a 16kB buffer. Most Linux drivers will reserve 3kB of that buffer (for two Tx buffers), leaving only 5kB of receive space for an 8 bit card. This is room enough for only three full sized (1500 bytes) ethernet packets.

4.2 ISA Bus Speed

As mentioned above, if the packets are removed from the card fast enough, then a drop or overrun condition won't occur even when the amount of Rx packet buffer memory is small. The factor that sets the rate at which packets are removed from the card to the computer's memory is the speed of the data path that joins the two—that being the ISA bus speed. (If the CPU is a dog-slow 386SX-16, then this will also play a role.)

The recommended ISA bus clock is about 8MHz, but many motherboards and peripheral devices can be run at higher frequencies. The clock frequency for the ISA bus can usually be set in the CMOS setup, by selecting a divisor of the main board/CPU clock frequency.

For example, here are some receive speeds as measured by the TTCP program on a 40MHz 486, with an 8 bit WD8003EP card, for different ISA bus speeds.

ISA Bus Speed (MHz)	Rx TTCP (kB/s)
6.7	740
13.4	970
20.0	1030
26.7	1075

You would be hard pressed to do better than 1075kB/s with any 10Mb/s Ethernet card, using TCP/IP. However, don't expect every system to work at fast ISA bus speeds. Most systems will not function properly at speeds above 13MHz. (Also, most PCI systems have the ISA bus speed fixed at 8MHz, so that the end user does not have the option of increasing it.)

In addition to faster transfer speeds, one will usually also benefit from a reduction in CPU usage due to the shorter duration memory and I/O cycles. (Note that hard disks and video cards located on the ISA bus will also usually experience a performance increase from an increased ISA bus speed.)

Be sure to back up your data prior to experimenting with ISA bus speeds in excess of 8MHz, and thouroughly test that all ISA peripherals are operating properly after making any speed increases.

4.3 Setting the TCP Rx Window

Once again, cards with small amounts of on-board RAM and relatively slow data paths between the card and the computer's memory run into trouble. The default TCP Rx window setting is 32kB, which means that a fast computer on the same subnet as you can dump 32k of data on you without stopping to see if you received any of it okay.

Recent versions of the `route` command have the ability to set the size of this window on the fly. Usually it is only for the local net that this window must be reduced, as computers that are behind a couple of routers or gateways are "buffered" enough to not pose a problem. An example usage would be:

```
route add <whatever> ... window <win_size>
```

where `win_size` is the size of the window you wish to use (in bytes). An 8-bit 3c503 card on an ISA bus operating at a speed of 8MHz or less would work well with a window size of about 4kB. Too large a window will cause overruns and dropped packets, and a drastic reduction in Ethernet throughput. You can check the operating status by doing a `cat /proc/net/dev` which will display any dropped or overrun conditions that occurred.

4.4 Increasing NFS performance

Some people have found that using 8-bit cards in NFS clients causes poorer than expected performance, when using 8kB (native Sun) NFS packet size.

The possible reason for this could be due to the difference in on board buffer size between the 8-bit and the 16-bit cards. The maximum ethernet packet size is about 1500 bytes. Now that 8kB NFS packet will arrive as about 6 back-to-back, maximum-size Ethernet packets. Both the 8- and 16-bit cards have no problem Rx'ing back-to-back packets. The problem arises when the machine doesn't remove the packets from the card buffer in time, and the buffer overflows. The fact that 8-bit cards take an extra ISA bus cycle per transfer doesn't help, either. What you *can* do if you have an 8-bit card is either set the NFS transfer size to 2kB (or even 1kB), or try increasing the ISA bus speed in order to get the card's buffer cleared out faster. I have found that an old WD8003E card at 8MHz (with no other system load) can keep up with a large receive at 2kB NFS size, but not at 4kB, where performance was degraded by a factor of three.

5 Vendor/Manufacturer/Model Specific Information

The following lists many cards in alphabetical order by vendor name and then product identifier. Beside each product ID, you will see either "Supported," "Semi-Supported," or "Not Supported."

Supported means that a driver for that card exists, and many people are happily using it and it seems quite reliable.

Semi-Supported means that a driver exists, but at least one of the following descriptions is true: (1) The driver or hardware is buggy, which may cause poor performance, failing connections, or even crashes. (2) The card is fairly uncommon, and hence the driver has seen very little use or testing, and the driver author has had very little feedback. Obviously (2) is preferable to (1), and the individual description of the card or driver should make it clear which one holds true. In either case, you will probably have to answer "Y" when asked "Prompt for development and/or incomplete code/drivers?" when running `make config`. For the older v1.2 kernels, the option was known as `CONFIG_NET_ALPHA`. It was changed to avoid confusion with the Alpha-AXP line of processors made by Digital, and to encompass all experimental drivers, not just Net drivers.

"Not Supported" means there is not a driver currently available for that card. This could be due to a lack of interest in hardware that is rare or uncommon, or because the vendors won't release the hardware documentation required to write a driver.

Note that the difference between "Supported" and "Semi-Supported" is rather subjective, and is based on user feedback observed in newsgroup postings and mailing list messages. (After all, it is impossible for one person to test all drivers with all cards for each kernel version.) So be warned that you may find a card listed as semi-supported that works perfectly for you (which is great), or that a card listed as supported gives you no end of troubles and problems (which is not so great).

5.1 3Com

If you are not sure what your card is, but you think it is a 3Com card, you can probably figure it out from the assembly number. 3Com has a document 'Identifying 3Com Adapters By Assembly Number' (ref 24500002) that would most likely clear things up. See Section 8.6 for info on how to get documents from 3Com.

Also note that 3Com has a FTP site with various goodies: `ftp.3Com.com` that you may want to check out.

For those of you browsing this document by a WWW browser, you can try 3Com's WWW site as well.

5.1.1 3c501

Status—*Semi-Supported*

Too brain damaged to use. Available surplus from many places. Avoid it like the plague. Again, do not purchase this card, even as a joke. It's performance is horrible, and it breaks in many ways.

Cameron L. Spitzer of 3Com said: "I'm speaking only for myself here, of course, but I believe 3Com advises against installing a 3C501 in a new system, mostly for the same reasons Donald has discussed. You probably won't be happy with the 3C501 in your Linux box. The data sheet is marked '(obsolete)' on 3Com's Developers' Order Form, and the board is not part of 3Com's program for sending free Technical Reference Manuals to people who need them. The decade-old things are nearly indestructible, but that's about all they've got going for them any more."

For those not yet convinced, the 3c501 can only do one thing at a time—while you are removing one packet from the single-packet buffer it cannot receive another packet, nor can it receive a packet while loading a transmit packet. This was fine for a network between two, 8088 based computers, where processing each packet and replying took 10's of msecs, but modern networks send back-to-back packets for almost every transaction.

Auto-IRQ works, DMA isn't used, the auto probe only looks at `0x280` and `0x300`, and the debug level is set with the third boot-time argument.

Once again, the use of a 3c501 is *strongly discouraged.* Even more so with a IP multicast kernel, as you will grind to a halt while listening to *all* multicast packets. See the comments at the top of the source code for more details.

5.1.2 3c503, 3c503/16

Status—*Supported*

If you have a 3c503/16 you may be interested to know that as of 1.3.37 the driver has the facility to use the full 16kB RAM on your card. Previous versions treated the 16-bit cards as 8-bit cards, and only used half of the available RAM. This update also detects the newer 3Com prefix found on newly manufactured cards mentioned below.

Recently made 3c503/16 cards have a new base hardware address because 3Com ran out of numbers (they made too many cards) The cards used to start with 02 60 8C and the newer ones use 00 20 AF. Up to 1.3.37, the driver will only check for the old address, and skip over the newer cards. You can upgrade to a kernel newer than 1.3.37, or change the numbers in 3c503.c for older kernels.

These cards should be about the same speed as the same bus width WD80x3, but turn out to be actually a bit slower. The 3c503 does not have "EEPROM setup," so a diagnostic or setup program isn't needed before running the card with Linux. The shared memory address of the 3c503 is set using jumpers that are shared with the boot PROM address. This is confusing to people familiar with other ISA cards, where you always leave the jumper set to "disable" unless you have a boot PROM.

These shared-memory Ethercards also have a programmed I/O mode that doesn't use the 8390 facilities (their engineers found too many bugs). The Linux 3c503 driver can also work with the 3c503 in programmed I/O mode, but this is slower and less reliable than shared memory mode. Also, programmed I/O mode is not as well tested when updating the drivers. You shouldn't use the programmed I/O mode unless you need it for MS-DOS compatibility.

The 3c503's IRQ line is set in software, with no hints from an EEPROM. Unlike the MS-DOS drivers, the Linux driver has capability to auto-IRQ: it uses the first available IRQ line in {5,2/9,3,4}, selected each time the card is `ifconfig`'ed. (Older driver versions selected the IRQ at boot time.) The ioctl() call in `ifconfig` will return EAGAIN if no IRQ line is available at that time.

Some common problems that people have with the 503 are discussed in Section 3.6.

If you intend on using this driver as a loadable module you should probably see Section 10.2 and also Section 10.2.1 for module specific information.

5.1.3 3c505

Status—*Semi-Supported*

This is a driver that was written by Craig Southeren `geoffw@extro.ucc.su.oz.au`. These cards also use the i82586 chip. There are not that many of these cards about. It is included in the standard kernel, but it is classed as an alpha driver. See Section 3.1 for important information on using alpha-test Ethernet drivers with Linux.

There is also the file `/usr/src/linux/drivers/net/README.3c505` that you should read if you are going to use one of these cards. It contains various options that you can enable or disable. Technical information is available in Section 8.5.

5.1.4 3c507

Status—*Semi-Supported*

This card uses one of the Intel chips, and the development of the driver is closely related to the development of the Intel Ether Express driver. The driver is included in the standard kernel release, but as an alpha driver.

See 3.1 for important information on using alpha-test Ethernet drivers with Linux. Technical information is available in 8.5.

5.1.5 3c509 / 3c509B

Status—*Supported*

This card is fairly inexpensive and has good performance for a non-bus-master design. The drawbacks are that the original 3c509 requires very low interrupt latency. The 3c509B shouldn't suffer from the same problem, due to having a larger buffer. (See below.) These cards use PIO transfers, similar to a NE2000 card, and so a shared memory card, such as a WD8013, will be more efficient in comparison.

The original 3c509 has a small packet buffer (4kB total, 2kB Rx, 2kB Tx), causing the driver to occasionally drop a packet if interrupts are masked for too long. To minimize this problem, you can try unmasking interrupts during IDE disk transfers (see `hdparm(8)`) and/or increasing your ISA bus speed so IDE transfers finish sooner.

The newer model 3c509B has 8kB on board, and the buffer can be split 4/4, 5/3 or 6/2 for Rx/Tx. This setting is changed with the DOS configuration utility, and is stored on the EEPROM. This should alleviate the above problem with the original 3c509. At this point in time, the Linux driver is not aware of this, and treats the 3c509B as an older 3c509.

3c509B users should use the supplied DOS utility to disable the plug-and-play support, *and* to set the output media to what they require. The Linux driver currently does *not* support the Auto-detect media setting, so you *have* to select 10Base-T or 10Base-2 or AUI. With regards to the media detection features, Cameron said: "Auto-select is a feature of the commercial drivers for 3C509(B). AFAIK nobody ever claimed the Linux driver attempts it. When `drivers/net/3c509.c` recognizes my 3C509B at boot time, it says: `eth0: 3c509 at 0x300 tag 1, 10baseT port, ...` revealing that the card is configured for 10BASE-T. It finds that out by reading the little EEPROM, which IMHO is the Right Way To Do It."

As for the plug-and-pray stuff, Cameron adds: "The 3C509B has 3Com's relocatable I/O port scheme, and Microsoft[tm] Plug-and-play ('PnP'). You can't use them both at the same time. Some (broken, IMHO) BIOSes begin a PnP sequence by writing to the PnP address (0x279 ?), which causes PnP adapters like 3C509B to enter the PnP state, but then they (these funny BIOSes) never come back to finish the job. The 3C509Bs hang there in the middle of the PnP ID Sequence, where they have no idea you didn't mean it and you're going to use the 3Com ID sequence after all. 3C5X9CFG /PNPRST clears this hang. Disable PnP if your drivers (e.g., Linux) don't use it.

It was a marketing decision to turn PnP on as a factory default setting. If it caused you a hassle, or not, please take the time to say so when you mail in your warranty card. The more information they have, the better decisions they can make. Also, check with your motherboard supplier to see if you need a BIOS upgrade."

It has been reported that you have to do a hard reset after doing the "3C5X9CFG /PNPRST" for the change to take effect.

Some people ask about the "Server or Workstation" and "Highest Modem Speed" settings presented in the DOS configuration utility. Donald writes "These are only hints to the drivers, and the Linux driver does not use these parameters: it always optimizes for high throughput rather than low latency ('Server'). Low latency was critically important for old, non-windowed, IPX throughput. To reduce the latency, the MS-DOS driver for the 3c509 disables interrupts for some operations, blocking serial port interrupts. Thus the need for the 'modem speed' setting. The Linux driver avoids the need to disable interrupts for long periods by operating only on whole packets; e.g., by not starting to transmit a packet until it is completely transferred to the card."

Note that the ISA card detection uses a different method than most cards. Basically, you ask the cards to respond by sending data to an ID_PORT (port `0x100`). This detection method means that a particular card will *always* get detected first in a multiple ISA 3c509 configuration. The card with the lowest hardware ethernet address will *always* end up being `eth0`. This shouldn't matter to anyone, except for those people who want to assign a 6-byte hardware address to a particular interface. If you have multiple 3c509 cards, it is best to append `ether=0,0,ethN` commands without the I/O port specified (i.e. use I/O=zero) and allow the probe to sort out which card is first; otherwise, it may not detect all of your cards.

If this really bothers you, have a look at Donald's latest driver, as you may be able to use a `0x3c509` value in the unused mem address fields to order the detection to suit.

5.1.6 3c515

Status—*Not Supported*

This is 3Com's fairly recent ISA 100Mbps offering, code named "CorkScrew." Donald is working on support for these cards, and it will probably appear in the near future on his WWW driver page. The driver will be incorporated into the 3c59x/3c90x driver, so you should probably expect to look for it on the Vortex page:
Vortex (`http://cesdis.gsfc.nasa.gov/linux/drivers/vortex.html`)

5.1.7 3c523

Status—*Semi-Supported*

This MCA-bus card uses the i82586, and now that people are actually running Linux on MCA machines, people have recycled parts of other i82586 drivers into a working driver for this card. Expect a driver for it to appear in v2.1.x along with a multitude of other MCA support.

More details can be found on the MCA-Linux page at `http://glycerine.cetmm.uni.edu/mca/`

5.1.8 3c527

Status—*Not Supported*

Yes, another MCA card. No, not too much interest in it. Better chances with the 3c529 if you are stuck with MCA.

5.1.9 3c529

Status—*Semi-Supported*

This card actually uses the same chipset as the 3c509. Donald actually put hooks into the 3c509 driver to check for MCA cards after probing for EISA cards, and before probing for ISA cards. But it hasn't evolved much further than that. Donald writes:

"I don't have access to a MCA machine (nor do I fully understand the probing code), so I never wrote the `mca_adaptor_select_mode()` or `mca_adaptor_id()` routines. If you can find a way to get the adaptor I/O address that assigned at boot time, you can just hard-wire that in place of the commented-out probe. Be sure to keep the code that reads the IRQ, if_port, and ethernet address."

Darrell Frappier (aa822@detroit.freenet.org) reports that you can get the I/O address from running the PS/2 reference diskette, and once you put that directly into the driver, it does actually work.

The required MCA probe code will probably appear in v2.1 sometime shortly after all the other MCA patches go in.

5.1.10 3c562

Status—*Supported*

This PCMCIA card is the combination of a 3c589B ethernet card with a modem. The modem appears as a standard modem to the end user. The only difficulty is getting the two separate Linux drivers to share one interrupt. There are a couple of new registers and some hardware interrupt sharing support. You need to use a v2.0 or newer kernel that has the support for interrupt sharing.

As a side note, the modem part of the card has been reported to be not well documented for the end user (the manual just says "supports the AT command set"), and it may not connect as well as other name-brand modems. The recommendation is to buy a 3c589B instead, and then get a PCMCIA modem card from a company that specializes in modems.

Thanks again to Cameron for getting a sample unit and documentation sent off to David Hinds. Look for support in David's PCMCIA package release.

5.1.11 3c579

Status—*Supported*

The EISA version of the 509. The current EISA version uses the same 16-bit wide chip rather than a 32-bit interface, so the performance increase isn't stunning. The EISA probe code was added to `3c509.c` for 0.99pl14. We would be interested in hearing progress reports from any 3c579 users. (Read the above 3c509 section for info on the driver.)

Cameron Spitzer writes: "The 3C579 (Etherlink III EISA) should be configured as an EISA card. The I/O Base Address (window 0 register 6 bits 4:0) should be 1f, which selects EISA addressing mode. Logic outside the ASIC decodes the IO address s000, where s is the slot number. I don't think it was documented real well. Except for its IO Base Address, the '579 should behave EXACTLY like the'509 (EL3 ISA), and if it doesn't, I want to hear about it (at my work address)."

5.1.12 3c589 / 3c589B

Status—*Semi-Supported*

Many people have been using this PCMCIA card for quite some time now. Note that support for it is not (at present) included in the default kernel source tree. You will also need a supported PCMCIA controller chipset. There are drivers available on Donald's FTP site:

```
cesdis.gsfc.nasa.gov:/pub/linux/pcmcia/README.3c589
cesdis.gsfc.nasa.gov:/pub/linux/pcmcia/3c589.c
cesdis.gsfc.nasa.gov:/pub/linux/pcmcia/dbether.c
```

Or, for those that are Net-surfing, you can try:

Don's PCMCIA Stuff (`http://cesdis.gsfc.nasa.gov/linux/pcmcia.html`)

You will still need a PCMCIA socket enabler as well.

See Section 9.3 for more info on PCMCIA chip sets, socket enablers, etc.

The "B" in the name means the same here as it does for the 3c509 case.

5.1.13 3c590 / 3c595

Status—*Supported*

These "Vortex" cards are for PCI bus machines, with the '590 being 10Mbps and the '595 being 3Com's 100Mbs offering. Also note that you can run the '595 as a '590 (i.e. in a 10Mbps mode). The driver is included in the v2.0 kernel source, but is also continually being updated. If you have problems with the driver in the v2.0 kernel, you can get an updated driver from the following URL:

Vortex (`http://cesdis.gsfc.nasa.gov/linux/drivers/vortex.html`)

Note that there are two different 3c590 cards out there: early models that had 32kB of on-board memory, and later models that only have 8kB (eeccch!) of memory. Chances are that you won't be able to buy a new 3c59x for much longer, as it is being replaced with the 3c90x card. If you are buying a used one off somebody, try and get the 32kB version. The 3c595 cards have 64kB, as you can't get away with only 8kB RAM at 100Mbps!

A thanks to Cameron Spitzer and Terry Murphy of 3Com for sending cards and documentation to Donald so he could write the driver.

Donald has set up a mailing list for Vortex driver support. To join the list, just do:

```
echo subscribe | /bin/mail linux-vortex-request@cesdis.gsfc.nasa.gov
```

5.1.14 3c592 / 3c597

Status—*Supported*

These are the EISA versions of the 3c59x series of cards. The 3c592/3c597 (aka Demon) should work with the Vortex driver discussed above.

5.1.15 3c900 / 3c905

Status—*Supported*

These cards (aka "Boomerang;" aka EtherLink III XL) have been recently released to take the place of the 3c590 and 3c595 cards. Cameron Spitzer of 3Com writes that the "3C900 has a scatter gather bus master controlled by a descriptor ring in main memory. Aside from that, it's a lot like 3C590."

You may still be able to get a couple of these cards at a reduced price through one of 3Com's evaluation deals, if you are quick.

To use this card with v2.0 kernels, you must obtain the updated `3c59x.c` driver from Donald's site at:

Vortex-Page (`http://cesdis.gsfc.nasa.gov/linux/drivers/vortex.html`)

This updated 3c59x driver allows you to use the 3c900 in a 3c59x compatible mode, and has been reported to be quite stable. Note that this updated driver may be sneaked into the v2.0 source tree at a later date.)

On the same WWW page, you will also find the experimental `boomerang.c` driver which uses some of the enhancements of the 3c900 over that which is available on the 3c59x cards. Since this is a new/experimental driver, you may be better off in using the updated `3c59x.c` if system stability is a primary concern.

Donald has set up a mailing list for Vortex driver support announcements and etc. To join the list, just do:

```
echo subscribe | /bin/mail linux-vortex-request@cesdis.gsfc.nasa.gov
```

5.2 Accton

5.2.1 Accton MPX

Status—*Supported*

Don't let the name fool you. This is still supposed to be a NE2000 compatible card. The MPX is supposed to stand for MultiPacket Accelerator, which, according to Accton, increases throughput substantially. But if you are already sending back-to-back packets, how can you get any faster...

5.2.2 Accton EN1203, EN1207, EtherDuo-PCI

Status—*Supported*

This is another implementation of the DEC 21040 PCI chip. The EN1207 card has the 21140, and also has a 10Base-2 connector, which has proved troublesome for some people in terms of selecting that media. Using the card with 10Base-T and 100Base-T media have worked for others, though. So as with all purchases, you should try and make sure you can return it if it doesn't work for you.

See Section 5.17.4 for more information on these cards, and the present driver situation.

5.2.3 Accton EN2212 PCMCIA Card

Status—*Semi-Supported*

David Hinds has been working on a driver for this card, and you are best to check the latest release of his PCMCIA package to see what the present status is.

5.3 Allied Telesyn/Telesis

5.3.1 AT1500

Status –*Supported*

These are a series of low-cost Ethercards using the 79C960 version of the AMD LANCE. These are bus-master cards, and hence one of the faster ISA-bus Ethercards available.

DMA selection and chip numbering information can be found in 5.4.1.

More technical information on AMD LANCE based Ethernet cards can be found in 8.7.

5.3.2 AT1700

Status—*Supported*

Note that to access this driver during `make config`, you still have to answer "Y" when asked "Prompt for development and/or incomplete code/drivers?" at the first. This is simply due to lack of feedback on the driver stability due to it being a relatively rare card. This will probably be changed for v2.1 kernels.

The Allied Telesis AT1700 series Ethercards are based on the Fujitsu MB86965. This chip uses a programmed I/O interface, and a pair of fixed-size transmit buffers. This allows small groups of packets to be sent back-to-back, with a short pause while switching buffers.

A unique feature is the ability to drive 150ohm STP (Shielded Twisted Pair) cable commonly installed for Token Ring, in addition to 10baseT 100ohm UTP (unshielded twisted pair). A fiber optic version of the card (AT1700FT) exists as well.

The Fujitsu chip used on the AT1700 has a design flaw: it can only be fully reset by doing a power cycle of the machine. Pressing the reset button doesn't reset the bus interface. This wouldn't be so bad, except that it can only be reliably detected when it has been freshly reset. The solution, or work-around, is to power-cycle the machine if the kernel has a problem detecting the AT1700.

Some production runs of the AT1700 had another problem: they are permanently wired to DMA channel 5. This is undocumented, there are no jumpers to disable the "feature," and no driver dares use the DMA capability because of compatibility problems. No device driver will be written using DMA if installing a second card into the machine breaks both, and the only way to disable the DMA is with a knife.

5.3.3 AT2450

Status—*Supported*

This is the PCI version of the AT1500, and it doesn't suffer from the problems that the Boca 79c970 PCI card does. Allied Telsyn was still "beta testing" the card in early-to-mid 1995, so it may not have spread to various retailers yet (but it doesn't hurt to ask).

DMA selection and chip numbering information can be found in Section 5.4.1.

More technical information on AMD LANCE based Ethernet cards can be found in Section 8.7.

5.4 AMD / Advanced Micro Devices

5.4.1 AMD LANCE (7990, 79C960, PCnet-ISA)

Status—*Supported*

There really is no AMD Ethernet card. You are probably reading this because the only markings you could find on your card said AMD and the above number. The 7990 is the original 'LANCE' chip, but most stuff (including this document) refer to all these similar chips as 'LANCE' chips. (incorrectly, I might add.)

These above numbers refer to chips from AMD that are the heart of many Ethernet cards. For example, the Allied Telesis AT1500 (see 5.3.1) the NE1500/2100 (see 5.26.4) and the Boca-VLB/PCI cards (see 5.10.1)

The 79C960 (a.k.a. PCnet-ISA) contains enhancements and bug fixes over the original 7990 LANCE design.

One common problem people have is the "busmaster arbitration failure" message. This is printed out when the LANCE driver can't get access to the bus after a reasonable amount of time has elapsed (50us). This usually indicates that the motherboard implementation of bus-mastering DMA is broken, or some other device is hogging the bus, or there is a DMA channel conflict. If your BIOS setup has the "GAT option" (for Guaranteed Access Time) then try toggling or altering that setting to see if it helps.

Chances are that the existing LANCE driver will work with all AMD LANCE based cards. (except perhaps some of the original 7990 designs with shared memory.) This driver should also work with NE1500 and NE2100 clones.

For the ISA bus master mode, all structures used directly by the LANCE, the initialization block, Rx and Tx rings, and data buffers, must be accessible from the ISA bus; i.e. in the lower 16M of real memory. If more than 16MB of memory is installed, low-memory "bounce-buffers" are used when needed.

The DMA channel can be set with the low bits of the otherwise-unused dev->mem_start value (a.k.a. PARAM_1). (see 10.1.1) If unset, it is probed for by enabling each free DMA channel in turn and checking if initialization succeeds.

The HP-J2405A board is an exception: with this board it's easy to read the EEPROM values for the IRQ, and DMA.

See Section 8.7 for more info on these chips.

5.4.2 AMD 79C961 (PCnet-ISA+)

Status—*Supported*

This is the PCnet-ISA+—an enhanced version of the 79C960. It has support for jumper-less configuration and Plug and Play. Also see the information in the above section.

Dave Platt writes: "The Lance driver may report recent versions of this chip as "PCnet (unknown)," as the ID number in newer '961s seems to have been revised (it's now 0x2261 rather than 0x2260). This misidentification shouldn't prevent the driver from working with it, though.

"I've been told of a problem with the '961—it will work correctly the first time you boot Linux after a hard reset, but will not work correctly after a soft reboot. From the data sheet, it looks as if the '961 disables itself upon reset, and won't "talk" again until the motherboard BIOS goes through the Plug+Play probe-and-enable sequence, and this might not be happening during a soft reboot. I do not yet know of a good workaround for this problem."

5.4.3 AMD 79C965 (PCnet-32)

Status—*Supported*

This is the PCnet-32–a 32-bit, bus-master version of the original LANCE chip for VL-bus and local bus systems. Minor cleanups were added to the original LANCE driver around v1.1.50 to support these 32-bit versions of the LANCE chip. The main problem was that the current versions of the '965 and '970 chips have a minor bug. They clear the Rx buffer length field in the Rx ring when they are explicitly documented not to. Again, see the above info.

5.4.4 AMD 79C970 (PCnet-PCI)

Status—*Supported*

This is the PCnet-PCI – similar to the PCnet-32, but designed for PCI bus based systems. Again, see the above info. Donald has modified the LANCE driver to use the PCI BIOS structure that was introduced by Drew Eckhardt for the PCI-NCR SCSI driver. This means that you need to build a kernel with PCI BIOS support enabled.

Note that the Boca implementation of the 79C970 fails on fast Pentium machines. This is a hardware problem, as it affects DOS users as well. See the Boca section for more details.

5.4.5 AMD 79C974 (PCnet-SCSI)

Status—*Supported*

This is the PCnet-SCSI – which is basically treated like a '970 from an Ethernet point of view. A minor, '974-specific fix was added to the 1.1.8x kernels, so get a 1.1.90 or newer kernel. Also see the above information. Don't ask if the SCSI half of the chip is supported—this is the Ethernet HOWTO, not the SCSI HOWTO.

5.5 Ansel Communications

5.5.1 AC3200 EISA

Status—*Semi-Supported*

Note that to access this driver during `make config`, you still have to answer "Y" when asked, "Prompt for development and/or incomplete code/drivers?" This is simply due to lack of feedback on the driver stability due to it being a relatively rare card.

This driver is included in the present kernel as an alpha test driver. It is based on the common NS8390 chip used in the NE2000 and WD80x3 cards. Please see Section 3.1 in this document for important information regarding alpha drivers.

If you use it, let one of us know how things work out, as feedback has been low, even though the driver has been in the kernel since v1.1.25.

If you intend on using this driver as a loadable module you should probably see 10.2 and also 10.2.1 for module specific information.

5.6 Apricot

5.6.1 Apricot Xen-II On Board Ethernet

Status—*Supported*

This on board Ethernet uses an i82596 bus-master chip. It can only be at I/O address `0x300`. The author of this driver is Mark Evans. By looking at the driver source, it appears that the IRQ is hardwired to 10.

Earlier versions of the driver had a tendency to think that anything living at `0x300` was an Apricot NIC. Since then, the hardware address is checked to avoid these false detections.

5.7 ArcNet

Status—*Supported*

With the very low cost and better performance of Ethernet, chances are that most places will be giving away their ArcNet hardware for free, resulting in a lot of home systems with ArcNet.

An advantage of ArcNet is that all of the cards have identical interfaces, so one driver will work for everyone. It also has built in error handling so that it supposedly never loses a packet. (Great for UDP traffic.)

Avery Pennarun's ArcNet driver has been in the default kernel sources since 1.1.80. The ArcNet driver uses 'arc0' as its name instead of the usual 'eth0' for Ethernet devices. Bug reports and success stories can be mailed to:

`apenwarr@foxnet.net`

There are information files contained in the standard kernel for setting jumpers and general hints.

Supposedly the driver also works with the 100Mbs ArcNet cards as well.

5.8 AT&T

Note that AT&T's StarLAN is an orphaned technology, like SynOptics LattisNet, and can't be used in a standard 10Base-T environment, without a hub that "speaks" both.

5.8.1 AT&T T7231 (LanPACER+)

Status—*Not Supported*

These StarLAN cards use an interface similar to the i82586 chip. At one point, Matthijs Melchior (matthijs.n.melchior@att.com) was playing with the 3c507 driver, and almost had something useable working. Haven't heard much since that.

5.9 AT-Lan-Tec / RealTek

5.9.1 AT-Lan-Tec / RealTek Pocket adaptor

Status—*Supported*

This is a generic, low-cost OEM pocket adaptor being sold by AT-Lan-Tec, and (likely) a number of other suppliers. A driver for it is included in the standard kernel. Note that there is substantial information contained in the driver source file `atp.c`. BTW, the adaptor (AEP-100L) has both 10baseT and BNC connections. You can reach AT-Lan-Tec at 1-301-948-7070. Ask for the model that works with Linux, or ask for tech support. Apparently there are various clones of this adaptor being sold here and there throughout Europe as well.

The adaptor is "normal size" for the product class, about 57mm wide, 22mm high tapering to 15mm high at the DB25 connector, and 105mm long (120mm including the BNC socket). It's switchable between the RJ45 and BNC jacks with a small slide switch positioned between the two: a very intuitive design.

Donald performed some power draw measurements, and determined that the average current draw was only about 100mA @ 5V. This power draw is low enough that you could buy or build a cable to take the 5V directly from the keyboard or mouse port available on many laptops. (Bonus points here for using a standardized power connector instead of a proprietary one.)

Note that the device name that you pass to `ifconfig` is *not* `eth0`, but `atp0` for this device.

5.9.2 RealTek 8029

Status—*Supported*

This is a PCI single chip implementation of a NE2000 clone. Various vendors are now selling cards with this chip. See Section 5.26.2 for information on using any of these cards.

5.10 Boca Research

Yes, they make more than just multi-port serial cards.

5.10.1 Boca BEN (PCI, VLB)

Status—*Supported*

These cards are based on AMD's PCnet chips, used in the AT1500 and the like. You can pick up a combo (10BaseT and 10Base2) PCI card for under $70 at the moment.

Prospective buyers should be warned that many users have had endless problems with these cards. Owners of fast Pentium systems have been especially hit. Note that this is not a driver problem, as it hits DOS/Win/NT users as well. Boca's technical support number is (407) 241-8088, and you can also reach them at `75300.2672@compuserve.com`.

Donald did a comparative test with the above Boca PCI card and a similar Allied Telsyn PCnet/PCI implementation, which showed that the problem lies in Boca's implementation of the PCnet/PCI chip. These test results can be accessed on Don's WWW server.

Linux at CESDIS (`http://cesdis.gsfc.nasa.gov/linux/`)

Also, Dave Platt has compared the recommended implementation given on the AMD data sheet with the Boca implementation, and has determined that Boca has left out a substantial number of important filtering capacitors. At the risk of being verbose, here is a quote from Dave, which will allow you to assess if the problem has been addressed yet, given a card for visual inspection.

"I just reviewed Appendix B in the 79c970 data sheet. It recommends a *minimum* of 8 high-frequency bypassing caps (.1 uF multilayer ceramic) around the chip, to keep ground and power bounce from causing unreliable operation. Looking at the card I have here, I see a total of 5 such caps on the entire card—only a couple of them are close enough to the chip to do a decent job of high-frequency bypassing.

If you hold the card with chips facing up, and the PCI pins pointed towards you, the lower-left corner of the '970 has the positioning dimple. The upper-left corner of the chip is the 'analog corner', where the analog power and ground pins are. Appendix B calls these "the most critical pins in the layout of a PCnet-PCI card." There are four analog power pins, and two analog ground pins... all of them are supposed to be connected, and properly bypassed.

On the left side of the chip, the uppermost pin is AVSS1 (analog ground 1). On the top edge, the fourth pin from the left is AVDD3 (analog power 3). The Appendix specifically recommends having a .1 uF bypass cap tied directly to these two pins (*not* going through the common ground plane). On the card I have, there is no such cap—the nearest bypass cap is about half-an-inch away over by the crystal, and is tied to the ground plane.

The Appendix also specifically recommends 'low-frequency bulk capacitors' (by which I assume that they mean multi-uF tantalum or aluminum electrolytics) as well as high-frequency bypass caps. I see only two bulk capacitors (one 10 μF in the AVSS2/AVDD2 filter circuit, and one 4.7 μF up above the chip which also appears to be part of a filter circuit). The Appendix recommends 'at least one low-frequency bulk (e.g., 22 μF) bypass capacitor... connected directly to the power and ground planes.' There is no capacitor on the board which matches this description.

It appears that Boca ignored *several* of AMD's recommendations, regarding the number, size, placement, and wiring of the power supply bypass capacitors."

(Thanks Dave.) Boca is offering a "warranty repair" for affected owners, which involves adding one of the missing capacitors, but it appears that this fix doesn't work 100 percent for most people, although it helps some.

If you are *still* thinking of buying one of these cards, then at least try and get a seven-day unconditional return policy, so that if it doesn't work properly in your system, you can return it.

More general information on the AMD chips can be found in 5.4.1.

More technical information on AMD LANCE based Ethernet cards can be found in 8.7.

5.11 Cabletron

Donald writes: 'Yes, another one of these companies that won't release its programming information. They waited for months before actually confirming that all their information was proprietary, deliberately wasting my time. Avoid their cards like the plague if you can. Also note that some people have phoned Cabletron, and have been told things like 'a D. Becker is working on a driver for linux'—making it sound like I work for them. This is NOT the case.'

If you feel like asking them why they don't want to release their low level programming info so that people can use their cards, write to support@ctron.com. Tell them that you are using Linux, and are disappointed that they don't support open systems. And no, the usual driver development kit they supply is useless. It is just a DOS object file that you are supposed to link against. Which you aren't allowed to even reverse engineer.

5.11.1 E10**, E10**-x, E20**, E20**-x

Status—*Semi-Supported*

These are NEx000 almost-clones that are reported to work with the standard NEx000 drivers, thanks to a ctron-specific check during the probe. If there are any problems, they are unlikely to be fixed, as the programming information is unavailable.

5.11.2 E2100

Status—*Semi-Supported*

Again, there is not much one can do when the programming information is proprietary. The E2100 is a poor design. Whenever it maps its shared memory in during a packet transfer, it maps it into the whole 128K region. That means you can't safely use another interrupt driven, shared-memory device in that region, including another E2100. It will work most of the time, but every once in a while it will bite you. (Yes, this problem can be avoided by turning off interrupts while transferring packets, but that will almost certainly lose clock ticks.) Also, if you mis-program the board, or halt the machine at just the wrong moment, even the reset button won't bring it back. You will have to turn it off and leave it off for about 30 seconds.

Media selection is automatic, but you can override this with the low bits of the dev->mem_end parameter. See Section 10.1.1. Module users can specify an `xcvr=N` value on the `insmod` command line to do the same.

Also, don't confuse the E2100 for a NE2100 clone. The E2100 is a shared memory NatSemi DP8390 design, roughly similar to a brain-damaged WD8013, whereas the NE2100 (and NE1500) use a bus-mastering AMD LANCE design.

There is an E2100 driver included in the standard kernel. However, seeing as programming info isn't available, don't expect bug fixes. Don't use one unless you are already stuck with the card.

If you intend on using this driver as a loadable module you should probably see sections 10.2 and 10.2.1 for module-specific information.

5.12 Cogent

Here is where and how to reach them:

```
Cogent Data Technologies, Inc.
175 West Street, P.O. Box 926
Friday Harbour, WA 98250, USA.

Cogent Sales
15375 S.E. 30th Place, Suite 310
Bellevue, WA 98007, USA.

Technical Support:
Phone (360) 378-2929 between 8am and 5pm PST
Fax (360) 378-2882
Compuserve GO COGENT
Bulletin Board Service (360) 378-5405
Internet: support@cogentdata.com
```

5.12.1 EM100-ISA/EISA

Status—*Semi-Supported*

These cards use the SMC 91c100 chip and may work with the SMC 91c92 driver, but this has yet to be verified.

5.12.2 Cogent eMASTER+, EM100-PCI, EM400, EM960, EM964

Status—*Supported*

These are yet another DEC 21040 implementation that should hopefully work fine with the standard 21040 driver.

The EM400 and the EM964 are four-port cards that use a DEC 21050 bridge and four 21040 chips.

See 5.17.4 for more information on these cards, and the present driver situation.

5.13 Compaq

Compaq isn't really in the business of making Ethernet cards, but a lot of their systems have embedded Ethernet controllers on the motherboard.

5.13.1 Compaq Deskpro / Compaq XL (Embedded AMD Chip)

Status—*Supported*

Machines such as the XL series have an AMD 79c97x PCI chip on the main board that can be used with the standard LANCE driver. But before you can use it, you have to do some trickery to get the PCI BIOS to a place where Linux can see it. Frank Maas was kind enough to provide the details:

"The problem with this Compaq machine however is that the PCI directory is loaded in high memory, at a spot where the Linux kernel can't (won't) reach. Result: the card is never detected nor is it usable (sideline: the mouse won't work either) The workaround (as described thoroughly in http://www-c724.uibk.ac.at/XL/) is to load MS-DOS, launch a little driver Compaq wrote and then load the Linux kernel using LOADLIN.EXE. Ok, I'll give you time to say "yuck, yuck," but for now this is the only working solution I know of. The little driver simply moves the PCI directory to a place where it is normally stored (and where Linux can find it)."

More general information on the AMD chips can be found in Section 5.4.1.

5.14 Danpex

5.14.1 Danpex EN9400

Status—*Supported*

Yet another card based on the DEC 21040 chip, reported to work fine, and at a relatively cheap price.

See Section 5.17.4 for more information on these cards, and the present driver situation.

5.15 D-Link

Some people have had difficulty in finding vendors that carry D-link stuff. This should help.

```
(714) 455-1688   in the US
(081) 203-9900   in the UK
(416) 828-0260   in Canada
(02) 916-1600    in Taiwan
```

5.15.1 DE-100, DE-200, DE-220-T, DE-250

Status—*Supported*

Some of the early D-Link cards didn't have the `0x57` PROM signature, but the NE2000 driver knows about them. For the software configurable cards, you can get the config program from `www.dlink.com`. The DE2** cards were the most widely reported as having the spurious transfer address mismatch errors with early versions of linux. Note that there are also cards from Digital (DEC) that are also named DE100 and DE200, but the similarity stops there.

5.15.2 DE-520

Status—*Supported*

This is a PCI card using the PCI version of AMD's LANCE chip. DMA selection and chip numbering information can be found in Section 5.4.1.

More technical information on AMD LANCE based Ethernet cards can be found in Section 8.7.

5.15.3 DE-530

Status—*Supported*

This is a generic DEC 21040 PCI chip implementation, and is reported to work with the generic 21040 Tulip driver. See 5.17.4 for more information on these cards, and the present driver situation.

5.15.4 DE-600

Status—*Supported*

Laptop users and other folk who might want a quick way to put their computer onto the Ethernet may want to use this. The driver is included with the default kernel source tree. Bjorn Ekwall `bj0rn@blox.se` wrote the driver. Expect about 180kb/s transfer speed from this via the parallel port. You should read the README.DLINK file in the kernel source tree.

Note that the device name that you pass to `ifconfig` is now `eth0` and not the previously used `dl0`.

If your parallel port is not at the standard `0x378` then you will have to recompile. Bjorn writes: "Since the DE-620 driver tries to sqeeze the last microsecond from the loops, I made the IRQ and port address constants instead of variables. This makes for a usable speed, but it also means that you can't change these assignements from e.g. LILO; you have to recompile.... " Also note that some laptops implement the on-board parallel port at `0x3bc` which is where the parallel ports on monochrome cards are.

5.15.5 DE-620

Status—*Supported*

Same as the DE-600, only with two output formats. Bjorn has written a driver for this model, for kernel versions 1.1 and above. See the above information on the DE-600.

5.15.6 DE-650

Status—*Semi-Supported*

Some people have been using this PCMCIA card for some time now with their notebooks. It is a basic 8390 design, much like a NE2000. The LinkSys PCMCIA card and the IC-Card Ethernet (available from Midwest Micro) are supposedly DE-650 clones as well. Note that at present, this driver is not part of the standard kernel, and so you will have to do some patching.

See 9.3 in this document, and if you can, have a look at:

Don's PCMCIA Stuff (`http://cesdis.gsfc.nasa.gov/linux/pcmcia.html`)

5.16 DFI

5.16.1 DFINET-300 and DFINET-400

Status—*Supported*

These cards are now detected (as of 0.99pl15) thanks to Eberhard Moenkeberg `emoenke@gwdg.de` who noted that they use "DFI" in the first 3 bytes of the PROM, instead of using `0x57` in bytes 14 and 15, which is what all the NE1000 and NE2000 cards use. (The 300 is an 8 bit pseudo NE1000 clone, and the 400 is a pseudo NE2000 clone.)

5.17 Digital / DEC

5.17.1 DEPCA, DE100/1, DE200/1/2, DE210, DE422

Status—*Supported*

As of linux v1.0, there is a driver included as standard for these cards. It was written by David C. Davies. There is documentation included in the source file `depca.c`, which includes info on how to use more than one of these cards in a machine. Note that the DE422 is an EISA card. These cards are all based on the AMD LANCE chip. See 5.4.1 for more info. A maximum of two of the ISA cards can be used, because they can only be set for `0x300` and `0x200` base I/O address. If you are intending to do this, please read the notes in the driver source file `depca.c` in the standard kernel source tree.

This driver will also work on Alpha CPU based machines, and there are various ioctl()s that the user can play with.

5.17.2 Digital EtherWorks 3 (DE203, DE204, DE205)

Status—*Supported*

Included into kernels v1.1.62 and above is this driver, also by David C. Davies of DEC. These cards use a proprietary chip from DEC, as opposed to the LANCE chip used in the earlier cards like the DE200. These cards support both shared memory or programmed I/O, although you take about a 50% performance hit if you use PIO mode. The shared memory size can be set to 2kB, 32kB or 64kB, but only 2 and 32 have been tested with this driver. David says that the performance is virtually identical between the 2kB and 32kB mode. There is more information (including using the driver as a loadable module) at the top of the driver file `ewrk3.c` and also in `README.ewrk3`. Both of these files come with the standard kernel distribution.

The standard driver has a number of interesting ioctl() calls that can be used to get or clear packet statistics, read/write the EEPROM, change the hardware address, and the like. Hackers can see the source code for more info on that one.

David has also written a configuration utility for this card (along the lines of the DOS program `NICSETUP.EXE`) along with other tools. These can be found on `sunsite.unc.edu` in the directory `/pub/Linux/system/Network/management` – look for the file `ewrk3tools-X.XX.tar.gz`.

The next release of this driver (v0.40) will have Alpha CPU support like `depca.c` does and is available from David now if you require it.

5.17.3 DE425 (EISA), DE434, DE435, DE500

Status—*Supported*

These cards are based on the 21040 chip mentioned below. Included into kernels v1.1.86 and above is this driver, also by David C. Davies of DEC. It sure is nice to have support from someone on the inside. The DE500 uses the newer 21140 chip to provide 10/100Mbs Ethernet connections. Have a read of the 21040 section below for extra information.

Note that as of 1.1.91, David has added a compile time option that will allow non-DEC cards to work with this driver. Have a look at `README.de4x5` for details.

All the Digital cards will auto probe for their media (except, temporarily, the DE500 due to a patent issue).

This driver is also Alpha CPU ready and supports being loaded as a module. Users can access the driver internals through ioctl() calls—see the "ewrk3" tools and the `de4x5.c` sources for information about how to do this.

5.17.4 DEC 21040, 21041, 2114x, Tulip

Status—*Supported*

The DEC 21040 is a bus-mastering, single chip Ethernet solution from Digital, similar to AMD's PCnet chip. The 21040 is specifically designed for the PCI bus architecture. SMC's new EtherPower PCI card uses this chip.

You have a choice of two drivers for cards based on this chip. There is the DE425 driver discussed above, and the generic 21040 driver that Donald has written.

Warning: Even though your card may be based upon this chip, *the drivers may not work for you.* David C. Davies writes:

"There are no guarantees that either 'tulip.c' OR 'de4x5.c' will run any DC2114x based card other than those they've been written to support. Why? You ask. Because there is a register, the General Purpose Register (CSR12) that (1) in the DC21140A is programmable by each vendor and they all do it differently (2) in the DC21142/3 this is now an SIA control register (a la DC21041). The only small ray of hope is that we can decode the SROM to help set up the driver. However, this is not a guaranteed solution since some vendors (e.g. SMC 9332 card) don't follow the Digital Semiconductor recommended SROM programming format."

In non-technical terms, this means that if you aren't sure that an unknown card with a DC2114x chip will work with the Linux driver(s), then make sure you can return the card to the place of purchase before you pay for it.

The updated 21041 chip is also found in place of the 21040 on most of the later SMC EtherPower cards. The 21140 is for supporting 100Base-x and works with the Linux drivers for the 21040 chip. To use David's DE4X5 driver with non-DEC cards, have a look at `README.de4x5` for details.

Donald has used SMC EtherPower-10/100 cards to develop the "Tulip" driver. Note that the driver that is in the standard kernel tree at the moment is not the most up-to-date version. If you are having trouble with this driver, you should get the newest version from Donald's FTP or WWW site.

Tulip Driver (`http://cesdis.gsfc.nasa.gov/linux/drivers/tulip.html`)

The above URL also contains a (non-exhaustive) list of various cards and vendors that use the 21040 chip.

Also note that the Tulip driver is still considered an *alpha* driver (see 3.1) at the moment, and should be treated as such. To use it, you will have to edit `arch/i386/config.in` and uncomment the line for `CONFIG_DEC_ELCP` support.

Donald has even set up a mailing list for Tulip driver support announcements, etc. To join it just type:

```
echo subscribe | /bin/mail linux-tulip-request@cesdis.gsfc.nasa.gov
```

5.18 Farallon

Farallon sells EtherWave adaptors and transceivers. This device allows multiple 10baseT devices to be daisy-chained.

5.18.1 Farallon Etherwave

Status—*Supported*

This is reported to be a 3c509 clone that includes the EtherWave transceiver. People have used these successfully with Linux and the present 3c509 driver. They are too expensive for general use, but are a great option for special cases. Hublet prices start at $125, and Etherwave adds $75–$100 to the price of the board—worth it if you have pulled one wire too few, but not if you are two network drops short.

5.19 Hewlett Packard

The 272** cards use programmed I/O, similar to the NE*000 boards, but the data transfer port can be "turned off" when you aren't accessing it, avoiding problems with auto-probing drivers.

Thanks to Glenn Talbott for helping clean up the confusion in this section regarding the version numbers of the HP hardware.

5.19.1 27245A

Status—*Supported*

8-bit, 8390 based, 10BaseT, not recommended for all of the usual 8-bit reasons. Redesigned a couple years back to be highly integrated which caused some changes in initialization timing that only affected testing programs, not LAN drivers. (The new card is not ready as soon after switching into and out of loopback mode.)

If you intend on using this driver as a loadable module you should probably see sections 10.2 and 10.2.1 for module-specific information.

5.19.2 HP PC Lan+ (27247, 27252A)

Status—*Supported*

The HP PC Lan+ is different to the standard HP PC Lan card. This driver was added to the list of drivers in the standard kernel during the v1.1.x development cycle. It can be operated in either a PIO mode like a NE2000, or a shared memory mode like a WD8013.

The 47B is a 16-bit 8390 based 10BaseT w/AUI, and the 52A is a 16-bit 8390 based ThinLAN w/AUI. These cards have 32K on-board RAM for Tx/Rx packet buffering instead of the usual 16KB, and they both offer LAN connector auto sense.

If you intend on using this driver as a loadable module you should probably see sections 10.2 and 10.2.1 for module-specific information.

5.19.3 HP-J2405A

Status—*Supported*

These are lower priced, and slightly faster, than the 27247/27252A, but are missing some features, such as AUI, ThinLAN connectivity, and boot PROM socket. This is a fairly generic LANCE design, but a minor design decision makes it incompatible with a generic "NE2100" driver. Special support for it (including reading the DMA channel from the board) is included thanks to information provided by HP's Glenn Talbott.

More technical information on LANCE based cards can be found in Section 8.7

5.19.4 HP-Vectra On Board Ethernet

Status—*Supported*

The HP-Vectra has an AMD PCnet chip on the motherboard. Earlier kernel versions would detect it as the HP-J2405A, but that would fail, as the Vectra doesn't report the IRQ and DMA channel like the J2405A. Get a kernel newer than v1.1.53 to avoid this problem.

DMA selection and chip numbering information can be found in Section 5.4.1.

More technical information on LANCE based cards can be found in Section 8.7

5.19.5 HP 10/100 VG Any LAN Cards (27248B, J2573, J2577, J2585)

Status—*Supported*

As of early 1.3.x kernels, this driver was made available by Jaroslav Kysela, (perex@pf.jcu.cz). Due to the newness of the driver and the relatively small number of VG cards in use, feedback on this driver has been low.

Donald has also written a driver for these cards. Unlike the above, it is not presently in the standard kernel source tree. Check out the following URL for more information on Donald's 100VG work.

Donald's 100VG Page (`http://cesdis.gsfc.nasa.gov/linux/drivers/100vg.html`)

5.20 International Business Machines (IBM)

5.20.1 IBM Thinkpad 300

Status—*Supported*

This is compatible with the Intel based Zenith Z-note. See Section 5.37.1 for more info.

Supposedly this site has a comprehensive database of useful stuff for newer versions of the Thinkpad. I haven't checked it out myself yet.

Thinkpad-info (`http://peipa.essex.ac.uk/html/linux-thinkpad.html`)

For those without a WWW browser handy, try `peipa.essex.ac.uk:/pub/tp750/`

5.20.2 IBM Credit Card Adaptor for Ethernet

Status—*Semi-Supported*

People have been using this PCMCIA card with Linux as well. Similar points apply, those being that you need a supported PCMCIA chipset on your notebook, and that you will have to patch the PCMCIA support into the standard kernel.

See Section 9.3 in this document, and if you can, have a look at http://cesdis.gsfc.nasa.gov/linux/pcmcia.html.

5.20.3 IBM Token Ring

Status—*Semi-Supported*

To support token ring requires more than only writing a device driver, it also requires writing the source routing routines for token ring. It is the source routing that would be the most time consuming to write.

Peter De Schrijver has been spending some time on Token Ring lately. and has worked with IBM ISA and MCA token ring cards.

The present token ring code has been included into the first of the 1.3.x series kernels.

Peter says that it was originally tested on an MCA 16/4 Megabit Token Ring board, but it should work with other Tropic based boards.

5.21 ICL Ethernet Cards

5.21.1 ICL EtherTeam 16i/32

Status—*Supported*

Mika Kuoppala (miku@pupu.elt.icl.fi) wrote this driver, and it was included into early 1.3.4x kernels. It uses the Fujitsu MB86965 chip that is also used on the AT1700 cards.

5.22 Intel Ethernet Cards

5.22.1 Ether Express

Status—*Supported*

This card uses the Intel i82586. (Surprise, huh?) Earlier versions of this driver (in v1.2 kernels) were classed as alpha-test, as it didn't work well for most people. The driver in the v2.0 kernel seems to work much better for those who have tried it. The comments at the top of the driver source list some of the problems associated with these cards.

There is also some technical information available on the i82586 in 8.5 and also in the source code for the driver `eexpress.c`. Don't be afraid to read it.

5.22.2 Ether Express PRO/10

Status—*Supported*

Bao Chau Ha has written a driver for these cards that has been included into early 1.3.x kernels. It may also work with some of the Compaq built-in Ethernet systems that are based on the i82595 chip.

5.22.3 Ether Express PRO/10 PCI (EISA)

Status—*Semi-Supported*

John Stalba (stalba@ultranet.com) has written a driver for the PCI version. These cards the PLX9036 PCI interface chip with the Intel i82596 LAN controller chip. If your card has the i82557 chip, then you *don't* have this card, but rather the "+" version discussed next, and hence want the EEPro100 driver instead.

You can get the alpha driver for the PRO/10 PCI card, along with instructions on how to use it at:

EEPro10 Driver (`http://www.ultranet.com/ stalba/eep10pci.html`)

If you have the EISA card, you will probably have to hack the driver a bit to account for the different (PCI vs. EISA) detection mechanisms that are used in each case.

5.22.4 Ether Express PRO/10+

Status—*Supported*

A slight change in name (from the above) but a different design. This card uses the i82557 chip, and hence uses the EEPRO100 driver described below.

5.22.5 Ether Express PRO 10/100B

Status—*Supported*

A driver for this card is available on Donald's WWW and FTP site for v2.0 kernels. It is not included in the v2.0 kernel source tree, so you have to get it separately. Note that this driver will *not* work with the older 100A cards.

Drivers-Page (`http://cesdis.gsfc.nasa.gov/linux/drivers/`)

Apparently Donald had to sign a non-disclosure agreement that stated he could actually disclose the driver source code. How is that for silliness on Intel's part?

This driver will be included into the v2.1 source tree sometime in the future. There is also a mailing list for driver announcements. To join it, just do:

```
echo subscribe | /bin/mail linux-eepro100-request@cesdis.gsfc.nasa.gov
```

5.23 LinkSys

LinkSys make a handful of different NE2000 clones, some straight ISA cards, some ISA plug-and-play and even some NE2000 PCI clones based on one of the supported NE2000 PCI chip sets. There are too many models to list here.

5.23.1 LinkSys Etherfast 10/100 Cards.

Beware with these cards—apparently some use the DEC chipset, and some use a proprietary PNIC chipset. The drivers for the DEC chips will *not* work with the PNIC cards. Thanks to Blake Wright for reporting this useful bit of information.

5.23.2 LinkSys Pocket Ethernet Adapter Plus (PEAEPP)

Status—*Supported*

This is supposedly a DE-620 clone, and is reported to work well with that driver. See Section 5.15.5 for more information.

5.23.3 LinkSys PCMCIA Adaptor

Status—*Supported*

This is supposed to be a re-badged DE-650. See Section 5.15.6 for more information.

5.24 Microdyne

5.24.1 Microdyne Exos 205T

Status—*Semi-Supported*

Another i82586 based card. Dirk Niggemann `dabnl00@hermes.cam.ac.uk` has written a driver that he classes as "pre-alpha" that he would like people to test. Mail him for more details.

5.25 Mylex

Mylex can be reached at the following numbers, in case anyone wants to ask them anything.

```
MYLEX CORPORATION, Fremont
Sales:  800-77-MYLEX, (510) 796-6100
FAX:    (510) 745-8016.
```

They also have a web site: *Mylex WWW Site* (`http://www.mylex.com`)

5.25.1 Mylex LNE390A, LNE390B

Status—*Semi-Supported*

These are fairly old EISA cards that make use of a shared memory implementation similar to the WD80x3. If you are interested in testing a driver for this card, contact me.

5.25.2 Mylex LNP101

Status—*Supported*

This is a PCI card that is based on DEC's 21040 chip. It is selectable between 10BaseT, 10Base2 and 10Base5 output. The LNP101 card has been verified to work with the generic 21040 driver.

See the section on the 21040 chip (5.17.4) for more information.

5.25.3 Mylex LNP104

Status—*Semi-Supported*

The LNP104 uses the DEC 21050 chip to deliver *four* independent 10BaseT ports. It should work with recent 21040 drivers that know how to share IRQs, but nobody has reported trying it yet (that I am aware of).

5.26 Novell Ethernet, NExxxx and associated clones.

The prefix "NE" came from Novell Ethernet. Novell followed the cheapest National Semiconductor data book design and sold the manufacturing rights to Eagle, just to get reasonably priced Ethercards into the market. (The now-ubiquitous NE2000 card.)

5.26.1 NE1000, NE2000

Status—*Supported*

NOTE: If you are using a kernel that is older than v1.2.9, it is *strongly* recommended that you upgrade to a newer version. There was an important bug fix made to the NE driver in 1.2.7, and another important bug fix made to the upper layers (`dev.c`) in 1.2.9. Both of these bugs can cause a NE2000 card to hang your computer.

The NE2000 is now a generic name for a bare-bones design around the National Semiconductor 8390 chip. They use programmed I/O rather than shared memory, leading to easier installation but slightly lower performance and a few problems. Again, the savings of using an 8-bit NE1000 over the NE2000 are only warranted if you expect light use. Some problems can arise with poor NE2000 clones. You should see sections 3.4 and 3.3

Some recently introduced NE2000 clones use the National Semiconductor "AT/LANTic" 83905 chip, which offers a shared memory mode similar to the WD8013 and EEPROM software configuration. The shared memory mode will offer less CPU usage (i.e. more efficient) than the programmed I/O mode.

In general it is not a good idea to put a NE2000 clone at I/O address `0x300` because nearly *every* device driver probes there at boot. Some poor NE2000 clones don't take kindly to being prodded in the wrong areas, and will respond by locking your machine. Also `0x320` is bad because SCSI drivers probe into `0x330`.

Donald has written a NE2000 diagnostic program (`ne2k.c`) for all NE2000 cards. See Section 7.2 for more information.

If you intend on using this driver as a loadable module you should probably see sections 10.2 and 10.2.1 for module-specific information.

5.26.2 NE2000-PCI (RealTek/Winbond/Compex)

Status—*Supported*

Yes, believe it or not, people are making PCI cards based on the ten-year-old interface design of the NE2000. At the moment nearly all of these cards are based on the RealTek 8029 chip, and Linux kernel v2.0 has support to automatically detect these cards at boot and use them.

Note that you have to say "Y" to the "Other ISA cards" option when running `make config` as you are actually using the same NE2000 driver as the ISA cards use. (That should also give you a hint that these cards aren't anywhere as intelligent as, say, a DEC 21040 card.)

Recently, two other PCI NE2000 clones have appeared, those being cards based upon the Winbond 89C940 chip and the Compex ReadyLink-2000 cards. The NE2000 driver in v2.0.x doesn't know about the PCI ID's of these cards, and hence won't detect them without an explicit I/O address being given at boot. (See the FAQ section on NE2000 cards for more details on dealing with an undetected PCI card.) Support for these additional cards has already been written and will appear in a v2.1.x kernel sometime in the near future, so that they will then be auto detected as well.

If you have a NE2000 PCI card that is *not* a RealTek, Winbond, or Compex ReadyLink, please contact the maintainer of the NE2000 driver as listed in `/usr/src/linux/MAINTAINERS`. That way the ID of your card can also be added to the driver.

If you are using the driver in v2.0 as a module, you will have to supply the I/O address of the card (obtained from doing a `cat /proc/pci`) when loading the module. Note that this will not be necessary for future v2.1 kernels.

5.26.3 NE-10/100

Status—*Not Supported*

These are ISA 100Mbps cards based on the National Semiconductor DP83800 and DP83840 chips. There is currently no driver support, nor is anyone reported that they are working on a driver.

5.26.4 NE1500, NE2100

Status—*Supported*

These cards use the original 7990 LANCE chip from AMD and are supported using the Linux LANCE driver. Newer NE2100 clones use the updated PCnet/ISA chip from AMD.

Some earlier versions of the LANCE driver had problems with getting the IRQ line via auto-IRQ from the original Novell and Eagle 7990 cards. Hopefully this is now fixed. If not, then specify the IRQ via LILO, and let us know that it still has problems.

DMA selection and chip numbering information can be found in Section 5.4.1.

More technical information on LANCE based cards can be found in Section 8.7

5.26.5 NE3200

Status—*Not Supported*

This card uses a lowly 8MHz 80186, and hence you are better off using a cheap NE2000 clone. Even if a driver was available, the NE2000 card would most likely be faster.

5.26.6 NE5500

Status—*Supported*

These are just AMD PCnet-PCI cards ('970A) chips. More information on LANCE and PCnet based cards can be found in Section 5.4.1.

5.27 Proteon

5.27.1 Proteon P1370-EA

Status—*Supported*

Apparently this is a NE2000 clone and works fine with Linux.

5.27.2 Proteon P1670-EA

Status—*Supported*

This is yet another PCI card that is based on DEC's Tulip chip. It has been reported to work fine with Linux. See the section on the 21040 chip (5.17.4) for more driver information.

5.28 Pure Data

5.28.1 PDUC8028, PDI8023

Status—*Supported*

The PureData PDUC8028 and PDI8023 series of cards are reported to work, thanks to special probe code contributed by Mike Jagdis `jaggy@purplet.demon.co.uk`. The support is integrated with the WD driver.

5.29 Racal Interlan

Racal Interlan can be reached via WWW at `www.interlan.com`. I believe they were also known as MiCom Interlan at one point in the past.

5.29.1 ES3210

Status—*Semi-Supported*

This is an EISA 8390 based, shared memory card. An experimental driver for v2.0 is available (from me, pg). It is reported to work fine, but the EISA IRQ and shared memory address detection appears not to work with (at least) the early revision cards. In that case, you have to supply them at boot; e.g. `ether=5,0,0xd0000,eth0` for IRQ 5 and shared memory at `0xd0000`. The I/O base is automatically detected and hence a value of zero should be used.

This driver will appear in the v2.1 kernels at some time in the near future.

5.29.2 NI5010

Status—*Semi-Supported*

This driver, by Jan-Pascal van Best (jvbest@qv3pluto.leidenuniv.nl) supports the old 8-bit MiCom-Interlan cards. You can get the driver from:

NI5010 Driver `(http://qv3pluto.leidenuniv.nl/jvbest/ni5010/ni5010.html)`

Jan-Pascal has got very little feedback on this driver and would appreciate it if you dropped him a note saying if it worked or not.

5.29.3 NI5210

Status—*Semi-Supported*

Michael Hipp has written a driver for this card. It is included in the standard kernel as an "alpha" driver. Michael would like to hear feedback from users who have this card. See 3.1 for important information on using alpha-test Ethernet drivers with Linux.

Michael says that "the internal sysbus seems to be slow. So we often lose packets because of overruns while receiving from a fast remote host."

This card also uses one of the Intel chips. See 8.5 for more technical information.

5.29.4 NI6510 (not EB)

Status—*Semi-Supported*

There is also a driver for the LANCE based NI6510, and it is also written by Michael Hipp. Again, it is also an "alpha" driver. For some reason, this card is not compatible with the generic LANCE driver. See 3.1 for important information on using alpha-test ethernet drivers with Linux.

5.29.5 EtherBlaster (aka NI6510EB)

Status—*Supported*

As of kernel 1.3.23, the generic LANCE driver had a check added to it for the `0x52, 0x44` NI6510EB specific signature. Others have reported that this signature is not the same for all NI6510EB cards however, which will cause the lance driver to not detect your card. If this happens to you, you can change the probe (at about line 322 in `lance.c`) to printk() out what the values are for your card and then use them instead of the `0x52, 0x44` defaults.

The cards should probably be run in "high-performance" mode and not in the NI6510 compatible mode when using the LANCE driver.

5.30 Sager

5.30.1 Sager NP943

Status—*Semi-Supported*

This is a 3c501 clone, with a different S.A. PROM prefix. I assume it is equally as brain dead as the original 3c501 as well. Kernels 1.1.53 and up check for the NP943 I.D. and then just treat it as a 3c501 after that. See 5.1.1 for all the reasons as to why you really don't want to use one of these cards.

5.31 Schneider & Koch

5.31.1 SK G16

Status—*Supported*

This driver was included into the v1.1 kernels, and it was written by P.J.D. Weichmann and S.W.S. Bern. It appears that the SK G16 is similar to the NI6510, in that it is based on the first edition LANCE chip (the 7990). Once again, it appears as though this card won't work with the generic LANCE driver.

5.32 SEEQ

5.32.1 SEEQ 8005

Status—*Supported*

This driver was included into early 1.3.x kernels, and was written by Hamish Coleman. There is little information about the card included in the driver, and hence little information to be put here. If you have a question, you are probably best off e-mailing hamish@zot.apana.org.au

5.33 SMC (Standard Microsystems Corp.)

Please see 5.35 for information on SMC cards. (SMC bought out Western Digital's network card section quite a while ago.)

5.34 Thomas Conrad

5.34.1 Thomas Conrad TC-5048

This is yet another PCI card that is based on DEC's 21040 chip.

See the section on the 21040 chip (5.17.4) for more information.

5.35 Western Digital / SMC

The Ethernet part of Western Digital has been bought out by SMC. One common mistake people make is that the relatively new SMC Elite Ultra is the same as the older SMC Elite16 models—this is not the case. They have separate drivers.

Here is how to contact SMC (not that you should need to.)

SMC / Standard Microsystems Corp., 80 Arkay Drive, Hauppage, New York, 11788, USA.

Technical Support via phone:

```
800-992-4762 (USA)
800-433-5345 (Canada)
516-435-6250 (Other Countries)
```

Literature requests:

```
800-SMC-4-YOU (USA)
800-833-4-SMC (Canada)
516-435-6255  (Other Countries)
```

Technical Support via E-mail:

```
techsupt@ccmail.west.smc.com
```

FTP Site:

```
ftp.smc.com
```

WWW Site:

```
http://www.smc.com
```

5.35.1 WD8003, SMC Elite

Status—*Supported*

These are the 8-bit versions of the card. The 8-bit, 8003 is slightly less expensive, but only worth the savings for light use. Note that some of the non-EEPROM cards (clones with jumpers, or old WD8003 cards) don't have a way to report the IRQ line used. In this case, auto-IRQ is used, and if that fails, the driver silently assings IRQ 5. You can get the SMC setup and driver disks from SMC's FTP site. Note that some of the newer SMC "SuperDisk" programs will fail to detect the real old EEPROM-less cards. The file `SMCDSK46.EXE` seems to be a good all-round choice. Also the jumper settings for all their cards are in an ASCII text file in the aforementioned archive. The latest (greatest?) version can be obtained from `ftp.smc.com`.

As these are basically the same as their 16-bit counterparts (WD8013 / SMC Elite16), you should see the next section for more information.

5.35.2 WD8013, SMC Elite16

Status—*Supported*

Over the years the design has added more registers and an EEPROM. (The first WD8003 cards appeared about ten years ago.) Clones usually go by the "8013" name, and usually use a non-EEPROM (jumpered) design. Late-model SMC cards have the SMC 83c690 chip instead of the original National Semiconductor DP8390 found on earlier cards. The shared memory design makes the cards a bit faster than PIO cards, especially with larger packets. More importantly, from the driver's point of view, it avoids a few bugs in the programmed I/O mode of the 8390, allows safe, multi-threaded access to the packet buffer, and it doesn't have a programmed I/O data register that hangs your machine during warm-boot probes.

Non-EEPROM cards that can't just read the selected IRQ will attempt auto-IRQ, and if that fails, they will silently assign IRQ 10. (8-bit versions will assign IRQ 5)

Cards with a non-standard amount of memory on-board can have the memory size specified at boot (or at '`insmod` time' if using modules). The standard memory size is 8kB for an 8-bit card and 16kB for a 16-bit card. For example, the older WD8003EBT cards could be jumpered for 32kB memory. To make full use of that RAM, you would use something like (for I/O=0x280 and IRQ 9):

```
LILO: linux ether=9,0x280,0xd0000,0xd8000,eth0
```

Also see Section 3.5 for some of the more common problems and frequently asked questions that pop up often.

If you intend on using this driver as a loadable module you should probably see sections 10.2 and 10.2.1 for module-specific information.

5.35.3 SMC Elite Ultra

Status—*Supported*

This Ethercard is based on a new chip from SMC, the 83c790, which has a few new features. While it has a mode that is similar to the older SMC Ethercards, it's not entirely compatible with the old WD80*3 drivers. However, in this mode, it shares most of its code with the other 8390 drivers, while operating slightly faster than a WD8013 clone.

Since part of the Ultra looks like an 8013, the Ultra probe is supposed to find an Ultra before the WD8013 probe has a chance to mistakenly identify it.

Donald mentioned that it is possible to write a separate driver for the Ultra's 'Altego' mode which allows chaining transmits at the cost of inefficient use of receive buffers, but that will probably not happen.

Bus-Master SCSI host adaptor users take note: In the manual that ships with Interactive UNIX, it mentions that a bug in the SMC Ultra will cause data corruption with SCSI disks being run from an AHA-154X host adaptor. This will probably bite AHA-154X compatible cards, such as the BusLogic boards, and the AMI-FastDisk SCSI host adaptors as well.

SMC has acknowledged that the problem occurs with Interactive and with older Windows NT drivers. It is due to a hardware conflict with early revisions of the card that can be worked around in the driver design. The current Ultra driver protects against this by only enabling the shared memory during data transfers with the card. Make sure that your kernel version is at least 1.1.84, or that the driver version reported at boot is at least `SMC-ultra.c:v1.12` otherwise you are vulnerable.

If you intend on using this driver as a loadable module you should probably see sections 10.2 and 10.2.1 for module-specific information.

5.35.4 SMC Elite Ultra32 EISA

Status—*Semi-Supported*

This EISA card shares a lot in common with its ISA counterpart. A working (and stable) driver is available for v2.0 kernels upon request from the author of this document. Thanks go to Leonard Zubkoff for purchasing some of these cards so that Leonard and myself could add linux support for them. The driver will be included with a future release of the v2.1.x Linux kernel as well.

5.35.5 SMC EtherEZ (8416)

Status—*Supported*

This card uses SMC's 83c795 chip and supports the Plug 'n Play specification. It also has an SMC Ultra compatible mode, which allows it to be used with the Linux Ultra driver. Be sure to set your card for this compatibility mode. See the above information for notes on the Ultra driver.

For v1.2 kernels, the card had to be configured for shared memory operation. However v2.0 kernels can use the card in shared memory or programmed I/O mode. Shared memory mode will be slightly faster, and use considerably less CPU resources as well.

Note that the EtherEZ specific checks were added to the SMC Ultra driver in 1.1.84, and hence earlier kernel versions will not detect or handle these cards correctly.

5.35.6 SMC EtherPower PCI (8432)

Status—*Supported*

These cards are a basic DEC 21040 implementation; i.e., one big chip and a couple of transceivers. Donald has used one of these cards for his development of the generic 21040 driver (aka `tulip.c`). Thanks to Duke Kamstra, once again, for supplying a card to do development on.

Some of the later revisons of this card use the newer DEC 21041 chip, which may cause problems with older versions of the Tulip driver. If you have problems, make sure that you are using the latest driver release, which may not yet be included in the current kernel source tree.

See Section 5.17.4 for more details on using one of these cards, and the current status of the driver.

Apparently, the latest revision of the card, the EtherPower-II, uses the 9432 chip. It is unclear at the moment if this one will work with the present driver. As always, if unsure, check that you can return the card if it doesn't work with the Linux driver before paying for the card.

5.35.7 SMC 3008

Status—*Not Supported*

These 8-bit cards are based on the Fujitsu MB86950, which is an ancient version of the MB86965 used in the Linux AT1700 driver. Russ says that you could probably hack up a driver by looking at the `at1700.c` code and his DOS packet driver for the Tiara card (`tiara.asm`). They are not very common.

5.35.8 SMC 3016

Status—*Not Supported*

These are 16-bit, I/O mapped 8390 cards, much similar to a generic NE2000 card. If you can get the specifications from SMC, then porting the NE2000 driver would probably be quite easy. They are not very common.

5.35.9 SMC-9000 / SMC 91c92/4

Status—*Supported*

The SMC9000 is a VLB card based on the 91c92 chip. The 91c92 appears on a few other brand cards as well, but is fairly uncommon. Erik Stahlman (erik@vt.edu) has written this driver which is in v2.0 kernels, but not in the older v1.2 kernels. You may be able to drop the driver into a v1.2 kernel source tree with minimal difficulty.

5.35.10 SMC 91c100

Status—*Semi-Supported*

The SMC 91c92 driver is supposed to work for cards based on this 100Base-T chip, but at the moment this is unverified.

5.36 Xircom

For the longest time, Xircom wouldn't release the programming information required to write a driver, unless you signed your life away. Apparently enough Linux users have pestered them for driver support. (They claim to support all popular networking operating systems.) So they have changed their policy to allow documentation to be released without having to sign a non-disclosure agreement, and apparently they will release the source code to the SCO driver as well. If you want to verify that this is the case, you can reach Xircom at 1-800-874-7875, 1-800-438-4526 or +1-818-878-7600.

However, at the moment nobody has rushed forth offering to write any drivers, so all their products are still unsupported.

5.36.1 PE1, PE2, PE3-10B*

Status—*Not Supported*

Not to get your hopes up, but if you have one of these parallel port adaptors, you may be able to use it in the DOS emulator with the Xircom-supplied DOS drivers. You will have to allow DOSEMU access to your parallel port, and will probably have to play with SIG (DOSEMU's Silly Interrupt Generator).

5.37 Zenith

5.37.1 Z-Note

Status—*Supported*

The built-in Z-Note network adaptor is based on the Intel i82593 using *two* DMA channels. There is an (alpha?) driver available in the present kernel version. As with all notebook and pocket adaptors, it is under the 'Pocket and portable adaptors' section when running `make config`. See Section 8.5 for more technical information. Also note that the IBM ThinkPad 300 is compatible with the Z-Note.

5.38 Znyx

5.38.1 Znyx ZX342 (DEC 21040 based)

Status—*Supported*

You have a choice of *two* drivers for cards based on this chip. There is the DE425 driver written by David, and the generic 21040 driver that Donald has written.

Note that as of 1.1.91, David has added a compile time option that may allow non-DEC cards (such as the Znyx cards) to work with this driver. Have a look at `README.de4x5` for details.

See Section 5.17.4 for more information on these cards, and the present driver situation.

5.39 Identifying an Unknown Card

Okay, so your uncle's cousin's neighbor's friend had a brother who found an old ISA Ethernet card in the AT case he was using as a cage for his son's pet hamster. Somehow, you ended up with the card and want to try and use it with Linux, but nobody has a clue what the card is and there isn't any documentation.

First of all, look for any obvious model numbers that might give a clue. Any model number that contains 2000 will most likely be a NE2000 clone. Any cards with 8003 or 8013 on them somewhere will be Western Digital WD80x3 cards or SMC Elite cards or clones of them.

5.39.1 Identifying the Network Interface Controller

Look for the biggest chip on the card. This will be the network controller (NIC) itself, and most can be identified by the part number. If you know which NIC is on the card, the following might be able to help you figure out what card it is.

Probably still the most common NIC is the National Semiconductor DP8390 aka NS32490 aka DP83901 aka DP83902 aka DP83905 aka DP83907. And those are just the ones made by National. Other companies such as Winbond and UMC make DP8390 and DP83905 clone parts, such as the Winbond 89c904 (DP83905 clone) and the UMC 9090. If the card has some form of 8390 on it, then chances are it is a NE1000 or NE2000 clone card. The second most common 8390 based card are WD80x3 cards and clones. Cards with a DP83905 can be configured to be an NE2000 *or* a WD8013. Never versions of the genuine WD80x3 and SMC Elite cards have an 83c690 in place of the original DP8390. The SMC Ultra cards have an 83c790, and use a slightly different driver than the WD80x3 cards. The SMC EtherEZ cards have an 83c795, and use the same driver as the SMC Ultra. All BNC cards based on some sort of 8390 or 8390 clone will usually have an 8392 (or 83c692, or XXX392) 16-pin DIP chip very close to the BNC connector.

Another common NIC found on older cards is the Intel i82586. Cards having this NIC include the 3c505, 3c507, 3c523, Intel EtherExpress-ISA, Microdyne Exos-205T, and the Racal-Interlan NI5210.

The original AMD LANCE NIC was numbered AM7990, and newer revisions include the 79c960, 79c961, 79c965, 79c970, and 79c974. Most cards with one of the above will work with the Linux LANCE driver, with the exception of the old Racal-Interlan NI6510 cards that have their own driver.

Newer PCI cards having a DEC 21040, 21041, 21140, or similar number on the NIC should be able to use the Linux Tulip or DE4x5 driver.

Other PCI cards having a big chip marked RTL8029 are NE2000 clone cards, and the NE driver in Linux version v2.0 and up should automatically detect these cards at boot.

5.39.2 Identifying the Ethernet Address

Each Ethernet card has its own, six-byte address that is unique to that card. The first three bytes of that address are the same for each card made by that particular manufacturer. For example, all SMC cards start with `00:00:c0`. The last three are assigned by the manufacturer uniquely to each individual card as they are produced.

If your card has a sticker on it giving all six bits of its address, you can look up the vendor from the first three. However it is more common to see only the last three bytes printed onto a sticker attached to a socketed PROM, which tells you nothing.

You can determine which vendors have which assigned addresses from RFC-1340. Apparently there is a more up to date listing available in various places as well. Try a WWW or FTP search for `EtherNet-codes` or `Ethernet-codes` and you will find something.

5.39.3 Tips on Trying to Use an Unknown Card

If you are still not sure what the card is, but have at least narrowed it down some, then you can build a kernel with a whole bunch of drivers included, and see if any of them auto detect the card at boot.

If the kernel doesn't detect the card, it may be that the card is not configured to one of the addresses that the driver probes when looking for a card. In this case, you might want to try getting `scanport.tar.gz` from your local Linux FTP site, and see if that can locate where your card is jumpered for. It scans ISA I/O space from 0x100 to 0x3ff looking for devices that aren't registered in `/proc/ioports`. If it finds an unknown device starting at some particular address, you can then explicitly point the Ethernet probes at that address with an `ether=` boot argument.

If you manage to get the card detected, you can then usually figure out the unknown jumpers by changing them one at a time and seeing at what I/O base and IRQ that the card is detected at. The IRQ settings can also usually be determined by following the traces on the back of the card to where the jumpers are soldered through. Counting the "gold fingers" on the backside, from the end of the card with the metal bracket, you have IRQ 9, 7, 6, 5, 4, 3, 10, 11, 12, 15, 14 at fingers 4, 21, 22, 23, 24, 25, 34, 35, 36, 37, 38 respectively. Eight-bit cards only have up to finger 31.

Jumpers that appear to do nothing usually are for selecting the memory address of an optional boot ROM. Other jumpers that are located near the BNC or RJ-45 or AUI connectors are usually to select the output media. These are also typically near the "black box" voltage converters marked YCL, Valor, or Fil-Mag.

A nice collection of jumper settings for various cards can be found at the following URL: http://www.syd.dit.csiro.au/staff/ken/personal/NIC/.

5.40 Drivers for Non-Ethernet Devices

There are a few other drivers that are in the :Linux source, that present an Ethernet-like device to network programs, while not really being ethernet. These are briefly listed here for completeness.

`dummy.c`—The purpose of this driver is to provide a device to point a route through, but not to actually transmit packets.

`eql.c`—Load Equalizer that controls multiple devices (usually modems) and balances the Tx load across them while presenting a single device to the network programs.

`ibmtr.c`—IBM Token Ring, which is not really Ethernet. Broken-Ring requires source routing and other uglies.

`loopback.c`—Loopback device, for which all packets from you machine and destined for your own machine go. It essentially just moves the packet off the Tx queue and onto the Rx queue.

`pi2.c`—Ottawa Amateur Radio Club PI and PI2 interface.

`plip.c`—Parallel Line Internet Protocol, allows two computers to send packets to each other over two joined parallel ports in a point-to-point fashion.

`ppp.c`—Point-to-Point Protocol (RFC1331), for the Transmission of Multi-protocol Datagrams over a Point-to-Point Link (usually modems).

`slip.c`—Serial Line Internet Protocol, allows two computers to send packets to each other over two joined serial ports (usually modems) in a point-to-point fashion.

`tunnel.c`—Provides an IP tunnel through which you can tunnel network traffic transparently across subnets

`wavelan.c`—An Ethernet-like radio transceiver controlled by the Intel 82586 coprocessor which is used on other Ethercards such as the Intel EtherExpress.

6 Cables, Coax, Twisted Pair

If you are starting a network from scratch, it's considerably less expensive to use thin ethernet, RG58 co-ax cable with BNC connectors, than old-fashioned thick ethernet, RG-5 cable with N connectors, or 10baseT, twisted pair TELCO-style cables with RJ-45 eight wire "phone" connectors. See Section 2.7 for an introductory look at cables.

Also note that the FAQ from *comp.dcom.lans.ethernet* has a lot of useful information on cables and such. Look in *Usenet FAQs* (`ftp://rtfm.mit.edu/pub/usenet-by-hierarchy/`) for the FAQ for that newsgroup.

6.1 Thin Ethernet (thinnet)

Thin Ethernet is the "ether of choice." The cable is inexpensive. If you are making your own cables, solid-core RG58A is $0.27/m., and stranded RG58AU is $0.45/m. Twist-on BNC connectors are < $2 ea., and other miscellaneous pieces are similarly inexpensive. It is essential that you properly terminate each end of the cable with 50-ohm terminators, so budget $2 ea. for a pair. It's also vital that your cable have no "stubs"—the "T" connectors must be attached directly to the Ethercards.

The only drawback is that if you have a big loop of machines connected together, and some bone head breaks the loop by taking one cable off the side of his tee, the whole network goes down because it sees an infinite impedance (open circuit) instead of the required 50-ohm termination. Note that you can remove the tee piece from the card itself without killing the whole subnet, as long as you don't remove the cables from the tee. Of course this will disturb the machine that you pull the actual tee from. And if you are doing a small network of two machines, you *still* need the tees and the 50-ohm terminators—you can't just cable them together.

Note that there are a few cards out there with "on-board termination." These cards have a jumper which when closed, puts a 50-ohm resistor across the BNC input. With these cards, you can use a BNC T and terminator like normal, or put the cable directly onto the card and close the jumper to enable the on-board termination.

There are also some fancy cable systems which look like a single lead going to the card, but the lead is actually a loop, with the two runs of cable lying side-by-side, covered by an outer sheath, giving the lead an oval cross-section. At the turnaround point of the loop, a BNC connector is spliced in that connects to your card. So you have the equivalent of two runs of cable and a BNC T, but in this case, it is impossible for the user to remove a cable from one side of the T and disturb the network.

6.2 Twisted Pair

Twisted pair networks require active hubs, which start around $200, and the raw cable cost can actually be higher than thinnet. They are usually sold using the claim that you can use your existing telephone wiring, but it's a rare installation where that turns out to be the case. The claim that you can upgrade to higher speeds is also suspect, as most proposed schemes use higher-grade (read $$) cable and more sophisticated termination ($$$) than you would likely install on speculation.

New gizmos are floating around which allow you to daisy-chain machines together, and the like. For example, Farallon sells EtherWave adaptors and transceivers. This device allows multiple 10baseT devices to be daisy-chained. They also sell a 3c509 clone that includes the EtherWave transceiver. The drawback is that it's more expensive and less reliable than a cheap ($100-$150) mini-hub and another Ethercard. You probably should either go for the hub approach or switch over to 10base2 thinnet.

On the other hand, hubs are rapidly dropping in price, all 100Mb/sec Ethernet proposals use twisted pair, and most new business installations use twisted pair. (This is probably to avoid the problem with idiots messing with the BNC's as described above.)

Also, Russ Nelson adds that "New installations should use Category 5 wiring. Anything else is a waste of your installer's time, as 100Base-whatever is going to require Cat 5."

If you are only connecting two machines, it is possible to avoid using a hub, by swapping the Rx and Tx pairs (1-2 and 3-6).

If you hold the RJ-45 connector facing you (as if you were going to plug it into your mouth) with the lock tab on the top, then the pins are numbered 1 to 8 from left to right. The pin usage is as follows:

```
Pin Number              Assignment
----------              ----------
1                       Output Data (+)
2                       Output Data (-)
3                       Input Data (+)
4                       Reserved for Telephone use
5                       Reserved for Telephone use
6                       Input Data (-)
7                       Reserved for Telephone use
8                       Reserved for Telephone use
```

If you want to make a cable, the following should spell it out for you. Differential signal pairs must be on the same twisted pair to get the required minimal impedance/loss of a UTP cable. If you look at the above table, you will see that 1+2 and 3+6 are the two sets of differential signal pairs. Not 1+3 and 2+6. At 10MHz, with short lengths, you *may* get away with such errors, if it is only over a short length. Don't even think about it at 100MHz.

For a normal patch cord, with ends 'A' and 'B', you want straight through pin-to-pin mapping, with the input and output each using a pair of twisted wires (for impedance issues). That means 1A goes to 1B, 2A goes to 2B, 3A goes to 3B and 6A goes to 6B. The wires joining 1A-1B and 2A-2B must be a twisted pair. Also the wires joining 3A-3B and 6A-6B must be another twisted pair.

Now if you don't have a hub, and want to make a "null cable," what you want to do is make the input of "A" be the output of "B" and the output of "A" be the input of "B," without changing the polarity. That means connecting 1A to 3B (out+ A to in+ B) and 2A to 6B (out- A to in- B). These two wires must be a twisted pair. They carry what card/plug "A" considers output, and what is seen as input for card/plug "B." Then connect 3A to 1B (in+ A to out+ B) and also connect 6A to 2B (in- A to out- B). These second two must also be a twisted pair. They carry what card-plug "A" considers input, and what card-plug "B" considers output.

So, if you consider a normal patch cord, chop one end off of it, swap the places of the Rx and Tx twisted pairs into the new plug, and crimp it down, you then have a "null" cable. Nothing complicated. You just want to feed the Tx signal of one card into the Rx of the second and vice versa.

Note that before 10BaseT was ratified as a standard, there existed other network formats using RJ-45 connectors, and the same wiring scheme as above. Examples are SynOptics' LattisNet, and AT&T's StarLAN. In some cases, (as with early 3C503 cards) you could set jumpers to get the card to talk to hubs of different types, but in most cases cards designed for these older types of networks will not work with standard 10BaseT networks/hubs. (Note that if the cards also have an AUI port, then there is no reason as to why you can't use that, combined with an AUI to 10BaseT transceiver.)

6.3 Thick Ethernet

Thick Ethernet is mostly obsolete, and is usually used only to remain compatible with an existing implementation. You can stretch the rules and connect short spans of thick and thin Ethernet together with a passive $3 N-to-BNC connector, and that's often the best solution to expanding an existing thicknet. A correct (but expensive) solution is to use a repeater in this case.

7 Software Configuration and Card Diagnostics

In most cases, if the configuration is done by software, and stored in an EEPROM, you will usually have to boot DOS, and use the supplied DOS program to set the cards IRQ, I/O, memory address, and whatnot. Besides, hopefully it is something you will only be setting once. If you don't have the DOS software for your card, try looking on the WWW site of your card manufacturer. If you don't know the site name, take a guess at it; i.e., "www.my_vendor.com," where, "my_vendor," is the name of your card manufacturer. This works for SMC, 3Com, and many other manufacturers.

There are some cards for which Linux versions of the config utilities exist, and they are listed here. Donald has written a few, small, card diagnostic programs that run under Linux. Most of these are a result of debugging tools that he has created while writing the various drivers. Don't expect fancy, menu driven interfaces. You will have to read the source code to use most of these. Even if your particular card doesn't have a corresponding diagnostic, you can still get some information just by typing `cat /proc/net/dev`—assuming that your card was at least detected at boot.

In either case, you will have to run most of these programs as root (to allow I/O to the ports) and you probably want to shut down the Ethercard before doing so by typing `ifconfig eth0 down` (Note: replace `eth0` with `atp0` or whatever when appropriate.)

7.1 Configuration Programs for Ethernet Cards

7.1.1 WD80x3 Cards

For people with WD80x3 cards, there is the program `wdsetup` that can be found in `wdsetup-0.6a.tar.gz` on Linux FTP sites. I am not sure if it is being actively maintained or not, as it has not been updated for quite a while. If it works fine for you then, great; if not, use the DOS version that you should have received with your card. If you don't have the DOS version, you will be glad to know that the SMC setup and driver disks are available at SMC's FTP site. Of course, you *have* to have an EEPROM card to use this utility. Old WD8003 cards, and some WD8013 clones, use jumpers to set up the card instead.

7.1.2 Digital (DEC) Cards

The Digital EtherWorks 3 card can be configured in a similar fashion to the DOS program `NICSETUP.EXE`. David C. Davies wrote this and other tools for the EtherWorks 3 in conjunction with the driver. Look on `sunsite.unc.edu` in the directory `/pub/linux/system/Network/management` for the file that is named `ewrk3tools-X.XX.tar.gz`.

7.1.3 NE2000+ or AT/LANTIC Cards

Some National Semiconductor DP83905 implementations (such as the AT/LANTIC and the NE2000+) are software configurable. (Note that these cards can also emulate a WD8013 card!) You can get the file `/pub/linux/setup/atlantic.c` from Donald's FTP server, `cesdis.gsfc.nasa.gov` to configure this card. In addition, the configuration programs for the Kingston DP83905 cards seem to work with all cards, as they don't check for a vendor specific address before allowing you to use them. Follow the following URL: *Kingston Software* (`http://www.kingston.com/download/etherx/etherx.htm`) and get `20XX12.EXE` and `INFOSET.EXE`.

Be careful when configuring NE2000+ cards, because you can give them bad setting values which can cause problems. A typical example is accidentally enabling the boot ROM in the EEPROM (even if no ROM is installed) to a setting which conflicts with the VGA card. The result is a computer that just beeps at you (AMI beeps eight times for VGA failure) when you turn it on and nothing appears on the screen.

You can typically recover from this by doing the following: Remove the card from the machine, and then boot and enter the CMOS setup. Change the "Display Adapter" to "Not Installed" and change the default boot drive to "A:" (your floppy drive). Also change the "Wait for F1 if any Error" to "Disabled." This way, the computer should boot without user intervention. Now create a bootable DOS floppy (`format a: /s /u`) and copy the program `DEFAULT.EXE` from the `20XX12.EXE` archive above onto that floppy. Then type `echo default > a:AUTOEXEC.bat` so that the program to set the card back to sane defaults will be run automatically when you boot from this floppy. Shut the machine off, re-install the NE2000+ card, insert your new boot floppy, and power it back up. It will still probably beep at you, but eventually you should see the floppy light come on as it boots from the floppy. Wait a minute or two for the floppy to stop, indicating that it has finished running the `DEFAULT.EXE` program, and then power down your computer. When you then turn it on again, you should hopefully have a working display again, allowing you to change your CMOS settings back, and to change the card's EEPROM settings back to the values you want.

Note that if you don't have DOS handy, you can do the whole method above with a Linux boot disk that automatically runs Donald's `atlantic` program (with the right command line switches) instead of a DOS boot disk that automatically runs the `DEFAULT.EXE` program.

7.1.4 3Com Cards

The 3Com Etherlink III family of cards (i.e. 3c5x9) can be configured by using another configuration utility from Donald. You can get the file `/pub/linux/setup/3c5x9setup.c` from Donald's FTP server, `cesdis.gsfc.nasa.gov` to configure these cards. (Note that the DOS 3c5x9B config utility may have more options pertaining to the new "B" series of the Etherlink III family.)

7.2 Diagnostic Programs for Ethernet Cards

Any of the diagnostic programs that Donald has written can be obtained from this URL.

Ethercard Diagnostics (`http://cesdis.gsfc.nasa.gov/pub/linux/diag/diagnostic.html`)

Allied Telesis AT1700—look for the file `/pub/linux/diag/at1700.c` on `cesdis.gsfc.nasa.gov`.

Cabletron E21XX—look for the file `/pub/linux/diag/e21.c` on `cesdis.gsfc.nasa.gov`.

HP PCLAN+—look for the file `/pub/linux/diag/hp+.c` on `cesdis.gsfc.nasa.gov`.

Intel EtherExpress—look for the file `/pub/linux/diag/eexpress.c` on `cesdis.gsfc.nasa.gov`.

NE2000 cards—look for the file `/pub/linux/diag/ne2k.c` on `cesdis.gsfc.nasa.gov`.

RealTek (ATP) Pocket adaptor—look for the file `/pub/linux/diag/atp-diag.c` on `cesdis.gsfc.nasa.gov`.

All Other Cards—try typing `cat /proc/net/dev` and `dmesg` to see what useful info the kernel has on the card in question.

8 Technical Information

For those who want to play with the present drivers, or try to make up their own driver for a card that is presently unsupported, this information should be useful. If you do not fall into this category, then perhaps you will want to skip this section.

8.1 Probed Addresses

While trying to determine what Ethernet card is there, the following addresses are auto probed, assuming the type and specs of the card have not been set in the kernel. The file names below are in `/usr/src/linux/drivers/net/`.

```
3c501.c       0x280, 0x300
3c503.c:      0x300, 0x310, 0x330, 0x350, 0x250, 0x280, 0x2a0, 0x2e0
3c505.c:      0x300, 0x280, 0x310
3c507.c:      0x300, 0x320, 0x340, 0x280
3c509.c:      Special ID Port probe
apricot.c     0x300
at1700.c:     0x300, 0x280, 0x380, 0x320, 0x340, 0x260, 0x2a0, 0x240
atp.c:        0x378, 0x278, 0x3bc
depca.c       0x300, 0x200
de600.c:      0x378
de620.c:      0x378
eexpress.c:   0x300, 0x270, 0x320, 0x340
hp.c:         0x300, 0x320, 0x340, 0x280, 0x2C0, 0x200, 0x240
hp-plus.c     0x200, 0x240, 0x280, 0x2C0, 0x300, 0x320, 0x340
```

```
lance.c:        0x300, 0x320, 0x340, 0x360
ne.c:           0x300, 0x280, 0x320, 0x340, 0x360
ni52.c          0x300, 0x280, 0x360, 0x320, 0x340
ni65.c          0x300, 0x320, 0x340, 0x360
smc-ultra.c:    0x200, 0x220, 0x240, 0x280, 0x300, 0x340, 0x380
wd.c:           0x300, 0x280, 0x380, 0x240
```

There are some NE2000 clone Ethercards out there that are waiting, black holes for auto-probe drivers. While many NE2000 clones are safe until they are enabled, some can't be reset to a safe mode. These dangerous Ethercards will hang any I/O access to their "data ports." The typical dangerous locations are:

```
Ethercard jumpered base     Dangerous locations (base + 0x10 - 0x1f)
        0x300 *                         0x310-0x317
        0x320                           0x330-0x337
        0x340                           0x350-0x357
        0x360                           0x370-0x377
```

* The 0x300 location is the standard Ethercard address, but it is also a popular address for other devices (often SCSI controllers). The 0x320 location is often the next one chosen, but that's bad for for the AHA-1542 driver probe. The 0x360 location is bad, because it conflicts with the parallel port at 0x378. If you have two IDE controllers, or two floppy controllers, then `0x360` is also a bad choice, as a NE2000 card will clobber them as well.

Note that kernels > 1.1.7X keep a log of what card uses which I/O ports, and will not allow a driver to use I/O ports registered by an earlier driver. This may result in probes silently failing. You can view who is using what I/O ports by typing `cat /proc/ioports` if you have the `/proc` filesystem enabled.

To avoid these lurking Ethercards, here are the things you can do:

- Probe for the device's BIOS in memory space. This is easy and always safe, but it only works for cards that always have BIOSes, like primary SCSI controllers.
- Avoid probing any of the above locations until you think that you've located your device. The NE2000 clones have a reset range from <base>+0x18 to <base>+0x1f that will read as 0xff, so probe there first if possible. It's also safe to probe in the 8390 space at <base>+0x00 - <base>+0x0f, but that area will return quasi-random values
- If you must probe in the dangerous range, for instance if your target device has only a few port locations, first check that there isn't an NE2000 there. You can see how to do this by looking at the probe code in `/usr/src/linux/net/inet/ne.c`.
- Use the "reserve" boot-time argument to protect volatile areas from being probed. See the information on using boot time arguments with LILO in 10.1.2

8.2 Writing a Driver

The only thing that one needs to use an Ethernet card with Linux is the appropriate driver. For this, it is essential that the manufacturer release the technical programming information to the general public without you (or anyone) having to sign your life away. A good guide for the likelihood of getting documentation (or, if you aren't writing code, the likelihood that someone else will write that driver you really, really need) is the availability of the Crynwr (*nee* Clarkson) packet driver. Russ Nelson runs this operation, and has been very helpful in supporting the development of drivers for Linux. Net surfers can try this URL to look up Russ' software.

Russ Nelson's Packet Drivers (`http://www.crynwr.com/crynwr/home.html`)

Given the documentation, you can write a driver for your card and use it for Linux (at least, in theory). Keep in mind that some old hardware that was designed for XT-type machines will not function very well in a multitasking environment such as Linux. Use of these will lead to major problems if your network sees a reasonable amount of traffic.

Most cards come with drivers for MS-DOS interfaces such as NDIS and ODI, but these are useless for Linux. Many people have suggested directly linking them in or automatic translation, but this is nearly impossible. The MS-DOS drivers expect to be in 16-bit mode and hook into "software interrupts," both incompatible with the Linux kernel. This incompatibility is actually a feature, as some Linux drivers are considerably better than their MS-DOS counterparts. The "8390" series drivers, for instance, use ping-pong transmit buffers, which are only now being introduced in the MS-DOS world.

(Ping-pong Tx buffers use at least 2 maximum size packet buffers for Tx packets. One is loaded while the card is transmitting the other. The second is then sent as soon as the first finished, and so on. In this way, most cards are able to continuously send back-to-back packets onto the wire.)

OK. So you have decided that you want to write a driver for the Foobar Ethernet card, as you have the programming information, and it hasn't been done yet. (These are the two main requirements.) You should start with the skeleton network driver that is provided with the Linux kernel source tree. It can be found in the file `/usr/src/linux/drivers/net/skeleton.c` in all recent kernels. Also have a look at the Kernel Hackers Guide, at the following URL: *KHG* (`http://www.redhat.com:8080/HyperNews/get/khg.html`)

8.3 Driver interface to the kernel

Here are some notes on the functions that you would have to write if creating a new driver. Reading this in conjunction with the above skeleton driver may help clear things up.

8.3.1 Probe

Called at boot to check for existence of card. Best if it can check un-obtrusively by reading from memory, etc. Can also read from I/O ports. Initial writing to I/O ports in a probe is not good as it may kill another device. Some device initialization is usually done here (allocating I/O space, IRQs,filling in the dev->??? fields etc.) You need to know what io ports/mem the card can be configured to, how to enable shared memory (if used) and how to select or enable interrupt generation and so forth.

8.3.2 Interrupt handler

Called by the kernel when the card posts an interrupt. This has the job of determining why the card posted an interrupt, and acted accordingly. Usual interrupt conditions are data to be received, transmit completed, and error conditions being reported. You must know any relevant interrupt status bits so that the handler can act accordingly.

8.3.3 Transmit function

Linked to dev->hard_start_xmit() and is called by the kernel when there is some data that the kernel wants to put out over the device. This puts the data onto the card and triggers the transmit. You must how to bundle the data and how to get it onto the card (shared memory copy, PIO transfer, and perhaps DMA) and in the right place on the card. Then you need to know how to tell the card to send the data down the wire, and possibly how to post an interrupt when done. When the hardware can't accept additional packets, it should set the dev->tbusy flag. When additional room is available, usually during a transmit-complete interrupt, dev->tbusy should be cleared and the higher levels informed with `mark_bh(INET_BH)`.

8.3.4 Receive function

Called by the kernel interrupt handler when the card reports that there is data on the card. It pulls the data off the card, packages it into a sk_buff and lets the kernel know that the data is there by doing a netif_rx(sk_buff). You need to know how to enable interrupt generation upon Rx of data, how to check any relevant Rx status bits, and how to get that data off the card (again sh mem, PIO, DMA, etc.)

8.3.5 Open function

Linked to dev->open and called by the networking layers when somebody does `ifconfig eth0 up`—this puts the device on line and enables it for Rx/Tx of data. Any special initialization incantations that were not done in the probe sequence (enabling IRQ generation, etc.) go here.

8.3.6 Close function (optional)

This puts the card in a sane state when someone does `ifconfig eth0 down`. It should free the IRQs and DMA channels if the hardware permits, and turn off anything that saves power (like the transceiver).

8.3.7 Miscellaneous functions

These are things like a reset function, so that if things go south, the driver can try resetting the card as a last ditch effort. Usually done when a Tx times out or under similar conditions. Also there may be function to read the statistics registers of the card if so equipped.

8.4 Interrupts and Linux

There are two kinds of interrupt handlers in Linux: fast ones and slow ones. You decide what kind you are installing by the flags you pass to irqaction(). The fast ones, such as the serial interrupt handler, run with all interrupts disabled. The normal interrupt handlers, like the one for Ethercard drivers, runs with other interrupts enabled.

There is a two-level interrupt structure. The 'fast' part handles the device register, removes the packets, and perhaps sets a flag. After it is done, and interrupts are re-enabled, the slow part is run if the flag is set.

The flag between the two parts is set by:

```
mark_bh(INET_BH);
```

Usually this flag is set within dev_rint() during a received-packet interrupt, and set directly by the device driver during a transmit-complete interrupt.

You might wonder why all interrupt handlers cannot run in "normal mode" with other interrupts enabled. Ross Biro uses this scenario to illustrate the problem:

- You get a serial interrupt, and start processing it. The serial interrupt is now masked.
- You get a network interrupt, and you start transferring a maximum-sized 1500 byte packet from the card.
- Another character comes in, but this time the interrupts are masked!

The "fast" interrupt structure solves this problem by allowing bounded-time interrupt handlers to run without the risk of leaving their interrupt lines masked by another interrupt request.

There is an additional distinction between fast and slow interrupt handlers—the arguments passed to the handler. A "slow" handler is defined as

```
static void
handle_interrupt(int reg_ptr)
{
    int irq = -(((struct pt_regs *)reg_ptr)->orig_eax+2);
    struct device *dev = irq2dev_map[irq];
...
```

While a fast handler gets the interrupt number directly

```
static void
handle_fast_interrupt(int irq)
{
...
```

A final aspect of network performance is latency. The only board that really addresses this is the 3c509, which allows a predictive interrupt to be posted. It provides an interrupt response timer so that the driver can fine-tune how early an interrupt is generated.

8.5 Programming the Intel chips (i82586 and i82593)

These chips are used on a number of cards, namely the 3c507 ('86), the Intel EtherExpress 16 ('86), Microdyne's exos205t ('86), the Z-Note ('93), and the Racal-Interlan ni5210 ('86).

Russ Nelson writes that 'Most boards based on the 82586 can reuse quite a bit of their code. More, in fact, than the 8390-based adapters. There are only three differences between them:

- The code to get the Ethernet address,
- The code to trigger CA on the 82586, and
- The code to reset the 82586.

The Intel EtherExpress 16 is an exception, as it I/O maps the 82586. Yes, I/O maps it. Fairly clunky, but it works.

Garrett Wollman did an AT&T driver for BSD that uses the BSD copyright. The latest version I have (Sep '92) only uses a single transmit buffer. You can and should do better than this if you've got the memory. The AT&T and 3c507 adapters do; the ni5210 doesn't.

The people at Intel gave me a very big clue on how you queue up multiple transmit packets. You set up a list of NOP-> XMIT-> NOP-> XMIT-> NOP-> XMIT-> beginning) blocks, then you set the "next" pointer of all the NOP blocks to themselves. Now you start the command unit on this chain. It continually processes the first NOP block. To transmit a packet, you stuff it into the next transmit block, then point the NOP to it. To transmit the next packet, you stuff the next transmit block and point the previous NOP to it. In this way, you don't have to wait for the previous transmit to finish, you can queue up multiple packets without any ambiguity as to whether it got accepted, and you can avoid the command unit start-up delay.

8.6 Technical information from 3Com

If you are interested in working on drivers for 3Com cards, you can get technical documentation from 3Com. Cameron has been kind enough to tell us how to go about it below:

> 3Com's Ethernet Adapters are documented for driver writers in our "Technical References" (TRs). These manuals describe the programmer interfaces to the boards but they don't talk about the diagnostics, installation programs, etc that end users can see.
>
> The Network Adapter Division marketing department has the TRs to give away. To keep this program efficient, we centralized it in a thing called "CardFacts." CardFacts is an automated phone system. You call it with a touch-tone phone and it faxes you stuff. To get a TR, call CardFacts at 408-727-7021. Ask it for Developer's Order Form, document number 9070. Have your fax number ready when you call. Fill out the order form and fax it to 408-764-5004. Manuals are shipped by Federal Express 2nd Day Service.
>
> After you get a manual, if you still can't figure out how to program the board, try our 'CardBoard' BBS at 1-800-876-3266, and if you can't do that, write Andy_Chan@3Mail.3com.com and ask him for alternatives. If you have a real stumper that nobody has figured out yet, the fellow who needs to know about it is Steve_Lebus@3Mail.3com.com.
>
> There are people here who think we are too free with the manuals, and they are looking for evidence that the system is too expensive, or takes too much time and effort. That's why it's important to try to use CardFacts before you start calling and mailing the people I named here.
>
> There are even people who think we should be like Diamond and Xircom, requiring tight "partnership" with driver writers to prevent poorly performing drivers from getting written. So far, 3Com customers have been really good about this, and there's no problem with the level of requests we've been getting. We need your continued cooperation and restraint to keep it that way.

```
Cameron Spitzer, 408-764-6339
3Com NAD
Santa Clara
work: camerons@nad.3com.com
home: cls@truffula.sj.ca.us
```

8.7 Notes on AMD PCnet / LANCE Based cards

The AMD LANCE (Local Area Network Controller for Ethernet) was the original offering, and has since been replaced by the "PCnet-ISA" chip, otherwise known as the 79C960. A relatively new chip from AMD, the 79C960, is the heart of many new cards being released at present. Note that the name "LANCE" has stuck, and some people will refer to the new chip by the old name. Dave Roberts of the Network Products Division of AMD was kind enough to contribute the following information regarding this chip:

> As for the architecture itself, AMD developed it originally and reduced it to a single chip—the PCnet(tm)-ISA—over a year ago. It's been selling like hot cakes ever since.
>
> Functionally, it is equivalent to a NE1500. The register set is identical to the old LANCE with the 1500/2100 architecture additions. Older 1500/2100 drivers will work on the PCnet-ISA. The NE1500 and NE2100 architecture is basically the same. Initially Novell called it the 2100, but then tried to distinguish between coax and 10BASE-T cards. Anything that was 10BASE-T only was to be numbered in the 1500 range. That's the only difference.
>
> Many companies offer PCnet-ISA based products, including HP, Racal-Datacom, Allied Telesis, Boca Research, Kingston Technology, etc. The cards are basically the same except that some manufacturers have added "jumper less" features that allow the card to be configured in software. Most have not. AMD offers a standard design package for a card that uses the PCnet-ISA and many manufacturers use our design without change. What this means is that anybody who wants to write drivers for most PCnet-ISA based cards can just get the data-sheet from AMD. Call our literature distribution center at (800)222-9323 and ask for the Am79C960, PCnet-ISA data sheet. It's free.
>
> A quick way to understand whether the card is a "stock" card is to just look at it. If it's stock, it should just have one large chip on it, a crystal, a small IEEE address PROM, possibly a socket for a boot ROM, and a connector (1, 2, or 3, depending on the media options offered). Note that if it's a coax card, it will have some transceiver stuff built onto it as well, but that should be near the connector and away from the PCnet-ISA.

There is also some info regarding the LANCE chip in the file `lance.c`, which is included in the standard kernel.

A note to would-be card hackers is that different LANCE implementations do "restart" in different ways. Some pick up where they left off in the ring, and others start right from the beginning of the ring, as if just initialized. This is a concern when setting the multicast list.

8.8 Multicast and Promiscuous Mode

Another one of the things Donald has worked on is implementing multicast and promiscuous mode hooks. All of the released (i.e., non-alpha) ISA drivers now support promiscuous mode.

Donald writes: "At first was planning to do it while implementing either the `/dev/*` or DDI interface, but that's not really the correct way to do it. I could only enable multicast or promiscuous modes when something wants to look at the packets, and shut it down when that application is finished, neither of which is strongly related to when the hardware is opened or released.

I'll start by discussing promiscuous mode, which is conceptually easy to implement. For most hardware you only have to set a register bit, and from then on you get every packet on the wire. Well, it's almost that easy; for some hardware you have to shut the board (potentially dropping a few packet), reconfigure it, and then re-enable the Ethercard. This is grungy and risky, but the alternative seems to be to have every application register before you open the Ethercard at boot-time.

OK, so that's easy, so I'll move on something that's not quite so obvious: Multicast. It can be done two ways:

1. Use promiscuous mode, and a packet filter like the Berkeley packet filter (BPF). The BPF is a pattern matching stack language, where you write a program that picks out the addresses you are interested in. Its advantage is that it's very general and programmable. Its disadvantage is that there is no general way for the kernel to avoid turning on promiscuous mode and running every packet on the wire through every registered packet filter. See Section 8.9 for more info.
2. Using the built-in multicast filter that most Etherchips have.

I guess I should list what a few Ethernet cards and chips provide:

```
Chip/card   Promiscuous  Multicast filter
----------------------------------------
Seeq8001/3c501  Yes      Binary filter (1)
3Com/3c509      Yes      Binary filter (1)
8390            Yes      Autodin II six bit hash (2) (3)
LANCE           Yes      Autodin II six bit hash (2) (3)
i82586          Yes      Hidden Autodin II six bit hash (2) (4)
```

1. These cards claim to have a filter, but it's a simple yes or no 'accept all multicast packets,' or 'accept no multicast packets.'
2. AUTODIN II is the standard ethernet CRC (checksum) polynomial. In this scheme multicast addresses are hashed and looked up in a hash table. If the corresponding bit is enabled, this packet is accepted. Ethernet packets are laid out so that the hardware to do this is trivial—you just latch six (usually) bits from the CRC circuit (needed anyway for error checking) after the first six octets (the destination address), and use them as an index into the hash table (six bits—a 64-bit table).
3. These chips use the six-bit hash, and must have the table computed and loaded by the host. This means the kernel must include the CRC code.
4. The 82586 uses the six-bit hash internally, but it computes the hash table itself from a list of multicast addresses to accept.

Note that none of these chips do perfect filtering, and we still need a middle-level module to do the final filtering. Also note that in every case we must keep a complete list of accepted multicast addresses to recompute the hash table when it changes.

My first pass at device-level support is detailed in the outline driver `skeleton.c`

It looks like the following:

```
#ifdef HAVE_MULTICAST
static void set_multicast_list(struct device *dev, int num_addrs,
                               void *addrs);
#endif
.
.
```

```
ethercard_open() {
...
#ifdef HAVE_MULTICAST
        dev->set_multicast_list = &set_multicast_list;
#endif
...

#ifdef HAVE_MULTICAST
/* Set or clear the multicast filter for this adaptor.
   num_addrs -- -1      Promiscuous mode, receive all packets
   num_addrs -- 0       Normal mode, clear multicast list
   num_addrs > 0        Multicast mode, receive normal and
        MC packets, and do best-effort filtering.
 */
static void
set_multicast_list(struct device *dev, int num_addrs, void *addrs)
{
...
```

Any comments, criticism, etc. are welcome."

8.9 The Berkeley Packet Filter (BPF)

The general idea of the developers is that the BPF functionality should not be provided by the kernel, but should be in a (hopefully little used) compatibility library.

For those not in the know: BPF (the Berkeley Packet Filter) is a mechanism that specifies to the kernel networking layers what packets you are interested in. It's implemented as a specialized, stack-language interpreter built into a low level of the networking code. An application passes a program written in this language to the kernel, and the kernel runs the program on each incoming packet. If the kernel has multiple BPF applications, each program is run on each packet.

The problem is that it is hard to determine the type of packets the application is really interested in from the packet filter program. The common solution is to always run the filter. Imagine a program that registers a BPF program to pick up a low-data-rate stream sent to a multicast address. Most Ethernet cards have a hardware multicast address filter implemented as a 64-entry hash table which ignores most unwanted multicast packets. It is possible to make this a cheap operation. But with the BFP, the kernel must switch the interface to promiscuous mode, receive all packets, and run them through this filter. This process is very hard to account to the process which originally requested the packets.

9 Networking with a Laptop or Notebook Computer

There are currently only a few ways to put your laptop on a network. You can use the SLIP code (and run at serial line speeds); you can buy one of the few laptops that come with a NE2000-compatible Ethercard; you can get a notebook with a supported PCMCIA slot built-in; you can get a laptop with a docking station and plug in an ISA ethercard; or you can use a parallel-port Ethernet adapter like the D-Link DE-600.

9.1 Using SLIP

This is the cheapest solution, but by far the most difficult. Also, you will not get very high transmission rates. Since SLIP is not really related to Ethernet cards, it will not be discussed further here. See the NET-2 HOWTO.

9.2 Built-in NE2000

This solution severely limits your laptop choices and is fairly expensive. Be sure to read the specifications carefully, as you may find that you will have to buy an additional non-standard transceiver to actually put the machine on a network. A good idea might be to boot the notebook with a kernel that has NE2000 support, and make sure it gets detected and works before you lay down your cash.

9.3 PCMCIA Support

As this area of Linux development is fairly young, I'd suggest that you join the LAPTOPS mailing channel. See Section 10.3 which describes how to join a mailing list channel.

Try and determine exactly what hardware you have (i.e., card manufacturer, PCMCIA chip controller manufacturer) and then ask on the laptops channel. Regardless, don't expect things to be all that simple. Expect to have to fiddle around a bit, and patch kernels, etc. Maybe someday you will be able to type "`make config`."

At present, the two PCMCIA chip sets that are supported are the Data book TCIC/2 and the Intel i82365.

There is a number of programs on tsx-11.mit.edu in `/pub/linux/packages/laptops/` that you may find useful. These range from PCMCIA Ethercard drivers to programs that communicate with the PCMCIA controller chip. Note that these drivers are usually tied to a specific PCMCIA chip (ie. the Intel 82365 or the TCIC/2)

For NE2000 compatible cards, some people have had success with just configuring the card under DOS, and then booting Linux from the DOS command prompt via `LOADLIN.EXE`.

Those Net-surfing can try:

Don's PCMCIA Stuff (`http://cesdis.gsfc.nasa.gov/linux/pcmcia.html`)

Anyway, the PCMCIA driver problem isn't specific to the Linux world. It's been a real disaster in the MS-DOS world. In that world people expect the hardware to work if they just follow the manual. They might not expect it to inter-operate with any other hardware or software, or operate optimally, but they do expect that the software shipped with the product will function. Many PCMCIA adaptors don't even pass this test.

Things are looking up for Linux users that want PCMCIA support, as substantial progress is being made. Pioneering this effort is David Hinds. His latest PCMCIA support package can be obtained from `cb-iris.stanford.edu` in the directory `/pub/pcmcia/`. Look for a file like `pcmcia-cs-X.Y.Z.tgz` where X.Y.Z will be the latest version number. This is most likely uploaded to `tsx-11.mit.edu` as well.

Note that Donald's PCMCIA enabler works as a user-level process, and David Hinds' is a kernel-level solution. You may be best served by David's package as it is much more widely used.

9.4 ISA Ethercard in the Docking Station.

Docking stations for laptops typically cost about $250 and provide two, full-size ISA slots, two serial, and one parallel port. Most docking stations take power from the laptop battery, and a few allow extra batteries to be added in the docking station if you use short ISA cards. You can add an inexpensive Ethercard and enjoy full-speed Ethernet performance.

9.5 Pocket / parallel port adaptors.

The "pocket" Ethernet adaptors may also fit your need. Until recently, they actually costed more than a docking station and cheap Ethercard, and most tie you down with a wall-brick power supply. At present, you can choose from the D-Link, or the RealTek adaptor. Most other companies treat the programming information as a trade secret, so support will likely be slow in coming. (if ever) Xircom (see Section 5.36) apparently is now releasing their specs, but nobody is currently working on a driver.

Note that the transfer speed will not be all that great (perhaps 200kB/s maximum) due to the limitations of the parallel interface.

See sections 5.15.4 and 5.9.1 for supported pocket adaptors.

You can sometimes avoid the wall brick with the adaptors by buying or making a cable that draws power from the laptop keyboard port. (See Section 5.9.1)

10 Miscellaneous.

Any other associated stuff that didn't fit in anywhere else gets dumped here. It may not be relevant, and it may not be of general interest, but it is here anyway.

10.1 Passing Ethernet Arguments to the Kernel

Here are two generic kernel commands that can be passed to the kernel at boot time. This can be done with LILO, `LOADLIN.EXE`, or any other booting utility that accepts optional arguments.

For example, if the command was "blah" and it expected 3 arguments (say 123, 456, and 789) then, with LILO, you would use:

```
LILO: linux blah=123,456,789
```

Note: PCI cards have their I/O and IRQ assigned by the BIOS at boot. This means that any boot time arguments for a PCI card's IRQ or I/O ports are usually ignored.

For more information on (and a complete list of) boot time arguments, please see the BootPrompt-HOWTO, http://sunsite.unc.edu/LDP/.

10.1.1 The `ether` command

In its most generic form, it looks something like this:

```
ether=IRQ,BASE_ADDR,PARAM_1,PARAM_2,NAME
```

All arguments are optional. The first non-numeric argument is taken as the NAME.

IRQ: Obvious. An IRQ value of '0' (usually the default) means to auto-IRQ. It's a historical accident that the IRQ setting is first rather than the base_addr—this will be fixed whenever something else changes.

BASE_ADDR: Also obvious. A value of "0" (usually the default) means to probe a card-type-specific address list for an ethercard.

PARAM_1: It was originally used as an override value for the memory start for a shared-memory ethercard, like the WD80*3. Some drivers use the low four bits of this value to set the debug message level. 0—default, 1–7—level 1..7, (7 is maximum verbosity) 8—level 0 (no messages). Also, the LANCE driver uses the low four bits of this value to select the DMA channel. Otherwise it uses auto-DMA.

PARAM_2: The 3c503 driver uses this to select between the internal and external transceivers. 0—default/internal, 1—AUI external. The Cabletron E21XX card also uses the low 4 bits of PARAM_2 to select the output media. Otherwise it detects automatically.

NAME: Selects the network device the values refer to. The standard kernel uses the names "eth0," "eth1," "eth2," and "eth3" for bus attached Ethercards, and "atp0" for the parallel port "pocket" Ethernet adaptor. The ArcNet driver uses "arc0" as its name. The default setting is for a single Ethercard to be probed for as "eth0." Multiple cards can only be enabled by explicitly setting up their base address using these LILO parameters. The 1.0 kernel has LANCE-based Ethercards as a special case. LILO arguments are ignored, and LANCE cards are always assigned 'eth<n>' names starting at 'eth0'. Additional non-LANCE Ethercards must be explicitly assigned to 'eth<n+1>', and the usual "eth0" probe disabled with something like "ether=0,-1,eth0." (Yes, this is bug.)

10.1.2 The `reserve` command

This next LILO command is used just like "ether=" above i.e., it is appended to the name of the boot select specified in lilo.conf

```
reserve=IO-base,extent{,IO-base,extent...}
```

In some machines it may be necessary to prevent device drivers from checking for devices (auto-probing) in a specific region. This may be because of poorly designed hardware that causes the boot to *freeze* (such as some Ethercards), hardware that is mistakenly identified, hardware whose state is changed by an earlier probe, or merely hardware you don't want the kernel to initialize.

The `reserve` boot-time argument addresses this problem by specifying an I/O port region that shouldn't be probed. That region is reserved in the kernel's port registration table as if a device has already been found in that region. Note that this mechanism shouldn't be necessary on most machines. Only when there is a problem or special case would it be necessary to use this.

The I/O ports in the specified region are protected against device probes. This was put in to be used when some driver was hanging on a NE2000, or misidentifying some other device as its own. A correct device driver shouldn't probe a reserved region, unless another boot argument explicitly specifies that it do so. This implies that `reserve` will most often be used with some other boot argument. Hence if you specify a `reserve` region to protect a specific device, you must generally specify an explicit probe for that device. Most drivers ignore the port registration table if they are given an explicit address.

For example, the boot line

```
LILO: linux reserve=0x300,32 ether=0,0x300,eth0
```

keeps all device drivers except the Ethercard drivers from probing 0x300-0x31f.

As usual with boot-time specifiers, there is an 11-parameter limit. Thus, you can only specify 5 reserved regions per `reserve` keyword. Multiple `reserve` specifiers will work if you have an unusually complicated request.

10.2 Using the Ethernet Drivers as Modules

See the `insmod(8)` manual page for information on passing arguments to the module as it is being loaded. The command `lsmod` will show you what modules are loaded, and `rmmod` will remove them.

At present, all the modules are put in the subdirectory `modules` in your Linux kernel source tree (usually in the form of symbolic links). To actually generate the modules, you have to type `make modules` after you have finished building the kernel proper. Earlier kernels built them automatically, which wasn't fair to those compiling on 4MB 386sx-16 machines.

Most modules accept parameters like io=0x340 and irq=12 on the insmod command line. It is strongly advised that you supply these parameters to avoid probing for the card. Unlike PCI and EISA devices, there is no real safe way to do auto-probing for ISA devices, and so it should be avoided when using drivers as modules.

A list of all the parameters that each module accepts can be found in the file:

/usr/src/linux/Documentation/networking/net-modules.txt

It is recommended that you read that to find out what options you can use for your particular card.

Once you have figured out the arguments and options you are going to use, you can insert the module by typing as root:

```
insmod mod_name.o [io=val1[,val2,...]] [irq=val7[,val8,...]]
```

The comma separated value lists are used for modules that have the capability to handle multiple devices from a single module, such as all the 8390 drivers, and the PLIP driver.

Once a module is inserted, then you can use it just like normal, and give ifconfig commands. If you set up your networking at boot, then make sure your /etc/rc* files run the insmod command(s) before getting to the ifconfig command.

Also note that a busy module can't be removed. That means that you will have to ifconfig eth0 down (shut down the Ethernet card) before you can remove the module(s).

10.2.1 8390 Based Cards as Modules

The present list of 8390 based drivers is: 3c503, ac3200, e2100, HP, HP-Plus, NE, SMC-Ultra and WD. These cards were not supported as modules for kernel versions prior to 1.3.42. (This does not include some of the separately distributed PCMCIA drivers (e.g., the DE-650) that are also 8390 based, that have had module support for quite some time now.)

If you have an 8390 based card, you may have to insert *two* modules, 8390.o and then the module for your card. If 8390 support has been built into your kernel, then you will not need to insert the 8390 module. (8390 support is built in whenever an 8390 based card is selected to be built into the kernel.) Doing a cat /proc/ksyms | grep 8390 will tell you if 8390 support is in your kernel.

For an 8390 based card, you will have to remove the card module before removing the 8390 module, as the 8390 module is used by the card module, and thus marked as busy.

The 8390 series of network drivers now support multiple card systems without reloading the same module multiple times (memory efficient!) This is done by specifying multiple comma separated values, such as:

```
insmod 3c503.o io=0x280,0x300,0x330,0x350 xcvr=0,1,0,1
```

The above would have the one module controlling four 3c503 cards, with card 2 and 4 using external transceivers.

It is strongly recommended that you supply "io=" instead of auto-probing. If an "io=" argument is not supplied, then the ISA 8390 drivers will complain about auto-probing being not recommended, and begrudgingly auto probe for a single card only—if you want to use multiple cards you have to supply an "io=0xNNN,0xQQQ,..." argument.

The NE module is an exception to the above. A NE2000 is essentially an 8390 chip, some bus glue and some RAM. Because of this, the NE probe is more invasive than the rest, and so at boot we make sure the ne probe is done last of all the 8390 cards (so that it won't trip over other 8390-based cards) With modules we can't ensure that all other non-NE 8390 cards have already been found. Because of this, the NE module requires an io=0xNNN argument passed via insmod. It will refuse to auto probe.

It is also worth noting that auto-IRQ probably isn't as reliable during the flurry of interrupt activity on a running machine. Cards such as the NE2000 that can't get the IRQ setting from an EEPROM or configuration register are probably best supplied with an irq=M argument as well. The file

/usr/src/linux/Documentation/networking/net-modules.txt

also lists how the interrupt settings are determined for the various cards if an irq=N value is not given.

10.3 Mailing Lists and the Linux Newsgroups

If you have questions about your Ethernet card, please read this document first. You may also want to join the Net channel of the Linux mailing lists by sending mail to majordomo@vger.rutgers.edu to get help with what lists are available, and how to join them.

Furthermore, keep in mind that the Net channel is for development discussions only. General questions on how to configure your system should be directed to comp.os.linux.setup unless you are actively involved in the development of part of the networking for Linux. We ask that you please respect this general guideline for content.

Also, the news groups comp.sys.ibm.pc.hardware.networking and comp.dcom.lans.ethernet should be used for questions that are not Linux specific.

10.4 Related Documentation

Much of this information came from saved postings from the comp.os.linux.* groups, which shows that it is a valuable resource of information. Other useful information came from a bunch of small files by Donald himself. Of course, if you are setting up an Ethernet card, then you will want to read the NET-2 HOWTO so that you can actually configure the software you will use. Also, if you fancy yourself as a bit of a hacker, you can always scrounge some additional information from the driver source files as well. There is usually a paragraph or two in there describing any important points before any actual code starts..

For those looking for information that is not specific in any way to Linux (i.e. what is 10BaseT, what is AUI, what does a hub do, etc.) I strongly recommend the **Ethernet FAQ** that is posted regularly to the newsgroup comp.dcom.lans.ethernet. You can grab it from rtfm.mit.edu, which holds all the newsgroup FAQs at the following URL:

Usenet FAQs `(ftp://rtfm.mit.edu/pub/usenet-by-hierarchy/)`

You can also have a look at the "Ethernet Home Page," so to speak, which is at the following URL:

http://wwwhost.ots.utexas.edu/ethernet/ethernet-home.html

10.5 Contributors

Other people who have contributed (directly or indirectly) to the Ethernet HOWTO are, in alphabetical order:

```
Ross Biro               <bir7@leland.stanford.edu>
Alan Cox                <iialan@www.linux.org.uk>
David C. Davies         <davies@wanton.enet.dec.com>
Bjorn Ekwall            <bj0rn@blox.se>
David Hinds             <dhinds@allegro.stanford.edu>
Michael Hipp            <mhipp@student.uni-tuebingen.de>
Mike Jagdis             <jaggy@purplet.demon.co.uk>
Duke Kamstra            <kamstra@ccmail.west.smc.com>
Russell Nelson          <nelson@crynwr.com>
Cameron Spitzer         <camerons@NAD.3Com.com>
Dave Roberts            <david.roberts@amd.com>
Glenn Talbott           <gt@hprnd.rose.hp.com>
```

These mail addresses are intentionally not "mailto" links so as to protect these people from WWW "spambot" filters. Many thanks to the above people, and all the other unmentioned testers out there.

10.6 Disclaimer and Copyright

This document is *not* gospel. However, it is probably the most up to date info that you will be able to find. Nobody is responsible for what happens to your hardware but yourself. If your ethercard or any other hardware goes up in smoke (...nearly impossible!) we take no responsibility. ie. THE AUTHORS ARE NOT RESPONSIBLE FOR ANY DAMAGES INCURRED DUE TO ACTIONS TAKEN BASED ON THE INFORMATION INCLUDED IN THIS DOCUMENT.

This document is Copyright (c) 1993, 1994, 1995 1996 by Donald Becker and Paul Gortmaker. Permission is granted to make and distribute verbatim copies of this manual provided the copyright notice and this permission notice are preserved on all copies.

Permission is granted to copy and distribute modified versions of this document under the conditions for verbatim copying, provided that this copyright notice is included exactly as in the original, and that the entire resulting derived work is distributed under the terms of a permission notice identical to this one.

Permission is granted to copy and distribute translations of this document into another language, under the above conditions for modified versions.

If you are intending to incorporate this document into a published work, please contact me, and I will make an effort to ensure that you have the most up-to-date information available. In the past, out-of-date versions of the Linux HOWTO documents have been published, which caused the developers undue grief from being plagued with questions that were already answered in the up-to-date versions.

10.7 Closing

If you have found any glaring typos, or outdated info in this document, please let one of us know. It's getting big, and it is easy to overlook stuff.

Thanks,
Paul Gortmaker, `Paul.Gortmaker@anu.edu.au`
Donald J. Becker, `becker@cesdis.gsfc.nasa.gov`

Part XXI

"Firewalling and Proxy Server HOWTO" by Mark Grennan,

markg@netplus.net

The Linux Documentation Project
The original, unaltered edition of this, and other, LDP documents, is on line at http://sunsite.unc.edu/LDP/.

Contents

Abstract

v0.4, 8 November 1996

This document is designed to teach the basics of firewall systems and give you some detail on setting up both a filtering and proxy firewall on a Linux based PC. An HTML version of this document is available at *http://okcforum.org/~markg/Firewall-HOWTO.html*

1 Introduction

This original Firewall HOWTO was written by David Rudder, drig@execpc.com. I'd like to thank him for allowing me to update his work.

Firewalls have gained great fame recently as the ultimate in Internet Security. Like most things that gain fame, with that fame has come misunderstanding. This HOWTO will go over the basics of what a firewall is, how to set one up, what proxy servers are, how to set up proxy servers, and the applications of this technology outside of the security realm.

1.1 Feedback

Any feedback is very welcome. **Please report any inaccuracies in this paper!** I am human, and prone to making mistakes. If you find any, fixing them is of my highest interest. I will try to answer all e-mail, but I am busy, so don't get insulted if I don't.

My email address is markg@netplus.net.

1.2 Disclaimer

I am not responsible for any damages incurred due to actions taken based on this document. This document is meant as an introduction to how firewalls and proxy servers work. I am not, nor do I pretend to be, a security expert. I am just some guy who has read to much and likes computers more than most people. Please, I am writing this to help get people acquainted with this subject, and I am not ready to stake my life on the accuracy of what is in here.

1.3 Copyright

1.4 My Reasons for Writing This

Even though there were a lot of discussions on comp.os.linux.* over the past year about firewalling, I found it difficult to find the information I needed to set up a firewall. The original version of this HOWTO was helpful but still lacking. I hope this beefed-up version of David Rudder's Firewall HOWTO will give everyone the information they need to create a functioning firewall in hours, not weeks.

I also feel I should return something to the Linux community.

1.5 Further Readings

- The NET-2 HOWTO.
- The Ethernet HOWTO.
- The Multiple Ethernet Mini HOWTO.
- Networking with Linux.
- The PPP HOWTO.
- TCP/IP Network Administrator's Guide by O'Reilly and Associates.

- The Documentation for the TIS Firewall Toolkit.

Trusted Information System's (TIS) web site has a great collection of documentation on firewalls and related material. See http://www.tis.com/.

Also, I am working on a security project called I am calling *Secure Linux*. On the *Secure Linux* web site I am gathering all the information, documentation and programs you need to create a trusted Linux system. Email me if you would like information.

2 Understanding Firewalls

A firewall is a term used for a part of a car. In cars, firewalls are physical objects that separate the engine from the passengers. They are meant to protect the passenger in case the car's engine catches fire while still providing the driver access to the engine's controls.

A firewall in computers is a device that protects a private network from the public part (the Internet as a whole).

The firewall computer, from now on named, "firewall," can reach both the protected network and the Internet. The protected network can't reach the Internet, and the Internet can not reach the protected network.

For someone to reach the Internet from inside the protected network, they must telnet to firewall, and use the Internet from there.

The simplest form of a firewall is a dual homed system. (a system with two network connections) If you can trust all your users, you can simple set up Linux (*Compile it with IP forwarding/gatewaying turned off.*) and give everyone accounts on it. They can then log in to this system and telnet, FTP, read mail, and use any other service you provide. With this setup, the only computer on your private network that knows anything about the outside world is the firewall. The other system on your protected network don't even need a default route.

This needs re-stating. For the above firewall to work **ou must trust all your users.** I don't recommend it.

2.1 Drawbacks with Firewalls

The problem with filtering firewalls are they inhibit the access to your network from the Internet. Only services on systems that have pass filters can be accessed. With a proxy server, users can log in to the firewall and then access any system within the private network they have access to.

Also, new types of network clients and servers a coming out almost daily. When they do you must find a new way to allow controlled access before these services can be used.

2.2 Types of Firewalls

There are two types of firewalls.

1. IP or Filtering Firewalls—that block all but selected network traffic.
2. Proxy Servers—that make the network connections for you.

2.2.1 IP Filtering Firewalls

An IP filtering firewall works at the packet level. It is designed to control the flow of packets based the source, destination, port, and packet type information contained in each packet.

This type of firewall is very secure but lacks any sort of useful logging. It can block people from accessing private systems, but it will not tell you who accessed your public systems or who accessed the internet from the inside.

Filtering firewalls are absolute filters. Even if you want to give someone on outside access to your private servers you can not without giving everyone access to the servers.

Linux has included packet filtering software in the kernel starting with version 1.3.x.

2.2.2 Proxy Servers

Proxy servers allow indirect internet access through the firewall. The best example of how this works is a person telneting to a system and then telneting from there to another. Only with a proxy server the process is automatic. When you connect to a proxy server with your client software, the proxy server starts it's client (proxy) software and passes you the data.

Because proxy servers are duplicating all the communications, they can log every thing they do.

The great thing about proxy servers is that they are completely secure, when configured correctly. They will not allow someone in through them. There are no direct IP routes.

3 Setting up the Firewall

3.1 Hardware requirements

For our example, the computer is a 486-DX66 with 16 Mb of memory and a 500 Mb Linux hard drive partition. This system has two network cards: one connected to our private LAN and the other connected to the a LAN we will call the de-militarized zone (DMZ). The DMZ has a router connected to it with a connection to the Internet.

This is a pretty standard setup for a business. You could use one network card and a modem with PPP to the Internet. The point is, the firewall must have two IP network numbers.

I know a lot of people have small LANs at home with two or three computers on them. Something you might consider is putting all your modems in on Linux box (maybe an old 386) and connecting all of them to the Internet with load balancing. With this setup when only one person is pulling data they would get both modems doubling the throughput.

4 Firewalling Software

4.1 Available packages

If all you want is a filtering firewall, you only need Linux and the basic networking packages. One package that might not come with your distribution is the IP Firewall Administration tool, IPFWADM, which from http://www.xos.nl/linux/ipfwadm/.

If you want to set up a proxy server, you will need one of these packages.

1. SOCKS
2. TIS Firewall Toolkit (FWTK)

4.2 The TIS Firewall Toolkit vs SOCKS

Trusted Information System (**http://www.tis.com**) has put out a collection of programs designed to facilitate firewalling. The programs do basically the same thing as the SOCKS package, but with a different design strategy. Where SOCKS has one program that covers all Internet transactions, TIS has provided one program for each utility that wishes to use the firewall.

To contrast the two, let's use the example of World Wide Web and telnet access. With SOCKS, you set up one configuration file and one daemon. Through this file and daemon, both telnet and WWW are enabled, as well as any other service that you have not disabled.

With the TIS toolkit, you set up one daemon for each WWW and telnet, as well as configuration files for each. After you have done this, other Internet access is still prohibited until explicitly set up. If a daemon for a specific utility has not been provided (like talk), there is a "plug-in" daemon, but it is neither as flexible, nor as easy to set up, as the other tools.

This might seem a minor, but it makes a major difference. SOCKS allows you to be sloppy. With a poorly set up SOCKS server, someone from the inside could gain more access to the Internet than was originally intended. With the TIS toolkit, the people on the inside have only the access the system administrator wants them to have.

SOCKS is easier to set up, easier to compile and allows for greater flexibility. The TIS toolkit is more secure if you want to regulate the users inside the protected network. Both provide absolute protection from the outside.

I will cover the installation and setup of both.

5 Preparing the Linux system

5.1 Compiling the Kernel

Start with a clean installation of your Linux distribution. (I use RedHat 3.0.3 and the examples here are based on this distribution.) The less software you have loaded the less holes, back doors, or bugs there will be to introduce security problems in your system, so load only a minimal set of applications.

Pick a stable kernel. I used the Linux 2.0.14 kernel for my system. So this documentation is based on its settings.

You well need to recompile the Linux kernel with the appropriate options. At this point, you should look at the Kernel HOWTO, the Ethernet HOWTO, and the NET-2 HOWTO if you haven't done this before.

Here are the network related settings I know work in `make config`.

1. Under General Setup.
   (a) Turn Networking Support ON.

2. Under Networking Options.
   (a) Turn Network firewalls ON.
   (b) Turn TCP/IP Networking ON.
   (c) Turn IP forwarding/gatewaying OFF (UNLESS you wish to use IP filtering).
   (d) Turn IP Firewalling ON.
   (e) Turn IP firewall packet logging ON (this is not required but it is a good idea).
   (f) Turn IP: masquerading OFF. (I am not covering this subject here.)
   (g) Turn IP: accounting ON.
   (h) Turn IP: tunneling OFF.
   (i) Turn IP: aliasing OFF.
   (j) Turn IP: PC/TCP compatibility mode OFF.
   (k) Turn IP: Reverse ARP OFF.
   (l) Turn Drop source routed frames ON.
3. Under Network Device Support.
   (a) Turn Network device support ON.
   (b) Turn Dummy net driver support ON.
   (c) Turn Ethernet (10 or 100Mbit) ON.
   (d) Select your network card.

Now you can recompile, reinstall the kernel and reboot. Your network card(s) should show up in the boot-up sequence. If not, go over the other HOWTOs again until it is working.

5.2 Configuring two network cards

If you have two network cards in your computer, you most likely will need to add an `append` statement to your `/etc/lilo.conf` file to describe the IRQ and address of both cards. My LILO `append` statement looks like this:

```
append="ether=12,0x300,eth0 ether=15,0x340,eth1"
```

5.3 Configuring the Network Addresses

This is the real interesting part. Now you have a few decisions to make. Since we don't want the Internet to have access to any part of the private network, we do not need to use real addresses. There are a number of Internet addresses set aside for private networks. Because everyone needs more addresses, and because these addresses can not cross the Internet, they are a good choice.

Of these, 192.168.2.xxx, is set aside, and we will use it in our examples.

Your proxy firewall will be a member of both networks, and so it can pass the data through to and from the private network.

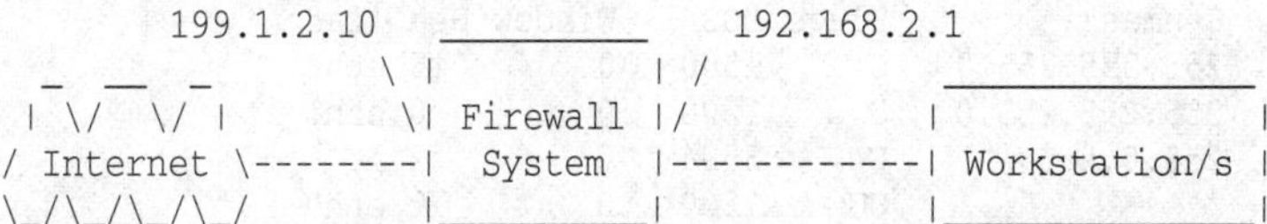

```
         199.1.2.10   __________    192.168.2.1
  _  __  _          \ |          | /           ______________
 | \/  \/ |          \| Firewall |/           |              |
/ Internet \--------|  System   |------------| Workstation/s |
\_/\_/\_/\_/         |__________|            |______________|
```

If your going to use a filtering firewall you can still use these numbers. You will need to use IP masquerading to make this happen. With this process the firewall will forward packets and translate them into "real" IP address to travel on the Internet.

You must assign the real IP address to the network card on the Internet (out) side. And, assign 192.168.2.1 to the Ethernet card on inside. This will be your proxy gateway IP address. You can assign all the other machines in the protected network some number in that 192.168.2.xxx range. (192.168.2.2 through 192.168.2.254)

Since I use Red Hat Linux (Hey guys, want to give me a copy for the plugs?) to configure the network at boot time I added a `ifcfg-eth1` file in the `/etc/sysconfig/network-scripts` directory. This file is read during the boot process to set your network and routing tables.

Here is what my `/etc/sysconfig/network-scripts/ifcfg-eth1` file looks like;

```
#!/bin/sh
#>>>Device type: ethernet
#>>>Variable declarations:
DEVICE=eth1
IPADDR=192.168.2.1
NETMASK=255.255.255.0
NETWORK=192.168.2.0
BROADCAST=192.168.2.255
GATEWAY=199.1.2.10
ONBOOT=yes
#>>>End variable declarations
```

You can also use these scripts to automatically connect by modem to your provider. Look at the ipup-ppp script.

If you're going to use a modem for your Internet connection, your outside IP address will be assigned for you by your provider at connect time.

5.4 Testing your network

Start by checking ifconfig and route. If you have two network cards, your ifconfig output should look something like:

```
#ifconfig
lo        Link encap:Local Loopback
          inet addr:127.0.0.0  Bcast:127.255.255.255  Mask:255.0.0.0
          UP BROADCAST LOOPBACK RUNNING  MTU:3584  Metric:1
          RX packets:1620 errors:0 dropped:0 overruns:0
          TX packets:1620 errors:0 dropped:0 overruns:0

eth0      Link encap:10Mbps Ethernet  HWaddr 00:00:09:85:AC:55
          inet addr:199.1.2.10 Bcast:199.1.2.255  Mask:255.255.255.0
          UP BROADCAST RUNNING MULTICAST  MTU:1500  Metric:1
          RX packets:0 errors:0 dropped:0 overruns:0
          TX packets:0 errors:0 dropped:0 overruns:0
          Interrupt:12 Base address:0x310

eth1      Link encap:10Mbps Ethernet  HWaddr 00:00:09:80:1E:D7
          inet addr:192.168.2.1  Bcast:192.168.2.255  Mask:255.255.255.0
          UP BROADCAST RUNNING MULTICAST  MTU:1500  Metric:1
          RX packets:0 errors:0 dropped:0 overruns:0
          TX packets:0 errors:0 dropped:0 overruns:0
          Interrupt:15 Base address:0x350
```

and your route table should look like:

```
#route -n
Kernel routing table
Destination     Gateway         Genmask         Flags MSS    Window Use Iface
199.1.2.0       *               255.255.255.0   U     1500   0        15 eth0
192.168.2.0     *               255.255.255.0   U     1500   0         0 eth1
127.0.0.0       *               255.0.0.0       U     3584   0         2 lo
default         199.1.2.10      *               UG    1500   0        72 eth0
```

Note: 199.1.2.0 is the Internet side of this firewall and 192.168.2.0 is the private side.

Now try to ping the Internet from the firewall. I used to use nic.ddn.mil as my test point. It's still a good test, but has proven to be less reliable than I had hoped. If it doesn't work at first, try pinging a couple other places that are not connected to your LAN. If this doesn't work, then your PPP is incorrectly setup. Reread the Net-2 HOWTO, and try again.

Next, try pinging a host within the protected network from the firewall. All the computers should be able to ping each other. If not, go over the NET-2 HOWTO again and work on the network some more.

Then, try to ping the outside address of firewall from inside the protected network. (NOTE: this is not any of the 192.168.2.xxx IP numbers.) If you can, then you have not turned off IP Forwarding. Make sure this is the way you want it. If you leave it turned on you will have to go through the IP filtering section of this document as well.

Now try pinging the Internet from behind your firewall. Use the same address that worked for you before. (I.E. nic.ddn.mil) Again, if you have IP Forwarding turned off, this should not work. But, if you have it turned on, it should.

If have IP forwarding turned on and your using a "real" (not 192.168.2.*) IP address for your private network, and you can't ping the Internet but you can ping the Internet side your firewall, check if the next router upstream is routing packets for your private network address. (Your provider may have to do this for you.)

If you have assigned your protected network to 192.168.2.*, then no packets can be routed to it anyway. If you have skipped ahead and you already have IP masquerading turned on, this test should work.

Now, you have your basic system setup.

5.5 Securing the Firewall

A firewall isn't any good if it is left wide-open to attacks through a unused service. A "bad guy" could gain access to the firewall and modify it for their own needs.

Start by turning off any unneeded services. Look at /etc/inetd.conf file. This file controls what is called the "super server." It controls a bunch of the server daemons and starts them as they are requested.

Definitely turn off netstat, systat, tftp, bootp, and finger. To turn a service off, put # as the first character of the service line. When your done, send a SIG-HUP to the process with

kill -HUP ⟨*pid*⟩

where *pid* is the process number of inetd. This will make inetd re-read its configuration file (/etc/inetd.conf) and restart.

Test it out by telneting to port 15 on firewall, the netstat port. If you get an output of netstat, you have not restarted it correctly.

6 IP filtering setup (IPFWADM)

To start, you should have IP forwarding turned on in your kernel, and your system should be up and forwarding everything you send it. Your routing tables should be in place, and you should be able to access everything, both from the inside out and from the outside in.

But, we're building a firewall, so we need to start chocking down what everyone has access to.

In my system, I created a couple of scripts to set the firewall forwarding policy and accounting policy. I call theses scripts from the /etc/rc.d scripts so my system is configured at boot time.

By default, the IP forwarding system in the Linux kernel forwards everything. Because of this, your firewall script should start by denying access to everything and flushing any ipfw rules in place from the last time it was run. This script will do the trick.

```
#
# setup IP packet Accounting and Forwarding
#
#   Forwarding
#
# By default DENY all services
ipfwadm -F -p deny
# Flush all commands
ipfwadm -F -f
ipfwadm -I -f
ipfwadm -O -f
```

Now we have the ultimate firewall. Nothing can get through. No doubt you have some services you need to forward so here are a few examples you should find useful.

```
# Forward email to your server
ipfwadm -F -a accept -b -P tcp -S 0.0.0.0/0 1024:65535 -D 192.1.2.10 25

# Forward email connections to outside email servers
ipfwadm -F -a accept -b -P tcp -S 196.1.2.10 25 -D 0.0.0.0/0 1024:65535

# Forward Web connections to your Web Server
/sbin/ipfwadm -F -a accept -b -P tcp -S 0.0.0.0/0 1024:65535 -D 196.1.2.11 80
```

```
# Forward Web connections to outside Web Server
/sbin/ipfwadm -F -a accept -b -P tcp -S 196.1.2.* 80 -D 0.0.0.0/0 1024:65535

# Forward DNS traffic
/sbin/ipfwadm -F -a accept -b -P udp -S 0.0.0.0/0 53 -D 196.1.2.0/24
```

You might also be interested in accounting for traffic going through your firewall. This script will count every packet. You could add a line or two to account for packets going to just a single system.

```
# Flush the current accounting rules
ipfwadm -A -f
# Accounting
/sbin/ipfwadm -A -f
/sbin/ipfwadm -A out -i -S 196.1.2.0/24 -D 0.0.0.0/0
/sbin/ipfwadm -A out -i -S 0.0.0.0/0 -D 196.1.2.0/24
/sbin/ipfwadm -A in -i -S 196.1.2.0/24 -D 0.0.0.0/0
/sbin/ipfwadm -A in -i -S 0.0.0.0/0 -D 196.1.2.0/24
```

If all you wanted was a filtering firewall you can stop here. Enjoy.

7 Installing the TIS Proxy server

7.1 Getting the software

The TIS FWTK is available at ftp://ftp.tis.com/.

Don't make the mistake I did. When you FTP files from TIS, read the `readme` files. The TIS FWTK is locked up in a hidden directory on their server. TIS requires you **send email to fwtk-request@tis.com** with only the word `send` in the body of the message to learn the name of this hidden directory. No subject is needed in the message. Their system will then mails you back the directory name (good for 12 hours) to download the source.

As I'm writing this TIS is releasing version 2.0 (beta) of the FWTK. This version seems to compile well (with a few exceptions) and everything is working for me. This is the version I will be covering here. When they release the final code I'll update the HOWTO.

To install the FWTK, create a `fwtk-2.0` directory in your `/usr/src` directory. Move your copy of the FWTK (fwtk-2.0.tar.gz) to this directory and un`tar` it (`tar zxf fwtk-2.0.tar.gz`).

The FWTK does not proxy SSL Web documents but there is an add-on for it written by Jean-Christophe Touvet. It is available at ftp://ftp.edelweb.fr/pub/contrib/fwtk/ssl-gw.tar.Z. Touvet does not support this code.

I am using a modified version that includes access to Netscape secure news servers written by Eric Wedel. It is available at ftp://mdi.meridian-data.com/pub/tis.fwtk/ssl-gw/ssl-gw2.tar.Z.

In our example, I will use Eric Wedel's version.

To install it, simply create a `ssl-gw` directory in your `/usr/src/fwtk-2.0` directory and put the files in it.

When I installed this gateway it required a few changes before it would compile with the rest of the toolkit.

The first change was to the `ssl-gw.c` file. I found it didn't include a needed include file.

```
#if defined(__linux)
#include        <sys/ioctl.h>
#endif
```

Second, it didn't come with a `Makefile`. I copied one out of the other gateway directories and replaced the gateway's name with `ssl-gw`.

7.2 Compiling the TIS FWTK

Version 2.0 of the FWTK compiles much easier than any of the older versions. I still found a couple of things that needed to be changed before the Beta version would compile cleanly. Hopefully these changes will be made in the final version.

To fix it up, start by changing to the `/usr/src/fwtk/fwtk` directory and copying the `Makefile.config.linux` file over the `Makefile.config` file.

Don't run `fixmake`. The instructions tell you to run this. If you do it will break the `Makefile`(s) in each directory.

I do have a fix for `fixmake`. The problem is the `sed` script. Add a '.' and " to the `include` line of every `Makefile`. This sed script works.

```
sed 's/^include[        ]*\([^  ].*\)/include \1/' $name .proto > $name
```

Next, we need to edit the `Makefile.config` file. There are two changes you may need to make.

The author set the source directory to his home directory. We are compiling our code in `/usr/src` so you should changed the `FWTKSRCDIR` variable to reflect this.

```
FWTKSRCDIR=/usr/src/fwtk/fwtk
```

Second, at least some Linux systems use the gdbm database. The `Makefile.config` is using dbm. You might need to change this. I had to for RedHat 3.0.3.

```
DBMLIB=-lgdbm
```

The last fix is in the x-gw. The bug in the Beta version is in the `socket.c` code. To fix it remove these lines of code.

```
#ifdef SCM_RIGHTS  /* 4.3BSD Reno and later */
                     + sizeof(un_name->sun_len) + 1
#endif
```

If you added the `ssl-gw` to your FWTK source directory you will need to add it to the list of directory in the `Makefile`.

```
DIRS=   smap smapd netacl plug-gw ftp-gw tn-gw rlogin-gw http-gw x-gw ssl-gw
```

Now run `make`.

7.3 Installing the TIS FWTK

Run `make install`.

The default installation directory is `/usr/local/etc`. You could change this (I didn't) to a more secure directory. I chose to change the access to this directory with `chmod 700`.

All that is left now is to configure the firewall.

7.4 Configuring the TIS FWTK

Now the fun really begins. We must teach the system to call theses new services and create the tables to control them.

I'm not going to try to re-write the TIS FWTK manual here. I will show you the setting I found that worked and explain the problems I ran into and how I got around them.

There are three files that make up these controls.

- `/etc/services`
  - Tells the system what ports services are on.
- `/etc/inetd.conf`
  - Tells inetd what program to call when someone knocks on a service port.
- `/usr/local/etc/netperm-table`
  - Tells the FWTK services who to allow and deny service to.

To get the FWTK functioning, you should edit these files from the bottom up. Editing the `/etc/services` file without the `/etc/inetd.conf` or `/etc/netperm-table` file set correctly could make your system inaccessible.

7.4.1 The `/etc/netperm-table` file

This file controls who can access the services of the TIS FWTK. You should think about the traffic using the firewall from both sides. People outside your network should identify themselves before gaining access, but the people inside your network might be allowed to just pass through.

So people can identify themselves, the firewall uses a program called `authsrv` to keep a database of user IDs and passwords. The authentication section of the `/etc/netperm-table` file controls where the database is kept and who can access it.

I had some trouble closing the access to this service. Note the `permit-hosts` line I show uses a `*` to give everyone access. The correct setting for this line is "`authsrv:   premit-hosts localhost`" if you can get it working.

```
#
# Proxy configuration table
#
# Authentication server and client rules
authsrv:       database /usr/local/etc/fw-authdb
authsrv:       permit-hosts *
authsrv:       badsleep 1200
authsrv:       nobogus true
# Client Applications using the Authentication server
*:             authserver 127.0.0.1 114
```

To initialize the database, su to root, and run `./authsrv` in the `/var/local/etc` directory to create the administrative user record. Here is a sample session.

Read the FWTK documentation to learn how to add users and groups.

```
#
# authsrv
authsrv# list
authsrv# adduser admin {\tt "}Auth DB admin{\tt "}
ok - user added initially disabled
authsrv# ena admin
enabled
authsrv# proto admin pass
changed
authsrv# pass admin {\tt "}plugh{\tt "}
Password changed.
authsrv# superwiz admin
set wizard
authsrv# list
Report for users in database
user   group  longname          ok?   proto  last
------ ------ ----------------- ----- ------ -----
admin         Auth DB admin     ena   passw  never
authsrv# display admin
Report for user admin (Auth DB admin)
Authentication protocol: password
Flags: WIZARD
authsrv# ^D
EOT
#
```

The telnet gateway (`tn-gw`) controls are straightforward and the first you should set up.

In my example, I premit hosts from inside the private network to pass through without authenticating themselves. (`permit-hosts 199.61.2.* -passok`) But, any other user must enter their user ID and password to use the proxy. (`permit-hosts * -auth`)

I also allow one other system (196.1.2.202) to access the firewall directly without going through the firewall at all. The two `inetacl-in.telnetd` lines do this. I will explain how these lines are called latter.

The telnet timeout should be kept short.

```
# telnet gateway rules:
tn-gw:               denial-msg      /usr/local/etc/tn-deny.txt
tn-gw:               welcome-msg     /usr/local/etc/tn-welcome.txt
tn-gw:               help-msg        /usr/local/etc/tn-help.txt
tn-gw:               timeout 90
tn-gw:               permit-hosts 196.1.2.* -passok -xok
tn-gw:               permit-hosts * -auth
# Only the Administrator can telnet directly to the Firewall via Port 24
netacl-in.telnetd: permit-hosts 196.1.2.202 -exec /usr/sbin/in.telnetd
```

The r-commands work the same way as telnet.

```
# rlogin gateway rules:
rlogin-gw:    denial-msg      /usr/local/etc/rlogin-deny.txt
rlogin-gw:    welcome-msg     /usr/local/etc/rlogin-welcome.txt
rlogin-gw:    help-msg        /usr/local/etc/rlogin-help.txt
rlogin-gw:    timeout 90
rlogin-gw:    permit-hosts 196.1.2.* -passok -xok
rlogin-gw:    permit-hosts * -auth -xok
# Only the Administrator can telnet directly to the Firewall via Port
netacl-rlogind: permit-hosts 196.1.2.202 -exec /usr/libexec/rlogind -a
```

You shouldn't have anyone accessing your firewall directly and that includes FTP, so don't put an FTP server on your firewall.

Again, the `permit-hosts` line allows anyone in the protected network free access to the Internet, and all others must authenticate themselves. I included logging of every file sent and received to my controls. (`-log { retr stor }`)

The FTP timeout controls how long it will take to drop a bad connections as well as how long a connection will stay open without activity.

```
# ftp gateway rules:
ftp-gw:              denial-msg      /usr/local/etc/ftp-deny.txt
ftp-gw:              welcome-msg     /usr/local/etc/ftp-welcome.txt
ftp-gw:              help-msg        /usr/local/etc/ftp-help.txt
ftp-gw:              timeout 300
ftp-gw:              permit-hosts 196.1.2.* -log { retr stor }
ftp-gw:              permit-hosts * -authall -log { retr stor }
```

Web, gopher and browser based FTP are contorted by the `http-gw`. The first two lines create a directory to store FTP and Web documents as they are passing through the firewall. I make these files owned by root and put them in a directory accessible only by root.

The Web connection should be kept short. It controls how long the user will wait on a bad connections.

```
# www and gopher gateway rules:
http-gw:      userid          root
http-gw:      directory       /jail
http-gw:      timeout 90
http-gw:      default-httpd   www.afs.net
http-gw:      hosts           196.1.2.* -log { read write ftp }
http-gw:      deny-hosts      *
```

The `ssl-gw` is really just a pass-anything gateway. Be careful with it. In this example I allow anyone inside the protected network to connect to any server outside the network except the addresses 127.0.0.* and 192.1.1.*, and then only on ports 443 through 563. Ports 443 through 563 are known SSL ports.

```
# ssl gateway rules:
ssl-gw: timeout 300
ssl-gw: hosts       196.1.2.* -dest { !127.0.0.* !192.1.1.* *:443:563 }
ssl-gw: deny-hosts  *
```

Here is an example of how to use the `plug-gw` to allow connections to a news server. In this example I allow anyone inside the protected network to connect to only one system and only to its news port.

The "seconded" line allows the news server to pass its data back to the protected network.

Because most clients expect to stay connected while the user reads news, the timeout for a news server should be long.

```
# NetNews Pluged gateway
plug-gw:          timeout 3600
plug-gw: port nntp 196.1.2.* -plug-to 199.5.175.22 -port nntp
plug-gw: port nntp 199.5.175.22 -plug-to 196.1.2.* -port nntp
```

The `finger` gateway is simple. Anyone inside the protected network must log in first, and then we allow them to use the `finger` program on the firewall. Anyone else just gets a message.

```
# Enable finger service
netacl-fingerd: permit-hosts 196.1.2.* -exec /usr/libexec/fingerd
```

```
netacl-fingerd: permit-hosts * -exec /bin/cat /usr/local/etc/finger.txt
```

I haven't set up the mail and X services, so I'm not including examples. If anyone has a working example, please send me email.

7.4.2 The /etc/inetd.conf file

Here is a complete /etc/inetd.conf file. All unneeded services have been commented out. I have included the complete file to show what to turn off, as well as how to set up the new firewall services.

```
#echo stream  tcp  nowait  root       internal
#echo dgram   udp  wait    root       internal
#discard      stream  tcp  nowait  root      internal
#discard      dgram   udp  wait    root      internal
#daytime      stream  tcp  nowait  root      internal
#daytime      dgram   udp  wait    root      internal
#chargen      stream  tcp  nowait  root      internal
#chargen      dgram   udp  wait    root      internal
# FTP firewall gateway
ftp-gw      stream  tcp  nowait.400  root  /usr/local/etc/ftp-gw  ftp-gw
# Telnet firewall gateway
telnet stream tcp nowait root /usr/local/etc/tn-gw /usr/local/etc/tn-gw
# local telnet services
telnet-a    stream  tcp  nowait root  /usr/local/etc/netacl in.telnetd
# Gopher firewall gateway
gopher stream tcp nowait.400 root /usr/local/etc/http-gw \
/usr/local/etc/http-gw

# WWW firewall gateway
http stream tcp nowait.400 root /usr/local/etc/http-gw \
/usr/local/etc/http-gw
# SSL firewall gateway
ssl-gw  stream  tcp     nowait  root /usr/local/etc/ssl-gw   ssl-gw
# NetNews firewall proxy (using plug-gw)
nntp    stream  tcp     nowait  root     /usr/local/etc/plug-gw plug-gw nntp
#nntp stream  tcp     nowait  root     /usr/sbin/tcpd  in.nntpd
# SMTP (email) firewall gateway
#smtp stream  tcp     nowait  root     /usr/local/etc/smap smap
#
# Shell, login, exec and talk are BSD protocols.
#
#shell        stream  tcp     nowait  root     /usr/sbin/tcpd  in.rshd
#login        stream  tcp     nowait  root     /usr/sbin/tcpd  in.rlogind
#exec stream  tcp     nowait  root     /usr/sbin/tcpd  in.rexecd
#talk dgram   udp     wait    root     /usr/sbin/tcpd  in.talkd
#ntalk        dgram   udp     wait    root     /usr/sbin/tcpd  in.ntalkd
#dtalk        stream  tcp     waut    nobody /usr/sbin/tcpd  in.dtalkd
#
# Pop and imap mail services et al
#
#pop-2    stream  tcp  nowait  root  /usr/sbin/tcpd    ipop2d
#pop-3    stream  tcp  nowait  root  /usr/sbin/tcpd    ipop3d
#imap     stream  tcp  nowait  root  /usr/sbin/tcpd    imapd
#
# The Internet UUCP service.
#
#uucp    stream  tcp  nowait  uucp  /usr/sbin/tcpd  /usr/lib/uucp/uucico -l
#
# Tftp service is provided primarily for booting.  Most sites
```

```
# run this only on machines acting as {\tt "}boot servers.{\tt "}
# Do not uncomment this unless you *need* it.
#
#tftp dgram   udp    wait    root    /usr/sbin/tcpd  in.tftpd
#bootps       dgram  udp     wait    root    /usr/sbin/tcpd  bootpd
#
# Finger, systat and netstat give out user information which may be
# valuable to potential "system crackers."  Many sites choose to disable
# some or all of these services to improve security.
#
# cfinger is for GNU finger, which is currently not in use in RHS Linux
#
 finger       stream  tcp  nowait  root   /usr/sbin/tcpd  in.fingerd
#cfinger      stream  tcp  nowait  root   /usr/sbin/tcpd  in.cfingerd
#systat       stream  tcp  nowait  guest  /usr/sbin/tcpd  /bin/ps -auwwx
#netstat      stream  tcp  nowait  guest  /usr/sbin/tcpd  /bin/netstat -f inet
#
# Time service is used for clock syncronization.
#
#time stream  tcp  nowait  root  /usr/sbin/tcpd  in.timed
#time dgram   udp  wait    root  /usr/sbin/tcpd  in.timed
#
# Authentication
#
 auth         stream  tcp  wait    root  /usr/sbin/tcpd in.identd -w -t120
 authsrv      stream  tcp  nowait  root  /usr/local/etc/authsrv authsrv
#
# End of inetd.conf
```

7.4.3 The /etc/services file

This is where it all begins. When a client connects to the firewall it connects on a known port (less than 1024). For example, telnet connects on port 23. The inetd daemon hears this connection and looks up the name of these service in the /etc/services file. It then calls the program assigned to the name in the /etc/inetd.conf file.

Some of the services we are creating are not normally in the /etc/services file. You can assign some of them to any port you want. For example, I have assigned the administrator's telnet port (telnet-a) to port 24. You could assign it to port 2323 if you wished. For the administrator (you) to connect directly to the firewall, you need to telnet to port 24 not 23, and if you setup your /etc/netperm-table file like I did, you will only be able to this from one system inside your protected network.

```
telnet-a        24/tcp
ftp-gw          21/tcp                # this named changed
auth            113/tcp  ident        # User Verification
ssl-gw          443/tcp
```

8 The SOCKS Proxy Server

8.1 Setting up the Proxy Server

The SOCKS proxy server available from ftp://sunsite.unc.edu/pub/Linux/system/Network/misc/socks-linux-src.tgz. There is also an example config file in that directory called socks-conf. Uncompress and untar the files into a directory on your system, and follow the instructions on how to make it. I had a couple problems when I made it. Make sure that your Makefiles are correct.

One important thing to note is that the proxy server needs to be added to /etc/inetd.conf. You must add a line:

```
socks  stream  tcp  nowait  nobody  /usr/local/etc/sockd  sockd
```

to tell the server to run when requested.

8.2 Configuring the Proxy Server

The SOCKS program needs two separate configuration files: one to tell the access allowed, and one to route the requests to the appropriate proxy server. The access file should be housed on the server. The routing file should be housed on every Un*x machine. The DOS and, presumably, Macintosh computers do their own routing.

8.2.1 The Access File

With SOCKS 4.2 Beta, the access file is called `sockd.conf"`. It should contain two lines, a `permit` and a `deny` line. Each line will have three entries:

- The Identifier (permit/deny).
- The IP address.
- The address modifier.

The identifier is either `permit` or `deny`. You should have both a `permit` and a `deny` line.

The IP address holds a four-byte address in typical IP dot notation. I.E. 192.168.2.0.

The address modifier is also a typical, four-byte IP address number. It works like a netmask. Envision this number to be 32 bits (1s or 0s). If the bit is a 1, the corresponding bit of the address that it is checking must match the corresponding bit in the IP address field. For instance, if the line is:

```
permit 192.168.2.23 255.255.255.255
```

it will permit only the IP address that matches every bit in 192.168.2.23; e.g., only 192.168.2.3. The line:

```
permit 192.168.2.0 255.255.255.0
```

will permit every number within group 192.168.2.0 through 192.168.2.255, the whole C Class domain. One should not have the line:

```
permit 192.168.2.0 0.0.0.0
```

as this will permit every address, regardless.

So, first permit every address you want to permit, and then deny the rest. To allow everyone in the domain 192.168.2.xxx, the lines:

```
permit 192.168.2.0 255.255.255.0
deny 0.0.0.0 0.0.0.0
```

will work nicely. Notice the first `0.0.0.0` in the deny line. With a modifier of 0.0.0.0, the IP address field does not matter. All 0's is the norm because it is easy to type.

More than one entry of each is allowed.

Specific users can also be granted or denied access. This is done via `ident` authentication. Not all systems support `ident`, including Trumpet Winsock, so I will not go into it here. The documentation with SOCKS is quite adequate on this subject.

8.2.2 The Routing File

The routing file in SOCKS is poorly named `socks.conf`. I say "poorly named" because it is so close to the name of the access file that it is easy to get the two confused.

The routing file is there to tell the SOCKS clients when to use socks and when not to. For instance, in our network, 192.168.2.3 will not need to use SOCKS to talk with 192.168.2.1, the firewall. It has a direct connection in via Ethernet. It defines 127.0.0.1, the loopback, automatically. Of course you do not need SOCKS to talk to yourself. There are three entries:

- deny
- direct
- sockd

Deny tells SOCKS when to reject a request. This entry has the same three fields as in `/etc/sockd.conf`: `identifier`, `address` and `modifier`. Generally, since this is also handled by `/etc/sockd.conf`, the access file, the `modifier` field is set to 0.0.0.0. If you want to preclude yourself from calling anyplace, you can do it here.

The direct entry tells which addresses to not use SOCKS for. These are all the addresses that can be reached without the proxy server. Again we have the three fields: `identifier`, `address`, and `modifier`. Our example would have

```
direct 192.168.2.0 255.255.255.0
```

Thus going direct for any on our protected network.

The `sockd` entry tells the computer which host has the SOCKS server daemon on it. The syntax is:

```
sockd @=<serverlist> <IP address> <modifier>
```

Notice the `@=` entry. This allows you to set the IP addresses of a list of proxy servers. In our example, we only use one proxy server. But, you can have many to allow a greater load, and for redundancy in case of failure.

The IP address and `modifier` fields work just like in the other examples. You specify which addresses go where through these.

8.2.3 DNS from behind a Firewall

Setting up Domain Name service from behind a firewall is a relatively simple task. You need merely to set up the DNS on the firewalling machine. Then, set each machine behind the firewall to use this DNS.

8.3 Working With a Proxy Server

8.3.1 Unix

To have your applications work with the proxy server, they need to be "SOCKified." You will need two different `telnets`, one for direct communication, one for communication via the proxy server. SOCKS comes with instructions on how to SOCKify a program, as well as a couple pre-SOCKified programs. If you use the SOCKified version to go somewhere direct, SOCKS will automatically switch over to the direct version for you. Because of this, we want to rename all the programs on our protected network and replace them with the SOCKified programs. `finger` becomes `finger.orig`, `telnet` becomes `telnet.orig`, etc. You must tell SOCKS about each of these via the `include/socks.h` file.

Certain programs will handle routing and SOCKifying itself. Netscape is one of these. You can use a proxy server under Netscape by entering the server's address (192.168.2.1 in our case) in the SOCKs field under Proxies. Each application will need at least a little messing with, regardless of how it handles a proxy server.

8.3.2 MS Windows with Trumpet Winsock

Trumpet Winsock comes with built-in proxy server capabilities. In the `setup` menu, enter the IP address of the server and the addresses of all the computers reachable directly. Trumpet will then handle all outgoing packets.

8.3.3 Getting the Proxy Server to work with UDP Packets

The SOCKS package works only with TCP packets, not UDP. This makes it quite a bit less useful. Many useful programs, like `talk` and `archie`, use UDP. There is a package designed to be used as a proxy server for UDP packets called UDPrelay, by Tom Fitzgerald fitz@wang.com. Unfortunately, at the time of this writing, it is not compatible with Linux.

8.4 Drawbacks with Proxy Servers

The proxy server is, above all, a security device. Using it to increase Internet access with limited IP addresses will have many drawbacks. A proxy server will allow greater access from inside the protected network to the outside, but will keep the inside completely unaccessible from the outside. This means no servers, talk or Archie connections, or direct mailing to the inside computers. These drawbacks might seem slight, but think of it this way:

- You have left a report you are doing on your computer inside a protected network. You are at home and decide that you would like to go over it. You can not. You can not reach your computer because it is behind the firewall. You try to log into the firewall first, but since everyone has proxy server access, no one has set up an account for you on it.
- Your daughter goes to college. You want to email her. You have some private things to talk about, and would rather have your mail sent directly to your machine. You trust your systems administrator completely, but still, this is private mail.
- The inability to use UDP packets represents a big drawback with the proxy servers. I imagine UDP capabilities will be coming shortly.

FTP causes another problem with a proxy server. When getting or doing an `ls`, the FTP server opens a socket on the client machine and sends the information through it. A proxy server will not allow this, so FTP doesn't particularly work.

And, proxy servers run slowly. Because of the greater overhead, almost any other means of getting this access will be faster.

Basically, if you have the IP addresses, and you are not worried about security, do not use a firewall or proxy server. If you do not have the IP addresses, but you are also not worried about security, you might also want to look into using an IP emulator, like `term`, `slirp`, or TIA. `term` is available from ftp://sunsite.unc.edu, `slirp` is available from ftp://blitzen.canberra.edu.au/pub/slirp, and TIA is available from marketplace.com. These packages run faster, allow better connections, and provide a greater level of access to the inside network from the Internet. Proxy servers are good for those networks which have a lot of hosts that will want to connect to the Internet on the fly, with one setup and little work after that.

9 Advanced Configurations

There is one configuration I would like to go over before wrapping this document up. The one I have just outlined will probably suffice for most people. However, I think the next outline will show a more advanced configuration that can clear up some questions. If you have questions beyond what I have just covered, or are just interested in the versatility of proxy servers and firewalls, read on.

9.1 A large network with emphasis on security

Say, for instance, you are the leader of a militia and you wish to network your site. You have 50 computers and a subnet of 32 (5 bits) IP numbers. You need various levels of access within your network because you tell your followers different things. Therefore, you'll need to protect certain parts of the network from the rest.

The levels are:

1. The external level. This is the level that gets shown to everybody. This is where you rant and rave to get new volunteers.
2. **Troop** This is the level of people who have gotten beyond the external level. Here is where you teach them about the evil government and how to make bombs.
3. **Mercenary** Here is where the real plans are kept. In this level is stored all the information on how the 3rd world government is going to take over the world, your plans involving Newt Gingrich, Oklahoma City, lawn care products, and what really is stored in those hangers at area 51.

9.1.1 The Network Setup

The IP numbers are arranged as:

- One number is 192.168.2.255, which is the broadcast address and is not usable.
- Twenty-three of the 32 IP addresses are allocated to 23 machines that will be accessible to the internet.
- One extra IP goes to a linux box on that network.
- One extra goes to a different linux box on that network.
- Two IP #'s go to the router.
- Four are left over, but given domain names paul, ringo, john, and george, just to confuse things a bit.
- The protected networks both have the addresses 192.168.2.xxx.

Then, two separate networks are built, each in different rooms. They are routed via infrared Ethernet so that they are completely invisible to the outside room. Luckily, infrared Ethernet works just like normal Ethernet.

These networks are each connected to one of the Linux boxes with an extra IP address.

There is a file server connecting the two protected networks. This is because the plans for taking over the world involves some of the higher Troops. The file server holds the address 192.168.2.17 for the Troop network and 192.168.2.23 for the Mercenary network. It has to have different IP addresses because it has to have different Ethernet cards. IP Forwarding on it is turned off.

IP Forwarding on both Linux boxes is also turned off. The router will not forward packets destined for 192.168.2.xxx unless explicitly told to do so, so the Internet will not be able to get in. The reason for turning off IP Forwarding here is so that packets from the Troop's network will not be able to reach the Mercenary network, and vice versa.

The NFS server can also be set to offer different files to the different networks. This can come in handy, and a little trickery with symbolic links can make it so that the common files can be shared with all. Using this setup and another Ethernet card can offer this one file server for all three networks.

9.1.2 The Proxy Setup

Now, since all three levels want to be able to monitor the network for their own devious purposes, all three need to have net access. The external network is connected directly into the Internet, so we don't have to mess with proxy servers here. The Mercenary and Troop networks are behind firewalls, so it is necessary to set up proxy servers here.

Both networks will be set up very similarly. They both have the same IP addresses assigned to them. I will throw in a couple of parameters, just to make things more interesting, though.

1. No one can use the file server for Internet access. This exposes the file server to viruses and other nasty things, and it is rather important, so it's off limits.
2. We will not allow troop access to the World Wide Web. They are in training, and this kind of information retrieval power might prove to be damaging.

So, the `/etc/sockd.conf` file on the Troop's Linux box will have this line:

```
deny 192.168.2.17 255.255.255.255
```

and on the Mercenary machine:

```
deny 192.168.2.23 255.255.255.255
```

And, the Troop's Linux box will have this line

```
deny 0.0.0.0 0.0.0.0 eq 80
```

This says to deny access to all machines trying to access the port equal (eq) to 80, the `http` port. This will still allow all other services, just deny Web access.

Then, both files will have:

```
permit 192.168.2.0 255.255.255.0
```

to allow all the computers on the 192.168.2.xxx network to use this proxy server except for those that have already been denied (i.e.; the file server and Web access from the Troop network).

The Troop's `/etc/sockd.conf` file will look like:

```
deny 192.168.2.17 255.255.255.255
deny 0.0.0.0 0.0.0.0 eq 80
permit 192.168.2.0 255.255.255.0
```

and the Mercenary file will look like:

```
deny 192.168.2.23 255.255.255.255
permit 192.168.2.0 255.255.255.0
```

This should configure everything correctly. Each network is isolated accordingly, with the proper amount of interaction. Everyone should be happy.

Now, take over the world!

Part XXII

"Linux GCC-HOWTO" by Daniel Barlow,

dan@detached.demon.co.uk

Contents

Abstract

v1.17, 28 February 1996
This document covers how to set up the GNU C compiler and development libraries under Linux, and gives an overview of compiling, linking, running and debugging programs under it. Most of the material in it has been taken from Mitch D'Souza's GCC-FAQ, which it replaces, or the ELF-HOWTO, which it will eventually largely replace. This is the first publicly released version (despite the version number; that's an artifact of RCS). Feedback is welcomed.

1 Preliminaries

1.1 ELF vs. a.out

Linux development is in a state of flux right now. Briefly, there are two formats for the binaries that Linux knows how to execute, and depending on how your system is put together, you may have either. When reading this HOWTO, it helps to know which.

How to tell? Use the `file` utility (eg `file /bin/bash`). For an ELF program, it will say something with ELF in it, for an a.out program it will say something involving `Linux/i386`.

The differences between ELF and a.out are covered (extensively) later in this document. ELF is the newer format, and generally accepted as better.

1.1.1 Administrata

The copyright information and like legalese can be found at the end of this document, together with the statutory warnings about asking dumb questions on Usenet, revealing your ignorance of the C language by reporting bugs which aren't, and picking your nose while chewing gum.

1.2 Typography

If you're reading this in Postscript, dvi, or html format, you get to see a little more font variation than people with the plain text version. In particular, filenames, commands, command output and source code excerpts are set in some form of `typewriter` font, whereas variables and random things that need emphasizing are *emphasized*.

You also get a usable index. In dvi or PostScript, the numbers in the index are section numbers. In HTML they're just sequentially assigned numbers that you can click on. In the plain text version, they really are just numbers. Get an upgrade.

The Bourne (rather than C) shell syntax is used in examples. C shell users will want to use

```
% setenv FOO bar
```

where I have written

```
$ FOO=bar; export FOO
```

If the prompt shown is `#` rather than `$`, the command shown will probably only work as root. Of course, I accept no responsibility for anything that happens to your system as a result of trying these examples. Have a nice day.

2 Where to get things

2.1 This document

This document is one of the Linux HOWTO series, so is available from all Linux HOWTO repositories, such as

```
http://sunsite.unc.edu/pub/linux/docs/HOWTO/
```

The HTML version can also be found (possibly in a slightly newer version) from

```
http://ftp.linux.org.uk/\verb+~+barlow/howto/gcc-howto.html
```

2.2 Other documentation

The official documentation for gcc is in the source distribution (see below) as texinfo files, and as `.info` files. If you have a fast network connection, a cdrom, or a reasonable amount of patience, you can just untar it and copy the relevant bits into `/usr/info`. If not, you may find them at

```
ftp://tsx-11.mit.edu:/pub/linux/packages/GCC/
```

but not necessarily always the latest version.

There are two source of documentation for libc. GNU libc comes with info files which describe Linux libc fairly accurately except for stdio. Also, the manual pages archive at

```
ftp://sunsite.unc.edu/pub/Linux/docs/
```

are written for Linux and describe a lot of system calls (Section 2) and libc functions (Section 3).

2.3 GCC

There are two answers.

(a) The official Linux GCC distribution can always be found in binary (ready-compiled) form at

```
ftp://tsx-11.mit.edu:/pub/linux/packages/GCC/
\index{FTP!archive sites!tsx-11.mit.edu@{\tt tsx-11.mit.edu}}%
\index{tsx-11.mit.edu@{\tt tsx-11.mit.edu}}%
```

At the time of writing, 2.7.2 (`gcc-2.7.2.bin.tar.gz`) is the latest version.

(b) The latest source distribution of GCC from the Free Software Foundation can be had from the GNU archives

```
ftp://prep.ai.mit.edu/pub/gnu/
```

This is not necessarily always the same version as above, though it is just now. The Linux GCC maintainer(s) have made it easy for you to compile the latest version available yourself — the `configure` script should set it all up for you. Check ftp://tsx-11.mit.edu:/pub/linux/packages/GCC/ as well, for patches which you may want to apply.

To compile anything non-trivial (and quite a few trivial things also) you will also need the

2.4 C library and header files

What you want here depends on (i) whether your system is ELF or a.out, and (ii) which you want it to be. If you're upgrading from libc 4 to libc 5, you are recommended to look at the ELF-HOWTO from approximately the same place as you found this document.

These are available from ftp://tsx-11.mit.edu:/pub/linux/packages/GCC/ as above:

`libc-5.2.18.bin.tar.gz`

—ELF shared library images, static libraries and include files for the C and maths libraries.

`libc-5.2.18.tar.gz`

— Source for the above. You will also need the `.bin.` package for the header files. If you are deliberating whether to compile the C library yourself or use the binaries, the right answer in nearly all cases is to use the binaries. You will however need to roll your own if you want NYS or shadow password support.

`libc-4.7.5.bin.tar.gz`

— a.out shared library images and static libraries for version 4.7.5 of the C library and friends. This is designed to coexist with the libc 5 package above, but is only really necessary if you wish to keep using or developing a.out format programs.

2.5 Associated tools (`as`, `ld`, `ar`, `strings`, etc.)

From ftp://tsx-11.mit.edu:/pub/linux/packages/GCC/, just like everything else so far. The current version is `binutils-2.6.0.2.bin.tar.gz`.

Note that the binutils are only available in ELF, the current libc version is in ELF and the a.out libc is happiest when used in conjunction with an ELF libc. C library development is moving emphatically ELFwards, and unless you have really good reasons for needing a.out things you're encouraged to follow suit.

3 GCC installation and setup

3.1 GCC versions

You can find out what GCC version you're running by typing `gcc -v` at the shell prompt. This is also a fairly reliable way to find out whether you are set up for ELF or a.out. On my system it does

```
$ gcc -v
Reading specs from /usr/lib/gcc-lib/i486-box-linux/2.7.2/specs
gcc version 2.7.2
```

The key things to note here are

- `i486`. This indicates that the gcc you are using was built for a 486 processor — you might have 386 or 586 instead. All of these chips can run code compiled for each of the others; the difference is that the 486 code has added padding in some places so runs faster on a 486. This has no detrimental performance effect on a 386, but does make the binaries slightly larger.
- `box`. This is *not* at all important, and may say something else (such as `slackware` or `debian`) or nothing at all (so that the complete directory name is `i486-linux`). If you build your own gcc, you can set this at build time for cosmetic effect. Just like I did.
- `linux`. This may instead say `linuxelf` or `linuxaout`, and, confusingly, the meaning of each varies according to the version that you are using.
  - `linux` means ELF if the version is 2.7.0 or newer, a.out otherwise.
  - `linuxaout` means a.out. It was introduced as a target when the definition of `linux` was changed from a.out to ELF, so you won't see any `linuxaout` gcc older than 2.7.0.
  - `linuxelf` is obsolete. It is generally a version of gcc 2.6.3 set to produce ELF executables. Note that gcc 2.6.3 has known bugs when producing code for ELF — an upgrade is advisable.
- `2.7.2` is the version number.

So, in summary, I have GCC 2.7.2 producing ELF code. *Quelle surprise.*

3.2 Where did it go?

If you installed gcc without watching, or if you got it as part of a distribution, you may like to find out where it lives in the filesystem. The key bits are

- `/usr/lib/gcc-lib/`*target*`/`*version*`/` (and subdirectories) is where most of the compiler lives. This includes the executable programs that do actual compiling, and some version-specific libraries and include files.
- `/usr/bin/gcc` is the compiler driver — the bit that you can actually run from the command line. This can be used with multiple versions of GCC provided that you have multiple compiler directories (as above) installed. To find out the default version it will use, type `gcc -v`. To force it to another version, type `gcc -V` *version*. For example

```
# gcc -v
Reading specs from /usr/lib/gcc-lib/i486-box-linux/2.7.2/specs
gcc version 2.7.2
# gcc -V 2.6.3 -v
Reading specs from /usr/lib/gcc-lib/i486-box-linux/2.6.3/specs
gcc driver version 2.7.2 executing gcc version 2.6.3
```

- `/usr/`*target*`/(bin|lib|include)`. If you have multiple targets installed (for example, a.out and ELF, or a cross-compiler of some sort, the libraries, binutils (`as`, `ld` and so on) and header files for the non-native target(s) can be found here. Even if you only have one kind of gcc installed you might find anyway that various bits for it are kept here. If not, they're in `/usr/(bin|lib|include)`.
- `/lib/`,`/usr/lib` and others are library directories for the native system. You will also need `/lib/cpp` for many applications (X makes quite a lot of use of it)—either copy it from `/usr/lib/gcc-lib/`*target*`/`*version*`/` or make a symlink pointing there.

3.3 Where are the header files?

Apart from whatever you install yourself under `/usr/local/include`, there are three main sources of header files in Linux:

- Most of `/usr/include/` and its subdirectories are supplied with the libc binary package from H J Lu. I say "most" because you may also have files from other sources (`curses` and `dbm` libraries, for example) in here, especially if you are using the newest libc distribution (which doesn't come with `curses` or `dbm`, unlike the older ones).
- `/usr/include/linux` and `/usr/include/asm` (for the files `<linux/*.h>` and `<asm/*.h>`) should be symbolic links to the directories `linux/include/linux` and `linux/include/asm` in the kernel source distribution. You need to install these if you plan to do any non-trivial development; they are not just there for compiling the kernel. You might find also that you need to do `make config` in the kernel directory after unpacking the sources. Many files depend on `<linux/autoconf.h>` which otherwise may not exist, and in some kernel versions `asm` is a symbolic link itself and only created at `make config` time.

  So, if you unpack your kernel sources under `/usr/src/linux`, that's

  ```
  $ cd /usr/src/linux
  $ su
  # make config
  [answer the questions.  Unless you're going to go on and build the kernel
  it doesn't matter _too_ much what you say]
  # cd /usr/include
  # ln -s ../src/linux/include/linux .
  # ln -s ../src/linux/include/asm .
  ```
- Files such as `<float.h>`, `<limits.h>`, `<varargs.h>`, `<stdarg.h>` and `<stddef.h>` vary according to the compiler version, so are found in `/usr/lib/gcc-lib/i486-box-linux/2.7.2/include/` and places of that ilk.

3.4 Building cross compilers

3.4.1 Linux as the target platform

Assuming you have obtained the source code to GCC, usually you can just follow the instructions given in the INSTALL file for GCC. A `configure -target=i486-linux -host=XXX` on platform `XXX` followed by a `make` should do the trick. Note that you will need the Linux includes, the kernel includes, and also to build the cross assembler and cross linker from the sources in `ftp://tsx-11.mit.edu/pub/linux/packages/GCC/`.

3.4.2 Linux as the source platform, MSDOS as the target

Ugh. Apparently this is somewhat possible by using the "emx" package or the "go" extender. Please look at

`ftp://sunsite.unc.edu/pub/Linux/devel/msdos`

I have not tested this and cannot vouch for its abilities.

4 Porting and Compiling

4.1 Automatically defined symbols

You can find out what symbols your version of GCC defines automatically by running it with the `-v` switch. For example, mine does:

```
$ echo 'main(){printf("hello world\n");}' | gcc -E -v -
Reading specs from /usr/lib/gcc-lib/i486-box-linux/2.7.2/specs
gcc version 2.7.2
 /usr/lib/gcc-lib/i486-box-linux/2.7.2/cpp -lang-c -v -undef
-D__GNUC__=2 -D__GNUC_MINOR__=7 -D__ELF__ -Dunix -Di386 -Dlinux
-D__ELF__ -D__unix__ -D__i386__ -D__linux__ -D__unix -D__i386
-D__linux -Asystem(unix) -Asystem(posix) -Acpu(i386)
-Amachine(i386) -D__i486__ -
```

If you are writing code that uses Linux-specific features, it is a good idea to enclose the nonportable bits in

```
#ifdef __linux__
/* ... funky stuff ... */
#endif /* linux */
```

Use `__linux__` for this purpose, *not* `linux`. Although the latter is defined, it is not POSIX compliant.

4.2 Compiler invocation

The documentation for compiler switches is the GCC info page (in Emacs, use `C-h i` then select the "gcc" option). Your distributor may not have packed this with your system, or you may have an old version; the best thing to do in this case is to download the GCC source archive from `ftp://prep.ai.mit.edu/pub/gnu` or one of its mirrors, and copy them out of it.

The `gcc` manual page (`gcc.1`) is, generally speaking, out of date. It will warn you of this when you try to look at it.

4.2.1 Compiler flags

`gcc` can be made to optimize its output code by adding `-O`*n* to its command line, where *n* is an optional small integer. Meaningful values of *n*, and their exact effect, vary according to the exact version, but typically it ranges from 0 (no optimization) to 2 (lots) or 3 (lots and lots).

Internally, GCC translates these to a series of `-f` and `-m` options. You can see exactly which `-O` levels map to which options by running `gcc` with the `-v` flag and the (undocumented) `-Q` flag. For example, for `-O2`, mine says

```
enabled: -fdefer-pop -fcse-follow-jumps -fcse-skip-blocks
-fexpensive-optimizations
         -fthread-jumps -fpeephole -fforce-mem -ffunction-cse -finline
         -fcaller-saves -fpcc-struct-return -frerun-cse-after-loop
         -fcommon -fgnu-linker -m80387 -mhard-float -mno-soft-float
         -mno-386 -m486 -mieee-fp -mfp-ret-in-387
```

Using an optimization level higher than your compiler supports (e.g. `-O6`) will have exactly the same effect as using the highest level that it *does* support. Distributing code which is set to compile this way is a poor idea though — if further optimisations are incorporated into future versions, you (or your users) may find that they break your code.

Users of GCC 2.7.0 thru 2.7.2 should note that there is a bug in `-O2` on these. Specifically, strength reduction doesn't work. A patch can be had to fix this if you feel like recompiling GCC, otherwise make sure that you always compile with `-fno-strength-reduce`

4.2.2 Processor-specific

There are other `-m` flags which aren't turned on by any variety of `-O` but are nevertheless useful. Chief among these are `-m386` and `-m486`, which tell gcc to favour the 386 or 486 respectively. Code compiled with one of these will still work on the other; 486 code is bigger, but otherwise not slower on the 386.

There is currently no `-mpentium` or `-m586`. Linus suggests using `-m486 -malign-loops=2 -malign-jumps=2 -malign-functions=2`, to get 486 code optimisations but without the big gaps for alignment (which the Pentium doesn't need). Michael Meissner (of Cygnus) says:

> My hunch is that `-mno-strength-reduce` also results in faster code on the x86 (note, I'm not talking about the strength reduction bug, which is another issue). This is because the x86 is rather register starved (and GCC's method of grouping registers into spill registers vs. other registers doesn't help, either). Strength reduction typically results in using additional registers to replace multiplications with addition. I also suspect `-fcaller-saves` may also be a loss.
>
> Another hunch is that `-fomit-frame-pointer` might or might not be a win. On the one hand, it can mean that another register is available for allocation. On the other hand, the way the x86 encodes its instruction set, means that stack relative addresses take more space instead of frame relative addresses, which means slightly less Icache availble to the program. Also, `-fomit-frame-pointer`, means that the compiler has to constantly adjust the stack pointer after calls, while with a frame, it can let the stack accumulate for a few calls.

The final word on this subject is from Linus again:

> Note that if you want to get optimal performance, don't believe me: test. There are lots of GCC compiler switches, and it may be that a particular set gives the best optimizations for you.

4.2.3 `Internal compiler error: cc1 got fatal signal 11`

Signal 11 is SIGSEGV, or "segmentation violation." Usually it means that the program got its pointers confused and tried to write to memory it didn't own. So, it could be a `gcc` bug.

GCC is however, a well tested and reliable piece of software, for the most part. It also uses a large number of complex data structures, and an awful lot of pointers. In short, it's the pickiest RAM tester commonly available. If you can't duplicate the bug—if it doesn't stop in the same place when you restart the compilation—it's almost certainly a problem with your hardware (CPU, memory, motherboard or cache). Don't claim it as a bug because your computer passes the power-on checks or runs MS Windows ok or whatever; these 'tests' are commonly and rightly held to be worthless. And don't claim it's a bug because a kernel compile always stops during `make zImage`—of course it will! `make zImage` is probably compiling over 200 files; we're looking for a slightly smaller place than that.

If you can duplicate the bug, and (better) can produce a short program that exhibits it, you can submit it as a bug report to the FSF, or to the linux-gcc mailing list. See the GCC documentation for details of exactly what information they need.

4.3 Portability

It has been said that, these days, if something hasn't been ported to Linux then it is not worth having.

Seriously though, in general only minor changes are needed to the sources to get over Linux's 100% POSIX compliance. It is also worthwhile passing back any changes to authors of the code such that in the future only `make` need be called to provide a working executable.

4.3.1 BSDisms (including `bsd_ioctl`, `daemon` and `<sgtty.h>`)

You can compile your program with `-I/usr/include/bsd` and link it with `-lbsd` (i.e. add `-I/usr/include/bsd` to `CFLAGS` and `-lbsd` to the `LDFLAGS` line in your `Makefile`). There is *no* need to add `-D__USE_BSD_SIGNAL` any more if you want BSD-type signal behavior, as you get this automatically when you have `-I/usr/include/bsd` and include `<signal.h>`.

4.3.2 "Missing" signals (`SIGBUS`, `SIGEMT`, `SIGIOT`, `SIGTRAP`, `SIGSYS`, etc.)

Linux is POSIX compliant. These are not POSIX-defined signals — ISO/IEC 9945-1:1990 (IEEE Std 1003.1-1990), paragraph B.3.3.1.1 sez:

> "The signals SIGBUS, SIGEMT, SIGIOT, SIGTRAP, and SIGSYS were omitted from POSIX.1 because their behavior is implementation dependent and could not be adequately categorized. Conforming implementations may deliver these signals, but must document the circumstances under which they are delivered and note any restrictions concerning their delivery."

The cheap and cheesy way to fix this is to redefine these signals to `SIGUNUSED`. The *correct* way is to bracket the code that handles them with appropriate `#ifdefs`:

```
#ifdef SIGSYS
/* ... non-posix SIGSYS code here .... */
#endif
```

4.3.3 K & R Code

GCC is an ANSI compiler; much existing code is not ANSI. There's really not much that can be done about this, except to add `-traditional` to the compiler flags. There is a certain amount of finer-grained control over which varieties of brain damage to emulate; consult the GCC info page.

Note that `-traditional` has effects beyond just changing the language that GCC accepts. For example, it turns on `-fwritable-strings`, which moves string constants into data space (from text space, where they cannot be written to). This increases the memory footprint of the program.

4.3.4 Preprocessor symbols conflict with prototypes in the code

One of the most frequent problems is that some common functions are defined as macros in Linux's header files and the preprocessor will refuse to parse similar prototype definitions in the code. Common ones are `atoi()` and `atol()`.

4.3.5 `sprintf()`

Something to be aware of, especially when porting from SunOS, is that `sprintf(string, fmt, ...)` returns a pointer to `string` on many Unices, whereas Linux (following ANSI) returns the number of characters which were put into the string.

4.3.6 `fcntl` and friends. Where are the definitions of `FD_*` stuff?

In `<sys/time.h>`. If you are using `fcntl` you probably want to include `<unistd.h>` too, for the actual prototype.

Generally speaking, the manual page for a function lists the necessary `#includes` in its SYNOPSIS section.

4.3.7 The `select()` timeout. Programs start busy-waiting.

Once upon a time, the timeout parameter to `select()` was used read-only. Even then, manual pages warned:

> select() should probably return the time remaining from the original timeout, if any, by modifying the time value in place. This may be implemented in future versions of the system. Thus, it is unwise to assume that the timeout pointer will be unmodified by the select() call.

The future has arrived! At least, it has here. On return from a `select()`, the timeout argument will be set to the remaining time that it would have waited had data not arrived. If no data has arrived, this will be zero, and future calls using the same timeout structure will immediately return.

To fix, put the timeout value into that structure every time you call `select()`. Change code like

```
struct timeval timeout;
timeout.tv_sec = 1; timeout.tv_usec = 0;
while (some_condition)
        select(n,readfds,writefds,exceptfds,&timeout);
```

to, say,

```
struct timeval timeout;
while (some_condition) {
        timeout.tv_sec = 1; timeout.tv_usec = 0;
        select(n,readfds,writefds,exceptfds,&timeout);
}
```

Some versions of Mosaic were at one time notable for this problem. The speed of the spinning globe animation was inversely related to the speed that the data was coming in from the network at.

4.3.8 Interrupted system calls.

4.3.9 Symptom:

When a program is stopped using Ctrl-Z and then restarted—or in other situations that generate signals: Ctrl-C interruption, termination of a child process, etc.—it complains about "interrupted system call" or "write: unknown error," or things like that.

4.3.10 Problem:

POSIX systems check for signals a bit more often than some older unices. Linux may execute signal handlers

- asynchronously (at a timer tick);
- on return from any system call;
- during the execution of the following system calls: `select()`, `pause()`, `connect()`, `accept()`, `read()` on terminals, sockets, pipes or files in `/proc`, `write()` on terminals, sockets, pipes or the line printer, `open()` on FIFOs, PTYs or serial lines, `ioctl()` on terminals, `fcntl()` with command `F_SETLKW`, `wait4()`, `syslog()`, any TCP or NFS operations.

For other operating systems you may have to include the system calls `creat()`, `close()`, `getmsg()`, `putmsg()`, `msgrcv()`, `msgsnd()`, `recv()`, `send()`, `wait()`, `waitpid()`, `wait3()`, `tcdrain()`, `sigpause()`, `semop()` to this list.

If a signal (that the program has installed a handler for) occurs during a system call, the handler is called. When the handler returns (to the system call) it detects that it was interrupted, and immediately returns with -1 and `errno = EINTR`. The program is not expecting that to happen, so bottles out.

You may choose between two fixes.

(1) For every signal handler that you install, add `SA_RESTART` to the sigaction flags. For example, change

```
    signal (sig_nr, my_signal_handler);
```

to

```
    signal (sig_nr, my_signal_handler);
    { struct sigaction sa;
      sigaction (sig_nr, (struct sigaction *)0, &sa);
  #ifdef SA_RESTART
      sa.sa_flags |= SA_RESTART;
  #endif
  #ifdef SA_INTERRUPT
      sa.sa_flags &= ~ SA_INTERRUPT;
  #endif
      sigaction (sig_nr, &sa, (struct sigaction *)0);
    }
```

Note that while this applies to most system calls, you must still check for `EINTR` yourself on `read()`, `write()`, `ioctl()`, `select()`, `pause()` and `connect()`. See below.

(2) Check for `EINTR` explicitly, yourself:

Here are two examples for `read()` and `ioctl()`,

Original piece of code using `read()`

```
  int result;
  while (len > 0) {
    result = read(fd,buffer,len);
    if (result {$<$} 0) break;
    buffer += result; len -= result;
  }
```

becomes

```
  int result;
  while (len > 0) {
    result = read(fd,buffer,len);
    if (result {$<$} 0) { if (errno != EINTR) break; }
    else { buffer += result; len -= result; }
  }
```

and a piece of code using `ioctl()`

```
  int result;
  result = ioctl(fd,cmd,addr);
```

becomes

```
  int result;
  do { result = ioctl(fd,cmd,addr); }
  while ((result == -1) && (errno == EINTR));
```

Note that in some versions of BSD Unix, the default behaviour is to restart system calls. To get system calls interrupted, you have to use the `SV_INTERRUPT` or `SA_INTERRUPT` flag.

4.3.11 Writable strings (program seg faults randomly)

GCC has an optimistic view of its users, believing that they intend string constants to be exactly that — constant. Thus, it stores them in the text (code) area of the program, where they can be paged in and out from the program's disk image (instead of taking up swap space), and any attempt to rewrite them will cause a segmentation fault. This is a feature!

It may cause a problem for old programs that, for example, call `mktemp()` with a string constant as argument. `mktemp()` attempts to rewrite its argument in place.

To fix, either (a) compile with `-fwritable-strings`, to get `gcc` to put constants in data space, or (b) rewrite the offending parts to allocate a non-constant string and strcpy the data into it before calling.

4.3.12 Why does the `execl()` call fail?

Because you're calling it wrong. The first argument to `execl` is the program that you want to run. The second and subsequent arguments become the `argv` array of the program you're calling. Remember: `argv[0]` is traditionally set even when a program is run with 'no' arguments. So, you should be writing

```
execl("/bin/ls","ls",NULL);
```

not just

```
execl("/bin/ls", NULL);
```

Executing the program with no arguments at all is construed as an invitation to print out its dynamic library dependencies, at least using a.out. ELF does things differently.

(If you want this library information, there are simpler interfaces; see the section on dynamic loading, or the manual page for `ldd`).

5 Debugging and Profiling

5.1 Preventative maintenance (`lint`)

There is no widely-used `lint` for Linux, as most people are satisfied with the warnings that gcc can generate. Probably the most useful is the `-Wall` switch — this stands for 'Warnings, all' but probably has more mnemonic value if thought of as the thing you bang your head against.

There is a public domain `lint` available from `ftp://larch.lcs.mit.edu/pub/Larch/lclint`. I don't know how good it is.

5.2 Debugging

5.2.1 How do I get debugging information into a program?

You need to compile and link all its bits with the `-g` switch, and without the `-fomit-frame-pointer` switch. Actually, you don't need to recompile all of it, just the bits you're interested in debugging.

On a.out configurations the shared libraries are compiled with `-fomit-frame-pointer`, which `gdb` won't get on with. Giving the `-g` option when you link should imply static linking; this is why.

If the linker fails with a message about not finding libg.a, you don't have `/usr/lib/libg.a`, which is the special debugging-enabled C library. It may be supplied in the libc binary package, or (in newer C library versions) you may need to get the libc source code and build it yourself. You don't actually need it though; you can get enough information for most purposes simply by symlinking it to `/usr/lib/libc.a`

5.2.2 How do I get it out again?

A lot of GNU software comes set up to compile and link with `-g`, causing it to make very big (and often static) executables. This is not really such a hot idea.

If the program has an `autoconf`-generated `configure` script, you can usually turn off debugging information by doing `./configure CFLAGS=` or `./configure CFLAGS=-O2`. Otherwise, check the `Makefile`. Of course, if you're using ELF, the program is dynamically linked regardless of the `-g` setting, so you can just `strip` it.

5.2.3 Available software

Most people use gdb, which you can get in source form from

ftp://prep.ai.mit.edu/pub/gnu/

or as a binary from

ftp://tsx-11.mit.edu/pub/linux/packages/GCC/

or sunsite. xxgdb is an X debugger based on this (i.e., you need gdb installed first). The source may be found at

ftp://ftp.x.org/contrib/xxgdb-1.08.tar.gz

Also, the UPS debugger has been ported by Rick Sladkey. It runs under X as well, but unlike xxgdb, it is not merely an X front end for a text based debugger. It has quite a number of nice features, and if you spend any time debugging stuff, you probably should check it out. The Linux precompiled version and patches for the stock UPS sources can be found in

ftp://sunsite.unc.edu/pub/Linux/devel/debuggers/

and the original source at

ftp://ftp.x.org/contrib/ups-2.45.2.tar.Z

Another tool you might find useful for debugging is strace, which displays the system calls that a process makes. It has a multiplicity of other uses too, including figuring out what path names were compiled into binaries that you don't have the source for, exacerbating race conditions in programs that you suspect contain them, and generally learning how things work. The latest version of strace (currently 3.0.8) can be found at ftp://ftp.std.com/pub/jrs/.

5.2.4 Background (daemon) programs

Daemon programs typically execute fork() early, and terminate the parent. This makes for a short debugging session.

The simplest way to get around this is to set a breakpoint for fork, and when the program stops, force it to return 0.

```
(gdb) list
1       #include <stdio.h>
2
3       main()
4       {
5         if(fork()==0) printf("child\n");
6         else printf("parent\n");
7       }
(gdb) break fork
Breakpoint 1 at 0x80003b8
(gdb) run
Starting program: /home/dan/src/hello/./fork
Breakpoint 1 at 0x400177c4

Breakpoint 1, 0x400177c4 in fork ()
(gdb) return 0
Make selected stack frame return now? (y or n) y
#0  0x80004a8 in main ()
    at fork.c:5
5         if(fork()==0) printf("child\n");
(gdb) next
Single stepping until exit from function fork,
which has no line number information.
child
7       }
```

5.2.5 Core files

When Linux boots it is usually configured not to produce core files. If you like them, use your shell's builtin command to re-enable them: for C-shell compatibles (e.g., tcsh) this is

```
% limit core unlimited
```

while Bourne-like shells (sh, bash, zsh, pdksh) use

```
$ ulimit -c unlimited
```

If you want a bit more versatility in your core file naming (for example, if you're trying to conduct a post-mortem using a debugger that's buggy itself) you can make a simple mod to your kernel. Look for the code in fs/binfmt_aout.c and fs/binfmt_elf.c (in newer kernels, you'll have to grep around a little in older ones) that says

```
        memcpy(corefile,"core.",5);
#if 0
        memcpy(corefile+5,current->comm,sizeof(current->comm));
#else
        corefile[4] = '\0';
#endif
```

and change the 0s to 1s.

5.3 Profiling

Profiling is a way to examine which bits of a program are called most often or run for longest. It is a good way to optimize code and look at where time is being wasted. You must compile all object files that you require timing information for with -p, and to make sense of the output file you will also need gprof (from the binutils package). See the gprof manual page for details.

6 Linking

Between the two incompatible binary formats, the static vs shared library distinction, and the overloading of the verb "link" to mean both "what happens after compilation" and "what happens when a compiled program is invoked" (and, actually, the overloading of the word "load" in a comparable but opposite sense), this section is complicated. Little of it is much more complicated than that sentence, though, so don't worry too much about it.

To alleviate the confusion somewhat, we refer to what happens at runtime as "dynamic loading" and cover it in the next section. You will also see it described as "dynamic linking," but not here. This section, then, is exclusively concerned with the kind of linking that happens at the end of a compilation.

6.1 Shared vs static libraries

The last stage of building a program is to "link" it; to join all the pieces of it together and see what is missing. Obviously there are some things that many programs will want to do—open files, for example, and the pieces that do these things are provided for you in the form of libraries. On the average Linux system these can be found in /lib and /usr/lib/, among other places.

When using a static library, the linker finds the bits that the program modules need, and physically copies them into the executable output file that it generates. For shared libraries, it doesn't—instead it leaves a note in the output saying "when this program is run, it will first have to load this library." Obviously shared libraries tend to make for smaller executables; they also use less memory and mean that less disk space is used. The default behaviour of Linux is to link shared if it can find the shared libraries, static otherwise. If you're getting static binaries when you want shared, check that the shared library files (*.sa for a.out, *.so for ELF) are where they should be, and are readable.

On Linux, static libraries have names like libname.a, while shared libraries are called libname.so.x.y.z where x.y.z is some form of version number. Shared libraries often also have links pointing to them, which are important, and (on a.out configurations) associated .sa files. The standard libraries come in both shared and static formats.

You can find out what shared libraries a program requires by using ldd (List Dynamic Dependencies)

```
$ ldd /usr/bin/lynx
        libncurses.so.1 => /usr/lib/libncurses.so.1.9.6
        libc.so.5 => /lib/libc.so.5.2.18
```

This shows that on my system the WWW browser lynx depends on the presence of libc.so.5 (the C library) and libncurses.so.1 (used for terminal control). If a program has no dependencies, ldd will say "statically linked" or "statically linked (ELF)."

6.2 Interrogating libraries ("which library is `sin()` in?")

`nm` *libraryname* should list all the symbols that *libraryname* has references to. It works on both static and shared libraries. Suppose that you want to know where `tcgetattr()` is defined: you might do

```
$ nm libncurses.so.1 |grep tcget
        U tcgetattr
```

The `U` stands for "undefined"—it shows that the ncurses library uses but does not define it. You could also do

```
$ nm libc.so.5 | grep tcget
00010fe8 T __tcgetattr
00010fe8 W tcgetattr
00068718 T tcgetpgrp
```

The "`W`" stands for "weak," which means that the symbol is defined, but in such a way that it can be overridden by another definition in a different library. A straightforward "normal" definition (such as the one for `tcgetpgrp`) is marked by a "`T`."

The short answer to the question in the title, by the way, is `libm.(so|a)`. All the functions defined in `<math.h>` are kept in the maths library; thus you need to link with `-lm` when using any of them.

6.3 Finding files

`ld: Output file requires shared library 'libfoo.so.1'`

The file search strategy of `ld` and friends varies according to version, but the only default you can reasonably assume is `/usr/lib`. If you want libraries elsewhere to be searched, specify their directories with the `-L` option to `gcc` or `ld`.

If that doesn't help, check that you have the right file in that place. For a.out, linking with `-lfoo` makes `ld` look for `libfoo.sa` (shared stubs), and if unsuccessful then for `libfoo.a` (static). For ELF, it looks for `libfoo.so` then `libfoo.a`. `libfoo.so` is usually a symbolic link to `libfoo.so.x`.

6.4 Building your own libraries

6.4.1 Version control

As any other program, libraries tend to have bugs which get fixed over time. They also may introduce new features, change the effect of existing ones, or remove old ones. This could be a problem for programs using them; what if it was depending on that old feature?

So, we introduce library versioning. We categorise the changes that might be made to a library as "minor" or "major," and we rule that a "minor" change is not allowed to break old programs that are using the library. You can tell the version of a library by looking at its filename (actually, this is, strictly speaking, a lie for ELF; keep reading to find out why): `libfoo.so.1.2` has major version 1, minor version 2. The minor version number can be more or less anything—libc puts a "patchlevel" in it, giving library names like `libc.so.5.2.18`, and it's also reasonable to put letters, underscores, or more or less any printable ASCII in it.

One of the major differences between ELF and a.out format is in building shared libraries. We look at ELF first, because it's simpler.

6.4.2 ELF? What is it then, anyway?

ELF (Executable and Linking Format) is a binary format originally developed by USL (UNIX System Laboratories) and currently used in Solaris and System V Release 4. Because of its increased flexibility over the older a.out format that Linux was using, the GCC and C library developers decided last year to move to using ELF as the Linux standard binary format also.

6.4.3 Come again?

This section is from the document `/news-archives/comp.sys.sun.misc`.

> ELF ("Executable Linking Format") is the "new, improved" object file format introduced in SVR4. ELF is much more powerful than straight COFF, in that it is user-extensible. ELF views an object-file as an arbitarily long list of sections (rather than an array of fixed size entities), these sections, unlike in COFF, do not HAVE to be in a certain place and do not HAVE to come in any specific order etc. Users can add new sections to object-files if they wish to capture new data. ELF also has a far more powerful debugging format called DWARF (Debugging With Attribute Record Format)—not currently fully supported on linux (but work is underway). A linked list of DWARF DIEs (or Debugging Information Entries) forms the .debug

section in ELF. Instead of being a collection of small, fixed-size information records, DWARF DIEs each contain an arbitrarily long list of complex attributes and are written out as a scope-based tree of program data. DIEs can capture a large amount of information that the COFF .debug section simply couldn't (like C++ inheritance graphs etc.).

ELF files are accessed via the SVR4 (Solaris 2.0 ?) ELF access library, which provides an easy and fast interface to the more gory parts of ELF. One of the major boons in using the ELF access library is that you will never need to look at an ELF file qua. UNIX file, it is accessed as an Elf *, after an elf_open() call and from then on, you perform elf_foobar() calls on its components instead of messing about with its actual on-disk image (something many COFFers did with impunity).

The case for or against ELF, and the necessary contortions to upgrade an a.out system to support it, are covered in the ELF HOWTO, and I don't propose to cut and paste them here. The HOWTO should be available in the same place that you found this one.

6.4.4 ELF shared libraries

To build `libfoo.so` as a shared library, the basic steps look like this:

```
$ gcc -fPIC -c *.c
$ gcc -shared -Wl,-soname,libfoo.so.1 -o libfoo.so.1.0 *.o
$ ln -s libfoo.so.1.0 libfoo.so.1
$ ln -s libfoo.so.1 libfoo.so
$ LD_LIBRARY_PATH='pwd':$LD_LIBRARY_PATH ; export LD_LIBRARY_PATH
```

This will generate a shared library called `libfoo.so.1.0`, and the appropriate links for `ld` (`libfoo.so`) and the dynamic loader (`libfoo.so.1`) to find it. To test, we add the current directory to `LD_LIBRARY_PATH`.

When you're happpy that the library works, you'll have to move it to, say, `/usr/local/lib`, and recreate the appropriate links. The link from `libfoo.so.1` to `libfoo.so.1.0` is kept up to date by `ldconfig`, which on most systems is run as part of the boot process. The `libfoo.so` link must be updated manually. If you are scrupulous about upgrading all the parts of a library (e.g. the header files) at the same time, the simplest thing to do is make `libfoo.so -> libfoo.so.1`, so that `ldconfig` will keep both links current for you. If you aren't, you're setting yourself up to have all kinds of weird things happen at a later date. Don't say you weren't warned.

```
$ su
# cp libfoo.so.1.0 /usr/local/lib
# /sbin/ldconfig
# ( cd /usr/local/lib ; ln -s libfoo.so.1 libfoo.so )
```

6.4.5 Version numbering, sonames and symlinks

Each library has a **soname**. When the linker finds one of these in a library it is searching, it embeds the soname into the binary instead of the actual filename it is looking at. At runtime, the dynamic loader will then search for a file with the name of the soname, not the library filename. Thus a library called `libfoo.so` could have a soname `libbar.so`, and all programs linked to it would look for `libbar.so` instead when they started.

This sounds like a pointless feature, but it is key to understanding how multiple versions of the same library can coexist on a system. The de facto naming standard for libraries in Linux is to call the library, say, `libfoo.so.1.2`, and give it a soname of `libfoo.so.1`. If it's added to a "standard" library directory (e.g. `/usr/lib`), `ldconfig` will create a symlink `libfoo.so.1 -> libfoo.so.1.2` so that the appropriate image is found at runtime. You also need a link `libfoo.so -> libfoo.so.1` so that `ld` will find the right soname to use at link time.

So, when you fix bugs in the library, or add new functions (any changes that won't adversely affect existing programs), you rebuild it, keeping the soname as it was, and changing the filename. When you make changes to the library that would break existing binaries, you simply increment the number in the soname — in this case, call the new version `libfoo.so.2.0`, and give it a soname of `libfoo.so.2`. Now switch the `libfoo.so` link to point to the new version and all's well with the world again.

Note that you don't have to name libraries this way, but it's a good convention. ELF gives you the flexibility to name libraries in ways that will confuse the pants off people, but that doesn't mean you have to use it.

Executive summary: supposing that you observe the tradition that major upgrades may break compatibility, minor upgrades may not, then link with

```
gcc -shared -Wl,-soname,libfoo.so.major -o libfoo.so.major.minor
```

and everything will be all right.

6.4.6 a.out. Ye olde traditional format

The ease of building shared libraries is a major reason for upgrading to ELF. That said, it's still possible in a.out. Get `ftp://tsx-11.mit.edu/pub/linux/packages/GCC/src/tools-2.17.tar.gz` and read the 20-page document that you will find after unpacking it. I hate to be so transparently partisan, but it should be clear from context that I never bothered myself.

6.4.7 ZMAGIC vs QMAGIC

QMAGIC is an executable format just like the old a.out (also known as ZMAGIC) binaries, but which leaves the first page unmapped. This allows for easier NULL dereference trapping as no mapping exists in the range 0-4096. As a side effect your binaries are nominally smaller as well (by about 1K).

Obsolescent linkers support ZMAGIC-only, semi-obsolescent support both formats, and current versions support QMAGIC only. This doesn't actually matter, though, as the kernel can still run both formats.

Your `file` command should be able to identify whether a program is QMAGIC.

6.4.8 File Placement

An a.out (DLL) shared library consists of two real files and a symlink. For the "foo" library used throughout this document as an example, these files would be `libfoo.sa` and `libfoo.so.1.2`; the symlink would be `libfoo.so.1` and would point at the latter of the files. What are these for?

At compile time, `ld` looks for `libfoo.sa`. This is the "stub" file for the library, and contains all exported data and pointers to the functions required for run time linking.

At run time, the dynamic loader looks for `libfoo.so.1`. This is a symlink rather than a real file so that libraries can be updated with newer, bug-fixed versions without crashing any application that was using the library at the time. After the new version—say, `libfoo.so.1.3`—is completely there, running `ldconfig` will switch the link to point to it in one atomic operation, leaving any program which had the old version still perfectly happy.

DLL libraries (I know that's a tautology—so sue me) often appear bigger than their static counterparts. They reserve space for future expansion in the form of "holes" which can be made to take no disk space. A simple `cp` call or using the program `makehole` will achieve this. You can also strip them after building, as the addresses are in fixed locations.

◇ Do not attempt to strip ELF libraries.

6.4.9 "libc-lite"?

A libc-lite is a light-weight version of the libc library built such that it will fit on a floppy and suffice for all of the most menial of UNIX tasks. It does not include curses, dbm, or termcap, etc., code. If your `/lib/libc.so.4` is linked to a lite lib, you are advised to replace it with a full version.

6.4.10 Linking: common problems

Send me your linking problems! I probably won't do anything about them, but I will write them up if I get enough ...

Programs link static when you wanted them shared

Check that you have the right links for `ld` to find each shared library. For ELF this means a `libfoo.so` symlink to the image, for a.out a `libfoo.sa` file. A lot of people had this problem after moving from ELF binutils 2.5 to 2.6—the earlier version searched more "intelligently" for shared libraries, so they hadn't created all the links. The intelligent behaviour was removed for compatibility with other architectures, and because quite often it got its assumptions wrong and caused more trouble than it solved.

The DLL tool `mkimage` fails to find libgcc, or

As of `libc.so.4.5.x` and above, libgcc is no longer shared. Hence you must replace occurrences of `-lgcc` on the offending line with `` `gcc -print-libgcc-file-name` `` (complete with the grave accents).

Also, delete all `/usr/lib/libgcc*` files. This is important.

`__NEEDS_SHRLIB_libc_4 multiply defined` **messages**

are another consequence of the same problem.

"Assertion failure" message when rebuilding a DLL ?

This cryptic message most probably means that one of your jump table slots has overflowed because too little space has been reserved in the original `jump.vars` file. You can locate the culprit(s) by running the `getsize` command provided in the tools-2.17.tar.gz package. Probably the only solution, though, is to bump the major version number of the library, forcing it to be backward incompatible.

`ld: output file needs shared library libc.so.4`

This usually happens when you are linking with libraries other than libc (e.g. X libraries), and use the `-g` switch on the link line without also using `-static`.

The `.sa` stubs for the shared libraries usually have an undefined symbol `_NEEDS_SHRLIB_libc_4` which gets resolved from the `libc.sa` stub. However with `-g` you end up linking with `libg.a` or `libc.a` and thus this symbol never gets resolved, leading to the above error message.

In conclusion, add `-static` when compiling with the `-g` flag, or don't link with `-g`. Quite often you can get enough debugging information by compiling the individual files with `-g`, and linking without it.

7 Dynamic Loading

This section is a bit short right now; it will be expanded over time as I gut the ELF howto

7.1 Concepts

Linux has shared libraries, as you will by now be sick of hearing if you read the whole of the last section at a sitting. Some of the matching-names-to-places work which was traditionally done at link time must be deferred to load time.

7.2 Error messages

Send me your link errors. I won't do anything about them, but I might write them up—

`can't load library: /lib/libxxx.so, Incompatible version`

(a.out only) This means that you don't have the correct major version of the xxx library. No, you can't just make a symlink to another version that you do have; if you are lucky this will cause your program to die with a segmentation fault. Get the new version. A similar situation with ELF will result in a message like

```
ftp: can't load library 'libreadline.so.2'
```

`warning using incompatible library version xxx`

(a.out only) You have an older minor version of the library than the person who compiled the program used. The program will still run. Probably. An upgrade wouldn't hurt, though.

7.3 Controlling the operation of the dynamic loader

There are a range of environment variables that the dynamic loader will respond to. Most of these are more use to `ldd` than they are to the average user, and can most conveniently be set by running `ldd` with various switches. They include

- `LD_BIND_NOW`—normally, functions are not "looked up" in libraries until they are called. Setting this flag causes all the lookups to happen when the library is loaded, giving a slower startup time. It's useful when you want to test a program to make sure that everything is linked.
- `LD_PRELOAD` can be set to a file containing "overriding" function definitions. For example, if you were testing memory allocation strategies, and wanted to replace "malloc," you could write your replacement routine, compile it into `malloc.o` and then

  ```
  $ LD_PRELOAD=malloc.o; export LD_PRELOAD
  $ some_test_program
  ```

  `LD_ELF_PRELOAD` and `LD_AOUT_PRELOAD` are similar, but only apply to the appropriate type of binary. If `LD_`*something*`_PRELOAD` and `LD_PRELOAD` are set, the more specific one is used.
- `LD_LIBRARY_PATH` is a colon-separated list of directories in which to look for shared libraries. It does *not* affect `ld`; it only has effect at runtime. Also, it is disabled for programs that run setuid or setgid. Again, `LD_ELF_LIBRARY_PATH` and `LD_AOUT_LIBRARY_PATH` can also be used to direct the search differently for different flavors of binary. `LD_LIBRARY_PATH` shouldn't be necessary in normal operation; add the directories to `/etc/ld.so.conf/` and rerun `ldconfig` instead.

- `LD_NOWARN` applies to a.out only. When set (e.g. with `LD_NOWARN=true; export LD_NOWARN`) it stops the loader from issuing non-fatal warnings (such as minor version incompatibility messages).
- `LD_WARN` applies to ELF only. When set, it turns the usually fatal "Can't find library" messages into warnings. It's not much use in normal operation, but important for `ldd`.
- `LD_TRACE_LOADED_OBJECTS` applies to ELF only, and causes programs to think they're being run under `ldd`:

```
$ LD_TRACE_LOADED_OBJECTS=true /usr/bin/lynx
        libncurses.so.1 => /usr/lib/libncurses.so.1.9.6
        libc.so.5 => /lib/libc.so.5.2.18
```

7.4 Writing programs with dynamic loading

This is very close to the way that Solaris 2.x dynamic loading support works, if you're familiar with that. It is covered extensively in H.J. Lu's ELF programming document, and the `dlopen(3)` manual page, which can be found in the `ld.so` package. Here's a nice simple example though: link it with `-ldl`

```
#include <dlfcn.h>
#include <stdio.h>

main()
{
  void *libc;
  void (*printf_call)();

  if(libc=dlopen("/lib/libc.so.5",RTLD_LAZY))
  {
    printf_call=dlsym(libc,"printf");
    (*printf_call)("hello, world\n");
  }

}
```

8 Contacting the developers

8.1 Bug reports

Start by *narrowing the problem down.* Is it specific to Linux, or does it happen with GCC on other systems? Is it specific to the kernel version? Library version? Does it go away if you link static? Can you trim the program down to something *short* that demonstrates the bug?

Having done that, you'll know what program(s) the bug is in. For GCC, the bug reporting procedure is explained in the info file. For `ld.so` or the C or maths libraries, send mail to `linux-gcc@vger.rutgers.edu`. If possible, include a short and self contained program that exhibits the bug, and a description both of what you want it to do, and what it actually does.

8.2 Helping with development

If you want to help with the development effort for GCC or the C library, the first thing to do is join the `linux-gcc@vger.rutgers.edu` mailing list. If you just want to see what the discussion is about, there are list archives at `http://homer.ncm.com/linux-gcc/`. The second and subsequent things depend on what you want to do!

9 The Remains

9.1 The Credits

Only presidents, editors, and people with tapeworms have the right to use the editorial "we."

—Mark Twain

This HOWTO is based very closely on Mitchum DSouza's GCC-FAQ; most of the information (not to mention a reasonable amount of the text) in it comes directly from that document. Instances of the first person pronoun in this HOWTO could refer to either of us; generally the ones that say "I have not tested this; don't blame me if it toasts your hard disk/system/spouse" apply to both of us.

Contributors to this document have included (in ASCII ordering by first name)
Andrew Tefft,
Axel Boldt,
Bill Metzenthen,
Bruce Evans,
Bruno Haible,
Daniel Barlow,
Daniel Quinlan,
David Engel,
Dirk Hohndel,
Eric Youngdale,
Fergus Henderson,
H.J. Lu,
Jens Schweikhardt,
Kai Petzke,
Michael Meissner,
Mitchum DSouza,
Olaf Flebbe,
Paul Gortmaker,
Rik Faith,
Steven S. Dick,
Tuomas J Lukka,
and of course Linus Torvalds, without whom the whole exercise would have been pointless, let alone impossible.

Please do not feel offended if your name has not appeared here and you have contributed to this document (either as HOWTO or as FAQ). Email me and I will rectify it.

9.2 Translations

At this time, there are no known translations of this work. If you wish to produce one, please go right ahead, but do tell me about it! The chances are (sadly) several hundred to one against that I speak the language you wish to translate to, but that aside I am happy to help in whatever way I can.

`dan@detached.demon.co.uk` . My PGP public key (ID 5F263625) is available from my web pages

`http://ftp.linux.org.uk/~barlow/`

if you feel the need to be secretive about things.

9.3 Legalese

All trademarks used in this document are acknowledged as being owned by their respective owners.

In short, we wish to promote dissemination of this information through as many channels as possible. However, we do wish to retain copyright on the HOWTO documents, and would like to be notified of any plans to redistribute the HOWTOs.

If you have questions, please contact Greg Hankins, the Linux HOWTO coordinator, at gregh@sunsite.unc.edu via email.

This HOWTO is based very closely on Mitchum DSouza's GCC-FAQ; most of the information (not to mention a reasonable amount of the text) in it comes directly from that document. Instances of the first person pronoun in this HOWTO could refer to either of us; generally the ones that say "I have not tested this; don't blame me if it toasts your hard disk/system/spouse" apply to both of us.

Contributors to this document have included (in ASCII ordering by first name)

Andrew Tefft
Axel Boldt
Bill Metzenthen
Bruce Evans
Bruno Haible
Daniel Barlow
Daniel Quinlan
David Engel
Dirk Hohndel
Eric Youngdale
Fergus Henderson
H.J. Lu
Jens Schweikhardt
Kai Petzke
Michael Meissner
Mitchum DSouza
Olaf Flebbe
Paul Gortmaker
Rik Faith
Steven S. Dick
Tuomas J Lukka

and of course Linus Torvalds, without whom the whole exercise would have been pointless, let alone impossible :-)

Please do not feel offended if your name has not appeared here and you have contributed to this document (either as HOWTO or as FAQ). Email me and I will correct it.

9.2 Translations

At this time, there are no known translations of this work. If you wish to produce one, please go right ahead, but do tell me about it! The chances are (sadly) several hundred to one against that I speak the language you wish to translate to, but that aside I am happy to help in whatever way I can.

The author's PGP public key (ID 5F263625) is available from my web pages,

[illegible]

if you feel the need to be secretive about things.

9.3 Legalese

All trademarks used in this document are acknowledged as being owned by their respective owners.

Part XXIII

"Glibc 2 HOWTO" by Eric Green,

thrytis@imaxx.net

Contents

v1.2, 26 October 1997
The glibc 2 HOWTO covers installing and using the GNU C Library version 2 (libc 6) on Linux systems.

1 Introduction

1.1 About glibc 2

Glibc 2 is the latest version of the GNU C Library. It currently runs unmodified on GNU Hurd systems and Linux i386, m68k, and Alpha systems. Ports to Linux PowerPC, MIPS, and Sparc are actively being developed. In the future support for other architectures and operating systems will be added.

On Linux, glibc 2 is used as the libc with major version 6, the successor of the Linux libc 5. It is intended by the Linux libc developers to eventually replace libc 5. It is currently experimental, but is stable enough to be used by people interested in testing it and willing to put a little extra effort to get things working. The latest version is actually quite stable if the program you are using supports it. Version 2.1 (due out in the near future) will be ready for main stream use.

There are three optional add-ons available for glibc 2:

Crypt
The UFC-crypt package. It is separate because of export restrictions.

LinuxThreads
An implementation of the Posix 1003.1c "pthread" interface.

Locale data
Contains the data needed to build the locale data files to use the internationalization features of the glibc.

1.2 About this document

This HOWTO covers installing the glibc 2 library on an existing Linux system. It is tailored for users of Intel based systems currently using libc 5, but users of other systems and alternate libraries (such as glibc 1) should be able to use this information by substituting the proper filenames and architecture names in the appropriate places.

The latest copy of this HOWTO can be found as part of the Linux Documentation Project

```
http://sunsite.unc.edu/LDP
```

or from

```
http://www.imaxx.net/~thrytis/glibc/Glibc2-HOWTO.html
```

2 Choosing your installation method

There are a few ways to install glibc. You can install the libraries as a test, using the existing libraries as the default but letting you try the new libraries by using different options when compiling your program. Installing in this way also makes it easy to remove glibc in the future (though any program linked with glibc will no longer work after the libraries are removed). Using glibc as a test library requires you to compile the libraries from source. There is no binary distribution for installing libraries this way. This installation is described in Section 4.

The other way described in this document to install is using glibc as your primary library. All new programs that you compile on your system will use glibc, though you can link programs with your old libraries using different options while compiling. You can either install the libraries from binaries, or compile the library yourself. If you want to change optimization or configuration options, or use an add-on which is not distributed as a binary package, you must get the source distribution and compile. This installation procedure is described in section 5.

Frodo Looijaard describes yet another way of installing glibc. His method involves installing glibc as a secondary library and setting up a cross compiler to compile using glibc. The installation procedure for this method is more complicated then the test library install described in this document, but allows for easier compiling when linking to glibc. This method is described in his "Installing glibc-2 on Linux" document, http://huizen.dds.nl/~frodol/glibc/.

If you are currently running Debian 1.3 but do not want to upgrade to the unstable version of Debian to use glibc, the "Debian libc5 to libc6 Mini-HOWTO," http://www.gate.net/~storm/FAQ/libc5-libc6-Mini-HOWTO.html describes how to use Debian packages to upgrade your system.

◇ **If you are installing glibc 2 on an important system, you should not install it as your primary library.** Use the test install, or better, try it on a spare system. Even if there are no bugs, some programs will need to be modified before they will compile due to changes in function prototypes and types.

3 Getting the library

The glibc 2 consists of the glibc package and three optional add-on packages: LinuxThreads, Locale, and Crypt. The source can be found at

- (ftp://prep.ai.mit.edu/pub/gnu/glibc-2.0.5.tar.gz)
- (ftp://prep.ai.mit.edu/pub/gnu/glibc-linuxthreads-2.0.5.tar.gz)
- (ftp://prep.ai.mit.edu/pub/gnu/glibc-localedata-2.0.5.tar.gz)
- (ftp://prep.ai.mit.edu/pub/gnu/glibc-crypt-2.0.5.tar.gz)

Version 2.0.5c requires an additional patch, which can be found at

```
ftp://prep.ai.mit.edu/pub/gnu/glibc-2.0.5-2.0.5c.diff.gz
```

It will take about 150 MB of disk space for the full compile and install. The basic binary install of just the core library package is about 50 MB.

Binary packages for 2.0.5c are not available. Version 2.0.4 binary packages are available for i386, Alpha, and 68k, and can be found at

- Intel x86:
  - (ftp://prep.ai.mit.edu/pub/gnu/glibc-2.0.4.bin.i386.tar.gz)
  - (ftp://prep.ai.mit.edu/pub/gnu/glibc-crypt-2.0.4.bin.i386.tar.gz)
- Alpha:
  - (ftp://prep.ai.mit.edu/pub/gnu/glibc-2.0.1.bin.alpha-linux.tar.gz)
  - (ftp://prep.ai.mit.edu/pub/gnu/glibc-crypt-2.0.1.bin.alpha-linux.tar.gz)
- m68k:
  - (ftp://prep.ai.mit.edu/pub/gnu/glibc-2.0.4-m68k-linux.bin.tar.gz)
  - (ftp://prep.ai.mit.edu/pub/gnu/glibc-crypt-2.0.4-m68k-linux.bin.tar.gz)

There are export restrictions on the crypt add-on. Non-US users should get it from

```
ftp://ftp.ifi.uio.no/pub/gnu
```

If you are running a Red Hat distribution, you can get RPMs for glibc 2 from

```
ftp://ftp.redhat.com/pub/redhat/tbird/RedHat/RPMS/
```

Glibc 2 is the primary C library since the beta Red Hat distribution 4.8.

If you are running a Debian distribution, you can get the packages for glibc 2 from

```
ftp://ftp.debian.org/debian/unstable/binary-i386/devel/
ftp://ftp.debian.org/debian/unstable/binary-m68k/devel/
```

or

```
ftp://ftp.debian.org/debian/unstable/binary-alpha/devel/
```

The files are named libc6. Glibc 2 is now part of the base package of the hamm version of Debian, and will be the primary libc when Debian 2.0 is released.

4 Installing as a test library

This section covers installing glibc 2 as a test library. Anything you compile will be linked to your existing libraries unless you give some extra parameters to link to the new libraries. It appears that the paths are compiled into quite a few files, so you probably have to install the library from source.

4.1 Compiling and installing

4.1.1 Prerequisites

- About 150 MB free disk space;
- GNU `make` 3.75;
- GCC >= 2.7.2 (better 2.7.2.1);
- binutils 2.8.1 (for Alpha you need a snapshot);
- `bash` 2.0;
- `autoconf` 2.12 (if you change `configure.in`).

On an i586 at 133 MHz with 64 MB of RAM, it takes about 3 hours to compile with full libraries with add-ons. On a loaded i686 at 200 MHz, it takes about half an hour.

4.1.2 Extracting the source

You need to extract the source from the archives so you can compile it. The best way to do this is:

```
tar xzf glibc-2.0.5.tar.gz
cd glibc-2.0.5
cat ../glibc-2.0.5-2.0.5c.diff.gz | gzip -d | patch -p0
tar xzf ../glibc-linuxthreads-2.0.5.tar.gz
tar xzf ../glibc-crypt-2.0.5.tar.gz
tar xzf ../glibc-localedata-2.0.5.tar.gz
```

This will put linuxthreads, crypt, and localedata directories in the `glibc-2.0.5` directory where configure can find these add-ons.

4.1.3 Configuring

In the `glibc-2.0.5` directory, create a directory named compile, and `cd` into it. All work will be done in this directory, which will simplify cleaning up. (The developers have not been very concerned with getting `make clean` perfect yet.)

```
mkdir compile
cd compile
```

Run `../configure`. To use the add-on packages, you need to specify them with `-enable-add-ons`, such as `-enable-add-ons=linuxthreads,crypt,localedata`. You also need to choose a destination directory to install to. `/usr/i486-linuxglibc2` is a good choice. The configure line for this would be:

```
../configure --enable-add-ons=linuxthreads,crypt,localedata --prefix=/usr/i486-linuxglibc2
```

4.1.4 Compiling and installing

To compile and verify, run:

```
make
make check
```

If the `make check` succeeds, install the library:

```
make install
```

4.2 Updating the dynamic loader

1. Create a link from the new ld.so to /lib/ld-linux.so.2:

```
ln -s /usr/i486-linuxglibc2/lib/ld-linux.so.2 /lib/ld-linux.so.2
```

   This is the only library where the location is fixed once a program is linked, and using a link in `/lib` will ease upgrading to glibc as your primary C library when the stable version is released.

2. Edit `/etc/ld.so.conf`. You need to add path to the `lib` directory the new libraries reside in at the end of the file, which will be *prefix*`/lib`, such as `/usr/i486-linuxglibc2/lib` for the choice above. After you have modified `/etc/ld.so.conf`, run

```
ldconfig -v
```

4.3 Configuring for GCC

The last step of installation is updating `/usr/lib/gcc-lib` so GCC knows how to use the new libraries. First you need to duplicate the existing configuration. To find out which configuration is current, use the -v option of `gcc`:

```
% gcc -v
Reading specs from /usr/lib/gcc-lib/i486-unknown-linux/2.7.2.2/specs
gcc version 2.7.2.2
```

In this case, `i486-unknown-linux` is the system, and 2.7.2.2 is the version. You need to copy the `/usr/lib/gcc-lib/`*system* to the new test system directory:

```
cd /usr/lib/gcc-lib/
cp -r i486-unknown-linux i486-linuxglibc2
```

Change into your new test system directory and version directory

```
cd /usr/lib/gcc-lib/i486-linuxglibc2/2.7.2.2
```

and edit the file `specs` found in this directory. In this file, change `/lib/ld-linux.so.1` to `/lib/ld-linux.so.2`. You also need to remove all expressions `%{...:-lgmon}` in the file, since glibc does not use the gmon library for profiling. A sample `specs` file can be found in Section 9.

4.4 Updating header file links

You need create links in your new include directory to other include directories:

```
cd /usr/i486-linuxglibc2/include
ln -s /usr/src/linux/include/linux
ln -s /usr/src/linux/include/asm
ln -s /usr/X11R6/include/X11
```

You might also have other libraries such as ncurses which need their header files put in this directory. You should copy or link the files from `/usr/include`. (Some libraries may need to be recompiled with glibc2 in order to work with it. In these cases, just compile and install the package to `/usr/i486-linuxglibc2`.)

4.5 Testing your installation

To test the installation, create the following program in a file glibc.c:

```
#include <stdio.h>

main()
{
    printf("hello world!\n");
}
```

and compile with the options of

`-b` <*base install directory*> `-nostdinc -I`<*install directory*>`/include -I/usr/lib/gcc-lib/`<*new system dir*>`/`<*gcc version*>`/include`

The example would be,

```
% gcc -b i486-linuxglibc2 -nostdinc -I/usr/i486-linuxglibc2/include \
  -I/usr/lib/gcc-lib/i486-linuxglibc2/2.7.2.2/include glibc.c -o glibc
```

Use `ldd` to verify the program was linked with glibc2, and not your old libc:

```
% ldd glibc
libc.so.6 => /usr/i486-linuxglibc2/lib/libc-2.0.5.so (0x4000d000)
/lib/ld-linux.so.2 => /lib/ld-linux.so.2 (0x40000000)
```

If it compiles, the links check out, and it generates `hello world!` when run, the installation succeeded.

5 Installing as the primary C library

This section covers installing glibc 2 as your primary C library. Any new programs you compile will be linked with this library, unless you use special compile options to link with another version.

If you are are using Redhat or Debian and have downloaded the appropriate RPM or DEB files, see the Redhat or Debian installion instructions. You can then skip this section.

5.1 Building the library from source

This section explains how to compile glibc 2 and add-ons from the sources. You must compile the library if you want to change optimization or configuration options or use a package you do not have the binaries for.

5.1.1 Prerequisites

- About 150 MB free disk space;
- GNU `make` 3.75;
- GCC >= 2.7.2 (better 2.7.2.1);
- binutils 2.8.1 (for Alpha you need a snapshot);
- `bash` 2.0;
- `autoconf` 2.12 (if you change `configure.in`).

On an i586 at 133 MHz with 64 MB of RAM, it takes about 3 hours to compile with full libraries with add-ons. On a loaded i686 at 200 MHz, it takes about half an hour.

5.1.2 Extracting the source

You need to extract the source from the archives so you can compile it. The best way to do this is:

```
tar xzf glibc-2.0.5.tar.gz
cd glibc-2.0.5
cat ../glibc-2.0.5-2.0.5c.diff.gz | gzip -d | patch -p0
tar xzf ../glibc-linuxthreads-2.0.5.tar.gz
tar xzf ../glibc-crypt-2.0.5.tar.gz
tar xzf ../glibc-localedata-2.0.5.tar.gz
```

This will put linuxthreads, crypt, and localedata directories in the `glibc-2.0.5` directory where configure can find these add-ons.

5.1.3 Configuring

In the `glibc-2.0.5` directory, create a directory named `compile`, and `cd` into it. All work will be done in this directory, which will simplify cleaning up. (The developers have not been very concerned with getting `make clean` perfect yet.)

```
mkdir compile
cd compile
```

Run `../configure`. To use the add-on packages, you need to specify them with `-enable-add-ons`, such as `-enable-add-ons=linuxthreads,crypt,localedata`. You probably will also want to specify paths where it will be installed. To match the standard linux distributions, specify `-prefix=/usr`. (When a prefix of `/usr` is specified on a Linux system, `configure` knows to adjust other paths to place `libc.so` and other important libraries in `/lib`.) The whole configure line would be:

```
../configure --enable-add-ons=linuxthreads,crypt,localedata --prefix=/usr
```

5.1.4 Compiling

To compile and verify, run:

```
make
make check
```

5.2 Preparing for installation

Now you need to move some files around to prepare for the new library, whether you are installing from source or binaries. Any new program compiled will be linked to glibc, but old programs which are not statically linked will still depend on libc 5, so you can not just overwrite the old version.

1. Create a new directory to hold the old files to:

   ```
   mkdir -p /usr/i486-linuxlibc5/lib
   ```

2. The old header files must be evacuated from `/usr/include`:

   ```
   mv /usr/include /usr/i486-linuxlibc5/include
   ```

3. Create a new include directory and set up the links to other include directories:

   ```
   mkdir /usr/include

   ln -s /usr/src/linux/include/linux /usr/include/linux
   ln -s /usr/src/linux/include/asm /usr/include/asm
   ln -s /usr/X11R6/include/X11 /usr/include/X11
   ln -s /usr/lib/g++-include /usr/include/g++
   ```

   The links may need adjusting according to your distribution. At least Slackware puts g++ headers in `/usr/local/g++-include`, while Debian puts the headers in `/usr/include/g++`, and links `/usr/lib/g++-include` to `/usr/include/g++`. In the later case, you probably will want to move the original `g++` include directory back to `/usr/include`.

4. Restore any extra header files and links. Some non-standard libraries such as ncurses put files in `/usr/include` or put a link to their include directories in the `/usr/include`. These files and links need to be restored in order to use the extra libraries properly.

5. Add your new library directory (such as `/usr/i486-linuxlibc5/lib`) *at the top* of your `/etc/ld.so.conf` file. You should have `ld.so` 1.8.8, or later, installed, to avoid getting strange messages once glibc is installed.

6. Move/copy all the old C libraries into the new directory.

```
mv /usr/lib/libbsd.a /usr/i486-linuxlibc5/lib
mv /usr/lib/libc.a /usr/i486-linuxlibc5/lib
mv /usr/lib/libgmon.a /usr/i486-linuxlibc5/lib
mv /usr/lib/libm.a /usr/i486-linuxlibc5/lib
mv /usr/lib/libmcheck.a /usr/i486-linuxlibc5/lib
mv /usr/lib/libc.so /usr/i486-linuxlibc5/lib
mv /usr/lib/libm.so /usr/i486-linuxlibc5/lib
cp /lib/libm.so.5.* /usr/i486-linuxlibc5/lib
cp /lib/libc.so.5.* /usr/i486-linuxlibc5/lib
```

`libm.so.5` and `libc.so.5` should be copied and not moved if `/usr` is a separate partition from `/`, because they are required by programs used to start Linux and must be located on the root drive partition.

7. Move the `/usr/lib/*.o` files into the new directory.

```
mv /usr/lib/crt1.o /usr/i486-linuxlibc5/lib
mv /usr/lib/crti.o /usr/i486-linuxlibc5/lib
mv /usr/lib/crtn.o /usr/i486-linuxlibc5/lib
mv /usr/lib/gcrt1.o /usr/i486-linuxlibc5/lib
```

8. Update your library cache after your libraries are moved.

```
ldconfig -v
```

5.3 Installing from the binary package

If you are installing glibc from pre-compiled binaries, you must:

```
cd /
gzip -dc glibc-2.0.bin.i386.tar.gz | tar tvvf -
gzip -dc glibc-crypt-2.0.bin.i386.tar.gz | tar tvvf -
ldconfig -v
```

If you have a different architecture or version, substitute the proper file names.

5.4 Installing from the source

To install the library from source, run:

```
make install
ldconfig -v
```

5.5 Updating the GCC `specs` file

The final step of the installation (for both binary and source installs) is to update the GCC `specs` file so you can link your programs properly. To determine which `specs` file is the one used by GCC, use:

```
% gcc -v
reading specs from /usr/lib/gcc-lib/i486-unknown-linux/2.7.2.2/specs
gcc version 2.7.2.2
```

In this case, i486-unknown-linux is the system, and 2.7.2.2 is the version. You need to copy the `/usr/lib/gcc-lib/`*system* to the old system directory:

```
cd /usr/lib/gcc-lib/
cp -r i486-unknown-linux i486-linuxlibc5
```

Change into the original directory and version directory

```
cd /usr/lib/gcc-lib/i486-unknown-linux/2.7.2.2
```

and edit the file `specs` found in this directory. In this file, change `/lib/ld-linux.so.1` to `/lib/ld-linux.so.2`. You also need to remove all expressions `%{...:-lgmon}` in the file, since glibc does not use the gmon library for profiling. A sample `specs` file can be found in the 9 section.

5.6 Testing your installation

To test the installation, create the following program in a file glibc.c:

```
#include <stdio.h>

main()
{
    printf("hello world!\n");
}
```

and compile the program.

```
% gcc glibc.c -o glibc
```

Use `ldd` to verify that the program was linked with glibc2, and not your old libc:

```
% ldd glibc
libc.so.6 => /lib/libc.so.6 (0x4000e000)
/lib/ld-linux.so.2 => /lib/ld-linux.so.2 (0x40000000)
```

If this compiles and generates `hello world!` when run, the installation was successful.

6 Compiling with the non-primary libc

There are times you will want to use an alternate library to compile your programs with. This section explains how to accomplish this, using the directories and installation names used in the examples in the previous two sections. Remember to change the names to fit your setup.

6.1 A warning when using non-primary libcs

Before compiling any program which is used in the system boot process, remember that if the program is dynamically linked and is used before the non-root partitions are mounted, all linked libraries must be on the root partition. Following the installation process in the previous section for installing glibc as your primary C library, the old libc is left in `/lib`, which will be on your root partition. This means all of your programs will still work during booting. However, if `/usr` is on a different partition and you install glibc as a test library in `/usr/i486-linuxglibc2`, any new programs you compile with glibc will not work until your `/usr` partition is mounted.

6.2 Compiling programs with a test glibc

To compile a program with a test-install glibc, you need to reset the include paths to point to the glibc includes. Specifying `-nostdinc` will negate the normal paths, and `-I/usr/i486-linuxglibc2/include` will point to the glibc includes. You will also need to specify the GCC includes, which are found in `/usr/lib/gcc-lib/i486-linuxglibc2/2.7.2.2/include` (assuming you installed the test lib in `i486-linuxglibc2` with GCC version 2.7.2.2).

To link a program with a test-install glibc, you need to specify the gcc setup. This is done by using the option `-b i486-linuxglibc2`.

For most programs, you can specify these new options by adding them to the `CFLAGS` and `LDFLAGS` makefile options:

```
CFLAGS = -nostdinc -I/usr/i486-linuxglibc2/include \
-I/usr/lib/gcc-lib/i486-linuxglibc2/2.7.2.2/include \
-b i486-linuxglibc2
LDFLAGS = -b i486-linuxglibc2
```

If you are using a `configure` script, define the `$CFLAGS` and `$LDFLAGS` shell variables (by using `env` or `setenv` for `csh` or `tcsh`, or `set` or `export` for `sh`, `bash`, or similar shells, before running configure. The `makefiles` generated by this should contain the proper `CFLAGS` and `LDFLAGS`. Not all `configure` scripts will pick up the variables, so you should check after running `configure` and edit the `makefiles` by hand if necessary.

If the programs you are compiling only call `gcc` (and not `cpp` or binutils directly), you can use the following script to save having to specify all of the options each time:

```
#!/bin/bash
/usr/bin/gcc -b i486-linuxglibc2 -nostdinc \
             -I/usr/i486-linuxglibc2/include \
             -I/usr/lib/gcc-lib/i486-linuxglibc2/2.7.2.2/include "$@"
```

You can then use this script instead of `gcc` when compiling.

6.3 Compiling programs with libc 5 when glibc is primary library

To compile a program with your old libraries when you have installed glibc as your main library, you need to reset the include paths to the old includes. Specifying `-nostdinc` will negate the normal paths, and `-I/usr/i486-linuxlibc5/include` will point to the glibc includes. You must also specify `-I/usr/lib/gcc-lib/i486-linuxlibc5/2.7.2.2/include` to include the GCC-specific includes. Remember to adjust these paths based on the what you named the new directories and your GCC version.

To link a program with your old libc, you need to specify the GCC setup. This is done by using the option `-b i486-linuxlibc5`.

For most programs, you can specify these new options by appending them to the `CFLAGS` and `LDFLAGS` `makefile` options:

```
 CFLAGS = -nostdinc -I/usr/i486-linuxlibc5/include \
-I/usr/lib/gcc-lib/i486-linuxlibc5/2.7.2.2/include \
-b i486-linuxlibc5
 LDFLAGS = -b i486-linuxlibc5
```

If you are using a `configure` script, define the `$CFLAGS` and `$LDFLAGS` shell variables (by using `env` or `setenv` for `csh` or `tcsh`, or `set` or `export` for `sh`, `bash`, or similar shells, before running `configure`. The `makefiles` generated by this should contain the proper `CFLAGS` and `LDFLAGS`. Not all `configure` scripts will pick up the variables, so you should check after running `configure` and edit the makefiles by hand if necessary.

If the programs you are compiling only call `gcc` (and not `cpp` or binutils directly), you can use the following script to save having to specify all of the options each time:

```
#!/bin/bash
/usr/bin/gcc -b i486-linuxlibc5 -nostdinc \
             -I/usr/i486-linuxlibc5/include \
             -I/usr/lib/gcc-lib/i486-linuxlibc5/2.7.2.2/include "$@"
```

You can then use this script instead of `gcc` when compiling.

7 Compiling C++ programs

Libg++ uses parts of the math library, so is linked to libm. Since your existing libg++ will be compiled with your old library, you will have to recompile libg++ with glibc or get a binary copy. The latest source for libg++ along with a binary linked with glibc (for x86) can be found at `ftp://ftp.yggdrasil.com/private/hjl/`.

7.1 Installing libg++ for a test glibc install

If you have installed glibc as a test library, you need to install the files into the directory you installed glibc into (such as `/usr/i486-linuxglibc2` for the example in the previous sections). If you are installing from the binary package (which I would recommend, since I never had any luck compiling libg++ this way), you need to extract the files into a temporary directory and move all the `usr/lib/` files into the *install directory*`/lib/` directory, the `usr/include/` files into the *install directory*`/include/` directory (remember to delete your `include/g++` link first!), and the `usr/bin/` files into the *install directory*`/bin/` directory.

7.2 Installing libg++ for a primary glibc install

If you have installed glibc as the primary library, you first need to move your old libg++ files into your old libc directory if you still want to be able to compile g++ programs with your old libc. Probably the easiest way to do this is by installing a new copy of the libg++ compiled with libc 5 as in the previous section, and then installing the glibc version normally.

7.3 Compiling C++ programs with the non-primary libc

If you are trying to compile a C++ program with a non-primary libc, you will need to include the g++ include dir, which in the examples above would be `/usr/i486-linuxglibc2/include/g++` for a test glibc install or `/usr/i486-linuxlibc5/include/g++` for a primary glibc install. This can usually be done by appending the `CXXFLAGS` variable:

```
CXXFLAGS = -nostdinc -I/usr/i486-linuxglibc2/include \
-I/usr/lib/gcc-lib/i486-linuxglibc2/2.7.2.2/include \
-I/usr/i486-linuxlibc5/include/g++ \
-b i486-linuxglibc2
```

8 Reporting bugs

If you think the lib is buggy, please read the FAQ first. It might be that others had the same problem and there's an easy solution. You should also check the section "Recommended Tools to Install the GNU C Library" in the `INSTALL` file since some bugs are bugs of the tools and not of glibc.

Once you've found a bug, make sure it's really a bug. A good way to do this is to see if the GNU C library behaves the same way some other C library does. If so, probably you are wrong and the libraries are right (but not necessarily). If not, one of the libraries is probably wrong.

Next, go to `http://www-gnats.gnu.org:8080/cgi-bin/wwwgnats.pl`, and look through the bug database. Check here to verify the problem has not already be reported. You should also look at the file `BUGS` (distributed with libc) to check for known bugs.

Once you're sure you've found a new bug, try to narrow it down to the smallest test case that reproduces the problem. In the case of a C library, you really only need to narrow it down to one library function call, if possible. This should not be too difficult.

The final step when you have a simple test case is to report the bug. When reporting a bug, send your test case, the results you got, the results you expected, what you think the problem might be (if you've thought of anything), your system type, the versions of the GNU C library, the GNU CC compiler, and the GNU Binutils which you are using. Also include the files `config.status` and `config.make` which are created by running `configure`; they will be in whatever directory was current when you ran `configure`.

All bug reports for the GNU C library should be sent using the `glibcbug` shell script which comes with the GNU libc to `bugs@gnu.org` (the older address `bugs@gnu.ai.mit.edu` is still working), or submitted through the GNATS web interface at `http://www-gnats.gnu.org:8080/cgi-bin/wwwgnats.pl`.

Suggestions and questions should be sent to the mailing list at `bugs-glibc@prep.ai.mit.edu`. If you don't read the gnewsgroup gnu.bug.glibc, you can subscribe to the list by asking `bug-glibc-request@prep.ai.mit.edu`.

Please do not send bug report for the GNU C library to `bug-gcc@prep.ai.mit.edu`. That list is for bug reports for GNU CC. GNU CC and the GNU C library are separate entities maintained by separate people.

9 Sample specs file

Included here is a sample "specs" file for glibc 2 which is used by GCC for compiling and linking. It should be found in the directory `/usr/lib/gcc-lib/`*new-system-dir*`/`*gcc-version*. If you are running an x86 system, you probably can copy this section to the file exactly (but without the line breaks).

```
*asm:
%{V} %{v:%{!V:-V}} %{Qy:} %{!Qn:-Qy} %{n} %{T} %{Ym,*} %{Yd,*} %{Wa,*:%*}

*asm_final:
%{pipe:-}

*cpp:
```

```
%{fPIC:-D__PIC__ -D__pic__} %{fpic:-D__PIC__ -D__pic__} \
%{!m386:-D__i486__} %{posix:-D_POSIX_SOURCE} \
%{pthread:-D_REENTRANT}

*cc1:
%{profile:-p}

*cc1plus:


*endfile:
%{!shared:crtend.o%s} %{shared:crtendS.o%s} crtn.o%s

*link:
-m elf_i386 %{shared:-shared}   %{!shared:    %{!ibcs:        \
%{!static:       %{rdynamic:-export-dynamic}        \
%{!dynamic-linker:-dynamic-linker /lib/ld-linux.so.2}}  \
%{static:-static}}}

*lib:
%{!shared: %{pthread:-lpthread}     %{profile:-lc_p} %{!profile: -lc}}

*libgcc:
-lgcc

*startfile:
%{!shared:     %{pg:gcrt1.o%s} %{!pg:%{p:gcrt1.o%s}        \
%{!p:%{profile:gcrt1.o%s}                          \
%{!profile:crt1.o%s}}}}     crti.o%s \
%{!shared:crtbegin.o%s} %{shared:crtbeginS.o%s}
*switches_need_spaces:


*signed_char:
%{funsigned-char:-D__CHAR_UNSIGNED__}

*predefines:
-D__ELF__ -Dunix -Di386 -Dlinux -Asystem(unix) -Asystem(posix) \
-Acpu(i386) -Amachine(i386)

*cross_compile:
0

*multilib:
 . ;
```

10 Miscellaney

10.1 Further information

10.1.1 Web Pages

- *FSF's GNU C Library Home Page* (http://www.gnu.org/software/libc/libc.html)
- *Using GNU Libc 2 with Linux* (http://www.imaxx.net/~thrytis/glibc/)
- *Installing glibc-2 on Linux* (http://huizen.dds.nl/~frodol/glibc/).

- *Debian libc5 to libc6 Mini-HOWTO* (http://www.gate.net/~storm/FAQ/libc5-libc6-Mini-HOWTO.html).

10.1.2 Newsgroups

- comp.os.linux.development.system
- comp.os.linux.development.apps
- linux.dev.kernel
- gnu.bugs.glibc

10.2 Credits

Most of this information was stolen from the

GNU Libc web page (http://www.gnu.org/software/libc/libc.html)

and from Ulrich Drepper's drepper@gnu.ai.mit.edu glibc 2 announcement and his comments. Andreas Jaeger aj@arthur.rhein-neckar.de provided some of the Reporting bugs section.

The following people have provided information and feedback for this document:

- Mark Brown <M.A.Brown-4@sms.ed.ac.uk>
- Ulrich Drepper <drepper@gnu.ai.mit.edu>
- Scott K. Ellis <ellis@valueweb.net>
- Aron Griffis <agriffis@coat.com>
- Andreas Jaeger <aj@arthur.rhein-neckar.de>
- Frodo Looijaard <frodol@dds.nl>
- Ryan McGuire <rmcguire@freenet.columbus.oh.us>
- Shaya Potter <spotter@capaccess.org>
- Les Schaffer <godzilla@futuris.net>
- Andy Sewell <puck@pookhill.demon.co.uk>
- Stephane <sr@adb.fr>
- Jan Vandenbos <jan@imaxx.net>

Translations of this document are being done by:

- French: Olivier Tharan <tharan@int-evry.fr>
- Japanese: Kazuyuki Okamoto <ikko-@pacific.rim.or.jp>

10.3 Feedback

Besides writing this HOWTO, maintaining the

glibc 2 for Linux (http://www.imaxx.net/~thrytis/glibc)

page, and using it on my machine, I have nothing to do with the glibc project. I am far from knowledgeable on this topic, though I try to help with problems mailed to me. I welcome any feedback, corrections, or suggestions you have to offer. Please send them to thrytis@imaxx.net.

[illegible]

10.1.2 Newsgroups

- comp.os.linux.[illegible]
- comp.os.linux.development.[illegible]
- [illegible]
- [illegible]

10.2 Credits

Most of this information was learnt from the [illegible]

[illegible]

The following people have provided information and feedback for this document:

- [illegible]
- [illegible]
- [illegible]
- [illegible]
- [illegible]
- [illegible]
- [illegible]
- [illegible]
- [illegible]
- [illegible]
- [illegible]
- [illegible]

Translations of this document are being done by:

- French: [illegible]
- Japanese: [illegible]

10.3 Feedback

[illegible]

Part XXIV

"Hebrew HOWTO"
by Yair G. Rajwan,
yair@hobbes.jct.ac.il

Contents

Abstract

v0.4, 12 September 1995
This "Frequently Asked Questions" (FAQ) and HOWTO document describes how to configure your Linux machine to use Hebrew characters on the X Window System and Virtual Consoles. The most up-to-date version of the Hebrew-HOWTO may be obtained from my Web page,

http://shekel.jct.ac.il/ rajwan/Hebrew.html
or from
ftp://hobbes.jct.ac.il

1 Introduction

Any language setup, other than the original American English, has two issues:

1. Displaying the right characters (fonts) - for Hebrew it's the ISO 8859-8 standard.
2. Mapping the keyboard.

There is much more to Hebrew than that (like right to left, geometry in the X Window System, etc.), but this HOWTO (at least for the first draft) deals only with the basic issues.

More information can be found in the various "national" HOWTOs (German, Danish, etc.) and in the ISO 8859-1 HOWTO (`ftp://ftp.vlsivie.tuwien.ac.at/pub/8bit` FAQ ISO-8859-1).

1.1 Thanks

This `HOWTO` prepared by the help of all the group: Linux-il—"The Israeli Linux users group" and especially by:

The Linux-il group (Linux-il@hagiga.jct.ac.il)
Vlad Moseanu (vlad@actcom.co.il)
Gili Granot (gil@csc.cs.technion.ac.il)
Harvey J. Stein (hjstein@math.huji.ac.il)
Dovie Adler (dadler@hobbes.jct.ac.il)
Gavrie Philipson (gavrie@shekel.jct.ac.il)

2 Standards for representation of Hebrew characters

2.1 ASCII

To make one thing clear, for once and forever: There is no such thing as 8-bit ASCII. ASCII is only 7 bits. Any 8-bit code is not ASCII, but that doesn't mean it's not standard. ISO 8859-8 is standard, but not ASCII. Thanks!

2.2 DOS Hebrew

The Hebrew encoding starts at 128d for Aleph. Therefore, encoding requires 8 bits. This is what you have on the Video card EPROM hardware fonts, all of the Hebrew DOS based editors use this table (Qtext, HED, etc.).

2.3 ISO Hebrew

The Hebrew encoding starts at 224 for Aleph. This is the Internet standard, international standard and basically the standard for MS Windows and for Macintosh (Dagesh, etc...).

2.4 OLD PC Hebrew

This is 7 bit, and obsolete, as it occupies essentially the same ASCII range as English lowercase letters. So, it is best avoided. However, when ISO Hebrew gets its eighth bit stripped off by some ignorant Unix mail program (so you get a jumble of English letters for the Hebrew part of your message and the regular English, reversed or not, mixed in), you will get this, and will need to transform it to PC or ISO. If there was English mixed in with the Hebrew, this will be a sad situation, as you will either get Hebrew plus jumble, or English plus jumble.

2.5 Conversions

Here are some simple scripts to convert from each standard to the other:

```
DOS - ISO:      tr '\200-\232' '\340-\372' < {dos_file} > {iso_file}
ISO - DOS:      tr '\340-\372' '\200-\232' < {iso_file} > {dos_file}
OLD - DOS:      tr -z '\200-\232' < {old_Hebrew_file} > {dos_file}
```

NOTE: The numbers use by `tr` are in octal!

3 Virtual Consoles (VCs)

Every distribution of Slackware comes with kbd; the package is called keytbls under Slackware (a4 in 2.3.0—kbd 0.90). Joel Hoffman has contributed Hebrew fonts and keymaps from his original `codepage.tar.Z` file. Look under `/usr/lib/kbd` for `iso08.*` files. It follows ISO 8859-8 and the Hebrew keytables and maps.

Put the following lines in `/etc/rc.d/rc.local`:

```
-----
#!/bin/sh
#       Put any local setup commands in here
#
INITTY=/dev/tty[1-6]
PATH=/sbin:/etc:/bin:/usr/sbin:/usr/bin
#
#       kbd - Set the the console font and keyboard
#       set numlock and set metabit mode on tty1 .. tty8
for tty in $INITTY
do
#       setleds -D +num < $tty > /dev/null
        setmetamode metabit < $tty > /dev/null
done
#       Latin8(Hebrew) keyboard/console
setfont iso08.f16
mapscrn trivial
loadkeys Hebrew
#       enable mapping
for tty in $INITTY
do
        echo -n -e "\\033(K" >$tty
done
-----
```

NOTE: If you are using X be careful with `setleds`. It may hang the X server.

The above setup works fine with the Hebrew version of `pico` (`pine`) and displays correctly ISO 8859-8 Hebrew (X, MS Windows).

4 X Windows setup—XFree86 3.1

4.1 Hebrew fonts.

XFree86 3.1 comes with two Hebrew fonts: heb6x13, heb8x13. Additional Hebrew fonts can be found on the Net:

- The web Type 1 fonts (Helvetica/David style (proportional) and Courier/Shalom Stick style (fixed space)) from the snunit-project archive at `ftp://snunit.huji.ac.il/pub/fonts/`, it's good for Netscape Hebrew pages.
- Avner Lottem, (lottem@techUnix.technion.ac.il) put some Hebrew-ISO 8859-8 fonts on archive at `ftp://sunsite.unc.edu/pub/Linux/X11/fonts/`, it has a font that's good for dosemu under X (read his README file).

4.2 Installing fonts

- Fonts installable: PCF (Portable Compiled Format), BDF (Bitmap Distribution Format), PFB (Type 1 fonts).
- Move the fonts to some existing directory (`/usr/lib/X11/fonts/misc`) or create a new one (`/usr/lib/X11/fonts/Hebrew`). `compress` (to *.Z) the fonts to save space (not `gzip`).
- Run `mkfontdir` to create or re-create the `fonts.dir` file and edit `fonts.alias` (optional) to define new aliases.
- For Type 1 fonts, `mkfontdir` does nothing. You have to add these fonts to `fonts.dir` manually.
- Make sure that the directory is in the X server path. Edit the `XF86Config` file and add the appropriate path—FontPath; e.g., `/usr/X11R6/lib/X11/fonts/`.

4.3 Making an X application use Hebrew fonts.

In short, you need to set the appropriate resource.

4.3.1 `xterm`

Put the following line in the `$HOME/.Xresources` file:

```
xterm*font:  heb8x13
```

or simply start `xterm` with `xterm -fn heb8x13` The above font is 'way too small, so search for a better one— See the comments and examples on starting X11.

4.3.2 Netscape

Usaly you can use the Hebrew fonts from Section 4.1, Install it Section 4.2, and then put the next defaults in your local `.Xdefaults` or in the `app-defaults/Netscape` directory.

```
----
*documentFonts.latin1.variable.italic*slant:         r
*documentFonts.latin1.variable.boldItalic*slant:     r
*documentFonts.latin1.variable*family:               web
*documentFonts.latin1.fixed*family:                  webmono
*documentFonts.latin1*registry:                      iso8859
*documentFonts.latin1*encoding:                      8
----
```

In general, you can specify any font instead of the Web font files as long as its supported by X11 4.2.

4.4 Mapping the keyboard.

For some reason, the X server doesn't inherit the keymap from the previous paragraph, and anyway I would like to define ALT Left and ALT Right and Scroll Lock. When pressing ALT together with some key it will generate a Hebrew character, Scroll Lock will lock in Hebrew mode.

To do that we need to use `xmodmap`. Following is a Xmodmap which also corrects the bugs with the "Num Lock:"

```
-----
! Hebrew key mapping for XFree86 (for US/Hebrew keyboards).
! By Vlad Moseanu
!
keysym Alt_L = Mode_switch
keysym Alt_R = Mode_switch
!clear Mod1
clear Mod2
!add Mod1 = Alt_L
add Mod2 = Mode_switch
!
! Set the mapping for each key
!
keycode   8 =
keycode   9 = Escape
keycode  10 = 1 exclam
```

```
keycode  11 = 2 at
keycode  12 = 3 numbersign
keycode  13 = 4 dollar
keycode  14 = 5 percent
keycode  15 = 6 asciicircum
keycode  16 = 7 ampersand
keycode  17 = 8 asterisk
keycode  18 = 9 parenleft
keycode  19 = 0 parenright
keycode  20 = minus underscore
keycode  21 = equal plus
keycode  22 = Delete
keycode  23 = Tab
keycode  24 = q Q slash Q
keycode  25 = w W apostrophe W
keycode  26 = e E 0x00f7 E
keycode  27 = r R 0x00f8 R
keycode  28 = t T 0x00e0 T
keycode  29 = y Y 0x00e8 Y
keycode  30 = u U 0x00e5 U
keycode  31 = i I 0x00ef I
keycode  32 = o O 0x00ed O
keycode  33 = p P 0x00f4 P
keycode  34 = bracketleft braceleft
keycode  35 = bracketright braceright
keycode  36 = Return
keycode  37 = Control_L
keycode  38 = a A 0x00f9 A
keycode  39 = s S 0x00e3 S
keycode  40 = d D 0x00e2 D
keycode  41 = f F 0x00eb F
keycode  42 = g G 0x00f2 G
keycode  43 = h H 0x00e9 H
keycode  44 = j J 0x00e7 J
keycode  45 = k K 0x00ec K
keycode  46 = l L 0x00ea L
keycode  47 = semicolon colon 0x00f3 colon
keycode  48 = apostrophe quotedbl comma quotedbl
keycode  49 = grave asciitilde semicolon asciitilde
keycode  50 = Shift_L
keycode  51 = backslash bar
keycode  52 = z Z 0x00e6 Z
keycode  53 = x X 0x00f1 X
keycode  54 = c C 0x00e1 C
keycode  55 = v V 0x00e4 V
keycode  56 = b B 0x00f0 B
keycode  57 = n N 0x00ee N
keycode  58 = m M 0x00f6 M
keycode  59 = comma less 0x00fa less
keycode  60 = period greater 0x00f5 greater
keycode  61 = slash question period question
keycode  62 = Shift_R
keycode  63 = KP_Multiply
!keycode  64 = Alt_L Meta_L
keycode  65 = space
keycode  66 = Caps_Lock
keycode  67 = F1
keycode  68 = F2
```

```
keycode  69 = F3
keycode  70 = F4
keycode  71 = F5
keycode  72 = F6
keycode  73 = F7
keycode  74 = F8
keycode  75 = Escape
keycode  76 = F10
keycode  77 = Num_Lock
keycode  78 = Scroll_Lock
keycode  79 = KP_7
keycode  80 = KP_8
keycode  81 = KP_9
keycode  82 = KP_Subtract
keycode  83 = KP_4
keycode  84 = KP_5
keycode  85 = KP_6
keycode  86 = KP_Add
keycode  87 = KP_1
keycode  88 = KP_2
keycode  89 = KP_3
keycode  90 = KP_0
keycode  91 = KP_Decimal
keycode  92 = Sys_Req
keycode  93 =
keycode  94 =
keycode  95 = F11
keycode  96 = F12
keycode  97 = Home
keycode  98 = Up
keycode  99 = Prior
keycode 100 = Left
keycode 101 = Begin
keycode 102 = Right
keycode 103 = End
keycode 104 = Down
keycode 105 = Next
keycode 106 = Insert
keycode 107 = Delete
keycode 108 = KP_Enter
keycode 109 = Control_R
keycode 110 = Pause
keycode 111 = Print
keycode 112 = KP_Divide
!keycode 113 = Alt_R Meta_R
keycode 114 = Break
!
! This xmodmap file can be use to set the correct numerical keypad mapping
! when "ServerNumLock" is set in the XF86Config file.  In this case the
! Xserver takes care of the Num Lock processing.
!
!
keycode  136 = KP_7
keycode  137 = KP_8
keycode  138 = KP_9
keycode  139 = KP_4
keycode  140 = KP_5
keycode  141 = KP_6
```

```
keycode  142 = KP_1
keycode  143 = KP_2
keycode  144 = KP_3
keycode  145 = KP_0
keycode  146 = KP_Decimal
keycode  147 = Home
keycode  148 = Up
keycode  149 = Prior
keycode  150 = Left
keycode  151 = Begin
keycode  152 = Right
keycode  153 = End
keycode  154 = Down
keycode  155 = Next
keycode  156 = Insert
keycode  157 = Delete
-----
```

To use the Xmodmap above define "Scroll-Lock Mode-Lock" in the `XF86Config`.

4.5 Integrating all the above, examples.

If you are using `xdm`, a `$HOME/.xsession` should look like the following:

```
-----
#!/bin/sh
# $XConsortium: Xsession,v 1.9 92/08/29 16:24:57 gildea Exp $
#
# General defs
#
export OPENWINHOME=/usr/openwin
export MANPATH=/usr/local/man:/usr/man/preformat:/usr/man:/usr/X11R6/man
#export HOSTNAME="'cat /etc/HOSTNAME'"
export PATH="/bin: /usr/bin: /usr/X11/bin: /usr/X386/bin: /usr/TeX/bini: /usr/local/bin: /usr/game
LESS=-MM
if [ -z $XAPPLRESDIR ]; then
        XAPPLRESDIR=/usr/lib/X11/app-defaults:/usr/local/lib/X11/app-defaults
else
        XAPPLRESDIR=$XAPPLRESDIR:/usr/lib/X11/app-defaults
fi
export XAPPLRESDIR
#
sysresources=/usr/lib/X11/Xresources
sysmodmap=/usr/lib/X11/Xmodmap
resources=$HOME/.Xresources
xmodmap=$HOME/.Xmodmap
if [ -f $sysresources ]; then
        xrdb -merge $sysresources
fi
if [ -f $sysmodmap ]; then
        xmodmap $sysmodmap
fi
if [ -f $resources ]; then
        xrdb -merge $resources
fi
if [ -f $xmodmap ]; then
        xmodmap $xmodmap
fi
#
# Start applications
```

```
#
# xterm -ls -sb &
xhost +                 # look out !!!
exec fvwm
-----
```

If you prefer `startx` use the above as an example for `.xinitrc`.

5 Shells setup.

For more details read the ISO 8859 HOWTO.

5.1 bash

Create a `$HOME/.inputrc` which contains the following:

```
-----
set meta-flag On
set convert-meta Off
set output-meta On
-----
```

5.2 tcsh

Define the following in the `$HOME/.login` or `/etc/csh.login`: `setenv LANG iw_IL.ISO8859-8 (or iw_IL)` Actually, because the binary version of `tcsh` is complied without nls, the `LANG` variable can be set to anything, and it will still work (no need for `/usr/lib/nls`...). The language name also shows my Digital bias.

6 Applications

6.1 Vim

- Vim is a Vi IMproved editor with some enhanced commands. The Hebrew support was made by Dov Grobgeld (HED developer).
- Another Vim patch announced by Avner Lottem, lottem@techunix.technion.ac.il and can be obtained from `ftp://sunsite.unc.edu/pub/Linux/apps/editors/vi/vim3.0-rlh0.1.tgz`.
- For more info, you can look at `http://www.cs.technion.ac.il/ gil/var.html`.

6.2 Hebrew pine and pico

`pine` and its additional editor `pico` had been changed by Helen Zommer from CC-huji and has a bug-report mail: pineh-bug@horizon.cc.huji.ac.il. It can be downloaded from `ftp://horizon.cc.huji.ac.il/pub`.

6.3 Some emacs Hebrew ports.

- Hebrew package by Joseph Friedman. It includes some Hebrew fonts in BDF format, patch for `emacs` 18.58 and an elisp package. It is fine, but nobody uses `emacs` 18.* anymore. It can be obtained from:

  `ftp://archive.cis.ohio-state.edu/pub/gnu/emacs/elisp-archive/misc/Hebrew.tar.Z`

- A very simple Hebrew package. Includes only right-to-left cursor movement support and right-to-left sorting. Works without any patches with FSF `emacs` 19. Can be obtained from

  `ftp://archive.cis.ohio-state.edu/pub/gnu/emacs/elisp-archive/misc/Hebrew.el.Z`

- One of `emacs` branches—MULE (Multi Lingual Emacs) supports a lot of languages, including Hebrew. It compiles and runs under Linux with no problem. It is full `emacs`, with Hebrew support and bi-directional handling. It can be obtained from: `ftp://kelim.jct.ac.il/pub/Hebrew`

6.4 Dosemu

For a VC dosemu you can use your Hebrew from the Video card EPROM, and if you don't have it, there are plenty of Hebrew MS-DOS fonts from EGA support to the VGA Hebrew support.

For X support you should download the file:

```
ftp://sunsite.unc.edu/pub/Linux/X11/fonts/hebxfonts-0.1.tgz
```

it contains some fonts including one called `vgah.pcf` that you should install in your fonts directory as described in 4.2

6.5 XHTerm

There is a main port of the regular `xterm` program for use with a Hebrew fonts—XHTerm = xterm + Hebrew support. The port for a Sun Microsystems machine was made avalaible by the help of Danny, danny@cs.huji.ac.il. Evgeny has some patches for use with this port under Linux. His version should come with a pre-compiled XHTerm for both X11R5 and X11R6. You should use `xhterm` with the option `-fn` and a Hebrew font from Section 4.3.1. Danny's port (for Sun) can be obtained from:

```
ftp://ftp.huji.ac.il/pub/local/xhterm
```

and the patched version by Evgeny Stambulchik is on:

```
ftp://plasma-gate.weizmann.ac.il/pub/software/linux
```

Get it from there and you'll get five fonts: `(heb10x20.pcf, heb6x13.bdf, heb6x13.pcf, heb8x13.bdf, heb8x13.pcf)`

6.6 TeX–XeT—Hebrew Tex.

The bigest problem with TEX with Hebrew is that the characters should go backwards relative to Visual look (i.e. `pico` inserts the charecters from right to left), so the best thing is to get XHterm with a regular `emacs` and write the Hebrew left to right, backwards as well.

If you want to use LATEX 2ε (the current de facto standard) you have a problem. Alon Ziv (alonz@csa.cs.technion.ac.il) is currently working in support for LATEX 2ε with Hebrew, using the Babel package. I don't know the current status of his work—ask him!

7 Printer setup

Mainly there is not much to say. If you have a regular ASCII line printer (who does, these days?) there is a good chance that there are Hebrew fonts in it on the EPROM chip.

If you use PostScript, you should download soft fonts to the printer (you can always use the 4.1 Web fonts for that. These fonts are also usable with Ghostscript).

If you have a PCL printer (LaserJet, etc.), you can either use font cartridges or use Ghostscript.

8 Commercial products.

8.1 El-Mar software.

The Hebrew Support for X and Motif, is a product of El-Mar Software, which adds Hebrew functionality to many of the parts and layers of X and Motif, including Xlib, all of the widgets of Motif, `hterm` (Hebrew `xterm`), demos and simple useful applications (e.g. bi-lingual Motif-based editor), fonts (including scalable Type 1), a keyboard manager in order to allow Hebrew and push-mode for non-Motif applications, etc.

Despite allowing many new features and variations for Motif widgets, the support doesn't have any modifications to internal data structures of Motif, so existing applications which were compiled and linked for non-Hebrew environments and libraries can be relinked (without compilation!) and run with Hebrew (you can replace shared libraries, so even the relink is not needed!)

With Motif/Xplorer, you can take commercial applications (without their source) and translate them to Hebrew. This was the way of giving Hebrew support for Oracle Forms 4, Intellicorp's Kappa and OMW, CA-Unicenter, and many other leading UNIX tools sold in Israel. This product was purchased and adopted by most of the workstation vendors (nine of them, including the biggest: Sun, HP, SGI), and many other software houses. There are Makefiles for more than 30 platforms and operating systems.

We believe only in open software, so all the customers get the compelete source code. We have good relations with the leading forces in this industry, including the technical staff of the X Consortium and the technical staff of COSE.

Eli Marmor
El-Mar Software Ltd.
Voice: 050-237338
FAX: 09-984279

marmor@sunshine.cs.biu.ac.il

P.S.: The announcement of the Arabic Support for X-Windows & Motif, is expected in January. English, Hebrew, and Arabic will be handled by 8 bits (!), including the full set of Arabic glyphes.

9 Hebrew around the Internet.

9.1 WWW

- Jerusalem 1—has many program and FAQ files about Hebrew on Unix and other platforms *http://www.jer1.co.il* (http://www.jer1.co.il).
- Gili Granot's Hebrew archive page—summaries of all Hebrew related issues around the Web (include all kind of files) http://www.cs.technion.ac.il/~gil.
- Gavrie has some info about Hebrew on his FTP site: ftp://kelim.jct.ac.il

9.2 Gopher

- A one-word testing for Hebrew gopher can be found on gopher://shekel.jct.ac.il.

9.3 FTP

- Some Tex-Xet programs and the main FTP site for TEX Hebrew support for PC and Unix is at ftp://noa.huji.ac.il/tex.
- Horizon site as 6.2 contains the main site of pine and pico Hebrew support— ftp://horizon.huji.ac.il/pub.
- Gili Granot's Hebrew archive page FTP site is at ftp://ssl.cs.technion.ac.il/pub.

Part XXV

"ISP-Hookup-HOWTO" by Egil Kvaleberg,

egilk@sn.no

Contents

Abstract

v1.24, 14 February 1997
This document describes how to use Linux to connect to an Internet Service Provider via a dial-up modem connection. As well as the basic dial-up procedure and IP establishment, email and news handling is covered.

1 Introduction

This description has been made to answer a few questions about how dial-up ISP (Internet Service Provider) subscribers may configure and use Linux.

To aid those who will connect their Linux based machines to an ISP for the first time, an attempt has been made to cover most issues encountered. This quite unavoidably will create a certain degree of overlap with other Linux HOWTO documents and LDP books. Reference should be made to these documents to provide better understanding and detail.

Much of the existing documentation is targeted towards users with a certain degree of experience, and first time users will often have trouble sorting out the relevant information.

To simplify, the examples given will assume the following:

- User name: `dirk`
- Password: `PrettySecret`
- Internet service provider: `acme.net`
- Email server: `mail.acme.net`
- News server: `news.acme.net`
- Name server: `193.212.1.0`
- Phone number: `12345678`

Our `dirk` will be calling his machine `roderick`.

All references in the table above should naturally be replaced by whatever is valid for the ISP one is using. Often, just a minimum of changes will otherwise be required for users with different ISPs. I would like to be informed about what problems you encounter on this account.

1.1 New versions of this document

New versions of this document will be periodically posted to comp.os.linux.answers. They will also be added to the various anonymous FTP sites who archive such information, including:

`ftp://sunsite.unc.edu/pub/Linux/docs/HOWTO`

In addition, you should generally be able to find this document on the Linux Documentation Project page via:

`http://sunsite.unc.edu/LDP/`

Finally, the very latest version of this document should also be available in various formats from:

`ftp://ftp.sn.no/user/egilk/ISP-Hookup-HOWTO.txt`
`ftp://ftp.sn.no/user/egilk/ISP-Hookup-HOWTO.ps.gz`
`ftp://ftp.sn.no/user/egilk/ISP-Hookup-HOWTO.tar.gz`
`http://home.sn.no/home/egilk/ISP-Hookup-HOWTO.html`

1.2 Feedback

All comments, error reports, additional information and criticism of all sorts should be directed to:

`egil@kvaleberg.no`
`http://home.sn.no/home/egilk/`

1.3 Disclaimer

No liability for the contents of this documents can be accepted. Use the concepts, examples and other content at your own risk. Additionally, this is an early version, with many possibilities for inaccuracies and errors.

One of many possible setups will be described. In the Linux world, there is usually a number of ways in which to accomplish things. Paragraphs containing hints to alternatives are marked by **ALT:** Please also note that FTP-references often will change slightly as new versions of programs arrive.

As far as I know, only programs that under certain terms may be used or evaluated for personal purposes will be described. Most of the programs will be available complete with source under GNU-like terms.

1.4 Copyright information

2 How do I connect to the rest of the world?

It will be assumed that we have installed the essential networking software modules (e.g. essential parts of the Slackware N-series), and that you have set up which serial port that is to be used for the `/dev/modem`.

The default configuration will usually only allow direct access to `/dev/modem` as user `root`.

To connect to ISP shell accounts directly, and to experiment with connection sequences, you may use the `minicom` program. It is pretty straight forward to use.

2.1 The basic configuration

Configuration of the machine for use on the net should be done as user `root`. Before proceeding any further, ensure that the file `/etc/hosts.deny` contains the following line:

```
ALL: ALL
```

You would normally want to allow yourself, so add the following line to `/etc/hosts.allow`:

```
ALL: LOCAL
```

Or if you insist:

```
ALL: 127.0.0.1
```

For the following, note that it is meant for those connected via PPP and with a dynamic IP address. If you have the benefit of a fixed connection, there will be some differences.

It is nice to have a name connected to the machine, a name that the dynamic IP user really can select as he or she pleases. Put the name in `/etc/HOSTNAME`:

```
roderick
```

The next step is to set up the name server in `/etc/resolv.conf`:

```
search .
nameserver 193.212.1.0
```

The name server must be specified by a numeric IP address, and will be different from ISP to ISP. If required, you can have up to three different servers, each on a separate line. They will be requested in the sequence in which they are listed.

If you want to be able to use names like `somemachine` as an abbreviation for `somemachine.acme.net`, you must replace the first line with:

```
search acme.net
```

A certain minimum of configuration will also be required in `/etc/hosts`. Most users will be able to manage with:

```
127.0.0.1 localhost
0.0.0.0   roderick
```

Those with a fixed IP-address will obviously replace 0.0.0.0 with this.

Likewise, a minimum `/etc/networks` is:

```
loopback  127.0.0.0
localnet  0.0.0.0
```

You should also set your external mail domain in /etc/mailname:

```
acme.net
```

The user name and password at the ISP must be specified in /etc/ppp/pap-secrets

```
dirk * PrettySecret
```

For those ISPs using CHAP instead of PAP, the filename is /etc/ppp/chap-secrets.

Finally, the nitty gritty regarding the connection procedure itself must be specified before PPP can be initiated. This is done in /etc/ppp/chatscript:

```
TIMEOUT 5
"" ATZ
OK ATDT12345678
ABORT "NO CARRIER"
ABORT BUSY
ABORT "NO DIALTONE"
ABORT WAITING
TIMEOUT 45
CONNECT ""
TIMEOUT 5
"name:" ppp
```

Details here may have to be tuned somewhat. The phone number in the third line must of course be set as required. Some users may need to replace the ATZ modem initialization string with something more tailored for the modem being used. The last line specifies that one is expecting the prompt name:, and that the response should be ppp when it arrives. Other systems may have other login procedures.

To actually initiate a call, the PPP protocol may be initiated by issuing the following command:

```
exec pppd connect \
      'chat -v -f /etc/ppp/chatscript' \
       -detach crtscts modem defaultroute \
       user dirk \
       /dev/modem 38400
```

We should now be on-air, and stay up until the program is killed by typing a Ctrl-C. Any messages concerning the connection will be appended to the system logs. To read them, try:

```
tail /var/adm/messages
```

As long as PPP is up, you will have direct access to the Internet, and may use programs like ftp, ncftp, rlogin, telnet, finger etc. All these programs should be part of the network package.

Further information concerning PPP is also available from:

/usr/lib/ppp/README.linux

/usr/lib/ppp/README.linux-chat

Finally, an additional word about safety. The file /etc/inetd.conf lists all services that your machine will offer externally. With the /etc/hosts.deny file we have made, no external access will be allowed. For those who need it, access must be allowed explicitly in /etc/hosts.allow. Local traffic may be allowed by:

```
ALL: LOCAL
```

See also man 5 hosts_access.

A final small issue: A certain confusion exists regarding the names of the POP-protocols. A definition in /etc/services compatible with just about everything is:

```
pop2      109/tcp   pop-2          # PostOffice V.2
pop3      110/tcp   pop-3 pop # PostOffice V.3
```

ALT: Instead of chatscript, one might use the much more flexible dip. But not in connection with diald.

ALT: Those fortunate enough to have a permanent TCP/IP connection via e.g. an Ethernet may safely ignore anything about PPP, and rather start concentrating about setting up their network card.

ALT: Others may not have the possibility of using PPP, but may be able to use SLIP instead, for which there is support in much the same manner as for PPP. Another possibility is UUCP. Others again may have to rely on exchange of news and email be means of SOUP. A description for the latter case may be found in:

ftp://ftp.sn.no/user/bjorn/Linux-offline.tgz

The TERM program is also an option. Refer to the Term HOWTO.

3 How do I surf?

If you think that text is the most important, you might want to use the Lynx Web-browser. It is available from:

`ftp://sunsite.unc.edu/pub/Linux/system/Network/info-systems/lynx-2.3.bin2.tar.gz`

If you have installed X-windows, you can also use one of the many graphical browsers. Chimera may be found at:

`ftp://sunsite.unc.edu/pub/Linux/system/Network/info-systems/chimera-1.65.bin.ELF.tar.gz`
`http://www.unlv.edu/chimera/`

Mosaic:

`ftp://sunsite.unc.edu/pub/Linux/system/Network/info-systems/Mosaic-2.7b1-aout.tgz`
`ftp://ftp.NCSA.uiuc.edu/Web/Mosaic/Unix/binaries/2.6`

Mozilla (Netscape):

`ftp://sunsite.unc.edu/pub/Linux/system/Network/info-systems/netscape-v11b3.tar.gz`
`ftp://ftp.cs.uit.no/pub/www/netscape`

These browsers are constantly available in new and in various ways *exciting* versions.

Use and evaluation of these programs is subject to certain terms. Please observe them.

4 How do I send and receive email?

First of all, ensure that `sendmail` is installed. Sendmail sorts internal and out-bound mail, and will buffer out-bound mail until such time it is possible to forward it.

Sendmail is based on a configuration found in `/etc/sendmail.cf`. An example suitable for ISP users can be found in:

`ftp://ftp.sn.no/user/egilk/sendmail.cf` This is based on procmail as a delivery agent, but may easily be changed to use deliver.

It is if course required to have an **official** domain address for out-bound mail, something which is specified in `/etc/sendmail.cf`:

```
# who I masquerade as (null for no masquerading)
DMacme.net
```

This assumes that you have the same user name locally as you have at your ISP. Sendmail is now configured for sending **directly** to the recipient. To avoid long and repeated connections in those cases where the connection to the receiving end is slow and irregular, is is usually nice to use one's ISP as a buffer store. This can be specified by the DS specification:

```
# "Smart" relay host (may be null)
DSmail.acme.net
```

Beware that sendmail is somewhat sensitive to handling of tab stop characters in `sendmail.cf`. You might want to use the `vi` editor to ensure that these tab characters are retained unchanged.

Email reception can often be performed via the POP3 protocol, which can be initiated every time the connection is brought up. A script for testing this is:

```
sendmail -q
popclient -3 -v mail.acme.net -u dirk -p "PrettySecret" \
    -k -o /usr/spool/mail/dirk
```

This script may be started after PPP connection has been established. Beware that this script is just for testing, so ensure that the local mailbox is left untouched while it runs. The `-k` option means that the mail is **kept** in the ISP mailbox, and you are simply given a copy of the mail. You would of course want to remove this option once you are confident that your setup is working.

Beware that the password will show on the command line. This really should be fixed ASAP.

A safe and better version of this script may be found at:

`ftp://ftp.sn.no/user/egilk/pop-script.tar.gz`

This version of the script requires that `procmail` is installed, but that is something you'll never regret anyway:

`ftp://sunsite.unc.edu/pub/Linux/system/Mail/mailhandlers/procmail-3.10-2.tar.gz`

Procmail is a simple and flexible tool that can sort incoming email based on a large range of criteria. In addition to being able to handle automated tasks like vacation messages and such.

Note that when we use procmail directly as in this case, the situation is somewhat different from what is described in the procmail documentation. A `.forward` is **not** required, and we also don't need a `.procmailrc`. The latter is only required if we want to sort the mail.

The user interface for reading and sending of email can be found in programs like Pine or Elm.

ALT: Fetchmail has recently become a most interesting alternative to popclient. The latest version is available from: ftp://ftp.ccil.org/pub/esr/fetchmail/fetchmail-3.3.tar.gz

ALT: For an ordinary dial-up ISP user it is not really necessary to have the sendmail daemon active. To reduce the resource usage, one may thus comment out any startup of sendmail, as is usually found in /etc/rc.d/rc.M.

ALT: In place of sendmail one might use the simpler **smail**. You'll find a good description of it (as well as most other things mentioned here) in the *Linux Network Administrator's Guide*.

ALT: There is also an m4 macro package for making a fresh sendmail.cf. For a simple installation it might be just as well to modify an existing configuration.

ALT: There are also simpler although less flexible alternatives. Pine may run stand-alone as long as it is configured properly, for instance. It might even be possible to use newer versions of some web-browsers.

ALT: Many are very enthusiastic regarding the Emacs companion Gnus as an email and news handler. Further information can be found at:
http://www.ifi.uio.no/~larsi/

ALT: An alternative to popclient is pop-perl5. It is available from:
ftp://sunsite.unc.edu/pub/Linux/System/Mail/pop-perl5-1.1.tar.gz

5 News

5.1 How do I set up an online news-reader?

As long as PPP is active, it will be possible to read news **online**. There are lots of available programs. Two simple alternatives are rtin and trn.

To start reading news, the only thing required in terms of configuration in most cases is to do (usually once and for all in the file .profile):

```
export NNTPSERVER=news.acme.net
```

To get the *From*-address correct in postings, some programs *may* require:

```
export NNTP_INEWS_DOMAIN=acme.net
```

5.2 How do I set up an offline news-reader?

To be able to read news while offline, and thus reduce phone bills and give greater flexibility, one must set up a local news-spool of one sort or the other. This requires some configuration, and there will also be a certain amount of disk space involved. After initial setup, things should run more or less by themselves, with only some attention needed from time to time.

Two different solutions will be described here.

5.3 How do I set up C News?

The solution described here is based on the news-server **C News** and the NNTP protocol. C News was originally targeted towards another sort of configuration, but is flexible enough to handle our situation too. One might also use the more recent **INN** news server, but it might require a bit more in terms of resources. Any way, be careful **not** to install both; they don't live together easily.

It is crucial that all maintenance of news is done while logged in as user news, and that all configuration files is placed in /usr/lib/news. One way of handling this is, while logged in as root to write su news; cd.

The most important files in the configuration are:

- active is an overview over active newsgroups. It is updated as required by the command addgroup, e.g. addgroup comp.os.linux.networking y.
- organization should simply contain whatever you want in the *Organization:* header field, in our case:

  ```
  Dirk Gently's Holistic Detective Agency
  ```
- mailname should in our case be set to acme.net.
- whoami is set to the name of your site in the *Path:* thread. In a setup as described here, using NewsX, this name will never leave the machine, so you can set this to whatever you like as long as you are pretty sure it is unique. In this case roderick.

- `sys` controls fetching and further distribution of news. We will assume the ISP in our case adds `acme.net` to the Path, and that this is the only news source we have. The example given really tells that we will accept everything that arrives, and that we will only post news to `acme.net` that it hasn't seen before, and is originally posted at our own site. In this simplified setup we assume that the all groups will come from a single source. `/all` specifies the distribution, and **must** be included. The letter `F` says that (pointers to) outgoing news articles will be collected in a file.

```
ME:all/all::
acme/acme.net:all,!junk/all:FL:
```

- A subdirectory for the outgoing news must be created, in our case:
  `mkdir /var/spool/news/out.going/acme`
- `mailpaths` controls posting in moderated groups, although this task may usually be left to the ISP.

C News needs a certain degree of daily maintenance, but this can be specified once and for all via the command `crontab -e` issued as user `news`. A suggested setup follows; it can be tuned as required:

```
# maintain incoming and outgoing batches
10,40 *  * * * /usr/lib/newsbin/input/newsrun

# expire C News, once a day
30 0  * * * /usr/lib/newsbin/expire/doexpire

# monitor and report if needed
00 2  * * sat /usr/lib/newsbin/maint/addmissing
40 3  * * * /usr/lib/newsbin/maint/newswatch
50 3  * * * /usr/lib/newsbin/maint/newsdaily
```

`/usr/lib/newsbin/input/newsrun` moves articles in and out (twice every hour), `/usr/lib/newsbin/expire/doexpire` will delete articles as they get old (every night at 00:30), and the three last commands does various supervisory and error correcting tasks.

One should also ensure that things are cleaned up when starting the machine. As user root, add the following line to `/etc/rc.d/rc.local`:

```
su news -c /usr/lib/newsbin/maint/newsboot
```

News may be collected via the program **NewsX**, picking news from an NNTP server. The program can be found at:
`ftp://sunsite.unc.edu/pub/Linux/system/news/transport/newsx-0.9.tar.gz`
Or:
`ftp://ftp.sn.no/user/egilk/newsx-0.9.tar.gz`
Setting up `NewsX` is quite simple. Installation is a classic case of:

```
make
su
make install
exit
```

With the setup outlined here, all you have to do is to create the groups you want to read using the "addgroup" command.

To fetch articles, user `news` issues the following commands (assuming communication via PPP or similar is up):

```
newsrun
newsx acme news.acme.net
newsrun
```

The option `-d` gives continuous printout to the screen. Refer to the NewsX documentation for further information. NewsX will also take care of posting of outgoing news.

To control disposal of articles as they get old, a file `explist` is required. The comments in this example should explain what we want to do:

```
# hold onto history lines 14 days, nobody gets {$>$}120 days
/expired/            x     14 -
/bounds/             x     0-1-120 -

# retain these for 2 months
```

```
comp.sources,comp.os.linux.all     x   60   -
# noise gets thrown away fast
junk,control             x   2   -

# default:  14 days, no archive
all              x    14    -
```

ALT: In a small news-spool, one will often not need the newsgroup `control`. The traffic is **huge** compared to the usefulness. The main point is that articles will be canceled, and that groups may be created automatically. To ensure that control messages containing `newgroup` not shall mess up things for us, a file called `newgroupperm` specifies what we will allow:

```
comp.os.linux  tale@uunet.com yv
all     any        nq
```

In this example, all proper groups under comp.os.linux will be created (y), and the user `news` will be notified (v). Everything else will be silently (q) ignored (n). The last line is sufficient if you want to create all groups manually.

ALT: Alternatives to NewsX are `suck`, or `slurp` combined with `postit`. Slurp uses the NNTP NEWNEWS which will put severe loads on many news servers.

5.4 How do I set up Leafnode?

A different solution altogether is to install the integrated package `leafnode`. This will handle all tasks required for a personal news spool, and is easy to configure. It is available via:

`http://www.troll.no/freebies/leafnode.html`

As for C News, all news maintenance should be performed as user `news`.

The home directory for leafnode is in `/usr/lib/leafnode`. To install, write:

```
cd /usr/lib/leafnode
tar -xzvf leafnode-0.8.tgz
cd leafnode-0.8
make
su
make install
```

While still being logged in as `root`, change the line that controls NNTP in `/etc/inetd.conf`:

```
nntp  stream  tcp  nowait  news  /usr/sbin/tcpd /usr/local/sbin/leafnode
```

Activate it by:

```
killall -HUP inetd
```

Return to user `news` by writing `exit`. In `/usr/lib/leafnode/config` change the line that defines the NNTP server. In our case:

```
server = news.acme.net
```

Leafnode will look after itself by adding the following command via `crontab -e` as user `news`:

```
# expire Leafnode, once a day
0 4 * * * /usr/local/sbin/texpire
```

The news exchange is also done as user `news` by the following command (assuming PPP is up and running):

```
/usr/local/sbin/fetch
```

Users who wants to read news should then use the recipe in *How do I set up an online news-reader?*, except that they configure for the local machine, i.e:

```
export NNTPSERVER=localhost
```

That should be all there is to it. The first `fetch` will transfer a list of available newsgroups. Leafnode will then monitor what groups the users are requesting, and adapt to this the **next** time it is activated.

ALT: An alternative to `leafnode` is `nntpcache`, available from:

`ftp://ftp.suburbia.net/pub/nntpcache/nntpcache.tgz`

6 How do I automate the connection procedure?

Automated handling of news and email is quite easy to implement in Linux.

First and foremost one should make a /usr/lib/ppp/ppp-on that initiates the ISP connection. Often, this file will simply contain the following:

```
/usr/sbin/pppd
```

Further specification will be performed in /etc/ppp/options:

```
connect "/usr/lib/ppp/chat -v -f /etc/ppp/chatscript"
crtscts
modem
defaultroute
asyncmap 00000000
user dirk
/dev/modem 38400
```

To end a connection, use the supplied version of /usr/lib/ppp/ppp-off.

Having tested the functionality of these two scripts, one must then write scripts that perform the various tasks. The script to collect email has been described before, and we will here assume it is located at /home/dirk/pop.

A script for exchange of email can then be produced in /root/mail:

```
#! /bin/sh
#
# exchange mail
# 10 minutes timeout:
TIMEOUT=600
DT=10

# kick sendmail:
sendmail -q \&

# retrieve mail:
su dirk -c /home/dirk/pop

# wait for sendmail to terminate:
t=0
while ! mailq | grep -q "Mail queue is empty"; do
    t=$[$t+$DT]
    if [ $t -gt $TIMEOUT ] ; then
     echo "sendmail -q timeout ($TIMEOUT).."
     exit 1
    fi
    sleep $DT
done

exit 0
```

The script to exchange news may be placed in /usr/lib/news/news:

```
#!/bin/sh
#
# exchange news
# must be run as news:
cd /usr/lib/news

#update the outgoing batch (C News):
/usr/lib/newsbin/input/newsrun < /dev/null

#exchange news:
/usr/lib/newsbin/newsx acme news.acme.net
```

```
#and flush the incoming batch:
/usr/lib/newsbin/input/newsrun < /dev/null
```

A script to connect the various bits and pieces remains, and can be placed in /root/news+mail:

```
#!/bin/sh
#
# exchange news and email
# must be run as root
#
if ! /usr/lib/ppp/ppp-on; then
    exit 1
fi
trap "/usr/lib/ppp/ppp-off" 1 2 3 15

#exchange news+mail:
/root/mail \&
su news -c ~news/news
wait

#disconnect..
/usr/lib/ppp/ppp-off

#update the incoming batch (C News):
su news -c /usr/lib/newsbin/input/newsrun < /dev/null \&

exit 0
```

It is quite easy to make an extension to the above that only will establish a connection if outgoing email and news is present. Lets call it /root/news+mail.cond, and keep in mind that the name of the outgoing news-spool must be updated to suit:

```
#!/bin/sh
#
# exchange news and email, only if outgoing news or mail
# (C News spool)
if [ -s /var/spool/news/out.going/acme/togo ] ||
    ! ( mailq | grep -q "Mail queue is empty"); then
     /root/news+mail
fi
```

The only thing remaining is to specify when all this is going to happen. This is done using the command crontab -e as root. Let us assume that we always want to exchange news and mail at 07:00 in the morning, and after that every 4th hour assuming there are outgoing email and news:

```
00 7      * * *     /root/news+mail
00 11,15,19,23 * * *     /root/news+mail.cond
```

Ensure that every component is tested well before you connect them together. One may later add several other tasks, such as adjustment of the time of day (using ntpdate), and automatic update (mirroring) of locally maintained WWW and FTP files up to the ISP (using make and ftp).

ALT: Depending on ones preferences, it is also possible to turn the process upside down. Every time a PPP link is initiated, the script /etc/ppp/ip-up will be started. One may here add whatever magic is required to start exchange of email and news. See man pppd for further detail.

ALT: It is also possible to automatically connect PPP whenever network traffic is detected. This is in many ways the more elegant solution, but it is quite dependent on a good configuration to avoid frequent (and costly) connections being made. More information can be found at:

http://www.dna.lth.se/ erics/diald.html

The diald utility is available from:

ftp://sunsite.unc.edu/pub/Linux/system/network/serial/diald-0.16.tar.gz

At the same location one will also find other variations on the theme PPP connections.

7 Final words

7.1 Other things I should know about?

- Various error messages in the system will normally be issued as internal email. To ensure that these will actually be read, one should create an `/etc/aliases`. Remember the command `newaliases` every time you change this. An example that should cover most eventualities is:

```
PostMaster: root
ftp: root
news: root
usenet: root
FaxMaster: root
fax: root
WebMaster: root
MAILER.DAEMON: root
```

- Many programs for Linux may be found at **Sunsite**, which is usually quite busy. But there are many mirrors, and every time there is a reference to `ftp://sunsite.unc.edu/pub/Linux/`. One should try to use a mirror close to home, e.g. `ftp://ftp.nvg.unit.no/pub/linux/sunite/`.
- If you happen to be migrating from Yarn, it should be possible to convert these to standard folders using the `yarn2mf` available at:

`ftp://ftp.sn.no/user/egilk/yarn2mf.zip`

8 ISP-specific information

More specific information for certain ISPs is available from a variety of sources:

Demon Internet (demon.co.uk)
`ftp://ftp.demon.co.uk/pub/unix/linux/Demon/slack3.0.help.tgz`
Easynet TBA
Netcom http://www.netcom.com/bin/webtech/NetCruiser/Operating_Systems/Linux/linux.cfg.html
PowerTech, Schibstednett, Telenor Online
`http://home.sn.no/home/egilk/no-isp.html`
Primenet TBA
Stanford
`http://www-leland.stanford.edu/ wkn/Linux/network/network.html`
If you know of ISP-specific information not listed here, please get in touch.

8.1 How do I learn more?

The *Linux Documentation Project* book called *Linux Network Administrator's Guide* by Olaf Kirch is pretty mandatory for anyone that will set up and maintain anything involving TCP/IP and Internet:

`ftp://sunsite.unc.edu/pub/Linux/docs/linux-doc-project/network-guide/nag-1.0.ascii.tar.gz`

The documentation that follows each software package will normally give you all the detailed information you need, if not always the overview. The manual pages will be the first place to look. Try for instance:

```
man pppd
```

You will also find some documentation about certain programs in the `/usr/doc` tree, although this is not always well structured.

The following HOWTOs will be highly relevant:

- **Installation-HOWTO** will get the basics sorted.
- **NET-2-HOWTO** is a very thorough description of installation and setup of the NET code. Much of this should already have been done if you use a standard Linux distribution (e.g. Slackware, Red Hat, Debian). But many sections on setup and troubleshooting will be very worthwhile.
- **Mail-HOWTO** explains how to configure various tools. Again, much of this will already have been done for you when you install a standard Linux distribution.
- **News-HOWTO** is for setting up a (conventional) news spool.
- **Tiny-News** covers yet another alternative for collecting news.

- **PPP-HOWTO** is a good description of problems you may encounter when setting up a PPP connection.
- **Serial-HOWTO** contains everything you need to know about setting up serial ports.
- **Mail-Queue** tells you how to send up *sendmail* to always queue remote mail but deliver local mail at once.

Red Hat has a mailing list for PPP issues; to join send an email to `redhat-ppp-list-request` with the subject line

```
subscribe
```

8.2 Thanks to

Information here is collected from many sources. Thanks to the following that either indirectly or directly have contributed:

```
Adam Holt <holt@graphics.lcs.mit.edu>
Arne Coucheron <arneco@oslonett.no>
Arne Riiber <riiber@oslonett.no>
Arnt Gulbrandsen <agulbra@troll.no>
Bjorn Steensrud <bjornst@powertech.no>
Gisle Hannemyr <gisle@a.sn.no>
Hans Amund Rosbach <haro@sesam.dnv.no>
Hans Peter Verne <hpv@ulrik.uio.no>
Harald T Alvestrand <Harald.T.Alvestrand@uninett.no>
Harald Terkelsen  <Harald.Terkelsen@adm.hioslo.no>
Haavard Engum <hobbes@interlink.no>
James Youngman <JYoungman@vggas.com>
Johan S. Seland <johanss@sn.no>
John Phillips <john@linux.demon.co.uk>
Jorn Lokoy <jorn@oslonett.no>
Kenneth Tjostheim <kenneth.tjostheim@asplanviak.no>
Kjell M. Myksvoll <kjell.myksvoll@fou.telenor.no>
Kjetil T. Homme <kjetilho@math.uio.no>
Michael Meissner <meissner@cygnus.com>
N J Bailey <N.J.Bailey@leeds.ac.uk>
Nicolai Langfeldt <janl@math.uio.no>
Ove Ruben R Olsen <Ove.R.Olsen@ub.uib.no>
R. Bardarson <ronb@powernet.net>
Steinar Fremme <steinar@fremme.no>
Sverre H. Huseby <sverrehu@ifi.uio.no>
Trond Eivind Glomsrod <teg@stud.imf.unit.no>
Tommy Larsen <tommy@mix.hive.no>
```

Part XXVI

"Linux Intranet Server HOWTO" by Pramod Karnad,

karnad@indiamail.com

Contents

Abstract

v2.11, 7 August 1997
This document describes how to set up an Intranet using Linux as the server which binds Unix, Netware, NT and Windows together. Hence by just establishing the connection to the Linux box you are provided transparent access to all the various platforms. Detailed explanations are provided for setting up HTTP using the NCSA server and connect to it using TCP/IP clients from Novell, Microsoft under Windows3.1, WFWG,Win95 and WinNT and MacTCP on the Apple PowerMac.

1 Introduction

In simple terms, the **Intranet** is the descriptive term being used for the implementation of Internet technologies within a corporate organization, rather than for external connection to the global Internet. This implementation is performed in such a way as to transparently deliver the immense informational resources of an organization to each individual's desktop with minimal cost, time and effort. This document attempts to explain in simple terms how to set up an Intranet using tools which are readily available and are generally costing little or are free.

This document assumes that you already know how to install TCP/IP on your Linux server and connect it physically to your LAN using an Ethernet network card. This also assumes you have some basic knowledge of Netware, WinNT and Mac systems. The configuration of the Netware server has been shown using version 3.1x as the basis. You can also use INETCFG to achieve the same result. On the client side the discussion is with respect to Windows 3.1x, Windows for Work groups and Win95, WinNT and the Apple PowerMac.

I am using the private network addresses (RFC-1918) of 172.16.0.0 and 172.17.0.0 only as examples. You may choose suitable addresses depending on your configuration.

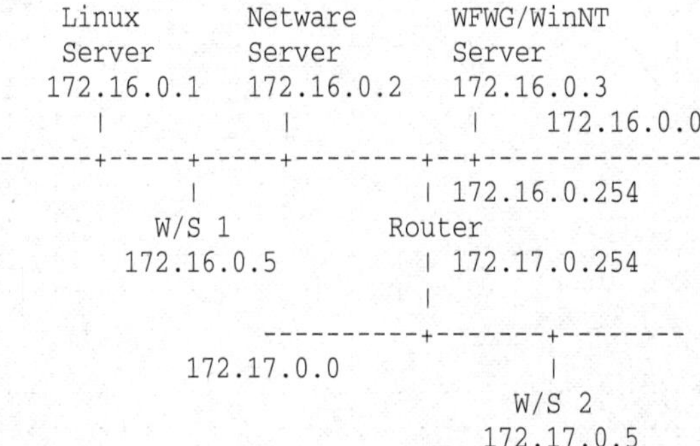

1.1 What is required

You will need the following software before attempting the installation.

- The HTTP server software which can be downloaded from OneStep NCSA HTTPd Downloader at http://hoohoo.ncsa.uiuc.edu/docs/setup/OneStep.html page.
- The Novell Netware Client available from HTTP://support.novell.com/ (The TCP/IP files are included with the client).
- The Microsoft TCP/IP client available from HTTP://www.microsoft.com/
- The Apple MacTCP client available from HTTP://www.apple.com/
- WWW Browsers like Netscape at HTTP://home.netscape.com/ or MS Internet Explorer at HTTP://www.microsoft.com/ or NCSA Mosaic from http://www.ncsa.uiuc.edu/SDG/Software/Mosaic/NCSAMosaicHome.html

1.2 New versions of this document

New versions of the Linux Intranet Server HOWTO will be periodically posted to comp.os.linux.announce and comp.os.linux.help. They will also be uploaded to various Linux FTP sites, including sunsite.unc.edu.

The Latest version of this document is available in HTML format at http://www.inet.co.th/cyberclub/karnadp/http.html

1.3 Feedback

If you have questions or comments about this document, please feel free to mail Pramod Karnad, at karnad@indiamail.com. Suggestions, criticism and mail are always welcome. If you find a mistake with this document, please let me know so I can correct it in the next version. Thanx.

2 Install the HTTP server

When you download the server you have two options: To get the source and compile it yourself, or get the pre-compiled binaries. The pre-compiled binaries for Linux (ELF) version are available at NCSA but not the older versions.

2.1 Preparation before downloading

The server at NCSA will guide you through the steps for configuration options and prepare the various files for you. But before you attempt to download HTTPd be prepared with answers to the following questions

2.1.1 The Operating System

First, you must choose whether to download the source or a pre-compiled version of the software. If your particular system doesn't appear in the menu, then you will have to get the default source, and compile it yourself.

To check the version of your Linux go to the command prompt on your Linux machine and type

```
linux:~$  uname -a
```

which will respond with a line which looks similar to this

```
linux:~$  uname -a
Linux linux 2.0.29 #4 Tue Sep 13 04:05:51 CDT 1994 i586
linux:~$
```

The version of Linux is 2.0.29.

The remaining parameters can be specified before downloading or configured later by modifying the file `srm.conf` in the `/usr/local/etc/httpd/conf` directory. The names of the actual directives that appear in the file `httpd.conf` are shown in brackets. The only exception is the directive DocumentRoot which appears in the file `srm.conf`

2.1.2 Process type (ServerType)

This specifies how your machine will run your HTTPd server. The preferred method is "standalone." This makes the HTTP daemon to be running constantly. If you choose to load HTTPd under `inetd`, the server binary will be reloaded into memory for every request, which may slow your server down.

2.1.3 Binding Port (Port)

This specifies which port of your machine that the HTTPd daemon will bind to and listen for HTTP requests. If you can login as "root," use the default setting of 80. Otherwise choose a setting between 1025 and 65535.

2.1.4 Server user identity (User)

This is the user id the server will change to when answering requests and acting on files.This question needs to be answered only if you are running the server as "standalone." If you are someone without root permissions, just use your own login name. If you are system administrator, you might want to create a special user so you can control file permissions.

2.1.5 Server group identity (Group)

This is the group id the server will change to when answering requests and acting on files. This is similar to Server User identity and is applicable only if you are running the server as standalone.

If you do not have root permissions, just use the name of your primary group. You can find out your group by typing **groups** at the Linux command prompt.

2.1.6 Server administrator email address (ServerAdmin)

This is the email address that the user should send an email message to when reporting a problem with the server. You can put your personal e-mail address.

2.1.7 Location of server directory (ServerRoot)

This is where the server resides on your system. If you have root permissions leave it in its recommended location /usr/local/etc/httpd. If you cannot login as root, choose a subdirectory in your home path. You can find out the path of your home directory with the **pwd** command.

2.1.8 Location of HTML files (DocumentRoot)

This is where the HTML files to be served are located. The default location is /usr/local/etc/httpd/htdocs. You could however set it to be the home directory of the special user you chose in Server user identity, or a subdirectory in your home directory if you can't login as root.

When in doubt, use the default settings. Now that you have answers to the above questions you can Download NCSA HTTPd at http://hoohoo.ncsa.uiuc.edu/docs/setup/OneStep.html. You should read the HTTPd Documentation at http://hoohoo.ncsa.uiuc.edu/docs/ before you attempt installation. If you are planning to compile the code then you need to modify the makefiles in each of the th ree directories support, src, cgi-src. If your version of Linux is already supported then you just have to type make linux at the top level directory (i.e. /usr/local/etc/httpd)

2.2 Compiling HTTPd

Compiling is simple, just type make linux at the prompt in the server root directory. **Note:** Users of pre-ELF Linux have to uncomment #define NO_PASS in file portability.h and set DBM_LIBS= -ldbm in the Makefile before compiling HTTPd.

3 Testing HTTPd

After you have installed HTTPd, login as root and start it by typing httpd &. (Assuming you have installed as standalone.) You should now be able to see it in the list generated by ps. The simplest way to test HTTPd is by Telnet. At the Linux command prompt type

```
linux:~$ telnet 172.16.0.1 80
```

where 80 is the default port for HTTP. If you have configured "Port" as something different then type that number instead. You should get a response which looks like this

```
Trying 172.16.0.1...
Connected to linux.mydomain.
Escape character is '^]'.
```

Now if you type in any character and press Enter you should get a response similar to the one shown below.

```
HTTP/1.0 400 Bad Request
Date: Wed, 10 Jan 1996 10:24:37 GMT
Server: NCSA/1.5
Content-type: text/html

<HEAD><TITLE>400 Bad Request < /TITLE> < /HEAD>
<BODY><H1>400 Bad Request < /H1>
Your client sent a query that this server could
not understand.<P>
Reason: Invalid or unsupported method.<P>
< /BODY>
```

Now we are ready to connect to this server using another PC and a WWW Browser.

4 Connecting to the Linux Server

Please refer to the diagram shown in the Section 1 for the addressing scheme used. Workstation 1 (W/S1) is on network 172.16.0.0 and can access the Linux server directly whereas Workstation 2 (W/S2) is on network 172.17.0.0 and needs to use the gateway (router) 172.17.0.254 to access the Linux box. This gateway information needs to be provided while configuring the clients only on W/S2. Netware refers to the gateway as 'ip_router'.

I am using W/S2 to illustrate the client setup. To set up W/S1 just change the address 172.17.0.5 to 172.16.0.5 and ignore all references to the gateway/router.

If you do not have a router you can skip the next section and proceed to

- 4.2 if you use a Netware server.
- 4.4 if you use the Microsoft Client.

4.1 Set up the Linux server

You may skip this section if you do not have a router.

You have to configure the Linux server to recognize the router thus allowing Workstation 2 to connect to the Web server. In order to set up the Linux server you should login as root. At the server prompt type

```
route add gw default 172.16.0.254
```

To use this gateway every time you boot the Linux server edit the file `/etc/rc.d/rc.inet1` and change the line containing the gateway definition to `GATEWAY = "172.16.0.254"`. Make sure the line for adding the gateway is not commented out.

ALT: You can add routes to the networks on the other side of the router. This would be done as

```
route add -net 172.17.0.0 gw 172.16.0.254
```

To add this route every time you boot Linux add the command to your `/etc/rc.d/rc.local` file.

4.2 Set up the Netware server

In order to set up the Netware server you should have Supervisor permissions or at least Console operator permissions. If these cannot be got, try asking your Network Administrator to help you with the setup. At the Server enable the Ethernet_II frame type on the LAN by typing these commands or include them in the `AUTOEXEC.NCF` file.

```
load NE2000 frame=Ethernet_II name=IPNET
load TCPIP
bind IP to IPNET addr=172.16.0.2 mask=FF.FF.FF.0
```

You might have to specify the slot or board number while loading the NE2000 driver depending on your machine configuration (eg: `load NE2000 slot=3 frame=...`).

4.3 Set up the Netware Client

On the PC you have the choice of Win3.1,WFWG or Win95. The installation procedure differs between Win95 and the older windows if you are using the 32-bit client from Microsoft or Novell. If you are going to use the 16-bit client, the procedure is the same and you can refer to the Windows 3.x installation instructions. For installing the 32-bit client for Win95 skip to 4.3.2.

4.3.1 Windows 3.x

If you are using Win3.1 or WFWG you can install the Netware Client (VLMs) and some additional files which are provided with the TCP/IP diskette, namely

TCPIP.exe, VTCPIP.386, WINSOCK.dll and WLIBSOCK.dll

Note that the WINSOCK.dll file is different from the ones provided with Win95 and Trumpet. Install the Netware Client with the support for windows. Copy VTCPIP.386, WINSOCK.dll and WLIBSOCK.dll to the SYSTEM directory and TCPIP.exe to the NWCLIENT directory. Now modify the STARTNET.bat in the NWCLIENT directory to

```
lsl
ne2000      ---> your network card driver
c:\windows\odihlp.exe     ---->if you are using WFWG
ipxodi
tcpip        ---> add this line
nwip         ---> if you use Netware/IP
vlm
```

Create a subdirectory (say) `\NET\TCP` and copy the files HOSTS, NETWORKS, PROTOCOLS and SERVICES from `/etc` on your Linux server or the directory `SYS:ETC` on your Netware server. Edit the copied HOSTS file to add the line for your new Linux server. This will enable you to refer to the Linux server as `http://linux.mydomain/` instead of `http://172.16.0.1/`in your WWW browser

```
127.0.0.1      localhost
172.16.0.1     linux.mydomain
```

Edit the NET.cfg file in NWCLIENT directory

```
Link Driver NE2000
    port 300
    int 3
    MEM D0000
    FRAME Ethernet_802.2

; ---- add these lines ----

    FRAME Ethernet_II

Protocol TCPIP
   PATH TCP_CFG C:\NET\TCP
   ip_address  172.17.0.5
   ip_netmask  255.255.255.0
   ip_router   172.17.0.254     ---> add the address of your gateway only
                               ---> if you have to use this
                               ---> gateway to reach your HTTP server

Link Support
   MemPool 6192         ---> the minimum is 1024. Try with different values
   Buffers 10 1580      ---> this again can be fine tuned

;---------------------------------
; You may need to add lines like these if you are using Netware/IP
;
NWIP
   NWIP_DOMAIN_NAME  mydomain
   NSQ_BROADCAST    ON
   NWIP1_1 COMPATIBILITY    OFF
   AUTORETRIES      1
   AUTORETRY SECS   10
```

Edit the SYSTEM.ini file in the WINDOWS directory and add this entry for VTCPIP.386

```
[386Enh]
.....
network=*vnetbios, vipx.386, vnetware.386, VTCPIP.386
.....
```

Reboot your PC, run STARTNET.bat and you can now use your favorite WWW browser to access your Web pages. You need not login to Netware and you don't have to run TCPMAN (if you use Trumpet Winsock).

4.3.2 Windows 95

This section explains how to install the 32-bit client on Win95. Firstly, you must install the following:

```
Client for Netware Networks (from Microsoft or Novell)
Microsoft TCP/IP Protocol
Network Adapter
```

To install these items, click on My Computer, Control Panel, Networks. Click Add. You will now be in a window that displays Client, Adapter, Protocol and Service. To install the Client for Netware Networks:

```
1. DoubleClick on Client
2. Click on Microsoft or Novell
3. DoubleClick on Client for Netware Networks
```

To install the TCP/IP Protocol:

```
1. DoubleClick on Protocol
2. Click on Microsoft
3. DoubleClick on TCP/IP
```

Windows 95 by default installs several other protocols automatically. Remove them by clicking on them and clicking the Remove button. Typically Win95 installs the Microsoft NetBeui protocol, and IPX/SPX compatible protocol. You can delete the NetBEUI protocol, but you will need the IPX/SPX protocol if you wish to login to the Netware Server.

To set up TCP/IP click on TCP/IP, click on Properties, click on the tab IP address

```
Enter your IP address in the {\tt '}Specify an IP address {\tt '}
                      box as 172.17.0.5
In the Subnet Mask box enter 255.255.255.0
```

select the tab Gateway

```
Enter your gateway (router) address in the box New gateway
   as 172.17.0.254
Click the Add button
```

The gateway address should now appear under the installed gateways box. Now Click OK.

You should get a message to reboot. Do so. You should now be able to use the Browser to connect to your HTTP Server.

4.4 Set up Microsoft Client

If you are using the Microsoft Client for accessing your network, then this section details how to install TCP/IP for

- MS Windows for Work groups;
- MS Windows 95;
- MS Windows NT.

Note: To enable you to refer to the Linux server as `http://linux.mydomain/` instead of `http://172.16.0.1/` in the WWW browser and all your intranet commands you need to edit the `hosts` file. You can add more entries for each of your other hosts (Netware, Unix, WinNT) as well. The Windows family keeps its HOSTS file in `\WINDOWS` or in `\WINDOWS\SYSTEM` depending on the version. Edit this file and add a line for your Linux server as:

```
127.0.0.1       localhost
172.16.0.1      linux.mydomain

172.16.0.2      netware.mydomain
172.16.0.3      winNT.mydomain
172.16.0.5      ws_1
```

4.4.1 Windows for Work groups

This section explains how to install the 32-bit client on WFWG. Firstly you must download the TCP/IP drivers for Windows from Microsoft. The current version is 3.11b and is available at ftp://ftp.microsoft.com or other sites as `tcp32b.exe`. Make sure that you have loaded Win32s before trying to load the TCP/IP 32-bit driver.

Having expanded the TCP/IP files into a temporary directory (say `C:\TEMP`), check your `\WINDOWS\SYSTEM` directory for copies of `OEMSETUP.INF`. If there are any, rename them. Now copy the `OEMSETUP.INF` file from the TEMP directory to the `\WINDOWS\SYSTEM` directory. If you have loaded any other TCP/IP stacks on your system, please remove them before you proceed.

Start Network Setup or Windows Setup/Change Network settings

```
Click the Networks button
Click Install Microsoft Windows Network.
  Choose support for additional networks (if required)
Click OK
```

You should be prompted for your network adapter—select the appropriate one. If you are not prompted, then

```
Click the Adapter button
    select an adapter (say NE2000)
    Click OK
Click the Protocol button
    select the MS TCP/IP-32 protocol
    click OK
```

You will now be prompted to configure the TCP/IP protocol stack. You can always reconfigure this by highlighting the TCP/IP protocol shown in the box Adapters and clicking the Setup button.

```
In the IP address box enter 172.17.0.5
In the Subnet Mask box enter 255.255.255.0
Enter your gateway (router) address in the box default gateway
  as 172.17.0.254
```

Click OK. The computer will ask you to restart. Do so. You should now be able to use the Browser to connect to your HTTP Server.

4.4.2 Windows 95

This section explains how to install the 32-bit client for Microsoft on Win95. Firstly, you must install the following

```
Client for Microsoft Networks
Microsoft TCP/IP Protocol
Network Adapter
```

To install these items, click on My Computer, Control Panel, Networks. Click Add. You will now be in a window that displays Client, Adapter, Protocol and Service. To install the Client for Microsoft Networks:

```
1. DoubleClick on Client
2. Click on Microsoft
3. DoubleClick on Client for Microsoft Networks
```

To install the TCP/IP Protocol:

```
1. DoubleClick on Protocol
2. Click on Microsoft
3. DoubleClick on TCP/IP
```

Windows 95 by default installs several protocols automatically. Remove them by clicking on them and clicking the Remove button. Typically Win95 installs the Microsoft NetBeui protocol.

To set up TCP/IP click on TCP/IP, click on Properties, click on the tab IP address

```
Enter your IP address in the {\tt '}Specify an IP address {\tt '}
                      box as 172.17.0.5
In the Subnet Mask box enter 255.255.255.0
```

select the tab Gateway

```
Enter your gateway (router) address in the box New gateway
   as 172.17.0.254
Click the Add button
```

The gateway address should now appear under the installed gateways box. Now Click OK.

You should get a message to reboot. Do so. You should now be able to use the Browser to connect to your HTTP Server.

4.4.3 Windows NT

This section details how to Install the TCP/IP client for WinNT 4.0. Start Control Panel/ Network

```
Select the Adapter tab.
    Click Add to add a new adapter (if you don't have one)
```

You should be prompted for your network adapter—select the appropriate one. To add the protocols.

```
Select the Protocols tab
    Click Add
    Select the TCP/IP protocol
    Click OK
```

You will now be prompted to configure the TCP/IP protocol stack. You can always reconfigure this by highlighting the TCP/IP protocol and clicking the Properties button.

```
Select the tab IP Address
   Mark the check box 'Specify an IP address'
   In the IP address box enter 172.17.0.5
   In the Subnet Mask box enter 255.255.255.0
   Enter your gateway (router) address in the box Default Gateway
       as 172.17.0.254
```

Click OK. The computer will ask you to restart. You can now use any Browser to connect to your HTTP Server.

4.5 Set up TCP/IP on Macintosh

If you are using the Macintosh for accessing your network, then this section details how to install MacTCP for the PowerMacs.

Note: To enable you to refer to the Linux server as `http://linux.mydomain/` instead of `http://172.16.0.1/` in the WWW browser and all your intranet commands you need to edit the `hosts` file. The format of the hosts file is different from the one used in Unix. The Mac hosts file is based on RFC-1035. You can add more entries for each of your other hosts (Netware, Unix, WinNT) as well. The MacOS keeps its HOSTS file in the `Preferences folder` under the `System folder`. Edit this file and add a line for your Linux server as:

```
linux.mydomain     A  172.16.0.1

netware.mydomain  A  172.16.0.2
winNT.mydomain    A  172.16.0.3
ws_1              A  172.16.0.5
```

4.5.1 MacTCP

This section explains how to install MacTCP. Firstly you must download the MacTCP files from Apple or install it from the Internet Connection CD. To configure MacTCP, click the Apple Menu/ Control Panels/ TCP/IP. In the screen change the setting for 'Connect via:' to 'Ethernet'

Change the 'Configure' setting to 'Manually'

```
In the IP address box enter 172.17.0.5
In the Subnet Mask box enter 255.255.255.0
Enter your gateway (router) address in the box
  Router address as 172.17.0.254
```

Click OK. You should now be able to use the Browser to connect to your HTTP Server.

5 Setting up the Intranet

An Intranet cannot be complete without sharing the resources on the different platforms. You will need support for other file systems, so that you can access the data available on them. This document provides instructions to connect Linux to the following popular file systems.

- NCP;
- SMB file system;
- Network File System (NFS).

These file systems can be compiled into the Linux kernel or added as modules, depending on the version of Linux. If you are not familiar with compiling the kernel you can refer to the Kernel HOWTO http://sunsite.unc.edu/mdw/HOWTO/Kernel-HOWTO.html and the Module HOWTO http://sunsite.unc.edu/mdw/HOWTO/Module-HOWTO.html for compiling the kernel with modules.

5.1 NCPFS

To share the files on the Netware server you will need support for NCP (ncpfs). NCPFS works with kernel version 1.2.x and 1.3.71 upwards. It does not work with any earlier 1.3.x kernel. It cannot access the NDS database in Netware 4.x, but can make use of the bindery. If you are using Netware 4.x you can enable bindery support for specific containers using the command `Set Bindery Context` at the console as:

```
set Bindery Context = CORP.MYDOM;WEBUSER.MYDOM
```

In the above example two containers have bindery support enabled.

You will need to download the NCP file system utilities using the URL ftp://sunsite.unc.edu/pub/Linux/system/filesystems/ncpfs/ncpfs.tgz (currently ncpfs-2.0.10) from Sunsite.

5.1.1 Installation

To install the ncpfs utilities, type

```
zcat ncpfs.tgz | tar xvf -
```

to expand the files into its own directory. In this case you will get a directory `ncpfs-2.0.10` Change your directory to this ncpfs directory before proceeding with the installation. Read the README and edit the Makefile if necessary.

The installation of ncpfs depends on the kernel version you are using. For kernel 1.2, you should simply type `make`. Subsequently typing `make install` will install the executables and manual pages.

If you use Kernel 1.3.71 or later, you might have to recompile your kernel. With these kernels, the kernel part of ncpfs is already included in the main source tree. To check if the kernel needs to be recompiled type

```
cat /proc/filesystems
```

It should show you a line saying that the kernel knows ncpfs.

If ncpfs is not there, you can either recompile the kernel or add ncpfs as a module. For recompiling the kernel you should type `make config` and when it asks you for

`The IPX protocol (CONFIG_IPX) [N/y/?]` simply answer "y." Probably you do not need the full internal net that you are asked for next. Once the kernel is successfully installed, reboot, check `/proc/filesystems` and if everything is OK proceed with the installation of the ncpfs utilities. Change directory to the location holding your downloaded ncpfs files, and type `make`. After the compilation is finished type `make install` to install the various utilities and man pages.

5.1.2 Mounting NCPFS

To check the installation type

```
ipx_configure --auto_interface=on --auto_primary=on
```

... wait for 10 seconds and type:

```
slist
```

You should be able to see a list of your Netware servers. Now we are ready to share files from the Netware server.

Suppose we need to access HTML files from directory `\home\htmldocs` on volume VOL1: on the server MYDOM_NW, I recommend that you create a new user (say) 'EXPORT' with password 'EXP123' on this server to whom you grant appropriate access rights to this directory using SYSCON or NWADMIN.

On the Linux machine create a new directory `/mnt/MYDOM_NW`. Now type the command

```
ncpmount -S MYDOM_NW -U EXPORT -P EXP123 /mnt/MYDOM_NW
```

to mount the netware file system. Typing the command

```
ls /mnt/MYDOM_NW/vol1/home/htmldocs
```

will show you a list of all the files in `MYDOM_NW/VOL1:\HOME\HTMLDOCS` (using Netware file notation). If you have any problems please read the IPX HOWTO at http://sunsite.unc.edu/mdw/HOWTO/IPX-HOWTO.html for more insights into the IPX system.

5.2 SMBFS

To share the files on the Windows server you will need support for SMB (smbfs).

You will need to download the SMB file system utilities from ftp://sunsite.unc.edu/pub/Linux/system/filesystems/smbfs/smbfs. (currently smbfs-2.0.1) from Sunsite.

5.2.1 Installation

To install the smbfs utilities, type

```
zcat smbfs.tgz | tar xvf -
```

to expand the files into its own directory. In this case you will get a directory `smbfs-2.0.1` Change your directory to this smbfs directory before proceeding with the installation. Read the README and edit the Makefile if necessary.

The installation of smbfs depends on the kernel version you are using. For kernel 1.2, you should simply type `make`. Subsequently typing `make install` will install the executables and manual pages.

If you use Kernel 2.0 or later, you might have to recompile your kernel. With these kernels, the kernel part of smbfs is already included in the main source tree. To check if the kernel needs to be recompiled type

```
cat /proc/filesystems
```

It should show you a line saying that the kernel knows smbfs.

If smbfs is not there, you can either recompile the kernel or add smbfs as a module. For recompiling the kernel you should type 'make config' and when it asks you for adding SMB file system support simply answer yes. Once the kernel is successfully installed, reboot, check `/proc/filesystems` and if everything is OK proceed with the installation of the smbfs utilities. Change directory to the location holding your downloaded smbfs files, and type 'make'. After the compilation is finished type `make install` to install the various utilities and man pages.

5.2.2 Mounting SMBFS

In our example let us assume that the WinNT server is called 'MYDOM_NT' and is sharing its directory `C:\PUB\HTMLDOCS` with a share name of 'HTMLDOCS' without a password. On the Linux machine create a new directory `/mnt/MYDOM_NT`. Now type the command

```
smbmount //MYDOM_NT/HTMLDOCS /mnt/MYDOM_NT -n
```

to mount the SMB (windows share) file system. If this does not work try

```
smbmount //MYDOM_NT/COMMON /mnt/MYDOM_NT -n -I 172.16.0.3
```

Typing the command

```
ls /mnt/MYDOM_NT
```

will show you a list of all the files in `bsol;bsol;MYDOM_NT\PUB\HTMLDOCS` (using Windows file notation).

5.3 NFS

First you will need a kernel with the NFS file system either compiled in or available as a module.

Suppose you have a Unix host running NFS with the name MYDOM_UNIX and an IP address of 172.16.0.4. You can check the directories that are being exported (shared) by this host by typing the command

```
showmount -e 172.16.0.4
```

Once we know the exported directories you can mount them by entering a appropriate mount command. I recommend that you create a subdirectory under `/mnt` (say) 'MYDOM_UNIX' and use that as your mount point.

```
mount -o rsize=1024,wsize=1024 172.16.0.4:/pub/htmldocs /mnt/MYDOM_UNIX
```

The `rsize` and `wsize` may have to be changed depending on your environment.

If you have any problems please read the NFS HOWTO at http://sunsite.unc.edu/mdw/HOWTO/NFS-HOWTO.html for more insights into the NFS system.

6 Accessing the Web

Now that we have set up the HTTP server, the clients, and interconnected the Linux server with the other servers, we need to make some small adjustments on the Linux server to be able to access these mounted filesystems from the Web Browser.

6.1 Accessing the mounted filesystems

To access the mounted directories in your HTML pages you have two methods:

- Create a link in DocumentRoot (`/usr/local/etc/httpd/htdocs`) to refer to the mounted directory as

```
ln -s /mnt/MYDOM_NW/vol1/home/htmldocs netware
                                 or

ln -s /mnt/MYDOM_NT     winNT
                                 or

ln -s /mnt/MYDOM_UNIX     unix
```

- to edit the file `srm.conf` in your `/usr/local/etc/httpd/conf` directory and add a new alias.

```
# Alias fakename realname
Alias /icons/      /usr/local/etc/httpd/icons/

# alias for netware server
Alias /netware/    /mnt/MYDOM_NW/vol1/home/htmldocs/
Alias /winNT/      /mnt/MYDOM_NT/
Alias /unix/       /mnt/MYDOM_UNIX
```

And restart your HTTPd. You can access the documents on the netware server by referring to them as `http://linux.mydomain/netware/index.htm` for the netware files and similar notations for the others.

6.2 Connecting to the Internet

You can finally connect your Intranet to the Internet to access E-Mail and all the wonderful information out there. I propose to write a brief note on how to do this in a future revision. Detailed explanations are available in the ISP Hookup HOWTO from http://sunsite.unc.edu/mdw/HOWTO/ISP-Hookup-HOWTO.html and Diald Mini-HOWTO at http://sunsite.unc.edu/mdw/HOWTO/mini/Diald for setting up these connections.

6.3 Other uses

The HTTP server can be used in the office to provide transparent access to information residing on different servers, at several locations and directories. The data can be simple documents in Word, Lotus spreadsheets, or complex databases.

The application of this technology is being typically used as follows:-

- Publishing corporate documents. These documents can include newsletters, annual reports, maps, company facilities, price lists, product information literature, and any document which is of value within the corporate entity.
- Access into searchable directories. Rapid access to corporate phone books and the like. This data can be mirrored at a Web site or, via CGI scripts, the Web server can serve as a gateway to back-end pre-existing or new applications. This means that, using the same standard access mechanisms, information can be made more widely available and in a simpler manner. This means that it can be used to create an interface with RDBMS like ORACLE and SYBASE for generating real-time information. Here is a list of links to such sites on the Web.

  - Web Access - http://cscsun1.larc.nasa.gov/~beowulf/db/web_access.html - CGI gateways - HTTP://www.w3.org/hypertext/WWW/RDBGate/Overview.html
- Corporate/Department/Individual pages

  As cultures change within organizations to the point where even each department moves towards their own individual mission statements, the Intranet technology provides the ideal medium to communicate current information to the Department or Individual. Powerful search engines provide the means for people to find the group or individual who has the answers to the continuous questions which arise in the normal day-to-day course of doing business.
- Simple Groupware applications With HTML forms support, sites can provide sign-up sheets, surveys and simple scheduling.
- Software distribution. Administrators can use the Intranet to deliver software and updates "on-demand" to users across the corporate network. This can be done with Java, which allows the creation and transparent distribution of objects on-demand rather than just data or applications. This is indeed possible more easily with the newer versions of Linux which has builtin support for Java.

- MailWith the move to the use of Intranet mail products with standard and simple methods for attachment of documents, sound, vision and other multimedia between individuals, mail is being pushed further forward as a simple, de facto communications method. Mail is essentially individual to individual, or individual to small group, communication. Several utilities are available on the Linux platform to set up an E-mail system like `sendmail`, `pop3d`, and `imapd`.
- User Interface

  Intranet technology evolves so rapidly, the HTML tools available can be used to dramatically change the way we interface with systems. With HTML you can build an Interface which is only limited by the programmer's imagination. The beauty about using Intranet technologies for this is that it is so simple. Clicking a hyperlink from HTML can take you to another page, it could ring an alarm, run a yearend procedure or anything else that a computer program can do.

7 More things to do

Here is a list of other interesting things to do with your Linux Intranet server. All the software mentioned below is freeware or shareware.

- Browse the Linux server using Network Neighborhood in Win95/ NT; Set up a WINS like NBT server. Check out the SAMBA Web page at http://lake.canberra.edu.au/pub/samba/samba.html
- Implement a search engine on your Intranet. Connect to ht://Dig at http://htdig.sdsu.edu/
- Use CUSeeMe by setting up a local reflector. Refer to their page at Cornell http://cu-seeme.cornell.edu/
- Set up Web Conferencing. Use COW from http://thecity.sfsu.edu/COW/
- Deploy a SQL database. Refer to the mSQL Home page at http://Hughes.com.au/
- Set up FTP, Gopher, Finger, Bootp servers on the Netware server. Get them at http://mft.ucs.ed.ac.uk/
- Emulate a Netware server. Check out the NCP Utilities at ftp://sunsite.unc.edu/pub/Linux/system/filesystems/ncpfs/

If you find other interesting things to do with your Linux Intranet server, please feel free to mail me.

8 Credits and Legalities

8.1 Thanks

Thanks to the people at NCSA for providing such excellent documentation, David Anderson and all others for trying out this HOWTO and sending in their comments. The details on Netware/IP are courtesy Romel Flores (rom@mnl.sequel.net).

8.2 Copyright information

Part XXVII

"Java CGI HOWTO"
by David H. Silber,

dhs@orbits.com

Contents

Abstract

v0.4, 18 November 1996 v0.4, 18 November 1996
This HOWTO document explains how to set up your server to allow CGI programs written in Java and how to use Java to write CGI programs. Although HOWTO documents are targeted towards use with the Linux operating system, this particular one is not dependent on the particular version of Unix used.

1 Introduction

Because of the way that Java is designed the programmer does not have easy access to the system's environment variables. Because of the way that the Java Development Kit (JDK) is set up, it is necessary to use multiple tokens to invoke a program, which does not mesh very well with the standard HTML forms/CGI manner of operations. There are ways around these limitations, and I have implemented one of them. Read further for details.

1.1 Prior Knowledge

I am assuming that you have a general knowledge of HTML and CGI concepts and at least a minimal knowledge of your HTTP server. You should also know how to program in Java, or a lot of this will not make sense.

1.2 This Document

The latest version of this document can be read at http://www.orbits.com/software/Java_CGI.html.

1.3 The Package

The latest version of the package described here can be accessed via anonymous FTP at

ftp://ftp.orbits.com/pub/software/java_cgi-0.4.tgz.

The package distribution includes SGML source for this document.

If you use this software, please make some reference to http://www.orbits.com/software/Java_CGI.html, so that others will be able to find the Java CGI classes.

2 Setting Up Your Server to Run Java CGI Programs (With Explanations)

This section will lead you through installing my Java CGI package with copious explanations so that you know what the effects of your actions will be. If you just want to install the programs and don't care about the whys and wherefores, skip to Section 3.

2.1 System Requirements

This software should work on any Unix-like web server that has the Java Development Kit installed. I am using it on a *Debian Linux* system running *apache* as the HTTP daemon. If you find that it does not run on your server, please contact me at `dhs@orbits.com`.

Unfortunately, the Java run-time interpreter seems to be something of a memory hog—you may want to throw another few megabytes of RAM onto your server if you will be using Java CGI programs a lot.

2.2 Java CGI Add-On Software

The software that I wrote to aid in this is called Java CGI. You can get it from

ftp://www.orbits.com/pub/software/java_cgi-0.4.tgz.

(The version number may have changed.)

2.3 Unpacking the Source

Find a convenient directory to unpack this package into. (If you don't already have a standard place to put packages, I suggest that you use /usr/local/src.) Unpack the distribution with this command:

```
gzip -dc java_cgi-0.4.tgz | tar -xvf -
```

This will create a directory called java_cgi-0.4. In there you will find the files referenced in the rest of this document. (If the version number has changed, use the instructions from within that distribution from this point on.)

2.4 Decide On Your Local Path Policies

You need to decide where you want your Java CGI programs to live. Generally, you will want to put them in a directory in parallel with your cgi-bin directory. My Apache server came configured to use /var/web/cgi-bin as the cgi-bin directory, so I use /var/web/javacgi as the directory to put Java CGI programs in. You probably do not want to put your Java CGI programs into one of the existing CLASSPATH directories. Edit the Makefile to reflect your system configuration. Make sure that you are logged in as the root user and run make install. This will compile the Java programs, modify the java.cgi script to fit in with your system, and install the programs in the appropriate places. If you want the HTML version of this documentation and an HTML test document in addition, run make all instead.

2.5 Testing your installation.

Installed from the distribution are HTML documents called javacgitest.html, javaemailtest.html and javahtmltest.html. If you installed all in the previous section, it will be in the directory you specified for WEBDIR in the Makefile. If you didn't, you can run make test to build them from javacgitest.html-dist, javaemailtest.html-dist and javahtmltest.html-dist.

When you are sure that your installation is working correctly, you may wish to remove CGI_Test.class, Email_Test.class and HTML_Test.class from your JAVACGI directory and javacgitest.html, javaemailtest.html and javahtmltest.html from your WEBDIR directory as they show the user information that is normally only available to the server.

3 Setting Up Your Server to Run Java CGI Programs (The Short Form)

- Get the Java CGI package from ftp://www.orbits.com/pub/software/java_cgi-0.4.tgz. (The version number may have changed.)
- Unpack the distribution with this command:

  ```
  gzip -dc java_cgi-0.4.tgz | tar -xvf -
  ```

  (If the version number has changed, use the instructions from within that distribution from this point on.)
- Edit the Makefile you will find in the newly created directory java_cgi-0.4 as appropriate to your system.
- As root, run make install. This will compile the Java programs, apply your system-specific information, and install the various files. If you want the HTML version of this documentation and an HTML test document, run make all instead.
- You should be ready to go.

4 Executing a Java CGI Program

4.1 Obstacles to Running Java Programs Under the CGI Model

There are two main problems in running a Java program from a web server:

4.1.1 You can't run Java programs like ordinary executables.

You need to run the Java run-time interpreter and provide the initial class (program to run) on the command line. With an HTML form, there is no provision for sending a command line to the web server.

4.1.2 Java does not have general access to the environment.

Every environment variable that will be needed by the Java program must be explicitly passed in. There is no method similar to the C `getenv()` function.

4.2 Overcoming Problems in Running Java CGI Programs

To deal with these obstacles, I wrote a shell CGI program that provides the information needed by the Java interpreter.

4.2.1 The `java.cgi` script.

This shell script manages the interaction between the HTTP daemon and the Java CGI program that you wish to use. It extracts the name of the program that you want to run from the data provide by the server. It collects all of the environment data into a temporary file. Then, it runs the Java run-time interpreter with the name of the file of environment information and the program name added to the command line.

The `java.cgi` script was configured and installed in Section 2.4.

4.2.2 Invoking `java.cgi` from an HTML form.

My forms that use Java CGI programs specify a form action as follows:

```
<form action="/cgi-bin/java.cgi/CGI\_Test" method="POST">
```

Where `/cgi-bin/` is your local CGI binary directory, `java.cgi` is the Java front-end that allows us to run Java programs over the web and `CGI_Test` is an example of the name of the Java program to run.

5 Using the Java CGI Classes.

There are currently three main classes supported—CGI (Section cgi-class), E-mail (Section email-class); and HTML (Section html-class). I am considering adding classes to deal with MIME-formatted input and output—MIMEin and MIMEout, respectively.

There are also a few support and test classes. A CGI test class (Section 5.2), and and e-mail test class (Section 5.4) can be used to test your installation. They can also be used as a starting point for your own Java programs which use this class library. The Section 5.7 text class is the superclass for both the `Email` and the `HTML` classes.

5.1 CGI

5.1.1 Class Syntax

```
public class CGI
```

5.1.2 Class Description

The CGI class holds the "CGI Information"—Environment variables set by the web server and the name/value sent from a form when its `submit` action is selected. All information is stored in a `Properties` class object.

This class is in the "Orbits.net" package.

5.1.3 Member Summary

```
CGI()          //  Constructor.
getNames()     //  Get the list of names.
getValue()     //  Get form value by specifying name.
```

5.1.4 See Also

`CGI_Test`.

5.1.5 CGI()

Purpose

Constructs an object which contains the available CGI data.

Syntax

```
public CGI()
```

Description

When a CGI object is constructed, all available CGI information is sucked-up into storage local to the new object.

5.1.6 getNames()

Purpose

List the names which are defined to have corresponding values.

Syntax

```
public Enumeration getKeys ()
```

Description

Provides the full list of names for which coresponding values are defined.

Returns

An `Enumeration` of all the names defined.

5.1.7 getValue()

Purpose

Retrieves the value associated with the name specified.

Syntax

```
public String getValue ( String name )
```

Description

This method provides the correspondence between the `names` and `values` sent from an HTML form.

Parameter

name

The key by which values are selected.

Returns

A `String` containing the value.

5.2 CGI_Test

This class provides both an example of how to use the `CGI` class and a test program which can be used to confirm that the Java CGI package is functioning correctly.

5.2.1 Member Summary

```
main()      //  Program main().
```

5.2.2 See Also

`CGI`.

5.2.3 main()

Purpose

Provide a `main()` method.

Syntax

```
public static void main( String argv[] )
```

Description

This is the entry point for a CGI program which does nothing but return a list of the available name/value pairs and their current values.

Parameter

argv[ ]

Arguments passed to the program by the `java.cgi` script. Currently unused.

5.3 Email

5.3.1 Class Syntax

```
public class Email extends Text
```

5.3.2 Class Description

Messages are built up with the `Text` class `add*()` methods and the e-mail specific methods added by this class. When complete, the message is sent to its destination.

This class is in the "Orbits.net" package.

5.3.3 Member Summary

```
Email()      //  Constructor.
send()       //  Send the e-mail message.
sendTo()     //  Add a destination for message.
subject()    //  Set the Subject: for message.
```

5.3.4 See Also

`Email_Test, Text.`

5.3.5 Email()

Purpose

Constructs an object which will contain an email message.

Syntax

```
public Email()
```

Description

Sets up an empty message to be completed by the Email methods.

See Also

`Text.`

5.3.6 send()

Purpose

Send the e-mail message.

Syntax

```
public void send ()
```

Description

This formats and sends the message. If no destination address has been set, there is no action taken.

5.3.7 sendTo()

Purpose

Add a destination for this message.

Syntax

```
public String sendTo ( String address )
```

Description

Add `address` to the list of destinations for this method. There is no set limit to the number of destinations an e-mail message may have. I'm sure that if you build up the list large enough, you can exceed the size of the parameter list that the Mail Transport Agent can accept or use up your memory.

Parameter/

address

A destination to send this message to.

5.3.8 subject()

Purpose

Set the subject for this message.

Syntax

```
public void subject ( String subject )
```

Description

This method sets the text for the e-mail's `Subject:` line. If called more than once, the latest subject set is the one that is used.

Parameter

subject

The text of this message's `Subject:` line.

5.4 Email_Test

This class provides both an example of how to use the `Email` class and a test program which can be used to confirm that the *Java CGI* package is functioning correctly.

5.4.1 Member Summary

```
main()      // Program main().
```

5.4.2 See Also

`Email`.

5.4.3 main()

Purpose

Provide a `main()` method.

Syntax

```
public static void main( String argv[] )
```

Description

This is the entry point for a CGI program which returns a list of the available name/value pairs and their current values. It will also send this list to the address specified in the `Email` variable.

Parameter

argv[ ]

Arguments passed to the program by the `java.cgi` script. Currently unused.

5.5 HTML

5.5.1 Class Syntax

```
public class HTML extends Text
```

5.5.2 Class Description

Messages are built up with the `Text` class `add*()` methods and the HTML-specific methods added by this class. When complete, the message is sent to its destination.

Currently, there is no error checking to confirm that the list-building methods are being used in a correct order, so the programmer must take pains not to violate HTML syntax.

This class is in the "Orbits.net" package.

5.5.3 Member Summary

```
HTML()                    // Constructor.
author()                  // Set the name of the document author.
definitionList()          // Start a definition list.
definitionListTerm()      // Add a term to a definition list.
endList()                 // End a list.
listItem()                // Add an entry to a list.
send()                    // Send the HTML message.
title()                   // Set the text for the document title.
```

5.5.4 See Also

`HTML_Test`, `Text`.

5.5.5 HTML()

Purpose

Constructs an object which will contain an HTML message.

Syntax

```
public HTML()
```

Description

Sets up an empty message to be completed by the HTML methods.

See Also

`Text`.

5.5.6 author()

Purpose

Set the name of the document author.

Syntax

```
public void author ( String author )
```

Description

Set the name of the document author to `author`.

Parameter/

author

The text to use as the author of this message.

See Also

`title()`.

5.5.7 definitionList()

Purpose

Start a definition list.

Syntax

```
public void definitionList ()
```

Description

Start a definition list. A definition list is a list specialized so that each entry in the list is a **term** followed by the definition **text** for that term. The start of a definition list should be followed by the creation of (at least) one term/text pair and a call to the `endList()` method. Note that, currently, lists cannot be nested.

See Also

`definitionListTerm()`, `endList()`, `listItem()`.

5.5.8 definitionListTerm()

Purpose

Add a term to a definition list.

Syntax

```
public void definitionListTerm ()
```

Description

Add a term to a definition list. The text for the term part of the current list entry should be appended to the message after this method is called and before a corresponding `listItem` method is called.

See Also

`definitionList()`, `listItem()`.

5.5.9 endList()

Purpose

End a list.

Syntax

```
public void endList ()
```

Description

End a list. This method closes out a list. *Note that, currently, lists cannot be nested.*

See Also

`definitionList()`.

5.5.10 listItem()

Purpose

Add an entry to a list.

Syntax

```
public void listItem ()

public void listItem ( String item )

public boolean listItem ( String term, String item )
```

Description

Add an entry to a list. If the first form is used, the text for the current list item should be appended to the message after this method is called and before any other list methods are called. In the second and third forms, the `item` text is specified as a parameter to the method instead of (or in addition to) being appended to the message. The third form is specific to definition lists and provides both the term and the definition of the list entry.

Parameters

item

The text of this list entry.

term

The text of this definition list entry's term part.

See Also

`definitionList()`, `definitionListTerm()`, `endList()`.

5.5.11 send()

Purpose

Send the HTML message.

Syntax

```
public void send ()
```

Description

Send the HTML message.

5.5.12 title()

Purpose

Set the text for the document title.

Syntax

```
public void title ( String title )
```

Description

Set the text for the document title.

Parameter

title

The text of this message's title.

See Also

`author()`.

5.6 HTML_Test

This class provides both an example of how to use the `HTML` class and a test program which can be used to confirm that the Java CGI package is functioning correctly.

5.6.1 Member Summary

```
main()      //  Program main().
```

5.6.2 See Also

`HTML`.

5.6.3 main()

Purpose

Provide a `main()` method.

Syntax

```
public static void main( String argv[] )
```

Description

This is the entry point for a CGI program which returns a list of the available name/value pairs in an HTML document, with each name/value pair displayed in a definition list element.

Parameter

argv[ ]

Arguments passed to the program by the `java.cgi` script. Currently unused.

5.7 Text

5.7.1 Class Syntax

```
public abstract class Text
```

5.7.2 Class Description

This class is the superclass of the `Email` and `HTML` classes. Messages are built up with the methods in this class and completed and formatted with the methods in subclasses.

This class is in the "Orbits.text" package.

5.7.3 Member Summary

```
Text()              //  Constructor.
add()               //  Add text to this object.
addLineBreak()      //  Add a line break.
addParagraph()      //  Add a paragraph break.
```

5.7.4 See Also

`Email`, `HTML`.

5.7.5 add()

Purpose

Add text to this item.

Syntax

```
public void add ( char addition )


public void add ( String addition )

public void add ( StringBuffer addition )
```

Description

Add `addition` to the contents of this text item.

Parameter

addition

Text to be added to the text item.

See Also

`addLineBreak()`, `addParagraph()`.

5.7.6 addLineBreak()

Purpose

Force a line break at this point in the text.

Syntax

```
public void addLineBreak ()
```

Description

Add a line break to the text at the current point.

See Also

`add()`, `addParagraph()`.

5.7.7 addParagraph()

Purpose

Start a new paragraph.

Syntax

```
public void add ()
```

Description

Start a new paragraph at this point in the text flow.

See Also

`add()`, `addLineBreak()`.

6 Future Plans

- Add to the Email class:

  Email(int capacity)
  Used when we know how much space the message will need to have allocated.

  sendTo(String address)
  Add a list of primary destinations to the e-mail message.

  sendCc(String address)
  Add a Carbon-Copy destination to the e-mail message.

  sendCc(String address)
  Add a list of Carbon-Copy destinations to the e-mail message.

  sendBcc(String address)
  Add a Blind Carbon-Copy destination to the e-mail message.

  sendBcc(String address)
  Add a list of Blind Carbon-Copy destinations to the e-mail message.

- Add to the HTML class:

  HTML(int capacity)
  Used when we know how much space the message will need to have allocated.

  public void unorderedList()
  Start an unordered list.

  public void orderedList()
  Start an ordered list.

  public void directoryList()
  Start a directory list.

public void menuList()
Start a menu list.

void anchor(String anchorName)
Specify an anchor.

void link(String url, String text)
Specify a link.

void applet(String url, String altText)
Specify an applet link.

- Allow HTML lists to be nested.
- Add error checking code to enforce correct ordering of HTML list formatting codes.
- The location of the file of environment data should be configurable from the `Makefile`.
- Get rid of the spurious empty name/value pair that appears in the list when we are dealing with the GET method of data transfer.
- Consider having CGI implement the java.util.Enumeration interface to successively provide variable names.
- Add a `Test` class, which would use every method in this package.
- Document how `CGI_Test`, `Email_Test` and `HTML_Test` build on each other to provide incremental tests for debugging purposes.
- Document how Test uses every feature available in this package.

Part XXVIII

"Linux Kernel HOWTO" by Brian Ward,

bri@blah.math.tu-graz.ac.at

Contents

Abstract

v0.80, 26 May 1997
This is a detailed guide to kernel configuration, compilation, upgrades, and troubleshooting for ix86-based systems.

1 Introduction

Should you read this document? Well, see if you've got any of the following symptoms:

- "Arg! This wizzo-46.5.6 package says it needs kernel release 1.8.193 and I still only have release 1.0.9!"
- There's a device driver in one of the newer kernels that you just gotta have.
- You really have no idea at all how to compile a kernel.
- "Is this stuff in the README *really* the whole story?"
- You came, you tried, it didn't work.
- You need something to give to people who insist on asking you to install their kernels for them.

1.1 Read this first! (I mean it)

Some of the examples in this document assume that you have GNU `tar`, `find`, and `xargs`. These are quite standard; this should not cause problems. It is also assumed that you know your system's file system structure; if you don't, it is critical that you keep a written copy of the `mount` command's output during normal system operation (or a listing of `/etc/fstab`, if you can read it). This information is important, and does not change unless you repartition your disk, add a new one, reinstall your system, or something similar.

The latest "production" kernel version at the time of this writing is 2.0.30, meaning that the references and examples correspond to that release. Even though I try to make this document as version-independent as possible, the kernel is constantly under development, so if you get a newer release, it will inevitably have some differences. Again, this should not cause major problems, but it may create some confusion.

There are two versions of the Linux kernel source, "production" and "development." Production releases begin with 1.0.x and are currently the even-numbered releases; 1.0.x was production, 1.2.x is production, as well as 2.0.x. These kernels are considered to be the most stable, bug-free versions available at the time of release. The development kernels (1.1.x, 1.3.x, etc) are meant as testing kernels, for people willing to test out new and possibly very buggy kernels. You have been warned.

2 Important questions and their answers

2.1 What does the kernel do, anyway?

The Unix kernel acts as a mediator for your programs and your hardware. First, it does (or arranges for) the memory management for all of the running programs (processes), and makes sure that they all get a fair (or unfair, if you please) share of the processor's cycles. In addition, it provides a nice, fairly portable interface for programs to talk to your hardware.

There is certainly more to the kernel's operation than this, but these basic functions are the most important to know.

2.2 Why would I want to upgrade my kernel?

Newer kernels generally offer the ability to talk to more types of hardware (that is, they have more device drivers), they can have better process management, they can run faster than the older versions, they could be more stable than the older versions, and they fix silly bugs in the older versions. Most people upgrade kernels because they want the device drivers and the bug fixes.

2.3 What kind of hardware do the newer kernels support?

See the Hardware-HOWTO. Alternatively, you can look at the `config.in` file in the linux source, or just find out when you try `make config`. This shows you all hardware supported by the standard kernel distribution, but not everything that Linux supports; many common device drivers (such as the PCMCIA drivers and some tape drivers) are loadable modules maintained and distributed separately.

2.4 What version of GCC and libc do I need?

Linus recommends a version of GCC in the `README` file included with the Linux source. If you don't have this version, the documentation in the recommended version of GCC should tell you if you need to upgrade your libc. This is not a difficult procedure, but it is important to follow the instructions.

2.5 What's a loadable module?

These are pieces of kernel code which are not linked (included) directly in the kernel. One compiles them separately, and can insert and remove them into the running kernel at almost any time. Due to its flexibility, this is now the preferred way to code certain kernel features. Many popular device drivers, such as the PCMCIA drivers and the QIC-80/40 tape driver, are loadable modules.

2.6 How much disk space do I need?

It depends on your particular system configuration. First, the compressed Linux source is nearly 6 MB in version 2.0.10. Most sites keep this even after unpacking. Uncompressed, it occupies 24 MB. But that's not the end—you need more to actually compile the thing. This depends on how much you configure into your kernel. For example, on one particular machine, I have networking, the 3Com 3C509 driver, and three file systems configured, using close to 30 MB. Adding the compressed linux source, you need about 36 MB for this particular configuration. On another system, without network device support (but still with networking support), and sound card support, it consumes even more. Also, a newer kernel is certain to have a larger source tree than an older one, so, in general, if you have a lot of hardware, make sure that you have a big enough hard disk in that mess (and at today's prices, I cannot help but recommend that you get another disk as an answer to your storage problems).

2.7 How long does it take?

For most people, the answer is "fairly long." The speed of your system and the amount of memory you have ultimately determines the time, but there is a small bit to do with the amount of stuff you configure into the kernel. On a 486DX4/100 with 16 MB of RAM, on a v1.2 kernel with five file systems, networking support, and sound card drivers, it takes around 20 minutes. On a 386DX/40 (8 MB RAM) with a similar configuration, compilation lasts nearly 1.5 hours. It is a generally good recommendation to make a little coffee, watch some TV, knit, or whatever you do for fun while your machine compiles the kernel. You can have someone else with a faster machine compile it for you if you really have a slow machine.

3 How to actually configure the kernel

3.1 Getting the source

You can obtain the source via anonymous ftp from `ftp.funet.fi` in `/pub/Linux/PEOPLE/Linus`, a mirror, or other sites. It is typically labelled `linux-x.y.z.tar.gz`, where `x.y.z` is the version number. Newer (better?) versions and the patches are typically in subdirectories such as `v1.1` and `v1.2` The highest number is the latest version, and is usually a "test release," meaning that if you feel uneasy about beta or alpha releases, you should stay with a major release.

I strongly suggest that you use a mirror FTP site instead of ftp.funet.fi. Here is a short list of mirrors and other sites:

```
USA:          sunsite.unc.edu:/pub/Linux/kernel
USA:          tsx-11.mit.edu:/pub/linux/sources/system
UK:           sunsite.doc.ic.ac.uk:/pub/unix/Linux/sunsite.unc-mirror/kernel
Austria:      ftp.univie.ac.at:/systems/linux/sunsite/kernel
Germany:      ftp.Germany.EU.net:/pub/os/Linux/Local.EUnet/Kernel/Linus
Germany:      sunsite.informatik.rwth-aachen.de:/pub/Linux/PEOPLE/Linus
France:       ftp.ibp.fr:/pub/linux/sources/system/patches
Australia:    sunsite.anu.edu.au:/pub/linux/kernel
```

In general, a mirror of `sunsite.unc.edu` is a good place to look. The file `/pub/Linux/MIRRORS` contains a list of known mirrors. If you do not have FTP access, a list of BBS systems which carry Linux is posted periodically to comp.os.linux.announce; try to obtain this.

If you were looking for general Linux information and distributions, try `http://www.linux.org`.

3.2 Unpacking the source

Log in as or su to root, and cd to /usr/src. If you installed kernel source when you first installed linux (as most do), there will already be a directory called linux there, which contains the entire old source tree. If you have the disk space and you want to play it safe, preserve that directory. A good idea is to figure out what version your system runs now and rename the directory accordingly. The command uname -r prints the current kernel version. Therefore, if uname -r said 1.0.9, you would rename (with mv) linux to linux-1.0.9. If you feel mildly reckless, just wipe out the entire directory. In any case, make certain there is no linux directory in /usr/src before unpacking the full source code.

Now, in /usr/src, unpack the source with tar zxpvf linux-x.y.z.tar.gz (if you've just got a .tar file with no .gz at the end, tar xpvf linux-x.y.z.tar works.). The contents of the source will fly by. When finished, there will be a new linux directory in /usr/src. cd to linux and look over the README file. There will be a section with the label INSTALLING the kernel. Carry out the instructions when appropriate – symbolic links that should be in place, removal of stale .o files, etc.

3.3 Configuring the kernel

Note: Some of this is reiteration and clarification of a similar section in Linus' README file.

The command make config while in /usr/src/linux starts a configure script which asks you many questions. It requires bash, so verify that bash is /bin/bash, /bin/sh, or $BASH.

There are some alternatives to make config and you may very well find them easier and more comfortable to use. For those running X, you can try make xconfig if you have Tk installed ('click-o-rama'—Nat). make menuconfig is for those who have (n)curses and would prefer a text based menu. These interfaces have one clear advantage: If you goof up and make a wrong choice during configuration, it is simple to go back and fix it.

You are ready to answer the questions, usually with y (yes) or n (no). Device drivers typically have an m option. This means "module," meaning that the system will compile it, but not directly into the kernel, but as a loadable module. A more comical way to describe it is as "maybe." Some of the more obvious and non-critical options are not described here; see the section "Other configuration options" for short descriptions of a few others.

In 2.0.x and later, there is a '?' option, which provides a brief description of the configuration parameter. That information is likely to be the most up-to-date.

3.3.1 Kernel math emulation

If you don't have a math coprocessor (you have a bare 386 or 486SX), you must say "y" to this. If you do have a coprocessor and you still say "y," don't worry too much—the coprocessor is still used and the emulation ignored. The only consequence is that the kernel will be larger (costing RAM). I have been told that the math emulation is slow; although this does not have much to do with this section, it might be something to keep in mind when faced with sluggish X window system performance.

3.3.2 Normal (MFM/RLL) disk and IDE disk/cdrom support

You probably need to support this; it means that the kernel will support standard PC hard disks, which most people have. This driver does not include SCSI drives; they come later in the configuration.

You will then be asked about the "old disk-only" and "new IDE" drivers. You want to choose one of them; the main difference is that the old driver only supports two disks on a single interface, and the new one supports a secondary interface and IDE/ATAPI cdrom drives. The new driver is 4k larger than the old one and is also supposedly "improved," meaning that aside from containing a different number of bugs, it might improve your disk performance, especially if you have newer (EIDE-type) hardware.

3.3.3 Networking support

In principle, you would only say "y" if your machine is on a network such as the Internet, or you want to use SLIP, PPP, term, etc to dial up for Internet access. However, as many packages (such as the X window system) require networking support even if your machine does not live on a real network, you should say "y." Later on, you will be asked if you want to support TCP/IP networking; again, say "y" here if you are not absolutely sure.

3.3.4 Limit memory to low 16MB

There exist buggy '386 DMA controllers which have problems with addressing anything more than 16 MB of RAM; you want to say "y" in the (rare) case that you have one.

3.3.5 System V IPC

One of the best definitions of IPC (Interprocess Communication) is in the Perl book's glossary. Not surprisingly, some Perl programmers employ it to let processes talk to each other, as well as many other packages (DOOM, most notably), so it is not a good idea to say "n" unless you know exactly what you are doing.

3.3.6 Processor type (386, 486, Pentium, PPro)

(in older kernels: Use `-m486` flag for 486-specific optimizations)

Traditionally, this compiled in certain optimizations for a particular processor; the kernels ran fine on other chips, but the kernel was perhaps a bit larger. In newer kernels, however, this is no longer true, so you should enter the processor for which you are compiling the kernel. A "386" kernel will work on all machines.

3.3.7 SCSI support

If you have SCSI devices, say "y." You will be prompted for further information, such as support for CD-ROM, disks, and what kind of SCSI adapter you have. See the SCSI-HOWTO for greater detail.

3.3.8 Network device support

If you have a network card, or you would like to use SLIP, PPP, or a parallel port adapter for connecting to the Internet, say "y." The config script will prompt for which kind of card you have, and which protocol to use.

3.3.9 Filesystems

The configure script then asks if you wish to support the following filesystems:

Standard (Minix)—Newer distributions don't create minix file systems, and many people don't use it, but it may still be a good idea to configure this one. Some "rescue disk" programs use it, and still more floppies may have a Minix file system, since the Minix file system is less painful to use on a floppy.

Extended file system—This was the first version of the extended file system, which is no longer in widespread use. Chances are that you'll know it if you need it and that if you are doubt, you do not need it.

Second extended—This is widely used in new distributions. You probably have one of these, and need to say "y."

xiafs file system—At one time, this was not uncommon, but at the time of this writing, I did not know of anyone using it.

MS-DOS—If you want to use your MS-DOS hard disk partitions, or mount MS-DOS formatted floppy disks, say "y."

UMSDOS—This file system expands an MS-DOS file system with usual Unix-like features such as long filenames. It is not useful for people (like me) who "don't do DOS."

/proc—Another one of the greatest things since powdered milk (idea shamelessly stolen from Bell Labs, I guess). One doesn't make a proc file system on a disk; this is a file system interface to the kernel and processes. Many process listers (such as `ps`) use it. Try `cat /proc/meminfo` or `cat /proc/devices` sometime. Some shells (rc, in particular) use `/proc/self/fd` (known as `/dev/fd` on other systems) for I/O. You should almost certainly say "y" to this; many important Linux tools depend on it.

NFS—If your machine lives on a network and you want to use file systems which reside on other systems with NFS, say "y."

ISO9660—Found on most CD-ROMs. If you have a CD-ROM drive and you wish to use it under Linux, say "y."

OS/2 HPFS—At the time of this writing, a read-only file system for OS/2 HPFS.

System V and Coherent—for partitions of System V and Coherent systems (These are other PC Unix variants).

But I don't know which file systems I need! Okay, type "`mount`." The output will look something like this:

```
blah# mount
/dev/hda1 on / type ext2 (defaults)
/dev/hda3 on /usr type ext2 (defaults)
none on /proc type proc (defaults)
/dev/fd0 on /mnt type msdos (defaults)
```

Look at each line; the word next to "`type`" is the file system type. In this example, my `/` and `/usr` file systems are second extended, I'm using `/proc`, and there's a floppy disk mounted using the msdos (bleah) file system.

You can try "`cat /proc/filesystems`" if you have `/proc` currently enabled; it will list your current kernel's file systems.

The configuration of rarely-used, non-critical file systems can cause kernel bloat; see the section on modules for a way to avoid this and the "Pitfalls" section on why a bloated kernel is undesirable.

3.3.10 Character devices

Here, you enable the drivers for your printer (parallel printer, that is), bus mouse, PS/2 mouse (many notebooks use the PS/2 mouse protocol for their built-in track balls), some tape drives, and other such "character" devices. Say "y" when appropriate.

Note: Selection is a program which allows the use of the mouse outside of the X Window System for cut and paste between virtual consoles. It's fairly nice if you have a serial mouse, because it coexists well with X, but you need to do special tricks for others. Selection support was a configuration option at one time, but is now standard.

Note 2: Selection is now considered obsolete. `gpm` is the name of the new program. It can do fancier things, such translate mouse protocols and handle multiple mice.

3.3.11 Sound card

If you feel a great desire to hear `biff` bark, say "y," and later on, another configuration program will compile and ask you all about your sound board. (A note on sound card configuration: when it asks you if you want to install the full version of the driver, you can say "n" and save some kernel memory by picking only the features which you deem necessary.) I highly recommend looking at the Sound HOWTO for more detail about sound support if you have a sound card.

3.3.12 Other configuration options

Not all of the configuration options are listed here because they change too often or fairly self-evident (for instance, 3Com 3C509 support to compile the device drive for this particular ethernet card). There exists a fairly comprehensive list of all the options (plus a way to place them into the `Configure` script) put together by Axel Boldt (`axel@uni-paderborn.de`) with the following URL:

```
http://math-www.uni-paderborn.de/~axel/config_help.html
```

or via anonymous FTP at:

```
ftp://sunsite.unc.edu/pub/Linux/kernel/config/krnl_cnfg_hlp.x.yz.tgz
```

where the `x.yz` is the version number.

For later (2.0.x and later) kernels, this has been integrated into the source tree.

3.3.13 Kernel hacking

From Linus' README:

The "kernel hacking" configuration details usually result in a bigger or slower kernel (or both), and can even make the kernel less stable by configuring some routines to actively try to break bad code to find kernel problems (kmalloc()). Thus you should probably answer "n" to the questions for a "production" kernel.

3.4 Now what? (The Makefile)

After you `make config`, a message tells you that your kernel has been configured, and to "check the top-level `Makefile` for additional configuration," etc.

So, look at the `Makefile`. You probably will not need to change it, but it never hurts to look. You can also change its options with the `rdev` command once the new kernel is in place.

4 Compiling the kernel

4.1 Cleaning and depending

When the configure script ends, it also tells you to `make dep` and (possibly) `clean`. So, do the `make dep`. This insures that all of the dependencies, such the include files, are in place. It does not take long, unless your computer is fairly slow to begin with. For older versions of the kernel, when finished, you should do a `make clean`. This removes all of the object files and some other things that an old version leaves behind. In any case, do not forget this step before attempting to recompile a kernel.

4.2 Compile time

After depending and cleaning, you may now make zImage or make zdisk (this is the part that takes a long time.). make zImage will compile the kernel, and leave a file in arch/i386/boot called zImage (among other things). This is the new compressed kernel. make zdisk does the same thing, but also places the new zImage on a floppy disk which you hopefully put in drive 'A:'. zdisk is fairly handy for testing new kernels; if it bombs (or just doesn't work right), just remove the floppy and boot with your old kernel. It can also be a handy way to boot if you accidentally remove your kernel (or something equally as dreadful). You can also use it to install new systems when you just dump the contents of one disk onto the other ("all this and more! *Now* how much would you pay?").

All even halfway reasonably recent kernels are compressed, hence the "z" in front of the names. A compressed kernel automatically decompresses itself when executed.

4.3 Other make-ables

make mrproper will do a more extensive cleaning. It is sometimes necessary; you may wish to do it at every patch. make mrproper will also delete your configuration file, so you might want to make a backup of it (.config) if you see it as valuable.

make oldconfig will attempt to configure the kernel from an old configuration file; it will run through the make config process for you. If you haven't ever compiled a kernel before or don't have an old configuration file, then you probably shouldn't do this, as you will most likely want to change the default configuration.

See the section on modules for a description of make modules.

4.4 Installing the kernel

After you have a new kernel that seems to work the way you want it to, it's time to install it. Most people use LILO (Linux Loader) for this. make zlilo will install the kernel, run LILO on it, and get you all ready to boot, BUT ONLY if lilo is configured in the following way on your system: kernel is /vmlinuz, lilo is in /sbin, and your lilo config (/etc/lilo.conf) agrees with this.

Otherwise, you need to use LILO directly. It's a fairly easy package to install and work with, but it has a tendency to confuse people with the configuration file. Look at the config file (either /etc/lilo/config for older versions or /etc/lilo.conf for new versions), and see what the current setup is. The config file looks like this:

```
image = /vmlinuz
    label = Linux
    root = /dev/hda1
    ...
```

The "image =" is set to the currently installed kernel. Most people use /vmlinuz. "label" is used by LILO to determine which kernel or operating system to boot, and "root" is the / of that particular operating system. Make a backup copy of your old kernel and copy the zImage which you just made into place (you would say "cp zImage /vmlinuz" if you use "/vmlinuz"). Then, rerun lilo—on newer systems, you can just run "lilo," but on older stuff, you might have to do an /etc/lilo/install or even an /etc/lilo/lilo -C /etc/lilo/config.

If you would like to know more about LILO's configuration, or you don't have LILO, get the newest version from your favorite FTP site and follow the instructions.

To boot one of your old kernels off the hard disk (another way to save yourself in case you screw up the new kernel), copy the lines below (and including) "image = xxx" in the LILO config file to the bottom of the file, and change the "image = xxx" to "image = yyy," where "yyy" is the full pathname of the file you saved your backup kernel to. Then, change the "label = zzz" to "label = linux-backup" and rerun lilo. You may need to put a line in the config file saying "delay=x," where x is an amount in tenths of a second, which tells LILO to wait that much time before booting, so that you can interrupt it (with the shift key, for example), and type in the label of the backup boot image (in case unpleasant things happen).

5 Patching the kernel

5.1 Applying a patch

Incremental upgrades of the kernel are distributed as patches. For example, if you have version 1.1.45, and you notice that there's a patch46.gz out there for it, it means you can upgrade to version 1.1.46 through application of the patch. You might want to make a backup of the source tree first (make clean and then cd /usr/src; tar zcvf old-tree.tar.gz linux will make a compressed tar archive for you.).

So, continuing with the example above, let's suppose that you have `patch46.gz` in `/usr/src`. `cd` to `/usr/src` and do a `zcat patch46.gz | patch -p0` (or `patch -p0 < patch46` if the patch isn't compressed). You'll see things whizz by (or flutter by, if your system is that slow) telling you that it is trying to apply hunks, and whether it succeeds or not. Usually, this action goes by too quickly for you to read, and you're not too sure whether it worked or not, so you might want to use the `-s` flag to `patch`, which tells `patch` to only report error messages. (You don't get as much of the "hey, my computer is actually doing something for a change!" feeling, but you may prefer this.) To look for parts which might not have gone smoothly, `cd` to `/usr/src/linux` and look for files with a `.rej` extension. Some versions of `patch` (older versions which may have been compiled with on an inferior filesystem) leave the rejects with a # extension. You can use `find` to look for you;

```
find .  -name '*.rej' -print
```

prints all files who live in the current directory or any subdirectories with a `.rej` extension to the standard output.

If everything went right, do a `make clean`, `config`, and `dep` as described in sections 3 and 4.

There are quite a few options to the `patch` command. As mentioned above, `patch -s` will suppress all messages except the errors. If you keep your kernel source in some other place than `/usr/src/linux`, `patch -p1` (in that directory) will patch things cleanly. Other `patch` options are well-documented in the manual page.

5.2 If something goes wrong

(Note: this section refers mostly to quite old kernels)

The most frequent problem that used to arise was when a patch modified a file called "`config.in`," and it didn't look quite right, because you changed the options to suit your machine. This has been taken care of, but one still might encounter it with an older release. To fix it, look at the `config.in.rej` file, and see what remains of the original patch. The changes will typically be marked with "+" and "-" at the beginning of the line. Look at the lines surrounding it, and remember if they were set to "y" or "n." Now, edit `config.in`, and change "y" to "n" and "n" to "y" when appropriate. Do a

```
patch -p0 < config.in.rej
```

and if it reports that it succeeded (no fails), then you can continue on with a configuration and compilation. The `config.in.rej` file will remain, but you can delete it.

If you encounter further problems, you might have installed a patch out of order. If patch says "`previously applied patch detected:  Assume -R?`" you are probably trying to apply a patch which is below your current version number; if you answer "y," it will attempt to degrade your source, and will most likely fail; thus, you will need to get a whole new source tree (which might not have been such a bad idea in the first place).

To back out (unapply) a patch, use `patch -R` on the original patch.

The best thing to do when patches really turn out wrong is to start over again with a clean, out-of-the-box source tree (for example, from one of the `linux-x.y.z.tar.gz` files), and start again.

5.3 Getting rid of the .orig files

After just a few patches, the `.orig` files will start to pile up. For example, one 1.1.51 tree I had was once last cleaned out at 1.1.48. Removing the .orig files saved over a half a meg.

```
find .  -name '*.orig' -exec rm -f {} ';'
```

will take care of it for you. Versions of `patch` which use # for rejects use a tilde instead of `.orig`.

There are better ways to get rid of the `.orig` files, which depend on GNU `xargs`:

```
find .  -name '*.orig' | xargs rm
```

or the "quite secure but a little more verbose" method:

```
find . -name '*.orig' -print0 | xargs --null rm --
```

5.4 Other patches

There are other patches (I'll call them "nonstandard") than the ones Linus distributes. If you apply these, Linus' patches may not work correctly and you'll have to either back them out, fix the source or the patch, install a new source tree, or a combination of the above. This can become very frustrating, so if you do not want to modify the source (with the possibility of a very bad outcome), back out the nonstandard patches before applying Linus', or just install a new tree. Then, you can see if the nonstandard patches still work. If they don't, you are either stuck with an old kernel, playing with the patch or source to get it to work, or waiting (possibly begging) for a new version of the patch to come out.

How common are the patches not in the standard distribution? You will probably hear of them. I used to use the noblink patch for my virtual consoles because I hate blinking cursors (This patch is (or at least was) frequently updated for new kernel releases.). With most newer device drivers being developed as loadable modules, though, the frequency of "nonstandard" patches is decreasing significantly.

6 Additional packages

Your Linux kernel has many features which are not explained in the kernel source itself; these features are typically utilized through external packages. Some of the most common are listed here.

6.1 kbd

The linux console probably has more features than it deserves. Among these are the ability to switch fonts, remap your keyboard, switch video modes (in newer kernels), etc. The kbd package has programs which allow the user to do all of this, plus many fonts and keyboard maps for almost any keyboard, and is available from the same sites that carry the kernel source.

6.2 util-linux

Rik Faith (`faith@cs.unc.edu`) put together a large collection of linux utilities which are, by odd coincidence, called util-linux. These are now maintained by Nicolai Langfeldt (`util-linux@math.uio.no`). Available via anonymous ftp from sunsite.unc.edu in `/pub/Linux/system/misc`, it contains programs such as `setterm`, `rdev`, and `ctrlaltdel`, which are relevant to the kernel. As Rik says, *do not install without thinking;* you do not need to install everything in the package, and it could very well cause serious problems if you do.

6.3 `hdparm`

As with many packages, this was once a kernel patch and support programs. The patches made it into the official kernel, and the programs to optimize and play with your hard disk are distributed separately.

6.4 `gpm`

`gpm` stands for general purpose mouse. This program allows you to cut and paste text between virtual consoles and do other things with a large variety of mouse types.

7 Some pitfalls

7.1 make clean

If your new kernel does really weird things after a routine kernel upgrade, chances are you forgot to `make clean` before compiling the new kernel. Symptoms can be anything from your system outright crashing, strange I/O problems, to crummy performance. Make sure you do a `make dep`, too.

7.2 Huge or slow kernels

If your kernel is sucking up a lot of memory, is too large, or just takes forever to compile even when you've got your new 786DX6/440 working on it, you've probably got lots of unneeded stuff (device drivers, file systems, etc) configured. If you don't use it, don't configure it, because it does take up memory. The most obvious symptom of kernel bloat is extreme swapping in and out of memory to disk; if your disk is making a lot of noise and it's not one of those old Fujitsu Eagles that sound like like a jet landing when turned off, look over your kernel configuration.

You can find out how much memory the kernel is using by taking the total amount of memory in your machine and subtracting from it the amount of "total mem" in `/proc/meminfo` or the output of the command `free`. You can also find out by doing a `dmesg` (or by looking at the kernel log file, wherever it is on your system). There will be a line which looks like this:

```
Memory:  15124k/16384k available (552k kernel code, 384k reserved, 324k data)
```

My '386 (which has slightly less junk configured) says this:

```
Memory:  7000k/8192k available (496k kernel code, 384k reserved, 312k data)
```

If you "just gotta" have a big kernel but the system won't let you, you can try "`make bzimage`." You may very well have to install a new version of LILO if you do this.

7.3 Kernel doesn't compile

If it does not compile, then it is likely that a patch failed, or your source is somehow corrupt. Your version of GCC also might not be correct, or could also be corrupt (for example, the include files might be in error). Make sure that the symbolic links which Linus describes in the README are set up correctly. In general, if a standard kernel does not compile, something is seriously wrong with the system, and re-installation of certain tools is probably necessary.

Or perhaps you're compiling a 1.2.x kernel with an ELF compiler (GCC 2.6.3 and higher). If you're getting a bunch of so-and-so undefined messages during the compilation, chances are that this is your problem. The fix is in most cases very simple. Add these lines to the top of arch/i386/Makefile:

```
AS=/usr/i486-linuxaout/bin/as
LD=/usr/i486-linuxaout/bin/ld -m i386linux
CC=gcc -b i486-linuxaout -D__KERNEL__ -I$(TOPDIR)/include
```

Then make dep and zImage again.

In rare cases, GCC can crash due to hardware problems. The error message will be something like "xxx exited with signal 15" and it will generally look very mysterious. I probably would not mention this, except that it happened to me once—I had some bad cache memory, and the compiler would occasionally barf at random. Try reinstalling GCC first if you experience problems. You should only get suspicious if your kernel compiles fine with external cache turned off, a reduced amount of RAM, etc.

It tends to disturb people when it's suggested that their hardware has problems. Well, I'm not making this up. There is an FAQ for it—it's at http://www.bitwizard.nl/sig11/.

7.4 New version of the kernel doesn't seem to boot

You did not run LILO, or it is not configured correctly. One thing that "got" me once was a problem in the config file; it said 'boot = /dev/hda1' instead of 'boot = /dev/hda' (This can be really annoying at first, but once you have a working config file, you shouldn't need to change it.).

7.5 You forgot to run LILO, or system doesn't boot at all

Ooops! The best thing you can do here is to boot off of a floppy disk and prepare another bootable floppy (such as "make zdisk" would do). You need to know where your root (/) file system is and what type it is (e.g. second extended, Minix). In the example below, you also need to know what file system your /usr/src/linux source tree is on, its type, and where it is normally mounted.

In the following example, / is /dev/hda1, and the filesystem which holds /usr/src/linux is /dev/hda3, normally mounted at /usr. Both are second extended file systems. The working kernel image in /usr/src/linux/arch/i386/boot is called zImage.

The idea is that if there is a functioning zImage, it is possible to use that for the new floppy. Another alternative, which may or may not work better (it depends on the particular method in which you messed up your system) is discussed after the example.

First, boot from a boot/root disk combo or rescue disk, and mount the file system which contains the working kernel image:

```
mkdir /mnt
mount -t ext2 /dev/hda3 /mnt
```

If mkdir tells you that the directory already exists, just ignore it. Now, cd to the place where the working kernel image was. Note that

```
/mnt + /usr/src/linux/arch/i386/boot - /usr = /mnt/src/linux/arch/i386/boot
```

Place a formatted disk in drive "A:" (not your boot or root disk), dump the image to the disk, and configure it for your root file system:

```
cd /mnt/src/linux/arch/i386/boot
dd if=zImage of=/dev/fd0
rdev /dev/fd0 /dev/hda1
```

cd to / and unmount the normal /usr file system:

```
cd /
umount /mnt
```

You should now be able to reboot your system as normal from this floppy. Don't forget to run `lilo` (or whatever it was that you did wrong) after the reboot.

As mentioned above, there is another common alternative. If you happen to have a working kernel image in / (`/vmlinuz` for example), you can use that for a boot disk. Supposing all of the above conditions, and that my kernel image is `/vmlinuz`, just make these alterations to the example above: change `/dev/hda3` to `/dev/hda1` (the / file system), `/mnt/src/linux` to `/mnt`, and `if=zImage` to `if=vmlinuz`. The note explaining how to derive `/mnt/src/linux` may be ignored.

Using LILO with big drives (more than 1024 cylinders) can cause problems. See the LILO mini-HOWTO or documentation for help on that.

7.6 It says "`warning: bdflush not running`"

This can be a severe problem. Starting with a kernel release after 1.0 (around 20 Apr 1994), a program called "`update`" which periodically flushes out the file system buffers, was upgraded or replaced. Get the sources to `bdflush` (you should find it where you got your kernel source), and install it (you probably want to run your system under the old kernel while doing this). It installs itself as `update` and after a reboot, the new kernel should no longer complain.

7.7 It says stuff about undefined symbols and does not compile

You probably have an ELF compiler (GCC 2.6.3 and up) and the 1.2.x (or earlier) kernel source. The usual fix is to add these three lines to the top of `arch/i386/Makefile`:

```
AS=/usr/i486-linuxaout/bin/as
LD=/usr/i486-linuxaout/bin/ld -m i386linux
CC=gcc -b i486-linuxaout -D__KERNEL__ -I$(TOPDIR)/include
```

This will compile a 1.2.x kernel with the a.out libraries.

7.8 I can't get my IDE/ATAPI CD-ROM drive to work

Strangely enough, lots of people cannot get their ATAPI drives working, probably because there are a number of things that can go wrong.

If your CD-ROM drive is the only device on a particular IDE interface, it must be jumpered as "master" or "single." Supposedly, this is the most common error.

Creative Labs (for one) has put IDE interfaces on their sound cards now. However, this leads to the interesting problem that while some people only have one interface to being with, many have two IDE interfaces built-in to their motherboards (at IRQ15, usually), so a common practice is to make the SoundBlaster interface a third IDE port (IRQ11, or so I'm told).

This causes problems with linux in that versions 1.2.x don't support a third IDE interface (there is support in starting somewhere in the 1.3.x series but that's development, remember, and it doesn't auto-probe). To get around this, you have a few choices.

If you have a second IDE port already, chances are that you are not using it or it doesn't already have two devices on it. Take the ATAPI drive off the sound card and put it on the second interface. You can then disable the sound card's interface, which saves an IRQ anyway.

If you don't have a second interface, jumper the sound card's interface (not the sound card's sound part) as IRQ15, the second interface. It should work.

If for some reason it absolutely has to be on a so-called "third" interface, or there are other problems, get a 1.3.x kernel (1.3.57 has it, for example), and read over `drivers/block/README.ide`. There is much more information here.

7.9 It says weird things about obsolete routing requests

Get new versions of the `route` program and any other programs which do route manipulation. `/usr/include/linux/route.h` (which is actually a file in `/usr/src/linux`) has changed.

7.10 Firewalling not working in 1.2.0

Upgrade to at least version 1.2.1.

7.11 "`Not a compressed kernel Image file`"

Don't use the `vmlinux` file created in `/usr/src/linux` as your boot image; `[..]/arch/i386/boot/zImage` is the right one.

7.12 Problems with console terminal after upgrade to 1.3.x

Change the word `dumb` to `linux` in the console termcap entry in `/etc/termcap`. You may also have to make a terminfo entry.

7.13 Can't seem to compile things after kernel upgrade

The linux kernel source includes a number of include files (the things that end with `.h`) which are referenced by the standard ones in `/usr/include`. They are typically referenced like this (where `xyzzy.h` would be something in `/usr/include/linux`:

```
#include <linux/xyzzy.h>
```

Normally, there is a link called `linux` in `/usr/include` to the `include/linux` directory of your kernel source (`/usr/src/linux/include/linux` in the typical system). If this link is not there, or points to the wrong place, most things will not compile at all. If you decided that the kernel source was taking too much room on the disk and deleted it, this will obviously be a problem. Another way it might go wrong is with file permissions; if root has a `umask` which doesn't allow other users to see its files by default, and you extracted the kernel source without the `p` (preserve file modes) option, those users also won't be able to use the C compiler. Although you could use the `chmod` command to fix this, it is probably easier to re-extract the include files. You can do this the same way you did the whole source at the beginning, only with an additional argument:

```
blah# tar zxvpf linux.x.y.z.tar.gz linux/include
```

Note: `make config` will recreate the `/usr/src/linux` link if it isn't there.

7.14 Increasing limits

The following few example commands may be helpful to those wondering how to increase certain soft limits imposed by the kernel:

```
echo 4096 > /proc/sys/kernel/file-max
echo 12288 > /proc/sys/kernel/inode-max
echo 300 400 500 > /proc/sys/vm/freepages
```

8 Note for upgrade to version 2.0.x

Kernel version 2.0.x introduced quite a bit of changes for kernel installation. The file `Documentation/Changes` in the 2.0.x source tree contains information that you should know when upgrading to version 2.0.x. You will most likely need to upgrade several key packages, such as gcc, libc, and SysVInit, and perhaps alter some system files, so expect this. Don't panic, though.

9 Modules

Loadable kernel modules can save memory and ease configuration. The scope of modules has grown to include file systems, ethernet card drivers, tape drivers, printer drivers, and more.

9.1 Installing the module utilities

The module utilities are available from wherever you got your kernel source as `modules-x.y.z.tar.gz`; choose the highest patch level `x.y.z` that is equal to or below that of your current kernel. Unpack it with `tar zxvf modules-x.y.z.tar.gz`, `cd` to the directory it creates (`modules-x.y.z`), look over the `README`, and carry out its installation instructions (which is usually something simple, such as `make install`). You should now have the programs `insmod`, `rmmod`, `ksyms`, `lsmod`, `genksyms`, `modprobe`, and `depmod` in `/sbin`. If you wish, test out the utilities with the "hw" example driver in `insmod`; look over the `INSTALL` file in that subdirectory for details.

`insmod` inserts a module into the running kernel. Modules usually have a `.o` extension; the example driver mentioned above is called `drv_hello.o`, so to insert this, one would say `insmod drv_hello.o`. To see the modules that the kernel is currently using, use `lsmod`. The output looks like this:

```
blah# lsmod
Module:         #pages:  Used by:
drv_hello          1
```

drv_hello is the name of the module, it uses one page (4k) of memory. No other kernel modules depend on it at the moment. To remove this module, use `rmmod drv_hello`. Note that rmmod wants a module name, not a file name. You get this from lsmod's listing. The other module utilities' purposes are documented in their manual pages.

9.2 Modules distributed with the kernel

As of version 2.0.30, most of everything is available as a loadable modules. To use them, first make sure that you don't configure them into the regular kernel; that is, don't say "y" to it during `make config`. Compile a new kernel and reboot with it. Then, cd to /usr/src/linux again, and do a `make modules`. This compiles all of the modules which you did not specify in the kernel configuration, and places links to them in /usr/src/linux/modules. You can use them straight from that directory or execute `make modules_install`, which installs them in /lib/modules/x.y.z, where x.y.z is the kernel release.

This can be especially handy with file systems. You may not use the minix or msdos file systems frequently. For example, if I encountered an MS-DOS (shudder) floppy, I would `insmod /usr/src/linux/modules/msdos.o`, and then `rmmod msdos` when finished. This procedure saves about 50k of RAM in the kernel during normal operation. A small note is in order for the Minix file system: you should *always* configure it directly into the kernel for use in "rescue" disks.

10 Other configuration options

This section contains descriptions of selected kernel configuration options (in `make config`) which are not listed in the configuration section. Most device drivers are not listed here.

10.1 General setup

`Normal floppy disk support`—is exactly that. You may wish to read over the file drivers/block/README.fd; this is especially important for IBM Thinkpad users.

`XT harddisk support`—if you want to use that 8-bit XT controller collecting dust in the corner.

`PCI bios support`—if you have PCI, you may want to give this a shot; be careful, though, as some old PCI motherboards could crash with this option. More information about the PCI bus under Linux is found in the PCI-HOWTO.

`Kernel support for ELF binaries`—ELF is an effort to allow binaries to span architectures and operating systems; linux seems is headed in that direction and so you most likely want this.

`Set version information on all symbols for modules`—in the past, kernel modules were recompiled along with every new kernel. If you say "y," it will be possible to use modules compiled under a different patch level. Read README.modules for more details.

10.2 Networking options

Networking options are described in the NET-3 HOWTO (or NET-something-HOWTO).

11 Tips and tricks

11.1 Redirecting output of the `make` or `patch` commands

If you would like logs of what those make or patch commands did, you can redirect output to a file. First, find out what shell you're running: `grep root /etc/passwd` and look for something like /bin/csh.

If you use sh or bash,

```
(command) 2>&1 | tee (output file)
```

will place a copy of (command)'s output in the file '(output file)'.

For csh or tcsh, use

```
(command) |& tee (output file)
```

For rc (Note: you probably do not use rc) it's

```
(command) >[2=1] | tee (output file)
```

11.2 Conditional kernel install

Other than using floppy disks, there are several methods of testing out a new kernel without touching the old one. Unlike many other Unix flavors, LILO has the ability to boot a kernel from anywhere on the disk (if you have a large (500 MB or above) disk, please read over the LILO documentation on how this may cause problems). So, if you add something similar to

```
image = /usr/src/linux/arch/i386/boot/zImage
    label = new_kernel
```

to the end of your LILO configuration file, you can choose to run a newly compiled kernel without touching your old `/vmlinuz` (after running `lilo`, of course). The easiest way to tell LILO to boot a new kernel is to press the shift key at boot-up time (when it says `LILO` on the screen, and nothing else), which gives you a prompt. At this point, you can enter "`new_kernel`" to boot the new kernel.

If you wish to keep several different kernel source trees on your system at the same time (this can take up a lot of disk space; be careful), the most common way is to name them `/usr/src/linux-x.y.z`, where `x.y.z` is the kernel version. You can then "select" a source tree with a symbolic link; for example, `ln -sf linux-1.2.2 /usr/src/linux` would make the 1.2.2 tree current. Before creating a symbolic link like this, make certain that the last argument to `ln` is not a real directory (old symbolic links are fine); the result will not be what you expect.

11.3 Kernel updates

Russell Nelson (`nelson@crynwr.com`) summarizes the changes in new kernel releases. These are short, and you might like to look at them before an upgrade. They are available with anonymous FTP from `ftp.emlist.com` in `pub/kchanges` or through the URL

```
http://www.crynwr.com/kchanges
```

12 Other relevant HOWTOs that might be useful

- Sound HOWTO: sound cards and utilities.
- SCSI HOWTO: all about SCSI controllers and devices.
- NET-2 HOWTO: networking.
- PPP HOWTO: PPP networking in particular.
- PCMCIA HOWTO: about the drivers for your notebook.
- ELF HOWTO: ELF: what it is, converting.
- Hardware HOWTO: overview of supported hardware.
- Module HOWTO: more on kernel modules.
- Kerneld Mini-HOWTO: about `kerneld`.
- BogoMips Mini-HOWTO: in case you were wondering.

13 Misc

13.1 Author

The author and maintainer of the Linux Kernel-HOWTO is Brian Ward (`bri@blah.math.tu-graz.ac.at`). Please send me any comments, additions, corrections (Corrections are, in particular, the most important to me.).

You can take a look at my "home page" at one of these URLs:

```
http://www.math.psu.edu/ward/
http://blah.math.tu-graz.ac.at/~bri/
```

Even though I try to be attentive as possible with mail, please remember that I get a lot of it every day, so it may take a little time to get back to you. Especially when emailing me with a question, please try extra hard to be clear and detailed in your message. If you're writing about non-working hardware (or something like that), I need to know what your hardware configuration is. If you report an error, don't just say "I tried this but it gave an error;" I need to know what the error was. I would also like to know what versions of the kernel, GCC, and libc you're using. If you just tell me you're using this-or-that distribution, it won't tell me much at all. I don't care if you ask simple questions; remember, if you don't ask, you may never get an answer! I'd like to thank everyone who gave me feedback.

If you mailed me and did not get an answer within a reasonable amount of time (three weeks or more), then chances are that I accidentally deleted your message or something (sorry). Please try again.

I get a lot of mail about things which are actually hardware problems or issues. That's OK, but please try to keep in mind that I'm not familiar with all of the hardware in the world and I don't know how helpful I can be; I personally use machines with IDE and SCSI disks, SCSI CD-ROMs, 3Com and WD ethernet cards, serial mice, motherboards with PCI, NCR 810 SCSI controllers, AMD 386DX40 w/Cyrix copr., AMD 5x86, AMD 486DX4, and Intel 486DX4 processors. (This is an overview of what I use and am familiar with, certainly not a recommendation, but if you want that, you're more than welcome to ask.)

Version -0.1 was written on October 3, 1994. This document is available in SGML, PostScript, TEX, roff, and plain text formats.

13.2 Contributions

A small part of Linus' README (kernel hacking options) is inclusive. (Thanks, Linus!)

`uc@brian.lunetix.de` (Ulrich Callmeier): `patch -s` and `xargs`.

`quinlan@yggdrasil.com` (Daniel Quinlan): corrections and additions in many sections.

`nat@nat@nataa.fr.eu.org` (Nat Makarevitch): `mrproper`, `tar -p`, many other things.

`boldt@math.ucsb.edu` (Axel Boldt): collected descriptions of kernel configuration options on the Net; then provided me with the list.

`lembark@wrkhors.psyber.com` (Steve Lembark): multiple boot suggestion.

`kbriggs@earwax.pd.uwa.edu.au` (Keith Briggs): some corrections and suggestions.

`rmcguire@freenet.columbus.oh.us` (Ryan McGuire): makeables additions.

`dumas@excalibur.ibp.fr` (Eric Dumas): French translation.

`simazaki@ab11.yamanashi.ac.jp` (Yasutada Shimazaki): Japanese translation.

`jjamor@lml.ls.fi.upm.es` (Juan Jose Amor Iglesias): Spanish translation.

`mva@sbbs.se` (Martin Wahlen): Swedish translation.

`jzp1218@stud.u-szeged.hu` (Zoltan Vamosi): Hungarian translation.

`bart@mat.uni.torun.pl` (Bartosz Maruszewski): Polish translation.

`donahue@tiber.nist.gov` (Michael J Donahue): typos, winner of the "sliced bread competition."

`rms@gnu.ai.mit.edu` (Richard Stallman): "free" documentation concept and distribution notice.

`dak@Pool.Informatik.RWTH-Aachen.DE` (David Kastrup): NFS thing.

`esr@snark.thyrsus.com` (Eric Raymond): various tidbits.

The people who have sent me mail with questions and problems have also been quite helpful.

13.3 Copyright notice, License, and all that stuff

Recommendations: Commercial redistribution is allowed and encouraged; however, it is strongly recommended that the redistributor contact the author before the redistribution, in the interest of keeping things up-to-date (you could send me a copy of the thing you're making while you're at it). Translators are also advised to contact the author before translating. The printed version looks nicer. Recycle.

Part XXIX

"Linux Keyboard and Console HOWTO" by Andries Brouwer,

aeb@cwi.nl

The Linux Documentation Project
The original, unaltered edition of this, and other, LDP documents, is on line at http://sunsite.unc.edu/LDP/.

Contents

Abstract

v2.7, 16 November 1997
This note contains some information about the Linux keyboard and console, and the use of non-ASCII characters. It describes Linux 2.0.

1 Copyright

2 Useful programs

The following packages contain keyboard or console related programs.

`kbd-0.95.tar.gz` contains `loadkeys`, `dumpkeys`, `showkey`, `setmetamode`, `setleds`, `setfont`, `showfont`, `mapscrn`, `kbd_mode`, `loadunimap`, `chvt`, `resizecons`, `deallocvt`, `getkeycodes`, `setkeycodes`.

util-linux-2.6 contains `setterm`, `kbdrate`. (Yes, the `more` in util-linux-2.6 dumps core due to a name conflict. Preserve your old copy, or use util-linux-2.5, or change "savetty" to "my_savetty" in `more.c`.)

sh-utils-1.12 contains `stty`.

`open-1.4.tgz` contains `open` (that should be renamed to `openvt`). (See also `dynamic-vc-1.1.tar.gz`.)

`SVGATextMode-1.6.tar.gz` contains `SVGATextMode`, a program that obsoletes `resizecons`.

The X distribution contains `xmodmap`, `xset`, `kbd_mode`. (See also `X386keybd(1)` for the situation under XFree86 1.3, and `Xserver(1)` for the `XKEYBOARD` extension under X11R6.)

`termcap-2.0.8.tar.gz` contains `termcap`, an old terminal capabilities data base. `ncurses-1.9.9e.tar.gz` contains the `termlib` data base which obsoletes `termcap`. (However, there are still many programs using `termcap`.)

See `loadkeys(1)`, `setleds(1)` and `setmetamode(1)` for the codes generated by the various keys and the setting of leds when not under X. Under X, see `xmodmap(1)` and `xset(1)`.

See `setfont(8)` for loading console fonts. Many people will want to load a font like `iso01.f16` because the default font is the hardware font of the video card, and often is a 'Code Page 437' font missing accented characters and other Latin-1 symbols.

See `setterm(1)` and `kbdrate(8)` for properties such as foreground and background colors, screen blanking and character repeat rate when not under X. Under X, see `xset(1)`, also for key click and bell volume.

The file `/etc/termcap` defines the escape sequences used by many programs addressing the console (or any other terminal). See `termcap(5)`. A more modern version is found in `/usr/lib/terminfo`. See `terminfo(5)`. Terminfo files are compiled by the terminfo compiler `/usr/lib/terminfo/tic`, see `tic(1)`. Their contents can be examined using the program `infocmp`, see `infocmp(1)`. The Linux console sequences are documented in `console_codes(4)`.

3 Keyboard generalities

You press a key, and the keyboard controller sends scan codes to the kernel keyboard driver. Some keyboards can be programmed, but usually the scan codes corresponding to your keys are fixed. The kernel keyboard driver just transmits whatever it receives to the application program when it is in **scan code mode**, like when X is running. Otherwise, it parses the stream of scan codes into key codes, corresponding to key press or key release events. (A single key press can generate up to 6 scan codes.) These key codes are transmitted to the application program when it is in **key code mode** (as used, for example, by `showkey`). Otherwise, these key codes are looked up in the key map, and the character or string found there is transmitted to the application, or the action described there is performed. (For example, if one presses and releases the `a` key, then the keyboard produces scan codes 0x1e and 0x9e, this is converted to key codes 30 and 158, and then transmitted as 0141, the ASCII or Latin-1 code for "a;" if one presses and releases `Delete`, then the keyboard produces scan codes 0xe0 0x53 0xe0 0xd3, these are converted to key codes 111 and 239, and then transmitted as the 4-symbol sequence ESC [3 ~, all assuming a US keyboard and a default key map. An example of a key combination to which an action is assigned is Ctrl-Alt-Del.)

The translation between unusual scan codes and key codes can be set using the utility `setkeycodes`—only very few people will need it. The translation between key codes and characters or strings or actions, that is, the key map, is set using the utilities `loadkeys` and `setmetamode`. For details, see `getkeycodes(8)`, `setkeycodes(8)`, `dumpkeys(1)`, `loadkeys(1)`, `setmetamode(1)`. The format of the files output by `dumpkeys` and read by `loadkeys` is described in `keytables(5)`.

Where it says "transmitted to the application" in the above description, this really means "transmitted to the terminal driver." That is, further processing is just like that of text that comes in over a serial line. The details of this processing are set by the program `stty`.

4 Console generalities

Conversely, when you output something to the console, it first undergoes the standard tty processing, and then is fed to the console driver. The console driver emulates a VT100, and parses the input in order to recognize VT100 escape sequences (for cursor movement, clear screen, etc.). The characters that are not part of an escape sequence are first converted into Unicode, using one of four mapping tables if the console was not in UTF-8 mode to start with, then looked up in the table describing the correspondence between Unicode values and font positions, and the obtained 8- or 9-bit font indices are then written to video memory, where they cause the display of character shapes found in the video card's character ROM. One can load one's own fonts into character ROM using `setfont`, load the corresponding Unicode map with `loadunimap`, and load a user mapping table using `mapscrn`. More details will be given below.

There are many consoles (called **Virtual Consoles** or **Virtual Terminals**, abbreviated VCs or VTs) that share the same screen. You can use them as independent devices, either to run independent login sessions, or just to send some output to, perhaps from `top`, or the tail of the system log or so. See below ("Console switching") on how to set them up and switch between them.

5 Resetting your terminal

There is garbage on the screen, or all your keystrokes are echoed as line drawing characters. What to do?

Many programs will redraw the screen when Ctrl-L is typed. This might help when there is some modem noise or broadcast message on your screen. The command `clear` will clear the screen.

The command `reset` will reset the console driver. This helps when the screen is full of funny graphic characters, and also if it is reduced to the bottom line. If you don't have this command, or if it does something else, make your own by putting the following two lines in an executable file `reset` in your `PATH`:

```
#!/bin/sh
echo -e \\033c
```

that is, you want to send the two characters ESC c to the console.

Why is it that the display sometimes gets confused and gives you a 24-line or 1-line screen, instead of the usual 25 lines? Well, the main culprit is the use of `TERM=VT100` (or some other entry with 24 lines) instead of `TERM=linux` when logged in remotely. If this happens on `/dev/tty2` then typing

```
% cat > /dev/tty2
^[c
^D
```

on some other VT (where 4 symbols are typed to `cat`: ESC, c, ENTER, Ctrl-D) and refreshing the screen on `/dev/tty2` (perhaps using ^L) will fix things. Of course the permanent fix is to use the right termcap or terminfo entry.

Why is it that you sometimes get a lot of line-drawing characters, e.g., after `cat`ing a binary to the screen? Well, there are various character set changing escape sequences, and by accident your binary might contain some of these. The ESC c is a general reset, a cure for all, but if you know precisely what went wrong you can repair it without resetting other console attributes. For example, after

```
% cat
^N
^D
```

your shell prompt will be all line-drawing characters. Now do (typing blindly)

```
% cat
^O
^D
```

and all is well again. (Three symbols typed to each `cat`: ^N (or ^O), ENTER, Ctrl-D.) To understand what is happening, see "The console character sets" below.

If you loaded some strange font, and want to return to the default,

```
% setfont
```

will do (provided you stored the default font in the default place). If this default font does not contain an embedded Unicode map (and gives the wrong symbols for accented characters), then say

```
% loadunimap
```

For example, if I do

```
% loadkeys de-latin1
```

then I have a German keyboard, and the key left of the Enter key gives me a-umlaut. This works, because the a-umlaut occurs on the CP437 code page and the kernel Unicode map is initialized to CP437, and my video card has a CP437 font built-in. If I now load an ISO 8859-1 font with

```
% setfont iso01.f16
```

then everything still works, because `setfont` invalidates the kernel Unicode map (if there is no Unicode map attached to the font), and without map the kernel goes directly to the font, and that is precisely correct for an ISO 8859-1 system with `iso01.f16` font. But going back to the previous font with

```
% setfont
```

gives capital Sigma's instead of a-umlaut—all accented letters are mixed up because also this font has no embedded Unicode map. After

```
% loadunimap
```

which loads the default Unicode map (which is right for the default font) all works correctly again. Usually `loadunimap` is not invoked directly, but via `setfont`. Thus, the previous two commands may be replaced by

```
% setfont -u def
```

The Ethiopian fonts and the `lat1u*.psf` fonts have embedded Unicode code map. Most of the others don't.

On old terminals output involving tabs may require a delay, and you have to say

```
% stty tab3
```

(see `stty(1)`).

You can change the video mode using `resizecons` or `SVGATextMode`. This usually settles the output side. On the input side there are many things that might be wrong. If `X` or `DOOM` or some other program using raw mode crashed, your keyboard may still be in raw (or mediumraw) mode, and it is difficult to give commands. (See "How to get out of raw mode," below.) If you loaded a bad key map, then

```
% loadkeys -d
```

loads the default map again, but it may well be difficult to type '-'. An alternative is

```
% loadkeys defkeymap
```

Sometimes even the letters are garbled. It is useful to know that there are four main types of keyboards: QWERTY, QWERTZ, AZERTY and DVORAK. The first three are named after the first six letter keys, and roughly represent the English, German and French speaking countries. Compared to QWERTY, the QWERTZ map interchanges Y and Z. Compared to QWERTY, the AZERTY map interchanges Q and A, W and Z, and has its M right of the L, at the semicolon position. DVORAK has an entirely different letter ordering.

5.1 Keyboard hardware reset

Things may be wrong on a lower level than Linux knows about. There are at least two distinct lower levels (keyboard and keyboard controller) where one can give the command "keyboard disable" to the keyboard hardware. Keyboards can often be programmed to use one out of three different sets of scan codes.

However, I do not know of cases where this turned out to be a problem.

Some keyboards have a remapping capability built in. Stormy Henderson (`stormy@Ghost.Net`) writes: "If it's your keyboard accidently being reprogrammed, you can (on a Gateway AnyKey keyboard) press control-alt-suspend_macro to reset the keys to normal."

6 Delete and Backspace

Getting Delete and Backspace to work just right is nontrivial, especially in a mixed environment, where you talk to console, to X, to `bash`, to `emacs`, login remotely, etc. You may have to edit several configuration files to tell all of the programs involved precisely what you want. On the one hand, there is the matter of which keys generate which codes (and how these codes are remapped by e.g. `kermit` or `emacs`), and on the other hand the question of what functions are bound to what codes.

People often complain "my backspace key does not work," as if this key had a built-in function "delete previous character." Unfortunately, all this key, or any key, does is producing a code, and one only can hope that the kernel tty driver and all application programs can be configured such that the backspace key indeed does function as a "delete previous character" key.

Most Unix programs get their tty input via the kernel tty driver in "cooked" mode, and a simple `stty` command determines the erase character. However, programs like `bash` and `emacs` and X do their own input handling, and have to be convinced one by one to do the right thing.

6.1 How to tell Unix what character you want to use to delete the last typed character

```
% stty erase ^?
```

If the character is erased, but in a funny way, then something is wrong with your tty settings. If `echoprt` is set, then erased characters are enclosed between \ and /. If `echoe` is not set, then the erase char is echoed (which is reasonable when it is a printing character, like #). Most people will want `stty echoe -echoprt`. Saying `stty sane` will do this and more. Saying `stty -a` shows your current settings. How come this is not right by default? It is, if you use the right `getty`.

Note that many programs (like `bash`, `emacs` etc.) have their own key bindings (defined in `~/.inputrc`, `~/.emacs` etc.) and are unaffected by the setting of the erase character.

The standard Unix tty driver does not recognize a cursor, or keys (like the arrow keys) to move the current position, and hence does not have a command 'delete current character' either. But for example you can get `bash` on the console to recognize the Delete key by putting

```
set editing-mode emacs
"\e[3\~{}":delete-char
```

into `~/.inputrc`.

6.1.1 'Getty used to do the right thing with DEL and BS but is broken now?'

Earlier, the console driver would do BS Space BS (`\010\040\010`) when it got a DEL (`\177`). Nowadays, DEL's are ignored (as they should be, since the driver emulates a vt100). Get a better getty, i.e., one that does not output DEL.

6.1.2 'Login behaves differently at the first and second login attempts?'

At the first attempt, you are talking to `getty`. At the second attempt, you are talking to `login`, a different program.

6.2 How to tell Linux what code to generate when a key is pressed

On the console, or, more precisely, when not in (MEDIUM)RAW mode, use

```
% loadkeys mykeys.map
```

and under X use

```
% xmodmap mykeys.xmap
```

Note that (since XFree86-2.1) X reads the Linux settings of the keymaps when initializing the X key map. Although the two systems are not 100% compatible, this should mean that in many cases the use of `xmodmap` has become superfluous.

For example, suppose that you would like the Backspace key to send a BackSpace (^H, octal 010) and the grey Delete key a DEL (octal 0177). Add the following to `/etc/rc.local` (or wherever you keep your local boot-time stuff):

```
/usr/bin/loadkeys << EOF
keycode 14 = BackSpace
keycode 111 = Delete
EOF
```

Note that this will only change the function of these keys when no modifiers are used. (You need to specify a keymaps line to tell which keymaps should be affected if you want to change bindings on more keymaps.) The Linux kernel default lets Ctrl-Backspace generate BackSpace—this is sometimes useful as emergency escape, when you find you can only generate DELs.

The left Alt key is sometimes called the Meta key, and by default the combinations AltL-X are bound to the symbol MetaX. But what character sequence is MetaX? That is determined (per-tty) by the Meta flag, set by the command `setmetamode`. The two choices are: ESC X or X or-ed with 0200.

6.2.1 'Why doesn't the Backspace key generate BackSpace by default?'

(i) Because the VT100 had a Delete key above the Enter key, and (ii), because Linus decided so.

6.3 How to tell X to interchange Delete and Backspace

```
% xmodmap -e "keysym BackSpace = Delete" -e "keysym Delete = BackSpace"
```

Or, if you just want the Backspace key to generate a BackSpace:

```
% xmodmap -e "keycode 22 = BackSpace"
```

Or, if you just want the Delete key to generate a Delete:

```
% xmodmap -e "keycode 107 = Delete"
```

(but usually this is the default binding already).

6.4 How to tell `emacs` what to do when it receives a Delete or Backspace

Put in your `.emacs` file lines like

```
(global-set-key "\?" 'help-command)
(global-set-key "\C-h" 'delete-backward-char)
```

Of course you can bind other commands to other keys in the same way. Note that various major and minor modes redefine key bindings. For example, in incremental search mode one finds the code

```
(define-key map "\177" 'isearch-delete-char)
(define-key map "\C-h" 'isearch-mode-help)
```

This means that it may be a bad idea to use the above two global-set-key commands. There are too many places where there are built-in assumptions about ^H = help and DEL = delete. That doesn't mean that you have to set up keys so that Backspace generates DEL. But if it doesn't then it is easiest to remap them at the lowest possible level in `emacs`.

6.5 How to tell emacs to interchange Delete and Backspace

Put in your `.emacs` file lines

```
(setq keyboard-translate-table (make-string 128 0))
(let ((i 0))
  (while (< i 128)
    (aset keyboard-translate-table i i)
    (setq i (1+ i))))
(aset keyboard-translate-table ?\b ?\^?)
(aset keyboard-translate-table ?\^? ?\b)
```

Recent versions of `emacs` have a function `keyboard-translate` and one may simplify the above to

```
(keyboard-translate ?\C-h ?\C-?)
(keyboard-translate ?\C-? ?\C-h)
```

Note that under X, `emacs` can distinguish between Ctrl-h and the Backspace key (regardless of what codes these produce on the console), and by default emacs will view the Backspace key as DEL (and do deletion things, as bound to that character, rather than help things, bound to ^H). One can distinguish Backspace and Delete, e.g. by

```
(global-unset-key [backspace] )
(global-set-key [backspace] 'delete-backward-char)
(global-unset-key [delete] )
(global-set-key [delete] 'delete-char)
```

6.6 How to tell kermit to interchange Delete and Backspace

Put in your `.kermrc` file the lines

```
set key \127 \8
set key \8 \127
```

6.7 How to tell `xterm` about your favorite tty modes

Normally `xterm` will inherit the tty modes from its invoker. Under `xdm`, the default erase and kill characters are `#` and `@`, as in good old Unix Version 6. If you don't like that, you might put something like

```
XTerm*ttymodes: erase ^? kill ^U intr ^C quit ^\ eof ^D \
                susp ^Z start ^Q stop ^S eol ^@
```

in `/usr/lib/X11/app-defaults/XTerm` or in `$HOME/.Xresources`, assuming that you have a line

```
xrdb $HOME/.Xresources
```

in your `$HOME/.xinitrc` or `$HOME/.xsession`.

6.8 How to tell `xmosaic` that the Backspace key generates a DEL

Putting

```
*XmText.translations: #override\n\
   <Key>osfDelete: delete-previous-character()
*XmTextField.translations: #override\n\
   <Key>osfDelete: delete-previous-character()
```

in your `$HOME/.Xresources` helps.

The Netscape FAQ, however, says:

```
Why doesn't my Backspace key work in text fields?
By default, Linux and XFree86 come with the Backspace and Delete keys
misconfigured. All Motif programs (including, of course, Netscape
Navigator) will malfunction in the same way.

The Motif spec says that Backspace is supposed to delete the previous
character and Delete is supposed to delete the following character.
Linux and XFree86 come configured with both the Backspace and Delete
keys generating Delete.

You can fix this by using any one of the xmodmap, xkeycaps, or
loadkeys programs to make the key in question generate the BackSpace
keysym instead of Delete.

You can also fix it by having a .motifbind file; see the man page
for VirtualBindings(3).

Note: Don't use the *XmText.translations or *XmTextField.translations
resources to attempt to fix this problem. If you do, you will blow
away Netscape Navigator's other text-field key bindings.
```

6.9 A better solution for Motif-using programs, like Netscape

Ted Kandell (`ted@tcg.net`) suggests the following:

Somewhere in your .profile add the following:

```
stty erase ^H
```

If you are using `bash`, add the following lines to your `.inputrc`:

```
"\C-?": delete-char
"\C-h": backward-delete-char
```

Add the following lines to your .xinitrc file:

```
xmodmap <<-EOF
keycode 22  =  BackSpace osfBackSpace
keycode 107 =  Delete
EOF

# start your window manager here,  for example:
#(fvwm) 2>&1 | tee /dev/tty /dev/console

stty sane
stty erase ^H
loadmap <<-EOF
keycode 14  = BackSpace
keycode 111 = Delete
EOF
```

This will definitely work for a PC 101 or 102-key keyboard with any Linux and XFree86 layout.

The important part to making Motif apps like Netscape work properly is adding osfBackSpace to keycode 22 in addition to BackSpace.

Note that there must be spaces on either side of the = sign.

6.10 What about termcap and terminfo?

When people have problems with backspace, they tend to look at their termcap (or terminfo) entry for the terminal, and indeed, there does exist a kb (or kbs) capability describing the code generated by the Backspace key. However, not many programs use it, so unless you are having problems with one particular program only, probably the fault is elsewhere. Of course it is a good idea anyway to correct your termcap (terminfo) entry. See also below under "The `TERM` variable."

7 The console character sets

The kernel first tries to figure out what symbol is meant by any given user byte, and next where this symbol is located in the current font.

The kernel knows about 5 translations of bytes into console-screen symbols. In Unicode (UTF-8) mode, the UTF-8 code is just converted directly into Unicode. The assumption is that almost all symbols one needs are present in Unicode, and for the cases where this does not hold the codes 0xff** are reserved for direct font access. When not in Unicode mode, one of four translation tables is used. The four tables are: a) Latin1 -> Unicode, b) VT100 graphics -> Unicode, c) PC -> Unicode, d) user-defined.

There are two character sets, called G0 and G1, and one of them is the current character set. (Initially G0.) Typing ^N causes G1 to become current, ^O causes G0 to become current.

These variables G0 and G1 point at a translation table, and can be changed by the user. Initially they point at tables a) and b), respectively. The sequences ESC (B and ESC (0 and ESC (U and ESC (K cause G0 to point at translation table a), b), c) and d), respectively. The sequences ESC) B and ESC) 0 and ESC) U and ESC) K cause G1 to point at translation table a), b), c) and d), respectively.

The sequence ESC c causes a terminal reset, which is what you want if the screen is all garbled. The oft-advised `echo ^V^O` will only make G0 current, but there is no guarantee that G0 points at table a). In some distributions there is a program reset(1) that just does `echo ^[c`. If your termcap entry for the console is correct (and has an entry `:rs=\Ec:`), then also `setterm -reset` will work.

The user-defined mapping table can be set using `mapscrn(8)`. The result of the mapping is that if a symbol c is printed, the symbol `s = map[c]` is sent to the video memory. The bitmap that corresponds to `s` is found in the character ROM, and can be changed using `setfont(8)`.

8 Console switching

By default, console switching is done using Alt-Fn or Ctrl-Alt-Fn. Under X (or recent versions of dosemu), only Ctrl-Alt-Fn works. Many keymaps will allow cyclic walks through all allocated consoles using Alt-RightArrow and Alt-LeftArrow.

XFree86 1.3 does not know that Alt is down when you switch to the X window. Thus, you cannot switch immediately to some other VT again but have to release Alt first. In the other direction this should work: the kernel always keeps track of the up/down status of all keys. (As far as possible: on some keyboards some keys do not emit a scancode when pressed (e.g.: the PFn keys of a FOCUS 9000) or released (e.g.: the Pause key of many keyboards).)

XFree86 1.3 saves the fonts loaded in the character ROMs when started, and restores it on a console switch. Thus, the result of `setfont` on a VT is wiped out when you go to X and back. Using `setfont` under X will lead to funny results.

One can change VT under program control using the `chvt` command.

8.1 Changing the number of Virtual Consoles

This question still comes up from time to time, but the answer is: you already have enough of them. Since kernel version 1.1.54, there are between 1 and 63 virtual consoles. A new one is created as soon as it is opened. It is removed by the utility `deallocvt` (but it can be removed only when no processes are associated to it anymore, and no text on it has been selected by programs like `selection` or `gpm`).

For older kernels, change the line

```
#define NR_CONSOLES      8
```

in `include/linux/tty.h` (don't increase this number beyond 63), and recompile the kernel.

If they do not exist yet, create the tty devices with `MAKEDEV` or `mknod ttyN c 4 N` where N denotes the tty number. For example,

```
for i in 9 10 11 12; do mknod /dev/tty$i c 4 $i; done
```

or, better (since it also takes care of owner and permissions),

```
for i in 9 10 11 12; do /dev/MAKEDEV tty$i; done
```

If you want the new VCs to run `getty`, add lines in `/etc/inittab`. (But it is much better to have only two `getty`'s running, and to create more consoles dynamically as the need arises. That way you'll have more memory when you don't use all these consoles, and also more consoles, in case you really need them. Edit `/etc/inittab` and comment out all `getty`'s except for the first two.)

When the consoles are allocated dynamically, it is usually easiest to have only one or two running `getty`. More are opened by `open -l -s bash`. Unused consoles (without associated processes) are deallocated using `deallocvt` (formerly `disalloc`). But, you say, I am involved in activities when I suddenly need more consoles, and do not have a bash prompt available to give the `open` command. Fortunately it is possible to create a new console upon a single keystroke, regardless of what is happening at the current console.

If you have `spawn_login` from `kbd-0.95.tar.gz` and you put

```
loadkeys << EOF
alt keycode 103 = Spawn_Console
EOF
spawn_login &
```

in `/etc/rc.local`, then typing Alt-UpArrow will create a fresh VC running `login` (and switch to it). With `spawn_console &` instead of `spawn_login &` you'll have bash running there. See also `open-1.4.tgz` and `dynamic-vc-1.1.tar.gz`.

What action should be taken upon this Spawn_Console key press can also be set in `/etc/inittab` under `kbrequest`, if you have a recent `init`. See `inittab(5)`.

(This action can be something entirely different—I just called the key `Spawn_Console` because that is what I used it for. When used for other purposes it is less confusing to use its synonym `KeyboardSignal`. For example, some people like to put the lines

```
kb::kbrequest:/sbin/shutdown -h now
```

in `/etc/inittab`, and

```
control alt keycode 79 = KeyboardSignal
control alt keycode 107 = KeyboardSignal
```

in their key map. Now Ctrl-Alt-End will do a system shutdown.)

You can only login as root on terminals listed in `/etc/securetty`. There exist programs that read terminal settings from files `/etc/ttys` and `/etc/ttytype`. If you have such files, and create additional consoles, then it might be a good idea to also add entries for them in these files.

9 Ctrl-Alt-Del and other special key combinations

9.1 Ctrl-Alt-Del (Boot)

If you press Ctrl-Alt-Del (or whatever key was assigned the keysym Boot by loadkeys) then either the machine reboots immediately (without sync), or `init` is sent a SIGINT. The former behavior is the default. The default can be changed by root, using the system call reboot(), see `ctrlaltdel(8)`. Some `init`'s change the default. What happens when `init` gets SIGINT depends on the version of `init` used - often it will be determined by the pf entry in `/etc/inittab` (which means that you can run an arbitrary program in this case). In the current kernel Ctrl-AltGr-Del is no longer by default assigned to Boot.

9.2 Other combinations

```
Name              Default binding
--------------------------------
Show_Memory       Shift-Scrollock
Show_Registers    AltGr-ScrollLock
Show_State        Ctrl-ScrollLock
Console_n         Alt-Fn and Ctrl-Alt Fn   (1 <= n <= 12)
Console_{n+12}    AltGr-Fn                 (1 <= n <= 12)
Incr_Console      Alt-RightArrow
Decr_Console      Alt-LeftArrow
Last_Console      Alt[Gr]-PrintScreen
Scroll_Backward   Shift-PageUp
Scroll_Forward    Shift-PageDown
Caps_On                                    (CapsLock is a toggle; this key sets)
Compose           Ctrl-.
```

9.3 X Combinations

```
Ctrl-Alt-Fn       Switch to VT n
Ctrl-Alt-KP+      Next mode
Ctrl-Alt-KP-      Previous mode
Ctrl-Alt-Backspace        Kill X
```

On some motherboards, Ctrl-Alt-KP- and Ctrl-Alt-KP+ will be equivalent to pressing the Turbo button. That is, both will produce the scancodes 1d 38 4a ca b8 9d and 1d 38 4e ce b8 9d, and both will switch between Turbo (>= 25MHz) and non-Turbo (8 or 12 MHz). (Often these key combinations only function this way when enabled by jumpers on the motherboard.)

Perry F Nguyen (`pfnguyen@netcom22.netcom.com`) writes: AMI BIOS has a feature that locks up the keyboard and flashes the LED's if the Ctrl-Alt-Backspace combination is pressed while a BIOS password is enabled, until the CMOS/BIOS password is typed in.

9.4 DOSEMU Combinations

```
Ctrl-Alt-Fn       Switch to VT n (from version 0.50; earlier Alt-Fn)
Ctrl-Alt-PgDn     Kill DOSEMU (when in RAW keyboard mode)
(and many other combinations - see the DOSEMU documentation)
```

9.5 Composing symbols

One symbol may be constructed using several keystrokes.

- LeftAlt-press, followed by a decimal number typed on the keypad, followed by LeftAlt-release, yields the symbol with code given by this number. (In Unicode mode this same mechanism, but then with 4 hexadecimal digits, may be used to define a Unicode symbol.)
- A dead diacritic followed by a symbol, yields that symbol adorned with that diacritic. If the combination is undefined, both keys are taken separately. Which keys are dead diacritics is user settable; none is by default. Five (since 2.0.25, six) dead diacritics can be defined (using `loadkeys(1)`): `dead_grave`, `dead_acute`, `dead_circumflex`, `dead_tilde`, `dead_diaeresis` (and `dead_cedilla`). Precisely what this adorning means is also user-settable: `dead-diacritic` symbol is equivalent to Compose + diacritic + symbol.
- Compose followed by two symbols yields a combination symbol. These combinations are user-settable. Today there are 68 combinations defined by default; you can see them by saying `dumpkeys | grep compose`.

- Then there are "Sticky" modifier keys (since 1.3.33). For example, one can type Ctrl-C as SControl, C and Ctrl-Alt-BackSpace as SControl, SAlt, BackSpace.

Note that there are at least three such composition mechanisms:

1. The Linux keyboard driver mechanism, used in conjunction with loadkeys.
2. The X mechanism—see `X386keybd(1)`, later `XFree86kbd(1)`. Under X11R6: edit `/usr/X11R6/lib/X11/locale/iso8859-1/Compose`.See also Andrew D. Balsa's comments at http://wauug.erols.com/ balsa/linux/deadkeys/index.html.
3. The emacs mechanism obtained by loading `iso-insert.el` or calling `iso-accents-mode`.

For X the order of the two symbols is arbitrary: both Compose-,-c and Compose-c-, yield a c-cedilla; for Linux and emacs only the former sequence works by default. For X the list of compose combinations is fixed. Linux and `emacs` are flexible. The three default lists are somewhat similar, but the details are different.

10 How to get out of raw mode

If some program using K_RAW keyboard mode exits without restoring the keyboard mode to K_XLATE, then it is difficult to do anything—not even Ctrl-Alt-Del works. However, it is sometimes possible to avoid hitting the reset button. (And desirable as well: your users may get angry if you kill their Hack game by rebooting; you might also damage your file system.) Easy solutions involve logging in from another terminal or another machine and doing `kbd_mode -a`. The procedure below assumes that no X is running, that the display is in text mode, and that you are at your bash prompt, that you are using a US keyboard layout, and that your interrupt character is Ctrl-C.

Step 1. Start X. As follows: press 2 (and don't release), press F12 (and don't release) and immediately afterwards press = . This starts X. (Explanation: if a key press produces keycode K, then the key release produces keycode K+128. Probably your shell does not like these high characters, so we avoid generating them by not releasing any key. However, we have to be quick, otherwise key repeat starts. The digit 2 produces a Ctrl-C that discards previous junk, the F12 produces an X and the = a Return.) Probably your screen will be grey now, since no `.xinitrc` was specified. However, Ctrl-Alt-Fn will work and you can go to another VT. (Ctrl-Alt-Backspace also works, but that exits X, and gets you back into the previous state, which is not what you want.)

Step 2. Setup to change the keyboard mode. (For example, by `sleep 5; kbd_mode -a`.)

Step 3. Leave X again. Alt-Fx (often Alt-F7) brings you back to X, and then Ctrl-Alt-Backspace exits X. Within 5 seconds your keyboard will be usable again.

If you want to prepare for the occasion, then make `\215A\301` (3 symbols) an alias for `kbd_mode -a`. Now just hitting = F7 = (3 symbols) will return you to sanity.

11 The keyboard LEDs

1. There are per-tty keyboard flags: each VC has its own NumLock, CapsLock, ScrollLock. By default these keyboard flags are shown in the LEDs. The usual way to change them is by pressing the corresponding key. (Side remark: pressing the NumLock key when in application key mode will not change the NumLock status, but produce an escape sequence. If you want the NumLock key to always change the Numlock status, bind it to Bare_Num_Lock.)

2. Next, there are per-tty default keyboard flags, to initialize the keyboard flags when a reset occurs. Thus if you want NumLock on all the time, that is possible. The usual way to change them is by `setleds -D ...`.

3. There is the possibility that the LEDs do not reflect the keyboard flags, but something else.

3A. This something else can be three bits somewhere in the kernel—which can be used if you want to monitor some hardware or software status bit(s). If you want this, edit the kernel source to call `register_leds()` somewhere.

3B. This something else can also be whatever some user program wants to show in the LEDs. Thus, people who like such things can make nice patterns of lights. If you want this, use the KDSETLED ioctl.

This latter use is not per-tty, but the choice between former and latter use is per-tty.

Summarizing: Each tty has a flag `kbd->ledmode`. If this has the value LED_SHOW_FLAGS then the keyboard flags (NumLock etc.) of that tty are shown. If this has the value LED_SHOW_MEM then three selected memory addresses are shown. If this has the value LED_SHOW_IOCTL then the leds show whatever value was last assigned to them using the KDSETLED ioctl.

One may add that X uses ioctl's to set the LEDs, but fails to reset its VT when it exits, so after using X there may be one VT that is not in the default LED_SHOW_FLAGS state. This can be fixed by doing `setleds -L` on that VT. See `setleds(1)`.

12 The `TERM` variable

Many programs use the `TERM` variable and the database `/etc/termcap` or `/usr/lib/terminfo/*` to decide which strings to send for clear screen, move cursor, etc., and sometimes also to decide which string is sent by the users backspace key, function keys etc. This value is first set by the kernel (for the console). Usually, this variable is re-set by `getty`, using `/etc/ttytype` or the argument specified in `/etc/inittab`. Sometimes, it is also set in `/etc/profile`.

Older systems use `TERM=console` or `TERM=con80x25`. Newer systems (with ncurses 1.8.6) use the more specific `TERM=linux` or `TERM=linux-80x25`. However, old versions of `setterm` test for `TERM=con*` and hence fail to work with `TERM=linux`.

Since kernel version 1.3.2, the kernel default for the console is `TERM=linux`.

If you have a termcap without entry for linux, add the word linux to the entry for the console:

```
console|con80x25|linux:\
```

and make `/usr/lib/terminfo/l/linux` a copy of or symbolic link to `/usr/lib/terminfo/c/console`.

12.1 Terminfo

The terminfo entry for the linux console from ncurses 1.8.6 misses the entry `kich1=\E[2~`, needed by some programs. Edit the file and `tic` it.

13 How to make other programs work with non-ASCII chars

In the bad old days this used to be quite a hassle. Every separate program had to be convinced individually to leave your bits alone. Not that all is easy now, but recently a lot of gnu utilities have learned to react to `LC_CTYPE=iso_8859_1` or `LC_CTYPE=iso-8859-1`. Try this first, and if it doesn't help look at the hints below. Note that in recent versions of libc the routine `setlocale()` only works if you have installed the locale files (e.g. in `/usr/lib/locale`).

First of all, the 8th bit should survive the kernel input processing, so make sure to have `stty cs8 -istrip -parenb` set.

A. For `emacs` the details strongly depend on the version. The information below is for version 19.34. Put lines

```
(set-input-mode nil nil 1)
(standard-display-european t)
(require 'iso-syntax)
```

into your `$HOME/.emacs`. The first line (to be precise: the final 1) tells `emacs` not to discard the 8th bit from input characters. The second line tells `emacs` not to display non-ASCII characters as octal escapes. The third line specifies the syntactic properties and case conversion table for the Latin-1 character set These last two lines are superfluous if you have something like `LC_CTYPE=ISO-8859-1` in your environment. (The variable may also be `LC_ALL` or even `LANG`. The value may be anything with a substring "88591" or "8859-1" or "8859_1.")

This is a good start. On a terminal that cannot display non-ASCII ISO 8859-1 symbols, the command

```
(load-library "iso-ascii")
```

will cause accented characters to be displayed like {,c}a. If your keymap does not make it easy to produce non-ASCII characters, then

```
(load-library "iso-transl")
```

will make the 2-character sequence Ctrl-X 8 a compose character, so that the 4-character sequence Ctrl-X 8 , c produces c-cedilla. Very inconvenient.

The command

```
(iso-accents-mode)
```

will toggle ISO-8859-1 accent mode, in which the six characters ', `, ", ^, ~, / are dead keys modifying the following symbol. Special combinations: ~c gives a c with cedilla, ~d gives an Icelandic eth, ~t gives an Icelandic thorn, "s gives German sharp s, /a gives a with ring, /e gives an a-e ligature, ~< and ~> give guillemots, ~! gives an inverted exclamation mark, ~? gives an inverted question mark, and '' gives an acute accent. This is the default mapping of accents. The variable `iso-languages` is a list of pairs (language name, accent mapping), and a non-default mapping can be selected using

```
(iso-accents-customize LANGUAGE)
```

Here LANGUAGE can be one of `portuguese`, `irish`, `french`, `latin-2`, or `latin-1`.

Since the Linux default compose character is Ctrl-. it might be convenient to use that everywhere. Try

```
(load-library "iso-insert.el")
(define-key global-map [?\C-.] 8859-1-map)
```

The latter line will not work under `xterm`, if you use `emacs -nw`, but in that case you can put

```
XTerm*VT100.Translations:       #override\n\
      Ctrl <KeyPress> . : string("\0308")
```

in your `.Xresources`.)

B. For `less`, put `LESSCHARSET=latin1` in the environment. This is also what you need if you see `\255` or `<AD>` in `man` output: some versions of `less` will render the soft hyphen (octal 0255, hex 0xAD) this way when not given permission to output Latin-1.

C. For `ls`, give the option `-N`. (Probably you want to make an alias.)

D. For `bash` (version 1.13.*), put

```
set meta-flag on
set convert-meta off
```

and, according to the Danish HOWTO,

```
set output-meta on
```

into your `$HOME/.inputrc`.

E. For `tcsh`, use

```
setenv LANG      US_en
setenv LC_CTYPE iso_8859_1
```

If you have nls on your system, then the corresponding routines are used. Otherwise `tcsh` will assume `iso_8859_1`, regardless of the values given to `LANG` and `LC_CTYPE`. See the section NATIVE LANGUAGE SYSTEM in `tcsh(1)`. (The Danish HOWTO says: `setenv LC_CTYPE ISO-8859-1; stty pass8`)

F. For `flex`, give the option `-8` if the parser it generates must be able to handle 8-bit input. (Of course it must.)

G. For `elm`, set `displaycharset` to `ISO-8859-1`. (Danish HOWTO: `LANG=C` and `LC_CTYPE=ISO-8859-1`)

H. For programs using curses (such as `lynx`) David Sibley reports: The regular curses package uses the high-order bit for reverse video mode (see flag _STANDOUT defined in `/usr/include/curses.h`). However, `ncurses` seems to be 8-bit clean and does display iso-latin-8859-1 correctly.

I. For programs using `groff` (such as `man`), make sure to use `-Tlatin1` instead of `-Tascii`. Old versions of the program `man` also use `col`, and the next point also applies.

J. For `col`, make sure 1) that it is fixed so as to do `setlocale(LC_CTYPE,"");` and 2) put `LC_CTYPE=ISO-8859-1` in the environment.

K. For `rlogin`, use option `-8`.

L. For `joe`, `sunsite.unc.edu:/pub/Linux/apps/editors/joe-1.0.8-linux.tar.gz` is said to work after editing the configuration file. Someone else said: `joe`: Put the `-asis` option in `/isr/lib/joerc` in the first column.

M. For LaTeX: `\documentstyle[isolatin]{article}`. For LaTeX 2ε: `\documentclass{article}\usepackage{isolatin}` where `isolatin.sty` is available from `ftp://ftp.vlsivie.tuwien.ac.at/pub/8bit`.

A nice discussion on the topic of ISO 8859-1 and how to manage 8-bit characters is contained in the file `grasp.insa-lyon.fr:/pub/faq/fr/accents` (in French). Another fine discussion (in English) can be found in `ftp.vlsivie.tuwien.ac.at:/pub/8bit/FAQ-ISO-8859-1`, which is mirrored in `rtfm.mit.edu:pub/usenet-by-group/comp.answers/character-sets/iso-8859-1-faq`.

If you need to fix a program that behaves badly with 8-bit characters, one thing to keep in mind is that if you have a signed char type then characters may be negative, and using them as an array index will fail. Several programs can be fixed by judiciously adding (unsigned char) casts.

14 What precisely does XFree86-2.1 do when it initializes its keymap?

Since version 2.1, XFree86 will initialize its keymap from the Linux keymap, as far as possible. However, Linux had 16 entries per key (one for each combination of the Shift, AltGr, Ctrl, Alt modifiers) and presently has 256 entries per key, while X has 4 entries per key (one for each combination of Shift, Mod), so some information is necessarily lost.

First X reads the `Xconfig` file, where definitions of the LeftAlt, RightAlt, RightCtl, ScrollLock keys as Meta, ModeShift, Compose, ModeLock or ScrollLock might be found—see `X386keybd(1)`, later `XFree86kbd(1)`.

For Mod the LeftAlt key is taken, unless RightCtl was defined as ModeShift or ModeLock, in which case RightCtl is taken, or RightAlt was so defined, in which case RightAlt is taken. This determines how the 4 XFree86 meanings of a key are selected from the 16 Linux meanings. Note that Linux today does not distinguish by default between the two Ctrl keys or between the two Shift keys. X does distinguish.

Now the kernel keymap is read and the usually obvious corresponding X bindings are made. The bindings for the "action keys" Show_Memory, Show_State, Show_Registers, Last_Console, Console_n, Scroll_Backward, Scroll_Forward, Caps_On and Boot are ignored, as are the dead diacriticals, and the locks (except for ShiftLock), and the "ASCII-x" keys.

Next, the definitions in the `XF86config` file are used. (Thus, a definition of Compose in `XF86config` will override its value as found in the Linux keymap.)

What happens to the strings associated with the function keys? Nothing, X does not have such a concept. (But it is possible to define strings for function keys in `xterm`—note however that the window manager gets the keys first.)

I don't know how to convince `xterm` that it should use the X keymap when Alt is pressed; it seems just to look at its resource `eightBitInput`, and depending on whether that is true or false either set the high order bit of the character, or generate an additional Escape character (just like `setmetamode(1)` does for the console).

15 Unusual keys and keyboards

The two keys PrintScrn/SysRq, and Pause/Break, are special in that they have two keycodes: the former has keycode 84 when Alt is pressed simultaneously, and keycode 99 otherwise; the latter has keycode 101 when Ctrl is pressed simultaneously, and keycode 119 otherwise. (Thus, it makes no sense to bind functions to Alt keycode 99 or Ctrl keycode 119.)

If you have strange keys that do not generate any code under Linux (or generate messages like "unrecognized scancode"), and your kernel is 1.1.63 or later, then you can use `setkeycodes(1)` to tell the kernel about them. They won't work under X, however. Once they have gotten a keycode from `setkeycodes`, they can be assigned a function by `loadkeys`.

16 Examples of use of `loadkeys` and `xmodmap`

Switching Caps Lock and Control on the keyboard (assuming you use keymaps 0-15; check with `dumpkeys | head -1`)

```
% loadkeys
keymaps 0-15
keycode 58 = Control
keycode 29 = Caps_Lock
%
```

Switching them under X only:

```
% xmodmap .xmodmaprc
```

where `.xmodmaprc` contains lines

```
remove Lock = Caps_Lock
remove Control = Control_L
keysym Control_L = Caps_Lock
keysym Caps_Lock = Control_L
add Lock = Caps_Lock
add Control = Control_L
```

What is this about the key numbering? Backspace is 14 under Linux, 22 under X? Well, the numbering can best be regarded as arbitrary; the Linux number of a key can be found using `showkey(1)`, and the X number using `xev(1)`. Often the X number will be 8 more than the Linux number.

Something else people like to change are the bindings of the function keys. Suppose that you want to make F12 produce the string 'emacs '. Then

```
% loadkeys
keycode 88 = F12
string F12 = "emacs "
%
```

will do this. More explicitly, the procedure is like this: (i) find the keycodes of the keys to be remapped, using `showkey(1)`. (ii) save the current keymap, make a copy and edit that:

```
% dumpkeys > my_keymap
% cp my_keymap trial_keymap
% emacs trial_keymap
% loadkeys trial_keymap
%
```

The format of the table can be guessed by looking at the output of dumpkeys, and is documented in keytables(5). When the new keymap functions as desired, you can put an invocation

```
loadkeys my_new_keymap
```

in /etc/rc.local or so, to execute it automatically at boot-up. Note that changing modifier keys is tricky, and a newbie can easily get into a situation only an expert can get out of.

The default directory for keymaps is /usr/lib/kbd/keytables. The default extension for keymaps is .map. Thus, loadkeys uk would probably load /usr/lib/kbd/keytables/uk.map.

(On my machine) /dev/console is a symbolic link to /dev/tty0, and the kernel regards /dev/tty0 as a synonym for the current VT. XFree86 1.3 changes the owner of /dev/tty0, but does not reset this after finishing. Thus, loadkeys or dumpkeys might fail because someone else owns /dev/tty0; in such a case you might run X first. Note that you cannot change keyboard mappings when not at the console (and not superuser).

16.1 "I can use only one finger to type with"

"Can the Shift, Ctrl and Alt keys be made to behave as toggles?"

Yes, after saying

```
% loadkeys
keymaps 0-15
keycode 29 = Control_Lock
keycode 42 = Shift_Lock
keycode 56 = Alt_Lock
%
```

the left Control, Shift and Alt keys will act as toggles. The numbers involved are revealed by showkey (and usually are 29, 97, 42, 54, 56, 100 for left and right control, shift and alt, respectively), and the functions are Control_Lock, Shift_Lock, Alt_Lock, ALtGr_Lock.

"What about 'sticky' modifier keys?"

Since version 1.3.33, the kernel knows about "sticky" modifier keys. These act on the next key pressed. So, where one earlier needed the 3-symbol sequence Shift_Lock a Shift_Lock to type 'A', one can now use the 2-symbol sequence SShift_Lock a. Versions of the kbd package older than 0.93 do not yet include code for these sticky modifiers, and have to invoke them using their hexadecimal codes. For example,

```
% loadkeys
keymaps 0-15
keycode 54 = 0x0c00
keycode 97 = 0x0c02
keycode 100 = 0x0c03
%
```

will make the right Shift, Ctrl, and Alt into sticky versions of the left ones. From 0.93 on you can say

```
% loadkeys
keymaps 0-15
keycode 54 = SShift
keycode 97 = SCtrl
keycode 100 = SAlt
%
```

to obtain the same result. This will allow you to type Ctrl-Alt-Del in three keystrokes with one hand.

The keymaps line in these examples should cover all keymaps you have in use. You find what keymaps you have in use by

```
% dumpkeys | head -1
```

17 Changing the video mode

As far as I know, there are six ways to change resolution:

1. At compile time: change the line

```
SVGA_MODE=       -DSVGA_MODE=NORMAL_VGA
```

in /usr/src/linux/Makefile.

1A. After compilation: use rdev -v—a terrible hack, but it exists.

2. At boot time: put vga=ask in the LILO configuration file, and LILO will ask you what video mode you want. Once you know, put vga=mypreference.

3. At run time: A. Use the resizecons command. (This is a very primitive wrapper around the VT_RESIZE ioctl.) B. Use the SVGATextMode command. (This is a less primitive wrapper around the VT_RESIZE ioctl.)

4. Not "on the console:" Under DOSEMU, or with svgalib etc. you can change the hardware video mode without the console driver being aware of it. Sometimes this is useful in getting resizecons or SVGATextMode set up: use DOSEMU and some DOS program to get into the desired video mode, dump (say from another VT) the contents of all video hardware registers, and use that in the initialization that resizecons and SVGATextMode require. In some cases where the video mode has gotten into some unusable state, starting DOSEMU, relying on the BIOS to set up the video mode, and then killing DOSEMU (with kill -9), is the easiest way to get into shape again.

17.1 Instructions for the use of resizecons

Get svgalib and compile the program restoretextmode. Boot up your machine in all possible video modes (using vga=ask in the LILO configuration file), and write the video hardware register contents to files CxR (C=cols, R=rows), e.g., 80x25, 132x44, etc. Put these files in /usr/lib/kbd/videomodes. Now resizecons 132x44 will change videomode for you (and send SIGWINCH to all processes that need to know about this, and load another font if necessary).

At present, resizecons only succeeds when there is memory enough for both the old and the new consoles at the same time.

18 Changing the keyboard repeat rate

At startup, the Linux kernel sets the repeat rate to its maximal value. For most keyboards this is reasonable, but for some it means that you can hardly touch a key without getting three copies of the corresponding symbol. Use the program kbdrate(8) to change the repeat rate, or, if that doesn't help, edit or remove the section

```
! set the keyboard repeat rate to the max

        mov     ax,#0x0305
        xor     bx,bx           ! clear bx
        int     0x16
```

of /usr/src/linux/[arch/i386/]boot/setup.S.

19 Scrolling

There are two ways to get a screen to scroll. The first, called "hard scrolling," is to leave the text in video memory as it is, but change the viewing origin. This is very fast. The second, called "soft scrolling," involves moving all screen text up or down. This is much slower. The kernel console driver will write text starting at the top of the video memory, continuing to the bottom, then copy the bottom part to the top again, and continue, all the time using hard scrolling to show the right part on the screen. You can scroll back until the top of the video memory by using Shift-PageUp (the grey PageUp) and scroll down again using Shift-PageDown (the grey PageDown), assuming a default keymap. The amount of scrollback is thus limited to the amount of video memory you happen to have, and you cannot increase this amount. If you need more scrollback, use some program that buffers the text, like less or screen—by using a buffer on disk you can go back to what you did last week. (One can set the amount of scrollback for xterm by adding a line like XTerm*saveLines: 2500 in .Xresources.)

Upon changing virtual consoles, the screen content of the old VT is copied to kernel memory, and the screen content of the new VT is copied from kernel memory to video memory. Only the visible screen is copied, not all of video memory, so switching consoles means losing the scrollback information.

Sometimes, hard scrolling is undesirable, for example when the hardware does not have the possibility to change viewing origin. The first example was a Braille machine that would render the top of video memory in Braille. There is a kernel boot-time option no-scroll to tell the console driver not to use hard scrolling. See bootparam(7).

20 Screensaving

`setterm -blank` **nn** will tell the console driver to blank the screen after **nn** minutes of inactivity. (With **nn** = 0, screen-saving is turned off. In some old kernels this first took effect after the next keyboard interrupt.)

The `s` option of `xset(1)` will set the X screensaving parameters: `xset s off` turns off the screen saver, `xset s 10` blanks the screen after 10 minutes.

The video hardware power saving modes can be enabled and disabled using the `setvesablank` program given in the starting comment of `/usr/src/linux/drivers/char/vesa_blank.c`.

21 Screen dumps

`setterm -dump` *N* will dump the contents of the screen of `/dev/tty`*N* to a file `screen.dump` in the current directory. See `setterm(1)`.

The current contents of the screen of `/dev/tty`*N* can be accessed using the device `/dev/vcs`*N* (where "vcs" stands for "virtual console screen"). For example, you could have a clock program that displays the current time in the upper right hand corner of the console screen (see the program `vcstime` in `kbd-0.95.tar.gz`). Just dumping the contents goes with `cat /dev/vcs`*N*. These device files `/dev/vcs`*N* do not contain newlines, and do not contain attributes, like colors. From a program it is usually better to use `/dev/vcsa`*N* ("virtual console screen with attributes") instead—it starts with a header giving the number of rows and columns and the location of the cursor. See `vcs(4)`.

22 Some properties of the VT100 application-key mode

Sometimes my cursor keys or keypad keys produce strange codes

When the terminal is in application-cursor key mode, the cursor keys produce Esc O x and otherwise Esc [x where x is one of A,B,C,D. Certain programs put the terminal in application cursor key mode; if you kill them with `kill -9`, or if they crash, then the mode will not be reset.

```
% echo -e '\033c'
```

resets all properties of the current VC. Just changing the cursor application key mode is done by

```
% echo -e '\033[?1h'
```

(set) and

```
% echo -e '\033[?1l'
```

(clear).

When the terminal is in application keypad key mode the keypad keys produce Esc O y and otherwise Esc [z ˜ for certain y and z. Setting application keypad key mode is done by

```
% echo -e '\033='
```

and

```
% echo -e '\033{$>$}'
```

clears it again.

23 Hardware incompatibility

Several people have noticed that they lose typed characters when a floppy disk is active. It seems that this might be a problem with Uni-486WB motherboards. Please mail me at `aeb@cwi.nl`) to confirm (yes, I have the same problem), deny (no, nothing wrong with my Uni-486WB), modify (My Xyzzy machine has the same problem).

Tjalling Tjalkens (`tjalling@ei.ele.tue.nl`) reports very similar problems with "a no-brand GMB-486 UNP Vesa motherboard with AMD 486DX2-66 CPU"—during floppy activity some keystrokes are lost, during floppy tape streamer (Conner C 250 MQ) activity many keystrokes are lost.

Some people experience sporadic lockups—sometimes associated to hard disk activity or other I/O.

Ulf Tietz (`ulf@rio70.bln.sni.de`) wrote: "I have had the same problems, when I had my motherboard tuned too fast. So I reset all the timings (CLK, wait statements etc) to more conventional values, and the problems are gone."

Bill Hogan (`bhogan@crl.com`) wrote, "If you have an AMI BIOS, you might try setting the Gate A20 emulation parameter to "chipset" (if you have that option). Whenever I have had that parameter set to any of the other options on my machine ('fast,' 'both,' 'disabled') I have had frequent keyboard lockups."

Additions and corrections are welcome. Andries Brouwer - `aeb@cwi.nl`

Part XXX

"A mSQL and perl Web Server Mini HOWTO"

by Oliver Corff,

corff@zedat.fu-berlin.de

The Linux Documentation Project
The original, unaltered edition of this, and other, LDP documents, is on line at http://sunsite.unc.edu/LDP/.

Contents

Abstract

v 0.1, 17 September 1997
This HOWTO, highly inspired by Michael Schilli's article "Gebunkert: Datenbankbedienung mit Perl und CGI," published in the German computer magazine *iX* 8/1997, describes how to build a SQL client/server database using WWW and HTML for the user interface.

1 About this Document

1.1 Intended Audience

Everybody who wants to install a web server database but does not know which software is necessary and how it is installed should benefit from reading this text. This text provides all information necessary to get a SQL database for a web server going; it does not go into any detail of CGI programming, nor does it explain the SQL database language. Excellent books are available on both topics, and it is the intention of this text to provide a working platform based on which a user can then study CGI programming and SQL.

For getting a small-scale SQL system running (not the notorious example of a major airline booking system, or space mission management database) it will be sufficient to have the software described in this text and the documentation accompanying it. The user manual of mSQL (a database introduced in this text) provides sufficient information on SQL for building your own database.

The reader of this text should have a working knowledge of how to obtain files via FTP if he has no access to CD-ROMs, and a basic understanding of how to build binaries from sources. Anyway, all steps explained in this text were tested on a real life system and should also work on the reader's system.

1.2 Conventions used in this text

A user command:

```
# make install
```

Screen output from a program:

```
Program installed. Read README for details on how to start.
```

Sample code of a file:

```
# My comment
char letter;
```

2 Introduction

It can be safely assumed that databases with a high volume of data or a complicated relational setup (like, perhaps, a lexical database for a living language) must be accessible to many users and operators at the same time. Ideally, it should be possible to use existing different hardware and software platforms that can be combined into the actual system. In order to reduce the implementation cost, only one system, the database server, needs to be powerful; the user stations typically just display data and accept user commands, but the processing is done on one machine only which led to the name client-server database. In addition, the user interface should be easy to maintain and should require as little as possible on the client side.

A system which meets these criteria can be built around the following items of protocols, concepts, and software:

Linux

supplies the operating system. It is a stable Unix implementation providing true multi-user, multi-tasking services with full network (TCP/IP e. a.) support. Except from the actual media and transmission cost, it is available free of charge and comes in form of so-called distributions which usually include everything needed from the basic OS to text processing, scripting, software development, interface builders, etc.

HTML

is the Hypertext Markup Language used to build interfaces to network systems like Intranets and the WWW, the World Wide Web. HTML is very simple and can be produced with any ASCII-capable text editor.

Browsers
: are text-based (e.g., Lynx) or graphical (e.g. Mosaic, Netscape, Arena, etc.) applications accepting, evaluating and displaying HTML documents. They are the only piece of software which is directly operated by the database user. Using browsers, it is possible to display various types of data (text, possibly images) and communicate with http servers (see next) on about every popular computer model for which a browser has been made available.

http servers
: provide access to the area of a host computer where data intended for public use in a network are stored. They understand the http protocol and procure the information the user requests.

SQL Structured Query Language is a language for manipulating data in relational databases. It has a very simple grammar and is a standard with wide industry support. SQL based databases have become the core of the classical client/server database concept. There are many famous SQL systems available, like Oracle and Informix, etc., and then there is also mSQL which comes with a very low or even zero price tag if it is used in academic and educational environments.

CGI Common Gateway Interface is the programming interface between the system holding the data (in our case a SQL based system) and the network protocol (HTML, of course). CGIs can be built around many programming languages, but a particularly popular language is Perl.

Perl is an extremely powerful scripting language which combines all merits of C, various shell languages, and stream manipulation languages like awk and sed. Perl has a lot of modularized interfaces and can be used to control SQL databases, for example.

3 Installation Procedure

3.1 Hardware Requirements

No general statement can be made about the hardware requirements of a database server. Too much depends on the expected number of users, the kind of application, the network load etc. In a small environment with only a few users and little network traffic a i486-equivalent machine with 16 MB of RAM can be completely sufficient. Linux, the operating system, is very efficient in terms of resources, and can supply enough horse-power for running a broad variety of applications at the same time. Of course, faster processors and more RAM mean more speed, but much more important than the processor is the amount of RAM. The more RAM the system has, the less it is forced to swap memory intensive processes to disk in case a bottleneck occurs.

Given anything like 32 MB RAM and a PCI bus, searches and sorting operations can be done without much resorting to swap files etc., resulting in lightning-fast speed.

The model installation described in this article was made on a IBM 686 (133MHz) with 32 MB RAM and a 1.2 GB IDE hard disk. Assuming that the installation process starts from scratch, here is a list of the necessary steps.

3.2 Software Requirements

The software described in this article is available from the Internet or from CD-ROM. The following products were used:

- Red Hat Linux PowerTools: 6 CD's Complete Easy-to-Use Red Hat 4.2, Summer '97; alternatively from `http://www.redhat.com`;
- mSQL SQL database server: it is now available in two versions. The versions have differences in the number of transactions they can handle, the administration interface, etc. The elder version, 1.0.16, is available from Sunsite mirrors. The ELF executable can be found at `sunsite:apps/database/sql/msql-1.0.16` or on CD-ROM (here: disc 4 of InfoMagic Linux Developer's Resource, 6-CD set, December 1996) or alternatively from the following URL: `http://www.infomagic.com`.

  The newer version, 2.0.1, can be directly obtained from Hughes' home page in Australia (`http://www.hughes.com.au`) or from numerous mirror sites around the world;
- Perl from CPAN: The Comprehensive Perl Archive Network. Walnut Creek CDROM, ISBN 1-57176-077-6, May 1997;
- Michael Schilli's CGI example program from computer journal iX 8/1997, pages 150–152, available via FTP from `ftp.uni-paderborn.de:/doc/magazin/iX`;

3.3 Installing the Operating System

Linux is installed in form of the Red Hat Linux Distribution 4.2. In order to install successfully, the machine must either have a DOS-accessible CD-ROM drive, a bootable CD-ROM drive, or else a boot disk must be made following the instructions on the Linux CD.

During installation the user has the choice to select and configure numerous software packages. It is convenient to select the following items now:

- TCP/IP network support,
- the http server Apache,
- the scripting language Perl,
- the X Window System, as well as
- the browsers Arena (graphical) and Lynx (text-based).

All these packages are provided with the Linux distribution. If you do not install these packages now you still have the chance to do this later with the assistance of `glint`, the graphical and intuitive software package installation manager. Be sure to be root when installing these packages.

It is beyond the scope of this article to describe the network installation and initialization procedure. Please consult the online (manual pages, HTML, texinfo) and printed (Linux Bible, etc.) documentation.

The installation procedure of Red Hat is very mature and requires only a little user attention besides the usual choices (like providing host names, etc.). Once the installation ends successfully, the system is basically ready to go.

Installing the X Window System is not mandatory for a pure server but it makes local access and testing much easier. The X installation procedure is done by any of several programs; `XF86Setup` offers the most extensive self-testing facilities and needs the least handling of hairy details (like video clock programming, etc.). The only requirement is that the software can detect the video adapter. A cheap accelerated graphics adapter (like Trio S64 based cards prior to S64UV+) usually works "out of the box."

At this point we assume that our system is up and running and that Apache, Perl and the X Window System have been successfully installed. We further assume that all standard structures like the file and directory structure are kept as they are defined in the installation. Last but not least, we leave the host name as it is, and do at this moment accept the name `localhost`. We'll use this name for testing the installation; once the whole system works the true name can be added. Please note that the network setup also requires editing the files `/etc/hosts`, among others. Ideally this should be done with the administration tools provided to user root.

3.4 The http Server

The http server supplied with Linux is known as Apache to humans and as httpd to the system. The manual page for `httpd` explains how to install and start the http daemon (http*d*) but, as mentioned, if the installation went without problems then the server should be running. You can verify the directory tree: there must be a directory `/home/httpd/` with three subdirectories: `../cgi-bin/`, `../html/` and `../icons/`. In `../html/` there must be a file `index.html`. Later we will manipulate or replace this file by our own `index.html`. All configuration information is stored in `/etc/httpd/conf/`. The system is well pre-configured and does not need further setup provided the installation went without error.

3.5 The Browsers

There are essentially three types of browsers available for Linux: pure text-based systems like Lynx, experimental and simple ones like Arena (free!) and commercial ones like Netscape (shareware!) with Java support. While Lynx and Arena come with Linux, Netscape must be procured from other sources. Netscape is available as a pre-compiled binary for Linux on ix86 architectures and will run "out of the box" as soon as the archive is unpacked.

3.5.1 Configuring Lynx

Once Lynx is started it will look for a "default URL" which is usually not very meaningful if the system does not have permanent Internet access. In order to change the default URL (and lots of other configuration details) the system administrator should edit `/usr/lib/lynx.cfg`. The file is big, around 57000 bytes and contains occasionally contradicting information. It states its own home as `/usr/local/lib/`. Not far from top is a line beginning with `STARTFILE`. We replace this line by the following entry: `STARTFILE:http://localhost` and make sure that no spacing etc. is inserted:

```
# STARTFILE:http://www.nyu.edu/pages/wsn/subir/lynx.html
STARTFILE:http://localhost
```

After saving the file, Lynx should now display our `index.html` document if started without arguments.

3.5.2 Configuring Arena

Arena first looks for its own default URL when started without arguments. This URL is hard-wired into the executable but can be overridden by the environment variable `WWW_HOME`. The system administrator can place a line saying `WWW_HOME="http://localhost"` in `/etc/profile`. The variable must then be exported, either by a separate statement (`export WWW_HOME`) or by appending `WWW_HOME` to the existing export statement:

```
WWW_HOME="http://localhost"
export WWW_HOME
```

After relaunching a login shell, the new default URL is now system-wide known to Arena.

3.5.3 Installing and Configuring Netscape

Netscape is a commercial product and thus not included with the Linux distributions. It is either downloadable from the Internet or available from software collections on CDROM. Netscape comes in form of pre-compiled binaries for every important hardware platform. For installation purposes, it is useful to create a directory `/usr/local/Netscape/` where the archive is unpacked. The files can be kept in place (except for the Java library: follow the instructions in the `README` file that comes with the Netscape binary), and it is sufficient to create a soft link in `/usr/local/bin/` by issuing the command

```
# ln -s /usr/local/Netscape/netscape .
```

from within `/usr/local/bin/`.

Netscape is now ready for use and can be configured via the "Options" menu. In "General Preferences" there is a card "Appearance" with the entry "Home Page Location." Enter `http://localhost` here and do not forget to save the options (via "Options"—"Save Options") before exiting Netscape. At the next startup, Netscape will now show the Apache "home page."

3.6 Cooperation of Apache and Browsers

You can now conduct the first real test of both the browser and the http server: simply start any of the available browsers and the `Apache: Red Hat Linux Web Server` page will pop up. This page shows the file locations and other basics of http server installation. If this page is not displayed please check whether the files mentioned above are in place and whether the browser configuration is correct. Close edited configuration files before you start the browser again. If all files are in place and the browsers seem to be configured correctly then examine the network setup of your machine. Either the host name is different from what was entered in the configuration, or the network setup as such is not correct. It is utterly important that `/etc/hosts` contains at least a line like

```
127.0.0.1          localhost localhost.localdomain
```

which implies that you can connect locally to your machine. One can verify this by issuing any network-sensitive command requiring a host name as argument, like `telnet localhost` (provided `telnet` is installed). If that does not work then the network setup must be verified before continuing with the main task.

3.7 The Database Engine and its Installation

Installing the database requires only little more preparation than the previous installation steps. There are a few SQL database engines available with different runtime and administrative requirements, and possibly one of the most straightforward systems is mSQL, or "Mini-SQL" by David Hughes. mSQL is shareware. Depending on the version used, commercial sites are charged USD 250.00 and more, private users are charged USD 65.00 and more, and only educational institutions and registered non-profit organizations can use this software free of charge. Please note that the exact figures are provided in the license notes of the database documentation. The figures given here serve as a rough indicator only.

A few words are in place here why the author chose mSQL. First of all, there is personal experience. While searching for a database engine, the author found mSQL to be about the easiest to install and maintain, and it provides enough coverage of the SQL language to meet general needs. Only when writing these lines, the author discovered the following words of praise in Alligator Descartes' DBI FAQ (Perl Database Interface FAQ):

> From the current author's point of view, if the dataset is relatively small, being tables of less than 1 million rows, and less than 1000 tables in a given database, then mSQL is a perfectly acceptable solution to your problem. This database is extremely cheap, is wonderfully robust and has excellent support. [...]

mSQL is available in two versions now, msql-1.0.16 and msql-2.0.1, which differ in performance (not noticeable in small scale projects) and accompanying software (the newer version comes with more tools, its own scripting language, etc.). We will describe both versions of mSQL since their installion differs in a few points.

3.7.1 Installing msql-1.0.16

mSQL is available as source and as compiled executable with ELF support. Using the ELF binaries makes installation easy since the archive file `msql-1.0.16.ELF.tgz` contains a complete absolute directory tree so that all directories are generated properly when unpacked from `/`.

If you decide to compile mSQL 1.0.16 yourself and are going to use the MsqlPerl package rather than the DBI interface (see a detailed discussion on the difference between these two further down) then be prepared that MsqlPerl might complain during the test suites that some instruction inside mSQL failed. In this case a patch may be necessary which is described in the MsqlPerl documentation (file `patch.lost.tables`). Notably, this demands including three lines in `msqldb.c` after line 1400 which says `entry->def = NULL;`:

```
*(entry->DB) = 0;
*(entry->table) = 0;
entry->age = 0;
```

The code fragment should now look like

```
freeTableDef(entry->def);
safeFree(entry->rowBuf);
safeFree(entry->keyBuf);
entry->def = NULL;
*(entry->DB) = 0;
*(entry->table) = 0;
entry->age = 0;
```

Compiling mSQL involves several steps. After unpacking the source archive, it is necessary to build a target directory. This is done by saying

```
# make target
```

If successful, the system will then answer with

```
Build of target directory for Linux-2.0.30-i486 complete
```

You must now change into this newly created directory and run a

```
# ./setup
```

command first. The `./` sequence is necessary to make sure that really the command `setup` in this directory and not another command which happens to have the same name is executed. You will then be asked questions on the location of the source directory and whether a root installation is desired. These questions answered, the system should then run a number of tests checking for available software (compilers, utilities etc.) and finally say

```
Ready to build mSQL.

You may wish to check "common/site.h" although the defaults should be
fine.  When you're ready, type "make all" to build the software
```

We say

```
# make all
```

If everything went as intended, we'll read:

```
make[2]: Leaving directory '/usr/local/Minerva/src/msql'
<-- [msql] done

Make of mSQL complete.
You should now mSQL using make install

NOTE : mSQL cannot be used free of charge at commercial sites.
       Please read the doc/License file to see what you have to do.
```

```
make[1]: Leaving directory '/usr/local/Minerva/src'
```

All binaries must then be made visible to the search paths by creating soft links in `/usr/local/bin/`. Change to that directory and issue the command

```
# ln -s /usr/local/Minerva/bin/* .
```

after which the links will be properly set.

3.7.2 Testing mSQL 1

After the installation it is now possible to test whether the database works. Before anything else is done, the server daemon must be started. The system administrator holding root privileges issues the command

```
# msqld &
```

(Do not forget to add the `&`, otherwise mSQL won't run in the background.) after which the following screen message appears:

```
mSQL Server 1.0.16 starting ...

Warning : Couldn't open ACL file: No such file or directory
Without an ACL file global access is Read/Write
```

This message tells us that everything so far worked since we did not set up any access restrictions. For the moment it is sufficient to start the mSQL daemon from within a shell but later we may want to have the system startup automatically execute this command for us. The command must then be mentioned in a suitable `rc.d` script. Only now the administrator can issue the first genuine database command:

```
# msqladmin create inventur
```

mSQL replies by saying `Database "inventur" created..` As a further proof, we find that the directory `/usr/local/Minerva/msqldb/` contains now the empty subdirectory `../inventur/`. We could manipulate the newly created database with the administration tools; these procedures are all covered in detail in the mSQL documentation.

3.7.3 Installing mSQL 2.0.1

There is now a newer, more powerful version of Hughes' mSQL server available the installation of which is different in a few points. Installing mSQL 2 from scratch involves the following steps. Copy the archive to your extraction point, e.g. `/usr/local/msql-2/`, then untar the archive:

```
# tar xfvz msql-2.0.1.tar.gz
```

Change to the root direction of the install tree and issue a

```
# make target
```

Change to `targets` and look for your machine type. There should be a new subdirectory `Linux`-***(your version)-(your cpu)/***. Change to that directory and start the setup facility located here:

```
# ./setup
```

There is also a file `site.mm` which can be edited. Maybe you have got used to the directory name `/usr/local/Minerva/` and want to preserve it? In this case change the `INST_DIR=...` line to your desired target directory. Otherwise, leave everything as it is.

Now you can start building the database:

```
# make
# make install
```

If everything went successfully, we'll see a message like:

```
[...]

Installation of mSQL-2 complete.

*********
**   This is the commercial, production release of mSQL-2.0
```

```
**   Please see the README file in the top directory of the
**   distribution for license information.
*********
```

After all is installed properly, we have to take care of the administration details. Here, the real differences from msql-1 begin. First, a user `msql` is created which is responsible for database administration.

```
# adduser msql
```

Then we have to change all ownerships in the mSQL directory to `msql` by saying:

```
# cd /usr/local/Minerva
# chown -R msql:msql *
```

Then we create soft links for all database binaries in `/usr/local/bin/` by saying:

```
# ln -s /usr/local/Minerva/bin/* .
```

3.7.4 Testing msql-2

We can now start the database server by issuing the command `msql2d &` and should get a response similar to this one:

```
Mini SQL Version 2.0.1
Copyright (c) 1993-4 David J. Hughes
Copyright (c) 1995-7 Hughes Technologies Pty. Ltd.
All rights reserved.

        Loading configuration from '/usr/local/Minerva/msql.conf'.
        Server process reconfigured to accept 214 connections.
        Server running as user 'msql'.
        Server mode is Read/Write.

Warning : No ACL file. Using global read/write access.
```

That looks perfect. The database is compiled and in place, and we can now continue with the perl modules since these rely partially on the presence of a working database server for testing.

Incidentally, this is also a good moment to print the complete manual that comes with msql-2.0.1:

```
# gzip -d manual.ps.gz
# lpr manual.ps
```

We can proceed to building the interfaces now, but it is a good idea to keep the newly created SQL server up and running since that makes testing the interface libraries somewhat simpler.

3.8 Choice of Interfaces: DBI/mSQL, MsqlPerl, and Lite

A frequently quoted saying in the Camel Book (the authoritative Perl documentation) states that there is more than one way to achieve a result when using Perl. This, alas, holds true for our model application, too. Basically there are three ways to access an mSQL database via CGI. First of all the question is whether or not perl shall be used. If we use Perl (on which this article focuses) then we still have the choice between two completely different interface models. Besides using Perl, we can also employ mSQL's own scripting language, called Lite, which is reasonably simple and a close clone of C.

3.8.1 DBI and DBD mSQL

By the time of this writing, using Perl's generic database interface called DBI is the method of choice. DBI has a few advantages: It provides unified access control to a number of commercial databases with a single command set. The actual database in use on a given system is then contacted through a driver which effectively hides the peculiarities of that database from the programmer. Being such, using DBI provides for a smooth transition between different databases by different makers. In one single script it is even possible to contact several different databases. Please refer to the DBI-FAQ for details. There is, however, one drawback: The DBI interface is still under development and shows rapidly galloping version numbers (sometimes with updates taking place within less than a month). Similarly, the individual database drivers are also frequently updated and may rely on specific versions of the database interface. Users making first-time installations should stick to the version numbers given in this article since other versions may cause compilation and testing problems the trouble shooting of which is nothing for the faint-hearted.

3.8.2 MsqlPerl

MsqlPerl is a library for directly accessing mSQL from perl scripts. It bypasses the DBI interface and is fairly compact. Though it works fine with both versions of mSQL, its usage is not promoted anymore in favor of the generalized DBI interface. Nonetheless, in a given installation it may prove to be the interface of choice since it is small and easy to install. Notably, it has less version dependencies than revealed by the interaction of DBI and particular database drivers.

3.8.3 mSQL's own scripting language: Lite

Last but not least mSQL 2 comes with its own scripting language: Lite. The language is a close relative of C stripped of its oddities with additional shell-like features (in a way, something like a very specialized version of Perl). Lite is a simple language and is well documented in the mSQL 2 manual. The mSQL 2 package also comes with a sample application sporting Lite.

We will not describe Lite here because it is well documented but fairly specific to msql-2, and because it is assumed that the readers of this article have a basic interest in and a basic understanding of perl. Nonetheless it is highly recommended to have a closer look at Lite: it may well be the case that Lite offers the solution of choice in an exclusive mSQL 2 environment (implying no other databases are involved) due to its simplicity and straightforward concept.

3.9 Going the generic way: DBI and DBD mSQL

We assume that Perl was installed during the system setup or via the package manager mentioned above. No further details will be given here. Nonetheless we first test whether our version of Perl is up to date:

```
# perl -v
```

Perl should respond with the following message:

```
This is perl, version 5.003 with EMBED
        Locally applied patches:
          SUIDBUF - Buffer overflow fixes for suidperl security

        built under linux at Apr 22 1997 10:04:46
        + two suidperl security patches

Copyright 1987-1996, Larry Wall
[...]
```

So far, everything is fine. The next step includes installing the perl libraries for databases in general (DBI), the mSQL driver (DBD-mSQL) and CGI. The CGI driver is necessary in any case. The following archives are necessary:

1. DBI-0.81.tar.gz
2. DBD-mSQL-0.65.tar.gz
3. CGI.pm-2.31.tar.gz (or higher)

A caveat is necessary here for beginners: the test installation described here works fine using software with exactly these version numbers, and combinations of other versions failed in one or the other way. Debugging flawed version combinations is nothing for those who are not very familiar with the intimate details of the calling conventions, etc. of the interfaces. Sometimes only a method is renamed while performing the same task, but sometimes the internal structure changes significantly. So, again, stick with these version numbers if you want to be on the safe side, even if you discover that version numbers have increased in the meantime. Frequent updates of these interfaces are the rule rather than the exception, so you should really anticipate problems when installing other versions than those indicated here.

It is very important that the database driver for mSQL (DBD mSQL) is installed after the generic interface DBI.

We start by creating the directory `/usr/local/PerlModules/` as it is very important to keep the original perl directory tree untouched. We could also choose a different directory name since the name is completely uncritical, and unfortunately that is not really mentioned in the README files of the various perl modules. Having copied the above-mentioned archives to `/usr/local/PerlModules/` we unpack them saying

```
# tar xzvf [archive-file]
```

for every single of the three archives. Do not forget to supply the real archive name to `tar`. The installation process for the three modules is essentially standardized; only the screen messages showing important steps of individual packages are reproduced here.

3.9.1 Installing Perl's Database Interface DBI

The database interface must always be installed before installing the specific database driver. Unpacking the DBI archive creates the directory /usr/local/PerlModules/DBI-0.81/. Change to that directory. There are a README file (you should read it) and a Perl-specific makefile. Now issue the command

```
# perl Makefile.PL
```

The system should answer with a lengthy message of which the most important part is shown here:

```
[...]
MakeMaker (v5.34)
Checking if your kit is complete...
Looks good
        NAME => q[DBI]
        PREREQ_PM => { }
        VERSION_FROM => q[DBI.pm]
        clean => { FILES=>q[$(DISTVNAME)/] }
        dist => { DIST_DEFAULT=>q[clean distcheck disttest [...]
Using PERL=/usr/bin/perl

WARNING! By default new modules are installed into your 'site_lib'
directories. Since site_lib directories come after the normal library
directories you MUST delete old DBI files and directories from your
'privlib' and 'archlib' directories and their auto subdirectories.

Writing Makefile for DBI
```

This looks good, as the program says, and we can proceed with the next step:

```
# make
```

If no error message occurs (the detailed protocol dumped on screen is not an error message) we test the newly installed library with the command

```
# make test
```

Watch the output for the following lines (you can always scroll back with [Shift]-[PgUp]):

```
[...]
t/basics...........ok
t/dbidrv...........ok
t/examp............ok
All tests successful.
[...]
DBI test application $Revision: 1.6 $
Switch: DBI-0.81 Switch by Tim Bunce, 0.81
Available Drivers: ExampleP, NullP, Sponge
ExampleP: testing 2 sets of 5 connections:
Connecting... 1 2 3 4 5
Disconnecting...
Connecting... 1 2 3 4 5
Disconnecting...
Made 10 connections in  0 secs ( 0.00 usr  0.00 sys =  0.00 cpu)

test.pl done
```

The final step is to install all files in their proper directories. The following command will take care of it:

```
# make install
```

No more duties are left. If for some reason the installation failed and you want to redo it, do not forget to issue

```
# make realclean
```

first. This will remove stale leftovers of the previous installation. You can also remove the files which were installed by copying the screen contents (shown abbreviated)

```
Installing /usr/lib/perl5/site_perl/i386-linux/./auto/DBI/DBIXS.h
Installing /usr/lib/perl5/site_perl/i386-linux/./auto/DBI/DBI.so
Installing /usr/lib/perl5/site_perl/i386-linux/./auto/DBI/DBI.bs
[...]
Writing /usr/lib/perl5/site_perl/i386-linux/auto/DBI/.packlist
Appending installation info to /usr/lib/perl5/i386-linux/5.003/perllocal.pod
```

into a file, replacing every `Installing` with `rm`. Provided you named the file `uninstall` you can then say

```
# ./uninstall
```

which will remove the recently installed files.

3.9.2 Perl's mSQL Driver DBD-mSQL

The mSQL driver can only be installed after a successful installation of Perl's generic database interface.

The basic steps are the same as above; so first go through

```
# perl Makefile.PL
```

Here, the system should answer with an urgent warning to read the accompanying documentation. It will then detect where mSQL resides, and asks which version you use:

```
$MSQL_HOME not defined. Searching for mSQL...
Using mSQL in /usr/local/Hughes

 -> Which version of mSQL are you using [1/2]?
```

state your correct version number. Quite a few lines of text will follow. Watch for the following ones:

```
Splendid! Your mSQL daemon is running. We can auto-detect your configuration!

I've auto-detected your configuration to be running on port: 1114
```

You can now test the driver by saying

```
# make test
```

Again, a lengthy output follows. If it ends with

```
Testing: $cursor->func( '_ListSelectedFields' ). This will fail.
        ok: not a SELECT in msqlListSelectedFields!
Re-testing: $dbh->do( 'DROP TABLE testaa' )
        ok
*** Testing of DBD::mSQL complete! You appear to be normal! ***
```

you are on the safe side of life and can install your driver by saying

```
# make install
```

You are now ready to go and can skip the next paragraph.

3.10 The MsqlPerl Interface

If you decide to use the exclusive MsqlPerl interface then no generic database driver is needed, only `MsqlPerl-1.15.tar.gz`, since, as mentioned earlier, MsqlPerl provides a direct interface between perl and the database server without using the DBI interface. Installing and testing is straightforward.

After saying `perl Makefile.PL` the make utility can be started. First you have to answer the question where mSQL resides. If it resides in `/usr/local/Minerva/` the default answer can be confirmed.

Then do a `make test`. Before doing so you must ensure that you have a database named `test` and that you have read and write permissions for it. This can be done by

```
# msqladmin create test
```

3.11 Perl's CGI library

Installing Perl's CGI part is the simplest of the three steps. Execute the following commands in the given order and everything is done:

```
# perl Makefile.PL
# make
# make install
```

Unlike the previous drivers, this interface does not have a test option (`# make test`) whereas the other modules *should* be tested in any case.

A subdirectory with CGI example scripts is also created. You can copy the contents of this directory into `/home/http/cgi-bin/` and use the browser to experiment with the scripts.

3.12 Installation Checklist

We went through the following steps, in this order:

1. Install Linux with networking support.
2. Install a http server, e.g., Apache.
3. Install a browser, e.g., Arena, Lynx or Netscape.
4. Install an SQL server, e.g., mSQL.
5. Install a suitable perl SQL interface.
6. Install the CGI files.

Finally, you can do some clean up. All source trees for mSQL and the Perl modules can be safely deleted. (However, you should not delete your archive files.) Since the binaries and documentation are now based in different directories.

4 Running an Example Database

After completing the system installation we can now finally run a model application. Depending on the version of mSQL installed and the perl database interface used, we have to modify the sample programs in a few points.

First however, the file `index.html` residing in `/home/httpd/html/` must be modified to allow calling a sample database application. We can place our database (which we call `database.cgi` or `inventur.cgi` here despite its archive name `perl.lst.ck`) in `/home/httpd/html/test/`.

We add one line (of course, depending on your installation choices) similar to the following to `index.html`:

```
<LI>Test the <A HREF="test/database.cgi">Database, DBI:DBD-mSQL style!</A>
<LI>Test the <A HREF="test/inventur.cgi">Database, MsqlPerl style!</A>
```

Usually you should only pick one of these two choices, but if you have both types of database interface installed you can leave both lines here as they are. You can then compare performance.

4.1 Adapting the sample script for MsqlPerl

Our sample script has to be told to use the MsqlPerl interface. The modification takes place in several locations. First, near the beginning of the file, we change the `use` clause:

```
#
# use DBI;                # Generisches Datenbank-Interface
use Msql;
```

Then, near line 27, the MsqlPerl syntax does not require the mentioning of a specific driver:

```
# $dbh = DBI->connect($host, $database, '', $driver) ||
$dbh = Msql->connect($host, $database) ||
```

Then, from line 33 onward throughout the whole script, we have to change all instances of `do` against `query`:

```
# $dbh->do("SELECT * FROM hw") || db_init($dbh);
$dbh->query("SELECT * FROM hw") || db_init($dbh);
```

Finally, in MsqlPerl speak, line 207 can be commented out:

```
# $sth->execute || msg("SQL Error:", $sth->errstr);
```

In addition, it may become necessary to swap all `errstr` calls like the one in the preceding code fragment against `errmsg`. This is also version dependent.

After these modifications, the script should run smoothly.

4.2 Adapting the sample script for mSQL 2

The SQL syntax was redefined during the development of mSQL 2. The original script will fail to execute the table initialization statements in lines 45–58. The `primary key` modifier is no longer supported by mSQL 2, and should simply be skipped:

```
    $dbh->do(<<EOT) || die $dbh->errstr; # Neue Personen-Tabelle
        create table person (
# We do not need the 'primary key' modifier anymore in msql-2!
#           pn        int primary key,    # Personalnummer
            pn        int,                # Personalnummer
            name      char(80),           # Nachname, Vorname
            raum      int                 # Raumnummer
        )
EOT
    $dbh->do(<<EOT) || die $dbh->errstr; # Neue Hardware-Tabelle
        create table hw (
# We do not need the 'primary key' modifier anymore in msql-2!
#           asset int primary key,        # Inventurnummer
            asset int,                    # Inventurnummer
            name   char(80),              # Bezeichnung
            person int                    # Besitzer
        )
EOT
```

Unfortunately, this specific script will then accept new entries with identical personnel numbers; the mSQL 1 modifier `primary key` intends to prevent exactly this behaviour. The mSQL 2 documentation shows how to use the `CREATE INDEX` clause to create unique entries.

5 Conclusion and Outlook

If you have installed mSQL 2 on your system then you can have a look at the sample programs written in Lite, mSQL 2's own scripting language.

Either version of mSQL comes with a basic set of administration tools which allow the user to create and drop tables (`msqladmin`) and examine database structures (`relshow`).

The second generation mSQL (i.e. mSQL 2) has a few more genuinely useful utilities: `msqlimport` and `msqlexport`. These allow the dumping of flat line data files into and out of the SQL database. They can be used for loading quantities of existing data *d'un coup* into existing tables, or extract flat data from tables, and the user does not have to deal with writing a single line of perl or SQL or whatever code for this task.

If you want to write your own Perl scripts dealing with databases you'll find sufficient support in the example files and the extensive on-line documentation that comes with the DBI module.

Anyway, you are now ready to go and present your data to the users of your own network, or even the WWW.

[illegible]

Adapting the sample script for mSQL 2

[illegible]

5 Conclusion and Outlook

[illegible]

Part XXXI

"Linux NET-3-HOWTO, Linux Networking"

by Terry Dawson, VK2KTJ

terry@perf.no.itg.telstra.com.au

Contents

Abstract

v1.1, 29 March 1997
The Linux Operating System boasts kernel based networking support written almost entirely from scratch. The performance of the TCP/IP implementation in recent kernels makes it a worthy alternative to even the best of its peers. This document aims to describe how to install and configure the Linux networking software and associated tools.

1 Introduction.

The original NET FAQ was written by Matt Welsh and I to answer frequently asked questions about networking for Linux at a time before the Linux Documentation Project had formally started. It covered the very early development versions of the Linux Networking Kernel. The NET-2 HOWTO superseded the NET FAQ and was one of the original LDP HOWTO documents, it covered what was called version 2 and later version 3 of the Linux kernel Networking software. This document in turn supersedes it and relates only to version 3 of the Linux Networking Kernel.

Previous versions of this document became quite large because of the enormous amount of material that fell within its scope. To help reduce this problem a number of HOWTOs dealing with specific networking topics have been produced. This document will provide pointers to them where relevant and cover those areas not yet covered by other documents.

1.1 Feedback

I always appreciate feedback and especially contributions. Please direct any feedback or contributions to me by *email* (`mailto:terry@perf.no.itg.telstra.com.au`).

2 How to use this HOWTO document (NET-3-HOWTO-HOWTO?).

The format of this document differs from earlier versions. I've now regrouped the sections so that there is informative material at the beginning which you can skip if you are not interested, generic material next which you must understand before proceeding to the technology-specific sections in the rest of the document.

Read the generic sections
: These sections apply to every, or nearly every, technology described later, and so are very important for you to understand.

Consider your network
: You should know how your network is, or will be, designed, and exactly what hardware and technology types you will be implementing.

Read the technology specific sections related to your requirements
: When you know what you want, you can address each component in turn. These sections cover only details specific to a particular technology.

Do the configuration work
: You should actually try to configure your network and take careful note of any problems you have.

Look for further help if needed
: If you experience problems that this document does not help you to resolve, then read the section related to where to get help or where to report bugs.

Have fun!
: Networking is fun, enjoy it.

3 General Information about Linux Networking.

3.1 A brief history of Linux Networking Kernel Development.

Developing a brand-new kernel implementation of the TCP/IP protocol stack that would perform as well as existing implementations was not an easy task. The decision not to port one of the existing implementations was made at a time when there was some uncertainty as to whether the existing implementations may become encumbered by restrictive copyrights because of the court case put by U.S.L. (Unix Systems Laboratories), and when there was a lot of fresh enthusiasm for doing it differently and perhaps even better than had already been done.

The original volunteer to lead development of the kernel network code was Ross Biro, biro@yggdrasil.com. Ross produced a simple and incomplete, but mostly usable, implementation set of routines that were complemented by an Ethernet driver for the WD-8003 network interface card. This was enough to get many people testing and experimenting with the software, and some people even managed to connect machines in this configuration to live Internet connections. The pressure within the Linux community driving development for networking support was building, and eventually the cost of a combination of some unfair pressure applied to Ross and his own personal commitments outweighed the benefit he was deriving and he stepped down as lead developer. Ross's efforts in getting the project started and accepting the responsibility for actually producing something useful in such controversial circumstances were what catalyzed all future work and were therefore an essential component of the success of the current product.

Orest Zborowski, obz@Kodak.COM, produced the original BSD socket programming interface for the Linux kernel. This was a big step forward as it allowed many of the existing network applications to be ported to Linux without serious modification.

Somewhere about this time Laurence Culhane, loz@holmes.demon.co.uk developed the first drivers for Linux to support the SLIP protocol. These enabled many people who did not have access to Ethernet networking to experiment with the new networking software. Again, some people took this driver and pressed it into service to connect them to the Internet. This gave many more people a taste of the possibilities that could be realized if Linux had full networking support and grew the number of users actively using and experimenting with the networking software that existed.

One of the people that had also been actively working on the task of building networking support was Fred van Kempen waltje@uwalt.nl.mugnet.org. After a period of some uncertainty following Ross's resignation from the lead developer position Fred offered his time and effort and accepted the role essentially unopposed. Fred had some ambitious plans for the direction that he wanted to take the Linux networking software and he set about progressing in those directions. Fred produced a series of networking code called the "NET-2" kernel code (the "NET" code being Ross's) which many people were able to use pretty much usefully. Fred formally put a number of innovations on the development agenda, such as the dynamic device interface, Amateur Radio AX.25 protocol support and a more modularly designed networking implementation. Fred's NET-2 code was used by a fairly large number of enthusiasts, the number increasing all the time as word spread that the software was working. The networking software at this time was still a large number of patches to the standard release of kernel code and was not included in the normal release. The NET FAQ and subsequent NET-2 HOWTOs described the then fairly complex procedure to get it all working. Fred's focus was on developing innovations to the standard network implementations and this was taking time. The community of users was growing impatient for something that worked reliably and satisfied the 80% of users and, as with Ross, the pressure on Fred as lead developer rose.

Alan Cox, iialan@www.uk.linux.org, proposed a solution to the problem designed to resolve the situation. He proposed that he would take Fred's NET-2 code and debug it, making it reliable and stable so that it would satisfy the impatient user base while relieving that pressure from Fred allowing him to continue his work. Alan set about doing this, with some good success and his first version of Linux networking code was called "Net-2D (debugged)." The code worked reliably in many typical configurations and the user base was happy. Alan clearly had ideas and skills of his own to contribute to the project and many discussions relating to the direction the NET-2 code was heading ensued. There developed two distinct schools within the Linux networking community, one that had the philosophy of "make it work first, then make it better" and the other of "make it better first." Linus ultimately arbitrated and offered his support to Alan's development efforts and included Alan's code in the standard kernel source distribution. This placed Fred in a difficult position. Any continued development would lack the large user base actively using and testing the code and this would mean progress would be slow and difficult. Fred continued to work for a short time and eventually stood down and Alan came to be the new leader of the Linux networking kernel development effort.

Donald Becker, becker@cesdis.gsfc.nasa.gov, soon revealed his talents in the low-level aspects of networking and produced a huge range of Ethernet drivers. Nearly all of those included in the current kernels were developed by Donald. There have been other people that have made significant contributions, but Donald's work is prolific and so warrants special mention.

Alan continued refining the NET-2-Debugged code for some time while working on progressing some of the matters that remained unaddressed on the "To Do" list. By the time the Linux `1.3.*` kernel source had grown its teeth, the kernel networking code had migrated to the NET-3 release on which current versions are based. Alan worked on many different aspects of the networking code and with the assistance of a range of other talented people from the Linux networking community grew the code in all sorts of directions. Alan produced dynamic network devices and the first standard AX.25 and IPX implementations. Alan has continued tinkering with the code, slowly restructuring and enhancing it to the state it is in today.

PPP support was added by Michael Callahan, callahan@maths.ox.ac.uk, and Al Longyear, longyear@netcom.com. This, too, was critical to increasing the number of people actively using Linux for networking.

Jonathon Naylor, jsn@cs.nott.ac.uk, has contributed by significantly enhancing Alan's AX.25 code, adding NetRom and Rose protocol support. The AX.25/NetRom/Rose support itself is quite significant, because no other operating system can boast standard native support for these protocols beside Linux.

There have, of course, been hundreds of other people who have made significant contribution to the development of the Linux networking software. Some of these you will encounter later in the technology specific sections, other people have contributed modules, drivers, bug-fixes, suggestions, test reports and moral support. In all cases each can claim to have played a part and offered what they could. The Linux kernel networking code is an excellent example of the results that can be obtained from the Linux style of anarchic development, if it hasn't yet surprised you, it is bound to soon enough, the development hasn't stopped.

3.2 Where to get other information about Linux Networking.

There are a number of places where you can find good information about Linux networking.

Alan Cox, the current maintainer of the Linux kernel networking code, maintains a World Wide Web page that contains highlights of current and new developments in linux Networking at:

```
http://www.uk.linux.org/NetNews.html
```

Another good place is a book written by Olaf Kirch entitled the *Network Administrators Guide.* It is a work of the Linux Documentation Project, at

```
http://sunsite.unc.edu/LDP/
```

and you can read it interactively at

```
http://sunsite.unc.edu/LDP/LDP/nag/nag.html
```

or you can obtain it in various formats by FTP from the

```
ftp://sunsite.unc.edu/pub/Linux/docs/LDP/network-guide/
```

Olaf's book is quite comprehensive and provides a good, high-level overview of network configuration under Linux.

There is a newsgroup in the Linux news hierarchy dedicated to networking and related matters, comp.os.linux.networking.

There is a mailing list to which you can subscribe, where you may ask questions relating to Linux networking. To subscribe you should send a mail message:

```
To: majordomo@vger.rutgers.edu
Subject: anything at all
Message:

subscribe linux-net
```

On the various IRC networks there are often `#linux` channels on which people will be able to answer questions on Linux networking.

Please remember when reporting any problem to include as much relevant detail about the problem as you can. Specifically you should the versions of software that you are using, especially the kernel version, the version of tools such as `pppd` or `dip`, and the exact nature of the problem you are experiencing. This means taking note of the exact syntax of any error messages you receive, and of any commands that you are issuing.

3.3 Where to get some non-Linux specific network information.

If you are after some basic tutorial information on TCP/IP networking generally, then I recommend that you take a look at the following documentation:

TCP/IP introduction

this document comes as both a text version,

```
ftp://athos.rutgers.edu/runet/tcp-ip-intro.doc
```

and a PostScript version.

```
ftp://athos.rutgers.edu/runet/tcp-ip-intro.ps
```

TCP/IP administration

this document comes as both a text version,

```
ftp://athos.rutgers.edu/runet/tcp-ip-admin.doc
```

and a PostScript version.

```
ftp://athos.rutgers.edu/runet/tcp-ip-admin.ps
```

If you are after some more detailed information on TCP/IP networking, then I highly recommend:

```
"Internetworking with TCP/IP"
by Douglas E. Comer

ISBN 0-13-474321-0
Prentice Hall publications.
```

If you want to learn about how to write network applications in a Unix compatible environment, then I also highly recommend:

```
"Unix Network Programming"
by W. Richard Stevens

ISBN 0-13-949876-1
Prentice Hall publications.
```

You might also try the comp.protocols.tcp-ip newsgroup.

```
news:comp.protocols.tcp-ip
```

An important source of specific technical information relating to the Internet and the TCP/IP suite of protocols are RFCs. RFC means "Request For Comment," and is the standard method of submitting and documenting Internet protocol standards. There are many RFC repositories. Many of these sites are FTP sites and other provide World Wide Web access with an associated search engine that allows you to search the RFC database for particular keywords.

One possible source of RFCs is the Nexor RFC database.

```
http://pubweb.nexor.co.uk/public/rfc/index/rfc.html
```

4 Generic Network Configuration Information.

The following subsections you will pretty much need to know and understand before you actually try to configure your network. They are fundamental principles that apply regardless of the exact nature of the network you wish to deploy.

4.1 What do I need to start?

Before you start building or configuring your network, you will need some things. The most important of these are:

4.1.1 Current Kernel source.

Because the kernel that you are running now might not yet have support for the network types or cards that you wish to use, you will probably need the kernel source so that you can recompile the kernel with the appropriate options.

You can always obtain the latest kernel source from ftp.funet.fi.

```
ftp://ftp.funet.fi/pub/Linux/PEOPLE/Linus/v2.0
```

Normally, the kernel source will be untarred into the `/usr/src/linux` directory. For information on how to apply patches and build the kernel you should read the Kernel HOWTO (see page 1019). For information on how to configure kernel modules, you should read the Module HOWTO.

Unless specifically stated otherwise, I recommend that you stick with the standard kernel release (the one with the even number as the second digit in the version number). Development-release kernels (the ones with the oddly numbered second digit) may have structural or other changes that may cause problems with the other software on your system. If you are uncertain that you could resolve those sorts of problems in addition to the potential for there being other software errors, then don't use them.

4.1.2 Current Network tools.

The network tools are the programs that you use to configure Linux network devices. These tools allow you to assign addresses to devices and configure routes, for example.

Most modern Linux distributions are supplied with the network tools, so if you have installed from a distribution and haven't yet installed the network tools, then you should do so.

If you haven't installed from a distribution, then you will need to source and compile the tools yourself. This isn't difficult.

The network tools are now maintained by Bernd Eckenfels and are available at ftp.inka.de:

```
ftp://ftp.inka.de/pub/comp/Linux/networking/NetTools/
```

and are mirrored at ftp.uk.linux.uk.

```
ftp://ftp.uk.linux.org/pub/linux/Networking/PROGRAMS/NetTools/
```

Be sure to choose the version that is most appopriate for the kernel you wish to use and follow the instructions in the package to install.

To install and configure the version that is current at the time of this writing, you need do the following:

```
#
# cd /usr/src
# tar xvfz net-tools-1.32-alpha.tar.gz
# cd net-tools-1.32-alpha
# make config
# make
# make install
#
```

Additionally, if you intend configuring a firewall or using the IP masquerade feature, you will need the `ipfwadm` command. The latest version of IPFWADM may be obtained from ftp.xos.nl.

```
ftp:/ftp.xos.nl/pub/linux/ipfwadm
```

Again, there are a number of versions available. Be sure to pick the version that most closely matches the version of your kernel.

To install and configure the version current at the time of this writing, you need do the following:

```
#
# cd /usr/src
# tar xvfz ipfwadm-2.3.0.tar.gz
# cd ipfwadm-2.3.0
# make
# make install
#
```

4.1.3 Network Application Programs.

Network application programs are programs like `telnet` and `ftp`, and their respective server programs. David Holland, dholland@hcs.harvard.edu, now manages a distribution of the most common of these. You may obtain it from ftp.uk.linux.org.

```
ftp://ftp.uk.linux.org/pub/linux/Networking/base
```

To install and configure the version current at the time of this writing, you need do the following:

```
#
# cd /usr/src
# tar xvfz /pub/net/NetKit-B-0.08.tar.gz
# cd NetKit-B-0.08
# more README
# vi MCONFIG
# make
# make install
#
```

4.1.4 Addresses.

Internet Protocol Addresses are composed of four bytes. The convention is to write addresses in what is called **dotted decimal notation**. In this form, each byte is converted to a decimal number (0-255), dropping any leading zeroes, unless the number is zero, and written with each byte separated by a period. By convention, each interface of a host or router has an IP address. It is legal for the same IP address to be used on each port of a single machine in some circumstances, but usually each interface will have its own address.

Internet Protocol Networks are contiguous sequences of IP addresses. All addresses within a network have a number of digits within the address in common. The portion of the address that is common among all addresses within the network is called the **network portion** of the address. The remaining digits are called the **host portion**. The number of bits that are shared by all addresses within a network is called the netmask, and it is role of the netmask to determine which addresses belong to the network it is applied to and which don't. For example, consider the following:

```
-----------------  ---------------
Host Address       192.168.110.23
Network Mask       255.255.255.0
Network Portion    192.168.110.
Host portion                  .23
-----------------  ---------------
Network Address    192.168.110.0
Broadcast Address  192.168.110.255
-----------------  ---------------
```

Any address that is "bitwise ANDed" with its netmask will reveal the address of the network it belongs to. The network address is therefore always the lowest numbered address within the range of addresses on the network, and always has the host portion of the address coded all zeroes.

The broadcast address is a special address that every host on the network listens to in addition to its own unique address. This address is the one that datagrams are sent to if every host on the network is meant to receive it. Certain types of data, like routing information and warning messages, are transmitted to the broadcast address so that every host on the network can receive it simultaneously. There are two commonly used standards for what the broadcast address should be. The most widely accepted one is to use the highest possible address on the network as the broadcast address. In the example above, this would be `192.168.110.255`. For some reason, other sites have adopted the convention of using the network address as the broadcast address. In practice, it doesn't matter very much which you use, but you must make sure that every host on the network is configured with the same broadcast address.

For administrative reasons, some time early in the development of the IP protocol, some arbitrary groups of addresses were formed into networks and these networks were grouped into what are called **classes**. These classes provide a number of standard size networks that could be allocated. The ranges allocated are:

```
----------------------------------------------------------
| Network | Netmask        | Network Addresses            |
| Class   |                |                              |
----------------------------------------------------------
|    A    | 255.0.0.0      | 0.0.0.0     - 127.255.255.255 |
|    B    | 255.255.0.0    | 128.0.0.0   - 191.255.255.255 |
|    C    | 255.255.255.0  | 192.0.0.0   - 223.255.255.255 |
|Multicast| 240.0.0.0      | 224.0.0.0   - 239.255.255.255 |
----------------------------------------------------------
```

What addresses you should use depends on exactly what it is that you are doing. You may have to use a combination of the following activities to get all the addresses you need:

Installing a Linux machine on an existing IP network

If you wish to install a Linux machine onto an existing IP network, then you should contact whoever administers the network and ask them for the following information:

- Host IP Address,
- IP network address,
- IP broadcast address,
- IP netmask,
- Router address,

- Domain Name Server Address.

You should then configure your Linux network device with those details. You cannot make them up and expect that your configuration will work.

Building a brand-new network that will never connect to the Internet

If you are building a private network, and you never intend the network to be connected to the Internet, then you can choose whatever addresses you like. However, for safety and consistency reasons, there have been some IP network addresses that have been reserved specifically for this purpose. These are specified in RFC1597 and are as follows:

```
-----------------------------------------------------------
|         RESERVED PRIVATE NETWORK ALLOCATIONS            |
-----------------------------------------------------------
| Network | Netmask         | Network Addresses           |
| Class   |                 |                             |
-----------------------------------------------------------
|    A    | 255.0.0.0       | 10.0.0.0    - 10.255.255.255  |
|    B    | 255.255.0.0     | 172.16.0.0  - 172.31.255.255  |
|    C    | 255.255.255.0   | 192.168.0.0 - 192.168.255.255 |
-----------------------------------------------------------
```

You should first decide how large you want your network to be and then choose as many of the addresses as you require.

4.2 Where should I put the configuration commands?

There are a few different approaches to Linux system boot procedures. After the kernel boots, it always executes a program called "init," which then reads its configuration file called /etc/inittab and commences the boot process. There are a few different flavors of init, and it is this variation that is the largest cause of variation between distributions or machines.

Usually the /etc/inittab file contains an entry looking something like:

```
si::sysinit:/etc/init.d/boot
```

This line specifies the name of the shell script file that actually manages the boot sequence. This file is somewhat equivalent to the AUTOEXEC.BAT file in MS-DOS.

There are usually other scripts that are called by the boot script, and often the network is configured within one of many of these.

The following table may be used as a guide for your system:

```
-------------------------------------------------------------------------------
Distrib.  |Interface Config/Routing                  |Server Initialisation
-------------------------------------------------------------------------------
Debian    |/etc/init.d/network                       |/etc/init.d/netbase
          |                                          |/etc/init.d/netstd_init
          |                                          |/etc/init.d/netstd_nfs
          |                                          |/etc/init.d/netstd_misc
-------------------------------------------------------------------------------
Slackware |/etc/rc.d/rc.inet1                        |/etc/rc.d/rc.inet2
-------------------------------------------------------------------------------
RedHat    |/etc/sysconfig/network-scripts/ifup-<ifname>|/etc/rc.d/init.d/network
-------------------------------------------------------------------------------
```

Most modern distributions include a program that will allow you to configure many of the common network interfaces. If you have one of these, then you should see if it will do what you want before attempting a manual configuration.

```
-----------------------------------------
Distrib    | Network configuration program
-----------------------------------------
RedHat     | /sbin/netcfg
Slackware  | /sbin/netconfig
-----------------------------------------
```

4.3 Creating your network interfaces.

In many Unix operating systems, the network devices have appearances in the /dev directory. This is not so in Linux. In Linux the network devices are created dynamically in software and thus do not require device files to be present.

In the majority of cases, the network devices are automatically created by the device driver while it is initializing and has located your hardware. For example, the Ethernet device driver creates eth*0...n* interfaces sequentially as it locates your Ethernet hardware. The first Ethernet card found becomes eth0, the second eth1, and so on.

In some cases though, notably SLIP and PPP, the network devices are created through the action of some user program. The same sequential device numbering applies, but the devices are not created automatically at boot time. The reason for this is that unlike Ethernet devices, the number of active SLIP or PPP devices may vary during the uptime of the machine. These cases will be covered in more detail in later sections.

4.4 Configuring a network interface.

When you have all of the programs you need, and your address and network information, you can configure your network interfaces. When we talk about configuring a network interface, we are talking about the process of assigning the appropriate addresses to a network device and to setting appropriate values for other configurable parameters of a network device. The program most commonly used to do this is ifconfig, the **interface configure** command.

Typically, you would use a command similar to the following:

```
# ifconfig eth0 192.168.0.1 netmask 255.255.255.0 up
```

In this case, I'm configuring an Ethernet interface eth0 with the IP address 192.168.0.1 and a network mask of 255.255.255.0. The up that trails the command tells the interface that it should become active.

The kernel assumes certain defaults when configuring interfaces. For example, you may specify the network address and broadcast address for an interface, but if you don't, as in my example above, then the kernel will make reasonable guesses as to what they should be, based on the class of the IP address configured. In my example, the kernel would assume that it is a class-C network being configured on the interface and configure a network address of 192.168.0.0 and a broadcast address of 192.168.0.255 for the interface.

There are many other options to the ifconfig command. The most important of these are:

up
: this option activates an interface.

down
: this option deactivates an interface.

−arp
: this option enables or disables use of the address resolution protocol on this interface

−allmulti
: this option enables or disables the use of promiscuous mode on this interface. Promiscuous mode is where a device can be commanded to accept packets, even if they are not destined for this device. This is very important for programs like tcpdump and other packet snoopers.

mtu N
: this parameter allows you to set the *MTU* of this device.

netmask addr
: this parameter allows you to set the network mask of the network this device belongs to.

irq addr
: this parameter only works on certain types of hardware, but allows you to set the IRQ of the hardware of this device.

−broadcast *addr*
: this parameter allows you to enable and set the accepting of datagrams destined to the broadcast address, or to disable reception of these datagrams.

−pointopoint *addr*
: this parameter allows you to set the address of the machine at the remote end of a point-to-point link such as for SLIP or PPP.

hw <type> <addr>
: this parameter allows you to set the hardware address of certain types of network devices. This is not often useful for Ethernet, but is useful for other network types such as AX.25.

You may use the ifconfig command on any network interface. Some user programs such as pppd and dip automatically configure the network devices as they create them, so manual use of ifconfig is unnecessary.

4.5 Configuring your Name Resolver.

The **Name Resolver** is a part of the Linux standard library. Its prime function is to provide a service to convert human-friendly host names like `ftp.funet.fi` into machine friendly IP addresses such as `128.214.248.6`.

4.5.1 What's in a name ?

You will probably be familiar with the appearance of Internet host names, but may not understand how they are constructed, or deconstructed. Internet domain names are hierarchical in nature; that is, they have a tree-like structure. A **domain** is a family, or group of names. A **domain** may be broken down into **subdomain**. A **top-level domain** is a domain that is not a subdomain. The Top Level Domains are specified in RFC-920. Some examples of the most common top level domains are:

COM
: Commercial Organizations

EDU
: Educational Organizations

GOV
: Government Organizations

MIL
: Military Organizations

ORG
: Other organizations

Country Designator
: these are two-letter codes that represent a particular country.

Each of these top-level domains has subdomains. The top level domains based on country name are used next broken down into subdomains based on the `com`, `edu`, `gov`, `mil`, and `org` domains. So, for example, you end up with: `com.au` and `gov.au` for commercial and government organizations in Australia. For historical reasons most domains belonging to one of the non-country based, top-level domains are for organizations within the United States, although the United States also has its own country code, "`us`."

The next level of division usually represents the name of the organization. Further subdomains vary in nature, often the next level of subdomain is based on the departmental structure of the organization but it may be based on any criterion considered reasonable and meaningful by the network administrators for the organization.

The very left-most portion of the name is always the unique name assigned to the host machine and is called the **hostname**, the portion of the name to the right of the hostname is called the **domain name**, and the complete name is called the **Fully Qualified Domain Name** (FQDN).

To use my own email host as an example, the fully qualified domain name is `perf.no.itg.telstra.com.au`. This means that the host name is `perf` and the domain name is `no.itg.telstra.com.au`. The domain name is based on a top-level domain based on my country, Australia and as my email address belongs to a commercial organization, we have `.com` as the next-level domain. The name of the company is (was) `telstra`, and our internal naming structure is based on organizational structure, in my case, my machine belongs to the Information Technology Group, Network Operations section.

4.5.2 What information you will need.

You will need to know what domain your host's name belongs to. The name resolver software provides this name translation service by making requests to a **Domain Name Server**, so you will need to know the IP address of a local nameserver that you can use.

There are three files you need to edit, and I'll cover each of these in turn.

4.5.3 `/etc/resolv.conf`

The `/etc/resolv.conf` file is the main configuration file for the name resolver code. Its format is quite simple. It is a text file with one keyword per line. There are three keywords typically used, they are:

domain
: this keyword specifies the local domain name.

search

this keyword specifies a list of alternate domain names to search for a hostname

nameserver

this keyword, which may be used many times, specifies an IP address of a domain name server to query when resolving names

An example /etc/resolv.conf might look something like:

```
domain maths.wu.edu.au
search maths.wu.edu.au wu.edu.au
nameserver 192.168.10.1
nameserver 192.168.12.1
```

This example specifies that the default domain name to append to unqualified names (i.e., host names supplied without a domain) is maths.wu.edu.au, and that if the host is not found in that domain, to also try the wu.edu.au domain directly. Two name servers entry are supplied, each of which may be called upon by the name resolver code to resolve the name.

4.5.4 /etc/host.conf

The /etc/host.conf file is where you configure some items that govern the behaviors of the name resolver code. The format of this file is described in detail in the resolv+ manual page. In nearly all circumstances, the following example will work for you:

```
order hosts,bind
multi on
```

This configuration tells the name resolver to check the /etc/hosts file before attempting to query a nameserver and to return all valid addresses for a host found in the /etc/hosts file instead of just the first.

4.5.5 /etc/hosts

The /etc/hosts file is where you put the name and IP address of local hosts. If you place a host in this file then, you do not need to query the Domain Name Server to get its IP Address. The disadvantage of doing this is that you must keep this file up to date yourself if the IP address for that host changes. In a well managed system, the only host names that usually appear in this file are an entry for the loopback interface, and the local host's name.

```
# /etc/hosts
127.0.0.1       localhost loopback
192.168.0.1     this.host.name
```

You may specify more than one host name per line, as demonstrated by the first entry, which is a standard entry for the loopback interface.

4.6 Configuring your loopback interface.

The **loopback** interface is a special type of interface that allows you to make connections to yourself. There are various reasons why you might want to do this, for example, you may wish to test some network software without interfering with anybody else on your network. By convention the IP address 127.0.0.1 has been assigned specifically for loopback. So no matter what machine you go to, if you open a telnet connection to 127.0.0.1, you will always reach the local host.

Configuring the loopback interface is simple, and you should ensure you do.

```
# ifconfig lo 127.0.0.1
# route add -host 127.0.0.1 lo
```

We'll talk more about the route command in the next section.

4.7 Routing.

Routing is a big topic. It is easily possible to write large volumes of text about it. Most of you will have fairly simple routing requirements, some of you will not. I will cover some basic fundamentals of routing only. If you are interested in more detailed information, then I suggest that you refer to the references provided at the start of the document.

Let's start with a definition. What is IP routing? Here is one that I'm using:

> IP Routing is the process by which a host with multiple network connections decides where to deliver IP datagrams it has received.

It might be useful to illustrate this with an example. Imagine a typical office router. It might have a PPP link from the Internet, a number of Ethernet segments feeding the workstations, and another PPP link to another office. When the router receives a datagram on any of its network connections, routing is the mechanism that it uses to determine which port it should send the datagram to next. Simple hosts also need to route, all Internet hosts have two network devices, one is the loopback interface described above, and the other is the one it uses to talk to the rest of the network, perhaps an Ethernet, perhaps a PPP or SLIP serial port.

Okay, so how does routing work? Each host keeps a special list of routing rules, called a **routing table**. This table contains rows which typically contain at least at least three fields. The first is a destination address, the second is the name of the interface to which the datagram is to be routed, and the third is optionally the IP address of another machine which will carry the datagram on its next step through the network. In Linux, you can see this table by using the following command:

```
# cat /proc/net/route
```

The routing process is fairly simple: an incoming datagram is received, the destination address (who it is for) is examined and compared with each entry in the table. The entry which best matches that address is selected, and the datagram is forwarded to the specified interface. If the gateway field is filled, then the datagram is forwarded to that host via the specified interface; otherwise, the destination address is assumed to be on the network supported by the interface.

To manipulate this table, a special command is used. This command takes command line arguments and converts them into kernel system calls that request the kernel to add, delete or modify entries in the routing table. The command is called `route`'

A simple example. Imagine that you have an Ethernet network. You've been told it is a class-C network with an address of `192.168.1.0`. You've been supplied with an IP address of `192.168.1.10` for your use and have been told that `192.168.1.1` is a router connected to the Internet.

The first step is to configure the interface as described earlier. You would use a command like:

```
# ifconfig eth0 192.168.1.10 netmask 255.255.255.0 up
```

You now need to add an entry into the routing table to tell the kernel that datagrams for all hosts with addresses that match `192.168.1.*` should be sent to the Ethernet device. You would use a command similar to:

```
# route add -net 192.168.0.0 netmask 255.255.255.0 eth0
```

Note the use of the `-net` argument to tell the route program that this entry is a network route. Your other choice here is a `host` route which is a route that is specific to one IP address.

This route enables you to establish IP connections with all of the hosts on your Ethernet segment. But what about all of the IP hosts that aren't on your Ethernet segment?

It would be a very difficult job to have to add routes to every possible destination network, so there is a special trick that is used to simplify this task. The trick is called the **default route**. The `default` route matches every possible destination, but poorly, so that if any other entry exists which matches the required address, it will be used, instead of the `default` route. The idea of the `default` route is simply to enable you to say "and everything else should go here." In the example I've contrived you would use an entry like:

```
# route add default gw 192.168.1.1 eth0
```

The "`gw`" argument tells the route command that the next argument is the IP address, or name, of a gateway or router machine which all datagrams matching this entry should be directed on to for further routing.

So, your complete configuration would look like:

```
# ifconfig eth0 192.168.1.10 netmask 255.255.255.0 up
# route add -net 192.168.0.0 netmask 255.255.255.0 eth0
# route add default gw 192.168.1.1 eth0
```

If you take a close look at your network `rc` files, you will find that at least one of them looks very similar to this. This is a very common configuration.

Let's now look at a slightly more complicated routing configuration. Imagine that we are configuring the router that we looked at earlier, the one that supports the PPP link to the Internet, and the LAN segments feeding the workstations in the office. Let's imagine that the router has three Ethernet segments and one PPP link. Our routing configuration would look something like:

```
# route add 192.168.1.0 netmask 255.255.255.0 eth0
# route add 192.168.2.0 netmask 255.255.255.0 eth1
# route add 192.168.3.0 netmask 255.255.255.0 eth2
# route add default ppp0
```

Each of the workstations would use the simpler form presented above. Only the router needs to specify each of the network routes separately because for the workstations. The `default` route mechanism will capture all of them, letting the router worry about splitting them up appropriately. You may be wondering why the default route presented doesn't specify a `gw`. The reason for this is simple. Serial link protocols such as PPP and SLIP only ever have two hosts on their network, one at each end. To specify the host at the other end of the link as the gateway is pointless and redundant as there is no other choice, so you do not need to specify a gateway for these types of network connections. Other network types such as Ethernet, ArcNet or Token Ring do require that the gateway be specified, as these networks support large numbers of hosts.

4.7.1 So what does the `routed` program do?

The routing configuration described above is best suited to simple network arrangements where there is only ever a single possible path to destinations. When you have a more complex network arrangement, things get a little more complicated. Fortunately, for most of you this won't be an issue.

The big problem with **manual routing** or **static routing** as described above, is that if a machine or link fails in your network, then the only way that you can direct your datagrams another way, if another way exists, is by manually intervening and executing the appopriate commands. Naturally, this is clumsy, slow, impractical, and hazard prone. Various techniques have been developed to automatically adjust routing tables in the event of network failures where there are alternate routes, all of these techniques are loosely grouped by the term **dynamic routing protocols**.

You may have heard of some of the more common dynamic routing protocols. The most common are probably **RIP (Routing Information Protocol)** and **OSPF (Open Shortest Path First Protocol)**.

The Routing Information Protocol is very common on small networks, such as small-medium sized corporate networks, or building networks. OSPF is more modern and more capable at handling large network configurations, and better suited to environments where there are a large number of possible paths through the network. Common implementations of these protocols are: `routed` (RIP), and `gated` (RIP, OSPF and others). The `routed` program is normally supplied with your Linux distribution or is included in the NetKit package, described above.

An example of where and how you might use a dynamic routing protocol might look something like the following:

```
    192.168.1.0 /                          192.168.2.0 /
       255.255.255.0                          255.255.255.0
     -                                     -
     |                                     |
     |   /-----\                 /-----\   |
     |   |     |ppp0   //    ppp0|     |   |
eth0 |---|  A  |------//---------|  B  |---| eth0
     |   |     |     //          |     |   |
     |   \-----/                 \-----/   |
     |      \ ppp1             ppp1 /      |
     -       \                     /       -
              \                   /
               \                 /
                \               /
                 \             /
                  \           /
                   \         /
                    \       /
                     \     /
                  ppp0\   /ppp1
                      /-----\
                      |     |
                      |  C  |
                      |     |
```

```
          \-----/
              |eth0
              |
          |---------|
          192.168.3.0 /
              255.255.255.0
```

We have three routers A, B and C. Each supports one Ethernet segment with a Class C IP network (netmask 255.255.255.0). Each router also has a PPP link to each of the other routers. The network forms a triangle.

It should be clear from the diagram and the text above, that the routing table at router A could look like:

```
# route add -net 192.168.1.0 netmask 255.255.255.0 eth0
# route add -net 192.168.2.0 netmask 255.255.255.0 ppp0
# route add -net 192.168.3.0 netmask 255.255.255.0 ppp1
```

This would work just fine until the link between router A and B fails. If that link fails, then, with the routing entry shown above, hosts on the Ethernet segment of A could not reach hosts on the Ethernet segment on B because their datagram would be directed to router A's `ppp0` link, which is broken. They could still continue to talk to hosts on the Ethernet segment of C, and hosts on the C's Ethernet segment could still talk to hosts on B's Ethernet segment, because the link between B and C is still intact.

But wait. If A can talk to C, and C can still talk to B, why shouldn't A route its datagrams for B via C, and let C send them to B? This is exactly the sort of problem that dynamic routing protocols like RIP are designed to solve. If each of the routers A, B and C run a routing daemon, then their routing tables would be automatically adjusted to reflect the new state of the network, should any one of the links in the network fail. To configure such a network is simple. At each router you need only do two things. In this case for Router A:

```
# route add -net 192.168.1.0 netmask 255.255.255.0 eth0
# /usr/sbin/routed
```

The `routed` routing daemon automatically finds all active network ports when it starts, and sends and listens for messages on each of the network devices to allow it to determine and update the routing table on the host.

This has been a very brief explanation of dynamic routing, and where you would use it. If you want more information then you should refer to the suggested references that are listed at the top of the document.

The important points related to dynamic routing are:

1. You only need to run a dynamic routing protocol daemon when your Linux machine has the possibility of selecting multiple possible routes to a destination.
2. The dynamic routing daemon will automatically modify your routing table to adjust to changes in your network.
3. RIP is suited to small-to-medium-sized networks.

4.8 Configuring your network servers and services.

Network servers and services are those programs that allow a remote user to make use of your Linux machine. The remote user establishes a network connection to your machine and the server program, or network daemon. Listening on that port accepts the connection and executes. There are two ways that network daemons may operate. Both are commonly employed in practice. The two ways are:

stand-alone

the network daemon program listens on the designated network port and when an incoming connection is made it manages the network connection itself to provide the service.

slave to the `inetd` server

the `inetd` server is a special network daemon program that specializes in managing incoming network connections. It has a configuration file which tells it what program needs to be run when an incoming connection is received on a particular combination of TCP or UDP and service port. The ports are described in another file that we will talk about soon.

There are two important files that we need to configure. They are the `/etc/services` file which assigns names to port numbers and the `/etc/inetd.conf` file which is the configuration file for the `inetd` network daemon.

4.8.1 /etc/services

The /etc/services file is a simple database that associates a human-friendly name to a machine-friendly service port. Its format is quite simple. The file is a text file with each line representing and entry in the database. Each entry is comprised of three fields separated by any number of white space (tab or space) characters. The fields are:

```
name      port/protocol      aliases    # comment
```

name a single-word name that represents the service being described.

port/protocol

this field is split into two subfields.

port

a number that specifies the port number that the named service will be available on. Most of the common services have assigned service numbers. These are described in RFC-1340.

protocol

this subfield may be set to either TCP or UDP.

It is important to note that an entry of 18/tcp is very different from an entry of 18/udp, and that there is no technical reason why the same service needs to exist on both. Normally, common sense prevails, and it is only if a particular service is available via both tcp and udp that you will see an entry for both.

aliases

other names that may be used to refer to this service entry.

Any text appearing in a line after a '#' character is ignored and treated as a comment.

An example /etc/services file. All modern Linux distributions provide a good /etc/services file. Just in case you happen to be building a machine from the ground up, here is a copy of the /etc/services file supplied with the Debian (http://www.debian.org/) distribution.

```
# /etc/services:
# $Id: NET-3-HOWTO.tex,v 1.10 1998/03/07 22:28:24 rak Exp $
#
# Network services, Internet style
#
# Note that it is presently the policy of IANA to assign a single well-known
# port number for both TCP and UDP; hence, most entries here have two entries
# even if the protocol doesn't support UDP operations.
# Updated from RFC 1340, ''Assigned Numbers'' (July 1992).  Not all ports
# are included, only the more common ones.

tcpmux          1/tcp                           # TCP port service multiplexer
echo            7/tcp
echo            7/udp
discard         9/tcp           sink null
discard         9/udp           sink null
systat          11/tcp          users
daytime         13/tcp
daytime         13/udp
netstat         15/tcp
qotd            17/tcp          quote
msp             18/tcp                          # message send protocol
msp             18/udp                          # message send protocol
chargen         19/tcp          ttytst source
chargen         19/udp          ttytst source
ftp-data        20/tcp
ftp             21/tcp
ssh             22/tcp                          # SSH Remote Login Protocol
ssh             22/udp                          # SSH Remote Login Protocol
telnet          23/tcp
# 24 - private
```

```
smtp            25/tcp          mail
# 26 - unassigned
time            37/tcp          timserver
time            37/udp          timserver
rlp             39/udp          resource        # resource location
nameserver      42/tcp          name            # IEN 116
whois           43/tcp          nicname
re-mail-ck      50/tcp                          # Remote Mail Checking Protocol
re-mail-ck      50/udp                          # Remote Mail Checking Protocol
domain          53/tcp          nameserver      # name-domain server
domain          53/udp          nameserver
mtp             57/tcp                          # deprecated
bootps          67/tcp                          # BOOTP server
bootps          67/udp
bootpc          68/tcp                          # BOOTP client
bootpc          68/udp
tftp            69/udp
gopher          70/tcp                          # Internet Gopher
gopher          70/udp
rje             77/tcp          netrjs
finger          79/tcp
www             80/tcp          http            # WorldWideWeb HTTP
www             80/udp                          # HyperText Transfer Protocol
link            87/tcp          ttylink
kerberos        88/tcp          kerberos5 krb5  # Kerberos v5
kerberos        88/udp          kerberos5 krb5  # Kerberos v5
supdup          95/tcp
# 100 - reserved
hostnames       101/tcp         hostname        # usually from sri-nic
iso-tsap        102/tcp         tsap            # part of ISODE.
csnet-ns        105/tcp         cso-ns          # also used by CSO name server
csnet-ns        105/udp         cso-ns
rtelnet         107/tcp                         # Remote Telnet
rtelnet         107/udp
pop-2           109/tcp         postoffice      # POP version 2
pop-2           109/udp
pop-3           110/tcp                         # POP version 3
pop-3           110/udp
sunrpc          111/tcp         portmapper      # RPC 4.0 portmapper TCP
sunrpc          111/udp         portmapper      # RPC 4.0 portmapper UDP
auth            113/tcp         authentication tap ident
sftp            115/tcp
uucp-path       117/tcp
nntp            119/tcp         readnews untp   # USENET News Transfer Protocol
ntp             123/tcp
ntp             123/udp                         # Network Time Protocol
netbios-ns      137/tcp                         # NETBIOS Name Service
netbios-ns      137/udp
netbios-dgm     138/tcp                         # NETBIOS Datagram Service
netbios-dgm     138/udp
netbios-ssn     139/tcp                         # NETBIOS session service
netbios-ssn     139/udp
imap2           143/tcp                         # Interim Mail Access Proto v2
imap2           143/udp
snmp            161/udp                         # Simple Net Mgmt Proto
snmp-trap       162/udp         snmptrap        # Traps for SNMP
cmip-man        163/tcp                         # ISO mgmt over IP (CMOT)
cmip-man        163/udp
```

```
cmip-agent      164/tcp
cmip-agent      164/udp
xdmcp           177/tcp                         # X Display Mgr. Control Proto
xdmcp           177/udp
nextstep        178/tcp         NeXTStep NextStep       # NeXTStep window
nextstep        178/udp         NeXTStep NextStep       # server
bgp             179/tcp                         # Border Gateway Proto.
bgp             179/udp
prospero        191/tcp                         # Cliff Neuman's Prospero
prospero        191/udp
irc             194/tcp                         # Internet Relay Chat
irc             194/udp
smux            199/tcp                         # SNMP Unix Multiplexer
smux            199/udp
at-rtmp         201/tcp                         # AppleTalk routing
at-rtmp         201/udp
at-nbp          202/tcp                         # AppleTalk name binding
at-nbp          202/udp
at-echo         204/tcp                         # AppleTalk echo
at-echo         204/udp
at-zis          206/tcp                         # AppleTalk zone information
at-zis          206/udp
z3950           210/tcp         wais            # NISO Z39.50 database
z3950           210/udp         wais
ipx             213/tcp                         # IPX
ipx             213/udp
imap3           220/tcp                         # Interactive Mail Access
imap3           220/udp                         # Protocol v3
ulistserv       372/tcp                         # UNIX Listserv
ulistserv       372/udp
#
# UNIX specific services
#
exec            512/tcp
biff            512/udp         comsat
login           513/tcp
who             513/udp         whod
shell           514/tcp         cmd             # no passwords used
syslog          514/udp
printer         515/tcp         spooler         # line printer spooler
talk            517/udp
ntalk           518/udp
route           520/udp         router routed   # RIP
timed           525/udp         timeserver
tempo           526/tcp         newdate
courier         530/tcp         rpc
conference      531/tcp         chat
netnews         532/tcp         readnews
netwall         533/udp                         # -for emergency broadcasts
uucp            540/tcp         uucpd           # uucp daemon
remotefs        556/tcp         rfs_server rfs  # Brunhoff remote filesystem
klogin          543/tcp                         # Kerberized 'rlogin' (v5)
kshell          544/tcp         krcmd           # Kerberized 'rsh' (v5)
kerberos-adm    749/tcp                         # Kerberos 'kadmin' (v5)
#
webster         765/tcp                         # Network dictionary
webster         765/udp
#
```

```
# From ''Assigned Numbers'':
#
#> The Registered Ports are not controlled by the IANA and on most systems
#> can be used by ordinary user processes or programs executed by ordinary
#> users.
#
#> Ports are used in the TCP [45,106] to name the ends of logical
#> connections which carry long term conversations.  For the purpose of
#> providing services to unknown callers, a service contact port is
#> defined.  This list specifies the port used by the server process as its
#> contact port.  While the IANA can not control uses of these ports it
#> does register or list uses of these ports as a convenience to the
#> community.
#
ingreslock      1524/tcp
ingreslock      1524/udp
prospero-np     1525/tcp                    # Prospero non-privileged
prospero-np     1525/udp
rfe             5002/tcp                    # Radio Free Ethernet
rfe             5002/udp                    # Actually uses UDP only
bbs             7000/tcp                    # BBS service
#
#
# Kerberos (Project Athena/MIT) services
# Note that these are for Kerberos v4, and are unofficial.  Sites running
# v4 should uncomment these and comment out the v5 entries above.
#
kerberos4       750/udp         kdc         # Kerberos (server) udp
kerberos4       750/tcp         kdc         # Kerberos (server) tcp
kerberos_master 751/udp                     # Kerberos authentication
kerberos_master 751/tcp                     # Kerberos authentication
passwd_server   752/udp                     # Kerberos passwd server
krb_prop        754/tcp                     # Kerberos slave propagation
krbupdate       760/tcp         kreg        # Kerberos registration
kpasswd         761/tcp         kpwd        # Kerberos "passwd"
kpop            1109/tcp                    # Pop with Kerberos
knetd           2053/tcp                    # Kerberos de-multiplexor
zephyr-srv      2102/udp                    # Zephyr server
zephyr-clt      2103/udp                    # Zephyr serv-hm connection
zephyr-hm       2104/udp                    # Zephyr hostmanager
eklogin         2105/tcp                    # Kerberos encrypted rlogin
#
# Unofficial but necessary (for NetBSD) services
#
supfilesrv      871/tcp                     # SUP server
supfiledbg      1127/tcp                    # SUP debugging
#
# Datagram Delivery Protocol services
#
rtmp            1/ddp                       # Routing Table Maintenance Protocol
nbp             2/ddp                       # Name Binding Protocol
echo            4/ddp                       # AppleTalk Echo Protocol
zip             6/ddp                       # Zone Information Protocol
#
# Debian GNU/Linux services
rmtcfg          1236/tcp                    # Gracilis Packeten remote config server
xtel            1313/tcp                    # french minitel
cfinger         2003/tcp                    # GNU Finger
```

```
postgres        4321/tcp                   # POSTGRES
mandelspawn     9359/udp        mandelbrot      # network mandelbrot

# Local services
```

4.8.2 /etc/inetd.conf

The /etc/inetd.conf file is the configuration file for the inetd server daemon. Its function is to tell inetd what to do when it receives a connection request for a particular service. For each service that you wish to accept connections for, you must tell inetd what network server daemon to run, and how to run it.

Its format is also fairly simple. It is a text file with each line describing a service that you wish to provide. Any text in a line following a '#' is ignored and considered a comment. Each line contains seven fields separated by any number of white space (tab or space) characters. The general format is as follows:

```
service  socket_type  proto  flags  user  server_path  server_args
```

service
: is the service relevant to this configuration as taken from the /etc/services file.

socket_type
: this field describes the type of socket that this entry will consider relevant. Allowable values are: stream, dgram, raw, rdm, or seqpacket. This is a little technical in nature, but as a rule of thumb nearly all tcp based services use stream and nearly all udp based services use dgram. It is only very special types of server daemons that would use any of the other values.

proto
: the protocol to considered valid for this entry. This should match the appropriate entry in the /etc/services file and will typically be either tcp or udp. Sun RPC (Remote Procedure Call) based servers will use rpc/tcp or rpc/udp.

flags
: there are really only two possible settings for this field. This field setting tells inetd whether the network server program frees the socket after it has been started, and therefore whether inetd can start another one on the next connection request, or whether inetd should wait and assume that any server daemon already running will handle the new connection request. Again, this is a little tricky to work out, but as a rule of thumb, all tcp servers should have this entry set to nowait, and most udp servers should have this entry set to wait. Be warned that there are some notable exceptions to this, so let the example guide you if you are not sure.

user
: this field describes which user account from /etc/passwd will be set as the owner of the network daemon when it is started. This is often useful if you want to safeguard against security risks. You can set the user of an entry to the nobody user so that if the network server security is breached the possible damage is minimized. Typically this field is set to root though, because many servers require root privileges in order to function correctly.

server_path
: this field is pathname to the actual server program to execute for this entry.

server_args
: this field comprises the rest of the line and is optional. This field is where you place any command line arguments that you wish to pass to the server daemon program when it is launched.

An example /etc/inetd.conf As for the /etc/services file, all modern distributions include a good /etc/inetd.conf file for you to work with. Here, for completeness, is the /etc/inetd.conf file from the Debian (http://www.debian.org) distribution.

```
# /etc/inetd.conf:  see inetd(8) for further informations.
#
# Internet server configuration database
#
#
# Modified for Debian by Peter Tobias <tobias@et-inf.fho-emden.de>
#
# <service_name> <sock_type> <proto> <flags> <user> <server_path> <args>
```

```
#
# Internal services
#
#echo          stream  tcp     nowait  root    internal
#echo          dgram   udp     wait    root    internal
discard        stream  tcp     nowait  root    internal
discard        dgram   udp     wait    root    internal
daytime        stream  tcp     nowait  root    internal
daytime        dgram   udp     wait    root    internal
#chargen       stream  tcp     nowait  root    internal
#chargen       dgram   udp     wait    root    internal
time           stream  tcp     nowait  root    internal
time           dgram   udp     wait    root    internal
#
# These are standard services.
#
telnet  stream  tcp     nowait  root    /usr/sbin/tcpd  /usr/sbin/in.telnetd
ftp     stream  tcp     nowait  root    /usr/sbin/tcpd  /usr/sbin/in.ftpd
#fsp    dgram   udp     wait    root    /usr/sbin/tcpd  /usr/sbin/in.fspd
#
# Shell, login, exec and talk are BSD protocols.
#
shell   stream  tcp     nowait  root    /usr/sbin/tcpd  /usr/sbin/in.rshd
login   stream  tcp     nowait  root    /usr/sbin/tcpd  /usr/sbin/in.rlogind
#exec   stream  tcp     nowait  root    /usr/sbin/tcpd  /usr/sbin/in.rexecd
talk    dgram   udp     wait    root    /usr/sbin/tcpd  /usr/sbin/in.talkd
ntalk   dgram   udp     wait    root    /usr/sbin/tcpd  /usr/sbin/in.ntalkd
#
# Mail, news and uucp services.
#
smtp    stream  tcp     nowait  root    /usr/sbin/tcpd  /usr/sbin/in.smtpd
#nntp   stream  tcp     nowait  news    /usr/sbin/tcpd  /usr/sbin/in.nntpd
#uucp   stream  tcp     nowait  uucp    /usr/sbin/tcpd  /usr/lib/uucp/uucico
#comsat dgram   udp     wait    root    /usr/sbin/tcpd  /usr/sbin/in.comsat
#
# Pop et al
#
#pop-2  stream  tcp     nowait  root    /usr/sbin/tcpd  /usr/sbin/in.pop2d
#pop-3  stream  tcp     nowait  root    /usr/sbin/tcpd  /usr/sbin/in.pop3d
#
# 'cfinger' is for the GNU finger server available for Debian.  (NOTE: The
# current implementation of the 'finger' daemon allows it to be run as 'root'.)
#
#cfinger stream tcp     nowait  root    /usr/sbin/tcpd  /usr/sbin/in.cfingerd
#finger stream  tcp     nowait  root    /usr/sbin/tcpd  /usr/sbin/in.fingerd
#netstat        stream  tcp     nowait  nobody  /usr/sbin/tcpd  /bin/netstat
#systat stream  tcp     nowait  nobody  /usr/sbin/tcpd  /bin/ps -auwwx
#
# Tftp service is provided primarily for booting.  Most sites
# run this only on machines acting as "boot servers."
#
#tftp   dgram   udp     wait    nobody  /usr/sbin/tcpd  /usr/sbin/in.tftpd
#tftp   dgram   udp     wait    nobody  /usr/sbin/tcpd  /usr/sbin/in.tftpd /boot
#bootps dgram   udp     wait    root    /usr/sbin/bootpd        \
 bootpd -i -t 120
#
# Kerberos authenticated services (these probably need to be corrected)
#
```

```
#klogin         stream  tcp     nowait  root    /usr/sbin/tcpd  \
/usr/sbin/in.rlogind -k
#eklogin        stream  tcp     nowait  root    /usr/sbin/tcpd  \
/usr/sbin/in.rlogind -k -x
#kshell         stream  tcp     nowait  root    /usr/sbin/tcpd  \
/usr/sbin/in.rshd -k
#
# Services run ONLY on the Kerberos server (these probably need to be corrected)
#
#krbupdate      stream tcp      nowait  root    /usr/sbin/tcpd  \
/usr/sbin/registerd
#kpasswd        stream  tcp     nowait  root    /usr/sbin/tcpd  \
/usr/sbin/kpasswdd
#
# RPC based services
#
#mountd/1       dgram   rpc/udp wait    root    /usr/sbin/tcpd  \
/usr/sbin/rpc.mountd
#rstatd/1-3     dgram   rpc/udp wait    root    /usr/sbin/tcpd  \
/usr/sbin/rpc.rstatd
#rusersd/2-3    dgram   rpc/udp wait    root    /usr/sbin/tcpd  \
/usr/sbin/rpc.rusersd
#walld/1        dgram   rpc/udp wait    root    /usr/sbin/tcpd  \
/usr/sbin/rpc.rwalld
#
# End of inetd.conf.
ident           stream  tcp     nowait  nobody  /usr/sbin/identd   \
     identd -i
```

4.9 Miscellaneous network related configuration files.

There are a number of miscellaneous files related to network configuration under Linux that you might be interested in. You may never have to modify these files, but they are worth describing so you know what they contain and what they are for.

4.9.1 /etc/protocols

The /etc/protocols file is a database that maps protocol ID numbers against protocol names. The file allows programmers to specify protocols by name in their programs and also by some programs such as tcpdump to allow them to display names instead of numbers in their output. The general syntax of the file is:

```
protocolname  number  aliases
```

The /etc/protocols file supplied with the *Debian* (http://www.debian.org/) distribution is as follows:

```
# /etc/protocols:
# $Id: NET-3-HOWTO.tex,v 1.10 1998/03/07 22:28:24 rak Exp $
#
# Internet (IP) protocols
#
#       from: @(#)protocols     5.1 (Berkeley) 4/17/89
#
# Updated for NetBSD based on RFC 1340, Assigned Numbers (July 1992).

ip      0       IP              # internet protocol, pseudo protocol number
icmp    1       ICMP            # internet control message protocol
igmp    2       IGMP            # Internet Group Management
ggp     3       GGP             # gateway-gateway protocol
ipencap 4       IP-ENCAP        # IP encapsulated in IP (officially ''IP'')
st      5       ST              # ST datagram mode
```

```
tcp      6       TCP              # transmission control protocol
egp      8       EGP              # exterior gateway protocol
pup      12      PUP              # PARC universal packet protocol
udp      17      UDP              # user datagram protocol
hmp      20      HMP              # host monitoring protocol
xns-idp 22       XNS-IDP          # Xerox NS IDP
rdp      27      RDP              # "reliable datagram" protocol
iso-tp4 29       ISO-TP4          # ISO Transport Protocol class 4
xtp      36      XTP              # Xpress Tranfer Protocol
ddp      37      DDP              # Datagram Delivery Protocol
idpr-cmtp        39      IDPR-CMTP        # IDPR Control Message Transport
rspf     73      RSPF             # Radio Shortest Path First.
vmtp     81      VMTP             # Versatile Message Transport
ospf     89      OSPFIGP          # Open Shortest Path First IGP
ipip     94      IPIP             # Yet Another IP encapsulation
encap    98      ENCAP            # Yet Another IP encapsulation
```

4.9.2 /etc/networks

The /etc/networks file has a similar function to that of the /etc/hosts file. It provides a simple database of network names against network addresses. Its format differs in that there may be only two fields per line, and that the fields are coded as:

```
# networkname networkaddress
```

An example might look like:

```
loopnet    127.0.0.0
localnet   192.168.0.0
amprnet    44.0.0.0
```

When you use commands like the route command, if a destination is a network, and that network has an entry in the /etc/networks file then the route command will display that network name instead of its address.

4.10 Network Security and access control.

Let me start this section by warning you that securing your machine and and network against malicious attack is a complex art. I do not consider myself an expert in this field at all, and while the following mechanisms I describe will help, if you are serious about security, then I recommend that you do some research of your own into the subject. There are many good references on the Internet relating to the subject.

An important rule of thumb is: **"Don't run servers you don't intend to use."**

Many distributions come configured with all sorts of services configured and automatically started. To ensure even a minimum level of safety, you should go through your /etc/inetd.conf file and comment out (*place a' #' at the start of the line*) any entries for services you don't intend to use. Good candidates are shell, login, exec, uucp, ftp, and informational services like finger, netstat and systat.

There are all sorts of security and access control mechanisms, I'll describe the most elementary of them.

4.10.1 /etc/ftpusers

The /etc/ftpusers file is a simple mechanism that allows you to deny certain users from logging into your machine via FTP. The /etc/ftpusers is read by the FTP daemon (ftpd) when an incoming FTP connection is received. The file is a simple list of those users who are disallowed from logging in. It might looks something like:

```
# /etc/ftpusers - users not allowed to login via ftp
root
uucp
bin
mail
```

4.10.2 /etc/securetty

The /etc/securetty file allows you to specify which tty devices root is allowed to login on. The /etc/securetty file is read by the login program (usually /bin/login). Its format is a list of the tty device names. root login is disallowed on all other devices.

```
# /etc/securetty - tty's on which root is allowed to login
tty1
tty2
tty3
tty4
```

4.10.3 The tcpd host access control mechanism.

The tcpd program you will have seen listed in the same /etc/inetd.conf provides logging and access control mechanisms to services it is configured to protect.

When it is invoked by inetd, it reads two files that contain access rules and either allows or denies access to the server it is protecting accordingly.

It searches the rules files until the first match is found. If no match is found, then it assumes that access should be allowed to anyone. The files it searches in sequence are: /etc/hosts.allow, /etc/hosts.deny. I'll describe each of these in turn. For a complete description of this facility, you should refer to the appopriate manual pages (hosts_access(5) is a good starting point).

/etc/hosts.allow The /etc/hosts.allow file is a configuration file of the /usr/sbin/tcpd program. The hosts.allow file contains rules describing which hosts are allowed access to a service on your machine.

The file format is quite simple:

```
# /etc/hosts.allow
#
# <service list>: <host list> [: command]
```

service list

is a comma delimited list of server names that this rule applies to. Example server names are: ftpd, telnetd, and fingerd.

host list

is a comma delimited list of host names. You may also use IP addresses here. You may additionally specify hostnames or addresses using wildcard characters to match groups of hosts. Examples include: gw.vk2ktj.ampr.org to match a specific host, .uts.edu.au to match any hostname ending in that string, 44. to match any IP address commencing with those digits. There are some special tokens to simplify configuration, some of these are: ALL matches every host, LOCAL matches any host whose name does not contain a '.'; i.e., is in the same domain as your machine, and PARANOID matches any host whose name does not match its address (**name spoofing**). There is one last token that is also useful. The EXCEPT token allows you to provide a list with exceptions. This will be covered in an example later.

command

is an optional parameter. This parameter is the full pathname of a command that would be executed every time this rule is matched. It could, for example, run a command that would attempt to identify who is logged onto the connecting host, or to generate a mail message or some other warning to a system administrator that someone is attempting to connect. There are a number of expansions that may be included. Some common examples are: %h expands to the name of the connecting host or address if it doesn't have a name, %d, the daemon name being called.

An example:

```
# /etc/hosts.allow
#
# Allow mail to anyone
in.smtpd: ALL
# All telnet and ftp to only hosts within my domain and my host at home.
telnetd, ftpd: LOCAL, myhost.athome.org.au
# Allow finger to anyone but keep a record of who they are.
fingerd: ALL: (finger @%h | mail -s "finger from %h" root)
```

`/etc/hosts.deny` The `/etc/hosts.deny` file is a configuration file of the `/usr/sbin/tcpd` program. The `/etc/hosts.deny` file contains rules describing which hosts are disallowed access to a service on your machine.

A simple, sample script would look something like this:

```
# /etc/hosts.deny
#
# Disallow all hosts with suspect hostnames
ALL: PARANOID
#
# Disallow all hosts.
ALL: ALL
```

The `PARANOID` entry is really redundant because the other entry traps everything in any case. Either of these entries would make a reasonable default depending on your particular requirement.

Having an `ALL: ALL` default in the `/etc/hosts.deny` and then specifically enabling on those services and hosts that you want in the `/etc/hosts.allow` file is the safest configuration.

4.10.4 `/etc/hosts.equiv`

The `/etc/hosts.equiv` file is used to grant certain hosts and users access rights to accounts on your machine without having to supply a password. This is useful in a secure environment where you control all machines, but is a security hazard otherwise. Your machine is only as secure as the least secure of the trusted hosts. To maximize security, don't use this mechanism and encourage your users not to use the `.rhosts` file as well.

4.10.5 Configure your `ftp` daemon properly.

Many sites will be interested in running an anonymous FTP server to allow other people to upload and download files without requiring a specific user ID. If you decide to offer this facility, make sure that you configure the FTP daemon properly for anonymous access. Most manual pages for `ftpd(8)` describe in some length how to go about this. You should always follow these instructions. An important hint is to not use a copy of your `/etc/passwd` file in the anonymous account `/etc` directory. Make sure that you strip out all account details except those that you must have; otherwise, you will be vulnerable to brute force password cracking techniques.

4.10.6 Network Firewalling.

Not allowing datagrams to even reach your machine or servers is an excellent means of security. This is covered in depth in the Firewall HOWTO (page 902).

4.10.7 Other suggestions.

Here are some other, potentially religious suggestions for you to consider.

sendmail despite its popularity, the `sendmail` daemon appears with frightening regularity on security warning announcements. Its up to you, but I choose not to run it.

NFS and other Sun RPC services be wary of these. There are all sorts of possible exploits for these services. It is difficult finding an option to services like NFS, but if you configure them, make sure you are careful with who you allow mount rights to.

5 Network Technology Specific Information.

The following subsections are specific to particular network technologies. The information contained in these sections does not necessarily apply to any other type of network technology.

5.1 ArcNet

ArcNet device names are arc0s, arc1e, arc2e etc. The first card detected by the kernel is assigned eth0 and the rest are assigned sequentially in the order they are detected. The letter at the end signifies whether you've selected Ethernet encapsulation packet format or RFC1051 packet format.

Kernel Compile Options:

```
Network device support  --->
    [*] Network device support
    <*> ARCnet support
    [ ]   Enable arc0e (ARCnet "Ether-Encap" packet format)
    [ ]   Enable arc0s (ARCnet RFC1051 packet format)
```

Once you have your kernel properly built to support your Ethernet card, then its configuration is easy.

Typically you would use something like:

```
# ifconfig arc0e 192.168.0.1 netmask 255.255.255.0 up
# route add 192.168.0.0 netmask 255.255.255.0 arc0e
```

Please refer to the /usr/src/linux/Documentation/networking/arcnet-hardware.txt file for further information.

Arcnet support was developed by Avery Pennarun, apenwarr@foxnet.net.

5.2 AppleTalk (AF_APPLETALK)

The AppleTalk support has no special device names as it uses existing network devices.

Kernel Compile Options:

```
Networking options  --->
    <*> Appletalk DDP
```

Appletalk support allows your Linux machine to internetwork with Apple networks. An important use for this is to share resources such as printers and disks between both your Linux and Apple computers. Additional software is required, and this is called **netatalk**. Wesley Craig, netatalk@umich.edu, represents a team called the "Research Unix Group" at the University of Michigan, and they have produced the netatalk package that implements the Appletalk protocol stack and some useful utilities. The netatalk package will either have been supplied with your Linux distribution, or you will have to FTP it from its home site:

```
ftp://terminator.rs.itd.umich.edu/unix/netatalk/
```

To build and install the package, do something like:

```
# cd /usr/src
# tar xvfz .../netatalk-1.4b2.tar.Z
- You may want to edit the 'Makefile' at this point, specifically to change
  the DESTDIR variable which defines where the files will be installed later.
  The default of /usr/local/atalk is fairly safe.
# make
- as root:
# make install
```

5.2.1 Configuring the Appletalk software.

The first thing you need to do to make it all work is add some new entries to your /etc/services file. The entries to add are:

```
rtmp    1/ddp   # Routing Table Maintenance Protocol
nbp     2/ddp   # Name Binding Protocol
echo    4/ddp   # AppleTalk Echo Protocol
zip     6/ddp   # Zone Information Protocol
```

The next step is to create the Appletalk configuration files in the /usr/local/atalk/etc directory (or wherever you installed the package).

The first file to create is the /usr/local/atalk/etc/atalkd.conf file. Initially this file needs only one line that gives the name of the network device that supports the network that your Apple machines are on:

```
eth0
```

The Appletalk daemon program will add extra details after it is run.

5.2.2 Exporting Linux file systems via Appletalk.

You can export file systems from your Linux machine to the network so that Apple machines on the network can share them.

To do this, you must configure the /usr/local/atalk/etc/AppleVolumes.system file. There is another configuration file called /usr/local/atalk/etc/AppleVolumes.default which has exactly the same format and describes which file system users connecting with "guest" privileges will receive.

Full details on how to configure these files and what the various options are can be found in the afpd manual page.

A simple example might look like:

```
/tmp Scratch
/home/ftp/pub "Public Area"
```

Which would export your /tmp filesystem as AppleShare Volume "Scratch" and your FTP public directory as AppleShare Volume "Public Area." The volume names are not mandatory; the daemon will choose some for you, but it won't hurt to specify them, anyway.

5.2.3 Sharing your Linux printer across an Appletalk network.

You can share your Linux printer with your Apple machines quite simply. You need to run the papd program, which is the Appletalk Printer Access Protocol daemon. When you run this program it accepts requests from your Apple machines, and spools the print job to your local line printer daemon for printing.

You need to edit the /usr/local/atalk/etc/papd.conf file to configure the daemon. The syntax of this file is the same as that of your usual /etc/printcap file. The name you give to the definition is registered with the Appletalk naming protocol, NBP.

A sample configuration might look like:

```
TricWriter:\
    :pr=lp:op=cg:
```

which would make a printer named "TricWriter" available to your Appletalk network, and all accepted jobs would be printed to the Linux printer lp (as defined in the /etc/printcap file) using lpd. The entry "op=cg" says that the Linux user "cg" is the operator of the printer.

5.2.4 Starting the Appletalk software.

Okay, you should now be ready to test this basic configuration. There is a rc.atalk file supplied with the netatalk package that should work okay for you, so all you should have to do is:

```
# /usr/local/atalk/etc/rc.atalk
```

and all should start up and run okay. You should see no error messages, and the software will send messages to the console indicating each stage as it starts.

5.2.5 Testing the Appletalk software.

To test that the software is functioning properly, go to one of your Apple machines, pull down the Apple menu, select the Chooser, click on AppleShare, and your Linux box should appear.

5.2.6 Caveats of the Appletalk software.

- You may need to start the Appletalk support before you configure your IP network. If you have problems starting the Appletalk programs, or if after you start them, you have trouble with your IP network, then try starting the Appletalk software before you run your /etc/rc.d/rc.inet1 file.
- The afpd (Apple Filing Protocol Daemon) severely messes up your hard disk. Below the mount points it creates a couple of directories: .AppleDesktop and Network Trash Folder. Then, for each directory you access, it will create a .AppleDouble below it so it can store resource forks, etc. So think twice before exporting /. You will have a great time cleaning up afterwards.
- The afpd program expects clear text passwords from the Macs. Security could be a problem, so be very careful when you run this daemon on a machine connected to the Internet. You have yourself to blame if somebody nasty does something bad.
- The existing diagnostic tools such as netstat and ifconfig don't support Appletalk. The raw information is available in the /proc/net/ directory if you need it.

5.2.7 More information

For a much more detailed description of how to configure Appletalk for Linux refer to Anders Brownworth's Linux Netatalk-HOWTO page at

```
http://thehamptons.com/anders/netatalk/
```

5.3 ATM

Werner Almesberger, werner.almesberger@lrc.di.epfl.ch, is managing a project to provide Asynchronous Transfer Mode support for Linux. Current information on the status of the project may be obtained from

```
http://lrcwww.epfl.ch/linux-atm/
```

5.4 AX.25 (AF_AX25)

AX.25 device names are `sl0`, `sl1`, etc., in `2.0.*` kernels, or 'ax0', 'ax1', etc., in `2.1.*` kernels.

Kernel Compile Options:

```
Networking options  --->
    [*] Amateur Radio AX.25 Level 2
```

The AX25, Netrom and Rose protocols are covered by the AX25 HOWTO (page 568). These protocols are used by amateur radio operators world wide in packet radio experimentation.

Most of the work for implementation of these protocols has been done by Jonathon Naylor, `jsn@cs.nott.ac.uk`.

5.5 DECNet

Support for DECNet is currently being worked on. You should expect it to appear in a late `2.1.*` kernel.

5.6 EQL—multiple-line traffic equaliser

The EQL device name is `eql`. With the standard kernel source you may have only one EQL device per machine. EQL provides a means of utilising multiple point-to-point lines such as PPP, SLIP or PLIP as a single, logical link to carry TCP/IP. Often it is cheaper to use multiple, lower-speed lines, than to have one, high-speed line installed.

Kernel Compile Options:

```
Network device support  --->
    [*] Network device support
    <*> EQL (serial line load balancing) support
```

To support this mechanism, the machine at the other end of the lines must also support EQL. Linux, Livingstone Portmasters and newer dial-in servers support compatible facilities.

To configure EQL, you will need the eql tools which are available from:

```
ftp://sunsite.unc.edu/pub/linux/system/Serial/eql-1.2.tar.gz
```

Configuration is fairly straightforward. You start by configuring the eql interface. The eql interface is just like any other network device. You configure the IP address and mtu using the `ifconfig` utility, so something like:

```
ifconfig eql 192.168.10.1 mtu 1006
route add default eql
```

Next, you need to manually initiate each of the lines you will use. These may be any combination of point-to-point network devices. How you initiate the connections depends on what sort of link they are. Refer to the appropriate sections for further information.

Lastly, you need to associate the serial link with the EQL device, this is called **enslaving** and is done with the `eql_enslave` command as shown:

```
eql_enslave eql sl0 28800
eql_enslave eql ppp0 14400
```

The "estimated speed" parameter you supply to `eql_enslave` doesn't do anything directly. It is used by the EQL driver to determine what share of the datagrams that device should receive, so you can fine tune the balancing of the lines by playing with this value.

To disassociate a line from an EQL device, you use the `eql_emancipate` command as shown:

```
eql_emancipate eql sl0
```

You add routing as you would for any other point-to-point link, except your routes should refer to the `eql` device rather than the actual serial devices themselves. Typically, you would use:

```
route add default eql0
```

The EQL driver was developed by Simon Janes, `simon@ncm.com`.

5.7 Ethernet

Ethernet device names are `eth0`, `eth1`, `eth2`, etc. The first card detected by the kernel is assigned `eth0`, and the rest are assigned sequentially in the order they are detected.

To learn how to make your Ethernet card working under Linux you should refer to the Ethernet-HOWTO (page 843).

Once you have your kernel properly built to support your Ethernet card, then configuration of the card is easy. Typically, you would use something like:

```
# ifconfig eth0 192.168.0.1 netmask 255.255.255.0 up
# route add 192.168.0.0 netmask 255.255.255.0 eth0
```

Most of the Ethernet drivers were developed by Donald Becker, `becker@CESDIS.gsfc.nasa.gov`.

5.8 FDDI

FDDI device names are `fddi0`, `fddi1`, `fddi2`, etc. The first card detected by the kernel is assigned `fddi0`, and the rest are assigned sequentially in the order they are detected.

Lawrence V. Stefani, stefani@lkg.dec.com, has developed a driver for the Digital Equipment Corporation FDDI EISA and PCI cards.

Kernel Compile Options:

```
Network device support  --->
    [*] FDDI driver support
    [*] Digital DEFEA and DEFPA adapter support
```

When you have your kernel built to support the FDDI driver and installed, configuration of the FDDI interface is almost identical that for an Ethernet interface. You just specify the appropriate FDDI interface name in the `ifconfig` and `route` commands.

5.9 Frame Relay

The Frame Relay device names are `dlci00`, `dlci01`, etc., for the DLCI encapsulation devices, and `sdla0`, `sdla1`, and so forth, for the FRAD(s).

Frame Relay is a new networking technology that is designed to suit data communications traffic that is of a "bursty" or intermittent nature. You connect to a Frame Relay network using a Frame Relay Access Device (FRAD). The Linux Frame Relay supports IP over Frame Relay as described in RFC-1490.

Kernel Compile Options:

```
Network device support  --->
    <*> Frame relay DLCI support (EXPERIMENTAL)
    (24)   Max open DLCI
    (8)   Max DLCI per device
    <*>   SDLA (Sangoma S502/S508) support
```

Mike McLagan, mike.mclagan@linux.org, developed the Frame Relay support and configuration tools.

Currently, the only FRAD supported are the `S502A`, `S502E` and `S508`, by Sangoma Technologies, http://www.sangoma.com/.

To configure the FRAD and DLCI devices after you have rebuilt your kernel, you will need the Frame Relay configuration tools. These are available at

```
ftp://ftp.invlogic.com/pub/linux/fr/frad-0.15.tgz
```

Compiling and installing the tools is straightforward, but the lack of a top-level `Makefile` makes it a fairly manual process:

```
# cd /usr/src
# tar xvfz .../frad-0.15.tgz
# cd frad-0.15
# for i in common dlci frad; do cd $i; make clean; make; cd ..; done
```

```
# mkdir /etc/frad
# install -m 644 -o root -g root bin/*.sfm /etc/frad
# install -m 700 -o root -g root frad/fradcfg /sbin
# install -m 700 -o root -g root dlci/dlcicfg /sbin
```

After installing the tools, you need to create a /etc/frad/router.conf file. You can use this template, which is a modified version of one of the example files:

```
# /etc/frad/router.conf
# This is a template configuration for frame relay.
# All tags are included. The default values are based on the code
# supplied with the DOS drivers for the Sangoma S502A card.
#
# A '#' anywhere in a line constitutes a comment
# Blanks are ignored (you can indent with tabs too)
# Unknown [] entries and unknown keys are ignored
#


[Devices]
Count=1                 # number of devices to configure
Dev_1=sdla0             # the name of a device
#Dev_2=sdla1            # the name of a device

# Specified here, these are applied to all devices, and can be overriden for
# each individual board.
#
Access=CPE
Clock=Internal
KBaud=64
Flags=TX
#
# MTU=1500              # Maximum transmit IFrame length, default is 4096
# T391=10               # T391 value    5 - 30, default is 10
# T392=15               # T392 value    5 - 30, default is 15
# N391=6                # N391 value    1 - 255, default is 6
# N392=3                # N392 value    1 - 10, default is 3
# N393=4                # N393 value    1 - 10, default is 4

# Specified here, these set the defaults for all boards
# CIRfwd=16             # CIR forward   1 - 64
# Bc_fwd=16             # Bc forward    1 - 512
# Be_fwd=0              # Be forward    0 - 511
# CIRbak=16             # CIR backward  1 - 64
# Bc_bak=16             # Bc backward   1 - 512
# Be_bak=0              # Be backward   0 - 511


#
#
# Device specific configuration
#
#

#
# The first device is a Sangoma S502E
#
[sdla0]
Type=Sangoma            # Type of the device to configure, currently only
                        # SANGOMA is recognised
#
```

```
# These keys are specific to the 'Sangoma' type
#
# The type of Sangoma board - S502A, S502E, S508
Board=S502E
#
# The name of the test firmware for the Sangoma board
# Testware=/usr/src/frad-0.10/bin/sdla_tst.502
#
# The name of the FR firmware
# Firmware=/usr/src/frad-0.10/bin/frm_rel.502
#
Port=360                # Port for this particular card
Mem=C8                  # Address of memory window, A0-EE, depending on card
IRQ=5                   # IRQ number, do not supply for S502A
DLCIs=1                 # Number of DLCI's attached to this device
DLCI_1=16               # DLCI #1's number, 16 - 991
# DLCI_2=17
# DLCI_3=18
# DLCI_4=19
# DLCI_5=20
#
# Specified here, these apply to this device only,
# and override defaults from above
#
# Access=CPE            # CPE or NODE, default is CPE
# Flags=TXIgnore,RXIgnore,BufferFrames,DropAborted,Stats,MCI,AutoDLCI
# Clock=Internal        # External or Internal, default is Internal
# Baud=128              # Specified baud rate of attached CSU/DSU
# MTU=2048              # Maximum transmit IFrame length, default is 4096
# T391=10               # T391 value    5 - 30, default is 10
# T392=15               # T392 value    5 - 30, default is 15
# N391=6                # N391 value    1 - 255, default is 6
# N392=3                # N392 value    1 - 10, default is 3
# N393=4                # N393 value    1 - 10, default is 4

#
# The second device is some other card
#
# [sdla1]
# Type=FancyCard        # Type of the device to configure.
# Board=                # Type of Sangoma board
# Key=Value             # values specific to this type of device


#
# DLCI Default configuration parameters
# These may be overridden in the DLCI specific configurations
#
CIRfwd=64               # CIR forward   1 - 64
# Bc_fwd=16             # Bc forward    1 - 512
# Be_fwd=0              # Be forward    0 - 511
# CIRbak=16             # CIR backward  1 - 64
# Bc_bak=16             # Bc backward   1 - 512
# Be_bak=0              # Be backward   0 - 511

#
# DLCI Configuration
# These are all optional. The naming convention is
```

```
# [DLCI_D<devicenum>_<DLCI_Num>]
#

[DLCI_D1_16]
# IP=
# Net=
# Mask=
# Flags defined by Sangoma: TXIgnore,RXIgnore,BufferFrames
# DLCIFlags=TXIgnore,RXIgnore,BufferFrames
# CIRfwd=64
# Bc_fwd=512
# Be_fwd=0
# CIRbak=64
# Bc_bak=512
# Be_bak=0

[DLCI_D2_16]
# IP=
# Net=
# Mask=
# Flags defined by Sangoma: TXIgnore,RXIgnore,BufferFrames
# DLCIFlags=TXIgnore,RXIgnore,BufferFrames
# CIRfwd=16
# Bc_fwd=16
# Be_fwd=0
# CIRbak=16
# Bc_bak=16
# Be_bak=0
```

When you've built your /etc/frad/router.conf file, the only step remaining is to configure the actual devices themselves. This is only a little trickier than a normal network device configuration. You need to remember to bring up the FRAD device before the DLCI encapsulation devices.

```
# Configure the frad hardware and the DLCI parameters
/sbin/fradcfg /etc/frad/router.conf || exit 1
/sbin/dlcicfg file /etc/frad/router.conf
#
# Bring up the FRAD device
ifconfig sdla0 up
#
# Configure the DLCI encapsulation interfaces and routing
ifconfig dlci00 192.168.10.1 pointopoint 192.168.10.2 up
route add 192.168.10.0 netmask 255.255.255.0 dlci00
#
ifconfig dlci01 192.168.11.1 pointopoint 192.168.11.2 up
route add 192.168.11.0 netmask 255.255.255.0 dlci00
#
route add default dev dlci00
#
```

5.10 IP Accounting

The IP accounting features of the Linux kernel allow you to collect and analyse some network usage data. The data comprises the number of packets and the number of bytes accumulated since the figures were last reset. You may specify a variety of rules to categorise the figures to suit whatever purpose you may have.

Kernel Compile Options:

```
Networking options  --->
    [*] IP: accounting
```

After you have compiled and installed the kernel you need to use the `ipfwadm` command to configure IP accounting. There are many different ways of breaking down the accounting information that you might choose. I've picked a simple example of what might be useful to use, you should read the `ipfwadm` man page for more information.

Scenario: You have a Ethernet network that is linked to the Internet via a PPP link. On the Ethernet, you have a machine that offers a number of services and that you are interested in knowing how much traffic is generated by each of telnet, rlogin, FTP and World Wide Web connection.

You might use a command set that looks like the following:

```
#
# Flush the accounting rules
ipfwadm -A -f
#
# Add rules for local Ethernet segment
ipfwadm -A in -a -P tcp -D 44.136.8.96/29 20
ipfwadm -A out -a -P tcp -S 44.136.8.96/29 20
ipfwadm -A in -a -P tcp -D 44.136.8.96/29 23
ipfwadm -A out -a -P tcp -S 44.136.8.96/29 23
ipfwadm -A in -a -P tcp -D 44.136.8.96/29 80
ipfwadm -A out -a -P tcp -S 44.136.8.96/29 80
ipfwadm -A in -a -P tcp -D 44.136.8.96/29 513
ipfwadm -A out -a -P tcp -S 44.136.8.96/29 513
ipfwadm -A in -a -P tcp -D 44.136.8.96/29
ipfwadm -A out -a -P tcp -D 44.136.8.96/29
ipfwadm -A in -a -P udp -D 44.136.8.96/29
ipfwadm -A out -a -P udp  -D 44.136.8.96/29
ipfwadm -A in -a -P icmp -D 44.136.8.96/29
ipfwadm -A out -a -P icmp -D 44.136.8.96/29
#
# Rules for default
ipfwadm -A in -a -P tcp -D 0/0 20
ipfwadm -A out -a -P tcp -S 0/0 20
ipfwadm -A in -a -P tcp -D 0/0 23
ipfwadm -A out -a -P tcp -S 0/0 23
ipfwadm -A in -a -P tcp -D 0/0 80
ipfwadm -A out -a -P tcp -S 0/0 80
ipfwadm -A in -a -P tcp -D 0/0 513
ipfwadm -A out -a -P tcp -S 0/0 513
ipfwadm -A in -a -P tcp -D 0/0
ipfwadm -A out -a -P tcp -D 0/0
ipfwadm -A in -a -P udp -D 0/0
ipfwadm -A out -a -P udp  -D 0/0
ipfwadm -A in -a -P icmp -D 0/0
ipfwadm -A out -a -P icmp -D 0/0
#
# List the rules
ipfwadm -A -l -n
#
```

The last command lists each of the accounting rules and displays the collected statistics.

An important point to note when analysing IP accounting is that **totals for all rules that match will be incremented**, so that to obtain differential figures, you need to perform appropriate maths. For example, if I wanted to know how much data was not FTP, telnet, rlogin, or WWW, I would substract the individual totals from the rule that matches all ports.

```
# ipfwadm -A -l -n
IP accounting rules
 pkts bytes dir prot source            destination         ports
    0     0 in  tcp  0.0.0.0/0         44.136.8.96/29      * -> 20
    0     0 out tcp  44.136.8.96/29    0.0.0.0/0           20 -> *
    0     0 in  tcp  0.0.0.0/0         44.136.8.96/29      * -> 23
    0     0 out tcp  44.136.8.96/29    0.0.0.0/0           23 -> *
```

```
    10  1166 in  tcp 0.0.0.0/0          44.136.8.96/29      * -> 80
    10   572 out tcp 44.136.8.96/29     0.0.0.0/0           80 -> *
   242  9777 in  tcp 0.0.0.0/0          44.136.8.96/29      * -> 513
   220 18198 out tcp 44.136.8.96/29     0.0.0.0/0           513 -> *
   252 10943 in  tcp 0.0.0.0/0          44.136.8.96/29      * -> *
   231 18831 out tcp  0.0.0.0/0         44.136.8.96/29      * -> *
     0     0 in  udp  0.0.0.0/0         44.136.8.96/29      * -> *
     0     0 out udp  0.0.0.0/0         44.136.8.96/29      * -> *
     0     0 in  icmp 0.0.0.0/0         44.136.8.96/29      *
     0     0 out icmp 0.0.0.0/0         44.136.8.96/29      *
     0     0 in  tcp  0.0.0.0/0         0.0.0.0/0           * -> 20
     0     0 out tcp  0.0.0.0/0         0.0.0.0/0           20 -> *
     0     0 in  tcp  0.0.0.0/0         0.0.0.0/0           * -> 23
     0     0 out tcp  0.0.0.0/0         0.0.0.0/0           23 -> *
    10  1166 in  tcp  0.0.0.0/0         0.0.0.0/0           * -> 80
    10   572 out tcp  0.0.0.0/0         0.0.0.0/0           80 -> *
   243  9817 in  tcp  0.0.0.0/0         0.0.0.0/0           * -> 513
   221 18259 out tcp  0.0.0.0/0         0.0.0.0/0           513 -> *
   253 10983 in  tcp  0.0.0.0/0         0.0.0.0/0           * -> *
   231 18831 out tcp  0.0.0.0/0         0.0.0.0/0           * -> *
     0     0 in  udp  0.0.0.0/0         0.0.0.0/0           * -> *
     0     0 out udp  0.0.0.0/0         0.0.0.0/0           * -> *
     0     0 in  icmp 0.0.0.0/0         0.0.0.0/0           *
     0     0 out icmp 0.0.0.0/0         0.0.0.0/0           *
#
```

5.11 IP Aliasing

There are some applications where being able to configure multiple IP addresses to a single network device is useful. Internet Service Providers often use this facility to provide a 'customised' to their World Wide Web and FTP offerings for their customers.

Kernel Compile Options:

```
Networking options  --->
    ....
    [*] Network aliasing
    ....
    <*> IP: aliasing support
```

After compiling and installing your kernel with IP_Alias support, configuration is very simple. The aliases are added to virtual network devices associated with the actual network device. A simple naming convention applies to these devices, being *devname:virtual dev num*; e.g., `eth0:0`, `ppp0:10`, etc.

For example, assume you have an Ethernet network that supports two different IP subnetworks simultaneously, and you wish your machine to have direct access to both, you could use something like:

```
#
# ifconfig eth0:0 192.168.1.1 netmask 255.255.255.0 up
# route add -net 192.168.1.0 netmask 255.255.255.0 eth0:0
#
# ifconfig eth0:1 192.168.10.1 netmask 255.255.255.0 up
# route add -net 192.168.10.0 netmask 255.255.255.0 eth0:0
#
```

To delete an alias you simply add a '-' to the end of its name and refer to it as simply as:

```
# ifconfig eth0:0- 0
```

All routes associated with that alias will also be deleted automatically.

5.12 IP Firewall

IP Firewall and Firewalling issues are covered in more depth in the Firewall HOWTO (page 902). IP Firewalling allows you to secure your machine against unauthorized network access by filtering or allowing datagrams from or to IP addresses that you nominate. There are three different classes of rules: incoming filtering, outgoing filtering, and forwarding filtering. Incoming rules are applied to datagrams that are received by a network device. Outgoing rules are applied to datagrams that are to be transmitted by a network device. Forwarding rules are applied to datagrams that are received and are not for this machine, ie datagrams that would be routed.

Kernel Compile Options:

```
Networking options  --->
    [*] Network firewalls
    ....
    [*] IP: forwarding/gatewaying
    ....
    [*] IP: firewalling
    [ ] IP: firewall packet logging
```

Configuration of the IP firewall rules is performed using the `ipfwadm` command. As I mentioned earlier, security is not something I am expert at, so while I will present an example you can use, you should do your own research and develop your own rules if security is important to you.

Probably the most common use of IP firewalls is when you are using your Linux machine as a router and firewall gateway to protect your local network from unauthorised access from outside your network.

The following configuration is based on a contribution from Arnt Gulbrandsen, agulbra@troll.no.

The example describes the configuration of the firewall rules on the Linux firewall or router machine illustrated in this diagram:

```
-                                   -
 \                                  | 172.16.37.0
  \                                 |   /255.255.255.0
   \                 ---------      |
    |  172.16.174.30 | Linux |      |
NET =================|  f/w  |------|    ..37.19
    |    PPP         | router|      |  --------
   /                 ---------      |--| Mail |
  /                                 |  | /DNS |
 /                                  |  --------
-                                   -
```

The following commands would normally be placed in a `rc` file so that they are automatically started each time the system boots. For maximum security, they are performed after the network interfaces are configured, but before the interfaces are actually brought up, to prevent anyone gaining access while the firewall machine is rebooting.

```
#!/bin/sh

# Flush the 'Forwarding' rules table
# Change the default policy to 'accept'
#
/sbin/ipfwadm -F -f
/sbin/ipfwadm -F -p accept
#
# .. and for 'Incoming'
#
/sbin/ipfwadm -I -f
/sbin/ipfwadm -I -p accept

# First off, seal off the PPP interface
# I'd love to use '-a deny' instead of '-a reject -y' but then it
# would be impossible to originate connections on that interface too.
# The -o causes all rejected datagrams to be logged. This trades
# disk space against knowledge of an attack of configuration error.
#
/sbin/ipfwadm -I -a reject -y -o -P tcp -S 0/0 -D 172.16.174.30

# Throw away certain kinds of obviously forged packets right away:
```

```
# Nothing should come from multicast/anycast/broadcast addresses
#
/sbin/ipfwadm -F -a deny -o -S 224.0/3 -D 172.16.37.0/24
#
# and nothing coming from the loopback network should ever be
# seen on a wire
#
/sbin/ipfwadm -F -a deny -o -S 127.0/8 -D 172.16.37.0/24

# accept incoming SMTP and DNS connections, but only
# to the the Mail/Name Server
#
/sbin/ipfwadm -F -a accept -P tcp -S 0/0 -D 172.16.37.19 25 53
#
# DNS uses UDP as well as TCP, so allow that too
# for questions to our name server
#
/sbin/ipfwadm -F -a accept -P udp -S 0/0 -D 172.16.37.19 53
#
# but not "answers" coming to dangerous ports like NFS and
# Larry McVoy's NFS extension.  If you run squid, add its port here.
#
/sbin/ipfwadm -F -a deny -o -P udp -S 0/0 53 \
        -D 172.16.37.0/24 2049 2050

# answers to other user ports are okay
#
/sbin/ipfwadm -F -a accept -P udp -S 0/0 53 \
        -D 172.16.37.0/24 53 1024:65535

# Reject incoming connections to identd
# We use 'reject' here so that the connecting host is told
# straight away not to bother continuing, otherwise we'd experience
# delays while ident timed out.
#
/sbin/ipfwadm -F -a reject -o -P tcp -S 0/0 -D 172.16.37.0/24 113

# Accept some common service connections from the 192.168.64 and
# 192.168.65 networks, they are friends that we trust.
#
/sbin/ipfwadm -F -a accept -P tcp -S 192.168.64.0/23 \
        -D 172.16.37.0/24 20:23

# accept and pass through anything originating inside
#
/sbin/ipfwadm -F -a accept -P tcp -S 172.16.37.0/24 -D 0/0

# deny most other incoming TCP connections, and log them
# (append 1:1023 if you have problems with ftp not working)
#
/sbin/ipfwadm -F -a deny -o -y -P tcp -S 0/0 -D 172.16.37.0/24

# ... for UDP too
#
/sbin/ipfwadm -F -a deny -o -P udp -S 0/0 -D 172.16.37.0/24
```

Good firewall configurations are a little tricky. This example should be a reasonable starting point for you. The ipfwadm manual page offers some assistance in how to use the tool. If you intend to configure a firewall, be sure to ask around and get as much advice from sources you consider reliable, and get someone to test and sanity-check your configuration from the outside.

5.13 IPIP Encapsulation

Why would you want to encapsulate IP datagrams within IP datagrams? It must seem an odd thing to do if you've never seen an application of it before. Ok, here are a couple of common places where it is used: Mobile-IP and IP-Multicast. What is perhaps the most widespread use of it, though also the least well known, is amateur radio.

Kernel Compile Options:

```
Networking options  --->
      [*] TCP/IP networking
      [*] IP: forwarding/gatewaying
      ....
      <*> IP: tunneling
```

IP tunnel devices are called `tunl0`, `tunl1`, etc.

"But why ?" Okay, okay. Conventional IP routing rules mandate that an IP network comprises a network address and a network mask. This produces a series of contiguous addresses that may all be routed via a single routing entry. This is very convenient, but it means that you may only use any particular IP address while you are connected to the particular piece of network to which it belongs. In most instances this is okay, but if you are a mobile netizen, you may not be able to stay connected to one place all the time. IP/IP encapsulation (IP tunneling) allows you to overcome this restriction by allowing datagrams destined for your IP address to be wrapped up and redirected to another IP address. If you know that you're going to be operating from some other IP network for some time, you can set up a machine on your home network to accept datagrams to your IP address and redirect them to the address that you will actually be using temporarily.

5.13.1 A tunneled network configuration.

As always, I believe a diagram will save me lots of confusing text, so here is one:

```
 192.168.1/24                                          192.168.2/24

      -                                                     -
      |        ppp0 =                ppp0 =                 |
      |  aaa.bbb.ccc.ddd  fff.ggg.hhh.iii                   |
      |                                                     |
      |   /-----\                       /-----\             |
      |   |     |       //              |     |             |
      |---|  A  |------//---------------|  B  |---|
      |   |     |     //                |     |             |
      |   \-----/                       \-----/             |
      |                                                     |
      -                                                     -
```

The diagram illustrates another possible reason to use IPIP encapsulation, virtual private networking. This example presupposes that you have two machines, each with a simple dial-up internet connection. Each host is allocated only a single IP address. Behind each of these machines are some private local area networks configured with reserved IP network addresses. Suppose that you want to allow any host on network A to connect to any host on network B, just as if they were properly connected to the Internet with a network route. IPIP encapsulation allows you to do this. Note, encapsulation does not solve the problem of how you get the hosts on networks A and B to talk to any other on the Internet. You still need tricks like IP Masquerade for that. Encapsulation is normally performed by machines functioning as routers.

Linux router '`A`' would be configured with:

```
#
PATH=/sbin:/usr/sbin
#
# Ethernet configuration
ifconfig eth0 192.168.1.1 netmask 255.255.255.0 up
route add 192.168.1.0 netmask 255.255.255.0 eth0
#
# ppp0 configuration (start ppp link, set default route)
pppd
```

```
route add default ppp0
#
# Tunnel device configuration
ifconfig tunl0 192.168.1.1 up
route add -net 192.168.2.0 netmask 255.255.255.0 gw fff.ggg.hhh.iii tunl0
```

Linux router 'B' would be configured with:

```
#
PATH=/sbin:/usr/sbin
#
# Ethernet configuration
ifconfig eth0 192.168.2.1 netmask 255.255.255.0 up
route add 192.168.2.0 netmask 255.255.255.0 eth0
#
# ppp0 configuration (start ppp link, set default route)
pppd
route add default ppp0
#
# Tunnel device configuration
ifconfig tunl0 192.168.2.1 up
route add -net 192.168.1.0 netmask 255.255.255.0 gw aaa.bbb.ccc.ddd tunl0
```

The command:

```
route add -net 192.168.1.0 netmask 255.255.255.0 gw aaa.bbb.ccc.ddd tunl0
```

reads: "Send any datagrams destined for `192.168.1.0/24` inside an IPIP encap datagram with a destination address of `aaa.bbb.ccc.ddd`."

Note that the configurations are reciprocated at either end. The tunnel device uses the `gw` in the route as the destination of the IP datagram in which it will place the datagram it has received to route. That machine must know how to decapsulate IPIP datagrams, that is, it must also be configured with a tunnel device.

5.13.2 A tunneled host configuration.

It doesn't have to be a whole network you route. You could for example route just a single IP address. In that instance, you might configure the `tunl` device on the remote machine with its home IP address and at the A end just use a host route (and proxy ARP) rather than a network route via the tunnel device. Let's redraw and modify our configuration appropriately. Now we have just host 'B' which to want to act and behave as if it is both fully connected to the Internet and also part of the remote network supported by host 'A':

```
192.168.1/24

    -
    |      ppp0 =                ppp0 =
    |  aaa.bbb.ccc.ddd      fff.ggg.hhh.iii
    |
    |   /-----\                 /-----\
    |   |     |        //       |     |
    |---|  A  |------//---------|  B  |
    |   |     |     //          |     |
    |   \-----/                 \-----/
    |                      also: 192.168.1.12
    -
```

Linux router 'A' would be configured with:

```
#
PATH=/sbin:/usr/sbin
#
# Ethernet configuration
ifconfig eth0 192.168.1.1 netmask 255.255.255.0 up
route add 192.168.1.0 netmask 255.255.255.0 eth0
```

```
#
# ppp0 configuration (start ppp link, set default route)
pppd
route add default ppp0
#
# Tunnel device configuration
ifconfig tunl0 192.168.1.1 up
route add -host 192.168.1.12 gw fff.ggg.hhh.iii tunl0
#
# Proxy ARP for the remote host
arp -s 192.168.1.12 xx:xx:xx:xx:xx:xx pub
```

Linux host 'B' would be configured with:

```
#
PATH=/sbin:/usr/sbin
#
# ppp0 configuration (start ppp link, set default route)
pppd
route add default ppp0
#
# Tunnel device configuration
ifconfig tunl0 192.168.1.12 up
route add -net 192.168.1.0 netmask 255.255.255.0 gw aaa.bbb.ccc.ddd tunl0
```

This sort of configuration is more typical of a Mobile IP application. Where a single host wants to roam around the Internet and maintain a single usable IP address the whole time. You should refer to the Mobile IP section for more information on how that is handled in practice.

5.14 IPX (AF_IPX)

The IPX protocol is most commonly utilised in Novell NetWare(tm) local area network environments. Linux includes support for this protocol, and may be configured to act as a network endpoint, or as a router for IPX.

Kernel Compile Options:

```
Networking options --->
    [*] The IPX protocol
    [ ] Full internal IPX network
```

The IPX protocol and the NCPFS are covered in greater depth in the IPX-HOWTO.

5.15 IPv6

Just when you thought you were beginning to understand IP networking the rules get changed! IPv6 is the shorthand notation for Version 6 of the Internet Protocol. IPv6 was developed primarily to overcome the concerns in the Internet community that there would soon be a shortage of IP addresses to allocate. IPv6 addresses are 32 bytes long (128 bits). IPv6 incorporates a number of other changes, mostly simplifications, that will make IPv6 networks more managable than IPv4 networks.

Linux already has a working, but not completed, IPv6 implementation in the `2.1.*` series kernels.

If you wish to experiment with this new generation Internet technology, or have a requirement for it, then you should read the IPv6-FAQ which is available at

`http://www.terra.net/ipv6/`

5.16 ISDN

The Integrated Services Digital Network (ISDN) is a series of standards that specify a general-purpose, switched, digital data network. An ISDN "call" creates a synchronous point to point data service to the destination. ISDN is generally delivered on a high-speed link that is broken down into a number of discreet channels. There are two different types of channels, the "B Channels" which will actually carry the user data, and a single channel called the "D channel" which is used to send control information to the ISDN exchange to establish calls and other functions. In Australia, for example, ISDN may be delivered on a 2Mbps link that is broken into 30 discreet 64kbps B channels with one 64kbps D channel. Any number of channels may be used at a time and in any combination. You could, for example, establish 30 seperate calls to 30 different destinations at 64kbps each, or you could establish 15 calls to 15 different destinations at 128kbps each (two channels used per call), or just a small number of calls and leave the rest idle. A channel may be used for either incoming or outgoing calls. The original intention of ISDN was to allow Telecommunications companies to provide a single data service which could deliver either telephone (via digitized voice) or data services to your home or business, without requiring you to make any special configuration changes.

There are a few different ways to connect your computer to an ISDN service. One way is to use a device called a "Terminal Adaptor" which plugs into the Network Terminating Unit that you telecommunications carrier will have installed when you got your ISDN service, and presents a number of serial interfaces. One of those interfaces is used to enter commands to establish calls and configuration, and the others are actually connected to the network devices that will use the data circuits when they are established. Linux will work in this sort of configuration without modification. You just treat the port on the Terminal Adaptor like you would treat any other serial device. Another way, which is the way that kernel ISDN support is designed, allows you to install an ISDN card into your Linux machine, and then has your Linux software handle the protocols and make the calls itself.

Kernel Compile Options:

```
ISDN subsystem  --->
        <*> ISDN support
        [ ] Support synchronous PPP
        [ ] Support audio via ISDN
        < > ICN 2B and 4B support
        < > PCBIT-D support
        < > Teles/NICCY1016PC/Creatix support
```

The Linux implementation of ISDN supports a number of different types of internal ISDN cards. Those listed in the kernel configuration options are:

- ICN 2B and 4B
- Octal PCBIT-D
- Teles ISDN-cards and compatibles

Some of these cards require software to be downloaded to them to make them operational. There is a separate utility for this.

Full details on how to configure the Linux ISDN support is available from the `/usr/src/linux/Documentation/isdn/` directory, and a FAQ dedicated to isdn4linux is available at

```
http://www.lrz-muenchen.de/ ui161ab/www/isdn/
```

(You can click on the British flag to get an English version).

A note about PPP. The PPP suite of protocols will operate over either asynchronous or synchronous serial lines. The commonly distributed PPP daemon for Linux, `pppd`, supports only asynchronous mode. If you wish to run the PPP protocols over your ISDN service, you need a specially modified version. Details of where to find it are available in the documentation referred to above.

5.17 IP Masquerade

Many people have a simple dialup account to connect to the Internet. Nearly everybody using this sort of configuration is allocated a single IP address by the Internet Service Provider. This is normally enough to allow only one host full access to the network. IP Masquerade is a clever trick that enables you to have many machines make use of that one IP address, by causing the other hosts to look like, hence the term **masquerade** the machine supporting the dialup connection. There is a small caveat, and that is that the masqerade function nearly always works only in one direction: that is, the masqueraded hosts can make calls out, but they cannot accept or receive network connections from remote hosts. This means that some network services do not work, such as talk, and others, such as FTP, must be configured to operate in passive (PASV) mode. Fortunately, the most common network services such as telnet, HTTP, and IRC, do work just fine.

Kernel Compile Options:

```
Code maturity level options  --->
    [*] Prompt for development and/or incomplete code/drivers
Networking options  --->
    [*] Network firewalls
    ....
    [*] TCP/IP networking
    [*] IP: forwarding/gatewaying
    ....
    [*] IP: masquerading (EXPERIMENTAL)
```

Normally, you have your Linux machine support a SLIP or PPP dialup line just as it would if it were a standalone machine. Additionally, it would have another network device configured, perhaps an Ethernet, with one of the reserved network addresses. The hosts to be masqueraded would be connected to this second network. Each of these hosts would have the IP address of the Ethernet port of the Linux machine set as their default gateway or router.

A typical configuration might look something like this:

```
 -                                    -
  \                                   | 192.168.1.0
   \                                  |   /255.255.255.0
    \                 ---------       |
     |                | Linux | .1.1 |
NET =================| masq  |------|
     |    PPP/slip    | router|       |  --------
    /                 ---------       |--| host |
   /                                  |  |      |
  /                                   |  --------
 -                                    -
```

The most relevant commands for this configuration are.

```
# Network route for ethernet
route add 192.168.1.0 netmask 255.255.255.0 eth0
#
# Default route to the rest of the internet.
route add default ppp0
#
# Cause all hosts on the 192.168.1/24 network to be masqueraded.
ipfwadm -F -a m -S 192.168.1.0/24 -D 0.0.0.0/0
```

You can get more information on the Linux IP Masquerade feature from the IP Masquerade Resource Page:

```
http://www.hwy401.com/achau/ipmasq/
```

5.18 IP Transparent Proxy

IP transparent proxy is a feature that enables you to redirect servers or services destined for another machine to those services on this machine. Typically, this would be useful where you have a Linux machine as a router and also provides a proxy server. You would redirect all connections destined for that service remotely to the local proxy server.

Kernel Compile Options:

```
Code maturity level options  --->
        [*] Prompt for development and/or incomplete code/drivers
Networking options  --->
        [*] Network firewalls
        ....
        [*] TCP/IP networking
        ....
        [*] IP: firewalling
        ....
        [*] IP: transparent proxy support (EXPERIMENTAL)
```

Configuration of the transparent proxy feature is performed using the `ipfwadm` command. An example that might useful is as follows:

```
ipfwadm -I -a accept -D 0/0 80 -r 8080
```

This example causes any connection attempts to port 80 (WWW) on any host to be redirected to port 8080 on this host. This could be used to insure that all WWW traffic from your network is automatically directed to a local WWW cache program.

5.19 Mobile IP

The term **IP mobility** describes the ability of a host that is able to move its network connection from one point on the Internet to another without changing its IP address or losing connectivity. Usually when an IP host changes its point of connectivity it must also change its IP address. IP mobility overcomes this problem by allocating a fixed IP address to the mobile host and using IP encapsulation (tunnelling) with automatic routing to insure that datagrams destined for it are routed to the actual IP address it is currently using.

A project is underway to provide a complete set of IP mobility tools for Linux. The status of the project and tools may be obtained from the Linux Mobile IP Home Page.

```
http://anchor.cs.binghamton.edu/ mobileip/
```

5.20 Multicast

IP Multicast allows an arbitrary number of IP hosts on disparate IP networks to have IP datagrams simultaneously routed to them. This mechanism is exploited to provide Internet-wide "broadcast" material, such as audio and video transmissions and other "novel" applications.

Kernel Compile Options:

```
Networking options  --->
        [*] TCP/IP networking
        ....
        [*] IP: multicasting
```

A suite of tools and some minor network configuration is required. One source of information on how to install and configure these for Linux is provided at

```
http://www.teksouth.com/linux/multicast/
```

5.21 NetRom (AF_NETROM)

NetRom device names are 'nr0', 'nr1', etc.

Kernel Compile Options:

```
Networking options  --->
    [*] Amateur Radio AX.25 Level 2
    [*] Amateur Radio NET/ROM
```

The AX.25, Netrom and Rose protocols are covered by the AX25-HOWTO (page 568). These protocols are used by amateur radio operators world wide in packet radio experimentation.

Most of the work for implementation of these protocols has been done by Jonathon Naylor, jsn@cs.nott.ac.uk.

5.22 PLIP

PLIP device names are plip0, plip1, etc. The first device configured is numbered 0 and the others are numbered sequentially.

Kernel Compile Options:

```
Networking options  --->
    <*> PLIP (parallel port) support
```

PLIP (Parallel Line IP), is like SLIP in that it is used for providing a point-to-point network connection between two machines, but it uses the parallel printer ports on your machine instead of the serial ports (a cabling diagram in included in the cabling diagram section later in this document). Because it is possible to transfer more than one bit at a time with a parallel port, it is possible to attain higher speeds with the PLIP interface than with a standard serial device. In addition, even the simplest of parallel ports, printer ports, can be used, in lieu of you having to purchase comparatively expensive 16550AFN UART's for your serial ports.

Please note that some lap tops use chipsets that will not work with PLIP because they do not allow some combinations of signals that PLIP relies on which printers don't use.

The Linux PLIP interface is compatible with Crynwyr Packet Driver PLIP, and this will mean that you can connect your Linux machine to a DOS machine running any other sort of TCP/IP software via PLIP.

When compiling the kernel, there is only one file that might need to be looked at to configure PLIP. That file is /usr/src/linux/driver/net/CONFIG, and it contains PLIP timers in mS. The defaults are probably okay in most cases. You will probably need to increase them if you have an especially slow computer, in which case the timers to increase are actually on the other computer.

The driver assumes the following defaults:

```
device  i/o addr    IRQ
------  --------    -----
plip0   0x3BC           5
plip1   0x378           7
plip2   0x278           2 (9)
```

If your parallel ports don't match any of the above combinations, then you can change the IRQ of a port using the `ifconfig` command's *IRQ* parameter. Be sure to enable IRQs on your printer ports in your ROM BIOS if it supports this option.

To configure a PLIP interface, you will need to add the following lines to your network `rc` file:

```
#
# Attach a PLIP interface
#
#  configure first parallel port as a plip device
/sbin/ifconfig plip0 IPA.IPA.IPA.IPA pointopoint IPR.IPR.IPR.IPR up
#
# End plip
```

Where:

IPA.IPA.IPA.IPA
represents your IP address.

IPR.IPR.IPR.IPR
represents the IP address of the remote machine.

The *pointopoint* parameter has the same meaning as for SLIP, in that it specifies the address of the machine at the other end of the link.

In almost all respects, you can treat a PLIP interface as though it were a SLIP interface, except that neither `dip` nor `slattach` need be, nor can be, used.

5.23 PPP

PPP devices names are `ppp0`, `ppp1`, etc. Devices are numbered sequentially with the first device configured receiving `0`.

Kernel Compile Options:

```
Networking options  --->
    <*> PPP (point-to-point) support
```

PPP configuration is covered in detail in the PPP HOWTO, page 1197.

5.23.1 Maintaining a permanent connection to the net with `pppd`.

If you are fortunate enough to have a semi-permanent connection to the net and would like to have your machine automatically redial your PPP connection if it is lost, then here is a simple trick to do so.

Configure PPP such that it can be started by the `root` user by issuing the command:

```
# pppd
```

Be sure that you have the `-detach` option configured in your `/etc/ppp/options` file. Then, insert the following line into your `/etc/inittab` file, down with the `getty` definitions:

```
pd:23:respawn:/usr/sbin/pppd
```

This will cause the `init` program to spawn and monitor the `pppd` program, and automatically restart it if it dies.

5.24 Rose protocol (`AF_ROSE`)

Rose device names are `rs0`, `rs1`, etc., in `2.1.*` kernels. Rose is available in the `2.1.*` kernels.

Kernel Compile Options:

```
Networking options  --->
    [*] Amateur Radio AX.25 Level 2
    <*> Amateur Radio X.25 PLP (Rose)
```

The AX25, Netrom, and Rose protocols are covered by the AX25-HOWTO (see page 568). These protocols are used by amateur radio operators world wide in packet radio experimentation.

Most of the work for implementation of these protocols has been done by Jonathon Naylor, `jsn@cs.nott.ac.uk`.

5.25 SAMBA—"NetBEUI," and "NetBios" support.

SAMBA is an implementation of the Session Management Block protocol. Samba allows Microsoft and other systems to mount and use your disks and printers.

SAMBA and its configuration are covered in detail in the SMB-HOWTO (page 1437).

5.26 SLIP client

SLIP devices are named `sl0`, `sl1`, etc., with the first device configured being assigned `0` and the rest incrementing sequentially as they are configured.

Kernel Compile Options:

```
Network device support  --->
    [*] Network device support
    <*> SLIP (serial line) support
    [ ]  CSLIP compressed headers
    [ ]  Keepalive and linefill
    [ ]  Six bit SLIP encapsulation
```

SLIP (Serial Line Internet Protocol) allows you to use TCP/IP over a serial line, be that a phone line with a dialup modem, or a leased line of some sort. Of course, to use SLIP, you need access to a **SLIP server** in your area. Many universities and businesses provide SLIP access all over the world.

Slip uses the serial ports on your machine to carry IP datagrams. To do this, it must take control of the serial device. SLIP device names are named `sl0`, `sl1`, etc. How do these correspond to your serial devices? The networking code uses what is called an **ioctl (I/O control)** call to change the serial devices into SLIP devices. There are two programs supplied that can do this. They are called `dip` and `slattach`.

5.26.1 dip

`dip` (Dialup IP) is a smart program that is able to set the speed of the serial device, command your modem to dial the remote end of the link, automatically log you into the remote server, search for messages sent to you by the server and extract information for them such as your IP address and perform the `ioctl` call necessary to switch your serial port into SLIP mode. `dip` has a powerful scripting ability, and it is this which you can exploit to automate your log-on procedure.

You can find `dip` at:

```
ftp://sunsite.unc.edu/pub/Linux/system/Network/serial/dip/dip337o-uri.tgz
```

To install `dip` try the following:

```
#
# cd /usr/src
# gzip -dc dip337o-uri.tgz | tar xvf -
# cd dip-3.3.7o
<edit Makefile>

# make install
#
```

The `Makefile` assumes the existence of a group called `uucp`, but you might like to change this to either `dip` or `slip`, depending on your configuration.

5.26.2 slattach

`slattach`, as contrasted with `dip`, is a very simple program that is very easy to use but does not have the sophistication of `dip`. It does not have the scripting ability: all it does is configure your serial device as a SLIP device. It assumes you have all the information you need and that the serial line is established before you invoke `slattach`. It is ideal where you have a permanent connection to your server like a physical cable or leased line.

5.26.3 When do I use which?

You would use dip when your link to the machine that is your SLIP server is a dialup modem or some other temporary link. You would use slattach when you have a leased line, perhaps a cable, between your machine and the server, and there is no special action needed to get the link working. See the section "Permanent Slip connection" for more information.

Configuring SLIP is much like configuring an Ethernet interface (read section "Configuring an Ethernet device," above). However, there are a few key differences.

First of all, SLIP links are unlike Ethernet networks in that there is only ever two hosts on the network, one at each end of the link. Unlike an Ethernet that is available for use as soon are you are cabled, with SLIP, depending on the type of link you have, you may have to initialize your network connection in some special way.

If you use dip, then this would not normally be done at boot time, but at some time later, when you are ready to use the link. It is possible to automate this procedure. If you use slattach, then you will probably want to add a section to your rc.inet1 file. This is described below.

There are two major types of SLIP servers: Dynamic IP address servers and static IP address servers. Almost every SLIP server will prompt you to login using a user name and password when dialing in. dip can handle automatic logins.

5.26.4 Static SLIP server with a dialup line and DIP.

A static SLIP server is one in which you have been supplied an IP address that is exclusively yours. Each time you connect to the server, you configure your SLIP port with that address. The static SLIP server answers your modem call, possibly prompts you for a user name and password, and routes any datagrams destined for your address to you via that connection. If you have a static server, you may want to put entries for your hostname and IP address (since you know what that will be) into your /etc/hosts file. You should also configure some other files like: rc.inet2, host.conf, resolv.conf, /etc/HOSTNAME, and rc.local. Remember that when configuring rc.inet1, you don't need to add any special commands for your SLIP connection, since it is dip that does all of the hard work for you in configuring your interface. You will need to give dip the appropriate information and it will configure the interface for you after commanding the modem to establish the call and logging you into your SLIP server.

If this is how your SLIP server works, then you can move to section "Using Dip" to learn how to configure dip appropriately.

5.26.5 Dynamic SLIP server with a dialup line and dip.

A **dynamic SLIP server** allocates you an IP address randomly, from a pool of addresses, each time you log on. This means that there is no guarantee that you will have any particular address each time, and that address may well be used by someone else after you have logged off. The network administrator who configured the SLIP server will have assigned a pool of address for the SLIP server to use, when the server receives a new incoming call, it finds the first unused address, guides the caller through the login process and then prints a welcome message that contains the IP address it has allocated and will proceed to use that IP address for the duration of that call.

Configuring for this type of server is similar to configuring for a static server, except that you must add a step where you obtain the IP address that the server has allocated for you and configure your SLIP device with that.

Again, dip does the hard work, and new versions are smart enough to not only log you in, but to also to be able to automatically read the IP address printed in the welcome message and store it so that you can have it configure your SLIP device with it.

If this is how your SLIP server works, then you can move to section, "Using dip," to learn how to configure dip appropriately.

5.26.6 Using dip.

As explained earlier, dip is a powerful program that can simplify and automate the process of dialing into the SLIP server, logging you in, starting the connection, and configuring your SLIP devices with the appropriate ifconfig and route commands.

Essentially, to use dip, you'll write a "dip script," which is basically a list of commands that dip understands which tell dip how to perform each of the actions you want it to perform. See sample.dip that comes supplied with dip to get an idea of how it works. dip is quite a powerful program, with many options. Instead of going into all of them here you should look at the manaul page, README, and sample files that come with your version of dip.

You may notice that the sample.dip script assumes that you're using a static SLIP server, so you know what your IP address is beforehand. For dynamic SLIP servers, the newer versions of dip include a command that you can use to automatically read and configure your SLIP device with the IP address that the dynamic server allocates for you. The following sample is a modified version of the `sample.dip` that came supplied with `dip337j-uri.tgz`, and is probably a good starting point for you. You might like to save it as `/etc/dipscript` and edit it to suit your configuration:

```
#
# sample.dip    Dialup IP connection support program.
#
#               This file (should show) shows how to use the DIP
#       This file should work for Annex type dynamic servers, if you
#       use a static address server then use the sample.dip file that
#       comes as part of the dip337-uri.tgz package.
#
#
# Version:      @(#)sample.dip  1.40    07/20/93
#
# Author:       Fred N. van Kempen, <waltje@uWalt.NL.Mugnet.ORG>
#

main:
# Next, set up the other side's name and address.
# My dialin machine is called 'xs4all.hacktic.nl' (== 193.78.33.42)
get $remote xs4all.hacktic.nl
# Set netmask on sl0 to 255.255.255.0
netmask 255.255.255.0
# Set the desired serial port and speed.
port cua02
speed 38400

# Reset the modem and terminal line.
# This seems to cause trouble for some people!
reset

# Note! "Standard" pre-defined "errlevel" values:
#  0 - OK
#  1 - CONNECT
#  2 - ERROR
#
# You can change those grep'ping for "addchat()" in *.c...

# Prepare for dialing.
send ATQ0V1E1X4\r
wait OK 2
if $errlvl != 0 goto modem_trouble
dial 555-1234567
if $errlvl != 1 goto modem_trouble

# We are connected.  Login to the system.
login:
sleep 2
wait ogin: 20
if $errlvl != 0 goto login_trouble
send MYLOGIN\n
wait ord: 20
if $errlvl != 0 goto password_error
send MYPASSWD\n
loggedin:

# We are now logged in.
wait SOMEPROMPT 30
```

```
if $errlvl != 0 goto prompt_error

# Command the server into SLIP mode
send SLIP\n
wait SLIP 30
if $errlvl != 0 goto prompt_error

# Get and Set your IP address from the server.
#   Here we assume that after commanding the SLIP server into SLIP
#   mode that it prints your IP address
get $locip remote 30
if $errlvl != 0 goto prompt_error

# Set up the SLIP operating parameters.
get $mtu 296
# Ensure "route add -net default xs4all.hacktic.nl" will be done
default

# Say hello and fire up!
done:
print CONNECTED $locip ---> $rmtip
mode CSLIP
goto exit

prompt_error:
print TIME-OUT waiting for sliplogin to fire up...
goto error

login_trouble:
print Trouble waiting for the Login: prompt...
goto error

password:error:
print Trouble waiting for the Password: prompt...
goto error

modem_trouble:
print Trouble occurred with the modem...
error:
print CONNECT FAILED to $remote
quit

exit:
exit
```

The above example assumes that you are calling a dynamic SLIP server. If you are calling a static SLIP server, then the `sample.dip` file that comes with `dip337j-uri.tgz` should work for you.

When `dip` is given the `get $local` command, it searches the incoming text from the remote end for a string that looks like an IP address; i.e., strings of numbers separated by '.' characters. This modification was put in place specifically for dynamic SLIP servers, so that the process of reading the IP address granted by the server could be automated.

The example above will automatically create a default route via your SLIP link. If this is not what you want, you might have an Ethernet connection that should be your default route, then remove the `default` command from the script. After this script has finished running, if you do an `ifconfig` command, you will see that you have a device `sl0`. This is your SLIP device. Should you need to, you can modify its configuration manually, after the `dip` command has finished, using the `ifconfig` and `route` commands.

Please note that `dip` allows you to select a number of different protocols to use with the `mode` command. The most common example is cSLIP for SLIP with compression. Please note that both ends of the link must agree, so you should ensure that whatever you select agrees with what your server is set to.

The above example is fairly robust and should cope with most errors. Please refer to the `dip` manual page for more information. Naturally you could, for example, code the script to do such things as redial the server if it doesn't get a connection within a prescribed period of time, or even try a series of servers if you have access to more than one.

5.26.7 Permanent SLIP connection using a leased line and `slattach`.

If you have a cable between two machines, or are fortunate enough to have a leased line, or some other permanent serial connection between your machine and another, then you don't need to go to all the trouble of using `dip` to set up your serial link. `slattach` is a very simple to use utility that will allow you just enough functionality to configure your connection.

Since your connection will be a permanent one, you will want to add some commands to your `rc.inet1` file. In essence all you need to do for a permanent connection is ensure that you configure the serial device to the correct speed and switch the serial device into SLIP mode. `slattach` allows you to do this with one command. Add the following to your `rc.inet1` file:

```
#
# Attach a leased line static SLIP connection
#
#  configure /dev/cua0 for 19.2kbps and cslip
/sbin/slattach -p cslip -s 19200 /dev/cua0 &
/sbin/ifconfig sl0 IPA.IPA.IPA.IPA pointopoint IPR.IPR.IPR.IPR up
#
# End static SLIP.
```

Where:

IPA.IPA.IPA.IPA
: represents your IP address.

IPR.IPR.IPR.IPR
: represents the IP address of the remote end.

`slattach` allocates the first unallocated SLIP device to the serial device specified. `slattach` starts with `sl0`. Therefore, the first `slattach` command attaches SLIP device `sl0` to the serial device specified and `sl1` the next serial device.

`slattach` allows you to configure a number of different protocols with the `-p` argument. In your case you will use either SLIP or cSLIP, depending on whether you want to use compression or not. Note: both ends must agree on whether you want compression or not.

5.27 SLIP server.

If you have a machine that is perhaps network connected, which you'd like other people be able to dial into and provide network services, then you need to configure your machine as a server. If you want to use SLIP as the serial line protocol, then currently you have three options as to how to configure your Linux machine as a SLIP server. My preference would be to use the first presented, `sliplogin`, as it seems the easiest to configure and understand, but I will present a summary of each, so you can make your own decision.

5.27.1 Slip Server using `sliplogin`.

`sliplogin` takes the place of the normal login shell for SLIP users and converts the terminal line into a SLIP line. It allows you to configure your Linux machine as either a **static address server**; that is, users get the same address everytime they call in, or a **dynamic address server**, where users get an address allocated for them which will not necessarily be the same as the last time they called.

The caller logs in with the standard login process, enters his or her user name and password. But instead of being presenting the user with a shell, the machine starts `sliplogin`, which searches its configuration file (`/etc/slip.hosts`) for an entry with a login name which matches that of the caller. If it locates one, it configures the line as 8-bit clean and uses an `ioctl` call to convert the line discipline to SLIP. When this process is complete, the last stage of configuration takes place, where `sliplogin` invokes a shell script which configures the SLIP interface with the relevant IP address, netmask, and sets appropriate routing in place. This script is usually called `/etc/slip.login`, but in a similar manner to `getty`, if you have certain callers that require special initialization, then you can create configuration scripts called `/etc/slip.login.loginname`, and they will be run specifically for them.

There are either three or four files that you need to configure to get `sliplogin` working for you. I will detail how and where to get the software and how each is configured in detail. The files are:

- /etc/passwd, for the dial-in user accounts.
- /etc/slip.hosts, to contain the information unique to each dial-in user.
- /etc/slip.login, which manages the configuration of the routing that needs to be performed for the user.
- /etc/slip.tty, which is required only if you are configuring your server for dynamic address allocation and contains a table of addresses to allocate.
- /etc/slip.logout, which contains commands to clean up after the user has hung up or logged out.

Where to get sliplogin. You may already have sliplogin installed as part of your distribution, if not then sliplogin can be obtained as:

```
ftp://sunsite.unc.edu/pub/linux/system/Network/serial/sliplogin-2.1.1.tar.gz
```

The tar file, at the time of this writing, contains source code, precompiled binaries, and a manual page.

To insure that only authorized users can run sliplogin, you should add an entry to your /etc/group file similar to the following:

```
..
slip::13:radio,fred
..
```

When you install sliplogin, the Makefile will change the group ownership of the sliplogin program to slip, and this will mean that only users who belong to that group will be able to execute it. The example above will allow only users radio and fred to execute sliplogin.

To install the binaries into your /sbin directory and the manual page into /usr/man/man8, do the following:

```
# cd /usr/src
# gzip -dc .../sliplogin-2.1.1.tar.gz | tar xvf -
# cd sliplogin-2.1.1
# <..edit the Makefile if you don't use shadow passwords..>
# make install
```

If you want to recompile the binaries before installation, execute a make clean before the make install. If you want to install the binaries somewhere else, you will need to edit the Makefile install rule.

Please read the README files that come with the package for more information.

Configuring /etc/passwd **for SLIP hosts.** Normally you would create some special logins for SLIP callers in your /etc/passwd file. A convention commonly followed is to use the host name of the calling host with a capital 'S' prefixed to it. So, for example, if the calling host is called radio then you could create a /etc/passwd entry that looked like:

```
Sradio:FvKurok73:1427:1:radio SLIP login:/tmp:/sbin/sliplogin
```

It doesn't really matter what the account is called, so long as it is meaningful to you.

Note: the caller doesn't need any special home directory, as they will not be presented with a shell from this machine, so /tmp is a good choice. Also note that sliplogin is used in place of the normal login shell.

Configuring /etc/slip.hosts The /etc/slip.hosts file is the file that sliplogin searches for entries matching the login name to obtain configuration details for this caller. It is this file where you specify the ip address and netmask that will be assigned to the caller and configured for their use. Sample entries for two hosts, one a static configuration for host radio and another, a dynamic configuration for user host albert might look like:

```
#
Sradio  44.136.8.99  44.136.8.100  255.255.255.0  normal      -1
Salbert 44.136.8.99  DYNAMIC       255.255.255.0  compressed  60
#
```

The /etc/slip.hosts file entries are:

1. the login name of the caller.
2. IP address of the server machine; i.e., this machine;
3. IP address that the caller will be assigned. If this field is coded DYNAMIC, an IP address will be allocated based on the information contained in the /etc/slip.tty file, discussed below. **Note:** you must be using at least version 1.3 of sliplogin for this to work;
4. the netmask assigned to the calling machine in dotted decimal notation; e.g., 255.255.255.0 for a Class C network mask;

5. SLIP mode setting which allows you to enable and disable compression and other SLIP features;
6. the timeout parameter specifies how long the line can remain idle (no datagrams received) before the line is automatically disconnected. A negative value disables this feature.
7. optional arguments.

Note: You can use either host names or IP addresses in dotted decimal notation for fields 2 and 3. If you use host names, then those hosts must be resolvable; that is, your machine must be able to locate an IP address for those host names; otherwise, the script will fail when it is called. You can test this by trying to telnet to the host. If you get the "`Trying nnn.nnn.nnn...`" message, then your machine is able to find an IP address for that name. If you get the message "`Unknown host`," then it has not. If not, either use IP addresses in dotted decimal notation, or fix up your name resolver configuration (See section `Name Resolution`).

The most common SLIP modes are:

normal
to enable normal, uncompressed SLIP.

compressed
to enable van Jacobsen header compression (cSLIP)

Naturally, these are mutually exclusive, you can use one or the other. For more information on the other options available, refer to the manual pages.

Configuring the `/etc/slip.login` file. After `sliplogin` has searched the `/etc/slip.hosts` and found a matching entry, it will attempt to execute the `/etc/slip.login` file to actually configure the SLIP interface with its IP address and netmask.

The sample `/etc/slip.login` file supplied with `sliplogin` looks like this:

```
#!/bin/sh -
#
#       @(#)slip.login  5.1 (Berkeley) 7/1/90
#
# generic login file for a SLIP line.  sliplogin invokes this with
# the parameters:
#      $1      $2      $3    $4, $5, $6 ...
#   SLIPunit ttyspeed   pid   the arguments from the slip.host entry
#
/sbin/ifconfig $1 $5 pointopoint $6 mtu 1500 -trailers up
/sbin/route add $6
arp -s $6 <hw_addr> pub
exit 0
#
```

Note that this script simply uses the `ifconfig` and `route` commands to configure the SLIP device with its IP address, remote IP address and netmask, and creates a route for the remote address via the SLIP device. This is just the same as using the `slattach` command.

Note also the use of proxy ARP to insure that other hosts on the same Ethernet as the server machine know how to reach the dial-in host. The *hw_addr* field should be the hardware address of the Ethernet card in the machine. If your server machine isn't on an Ethernet network, then you can omit the line completely.

Configuring the `/etc/slip.logout` file. When the call drops out, you want to insure that the serial device is restored to its normal state so that future callers will be able to log in correctly. This is achieved with the use of the `/etc/slip.logout` file. It is quite simple in format and is called with the same argument as the `/etc/slip.login` file.

```
#!/bin/sh -
#
#               slip.logout
#
/sbin/ifconfig $1 down
arp -d $6
exit 0
#
```

All it does is "down" the interface, which deletes the manual route previously created. It also uses the `arp` command to delete any proxy ARP put in place; again, you don't need the `arp` command in the script if your server machine does not have an Ethernet port.

Configuring the `/etc/slip.tty` **file.** If you are using a dynamic IP address allocation (have any hosts configured with the `DYNAMIC` keyword in the `/etc/slip.hosts` file, then you must configure the `/etc/slip.tty` file to list what addresses are assigned to what port. You only need this file if you wish your server to dynamically allocate addresses to users.

The file is a table that lists the *tty* devices that will support dial-in SLIP connections and the IP address that should be assigned to users who call in on that port.

Its format is as follows:

```
# slip.tty    tty -> IP address mappings for dynamic SLIP
# format: /dev/tty?? xxx.xxx.xxx.xxx
#
/dev/ttyS0       192.168.0.100
/dev/ttyS1       192.168.0.101
#
```

What this table says is that callers that dial in on port `/dev/ttyS0` who have their remote address field in the `/etc/slip.hosts` file set to `DYNAMIC` will be assigned an address of `192.168.0.100`.

In this way you need only allocate one address per port for all users who do not require an dedicated address for themselves. This helps you keep the number of addresses you need down to a minimum to avoid wastage.

5.27.2 Slip Server using `dip`.

Let me start by saying that some of the information below came from the `dip` manual pages, where how to run Linux as a SLIP server is briefly documented. Please also be aware that the following has been based on the `dip337o-uri.tgz` package and probably will not apply to other versions of `dip`.

`dip` has an input mode of operation, where it automatically locates an entry for the user who invoked it and configures the serial line as a SLIP link according to information it finds in the `/etc/diphosts` file. This input mode of operation is activated by invoking `dip` as `diplogin`. This therefore is how you use `dip` as a SLIP server, by creating special accounts where `diplogin` is used as the login shell.

The first thing you need to do is to make a symbolic link:

```
# ln -sf /usr/sbin/dip /usr/sbin/diplogin
```

You then need to add entries to both your `/etc/passwd` and your `/etc/diphosts` files. The entries you need to make are formatted as follows:

To configure Linux as a SLIP server with `dip`, you need to create some special SLIP accounts for users, where `dip` (in input mode) is used as the login shell. A suggested convention is that of having all SLIP accounts begin with a capital "S"; e.g., "Sfredm."

A sample `/etc/passwd` entry for a SLIP user looks like:

```
Sfredm:ij/SMxiTlGVCo:1004:10:Fred:/tmp:/usr/sbin/diplogin
^^     ^^            ^^   ^^  ^^   ^^   ^^
|      |             |    |   |    |    \__ diplogin as login shell
|      |             |    |   |    \_______ Home directory
|      |             |    |   \____________ User Full Name
|      |             |    \________________ User Group ID
|      |             \_____________________ User ID
|      \___________________________________ Encrypted User Password
\__________________________________________ Slip User Login Name
```

After the user logs in, the `login(1)` program, if it finds and verifies the user as correct, will execute the `diplogin` command. `dip`, when invoked as `diplogin`, knows that it should automatically assume it is being used a login shell. When it is started as `diplogin`, the first thing it does is use the `getuid()` function call to get the user ID of whoever invoked it. It then searches the `/etc/diphosts` file for the first entry that matches either the user ID or the name of the `tty` device that the call has come in on, and configures itself appropriately. By judicious decision as to whether to give a user an entry in the `diphosts` file, or whether to let the user be given the default configuration, you can build your server in such a way that you can have a mix of static and dynamic addressed users.

`dip` will automatically add a "Proxy ARP" entry if invoked in input mode, so you do not need to worry about manually adding such entries.

Configuring /etc/diphosts /etc/diphosts is used by dip to look up preset configurations for remote hosts. These remote hosts might be users dialing into your Linux machine, or they might be for machines that you dial into with your Linux machine.

The general format for /etc/diphosts is as follows:

```
..
Suwalt::145.71.34.1:145.71.34.2:255.255.255.0:SLIP uwalt:CSLIP,1006
ttyS1::145.71.34.3:145.71.34.2:255.255.255.0:Dynamic ttyS1:CSLIP,296
..
```

The fields are:

1. login name: as returned by getpwuid(getuid()) or tty name;
2. unused: compat. with passwd;
3. Remote Address: IP address of the calling host, either numeric or by name;
4. Local Address: IP address of this machine, again numeric or by name;
5. Netmask: in dotted decimal notation;
6. Comment field: put whatever you want here;
7. protocol: Slip, CSlip, etc.;
8. MTU: decimal number.

An example /etc/net/diphosts entry for a remote SLIP user might be:

```
Sfredm::145.71.34.1:145.71.34.2:255.255.255.0:SLIP uwalt:SLIP,296
```

which specifies a SLIP link with remote address of 145.71.34.1 and MTU of 296, or:

```
Sfredm::145.71.34.1:145.71.34.2:255.255.255.0:SLIP uwalt:CSLIP,1006
```

which specifies a cSLIP-capable link with remote address 145.71.34.1 and MTU of 1006.

Therefore, all users who you wish to be allowed a statically allocated dial-up IP access, should have an entry in /etc/diphosts, and if you want users who call a particular port to have their addresses dynamically allocated, you must have an entry for the tty device, and must not configure a user based entry. You should remember to configure at least one entry for each dialup tty device to insure that a suitable configuration is available regardless of which modem a user calls in on.

When a user logs in, they will receive a normal login and password prompt, at which they should enter their SLIP login user ID and password. If they check out okay, then the user will see no special messages, they should just change into SLIP mode, and then be able to connect okay with the line configured with the parameters in the diphosts file.

5.27.3 SLIP server using the dSLIP package.

Matt Dillon, dillon@apollo.west.oic.com, has written a package that does not only dial in but also dials out on a SLIP line. Matt's package is a combination of small programs and scripts that manage your connections for you. You need to have tcsh installed—at least one of the scripts requires it. Matt supplies a binary copy of the expect utility. It, too is needed by one of the scripts. You will most likely need some experience with expect to get this package working to your liking, but don't let that put you off.

Matt has written a good set of installation instructions in the README file, so I won't bother repeating them.

You can get the dSLIP package from its home site at:
apollo.west.oic.com

```
/pub/linux/dillon_src/dSLIP203.tgz
```

or from: sunsite.unc.edu

```
/pub/Linux/system/Network/serial/dSLIP203.tgz
```

Read the README file and create the /etc/passwd and /etc/group entries before doing a make install.

5.28 STRIP support (Starmode Radio IP)

STRIP device names are st0, st1, and so on.

Kernel Compile Options:

```
Network device support  --->
        [*] Network device support
        ....
        [*] Radio network interfaces
        < > STRIP (Metricom starmode radio IP)
```

STRIP is a protocol designed specifically for a range of Metricom radio modems for a research project being conducted by Stanford University called the MosquitoNet Project:

```
http://mosquitonet.Stanford.EDU/mosquitonet.html
```

There is a lot of interesting reading here, even if you aren't directly interested in the project.

The Metricom radios connect to a serial port, employ spread-spectrum technology, and are typically capable of about 100kbps. Information on the Metricom radios is available from

http://www.metricom.com/ Metricom Web Server

At present, the standard network tools and utilities do not support the STRIP driver, so you will have to download some customized tools from the MosquitoNet web server. Details on what software you need is available at the MosquitoNet STRIP Page:

```
http://mosquitonet.Stanford.EDU/strip.html
```

In summary, you use a modified slattach program to set the line discipline of a serial tty device to STRIP, and then configure the resulting "st[0-9]" device as you would for Ethernet, with one important exception: for technical reasons STRIP does not support the ARP protocol, so you must manually configure the ARP entries for each of the hosts on your subnet. This shouldn't prove too onerous.

5.29 Token Ring

Token ring device names are tr0, tr1, and so on. Token Ring is an IBM-standard LAN protocol that avoids collisions by providing a mechanism that allows only one node station on the LAN the right to transmit at a time. A "token" is held by one station at a time, and the station holding the token is the only station allowed to transmit. When it has transmitted its data it passes the token onto the next station. The token loops amongst all active stations, hence the name "Token Ring."

Kernel Compile Options:

```
Network device support  --->
        [*] Network device support
        ....
        [*] Token Ring driver support
        < > IBM Tropic chipset based adaptor support
```

Configuration of token ring is identical to that of Ethernet with the exception of the network device name to configure.

5.30 X.25

X.25 is a circuit based packet switching protocol defined by the C.C.I.T.T. (a standards body recognized by Telecommunications companies in most parts of the world). An implementation of X.25 and LAPB are being worked on, and recent 2.1.* kernels include the work in progress.

Jonathon Naylor jsn@cs.nott.ac.uk is leading the development and a mailing list has been established to discuss Linux X.25 related matters. To subscribe send a message to: majordomo@vger.rutgers.edu with the text "subscribe linux-x25" in the body of the message.

Early versions of the configuration tools may be obtained from Jonathon's FTP site at

```
ftp://ftp.cs.nott.ac.uk/jsn/
```

5.31 WaveLan Card

Wavelan device names are `eth0`, `eth1`, and so on.

Kernel Compile Options:

```
Network device support  --->
        [*] Network device support
        ....
        [*] Radio network interfaces
        ....
        <*> WaveLAN support
```

The WaveLAN card is a spread-spectrum, wireless LAN card. The card looks very much like an Ethernet card in practice and is configured in much the same manner.

You can get information on the Wavelan card from

```
http://www.wavelan.com/
```

6 Cables and Cabling

Those of you handy with a soldering iron may want to build your own cables to interconnect two Linux machines. The following cabling diagrams should assist you in this.

6.1 Serial Null Modem cable

Not all NULL modem cables are alike. Many null modem cables do little more than trick your computer into thinking all the appropriate signals are present and swap transmit and receive data. This is okay, but means that you must use software flow control (XON/XOFF) which is less efficient than hardware flow control. The following cable provides the best possible signalling between machines and allows you to use hardware (RTS/CTS) flow control.

```
Pin Name Pin                              Pin
Tx Data     2  -----------------------------  3
Rx Data     3  -----------------------------  2
RTS         4  -----------------------------  5
CTS         5  -----------------------------  4
Ground      7  -----------------------------  7
DTR        20 -\----------------------------  8
DSR         6 -/
RLSD/DCD    8  ---------------------------/ 20
                                          \-  6
```

6.2 Parallel port cable (PLIP cable)

If you intend to use PLIP between two machines, this cable will work for you, regardless of what sort of parallel ports your machines have.

```
Pin Name     pin            pin
STROBE       1*
D0->ERROR    2  ----------- 15
D1->SLCT     3  ----------- 13
D2->PAPOUT   4  ----------- 12
D3->ACK      5  ----------- 10
D4->BUSY     6  ----------- 11
D5           7*
D6           8*
D7           9*
ACK->D3      10 ----------- 5
BUSY->D4     11 ----------- 6
PAPOUT->D2   12 ----------- 4
SLCT->D1     13 ----------- 3
FEED         14*
ERROR->D0    15 ----------- 2
```

```
INIT       16*
SLCTIN     17*
GROUND     25 ----------- 25
```

Notes:

- Do not connect the pins marked with an asterisk '*'.
- Extra grounds are 18,19,20,21,22,23 and 24.
- If the cable you are using has a metallic shield, it should be connected to the metallic DB-25 shell at **one end only**.

◇ **Warning: A miswired PLIP cable can destroy your controller card.** Be very careful and double check every connection to insure you don't cause yourself any unnecessary work or heartache.

While you may be able to run PLIP cables for long distances, you should avoid it if you can. The specifications for the cable allow for a cable length of about 1 meter or so. Please be very careful when running long PLIP cables as sources of strong electromagnetic fields such as lightning, power lines and radio transmitters can interfere with and sometimes even damage your controller. If you really want to connect two of your computers over a large distance you really should be looking at obtaining a pair of thin-net Ethernet cards and running some coaxial cable.

6.3 10base2 (thin coax) Ethernet Cabling

10base2 is an Ethernet cabling standard that specifies the use of 52-ohm coaxial cable with a diameter of about 5 millimeters. There are a couple of important rules to remember when interconnecting machines with 10base2 cabling. The first is that you must use terminators at both ends of the cabling. A terminator is a 52-ohm resistor that helps insure that the signal is absorbed and not reflected when it reaches the end of the cable. Without a terminator at each end of the cabling, you may find that the Ethernet is unreliable or doesn't work at all. Normally, you'd use "T pieces" to interconnect the machines, so that you end up with something that looks like:

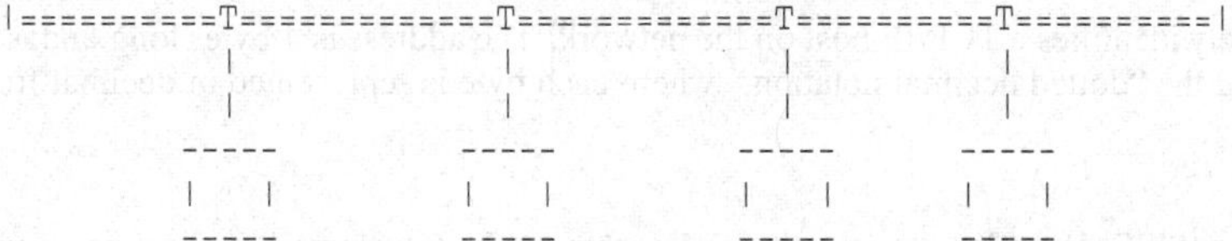

where the "|" at either end represents a terminator, the "======" represents a length of coaxial cable with BNC plugs at either end and the "T" represents a "T piece" connector. You should keep the length of cable between the "T piece" and the actual Ethernet card in the PC as short as possible, ideally the "T piece" will be plugged directly into the Ethernet card.

6.4 Twisted Pair Ethernet Cable

If you have only two twisted pair Ethernet cards, and you wish to connect them, you do not require a hub. You can cable the two cards directly together. A diagram showing how to do this is included in the Ethernet HOWTO (page 843).

7 Glossary of Terms used in this document.

The following is a list of some of the most important terms used in this document.

ARP

This is an abbreviation for **Address Resolution Protocol**, the way a network machine associates an IP Address with a hardware address.

ATM

This is an abbreviation for **Asynchronous Transfer Mode**. ATM networks package data into standard size blocks which they convey efficiently from point to point. ATM is a circuit switched packet network technology.

client

This is usually the piece of software at the end of a system where the user is. There are exceptions to this; for example, in the X11 window system it is actually the server with the user and the client runs on the remote machine. The client is the program or end of a system that is receiving the service provided by the server. In the case of **peer-to-peer** systems like SLIP or PPP, the client is taken to be the end that initiates the connection and the remote end, being called, is taken to be the server.

datagram

A datagram is a discrete package of data and headers which contain addresses, which is the basic unit of transmission across an IP network. You might also hear this called a "packet."

DLCI

The DLCI is the Data Link Connection Identifier, and is used to identify a unique, virtual, point-to-point connection via a Frame Relay network. The DLCI's are normally assigned by the Frame Relay network provider.

Frame Relay

Frame Relay is a network technology ideally suited to carrying traffic that is of bursty or sporadic nature. Network costs are reduced by having many Frame Relay customers sharing the same network capacity and relying on them wanting to make use of the network at slightly different times.

Hardware address

This is a number that uniquely identifies a host in a physical network at the media access layer. Examples of this are Ethernet addresses and AX.25 addresses.

ISDN

This is an abbreviation for **Integrated Services Dedicated Network**. ISDN provides a standard means by which telecommunications companies may deliver either voice or data information to a customer's premises. Technically, ISDN is a circuit switched data network.

ISP

This is an abbreviation of **Internet Service Provider**. These are organizations or companies that provide people with network connectivity to the Internet.

IP address

This is a number that uniquely identifies a TCP/IP host on the network. The address is 4 bytes long and is usually represented in what is called the "dotted decimal notation," where each byte is represented in decimal from with periods '.' between them.

MSS

The Maximum Segment Size (MSS) is the largest quantity of data that can be transmitted at one time. If you want to prevent local fragmentation, MSS would equal MTU-IP header.

MTU

The Maximum Transmission Unit (MTU) is a parameter that determines the largest datagram than can be transmitted by an IP interface without it needing to be broken down into smaller units. The MTU should be larger than the largest datagram you wish to transmit unfragmented. Note, this only prevents fragmentation locally, some other link in the path may have a smaller MTU and the datagram will be fragmented there. Typical values are 1500 bytes for an Ethernet interface, or 576 bytes for a SLIP interface.

route

The **route** is the path that your datagrams take through the network to reach their destination.

server

This is usually the piece of software or end of a system remote from the user. The server provides some service to one or many clients. Examples of servers include FTP, Network File System (NFS), or Domain Name Server (DNS). In the case of peer-to-peer systems, like SLIP or PPP, the server is taken to be the end of the link that is called, and the end calling is taken to be the client.

window

The **window** is the largest amount of data that the receiving end can accept at a given point in time.

8 Linux for an ISP?

If you are interested in using Linux for ISP purposes, I recommend you take a look at the Linux ISP home page

```
http://www.anime.net/linuxisp/
```

for a good list of pointers to information you might need and use.

9 Acknowledgements

I'd like to thank the following people for their contributions to this document (in no particular order): Axel Boldt, Arnt Gulbrandsen, Gary Allpike, Cees de Groot, Alan Cox, Jonathon Naylor.

10 Copyright.

Part XXXII

"NFS HOWTO"
by Nicolai Langfeldt,

`janl@math.uio.no`

The Linux Documentation Project
The original, unaltered edition of this, and other, LDP documents, is on line at http://sunsite.unc.edu/LDP/.

Contents

Abstract

v0.7, 3 November 1997
HOWTO set up NFS clients and servers.

1 Preamble

1.1 Legal stuff

1.2 Other stuff

This will never be a finished document. Please send me mail about your problems and successes because it can make this a better HOWTO. Please send money, comments, and questions to janl@math.uio.no. If you send E-mail, please make sure that the return address is correct and working, I get a lot of e-mail and figuring out your e-mail address can be a lot of work. Please.

If you want to translate this HOWTO, please notify me so I can keep track of what languages I have been published in.

Curses and Thanks to Olaf Kirch who got me to write this and then gave good suggestions for it.

This HOWTO covers NFS in the 2.0 versions of the kernel. There are significant enhancements, and changes, to NFS in the 2.1 versions of the kernel.

1.3 Dedication

This HOWTO is dedicated to Anne Line Norheim Langfeldt. Though she will probably never read it since she's not that kind of girl.

2 README.first

NFS, the Network File System, has three important characteristics:

- It makes sharing of files over a network possible.
- It mostly works well enough.
- It opens a can of security risks that are well understood by crackers, and easily exploited to get access (read, write, and delete) to all of your files.

I'll say something on these issues in this HOWTO. Please make sure you read the security section of this HOWTO, and you will be vulnerable to fewer silly security risks. The passages about security will at times be pretty technical and require some knowledge about IP networking and the terms used. If you don't recognize the terms, you can either go back and check the Networking HOWTO, wing it, or get a book about TCP/IP network administration to familiarize yourself with TCP/IP. That's a good idea anyway if you're administering UNIX or Linux machines. A very good book on the subject is *TCP/IP Network Administration* by Craig Hunt, published by O'Reilly & Associates, Inc. And after you've read it and understood it you'll have higher value on the job market. You can't lose.

There are two sections to help you troubleshoot NFS, called "Mount Checklist" and "FAQs." Please refer to them if something doesn't work as advertised.

3 Setting up a NFS server

3.1 Prerequisites

Before you continue to read this HOWTO, you will need to be able to telnet back and forth between the machine you're using as server and the client. If that does not work, you need to check the networking/NET-2 HOWTO and set up networking properly.

3.2 First step

Before we can do anything else, we need a NFS server set up. If you're part of a department or university network there are likely numerous NFS servers already set up. If they will let you get access to them, or indeed, if you're reading this HOWTO to get access to one of them, you obviously don't need to read this section and can just skip ahead to Section 4

If you need to set up a non-Linux box as server, you will have to read the system manual(s) to discover how to enable NFS serving and export of file systems through NFS. There is a separate section in this HOWTO on how to do it on many different systems. After you have figured all of that out, you can continue reading the next section of this HOWTO. Or, read more of this section, since some of the things that I will say are relevant no matter what kind of machine you use as server.

Those of you still reading will need to set up a number of programs.

3.3 The portmapper

The portmapper on Linux is called either `portmap` or `rpc.portmap`. The manual page on my system says it is a "DARPA port to RPC program number mapper." It is the first security hole you'll open by applying this HOWTO. Description of how to close one of the holes is in Section 6, which I, again, urge you to read.

Start the portmapper. It's either called `portmap` or `rpc.portmap`, and it should live in the `/usr/sbin` directory (on some machines it's called `rpcbind`). You can start it by hand now, but it will need to be started every time you boot your machine so you need to make or edit the `rc` scripts. Your `rc` scripts are explained more closely in the `init` manual page, they usually reside in `/etc/rc.d`, `/etc/init.d` or `/etc/rc.d/init.d`. If there is a script called something like `inet`, it's probably the right script to edit. But, what to write or do is outside the scope of this HOWTO. Start portmap, and check that it lives by running `ps aux`. It does? Good.

3.4 `mountd` and `nfsd`

The next programs we need running are `mountd` and `nfsd`. But first, we'll edit another file, `/etc/exports` this time. Say I want the file system `/mn/eris/local`, which lives on the machine `eris` to be available to the machine called `apollon`. Then I'd put this in `/etc/exports` on eris:

```
/mn/eris/local  apollon(rw)
```

The above line gives `apollon` read/write access to `/mn/eris/local`. Instead of `rw` it could say `ro` which means "read only" (if you put nothing in, it defaults to read only). There are other options you can give it, and I will discuss some security related ones later. They are all enumerated in the `exports` man page which you should have read at least once in your life. There are also better ways than listing all the hosts in the exports file. You can for example use net groups if you are running NIS (or NYS) (NIS was known as YP), and always specify domain wild cards and IP-subnets as hosts that are allowed to mount something. But you should consider who can get access to the server in unauthorized ways if you use such blanket authorizations.

Note: This `/etc/exports` file is not the same syntax that other Unices use. There is a separate section in this HOWTO about other Unices `/etc/exports` files.

Now we're set to start `mountd` (or maybe it's called `rpc.mountd`), and then `nfsd` (which could be called `rpc.nfsd`). They will both read the `/etc/exports` file.

If you edit `/etc/exports`, you will have to make sure that `nfsd` and `mountd` know that the files have changed. The traditional way is to run `exportfs`. Many Linux distributions lack an `exportfs` program. If you're `exportfs`-less, you can install this script on your machine:

```
#!/bin/sh
killall -HUP /usr/sbin/rpc.mountd
killall -HUP /usr/sbin/rpc.nfsd
echo re-exported file systems
```

Save it in, say, `/usr/sbin/exportfs`, and don't forget to `chmod a+rx` it. Now, whenever you change your `/etc/exports` file, you run `exportfs` after, as root.

Now you should check that `mountd` and `nfsd` are running properly, first with `rpcinfo -p`. It should show something like this:

```
   program vers proto   port
    100000    2   tcp    111  portmapper
    100000    2   udp    111  portmapper
    100005    1   udp    745  mountd
    100005    1   tcp    747  mountd
    100003    2   udp   2049  nfs
```

```
100003    2   tcp   2049  nfs
```

As you see, the portmapper has announced it's services, and so has `mountd` and `nfsd`.

If you get `rpcinfo: can't contact portmapper: RPC: Remote system error - Connection refused` or something similar instead, then the portmapper isn't running. Fix it. If you get `No remote programs registered.` then either the portmapper doesn't want to talk to you, or something is broken. Kill `nfsd`, `mountd`, and the portmapper and try the ignition sequence again.

After checking that the portmapper reports the services, you can check with `ps`, too. The portmapper will continue to report the services even after the programs that extend them have crashed. So a `ps` check can be smart if something seems broken.

Of course, you will need to modify your system `rc` files to start `mountd` and `nfsd` as well as the portmapper when you boot. It is very likely that the scripts already exist on your machine, and you just have to uncomment the critical section or activate it for the correct `init` run levels.

Manual pages you should be familiar with now: `portmap`, `mountd`, `nfsd`, and `exports`.

Well, if you did everything exactly like I said you should, you're all set to start on the NFS client.

4 Setting up a NFS client

First you will need a kernel with the NFS file system either compiled in or available as a module. This is configured before you compile the kernel. If you have never compiled a kernel before, you might need to check the kernel HOWTO and figure it out. If you're using a very cool distribution (like Red Hat) and you've never fiddled with the kernel or modules on it (and thus ruined it), NFS is likely automagically available to you.

You can now, at a root prompt, enter an appropriate `mount` command and the file system will appear. Continuing the example in the previous section, we want to mount `/mn/eris/local` from `eris`. This is done with this command:

```
mount -o rsize=1024,wsize=1024 eris:/mn/eris/local /mnt
```

(We'll get back to the `rsize` and `wsize` options.) The file system is now available under `/mnt` and you can `cd` there, and `ls` in it, and look at the individual files. You will notice that it's not as fast as a local file system, but a lot more convenient than FTP. If, instead of mounting the file system, `mount` produces a error message like `mount: eris:/mn/eris/local failed, reason given by server: Permission denied` then the `/etc/exports` file is wrong, or you forgot to run `exportfs` after editing the `/etc/exports` file. If it says `mount clntudp_create: RPC: Program not registered` it means that `nfsd` or `mountd` is not running on the server.

To get rid of the file system you can say

```
umount /mnt
```

To make the system mount a NFS file system upon boot, you edit `/etc/fstab` in the normal manner. For our example, a line such as this is required:

```
# device          mountpoint      fs-type     options                 dump fsckorder
...
eris:/mn/eris/local   /mnt        nfs         rsize=1024,wsize=1024 0    0
...
```

That's all there is too it, almost. Read on please.

4.1 Mount options

There are some options you should consider adding at once. They govern the way the NFS client handles a server crash or network outage. One of the cool things about NFS is that it can handle this gracefully, if you set the clients up right. There are two distinct failure modes:

soft

The NFS client will report an error to the process accessing a file on a NFS mounted file system. Some programs can handle this with composure, most won't. I cannot recommend using this setting.

hard

The program accessing a file on a NFS mounted file system will hang when the server crashes. The process cannot be interrupted or killed unless you also specify `intr`. When the NFS server is back online, the program will continue undisturbed from where it was. This is probably what you want. I recommend using `hard,intr` on all NFS mounted file systems.

Picking up the previous example, this is now your `/etc/fstab` entry:

```
# device          mountpoint    fs-type    options                          dump fsckorder
...
eris:/mn/eris/local   /mnt     nfs        rsize=1024,wsize=1024,hard,intr 0 0
...
```

4.2 Optimizing NFS

Normally, if no `rsize` and `wsize` options are specified, NFS will read and write in chunks of 4096 or 8192 bytes. Some combinations of Linux kernels and network cards cannot handle blocks that large, and it might not be optimal, anyway. So we'll want to experiment and find a `rsize` and `wsize` that works and is as fast as possible. You can test the speed of your options with some simple commands. Given the `mount` command above and that you have write access to the disk, you can do this to test the sequential write performance:

```
time dd if=/dev/zero of=/mnt/testfile bs=16k count=4096
```

This creates a 64Mb file of zeroed bytes, which should be large enough that caching is no significant part of any performance perceived. Use a larger file if you have a lot of memory. Do it a couple (5-10?) of times and average the times. It is the "elapsed" or "wall clock" time that's most interesting in this connection. Then you can test the read performance by reading back the file:

```
time dd if=/mnt/testfile of=/dev/null bs=16k
```

Do that a couple of times and average. Then `umount`, and `mount` again with a larger `rsize` and `wsize`. They should probably be multiples of 1024, and not larger than 16384 bytes, since that's the maximum size in NFS version 2. Directly after mounting with a larger size, `cd` into the mounted file system and do things like `ls`, explore the fs a bit to make sure everything is as it should. If the `rsize` and `wsize` is too large, the symptoms are *very* odd and not 100% obvious. A typical symptom is incomplete file lists when doing `ls`, and no error messages. Or reading files failing mysteriously with no error messages. After establishing that the given `rsize` and `wsize` works, you can do the speed tests again. Different server platforms are likely to have different optimal sizes. SunOS and Solaris is reputedly a lot faster with 4096-byte blocks than with anything else.

Newer Linux kernels (since 1.3 sometime) perform read-ahead for `rsizes` larger or equal to the machine page size. On Intel CPUs, the page size is 4096 bytes. Read ahead will *significantly* increase the NFS read performance. So on a Intel machine you will want a 4096-byte `rsize` if at all possible.

Remember to edit `/etc/fstab` to reflect the `rsize` and `wsize` you found.

A trick to increase NFS write performance is to disable synchronous writes on the server. The NFS specification states that NFS write requests shall not be considered finished before the data written is on a non-volatile medium (normally the disk). This restricts the write performance somewhat. Asynchronous writes will speed NFS writes up. The Linux `nfsd` has never done synchronous writes since the Linux file system implementation does not lend itself to this, but on non-Linux servers you can increase the performance this way with this in your `exports` file:

```
/dir     -async,access=linuxbox
```

or something similar. Please refer to the `exports` manual page on the machine in question. Please note that this increases the risk of data loss.

5 NFS over slow lines

Slow lines include modems, ISDN, and quite possibly other long-distance connections.

This section is based on knowledge about the protocols but no actual experiments. My home computer was down for 6 months (bad HD, low on cash) and so I have had no modem connection to test this with. Please let me hear from you if try this.

The first thing to remember is that NFS is a slow protocol. It has high overhead. Using NFS is almost like using kermit to transfer files. It's *slow*. Almost anything is faster than NFS. FTP is faster. HTTP is faster. `rcp` is faster. `ssh` is faster.

Still determined to try it out? Okay.

NFS' default parameters are for quite fast, low latency, lines. If you use these default parameters over high latency lines it can cause NFS to report errors, abort operations, pretend that files are shorter than they really are, and act mysteriously in other ways.

The first thing to do is *not* to use the `soft` mount option. This will cause timeouts to return errors to the software, which will, most likely not handle the situation at all well. This is a good way to get mysterious failures. Instead, use the `hard` mount option. When `hard` is active timeouts causes infinite retries instead of aborting whatever it was the software wanted to do. This is what you want. Really.

The next thing to do is to tweak the timeout and retrans mount options. They are described in the `nfs(5)` manual page, but here is a copy:

```
timeo=n        The  value  in  tenths  of  a second before
               sending the first retransmission  after  an
               RPC timeout.  The default value is 7 tenths
               of a second.  After the first timeout,  the
               timeout  is  doubled  after each successive
               timeout until a maximum timeout of 60  sec-
               onds  is  reached or the enough retransmis-
               sions have occured to cause a  major  time-
               out.   Then,  if  the  filesystem  is  hard
               mounted, each new timeout cascade  restarts
               at  twice the initial value of the previous
               cascade, again doubling at each retransmis-
               sion.   The  maximum  timeout  is always 60
               seconds.  Better overall performance may be
               achieved  by  increasing  the  timeout when
               mounting on  a  busy  network,  to  a  slow
               server, or through several routers or gate-
               ways.

retrans=n      The number of minor timeouts  and  retrans-
               missions  that  must  occur  before a major
               timeout occurs.  The default is 3 timeouts.
               When a major timeout occurs, the file oper-
               ation is either aborted or  a  "server  not
               responding"  message is printed on the con-
               sole.
```

In other words: If a reply is not received within the 0.7 second (700ms) timeout the NFS client will repeat the request and double the timeout to 1.4 seconds. If the reply does not appear within the 1.4 seconds the request is repeated again and the timeout doubled again, to 2.8 seconds.

A line's speed can be measured with `ping` with the same packet size as your `rsize` and `wsize` options.

```
$ ping -s 8192 lugulbanda
PING lugulbanda.uio.no (129.240.222.99): 8192 data bytes
8200 bytes from 129.240.222.99: icmp_seq=0 ttl=64 time=15.2 ms
8200 bytes from 129.240.222.99: icmp_seq=1 ttl=64 time=15.9 ms
8200 bytes from 129.240.222.99: icmp_seq=2 ttl=64 time=14.9 ms
8200 bytes from 129.240.222.99: icmp_seq=3 ttl=64 time=14.9 ms
8200 bytes from 129.240.222.99: icmp_seq=4 ttl=64 time=15.0 ms

--- lugulbanda.uio.no ping statistics ---
5 packets transmitted, 5 packets received, 0% packet loss
round-trip min/avg/max = 14.9/15.1/15.9 ms
```

The time here is how long the `ping` packet took to get back and forth to `lugulbanda`. 15ms is quite fast. Over a 28.000 bps line you can expect something like 4000-5000ms, and if the line is otherwise loaded this time will be even higher, easily double. When this time is high we say that there is "high latency." Generally, for larger packets and for more loaded lines, the latency will tend to increase. Increase `timeo` suitably for your line and load. And since the latency increases when you use the line for other things: If you ever want to use FTP and NFS at the same time, you should try measuring `ping` times while using FTP to transfer files.

6 Security and NFS

I am by no means a computer security expert. But I do have a little advice for the security conscious. But be warned: This is by no means a complete list of NFS related problems, and if you think you're safe once you're read and implemented all this I have a bridge I want to sell you.

This section is probably of no concern if you are on a closed network where you trust all the users, and no one you don't trust can get access to machines on the network. I.e., there should be no way to dial into the network, and it should in no way be connected to other networks where you don't trust everyone using it as well as the security. Do you think I sound paranoid? I'm not at all paranoid. This is just *basic* security advice. And remember, the things I say here is just the start of it. A secure site needs a diligent and knowledgeable administrator that knows where to find information about current and potential security problems.

NFS has a basic problem in that the client, if not told otherwise, will trust the NFS server and vice versa. This can be bad. It means that if the server's root account is broken into it can be quite easy to break into the client's root account as well. And vice versa. There are a couple of coping strategies for this, which we'll get back to.

Something you should read is the CERT advisories on NFS. Most of the text below deals with issues CERT has written advisories about. See ftp.cert.org/01-README for a up to date list of CERT advisories. Here are some NFS related advisories:

```
CA-91:21.SunOS.NFS.Jumbo.and.fsirand                              12/06/91
    Vulnerabilities concerning Sun Microsystems, Inc. (Sun) Network
    File System (NFS) and the fsirand program.  These vulnerabilities
    affect SunOS versions 4.1.1, 4.1, and 4.0.3 on all architectures.
    Patches are available for SunOS 4.1.1.  An initial patch for SunOS
    4.1 NFS is also available. Sun will be providing complete patches
    for SunOS 4.1 and SunOS 4.0.3 at a later date.

CA-94:15.NFS.Vulnerabilities                                      12/19/94
    This advisory describes security measures to guard against several
    vulnerabilities in the Network File System (NFS). The advisory was
    prompted by an increase in root compromises by intruders using tools
    to exploit the vulnerabilities.

CA-96.08.pcnfsd                                                   04/18/96
    This advisory describes a vulnerability in the pcnfsd program (also
    known as rpc.pcnfsd). A patch is included.
```

6.1 Client Security

On the client we can decide that we don't want to trust the server too much in a couple of ways with options to mount. For example, we can forbid `suid` programs to work from the NFS file system with the `nosuid` option. This is a good idea and you should consider using this with all NFS mounted disks. It means that the server's root user cannot make a `suid` root program on the file system, log in to the client as a normal user and then use the `suid` root program to become root on the client, too. We could also forbid execution of files on the mounted file system altogether with the `noexec` option. But this is more likely to be impractical than `nosuid`, since a file system is likely to at least contain *some* scripts or programs that need to be executed. You enter these options in the `options` column, with the `rsize` and `wsize`, separated by commas.

6.2 Server security: `nfsd`

On the server, we can decide that we don't want to trust the client's root account. We can do that by using the root_squash option in exports:

```
/mn/eris/local apollon(rw,root_squash)
```

Now, if a user with UID 0 on the client attempts to access (read, write, delete) the file system the server substitutes the UID of the server's "nobody" account. Which means that the root user on the client can't access or change files that only root on the server can access or change. That's good, and you should probably use `root_squash` on all the file systems you export. "But the root user on the client can still use `su` to become any other user and access and change that user's files!" say you. To which the answer is: "Yes, and that's the way it is, and has to be with Unix and NFS." This has one important implication: All important binaries and files should be owned by `root`, and not `bin` or other non-root account, since the only account the client's root user cannot access is the servers root account. In the `nfsd` manual page, there are several other squash options listed, so that you can decide to mistrust whomever you (don't) like on the clients. You also have options to squash any UID and GID range you want to. This is described in the Linux `nfsd` manual page.

`root_squash` is in fact the default with the Linux `nfsd`, to grant root access to a filesystem use `no_root_squash`.

Another important thing is to insure that `nfsd` checks that all its requests come from a privileged port. If it accepts requests from any old port on the client, a user with no special privileges can run a program that is is easy to obtain over the Internet. It talks NFS protocol and will claim that the user is anyone the user wants to be. Spooky. The Linux `nfsd` does this check by default, but on other OSes you have to enable this check yourself. This should be described in the `nfsd` manual page for the OS.

Another thing. Never export a file system to 'localhost' or 127.0.0.1. Trust me.

6.3 Server security: the portmapper

The basic portmapper, in combination with `nfsd`, has a design problem that makes it possible to get to files on NFS servers without any privileges. Fortunately, the portmapper Linux uses is relatively secure against this attack, and can be made more secure by configuring up access lists in two files.

First we edit `/etc/hosts.deny`. It should contain the line

```
portmap: ALL
```

which will deny access to everyone. That's a bit drastic perhaps, so we open it again by editing `/etc/hosts.allow`. But first we need to figure out what to put in it. It should basically list all machines that should have access to your portmapper. On a run of the mill Linux system, there are very few machines that need any access for any reason. The portmapper administrates `nfsd`, `mountd`, `ypbind` and `ypserv`, `pcnfsd`, and "r" services like `ruptime` and `rusers`. Of these, only `nfsd`, `mountd`, `ypbind` and `ypserv`, and perhaps `pcnfsd` are of any consequence. All machines that need to access services on your machine should be allowed to do that. Let's say that your machine's address is 129.240.223.254 and that it lives on the subnet 129.240.223.0 which should have access to it (those are terms introduced by the NET-3 HOWTO, go back and refresh your memory if you need to). Then we write

```
portmap: 129.240.223.0/255.255.255.0
```

in `hosts.allow`. This is the same as the network address you give to `route`, and the subnet mask you give to `ifconfig`. For the device `eth0` on this machine, `ifconfig` should show

```
...
eth0      Link encap:10Mbps Ethernet  HWaddr 00:60:8C:96:D5:56
          inet addr:129.240.223.254  Bcast:129.240.223.255  Mask:255.255.255.0
          UP BROADCAST RUNNING MULTICAST  MTU:1500  Metric:1
          RX packets:360315 errors:0 dropped:0 overruns:0
          TX packets:179274 errors:0 dropped:0 overruns:0
          Interrupt:10 Base address:0x320
...
```

and `netstat -rn` should show

```
Kernel routing table
Destination     Gateway         Genmask         Flags Metric Ref Use    Iface
...
129.240.223.0   0.0.0.0         255.255.255.0   U     0      0   174412 eth0
...
```

(Network address in first column).

The `/etc hosts.deny` and `/etc/hosts.allow` files are described in the manual pages of the same names.

IMPORTANT: Do *not* put *anything* but *IP NUMBERS* in the portmap lines of these files. Host name lookups can indirectly cause portmap activity which will trigger host name lookups which can indirectly cause portmap activity which will trigger...

The above things should make your server tighter. The only remaining problem (Yeah, right!) is someone breaking root (or boot MS-DOS) on a trusted machine and using that privilege to send requests from a secure port as any user they want to be.

6.4 NFS and firewalls

It's a very good idea to firewall the NFS and portmap ports in your router or firewall. The `nfsd` operates at port 2049, both UDP and TCP protocols. The portmapper at port 111, TCP and UDP, and `mountd` at port 745 and and 747, TCP and UDP. Normally. You should check the ports with the `rpcinfo -p` command.

If on the other hand you want NFS to go through a firewall there are options for newer `nfsds` and `mountds` to make them use a specific (nonstandard) port which can be open in the firewall.

6.5 Summary

If you use the `/etc/hosts.allow` or `/etc/hosts.deny` files, `root_squash`, `nosuid`, and privileged port features in the portmapper and NFS software, you avoid many of the presently known bugs in NFS and can almost feel secure about that at least. But still, after all that: when an intruder has access to your network, she or he can make strange commands appear in your `.forward` or mailbox file when `/home` or `/var/spool/mail` are mounted over NFS. For the same reason, you should never access your PGP private key over NFS. Or at least you should know the risk involved. And now you know a bit of it.

NFS and the portmapper makes up a complex subsystem, and therefore it's not totally unlikely that new bugs will be discovered, either in the basic design or the implementation we use. There might even be holes known now, which someone is abusing. But that's life. To keep abreast of things like this you should at least read the newsgroups comp.os.linux.announce and comp.security.announce at a absolute minimum.

7 Mount Checklist

This section is based on IBM Corp. NFS mount problem checklist. My thanks to them for making it available for this HOWTO. If you experience a problem mounting a NFS file system, please refer to this list before posting your problem. Each item describes a failure mode and the fix.

1. File system not exported, or not exported to the client in question.

   Fix: Export it

2. Name resolution doesn't jibe with the exports list.

   E.g.: export list says export to `johnmad` but `johnmad`'s name is resolved as `johnmad.austin.ibm.com`. mount permission is denied.

   Fix: Export to both forms of the name.

   It can also happen if the client has 2 interfaces with different names for each of the two adapters and the export only specifies one.

   Fix: export both interfaces.

   This can also happen if the server can't do a lookuphostbyname or lookuphostbyaddr (these are library functions) on the client. Make sure the client can do host <name>; host <ip_addr>; and that both shows the same machine.

   Fix: straighten out name resolution.

3. The file system was mounted after NFS was started (on that server). In that case the server is exporting underlying mount point, not the mounted filesystem.

   Fix: Shut down `nfsd` and then restart it.

   Note: The clients that had the underlying mount point mounted will get problems accessing it after the restart.

4. The date is wildly off on one or both machines (this can mess up `make`)

   Fix: Get the date set right.

   The HOWTO author recommends using NTP to synchronize clocks. Since there are export restrictions on NTP in the US, you have to get NTP for Debian, Red Hat, or Slackware from ftp://ftp.hacktic.nl/pub/replay/pub/linux, or a mirror.

5. The server can not accept a mount from a user that is in more than 8 groups.

   Fix: decrease the number of groups the user is in or mount via a different user.

8 FAQs

This is the FAQ section. Most of it was written by Alan Cox.

1. I get a lot of "stale NFS handle" errors when using Linux as a NFS server.

   This is caused by a bug in some oldish `nfsd` versions. It is fixed in NFS-server2.2beta16 and later.

2. When I try to mount a file system I get

   ```
   can't register with portmap: system error on send
   ```

You are probably using a Caldera system. There is a bug in the `rc` scripts. Please contact Caldera to obtain a fix.

3. Why can't I execute a file after copying it to the NFS server?
   The reason is that `nfsd` caches open file handles for performance reasons (remember, it runs in user space). While `nfsd` has a file open (as is the case after writing to it), the kernel won't allow you to execute it. A `nfsd` newer than Spring '95 release open files after a few seconds, while older ones would cling to them for days.
4. My NFS files are all read-only
   The Linux NFS server defaults to read only. RTFM the `exports` and `nfsd` manual pages. You will need to alter `/etc/exports`.
5. I mount from a Linux NFS server and while `ls` works, I can't read or write files.
   On older versions of Linux you must mount NFS volumes with `rsize=1024,wsize=1024`.
6. I mount from a Linux NFS server with a block size of between 3500–4000, and it crashes the Linux box regularly.
   Basically don't do it then.
7. Can Linux do NFS over TCP?
   No, not at present.
8. I get loads of strange errors trying to mount a remote volume from a Linux box.
   Make sure your users are in 8 groups or less. Older servers require this.
9. When I reboot my machine, it sometimes hangs when trying to unmount a hung NFS server.
   Do *not* unmount NFS servers when rebooting or halting, just ignore them, it will not hurt anything if you don't unmount them. The command is `umount -avt nonfs`.
10. Linux NFS clients are very slow when writing to Sun and BSD systems
    NFS writes are normally synchronous (you can disable this if you don't mind risking losing data). Worse still, BSD derived kernels tend to be unable to work in small blocks. Thus, when you write 4K of data from a Linux box in the 1K packets it uses, BSD does this

```
read 4K page
alter 1K
write 4K back to physical disk
read 4K page
alter 1K
write 4K page back to physical disk
etc..
```

9 Exporting filesystems

The way to export filesytems with NFS is not completely consistent across platforms of course. In this case Linux and Solaris 2 are the deviants. This section lists, superficially, the way to do it on most systems. If the kind of system you have is not covered, you must check your OS man-pages. Keywords are: nfsd, system administration tool, rc scripts, boot scripts, boot sequence, /etc/exports, exportfs. I'll use one example throughout this section: How to export /mn/eris/local to apollon read/write.

9.1 IRIX, HP-UX, Digital-UNIX, Ultrix, SunOS 4 (Solaris 1), AIX

These OSes use the traditional Sun export format. In `/etc/exports` write:

```
/mn/eris/local -rw=apollon
```

The complete documentation is in the `exports` manual page. After editing the file, run `exportfs -av` to export the file systems.

How strict the `exportfs` command is about the syntax varies. On some OSes you will find that previously entered line reads:

```
/mn/eris/local apollon
```

or even something degenerate like:

```
/mn/eris/local rw=apollon
```

I recommend being formal. You risk that the next version of `exportfs` is much stricter, and then suddenly everything will stop working.

9.2 Solaris 2

Sun completely re-invented the wheel when they did Solaris 2. So this is completely different from all other OSes. What you do is edit the file `/etc/dfs/dfstab`. In it, you place `share` commands as documented in the `share(1M)` manual page. Like this:

```
share -o rw=apollon -d "Eris Local" /mn/eris/local
```

After editing run the program `shareall` to export the file systems.

10 PC-NFS

You should not run PC-NFS. You should run SAMBA.

[Sorry: I don't know anything about PC-NFS. If someone feels like writing something about it please do and I'll include it here.]

Part XXXIII

"Linux NIS(YP)/NIS+/NYS HOWTO" by Thorsten Kukuk,

kukuk@vt.uni-paderborn.de

Contents

Abstract

v0.8, 9 November 1997
This document describes how to configure Linux as NIS(YP) or NIS+ client and how to install as NIS server.

1 Introduction

More and more, Linux machines are installed as part of a network of computers. To simplify network administration, most networks (mostly Sun-based networks) run the Network Information Service. Linux machines can take full advantage of existing NIS service or provide NIS service themselves. Linux machines can also act as full NIS+ clients, this support is in beta stage.

This document tries to answer questions about setting up NIS(YP) and NIS+ on your Linux machine. Don't forget to read the section about portmappers, 5

The NIS-HOWTO is edited and maintained by:

Thorsten Kukuk, `kukuk@vt.uni-paderborn.de`

The primary source of the information for the initial NIS-HOWTO was from:

```
Andrea Dell'Amico       <adellam@ZIA.ms.it>
Mitchum DSouza          <Mitch.DSouza@NetComm.IE>
Erwin Embsen            <erwin@nioz.nl>
Peter Eriksson          <peter@ifm.liu.se>
```

who we should thank for writing the first versions of this document.

1.1 New versions of this document

New versions of this document will be posted periodically to the newsgroups news:comp.os.linux.help and news:comp.os.linux.announce. They will also be uploaded to various Linux WWW and FTP sites, including the LDP home page.

You can always view the latest version of this on the World Wide Web via the URL

```
http://sunsite.unc.edu/mdw/HOWTO/NIS-HOWTO.html
```

1.2 Disclaimer

Although this document has been put together to the best of our knowledge, it may, and probably does, contain errors. Please read any README files that are bundled with any of the various pieces of software described in this document for more detailed and accurate information. We will attempt to keep this document as error free as possible.

1.3 Feedback and Corrections

If you have questions or comments about this document, please feel free to mail Thorsten Kukuk, at kukuk@vt.uni-paderborn.de. I welcome any suggestions or criticisms. If you find a mistake with this document, please let me know so I can correct it in the next version. Thanks.

Please do *not* mail me questions about special problems with your Linux distributions! I don't know every Linux Distribution. But I will try to add every solution you send me.

1.4 Acknowledgements

We would like to thank all the people who have contributed (directly or indirectly) to this document. In alphabetical order:

```
Byron A Jeff            <byron@cc.gatech.edu>
Miquel van Smoorenburg  <miquels@cistron.nl>
```

Theo de Raadt <deraadt@theos.com> is responsible for the original yp-clients code. Swen Thuemmler <swen@uni-paderborn.de> ported the yp-clients code to Linux and also ported the yp-routines in libc (again based on Theo's work). Thorsten Kukuk has written the NIS(YP) and NIS+ routines for GNU libc 2.x from scratch.

2 Glossary and General Information

2.1 Glossary of Terms

In this document a lot of abbreviations are used. Here are the most important of them and brief explanations:

DBM
: DataBase Management, a library of functions which maintain key-content pairs in a data base.

DLL
: Dynamically Linked Library, a library linked to an executable program at run-time.

domain name
: A name "key" that is used by NIS clients to be able to locate a suitable NIS server that serves that domain name key. Please note that this does not necessarily have anything at all to do with the DNS "domain" (machine name) of the machine(s).

FTP
: File Transfer Protocol, a protocol used to transfer files between two computers.

libnsl
: Name services library, a library of name service calls (getpwnam, getservbyname, etc...) on SVR4 Unixes. GNU libc uses this for the NIS (YP) and NIS+ functions.

libsocket
: Socket services library, a library for the socket service calls (socket, bind, listen, etc...) on SVR4 Unixes.

NIS
: Network Information Service, a service that provides information, that has to be known throughout the network, to all machines on the network. There is support for NIS in Linux's standard libc library, which in the following text is referred to as **traditional NIS.**

NIS+
: Network Information Service (Plus), essentially NIS on steroids. NIS+ is designed by Sun Microsystems Inc. as a replacement for NIS with better security and better handling of large installations.

NYS
: This is the name of a project and stands for NIS+, YP, and Switch and is managed by Peter Eriksson, peter@ifm.liu.se. It contains, among other things, a complete re-implementation of the NIS (= YP) code that uses the Name Services Switch functionality of the NYS library.

NSS
: Name Service Switch. The `/etc/nsswitch.conf` file determines the order of lookups performed when a certain piece of information is requested.

RPC
: Remote Procedure Call. RPC routines allow C programs to make procedure calls on other machines across the network. When people talk about RPC they most often mean the Sun RPC variant.

YP
: Yellow Pages(tm), a registered trademark in the UK of British Telecom plc.

TCP/IP
: Transmission Control Protocol/Internet Protocol. It's the data communication protocol most often used on Unix machines.

2.2 Some General Information

The next four lines are quoted from the Sun(tm) System & Network Administration Manual:

```
"NIS was formerly known as Sun Yellow Pages (YP) but
 the name Yellow Pages(tm) is a registered trademark
 in the United Kingdom of British Telecom plc and may
 not be used without permission."
```

NIS stands for Network Information Service. It's purpose is to provide information that has to be known throughout the network to all machines on the network. Information likely to be distributed by NIS is:

- login names/passwords/home directories (`/etc/passwd`);
- group information (`/etc/group`).

So, for example, if your password entry is recorded in the NIS passwd database, you will be able to login on all machines on the net which have the NIS client programs running.

Sun is a trademark of Sun Microsystems, Inc. licensed to SunSoft, Inc.

3 NIS or NIS+ ?

The choice between NIS and NIS+ is easy—use NIS if you don't have to use NIS+ or have severe security needs. NIS+ is much more problematic to administer (it's pretty easy to handle on the client side, but the server side is horrible). Another problem is that the support for NIS+ under Linux is still under development—you need the latest glibc snapshot for it, or have to wait for glibc 2.1. There is a port of the glibc NIS+ support for libc5 as drop-in replacement.

3.1 libc 4 or 5 with traditional NIS or NYS?

The choice between "traditional NIS" or the NIS code in the NYS library is a choice between laziness and maturity, vs. flexibility and love of adventure.

The "traditional NIS" code is in the standard C library and has been around longer and sometimes suffers from its age and slight inflexibility.

The NIS code in the NYS library requires you to recompile the libc library to include the NYS code into the libc library (or maybe you can go get a pre-compiled version of libc from someone who has already done it).

Another difference is that the traditional NIS code has some support for NIS net groups, which the NYS code doesn't (yet). On the other hand, the NYS code allows you to handle Shadow Passwords in a transparent manner. The "traditional NIS" code doesn't support Shadow Passwords over NIS.

Forget this all if you use the new GNU C Library 2.x (a.k.a., libc6). It supports NSS (name switch service), which makes it very flexible, and contains support for the following NIS/NIS+ maps: aliases, ethers, group, hosts, net groups, networks, protocols, public key, passwd, rpc, services, and shadow.

4 How it works

4.1 How NIS(YP) works

Within a network there must be at least one machine acting as a NIS server. You can have multiple NIS servers, each serving different NIS "domains," or you can have cooperating NIS servers, where one is said to be the master NIS server, and all the other are so-called slave NIS servers (for a certain NIS "domain," that is!)—or you can have a mix of them...

Slave servers only have copies of the NIS databases and receive these copies from the master NIS server whenever changes are made to the masters' databases. Depending on the number of machines in your network and the reliability of your network, you might decide to install one or more slave servers. Whenever a NIS server goes down or is too slow in responding to requests, a NIS client connected to that server will try to find one that is up or quicker.

NIS databases are in so-called DBM format, derived from ASCII databases. For example, the files `/etc/passwd` and `/etc/group` can be directly converted to DBM format using ASCII-to-DBM translation software (`makedbm` is included with the server software). The master NIS server should have both, the ASCII databases and the DBM databases.

Slave servers will be notified of any change to the NIS maps, (via the `yppush` program), and automatically retrieve the necessary changes in order to synchronize their databases. NIS clients do not need to do this since they always talks to the NIS server to read the information stored in it's DBM databases.

The author of the YP clients for linux has informed us that the newest `ypbind` (ypbind-3.3.tar.gz) is able to get the server from a configuration file—thus no need to broadcast. (Which is insecure due to the fact that anyone may install a NIS server and answer the broadcast queries.)

4.2 How NIS+ works

NIS+ is a new version of the network information name service from Sun. The biggest difference between NIS and NIS+ is, that NIS+ has support for data encryption and authentication over secure RPC.

The naming model of NIS+ is based upon a tree structure. Each node in the tree corresponds to an NIS+ object, from which we have six types: directory, entry, group, link, table and private.

The NIS+ directory that forms the root of the NIS+ name space is called the root directory. There are two special NIS+ directories: `org_dir` and `groups_dir`. The `org_dir` directory consists of all administration tables, such as passwd, hosts, and `mail_aliases`. The `groups_dir` directory consists of NIS+ group objects which are used for access control. The collection of `org_dir`, `groups_dir` and their parent directory is referred to as an NIS+ domain.

5 The RPC Portmapper

To run any of the software mentioned below, you will need to run the program /usr/sbin/portmap. Some Linux distributions already have the code in the /etc/rc.d/ files to start up this daemon. All you have to do is to activate it and reboot your Linux machine. Read your Linux Distribution Documentation how to do this.

The RPC portmapper (portmap(8)) is a server that converts RPC program numbers into TCP/IP (or UDP/IP) protocol port numbers. It must be running in order to make RPC calls (which is what the NIS/NIS+ client software does) to RPC servers (like a NIS or NIS+ server) on that machine. When an RPC server is started, it will tell portmap what port number it is listening to, and what RPC program numbers it is prepared to serve. When a client wishes to make an RPC call to a given program number, it will first contact portmap on the server machine to determine the port number where RPC packets should be sent.

Normally, standard RPC servers are started by inetd(8), so portmap must be started before inetd is invoked.

For secure RPC, the portmapper needs the Time Service. Make sure that the Time Service is enabled in /etc/inetd.conf on all hosts:

```
#
# Time service is used for clock synchronization.
#
time    stream  tcp     nowait  nobody  /usr/sbin/tcpd  in.timed
time    dgram   udp     wait    nobody  /usr/sbin/tcpd  in.timed
```

IMPORTANT: Don't forget to restart inetd after making changes on this file!

6 What do you need to set up NIS?

6.1 Determine whether you are a Server, Slave, or Client.

To answer this question, you have to consider two cases:

1. Your machine is going to be part of a network with existing NIS servers.
2. You do not have any NIS servers in the network yet.

In the first case, you only need the client programs (ypbind, ypwhich, ypcat, yppoll, ypmatch). The most important program is ypbind. This program must be running at all times, that is, it should always appear in the list of processes. It's a so-called daemon process and needs to be started from the system's startup file (eg. /etc/rc.local, /etc/init.d/nis, /etc/rc.d/init.d/ypbind). As soon as ypbind is running, your system has become a NIS client.

In the second case, if you don't have NIS servers, then you will also need a NIS server program (usually called ypserv). Section 8 describes how to set up a NIS server on your Linux machine using the "ypserv" implementation by Peter Eriksson and Thorsten Kukuk. Note that from version 0.14 this implementation supports the master-slave concept talked about in Section 4.1.

There is also another free NIS server available, called "yps," written by Tobias Reber in Germany which does support the master-slave concept, but has other limitations and isn't supported any longer.

6.2 The Software

The system library /usr/lib/libc.a (version 4.4.2 and better) or the shared library "/lib/libc.so.x" contain all necessary system calls to successfully compile the NIS client and server software. For glibc 2.x, you also need /lib/libnsl.so.1.

Some people report that NIS only works with /usr/lib/libc.a version 4.5.21 and better so if you want to play it safe, don't use older libc's. The NIS client software can be obtained from:

Site	Directory	File Name
ftp.uni-paderborn.de	/linux/local/yp	yp-clients-2.2.tar.gz
ftp.uni-paderborn.de	/linux/local/yp	ypbind-3.3.tar.gz
wauug.erols.com	/pub/net/nis	yp-tools-1.2.tar.gz
wauug.erols.com	/pub/net/nis	ypbind-3.3.tar.gz
ftp.lysator.liu.se	/pub/NYS/clients	yp-tools-1.2.tar.gz
sunsite.unc.edu	/pub/Linux/system/Network/admin	yp-clients-2.2.tar.gz

Once you obtained the software, please follow the instructions which come with the software. yp-clients 2.2 are for use with libc4 and libc5 until 5.4.20. libc 5.4.21 and glibc 2.x needs yp-tools 1.2. ypbind 3.3 will work with all libraries. You should never use the ypbind from yp-clients 2.2.

6.3 The ypbind daemon

Assuming you have successfully compiled the software, you are now ready to install the software. A suitable place for the ypbind daemon is the directory /usr/sbin. Some people may tell you, that you don't need ypbind on a system with NYS. This is wrong: ypwhich and ypcat need it.

You'll need to do this as root of course. The other binaries (ypwhich, ypcat, yppoll, ypmatch) should go in a directory accessible by all users, normally /usr/bin.

The ypbind process has a configuration file called /etc/yp.conf. You can hard code a NIS server there—for more information, see the manual page for ypbind(8). You also need this file for NYS. An example:

```
ypserver voyager
ypserver ds9
```

If the system could resolve the hostnames without NIS, you could use the name, otherwise you have to use the IP address.

It might be a good idea to test ypbind before incorporating it in the /etc/rc.d/ files. To test ypbind, do the following:

- Make sure you have your domain name set. If it is not set then issue the command:

  ```
  /bin/domainname nis.domain
  ```

  where nis.domain should be some string, not normally associated with the domain name of your machine! The reason for this is that it makes it a little harder for external crackers to retrieve the password database from your NIS servers. If you don't know what the NIS domain name is on your network, ask your system or network administrator.
- Start up /usr/sbin/portmap if it is not already running.
- Create the directory /var/yp if it does not exist.
- Start up /usr/sbin/ypbind.
- Use the command rpcinfo -p localhost to check if ypbind was able to register its service with the portmapper. rpcinfo should produce something like:

  ```
  program vers proto   port
   100000    2   tcp    111  portmapper
   100000    2   udp    111  portmapper
   100007    2   udp    637  ypbind
   100007    2   tcp    639  ypbind
   300019    1   udp    660
  ```

- You may also run rpcinfo -u localhost ypbind. This command should produce something like:

  ```
  program 100007 version 2 ready and waiting
  ```

At this point you should be able to use NIS client programs like ypcat, etc. For example, ypcat passwd will give you the entire NIS password database.

IMPORTANT: If you skipped the test procedure, then make sure you have set the domain name, and created the directory:

```
/var/yp
```

This directory must exist for ypbind to start up successfully.

If the test worked, you may now want to change the files in /etc/rc.d/ on your system, so that ypbind will be started up at boot time and your system will act as a NIS client. Make sure, that the domainname will be set at boot time.

Well, that's it. Reboot the machine and watch the boot messages to see if ypbind is actually started.

6.4 Setting up a NIS Client using Traditional NIS

For host lookups you must set (or add) "nis" to the lookup order line in your `/etc/host.conf` file. Please read the manual page `resolv+.8` for more details.

Add the following line to `/etc/passwd` on your NIS clients:

```
+::::::
```

You can also use the `+` and `-` characters to include, exclude, or change users. If you want to exclude the user "guest," just add -guest to your `/etc/passwd` file. You want to use a different shell (e.g. `ksh`) for the user "linux?" No problem, just add `+linux::::::/bin/ksh` to your `/etc/passwd` file. Fields that you don't want to change have to be left empty. You could also use net groups for user control.

For example, to only allow login-access to miquels, dth and ed, and all members of the sysadmin net group, but to have the account data of all other users available:

```
+miquels:::::::
+ed:::::::
+dth:::::::
+@sysadmins:::::::
-ftp
+:*::::::/etc/NoShell
```

Note that in Linux you can also override the password field, as we did in this example. In this example, we also remove the login "ftp," so it isn't known any longer, and anonymous FTP will not work.

The net group would be look like

```
sysadmins (-,software,) (-,kukuk,)
```

IMPORTANT: Note that the net group feature is implemented starting from libc 4.5.26. But if you have a version of libc earlier than 4.5.26, every user in the NIS password database can access your Linux machine if you run `ypbind`.

6.5 Setting up a NIS Client using NYS

All that is required is that the NIS configuration file (`/etc/yp.conf`) points to the correct server(s) for its information. Also, the Name Services Switch configuration file (`/etc/nsswitch.conf`) must be correctly set up.

You should install `ypbind`. It isn't needed by the libc, but the NIS(YP) tools need it.

If you wish to use the include or exclude user feature (+/-guest/+@admins), you have to use "passwd: compat" and "group: compat." Note, that there is no "shadow: compat." You have to use "shadow: files nis" in this case.

6.6 Setting up a NIS Client using glibc 2.x

The glibc uses "traditional NIS," so you need to start `ypbind`. The Name Services Switch configuration file (`/etc/nsswitch.conf`) must be correctly set up. If you use the compat mode for passwd, shadow or group, you have to add the "+" at the end of this file, and you could use the include and exclude user features. The configuration is exactly the same as under Solaris 2.x.

6.7 The `/etc/nsswitch.conf` file

The Network Services switch file `/etc/nsswitch.conf` determines the order of lookups performed when a certain piece of information is requested, just like the `/etc/host.conf` file, which determines the way host lookups are performed. For example, the line

```
hosts: files nis dns
```

specifies that host lookup functions should first look in the local `/etc/hosts` file, followed by a NIS lookup and finally thru the domain name service (`/etc/resolv.conf` and `named`), at which point if no match is found an error is returned.

A good `/etc/nsswitch` file for NIS is:

```
#
# /etc/nsswitch.conf
#
# An example Name Service Switch config file. This file should be
# sorted with the most-used services at the beginning.
#
# The entry '[NOTFOUND=return]' means that the search for an
# entry should stop if the search in the previous entry turned
# up nothing. Note that if the search failed due to some other reason
```

```
# (like no NIS server responding) then the search continues with the
# next entry.
#
# Legal entries are:
#
#       nisplus                  Use NIS+ (NIS version 3)
#       nis                      Use NIS (NIS version 2), also called YP
#       dns                      Use DNS (Domain Name Service)
#       files                    Use the local files
#       db                       Use the /var/db databases
#       [NOTFOUND=return]        Stop searching if not found so far
#

passwd:     compat
group:      compat
shadow:     compat

passwd_compat: nis
group_compat: nis
shadow_compat: nis

hosts:      nis files dns

services:   nis [NOTFOUND=return] files
networks:   nis [NOTFOUND=return] files
protocols:  nis [NOTFOUND=return] files
rpc:        nis [NOTFOUND=return] files
ethers:     nis [NOTFOUND=return] files
netmasks:   nis [NOTFOUND=return] files
netgroup:   nis
bootparams: nis [NOTFOUND=return] files
publickey:  nis [NOTFOUND=return] files
automount:  files
aliases:    nis [NOTFOUND=return] files
```

`passwd_compat`, `group_compat`, and `shadow_compat` are only supported by glibc 2.x. If there are no shadow rules in `/etc/nsswitch.conf`, glibc will use the `passwd` rule for lookups. There are some more lookup module for glibc like hesoid. For more information, read the glibc documentation.

7 What do you need to set up NIS+ ?

7.1 The Software

You need to retrieve and compile the latest GNU C library 2 snapshot. And you need a glibc based system like Red Hat Mustang or the unstable Debian. But be warned: This is all beta Software! Read the documentation about glibc snapshots and the distributions! glibc 2.0.x doesn't contain the NIS+ support, and will never contain it. The first public version with NIS+ support will be 2.1.

The NIS+ client software can be obtained from:

Site	Directory	File Name
ftp.kernel.org	/pub/software/libs/glibc	libc-*, glibc-crypt-*, glibc-linuxthreads-*, glibc-localedata-*
wauug.erols.com	/pub/net/nis	nis-tools-1.4.tar.gz
wauug.erols.com	/pub/net/nis	pam_keylogin-1.0.tar.gz

Distributions based on glibc can be fetched from:

Site	Directory

```
ftp.redhat.com          /pub/redhat/mustang
ftp.debian.org          /pub/debian/hamm
```

For compilation of the GNU C Library, please follow the instructions which come with the software. There is a patched libc5, based on NYS and the glibc sources. ad drop in replacement for the standard libc5.

You should also look at http://www-vt.uni-paderborn.de/ kukuk/linux/nisplus.html for more information and the latest sources.

7.2 Setting up a NIS+ client

IMPORTANT: For setting up a NIS+ client, read your Solaris NIS+ docs what to do on the server side. This document only describes what to do on the client side.

After installing the new libc and nis-tools, run

```
domainname nisplus.domain.
nisinit -c -H <NIS+ server>
```

to initialize the cold Start File. Read the `nisinit` manual page for more options. Make sure, that the domain name will always be set after a reboot. If you don't know what the NIS+ domain name is on your network, ask your system or network administrator.

Now you should change your `/etc/nsswitch.conf` file. Make sure that the only service after publickey is nisplus ("publickey: nisplus"), and nothing else!

After this, start keyserv and make sure, that it will always be started at boot time. Run

```
keylogin -r
```

to store the root secretkey on your system. (I hope you have added the publickey for the new host on the NIS+ server.)

`niscat passwd.org_dir` should now show you all entries in the passwd database.

7.3 NIS+, keylogin, login and PAM

When the user logs in, he needs to set his secretkey to keyserv. This is done by calling `keylogin`. The `login` from the shadow package will do this for the user. For a PAM-aware `login`, you have to install `pam_keylogin-1.0.tar.gz`, and change the `/etc/pam.d/login` file to use `pam_unix_auth`, not pwdb, which doesn't support NIS+. An example:

```
#%PAM-1.0
auth       required    /lib/security/pam_securetty.so
auth       required    /lib/security/pam_keylogin.so
auth       required    /lib/security/pam_unix_auth.so
auth       required    /lib/security/pam_nologin.so
account    required    /lib/security/pam_unix_acct.so
password   required    /lib/security/pam_unix_passwd.so
session    required    /lib/security/pam_unix_session.so
```

8 Setting up a NIS Server

8.1 The Server Program `ypserv`

This document only describes how to set up the `ypserv` NIS server.

The NIS server software can be found on:

```
Site                     Directory              File Name

waaug.erols.com          /pub/net/nis           ypserv-1.2.5.tar.gz
ftp.lysator.liu.se       /pub/NYS/servers       ypserv-1.2.5.tar.gz
ftp.uni-paderborn.de     /linux/local/yp        ypserv-1.2.5.tar.gz
```

You could also look at http://www-vt.uni-paderborn.de/ kukuk/linux/nis.html for more information and the latest sources.

The server setup is the same for both traditional NIS and NYS.

Compile the software to generate the `ypserv` and `makedbm` programs. If you run your server as master, determine what files you require to be available via NIS and then add or remove the appropriate entries to the `/var/yp/Makefile`.

Now edit `/var/yp/securenets` and `/etc/ypserv.conf`. For more information, read the `ypserv(8)` and `ypserv.conf(5)` manual pages.

Make sure the portmapper (`portmap(8)`) is running, and start the server `ypserv`. The command

```
% rpcinfo -u localhost ypserv
```

should output something like

```
program 100004 version 2 ready and waiting
```

Now generate the NIS (YP) database. On the master, run

```
% /usr/lib/yp/ypinit -m
```

on a slave, make sure that ypwhich -m works. Then run

```
% /usr/lib/yp/ypinit -s masterhost
```

That's it, your server is up and running. You might want to edit root's `crontab` on the slave server and add the following lines:

```
20 *     * * *    /usr/lib/yp/ypxfr_1perhour
40 6     * * *    /usr/lib/yp/ypxfr_1perday
55 6,18 * * *    /usr/lib/yp/ypxfr_2perday
```

This will ensure that most NIS maps are kept up to date, even if an update is missed because the slave was down at the time the update was done on the master.

If you want to restrict access to your NIS server, you'll have to set up the NIS server as a client as well by running ypbind and adding the plus-entries to `/etc/passwd` *halfway* through the password file. The library functions will ignore all normal entries after the first NIS entry, and will get the rest of the info through NIS. This way, the NIS access rules are maintained. For example:

```
root:x:0:0:root:/root:/bin/bash
daemon:*:1:1:daemon:/usr/sbin:
bin:*:2:2:bin:/bin:
sys:*:3:3:sys:/dev:
sync:*:4:100:sync:/bin:/bin/sync
games:*:5:100:games:/usr/games:
man:*:6:100:man:/var/catman:
lp:*:7:7:lp:/var/spool/lpd:
mail:*:8:8:mail:/var/spool/mail:
news:*:9:9:news:/var/spool/news:
uucp:*:10:50:uucp:/var/spool/uucp:
nobody:*:65534:65534:noone at all,,,,:/dev/null:
+miquels::::::
+:*:::::/etc/NoShell
[ All normal users AFTER this line! ]
tester:*:299:10:Just a test account:/tmp:
miquels:1234567890123:101:10:Miquel van Smoorenburg:/home/miquels:/bin/zsh
```

The user `tester` will exist, but have a shell of `/etc/NoShell`. `miquels` will have normal access.

Alternatively, you could edit the `/var/yp/Makefile` file and set NIS to use another source password file. On big systems, the NIS password and group files are usually stored in `/var/yp/ypfiles/`. If you do this the normal tools to administer the password file such as `passwd`, `chfn`, and `adduser` will not work anymore and you will need special, homemade tools for this.

However `yppasswd`, `ypchsh`, and `ypchfn` will work, of course.

8.2 The Server Program `yps`

To set up the `yps` NIS server please refer to the previous paragraph. The `yps` server setup is similar, but not exactly the same, so beware if you try to apply the `ypserv` instructions to `yps`. `yps` is not supported by any author, and contains some security leaks. You shouldn't really use it.

The `yps` NIS server software can be found at:

Site	Directory	File Name
ftp.lysator.liu.se	/pub/NYS/servers	yps-0.21.tar.gz
ftp.funet.fi	/pub/Linux/BETA/NYS/servers	yps-0.21.tar.gz

8.3 The Program `rpc.yppasswdd`

Whenever users change their passwords, the NIS password database, and probably other NIS databases which depend on the NIS password database, should be updated. The program `rpc.yppasswdd` is a server that handles password changes and makes sure that the NIS information will be updated accordingly. `rpc.yppasswdd` is now integrated in `ypserv` 1.2.5. You don't need the older, separate yppasswd-0.9.tar.gz or yppasswd-0.10.tar.gz, and you shouldn't use them any longer. The `rpc.yppasswdd` in `ypserv` 1.2.5 has full shadow support. `yppasswd` is now part of yp-tools-1.2.tar.gz, ypserv-1.2.5.tar.gz contains the sources for the same version.

9 Verifying the NIS/NYS Installation

If everything is fine (as it should be), you should be able to verify your installation with a few simple commands. Assuming, for example, your `passwd` file is being supplied by NIS, the command

```
% ypcat passwd
```

should give you the contents of your NIS `passwd` file. The command

```
% ypmatch userid passwd
```

(where *user ID* is the login name of an arbitrary user) should give you the user's entry in the NIS passwd file. The `ypcat` and `ypmatch` programs should be included with your distribution of traditional NIS or NYS.

If a user can't log in, run the following program on the client:

```
#include <stdio.h>
#include <pwd.h>
#include <sys/types.h>

int
main(int argc, char *argv[])
{
  struct passwd *pwd;

  if(argc != 2)
    {
      fprintf(stderr,"Usage: getwpnam username\n");
      exit(1);
    }

  pwd=getpwnam(argv[1]);

  if(pwd != NULL)
    {
      printf("name.....: [%s]\n",pwd->pw_name);
      printf("password.: [%s]\n",pwd->pw_passwd);
      printf("user id..: [%d]\n", pwd->pw_uid);
      printf("group id.: [%d]\n",pwd->pw_gid);
      printf("gecos....: [%s]\n",pwd->pw_gecos);
      printf("directory: [%s]\n",pwd->pw_dir);
      printf("shell....: [%s]\n",pwd->pw_shell);
    }
  else
    fprintf(stderr,"User \"%s\" not found!\n",argv[1]);

  exit(0);
}
```

Running this program with the user name as parameter will print all the information the `getpwnam` function will give back for this user. This should show you which entry is incorrect. The most common problem is that the password field is overwritten with a "*".

10 Common Problems and Troubleshooting NIS

Here are some common problems reported by various users:

1. The libraries for 4.5.19 are broken. NIS won't work with it.
2. If you upgrade the libraries from 4.5.19 to 4.5.24 then the su command breaks. You need to get the su command from the slackware 1.2.0 distribution. Incidentally, that's where you can get the updated libraries.
3. You could run into trouble with NIS and DNS on the same machine. My DNS server occasionally will not bring up NIS. Haven't yet tracked down why.
4. When a NIS server goes down and comes up again ypbind starts complaining with messages like:

   ```
   yp_match: clnt_call:
                   RPC: Unable to receive; errno = Connection refused
   ```

   and logins are refused for those who are registered in the NIS database. Try to login as root and if you succeed, then kill `ypbind` and start it up again.
5. Afterward, upgrade the libc to a version greater then 5.4.20, the YP tools will not work any longer. You need yp-tools 1.2 or later for libc >= 5.4.21 and glibc 2.x and yp-clients 2.2. for earlier versions.

11 Frequently Asked Questions

Most of your questions should be answered by now. If there are still questions unanswered you might want to post a message to

```
comp.os.linux.help
```

or

```
comp.os.linux.networking
```

or contact one of the authors of this HOWTO.

Part XXXIV

"Linux PCMCIA HOWTO" by David Hinds,

dhinds@hyper.stanford.edu

Contents

Abstract

v1.106, 14 November 1997
This document describes how to install and use PCMCIA Card Services for Linux, and answers some frequently asked questions. The latest version of this document can always be found at `hyper.stanford.edu` in `/pub/pcmcia/doc`. An HTML version is at `http://hyper.stanford.edu/HyperNews/get/pcmcia/home.html`

1 General information and hardware requirements

1.1 Introduction

Card Services for Linux is a complete PCMCIA support package. It includes a set of loadable kernel modules that implement a version of the PCMCIA Card Services applications program interface, a set of client drivers for specific cards, and a card manager daemon that can respond to card insertion and removal events, loading and unloading drivers on demand. It supports "hot swapping" of PCMCIA cards, so cards can be inserted and ejected at any time.

This software is still under development. It probably contains bugs, and should be used with caution. I'll do my best to fix problems that are reported to me, but if you don't tell me, I may never know. If you use this code, I hope you will send me your experiences, good or bad!

If you have any suggestions for how this document could be improved, please let me know (`dhinds@hyper.stanford.edu`).

1.2 Copyright notice and disclaimer

1.3 What is the latest version, and where can I get it?

The current major release of Card Services is Version 2.9, and minor updates or bug fixes are numbered 2.9.1, 2.9.2, and so on.

Source code for the latest version is available from `hyper.stanford.edu` in the `/pub/pcmcia` directory, as `pcmcia-cs-2.9.?.tar.gz`. There will usually be several versions here. I generally only keep the latest minor release for a given major release. New major releases may contain relatively untested code, so I also keep the latest version of the previous major release as a relatively stable fall back; the current fall back is 2.8.23. It is up to you to decide which version is more appropriate, but the `CHANGES` file will summarize the most important differences.

`hyper.stanford.edu` is mirrored at `sunsite.unc.edu` in `/pub/Linux/kernel/pcmcia`. I'll also try to upload major releases to `tsx-11.mit.edu` under `/pub/linux/packages/laptops/pcmcia` now and then.

If you do not feel up to compiling the PCMCIA drivers from scratch, pre-compiled drivers are included with current releases of most of the major Linux distributions, including Slackware, Red Hat, Caldera, and Yggdrasil, among others.

1.4 What systems are supported?

This code should run on almost any Linux-capable laptop. All common PCMCIA controllers are supported, including Intel, Cirrus, Vadem, VLSI, Ricoh, and Databook chips. Custom controllers used in IBM and Toshiba laptops are also supported. PCMCIA card docks for desktop systems should work as long as they are the type that plugs directly into the ISA bus, rather than SCSI-to-PCMCIA or IDE-to-PCMCIA adapters.

The Motorola 6AHC05GA controller used in some Hyundai laptops is not supported. The custom PCMCIA controller in the HP Omnibook 600 is unsupported. PCI to CardBus bridge controllers (from SMC, Ricoh, Cirrus, and TI) are currently supported only in legacy 16-bit mode, and this support is still somewhat experimental.

1.5 What PCMCIA cards are supported?

The current release includes drivers for a variety of ethernet cards, a driver for modem and serial port cards, several SCSI adapter drivers, a driver for ATA/IDE drive cards, and memory card drivers that should support most SRAM cards and some flash cards. The `SUPPORTED.CARDS` file included with each release of Card Services lists all cards that are known to work in at least one actual system.

The likelihood that a card not on the supported list will work depends on the type of card. Essentially all modems should work with the supplied driver. Some network cards may work if they are OEM versions of supported cards. Other types of IO cards (frame buffers, sound cards, etc) will not work until someone writes the appropriate drivers.

1.6 When will my new card be supported?

Unfortunately, they usually don't pay me to write device drivers, so if you would like to have a driver for your favorite card, you are probably going to have to do at least some of the work. Ideally, I'd like to work towards a model like the Linux kernel, where I would be responsible mainly for the "core" PCMCIA code and other authors would contribute and maintain drivers for specific cards. The `SUPPORTED.CARDS` file mentions some cards for which driver work is currently in progress. I will try to help where I can, but be warned that debugging kernel device drivers by email is not particularly effective.

Manufacturers interested in helping provide Linux support for their products can contact me about consulting arrangements.

1.7 Mailing lists

I used to maintain a database and mailing list of Linux PCMCIA users. More recently, I've turned my web page for Linux PCMCIA information into a "HyperNews" site, with a set of message lists for Linux PCMCIA issues. There are lists for installation and configuration issues, for different types of cards, and for PCMCIA programming and debugging. The Linux PCMCIA information page is at `http://hyper.stanford.edu/HyperNews/get/pcmcia/home.html`. Users can request email notification of new responses to particular questions, or notification for all new messages in a given category. I hope that this will become a useful repository of information, for questions that go beyond the scope of the HOWTO.

There is a Linux mailing list devoted to laptop issues, the "linux-laptop" list. For more information, send a message containing the word "help" to `majordomo@vger.rutgers.edu`. To subscribe, send a message containing "subscribe linux-laptop" to the same address. This mailing list might be a good forum for discussion of Linux PCMCIA issues.

The Linux Laptop Home Page at `http://www.cs.utexas.edu/users/kharker/linux-laptop` has links to many sites that have information about configuring specific types of laptops for Linux (and PCMCIA). There is also a searchable database of system configuration information.

2 Compilation, installation, and configuration

2.1 Prerequisites and kernel setup

Before starting, you should think about whether you really need to compile the PCMCIA package yourself. All common Linux distributions come with pre-compiled PCMCIA driver packages. Generally, you only need to install the drivers from scratch if you need a new feature of the current drivers, or if you've updated or reconfigured your kernel in a way that is incompatible with the drivers included with your Linux distribution. While compiling the PCMCIA package is not technically difficult, it does require some general Linux familiarity.

The following things should be installed on your system before you start installing PCMCIA:

- One of the following kernels: 1.2.8 through 1.2.13, 1.3.30, 1.3.37, 1.3.39 through 1.3.99, 1.99.* (i.e., pre-2.0), 2.0.*, or 2.1.*.
- A current set of module utilities.
- (Optional) the "Forms" X11 user interface toolkit.

The latest version requires a kernel version 1.2.8 or higher, or a development kernel 1.3.30 or higher. 1.3.38 is definitely broken, and 1.3.31 to 1.3.36 are untested. It also requires a relatively recent set of module utilities. There are no kernel patches specifically for PCMCIA.

You need to have a complete linux source tree for your kernel, not just an up-to-date kernel image, to compile the PCMCIA package. The PCMCIA modules contain some references to kernel source files. While you may want to build a new kernel to remove unnecessary drivers, installing PCMCIA does not require you to do so.

Current "stable" kernel sources and patches are available from sunsite.unc.edu in /pub/Linux/kernel/v2.0, or from tsx-11.mit.edu in /pub/linux/sources/system/v2.0. Current module utilities can be found in the same place, in modules-2.0.0.tgz. Development kernels can be found in the corresponding v2.1 subdirectories.

In the Linux source tree for 2.0 and 2.1 kernels, the Documentation/Changes file describes the versions of all sorts of other system components that are required for that kernel release. You may want to check through this and verify that your system is up to date, especially if you have updated your kernel. If you are using a 2.1 kernel, be sure that you are using the right combination of shared libraries and module tools. The latest versions of the module utilities, as well as versions for older kernels, can be found at <http://www.pi.se/blox/modules>.

When configuring your kernel, if you plan on using a PCMCIA ethernet card, you should turn on networking support but turn off the normal Linux network card drivers, including the "pocket and portable adapters". The PCMCIA network card drivers are all implemented as loadable modules. Any drivers compiled into your kernel will only waste space.

If you want to use SLIP, PPP, or PLIP, you do need to either configure your kernel with these enabled, or use the loadable module versions of these drivers. There is an unfortunate deficiency in the kernel config process in 1.2.X kernels, in that it is not possible to set configuration options (like SLIP compression) for a loadable module, so it is probably better to just link SLIP into the kernel if you need it.

If you want to use a PCMCIA token ring adapter, your kernel needs to be configured with "Token Ring driver support" (CONFIG_TR) enabled, though you should leave CONFIG_IBMTR off.

If you want to use a PCMCIA IDE adapter, your kernel should be configured with CONFIG_BLK_DEV_IDE_PCMCIA enabled, for 1.3.72 through 2.1.7 kernels. Older kernels do not support removable IDE devices; newer kernels do not require a special configuration setting.

If you will be using a PCMCIA SCSI adapter, you should enable CONFIG_SCSI when configuring your kernel. Also, enable any top level drivers (SCSI disk, tape, cdrom, generic) that you expect to use. All low-level drivers for particular host adapters should be disabled, as they will just take up space.

If you want to modularize a driver that is needed for a PCMCIA device, you must modify /etc/pcmcia/config to specify what modules need to be loaded for what card types. For example, if the serial driver is modularized, then you could change the serial device definition to:

```
device "serial_cs"
  class "serial" module "misc/serial", "serial_cs"
```

This package includes an X-based card status utility called cardinfo. This utility is based on a freely distributed user interface toolkit called the Forms Library, which you will need to install before building cardinfo. A binary distribution is on hyper.stanford.edu in /pub/pcmcia/extras: there are both a.out and ELF versions of the library. You will also need to have all the normal X header files and libraries installed.

2.2 Installation

Here is a synopsis of the installation process:

- Unpack pcmcia-cs-2.9.?.tar.gz in /usr/src.
- Run "make config" in the new pcmcia-cs-2.9.? directory.
- Run "make all", then "make install".
- Customize the PCMCIA startup script and the option files in /etc/pcmcia for your site.

If you plan to install any contributed client drivers not included in the core PCMCIA distribution, unpack each of them in the top-level directory of the PCMCIA source tree. Then follow the normal build instructions. The extra drivers will be compiled and installed automatically.

Running "make config" prompts for a few configuration options, and checks out your system to verify that it satisfies all prerequisites for installing PCMCIA support. In most cases, you'll be able to just accept all the default configuration options. Be sure to carefully check the output of this command in case there are problems.

If you are compiling the PCMCIA package for installation on another machine, specify an alternate target directory when prompted by the configure script. This should be an absolute path. All the PCMCIA tools will be installed relative to this directory. You will then be able to tar this directory tree and copy to your target machine, and unpack relative to its root directory to install everything in the proper places.

If you are cross compiling on another machine, you may want to specify alternate names for the compiler and linker. This may also be helpful on mixed a.out and ELF systems. The script will also prompt for additional compiler flags for debugging.

Some of the support utilities (cardctl and cardinfo) can be compiled either in "safe" or "trusting" forms. The "safe" forms prevent non-root users from modifying card configurations. The "trusting" forms permit ordinary users to issue commands to suspend and resume cards, reset cards, and change the current configuration scheme. The configuration script will ask if you want the utilities compiled as safe or trusting: the default is to be safe.

There are a few kernel configuration options that affect the PCMCIA tools. The configuration script can deduce these from the running kernel (the most common case). Alternatively, if you are compiling for installation on another machine, it can read the configuration from a kernel source tree, or each option can be set interactively.

Running "make all" followed by "make install" will build and then install the kernel modules and utility programs. Kernel modules are installed under /lib/modules/<version>/pcmcia. The cardmgr and cardctl programs are installed in /sbin. If cardinfo is built, it is installed in /usr/bin/X11.

Configuration files will be installed in the /etc/pcmcia directory. If you are installing over an older version, your old config scripts will be backed up before being replaced. The saved scripts will be given extensions like *.~1~, *.~2~, and so on.

If you don't know what kind of PCMCIA controller chip you have, you can use the probe utility in the cardmgr/ subdirectory to determine this. There are two major types: the Databook TCIC-2 type and the Intel i82365SL-compatible type.

A user-level daemon processes card insertion and removal events. This is called cardmgr. It is similar in function to Barry Jaspan's pcmciad in earlier PCMCIA releases. Cardmgr reads a configuration file describing known PCMCIA cards from /etc/pcmcia/config. This file also specifies what resources can be allocated for use by PCMCIA devices, and may need to be customized for your system. See the pcmcia man page for more information about this file.

2.3 Post-installation for systems using BSD init scripts

Some Linux distributions, including Slackware, use a BSD arrangement for system startup scripts. If /etc/rc.d/rc.M exists, your system is in this group. The script rc.pcmcia, installed in /etc/rc.d, controls starting up and shutting down the PCMCIA system. "make install" will use the probe command to determine your controller type and modify rc.pcmcia appropriately. You should add a line to your system startup file /etc/rc.d/rc.M to invoke the PCMCIA startup script, like:

```
/etc/rc.d/rc.pcmcia start
```

It does not really matter where you insert this line, as long as the PCMCIA drivers are started after syslogd.

2.4 Post-installation for systems using System V init scripts

Red Hat, Caldera, and Debian Linux have a System V-ish arrangement for system startup files. If you have a directory called /etc/init.d or /etc/rc.d/init.d, then your system is in this group. The rc.pcmcia script will be installed as /etc/rc.d/init.d/pcmcia, or /etc/init.d/pcmcia, as appropriate. There is no need to edit any of the startup scripts to enable PCMCIA: it will happen automatically.

If the /etc/sysconfig directory exists, then a separate configuration file, /etc/sysconfig/pcmcia, will be created for startup options. If you need to change any module options (like the PCIC= or PCIC_OPTS= settings), edit this config file rather than the actual PCMCIA startup script. This file will not be overwritten by subsequent installs.

Some previous releases used the /etc/sysconfig/pcmcia-scripts directory in place of /etc/pcmcia on these platforms. The current release instead uses /etc/pcmcia for all systems, and will move an existing /etc/sysconfig/pcmcia-scripts to /etc/pcmcia.

2.5 Site-specific configuration options

Card Services should automatically avoid allocating I/O ports and interrupts already in use by other standard devices. It will also attempt to detect conflicts with unknown devices, but this is not completely reliable. In some cases, you may need to explicitly exclude resources for a device in /etc/pcmcia/config.opts.

Here are some resource settings for specific laptop types.

- On the AMS SoundPro, exclude IRQ 10.
- On some AMS TravelPro 5300 models, use memory 0xc8000-0xcffff.
- On the BMX 486DX2-66, exclude IRQ 5 and IRQ 9.
- On the Chicony NB5, use memory 0xda000-0xdffff.
- On the Compaq Presario 1020, exclude port 0x2f8-0x2ff, IRQ 3 and IRQ 5.
- On the HP Omnibook 4000C, exclude port 0x300-0x30f.
- On the Micron Millenia Transport, exclude IRQ 5 and IRQ 9.
- On the NEC Versa M, exclude IRQ 9, port 0x2e0-2ff.
- On the NEC Versa P/75, exclude IRQ 5 and IRQ 9.
- On the NEC Versa S, exclude IRQ 9 and IRQ 12.

- On the NEC Versa 6000 series, exclude port 0x300-0x33f, IRQ 9 and IRQ 10.
- On the ProStar 9200, Altima Virage, and Acquiline Hurricane DX4-100, exclude IRQ 5, port 0x330-0x35f. Maybe use memory 0xd8000-0xdffff.
- On the Siemens Nixdorf SIMATIC PG 720C, use memory 0xc0000-0xcffff, port 0x300-0x3bf.
- On the TI TravelMate 5000, use memory 0xd4000-0xdffff.
- On the Toshiba T4900 CT, exclude IRQ 5, port 0x2e0-0x2e8, port 0x330-0x338.
- On the Twinhead 5100, HP 4000, Sharp PC-8700 and PC-8900, exclude IRQ 9 (sound), IRQ 12.
- On an MPC 800 Series, exclude IRQ 5, port 0x300-0x30f for the CD-ROM.

Some PCMCIA controllers have optional features that may or may not be implemented in a particular system. It is generally impossible for a socket driver to detect if these features are implemented. Check the man page for your driver to see what optional features may be enabled.

In a few cases, the `probe` command will be unable to determine your controller type automatically. If you have a Halikan NBD 486 system, it has a TCIC-2 controller at an unusual location: you'll need to edit `rc.pcmcia` to load the `tcic` module, as well as setting the `PCIC_OPTS` parameter to "`tcic_base=0x02c0`".

The low level socket drivers, `tcic` and `i82365`, have numerous bus timing parameters that may need to be adjusted for systems with particularly fast processors. Symptoms of timing problems include card recognition problems, lock-ups under heavy loads, high error rates, or poor device performance. Check the corresponding man pages for more details, but here is a brief summary:

- Cirrus controllers have numerous configurable timing parameters. The most important seems to be the `cmd_time` flag, which determines the length of PCMCIA bus cycles. Fast 486 systems (i.e., DX4-100) seem to often benefit from increasing this from 6 (the default) to 12 or 16.
- The Cirrus PD6729 PCI controller has the `fast_pci` flag, which should be set if the PCI bus speed is greater than 25 MHz.
- For Vadem VG-468 controllers and Databook TCIC-2 controllers, the `async_clock` flag changes the relative clocking of PCMCIA bus and host bus cycles. Setting this flag adds extra wait states to some operations. However, I have yet to hear of a laptop that needs this.
- The `pcmcia_core` module has the `cis_speed` parameter for changing the memory speed used for accessing a card's Card Information Structure (CIS). On some systems with fast bus clocks, increasing this parameter (i.e., slowing down card accesses) may be beneficial for card recognition problems.
- This isn't a timing issue, but if you have more than one PCMCIA controller in your system or extra sockets in a docking station, the `i82365` module should be loaded with the `extra_sockets` parameter set to 1.

All these options should be configured by modifying the top of `/etc/rc.d/rc.pcmcia`. For example:

```
# Should be either i82365 or tcic
PCIC=i82365
# Put socket driver timing parameters here
PCIC_OPTS="cmd_time=12"
# Put pcmcia_core options here
CORE_OPTS="cis_speed=500"
```

Here are some timing settings for specific systems:

- On the ARM Pentium-90 or Midwest Micro Soundbook Plus, use "`freq_bypass=1 cmd_time=8`".
- On a Midwest Micro Soundbook Elite, use "`cmd_time=12`".
- On a Gateway Liberty, try "`cmd_time=16`".

On some systems using Cirrus controllers, including the NEC Versa M, the BIOS puts the controller in a special suspended state at system startup time. On these systems, the `probe` command will fail to find any known PCMCIA controller. If this happens, edit `/etc/rc.d/rc.pcmcia` by hand as follows:

```
# Should be either i82365 or tcic
PCIC=i82365
# Put socket driver timing parameters here
PCIC_OPTS="wakeup=1"
```

2.6 Problems loading kernel modules

The configure script will normally ensure that the PCMCIA modules are compatible with your kernel. So, module loading problems generally indicate that the user has interfered with the normal installation process in some way. Some module loading errors are sent directly to the Linux console. Other errors are recorded in the system log file, normally `/usr/adm/messages` or `/var/log/messages`. Depending on your syslogd configuration, some messages may be written to other files, but they will usually still be under `/usr/adm` or `/var/log`. To track down a problem, be sure to check both locations, to pin down which module is actually causing trouble.

Some of the PCMCIA modules require kernel services that may or may not be present, depending on kernel configuration. For instance, the SCSI card drivers require that the kernel be configured with SCSI support, and the network drivers require a networking kernel. If a kernel lacks a necessary feature, `insmod` may report undefined symbols and refuse to load a module.

If `insmod` reports "wrong version" errors, it means that the module was compiled for a different kernel version than your system is actually running. This might occur if modules compiled on one machine are copied to another machine with a different configuration, or if the kernel is reconfigured after PCMCIA is installed.

Another source of module loading errors is when the modules and kernel were compiled with different settings of `CONFIG_MODVERSIONS`. If a module with version checking is loaded against a kernel without version checking, `insmod` will complain about undefined symbols.

Finally, relatively recent binutils releases are incompatible with older versions of the module utilities, and can cause module version incompatibilities to be reported. The most common symptom is complaints about "`gcc_compiled`" being undefined. If you get these errors, upgrade to the latest module utilities, available from <http://www.pi.se/blox/modules>.

2.7 Problems with the card status change interrupt

In most cases, the socket driver (`i82365` or `tcic`) will automatically probe and select an appropriate interrupt to signal card status changes. The automatic interrupt probe doesn't work on some Intel-compatible controllers, including Cirrus chips and the chips used in some IBM ThinkPads. If a device is inactive at probe time, its interrupt may also appear to be available. In these cases, the socket driver may pick an interrupt that is used by another device.

With the `i82365` and `tcic` drivers, the `irq_list` option can be used to limit the interrupts that will be tested. This list limits the set of interrupts that can be used by PCMCIA cards as well as for monitoring card status changes. The `cs_irq` option can also be used to explicitly set the interrupt to be used for monitoring card status changes.

If you can't find an interrupt number that works, there is also a polled status mode: both `i82365` and `tcic` will accept a `poll_interval=100` option, to poll for card status changes once per second. This option should also be used if your system has a shortage of interrupts available for use by PCMCIA cards. Especially for systems with more than one PCMCIA controller, there is little point in dedicating interrupts for monitoring card status changes.

All these options should be set in the `PCIC_OPTS=` line in either `/etc/rc.d/rc.pcmcia` or `/etc/sysconfig/pcmcia`, depending on your site setup.

2.8 Card identification problems

By default, the PCMCIA drivers allocate memory windows in the region 0xc0000-0xfffff, after probing this region for conflicts with ROM or other devices. This memory window is specified in `/etc/pcmcia/config.opts`. The probe is done when the drivers first attempt to configure a new card. The probe procedure is not foolproof, so it is possible for a conflict to go unrecognized. If an address region that passes the probe is used by other devices in your system, cards may not be identified correctly. With chip sets that support it, conflicts can also result from BIOS shadowing in this region.

The classic symptom of a memory window configuration problem is that all cards will be misidentified as memory cards. In unusual cases, a memory window conflict can interfere with a crucial system service, resulting in lock-ups or reboots. If you suspect a memory window problem, first verify that ROM shadowing is disabled in your system's hardware setup. Finding a good window may require some experimentation. Some alternative windows to try are 0xd0000-0xdffff, 0xc0000-0xc7fff, 0xc8000-0xcffff, or 0xd8000-0xdffff.

If you have DOS PCMCIA drivers, you may be able to deduce what memory region those drivers use. Note that DOS memory addresses are often specified in "segment" form, which leaves off the final hex digit (so an absolute address of 0xd0000 might be given as 0xd000). Be sure to add the extra digit back when making changes to `/etc/pcmcia/config.opts`.

If adjusting the memory window fails to solve a card identification problem, then it is likely to be due to a timing problem.

2.9 Why don't you distribute PCMCIA binaries?

For me, distributing binaries is a significant hassle. It is complicated because some features can only be selected at compile time, and because the PCMCIA modules are somewhat dependent on having the "right" kernel configuration. So, I would probably need to distribute pre-compiled modules along with matching kernels. Beyond this, the greatest need for pre-compiled modules is when installing Linux on a clean system. This typically requires setting up PCMCIA so that it can be used in the installation process for a particular Linux distribution. Each Linux distribution has its own procedures, and it is not feasible for me to provide boot and root disks for even just the common combinations of drivers and distributions.

PCMCIA is now a part of many of the major Linux distributions, including Red Hat, Caldera, Slackware, Yggdrasil, Craftworks, and Nascent Technology.

2.10 Why is the PCMCIA package so darned big?

Well, first of all, it isn't actually that large. All the driver modules together take up about 200K of disk space. The utility programs add up to about 70K, and the stuff in /etc/pcmcia is about 30K. When running, the core PCMCIA modules take up 48K of system memory. The `cardmgr` daemon will generally be swapped out except when cards are inserted or removed. The total package size is not much different from DOS Card Services implementations.

Compared to DOS "point enablers," this may still seem like a lot of overhead, especially for people that don't plan on using many of the features of PCMCIA, such as power management or hot swapping. Point enablers can be tiny because they generally support only one or a small set of cards, and also generally support a restricted set of PCMCIA controllers. If someone were to write a genuinely "generic" modem enabler, it would end up incorporating much of the functionality of Card Services, to handle cards from different vendors and the full range of PCMCIA controller variants.

3 Usage and features

3.1 Tools for monitoring PCMCIA devices

The `cardmgr` daemon normally beeps when a card is inserted, and the tone of the beeps indicates the status of the newly inserted card. Two high beeps indicate the card was identified and configured successfully. A high beep followed by a lower beep indicates that the card was identified, but could not be configured for some reason. One low beep indicates that the card could not be identified.

If the modules are all loaded correctly, the output of the `lsmod` command should look like the following, with no cards inserted:

```
Module:         #pages:  Used by:
ds                 2
i82365             3
pcmcia_core        7     [ds i82365]
```

All the PCMCIA modules and the `cardmgr` daemon send status messages to the system log. This will usually be `/var/log/messages` or `/usr/adm/messages`. This file should be the first place to look when tracking down a problem. When submitting a bug report, always include the contents of this file. If you are having trouble finding your system messages, check `/etc/syslogd.conf` to see how different classes of messages are handled.

`cardmgr` also records some current device information for each socket in `/var/run/stab`. Here is a sample `/var/run/stab` listing:

```
Socket 0: Adaptec APA-1460 SlimSCSI
0       scsi    aha152x_cs      0       sda     8       0
0       scsi    aha152x_cs      1       scd0    11      0
Socket 1: Serial or Modem Card
1       serial  serial_cs       0       ttyS1   5       65
```

For the lines describing devices, the first field is the socket, the second is the device class, the third is the driver name, the fourth is used to number multiple devices associated with the same driver, the fifth is the device name, and the final two fields are the major and minor device numbers for this device (if applicable).

The `cardctl` command can be used to check the status of a socket, or to see how it is configured. Here is an example of the output of the `cardctl config` command:

```
Socket 0:
Socket 1:
  Vcc = 5.0, Vpp1 = 0.0, Vpp2 = 0.0
```

```
Card type is memory and I/O
IRQ 3 is dynamic shared, level mode, enabled
Speaker output is enabled
Function 0:
  Config register base = 0x0800
    Option = 0x63, status = 0x08
  I/O window 1: 0x0280 to 0x02bf, auto sized
  I/O window 2: 0x02f8 to 0x02ff, 8 bit
```

If you are running X, the `cardinfo` utility produces a graphical display showing the current status of all PCMCIA sockets, similar in content to `cardctl config`.

3.2 Overview of the PCMCIA configuration scripts

Each PCMCIA device has an associated **class** that describes how it should be configured and managed. Classes are associated with device drivers in `/etc/pcmcia/config`. There are currently five IO device classes (network, SCSI, cdrom, fixed disk, and serial) and two memory device classes (memory and FTL). For each class, there are two scripts in `/etc/pcmcia/config`: a main configuration script (i.e., `/etc/pcmcia/scsi` for SCSI devices), and an options script (i.e., `/etc/pcmcia/scsi.opts`). The main script for a device will be invoked to configure that device when a card is inserted, and to shut down the device when the card is removed. For cards with several associated devices, the script will be invoked for each device.

The config scripts start by extracting some information about a device from `/var/run/stab`. Each script constructs a "device address," that uniquely describes the device it has been asked to configure, in the `ADDRESS` variable. This is passed to the `*.opts` script, which should return information about how a device at this address should be configured. For some devices, the device address is just the socket number. For others, it includes extra information that may be useful in deciding how to configure the device. For example, network devices pass their hardware ethernet address as part of the device address, so the `network.opts` script could use this to select from several different configurations.

The first part of all device addresses is the current PCMCIA "scheme." This parameter is used to support multiple sets of device configurations based on a single external user-specified variable. One use of schemes would be to have a "home" scheme, and a "work" scheme, which would include different sets of network configuration parameters. The current scheme is selected using the `cardctl` command. The default if no scheme is set is "default."

As a general rule, when configuring Linux for a laptop, PCMCIA devices should only be configured from the PCMCIA device scripts. Do not try to configure a PCMCIA device the same way you would configure a permanently attached device.

3.3 PCMCIA network adapters

Linux ethernet-type network interfaces normally have names like `eth0`, `eth1`, and so on. Token-ring adapters are handled similarly, however they are named `tr0`, `tr1`, and so on. The `ifconfig` command is used to view or modify the state of a network interface. A peculiarity of Linux is that network interfaces do not have corresponding device files under `/dev`, so don't be surprised when you can't find them.

When a PCMCIA ethernet card is detected, it will be assigned the first free interface name, which will probably be `eth0`. `cardmgr` will run the `/etc/pcmcia/network` script to configure the interface.

Do not configure your PCMCIA ethernet card in `/etc/rc.d/rc.inet1`, since the card may not be present when this script is executed. Comment out everything except the loopback stuff in `rc.inet1`. If your system has an automatic network configuration procedure, you should generally indicate that you do not have a network card installed. Instead, edit the `/etc/pcmcia/network.opts` file to match your local network setup. The `network` and `network.opts` scripts will be executed only when your ethernet card is actually present.

The device address passed to `network.opts` consists of four comma-separated fields: the scheme, the socket number, the device instance, and the card's hardware ethernet address. The device instance is used to number devices for cards that have several network interfaces, so it will usually be 0. If you have several network cards used for different purposes, one option would be to configure the cards based on socket position, as in:

```
case "$ADDRESS" in
*,0,*,*)
    # definitions for network card in socket 0
    ;;
*,1,*,*)
    # definitions for network card in socket 1
    ;;
esac
```

Alternatively, they could be configured using their hardware addresses, as in:

```
case "$ADDRESS" in
*,*,*,00:80:C8:76:00:B1)
    # definitions for a D-Link card
    ;;
*,*,*,08:00:5A:44:80:01)
    # definitions for an IBM card
esac
```

To automatically mount and unmount NFS file systems, first add all these file systems to `/etc/fstab`, but include `noauto` in the mount options. In `network.opts`, list the file system mount points in the `MOUNTS` variable. It is especially important to use either `cardctl` or `cardinfo` to shut down a network card when NFS mounts are configured this way. It is not possible to cleanly unmount NFS file systems if a network card is simply ejected without warning.

In addition to the usual network configuration parameters, the `network.opts` script can specify extra actions to be taken after an interface is configured, or before an interface is shut down. If `network.opts` defines a shell function called `start_fn`, it will be invoked by the network script after the interface is configured, and the interface name will be passed to the function as its first (and only) argument. Similarly, if it is defined, `stop_fn` will be invoked before shutting down an interface.

3.3.1 Transceiver selection

The transceiver type can be selected in `network.opts` using the `IF_PORT` setting. This can either be a numeric value as in previous PCMCIA releases, or a keyword identifying the transceiver type. All the network drivers default to either auto detect the interface if possible, or 10baseT otherwise. The `ifport` command can be used to check or set the current transceiver type. For example:

```
# ifport eth0 10base2
#
# ifport eth0
eth0    2 (10base2)
```

Current releases of the 3c589 driver attempt to auto detect the network connection, but this doesn't seem to be completely functional yet. For auto detection to work, the network cable should be connected to the card when the card is configured. Alternatively, once the network is connected, you can force the driver to check the connection with:

```
ifconfig eth0 down up
```

3.3.2 Comments about specific cards

- With IBM CCAE and Socket EA cards, you need to pick the transceiver type (10base2, 10baseT, AUI) when the network device is configured. Make sure that the transceiver type reported in the system log matches your connection.
- The drivers for SMC, Megahertz, Ositech, and 3Com cards should auto detect the attached network type (10base2 or 10baseT). Setting the transceiver type when the driver is loaded serves to define the card's "first guess."
- The Farallon EtherWave is actually based on the 3Com 3c589, with a special transceiver. Though the EtherWave uses 10baseT-style connections, its transceiver requires that the 3c589 be configured in 10base2 mode.
- If you have trouble with an IBM CCAE, NE4100, Thomas Conrad, or Kingston adapter, try increasing the memory access time with the `mem_speed=#` option to the `pcnet_cs` module. An example of how to do this is given in the standard `config.opts` file. Try speeds of up to 1,000 (in nanoseconds).
- For the New Media Ethernet adapter, on some systems, it may be necessary to increase the IO port access time with the `io_speed=#` option when the `pcmcia_core` module is loaded. Edit `CORE_OPTS` in the startup script to set this option.
- The multicast support in the New Media Ethernet driver is incomplete. The latest driver will function with multicast kernels, but will ignore multicast packets. Promiscuous mode should work properly.
- The driver used by the IBM and 3Com token ring adapters seems to behave very badly if the cards are not connected to a ring when they get initialized. Always connect these cards to the net before they are powered up. This driver also requires free IO ports in the range of 0xa20-0xa27. On some systems, the automatic IO port conflict checker will incorrectly determine that this port range is unavailable. In that case, the port check can be disabled by loading the `pcmcia_core` module with `probe_io=0`.

- Newer Linksys and D-Link cards have a unique way of selecting the transceiver type that isn't handled by the Linux drivers. One workaround is to boot DOS and use the vendor-supplied utility to select the transceiver, then warm boot Linux. I am looking for beta testers for a Linux utility to perform this function.
- For WaveLAN wireless network adapters, Jean Tourrilhes (`jt@hplb.hpl.hp.com`) has put together a wireless HOWTO at `http://www-uk.hpl.hp.com/people/jt/Linux/Wavelan.html`.

3.3.3 Diagnosing problems with network adapters

- Is your card recognized as an Ethernet card? Check the system log and make sure that `cardmgr` identifies the card correctly and starts up one of the network drivers. If it doesn't, your card might still be usable if it is compatible with a supported card. This will be most easily done if the card claims to be "NE2000 compatible."
- Is the card configured properly? If you are using a supported card, and it was recognized by `cardmgr`, but still doesn't work, there might be an interrupt or port conflict with another device. Find out what resources the card is using (from the system log), and try excluding these in `/etc/pcmcia/config.opts` to force the card to use something different.
- If your card seems to be configured properly, but sometimes locks up, particularly under high load, you may need to try changing your socket driver timing parameters. See Section 2.5 for more information.
- If you get messages like "network unreachable" when you try to access the network, then you have probably set up `/etc/pcmcia/network.opts` incorrectly. On the other hand, mis-configured cards will usually fail silently.
- To diagnose problems in `/etc/pcmcia/network.opts`, start by trying to ping other systems on the same subnet using their IP addresses. Then try to ping your gateway, and then machines on other subnets. Ping machines by name only after trying these simpler tests.
- Make sure your problem is really a PCMCIA one. It may help to see see if the card works under DOS with the vendor's drivers. Double check your modifications to the `/etc/pcmcia/network.opts` script. Make sure your drop cable, "T" jack, terminator, etc., are working.

3.4 PCMCIA serial and modem devices

Linux serial devices are accessed via the `/dev/cua*` and `/dev/ttyS*` special device files. The `ttyS*` devices are for incoming connections, such as directly connected terminals. The `cua*` devices are for outgoing connections, such as modems. Each physical serial port has both a `ttyS` and a `cua` device file: it is up to you to pick the appropriate device for your application. The configuration of a serial device can be examined and modified with the `setserial` command.

When a PCMCIA serial or modem card is detected, it will be assigned to the first available serial device slot. This will usually be `/dev/ttyS1` (`cua1`) or `/dev/ttyS2` (`cua2`), depending on the number of built-in serial ports. The `ttyS*` device is the one reported in `/var/run/stab`. The default serial device option script, `/etc/pcmcia/serial.opts`, will link the corresponding `cua*` device file to `/dev/modem` as a convenience.

Do not try to use `/etc/rc.d/rc.serial` to configure a PCMCIA modem. This script should only be used to configure non-removable devices. Modify `/etc/pcmcia/serial.opts` if you want to do anything special to set up your modem. Also, do not try to change the I/O port and interrupt settings of a PCMCIA serial device using `setserial`. This would tell the serial driver to look for the device in a different place, but would not change how the card hardware is actually configured. The serial configuration script allows you to specify other `setserial` options, as well as whether a line should be added to `/etc/inittab` for this port.

The device address passed to `serial.opts` has three comma-separated fields: the first is the scheme, the second is the socket number, and the third is the device instance. The device instance may take several values for cards that support multiple serial ports, but for single-port cards, it will always be 0. If you commonly use more than one PCMCIA modem, you may want to specify different settings based on socket position, as in:

```
case "$ADDRESS" in
*,0,*)
    # Options for modem in socket 0
    LINK=/dev/modem0
    ;;
*,1,*)
    # Options for modem in socket 1
    LINK=/dev/modem1
    ;;
esac
```

If a PCMCIA modem is already configured when Linux boots, it may be incorrectly identified as an ordinary built-in serial port. This is harmless, however, when the PCMCIA drivers take control of the modem, it will be assigned a different device slot. It is best to either parse `/var/run/stab` or use `/dev/modem`, rather than expecting a PCMCIA modem to always have the same device assignment.

If you configure your kernel to load the basic Linux serial port driver as a module, you must edit `/etc/pcmcia/config` to indicate that this module must be loaded. Edit the serial device entry to read:

```
device "serial_cs"
  class "serial" module "misc/serial", "serial_cs"
```

3.4.1 Diagnosing problems with serial devices

- Is your card recognized as a modem? Check the system log and make sure that `cardmgr` identifies the card correctly and starts up the `serial_cs` driver. If it doesn't, you may need to add a new entry to your `/etc/pcmcia/config` file so that it will be identified properly. See Section 5.1 for details.
- Is the modem configured successfully by `serial_cs`? Again, check the system log and look for messages from the `serial_cs` driver. If you see "`register_serial() failed`", you may have an I/O port conflict with another device. Another tip-off of a conflict is if the device is reported to be an 8250; most modern PCMCIA modems should be identified as 16550A UART's. If you think you're seeing a port conflict, edit `/etc/pcmcia/config.opts` and exclude the port range that was allocated for the modem.
- Is there an interrupt conflict? If the system log looks good, but the modem just doesn't seem to work, try using `setserial` to change the IRQ to 0, and see if the modem works. This causes the serial driver to use a slower polled mode instead of using interrupts. If this seems to fix the problem, it is likely that some other device in your system is using the interrupt selected by serial_cs. You should add a line to `/etc/pcmcia/config.opts` to exclude this interrupt.
- If the modem seems to work only very slowly, this is an almost certain indicator of an interrupt conflict.
- Make sure your problem is really a PCMCIA problem. It may help to see if the card works under DOS with the vendor's drivers. Also, don't test the card with something complex like SLIP or PPP until you are sure you can make simple connections. If simple things work but SLIP does not, your problem is most likely with SLIP, not with PCMCIA.
- If you get kernel messages indicating that the `serial_cs` module cannot be loaded, it means that your kernel does not have serial device support. If you have compiled the serial driver as a module, you must modify `/etc/pcmcia/config` to indicate that the `serial` module should be loaded before `serial_cs`.

3.5 PCMCIA SCSI adapters

All the currently supported PCMCIA SCSI cards are work-alikes of one of the following ISA bus cards: the Qlogic, the Adaptec AHA-152X, or the Future Domain TMC-16x0. The PCMCIA drivers are built by linking some PCMCIA-specific code (in `qlogic_cs.c`, `toaster_cs.c`, or `fdomain_cs.c`) with the normal Linux SCSI driver.

When a new SCSI host adapter is detected, the SCSI drivers will probe for devices. Check the system log to make sure your devices are detected properly. New SCSI devices will be assigned to the first available SCSI device files. The first SCSI disk will be `/dev/sda`, the first SCSI tape will be `/dev/st0`, and the first CD-ROM will be `/dev/scd0`.

With 1.3.X and later kernels, the PCMCIA core drivers are able to find out from the kernel which SCSI devices are connected to a card. They will be listed in `/var/run/stab`, and the SCSI configuration script, `/etc/pcmcia/scsi`, will be called once for each attached device, to either configure or shut down that device. The default script does not take any actions to configure SCSI devices, but will properly unmount file systems on SCSI devices when a card is removed.

With 1.2.X kernels, the PCMCIA drivers cannot automatically deduce which devices are associated with a particular SCSI adapter. Instead, if you have one normal SCSI device configuration, you may list these devices in `/etc/pcmcia/scsi.opts`. For example, if you normally have a SCSI disk and a CD-ROM, you would use:

```
# For 1.2 kernels: list of attached devices
SCSI_DEVICES="sda scd0"
```

The device addresses passed to `scsi.opts` are complicated, because of the variety of things that can be attached to a SCSI adapter. Addresses consist of either six or seven comma-separated fields: the current scheme, the device type, the socket number, the SCSI channel, ID, and logical unit number, and optionally, the partition number. The device type will be "sd" for disks, "st" for tapes, "sr" for CD-ROM devices, and "sg" for generic SCSI devices. For most setups, the SCSI channel and logical unit number will be 0. For disk devices with several partitions, `scsi.opts` will first be called for the whole device, with a five-field address. The script should set the `PARTS` variable to a list of partitions. Then, `scsi.opts` will be called for each partition, with the longer seven-field addresses. For example, here is a script for configuring a disk device at SCSI ID 3, with two partitions, and a CD-ROM at SCSI ID 6:

```
case "$ADDRESS" in
*,sd,*,0,3,0)
    # This device has two partitions...
    PARTS="1 2"
    ;;
*,sd,*,0,3,0,1)
    # Options for partition 1:
    #  update /etc/fstab, and mount an ext2 fs on /usr1
    DO_FSTAB="y" ; DO_FSCK="y" ; DO_MOUNT="y"
    FSTYPE="ext2"
    OPTS=""
    MOUNTPT="/usr1"
    ;;
*,sd,*,0,3,0,2)
    # Options for partition 2:
    #  update /etc/fstab, and mount an MS-DOS fs on /usr2
    DO_FSTAB="y" ; DO_FSCK="y" ; DO_MOUNT="y"
    FSTYPE="msdos"
    OPTS=""
    MOUNTPT="/usr2"
    ;;
*,sr,*,0,6,0)
    # Options for CD-ROM at SCSI ID 6
    PARTS=""
    DO_FSTAB="y" ; DO_FSCK="n" ; DO_MOUNT="y"
    FSTYPE="iso9660"
    OPTS="ro"
    MOUNTPT="/cdrom"
    ;;
esac
```

If your kernel does not have a top-level driver (disk, tape, etc.) for a particular SCSI device, then the device will not be configured by the PCMCIA drivers. As a side effect, the device's name in `/var/run/stab` will be something like "sd#nnnn" where "nnnn" is a four-digit hex number. This happens when `cardmgr` is unable to translate a SCSI device ID into a corresponding Linux device name.

It is possible to modularize the top-level SCSI drivers so that they are only loaded when a PCMCIA SCSI adapter is detected. To do so, you need to edit `/etc/pcmcia/config` to tell `cardmgr` which extra modules need to be loaded when your adapter is configured. For example:

```
device "aha152x_cs"
  class "scsi" module "scsi/scsi_mod", "scsi/sd_mod", "aha152x_cs"
```

would say to load the core SCSI module and the top-level disk driver module before loading the regular PCMCIA driver module. The PCMCIA Configure script will not automatically detect modularized SCSI modules, so you will need use the manual configure option to enable SCSI support.

Always turn on SCSI devices before powering up your laptop, or before inserting the adapter card, so that the SCSI bus is properly terminated when the adapter is configured. Also be very careful about ejecting a SCSI adapter. Be sure that all associated SCSI devices are unmounted and closed before ejecting the card. The best way to ensure this is to use either `cardctl` or `cardinfo` to request card removal before physically ejecting the card. For now, all SCSI devices should be powered up before plugging in a SCSI adapter, and should stay connected until after you unplug the adapter or power down your laptop.

There is a potential complication when using these cards that does not arise with ordinary ISA bus adapters. The SCSI bus carries a "termination power" signal that is necessary for proper operation of ordinary passive SCSI terminators. PCMCIA SCSI adapters do not supply termination power, so if it is required, an external device must supply it. Some external SCSI devices may be configured to supply termination power. Others, such as the Zip Drive and the Syquest EZ-Drive, use active terminators that do not depend on it. In some cases, it may be necessary to use a special terminator block such as the APS SCSI Sentry 2, which has an external power supply. When configuring your SCSI device chain, be aware of whether or not any of your devices require or can provide termination power.

The Adaptec APA-460 SlimSCSI adapter is not supported. This card was originally sold under the Trantor name, and when Adaptec merged with Trantor, they continued to sell the Trantor card with an Adaptec label. The APA-460 is not compatible with any existing Linux driver. I'm not sure how hard it would be to write a driver; I don't think anyone has been able to obtain the technical information from Adaptec.

The (unsupported) Trantor SlimSCSI can be identified by the following:

```
Trantor / Adaptec APA-460 SlimSCSI
FCC ID: IE8T460
Shipped with SCSIworks! driver software
```

The (supported) Adaptec SlimSCSI can be identified by the following:

```
Adaptec APA-1460 SlimSCSI
FCC ID: FGT1460
P/N: 900100
Shipped with EZ-SCSI driver software
```

3.5.1 Diagnosing problems with SCSI adapters

- With the `aha152x_cs` driver (used by Adaptec, New Media, and a few others), it seems that SCSI disconnect/reconnect support is a frequent source of trouble with tape drives. To disable this "feature," add the following to `/etc/pcmcia/config.opts`:

  ```
  module "aha152x_cs" opts "reconnect=0"
  ```

- If you have compiled SCSI support as modules (`CONFIG_SCSI` is "m"), when configuring PCMCIA, you must explicitly specify that you want the SCSI drivers to be built. You must also modify `/etc/pcmcia/config` to load the SCSI modules before the appropriate `*_cs` driver is loaded.

3.6 PCMCIA memory cards

The `memory_cs` driver handles all types of memory cards, as well as providing direct access to the PCMCIA memory address space for cards that have other functions. When loaded, it creates a combination of character and block devices. See the man page for the module for a complete description of the device naming scheme. Block devices are used for disk-like access (creating and mounting file systems, etc.). The character devices are for "raw" unbuffered reads and writes at arbitrary locations.

The device address passed to `memory.opts` consists of two fields: the scheme, and the socket number. The options are applied to the first common memory partition on the corresponding memory card. Here is an example of a script that will automatically mount memory cards based on which socket they are inserted into:

```
case "$ADDRESS" in
*,0,0)
    # Mount file system, but don't update /etc/fstab
    DO_FSTAB="n" ; DO_FSCK="y" ; DO_MOUNT="y"
    FSTYPE="ext2" ; OPTS=""
    MOUNTPT="/mem0"
    ;;
*,1,0)
    # Mount file system, but don't update /etc/fstab
    DO_FSTAB="n" ; DO_FSCK="y" ; DO_MOUNT="y"
    FSTYPE="ext2" ; OPTS=""
    MOUNTPT="/mem1"
    ;;
esac
```

Some older memory cards, and most simple static RAM cards, lack a "Card Information Structure" (CIS), which is the scheme PCMCIA cards use to identify themselves. Normally, `cardmgr` will assume that any card that lacks a CIS is a simple memory card, and load the `memory_cs` driver. Thus, a common side effect of a general card identification problem is that other types of cards may be misdetected as memory cards.

The `memory_cs` driver uses a heuristic to guess the capacity of these cards. The heuristic does not work for write protected cards, and may make mistakes in some other cases as well. If a card is misdetected, its size should then be explicitly specified when using commands such as `dd` or `mkfs`.

3.6.1 Using flash memory cards

The device address passed to `ftl.opts` consists of three or four fields: the scheme, the socket number, the region number, and optionally, the partition number. Most flash cards have just one flash memory region, so the region number will generally always be zero.

To use a flash memory card as an ordinary disk-like block device, first create a "flash translation layer" partition on the device with the `ftl_format` command:

```
ftl_format -i /dev/mem0c0c
```

Note that this command accesses the card through the "raw" memory card interface. Once formatted, the card can be accessed as an ordinary block device via the `ftl_cs` driver. For example:

```
mke2fs /dev/ftl0c0
mount -t ext2 /dev/ftl0c0 /mnt
```

Device naming for FTL devices is tricky. Minor device numbers have three parts: the card number, the region number on that card, and optionally, the partition within that region. A region can either be treated as a single block device with no partition table (like a floppy), or it can be partitioned like a hard disk device. The "ftl0c0" device is card 0, common memory region 0, the entire region. The "ftl0c0p1" through "ftl0c0p4" devices are primary partitions 1 through 4 if the region has been partitioned.

There are two major formats for flash memory cards: the "flash translation layer" style, and the Microsoft Flash File System. The FTL format is generally more flexible because it allows any ordinary high-level file system (ext2, ms-dos, etc) to be used on a flash card as if it were an ordinary disk device. The FFS is a completely different file system type. Linux cannot currently handle cards formated with FFS.

3.7 PCMCIA ATA/IDE card drives

ATA/IDE drive support requires a 1.3.72 or higher kernel. The PCMCIA-specific part of the driver is `fixed_cs`. Be sure to use `cardctl` or `cardinfo` to shut down an ATA/IDE card before ejecting it, as the driver has not been made "hot-swap-proof."

The device addresses passed to `fixed.opts` consist of either three or four fields: the current scheme, the socket number, the drive's serial number, and an optional partition number. As with SCSI devices, `fixed.opts` is first called for the entire device. If `fixed.opts` returns a list of partitions in the `PARTS` variable, the script will then be called for each partition.

Here is an example `fixed.opts` file to mount the first partition of any ATA/IDE card on `/mnt`.

```
case "$ADDRESS" in
*,*,*)
    PARTS="1"
    ;;
*,*,*,1)
    DO_FSTAB="y" ; DO_FSCK="y" ; DO_MOUNT="y"
    FSTYPE="msdos"
    OPTS=""
    MOUNTPT="/mnt"
    ;;
esac
```

Note that the default `fixed.opts` file has these lines but they are commented out. If you wish, you can have separate configurations for specific cards based on their serial numbers. To find out a drive's serial number, use the `ide_info` utility. Then, part of `fixed.opts` might look like:

```
case "$ADDRESS" in
*,*,Z4J60542)
    # This is my DOS stuff
    PARTS="1"
    ;;
*,*,Z4J60542,1)
    DO_FSTAB="y" ; DO_FSCK="y" ; DO_MOUNT="y"
    FSTYPE="msdos"
    OPTS=""
    MOUNTPT="/mnt"
    ;;
esac
```

3.7.1 Diagnosing problems with ATA/IDE adapters

- Some IDE drives violate the PCMCIA specification by requiring a longer time to spin up than the maximum allowed card setup time. To use these cards, load the `pcmcia_core` module with:

```
CORE_OPTS="unreset_delay=400"
```

- To use an ATA/IDE CD-ROM device, your kernel must be compiled with `CONFIG_BLK_DEV_IDECD` enabled. This will normally be the case for standard kernels, however it is something to be aware of if you compile a custom kernel.

3.8 Multifunction cards

Starting with the 1.3.73 Linux kernel, a single interrupt can be shared by several drivers, such as the serial driver and an Ethernet driver. When using a multifunction card under a newer kernel, all card functions can be used without loading and unloading drivers.

Simultaneous use of two card functions is "tricky" and various hardware vendors have implemented interrupt sharing in their own incompatible (and sometimes proprietary) ways. The drivers for some cards (Ositech Jack of Diamonds, 3Com 3c562, Linksys) properly support simultaneous access, but others (Megahertz in particular) do not.

Earlier kernels do not support interrupt sharing between different device drivers, so it is not possible for the PCMCIA drivers to configure this card for simultaneous Ethernet and modem access. The Ethernet and serial drivers are both loaded automatically. However, the Ethernet driver "owns" the card interrupt by default. To use the modem, you can unload the ethernet driver and reconfigure the serial port by doing something like:

```
ifconfig eth0 down
rmmod 3c589_cs
setserial /dev/modem autoconfig auto_irq
setserial /dev/modem
```

The second `setserial` should verify that the port has been configured to use the interrupt previously used by the ethernet driver.

3.9 When is it safe to insert or eject a PCMCIA card?

In theory, you can insert and remove PCMCIA cards at any time. However, it is a good idea not to eject a card that is currently being used by an application program. Kernels older than 1.1.77 would often lock up when serial/modem cards were ejected, but this should be fixed now.

3.10 Card Services and Advanced Power Management

Card Services can be compiled with support for APM (Advanced Power Management) if you've installed this package on your system. APM is incorporated into 1.3.46 and later kernels. It is currently being maintained by Rick Faith (faith@cs.unc.edu), and APM tools can be obtained from `ftp.cs.unc.edu` in `/pub/users/faith/linux`. The PCMCIA modules will automatically be configured for APM if a compatible version is detected on your system.

Without resorting to APM, you can do `cardctl suspend` before suspending your laptop, and `cardctl resume` after resuming, to properly shut down and restart your PCMCIA cards. This will not work with a PCMCIA modem that is in use, because the serial driver isn't able to save and restore the modem operating parameters.

APM seems to be unstable on some systems. If you experience trouble with APM and PCMCIA on your system, try to narrow down the problem to one package or the other before reporting a bug.

Some drivers, notably the PCMCIA SCSI drivers, cannot recover from a suspend/resume cycle. When using a PCMCIA SCSI card, use cardctl eject prior to suspending the system.

3.11 How do I turn off a PCMCIA card without ejecting it?

Use either the `cardctl` or `cardinfo` command. `cardctl suspend #` will suspend one socket, and turn off its power. The corresponding `resume` command will wake up the card in its previous state.

3.12 How do I unload the PCMCIA drivers?

To unload the entire PCMCIA package, invoke `rc.pcmcia` with:

```
/etc/rc.d/rc.pcmcia stop
```

This script will take several seconds to run, to give all client drivers time to shut down gracefully. If a PCMCIA device is currently in use, the shutdown will be incomplete, and some kernel modules may not be unloaded. To avoid this, use `cardctl eject` to shut down all sockets before invoking `rc.pcmcia`. The exit status of the `cardctl` command will indicate if any sockets could not be shut down.

4 Advanced topics

4.1 Resource allocation for PCMCIA devices

In theory, it should not really matter which interrupt is allocated to which device, as long as two devices are not configured to use the same interrupt. In /etc/pcmcia/config.opts you'll find a place for excluding interrupts that are used by non-PCMCIA devices.

Similarly, there is no way to directly specify the I/O addresses for a PCMCIA card to use. The /etc/pcmcia/config.opts file allows you to specify ranges of ports available for use by all PCMCIA devices, or to exclude ranges that conflict with other devices.

After modifying /etc/pcmcia/config.opts, you can restart cardmgr with kill -HUP.

The interrupt used to monitor card status changes is chosen by the low-level socket driver module (i82365 or tcic) before cardmgr parses /etc/pcmcia/config, so it is not affected by changes to this file. To set this interrupt, use the cs_irq= option when the socket driver is loaded, by setting the PCIC_OPTS variable in /etc/rc.d/rc.pcmcia.

All the client card drivers have a parameter called irq_list for specifying which interrupts they may try to allocate. These driver options should be set in your /etc/pcmcia/config file. For example:

```
device "serial_cs"
  module "serial_cs" opts "irq_list=8,12"
  ...
```

would specify that the serial driver should only use irq 8 or irq 12. Regardless of irq_list settings, Card Services will never allocate an interrupt that is already in use by another device, or an interrupt that is excluded in the configuration file.

4.2 How can I have separate device setups for home and work?

This is fairly easy using PCMCIA "scheme" support. Use two configuration schemes, called "home" and "work." Here is an example of a network.opts script with scheme-specific settings:

```
case "$ADDRESS" in
work,*,*,*)
    # definitions for network card in work scheme
    ...
    ;;
home,*,*,*|default,*,*,*)
    # definitions for network card in home scheme
    ...
    ;;
esac
```

The first part of a PCMCIA device address is always the configuration scheme. In this example, the second "case" clause will select for both the "home" and "default" schemes. So, if the scheme is unset for any reason, it will default to the "home" setup.

Now, to choose between the two sets of settings, run either:

```
cardctl scheme home
```

or

```
cardctl scheme work
```

The cardctl command does the equivalent of shutting down all your cards and restarting them. The command can be safely executed whether or not the PCMCIA system is loaded, but the command may fail if you are using other PCMCIA devices at the time (even if their configurations are not explicitly dependent on the scheme setting).

To find out the current PCMCIA scheme setting, run:

```
cardctl scheme
```

4.3 Booting from a PCMCIA device

Having the root file system on a PCMCIA device is tricky because the Linux PCMCIA system is not designed to be linked into the kernel. Its core components, the loadable kernel modules and the user mode `cardmgr` daemon, depend on an already running system. The kernel's `initrd` facility works around this requirement by allowing Linux to boot using a temporary ram disk as a minimal root image, load drivers, and then re-mount a different root file system. The temporary root can configure PCMCIA devices and then re-mount a PCMCIA device as root.

Some Linux distributions will allow installation to a device connected to a PCMCIA SCSI adapter, as an unintended side-effect of their support for installs from PCMCIA SCSI CD-ROM devices. However, at present, no Linux installation tools support configuring an appropriate `initrd` to boot Linux with a PCMCIA root file system. Setting up a system with a PCMCIA root thus requires that you use another Linux system to create the `initrd` image. If another Linux system is not available, another option would be to temporarily install a minimal Linux setup on a non-PCMCIA drive, create an initrd image, and then reinstall to the PCMCIA target.

The Linux Bootdisk-HOWTO has some general information about setting up boot disks but nothing specific to initrd. The main initrd document is included with recent kernel source code distributions, in `linux/Documentation/initrd.txt`. Before beginning, you should read this document. A familiarity with `lilo` is also helpful. Using initrd also requires that you have a kernel compiled with `CONFIG_BLK_DEV_RAM` and `CONFIG_BLK_DEV_INITRD` enabled.

4.3.1 The `pcinitrd` helper script

The `pcinitrd` script creates a basic `initrd` image for booting with a PCMCIA root partition. The image includes a minimal directory hierarchy, a handful of device files, a few binaries, shared libraries, and a set of PCMCIA driver modules. When invoking `pcinitrd`, you specify the driver modules that you want to be included in the image. The core PCMCIA components, `pcmcia_core` and `ds`, are automatically included.

As an example, say that your laptop uses an i82365-compatible PCMCIA host controller, and you want to boot Linux with the root file system on a hard drive attached to an Adaptec SlimSCSI adapter. You could create an appropriate `initrd` image with:

```
pcinitrd -v initrd pcmcia/i82365.o pcmcia/aha152x_cs.o
```

To customize the `initrd` startup sequence, you could mount the image using the loopback device with a command like:

```
mount -o loop -t ext2 initrd /mnt
```

and then edit the `linuxrc` script. The PCMCIA configuration files will be installed under `/etc` in the image, and can also be customized. See the manual page for `pcinitrd` for more information.

4.3.2 Creating an initrd boot floppy

After creating an image with `pcinitrd`, you can create a boot floppy by copying the kernel, the compressed initrd image, and a few support files for `lilo` to a clean floppy. In the following example, we assume that the desired PCMCIA root device is `/dev/sda1`:

```
mke2fs /dev/fd0
mount /dev/fd0 /mnt
mkdir /mnt/etc /mnt/boot /mnt/dev
cp -a /dev/fd0 /dev/sda1 /mnt/dev
cp [kernel-image] /mnt/vmlinuz
gzip < [initrd-image] > /mnt/initrd
```

Create `/mnt/etc/lilo.conf` with the contents:

```
boot=/dev/fd0
compact
image=/vmlinuz
    label=linux
    initrd=/initrd
    read-only
    root=/dev/sda1
```

Finally, invoke lilo with:

```
lilo -r /mnt
```

When lilo is invoked with -r, it performs all actions relative to the specified alternate root directory. The reason for creating the device files under /mnt/dev was that lilo will not be able to use the files in /dev when it is running in this alternate-root mode.

4.3.3 Installing an initrd image on a non-Linux drive

One common use of the initrd facility would be on systems where the internal hard drive is dedicated to another operating system. The Linux kernel and initrd image can be placed in a non-Linux partition, and lilo or LOADLIN can be set up to boot Linux from these images.

Assuming that you have a kernel has been configured for the appropriate root device, and an initrd image created on another system, the easiest way to get started is to boot Linux using LOADLIN.EXE, as:

```
LOADLIN <kernel> initrd=<initrd-image>
```

Once you can boot Linux on your target machine, you could then install LILO to allow booting Linux directly. For example, say that /dev/hda1 is the non-Linux target partition and /mnt can be used as a mount point. First, create a subdirectory on the target for the Linux files:

```
mount /dev/hda1 /mnt
mkdir /mnt/linux
cp [kernel-image] /mnt/linux/vmlinuz
cp [initrd-image] /mnt/linux/initrd
```

In this example, say that /dev/sda1 is the desired Linux root partition, a SCSI hard drive mounted via a PCMCIA SCSI adapter. To install LILO, create a lilo.conf file with the contents:

```
boot=/dev/hda
map=/mnt/linux/map
compact
image=/mnt/linux/vmlinuz
        label=linux
        root=/dev/sda1
        initrd=/mnt/linux/initrd
        read-only
other=/dev/hda1
        table=/dev/hda
        label=windows
```

The boot= line says to install the boot loader in the master boot record of the specified device. The root= line identifies the desired root file system to be used after loading the initrd image, and may be unnecessary if the kernel image is already configured this way. The other= section is used to describe the other operating system installed on /dev/hda1.

To install lilo in this case, use:

```
lilo -C lilo.conf
```

Note that in this case, the lilo.conf file uses absolute paths that include /mnt. I did this in the example because the target file system may not support the creation of Linux device files for the boot= and root= options.

5 Dealing with unsupported cards

5.1 Configuring unrecognized cards

Assuming that your card is supported by an existing driver, all that needs to be done is to add an entry to /etc/pcmcia/config to tell cardmgr how to identify the card, and which driver(s) need to be linked up to this card. Check the man page for pcmcia for more information about the config file format. If you insert an unknown card, cardmgr will normally record some identification information in the system log that can be used to construct the config entry.

Here is an example of how cardmgr will report an unsupported card in /usr/adm/messages.

```
cardmgr[460]: unsupported card in socket 1
cardmgr[460]: version info: "MEGAHERTZ", "XJ2288", "V.34 PCMCIA MODEM"
```

The corresponding entry in /etc/pcmcia/config would be:

```
card "Megahertz XJ2288 V.34 Fax Modem"
  version "MEGAHERTZ", "XJ2288", "V.34 PCMCIA MODEM"
  bind "serial_cs"
```

You can use "*" to match strings that don't need to match exactly, like version numbers. When making new configuration entries, be careful to copy the strings exactly, preserving case and blank spaces. Also be sure that the configuration entry has the same number of strings as are reported in the log file.

After editing /etc/pcmcia/config, you can signal cardmgr to reload the file with:

```
kill -HUP 'cat /var/run/cardmgr.pid'
```

If you do set up an entry for a new card, please send me a copy so that I can include it in the standard configuration file.

5.2 Adding support for an NE2000-compatible ethernet card

First, see if the card is already recognized by cardmgr. Some cards not listed in SUPPORTED.CARDS are actually OEM versions of cards that are supported. If you find a card like this, let me know so I can add it to the list.

If your card is not recognized, follow the instructions in section 5.1 to create a config entry for your card, and bind the card to the pcnet_cs driver. Restart cardmgr to use the updated config file.

If the pcnet_cs driver says that it is unable to determine your card's hardware ethernet address, then edit your new config entry to bind the card to the memory card driver, memory_cs. Restart cardmgr to use the new updated config file. You will need to know your card's hardware ethernet address. This address is a series of six, two-digit hex numbers, often printed on the card itself. If it is not printed on the card, you may be able to use a DOS driver to display the address. In any case, once you know it, run:

```
dd if=/dev/mem0a count=20 | od -Ax -t x1
```

and search the output for your address. Only the even bytes are defined, so ignore the odd bytes in the dump. Record the hex offset of the first byte of the address. Now, edit modules/pcnet_cs.c and find the hw_info structure. You'll need to create a new entry for your card. The first field is the memory offset. The next three fields are the first three bytes of the hardware address. The final field contains some flags for specific card features; to start, try setting it to 0.

After editing pcnet_cs.c, compile and install the new module. Edit /etc/pcmcia/config again, and change the card binding from memory_cs to pcnet_cs. Follow the instructions for reloading the configuration file, and you should be all set. Please send me copies of your new hw_info and configuration entries.

If you can't find your card's hardware address in the hex dump, as a method of last resort, it is possible to "hard-wire" the address when the pcnet_cs module is initialized. Edit /etc/pcmcia/config and add a hw_addr= option, like so:

```
module "pcnet_cs" opts "hw_addr=0x00,0x80,0xc8,0x01,0x02,0x03"
```

Substitute your own card's hardware address in the appropriate spot, of course.

5.3 PCMCIA floppy interface cards

The PCMCIA floppy interface used in the Compaq Aero and a few other laptops is not yet supported by this package. The snag in supporting the Aero floppy is that the Aero seems to use a customized PCMCIA controller to support DMA to the floppy. Without knowing exactly how this is done, there isn't any way to implement support under Linux.

If the floppy adapter card is present when an Aero is booted, the Aero BIOS will configure the card, and Linux will identify it as a normal floppy drive. When the Linux PCMCIA drivers are loaded, they will notice that the card is already configured and attached to a Linux driver, and this socket will be left alone. So, the drive can be used if it is present at boot time, but the card is not hot swappable.

5.4 What's up with support for Xircom cards?

A driver for Xircom ethernet and ethernet/modem cards is included in the current PCMCIA package, thanks to the work of Werner Koch. I've set up a HyperNews forum specifically for discussion of Xircom driver development, at http://hyper.stanford.edu/HyperNews/get/pcmcia/xircom.html.

For a long time, Xircom cards were not supported because Xircom had a company policy of not disclosing technical information about their cards. However, they have relaxed their rules, and now, they do distribute driver information.

6 Debugging tips and programming information

6.1 How can I submit a helpful bug report?

The best way to submit bug reports is to use the HyperNews message lists on the Linux PCMCIA information site. That way, other people can see current problems (and fixes or workarounds, if available). Here are some things that should be included in all bug reports:

- Your system type, and the output of the `probe` command.
- What PCMCIA cards you are using.
- Your Linux kernel version, and PCMCIA driver version.
- Any changes you've made to the startup files in `/etc/pcmcia`, or to the PCMCIA startup script.
- All PCMCIA-related messages in your system log file.

Before submitting a bug report, please check to make sure that you are using an up-to-date copy of the driver package. While it is somewhat gratifying to read bug reports for things I've already fixed, it isn't a particularly constructive use of my time.

If your problem involves a kernel fault, the register dump from the fault is only useful if you can track down the fault address, EIP. If it is in the main kernel, look up the address in `System.map` to identify the function at fault. If the fault is in a loadable module, it is a bit harder to trace. With the current module tools, "`ksyms -m`" will report the base address of each loadable module. Pick the module that contains the EIP address, and subtract its base address from EIP to get an offset inside that module. Then, run `gdb` on that module, and look up the offset with the `list` command. This will only work if you've compiled that module with `-g` to include debugging information.

If you do not have web access, bug reports can be sent to me at `dhinds@hyper.stanford.edu`. However, I prefer that bug reports be posted to my Web site, so that they can be seen by others.

6.2 Low level PCMCIA debugging aids

The PCMCIA modules contain a lot of conditionally-compiled debugging code. Most of this code is under control of the `PCMCIA_DEBUG` preprocessor define. If this is undefined, debugging code will not be compiled. If set to 0, the code is compiled but inactive. Larger numbers specify increasing levels of verbosity. Each module built with `PCMCIA_DEBUG` defined will have an integer parameter, `pc_debug`, that controls the verbosity of its output. This can be adjusted when the module is loaded, so output can be controlled on a per-module basis without recompiling.

There are a few debugging tools in the `debug_tools/` subdirectory of the PCMCIA distribution. The `dump_tcic` and `dump_i365` utilities generate complete register dumps of the PCMCIA controllers, and decode a lot of the register information. They are most useful if you have access to a data sheet for the corresponding controller chip. The `dump_tuples` utility lists a card's CIS (Card Information Structure), and decodes some of the important bits. And the `dump_cisreg` utility displays a card's local configuration registers.

The `memory_cs` memory card driver is also sometimes useful for debugging. It can be bound to any PCMCIA card, and does not interfere with other drivers. It can be used to directly access any card's attribute memory or common memory.

6.3 How do I write a Card Services driver for a new card?

The Linux PCMCIA Programmer's Guide is the best documentation for the Linux PCMCIA interface. The latest version is always available from `hyper.stanford.edu` in `/pub/pcmcia/doc`, or on the web at `http://hyper.stanford.edu/HyperNews/get/pcmcia/home.html`.

For devices that are close relatives of normal ISA devices, you'll probably be able to use parts of existing Linux drivers. In some cases, the biggest stumbling block will be modifying an existing driver so that it can handle adding and removing devices after boot time. Of the current drivers, the memory card driver is the only "self-contained" driver that does not depend on other parts of the Linux kernel to do most of the dirty work.

I've written a skeleton driver with lots of comments that explains a lot of how a driver communicates with Card Services; you'll find this in the PCMCIA source distribution in `modules/skeleton.c`.

6.4 Guidelines for PCMCIA client driver authors

I have decided that it is not really feasible for me to distribute all PCMCIA client drivers as part of the PCMCIA package. Each new driver makes the main package incrementally harder to maintain, and including a driver inevitably transfers some of the maintenance work from the driver author to me. Instead, I will decide on a case by case basis whether or not to include contributed drivers, based on user demand as well as maintainability. For drivers not included in the core package, I suggest that driver authors adopt the following scheme for packaging their drivers for distribution.

Driver files should be arranged in the same directory scheme used in the PCMCIA source distribution, so that the driver can be unpacked on top of a complete PCMCIA source tree. A driver should include source files (in `./modules/`), a manual page (in `./man/`), and configuration files (in `./etc/`). The top level directory should also include a README file.

The top-level directory should include a makefile, set up so that `make -f ... all` and `make -f ... install` compile the driver and install all appropriate files. If this makefile is given an extension of `.mk`, then it will automatically be invoked by the top-level `Makefile` for the `all` and `install` targets. Here is an example of how such a makefile could be constructed:

```
# Sample Makefile for contributed client driver
FILES = sample_cs.mk README.sample_cs \
        modules/sample_cs.c modules/sample_cs.h \
        etc/sample etc/sample.opts man/sample_cs.4
all:
        $(MAKE) -C modules MODULES=sample_cs.o
install:
        $(MAKE) -C modules install-modules MODULES=sample_cs.o
        $(MAKE) -C etc install-clients CLIENTS=sample
        $(MAKE) -C man install-man4 MAN4=sample_cs.4
dist:
        tar czvf sample_cs.tar.gz $(FILES)
```

This makefile uses install targets defined in 2.9.10 and later versions of the PCMCIA package. This makefile also includes a "dist" target for the convenience of the driver author. You would probably want to add a version number to the final package filename (for example, `sample_cs-1.5.tar.gz`). A complete distribution could look like:

```
sample_cs.mk
README.sample_cs
modules/sample_cs.c
modules/sample_cs.h
etc/sample
etc/sample.opts
man/sample_cs.4
```

With this arrangement, when the contributed driver is unpacked, it becomes essentially part of the PCMCIA source tree. It can make use of the PCMCIA header files, as well as the machinery for checking the user's system configuration, and automatic dependency checking, just like a "normal" client driver.

I will accept client drivers prepared according to this specification and place them in the `/pub/pcmcia/contrib` directory on my FTP server, `hyper.stanford.edu`. The README in this directory will describe how to unpack a contributed driver.

The PCMCIA client driver interface has not changed much over time, and has almost always preserved backwards compatibility. A client driver will not normally need to be updated for minor revisions in the main PCMCIA package. I will try to notify authors of contributed drivers of changes that require updates to their drivers.

6.5 Guidelines for Linux distribution maintainers

If your distribution has system configuration tools that you would like to be PCMCIA-aware, please use the `*.opts` files in `/etc/pcmcia` for your "hooks." These files will not be modified if a user compiles and installs a new release of the PCMCIA package. If you modify the main configuration scripts, then a fresh PCMCIA install will silently overwrite your custom scripts and break the connection with your configuration tools. Contact me if you are not sure how to write an appropriate option script.

When building PCMCIA for distribution, you should consider including contributed drivers that are not part of the main PCMCIA package. For reasons of maintainability, I am trying to limit the core package size, by only adding new drivers if I think they are of particularly broad interest. Other drivers will be distributed separately, as described in the previous section. The split between integral and separate drivers is somewhat arbitrary and partly historical, and should not imply a difference in quality.

Part XXXV

"Pilot HOWTO"
by David H. Silber,
pilot@orbits.com

The Linux Documentation Project
The original, unaltered edition of this, and other, LDP documents, is on line at http://sunsite.unc.edu/LDP/.

Contents

Abstract

This HOWTO document explains how to use your Pilot with a Linux system. Although HOWTO documents are targeted towards use with the Linux operating system, this one is not dependent on the version of UNIX used.

1 Introduction

The Pilot comes with software to synchronize its memory with data on a Microsoft Windows system. There is optional software you can buy to synchronize with an Apple Macintosh. The Linux and Unix community has been ignored by the manufacturers of the Pilot. Fortunately, a suite of free software has been developed to fill this need. This document describes this software, where to get it, and how to install and use it.

1.1 This Document

The latest version of this document can be read at `http://www.orbits.com/Pilot/Pilot-HOWTO.html`, and is part of the Linux Documentation Project (LDP). See `http://sunsite.unc.edu/LDP/` for further information about the LDP and other HOWTO documents.

Future versions will cover more UNIX tools for writing application programs to run on the Pilot and conduits to transfer data between the UNIX system and the Pilot.

If you find anything in this document which needs to be corrected or better explained, please send me e-mail at the address above and specify which version of this document you are referring to.

1.2 Mailing List

The pilot-unix mailing list is maintained by Matthew Cravit, pilot-unix-owner@lists.best.com. Its mandate is:

```
The pilot-unix mailing list is for discussion and idea-sharing for those
interested in using the US Robotics Pilot PDAs with UNIX systems. This
includes people who are interested in helping to develop tools to allow the
Pilot to operate with UNIX, and possibly to develop an SDK for the Pilot
for Unix.
```

For more information, including how to subscribe to the list, send mail containing the word "`INFO`" to `pilot-unix-request@lists.best.com`. The subject line does not matter.

1.3 Mailing List Archives

An archive of the pilot-unix mailing list can be found at `http:///www.acm.rpi.edu/~albert/pilot/`. It is maintained by Chris Stevens, albert@acm.rpi.edu.

1.4 FTP Site

An FTP site containing an archive of Pilot tools for use on unix systems is located at `ftp://ryeham.ee.ryerson.ca/pub/PalmOS/`. It is maintained by Jeff Dionne, jeff@ryeham.ee.ryerson.ca.

2 General Information

2.1 What is a Pilot?

The Pilot is a small, pen based Personal Digital Assistant (PDA). It is made by U. S. Robotics, now part of 3Com.

For those of you unfamiliar with the term, a **Personal Digital Assistant** is one of those small electronic devices which typically contain various types of personal information, such as addresses and telephone numbers, a calendar, checkbook registry, lists of reminders or memos, and is designed to be conveniently carried so as to be handy when the information is needed.

The more adaptable PDAs, such as the Pilot, allow for the data stored on the PDA to be backed up to another computer and for data and new programs to be loaded onto the PDA from another computer.

2.2 Different types of Pilots

There are four versions of the Pilot. The earlier two, the 1000 and the 5000 have 128k and 512k of RAM, respectively.

The more recent two, the PalmPilot Personal and the PalmPilot Professional have 512k and 1 Meg of RAM, respectively. They also have a backlighting feature for the LCD panel and version 2.0 of the operating system. The Professional also comes with a TCP/IP stack and a few extra programs built-in.

It is possible to upgrade any Pilot by swapping out the memory card, which includes both RAM & ROM. Of course, this doesn't get you backlighting for the older pilots.

2.3 Hardware Installation

Pilots come with a "cradle" for exchanging data with the desktop computer. This device is actually a serial cable with a custom holder for the Pilot end and a HotSync button. Plug your cradle into a spare serial port on your computer. When you run each of the stand-alone programs, you will need to place your Pilot in the cradle and push the HotSync button so the Pilot knows that it has to communicate. If the Pilot happens to be off when the button is pushed, it will turn itself on.

For convenience, create a device, `/dev/pilot` which will be an alternate name for the serial port to which your Pilot cradle is connected. As the root user, enter the following at the shell prompt:

```
ln /dev/cua0 /dev/pilot
```

Replace `cua0` with the name of the port to which you connected your Pilot's cradle.

3 Sharing Pilot Data with your Linux System

3.1 The pilot-link software

The pilot-link suite of software tools allows you to download programs onto your Pilot, and transfer data for the Pilot's various built-in programs between the linux system and the Pilot. While these programs are not quite as seamless as the desktop software that comes with the Pilot, they do allow you to copy your data in both directions. In general, each separate program in the `pilot-link` suite manages one type of data. The PilotManager software is built on top of `pilot-link` and provides a more integrated solution, which typically includes full synchronization of the various types of data.

3.1.1 Installing the pilot-link software

The prepackaged versions will inevitably lag slightly behind the master distribution, but will be easier to install and not require configuration. The master distribution might be a better choice in those rare occasions when you have been waiting for a particular feature or bug fix.

You can get the Debian GNU/Linux port of *pilot-link* version 0.7.2 from ftp://ftp.debian.org/pub/debian/hamm/hamm/binary-i386/otherosfs/ as `pilot-link_0.7.2-1.deb`. Install this file in the normal manner and skip to *Using the pilot-link software*.

You can get the Red Hat Linux port of pilot-link version 0.7.6 from ftp://ftp.redhat.com/pub/contrib/i386/ `pilot-link-0.7.6-2.i386.rpm`. Install this file in the normal manner and skip to *Using the pilot-link software*.

For other versions of Linux or Unix, download the version 0.8.2 of pilot-link from ftp://ryeham.ee.ryerson.ca/pub/PalmOS/ as `pilot-link.0.8.2.tar.gz`. The version number is likely to change, but new versions should end up in the same location with a similar name.

Once you have the software distribution, unpack it with:

```
tar -xvzf pilot-link.0.8.2.tar.gz
```

This creates a directory (`pilot-link.0.8.2`) containing the source.

Run `./configure`. This will search through your system for information needed to compile the software. `configure` will set things up to be installed in `/usr/local` by default. If you want to change it, run `./configure -prefix=DIR`, where `DIR` is replaced with the name of the directory to which the software will be installed.

Run `make`. This will compile the software. The software will not be installed until later, so that you have a chance to try it out first. (If you are replacing an older version with a newer release, you may wish to check and make sure that no functionality that you need has been broken. Generally, this is not a problem.)

As the root user, run `make install`. This will copy the software into directories under `/usr/local` (or wherever you specified with the `-prefix` option). If you can not log in as root, you can install the software to some directory where you have write access.

Don't forget to add any new directories of executables to your search path.

3.1.2 Using the pilot-link software

Most of the programs in the `pilot-link` suite are **conduits**, that is they transfer data into or out of your Pilot.

Each time you use of one of these programs, press the HotSync button on your Pilot's cradle. This will initiate the Pilot side of the data transfer. Note that not all of these programs prompt you to press the HotSync button, so you may have to remember to do it yourself.

For more details, and other options to these programs, view the corresponding manual page. For the `pilot-xfer` program, for example, type `man pilot-xfer` at your unix shell prompt.

If you are going to use `PilotManager`, you may not need to bother learning to use these (more primitive) tools.

`pilot-xfer` Possibly the most useful program in the pilot-link suite, `pilot-xfer` allows you to install programs on your Pilot, make a backup, and restore that backup.

To install a program:

```
pilot-xfer /dev/pilot -i program.prc
```

To backup your Pilot:

```
pilot-xfer /dev/pilot -b backup-directory
```

This will copy all of the databases on your Pilot to a directory called *backup-directory*, creating it if it does not already exist.

To restore data to Pilot:

```
pilot-xfer /dev/pilot -r backup-directory
```

Generally, you will only need to do this if your Pilot loses power or if you have to do a hard reset.

To list the programs on your Pilot:

```
pilot-xfer /dev/pilot -l
```

`install-memo`. Install a linux file onto the Pilot as a memo.

To install a memo into your (already existing) *project* category:

```
install-memo /dev/pilot -c project project.memo
```

The name of the file will be inserted into the memo as its first line and will appear in the directory of memos on your Pilot.

`memos`. This program grabs each memo from the Pilot and prints it out in standard mailbox format.

To view your memos:

```
memos /dev/pilot
```

`pilot-addresses`. Transfer the address database to or from the Pilot.

To write your address data to a linux file from your Pilot:

```
pilot-addresses /dev/pilot -w storage.file
```

To read your address data from a linux file onto your Pilot:

```
pilot-addresses /dev/pilot -r storage.file
```

3.2 MakeDoc

One shortcoming of the Pilot's built-in memo program is that it does not deal well with large documents. To compensate for this, Rick Bram, rbram@concentric.net, wrote Doc, a document reader for the Pilot. (See http://www.concentric.net/~rbram/doc.shtml). Documents can be converted to the Doc format with MakeDoc, by Pat Beirne, pat.beirne@sympatico.ca.

3.2.1 Installing MakeDoc

MakeDoc can be downloaded from `http://www.concentric.net/~rbram/makedoc7.cpp`. Compile it with your C++ compiler and install the resulting executable as `makedoc` in a directory in your search path. There seems to be a small bug in `makedoc` (version 0.7a) in that it does not output a newline as the last character displayed to the user. This does not seem to affect the resulting document file, but it is annoying.

There is a new version out, but it requires Java. Take a look at Pat Beirne's MakeDoc web page at `http://cpu563.adsl.sympatico.ca/MakeDocJ.htm`.

3.2.2 Using MakeDoc

Use MakeDoc as follows:

```
makedoc data.txt data.prc "Data to display with Doc"
```

This will create a file `data.prc`, which can be installed on your Pilot with `pilot-xfer`. The text "Data to display with Doc" will be displayed in the directory of documents that Doc manages.

The syntax for `MakeDoc` is as follows:

```
makedoc [-n] [-b] <text-file> <prc-file> <story-name>
or
makedoc -d [-b] <prc-file> <text-file>
```

<text-file>
The file that you wish to convert.

<prc-file>
The name of the resulting file. (End the name with "`.prc`".)

<story-name>
The name you want displayed in the Doc or Jdoc directory of documents.

There are also options to decode the resulting `.prc` file and manage various compression options.

3.3 PilotManager

PilotManager is a generalized tool which allows multiple databases to be synchronized in a single HotSync session.

I have not been able to build and install PilotManager in time to write about it for this version of the Pilot-HOWTO.

A few links that might be helpful:

- The PilotManager package:
  `http://playground.sun.com/~bharat/pilotmgr.html`
- A patch:
  `ftp://ftp.orbits.com/pub/Pilot/pilotmgr,v1.009-BETA-3.patch`

This patch for PilotManager is only intended for use with PilotManager version 1.009 Beta 3 when used with pilot-link version 0.8.0. Install the PilotManager source and apply the patch with the commands:

```
tar -xvzf pilotmgr,v1.009-BETA-3.dev.tar.gz
cd pilotmgr,v1.009-BETA-3
patch -p1 < ../pilotmgr,v1.009-BETA-3.patch
```

I hope to be able to install this software soon and report about it in a future version of this document.

4 Tools for Developing Pilot Software

4.1 prc-tools

The prc-tools package is a complete development environment built from the FSF GNU utilities, compiler and debugger with the addition of a few special tools.

There is not much in the way of documentation, but you might want to look at the Pilot Software Development web page at `http://www.massena.com/darrin/pilot/`.

4.1.1 Installing prc-tools

Download the most recent version of prc-tools from `ftp://ryeham.ee.ryerson.ca/pub/PalmOS`. The GNU tools can be retrieved from `ftp://prep.ai.mit.edu/pub/gnu`. Get `binutils-2.7.tar.gz`, `gcc-2.7.2.2.tar.gz` and `gdb-4.16.tar.gz`. The version numbers specified for the GNU tools are correct as of prc-tools release 0.5.0. Later releases of prc-tools may require newer versions of the GNU tools.

Put all of the distribution packages in one directory. Unpack only the prc-tools distribution. The prc-tools `Makefile` will take care of the other packages. By default, prc-tools will be installed in `/usr/local/gnu`. If you want them installed somewhere else, you need to change the value of `INSTALLDIR` in `Makefile`. The steps are:

```
tar -xvzf prc-tools.0.5.0.tar.gz
cd prc-tools-0.5.0
(Edit Makefile, if necessary.)
make doeverything
```

4.1.2 Using prc-tools

One good reference for general use of `prc-tools` is the `example` directory, particularly the `Makefile`. Documentation for PilRC is provided in the file `pilrc1.5/doc/pilrc.htm` included as part of prc-tool version 0.5.0.

5 People

Kenneth Albanowski (`mailto:kjahds@kjahds.com`) Maintains the pilot-link suite of tools.

Donnie Barnes (`mailto:djb@redhat.com`) Packaged pilot-link suite as Red Hat RPM files.

Rick Bram (`mailto:rbram@concentric.net`) Author of Doc.

Matthew Cravit (`mailto:pilot-unix-owner@lists.best.com`) List owner for the pilot-unix mailing list.

Jeff Dionne (`mailto:jeff@ryeham.ee.ryerson.ca`) Original author of the pilot-link suite of tools. Manages the FTP area for the UNIX PalmOS/Pilot development project.

Mark W. Eichin (`mailto:eichen@kitten.gen.ma.us`) Ported pilot-link suite to Debian Linux.

David H. Silber (`mailto:pilot@orbits.com`) Author of this document.

Chris Stevens (`mailto:albert@acm.rpi.edu`) Maintains the pilot-unix mailing list archives.

Part XXXVI

"Linux PPP HOWTO"
by Robert Hart,

hartr@hedland.edu.au

Contents

Abstract

v3.0, 31 March 1997

This document shows how to connect your Linux PC to a PPP server, how to use PPP to link two LANs together, and provides one method of setting up your Linux computer as a PPP server. The document also provides help in debugging non-functional PPP connections.

Copyright

Distribution

This document will be posted to comp.os.linux.answers as new versions of the document are produced. It is also available in HTML format at:

- http://sunsite.unc.edu/mdw/linux.html#howto
- http://www.interweft.com.au/other/ppp-howto/ppp-howto.html

Other formats (SGML, ASCII, PostScript, DVI) are available from ftp://sunsite.unc.edu in the directory /pub/Linux/docs/HOWTO/other-formats/.

As sunsite.unc.edu carries a very heavy load, please use an appropriate mirror site close to you.

Acknowledgements

A growing number of people have provided me with assistance in preparing this document. Special thanks go to Al Longyear for the guidance on PPP itself (if there are mistakes here, they are mine not his), Greg Hankins (maintainer of the Linux HOWTOs) and Debi Tackett (of MaximumAccess.com) for many helpful suggestions on style, content order, logic, and clarity of explanations.

Finally, to the many people who have contacted me by e-mail offering comments—my thanks. As with all HOWTO authors, the satisfaction of helping is all the payment we receive and it is enough. By writing this HOWTO, I am repaying in a small way the debt I—and all other Linux users—owe to the people who write and maintain our OS of choice.

1 Introduction

PPP (the Point-to-Point Protocol) is a mechanism for creating and running the Internet Protocol (IP) and other network protocols over a serial link—be that a direct serial connection (using a null modem cable), over a telnet established link or a link made using modems and telephone lines (and of course using digital lines such as ISDN).

Using PPP, you can connect your Linux PC to a PPP server and access the resources of the network to which the server is connected (almost) as if you were directly connected to that network.

You can also set up your Linux PC as a PPP server, so that other computers can dial in to your computer and access the resources on your local PC or network.

As PPP is a peer-to-peer system, you can also use PPP on two Linux PCs to link together two networks (or a local network to the Internet), creating a Wide Area Network (WAN).

One major difference between PPP and an Ethernet connection is, of course speed—a standard Ethernet connection operates at 10 Mbs (Mega: million bits per second) maximum theoretical throughput, whereas an analogue modem operates at speeds up to 56 kbps (kilo: thousand bits per second).

Also, depending on the type of PPP connection, there may be some limitations in usage of some applications and services.

1.1 Clients and Servers

PPP is strictly a **peer-to-peer** protocol; there is (technically) no difference between the machine that dials in and the machine that is dialed into. However, for clarity's sake, it is useful to think in terms of **servers** and **clients**.

When you dial into a site to establish a PPP connection, you are a **client**. The machine to which you connect is the **server**.

When you are setting up a Linux box to receive and handle dial-in PPP connections, you are setting up a PPP **server**.

Any Linux PC can be both a PPP server and client—even simultaneously, if you have more than one serial port (and modem if necessary). As stated above, there is no real difference between clients and servers as far as PPP is concerned, once the connection is made.

This document refers to the machine that initiates the call (that dials in) as the **client**, while the machine that answers the telephone, checks the authentication of the dial in request (using user names, passwords and possibly other mechanisms) is referred to as the **server**.

The use of PPP as a client to link one or more machines at a location into the Internet is, probably, the one in which most people are interested—that is, using their Linux PC as a client.

The procedure described in this document will allow you to establish and automate your Internet connection.

This document will also give you guidance in setting up your Linux PC as a PPP server and in linking two LANs together (with full routing) using PPP (this is frequently characterized as establishing a WAN—wide area network—link).

1.2 Differences between Linux distributions

There are many different Linux distributions, and they all have their own idiosyncrasies and ways of doing things.

In particular, there are two different ways a Linux (and Unix) computer actually starts up, configures its interfaces, and so forth.

These are **BSD system initialization** and **System V system initialization**. If you dip into some of the Unix news groups, you will find occasional religious wars between proponents of these two systems. If that sort of thing amuses you, have fun burning bandwidth and join in.

Possibly the most widely used distributions are

- Slackware
  which uses BSD-style system initialization.
- Red Hat (and its former associate Caldera)
  which use SysV system initialization (although in a slightly modified form).
- Debian
  which uses SysV system initialization.

BSD-style initialization typically keeps its initialization files in `/etc/...` and these files are:

```
/etc/rc
/etc/rc.local
/etc/rc.serial
        (and possibly other files)
```

Of recent times, some BSD system initialization schemes use a `/etc/rc.d...` directory to hold the start up file rather than putting everything into `/etc`.

System V initialization keeps its initialization files in directories under `/etc/...` or `/etc/rc.d/...` and a number of subdirectories under there:

```
drwxr-xr-x   2 root     root         1024 Jul  6 15:12 init.d
-rwxr-xr-x   1 root     root         1776 Feb  9 05:01 rc
-rwxr-xr-x   1 root     root          820 Jan  2  1996 rc.local
-rwxr-xr-x   1 root     root         2567 Jul  5 20:30 rc.sysinit
drwxr-xr-x   2 root     root         1024 Jul  6 15:12 rc0.d
drwxr-xr-x   2 root     root         1024 Jul  6 15:12 rc1.d
drwxr-xr-x   2 root     root         1024 Jul  6 15:12 rc2.d
drwxr-xr-x   2 root     root         1024 Jul 18 18:07 rc3.d
drwxr-xr-x   2 root     root         1024 May 27  1995 rc4.d
drwxr-xr-x   2 root     root         1024 Jul  6 15:12 rc5.d
drwxr-xr-x   2 root     root         1024 Jul  6 15:12 rc6.d
```

If you are trying to track down where your Ethernet interface and associated network routes are actually configured, you will need to track through these files to actually find where the commands are that do this.

1.3 Distribution specific PPP configuration tools

On some installations (for example Red Hat and Caldera), there is a X Window System configured PPP dial-up system. This HOWTO does not cover these distribution-specific tools. If you are having problems with them, contact the distributors directly.

For Red Hat 4.x users, there is now a Red Hat PPP-TIP, http://www.interweft.com.au, in the Linux resources area and also from Red Hat Software, http://www.redhat.com in the support area.

2 IP Numbers

Every device that connects to the Internet must have its own, unique IP number. These are assigned centrally by a designated authority for each country.

If you are connecting a local area network (LAN) to the Internet, you must use an IP number from your own assigned network range for all the computers and devices you have on your LAN. You must not pick IP numbers out of the air and use these while connecting to another LAN (let alone the Internet). At worst this will simply not work at all and could cause total havoc as your "stolen" IP number starts interfering with the communications of another computer that is already using the IP number you have picked out of the air.

Please note that the IP numbers used throughout this document (with some exceptions) are from the "unconnected network numbers" series that are reserved for use by networks that are not (ever) connected to the Internet.

There are IP numbers that are specifically dedicated to LANs that do not connect to the Internet. The IP number sequences are:

- One A Class Network Address
  10.0.0.0 (netmask 255.0.0.0)
- 16 B Class Network Addresses
  172.16.0.0—172.31.0.0 (netmask 255.255.0.0)
- 256 C Class Network Addresses
  192.168.0.0—192.168.255.0 (netmask 255.255.255.0)

If you have a LAN for which you have not been allocated IP numbers by the responsible authority in your country, you should use one of the network numbers from the above sequences for your machines.

◇ These numbers should never be used on the Internet.

However, they can be used for the local Ethernet on a machine that is connecting to the Internet. This is because IP numbers are actually allocated to a network interface, not to a computer. So while your Ethernet interface may use 10.0.0.1 (for example), when you hook onto the Internet using PPP, your PPP interface will be given another (and valid) IP number by the server. Your PC will have Internet connectivity, but the other computers on your LAN will not.

However, using Linux and the IP Masquerade (also known as NAT—Network Address Translation) capabilities of the Linux and the `ipfwadm` software, you can connect your LAN to the Internet (with some restriction of services), even if you do not have valid IP numbers for the machines on your Ethernet.

For more information on how to do this see the IP Masquerade mini-HOWTO at http://sunsite.unc.edu/LDP/HOWTO/mini/IP-Masquerade.

For most users, who connect a single machine to an Internet service provider via PPP, obtaining an IP number (or more accurately, a network number) will not be necessary.

If you wish to connect a small LAN to the Internet, many Internet Service Providers (ISPs) can provide you with a dedicated subnet (a specific sequence of IP numbers) from their existing IP address space. Alternatively, use IP Masquerading.

For users who are connecting a single PC to the Internet via an ISP, most providers use **dynamic** IP number assignment. That is, as part of the connection process, the PPP service that you contact will tell your machine what IP number to use for the PPP interface during the current session. This number will not be the same every time you connect to your ISP.

With dynamic IP numbers, you are not given the same IP number each time you connect. This has implications for server type applications on your Linux machine such as `sendmail`, `ftpd`, `httpd`, and so forth. These services are based on the premise that the computer offering the service is accessible at the same IP number all the time (or at least the same fully qualified domain name—FQDN— and that DNS resolution of the name to IP address is available).

The limitations of service due to dynamic IP number assignment (and ways to work around these, where possible) are discussed later in the document.

3 Aims of this Document

3.1 Setting up a PPP Client

This document provides guidance to people who wish to use Linux and PPP to dial in to a PPP server and set up an IP connection using PPP. It assumes that PPP has been compiled and installed on your Linux machine (but does briefly cover reconfiguring and recompiling your kernel to include PPP support).

Whilst `dip` (the standard way of creating a SLIP connection) can be used to set up a PPP connection, `dip` scripts are generally quite complex. For this reason, this document does not cover using `dip` to set up a PPP connection.

Instead, this document describes the standard Linux PPP software, `chat` and `pppd`.

3.2 Linking two LANs or a LAN to the Internet using PPP

This document provides (basic) information on linking two LANs or a LAN to the Internet using PPP.

3.3 Setting up a PPP server

This document provides guidance on how to configure your Linux PC as a PPP server (allowing other people to dial into your Linux PC and establish a PPP connection).

You should note that there are a myriad of ways of setting up Linux as a PPP server. This document gives one method—that used by the author to set up several small PPP servers (each of 16 modems).

This method is known to work well. However, it is not necessarily the best method.

3.4 Using PPP over a direct null modem connection

This document provides a brief overview of using PPP to link two Linux PCs via a null modem cable. It is possible to link other OS's to Linux this way as well. To do so, you will need to consult the documentation for the operating system you are interested in.

3.5 This document at present does NOT cover...

- Compiling the PPP daemon software
  See the documentation that comes with the version of `pppd` you are using.
- Connecting and configuring a modem to Linux (in detail) See the Serial-HOWTO and for modem-specific initialisation, see

  http://www.in.net/info/modems/index.html

  for information that may help you to configure your modem.
- Using `dip` to make PPP connections.
  Use `chat` instead.
- Using SOCKS or IP Masquerade.
  There are perfectly good documents already covering these two packages.
- Using `diald` to set up an automated connection.
  See the `diald` documentation for information on this.
- Using EQL to gang together two modems into a single PPP link.
- Distribution specific PPP connection methods such as the Red Hat 4.x network configuration tool.
  See the distribution for documentation on the methods used.
- The growing number of tools available to automate PPP setup.
  See the appropriate documentation.

4 Software versions covered

This HOWTO assumes that you are using a Linux 1.2.x kernel with the PPP 2.1.2 software or Linux 1.3.*x*/2.0.*x* and PPP 2.2.

At the time of this writing, the latest official version of PPP available for Linux is ppp-2.2f. The new version (ppp-2.3) is still in Beta testing.

It is possible to use PPP 2.2.0 with kernel 1.2.13. This requires kernel patches. It is recommended that version 1.2.13 kernel users move up to ppp-2.2 as it includes several bug fixes and enhancements.

Note: You should particularly note that you cannot use the PPP 2.1.2 software with Linux kernel version 2.0.*x*.

Please note that this document does not cover problems arising from the use of loadable modules for Linux kernel 2.0.*x*. Please see the kerneld mini-HOWTO and the kernel module 2.0.*x* documentation (in the Linux 2.0.x source tree at `/usr/src/linux/Documentation/...`).

Note: As this document is designed to assist new users, it is highly recommended that you use a version of the Linux kernel and the appropriate PPP version that are known to be stable together.

5 Other Useful and Important Documents

Users are advised to read :

- the documentation that comes with the PPP package;
- the `pppd` and `chat` manual pages;
  (use `man chat` and `man pppd`);

- The Linux Network Administration Guide (NAG): http://sunsite.unc.edu/mdw/LDP-books/nag-1.0/nag.html;
- the Net-3 HOWTO: http://sunsite.unc.edu/mdw/HOWTO/NET-3-HOWTO.html;
- Linux kernel documentation installed in `/usr/src/linux/Documentation` when you install the Linux source code;
- The modem setup information page—see http://www.in.net/info/modems/index.html
- The excellent Unix and Linux books published by O'Reilly and Associates. See http://www.ora.com/. If you are new to Unix or Linux, run (don't walk) to your nearest computer book shop and invest in a number of these immediately;
- The PPP-FAQ maintained by Al Longyear, available from

  ftp://sunsite.unc.edu/pub/Linux/docs/faqs;

  This contains a great deal of useful information in question-and-answer format that is very useful when working out why PPP is not working (properly).
- The growing number of Linux books from various publishing houses and authors; You are actively encouraged to check the currency of these books. Linux development and distributions tend to evolve fairly rapidly, while the revision of books move (generally) much more slowly. Buying an excellent book (and there are many) which is now out of date will cause new users considerable confusion and frustration.

The best general starting point for Linux documentation is http://sunsite.unc.edu/LDP/ The HOWTOS tend to be revised reasonably regularly.

While you can use this document to create your PPP link without reading any of these documents, you will have a far better understanding of what is going on if you do so. You will also be able to address problems yourself (or at least ask more intelligent questions on the comp.os.linux.* newsgroups or Linux mailing lists).

These documents (as well as various others, including the relevant RFCs) provide additional and more detailed explanation than is possible in this HOWTO.

If you are connecting a LAN to the Internet using PPP, you will need to know a reasonable amount about TCP/IP networking. In addition to the documents above, you will find the O'Reilly books *TCP/IP Network Administration* and *Building Internet Firewalls* of considerable benefit.

5.1 Useful Linux Mailing Lists

There are many Linux mailing lists that operate as a means of communication between users of many levels of ability. By all means, subscribe to those that interest you and contribute your expertise and views.

A word to the wise: some lists are specifically aimed at "high powered" users or specific topics. Whilst no one will complain if you "lurk" (subscribe but don't post messages), you are likely to earn heated comments (if not outright flames) if you post "newbie" questions to inappropriate lists.

This is not because guru-level users hate new users, but because these lists are there to handle the specific issues at particular levels of difficulty.

By all means join the lists that offer open subscription, but keep your comments relevant to the subject of the list.

A good starting point for Linux mailing lists is

http://summer.snu.ac.kr/~djshin/linux/mail-list/index.shtml

6 Overview of what has to be done to get PPP working as a client

This document contains a great deal of information—and with each version it grows.

As a consequence, this section aims to provide a concise overview of the actions you will need to take to get your Linux system connected as a client to a PPP server.

6.1 Obtaining and Installing the software

If your Linux distribution does not include the PPP software, you will need to obtain this from ftp://sunsite.unc.edu/pub/Linux/system/Network/serial/ppp/ppp-2.2.0f.tar.gz.

This is the latest official version at the time of writing. However, choose the latest version available from this site (ppp-2.3 is in Beta testing at the time of writing and should be released soon).

The PPP package contains instructions on how to compile and install the software, so this HOWTO does not.

6.2 Compiling PPP support into the kernel

Linux PPP operations come in two parts:

- the PPP daemon mentioned above;
- kernel support for PPP.

Many distributions seem to provide PPP kernel support in their default installation kernels, but others do not. If at boot your kernel reports messages like

```
PPP Dynamic channel allocation code copyright 1995 Caldera, Inc.
PPP line discipline registered.
```

your kernel has PPP support compiled in.

That said, you will probably want to compile your own kernel, whatever your distribution, to provide the most efficient use of system resources given your particular hardware configuration. It is worth remembering that the kernel cannot be swapped out of memory, and so keeping the kernel as small as possible has advantages on a limited memory machine.

This document provides minimal kernel re-compilation instructions in Section 7.

For greater detail, see the Kernel HOWTO (page 1019).

6.3 Obtaining information from your ISP

There are an almost-infinite number of ways in which a PPP server can be set up. In order to connect to your ISP (or corporate PPP server to access your intranet), you need to obtain information on how the PPP server operates.

Because you are using Linux, you may have some difficulty with some ISP help desks (and worksite based PPP intranet servers) which know only about MS Windows clients.

However, a rapidly growing number of ISPs use Linux to provide their service—and Linux is also penetrating the corporate environment as well, so you may be lucky if you do run into problems.

Section 8 tells you what you need to know about the PPP server to which you are going to connect—and how to find out the information you need to know.

6.4 Configuring your modem and serial port

In order to connect to a PPP server and to obtain the best possible data transfer rate, your modem needs to be configured correctly.

Similarly, the serial ports on your modem and computer need to be set up correctly.

Section 9 provides information on this.

6.5 Setting up Name-to-Address Resolution (DNS)

In addition to the files that run PPP and perform the automated log in to the PPP server, there are a number of text configuration files that have to be set up for your computer to be able to resolve names like `www.interweft.com.au` to the IP address that is actually used to contact that computer. These are:

- `/etc/resolv.conf`
- `/etc/host.conf`

Section 10 has details on setting this up.

In particular, you do not need to run a name server on your Linux PC in order to connect to the Internet (although you may wish to). All you need is to know the IP number of at least one name server that you can use (preferably one at your ISP's site).

6.6 PPP and Root Privileges

As establishing a PPP link between you Linux computer and another PPP server requires manipulation of network devices (the PPP interface is a network interface) and the kernel routing table, `pppd` requires root privileges.

For details on this, see Section 11.

6.7 Checking your distribution PPP Files and setting up the PPP Options

There are a number of configuration and dialer files that need to be set up to make PPP operational. There are examples as part of the PPP distribution, and this section shows what files you should have:

```
/etc/ppp/options
/etc/ppp/scripts/ppp-on
/etc/ppp/scripts/ppp-on-dialer
/etc/ppp/options.tpl
```

You may need to create some additional files, depending on exactly what you are aiming to achieve with PPP:

```
/etc/ppp/options.ttyXX
/etc/ppp/ip-up
/etc/ppp/pap-secrets
/etc/ppp/chap-secrets
```

In addition, the PPP daemon can use a large number of command-line options, and it is important to use the right ones. This section takes you through the standard PPP options and helps you choose the options that you should use.

For details on this, see Section 12.

6.8 If your PPP server uses PAP (Password Authentication Protocol)

Many ISPs and corporate PPP servers use PAP. If your server does not require you to use PAP (i.e., you can log in manually and receive the standard user name and password text prompts, it does not use PAP), you can safely ignore this section.

Instead of logging in to such a server using a user name and password when prompted to enter them by the server, a PPP server using PAP does not require a text based login.

The user authentication information instead is exchanged as part of the Link Control Protocol (LCP), which is the first part of establishing a PPP link.

Section 13 provides information on the files you need to set up to establish a PPP link using PAP.

6.9 Connecting to the PPP server by hand

Having set up the basic files, it is a good idea to test these by connecting (using `minicom` or `seyon`) and starting `pppd` on your Linux PC by hand.

See Section 14 for full details of setting this up.

6.10 Automating your PPP Connection

Once you are able to log in by hand, you can now move to setting up a set of scripts that will automate the establishment of the connection.

Section 15 covers setting up the necessary scripts, with considerable attention paid to `chat` and scripting the login process to the PPP server.

This section discusses scripts for user name and password authentication, as well as scripts for PAP and CHAP authenticating servers.

6.11 Shutting down the link

Once your link is up and working, you need to be able to deactivate the link.

This is covered in Section 17.

6.12 If you have problems

Many people have problems getting PPP to work straight away. The variation in PPP servers and how they require you to set up the connection is enormous. Similarly, there are many options to PPP—and some combinations of these just do not work together, ever.

In addition to the problems of logging in and starting the PPP service, there are problems with the modems and the actual telephone lines as well.

Section 18 provides some basic information about common errors, and how to isolate and fix them.

This is not intended to provide more than just the basics. Al Longyear maintains the PPP FAQ which contains much more information on this topic.

6.13 After the link comes up

Once a PPP link is operational (specifically, once the IP layer is operational), Linux PPP can automatically run (as the root user), a script to perform any function you can write a script to accomplish.

Section 23 provides information on the `/etc/ppp/ip-up` script, the parameters it receives from PPP, and how to use it to do things like acquire your e-mail from your ISP account, send any queued e-mail waiting transmission on your machine and such.

6.14 Problems with standard IP services on a Dynamic IP number PPP link

As noted in the introduction, dynamic IP numbers affect the ability of your Linux PC to act as a server on the Internet.

Section 21 provides information on the (main) services affected and what you can do (if anything) to overcome this.

7 Configuring your Linux Kernel

In order to use PPP, your Linux kernel must be compiled to include PPP support. Obtain the Linux source code for your kernel if you do not already have this—it belongs in `/usr/src/linux` on Linux's standard file system.

Check out this directory—many Linux distributions install the source tree (the files and subdirectories) as part of their installation process.

At boot up, your Linux kernel prints out a great deal of information. Amongst this is information about PPP support if the kernel includes this. To view this information, look at your syslog file or use `dmesg | less` to display the information to the screen. If your kernel includes PPP support, you will see lines like

```
PPP Dynamic channel allocation code copyright 1995 Caldera, Inc.
PPP line discipline registered.
```

(This is for the Linux 2.0.x kernel series.)

Linux kernel sources can be obtained by FTP from `sunsite.unc.edu` or its mirror sites.

7.1 Installing the Linux Kernel source

The following are brief instructions for obtaining and installing the Linux kernel sources. Full information can be obtained from The Linux Kernel HOWTO (page 1019).

In order to install and compile the Linux kernel, you need to be logged in as root.

1. Change directory to the `/usr/src` directory
   `cd /usr/src`
2. Check in `/usr/src/linux` to see if you already have the sources installed.
3. If you don't have the sources, get them from
   ftp://sunsite.unc.edu/pub/Linux/kernel/v2.0
   or your nearest mirror.

   If you are looking for earlier versions of the kernel (such as 1.2.x), these are kept in ftp://sunsite.unc.edu/pub/Linux/kernel/old/.
4. Choose the appropriate kernel—usually the most recent one available is what you are looking for. Retrieve this and put the source tar file in `/usr/src`.
   Note: a "tar" file is an archive—possibly compressed (as are the Linux kernel source tar files) containing many files in a number of directories. It is the Linux equivalent of a MSDOS multi-directory ZIP file.
5. If you already have the Linux sources installed but are upgrading to a new kernel, you must remove the old sources. Use the command:
   `rm -rf /usr/src/linux`
6. Now uncompress and extract the sources using the command:
   `tar xzf linux-2.0.XX.tar.gz`
7. Now, `cd /usr/src/linux` and read the `README` file. This contains an excellent explanation of how to go about configuring and compiling a new kernel. Read this file. (It's a good idea to print it out and have a copy handy whilst you are compiling, until you have done this enough times to know your way around.)

7.2 Knowing your hardware

You must know what cards and devices you have inside your PC if you are going to recompile your kernel. For some devices (such as sound cards) you will also need to know various settings (such as IRQ's, I/O addresses, and such).

7.3 Kernel compilation—the Linux 1.2.13 kernel

To start the configuration process, follow the instructions in the README file to properly install the sources. You start the kernel configuration process with

```
make config
```

In order to use PPP, you must configure the kernel to include PPP support (PPP requires BOTH pppd *and* kernel support for PPP).

```
PPP (point-to-point) support (CONFIG_PPP) [n] y
```

Answer the other questions of the make config process according to the hardware in your PC and the features of the Linux operating system you want. Then, continue to follow the README to compile and install your new kernel.

The 1.2.13 kernel creates only four PPP devices. For multi-port serial cards, you will need to edit the kernel PPP sources to obtain more ports. (See the README.linux file that comes as part of the PPP-2.1.2 distribution for full details of the simple edits you need to make).

Note: the 1.2.13 configuration dialogue does not allow you to go backwards—so if you make a mistake in answering one of the questions in the make config dialogue, exit by typing Ctrl-C and start again.

7.4 Kernel compilation—the Linux 1.3.x and 2.0.x kernels

For Linux 1.3.x and 2.0.x, you can use a similar process as for Linux 1.2.13. Again, follow the instructions in the README file to properly install the sources. You start the kernel configuration process with

```
make config
```

However, you also have the choice of

```
make menuconfig
```

This provides a menu based configuration system with online help that allows you to move backwards and forwards in the configuration process.

There is also a highly recommended X based configuration interface

```
make xconfig
```

You can compile PPP support directly into your kernel or as a loadable module.

If you only use PPP some of the time that your Linux machine is operating, then compiling PPP support as a loadable module is recommended. Using kerneld, your kernel will automatically load the module(s) required to provide PPP support when you start your PPP link process. This saves valuable memory space: no part of the kernel can be swapped out of memory, but loadable modules are automatically removed if they are not in use.

To do this, you need to enable loadable module support:

```
Enable loadable module support (CONFIG_MODULES) [Y/n/?] y
```

To add PPP kernel support, answer the following question:

```
PPP (point-to-point) support (CONFIG_PPP) [M/n/y/?]
```

For a PPP loadable module, answer M, otherwise for PPP compiled in as part of the kernel, answer Y.

Unlike kernel 1.2.13, kernel 2.0.x creates PPP devices on the fly as needed, and it is not necessary to hack the sources to increase available PPP device numbers at all.

7.5 Note on PPP-2.2 and /proc/net/dev

If you use PPP-2.2, you will find that a side effect of the "on the fly' creation of the PPP devices is that no devices show up if you look in the /proc/net file system until a device is created by starting up pppd:

```
[hartr@archenland hartr]$ cat /proc/net/dev
Inter-|   Receive                           |  Transmit
 face |packets errs drop fifo frame|packets errs drop fifo colls carrier
    lo:  92792    0    0    0    0    92792    0    0    0    0    0
  eth0: 621737   13   13    0   23   501621    0    0    0 1309    0
```

Once you have one (or more) PPP services started, you will see entries such as this (from a PPP server):

```
[root@kepler /root]# cat /proc/net/dev
Inter-|   Receive                           |  Transmit
 face |packets errs drop fifo frame|packets errs drop fifo colls carrier
    lo: 428021    0    0    0    0   428021    0    0    0     0    0
  eth0:4788257  648  648  319  650  1423836    0    0    0  4623    5
  ppp0:   2103    3    3    0    0     2017    0    0    0     0    0
  ppp1:  10008    0    0    0    0     8782    0    0    0     0    0
  ppp2:    305    0    0    0    0      297    0    0    0     0    0
  ppp3:   6720    7    7    0    0     7498    0    0    0     0    0
  ppp4: 118231  725  725    0    0   117791    0    0    0     0    0
  ppp5:  38915    5    5    0    0    28309    0    0    0     0    0
```

7.6 General kernel config considerations for PPP

If you set up your Linux PC as a PPP server, you must compile in IP forwarding support. This is also necessary if you want to use Linux to link to LANs together, or your LAN to the Internet.

If you are linking a LAN to the Internet (or linking together two LANs), you should be concerned about security. Adding support for IP fire walls to the kernel is probably a must.

You will also need this if you want to use IP masquerade to connect a LAN that uses any of the above mentioned "unconnected" IP network numbers.

To enable IP Masquerade and IP firewalling, you *must* answer "Y" to the first question in the `make config` process:

```
Prompt for development and/or incomplete code/drivers (CONFIG_EXPERIMENTAL)?
```

While this may sound a bit off-putting to new users, many users are actively using the IP Masquerade and IP firewalling features of the Linux 2.0.*xx* kernel with no problems.

Once you have installed and rebooted your new kernel, you can start configuring and testing your PPP link(s).

8 Getting the Information you need about the PPP server

Before you can establish a PPP connection with a server, you need to obtain the following information (from the system administrator or user support people of the PPP server):

- The telephone number(s) to dial for the service
  If you are behind a PABX, you also need the PABX number that gives you an outside dial tone—this is frequently digit zero (0) or nine (9).
- Does the server use dynamic or static IP numbers?
  If the server uses static IP numbers, then you may need to know what IP number to use for your end of the PPP connection. If your ISP is providing you with a subnet of valid IP numbers, you will need to know the IP numbers you can use and the network mask (netmask).

  Most Internet Service Providers use dynamic IP numbers. As mentioned above, this has some implications in terms of the services you can use.

  However, even if you are using static IP numbers, most PPP servers will never (for security reasons) allow the client to specify an IP number as this is a security risk. You still need to know this information.
- What are the IP numbers of the ISPs Domain Name Servers?
  There should be at least two, although only one is needed.

  There could be a problem here. The MS Windows 95 PPP setup allows the DNS address to be passed to the client as part of its connection process. So your ISP (or corporate help desk) may well tell you you don't need the IP address of the DNS server(s).

  For Linux, you need the address of at least one DNS. The Linux implementation of PPP does not allow the setting of the DNS IP number dynamically at connection time—and quite possibly will never do so.

  Note: while Linux (as a PPP client) cannot accept the DNS address from a server, it can, when acting as a server, pass this information to clients using the `dns-addr` pppd option.

- Does the server require the use of PAP or CHAP?
  If this is the case you need to know the "id" and "secret" you are to use in connecting. (These are probably your user name and password at your ISP).

- Does the server automatically start PPP or do you need to issue any commands to start PPP on the server once you are logged in?
  If you must issue a command to start PPP, what is it?

- Is the server a Microsoft Windows NT system and, if so, is it using the MS PAP or CHAP system?
  Many corporate LANs seem to use MS Windows NT this way for increased security.

Carefully note down this information—you are going to use it.

9 Configuring your modem and serial port

You should make sure that your modem is correctly set up and that you know which serial port it is connected to.
Remember:

- DOS COM1: = Linux `/dev/cua0` (and `/dev/ttyS0`);
- DOS COM2: = Linux `/dev/cua1` (and `/dev/ttyS1`);
  et cetera.

It is also worth remembering that if you have four serial ports, the standard PC setup is to have COM1 and COM3 share IRQ4 and COM2 and COM4 share IRQ3.

If you have devices on standard serial ports that share an IRQ with your modem, you are going to have problems. You need to make sure that your modem serial port is on its own, unique IRQ. Many modern serial cards (and better quality motherboard serial ports) allow you to move the IRQ of the serial ports around.

If you are running Linux kernel 2, you can check the in-use IRQs using `cat /proc/interrupts`, which will produce output like

```
 0:    6766283   timer
 1:      91545   keyboard
 2:          0   cascade
 4:     156944 + serial
 7:     101764   WD8013
10:     134365 + BusLogic BT-958
13:          1   math error
15:    3671702 + serial
```

This shows a serial port on IRQ4 (a mouse) and a serial port on IRQ15, the permanent, modem based PPP link to the Internet. (There is also a serial port on COM2, IRQ3 and COM4 is on IRQ14, but as they are not in use, they do not show up.)

Be warned—you need to know what you are doing if you are going to play with your IRQs. Not only do you have to open up you computer, pull out cards and play with jumpers, but you need to know what is on which IRQ. In my case, this is a totally SCSI based PC, and so I can disable the motherboard IDE interfaces that normally use IRQs 14 and 15.

You should also remember that if your PC boots other operating systems, moving IRQs around may well mean that OS cannot boot properly—or at all!

If you move your serial ports to non-standard IRQs, then you need to tell Linux which IRQ each port is using. This is done using `setserial` and is best done as part of the boot process in `rc.local` or `rc.serial` which is called from `rc.local` or as part of the SysV initialisation. For the machine illustrated above, the commands used are

```
/bin/setserial -b /dev/ttyS2 IRQ 11
/bin/setserial -b /dev/ttyS3 IRQ 15
```

However, if you use serial modules dynamically loaded when required by the `kerneld` process, you cannot set and forget the IRQ and port addresses once at boot time. This is because once the serial module is unloaded, Linux forgets the modified settings.

So if you are loading the serial module on demand, you will need to reconfigure the IRQ and port address each time the module is loaded.

9.1 A note about serial ports and speed capabilities

If you are using a high speed (external) modem (14,400 Baud or above), your serial port needs to be capable of handling the throughput that such a modem is capable of producing, particularly when the modems are compressing the data.

This requires your serial port to use a modern UART (Universal Asynchronous Receiver Transmitter) such as a 16550(A). If you are using an old machine (or old serial card), it is quite possible that your serial port has only an 8250 UART, which will cause you considerable problems when used with a high speed modem.

Use the command

```
setserial -a /dev/ttySx
```

to get Linux to report to you the type of UART you have. If you do not have a 16550A type UART, invest in a new serial card (available for under $50). When you purchase a new card, make sure you can move the IRQs around on it!

Note: the first versions of the 16550 UART chip had an error. This was rapidly discovered and a revision of the chip was released—the 16550A UART. A relatively small number of the faulty chips did however get into circulation. It is unlikely that you will encounter one of these but you should look for a response that says 16550A, particularly on serial cards of some vintage.

9.2 Serial Port Names

Historically, Linux used `cuax` devices for dial out and `ttySx` devices for dial in.

The kernel code that required this was changed in kernel version 2.0.x and you should now use `ttySx` for both dial in and dial out. I understand that the `cuax` device names may well disappear in future kernel versions.

9.3 Configuring your modem

You will need to configure your modem correctly for PPP—to do this

Read Your Modem Manual.

Most modems come with a factory default setting that selects the options required for PPP. The minimum configuration specifies:

- Hardware flow control (RTS/CTS) (`&`K3 on many Hayes modems).

Other settings (in standard Hayes commands) you should investigate are:

- `E1`: Command/usr/src/linux-2.0.27/include/linux/serial.h Echo ON (required for chat to operate).
- `Q0`: Report result codes (required for chat to operate).
- `S0=0`: Auto Answer OFF (unless you want your modem to answer the phone).
- `&C1`: Carrier Detect ON only after connect.
- `&S0`: Data Set Ready (DSR) always ON.
- (depends) Data Terminal Ready.

There is a site offering modem setups for a growing variety of modem makes and models at http://www.in.net/info/modems/index.html which may assist you.

It is also worth while investigating how the modem's serial interface between your computer and modem operates. Most modern modems allow you to run the serial interface at a fixed speed whilst allowing the telephone line interface to change its speed to the highest speed it and the remote modem can both handle.

This is known as split-speed operation. If your modem supports this, lock the modem's serial interface to its highest available speed (usually 115,200 baud, but maybe 38,400 baud for 14,400 baud modems).

Use your communications software (e.g., `minicom` or `seyon`) to find out about your modem configuration and set it to what is required for PPP. Many modems report their current settings in response to AT`&V`, but you should consult your modem manual.

If you completely mess up the settings, you can return to sanity (usually) by issuing an AT`&F`—return to factory settings. (For most modem modems I have encountered, the factory settings include all that you need for PPP—but you should check).

Once you have worked out the modem setup string required, write it down. You now have a decision: you can store these settings in your modem non-volatile memory so they can be recalled by issuing the appropriate AT command. Alternatively, you can pass the correct settings to your modem as part of the PPP dialing process.

If you only use your modem from Linux to call into your ISP or corporate server, the simplest setup will have you save your modem configuration in non-volatile RAM.

If on the other hand, your modem is used by other applications and operating systems, it is safest to pass this information to the modem as each call is made so that the modem is guaranteed to be in the correct state for the call. (This has the added advantage also of recording the modem setup string in case the modem looses the contents of its NV-RAM, which can indeed happen.)

9.4 Note on Serial Flow Control

When data is traveling on serial communication lines, it can happen that data arrives faster than a computer can handle it (the computer may be busy doing something else. Linux is a multi-user, multi- tasking operating system). In order to ensure that data is not lost (data does not overrun in the input buffer and hence get lost), some method of controlling the flow of data is necessary.

There are two ways of doing this on serial lines:

- Using hardware signals (Clear To Send/Request to Send—CTS/RTS);
- Using software signals (control S and control Q, also known as XON/XOFF).

While the latter may be fine for a terminal (text) link, data on a PPP link uses all 8 bits—and it is quite probable that somewhere in the data there will be data bytes that translate as Control-S and Control-Q. So, if a modem is set up to use software flow control, things can rapidly go berserk!

For high speed links using PPP (which uses 8 bits of data) hardware flow control is vital and it is for this reason that you must use hardware flow control.

9.5 Testing your modem for dial out

Now that you have sorted out the serial port and modem settings, it is a good idea to make sure that these setting do indeed work by dialing you ISP and seeing if you can connect.

Using you terminal communications package (like `minicom`), set up the modem initialisation required for PPP and dial into the PPP server you want to connect to with a PPP session.

(**Note:** At this stage we are not trying to make a PPP connection—just establishing that we have the correct phone number and also to find out *exactly* what the server sends to us in order to get logged in and start PPP).

During this process, either capture (log to a file) the entire login process or carefully (very carefully) write down exactly what prompts the server gives to let you know it is time to enter your user name and password (and any other commands needed to establish the PPP connection).

If your server uses PAP, you should not see a login prompt, but should instead see the (text representation) of the link control protocol (which looks like garbage) starting on your screen.

A few words of warning:

- some servers are quite intelligent. You can log in using a text based user name and passwords, or using PAP. So if your ISP or corporate site uses PAP, but you do not see the garbage start up immediately, this may not mean you have done anything wrong:
- some servers require that you enter some text initially and then start a standard PAP sequence;
- Some PPP servers are passive. That is, they simply sit there sending nothing until the client that is dialing in sends them a valid LCP packet. If the PPP server that you are connecting to operates in passive mode, you will never see the garbage;
- Some servers do not start PPP until you press ENTER, so it is worth trying this if you correctly log in and do not see the garbage.

It is worth dialing in at least twice—some servers change their prompts (for example, with the time) every time you log in. The two critical prompts your Linux box needs to be able to identify every time you dial in are:

- the prompt that requests you to enter your user name;
- the prompt that requests you to enter your password.

If you have to issue a command to start PPP on the server, you also need to find out the prompt the server gives you once you are logged in to tell you that you can now enter the command to start ppp.

If your server automatically starts PPP once you have logged in, you will start to see garbage on your screen—this is the PPP server sending your machine information to start up and configure the PPP connection.

This should look something like this :

```
~y}#.!}!}!} }8}!}$}%U}"}&} } } }%}& ...}'}"}(}"} .~~y}
```

(And it just keeps on coming!)

On some systems PPP must be explicitly started on the server. This is usually because the server has been set up to allow PPP logins and shell logins using the same user name and password pair. If this is the case, issue this command once you have logged in. Again, you will see the garbage as the server end of the PPP connection starts up.

If you do not see this immediately after connecting (and logging in and starting the PPP server if required), press Enter to see if this starts the PPP server.

At this point, you can hang up your modem (usually, type +++ quickly and then issue the ATH0 command once your modem responds with OK).

If you can't get your modem to work, read your modem manual, the manual pages for your communications software and the Serial HOWTO (page 1374). Once you have this sorted out, carry on as above.

10 Setting up Name to Address Resolution (DNS)

Whilst we humans like to give names to things, computers really like numbers. On a TCP/IP network (which is what the Internet is), we call machines by a particular name—and every machine lives in a particular `domain`. For example, my Linux workstation is called `archenland` and it resides in the `interweft.com.au` domain. Its human readable address is thus archenland.interweft.com.au (which is known as the **FQDN**—fully qualified domain name).

However, for this machine to be found by other computers on the Internet, it is actually known by its IP number when computers are communicating across the Internet.

Translating (resolving) machine (and domain) names into the numbers actually used on the Internet is the business of machines that offer the Domain Name Service.

What happens is this:

- your machine needs to know the IP address of a particular computer. The application requiring this information asks the **resolver** on your Linux PC to provide this information;
- the resolver queries the local host file (`/etc/hosts` and/or the domain name servers it knows about (the exact behaviour of the resolver is determined by `/etc/host.conf`);
- if the answer is found in the host file, this answer is returned;
- if a domain name server is specified, your PC queries this machine;
- if the DNS machine already knows the IP number for the required name, it returns it. If it does not, it queries other name servers across the Internet to find the information. The name server than passes this information back to the requesting resolver—which gives the information to the requesting application.

When you make a PPP connection, you need to tell your Linux machine where it can get host name to IP number (address resolution) information so that **you** can use the machine names but your **computer** can translate these to the IP numbers it needs to do its work.

One way is to enter every host that you want to talk to into the `/etc/hosts` file (which is in reality totally impossible if you are connecting to the Internet); another is to use the machine IP numbers as opposed to the names (an impossible memory task for all but the smallest LANs).

The best way is to set up Linux so that it knows where to go to get this name to number information—automatically. This service is provided by the Domain Name Server (DNS) system. All that is necessary is to enter the IP number(s) for the domain name servers into your `/etc/resolv.conf` file.

10.1 The `/etc/resolv.conf` file

Your PPP server sysadmin/user support people should provide you with two DNS IP numbers (only one is necessary—but two gives some redundancy in the event of failure).

As previously mentioned, Linux cannot set its name server IP number in the way that MS Windows 95 does. So you must **insist** (politely) that your ISP provide you with this information!

Your `/etc/resolv.conf` should look something like :

```
domain your.isp.domain.name
nameserver 10.25.0.1
nameserver 10.25.1.2
```

Edit this file (creating it if necessary) to represent the information that your ISP has provided. It should have ownership and permissions as follows :

```
-rw-r--r--   1 root     root             73 Feb 19 01:46 /etc/resolv.conf
```

If you have already set up a `/etc/resolv.conf` because you are on a LAN, simply add the IP numbers of the PPP DNS servers to your existing file.

10.2 The /etc/host.conf file

You should also check that your /etc/host.conf file is correctly set up. This should look like

```
order hosts,bind
multi on
```

This tells the resolver to use information in the host file before it sends queries to the DNS for resolution.

11 Using PPP and root privileges

Because PPP needs to set up networking devices, change the kernel routing table and so forth, it requires root privileges to do this.

If users other than root are to set up PPP connections, the pppd program should be setuid root :

```
-rwsr-xr-x   1 root     root          95225 Jul 11 00:27 /usr/sbin/pppd
```

If /usr/sbin/pppd is not set up this way, then as root issue the command:

```
chmod u+s /usr/sbin/pppd
```

root privileges even if the binary is run by an ordinary user. This allows a normal user to run pppd with the necessary privileges to set up the network interfaces and the kernel routing table.

Programs that run set UID root are potential security holes and you should be extremely cautious about making programs suid root. A number of programs (including pppd) have been carefully written to minimise the danger of running suid root, so you should be safe with this one (but no guarantees).

Depending on how you want your system to operate—specifically if you want ANY user on your system to be able to initiate a PPP link, you should make your ppp-on and ppp-off scripts world read and world execute. (This is probably fine if your PC is used only by you).

However, if you do not want just anyone to be able to start up a PPP connection (for example, your children have accounts on your Linux PC and you do not want them hooking into the Internet without your supervision), you will need to establish a PPP group (as root, edit /etc/group) and :

- Make pppd suid root, owned by user root and group PPP, with the "other" permissions on this file empty. It should then look like

  ```
  -rwsr-x---   1 root     PPP           95225 Jul 11 00:27 /usr/sbin/pppd
  ```

- Make the ppp-on/off scripts owned by user root and group PPP
- Make the ppp-on/off scripts read/executable by group PPP

  ```
  -rwxr-x---   1 root     PPP             587 Mar 14  1995 /usr/sbin/ppp-on
  -rwxr-x---   1 root     PPP             631 Mar 14  1995 /usr/sbin/ppp-off
  ```

- Make the other access rights for ppp-on/off nil.
- add the users who will be firing up PPP to the PPP group in /etc/group.

Even if you do this, ordinary users will still not be able to shut down the link under software control. Running the ppp-off script requires root privileges. However, any user can just turn off the modem (or disconnect the telephone line from an internal modem).

An alternative (and better method) to this set up is to use the sudo program. This offers superior security and will allow you to set things up so that any (authorised) user can activate/deactivate the link using the scripts. Using sudo will allow an authorised user to activate/deactivate the PPP link cleanly and securely.

12 Setting up the PPP connection files

You now need to be logged in as root to create the directories and edit the files needed to set up PPP, even if you want PPP to be accessible to all users.

PPP uses a number of files to connect and set up a PPP connection. These differ in name and location between PPP 2.1.2 and 2.2.

For PPP 2.1.2 the files are:

```
/usr/sbin/pppd          # the PPP binary
/usr/sbin/ppp-on        # the dialer/connection script
/usr/sbin/ppp-off       # the disconnection script
/etc/ppp/options        # the options pppd uses for all connections
/etc/ppp/options.ttyXX  # the options specific to a connection on this port
```

For PPP 2.2 the files are:

```
/usr/sbin/pppd                  # the PPP binary
/etc/ppp/scripts/ppp-on         # the dialer/connection script
/etc/ppp/scripts/ppp-on-dialer  # part 1 of the dialer script
/etc/ppp/scripts/ppp-off        # the actual chat script itself
/etc/ppp/options                # the options pppd uses for all connections
/etc/ppp/options.ttyXX          # the options specific to a connection on this port
```

Red Hat Linux users should note that the standard Red Hat 4.*x* installation places these scripts in `/usr/doc/ppp-2.2.0f-2/scripts`.

In your `/etc` directory there should be a ppp directory:

```
drwxrwxr-x   2 root     root         1024 Oct  9 11:01 ppp
```

If it does not exist—create it with these ownerships and permissions.

If the directory already existed, it should contain a template options file called `options.tpl`. This file is included below in case it does not.

Print it out as it contains an explanation of nearly all the PPP options (these are useful to read in conjunction with the `pppd` manual pages). Whilst you can use this file as the basis of your `/etc/ppp/options` file, it is probably better to create your own options file that does not include all the comments in the template—it will be much shorter and easier to read and maintain.

If you have multiple serial lines or modems (typically the case for PPP servers), create a general `/etc/ppp/options` file containing the options that are common for all the serial ports on which you are supporting dial in and out and set up individual option files for each serial line on which you will be establishing a PPP connection with the individual settings required for each port.

These port specific option files are named `options.tty`*x*`1`, `options.tty`*x*`2` and so forth (where *x* is the appropriate letter for your serial ports).

However, for a single PPP connection, you can happily use the `/etc/ppp/options` file. Alternatively, you can put all the options as arguments in the `pppd` command itself.

It is easier to maintain a setup that uses `/etc/ppp/options.ttyS`*x* files. If you use PPP to connect to a number of different sites, you can create option files for each site in `/etc/ppp/options.site` and then specify the option file as a parameter to the PPP command as you connect (using the `file option-file` pppd option to pppd on the command line).

12.1 The supplied `options.tpl` file

Some distributions of PPP seem to have lost the options.tpl file, so here is the complete file. I suggest that you do not edit this file to create your `/etc/ppp/options` file(s). Rather, copy this to a new file and then edit that. If you mess up your edits, you can then go back to the original and start again.

```
# /etc/ppp/options -*- sh -*- general options for pppd
# created 13-Jul-1995 jmk
# autodate: 01-Aug-1995
# autotime: 19:45

# Use the executable or shell command specified to set up the serial
# line.  This script would typically use the "chat" program to dial the
# modem and start the remote ppp session.
#connect "echo You need to install a connect command."

# Run the executable or shell command specified after pppd has
# terminated the link.  This script could, for example, issue commands
# to the modem to cause it to hang up if hardware modem control signals
# were not available.
#disconnect "chat -- \d+++\d\c OK ath0 OK"
```

```
# async character map -- 32-bit hex; each bit is a character
# that needs to be escaped for pppd to receive it.  0x00000001
# represents '\x01', and 0x80000000 represents '\x1f'.
#asyncmap 0

# Require the peer to authenticate itself before allowing network
# packets to be sent or received.
#auth

# Use hardware flow control (i.e. RTS/CTS) to control the flow of data
# on the serial port.
#crtscts

# Use software flow control (i.e. XON/XOFF) to control the flow of data
# on the serial port.
#xonxoff

# Add a default route to the system routing tables, using the peer as
# the gateway, when IPCP negotiation is successfully completed.  This
# entry is removed when the PPP connection is broken.
#defaultroute

# Specifies that certain characters should be escaped on transmission
# (regardless of whether the peer requests them to be escaped with its
# async control character map).  The characters to be escaped are
# specified as a list of hex numbers separated by commas.  Note that
# almost any character can be specified for the escape option, unlike
# the asyncmap option which only allows control characters to be
# specified.  The characters which may not be escaped are those with hex
# values 0x20---0x3f or 0x5e.
#escape 11,13,ff

# Don't use the modem control lines.
#local

# Specifies that pppd should use a UUCP-style lock on the serial device
# to ensure exclusive access to the device.
#lock

# Use the modem control lines.  On Ultrix, this option implies hardware
# flow control, as for the crtscts option.  (This option is not fully
# implemented.)
#modem

# Set the MRU [Maximum Receive Unit] value to <n> for negotiation.  pppd
# will ask the peer to send packets of no more than <n> bytes. The
# minimum MRU value is 128.  The default MRU value is 1500.  A value of
# 296 is recommended for slow links (40 bytes for TCP/IP header + 256
# bytes of data).
#mru 542

# Set the interface netmask to <n>, a 32 bit netmask in "decimal dot"
# notation (e.g. 255.255.255.0).
#netmask 255.255.255.0

# Disables the default behaviour when no local IP address is specified,
# which is to determine (if possible) the local IP address from the
```

```
# hostname. With this option, the peer will have to supply the local IP
# address during IPCP negotiation (unless it specified explicitly on the
# command line or in an options file).
#noipdefault

# Enables the "passive" option in the LCP.  With this option, pppd will
# attempt to initiate a connection; if no reply is received from the
# peer, pppd will then just wait passively for a valid LCP packet from
# the peer (instead of exiting, as it does without this option).
#passive

# With this option, pppd will not transmit LCP packets to initiate a
# connection until a valid LCP packet is received from the peer (as for
# the "passive" option with old versions of pppd).
#silent

# Don't request or allow negotiation of any options for LCP and IPCP
# (use default values).
#-all

# Disable Address/Control compression negotiation (use default, i.e.
# address/control field disabled).
#-ac

# Disable asyncmap negotiation (use the default asyncmap, i.e. escape
# all control characters).
#-am

# Don't fork to become a background process (otherwise pppd will do so
# if a serial device is specified).
#-detach

# Disable IP address negotiation (with this option, the remote IP
# address must be specified with an option on the command line or in an
# options file).
#-ip

# Disable magic number negotiation.  With this option, pppd cannot
# detect a looped-back line.
#-mn

# Disable MRU [Maximum Receive Unit] negotiation (use default, i.e.
# 1500).
#-mru

# Disable protocol field compression negotiation (use default, i.e.
# protocol field compression disabled).
#-pc

# Require the peer to authenticate itself using PAP.
# This requires TWO WAY authentication---do NOT use this for a standard
# PAP authenticated link to an ISP as this will require the ISP machine
# to authenticate itself to your machine (and it will not be able to).
#+pap

# Don't agree to authenticate using PAP.
#-pap
```

```
# Require the peer to authenticate itself using CHAP [Cryptographic
# Handshake Authentication Protocol] authentication.
# This requires TWO WAY authentication---do NOT use this for a standard
# CHAP authenticated link to an ISP as this will require the ISP machine
# to authenticate itself to your machine (and it will not be able to).
#+chap

# Don't agree to authenticate using CHAP.
#-chap

# Disable negotiation of Van Jacobson style IP header compression (use
# default, i.e. no compression).
#-vj

# Increase debugging level (same as -d).  If this option is given, pppd
# will log the contents of all control packets sent or received in a
# readable form.  The packets are logged through syslog with facility
# daemon and level debug. This information can be directed to a file by
# setting up /etc/syslog.conf appropriately (see syslog.conf(5)).  (If
# pppd is compiled with extra debugging enabled, it will log messages
# using facility local2 instead of daemon).
#debug

# Append the domain name <d> to the local host name for authentication
# purposes.  For example, if gethostname() returns the name porsche,
# but the fully qualified domain name is porsche.Quotron.COM, you would
# use the domain option to set the domain name to Quotron.COM.
#domain <d>

# Enable debugging code in the kernel-level PPP driver.  The argument n
# is a number which is the sum of the following values: 1 to enable
# general debug messages, 2 to request that the contents of received
# packets be printed, and 4 to request that the contents of transmitted
# packets be printed.
#kdebug n

# Set the MTU [Maximum Transmit Unit] value to <n>. Unless the peer
# requests a smaller value via MRU negotiation, pppd will request that
# the kernel networking code send data packets of no more than n bytes
# through the PPP network interface.
#mtu <n>

# Set the name of the local system for authentication purposes to <n>.
# This will probably have to be set to your ISP user name if you are
# using PAP/CHAP.
#name <n>

# Set the user name to use for authenticating this machine with the peer
# using PAP to <u>.
# Do NOT use this if you are using 'name' above!
#user <u>

# Enforce the use of the host name as the name of the local system for
# authentication purposes (overrides the name option).
#usehostname

# Set the assumed name of the remote system for authentication purposes
# to <n>.
```

```
#remotename <n>

# Add an entry to this system's ARP [Address Resolution Protocol]
# table with the IP address of the peer and the Ethernet address of this
# system.
#proxyarp

# Use the system password database for authenticating the peer using
# PAP.
#login

# If this option is given, pppd will send an LCP echo-request frame to
# the peer every n seconds. Under Linux, the echo-request is sent when
# no packets have been received from the peer for n seconds. Normally
# the peer should respond to the echo-request by sending an echo-reply.
# This option can be used with the lcp-echo-failure option to detect
# that the peer is no longer connected.
#lcp-echo-interval <n>

# If this option is given, pppd will presume the peer to be dead if n
# LCP echo-requests are sent without receiving a valid LCP echo-reply.
# If this happens, pppd will terminate the connection.  Use of this
# option requires a non-zero value for the lcp-echo-interval parameter.
# This option can be used to enable pppd to terminate after the physical
# connection has been broken (e.g., the modem has hung up) in
# situations where no hardware modem control lines are available.
#lcp-echo-failure <n>

# Set the LCP restart interval (retransmission timeout) to <n> seconds
# (default 3).
#lcp-restart <n>

# Set the maximum number of LCP terminate-request transmissions to <n>
# (default 3).
#lcp-max-terminate <n>

# Set the maximum number of LCP configure-request transmissions to <n>
# (default 10).
# Some PPP servers are slow to start up. You may need to increase this
# if you keep getting 'serial line looped back' errors and your are SURE
# that you have logged in correctly and PPP should be starting on the server.
#lcp-max-configure <n>

# Set the maximum number of LCP configure-NAKs returned before starting
# to send configure-Rejects instead to <n> (default 10).
#lcp-max-failure <n>

# Set the IPCP restart interval (retransmission timeout) to <n>
# seconds (default 3).
#ipcp-restart <n>

# Set the maximum number of IPCP terminate-request transmissions to <n>
# (default 3).
#ipcp-max-terminate <n>

# Set the maximum number of IPCP configure-request transmissions to <n>
# (default 10).
#ipcp-max-configure <n>
```

```
# Set the maximum number of IPCP configure-NAKs returned before starting
# to send configure-Rejects instead to <n> (default 10).
#ipcp-max-failure <n>

# Set the PAP restart interval (retransmission timeout) to <n> seconds
# (default 3).
#pap-restart <n>

# Set the maximum number of PAP authenticate-request transmissions to
# <n> (default 10).
#pap-max-authreq <n>

# Set the CHAP restart interval (retransmission timeout for
# challenges) to <n> seconds (default 3).
#chap-restart <n>

# Set the maximum number of CHAP challenge transmissions to <n>
# (default 10).
#chap-max-challenge

# If this option is given, pppd will re-challenge the peer every <n>
# seconds.
#chap-interval <n>

# With this option, pppd will accept the peer's idea of our local IP
# address, even if the local IP address was specified in an option.
#ipcp-accept-local

# With this option, pppd will accept the peer's idea of its (remote) IP
# address, even if the remote IP address was specified in an option.
#ipcp-accept-remote
```

12.2 What options should I use? (No PAP/CHAP)

Well, as in all things that depends (sigh). The options specified here should work with most servers.

However, if it does not work, read the template file (`/etc/ppp/options.tpl`) **and** the pppd manual pages and speak to the system administration or user support people who run the server to which you are connecting.

You should also note that the connect scripts presented here also use some command line options to pppd to make things a bit easier to change.

```
# /etc/ppp/options (NO PAP/CHAP)
#
# Prevent pppd from forking into the background
-detach
#
# use the modem control lines
modem
# use uucp style locks to ensure exclusive access to the serial device
lock
# use hardware flow control
crtscts
# create a default route for this connection in the routing table
defaultroute
# do NOT set up any "escaped" control sequences
asyncmap 0
# use a maximum transmission packet size of 552 bytes
mtu 552
# use a maximum receive packet size of 552 bytes
```

```
mru 552
#
#-------END OF SAMPLE /etc/ppp/options (no PAP/CHAP)
```

13 If your PPP server uses PAP (Password Authentication Protocol)

If the server to which you are connecting requires PAP or CHAP authentication, you have a little bit more work.

To the above options file, add the following lines:

```
#
# force pppd to use your ISP user name as your 'host name' during the
# authentication process
name <your ISP user name>       # you need to edit this line
#
# If you are running a PPP *server* and need to force PAP or CHAP
# uncomment the appropriate one of the following lines. Do NOT use
# these is you are a client connecting to a PPP server (even if it uses PAP
# or CHAP) as this tells the SERVER to authenticate itself to your
# machine (which almost certainly can't do---and the link will fail).
#+chap
#+pap
#
# If you are using ENCRYPTED secrets in the /etc/ppp/pap-secrets
# file, then uncomment the following line.
# Note: this is NOT the same as using MS encrypted passwords as can be
# set up in MS RAS on Windows NT.
#+papcrypt
```

13.1 Using MSCHAP

Microsoft Windows NT RAS can be set up to use a variation on CHAP (Challenge/Handshake Authentication Protocol). In your PPP sources tarball, you will find a file called `README.MSCHAP80` that discusses this.

You can determine if the server is requesting authentication using this protocol by enabling debugging for `pppd`. If the server is requesting MS CHAP authentication, you will see lines like

```
rcvd [LCP ConfReq id=0x2 <asyncmap 0x0> <auth chap 80> <magic 0x46a3>]
```

The critical information here is "`auth chap 80`."

In order to use MS CHAP, you will need to recompile pppd to support this. Please see the instructions in the `README.MSCHAP80` file in the PPP source file for instructions on how to compile and use this variation.

You should note that at present this code supports only Linux PPP clients connecting to an MS Windows NT server. It does not support setting up a Linux PPP server to use MSCHAP80 authentication from clients.

13.2 The PAP/CHAP secrets file

If you are using PAP or CHAP authentication, then you also need to create the secrets file. These are:

```
/etc/ppp/pap-secrets
/etc/ppp/chap-secrets
```

They must be owned by user root, group root and have file permissions 740 for security.

The first point to note about PAP and CHAP is that they are designed to authenticate computer systems, not users.

"Huh? What's the difference?" I hear you ask.

Well now, once your computer has made its PPP connection to the server, any user on your system can use that connection—not just you. This is why you can set up a WAN (wide area network) link that joins two LANs (local area networks) using PPP.

PAP can (and for CHAP, DOES) require bidirectional authentication—that is a valid name and secret is required on each computer for the other computer involved. However, this is not the way most PPP servers offering dial up PPP PAP-authenticated connections operate.

That being said, your ISP will probably have given you a user name and password to allow you to connect to their system and thence the Internet. Your ISP is not interested in your computer's name at all, so you will probably need to use the user name at your ISP as the name for your computer.

This is done using the `name user name` option to `pppd`. So, if you are to use the user name given you by your ISP, add the line

```
name your_user name_at_your_ISP
```

to your `/etc/ppp/options` file.

Technically, you should really use `user our_user name_at_your_ISP` for PAP, but `pppd` is sufficiently intelligent to interpret `name` as `user` if it is required to use PAP. The advantage of using the `name` option is that this is also valid for CHAP.

As PAP is for authenticating computers, technically you need also to specify a remote computer name. However, as most people only have one ISP, you can use a wild card (*) for the remote host name in the secrets file.

It is also worth noting that many ISPs operate multiple modem banks connected to different terminal servers—each with a different name, but accessed from a single (rotary) dial in number. It can therefore be quite difficult in some circumstances to know ahead of time what the name of the remote computer is, as this depends on which terminal server you connect to.

13.3 The PAP secrets file

The `/etc/ppp/pap-secrets` file looks like

```
# Secrets for authentication using PAP
# client        server       secret     acceptable_local_IP_addresses
```

The four fields are white-space delimited and the last one can be blank (which is what you want for a dynamic and probably static IP allocation from your ISP).

Suppose your ISP gave you a user name of `fred` and a password of `flintstone`, you would set the `name fred` option in `/etc/ppp/options[.ttySx]` and set up your `/etc/ppp/pap-secrets` file as follows

```
# Secrets for authentication using PAP
# client        server  secret          acceptable local IP addresses
fred            *       flintstone
```

This says for the local machine name `fred` (which we have told pppd to use even though it is not our local machine name) and for any server, use the password (secret) of `flintstone`.

Note that we do not need to specify a local IP address, unless we are required to force a particular local, static IP address. Even if you try this, it is unlikely to work as most PPP servers (for security reasons) do not allow the remote system to set the IP number they are to be given.

13.4 The CHAP secrets file

This requires that you have mutual authentication methods—that is you must allow for both your machine to authenticate the remote server and the remote server to authenticate your machine.

So, if your machine is `fred` and the remote is `barney`, your machine would set `name fred remotename barney` and the remote machine would set `name barney remotename fred` in their respective `/etc/ppp/options.ttySx` files.

The `/etc/chap-secrets` file for `fred` would look like

```
# Secrets for authentication using CHAP
# client        server  secret            acceptable local IP addresses
fred            barney  flintstone
barney          fred    wilma
```

and for `barney`

```
# Secrets for authentication using CHAP
# client        server  secret            acceptable local IP addresses
barney          fred    flintstone
fred            barney  wilma
```

Note in particular that both machines must have entries for bidirectional authentication. This allows the local machine to authenticate itself to the remote and the remote machine to authenticate itself to the local machine.

13.5 Handling multiple PAP-authenticated connections

Some users have more than one server to which they connect that use PAP. Provided that your user name is different on each machine to which you want to connect, this is not a problem.

However, many users have the same user name on two (or more—even all) systems to which they connect. This then presents a problem in correctly selecting the appropriate line from /etc/ppp/pap-secrets.

As you might expect, PPP provides a mechanism for overcoming this. PPP allows you to set an 'assumed name' for the remote (server) end of the connection using the **remotename** option to pppd.

Let us suppose that you connect to two PPP servers using the user name fred. You set up your /etc/ppp/pap-secrets something like

```
fred    pppserver1      barney
fred    pppserver2      wilma
```

Now, to set connect to pppserver1, you would use name fred remotename pppserver1 in your ppp-options and for pppserver2 name fred remotename pppserver2.

As you can select the ppp options file to use with pppd using the file filename option, you can set up a script to connect to each of your PPP servers, correctly picking the options file to use and hence selecting the right remotename option.

14 Setting up the PPP connection manually

Now that you have created your /etc/ppp/options and /etc/resolv.conf files (and, if necessary, the /etc/ppp/pap|chap-secrets file), you can test the settings by manually establishing a PPP connection. (Once we have the manual connection working, we will automate the process.)

To do this, your communications software must be capable of quitting WITHOUT resetting the modem. minicom can do this—Alt-Q (or in older versions of minicom CTRL A Q)

Make sure you are logged in as root.

Fire up you communications software (such as minicom), dial into the PPP server and log in as normal. If you need to issue a command to start up PPP on the server, do so. You will now see the garbage you saw before.

If you are using PAP or CHAP, then merely connecting to the remote system should start ppp on the remote and you will see the garbage without logging in (although this may not happen for some servers—try pressing Enter and see if the garbage starts up).

Now quit the communications software without resetting the modem (Alt-Q or Ctrl-A Q in minicom) and at the Linux prompt (as root) type

```
pppd -d -detach /dev/ttySx 38400 &
```

The -d option turns on debugging—the PPP connection start-up conversation will be logged to your system log—which is useful if you are having trouble.

Your modem lights should now flash as the PPP connection is established. It will take a short while for the PPP connection to be made.

At this point you can look at the PPP interface by issuing the command

```
ifconfig
```

In addition to any Ethernet and loopback devices you have, you should see something like :

```
ppp0      Link encap:Point-Point Protocol
          inet addr:10.144.153.104  P-t-P:10.144.153.51 Mask:255.255.255.0
          UP POINTOPOINT RUNNING  MTU:552  Metric:1
          RX packets:0 errors:0 dropped:0 overruns:0
          TX packets:0 errors:0 dropped:0 overruns:0
```

Where

- inet addr:10.144.153.10 is the IP number of your end of the link.
- P-t-P:10.144.153.5 is the SERVER's IP number.

(Naturally, ifconfig will not report these IP numbers, but the ones used by your PPP server.)

Note: ifconfig also tells you that the link is UP and RUNNING!

If you get no ppp device listed or something like

```
ppp0      Link encap:Point-Point Protocol
          inet addr:0.0.0.0  P-t-P:0.0.0.0  Mask:0.0.0.0
          POINTOPOINT  MTU:1500  Metric:1
          RX packets:0 errors:0 dropped:0 overruns:0
          TX packets:0 errors:0 dropped:0 overruns:0
```

Your PPP connection has not been made. See the later section on debugging.

You should also be able to see a route to the the remote host (and beyond). To do this, issue the command

```
route -n
```

You should se something like:

```
Kernel routing table
Destination     Gateway         Genmask         Flags MSS    Window Use Iface
10.144.153.3    *               255.255.255.255 UH    1500   0        1 ppp0
127.0.0.0       *               255.0.0.0       U     3584   0       11 lo
10.0.0.0        *               255.0.0.0       U     1500   0       35 eth0
default         10.144.153.3    *               UG    1500   0        5 ppp0
```

Of particular importance here, notice we have two entries pointing to our PPP interface.

The first is a host route (indicated by the H flag) and that allows us to see the host to which we are connected to—but no further.

The second is the default route (established by giving `pppd` the option `defaultroute`. This is the route that tells our Linux PC to send any packets not destined for the local Ethernet(s)—to which we have specific network routes—to the PPP server itself. The PPP server then is responsible for routing our packets out onto the Internet and routing the return packets back to us.

◇ If you do not see a routing table with two entries, something is wrong. In particular if your syslog shows a message telling you pppd is not replacing an existing default route, then you have a default route pointing at your Ethernet interface—which must be replaced by a specific network route: you can only have one default route.

You will need to explore your system initialisation files to find out where this default route is being set up (it will use a `route add default...` command). Change this command to something like `route add net....`

Now test the link by pinging the server at its IP number as reported by the ifconfig output, i.e.

```
ping 10.144.153.51
```

You should receive output like

```
PING 10.144.153.51 (10.144.153.51): 56 data bytes
64 bytes from 10.144.153.51: icmp_seq=0 ttl=255 time=328.3 ms
64 bytes from 10.144.153.51: icmp_seq=1 ttl=255 time=190.5 ms
64 bytes from 10.144.153.51: icmp_seq=2 ttl=255 time=187.5 ms
64 bytes from 10.144.153.51: icmp_seq=3 ttl=255 time=170.7 ms
```

This listing will go on forever—to stop it press Ctrl-C, at which point you will receive some more information:

```
--- 10.144.153.51 ping statistics ---
4 packets transmitted, 4 packets received, 0% packet loss
round-trip min/avg/max = 170.7/219.2/328.3 ms
```

So far so good.

Now try pinging a host by name (not the name of the PPP server itself) but a host at another site that you know is probably going to be up and running. For example:

```
ping sunsite.unc.edu
```

This time there will be a bit of a pause as Linux obtains the IP number for the fully qualified host name you have pinged from the DNS you specified in `/etc/resolv.conf`—so don't worry (but you will see your modem lights flash). Shortly you will receive output like

```
 PING sunsite.unc.edu (152.2.254.81): 56 data bytes
64 bytes from 152.2.254.81: icmp_seq=0 ttl=254 time=190.1 ms
64 bytes from 152.2.254.81: icmp_seq=1 ttl=254 time=180.6 ms
64 bytes from 152.2.254.81: icmp_seq=2 ttl=254 time=169.8 ms
64 bytes from 152.2.254.81: icmp_seq=3 ttl=254 time=170.6 ms
64 bytes from 152.2.254.81: icmp_seq=4 ttl=254 time=170.6 ms
```

Again, stop the output by pressing Ctrl-C and get the statistics.

```
--- sunsite.unc.edu ping statistics ---
5 packets transmitted, 5 packets received, 0% packet loss
round-trip min/avg/max = 169.8/176.3/190.1 ms
```

If you don't get any response, try pinging the IP address of the DNS server at your ISP's site. If you get a result from this, then it looks like you have a problem with `/etc/resolv.conf`.

If this doesn't work, you have a routing problem, or your ISP has a problem routing packets back to you. Check your routing table as shown above and if that is okay, contact your ISP. A good test of the ISP is to use another operating system to connect. If you can get beyond your ISP with that, then the problem is at your end.

If everything works, shut down the connection by typing

```
ppp-off
```

After a short pause, the modem should hang itself up.

If that does not work, either turn off your modem or fire up your communications software and interrupt the modem with +++ and then hang up with ATH0 when you receive the modem's OK prompt.

You may also need to clean up the lock file created by `pppd`

```
rm -f /var/lock/LCK..ttySx
```

15 Automating your connections—creating the connection scripts

While you can continue to log in by hand as shown above, it is much neater to set up some scripts to do this automatically for you.

A set of scripts automates the log in and PPP start up so all you have to do (as root or as a member of the PPP group) is issue a single command to fire up your connection.

15.1 Connection scripts for User name/Password Authentication

If your ISP does not require the use of PAP/CHAP, these are the scripts for you.

If the PPP package installed correctly, you should have two example files. For PPP 2.1.2 they are in `/usr/sbin` and for PPP 2.2 they are in `/etc/ppp/scripts`. They are called

for PPP-2.1.2

```
ppp-on
ppp-off
```

and for PPP-2.2

```
ppp-off
ppp-on
ppp-on-dialer
```

Now, if you are using PPP 2.1.2, I strongly urge you to delete the sample files. There are potential problems with these—and don't tell me they work fine—I used them for ages, too (and recommended them in the first version of this HOWTO).

For the benefit of PPP 2.1.2 users, here are better template versions, taken from the PPP 2.2 distribution. I suggest you copy and use these scripts **instead of** the old PPP-2.1.2 scripts.

15.2 The `ppp-on` script

This is the first of a pair of scripts that actually fire up the connection.

```
#!/bin/sh
#
# Script to initiate a PPP connection. This is the first part of the
# pair of scripts. This is not a secure pair of scripts as the codes
# are visible with the 'ps' command.  However, it is simple.
#
# These are the parameters. Change as needed.
TELEPHONE=555-1212       # The telephone number for the connection
ACCOUNT=george           # The account name for logon (as in 'George Burns')
PASSWORD=gracie          # The password for this account (and 'Gracie Allen')
```

```
LOCAL_IP=0.0.0.0         # Local IP address if known. Dynamic = 0.0.0.0
REMOTE_IP=0.0.0.0        # Remote IP address if desired. Normally 0.0.0.0
NETMASK=255.255.255.0    # The proper netmask if needed
#
# Export them so that they will be available to 'ppp-on-dialer'
export TELEPHONE ACCOUNT PASSWORD
#
# This is the location of the script which dials the phone and logs
# in.  Please use the absolute file name as the $PATH variable is not
# used on the connect option.  (To do so on a 'root' account would be
# a security hole so don't ask.)
#
DIALER_SCRIPT=/etc/ppp/ppp-on-dialer
#
# Initiate the connection
#
#
exec /usr/sbin/pppd debug /dev/ttySx 38400 \
        $LOCAL_IP:$REMOTE_IP \
        connect $DIALER_SCRIPT
```

Here is the ppp-on-dialer script:

```
#!/bin/sh
#
# This is part 2 of the ppp-on script. It will perform the connection
# protocol for the desired connection.
#
/usr/sbin/chat -v                                                   \
        TIMEOUT         3                               \
        ABORT           '\nBUSY\r'                      \
        ABORT           '\nNO ANSWER\r'                 \
        ABORT           '\nRINGING\r\n\r\nRINGING\r'    \
        ''              \rAT                            \
        'OK-+++\c-OK'   ATH0                            \
        TIMEOUT         30                              \
        OK              ATDT$TELEPHONE                  \
        CONNECT         ''                              \
        ogin:--ogin:    $ACCOUNT                        \
        assword:        $PASSWORD
```

For PPP-2.2, the ppp-off script looks like:

```
#!/bin/sh
######################################################################
#
# Determine the device to be terminated.
#
if [ "$1" = "" ]; then
        DEVICE=ppp0
else
        DEVICE=$1
fi

######################################################################
#
# If the ppp0 pid file is present then the program is running. Stop it.
if [ -r /var/run/$DEVICE.pid ]; then
        kill -INT 'cat /var/run/$DEVICE.pid'
#
```

```
# If the kill did not work then there is no process running for this
# pid. It may also mean that the lock file will be left. You may wish
# to delete the lock file at the same time.
        if [ ! "$?" = "0" ]; then
                rm -f /var/run/$DEVICE.pid
                echo "ERROR: Removed stale pid file"
                exit 1
        fi
#
# Success. Let pppd clean up its own junk.
        echo "PPP link to $DEVICE terminated."
        exit 0
fi
#
# The ppp process is not running for ppp0
echo "ERROR: PPP link is not active on $DEVICE"
exit 1
```

15.3 Editing the supplied PPP startup scripts

As the new scripts come in two parts, we will edit them in turn.

15.3.1 The `ppp-on` script

You will need to edit the script to reflect your user name at your ISP, your password at your ISP, and the telephone number of your ISP.

Each of the lines like `TELEPHONE=` actually set up shell variables that contain the information to the right of the '=' (excluding the comments of course). So edit each of these lines so it is correct for your ISP and connection.

Also, as you are setting the IP number (if you need to) in the `/etc/ppp/options` file, delete the line that says

```
$LOCAL_IP:$REMOTE_IP \
```

Also, make sure that the shell variable `DIALER_SCRIPT` points at the full path and name of the dialer script that you are actually going to use. So, if you have moved this or renamed the script, make sure you edit this line correctly in the `ppp-on` script.

15.3.2 The `ppp-on-dialer` script

This is the second of the scripts that actually brings up our PPP link.

Note: a chat script is normally all on one line. the backslashes are used to allow line continuations across several physical lines (for human readability) and do not form part of the script itself.

However, it is very useful to look at it in detail so that we understand what it is actually (supposed) to be doing.

15.4 What a Chat script means...

A chat script is a sequence of "expect string" "send string" pairs. In particular, note that we always expect something before we send something.

If we are to send something without receiving anything first, we must use an empty expect string (indicated by " and similarly for expecting something without sending anything. Also, if a string consists of several words, (e.g. NO CARRIER), you must quote the string so that it is seen as a single entity by chat.

The chat line in our template is:

```
exec /usr/sbin/chat -v
```

Invoke `chat`, the `-v` tells chat to copy all its I/O into the system log (usually /var/log/messages). Once you are happy that the chat script is working reliably, edit this line to remove the `-v` to save unnecessary clutter in your syslog.

```
TIMEOUT         3
```

This sets the timeout for the receipt of expected input to three seconds. You may need to increase this to, say, 5 or 10 seconds if you are using a really slow modem.

```
ABORT           '\nBUSY\r'
```

If the string BUSY is received, abort the operation.

```
ABORT           '\nNO ANSWER\r'
```

If the string NO ANSWER is received, abort the operation

```
ABORT           '\nRINGING\r\n\r\nRINGING\r'
```

If the (repeated) string RINGING is received, abort the operation. This is because someone is ringing your phone line.

```
''              \rAT
```

Expect nothing from the modem and send the string AT.

```
OK-+++\c-OK   ATH0
```

This one is a bit more complicated as it uses some of `chat`'s error recovery capabilities.

What is says is: expect OK, if it is not received (because the modem is not in command mode) then send +++ (the standard Hayes-compatible modem string that returns the modem to command mode) and expect OK. Then send ATH0 (the modem hang-up string). This allows your script to cope with the situation of your modem being stuck on-line.

```
TIMEOUT         30
```

Set the timeout to 30 seconds for the remainder of the script. If you experience trouble with the chat script aborting due to timeouts, increase this to 45 seconds or more.

```
OK              ATDT$TELEPHONE
```

Expect OK (the modem's response to the ATH0 command), and dial the number we want to call.

```
CONNECT         ''
```

Expect CONNECT (which our modem sends when the remote modem answers) and send nothing in reply.

```
ogin:--ogin:    $ACCOUNT
```

Again, we have some error recovery built in here. Expect the login prompt (`ogin:`) but if we don't receive it by the timeout, send a return and then look for the login prompt again. When the prompt is received, send the user name (stored in the shell variable $ACCOUNT).

```
assword:        $PASSWORD
```

Expect the password prompt and send our password (again, stored in a shell variable).

This chat script has reasonable error recovery capability. Chat has considerably more features than demonstrated here. For more information consult the chat manual page (`man 8 chat`).

15.4.1 Starting PPP at the server end

While the `ppp-on-dialer` script is fine for servers that automatically start `pppd` at the server end once you have logged in, some servers require that you explicitly start PPP on the server.

If you need to issue a command to start up PPP on the server, you do need to edit the `ppp-on-dialer` script.

At the end of the script (after the password line) add an additional expect send pair—this one would look for your login prompt (beware of characters that have a special meaning in the Bourne shell—such as $ and []).

Once `chat` has found the shell prompt, chat must issue the ppp start up command required for your ISPs PPP server.

In my case, my PPP server uses the standard Linux Bash prompt

```
[hartr@kepler hartr]$
```

and requires that I type

```
ppp
```

to start up PPP on the server.

It is a good idea to allow for a bit of error recovery here, so in my case I use

```
    hartr--hartr  ppp
```

This says, if we don't receive the prompt within the timeout, send a carriage return and looks for the prompt again.

Once the prompt is received, then send the string `ppp`.

Note: don't forget to add a \ to the end of the previous line so `chat` still thinks the entire chat script is on one line!

Unfortunately, some servers produce a very variable set of prompts. You may need to log in several times using `minicom` to understand what is going on and pick the stable expect strings.

15.5 A chat script for PAP/CHAP authenticated connections

If your ISP is using PAP/CHAP, then your chat script is much simpler. All your chat script needs to do is dial the telephone, wait for a connect and then let pppd handle the logging in.

```
#!/bin/sh
#
# This is part 2 of the ppp-on script. It will perform the connection
# protocol for the desired connection.
#
exec /usr/sbin/chat -v                                          \
        TIMEOUT         3                                       \
        ABORT           '\nBUSY\r'                              \
        ABORT           '\nNO ANSWER\r'                         \
        ABORT           '\nRINGING\r\n\r\nRINGING\r'            \
        ''              \rAT                                    \
        'OK-+++\c-OK'   ATH0                                    \
        TIMEOUT         30                                      \
        OK              ATDT$TELEPHONE                          \
        CONNECT         ''                                      \
```

15.6 The pppd debug and file option_file options

As we have already seen, you can turn on debug information logging with the -d option to pppd. The debug option is equivalent to this.

As we are establishing a new connection with a new script, leave in the debug option for now. (Warning: if your disk space is tight, logging pppd exchanges can rapidly extend your syslog file and run you into trouble—but to do this you must fail to connect and keep on trying for quite a few minutes).

Once you are happy that all is working properly, then you can remove this option.

If you have called your PPP options file anything other than /etc/ppp/options or /etc/ppp/options.ttySx, specify the file name with the file option to pppd—e.g.

```
exec /usr/sbin/pppd debug file options.myserver /dev/ttyS0 38400 \
```

16 Testing your connection script

Open a new root Xterm (if you are in X) or open a new virtual console and log in as root.

In this new session, issue the command

```
tail -f /var/log/messages
```

(or whatever your system log file is).

In the first window (or virtual console) issue the command

```
ppp-on &
```

(or whatever name you have called your edited version of /usr/sbin/ppp- on). If you do not put the script into the background by specifying & at the end of the command, you will not get your terminal prompt back until PPP exits (when the link terminates).

Now switch back to the window that is tracking your system log.

(Note—I am using static IP numbers—hence my machine sent that to the PPP server—you won't see this if you are using dynamic IP numbers.) Also, this server requires a specific command to start PPP at its end.

This looks OK—so test it out as before with pings to IP numbers and host names.

Fire up you web browser or whatever and go surfing—you are connected!

17 Shutting down the PPP link

When you have finished with the PPP link, use the standard ppp-off command to shut it down (remember—you need to be root or a member of the PPP group).

In your system log you will see something like:

```
Oct 21 16:10:45 hwin pppd[19873]: Interrupt received: terminating link
Oct 21 16:10:45 hwin pppd[19873]: ipcp: down
Oct 21 16:10:45 hwin pppd[19873]: default route ioctl(SIOCDELRT): Bad address
Oct 21 16:10:45 hwin pppd[19873]: fsm_sdata(LCP): Sent code 5, id 2.
Oct 21 16:10:46 hwin pppd[19873]: fsm_rtermack(LCP).
Oct 21 16:10:46 hwin pppd[19873]: Connection terminated.
Oct 21 16:10:46 hwin pppd[19873]: Exit.
```

Don't worry about the `SIOCDELRT`—this is just `pppd` noting that it is terminating and is nothing to worry about.

18 Debugging

There are any number of reasons that your connection does not work—chat has failed to complete correctly, you have a dirty line, etc. So check your syslog for indications.

18.1 I have compiled PPP support into the kernel, but—

A very common problem is that people compile PPP support into the kernel and yet when they try to run `pppd`, the kernel complains that it does not support PPP. There are a variety of reasons this can occur.

18.1.1 Are you booting the right kernel?

While you have recompiled your kernel to support PPP, you are not booting the new kernel. This can happen if you do not update `/etc/lilo.conf` and rerun `lilo`.

A good check on the kernel can be obtained by issuing the command `uname -a`, which should produce a line like

```
Linux archenland 2.0.28 #2 Thu Feb 13 12:31:37 EST 1997 i586
```

This gives the kernel version and the date on which this kernel was compiled—which should give you a pretty good idea of what is going on.

18.1.2 Did you compile PPP kernel support as a module?

If you compiled your kernel ppp support as a module, but did not make and install the modules, then you can get this error. Check the Kernel HOWTO (page 1019) and the `README` file in `/usr/src/linux`!

Another module connected possibility is that you are expecting required modules to be automatically loaded, but are not running the `kerneld` daemon (which auto-loads and unloads modules on the fly). Check the `kerneld` Mini-HOWTO (on the LDP Home Page) for information on setting up `kerneld`.

18.1.3 Are you using the correct version of PPP for your kernel?

You must use PPP 2.2 with kernel version 2.0.x. You can use PPP 2.2 with kernel version 1.2.x (if you patch the kernel) otherwise you must use PPP 2.1.2.

18.2 My modem connects but ppp never starts up

There are innumerable variations on this (take a look in comp.os.linux.*).

A very common mistake is that you have mistyped something in your scripts. The only thing to do here is to make sure you are logging the chat conversation between you Linux PC and the server into your syslog `/var/log/messages` and then go through this line by line to make. You may need to dial into the PPP server manually to check things out again.

You need to check the log against the actual prompts very carefully—and bear in mind that we humans have a tendency to read what we think we have typed—not what is actually there!

18.3 The syslog says "`serial line is not 8 bit clean`"

There are variations on this too—such as `serial line looped back` etc., and the cause can be one (or a sequence) of a number of things.

To understand what is going on here, it is necessary to grasp a bit of what is going on behind the scenes in `pppd` itself.

When `pppd` starts up, it sends LCP (link control protocol) packets to the remote machine. If it receives a valid response it then goes on to the next stage (using IPCP—IP control protocol packets) and only when this negotiation completes is the actual IP layer started so that you can use the PPP link.

If there is no PPP server operating at the remote end when your PC sends lcp packets, these get reflected by the login process at the far end. As these packets use 8 bits, reflecting them strips the 8th bit (remember, ASCII is a 7-bit encoding). PPP sees this and complains accordingly.

There are several reasons this reflection can occur.

18.3.1 You are not correctly logging into the server

When your chat script completes, pppd starts on your PC. However, if you have not completed the log in process to the server (including sending any command required to start PPP on the server), PPP will not start.

So, the LCP packets are reflected and you receive this error.

You need to carefully check and correct (if necessary) your chat script (see above).

18.3.2 You are not starting PPP on the server

Some PPP servers require you to enter a command or a Return after completing the log in process before the remote end starts PPP.

Check your chat script (see above).

If you log in manually and find you need to send a Return after this to start PPP, simply add a blank expect send pair to the end of your chat script (an empty send string actually sends a RETURN).

18.3.3 The remote PPP process is slow to start

This one is a bit tricky.

By default, your Linux pppd is compiled to send a maximum of 10 LCP configuration requests. If the server is a bit slow to start up, all 10 such requests can be sent before the remote PPP is ready to receive them.

On your machine, pppd sees all 10 requests reflected back (with the 8th bit stripped) and exits.

There are two ways around this:

Add `lcp-max-configure 30` to your PPP options. This increases the maximum number of LCP configure packets pppd sends before giving up. For really slow server, you may need even more than this.

Alternatively, you can get a bit tricky in return. You may have noticed that when you logged in by hand to the PPP server and PPP started there, the first character of the PPP garbage that appears was always the tilde character (~).

Using this knowledge we can add a new expect send pair to the end of the chat script which expects a tilde and sends nothing. This would look like:

```
\~          ''
```

Note: as the tilde character has a special meaning in the shell, it must be escaped (and hence the leading backslash).

18.4 Default route not set

If pppd refuses to set up a default route, it is because (quite correctly) it refuses remove or replace an existing default route.

The usual reason that this error occurs is that some distributions set up a default route via your Ethernet card as opposed to setting up a specific network route.

See the Linux Network Administrator's Guide and the Net-3 HOWTO (page 1074) for information on correctly setting up your Ethernet card and associated routes.

An alternative to this is that your LAN uses a gateway or router already and your routing table has been set up to point the default route at this.

Fixing up this last situation can require a fair bit of IP networking knowledge and is beyond the scope of this HOWTO. It is suggested that you obtain some expert advice (via the news groups of from someone locally you can ask).

18.5 Other Problems

There are many reasons apart from these that PPP fails to connect or operate properly.

Look in the PPP FAQ (which is really a series of questions and answers). This is a very comprehensive document and the answers are there! From my own experience, if the answer to your problems is not there, the problem is not PPP's fault! In my case I was using an ELF kernel that I had not upgraded to the appropriate kernel modules. I only wasted about 2 days (and most of one night) cursing what had been a perfect PPP server before the light dawned!

19 Getting Help when totally stuck

If you can't get your PPP link to work, go back through this document and check everything—in conjunction with the output created by `chat -v` and `pppd -d` in you system log.

Also consult the PPP documentation and FAQ plus the other documents mention herein!

If you are still stuck, try the comp.os.linux.misc and comp.os.linux.networking newsgroups are reasonably regularly scanned by people that can help you with PPP as is comp.protocols.ppp

You can try sending me personal email, but I do have a day job (and a life) and I do not guarantee to respond quickly (if at all) as this depends on my current work load and the state of my private life!

20 Common Problems once the link is working

One problem you will find is that many service providers will only support the connection software package that they distribute to new accounts. This is (typically) for Microsoft Windows: (—and many service provider help desks seem to know nothing about Unix (or Linux). So, be prepared for limited assistance from them!

You could of course do the individual a favour and educate then about Linux (any ISP help desk person should be reasonably 'with it' in Internet terms and that means they should have a home Linux box—of course it does)!

20.1 I can't see beyond the PPP server I connect to

OK—your PPP connection is up and running and you can ping the PPP server by IP number (the second or remote IP number shown by `ifconfig ppp0`), but you can't reach anything beyond this.

First of all, try pinging the IP numbers you have specified in `/etc/resolv.conf` as name servers. If this works, you can see beyond your PPP server (unless this has the same IP number as the remote IP number of your connection). So now try pinging the full Internet name of your service provider—eg

```
ping my.provider.net.au
```

If this does not work, you have a problem with the name resolution. This is probably because of a typo in your /etc/resolv.conf file. Check this carefully against the information you acquired by ringing your service provider. If all looks OK, ring your service provider and check that you wrote down the IP numbers correctly.

If it still doesn't work (and your service provider confirms that his name servers are up and running), you have a problem somewhere else—and I suggest you check carefully through your Linux installation (looking particularly for file permissions).

If you still can't ping your service provider's IP name servers by IP number, either they are down (give them a voice call and check) or there is a routing problem at your service provider's end. Again, ring them and check this out.

One possibility is that the remote end is a Linux PPP server where the IP forwarding option has not been specified in the kernel.

A good general test is to try connecting to your service provider using the software that most supply for (gulp) Microsoft Windows. If everything works from another operating system to exactly the same account, then the problem is with your Linux system and not your service provider.

20.2 I can send email, but not receive it

If you are using dynamic IP numbers, this is perfectly normal. See "Setting up Services" below.

20.3 Why can't people finger, WWW, gopher, talk, etc. to my machine?

Again, if you are using dynamic IP numbers, this is perfectly normal. See "Setting up Services" below.

21 Using Internet services with Dynamic IP numbers

If you are using dynamic IP numbers (and many service providers will only give you a dynamic IP number unless you pay significantly more for your connection), then you have to recognize the limitations this imposes.

First of all, outbound service requests will work just fine. That is, you can send email using `sendmail` (provided you have correctly set up `sendmail`), FTP files from remote sites, finger users on other machines, browse the Web etc.

In particular, you can answer email that you have brought down to your machine whilst you are off line. Mail will simply sit in your mail queue until you dial back into your ISP.

However, your machine is not connected to the Internet 24 hours a day, nor does it have the same IP number every time it is connected. So it is impossible for you to receive email directed to your machine, and very difficult to set up a Web or FTP server that your friends can access. As far as the Internet is concerned your machine does not exist as a unique, permanently contactable machine as it does not have a unique IP number (remember—other machines will be using the IP number when they are allocated it on dial in).

If you set up a WWW (or any other server), it is totally unknown by any user on the Internet unless they know that your machine is connected and its actual (current) IP number. There are a number of ways they can get this info, ranging from you ringing them, sending them email to tell them or cunning use of ".plan" files on a shell account at your service provider (assuming that your provider allows shell and finger access).

Now, for most users, this is not a problem—all that most people want is to send and receive email (using your account on your service provider) and make outbound connections to WWW, FTP and other servers on the Internet. If you must have inbound connections to your server, you should really get a static IP number. Alternatively you can explore the methods hinted at above.

21.1 Setting up email

Even for dynamic IP numbers, you can certainly configure `sendmail` on your machine to send out any email that you compose locally. Configuration of sendmail can be obscure and difficult—so this document does not attempt to tell you how to do this. However, you should probably configure `sendmail` so that your Internet service provider is designated as your "smart relay" host (the `sendmail.cf` DS option). (For more `sendmail` configuration info, see the `sendmail` documents—and look at the m4 configurations that come with `sendmail`. There is almost certain to be one there that will meet your needs).

There are also excellent books on `sendmail` (notably the "bible" from O'Reilly and Associates), but these are almost certainly overkill for most users.

Once you have `sendmail` configured, you will probably want to have it dispatch any messages that have been sitting in the outbound mail queue as soon as the PPP connection comes up. To do this, add the command

```
sendmail -q &
```

to your `/etc/ppp/ip-up script` (see below).

Inbound email is a problem for dynamic IP numbers. The way to handle this is to:

- configure your mail user agent so that all mail is sent out with a "reply to" header giving your email address at your Internet Service provider.
  If you can, you should also set your "From:" address to be your email address at your ISP as well.
- use the `popclient` or `fetchmail` programs to retrieve your email from your service provider. Alternatively, if your ISP is using IMAP, use an IMAP enabled mail user agent (such as `pine`).

You can automate this process at dial up time by putting the necessary commands in the `/etc/ppp/ip-up` script (see below).

21.2 Setting up a local name server

While you can quite happily use the domain name servers located at your ISP, you can also set up a local caching only (secondary) name server that is brought up by the `ip-up` script. The advantage of running a local (caching only) name server is that it will save you time (and bandwidth) if you frequently contact the same sites during a long on-line session.

DNS configuration for a caching only nameserver (that uses a "forwarders" line in the `named.boot` file pointing at your ISPs DNS) is relatively simple. The O'Reilly book (DNS and Bind) explains all you want to know about this.

See also the DNS HOWTO (page 762).

If you are running a small LAN that can access the Internet through you Linux PC (using IP Masquerade for example), it is probably a good idea to run a local name server (with a forwarders directive) while the link is up as this will minimize the bandwidth and delays associated with name resolution.

One point of Netiquette: ask permission from your ISP before you start using a secondary, caching only name server in your ISP's domain. Properly configured, your DNS will not cause any problems to your ISP at all, but if you get things wrong, it can cause problems.

22 Linking two networks using PPP

There is basically no difference between linking a single Linux PC to a PPP server and linking two LANs using PPP on a machine on each LAN. Remember, PPP is a peer-to-peer protocol.

However, you definitely need to understand about how routing is established. Read the NET-3 HOWTO and the Linux Network Administrator Guide (NAG).

You will also find *TCP/IP Network Administration* (published by O'Reilly & Associates—ISBN 0-937175-82-X) to be of invaluable assistance.

If you are going to be subnetworking an IP network number on either side of the link, you will also find the Linux IP Sub-Networking Mini-Howto) to be of use. This is available at http://www.interweft.com.au/other/.

In order to link two LANs, you must be using different IP network numbers (or subnets of the same network number) and you will need to use static IP numbers—or use IP masquerade. If you want to use IP masquerade, see the IP Masquerade Mini-HOWTO for instructions on setting that up.

22.1 Setting up the IP numbers

Arrange with the network administrator of the other LAN the IP numbers that will be used for each end of the PPP interface. If you are using static IP numbers, this will also probably require you to dial into a specific telephone number.

Now edit the appropriate `/etc/ppp/options.tty`*xx* file—it's a good idea to have a specific modem and port at your end for this connection. This may well require you to change your `/etc/ppp/options` file—and create appropriate `options.tty`*xx* files for any other connections.

Specify the IP numbers for your end of the PPP link in the appropriate options file exactly as shown above for static IP numbers.

22.2 Setting up the routing

You must arrange that packets on your local LAN are routed across the interface that the PPP link establishes. This is a two-stage process.

First of all, you need to establish a route from the machine running the PPP link to the network(s) at the far end of the link. If the link is to the Internet, this can be handled by a default route established by pppd itself at your end of the connection using the `defaultroute` option to `pppd`.

If however, the link is only linking two LANs, then a specific network route must be added for each network that is accessible across the link. This is done using a `route` command for each network in the `/etc/ppp/ip-up script` (see "After the link comes up") for instructions on doing this.

The second thing you need to do is to tell the other computers on your LAN that your Linux computer is actually the gateway for the network(s) at the far end of the PPP link.

Of course, the network administrator at the other end of the link has to do all this too. However, as she or he will be routing packets to your specific networks, a specific network route will be required, not a default route (unless the LANs at the far and of the link are linking into you to access the Internet across your connection).

22.3 Network security

If you are linking you LAN to the Internet using PPP—or even just to a "foreign" LAN, you need to think about security issues. I strongly urge you to think about setting up a firewall.

You should also speak to the LAN administrator at your site before you start linking to foreign LANs or the Internet this way. Failure to do so could earn you anything from no reaction to really serious trouble.

23 After the link comes up—the `/etc/ppp/ip-up` script

Once the PPP link is established, `pppd` looks for `/etc/ppp/ip-up`. If this script exists and is executable, the PPP daemon executes the script. This allows you to automate any special routing commands that may be necessary and any other actions that you want to occur every time the PPP link is activated.

This is just a shell script and can do anything that a shell script can do (i.e., virtually anything you want).

For example, you can get `sendmail` to dispatch any waiting outbound messages in the mail queue.

Similarly, you can insert the commands into `ip-up` to collect (using POP) any email waiting for you at your ISP.

There are restrictions on `/etc/ppp/ip-up`:

- It runs in a deliberately restricted environment to enhance security. This means you must give a full path to binaries etc.
- Technically, `/etc/ppp/ip-up` is a program, not a script. This means it can be directly executed—and hence it requires the standard file magic (`#!/bin/bash`) at the start of the first line and must be readable and executable by root.

23.1 Special routing

If you are linking two LANs, you will need to set up specific routes to the "foreign" LANs. This is easily done using the `/etc/ppp/ip-up` script. The only difficulty arises if your machine handles multiple PPP links.

This is because the `/etc/ppp/ip-up` is executed for every ppp connection that comes up, so you need to carefully execute the correct routing commands for the particular link that comes up—and not when any other link comes up.

23.2 Handling email queues

When the link between two LANs comes up, you may well want to make sure that email that is queued at either end is flushed—sent out to its destination. This is done by adding the appropriate `sendmail` invocation.

Using the bash "case" statement on an appropriate parameter that pppd passes into the script accomplishes this. For example, this is the `/etc/ppp/ip-up` script I use to handle our WAN links and the link to my home Ethernet (also handled on the same PPP server).

23.3 A sample `/etc/ppp/ip-up` script

The example below provides a variety of example uses.

```
#!/bin/bash
#
# Script which handles the routing issues as necessary for pppd
# Only the link to Newman requires this handling.
#
# When the ppp link comes up, this script is called with the following
# parameters
#       $1      the interface name used by pppd (e.g. ppp3)
#       $2      the tty device name
#       $3      the tty device speed
#       $4      the local IP address for the interface
#       $5      the remote IP address
#       $6      the parameter specified by the 'ipparam' option to pppd
#
case "$5" in
# Handle the routing to the Newman Campus server
        202.12.126.1)
                /sbin/route add -net 202.12.126.0 gw 202.12.126.1
# and flush the mail queue to get their email there asap!
                /usr/sbin/sendmail -q &
                ;;
        139.130.177.2)
# Our Internet link
# When the link comes up, start the time server and synchronise to the world
# provided it is not already running
                if [ ! -f /var/lock/subsys/xntpd ]; then
                        /etc/rc.d/init.d/xntpd.init start &
                fi
# Start the news server (if not already running)
                if [ ! -f /var/lock/subsys/news ]; then
                        /etc/rc.d/init.d/news start &
                fi
                ;;
        203.18.8.104)
# Get the email down to my home machine as soon as the link comes up
# No routing is required as my home Ethernet is handled by IP
# masquerade and proxyarp routing.
                /usr/sbin/sendmail -q &
                ;;
        *)
esac
exit 0
```

As a result of bringing up the PPP link to our campus and this script, we end up with the following routing table entries (this machine also is our general dial-up PPP server and handles our Internet link). I have interspersed comments in the output to help explain what each entry is:

```
[root@kepler /root]# route -n
Kernel routing table
```

```
Destination     Gateway         Genmask          Flags MSS    Window Use Iface
# the HOST route to our remote internet gateway
139.130.177.2   *               255.255.255.255 UH    1500   0       134 ppp4
# the HOST route to our Newman campus server
202.12.126.1    *               255.255.255.255 UH    1500   0        82 ppp5
# the HOST route to my home ethernet
203.18.8.104    *               255.255.255.255 UH    1500   0        74 ppp3
# two of our general dial up PPP lines
203.18.8.64     *               255.255.255.255 UH    552    0         0 ppp2
203.18.8.62     *               255.255.255.255 UH    552    0         1 ppp1
# the specific network route to the Newman campus LAN
202.12.126.0    202.12.126.1    255.255.255.0   UG    1500   0         0 ppp5
# the route to our local Ethernet (super-netting two adjacent C classes)
203.18.8.0      *               255.255.254.0   U     1500   0      1683 eth0
# the route to the loop back device
127.0.0.0       *               255.0.0.0       U     3584   0       483 lo
# the default route to the Internet
default         139.130.177.2   *               UG    1500   0      3633 ppp4
```

23.4 Handling email

The previous section shows how to handle the outgoing mail—simply by flushing the mail queue once the link is up.

If you are running a WAN link, you can arrange with the network administrator of the remote LAN to do exactly the same thing. For example, at the other end of our WAN link, the `/etc/ppp/ip-up` script looks like :

```
#!/bin/bash
#
# Script which handles the routing issues as necessary for pppd
# Only the link to Hedland requires this handling.
#
# When the ppp link comes up, this script is called with the following
# parameters
#       $1      the interface name used by pppd (e.g. ppp3)
#       $2      the tty device name
#       $3      the tty device speed
#       $4      the local IP address for the interface
#       $5      the remote IP address
#       $6      the parameter specified by the 'ipparam' option to pppd
#
case "$5" in
        203.18.8.4)
                /usr/sbin/sendmail -q
                ;;
        *)
esac
exit 0
```

If, however, you have only a dynamic IP PPP link to your ISP, you need to get your email from the account on your ISP's machine. This is usually done using the POP (Post Office Protocol). This process can be handled using `popclient`—and the `ip-up` script can automate this process for you, too.

Simply create a `/etc/ppp/ip-up` script that contains the appropriate invocation of `popclient`. For my laptop that runs Red Hat Linux (which I take on any travels), this is

```
popclient -3 -c -u hartr -p <password> kepler.hedland.edu.au |formail -s procmail
```

You could use `slurp` or whatever to do the same for news, and so forth. Remember, the `ip-up` script is just a standard bash script and so can be used to automate any function that needs to be accomplished every time the appropriate PPP link comes up.

24 Using /etc/ppp/ip-down

You can create a script that will be executed once the link has been terminated. This is stored in /etc/ppp/ip-down. It can be used to undo anything special that you did in the corresponding /etc/ppp/ip-up script.

25 Routing issues on a LAN

If you are connected to a LAN but still want to use PPP on your personal Linux machine , you need to address some issues of the routes packets need to take from your machine to reach your LAN (through your Ethernet interface) and also to the remote PPP server and beyond.

This section does not attempt to teach you about routing—it deals only with a simple, special case of (static) routing. I strongly urge you to read the Linux Network Administrator Guide (NAG) if you are not familiar with routing. Also the O'Reilly book *TCP/IP Network Administration* covers this topic in a very understandable form.

The basic rule of static routing is that the default route should be the one that points to the most number of network addresses. For other networks, enter specific routes to the routing table.

The only situation I am going to cover here is where your Linux box is on a LAN that is not connected to the Internet—and you want to dial out to the Internet for personal use whilst still connected to the LAN.

First of all, make sure that your Ethernet route is set up to the specific network addresses available across your LAN—not set to the default route.

Check this by issuing a route command, you should see something like the following:

```
[root@hwin /root]# route -n
Kernel routing table
Destination     Gateway         Genmask         Flags MSS    Window Use Iface
loopback        *               255.255.255.0   U     1936   0        50 lo
10.0.0.0        *               255.255.255.0   U     1436   0       565 eth0
```

If your Ethernet interface (eth0) is pointing at the default route, (the first column will show "default" in the eth0 line) you need to change your Ethernet initialisation scripts to make it point at the specific network numbers rather than the default route (consult the NET-3 HOWTO and *Network Administrator's Guide*).

This will allow pppd to set up your default route as shown below.

```
[root@hwin /root]# route -n
Kernel routing table

Destination     Gateway         Genmask           Flags MSS    Window Use Iface
10.144.153.51   *               255.255.255.255 UH    488    0         0 ppp0
127.0.0.0       *               255.255.255.0   U     1936   0        50 lo
10.1.0.0        *               255.255.255.0   U     1436   0       569 eth0
default         10.144.153.51   *               UG    488    0         3 ppp0
```

As you can see, we have a host route to the PPP server (10.144.153.51) via ppp0 and also a default network route that uses the PPP server as its gateway.

If your setup needs to be more complex than this—read the routing documents already mentioned and consult an expert at your site.

If your LAN already has routers on it, you will already have gateways established to the wider networks available at your site. You should still point your default route at the PPP interface—and make the other routes specific to the networks they serve.

25.1 Note on Security

When you set up a Linux box on an existing LAN to link into the Internet, you are potentially opening your entire LAN to the Internet—and the hackers that reside there. Before you do this, I strongly urge you to consult your network administrator and site security policy. If your PPP connection to the Internet is used to successfully attack your site, you will at the very least earn the intense anger of your fellow users, network and system administrators. You may also find yourself in very much more serious trouble!

Before you connect a LAN to the Internet, you should consider the security implications of even a DYNAMIC connection—hence the earlier reference to the O'Reilly *Building Internet Firewalls*.

26 Setting up a PPP server

As already mentioned, there are many ways to do this. What I present here is the way I do it (using a Cyclades multi-port serial card) and a rotary dial-in set of telephone lines.

If you don't like the method I present here, please feel free to go your own way. I would however, be pleased to include additional methods in future versions of the HOWTO. So, please send me your comments and methods.

Please note, this section only concerns setting up Linux as a PPP server. I do not (ever) intend to include information on setting up special terminal servers and such.

Also, I have yet to experiment with shadow passwords (but will be doing so sometime). Information currently presented does NOT therefore include any bells and whistles that are required by the shadow suite.

26.1 Kernel compilation

All the earlier comments regarding kernel compilation and kernel versions versus `pppd` versions apply. This section assumes that you have read the earlier sections of this document.

For a PPP server, you must include IP forwarding in your kernel. You may also wish to include other capabilities (such as IP fire walls, accounting etc etc).

If you are using a multi-port serial card, then you must obviously include the necessary drivers in your kernel too.

26.2 Overview of the server system

We offer dial up PPP (and SLIP) accounts and shell accounts using the same user name and password pair. This has the advantage (for us) that a user requires only one account and can use it for all types of connectivity.

As we are an educational organisation, we do not charge our staff and students for access, and so do not have to worry about accounting and charging issues.

We operate a fire wall between our site and the Internet, and this restricts some user access as the dial-up lines are inside our (Internet) firewall (for fairly obvious reasons, details of our other internal fire walls are not presented here and are irrelevant in any case).

The process a user goes through to establish a PPP link to our site (once they have a valid account, of course) is :

- Dial into our rotary dialer (this is a single phone number that connects to a bank of modems—the first free modem is then used).
- Log in using a valid user name and password pair.
- At the shell prompt, issue the command `ppp` to start PPP on the server.
- Start PPP on their PC (be it running Windows, DOS, Linux, MAC OS or whatever—that is their problem).

The server uses individual `/etc/ppp/options.tty`*xx* files for each dial-in port that set the remote IP number for dynamic IP allocation. The server users proxy ARP routing for the remote clients (set via the appropriate option to `pppd`). This obviates the need for `routed` or `gated`.

When the user hangs up at their end, `pppd` detects this and tells the modem to hang up, bringing down the PPP link at the same time.

26.3 Getting the software together

You will need the following software:

- Linux, properly compiled to include the necessary options.
- The appropriate version of `pppd` for your kernel.
- A `getty` program that intelligently handles modem communications.
  We use getty_ps2.0.7h, but mgetty is highly thought of. I understand that mgetty can detect a call that is using PAP/CHAP. (PAP is the standard for Windows95), and invoke `pppd` automatically, but I have yet to explore this.
- An operational domain name server (DNS) that is accessible to your dial up users.
  You should really be running your own DNS if possible...

26.4 Setting up standard (shell access) dialup.

Before you can set up your PPP server, your Linux box must be capable of handling standard dial-up access.

This HOWTO does not cover setting this up. Please see the documentation of the `getty` of your choice and Serial HOWTO for information on this.

26.5 Setting up the PPP options files

You will need to set up the overall `/etc/ppp/options` with the common options for all dial-up ports. The options we use are:

```
asyncmap 0
netmask 255.255.254.0
proxyarp
lock
crtscts
modem
```

Note: We do not use any (obvious) routing—and in particular there is no defaultroute option. The reason for this is that all you (as a PPP server) are required to do is to route packets from the PPP client out across your LAN or Internet and route packets to the client from your LAN and beyond.

All that is necessary for this is a host route to the client machine and the use of the `proxyarp` option to `pppd`.

The `proxyarp` option sets up (surprise) a proxy ARP entry in the PPP server's ARP table that basically says 'send all packets destined for the PPP client to me'. This is the easiest way to set up routing to a single PPP client—but you cannot use this if you are routing between two LANs—ou must add proper network routes which can't use proxy ARP.

You will almost certainly wish to provide dynamic IP number allocation to your dial up users. You can accomplish this by allocating an IP number to each dial up port. Now, create a `/etc/ppp/options.tty`*xx* for each dial up port.

In this, simply put the local (server) IP number and the IP number that is to be used for that port. For example

```
kepler:slip01
```

In particular, note that you can use valid host names in this file (I find that I only remember the IP numbers of critical machines and devices on my networks—names are more meaningful). Before you can set up your PPP server, your Linux box must be capable of handling standard dial up access.

This HOWTO does not cover setting this up. Please see the documentation of the `getty` of your choice and Serial HOWTO for information on this.

26.6 Setting up the PPP options files

26.7 Setting `pppd` up to allow users to (successfully) run it

As starting a PPP link implies configuring a kernel device (a network interface) and manipulating the kernel routing tables, special privileges are required—in fact full root privileges.

Fortunately, pppd has been designed to be "safe" to run set uid to root. So you will need to

```
chmod u+s /usr/sbin/pppd
```

When you list the file, it should then appear as

```
-rwsr-xr-x   1 root     root        74224 Apr 28 07:17 /usr/sbin/pppd
```

If you do not do this, users will be unable to set up their PPP link.

26.8 Setting up the global alias for pppd

In order to simplify things for our dial up PPP users, we create a global alias (in `/etc/bashrc`) so that one simple command will start PPP on the server once they are logged in.

This looks like

```
alias ppp="exec /usr/sbin/pppd -detach"
```

What this does is

- `exec`: this means replace the running program (in this case the shell) with the program that is run.
- `pppd -detach`: start up `pppd` and do not fork into the background. This ensures that when `pppd` exits there is no process hanging around.

When a user logs in like this, they will appear in the output of 'w' as

```
  6:24pm  up 3 days,  7:00,  4 users,  load average: 0.05, 0.03, 0.00
User     tty       login@  idle   JCPU   PCPU  what
hartr    ttyC0     3:05am  9:14                -
```

And that is it.. . I told you this was a simple, basic PPP server system.

Robert Hart

Port Hedland, Western Australia

Melbourne, Victoria, Australia August/October 1996 January/March 1997

Part XXXVII

"Linux Printing HOWTO" by Grant Taylor,

gtaylor+pht@picante.com

Contents

Abstract

v3.14, 23 September 1997
This is the Linux Printing HOWTO, a collection of information on how to generate, preview, print, and fax anything under Linux (and other Unices in general).

1 Introduction

The Printing HOWTO should contain everything you need to know to help you set up printing services on your Linux box(en). As life would have it, it's a bit more complicated than in the point-and-click world of Microsoft and Apple, but it's also a bit more flexible and certainly easier to administer for large LANs.

This document is ordered so most people will only need to read the first half or so. Much of the more obscure and situation-dependent information in here is in the last half, and can be easily located in the Table of Contents, whereas most of the information through sections 9 or 10 is probably needed by most people.

Since version 3.*x* is a complete rewrite, much information from previous editions has been lost. This is by design, as the previous HOWTOs were so large as to be 60 typeset pages, and had the narrative flow of a dead turtle. If you do not find the answer here, you are encouraged to a) scan the previous version at the Printing HOWTO Home Page:

```
http://www.picante.com/~gtaylor/pht/
```

and b) drop me a note saying what ought to be here but isn't.

The PHT Home Page is a good place to find the latest version; it is also, of course, distributed from SunSite (`sunsite.unc.edu`) and your friendly local LDP mirror.

1.1 Copyright

2 How to print

If you've already got lpd set up to print to your printer, or your system administrator already did so, or your vendor did so for you, then all you need to do is learn how to use the lpr command. The Printing Usage HOWTO (page 1260) covers this, and a few other queue manipulation commands you should probably know.

If, however, you have a new system or new printer, then you'll have to set up printing services one way or another before you can print. Read on!

3 Kernel printer devices

3.1 The lp device

The Linux kernel (<=2.1.32), assuming you have compiled in or loaded the lp device (the output of `cat /proc/devices` should include the device lp), provides one or more of `/dev/lp0`, `/dev/lp1`, and `/dev/lp2`. These are not assigned dynamically, rather, each corresponds to a specific hardware I/O address. This means that your first printer may be `lp0` or `lp1` depending on your hardware. Try both.

A few users have reported that their bidirectional lp ports aren't detected if they use an older unidirectional printer cable. Check that you've got a decent cable.

One cannot run the PLIP and lp drivers at the same time on any given port. You can, however, have one or the other driver loaded at any given time either manually, or by `kerneld` with version 2.*x* (and later 1.3.*x*) kernels. By carefully setting the interrupts and such, you can supposedly run PLIP on one port and lp on the other. One person did so by editing the drivers; I eagerly await a success report of someone doing so with only a clever command line.

There is a little utility called `tunelp` floating about with which you, as root, can tune the Linux lp device's interrupt usage, polling rate, and other options.

When built in to some 1.3.*x* and later kernels, the kernel will accept an `lp=` option to set interrupts and io addresses:

```
When the lp driver is built in to the kernel, you may use the
LILO/LOADLIN.EXE command line to set the port addresses and interrupts
that the driver will use.

Syntax:     lp=port0[,irq0[,port1[,irq1[,port2[,irq2]]]]]
```

```
For example:   lp=0x378,0   or   lp=0x278,5,0x378,7 **

Note that if this feature is used, you must specify {\em all} the ports
you want considered, there are no defaults.  You can disable a
built-in driver with lp=0.
```

When loaded as a module in version 2 and late-model 1.3.x kernels, it is possible to specify I/O addresses and interrupt lines on the `insmod` command line (or in `/etc/conf.modules` so as to affect `kerneld`) using the usual syntax. The parameters are `io=port0,port1,port2` and `irq=irq0,irq1,irq2`. Read the manual page for `insmod` for more information on this.

For those of you who can never find the standard port numbers when you need them, they are as in the second example above. The other port (`lp0`) is at 0x3bc. I've no idea what interrupt it usually uses.

The source code for the Linux parallel port driver is in `/usr/src/linux/drivers/char/lp.c`.

3.2 The parport device (kernels >= 2.1.33)

Beginning with kernel 2.1.33 (and available as a patch for kernel 2.0.30), the lp device is merely a client of the new parport device. The addition of the parport device corrects a number of the problems that plague the old lp device driver—it can share the port with other drivers, it dynamically assigns available parallel ports to device numbers rather than enforcing a fixed correspondence between I/O addresses and port numbers, and so forth.

I'll cover the parport driver more completely when I find myself using one, but in the meantime you can read the file `Documentation/parport.txt` in your kernel sources, or look at http://www.cyberelk.demon.co.uk/parport.html.

3.3 Serial devices

Serial devices are usually called something like `/dev/ttyS1` under Linux. The utility `stty` will allow you to interactively view or set the settings for a serial port; `setserial` will allow you to control a few extended attributes and configure IRQs and I/O addresses for non-standard ports. Further discussion of serial ports under Linux may be found in the Serial HOWTO (page 1374).

When using a slow serial printer with flow control, you may find that some of your print jobs get truncated. This may be due to the serial port, whose default behavior is to purge any untransmitted characters from its buffer 30 seconds after the port device is closed. The buffer can hold up to 4096 characters, and if your printer uses flow control and is slow enough that it can't accept all the data from the buffer within 30 seconds after printing software has closed the serial port, the tail end of the buffer's contents will be lost. If the command `cat file > /dev/ttyS2` produces complete printouts for short files but truncated ones for longer files, you may have this condition.

The 30-second interval can be adjusted through the "closing_wait" command line option of `setserial` (version 2.12 and later). A machine's serial ports are usually initialized by a call to setserial in the rc.serial boot file. The call for the printing serial port can be modified to set the `closing_wait` at the same time as it sets that port's other parameters.

4 Supported Printers

The Linux kernel mostly supports any printer that you can plug into a serial or parallel port, but there are things to look out for, and printers that you won't be able to use, even though they can (electrically speaking) communicate with Linux. Primary among these incompatible printers are those that rely on the "Windows Printing System." (They're often vaguely labelled "for Windows.") These printers do not work with Linux. They haven't any "smarts" at all, and rely on the computer CPU to do much of the tasks that have been traditionally done by the printer's CPU. Unfortunately, these tasks can only be done by the vendor-supplied drivers, which only run under Windows. So don't buy one to use with Linux.

As for what printers do work with Linux, the best choice is to buy a printer with native PostScript support. Nearly all UNIX software that produces printable output produces it in PostScript, so obviously it'd be nice to get a printer that supports PostScript directly. Unfortunately, PostScript support is scarce outside the laser printer domain.

Failing the (larger) budget necessary to buy a PostScript printer, you can use any printer supported by Ghostscript, the free PostScript interpreter used in lieu of actual printer PostScript support. The Ghostscript Home Page, http://cs.wisc.edu/~ghost/, has a list of supported printers and information on the status of new and experimental drivers. Please help improve the Ghostscript printer support page by reporting your successes and failures as it asks.

5 Which spooling software?

Until recently, the choice for Linux users was simple—everyone ran the same old `lpd` lifted mostly verbatim out of BSD's Net-2 code. Even today, most vendors ship this software. But this is beginning to change. SVR4-like systems including Sun's Solaris come with a completely different print spooling package, centered around `lpsched`. And there are signs that some Linux vendors will shift to providing LPRng, a far less ancient print spooling implementation that is freely available. LPRng is far easier to administer for large installations and has a less frightfully haphazard code base than does stock `lpd`.

For the moment, even in light of the new options, `lpd` is probably fine for most Linux users. While it isn't the snazziest system, it works fine once set up, and it is well understood and extensively documented in third-party UNIX books.

If you'd like more information on LPRng, check out http://ltpwww.gsfc.nasa.gov/ltpcf/about/unix/Depotdoc/LPRng/ Future versions of this HOWTO will include information on using both LPRng and regular `lpd`.

6 How it works, basic

In order to get printing working well, you need to understand how the `lpd` system works.

`lpd` stands for Line Printer Daemon, and refers in different contexts to both the daemon and the whole collection of programs which run print spooling. These are:

lpd The spooling daemon. One of these runs to control everything on a machine, AND one is run per printer while the printer is printing.

lpr
The user spooling command. `lpr` contacts `lpd` and injects a new print job into the spool.

lpq Lists the jobs in a print queue.

lpc The lpd system control command. With `lpc` you can stop, start, reorder, etc, the print queues.

lprm `lprm` will remove a job from the print spool.

So how does it fit together? Well, when the system boots, `lpd` is run. It scans the file `/etc/printcap` to learn which printers it will be managing spools for. Each time someone runs `lpr`, `lpr` contacts lpd through the named socket `/dev/printer`, and feeds `lpd` both the file to print and some information about who is printing and how to print it. `lpd` then prints the file on the appropriate printer in turn.

The lp system was originally designed when most printers were line printers—that is, people mostly printed plain ASCII. As it turns out, only a little extra scripting is needed to make `lpd` work quite well for today's print jobs, which are often in PostScript, or text, or dvi, or—

7 How to set things up, basic

7.1 Traditional lpd configuration

The minimal setup for lpd results in a system that can queue files and print them. It will not pay any attention to whether or not your printer will understand them, and will probably not let you produce attractive output. Nevertheless, it is the first step to understanding, so read on!

Basically, to add a print queue to `lpd`, you must add an entry in `/etc/printcap`, and make the new spool directory under `/var/spool/lpd`.

An entry in `/etc/printcap` looks like:

```
# LOCAL djet500
lp|dj|deskjet:\
        :sd=/var/spool/lpd/dj:\
        :mx#0:\
        :lp=/dev/lp0:\
        :sh:
```

This defines a spool called `lp`, `dj`, or `deskjet`, spooled in the directory `/var/spool/lpd/dj`, with no per-job maximum size limit, which prints to the device `/dev/lp0`, and which does not have a banner page (with the name of the person who printed, etc) added to the front of the print job.

Go now and read the man page for `printcap`.

The above looks very simple, but there a catch—unless I send in files a DeskJet 500 can understand, this DeskJet will print strange things. For example, sending an ordinary Unix text file to a deskjet results in literally interpreted newlines, and gets me:

```
This is line one.
                  This is line two.
                                    This is line three.
```

ad nauseam. Printing a PostScript file to this spool would get a beautiful listing of the PostScript commands, printed out with this "staircase effect," but no useful output.

Clearly more is needed, and this is the purpose of filtering. The more observant of you who read the `printcap` manual page might have noticed the spool attributes `if` and `of`. Well, `if`, or the input filter, is just what we need here.

If we write a small shell script called `filter` that adds carriage returns before newlines, the staircasing can be eliminated. So we have to add in an `if` line to our printcap entry above:

```
lp|dj|deskjet:\
        :sd=/var/spool/lpd/dj:\
        :mx#0:\
        :lp=/dev/lp0:\
        :if=/var/spool/lpd/dj/filter:\
        :sh:
```

A simple filter script might be:

```
#!perl
# The above line should really have the whole path to perl
# This script must be executable: chmod 755 filter
while(<STDIN>){chop $_; print "$_\r\n";};
# You might also want to end with a form feed: print "\f";
```

If we were to do the above, we'd have a spool to which we could print regular Unix text files and get meaningful results. (Yes, there are four million better ways to write this filter, but few so illustrative. You are encouraged to do this more efficiently.)

The only remaining problem is that printing plain text is really not too hot—surely it would be better to be able to print PostScript and other formatted or graphic types of output. Well, yes, it would, and it's easy to do. The method is simply an extension of the above linefeed-fixing filter. If you write a filter than can accept arbitrary file types as input and produce DeskJet-kosher output for each case, then you've got a clever print spooler indeed.

Such a filter is called a **magic** filter. Don't bother writing one yourself unless you print strange things—there are a good many written for you already on the net.

7.2 File Permissions

By popular demand, I include below a listing of the permissions on interesting files on my system. There are a number of better ways to do this, ideally using only SGID binaries and not making everything SUID root, but this is how my system came out of the box, and it works for me. (Quite frankly, if your vendor can't even ship a working lpd you're in for a rough ride).

```
-r-sr-sr-x   1 root    lp    /usr/bin/lpr*
-r-sr-sr-x   1 root    lp    /usr/bin/lprm*
-rwxr--r--   1 root    root  /usr/sbin/lpd*
-r-xr-sr-x   1 root    lp    /usr/sbin/lpc*
drwxrwxr-x   4 root    lp    /var/spool/lpd/
drwxr-xr-x   2 root    lp    /var/spool/lpd/lp/
```

`lpd` must currently be run as root so that it can bind to the low-numbered lp service port. It should probably become UID lp.lp or something after binding, but I don't think it does. Bummer.

8 Getting Printing Software

Many pre-written filter packages (and other printer-related software) are available from ftp://sunsite.unc.edu/pub/Linux/system/printing/. Such utilities as psutils, `a2ps`, `mpage`, `dvitodvi`, `flpr`, etc. can all be found there.

8.1 Magicfilter

Magicfilter is one of the fully-featured filter packages out there; it is designed to be installed in 10 minutes. I'm told it also includes special support for LPRng.

```
Title:          magicfilter
Version:        1.1b
Entered-date:   04APR95
Description:    A customizable, extensible automatic printer filter.
                Lets you automatically detect and print just about any
                data type you can find a conversion utility for.  This
                filter is written in C and is controlled completely
                from an external printer configuration file.
                This version adds automagic creation of configuration
                files based on the installed software on your system,
                courtesy of GNU Autoconf.
                This version is a bug fix from 1.1/1.1a; filters for
                non-ASCII capable PostScript printers have been added.
Author:         H. Peter Anvin <hpa@zytor.com>
Primary-site:   sunsite.unc.edu
                53000 /pub/Linux/system/printing/magicfilter-1.1b.tar.gz
Copying-policy: GPL
```

8.2 APSFILTER

Another of the many magic filter packages is APSFILTER, by Andreas Klemm. The Linux Software Map entry goes something like this:

```
Begin3
Title:          apsfilter
Version:        4.9.1
Entered-date:   Montag, 10. Juli 1995, 21:22:35 Uhr MET DST
Description:    magicfilter for lpd with auto filetype detection
Keywords:       lpd magicfilter aps apsfilter
Original-site:  sunsite.unc.edu
                /pub/Linux/system/printing/
                211KB aps-491.tgz
Platforms:      C-Compiler, gs Postscript emulator, pbmutils
Copying-policy: GPL
End
```

APSFILTER installs as an `if` filter for a print queue, and will translate from many common file types into your printer's command set. It understands, for example, text, PostScript, dvi, gif, and others.

8.3 EZ-Magic

EZ-Magic is another filter package, written as a bash script, available on sunsite.

```
Title:          ez-magic printer filter
Version:        1.0.5
Entered-date:   January 26, 1997
Description:    ez-magic is a printer filter that supports 8 common file
                formats (txt,ps,gif,bmp,pcx,png,jpg,tif) for printing.
                It can print over a network (SMB), or to a local printer.
                Reads from a file, STDIN, or lpd. Simple to use and
                configure. Just one script file, no huge manuals and
                multibillion drivers. The only catch is that you need a
                few common helper programs like netpbm and ghostscript.
                Written in bash. Easy to add formats and code. Still more
                bugs than I have appendages, but less than the number of
                grams of fat in a hot dog. Pre-configured for HP DeskJet
                870Cse over network. Comparable to apsfilter and others.
Keywords:       magic filter, print, graphics, samba, network, smb,
```

```
                  ghostscript, postscript, gif, jpg, simple
Author:           toby@eskimo.com (Toby Reed)
Maintained-by:    toby@eskimo.com (Toby Reed)
Primary-site:     http://www.eskimo.com/~toby/ez-magic-1.0.5.tar.gz
                           38 kb ez-magic-1.0.5.tar.gz
Alternate-site:   sunsite.unc.edu /pub/Linux/system/printing
                           38 kb ez-magic-1.0.5.tar.gz
Copying-policy:   Copyrighted, full manipulation rights, with one or two
                  restrictions.
```

9 Vendor Solutions

This section is, by definition, incomplete. Feel free to send in details of your favorite distribution.

9.1 Red Hat

Red Hat has a GUI printer administration tool which can add remote printers and printers on local devices. It lets you choose a ghostscript-supported printer type and Unix device file to print to, then installs a print queue in `/etc/printcap` and writes a short PostScript and ASCII magic filter based around `gs` and `enscript`. This solution works fairly well, and is trivial to setup for common cases.

9.2 Other Distributions

Please send me information on what other distributions do.

10 Ghostscript.

Ghostscript is an incredibly significant program for Linux printing. Most printing software under Unix generates PostScript, which is typically a $100 option on a printer. Ghostscript, however, is free, and will generate the language of your printer from PostScript. When tied in with your `lpd` input filter, it gives you a virtual PostScript printer and simplifies life immensely.

Ghostscript is available in two forms. The commercial version of Ghostscript, called Aladdin Ghostscript, may be used freely for personal use but may not be distributed by commercial Linux distributions. It is generally a year or so ahead of the free Ghostscript; at the moment, for example, it supports Adobe Acrobat's Portable Document Format, while the older Ghostscripts do not.

The free version of Ghostscript is GNU Ghostscript, and is simply an aged version of Aladdin Ghostscript kindly given to GNU. (Kudos to Aladdin for this arrangement; more software vendors should support free software in this way).

Whatever you do with `gs`, be very sure to run it with the option for disabling file access (`-dSAFER`). PostScript is a fully functional language, and a bad PostScript program could give you quite a headache.

Speaking of PDF, Adobe's Portable Document Format is actually little more than organized PostScript in a compressed file. Ghostscript can handle PDF input just as it does PostScript. So you can be the first on your block with a PDF-capable printer.

10.1 Invoking Ghostscript

Typically, Ghostscript will be run by whatever magic filter you settle upon, but for debugging purposes it's often handy to run it directly.

`gs -help` will give a brief, informative listing of options and available drivers (note that this list is the list of drivers compiled in, not the master list of all available drivers).

You might run `gs` for testing purposes like: `gs` *`options`* `-q -dSAFER -sOutputFile=/dev/lp1 test.ps`.

10.2 Ghostscript output tuning

There are a number of things one can do if `gs`'s output is not satisfactory. (Actually, you can do anything you darn well please, since you have the source.)

10.2.1 Output location and size

The location, size, and aspect ratio of the image on a page is controlled by the printer-specific driver in Ghostscript. If you find that your pages are coming out scrunched too short, or too long, or too big by a factor of two, you might want to look in your driver's source module and adjust whatever parameters jump out at you. Unfortunately, each driver is different, so I can't really tell you what to adjust, but most of them are reasonably well commented.

10.2.2 Gamma, dot sizes, etc.

Most non-laser printers suffer from the fact that their dots are rather large. This results in pictures coming out too dark. If you experience this problem you should use your own transfer function. Simply create the following file in the ghostscript lib-dir and add its name to the gs call just before the actual file. You may need to tweak the actual values to fit your printer. Lower values result in a brighter print. Especially if your driver uses a Floyd-Steinberg algorithm to rasterize colors, lower values (0.2–0.15) are probably a good choice.

```
---8<---- gamma.ps ----8<---
%!
%transfer functions for cyan magenta yellow black
{0.3 exp} {0.3 exp} {0.3 exp} {0.3 exp} setcolortransfer
---8<------------------8<---
```

It is also possible to mend printers that have some kind of color fault by tweaking these values. If you do that kind of thing, I recommend using the file `colorcir.ps`, that comes with Ghostscript (in the `examples` subdirectory), as a test page.

11 How to print to a printer over the network

One of the features of `lpd` is that it supports printing over the network to printers physically connected to a different machine. With the careful combination of filter scripts and assorted utilities, you can make `lpr` print transparently to printers on all sorts of networks.

11.1 To a UNIX `lpd` host

To allow remote machines to print to your printer, you must list the machines in `/etc/hosts.equiv` or `/etc/hosts.lpd`. (Note that `/etc/hosts.equiv` has a host of other effects; be sure you know what you are doing if you list any machine there). You can allow only certain users on the other machines to print to your printer by using the *rs* attribute; read the `lpd` manual page for information on this.

11.1.1 With `lpd`

To print to another machine, you make an `/etc/printcap` entry like this:

```
# REMOTE djet500
lp|dj|deskjet:\
        :sd=/var/spool/lpd/dj:\
        :rm=machine.out.there.com:\
        :rp=printername:\
        :lp=/dev/null:\
        :sh:
```

Note that there is still a spool directory on the local machine managed by `lpd`. If the remote machine is busy or offline, print jobs from the local machine wait in the spool area until they can be sent.

11.1.2 With `rlpr`

You can also use `rlpr` to send a print job directly to a queue on a remote machine without going through the hassle of configuring `lpd` to handle it. This is mostly useful in situations where you print to a variety of printers only occasionally. From the announcement for `rlpr`:

`rlpr` uses TCP/IP to send print jobs to `lpd` servers anywhere on a network.

Unlike `lpr`, it does not require that the remote printers be explicitly known to the machine you wish to print from, (e.g. through `/etc/printcap`) and thus is considerably more flexible and requires less administration.

rlpr can be used anywhere a traditional lpr command might be used, and is backwardly compatible with traditional BSD lpr.

The main advantage you gain with rlpr is the power to print remotely from anywhere to anywhere without regard for how the system you wish to print from was configured. It can work as a filter just like traditional lpr so that clients executing on a remote machine like netscape, and XEmacs, can print to your local machine with little effort.

rlpr is available from ftp://sunsite.unc.edu/pub/Linux/system/printing/.

11.2 To a Win95, WinNT, LanManager, or Samba printer

There is a Printing to Windows mini-HOWTO out there which has more info than there is here. It is possible to direct an lpd queue through the smbclient program (part of the SAMBA suite) to a TCP/IP based SMB print service. Samba includes a script to do this called smbprint. In short, you put a configuration file for the specific printer in question in the spool directory, and install the smbprint script as the if.

The /etc/printcap entry goes like this:

```
lp|remote-smbprinter:\
        :lp=/dev/null:sh:\
        :sd=/var/spool/lpd/lp:\
        :if=/usr/local/sbin/smbprint:
```

You should read the documentation inside the smbprint script for more information on how to set this up.

You can also use smbclient to submit a file directly to an SMB printing service without involving lpd. See the man page.

11.3 To a NetWare Printer

The ncpfs suite includes a utility called nprint which provides the same functionality as smbprint but for NetWare. You can get ncpfs from SunSite. From the LSM entry for version 0.16:

> With ncpfs you can mount volumes of your Netware server under Linux. You can also print to netware print queues and spool netware print queues to the Linux printing system. You need kernel 1.2.x or 1.3.54 and above. ncpfs does NOT work with any 1.3.x kernel below 1.3.54.

To make nprint work via lpd, you write a little shell script to print stdin on the NetWare printer, and install that as the if for an lpd print queue. You'll get something like:

```
sub2|remote-NWprinter:\
            :lp=/dev/null:sh:\
            :sd=/var/spool/lpd/sub2:\
            :if=/var/spool/lpd/nprint-script:
```

The nprint-script might look approximately like:

```
#! /bin/sh
# You should try the guest account with no password first!
/usr/local/bin/nprint -S net -U name -P passwd -q printq-name -
```

11.4 To an EtherTalk (Apple) printer

The netatalk package includes something like nprint and smbclient. Others have documented the procedure for printing to and from an Apple network far better than I ever will; see the Linux Netatalk HOWTO, http://thehamptons.com/anders/netatalk/.

Obscure caveat of the week: Netatalk does not work with SMC Etherpower PCI Card with a DEC tulip chip.

11.5 To a Hewlett Packard or other Ethernet printer

HPs and some other printers come with an Ethernet interface which you can print to directly using lpd. You should follow the instructions that came with your printer or its network adaptor, but in general, such printers are running lpd, and provide one or more queues which you can print to. An HP, for example, might work with a printcap like:

```
lj-5|remote-hplj:\
            :lp=/dev/null:sh:\
            :sd=/var/spool/lpd/lj-5:\
            :rm=printer.name.com:rp=raw:
```

HP Laserjet printers with Jet Direct interfaces generally support two built-in `lpd` queues—"raw," which accepts PCL (and possibly PostScript) and "text," which accepts straight ASCII (and copes automatically with the staircase effect).

In a large-scale environment, especially a large environment where some printers do not support PostScript, it may be useful to establish a dedicated print server to which all machines print and on which all Ghostscript jobs are run.

This also allows your Linux box to act as a spool server for the printer so that your network users can complete their print jobs quickly and get on with things without waiting for the printer to print any other job that someone else has sent.

To do this, set up a queue on you Linux box that points at the Ethernet equipped HP LJ (as above). Now set up all the clients on your LAN to point at the Linux queue (e.g., lj-5 in the example above).

Some HP network printers apparently don't heed the banner page setting sent by clients; you can turn off their internally generated banner page by telnetting to the printer, pressing return twice, typing "banner: 0" followed by "quit." There are other settings you can change this way, as well; type "?" to see a list.

11.5.1 To older HPs

Some printers (and printer networking "black boxes"), support only a cheesy little non-protocol involving plain TCP connections. Notable in this category are early-model JetDirect (including some JetDirectEx) cards. Basically, to print to the printer, you must open a TCP connection to the printer on a specified port (typically 9100) and stuff your print job into it. This can be implemented, among other ways, in Perl:

```
#!/usr/bin/perl
# Thanks to Dan McLaughlin for writing the original version of this
# script (And to Jim W. Jones for sitting next to Dan when writing me
# for help ;)

$fileName = @ARGV[0];

open(IN,"$fileName") || die "Can't open file $fileName";

$dpi300     = "\x1B*t300R";
$dosCr      = "\x1B&k3G";
$ends = "\x0A";

$port =  9100 unless $port;
$them = "bach.sr.hp.com" unless $them;

$AF_INET = 2;
$SOCK_STREAM = 1;
$SIG{'INT'} = 'dokill';
$sockaddr = 'S n a4 x8';

chop($hostname = 'hostname');
($name,$aliases,$proto) = getprotobyname('tcp');
($name,$aliases,$port) = getservbyname($port,'tcp')
    unless $port =~ /^\d+$/;;
($name,$aliases,$type,$len,$thisaddr) =
        gethostbyname($hostname);
($name,$aliases,$type,$len,$thataddr) = gethostbyname($them);
$this = pack($sockaddr, $AF_INET, 0, $thisaddr);
$that = pack($sockaddr, $AF_INET, $port, $thataddr);

if (socket(S, $AF_INET, $SOCK_STREAM, $proto)) {
#    print "socket ok\n";
}
else {
    die $!;
}
# Give the socket an address.
if (bind(S, $this)) {
#    print "bind ok\n";
```

```
}
else {
    die $!;
}

# Call up the server.

if (connect(S,$that)) {
#   print "connect ok\n";
}
else {
    die $!;
}

# Set socket to be command buffered.

select(S); $| = 1; select(STDOUT);

#    print S "@PJL ECHO Hi $hostname! $ends";
#    print S "@PJL OPMSG DISPLAY=\"Job $whoami\" $ends";
#    print S $dpi300;

# Avoid deadlock by forking.

if($child = fork) {
    print S $dosCr;
    print S $TimesNewR;

    while (<IN>) {
        print S;
    }
    sleep 3;
    do dokill();
} else {
    while(<S>) {
        print;
    }
}

sub dokill {
    kill 9,$child if $child;
}
```

11.6 Running an `if` for remote printers

One oddity of `lpd` is that the `if` is not run for remote printers. If you find that you need to run an `if`, you can do so by setting up a double queue and requeueing the job. As an example, consider this `/etc/printcap`:

```
lj-5:remote-hplj:\
        :lp=/dev/null:sh:\
        :sd=/var/spool/lpd/lj-5:\
        :if=/usr/lib/lpd/filter-lj-5:
lj-5-remote:lp=/dev/null:sh:rm=printer.name.com:\
        :rp=raw:sd=/var/spool/lpd/lj-5-raw:
```

in light of this `filter-lj-5` script:

```
#!/bin/sh
gs <options> -q -dSAFER -sOutputFile=- - | \
        lpr -Plj-5-remote -U$5
```

The `-U` option to `lpr` only works if `lpr` is run as daemon, and it sets the submitter's name for the job in the resubmitted queue correctly. You should probably use a more robust method of getting the username, since in some cases it is not argument 5. See the manual page for `printcap`.

11.7 From Windows.

Printing from a Windows (or presumably, OS/2) client to a Linux server is directly supported over SMB through the use of the SAMBA package, which also supports file sharing of your Linux filesystem to Windows clients.

Samba includes fairly complete documentation. You can either configure a magic filter on the Linux box and print PostScript to it, or run around installing printer-specific drivers on all the Windows machines and having a queue for them with no filters at all. Relying on the Windows drivers may in some cases produce better output, but is a bit more of an administrative hassle if there are many Windows boxen. So try PostScript first.

11.8 From an Apple.

Netatalk supports printing from Apple clients over EtherTalk. See the Netatalk HOWTO Page, http://thehamptons.com/anders/netatalk/ for more information.

11.9 From Netware.

There is some Netware service support available for Linux from or because of Caldera, but I have no idea if you can offer print services to Netware clients.

12 How to print to a fax machine.

12.1 Using a faxmodem

There are a number of fax programs out there that will let you fax and receive documents. One of the most complex is Sam Leffler's HylaFax, available from `ftp.sgi.com`. It supports all sorts of things from multiple modems to broadcasting.

Also available, and a better choice for most Linux boxen, is `efax`, a simple program which sends faxes. The getty program `mgetty` can receive faxes (and even do voicemail on some modems!).

12.2 Using the Remote Printing Service

There is an experimental service offered that lets you send an email message containing something you'd like printed such that it will appear on a fax machine elsewhere. Nice formats like PostScript are supported, so even though global coverage is spotty, this can still be a very useful service. For more information on printing via the remote printing service, see the Remote Printing WWW Site, http://www.tpc.int/.

13 How to generate something worth printing.

Here we get into a real rat's-nest of software. Basically, Linux can run many types of binaries with varying degrees of success: Linux/x86, Linux/Alpha, Linux/Sparc, Linux/foo, iBCS, Win16/Win32s (with dosemu and, someday, with Wine), Mac/68k (with Executor), and Java. I'll just discuss native Linux and common Unix software, except to say that WordPerfect for SCO, and quite probably other commercial word processing software, runs fine under Linux's iBCS emulation, as does anything in pure Java (the Corel Office for Java Preview looked quite promising).

For Linux itself, choices are mostly limited to those available for Unix in general:

13.1 Markup languages

Most markup languages are more suitable for large or repetitive projects, where you want the computer to control the layout of the text to make things uniform. Trying to make a pretty sign in a markup language would probably hurt.

`nroff` This was one of the first Unix markup languages. Manual pages are the most common examples of things formatted in *roff macros; many people swear by them, but nroff has, to me at least, a more arcane syntax than needed, and probably makes a poor choice for new works. It is worth knowing, though, that you can typeset a manual page directly into PostScript with groff. Most man commands will do this for you with `man -t foo | lpr`.

TeX TeX, and the macro package LaTeX, is one of the most widely used markup languages on Unix. Technical works are frequently written in LaTeX because it greatly simplifies the layout issues and is still one of the few text processing systems to support mathematics both completely and well. TeX's output format is `dvi`, and is converted to PostScript or Hewlett Packard's PCL with `dvips` or `dvilj`.

SGML There is at least one free SGML parser available for Unix and Linux; it forms the basis of Linuxdoc-SGML's homegrown document system. It can support other DTD's, as well.

HTML Someone suggested that for simple projects, it may suffice to write it in HTML and print it out using Netscape. I disagree, but YMMV.

13.2 WYSIWYG Word Processors

There is no longer any shortage of WYSIWYG word processing software. Several complete office suites are available, including one that's free for personal use (StarOffice).

StarOffice A German company is distributing StarOffice 3.1 (as opposed to the newer version 4) on the Net, free for Linux. This full-blown office suite has all the features you'd expect, and you can't beat the price. There's a mini-HOWTO out there which describes how to obtain and install it. It generates PostScript or PCL, so should work with most any printer that works otherwise on Linux.

LyX LyX is a front-end to LaTeX which looks very promising. See the LyX Homepage http://www-pu.informatik.uni-tuebingen.de/users/ettrich/ for more information.

The Andrew User Interface System AUIS includes `ez`, a WYSIWYG-style editor with most basic word processor features, HTML capabilities, and full MIME email and newsgroup support.

Commercial offerings

At least Caldera and Red Hat ship packages containing the usual office apps like a WYSIWYGish word processor and a spreadsheet. I would assume they do a dandy job, but I've never used them. I think Caldera also ships Sun's WABI, so you could probably run something like MS Office under that if you had to integrate with other folks' files.

Jeff Phillips `<jeff@I_RATUS.org>` uses Caldera's WordPerfect for Linux (on Slackware, of all things) and says that it works well. It apparently includes built-in printer support, as one would expect. Caldera should have info on `(http://www.caldera.com/)`.

Red Hat ships a suite called Applixware; you can find their web site at `(http://www.redhat.com/)`.

Other vendors: feel free to drop me a line with your offerings.

14 On-screen previewing of printable things.

Nearly anything you can print can be viewed on the screen, too.

14.1 PostScript

Ghostscript has an X11 driver best used under the management of the PostScript previewer Ghostview. The latest versions of these programs should be able to view PDF files, as well.

14.2 TeX dvi

TeX device independant files may be previewed under X11 with `xdvi`. Modern versions of `xdvi` call Ghostscript to render PostScript specials.

A VT100 driver exists as well. It's called `dgvt`. `tmview` works with Linux and svgalib, if that's all you can do.

14.3 Adobe PDF

Adobe's Acrobat Reader is available for Linux. Just download it from their web site, http://www.adobe.com/.

You can also use `xpdf`, which is freeware and comes with source, and I should think Ghostview supports viewing PDF files with `gs` under X11 by now.

15 Serial printers under `lpd`

15.1 Setting up in `/etc/printcap`

`lpd` provides five attributes which you can set in `/etc/printcap` to control all the settings of the serial port a printer is on. Read the `printcap` manual page and note the meanings of `br#`, `fc#`, `xc#`, `fs#` and `xs#`. The last four of these attributes are bitmaps indicating the settings for use the port. The `br#` attribute is simply the baud rate, ie '`br#9600`'.

It is very easy to translate from `stty` settings to `printcap` flag settings. If you need to, see the manual page for `stty` now.

Use `stty` to set up the printer port so that you can `cat` a file to it and have it print correctly. Here's what "`stty -a`" looks like for my printer port:

```
dina:/usr/users/andy/work/lpd/lpd# stty -a < /dev/ttyS2
speed 9600 baud; rows 0; columns 0; line = 0;
intr = ^C; quit = ^\; erase = ^?; kill = ^U; eof = ^D; eol = <undef>;
eol2 = <undef>; start = ^Q; stop = ^S; susp = ^Z; rprnt = ^R; werase = ^W;
lnext = ^V; min = 1; time = 0;
-parenb -parodd cs8 hupcl -cstopb cread -clocal -crtscts
-ignbrk -brkint -ignpar -parmrk -inpck -istrip -inlcr
-igncr -icrnl ixon -ixoff -iuclc -ixany -imaxbel
-opost -olcuc -ocrnl -onlcr -onocr -onlret -ofill -ofdel nl0 cr0 tab0
bs0 vt0 ff0
-isig -icanon -iexten -echo -echoe -echok -echonl -noflsh -xcase
-tostop -echoprt -echoctl -echoke
```

The only changes between this and the way the port is initialized at bootup are `-clocal`, `-crtscts`, and `ixon`. Your port may well be different depending on how your printer does flow control.

You actually use `stty` in a somewhat odd way. Since `stty` operates on the terminal connected to it's standard input, you use it to manipulate a given serial port by using the '<' character as above.

Once you have your `stty` settings right, so that "`cat file > /dev/ttyS2`" (in my case) sends the file to the printer, look at the file `/usr/src/linux/include/asm-i386/termbits.h`. This contains a lot of #defines and a few structs (You may wish to `cat` this file to the printer (you do have that working, right?) and use it as scratch paper). Go to the section that starts out

```
/* c_cflag bit meaning */
#define CBAUD   0000017
```

This section lists the meaning of the `fc#` and `fs#` bits. You will notice that the names there (after the baud rates) match up with one of the lines of stty output. Didn't I say this was going to be easy?

Note which of those settings are preceded with a - in your stty output. Sum up all those numbers (they are octal). This represents the bits you want to clear, so the result is your `fc#` capability. Of course, remember that you will be setting bits directly after you clear, so you can just use '`fc#0177777`' (I do).

Now do the same for those settings (listed in this section) which do not have a—before them in your stty output. In my example the important ones are CS8 (0000060), HUPCL (0002000), and CREAD (0000200). Also note the flags for your baud rate (mine is 0000015). Add those all up, and in my example you get 0002275. This goes in your `fs#` capability ('`fs#02275`' works fine in my example).

Do the same with set and clear for the next section of the include file, "c_lflag bits." In my case I didn't have to set anything, so I just use "`xc#0157777`" and "`xs#0`."

15.2 Older serial printers that drop characters

Jon Luckey points out that some older serial printers with ten-cent serial interfaces and small buffers really mean stop when they say so with flow control. He found that disabling the FIFO in his Linux box's 16550 serial port with `setserial` corrected the problem of dropped characters (you apparently specify the UART type as an 8250 to do this).

16 Credits

The `smbprint` information is from an article by Marcel Roelofs <`marcel@paragon.nl`>.

The `nprint` information for using Netware printers was provided by Michael Smith <`mikes@bioch.ox.ac.uk`>.

The serial printers under lpd section is from Andrew Tefft <`teffta@engr.dnet.ge.com`>.

The blurb about gammas and such for gs was sent in by Andreas <`quasi@hub-fue.franken.de`>.

The two paragraphs about the 30 second closing_wait of the serial diver was contributed by Cris Johnson <`cdj@netcom.com`>.

Robert Hart sent a few excellent paragraphs about setting up a print server to networked HPs which I used verbatim.

And special thanks to the dozens upon dozens of you who've pointed out typos, bad URLs, and errors in the document over the years.

15.2 [illegible] printers that drop characters

16 Credits

Part XXXVIII

“Linux Printing Usage HOWTO” by Matt Foster,

markk@auratek.com

Contents

Abstract

v1.2, 10 September 1996

1 Introduction

This document describes how to use the line printer spooling system provided with the Linux operating system. This HOWTO is the supplementary document to the Linux Printing Setup HOWTO, which discusses the installation and setup of the Linux printing system. The material presented in this HOWTO should be equally relevant for all flavors of the BSD operating system in addition to the Linux operating system.

1.1 Copyrights and Trademarks

If you have questions, please contact Greg Hankins, the Linux HOWTO coordinator, at <gregh@sunsite.unc.edu>. You may finger this address for phone number and additional contact information.

1.2 Downloading the Linux Printing HOWTOs

I recommend that if you want to print a copy of this HOWTO that you download the PostScript version. It is formatted in a fashion that is aesthetically appealing and easier to read. You can get the PostScript version from one of the many Linux distribution sites.

1.3 Feedback

Questions, comments, or corrections for this HOWTO may be directed to <markk@auratek.com>.

1.4 Acknowledgments

Thanks go out to all of the people who took the time to read the alpha version of this HOWTO and respond with many helpful comments and suggestions—some of you may see your comments reflected in the version.

I'd also like to thank Matt Foster who did the original re-write.

2 Printing Under Linux

This section discusses how to print files, examine the print queue, remove jobs from the print queue, format files before printing them, and configure your printing environment.

2.1 History of Linux Printing

The Linux printing system—the lp system—is a port of the source code written by the Regents of the University of California for the Berkeley Software Distribution version of the UNIX operating system.

2.2 Printing a File Using `lpr`

By far, the most simplistic way to print in the Linux operating system is to send the file to be printed directly to the printing device. One way to do this is to use the `cat` command. As the root user, one could do something like

```
# cat thesis.txt > /dev/lp
```

In this case, `/dev/lp` is a symbolic link to the actual printing device—be it a dot-matrix, laser printer, typesetter, or plotter. (See `ln`(1) for more information on symbolic links.)

For the purpose of security, only the root user and users in the same group as the print daemon are able to write directly to the printer. This is why commands such as `lpr`, `lprm`, and `lpq` have to be used to access the printer.

Because of this, users have to use `lpr` to print a file. The `lpr` command takes care of all the initial work needed to print the file, and then it hands control over to another program, `lpd`, the line printing daemon. The line printing daemon then tells the printer how to print the file.

When `lpr` is executed, it first copies the specified file to a certain directory (the spool directory) where the file remains until `lpd` prints it. Once `lpd` is told that there is a file to print, it will spawn a copy of itself (what we programmers call forking). This copy will print our file while the original copy waits for more requests. This allows for multiple jobs to be queued at once.

The syntax of `lpr(1)` is a very familiar one,

```
$ lpr [ options ] [ filename ... ]
```

If `filename` is not specified, `lpr` expects input to come from standard input (usually the keyboard, or another program's output). This enables the user to redirect a command's output to the print spooler. As such,

```
$ cat thesis.txt | lpr
```

or,

```
$ pr -l60 thesis.txt | lpr
```

The `lpr` command accepts several command-line arguments that allow a user to control how it works. Some of the most widely used arguments are: `-P`printer specifies the printer to use, `h` suppresses printing of the burst page, `-s` creates a symbolic link instead of copying the file to the spool directory (useful for large files), and -*num* specifies the number of copies to print. An example interaction with `lpr` might be something like

```
$ lpr -#2 -sP dj thesis.txt
```

This command will create a symbolic link to the file `thesis.txt` in the spool directory for the printer named `dj`, where it would be processed by `lpd`. It would then print a second copy of `thesis.txt`.

For a listing of all the options that `lpr` will recognize, see `lpr`(1).

2.3 Viewing the Print Queue with `lpq`

To view the contents of the print queue, use the `lpq` command. Issued without arguments, it returns the contents of the default printer's queue.

The returned output of `lpq` can be useful for many purposes.

```
$ lpq
lp is ready and printing
Rank    Owner      Job  Files                                Total Size
active mwf         31   thesis.txt                           682048 bytes
```

2.4 Canceling a Print Job Using `lprm`

Another useful feature of any printing system is the ability to cancel a job that has been previously queued. To do this, use `lprm`.

```
$ lprm -
```

The above command cancels all of the print jobs that are owned by the user who issued the command. A single print job can be canceled by first getting the job number as reported by `lpq` and then giving that number to `lprm`. For example,

```
$ lprm 31
```

would cancel job 31 (`thesis.txt`) on the default printer.

2.5 Controlling the lpd program with `lpc`

The `lpc(8)` program is used to control the printers that `lpd` serves. you can enable or disable a printer or its queues, rearrange entries within a queue, and get a status report on the printers and their queues. `lpc` is mostly used in a setup where there are multiple printers hanging off one machine.

```
$ lpc
```

The above will start the `lpc` program. By default, this enters you into an interactive mode, and you can begin issuing commands. The other option is to issue an `lpc` command on the command line.

```
$ lpc status all
```

A list of the available commands are in the `lpd` manual page, but here are a few of the major commands you'll want to know about. Any commands marked with *option* can either be a printer name (lp, print, etc) or the keyword `all`, which means all printers.

- `disable` *option*—prevents any new printer job from being entered.
- `down` *option*—disables all printing on the printer.
- `enable` *option*—allow new jobs to enter the print queue.
- `quit` (or `exit`)—leave `lpc`.
- `restart` *option*—restarts `lpd` for that printer.
- `status` *option*—print status of printer.
- `up` *option*—enable everything and start a new `lpd`.

3 Miscellaneous Items

This section discusses some of the miscellaneous things that you may want to know about printing under Linux.

3.1 Formatting Before Printing

Since most ASCII files are not formatted for printing, it is useful to format them in some way before they are actually printed. This may include putting a title and page number on each page, setting the margins, double spacing, indenting, or printing a file in multiple columns. A common way to do this is to use a print preprocessor such as `pr`.

```
$ pr +4 -d -h"Ph.D. Thesis, 2nd Draft" -l60 thesis.txt | lpr
```

In the above example, `pr` would take the file `thesis.txt` and skip the first three pages (`+4`), set the page length to sixty lines (`-l60`), double space the output (`-d`), and add the phrase `Ph.D. Thesis, 2nd Draft` to the top of each page (`-h`). `lpr` would then queue `pr`'s output. See `pr`'s on-line manual page for more information.

3.2 The `PRINTER` environment variables

All of the commands in the Linux printing system accept the `-P` option. This option allows the user to specify which printer to use for output. If a user doesn't specify which printer to use, then the default printer will be assumed as the output device.

Instead of having to specify a printer to use every time that you print, you can set the `PRINTER` environment variable to the name of the printer that you want to use. This is accomplished in different ways for each shell. For `bash` you can do this with

```
$ PRINTER="printer_name"; export PRINTER
```

and `csh`, you can do it with

```
% setenv PRINTER "printer_name"
```

These commands can be placed in your login scripts (`.profile` for `bash`, or `.cshrc` for `csh`), are issued on the command line. (See `bash(1)` and `csh(1)` for more information on environment variables.)

3.3 Printing graphics files

Printing graphics files through a printer usually depends on the kind of graphics you're converting, and the kind of printer you want to send to. Dot matrix is usually out of the question due to differences in the way dot-matrix handles graphics. Your best bet in this situation is to see if your printer is compatable with an Epson or an IBM ProPrinter, then convert the graphics file to PostScript, then use Ghostscript (see next section) to print the graphics.

If you have a laser printer, things are a bit easier since many are compatable with PCL. This now gives you a few options. Some programs may output directly in PCL. If not, programs like `NetPBM` can convert into PCL. Last option is to use ghostscript (see next section).

Your absolutely best option is to install packages like NetPBM and Ghostscript then installing a magic filter to process the graphics files automagically.

3.4 Printing PostScript files

Printing PostScript files on a printer that has a PostScript interpreter is simple; just use `lpr`, and the printer will take care of all of the details for you. For those of us that don't have printers with PostScript capabilities, we have to resort to other means. Luckily, there are programs available that can make sense of PostScript, and translate it into a language that most printers will understand. Probably the most well known of these programs is Ghostscript.

Ghostscript's responsibility is to convert all of the descriptions in a PostScript file to commands that the printer will understand. To print a PostScript file using Ghostscript, you might do something like

```
$ gs -dSAFER -dNOPAUSE -sDEVICE=deskjet -sOutputFile=|lpr thesis.ps
```

Notice in the above example that we are actually piping the output of Ghostscript to the `lpr` command by using the `-sOutputFile` option.

Ghostview is an interface to Ghostscript for the X Window System. It allows you to preview a PostScript file before you print it.

3.5 Printing PDF files

While there is no Adobe PDF viewer, there is an `xpdf` program which will print out PostScript data.

3.6 Printing TeX files

One of the easiest ways to print TeX files is to convert them to PostScript and then print them using Ghostscript. To do this, you first need to convert them from TeX to a format known as DVI (which stands for device-independent). You can do this with the `tex(1)` command. Then you need to convert the DVI file to a PostScript file using `dvips`. All of this would look like the following when typed in.

```
$ tex thesis.tex
$ dvips thesis.dvi
```

Now you are ready to print the resulting PostScript file as described above.

3.7 Printing `troff` formatted files

```
$ groff -Tascii thesis.tr | lpr
```

or, if you prefer,

```
$ groff thesis.tr > thesis.ps
```

and then print the PostScript file as described above.

3.8 Printing `man` pages

```
$ man man | col -b | lpr
```

The manual pages contain pre-formatted `troff` data, so we have to strip out any highlighting, underlines, etc. The `col` program does this just nicely, and since we're piping data, the `man` program won't use `more`.

4 Answers to Frequently Asked Questions

Q1. How do I prevent the staircase effect?

A1. The staircase effect is caused by the way some printers expect lines to be terminated. Some printers want lines that end with a carriage-return/line-feed sequence (DOS-style) instead of the line-feed sequence used for UNIX-type systems. The easiest way to fix this is to see if your printer can switch between the two styles somehow—either by flipping a DIP switch, or by sending an escape sequence at the start of each print job. To do the latter, you need to create a filter (see Q2 and *Foster95b*).

A quick fix is to use a filter on the command-line. An example of this might be

```
$ cat thesis.txt | todos | lpr
```

Q2. What is a filter?

A2. A filter is a program that reads from standard input (stdin), performs some action on this input, and writes to standard output (stdout). Filters are used for a lot of things, including text processing.

Q3. What is a "magic filter"?

A3. A **magic filter** performs an action based on a file's type. For example, if the file is a plain, text file, it would simply print the file using the normal methods. If the file is a PostScript file, or any other format, it would print it using another method (Ghostscript). Two examples of this are magicfilter and APSfilter. One caveat of these filters is that the appropriate programs have to be installed before you install the filter.

The reason for this is that when the magicfilter gets installed, it queries your system for specific programs (such as ghostscript - if it finds it, then it knows it can handle PostScript data), then builds itself based on what it finds. To handle all the printer files, you should probably have at least the following installed:

- GhostScript,
- $\TeX$
- NetPBM,
- jpeg utilities,
- gzip.

Q4. What about Windows Printing System? Will Linux work with that?

A4. Maybe. Printers that accept only the WPS commands will not work with Linux. Printers that accept WPS and other commands (such as the Canon BJC 610) will work, as long as they're set to something other than WPS format.

Q5. What kinda cheey system is this? I can't print more than six pages or else I get a "file too large" error.

A5. One of the options in the `/etc/printcap` file relates to the maximum size of a print file. The default is 1000 disk blocks (about 500k?). For PostScript files and the like, this will give you maybe 6–8 pages with graphics and all. Be sure to add the following line in the printer definition:

```
mx=0
```

The primary reason for this is to keep the spool partition from getting filled. There is another way to do it, by making `lpr` create a soft link from the spool directory to your print file. But you have to remember to add the `-s` option to lpr every time.

5 Troubleshooting

This section covers some common things that can go wrong with your printing system.

If your printer doesn't work:

- Do other print jobs work (application)?
- Is `lpd` running? (check it using `lpc`);
- Can root send something directly to the printer (print services)?
- Can you print from MS-DOS (cable or printer problem)?

Answering these questions can help find a solution.

Send other suggestions for this section to <markk@auratek.com>.

6 References

This is a section of references on the Linux printing system. I have tried to keep the references section of this HOWTO as focused as possible. If you feel that I have forgotten a significant reference work, please do not hesitate to contact me.

Before you post your question to a USENET group, consider the following:

- Is the printer accepting jobs? (Use `lpc`(8) to verify.)
- Is the answer to your question covered in this HOWTO, or the Printing Setup HOWTO?

If any of the above are true, you may want to think twice before you post your question. And, when you do finally post to a newsgroup, try to include pertinent information. Try not to just say something like, "I'm having trouble with lpr, please help." These types of posts will most definitely be ignored by many. Also try to include the kernel version that you're running, how the error occured, and, if any, the specific error message that the system returned.

On-Line Manual Pages

- `cat(1)`. Concatenate and print files.
- `dvips(1)`. Convert a TeX DVI file to PostScript.
- `ghostview(1)`. View PostScript documents using Ghostscript.
- `groff(1)`. Front end for the groff document formatting system.
- `gs(1)`. Ghostscript PostScript interpreter/viewer.
- `lpc(8)`. Line printer control program.
- `lpd(8)`. Line printer spooler daemon.
- `lpq(1)`. Spool queue examination program.
- `lpr(1)`. Off-line printer.
- `lprm(1)`. Remove jobs from the line printer spooling queue.
- `pr(1)`. Convert text files for printing.
- `tex(1)`. Text formatting and typesetting.

USENET newsgroups

- `comp.os.linux.*` a plethora of information on Linux
- `comp.unix.*` discussions relating to the UNIX operating system

Part XXXIX

“RPM HOWTO”
by Donnie Barnes,

djb@redhat.com

Contents

1 Introduction

RPM is the Red Hat Package Manager. While it does contain Red Hat in the name, it is completely intended to be an open packaging system available for anyone to use. It allows users to take source code for new software and package it into source and binary form such that binaries can be easily installed and tracked and source can be rebuilt easily. It also maintains a database of all packages and their files that can be used for verifying packages and querying for information about files and/or packages.

Red Hat Software encourages other distribution vendors to take the time to look at RPM and use it for their own distributions. RPM is quite flexible and easy to use, though it provides the base for a very extensive system. It is also completely open and available, though we would appreciate bug reports and fixes. Permission is granted to use and distribute RPM royalty free under the GPL.

More complete documentation is available on RPM in the book by Ed Bailey, *Maximum RPM*. That book is available for download or purchase at http://www.redhat.com/.

2 Overview

First, let me state some of the philosophy behind RPM. One design goal was to allow the use of "pristine" sources. With RPP (our former packaging system of which none of RPM is derived), our source packages were the "hacked" sources that we built from. Theoretically, one could install a source RPP and then `make` it with no problems. But the sources were not the original ones, and there was no reference as to what changes we had to make to get it to build. One had to download the pristine sources separately. With RPM, you have the pristine sources along with a patch that we used to compile from. We see this as a big advantage. Why? Several reasons. For one, if a new version of a program comes out, you don't necessarily have to start from scratch to get it to compile under RHL. You can look at the patch to see what you might need to do. All the compile-in defaults are easily visible this way.

RPM is also designed to have powerful querying options. You can do searches through your entire database for packages or just certain files. You can also easily find out what package a file belongs to and where it came from. The RPM files themselves are compressed archives, but you can query individual packages easily and quickly because of a custom binary header added to the package with everything you could possibly need to know contained in uncompressed form. This allows for fast querying.

Another powerful feature is the ability to verify packages. If you are worried that you deleted an important file for some package, just verify it. You will be notified of any anomalies. At that point, you can reinstall the package if necessary. Any config files that you had are preserved as well.

We would like to thank the folks from the BOGUS distribution for many of their ideas and concepts that are included in RPM. While RPM was completely written by Red Hat Software, its operation is based on code written by BOGUS (PM and PMS).

3 General Information

3.1 Acquiring RPM

The best way to get RPM is to install Red Hat Linux. If you don't want to do that, you can still get and use RPM. It can be acquired from ftp://ftp.redhat.com/pub/redhat/code/rpm/.

3.2 RPM Requirements

The main requirement to run RPM is `cpio` 2.4.2 or greater. While this system is intended for use with Linux, it may very well be portable to other Unix systems. It has, in fact, been compiled on SunOS, Solaris, AIX, Irix, AmigaOS, and others. Be warned, the binary packages generated on a different type of Unix system will not be compatible.

Those are the minimal requirements to install RPMs. To build RPMs from source, you also need everything normally required to build a package, like `gcc`, `make`, etc.

4 Using RPM

In its simplest form, RPM can be used to install packages:

```
rpm -i foobar-1.0-1.i386.rpm
```

The next simplest command is to uninstall a package:

```
rpm -e foobar
```

One of the more complex but highly useful commands allows you to install packages via FTP. If you are connected to the net and want to install a new package, all you need to do is specify the file with a valid URL, like so:

```
rpm -i ftp://ftp.pht.com/pub/linux/redhat/rh-2.0-beta/RPMS/foobar-1.0-1.i386.rpm
```

Please note, that RPM will now query and install via FTP.

While these are simple commands, RPM can be used in a multitude of ways as seen from the Usage message:

```
RPM version 2.3.9
Copyright (C) 1997 - Red Hat Software
This may be freely redistributed under the terms of the GNU Public License

usage: rpm {--help}
       rpm {--version}
       rpm {--initdb}   [--dbpath <dir>]
       rpm {--install -i} [-v] [--hash -h] [--percent] [--force] [--test]
                        [--replacepkgs] [--replacefiles] [--root <dir>]
                        [--excludedocs] [--includedocs] [--noscripts]
                        [--rcfile <file>] [--ignorearch] [--dbpath <dir>]
                        [--prefix <dir>] [--ignoreos] [--nodeps]
                        [--ftpproxy <host>] [--ftpport <port>]
                        file1.rpm ... fileN.rpm
       rpm {--upgrade -U} [-v] [--hash -h] [--percent] [--force] [--test]
                        [--oldpackage] [--root <dir>] [--noscripts]
                        [--excludedocs] [--includedocs] [--rcfile <file>]
                        [--ignorearch] [--dbpath <dir>] [--prefix <dir>]
                        [--ftpproxy <host>] [--ftpport <port>]
                        [--ignoreos] [--nodeps] file1.rpm ... fileN.rpm
       rpm {--query -q} [-afpg] [-i] [-l] [-s] [-d] [-c] [-v] [-R]
                        [--scripts] [--root <dir>] [--rcfile <file>]
                        [--whatprovides] [--whatrequires] [--requires]
                        [--ftpuseport] [--ftpproxy <host>] [--ftpport <port>]
                        [--provides] [--dump] [--dbpath <dir>] [targets]
       rpm {--verify -V -y} [-afpg] [--root <dir>] [--rcfile <file>]
                        [--dbpath <dir>] [--nodeps] [--nofiles] [--noscripts]
                        [--nomd5] [targets]
       rpm {--setperms} [-afpg] [target]
       rpm {--setugids} [-afpg] [target]
       rpm {--erase -e} [--root <dir>] [--noscripts] [--rcfile <file>]
                        [--dbpath <dir>] [--nodeps] [--allmatches]
                        package1 ... packageN
       rpm {-b|t}[plciba] [-v] [--short-circuit] [--clean] [--rcfile  <file>]
                        [--sign] [--test] [--timecheck <s>] specfile
       rpm {--rebuild} [--rcfile <file>] [-v] source1.rpm ... sourceN.rpm
       rpm {--recompile} [--rcfile <file>] [-v] source1.rpm ... sourceN.rpm
       rpm {--resign} [--rcfile <file>] package1 package2 ... packageN
       rpm {--addsign} [--rcfile <file>] package1 package2 ... packageN
       rpm {--checksig -K} [--nopgp] [--nomd5] [--rcfile <file>]
                           package1 ... packageN
       rpm {--rebuilddb} [--rcfile <file>] [--dbpath <dir>]
       rpm {--querytags}
```

You can find more details on what those options do in the RPM manual page.

5 Now what can I *really* do with RPM?

RPM is a very useful tool and, as you can see, has several options. The best way to make sense of them is to look at some examples. I covered a simple install and uninstall above, so here are some more examples:

- Let's say you delete some files by accident, but you aren't sure what you deleted. If you want to verify your entire system and see what might be missing, you would do:

```
rpm -Va
```

- Let's say you run across a file that you don't recognize. To find out which package owns it, you would do:

```
rpm -qf /usr/X11R6/bin/xjewel
```

The output would be:

```
xjewel-1.6-1
```

- You find a new `koules` RPM, but you don't know what it is. To find out some information on it, do:

```
rpm -qpi koules-1.2-2.i386.rpm
```

The output would be:

```
Name        : koules                    Distribution: Red Hat Linux Colgate
Version     : 1.2                             Vendor: Red Hat Software
Release     : 2                           Build Date: Mon Sep 02 11:59:12 1996
Install date: (none)                      Build Host: porky.redhat.com
Group       : Games                       Source RPM: koules-1.2-2.src.rpm
Size        : 614939
Summary     : SVGAlib action game with multiplayer, network, and sound support
Description :
This arcade-style game is novel in conception and excellent in execution.
No shooting, no blood, no guts, no gore.  The play is simple, but you
still must develop skill to play.  This version uses SVGAlib to
run on a graphics console.
```

- Now you want to see what files the `koules` RPM installs. You would do:

```
rpm -qpl koules-1.2-2.i386.rpm
```

The output is:

```
/usr/doc/koules
/usr/doc/koules/ANNOUNCE
/usr/doc/koules/BUGS
/usr/doc/koules/COMPILE.OS2
/usr/doc/koules/COPYING
/usr/doc/koules/Card
/usr/doc/koules/ChangeLog
/usr/doc/koules/INSTALLATION
/usr/doc/koules/Icon.xpm
/usr/doc/koules/Icon2.xpm
/usr/doc/koules/Koules.FAQ
/usr/doc/koules/Koules.xpm
/usr/doc/koules/README
/usr/doc/koules/TODO
/usr/games/koules
/usr/games/koules.svga
/usr/games/koules.tcl
/usr/man/man6/koules.svga.6
```

These are just several examples. More creative ones can be thought of really easy once you are familiar with RPM.

6 Building RPMs

Building RPMs is fairly easy to do, especially if you can get the software you are trying to package to build on its own.
The basic procedure to build an RPM is as follows:

- Make sure your `/etc/rpmrc` is setup for your system.
- Get the source code you are building the RPM for to build on your system.

- Make a patch of any changes you had to make to the sources to get them to build properly.
- Make a spec file for the package.
- Make sure everything is in its proper place.
- Build the package using RPM.

Under normal operation, RPM builds both binary and source packages.

6.1 The rpmrc File

Right now, the only configuration of RPM is available via the /etc/rpmrc file. An example one looks like:

```
require_vendor: 1
distribution: I roll my own!
require_distribution: 1
topdir: /usr/src/me
vendor: Mickiesoft
packager:  Mickeysoft Packaging Account <packages@mickiesoft.com>

optflags: i386 -O2 -m486 -fno-strength-reduce
optflags: alpha -O2
optflags: sparc -O2

signature: pgp
pgp_name: Mickeysoft Packaging Account
pgp_path: /home/packages/.pgp

tmppath: /usr/tmp
```

The require_vendor line causes RPM to require that it find a vendor line. This can come from the /etc/rpmrc or from the header of the spec file itself. To turn this off, change the number to 0. The same holds true for the require_distribution and require_group lines.

The next line is the distribution line. You can define that here or later in the header of the spec file. When building for a particular distribution, it's a good idea to make sure this line is correct, even though it is not required. The vendor line works much the same way, but can be anything (i.e., Joe's Software and Rock Music Emporium).

RPM also now has support for building packages on multiple architectures. The rpmrc file can hold an optflags variable for building things that require architecture specific flags when building. See later sections for how to use this variable.

In addition to the above macros, there are several more. You can use:

```
rpm --showrc
```

to find out how your tags are set and what all the available flags are.

6.2 The spec file

We'll begin with discussion of the spec file. spec files are required to build a package. The spec file is a description of the software along with instructions on how to build it and a file list for all the binaries that get installed.

You'll want to name your spec file according to a standard convention. It should be the package name-dash-version number-dash-release number-dot-spec.

Here is a small spec file (vim-3.0-1.spec):

```
Summary: ejects ejectable media and controls auto ejection
Name: eject
Version: 1.4
Release: 3
Copyright: GPL
Group: Utilities/System
Source: sunsite.unc.edu:/pub/Linux/utils/disk-management/eject-1.4.tar.gz
Patch: eject-1.4-make.patch
Patch1: eject-1.4-jaz.patch
%description
This program allows the user to eject media that is auto-ejecting like
```

```
CD-ROMs, Jaz and Zip drives, and floppy drives on SPARC machines.

%prep
%setup
%patch -p1
%patch1 -p1

%build
make RPM_OPT_FLAGS="$RPM_OPT_FLAGS"

%install
install -s -m 755 -o 0 -g 0 eject /usr/bin/eject
install -m 644 -o 0 -g 0 eject.1 /usr/man/man1

%files
%doc README COPYING ChangeLog

/usr/bin/eject
/usr/man/man1/eject.1
```

6.3 The Header

The header has some standard fields in it that you need to fill in. There are a few caveats as well. The fields must be filled in as follows:

- `Summary`: This is a one line description of the package.
- `Name`: This must be the name string from the RPM file name you plan to use.
- `Version`: This must be the version string from the RPM file name you plan to use.
- `Release`: This is the release number for a package of the same version (i.e., if we make a package and find it to be slightly broken and need to make it again, the next package would be release number 2).
- `Icon`: This is the name of the icon file for use by other high level installation tools (like Red Hat's `glint`). It must be a GIF and resides in the `SOURCES` directory.
- `Source`: This line points at the `HOME` location of the pristine source file. It is used if you ever want to get the source again or check for newer versions. Caveat: The file name in this line must match the filename you have on your own system (i.e., don't download the source file and change its name). You can also specify more than one source file using lines like:

  ```
  Source0: blah-0.tar.gz
  Source1: blah-1.tar.gz
  Source2: fooblah.tar.gz
  ```

  These files would go in the `SOURCES` directory. (The directory structure is discussed in a later section, "The Source Directory Tree."
- `Patch`: This is the place you can find the patch if you need to download it again. Caveat: The file name here must match the one you use when you make your patch. You may also want to note that you can have multiple patch files much as you can have multiple sources. You would have something like:

  ```
  Patch0: blah-0.patch
  Patch1: blah-1.patch
  Patch2: fooblah.patch
  ```

  These files would go in the `SOURCES` directory.
- `Copyright`: This line tells how a package is copyrighted. You should use something like GPL, BSD, MIT, public domain, distributable, or commercial.
- `BuildRoot`: This line allows you to specify a directory as the "root" for building and installing the new package. You can use this to help test your package before having it installed on your machine.
- `Group`: This line is used to tell high level installation programs (such as Red Hat's `glint`) where to place this particular program in its hierarchical structure. The group tree currently looks something like this:

```
Applications
    Communications
    Editors
        Emacs
    Engineering
    Spreadsheets
    Databases
    Graphics
    Networking
    Mail
    Math
    News
    Publishing
        TeX
Base
    Kernel
Utilities
    Archiving
    Console
    File
    System
    Terminal
    Text
Daemons
Documentation
X11
    XFree86
        Servers
    Applications
        Graphics
        Networking
    Games
        Strategy
        Video
    Amusements
    Utilities
    Libraries
    Window Managers
Libraries
Networking
    Admin
    Daemons
    News
    Utilities
Development
    Debuggers
    Libraries
        Libc
    Languages
        Fortran
        Tcl
    Building
    Version Control
    Tools
Shells
Games
```

- `description` It's not really a header item, but should be described with the rest of the header. You need one description tag per package or subpackage. This is a multi-line field that should be used to give a comprehensive description of the package.

6.4 Prep

This is the second section in the spec file. It is used to get the sources ready to build. Here you need to do anything necessary to get the sources patched and set up like they need to be set up to do a make.

One thing to note: Each of these sections is really just a place to execute shell scripts. You could simply make an sh script and put it after the %prep tag to unpack and patch your sources. We have made macros to aid in this, however.

The first of these macros is the %setup macro. In its simplest form (no command line options), it simply unpacks the sources and cd's into the source directory. It also takes the following options:

- -n name will set the name of the build directory to the listed name. The default is $NAME-$VERSION. Other possibilities include $NAME, ${NAME}${VERSION}, or whatever the main tar file uses. (Please note that these "$" variables are not real variables available within the spec file. They are really just used here in place of a sample name. You need to use the real name and version in your package, not a variable.)
- -c will create and cd to the named directory before doing the untar.
- -b # will untar Source# before cd'ing into the directory (and this makes no sense with -c so don't do it). This is only useful with multiple source files.
- -a # will untar Source# after cd'ing into the directory.
- -T This option overrides the default action of untarring the Source and requires a -b 0 or -a 0 to get the main source file untarred. You need this when there are secondary sources.
- -D Do not delete the directory before unpacking. This is only useful where you have more than one setup macro. It should only be used in setup macros after the first one (but never in the first one).

The next of the available macros is the %patch macro. This macro helps automate the process of applying patches to the sources. It takes several options, listed below:

- # will apply Patch# as the patch file.
- -p # specifies the number of directories to strip for the patch(1) command.
- -P The default action is to apply Patch (or Patch0). This flag inhibits the default action and will require a 0 to get the main source file untarred. This option is useful in a second (or later) %patch macro that required a different number than the first macro.
- You can also do %patch# instead of doing the real command: %patch # -P

That should be all the macros you need. After you have those right, you can also do any other setup you need to do via sh type scripting. Anything you include up until the %build macro (discussed in the next section) is executed via sh. Look at the example above for the types of things you might want to do here.

6.5 Build

There aren't really any macros for this section. You should just put any commands here that you would need to use to build the software once you had untarred the source, patched it, and cd'ed into the directory. This is just another set of commands passed to sh, so any legal sh commands can go here (including comments). **Your current working directory is reset in each of these sections to the toplevel of the source directory**, so keep that in mind. You can cd into subdirectories if necessary.

6.6 Install

There aren't really any macros here, either. You basically just want to put whatever commands here that are necessary to install. If you have make install available to you in the package you are building, put that here. If not, you can either patch the makefile for a make install and just do a make install here, or you can hand install them here with sh commands. You can consider your current directory to be the top level of the source directory.

6.7 Optional pre- and post-install and uninstall Scripts

You can put scripts in that get run before and after the installation and uninstallation of binary packages. A main reason for this is to do things like run ldconfig after installing or removing packages that contain shared libraries. The macros for each of the scripts is as follows:

- %pre is the macro to do pre-install scripts.
- %post is the macro to do post-install scripts.

- `%preun` is the macro to do pre-uninstall scripts.
- `%postun` is the macro to do post-uninstall scripts.

The contents of these sections should just be any `sh` style script, though you do not need the `#!/bin/sh`.

6.8 Files

This is the section where you must list the files for the binary package. RPM has no way to know what binaries get installed as a result of `make install`. There is no way to do this. Some have suggested doing a `find` before and after the package install. With a multiuser system, this is unacceptable as other files may be created during a package building process that have nothing to do with the package itself.

There are some macros available to do some special things as well. They are listed and described here:

- `%doc` is used to mark documentation in the source package that you want installed in a binary install. The documents will be installed in `/usr/doc/$NAME-$VERSION-$RELEASE`. You can list multiple documents on the command line with this macro, or you can list them all separately using a macro for each of them.
- `%config` is used to mark configuration files in a package. This includes files like `sendmail.cf`, `passwd`, etc. If you later uninstall a package containing configuration files, any unchanged files will be removed and any changed files will get moved to their old name with a `.rpmsave` appended to the file name. You can list multiple files with this macro as well.
- `%dir` marks a single directory in a file list to be included as being owned by a package. By default, if you list a directory name without a `%dir` macro, everything in that directory is included in the file list and later installed as part of that package.
- `%files -f <filename>` will allow you to list your files in some arbitrary file within the build directory of the sources. This is nice in cases where you have a package that can build it's own filelist. You then just include that file list here and you don't have to specifically list the files.

The biggest caveat in the file list is listing directories. If you list `/usr/bin` by accident, your binary package will contain every file in `/usr/bin` on your system.

6.9 Building It

6.9.1 The Source Directory Tree

The first thing you need is a properly configured build tree. This is configurable using the `/etc/rpmrc` file. Most people will just use `/usr/src`.

You may need to create the following directories to make a build tree:

- `BUILD` is the directory where all building occurs by RPM. You don't have to do your test building anywhere in particular, but this is where RPM will do it's building.
- `SOURCES` is the directory where you should put your original source tar files and your patches. This is where RPM will look by default.
- `SPECS` is the directory where all spec files should go.
- `RPMS` is where RPM will put all binary RPMs when built.
- `SRPMS` is where all source RPMs will be put.

6.9.2 Test Building

The first thing you'll probably want to to is get the source to build cleanly without using RPM. To do this, unpack the sources, and change the directory name to `$NAME.orig`. Then unpack the source again. Use this source to build from. Go into the source directory and follow the instructions to build it. If you have to edit things, you'll need a patch. Once you get it to build, clean the source directory. Make sure and remove any files that get made from a `configure` script. Then `cd` back out of the source directory to its parent. Then you'll do something like:

```
diff -uNr dirname.orig dirname > ../SOURCES/dirname-linux.patch
```

This will create a patch for you that you can use in your spec file. Note that the "linux" that you see in the patch name is just an identifier. You might want to use something more descriptive like "config" or "bugs" to describe why you had to make a patch. It's also a good idea to look at the patch file you are creating before using it to make sure no binaries were included by accident.

6.9.3 Generating the File List

Now that you have source that will build and you know how to do it, build it and install it. Look at the output of the install sequence and build your file list from that to use in the spec file. We usually build the spec file in parallel with all of these steps. You can create the initial one and fill in the easy parts, and then fill in the other steps as you go.

6.9.4 Building the Package with RPM

Once you have a spec file, you are ready to try and build your package. The most useful way to do it is with a command like the following:

```
rpm -ba foobar-1.0.spec
```

There are other options useful with the `-b` switch as well:

- `p` means just run the `prep` section of the specfile.
- `l` is a list check that does some checks on `%files`.
- `c` do a prep and compile. This is useful when you are unsure of whether your source will build at all. It seems useless because you might want to just keep playing with the source itself until it builds and then start using RPM, but once you become accustomed to using RPM you will find instances when you will use it.
- `i` do a prep, compile, and install.
- `b` prep, compile, install, and build a binary package only.
- `a` build it all (both source and binary packages).

There are several modifiers to the `-b` switch. They are as follows:

- `-short-circuit` will skip straight to a specified stage (can only be used with c and i).
- `-clean` removes the build tree when done.
- `-keep-temps` will keep all the temp files and scripts that were made in `/tmp`. You can actually see what files were created in `/tmp` using the `-v` option.
- `-test` does not execute any real stages, but does keep-temp.

6.10 Testing It

Once you have a source and binary rpm for your package, you need to test it. The easiest and best way is to use a totally different machine from the one you are building on to test. After all, you've just done a lot of `make install`'s on your own machine, so it should be installed fairly well.

You can do an `rpm -u packagename` on the package to test, but that can be deceiving because in building the package, you did a `make install`. If you left something out of your file list, it will not get uninstalled. You'll then reinstall the binary package and your system will be complete again, but your rpm still isn't. Make sure and keep in mind that just because you do a `rpm -ba package`, most people installing your package will just be doing the `rpm -i package`. Make sure you don't do anything in the `build` or `install` sections that will need to be done when the binaries are installed by themselves.

6.11 What to do with your new RPMs

Once you've made your own RPM of something (assuming its something that hasn't already been RPM'ed), you can contribute your work to others (also assuming you RPM'ed something freely distributable). To do so, you'll want to upload it to ftp://ftp.redhat.com/.

6.12 What Now?

Please see the above sections on Testing and What to do with new RPMs. We want all the RPMs available we can get, and we want them to be good RPMs. Please take the time to test them well, and then take the time to upload them for everyone's benefit. Also, *please* make sure you are only uploading *freely available software*. Commercial software and shareware should *not* be uploaded unless they have a copyright expressly stating that this is allowed. This includes Netscape software, ssh, pgp, etc.

7 Multi-architectural RPM Building

RPM can now be used to build packages for the Intel i386, the Digital Alpha running Linux, and the Sparc. It has been reported to work on SGI's and HP workstations as well. There are several features that make building packages on all platforms easy. The first of these is the `optflags` directive in the `/etc/rpmrc`. It can be used to set flags used when building software to architecture specific values. Another feature is the `arch` macros in the `spec` file. They can be used to do different things depending on the architecture you are building on. Another feature is the `Exclude` directive in the header.

7.1 Sample `spec` File

The following is part of the `spec` file for the "fileutils" package. It is setup to build on both the Alpha and the Intel.

```
Summary: GNU File Utilities
Name: fileutils
Version: 3.16
Release: 1
Copyright: GPL
Group: Utilities/File
Source0: prep.ai.mit.edu:/pub/gnu/fileutils-3.16.tar.gz
Source1: DIR_COLORS
Patch: fileutils-3.16-mktime.patch

%description
These are the GNU file management utilities.  It includes programs
to copy, move, list, etc, files.

The ls program in this package now incorporates color ls!

%prep
%setup

%ifarch alpha
%patch -p1
autoconf
%endif
%build
configure --prefix=/usr --exec-prefix=/
make CFLAGS="$RPM_OPT_FLAGS" LDFLAGS=-s

%install
rm -f /usr/info/fileutils*
make install
gzip -9nf /usr/info/fileutils*

.
.
.
```

7.2 `optflags`

In this example, you see how the `optflags` directive is used from the `/etc/rpmrc`. Depending on which architecture you are building on, the proper value is given to `RPM_OPT_FLAGS`. You must patch the `Makefile` for your package to use this variable in place of the normal directives you might use (like `-m486` and `-O2`). You can get a better feel for what needs to be done by installing this source package and then unpacking the source and examine the `Makefile`. Then look at the patch for the `Makefile` and see what changes must be made.

7.3 Macros

The `%ifarch` macro is very important to all of this. Most times you will need to make a patch or two that is specific to one architecture only. In this case, RPM will allow you to apply that patch to just one architecture only.

In the above example, fileutils has a patch for 64 bit machines. Obviously, this should only be applied on the Alpha at the moment. So, we add an `%ifarch` macro around the 64 bit patch like so:

```
%ifarch axp
%patch1 -p1
%endif
```

This will insure that the patch is not applied on any architecture except the Alpha.

7.4 Excluding Architectures from Packages

So that you can maintain source RPMs in one directory for all platforms, we have implemented the ability to `exclude` packages from being built on certain architectures. This is so you can still do things like

```
rpm --rebuild /usr/src/SRPMS/*.rpm
```

and have the right packages build. If you haven't yet ported an application to a certain platform, all you have to do is add a line like:

```
ExcludeArch: axp
```

to the header of the spec file of the source package. Then rebuild the package on the platform that it does build on. You'll then have a source package that builds on an Intel and can easily be skipped on an Alpha.

7.5 Finishing Up

Using RPM to make multi-architectural packages is usually easier to do than getting the package itself to build both places. As more of the hard packages get built this is getting much easier, however. As always, the best help when you get stuck building an RPM is to look a similar source package.

8 Copyright Notice

Part XL

"Linux SCSI HOWTO"
by Drew Eckhardt,

drew@PoohSticks.ORG

Contents

Abstract

v2.30, 30 August 1996

1 Introduction

That said, I'd appreciate it if people would ask me, `drew@PoohSticks.ORG`, if there's a newer version available before they publish it. When people publish outdated versions, I get questions from users that are answered in newer versions, and it reflects poorly on the publisher. I'd also prefer that all references to free distribution sites, and possibly competing distributions/products be left intact.

IMPORTANT :

BUG REPORTS OR OTHER REQUESTS FOR HELP WHICH FAIL TO FOLLOW THE PROCEDURES OUTLINED IN THE 3 SECTION WILL BE IGNORED.

This HOWTO covers the Linux SCSI subsystem, as implemented in Linux kernel revision 1.2.10 and newer alpha code. Earlier revisions of the SCSI code are *unsupported,* and may differ significantly in terms of the drivers implemented, performance, and options available.

For additional information, you may wish to join the linux-scsi mailing list by mailing majordomo@vger.rutgers.edu with the line

```
subscribe linux-scsi
```

in the text. You can unsubscribe by sending mail to the same address and including

```
unsubscribe linux-scsi
```

in the text. Once you're subscribed, you can send mail to the list at

```
linux-scsi@vger.rutgers.edu
```

I'm aware that this document isn't the most user-friendly, and that there may be inaccuracies and oversights. If you have constructive comments on how to rectify the situation you're free to mail me about it.

2 Common Problems

This section lists some of the common problems that people have. If there is not anything here that answers your questions, you should also consult the sections for your host adapter and the devices in that are giving you problems.

2.1 General Flakiness

If you experience random errors, the most likely causes are cabling and termination problems.

Some products, such as those built around the newer NCR chips, feature digital filtering and active signal negation, and aren't very sensitive to cabling problems.

Others, such as the Adaptec 154xC, 154xCF, and 274x, are extremely sensitive and may fail with cables that work with other systems.

I reiterate : some host adapters are extremely sensitive to cabling and termination problems and therefore, cabling and termination should be the first things checked when there are problems.

To minimize your problems, you should use cables which

1. Claim SCSI-II compliance,
2. Have a characteristic impedance of 132 ohms,
3. All come from the same source to avoid impedance mismatches,
4. Come from a reputable vendor such as Amphenol.

Termination power should be provided by all devices on the SCSI bus, through a diode to prevent current back flow, so that sufficient power is available at the ends of the cable where it is needed. To prevent damage if the bus is shorted, TERMPWR should be driven through a fuse or other current limiting device.

If multiple devices, external cables, or FAST SCSI 2 are used, active or forced perfect termination should be used on both ends of the SCSI bus.

See the "SCSI FAQ: Frequently Asked Questions for comp.periphs.scsi" (available on tsx-11 in pub/linux/ALPHA/scsi) for more information about active termination.

2.2 The kernel command line

Other parts of the documentation refer to a "kernel command line."

The kernel command line is a set of options you may specify from either the LILO : prompt after an image name, or in the append field in your LILO configuration file (LILO .14 and newer use `/etc/lilo.conf`, older versions use `/etc/lilo/config`).

Boot your system with LILO, and hit one of the Alt, Control, or Shift keys when it first comes up to get a prompt. LILO should respond with

```
:
```

At this prompt, you can select a kernel image to boot, or list them with '?'.

```
:?

ramdisk floppy harddisk
```

To boot that kernel with the command line options you have selected, simply enter the name followed by a white space delimited list of options, terminating with a return.

Options take the form of

```
variable=valuelist
```

Where value list may be a single value or comma delimited list of values with no white space. With the exception of root device, individual values are numbers, and may be specified in either decimal or hexadecimal.

I.e., to boot Linux with an Adaptec 1520 clone not recognized at bootup, you might type

```
:floppy aha152x=0x340,11,7,1
```

If you don't care to type all of this at boot time, it is also possible to use the LILO configuration file `append` option with LILO .13 and newer.

I.e.,

```
append="aha152x=0x340,11,7,1"
```

2.3 A SCSI device shows up at all possible IDs

If this is the case, you have strapped the device at the same address as the controller (typically 7, although some boards use other addresses, with 6 being used by some Future Domain boards).

Please change the jumper settings.

2.4 A SCSI device shows up at all possible LUNs

The device has buggy firmware.

As an interim solution, you should try using the kernel command line option

```
max_scsi_luns=1
```

If that works, there is a list of buggy devices in the kernel sources in drivers/scsi/scsi.c in the variable blacklist. Add your device to this list and mail the patch to Linus Torvalds <`Linus.Torvalds@cs.Helsinki.FI`>.

2.5 You get sense errors when you know the devices are error free

Sometimes this is caused by bad cables or improper termination.

See Section 2.1

2.6 A kernel configured with networking does not work

The auto-probe routines for many of the network drivers are not passive, and will interfere with operation with some of the SCSI drivers.

2.7 Device detected, but unable to access

A SCSI device is detected by the kernel, but you are unable to access it—i.e., `mkfs /dev/sdc`, `tar xvf /dev/rst2`, etc. fails.

You don't have a special file in `/dev` for the device.

Unix devices are identified as either block or character (block devices go through the buffer cache, character devices do not) devices, a major number (ie which driver is used—block major 8 corresponds to SCSI disks) and a minor number. (I.e., which unit is being accessed through a given driver—i.e., character major 4, minor 0 is the first virtual console, minor 1 the next, etc.) However, accessing devices through this separate name space would break the Unix and Linux metaphor of "everything is a file," so character and block device special files are created under `/dev`. This lets you access the raw third SCSI disk device as `/dev/sdc`, the first serial port as `/dev/ttyS0`, etc.

The preferred method for creating a file is using the `MAKEDEV` script— `cd /dev` and run `MAKEDEV` (as root) for the devices you want to create—i.e.:

```
./MAKEDEV sdc
```

wild cards "should" work—i.e.:

```
./MAKEDEV sd\*
```

should create entries for all SCSI disk devices (doing this should create `/dev/sda` through `/dev/sdp`, with 15 partition entries for each)

```
./MAKEDEV sdc\*
```

should create entries for `/dev/sdc` and all 15 permissible partitions on `/dev/sdc`, etc.

I say "should" because this is the standard Unix behavior—the `MAKEDEV` script in your installation may not conform to this behavior, or may have restricted the number of devices it will create.

If `MAKEDEV` won't do the right magic for you, you'll have to create the device entries by hand with the `mknod` command.

The block/character type, major, and minor numbers are specified for the various SCSI devices in Section 6.3 in the appropriate section.

Take those numbers, and use (as root)

```
mknod /dev/device b|c major minor
```

i.e.,

```
mknod /dev/sdc b 8 32
mknod /dev/rst0 c 9 0
```

2.8 SCSI System Lockups

This could be one of a number of things. Also see the section for your specific host adapter for possible further solutions.

There are cases where the lockups seem to occur when multiple devices are in use at the same time. In this case, you can try contacting the manufacturer of the devices and see if firmware upgrades are available which would correct the problem. If possible, try a different SCSI cable, or try on another system. This can also be caused by bad blocks on disks, or by bad handling of DMA by the motherboard (for host adapters that do DMA). There are probably many other possible conditions that could lead to this type of event.

Sometimes these problems occur when there are multiple devices in use on the bus at the same time. In this case, if your host adapter driver supports more than one outstanding command on the bus at one time, try reducing this to 1 and see if this helps. If you have tape drives or slow CD-ROM drives on the bus, this might not be a practical solution.

2.9 Configuring and building the kernel

Unused SCSI drivers eat up valuable memory, aggravating memory shortage problems on small systems because kernel memory is unpageable.

So, you will want to build a kernel tuned for your system, with only the drivers you need installed.

```
cd to /usr/src/linux
```

If you are using a root device other than the current one, or something other than 80x25 VGA, and you are writing a boot floppy, you should edit the makefile, and make sure the

```
ROOT_DEV =
```

and

```
SVGA_MODE =
```

lines are the way you want them.

If you've installed any patches, you may wish to guarantee that all files are rebuilt. If this is the case, you should type

```
make mrproper
```

Regardless of whether you ran `make mrproper`, type

```
make config
```

and answer the configuration questions. Then run

```
make depend
```

and finally

```
make
```

Once the build completes, you may wish to update the LILO configuration, or write a boot floppy. A boot floppy may be made by running

```
make zdisk
```

2.10 LUNS other than 0 don't work

Many SCSI devices are horrendously broken, lock the SCSI bus up solid, and do other bad things when you attempt to talk to them at a logical unit someplace other than zero.

So, by default recent versions of the Linux kernel will not probe LUNS other than 0. To work around this, you need to the max_scsi_luns command line option, or recompile the kernel with the CONFIG_SCSI_MULTI_LUN option.

Usually, you'll put

```
max_scsi_luns=8
```

on your LILO command line.

If your multi-LUN devices still aren't detected correctly after trying one of these fixes (as the case will be with many old SCSI->MFM, RLL, ESDI, SMD, and similar bridge boards), you'll be thwarted by this piece of code

```
/* Some scsi-1 peripherals do not handle lun != 0.
   I am assuming that scsi-2 peripherals do better */
if((scsi_result[2] & 0x07) == 1 &&
   (scsi_result[3] & 0x0f) == 0) break;
```

in scan_scsis() in drivers/scsi/scsi.c. Delete this code, and you should be fine.

3 Reporting Bugs

The Linux SCSI developers don't necessarily maintain old revisions of the code due to space constraints. So, if you are not running the latest publicly released Linux kernel (note that many of the Linux distributions, such as MCC, SLS, Yggdrasil, etc. often lag one or even twenty patches behind this) chances are we will be unable to solve your problem. So, before reporting a bug, please check to see if it exists with the latest publicly available kernel.

If after upgrading, and reading this document thoroughly, you still believe that you have a bug, please mail a bug report to the SCSI channel of the mailing list where it will be seen by many of the people who've contributed to the Linux SCSI drivers.

In your bug report, please provide as much information as possible regarding your hardware configuration, the exact text of

all of the messages that Linux prints when it boots, when the error condition occurs, and where in the source code the error is. Use the procedures outlined in sections 3.1 and 3.2.

Failure to provide the maximum possible amount of information may result in mis-diagnosis of your problem, or developers deciding that there are other more interesting problems to fix.

The bottom line is that if we can't reproduce your bug, and you can't point at us what's broken, it won't get fixed.

3.1 Capturing messages

If you are not running a kernel message logging system :

Insure that the /proc file system is mounted.

```
grep proc /etc/mtab
```

If the /proc file system is not mounted, mount it

```
mkdir /proc
chmod 755 /proc
mount -t proc /proc /proc
```

Copy the kernel revision and messages into a log file

```
cat /proc/version > /tmp/log
cat /proc/kmsg >> /tmp/log
```

Type Ctrl-C after a second or two.

If you are running some logger, you'll have to poke through the appropriate log files (/etc/syslog.conf should be of some use in locating them), or use dmesg.

If Linux is not yet bootstrapped, format a floppy diskette under DOS. Note that if you have a distribution which mounts the root diskette off of floppy rather than RAM drive, you'll have to format a diskette readable in the drive not being used to mount root or use their ramdisk boot option.

Boot Linux off your distribution boot floppy, preferably in single user mode using a RAM disk as root.

```
mkdir /tmp/dos
```

Insert the diskette in a drive not being used to mount root, and mount it.

```
mount -t msdos /dev/fd0 /tmp/dos
```

or

```
mount -t msdos /dev/fd1 /tmp/dos
```

Copy your log to it

```
cp /tmp/log /tmp/dos/log
```

Unmount the DOS floppy

```
umount /tmp/dos
```

And shutdown Linux

```
shutdown
```

Reboot into DOS, and using your favorite communications software include the log file in your trouble mail.

3.2 Locating the source of a panic()

Like other Unices, when a fatal error is encountered, Linux calls the kernel panic() function. Unlike other Unices, Linux doesn't dump core to the swap or dump device and reboot automatically. Instead, a useful summary of state information is printed for the user to manually copy down. I.e.:

```
Unable to handle kernel NULL pointer dereference at virtual address c0000004
current->tss,cr3 = 00101000, %cr3 = 00101000
*pde = 00102027
*pte = 00000027
Oops: 0000
EIP:    0010:0019c905
EFLAGS: 00010002
eax: 0000000a   ebx: 001cd0e8   ecx: 00000006   edx: 000003d5
esi: 001cd0a8   edi: 00000000   ebp: 00000000   esp: 001a18c0
ds: 0018   es: 0018   fs: 002b   gs: 002b   ss: 0018
Process swapper (pid: 0, process nr: 0, stackpage=001a09c8)
Stack: 0019c5c6 00000000 0019c5b2 00000000 0019c5a5 001cd0a8 00000002 00000000
       001cd0e8 001cd0a8 00000000 001cdb38 001cdb00 00000000 001ce284 0019d001
       001cd004 0000e800 fbfff000 0019d051 001cd0a8 00000000 001a29f4 00800000
Call Trace: 0019c5c6 0019c5b2 0018c5a5 0019d001 0019d051 00111508 00111502
```

```
          0011e800 0011154d 00110f63 0010e2b3 0010ef55 0010ddb7
Code: 8b 57 04 52 68 d2 c5 19 00 e8 cd a0 f7 ff 83 c4 20 8b 4f 04
Aiee, killing interrupt handler
kfree of non-kmalloced memory: 001a29c0, next= 00000000, order=0
task[0] (swapper) killed: unable to recover
Kernel panic: Trying to free up swapper memory space
In swapper task---not syncing
```

Take the hexadecimal number on the EIP: line, in this case 19c905, and search through /usr/src/linux/zSystem.map for the highest number not larger than that address.

```
0019a000 T _fix_pointers
0019c700 t _intr_scsi
0019d000 t _NCR53c7x0_intr
```

That tells you what function its in. Recompile the source file which defines that function file with debugging enabled, or the whole kernel if you prefer by editing /usr/src/linux/Makefile and adding a -g to the CFLAGS definition.

```
#
# standard CFLAGS
#
```

For example:

```
CFLAGS = -Wall -Wstrict-prototypes -O2 -fomit-frame-pointer -pipe
```

becomes

```
CFLAGS = -g -Wall -Wstrict-prototypes -O2 -fomit-frame-pointer -pipe
```

Rebuild the kernel incrementally or by doing a

```
make clean
make
```

Make the kernel bootable by creating an entry in your /etc/lilo.conf for it

```
image = /usr/src/linux/zImage
label = experimental
```

and re-running LILO as root, or by creating a boot floppy

```
make zImage
```

Reboot and record the new EIP for the error.

If you have script installed, you may want to start it, as it will log your debugging session to the typescript file. Now, run

```
gdb /usr/src/linux/tools/zSystem
```

and enter

```
info line *<your EIP>
```

i.e.,

```
info line *0x19c905
```

To which gdb will respond something like

```
(gdb) info line *0x19c905
Line 2855 of ''53c7,8xx.c'' starts at address 0x19c905 <intr_scsi+641&>
   and ends at 0x19c913 <intr_scsi+655>.
```

Record this information. Then, enter

```
list <line number>
```

i.e.,

```
(gdb) list 2855
2850    /*    printk(''scsi\%d : target \%d lun \%d unexpected disconnect\n'',
2851              host->host_no, cmd->cmd->target, cmd->cmd->lun); */
2852          printk(''host : 0x\%x\n'', (unsigned) host);
2853          printk(''host->host_no : %d\n'', host->host_no);
2854          printk(''cmd : 0x%x\n'', (unsigned) cmd);
2855          printk(''cmd->cmd : 0x%x\n'', (unsigned) cmd->cmd);
2856          printk(''cmd->cmd->target : %d\n'', cmd->cmd->target);
2857          if (cmd) {;
2858              abnormal_finished(cmd, DID_ERROR << 16);
2859          }
2860          hostdata->dsp = hostdata->script + hostdata->E_schedule /
2861              sizeof(long);
2862          hostdata->dsp_changed = 1;
2863      /* SCSI PARITY error */
2864      }
2865
2866      if (sstat0_sist0 & SSTAT0_PAR) {
2867          fatal = 1;
2868          if (cmd && cmd->cmd) {
2869              printk(''scsi%d : target %d lun %d parity error.\n'',
```

Obviously, quit will take you out of gdb.

Record this information too, as it will provide a context in case the developers' kernels differ from yours.

4 Modules

This section gives specific details regarding the support for loadable kernel modules and how it relates to SCSI.

4.1 General Information

Loadable modules are a means by which the user or system administrator can load files into the kernel's memory in such a way that the kernel's capabilities are expanded. The most common usages of modules are for drivers to support hardware, or to load file systems.

There are several advantages of modules for SCSI. One is that a system administrator trying to maintain a large number of machines can use a single kernel image for all of the machines, and then load kernel modules to support hardware that is only present on some machines.

It is also possible for someone trying to create a distribution to use a script on the bootable floppy to query for which modules to be loaded. This saves memory that would otherwise be wasted on unused drivers, and it would also reduce the possibility that a probe for a non-existent card would screw up some other card on the system.

Modules also work out nicely on laptops, which tend to have less memory than desktop machines, and people tend to want to keep the kernel image as small as possible and load modules as required. Also, modules makes supporting PCMCIA SCSI cards on laptops somewhat easier, since you can load and unload the driver as the card is inserted or removed. (Note: currently the qlogic and 152x drivers support PCMCIA.)

Finally, there is the advantage that kernel developers can more easily debug and test their drivers, since testing a new driver does not require rebooting the machine (provided of course that the machine has not completely crashed as a result of some bug in the driver).

Although modules are very nice, there is one limitation. If your root disk partition is on a SCSI device, you will not be able to use modularized versions of SCSI code required to access the disk. This is because the system must be able to mount the root partition before it can load any modules from disk. There are people thinking about ways of fixing the loader and the kernel so that the kernel can self-load modules prior to attempting to mount the root filesystem, so at some point in the future this limitation may be lifted.

4.2 Module support in the 1.2.*n* kernel

In the 1.2.*n* series of kernels, there is partial support for SCSI kernel modules. While none of the high level drivers (such as disk, tape, etc) can be used as modules, most of the low level drivers (i.e. 1542, 1522) can be loaded and unloaded as required. Each time you load a low-level driver, the driver first searches for cards that can be driven. Next, the bus is scanned for each card that is found, and then the internal data structures are set up so as to make it possible to actually use the devices attached to the cards that the driver is managing.

When you are through with a low-level driver, you can unload it. You should keep in mind that usage counts are maintained based upon mounted filesystems, open files, etc, so that if you are still using a device that the driver is managing, the `rmmod` utility will tell you that the device is still busy and refuse to unload the driver. When the driver is unloaded, all of the associated data structures are also freed so that the system state should be back to where it was before the module was loaded. This means that the driver could be reloaded at a later time if required.

4.3 Module support in the 1.3.N kernel

In the 1.3 series of kernels, the SCSI code is completely modularized. This means that you can start with a kernel that has no SCSI support whatsoever, and start loading modules and you will eventually end up with complete support.

If you wish, you can compile some parts of the SCSI code into the kernel and then load other parts later—it is all up to you how much gets loaded at runtime and how much is linked directly into the kernel.

If you are starting with a kernel that has no support whatsoever for SCSI, then the first thing you will need to do is to load the scsi core into the kernel—this is in a module called "scsi_mod". You will not be able to load any other SCSI modules until you have this loaded into kernel memory. Since this does not contain any low-level drivers, the act of loading this module will not scan any busses, nor will it activate any drivers for SCSI disks, tapes, etc. If you answered "Y" to the CONFIG_SCSI question when you built your kernel, you will not need to load this module.

At this point you can add modules in more or less any order to achieve the desired functionality. Usage counts are interlocks are used to prevent unloading of any component which might still be in use, and you will get a message from rmmod if a module is still busy.

The high level drivers are in modules named "sd_mod", "sr_mod", "st", and "sg", for disk, cdrom, tape, and SCSI generic support respectively. When you load a high level driver, the device list for all attached hosts is examined for devices which the high level driver can drive, and these are automatically activated.

The use of modules with low level drivers were described in the section of the 4.2. When a low-level driver is loaded, the bus is scanned, and each device is examined by each of the high level drivers to see if they recognize it as something that they can drive—anything recognized is automatically attached and activated.

5 Hosts

This section gives specific information about the various host adapters that are supported in some way or another under Linux.

5.1 Supported and Unsupported Hardware

Drivers in the distribution kernel : Adaptec 152x, Adaptec 154x (DTC 329x boards usually work, but are unsupported), Adaptec 174x, Adaptec 274x/284x (294x support requires a newer version of the driver), BusLogic MultiMaster Host Adapters, EATA-DMA and EATA-PIO protocol compilant boards (DPT PM2001, PM2011, PM2012A, PM2012B, PM2021, PM2022, PM2024, PM2122, PM2124, PM2322, PM2041, PM2042, PM2044, PM2142, PM2144, PM2322, PM3021, PM3122, PM3222, PM3224, PM3334 some boards from NEC, AT&T, SNI, AST, Olivetti, and Alphatronix), Future Domain 850, 885, 950, and other boards in that series (but not the 840, 841, 880, and 881 boards unless you make the appropriate patch), Future Domain 16x0 with TMC-1800, TMC-18C30, or TMC-18C50 chips, NCR53c8xx,PAS16 SCSI ports, Seagate ST0x, Trantor T128/T130/T228 boards, Ultrastor 14F, 24F, and 34F, and Western Digital 7000.

MCA :

MCA boards which are compatible with a supported board (ie, Adaptec 1640 and BusLogic 640) will work.

Alpha drivers :

Many ALPHA drivers are available at

```
ftp://tsx-11.mit.edu/pub/linux/ALPHA/scsi
```

Drivers which will work with modifications NCR53c8x0/7x0:

```
   A NCR53c8xx driver has been developed, but currently will not work
with NCR53c700, NCR53c700-66, NCR53c710, and NCR53c720 chips.  A list
of changes needed to make each of these chips work follows, as well
as a summary of the complexity.

NCR53c720 (trivial)---detection changes, initialization changes, change
    fixup code to translate '810 register addresses to
    '7xx mapping.

NCR53c710 (trivial)---detection changes, initialization changes,
```

```
        of assembler, change fixup code to translate '810 register
        addresses to '7xx mapping, change interrupt handlers to treat
        IID interrupt from INTFLY instruction to emulate it.

    NCR53c700, NCR53c700-66 (very messy)---detection changes,
        initialization changes, modification of NCR code to not use DSA,
        modification of Linux code to handle context switches.
```

SCSI hosts that will not work : All parallel->SCSI adapters, Rancho SCSI boards, and Grass Roots SCSI boards. BusLogic FlashPoint boards, such as the BT-930/932/950, are currently unsupported.

SCSI hosts that will never work :

Non-Adaptec compatible, non-NCR53c8xx DTC boards (including the 3270 and 3280).

CMD SCSI boards.

Acquiring programming information requires a non-disclosure agreement with DTC/CMD. This means that it would be impossible to distribute a Linux driver if one were written, since complying with the NDA would mean distributing no source, in violation of the GPL, and complying with the GPL would mean distributing source, in violation of the NDA.

If you want to run Linux on some other unsupported piece of hardware, your options are to either write a driver yourself (Eric Youngdale and I are usually willing to answer technical questions concerning the Linux SCSI drivers) or to commission a driver. (Normal consulting rates mean that this will not be a viable option for personal use.)

5.1.1 Multiple host adapters

With some host adapters (see Section 10.7), you can use multiple host adapters of the same type in the same system. With multiple adapters of the same type in the same system, generally the one at the lowest address will be `scsi0`, the one at the next address `scsi1`, etc.

In all cases, it is possible to use multiple host adapters of different types, provided that none of their addresses conflict. SCSI controllers are scanned in the order specified in the builtin_scsi_hosts[] array in `drivers/scsi/hosts.c`, with the order currently being

> BusLogic, Ultrastor 14/34F, Ultrastor 14F,, Adaptec 151x/152x, Adaptec 154x, Adaptec 174x, AIC7XXX, AM53C974, Future Domain 16x0, Always IN2000, Generic NCR5380, QLOGIC, PAS16, Seagate, Trantor T128/T130, NCR53c8xx, EATA-DMA, WD7000, debugging driver.

In most cases (i.e., you aren't trying to use both BusLogic and Adaptec drivers), this can be changed to suit your needs (i.e., keeping the same devices when new SCSI devices are added to the system on a new controller) by moving the individual entries.

5.2 Common Problems

5.2.1 SCSI timeouts

Make sure interrupts are enabled correctly, and there are no IRQ, DMA, or address conflicts with other boards.

5.2.2 Failure of auto-probe routines on boards that rely on BIOS for auto probe.

If your SCSI adapter is one of the following :

> Adaptec 152x, Adaptec 151x, Adaptec AIC-6260, Adaptec AIC-6360, Future Domain 1680, Future Domain TMC-950, Future Domain TMC-8xx, Trantor T128, Trantor T128F, Trantor T228F, Seagate ST01, Seagate ST02, or a Western Digital 7000

and it is not detected on bootup, i.e. you get a

```
scsi : 0 hosts
```

message or a

```
scsi%d : type
```

message is not printed for each supported SCSI adapter installed in the system, you may have a problem with the auto-probe routine not knowing about your board.

Auto detection will fail for drivers using the BIOS for auto detection if the BIOS is disabled. Double check that your BIOS is enabled, and not conflicting with any other peripheral BIOSes.

Auto detection will also fail if the board's signature or BIOS address don't match known ones.

If the BIOS is installed, please use DOS and DEBUG to find a signature that will detect your board—i.e., if your board lives at 0xc8000, under DOS do

```
debug
d c800:0
q
```

and send a message to the SCSI channel of the mailing list with the ASCII message, with the length and offset from the base address (ie, 0xc8000). Note that the exact text is required, and you should provide both the hex and ASCII portions of the text.

If no BIOS is installed, and you are using an Adaptec 152x, Trantor T128, or Seagate driver, you can use command line or compile time overrides to force detection.

Please consult the appropriate subsection for your SCSI board as well as Section 2.1.

5.2.3 Failure of boards using memory mapped I/O

(This include the Trantor T128 and Seagate boards, but not the Adaptec, Generic NCR5380, PAS16, and Ultrastor drivers)

This is often caused when the memory mapped I/O ports are incorrectly cached. You should have the board's address space marked as uncacheable in the XCMOS settings.

If this is not possible, you will have to disable cache entirely.

If you have manually specified the address of the board, remember that Linux needs the actual address of the board, and not the 16-byte segment the documentation may refer to.

I.e., 0xc8000 would be correct, 0xc800 would not work and could cause memory corruption.

5.2.4 "kernel panic : cannot mount root device" when booting an ALPHA driver boot floppy

You'll need to edit the binary image of the kernel (before or after writing it out to disk), and modify a few two-byte fields (little endian) to guarantee that it will work on your system.

1. Default swap device at offset 502, this should be set to 0x00 0x00.
2. RAM disk size at offset 504, this should be set to the size of the boot floppy in K—ie, 5.25" = 1200, 3.5" = 1440.

```
This means the bytes are

3.5'' : 0xA0 0x05
5.25'' : 0xB0 0x04
```

3. Root device offset at 508, this should be 0x00 0x00, ie the boot device.

`dd` or `RAWRITE.EXE` the file to a disk. Insert the disk in the first floppy drive, wait until it prompts you to insert the root disk, and insert the root floppy from your distribution.

5.2.5 Installing a device driver not included with the distribution kernel

You need to start with the version of the kernel used by the driver author. This revision may be alluded to in the documentation included with the driver.

Various recent kernel revisions can be found at

```
nic.funet.fi:/pub/OS/Linux/PEOPLE/Linus
```

as `linux-version.tar.gz`

They are also mirrored at tsx-11.mit.edu and various other sites.

```
cd to /usr/src.
```

Remove your old Linux sources, if you want to keep a backup copy of them

```
mv linux linux-old
```

Untar the archive

```
gunzip < linux-0.99.12.tar.gz | tar xvfp -
```

Apply the patches. The patches will be relative to some directory in the filesystem. By examining the output file lines in the patch file (grep for ^—), you can tell where this is—i.e., patches with these lines

```
--- ./kernel/blk_drv/scsi/Makefile

--- ./config.in Wed Sep  1 16:19:33 1993
```

would have the files relative to /usr/src/linux.

Untar the driver sources at an appropriate place—you can type

```
tar tfv patches.tar
```

to get a listing, and move files as necessary. (The SCSI driver files should live in /usr/src/linux/kernel/drivers/scsi.)

Either cd to the directory they are relative to and type

```
patch -p0 < patch_file
```

or tell patch to strip off leading path components. I.e., if the files started with

```
--- linux-new/kernel/blk_drv/scsi/Makefile
```

and you wanted to apply them while in /usr/src/linux, you could cd to /usr/src/linux and type

```
patch -p1 < patches
```

to strip off the "linux-new" component.

After you have applied the patches, look for any patch rejects, which will be the name of the rejected file with a # suffix appended.

```
find /usr/src/linux/ -name ''*#'' -print
```

If any of these exist, look at them. In some cases, the differences will be in RCS identifiers and will be harmless, in other cases, you'll have to manually apply important parts. Documentation on diff files and patch is beyond the scope of this document.

See also Section 2.9.

5.2.6 Installing a driver that has no patches

In some cases, a driver author may not offer patches with the .c and .h files which comprise his driver, or the patches may be against an older revision of the kernel and not go in cleanly.

1. Copy the .c and .h files into /usr/src/linux/drivers/scsi.
2. Add the configuration option.
   Edit /usr/src/linux/config.in, and add a line in the

   ```
   *
   * SCSI low-level drivers
   *
   ```

   section, add a boolean configuration variable for your driver.

   ```
   bool 'Always IN2000 SCSI support' CONFIG_SCSI_IN2000 y
   ```

3. Add the makefile entries
   Edit /usr/src/linux/drivers/scsi/Makefile, and add an entry like

   ```
   ifdef CONFIG_SCSI_IN2000
   SCSI_OBS := $(SCSI_OBJS) in2000.o
   SCSI_SRCS := $(SCSI_SRCS) in2000.c
   endif
   ```

   before the

   ```
   scsi.a: $(SCSI_OBJS)
   ```

   line in the makefile, where the .c file is the .c file you copied in, and the .o file is the basename of the .c file with a .o suffixed.
4. Add the entry points
   Edit /usr/src/linux/drivers/scsi/hosts.c, and add a #include for the header file, conditional on the CONFIG_SCSI preprocessor define you added to the configuration file. I.e., after

   ```
   #ifdef CONFIG_SCSI_GENERIC_NCR5380
   #include "g_NCR5380.h"
   #endif
   ```

you might add

```
#ifdef CONFIG_SCSI_IN2000
#include "in2000.h"
#endif
```

You will also need to add the Scsi_Host_Template entry into the scsi_hosts[] array. Take a look into the .h file, and you should find a #define that looks something like this :

```
#define IN2000 {''Always IN2000'', in2000_detect, \
        in2000_info, in2000_command,          \
        in2000_queuecommand,                  \
        in2000_abort,                         \
        in2000_reset,                         \
        NULL,                                 \
        in2000_biosparam,                     \
        1, 7, IN2000_SG, 1, 0, 0}
```

the name of the preprocessor define, and add it into the scsi_hosts[] array, conditional on definition of the preprocessor symbol you used in the configuration file.
That is, after

```
#ifdef CONFIG_SCSI_GENERIC_NCR5380
        GENERIC_NCR5380,
#endif
```

you might add

```
#ifdef CONFIG_SCSI_IN2000
        IN2000,
#endif
```

See also Section 2.9.

5.2.7 Failure of a PCI board in a Compaq System

A number of Compaq systems map the 32-bit BIOS extensions used to probe for PCI devices into memory which is inaccessible to the Linux kernel due to the memory layout. If Linux is unable to detect a supported PCI SCSI board, and the kernel tells you something like

```
pcibios_init: entry in high memory, unable to access
```

Grab

```
ftp://ftp.compaq.com/pub/softpaq/Software-Solutions/sp0921.zip
```

which is a self-extracting archive of a program which will relocate the BIOS32 code.

5.2.8 A SCSI system with PCI boards hangs after the %d Hosts message

Some PCI systems have broken BIOSes which disable interrupts and fail to reenable them before returning control to the caller. The following patch fixes this

```
--- bios32.c.orig       Mon Nov 13 22:35:31 1995
+++ bios32.c    Thu Jan 18 00:15:09 1996
@@ -56,6 +56,7 @@
 #include <linux/pci.h>

 #include <asm/segment.h>
+#include <asm/system.h>

 #define PCIBIOS_PCI_FUNCTION_ID         0xb1XX
 #define PCIBIOS_PCI_BIOS_PRESENT        0xb101
@@ -125,7 +126,9 @@
```

```
        unsigned long address;          /* %ebx */
        unsigned long length;           /* %ecx */
        unsigned long entry;            /* %edx */
+       unsigned long flags;

+       save_flags(flags);
        __asm__("lcall (%%edi)"
                :"=a" (return_code),
                 "=b" (address),
@@ -134,6 +137,7 @@
                :"0" (service),
                 "1" (0),
                 "D" (&bios32_indirect));
+       restore_flags(flags);

        switch (return_code) {
                case 0:
@@ -161,11 +165,13 @@
        unsigned char present_status;
        unsigned char major_revision;
        unsigned char minor_revision;
+       unsigned long flags;
        int pack;

        if ((pcibios_entry = bios32_service(PCI_SERVICE))) {
                pci_indirect.address = pcibios_entry;

+               save_flags(flags);
                __asm__("lcall (%%edi)\n\t"
                        "jc 1f\n\t"
                        "xor %%ah, %%ah\n"
@@ -176,6 +182,7 @@
                        :"1" (PCIBIOS_PCI_BIOS_PRESENT),
                         "D" (&pci_indirect)
                        :"bx","cx");
+               restore_flags(flags);

                present_status = (pack >> 16) & 0xff;
                major_revision = (pack >> 8) & 0xff;
@@ -210,7 +217,9 @@
 {
        unsigned long bx;
        unsigned long ret;
+       unsigned long flags;

+       save_flags(flags);
        __asm__ ("lcall (%%edi)\n\t"
                "jc 1f\n\t"
                "xor %%ah, %%ah\n"
@@ -221,6 +230,7 @@
                "c" (class_code),
                "S" ((int) index),
                "D" (&pci_indirect));
+       restore_flags(flags);
        *bus = (bx >> 8) & 0xff;
        *device_fn = bx & 0xff;
        return (int) (ret & 0xff00) >> 8;
@@ -232,7 +242,9 @@
```

```
 {
        unsigned short bx;
        unsigned short ret;
+       unsigned long flags;

+       save_flags(flags);
        __asm__("lcall (%%edi)\n\t"
                "jc 1f\n\t"
                "xor %%ah, %%ah\n"
@@ -244,6 +256,7 @@
                  "d" (vendor),
                  "S" ((int) index),
                  "D" (&pci_indirect));
+       restore_flags(flags);
        *bus = (bx >> 8) & 0xff;
        *device_fn = bx & 0xff;
        return (int) (ret & 0xff00) >> 8;
@@ -254,7 +267,9 @@
 {
        unsigned long ret;
        unsigned long bx = (bus << 8) | device_fn;
+       unsigned long flags;

+       save_flags (flags);
        __asm__("lcall (%%esi)\n\t"
                "jc 1f\n\t"
                "xor %%ah, %%ah\n"
@@ -273,7 +288,9 @@
 {
        unsigned long ret;
        unsigned long bx = (bus << 8) | device_fn;
+       unsigned long flags;

+       save_flags(flags);
        __asm__("lcall (%%esi)\n\t"
                "jc 1f\n\t"
                "xor %%ah, %%ah\n"
@@ -292,7 +309,9 @@
 {
        unsigned long ret;
        unsigned long bx = (bus << 8) | device_fn;
+       unsigned long flags;

+       save_flags(flags);
        __asm__("lcall (%%esi)\n\t"
                "jc 1f\n\t''
                "xor %%ah, %%ah\n"
@@ -303,6 +322,7 @@
                  "b" (bx),
                  "D" ((long) where),
                  "S" (&pci_indirect));
+       restore_flags(flags);
        return (int) (ret & 0xff00) >> 8;
 }

@@ -311,7 +331,9 @@
 {
        unsigned long ret;
```

```
        unsigned long bx = (bus << 8) | device_fn;
+       unsigned long flags;

+       save_flags(flags);
        __asm__("lcall (%%esi)\n\t"
                "jc 1f\n\t''
                "xor %%ah, %%ah\n"
@@ -322,6 +344,7 @@
                  "b" (bx),
                  "D" ((long) where),
                  "S" (&pci_indirect));
+       restore_flags(flags);
        return (int) (ret & 0xff00) >> 8;
 }

@@ -330,7 +353,9 @@
 {
        unsigned long ret;
        unsigned long bx = (bus << 8) | device_fn;
+       unsigned long flags;

+       save_flags(flags);
        __asm__("lcall (%%esi)\n\t"
                "jc 1f\n\t"
                "xor %%ah, %%ah\n"
@@ -341,6 +366,7 @@
                  "b" (bx),
                  "D" ((long) where),
                  "S" (&pci_indirect));
+       restore_flags(flags);
        return (int) (ret & 0xff00) >> 8;
 }

@@ -349,7 +375,9 @@
 {
        unsigned long ret;
        unsigned long bx = (bus << 8) | device_fn;
+       unsigned long flags;

+       save_flags(flags);
        __asm__("lcall (%%esi)\n\t"
                "jc 1f\n\t"
                "xor %%ah, %%ah\n"
@@ -360,6 +388,7 @@
                  "b" (bx),
                  "D" ((long) where),
                  "S" (&pci_indirect));
+       restore_flags(flags);
        return (int) (ret & 0xff00) >> 8;
 }
```

5.3 Adaptec 152x, 151x, 1505, 282x, Sound Blaster 16 SCSI, SCSI Pro, Gigabyte, and other AIC 6260/6360 based products (Standard)

Supported Configurations :

```
BIOS addresses : 0xd8000, 0xdc000, 0xd0000, 0xd4000, 0xc8000, 0xcc000, 0xe0000,
                 0xe4000.
Ports          : 0x140, 0x340
```

```
IRQs            : 9, 10, 11, 12
DMA             : not used
IO              : port mapped
```

Autoprobe :

```
Works with many boards with an installed BIOS.  All
other boards, including the Adaptec 1510, and Sound Blaster16 SCSI
must use a kernel command line or compile time override.
```

Autoprobe Override :
Compile time :

```
Define PORTBASE, IRQ, SCSI_ID, RECONNECT, PARITY as appropriate, see Defines
```

Kernel command line :

```
aha152x=<PORTBASE>[,<IRQ>[,<SCSI-ID>[,<RECONNECT>[,<PARITY>]]]]
```

SCSI-ID is the SCSI ID of the host adapter, not of any devices you have installed on it. Usually, this should be 7.

To force detection at 0x340, IRQ 11, at SCSI-ID 7, allowing disconnect and reconnect, you would use the following command line option :

```
aha152x=0x340,11,7,1
```

Antiquity problems, fix by upgrading :

1. The driver fails with VLB boards. There was a timing problem in kernels older than revision 1.0.5.

Defines :

```
AUTOCONF        : use configuration the controller reports (only 152x)
IRQ             : override interrupt channel (9,10,11 or 12) (default 11)
SCSI_ID         : override SCSI ID of AIC-6260 (0-7) (default 7)
RECONNECT       : override target disconnect/reselect (set to non-zero to
                  allow, zero to disable)
DONT_SNARF      : Don't register ports (pl12 and below)
SKIP_BIOSTEST   : Don't test for BIOS signature (AHA-1510 or disabled BIOS)
PORTBASE        : Force port base. Don't try to probe
```

5.4 Adaptec 154x, AMI FastDisk VLB, DTC 329x (Standard)

Supported Configurations :

```
Ports           : 0x330 and 0x334
IRQs            : 9, 10, 11, 12, 14, 15
DMA channels    : 5, 6, 7
IO              : port mapped, bus master
```

Autoprobe :

```
will detect boards at 0x330 and 0x334 only.
```

Autoprobe override :

```
aha1542=<PORTBASE>[,<BUSON>,<BUSOFF>[,<DMASPEED>]]
```

Notes:

1. BusLogic makes a series of boards that are software compatible with the Adaptec 1542, and these come in ISA, VLB, EISA, and PCI flavors.
2. No-suffix boards, and early "A" suffix boards do not support scatter/gather, and thus don't work. However, they can be made to work for some definition of the word works if AHA1542_SCATTER is changed to 0 in drivers/scsi/aha1542.h.

Antiquity Problems, fix by upgrading :

1. Linux kernel revisions prior to .99.10 don't support the "C" revision.
2. Linux kernel revisions prior to .99.14k don't support the "C" revision options for
    - BIOS support for the extended mapping for disks > 1G;

- BIOS support for > 2 drives;
- BIOS support for auto scanning the SCSI bus.

3. Linux kernel revisions prior to .99.15e don't support the "C" with the BIOS support for > 2 drives turned on and the BIOS support for the extended mapping for disks > 1G turned off.
4. Linux kernel revisions prior to .99.14u don't support the "CF" revisions of the board.
5. Linux kernel revisions prior to 1.0.5 have a race condition when multiple devices are accessed at the same time.

Common problems :

1. There are unexpected errors with a 154xC or 154xCF board,

   Early examples of the 154xC boards have a high slew rate on one of the SCSI signals, which results in signal reflections when cables with the wrong impedance are used. Newer boards aren't much better, and also suffer from extreme cabling and termination sensitivity.

   See also Common Problems 2 and 3 and sections 5.2 and 2.1.
2. There are unexpected errors with a 154xC or 154x with both internal and external devices connected.

   This is probably a termination problem. In order to use the software option to disable host adapter termination, you must turn switch 1 off.

   See also Common Problems 1 and 3 and sections 5.2 and 2.1.
3. The SCSI subsystem locks up completely.

   There are cases where the lockups seem to occur when multiple devices are in use at the same time. In this case, you can try contacting the manufacturer of the devices and see if firmware upgrades are available which would correct the problem. As a last resort, you can go into aha1542.h and change AHA1542_MAILBOX to 1. This will effectively limit you to one outstanding command on the SCSI bus at one time, and may help the situation. If you have tape drives or slow CD-ROMdrives on the bus, this might not be a practical solution.

   See also Common Problems 1 and 2 and sections 5.2 and 2.8.
4. An "Interrupt received, but no mail" message is printed on bootup and your SCSI devices are not detected.

   Disable the BIOS options to support the extended mapping for disks > 1G, support for > 2 drives, and for auto scanning the bus. Or, upgrade to Linux .99.14k or newer.
5. If infinite timeout errors occur on "C" revision boards, you may need to go into the Adaptec setup program and enable synchronous negotiation.
6. Linux 1.2.x gives the message

   Unable to determine Adaptec DMA priority. Disabling board.

   This is due to a conflict on some systems with the obsolete BusLogic driver. Either rebuild your kernel without it, or give the BusLogic driver a command line option telling it to look somewhere other than where your controller is configured. I.e., if you have an Adaptec board at port 0x334, and nothing at 0x330, use a command line option like

   ```
   buslogic=0x330
   ```
7. The system locks up with simultaneous access to multiple devices on a 1542C or 1540C and disconnection enabled

   Some Adaptec firmware revisions have bugs. Upgrading to BIOS v2.11 purportedly fixes these problems.

5.5 Adaptec 174x

Supported Configurations :

```
Slots          : 1-8
Ports          : EISA board, not applicable
IRQs           : 9, 10, 11, 12, 14, 15
DMA Channels   : EISA board, not applicable
IO             : port mapped, bus master
```

Autoprobe :

```
works with all supported configurations
```

Autoprobe override :

```
none
```

Note:

1. This board has been discontinued by Adaptec.

Common Problems :

1. If the Adaptec 1740 driver prints the message "aha1740: Board detected, but EBCNTRL = %x, so disabled it." your board was disabled because it was not running in enhanced mode. Boards running in standard 1542 mode are not supported.

5.6 Adaptec 274x, 284x (Standard) 294x (ALPHA)

A newer version which also supports the Adaptec 294x boards is available at

```
ftp://ftp.ims.com/pub/Linux/aic7xxx
```

Supported Configurations :

```
                  274x           284x           294x
EISA Slots      : 1-12           N/A            N/A
Ports           : N/A            ALL            ALL
IRQs            : ALL            ALL            ALL
DMA Channels    : N/A            ALL            N/A

IO              : port mapped, bus master
```

Autoprobe Override :
kernel command line :

```
aha274x=extended
(to force extended mapping)
```

Notes:

1. BIOS must be enabled.
2. The B channel on 2742AT boards is ignored.
3. CONFIG_PCI must be set if you are using a PCI board.

5.7 Always IN2000 (Standard)

Supported Configurations :

```
Ports           : 0x100, 0x110, 0x200, 0x220
IRQs            : 10, 11, 14, 15
DMA             : not used
IO              : port mapped
```

Autoprobe :

```
BIOS not required
```

Autoprobe override :

```
none
```

Common Problems :

1. There are known problems in systems with IDE drives and with swapping.

5.8 BusLogic MultiMaster Host Adapters

(this section Copyright 1995 by Leonard N. Zubkoff <lnz@dandelion.com>) (see `README.BusLogic` for more complete BusLogic driver documentation)

```
                BusLogic MultiMaster SCSI Driver for Linux

                     Version 1.2.2 for Linux 1.2.13
                     Version 1.3.2 for Linux 1.3.88

                ftp://ftp.dandelion.com/BusLogic-1.2.2.tar.gz
                ftp://ftp.dandelion.com/BusLogic-1.3.2.tar.gz

                                16 April 1996

                             Leonard N. Zubkoff
                             Dandelion Digital
                             lnz@dandelion.com

BusLogic, Inc. designs and manufactures a variety of high performance SCSI host
adapters which share a common programming interface across a diverse collection
of bus architectures by virtue of their MultiMaster ASIC technology.  This
driver supports all present BusLogic MultiMaster Host Adapters, and should
support any future MultiMaster designs with little or no modification.  Host
adapters based on the new FlashPoint architecture are not supported by this
driver; consult the README.FlashPoint file for information about a program to
upgrade Linux users from the unsupported FlashPoint LT to the supported BT-948.

My primary goals in writing this completely new BusLogic driver for Linux are
to achieve the full performance that BusLogic SCSI Host Adapters and modern
SCSI peripherals are capable of, and to provide a highly robust driver that can
be depended upon for high performance mission critical applications.  All of
the major performance and error recovery features can be configured from the
Linux kernel command line, allowing individual installations to tune driver
performance and error recovery to their particular needs.

BusLogic has been an excellent company to work with and I highly recommend
their products to the Linux community.  In November 1995, I was offered the
opportunity to become a beta test site for their latest MultiMaster product,
the BT-948 PCI Ultra SCSI Host Adapter, and then again for the BT-958 PCI Wide
Ultra SCSI Host Adapter in January 1996.  This was mutually beneficial since
BusLogic received a degree and kind of testing that their own testing group
cannot readily achieve, and the Linux community has available high performance
host adapters that have been well tested with Linux even before being brought
to market.  This relationship has also given me the opportunity to interact
directly with their technical staff, to understand more about the internal
workings of their products, and in turn to educate them about the needs and
potential of the Linux community.  Their interest and support is greatly
appreciated.

Unlike some other vendors, if you contact BusLogic Technical Support with a
problem and are running Linux, they will not tell you that your use of their
products is unsupported.  Their latest product marketing literature even states
''BusLogic SCSI host adapters are compatible with all major operating systems
including: ... Linux ...''.

BusLogic, Inc. is located at 4151 Burton Drive, Santa Clara, California, 95054,
USA and can be reached by Voice at 408/492-9090 or by FAX at 408/492-1542.
BusLogic maintains a World Wide Web site at http://www.buslogic.com, an
```

```
anonymous FTP site at ftp.buslogic.com, and a BBS at 408/492-1984.  BusLogic
Technical Support can be reached by electronic mail at techsup@buslogic.com, by
Voice at 408/654-0760, or by FAX at 408/492-1542.  Contact information for
offices in Europe and Japan is available on the Web site.
```

SUPPORTED HOST ADAPTERS

The following list comprises the supported BusLogic SCSI Host Adapters as of the date of this document. It is recommended that anyone purchasing a BusLogic Host Adapter not in the following table contact the author beforehand to verify that it is or will be supported.

"W" Series Host Adapters:

BT-948 PCI Ultra Fast Single-ended SCSI-2 BT-958 PCI Ultra Wide Single-ended SCSI-2 BT-958D PCI Ultra Wide Differential SCSI-2

"C" Series Host Adapters:

BT-946C PCI Fast Single-ended SCSI-2 BT-956C PCI Fast Wide Single-ended SCSI-2 BT-956CD PCI Fast Wide Differential SCSI-2 BT-445C VLB Fast Single-ended SCSI-2 BT-747C EISA Fast Single-ended SCSI-2 BT-757C EISA Fast Wide Single-ended SCSI-2 BT-757CD EISA Fast Wide Differential SCSI-2 BT-545C ISA Fast Single-ended SCSI-2 BT-540CF ISA Fast Single-ended SCSI-2

"S" Series Host Adapters:

BT-445S VLB Fast Single-ended SCSI-2 BT-747S EISA Fast Single-ended SCSI-2 BT-747D EISA Fast Differential SCSI-2 BT-757S EISA Fast Wide Single-ended SCSI-2 BT-757D EISA Fast Wide Differential SCSI-2 BT-545S ISA Fast Single-ended SCSI-2 BT-542D ISA Fast Differential SCSI-2 BT-742A EISA Single-ended SCSI-2 (742A revision H) BT-542B ISA Single-ended SCSI-2 (542B revision H)

"A" Series Host Adapters:

BT-742A EISA Single-ended SCSI-2 (742A revisions A—G) BT-542B ISA Single-ended SCSI-2 (542B revisions A—G)

AMI FastDisk Host Adapters that are true BusLogic clones are supported by this driver.

BT-948/958/958D INSTALLATION NOTES

The BT-948/958/958D PCI Ultra SCSI Host Adapters have some features which may require attention in some circumstances when installing Linux.

o PCI I/O Port Assignments

When configured to factory default settings, the BT-948/958/958D will only recognize the PCI I/O port assignments made by the motherboard's PCI BIOS. The BT-948/958/958D will not respond to any of the ISA compatible I/O ports that previous BusLogic SCSI Host Adapters respond to. This driver supports the PCI I/O port assignments, so this is the preferred configuration. However, if the obsolete BusLogic driver must be used for any reason, such as a Linux distribution that does not yet use this driver in its boot kernel, BusLogic has provided an Auto SCSI configuration option to enable a legacy ISA compatible I/O port.

To enable this backward compatibility option, invoke the Auto SCSI utility via Ctrl-B at system startup and select "Adapter Configuration", "View/Modify Configuration", and then change the "ISA Compatible Port" setting from "Disable" to "Primary" or "Alternate". Once this driver has been installed, the "ISA Compatible Port" option should be set back to "Disable" to avoid possible future I/O port conflicts. The older BT-946C/956C/956CD also have this configuration option, but the factory default setting is "Primary".

o PCI Slot Scanning Order

In systems with multiple BusLogic PCI Host Adapters, the order in which the PCI slots are scanned may appear reversed with the BT-948/958/958D as compared to the BT-946C/956C/956CD. For booting from a SCSI disk to work correctly, it is necessary that the host adapter's BIOS and the kernel agree on which disk is the boot device, which requires that they recognize the PCI host adapters in the same order. The motherboard's PCI BIOS provides a standard way of enumerating the PCI host adapters, which is used by the Linux kernel. Some PCI BIOS implementations enumerate the PCI slots in order of increasing bus number and device number, while others do so in the opposite direction.

Unfortunately, Microsoft decided that Windows 95 would always enumerate the PCI slots in order of increasing bus number and device number regardless of the PCI BIOS enumeration, and requires that their scheme be supported by the host adapter's BIOS to receive Windows 95 certification. Therefore, the factory default settings of the BT-948/958/958D enumerate the host adapters by increasing bus number and device number. To disable this feature, invoke the Auto SCSI utility via Ctrl-B at system startup and select "Adapter Configuration", "View/Modify Configuration", press Ctrl-F10, and then change the "Use Bus And Device # For PCI Scanning Seq." option to OFF.

This driver will interrogate the setting of the PCI Scanning Sequence option so as to recognize the host adapters in the same order as they are enumerated by the host adapter's BIOS.

BUSLOGIC ANNOUNCEMENTS MAILING LIST

The BusLogic Announcements Mailing List provides a forum for informing Linux users of new driver releases and other announcements regarding Linux support for BusLogic SCSI Host Adapters. To join the mailing list, send a message to "BusLogic-announce-request@dandelion.com" with the line "subscribe" in the message body.

5.9 BusLogic FlashPoint Host Adapters

(this section Copyright 1995 by Leonard N. Zubkoff <lnz@dandelion.com>)

```
There are no Linux drivers for the FlashPoint LT/DL/LW (BT-930/932/950)
available and it is not clear when or if there will be any.  The FlashPoint
boards have a different architecture from the MultiMaster boards and have no
onboard CPU, only a SCSI sequencer engine.  They are positioned as a desktop
workstation product, and are not particularly well suited for a high
performance multitasking operating system like Linux.

The MultiMaster BT-948/958 have an onboard CPU and the mailbox programming
interface allows for parallelism and pipelining between the host operating
system and the host adapter, whereas the FlashPoint boards require frequent
host CPU intervention.  As interrupt latencies rise in a loaded multitasking
system, the BT-948/958 should maintain excellent performance whereas the
FlashPoint's performance will likely drop quite rapidly.  Furthermore, the
firmware on the BT-948/958 contains the low level knowledge for proper
interaction with the SCSI bus, whereas with a sequencer engine the Linux driver
must contain some or all of this information, and it often takes quite a long
time to get all the kinks worked out.  Given the relatively small difference in
the street price of these products, the BT-948 or BT-958 is clearly the better
choice for Linux.

<begin quotation>

                                ANNOUNCEMENT
                  BusLogic FlashPoint/BT-948 Upgrade Program
                               1 February 1996

Ever since its introduction last October, the BusLogic FlashPoint LT has
been problematic for members of the Linux community, in that no Linux
drivers have been available for this new Ultra SCSI product.  Despite it's
officially being positioned as a desktop workstation product, and not being
particularly well suited for a high performance multitasking operating
system like Linux, the FlashPoint LT has been touted by computer system
vendors as the latest thing, and has been sold even on many of their high
end systems, to the exclusion of the older MultiMaster products.  This has
caused grief for many people who inadvertently purchased a system expecting
that all BusLogic SCSI Host Adapters were supported by Linux, only to
discover that the FlashPoint was not supported and would not be for quite
some time, if ever.

After this problem was identified, BusLogic contacted its major OEM
customers to make sure the BT-946C/956C MultiMaster cards would still be
made available, and that Linux users who mistakenly ordered systems with
the FlashPoint would be able to upgrade to the BT-946C.  While this helped
many purchasers of new systems, it was only a partial solution to the
overall problem of FlashPoint support for Linux users.  It did nothing to
assist the people who initially purchased a FlashPoint for a supported
operating system and then later decided to run Linux, or those who had
ended up with a FlashPoint LT, believing it was supported, and were unable
to return it.

In the middle of December, I asked to meet with BusLogic's senior
```

management to discuss the issues related to Linux and free software support for the FlashPoint. Rumors of varying accuracy had been circulating publicly about BusLogic's attitude toward the Linux community, and I felt it was best that these issues be addressed directly. I sent an email message after 11pm one evening, and the meeting took place the next afternoon. Unfortunately, corporate wheels sometimes grind slowly, especially when a company is being acquired, and so it's taken until now before the details were completely determined and a public statement could be made.

BusLogic is not prepared at this time to release the information necessary for third parties to write drivers for the FlashPoint. The only existing FlashPoint drivers have been written directly by BusLogic Engineering, and there is no FlashPoint documentation sufficiently detailed to allow outside developers to write a driver without substantial assistance. While there are people at BusLogic who would rather not release the details of the FlashPoint architecture at all, that debate has not yet been settled either way. In any event, even if documentation were available today it would take quite a while for a usable driver to be written, especially since I'm not convinced that the effort required would be worthwhile.

However, BusLogic does remain committed to providing a high performance SCSI solution for the Linux community, and does not want to see anyone left unable to run Linux because they have a Flashpoint LT. Therefore, BusLogic has put in place a direct upgrade program to allow any Linux user worldwide to trade in their FlashPoint LT for the new BT-948 MultiMaster PCI Ultra SCSI Host Adapter. The BT-948 is the Ultra SCSI successor to the BT-946C and has all the best features of both the BT-946C and FlashPoint LT, including smart termination and a flash PROM for easy firmware updates, and is of course compatible with the present Linux driver. The price for this upgrade has been set at US \$45, and the upgrade program will be administered through BusLogic Technical Support, which can be reached by electronic mail at techsup@BusLogic.com, by Voice at +1 408 654-0760, or by FAX at +1 408 492-1542.

I was a beta test site for the BT-948 and versions 1.2.1 and 1.3.1 of my BusLogic driver already include latent support for the BT-948. Additional cosmetic support for the Ultra SCSI MultiMaster cards will be added in a subsequent release. As a result of this cooperative testing process, several firmware bugs were found and corrected (make sure you have firmware version 5.05R or later). My heavily loaded Linux test system provided an ideal environment for testing error recovery processes that are much more rarely exercised in production systems, but are crucial to overall system stability. It was especially convenient being able to work directly with their firmware engineer in demonstrating the problems under control of the firmware debugging environment; things sure have come a long way since the last time I worked on firmware for an embedded system. I am presently working on some performance testing and expect to have some data to report in the not too distant future.

BusLogic asked me to send this announcement since a large percentage of the questions regarding support for the FlashPoint have either been sent to me directly via email, or have appeared in the Linux newsgroups in which I participate. To summarize, BusLogic is offering Linux users an upgrade from the unsupported FlashPoint LT (BT-930) to the supported BT-948 for US \$45. Contact BusLogic Technical Support at techsup@BusLogic.com or +1 408 654-0760 to take advantage of their offer.

```
        Leonard N. Zubkoff
        lnz@dandelion.com
```

<end quotation>

5.10 EATA: DPT SmartCache, SmartCache Plus, SmartCache III, SmartCache IV and SmartRAID (Standard)

Supported boards: all, that support the EATA-DMA protocol.
Among them are:

```
DPT Smartcache (Plus) family:
PM2011      ISA      Fast Single-ended SCSI-2
PM2012B     EISA     Fast Single-ended SCSI-2

DPT Smartcache III family:
PM2021      ISA      Fast Single-ended SCSI-2
PM2021W     ISA      Wide Single-ended SCSI-2
PM2022      EISA     Fast Single-ended SCSI-2
PM2022W     EISA     Wide Single-ended SCSI-2
PM2024      PCI      Fast Single-ended SCSI-2
PM2024W     PCI      Wide Single-ended SCSI-2
PM2122      EISA     Fast Single-ended SCSI-2
PM2122W     EISA     Wide Single-ended SCSI-2
PM2124      PCI      Fast Single-ended SCSI-2
PM2124W     PCI      Wide Single-ended SCSI-2
PM2322      EISA     Fast Single-ended SCSI-2
PM2322W     EISA     Wide Single-ended SCSI-2

DPT Smartcache VI family:
PM2041W     ISA      Wide Single-ended SCSI-2
PM2041UW    ISA      Ultra Wide Single-ended SCSI-2
PM2042W     EISA     Wide Single-ended SCSI-2
PM2042UW    EISA     Ultra Wide Single-ended SCSI-2
PM2044W     PCI      Wide Single-ended SCSI-2
PM2044UW    PCI      Ultra Wide Single-ended SCSI-2
PM2142W     EISA     Wide Single-ended SCSI-2
PM2142UW    EISA     Ultra Wide Single-ended SCSI-2
PM2144W     PCI      Wide Single-ended SCSI-2
PM2144UW    PCI      Ultra Wide Single-ended SCSI-2
PM2322W     EISA     Wide Single-ended SCSI-2
PM2322UW    EISA     Ultra Wide Single-ended SCSI-2

DPT SmartRAID family:
PM3021      ISA      Fast Single-ended SCSI-2
PM3021W     ISA      Wide Single-ended SCSI-2
PM3122      EISA     Fast Single-ended SCSI-2
PM3122W     EISA     Wide Single-ended SCSI-2
PM3222      EISA     Fast Single-ended SCSI-2
PM3222W     EISA     Wide Single-ended SCSI-2
PM3224      PCI      Fast Single-ended SCSI-2
PM3224W     PCI      Wide Single-ended SCSI-2
PM3334W     PCI      Wide Single-ended SCSI-2
PM3334UW    PCI      Ultra Wide Single-ended SCSI-2
```

also the differential versions of the above controllers.
and some controllers from:
NEC, AT&T, SNI, AST, Olivetti, Alphatronix.
Supported Configurations :

```
Slots          : ALL
Ports          : ALL
IRQs           : ALL level & edge triggered
DMA Channels   : ISA ALL, EISA/PCI not applicable
IO             : port mapped, bus master
SCSI Channels  : ALL
```

Autoprobe :

```
works with all supported configurations
```

The latest version of the EATA-DMA driver is available on:

```
ftp.i-Connect.Net:/pub/Local/EATA/
```

Mailing list:

The EATA Mailing List provides a forum to Linux users of the EATA-DMA and EATA-PIO driver for discussions and announcements of new releases and other announcements. To join the mailing list, send a message to `linux-eata-request@i-connect.net` with the line subscribe in the message body.

`/proc/scsi` support:

To get advanced command statistics, do the following:

```
echo "eata_dma latency" >/proc/scsi/eata_dma/<driver_no>
and to switch it off again:
echo "eata_dma nolatency" >/proc/scsi/eata_dma/<driver_no>
```

Common Problems :

1. Slackware doesn't find the controller. Solution: Use one of the ascsi* bootdisks.
2. The IDE driver can detect the ST-506 interface of the EATA board in old kernels (<v1.3).
   (a) This will look like similar to one of the following 2 examples:

   ```
   hd.c: ST-506 interface disk with more than 16 heads detected,
     probably due to non-standard sector translation.  Giving up.
     (disk %d: cyl=%d, sect=63, head=64)

   hdc: probing with STATUS instead of ALTSTATUS
   hdc: MP0242 A, 0MB w/128KB Cache, CHS=0/0/0
   hdc: cannot handle disk with 0 physical heads
   hdd: probing with STATUS instead of ALTSTATUS
   hdd: MP0242 A, 0MB w/128KB Cache, CHS=0/0/0
   hdd: cannot handle disk with 0 physical heads
   ```

   If the IDE driver gets into trouble because of this, ie. you can't access your (real) IDE hardware, change the I/O Port or the IRQ of the EATA board, or both.

   (b) If the IDE driver finds hardware it can handle ie. hard disks with a capacity <=504MB, it will allocate the IO Port and IRQ, so that the eata driver can't utilize them. In this case also change I/O Port and IRQ (!= 14,15).
3. Some old SK2011 boards have a broken firmware. Please contact DPT's customer support for an update.

Notes:

1. `CONFIG_PCI` must be set if you are using a PCI board.

5.11 Future Domain 16x0 with TMC-1800, TMC-18C30, TMC-18C50, or TMC-36C70 chip

Supported Configurations :

```
BIOSs          : 2.0, 3.0, 3.2, 3.4, 3.5
BIOS Addresses : 0xc8000, 0xca000, 0xce000, 0xde000
Ports          : 0x140, 0x150, 0x160, 0x170
IRQs           : 3, 5, 10, 11, 12, 14, 15
DMA            : not used
IO             : port mapped
```

Autoprobe :

```
works with all supported configurations, requires installed BIOS
```

Autoprobe Override :

```
none
```

Antiquity Problems, fix by upgrading :

1. Old versions do not support the TMC-18C50 chip, and will fail with newer boards.
2. Old versions will not have the most current BIOS signatures for autodetection.
3. Versions prior to the one included in Linux 1.0.9 and 1.1.6 don't support the new SCSI chip or 3.4 BIOS.

Notes :

1. The Future Domain BIOS often scans for SCSI-devices from highest ID to 0, in reverse order of other SCSI BIOSes. sda will be the last "drive letter" (ie, D: rather than C:). You may also need to use a a disktab override for LILO.

5.12 Generic NCR5380 / T130B (Standard)

Supported and Unsupported Configurations :

```
Ports           : all
IRQs            : all
DMA channels    : DMA is not used
IO              : port mapped
```

Autoprobe :

```
none
```

Autoprobe Override :

```
Compile time : Define GENERIC_NCR5380_OVERRIDE to be an array of tuples
with port, irq, dma, board type---ie
#define GENERIC_NCR5380_OVERRIDE {{0x330, 5, DMA_NONE, BOARD_NCR5380}}

for a NCR5380 board at port 330, IRQ 5.

#define GENERIC_NCR5380_OVERRIDE {{0x350, 5, DMA_NONE, BOARD_NCR53C400}}

for a T130B at port 0x350.

Older versions of the code eliminate the BOARD_* entry.

The symbolic IRQs IRQ_NONE and IRQ_AUTO may be used.
```

Kernel command line :

```
ncr5380=port,irq
ncr5380=port,irq,dma
ncr53c400=port,irq

255 may be used for no irq, 254 for irq autoprobe.
```

Common Problems :

1. Using the T130B board with the old (pre public release 6) generic NCR5380 driver which doesn't support the ncr53c400 command line option. The NCR5380 compatible registers are offset eight from the base address. So, if your address is 0x350, use

   ```
   ncr5380=0x358,254
   ```

   on the kernel command line.

Antiquity problems, fix by upgrading :

1. The kernel locks up during disk access with T130B or other NCR53c400 boards. Pre-public release 6 versions of the Generic NCR5380 driver didn't support interrupts on these boards. Upgrade.

Notes :

1. The generic driver doesn't support DMA yet, and pseudo-DMA isn't supported in the generic driver.

5.13 NCR53c8xx (Standard)

Supported and Unsupported Configurations :

```
Base addresses : ALL
IRQs           : ALL
DMA channels   : PCI, not applicable
IO             : port mapped, busmastering
```

Autoprobe :

```
requires PCI BIOS, uses PCI BIOS routines to
search for devices and read configuration space
```

The driver uses the pre-programmed values in some registers for initialization, so a BIOS must be installed.
Antiquity problems, fix by upgrading :

1. Older versions of Linux had a problem with swapping. See Section 6.2.7
2. Older versions of Linux didn't recognize '815 and '825 boards.
3. Distribution kernels include release 4 or 5 of the driver, which does not support useful things like disconnect/reconnect (the most noticeable effect of this being attempts to re-tension/rewind/file space a tape lock you out of all SCSI devices), multiple host adapters, and BIOS-less operation. The latest release of the driver is available at

   ```
   ftp://tsx-11.mit.edu/pub/linux/ALPHA/scsi/ncr53c810
   ```

   Currently, this is a 1.2.10 and newer patch, although the next release will be 1.3.*x* exclusively. These patches are not entirely clean due to some ELF and other patches which were in the baseline revision of my source tree, and if you can't manually correct the (four) problems you should get, you shouldn't use them. Note that only the newest patch is needed; these are not incremental.

   If you wish to run the newer NCR driver with a 1.3.*x* kernel before then, Harald Evensen <Harald.Evensen@pvv.unit.no> has adapted the patches for 1.3.*x*

   ```
   ftp://ftp.pvv.unit.no/pub/Linux/ALPHA/ncr
   ```

   These patches should be clean.

   Please see all of the `README`s in these directories. You should also join the NCR mailing list if you are interested in running the Alpha code, since interim bug fixes and announcements of the next release are posted to this list.

   To subscribe, send mail to `majordomo@colorado.edu` with

   ```
   subscribe ncr53c810
   ```

   in the text. You can unsubscribe by sending mail to the same address and including

   ```
   unsubscribe ncr53c810
   ```

   in the text.

Common Problems :

1. Many people have encountered problems where the chip worked fine under DOS, but failed under Linux with a timeout on test 1 due to a lost interrupt. This is often due to a mismatch between the IRQ hardware jumper for a slot or main board device and the value set in the CMOS setup. Double check:

   - The IRQ you are using is used only by your onboard NCR chip, or the slot an NCR board is installed in;
   - Any main board jumpers selecting the IRQ for the onboard chip or slot match your CMOS setup;
   - Some PCI main boards have an "auto" assignment feature, which will not work.

   It may also be due to PCI INTB, INTC, or INTD being selected on a PCI board in a system which only supports PCI INTA. If you are using an NCR board which has jumpers to select between PCI interrupt lines, make sure you are using INTA.

   Finally, PCI should be using level-sensitive rather than edge triggered interrupts. Check that your board is jumpered for level-sensitive, and if that fails try edge-triggered because your system may be broken.

   This problem is especially common with Viglen some Viglen motherboards, where the main board IRQ jumper settings are NOT as documented in the manual. I've been told that what claims to be IRQ 5 is really IRQ 9, your mileage will vary.

2. Lockups or other problems occur when using an S3 928, or Tseng ET4000W32 PCI video board.

   There are hardware bugs in at least some revisions of these chips. Don't use them.

3. You get a message on boot up indicating that the I/O mapping was disabled because base address 0 bits 0..1 indicated a non-I/O mapping.

   This is due to a BIOS bug in some machines which results in dword reads of configuration registers returning the high and low 16-bit words swapped.

4. Some systems have problems if PCI write posting, or CPU-> PCI buffering are enabled. If you have problems, disable these options.

5. Some systems with the NCR SDMS software in an onboard BIOS.

   ROM and in the system BIOS are unable to boot DOS. Disabling the image in one place should rectify this problem.

6. If you encounter the message

   ```
   ''scsi%d: IRQ0 not free, detaching''
   ```

   or

   ```
   ''scsi%d: IRQ255 not free, detaching''
   ```

   The NCR chip has all 0 or 1 bits stored in the PCI configuration register. Either you have configuration problems (see 1), or you have a defective main board BIOS.

   As a work around, you could edit drivers/scsi/ncr53c7,8xx.c, and change pci_init() so that you have

   ```
   irq = my_irq;
   ```

   before

   ```
   return normal_init (tpnt, board, chip, (int) base,
       (int) io_port, (int) irq, DMA_NONE, 1, bus, device_fn,
       options);
   ```

7. Some systems have hideous, broken, BIOS chips. Don't make any bug reports until you've made sure you have the newest ROM from your vendor.

8. The command line overrides ncr53c810=xxx, etc. don't work.

   In stock kernels, this is because their entry points are not included in `init/main.c`, which is quite intentional : The driver makes no attempt to avoid auto probing for a board where a command line override was used, so if an override is used where the board actually showed up to the PCI configuration routines, you'll have big problems.

   The only reason you would need an override would be if the PCI hardware + BIOS were broken, in which case certain error recovery routines wouldn't work, rendering the override less than useful.

   Finally, nearly all of people who think they need a command line override do because they get configuration or other error messages from the driver. If the driver says you have a configuration problem, you have a broken system or a configuration problem and no override is going to fix this.

   If some one has gone and added the appropriate entry points to init/main.c for command line overrides, they are totally unsupported and may not work.

9. Certain NCR boards (most notably Nexstor) which don't use an NCR BIOS get timeouts. Some of these ROMs handle synchronous and transfers, negotiate for sync. transfers on power up, and leave the drives in an unknown state. When the distribution Linux NCR driver attempts to talk with them, it gets timeouts and cannot recover because it won't do a bus reset or renegotiate.

   If you run into this problem, you can either disable synchronous transfers in the board's setup program, or upgrade to a newer Alpha release of the NCR driver which will do synchronous negotiation.

10. Tyan S1365 '825 boards have problems with timeouts, especially when disconnects are enabled. Some of these boards have the documentation regarding the termination enable jumper reversed—so that termination is off when you need it, and on when it shouldn't be.

    Try reversing the position of the jumper.

Notes:

1. CONFIG_PCI must be set

5.14 Seagate ST0x/Future Domain TMC-8xx/TMC-9xx (Standard)

Supported and Unsupported Configurations :

```
Base addresses : 0xc8000, 0xca000, 0xcc000, 0xce000, 0xdc000, 0xde000
IRQs           : 3, 5
DMA channels   : DMA is not used
IO             : memory mapped
```

Autoprobe :

```
probes for address only, IRQ is assumed to be 5, requires installed BIOS.
```

Autoprobe Override :

Compile time :

```
Define OVERRIDE to be the base address, CONTROLLER to
FD or SEAGATE as appropriate, and IRQ to the IRQ.
```

Kernel command line :

```
st0x=address,irq or tmc8xx=address,irq (only works for .99.13b and newer)
```

Antiquity problems, fix by upgrading:

1. Versions prior to the one in the Linux .99.12 kernel had a problem handshaking with some slow devices, where This is what happens when you write data out to the bus
   (a) Write byte to data register, data register is asserted to bus;
   (b) time_remaining = 12μs;
   (c) wait while time_remaining > 0 and REQ is not asserted;
   (d) if time_remaining > 0, assert ACK;
   (e) wait while time remaining > 0 and REQ is asserted;
   (f) de-assert ACK.

   The problem was encountered in slow devices that do the command processing as they read the command, where the REQ/ACK handshake takes over 12μs—REQ didn't go false when the driver expected it to, so the driver ended up sending multiple bytes of data for each REQ pulse.
2. With Linux .99.12, a bug was introduced when I fixed the arbitration code, resulting in failed selections on some systems. This was fixed in .99.13.

Common Problems :

1. There are command timeouts when Linux attempts to read the partition table or do other disk access. The board ships with the defaults set up for MS-DOS, i.e., interrupts are disabled. To jumper the board for interrupts, on the Seagate use jumper W3 (ST01) or JP3 (ST02) and short pins F-G to select IRQ 5.
2. The driver can't handle some devices, particularly cheap SCSI tapes and Cd-ROMs.

   The Seagate ties the SCSI bus REQ/ACK handshaking into the PC bus I/O CHANNEL READY and (optionally) 0WS signals. Unfortunately, it doesn't tell you when the watchdog timer runs out, and you have no way of knowing for certain that REQ went low, and may end up seeing one REQ pulse as multiple REQ pulses.

   Dealing with this means using a tight loop to look for REQ to go low, with a timeout in case you don't catch the transition due to an interrupt, etc. This results in a performance decrease, so it would be undesirable to apply this to all SCSI devices. Instead, it is selected on a per-device basis with the "broken" field for the given SCSI device in the scsi_devices array. If you run into problems, you should try adding your device to the list of devices for which broken is not reset to zero (currently, only the TENEX CD-ROM drives).
3. A future domain board (specific examples include the 840, 841, 880, and 881) doesn't work.

   A few of the Future domain boards use the Seagate register mapping, and have the MSG and CD bits of the status register flipped.

   You should edit seagate.h, swapping the definitions for STAT_MSG and STAT_CD, and recompile the kernel with CONTROLLER defined to SEAGATE and an appropriate IRQ and OVERRIDE specified.
4. When attempting to fdisk your drive, you get error messages indicating that the HDIO_REQ or HDIO_GETGEO ioctl failed, or

```
You must set heads sectors and cylinders.
You can do this from the extra functions menu.
```

See Section 6.4

5. After manually specifying the drive geometry, subsequent attempts to read the partition table result in partition boundary not on a cylinder boundary, physical and logical boundaries don't match, etc. error messages.
   See Section 6.4
6. Some systems which worked prior to .99.13 fail with newer versions of Linux. Older versions of Linux assigned the CONTROL and DATA registers in an order different than that outlined in the Seagate documentation, which broke on some systems. Newer versions make the assignment in the correct way, but this breaks other systems.

The code in seagate.c looks like this now :

```
cli();
DATA = (unsigned char) ((1 << target) |
(controller_type == SEAGATE ? 0x80 : 0x40));
CONTROL = BASE_CMD | CMD_DRVR_ENABLE | CMD_SEL |
        (reselect ? CMD_ATTN : 0);
sti();
```

Changing this to

```
cli();
CONTROL = BASE_CMD | CMD_DRVR_ENABLE | CMD_SEL |
        (reselect ? CMD_ATTN : 0);
DATA = (unsigned char) ((1 {\(<\)}{\(<\)} target) |
(controller_type == SEAGATE ? 0x80 : 0x40));
sti();
```

may fix your problem.

Defines :

```
FAST or FAST32 will use blind transfers where possible

ARBITRATE will cause the host adapter to arbitrate for the
        bus for better SCSI-II compatibility, rather than just
        waiting for BUS FREE and then doing its thing.  Should
        let us do one command per Lun when I integrate my
        reorganization changes into the distribution sources.

SLOW_HANDSHAKE will allow compatibility with broken devices that don't
        handshake fast enough (ie, some CD ROM's) for the Seagate
        code.

SLOW_RATE=x, x some number will let you specify a default
        transfer rate if handshaking isn't working correctly.
```

5.15 PAS16 SCSI (Standard)

Supported and Unsupported Configurations :

```
Ports          : 0x388, 0x384, 0x38x, 0x288
IRQs           : 10, 12, 14, 15
     IMPORTANT : IRQ MUST be different from the IRQ used for the sound
                 portion of the board.
DMA            : is not used for the SCSI portion of the board
IO             : port mapped
```

Autoprobe :

```
does not require BIOS
```

Autoprobe Override :

```
Compile time : Define PAS16_OVERRIDE to be an array of port, irq
tuples.  Ie

#define PAS16_OVERRIDE {{0x388, 10}}

for a board at port 0x388, IRQ 10.
```

Kernel command line :

```
pas16=port,irq
```

Defines :

```
AUTOSENSE - if defined, REQUEST SENSE will be performed automatically
for commands that return with a CHECK CONDITION status.

PSEUDO_DMA---enables PSEUDO-DMA hardware, should give a 3-4X performance
increase compared to polled I/O.

PARITY---enable parity checking.  Not supported

SCSI2---enable support for SCSI-II tagged queuing.  Untested


UNSAFE---leave interrupts enabled during pseudo-DMA transfers.  You
         only really want to use this if you're having a problem with
         dropped characters during high speed communications, and even
         then, you're going to be better off twiddling with transfer size.

USLEEP---enable support for devices that don't disconnect.  Untested.
```

Common problems :

1. Command timeouts, aborts, etc. You should install the NCR5380 patches that I posted to the net some time ago, which should be integrated into some future alpha release. These patches fix a race condition in earlier NCR5380 driver cores, as well as fixing support for multiple devices on NCR5380 based boards.

   If that fails, you should disable the PSEUDO_DMA option by changing the #define PSEUDO_DMA line in `drivers/scsi/pas16.c` to `#undef PSEUDO_DMA`.

   Note that the later should be considered a last resort, because there will be a severe performance degradation.

5.16 Trantor T128/T128F/T228 (Standard)

Supported and Unsupported Configurations :

```
Base addresses :  0xcc000, 00xc8000, 0xdc000, 0xd8000
IRQs           : none, 3, 5, 7 (all boards)
                 10, 12, 14, 15 (T128F only)
DMA            : not used.
IO             : memory mapped
```

Autoprobe :

```
works for all supported configurations, requires installed BIOS.
```

Autoprobe Override :

```
Compile time : Define T128_OVERRIDE to be an array of address, irq
tuples.  Ie

#define T128_OVERRIDE {{0xcc000, 5}}

for a board at address 0xcc000, IRQ 5.

The symbolic IRQs IRQ_NONE and IRQ_AUTO may be used.
```

Kernel command line :

```
t128=address,irq
-1 may be used for no irq, -2 for irq autoprobe.
```

Defines :

```
AUTOSENSE---if defined, REQUEST SENSE will be performed automatically
for commands that return with a CHECK CONDITION status.

PSEUDO_DMA---enables PSEUDO-DMA hardware, should give a 3-4X performance
increase compared to polled I/O.

PARITY---enable parity checking.  Not supported

SCSI2---enable support for SCSI-II tagged queuing.  Untested

UNSAFE---leave interrupts enabled during pseudo-DMA transfers.  You
         only really want to use this if you're having a problem with
         dropped characters during high speed communications, and even
         then, you're going to be better off twiddling with transfer size.

USLEEP---enable support for devices that don't disconnect.  Untested.
```

Common Problems :

1. Command timeouts, aborts, etc.

   You should install the NCR5380 patches that I posted to the net some time ago, which should be integrated into some future alpha release. These patches fix a race condition in earlier NCR5380 driver cores, as well as fixing support for multiple devices on NCR5380 based boards. If that fails, you should disable the PSEUDO_DMA option by changing the #define PSEUDO_DMA line in `drivers/scsi/pas16.c` to `#undef PSEUDO_DMA`.

   Note that the later should be considered a last resort, because there will be a severe performance degradation.

5.17 Ultrastor 14f (ISA), 24f (EISA), 34f (VLB) (Standard)

Supported Configurations :

```
Ports          : 0x130, 0x140, 0x210, 0x230, 0x240, 0x310, 0x330, 0x340
IRQs           : 10, 11, 14, 15
DMA channels   : 5, 6, 7
IO             : port mapped, bus master
```

Autoprobe :

```
does not work for boards at port 0x310, BIOS not required.
```

Autoprobe override :

```
compile time only, define PORT_OVERRIDE
```

Common Problems :

1. The address 0x310 is not supported by the autoprobe code, and may cause conflicts if networking is enabled. Please use a different address.
2. Using an Ultrastor at address 0x330 may cause the system to hang when the sound drivers are auto probing. Please use a different address.
3. Various other drivers do unsafe probes at various addresses, if you are having problems with detection or the system is hanging at boot time, please try a different address.

   0x340 is recommended as an address that is known to work.
4. Linux detects no SCSI devices, but detects your SCSI hard disk on an Ultrastor SCSI board as a normal hard disk, and the hard disk driver refuses to support it. Note that when this occurs, you will probably also get a message `hd.c`: ST-506 interface disk with more than 16 heads detected, probably due to non-standard sector translation. Giving up. (disk %d: cyl=%d, sect=63, head=64)

   If this is the case, you are running the Ultrastor board in WD1003 emulation mode. You have

(a) Switch the Ultrastor into native mode. This is the recommended action, since the SCSI driver can be significantly faster than the IDE driver, especially with the clustered read/write patches installed. Some users have sustained in excess of 2M/sec through the file system using these patches.

Note that this will be necessary if you wish to use any non- hard disk, or more than two hard disk devices on the Ultrastor.

(b) Use the kernel command line switch

```
hd=cylinders,heads,sectors
```

to override the default setting to bootstrap yourself, keeping number of cylinders <= 2048, number of heads <= 16, and number of sectors <= 255 such that cylinders * heads * sectors is the same for both mappings.

You'll also have to manually specify the disk geometry when running fdisk under Linux. Failure to do so will result in incorrect partition entries being written, which will work correctly with Linux but fail under MS-DOS which looks at the cylinder/head/sector entries in the table.

Once Linux is up, you can avoid the inconvenience of having to boot by hand by recompiling the kernel with an appropriately defined HD_TYPE macro in `include/linux/config.h`.

5.18 Western Digital 7000 (Standard)

Supported Configurations :

```
BIOS Addresses : 0xce000
Ports          : 0x350
IRQs           : 15
DMA Channels   : 6
IO             : port mapped, bus master
```

Autoprobe :

```
requires installed BIOS
```

Common Problems :

1. There are several revisions of the chip and firmware. Supposedly, revision 3 boards do not work, revision 5 boards do, chips with no suffix do not work, chips with an 'A' suffix do.
2. The board supports a few BIOS addresses which aren't on the list of supported addresses. If you run into this situation, please use one of the supported addresses and submit a bug report as outlined in 3.

5.19 AM53/79C974 (ALPHA)

`ftp://tsx-11.mit.edu/pub/linux/ALPHA/scsi/AM53C974-0.3.tar.gz`

Supported Configurations :

```
Ports          : all
IRQs           : all
DMA Channels   : 6
IO             : port mapped, bus master (unintelligent)
```

6 Disks

This section gives information that is specific to disk drives.

6.1 Supported and Unsupported Hardware

All direct access SCSI devices with a block size of 256, 512, or 1024 bytes should work. Other block sizes will not work. (Note that this can often be fixed by changing the block or sector sizes using the MODE SELECT SCSI command.)

Sector size refers to the number of data bytes allocated per sector on a device, ie CD-ROMs use a 2048 byte sector size.

Block size refers to the size of the logical blocks used to interface with the device. Although this is usually identical to sector size, some devices map multiple smaller physical sectors (ie, 256 bytes in the case of 55M Syquest drives) to larger logical blocks or vice versa (ie, 512 byte blocks on SUN compatible CDROM drives).

Removable media devices, including Bernoulis, flopticals, MO drives, and Syquests.

In theory, drives up to a terabyte in size should work. There is definitely no problem with tiny 9G drives.

6.2 Common Problems

6.2.1 Cylinder > 1024 message

When partitioning, you get a warning message about "cylinder > 1024" or you are unable to boot from a partition including a logical cylinder past logical cylinder 1024.

This is a BIOS limitation.

See sections 6.5 and 6.4 for an explanation.

6.2.2 You are unable to partition "`/dev/hd*`"

`/dev/hd*` aren't SCSI devices, `/dev/sd*` are.

See sections 6.3, 6.5, and 6.4 for the correct device names and partitioning procedure.

6.2.3 Unable to eject media from a removable media drive

Linux attempts to lock the drive door when a piece of media is mounted to prevent file system corruption due to an inadvertent media change.

Please unmount your disks before ejecting them.

6.2.4 Unable to boot using LILO from a SCSI disk

In some cases, the SCSI driver and BIOS will disagree over the correct BIOS mapping to use, and will result in LILO hanging after "LI" at boot time or other problems.

To workaround this, you'll have to determine your BIOS geometry mapping used under DOS, and make an entry for your disk in `/etc/lilo/disktab`.

Alternatively, you may be able to use the "linear" configuration file option.

6.2.5 Fdisk responds with

```
You must set heads sectors and cylinders.
You can do this from the extra functions menu.
```

and disk geometry is not "remembered" when fdisk is rerun.

See Section 6.4.

6.2.6 Only one drive is detected on a bridge board with multiple drives connected.

Linux won't search LUNs past zero on SCSI devices which predate ANSI SCSI revision 1. If you wish devices on alternate LUNs to be recognized, you will have to modify `drivers/scsi/scsi.c:scan_scsis()`.

6.2.7 System hangs when swapping

We think this has been fixed, try upgrading to 1.1.38.

6.2.8 Connor CFP1060S disks get corrupted

This is due to a microcode bug in the read-ahead and caching code.

From Soenke Behrens of Conner tech. support :

```
During the past few weeks, we got several calls from customers stating
that they had severe problems with Conner CFP1060x 1GB SCSI drives
using the Linux operating system. Symptoms were corrupt filesystems
(damaged inodes) reported by e2fsck on each system boot and similar
errors.

There is now a fix available for customers with a CFP1060x (microcode
revisions 9WA1.62/1.66/1.68) and Linux. To apply the upgrade, you
will need a DOS boot disk and ASPI drivers that can access the hard
drive. The upgrade downloads new queuing and lookahead code into the
```

```
non-volatile SCSI RAM of the drive.

If you are experiencing problems with a disk that has microcode
revision 9WA1.60, you will have to contact your nearest Conner service
center to get the disk upgraded. The microcode revision can be found
on the label of the drive and on the underside of the drive on a label
on one of the ICs.

If you are confident that you can perform the upgrade yourself, please
contact Conner Technical Support and have your microcode revision
ready. Conner Technical Support Europe can be reached on +44 1294-315333,
Conner Technical Support in the USA can be reached on 1-800-4CONNER.

Regards
Soenke Behrens
European Technical Support
```

6.3 Device Files

SCSI disks use block device major 8, and there are no "raw" devices ala BSD.

16 minor numbers are allocated to each SCSI disk, with minor % 16 == 0 being the whole disk, minors 1 <= (minor % 16) <= 4 the four primary partitions, minors 5 <= (minor % 16) <= 15 any extended partitions.

That is, a configuration may work out like this (with one host adapter)

```
Device                  Target, Lun     SCSI disk
84M Seagate             0       0       /dev/sda
SCSI->SMD bridge disk 0 3       0       /dev/sdb
SCSI->SMD bridge disk 1 3       1       /dev/sdc
Wangtek tape            4       0       none
213M Maxtor             6       0       /dev/sdd
```

Etc.

The standard naming convention is

/dev/sd{letter} for the entire disk device ((minor % 16) == 0) /dev/sd{letter}{partition} for the partitions on that device (1 <= (minor % 16) <= 15)

That is,

```
/dev/sda        block device major 8 minor 0
/dev/sda1       block device major 8 minor 1
/dev/sda2       block device major 8 minor 2
/dev/sdb        block device major 8 minor 16
```

etc.

6.4 Partitioning

You can partition your SCSI disks using the partitioning program of your choice, under DOS, OS/2, Linux or any other operating system supporting the standard partitioning scheme.

The correct way to run the Linux `fdisk` program is by specifying the device on the command line. I.e., to partition the first SCSI disk,

```
fdisk /dev/sda
```

If you don't explicitly specify the device, the partitioning program may default to /dev/hda, which isn't a SCSI disk. In some cases, `fdisk` will respond with

```
You must set heads sectors and cylinders.
You can do this from the extra functions menu.

Command (m for help):
```

or give a message to the effect that the HDIO_REQ or HDIO_GETGEO ioctl failed. In these cases, you must manually specify the disk geometry as outlined in 6.5 when running `fdisk`, and also in `/etc/disktab` if you wish to boot kernels off that disk with LILO.

If you have manually specified the disk geometry, subsequent attempts to run fdisk will give the same error message. This is normal, since PCs don't store the disk geometry information in the partition table. In and of itself, will cause no problems, and you will have no problems accessing partitions you created on the drive with Linux. Some vendors' poor installation code will choke on this, in which case you should contact your vendor and insist that they fix the code.

In some cases, you will get a warning message about a partition ending past cylinder 1024. If you create one of these partitions, you will be unable to boot Linux kernels off of that partition using LILO. Note, however, that this restriction does not preclude the creation of a root partition partially or entirely above the 1024 cylinder mark, since it is possible to create a small `/boot` partition below the 1024 cylinder mark or to boot kernels off existing partitions.

6.5 Disk Geometry

Under Linux, each disk is viewed as the SCSI host adapter sees it : N blocks, numbered from 0 to N-1, all error free, whereas DOS/BIOS predate intelligent disks and apply an arbitrary head / cylinder / sector mapping to this linear addressing.

This can pose a problem when you partition the drives under Linux, since there is no portable way to get DOS/BIOS's idea of the mapped geometry. In most cases, a HDIO_GETGEO ioctl() can be implemented to return this mapping. Unfortunately, when the vendor (i.e., Seagate) has chosen a perverse, non-standard, and undocumented mapping, this is not possible and geometry must be manually specified.

If manual specification of the is required, you have one of several options:

1. If you don't care about using DOS, or booting kernels from the drive with LILO, create a translation such that heads * cylinders * sectors * 512 < size of your drive in bytes (a megabyte is defined as 2^20 bytes).

   ```
   1 <= heads <= 256
   1 <= cylinders <= 1024
   1 <= sectors <= 63
   ```

2. Use the BIOS mapping. In some cases, this will mean reconfiguring the disk so that it is at SCSI ID 0, and disabling the second IDE drive (if you have one).

You can either use a program like NU, or you can use the following program :

```
begin 664 dparam.com
MBAZ''##_B+^!'+N!'(H'0SP@=/D\,'5:@#]X='6'/UAU4(!_'3AU2H!_'P!U
M1(I7'H#J,(#Z'7<Y@,*'M'C-$PCD=3-14HC()#\PY.@R'.@J'%J(\/[',.3H
M)0#H'0!8AL2Q!M+L0.@7'+K"';0)S2'#NIP!ZR"ZQ0'K&[K5'>L6N]T!,=*Y
M"@#W\8#",$N(%PG'=>^)VK0)S2'#=7-A9V4Z(&1P87)A;2'P>#@P#0H@("!O
L<B'@9'!A<F%M(#!X.#$-"B1);G9A;&ED(&1R:79E#0HD("'D'''''''D''!O
'
end
```

When run, it prints the sectors, heads, and cylinders of the drive whose BIOS address was specified on the command line (0x80 is the first disk, 0x81 the second).

I.e., dparam 0x80

```
60      17      1007
```

Would mean that C: had 60 sectors, 17 heads, and 1007 cylinders.

7 CD ROMs

This section gives information that is specific to CD-ROM drives.

7.1 Supported and Unsupported Hardware

SCSI CDs with a block size of 512 or 2048 bytes should work. Other block sizes will not work.

7.2 Common Problems

7.2.1 Unable to mount CD-ROM

The correct syntax to mount an ISO 9660 CD-ROM is

```
mount -t iso9660 /dev/sr0 /mount_point -o ro
```

Note that for this to work, you must have the kernel configured with support for SCSI, your host adapter, the SCSI CD-ROM driver, and the ISO 9660 filesystem.

Note that as of Linux 1.1.32, read-only devices such as CD-ROMs cannot be mounted with the default read/write options.

7.2.2 Unable to eject CD-ROM

Linux attempts to lock the drive door when a piece of media is mounted to prevent file system corruption due to an inadvertent media change.

7.2.3 Unable to play audio

The programs `workman` or `xcdplayer` will do this for you.

7.2.4 `workman` or `xcdplayer` do not work

The functions to control audio functions are part of the SCSI-II command set, so any drive that is not SCSI-II will probably not work here. Also, many SCSI-I and some SCSI-II CDROM drives use a proprietary command set for accessing audio functions instead of the SCSI-II command set. For NEC drives, there is a version of xcdplayer specially adapted to use this command set floating around—try looking on tsx-11.mit.edu in `pub/linux/BETA/cdrom`.

These programs may work with some of the non-SCSI CD-ROMdrives if the driver implements the same ioctls as the SCSI drivers.

7.2.5 Additional drives on CD-ROM changers do not work

Most CD changers assign each disc to a logical unit. Insure that you have special files made for each platter (see sections 6.3 and 2.10).

7.3 Device Files

SCSI CD-ROMs use major 11.

Minors are allocated dynamically (See sections 6 and 6.3 for an example) with the first CDROM found being minor 0, the second minor 1, etc.

The standard naming convention is
/dev/sr{digit}, although some distributions have used /dev/scd{digit}, with examples being

```
/dev/sr0          /dev/scd0
/dev/sr1          /dev/scd1
```

8 Tapes

This section gives information that is specific to SCSI tape drives.

8.1 Supported and Unsupported Hardware

Drives using both fixed and variable length blocks smaller than the the driver buffer length (set to 32K in the distribution sources) are supported.

Parameters (block size, buffering, density) are set with ioctls (usually with the `mt` program), and remain in effect after the device is closed and reopened.

Virtually all drives should work, including :

- Archive Viper QIC drives, including the 150M and 525M models,
- Exabyte 8mm drives,
- Wangtek 5150S drives,
- Wangdat DAT drives.

8.2 Common Problems

8.2.1 Tape drive not recognized at boot time

Try booting with a tape in the drive.

8.2.2 Tapes with multiple files cannot be read properly

When reading a tape with multiple files, the first `tar` is successful, a second `tar` fails silently, and retrying the second `tar` is successful.

User level programs, such as `tar`, don't understand file marks. The first `tar` reads up until the end of the file. The second `tar` attempts to read at the file mark, gets nothing, but the tape spaces over the file mark. The third `tar` is successful since the tape is at the start of the next file.

Use `mt` on the no-rewind device to space forward to the next file.

8.2.3 Decompression fails

Decompressing programs cannot handle the zeros padding the last block of the file.

To prevent warnings and errors, wrap your compressed files in a .tar file—ie, rather than doing

```
tar cfvz /dev/nrst0 file.1 file.2 ...
```

do

```
tar cfvz tmp.tar.z file.1 file.2 ...

tar cf /dev/nrst0 tmp.tar.z
```

8.2.4 Problems taking tapes to or from other systems

You can't read a tape made with another operating system or another operating system can't read a tape written in Linux.

Different systems often use different block sizes. On a tape device using a fixed block size, you will get errors when reading blocks written using a different block size.

To read these tapes, you must set the block size of the tape driver to match the block size used when the tape was written, or to variable.

NOTE : this is the hardware block size, not the blocking factor used with `tar`, `dump`, etc.

You can do this with the `mt` command:

```
mt setblk <size>
```

or

```
mt setblk 0
```

to get variable block length support.

Note that these `mt` flags are not supported under the GNU version of `mt` which is included with some Linux distributions. Instead, you must use the BSD derived Linux SCSI mt command. Source should be available from

```
tsx-11.mit.edu:/pub/linux/ALPHA/scsi
```

Also note that by default, ST_BUFFER_BLOCKS (defined in `/usr/src/linux/drivers/scsi/st_options.h` in newer kernels, `st.c` in older kernels) is set to allow for a 32K maximum buffer size; you'll need to edit the source to use larger blocks.

8.2.5 "No such device" error message

All attempts to access the tape result in a

"No such device"

or similar error message. Check the type of your tape device—it must be a character device with major and minor numbers matching those specified in Section 6.3.

8.2.6 Tape reads at a given density work, writes fail

Many tape drives support reading at lower densities for compatibility with older hardware, but will not write at those same densities.

This is especially the case with QIC drives, which will read old 60M tapes but only write new 120, 150, 250, and 525M formats.

8.2.7 Repositioning the tape locks out access to all SCSI devices

This is most common with SCSI drivers which only support one outstanding command at a time (see Section 10.5 for an explanation, and Section 10.7 to see which drivers suffer from this limitation), although there may be a few tape drives out there which refuse to disconnect.

In either case, you can work around the problem by editing `drivers/scsi/st.c` and adding a

```
#define ST_NOWAIT
```

at the top and rebuilding the kernel.

Note that this will defer error condition reporting until the next SCSI command is executed. For this reason, you may want to do something like a

```
mt status
```

after a `mt` file positioning command so you don't overwrite tape files if the positioning command failed.

You may also wish to consider changing to a better-supported SCSI board or newer tape drive if you need to use this workaround and are writing multiple files to tapes.

8.3 Device Files

SCSI tapes use character device major 9.

Due to constraints imposed by Linux's use of a 16-bit dev_t with only eight bits allocated to the minor number, the SCSI tape minor numbers are assigned dynamically starting with the lowest SCSI HOST, ID, or LUN.

Rewinding devices are numbered from 0—with the first SCSI tape, `/dev/rst0` being `c 9 0`, the second `/dev/rst1`, `c 9 1`, etc. Non-rewinding devices have the high bit set in the minor number; i.e., `/dev/nrst0` is `c 9 128`.

The standard naming convention is

```
/dev/nst{digit}        for non-rewinding devices
/dev/st{digit}                for rewinding devices
```

9 Generic

This information gives information that is specific to the generic SCSI driver.

9.1 Supported Hardware

The Generic SCSI device driver provides an interface for sending SCSI commands to all SCSI devices—disks, tapes, Cd-ROMs, media changer robots, etc.

Everything electrically compatible with your SCSI board should work.

9.2 Common Problems

None.

9.3 Device Files

SCSI generic devices use character major 21. Due to constraints imposed by Linux's use of a 16-bit dev_t, minor numbers are dynamically assigned from 0, one per device, with

```
/dev/sg0
```

corresponding to the lowest numerical target/lun on the first SCSI board.

10 Buyers' Guide

A frequent question is:

"Linux supports quite a number of different boards, so which SCSI host adapter should I get?

The answer depends upon how much performance you expect or need, motherboard, and the SCSI peripherals that you plan on attaching to your machine.

10.1 Transfer types

The biggest factor affecting performance (in terms of throughput and interactive response time during SCSI I/O) is the transfer type used. The table below lists the various transfer types, the effects they have on performance, and some recommendations as to their use.

Transfer type

Description / Performance / Recommendations

Pure Polled

A pure polled I/O board will use the CPU to handle all of the SCSI processing, including the REQ/ACK handshaking.

Even a fast CPU will be slower handling the REQ/ACK handshake sequence than a simple finite state machine, resulting in peak transfer rates of about 150K/sec on a fast machine, perhaps 60K/sec on a slow machine (through the filesystem).

The driver also must sit in a tight loop as long as the SCSI bus is busy, resulting in near 100% CPU utilization and extremely poor responsiveness during SCSI I/O. Slow Cd-ROMs which don't disconnect/reconnect will kill interactive performance with these boards.

Not recommended.

Interlocked Polled

Boards using interlocked polled I/O are essentially the same as pure polled I/O boards, only the SCSI REQ/ACK handshaking signals are interlocked with the PC bus handshaking signals. All SCSI processing beyond the handshaking is handled by the CPU.

Peak transfer rates of 500-600K/sec through the filesystem are possible on these boards.

As with pure polled I/O boards, the driver must sit in a tight loop as long as the SCSI bus is busy, resulting in CPU utilization dependent on the transfer rates of the devices, and when they disconnect/reconnect. CPU utilization may vary between 25% for single speed CDs which handle disconnect/reconnect properly to 100% for faster drives or broken CD ROMs which fail to disconnect/reconnect.

On my 486-66, with a T128, I use 90% of my CPU time to sustain a throughput of 547K/sec on a drive with a head rate of 1080K/sec with a T128 board.

Sometimes acceptable for slow tapes and Cd-ROMs when low cost is essential.

FIFO Polled

Boards using FIFO polled I/O put a small (typically 8K) buffer between the CPU and the SCSI bus, and often implement some amount of intelligence. The net effect is that the CPU is only tied up when it is transferring data at top speed to the FIFO and when it's handling the rest of the interrupt processing for FIFO empty conditions, disconnect/reconnect, etc.

Peak transfer rates should be sufficient to handle most SCSI devices, and have been measured at up to 4M/sec using raw SCSI commands to read 64K blocks on a fast Seagate Barracuda with an Adaptec 1520.

CPU utilization is dependent on the transfer rates of the devices, with faster devices generating more interrupts per unit time which require more CPU processing time. Although CPU usage may be high (perhaps 75%) with fast devices, the system usually remains usable. These boards will provide excellent interactive performance with broken devices which don't disconnect/reconnect (typically cheap CD-ROM drives)

Recommended for persons on a budget.

Slave DMA

Drivers for boards using slave DMA program the PC's DMA controller for a channel when they do a data transfer, and return control to the CPU.

Peak transfer rates are usually handicapped by the poor DMA controller used on PCs, with one such 8-bit board having problems going faster than 140-150K/sec with one main board.

CPU utilization is very reasonable, slightly less than what is seen with FIFO polled I/O boards. These boards are very tolerant of broken devices which don't disconnect/reconnect (typically cheap CSG limitDROM drives).

Acceptable for slow CDROM drives, tapes, etc.

Busmastering DMA

These boards are intelligent. Drivers for these boards throw a SCSI command, the destination target and lun, and where the data should end up in a structure, and tell the board "Hey, I have a command for you." The driver returns control to various running programs, and eventually the SCSI board gets back and says that it's done.

Since the intelligence is in the host adapter firmware and not the driver, drivers for these boards typically support more features—synchronous transfers, tagged queuing, etc.

With the clustered read/write patches, peak transfer rates through the file system approach 100% of head rate writing, 75% reading.

CPU utilization is minimal, regardless of I/O load, with a measured 5% CPU usage while accessing a double speed CDROM on an Adaptec 1540 and 20% while sustaining a 1.2M/sec transfer rate on a SCSI disk.

Recommended in all cases where money is not extremely tight, the main board is not broken (some broken main boards do not work with bus masters), and applications where time to data is more important than throughput are not being run (bus master overhead may hit 3–4ms per command).

10.2 Scatter/gather

The second most important driver or hardware feature with respect to performance is support for scatter/gather I/O. The overhead of executing a SCSI command is significant—on the order of milliseconds. Intelligent bus masters like the Adaptec 1540 may take 3–4ms to process a SCSI command before the target even sees it. On unbuffered devices, this overhead is always enough to slip a revolution, resulting in a transfer rate of about 60K/sec (assuming a 3600 RPM drive) per block transfered at a time. So, to maximize performance, it is necessary to minimize the number of SCSI commands needed to transfer a given amount of data by transferring more data per command. Due to the design of the Linux buffer cache, contiguous disk blocks are not contiguous in memory. With the clustered read/write patches, 4K worth of buffers are contiguous. So, the maximum amount of data which can be transfered per SCSI command is going to be 1K * # of scatter/gather regions without the clustered read/write patches, 4K * # of regions with. Experimentally, we've determined that 64K is a reasonable amount to transfer with a single SCSI command—meaning 64 scatter/gather buffers with clustered read/write patches, 16 without. With the change from 16K to 64K transfers, we saw an improvement from 50% of head rate, through the file system, reading and writing, to 75% and 100% respectively using an Adaptec 1540 series board.

10.3 Mailbox vs. non-mailbox

A number of intelligent host adapters, such as the Ultrastor, WD7000, Adaptec 1540, 1740, and BusLogic boards have used a mailbox-metaphor interface, where SCSI commands are executed by putting a SCSI command structure in a fixed memory location (mailbox), signaling the board (i.e., raising the outgoing mail flag), and waiting for a return (incoming mail). With this high level programming interface, users can often upgrade to a newer board revision to take advantage of new features, such as FAST + WIDE SCSI, without software changes. Drivers tend to be simpler to implement, may implement a larger feature set, and may be more stable.

Other intelligent host adapters, such as the NCR53c7/8xx family, and Adaptec AIC-7770/7870 chips (including the 274x, 284x, and 2940 boards) use a lower level programming interface. This may prove faster since processing can be shifted between the board's processor and faster host CPU, allow better flexibility in implementing certain features (ie, target mode for arbitrary devices), and these boards can be built for less money (In some cases, this is passed on to the consumer (ie, most NCR boards)). On the down side, drivers tend to be more complex (read: there is more potential for bugs), and must be modified to take advantage of the features present on newer chips.

10.4 Bus types

Bus type is the next thing to consider, with choices including ISA, EISA, VESA, and PCI. Marketing types often spout of absurd bandwidth numbers based on burst transfer rates and fiction, which isn't very useful. Instead, I've chosen to state "real-world" numbers based on measured performance with various peripherals.

Bus

Bandwidth, description,

ISA

Bandwidth is slightly better than 5M/sec for bus mastering devices. With an ISA bus, arbitration for bus masters is performed by the venerable 8237 third party DMA controller, resulting in relatively high bus acquisition times. Interrupt drivers are tri-state and edge triggered, meaning interrupts cannot be shared. Generally, ISA is unbuffered, meaning the host/memory bus is tied up whenever a transfer is occurring. No mechanism is provided to prevent bus-hogging.

VESA

Bandwidth is about 30M/sec. Some VESA systems run the bus out of spec, rendering them incompatible with some boards, so this should be taken into consideration before purchasing hardware without a return guarantee. Generally, VESA is unbuffered, meaning meaning the host/memory bus is tied up whenever a transfer is occurring.

EISA

Bandwidth is about 30M/sec, with busmastering operations generally being faster than VESA. Some EISA systems buffer the bus, allowing burst transfers to the faster host/memory bus and minimizing impact on CPU performance. EISA interrupt drivers may be either tri-state edge-triggered or open collector level-active, allowing interrupt sharing with drivers that support it. Since EISA allocates a separate address space for each board, it is usually less prone to resource conflicts than ISA or VESA.

PCI

Bandwidth is about 60M/sec. Most PCI systems implement write posting buffers on the host bridge, allowing speed mismatches on either side to have a minimum impact on bus/CPU performance. PCI interrupt drivers are open collector level active, allowing interrupt sharing with drivers that support it. Mechanisms are provided to prevent bus hogging, and for both master and slave to suspend a bus-mastering operation.

Since PCI provides a plug-n-play mechanism with writable configuration registers on every board, in a separate address space, a properly implemented PCI system is plug-and play.

PCI is extremely strict as to trace length, loading, mechanical specifications, etc. and ultimately should be more reliable than VESA or ISA.

In summary, PCI is the best PC bus, although it does have its dark side. PCI is still in its infancy, and although most manufacturers have ironed out the problems, there is still stock of older, buggy PCI hardware and broken main BIOSes. For this reason, I strongly recommend a return guarantee on the hardware. While the latest PCI main boards are truly plug-and-play, older PCI boards may require the user to set options with both jumpers and in software (i.e., interrupt assignments). Although many users have resolved their PCI problems, it has taken time and for this reason I cannot recommend a PCI purchase if having the system operational is extremely time critical.

For many slower SCSI devices, such as disks with head rates around 2M/sec or less, CD-ROMs, and tapes, there will be little difference in throughput with the different PC bus interfaces. For faster contemporary SCSI drives (Typical high end multi-gigabyte drives have a head rate of 4-5M/sec, and at least one company is currently Alpha testing a parallel head unit with a 14M/sec head rate), throughput will often be significantly better with controllers on faster busses, with one user noting a 2.5 fold performance improvement when going from an Adaptec 1542 ISA board to a NCR53c810 PCI board.

With the exception of situations where PCI write-posting or a similar write-buffering mechanism is being used, when one of the busses in your system is busy, all of the busses will be unaccessible. So, although bus saturation may not be interfering with SCSI performance, it may have a negative effect on interactive performance. I.e., if you have a 4M/sec SCSI disk under ISA, you'll have lost 80% of your bandwidth, and in an ISA/VESA system would only be able to bitblt at 6M/sec. In most cases, a similar impact on processing jobs in the background would also be felt.

Note that having over 16M of memory does not preclude using an ISA busmastering SCSI board. Unlike various broken operating systems, Linux will double buffer when using a DMA with an ISA controller and a transfer is ultimately destined for an area above 16M. Performance on these transfers only suffers by about 1.5%, ie not noticeably.

Finally, the price difference between bus masters offered with the different bus interfaces is often minimal.

With all that in mind, based on your priorities you will have certain bus preferences

```
Stability, time critical installations,         EISA ISA VESA PCI
          and poor return policies
Performance, and typical hobbyist               PCI EISA VESA ISA
          installations
```

As I pointed out earlier, bus mastering versus other transfer modes is going to have a bigger impact on total system performance, and should be considered more important than bus type when purchasing a SCSI controller.

10.5 Multiple devices

If will you have multiple devices on your SCSI bus, you may want to see whether the host adapter/driver that you are considering supports more than one outstanding command at one time. This is almost essential if you'll be running a tape drive, and very desirable if you are mixing devices of different speeds, like a CD ROM and a disk drive. If the Linux driver only supports one outstanding command, you may be locked out of your disk drive while a tape in the tape drive is rewinding or seeking to end of media (perhaps for half an hour). With two disk drives, the problem will not be as noticeable, although throughput would approach the average of the two transfer rates rather than the sum of the two transfer rates.

10.6 SCSI-I, SCSI-II, SCSI-III FAST, and WIDE options, etc.

Over the years, SCSI has evolved, with new revisions of the standard introducing higher transfer rates, methods to increase throughput, standardized commands for new devices, and new commands for previously supported devices.

In and of themselves, the revision levels don't really mean anything. Excepting minor things like SCSI-II not allowing the single initiator option of SCSI-I, SCSI is backwards compatible, with new features being introduced as options and not mandatory. So, the decision to call a SCSI adapter SCSI, SCSI-II, or SCSI-III is almost entirely a marketing one.

10.7 Driver feature comparison

Driver feature comparison (supported chips are listed in parenthesis)

Driver	Transfer mode	Simultaneous Commands total/LUN	SG limit	> 1 Boards
AM53C974	Busmastering DMA	12s/1s	255s	Y
aha152x (AIC6260, AIC6360)	FIFO(8k) Polled	7s/1s	255s	N
aha1542	Busmastering DMA	8s/1s	16	Y
aha1740	Busmastering DMA	32s	16	N
aha274x	Busmastering DMA	4s/1s	255s	Y
BusLogic	Busmastering DMA	192/31	128s, 8192h	Y
(values are for BT-948/958/958D, older boards support fewer commands)				
eata_dma	Busmastering DMA	64s-8192h/2-64	512s, 8192h	Y
fdomain (TMC1800, TMC18c30, TMC18c50, TMC36c70)	FIFO(8k) Polled except TMC18c30 with 2k FIFO	1s	64s	N
in2000*	FIFO(2k) Polled	1s	255s	N
g_NCR5380 (NCR5380, NCR53c80, NCR5381, NCR53c400)	Pure Polled	16s/2s	255s	Y
gsi8* (NCR5380)	Slave DMA	16s/2s	255s	
PAS16 (NCR5380)	Pure Polled or Interlocked Polled (fails on some systems!)	16s/2s	255s	Y
seagate	Interlocked Polled	1s/1s	255s	N
wd7000	Busmastering DMA	16s/1s	16	Y
t128 (NCR5380)	Interlocked Polled	16s	255s	Y
qlogic	Interlocked Polled	1s/1s	255s	N
ultrastor	Busmastering DMA	16s/2s	32	Y
53c7,8xx (NCR53c810, NCR53c815, NCR53c820, NCR53c825)	Busmastering DMA			
rel5		1s/1s	127s	N
rel10		8s/1s	127s	Y

Notes :

1. Drivers flagged with an '*' are not included with the distribution kernel, and binary boot images may be unavailable.
2. Numbers suffixed with an 's' are arbitrary limits set in software which may be changed with a compile time define.

3. Hardware limits are indicated by an 'h' suffix, and may differ from the software limits currently imposed by the Linux drivers.
4. Unsuffixed numbers may indicate either hard or soft limits.
5. Release 5 of the NCR53c810 driver is included in the stock 1.2.x and 1.3.x kernels; rel10 is available via anonymous FTP.
6. With the exception of the AM53C974, the busmastering DMA boards are intelligent; with the NCR executing microcode from main memory, the AIC7770 executing microcode from on-chip RAM, and the rest using a mailbox-style interface.

10.8 Board comparison

Board	Driver	Bus	Price	Notes
Adaptec AIC-6260	aha152x	ISA		chip, not board
Adaptec AIC-6360 (Used in most VESA/ISA multi-IO boards with SCSI, Zenon mainboards)	aha152x	VLB		chip, not board
Adaptec 1520	aha152x	ISA		
Adaptec 1522	aha152x	ISA	$80	1520 w/FDC
Adaptec 1510	aha152x	ISA		1520 w/out boot ROM, won't autoprobe.
Adaptec 1540C	aha1542	ISA		
Adaptec 1542C	aha1542	ISA		1540C w/FDC
Adaptec 1540CF	aha1542	ISA		FAST SCSI-II
Adaptec 1542CF	aha1542	ISA	$200	1540CF w/FDC
Adaptec 1640	aha1542	MCA		
Adaptec 1740	aha1740	EISA		discontinued
Adaptec 1742	aha1740	EISA		discontinued, 1740 w/FDC
Adaptec 2740	aha274x	EISA		
Adaptec 2742	aha274x	EISA		w/FDC
Adaptec 2840	aha274x	VLB		
Adaptec 2842	aha274x	VLB		w/FDC
Adaptec 2940	aha274x	PCI		
Always IN2000	in2000	ISA		
BusLogic BT-948	BusLogic	PCI	$180	Ultra SCSI
BusLogic BT-958	BusLogic	PCI	$230	Wide Ultra SCSI

(See Section 5.8 for additional BusLogic board descriptions.)

Board	Driver	Bus	Price	Notes
DPT PM2011	eata_dma	ISA		FAST SCSI-II
PM2012A	eata_dma	EISA		FAST SCSI-II
PM2012B	eata_dma	EISA		FAST SCSI-II
PM2021	eata_dma	ISA		FAST SCSI-II
PM2022	eata_dma	EISA		FAST SCSI-II
PM2024	eata_dma	PCI		FAST SCSI-II
PM2122	eata_dma	EISA		FAST SCSI-II
PM2322	eata_dma	EISA		FAST SCSI-II
PM2124	eata_dma	PCI		FAST SCSI-II
PM2124	eata_dma	PCI		FAST SCSI-II
PM2124	eata_dma	PCI		FAST SCSI-II
PM2124	eata_dma	PCI		FAST SCSI-II
PM2124	eata_dma	PCI		FAST SCSI-II
PM2124	eata_dma	PCI		FAST SCSI-II
PM2041W	eata_dma	ISA		Wide Single-ended SCSI-II
PM2041UW	eata_dma	ISA		Ultra Wide Single-ended

PM2042W	eata_dma	EISA		Wide Single-ended
PM2042UW	eata_dma	EISA		Ultra Wide Single-ended
PM2044W	eata_dma	PCI		Wide Single-ended
PM2044UW	eata_dma	PCI		Ultra Wide Single-ended
PM2142W	eata_dma	EISA		Wide Single-ended
PM2142UW	eata_dma	EISA		Ultra Wide Single-ended
PM2144W	eata_dma	PCI		Wide Single-ended
PM2144UW	eata_dma	PCI		Ultra Wide Single-ended
PM3021	eata_dma	ISA		multichannel raid/simm sockets
PM3122	eata_dma	EISA		multichannel/raid
PM3222	eata_dma	EISA		multichannel raid/simm sockets
PM3224	eata_dma	PCI		multichannel raid/simm sockets
PM3334	eata_dma	PCI		Wide Ultra SCSI multichannel raid/simm sockets
DTC 3290	aha1542	EISA		Although it should work, due to documentation release polcies, DTC hardware is unsupported
DTC 3130	53c7,8xx	PCI		'810
DTC 3130B	53c7,8xx	PCI		'815
DTC 3292	aha1542	EISA		3290 w/FDC
DTC 3292	aha1542	EISA		3290 w/FDC
Future Domain 1680	fdomain	ISA		FDC
Future Domain 3260	fdomain	PCI		
NCR53c810 (boards sold by FIC, Chaintech, Nextor, Gigabyte, etc. Mainboards with chip by AMI, ASUS, J-Bond, etc. Common in DEC PCI systems)	53c7,8xx	PCI	$60 (board)	chip, not board. Boards don't include BIOS, although most non-NCR equipped main boards have the SDMS BIOS
NCR53c815 (Intel PCISCSIKIT, NCR8150S, etc)	53c7,8xx	PCI	$100	NCR53c810 plus bios
NCR53c825	53c7,8xx	PCI	$120	Wide variant of NCR53c815. Note that the current Linux driver does not negotiate for wide transfers.
Pro Audio Spectrum 16	pas16	ISA		Sound board w/SCSI
Seagate ST01	seagate	ISA	$20	BIOS only works with some drives
Seagate ST02	seagate	ISA	$40	ST01 w/FDC
Sound Blaster 16 SCSI	aha152x	ISA		Sound board w/SCSI
Western Digital 7000	wd7000	ISA		w/FDC
Trantor T128	t128	ISA		
Trantor T128F	t128	ISA		T128 w/FDC and support for high IRQs
Trantor T130B	g_NCR5380	ISA		
Ultrastor 14F	ultrastor	ISA		w/FDC
Ultrastor 24F	ultrastor	EISA		w/FDC
Ultrastor 34F	ultrastor	VLB		

Notes :

1. Trantor was recently purchased by Adaptec, and some products are being sold under the Adaptec name.
2. Ultrastor recently filed for Chapter 11 Bankruptcy, so technical support is non-existent at this time.
3. The price for the busmastering NCR53c810 boards is not a typo, includes the standard ASPI/CAM driver package for DOS, OS/2 and Windows (32 bit access), and other drivers are available for free download.

   Some people have had luck with the following companies :

   ```
   SW (swt@netcom.com) (214) 907-0871 fax (214) 907-9339
   ```

   As of 23 Dec 1995, their price was $53 on '810 boards.
4. Adaptec's recent SCSI chips show an unusual sensitivity to cabling and termination problems. For this reason, I cannot recommend the Adaptec 154x C and CF revisions or the 2xxx series.

   Note that the reliability problems do not apply to the older 154x B revision boards, 174x A revision boards, or to my knowledge AIC-6360/AIC-6260 based boards (1505, 1510, 1520, etc).

   Also, the quality of their technical support has slipped markedly, with long delays becoming more common, and their employees being ignorant (suggesting there were non-disclosure policies affecting certain literature when there were none), and hostile (ie, refusing to pass questions on to some one else when they couldn't answer them).

   If users desire handholding, or wish to make a political statement, they should take this point into consideration. Otherwise, the Adaptec 152x/1510/1505 are nicer than the other ISA boards in the same price range, and there are some excellent deals on used and surplus 154x B revision boards and 1742 boards which IMHO outweigh the support problems.
5. All DPT boards can be upgraded with cache and raid modules, most of the boards are also available in Wide or Differential versions.
6. The various NCR boards are not entirely equivalent. I.e., while the ASUS SC200 uses active termination, many other NCR53c810 boards use passive termination. Most '825 boards use active termination, but some use a ROM for BIOS and others have a FLASH ROM. Most '825 boards have a WIDE external connector, WIDE internal connector, and narrow internal connector, although a few (i.e., CSC's less expensive model) lack the narrow internal connector.

10.9 Summary

Most ISA, EISA, VESA, and PCI users will probably be served best by a BusLogic MultiMaster board, due to its performance, features such as active termination, and Adaptec 1540 compatibility. There are a number of models available with EISA, ISA, PCI, and VESA local bus interfaces, in single ended and differential, and 8 or 16-bit SCSI bus widths. The most recent Ultra SCSI PCI models, the BT-948/958/958D, also include Flash ROM for easy firmware updates, as well as automatic "smart" termination.

People with the need for the highest possible I/O performance at their fingertips should consider the boards from DPT, which are the only ones that support RAID, caching and more than one SCSI channel.

People with PCI systems should consider NCR53c8xx based boards. These are bus mastering SCSI controllers, '810s are available quantity one for $53 (ie, cheaper than the Adaptec 1520). C't magazine benchmarked the boards as faster than both the Adaptec 2940 and BusLogic BT-946C (under DOS), and they get reasonable performance under Linux (up to 6M/sec through the file system). The disadvantages of these boards versus the BusLogics are that they aren't Adaptec 1540 compatible, may or may not come with active termination, you'll need the latest driver revision (standard in 1.3.5x, also available via anonymous FTP for 1.2.x) to make full use of the hardware, and are more likely to have problems than with a mailbox interface board like a BusLogic or DPT.

Where everything working right on the first try is imperative, a BusLogic MultiMaster or DPT board is probably optimal due to the complexity and potential for problems in non-mailbox interface boards like the NCR53c8xx and Adaptec AIC7xxx.

People wanting non-PCI SCSI on a limited budget will probably be happiest finding a surplus or used Adaptec 154x B revision or 174x A revision, or an Adaptec 1520 clone of some sort (about $80) if they want new hardware. These boards offer reasonable throughput and interactive performance at a modest price.

11 Assignment of minor numbers

Due to constraints imposed by Linux's use of a 16-bit dev_t with only eight bits allocated to the minor number, SCSI disk, tape, CDROM, and generic minor numbers are assigned dynamically. according to the following procedure :

```
For all SCSI host adapters, from scsi0 through scsiN
 For all SCSI IDs on this bus, from 0 through 7, except for
   this host adapter's ID
      For all logical units, from 0 through max_scsi_luns
        ---Probe the bus, target, and LUN combination by
           issuing a TEST UNIT READY command.  If we don't
           think a unit was here, don't probe any more LUNs
           on this bus + SCSI ID.
        ---Send an INQUIRY command to determine what we've
           found; including the device type, vendor, model,
           firmware revision, etc.
        ---Pass the results of this to a special recognition
           function for each high level driver present (i.e. disk,
           tape, etc).  Attach this device to the next available
           unit for any drivers that are willing to drive this.
           The generic device will attach to all devices.
        ---If it was SCSI-I, or in a list of devices known
           not to handle multiple LUNs, don't probe any more
           LUNs on this bus + SCSI ID.
        ---If it is a device known to have multiple LUNs, then
           a scan of the full LUN spectrum is forced, overriding
           max_scsi_luns.
```

There are frequently problems with this approach, because if you have a system where some devices are only present some of the time, then the minor numbers for a given device will depend upon which devices were present at boot time. This can present problem, because `rc` scripts or the file `/etc/fstab` might contain instructions for mounting specific partitions which fails when the disk appears with a different minor number.

This problem has not yet been fully solved. There is a program which can be found on tsx-11 that creates a `/dev/scsi` hierarchy based upon host number, ID and LUN. This is a bit clumsy, but it would help to alleviate some of the problems.

A better solution will probably come out of the `/proc/scsi` pseudo directory. This is currently a work in progress, so at present we cannot say exactly the form of the solution, but at the time of this writing this appears to be a promising approach for resolving some of these issues.

Part XLI

"Linux SCSI Programming HOWTO" by Heiko Eißfeldt,

heiko@colossus.escape.de

Contents

Abstract

v1.5, 7 May 1996
This document deals with programming the Linux generic SCSI interface.

1 What's New?

Newer kernels have changed the interface a bit. This affects a section formerly entitled "rescanning the devices." Now it is possible to add/remove SCSI devices on the fly.

Since kernel 1.3.98 some important header files have been moved/split (sg.h and scsi.h).

Some stupid bugs have been replaced by newer ones.

2 Introduction

This document is a guide to the installation and programming of the Linux generic SCSI interface.

It covers kernel prerequisites, device mappings, and basic interaction with devices. Some simple C programming examples are included. General knowledge of the SCSI command set is required; for more information on the SCSI standard and related information, see the appendix to this document.

Note the plain text version of this document lacks cross references (they show up as "").

3 What is the generic SCSI interface?

The generic SCSI interface has been implemented to provide general SCSI access to (possibly exotic) pieces of SCSI hardware. It was developed by Lawrence Foard (`entropy@world.std.com`) and sponsored by Killy Corporation (see the comments in `scsi/sg.h`).

The interface makes special device handling possible from user level applications (i.e., outside the kernel). Thus, kernel driver development, which is more risky and difficult to debug, is not necessary.

However, if you don't program the driver properly it is possible to hang the SCSI bus, the driver, or the kernel. Therefore, it is important to properly program the generic driver and to first back up all files to avoid losing data. Another useful thing to do before running your programs is to issue a `sync` command to ensure that any buffers are flushed to disk, minimizing data loss if the system hangs.

Another advantage of the generic driver is that as long as the interface itself does not change, all applications are independent of new kernel development. In comparison, other low-level kernel drivers have to be synchronized with other internal kernel changes.

Typically, the generic driver is used to communicate with new SCSI hardware devices that require special user applications to be written to take advantage of their features (e.g., scanners, printers, CD-ROM juke boxes). The generic interface allows these to be written quickly.

4 What are the requirements to use it?

4.1 Kernel Configuration

You must have a supported SCSI controller, obviously. Furthermore, your kernel must have controller support as well as generic support compiled in. Configuring the Linux kernel (via `make config` under `/usr/src/linux`) typically looks like the following:

```
 ...
*
* SCSI support
*
SCSI support? (CONFIG_SCSI) [n] y
*
* SCSI support type (disk, tape, CDrom)
*
 ...
Scsi generic support (CONFIG_CHR_DEV_SG) [n] y
*
```

```
 * SCSI low-level drivers
 *
  ...
```

If available, modules can of course be built instead.

4.2 Device Files

The generic SCSI driver uses its own device files, separate from those used by the other SCSI device drivers. They can be generated using the `MAKEDEV` script, typically found in the `/dev` directory. Running `MAKEDEV sg` produces these files:

```
crw-------   1 root     system    21,   0 Aug 20 20:09 /dev/sga
crw-------   1 root     system    21,   1 Aug 20 20:09 /dev/sgb
crw-------   1 root     system    21,   2 Aug 20 20:09 /dev/sgc
crw-------   1 root     system    21,   3 Aug 20 20:09 /dev/sgd
crw-------   1 root     system    21,   4 Aug 20 20:09 /dev/sge
crw-------   1 root     system    21,   5 Aug 20 20:09 /dev/sgf
crw-------   1 root     system    21,   6 Aug 20 20:09 /dev/sgg
crw-------   1 root     system    21,   7 Aug 20 20:09 /dev/sgh
                                   |     |
                               major,   minor device numbers
```

Note that these are character devices for raw access. On some systems these devices may be called `/dev/{sg0,sg1,...}`, depending on your installation, so adjust the following examples accordingly.

4.3 Device Mapping

These device files are dynamically mapped to SCSI IDs or LUNs on your SCSI bus (LUN = logical unit). The mapping allocates devices consecutively for each LUN of each device on each SCSI bus found at time of the SCSI scan, beginning at the lower LUNs, IDs, or buses. It starts with the first SCSI controller and continues without interruption with all following controllers. This is currently done in the initialisation of the SCSI driver.

For example, assuming you had three SCSI devices hooked up with IDs 1, 3, and 5 on the first SCSI bus (each having one LUN), then the following mapping would be in effect:

```
/dev/sga -> SCSI ID 1
/dev/sgb -> SCSI ID 3
/dev/sgc -> SCSI ID 5
```

If you now add a new device with ID 4, then the mapping (after the next rescan) will be:

```
/dev/sga -> SCSI ID 1
/dev/sgb -> SCSI ID 3
/dev/sgc -> SCSI ID 4
/dev/sgd -> SCSI ID 5
```

Notice the change for ID 5—the corresponding device is no longer mapped to `/dev/sgc` but is now under `/dev/sgd`.

Luckily, newer kernels allow for changing this order.

4.3.1 Dynamically insert and remove SCSI devices

If a newer kernel and the `/proc` file system is running, a non-busy device can be removed and installed "on the fly."

To remove a SCSI device:

```
echo "scsi remove-single-device a b c d" > /proc/scsi/scsi
```

and similar. To add a SCSI device, do

```
echo "scsi add-single-device a b c d" > /proc/scsi/scsi
```

where

```
a == hostadapter ID (first one being 0)
b == SCSI channel on hostadapter (first one being 0)
c == ID
d == LUN (first one being 0)
```

So, in order to swap the `/dev/sgc` and `/dev/sgd` mappings from the previous example, we could do

```
echo "scsi remove-single-device 0 0 4 0" > /proc/scsi/scsi
echo "scsi remove-single-device 0 0 5 0" > /proc/scsi/scsi
echo "scsi add-single-device 0 0 5 0" > /proc/scsi/scsi
echo "scsi add-single-device 0 0 4 0" > /proc/scsi/scsi
```

since generic devices are mapped in the order of their insertion.

When adding more devices to the SCSI bus keep in mind there are limited spare entries for new devices. The memory has been allocated at boot time and has room for two more devices.

5 Programmers Guide

The following sections are for programmers who want to use the generic SCSI interface in their own applications. An example will be given showing how to access a SCSI device with the INQUIRY and the TESTUNITREADY commands.

When using these code examples, note the following:

- The location of the header files `sg.h` and `scsi.h` has changed in kernel version 1.3.98. Now these files are located at `/usr/src/linux/include/scsi`, which is hopefully linked to `/usr/include/scsi`. Previously they were in `/usr/src/linux/drivers/scsi`. We assume a newer kernel in the following text.
- The generic SCSI interface was extended in kernel version 1.1.68; the examples require at least this version. But please avoid kernel version 1.1.77 up to 1.1.89 and 1.3.52 up to 1.3.56 since they had a broken generic scsi interface.
- The constant DEVICE in the header section describing the accessed device should be set according to your available devices (see Section 8.

6 Overview Of Device Programming

The header file `include/scsi/sg.h` contains a description of the interface (this is based on kernel version 1.3.98):

```
struct sg_header
 {
  int pack_len;
                  /* length of incoming packet (including header) */
  int reply_len;  /* maximum length of expected reply */
  int pack_id;    /* ID number of packet */
  int result;     /* 0==ok, otherwise refer to errno codes */
  unsigned int twelve_byte:1;
              /* Force 12 byte command length for group 6 & 7 commands  */
  unsigned int other_flags:31;                  /* for future use */
  unsigned char sense_buffer[16]; /* used only by reads */
  /* command follows then data for command */
 };
```

This structure describes how a SCSI command is to be processed and has room to hold the results of the execution of the command. The individual structure components will be discussed later in Section 8.

The general way of exchanging data with the generic driver is as follows: to send a command to an opened generic device, `write()` a block containing these three parts to it:

```
struct sg_header
SCSI command
data to be sent with the command
```

To obtain the result of a command, `read()` a block with this (similar) block structure:

```
struct sg_header
data coming from the device
```

This is a general overview of the process. The following sections describe each of the steps in more detail.

NOTE: Up to recent kernel versions, it is necessary to block the SIGINT signal between the `write()` and the corresponding `read()` call (i.e., via `sigprocmask()`). A return after the `write()` part without any `read()` to fetch the results will block on subsequent accesses. This signal blocking has not yet been included in the example code. So better do not issue SIGINT (a la ^C) when running these examples.

7 Opening The Device

A generic device has to be opened for read and write access:

```
int fd = open (device_name, O_RDWR);
```

(This is the case even for a read-only hardware device such as a CD-ROM drive).

We have to perform a `write` to send the command and a `read` to get back any results. In the case of an error the return code is negative (see Section B for a complete list).

8 The Header Structure

The header structure `struct sg_header` serves as a controlling layer between the application and the kernel driver. We now discuss its components in detail.

int pack_len

defines the size of the block written to the driver. This is defined within the kernel for internal use.

int reply_len

defines the size of the block to be accepted at reply. This is defined from the application side.

int pack_id

This field helps to assign replies to requests. The application can supply a unique ID for each request. Suppose you have written several commands (say four) to one device. They may work in parallel, one being the fastest. When getting replies via four reads, the replies do not have to have the order of the requests. To identify the correct reply for a given request one can use the `pack_id` field. Typically its value is incremented after each request (and wraps eventually). The maximum amount of outstanding requests is limited by the kernel to SG_MAX_QUEUE (eg 4).

int result

The result code of a `read` or `write` call. This is (sometimes) defined from the generic driver (kernel) side. It is safe to set it to null before the `write` call. These codes are defined in `errno.h` (0 meaning no error).

unsigned int twelve_byte:1

This field is necessary only when using non-standard vendor specific commands (in the range 0xc0 - 0xff). When these commands have a command length of 12 bytes instead of 10, this field has to be set to one before the write call. Other command lengths are not supported. This is defined from the application side.

unsigned char sense_buffer[16]

This buffer is set after a command is completed (after a `read()` call) and contains the SCSI sense code. Some command results have to be read from here (e.g. for `TESTUNITREADY`). Usually it contains just zero bytes. The value in this field is set by the generic driver (kernel) side.

The following example function interfaces directly with the generic kernel driver. It defines the header structure, sends the command via `write`, gets the result via `read` and does some (limited) error checking. The sense buffer data is available in the output buffer (unless a NULL pointer has been given, in which case it's in the input buffer). We will use it in the examples which follow.

Note: Set the value of `DEVICE` to your device descriptor.

```
#define DEVICE "/dev/sgc"

/* Example program to demonstrate the generic SCSI interface */
#include <stdio.h>
#include <unistd.h>
#include <string.h>
#include <fcntl.h>
#include <errno.h>
#include <scsi/sg.h>


#define SCSI_OFF sizeof(struct sg_header)
static unsigned char cmd[SCSI_OFF + 18];      /* SCSI command buffer */
int fd;                               /* SCSI device/file descriptor */
```

```
/* process a complete SCSI cmd. Use the generic SCSI interface. */
static int handle_SCSI_cmd(unsigned cmd_len,         /* command length */
                           unsigned in_size,         /* input data size */
                           unsigned char *i_buff,    /* input buffer */
                           unsigned out_size,        /* output data size */
                           unsigned char *o_buff     /* output buffer */
                           )
{
    int status = 0;
    struct sg_header *sg_hd;

    /* safety checks */
    if (!cmd_len) return -1;            /* need a cmd_len != 0 */
    if (!i_buff) return -1;             /* need an input buffer != NULL */
#ifdef SG_BIG_BUFF
    if (SCSI_OFF + cmd_len + in_size > SG_BIG_BUFF) return -1;
    if (SCSI_OFF + out_size > SG_BIG_BUFF) return -1;
#else
    if (SCSI_OFF + cmd_len + in_size > 4096) return -1;
    if (SCSI_OFF + out_size > 4096) return -1;
#endif

    if (!o_buff) out_size = 0;      /* no output buffer, no output size */

    /* generic SCSI device header construction */
    sg_hd = (struct sg_header *) i_buff;
    sg_hd->reply_len   = SCSI_OFF + out_size;
    sg_hd->twelve_byte = cmd_len == 12;
    sg_hd->result = 0;
#if     0
    sg_hd->pack_len    = SCSI_OFF + cmd_len + in_size; /* not necessary */
    sg_hd->pack_id;       /* not used */
    sg_hd->other_flags; /* not used */
#endif

    /* send command */
    status = write( fd, i_buff, SCSI_OFF + cmd_len + in_size );
    if ( status < 0 || status != SCSI_OFF + cmd_len + in_size ||
                       sg_hd->result ) {
        /* some error happened */
        fprintf( stderr, "write(generic) result = 0x%x cmd = 0x%x\n",
                    sg_hd->result, i_buff[SCSI_OFF] );
        perror("");
        return status;
    }

    if (!o_buff) o_buff = i_buff;       /* buffer pointer check */

    /* retrieve result */
    status = read( fd, o_buff, SCSI_OFF + out_size);
    if ( status < 0 || status != SCSI_OFF + out_size || sg_hd->result ) {
        /* some error happened */
        fprintf( stderr, "read(generic) status = 0x%x, result = 0x%x, "
                         "cmd = 0x%x\n",
                         status, sg_hd->result, o_buff[SCSI_OFF] );
        fprintf( stderr, "read(generic) sense "
                "%x %x %x %x %x %x %x %x %x %x %x %x %x %x %x %x\n",
                sg_hd->sense_buffer[0],         sg_hd->sense_buffer[1],
```

```
                sg_hd->sense_buffer[2],        sg_hd->sense_buffer[3],
                sg_hd->sense_buffer[4],        sg_hd->sense_buffer[5],
                sg_hd->sense_buffer[6],        sg_hd->sense_buffer[7],
                sg_hd->sense_buffer[8],        sg_hd->sense_buffer[9],
                sg_hd->sense_buffer[10],       sg_hd->sense_buffer[11],
                sg_hd->sense_buffer[12],       sg_hd->sense_buffer[13],
                sg_hd->sense_buffer[14],       sg_hd->sense_buffer[15]);
        if (status < 0)
            perror("");
    }
    /* Look if we got what we expected to get */
    if (status == SCSI_OFF + out_size) status = 0; /* got them all */

    return status;  /* 0 means no error */
}
```

While this may look somewhat complex at first appearance, most of the code is for error checking and reporting (which is useful even after the code is working).

`Handle_SCSI_cmd` has a generalized form for all SCSI commands types, falling into each of these categories:

```
     Data Mode                | Example Command
===============================================
neither input nor output data | test unit ready
 no input data, output data   | inquiry, read
 input data, no output data   | mode select, write
   input data, output data    | mode sense
```

9 Inquiry Command Example

One of the most basic SCSI commands is the `INQUIRY` command, used to identify the type and make of the device. Here is the definition from the SCSI-2 specification (for details refer to the SCSI-2 standard).

```
                         Table 44: INQUIRY Command
+=====-========-========-========-========-========-========-========-========+
|  Bit|   7    |   6    |   5    |   4    |   3    |   2    |   1    |   0    |
|Byte |        |        |        |        |        |        |        |        |
|=====+=======================================================================|
| 0   |                           Operation Code (12h)                        |
|-----+-----------------------------------------------------------------------|
| 1   | Logical Unit Number      |                  Reserved         | EVPD   |
|-----+-----------------------------------------------------------------------|
| 2   |                           Page Code                                   |
|-----+-----------------------------------------------------------------------|
| 3   |                           Reserved                                    |
|-----+-----------------------------------------------------------------------|
| 4   |                           Allocation Length                           |
|-----+-----------------------------------------------------------------------|
| 5   |                           Control                                     |
+=============================================================================+
```

The output data are as follows:

```
                  Table 45: Standard INQUIRY Data Format
+=====-========-========-========-========-========-========-========-========+
|  Bit|   7    |   6    |   5    |   4    |   3    |   2    |   1    |   0    |
|Byte |        |        |        |        |        |        |        |        |
|=====+==========================+============================================|
| 0   | Peripheral Qualifier     |           Peripheral Device Type           |
|-----+-----------------------------------------------------------------------|
| 1   |  RMB   |                  Device-Type Modifier                        |
```

```
|-----+-----------------------------------------------------------------------|
| 2   |   ISO Version    |       ECMA Version        | ANSI-Approved Version   |
|-----+------------------+----------------------------------------------------|
| 3   |  AENC   | TrmIOP |     Reserved     |        Response Data Format      |
|-----+-----------------------------------------------------------------------|
| 4   |                          Additional Length (n-4)                       |
|-----+-----------------------------------------------------------------------|
| 5   |                          Reserved                                      |
|-----+-----------------------------------------------------------------------|
| 6   |                          Reserved                                      |
|-----+-----------------------------------------------------------------------|
| 7   | RelAdr | WBus32 | WBus16 |  Sync   | Linked |Reserved| CmdQue | SftRe  |
|-----+-----------------------------------------------------------------------|
| 8   | (MSB)                                                                  |
|- - -+---                       Vendor Identification                      ---|
| 15  |                                                                 (LSB) |
|-----+-----------------------------------------------------------------------|
| 16  | (MSB)                                                                  |
|- - -+---                       Product Identification                     ---|
| 31  |                                                                 (LSB) |
|-----+-----------------------------------------------------------------------|
| 32  | (MSB)                                                                  |
|- - -+---                       Product Revision Level                     ---|
| 35  |                                                                 (LSB) |
|-----+-----------------------------------------------------------------------|
| 36  |                                                                        |
|- - -+---                       Vendor Specific                            ---|
| 55  |                                                                        |
|-----+-----------------------------------------------------------------------|
| 56  |                                                                        |
|- - -+---                       Reserved                                   ---|
| 95  |                                                                        |
|=====+=======================================================================|
|     |                   Vendor-Specific Parameters                           |
|=====+=======================================================================|
| 96  |                                                                        |
|- - -+---                       Vendor Specific                            ---|
| n   |                                                                        |
+=============================================================================+
```

The next example uses the low-level function `handle_SCSI_cmd` to perform the Inquiry SCSI command.

We first append the command block to the generic header, then call `handle_SCSI_cmd`. Note that the output buffer size argument for the `handle_SCSI_cmd` call excludes the generic header size. After command completion the output buffer contains the requested data, unless an error occurred.

```
#define INQUIRY_CMD     0x12
#define INQUIRY_CMDLEN  6
#define INQUIRY_REPLY_LEN 96
#define INQUIRY_VENDOR  8       /* Offset in reply data to vendor name */

/* request vendor brand and model */
static unsigned char *Inquiry ( void )
{
  unsigned char Inqbuffer[ SCSI_OFF + INQUIRY_REPLY_LEN ];
  unsigned char cmdblk [ INQUIRY_CMDLEN ] =
      { INQUIRY_CMD,  /* command */
                  0,  /* lun/reserved */
                  0,  /* page code */
                  0,  /* reserved */
```

```
    INQUIRY_REPLY_LEN,  /* allocation length */
                    0 };/* reserved/flag/link */

    memcpy( cmd + SCSI_OFF, cmdblk, sizeof(cmdblk) );

    /*
     * +------------------+
     * | struct sg_header | <- cmd
     * +------------------+
     * | copy of cmdblk   | <- cmd + SCSI_OFF
     * +------------------+
     */

    if (handle_SCSI_cmd(sizeof(cmdblk), 0, cmd,
                        sizeof(Inqbuffer) - SCSI_OFF, Inqbuffer )) {
        fprintf( stderr, "Inquiry failed\n" );
        exit(2);
    }
    return (Inqbuffer + SCSI_OFF);
  }
```

The example above follows this structure. The inquiry function copies its command block behind the generic header (given by `SCSI_OFF`). Input data is not present for this command. `Handle_SCSI_cmd` will define the header structure. We can now implement the function `main` to complete this working example program.

```
  void main( void )
  {
    fd = open(DEVICE, O_RDWR);
    if (fd < 0) {
      fprintf( stderr, "Need read/write permissions for "DEVICE".\n" );
      exit(1);
    }

    /* print some fields of the Inquiry result */
    printf( "%s\n", Inquiry() + INQUIRY_VENDOR );
  }
```

We first open the device, check for errors, and then call the higher level subroutine. Then we print the results in human readable format including the vendor, product, and revision.

Note: There is more information in the Inquiry result than this little program gives. You may want to extend the program to give device type, ANSI version etc. The device type is of special importance, since it determines the mandatory and optional command sets for this device. If you don't want to program it yourself, you may want to use the scsiinfo program from Eric Youngdale, which requests nearly all information about an SCSI device. Look at tsx-11.mit.edu in `pub/Linux/ALPHA/scsi`.

10 The Sense Buffer

Commands with no output data can give status information via the sense buffer (which is part of the header structure). Sense data is available when the previous command has terminated with a CHECK CONDITION status. In this case the kernel automatically retrieves the sense data via a REQUEST SENSE command. Its structure is:

```
+=====-========-========-========-========-========-========-========-========+
|  Bit|   7    |   6    |   5    |   4    |   3    |   2    |   1    |   0    |
|Byte |        |        |        |        |        |        |        |        |
|=====+========+==============================================================|
| 0   | Valid  |                  Error Code (70h or 71h)                     |
|-----+-----------------------------------------------------------------------|
| 1   |                           Segment Number                              |
|-----+-----------------------------------------------------------------------|
| 2   |Filemark|  EOM   |  ILI   |Reserved|          Sense Key                |
```

```
|-----+-----------------------------------------------------------------------|
| 3   | (MSB)                                                                 |
|- - -+---                        Information                              ---|
| 6   |                                                                 (LSB) |
|-----+-----------------------------------------------------------------------|
| 7   |                     Additional Sense Length (n-7)                     |
|-----+-----------------------------------------------------------------------|
| 8   | (MSB)                                                                 |
|- - -+---                 Command-Specific Information                    ---|
| 11  |                                                                 (LSB) |
|-----+-----------------------------------------------------------------------|
| 12  |                        Additional Sense Code                          |
|-----+-----------------------------------------------------------------------|
| 13  |                  Additional Sense Code Qualifier                      |
|-----+-----------------------------------------------------------------------|
| 14  |                    Field Replaceable Unit Code                        |
|-----+-----------------------------------------------------------------------|
| 15  |  SKSV  |                                                              |
|- - -+------------                Sense-Key Specific                      ---|
| 17  |                                                                       |
|-----+-----------------------------------------------------------------------|
| 18  |                                                                       |
|- - -+---                     Additional Sense Bytes                      ---|
| n   |                                                                       |
+=============================================================================+
```

Note: The most useful fields are Sense Key (see section B.3), Additional Sense Code and Additional Sense Code Qualifier (see section C). The latter two are used combined as a pair.

11 Example Using Sense Buffer

Here we will use the TEST UNIT READY command to check whether media is loaded into our device. The header declarations and function `handle_SCSI_cmd` from the inquiry example will be needed as well.

```
                       Table 73: TEST UNIT READY Command
+=====-========-========-========-========-========-========-========-========+
|  Bit|   7    |   6    |   5    |   4    |   3    |   2    |   1    |   0    |
|Byte |        |        |        |        |        |        |        |        |
|=====+=======================================================================|
| 0   |                        Operation Code (00h)                           |
|-----+-----------------------------------------------------------------------|
| 1   | Logical Unit Number      |                  Reserved                  |
|-----+-----------------------------------------------------------------------|
| 2   |                           Reserved                                    |
|-----+-----------------------------------------------------------------------|
| 3   |                           Reserved                                    |
|-----+-----------------------------------------------------------------------|
| 4   |                           Reserved                                    |
|-----+-----------------------------------------------------------------------|
| 5   |                           Control                                     |
+=============================================================================+
```

Here is the function which implements it:

```
#define TESTUNITREADY_CMD 0
#define TESTUNITREADY_CMDLEN 6

#define ADD_SENSECODE 12
#define ADD_SC_QUALIFIER 13
#define NO_MEDIA_SC 0x3a
```

```
#define NO_MEDIA_SCQ 0x00

int TestForMedium ( void )
{
  /* request READY status */
  static unsigned char cmdblk [TESTUNITREADY_CMDLEN] = {
      TESTUNITREADY_CMD, /* command */
                      0, /* lun/reserved */
                      0, /* reserved */
                      0, /* reserved */
                      0, /* reserved */
                      0};/* control */

  memcpy( cmd + SCSI_OFF, cmdblk, sizeof(cmdblk) );

  /*
   * +------------------+
   * | struct sg_header | <- cmd
   * +------------------+
   * | copy of cmdblk   | <- cmd + SCSI_OFF
   * +------------------+
   */

  if (handle_SCSI_cmd(sizeof(cmdblk), 0, cmd,
                            0, NULL)) {
      fprintf (stderr, "Test unit ready failed\n");
      exit(2);
  }

  return
   *(((struct sg_header*)cmd)->sense_buffer +ADD_SENSECODE) !=
                                                  NO_MEDIA_SC ||
   *(((struct sg_header*)cmd)->sense_buffer +ADD_SC_QUALIFIER) !=
                                                  NO_MEDIA_SCQ;
}
```

Combined with this `main` function we can do the check.

```
void main( void )
{
  fd = open(DEVICE, O_RDWR);
  if (fd < 0) {
    fprintf( stderr, "Need read/write permissions for "DEVICE".\n" );
    exit(1);
  }

  /* look if medium is loaded */

  if (!TestForMedium()) {
    printf("device is unloaded\n");
  } else {
    printf("device is loaded\n");
  }
}
```

The file `generic_demo.c` from the appendix contains both examples.

12 Ioctl Functions

There are two ioctl functions available:

- `ioctl(fd, SG_SET_TIMEOUT, &Timeout);` sets the timeout value to `Timeout` * 10 milliseconds. `Timeout` has to be declared as int.
- `ioctl(fd, SG_GET_TIMEOUT, &Timeout);` gets the current timeout value. `Timeout` has to be declared as int.

13 Driver Defaults

13.1 Transfer Lengths

Currently (at least up to kernel version 1.1.68) input and output sizes have to be less than or equal than 4096 bytes unless the kernel has been compiled with `SG_BIG_BUFF` defined, if which case it is limited to `SG_BIG_BUFF` (e.g. 32768) bytes. These sizes include the generic header as well as the command block on input. `SG_BIG_BUFF` can be safely increased upto (131072 - 512). To take advantage of this, a new kernel has to be compiled and booted, of course.

13.2 Timeout And Retry Values

The default timeout value is set to one minute (`Timeout` = 6000). It can be changed through an ioctl call (see Section 12). The default number of retries is one.

14 Obtaining The Scsi Specifications

There are standards entitled SCSI-1 and SCSI-2 (and possibly soon SCSI-3). The standards are mostly upward compatible.

The SCSI-1 standard is (in the author's opinion) mostly obsolete, and SCSI-2 is the most widely used. SCSI-3 is very new and very expensive. These standardized command sets specify mandatory and optional commands for SCSI manufacturers and should be preferred over the vendor specific command extensions which are not standardized and for which programming information is seldom available. Of course sometimes there is no alternative to these extensions.

Electronic copies of the latest drafts are available via anonymous ftp from:

- ftp.cs.tulane.edu:pub/scsi
- ftp.symbios.com:/pub/standards
- ftp.cs.uni-sb.de:/pub/misc/doc/scsi

(I got my SCSI specification from the Yggdrasil Linux CD-ROM in the directory /usr/doc/scsi-2 and /usr/doc/scsi-1).
The SCSI FAQ also lists the following sources of printed information:
The SCSI specification: Available from:

```
      Global Engineering Documents
      15 Inverness Way East
      Englewood Co  80112-5704
      (800) 854-7179
        SCSI-1: X3.131-1986
        SCSI-2: X3.131-199x
        SCSI-3 X3T9.2/91-010R4 Working Draft

(Global Engineering Documentation in Irvine, CA (714)261-1455??)

SCSI-1: Doc \# X3.131-1986 from ANSI, 1430 Broadway, NY, NY 10018

IN-DEPTH EXPLORATION OF SCSI can be obtained from
Solution Technology, Attn: SCSI Publications, POB 104, Boulder Creek,
CA 95006, (408)338-4285, FAX (408)338-4374

THE SCSI ENCYLOPEDIA and the SCSI BENCH REFERENCE can be obtained from
ENDL Publishing, 14426 Black Walnut Ct., Saratoga, CA 95090,
(408)867-6642, FAX (408)867-2115

SCSI: UNDERSTANDING THE SMALL COMPUTER SYSTEM INTERFACE was published
by Prentice-Hall, ISBN 0-13-796855-8
```

15 Related Information Sources

15.1 HOWTOs and FAQs

The Linux **SCSI-HOWTO** by Drew Eckhardt covers all supported SCSI controllers as well as device specific questions. A lot of troubleshooting hints are given. It is available from sunsite.unc.edu in `/pub/Linux/docs/LDP` and its mirror sites.

General questions about SCSI are answered in the *SCSI FAQ: Frequently Asked Questions for comp.periphs.scsi* from the newsgroup `comp.periphs.scsi` (available on tsx-11 in pub/linux/ALPHA/scsi and mirror sites).

15.2 Mailing list

There is a **mailing list** for bug reports and questions regarding SCSI development under Linux. To join, send email to `majordomo@vger.rutgers.edu` with the line `subscribe linux-scsi` in the body of the message. Messages should be posted to `linux-scsi@vger.rutgers.edu`. Help text can be requested by sending the message line "help" to `majordomo@vger.rutgers.edu`.

15.3 Example code

`sunsite.unc.edu: apps/graphics/hpscanpbm-0.3a.tar.gz`

This package handles a HP scanjet scanner through the generic interface.

`tsx-11.mit.edu: BETA/cdrom/private/mkisofs/cdwrite-1.3.tar.gz`

The cdwrite package uses the generic interface to write a cd image to a CD writer.

`sunsite.unc.edu: apps/sound/cds/cdda2wav*.src.tar.gz`

A shameless plug for my own application, which copies audio CD tracks into WAV files.

16 Other useful stuff

Things that may come in handy. I don't have no idea if there are newer or better versions around. Feedback is welcome.

16.1 Device driver writer helpers

These documents can be found at the sunsite.unc.edu ftp server and its mirrors.

`/pub/Linux/docs/kernel/kernel-hackers-guide`

The LDP kernel hackers guide. May be a bit outdated, but covers the most fundamental things.

`/pub/Linux/docs/kernel/drivers.doc.z`

This document covers writing character drivers.

`/pub/Linux/docs/kernel/tutorial.doc.z`

Tutorial on writing a character device driver with code.

`/pub/Linux/docs/kernel/scsi.paper.tar.gz`

A LaTeX document describing howto write a SCSI driver.

`/pub/Linux/docs/hardware/DEVICES`

A list of device majors and minors used by Linux.

16.2 Utilities

`tsx-11.mit.edu: ALPHA/scsi/scsiinfo*.tar.gz` Program to query a SCSI device for operating parameters, defect lists, etc. An X-based interface is available which requires you have Tk/Tcl and `wish` installed. With the X based interface you can easily alter the settings on the drive.

`tsx-11.mit.edu: ALPHA/kdebug` A gdb extension for kernel debugging.

17 Other SCSI Access Interfaces

In Linux there is also another SCSI access method via SCSI_IOCTL_SEND_COMMAND ioctl calls, which is deprecated. Special tools like `scsiinfo` utilize it.

There are some other similar interfaces in use in the un*x world, but not available for Linux:

1. CAM (Common Access Method) developed by Future Domain and other SCSI vendors. Linux has little support for a SCSI CAM system yet (mainly for booting from hard disk). CAM even supports target mode, so one could disguise ones computer as a peripheral hardware device (e.g. for a small SCSI net).
2. ASPI (Advanced SCSI Programming Interface) developed by Adaptec. This is the de facto standard for MS-DOS machines.

There are other application interfaces from SCO(TM), NeXT(TM), Silicon Graphics(TM) and SUN(TM) as well.

18 Final Comments

The generic SCSI interface bridges the gap between user applications and specific devices. But rather than bloating a lot of programs with similar sets of low-level functions, it would be more desirable to have a shared library with a generalized set of low-level functions for a particular purpose. The main goal should be to have independent layers of interfaces. A good design would separate an application into low-level and hardware independent routines. The low-level routines could be put into a shared library and made available for all applications. Here, standardized interfaces should be followed as much as possible before making new ones.

By now you should know more than I do about the Linux generic SCSI interface. So you can start developing powerful applications for the benefit of the global Linux community now...

19 Acknowledgments

Special thanks go to Jeff Tranter for proofreading and enhancing the text considerably as well as to Carlos Puchol for useful comments. Drew Eckhardt's and Eric Youngdale's help on my first (dumb) questions about the use of this interface has been appreciated.

A Appendix

B Error handling

The functions `open`, `ioctl`, `write`, and `read` can report errors. In this case their return value is -1 and the global variable errno is set to the error number. The errno values are defined in `/usr/include/errno.h`. Possible values are:

```
Function | Error         | Description
=========|===============|=============================================
open     | ENXIO         | not a valid device
         | EACCES        | access mode is not read/write (O_RDWR)
         | EBUSY         | device was requested for nonblocking access,
         |               | but is busy now.
         | ERESTARTSYS   | this indicates an internal error. Try to
         |               | make it reproducible and inform the SCSI
         |               | channel (for details on bug reporting
         |               | see Drew Eckhardts SCSI-HOWTO).
ioctl    | ENXIO         | not a valid device
read     | EAGAIN        | the device would block. Try again later.
         | ERESTARTSYS   | this indicates an internal error. Try to
         |               | make it reproducible and inform the SCSI
         |               | channel (for details on bug reporting
         |               | see Drew Eckhardts SCSI-HOWTO).
write    | EIO           | the length is too small (smaller than the
         |               | generic header struct). Caution: Currently
         |               | there is no overlength checking.
         | EAGAIN        | the device would block. Try again later.
```

```
          | ENOMEM         | memory required for this request could not be
          |                | allocated. Try later again unless you
          |                | exceeded the maximum transfer size (see above)
select    |                | none
close     |                | none
```

For read/write positive return values indicate as usual the amount of bytes that have been successfully transferred. This should equal the amount you requested.

B.1 Error status decoding

Furthermore a detailed reporting is done via the kernels `hd_status` and the devices `sense_buffer` (see Section 10) both from the generic header structure.

The meaning of `hd_status` can be found in `drivers/scsi/scsi.h`: This `unsigned int` is composed out of different parts:

```
  lsb  |    ...     |    ...     | msb
=======|============|============|============
status | sense key  | host code  | driver byte
```

These macros from `drivers/scsi/scsi.h` are available, but unfortunately cannot be easily used due to weird header file interdependencies. This has to be cleaned.

```
       Macro                | Description
============================|================================================
status_byte(hd_status)      | The SCSI device status. See section Status codes
msg_byte(hd_status)         | From the device. See section SCSI sense keys
host_byte(hd_status)        | From the kernel. See section Hostcodes
driver_byte(hd_status)      | From the kernel. See section midlevel codes
```

B.2 Status codes

The following status codes from the SCSI device (defined in `scsi/scsi.h`) are available.

```
Value | Symbol
======|=====================
0x00  | GOOD
0x01  | CHECK_CONDITION
0x02  | CONDITION_GOOD
0x04  | BUSY
0x08  | INTERMEDIATE_GOOD
0x0a  | INTERMEDIATE_C_GOOD
0x0c  | RESERVATION_CONFLICT
```

Note that these symbol values have been **shifted right once**. When the status is CHECK_CONDITION, the sense data in the sense buffer is valid (check especially the additional sense code and additional sense code qualifier).

These values carry the meaning from the SCSI-2 specification:

```
                    Table 27: Status Byte Code

+=================================================================+
|       Bits of Status Byte        |  Status                      |
|  7    6    5    4    3    2    1    0 |                         |
|----------------------------------+------------------------------|
|  R    R    0    0    0    0    0    R |  GOOD                   |
|  R    R    0    0    0    0    1    R |  CHECK CONDITION        |
|  R    R    0    0    0    1    0    R |  CONDITION MET          |
|  R    R    0    0    1    0    0    R |  BUSY                   |
|  R    R    0    1    0    0    0    R |  INTERMEDIATE           |
|  R    R    0    1    0    1    0    R |  INTERMEDIATE-CONDITION MET |
|  R    R    0    1    1    0    0    R |  RESERVATION CONFLICT   |
|  R    R    1    0    0    0    1    R |  COMMAND TERMINATED     |
|  R    R    1    0    1    0    0    R |  QUEUE FULL             |
|                                  |                              |
```

```
|       All Other Codes            |  Reserved                       |
|------------------------------------------------------------------|
|  Key: R = Reserved bit                                           |
+==================================================================+
```

```
A definition of the status byte codes is given below.

GOOD.  This status indicates that the target has successfully completed the
command.

CHECK CONDITION.  This status indicates that a contingent allegiance condition
has occurred (see 6.6).

CONDITION MET.  This status or INTERMEDIATE-CONDITION MET is returned whenever
the requested operation is satisfied (see the SEARCH DATA and PRE-FETCH
commands).

BUSY.  This status indicates that the target is busy.  This status shall be
returned whenever a target is unable to accept a command from an otherwise
acceptable initiator (i.e., no reservation conflicts).  The recommended
initiator recovery action is to issue the command again at a later time.

INTERMEDIATE.  This status or INTERMEDIATE-CONDITION MET shall be returned for
every successfully completed command in a series of linked commands (except
the last command), unless the command is terminated with CHECK CONDITION,
RESERVATION CONFLICT, or COMMAND TERMINATED status.  If INTERMEDIATE or
INTERMEDIATE-CONDITION MET status is not returned, the series of linked
commands is terminated and the I/O process is ended.

INTERMEDIATE-CONDITION MET.  This status is the combination of the CONDITION
MET and INTERMEDIATE statuses.

RESERVATION CONFLICT.  This status shall be returned whenever an initiator
attempts to access a logical unit or an extent within a logical unit that is
reserved with a conflicting reservation type for another SCSI device (see the
RESERVE and RESERVE UNIT commands).  The recommended initiator recovery action
is to issue the command again at a later time.

COMMAND TERMINATED.  This status shall be returned whenever the target
terminates the current I/O process after receiving a TERMINATE I/O PROCESS
message (see 5.6.22).  This status also indicates that a contingent allegiance
condition has occurred (see 6.6).

QUEUE FULL.  This status shall be implemented if tagged queuing is
implemented.  This status is returned when a SIMPLE QUEUE TAG, ORDERED QUEUE
TAG, or HEAD OF QUEUE TAG message is received and the command queue is full.
The I/O process is not placed in the command queue.
```

B.3 SCSI Sense Keys

These kernel symbols (from `scsi/scsi.h`) are predefined:

```
Value | Symbol
======|================
0x00  | NO_SENSE
0x01  | RECOVERED_ERROR
0x02  | NOT_READY
0x03  | MEDIUM_ERROR
0x04  | HARDWARE_ERROR
0x05  | ILLEGAL_REQUEST
```

```
0x06  | UNIT_ATTENTION
0x07  | DATA_PROTECT
0x08  | BLANK_CHECK
0x0a  | COPY_ABORTED
0x0b  | ABORTED_COMMAND
0x0d  | VOLUME_OVERFLOW
0x0e  | MISCOMPARE
```

A verbatim list from the SCSI-2 doc follows (from section 7.2.14.3):

```
                  Table 69: Sense Key (0h-7h) Descriptions
+========-=====================================================================+
| Sense  | Description                                                         |
| Key    |                                                                     |
|--------+---------------------------------------------------------------------|
|   0h   | NO SENSE.  Indicates that there is no specific sense key            |
|        | information to be reported for the designated logical unit.  This   |
|        | would be the case for a successful command or a command that        |
|        | received CHECK CONDITION or COMMAND TERMINATED status because one   |
|        | of the filemark, EOM, or ILI bits is set to one.                    |
|--------+---------------------------------------------------------------------|
|   1h   | RECOVERED ERROR.  Indicates that the last command completed         |
|        | successfully with some recovery action performed by the target.     |
|        | Details may be determinable by examining the additional sense       |
|        | bytes and the information field.  When multiple recovered errors    |
|        | occur during one command, the choice of which error to report       |
|        | (first, last, most severe, etc.) is device specific.                |
|--------+---------------------------------------------------------------------|
|   2h   | NOT READY.  Indicates that the logical unit addressed cannot be     |
|        | accessed.  Operator intervention may be required to correct this    |
|        | condition.                                                          |
|--------+---------------------------------------------------------------------|
|   3h   | MEDIUM ERROR.  Indicates that the command terminated with a non-    |
|        | recovered error condition that was probably caused by a flaw in     |
|        | the medium or an error in the recorded data.  This sense key may    |
|        | also be returned if the target is unable to distinguish between a   |
|        | flaw in the medium and a specific hardware failure (sense key 4h).|
|--------+---------------------------------------------------------------------|
|   4h   | HARDWARE ERROR.  Indicates that the target detected a non-          |
|        | recoverable hardware failure (for example, controller failure,      |
|        | device failure, parity error, etc.) while performing the command    |
|        | or during a self test.                                              |
|--------+---------------------------------------------------------------------|
|   5h   | ILLEGAL REQUEST.  Indicates that there was an illegal parameter in|
|        | the command descriptor block or in the additional parameters        |
|        | supplied as data for some commands (FORMAT UNIT, SEARCH DATA,       |
|        | etc.).  If the target detects an invalid parameter in the command   |
|        | descriptor block, then it shall terminate the command without       |
|        | altering the medium.  If the target detects an invalid parameter    |
|        | in the additional parameters supplied as data, then the target may|
|        | have already altered the medium.  This sense key may also indicate|
|        | that an invalid IDENTIFY message was received (5.6.7).              |
|--------+---------------------------------------------------------------------|
|   6h   | UNIT ATTENTION.  Indicates that the removable medium may have been|
|        | changed or the target has been reset.  See 6.9 for more detailed    |
|        | information about the unit attention condition.                     |
|--------+---------------------------------------------------------------------|
|   7h   | DATA PROTECT.  Indicates that a command that reads or writes the    |
|        | medium was attempted on a block that is protected from this         |
```

```
|     | operation. The read or write operation is not performed.      |
+=====================================================================+
```

Table 70: Sense Key (8h-Fh) Descriptions

Sense Key	Description
8h	BLANK CHECK. Indicates that a write-once device or a sequential-access device encountered blank medium or format-defined end-of-data indication while reading or a write-once device encountered a non-blank medium while writing.
9h	Vendor Specific. This sense key is available for reporting vendor specific conditions.
Ah	COPY ABORTED. Indicates a COPY, COMPARE, or COPY AND VERIFY command was aborted due to an error condition on the source device, the destination device, or both. (See 7.2.3.2 for additional information about this sense key.)
Bh	ABORTED COMMAND. Indicates that the target aborted the command. The initiator may be able to recover by trying the command again.
Ch	EQUAL. Indicates a SEARCH DATA command has satisfied an equal comparison.
Dh	VOLUME OVERFLOW. Indicates that a buffered peripheral device has reached the end-of-partition and data may remain in the buffer that has not been written to the medium. A RECOVER BUFFERED DATA command(s) may be issued to read the unwritten data from the buffer.
Eh	MISCOMPARE. Indicates that the source data did not match the data read from the medium.
Fh	RESERVED.

B.4 Host codes

The following host codes are defined in `drivers/scsi/scsi.h`. They are set by the kernel driver.

Value	Symbol	Description
0x00	DID_OK	No error
0x01	DID_NO_CONNECT	Couldn't connect before timeout period
0x02	DID_BUS_BUSY	BUS stayed busy through time out period
0x03	DID_TIME_OUT	TIMED OUT for other reason
0x04	DID_BAD_TARGET	BAD target
0x05	DID_ABORT	Told to abort for some other reason
0x06	DID_PARITY	Parity error
0x07	DID_ERROR	internal error
0x08	DID_RESET	Reset by somebody
0x09	DID_BAD_INTR	Got an interrupt we weren't expecting

B.5 Driver codes

The midlevel driver categorizes the returned status from the lowlevel driver based on the sense key from the device. It suggests some actions to be taken such as retry, abort or remap. The routine scsi_done from scsi.c does a very differentiated handling based on host_byte(), status_byte(), msg_byte() and the suggestion. It then sets the driver byte to show what it has done. The driver byte is composed out of two nibbles: the driver status and the suggestion. Each half is composed from the below values being "or"ed together (found in scsi.h).

```
Value | Symbol          | Description of Driver status
======|=================|========================================
0x00  | DRIVER_OK       | No error
0x01  | DRIVER_BUSY     | not used
0x02  | DRIVER_SOFT     | not used
0x03  | DRIVER_MEDIA    | not used
0x04  | DRIVER_ERROR    | internal driver error
0x05  | DRIVER_INVALID  | finished (DID_BAD_TARGET or DID_ABORT)
0x06  | DRIVER_TIMEOUT  | finished with timeout
0x07  | DRIVER_HARD     | finished with fatal error
0x08  | DRIVER_SENSE    | had sense information available

Value | Symbol          | Description of suggestion
======|=================|========================================
0x10  | SUGGEST_RETRY   | retry the SCSI request
0x20  | SUGGEST_ABORT   | abort the request
0x30  | SUGGEST_REMAP   | remap the block (not yet implemented)
0x40  | SUGGEST_DIE     | let the kernel panic
0x80  | SUGGEST_SENSE   | get sense information from the device
0xff  | SUGGEST_IS_OK   | nothing to be done
```

C Additional sense codes and additional sense code qualifiers

When the status of the executed SCSI command is CHECK_CONDITION, sense data is available in the sense buffer. The additional sense code and additional sense code qualifier are contained in that buffer.

From the SCSI-2 specification I include two tables. The first is in lexical, the second in numerical order.

C.1 ASC and ASCQ in lexical order

The following table list gives a list of descriptions and device types they apply to.

```
+=============================================================================+
|           D - DIRECT ACCESS DEVICE                                          |
|           .T - SEQUENTIAL ACCESS DEVICE                                     |
|           . L - PRINTER DEVICE                                              |
|           .  P - PROCESSOR DEVICE                                           |
|           .  .W - WRITE ONCE READ MULTIPLE DEVICE                           |
|           .  . R - READ ONLY (CD-ROM) DEVICE                                |
|           .  .  S - SCANNER DEVICE                                          |
|           .  .  .O - OPTICAL MEMORY DEVICE                                  |
|           .  .  . M - MEDIA CHANGER DEVICE                                  |
|           .  .  .  C - COMMUNICATION DEVICE                                 |
|           .  .  .  .                                                        |
| ASC ASCQ  DTLPWRSOMC  DESCRIPTION                                           |
| --- ----              ----------------------------------------------------- |
| 13h  00h  D   W  O    ADDRESS MARK NOT FOUND FOR DATA FIELD                 |
| 12h  00h  D   W  O    ADDRESS MARK NOT FOUND FOR ID FIELD                   |
| 00h  11h       R      AUDIO PLAY OPERATION IN PROGRESS                      |
| 00h  12h       R      AUDIO PLAY OPERATION PAUSED                           |
| 00h  14h       R      AUDIO PLAY OPERATION STOPPED DUE TO ERROR             |
| 00h  13h       R      AUDIO PLAY OPERATION SUCCESSFULLY COMPLETED           |
| 00h  04h   T    S     BEGINNING-OF-PARTITION/MEDIUM DETECTED                |
| 14h  04h   T          BLOCK SEQUENCE ERROR                                  |
| 30h  02h  DT  WR O    CANNOT READ MEDIUM - INCOMPATIBLE FORMAT              |
| 30h  01h  DT  WR O    CANNOT READ MEDIUM - UNKNOWN FORMAT                   |
| 52h  00h   T          CARTRIDGE FAULT                                       |
```

```
| 3Fh  02h  DTLPWRSOMC  CHANGED OPERATING DEFINITION                             |
| 11h  06h      WR O    CIRC UNRECOVERED ERROR                                   |
| 30h  03h  DT          CLEANING CARTRIDGE INSTALLED                             |
| 4Ah  00h  DTLPWRSOMC  COMMAND PHASE ERROR                                      |
| 2Ch  00h  DTLPWRSOMC  COMMAND SEQUENCE ERROR                                   |
| 2Fh  00h  DTLPWRSOMC  COMMANDS CLEARED BY ANOTHER INITIATOR                    |
| 2Bh  00h  DTLPWRSO C  COPY CANNOT EXECUTE SINCE HOST CANNOT DISCONNECT         |
| 41h  00h  D           DATA PATH FAILURE (SHOULD USE 40 NN)                     |
| 4Bh  00h  DTLPWRSOMC  DATA PHASE ERROR                                         |
| 11h  07h      W  O    DATA RESYCHRONIZATION ERROR                              |
| 16h  00h  D   W  O    DATA SYNCHRONIZATION MARK ERROR                          |
| 19h  00h  D      O    DEFECT LIST ERROR                                        |
| 19h  03h  D      O    DEFECT LIST ERROR IN GROWN LIST                          |
| 19h  02h  D      O    DEFECT LIST ERROR IN PRIMARY LIST                        |
| 19h  01h  D      O    DEFECT LIST NOT AVAILABLE                                |
| 1Ch  00h  D      O    DEFECT LIST NOT FOUND                                    |
| 32h  01h  D   W  O    DEFECT LIST UPDATE FAILURE                               |
| 40h  NNh  DTLPWRSOMC  DIAGNOSTIC FAILURE ON COMPONENT NN (80H-FFH)             |
| 63h  00h       R      END OF USER AREA ENCOUNTERED ON THIS TRACK               |
| 00h  05h   T    S     END-OF-DATA DETECTED                                     |
| 14h  03h   T          END-OF-DATA NOT FOUND                                    |
| 00h  02h   T    S     END-OF-PARTITION/MEDIUM DETECTED                         |
| 51h  00h   T     O    ERASE FAILURE                                            |
| 0Ah  00h  DTLPWRSOMC  ERROR LOG OVERFLOW                                       |
| 11h  02h  DT  W SO    ERROR TOO LONG TO CORRECT                                |
| 03h  02h   T          EXCESSIVE WRITE ERRORS                                   |
| 3Bh  07h    L         FAILED TO SENSE BOTTOM-OF-FORM                           |
| 3Bh  06h    L         FAILED TO SENSE TOP-OF-FORM                              |
| 00h  01h   T          FILEMARK DETECTED                                        |
| 14h  02h   T          FILEMARK OR SETMARK NOT FOUND                            |
| 09h  02h      WR O    FOCUS SERVO FAILURE                                      |
| 31h  01h  D L    O    FORMAT COMMAND FAILED                                    |
| 58h  00h         O    GENERATION DOES NOT EXIST                                |
+================================================================================+
```

Table 71: (continued)

```
+================================================================================+
| ASC ASCQ  DTLPWRSOMC  DESCRIPTION                                              |
| --- ----              ---------------------------------------------------      |
| 1Ch  02h  D      O    GROWN DEFECT LIST NOT FOUND                              |
| 00h  06h  DTLPWRSOMC  I/O PROCESS TERMINATED                                   |
| 10h  00h  D   W  O    ID CRC OR ECC ERROR                                      |
| 22h  00h  D           ILLEGAL FUNCTION (SHOULD USE 20 00, 24 00, OR 26 00)     |
| 64h  00h       R      ILLEGAL MODE FOR THIS TRACK                              |
| 28h  01h          M   IMPORT OR EXPORT ELEMENT ACCESSED                        |
| 30h  00h  DT  WR OM   INCOMPATIBLE MEDIUM INSTALLED                            |
| 11h  08h   T          INCOMPLETE BLOCK READ                                    |
| 48h  00h  DTLPWRSOMC  INITIATOR DETECTED ERROR MESSAGE RECEIVED                |
| 3Fh  03h  DTLPWRSOMC  INQUIRY DATA HAS CHANGED                                 |
| 44h  00h  DTLPWRSOMC  INTERNAL TARGET FAILURE                                  |
| 3Dh  00h  DTLPWRSOMC  INVALID BITS IN IDENTIFY MESSAGE                         |
| 2Ch  02h        S     INVALID COMBINATION OF WINDOWS SPECIFIED                 |
| 20h  00h  DTLPWRSOMC  INVALID COMMAND OPERATION CODE                           |
| 21h  01h          M   INVALID ELEMENT ADDRESS                                  |
| 24h  00h  DTLPWRSOMC  INVALID FIELD IN CDB                                     |
| 26h  00h  DTLPWRSOMC  INVALID FIELD IN PARAMETER LIST                          |
| 49h  00h  DTLPWRSOMC  INVALID MESSAGE ERROR                                    |
| 11h  05h      WR O    L-EC UNCORRECTABLE ERROR                                 |
| 60h  00h        S     LAMP FAILURE                                             |
```

```
| 5Bh  02h  DTLPWRSOM   LOG COUNTER AT MAXIMUM
| 5Bh  00h  DTLPWRSOM   LOG EXCEPTION
| 5Bh  03h  DTLPWRSOM   LOG LIST CODES EXHAUSTED
| 2Ah  02h  DTL WRSOMC  LOG PARAMETERS CHANGED
| 21h  00h  DT  WR OM   LOGICAL BLOCK ADDRESS OUT OF RANGE
| 08h  00h  DTL WRSOMC  LOGICAL UNIT COMMUNICATION FAILURE
| 08h  02h  DTL WRSOMC  LOGICAL UNIT COMMUNICATION PARITY ERROR
| 08h  01h  DTL WRSOMC  LOGICAL UNIT COMMUNICATION TIME-OUT
| 4Ch  00h  DTLPWRSOMC  LOGICAL UNIT FAILED SELF-CONFIGURATION
| 3Eh  00h  DTLPWRSOMC  LOGICAL UNIT HAS NOT SELF-CONFIGURED YET
| 04h  01h  DTLPWRSOMC  LOGICAL UNIT IS IN PROCESS OF BECOMING READY
| 04h  00h  DTLPWRSOMC  LOGICAL UNIT NOT READY, CAUSE NOT REPORTABLE
| 04h  04h  DTL    O    LOGICAL UNIT NOT READY, FORMAT IN PROGRESS
| 04h  02h  DTLPWRSOMC  LOGICAL UNIT NOT READY, INITIALIZING COMMAND REQUIRED
| 04h  03h  DTLPWRSOMC  LOGICAL UNIT NOT READY, MANUAL INTERVENTION REQUIRED
| 25h  00h  DTLPWRSOMC  LOGICAL UNIT NOT SUPPORTED
| 15h  01h  DTL WRSOM   MECHANICAL POSITIONING ERROR
| 53h  00h  DTL WRSOM   MEDIA LOAD OR EJECT FAILED
| 3Bh  0Dh          M   MEDIUM DESTINATION ELEMENT FULL
| 31h  00h  DT  W  O    MEDIUM FORMAT CORRUPTED
| 3Ah  00h  DTL WRSOM   MEDIUM NOT PRESENT
| 53h  02h  DT  WR OM   MEDIUM REMOVAL PREVENTED
| 3Bh  0Eh          M   MEDIUM SOURCE ELEMENT EMPTY
| 43h  00h  DTLPWRSOMC  MESSAGE ERROR
| 3Fh  01h  DTLPWRSOMC  MICROCODE HAS BEEN CHANGED
| 1Dh  00h  D   W  O    MISCOMPARE DURING VERIFY OPERATION
| 11h  0Ah  DT     O    MISCORRECTED ERROR
| 2Ah  01h  DTL WRSOMC  MODE PARAMETERS CHANGED
| 07h  00h  DTL WRSOM   MULTIPLE PERIPHERAL DEVICES SELECTED
| 11h  03h  DT  W SO    MULTIPLE READ ERRORS
| 00h  00h  DTLPWRSOMC  NO ADDITIONAL SENSE INFORMATION
| 00h  15h       R      NO CURRENT AUDIO STATUS TO RETURN
| 32h  00h  D   W  O    NO DEFECT SPARE LOCATION AVAILABLE
| 11h  09h   T          NO GAP FOUND
| 01h  00h  D   W  O    NO INDEX/SECTOR SIGNAL
| 06h  00h  D   WR OM   NO REFERENCE POSITION FOUND
+==============================================================================+

Table 71: (continued)
+==============================================================================+
| ASC ASCQ  DTLPWRSOMC  DESCRIPTION
| --- ----              -----------------------------------------------------
| 02h  00h  D   WR OM   NO SEEK COMPLETE
| 03h  01h   T          NO WRITE CURRENT
| 28h  00h  DTLPWRSOMC  NOT READY TO READY TRANSITION, MEDIUM MAY HAVE CHANGED
| 5Ah  01h  DT  WR OM   OPERATOR MEDIUM REMOVAL REQUEST
| 5Ah  00h  DTLPWRSOM   OPERATOR REQUEST OR STATE CHANGE INPUT (UNSPECIFIED)
| 5Ah  03h  DT  W  O    OPERATOR SELECTED WRITE PERMIT
| 5Ah  02h  DT  W  O    OPERATOR SELECTED WRITE PROTECT
| 61h  02h        S     OUT OF FOCUS
| 4Eh  00h  DTLPWRSOMC  OVERLAPPED COMMANDS ATTEMPTED
| 2Dh  00h   T          OVERWRITE ERROR ON UPDATE IN PLACE
| 3Bh  05h    L         PAPER JAM
| 1Ah  00h  DTLPWRSOMC  PARAMETER LIST LENGTH ERROR
| 26h  01h  DTLPWRSOMC  PARAMETER NOT SUPPORTED
| 26h  02h  DTLPWRSOMC  PARAMETER VALUE INVALID
| 2Ah  00h  DTL WRSOMC  PARAMETERS CHANGED
| 03h  00h  DTL W SO    PERIPHERAL DEVICE WRITE FAULT
| 50h  02h   T          POSITION ERROR RELATED TO TIMING
```

```
| 3Bh  0Ch        S     POSITION PAST BEGINNING OF MEDIUM                     |
| 3Bh  0Bh        S     POSITION PAST END OF MEDIUM                           |
| 15h  02h  DT  WR O    POSITIONING ERROR DETECTED BY READ OF MEDIUM          |
| 29h  00h  DTLPWRSOMC  POWER ON, RESET, OR BUS DEVICE RESET OCCURRED         |
| 42h  00h  D           POWER-ON OR SELF-TEST FAILURE (SHOULD USE 40 NN)      |
| 1Ch  01h  D      O    PRIMARY DEFECT LIST NOT FOUND                         |
| 40h  00h  D           RAM FAILURE (SHOULD USE 40 NN)                        |
| 15h  00h  DTL WRSOM   RANDOM POSITIONING ERROR                              |
| 3Bh  0Ah        S     READ PAST BEGINNING OF MEDIUM                         |
| 3Bh  09h        S     READ PAST END OF MEDIUM                               |
| 11h  01h  DT  W SO    READ RETRIES EXHAUSTED                                |
| 14h  01h  DT  WR O    RECORD NOT FOUND                                      |
| 14h  00h  DTL WRSO    RECORDED ENTITY NOT FOUND                             |
| 18h  02h  D   WR O    RECOVERED DATA - DATA AUTO-REALLOCATED                |
| 18h  05h  D   WR O    RECOVERED DATA - RECOMMEND REASSIGNMENT               |
| 18h  06h  D   WR O    RECOVERED DATA - RECOMMEND REWRITE                    |
| 17h  05h  D   WR O    RECOVERED DATA USING PREVIOUS SECTOR ID               |
| 18h  03h       R      RECOVERED DATA WITH CIRC                              |
| 18h  01h  D   WR O    RECOVERED DATA WITH ERROR CORRECTION & RETRIES APPLIED|
| 18h  00h  DT  WR O    RECOVERED DATA WITH ERROR CORRECTION APPLIED          |
| 18h  04h       R      RECOVERED DATA WITH L-EC                              |
| 17h  03h  DT  WR O    RECOVERED DATA WITH NEGATIVE HEAD OFFSET              |
| 17h  00h  DT  WRSO    RECOVERED DATA WITH NO ERROR CORRECTION APPLIED       |
| 17h  02h  DT  WR O    RECOVERED DATA WITH POSITIVE HEAD OFFSET              |
| 17h  01h  DT  WRSO    RECOVERED DATA WITH RETRIES                           |
| 17h  04h      WR O    RECOVERED DATA WITH RETRIES AND/OR CIRC APPLIED       |
| 17h  06h  D   W  O    RECOVERED DATA WITHOUT ECC - DATA AUTO-REALLOCATED    |
| 17h  07h  D   W  O    RECOVERED DATA WITHOUT ECC - RECOMMEND REASSIGNMENT   |
| 17h  08h  D   W  O    RECOVERED DATA WITHOUT ECC - RECOMMEND REWRITE        |
| 1Eh  00h  D   W  O    RECOVERED ID WITH ECC CORRECTION                      |
| 3Bh  08h   T          REPOSITION ERROR                                      |
| 36h  00h    L         RIBBON, INK, OR TONER FAILURE                         |
| 37h  00h  DTL WRSOMC  ROUNDED PARAMETER                                     |
| 5Ch  00h  D      O    RPL STATUS CHANGE                                     |
| 39h  00h  DTL WRSOMC  SAVING PARAMETERS NOT SUPPORTED                       |
| 62h  00h        S     SCAN HEAD POSITIONING ERROR                           |
| 47h  00h  DTLPWRSOMC  SCSI PARITY ERROR                                     |
| 54h  00h     P        SCSI TO HOST SYSTEM INTERFACE FAILURE                 |
| 45h  00h  DTLPWRSOMC  SELECT OR RESELECT FAILURE                            |
+=============================================================================+

Table 71: (concluded)
+=============================================================================+
| ASC ASCQ  DTLPWRSOMC  DESCRIPTION                                           |
| --- ----              ----------------------------------------------------- |
| 3Bh  00h   TL         SEQUENTIAL POSITIONING ERROR                          |
| 00h  03h   T          SETMARK DETECTED                                      |
| 3Bh  04h    L         SLEW FAILURE                                          |
| 09h  03h      WR O    SPINDLE SERVO FAILURE                                 |
| 5Ch  02h  D      O    SPINDLES NOT SYNCHRONIZED                             |
| 5Ch  01h  D      O    SPINDLES SYNCHRONIZED                                 |
| 1Bh  00h  DTLPWRSOMC  SYNCHRONOUS DATA TRANSFER ERROR                       |
| 55h  00h     P        SYSTEM RESOURCE FAILURE                               |
| 33h  00h   T          TAPE LENGTH ERROR                                     |
| 3Bh  03h    L         TAPE OR ELECTRONIC VERTICAL FORMS UNIT NOT READY      |
| 3Bh  01h   T          TAPE POSITION ERROR AT BEGINNING-OF-MEDIUM            |
| 3Bh  02h   T          TAPE POSITION ERROR AT END-OF-MEDIUM                  |
| 3Fh  00h  DTLPWRSOMC  TARGET OPERATING CONDITIONS HAVE CHANGED              |
| 5Bh  01h  DTLPWRSOM   THRESHOLD CONDITION MET                               |
```

```
| 26h  03h  DTLPWRSOMC  THRESHOLD PARAMETERS NOT SUPPORTED                        |
| 2Ch  01h        S     TOO MANY WINDOWS SPECIFIED                                |
| 09h  00h  DT  WR O    TRACK FOLLOWING ERROR                                     |
| 09h  01h      WR O    TRACKING SERVO FAILURE                                    |
| 61h  01h        S     UNABLE TO ACQUIRE VIDEO                                   |
| 57h  00h       R      UNABLE TO RECOVER TABLE-OF-CONTENTS                       |
| 53h  01h   T          UNLOAD TAPE FAILURE                                       |
| 11h  00h  DT  WRSO    UNRECOVERED READ ERROR                                    |
| 11h  04h  D   W  O    UNRECOVERED READ ERROR - AUTO REALLOCATE FAILED           |
| 11h  0Bh  D   W  O    UNRECOVERED READ ERROR - RECOMMEND REASSIGNMENT           |
| 11h  0Ch  D   W  O    UNRECOVERED READ ERROR - RECOMMEND REWRITE THE DATA       |
| 46h  00h  DTLPWRSOMC  UNSUCCESSFUL SOFT RESET                                   |
| 59h  00h         O    UPDATED BLOCK READ                                        |
| 61h  00h        S     VIDEO ACQUISITION ERROR                                   |
| 50h  00h   T          WRITE APPEND ERROR                                        |
| 50h  01h   T          WRITE APPEND POSITION ERROR                               |
| 0Ch  00h   T    S     WRITE ERROR                                               |
| 0Ch  02h  D   W  O    WRITE ERROR - AUTO REALLOCATION FAILED                    |
| 0Ch  01h  D   W  O    WRITE ERROR RECOVERED WITH AUTO REALLOCATION              |
| 27h  00h  DT  W  O    WRITE PROTECTED                                           |
|                                                                                 |
| 80h  XXh     \                                                                  |
| THROUGH       >       VENDOR SPECIFIC.                                          |
| FFh  XX      /                                                                  |
|                                                                                 |
| XXh  80h     \                                                                  |
| THROUGH       >       VENDOR SPECIFIC QUALIFICATION OF STANDARD ASC.            |
| XXh  FFh     /                                                                  |
|                       ALL CODES NOT SHOWN ARE RESERVED.                         |
|---------------------------------------------------------------------------------|
```

C.2 ASC and ASCQ in numerical order

Table 364: ASC and ASCQ Assignments

```
+=================================================================================+
|           D - DIRECT ACCESS DEVICE                                              |
|           .T - SEQUENTIAL ACCESS DEVICE                                         |
|           . L - PRINTER DEVICE                                                  |
|           .  P - PROCESSOR DEVICE                                               |
|           .  .W - WRITE ONCE READ MULTIPLE DEVICE                               |
|           .  . R - READ ONLY (CD-ROM) DEVICE                                    |
|           .  .  S - SCANNER DEVICE                                              |
|           .  .  .O - OPTICAL MEMORY DEVICE                                      |
|           .  .  . M - MEDIA CHANGER DEVICE                                      |
|           .  .  .  C - COMMUNICATION DEVICE                                     |
|           .  .  .  .                                                            |
| ASC ASCQ  DTLPWRSOMC  DESCRIPTION                                               |
| --- ----              ----------------------------------------------------------|
|  00  00   DTLPWRSOMC  NO ADDITIONAL SENSE INFORMATION                           |
|  00  01    T          FILEMARK DETECTED                                         |
|  00  02    T    S     END-OF-PARTITION/MEDIUM DETECTED                          |
|  00  03    T          SETMARK DETECTED                                          |
|  00  04    T    S     BEGINNING-OF-PARTITION/MEDIUM DETECTED                    |
|  00  05    T    S     END-OF-DATA DETECTED                                      |
|  00  06   DTLPWRSOMC  I/O PROCESS TERMINATED                                    |
|  00  11   R           AUDIO PLAY OPERATION IN PROGRESS                          |
|  00  12   R           AUDIO PLAY OPERATION PAUSED                               |
|  00  13   R           AUDIO PLAY OPERATION SUCCESSFULLY COMPLETED               |
```

```
|  00  14   R           AUDIO PLAY OPERATION STOPPED DUE TO ERROR              |
|  00  15   R           NO CURRENT AUDIO STATUS TO RETURN                      |
|  01  00   DW  O       NO INDEX/SECTOR SIGNAL                                 |
|  02  00   DWR OM      NO SEEK COMPLETE                                       |
|  03  00   DTL W SO    PERIPHERAL DEVICE WRITE FAULT                          |
|  03  01    T          NO WRITE CURRENT                                       |
|  03  02    T          EXCESSIVE WRITE ERRORS                                 |
|  04  00   DTLPWRSOMC  LOGICAL UNIT NOT READY, CAUSE NOT REPORTABLE           |
|  04  01   DTLPWRSOMC  LOGICAL UNIT IS IN PROCESS OF BECOMING READY           |
|  04  02   DTLPWRSOMC  LOGICAL UNIT NOT READY, INITIALIZING COMMAND REQUIRED  |
|  04  03   DTLPWRSOMC  LOGICAL UNIT NOT READY, MANUAL INTERVENTION REQUIRED   |
|  04  04   DTL    O    LOGICAL UNIT NOT READY, FORMAT IN PROGRESS             |
|  05  00   DTL WRSOMC  LOGICAL UNIT DOES NOT RESPOND TO SELECTION             |
|  06  00   DWR OM  NO  REFERENCE POSITION FOUND                               |
|  07  00   DTL WRSOM   MULTIPLE PERIPHERAL DEVICES SELECTED                   |
|  08  00   DTL WRSOMC  LOGICAL UNIT COMMUNICATION FAILURE                     |
|  08  01   DTL WRSOMC  LOGICAL UNIT COMMUNICATION TIME-OUT                    |
|  08  02   DTL WRSOMC  LOGICAL UNIT COMMUNICATION PARITY ERROR                |
|  09  00   DT  WR O    TRACK FOLLOWING ERROR                                  |
|  09  01       WR O    TRA CKING SERVO FAILURE                                |
|  09  02       WR O    FOC US SERVO FAILURE                                   |
|  09  03       WR O    SPI NDLE SERVO FAILURE                                 |
+==============================================================================+
```

Table 364: (continued)

```
+==============================================================================+
|           D - DIRECT ACCESS DEVICE                                           |
|           .T - SEQUENTIAL ACCESS DEVICE                                      |
|           . L - PRINTER DEVICE                                               |
|           .  P - PROCESSOR DEVICE                                            |
|           .  .W - WRITE ONCE READ MULTIPLE DEVICE                            |
|           .  . R - READ ONLY (CD-ROM) DEVICE                                 |
|           .  .  S - SCANNER DEVICE                                           |
|           .  .  .O - OPTICAL MEMORY DEVICE                                   |
|           .  .  . M - MEDIA CHANGER DEVICE                                   |
|           .  .  .  C - COMMUNICATION DEVICE                                  |
|           .  .  .  .                                                         |
| ASC ASCQ  DTLPWRSOMC  DESCRIPTION                                            |
| --- ----              ----------------------------------------------------- |
|  0A  00   DTLPWRSOMC  ERROR LOG OVERFLOW                                     |
|  0B  00                                                                      |
|  0C  00    T    S     WRITE ERROR                                            |
|  0C  01   D   W  O    WRITE ERROR RECOVERED WITH AUTO REALLOCATION           |
|  0C  02   D   W  O    WRITE ERROR - AUTO REALLOCATION FAILED                 |
|  0D  00                                                                      |
|  0E  00                                                                      |
|  0F  00                                                                      |
|  10  00   D   W  O    ID CRC OR ECC ERROR                                    |
|  11  00   DT  WRSO    UNRECOVERED READ ERROR                                 |
|  11  01   DT  W SO    READ RETRIES EXHAUSTED                                 |
|  11  02   DT  W SO    ERROR TOO LONG TO CORRECT                              |
|  11  03   DT  W SO    MULTIPLE READ ERRORS                                   |
|  11  04   D   W  O    UNRECOVERED READ ERROR - AUTO REALLOCATE FAILED        |
|  11  05       WR O    L-EC UNCORRECTABLE ERROR                               |
|  11  06       WR O    CIRC UNRECOVERED ERROR                                 |
|  11  07       W  O    DATA RESYCHRONIZATION ERROR                            |
|  11  08    T          INCOMPLETE BLOCK READ                                  |
|  11  09    T          NO GAP FOUND                                           |
|  11  0A   DT     O    MISCORRECTED ERROR                                     |
```

```
|  11  0B  D   W  O   UNRECOVERED READ ERROR - RECOMMEND REASSIGNMENT          |
|  11  0C  D   W  O   UNRECOVERED READ ERROR - RECOMMEND REWRITE THE DATA      |
|  12  00  D   W  O   ADDRESS MARK NOT FOUND FOR ID FIELD                      |
|  13  00  D   W  O   ADDRESS MARK NOT FOUND FOR DATA FIELD                    |
|  14  00  DTL WRSO   RECORDED ENTITY NOT FOUND                                |
|  14  01  DT  WR O   RECORD NOT FOUND                                         |
|  14  02   T         FILEMARK OR SETMARK NOT FOUND                            |
|  14  03   T         END-OF-DATA NOT FOUND                                    |
|  14  04   T         BLOCK SEQUENCE ERROR                                     |
|  15  00  DTL WRSOM  RANDOM POSITIONING ERROR                                 |
|  15  01  DTL WRSOM  MECHANICAL POSITIONING ERROR                             |
|  15  02  DT  WR O   POSITIONING ERROR DETECTED BY READ OF MEDIUM             |
|  16  00  DW     O   DATA SYNCHRONIZATION MARK ERROR                          |
|  17  00  DT  WRSO   RECOVERED DATA WITH NO ERROR CORRECTION APPLIED          |
|  17  01  DT  WRSO   RECOVERED DATA WITH RETRIES                              |
|  17  02  DT  WR O   RECOVERED DATA WITH POSITIVE HEAD OFFSET                 |
|  17  03  DT  WR O   RECOVERED DATA WITH NEGATIVE HEAD OFFSET                 |
|  17  04      WR O   RECOVERED DATA WITH RETRIES AND/OR CIRC APPLIED          |
|  17  05  D   WR O   RECOVERED DATA USING PREVIOUS SECTOR ID                  |
|  17  06  D   W  O   RECOVERED DATA WITHOUT ECC - DATA AUTO-REALLOCATED       |
|  17  07  D   W  O   RECOVERED DATA WITHOUT ECC - RECOMMEND REASSIGNMENT      |
|  17  08  D   W  O   RECOVERED DATA WITHOUT ECC - RECOMMEND REWRITE           |
|  18  00  DT  WR O   RECOVERED DATA WITH ERROR CORRECTION APPLIED             |
|  18  01  D   WR O   RECOVERED DATA WITH ERROR CORRECTION & RETRIES APPLIED   |
|  18  02  D   WR O   RECOVERED DATA - DATA AUTO-REALLOCATED                   |
|  18  03       R     RECOVERED DATA WITH CIRC                                 |
|  18  04       R     RECOVERED DATA WITH LEC                                  |
|  18  05  D   WR O   RECOVERED DATA - RECOMMEND REASSIGNMENT                  |
|  18  06  D   WR O   RECOVERED DATA - RECOMMEND REWRITE                       |
+==============================================================================+
```

Table 364: (continued)

```
+==============================================================================+
|          D - DIRECT ACCESS DEVICE                                            |
|          .T - SEQUENTIAL ACCESS DEVICE                                       |
|          . L - PRINTER DEVICE                                                |
|          .  P - PROCESSOR DEVICE                                             |
|          .  .W - WRITE ONCE READ MULTIPLE DEVICE                             |
|          .  . R - READ ONLY (CD-ROM) DEVICE                                  |
|          .  .  S - SCANNER DEVICE                                            |
|          .  .  .O - OPTICAL MEMORY DEVICE                                    |
|          .  .  . M - MEDIA CHANGER DEVICE                                    |
|          .  .  .  C - COMMUNICATION DEVICE                                   |
|          .  .  .  .                                                          |
| ASC ASCQ  DTLPWRSOMC  DESCRIPTION                                            |
| --- ----              -----------------------------------------------------  |
|  19  00   D      O    DEFECT LIST ERROR                                      |
|  19  01   D      O    DEFECT LIST NOT AVAILABLE                              |
|  19  02   D      O    DEFECT LIST ERROR IN PRIMARY LIST                      |
|  19  03   D      O    DEFECT LIST ERROR IN GROWN LIST                        |
|  1A  00   DTLPWRSOMC  PARAMETER LIST LENGTH ERROR                            |
|  1B  00   DTLPWRSOMC  SYNCHRONOUS DATA TRANSFER ERROR                        |
|  1C  00   D      O    DEFECT LIST NOT FOUND                                  |
|  1C  01   D      O    PRIMARY DEFECT LIST NOT FOUND                          |
|  1C  02   D      O    GROWN DEFECT LIST NOT FOUND                            |
|  1D  00   D   W  O    MISCOMPARE DURING VERIFY OPERATION                     |
|  1E  00   D   W  O    RECOVERED ID WITH ECC                                  |
|  1F  00                                                                      |
|  20  00   DTLPWRSOMC  INVALID COMMAND OPERATION CODE                         |
```

```
| 21  00   DT  WR OM   LOGICAL BLOCK ADDRESS OUT OF RANGE                      |
| 21  01          M    INVALID ELEMENT ADDRESS                                 |
| 22  00   D           ILLEGAL FUNCTION (SHOULD USE 20 00, 24 00, OR 26 00)    |
| 23  00                                                                       |
| 24  00   DTLPWRSOMC  INVALID FIELD IN CDB                                    |
| 25  00   DTLPWRSOMC  LOGICAL UNIT NOT SUPPORTED                              |
| 26  00   DTLPWRSOMC  INVALID FIELD IN PARAMETER LIST                         |
| 26  01   DTLPWRSOMC  PARAMETER NOT SUPPORTED                                 |
| 26  02   DTLPWRSOMC  PARAMETER VALUE INVALID                                 |
| 26  03   DTLPWRSOMC  THRESHOLD PARAMETERS NOT SUPPORTED                      |
| 27  00   DT  W  O    WRITE PROTECTED                                         |
| 28  00   DTLPWRSOMC  NOT READY TO READY TRANSITION(MEDIUM MAY HAVE CHANGED)  |
| 28  01          M    IMPORT OR EXPORT ELEMENT ACCESSED                       |
| 29  00   DTLPWRSOMC  POWER ON, RESET, OR BUS DEVICE RESET OCCURRED           |
| 2A  00   DTL WRSOMC  PARAMETERS CHANGED                                      |
| 2A  01   DTL WRSOMC  MODE PARAMETERS CHANGED                                 |
| 2A  02   DTL WRSOMC  LOG PARAMETERS CHANGED                                  |
| 2B  00   DTLPWRSO C  COPY CANNOT EXECUTE SINCE HOST CANNOT DISCONNECT        |
| 2C  00   DTLPWRSOMC  COMMAND SEQUENCE ERROR                                  |
| 2C  01         S     TOO MANY WINDOWS SPECIFIED                              |
| 2C  02         S     INVALID COMBINATION OF WINDOWS SPECIFIED                |
| 2D  00    T          OVERWRITE ERROR ON UPDATE IN PLACE                      |
| 2E  00                                                                       |
| 2F  00   DTLPWRSOMC  COMMANDS CLEARED BY ANOTHER INITIATOR                   |
| 30  00   DT  WR OM   INCOMPATIBLE MEDIUM INSTALLED                           |
| 30  01   DT  WR O    CANNOT READ MEDIUM - UNKNOWN FORMAT                     |
| 30  02   DT  WR O    CANNOT READ MEDIUM - INCOMPATIBLE FORMAT                |
| 30  03   DT          CLEANING CARTRIDGE INSTALLED                            |
| 31  00   DT  W  O    MEDIUM FORMAT CORRUPTED                                 |
| 31  01   D L    O    FORMAT COMMAND FAILED                                   |
| 32  00   D   W  O    NO DEFECT SPARE LOCATION AVAILABLE                      |
| 32  01   D   W  O    DEFECT LIST UPDATE FAILURE                              |
| 33  00    T          TAPE LENGTH ERROR                                       |
| 34  00                                                                       |
| 35  00                                                                       |
| 36  00     L         RIBBON, INK, OR TONER FAILURE                           |
+=============================================================================+
```

Table 364: (continued)

```
+=============================================================================+
|          D - DIRECT ACCESS DEVICE                                           |
|          .T - SEQUENTIAL ACCESS DEVICE                                      |
|          . L - PRINTER DEVICE                                               |
|          .  P - PROCESSOR DEVICE                                            |
|          .  .W - WRITE ONCE READ MULTIPLE DEVICE                            |
|          .  . R - READ ONLY (CD-ROM) DEVICE                                 |
|          .  .  S - SCANNER DEVICE                                           |
|          .  .  .O - OPTICAL MEMORY DEVICE                                   |
|          .  .  . M - MEDIA CHANGER DEVICE                                   |
|          .  .  .  C - COMMUNICATION DEVICE                                  |
|          .  .  .  .                                                         |
| ASC ASCQ DTLPWRSOMC  DESCRIPTION                                            |
| --- ----             ----------------------------------------------------   |
| 37  00   DTL WRSOMC  ROUNDED PARAMETER                                      |
| 38  00                                                                      |
| 39  00   DTL WRSOMC  SAVING PARAMETERS NOT SUPPORTED                        |
| 3A  00   DTL WRSOM   MEDIUM NOT PRESENT                                     |
| 3B  00    TL         SEQUENTIAL POSITIONING ERROR                           |
| 3B  01    T          TAPE POSITION ERROR AT BEGINNING-OF-MEDIUM             |
```

```
|  3B  02    T          TAPE POSITION ERROR AT END-OF-MEDIUM
|  3B  03     L         TAPE OR ELECTRONIC VERTICAL FORMS UNIT NOT READY
|  3B  04     L         SLEW FAILURE
|  3B  05     L         PAPER JAM
|  3B  06     L         FAILED TO SENSE TOP-OF-FORM
|  3B  07     L         FAILED TO SENSE BOTTOM-OF-FORM
|  3B  08    T          REPOSITION ERROR
|  3B  09         S     READ PAST END OF MEDIUM
|  3B  0A         S     READ PAST BEGINNING OF MEDIUM
|  3B  0B         S     POSITION PAST END OF MEDIUM
|  3B  0C         S     POSITION PAST BEGINNING OF MEDIUM
|  3B  0D           M   MEDIUM DESTINATION ELEMENT FULL
|  3B  0E           M   MEDIUM SOURCE ELEMENT EMPTY
|  3C  00
|  3D  00   DTLPWRSOMC  INVALID BITS IN IDENTIFY MESSAGE
|  3E  00   DTLPWRSOMC  LOGICAL UNIT HAS NOT SELF-CONFIGURED YET
|  3F  00   DTLPWRSOMC  TARGET OPERATING CONDITIONS HAVE CHANGED
|  3F  01   DTLPWRSOMC  MICROCODE HAS BEEN CHANGED
|  3F  02   DTLPWRSOMC  CHANGED OPERATING DEFINITION
|  3F  03   DTLPWRSOMC  INQUIRY DATA HAS CHANGED
|  40  00   D           RAM FAILURE (SHOULD USE 40 NN)
|  40  NN   DTLPWRSOMC  DIAGNOSTIC FAILURE ON COMPONENT NN (80H-FFH)
|  41  00   D           DATA PATH FAILURE (SHOULD USE 40 NN)
|  42  00   D           POWER-ON OR SELF-TEST FAILURE (SHOULD USE 40 NN)
|  43  00   DTLPWRSOMC  MESSAGE ERROR
|  44  00   DTLPWRSOMC  INTERNAL TARGET FAILURE
|  45  00   DTLPWRSOMC  SELECT OR RESELECT FAILURE
|  46  00   DTLPWRSOMC  UNSUCCESSFUL SOFT RESET
|  47  00   DTLPWRSOMC  SCSI PARITY ERROR
|  48  00   DTLPWRSOMC  INITIATOR DETECTED ERROR MESSAGE RECEIVED
|  49  00   DTLPWRSOMC  INVALID MESSAGE ERROR
|  4A  00   DTLPWRSOMC  COMMAND PHASE ERROR
|  4B  00   DTLPWRSOMC  DATA PHASE ERROR
|  4C  00   DTLPWRSOMC  LOGICAL UNIT FAILED SELF-CONFIGURATION
|  4D  00
|  4E  00   DTLPWRSOMC  OVERLAPPED COMMANDS ATTEMPTED
|  4F  00
|  50  00    T          WRITE APPEND ERROR
|  50  01    T          WRITE APPEND POSITION ERROR
|  50  02    T          POSITION ERROR RELATED TO TIMING
|  51  00    T     O    ERASE FAILURE
|  52  00    T          CARTRIDGE FAULT
+==============================================================================+

Table 364: (continued)
+==============================================================================+
|           D - DIRECT ACCESS DEVICE
|           .T - SEQUENTIAL ACCESS DEVICE
|           . L - PRINTER DEVICE
|           .  P - PROCESSOR DEVICE
|           .  .W - WRITE ONCE READ MULTIPLE DEVICE
|           .  . R - READ ONLY (CD-ROM) DEVICE
|           .  .  S - SCANNER DEVICE
|           .  .  .O - OPTICAL MEMORY DEVICE
|           .  .  . M - MEDIA CHANGER DEVICE
|           .  .  .  C - COMMUNICATION DEVICE
|           .  .  .  .
| ASC ASCQ  DTLPWRSOMC  DESCRIPTION
| --- ----              ----------------------------------------------------
```

```
|  53  00   DTL WRSOM   MEDIA LOAD OR EJECT FAILED                          |
|  53  01    T          UNLOAD TAPE FAILURE                                 |
|  53  02   DT  WR OM   MEDIUM REMOVAL PREVENTED                            |
|  54  00      P        SCSI TO HOST SYSTEM INTERFACE FAILURE               |
|  55  00      P        SYSTEM RESOURCE FAILURE                             |
|  56  00                                                                   |
|  57  00        R      UNABLE TO RECOVER TABLE-OF-CONTENTS                 |
|  58  00          O    GENERATION DOES NOT EXIST                           |
|  59  00          O    UPDATED BLOCK READ                                  |
|  5A  00   DTLPWRSOM   OPERATOR REQUEST OR STATE CHANGE INPUT (UNSPECIFIED)  |
|  5A  01   DT  WR OM   OPERATOR MEDIUM REMOVAL REQUEST                     |
|  5A  02   DT  W  O    OPERATOR SELECTED WRITE PROTECT                     |
|  5A  03   DT  W  O    OPERATOR SELECTED WRITE PERMIT                      |
|  5B  00   DTLPWRSOM   LOG EXCEPTION                                       |
|  5B  01   DTLPWRSOM   THRESHOLD CONDITION MET                             |
|  5B  02   DTLPWRSOM   LOG COUNTER AT MAXIMUM                              |
|  5B  03   DTLPWRSOM   LOG LIST CODES EXHAUSTED                            |
|  5C  00   D      O    RPL STATUS CHANGE                                   |
|  5C  01   D      O    SPINDLES SYNCHRONIZED                               |
|  5C  02   D      O    SPINDLES NOT SYNCHRONIZED                           |
|  5D  00                                                                   |
|  5E  00                                                                   |
|  5F  00                                                                   |
|  60  00         S     LAMP FAILURE                                        |
|  61  00         S     VIDEO ACQUISITION ERROR                             |
|  61  01         S     UNABLE TO ACQUIRE VIDEO                             |
|  61  02         S     OUT OF FOCUS                                        |
|  62  00         S     SCAN HEAD POSITIONING ERROR                         |
|  63  00        R      END OF USER AREA ENCOUNTERED ON THIS TRACK          |
|  64  00        R      ILLEGAL MODE FOR THIS TRACK                         |
|  65  00                                                                   |
|  66  00                                                                   |
|  67  00                                                                   |
|  68  00                                                                   |
|  69  00                                                                   |
|  6A  00                                                                   |
|  6B  00                                                                   |
|  6C  00                                                                   |
|  6D  00                                                                   |
|  6E  00                                                                   |
|  6F  00                                                                   |
+===========================================================================+
Table 364: (concluded)
+===========================================================================+
|           D - DIRECT ACCESS DEVICE                                        |
|           .T - SEQUENTIAL ACCESS DEVICE                                   |
|           . L - PRINTER DEVICE                                            |
|           .  P - PROCESSOR DEVICE                                         |
|           .  .W - WRITE ONCE READ MULTIPLE DEVICE                         |
|           .  . R - READ ONLY (CD-ROM) DEVICE                              |
|           .  .  S - SCANNER DEVICE                                        |
|           .  .  .O - OPTICAL MEMORY DEVICE                                |
|           .  .  . M - MEDIA CHANGER DEVICE                                |
|           .  .  .  C - COMMUNICATION DEVICE                               |
|           .  .  .  .                                                     |
| ASC ASCQ  DTLPWRSOMC  DESCRIPTION                                         |
| --- ----              ----------------------------------------------------|
|  70  00                                                                   |
```

```
|  71  00                                                                 |
|  72  00                                                                 |
|  73  00                                                                 |
|  74  00                                                                 |
|  75  00                                                                 |
|  76  00                                                                 |
|  77  00                                                                 |
|  78  00                                                                 |
|  79  00                                                                 |
|  7A  00                                                                 |
|  7B  00                                                                 |
|  7C  00                                                                 |
|  7D  00                                                                 |
|  7E  00                                                                 |
|  7F  00                                                                 |
|                                                                         |
|  80  xxh \                                                              |
|   THROUGH >  VENDOR SPECIFIC.                                           |
|  FF  xxh /                                                              |
|                                                                         |
|  xxh 80 \                                                               |
|  THROUGH >  VENDOR SPECIFIC QUALIFICATION OF STANDARD ASC.              |
|  xxh FF /                                                               |
|              ALL CODES NOT SHOWN OR BLANK ARE RESERVED.                 |
+=========================================================================+
```

D A SCSI command code quick reference

Table 365 is a numerical order listing of the command operation codes.

Table 365: SCSI-2 Operation Codes

```
+=========================================================================+
|           D - DIRECT ACCESS DEVICE                   Device Column Key  |
|           .T - SEQUENTIAL ACCESS DEVICE              M = Mandatory      |
|           . L - PRINTER DEVICE                       O = Optional       |
|           .  P - PROCESSOR DEVICE                    V = Vendor Specific|
|           .  .W - WRITE ONCE READ MULTIPLE DEVICE    R = Reserved       |
|           .  . R - READ ONLY (CD-ROM) DEVICE                            |
|           .  .  S - SCANNER DEVICE                                      |
|           .  .  .O - OPTICAL MEMORY DEVICE                              |
|           .  .  . M - MEDIA CHANGER DEVICE                              |
|           .  .  .  C - COMMUNICATION DEVICE                             |
|           .  .  .  .                                                    |
|        OP DTLPWRSOMC Description                                        |
|----------+----------+---------------------------------------------------|
|        00 MMMMMMMMMM TEST UNIT READY                                    |
|        01  M         REWIND                                             |
|        01 O V OO OO  REZERO UNIT                                        |
|        02 VVVVVV  V                                                     |
|        03 MMMMMMMMMM REQUEST SENSE                                      |
|        04   O        FORMAT                                             |
|        04 M      O   FORMAT UNIT                                        |
|        05 VMVVVV  V  READ BLOCK LIMITS                                  |
|        06 VVVVVV  V                                                     |
|        07         O  INITIALIZE ELEMENT STATUS                          |
|        07 OVV O  OV  REASSIGN BLOCKS                                    |
```

```
|      08          M GET MESSAGE(06)                                        |
|      08 OMV OO OV  READ(06)                                               |
|      08    O       RECEIVE                                                |
|      09 VVVVVV  V                                                         |
|      0A   M        PRINT                                                  |
|      0A          M SEND MESSAGE(06)                                       |
|      0A    M       SEND(06)                                               |
|      0A OM  O  OV  WRITE(06)                                              |
|      0B O   OO OV  SEEK(06)                                               |
|      0B   O        SLEW AND PRINT                                         |
|      0C VVVVVV  V                                                         |
|      0D VVVVVV  V                                                         |
|      0E VVVVVV  V                                                         |
|      0F VOVVVV  V  READ REVERSE                                           |
|      10   O O      SYNCHRONIZE BUFFER                                     |
|      10 VM VVV     WRITE FILEMARKS                                        |
|      11 VMVVVV     SPACE                                                  |
|      12 MMMMMMMMMM INQUIRY                                                |
|      13 VOVVVV     VERIFY(06)                                             |
|      14 VOOVVV     RECOVER BUFFERED DATA                                  |
|      15 OMO OOOOOO MODE SELECT(06)                                        |
|      16 M   MM MO  RESERVE                                                |
|      16  MM   M    RESERVE UNIT                                           |
|      17 M   MM MO  RELEASE                                                |
|      17  MM   M    RELEASE UNIT                                           |
|      18 OOOOOOOO   COPY                                                   |
|      19 VMVVVV     ERASE                                                  |
|      1A OMO OOOOOO MODE SENSE(06)                                         |
|      1B  O         LOAD UNLOAD                                            |
|      1B      O     SCAN                                                   |
|      1B   O        STOP PRINT                                             |
|      1B O   OO O   STOP START UNIT                                        |
+===========================================================================+
```

Table 365: (continued)

```
+===========================================================================+
|        D - DIRECT ACCESS DEVICE                        Device Column Key  |
|        .T - SEQUENTIAL ACCESS DEVICE                   M = Mandatory      |
|        . L - PRINTER DEVICE                            O = Optional       |
|        .  P - PROCESSOR DEVICE                         V = Vendor Specific|
|        .  .W - WRITE ONCE READ MULTIPLE DEVICE         R = Reserved       |
|        .  . R - READ ONLY (CD-ROM) DEVICE                                 |
|        .  .  S - SCANNER DEVICE                                           |
|        .  .  .O - OPTICAL MEMORY DEVICE                                   |
|        .  .  . M - MEDIA CHANGER DEVICE                                   |
|        .  .  .  C - COMMUNICATION DEVICE                                  |
|        .  .  .  .                                                         |
|      OP DTLPWRSOMC Description                                            |
|----------+----------+-----------------------------------------------------|
|      1C OOOOOOOOOO RECEIVE DIAGNOSTIC RESULTS                             |
|      1D MMMMMMMMMM SEND DIAGNOSTIC                                        |
|      1E OO  OO OO  PREVENT ALLOW MEDIUM REMOVAL                           |
|      1F                                                                   |
|      20 V   VV V                                                          |
|      21 V   VV V                                                          |
|      22 V   VV V                                                          |
|      23 V   VV V                                                          |
|      24 V   VVM     SET WINDOW                                            |
|      25       O     GET WINDOW                                            |
```

```
|      25  M   M  M   READ CAPACITY                                      |
|      25       M      READ CD-ROM CAPACITY                               |
|      26  V   VV                                                         |
|      27  V   VV                                                         |
|      28           O  GET MESSAGE(10)                                    |
|      28  M   MMMM    READ(10)                                           |
|      29  V   VV O    READ GENERATION                                    |
|      2A           O  SEND MESSAGE(10)                                   |
|      2A        O     SEND(10)                                           |
|      2A  M   M  M    WRITE(10)                                          |
|      2B   O          LOCATE                                             |
|      2B          O   POSITION TO ELEMENT                                |
|      2B  O   OO O    SEEK(10)                                           |
|      2C  V      O    ERASE(10)                                          |
|      2D  V   O  O    READ UPDATED BLOCK                                 |
|      2E  O   O  O    WRITE AND VERIFY(10)                               |
|      2F  O   OO O    VERIFY(10)                                         |
|      30  O   OO O    SEARCH DATA HIGH(10)                               |
|      31        O     OBJECT POSITION                                    |
|      31  O   OO O    SEARCH DATA EQUAL(10)                              |
|      32  O   OO O    SEARCH DATA LOW(10)                                |
|      33  O   OO O    SET LIMITS(10)                                     |
|      34        O     GET DATA BUFFER STATUS                             |
|      34  O   OO O    PRE-FETCH                                          |
|      34   O          READ POSITION                                      |
|      35  O   OO O    SYNCHRONIZE CACHE                                  |
|      36  O   OO O    LOCK UNLOCK CACHE                                  |
|      37  O      O    READ DEFECT DATA(10)                               |
|      38      O  O    MEDIUM SCAN                                        |
|      39  OOOOOOOO    COMPARE                                            |
|      3A  OOOOOOOO    COPY AND VERIFY                                    |
|      3B  OOOOOOOOOO  WRITE BUFFER                                       |
|      3C  OOOOOOOOOO  READ BUFFER                                        |
|      3D      O  O    UPDATE BLOCK                                       |
|      3E  O   OO O    READ LONG                                          |
|      3F  O   O  O    WRITE LONG                                         |
+=========================================================================+
Table 365: (continued)
+=========================================================================+
|         D - DIRECT ACCESS DEVICE                   Device Column Key     |
|         .T - SEQUENTIAL ACCESS DEVICE              M = Mandatory         |
|         . L - PRINTER DEVICE                       O = Optional          |
|         .  P - PROCESSOR DEVICE                    V = Vendor Specific   |
|         .  .W - WRITE ONCE READ MULTIPLE DEVICE    R = Reserved          |
|         .  . R - READ ONLY (CD-ROM) DEVICE                               |
|         .  .  S - SCANNER DEVICE                                         |
|         .  .  .O - OPTICAL MEMORY DEVICE                                 |
|         .  .  . M - MEDIA CHANGER DEVICE                                 |
|         .  .  .  C - COMMUNICATION DEVICE                                |
|         .  .  .  .                                                       |
|      OP DTLPWRSOMC Description                                           |
|----------+----------+---------------------------------------------------|
|      40  OOOOOOOOOO  CHANGE DEFINITION                                  |
|      41  O           WRITE SAME                                         |
|      42       O      READ SUB-CHANNEL                                   |
|      43       O      READ TOC                                           |
|      44       O      READ HEADER                                        |
|      45       O      PLAY AUDIO(10)                                     |
```

```
|       46                                                                |
|       47       O      PLAY AUDIO MSF                                    |
|       48       O      PLAY AUDIO TRACK INDEX                            |
|       49       O      PLAY TRACK RELATIVE(10)                           |
|       4A                                                                |
|       4B       O      PAUSE RESUME                                      |
|       4C OOOOOOOOOO LOG SELECT                                          |
|       4D OOOOOOOOOO LOG SENSE                                           |
|       4E                                                                |
|       4F                                                                |
|       50                                                                |
|       51                                                                |
|       52                                                                |
|       53                                                                |
|       54                                                                |
|       55 OOO OOOOOO MODE SELECT(10)                                     |
|       56                                                                |
|       57                                                                |
|       58                                                                |
|       59                                                                |
|       5A OOO OOOOOO MODE SENSE(10)                                      |
|       5B                                                                |
|       5C                                                                |
|       5D                                                                |
|       5E                                                                |
|       5F                                                                |
+=========================================================================+
```

Table 365: (concluded)

```
+=========================================================================+
|          D - DIRECT ACCESS DEVICE                  Device Column Key   |
|          .T - SEQUENTIAL ACCESS DEVICE             M = Mandatory       |
|          . L - PRINTER DEVICE                      O = Optional        |
|          .  P - PROCESSOR DEVICE                   V = Vendor Specific |
|          .  .W - WRITE ONCE READ MULTIPLE DEVICE   R = Reserved        |
|          .  . R - READ ONLY (CD-ROM) DEVICE                            |
|          .  .  S - SCANNER DEVICE                                      |
|          .  .  .O - OPTICAL MEMORY DEVICE                              |
|          .  .  . M - MEDIA CHANGER DEVICE                              |
|          .  .  .  C - COMMUNICATION DEVICE                             |
|          .  .  .  .                                                    |
|       OP DTLPWRSOMC Description                                        |
|----------+----------+-------------------------------------------------|
|       A0                                                               |
|       A1                                                               |
|       A2                                                               |
|       A3                                                               |
|       A4                                                               |
|       A5         M  MOVE MEDIUM                                        |
|       A5     O      PLAY AUDIO(12)                                     |
|       A6          O EXCHANGE MEDIUM                                    |
|       A7                                                               |
|       A8           O GET MESSAGE(12)                                   |
|       A8    OO O    READ(12)                                           |
|       A9     O      PLAY TRACK RELATIVE(12)                            |
|       AA           O SEND MESSAGE(12)                                  |
|       AA    O  O    WRITE(12)                                          |
|       AB                                                               |
|       AC         O  ERASE(12)                                          |
```

```
|     AD                                                                    |
|     AE      O  O   WRITE AND VERIFY(12)                                   |
|     AF      OO O   VERIFY(12)                                             |
|     B0      OO O   SEARCH DATA HIGH(12)                                   |
|     B1      OO O   SEARCH DATA EQUAL(12)                                  |
|     B2      OO O   SEARCH DATA LOW(12)                                    |
|     B3      OO O   SET LIMITS(12)                                         |
|     B4                                                                    |
|     B5                                                                    |
|     B5         O   REQUEST VOLUME ELEMENT ADDRESS                         |
|     B6                                                                    |
|     B6         O   SEND VOLUME TAG                                        |
|     B7        O    READ DEFECT DATA(12)                                   |
|     B8                                                                    |
|     B8         O   READ ELEMENT STATUS                                    |
|     B9                                                                    |
|     BA                                                                    |
|     BB                                                                    |
|     BC                                                                    |
|     BD                                                                    |
|     BE                                                                    |
|     BF                                                                    |
+===========================================================================+
```

E Example programs

Here is the C example program, which requests manufacturer and model and reports if a medium is loaded in the device.

```
#define DEVICE "/dev/sgc"
/* Example program to demonstrate the generic SCSI interface */
#include <stdio.h>
#include <unistd.h>
#include <string.h>
#include <fcntl.h>
#include <errno.h>
#include <scsi/sg.h>

#define SCSI_OFF sizeof(struct sg_header)
static unsigned char cmd[SCSI_OFF + 18];       /* SCSI command buffer */
int fd;                                /* SCSI device/file descriptor */

/* process a complete SCSI cmd. Use the generic SCSI interface. */
static int handle_scsi_cmd(unsigned cmd_len,         /* command length */
                           unsigned in_size,         /* input data size */
                           unsigned char *i_buff,    /* input buffer */
                           unsigned out_size,        /* output data size */
                           unsigned char *o_buff     /* output buffer */
                           )
{
    int status = 0;
    struct sg_header *sg_hd;

    /* safety checks */
    if (!cmd_len) return -1;            /* need a cmd_len != 0 */
    if (!i_buff) return -1;             /* need an input buffer != NULL */
#ifdef SG_BIG_BUFF
    if (SCSI_OFF + cmd_len + in_size > SG_BIG_BUFF) return -1;
    if (SCSI_OFF + out_size > SG_BIG_BUFF) return -1;
```

```
#else
    if (SCSI_OFF + cmd_len + in_size > 4096) return -1;
    if (SCSI_OFF + out_size > 4096) return -1;
#endif

    if (!o_buff) out_size = 0;

    /* generic SCSI device header construction */
    sg_hd = (struct sg_header *) i_buff;
    sg_hd->reply_len   = SCSI_OFF + out_size;
    sg_hd->twelve_byte = cmd_len == 12;
    sg_hd->result = 0;
#if     0
    sg_hd->pack_len    = SCSI_OFF + cmd_len + in_size; /* not necessary */
    sg_hd->pack_id;     /* not used */
    sg_hd->other_flags; /* not used */
#endif

    /* send command */
    status = write( fd, i_buff, SCSI_OFF + cmd_len + in_size );
    if ( status < 0 || status != SCSI_OFF + cmd_len + in_size ||
                       sg_hd->result ) {
        /* some error happened */
        fprintf( stderr, "write(generic) result = 0x%x cmd = 0x%x\n",
                    sg_hd->result, i_buff[SCSI_OFF] );
        perror("");
        return status;
    }

    if (!o_buff) o_buff = i_buff;       /* buffer pointer check */

    /* retrieve result */
    status = read( fd, o_buff, SCSI_OFF + out_size);
    if ( status < 0 || status != SCSI_OFF + out_size || sg_hd->result ) {
        /* some error happened */
        fprintf( stderr, "read(generic) result = 0x%x cmd = 0x%x\n",
                sg_hd->result, o_buff[SCSI_OFF] );
        fprintf( stderr, "read(generic) sense "
                "%x %x %x %x %x %x %x %x %x %x %x %x %x %x %x %x\n",
                sg_hd->sense_buffer[0],         sg_hd->sense_buffer[1],
                sg_hd->sense_buffer[2],         sg_hd->sense_buffer[3],
                sg_hd->sense_buffer[4],         sg_hd->sense_buffer[5],
                sg_hd->sense_buffer[6],         sg_hd->sense_buffer[7],
                sg_hd->sense_buffer[8],         sg_hd->sense_buffer[9],
                sg_hd->sense_buffer[10],        sg_hd->sense_buffer[11],
                sg_hd->sense_buffer[12],        sg_hd->sense_buffer[13],
                sg_hd->sense_buffer[14],        sg_hd->sense_buffer[15]);
        if (status < 0)
            perror("");
    }
    /* Look if we got what we expected to get */
    if (status == SCSI_OFF + out_size) status = 0; /* got them all */

    return status;  /* 0 means no error */
}

#define INQUIRY_CMD     0x12
#define INQUIRY_CMDLEN  6
```

```
#define INQUIRY_REPLY_LEN 96
#define INQUIRY_VENDOR  8       /* Offset in reply data to vendor name */

/* request vendor brand and model */
static unsigned char *Inquiry ( void )
{
  unsigned char Inqbuffer[ SCSI_OFF + INQUIRY_REPLY_LEN ];
  unsigned char cmdblk [ INQUIRY_CMDLEN ] =
      { INQUIRY_CMD,  /* command */
                  0,  /* lun/reserved */
                  0,  /* page code */
                  0,  /* reserved */
  INQUIRY_REPLY_LEN,  /* allocation length */
                  0 };/* reserved/flag/link */

  memcpy( cmd + SCSI_OFF, cmdblk, sizeof(cmdblk) );

  /*
   * +------------------+
   * | struct sg_header | <- cmd
   * +------------------+
   * | copy of cmdblk   | <- cmd + SCSI_OFF
   * +------------------+
   */

  if (handle_scsi_cmd(sizeof(cmdblk), 0, cmd,
                      sizeof(Inqbuffer) - SCSI_OFF, Inqbuffer )) {
      fprintf( stderr, "Inquiry failed\n" );
      exit(2);
  }
  return (Inqbuffer + SCSI_OFF);
}

#define TESTUNITREADY_CMD 0
#define TESTUNITREADY_CMDLEN 6

#define ADD_SENSECODE 12
#define ADD_SC_QUALIFIER 13
#define NO_MEDIA_SC 0x3a
#define NO_MEDIA_SCQ 0x00
int TestForMedium ( void )
{
  /* request READY status */
  static unsigned char cmdblk [TESTUNITREADY_CMDLEN] = {
      TESTUNITREADY_CMD, /* command */
                      0, /* lun/reserved */
                      0, /* reserved */
                      0, /* reserved */
                      0, /* reserved */
                      0};/* reserved */

  memcpy( cmd + SCSI_OFF, cmdblk, sizeof(cmdblk) );

  /*
   * +------------------+
   * | struct sg_header | <- cmd
   * +------------------+
   * | copy of cmdblk   | <- cmd + SCSI_OFF
```

```
   * +------------------+
   */

  if (handle_scsi_cmd(sizeof(cmdblk), 0, cmd,
                          0, NULL)) {
      fprintf (stderr, "Test unit ready failed\n");
      exit(2);
  }

  return
   *(((struct sg_header*)cmd)->sense_buffer +ADD_SENSECODE) !=
                                                  NO_MEDIA_SC ||
   *(((struct sg_header*)cmd)->sense_buffer +ADD_SC_QUALIFIER) !=
                                                  NO_MEDIA_SCQ;
}

void main( void )
{
  fd = open(DEVICE, O_RDWR);
  if (fd < 0) {
    fprintf( stderr, "Need read/write permissions for "DEVICE".\n" );
    exit(1);
  }

  /* print some fields of the Inquiry result */
  printf( "%s\n", Inquiry() + INQUIRY_VENDOR );

  /* look if medium is loaded */
  if (!TestForMedium()) {
    printf("device is unloaded\n");
  } else {
    printf("device is loaded\n");
  }
}
```

Part XLII

“Linux Serial HOWTO” by Greg Hankins, gregh@cc.gatech.edu

Contents

Abstract

v1.11, 15 November 1997
This document describes how to set up serial communications devices on a Linux box.

1 Introduction

This is the Linux Serial HOWTO. All about how to set up modems and terminals under Linux, some serial tips, and troubleshooting. This HOWTO addresses Linux running on Intel x86 hardware, although it might work for other architectures.

1.1 Copyright

1.2 New Versions Of This Document

New versions of the Serial HOWTO will be available at `ftp://sunsite.unc.edu:/pub/Linux/docs/HOWTO/Serial-HOWTO` and mirror sites. There are other formats, such as PostScript and DVI versions in the `other-formats` directory. The Serial HOWTO is also available at `http://sunsite.unc.edu/LDP/HOWTO/Serial-HOWTO.html` and will be posted to `comp.os.linux.answers` monthly.

1.3 Feedback

Please send me any questions, comments, suggestions, or additional material. I'm always eager to hear about what you think about the HOWTO. I'm also always on the lookout for improvements. Tell me exactly what you don't understand, or what could be clearer. You can reach me at `greg.hankins@cc.gatech.edu` via email. All email will be answered, although it may take me a week or so depending on how busy I am. I get a lot of email from `root` and mis-configured sites. Please send me email as a real person, and make sure that your email system is working so that I will be able to reply to you. If you don't hear back from me within two weeks, please try sending your email again.

I can also be reached at:
Greg Hankins
College of Computing
801 Atlantic Drive
Atlanta, GA 30332-0280
via snail mail, and at `http://www.cc.gatech.edu/staff/h/Greg.Hankins/`.

Please include the version number of the Serial HOWTO when writing, this is version 1.11.

1.4 Disclaimer

Your mileage may vary. The answers given may not work for all systems and all setup combinations.

2 Supported Serial Hardware

Linux is known to work with the following serial hardware.

2.1 Standard PC Serial Boards

- Standard PC serial boards (COM1–COM4), to which external serial devices (modems, serial mice, etc...) can be connected.
- Standard PC internal modems (COM1–COM4).
- Quickpath Systems Port-Folio 550e (allows IRQs of 3, 4, 5, 9, 10, 11, 12, and 15).

Note: due to address conflicts, you cannot use COM4 and IBM8514 video board simultaneously. This is due to a bug in the IBM8514 board.

2.2 Plug And Play (PnP) Modems

PnP modems will work with Linux. However, I recommend against using them because they are difficult. There are a couple things you can try;

- Try to disable the PnP features in the BIOS on your computer and modem.
- Boot Win95, configure the modem, and see if the settings are preserved when you boot Linux. If not, then:
- Boot Win95, configure the modem, and then *warm boot* Linux so that the settings are preserved. You can do this with the `loadlin` boot loader.
- Get the PnP tools from `http://www.redhat.com/linux-info/pnp`.
- And of course you can get a real modem.

2.3 Dumb Multiport Serial Boards (with 8250/16450/16550A UARTs)

- AST FourPort and clones (4 ports).
- Accent Async-4 (4 ports).
- Arnet Multiport-8 (8 ports).
- Bell Technologies HUB6 (6 ports).
- Boca BB-1004 (4 ports), BB-1008 (8 ports), BB-2016 (16 ports).
- Boca IOAT66 (6 ports).
- Boca 2by4 (4 serial ports, 2 parallel ports).
- Computone ValuePort V4-ISA (AST FourPort compatible).
- Digi PC/8 (8 ports).
- GTEK BBS-550 (8 ports).
- Longshine LCS-8880, Longshine LCS-8880+ (AST FourPort compatible).
- Moxa C104, Moxa C104+ (AST FourPort compatible).
- PC-COMM (4 ports).
- Sealevel Systems, http://www.sealevel.com, COMM-2 (2 ports), COMM-4 (4 ports) and COMM-8 (8 ports).
- SIIG I/O Expander 2S IO1812 (4 ports).
- STB-4COM (4 ports).
- Twincom ACI/550.
- Usenet Serial Board II (4 ports).

In general, Linux will support any serial board which uses a 8250, 16450, 16550, 16550A (or compatible) UART, or an internal modem which emulates one of the above UARTs.

Note: the BB-1004 and BB-1008 do not support DCD and RI lines, and thus are not usable for dial-in modems. They will work fine for all other purposes.

2.4 Intelligent Multiport Serial Boards

- Comtrol RocketPort (36MHz ASIC; 4, 8, 16 or 32 ports)
  contact: `info@comtrol.com` or `http://www.comtrol.com`
  driver status: supported by Comtrol
  driver location: `ftp://tsx-11.mit.edu/pub/linux/packages/comtrol`
- Computone IntelliPort II (16MHz 80186; 4, 8, or 16 ports),
  IntelliPort II EXpandable (20MHz 80186; 16—64 ports)
  contact: Michael H. Warfield, `mhw@wittsend.atl.ga.us`
  driver status: pre-ALPHA
- Cyclades Cyclom-Y (Cirrus Logic CD1400 UARTs; 8—32 ports),
  Cyclom-Z (25MHz MIPS R3000; 8—128 ports)
  contact: `sales@cyclades.com` or `http://www.cyclades.com`
  driver status: supported by Cyclades
  driver location: `ftp://ftp.cyclades.com/pub/cyclades` and included in Linux kernel since version 1.1.75

- Decision PCCOM8 (8 ports)
  contact: `pccom8@signum.se`
  driver location: `ftp://ftp.signum.se/pub/pccom8`
- Digi PC/Xi (12.5MHz 80186; 4, 8, or 16 ports),
  PC/Xe (12.5/16MHz 80186; 2, 4, or 8 ports),
  PC/Xr (16MHz IDT3041; 4 or 8 ports),
  PC/Xem (20MHz IDT3051; 8—64 ports)
  contact: `sales@dgii.com` or `http://www.dgii.com`
  driver status: supported by Digi
  driver location: `ftp://ftp.dgii.com/drivers/linux` and included in Linux kernel since version 2.0
- Digi COM/Xi (10MHz 80188; 4 or 8 ports)
  contact: Simon Park, `si@wimpol.demon.co.uk`
  driver status: ALPHA
  note: Simon is often away from email for months at a time due to his job. Mark Hatle, `fray@krypton.mankato.msus.edu` has graciously volunteered to make the driver available if you need it. Mark is not maintaining or supporting the driver.
- Equinox SuperSerial Technology (30MHz ASIC; 2—128 ports)
  contact: `sales@equinox.com` or `http://www.equinox.com`
  driver status: supported by Equinox
  driver location: `ftp://ftp.equinox.com/library/sst`
- GTEK Cyclone (16C654 UARTs; 6, 16 and 32 ports),
  SmartCard (24MHz Dallas DS80C320; 8 ports),
  BlackBoard-8A (16C654 UARTs; 8 ports),
  PCSS (15/24MHz 8032; 8 ports)
  contact: `spot@gtek.com` or `http://www.gtek.com`
  driver status: supported by GTEK
  driver location: `ftp://ftp.gtek.com/pub`
- Hayes ESP (COM-bic; 1—8 ports)
  contact: Andrew J. Robinson, `arobinso@nyx.net` or `http://www.nyx.net/~arobinso`
  driver status: supported by author
  driver location: `http://www.nyx.net/~arobinso` and included in Linux kernel since version 2.1.15
- Maxpeed SS (Toshiba; 4, 8 and 16 ports)
  contact: `info@maxpeed.com` or `http://www.maxpeed.com`
  driver status: supported by Maxpeed
  driver location: `ftp://maxpeed.com/pub/ss`
- Moxa C218 (12MHz 80286; 8 ports),
  Moxa C320 (40MHz TMS320; 8—32 ports)
  contact: `info@moxa.com.tw` or `http://www.moxa.com.tw`
  driver status: supported by Moxa
  driver location: `ftp://ftp.moxa.com.tw/drivers/c218-320/linux`
- SDL RISCom/8 (Cirrus Logic CD180; 8 ports)
  contact: `sales@sdlcomm.com` or `http://www.sdlcomm.com`
  driver status: supported by SDL
  driver location: `ftp://ftp.sdlcomm.com/pub/drivers`
- Specialix SIO (20MHz Zilog Z280; 4—32 ports),
  XIO (25MHz Zilog Z280; 4—32 ports)
  contact: Simon Allen, `simonallen@cix.compulink.co.uk`
  driver status: BETA
  driver location: `ftp://sunsite.unc.edu/pub/Linux/kernel/patches/serial`
- Stallion EasyIO-4 (4 ports), EasyIO-8 (8 ports), and
  EasyConnection (8—32 ports)—each with Cirrus Logic CD1400 UARTs,
  Stallion (8MHz 80186 CPU; 8 or 16 ports),
  Brumby (10/12 MHz 80186 CPU; 4, 8 or 16 ports),
  ONboard (16MHz 80186 CPU; 4, 8, 12, 16 or 32 ports),
  EasyConnection 8/64 (25MHz 80186 CPU; 8—64 ports)

contact: sales@stallion.com or http://www.stallion.com
driver status: supported by Stallion
driver location: ftp://ftp.stallion.com/drivers/ata5/Linux and included in linux kernel since 1.3.27

A review of Comtrol, Cyclades, Digi, and Stallion products was printed in the June 1995 issue of the *Linux Journal*. The article is available at http://www.ssc.com/lj/issue14.

2.5 Unsupported Serial Hardware

Modems that claim to be "Winmodems," for example, the USR Sportster Winmodem, and IBM Aptiva MWAVE, are not supported under Linux. These modems use proprietary designs that require special Windows drivers. Avoid these types of modems. In addition, stay away from modems that require Rockwell RPI drivers for the same reason.

Intelligent serial boards that require drivers not available for Linux won't work either.

3 What Are The Names Of The Serial Ports?

An I/O port is a way to get data into and out of a computer. There are many types of I/O ports such as serial ports, parallel ports, disk drive controllers, ethernet boards, etc. We will be dealing with serial ports since modems and terminals are serial devices. Each serial port must have an I/O address, and an interrupt (IRQ). There are the four serial ports corresponding to COM1–COM4:

```
ttyS0 (COM1) address 0x3f8 IRQ 4
ttyS1 (COM2) address 0x2f8 IRQ 3
ttyS2 (COM3) address 0x3e8 IRQ 4
ttyS3 (COM4) address 0x2e8 IRQ 3
```

If Linux does not detect any serial ports when it boots, then make sure that serial support is enabled and compiled into the kernel. In this document, I refer to COM1 as ttyS0, COM2 as ttyS1, COM3 as ttyS2, and COM4 as ttyS3. Notice that by default these devices have overlapping IRQs. You cannot use all of the ports in this default configuration, and you must reassign different IRQs. See Section 8 on setting IRQs.

On some installations, two extra devices will be created, /dev/modem for your modem and /dev/mouse for your mouse. Both of these are symbolic links to the appropriate device in /dev which you specified during the installation (unless you have a bus mouse, then /dev/mouse will point to the bus mouse device).

There has been some discussion on the merits of /dev/mouse and /dev/modem. I *strongly* discourage the use of these links. In particular, if you are planning on using your modem for dial-in you may run into problems because the lock files may not work correctly if you use /dev/modem. Use them if you like, but be sure they point to the right device. However, if you change or remove this link, some applications (minicom for example) might need reconfiguration.

3.1 Serial Port Devices and Numbers In /dev

```
/dev/ttyS0 major 4, minor 64      /dev/cua0 major 5, minor 64
/dev/ttyS1 major 4, minor 65      /dev/cua1 major 5, minor 65
/dev/ttyS2 major 4, minor 66      /dev/cua2 major 5, minor 66
/dev/ttyS3 major 4, minor 67      /dev/cua3 major 5, minor 67
```

Note that all distributions should come with these devices already made correctly. You can verify this by typing:

```
linux% ls -l /dev/cua*
linux% ls -l /dev/ttyS*
```

3.1.1 Creating Devices In /dev

If you don't have a device, you will have to create it with the mknod command. Example, suppose you needed to create devices for ttyS0:

```
linux# mknod -m 666 /dev/cua0 c 5 64
linux# mknod -m 666 /dev/ttyS0 c 4 64
```

You can use the MAKEDEV script, which lives in /dev. This simplifies the making of devices. For example, if you needed to make the devices for ttyS0 you would type:

```
linux# cd /dev
linux# ./MAKEDEV ttyS0
```

This handles the devices creation for the incoming and outgoing devices, and should set the correct permissions.

3.2 Notes For Dumb Multiport Boards

The devices your multiport board uses depends on what kind of board you have. These are listed in detail in `rc.serial` which comes with the `setserial` program. I highly recommend getting the latest version of `setserial` if you are trying to use multiport boards. You will probably need to create these devices. Either use the `mknod` command, or the `MAKEDEV` script. Devices for multiport boards are made by adding "64 + port number". So, if you wanted to create devices for `ttyS17`, you would type:

```
linux# mknod -m 666 /dev/cua17 c 5 81
linux# mknod -m 666 /dev/ttyS17 c 4 81
```

Note that "64 + 17 = 81." Using the `MAKEDEV` script, you would type:

```
linux# cd /dev
linux# ./MAKEDEV ttyS17
```

Note: the SIIG manual for the IO1812 listing for COM5–COM8 is wrong. They should be COM5=0x250, COM6=0x258, COM7=0x260, and COM8=0x268.

Note: the Digi PC/8 Interrupt Status Register is at 0x140.

Note: for an AST Fourport, you might need to specify `skip_test` in `rc.serial`.

3.3 Notes For Intelligent Multiport Boards

Read the information that comes with the driver. These boards use special devices, and not the standard ones. This information varies depending on your hardware.

4 Interesting Programs You Should Know About

4.1 What is `getty`?

`getty` is a program that handles the login process when you log onto a Unix box. You will need to use `getty` if you want to be able to dial in to your Linux machine with a modem. You do not need to use `getty` if you only want to dial out with your modem. There are three versions that are commonly used with Linux: `getty_ps`, `mgetty` and `agetty`. The syntax for these programs differs, so be sure to check and make sure that you are using the correct syntax for whatever `getty` you use.

4.1.1 About `getty_ps`

Most distributions come with the `getty_ps` package installed. It contains two programs: `getty` is used for console and terminal devices, and `uugetty` for modems. I use this version of `getty`, so that is what I will focus on.

4.1.2 About `mgetty`

`mgetty` is a version of `getty` for use with modems. In addition to allowing dialup logins, `mgetty` also provides FAX support and auto PPP detection. The `mgetty` documentation is very good, and does not need supplementing. Please refer to it for installation instructions. You can find the latest information on `mgetty` at `http://www.leo.org/~doering/mgetty/`.

4.1.3 About `agetty`

`agetty` is the third variation of `getty`. It's a simple, completely functional implementation of `getty` which is best suited for virtual consoles or terminals rather than modems.

4.2 What is `setserial`?

`setserial` is a program which allows you to look at and change various attributes of a serial device, including its port address, its interrupt, and other serial port options. You can find out what version you have by running `setserial` with no arguments.

When your Linux system boots, only `ttyS{0-3}` are configured, using the default IRQs of 4 and 3. So, if you have any other serial ports provided by other boards or if `ttyS{0-3}` have a non-standard IRQ, you *must* use this program in order to configure those serial ports. For the full listing of options, consult the man page.

5 How Do I Dial Out With My Modem?

5.1 Hardware Requirements

First, make sure you have the right cable. Your modem requires a straight through cable, with no pins crossed. Any computer store should have these. Make sure you get the correct gender. If you are using the DB25 serial port, it will always be the male DB25. Do not confuse it with the parallel port, which is the female DB25. Hook up your modem to one of your serial ports. Consult your modem manual on how to do this if you need help.

5.1.1 Notes On Internal Modems

For an internal modem, you will not need a cable. An internal modem does not need a serial port, it has one built in. All you need to do is configure it to use an interrupt that is not being used, and configure the port I/O address. Consult your modem manual if you get stuck. Also, see Section 8 if you need help on choosing interrupts or addresses.

On some motherboards you will have to disable the serial port that the modem is replacing in order to avoid conflicts. This may be done with jumpers or in the BIOS settings, depending on your motherboard. Consult your motherboard manual.

Due to a bug in IBM8514 video boards, you may encounter problems if you want your internal modem to be on `ttyS3`. If Linux does not detect your internal modem on `ttyS3`, you can use `setserial` and the modem will work fine. Internal modems on `ttyS{0-2}` should not have any problems being detected. Linux does not do any auto configuration on `ttyS3` due to this video board bug.

5.2 Talking To Your Modem

Use `kermit` or some other communications program to test the setup, before you go jumping into complex things like SLIP and PPP. You can find the latest version of `kermit` at `http://www.columbia.edu/kermit/`. For example, say your modem was on `ttyS3`, and its speed was 115200 bps. You would do the following:

```
linux# kermit
C-Kermit 6.0.192, 6 Sep 96, for Linux
 Copyright (C) 1985, 1996,
  Trustees of Columbia University in the City of New York.
Default file-transfer mode is BINARY
Type ? or HELP for help.
C-Kermit>set line /dev/ttyS3
C-Kermit>set carrier-watch off
C-Kermit>set speed 115200
/dev/ttyS3, 115200 bps
C-Kermit>c
Connecting to /dev/ttyS3, speed 115200.
The escape character is Ctrl-\ (ASCII 28, FS)
Type the escape character followed by C to get back,
or followed by ? to see other options.
ATE1Q0V1                        ; you type this and then the Enter key
OK                              ; modem should respond with this
```

If your modem responds to `AT` commands, you can assume your modem is working correctly on the Linux side. Now try calling another modem by typing:

```
ATDT7654321
```

where 7654321 is a phone number. Use ATDP instead of ATDT if you have a pulse line. If the call goes through, your modem is working.

To get back to the `kermit` prompt, hold down the Ctrl key, press the backslash key, then let go of the Ctrl key, then press the C key:

```
Ctrl-\-C
(Back at linux)
C-Kermit>quit
linux#
```

This was just a test using the primitive, "by hand" dialing method. The normal method is to let `kermit` do the dialing for you with its built-in modem database and automatic dialing features, for example using a US Robotics (USR) modem:

```
linux# kermit
C-Kermit 6.0.192, 6 Sep 1997, for Linux
 Copyright (C) 1985, 1996,
  Trustees of Columbia University in the City of New York.
Default file-transfer mode is BINARY
Type ? or HELP for help
C-Kermit>set modem type usr          ; Select modem type
C-Kermit>set line /dev/ttyS3         ; Select communication device
C-Kermit>set speed 115200            ; Set the dialing speed
C-Kermit>dial 7654321                ; Dial
 Number: 7654321
 Device=/dev/ttyS3, modem=usr, speed=115200
 Call completed.<BEEP>
Connecting to /dev/ttyS3, speed 115200
The escape character is Ctrl-\ (ASCII 28, FS).
Type the escape character followed by C to get back,
or followed by ? to see other options.

Welcome to ...

login:
```

See Section 10 about communications programs if you need some pointers.

When you dial out with your modem, set the speed to the highest bps rate that your modem supports. Versions of Linux with a `libc` version greater then 5.x have support for speeds up to 115200 bps. `libc` usually lives in `/lib`, so look there for what version you have. If Linux does not recognize a speed of 57600 or 115200 bps, then you must use the `setserial` program to set your serial port to a higher speed. See Section 9 for how to do this. Then, set the speed to 38400 bps in your comm program.

5.3 Dial-out Modem Configuration

For dial-out use only, you can configure your modem however you want. If you intend to use your modem for dial-in, you *must* configure your modem at the same speed that you intend to run `getty` at. So, if you want to run `getty` at 38400 bps, set your speed to 38400 bps when you configure your modem. This is done to prevent speed mismatches between your computer and modem. In general, factory defaults that enable error correction and hardware flow control are the best setting for dial out modems, consult your modem manual for these settings.

5.4 Hardware Flow Control

If your modem supports hardware flow control (RTS/CTS), I highly recommend that you use it. This is particularly important for modems that support data compression. First, you have to enable RTS/CTS flow control on the serial port itself. This is best done on startup, like in `/etc/rc.d/rc.local` or `/etc/rc.d/rc.serial`. Make sure that these files are being run from the main `rc.sysinit` file. You need to do the following for each serial port you want to enable hardware flow control on:

```
stty crtscts < /dev/ttyS3
```

You must also enable RTS/CTS flow control on your modem. Consult your modem manual on how to do this, as it varies between modem manufacturers. Be sure to save your modem configuration if your modem supports stored profiles.

6 How Do I Dial In And Out With My Modem Using `getty_ps`?

Get your modem to dial out correctly. If you haven't read Section 5 go read it now. It contains very important setup information. You do not need to read this section if you only want to dial out with your modem.

6.1 Dial-in And Dial-out Modem Configuration

For dial-in and dial-out use, you have to set up your modem a certain way (again, using `AT` commands on your modem):

```
E1      command echo ON
Q0      result codes are reported
V1      verbose ON
S0=0    never answer (uugetty handles this with the WAITFOR option)
```

If you don't set these correctly, your `INIT` string in your config file may fail, hosing the whole process. But, more on config files below...

```
&C1     DCD is on after connect only
&S0     DSR is always on
        DTR on/off resets modem (depends on manufacturer---RTFM)
```

These affect what your modem does when calls start and end.

If your modem does not support a stored profile, you can set these through the `INIT` string in your config file. See below. Some modems come with DIP switches that affect register settings. Be sure these are set correctly, too.

I have started a collection of modem setups for different types of modems. So far, I only have a few of them, if you would like to send me your working configuration, please do so. You can get them at `ftp://ftp.cc.gatech.edu/pub/people/gregh/modem-configs`.

Note: to get my USR Courier V.34 modem to reset correctly when DTR drops, I had to set `&D2` and `S13=1` (this sets bit 0 of register S13). This has been confirmed to work on USR Sportster V.34 modems as well.

Note: some Supra modems treat DCD differently than other modems. If you are using a Supra, try setting `&C0` and not `&C1`. You must also set `&D2` to handle DTR correctly.

6.2 Installing `getty_ps`

Get the latest version from `sunsite.unc.edu:/pub/Linux/system/serial`. In particular, if you want to use high speeds (57600 and 115200 bps), you must get version 2.0.7j or later. You must also have libc 5.x or greater.

By default, `getty_ps` will be configured to be Linux FSSTND (File System Standard) compliant, which means that the binaries will be in `/sbin`, and the config files will be named `/etc/conf.{uu}getty.ttyS`*N*. This is not apparent from the documentation. It will also expect lock files to go in `/var/lock`. Make sure you have the `/var/lock` directory.

If you don't want FSSTND compliance, binaries will go in `/etc`, config files will go in `/etc/default/{uu}getty.ttyS`*N*, and lock files will go in `/usr/spool/uucp`. I recommend doing things this way if you are using UUCP, because UUCP will have problems if you move the lock files to where it isn't looking for them.

`getty_ps` can also use `syslogd` to log messages. See the man pages for `syslogd(1)` and `syslog.conf(5)` for setting up `syslogd`, if you don't have it running already. Messages are logged with priority LOG_AUTH, errors use LOG_ERR, and debugging uses LOG_DEBUG. If you don't want to use `syslogd` you can edit `tune.h` in the `getty_ps` source files to use a log file for messages instead, namely `/var/adm/getty.log` by default.

Decide on if you want FSSTND compliance and syslog capability. You can also choose a combination of the two. Edit the `Makefile`, `tune.h` and `config.h` to reflect your decisions. Then compile and install according to the instructions included with the package.

From this point on, all references to `getty` will refer to `getty_ps`. References to `uugetty` will refer to the `uugetty` that comes with the `getty_ps` package. These instructions will not work for `mgetty` or `agetty`.

6.3 Setting up `uugetty`

For dialing into, and out from your modem, we want to use `uugetty`. `uugetty` does important lock file checking. Update `/etc/gettydefs` to include entries for modems if they aren't already there (note that the entries point to each other, these are not for fixed speed—blank lines are needed between each entry):

```
# Modem entries
115200# B115200 CS8 # B115200 SANE -ISTRIP HUPCL #@S @L @B login: #57600

57600# B57600 CS8 # B57600 SANE -ISTRIP HUPCL #@S @L @B login: #38400

38400# B38400 CS8 # B38400 SANE -ISTRIP HUPCL #@S @L @B login: #19200

19200# B19200 CS8 # B19200 SANE -ISTRIP HUPCL #@S @L @B login: #9600

9600# B9600 CS8 # B9600 SANE -ISTRIP HUPCL #@S @L @B login: #2400

2400# B2400 CS8 # B2400 SANE -ISTRIP HUPCL #@S @L @B login: #115200
```

If you have a 9600 bps or faster modem with data compression, you can lock your serial port speed and let the modem handle the transitions to other speeds. Then, instead of the step down series of lines listed above `/etc/gettydefs` only needs to contain one line for the modem, for example:

```
# 115200 fixed speed
F115200# B115200 CS8 # B115200 SANE -ISTRIP HUPCL #@S @L @B login: #F115200
```

If you have your modem set up to do RTS/CTS hardware flow control, you can add `CRTSCTS` to the entries:

```
# 115200 fixed speed with hardware flow control
F115200# B115200 CS8 CRTSCTS # B115200 SANE -ISTRIP HUPCL CRTSCTS #@S @L @B login: #F115200
```

If you want, you can make `uugetty` print interesting things in the login banner. In my examples, I have the system name, the serial line, and the current bps rate. You can add other things:

```
@B    The current (evaluated at the time the @B is seen) bps rate.
@D    The current date, in MM/DD/YY.
@L    The serial line to which getty is attached.
@S    The system name.
@T    The current time, in HH:MM:SS (24-hour).
@U    The number of currently signed-on users.  This is  a
      count of the number of entries in the /etc/utmp file
      that have a non-null ut_name field.
@V    The value of VERSION, as given in the defaults file.
To display a single '@' character, use either '\@' or '@@'.
```

Next, make sure that you have an outgoing and incoming device for the serial port your modem is on. If you have your modem on `ttyS3` you will need the `/dev/cua3`, and `/dev/ttyS3` devices. If you don't have the correct devices, see section 3.1.1 on how to create devices, and create the devices. If you want to be able to dial out with your modem while `uugetty` is watching the port for logins, use the `/dev/cua`*N* device instead of the `/dev/ttyS`*N* device.

When you are done editing `/etc/gettydefs`, you can verify that the syntax is correct by doing:

```
linux# getty -c /etc/gettydefs
```

6.4 Customizing `uugetty`

There are lots of parameters you can tweak for each port you have. These are implemented in separate config files for each port. The file `/etc/conf.uugetty` will be used by all instances of `uugetty`, and `/etc/conf.uugetty.ttyS`*N* will only be used by that one port. Sample default config files can be found with the `getty_ps` source files, which come with most Linux distributions. Due to space concerns, they are not listed here. Note that if you are using older versions of `getty` (older than 2.0.7e), or aren't using FSSTND, then the default file will be `/etc/default/uugetty.ttyS`*N*. My `/etc/conf.uugetty.ttyS3` looks like this:

```
# sample uugetty configuration file for a Hayes compatible modem to allow
# incoming modem connections
#
# alternate lock file to check... if this lock file exists, then uugetty is
# restarted so that the modem is re-initialized
ALTLOCK=cua3
ALTLINE=cua3
# line to initialize
INITLINE=cua3
# timeout to disconnect if idle...
TIMEOUT=60
# modem initialization string...
# format: <expect> <send> ... (chat sequence)
INIT="" AT\r OK\r\n
WAITFOR=RING
CONNECT="" ATA\r CONNECT\s\A
# this line sets the time to delay before sending the login banner
DELAY=1
#DEBUG=010
```

Add the following line to your `/etc/inittab`, so that `uugetty` is run on your serial port (substituting in the correct information for your environment—config file location, port, speed, and default terminal type):

```
S3:456:respawn:/sbin/uugetty -d /etc/default/uugetty.ttyS3 ttyS3 F115200 vt100
```

Restart `init`:

```
linux# init q
```

For the speed parameter in your /etc/inittab, you want to use the highest bps rate that your modem supports.

Now Linux will be watching your serial port for connections. Dial in from another machine and log in to you Linux system.

uugetty has a lot more options, see the man page for getty(1m) for a full description. Among other things there is a scheduling feature, and a ring-back feature.

7 How Do I Set Up A Terminal Connected To My PC?

The instructions in this section will work for connecting terminals, as well as other computers to the serial port on your Linux box.

7.1 Hardware Requirements

Make sure you have the right kind of cable. A null modem cable bought at a computer store will do it. But it must be a **null modem** cable. Many computer stores advertise this kind of cable as a serial printer cable. Make sure you are using your serial port, the male DB25 or the DB9, and not your parallel port (female DB25 or Centronics).

For a DB25 connector, you need a minimum of:

```
PC male DB25                            Terminal DB25
TxD    Transmit Data          2 --> 3   RxD    Receive Data
RxD    Receive Data           3 <-- 2   TxD    Transmit Data
SG     Signal Ground          7 --- 7   SG     Signal Ground
```

If you want to have hardware handshaking signals, you must have a full null modem cable:

```
PC male DB25                            Terminal DB25
TxD    Transmit Data          2 --> 3   RxD    Receive Data
RxD    Receive Data           3 <-- 2   TxD    Transmit Data
RTS    Request To Send        4 --> 5   CTS    Clear To Send
CTS    Clear To Send          5 <-- 4   RTS    Request To Send
DSR    Data Set Ready         6
                              |
DCD    Carrier Detect         8 <-- 20  DTR    Data Terminal Ready
SG     Signal Ground          7 --- 7   SG     Signal Ground
                                    6   DSR    Data Set Ready
                                    |
DTR    Data Terminal Ready   20 --> 8   DCD    Carrier Detect
```

If you have a DB9 connector on your serial port, try the following:

```
PC DB9                                  Terminal DB25
RxD    Receive Data           2 <-- 2   TxD    Transmit Data
TxD    Transmit Data          3 --> 3   RxD    Receive Data
SG     Signal Ground          5 --- 7   SG     Signal Ground
```

Alternatively, a full DB9 to DB25 null modem cable:

```
PC DB9                                  Terminal DB25
RxD    Receive Data           2 <-- 2   TxD    Transmit Data
TxD    Transmit Data          3 --> 3   RxD    Receive Data
                                    6   DSR    Data Set Ready
                                    |
DTR    Data Terminal Ready    4 --> 8   DCD    Carrier Detect
GND    Signal Ground          5 --- 7   GND    Signal Ground
DCD    Carrier Detect         1
                              |
DSR    Data Set Ready         6 <-- 20  DTR    Data Terminal Ready
RTS    Request To Send        7 --> 5   CTS    Clear To Send
CTS    Clear To Send          8 <-- 4   RTS    Request To Send
(RI    Ring Indicator         9 not needed)
```

(Yes, the pins 2 and 3 really do have the opposite meanings in DB9 connectors than in DB25 connectors.)

If you are not using a full null modem cable, you might have to do the following trick: on your computer side of the connector, connect RTS and CTS together, and also connect DSR, DCD and DTR together. This way, when the computer wants a certain handshaking signal, it will get it (from itself).

Now that you have the right kind of cable, connect your terminal to your computer. If you can, tell the terminal to ignore modem control signals. Try using 9600 bps, 8 data bits, 1 stop bit, no parity bits for the terminal's setup.

7.2 Setting up `getty`

Add entries for `getty` to use for your terminal in `/etc/gettydefs` if there they aren't already there:

```
# 38400 bps Dumb Terminal entry
DT38400# B38400 CS8 CLOCAL # B38400 SANE -ISTRIP CLOCAL #@S @L login: #DT38400

# 19200 bps Dumb Terminal entry
DT19200# B19200 CS8 CLOCAL # B19200 SANE -ISTRIP CLOCAL #@S @L login: #DT19200

# 9600 bps Dumb Terminal entry
DT9600# B9600 CS8 CLOCAL # B9600 SANE -ISTRIP CLOCAL #@S @L login: #DT9600
```

If you want, you can make `getty` print interesting things in the login banner. In my examples, I have the system name and the serial line printed. You can add other things:

```
@B    The current (evaluated at the time the @B is seen) bps rate.
@D    The current date, in MM/DD/YY.
@L    The serial line to which getty is attached.
@S    The system name.
@T    The current time, in HH:MM:SS (24-hour).
@U    The number of currently signed-on users.  This is  a
      count of the number of entries in the /etc/utmp file
      that have a non-null ut_name field.
@V    The value of VERSION, as given in the defaults file.
To display a single '@' character, use either '\@' or '@@'.
```

When you are done editing `/etc/gettydefs`, you can verify that the syntax is correct by doing:

```
linux# getty -c /etc/gettydefs
```

Make sure there is no `getty` or `uugetty` configuration file for the serial port that your terminal is attached to (`/etc/default/{uu}getty.ttyS`*N* or `/etc/conf.{uu}getty.ttyS`*N*), as this will probably interfere with running `getty` on a terminal. Remove the file if it exits.

Edit your `/etc/inittab` file to run `getty` on the serial port (substituting in the correct information for your environment— port, speed, and default terminal type):

```
S1:456:respawn:/sbin/getty ttyS1 DT9600 vt100
```

Restart `init`:

```
linux# init q
```

At this point, you should see a login prompt on your terminal. You may have to hit Return to get the terminal's attention.

7.3 Notes On Setting Up A PC As A Terminal

Many people set up other PCs as terminals connected to Linux boxen. For example, old 8088 or 80286 PCs are perfect for this purpose. All you need is a DOS boot disk containing a version of DOS suitable for your terminal-PC, and a communications program for your terminal-PC to run. `kermit` works very well for this purpose. You can find precompiled versions of `kermit` for every OS in existence at `http://www.columbia.edu/kermit/`. Other popular DOS comm programs such as `Telix` and `Procomm` will work equally well. Be sure to input correct serial port information into your terminal-PC's communications setup.

8 Can I Use More Than Two Serial Devices?

You don't need to read this section, unless you want to use three or more serial devices... (assuming you don't have a multiport board).

Providing you have another spare serial port, yes you can. The number of serial ports you can use is limited by the number of interrupts (IRQs) and port I/O addresses we have to use. This is not a Linux limitation, but a limitation of the PC bus. Each serial devices must be assigned it's own interrupt and address. A serial device can be a serial port, an internal modem, or a multiport serial board.

Multiport serial boards are specially designed to have multiple serial ports that share the same IRQ for all serial ports on the board. Linux gets data from them by using a different I/O address for each port on the board.

8.1 Choosing Serial Device Interrupts

Your PC will normally come with `ttyS0` and `ttyS2` at IRQ 4, and `ttyS1` and `ttyS3` at IRQ 3. You can see what IRQs are in use by looking at `/proc/interrupts`. To use more than two serial devices, you will have to reassign an interrupt. A good choice is to reassign an interrupt from your parallel port. Your PC normally comes with IRQ 5 and IRQ 7 set up as interrupts for your parallel ports, but few people use two parallel ports. You can reassign one of the interrupts to a serial device, and still happily use a parallel port. You will need the `setserial` program to do this. In addition, you have to play with the jumpers on your boards, check the documentation for your board. Set the jumpers to the IRQ you want for each port.

You will need to set things up so that there is one, and only one interrupt for each serial device. Here is how I set mine up in `/etc/rc.d/rc.local`—you should do it upon startup somewhere:

```
/sbin/setserial /dev/ttyS0 irq 3        # my serial mouse
/sbin/setserial /dev/ttyS1 irq 4        # my Wyse dumb terminal
/sbin/setserial /dev/ttyS2 irq 5        # my Zoom modem
/sbin/setserial /dev/ttyS3 irq 9        # my USR modem
```

Standard IRQ assignments:

```
IRQ  0    Timer channel 0
IRQ  1    Keyboard
IRQ  2    Cascade for controller 2
IRQ  3    Serial port 2
IRQ  4    Serial port 1
IRQ  5    Parallel port 2
IRQ  6    Floppy diskette
IRQ  7    Parallel port 1
IRQ  8    Real-time clock
IRQ  9    Redirected to IRQ2
IRQ 10    not assigned
IRQ 11    not assigned
IRQ 12    not assigned
IRQ 13    Math coprocessor
IRQ 14    Hard disk controller 1
IRQ 15    Hard disk controller 2
```

There is really no Right Thing To Do when choosing interrupts. Just make sure it isn't being used by the motherboard, or any other boards. 2, 3, 4, 5, or 7 is a good choice. "Not assigned" means that currently nothing standard uses these IRQs. Also note that IRQ 2 is the same as IRQ 9. You can call it either 2 or 9, the serial driver is very understanding. If you have a serial board with a 16-bit bus connector, you can also use IRQ 10, 11, 12 or 15.

◇ Just make sure you don't use IRQ 0, 1, 6, 8, 13 or 14. These are used by your mother board. You will make her very unhappy by taking her IRQs. When you are done, double-check `/proc/interrupts` and make sure there are no conflicts.

8.2 Setting Serial Device Addresses

Next, you must set the port address. Check the manual on your board for the jumper settings. Like interrupts, there can only be one serial device at each address. Your ports will usually come configured as follows:

```
ttyS0 address 0x3f8
ttyS1 address 0x2f8
ttyS2 address 0x3e8
ttyS3 address 0x2e8
```

Choose which address you want each serial device to have and set the jumpers accordingly. I have my modem on `ttyS3`, my mouse on `ttyS0`, and my terminal on `ttyS2`.

When you reboot, Linux should see your serial ports at the address you set them. The IRQ Linux sees may not correspond to the IRQ you set with the jumpers. Don't worry about this. Linux does not do any IRQ detection when it boots, because IRQ detection is dicy and can be fooled. Use `setserial` to tell Linux what IRQ the port is using. You can check `/proc/ioports` to see what I/O port addresses are in use after Linux boots.

9 How Do I Set Up My Serial Ports For Higher Speeds? What Speed Should I Use With My Modem?

This section should help you figure out what speed to use when using your modem with a communications program, or with a `getty` program.

- If you have something slower than a 9600 bps (V.32) modem, set your speed to the highest speed your modem supports. For example 300 bps (V.21/Bell 103), 1200 bps (V.22/Bell 212A), or 2400 bps (V.22bis).
- If you have a 9600 bps (V.32) modem, with V.42bis data compression, use 38400 bps as your speed. V.42bis compression has a *theoretical* rate of 4:1, thus "4 * 9600 = 38400."
- If you have a 14400 bps (V.32bis) modem, with V.42bis data compression, use `setserial` with the `spd_hi` flag to configure your serial port to use 57600 bps (4 * 14400 = 57600). Use the `spd_vhi` flag if you have a 28800 or 33600 bps (V.FC or V.34) modem (4 * 28800 = 115200).

  Then, use 38400 bps as the speed in your communication program, or `/etc/inittab`. This is now the high speed you have set. Make sure you have 16550A UARTs.

  If your libc version is at least 5.x, there will be speeds named 57600 and 115200. `libc` lives in `/lib`, so look there for what version you have. You can use these directly (without using `setserial`), if your applications have been compiled to take advantage of this. There are many distributions out there, so the best thing to do would be to try using these higher speeds if you have a recent version of a Linux distribution.

Test your `setserial` setting on the command line first, and then when you have them working, put them into `/etc/rc.d/rc.serial` or `/etc/rc.d/rc.local` so that they are done at startup. In my `/etc/rc.d/rc.local`, I set `ttyS3` to 115200 bps by doing:

```
/sbin/setserial /dev/ttyS3 spd_vhi
```

Make sure that you are using a valid path for `setserial`, and a valid device name. You can check the settings of a serial port by running:

```
setserial -a /dev/ttyS3
```

10 Communications Programs And Utilities

Here is a list of some communication software you can choose from, available via FTP, if they didn't come with your distribution.

- `ecu`—a communications program
- C Kermit, http://www.columbia.edu/kermit/: portable, scriptable, serial and TCP/IP communications, including file transfer and character-set translation
- `minicom`—`telix`-like communications program
- `procomm`—`procomm`-like communications program with zmodem
- `seyon`—X based communication program
- `xc`—xcomm communication package
- Other useful programs are `term` and `SLiRP`. They offer TCP/IP functionality using a shell account.
- `screen` is another multi-session program. This one behaves like the virtual consoles.
- `callback` is a program that will have your modem call you back.
- `mgetty+fax` handles FAX stuff, and provides an alternate `getty`.

- ZyXEL is a control program for ZyXEL U-1496 modems. It handles dial-in, dial-out, dial-back security, FAXing, and voice mailbox functions.
- SLIP and PPP software can be found at ftp://sunsite.unc.edu/pub/Linux/system/network/serial.
- Other things can be found on ftp://sunsite.unc.edu/pub/Linux/system/serial and ftp://sunsite.unc.edu/pub/Linux/apps/serialcomm or one of the many mirrors. These are the directories where serial programs are kept.

11 Serial Tips And Miscellany

Here are some serial tips you might find helpful...

11.1 kermit and zmodem

To use zmodem with kermit, add the following to your .kermrc:

```
define rz !rz < /dev/ttyS3 > /dev/ttyS3
define sz !sz \%0 > /dev/ttyS3 < /dev/ttyS3
```

Be sure to put in the correct port your modem is on. Then, to use it, just type rz or sz <filename> at the kermit prompt.

11.2 Setting Terminal Types Automagically

To set your terminal type automagically when you log in, add the terminal type to the entry in /etc/inittab. If I have a vt100 terminal on ttyS1, I would add "vt100" to the getty command:

```
S1:456:respawn:/sbin/getty ttyS1 DT9600 vt100
```

You can also use tset, which can establish terminal characteristics when you log in, and doesn't depend on any defaults.

11.3 Color ls On Serial Connections

If ls is screwing up your terminal emulation with the color feature, turn it off. ls -color, and ls -colour all use the color feature. Some installations have ls set to use color by default. Check /etc/profile and /etc/csh.cshrc for ls aliases. You can also alias ls to ls -no-color, if you don't want to change the system defaults.

11.4 Printing To A Printer Connected To A Terminal

There is a program called vtprint, available from ftp://ftp.sdsu.edu/pub/vtprint, and from http://www.sdsu.edu/~garrett.

Another program that will do this is called xprt. It can be found at ftp://sunsite.unc.edu/pub/Linux/system/printing.

11.5 Can Linux Configure The Serial Devices Automagically?

Yes. To get Linux to detect and set up the serial devices automatically on startup, add the line:

```
/sbin/setserial /dev/ttyS3 auto_irq skip_test autoconfig
```

to your /etc/rc.d/rc.local or /etc/rc.d/rc.serial file. Do this for every serial port you want to auto configure. Be sure to give a device name that really does exist on your machine.

11.5.1 Notes For Multiport Boards

For board addresses, and IRQs, look at the rc.serial that comes with the setserial program. It has a lot of detail on multiport boards, including I/O addresses and device names.

11.6 Using A Serial Console

There is an article in issue 36 of the *Linux Journal*, http://www.ssc.com/lj/issue36/index.html that explains how to use a serial console. Unfortunately, email to the author bounces. I hope that the article will be on the *Linux Journal* web site at the above URL soon.

11.7 Higher Serial Throughput

If you are seeing slow throughput and serial port overruns on a system with (E)IDE disk drives, you can get `hdparm`. This is a utility that can modify (E)IDE parameters, including unmasking other IRQs during a disk IRQ. This will improve repsonsiveness and will help eliminate overruns. Be sure to read the man page very carefully, since some drive/controller combinations don't like this and may corrupt the filesystem.

Also have a look at a utility called `irqtune` that will change the IRQ priority of a device, for example the serial port that your modem is on. This may improve the serial throughput on your system. The `irqtune` FAQ is at `http://www.best.com/~cae/irqtune`.

12 One Step Further...

This section is not required reading, but may give you some further insight into Unix, and the world of telecommunications.

12.1 What Are Lock Files?

Lock file are simply a file saying that a particular device is in use. They are kept in `/usr/spool/uucp`, or `/var/lock`. Linux lock files are named `LCK..`*name*, where *name* is either a device name, or a UUCP site name. Certain processes create these locks so that they can have exclusive access to devices, for instance if you dial out on your modem, a lock will appear telling other processes that someone is using the modem already. Locks mainly contain the PID of the process that has locked the device. Most programs look at the lock, and try to determine if that lock is still valid by checking the process table for the process that has locked the device. If the lock is found to be valid, the program (should) exit. If not, some programs remove the stale lock, and use the device, creating their own lock in the process. Other programs just exit and tell you that the device is in use.

12.2 "baud" Vs. "bps"

"baud" and "bps" are perhaps two of the most confused terms in the computing and telecommunications field. Many people use these terms interchangeably, when in fact they are not.

baud

The baud rate is a measure of how many times per second a signal, for instance one sent by a modem (**mo**dulator-**dem**odulator) changes. For example, a baud rate of 1200 implies one signal change every 833 microseconds. Common modem baud rates are 50, 75, 110, 300, 600, 1200, and 2400. Most high speed modems run at 2400 baud. Because of the bandwidth limitations on voice-grade phone lines, baud rates greater than 2400 are harder to achieve, and only work under very pristine phone line quality. Multiple bits can be encoded per baud, to get bit rates that exceed the baud rate. "baud" is named after Emile Baudot, the inventor of the asynchronous telegraph printer.

bps

The bps rate is a measure of how many bits per second are transmitted. Common modem bps rates are 50, 75, 110, 300, 1200, 2400, 9600, ... 115200. Using modems with V.42bis compression (max 4:1 compression), theoretical rates up to 115200 bps are possible. This is what most people mean when they misuse the word "baud."

So, if high-speed modems are running at 2400 baud, how can they send 14400 bps? The modems achieve a bps rate greater than baud rate by encoding many bits in each signal change, or phase change. Thus, when 2 or more bits are encoded per baud, the bps rate exceeds the baud rate. If your modem connects at 14400 bps, it's going to be sending 6 bits per phase change, at 2400 baud.

How did this confusion start? Well, back when low speed modems were high-speed modems, the bps rate actually did equal the baud rate. One bit would be encoded per phase change. People would use bps and baud interchangeably, because they were the same number. For example, a 300 bps modem also had a baud rate of 300. This all changed when faster modems came around, and the bit rate exceeded the baud rate.

12.3 What Are UARTs? How Do They Affect Performance?

UARTs (Universal Asynchronous Receiver Transmitters) are chips on your PC serial board. Their purpose is to convert data to bits, send the bits down the serial line, and then rebuild the data again on the other end. UARTs deal with data in byte sized pieces, which is conveniently also the size of ASCII characters.

Say you have a terminal hooked up to your PC. When you type a character, the terminal gives that character to it's transmitter (also a UART). The transmitter sends that byte out onto the serial line, one bit at a time, at a specific rate. On the PC end, the receiving UART takes all the bits and rebuilds the byte and puts it in a buffer.

There are two different types of UARTs. You have probably heard of dumb UARTs—the 8250 and 16450, and FIFO UARTs—the 16550A. To understand their differences, first let's examine what happens when a UART has sent or received a byte.

The UART itself can't do anything with the data, it just sends and receives it. The CPU gets an interrupt from the serial device every time a byte has been sent or received. The CPU then moves the received byte out of the UART's buffer and into memory somewhere, or gives the UART another byte to send. The 8250 and 16450 UARTs only have a 1 byte buffer. That means, that every time 1 byte is sent or received, the CPU is interrupted. At low rates, this is OK. But, at high transfer rates, the CPU gets so busy dealing with the UART, that is doesn't have time to tend to other tasks. In some cases, the CPU does not get around to servicing the interrupt in time, and the byte is overwritten, because they are coming in so fast.

That's where the 16550A UARTs are useful. These chips come with 16 byte FIFOs. This means that it can receive or transmit up to 16-bytes before it has to interrupt the CPU. Not only can it wait, but the CPU then can transfer all 16 bytes at a time. Although the interrupt threshold is seldom set at 16, this is still a significant advantage over the other UARTs, which only have the 1-byte buffer. The CPU receives less interrupts, and is free to do other things. Data is not lost, and everyone is happy. (There is also a 16550 UART, but it is treated as a 16450 since it is broken.)

In general, the 8250 and 16450 UARTs should be fine for speeds up to 38400 bps. At speeds greater than 38400 bps, you might start seeing data loss. Other PC operating systems (definition used loosely here), like MS-DOS aren't multitasking, so they might be able to cope better with 8250 or 16450s. That's why some people don't see data loss, until they switch to Linux.

Non-UART, and intelligent multiport boards use DSP chips to do additional buffering and control, thus relieving the CPU even more. For example, the Cyclades Cyclom, and Stallion EasyIO boards use a Cirrus Logic CD1400 RISC UART, and many boards use 80186 CPUs or even special RISC CPUs, to handle the serial I/O.

Keep in mind that these dumb UART types are not bad, they just aren't good for high speeds. You should have no problem connecting a terminal, or a mouse to these UARTs. But, for a high speed modem, the 16550A is definitely a must.

You can buy serial boards with the 16550A UARTs for a little more money, just ask your dealer what type of UART is on the board. Or if you want to upgrade your existing board, you can simply purchase 16550A chips and replace your existing 16450 UARTs. They are pin-to-pin compatible. Some boards come with socketed UARTs for this purpose, if not you can solder. Note that you'll probably save yourself a lot of trouble by just getting a new board, if you've got the money, they are under US$50.

13 Troubleshooting

13.1 I Keep Getting "line *NNN* of inittab invalid"

Make sure you are using the correct syntax for your version of `init`. The different `init`'s that are out there use different syntax in the `/etc/inittab` file. Make sure you are using the correct syntax for your version of `getty`.

13.2 When I Try To Dial Out, It Says "/dev/cua*N*: Device or resource busy"

This problem can arise when DCD or DTR are not set correctly. DCD should only be set when there is an actual connection (i.e., someone is dialed in), not when `getty` is watching the port. Check to make sure that your modem is configured to only set DCD when there is a connection. DTR should be set whenever something is using, or watching the line, like `getty`, `kermit`, or some other comm program.

Another common cause of "device busy" errors is that you set up your serial port with an interrupt already taken by something else. As each device initializes, it asks Linux for permission to use its hardware interrupt. Linux keeps track of which interrupt is assigned to whom, and if your interrupt is already taken, your device won't be able to initialize properly. The device really doesn't have much of any way to tell you that this happened, except that when you try to use it, it will return a "device-busy" error. Check the interrupts on all of your boards (serial, Ethernet, SCSI, etc.). Look for IRQ conflicts.

13.3 I Keep Getting "Id S*N* respawning too fast: disabled for 5 minutes"

Make sure your modem is configured correctly. Look at registers `E` and `Q`. This can occur when your modem is chatting with `getty`.

Make sure you are calling `getty` correctly from your `/etc/inittab`. Using the wrong syntax or device names will cause serious problems.

Verify that your `/etc/gettydefs` syntax is correct by doing the following:

```
linux# getty -c /etc/gettydefs
```

This can also happen when the `uugetty` initialization is failing. See section 13.11.

13.4 Serial Devices Are Slow, Or Serial Devices Can Only Send In One Direction

You probably have an IRQ conflict. Make sure there are no IRQs being shared. Check all your boards (serial, ethernet, SCSI, etc...). Make sure the jumper settings, and the `setserial` parameters are correct for all your serial devices. Also check `/proc/ioports` and `/proc/interrupts` for conflicts.

13.5 My Modem Is Hosed After Someone Hangs Up, Or `uugetty` doesn't respawn

This can happen when your modem doesn't reset when DTR is dropped. I saw my RD and SD LEDs go crazy when this happened to me. You need to have your modem reset. Most Hayes compatible modems do this with `&D3`, but on my USR Courier, I had to set `&D2` and `S13=1`. Check your modem manual.

13.6 I Havc My Terminal Connected To My PC, But After I Type In A Login Name, It Just Locks Up

- If you are using `getty`: You probably don't have `CLOCAL` in your `/ctc/gettydefs` entry for the terminal, and you're probably not using a full null modem cable. You need `CLOCAL`, which tells Linux to ignore modem control signals. Here is what it should look like:

```
# 38400 bps Dumb Terminal entry
DT38400# B38400 CS8 CLOCAL # B38400 SANE -ISTRIP CLOCAL #@S @L login: #DT38400

# 19200 bps Dumb Terminal entry
DT19200# B19200 CS8 CLOCAL # B19200 SANE -ISTRIP CLOCAL #@S @L login: #DT19200

# 9600 bps Dumb Terminal entry
DT9600# B9600 CS8 CLOCAL # B9600 SANE -ISTRIP CLOCAL #@S @L login: #DT9600
```

  Next, `kill` the `getty` process so a new one will be spawned with the new entry.

- If you are using `agetty`: Add the `-L` flag to the `agetty` line in your `/etc/inittab`. This will make it ignore modem control signals. Then restart `init` by typing `init q`. The entry should look like this:

```
s1:345:respawn:/sbin/agetty -L 9600 ttyS1 vt100
```

13.7 At High Speeds, My Modem Looses Data

If you are trying to run your modem faster than 38400 bps, and you don't have 16550A UARTs, you should upgrade them. See Section 12.3 about UARTs.

13.8 On Startup, Linux Doesn't Report The Serial Devices The Way I Have Them Configured

This is true. Linux does not do any IRQ detection on startup, it only does serial device detection. Thus, disregard what it says about the IRQ, because it's just assuming the standard IRQs. This is done, because IRQ detection is unreliable, and can be fooled.

So, even though I have my `ttyS2` set at IRQ 5, I still see

```
Jan 23 22:25:28 misfits vmunix: tty02 at 0x03e8 (irq = 4) is a 16550A
```

when Linux boots. You have to use `setserial` to tell Linux the IRQ you are using. After Linux boots, you can look at the `/proc/interrupts` file, to see what IRQs are really configured.

13.9 `rz` or `sz` Don't Work When I Call My Linux Box On A Modem

If Linux looks for `/dev/modem` when you try to transfer files, look at `/etc/profile`, and `/etc/csh.cshrc`. There are a bunch of aliases defined there on some distributions, most notably Slackware. These aliases mess up the zmodem programs. Take them out, or correct them.

13.10 My Screen Is Printing Funny Looking Characters

This happens on virtual consoles when you send binary data to your scrèen, or sometimes on serial connections. The way to fix this is to type `echo ^v^[c`. For the control-character-impaired, thats:

```
linux% echo <ctrl>v<esc>c
```

13.11 `getty` Or `uugetty` Still Doesn't Work

There is a `DEBUG` option that comes with `getty_ps`. Edit your config file `/etc/conf.{uu}getty.ttyS`*N* and add `DEBUG=`*NNN*. Where *NNN* is one of the following combination of numbers according to what you are trying to debug:

```
D_OPT   001        option settings
D_DEF   002        defaults file processing
D_UTMP  004        utmp/wtmp processing
D_INIT  010        line initialization (INIT)
D_GTAB  020        gettytab file processing
D_RUN   040        other runtime diagnostics
D_RB    100        ringback debugging
D_LOCK  200        uugetty lockfile processing
D_SCH   400        schedule processing
D_ALL   777        everything
```

Setting `DEBUG=010` is a good place to start.

If you are running `syslogd`, debugging info will appear in your log files. If you aren't running `syslogd` info will appear in `/tmp/getty:ttyS`*N* for debugging `getty` and `/tmp/uugetty:ttyS`*N* for `uugetty`, and in `/var/adm/getty.log`. Look at the debugging info and see what is going on. Most likely, you will need to tune some of the parameters in your config file, and reconfigure your modem.

You could also try `mgetty`. Some people have better luck with it.

14 Other Sources Of Information

- manual pages for: `agetty(8)`, `getty(1m)`, `gettydefs(5)`, `init(1)`, `login(1)`, `mgetty(8)`, `setserial(8)`
- Your modem manual.
- NET-3 HOWTO: all about networking, including SLIP, CSLIP, and PPP.
- PPP HOWTO: help with PPP.
- Printing HOWTO: for setting up a serial printer.
- Term HOWTO: everything you wanted to know about the `term` program.
- UPS HOWTO: setting up UPS boxen connected to your serial port.
- UUCP HOWTO: for information on setting up UUCP.
- Usenet newsgroups:

```
comp.os.linux.answers.
        FAQs, How-To's, READMEs, etc. about Linux.
comp.os.linux.hardware.
        Hardware compatibility with the Linux operating system.
comp.os.linux.networking.
        Networking and communications under Linux.
comp.os.linux.setup.
        Linux installation and system administration.
```

- The Linux serial mailing list. To join, send email to `majordomo@vger.rutgers.edu`, with "`subscribe linux-serial`" in the message body. If you send "`help`" in the message body, you get a help message. The server also serves many other Linux lists. Send the "`lists`" command for a list of mailing lists.
- A white paper discussing serial communications and multiport serial boards is available from Cyclades at `http://www.cyclades.com`.
- Modem FAQs:
  Navas 28800 Modem FAQ (`http://web.aimnet.com/~jnavas/modem/faq.html`)
  Curt's High Speed Modem Page (`http://www.teleport.com/~curt/modems.html`)
- Serial programming: *Advanced Programming in the UNIX Environment* (`http://heg-school.aw.com/cseng/authors/stevens/advanced/advanced.nclk`), by W. Richard Stevens (ISBN 0-201-56317-7; Addison-Wesley)
  POSIX Programmer's Guide, by Donald Lewine (ISBN 0-937175-73-0; O'Reilly, http://www.ora.com/catalog/posix/.

15 Contributions

There was no possible way to write this HOWTO alone. Although a lot of the HOWTO is my writing, I have rewritten many contributions to maintain continuity in the writing style and flow. Thanks to everyone who has contributed or commented, the list of people has gotten too long to list (somewhere over one hundred). Special thanks to Ted T'so for answering questions about the serial drivers, Kris Gleason who used to maintain `getty_ps`, and Gert Döring who maintains `mgetty`.

END OF SERIAL HOWTO

Part XLIII

"Linux Serial Programming HOWTO" by Peter H. Baumann,

Peter.Baumann@dlr.de

Contents

Abstract

v0.3, 14 June 1997
This document describes how to program communications with devices over a serial port on a Linux box.

1 Introduction

Programming HOWTO, all about how to program communications with other devices and computers over a serial line under Linux. Different techniques are explained: Canonical I/O (only complete lines are transmitted and received), asynchronous I/O, and waiting for input from multiple sources.

This document does not describe how to set up serial ports, because this has been described by Greg Hankins in the Serial-HOWTO.

I have to emphasize that I am not an expert in this field, but have had problems with a project that involved such communication. The code examples presented here were derived from the `miniterm` code available from the Linux Programmer's Guide on sunsite.unc.edu and mirrors, as: `/pub/Linux/docs/LDP/programmers-guide/lpg-0.4.tar.gz.` in the examples directory. If anybody has any comments, I will gladly incorporate them into this document (see Feedback section).

All examples were tested using a i386 Linux Kernel 2.0.29.

1.1 Copyright

1.2 New Versions Of This Document

New versions of the Serial-Programming-HOWTO will be available at sunsite.unc.edu and mirrors as `/pub/Linux/docs/HOWTO/Serial-Programming-HOWTO` There are other formats, such as PostScript and DVI versions in the `other-formats` directory. The Serial-Programming-HOWTO is also available at http://sunsite.unc.edu/LDP/HOWTO/Serial-Programming-HOWTO.html

and will be posted to `comp.os.linux.answers` monthly.

1.3 Feedback

Please send me any corrections, questions, comments, suggestions, or additional material. I would like to improve this HOWTO. Tell me exactly what you don't understand, or what could be clearer. You can reach me at `Peter.Baumann@dlr.de` via email. Please include the version number of the Serial-Programming-HOWTO when writing, this is version 0.3.

2 Getting started

2.1 Debugging

The best way to debug your code is to set up another Linux box, and connect the two computers via a null modem cable. Use `miniterm` (available from the Linux Programmer's Guide (`ftp://sunsite.unc.edu/pub/Linux/docs/LDP/programmers-guide/lpg-0.4.tar.gz` in the examples directory) to transmit characters to your Linux box. `miniterm` can be compiled very easily and will transmit all keyboard input raw over the serial port. Only the define statement `#define MODEMDEVICE "/dev/ttyS0"` has to be checked. Set it to `ttyS0` for COM1, `ttyS1` for COM2, etc.. It is essential for testing, that all characters are transmitted raw (without output processing) over the line. To test your connection, start `miniterm` on both computers and just type away. The characters input on one computer should appear on the other computer and vice versa. The input will not be echoed to the attached screen.

To make a null modem cable, you have to cross the TxD (transmit) and RxD (receive) lines. For a description of a cable see Section 7 of the Serial HOWTO.

It is also possible to perform this testing with only one computer, if you have two unused serial ports. You can then run two `miniterm` in two virtual consoles. If you free a serial port by disconnecting the mouse, remember to redirect `/dev/mouse`, if it exists. If you use a multiport serial card, be sure to configure it correctly. I had mine configured wrong and everything worked fine as long as I was testing only on my computer. When I connected to another computer, the port started losing characters. Executing two programs on one computer just isn't fully asynchronous.

2.2 Port Settings

The devices `/dev/ttyS*` are intended to hook up terminals to your Linux box, and are configured for this use after startup. This has to be kept in mind when programming communication with a raw device. E.g. the ports are configured to echo characters sent from the device back to it, which normally has to be changed for data transmission.

All parameters can be easily configured from within a program. The configuration is stored in a structure `struct termios`, which is defined in `<asm/termbits.h>`:

```
#define NCCS 19
struct termios {
        tcflag_t c_iflag;               /* input mode flags */
        tcflag_t c_oflag;               /* output mode flags */
        tcflag_t c_cflag;               /* control mode flags */
        tcflag_t c_lflag;               /* local mode flags */
        cc_t c_line;                    /* line discipline */
        cc_t c_cc[NCCS];                /* control characters */
};
```

This file also includes all flag definitions. The input mode flags in `c_iflag` handle all input processing, which means that the characters sent from the device can be processed before they are read with `read`. Similarly `c_oflag` handles the output processing. `c_cflag` contains the settings for the port, as the baud rate, bits per character, stop bits, etc.. The local mode flags stored in `c_lflag` determine if characters are echoed, signals are sent to your program, etc.. Finally, the array `c_cc` defines the control characters for end-of-file, stop, and so on. Default values for the control characters are defined in `<asm/termios.h>`. The flags are described in the manual page `termios(3)`.

The structure `termios` contains the `c_line` element. This element is neither mentioned in the manual page for termios of Linux, nor in the manual page of Solaris 2.5. Could somebody shed some light on this? Shouldn't it be only included in the structure `termio`?

2.3 Input Concepts for Serial Devices

Here, three different input concepts will be presented. The appropriate concept has to be chosen for the intended application. Whenever possible, do not loop reading single characters to get a complete string. When I did this, I lost characters, whereas a `read` for the whole string did not show any errors.

2.3.1 Canonical Input Processing

This is the normal processing mode for terminals, but can also be useful for communicating with other devices. All input is processed in units of lines, which means that a `read` will only return a full line of input. A line is by default terminated by a `NL` (ASCII `LF`), an end of file, or an end-of-line character. A `CR` (the MS-DOS and MS-Windows default end-of-line) will not terminate a line with the default settings.

Canonical input processing can also handle the erase, delete word, and reprint characters, translate `CR` to `NL`, etc..

2.3.2 Non-Canonical Input Processing

Non-canonical input processing handles a fixed amount of characters per read, and allows for a character timer. This mode should be used if your application will always read a fixed number of characters, or if the connected device sends bursts of characters.

2.3.3 Asynchronous Input

The two modes described above can be used in synchronous and asynchronous mode. Synchronous is the default, where a `read` statement will block, until the read is satisfied. In asynchronous mode, the `read` statement will return immediately and send a signal to the calling program upon completion. This signal can be received by a signal handler.

2.3.4 Waiting for Input from Multiple Sources

This is not a different input mode, but might be useful, if you are handling multiple devices. In my application I was handling input over a TCP/IP socket and input over a serial connection from another computer quasi-simultaneously. The program example given below will wait for input from two different input sources. If input from one source becomes available, it will be processed, and the program will then wait for new input.

The approach presented below seems rather complex, but it is important to keep in mind that Linux is a multi-processing operating system. The `select` system call will not load the CPU while waiting for input, whereas looping until input becomes available would slow down other processes executing at the same time.

3 Program Examples

All examples have been derived from `miniterm.c`. The type-ahead buffer is limited to 255 characters, just like the maximum string length for canonical input processing (<linux/limits.h> or <posix1_lim.h>).

See the comments in the code for explanation of the use of the different input modes. I hope that the code is understandable. The example for canonical input is commented best, the other examples are commented only where they differ from the example for canonical input to emphasize the differences.

The descriptions are not complete, but you are encouraged to experiment with the examples to derive the best solution for your application.

Don't forget to give the appropriate serial ports the right permissions (e. g.: `chmod a+rw /dev/ttyS1`).

3.1 Canonical Input Processing

```
#include <sys/types.h>
#include <sys/stat.h>
#include <fcntl.h>
#include <termios.h>
#include <stdio.h>

/* baudrate settings are defined in <asm/termbits.h>, which is
included by <termios.h> */
#define BAUDRATE B38400
/* change this definition for the correct port */
#define MODEMDEVICE "/dev/ttyS1"
#define _POSIX_SOURCE 1 /* POSIX compliant source */

#define FALSE 0
#define TRUE 1

volatile int STOP=FALSE;

main()
{
  int fd,c, res;
  struct termios oldtio,newtio;
  char buf[255];
/*
  Open modem device for reading and writing and not as controlling tty
  because we don't want to get killed if linenoise sends CTRL-C.
*/
 fd = open(MODEMDEVICE, O_RDWR | O_NOCTTY );
 if (fd <0) {perror(MODEMDEVICE); exit(-1); }
```

```
 tcgetattr(fd,&oldtio); /* save current serial port settings */
 bzero(newtio, sizeof(newtio)); /* clear the struct for new port settings */

/*
  BAUDRATE: Set bps rate. You could also use cfsetispeed and cfsetospeed.
  CRTSCTS : output hardware flow control (only used if the cable has
            all necessary lines. See sect. 7 of Serial-HOWTO)
  CS8     : 8n1 (8bit,no parity,1 stopbit)
  CLOCAL  : local connection, no modem contol
  CREAD   : enable receiving characters
*/
 newtio.c_cflag = BAUDRATE | CRTSCTS | CS8 | CLOCAL | CREAD;

/*
  IGNPAR  : ignore bytes with parity errors
  ICRNL   : map CR to NL (otherwise a CR input on the other computer
            will not terminate input)
  otherwise make device raw (no other input processing)
*/
 newtio.c_iflag = IGNPAR | ICRNL;

/*
 Raw output.
*/
 newtio.c_oflag = 0;

/*
  ICANON  : enable canonical input
  disable all echo functionality, and don't send signals to calling program
*/
 newtio.c_lflag = ICANON;

/*
  initialize all control characters
  default values can be found in /usr/include/termios.h, and are given
  in the comments, but we don't need them here
*/
 newtio.c_cc[VINTR]    = 0;     /* Ctrl-c */
 newtio.c_cc[VQUIT]    = 0;     /* Ctrl-\ */
 newtio.c_cc[VERASE]   = 0;     /* del */
 newtio.c_cc[VKILL]    = 0;     /* @ */
 newtio.c_cc[VEOF]     = 4;     /* Ctrl-d */
 newtio.c_cc[VTIME]    = 0;     /* inter-character timer unused */
 newtio.c_cc[VMIN]     = 1;     /* blocking read until 1 character arrives */
 newtio.c_cc[VSWTC]    = 0;     /* '\0' */
 newtio.c_cc[VSTART]   = 0;     /* Ctrl-q */
 newtio.c_cc[VSTOP]    = 0;     /* Ctrl-s */
 newtio.c_cc[VSUSP]    = 0;     /* Ctrl-z */
 newtio.c_cc[VEOL]     = 0;     /* '\0' */
 newtio.c_cc[VREPRINT] = 0;     /* Ctrl-r */
 newtio.c_cc[VDISCARD] = 0;     /* Ctrl-u */
 newtio.c_cc[VWERASE]  = 0;     /* Ctrl-w */
 newtio.c_cc[VLNEXT]   = 0;     /* Ctrl-v */
 newtio.c_cc[VEOL2]    = 0;     /* '\0' */

/*
  now clean the modem line and activate the settings for the port
*/
```

```
 tcflush(fd, TCIFLUSH);
 tcsetattr(fd,TCSANOW,&newtio);

/*
  terminal settings done, now handle input
  In this example, inputting a 'z' at the beginning of a line will
  exit the program.
*/
 while (STOP==FALSE) {     /* loop until we have a terminating condition */
 /* read blocks program execution until a line terminating character is
    input, even if more than 255 chars are input. If the number
    of characters read is smaller than the number of chars available,
    subsequent reads will return the remaining chars. res will be set
    to the actual number of characters actually read */
    res = read(fd,buf,255);
    buf[res]=0;            /* set end of string, so we can printf */
    printf(":%s:%d\n", buf, res);
    if (buf[0]=='z') STOP=TRUE;
 }
 /* restore the old port settings */
 tcsetattr(fd,TCSANOW,&oldtio);
}
```

3.2 Non-Canonical Input Processing

In non-canonical input processing mode, input is not assembled into lines and input processing (erase, kill, delete, and so on) does not occur. Two parameters control the behavior of this mode: `c_cc[VTIME]` sets the character timer, and `c_cc[VMIN]` sets the minimum number of characters to receive before satisfying the read.

If MIN > 0 and TIME = 0, MIN sets the number of characters to receive before the read is satisfied. As TIME is zero, the timer is not used.

If MIN = 0 and TIME > 0, TIME serves as a timeout value. The read will be satisfied if a single character is read, or TIME is exceeded (t = TIME *0.1 s). If TIME is exceeded, no character will be returned.

If MIN > 0 and TIME > 0, TIME serves as an inter-character timer. The read will be satisfied if MIN characters are received, or the time between two characters exceeds TIME. The timer is restarted every time a character is received and only becomes active after the first character has been received.

If MIN = 0 and TIME = 0, read will be satisfied immediately. The number of characters currently available, or the number of characters requested will be returned. According to Antonino (see contributions), you could issue a `fcntl(fd, F_SETFL, FNDELAY);` before reading to get the same result.

By modifying `newtio.c_cc[VTIME]` and `newtio.c_cc[VMIN]` all modes described above can be tested.

```
#include <sys/types.h>
#include <sys/stat.h>
#include <fcntl.h>
#include <termios.h>
#include <stdio.h>

#define BAUDRATE B38400
#define MODEMDEVICE "/dev/ttyS1"
#define _POSIX_SOURCE 1 /* POSIX compliant source */
#define FALSE 0
#define TRUE 1

volatile int STOP=FALSE;

main()
{
  int fd,c, res;
  struct termios oldtio,newtio;
```

```
  char buf[255];

 fd = open(MODEMDEVICE, O_RDWR | O_NOCTTY );
 if (fd <0) {perror(MODEMDEVICE); exit(-1); }

 tcgetattr(fd,&oldtio); /* save current port settings */

 bzero(newtio, sizeof(newtio));
 newtio.c_cflag = BAUDRATE | CRTSCTS | CS8 | CLOCAL | CREAD;
 newtio.c_iflag = IGNPAR;
 newtio.c_oflag = 0;

 /* set input mode (non-canonical, no echo,...) */
 newtio.c_lflag = 0;

 newtio.c_cc[VTIME]    = 0;   /* inter-character timer unused */
 newtio.c_cc[VMIN]     = 5;   /* blocking read until 5 chars received */

 tcflush(fd, TCIFLUSH);
 tcsetattr(fd,TCSANOW,&newtio);


 while (STOP==FALSE) {       /* loop for input */
   res = read(fd,buf,255);   /* returns after 5 chars have been input */
   buf[res]=0;               /* so we can printf... */
   printf(":%s:%d\n", buf, res);
   if (buf[0]=='z') STOP=TRUE;
 }
 tcsetattr(fd,TCSANOW,&oldtio);
}
```

3.3 Asynchronous Input

```
#include <termios.h>
#include <stdio.h>
#include <unistd.h>
#include <fcntl.h>
#include <sys/signal.h>
#include <sys/types.h>

#define BAUDRATE B38400
#define MODEMDEVICE "/dev/ttyS1"
#define _POSIX_SOURCE 1 /* POSIX compliant source */
#define FALSE 0
#define TRUE 1

volatile int STOP=FALSE;

void signal_handler_IO (int status);   /* definition of signal handler */
int wait_flag=TRUE;                    /* TRUE while no signal received */

main()
{
  int fd,c, res;
  struct termios oldtio,newtio;
  struct sigaction saio;           /* definition of signal action */
  char buf[255];

  /* open the device to be non-blocking (read will return immediatly) */
```

```
  fd = open(MODEMDEVICE, O_RDWR | O_NOCTTY | O_NONBLOCK);
  if (fd <0) {perror(MODEMDEVICE); exit(-1); }

  /* install the signal handler before making the device asynchronous */
  saio.sa_handler = signal_handler_IO;
  saio.sa_mask = 0;
  saio.sa_flags = 0;
  saio.sa_restorer = NULL;
  sigaction(SIGIO,&saio,NULL);

  /* allow the process to receive SIGIO */
  fcntl(fd, F_SETOWN, getpid());
  /* Make the file descriptor asynchronous (the manual page says only
     O_APPEND and O_NONBLOCK, will work with F_SETFL...) */
  fcntl(fd, F_SETFL, FASYNC);

  tcgetattr(fd,&oldtio); /* save current port settings */
  /* set new port settings for canonical input processing */
  newtio.c_cflag = BAUDRATE | CRTSCTS | CS8 | CLOCAL | CREAD;
  newtio.c_iflag = IGNPAR | ICRNL;
  newtio.c_oflag = 0;
  newtio.c_lflag = ICANON;
  newtio.c_cc[VMIN]=1;
  newtio.c_cc[VTIME]=0;
  tcflush(fd, TCIFLUSH);
  tcsetattr(fd,TCSANOW,&newtio);

  /* loop while waiting for input. normally we would do something
     useful here */
  while (STOP==FALSE) {
    printf(".\n");usleep(100000);
    /* after receiving SIGIO, wait_flag = FALSE, input is available
       and can be read */
    if (wait_flag==FALSE) {
      res = read(fd,buf,255);
      buf[res]=0;
      printf(":%s:%d\n", buf, res);
      if (res==1) STOP=TRUE; /* stop loop if only a CR was input */
      wait_flag = TRUE;      /* wait for new input */
    }
  }
  /* restore old port settings */
  tcsetattr(fd,TCSANOW,&oldtio);
}

/***************************************************************************
* signal handler. sets wait_flag to FALSE, to indicate above loop that     *
* characters have been received.                                           *
***************************************************************************/

void signal_handler_IO (int status)
{
  printf("received SIGIO signal.\n");
  wait_flag = FALSE;
}
```

3.4 Waiting for Input from Multiple Sources

This section is kept to a minimum. It is just intended to be a hint, and therefore the example code is kept short. This will not only work with serial ports, but with any set of file descriptors.

The select call and acompanying macros use a `fd_set`. This is a bit array, which has a bit entry for every valid file descriptor number. `select` will accept a `fd_set` with the bits set for the relevant file descriptors and returns a `fd_set`, in which the bits for the file descriptors are set where input, output, or an exception occurred. All handling of `fd_set` is done with the provided macros. See also the manual page `select(2)`.

```
#include <sys/time.h>
#include <sys/types.h>
#include <unistd.h>

main()
{
  int     fd1, fd2; /* input sources 1 and 2 */
  fd_set readfs;    /* file descriptor set */
  int    maxfd;     /* mixmum file desciptor used */
  int    loop=1;    /* loop while TRUE */

  /* open_input_source opens a device, sets the port correctly, and
     returns a file descriptor */
  fd1 = open_input_source("/dev/ttyS1");   /* COM2 */
  if (fd1<0) exit(0);
  fd2 = open_input_source("/dev/ttyS2");   /* COM3 */
  if (fd2<0) exit(0);
  maxfd = MAX (fd1, fd2)+1;  /* maximum bit entry (fd) to test */

  /* loop for input */
  while (loop) {
    FD_SET(fd1, &readfs);  /* set testing for source 1 */
    FD_SET(fd2, &readfs);  /* set testing for source 2 */
    /* block until input becomes available */
    select(maxfd, &readfs, NULL, NULL, NULL);
    if (FD_ISSET(fd1))         /* input from source 1 available */
      handle_input_from_source1();
    if (FD_ISSET(fd2))         /* input from source 2 available */
      handle_input_from_source2();
  }

}
```

The example given blocks indefinitely, until input from one of the sources becomes available. If you need to time out on input, just replace the select call by:

```
int res;
struct timeval Timeout;

/* set timeout value within input loop */
Timeout.tv_usec = 0;  /* milliseconds */
Timeout.tv_sec  = 1;  /* seconds */
res = select(maxfd, &readfs, NULL, NULL, &Timeout);
if (res==0)
/* number of filedescriptors with input = 0, timeout occurred. */
```

This example will time out after 1 second. If a timeout occurs, select will return 0, but beware that `Timeout` is decremented by the time actually waited for input by `select`. If the timeout value is zero, select will return immediately.

4 Other Sources of Information

- The Linux Serial-HOWTO describes how to set up serial ports and contains hardware information.
- "Serial Programming Guide for POSIX Compliant Operating Systems", http://www.easysw.com/ mike/serial/, by Michael Sweet.
- The manual page `termios(3)` describes all flags for the `termios` structure.

5 Contributions

As mentioned in the introduction, I am no expert in this field, but had problems myself, and found a solution with the help of others. Thanks for the help from Mr. Strudthoff from the European Transonic Windtunnel, Cologne, Michael Carter (`mcarter@rocke.electro.swri.edu`, and Peter Waltenberg (`p.waltenberg@karaka.chch.cri.nz`)

Antonino Ianella (`antonino@usa.net` wrote the Serial-Port-Programming Mini HOWTO, at the same time I prepared this document. Greg Hankins asked me to incorporate Antonino's Mini-HOWTO into this document.

The structure of this document and SGML formatting was derived from the Serial-HOWTO by Greg Hankins.

Part XLIV

“Linux Shadow Password HOWTO”
by Michael H. Jackson,

mhjack@tscnet.com

Contents

Abstract

v1.3, 3 April 1996
This document aims to describe how to obtain, install, and configure the Linux password Shadow Suite. It also discusses obtaining, and re-installing other software and network daemons that require access to user passwords. This other software is not actually part of the Shadow Suite, but these programs will need to be recompiled to support the Shadow Suite. This document also contains a programming example for adding shadow support to a program. Answers to some of the more frequently asked questions are included near the end of this document.

1 Introduction.

This is the Linux Shadow-Password-HOWTO. This document describes why and how to add shadow password support on a Linux system. Some examples of how to use some of the Shadow Suite's features is also included.

When installing the Shadow Suite and when using many of the utility programs, you must be logged in as `root`. When installing the Shadow Suite, you will be making changes to system software, and it is highly recommended that you make backup copies of programs as indicated. I also recommend that you read and understand all of the instructions before you begin.

1.1 New versions of this document.

The latest released version of this document can always be retrieved by anonymous FTP from:

`ftp//sunsite.unc.edu/pub/Linux/docs/HOWTO/Shadow-Password-HOWTO`

or

`/pub/Linux/docs/HOWTO/other-formats/Shadow-Password-HOWTO{-html.tar,ps,dvi}.gz`

or via the World Wide Web from the Linux Documentation Project Web Server,

`http://sunsite.unc.edu/mdw/linux.html`

at page Shadow-Password-HOWTO

`http://sunsite.unc.edu/linux/HOWTO/Shadow-Password-HOWTO.html`

or directly from me, mhjack@tscnet.com.

This document is now packaged with the Shadow-YYDDMM packages.

1.2 Feedback.

Please send any comments, updates, or suggestions to me: Michael H. Jackson, mhjack@tscnet.com. The sooner I get feedback, the sooner I can update and correct this document. If you find any problems with it, please mail me directly as I very rarely stay up to date on the newsgroups.

2 Why shadow your passwd file?

By default, most current Linux distributions do not contain the Shadow Suite installed. This includes Slackware 2.3, Slackware 3.0, and other popular distributions. One of the reasons for this is that the copyright notices in the original Shadow Suite were not clear on redistribution if a fee was charged. Linux uses a GNU Copyright (sometimes refereed to as a Copyleft) that allows people to package it into a convenient package (like a CD-ROM distribution) and charge a fee for it.

The current maintainer of the Shadow Suite, Marek Michalkiewicz, marekm@i17linuxb.ists.pwr.wroc.pl, received the source code from the original author under a BSD-style copyright that allowed redistribution. Now that the copyright issues are resolved, it is expected that future distributions will contain password shadowing by default. Until then, you will need to install it yourself.

If you installed your distribution from a CD-ROM, you may find that, even though the distribution did not have the Shadow Suite installed, some of the files you need to install the Shadow Suite may be on the CD-ROM.

However, Shadow Suite versions 3.3.1, 3.3.1-2, and shadow-mk all have security problems with their login program and several other suid root programs that came with them, and should no longer be used.

All of the necessary files may be obtained via anonymous FTP or through the World Wide Web.

On a Linux system without the Shadow Suite installed, user information including the passwords are stored in the `/etc/passwd` file. The password is stored in an encrypted format. If you ask a cryptography expert, however, he or she will tell you that the password is actually in an encoded rather than encrypted format because when using `crypt(3)`, the text is set to `/dev/null` and the password is the key. Therefore, from here on, I will use the term "encoded."

The algorithm used to encode the password field is technically referred to as a one-way hash function. This is an algorithm that is easy to compute in one direction, but very difficult to calculate in the reverse direction. More about the actual algorithm used can be found in Section 2.4 or your `crypt(3)` manual page.

When a user picks or is assigned a password, it is encoded with a randomly generated value called the "salt." This means that any particular password could be stored in 4096 different ways. The salt value is then stored with the encoded password.

When a user logs in and supplies a password, the salt is first retrieved from the stored encoded password. Then the supplied password is encoded with the salt value, and then compared with the encoded password. If there is a match, then the user is authenticated.

It is computationally difficult (but not impossible) to take a randomly encoded password and recover the original password. However, on any system with more than just a few users, at least some of the passwords will be common words (or simple variations of common words).

System crackers know all this, and will simply encrypt a dictionary of words and common passwords using all possible 4096 salt values. Then they will compare the encoded passwords in your `/etc/passwd` file with their database. Once they have found a match, they have the password for another account. This is referred to as a "**dictionary attack**," and is one of the most common methods for gaining or expanding unauthorized access to a system.

If you think about it, an 8-character password encodes to 4096 * 13 character strings. So a dictionary of say 400,000 common words, names, passwords, and simple variations would easily fit on a 4GB hard drive. The attacker need only sort them, and then check for matches. Since a 4GB hard drive can be had for under $1000.00, this is well within the means of most system crackers.

Also, if a cracker obtains your `/etc/passwd` file first, they only need to encode the dictionary with the salt values actually contained in your `/etc/passwd` file. This method is usable by your average teenager with a couple of hundred spare Megabytes and a 80486-class computer.

Even without lots of drive space, utilities like `crack(1)` can usually break at least a couple of passwords on a system with enough users (assuming the users of the system are allowed to pick their own passwords).

The `/etc/passwd` file also contains information like user IDs and group IDs that are used by many system programs. Therefore, the `/etc/passwd` file must remain world readable. If you were to change the `/etc/passwd` file so that nobody can read it, the first thing that you would notice is that the `ls -l` command now displays user IDs instead of names.

The Shadow Suite solves the problem by relocating the passwords to another file (usually `/etc/shadow`). The `/etc/shadow` file is set so that it cannot be read by just anyone. Only root will be able to read and write to the `/etc/shadow` file. Some programs (like `xlock`) don't need to be able to change passwords, they only need to be able to verify them. These programs can either be run suid root or you can set up a group, `shadow` that is allowed read-only access to the `/etc/shadow` file. Then the program can be run sgid shadow.

By moving the passwords to the `/etc/shadow` file, we effectively keep the attacker from having access to the encoded passwords with which to perform a dictionary attack.

Additionally, the Shadow Suite adds lots of other nice features:

- A configuration file to set login defaults (`/etc/login.defs`)
- Utilities for adding, modifying, and deleting user accounts and groups.
- Password aging and expiration.
- Account expiration and locking.
- Shadowed group passwords (optional).
- Double length passwords (16 character passwords). Not recommended.
- Better control over user's password selection.
- Dial-up passwords.
- Secondary authentication programs Not recommended.

Installing the Shadow Suite contributes toward a more secure system, but there are many other things that can also be done to improve the security of a Linux system, and there will eventually be a series of Linux Security HOWTO's that will discuss other security measures and related issues.

For current information on other Linux security issues, including warnings on known vulnerabilities see the Linux Security home page, http://bach.cis.temple.edu/linux/linux-security/.

2.1 Why you might not want to shadow your passwd file.

There are a few circumstances and configurations in which installing the Shadow Suite would not be a good idea:

- The machine does not contain user accounts.
- Your machine is running on a LAN and is using NIS (Network Information Services) to get or supply user names and passwords to other machines on the network. (This can actually be done, but is beyond the scope of this document, and really won't increase security much anyway).
- Your machine is being used by terminal servers to verify users via NFS (Network File System), NIS, or some other method.
- Your machine runs other software that validates users, and there is no shadow version available, and you don't have the source code.

2.2 Format of the `/etc/passwd` file

A non-shadowed `/etc/passwd` file has the following format:

```
username:passwd:UID:GID:full_name:directory:shell
```

Where:

username
: The user (login) name.

passwd
: The encoded password.

UID
: Numerical user ID.

GID
: Numerical default group ID.

full_name
: The user's full name—Actually this field is called the GECOS (General Electric Comprehensive Operating System) field and can store information other than just the full name. The Shadow commands and manual pages refer to this field as the comment field.

directory
: User's home directory (full pathname).

shell
: User's login shell (full pathname).

For example:

```
username:Npge08pfz4wuk:503:100:Full Name:/home/username:/bin/sh
```

Where `Np` is the salt and `ge08pfz4wuk` is the encoded password. The encoded salt/password could just as easily have been `kbeMVnZM0oL7I` and the two are exactly the same password. There are 4096 possible encodings for the same password. (The example password in this case is 'password', a really bad password).

Once the shadow suite is installed, the `/etc/passwd` file would instead contain:

```
username:x:503:100:Full Name:/home/username:/bin/sh
```

The `x` in the second field in this case is now just a place holder. The format of the `/etc/passwd` file really didn't change, it just no longer contains the encoded password. This means that any program that reads the `/etc/passwd` file but does not actually need to verify passwords will still operate correctly.

The passwords are now relocated to the shadow file (usually `/etc/shadow` file).

2.3 Format of the shadow file

The `/etc/shadow` file contains the following information:

```
username:passwd:last:may:must:warn:expire:disable:reserved
```

Where:

`username`
The User Name

`passwd`
The Encoded password

`last`
Days since Jan 1, 1970 that password was last changed

`may`
Days before password may be changed

`must`
Days after which password must be changed

`warn`
Days before password is to expire that user is warned

`expire`
Days after password expires that account is disabled

`disable`
Days since Jan 1, 1970 that account is disabled

`reserved`
A reserved field

The previous example might then be:

```
username:Npge08pfz4wuk:9479:0:10000::::
```

2.4 Review of `crypt(3)`.

From the `crypt(3)` manual page:

`crypt` is the password encryption function. It is based on the Data Encryption Standard algorithm with variations intended (among other things) to discourage use of hardware implementations of a key search.

The key is a user's typed password.

The salt is a two-character string chosen from the set `a-zA-Z0-9./`. This string is used to perturb the algorithm in one of 4096 different ways.

By taking the lowest 7 bits of each character of the key, a 56-bit key is obtained. This 56-bit key is used to encrypt repeatedly a constant string (usually a string consisting of all zeros). The returned value points to the encrypted password, a series of 13 printable ASCII characters (the first two characters represent the salt itself). The return value points to static data whose content is overwritten by each call.

The key space consists of 2**56 equal 7.2e16 possible values. Exhaustive searches of this key space **are possible** using massively parallel computers. Software, such as `crack(1)`, is available which will search the portion of this key space that is generally used by humans for passwords. Hence, password selection should, at minimum, avoid common words and names.

◇ The use of a `passwd(1)` program that checks for crackable passwords during the selection process is recommended.

The DES algorithm itself has a few quirks which make the use of the `crypt(3)` interface a very poor choice for anything other than password authentication. If you are planning on using the `crypt(3)` interface for a cryptography project, don't do it: get a good book on encryption and one of the widely available DES libraries.

Most Shadow Suites contain code for doubling the length of the password to 16-characters. Experts in DES recommend against this, as the encoding is simply applied first to the left half and then to the right half of the longer password. Because of the way `crypt` works, this may make for a less secure encoded password then if double length passwords were not used in the first place. Additionally, it is less likely that a user will be able to remember a 16-character password.

There is development work under way that would allow the authentication algorithm to be replaced with something more secure and with support for longer passwords (specifically the MD5 algorithm) and retain compatibility with the `crypt` method.

If you are looking for a good book on encryption, I recommend:

```
"Applied Cryptography: Protocols, Algorithms, and Source Code in C"
by Bruce Schneier <schneier@chinet.com>
ISBN: 0-471-59756-2
```

3 Getting the Shadow Suite.

3.1 History of the Shadow Suite for Linux

DO NOT USE THE PACKAGES IN THIS SECTION, THEY HAVE SECURITY PROBLEMS

The original Shadow Suite was written by `John F. Haugh II`.

There are several versions that have been used on Linux systems:

- `shadow-3.3.1` is the original.
- `shadow-3.3.1-2` is Linux specific patch made by Florian La Roche flla@stud.uni-sb.de and contains some further enhancements.
- `shadow-mk` was specifically packaged for Linux.

The `shadow-mk` package contains the `shadow-3.3.1` package distributed by `John F. Haugh II` with the `shadow-3.3.1-2 patch` installed, a few fixes made by Mohan Kokal magnus@texas.net that make installation a lot easier, a patch by `Joseph R.M. Zbiciak` for `login1.c` (login.secure) that eliminates the -f, -h security holes in /bin/login, and some other miscellaneous patches.

The `shadow.mk` package was the previously recommended package, but should be replaced due to a security problem with the `login` program.

There are security problems with Shadow versions 3.3.1, 3.3.1-2, and shadow-mk involving the `login` program. This `login` bug involves not checking the length of a login name. This causes the buffer to overflow causing crashes or worse. It has been rumored that this buffer overflow can allow someone with an account on the system to use this bug and the shared libraries to gain root access. I won't discuss exactly how this is possible because there are a lot of Linux systems that are affected, but systems with these Shadow Suites installed, and most pre-ELF distributions without the Shadow Suite are vulnerable.

For more information on this and other Linux security issues, see the
Linux Security home page (Shared Libraries and login Program Vulnerability)
http://bach.cis.temple.edu/linux/linux-security/Linux-Security-FAQ/Linux-telnetd.html

3.2 Where to get the Shadow Suite.

The only recommended Shadow Suite is still in BETA testing, however the latest versions are safe in a production environment and don't contain a vulnerable `login` program.

The package uses the following naming convention:

```
shadow-YYMMDD.tar.gz
```

where `YYMMDD` is the issue date of the Suite.

This version will eventually be Version 3.3.3 when it is released from Beta testing, and is maintained by Marek Michalkiewicz marekm@i17linuxb.ists.pwr.wroc.pl. It's available as shadow-current.tar.gz:

ftp://i17linuxb.ists.pwr.wroc.pl/pub/linux/shadow/shadow-current.tar.gz

The following mirror sites have also been established:

- ftp://ftp.icm.edu.pl/pub/Linux/shadow/shadow-current.tar.gz
- ftp://iguana.hut.fi/pub/linux/shadow/shadow-current.tar.gz
- ftp://ftp.cin.net/usr/ggallag/shadow/shadow-current.tar.gz
- ftp://ftp.netural.com/pub/linux/shadow/shadow-current.tar.gz

You should use the currently available version.

You should not use a version older than `shadow-960129` as they also have the `login` security problem discussed above.

When this document refers to the Shadow Suite I am referring to the this package. It is assumed that this is the package that you are using.

For reference, I used `shadow-960129` to make these installation instructions.

If you were previously using `shadow-mk`, you should upgrade to this version and rebuild everything that you originally compiled.

3.3 What is included with the Shadow Suite.

The Shadow Suite contains replacement programs for:

`su, login, passwd, newgrp, chfn, chsh,` and `id`. The package also contains the new programs:

`chage, newusers, dpasswd, gpasswd, useradd, userdel, usermod, groupadd, groupdel, groupmod, groups, pwck, grpck, lastlog, pwconv,` and `pwunconv`.

Additionally, the library: `libshadow.a` is included for writing or compiling programs that need to access user passwords.

Also, manual pages for the programs are included.

There is also a configuration file for the login program which will be installed as `/etc/login.defs`.

4 Compiling the programs.

4.1 Unpacking the archive.

The first step after retrieving the package is unpacking it. The package is in the tar (tape archive) format and compressed using gzip, so first move it to `/usr/src`, then type:

```
tar -xzvf shadow-current.tar.gz
```

This will unpack it into the directory: `/usr/src/shadow-YYMMDD`

4.2 Configuring with the config.h file

The first thing that you need to do is to copy over the `Makefile` and the `config.h` file:

```
cd /usr/src/shadow-YYMMDD
cp Makefile.linux Makefile
cp config.h.linux config.h
```

You should then take a look at the `config.h` file. This file contains definitions for some of the configuration options. If you are using the recommended package, I recommend that you disable group shadow support for your first time around.

By default shadowed group passwords are enabled. To disable these edit the `config.h` file, and change the `#define SHADOWGRP` to `#undef SHADOWGRP`. I recommend that you disable them to start with, and then if you really want group passwords and group administrators that you enable it later and recompile. If you leave it enabled, you must create the file `/etc/gshadow`.

Enabling the long passwords option is not recommended as discussed above.

Do not change the setting: `#undef AUTOSHADOW`

The `AUTOSHADOW` option was originally designed so that programs that were shadow ignorant would still function. This sounds good in theory, but does not work correctly. If you enable this option, and the program runs as root, it may call `getpwnam()` as root, and later write the modified entry back to the `/etc/passwd` file (with the no-longer-shadowed password). Such programs include `chfn` and `chsh`. (You can't get around this by swapping real and effective uid before calling `getpwnam()` because root may use `chfn` and `chsh` too.)

The same warning is also valid if you are building libc, it has a `SHADOW_COMPAT` option which does the same thing. It should not be used. If you start getting encoded passwords back in your `/etc/passwd` file, this is the problem.

If you are using a `libc` version prior to 4.6.27, you will need to make a couple more changes to `config.h` and the `Makefile`. To `config.h` edit and change:

```
#define HAVE_BASENAME
```

to:

```
#undef HAVE_BASENAME
```

And then in the `Makefile`, change:

```
SOBJS = smain.o env.o entry.o susetup.o shell.o \
        sub.o mail.o motd.o sulog.o age.o tz.o hushed.o

SSRCS = smain.c env.c entry.c setup.c shell.c \
        pwent.c sub.c mail.c motd.c sulog.c shadow.c age.c pwpack.c rad64.c \
        tz.c hushed.c
```

```
SOBJS = smain.o env.o entry.o susetup.o shell.o \
        sub.o mail.o motd.o sulog.o age.o tz.o hushed.o basename.o

SSRCS = smain.c env.c entry.c setup.c shell.c \
        pwent.c sub.c mail.c motd.c sulog.c shadow.c age.c pwpack.c rad64.c \
        tz.c hushed.c basename.c
```

These changes add the code contained in `basename.c` which is contained in `libc 4.6.27` and later.

4.3 Making backup copies of your original programs.

It would also be a good idea to track down and make backup copies of the programs that the shadow suite will replace. On a Slackware 3.0 system these are:

- `/bin/su`
- `/bin/login`
- `/usr/bin/passwd`
- `/usr/bin/newgrp`
- `/usr/bin/chfn`
- `/usr/bin/chsh`
- `/usr/bin/id`

The beta package has a save target in the `Makefile`, but it's commented out because different distributions place the programs in different places.

You should also make a backup copy of your `/etc/passwd` file, but be careful to name it something else if you place it in the same directory so you don't overwrite the `passwd` command.

4.4 Running make

You need to be logged as root to do most of the installation.

Run make to compile the executables in the package:

```
make all
```

You may see the warning: `rcsid defined but not used`. This is fine, it just happens because the author is using a version control package.

5 Installing

5.1 Have a boot disk handy in case you break anything.

If something goes terribly wrong, it would be handy to have a boot disk. If you have a boot/root combination from your installation, that will work, otherwise see the Bootdisk HOWTO,

http://sunsite.unc.edu/mdw/HOWTO/Bootdisk-HOWTO.html

which describes how to make a bootable disk.

5.2 Removing duplicate man pages

You should also move the manual pages that are about to be replaced. Even if you are brave enough install the Shadow Suite without making backups, you will still want to remove the old manual pages. The new manual pages won't normally overwrite the old ones because the old ones are probably compressed.

You can use a combination of: `man -aW command` and `locate command` to locate the manual pages that need to be (re)moved. It's generally easier to figure out which are the older pages before you run `make install`.

If you are using the Slackware 3.0 distribution, then the manual pages you want to remove are:

- `/usr/man/man1/chfn.1.gz`
- `/usr/man/man1/chsh.1.gz`
- `/usr/man/man1/id.1.gz`
- `/usr/man/man1/login.1.gz`
- `/usr/man/man1/passwd.1.gz`

- /usr/man/man1/su.1.gz
- /usr/man/man5/passwd.5.gz

There may also be man pages of the same name in the /var/man/cat[1-9] subdirectories that should also be deleted.

5.3 Running make install

You are now ready to type: (do this as root)

```
make install
```

This will install the new and replacement programs and fix-up the filc permissions. It will also install the man pages.

This also takes care of installing the Shadow Suite include files in the correct places in /usr/include/shadow.

Using the BETA package you must manually copy the file login.defs to the /etc subdirectory and make sure that only *root* can make changes to it.

```
cp login.defs /etc
chmod 700 /etc/login.defs
```

This file is the configuration file for the login program. You should review and make changes to this file for your particular system. This is where you decide which tty's root can login from, and set other security policy settings (like password expiration defaults).

5.4 Running pwconv

The next step is to run pwconv. This must also be done as root, and is best done from the /etc subdirectory:

```
cd /etc
/usr/sbin/pwconv
```

pwconv takes your /etc/passwd file and strips out the fields to create two files: /etc/npasswd and /etc/nshadow.

A pwunconv program is also provided if you need to make a normal /etc/passwd file out of an /etc/passwd and /etc/shadow combination.

5.5 Renaming npasswd and nshadow

Now that you have run pwconv you have created the files /etc/npasswd and /etc/nshadow. These need to be copied over to /etc/passwd and /etc/shadow. We also want to make a backup copy of the original /etc/passwd file, and make sure only root can read it. We'll put the backup in root's home directory:

```
cd /etc
cp passwd ~passwd
chmod 600 ~passwd
mv npasswd passwd
mv nshadow shadow
```

You should also ensure that the file ownerships and permissions are correct. If you are going to be using X, the xlock and xdm programs need to be able to read the shadow file (but not write it).

There are two ways that this can be done. You can set xlock to suid root (xdm is usually run as root anyway). Or you can make the shadow file owned by root with a group of shadow, but before you do this, make sure that you have a shadow group (look in /etc/group). None of the users on the system should actually be in the shadow group.

```
chown root.root passwd
chown root.shadow shadow
chmod 0644 passwd
chmod 0640 shadow
```

Your system now has the password file shadowed. You should now pop over to another virtual terminal and verify that you can login.

◇ **Really, do this now.**

If you can't, then something is wrong. To get back to a non-shadowed state, do the following the following:

```
cd /etc
cp ~passwd passwd
chmod 644 passwd
```

You would then restore the files that you saved earlier to their proper locations.

6 Other programs you may need to upgrade or patch

Even though the shadow suite contains replacement programs for most programs that need to access passwords, there are a few additional programs on most systems that require access to passwords.

If you are running a Debian Distribution (or even if you are not), you can obtain Debian sources for the programs that need to be rebuild from: `ftp://ftp.debian.org/debian/stable/source/`

The remainder of this section discusses how to upgrade `adduser`, `wu_ftpd`, `ftpd`, `pop3d`, `xlock`, `xdm` and `sudo` so that they support the shadow suite.

See Section 8 for a discussion on how to put shadow support into any other program that needs it (although the program must then be run SUID root or SGID shadow to be able to actually access the shadow file).

6.1 Slackware `adduser` program

Slackware distributions (and possibly some others) contain a interactive program for adding users called `/sbin/adduser`. A shadow version of this program can be obtained from ftp://sunsite.unc.edu/pub/Linux/system/Admin/accounts/adduser.shadow-1.4.tar.gz.

I would encourage you to use the programs that are supplied with the Shadow Suite (`useradd`, `usermod`, and `userdel`) instead of the slackware `adduser` program. They take a little time to learn how to use, but it's well worth the effort because you have much more control and they perform proper file locking on the `/etc/passwd` and `/etc/shadow` file (`adduser` doesn't).

See the section on 7 for more information.

But if you gotta have it, here is what you do:

```
tar -xzvf adduser.shadow-1.4.tar.gz
cd adduser
make clean
make adduser
chmod 700 adduser
cp adduser /sbin
```

6.2 The `wu_ftpd` Server

Most Linux systems some with the `wu_ftpd` server. If your distribution does not come with shadow installed, then your `wu_ftpd` will not be compiled for shadow. `wu_ftpd` is launched from `inetd/tcpd` as a root process. If you are running an old `wu_ftpd` daemon, you will want to upgrade it anyway because older ones had a bug that would allow the root account to be compromised (For more info see the Linux security home page
http://bach.cis.temple.edu/linux/linux-security/Linux-Security-FAQ/
Linux-wu.ftpd-2.4-Update.html).

Fortunately, you only need to get the source code and recompile it with shadow enabled.

The `wu_ftp` server can be found on Sunsite as
ftp://sunsite.unc.edu/pub/Linux/system/Network/file-transfer
/wu-ftpd-2.4-fixed.tar.gz.

Once you retrieve the server, put it in `/usr/src`, then type:

```
cd /usr/src
tar -xzvf wu-ftpd-2.4-fixed.tar.gz
cd wu-ftpd-2.4-fixed
cp ./src/config/config.lnx.shadow ./src/config/config.lnx
```

Then edit `./src/makefiles/Makefile.lnx`, and change the line:

```
LIBES    = -lbsd -support
```

to:

```
LIBES    = -lbsd -support -lshadow
```

Now you are ready to run the build script and install:

```
cd /usr/src/wu-ftpd-2.4-fixed
/usr/src/wu-ftp-2.4.fixed/build lnx
cp /usr/sbin/wu.ftpd /usr/sbin/wu.ftpd.old
cp ./bin/ftpd /usr/sbin/wu.ftpd
```

This uses the Linux shadow configuration file, compiles and installs the server.

On my Slackware 2.3 system I also had to do the following before running `build`:

```
cd /usr/include/netinet
ln -s in_systm.h in_system.h
cd -
```

Problems have been reported compiling this package under ELF systems, but the Beta version of the next release works fine. It can be found as `wu-ftp-2.4.2-beta-10.tar.gz`

ftp://tscnet.com/pub/linux/network/ftp/wu-ftpd-2.4.2-beta-10.tar.gz

Once you retrieve the server, put it in `/usr/src`, then type:

```
cd /usr/src
tar -xzvf wu-ftpd-2.4.2-beta-9.tar.gz
cd wu-ftpd-beta-9
cd ./src/config
```

Then edit `config.lnx`, and change:

```
#undef SHADOW.PASSWORD
```

to:

```
#define SHADOW.PASSWORD
```

Then,

```
cd ../Makefiles
```

and edit the file `Makefile.lnx` and change:

```
LIBES = -lsupport -lbsd # -lshadow
```

to:

```
LIBES = -lsupport -lbsd -lshadow
```

Then build and install:

```
cd ..
build lnx
cp /usr/sbin/wu.ftpd /usr/sbin/wu.ftpd.old
cp ./bin/ftpd /usr/sbin/wu.ftpd
```

Note that you should check your `/etc/inetd.conf` file to make sure that this is where your `wu.ftpd` server really lives. It has been reported that some distributions place the server daemons in different places, and then `wu.ftpd` in particular may be named something else.

6.3 Standard `ftpd`

If you are running the standard `ftpd` server, I would recommend that you upgrade to the `wu_ftpd` server. Aside from the known bug discussed above, it's generally thought to be more secure.

If you insist on the standard one, or you need NIS support, Sunsite has *ftpd-shadow-nis.tgz*

ftp://sunsite.unc.edu/pub/Linux/system/Network/file-transfer/ftpd-shadow-nis.tgz

6.4 `pop3d` (Post Office Protocol 3)

If you need to support the third Post Office Protocol (POP3), you will need to recompile a `pop3d` program. `pop3d` is normally run by `inetd/tcpd` as `root`.

There are two versions available from Sunsite:

pop3d-1.00.4.linux.shadow.tar.gz
ftp://sunsite.unc.edu/pub/Linux/system/Mail/pop/pop3d-1.00.4.linux.shadow.tar.gz

and

pop3d+shadow+elf.tar.gz
ftp://sunsite.unc.edu/pub/Linux/system/Mail/pop/pop3d+shadow+elf.tar.gz

Both of these are fairly straight forward to install.

6.5 xlock

If you install the shadow suite, and then run X and lock the screen without upgrading your `xlock`, you will have to use `Ctrl-Alt-Fx` to switch to another tty, log in, and kill the `xlock` process (or use `Ctrl-Alt-BS` to kill the X server). Fortunately it's fairly easy to upgrade your `xlock` program.

If you are running XFree86 Versions 3.*x.x*, you are probably using `xlockmore` (which is a great screen-saver in addition to a lock). This package supports shadow with a recompile. If you have an older `xlock`, I recommend that you upgrade to this one.

`xlockmore-3.5.tgz` is available at:
ftp://sunsite.unc.edu/pub/Linux/X11/xutils/screensavers/xlockmore-3.7.tgz

Basically, this is what you need to do:

Get the `xlockmore-3.7.tgz` file and put it in `/usr/src` unpack it:

```
tar -xzvf xlockmore-3.7.tgz
```

Edit the file: `/usr/X11R6/lib/X11/config/linux.cf`, and change the line:

```
#define HasShadowPasswd     NO
to
#define HasShadowPasswd     YES
```

Then build the executables:

```
cd /usr/src/xlockmore
xmkmf
make depend
make
```

Then move everything into place and update file ownerships and permissions:

```
cp xlock /usr/X11R6/bin/
cp XLock /var/X11R6/lib/app-defaults/
chown root.shadow /usr/X11R6/bin/xlock
chmod 2755 /usr/X11R6/bin/xlock
chown root.shadow /etc/shadow
chmod 640 /etc/shadow
```

Your xlock will now work correctly.

6.6 xdm

`xdm` is a program that presents a login screen for X. Some systems start `xdm` when the system is told to goto a specified run level (see `/etc/inittab`.

With the Shadow Suite installed, `xdm` will need to be updated. Fortunately it's fairly easy to upgrade your `xdm` program.

`xdm.tar.gz` is available at: ftp://sunsite.unc.edu/pub/Linux/X11/xutils/xdm.tar.gz

Get the `xdm.tar.gz` file and put it in `/usr/src`, then to unpack it:

```
tar -xzvf xdm.tar.gz
```

Edit the file: `/usr/X11R6/lib/X11/config/linux.cf`, and change the line:

```
#define HasShadowPasswd     NO
to
#define HasShadowPasswd     YES
```

Then build the executables:

```
cd /usr/src/xdm
xmkmf
make depend
make
```

Then move everything into place:

```
cp xdm /usr/X11R6/bin/
```

`xdm` is run as root so you don't need to change it file permissions.

6.7 sudo

The program sudo allows a system administrator to let users run programs that would normally require root access. This is handy because it lets the administrator limit access to the root account itself while still allowing users to do things like mounting drives.

sudo needs to read passwords because it verifies the users password when it's invoked. sudo already runs SUID root, so accessing the /etc/shadow file is not a problem.

sudo for the shadow suite, is available as at:

ftp://sunsite.unc.edu/pub/Linux/system/Admin/sudo-1.2-shadow.tgz

Warning: When you install sudo your /etc/sudoers file will be replaced with a default one, so you need to make a backup of it if you have added anything to the default one. (you could also edit the Makefile and remove the line that copies the default file to /etc).

The package is already setup for shadow, so all that's required is to recompile the package (put it in /usr/src):

```
cd /usr/src
tar -xzvf sudo-1.2-shadow.tgz
cd sudo-1.2-shadow
make all
make install
```

6.8 imapd (E-Mail pine package)

imapd is an e-mail server similar to pop3d. imapd comes with the Pine E-mail package. The documentation that comes with the package states that the default for Linux systems is to include support for shadow. However, I have found that this is not true. Furthermore, the build script-Makefile combination on this package is makes it very difficult to add the libshadow.a library at compile time, so I was unable to add shadow support for imapd.

If anyone has this figured out, please E-mail me, and I'll include the solution here.

6.9 pppd (Point-to-Point Protocol Server)

The pppd server can be setup to use several types of authentication: Password Authentication Protocol (PAP) and Cryptographic Handshake Authentication Protocol (CHAP). The pppd server usually reads the password strings that it uses from /etc/ppp/chap-secrets or /etc/ppp/pap-secrets. If you are using this default behavior of pppd, it is not necessary to re-install pppd.

pppd also allows you to use the login parameter (either on the command line, or in the configuration or options file). If the login option is given, then pppd will use the /etc/passwd file for the username and passwords for the PAP. This, of course, will no longer work now that our password file is shadowed. For pppd-1.2.1d this requires adding code for shadow support.

The example given in the next section is adding shadow support to pppd-1.2.1d (an older version of pppd).

pppd-2.2.0 already contains shadow support.

7 Putting the Shadow Suite to use.

This section discusses some of the things that you will want to know now that you have the Shadow Suite installed on your system. More information is contained in the manual pages for each command.

7.1 Adding, Modifying, and deleting users

The Shadow Suite added the following command line oriented commands for adding, modifying, and deleting users. You may also have installed the adduser program.

7.1.1 useradd

The useradd command can be used to add users to the system. You also invoke this command to change the default settings.

The first thing that you should do is to examine the default settings and make changes specific to your system:

```
useradd -D
```

```
GROUP=1
HOME=/home
INACTIVE=0
EXPIRE=0
SHELL=
SKEL=/etc/skel
```

The defaults are probably not what you want, so if you started adding users now you would have to specify all the information for each user. However, we can and should change the default values.

On my system:

- I want the default group to be 100.
- I want passwords to expire every 60 days.
- I don't want to lock an account because the password is expired.
- I want to default shell to be /bin/bash.

To make these changes I would use:

```
useradd -D -g100 -e60 -f0 -s/bin/bash
```

Now running `useradd -D` will give:

```
GROUP=100
HOME=/home
INACTIVE=0
EXPIRE=60
SHELL=/bin/bash
SKEL=/etc/skel
```

Just in case you wanted to know, these defaults are stored in the file /etc/default/useradd.

Now you can use useradd to add users to the system. For example, to add the user fred, using the defaults, you would use the following:

```
useradd -m -c "Fred Flintstone" fred
```

This will create the following entry in the /etc/passwd file:

```
fred:*:505:100:Fred Flintstone:/home/fred:/bin/bash
```

And the following entry in the /etc/shadow file:

```
fred:!:0:0:60:0:0:0:0
```

fred's home directory will be created and the contents of /etc/skel will be copied there because of the -m switch. Also, since we did not specify a UID, the next available one was used.

fred's account is created, but fred still won't be able to login until we unlock the account. We do this by changing the password.

```
passwd fred
```

```
Changing password for fred
Enter the new password (minimum of 5 characters)
Please use a combination of upper and lower case letters and numbers.
New Password: *******
Re-enter new password: *******
```

Now the /etc/shadow will contain:

```
fred:J0C.WDR1amIt6:9559:0:60:0:0:0:0
```

And fred will now be able to login and use the system. The nice thing about useradd and the other programs that come with the Shadow Suite is that they make changes to the /etc/passwd and /etc/shadow files atomically. So if you are adding a user, and another user is changing their password at the same time, both operations will be performed correctly.

You should use the supplied commands rather than directly editing /etc/passwd and /etc/shadow. If you were editing the /etc/shadow file, and a user were to change his password while you are editing, and then you were to save the file you were editing, the user's password change would be lost.

Here is a small interactive script that adds users using useradd and passwd:

```
#!/bin/bash
#
# /sbin/newuser - A script to add users to the system using the Shadow
#                 Suite's useradd and passwd commands.
#
# Written my Mike Jackson <mhjack@tscnet.com> as an example for the Linux
# Shadow Password Howto.  Permission to use and modify is expressly granted.
#
# This could be modified to show the defaults and allow modification similar
# to the Slackware Adduser program.  It could also be modified to disallow
# stupid entries.  (i.e. better error checking).
#
##
#  Defaults for the useradd command
##
GROUP=100          # Default Group
HOME=/home         # Home directory location (/home/username)
SKEL=/etc/skel     # Skeleton Directory
INACTIVE=0         # Days after password expires to disable account (0=never)
EXPIRE=60          # Days that a passwords lasts
SHELL=/bin/bash    # Default Shell (full path)
##
#  Defaults for the passwd command
##
PASSMIN=0          # Days between password changes
PASSWARN=14        # Days before password expires that a warning is given
##
#  Ensure that root is running the script.
##
WHOAMI='/usr/bin/whoami'
if [ $WHOAMI != "root" ]; then
        echo "You must be root to add news users!"
        exit 1
fi
##
#  Ask for username and fullname.
##
echo ""
echo -n "Username: "
read USERNAME
echo -n "Full name: "
read FULLNAME
#
echo "Adding user: $USERNAME."
#
# Note that the "" around $FULLNAME is required because this field is
# almost always going to contain at least on space, and without the "'s
# the useradd command would think that you we moving on to the next
# parameter when it reached the SPACE character.
#
/usr/sbin/useradd -c"$FULLNAME" -d$HOME/$USERNAME -e$EXPIRE \
        -f$INACTIVE -g$GROUP -m -k$SKEL -s$SHELL $USERNAME
##
#  Set password defaults
##
/bin/passwd -n $PASSMIN -w $PASSWARN $USERNAME >/dev/null 2>&1
##
#  Let the passwd command actually ask for password (twice)
```

```
##
/bin/passwd $USERNAME
##
#  Show what was done.
##
echo ""
echo "Entry from /etc/passwd:"
echo -n "    "
grep "$USERNAME:" /etc/passwd
echo "Entry from /etc/shadow:"
echo -n "    "
grep "$USERNAME:" /etc/shadow
echo "Summary output of the passwd command:"
echo -n "    "
passwd -S $USERNAME
echo ""
```

Using a script to add new users is really much more preferable than editing the /etc/passwd or /etc/shadow files directly or using a program like the Slackware adduser program. Feel free to use and modify this script for your particular system.

For more information on the useradd see the online manual page.

7.1.2 usermod

The usermod program is used to modify the information on a user. The switches are similar to the useradd program.

Let's say that you want to change fred's shell, you would do the following:

```
usermod -s /bin/tcsh fred
```

Now fred's /etc/passwd file entry would be change to this:

```
fred:*:505:100:Fred Flintstone:/home/fred:/bin/tcsh
```

Let's make fred's account expire on 09/15/97:

```
usermod -e 09/15/97 fred
```

Now fred's entry in /etc/shadow becomes:

```
fred:J0C.WDR1amIt6:9559:0:60:0:0:10119:0
```

For more information on the usermod command see the online manual page.

7.1.3 userdel

userdel does just what you would expect, it deletes the user's account. You simply use:

```
userdel -r username
```

The -r causes all files in the user's home directory to be removed along with the home directory itself. Files located in other file system will have to be searched for and deleted manually.

If you want to simply lock the account rather than delete it, use the passwd command instead.

7.2 The passwd command and passwd aging.

The passwd command has the obvious use of changing passwords. Additionally, it is used by the root user to:

- Lock and unlock accounts (-l and -u)
- Set the maximum number of days that a password remains valid (-x)
- Set the minimum days between password changes (-n)
- Sets the number of days of warning that a password is about to expire (-w)
- Sets the number of days after the password expires before the account is locked (-i)
- Allow viewing of account information in a clearer format (-S)

For example, let look again at fred

```
passwd -S fred
fred P 03/04/96 0 60 0 0
```

This means that fred's password is valid, it was last changed on 03/04/96, it can be changed at any time, it expires after 60 days, fred will not be warned, and and the account won't be disabled when the password expires.

This simply means that if fred logs in after the password expires, he will be prompted for a new password at login.

If we decide that we want to warn fred 14 days before his password expires and make his account inactive 14 days after he lets it expire, we would need to do the following:

```
passwd -w14 -i14 fred
```

Now fred is changed to:

```
fred P 03/04/96 0 60 14 14
```

For more information on the passwd command see the online manual page.

7.3 The /etc/login.defs file.

The file /etc/login is the configuration file for the login program and also for the Shadow Suite as a whole.

/etc/login contains settings from what the prompts will look like to what the default expiration will be when a user changes his password.

The /etc/login.defs file is quite well documented just by the comments that are contained within it. However, there are a few things to note:

- It contains flags that can be turned on or off that determine the amount of logging that takes place.
- It contains pointers to other configuration files.
- It contains defaults assignments for things like password aging.

From the above list you can see that this is a rather important file, and you should make sure that it is present, and that the settings are what you desire for your system.

7.4 Group passwords.

The /etc/group file may contain passwords that permit a user to become a member of a particular group. This function is enabled if you define the constant SHADOWGRP in the /usr/src/shadow-YYMMDD/config.h file.

If you define this constant and then compile, you must create an /etc/gshadow file to hold the group passwords and the group administrator information.

When you created the /etc/shadow, you used a program called pwconv, there no equivalent program to create the /etc/gshadow file, but it really doesn't matter, it takes care of itself.

To create the initial /etc/gshadow file do the following:

```
touch /etc/gshadow
chown root.root /etc/gshadow
chmod 700 /etc/gshadow
```

Once you create new groups, they will be added to the /etc/group and the /etc/gshadow files. If you modify a group by adding or removing users or changing the group password, the /etc/gshadow file will be changed.

The programs groups, groupadd, groupmod, and groupdel are provided as part of the Shadow Suite to modify groups.

The format of the /etc/group file is as follows:

```
groupname:!:GID:member,member,...
```

Where:

groupname
: The name of the group

!
: The field that normally holds the password, but that is now relocated to the /etc/gshadow file.

GID
: The numerical group ID number

member
: List of group members

The format of the /etc/gshadow file is as follows:

```
groupname:password:admin,admin,...:member,member,...
```

Where:

groupname
The name of the group

password
The encoded group password.

admin
List of group administrators

member
List of group members

The command gpasswd is used only for adding or removing administrators and members to or from a group. root or someone in the list of administrators may add or remove group members.

The groups password can be changed using the passwd command by root or anyone listed as an administrator for the group.

Despite the fact that there is not currently a manual page for gpasswd, typing gpasswd without any parameters gives a listing of options. It's fairly easy to grasp how it all works once you understand the file formats and the concepts.

7.5 Consistency checking programs

7.5.1 pwck

The program pwck is provided to provide a consistency check on the /etc/passwd and /etc/shadow files. It will check each username and verify that it has the following:

- the correct number of fields,
- unique user name,
- valid user and group identifier,
- valid primary group,
- valid home directory,
- valid login shell.

It will also warn of any account that has no password.

It's a good idea to run pwck after installing the Shadow Suite. It's also a good idea to run it periodically, perhaps weekly or monthly. If you use the -r option, you can use cron to run it on a regular basis and have the report mailed to you.

7.5.2 grpck

grpck is the consistency checking program for the /etc/group and /etc/gshadow files. It performs the following checks:

- the correct number of fields
- unique group name
- valid list of members and administrators

It also has the -r option for automated reports.

7.6 Dial-up passwords.

Dial-up passwords are another optional line of defense for systems that allow dial-in access. If you have a system that allows many people to connect locally or via a network, but you want to limit who can dial in and connect, then dial-up passwords are for you. To enable dial-up passwords, you must edit the file `/etc/login.defs` and ensure that `DIALUPS_CHECK_ENAB` is set to `yes`.

Two files contain the dial-up information, `/etc/dialups` which contains the ttys (one per line, with the leading "`/dev/` removed). If a tty is listed then dial-up checks are performed.

The second file is the `/etc/d_passwd` file. This file contains the fully qualified path name of a shell, followed by an optional password.

If a user logs into a line that is listed in `/etc/dialups`, and his shell is listed in the file `/etc/d_passwd` he will be allowed access only by suppling the correct password.

Another useful purpose for using dial-up passwords might be to setup a line that only allows a certain type of connect (perhaps a PPP or UUCP connection). If a user tries to get another type of connection (i.e. a list of shells), he must know a password to use the line.

Before you can use the dial-up feature, you must create the files.

The command `dpasswd` is provided to assign passwords to the shells in the `/etc/d_passwd` file. See the manual page for more information.

8 Adding shadow support to a C program

Adding shadow support to a program is actually fairly straightforward. The only problem is that the program must be run by root (or suid root) in order for the the program to be able to access the `/etc/shadow` file.

This presents one big problem: very careful programming practices must be followed when creating suid programs. For instance, if a program has a shell escape, this must not occur as root if the program is suid root.

For adding shadow support to a program so that it can check passwords, but otherwise does need to run as root, it's a lot safer to run the program suid shadow instead. The `xlock` program is an example of this.

In the example given below, `pppd-1.2.1d` already runs suid as root, so adding shadow support should not make the program any more vulnerable.

8.1 Header files

The header files should reside in `/usr/include/shadow`. There should also be a `/usr/include/shadow.h`, but it will be a symbolic link to `/usr/include/shadow/shadow.h`.

To add shadow support to a program, you need to include the header files:

```
#include <shadow/shadow.h>
#include <shadow/pwauth.h>
```

It might be a good idea to use compiler directives to conditionally compile the shadow code (I do in the example below).

8.2 `libshadow.a` library

When you installed the Shadow Suite the `libshadow.a` file was created and installed in `/usr/lib`.

When compiling shadow support into a program, the linker needs to be told to include the `libshadow.a` library into the link.

This is done by:

```
gcc program.c -o program -lshadow
```

However, as we will see in the example below, most large programs use a `Makefile`, and usually have a variable called `LIBS=...` that we will modify.

8.3 Shadow Structure

The `libshadow.a` library uses a structure called `spwd` for the information it retrieves from the `/etc/shadow` file. This is the definition of the `spwd` structure from the `/usr/include/shadow/shadow.h` header file:

```
struct spwd
{
  char *sp_namp;                /* login name */
  char *sp_pwdp;                /* encrypted password */
```

```
  sptime sp_lstchg;              /* date of last change */
  sptime sp_min;                 /* minimum number of days between changes */
  sptime sp_max;                 /* maximum number of days between changes */
  sptime sp_warn;                /* number of days of warning before password
                                    expires */
  sptime sp_inact;               /* number of days after password expires
                                    until the account becomes unusable. */
  sptime sp_expire;              /* days since 1/1/70 until account expires
*/
  unsigned long sp_flag;         /* reserved for future use */
};
```

The Shadow Suite can put things into the sp_pwdp field besides just the encoded passwd. The password field could contain:

```
username:Npge08pfz4wuk;@/sbin/extra:9479:0:10000::::
```

This means that in addition to the password, the program /sbin/extra should be called for further authentiaction. The program called will get passed a the username and a switch that indicates why it's being called. See the file /usr/include/shadow/pwauth.h and the source code for pwauth.c for more information.

What this means is that we should use the function pwauth to perform the actual authentication, as it will take care of the secondary authentication as well. The example below does this.

The author of the Shadow Suite indicates that since most programs in existence don't do this, and that it may be removed or changed in future versions of the Shadow Suite.

8.4 Shadow Functions

The shadow.h file also contains the function prototypes for the functions contained in the libshadow.a library:

```
extern void setspent __P ((void));
extern void endspent __P ((void));
extern struct spwd *sgetspent __P ((__const char *__string));
extern struct spwd *fgetspent __P ((FILE *__fp));
extern struct spwd *getspent __P ((void));
extern struct spwd *getspnam __P ((__const char *__name));
extern int putspent __P ((__const struct spwd *__sp, FILE *__fp));
```

The function that we are going to use in the example is: getspnam which will retrieve for us a spwd structure for the supplied name.

8.5 Example

This is an example of adding shadow support to a program that needs it, but does not have it by default.

This example uses the Point-to-Point Protocol Server (pppd-1.2.1d), which has a mode in which it performs *PAP* authentication using user names and passwords from the /etc/passwd file instead of the PAP or CHAP files. You would not need to add this code to pppd-2.2.0 because it's already there.

This feature of pppd probably isn't used very much, but if you installed the Shadow Suite, it won't work anymore because the passwords are no longer stored in /etc/passwd.

The code for authenticating users under pppd-1.2.1d is located in the /usr/src/pppd-1.2.1d/pppd/auth.c file.

The following code needs to be added to the top of the file where all the other #include directives are. We have surrounded the #includes with conditional directives (i.e. only include if we are compiling for shadow support).

```
#ifdef HAS_SHADOW
#include <shadow.h>
#include <shadow/pwauth.h>
#endif
```

The next thing to do is to modify the actual code. We are still making changes to the auth.c file.

Function auth.c before modifications:

```
/*
 * login - Check the user name and password against the system
 * password database, and login the user if OK.
 *
```

```
 * returns:
 *      UPAP_AUTHNAK: Login failed.
 *      UPAP_AUTHACK: Login succeeded.
 * In either case, msg points to an appropriate message.
 */
static int
login(user, passwd, msg, msglen)
    char *user;
    char *passwd;
    char **msg;
    int *msglen;
{
    struct passwd *pw;
    char *epasswd;
    char *tty;

    if ((pw = getpwnam(user)) == NULL) {
        return (UPAP_AUTHNAK);
    }
     /*
      * XXX If no passwd, let them login without one.
      */
    if (pw->pw_passwd == '\0') {
        return (UPAP_AUTHACK);
    }

    epasswd = crypt(passwd, pw->pw_passwd);
    if (strcmp(epasswd, pw->pw_passwd)) {
        return (UPAP_AUTHNAK);
    }

    syslog(LOG_INFO, "user %s logged in", user);

    /*
     * Write a wtmp entry for this user.
     */
    tty = strrchr(devname, '/');
    if (tty == NULL)
        tty = devname;
    else
        tty++;
    logwtmp(tty, user, "");             /* Add wtmp login entry */
    logged_in = TRUE;

    return (UPAP_AUTHACK);
}
```

The user's password is placed into pw-pw_passwd, so all we really need to do is add the function getspnam. This will put the password into spwd-sp_pwdp.

We will add the function pwauth to perform the actual authentication. This will automatically perform secondary authentication if the shadow file is setup for it.

Function auth.c after modifications to support shadow:

```
/*
 * login - Check the user name and password against the system
 * password database, and login the user if OK.
 *
 * This function has been modified to support the Linux Shadow Password
 * Suite if USE_SHADOW is defined.
```

```
 *
 * returns:
 *      UPAP_AUTHNAK: Login failed.
 *      UPAP_AUTHACK: Login succeeded.
 * In either case, msg points to an appropriate message.
 */
static int
login(user, passwd, msg, msglen)
    char *user;
    char *passwd;
    char **msg;
    int *msglen;
{
    struct passwd *pw;
    char *epasswd;
    char *tty;

#ifdef USE_SHADOW
    struct spwd *spwd;
    struct spwd *getspnam();
#endif

    if ((pw = getpwnam(user)) == NULL) {
        return (UPAP_AUTHNAK);
    }

#ifdef USE_SHADOW
        spwd = getspnam(user);
        if (spwd)
                pw->pw_passwd = spwd->sp-pwdp;
#endif

     /*
      * XXX If no passwd, let NOT them login without one.
      */
    if (pw->pw_passwd == '\0') {
        return (UPAP_AUTHNAK);
    }
#ifdef HAS_SHADOW
    if ((pw->pw_passwd && pw->pw_passwd[0] == '@'
         && pw_auth (pw->pw_passwd+1, pw->pw_name, PW_LOGIN, NULL))
        || !valid (passwd, pw)) {
        return (UPAP_AUTHNAK);
    }
#else
    epasswd = crypt(passwd, pw->pw_passwd);
    if (strcmp(epasswd, pw->pw_passwd)) {
        return (UPAP_AUTHNAK);
    }
#endif

    syslog(LOG_INFO, "user %s logged in", user);

    /*
     * Write a wtmp entry for this user.
     */
    tty = strrchr(devname, '/');
    if (tty == NULL)
```

```
        tty = devname;
    else
        tty++;
    logwtmp(tty, user, "");              /* Add wtmp login entry */
    logged_in = TRUE;

    return (UPAP_AUTHACK);
}
```

Careful examination will reveal that we made another change as well. The original version allowed access (returned `UPAP_AUTHACK` if there was NO password in the `/etc/passwd` file. This is *not* good, because a common use of this login feature is to use one account to allow access to the PPP process and then check the username and password supplied by PAP with the username in the `/etc/passwd` file and the password in the `/etc/shadow` file.

So if we had set the original version up to run as the shell for a user i.e. `ppp`, then anyone could get a PPP connection by setting their PAP to user `ppp` and a password of null.

We fixed this also by returning `UPAP_AUTHNAK` instead of `UPAP_AUTHACK` if the password field was empty.

Interestingly enough, `pppd-2.2.0` has the same problem.

Next we need to modify the Makefile so that two things occur: `USE_SHADOW` must be defined, and `libshadow.a` needs to be added to the linking process.

Edit the Makefile, and add:

```
LIBS = -lshadow
```

Then we find the line:

```
COMPILE_FLAGS = -I.. -D_linux_=1 -DGIDSET_TYPE=gid_t
```

And change it to:

```
COMPILE_FLAGS = -I.. -D_linux_=1 -DGIDSET_TYPE=gid_t -DUSE_SHADOW
```

Now make and install.

9 Copyright Message.

10 Miscellaneous and Acknowledgments.

The code examples for `auth.c` are taken from pppd-1.2.1d and ppp-2.1.0e, Copyright (c) 1993 and The Australian National University and Copyright (c) 1989 Carnegie Mellon University.

Thanks to Marek Michalkiewicz, marekm@i17linuxb.ists.pwr.wroc.pl, for writing and maintaining the Shadow Suite for Linux, and for his review and comments on this document.

Thanks to Ron Tidd rtidd@tscnet.com for his helpful review and testing.

Thanks to everyone who has sent me feedback to help improve this document.

Please, if you have any comments or suggestions then mail them to me.

regards

Michael H. Jackson mhjack@tscnet.com

Part XLV

"SMB HOWTO" by David Wood,

dwood@plugged.net.au

Contents

Abstract

v1.0, 10 August 1996
This is the SMB HOWTO. This document describes how to use the Session Message Block (SMB) protocol, also called the NetBIOS or LanManager protocol, with Linux.

1 Introduction

This is the SMB HOWTO. This document describes how to use the Session Message Block (SMB) protocol, also called the NetBIOS or LanManager protocol, with Linux.

This document is maintained by David Wood (dwood@plugged.net.au). Additions, modifications or corrections may be mailed there for inclusion in the next release.

The SMB protocol is used by Microsoft Windows 3.11, NT and 95 to share disks and printers. Using the Samba suite of tools by Andrew Tridgell, UNIX (including Linux) machines can share disk and printers with Windows hosts.

There are four things that one can do with Samba:

1. Share a Linux drive with Windows machines.
2. Share a Windows drive with Linux machines.
3. Share a Linux printer with Windows machines.
4. Share a Windows printer with Linux machines.

All of these are covered in this document.

Disclaimer: The procedures and scripts either work for the author or have been reported to work by the people that provided them. Different configurations may not work with the information given here. If you encounter such a situation, you may e-mail the author with suggestions for improvement in this document, but the author guarantees nothing. What did you expect? The author is, after all, a consultant.

2 Further Information

This HOWTO attempts to explain how to configure basic SMB file and print services on a Linux machine. Samba is a very complex and complete package. There would be no point in attempting to duplicate all of the documentation for Samba here.

For further information, please see the following documents:

- The Samba documentation, available as part of the Samba distribution. The distribution is available at ftp://nimbus.anu.edu.au/pub/tridge/samba/.
- The Linux Printing HOWTO by Grant Taylor.
- The Print2Win Mini-HOWTO by Harish Pillay.

3 Installation

The latest source version of Samba is available from:

ftp://nimbus.anu.edu.au/pub/tridge/samba/.

However, if you have installed the Red Hat distribution of linux, you have the option of installing it as a package. Some other distributions also include the Samba binaries.

The following two daemons are required for the Samba package. They are typically installed in `/usr/sbin` and run either on boot from the systems startup scripts or from inetd. Example scripts are shown in 4.

```
smbd (The SMB daemon)
nmbd (Provides NetBIOS name server support to clients)
```

Typically, the following Samba binaries are installed in /usr/bin, although the location is optional.

```
smbclient       (An SMB client for UNIX machines)
smbprint        (A script to print to a printer on an SMB host)
smbprint.sysv   (As above, but for SVR4 UNIX machines)
smbstatus       (Lists the current SMB connections for the local host)
smbrun          (A 'glue' script to facilitate running applications
                 on SMB hosts)
```

Additionally, a script called "print" is included with this HOWTO, which serves as a useful front end to the smbprint script.

The Samba package is simple to install. Simply retrieve the source from the location mentioned above, and read the file README in the distribution. There is also a file called `docs/INSTALL.txt` in the distribution that provides a simple step-by-step set of instructions.

Following installation, place the daemons in `/usr/sbin` and the binaries in `/usr/bin`. Install the manual pages in `/usr/local/man`.

When you made the Samba package, you would have specified in the Makefile the location for the configuration file, `smb.conf`. This is generally in `/etc`, but you can put it anywhere you like. For these directions, we will presume that you specified the location of the configuration file as `/etc/smb.conf`, the log file location as `log file = /var/log/samba-log` and the lock directory as lock directory = /var/lock/samba.

Install the configuration file, `smb.conf`. Go to the directory where Samba was built. Look in the subdirectory `examples/simple` and read the file `README`. Copy the file `smb.conf` found in that directory to `/etc`. Be careful. If you have a Linux distribution that already has Samba installed, you may already have a Samba configuration file in `/etc`. You should probably start with that one.

If you don't want to have your configuration file in `/etc`, put it wherever you want to, then put a symlink in `/etc`:

```
ln -s /path/to/smb.conf /etc/smb.conf
```

4 Running The Daemons

The two SMB daemons are `/usr/sbin/smbd` and `/usr/sbin/nmbd`.

You can run the Samba daemons from `inetd` or as stand-alone processes. If you are configuring a permanent file server, they should be run from `inetd` so that they will be restarted if they die. If you just want to use SMB services occasionally or to assist with systems administration, you can start them with an `/etc/rc.d/init.d` script or even by hand when you need them.

To run the daemons from inetd, place the following lines in the inetd configuration file, `/etc/inetd.conf`

```
# SAMBA NetBIOS services (for PC file and print sharing)
netbios-ssn stream tcp nowait root /usr/sbin/smbd smbd
netbios-ns dgram udp wait root /usr/sbin/nmbd nmbd
```

Then restart the `inetd` daemon by running the command:

```
kill -HUP 1
```

To run the daemons from the system startup scripts, put the following script in file called `/etc/rc.d/init.d/smb` and symbolically link it to the files specified in the comments:

```
#!/bin/sh

#
# /etc/rc.d/init.d/smb - starts and stops SMB services.
#
# The following files should be synbolic links to this file:
# symlinks: /etc/rc.d/rc1.d/K35smb  (Kills SMB services on
#    shutdown)
#  /etc/rc.d/rc3.d/S91smb  (Starts SMB services in
#    multiuser mode)
#  /etc/rc.d/rc6.d/K35smb  (Kills SMB services on reboot)
#

# Source function library.
. /etc/rc.d/init.d/functions

# Source networking configuration.
. /etc/sysconfig/network

# Check that networking is up.
[ ${NETWORKING} = "no" ] && exit 0
```

```
# See how we were called.
case "$1" in
  start)
    echo -n "Starting SMB services: "
      daemon smbd -D
      daemon nmbd -D
      echo
      touch /var/lock/subsys/smb
      ;;
    stop)
      echo -n "Shutting down SMB services: "
      killproc smbd
      killproc nmbd
      rm -f /var/lock/subsys/smb
      echo ""
      ;;
   *)
      echo "Usage: smb {start|stop}"
      exit 1
  esac
```

5 General Configuration (/etc/smb.conf)

Samba configuration on a Linux (or other UNIX machine) is controlled by a single file, `/etc/smb.conf`. This file determines which system resources you want to share with the outside world and what restrictions you wish to place on them.

Since the following sections will address sharing Linux drives and printers with Windows machines, the smb.conf file shown in this section is as simple as you can get, just for introductory purposes.

Don't worry about the details, yet. Later sections will introduce the major concepts.

Each section of the file starts with a section header such as "Global," "homes," and "printers"

The "global" section defines a few variables that Samba will use to define sharing for all resources.

The *homes* section allows a remote users to access their (and only their) home directory on the local (linux) machine). That is, if a Windows user trys to connect to this share from their Windows machines, they will be connected to their personal home directory. Note that to do this, they must have an account on the linux box.

The sample smb.conf file below allows remote users to get to their home directories on the local machine and to write to a temporary directory. For a Windows user to see these shares, the linux box has to be on the local network. Then the user simply connects a network drive from the Windows File Manager or Windows Explorer.

Note that in the following sections, additional entries for this file will be given to allow more resources to be shared.

```
; /etc/smb.conf
;
; Make sure and restart the server after making changes
; to this file, ex:
; /etc/rc.d/init.d/smb stop
; /etc/rc.d/init.d/smb start

[global]
; Uncomment this if you want a guest account
; guest account = nobody
   log file = /var/log/samba-log.%m
   lock directory = /var/lock/samba
   share modes = yes

[homes]
   comment = Home Directories
   browseable = no
   read only = no
   create mode = 0750
```

```
[tmp]
   comment = Temporary file space
   path = /tmp
   read only = no
   public = yes
```

6 Sharing A Linux Drive With Windows Machines

As shown in the simple smb.conf above, sharing linux drives with Windows users is easy. However, like everything else with Samba, you can control things to a large degree. Here are some examples:

To share a directory with the public, create a clone of the tmp section above by adding something like this to smb.conf:

```
[public]
   comment = Public Stuff
   path = /home/public
   public = yes
   writable = yes
   printable = yes
```

To make the above directory readable by the public, but only writable by people in group staff, modify the entry like this:

```
[public]
   comment = Public Stuff
   path = /home/public
   public = yes
   writable = yes
   printable = no
   write list = @staff
```

For other tricks to play with drive shares, see the Samba documentation or manual pages.

7 Sharing A Windows Drive With Linux Machines

An SMB client program for UNIX machines is included with the Samba distribution. It provides an FTP-like interface on the command line. You can use this utility to transfer files between a Windows server and a Linux client.

To see which shares are available on a given host, run:

```
/usr/sbin/smbclient -L host
```

where host is the name of the machine that you wish to view. this will return a list of service names—that is, names of drives or printers that it can share with you. Unless the SMB server has no security configured, it will ask you for a password. Get it the password for the guest account or for your personal account on that machine.

For example:

```
smbclient -L zimmerman
```

The output of this command should look something like this:

```
Server time is Sat Aug 10 15:58:27 1996
Timezone is UTC+10.0
Password:
Domain=[WORKGROUP] OS=[Windows NT 3.51]\
 Server=[NT LAN Manager 3.51]

Server=[ZIMMERMAN] User=[] Workgroup=[WORKGROUP] Domain=[]

        Sharename      Type      Comment
        ---------      ----      -------
        ADMIN$         Disk      Remote Admin
        public         Disk      Public
```

```
        C$              Disk      Default share
        IPC$            IPC       Remote IPC
        OReilly         Printer   OReilly
        print$          Disk      Printer Drivers


This machine has a browse list:

        Server              Comment
        ---------           -------
        HOPPER              Samba 1.9.15p8
        KERNIGAN            Samba 1.9.15p8
        LOVELACE            Samba 1.9.15p8
        RITCHIE             Samba 1.9.15p8
        ZIMMERMAN
```

The browse list shows other SMB servers with resources to share on the network.

To use the client, run:

```
/usr/sbin/smbclient service <password>
```

where "service" is a machine and share name. For example, if you are trying to reach a directory that has been shared as "public" on a machine called zimmerman, the service would be called \\zimmerman\public. However, due to shell restrictions, you will need to escape the backslashes, so you end up with something like this:

```
/usr/sbin/smbclient \\\\zimmerman\\public mypasswd
```

where *mypasswd* is the literal string of your password.

You will get the smbclient prompt:

```
Server time is Sat Aug 10 15:58:44 1996
Timezone is UTC+10.0
Domain=[WORKGROUP] OS=[Windows NT 3.51] Server=[NT LAN Manager 3.51]
smb: \>
```

Type "h" to get help using smbclient:

```
smb: \> h
ls          dir         lcd       cd          pwd
get         mget        put       mput        rename
more        mask        del       rm          mkdir
md          rmdir       rd        prompt      recurse
translate   lowercase   print     printmode   queue
cancel      stat        quit      q           exit
newer       archive     tar       blocksize   tarmode
setmode     help        ?         !
smb: \>
```

If you can use FTP, you shouldn't need the manual pages for `smbclient`.

8 Sharing A Linux Printer With Windows Machines

To share a Linux printer with Windows machines, you need to make certain that your printer is set up to work under linux. If you can print from Linux, setting up an SMB share of the printer is straight forward.

See the Printing HOWTO to set up local printing.

Since the author uses a printer connected to a Windows NT machine, this section should not be taken as definitive, but merely a suggestion. Anyone with details to share, please send them to dwood@plugged.net.au so this section can be completed.

Add printing configuration to your smb.conf:

```
[global]
    printing = bsd
    printcap name = /etc/printcap
```

```
    load printers = yes
    log file = /var/log/samba-log.%m
    lock directory = /var/lock/samba

[printers]
    comment = All Printers
    security = server
    path = /var/spool/lpd/lp
    browseable = no
    printable = yes
    public = yes
    writable = no
    create mode = 0700

[ljet]
    security = server
    path = /var/spool/lpd/lp
    printer name = lp
    writable = yes
    public = yes
    printable = yes
    print command = lpr -r -h -P %p %s
```

Make certain that the printer path (in this case under `ljet`) matches the spool directory in `/etc/printcap`.

NOTE: There are some problems sharing printers on UNIX boxes with Windows NT machines using Samba. One problem is with NT seeing the shared printer properly. To fix this, see the notes in the Samba distribution in the file `docs/WinNT.txt`. The other deals with password problems. See the comments in the same file for an annoying gain of understanding and failure to fix the problem.

9 Sharing A Windows Printer With Linux Machines

To share a printer on a Windows machine, you must do the following:

- You must have the proper entries in `/etc/printcap` and they must correspond to the local directory structure (for the spool directory, etc)
- You must have the script `/usr/bin/smbprint`. This comes with the Samba source, but not with all Samba binary distributions. A slightly modified copy is discussed below.
- If you want to convert ASCII files to PostScript, you must have `nenscript`, or its equivalent. `nenscript` is a PostScript converter and is generally installed in `/usr/bin`.
- You may wish to make Samba printing easier by having an easy-to-use front end. A simple Perl script to handle ASCII, PostScript or created PostScript is given below.

The `/etc/printcap` entry below is for an HP 5MP printer on a Windows NT host. The entries are as follows:

```
cm - comment
lp - device name to open for output
sd - the printer's spool directory (on the local machine)
af - the accounting file
mx - the maximum file size (zero is unlimited)
if - name of the input filter (script)
```

For more information, see the Printing HOWTO page 1243) or the manual page for `/etc/printcap`.

```
# /etc/printcap
#
# //zimmerman/oreilly via smbprint
#
lp:\
        :cm=HP 5MP Postscript OReilly on zimmerman:\
        :lp=/dev/lp1:\
```

```
        :sd=/var/spool/lpd/lp:\
        :af=/var/spool/lpd/lp/acct:\
        :mx#0:\
        :if=/usr/bin/smbprint:
```

Make certain that the spool and accounting directories exist and are writable. Ensure that the "if line holds the proper path to the smbprint script (given below) and make sure that the proper device is pointed to the /dev special file.

Next is the smbprint script itself. It is usually placed in /usr/bin and is attributable to Andrew Tridgell, the person who created Samba as far as I know. It comes with the Samba source distribution, but is absent from some binary distributions, so I have recreated it here.

You may wish to look at this carefully. There are some minor alterations that have shown themselves to be useful.

```
#!/bin/sh -x

# This script is an input filter for printcap printing on a
# unix machine. It uses the smbclient program to print the
# file to the specified smb-based server and service.
# For example you could have a printcap entry like this
#
# smb:lp=/dev/null:sd=/usr/spool/smb:\
#  sh:if=/usr/local/samba/smbprint
#
# which would create a unix printer called "smb" that will
# print via this script. You will need to create the spool
# directory /usr/spool/smb with appropriate permissions and
# ownerships for your system.

# Set these to the server and service you wish to print to
# In this example I have a WfWg PC called "lapland" that has
# a printer exported called "printer" with no password.


#
# Script further altered by hamiltom@ecnz.co.nz
# (Michael Hamilton) so that the server, service,
# and password can be read from a
# /usr/var/spool/lpd/PRINTNAME/.config file.
#
# In order for this to work the /etc/printcap entry must
# include an accounting file (af=...):
#
#    cdcolour:\
#        :cm=CD IBM Colorjet on 6th:\
#        :sd=/var/spool/lpd/cdcolour:\
#        :af=/var/spool/lpd/cdcolour/acct:\
#        :if=/usr/local/etc/smbprint:\
#        :mx=0:\
#        :lp=/dev/null:
#
# The /usr/var/spool/lpd/PRINTNAME/.config file
# should contain:
#    server=PC_SERVER
#    service=PR_SHARENAME
#    password="password"
#
# E.g.
#    server=PAULS_PC
#    service=CJET_371
#    password=""


#
```

```
# Debugging log file, change to /dev/null if you like.
#
logfile=/tmp/smb-print.log
# logfile=/dev/null


#
# The last parameter to the filter is the accounting
# file name.
spool_dir=/var/spool/lpd/lp
config_file=$spool_dir/.config

# Should read the following variables set in the config file:
#   server
#   service
#   password
#   user
eval 'cat $config_file'

#
# Some debugging help, change the >> to > if you
# want to same space.
#
echo "server $server, service $service" >> $logfile

(
# NOTE You may wish to add the line 'echo translate'
# if you want automatic CR/LF translation when printing.
        echo translate
        echo "print -"
        cat
) | /usr/bin/smbclient \
   "\\\\$server\\$service" $password -U $user -N -P \
>> $logfile
```

Most linux distributions come with nenscript for converting ASCII documents to PostScript. The following Perl script makes life easier be providing a simple interface to linux printing via smbprint.

```
Usage: print [-a|c|p] <filename>
       -a prints <filename> as ASCII
       -c prints <filename> formatted as source code
       -p prints <filename> as Postscript
        If no switch is given, print attempts to
        guess the file type and print appropriately.
```

Using `smbprint` to print ASCII files tends to truncate long lines. This script breaks long lines on whitespace (instead of in the middle of a word), if possible.

The source code formatting is done with `nenscript`. It takes an ASCII file and foramts it in two columns with a fancy header (date, filename, etc.). It also numbers the lines. Using this as an example, other types of formatting can be accomplished.

PostScript documents are already properly formatted, so they pass through directly.

```
#!/usr/bin/perl

# Script:   print
# Authors:  Brad Marshall, David Wood
#           Plugged In Communications
# Date:     960808
#
# Script to print to oreilly which is currently on zimmerman
# Purpose:  Takes files of various types as arguments and
```

```
# processes them appropriately for piping to a Samba print script.
#
# Currently supported file types:
#
# ASCII      - ensures that lines longer than $line_length characters wrap on
#              whitespace.
# Postscript - Takes no action.
# Code       - Formats in Postscript (using nenscript) to display
#              properly (landscape, font, etc).
#

# Set the maximum allowable length for each line of ASCII text.
$line_length = 76;

# Set the path and name of the Samba print script
$print_prog = "/usr/bin/smbprint";

# Set the path and name to nenscript (the ASCII-->Postscript converter)
$nenscript = "/usr/bin/nenscript";

unless ( -f $print_prog ) {
        die "Can't find $print_prog!";
}
unless ( -f $nenscript ) {
        die "Can't find $nenscript!";
}

&ParseCmdLine(@ARGV);

# DBG
print "filetype is $filetype\n";

if ($filetype eq "ASCII") {
        &wrap($line_length);
} elsif ($filetype eq "code") {
        &codeformat;
} elsif ($filetype eq "ps") {
        &createarray;
} else {
        print "Sorry..no known file type.\n";
        exit 0;
}
# Pipe the array to smbprint
open(PRINTER, "|$print_prog") || die "Can't open $print_prog: $!\n";
foreach $line (@newlines) {
        print PRINTER $line;
}
# Send an extra linefeed in case a file has an incomplete last line.
print PRINTER "\n";
close(PRINTER);
print "Completed\n";
exit 0;

# ---------------------------------------------------- #
#        Everything below here is a subroutine         #
# ---------------------------------------------------- #

sub ParseCmdLine {
```

```
        # Parses the command line, finding out what file type the file is

        # Gets $arg and $file to be the arguments (if the exists)
        # and the filename
        if ($#_ < 0) {
                &usage;
        }
        # DBG
#       foreach $element (@_) {
#               print "*$element* \n";
#       }

        $arg = shift(@_);
        if ($arg =~ /\-./) {
                $cmd = $arg;
        # DBG
#       print "\$cmd found.\n";

                $file = shift(@_);
        } else {
                $file = $arg;
        }

        # Defining the file type
        unless ($cmd) {
                # We have no arguments

                if ($file =~ /\.ps$/) {
                        $filetype = "ps";
                } elsif ($file =~ /\.java$|\.c$|\.h$|\.pl$|\
\.sh$|\.csh$|\.m4$|\.inc$|\
\.html$|\.htm$/) {
                        $filetype = "code";
                } else {
                        $filetype = "ASCII";
                }

                # Process $file for what type is it and
# return $filetype
        } else {
                # We have what type it is in $arg
                if ($cmd =~ /^-p$/) {
                        $filetype = "ps";
                } elsif ($cmd =~ /^-c$/) {
                        $filetype = "code";
                } elsif ($cmd =~ /^-a$/) {
                        $filetype = "ASCII"
                }
        }
}

sub usage {
        print "
Usage: print [-a|c|p] <filename>
       -a prints <filename> as ASCII
       -c prints <filename> formatted as source code
       -p prints <filename> as Postscript
        If no switch is given, print attempts to
```

```
        guess the file type and print appropriately.\n
";
        exit(0);
}

sub wrap {
   # Create an array of file lines, where each line is
   # < the number of characters specified, and wrapped
   # only on whitespace

   # Get the number of characters to limit the line to.
   $limit = pop(@_);

   # DBG
   #print "Entering subroutine wrap\n";
   #print "The line length limit is $limit\n";

   # Read in the file, parse and put into an array.
   open(FILE, "<$file") || die "Can't open $file: $!\n";
   while(<FILE>) {
      $line = $_;

         # DBG
         #print "The line is:\n$line\n";

         # Wrap the line if it is over the limit.
         while ( length($line) > $limit ) {

            # DBG
            #print "Wrapping...";

            # Get the first $limit +1 characters.
               $part = substr($line,0,$limit +1);

               # DBG
               #print "The partial line is:\n$part\n";

               # Check to see if the last character is
       # a space.
               $last_char = substr($part,-1, 1);
               if ( " " eq $last_char ) {
                  # If it is, print the rest.

                  # DBG
          #print "The last character was a space\n";

                  substr($line,0,$limit + 1) = "";
                  substr($part,-1,1) = "";
                  push(@newlines,"$part\n");
               } else {
               # If it is not, find the last space in the
               # sub-line and print up to there.

               # DBG
          #print "The last character was not a space\n";

          # Remove the character past $limit
                    substr($part,-1,1) = "";
```

```
                    # Reverse the line to make it easy to find
                    # the last space.
                      $revpart = reverse($part);
                      $index = index($revpart," ");
                      if ( $index > 0 ) {
                      substr($line,0,$limit-$index) = "";
                      push(@newlines,
                          substr($part,0,$limit-$index) . "\n");
                      } else {
                    # There was no space in the line, so
                    # print it up to $limit.
                      substr($line,0,$limit) = "";
                      push(@newlines,substr($part,0,$limit)
                           . "\n");
                }
            }
        }
        push(@newlines,$line);
    }
    close(FILE);
}

sub codeformat {
    # Call subroutine wrap then filter through nenscript
    &wrap($line_length);

    # Pipe the results through nenscript to create a Postscript
    # file that adheres to some decent format for printing
    # source code (landscape, Courier font, line numbers).
    # Print this to a temporary file first.
    $tmpfile = "/tmp/nenscript$$";
    open(FILE, "|$nenscript -2G -i$file -N -p$tmpfile -r") ||
            die "Can't open nenscript: $!\n";
    foreach $line (@newlines) {
            print FILE $line;
    }
   close(FILE);

   # Read the temporary file back into an array so it can be
   # passed to the Samba print script.
   @newlines = ("");
   open(FILE, "<$tmpfile") || die "Can't open $file: $!\n";
   while(<FILE>) {
           push(@newlines,$_);
   }
    close(FILE);
    system("rm $tmpfile");
}

sub createarray {
   # Create the array for postscript
   open(FILE, "<$file") || die "Can't open $file: $!\n";
   while(<FILE>) {
            push(@newlines,$_);
    }
    close(FILE);
}
```

10 Copyright

11 Acknowledgements

As soon as you mail me with suggestions, I'll acknowledge you here in the next release.

Part XLVI

"Linux Sound HOWTO"
by Jeff Tranter,

jeff_tranter@pobox.com

Contents

Abstract

v1.18, 1 November 1997
This document describes sound support for Linux. It lists the supported sound hardware, describes how to configure the kernel drivers, and answers frequently asked questions. The intent is to bring new users up to speed more quickly and reduce the amount of traffic in the Usenet news groups and mailing lists.

1 Introduction

This is the Linux Sound HOWTO. It is intended as a quick reference covering everything you need to know to install and configure sound support under Linux. Frequently asked questions about sound under Linux are answered, and references are given to some other sources of information on a variety of topics related to computer generated sound and music.

The scope is limited to the aspects of sound cards pertaining to Linux. See the other documents listed in the References section for more general information on sound cards and computer sound and music generation.

1.1 Acknowledgments

Much of this information came from the documentation provided with the sound driver source code, by Hannu Savolainen (hannu@voxware.pp.fi). Thanks go to Hannu and the many other people who developed the Linux kernel sound drivers and utilities.

Thanks to the SGML Tools package, this HOWTO is available in several formats, all generated from a common source file.

1.2 New versions of this document

New versions of this document will be periodically posted to the comp.os.linux.answers newsgroup. They will also be uploaded to various anonymous ftp sites that archive such information including ftp://sunsite.unc.edu/pub/Linux/docs/HOWTO/.

Hypertext versions of this and other Linux HOWTOs are available on many World-Wide-Web sites, including http://sunsite.unc.edu/LDP/. Most Linux CD-ROM distributions include the HOWTOs, often under the `/usr/doc` directory, and you can also buy printed copies from several vendors. Sometimes the HOWTOs available from CD-ROM vendors, FTP sites, and printed format are out of date. If the date on this HOWTO is more than six months in the past, then a newer copy is probably available on the Internet.

A French translation of this document is available at

```
ftp://ftp.ibp.fr/pub2/linux/french/docs/HOWTO/
```

A Japanese translation is available from

```
http://yebisu.ics.es.osaka-u.ac.jp/linux/
```

An Italian translation is available from

```
http://www.psy.unipd.it/ildp/docs/HOWTO/Sound-HOWTO.html
```

A Spanish translation is available from

```
http://www.insflug.nova.es/howtos/online/sonido/sonido-COMO.html
```

A Chinese translation is available from

```
http://linux.ntcic.edu.tw/ yorkwu/linux/howto/sound/
```

A Hangul (Korean) translation is available from

```
http://members.iWorld.net/mangchi/HOWTO/Sound-HOWTO.html
```

Most translations of this and other Linux HOWTOs can also be found at

```
http://sunsite.unc.edu/pub/Linux/docs/HOWTO/translations/
```

and

```
ftp://sunsite.unc.edu/pub/Linux/docs/HOWTO/translations/
```

If you make a translation of this document into another language, let me know and I'll include a reference to it here.

1.3 Feedback

I rely on you, the reader, to make this HOWTO useful. If you have any suggestions, corrections, or comments, please send them to me, jeff_tranter@pobox.com, and I will try to incorporate them in the next revision.

I am also willing to answer general questions on sound cards under Linux, as best I can. Before doing so, please read all of the information in this HOWTO, and send me detailed information about the problem. Please do not ask me about using sound cards under operating systems other than Linux.

If you publish this document on a CD-ROM or in hardcopy form, a complimentary copy would be appreciated. Mail me for my postal address. Also consider making a donation to the Linux Documentation Project to help support free documentation for Linux. Contact the Linux HOWTO coordinator, Greg Hankins, gregh@sunsite.unc.edu, for more information.

1.4 Distribution Policy

2 Sound Card Technology

This section gives a very cursory overview of computer audio technology, in order to help you understand the concepts used later in the document. You should consult a book on digital audio or digital signal processing in order to learn more.

Sound is an analog property; it can take on any value over a continuous range. Computers are digital; they like to work with discrete values. Sound cards use a device known as an **Analog to Digital Converter** (A/D or ADC) to convert voltages corresponding to analog sound waves into digital or numeric values which can be stored in memory. Similarly, a **Digital to Analog Converter** (D/A or DAC) converts numeric values back to an analog voltage which can in turn drive a loudspeaker, producing sound.

The process of analog to digital conversion, known as sampling, introduces some error. Two factors are key in determining how well the sampled signal represents the original. **Sampling rate** is the number of samples made per unit of time (usually expresses as samples per second or Hertz). A low sampling rate will provide a less accurate representation of the analog signal. Sample size is the range of values used to represent each sample, usually expressed in bits. The larger the sample size, the more accurate the digitized signal will be.

Sound cards commonly use 8 or 16 bit samples at sampling rates from about 4000 to 44,000 samples per second. The samples may also be contain one channel (mono) or two (stereo).

FM Synthesis is an older technique for producing sound. It is based on combining different waveforms (e.g. sine, triangle, square). FM synthesis is simpler to implement in hardware that D/A conversion, but is more difficult to program and less flexible. Many sound cards provide FM synthesis for backward compatibility with older cards and software. Several independent sound generators or **voices** are usually provided.

Wavetable Synthesis combines the flexibility of D/A conversion with the multiple channel capability of FM synthesis. With this scheme, digitized voices can be downloaded into dedicated memory, and then played, combined, and modified with little CPU overhead. State of the art sound cards all support wavetable synthesis.

Most sound cards provide the capability of **mixing**, combining signals from different input sources and controlling gain levels.

MIDI stands for Musical Instrument Digital Interface, and is a standard hardware and software protocol for allowing musical instruments to communicate with each other. The events sent over a MIDI bus can also be stored as MIDI files for later editing and playback. Many sound cards provide a MIDI interface. Those that do not can still play MIDI files using the on-board capabilities of the sound card.

MOD files are a common format for computer generated songs. As well as information about the musical notes to be played, the files contain digitized samples for the instruments (or voices). MOD files originated on the Amiga computer, but can be played on other systems, including Linux, with suitable software.

3 Supported Hardware

This section lists the sound cards and interfaces that are currently supported under Linux. The information here is based on the latest Linux kernels, at time of writing.

The sound driver has its own version numbering. The latest stable Linux kernel release was version 2.0.31, using sound driver version 3.5.4-960630.

The author of the sound driver, Hannu Savolainen, typically also makes available newer beta releases of the sound driver before they are included as part of the standard Linux kernel distribution. The most up to date list of supported cards is available at http://www.4front-tech.com/ossfree/new_cards.html (USA) or http://personal.eunet.fi/pp/voxware/new_cards.html (Europe). These pages indicate which sound driver version is required for a given type of sound card or if support for it is still under development. The file `/usr/src/linux/drivers/sound/Readme.cards` distributed with the kernel sound driver contains information on supported cards but it is not always up to date.

The information in this HOWTO is valid for Linux on the Intel platform.

The sound driver should also work with most sound cards on the Alpha platform. However, some cards may conflict with I/O ports of other devices on Alpha systems even though they work perfectly on i386 machines, so in general it's not possible to tell if a given card will work or not without actually trying it.

At the time of writing, the sound driver was not yet working on the PowerPC version of Linux, but it should be supported in future.

Sound can be configured into the kernel under the MIPs port of Linux, and some MIPs machines have EISA slots or built-in sound hardware. I'm told the Linux-MIPs group is interested in adding sound support in the future.

The Linux kernel includes a separate driver for the Atari and Amiga versions of Linux that implements a compatible subset of the sound driver on the Intel platform using the built-in sound hardware on these machines.

The SPARC port of Linux does not currently have sound support. Like the Amiga and Atari, SPARC machines have built in sound hardware, so it could be done with a new driver (this is somewhat ironic, as under Linux `/dev/dsp` emulates the SunOS sound device).

3.1 Sound Cards

The following sound cards are supported by the Linux kernel sound driver:

- ATI Stereo F/X (no longer manufactured);
- AdLib (no longer manufactured);
- Ensoniq SoundScape (and compatibles made by Reveal and Spea);
- Gravis Ultrasound;
- Gravis Ultrasound ACE;
- Gravis Ultrasound Max;
- Gravis Ultrasound with 16-bit sampling option;
- Logitech Sound Man 16;
- Logitech SoundMan Games;
- Logitech SoundMan Wave;
- MAD16 Pro (OPTi 82C928, 82C929, 82C930, 82C924 chipsets);
- Media Vision Jazz16;
- MediaTriX AudioTriX Pro;
- Microsoft Windows Sound System (MSS/WSS);
- Mozart (OAK OTI-601);
- Orchid SW32;
- Personal Sound System (PSS);
- Pro Audio Spectrum 16;
- Pro Audio Studio 16;
- Pro Sonic 16;
- Roland MPU-401 MIDI interface;

- Sound Blaster 1.0;
- Sound Blaster 16;
- Sound Blaster 16ASP;
- Sound Blaster 2.0;
- Sound Blaster AWE32;
- Sound Blaster Pro;
- TI TM4000M notebook;
- ThunderBoard;
- Turtle Beach Tropez ("classic" but not Plus);
- Turtle Beach Maui;
- Yamaha FM synthesizers (OPL2, OPL3 and OPL4);
- 6850 UART MIDI Interface;

It should be noted that Plug and Play (PnP) sound cards are not fully compatible with the older non-PnP models of the same device. For example, the SoundBlaster16 PnP is not fully compatible with the original SoundBlaster16. The same is true for the Soundscape PnP and GUS PnP cards. More information related to Plug and Play is found later in this document.

The following cards are not supported, either because they are obsolete or because the vendor will not release the programming information needed to write a driver:

- Pro Audio Spectrum (original);
- Pro Audio Spectrum+;
- older (Sierra Aria based) sound cards made by Diamond;

Other sound cards that are claimed to be compatible with one of the supported sound cards may work if they are hardware (i.e., register level) compatible.

Even though most sound cards are claimed to be "SoundBlaster compatible," very few currently sold cards are compatible enough to work with the Linux SoundBlaster driver. These cards usually work better using the MSS/WSS or MAD16 driver. Only real SoundBlaster cards made by Creative Labs, which use Creative's custom chips (e.g. SoundBlaster16 Vibra), MV Jazz16 and ESS688/1688 based cards generally work with the SoundBlaster driver. Trying to use a "SoundBlaster Pro compatible 16-bit sound card" with the SoundBlaster driver is usually just a waste of time.

The Linux kernel supports the SCSI port provided on some sound cards (e.g., ProAudioSpectrum 16) and the proprietary interface for some CD-ROM drives (e.g., Soundblaster Pro). See the Linux SCSI HOWTO and CD-ROM HOWTO documents for more information.

A loadable kernel module to support joystick ports, including those provided on some sound cards, is also available.

Note that the kernel SCSI, CD-ROM, joystick, and sound drivers are completely independent of each other.

For the latest information on the sound card driver check Hannu Savolainen's World-Wide Web site listed in the References section.

3.2 Alternate Sound Drivers

There are some "unofficial" sound drivers available, not included in the standard Linux kernel distribution, and used in place of the standard sound driver.

A commercial version of the Linux sound driver is sold by 4Front Technologies. It offers a number of additional features over the free version included in the Linux kernel. For more information see the 4Front Technologies Web page at http://www.4front-tech.com/.

Markus Mummert (mum@mmk.e-technik.tu-muenchen.de) has written a driver package for the Turtle Beach MultiSound (classic), Tahiti, and Monterey sound cards. The documentation states:

> "It is designed for high quality hard disk recording/playback without losing sync even on a busy system. Other features such as wave synthesis, MIDI and digital signal processor (DSP) cannot be used. Also, recording and playback at the same time is not possible. It currently replaces VoxWare and was tested on several kernel versions ranging from 1.0.9 to 1.2.1. Also, it is installable on UN*X SysV386R3.2 systems."

It can be found at http://www.cs.colorado.edu/ mccreary/tbeach.

Kim Burgaard (burgaard@daimi.aau.dk) has written a device driver and utilities for the Roland MPU-401 MIDI interface. The Linux software map entry gives this description:

"A device driver for true Roland MPU-401 compatible MIDI interfaces (including Roland SCC-1 and RAP-10/ATW-10). Comes with a useful collection of utilities including a Standard MIDI File player and recorder.

"Numerous improvements have been made since version 0.11a. Among other things, the driver now features IRQ sharing policy and complies with the new kernel module interface. Metronome functionality, possibility for synchronizing e.g. graphics on a per beat basis without losing precision, advanced replay/record/overdub interface and much, much more."

It can be found at ftp://sunsite.unc.edu/pub/Linux/kernel/sound/mpu401-0.2.tar.gz

Jaroslav Kysela and others have written an alternate sound driver for the Gravis UltraSound Card. Information can be found at http://romeo.pf.jcu.cz/ perex/ultra, the home page of the Linux UltraSound Project.

Another novel use for a sound card under Linux is as a modem for amateur packet radio. The recent 2.1.x kernels include a driver that works with SoundBlaster and Windows Sound System compatible sound cards to implement 1200 bps AFSK and 9600 bps FSK packet protocols. See the Linux AX25 HOWTO for details (I'm a ham myself, by the way—callsign VE3ICH).

3.3 PC Speaker

An alternate sound driver is available that requires no additional sound hardware; it uses the internal PC speaker. It is mostly software compatible with the sound card driver, but, as might be expected, provides much lower quality output and has much more CPU overhead. The results seem to vary, being dependent on the characteristics of the individual loudspeaker. For more information, see the documentation provided with the release.

The current version is 1.1, and can be found at ftp://ftp.informatik.hu-berlin.de/pub/os/linux/hu-sound/.

3.4 Parallel Port

Another option is to build a digital to analog converter using a parallel printer port and some additional components. This provides better sound quality than the PC speaker but still has a lot of CPU overhead. The PC sound driver package mentioned above supports this, and includes instructions for building the necessary hardware.

4 Installation

Configuring Linux to support sound involves the following steps:

1. Installing the sound card.
2. Configuring and building the kernel for sound support.
3. Creating the device files.
4. Booting the Linux kernel and testing the installation.

The next sections will cover each of these steps in detail.

4.1 Installing the Sound Card

Follow the manufacturer's instructions for installing the hardware or have your dealer perform the installation.

Older sound cards usually have switch or jumper settings for IRQ, DMA channel, etc; note down the values used. If you are unsure, use the factory defaults. Try to avoid conflicts with other devices (e.g. Ethernet cards, SCSI host adaptors, serial, and parallel ports) if possible.

Usually you should use the same I/O port, IRQ, and DMA settings that work under MS-DOS. In some cases though (particularly with PnP cards) you may need to use different settings to get things to work under Linux. Some experimentation may be needed.

4.2 Configuring the Kernel

When initially installing Linux, you likely used a pre-compiled kernel. These kernels usually do not provide sound support. It is best to recompile the kernel yourself with the drivers you need. You may also want to recompile the kernel in order to upgrade to a newer version or to free up memory resources by minimizing the size of the kernel.

The Linux Kernel HOWTO (page 1019) should be consulted for the details of building a kernel. I will just mention here some issues that are specific to sound cards.

If you have never configured the kernel for sound support before it is a good idea to read all of the Readme files included with the kernel sound drivers, particularly information specific to your card type. The following documentation files can be found in the kernel sound driver directory, usually installed in `/usr/src/linux/drivers/sound`:

```
CHANGELOG          - description of changes in each release
COPYING            - copying and copyright restrictions
Readme             - latest and most important news
Readme.aedsp16     - information about Audio Excel DSP 16 sound card
Readme.cards       - notes on configuring specific cards
Readme.linux       - notes on installing separately release sound drivers
Readme.modules     - how to build driver as a loadable kernel module
Readme.v30         - new features in version 3.0 sound driver
experimental.txt   - notes on experimental features
```

Follow the usual procedure for building the kernel. There are currently three interfaces to the configuration process. A graphical user interface that runs under X11 can be invoked using `make xconfig`. A menu-based system that only requires text displays is available as `make menuconfig`. The original method, using `make config`, offers a simple text-based interface.

Special care must be taken when using `make xconfig` or `make menuconfig`. All Yes/No questions must be examined carefully. The default answer provided by these commands is always No which is not the proper one in all cases. In particular the `/dev/dsp` and `/dev/audio` support (CONFIG_AUDIO) option should usually be enabled.

In this document I will assume that you use the traditional command line configuration process invoked using `make config`, although the process is similar in each case.

There are also two different ways to configure sound. The first is the old way (the only one offered prior to the 2.0.0 kernels). It uses a stand-alone configuration program that is part of the sound driver. This method works with most sound cards except the rare few that require additional "low level" drivers (miroSOUND, AWE32, and AEDSP16 cards).

The second is the new method which is better integrated with the menu based configuration used for the rest of the kernel. This one doesn't work with sound cards that require a firmware download file. This includes the PSS, SM Wave, AudioTrix Pro and TurtleBeach Tropez/Maui cards. With these cards the old method has to be used.

The new method is always used by `make xconfig`. When using `make menuconfig` you can select between the old and new methods in the sound subscreen. When using `make config` you get the old method by default. However if you have used the new method once, it will be used by `make config` too. You can switch back to the old method by running `make menuconfig` and by selecting the old one.

The recommended method is to use `make menuconfig` together with the old sound config method. Many sound configuration problems are caused (at least partly) by incorrect use of the new method.

It is also possible to build the sound driver as a kernel loadable module. I recommend initially building the driver into the kernel. Once it is tested and working you can explore using the kernel module option.

When you run `make config`, enable sound support by answering "y" to the question

```
Sound card support (CONFIG_SOUND) [M/n/y/?]
```

At the end of the configuration questions, a sound configuration program will be compiled, run, and will then ask you what sound card options you want. Be careful when answering these questions since answering a question incorrectly may prevent some later ones from being asked. For example, don't answer "yes" to the first question (PAS16) if you don't really have a PAS16. Don't enable more cards than you really need, since they just consume memory. Also some drivers (like MPU-401) may conflict with your SCSI controller and prevent the kernel from booting.

I list here a brief description of each of the configuration dialog options. Answer "y" (yes) or "n" (no) to each question. The default answer is shown so that "[Y/n/?]" means "y" by default and "[N/y/?]" means the default is "n." To use the default value, just hit Enter, but remember that the default value isn't necessarily correct.

Entering a question mark ("?") will produce a short descriptive message describing that configuration option.

Note also that all questions may not be asked. The configuration program may disable some questions depending on the earlier choices. It may also select some options automatically as well.

Old configuration exists in /etc/soundconf. Use it Y/n/?

If you have previously compiled the kernel for sound support, then the previous configuration can be saved. If you want to use the previous setup, answer "y." If you are trying a different configuration or have upgraded to a newer kernel, you should answer "n" and go through the configuration process.

ProAudioSpectrum 16 support Y/n/?

Answer "y" only if you have a Pro Audio Spectrum 16, ProAudio Studio 16 or Logitech SoundMan 16. Don't answer "y" if you have some other card made by Media Vision or Logitech since they are not PAS16 compatible.

SoundBlaster support Y/n/?

Answer "y" if you have an original SoundBlaster card made by Creative Labs or a 100% hardware compatible clone (like the Thunderboard or SM Games). If your card was in the list of supported cards look at the card specific instructions in the `Readme.cards` file before answering this question. For an unknown card you may answer "y" if the card claims to be SoundBlaster compatible.

Gravis Ultrasound support Y/n/?

Answer "y" if you have a GUS or GUS MAX. Answer "n" if you don't have a GUS since the driver consumes a lot of memory.

MPU-401 support (NOT for SB16) Y/n/?

Be careful with this question. The MPU-401 interface is supported by almost all sound cards. However, some natively supported cards have their own driver for MPU-401. Enabling the MPU-401 option with these cards will cause a conflict. Also enabling MPU-401 on a system that doesn't really have a MPU-401 could cause some trouble. If your card was in the list of supported cards, look at the card specific instructions in the `Readme.cards` file. It's safe to answer "y" if you have a true MPU-401 MIDI interface card.

6850 UART Midi support Y/n/?

It's safe to answer "n" to this question in all cases. The 6850 UART interface is very rarely used.

PSS (ECHO-ADI2111) support Y/n/?

Answer "y" only if you have Orchid SW32, Cardinal DSP16 or some other card based on the PSS chipset (AD1848 codec + ADSP-2115 DSP chip + Echo ESC614 ASIC CHIP).

16 bit sampling option of GUS (not GUS MAX) Y/n/?

Answer "y" if you have installed the 16-bit sampling daughtercard on your GUS. Answer "n" if you have a GUS MAX. Enabling this option disables GUS MAX support.

GUS MAX support Y/n/?

Answer "y" only if you have a GUS MAX.

Microsoft Sound System support Y/n/?

Again think carefully before answering "y" to this question. It's safe to answer "y" if you have the original Windows Sound System card made by Microsoft or Aztech SG 16 Pro (or NX16 Pro). Also you may answer "y" in case your card was not listed earlier in this file. For cards having native support in VoxWare, consult the card specific instructions in `Readme.cards`. Some drivers have their own MSS support and enabling this option will cause a conflict.

Ensoniq Soundscape support Y/n/?

Answer "y" if you have a sound card based on the Ensoniq SoundScape chipset. Such cards are being manufactured at least by Ensoniq, Spea and Reveal (Reveal makes other cards also).

MediaTriX AudioTriX Pro support Y/n/?

Answer "y" if you have the AudioTriX Pro.

Support for MAD16 and/or Mozart based cards?

Answer "y" if your card has a Mozart (OAK OTI-601) or MAD16 (OPTi 82C928 or 82C929) audio interface chip. These chips are currently quite common so it's possible that many no-name cards have one of them. In addition the MAD16 chip is used in some cards made by known manufacturers such as Turtle Beach (Tropez), Reveal (some models) and Diamond (latest ones).

Support for Crystal CS4232 based (PnP) cards Y/n/?

Answer "y" if you have a card based on the Crystal CS4232 chip set.

Support for Turtle Beach Wave Front (Maui, Tropez) synthesizers Y/n/?

Answer "y" if you have any of these cards.

SoundBlaster Pro support Y/n/?

Enable this option if your card is a SoundBlaster Pro or SoundBlaster 16. Enable it also with any SoundBlaster Pro clones. Answering "n" saves some memory but "y" is the safe alternative.

SoundBlaster 16 support Y/n/?

Enable if you have a SoundBlaster 16 (including the AWE32).

Audio Excel DSP 16 initialization support Y/n/?

Enable this if you have an Audio Excel DSP16 card. See the file `Readme.aedsp16` for more information.

The configuration program then asks some questions about the higher level services. It's recommended to answer "y" to each of these questions. Answer "n" only if you know you will not need the option.

/dev/dsp and /dev/audio support (usually required) Y/n/?

Answering "n" disables `/dev/dsp` and `/dev/audio`, the A/D and D/A converter devices. Answer "y."

MIDI interface support Y/n/?

Answering "n" disables `/dev/midixx` devices and access to any MIDI ports using `/dev/sequencer` and `/dev/music`. This option also affects any MPU-401 and/or General MIDI compatible devices.

FM synthesizer (YM3812/OPL-3) support Y/n/?

Answer "y" here.

/dev/sequencer support Y/n/?

Answering "n" disables `/dev/sequencer` and `/dev/music`

Do you want support for the mixer of SG NX Pro ?

Answer "y" if you have a Sound Galaxy NX Pro sound card and want support for its extended mixer functions.

Do you want support for the MV Jazz16 (ProSonic etc.) ?

Answer "y" if you have an MV Jazz16 sound card.

Do you have a Logitech SoundMan Games Y/n/?

Answer "y" if you have a Logitech SoundMan Games sound card.

After the above questions the configuration program prompts for the card specific configuration information. Usually just a set of I/O address, IRQ and DMA numbers are asked. With some cards the program asks for some files to be used during initialization of the card. These are used by cards which have a DSP chip or microprocessor which must be initialized by downloading a program (microcode) file to the card. In some cases this file is written to a .h file by the config program and then included to the driver during compile. Again, read the information in the file `Readme.cards` pertaining to your card type.

At the end you will be prompted:

```
The sound driver is now configured.
Save copy of this configuration to /etc/soundconf [Y/n/?]
```

Normally you would enter "y," so that if you later need to recompile the kernel you have the option of using the same sound driver configuration.

If you are upgrading from an older sound driver, make sure that the files `/usr/include/sys/soundcard.h` and `/usr/include/sys/ultrasound.h` are symbolic links to the corresponding files in `/usr/include/linux`, or that they simply contain the lines `#include <linux/soundcard.h>` and `#include <linux/ultrasound.h>`, respectively.

You are now ready to compile and install the new kernel.

4.3 Creating the Device Files

For proper operation, device file entries must be created for the sound devices. These are normally created for you during installation of your Linux system. A quick check can be made using the command listed below. If the output is as shown (the date stamp will vary) then the device files are almost certainly okay.

```
% ls -l /dev/sndstat
crw-rw-rw-   1 root     root      14,   6 Apr 25  1995 /dev/sndstat
```

Note that having the right device files there doesn't guarantee anything on its own. The kernel driver must also be loaded or compiled in before the devices will work (more on that later).

In rare cases, if you believe the device files are wrong, you can recreate them using the short shell script from the end of the file `Readme.linux` in the directory `/usr/src/linux/drivers/sound`, running it as user `root`. Alternatively, most Linux distributions have a `/dev/MAKEDEV` script which can be used for this purpose.

If you are using the PC speaker sound driver, read the documentation that came with the package to determine if any device files need to be created.

4.4 Booting Linux and Testing the Installation

You should now be ready to boot the new kernel and test the sound drivers. Follow your usual procedure for installing and rebooting the new kernel (keep the old kernel around in case of problems, of course).

During booting, check for a message such as the following on power-up (if they scroll by too quickly to read, you may be able to retrieve them with the `dmesg` command):

```
Sound initialization started
<Sound Blaster 16 (4.13)> at 0x220 irq 5 dma 1,5
<Sound Blaster 16> at 0x330 irq 5 dma 0
<Yamaha OPL3 FM> at 0x388
Sound initialization complete
```

This should match your sound card type and jumper settings (if any).

Note that the above messages are not displayed when using loadable sound driver module (unless you enable it, e.g. using `insmod sound trace_init=1`).

When the sound driver is linked into the kernel, the "Sound initialization started" and "Sound initialization complete" messages should be displayed. If they are not printed, it means that there is no sound driver present in the kernel. In this case you should check that you actually installed the kernel you compiled when enabling the sound driver.

If nothing is printed between the "Sound initialization started" and the "Sound initialization complete" lines, it means that no sound devices were detected. Most probably it means that you don't have the correct driver enabled, the card is not supported, the I/O port is bad or that you have a PnP card that has not been configured.

The driver may also display some error messages and warnings during boot. Watch for these when booting the first time after configuring the sound driver.

Next you should check the device file `/dev/sndstat`. Reading the sound driver status device file should provide additional information on whether the sound card driver initialized properly. Sample output should look something like this:

```
% cat /dev/sndstat
Sound Driver:3.5.4-960630 (Sat Jan 4 23:56:57 EST 1997 root,
Linux fizzbin 2.0.27 #48 Thu Dec 5 18:24:45 EST 1996 i586)
Kernel: Linux fizzbin 2.0.27 #48 Thu Dec 5 18:24:45 EST 1996 i586
Config options: 0

Installed drivers:
Type 1: OPL-2/OPL-3 FM
Type 2: Sound Blaster
Type 7: SB MPU-401

Card config:
Sound Blaster at 0x220 irq 5 drq 1,5
SB MPU-401 at 0x330 irq 5 drq 0
OPL-2/OPL-3 FM at 0x388 drq 0

Audio devices:
0: Sound Blaster 16 (4.13)

Synth devices:
0: Yamaha OPL-3

Midi devices:
0: Sound Blaster 16

Timers:
0: System clock

Mixers:
0: Sound Blaster
```

The command above can report some error messages. "No such file or directory" indicates that you need to create the device files (see section 4.3). "No such device" means that sound driver is not loaded or linked into kernel. Go back to Section 4.2 to correct this.

If lines in the "Card config:" section of `/dev/sndstat` are listed inside parentheses (such as "(SoundBlaster at 0x220 irq 5 drq 1,5)"), it means that this device was configured but not detected.

Now you should be ready to play a simple sound file. Get hold of a sound sample file, and send it to the sound device as a basic check of sound output, e.g.

```
% cat endoftheworld >/dev/dsp
% cat crash.au >/dev/audio
```

(Make sure you don't omit the ">" in the commands above).

Note that, in general, using `cat` is not the proper way to play audio files, it's just a quick check. You'll want to get a proper sound player program (described later) that will do a better job.

This command will work only if there is at least one device listed in the audio devices section of `/dev/sndstat`. If the audio devices section is empty you should check why the device was not detected.

If the above commands return "I/O error," you should look at the end of the kernel messages listed using the "dmesg" command. It's likely that an error message is printed there. Very often the message is "Sound: DMA (output) timed out—IRQ/DRQ config error?" The above message means that the driver didn't get the expected interrupt from the sound card. In most cases it means that the IRQ or the DMA channel configured to the driver doesn't work. The best way to get it working is to try with all possible DMAs and IRQs supported by the device.

Another possible reason is that the device is not compatible with the device the driver is configured for. This is almost certainly the case when a supposedly "SoundBlaster (Pro/16) compatible" sound card doesn't work with the SoundBlaster driver. In this case you should try to find out the device your sound card is compatible with (by posting to the comp.os.linux.hardware newsgroup, for example).

Some sample sound files can be obtained from ftp://tsx-11.mit.edu/pub/linux/packages/sound/snd-data-0.1.tar.Z.

Now you can verify sound recording. If you have sound input capability, you can do a quick test of this using commands such as the following:

```
# record 4 seconds of audio from microphone
EDT% dd bs=8k count=4 </dev/audio >sample.au
4+0 records in
4+0 records out
# play back sound
% cat sample.au >/dev/audio
```

Obviously for this to work you need a microphone connected to the sound card and you should speak into it. You may also need to obtain a mixer program to set the microphone as the input device and adjust the recording gain level.

If these tests pass, you can be reasonably confident that the sound D/A and A/D hardware and software are working. If you experience problems, refer to the next section of this document.

4.5 Troubleshooting

If you still encounter problems after following the instructions in the HOWTO, here are some things to check. The checks are listed in increasing order of complexity. If a check fails, solve the problem before moving to the next stage.

4.5.1 Step 1: Make sure you are really running the kernel you compiled.

You can check the date stamp on the kernel to see if you are running the one that you compiled with sound support. You can do this with the `uname` command:

```
% uname -a
Linux fizzbin 2.0.0 #1 Tue Jun 4 16:57:55 EDT 1996 i386
```

or by displaying the file `/proc/version`:

```
% cat /proc/version
Linux version 2.0.0 (root@fizzbin) (gcc version 2.7.0) #1 Tue Jun 4 16:57:55 EDT 1996
```

If the date stamp doesn't seem to match when you compiled the kernel, then you are running an old kernel. Did you really reboot? If you use LILO, did you re-install it (typically by running `/etc/lilo/install`)? If booting from floppy, did you create a new boot floppy and use it when booting?

4.5.2 Step 2: Make sure the kernel sound drivers are compiled in.

The easiest way to do this is to check the output of `/dev/sndstat` as described earlier. If the output is not as expected then something went wrong with the kernel configuration or build. Start the installation process again, beginning with configuration and building of the kernel.

4.5.3 Step 3: Did the kernel detect your sound card during booting?

Make sure that the sound card was detected when the kernel booted. You should have seen a message on bootup. If the messages scrolled off the screen, you can usually recall them using the `dmesg` command:

```
% dmesg
```

or

```
% tail /var/adm/messages
```

If your sound card was not found then something is wrong. Make sure it really is installed. If the sound card works under DOS then you can be reasonably confident that the hardware is working, so it is likely a problem with the kernel configuration. Either you configured your sound card as the wrong type or wrong parameters, or your sound card is not compatible with any of the Linux kernel sound card drivers.

One possibility is that your sound card is one of the "compatible" type that requires initialization by the DOS driver. Try booting DOS and loading the vendor supplied sound card driver. Then soft boot Linux using `Control-Alt-Delete`. Make sure that card I/O address, DMA, and IRQ settings for Linux are the same as used under DOS. Read the `Readme.cards` file from the sound driver source distribution for hints on configuring your card type.

If your sound card is not listed in this document, it is possible that the Linux drivers do not support it. You can check with some of the references listed at the end of this document for assistance.

4.5.4 Step 4: Can you read data from the dsp device?

Try reading from the `/dev/audio` device using the `dd` command listed earlier in this document. The command should run without errors.

If it doesn't work, then chances are that the problem is an IRQ or DMA conflict or some kind of hardware incompatibility (the device is not supported by Linux or the driver is configured for a wrong device).

A remote possibility is broken hardware. Try testing the sound card under DOS, if possible, to eliminate that as a possibility.

4.5.5 When All Else Fails

If you still have problems, here are some final suggestions for things to try:

- carefully re-read this HOWTO document;
- read the references listed at the end of this document, especially Hannu Savolainen's web pages and the relevant kernel source Readme files;
- post a question to one of the `comp.os.linux` or other Usenet newsgroups (comp.os.linux.hardware is a good choice; because of the high level of traffic in these groups it helps to put the string "sound" in the subject header for the article so the right experts will see it);
- Using a Web/Usenet search engine with an intelligently selected search criteria can give very good results quickly. One such choice is http://www.altavista.digital.com;
- try using the latest Linux kernel (but only as a last resort, the latest development kernels can be unstable);
- send mail to the author of the sound driver;
- send mail to the author of the Sound HOWTO;
- fire up emacs and type `Esc-x doctor`. :-)

5 Applications Supporting Sound

I give here a sample of the types of applications that you likely want if you have a sound card under Linux. You can check the Linux Software Map, Internet archive sites, or files on your Linux CD-ROM for more up to date information.

As a minimum, you will likely want to obtain the following sound applications:

- audio file format conversion utility (e.g. `Sox`);
- mixer utility (e.g. `aumix` or `xmix`);
- digitized file player/recorder (e.g. `play` or ttfamily wavplay);
- MOD file player (e.g. `tracker`);

- MIDI file player (e.g. `playmidi`).

There are text based as well as GUI based versions of most of these tools. There are also some more esoteric applications (e.g., speech synthesis and recognition) that you may wish to try.

6 Answers To Frequently Asked Questions

This section answers some of the questions that have been commonly asked on the Usenet news groups and mailing lists. Answers to more questions can also be found at the OSS sound driver web page.

6.1 What are the various sound device files?

These are the most "standard" device file names, some Linux distributions may use slightly different names.

/dev/audio
normally a link to `/dev/audio0`;

/dev/audio0
Sun workstation-compatible audio device (only a partial implementation, does not support Sun ioctl interface, just u-law encoding);

/dev/audio1
second audio device (if supported by sound card or if more than one sound card installed);

/dev/dsp
normally a link to `/dev/dsp0`;

/dev/dsp0
first digital sampling device;

/dev/dsp1
second digital sampling device;

/dev/mixer
normally a link to `/dev/mixer0`;

/dev/mixer0
first sound mixer;

/dev/mixer1
second sound mixer;

/dev/music
high-level sequencer interface;

/dev/sequencer
low level MIDI, FM, and GUS access;

/dev/sequencer2
normally a link to `/dev/music`;

/dev/midi00
1st raw MIDI port;

/dev/midi01
2nd raw MIDI port;

/dev/midi02
3rd raw MIDI port;

/dev/midi03
4th raw MIDI port;

/dev/sndstat
displays sound driver status when read;

The PC speaker driver provides the following devices:

/dev/pcaudio
equivalent to /dev/audio;

/dev/pcsp
equivalent to /dev/dsp;

/dev/pcmixer
equivalent to /dev/mixer;

6.2 How can I play a sound sample?

Sun workstation (.au) sound files can be played by sending them to the `/dev/audio` device. Raw samples can be sent to `/dev/dsp`. This will generally give poor results though, and using a program such as `play` is preferable, as it will recognize most file types and set the sound card to the correct sampling rate, etc.

Programs like `wavplay` or `vplay` (in the snd-util package) will give best results with WAV files. However they don't recognize Microsoft ADPCM compressed WAV files. Also older versions of `play` (from the Lsox package) doesn't work well with 16-bit WAV files.

The `splay` command included in the snd-util package can be used to play most sound files if proper parameters are entered manually in the command line.

6.3 How can I record a sample?

Reading `/dev/audio` or `/dev/dsp` will return sampled data that can be redirected to a file. A program such as `vrec` makes it easier to control the sampling rate, duration, etc. You may also need a mixer program to select the appropriate input device.

6.4 Can I have more than one sound card?

With the current sound driver, it's possible to have several SoundBlaster, SoundBlaster/Pro, SoundBlaster16, MPU-401 or MSS cards at the same time on the system. Installing two SoundBlasters is possible but requires defining the macros SB2_BASE, SB2_IRQ, SB2_DMA and (in some cases) SB2_DMA2 by editing `local.h` manually. It's also possible to have a SoundBlaster at the same time as a PAS16.

With the newer 2.0.x kernels that configure sound using `make config`, instead of `local.h`, you need to edit the file `/usr/include/linux/autoconf.h`. After the section containing the lines:

```
#define SBC_BASE 0x220
#define SBC_IRQ (5)
#define SBC_DMA (1)
#define SB_DMA2 (5)
#define SB_MPU_BASE 0x0
#define SB_MPU_IRQ (-1)
```

add these lines (with values appropriate for your system):

```
#define SB2_BASE 0x330
#define SB2_IRQ (7)
#define SB2_DMA (2)
#define SB2_DMA2 (2)
```

The following drivers don't permit multiple instances:

- GUS (driver limitation);
- MAD16 (hardware limitation);
- AudioTrix Pro (hardware limitation);
- CS4232 (hardware limitation).

6.5 Error: No such file or directory for sound devices

You need to create the sound driver device files. See the section on creating device files. If you do have the device files, ensure that they have the correct major and minor device numbers (some older CD-ROM distributions of Linux may not create the correct device files during installation).

6.6 Error: No such device for sound devices

You have not booted with a kernel containing the sound driver or the I/O address configuration doesn't match your hardware. Check that you are running the newly compiled kernel and verify that the settings entered when configuring the sound driver match your hardware setup.

6.7 Error: No space left on device for sound devices

This can happen if you tried to record data to `/dev/audio` or `/dev/dsp` without creating the necessary device file. The sound device is now a regular file, and has filled up your disk partition. You need to run the script described in the "Creating the Device Files" section of this document.

This may also happen with Linux 2.0 and later if there is not enough free RAM on the system when the device is opened. The audio driver requires at least two pages (8k) of contiguous physical RAM for each DMA channel. This happens sometimes in machines with less than 16M of RAM or which have been running for very long time. It may be possible to free some RAM by compiling and running the following C program before trying to open the device again:

```
main() {
    int i;
    char mem[500000];
    for (i = 0; i < 500000; i++)
      mem[i] = 0;
    exit(0);
  }
```

6.8 Error: Device busy for sound devices

Only one process can open a given sound device at one time. Most likely some other process is using the device in question. One way to determine this is to use the `fuser` command:

```
% fuser -v /dev/dsp
/dev/dsp:            USER         PID ACCESS COMMAND
                     tranter      265 f....  tracker
```

In the above example, the `fuser` command showed that process 265 had the device open. Waiting for the process to complete or killing it will allow the sound device to be accessed once again. You should run the `fuser` command as root in order to report usage by users other than yourself.

6.9 I still get device busy errors—

According to Brian Gough, for the SoundBlaster cards which use DMA channel 1 there is a potential conflict with the QIC-02 tape driver, which also uses DMA 1, causing "device busy" errors. If you are using Ftape, you may have this driver enabled. According to the Ftape-HOWTO the QIC-02 driver is not essential for the use of Ftape; only the QIC-117 driver is required. Reconfiguring the kernel to use QIC-117 but not QIC-02 allows Ftape and the sound-driver to coexist.

6.10 Partial playback of digitized sound file

The symptom is usually that a sound sample plays for about a second and then stops completely or reports an error message about "missing IRQ" or "DMA timeout." Most likely you have incorrect IRQ or DMA channel settings. Verify that the kernel configuration matches the sound card jumper settings and that they do not conflict with some other card.

Another symptom is sound samples that "loop." This is usually caused by an IRQ conflict.

6.11 There are pauses when playing MOD files

Playing MOD files requires considerable CPU power. You may have too many processes running or your computer may be too slow to play in real time. Your options are to:

- try playing with a lower sampling rate or in mono mode;
- eliminate other processes;
- buy a faster computer;
- buy a more powerful sound card (e.g. Gravis UltraSound).

If you have a Gravis UltraSound card, you should use one of the mod file players written specifically for the GUS (e.g. `gmod`).

6.12 Compile errors when compiling sound applications

The version 1.0c and earlier sound driver used a different and incompatible `ioctl()` scheme. Obtain newer source code or make the necessary changes to adapt it to the new sound driver. See the sound driver `Readme` file for details.

Also ensure that you have used the latest version of `soundcard.h` and `ultrasound.h` when compiling the application. See the installation instructions at beginning of this text.

6.13 SEGV when running sound binaries that worked previously

This is probably the same problem described in the previous question.

6.14 What known bugs or limitations are there in the sound driver?

See the `Readme` and `CHANGELOG` files included with the sound driver kernel source.

6.15 Where are the sound driver ioctls() etc. documented?

These are partially documented in the *Hacker's Guide to VoxWare*, currently available in draft form. The latest version is draft 2, and can be found on ftp://nic.funet.fi/pub/Linux/ALPHA/sound/. Note that this directory is "hidden" and will not appear in directory listings. If you `cd` to the directory and use the `dir` command in `ftp`, the files are there.

At time of this writing, new documentation is becoming available on the 4Front Technologies Web site.

Another source of information is the Linux Multimedia Guide, described in the references section.

6.16 What CPU resources are needed to play or record without pauses?

There is no easy answer to this question, as it depends on:

- whether using PCM sampling or FM synthesis;
- sampling rate and sample size;
- which application is used to play or record;
- Sound Card hardware;
- disk I/O rate, CPU clock speed, cache size, etc.

In general, any 80386 machine should be able to play samples or FM synthesized music on an 8-bit sound card with ease.

Playing MOD files, however, requires considerable CPU resources. Some experimental measurements have shown that playing at 44kHz requires more than 40% of the speed of a 80486 at 50 MHz and a 80386 at 25 MHz can hardly play faster than 22 kHz (these are with an 8 bit card sound such as a SoundBlaster). A card such as the Gravis UltraSound card performs more functions in hardware, and will require less CPU resources.

These statements assume the computer is not performing any other CPU intensive tasks.

Converting sound files or adding effects using a utility such as `sox` is also much faster if you have a math coprocessor (or CPU with on board FPU). The kernel driver itself does not do any floating point calculations, though.

6.17 Problems with a PAS16 and an Adaptec 1542 SCSI host adaptor

(the following explanation was supplied by `seeker@indirect.com`)

Linux only recognizes the 1542 at address 330 (default) or 334, and the PAS only allows the MPU-401 emulation at 330. Even when you disable the MPU-401 under software, something still wants to conflict with the 1542 if it's at its preferred default address. Moving the 1542 to 334 makes everyone happy.

Additionally, both the 1542 and the PAS-16 do 16-bit DMA, so if you sample at 16-bit 44 KHz stereo and save the file to a SCSI drive hung on the 1542, you're about to have trouble. The DMAs overlap and there isn't enough time for RAM refresh, so you get the dread "PARITY ERROR—SYSTEM HALTED" message, with no clue to what caused it. It's made worse because a few second-party vendors with QIC-117 tape drives recommend setting the bus on/off times such that the 1542 is on even longer than normal. Get the `SCSISEL.EXE` program from Adaptec's BBS or several places on the Internet, and reduce the BUS ON time or increase the BUS OFF time until the problem goes away, then move it one notch or more further. SCSISEL changes the EEPROM settings, so it's more permanent than a patch to the DOS driver line in `CONFIG.SYS`, and will work if you boot right into Linux (unlike the DOS patch). Next problem solved.

Last problem—the older Symphony chip sets drastically reduced the timing of the I/O cycles to speed up bus accesses. None of various boards I've played with had any problem with the reduced timing except for the PAS-16. Media Vision's BBS has `SYMPFIX.EXE` that's supposed to cure the problem by twiddling a diagnostic bit in Symphony's bus controller, but it's not a hard guarantee. You may need to:

- get the motherboard distributor to replace the older version bus chip,

- replace the motherboard, or
- buy a different brand of sound card.

Young Microsystems will upgrade the boards they import for around $30 (US); other vendors may be similar if you can figure out who made or imported the motherboard (good luck). The problem is in ProAudio's bus interface chip as far as I'm concerned; nobody buys a $120 sound card and sticks it in a 6MHz AT. Most of them wind up in 25–40MHz 386/486 boxes, and should be able to handle at least 12MHz bus rates if the chips are designed right. Exit soapbox (stage left).

The first problem depends on the chip set used on your motherboard, what bus speed and other BIOS settings, and the phase of the moon. The second problem depends on your refresh option setting (hidden or synchronous), the 1542 DMA rate and (possibly) the bus I/O rate. The third can be determined by calling Media Vision and asking which flavor of Symphony chip is incompatible with their slow design. Be warned, though—3 of 4 techs I talked to were brain damaged. I would be very leery of trusting anything they said about someone else's hardware, since they didn't even know their own very well.

6.18 Is it possible to read and write samples simultaneously?

Due to hardware limitations, this is not possible with most sound cards. Some newer cards do support it. See the section on bidirectional mode in the *Hacker's Guide to Voxware* for more information.

6.19 My SB16 is set to IRQ 2, but configure does not allow this value.

On 80286 and later machines, the IRQ 2 interrupt is cascaded to the second interrupt controller. It is equivalent to IRQ 9.

6.20 Are the SoundBlaster AWE32 or SoundBlaster16 ASP supported?

In the past, Creative Labs was not willing to release programming information for these cards. They have since changed their policy and an AWE driver is now included in the Linux 2.1.x kernels.

6.21 If I run Linux, then boot DOS, I get errors, or sound applications do not work properly.

This happens after a soft reboot to DOS. Sometimes the error message misleadingly refers to a bad `CONFIG.SYS` file.

Most of the current sound cards have software programmable IRQ and DMA settings. If you use different settings between Linux and MS-DOS and MS Windows, this may cause problems. Some sound cards don't accept new parameters without a complete reset (i.e., cycle the power or use the hardware reset button).

The quick solution to this problem it to perform a full reboot using the reset button or power cycle rather than a soft reboot (e.g. Ctrl-Alt-Del).

The correct solution is to ensure that you use the same IRQ and DMA settings with MS-DOS and Linux (or not to use DOS).

6.22 Problems running DOOM under Linux

Users of the port of ID software's game DOOM for Linux may be interested in these notes.

For correct sound output you need version 2.90 or later of the sound driver; it has support for the real-time "DOOM mode."

The sound samples are 16 bit. If you have an 8-bit sound card, you can still get sound to work using one of several programs available in ftp://sunsite.unc.edu/pub/Linux/games/doom/.

If performance of DOOM is poor on your system, disabling sound (by renaming the file `sndserver`) may improve it.

By default, DOOM does not support music (as in the DOS version). The program `musserver` will add support for music to DOOM under Linux. It can be found at ftp://pandora.st.hmc.edu/pub/linux/musserver.tgz.

6.23 How can I reduce noise picked up by my sound card?

Using good quality shielded cables and trying the sound card in different slots may help reduce noise. If the sound card has a volume control, you can try different settings (maximum is probably best).

Using a mixer program you can make sure that undesired inputs (e.g. microphone) are set to zero gain.

Some sound cards are simply not designed with good shielding and grounding and are prone to noise pickup.

Finally, on my system I found that the kernel command line option `no-hlt` reduces the noise level. This tells the kernel not to use the halt instruction when running the idle process loop. You can try this manually when booting, or set it up using the command `append="no-hlt"` in your LILO configuration file.

6.24 I can play sounds, but not record.

If you can play sound but not record, try these steps:

- use a mixer program to select the appropriate device (e.g. microphone);
- use the mixer to set the input gains to maximum;
- If you can, try to test sound card recording under MS-DOS to determine if there is a hardware problem.

Sometimes a different DMA channel is used for recording than for playback. In this case the most probable reason is that the recording DMA is set up incorrectly.

6.25 My "compatible" sound card only works if I first initialize under MS-DOS.

In most cases a "SoundBlaster compatible" card will work better under Linux if configured with a driver other than the SoundBlaster one. Most sound cards claim to be compatible (e.g. 16 bit SB Pro compatible, or SB compatible 16 bit) but usually this SoundBlaster mode is just a hack provided for MS-DOS games compatibility. Most cards have a 16-bit native mode which is likely to be supported by recent Linux versions (2.0.1 and later).

Only with some (usually rather old) cards is it necessary to try to get them to work in the SoundBlaster mode. The only newer cards that are the exception to this rule are the Mwave-based cards.

6.26 My 16-bit SoundBlaster "compatible" sound card only works in 8-bit mode under Linux.

16-bit sound cards described as SoundBlaster compatible are really only compatible with the 8-bit SoundBlaster Pro. They typically have a 16-bit mode which is not compatible with the SoundBlaster 16 and not compatible with the Linux sound driver.

You may be able to get the card to work in 16-bit mode by using the MAD16 or MSS/WSS driver.

6.27 Where can I find sound applications for Linux?

Here are some good archive sites to search for Linux specific sound applications:

- ftp://sunsite.unc.edu:/pub/Linux/kernel/sound/;
- ftp://sunsite.unc.edu:/pub/Linux/apps/sound/;
- ftp://tsx-11.mit.edu:/pub/linux/packages/sound/;
- ftp://nic.funet.fi:/pub/Linux/util/sound/;
- ftp://nic.funet.fi:/pub/Linux/xtra/snd-kit/;
- ftp://nic.funet.fi:/pub/Linux/ALPHA/sound/.

6.28 Can the sound driver be compiled as a loadable module?

With recent kernels the sound driver is supported as a kernel loadable module. See the files `/usr/src/linux/drivers/sound/Readme.modules` and `/usr/src/linux/Documentation/modules.txt` (or `/usr/src/linux/README`) for details.

6.29 Can I use a sound card to replace the system console beep?

Try the `oplbeep` program, found at:
ftp://sunsite.unc.edu/pub/Linux/apps/sound/oplbeep-alpha.tar.gz.

Another variant is the `beep` program found at:
ftp://sunsite.unc.edu/pub/Linux/kernel/patches/misc/modreq_beep.tgz

The `modutils` package has an example program and kernel patch that supports calling an arbitrary external program to generate sounds when requested by the kernel.

Alternatively, with some sound cards, you can connect the PC speaker output to the sound card so that all sounds come from the sound card speakers.

6.30 What is VoxWare?

The kernel sound drivers support several different Intel based, Unix compatible operating systems, and can be obtained as a package separate from the Linux kernel. Up until February 1996, the author had called the software "VoxWare." Unfortunately this name has been registered by VoxWare Incorporated, and can not be used. The new name of the driver is OSS/Free.

The Open Sound System (OSS) is a commercially available kernel sound driver for various Unix systems, sold by 4Front Technologies. The free version, known as OSS/Free will continue to be made freely available for Linux systems.

Other names you may come across that have been used in the past to refer to the same sound driver are TASD (Temporarily Anonymous Sound Driver) and USS (Unix Sound System).

For more information see the 4Front Technologies Web page at
http://www.4front-tech.com/.
I wrote a review of OSS/Linux in the June 1997 issue of Linux Journal.

6.31 Are Plug and Play sound card supported?

Full Plug-and-Play support should be coming in Linux version 2.1. In the mean time, there are a number of workarounds for getting Plug and Play sound cards to work.

If you have a newer Pentium system with a Plug and Play BIOS, it should take care of configuring the cards for you. Make sure that you configure the Linux sound driver to use the same I/O address, IRQ, and DMA channel parameters as the BIOS.

There is a package of Plug and Play tools for Linux that can be used to set up the card. It can be found at Red Hat's Web site, http://www.redhat.com/. (It may also be included in your Linux distribution.)

If you use the card under MS Windows 95, you can use the device manager to set up the card, then soft boot into Linux using the LOADLIN program. Make sure MS Windows 95 and Linux use the same card setup parameters.

If you use the card under MS-DOS, you can use the `ICU.EXE` utility that comes with SoundBlaster16 PnP cards to configure it under MS-DOS, then soft boot into Linux using the LOADLIN.EXE program. Again, make sure DOS and Linux use the same card setup parameters.

The commercial OSS sound driver has support for the SoundBlaster16 PnP sound card. You can purchase this driver from 4Front Technologies.

6.32 Sox, Play, or Vplay reports "invalid block size 1024"

A change to the sound driver in version 1.3.67 broke some sound player programs which (incorrectly) checked that the result from the SNDCTL_DSP_GETBLKSIZE ioctl was greater than 4096. The utilities included in the latest snd-util-3.x.tar.gz package (at ftp://ftp.4front-tech.com/ossfree/) now handle this properly. The latest sound driver versions have also been fixed to avoid allocating fragments shorter than 4096 bytes which solves this problem with old utilities.

6.33 Why does the sound driver have its own configuration program?

The sound driver supports many different configuration parameters. The `configure` program included with the sound driver checks for many dependencies between parameters. The tools used to configure the kernel don't support this level of functionality.

That said, the latest kernels do optionally allow using the standard kernel configuration tools with the sound driver (see the earlier section on "Configuring the Kernel."

6.34 The mixer settings are reset whenever I load the sound driver module

You can build the sound driver as a loadable module and use `kerneld` to automatically load and unload it. This can present one problem—whenever the module is reloaded the mixer settings go back to their default values. For some sound cards this can be too loud (e.g. SoundBlaster16) or too quiet. Markus Gutschke (gutschk@uni-muenster.de) found this solution. Use a line in your `/etc/conf.modules` file such as the following:

```
options sound dma_buffsize=65536 \&\& /usr/bin/setmixer igain 0 ogain 0 vol 75
```

This causes your mixer program (in this case `setmixer`) to be run immediately after the sound driver is loaded. The `dma_buffsize` parameter is just a dummy value needed because the option command requires a command line option. Change the line as needed to match your mixer program and gain settings.

If you have compiled the sound driver into your kernel and you want to set the mixer gains at boot time you can put a call to your mixer program in a system startup file such as `/etc/rc.d/rc.local`.

6.35 Only user root can record sound

By default, the script in `Readme.linux` that creates the sound device files only allows the devices to be read by user `root`. This is to plug a potential security hole. In a networked environment, external users could conceivably log in remotely to a Linux PC with a sound card and microphone and eavesdrop. If you are not worried about this, you can change the permissions used in the script.

With the default setup, users can still play sound files. This is not a security risk but is a potential for nuisance.

6.36 Is the sound hardware on the IBM ThinkPad supported?

Information on how to use the mwave sound card on an IBM ThinkPad laptop computer under Linux can be found at http://www.screamin.demon.co.uk/.

7 References

If you have a sound card that supports a CD-ROM or SCSI interface, the Linux SCSI HOWTO (page 1285), and the Linux CD-ROM HOWTO (page 702) have additional information that may be useful to you.

The Sound Playing HOWTO (page 1477) describes how to play various types of sound and music files under Linux.

The Ultrasound Plug'n'play Mini-HOWTO describes how to get a plug and play Gravis Ultrasound card working under Linux.

The Linux SoundBlaster 16 PnP Mini-HOWTO describes how to get a plug and play SoundBlaster 16 card working under Linux.

The Linux SoundBlaster AWE64 PnP Mini-HOWTO describes how to get a plug and play SoundBlaster AWE64 card working under Linux.

There is an old document called the *Hacker's Guide to VoxWare*, available from ftp://nic.funet.fi/pub/Linux/ALPHA/sound/. Most of the information in there has been superseded by the documents at http://www.4front-tech.com/pguide/, but the section on `/dev/sequencer` may still be useful.

The following FAQs are regularly posted to the Usenet newsgroup news.announce as well as being archived at ftp://rtfm.mit.edu/pub/usenet/news.answers/.

- PCsoundcards/generic-faq (Generic PC Soundcard FAQ).
- PCsoundcards/soundcard-faq (comp.sys.ibm.pc.soundcard FAQ).
- PCsoundcards/gravis-ultrasound/faq (Gravis UltraSound FAQ).
- audio-fmts/part1 (Audio file format descriptions).
- audio-fmts/part2 (Audio file format descriptions).

The FAQs also list several product specific mailing lists and archive sites. The following Usenet news groups discuss sound r music related issues:

- alt.binaries.sounds.* (various groups for posting sound files);
- alt.binaries.multimedia (for posting Multimedia files);
- alt.sb.programmer (Soundblaster programming topics);
- comp.multimedia; (Multimedia topics);
- comp.music (Computer music theory and research);
- comp.sys.ibm.pc.soundcard.* (various IBM PC sound card groups).

A Web site dedicated to multimedia can be found at http://viswiz.gmd.de/MultimediaInfo/. Creative Labs has a Web site at http://www.creaf.com/. MediaTrix has a Web site at http://www.mediatrix.com/.

The Linux mailing list has a number of "channels" dedicated to different topics, including sound. To find out how to join, send a mail message with the word "help" as the message body to majordomo@vger.rutgers.edu. These mailing lists are not recommended for questions on sound card setup, etc., they are intended for development related discussion.

As mentioned several times before, the kernel sound driver includes a number of `Readme` files containing useful information about the sound card driver. These can typically be found in the directory `/usr/src/linux/drivers/sound`.

The author of the kernel sound driver, Hannu Savolainen, can be contacted by email at hannu@voxware.pp.fi. He also has a World-Wide Web site at http://personal.eunet.fi/pp/voxware. The Web site is the best source for finding out the latest status of supported sound cards, known problems, and bug fixes.

Information on OSS, the commercial sound driver for Linux and other Unix compatible operating systems, can be found on the 4Front Technologies Web page at http://www.4front-tech.com/.

The Linux Software Map (LSM) is an invaluable reference for locating Linux software. Searching the LSM for keywords such as "sound" is a good way to identify applications related to sound hardware. The LSM can be found on various anonymous FTP sites, including ftp://sunsite.unc.edu/pub/Linux/docs/LSM/.

The Linux Documentation Project has produced several books on Linux, including *Linux Installation and Getting Started* (see page 3). It is freely available by anonymous FTP from major Linux archive sites and can be purchased in hardcopy format.

Finally, a shameless plug: If you want to learn a lot more about multimedia under Linux (especially CD-ROM and sound card applications and programming), check out my book *Linux Multimedia Guide*, ISBN 1-56592-219-0, published by O'Reilly and Associates. As well as the original English version, French and Japanese translations are now in print. For details, call 800-998-9938 in North America or check the Web page

```
http://www.ora.com/catalog/multilinux/noframes.html
```

or my home page,

```
http://www.pobox.com/~tranter
```

Part XLVII

"Linux Sound Playing HOWTO" by Yoo C. Chung,

wacko@laplace.snu.ac.kr

Contents

Abstract

v1.5, 7 November 1997
This document lists applications for Linux that play various sound formats.

1 Introduction

This is the Sound Playing HOWTO. It lists the many sound formats and the applications that can be used to play them. It also lists some hacks and advice on using these applications. There are also some other interesting applications related to sound not directly related to playback. However, this document does not describe how one can setup a Linux system for sound support. Refer to the Linux Sound HOWTO by Jeff Tranter for instructions on setting up a Linux system for sound support and the supported sound hardware.

This deals with normal user sound applications. That is, it is only concerned about what the average user needs to know on the application side of sound, not exotic stuff like speech synthesis, or hardware stuff which is dealt in the Sound HOWTO.

1.1 Copyright of this document

1.2 Copyright of the listed applications

If there is no mention of any copyright, then the application is under the GNU General Public License.

1.3 Where to get this document

The most recent official version of this document can be obtained from

`http://sunsite.unc.edu/LDP/`

The most recent, unofficial version of this document can be obtained from

`http://laplace.snu.ac.kr/~wacko/howto/`

A Korean version of this document (very outdated) is available at

`http://laplace.snu.ac.kr/~wacko/howto/Sound-Playing-HOWTO.ks`

A Japanese version of this document is available at

`http://jf.gee.kyoto-u.ac.jp/JF/JF-ftp/euc/Sound-Playing-HOWTO.euc`

1.4 Feedback

I am not omniscient, and I don't use all the applications in here (a few I can't even try), so there are bound to be mistakes. Also, programs usually continuously evolve, so documentation tends to get out of date. Therefore, if you find anything wrong, please send me any corrections. Suggestions or additions to this document are welcome, too.

1.5 Acknowledgments

All the authors of the applications in this HOWTO. Also, Hannu Savolainen for the great sound driver and Linus Torvalds for the great underlying OS.

I'd also like to thank Raymond Nijssen (`raymond@es.ele.tue.nl`), Jeroen Rutten (`jeroen@es.ele.tue.nl`), Antonio Perez (`aperez@arrakis.es`), Ian Jackson (`ijackson@gnu.org`), and Peter Amstutz (`amstpi@freenet.tlh.fl.us`) for their information and help.

2 Playing Various Sound Formats

There are many kinds of sound formats (WAV, MIDI, MPEG etc.). Below, we list the various formats and the applications that can be used to play them.

2.1 MIDI

MIDI stands for "Musical Instrument Device Interface." MIDI files usually have the extension `.mid`. They contain sequencing information, that is, information on when to play what instrument in what way, etc. Depending on your hardware (and maybe the software you use to play them), the sound might be awesome, or it might not.

2.1.1 The adagio package

This package includes `mp` (a command-line MIDI file player) and `xmp` (an XView based MIDI file player, not to be confused with the module player also called `xmp`). You will need the SlingShot extensions to use `xmp`. It also contains other programs for playing Adagio scores.

If you have a GUS, `mp` can also play MOD files (see section 2.2 for more information on modules).

One little annoying bug (as of version 0.5 on some hardware) is that the sound breaks at the end. Namely, instead of ending the sound the way the MIDI file specifies, it ends by playing the note right before the last one in a long interval. It hasn't stopped me from using `mp`, but it might prevent someone from using it for "real" work. It also starts up relatively slowly.

The package does not mention any copyright (at least none that I can find), so I assume it can be freely redistributed and modified. (By a strict interpretation of copyright law, nothing gives one the right to do these things, but I somehow doubt that this was the intention of the author.)

It is a port of the CMU MIDI Toolkit to Linux (though there was enough added to make this questionable) by Greg Lee (`lee@uhunix.uhcc.hawaii.edu`).

It can be obtained by anonymous FTP from `tsx-11.mit.edu` at `/pub/linux/packages/sound/adagio05.tar.gz`. The binaries included here are in a.out format (linked with ancient libraries), and the `xmp` binary segfaults in a X11R6 environment (XFree86 3.1.1, libc 4.7.2). The `mp` binary works fine in an `a.out` environment.

You will need a bit of hackery to compile it. Actually, it's not much of a hackery. All you have to do is to include the `-lfl` switch at the end of `SHROBJ` and `XMPOBJ` in the Makefile. This is to link in the `flex` library, which is not linked in by default. Then follow the installation instructions. And don't forget to have XView and the SlingShot extensions installed if you want to compile `xmp`.

2.1.2 TiMidity

Some people recommend this experimental program because of good sound quality (which is very true, it's much better than `mp` on a Sound Blaster 16, though it probably won't be much different on soundcards with wavetable synthesis like the GUS). However, it suffers from high CPU loads. It plays MIDI by first converting MIDI to WAV and then plays the WAV (you can also convert a MIDI file to a WAV file without playing if you want). This is the reason for its CPU intensive nature.

It also has an optional ncurses, SLang, Tcl/Tk or Motif interface.

You need Gravis Ultrasound patch files to use this. Look into the FAQ included with TiMidity for more information.

The author is Tuukka Toivonen (`tt@cgs.fi`).

The latest version of TiMidity can be found at the http://www.cgs.fi/~tt/timidity/. This page also contains a link to a small library of GUS patches.

2.1.3 playmidi

This is a MIDI player that plays to FM, GUS, and external MIDI. It is supposed to have a faster startup time compared to other MIDI players. It is also able to play Creative Music Files, Microsoft RIFF files, and large MIDI archives from games such as Ultima 7.

It has an X interface and a SVGA interface. It also has an option for real time playback with tracking all the notes on each channel and the current playback clock (included automatically with `xplaymidi` and `splaymidi`).

You should do something like

```
$ splaymidi foo.mid; stty sane
```

if you are going to use the SVGA interface, since it doesn't reset the terminal tty mode properly. The SVGA interface may be removed in the near future.

It was written by Nathan Laredo (`laredo@gnu.org` or `laredo@ix.netcom.com`).

It can be obtained by anonymous FTP from `sunsite.unc.edu` at `/pub/Linux/apps/sound/players/playmidi-2.3.tar.gz`.

2.2 Modules

Modules (in computer music) are digital music files, made up of a set of samples and sequencing information, telling the player when to play which sample (instrument) on which track at what pitch, optionally performing an effect, like vibrato for example.

An advantage it has over MIDI is that it can include almost any kind of sound (including human voices). Another is that it sounds just about the same on any platform, because the samples are in the module. A disadvantage it has is that it has a much larger file size compared to MIDI. Another one is that it has no real standard format (the only "real" one is the ProTracker, which many modules aren't quite compatible with). It originated on the Amiga.

The most common format has the extension `.mod`. There are many other extensions depending on what format they are in.

2.2.1 `tracker`

This very portable program (it has been ported to many platforms) plays Soundtracker and Protracker music modules. It uses 16-bit stereo output, and I consider the quality to be very good. If you need a simple way to reduce CPU load use the `-mono` option.

This is a giftware program (quoting the author). It is by Marc Espie (`Marc.Espie@ens.fr`).

A version of this with the Makefile already tweaked for Linux can be obtained by anonymous FTP from `sunsite.unc.edu` at `/pub/Linux/apps/sound/players/tracker-4.3-linux.tar.gz`.

2.2.2 `gmod`

This is a music module player for the Gravis Ultrasound card. 4/6/8 channel MOD, 8 channel 669, MultiTracker (MTM), UltraTracker (ULT), FastTracker (XM), and ScreamTracker III (S3M) are the supported formats.

It requires a version 3.0 or later sound driver. And a GUS, of course. You may need to modify the kernel to make volume control work the way you want.

This has an X interface. It uses the QT toolkit (needs version 0.99 or greater). Check http://www.troll.no/ for information on QT.

This can be freely distributed. It was originally written by Hannu Savolainen, and now maintained by Andrew J. Robinson (`robinson@cnj.digex.net`).

It can be obtained by anonymous FTP from `sunsite.unc.edu` at `/pub/Linux/apps/sound/players/gmod-3.1.tar.gz`.

2.2.3 MikMod

This portable module player plays XM, ULT, STM, S3M, MTM, MOD and UNI formats. (The UNI format is an internal format used by MikMod.) It has support for zipped module files. It uses 16-bit stereo for the sound output. Use the `-m` option (for mono output) if you need a simple way to lower the CPU load.

The Unix version can either use ncurses or Tcl/Tk for its interface. It can also be used as a library, not just an independent program.

It was originally written by Jean-Paul Mikkers (`mikmak@via.nl`). It is now maintained by Jake Stine (`dracoirs@epix.net`). This is shareware that has to be registered if you want to use it commercially. You also need permission to redistribute it commercially (non-commercial redistribution does not need such permission).

This can be found at the MikMod home page,

`http://www.aics.net/~amstutz/mikmod.html`

2.2.4 `xmp`

This is a module player (not to be confused with Adagio's `xmp`) which can play MOD, S3M, STM, 669, and XM modules (other formats are also supported, but still experimental or incomplete) on soundcards with wavetable synthesis (GUS or SoundBlaster 32AWE), or on systems with SoftOSS (a driver that does software mixing). In the very near future ordinary DSP output should be possible as well.

An X front end to `xmp` is also available.

This was written by Claudio Matsuoka (`claudio@brasil.enemy.org`) and H. Carraro Jr.

This can found at the `xmp` home page,

`http://www.merdre.net/~claudio/xmp/`

2.2.5 s3mod

This plays 4/6/8 track MOD modules and Scream Tracker 3 modules. It uses 8-bit mono output with a sampling rate of 22000 Hz by default. You can use the option `-s` to enable stereo, `-b` to enable 16 bit output, and `-f` to set the sampling frequency. However, the sound output is worse than tracker (some noise), so I recommend using `tracker` instead of `s3mod` for playing ordinary MOD files (unless you have an underpowered machine). It has a much smaller CPU load compared to tracker.

It is copyrighted by Daniel Marks and David Jeske (`jeske@uiuc.edu`), but you can do anything you want with it (except that you can't claim you wrote it).

It can be obtained by anonymous FTP from `sunsite.unc.edu` at `/pub/Linux/apps/sound/players/s3mod-v1.09.tar.gz`.

2.2.6 mod

This beta program plays MODs (15/31-instrument, up to 32 voices), MTMs, ULTs and S3Ms on the Gravis Ultrasound card. It can also use packed modules if you have `gzip`, `lharc`, `unzip`, and `unarj` installed. It cannot play Powerpacked modules or modules packed with some Amiga composers ("PACK" signature).

This requires at least version 3.0 of the sound driver. It won't work with the 2.90-2 or earlier version of the sound driver. The text interface requires ncurses. There is also an X interface included, which uses Tcl/Tk.

It was written by Mikael Nordqvist (`mech@df.lth.se` or `d91mn@efd.lth.se`).

It can be obtained by anonymous FTP from `sunsite.unc.edu` at `/pub/Linux/apps/sound/players/mod-v0.81.tgz`.

2.2.7 nspmod

This is an alpha module player which can play MTM, S3M, and MOD modules. It is intended to be a module player for soundcards without a DSP (not to be confused with what Creative Labs calls a DSP). It has a CPU load somewhat similar compared to `tracker`.

It has a feature which lets modules loop if they want to. The number of loops can be limited by the `-l` option. It uses only 8 bit sound output (as of version 0.1).

This was written by Toru Egashira (`toru@jms.jeton.or.jp`).

It can be obtained by anonymous FTP from `sunsite.unc.edu` at `/pub/Linux/apps/sound/players/nspmod-0.1.tar.gz`.

2.2.8 yampmod

This program, still an alpha version, was designed to play 4-channel modules using the minimum of CPU resources. It was not designed to produce high quality sound. So the only sound output it produces is 22 kHz mono output. Also, the output isn't as clean as it should be, reflecting its alpha status.

It was written by David Groves (`djg@djghome.demon.co.uk`).

It can be obtained by anonymous FTP from `sunsite.unc.edu` at `/pub/Linux/apps/sound/players/yampmod-0.1.tar.gz`.

2.3 MPEG audio streams

MPEG is a standard specifying the coding of video and the associated audio for digital storage. MPEG is usually associated with video, but the audio part of the standard can be used separately. The audio part of the MPEG standard defines three layers, layer I, II, and III. Players that can decode higher layers can also decode lower layers (e.g. layer III players can play layer II files). Layer I MPEG audio files usually have the extension `.mpg` (so if there is a file with this extension that can't be played by a MPEG video player, it's probably an audio stream), layer II usually have the extension `.mp2`, and layer III usually have the extension `.mp3`. The audio compression is pretty good. A two megabyte layer II MPEG audio file will probably take up 25 megabytes for a raw PCM sample file with the same quality.

2.3.1 mpg123

This beta program is an efficient MPEG audio stream player, which has support for layers I, II, and III. It is based on code from many sources. It is able to play in real time streams that are read by HTTP (i.e., one can play an MPEG audio stream directly over the World Wide Web).

The main author is Michael Hipp (Michael.Hipp@student.uni-tuebingen.de). It may be used and distributed in unmodified form freely for non-commercial purposes. Inclusion in a collection of free software (such as CD-ROM images of FTP servers) is explicitly allowed.

The latest version can be obtained from Oliver Fromme's mpg123 page,

```
http://www.heim3.tu-clausthal.de/~olli/mpg123/
```

2.3.2 maplay 1.2

This MPEG audio stream player only has support for Layer I and Layer II streams, and lacks support for Layer III streams. It supports 16-bit sound cards on Linux.

It is pretty CPU intensive, taking up to about 55% CPU time on a 60MHz Pentium. The output is intolerable on a 66MHz 486 because the CPU just can't catch up with the sound. If this happens to you, try playing only one side of the audio stream (with the -l or -r option), instead of the default stereo.

A slight change in one of the files may be necessary in order to compile it. Namely, you may need to add the following line to the beginning of the file configuration.sh.

```
#! /bin/sh
```

The author is Tobias Bading (bading@cs.tu-berlin.de). maplay 1.2 can be obtained by anonymous FTP from ftp.cs.tu-berlin.de at /pub/multimedia/maplay1.2/maplay1_2.tar.

2.3.3 maplay 1.3b

This is an unofficial modification (i.e. not by the original author) of maplay 1.2, so that it can run with a much lower load on the CPU. It accomplishes this mainly by making u-law output actually work on other platforms besides the SPARC. Note that it uses u-law output by default, so the sound quality is lower.

The modifications were made by Orlando Andico (orly@gibson.eee.upd.edu.ph).

This can be obtained by anonymous FTP from sunsite.unc.edu at /pub/Linux/apps/sound/players/maplay-1.3b-Linux.tar.gz.

2.3.4 maplay3

This is another derivative of maplay 1.2. It adds support for MPEG Layer 3 audio streams. Currently it seems to have some bugs in its playback (you may hear some screeching noises). You may have to twiddle with the options to solve this.

The modifications were made by Timo Jantunen (timo.jantunen@hut.fi or jeti@cc.hut.fi). The copyright says that it can be used freely, but making money off of it is not allowed. However, I'm not entirely sure about the validity of this copyright, since the original maplay is under the GNU General Public License, which does not allow derivative works to have a different copyright.

This can be obtained by anonymous FTP from sunsite.unc.edu at /pub/Linux/apps/sound/players/maplay3.tar.gz.

2.3.5 splay

This beta player is another derivative of maplay 1.2 (actually, it is a derivative of maplay 1.2+, which is a MS Windows-only derivative of maplay 1.2). It adds support for MPEG Layer-3 audio streams. It is also able to play WAV files. It can also play audio streams received over an HTTP connection.

Another feature of splay is that it can be used as a library (under the LGPL), so that it can be used in other programs. It also tries to improve performance by using threading (you need pthread to use this feature) and a little inline assembly.

splay uses a command line interface and an optional X interface (which uses QT).

If after compiling it doesn't work (e.g. it segmentation faults), try compiling it again without threading.

This is by Jung Woo-jae (jwj95@eve.kaist.ac.kr).

It can be obtained from splay's home page,

```
http://adam.kaist.ac.kr/~jwj95/
```

2.3.6 Sajber Jukebox

This program is a MPEG audio player with a graphical user interface. It is based on `splay`, so it includes support for MPEG audio layers up to III. It is also able to play MPEG audio streams in real time with the stream being fed by HTTP. It is also easy to configure.

It uses the QT toolkit (at least version 1.2 is required). It also uses the LinuxThreads library (the included binary only works with version 0.5).

The author is Joel Lindholm (`wizball@kewl.campus.luth.se`).

The latest version can be obtained by anonymous FTP from `kewl.campus.luth.se` at `/pub/jukebox`.

2.3.7 `amp`

This beta MPEG audio player only has support for MPEG Layer 3 audio streams. It is able to play directly to the soundcard, and it can output to raw PCM or WAV files. This also gives quite a load on the CPU (about 60% on a 133MHz Pentium).

This was written by Tomislav Uzelac (`tuzelac@rasip.fer.hr`). It can be freely used and distributed, as long as it is not sold commercially without permission (including it in CD-ROMs that contain free software is explicitly permitted, though).

It can be obtained by anonymous FTP from `ftp.rasip.fer.hr` at `/pub/mpeg/amp-0.7.3.tgz`.

2.3.8 XAudio

This alpha-development library was written to be a fast implementation of an MPEG audio decoding library to be used by various GUI front-ends. It supports MPEG audio layers I, II, and III. It is capable of random access to bitstreams. A command-line interface is included. A Motif (Lesstif) front end is also included in the Linux version.

This is by Gilles Boccon-Gibod, Alain Jobart, and others. The front ends to the libary can be freely downloaded. The library itself must be licensed to be used (a source and binary license is available).

The front ends to the library can be obtained from the XAudio home page,

```
http://www.mpeg.org/xaudio/
```

2.3.9 Layer 3 Shareware Encoder/Decoder

This is actually a converter that converts MPEG Layer 3 audio streams to WAV, AIFF, SND, AIFC, or just raw PCM sample files. The Linux version does not directly output the sound to the soundcard. One has to first convert it to some other format.

However, when you try to play a converted file using `sox`, you'll probably just get noise because the word order in the PCM samples is not right (at least on Intel platforms). You need to give `sox` the option `-x` to solve this problem. But there are some players that don't have to be told that the word order is wrong, so you might not have to worry about this.

If you have a really fast computer (probably at least a 100Mhz Pentium), then you can try to play MPEG Layer 3 streams directly without having to first convert the audio file to another format like in the following example (this example assumes that you're using `sox` and playing a 44.1 kHz stereo sample).

```
$ l3dec foo.mp3 -sto | play -t raw -x -u -w -c 2 -r 44100 -
```

The number after `-r` is the sample rate of the audio stream, and the number after `-c` depends on whether it is mono or stereo (or even quad). If this looks too complicated, you can use something like a shell script or an alias.

This is shareware copyrighted by Fraunhofer-IIS. A demo version for Linux on x86 systems can be obtained by anonymous FTP from `ftp.fhg.de` at `/pub/layer3`. The demo version only converts Layer III audio streams.

2.4 WAV

Quote from the `sox` man page:

> These appear to be very similar to IFF files, but not the same. They are the native sound file format of Windows 3.1. Obviously, Windows 3.1 is of such incredible importance to the computer industry that it just had to have its own sound file format.

These usually have the extension `.wav`.

Also see section 2.5.1 and 2.5.2 for other WAV players besides the ones listed here.

2.4.1 wavplay

This program supports playing and recording with the WAV format. It uses locking so that only one sound may be played at a time. Its locking capabilities can also be used separately from its sound playing capabilities.

In addition to a command-line interface, it also has a Motif interface,which can be used with Lesstif.

It was originally written by Andre Fuechsel (`af1@irz.inf.tu-dresden.de`), but was evolved to the point of being completely rewritten by Warren W. Gay (`bx249@freenet.toronto.on.ca` or `wwg@ica.net`).

It can be obtained by anonymous FTP from `sunsite.unc.edu` at `/pub/Linux/apps/sound/players/wavplay-1.0.tar.gz`.

2.5 Other stuff

This section lists stuff that play sound formats that don't deserve a separate section (i.e. formats that have only one player available), or players that play more than one format.

2.5.1 sox

This program is actually a converter, that is, it converts one sound format to another. However, some versions of `sox`, when invoked as `play`, plays the sound (the `play` application in the Sound HOWTO probably refers to this). It supports raw (no header) binary and textual data, IRCAM Sound Files, Sound Blaster `.voc`, SPARC `.au` (w/header), Mac HCOM, PC/DOS `.sou`, Sndtool, and Sounder, NeXT `.snd`, Windows 3.1 RIFF/WAV, Turtle Beach `.smp`, CD-R, and Apple/SGI AIFF and 8SVX formats

Since somewhere in the 1.3.6x kernels, you might have to make a small change in one file to make it play the sound directly. Namely, you may have to change line 179 in `sbdsp.c` from

```
if (abuf_size < 4096 || abuf_size > 65536) {
```

to

```
if (abuf_size < 1 || abuf_size > 65536) {
```

But then again, you may not have to do this. But doing this won't break anything.

It is written and copyrighted by many people, and can be used for any purpose.

It can be obtained by anonymous FTP from `sunsite.unc.edu` at `/pub/Linux/apps/sound/convert/Lsox-linux.tar.gz`.

A more recent version by Chris Bagwell (`cbagwell@sprynet.com`) (based on the latest gamma version of the original `sox`, and includes the above fix) can be obtained by anonymous FTP from `sunsite.unc.edu` at `/pub/Linux/apps/sound/convert/sox-11gamma-cb3.tar.gz`.

2.5.2 bplay

This beta program plays raw audio, WAV, and VOC files. It's also able to record to these files. It uses a variety of techniques to get the highest speed possible so that it can run acceptably even on slow machines. One of these techniques require that the installed programs be setuid root. The paranoid hoping to use this may want to use the Debian package by Ian Jackson (`ijackson@gnu.org`), which disables the feature that needs the setuid bit.

The author is David Monro (`davidm@gh.cs.usyd.edu.au`).

It can be obtained by anonymous FTP from `sunsite.unc.edu` at `/pub/Linux/apps/sound/players/bplay-0.96.tar.gz`.

2.5.3 sidplay

This program emulates the Sound Interface Device chip (MOS 6581, commonly called SID) and the Micro Processor Unit (MOS 6510) of the Commodore 64. Therefore it is able to load and execute C64 machine code programs which produce music or sound. In general these are independent fragments of code and data which have been ripped from games and demonstration programs and have been transferred directly from the C64.

It uses a command line interface by default. There are also Tk and QT interfaces available separately from the main package.

It is maintained by Michael Schwendt (`sidplay@geocities.com`).

It can be obtained from SIDPLAY's home page,

```
http://www.geocities.com/SiliconValley/Lakes/5147/
```

2.5.4 RealAudio Player

This lets you listen to sound, which is stored in a proprietary format, in real time over the Internet without downloading the whole sound file first. It could be used stand alone, but it is really intended to be used along with a web browser (the explicitly supported ones are Mosaic and Netscape). It cannot be used without X (you wouldn't be able to get it working with Lynx in a text console).

This is by Progressive Networks, Inc. This cannot be redistributed, modified etc. Look at the license for exact details on what you can do. It can be obtained by registering with no cost at the RealAudio home page,

```
http://www.realaudio.com/
```

2.5.5 `cat`

One might think what `cat`, the sometimes overused concatenating utility, has to do with playing sounds. I'll show a use of it through an example.

```
$ cat sample.voc > /dev/dsp
$ cat sample.wav > /dev/dsp
$ cat sample.au > /dev/audio
```

Doing a `cat` of an `.au` file to `/dev/audio` will usually work, and if you're lucky enough that the file has the correct byte order (for your platform) etc., a `cat` of a sound file that uses PCM samples (like `.wav` or `.voc`) to `/dev/dsp` might even sound right.

This isn't a totally useless use of `cat`. It might be useful, for example, if you have a sound file that none of your programs recognize, and you know that it uses PCM samples, then you might be able to get a very approximate idea on how it sounds like this way (if you're lucky).

3 Other useful sound utilities

This section has nothing to do with the actual playing of sound files. Rather, it is a collection of some sound utilities that one might find useful.

3.1 volume

This is a simple command line interface for controlling the volume (what else could it be?). It also has a separate program with a Tcl/Tk interface included in the package for controlling the volume and playing `.au` sound files. A very simple Tcl/Tk CD player is also included.

This is Freeware and it is written by Sam Lantinga (`slouken@cs.ucdavis.edu`).

It can be obtained by anonymous FTP from `sunsite.unc.edu` at `/pub/Linux/apps/sound/soundcard/volume-2.1.tar.gz`.

3.2 Sound Studio

This is a Tcl/Tk application that supports playback, recording, and editing of digital sound using `sox`. It includes `sox` in the distribution to avoid compatibility problems.

This was written by Paul Sharpe and N. J. Bailey (`N.J.Bailey@leeds.ac.uk`). It may be freely used and redistributed if a postcard is sent.

It can be found at Sound Studio's home page,

```
http://www.elec-eng.leeds.ac.uk/staff/een6njb/Software/Studio/screens.html
```

3.3 Tickle Music

This beta Tcl/Tk program is a music file browser that allows you to play various sound formats as long as an appropriate program to play it is on your system. By default `gmod` is used for playing MOD files and `mp` for playing MIDI files (you can change the source to use other programs).

It is written and copyrighted by Shannon Hendrix (`shendrix@pcs.cnu.edu` or `shendrix@escape.widomaker.com`).

It can be obtained by anonymous FTP from `sunsite.unc.edu` at `/pub/Linux/apps/sound/players/tmusic-1.0.tar.gz`.

4 References

1. The documentation included with the applications in this document.
2. The Linux Sound HOWTO. It can be found at http://sunsite.unc.edu/LDP/.
3. The Linux MIDI and Sound Pages, http://www.digiserve.com/ar/linux-snd/.
4. MPEG Audio Layer 3 FAQ, http://www.iis.fhg.de/departs/amm/layer3/sw/.
5. Programmer's Guide to OSS, http://www.4front-tech.com/pguide/.
6. SoX home page, http://www.spies.com/Sox/.

Part XLVIII

“SRM Firmware HOWTO” by David Mosberger,

davidm@azstarnet.com

Contents

Abstract

v0.5, 17 August 1996
This document describes how to boot Linux/Alpha using the SRM firmware, which is the firmware normally used to boot DEC Unix. Generally, it is preferable to use MILO instead of aboot since MILO is perfectly adapted to the needs of Linux. However, MILO is not always available for a particular system, and MILO does not presently have the ability to boot over the network. In either case, using the SRM console may be the right solution.

Unless you're interested in technical details, you may want to skip right to Section 3.

1 How Does SRM Boot an OS?

All versions of SRM can boot from SCSI disks and the versions for recent platforms, such as the Noname or AlphaStations can boot from floppy disks as well. Network booting via `bootp` is supported. Note that older SRM versions (notably the one for the Jensen) *cannot* boot from floppy disks. Also, booting from IDE disk drives is unsupported.

Booting Linux with SRM is a two-step process: first, SRM loads and transfers control to the secondary bootstrap loader. Then the secondary bootstrap loader sets up the environment for Linux, reads the kernel image from a disk file system and finally transfers control to Linux.

Currently, there are two secondary bootstrap loaders for Linux: the raw loader that comes with the Linux kernel and `aboot` which is distributed separately. These two loaders are described in more detail below.

1.1 Loading The Secondary Bootstrap Loader

SRM knows nothing about file systems or disk partitions. It simply expects that the secondary bootstrap loader occupies a consecutive range of physical disk sector, starting from a given offset. The information on the size of the secondary bootstrap loader and the offset of its first disk sector is stored in the first 512-byte sector. Specifically, the long integer at offset 480 stores the size of the secondary bootstrap loader (in 512-byte blocks), and the long at offset 488 gives the sector number at which the secondary bootstrap loader starts. The first sector also stores a flag-word at offset 496 which is always 0 and a checksum at offset 504. The checksum is simply the sum of the first 63 long integers in the first sector.

If the checksum in the first sector is correct, SRM goes ahead and reads the size sectors starting from the sector given in the sector number field and places them in virtual memory at address `0x20000000`. If the reading completes successfully, SRM performs a jump to address `0x20000000`.

2 The Raw Loader

The sources for this loader can be found in directory

```
linux/arch/alpha/boot
```

of the Linux kernel source distribution. It loads the Linux kernel by reading `START_SIZE` bytes starting at disk offset `BOOT_SIZE+512` (also in bytes). The constants `START_SIZE` and `BOOT_SIZE` are defined in `linux/include/asm-alpha/system.h`. `START_SIZE` must be at least as big as the kernel image (i.e., the size of the `.text`, `.data`, and `.bss` segments). Similarly, `BOOT_SIZE` must be at least as big as the image of the raw bootstrap loader. Both constants should be an integer multiple of the sector size, which is 512 bytes. The default values are currently 2MB for `START_SIZE` and 16KB for `BOOT_SIZE`. Note that if you want to boot from a 1.44MB floppy disk, you have to reduce `START_SIZE` to 1400KB and make sure that the kernel you want to boot is no bigger than that.

To build a raw loader, simply type `make rawboot` in `/usr/src/linux`. This should produce the following files in `arch/alpha/boot`:

`tools/lxboot`:
: The first sector on the disk. It contains the offset and size of the next file in the format described above.

`tools/bootlx`:
: The raw boot loader that will load the file below.

`vmlinux.nh`:
: The raw kernel image consisting of the `.text`, `.data`, and `.bss` segments of the object file in `/usr/src/linux/vmlinux`. The extension `.nh` indicates that this file has no object-file header.

The concatenation of these three files should be written to the disk from which you want to boot. For example, to boot from a floppy, insert an empty floppy disk in, say, `/dev/fd0` and then type:

```
cat tools/lxboot tools/bootlx vmlinux >/dev/fd0
```

You can then shutdown the system and boot from the floppy by issuing the command `boot dva0`.

3 The `aboot` Loader

When using the SRM firmware, `aboot` is the preferred way of booting Linux. It supports:

- direct booting from various file systems (`ext2`, `ISO9660`, and `UFS`, the DEC Unix file system);
- booting of executable object files (both ELF and ECOFF);
- booting compressed kernels;
- network booting (using bootp);
- partition tables in DEC Unix format (which is compatible with BSD Unix partition tables)l
- interactive booting and default configurations for SRM consoles that cannot pass long option strings.

3.1 Getting and Building aboot

The latest sources for `aboot` are available from ftp://ftp.azstarnet.com/pub/linux/axp/aboot/. The description in this manual applies to `aboot` version 0.5 or newer.

Once you download and extract the latest tar file, take a look at the `README` and `INSTALL` files for installation hints. In particular, be sure to adjust the variables in `Makefile` and in `include/config.h` to match your environment. Normally, you won't need to change anything when building under Linux, but it is always a good idea to double check. If you're satisfied with the configuration, simply type `make` to build it (if you're not building under Linux, be advised that `aboot` requires GNU `make`).

After running `make`, the `aboot` directory should contain the following files:

aboot

This is the actual `aboot` executable (either an ECOFF or ELF object file).

bootlx

Same as above, but it contains only the text, data and bss segments—that is, this file is not an object file.

sdisklabel/writeboot

Utility to install `aboot` on a hard disk.

tools/e2writeboot

Utility to install `aboot` on an ext2 file system (usually used for floppies only).

tools/isomarkboot

Utility to install `aboot` on a iso9660 file system (used by CD-ROM distributors).

tools/abootconf

Utility to configure an installed `aboot`.

3.2 Floppy Installation

The boot loader can be installed on a floppy using the `e2writeboot` command (note: this can't be done on a Jensen since its firmware does not support booting from floppy). This command requires that the disk is not overly fragmented as it needs to find enough contiguous file blocks to store the entire `aboot` image (currently about 90KB). If `e2writeboot` fails because of this, reformat the floppy and try again (e.g., with `fdformat(1)`). For example, the following steps install `aboot` on floppy disk assuming the floppy is in drive `/dev/fd0`:

```
fdformat /dev/fd0
mke2fs /dev/fd0
e2writeboot /dev/fd0 bootlx
```

3.3 Hard disk Installation

Since the `e2writeboot` command may fail on highly fragmented disks, and since reformatting a hard disk is not without pain, it is generally safer to install `aboot` on a hard disk using the `swriteboot` command. `swriteboot` requires that the first few sectors be reserved for booting purposes. We suggest that the disk be partitioned such that the first partition starts at an offset of 2048 sectors. This leaves 1MB of space for storing `aboot`. On a properly partitioned disk, it is then possible to install `aboot` as follows (assuming the disk is `/dev/sda`):

```
swriteboot /dev/sda bootlx
```

On a Jensen, you will want to leave more space, since you need to write a kernel to this place, too—2MB should be sufficient when using compressed kernels. Use `swriteboot` as described in Section 3.6 to write `bootlx` together with the Linux kernel.

3.4 CD-ROM Installation

To make a CD-ROM bootable by SRM, simply build `aboot` as described above. Then, make sure that the `bootlx` file is present on the iso9660 file system (e.g., copy `bootlx` to the directory that is the file system master, then run `mkisofs` on that directory). After that, all that remains to be done is to mark the file system as SRM bootable. This is achieved with a command of the form:

```
isomarkboot ⟨file-system⟩ bootlx
```

The command above assumes that *file-system* is a file containing the ISO 9660 file system and that `bootlx` has been copied into the root directory of that file system.

3.5 Building the Linux Kernel

A bootable Linux kernel can be built with the following steps. During the `make config`, be sure to answer "yes" to the question whether you want to boot the kernel via SRM.

```
cd /usr/src/linux
make config
make dep
make boot
```

The last command will build the file `arch/alpha/boot/vmlinux.gz`, which can then be copied to the disk from which you want to boot from. In our floppy disk example above, this would entail:

```
mount /dev/fd0 /mnt
cp arch/alpha/boot/vmlinux.gz /mnt
umount /mnt
```

3.6 Booting Linux

With the SRM firmware and `aboot` installed, Linux is generally booted with a command of the form:

```
boot ⟨devicename⟩ -fi ⟨filename⟩ -fl ⟨flags⟩
```

The *filename* and *flags* arguments are optional. If they are not specified, SRM uses the default values stored in environment variables `BOOT_OSFILE` and `BOOT_OSFLAGS`. The syntax and meaning of these two arguments is described in more detail below.

3.6.1 Boot Filename

The filename argument takes the form:

[*n*/]*filename*

n is a single digit in the range 1..8 that gives the partition number from which to boot from. *filename* is the path of the file you want boot. For example, to boot from the second partition of SCSI device 6, you would enter:

```
boot dka600 -file 2/vmlinux.gz
```

To boot from floppy drive 0,

```
boot dva0 -file vmlinux.gz
```

If a disk has no partition table, `aboot` pretends that the disk contains one `ext2` partition starting at the first disk block. This allows booting from floppy disks.

As a special case, partition number 0 is used to request booting from a disk that does not (yet) contain a file system. When specifying "partition" number 0, `aboot` assumes that the Linux kernel is stored right behind the `aboot` image. Such a layout can be achieved with the `swriteboot` command. For example, to set up a file system-less boot from `/dev/sda`, one could use the command:

```
swriteboot /dev/sda bootlx vmlinux.gz
```

Booting a system in this way is not normally necessary. The reason this feature exists is to make it possible to get Linux installed on a systems that can't boot from a floppy disk (e.g., the Jensen).

3.6.2 Boot Flags

A number of bootflags can be specified. The syntax is:

```
-flags "options..."
```

Where "options..." is any combination the following options (separated by blanks). There are many more boot options, depending on what drivers your kernel has installed. The options listed below are therefore just examples to illustrate the general idea:

load_ramdisk=1

Copy root file system from a (floppy) disk to the RAM disk before starting the system. The RAM disk will be used in lieu of the root device. This is useful to bootstrap Linux on a system with only one floppy drive.

floppy=*str*

Sets floppy configuration to *str*.

root=*dev*

Select device *dev* as the root file system. The device can be specified as a major/minor hex number (e.g., 0x802 for /dev/sda2) or one of a few canonical names (e.g., `/dev/fd0`, `/dev/sda2`).

single

Boot system in single user mode.

kgdb

Enable kernel-gdb (works only if `CONFIG_KGDB` is enabled; a second Alpha system needs to be connected over the serial port in order to make this work)

Some SRM implementations (e.g., the one for the Jensen) are handicapped and allow only short option strings (e.g., at most 8 characters). In such a case, `aboot` can be booted with the single-character boot flag "i." With this flag, `aboot` will prompt the user to interactively enter a boot option string of up to 256 characters. For example:

```
boot dka0 -fl i
aboot> 3/vmlinux.gz root=/dev/sda3 single
```

Since booting in that manner quickly becomes tedious, `aboot` allows shortcuts for frequently used command lines. In particular, a single digit option (0-9) requests that `aboot` uses the corresponding option string stored in file `/etc/aboot.conf`. A sample `aboot.conf` is shown below:

```
#
# aboot default configurations
#
0:3/vmlinux.gz root=/dev/sda3
1:3/vmlinux.gz root=/dev/sda3 single
2:3/vmlinux.new.gz root=/dev/sda3
3:3/vmlinux root=/dev/sda3
8:- root=/dev/sda3              # fs-less boot of raw kernel
9:0/vmlinux.gz root=/dev/sda3 # fs-less boot of (compressed) ECOFF kernel
-
```

With this configuration file, the command

```
boot dka0 -fl 1
```

corresponds exactly to the boot command shown above. It is quite easy to forget what number corresponds to what option string. To alleviate this problem, boot with option "h" and `aboot` will print the contents of `/etc/aboot.conf` before issuing the prompt for the full option string.

Finally, whenever `aboot` prompts for an option string, it is possible to enter one of the single character flags ("i," "h," or "0"–"9") to get the same effect as if that flag had been specified in the boot command line. For example, you could boot with flag "i" and then type "h" (followed by return) to remind yourself of the contents of `/etc/aboot.conf`

Selecting the Partition of `/etc/aboot.conf` When installed on a hard disk, aboot needs to know what partition to search for the /etc/aboot.conf file. A newly compiled aboot will search the *second* partition (e.g., /dev/sda2). Since it would be inconvenient to have to recompile aboot just to change the partition number, abootconf allows to directly modify an installed aboot. Specifically, if you want to change aboot to use the third partition on disk /dev/sda, you'd use the command:

```
abootconf /dev/sda 3
```

You can verify the current setting by simply omitting the partition number. That is: abootconf /dev/sda will print the currently selected partition number. Note that aboot does have to be installed already for this command to succeed. Also, when installing a new aboot, the partition number will fall back to the default (i.e., it will be necessary to rerun abootconf).

Since aboot version 0.5, it is also possible to select the aboot.conf partition via the boot command line. This can be done with a command line of the form *a*:*b* where *a* is the partition that holds /etc/aboot.conf and *b* is a single-letter option as described above (0-9, i, or h). For example, if you type boot -fl "3:h" dka100 the system boots from SCSI ID 1, loads /etc/aboot.conf from the third partition, prints its contents on the screen and waits for you to enter the boot options.

3.7 Booting Over the Network

Two preliminary steps are necessary before Linux can be booted via a network. First, you need to set the SRM environment variables to enable booting via the bootp protocol, and second, you need to set up another machine as the your boot server. Please refer to the SRM documentation that came with your machine for information on how to enable bootp. Setting up the boot server is obviously dependent on what operating system that machine is running, but typically it involves starting the program bootpd in the background after configuring the /etc/bootptab file. The bootptab file has one entry describing each client that is allowed to boot from the server. For example, if you want to boot the machine myhost.cs.arizona.edu, then an entry of the following form would be needed:

```
myhost.cs.arizona.edu:\
        :hd=/remote/:bf=vmlinux.bootp:\
        :ht=ethernet:ha=08012B1C51F8:hn:vm=rfc1048:\
        :ip=192.12.69.254:bs=auto:
```

This entry assumes that the machine's Ethernet address is 08012B1C51F8 and that its IP address is 192.12.69.254. The Ethernet address can be found with the show device command of the SRM console or, if Linux is running, with the ifconfig command. The entry also defines that if the client does not specify otherwise, the file that will be booted is vmlinux.bootp in directory /remote. For more information on configuring bootpd, please refer to its manual page.

Next, build aboot with with the command make netboot. Make sure the kernel that you want to boot has been built already. By default, the aboot Makefile uses the kernel in /usr/src/linux/arch/alpha/boot/vmlinux.gz (edit the Makefile if you want to use a different path). The result of make netboot is a file called vmlinux.bootp which contains aboot and the Linux kernel, ready for network booting.

Finally, copy vmlinux.bootp to the boot server's directory. In the example above, you'd copy it into /remote/vmlinux.bootp. Next, power up the client machine and boot it, specifying the Ethernet adapter as the boot device. Typically, SRM calls the first Ethernet adapter ewa0, so to boot from that device, you'd use the command:

```
boot ewa0
```

The -fi and -fl options can be used as usual. In particular, you can ask aboot to prompt for Linux kernel arguments by specifying the option -fl i.

4 Sharing a Disk With DEC Unix

Unfortunately, DEC Unix doesn't know anything about Linux, so sharing a single disk between the two OSes is not entirely trivial. However, it is not a difficult task if you heed the tips in this section. The section assumes that you are using aboot version 0.5 or newer.

4.1 Partitioning the disk

First and foremost: *never* use any of the Linux partitioning programs (minlabel or fdisk) on a disk that is also used by DEC Unix. The Linux minlabel program uses the same partition table format as DEC Unix disklabel, but there are some incompatibilities in the data that minlabel fills in, so DEC Unix will simply refuse to accept a partition table generated by minlabel. To set up a Linux ext2 partition under DEC Unix, you'll have to change the disktab entry for your disk. For the purpose of this discussion, let's assume that you have an rz26 disk (a common 1GB drive) on which you want to install Linux. The disktab entry under DEC Unix v3.2 looks like this (see file /etc/disktab):

```
rz26|RZ26|DEC RZ26 Winchester:\
        :ty=winchester:dt=SCSI:ns#57:nt#14:nc#2570:\
        :oa#0:pa#131072:ba#8192:fa#1024:\
        :ob#131072:pb#262144:bb#8192:fb#1024:\
        :oc#0:pc#2050860:bc#8192:fc#1024:\
        :od#393216:pd#552548:bd#8192:fd#1024:\
        :oe#945764:pe#552548:be#8192:fe#1024:\
        :of#1498312:pf#552548:bf#8192:ff#1024:\
        :og#393216:pg#819200:bg#8192:fg#1024:\
        :oh#1212416:ph#838444:bh#8192:fh#1024:
```

The interesting fields here are `o?`, and `p?`, where *?* is a letter in the range `a`–`h` (first through eighth partition). The `o` value gives the starting offset of the partition (in sectors) and the `p` value gives the size of the partition (also in sectors). See `disktab(4)` for more info. Note that DEC Unix likes to define overlapping partitions. For the entry above, the partition layout looks like this (you can verify this by adding up the various `o` and `p` values):

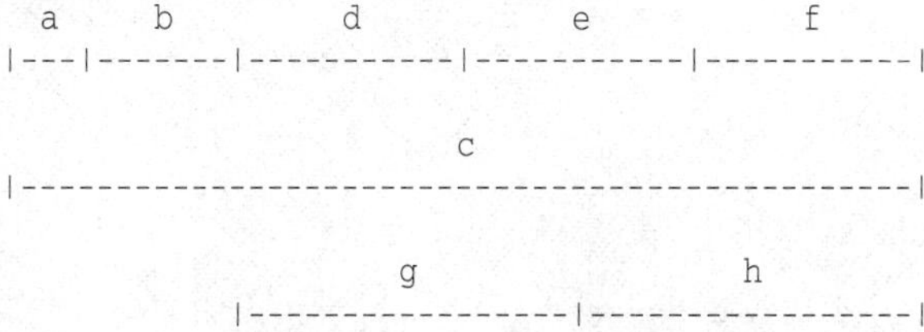

DEC Unix insists that partition `a` starts at offset 0 and that partition `c` spans the entire disk. Other than that, you can set up the partition table any way you like.

Let's suppose that you have DEC Unix using partition `g` and want to install Linux on partition `h` with partition `b` being a (largish) swap partition. To get this layout without destroying the existing DEC Unix partition, you need to set the partition types explicitly. You can do this by adding a `t` field for each partition. In our case, we add the following line to the above disktab entry.

```
:ta=unused:tb=swap:tg=4.2BSD:th=resrvd8:
```

Now why do we mark partition `h` as "reservd8" instead of "ext2"? Well, DEC Unix doesn't know about Linux. It so happens that partition type "ext2" corresponds to a numeric value of 8, and DEC Unix uses the string "reservd8" for that value. Thus, in DEC Unix speak, "reservd8" means "ext2." Okay, this was the hard part. Now we just need to install the updated disktab entry on the disk. Let's assume the disk has SCSI ID 5. In this case, we'd do:

```
disklabel -rw /dev/rrz5c rz26
```

You can verify that everything is all right by reading back the disklabel with `disklabel -r /dev/rrz5c`. At this point, you may want to reboot DEC Unix and make sure the existing DEC Unix partition is still alive and well. If that is the case, you can shut down the machine and start with the Linux installation. Be sure to skip the disk partitioning step during the install. Since we already installed a good partition table, you should be able to proceed and select the 8th partition as the Linux root partition and the 2nd partition as the swap partition. If the disk is, say, the second SCSI disk in the machine, then the device name for these partitions would be `/dev/sdb8` and `/dev/sdb2`, respectively (note that Linux uses letters to name the drives and numbers to name the partitions, which is exactly reversed from what DEC Unix does; the Linux scheme makes more sense, of course.

4.2 Installing `aboot`

First big caveat: with the SRM firmware, you can boot one, and only one, operating system per disk. For this reason, it is generally best to have at least two SCSI disks in a machine that you want to dual boot between Linux and DEC Unix. Of course, you could also boot Linux from a floppy if speed doesn't matter or over the network, if you have a `bootp`-capable server. But in this section we assume you want to boot Linux from a disk that contains one or more DEC Unix partitions.

Second big caveat: installing `aboot` on a disk shared with DEC Unix renders the first and third partition unusable (since those *must* have a starting offset of 0). For this reason, we recommend that you change the size of partition `a` to something that is just big enough to hold `aboot` (1MB should be plenty).

Once these two caveats are taken care of, installing `aboot` is almost as easy as usual: since partition `a` and `c` will overlap with `aboot`, we need to tell `swriteboot` that this is indeed OK. We can do this under Linux with a command line of the following form (again, assuming we're trying to install `aboot` on the second SCSI disk):

```
swriteboot -f1 -f3 /dev/sdb bootlx
```

The `-f1` means that we want to force writing `bootlx` even though it overlaps with partition 1. The corresponding applies for partition 3.

This is it. You should now be able to shutdown the system and boot Linux from the hard disk. In our example, the SRM command line to do this would be:

```
boot dka5 -fi 8/vmlinux.gz -fl root=/dev/sdb8
```

Part XLIX

"TeTeX HOWTO"
by Robert Kiesling,

kiesling@terracom.net

Contents

Abstract

$Id: TeTeX-HOWTO.tex,v 1.7 1998/03/01 16:21:04 rak Exp $
This document covers the basic installation and usage of the teTeX TEX and LATEX implementation, and auxiliary packages like Ghostscript. Contents of the teTeX HOWTO: The Linux-teTeX Local Guide are Copyright (c) 1997 by Robert A. Kiesling. Permission is granted to copy this document, in whole or in part, provided that credit is given to the author and the Linux Documentation Project. Registered trademarks are the property of their respective holders. Please send all complaints, suggestions, errata, and any miscellany to kiesling@terracom.net, so I can keep this document as complete and up to date as possible.

1 Introduction.

FAQ No. 1. My computer just ate NINE high density diskettes' worth of data. WHAT HAPPENED?

Answer: Installing teTeX on my Compaq laptop was like dropping a 20-foot concrete bridge section exactly into place from a height of 50 feet. TeTeX is a *big package.* Even so, it is a moderately complete implementation of TeX 3.1415 and LATEX 2ε for Linux systems. TEX is a big subject anyway, so you can expect to spend the rest of your computing career keeping up-to-date on the latest in the world of TEX. That is to say, installing and using teTeX is not for the faint of heart. Nor is it for daytrippers. This package requires serious quality time.

Thomas Esser, the author of teTeX, has gone to great lengths to make the package fast, complete, and easy to use. Because TEX is implemented for practically every serious computer system in the world – and quite a few "non-serious" ones – implementors must provide the installation facilities for all of them. This accounts in part for teTeX's size. It also accounts for the fact that the pieces necessary to make a workable teTeX installation are spread all over your friendly neighborhood CTAN archive.

CTAN is the Comprehensive TeX Archive Network, a series of anonymous FTP sites which archive TeX programs, macros, fonts, and documentation. You'll probably become familiar with at least one CTAN site. In this document, a pathname like `~CTAN/contrib/pstricks` means "look in the directory `contrib/pstricks` of your nearest CTAN site." See **Appendix A** for a current list of CTAN sites and their mirror sites.

Fortunately, some considerate Linux Distribution implementors have assembled the necessary pieces for us. teTeX comes with all the major Linux distributions.

However, if you don't have the Slackware, Red Hat, or Debian GNU/Linux distribution, you can install teTeX from its official CTAN distribution. In some cases this may be more desirable. See **Section 3** for details.

If you already have teTeX installed on your system and want to jump directly into figuring out how to use it, skip this section and the next, and go directly to section 5.

2 What is TEX? What is LATEX? What is teTeX?

"What is the difference?" you ask.

TeTeX is an implementation of TEX for UNIX systems. It is the work of Thomas Esser, te@informatik.uni-hannover.de. In the Linux versions of teTeX, the executable programs themselves run under Linux and the fonts are provided in form usable by the Linux-teTeX system. (The sections covering teTeX installation concentrate on the i386 versions of Linux. Installing MkLinux or Linux for the Alpha should require only substituting the appropriate binary-program archive in the installation process.) The rest of the code, TEX and LATEX itself, is portable across various machines.

In addition to the executable programs, the distribution includes all of the TEX and LATEX package, metafont and its sources, `bibtex(1)`, `makeindex(1)`, and *all* of the documentation... more than 4 megabytes' worth. The documentation covers everything you will forseeably need to know to get started. So, you should install all of the documents. Not only will you eventually read them, the documents themselves provide many examples of "live" TEX and LATEX code.

In comparison with other implementations of TEX, the installation of teTeX is almost trivial, even without the Linux distribution packages, if you don't count the effort necessary acquire the distributions via anonymous FTP or insert and remove several dozen distribution diskettes by hand. If your teTeX distribution arrived on a CD-ROM, even less effort is required to install it.

TEX is a typesetting system developed by Professor Donald Knuth of Stanford University. It is a lower-level typesetting language that powers all of the higher-level packages like LATEX. Essentially, LATEX is a set of TEX macros which provide convenient, predefined document formats for end users. If you like the formats provided by LaTeX, you may never need to learn bare-bones TEX programming. The difference between the two languages is like the difference between assembly language and C. You can have the speed and flexibility of TEX, or the convenience of LATEX. Which brings us to the next answer,

Answer: You have it backwards! I want to know what exactly I need to get before I can have TEX on my system!

It's important to remember that TEX only handles the typesetting part of the document preparation. Generating output with TEX is like compiling source code into object code, which still needs to be linked. You prepare an input file with a text editor – what most people think of as "word processing" – and typeset the input file document with TEX to produce a device-independent output file, called a `.dvi` file.

You also need output drivers for your printer and video display. These output drivers translate TEX's `.dvi` output to display your typeset document on the screen or on paper. This software is collectively known as "dviware." For example, TeX itself only makes requests for fonts. It is up to the `.dvi` output translator to provide the actual font to the display device if necessary, regardless of whether it is the screen or a printer. This extra step may seem overly complicated, but the abstraction allows documents to display the same on different devices with no change to the original document.

In fact, much of TEX's, and therefore LATEX's, complexity, arises from its implementation of various font systems, and the way these fonts are specified. A major improvement of LATEX 2ε over its predecessor was the way users specify fonts, the former New Font Selection Scheme. (See **Section 6.**)

TeTeX comes distributed with about a dozen standard fonts preloaded, which is enough to get you started. Also provided are the font metrics descriptions, in `.tfm` (TEX font metric) files. To generate the other fonts you will need, it is simply a matter of installing the `metafont` sources. Tetex's `.dvi` utilities will invoke `metafont` automatically and generate the Computer Modern fonts you need, on-the-fly.

By the way, the letters of the word "TeX" are Greek, tau-epsilon-chi. This is *not* a fraternity. Instead, it is the root of the Greek word, *techne,* which means art and/or science. (The and/or construct is itself untranslatable, unless the destination language is Japanese.) "TeX" is not pronounced like the first syllable in "Texas." The *chi* has no English equivalent, but TEX is generally pronounced so that it rhymes with "yecch," to use Professor Knuth's example from *The TeXBook* (see below). When writing, "TeX," on character devices, always use the standard capitalization, or the `\TeX{}` macro in typesetting. This is how TEX is distinguished from other typesetting systems.

Speaking of typing, any of the editors which work under Linux— `nvi(1)`, `jed(1)`, `joe(1)`, `jove(1)`, `vi(1)`, `vim(1)`, `stevie(1)`, `emacs(1)`, microemacs— will work to prepare a TEX input file, as long as the editor reads and writes plain-vanilla ASCII text. My preference is `emacs(1)`, the GNU version. There are several reasons for this:

- Emacs' TEX and LATEX modes obviate the need for a stand-alone TEX shell.
- Emacs can automatically insert TEX-style, "curly quotes," as you type, rather than the "ASCII-vanilla" kind.
- Emacs has integrated support for `texinfo` and `makeinfo`, a hypertext documentation system.
- Emacs is widely supported. Version 19.34, for example, is included in the major U.S. Linux distributions.
- Emacs does everything except butter the toast in the morning. Version 20.2, which is being added to the standard Linux distributions at this time, is even more capable.
- Emacs is free.

There's a lot of software to assemble. In the meantime, you can start in "learning" TEX and LATEX. Remember that teTeX and the font packages have been designed as two separate entities: The teTeX executable programs and shell scripts, as distributed with Linux, have been built specifically for the system, but the CM, DC, American Mathematical Society, or other font distributions work on many different platforms. While you are working on assembling the files, you can take a few breaks to locate some of the documentation you will need.

2.1 Resources for further information.

There are user manuals available both commercially and via the Internet. Judging by the number of mentions they receive in the Usenet `comp.text.tex` newsgroup, the most useful – and definitive – commercially available texts for beginners are:

LaTeX: A Document Preparation System, by Leslie Lamport, 272 pp. If you're using LATEX instead of plain TEX (highly recommended), this is the definitive reference.

If you must use plain TeX, *The TeXBook* by Donald Knuth, 483 pp., is the definitive reference. It is also necessary if you plan to do any serious class, package, or macro writing for LaTeX.

The LaTeX Companion, by Michel Goosens, Frank Mittelbach, and Alexander Samarin, 530 pp., is more advanced than the Lamport, above. If you are approaching TeX or LaTeX for the first time, you may feel lost reading this. (I was.) However, when you need to add extension packages, like PSNFSS (See **Section 6.**) or `bibtex(1)`, a bibliography indexing program, this book is one of the most highly regarded on the market.

At your nearest CTAN site you can retrieve these documents for free:

The Not So Short Introduction to LATEX 2epsilon, by Tobias Oetiker, Hubert Partl, Irene Hyna, and Elisabeth Schlegl, 69 pp. This wonderful document is located at `~CTAN/packages/TeX/info/lshort/*`.

You can get a PostScript or `.dvi` version of the document ready for printing, or the native LaTeX document. There is also a version available in German: `lkurz.*`. Make sure to read the `README` file before assembling!

Late news flash: a French translation has been released, available at the same locations above.

A Gentle Introduction to TeX: A Manual for Self-Study, by Michael Doob, 91 pp. You can find this document at: `~CTAN:packages/TeX/info/gentle.tex`. Almost of necessity, this document covers less ground than its LaTeX counterpart, above. However, it will get you to the same place as the LaTeX manuals. If you must use plain TeX for your documents, this document clarifies many of the complexities of plain TeX and makes its use almost easy.

The LaTeX Catalogue is a `bibtex(1)` database of available LaTeX packages, compiled and maintained by Graham Williams. It's included with teTeX, and the most recent version is available on the World Wide Web. Do you need a package that prints borders, or makes margin notes? You'll find that the package you need is listed here. *The LaTeX Catalogue* is located in your local teTeX library in the directory `teTeX/texmf/doc/Catalog`, and on the Web at http://cbr.dit.csiro.au/~gjw. See Section 5.3 for further details about LaTeX packages.

Thomas Merz's *Ghostscript Manual,* which is the Ghostscript appendix of his book, *PostScript & Acrobat/PDF: Applications, Troubleshooting, and Cross-Platform Publishing.* It is available from the Ghostscript Home Page (see section 3.2), or from Merz's home page, http://www.muc.de/~tm/.

There are, of course, other guides available to using TeX and LaTeX. They cover different aspects of these systems to varying degrees. The reference documents cited above, however, are the most comprehensive in scope that I have seen and are aimed at beginners (or near-beginners).

If the going gets especially tough, you can probably do a little extra shopping at Office Max, Office Depot, Staples, or your local stationer, and pick up several reams of three-hole punched, photocopy paper, two or three, three-inch binders, and some index tabs. When it comes time to print the documents, you'll need a place to keep them, and they seem to be more useful if they are kept on paper. This must be one of the stranger phenomena of technical documentation.

You will note, however, that the references mentioned above are hardware-independent. They won't tell you a thing about running teTeX specifically. Many of them, in fact, refer to some mythical *"Local Guide."* This, and several of the documents that come bundled with teTeX, comprise the less-than-mythical *Local Guide* to installing and operating teTeX with Linux.

3 Installation notes.

All of the major Linux distributions include packaged versions of teTeX, and each distribution has its own idiosyncracies. The packaging methods of each distribution are, for the most part, incompatible. You'll probably succeed in installing the package, but you're certain to mess up the package-management database on your system. The exception is Debian GNU/Linux, which in Version 1.3.1 supports RedHat and Slackware package formats.

The generic, CTAN distribution isn't any harder to install than the Linux packages. See section 3.1, below.

You should consider installing the generic teTeX distribution if:

- Your system isn't based on one of the standard Linux distributions.
- You don't have root privileges on your system.
- You want or need to have the very latest version of teTeX.
- You don't have enough disk space available for a full installation.
- You want to install teTeX somewhere instead of the `/usr` file system.
- You would like to share your teTeX installation with other UNIX variants or platforms on a network. In this case, you should strongly consider installing from the *source* distribution. See section 3.1.2, below.
- You want the latest versions of teTeX's public domain Type 1 fonts, which are significantly better than the fonts included in earlier releases.

In order to conserve space, and to prevent this HOWTO from becoming moribund, I'll cover in detail only the installation of the generic teTeX distribution. Installing the standard distribution packages is mostly a matter of running the package management software, after which you can proceed directly to the section on configuring teTeX, below.

A complete installation of the binary distribution requires 40–50 Mb of disk space, and building the distribution from the source code takes about 75 Mb, so you should make sure that the disk space is available before you start. You don't need to have the `gcc(1)` compiler or the X Window System installed (although X certainly helps because it is much easier to preview documents on-screen). All you need is an editor that is capable of producing plain ASCII, text (see Section 2). What could be simpler?

Ghostscript V. 5.03 allows printing of PostScript documents on non-PostScript printers, and allows previewing of PostScript documents on VGA monitors and X Window System displays. If you already have a PostScript printer, you won't need Ghostscript simply to print PostScript documents. Ghostscript has many other capabilities, however, which are beyond the scope of this HOWTO.

APSFILTER can automate document post processing and printing, and generally make life with your printer a lot easier. See Section 3.3.

For information on how to install a printer daemon and generally configure printers for Linux, see section 3.4, and consult the Printing HOWTO.

3.1 Generic CTAN distribution, V. 0.4.

You can retrieve the files from one of the CTAN archives listed in Section 8. In the examples below, the files were retrieved from the CTAN archive at ftp.tex.ac.uk.

3.1.1 Installing the binary distribution.

Minimal installation. First, FTP to ftp.tex.ac.uk and `cd` to the directory

```
ctan/tex-archive/systems/unix/teTeX/distrib/
```

Retrieve the files

```
INSTALL.bin
install.sh
```

and place them in the top-level directory where you want to install teTeX, for example, `/var/teTeX` if you plan to install teTeX in the `/var` file system.

Print out the `INSTALL.bin` file. Keep this file handy, because it describes how to install a minimal teTeX installation. The minimal installation requires only 10–15 Mb of disk space, but it is recommended that you install the complete teTeX package if at all possible. For a minimum installation, you'll need the files

```
ctan/tex-archive/systems/unix/teTeX/distrib/base/latex-base.tar.gz
ctan/tex-archive/systems/unix/teTeX/distrib/base/tetex-base.tar.gz
```

You'll also need one of two archives which contain the executable teTeX programs. Retrieve the archive file

```
ctan/tex-archive/systems/unix/teTeX/distrib/binaries/i386-linux.tar.gz
```

if your system uses the Linux ELF shared libraries, `ld.so(1)` of at least version 1.73, and clibs of at least version 5.09. If it doesn't, retrieve the archive

```
ctan/tex-archive/systems/unix/teTeX/distrib/binaries/i386-linuxaout.tar.gz
```

which is compiled for systems that use the older a.out-format static libraries.

Then, following the instructions in the file `INSTALL.bin`, execute the command

```
sh ./install.sh
```

while in the top-level teTeX installation directory. (Make sure that the teTeX archives are located there, too.) After a few moments the installation program will warn you that you are missing some of the teTeX packages. However, if you're planning only a minimal teTeX installation, you should ignore the warnings and proceed. To configure the basic teTeX system, see section 3.1.1, below.

To install the remaining packages, see the next section.

Complete installation. To perform a complete teTeX installation, retrieve the archive files listed in the previous section, as well as the following files:

```
ctan/tex-archive/systems/unix/teTeX/distrib/doc/ams-doc.tar.gz
ctan/tex-archive/systems/unix/teTeX/distrib/doc/bibtex-doc.tar.gz
ctan/tex-archive/systems/unix/teTeX/distrib/doc/eplain-doc.tar.gz
ctan/tex-archive/systems/unix/teTeX/distrib/doc/fonts-doc.tar.gz
ctan/tex-archive/systems/unix/teTeX/distrib/doc/general-doc.tar.gz
ctan/tex-archive/systems/unix/teTeX/distrib/doc/generic-doc.tar.gz
ctan/tex-archive/systems/unix/teTeX/distrib/doc/latex-doc.tar.gz
ctan/tex-archive/systems/unix/teTeX/distrib/doc/makeindex-doc.tar.gz
ctan/tex-archive/systems/unix/teTeX/distrib/doc/metapost-doc.tar.gz
ctan/tex-archive/systems/unix/teTeX/distrib/doc/programs-doc.tar.gz
ctan/tex-archive/systems/unix/teTeX/distrib/fonts/ams-fonts.tar.gz
ctan/tex-archive/systems/unix/teTeX/distrib/fonts/dc-fonts.tar.gz
```

```
ctan/tex-archive/systems/unix/teTeX/distrib/fonts/ec-fonts.tar.gz
ctan/tex-archive/systems/unix/teTeX/distrib/fonts/misc-fonts.tar.gz
ctan/tex-archive/systems/unix/teTeX/distrib/fonts/postscript-fonts.tar.gz
ctan/tex-archive/systems/unix/teTeX/distrib/fonts/sauter-fonts.tar.gz
ctan/tex-archive/systems/unix/teTeX/distrib/goodies/amstex.tar.gz
ctan/tex-archive/systems/unix/teTeX/distrib/goodies/bibtex.tar.gz
ctan/tex-archive/systems/unix/teTeX/distrib/goodies/eplain.tar.gz
ctan/tex-archive/systems/unix/teTeX/distrib/goodies/latex-extra.tar.gz
ctan/tex-archive/systems/unix/teTeX/distrib/goodies/metapost.tar.gz
ctan/tex-archive/systems/unix/teTeX/distrib/goodies/pictex.tar.gz
ctan/tex-archive/systems/unix/teTeX/distrib/goodies/pstricks.tar.gz
ctan/tex-archive/systems/unix/teTeX/distrib/goodies/texdraw.tar.gz
ctan/tex-archive/systems/unix/teTeX/distrib/goodies/xypic.tar.gz
```

All of these files should be placed in the top-level directory where you want teTeX to reside. As with the minimal installation, execute the command

```
sh ./install.sh
```

Base system configuration. The `install.sh` script, after determining which teTeX archive series are present, will present you with a menu of options. The only setting you need to make at this point is to set the top-level directory where you want teTeX installed, by selecting the "D" option. You must, of course, choose a directory in whose parent directory you have write permissions. For example, if you are installing teTeX in your home directory, you would specify the teTeX installation directory as

```
/home/john.q.public/teTeX
```

and, after returning to the main menu, select "I" to proceed with the installation. Note that the directory must not exist already: the `install.sh` script must be able to create it.

An option which you should consider enabling, is setting an alternative directory for generated fonts. Even if you plan to use only PostScript fonts, occasionally you'll process a file that requires the Computer Modern fonts. Enabling this option requires that you enter the directory to use. You must have write permissions for the parent directory. Following the example above, you could specify

```
/home/john.q.public/texfonts
```

or, if you want the generated fonts to be accessible by all users on the system, specify a directory like

```
/var/texfonts
```

I would recommend that you *not,* however, use the default `/var/tmp/texfonts` directory for this option, because the generated fonts could be deleted after the next reboot, and the fonts will need to be generated again the next time they're needed. After you've selected the option "I," and `install.sh` has installed the archives, set various permissions, and generated its links and format files, the program will exit with a message telling you to add the teTeX binary directory to your `$PATH` environment variable, and the directories where the man pages and info files reside to your `$MANPATH` and `$INFOPATH` environment variables. For example, add the statements

```
export PATH=$PATH:"/home/john.q.public/teTeX/bin"
export MANPATH=$MANPATH":/home/john.q.public/teTeX/man"
export INFOPATH$=INFOPATH":/home/john.q.public/teTeX/info"
```

to your `~/.bash_profile` if you use `bash(1)` as your shell, or to your `~/.profile` if you use another shell for logins.

Log out, and then log in again, so the environment variables are registered. Then, run the command

```
texconfig confall
```

to insure that the installation is correct.

Next, you can configure teTeX for you specific hardware. See Section 4, below.

3.1.2 Installing the source distribution.

To install teTeX V. 0.4 from the source code, FTP to a CTAN site like ftp://ftp.tex.ac.uk and retrieve the files

```
ctan/tex-archive/systems/unix/teTeX/distrib/INSTALL.src
ctan/tex-archive/systems/unix/teTeX/distrib/sources/README.texmf-src
ctan/tex-archive/systems/unix/teTeX/distrib/sources/teTeX-lib-0.4pl8.tar.gz
```

ctan/tex-archive/systems/unix/teTeX/distrib/sources/teTeX-src-0.4pl7.tar.gz

Read over the instructions in INSTALL.src, then su to root and unpack the files in a directory for which you have read-write-execute permissions.

Remember to use the p argument to tar(1), and also remember to unset the noclobber option of bash(1). You can do this with the counterintuitive command

```
set +o noclobber
```

Note that the argument +o to set *un*sets a variable, just exactly backwards from what you might expect.

The file teTeX-lib-0.4pl8.tar.gz will create the directory ./teTeX. The file teTeX-src-0.4pl7.tar.gz will create the directory teTeX-src-0.4 Print out the file INSTALL.src and keep it nearby for the following steps. cd to the ./teTeX-src-0.4 directory, and, per the instructions in the INSTALL.src file, edit ./Makefile. You need to set the TETEXDIR variable to the absolute path of the parent teTeX directory. This will be the subdirectory teTeX of the directory where you unpacked the source and library archives. For example, if you unpacked the archives in your home directory, you would set TETEXDIR to

```
/home/john.q.public/teTeX
```

The rest of the Makefile options are pretty generic. With gcc(1) version 2.7.2 and later, you should not need to make any further adjustments unless you have a non-standard compiler and library setup, or want the compiler to perform some further optimizations, or for some other reason. Check that the USE_DIALOG, USE_NCURSES, and HAVE_NCURSES variables are set correctly for your system, because the dialog program needs the ncurses library to be installed. A ncurses(3x) library is included in the source distribution, so the default values in the Makefile should work fine. If you can't get ncurses(3x) to compile or link, texconfig(1) can also be run from the command line.

If you've done everything correctly up to this point, you should be able to type make world in the top-level source directory, and relax until the teTeX executables are built. This can take a few hours.

After the build has completed, set the evironment variables $PATH, $MANPATH, $INFOPATH to include the teTeX directories. The statements which would be added to the file .bash_profile, in the example, above, would be

```
export PATH=$PATH":/home/john.q.public/teTeX/bin/i386-linux"
export MANPATH=$MANPATH":/home/john.q.public/teTeX/man"
export INFOPATH=$INFOPATH":/home/john.q.public/teTeX/info"
```

The $PATH variable is different in the source distribution than in the binary distribution. Note that here the path to the binaries is teTeX/bin/i386-linux instead of simply teTeX/bin as in the binary distribution.

At this point you can run texconfig confall to ensure that the paths have been set correctly, and then proceed to configure teTeX as in the binary distribution. See the Section 4, below.

3.2 Ghostscript V. 5.03.

Ghostscript development is rapid, and the changes which are incorporated into every new version are significant. Therefore, it's worth the effort to install the version of Ghostscript that is available on its home page, http://www.cs.wisc.edu/˜ghost.

At the time of this writing, the current version is 5.03. The Ghostscript archive for Linux is composed of the following files:

```
ghostscript-5.03gnu.tar.gz
ghostscript-5.03jpeg.tar.gz
ghostscript-5.03libpng.tar.gz
ghostscript-5.03zlib.tar.gz
ghostscript-fonts-std-5.03.tar.gz
ghostscript-fonts-other-5.03.tar.gz
```

What is Ghostscript, and why do you need it? Technically, Ghostscript is a Raster Image Processor. It translates PostScript code into many common, bit-mapped formats, like those understood by your printer or screen, whether or not they are equipped with PostScript. In practical terms, Ghostscript allows you to use Type 1 fonts, and mix text and graphics on any printer or video display that Ghostscript knows about.

The quality of the fonts which come with the program have improved steadily in the last several versions as well. Or maybe it's that more recent versions of Ghostscript have improved font rendering. In either case, this is of real benefit for Linux users, who may not be able to spend hundreds of dollars on commercial fonts. Because Ghostscript is able to read the font requests made by dvips(1), Ghostscript's font library provides the fonts, not teTeX. But the font metrics files for Ghostscript's font library, which have the extension .afm, are already included in the teTeX distribution.

For information about using Ghostscript, see the file `use.txt` in the Ghostscript distribution, and the Linux Documentation Project's Printing HOWTO. There's also a Ghostscript manual available from the Internet. See Section 2.1

Or, install APSFILTER and let that run Ghostscript automatically. (See Section 3.3.)

A final, significant note: I would recommend that you compile Ghostscript for your own system, if possible. Combining different versions of Ghostscript and svgalib can quickly become confusing. The version of Ghostscript which is included in the Slackware AP set is version 2.6.2 and does not have X support compiled in. You might also have trouble finding the correct svgalib versions for it. There is supposedly a version of Ghostscript with X11 support in the Slackware `XAP` distribution series, and presumably in the other Linux distributions, though I haven't tried them. Compiling Ghostscript for your own system is far easier, it seems to me.

It's also important to remember that there are two Ghostscript releases in distribution: the commercial, Aladdin Ghostscript, and GNU Ghostscript, which lags behind Aladdin Ghostscript by several years. This is due to Ghostscript's unique licensing arrangement. See the Printing HOWTO for more information about Ghostscript licensing.

svgalib support for GNU Ghostscript 3.33 is included in a small archive which contains a .diff file. Ghostscript 3.33 for X is also configured for JPEG support, so you should include the JPEG library sources as well. The relevant archives can be found at any GNU distribution site, like ftp://prep.ai.mit.edu/pub/gnu.

3.3 APSFILTER.

There are software packages which will simplify your life, and APSFILTER is one of them. Written by Andreas Klemm, APSFILTER works with any BSD-compatible printer daemon (which means that you have the `lpd(8)` program and an `/etc/printcap` file; see below), and provides transparent printer support for ASCII, `family .dvi`, and PostScript files, as well as files compressed by `gzip(1)`, `compress(1)`, and other data compression software.

Once you have successfully installed APSFILTER, you can print a PostScript file to whatever printer you have, by typing

```
lpr file.ps
```

Or, to print an ASCII file without PostScript translation, you can type

```
lpr -Praw file.asc
```

Amazing.

APSFILTER is surprisingly easy to install, considering that it works with many disparate elements of your system. Installing the generic APSFILTER distribution, however, does require that you have a current `gcc(1)` compiler on hand, because APSFILTER builds some of its filters during installation. Some distributions of Linux, however, provide a pre-built version, so check your specific distribution first.

In any event, you will need a correctly installed Ghostscript and `lpd(8)` installation for APSFILTER to work.

The most recent APSFILTER is located in the Linux Archives at ftp://sunsite.unc.edu/pub/Linux/system/printing/.

3.4 The `lpd(8)` daemon.

There are wide variations in printers and configurations. Setting up a working printer daemon is no mean feat. If you're using teTeX on an individual system, you could simply dump the output to the printer, but this is less than desirable. You lose the filtering capabilities of the printer daemon. If you're printing on a network, having a working printer daemon is a must.

The basic UNIX program for printer management on BSD-style systems is `lpd(8)`. When you print a file with `lpr(1)` you are really sending the file to a print queue. `lpd(8)` prints files in the order they're queued. Other printer utilities include `lpq(1)`, which displays the contents of the print queue, and `lprm(1)`, which removes (dequeues) files from the print queue.

The printer daemon can perform other tasks, like transparently filtering output from various programs (using filter programs like APSFILTER, above), accept print jobs from other machines on a network, send print jobs to various printers if you have more than one connected, and hold print output until you've refilled the paper feed tray.

Setting up a working printer daemon can be a challenge. The Printing HOWTO explains the process in detail. Many Linux distributions already have configured `lpd(8)` suites. Check there first, because it will save you considerable work. They're usually archived, strangely enough, using the name `lpr`, so search for that program. There is also a printer daemon suite available from the Linux archives, at ftp://sunsite.unc.edu/pub/Linux/system/printing.

4 Post-installation configuration details.

The first thing you'll want to do is look at Thomas Esser's `README` file. It contains a lot of hints on how to configure teTeX for your output device (i.e., printer). The `README` file is located in the directory

```
/usr/lib/teTeX/texmf/doc/tetex
```

Read the file over with the command (the path in the following examples is that of the Slackware distributions):

```
less /usr/lib/teTeX/texmf/doc/tetex/README
```

or even better, print it out with the command

```
cat /usr/lib/teTeX/texmf/doc/tetex/README >/dev/lp0
```

assuming that your printer is connected to `/dev/lp0`. Substitute the device driver file that your printer is connected to, as appropriate.

Or, better still, print it using the `lpr(1)` command:

```
lpr /usr/lib/teTeX/texmf/doc/tetex/README
```

You should have installed the printer daemon that is included with your distribution of Linux. If not, do that now, per the instructions that come with the package. If you don't have one of the packages, or want to install a printer daemon yourself, see Section 3.4

Print out the `teTeX-FAQ`. Keep the FAQ handy because it contains useful hints for configuring teTeX's output drivers for your printer. We'll get to that in a moment. In more recent releases of teTeX, the `teTeX-FAQ` is viewable via the `texconfig` utility.

Next, you want to define a directory to store your own TeX format files. TeTeX searches the directories listed by the `$TEXINPUTS` environment variable for local TEX input files. On Chanel3, I added the line

```
export TEXINPUTS=".:~/texinputs:"
```

to the system-wide `/etc/profile` file. Individual users can set their own local `$TEXINPUTS` directory, by adding the line in their `~/.profile` or `~/.bash_profile` if `bash(1)` is the default shell. The `$TEXINPUTS` environment variable tells teTeX to look for users' individual TeX style files in the `~/texinputs` directories under each user's home directory. It is *critical* that a colon appear before and after this directory. TeTeX is going to append its own directory searches to your own. You want to have teTeX search the local format files first, so it uses the local versions of any of the standard files you have edited.

Add the `/usr/lib/teTeX/bin` directory to the system-wide path if you're installing teTeX as root. Again, if you're installing a personal copy of teTeX, add the directory where the teTeX binaries are located to *the front* your `$PATH` with the following line in your `~/.profile` or `~/.bash_profile`:

```
export PATH="~/tetex/bin:"$PATH
```

Now, log in as `root` and run `texconfig` per the instructions in the `teTeX-FAQ` and choose the printer that is attached to your system. Make sure that you configure teTeX for both the correct printer and printer resolution.

Finally, run the `texhash` program. This ensures that teTeX's internal database is up to date. The database is actually a `ls-lR` file. You *must* run `texhash` every time you change the system configuration, or teTeX may not be able to locate your changes.

4.1 What if my printer isn't included?

The teTeX distribution comes with only a limited selection of DVI output drivers: `dvips(1)`, drivers for Hewlett Packard LaserJets, and nothing else. You have two options if you have a printer which isn't LaserJet-compatible: You can use `dvips(1)` and Ghostscript, which I would recommend anyway, for reasons already mentioned, or you can investigate other dviware sources.

A limited number of DVI drivers have been ported to Linux and are available as pre-built binaries. They are located in the Linux archives at ftp://sunsite.unc.edu/pub/Linux/apps/tex/dvi/.

The master dviware libraries are maintained at the University of Utah archives. If you can't find a DVI driver there which supports your printer, chances are that it doesn't exist. You can also write your *own* DVI driver using the templates available there. The library's URL is ftp://ftp.math.utah.edu/pub/tex/dvi/.

5 Using teTeX.

Theoretically, at least, everything is installed correctly and is ready to run. TeTeX is a very large software package. As with any complex software package, you'll want to start by learning teTeX slowly, instead of being overwhelmed by its complexity.

At the same time, we want the software to do something useful. So instead of watching TEX typeset

```
''Hello, World!''
```

as Professor Knuth suggests in the *The TeXBook,* we'll produce a couple of teTeX's own documents in order to test it.

The next section, 5.1, is really a tutorial for operating teTeX. It covers printing the documentation included with teTeX (which is in LaTeX and `.dvi` format, of course). The following section, 5.2, is more of a "cookbook" than a tutorial. It discusses how to format LaTeX documents, and covers a few of the commands and environments of the more commonly used document classes.

Section 5.3 tells how to use the many pre-existing LaTeX packages to customize documents to your specifications.

5.1 Printing the documentation.

You should be logged in as `root` the first few times you run teTeX. If you aren't, metafont may not be able to create the necessary directories for its fonts. The `texconfig` program includes an option to make the font directories world-writable, but if you're working on a multi-user system, security considerations may make this option impractical or undesirable.

In either instance, if you don't have the appropriate permissions to write to the directories where the fonts are stored, `metafont` will complain loudly because it can't make the directories, and you won't see any output because you have a bunch of zero-length font characters. This is no problem. Simply log out, re-login as `root,` and repeat the offending operation.

The nice thing about teTeX is that, if you blow it, no real harm is done. It's not like a compiler, where, say, you will trash the root partition if a pointer goes astray. What, you haven't read the teTeX manual yet? Of course you haven't. It's still in the distribution, in source code form, waiting to be output.

So, without further delay, you will want to read the teTeX manual. It's located in the directory

```
/usr/lib/teTeX/texmf/doc/tetex.
```

The LaTeX source for the manual is called `TETEXDOC.tex`. (The `.tex` extension is used for both TeX and LaTeX files. Some editors, like `emacs(1),` can tell the difference.) There is also a file `TETEXDOC.dvi` included with the distribution, which you might want to keep in a safe place—say, another directory—in case you want to test your `.dvi` drivers later. With that out of the way, type

```
latex TETEXDOC.tex
```

LaTeX will print several warnings. The first,

```
LaTeX Warning: Label(s) may have changed. Rerun to get the
cross-references right.
```

is standard. It's common to build a document's Table of Contents by LaTeXing the document twice. So, repeat the command. The other warnings can be safely ignored. They simply are informing you that some of the FTP paths mentioned in the documentation are too wide for their alloted spaces. (If you're really inquisitive, look at one of the TeX references for a discussion of `\hbox` and `\vbox.`)

TeTeX will have generated several files from `TETEXDOC.tex.` The one that we're interested in is `TETEXDOC.dvi.` This is the device-independent output which you can send either to the screen or the printer. If you're running teTeX under the X Windows System, you can preview the document with `xdvi(1).`

For the present, let's assume that you have a HP Laserjet II. You would give the command

```
dvilj2 TETEXDOC.dvi
```

which will write a PCL output file from `TETEXDOC.dvi,` including soft fonts which will be down loaded to the Laserjet. This is *not* a feature of TeX or LaTeX, but a feature provided by `dvilj2(1).` Other `.dvi` drivers provide features which are relevant to the devices they support. `dvilj2(1)` will fill the font requests which were made in the original LaTeX document with the the closest equivalents available on the system. In the case of a plain-text document like `TETEXDOC.tex,` there isn't much difficulty. All of the fonts requested by `TETEXDOC.tex` will be generated by metafont, which is automatically invoked by `dvilj2(1)` and generates the fonts if they aren't already present. (If you're running `dvilj2(1)` for the first time, the program needs to generate all of the fonts, which could take up to several days if you're using a *really* slow machine.) There are several options which control font generation via `dvilj2(1);` they're outlined in the manual page. At this point, you shouldn't need to operate metafont directly. If you do, then something has gone awry with your installation. All of the `.dvi` drivers will invoke `metafont` directly via the kpathsea path-searching library—also beyond the scope of this document—and you don't need to do any more work with metafont for the present—all of the metafont sources for the Computer Modern font library are provided.

You can print `TETEXDOC.lj` with the command

```
lpr TETEXDOC.lj
```

You may need to install a printer filter that understands PCL. Look at the Printing HOWTO for details.

The nine-page teTeX Users Manual provides some useful information for further configuring your system, some of which I have mentioned, much which this document doesn't cover.

Some of the information in the next section I haven't been able to test, because I have a non-PostScript HP Deskjet 400 color inkjet printer connected to Chanel3's parallel port. However, not owning a PostScript printer is no barrier to printing text and graphics from your text documents. See Section 3.2 to install Ghostscript, if it isn't already installed on your system.

5.2 TEX and LATEX commands.

5.2.1 Document structure.

Preparing documents for TEX typesetting is easy. Make sure there's a blank line between the paragraphs of a plain text file, and run file through the TEX program with the command

```
TeX your_text_file
```

The result will be a file of the same base name and the extension `.dvi`. The text is set in 10-point Computer Modern Roman, single-spaced, with justified left and right margins. If you receive error messages from special characters like dollar signs, escape them with a backslash character, \, and run TEX on the file again. You should be able to process the resulting file with the `.dvi` file translator of your choice (see above) to get printed output.

The only other peculiarity of TEX input files is to make sure that you use opening and closing quotes which are denoted in the input file with the grave accent and single quote characters. Emacs' TEX mode will do this for you automatically.

```
"These are ASCII-type quotes."
''These are 'TeX-style' quotes.''
```

You can consult a guide like *A Gentle Introduction to TEX,* described above, for hints on how to make modifications to the default TEX page format.

Documents formatted for LATEX have a few more rules, but with complex documents, LATEX can greatly simplify the formatting process.

Essentially, LATEX is a document markup language which tries to separate the output style from the document's logical content. For example, formatting a section heading with TEX would require specifying 36 points of white space above the heading, then the heading itself set in bold, 24-point type, then copying the heading text and page number to the Table of Contents, then leaving 24 points of white space after the heading. By contrast, LATEX has the `\section{}` command, which does all of the work for you. If you need to change the format of the section headings throughout your document, you can change the definition of `\section{}` instead of the text in the document. You can see where this would save hours of reformatting for documents of more than a dozen pages in length.

All LATEX documents have three sections: a **preamble**, the **body** text, and a **postamble**. These terms are standard jargon and are widely used by TEXperts.

The preamble, at a minimum, specifies the type of document to be produced—the **document class** and a statement which signals the beginning of the document's body text. For example:

```
\documentclass{article}
\begin{document}
```

The document's postamble is usually very simple. Except in specialized cases, it contains only the statement:

```
\end{document}
```

Note the `\begin{document}` and `\end{document}` pairing. In LaTeX, this is called an **environment**. All text must appear within an environment, and many commands are effective only in the environments in which they're called. The `document` environment is the only instance where LaTeX enforces this convention, however. That is, it's the only environment that is required in a document. (An exception is `letter` class, which also requires you to declare `\begin{letter}` and `\end{letter}`. See Section 5.2.4.) However, many formatting features are specified as environments. They're described in the following sections.

The document classes can be called with arguments. For example, instead of the default 10-point type used as the base point size, as in the previous example, we could have specified

```
\documentclass[12pt]{article}
```

to produce the document using 12 points as the base point size. The document class, *article,* makes the necessary adjustments for the new point size.

There are a few document classes which are commonly used. They're described below. The **report** class is similar to **article** class, but produces a title page and starts each section on a new page. The **letter** class includes special definitions for addresses, salutations, and closings, a few of which are described below.

You include canned LaTeX code, commonly known as a *package*, with the `\usepackage{}` command.

```
\usepackage{fancyhdr}
```

The command above would include the LaTeX style file `fancyhdr.sty` from one of the `TEXINPUTS` directories, which either you or teTeX specified during installation and setup processes.

With the addition of this statement, the example document preamble, above, would look like:

```
\documentclass{article}
\usepackage{fancyhdr}
\begin{document}
```

Note that the `\usepackage{}` declarations are given before the `\begin{document}` statement; that is, in the document preamble.

`fancyhdr.sty` extends the `\pagestyle{}` command so that you can create custom headers and footers. Most LaTeX document classes provide headers and footers of the following standard page styles:

```
\pagestyle{plain}      % default pages style -- page number centered at
                       % the bottom of the page.
\pagestyle{empty}      % no headers or footers
\pagestyle{headings}   % print section number and page number at the
                       % top of the page.
\pagestyle{myheadings} % print custom information in the page heading.
```

Everything on a line to the right of the percent sign is a comment.

The `\pagestyle{}` command doesn't take effect until the following page. To change the headers and footers of the current page, use the command

```
\thispagestyle{the_pagestyle}
```

5.2.2 Characters and type styles.

Character styles are partially a function of the fonts specified in the document. However, bold and italic character emphasis should be available for every font present on the system. Underlining, too, can be used, though its formatting presents special problems. See Section 5.3, below.

You can specify text to be emphasized in several ways. The most portable is the `\em` command. All text within its scope is italicized by default. For example:

```
This word will be {\em emphasized.}
```

If you have italicized text that runs into text which is not italicized, you can specify an italic correction factor to be used. The command for this is `\/`; that is, a backslash and a forward slash.

```
This example {\em will\/} print correctly.

This example will {\em not} print correctly.
```

Slightly less portable, but still acceptable in situations where they're used singly, are the commands `\it`, `\bf`, and `\tt`, which specify that the characters within their scope be printed using italic, bold and monospaced (teletype) typefaces, respectively.

```
{\tt This text will be printed monospaced,}
{\it this text will be italic,} and
{\bf this text will be bold\dots} all in one paragraph.
```

The command `\dots` prints a series of three periods for ellipses, which will not break across a line.

The most recent version of LaTeX, which is what you have, includes commands which account for instances where one emphasis command would supersede another.

```
This is {\it not {\bf bold italic!}}
```

What happens is that teTeX formats the text with the italic typeface until it encounters the `\bf` command, at which point it switches to boldface type.

To get around this, the NFSS scheme of selecting font shapes requires three parameters for each typeface: shape, series, and family. Not all font sets will include all of these styles. LaTeX will print a warning, however, if it needs to substitute another font.

You can specify the following font shapes:

```
\textup{text}           % upright shape (the default)
\textit{text}           % italic
\textsl{text}           % slanted
\textsc{text}           % small caps
```

These are the two series that most fonts have:

```
\textmd{text}           % medium series.  the default
\textbf{text}           % boldface series.
```

There are generally three families of type available.

```
\textrm{text}           % roman.  the default.
\textsf{text}           % sans serif
\texttt{text}           % typewriter (monospaced, Courier-like)
```

Setting font styles using these parameters, you can combine effects.

```
\texttt{\textit{This example likely will result in a font
substituition, because many fonts don't include a typewriter italic
typeface.}}
```

The font family defaults to Computer Modern, which is a bit-mapped font. Other font families are usually PostScript-format Type 1 fonts. See Section 7 for details how to specify them.

There are also many forms of accents and special characters that are available for typesetting. This is only a few of them. (Try typesetting these on your own printer.)

```
\'{o}   \'{e}   \^{o}   \"{u}   \={o}   \c{c}   '? '!
\copyright      \pounds         \dag
```

Finally, there are characters which are used as meta- or escape characters in TeX and LaTeX. One of them, the dollar sign, is mentioned above. The complete set of metacharacters, which need to be escaped with a backslash to be used literally, is:

```
# $ % & _ { } \
```

There are also different alphabets available, like Greek and Cyrillic. LaTeX provides many facilities for setting non-English text, which are covered by some of the other references mentioned here

5.2.3 Margins and line spacing.

Changing margins in a TeX or LaTeX document is not a straightforward task. A lot depends on the relative indent of the text you're trying to adjust the margin for. The placement of the margin changing command is also significant.

For document-wide changes to LaTeX documents, the `\evensidemargin` and `\oddsidemargin` commands are available. They affect the left-hand margins of the even-numbered and odd-numbered pages, respectively. For example,

```
\evensidemargin=1in
\oddsidemargin=1in
```

adds on inch to the left-hand margin of the even and odd pages in addition to the standard one-inch, left-hand margin. These commands affect the entire document and will shift the entire body of the text right and left across a page, regardless of any local indent, so they're safe to use with LaTeX environments like `verse` and `list`.

Below is a set of margin-changing macros which I wrote. They have a different effect than the commands mentioned above. Because they use plain TeX commands, they're not guaranteed to honor the margins of any LaTeX environments which may be in effect, but you can place them anywhere in a document and change the margins from that point on.

```
%%  margins.sty -- v. 0.1   by Robert Kiesling
%%  Copies of this code may be freely distributed in verbatim form.
%%
%%  Some elementary plain TeX margin-changing commands. Lengths are
%%  in inches:
%%  \leftmargin{1}   %% sets the document's left margin in 1 inch.
```

```
%%  \leftindent{1}    %% sets the following paragraphs' indent in
%%                      1 inch.
%%  \rightindent{1}  %% sets the following paragraphs' right margins
%%                   %% in 1 inch.
%%  \llength{3}      %% sets the following lines' lengths to 3 inches.
%%
\message{Margins macros...}
\def\lmargin#1{\hoffset = #1 in}
\def\lindent#1{\leftskip = #1 in}
\def\rindent#1{\rightskip = #1 in}
\def\llength#1{\hsize = #1 in}
%%
%% (End of margins macros.)
```

Place this code in a file called `margins.sty` in your local `$TEXINPUTS` directory. The commands are explained in the commented section of the file. To include them in a document, use the command

```
\usepackage{margins}
```

in the document preamble.

While we're on the subject, if you don't want the right margin to be justified, which is the default, you can tell LaTeX to use ragged right margins by giving the command:

```
\raggedright
```

Setting line spacing also has its complexities.

The *baselineskip* measurement is the distance between lines of text. It is given as an absolute measurement. For example,

```
\baselineskip=24pt
```

or even better:

```
\setlength{\baselineskip}{24pt}
```

The difference between the two forms is that *setlength* will respect any scoping rules that may be in effect when you use the command.

The problem with using baselineskip is that it also affects the distance between section headings, footnotes, and the like. You need to take care that baselineskip is correct for whatever text elements you're formatting. There are, however, LaTeX macro packages, like `setspace.sty`, which will help you in these circumstances. See Section 5.3.

5.2.4 Document classes.

LaTeX provides document classes which provide standardized formats for documents. They provide environments to format lists, quotations, footnotes, and other text elements. Commonly used document classes are covered in the following sections.

Articles and reports. As mentioned above, the `article` class and the `report` class are similar. The main differences are that the report class creates a title page by default and begins each section on a new page.

To create titles, abstracts, and bylines in these document classes, you can type, for example,

```
\title{The Breeding Habits of Cacti}
\author{John Q. Public}
\abstract{This paper describes how common varieties of desert cacti
search for the appropriate watering holes to perform their breeding
rituals.}
```

in the document preamble. Then, the command

```
\maketitle
```

given at the start of the text, will generate either a title page in the report class, or the title and abstract at the top of the first page, in the article class.

Sections can be defined with commands that include the following:

```
\section
\subsection
\subsubsection
```

These commands will produce the standard, numbered sections used in technical documents. For unnumbered sections, use

```
\section*
\subsection*
\subsubsection*
```

and so on.

LaTeX provides many environments for formatting displayed material. You can include quoted text with the `quotation` environment.

```
\begin{quotation}
Start of paragraph to be quoted...

... end of paragraph.
\end{quotation}
```

For shorter quotes, you can use the `quote` environment.

To format verse, use the `verse` environment.

```
\begin{verse}
Because I could not stop for death\\
He kindly stopped for me
\end{verse}
```

Notice that you must use the double backslashes to break lines in the correct places. Otherwise, LaTeX fills the lines in a verse environment, just like any other environment.

Lists come in several flavors. To format a bulleted list, the `list` environment is used:

```
\begin{list}
\item
This is the first item of the list.
\item
This is the second item of the list...
\item
... and so on.
\end{list}
```

A numbered list uses the `enumerate` environment:

```
\begin{enumerate}
\item
Item No. 1.
\item
Item No. 2.
\item
\dots
\end{enumerate}
```

A descriptive list uses the `description` environment.

```
\begin{description}
\item{Oven} Dirty, needs new burner.
\item{Refrigerator} Dirty. Sorry.
\item{Sink and drainboard} Stained, drippy, cold water faucet.
\end{description}
```

Letters. The `letter` class uses special definitions to format business letters.

The `letter` environment takes one argument, the address of the letter's addressee. The `address` command, which must appear in the document preamble, defines the return address. The `signature` command defines the sender's name as it appears after the closing.

The LaTeX source of a simple business letter might look like this.

```
\documentclass[12pt]{letter}
\signature{John Q. Public}
\address{123 Main St.\\Los Angeles, CA.  96005\\Tel: 123/456-7890}
\begin{document}
\begin{letter}{ACME Brick Co.\\100 Ash St.\\San Diego, CA 96403}
\opening{Dear Sir/Madam:}

With regard to one of your bricks that I found on my living room
carpet surrounded by shards of by broken front window...

(Remainder of the body of the letter.)

\closing{Sincerely,}

\end{letter}
\end{document}
```

Note that the addresses include double backslashes, which specify where the line breaks should occur.

5.3 LaTeX extension packages and other resources.

We mentioned above that using underlining as a form of text emphasis presents special problems. Actually, TeX has no problem underlining text, because it is a convention of mathematical typesetting. In LaTeX, you can underline a word with the command:

```
\underline{text to be underlined}
```

The problem is that underlining will not break across lines, and, in some circumstances, underlining can be uneven. However, there is a LaTeX macro package ready made that makes underlining the default mode of text emphasis. It's called `ulem.sty`, and is one of the many contributed LaTeX packages that are freely available via the Internet.

To use `ulem.sty`, include the command

```
\usepackage{ulem}
```

in the document preamble.

The LaTeX Catalogue provides one-line descriptions of every LaTeX package available, their names and CTAN paths. For the URL of the most current edition of the Catalogue, see Section 2.1.

The packages which are available for LaTeX include:

ifthen

Include conditional statements in your documents.

initials

Defines a font for initial dropped capitals.

sanskrit

Font and preprocessor for producing documents in Sanskrit.

recipe

A LaTeX 2ε class to typeset recipes.

refman

Variant report and article styles.

To make the path given in the Catalogue into a fully-qualified URL, concatenate the path to the hostname URL and top-level path of the CTAN archive you wish to contact. For example, the top-level CTAN directory of the site ftp.tex.ac.uk is `ctan/tex-archive`. The complete URL of the directory of the **refman** package would be:

```
ftp://ftp.tex.ac.uk/ctan/tex-archive/          +
macros/latex/contrib/supported/refman          =

ftp://ftp.tex.ac.uk/ctan/tex-archive/macros/latex/contrib/supported/refman/
```

Some packages have more than one file, so only the path to the package's directory is given.

When you have the URL in hand, you can retrieve the package from one of the CTAN archive sites listed in Section 8. You can download a complete list of the archives contents as the file `FILES.byname`, in the archive's top-level directory. You can also search the archive on line for a keyword with the `ftp(1)` command

```
quote site index <keyword>
```

6 Mixing text and graphics with dvips.

In general, this section applies to any TEX or LATEX document that mixes text and graphics. TeTeX, like most other TEX distributions, is configured to request Computer Modern fonts by default. When printing documents with Type 1 scalable fonts or graphics, font and graphics imaging is the job of `dvips(1)`. `dvips(1)` can use either Computer Modern bit mapped fonts or Type 1 scalable fonts, or any combination of the two. First, let's concentrate on printing and previewing some graphics.

In general, you will want to follow this procedure any time a LATEX source document has the statement

```
\usepackage{graphics}
```

in the document preamble. This statement tells LATEX to include the text of the `graphics.sty` package in the source document. There are other commands to perform graphics operations, and the statements in plain-TEX documents may not clue you in whether you need to use `dvips(1)`. The difference will be apparent in the output, though, when the document is printed with missing figures and other graphics.

So for now, we'll concentrate on printing documents which use the LATEX `graphics.sty` package. You might want to take a look at the original TEX input. It isn't included in the teTeX distribution, but it is available at

```
~CTAN/macros/latex/packages/graphics/grfguide.tex.
```

What the teTeX distribution does include is the `.dvi` output file, and it is already TeXed for you. There is a reason for this, and it has to do with the necessity of including Type 1 fonts in the output in order for the document to print properly. If you want to LATEX `grfguide.tex`, see the next section. For now, however, we'll work on getting usable output using `dvips(1)`.

This is where Ghostscript, `gs(1)`, comes into the picture. What `ghostscript` does is translate (actually, render) PostScript code into a form that bit mapped or rasterized output devices can understand. Even though my HP Deskjet doesn't understand PostScript, `ghostscript` allows me to scale, rotate, blend, or otherwise alter text, or include graphics or colors, just like the expensive printers. A discussion of color printing is a little beyond the scope of this document, though, along with most other effects. We're going to stick to the basics for the moment.

The file `grfguide.dvi` is located in the directory

```
/usr/lib/teTeX/texmf/doc/latex/graphics
```

The first step in outputting `grfguide.dvi` is to translate it to PostScript. The program `dvips(1)` is used for this. It does just exactly what its name implies. There are many options available for invoking `dvips(1)`, but the simplest (nearly) form is

```
dvips -f -r <grfguide.dvi >grfguide.ps
```

The `-f` command switch tells `dvips(1)` to operate as a filter, reading from standard input and writing to standard output. `dvips(1)` output can be configured so its output defaults to `lpr(1)`. (Mine does, which allows me to print directly from `dvips(1)`.) Post-processors like Ghostscript and printing filter like APSFILTER (see Section 3.3, can be configured for your own needs. If you need to feed the output manually to a post-processor, the `-f` option is generally the first you should include in the `dvips(1)` command line. This form also seems to be easier to use in shell scripts.

If you can print PostScript directly to your printer via `lpr(1)`, you can simply type

```
dvips -r grfguide.dvi
```

The `-r` option tells dvips to output the pages in reverse order so they stack correctly when they exit a printer. Use it or not, as appropriate for your output device.

Depending on whether you still have the fonts that `dvilj2(1)` generated from the last document, `dvips(1)` and `metafont` may or may not need to create new fonts needed by `grfguide.dvi`. Eventually, though, `dvips(1)` will output a list of the pages translated to PostScript, and you will have your PostScript output ready to be rendered on whatever output device you have available.

If you're lucky (and rich), then you have a PostScript-capable printer already and will be able to print `grfguide.ps` directly. You can either spool the output to the printer using `lpr(1)`. If for some reason your printer software doesn't work right with PostScript files, you can, in a pinch, simply dump the file to printer, with

```
cat grfguide.ps >/dev/lp0
```

or whichever port your printer is attached to, though this is not recommended for everyday use.

If you want or need to invoke Ghostscript manually, this is the standard procedure for its operation. The first thing you want to do is invoke Ghostscript to view its command line arguments, like this:

```
gs -help | less
```

You'll see a list of supported output devices and sundry other commands. Pick the output device which most nearly matches your printer. On Chanel3, because I generally produce black-and-white text, I use the `cdjmono` driver, which drives a color Deskjet in monochrome (black and white) mode.

The command line I would use is:

```
gs -dNOPAUSE -sDEVICE=cdjmono -sOutputFile=/tmp/gs.out grfguide.ps -c quit
```

This will produce my HP-compatible output in the `/tmp` directory. It's a good idea to use a directory like `/tmp`, because `gs(1)` can be particular about access permissions, and you can't (and shouldn't) always count on being logged in as `root` to perform these steps. Now you can print the file:

```
lpr /tmp/gs.out
```

Obviously, this can all go into a shell script. On my system, I have two simple scripts written, `pv` and `pr`, which simply outputs the PostScript file either to the display or the printer. Screen previewing is possible without X, but it's far from ideal. So, it's definitely worth the effort to install XFree86, or TinyX (which is what I did) to view the output on the screen.

The order of commands in a `gs(1)` command line is significant, because some of the options tell `ghostscript` to look for pieces of PostScript code from its library.

The important thing to remember is that `grfguide.dvi` makes requests for both Computer Modern bit mapped and Type 1 scaled fonts. If you can mix scalable and bit mapped fonts in a document, you're well on the way to becoming a TeXpert. It used to be that public domain, Type 1 fonts were much poorer quality than Computer Modern bit mapped fonts. This situation has improved in the last several years, though, but matching the fonts is up to you. Having several different font systems on one machine can seem redundant and an unnecessary waste of disk space. And the Computer Modern fonts can seem, well, a little too *formal* to be suitable for everyday use. It reminds me sometimes of bringing out the good China to feed the dog. At least you don't need to spend a bundle on professional quality fonts any longer.

7 Using PostScript fonts.

One of the major improvements of LATEX 2ε over its predecessor was the inclusion of the New Font Selection Scheme. (It's now called PSNFSS.) Formerly, TEX authors would specify fonts with commands like

```
\font=bodyroman = cmr10 scaled \magstep 1
```

which provides precision but requires the skills of a type designer and mathematician to make good use of. Also, it's not very portable. If another system didn't have the font `cmr10` (this is TeX nomenclature for Computer Modern Roman, 10 point, with the default medium stroke weight), somebody would have to re-code the fonts specifications for the entire document. PSNFSS, however, allows you specify fonts by family (Computer Modern, URW Nimbus, Helvetica, Utopia, and so forth), weight (light, medium, bold), orientation (upright or oblique), face (Roman, Italic), and base point size. Also, many fonts are packaged as families. For example, a Roman-type font may come packaged with a sans serif font, like Helvetica, and a monospaced font, like Courier. You, as the author of a LATEX document, can specify an entire font family with one command.

There are, as I said, several high-quality font sets available in the public domain. One of them is Adobe Utopia. Another is Bitstream Charter. Both are commercial quality fonts which have been donated to the public domain.

These happen to be two of my favorites. If you look around one of the CTAN sites, you will find these and other fonts archived there. There are enough fonts around that you'll be able to design documents the way you want them to look, and not just English text, either. TEX was originally designed for mathematical typesetting, so there is a full range of mathematical fonts available, as well as Cyrillic, Greek, Kana, and other alphabets too numerous to mention.

The important thing to look for is files which have either the `.pfa` or `.pfb` extension. They indicate that these are the scalable fonts themselves, not simply the metrics files. Type 1 fonts use `.pfm` metric files, as opposed to the `.tfm` metric files which bit mapped fonts use. The two font sets I mentioned above are included in teTeX distributions, as well as separately.

What I said above, concerning the ease of font selection under PSNFSS, is true in this instance. If we want to use the Charter fonts in our document instead of Computer Modern bit mapped, all that is necessary is include the LaTeX statement

```
\renewcommand{\familydefault}{bch}
```

where "bch" is the common designation for Bitstream Charter. The Charter fonts reside in the directory

```
/usr/lib/teTeX/texmf/fonts/type1/bitstrea/charter
```

There you'll see the `.pfb` files of the Charter fonts: `bchb8a.pfb` for Charter Bold, `bchr8a.pfb` for Charter Roman, `bchbi8a.pfb` for Charter Bold Italic. The "8a" in the font names indicates the character encoding. At this point you don't need to worry about them, because the encodings mostly differ for 8-bit characters, which have numeric values above 128 decimal. They mostly define accents, and foreign characters. You'll be concerned with them if you're typesetting documents in say, Spanish, but for now the default encodings are fine. The Type 1 fonts conform to the ISO standards for international character sets, so this is an added benefit of using them.

To typeset a document which has Charter fonts selected, you would give the command

```
pslatex document.tex
```

`pslatex` is a variant of teTeX's standard `latex(1)` command which defines the directories where the Type 1 fonts are, as well as some additional LaTeX code to load. You'll see the notice screen for `pslatex` followed by the status output of the TeX job itself. In a moment you'll have a .dvi file which includes the Charter font requests. You can then print the file with `dvips(1)`, and `gs(1)` if necessary

Installing a Type 1 font set is not difficult, as long as you follow a few basic steps. You should unpack the fonts in a subdirectory of the `/usr/lib/teTeX/texmf/fonts/type1` directory, where your other Type 1 fonts are located, and then run `texhash` to let the directory search routines know that the fonts have been added. Then you need to add the font descriptions to the file `psfonts.map` so `dvips(1)` knows they're on the system. The format of the `psfonts.map` file is covered in a couple different places in the references mentioned above. Again, remember to run the `texhash` program to update the teTeX directory database.

It is definitely an advantage to use the X Window System with teTeX under Linux, because it allows for superior document previewing. It's not required, but in general, anything that allows for easier screen previewing is going to benefit your work, in terms of the quality of the output. However, there is a tradeoff with speed of editing, which is much quicker on character-mode displays. Having an editor which is slower than molasses in Minnesota can definitely hinder your work.

Anyway, whether or not you are able to view documents easily on-screen, please recycle your paper, and use both sides of each sheet. If possible, purchase recycled photocopy paper to print on.

Remember: Save a tree... kill an editor.

Robert Kiesling
kiesling@terracom.net

8 Appendix: CTAN Site Listing

This is the text of the file `CTAN.sites`, which is available in the top-level directory of each CTAN archive or mirror site.

```
In order to reduce network load, it is recommended that you use the
Comprehensive TeX Archive Network (CTAN) host which is located in the
closest network proximity to your site.  Alternatively, you may wish to
obtain a copy of the CTAN via CD-ROM (see help/CTAN.cdrom for details).

Known mirrors of the CTAN reside on (alphabetically):
  cis.utovrm.it (Italia)                /TeX
  ctan.unsw.edu.au (NSW, Australia)     /tex-archive
  dongpo.math.ncu.edu.tw (Taiwan)       /tex-archive
  ftp.belnet.be (Belgium)               /packages/TeX
  ftp.ccu.edu.tw (Taiwan)               /pub/tex
  ftp.cdrom.com (West coast, USA)       /pub/tex/ctan
  ftp.comp.hkbu.edu.hk (Hong Kong)      /pub/TeX/CTAN
  ftp.cs.rmit.edu.au  (Australia)       /tex-archive
```

```
ftp.cs.ruu.nl (The Netherlands)          /pub/tex-archive
ftp.cstug.cz (The Czech Republic)        /pub/tex/CTAN
ftp.duke.edu (North Carolina, USA)       /tex-archive
ftp.funet.fi (Finland)                   /pub/TeX/CTAN
ftp.gwdg.de (Deutschland)                /pub/dante
ftp.jussieu.fr (France)                  /pub4/TeX/CTAN
ftp.kreonet.re.kr (Korea)                /pub/CTAN
ftp.loria.fr (France)                    /pub/unix/tex/ctan
ftp.mpi-sb.mpg.de (Deutschland)          /pub/tex/mirror/ftp.dante.de
ftp.nada.kth.se (Sweden)                 /pub/tex/ctan-mirror
ftp.oleane.net (France)                  /pub/mirrors/CTAN/
ftp.rediris.es (Espa\~na)                /mirror/tex-archive
ftp.rge.com (New York, USA)              /pub/tex
ftp.riken.go.jp (Japan)                  /pub/tex-archive
ftp.tu-chemnitz.de (Deutschland)         /pub/tex
ftp.u-aizu.ac.jp (Japan)                 /pub/tex/CTAN
ftp.uni-augsburg.de (Deutschland)        /tex-archive
ftp.uni-bielefeld.de (Deutschland)       /pub/tex
ftp.unina.it (Italia)                    /pub/TeX
ftp.uni-stuttgart.de (Deutschland)       /tex-archive (/pub/tex)
ftp.univie.ac.at (\"Osterreich)          /packages/tex
ftp.ut.ee (Estonia)                      /tex-archive
ftpserver.nus.sg (Singapore)             /pub/zi/TeX
src.doc.ic.ac.uk (England)               /packages/tex/uk-tex
sunsite.auc.dk (Denmark)                 /pub/tex/ctan
sunsite.cnlab-switch.ch (Switzerland)    /mirror/tex
sunsite.icm.edu.pl (Poland)              /pub/CTAN
sunsite.unc.edu (North Carolina, USA)    /pub/packages/TeX
wuarchive.wustl.edu (Missouri, USA)      /packages/TeX

Known partial mirrors of the CTAN reside on (alphabetically):
ftp.adfa.oz.au (Australia)               /pub/tex/ctan
ftp.fcu.edu.tw (Taiwan)                  /pub2/tex
ftp.germany.eu.net (Deutschland)         /pub/packages/TeX
ftp.gust.org.pl (Poland)                 /pub/TeX
ftp.jaist.ac.jp (Japan)                  /pub/TeX/tex-archive
ftp.uu.net (Virginia, USA)               /pub/text-processing/TeX
nic.switch.ch (Switzerland)              /mirror/tex
sunsite.dsi.unimi.it (Italia)            /pub/TeX
sunsite.snu.ac.kr (Korea)                /shortcut/CTAN

Please send updates to this list to <ctan@urz.uni-heidelberg.de>.

The participating hosts in the Comprehensive TeX Archive Network are:
 ftp.dante.de (Deutschland)
       -- anonymous ftp                  /tex-archive (/pub/tex /pub/archive)
       -- gopher on node gopher.dante.de
       -- e-mail via ftpmail@dante.de
       -- World Wide Web access on www.dante.de
       -- Administrator: <ftpmaint@dante.de>

 ftp.tex.ac.uk (England)
       -- anonymous ftp                  /tex-archive (/pub/tex /pub/archive)
       -- gopher on node gopher.tex.ac.uk
       -- NFS mountable from nfs.tex.ac.uk:/public/ctan/tex-archive
       -- World Wide Web access on www.tex.ac.uk
       -- Administrator: <ctan-uk@tex.ac.uk>
```

Part L

"Linux User Group HOWTO" by Kendall Grant Clark

Contents

Abstract

v1.5.2, 15 November 1997
The Linux User Group HOWTO is a guide to founding, maintaining, and growing a Linux User Group.

1 Introduction

1.1 Purpose of this document

The Linux User Group HOWTO is intended to serve as a guide to founding, maintaining, and growing a Linux User Group.

Linux is a freely-distributable implementation of Unix for personal computers, servers and workstations. It was developed on the i386 and now supports i486, Pentium, Pentium Pro, and Pentium II processors, as well as x86-clones from AMD, Cyrix, and others. It also supports many SPARC, DEC Alpha, PowerPC/PowerMac, Motorola 68x0 Mac/Amiga machines.

1.2 Other sources of information

If you want to learn more about Linux, the Linux Documentation Project, http://sunsite.unc.edu/LDP/ is a good place to start.

For general information about computer user groups, please see the Association of PC Users Groups, http://www.apcug.org/.

1.3 New versions of this document

New versions of the Linux User Group HOWTO will be periodically uploaded to various Linux WWW and FTP sites, principally http://www.cmpu.net/public/kclark/linux/ and the http://sunsite.unc.edu/LDP/.

1.4 How you can help me write this HOWTO

I **welcome** questions about and feedback on this document. Please send them to me at kclark@cmpu.net. *I am especially interested in hearing from leaders of LUGs from around the world*. I would like to include real-life examples of the things described here. I would also like to include a section on LUGs outside the United States, since this HOWTO as it stands now is rather US-centric. Please let me know if your group does things that should be mentioned in this HOWTO.

2 What is a Linux User Group?

2.1 What is Linux?

In order to appreciate and understand fully the significant role of LUGs in the Linux Movement, it is important to understand what makes Linux unique among computer operating systems.

Linux as an operating system is very efficient and very powerful. But, Linux as an ***idea*** about how software ought to be developed is even more powerful. Linux is a **free** operating system: it is licensed under the GNU Public License. The source code is freely available to anyone who wants it and always will be. It is developed by a unstructured group of programmers from around the world, under the technical direction of Linus Torvalds and other key developers. Linux is a world-wide movement without any central structure, bureaucracy, or entity to control, coordinate, or otherwise direct its affairs. While this situation is a powerful part of the appeal and technical quality of Linux as an computer operating system, it can make for inefficient allocation of human resources, ineffective and even detrimental advocacy, public relations, user education and training.

2.2 How is Linux unique?

This loose structure is not likely to change with regard to Linux as a software project. And it's a good thing, too. Linux works precisely because people are free to come and go as they please: **free programmers are happy programmers are effective programmers**.

But this loose structure can make the average Linux user's life a little complicated–especially if that user isn't a programmer by profession or by vocation. Who does she call for support, training, or education? How does she know the kinds of uses for which Linux is well-suited?

In large part local LUGs provide the answers to these kinds of question. This is why LUGs are a crucial part of the Linux Movement. Because there is no "regional office" of the Linux Corporation in your town or village or metropolis, the local LUG takes on many of the same roles that a regional office does for a large multi-national corporation..

Linux is unique because it does not have, nor is it burdened by, a central structure or bureaucracy to allocate its resources, train its users, or provide support for its products. These jobs get done in a variety of ways: the Internet, consultants, VARs, support companies, colleges and universities. But, increasingly, in many places around the globe, they get done by a local LUG.

2.3 What is a user group?

Computer user groups, at least in the United States, are not a new phenomenon; in fact, they played an important role in the history of the personal computer. The personal computer arose in large part to satisfy the demand of electronics, Ham Radio, and other hobbyist user groups, as well as trade shows and swap meets, for affordable, personal access to computing resources. Of course eventually giants like IBM discovered that the PC was a good and profitable thing, but the impetus for the PC came from the people, by the people, and for the people.

In the United States, user groups have changed, and many for the worse, with the times. The financial woes of the largest user group ever, the *Boston Computer Society* (http://www.bcs.org/) have been well-reported; but all over the U.S. most of the big PC user groups have seen a decline in real membership. American user groups in their heyday concentrated on the production of newsletters, the maintenance of shareware and diskette libraries, meetings, social events, and, sometimes, even Bulletin Board Systems. With the advent of the Internet, however, many of the services that user groups once provided were transferred to things like CompuServe, AOL, and the Web.

The rise of Linux, however, coincided with and was intensified by general public's "discovery" of the Internet. As the Internet grew more popular, so did Linux: the Internet brought new users, developers, and vendors to the Linux Movement.

So just when traditional PC user groups were declining because of the Internet's popularity, this popularity propelled Linux forward, creating new demand for new user groups dedicated exclusively to Linux. To give just one indication of the ways in which a LUG is different than a traditional user group, I call the reader's attention to a curious fact: traditional user groups have had to maintain a fairly tight control over the kinds of software that its users copy and trade at its meetings. While illegal copying of commercial software certainly occurred at these meetings, it was officially discouraged and for good reason.

At a LUG meeting, however, this entire mind set simply does not apply. Far from being the kind of thing that a LUG ought to discourage, the free copying of Linux itself ought to be one of the primary activities of a LUG. In fact there is anecdotal evidence that traditional user groups sometimes have a difficult time adapting to the fact that Linux can be freely copied as many times as one needs or wants.

2.4 Summary

In order for the Linux Movement to continue to flourish, the proliferation and success of local LUGs, along with other factors, is an absolute requirement. Because of the unique status of Linux, the local LUG must provide some of the same functions that a "regional office" provides for large computer corporations like IBM, Microsoft, or Sun. LUGs can and must train, support, and educate Linux users, coordinate Linux consultants, advocate Linux as a computing solution, and even serve as a liaison to local media outlets like newspapers and television.

3 What LUGs are there?

Since this document is meant as a guide not only to maintaining and growing LUGs but also to founding them, it would be well before we go much further to determine what LUGs there are.

3.1 Lists of LUGs

There are several lists of LUGs available on the Web. If you want to found a local LUG, one of the first things to do is to determine where the nearest LUG is. *Your best bet may be to join a LUG that is already established in your area rather than founding a new one.*

As of the mid-1997, there are LUGs in all 50 states, the District of Columbia, and 26 other countries, including India, Russia, and most of Western and Eastern Europe.

Note: the biggest untapped computing market on the planet, China, does not yet appear to have a LUG, and India, the second most populous country on the planet, has only a few.

- *Finding Groups of Linux Users Everywhere* (http://www.ssc.com/glue/groups/)
- *LUG List Project* (http://www.nllgg.nl/lugww/)

It appears that the GLUE list is more comprehensive for American LUGs, while the LUG List Project offers more comprehensive international coverage.

3.2 Solidarity versus convenience

While the lists of LUGs on the Web are well-maintained, it is likely that they do not list every LUG. In addition to consulting these lists, I suggest, if you are considering founding a LUG, that you post a short message asking about the existence of a local LUG to *comp.os.linux.announce* (`news:comp.os.linux.announce`), *comp.os.linux.misc* (`news:comp.os.linux.misc`), or an appropriate regional Usenet hierarchy. If there isn't a LUG already in your area, then posting messages to these groups will alert potential members of your plans.

If you plan to found a local LUG, you should carefully balance convenience against solidarity. In other words, if there is a LUG in your metropolitan area, but on the other side of the city, it may be better to start a new group for the sake of convenience. But it may be better to join the pre-existing group for the sake of unity and solidarity. Greater numbers almost always means greater power, influence, and efficiency. While it might be nice to have two groups of 100 members each, there are certain advantages to one group of 200 members. Of course if you live in a small town or village, any group is better than no group at all.

The point is that starting a LUG is an arduous undertaking, and one that ought to be entered into with all the relevant facts, and with some appreciation of the effect on other groups.

4 What does a LUG do?

The goals of local LUGs are as varied as the locales in which they operate. There is no master plan for LUGs, nor is this document meant to supply one. Remember: Linux is free from bureaucracy and centralized control and so are local LUGs.

It is possible, however, to identify a core set of goals for a local LUG:

- advocacy,
- education,
- support,
- socializing.

Each local LUG will combine these and other goals in a unique way in order to satisfy the unique needs of its membership.

4.1 Linux advocacy

The urge to advocate the use of Linux is as natural to computer users as is eating or sleeping. When you find something that works and works well, the natural urge is to tell as many people about it as you can. The role of LUGs in Linux advocacy cannot be overestimated, especially since the wide-scale commercial acceptance of Linux which it so richly deserves has not yet been achieved. While it is certainly beneficial to the Linux Movement each and every time a computer journalist writes a positive review of Linux, it is also beneficial every time satisfied Linux users tell their friends, colleagues, employees or employers about Linux.

There is effective advocacy and there is ineffective carping: as Linux users, we must be constantly vigilant to advocate Linux in such a way as to reflect positively on both the product, its creators and developers, and our fellow users. The Linux Advocacy Mini-HOWTO, available at the Linux Documentation Project, gives some helpful suggestions in this regard. Suffice it to say that advocacy is an important aspect of the mission of a local LUG.

There may come a time when Linux advocacy is pretty much beside the point because Linux has more or less won the day, when the phrase "No one ever got fired for using Linux" becomes a reality. Until that time, however, the local LUG plays an indispensable role in promoting the use of Linux. It does so because its advocacy is free, well-intentioned, and backed up by organizational commitment. If a person comes to know about Linux through the efforts of a local LUG, then that person, as a new Linux user, is already ahead of the game: *she is already aware of the existence of an organization that will help her install, configure, and even maintain Linux on whatever computers she is willing to dedicate to it.*

New Linux users who are already in contact with a local LUG are ahead of those whose interest in Linux has been piqued by a computer journalist, but who have no one to whom to turn to aid them in their quest to install, run, and learn Linux.

It is, therefore, important for local LUGs to advocate Linux because their advocacy is effective, well-supported, and free.

4.2 Linux education

Not only is it the business of a local LUG to advocate the use of Linux, it may also turn its efforts to training its member, as well as the computing public in its area, about Linux and associated components. In my own estimation, the goal of user education is the single most important goal a LUG may undertake. Of course, as I have already pointed out, LUGs are perfectly free to organize themselves and their activities around any of these, or other, goals. I believe, however, that LUGs can have the greatest impact on the Linux Movement by educating and training Linux users.

Local LUGs may choose to undertake the goal of education simply because there is no other local entity from which a Linux user may receive technically-oriented education. While it is certainly the case that universities, colleges, and junior colleges are increasingly turning to Linux as a way to educate their students, both efficiently and cheaply, about Unix-like operating systems, some Linux users are either unable or unwilling to register for courses in order to learn Linux. For these users the local LUG is a valuable resource for enhancement or creation of advanced computer skills: Unix-like system administration, system programming, support and creation of Internet and Intranet technologies, etc.

In an ironic twist, many local LUGs are even sharing the burden of worker training with large corporations. Every worker at Acme Corp that expands her computer skills by participating in a local LUG is one less worker Acme Corp has to train or pay to train. Even though using and administering a Linux PC at home isn't the same as administering a corporate data warehouse, call center, or similar high-availability facility, it is light years more complex, more rewarding, and more educational than using and administering a Windows 95 PC at home. As Linux itself advances toward things like journalling file systems, high-availability, real-time capacity, and other high-end Unix features, the already blurry line between Linux and the "real" Unixes will get even more indistinct.

Not only is such education a form of worker training, but it will also serve, as information technology becomes an increasingly vital part of the global economy, as a kind of community service. In most metropolitan areas in the United States, for example, it is possible for a local LUG to take Linux into local schools, small businesses, community and social organizations, and other non-corporate environments. This accomplishes the task of Linux advocacy and also helps train the general public about Linux as a Unix-like operating system. As more and more of these kinds of organizations seek to establish an Internet presence or provide dial-in access to their workers, students, and constituents, the opportunities arise for local LUGs to participate in the life of their community by educating it about a free and freely-available operating system. This kind of community service allows the average Linux user to emulate the kind of generosity that has characterized Linux, and the free software community, from the very beginning. Most Linux users can't program like Linus Torvalds, but we can all all give our time and abilities to other Linux users, the Linux community, and the broader community in which work and live.

Linux is a natural fit for these kinds of organization because deploying it doesn't commit them to expensive license, upgrade, or maintenance fees. Because Linux is also technically elegant and economical, it runs very well on the the kinds of disposable hardware that corporations typically cast off and that non-profit organizations are only too happy to use. As more and more people discover every day, that old 486 collecting dust in the closet can do real work if someone will install Linux on it.

In addition, Linux education has a cumulative effect on the other goals of a local LUG, in particular the goal of Linux support discussed below. Better Linux education means better Linux support. The more people that a LUG can count on to reach its support goals, the easier support becomes and, therefore, the more of it can be done. The more new and inexperienced users a local LUG can support and eventually educate about Linux, the larger and more effective the LUG can become. In other words, if a LUG focuses solely on Linux support to the neglect of Linux education, the natural barriers to organizational growth will be more restrictive. If only two or three percent of the members of a LUG take upon themselves the task of supporting the others, the growth of the LUG will be stifled. One thing you can count on: if new and inexperienced users don't get the help with Linux they need from a local LUG, they won't participate in that LUG for very long. If a larger percentage of members support the others, the LUG will be able to grow much larger. Linux education is the key to this dynamic: education turns new Linux users into experienced ones.

Free education about free Linux also highlights the degree to which Linux is part and parcel of the free software Community. So it seems appropriate that local LUGs focus not solely on Linux education but also education about all of the various software systems and technologies that run under Linux. These include, for instance, the GNU suite of programs and utilities, the Apache Web server, the XFree86 implementation of X, $\TeX$, $\LaTeX$, etc. Fortunately the list of free software that runs under Linux is a long and diverse one.

Finally, Linux is a self-documenting operating environment; in other words, if we don't write the documentation, nobody is going to do it for us. Toward that end, make sure that LUG members are well aware of the *Linux Documentation Project* (`http://sunsite.unc.edu/LDP/`), which can be found at mirrors worldwide. Consider providing an LDP mirror for the local Linux community and for LUG members. Also make sure to publicize—through `comp.os.linux.announce`, the LDP, and other pertinent sources of Linux information—any relevant documentation that is developed by the LUG: technical presentations, tutorials, local FAQs, etc. There is a lot of Linux documentation produced in LUGs that doesn't benefit the worldwide Linux community because no one outside the LUG knows about it. Don't let the LUGs efforts in this regard go to waste: it is highly probable that if someone at one LUG had a question or problem with something, then people at other LUGs around the world will have the same questions and problems.

4.3 Linux support

Of course for the desperate **newbie** the primary role of a local LUG is Linux support. But it is a mistake to suppose that Linux support only means *technical* support for new Linux users. It can and should mean much more.

Local LUGs have the opportunity to support:

- users,
- consultants,
- businesses, non-profit organizations, and schools,
- the Linux Movement,

4.3.1 Users

The most frequent complaint from new Linux users, once they have gotten Linux installed, is the steep learning curve which is not at all unique to Linux but is, rather, a characteristic of all modern Unixes. With the steepness of the learning curve, however, comes the power and flexibility of a complex operating system. A local LUG is often the only resource that a new Linux user has available to help flatten out the learning curve.

But even if a new Linux user doesn't know it yet, she needs more than just technical support: Linux and the free software worlds are both rapidly moving targets. The local LUGs form an invaluable conduit of information about Linux and other free software products. Not only does Linux lack a central bureaucracy, but it also for the most part lacks the kind of journalistic infrastructure from which users of other computer systems benefit. The Linux Movement does have resources like *Linux Journal* (`http://www.ssc.com/lj/`) and *Linux Gazette* (`http://www.ssc.com/lg/`), but many new Linux users are unaware of these resources. In addition, as monthly publications they are often already out of date about bug fixes, security problems, patches, new kernels, etc. This is where the local LUG as a source and conduit of timely information is so vital to new and experienced Linux users alike.

For example, until a new Linux user knows that the newest kernels are available from *ftp.kernel.org* (`ftp://ftp.kernel.org`) or that the Linux Documentation Project usually has newer versions of Linux HOWTOs than a CD-based Linux distribution, it is up to the local LUG, as the primary support entity, to be a conduit of timely and useful information.

In fact it may be just a bit misleading to focus on the support role that local LUGs provide to new users: intermediate and advanced users also benefit from the proliferation of timely and useful tips, facts, and secrets about Linux. Because of the complexity of Linux, even advanced users often learn new tricks or techniques simply by becoming involved in a local LUG. Sometimes they learn about software packages they didn't know existed, sometimes they just remember that arcane `vi` command sequence they've not used since college.

4.3.2 Consultants

It is, I think, rather obvious to claim that local LUGs ought to be in the business of supporting new Linux users. After all, if they're not supposed to be doing that, what are they to do? It may not be as obvious that local LUGs can play an important role in supporting local Linux consultants. Whether they do Linux consulting full-time or only part-time, consultants can be an important part of a local LUG. How can the LUG support them?

The answer to that question is just the answer to another question: what is it that Linux consultants want and need? They need someone for whom to consult. A local LUG provides the best way for those who offer Linux consulting to find those who need Linux consulting. The local LUG can informally broker connections between consulting suppliers and consulting consumers simply by getting all, or as many as possible, of the people interested in Linux in a local area together and talking with one another. How LUGs do that will occupy us below. What is important here is to point out that LUGs can and should play this role as well. The Linux Consultants HOWTO is an important document in this regard, but it is surely the case that only a fraction of the full-time and part-time Linux consultants worldwide are registered in the Consultants HOWTO.

The relationship is mutually beneficial. Consultants aid LUGs by providing experienced leadership, both technically and organizationally, while LUGs aid consultants by putting them in contact with the kinds of people who need their services. New and inexperienced users gain benefit from both LUGs and consultants since their routine or simple requests for support are handled by LUGs *gratis*, and their complex needs and problems—the kind that obviously require the services of a paid consultant—can be handled by the consultants whom the local LUG helps them contact.

The line between support requests that need a consultant and those that do not is sometimes indistinct; but in most cases the difference is clear. While a local LUG doesn't want to gain the reputation for pawning new users off unnecessarily on consultants–as this is simply rude and very anti-Linux behavior–there is no reason for LUGs not to help broker contacts between the users who need consulting services and the professionals who offer them.

Please see Martin Michlmayr's Consultant's HOWTO, at http://sunsite.unc.edu/LDP/HOWTO/Consultants-HOWTO.html for an international list of Linux consultants.

4.3.3 Businesses, non-profit organizations, and schools

LUGs also have the opportunity to support local businesses and organizations. This support has two aspects. First, LUGs can support businesses and organizations that want to use Linux as a part of their computing and IT efforts. Second, LUGs can support local businesses and organizations that develop for Linux, cater to Linux users, support or install Linux, etc.

The kinds of support that LUGs can provide to local businesses that want to use Linux as a part of their computing operations isn't really all that different from the kinds of support LUGs give to individuals who want to run Linux at home. For example, compiling the Linux kernel doesn't really vary from home to business. Supporting businesses using Linux, however, may mean that a LUG needs to concentrate on commercial software that runs on Linux, rather than concentrating solely on free software. If Linux is going to continue to maintain its momentum as a viable computing alternative, then it's going to take software vendors who are willing to write for and port to Linux as a commercially-viable platform. If local LUGs can play a role in helping business users evaluate commercial Linux solutions, then more software vendors will be encouraged to consider Linux in their development and planning.

This leads us directly to the second kind of support that a local LUG can give to local businesses. Local LUGs can serve as a clearing house for the kind of information that is available in very few other places. For example:

- Which local ISP is Linux-friendly?
- Are there any local hardware vendors that build Linux PCs?
- Does anyone sell Linux CDs locally?

Maintaining and making this kind of information public not only helps the members of a local LUG, but it also helps Linux-friendly local businesses as well, and it encourages them to continue to be Linux-friendly. It may even, in some cases, help contribute to a competitive atmosphere in which other businesses are encouraged to become Linux-friendly too.

4.3.4 Linux Movement

I have been referring throughout this HOWTO to something I call the **Linux Movement**. There really is no better way to describe the international Linux phenomenon than to call it a movement: it isn't a bureaucracy, but it is organized; it isn't a corporation, but it is important to businesses all over the world. The best way for a local LUG to support the international Linux movement is to work to insure that the local Linux community is robust, vibrant, and growing. Linux is *developed* internationally, which is easy enough to see by reading `/usr/src/linux/MAINTAINERS`. But Linux is also *used* internationally. And this ever-expanding user base is the key to Linux's continued success. And that is where the local LUG plays an incalculably important role.

The strength of the Linux Movement internationally is the simple fact that Linux offers unprecedented computing power and sophistication for its cost and for its freedom. The keys are value and independence from proprietary control. Every time a new person, group, business, or organization has the opportunity to be exposed to Linux's inherent value the Linux Movement grows in strength and numbers. Local LUGs can make that happen.

4.4 Linux socializing

The last goal of a local LUG that I will mention here is socializing. In some ways this is the most difficult goal to discuss because it is not clear how many or to what degree LUGs engage in it. While it would be strange to have a local LUG that didn't engage in the other goals, there very well may be local LUGs somewhere in the world for which socialization isn't an important consideration.

It seems, however, that whenever two or three Linux users get together fun, high jinks, and, often, beer are sure to follow. Linus Torvalds has always had one enduring goal for Linux: to have more fun. For hackers, kernel developers, and Linux users, there's nothing quite like downloading a new kernel, recompiling an old one, twittering with a window manager, or hacking some code. It is the sheer fun of Linux that keeps many LUGs together, and it is this kind of fun that leads many LUGs naturally to socializing.

By "socializing" here I mean primarily sharing experiences, forming friendships, and mutually-shared admiration and respect. There is another meaning, however, one that social scientists call "socialization." In any movement, institution, or human community, there is the need for some process or pattern of events in and by which, to put it in Linux terms, newbies are turned into hackers. In other words, socialization turns you from "one of them" to "one of us."

For armed forces in the U.S. and in most countries, this process is called boot camp or basic training. This is the process whereby civilians are transformed into soldiers. The Linux movement has analogous requirements. It is important that new Linux users come to learn what it means to be a Linux user, what is expected of them as a member of an international community, the special vocabulary of the Linux movement, its unique requirements and opportunities. This may be as simple as how Linux users in a particular locale pronounce "Linux." It may be as profound as the ways in which Linux users should advocate, and the ways in which they should, more importantly, itshapé refrain from advocating Linux.

Linux socialization, unlike "real world" socialization, can occur on mailing lists and Usenet, although the efficacy of the latter is constantly challenged precisely by poorly socialized users. In my view, socialization and socializing are both done best in the company of real, flesh-and-blood fellow human beings, and not by incorporeal voices on a mailing list or Usenet group.

5 Local LUG activities

In the previous section I focused exclusively on what LUGs do and what they ought to be doing. In this section the focus shifts to practical strategies for accomplishing these goals.

There are, despite the endless permutations of form, two basic things that local LUGs do: first, they meet together in physical space; second, they communicate with each other in cyberspace. Everything or nearly everything that LUGs do can be seen in terms of meetings and online resources.

5.1 Meetings

As I said above, physical meetings are synonymous with LUGs and with most computer user groups. LUGs have these kinds of meetings:

- social,
- technical presentations,
- informal discussion groups,
- user group business,
- Linux installation,
- configuration and bug-squashing.

What do LUGs do at these meetings?

- Install Linux for newbies and strangers;
- Teach members about Linux;
- Compare Linux to other operating systems;
- Teach members about the software that runs on Linux;
- Discuss the ways in which Linux can be advocated;
- Discuss the importance of the Free Software Movement;
- Discuss the business of the user group;
- Eat, drink, and be merry.

5.2 Online resources

The commercial rise of the Internet coincided roughly with the rise of Linux, and the latter in large part owes something to the former. The Internet has always been an important asset for Linux development. It is no different for LUGs. Most LUGs have web pages if not whole Web sites. In fact, I am not sure how else to find a local LUG but to check the Web.

It makes sense, then, for a local LUG to make use of whatever Internet technologies they can appropriate: Web sites, mailing lists, gopher, FTP, e-mail, WAIS, finger, news, etc. As the world of commerce is discovering, the Internet can be an effective way to advertise, inform, educate, and even sell. The other reason that LUGs make extensive use of Internet technologies is that it is the very essence of Linux to *provide* a stable and rich platform for the deployment of these technologies. So not only do LUGs benefit from, say, the establishment of a Web site because it advertises their existence and helps organize their members, but in deploying these technologies, the members of the LUG are provided an opportunity to learn about this technology and see Linux at work.

Some LUGs that use the Internet effectively:

- *Atlanta Linux Enthusiasts* (`http://www.ale.org/`)
- *North Texas Linux Users Group* (`http://www.ntlug.org/`)

- *Boston Linux and Unix* (http://www.blu.org/)
- *Colorado Linux Users and Enthusiasts* (http://spot.elfwerks.com/ clue/)
- *BLUG - BHZ Linux Users Group (Brazil)* (http://www.bhz.ampr.org/ linux/)
- *Ottawa Carleton Linux Users Group* (http://www.oclug.on.ca/)
- *Provence Linux Users Group* (http://www.pipo.com/plug/)
- *Duesseldorf Linux Users Group* (http://www.hsp.de/ dlug/)
- *Israeli Linux Users Group* (http://www.linux.org.il/)
- *Tokyo Linux Users Group* (http://www.twics.co.jp/ tlug/)
- *Linux in Mexico* (http://www.linux.org.mx/)
- *Netherlands Linux Users Group (NLLGG)* (http://www.nllgg.nl/)
- *St. Petersburg Linux User Group* (http://ethereal.ru/ mbravo/spblug/index.html)
- *Linux User Group of Singapore* (http://www.lugs.org.sg/)
- *Essex Linux User Group* (http://www.epos.demon.co.uk/)
- *Turkish Linux User Group* (http://www.linux.org.tr/)
- *Linux User Group of Rochester* (http://www.lugor.org/)
- *Korean Linux Users Group* (http://www.linux-kr.org)

Please let me know if your LUG uses the Internet in an important or interesting way; I'd like this list to include your group.

6 Practical suggestions

Finally, I want to make some very practical, even mundane, suggestions for anyone wanting to found, maintain, or grow a LUG.

6.1 LUG support organizations

There are several organizations that offer assistance to local LUGs.

GLUE

Groups of Linux Users Everywhere is a user group coordination and support program started by SSC, the same people who publish *Linux Journal*. The *GLUE program* (http://www.ssc.com/glue/) is an inexpensive way for a local LUG to provide some benefits to its membership.

Linux Systems Labs

LSL offers their Tri-Linux Disk set (Three Linux distributions on four CDs: Red Hat, Slackware, and Debian) to LUGs for resale at a considerable discount.

Linux Mall User Group Program

Sponsored by WorkGroup Solutions, the *Linux Mall User Group Program* (http://www.LinuxMall.com/usergrp.program.html) offers a range of benefits for participating User Groups. LUGs are also free to participate in *Linux Mall's Referral Program* (http://www.LinuxMall.com/mallrfr.html) as well.

Cleveland Linux User's Group

Owns the Internet domain, lug.net. They will provide your LUG an Internet domain name at lug.net: your-LUG-name-or-citylug.net. More information may be found at *LUG.NET* (http://www.lug.net/) or by e-mailing Jeff Garvas.

Red Hat Software's User Group Program

Assists LUGs to develop and grow. More information may be found at *Red Hat Web site* (http://www.redhat.com/redhat/rhug.html)

6.2 Founding a LUG

- Determine the nearest pre-existing LUG.
- Announce your intentions on `comp.os.linux.announce` and on an appropriate regional hierarchy.
- Announce your intention wherever computer users are in your area: bookstores, swap meets, cybercafes, colleges and universities, corporations, Internet service providers, etc.
- Find Linux-friendly businesses or institutions in your area that may be willing to help you form the LUG.
- Form a mailing list or some means of communication between the people who express an interest in forming a LUG.
- Ask key people specifically for help in spreading the word about your intention to form a LUG.
- Solicit space on a Web server to put a few HTML pages together about the group.
- Begin looking for a meeting place.
- Schedule an initial meeting.
- Discuss at the initial meeting the goals for the LUG.

6.3 Maintaining and growing a LUG

- Make the barriers to LUG membership as low as possible.
- Make the LUG's Web site a priority: keep all information current, make it easy to find details about meetings (who, what, and where), and make contact information and feedback mechanisms prominent.
- Install Linux for anyone who wants it.
- Post flyers, messages, or hand bills wherever computer users are in your area.
- Secure dedicated leadership.
- Follow Linus's benevolent dictator model of leadership.
- Take the big decisions to the members for a vote.
- Start a mailing list devoted to technical support and ask the "gurus" to participate on it.
- Schedule a mixture of advanced and basic, formal and informal, presentations.
- Support the software development efforts of your members.
- Find way to raise money without dues: for instance, selling Linux merchandise to your members and to others.
- Consider securing formal legal standing for the group, such as incorporation or tax-exempt status.
- Find out if your meeting place is restricting growth of the LUG.
- Meet in conjunction with swap meets, computer shows, or other community events where computer users—i.e., potential Linux converts—are likely to gather.
- Elect formal leadership for the LUG as soon as is practical: some helpful officers might include President, Treasurer, Secretary, Meeting Host (general announcements, speaker introductions, opening and closing remarks, etc.), Publicity Coordinator (handles Usenet and e-mail postings, local publicity), and Program Coordinator (organizes and schedules speakers at LUG meetings).
- Provide ways for members and others to give feedback about the direction, goals, and strategies of the LUG.
- Support Linux and Free Software development efforts by donating Web space, a mailing list, or FTP site.
- Establish an FTP site for relevant software.
- Archive everything the LUG does for the Web site.
- Solicit "door prizes" from Linux vendors, VARs, etc. to give away at meetings.
- Give credit where credit is due.
- Join SSC's GLUE (Groups of Linux Users Everywhere) but be aware they charge a membership fee.
- Submit your LUG's information to all of the Lists of LUGs.
- Publicize your meetings on appropriate Usenet groups and in local computer publications and newspapers.

- Compose promotional materials, like Postscript files, for instance, that members can use to help publicize the LUG at workplaces, bookstores, computer stores, etc.
- Make sure you know what LUG members want the LUG to do.
- Release press releases to local media outlets about any unusual LUG events like an Installation Fest, Net Day, etc.
- Use LUG resources and members to help local non-profit organizations and schools with their Information Technology needs.
- Advocate the use of Linux zealously but responsibly.
- Play to the strengths of LUG members.
- Maintain good relations with Linux vendors, VARs, developers, etc.
- Identity and contact Linux consultants in your area.
- Network with the leaders of other LUGs in your area, state, region, or country to share experiences, tricks, and resources.
- Keep LUG members advised on the state of Linux software—new kernels, bugs, fixes, patches, security advisories—and the state of the Linux world at large—new ports, trademark and licensing issues, where Linus is living and working, etc.
- Notify the Linux Documentation Project—and other pertinent sources of Linux information—about the documentation that the LUG produces: technical presentations, tutorials, local HOWTOs, etc.

7 Legal and organizational issues

7.1 United States legal issues

There is a strong case to be made for formal organization of local LUGs. I will not make that case here. If, however, you are interested in formally organizing your local LUG, then this section will introduce you to some of the relevant issues.

Note: this section should not be construed as competent legal counsel. These issues require the expertise of competent legal counsel; you should, before acting on any of the statements made in this section, consult an attorney.

There are at least two different legal statuses that a local LUG in the United States may attain:

1. incorporation as a non-profit entity,
2. tax-exemption.

Although the relevant statutes differ from state to state, most states allow user groups to incorporate as non-profit entities. The benefits of incorporation for a local LUG may include limitations of liability of LUG members and volunteers, as well as limitation or even exemption from state corporate franchise taxes.

While you should consult competent legal counsel before incorporating your LUG as a non-profit entity, you can probably reduce your legal fees if you are acquainted with the relevant issues before consulting with an attorney. I recommend the *Non-Lawyers Non-Profit Corporation Kit* (ISBN 0-937434-35-3).

As for the second status, tax-exemption, this is not a legal status so much as a judgment by the Internal Revenue Service. It is important for you to know that incorporation as a non-profit entity does not insure that the IRS will rule that your LUG is to be tax-exempt. It is possible to have a non-profit corporation that is not also tax-exempt.

The IRS has a relatively simple document that explains the criteria and process for tax-exemption. It is *Publication 557: Tax-Exempt Status for Your Organization*. It is available as an Adobe Acrobat file from the IRS's Web site. I strongly recommend that you read this document before filing for incorporation as a non-profit entity. While becoming a non-profit corporation cannot insure that your LUG will be declared tax-exempt by the IRS, there are ways to incorporate that will prevent the IRS from declaring your LUG to be tax-exempt. *Tax-Exempt Status for Your Organization* clearly sets out the necessary conditions for your LUG to be declared tax-exempt.

Finally, there are resources available on the Internet for non-profit and tax-exempt organizations. Some of the material is probably relevant to your local LUG.

7.2 International legal issues

I need input from LUG leaders around the world in order to flesh this section out.

8 About this document

8.1 Terms of Use

8.2 Acknowledgements

I want to thank all the wonderful people I met during 1996–1997 when I served as President of the North Texas Linux Users Group. They helped inspire me to use Linux full-time. The best thing about Linux really is the people you meet.

In addition, the following people have made helpful comments and suggestions:

- Hugo van der Kooij
- Greg Hankins
- Charles Lindahl
- Rick Moen
- Jeff Garvas

Part LI

"Virtual Services HOWTO" by Brian Ackerman,

brian@nycrc.net

The Linux Documentation Project
The original, unaltered edition of this, and other, LDP documents, is on line at http://sunsite.unc.edu/LDP/.

Contents

1 Introduction

1.1 Knowledge Required

Creating a virtual services machine is not all that difficult. However, more than fundamental knowledge is required. And this document is not a primer to how to fully configure a Linux machine.

In order to understand this HOWTO document it is assumed that you are thoroughly familiar with the following:

- Compiling a Linux kernel and adding IP aliasing support; IP Alias Mini-HOWTO.
- Setting up and configuring of network devices; NET-3 HOWTO.
- Setting up of `inetd`; NET-3 HOWTO.
- Compiling and installing various network packages like Sendmail, Site; Apache, Site, Wu-Ftpd FAQs.
- Setting up DNS; DNS HOWTO.

If you are uncertain of how to proceed with any of the above it is strongly recommended that you use the links provided to familiarize yourself with all packages. I will not reply to any mail regarding any of the above. Please direct any questions to the appropriate author of the HOWTO.

1.2 Purpose

The purpose of virtual services is to allow a single machine to recognize multiple IP addresses without multiple network cards. IP aliasing is a kernel option that allows you to assign each network device more than one IP address. The kernel then multiplexes (swaps between them very fast) in the background and to the user it appears like you have more than one network card.

This multiplexing allows multiple domains (www.domain1.com, www.domain2.com, etc.) to be hosted by the same machine for the same cost as hosting one domain. Unfortunately, most services (ftp, web, mail) were not designed to handle multiple domains. In order to make them work properly you must modify both configuration files and source code. This document describes how to make these modifications in the setting up of a virtual machine.

A daemon is also required in order to make virtual services function. The source for this daemon, `virtuald`, is provided later in this document.

1.3 Feedback

This document will expand as packages are updated and source or configuration modifications change. If there are any portions of this document that are unclear please feel free to email me with your suggestions or questions. So that I do not have to go searching through the entire HOWTO please make certain that all comments are as specific as possible and include the section where the uncertainty lies. It is important that all mail be addressed with "VIRTSERVICES HOWTO" in the subject line. Any other mail will be considered personal and all my friends know that I do not ever read my personal mail so it will probably get discarded with theirs.

Please note that my examples are just that, examples and should not be copied verbatim. You may have to insert your own values. If you are having trouble, send me mail, with all the pertinent configuration files and the error messages you get when installing, and I will look them over and mail my suggestions back.

1.4 Copyright/Distribution

2 IP aliasing

IP aliasing is a kernel option that needs to be set up in order to run a virtual hosting machine. There is already a Mini-HOWTO on IP aliasing. Consult that for any questions on how to set it up.

3 Virtuald

3.1 How it works

Every network connection is made up of two IP address/port pairs. The API (Applications Program Interface) for network programming is called the Sockets API. The socket acts like an open file and by reading/writing to it you can send data over a network connection. There is a function call `getsockname` that will return the IP address of the local socket. `irtuald` uses `getsockname` to determine which IP on the local machine is being accessed. Virtuald reads a config file to retrieve the directory associated with that IP. It will `chroot` to that directory and hand the connection off to the service. `chroot` resets / or the root directory to a new point so everything higher in the directory tree is cut off from the running program. Therefore, each IP address gets their own virtual file system. To the network program this is transparent and the program will behave like nothing happened. `virtuald` in conjunction with a program like `inetd` can then be used to virtualize any service.

3.2 inetd

`inetd` is a network super server that listens at multiple ports and when it receives a connection (for example, an incoming POP request), `inetd` performs the network negotiation and hands the network connection off to the specified program. This prevents servers from running idly when they are not needed.

A standard `/etc/inetd.conf` file looks like this:

```
ftp stream tcp nowait root /usr/sbin/tcpd wu.ftpd -l -a
pop-3 stream tcp nowait root /usr/sbin/tcpd in.qpop -s
```

A virtual `/etc/inetd.conf` file looks like this:

```
ftp stream tcp nowait root /usr/bin/virtuald virtuald /virtual/conf.ftp wu.ftpd -l -a
pop-3 stream tcp nowait root /usr/bin/virtuald virtuald /virtual/conf.pop in.qpop -s
```

3.3 virtual.conf

Each service gets a conf file that will control what IPs and directories are allowed for that service. You can have one master configuration file or several configuration files if you want each service to get a different list of domains. A `virtual.conf` file looks like this:

```
# This is a comment and so are blank lines

# Format IP <SPACE> dir <NOSPACES>
10.10.10.129 /virtual/foo.bar.com
10.10.10.130 /virtual/bar.foo.com
10.10.10.157 /virtual/boo.la.com
```

3.4 The source for virtuald

```
#include <netinet/in.h>
#include <sys/socket.h>
#include <arpa/inet.h>
#include <stdarg.h>
#include <string.h>
#include <syslog.h>
#include <stdio.h>

#define BUFSIZE 8192

main(int argc,char **argv)
{
        char buffer[BUFSIZE];
        char *ipaddr,*dir;
```

```
        logit("Virtuald Starting: $Revision: 1.6 $");
        if (!argv[1])
        {
                logit("invalid arguments: no conf file");
                quitting_virtuald(0);
        }
        if (!argv[2])
        {
                logit("invalid arguments: no program to run");
                quitting_virtuald(0);
        }
        if (getipaddr(&ipaddr))
        {
                logit("getipaddr failed");
                quitting_virtuald(0);
        }
        sprintf(buffer,"Incoming ip: %s",ipaddr);
        logit(buffer);
        if (iptodir(&dir,ipaddr,argv[1]))
        {
                logit("iptodir failed");
                quitting_virtuald(0);
        }
        if (chroot(dir)<0)
        {
                logit("chroot failed: %m");
                quitting_virtuald(0);
        }
        sprintf(buffer,"Chroot dir: %s",dir);
        logit(buffer);
        if (chdir("/")<0)
        {
                logit("chdir failed: %m");
                quitting_virtuald(0);
        }
        if (execvp(argv[2],argv+2)<0)
        {
                logit("execvp failed: %m");
                quitting_virtuald(0);
        }
}

int logit(char *buf)
{
        openlog("virtuald",LOG_PID,LOG_DAEMON);
        syslog(LOG_ERR,buf);
        closelog();
        return 0;
}

int quitting_virtuald(int retval)
{
        exit(retval);
        return 0;
}

int getipaddr(char **ipaddr)
```

```
{
        struct sockaddr_in virtual_addr;
        static char ipaddrbuf[BUFSIZE];
        int virtual_len;
        char *ipptr;

        virtual_len=sizeof(virtual_addr);
        if (getsockname(0,(struct sockaddr *)&virtual_addr,&virtual_len)<0)
        {
                logit("getipaddr: getsockname failed: %m");
                return -1;
        }
        if (!(ipptr=inet_ntoa(virtual_addr.sin_addr)))
        {
                logit("getipaddr: inet_ntoa failed: %m");
                return -1;
        }
        strncpy(ipaddrbuf,ipptr,sizeof(ipaddrbuf)-1);
        *ipaddr=ipaddrbuf;
        return 0;
}

int iptodir(char **dir,char *ipaddr,char *filename)
{
        char buffer[BUFSIZE],*bufptr;
        static char dirbuf[BUFSIZE];
        FILE *fp;

        if (!(fp=fopen(filename,"r")))
        {
                logit("iptodir: fopen failed: %m");
                return -1;
        }
        *dir=NULL;
        while(fgets(buffer,BUFSIZE,fp))
        {
                buffer[strlen(buffer)-1]=0;
                if (*buffer=='#' || *buffer==0)
                        continue;
                if (!(bufptr=strchr(buffer,' ')))
                {
                        logit("iptodir: strchr failed");
                        return -1;
                }
                *bufptr++=0;
                if (!strcmp(buffer,ipaddr))
                {
                        strncpy(dirbuf,bufptr,sizeof(dirbuf)-1);
                        *dir=dirbuf;
                        break;
                }
        }
        if (fclose(fp)==EOF)
        {
                logit("iptodir: fclose failed: %m");
                return -1;
        }
        if (!*dir)
```

```
        {
                logit("iptodir: ip not found in conf file");
                return -1;
        }
        return 0;
}
```

4 Virt scripts

4.1 virtfs

Each domain should get their own directory structure. Since you are using `chroot` you will require duplicate copies of the shared libraries, binaries, configuration files, etc. I use `/virtual/domain.com` for each domain that I create. I realize that you are taking up more disk space but it is cheaper than a whole new machine and network cards. If you really want to preserve space you can link the files together so only one copy of each binary exists.

Here is a sample `virtfs` script:

```
#!/bin/bash

echo '$Revision: 1.6 $'

echo -n "Enter the domain name: "
read domain

if [ "$domain" = "" ]
then
        echo Nothing entered: aborting
        exit 0
fi

leadingdir=/virtual

echo -n "Enter leading dir: (Enter for default: $leadingdir): "
read ans

if [ "$ans" != "" ]
then
        leadingdir=$ans
fi

newdir=$leadingdir/$domain

if [ -d "$newdir" ]
then
        echo New directory: $newdir: ALREADY exists
        exit 0
else
        echo New directory: $newdir
fi

echo Create $newdir
mkdir -p $newdir

echo Create bin
cp -pdR /bin $newdir

echo Create dev
cp -pdR /dev $newdir
```

```
echo Create dev/log
ln -f /virtual/log $newdir/dev/log

echo Create etc
mkdir -p $newdir/etc
for i in /etc/*
do
        if [ -d "$i" ]
        then
                continue
        fi
        cp -pd $i $newdir/etc
done

echo Create etc/skel
mkdir -p $newdir/etc/skel

echo Create home
for i in a b c d e f g h i j k l m n o p q r s t u v w x y z
do
        mkdir -p $newdir/home/$i
done

echo Create home/c/crc
mkdir -p $newdir/home/c/crc
chown crc.users $newdir/home/c/crc

echo Create lib
mkdir -p $newdir/lib
for i in /lib/*
do
        if [ -d "$i" ]
        then
                continue
        fi
        cp -pd $i $newdir/lib
done

echo Create proc
mkdir -p $newdir/proc

echo Create sbin
cp -pdR /sbin $newdir

echo Create tmp
mkdir -p -m 0777 $newdir/tmp
chmod +t $newdir/tmp

echo Create usr
mkdir -p $newdir/usr

echo Create usr/bin
cp -pdR /usr/bin $newdir/usr

echo Create usr/lib
mkdir -p $newdir/usr/lib
```

```
echo Create usr/lib/locale
cp -pdR /usr/lib/locale $newdir/usr/lib

echo Create usr/lib/terminfo
cp -pdR /usr/lib/terminfo $newdir/usr/lib

echo Create usr/lib/zoneinfo
cp -pdR /usr/lib/zoneinfo $newdir/usr/lib

echo Create usr/lib/\*.so\*
cp -pdR /usr/lib/*.so* $newdir/usr/lib

echo Create usr/sbin
cp -pdR /usr/sbin $newdir/usr

echo Linking usr/tmp
ln -s /tmp $newdir/usr/tmp

echo Create var
mkdir -p $newdir/var

echo Create var/lock
cp -pdR /var/lock $newdir/var

echo Create var/log
mkdir -p $newdir/var/log

echo Create var/log/wtmp
cp /dev/null $newdir/var/log/wtmp

echo Create var/run
cp -pdR /var/run $newdir/var

echo Create var/run/utmp
cp /dev/null $newdir/var/run/utmp

echo Create var/spool
cp -pdR /var/spool $newdir/var

echo Linking var/tmp
ln -s /tmp $newdir/var/tmp

echo Create var/www/html
mkdir -p $newdir/var/www/html
chown webmast.www $newdir/var/www/html
chmod g+s $newdir/var/www/html

echo Create var/www/master
mkdir -p $newdir/var/www/master
chown webmast.www $newdir/var/www/master

echo Create var/www/server
mkdir -p $newdir/var/www/server
chown webmast.www $newdir/var/www/server

exit 0
```

4.2 virtexec

To execute commands in a virtual environment you have to chroot to that directory and then run the command. I have written a special shell script called virtexec that handles this for any command:

```
#!/bin/sh

echo '$Revision: 1.6 $'

BNAME='basename $0'
FIRST4CHAR='echo $BNAME | cut -c1-4'
REALBNAME='echo $BNAME | cut -c5-'

if [ "$BNAME" = "virtexec" ]
then
        echo Cannot run virtexec directly: NEED a symlink
        exit 0
fi

if [ "$FIRST4CHAR" != "virt" ]
then
        echo Symlink not a virt function
        exit 0
fi

list=""
num=1
for i in /virtual/*
do
        if [ ! -d "$i" ]
        then
                continue
        fi
        if [ "$i" = "/virtual/lost+found" ]
        then
                continue
        fi
        list="$list $i $num"
        num='expr $num + 1'
done

if [ "$list" = "" ]
then
        echo No virtual environments exist
        exit 0
fi

dialog --clear --title 'Virtexec' --menu Pick 20 70 12 $list 2> /tmp/menu.$$
if [ "$?" = "0" ]
then
        newdir='cat /tmp/menu.$$'
else
        newdir=""
fi
tput clear
rm -f /tmp/menu.$$

echo '$Revision: 1.6 $'
```

```
if [ ! -d "$newdir" ]
then
        echo New directory: $newdir: NOT EXIST
        exit 0
else
        echo New directory: $newdir
fi

echo bname: $BNAME

echo realbname: $REALBNAME

if [ "$*" = "" ]
then
        echo args: none
else
        echo args: $*
fi

echo Changing to $newdir
cd $newdir

echo Running program $REALBNAME

chroot $newdir $REALBNAME $*

exit 0
```

Please note that you must have the `dialog` program installed on your system for this to work. To use `virtexec` just symlink a program to it. For example,

```
ln -s /usr/bin/virtexec /usr/bin/virtpasswd
ln -s /usr/bin/virtexec /usr/bin/virtvi
ln -s /usr/bin/virtexec /usr/bin/virtpico
ln -s /usr/bin/virtexec /usr/bin/virtemacs
ln -s /usr/bin/virtexec /usr/bin/virtmailq
```

Then if you type `virtvi` or `virtpasswd` or `virtmailq` it will allow you to `vi` a program, change a user's password, or check the mail queue on your virtual system. You can create as many `virtexec` symlinks as you want. However, note that if your program requires a shared library it has to be in the virtual filesystem. The binary has to exist on the virtual filesystem also.

4.3 Notes on `virtfs` and `virtexec`

I install all the scripts in `/usr/bin`. Anything that I do not want to put on the virtual filesystem I put in `/usr/local`. The script does not touch anything in there for copying. Any files that are important to not cross virtual filesystems should be removed. For example, `ssh` is installed on my system and I did not want the private key for the server available on all the virtual filesystems so I remove it from each virtual filesystem after I run virtfs. I also change `resolv.conf` and remove anything that has the name of another domain on it for legal reasons. For example, `/etc/hosts` and `/etc/HOSTNAME`.

The programs that I symlink to `virtexec` are:

- `virtpasswd`—change a user password.
- `virtadduser`—create a user.
- `virtdeluser`—delete a user.
- `virtsmbstatus`—see Samba status.
- `virtvi`—edit a file.
- `virtmailq`—check out the `mailq`.
- `virtnewaliases`—rebuild alias tables.

5 DNS

You can configure DNS normally. The beauty of this system is that all services will behave normally like they are on separate machines. There is a HOWTO on DNS.

6 Syslog

6.1 Problem

Syslog is the system logging utility commonly used on UNIX systems. Syslog is a daemon that opens a special file called a FIFO. A FIFO is a special file that is like a pipe. Anything that is written to the write side will come out the read side. The syslog daemon waits for data from the read side. There are C functions that write to the write side. If you write your program with these C functions your output will go to syslog. Remember that we have used a `chroot` environment and the FIFO `/dev/log` is not in the virtual environment. That means all the virtual environments will not log to syslog. We cannot simply copy the file since the programs use `/dev/log` instead of the new one we would create.

Beware that certain versions of syslog use a udp socket instead of the FIFO. However, this is usually not the case.

6.2 Solution

Syslog can look to a different FIFO if you tell it on the command line so run syslog with the argument:

```
syslog -p /virtual/log
```

Then link `/dev/log` to `/virtual/log` by symlinking:

```
ln -sf /virtual/log /dev/log
```

Then link all the `/dev/log` copies to this file by running (Note it is a hard link and not a symlink):

```
ln /virtual/log /virtual/domain.com/dev/log
```

The `virtfs` script above already does this. Since `/virtual` is one contiguous disk and the `/dev/log`'s are linked they have the same inode number and point to the same data. The `chroot` cannot stop this so all your virtual `/dev/log`'s will now function. Note that all the messages from all the environments will be logged in one place. However, you can write separate programs to filter out the data. If you do not want to write a program and require separate log files you can use a separate syslog for each virtual filesystem by running:

```
syslog -p /virtual/domain1.com/dev/log
syslog -p /virtual/domain2.com/dev/log
```

However that wastes process ID's so I do not recommend it. This version of the `syslog.init` file relinks the `/dev/log`'s each time you start it in case they have been improperly set up. Here is a modified `syslog.init` file:

```
#!/bin/sh

# Source function library.
. /etc/rc.d/init.d/functions

case "$1" in
  start)
        echo -n "Starting dev log: "
        ln -sf /virtual/log /dev/log
        echo done
        echo -n "Starting system loggers: "
        daemon syslogd -p /virtual/log
        daemon klogd
        echo
        echo -n "Starting virtual dev log: "
        for i in /virtual/*
        do
                if [ ! -d "$i" ]
                then
                        continue
                fi
```

```
                if [ "$i" = "/virtual/lost+found" ]
                then
                        continue
                fi
                ln -f /virtual/log $i/dev/log
                echo -n "."
        done
        echo " done"
        touch /var/lock/subsys/syslog
        ;;
  stop)
        echo -n "Shutting down system loggers: "
        killproc syslogd
        killproc klogd
        echo
        rm -f /var/lock/subsys/syslog
        ;;
  *)
        echo "Usage: syslog {start|stop}"
        exit 1
esac

exit 0
```

Note that you do not have to put all the virtual file systems on one disk. However, you will have to run a different syslog for each partition that has virtual file systems on it.

7 Virtual FTP

Wu-ftpd comes with built-in support to make it virtual. However, you cannot maintain separate password files for each domain. For example, if `bob@domain1.com` and `bob@domain2.com` both want an account you would have to make one of them bob2 or have one of the users choose a different user name. Since you now have a virtual filesystem for each domain you have separate password files and this problem goes away. Just create a virtnewuser script and virtpasswd script in the way mentioned above and you are all set. You can also have anonymous FTP in each virtual environment as that would be unaffected by the virtual file system as well.

The `inetd.conf` entries for wu-FTP:

```
ftp stream tcp nowait root /usr/bin/virtuald virtuald /virtual/conf.ftp wu.ftpd -l -a
```

8 Virtual Web

Apache has its own support for virtual domains. This is the only program I recommend using the internal virtual domain mechanism. When you run something through inetd there is a cost. The program now has to start up each time you run it. That means slower response times which is unacceptable for web service. Apache also has a mechanism for stopping connections when too many come in.

However, if you did want to run Apache through `inetd` then add the following line to your `inetd.conf` file:

```
# This is really one long line, but the '/' was inserted for formatting
# reasons.
www stream tcp nowait www /usr/bin/virtuald virtuald /virtual/conf.www \
httpd -f /var/www/conf/httpd.conf
```

In the `/var/www/conf/httpd.conf` file you have to specify:

```
ServerType inetd
```

Then configure each instance of the Apache server like you would normally for single domain use.

At the time of this writing there is no virtual web HOWTO. However, I am under the impression one is coming. Eventually I will just refer to that HOWTO and have some notes on it. If it does not come soon and I get enough requests I will write a small section on how to configure the Apache `virthost` directive.

9 Virtual Mail and POP

9.1 Qmail Notice

This section applies to `sendmail` only. A section for `qmail` will be added in the next version of this HOWTO document.

9.2 Problem

Virtual mail support is in ever increasing demand. `sendmail` says it supports virtual mail. What it does support is listening for incoming mail from different domains. You can then specify to have the mail forwarded somewhere. However, if you forward it to the local machine and have incoming mail to bob@domain1.com and bob@domain2.com they will go to the same mail folder. This is a problem since both bob's are different people with different mail.

9.3 Bad Solution

You can make sure that each user name is unique by using a numbering scheme: bob1, bob2, etc or prepending a few characters to each username dom1bob, dom2bob, etc. You could also hack mail and pop to do these conversions behind the scenes but that can get messy. Outgoing mail also has the banner maindomain.com and you want each subdomain's outgoing mail banner to be different.

9.4 Good Solution

Each virtual filesystem gives a domain its own `/etc/passwd`. This means that bob@domain1.com and bob@domain2.com are different users in different `/etc/passwds` so mail will be no problem. They also have their own spool directories so the mail folders will be different files on different virtual filesystems.

However, `sendmail` requires one minor source code modification. Sendmail has a file called `/etc/sendmail.cw`, and it contains all machine names that `sendmail` will deliver mail to locally rather than forwarding to another machine. `sendmail` does internal checking of all the devices on the machine to initialize this list with the local IPs. This presents a problem if you are mailing between virtual domains on the same machine. `sendmail` will be fooled into thinking another virtual domain is a local address and spool the mail locally. For example, bob@domain1.com sends mail to fred@domain2.com. Since domain1.com's sendmail thinks domain2.com is local, it will spool the mail on domain1.com and never send it to domain2.com. You have to modify `sendmail` (I did this on v8.8.5 without a problem):

```
vi v8.8.5/src/main.c # Approximately Line 494
It should say:

load_if_names();

Replace it with:

/* load_if_names(); Commented out since hurts virtual */
```

Note only do this if you need to send mail between virtual domains which I think is probable.

This will fix the problem. However, the main ethernet device eth0 is not removed. Therefore, if you send mail from a virtual IP to the one on eth0 on the same box it will delivery locally. Therefore, I just use this as a dummy IP virtual1.domain.com (10.10.10.157). I never send mail to this host so neither will the virtual domains. This is also the IP I would use to ssh into the box to check if the system is ok.

Edit `/etc/sendmail.cw` with the local hostnames.

```
vi /etc/sendmail.cw
mail.domain1.com
domain1.com
domain1
localhost
```

Create `/etc/sendmail.cf` like you would normally through m4. I used:

```
divert(0)dnl
VERSIONID('@(#)tcpproto.mc      8.5 (Berkeley) 3/23/96')
OSTYPE(linux)
FEATURE(redirect)
FEATURE(always_add_domain)
FEATURE(use_cw_file)
FEATURE(local_procmail)
```

```
MAILER(local)
MAILER(smtp)
```

Edit `/etc/sendmail.cf` to respond as your virtual domain:

```
vi /etc/sendmail.cf # Approximately Line 86
It should say:

#Dj$w.Foo.COM

Replace it with:

Djdomain1.com
```

`sendmail` cannot be started stand alone anymore so you have to run it through `inetd`. This is inefficient and will result in lower start up time but if you had such a high hit site you would not share it on a virtual box with other domains. Note that you are not running with the `-bd` flag. Also note that you need a `sendmail -q` running for each domain to queue up undelivered mail. The new `sendmail.init` file:

```
#!/bin/sh

# Source function library.
. /etc/rc.d/init.d/functions

case "$1" in
  start)
        echo -n "Starting sendmail: "
        daemon sendmail -q1h
        echo
        echo -n "Starting virtual sendmail: "
        for i in /virtual/*
        do
                if [ ! -d "$i" ]
                then
                        continue
                fi
                if [ "$i" = "/virtual/lost+found" ]
                then
                        continue
                fi
                chroot $i sendmail -q1h
                echo -n "."
        done
        echo " done"
        touch /var/lock/subsys/sendmail
        ;;
  stop)
        echo -n "Stopping sendmail: "
        killproc sendmail
        echo
        rm -f /var/lock/subsys/sendmail
        ;;
  *)
        echo "Usage: sendmail {start|stop}"
        exit 1
esac

exit 0
```

`pop` should install normally with no extra effort. It will just need the `inetd` entry for it with the `virtuald` part added. The `inetd.conf` entries for `sendmail` and `pop`:

```
pop-3 stream tcp nowait root /usr/bin/virtuald virtuald /virtual/conf.pop in.qpop -s
smtp stream tcp nowait root /usr/bin/virtuald virtuald /virtual/conf.mail sendmail -bs
```

10 Virtual other

Any other service should be a similar procedure.

- Add the binary and the libraries to the virtual file system.
- Add it to `/etc/inetd.conf`.
- Create a `/virtual/conf.service` file.
- Create any virtual scripts that need to be made.

I have experimented with both the Samba package and have written a virtual `poppassd` through Eudora. Both work without any problems. If there is enough interest, I will add a section on installing virtual Samba.

11 Conclusion

Those are all the steps you need. I hope that this article meets with a positive response. Again mail any responses to Computer Resource Center. If you have a question or an update to the document let me know and I will add it.

12 FAQ

Q1. Why are there no questions in this FAQ?
A1. Because nobody has asked any yet.

Part LII

"From VMS to Linux HOWTO" by Guido Gonzato,

guido@ibogfs.cineca.it

Contents

v1.0.1, 31 October 1997 This HOWTO is aimed at all those who have been using VMS and now need or want to switch to Linux, the free UNIX clone. The transition is made (hopefully) painless with a step—to—step comparison between commands and available tools.

1 Introduction

1.1 Why Linux?

You've heard that UNIX is difficult and balk at the prospect of leaving VMS, right? Don't worry. Linux, one of the finest UNIX clones, is not more difficult to use than VMS (actually, I find it much easier), and it's much more powerful and versatile.

Linux and VMS accomplish essentially the same tasks, but Linux's tools are superior, its syntax is much more concise, and has some features missing in VMS that help save a lot of time. (You'll often hear that VMS and UNIX have a different "philosophy.") Moreover, Linux is available for PCs while VMS is not, and a Pentium-based Linux box can outperform a VAX. I guess this is the reason why you want to swap VMS to Linux.

I imagine you're a university researcher or a student, and that you use VMS for the following everyday tasks:

- writing papers with TEX and LATEX;
- programming in Fortran;
- doing some graphics;
- using Internet services;
- et cetera.

In the following sections I'm going to explain to you how to do these tasks under Linux, exploiting your experience with VMS. Prerequisites:

- Linux and X Window System are properly installed;
- there's a system administrator to take care of the technical details (please get help from them, not from me;
- your shell—the equivalent of `DCL`—is `bash` (ask your sysadm).

Please note that this HOWTO is not enough to acquaint you fully with Linux: it only contains the bare essentials to get you started. You should learn more about Linux to make the most of it (advanced `bash` features; programming, regular expressions). From now on, RMP means "please read the manual pages for further details." The manual pages are the equivalent of the command `HELP`.

The Linux Documentation Project documents, available on `sunsite.unc.edu:/pub/Linux/docs/LDP`, are an important source of information.

And now, go ahead.

1.2 Comparing Commands and Files

This table attempts to compare VMS's and Linux's most used commands. Please keep in mind that the syntax is often very different; for more details, refer to the following sections.

```
VMS                         Linux                     Notes
----------------------------------------------------------------------------

@COMMAND                    command                   must be executable
COPY file1 file2            cp file1 file2
CREATE/DIR [.dirname]       mkdir dirname             only one at a time
CREATE/DIR [.dir1.dir2]     mkdirhier dir/name
DELETE filename             rm filename
DIFF file1 file2            diff -c file1 file2
DIRECTORY                   ls
DIRECTORY [...]file         find . -name file
DIRECTORY/FULL              ls -al
EDIT filename               vi filename,              you won't like it
                            emacs filename,           EDT compatible
                            jed filename              ditto---my favorite
FORTRAN prog.for            g77 prog.f,               no need to do LINK
                            f77 prog.f,
```

	fort77 prog.f	
HELP command	man command	must specify 'command'
	info command	ditto
LATEX file.tex	latex file.tex	
LOGIN.COM	.bash_profile,	'hidden' file
	.bashrc	ditto
LOGOUT.COM	.bash_logout	ditto
MAIL	mail,	crude
	elm,	much better
	pine	better still
PRINT file.ps	lpr file.ps	
PRINT/QUEUE=laser file.ps	lpr -Plaser file.ps	
PHONE user	talk user	
RENAME file1 file2	mv file1 file2	not for multiple files
RUN progname	progname	
SEARCH file "pattern"	grep pattern file	
SET DEFAULT [-]	cd ..	
SET DEFAULT [.dir.name]	cd dir/name	
SET HOST hostname	telnet hostname,	not exactly the same
	rlogin hostname	
SET FILE/OWNER_UIC=joe	chown joe file	completely different
SET NOBROADCAST	mesg	
SET PASSWORD	passwd	
SET PROT=(perm) file	chmod perm file	completely different
SET TERMINAL	export TERM=	different syntax
SHOW DEFAULT	pwd	
SHOW DEVICE	du, df	
SHOW ENTRY	lpq	
SHOW PROCESS	ps -ax	
SHOW QUEUE	lpq	
SHOW SYSTEM	top	
SHOW TIME	date	
SHOW USERS	w	
STOP	kill	
STOP/QUEUE	kill,	for processes
	lprm	for print queues
SUBMIT command	command &	
SUBMIT/AFTER=time command	at time command	
TEX file.tex	tex file.tex	
TYPE/PAGE file	more file	
	less file	much better

But of course it's not only a matter of different command names. Read on.

2 Short Intro

This is what you absolutely need to know before logging in the first time. Relax, it's not much.

2.1 Files

- Under VMS, filenames are in the form `filename.extension.version;`. Under Linux, the version number doesn't exist (big limitation, but see Section 10.2); the filename has normally a limit of 255 characters and can have as many dots as you like. Example of filename: `This.is_a_FILEname.txt`.
- Linux distinguishes between upper case and lower case characters: `FILENAME.txt` and `filename.txt` are two different files; `ls` is a command, `LS` is not.
- A filename starting with a dot is a "hidden" file (that is, it won't normally show up in dir listings), while filenames ending with a tilde "~" represent backup files.

Now, a table to sum up how to translate commands from VMS to Linux:

```
VMS                                    Linux
---------------------------------------------------------------------

$ COPY file1.txt; file2.txt;           $ cp file1.txt file2.txt
$ COPY [.dir]file.txt;1 []             $ cp dir/file.txt .
$ COPY [.dir]file.txt;1 [-]            $ cp dir/file.txt ..
$ DELETE *.dat.*                       $ rm *dat
$ DIFF file1 file2                     $ diff -c file1 file2
$ PRINT file                           $ lpr file
$ PRINT/queue=queuename file           $ lpr -Pprintername file
$ SEARCH *.tex.* "geology"             $ grep geology *tex
```

For other examples involving directories, see below; for details about protections, ownership, and advanced topics, see Section 8.

2.2 Directories

- Within the same node and device, directories names under VMS are in the form `[top.dir.subdir]`; under Linux, `/top/dir/subdir/`. On the top of the directory tree lies the so–called "root directory" called `/`; underneath there are other directories like `/bin`, `/usr`, `/tmp`, `/etc`, and others.
- The directory `/home` contains the so–called users' "home directories:" e.g., `/home/guido`, `/home/warner`, and so on. When a user logs in, they start working in their home directory; it's the equivalent of `SYS$LOGIN`. There's a shortcut for the home directory: the tilde "~." So, `cd ~/tmp` is the same as, say, `cd /home/guido/tmp`.
- Directory names follow the same rules as file names. Furthermore, each directory has two special entries: one is `.` and refers to the directory itself (like `[]`), and `..` that refers to the parent directory (like `[-]`).

And now for some other examples:

```
DOS                                    Linux
---------------------------------------------------------------------

$ CREATE/DIR [.dirname]                $ mkdir dirname
$ CREATE/DIR [.dir1.dir2.dir3]         $ mkdirhier dir1/dir2/dir3
   n/a                                 $ rmdir dirname
                                       (if dirname is empty)
                                       $ rm -R dirname
$ DIRECTORY                            $ ls
$ DIRECTORY [...]file.*.*              $ find . -name "file*"
$ SET DEF SYS$LOGIN                    $ cd
$ SET DEF [-]                          $ cd ..
$ SET DEF [top.dir.subdir]             $ cd /top/dir/subdir
$ SET DEF [.dir.subdir]                $ cd dir/subdir
$ SHOW DEF                             $ pwd
```

For protections, ownership, and advanced topics, see Section 8.

2.3 Programs

- Commands, compiled programs, and shell scripts (VMS' "command files") don't have compulsory extensions like `.EXE` or `.COM` and can be called whatever you like. Executable files are marked by an asterisk "*" when you issue `ls -F`.
- To run an executable file, just type its name (no `RUN PROGRAM.EXE` or `@COMMAND`). Caveat: it's essential that the file be located in a directory included in the *path of executables*, which is a list of directories. Typically, the path includes dirs like `/bin`, `/usr/bin`, `/usr/X11R6/bin`, and others. If you write your own programs, put them in a directory you have included in the path (see how in Section 9). As an alternative, you may run a program specifying its complete path: e.g., `/home/guido/data/myprog`; or `./myprog`, if the current directory isn't in the path.
- Command switches are obtained with `/OPTION=` under VMS, and with `-switch` or `-switch` under Linux, where `switch` is a letter, more letters combined, or a word. In particular, the switch `-R` (recursive) of many Linux commands performs the same action as `[...]` under VMS;

- You can issue several commands on the command line:

```
$ command1 ; command2 ; ... ; commandn
```

- Most of the flexibility of Linux comes from two features awkwardly implemented or missing in VMS: I/O redirection and piping. Redirection is a side feature under VMS (remember the switch `/OUTPUT=` of many commands), or a fastidious process, like:

```
$ DEFINE /USER SYS$OUTPUT OUT
$ DEFINE /USER SYS$INPUT IN
$ RUN PROG
```

  which has the simple Linux (UNIX) equivalent:

```
$ prog < in > out
```

  Piping is simply impossible under VMS, but has a key role under UNIX. A typical example:

```
$ myprog < datafile | filter_1 | filter_2 >> result.dat 2> errors.log &
```

  which means: the program `myprog` gets its input from the file `datafile` (via <), its output is piped (via `|`) to the program `filter_1` that takes it as input and processes it, the resulting output is piped again to `filter_2` for further processing, the final output is appended (via >>) to the file `result.dat`, and error messages are redirected (via `2>`) onto the file `errors.log`. All this in background (`&` at the end of the command line). More about this in Section 11.

For multitasking, "queues," and the like, see Section 8.

2.4 Quick Tour

Now you are ready to try Linux out. Enter your login name and password exactly as they are. For example, if your login name and password are `john` and `My_PassWd`, don't type `John` or `my_passwd`. Remember, UNIX distinguishes between capital and small letters.

Once you've logged in, you'll see a prompt; chances are it'll be something like `machinename:$`. If you want to change the prompt or make some programs start automatically, you'll have to edit a "hidden" file called `.profile` or `.bash_profile` (see example in Section 9). This is the equivalent of `LOGIN.COM`.

Pressing ALT–F1, ALT–F2, ... ALT–F6 switches between "virtual consoles." When one VC is busy with a full–screen application, you can flip over to another and continue to work. Try and log in to another VC.

Now you may want to start X Window System (from now on, X). X is a graphic environment very similar to DECWindows—actually, the latter derives from the former. Type the command `startx` and wait a few seconds; most likely you'll see an open `xterm` or equivalent terminal emulator, and possibly a button bar. (It depends on how your sysadm configured your Linux box.) Click on the desktop (try both mouse buttons) to see a menu.

While in X, to access the text mode ('console') sessions press CTRL–ALT–F1 ... CTRL–ALT–F6. Try it. When in console, go back to X pressing ALT–F7. To quit X, follow the menu instructions or press CTRL–ALT–BS.

Type the following command to list your home dir contents, including the hidden files:

```
$ ls -al
```

Press SHIFT–PAG UP to back-scroll. Now get help about the `ls` command typing:

```
$ man ls
```

pressing "q" to exit. To end the tour, type `exit` to quit your session. If now you want to turn off your PC, press CTRL–ALT–DEL and wait a few seconds (*never* switch off the PC while in Linux! You could damage the file system.)

If you think you're ready to work, go ahead, but if I were you I'd jump to Section 8.

3 Editing Files

Linux doesn't have `EDT`, but there are scores of editors available. The only one that's guaranteed to be included in every UNIX version is `vi`—forget it, your system administrator must have installed something better. Probably the most popular editor is `emacs`, which can emulate `EDT` to a certain degree; `jed` is another editor that provides `EDT` emulation.

These two editors are particularly useful for editing program sources, since they have two features unknown to `EDT`: syntax highlighting and automatic indentation. Moreover, you can compile your programs from within the editor (command `ESC-X compile`); in case of a syntax error, the cursor will be positioned on the offending line. I bet that you'll never want to use the true blue `EDT` again.

If you have `emacs`: start it, then type `ESC-X edt-emulation-on`. Pressing ALT–X or ESC-X is `emacs`' way of issuing commands, like `EDT`'s CTRL–Z. From now on, `emacs` acts like `EDT` apart from a few commands. Differences:

- *don't* press CTRL–Z to issue commands (if you did, you stopped emacs. Type fg to resume it);
- there's an extensive on-line help. Press CTRL-H ?, or CTRL-H T to start a tutorial;
- to save a file, press CTRL-X CTRL-S;
- to exit, press CTRL-X CTRL-C;
- to insert a new file in a buffer, press CTRL-X CTRL-F, then CTRL-X B to switch among buffers.

If you have jed: ask your sysadm to configure jed properly. Emulation is already on when you start it; use the normal keypad keys, and press CTRL–H CTRL–H or CTRL-? to get help. Commands are issued in the same way as emacs'. In addition, there are some handy key bindings missing in the original EDT; key bindings can also be tailored to your own taste. Ask your sysadm.

In alternative, you may use another editor with a completely different interface. emacs in native mode is an obvious choice; another popular editor is joe, which can emulate other editors like emacs itself (being even easier to use) or the MS-DOS editor. Invoke the editor as jmacs or jstar and press, respectively, CTRL-X H or CTRL-J to get online help. emacs and jed are *much* more powerful than good ol' EDT.

4 TEXing

TEX and LATEX are identical to their VMS counterparts—only quicker, but the tools to handle the .dvi and .ps files are superior:

- to run a .tex file through TEX, do as usual: tex file.tex;
- to turn a .dvi file into a .ps file, type dvips -o filename.ps filename.dvi;
- to visualize a .dvi file, type within an X session: xdvi filename.dvi &. Click on the page to magnify. This program is smart: if you edit and run TEX producing newer versions of the .dvi file, xdvi will update it automatically;
- to visualize a .ps file, type within an X session: ghostview filename.ps &. Click on the page to magnify. The whole document or selected pages can be printed. A newer and better program is gv.
- to print the .ps: usually the command lpr mypaper.ps will do, but if the PostScript printer is called, say, "ps" (ask your system administrator), you'll do: lpr -Pps mypaper.ps. For more information about print queues, go to Section 8.4.

5 Programming

Programming under Linux is much better: there are lots of tools that make programming easier and quicker. For instance, the drudgery of editing—saving—exiting—compiling—re-editing can be cut short by using editors like emacs or jed, as seen above.

5.1 Fortran

Not substantial differences here, but note that at the time of writing the available (free) compilers are not 100% compatible with VMS'; expect some minor quirks. (It's actually the VMS compiler which has non-standard extensions.) See /usr/doc/g77/DOC or /usr/doc/f2c/f2c.ps for details.

Your sysadm has installed a native compiler called g77 (good but, as of version 0.5.21, still not perfectly compatible with DEC Fortran) or possibly the Fortran to C translator, f2c, and one of the front-ends that make it mimic a native compiler. In my experience, the package yaf77 is the one that provides best results.

To compile a Fortran program with g77, edit the source, save it with extension .f, then do:

```
$ g77 myprog.f
```

which creates by default an executable called a.out (you don't have to link anything). To give the executable a different name and do some optimisation:

```
$ g77 -O2 -o myprog myprog.f
```

Beware of optimizations. Ask your system administrator to read the documentation that comes with the compiler and tell you if there are any problems.

To compile a subroutine:

```
$ g77 -c mysub.f
```

This creates a file `mysub.o`. To link this subroutine to a program, you'll do

```
$ g77 -o myprog myprog.f mysub.o
```

If you have many external subroutines and you want to make a library, do the following:

```
$ cd subroutines/
$ cat *f >mylib.f ; g77 -c mylib.f
```

This will create `mylib.o` that you can link to your programs.

Finally, to link an external library called, say, `libdummy.so`:

```
$ g77 -o myprog myprog.f -ldummy
```

If you have `f2c`, you only have to use `f77` or `fort77` instead of `g77`.

Another useful programming tool is `make`, described below.

5.2 Using `make`

The utility `make` is a tool to handle the compilation of programs that are split into several source files.

Let's suppose you have source files containing your routines, `file_1.f, file_2.f, file_3.f`, and a source file of the main program that uses the routines, `myprog.f`. If you compile your program manually, whenever you modify one of the source files you have to figure out which file depends on which, which file to recompile first, and so on.

Instead of getting mad, you can write a `makefile`. This is a text file containing the dependencies between your sources: when one is modified, only the ones that depend on the modified file will be recompiled.

In our example, you'd write a `makefile` like this:

```
# This is makefile
# Press the <TAB> key where you see <TAB>!
# It's important: don't use spaces instead.

myprog: myprog.o file_1.o file_2.o file_3.o
<TAB>g77 -o myprog myprog.o file_1.o file_2.o file_3.o
# myprog depends on four object files

myprog.o: myprog.f
<TAB>g77 -c myprog.f
# myprog.o depends on its source file

file_1.o: file_1.f
<TAB>g77 -c file_1.f
# file_1.o depends on its source file

file_2.o: file_2.f file_1.o
<TAB>g77 -c file_2.f file_1.o
# file_2.o depends on its source file and an object file

file_3.o: file_3.f file_2.o
<TAB>g77 -c file_3.f file_2.o
# file_3.o depends on its source file and an object file

# end of makefile.
```

Save this file as `Makefile` and type `make` to compile your program; alternatively, save it as `myprog.mak` and type `make -f myprog.mak`. And of course, RMP.

5.3 Shell Scripts

Shell scripts are the equivalent of VMS' command files and, for a change, are much more powerful.

To write a script, all you have to do is write a standard ASCII file containing the commands, save it, then make it executable with the command `chmod +x <scriptfile>`. To execute it, type its name.

Writing scripts under `bash` is such a vast subject it would require a book by itself, and I will not delve into the topic any further. I'll just give you a more-or-less comprehensive and (hopefully) useful example you can extract some basic rules from.

EXAMPLE: `sample.sh`

```
#!/bin/sh
# sample.sh
# I am a comment
# don't change the first line, it must be there
echo "This system is: 'uname -a'" # use the output of the command
echo "My name is $0" # built-in variables
echo "You gave me the following $# parameters: "$*
echo "First parameter is: "$1
echo -n "What's your name? " ; read your_name
echo notice the difference: "hi $your_name" # quoting with "
echo notice the difference: 'hi $your_name' # quoting with '
DIRS=0 ; FILES=0
for file in 'ls .' ; do
  if [ -d ${file} ] ; then # if file is a directory
    DIRS='expr $DIRS + 1'  # this means DIRS = DIRS + 1
  elif [ -f ${file} ] ; then
    FILES='expr $FILES + 1'
  fi
  case ${file} in
    *.gif|*jpg) echo "${file}: graphic file" ;;
    *.txt|*.tex) echo "${file}: text file" ;;
    *.c|*.f|*.for) echo "${file}: source file" ;;
    *) echo "${file}: generic file" ;;
  esac
done
echo "there are ${DIRS} directories and ${FILES} files"
ls | grep "ZxY--!!!WKW"
if [ $? != 0 ] ; then # exit code of last command
  echo "ZxY--!!!WKW not found"
fi
echo "enough... type 'man bash' if you want more info."
```

5.4 C

Linux is an excellent environment to program in C. Taken for granted that you know C, here are a couple of guidelines. To compile your standard `hello.c` you'll use the `gcc` compiler, which comes as part of Linux and has the same syntax as `g77`:

```
$ gcc -O2 -o hello hello.c
```

To link a library to a program, add the switch `-l<libname>`. For example, to link the math library and optimize do

```
$ gcc -O2 -o mathprog mathprog.c -lm
```

(The `-l<libname>` switch forces `gcc` to link the library `/usr/lib/lib<libname>.a`; so `-lm` links `/usr/lib/libm.a`).

When your program is made of several source files, you'll need to use the utility `make` described above. Just use `gcc` and C source files in the makefile.

You can invoke some help about the C functions, that are covered by man pages, section 3; for example,

```
$ man 3 printf
```

There are lots of libraries available out there; among the first you'll want to use are `ncurses`, to handle text mode effects, and `svgalib`, to do graphics.

6 Graphics

Among the scores of graphic packages available, `gnuplot` stands out for its power and ease of use. Go to X and type `gnuplot`, and have two sample data files ready: `2D-data.dat` (two data per line), and `3D-data.dat` (three data per line).

Examples of 2-D graphs:

```
gnuplot> set title "my first graph"
gnuplot> plot '2D-data.dat'
gnuplot> plot '2D-data.dat' with linespoints
gnuplot> plot '2D-data.dat', sin(x)
gnuplot> plot [-5:10] '2D-data.dat'
```

Example of 3-D graphs (each 'row' of X values is followed by a blank line):

```
gnuplot> set parametric ; set hidden3d ; set contour
gnuplot> splot '3D-data.dat' using 1:2:3 with linespoints
```

A single-column datafile (e.g., a time series) can also be plotted as a 2-D graph:

```
gnuplot> plot [-5:15] '2D-data-1col.dat' with linespoints
```

or as a 3-D graph (blank lines in the datafile, as above):

```
gnuplot> set noparametric ; set hidden3d
gnuplot> splot '3D-data-1col.dat' using 1 with linespoints
```

To print a graph: if the command to print on your Postscript printer is `lpr -Pps file.ps`, issue:

```
gnuplot> set term post
gnuplot> set out '| lpr -Pps'
gnuplot> replot
```

then type `set term x11` to restore. Don't get confused—the last print will come out only when you quit `gnuplot`.

For more info, type `help` or see the examples in directory `/usr/lib/gnuplot/demos/`, if you have it.

7 Mail and Internet Tools

Since Internet was born on UNIX machines, you find plenty of nice and easy-to-use applications under Linux. Here are just some:

- **Mail**: use `elm` or `pine` to handle your email; both programs have on-line help. For short messages, you could use `mail`, as in `mail -s "hello mate" user@somewhere < msg.txt`. You may like programs like `xmail` or some such.
- **Newsgroups**: use `tin` or `slrn`, both very intuitive and self-explanatory.
- **ftp**: apart from the usual character-based `ftp`, ask your sysadm to install the full-screen `ncftp` or a graphical ftp client like `xftp`.
- **WWW**: the ubiquitous `netscape`, or `xmosaic`, `chimera`, and `arena` are graphical web browsers; a character-based one is `lynx`, quick and effective.

8 Advanced Topics

Here the game gets tough. Learn these features, then you'll be ready to say that you "know something about Linux."

8.1 Permissions and Ownership

Files and directories have permissions ("protections") and ownership, just like under VMS. If you can't run a program, or can't modify a file, or can't access a directory, it's because you don't have the permission to do so, or because the file doesn't belong to you. Let's have a look at the following example:

```
$ ls -l /bin/ls
-rwxr-xr-x   1 root     bin         27281 Aug 15  1995 /bin/ls*
```

The first field shows the permissions of the file `ls` (owner root, group bin). There are three types of ownership: owner, group, and others (similar to VMS owner, group, world), and three types of permissions: read, write (and delete), and execute.

From left to right, `-` is the file type (`-` = ordinary file, `d` = directory, `l` = link, etc); `rwx` are the permissions for the file owner (read, write, execute); `r-x` are the permissions for the group of the file owner (read, execute); `r-x` are the permissions for all other users (read, execute).

To change a file's permissions:

```
$ chmod <whoXperm> <file>
```

where who is u (user, that is owner), g (group), o (other), X is either + or -, perm is r (read), w (write), or x (execute). Examples:

```
$ chmod u+x file
```

this sets the execute permission for the file owner. Shortcut: `chmod +x file`.

```
$ chmod go-wx file
```

this removes write and execute permission for everyone except the owner.

```
$ chmod ugo+rwx file
```

this gives everyone read, write, and execute permission.

A shorter way to refer to permissions is with numbers: `rwxr-xr-x` can be expressed as 755 (every letter corresponds to a bit: `--` is 0, `-x` is 1, `-w-` is 2...).

For a directory, `rx` means that you can `cd` to that directory, and `w` means that you can delete a file in the directory (according to the file's permissions, of course), or the directory itself. All this is only part of the matter—RMP.

To change a file's owner:

```
$ chown username file
```

To sum up, a table:

```
VMS                              Linux                    Notes
------------------------------------------------------------------------------

SET PROT=(O:RW) file.txt         $ chmod u+rw file.txt
                                 $ chmod 600 file.txt
SET PROT=(O:RWED,W) file         $ chmod u+rwx file
                                 $ chmod 700 file
SET PROT=(O:RWED,W:RE) file      $ chmod 755 file
SET PROT=(O:RW,G:RW,W) file      $ chmod 660 file
SET FILE/OWNER_UIC=JOE file      $ chown joe file
SET DIR/OWNER_UIC=JOE [.dir]     $ chown joe dir/
```

8.2 Multitasking: Processes and Jobs

More about running programs. There are no "batch queues" under Linux as you're used to; multitasking is handled very differently. Again, this is what the typical command line looks like:

```
$ command -s1 -s2 ... -sn par1 par2 ... parn < input > output &
```

where `-s1`, ..., `-sn` are the program switches, `par1`, ..., `parn` are the program parameters.

Now let's see how multitasking works. Programs, running in foreground or background, are called 'processes'.

- To launch a process in background:

  ```
  $ progname [-switches] [parameters] [< input] [> output] &
  [1] 234
  ```

  the shell tells you what the 'job number' (the first digit; see below) and PID (Process IDentifier) of the process are. Each process is identified by its PID.

- To see how many processes there are:

  ```
  $ ps -ax
  ```

  This will output a list of currently running processes.

- To kill a process:

  ```
  $ kill <PID>
  ```

  You may need to kill a process when you don't know how to quit it the right way... ;-). Sometimes, a process will only be killed by one of the following:

  ```
  $ kill -15 <PID>
  $ kill -9 <PID>
  ```

In addition to this, the shell allows you to stop or temporarily suspend a process, send a process to background, and bring a process from background to foreground. In this context, processes are called 'jobs'.

- To see how many jobs there are:

  ```
  $ jobs
  ```

  jobs are identified by the numbers the shell gives them, not by their PID.
- To stop a process running in foreground:

  ```
  $ CTRL-C
  ```

  (it doesn't always work)
- To suspend a process running in foreground:

  ```
  $ CTRL-Z
  ```

  (ditto)
- To send a suspended process into background (it becomes a job):

  ```
  $ bg <job>
  ```

- To bring a job to foreground:

  ```
  $ fg <job>
  ```

- To kill a job:

  ```
  $ kill <%job>
  ```

8.3 Files, Revisited

More information about files.

- **stdin, stdout, stderr**: under UNIX, every system component is treated as if it were a file. Commands and programs get their input from a 'file' called `stdin` (standard input; usually, the keyboard), put their output on a 'file' called `stdout` (usually, the screen), and error messages go to a 'file' called `stderr` (usually, the screen).

  Using < and > you redirect input and output to a different file. Moreover, >> appends the output to a file instead of overwriting it; 2> redirects error messages (stderr); 2>&1 redirects stderr to stdout, while 1>&2 redirects stdout to stderr. There's a 'black hole' called `/dev/null`: everything redirected to it disappears;
- **wildcards**: '`*`' is almost the same. Usage: * matches all files except the hidden ones; .* matches all hidden files; *.* matches only those that have a '.' in the middle, followed by other characters; p*r matches both 'peter' and 'piper'; *c* matches both 'picked' and 'peck'. '`%`' becomes '`?`'. There is another wildcard: the `[]`. Usage: `[abc]*` matches files starting with a, b, c; `*[I-N,1,2,3]` matches files ending with I, J, K, L, M, N, 1, 2, 3;
- `mv` (`RENAME`) doesn't work for multiple files; that is, `mv *.xxx *.yyy` won't work;
- use `cp -i` and `mv -i` to be warned when a file is going to be overwritten.

8.4 Print Queues

Your prints are queued, like under VMS. When you issue a print command, you may specify a printer name. Example:

```
$ lpr file.txt            # this goes to the standard printer
$ lpr -Plaser file.ps     # this goes to the printer named 'laser'
```

To handle the print queues, you use the following commands:

```
VMS                                    Linux
-------------------------------------------------------------------------------

$ PRINT file.ps                        $ lpr file.ps
$ PRINT/QUEUE=laser file.ps            $ lpr -Plaser file.ps
$ SHOW QUEUE                           $ lpq
$ SHOW QUEUE/QUEUE=laser               $ lpq -Plaser
$ STOP/QUEUE                           $ lprm <item>
```

9 Configuring

Your sysadm has already provided you with a number of configuration files like .xinitrc, .bash_profile, .inputrc, and many others. The ones you may want to edit are:

- .bash_profile or .profile: read by the shell at login time. It's like LOGIN.COM;
- .bash_logout: read by the shell at logout. It's like LOGOUT.COM;
- .bashrc: read by non–login shells.
- .inputrc: this file customises the key bindings and the behaviour of the shell.

To give you an example, I'll include my .bash_profile (abridged):

```
# $HOME/.bash_profile

# don't redefine the path if not necessary
echo $PATH | grep $LOGNAME > /dev/null
if [ $? != 0 ]
then
  export PATH="$PATH:/home/$LOGNAME/bin"  # add my dir to the PATH
fi

export PS1='LOGNAME:\w\$ '
export PS2='Continued...>'

# aliases

alias bin="cd ~/bin" ; alias cp="cp -i" ; alias d="dir"
alias del="delete" ; alias dir="/bin/ls $LS_OPTIONS --format=vertical"
alias ed="jed" ; alias mv='mv -i'
alias u="cd .." ; alias undel="undelete"
# A few useful functions

inst() # Install a .tar.gz archive in current directory.
{
  gzip -dc $1 | tar xvf -
}
cz() # List the contents of a .zip archive.
{
  unzip -l $*
}
ctgz() # List the contents of a .tar.gz archive.
{
  for file in $* ; do
    gzip -dc ${file} | tar tf -
  done
}
tgz() # Create a .tgz archive a la zip.
{
  name=$1 ; tar -cvf $1 ; shift
  tar -rf ${name} $* ; gzip -S .tgz ${name}
}
```

And this is my .inputrc:

```
# $HOME/.inputrc
# Last modified: 16 January 1997.
#
# This file is read by bash and defines key bindings to be used by the shell;
# what follows fixes the keys END, HOME, and DELETE, plus accented letters.
```

```
# For more information, man readline.

"\e[1~": beginning-of-line
"\e[3~": delete-char
"\e[4~": end-of-line

set bell-style visible
set meta-flag On
set convert-meta Off
set output-meta On
set horizontal-scroll-mode On
set show-all-if-ambiguous On

# (F1 .. F5) are "\e[[A" ... "\e[[E"

"\e[[A": "info "
```

10 Useful Programs

10.1 Browsing Files: less

You'll use this file browser every day, so I'll give you a couple of tips to use it at best. First of all, ask your sysadm to configure `less` so as it can display not only plain text files, but also compressed files, archives, and so on.

The main advantage of `less` over `TYPE` is that you can browse files in both directions. It also accepts several commands that are issued pressing a key. The most useful are:

- first of all, press `q` to leave the browser;
- `h` gives you extensive help;
- `g` to go to beginning of file, `G` to the end, number+`g` to go to line 'number' (e.g. `125g`), number+`%` to move to that percentage of the file;
- `/pattern` searches forwards for 'pattern'; `n` searches forwards for the next match; `?pattern` and `N` search backwards;
- `m`+letter marks current position (e.g. `ma`); `'`+letter go to the marked position;
- `:e` examines a new file;
- `!command` executes the shell command.

10.2 A brief introduction to RCS

The lack of version numbers in files can be easily overcome by using RCS (Revision Control System). This allows you to maintain several versions of the same file, and offers many more advantages. I'll only explain the very basics of this powerful version control system.

The most important commands are `ci` and `co`. The first ("check in") is used to commit the changes you have done to your file, and create a new version. The second ("check out") is used to obtain a working copy of your file from the RCS system, either to modify it or simply use it for browsing, printing, or whatever.

Let's see an example. First of all you create an *initial revision* of your file, using your favourite editor. Let's suppose that the file you'll have under RCS control is called `project.tex`. Follow these steps:

- make a subdirectory called `RCS/` in the directory containing `project.tex`. `RCS/` will contain the revision control file;
- to put `project.tex` under RCS control, issue the command

  ```
  $ ci project.tex
  RCS/project.tex,v  <-- project.tex
  enter description, terminated with a single '.' or end of file:
  NOTE: This is NOT the log message!
  >>
  ```

- you will write a line or more containing a description of the contents of your file. End it with a line containing a '.' by itself, and you'll see

```
initial revision: 1.1
done
```

Now the file `project.tex` has been taken over by RCS.

10.2.1 Using the latest version

Whenever you want to use, but not modify, the latest version of project.tex, you issue the command

```
$ co project.tex
RCS/project.tex,v  --> project.tex
revision 1.1
done
```

This extracts the latest version (read only) of your file. Now you can browse it, or compile it with tex, but you can't modify it.

10.2.2 Creating a new version

When you want to modify your file, you must obtain a "lock" on it. This means that RCS knows that you're about to make a newer version. In this case, you use the command

```
$ co project.tex
RCS/project.tex,v  --> project.tex
revision 1.1 (locked)
done
```

You now have a working copy you can modify with your editor. When you're done editing it, you check it in again to commit the changes:

```
$ ci project.tex
RCS/project.tex,v  <-- project.tex
new revision 1.2; previous revision: 1.1
enter log message, terminated with a single '.' or end of file:
>> (enter your description here)
>> .
done
```

If you want to change the version number, type `ci -f2.0 project.tex`.

10.2.3 Comparing versions

If you want to see the history of the changes in project.tex, issue

```
$ rlog project.tex
```

10.2.4 Using an old version

To extract an older version of your file (say, version 1.2 when you're working on 1.6), issue

```
$ co -r1.2 project.tex
```

Be aware that this overwrites your existing working file, if you have one. You may do:

```
$ co -r1.2 -p project.tex > project.tex.1.2
```

10.3 Archiving: tar & gzip

Under UNIX there are some widely used applications to archive and compress files. `tar` is used to make archives, that is collections of files. To make a new archive:

```
$ tar -cvf <archive_name.tar> <file> [file...]
```

To extract files from an archive:

```
$ tar -xpvf <archive_name.tar> [file...]
```

To list the contents of an archive:

```
$ tar -tf <archive_name.tar> | less
```

Files can be compressed to save disk space using compress, which is obsolete and shouldn't be used any more, or gzip:

```
$ compress <file>
$ gzip <file>
```

that creates a compressed file with extension .Z (compress) or .gz (gzip). These programs don't make archives, but compress files individually. To decompress, use:

```
$ compress -d <file.Z>
$ gzip -d <file.gz>
```

RMP.

The unarj, zip and unzip utilities are also available. Files with extension .tar.gz or .tgz (archived with tar, then compressed with gzip) are very common in the UNIX world. Here's how to list the contents of a .tar.gz archive:

```
$ gzip -dc <file.tar.gz> | tar tf - | less
```

To extract the files from a .tar.gz archive:

```
$ gzip -dc <file.tar.gz> | tar xvf -
```

11 Real Life Examples

UNIX's core idea is that there are many simple commands that can linked together via piping and redirection to accomplish even really complex tasks. Look at the following examples; I'll only explain the most complex ones, for the others, please study the above sections and the man pages.

Problem: ls is too quick and the file names fly away.
Solution:

```
$ ls | less
```

Problem: I have a file containing a list of words. I want to sort it in reverse order and print it.
Solution:

```
$ cat myfile.txt | sort -r | lpr
```

Problem: my datafile has some repeated lines! How do I get rid of them?
Solution:

```
$ sort datafile.dat | uniq > newfile.dat
```

Problem: I have a file called 'mypaper.txt' or 'mypaper.tex' or some such somewhere, but I don't remember where I put it. How do I find it?
Solution:

```
$ find ~ -name "mypaper*"
```

Explanation: find is a very useful command that lists all the files in a directory tree (starting from ~ in this case). Its output can be filtered to meet several criteria, such as -name.

Problem: I have a text file containing the word 'entropy' in this directory, is there anything like SEARCH?
Solution: yes, try

```
$ grep -l 'entropy' *
```

Problem: somewhere I have text files containing the word 'entropy', I'd like to know which and where they are. Under VMS I'd use search entropy [...]*.*.*, but grep can't recurse subdirectories. Now what?
Solution:

```
$ find . -exec grep -l "entropy" {} \; 2> /dev/null
```

Explanation: find . outputs all the file names starting from the current directory, -exec grep -l "entropy" is an action to be performed on each file (represented by {}), \ terminates the command. If you think this syntax is awful, you're right.

In alternative, write the following script:

```
#!/bin/sh
# rgrep: recursive grep
if [ $# != 3 ]
then
  echo "Usage: rgrep --switches 'pattern' 'directory'"
  exit 1
fi
find $3 -name "*" -exec grep $1 $2 {} \; 2> /dev/null
```

Explanation: `grep` works like `search`, and combining it with `find` we get the best of both worlds.

Problem: I have a data file that has two header lincs, then every line has 'n' data, not necessarily equally spaced. I want the 2nd and 5th data of each line. Shall I write a Fortran program?

Solution: nope. This is quicker:

```
$ awk 'NL > 2 {print $2, "\t", $5}' datafile.dat > newfile.dat
```

Explanation: the command `awk` is actually a programming language: for each line starting from the third in `datafile.dat`, print out the second and fifth field, separated by a tab. Learn some `awk`—it saves a lot of time.

Problem: I've downloaded an FTP site's `ls-lR.gz` to check its contents. For each subdirectory, it contains a line that reads "total xxxx", where xxxx is size in kbytes of the dir contents. I'd like to get the grand total of all these xxxx values.

Solution:

```
zcat ls-lR.gz | awk ' $1 == "total" { i += $2 } END {print i}'
```

Explanation: `zcat` outputs the contents of the `.gz` file and pipes to `awk`, whose man page you're kindly requested to read.

Problem: I've written a Fortran program, `myprog`, to calculate a parameter from a data file. I'd like to run it on hundreds of data files and have a list of the results, but it's a nuisance to ask each time for the file name. Under VMS I'd write a lengthy command file, and under Linux?

Solution: a very short script. Make your program look for the data file '`mydata.dat`' and print the result on the screen (stdout), then write the following script:

```
#!/bin/sh
# myprog.sh: run the same command on many different files
# usage: myprog.sh *.dat
for file in $*  # for all parameters (e.g. *.dat)
do
  # append the file name to result.dat
  echo -n "${file}:    " >> results.dat
  # copy current argument to mydata.dat, run myprog
  # and append the output to results.dat
  cp ${file} mydata.dat ; myprog >> results.dat
done
```

Problem: I want to replace "geology" with "geophysics" in all my text files. Shall I edit them all manually?

Solution: Nope. Write this shell script:

```
#!/bin/sh
# replace $1 with $2 in $*
# usage: replace "old-pattern" "new-pattern" file [file...]
OLD=$1          # first parameter of the script
NEW=$2          # second parameter
shift ; shift   # discard first two parameters: the next are the file names
for file in $*  # for all files given as parameters
do
# replace every occurrence of OLD with NEW, save on a temporary file
  sed "s/$OLD/$NEW/g" ${file} > ${file}.new
# rename the temporary file as the original file
  /bin/mv ${file}.new ${file}
done
```

Problem: I have some data files, I don't know their length and have to remove their last but one and last but two lines. Er... manually?

Solution: No, of course. Write this script:

```
#!/bin/sh
# prune.sh: removes n-1th and n-2th lines from files
# usage: prune.sh file [file...]
for file in $*   # for every parameter
do
  LINES=‘wc -l $file | awk '{print $1}'‘  # number of lines in file
  LINES=‘expr $LINES - 3‘                 # LINES = LINES - 3
  head -n $LINES $file > $file.new        # output first LINES lines
  tail -n 1 $file >> $file.new            # append last line
done
```

I hope these examples whetted your appetite.

12 Tips You Can't Do Without

- **Command completion**: pressing <Tab> when issuing a command will complete the command line for you. Example: you have to type `less this_is_a_long_name`; typing in `less thi<TAB>` will suffice. (If you have other files that start with the same characters, supply enough characters to resolve any ambiguity.)
- **Back-scrolling**: pressing SHIFT–PAG UP (the grey key) allows you to backscroll a few pages, depending on your PC's video memory.
- **Resetting the screen**: if you happen to `more` or `cat` a binary file, your screen may end up full of garbage. To fix things, blind type `reset` or this sequence of characters: `echo CTRL-V ESC c RETURN`.
- **Pasting text**: in console, see below; in X, click and drag to select the text in an `xterm` window, then click the middle button (or the two buttons together if you have a two-button mouse) to paste.
- **Using the mouse**: ask your sysadm to install `gpm`, a mouse driver for the console. Click and drag to select text, then right click to paste the selected text. It works across different VCs.

13 The End

13.1 Copyright

14 Disclaimer

This work was written following the experience we had at the Settore di Geofisica of Bologna University (Italy), where a VAX 4000 is being superseded and replaced by Linux-based Pentium PCs. Most of my colleagues are VMS users, and some of them have switched to Linux.

"From VMS to Linux HOWTO" was written by Guido Gonzato, `guido@ibogfs.cineca.it`, 1997. Many thanks to my colleagues and friends who helped me define the needs and habits of the average VMS user, especially to Dr. Warner Marzocchi.

Please help me improve this HOWTO. I'm not a VMS expert and never will be, so your suggestions and bug reports are more than welcome.

Enjoy,

Guido

Part LIII

"Linux WWW-HOWTO"
by Wayne Leister,

n3mtr@qis.net

Contents

Abstract

v0.82, 19 November 1997
This document contains information about setting up WWW services under Linux (both server and client). It tries not to be a detailed manual, but an overview and a good pointer to further information.

1 Introduction

Many people are trying Linux because they are looking for a really good, Internet capable operating system. Also, there are institutes, universities, non-profit and small businesses, that want to set up Internet sites on a small budget. This is where the WWW-HOWTO comes in. This document explains how to set up clients and servers for the largest part of the Internet—the World Wide Web.

All prices in this document are stated in US dollars. This document assumes you are running Linux on an Intel platform. Instructions and product availability my vary from platform to platform. There are many links for downloading software in this document. Whenever possible use a mirror site for faster downloading and to keep the load down on the main server.

The US government forbids US companies from exporting encryption stronger than 40 bit in strength. Therefore US companies will usually have two versions of software. The import version will usually support 128 bit, and the export only 40 bit. This applies to web browsers and servers supporting secure transactions. Another name for secure transactions is Secure Sockets Layer (SSL). We will refer to it as SSL for the rest of this document.

1.1 Copyright

1.2 Feedback

Any feedback is welcome. I do not claim to be an expert. Some of this information was taken from badly written web sites; there are bound to be errors and omissions. But make sure you have the latest version before you send corrections; It may be fixed in the next version (see the next section for where to get the latest version). Send feedback to n3mtr@qis.net.

1.3 New versions of this document

New versions of this document can be retrieved in text format from Sunsite at `(http://sunsite.unc.edu/pub/Linux/docs/HOWTO/WWW-HOWTO)` and almost any Linux mirror site. You can view the latest HTML version on the web at `(http://sunsite.unc.edu/LDP/HOWTO/WWW-HOWTO.html)`. There are also HTML versions available on Sunsite in a tar archive.

2 Setting up WWW client software

The following chapter is dedicated to the setting up web browsers. Please feel free to contact me, if your favorite web browser is not mentioned here. In this version of the document only a few of the browsers have their own section, but I tried to include all of them (all I could find) in the overview section. In the future those browsers that deserve there own section will have it.

The overview section is designed to help you decide which browser to use, and give you basic information on each browser. The detail section is designed to help you install, configure, and maintain the browser.

Personally, I prefer the Netscape; it is the only browser that keeps up with the latest things in HTML. For example, Frames, Java, Javascript, style sheets, secure transactions, and layers. Nothing is worse than trying to visit a web site and finding out that you can't view it because your browser doesn't support some new feature.

However, I use Lynx when I don't feel like firing up the X/Netscape monster.

3 Lynx

Lynx is one of the smaller (around 600 K executable) and faster web browsers available. It does not eat up much bandwidth nor system resources as it only deals with text displays. It can display on any console, terminal or xterm. You will not need X or additional system memory to run this browser.

3.1 Where to get

Both the Red Hat and Slackware distributions have Lynx in them. Therefore I will not bore you with the details of compiling and installing Lynx.

The latest version is 2.7.1 and can be retrieved from `(http://www.slcc.edu/lynx/fote/)` or from almost any friendly Linux FTP server like ftp://sunsite.unc.edu under /pub/Linux/apps/www/browsers/ or mirror site.

For more information on Lynx try these locations:

Lynx Links

`(http://www.crl.com/ subir/lynx.html)`

Lynx Pages

`(http://lynx.browser.org)`

Lynx Help Pages

`(http://www.crl.com/ subir/lynx/lynx_help/lynx_help_main.html)` (The same pages you get from lynx –help and typing ? in lynx.)

Note: The Lynx help pages have recently moved. If you have an older version of Lynx, you will need to change your lynx.cfg (in /usr/lib) to point to the new address(above).

I think the most special feature of Lynx against all other web browsers is the capability for batch mode retrieval. One can write a shell script which retrieves a document, file or anything like that via http, FTP, gopher, WAIS, NNTP or file://—url's and save it to disk. Furthermore, one can fill in data into HTML forms in batch mode by simply redirecting the standard input and using the -post_data option.

For more special features of Lynx just look at the help files and the man pages. If you use a special feature of Lynx that you would like to see added to this document, let me know.

4 Emacs-W3

There are several different flavors of Emacs. The two most popular are GNU Emacs and XEmacs. GNU Emacs is put out by the Free Software Foundation, and is the original Emacs. It is mainly geared toward text based terminals, but it does run in X-Windows. XEmacs (formerly Lucid Emacs) is a version that only runs on X. It has many special features that are X related (better menus, etc).

4.1 Where to get

Both the Red Hat and Slackware distributions include GNU Emacs.

The most recent GNU emacs at the time of this writing is 19.34. It doesn't seem to have a web site. The FTP site is at `(ftp://ftp.gnu.ai.mit.edu/pub/gnu/)`.

The latest version of XEmacs at the time of this writing is 20.2. The XEmacs FTP site is at `(ftp://ftp.xemacs.org/pub/xemacs)`. For more information about XEmacs goto see its web page at `(http://www.xemacs.org)`.

Both are available from the Linux archives at ftp://sunsite.unc.edu under /pub/Linux/apps/editors/emacs/

If you got GNU Emacs or XEmacs installed, you probably got the W3 browser running to.

The Emacs W3 mode is a nearly fully featured web browser system written in the Emacs Lisp system. It mostly deals with text, but can display graphics, too—at least—if you run the emacs under the X Window System.

To get XEmacs in to W3 mode, goto the apps menu and select browse the web.

I don't use Emacs, so if someone will explain how to get it into the W3 mode I'll add it to this document. Most of this information was from the original author. If any information is incorrect, please let me know. Also let me know if you think anything else should be added about Emacs.

5 Netscape Navigator/Communicator

5.1 Different versions and options.

Netscape Navigator is the king of WWW browsers. Netscape Navigator can do almost everything. But on the other hand, it is one of the most memory-hungry and resource eating program I've ever seen.

There are three different versions of the program:

Netscape Navigator includes the web browser, netcaster (push client) and a basic mail program.

Netscape Communicator includes the web browser, a web editor, an advanced mail program, a news reader, netcaster (push client), and a group conference utility.

Netscape Communicator Pro includes everything Communicator has plus a group calendar, IBM terminal emulation, and remote administration features (administrators can update thousands of copies of Netscape from their desk).

In addition to the three versions there are two other options you must pick.

The first is full install or base install. The full install includes everything. The base install includes enough to get you started. You can download the additional components as you need them (such as multimedia support and netcaster). These components can be installed by the Netscape smart update utility (after installing goto help->software updates). At this time the full install is not available for Linux.

The second option is import or export. If you are from the US are Canada you have the option of selecting the import version. This gives you the stronger 128 bit encryption for secure transactions (SSL). The export version only has 40 bit encryption, and is the only version allowed outside the US and Canada.

The latest version of the Netscape Navigator/Communicator/Communicator Pro is 4.03. There are two different versions for Linux. One is for the old 1.2 series kernels and one for the new 2.0 kernels. If you don't have a 2.0 kernel I suggest you upgrade; there are many improvements in the new kernel.

Beta versions are also available. If you try a beta version, they usually expire in a month or so!

5.2 Where to get

The best way to get Netscape software is to go through their web site at `(http://www.netscape.com/download/)`. They have menus to guide you through the selection. When it asks for the Linux version, it is referring to the kernel (most people should be using 2.0 by now). If your not sure which version kernel you have run 'cat /proc/version'. Going through the web site is the only way to get the import versions.

If you want an export version you can download them directly from the Netscape FTP servers. The FTP servers are also more up to date. For example when I first wrote this the web interface did not have the non-beta 4.03 for Linux yet, but it was on the FTP site. Here are the links to the export Linux 2.0 versions:

Netscape Navigator 4.03 is at ftp://ftp.netscape.com in

```
/pub/communicator/4.03/shipping/english/unix/linux20/navigator_standalone/
navigator-v403-export.x86-unknown-linux2.0.tar.gz
```

Netscape Communicator 4.03 for Linux 2.0 (kernel) is at ftp://ftp.netscape.com in

```
/pub/communicator/4.03/shipping/english/unix/linux20/base_install/
communicator-v403-export.x86-unknown-linux2.0.tar.gz
```

Communicator Pro 4.03 for Linux was not available at the time I wrote this.

These URL's will change as new versions come out. If these links break you can find them by fishing around at the FTP site, ftp://ftp.netscape.com/pub/communicator/.

These servers are heavily loaded at times. Its best to wait for off-peak hours or select a mirror site. Be prepared to wait, these archives are large. Navigator is almost 8 MB, and Communicator base install is 10 MB.

5.3 Installing

This section explains how to install Version 4 of Netscape Navigator, Communicator, and Communicator Pro.

First unpack the archive to a temporary directory. Then run the `ns-install` script (type `./ns-install`). Then make a symbolic link from the `/usr/local/netscape/netscape` binary to `/usr/local/bin/netscape` (type `ln -s /usr/local/netscape/netscape /usr/local/bin/netscape`). Finally set the system wide environment variable `$MOZILLA_HOME` to `/usr/local/netscape` so Netscape can find its files. If you are using bash for your shell edit your `/etc/profile` and add the lines:

```
MOZILLA_HOME="/usr/local/netscape"
export MOZILLA_HOME
```

After you have it installed the software can automatically update itself with smart update. Just run Netscape as root and goto help->software updates. If you only got the base install, you can also install the Netscape components from there.

Note: This will not remove any old versions of Netscape, you must manually remove them by deleting the Netscape binary and Java class file (for version 3).

6 Setting up WWW server systems

This section contains information on different http server software packages and additional server side tools like script languages for CGI programs etc. There are several dozen web servers, I only covered those that are fully functional. As some of these are commercial products, I have no way of trying them. Most of the information in the overview section was pieced together from various web sites. If there is any incorrect or missing information please let me know.

For a technical description on the http mechanism, take a look at the RFC documents mentioned in the section "For further reading" of this HOWTO.

I prefer to use the Apache server. It has almost all the features you would ever need and its free! I will admit that this section is heavily biased toward Apache. I decided to concentrate my efforts on the Apache section rather than spread it out over all the web servers. I may cover other web servers in the future.

6.1 Overview

Cern `httpd`

This was the first web server. It was developed by the European Laboratory for Particle Physics (CERN). CERN httpd is no longer supported. The CERN httpd server is reported to have some ugly bugs, to be quite slow and resource hungry. The latest version is 3.0. For more information visit the CERN httpd home page at `(http://www.w3.org/Daemon/Status.html)`. It is available for download at `(ftp://sunsite.unc.edu/pub/Linux/apps/www/servers/httpd-3.0.term.tpz)` (no it is not a typo, the extension is actually .tpz on the site; probably should be .tgz)

NCSA HTTPd

The NCSA HTTPd server is the father to Apache (The development split into two different servers). Therefore the setup files are very similar. NCSA HTTPd is free and the source code is available. This server not covered in this document, although reading the Apache section may give you some help. The NCSA server was once popular, but most people are replacing it with Apache. Apache is a drop in replacement for the NCSA server(same configuration files), and it fixes several shortcomings of the NCSA server. NCSA HTTPd accounts for 4.9% (and falling) of all web servers. (source September 1997 *Netcraft survey* `(http://www.netcraft.com/survey/)`). The latest version is 1.5.2a. For more information see the NCSA website at `(http://hoohoo.ncsa.uiuc.edu)`.

Apache

Apache is the king of all web servers. Apache and its source code is free. Apache is modular, therefore it is easy to add features. Apache is very flexible and has many, many features. Apache and its derivatives makes up 44% of all web domains (50% if you count all the derivatives). There are over 695,000 Apache servers in operation (source November 1997 *Netcraft survey* `(http://www.netcraft.com/survey/)`).

The official Apache is missing SSL, but there are two derivatives that fill the gap. Stronghold is a commercial product that is based on Apache. It retails for $995; an economy version is available for $495 (based on an old version of Apache). Stronghold is the number-two secure server behind Netscape (source *C2 net* `(http://www.c2.net/products/stronghold)` and *Netcraft survey* `(http://www.netcraft.com/survey/)`). For more information visit the Stronghold website at `(http://www.c2.net/products/stronghold/)`. It was developed outside the US, so it is available with 128-bit SSL everywhere.

Apache-SSL is a free implementation of SSL, but it is not for commercial use in the US (RSA has US patents on SSL technology). It can be used for non-commercial use in the US if you link with the free RSAREF library. For more information see the website at `(http://www.algroup.co.uk/Apache-SSL/)`.

Netscape Fast Track Server

Fast Track was developed by Netscape, but the Linux version is put out by Caldera. The Caldera site lists it as Fast Track for OpenLinux. I'm not sure if it only runs on Caldera OpenLinux or if any Linux distribution will do (E-mail me if you have the answer). Netscape servers account for 11.5% (and falling) of all web servers (source September 1997 `(http://www.netcraft.com/survey/)`). The server sells for $295. It is also included with the Caldera OpenLinux Standard distribution which sells for $399 ($199.50 educational). The web pages tell of a nice administration interface and a quick 10 minute setup. The server has support for 40-bit SSL. To get the full

128-bit SSL you need Netscape Enterprise Server. Unfortunately that is not available for Linux. The latest version available for Linux is 2.0. (Version 3 is in beta, but its not available for Linux yet.) To buy a copy, go to the Caldera web site at (http://www.caldera.com/products/netscape/netscape.html) For more information, go to the Fast Track page at (http://www.netscape.com/comprod/server_central/product/fast_track/)

WN

WN has many features that make it attractive. First it is smaller than the CERN, NCSA HTTPd, an Apache servers. It also has many built-in features that would require CGI's. For example site searches, enhanced server side includes. It can also decompress/compress files on the fly with its filter feature. It also has the ability to retrieve only part of a file with its ranges feature. It is released under the GNU public license. The current version is 1.18.3. For more information see the WN website at (http://hopf.math.nwu.edu/).

AOLserver

AOLserver is made by America Online. I'll admit that I was surprised by the features of a web server coming from AOL. In addition to the standard features it supports database connectivity. Pages can query a database by Structured Query Language (SQL) commands. The database is access through Open Database Connectivity (ODBC). It also has built-in search engine and TCL scripting. If that is not enough you can add your own modules through the c Application Programming Interface (API). I almost forgot to mention support for 40 bit SSL. And you get all this for free. For more information visit the AOLserver site at (http://www.aolserver.com/server/)

Zeus Server

Zeus Server was developed by Zeus Technology. They claim that they are the fastest web server (using WebSpec96 benchmark). The server can be configured and controlled from a web browser! It can limit processor and memory resources for CGI's, and it executes them in a secure environment (whatever that means). It also supports unlimited virtual servers. It sells for $999 for the standard version. If you want the secure server (SSL) the price jumps to $1699. They are based outside the US so 128 bit SSL is available everywhere. For more information visit the Zeus Technology website at (http://www.zeus.co.uk). The US website is at (http://www.zeus.com). I'll warn you they are cocky about the fastest web server thing. But they don't even show up under top web servers in the Netcraft Surveys.

CL-HTTP

CL-HTTP stands for Common Lisp Hypermedia Server. If you are a Lisp programmer this server is for you. You can write your CGI scripts in Lisp. It has a web based setup function. It also supports all the standard server features. CL-HTTP is free and the source code is available. For more information visit the CL-HTTP website at (http://www.ai.mit.edu/projects/iiip/doc/cl-http/home-page.html). (Could they make that URL any longer?)

If you have a commercial purpose (company web site, or ISP), I would strongly recommend that you use Apache. If you are looking for easy setup at the expense of advanced features then the Zeus Server wins hands down. I've also heard that the Netscape Server is easy to setup. If you have an internal use you can be a bit more flexible. But unless one of them has a feature that you just have to use, I would still recommend using one of the three above.

This is only a partial listing of all the servers available. For a more complete list visit Netcraft at (http://www.netcraft.com/survey/servers.html) or Web Compare at (http://webcompare.internet.com).

7 Apache

The current version of Apache is 1.2.4. Version 1.3 is in beta testing. The main Apache site is at (http://www.apache.org/). Another good source of information is Apacheweek at (http://www.apacheweek.com/). The Apache documentation is okay, so I'm not going to go into detail in setting up Apache. The documentation is on the website and is included with the source (in HTML format). There are also text files included with the source, but the HTML version is better. The documentation should get a whole lot better once the Apache Documentation Project gets under way. Right now most of the documents are written by the developers. Not to discredit the developers, but they are a little hard to understand if you don't know the terminology.

7.1 Where to get

Apache is included in the Red Hat, Slackware, and OpenLinux distributions. Although they may not be the latest version, they are very reliable binaries. The bad news is you will have to live with their directory choices (which are totally different from each other and the Apache defaults).

The source is available from the Apache web site at (http://www.apache.org/dist/) Binaries are are also available at apache at the same place. You can also get binaries from sunsite at (ftp://sunsite.unc.edu/pub/Linux/apps/www/servers/). And for those of us running Red Hat the latest binary RPM file can usually be found in the contrib directory at (ftp://ftp.redhat.com/pub/contrib/i386/)

If your server is going to be used for commercial purposes, it is highly recommended that you get the source from the Apache website and compile it yourself. The other option is to use a binary that comes with a major distribution. For example Slackware, Red Hat, or OpenLinux distributions. The main reason for this is security. An unknown binary could have a back door for hackers, or an unstable patch that could crash your system. This also gives you more control over what modules are compiled in, and allows you to set the default directories. It's not that difficult to compile Apache, and besides you not a real Linux user until you compile your own programs.

7.2 Compiling and Installing

First untar the archive to a temporary directory. Next change to the `src` directory. Then edit the Configuration file if you want to include any special modules. The most commonly used modules are already included. There is no need to change the rules or makefile stuff for Linux. Next run the Configure shell script (`./Configure`). Make sure it says Linux platform and gcc as the compiler. Next you may want to edit the httpd.h file to change the default directories. The server home (where the config files are kept) default is `/usr/local/etc/httpd/`, but you may want to change it to just `/etc/httpd/`. And the server root (where the HTML pages are served from) default is `/usr/local/etc/httpd/htdocs/`, but I like the directory `/home/httpd/html` (the Red Hat default for Apache). If you are going to be using su-exec (see special features below) you may want to change that directory too. The server root can also be changed from the config files too. But it is also good to compile it in, just encase Apache can't find or read the config file. Everything else should be changed from the config files. Finally run make to compile Apache.

If you run in to problems with include files missing, check the following things. Make sure you have the kernel headers (include files) installed for your kernel version. Also make sure you have these symbolic links in place:

```
/usr/include/linux should be a link to /usr/src/linux/include/linux
/usr/include/asm should be a link to /usr/src/linux/include/asm
/usr/src/linux should be a link to the Linux source directory (ex.linux-2.0.30)
```

Links can be made with `ln -s`, it works just like the cp command except it makes a link (`ln -s source-dir destination-link`)

When make is finished there should be an executable named httpd in the directory. This needs to be moved in to a bin directory. `/usr/sbin` or `/usr/local/sbin` would be good choices.

Copy the `conf`, `logs`, and `icons` sub-directories from the source to the server home directory. Next rename three of the files files in the `conf` sub-directory to get rid of the `-dist` extension (ex. `httpd.conf-dist` becomes `httpd.conf`)

There are also several support programs that are included with Apache. They are in the `support` directory and must be compiled and installed separately. Most of them can be make by using the `makefile` in that directory (which is made when you run the main `Configure` script). You don't need any of them to run Apache, but some of them make the administrator's job easier.

7.3 Configuring

Now you should have four files in your `conf` sub-directory (under your server home directory). The `httpd.conf` sets up the server daemon (port number, user, etc). The `srm.conf` sets the root document tree, special handlers, etc. The `access.conf` sets the base case for access. Finally `mime.types` tells the server what mime type to send to the browser for each extension.

The configuration files are pretty much self-documented (plenty of comments), as long as you understand the lingo. You should read through them thoroughly before putting your server to work. Each configuration item is covered in the Apache documentation.

The `mime.types` file is not really a configuration file. It is used by the server to translate file extensions into mime-types to send to the browser. Most of the common mime-types are already in the file. Most people should not need to edit this file. As time goes on, more mime types will be added to support new programs. The best thing to do is get a new mime-types file (and maybe a new version of the server) at that time.

Always remember when you change the configuration files you need to restart Apache or send it the SIGHUP signal with `kill` for the changes to take effect. Make sure you send the signal to the parent process and not any of the child processes. The parent usually has the lowest process ID number. The process id of the parent is also in the `httpd.pid` file in the log directory. If you accidently send it to one of the child processes the child will die and the parent will restart it.

I will not be walking you through the steps of configuring Apache. Instead I will deal with specific issues, choices to be made, and special features.

I highly recommend that all users read through the security tips in the Apache documentation. It is also available from the Apache website at (http://www.apache.org/docs/mics/security_tips.html).

7.4 Hosting virtual web sites

Virtual Hosting is when one computer has more than one domain name. The old way was to have each virtual host have its own IP address. The new way uses only one IP address, but it doesn't work correctly with browsers that don't support HTTP 1.1.

My recommendation for businesses is to go with the IP based virtual hosting until most people have browsers that support HTTP 1.1 (give it a year or two). This also gives you a more complete illusion of virtual hosting. While both methods can give you virtual mail capabilities (can someone confirm this?), only IP based virtual hosting can also give you virtual FTP as well.

If it is for a club or personal page, you may want to consider shared IP virtual hosting. It should be cheaper than IP based hosting and you will be saving precious IP addresses.

You can also mix and match IP and shared IP virtual hosts on the same server. For more information on virtual hosting visit Apacheweek at `(http://www.apacheweek.com/features/vhost)`.

7.4.1 IP based virtual hosting

In this method each virtual host has its own IP address. By determining the IP address that the request was sent to, Apache and other programs can tell what domain to serve. This is an incredible waste of IP space. Take for example the servers where my virtual domain is kept. They have over 35,000 virtual accounts, that means 35,000 IP addresses. Yet I believe at last count they had less than 50 servers running.

Setting this up is a two part process. The first is getting Linux setup to accept more than one IP address. The second is setting up Apache to serve the virtual hosts.

The first step in setting up Linux to accept multiple IP addresses is to make a new kernel. This works best with a 2.0 series kernel (or higher). You need to include IP networking and IP aliasing support. If you need help with compiling the kernel see the *kernel howto* `(http://sunsite.unc.edu/LDP/HOWTO/Kernel-HOWTO.html)`.

Next you need to set up each interface at boot. If you are using the Red Hat Distribution then this can be done from the control panel. Start X as root, you should see a control panel. Then double click on network configuration. Next goto the interfaces panel and select your network card. Then click alias at the bottom of the screen. Fill in the information and click done. This will need to be done for each virtual host/IP address.

If you are using other distributions you may have to do it manually. You can just put the commands in the `rc.local` file in `/etc/rc.d` (really they should go in with the networking stuff). You need to have a `ifconfig` and `route` command for each device. The aliased addresses are given a sub device of the main one. For example eth0 would have aliases eth0:0, eth0:1, eth0:2, etc. Here is an example of configuring a aliased device:

```
ifconfig eth0:0 192.168.1.57
route add -host 192.168.1.57 dev eth0:0
```

You can also add a broadcast address and a netmask to the ifconfig command. If you have alot of aliases you may want to make a for loop to make it easier. For more information see the IP Alias Mini-HOWTO, http://sunsite.unc.edu/LDP/HOWTO/mini/IP-Alias.html.

Then you need to setup your domain name server (DNS) to serve these new domains. And if you don't already own the domain names, you need to contact Internic, http://www.internic.net, to register the domain names. See the DNS HOWTO for information on setting up your DNS.

Finally, you need to set up Apache to server the virtual domain correctly. This is in the `httpd.conf` configuration file near the end. They give you an example to go by. All commands specific to that virtual host are put in between the `virtual host` directive tags. You can put almost any command in there. Usually you set up a different document root, script directory, and log files. You can have almost unlimited number of virtual hosts by adding more `virtual host` directive tags.

In rare cases you may need to run separate servers if a directive is needed for a virtual host, but is not allowed in the virtual host tags. This is done using the `bindaddress` directive. Each server will have a different name and setup files. Each server only responds to one IP address, specified by the bindaddress directive. This is an incredible waste of system resources.

7.4.2 Shared IP virtual hosting

This is a new way to do virtual hosting. It uses a single IP address, thus conserving IP addresses for real machines (not virtual ones). In the same example used above those 30,000 virtual hosts would only take 50 IP addresses (one for each machine). This is done by using the new HTTP 1.1 protocol. The browser tells the server which site it wants when it sends the request. The problem is browsers that don't support HTTP 1.1 will get the servers main page, which could be setup to provide a menu of virtual hosts available. That ruins the whole illusion of virtual hosting, the illusion that you have your own server.

The setup is much simpler than the IP based virtual hosting. You still need to get your domain from the Internic and setup your DNS. This time the DNS points to the same IP address as the original domain. Then Apache is setup the same as before. Since you are using the same IP address in the virtualhost tags, it knows you want Shared IP virtual hosting.

There are several work arounds for older browsers. I'll explain the best one. First you need to make your main pages a virtual host (either IP based or shared IP). This frees up the main page for a link list to all your virtual hosts. Next you need to make a back door for the old browsers to get in. This is done using the `ServerPath` directive for each virtual host inside the `virtualhost` directive. For example by adding `ServerPath /mysite/` to www.mysite.com old browsers would be able to access the site by www.mysite.com/mysite/. Then you put the default page on the main server that politely tells them to get a new browser, and lists links to all the back doors of all the sites you host on that machine. When an old browser accesses the site they will be sent to the main page, and get a link to the correct page. New browsers will never see the main page and will go directly to the virtual hosts. You must remember to keep all of your links relative within the web sites, because the pages will be accessed from two different URL's (www.mysite.com and www.mysite.com/mysite/).

I hope I didn't lose you there, but it's not an easy workaround. Maybe you should consider IP based hosting after all. A very similar workaround is also explained on the Apache web site at http://www.apache.org/manual/host.html.

If anyone has a great resource for Shared IP hosting, I would like to know about it. It would be nice to know what percent of browsers out there support HTTP 1.1, and to have a list of which browsers and versions support HTTP 1.1.

7.5 CGI scripts

There are two different ways to give your users CGI script capability. The first is make everything ending in `.cgi` a CGI script. The second is to make script directories (usually named `cgi-bin`). You could also use both methods. For either method to work the scripts must be world executable (`chmod 711`). By giving your users script access you are creating a big security risk. Be sure to do your homework to minimize the security risk.

I prefer the first method, especially for complex scripting. It allows you to put scripts in any directory. I like to put my scripts with the web pages they work with. For sites with allot of scripts it looks much better than having a directory full of scripts. This is simple to setup. First uncomment the `.cgi` handler at the end of the `srm.conf` file. Then make sure all your directories have the `option ExecCGI` or `All` in the `access.conf` file.

Making script directories is considered more secure. To make a script directory you use the ScriptAlias directive in the `srm.conf` file. The first argument is the Alias the second is the actual directory. For example `ScriptAlias /cgi-bin/ /usr/httpd/cgi-bin/` would make `/usr/httpd/cgi-bin` able to execute scripts. That directory would be used whenever someone asked for the directory `/cgi-bin/`. For security reasons you should also change the properties of the directory to `Options none, AllowOveride none` in the `access.conf` (just uncomment the example that is there). Also do not make your script directories subdirectories of your web page directories. For example if you are serving pages from `/home/httpd/html/`, don't make the script directory `/home/httpd/html/cgi-bin`; Instead make it `/home/httpd/cgi-bin`.

If you want your users to have there own script directories you can use multiple `ScriptAlias` commands. Virtual hosts should have there `ScriptAlias` command inside the `virtualhost` directive tags. Does anyone know a simple way to allow all users to have a cgi-bin directory without individual ScriptAlias commands?

7.6 Users Web Directories

There are two different ways to handle user web directories. The first is to have a subdirectory under the users home directory (usually `public_html`). The second is to have an entirely different directory tree for web directories. With both methods make sure set the access options for these directories in the `access.conf` file.

The first method is already setup in apache by default. Whenever a request for `/~bob/` comes in it looks for the `public_html` directory in bob's home directory. You can change the directory with the `UserDir` directive in the `srm.conf` file. This directory must be world readable and executable. This method creates a security risk because for Apache to access the directory the users home directory must be world executable.

The second method is easy to setup. You just need to change the `UserDir` directive in the `srm.conf` file. It has many different formats; you may want to consult the Apache documentation for clarification. If you want each user to have their own directory under `/home/httpd/`, you would use `UserDir /home/httpd`. Then when the request `/~bob/` comes in it would translate to `/home/httpd/bob/`. Or if you want to have a subdirectory under bob's directory you would use `UserDir /home/httpd/*/html`. This would translate to `/home/httpd/bob/html/` and would allow you to have a script directory too (for example `/home/httpd/bob/cgi-bin/`).

7.7 Daemon mode vs. Inetd mode

There are two ways that Apache can be run. One is as a daemon that is always running (Apache calls this stand-alone). The second is from the `inetd` super-server.

Daemon mode is far superior to `inetd` mode. Apache is setup for daemon mode by default. The only reason to use the `inetd` mode is for very low-use applications. Such as internal testing of scripts, small company Intranet, etc. Inetd mode will save memory because Apache will be loaded as needed. Only the `inetd` daemon will remain in memory.

If you don't use Apache that often you may just want to keep it in daemon mode and just start it when you need it. Then you can kill it when you are done (be sure to kill the parent and not one of the child processes).

To set up `inetd` mode you need to edit a few files. First in `/etc/services` see if http is already in there. If its not then add it:

```
http    80/tcp
```

Right after 79 (finger) would be a good place. Then you need to edit the `/etc/inetd.conf` file and add the line for Apache:

```
http    stream  tcp     nowait  root    /usr/sbin/httpd httpd
```

Be sure to change the path if you have Apache in a different location. And the second `httpd` is not a typo; the inet daemon requires that. If you are not currently using the inet daemon, you may want to comment out the rest of the lines in the file so you don't activate other services as well (FTP, finger, telnet, and many other things are usually run from this daemon).

If you are already running the inet daemon (`inetd`), then you only need to send it the SIGHUP signal (via kill; see kill's man page for more info) or reboot the computer for changes to take effect. If you are not running `inetd` then you can start it manually. You should also add it to your init files so it is loaded at boot (the `rc.local` file may be a good choice).

7.8 Allowing `put` and `delete` commands

The newer web publishing tools support this new method of uploading web pages by http (instead of FTP). Some of these products don't even support FTP anymore! Apache does support this, but it is lacking a script to handle the requests. This script could be a big security hole, be sure you know what you are doing before attempting to write or install one.

If anyone knows of a script that works let me know and I'll include the address to it here.

For more information goto Apacheweek's article at (`http://www.apacheweek.com/features/put`).

7.9 User Authentication/Access Control

This is one of my favorite features. It allows you to password protect a directory or a file without using CGI scripts. It also allows you to deny or grant access based on the IP address or domain name of the client. That is a great feature for keeping jerks out of your message boards and guest books (you get the IP or domain name from the log files).

To allow user authentication the directory must have `AllowOverrides AuthConfig` set in the `access.conf` file. To allow access control (by domain or IP address) AllowOverrides Limit must be set for that directory.

Setting up the directory involves putting an `.htaccess` file in the directory. For user authentication it is usually used with an `.htpasswd` and optionally a `.htgroup` file. Those files can be shared among multiple `.htaccess` files if you wish.

For security reasons I recommend that everyone use these directives in there `access.conf` file:

```
<files ~ "/\.ht">
order deny,allow
deny from all
</files>
```

If you are not the administrator of the system you can also put it in your `.htaccess` file if AllowOverride Limit is set for your directory. This directive will prevent people from looking into your access control files (`.htaccess`, `.htpasswd`, etc.)

There are many different options and file types that can be used with access control. Therefore it is beyond the scope of this document to describe the files. For information on how to setup User Authentication see the Apacheweek feature at http://www.apacheweek.com/features/userauth/ or the NCSA pages at http://hoohoo.ncsa.uiuc.edu/docs-1.5/tutorials/user.html

7.10 su-exec

The su-exec feature runs CGI scripts as the user of the owner. Normally it is run as the user of the web server (usually nobody). This allows users to access there own files in CGI scripts without making them world writable (a security hole). But if you are not careful you can create a bigger security hole by using the su-exec code. The su-exec code does security checks before executing the scripts, but if you set it up wrong you will have a security hole.

The su-exec code is not for amateurs. Don't use it if you don't know what you are doing. You could end up with a gaping security hole where your users can gain root access to your system. Do not modify the code for any reason. Be sure to read all the documentation carefully. The su-exec code is hard to set up on purpose, to keep the amateurs out (everything must be done manually, no make file no install scripts).

The su-exec code resides in the support directory of the source. First you need to edit the suexec.h file for your system. Then you need to compile the su-exec code with this command:

```
gcc suexec.c -o suexec
```

Then copy the suexec executable to the proper directory. The Apache default is /usr/local/etc/httpd/sbin/. This can be changed by editing httpd.h in the Apache source and recompiling Apache. Apache will only look in this directory, it will not search the path. Next the file needs to be changed to user root (chown root suexec) and the suid bit needs to be set (chmod 4711 suexec). Finally restart Apache, it should display a message on the console that su-exec is being used.

CGI scripts should be set world executable like normal. They will automatically be run as the owner of the CGI script. If you set the SUID (set user id) bit on the CGI scripts they will not run. If the directory or file is world or group writable the script will not run. Scripts owned by system users will not be run (root, bin, etc.). For other security conditions that must be met see the su-exec documentation. If you are having problems see the su-exec log file named cgi.log.

su-exec does not work if you are running Apache from inetd, it only works in daemon mode. It will be fixed in the next version because there will be no inetd mode. If you like playing around in source code, you can edit the http_main.c. You want to get rid of the line where Apache announces that it is using the su-exec wrapper (It wrongly prints this in front of the output of everything).

Be sure and read the Apache documentation on su-exec. It is included with the source and is available on the Apache web site at http://www.apache.org/docs/suexec.html.

7.11 Imagemaps

Apache has the ability to handle server-side imagemaps. Imagemaps are images on web pages that take users to different locations depending on where they click. To enable imagemaps first make sure the imagemap module is installed (its one of the default modules). Next you need to uncomment the .map handler at the end of the srm.conf file. Now all files ending in .map will be imagemap files. Imagemap files map different areas on the image to separate links. Apache uses map files in the standard NCSA format. Here is an example of using a map file in a web page:

```
<a href="/map/mapfile.map">
<img src="picture.gif" ISMAP>
</a>
```

In this example mapfile.map is the mapfile, and picture.gif is the image to click on.

There are many programs that can generate NCSA compatible map files or you can create them yourself. For a more detailed discussion of imagemaps and map files see the Apacheweek feature at (http://www.apacheweek.com/features/imagemaps).

7.12 SSI/XSSI

Server Side Includes (SSI) adds dynamic content to otherwise static web pages. The includes are embedded in the web page as comments. The web server then parses these includes and passes the results to the web server. SSI can add headers and footers to documents, add date the document was last updated, execute a system command or a CGI script. With the new eXtended Server Side Includes (XSSI) you can do a whole lot more. XSSI adds variables and flow control statements (if, else, etc). Its almost like having an programming language to work with.

Parsing all HTML files for SSI commands would waste allot of system resources. Therefore you need to distinguish normal HTML files from those that contain SSI commands. This is usually done by changing the extension of the SSI enhanced HTML files. Usually the .shtml extension is used.

To enable SSI/XSSI first make sure that the includes module is installed. Then edit srm.conf and uncomment the AddType and AddHandler directives for .shtml files. Finally you must set Options Includes for all directories where you want to run SSI/XSSI files. This is done in the access.conf file. Now all files with the extension .shtml will be parsed for SSI/XSSI commands.

Another way of enabling includes is to use the XBitHack directive. If you turn this on it looks to see if the file is executable by user. If it is and Options Includes is on for that directory, then it is treated as an SSI file. This only works for files with the mime type text/html (.html .htm files). This is not the preferred method.

There is a security risk in allowing SSI to execute system commands and CGI scripts. Therefore it is possible to lock that feature out with the Option IncludesNOEXEC instead of Option Includes in the access.conf file. All the other SSI commands will still work.

For more information see the Apache mod_includes documentation that comes with the source. It is also available on the website at (http://www.apache.org/docs/mod/mod_include.html).

For a more detailed discussion of SSI/XSSI implementation see the Apacheweek feature at (http://www.apacheweek.com/features/ssi).

For more information on SSI commands see the NCSA documentation at (http://hoohoo.ncsa.uiuc.edu/docs/tutorials/includes.html).

For more information on XSSI commands go to (ftp://pageplus.com/pub/hsf/xssi/xssi-1.1.html).

7.13 Module system

Apache can be extended to support almost anything with modules. There are allot of modules already in existence. Only the general interest modules are included with Apache. For links to existing modules go to the

Apache Module Registry at (http://www.zyzzyva.com/module_registry/).

For module programming information go to (http://www.zyzzyva.com/module_registry/reference/)

8 For further reading

8.1 O'Reilly & Associates Books

In my humble opinion O'Reilly & Associates make the best technical books on the planet. They focus mainly on Internet, Unix and programming related topics. They start off slow with plenty of examples and when you finish the book your an expert. I think you could get by if you only read half of the book. They also add some humor to otherwise boring subjects.

They have great books on HTML, PERL, CGI Programming, Java, JavaScript, C/C++, Sendmail, Linux and much much more. And the fast moving topics (like HTML) are updated and revised about every 6 months or so. So visit the *O'Reilly & Associates* (http://www.ora.com/) web site or stop by your local book store for more info.

And remember if it doesn't say O'Reilly & Associates on the cover, someone else probably wrote it.

8.2 Internet Request For Comments (RFC)

- RFC1866 written by T. Berners-Lee and D. Connolly, "Hypertext Markup Language - 2.0," 11/03/1995
- RFC1867 writtenm by E. Nebel and L. Masinter, "Form-based File Upload in HTML," 11/07/1995
- RFC1942 written by D. Raggett, "HTML Tables," 05/15/1996
- RFC1945 by T. Berners-Lee, R. Fielding, H. Nielsen, "Hypertext Transfer Protocol – HTTP/1.0," 05/17/1996.
- RFC1630 by T. Berners-Lee, "Universal Resource Identifiers in WWW: A Unifying Syntax for the Expression of Names and Addresses of Objects on the Network as used in the World-Wide Web," 06/09/1994
- RFC1959 by T. Howes, M. Smith, "An LDAP URL Format," 06/19/1996

Part LIV

"XFree86 Video Timings HOWTO" by Eric Raymond,

esr@snark.thyrsus.com

Contents

Abstract

v3.1, 31 October 1997
How to compose a mode line for your card/monitor combination under XFree86. The XFree86 distribution now includes good facilities for configuring most standard combinations; this document is mainly useful if you are tuning a custom mode line for a high-performance monitor or very unusual hardware. It may also help you in using `xvidtune` to tweak a standard mode that is not quite right for your monitor.

1 Disclaimer

You use the material herein SOLELY AT YOUR OWN RISK. It is possible to harm both your monitor and yourself when driving it outside the manufacturer's specs. Read section 11 for detailed cautions. Any damages to you or your monitor caused by overdriving it are your problem.

The most up-to-date version of this HOWTO can be found at the *Linux Documentation Project* (`http://sunsite.unc.edu/LDP`) web page.

Please direct comments, criticism, and suggestions for improvement to esr@snark.thyrsus.com. Please do not send email pleading for a magic solution to your special monitor problem, as doing so will only burn up my time and frustrate you—everything I know about the subject is already in here.

2 Introduction

The XFree86 server allows users to configure their video subsystem and thus encourages best use of existing hardware. This tutorial is intended to help you learn how to generate your own timing numbers to make optimum use of your video card and monitor.

We'll present a method for getting something that works, and then show you how you can experiment starting from that base to develop settings that optimize for your taste.

Starting with XFree86 3.2, XFree86 provides an XF86Setup program that makes it easy to generate a working monitor mode interactively, without messing with video timing number directly. So you shouldn't actually need to calculate a base monitor mode in most cases. Unfortunately, XF86Setup has some limitations; it only knows about standard video modes up to 1280x1024. If you have a very high-performance monitor capable of 1600x1200 or more you will still have to compute your base monitor mode yourself.

Recent versions of XFree86 provide a tool called `xvidtune` which you will probably find quite useful for testing and tuning monitor modes. It begins with a gruesome warning about the possible consequences of mistakes with it. If you pay careful attention to this document and learn what is behind the pretty numbers in xvidtune's boxes, you will become able to use xvidtune effectively and with confidence.

If you already have a mode that almost works (in particular, if one of predefined VESA modes gives you a stable display but one that's displaced right or left, or too small, or too large) you can go straight to Section 14. This will enlighten you on ways to tweak the timing numbers to achieve particular effects.

If you have `xvidtune`, you'll be able to test new modes on the fly, without modifying your X configuration files or even rebooting your X server. Otherwise, XFree86 allows you to hot-key between different modes defined in Xconfig (see XFree86.man for details). Use this capability to save yourself hassles! When you want to test a new mode, give it a unique mode label and add it to the end of your hot-key list. Leave a known-good mode as the default to fall back on if the test mode doesn't work.

3 How Video Displays Work

Knowing how the display works is essential to understanding what numbers to put in the various fields in the file `XF86Config`. Those values are used in the lowest levels of controlling the display by the XFree86 server.

The display generates a picture from a series of dots. The dots are arranged from left to right to form lines. The lines are arranged from top to bottom to form the picture. The dots emit light when they are struck by the electron beam inside the display. To make the beam strike each dot for an equal amount of time, the beam is swept across the display in a constant pattern.

The pattern starts at the top left of the screen, goes across the screen to the right in a straight line, and stops temporarily on the right side of the screen. Then the beam is swept back to the left side of the display, but down one line. The new line is swept from left to right just as the first line was. This pattern is repeated until the bottom line on the display has been swept. Then the beam is moved from the bottom right corner of the display to the top left corner, and the pattern is started over again.

there is one variation of this scheme known as interlacing: here only every second line is swept during one half-frame and the others are filled in in during a second half-frame.

Starting the beam at the top left of the display is called the beginning of a frame. The frame ends when the beam reaches the the top left corner again as it comes from the bottom right corner of the display. A frame is made up of all of the lines the beam traced from the top of the display to the bottom.

If the electron beam were on all of the time it was sweeping through the frame, all of the dots on the display would be illuminated. There would be no black border around the edges of the display. At the edges of the display the picture would become distorted because the beam is hard to control there. To reduce the distortion, the dots around the edges of the display are not illuminated by the beam even though the beam may be pointing at them. The viewable area of the display is reduced this way.

Another important thing to understand is what becomes of the beam when no spot is being painted on the visible area. The time the beam would have been illuminating the side borders of the display is used for sweeping the beam back from the right edge to the left and moving the beam down to the next line. The time the beam would have been illuminating the top and bottom borders of the display is used for moving the beam from the bottom-right corner of the display to the top-left corner.

The adapter card generates the signals which cause the display to turn on the electron beam at each dot to generate a picture. The card also controls when the display moves the beam from the right side to the left and down a line by generating a signal called the horizontal sync (for synchronization) pulse. One horizontal sync pulse occurs at the end of every line. The adapter also generates a vertical sync pulse which signals the display to move the beam to the top-left corner of the display. A vertical sync pulse is generated near the end of every frame.

The display requires that there be short time periods both before and after the horizontal and vertical sync pulses so that the position of the electron beam can stabilize. If the beam can't stabilize, the picture will not be steady.

In a later section, we'll come back to these basics with definitions, formulas and examples to help you use them.

4 Basic Things to Know about your Display and Adapter

There are some fundamental things you need to know before hacking an `XF86Config` entry. These are:

- your monitor's horizontal and vertical sync frequency options;
- your video adapter's driving clock frequency, or "dot clock;"
- your monitor's bandwidth.

The monitor sync frequencies:

The horizontal sync frequency is just the number of times per second the monitor can write a horizontal scan line; it is the single most important statistic about your monitor. The vertical sync frequency is the number of times per second the monitor can traverse its beam vertically.

Sync frequencies are usually listed on the specifications page of your monitor manual. The vertical sync frequency number is typically calibrated in Hz (cycles per second), the horizontal one in KHz (kilocycles per second). The usual ranges are between 50 and 150Hz vertical, and between 31 and 135KHz horizontal.

If you have a multisync monitor, these frequencies will be given as ranges. Some monitors, especially lower-end ones, have multiple fixed frequencies. These can be configured too, but your options will be severely limited by the built-in monitor characteristics. Choose the highest frequency pair for best resolution. And be careful—trying to clock a fixed-frequency monitor at a higher speed than it's designed for can easily damage it.

Earlier versions of this guide were pretty cavalier about overdriving multisync monitors, pushing them past their nominal highest vertical sync frequency in order to get better performance. We have since had more reasons pointed out to us for caution on this score; we'll cover those under Section 11 below.

The card driving clock frequency:

Your video adapter manual's specifcation page will usually give you the card's dot clock (that is, the total number of pixels per second it can write to the screen). If you don't have this information, the X server will get it for you. Even if your X locks up your monitor, it will emit a line of clock and other info to standard output. If you redirect this to a file, it should be saved even if you have to reboot to get your console back. (Recent versions of the X servers all support a `-probeonly` option that prints out this information and exits without actually starting up X or changing the video mode.)

Your X startup message should look something like one of the following examples:

If you're using XFree86:

```
{\tt XF86Config}: /usr/X11R6/lib/X11/{\tt XF86Config}
(**) stands for supplied, (--) stands for probed/default values
(**) Mouse: type: MouseMan, device: /dev/ttyS1, baudrate: 9600
Warning: The directory "/usr/andrew/X11fonts" does not exist.
```

```
    Entry deleted from font path.
(**) FontPath set to "/usr/lib/X11/fonts/misc/,/usr/lib/X11/fonts/75dpi/"
(--) S3: card type: 386/486 localbus
(--) S3: chipset:  924
                   ---
    Chipset -- this is the exact chip type; an early mask of the 86C911

(--) S3: chipset driver: s3_generic
(--) S3: videoram:  1024k
                    -----
          Size of on-board frame-buffer RAM

(**) S3: clocks:  25.00  28.00  40.00   3.00  50.00  77.00  36.00  45.00
(**) S3: clocks:   0.00   0.00  79.00  31.00  94.00  65.00  75.00  71.00
                 ----------------------------------------------------
                          Possible driving frequencies in MHz

(--) S3: Maximum allowed dot-clock: 110MHz
                                    ------
                                  Bandwidth
(**) S3: Mode "1024x768": mode clock =  79.000, clock used =  79.000
(--) S3: Virtual resolution set to 1024x768
(--) S3: Using a banksize of 64k, line width of 1024
(--) S3: Pixmap cache:
(--) S3: Using 2 128-pixel 4 64-pixel and 8 32-pixel slots
(--) S3: Using 8 pages of 768x255 for font caching
```

If you're using SGCS or X/Inside X:

```
WGA: 86C911 (mem: 1024k clocks: 25 28 40 3 50 77 36 45 0 0 79 31 94 65 75 71)
---  ------       -----        ------------------------------------------
 |     |            |                 Possible driving frequencies in MHz
 |     |            +-- Size of on-board frame-buffer RAM
 |     +-- Chip type
 +-- Server type
```

Note: do this with your machine unloaded (if at all possible). Because X is an application, its timing loops can collide with disk activity, rendering the numbers above inaccurate. Do it several times and watch for the numbers to stabilize; if they don't, start killing processes until they do. SVr4 users: the `mousemgr` process is particularly likely to mess you up.

In order to avoid the clock-probe inaccuracy, you should clip out the clock timings and put them in your `XF86Config` as the value of the Clocks property—this suppresses the timing loop and gives X an exact list of the clock values it can try. Using the data from the example above:

```
wga
        Clocks   25 28 40 3 50 77 36 45 0 0 79 31 94 65 75 71
```

On systems with a highly variable load, this may help you avoid mysterious X startup failures. It's possible for X to come up, get its timings wrong due to system load, and then not be able to find a matching dot clock in its config database—or find the wrong one.

4.1 The monitor's video bandwidth:

If you're running XFree86, your server will probe your card and tell you what your highest-available dot clock is.

Otherwise, your highest available dot clock is approximately the monitor's video bandwidth. There's a lot of give here, though—some monitors can run as much as 30% over their nominal bandwidth. The risks here have to do with exceeding the monitor's rated vertical-sync frequency; we'll discuss them in detail below.

Knowing the bandwidth will enable you to make more intelligent choices between possible configurations. It may affect your display's visual quality (especially sharpness for fine details).

Your monitor's video bandwidth should be included on the manual's spec page. If it's not, look at the monitor's highest rated resolution. As a rule of thumb, here's how to translate these into bandwidth estimates (and thus into rough upper bounds for the dot clock you can use):

```
640x480                  25
800x600                  36
1024x768                 65
1024x768 interlaced      45
1280x1024                110
1600x1200                185
```

BTW, there's nothing magic about this table; these numbers are just the lowest dot clocks per resolution in the standard XFree86 Modes database (except for the last, which I interpolated). The bandwidth of your monitor may actually be higher than the minimum needed for its top resolution, so don't be afraid to try a dot clock a few MHz higher.

Also note that bandwidth is seldom an issue for dot clocks under 65MHz or so. With an SVGA card and most high-resolution monitors, you can't get anywhere near the limit of your monitor's video bandwidth. The following are examples:

```
Brand                              Video Bandwidth
----------                         ---------------
NEC 4D                             75Mhz
Nano 907a                          50Mhz
Nano 9080i                         60Mhz
Mitsubishi HL6615                  110Mhz
Mitsubishi Diamond Scan            100Mhz
IDEK MF-5117                       65Mhz
IOCOMM Thinksync-17 CM-7126        136Mhz
HP D1188A                          100Mhz
Philips SC-17AS                    110Mhz
Swan SW617                         85Mhz
Viewsonic 21PS                     185Mhz
```

Even low-end monitors usually aren't terribly bandwidth-constrained for their rated resolutions. The NEC Multisync II makes a good example—it can't even display 800x600 per its specifications. It can only display 800x560. For such low resolutions you don't need high dot clocks or a lot of bandwidth; probably the best you can do is 32Mhz or 36Mhz, both of them are still not too far from the monitor's rated video bandwidth of 30Mhz.

At these two driving frequencies, your screen image may not be as sharp as it should be, but definitely of tolerable quality. Of course it would be nicer if NEC Multisync II had a video bandwidth higher than, say, 36Mhz. But this is not critical for common tasks like text editing, as long as the difference is not so significant as to cause severe image distortion (your eyes would tell you right away if this were so).

4.2 What these control:

The sync frequency ranges of your monitor, together with your video adapter's dot clock, determine the ultimate resolution that you can use. But it's up to the driver to tap the potential of your hardware. A superior hardware combination without an equally competent device driver is a waste of money. On the other hand, with a versatile device driver but less capable hardware, you can push the hardware's envelope a little. This is the design philosophy of XFree86.

5 Interpreting the Basic Specifications

This section explains what the specifications above mean, and some other things you'll need to know. First, some definitions. Next to each in parentheses is the variable name we'll use for it when doing calculations.

horizontal sync frequency (HSF)

Horizontal scans per second (see above).

vertical sync frequency (VSF)

Vertical scans per second (see above). Mainly important as the upper limit on your refresh rate.

dot clock (DCF)

More formally, 'driving clock frequency'; The frequency of the crystal or VCO on your adaptor — the maximum dots-per-second it can emit.

video bandwidth (VB)

The highest frequency you can feed into your monitor's video input and still expect to see anything discernible. If your adaptor produces an alternating on/off pattern, its lowest frequency is half the DCF, so in theory bandwidth starts making sense at DCF/2. For tolerably crisp display of fine details in the video image, however, you don't want it much below your highest DCF, and preferably higher.

frame length (HFL, VFL)

Horizontal frame length (HFL) is the number of dot-clock ticks needed for your monitor's electron gun to scan one horizontal line, including the inactive left and right borders. Vertical frame length (VFL) is the number of scan lines in the entire image, including the inactive top and bottom borders.

screen refresh rate (RR)

The number of times per second your screen is repainted (this is also called "frame rate"). Higher frequencies are better, as they reduce flicker. 60Hz is good, VESA-standard 72Hz is better. Compute it as

```
RR = DCF / (HFL * VFL)
```

Note that the product in the denominator is *not* the same as the monitor's visible resolution, but typically somewhat larger. We'll get to the details of this below.

The rates for which interlaced modes are usually specified (like 87Hz interlaced) are actually the half-frame rates: an entire screen seems to have about that flicker frequency for typical displays, but every single line is refreshed only half as often.

For calculation purposes we reckon an interlaced display at its full-frame (refresh) rate, i.e. 43.5Hz. The quality of an interlaced mode is better than that of a non-interlaced mode with the same full-frame rate, but definitely worse then the non-interlaced one corresponding to the half-frame rate.

5.1 About Bandwidth:

Monitor makers like to advertise high bandwidth because it constrains the sharpness of intensity and color changes on the screen. A high bandwidth means smaller visible details.

Your monitor uses electronic signals to present an image to your eyes. Such signals always come in in wave form once they are converted into analog form from digitized form. They can be considered as combinations of many simpler wave forms each one of which has a fixed frequency, many of them are in the Mhz range, eg, 20Mhz, 40Mhz, or even 70Mhz. Your monitor video bandwidth is, effectively, the highest-frequency analog signal it can handle without distortion.

For our purposes, video bandwidth is mainly important as an approximate cutoff point for the highest dot clock you can use.

5.2 Sync Frequencies and the Refresh Rate:

Each horizontal scan line on the display is just the visible portion of a frame-length scan. At any instant there is actually only one dot active on the screen, but with a fast enough refresh rate your eye's persistence of vision enables you to "see" the whole image.

Here are some pictures to help:

```
 _________________________
|                         |  The horizontal sync frequency
|->->->->->->->->->->->-> |  is the number of times per
|                        )|  second that the monitor's
|<-----<-----<-----<---   |  electron beam can trace
|                         |  a pattern like this
|                         |
|                         |
|                         |
|_________________________|

 _________________________
|          ^              |  The vertical sync frequency
|        ^ |              |  is the number of times per
|        | v              |  second that the monitor's
|        ^ |              |  electron beam can trace
|        | |              |  a pattern like this
|        ^ |              |
|        | v              |
|        ^ |              |
|________|_v______________|
```

Remember that the actual raster scan is a very tight zigzag pattern; that is, the beam moves left-right and at the same time up-down.

Now we can see how the dot clock and frame size relates to refresh rate. By definition, one hertz (hz) is one cycle per second. So, if your horizontal frame length is HFL and your vertical frame length is VFL, then to cover the entire screen takes (HFL * VFL) ticks. Since your card emits DCF ticks per second by definition, then obviously your monitor's electron gun(s) can sweep the screen from left to right and back and from bottom to top and back DCF / (HFL * VFL) times/sec. This is your screen's refresh rate, because it's how many times your screen can be updated (thus *refreshed*) per second!

You need to understand this concept to design a configuration which trades off resolution against flicker in whatever way suits your needs.

For those of you who handle visuals better than text, here is one:

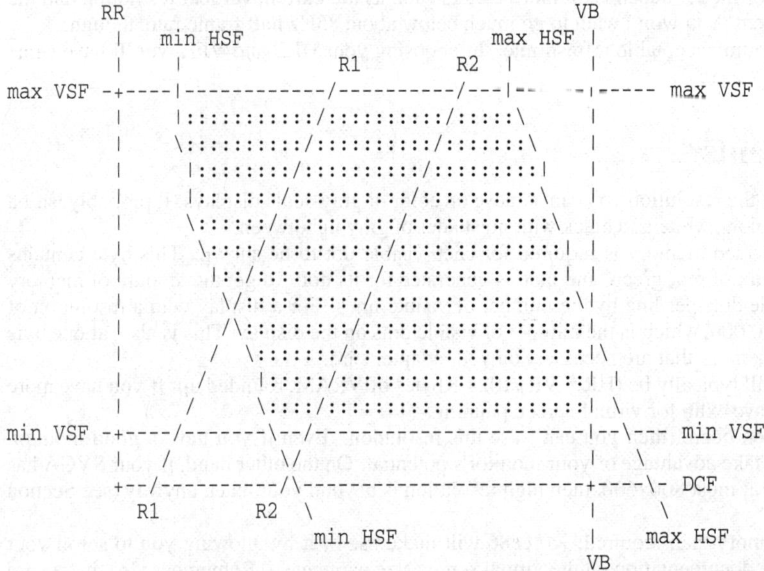

This is a generic monitor mode diagram. The x axis of the diagram shows the clock rate (DCF), the y axis represents the refresh rate (RR). The filled region of the diagram describes the monitor's capabilities: every point within this region is a possible video mode.

The lines labeled 'R1' and 'R2' represent a fixed resolutions (such as 640x480); they are meant to illustrate how one resolution can be realized by many different combinations of dot clock and refresh rate. The R2 line would represent a higher resolution than R1.

The top and bottom boundaries of the permitted region are simply horizontal lines representing the limiting values for the vertical sync frequency. The video bandwidth is an upper limit to the clock rate and hence is represented by a vertical line bounding the capability region on the right.

Under Section 15) you'll find a program that will help you plot a diagram like this (but much nicer, with X graphics) for your individual monitor. That section also discusses the interesting part; the derivation of the boundaries resulting from the limits on the horizontal sync frequency.

6 Tradeoffs in Configuring your System

Another way to look at the formula we derived above is

```
DCF = RR * HFL * VFL
```

That is, your dot clock is fixed. You can use those dots per second to buy either refresh rate, horizontal resolution, or vertical resolution. If one of those increases, one or both of the others must decrease.

Note, though, that your refresh rate cannot be greater than the maximum vertical sync frequency of your monitor. Thus, for any given monitor at a given dot clock, there is a minimum product of frame lengths below which you can't force it.

In choosing your settings, remember: if you set RR too low, you will get mugged by screen flicker.

You probably do not want to pull your refresh rate below 60Hz. This is the flicker rate of fluorescent lights; if you're sensitive to those, you need to hang with 72Hz, the VESA ergonomic standard.

Flicker is very eye-fatiguing, though human eyes are adaptable and peoples' tolerance for it varies widely. If you face your monitor at a 90% viewing angle, are using a dark background and a good contrasting color for foreground, and stick with low to medium intensity, you "may" be comfortable at as little as 45Hz.

The acid test is this: open a `xterm` with pure white background and black foreground using `xterm -bg white -fg black` and make it so large as to cover the entire viewable area. Now turn your monitor's intensity to 3/4 of its maximum setting, and turn your face away from the monitor. Try peeking at your monitor sideways (bringing the more sensitive peripheral-vision cells into play). If you don't sense any flicker or if you feel the flickering is tolerable, then that refresh rate is fine with you. Otherwise you better configure a higher refresh rate, because that semi-invisible flicker is going to fatigue your eyes like crazy and give you headaches, even if the screen looks OK to normal vision.

For interlaced modes, the amount of flicker depends on more factors such as the current vertical resolution and the actual screen contents. So just experiment. You won't want to go much below about 85Hz half frame rate, though.

So let's say you've picked a minimum acceptable refresh rate. In choosing your HFL and VFL, you'll have some room for maneuver.

7 Memory Requirements

Available frame-buffer RAM may limit the resolution you can achieve on color or gray-scale displays. It probably isn't a factor on displays that have only two colors, white and black with no shades of gray in between.

For 256-color displays, a byte of video memory is required for each visible dot to be shown. This byte contains the information that determines what mix of red, green, and blue is generated for its dot. To get the amount of memory required, multiply the number of visible dots per line by the number of visible lines. For a display with a resolution of 800x600, this would be 800 x 600 = 480,000, which is the number of visible dots on the display. This is also, at one byte per dot, the number of bytes of video memory that are necessary on your adapter card.

Thus, your memory requirement will typically be (HR * VR)/1024 Kbytes of VRAM, rounded up. If you have more memory than strictly required, you'll have extra for virtual-screen panning.

However, if you only have 512K on board, then you can't use this resolution. Even if you have a good monitor, without enough video RAM, you can't take advantage of your monitor's potential. On the other hand, if your SVGA has one meg, but your monitor can display at most 800x600, then high resolution is beyond your reach anyway (see Section 12 for a possible remedy).

Don't worry if you have more memory than required; XFree86 will make use of it by allowing you to scroll your viewable area (see the `XF86Config` file documentation on the virtual screen size parameter). Remember also that a card with 512K bytes of memory really doesn't have 512,000 bytes installed, it has 512 x 1024 = 524,288 bytes.

If you're running SGCS X (now called X/Inside) using an S3 card, and are willing to live with 16 colors (4 bits per pixel), you can set depth 4 in `XF86Config` and effectively double the resolution your card can handle. S3 cards, for example, normally do 1024x768x256. You can make them do 1280x1024x16 with depth 4.

8 Computing Frame Sizes

Warning: this method was developed for multisync monitors. It will probably work with fixed-frequency monitors as well, but no guarantees!

Start by dividing DCF by your highest available HSF to get a horizontal frame length.

For example; suppose you have a Sigma Legend SVGA with a 65MHz dot clock, and your monitor has a 55KHz horizontal scan frequency. The quantity (DCF / HSF) is then 1181 (65MHz = 65000KHz; 65000/55 = 1181).

Now for our first bit of black magic. You need to round this figure to the nearest multiple of 8. This has to do with the VGA hardware controller used by SVGA and S3 cards; it uses an 8-bit register, left-shifted 3 bits, for what's really an 11-bit quantity. Other card types such as ATI 8514/A may not have this requirement, but we don't know and the correction can't hurt. So round the usable horizontal frame length figure down to 1176.

This figure (DCF / HSF rounded to a multiple of 8) is the minimum HFL you can use. You can get longer HFLs (and thus, possibly, more horizontal dots on the screen) by setting the sync pulse to produce a lower HSF. But you'll pay with a slower and more visible flicker rate.

As a rule of thumb, 80% of the horizontal frame length is available for horizontal resolution, the visible part of the horizontal scan line (this allows, roughly, for borders and sweepback time—that is, the time required for the beam to move from the right screen edge to the left edge of the next raster line). In this example, that's 944 ticks.

Now, to get the normal 4:3 screen aspect ratio, set your vertical resolution to 3/4ths of the horizontal resolution you just calculated. For this example, that's 708 ticks. To get your actual VFL, multiply that by 1.05 to get 743 ticks.

The 4:3 is not technically magic; nothing prevents you from using a non-Golden-Section ratio if that will get the best use out of your screen real estate. It does make figuring frame height and frame width from the diagonal size convenient, you just multiply the diagonal by by 0.8 to get width and 0.6 to get height.

So, HFL=1176 and VFL=743. Dividing 65MHz by the product of the two gives us a nice, healthy 74.4Hz refresh rate. Excellent! Better than VESA standard. And you got 944x708 to boot, more than the 800 by 600 you were probably expecting. Not bad at all.

You can even improve the refresh rate further, to almost 76 Hz, by using the fact that monitors can often sync horizontally at 2khz or so higher than rated, and by lowering VFL somewhat (that is, taking less than 75% of 944 in the example above). But before you try this "overdriving" maneuver, if you do, make sure that your monitor electron guns can sync up to 76 Hz vertical. (the popular NEC 4D, for instance, cannot. It goes only up to 75 Hz VSF). (See Section 11 for more general discussion of this issue.)

So far, most of this is simple arithmetic and basic facts about raster displays. Hardly any black magic at all

9 Black Magic and Sync Pulses

OK, now you've computed HFL/VFL numbers for your chosen dot clock, found the refresh rate acceptable, and checked that you have enough VRAM. Now for the real black magic – you need to know when and where to place synchronization pulses.

The sync pulses actually control the horizontal and vertical scan frequencies of the monitor. The HSF and VSF you've pulled off the spec sheet are nominal, approximate maximum sync frequencies. The sync pulse in the signal from the adapter card tells the monitor how fast to actually run.

Recall the two pictures above? Only part of the time required for raster-scanning a frame is used for displaying viewable image (ie. your resolution).

9.1 Horizontal Sync:

By previous definition, it takes HFL ticks to trace the a horizontal scan line. Let's call the visible tick count (your horizontal screen resolution) HR. Then obviously, HR < HFL by definition. For concreteness, let's assume both start at the same instant as shown below:

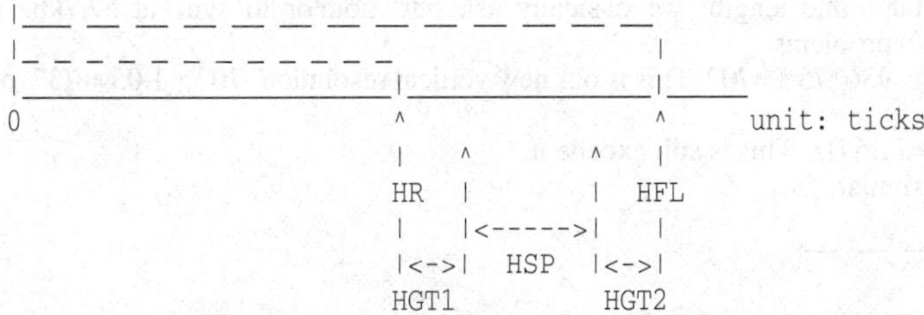

Now, we would like to place a sync pulse of length HSP as shown above, ie, between the end of clock ticks for display data and the end of clock ticks for the entire frame. Why so? because if we can achieve this, then your screen image won't shift to the right or to the left. It will be where it supposed to be on the screen, covering squarely the monitor's viewable area.

Furthermore, we want about 30 ticks of "guard time" on either side of the sync pulse. This is represented by HGT1 and HGT2. In a typical configuration HGT1 != HGT2, but if you're building a configuration from scratch, you want to start your experimentation with them equal (that is, with the sync pulse centered).

The symptom of a misplaced sync pulse is that the image is displaced on the screen, with one border excessively wide and the other side of the image wrapped around the screen edge, producing a white edge line and a band of "ghost image" on that side. A way-out-of-place vertical sync pulse can actually cause the image to roll like a TV with a mis-adjusted vertical hold (in fact, it's the same phenomenon at work).

If you're lucky, your monitor's sync pulse widths will be documented on its specification page. If not, here's where the real black magic starts...

You'll have to do a little trial and error for this part. But most of the time, we can safely assume that a sync pulse is about 3.5 to 4.0 microsecond in length.

For concreteness again, let's take HSP to be 3.8 microseconds (which btw, is not a bad value to start with when experimenting).

Now, using the 65Mhz clock timing above, we know HSP is equivalent to 247 clock ticks (= 65 * 10**6 * 3.8 * 10^-6) [recall M=10^6, micro=10^-6]

Some makers like to quote their horizontal framing parameters as timings rather than dot widths. You may see the following terms:

active time (HAT)
Corresponds to HR, but in milliseconds. HAT * DCF = HR.

blanking time (HBT)
Corresponds to (HFL - HR), but in milliseconds. HBT * DCF = (HFL - HR).

front porch (HFP)
This is just HGT1.

sync time
This is just HSP.

back porch (HBP)
This is just HGT2.

9.2 Vertical Sync:

Going back to the picture above, how do we place the 247 clock ticks as shown in the picture?

Using our example, HR is 944 and HFL is 1176. The difference between the two is 1176 - 944=232 < 247! Obviously we have to do some adjustment here. What can we do?

The first thing is to raise 1176 to 1184, and lower 944 to 936. Now the difference = 1184-936= 248. Hmm, closer.

Next, instead using 3.8, we use 3.5 for calculating HSP; then, we have 65*3.5=227. Looks better. But 248 is not much higher than 227. It's normally necessary to have 30 or so clock ticks between HR and the start of SP, and the same for the end of SP and HFL. AND they have to be multiple of eight! Are we stuck?

No. Let's do this, 936 % 8 = 0, (936 + 32) % 8 = 0 too. But 936 + 32 = 968, 968 + 227 = 1195, 1195 + 32 = 1227. Hmm.. this looks not too bad. But it's not a multiple of 8, so let's round it up to 1232.

But now we have potential trouble, the sync pulse is no longer placed right in the middle between h and H any more. Happily, using our calculator we find 1232 - 32 = 1200 is also a multiple of 8 and (1232 - 32) - 968 = 232 corresponding using a sync pulse of 3.57 μs long, still reasonable.

In addition, 936/1232 0.76 or 76%, still not far from 80%, so it should be all right.

Furthermore, using the current horizontal frame length, we basically ask our monitor to sync at 52.7khz (= 65Mhz/1232) which is within its capability. No problems.

Using rules of thumb we mentioned before, 936*75%=702, This is our new vertical resolution. 702 * 1.05 = 737, our new vertical frame length.

Screen refresh rate = 65Mhz/(737*1232)=71.6 Hz. This is still excellent.

Figuring the vertical sync pulse layout is similar:

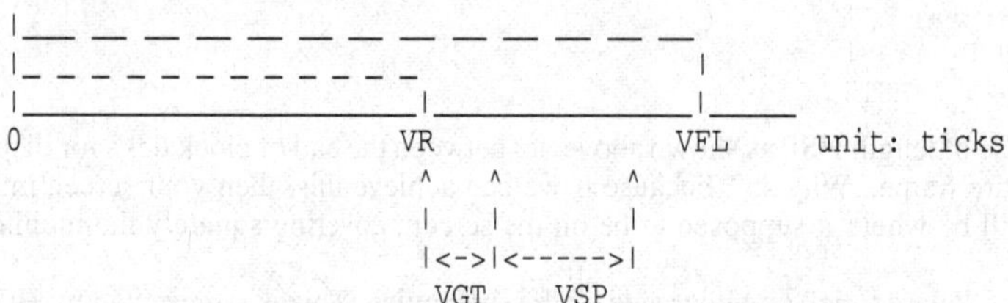

We start the sync pulse just past the end of the vertical display data ticks. VGT is the vertical guard time required for the sync pulse. Most monitors are comfortable with a VGT of 0 (no guard time) and we'll use that in this example. A few need two or three ticks of guard time, and it usually doesn't hurt to add that.

Returning to the example: since by the definition of frame length, a vertical tick is the time for tracing a complete HORIZONTAL frame, therefore in our example, it is 1232/65Mhz=18.95μs.

Experience shows that a vertical sync pulse should be in the range of 50μs and 300μs. As an example let's use 150μs, which translates into 8 vertical clock ticks (150μs/18.95μs 8).

Some makers like to quote their vertical framing parameters as timings rather than dot widths. You may see the following terms:

active time (VAT)
Corresponds to VR, but in milliseconds. VAT * VSF = VR.

blanking time (VBT)
Corresponds to (VFL - VR), but in milliseconds. VBT * VSF = (VFL - VR).

front porch (VFP)
This is just VGT.

sync time
This is just VSP.

back porch (VBP)
This is like a second guard time after the vertical sync pulse. It is often zero.

10 Putting it All Together

The `XF86Config` file Table of Video Modes contains lines of numbers, with each line being a complete specification for one mode of X-server operation. The fields are grouped into four sections, the name section, the clock frequency section, the horizontal section, and the vertical section.

The name section contains one field, the name of the video mode specified by the rest of the line. This name is referred to on the "Modes" line of the Graphics Driver Setup section of the `XF86Config` file. The name field may be omitted if the name of a previous line is the same as the current line.

The dot clock section contains only the dot clock (what we've called DCF) field of the video mode line. The number in this field specifies what dot clock was used to generate the numbers in the following sections.

The horizontal section consists of four fields which specify how each horizontal line on the display is to be generated. The first field of the section contains the number of dots per line which will be illuminated to form the picture (what we've called HR). The second field of the section indicates at which dot the horizontal sync pulse will begin. The third field indicates at which dot the horizontal sync pulse will end. The fourth field specifies the total horizontal frame length (HFL).

The vertical section also contains four fields. The first field contains the number of visible lines which will appear on the display (VR). The second field indicates the line number at which the vertical sync pulse will begin. The third field specifies the line number at which the vertical sync pulse will end. The fourth field contains the total vertical frame length (VFL).

Example:

```
#Modename     clock  horizontal timing  vertical timing

"752x564"     40     752 784  944 1088  564 567 569 611
              44.5   752 792  976 1240  564 567 570 600
```

(Note: stock X11R5 doesn't support fractional dot clocks.)

For `XF86Config`, all of the numbers just mentioned—the number of illuminated dots on the line, the number of dots separating the illuminated dots from the beginning of the sync pulse, the number of dots representing the duration of the pulse, and the number of dots after the end of the sync pulse - are added to produce the number of dots per line. The number of horizontal dots must be evenly divisible by eight.

Example horizontal numbers: 800 864 1024 1088

This sample line has the number of illuminated dots (800) followed by the number of the dot when the sync pulse starts (864), followed by the number of the dot when the sync pulse ends (1024), followed by the number of the last dot on the horizontal line (1088).

Note again that all of the horizontal numbers (800, 864, 1024, and 1088) are divisible by eight! This is not required of the vertical numbers.

The number of lines from the top of the display to the bottom form the frame. The basic timing signal for a frame is the line. A number of lines will contain the picture. After the last illuminated line has been displayed, a delay of a number of lines will occur before the vertical sync pulse is generated. Then the sync pulse will last for a few lines, and finally the last lines in the frame, the delay required after the pulse, will be generated. The numbers that specify this mode of operation are entered in a manner similar to the following example.

Example vertical numbers: 600 603 609 630

This example indicates that there are 600 visible lines on the display, that the vertical sync pulse starts with the 603rd line and ends with the 609th, and that there are 630 total lines being used.

Note that the vertical numbers don't have to be divisible by eight!

Let's return to the example we've been working. According to the above, all we need to do from now on is to write our result into `XF86Config` as follows:

```
<name>  DCF      HR  SH1 SH2    HFL   VR  SV1 SV2 VFL
```

where SH1 is the start tick of the horizontal sync pulse and SH2 is its end tick; similarly, SV1 is the start tick of the vertical sync pulse and SV2 is its end tick.

```
#name     clock   horizontal timing    vertical timing     flag
936x702   65      936 968 1200 1232    702 702 710 737
```

No special flag necessary; this is a non-interlaced mode. Now we are really done.

11 Overdriving Your Monitor

You should absolutely not try exceeding your monitor's scan rates if it's a fixed-frequency type. You can smoke your hardware doing this! There are potentially subtler problems with overdriving a multisync monitor which you should be aware of.

Having a pixel clock higher than the monitor's maximum bandwidth is rather harmless, in contrast. (Note: the theoretical limit of discernible features is reached when the pixel clock reaches double the monitor's bandwidth. This is a straightforward application of Nyquist's Theorem: consider the pixels as a spatially distributed series of samples of the drive signals and you'll see why.)

It's exceeding the rated maximum sync frequencies that's problematic. Some modern monitors might have protection circuitry that shuts the monitor down at dangerous scan rates, but don't rely on it. In particular there are older multisync monitors (like the Multisync II) which use just one horizontal transformer. These monitors will not have much protection against overdriving them. While you necessarily have high voltage regulation circuitry (which can be absent in fixed frequency monitors), it will not necessarily cover every conceivable frequency range, especially in cheaper models. This not only implies more wear on the circuitry, it can also cause the screen phosphors to age faster, and cause more than the specified radiation (including X-rays) to be emitted from the monitor.

Another importance of the bandwidth is that the monitor's input impedance is specified only for that range, and using higher frequencies can cause reflections probably causing minor screen interferences, and radio disturbance.

However, the basic problematic magnitude in question here is the slew rate (the steepness of the video signals) of the video output drivers, and that is usually independent of the actual pixel frequency, but (if your board manufacturer cares about such problems) related to the maximum pixel frequency of the board.

So be careful out there.

12 Using Interlaced Modes

(This section is largely due to David Kastrup <dak@pool.informatik.rwth-aachen.de>)

At a fixed dot clock, an interlaced display is going to have considerably less noticeable flicker than a non-interlaced display, if the vertical circuitry of your monitor is able to support it stably. It is because of this that interlaced modes were invented in the first place.

Interlaced modes got their bad repute because they are inferior to their non-interlaced companions at the same vertical scan frequency, VSF (which is what is usually given in advertisements). But they are definitely superior at the same horizontal scan rate, and that's where the decisive limits of your monitor/graphics card usually lie.

At a fixed refresh rate (or half frame rate, or VSF) the interlaced display will flicker more: a 90Hz interlaced display will be inferior to a 90Hz non-interlaced display. It will, however, need only half the video bandwidth and half the horizontal scan rate. If you compared it to a non-interlaced mode with the same dot clock and the same scan rates, it would be vastly superior: 45Hz non-interlaced is intolerable. With 90Hz interlaced, I have worked for years with my Multisync 3D (at 1024x768) and am very satisfied. I'd guess you'd need at least a 70Hz non-interlaced display for similar comfort.

You have to watch a few points, though: use interlaced modes only at high resolutions, so that the alternately lighted lines are close together. You might want to play with sync pulse widths and positions to get the most stable line positions. If alternating lines are bright and dark, interlace will jump at you. I have one application that chooses such a dot pattern for a menu background (XCept, no other application I know does that, fortunately). I switch to 800x600 for using XCept because it really hurts my eyes otherwise.

For the same reason, use at least 100dpi fonts, or other fonts where horizontal beams are at least two lines thick (for high resolutions, nothing else will make sense anyhow).

And of course, never use an interlaced mode when your hardware would support a non-interlaced one with similar refresh rate.

If, however, you find that for some resolution you are pushing either monitor or graphics card to their upper limits, and getting dissatisfactorily flickery or outwashed (bandwidth exceeded) display, you might want to try tackling the same resolution using an interlaced mode. Of course this is useless if the VSF of your monitor is already close to its limits.

Design of interlaced modes is easy: do it like a non-interlaced mode. Just two more considerations are necessary: you need an odd total number of vertical lines (the last number in your mode line), and when you specify the "interlace" flag, the actual vertical frame rate for your monitor doubles. Your monitor needs to support a 90Hz frame rate if the mode you specified looks like a 45Hz mode apart from the "Interlace" flag.

As an example, here is my modeline for 1024x768 interlaced: my Multisync 3D will support up to 90Hz vertical and 38kHz horizontal.

```
ModeLine "1024x768" 45 1024 1048 1208 1248 768 768 776 807 Interlace
```

Both limits are pretty much exhausted with this mode. Specifying the same mode, just without the "Interlace" flag, still is almost at the limit of the monitor's horizontal capacity (and strictly speaking, a bit under the lower limit of vertical scan rate), but produces an intolerably flickery display.

Basic design rules: if you have designed a mode at less than half of your monitor's vertical capacity, make the vertical total of lines odd and add the "Interlace" flag. The display's quality should vastly improve in most cases.

If you have a non-interlaced mode otherwise exhausting your monitor's specs where the vertical scan rate lies about 30% or more under the maximum of your monitor, hand-designing an interlaced mode (probably with somewhat higher resolution) could deliver superior results, but I won't promise it.

13 Questions and Answers

Q. The example you gave is not a standard screen size, can I use it?

A. Why not? There is no reason whatsoever why you have to use 640x480, 800x600, or even 1024x768. The XFree86 servers let you configure your hardware with a lot of freedom. It usually takes two to three tries to come up the right one. The important thing to shoot for is high refresh rate with reasonable viewing area. not high resolution at the price of eye-tearing flicker!

Q. It this the only resolution given the 65Mhz dot clock and 55Khz HSF?

A. Absolutely not! You are encouraged to follow the general procedure and do some trial-and-error to come up a setting that's really to your liking. Experimenting with this can be lots of fun. Most settings may just give you nasty video hash, but in practice a modern multi-sync monitor is usually not damaged easily. Be sure though, that your monitor can support the frame rates of your mode before using it for longer times.

Beware fixed-frequency monitors! This kind of hacking around can damage them rather quickly. Be sure you use valid refresh rates for every experiment on them.

Q. You just mentioned two standard resolutions. In `XF86Config`, there are many standard resolutions available, can you tell me whether there's any point in tinkering with timings?

A. Absolutely. Take, for example, the "standard" 640x480 listed in the current `XF86Config`. It employs 25Mhz driving frequency, frame lengths are 800 and 525 => refresh rate 59.5Hz. Not too bad. But 28Mhz is a commonly available driving frequency from many SVGA boards. If we use it to drive 640x480, following the procedure we discussed above, you would get frame lengths like 812 and 505. Now the refresh rate is raised to 68Hz, a quite significant improvement over the standard one.

Q. Can you summarize what we have discussed so far?

A. In a nutshell:

1. for any fixed driving frequency, raising max resolution incurs the penalty of lowering refresh rate and thus introducing more flicker;
2. if high resolution is desirable and your monitor supports it, try to get a SVGA card that provides a matching dot clock or DCF. The higher, the better.

14 Fixing Problems with the Image.

OK, so you've got your X configuration numbers. You put them in `XF86Config` with a test mode label. You fire up X, hot-key to the new mode—and the image doesn't look right. What do you do? Here's a list of common video image distortions and how to fix them.

You move the image by changing the sync pulse timing. You scale it by changing the frame length (you need to move the sync pulse to keep it in the same relative position, otherwise scaling will move the image as well). Here are some more specific recipes:

The horizontal and vertical positions are independent. That is, moving the image horizontally doesn't affect placement vertically, or vice-versa. However, the same is not quite true of scaling. While changing the horizontal size does nothing to the vertical size or vice versa, the total change in both may be limited. In particular, if your image is too large in both dimensions you will probably have to go to a higher dot clock to fix it. Since this raises the usable resolution, it is seldom a problem.

14.1 The image is displaced to the left or right

To fix this, move the horizontal sync pulse. That is, increment or decrement (by a multiple of 8) the middle two numbers of the horizontal timing section that define the leading and trailing edge of the horizontal sync pulse.

If the image is shifted left (right border too large, you want to move the image to the right) decrement the numbers. If the image is shifted right (left border too large, you want it to move left) increment the sync pulse.

14.2 The image is displaced up or down

To fix this, move the vertical sync pulse. That is, increment or decrement the middle two numbers of the vertical timing section that define the leading and trailing edge of the vertical sync pulse.

If the image is shifted up (lower border too large, you want to move the image down) decrement the numbers. If the image is shifted down (top border too large, you want it to move up) increment the numbers.

14.3 The image is too large both horizontally and vertically

Switch to a higher card clock speed. If you have multiple modes in your clock file, possibly a lower-speed one is being activated by mistake.

14.4 The image is too wide (too narrow) horizontally

To fix this, increase (decrease) the horizontal frame length. That is, change the fourth number in the first timing section. To avoid moving the image, also move the sync pulse (second and third numbers) half as far, to keep it in the same relative position.

14.5 The image is too deep (too shallow) vertically

To fix this, increase (decrease) the vertical frame length. That is, change the fourth number in the second timing section. To avoid moving the image, also move the sync pulse (second and third numbers) half as far, to keep it in the same relative position.

Any distortion that can't be handled by combining these techniques is probably evidence of something more basically wrong, like a calculation mistake or a faster dot clock than the monitor can handle.

Finally, remember that increasing either frame length will decrease your refresh rate, and vice-versa.

15 Plotting Monitor Capabilities

To plot a monitor mode diagram, you'll need the gnuplot package (a freeware plotting language for UNIX-like operating systems) and the tool `modeplot`, a shell/gnuplot script to plot the diagram from your monitor characteristics, entered as command-line options.

Here is a copy of `modeplot`:

```
#!/bin/sh
#
# modeplot -- generate X mode plot of available monitor modes
#
# Do 'modeplot -?' to see the control options.
#
# ($Id: XFree86-Video-Timings-HOWTO.tex,v 1.6 1998/03/07 21:08:08 rak Exp $)

# Monitor description. Bandwidth in MHz, horizontal frequencies in kHz
# and vertical frequencies in Hz.
TITLE="Viewsonic 21PS"
BANDWIDTH=185
MINHSF=31
MAXHSF=85
MINVSF=50
MAXVSF=160
ASPECT="4/3"
vesa=72.5          # VESA-recommended minimum refresh rate
```

```
while [ "$1" != "" ]
do
      case $1 in
      -t) TITLE="$2"; shift;;
      -b) BANDWIDTH="$2"; shift;;
      -h) MINHSF="$2" MAXHSF="$3"; shift; shift;;
      -v) MINVSF="$2" MAXVSF="$3"; shift; shift;;
      -a) ASPECT="$2"; shift;;
      -g) GNUOPTS="$2"; shift;;
      -?) cat <<EOF
modeplot control switches:

-t "<description>"       name of monitor            defaults to "Viewsonic 21PS"
-b <nn>                  bandwidth in MHz           defaults to 185
-h <min> <max>           min & max HSF (kHz)        defaults to 31 85
-v <min> <max>           min & max VSF (Hz)         defaults to 50 160
-a <aspect ratio>        aspect ratio               defaults to 4/3
-g "<options>"           pass options to gnuplot

The -b, -h and -v options are required, -a, -t, -g optional.  You can
use -g to pass a device type to gnuplot so that (for example) modeplot's
output can be redirected to a printer.  See gnuplot(1) for  details.

The modeplot tool was created by Eric S. Raymond <esr@thyrsus.com> based on
analysis and scratch code by Martin Lottermoser <Martin.Lottermoser@mch.sni.de>

This is modeplot $Revision: 1.6 $
EOF
            exit;;
      esac
      shift
done

gnuplot $GNUOPTS <<EOF
set title "$TITLE Mode Plot"

# Magic numbers.  Unfortunately, the plot is quite sensitive to changes in
# these, and they may fail to represent reality on some monitors.  We need
# to fix values to get even an approximation of the mode diagram.  These come
# from looking at lots of values in the ModeDB database.
F1 = 1.30         # multiplier to convert horizontal resolution to frame width
F2 = 1.05         # multiplier to convert vertical resolution to frame height

# Function definitions (multiplication by 1.0 forces real-number arithmetic)
ac = (1.0*$ASPECT)*F1/F2
refresh(hsync, dcf) = ac * (hsync**2)/(1.0*dcf)
dotclock(hsync, rr) = ac * (hsync**2)/(1.0*rr)
resolution(hv, dcf) = dcf * (10**6)/(hv * F1 * F2)

# Put labels on the axes
set xlabel 'DCF (MHz)'
set ylabel 'RR (Hz)' 6  # Put it right over the Y axis

# Generate diagram
set grid
set label "VB" at $BANDWIDTH+1, ($MAXVSF + $MINVSF) / 2 left
set arrow from $BANDWIDTH, $MINVSF to $BANDWIDTH, $MAXVSF nohead
```

```
set label "max VSF" at 1, $MAXVSF-1.5
set arrow from 0, $MAXVSF to $BANDWIDTH, $MAXVSF nohead
set label "min VSF" at 1, $MINVSF-1.5
set arrow from 0, $MINVSF to $BANDWIDTH, $MINVSF nohead
set label "min HSF" at dotclock($MINHSF, $MAXVSF+17), $MAXVSF + 17 right
set label "max HSF" at dotclock($MAXHSF, $MAXVSF+17), $MAXVSF + 17 right
set label "VESA $vesa" at 1, $vesa-1.5
set arrow from 0, $vesa to $BANDWIDTH, $vesa nohead # style -1
plot [dcf=0:1.1*$BANDWIDTH] [$MINVSF-10:$MAXVSF+20] \
  refresh($MINHSF, dcf) notitle with lines 1, \
  refresh($MAXHSF, dcf) notitle with lines 1, \
  resolution(640*480,   dcf) title "640x480  " with points 2, \
  resolution(800*600,   dcf) title "800x600  " with points 3, \
  resolution(1024*768,  dcf) title "1024x768 " with points 4, \
  resolution(1280*1024, dcf) title "1280x1024" with points 5, \
  resolution(1600*1280, dcf) title "1600x1200" with points 6

pause 9999
EOF
```

Once you know you have modeplot and the gnuplot package in place, you'll need the following monitor characteristics:

- video bandwidth (VB);
- range of horizontal sync frequency (HSF);
- range of vertical sync frequency (VSF).

The plot program needs to make some simplifying assumptions which are not necessarily correct. This is the reason why the resulting diagram is only a rough description. These assumptions are:

1. All resolutions have a single fixed aspect ratio AR = HR/VR. Standard resolutions have AR = 4/3 or AR = 5/4. The modeplot programs assumes 4/3 by default, but you can override this.
2. For the modes considered, horizontal and vertical frame lengths are fixed multiples of horizontal and vertical resolutions, respectively:

```
HFL = F1 * HR
VFL = F2 * VR
```

As a rough guide, take F1 = 1.30 and F2 = 1.05 (see Section 8 "Computing Frame Sizes").

Now take a particular sync frequency, HSF. Given the assumptions just presented, every value for the clock rate DCF already determines the refresh rate RR, i.e. for every value of HSF there is a function RR(DCF). This can be derived as follows.

The refresh rate is equal to the clock rate divided by the product of the frame sizes:

```
RR = DCF / (HFL * VFL)          (*)
```

On the other hand, the horizontal frame length is equal to the clock rate divided by the horizontal sync frequency:

```
HFL = DCF / HSF                 (**)
```

VFL can be reduced to HFL be means of the two assumptions above:

```
VFL = F2 * VR
    = F2 * (HR / AR)
    = (F2/F1) * HFL / AR        (***)
```

Inserting (**) and (***) into (*) we obtain:

```
RR = DCF / ((F2/F1) * HFL**2 / AR)
   = (F1/F2) * AR * DCF * (HSF/DCF)**2
   = (F1/F2) * AR * HSF**2 / DCF
```

For fixed HSF, F1, F2 and AR, this is a hyperbola in our diagram. Drawing two such curves for minimum and maximum horizontal sync frequencies we have obtained the two remaining boundaries of the permitted region.

The straight lines crossing the capability region represent particular resolutions. This is based on (*) and the second assumption:

```
RR = DCF / (HFL * VFL) = DCF / (F1 * HR * F2 * VR)
```

By drawing such lines for all resolutions one is interested in, one can immediately read off the possible relations between resolution, clock rate and refresh rate of which the monitor is capable. Note that these lines do not depend on monitor properties, but they do depend on the second assumption.

The `modeplot` tool provides you with an easy way to do this. Do `modeplot -?` to see its control options. A typical invocation looks like this:

```
modeplot -t "Swan SW617" -b 85 -v 50 90 -h 31 58
```

The `-b` option specifies video bandwidth; `-v` and `-h` set horizontal and vertical sync frequency ranges.

When reading the output of `modeplot`, always bear in mind that it gives only an approximate description. For example, it disregards limitations on HFL resulting from a minimum required sync pulse width, and it can only be accurate as far as the assumptions are. It is therefore no substitute for a detailed calculation (involving some black magic) as presented in 10. However, it should give you a better feeling for what is possible and which tradeoffs are involved.

16 Credits

The original ancestor of this document was by Chin Fang <fangchin@leland.stanford.edu>.

Eric S. Raymond <esr@snark.thyrsus.com> reworked, reorganized, and massively rewrote Chin Fang's original in an attempt to understand it. In the process, he merged in most of a different how-to by Bob Crosson <crosson@cam.nist.gov>.

The material on interlaced modes is largely by David Kastrup <dak@pool.informatik.rwth-aachen.de>

Martin Lottermoser <Martin.Lottermoser@mch.sni.de> contributed the idea of using gnuplot to make mode diagrams and did the mathematical analysis behind `modeplot`. The distributed `modeplot` was redesigned and generalized by ESR from Martin's original gnuplot code for one case.

Index

This book would not have been possible without the economies of free software developed in large part by the Linux community. The source text of the Linux Documentation Project HOWTOs was formatted with SGML Tools using the Linuxdoc DTD, and translated to LaTeX 2ε. Both GNU Emacs 20.2 and XEmacs 20.3 were used during editing. Formatting of the book was done with the teTeX distribution of LaTeX 2ε, version 0.4. For revision tracking, the GNU Revision Control System, RCS, was used. Throughout the editing and revision process, the authors, editors, and publishers communicated over the Internet, often with networking software developed under Linux. Imaging was done with Ghostscript 3.33 and the public domain Type 1 fonts of the Ghostscript library, and the proofs were printed on IBM and Hewlett Packard printers or previewed under XFree86. The final PostScript output was generated by dvips.

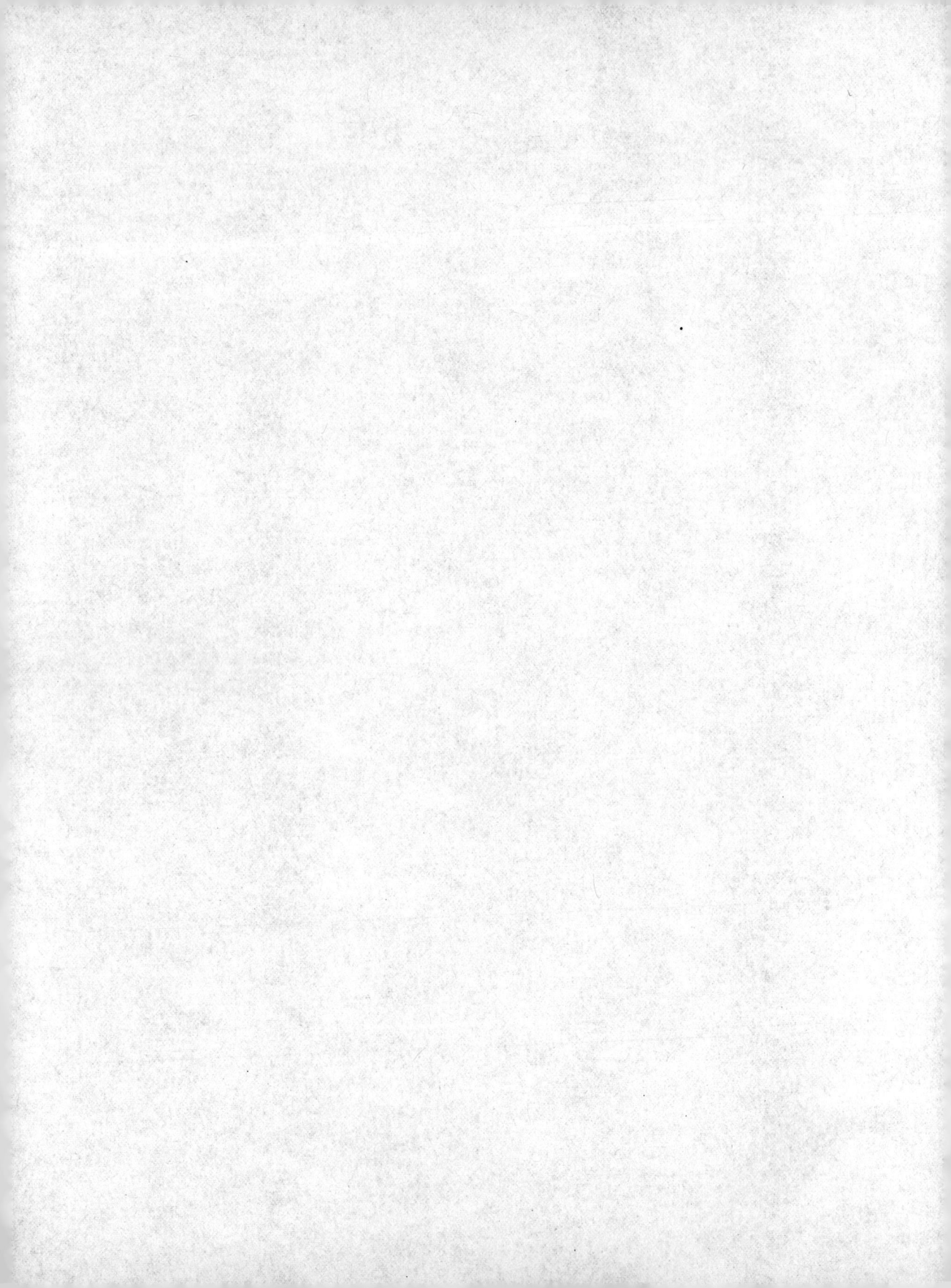